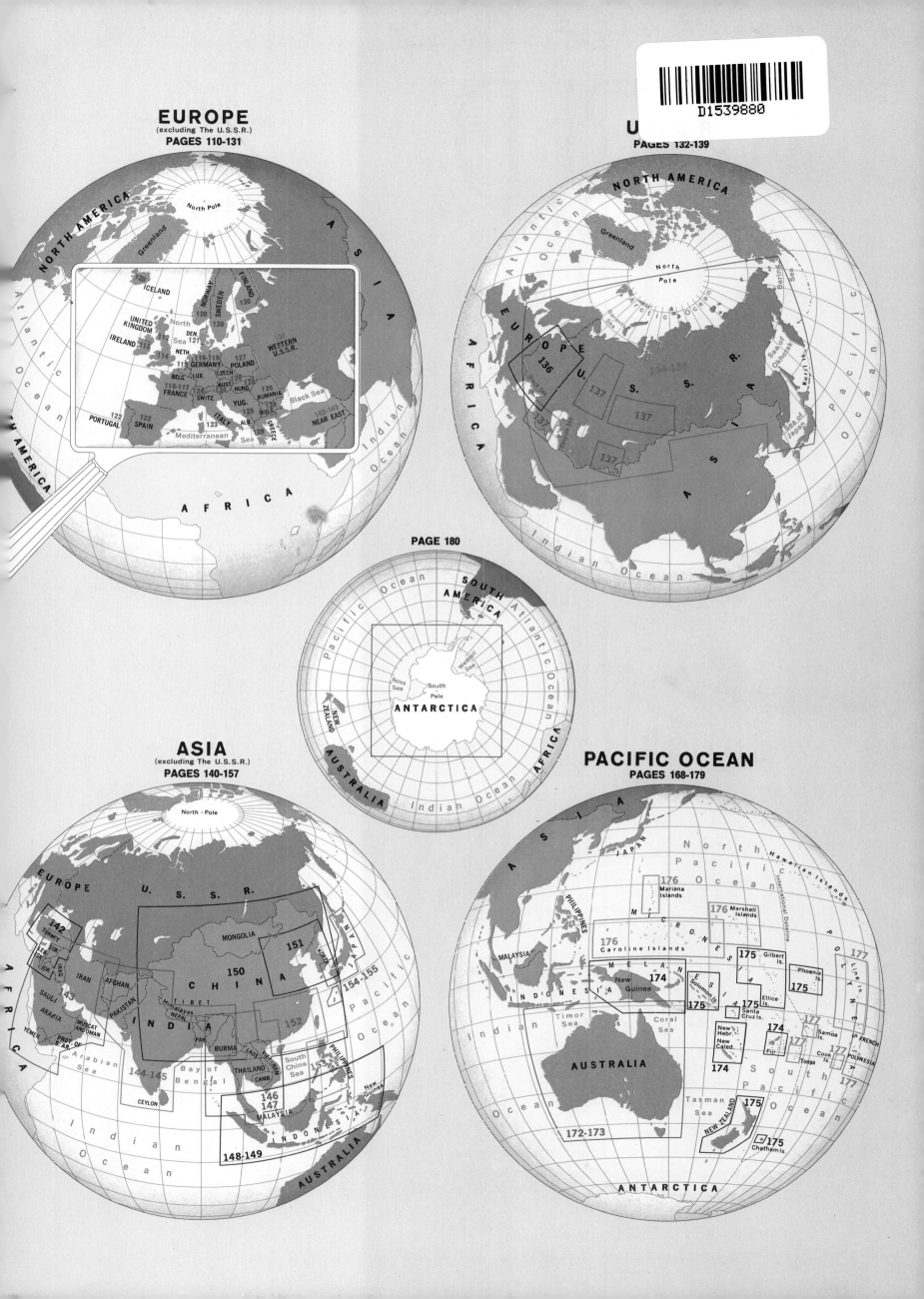

THE ODYSSEY

WORLD ATLAS

 # CONSULTANTS

JOHN E. BRUSH,
Professor, Department of Geography,
Rutgers—The State University

GEORGE F. DEASY,
Professor of Geography,
The Pennsylvania State University

HAROLD K. FAYE,
Cartographer,
New York, N.Y.

NORTON S. GINSBURG,
Professor of Geography,
University of Chicago

PHYLLIS R. GRIESS,
Professor Emerita, Department of Geography,
The Pennsylvania State University

WILLIAM A. HANCE,
Chairman, Department of Geography,
Columbia University

THEODORE HERMAN,
Professor and Chairman, Department of Geography,
Colgate University

ROBERT B. McNEE,
Head, Department of Geography,
University of Cincinnati

DONALD W. MEINIG,
Professor, Department of Geography,
Syracuse University

ALEXANDER MELAMID,
Professor of Economic Geography,
New York University

ABRAHAM MELEZIN,
Assistant Professor of Geography,
City College of New York

KEMPTON E. WEBB,
Associate Professor, Department of Geography,
Columbia University

GUIDO G. WEIGEND,
Professor and Chairman, Department of Geography,
Rutgers—The State University

HEROLD J. WIENS,
Professor of Geography,
University of Hawaii

 **RICHARD EDES HARRISON,**
Relief Renderings,
New York

GENERAL DRAFTING CO., INC.,
Cartography,
Convent Station, New Jersey

THE ODYSSEY
WORLD ATLAS

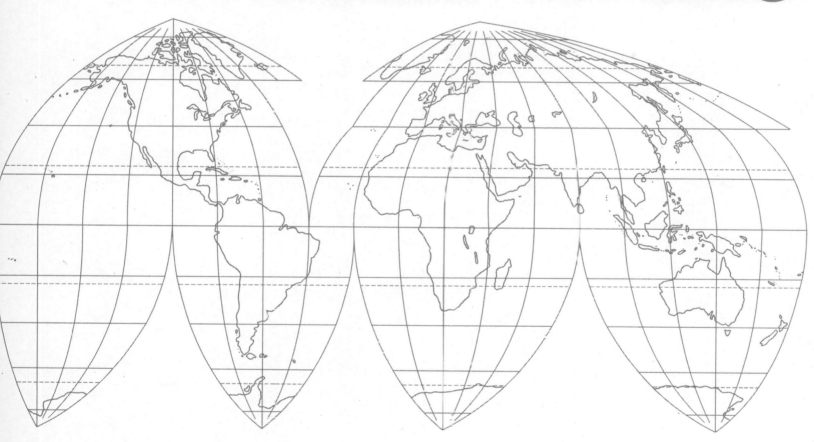

UNIVERSAL EDITION

GOLDEN PRESS · NEW YORK

ACKNOWLEDGMENTS

Many people and agencies have been of invaluable aid in the compilation and preparation of material for this atlas. In particular we should like to thank Dr. G. Etzel Pearcy, The Geographer, U.S. Department of State; Dr. Meredith F. Burrill, Office of Geography, U.S. Department of the Interior; and Dr. Arch C. Gerlach, Map Division, Library of Congress.

We should also like to acknowledge the cheerfulness and persistence of the staffs of the United Nations and American Geographical Society in tracking down information and source materials.

Too numerous to mention specifically have been all the governmental agencies, foreign and domestic, and private organizations who have supplied us with data.

Lastly, we should like to acknowledge the work of Lothar Roth in the preparation of the front end papers, and of Avery Johnson on various of the relief insets.

CONTENTS

QUICK REFERENCE INDEX

PROJECTIONS

INTRODUCTION

Map projections are necessary because the three-dimensional surface of the earth must be rearranged so that it can be printed on the two-dimensional surface of paper. There are many such rearrangements and these are called projections. The closest link between a map and a globe, which is a true representation of the earth, will be a map so designed that it can be fitted to a globe, such as globe gores. Even here the paper has to be dampened and stretched so that it can be fitted onto the spherical surface of the globe.

THE GLOBE AND THE MAP

Maps are plotted and constructed on grids composed of lines of latitude (parallels) and longitude (meridians). Both divide the circumference of the earth into 360 degrees (designated °); each degree is subdivided into 60 minutes (′); and each minute into 60 seconds (″). The location of Washington, D.C. is given by the crossing of latitude and longitude thus: Latitude 38° 54′ N Longitude 77°00′W. If the location were to be given precisely, the second (″) would also be indicated, but this is rarely used except when great accuracy is required, as in surveying. The Prime Meridian, passing through the Royal Observatory at Greenwich, England, is the starting point for east and west longitude. The Equator divides north and south latitudes.

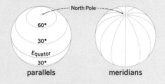

parallels   meridians

complete grid

A map such as that on the globe above (see first illustration) is not suited for ordinary flat maps because of the numerous interruptions, so other methods must be employed. In **true projections**, this is done by direct geometrical projection. Other projections, preferably referred to as **transformations**, may be modified from geometrically derived projections or arrived at through various mathematical formulae.

No single projection can present an entirely accurate map of a globe or even part of a globe; therefore, projections are devised to be true in selected properties or a compromise between selected properties. When a map is correct in one property, it cannot be completely correct in any other. The prime properties of maps are:

Equidistance or **true distance measuring.** This property can be fulfilled on a given map only from one point in any direction or along certain lines.

Equal area or **true comparison of surface.** This is true throughout such a map.

Conformality or **true shape.** From any point in maps such as the Mercator or the Stereographic, compass direction is true to any other point and the shape of any small geographical area is faithfully preserved. Thus they are most important in navigation.

Great circles (gnomonic). On these maps great circles are straight lines. Meridians are all great circles; of all the parallels, only the Equator is. Gnomonic maps supplement conformal maps in navigation. They are greatly distorted and limited to less than a hemisphere.

TRUE PROJECTIONS (Geometrically Projected)

True or direct projection is accomplished by drawing a line from a given point through the globe to a flat surface, or plane. Here are three examples:

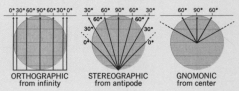

ORTHOGRAPHIC
from infinity

STEREOGRAPHIC
from antipode

GNOMONIC
from center

DIRECT PROJECTION ONTO A PLANE (as a map)

The above are three members of the Azimuthal group which are treated in the table of projections.

Lines from a given point may also be projected to a point on a developable surface such as a cone;

(central conic projection)

DIRECT PROJECTION ONTO A CONE

Or a cylinder;

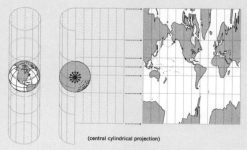

(central cylindrical projection)

DIRECT PROJECTION ONTO A CYLINDER

(cylindrical equal-area projection)

Note here that, although this is a precise equal-area by projection, it results in a very distorted map of the earth's surface.

In the three polar projections illustrated at the top of this column, the meridians are radial and identical; therefore, they differ only in the spacing of the parallels as below.

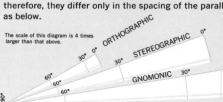

The scale of this diagram is 4 times larger than that above.

ORTHOGRAPHIC
STEREOGRAPHIC
GNOMONIC

We have shown the plane tangent at the pole in the interest of simplicity. But the plane may be tangent at any latitude as shown below. If this is done, the appearance of the grid is altered according to the latitude (and extremely so when tangent at the Equator), but the properties always remain the same.

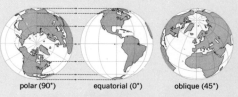

polar (90°)   equatorial (0°)   oblique (45°)

THE THREE CASES OF THE ORTHOGRAPHIC

Note that the cylinder, cone, and plane—all involved in the true projections—are closely related forms.

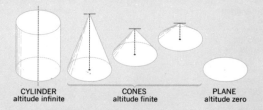

CYLINDER
altitude infinite

CONES
altitude finite

PLANE
altitude zero

TRANSFORMATIONS

These can perhaps be best explained by going back to our first illustration—the globe gores. As noted, these do not make an acceptable flat map because of the many interruptions of land surfaces. We can, however, transform globe gores easily to a useful map by coalescing several gores so that the remaining interruptions occur in the ocean areas and the land is continuous. The only prime property readily attained in this kind of map is that of equal area.

AITOFF'S INTERRUPTED EQUAL AREA PROJECTION

When maps are so designed (and there are unlimited variants), they are most frequently used for showing the distribution of anything, physical or cultural, on the surface of the earth.

Of the cylindrical projections which are transformations, the simplest of all is made by laying out a grid of squares 12 wide and 6 high using the 30° net shown on all the examples on this page.

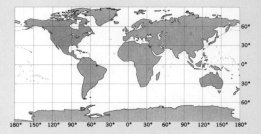

SIMPLE CYLINDRICAL PROJECTION

As in the polar azimuthals where the radii (meridians) are always the same and only the parallels vary, all cylindricals have equally spaced meridians and vary only in the spacing of the parallels. On the Mercator the parallel spacing increases from the Equator north and south according to formula so that the shapes of coasts and small geographical features are closely preserved and that all compass directions from one place to any other are correct throughout. This is the property which has made Mercator the standard navigation map from the time it was generally accepted (before 1600) up to now.

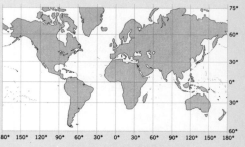

MERCATOR PROJECTION

A simple transformation is the globular "projection" which is used frequently on seals, trademarks, and hemispheres generally. The procedure is to draw a circle and its quadrants, the vertical line being the central meridian and the horizontal one the Equator. Each line and arc is divided equally according to the desired grid (in this case thirty degrees). The remaining meridians and the parallels are all arcs of circles and since three points on each are known, the centers of the arcs can be found readily by trial and error or by construction. This transformation does not possess any of the prime properties but represents a compromise between all of them.

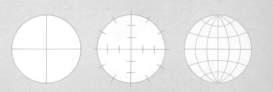

SOME USEFUL PROJECTIONS

Although several hundred projections have been devised, the majority of them are variants of the basic families described on this page. The notes about each family or group provide a clue to the purpose for which it is most commonly used and whether it is equal area, equidistant, or conformal.

THE AZIMUTHAL FAMILY (projections on a plane)

ORTHOGRAPHIC

polar   equatorial   oblique

A projection having no prime properties but effective as a visual link between globes and map. It shows one hemisphere only.

STEREOGRAPHIC

polar   equatorial   oblique

A conformal projection in which all great circles are arcs of circles. The complete world cannot be shown.

GNOMONIC

polar   equatorial   oblique

All great circles are straight lines. Less than one hemisphere can be shown.

AZIMUTHAL EQUIDISTANT

polar   equatorial   oblique

All radii are true to scale and great circles. The complete world can be shown.

AZIMUTHAL EQUAL AREA

polar   equatorial   oblique

The complete world can be shown.

BIPOLAR OBLIQUE CONIC CONFORMAL
(Miller, Briesemeister)

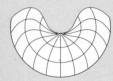

A projection devised particularly to show the Americas conformally with minimum distortion of area.

An equal-area projection showing less than the whole world and used mostly for temperate zone large countries, although it is sometimes used for full continents. It is easy to construct.

THE CONIC FAMILY

SIMPLE CONIC

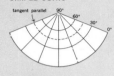

Parallels equally spaced. A projection with no special properties, it is fair for latitudes near tangent parallels. Can include the entire world.

CENTRAL CONIC

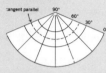

Parallels projected from the center of the globe. Easy to construct but of no special properties. Also called the perspective conic.

CONFORMAL CONIC (Lambert)

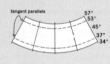

Constructed on two standard parallels, this projection was designed for mid-latitude countries such as France and the United States.

EQUAL AREA CONIC (Albers)

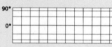

A projection used for minimal area distortion of large mid-latitude countries such as the United States and Australia.

THE CYLINDRICAL FAMILY

SIMPLE CYLINDRICAL (equatorial cases)

An easily constructed map showing the whole world but of no special properties or use.

CYLINDRICAL EQUAL AREA

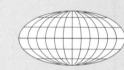

An easily constructed map showing the whole world but rarely used.

MERCATOR

A conformal projection on which the very high latitudes cannot be shown. It is the standard world navigation map (except for the polar areas), with shape and compass directions true throughout. It is weak as a general world map because of the great distortion in high latitudes.

GALL'S STEREOGRAPHIC

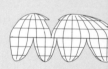

A true projection showing the complete world.

MILLER CYLINDRICAL

A complete world map like Mercator in the middle latitudes but increasingly compressed like Gall's in the higher latitudes. The poles can be shown.

TRANSVERSE MERCATOR

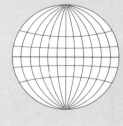

A conformal projection limited to less than the complete world, it is used for navigation along long north-south routes and for mapping areas of predominantly north-south extension.

OBLIQUE MERCATOR

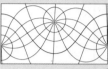

A conformal projection limited to less than the complete world and used for oblique long-range great circle lines such as London-Australia.

NOTE: All other cylindrical projections can be shown in transverse and oblique versions, maintaining the same properties as the equatorial versions.

THE ECKERT FAMILY

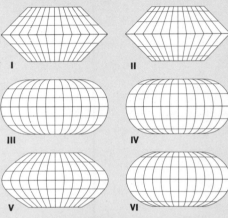

I   II

III   IV

V   VI

Poles equal ½ the equator. In each of the above pairs, all of which show the complete world, the first example is a compromise projection with parallels and meridians equally spaced, and in the second example the parallels have been respaced to make it equal area. Eckert IV is frequently used as a world distribution map.

ELLIPTICAL (Mollweide)

An equal-area projection showing the complete world. The central hemisphere is a circle and all meridians are ellipses. Also used in transverse and oblique cases.

EUMORPHIC (Boggs)

A compromise between the elliptical and sinusoidal projections showing the complete world.

HOMOLOSINE, INTERRUPTED (Goode)

An equal-area projection showing the complete world, it is used extensively for world distribution. The lobes are constructed as in the sinusoidal, and many variations are possible.

POLYCONIC

A compromise projection showing the entire world, it is used mainly, however, for continental areas such as North and South America which have more latitude than longitude.

SINUSOIDAL

This is an equal-area projection of the entire world. Its elements are often used to make an interrupted projection of the world.

VAN DER GRINTEN

A compromise projection showing the whole world, often used but having no special properties. La Grange is a conformal version of this projection.

MAP SYMBOLS

WATER FEATURES

- Rivers and Streams
- Rivers and Streams, Intermittent
- Lakes
- Lakes, Intermittent or Dry
- Salt Pans
- Swamps (on Physical Maps)
- Canals
- Falls
- Rapids
- Wells
- Glaciers, Ice Fields (on Physical Maps)
- Limits of Permanent Pack Ice
- •8097 ft. 2468 m. — Water Depths

LAND FEATURES

- 5633 ft. △1717 m. — Elevations above or below Sea Level
- Highest Elevations
- Volcanoes
- Craters and Depressions
- Passes
- Reefs
- Deserts (on Physical Maps)

BOUNDARIES

- International Boundaries or Limits of Administration
- Indefinite Boundaries
- State, Province, etc., Boundaries
- County Lines (U.S. and British Isles)

MISCELLANEOUS

- National Park
- National Monuments
- Other Parks and Reserves
- Dams
- Ruins and Antiquities
- LONDON — National Capitals
- TRENTON — Other Capitals

County seats in the U.S. are indicated by red town symbols. See individual maps for explanation of symbols for all populated places.

Solid red outlines Indicate extent of more detailed map coverage.

HOW TO RECOGNIZE MAP DISTORTION

All maps have distortions (areas, distances, shapes, or great circle deviations), having lost a dimension in the process of going from the globe to the map. Some distortions can be detected by inspection; others may require mathematical analysis or other research—but a few rules of thumb can help greatly with the former and much of it is surprisingly easy.

For example, all graticules (boxes formed by pairs of meridians and parallels) in the same latitude are identical on the globe. Therefore, any variation along such a row of graticules on a map is a direct indication of

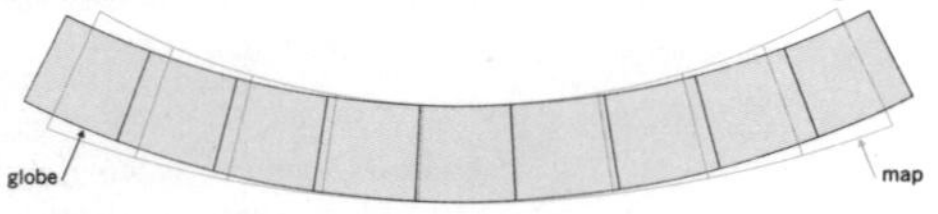

Distortion of shape does not necessarily mean distortion of area. The two graticules below have the same area.

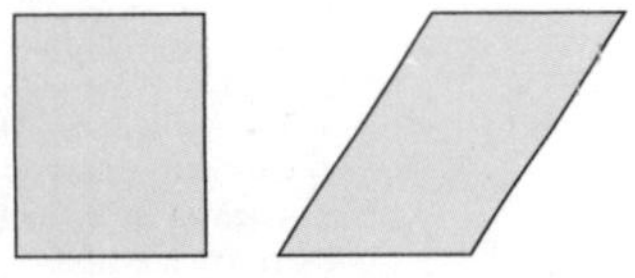

true shape distorted shape

In world maps the problem of distortion is at its greatest. The U.S. can be mapped on a projection with a maximum error of only $1\frac{1}{4}\%$. Large-scale maps often have less distortion than that caused by paper size changes resulting from humidity.

A globe may be used readily as a check on map distortions. Here is an extreme example from the Mercator projection comparing equatorial and arctic islands.

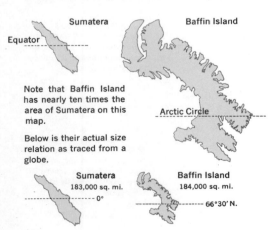

Sumatera

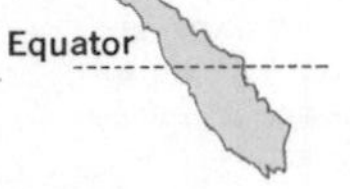

Baffin Island

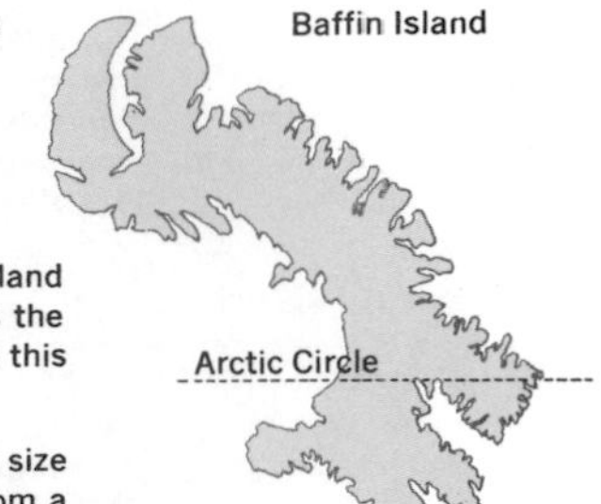

Note that Baffin Island has nearly ten times the area of Sumatera on this map.

Below is their actual size relation as traced from a globe.

Sumatera
183,000 sq. mi.

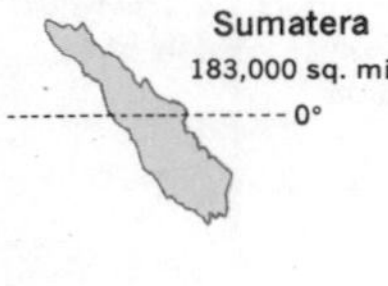

Baffin Island
184,000 sq. mi.

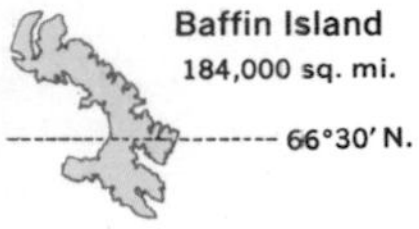

SCALE

A map represents the whole or part of the earth enormously reduced in size. The relationship of the map to the size of the earth is known as scale. If an object as drawn on a map—such as an air strip, or a factory, or a hill—is exactly one one-millionth the size of this object on the earth, then the map is said to be at a scale of 1:1,000,000. This way of stating it is called the **natural scale.** It is also correct to write it 1/1,000,000, a preferable method since it reminds us that the greater the figure below the line, the smaller the scale of the map. The difference between large- and small-scale maps has confused many, and the simplest way out is to remember that scale is preferably expressed as a fraction.

A second way of stating scale is in terms of miles per inch on the map. If you have only the natural scale on a map, divide it by 63,360 (the number of inches in a statute mile), to arrive at the miles per inch. For example, a map at the scale of 1/1,000,000 or 1:1,000,000 works out to 15.78 miles, or approximately 16 miles per inch.

The third way is by use of a linear or bar scale. This kind of scale should be on all reference maps because it is the only one of the three methods that remains accurate when a map is enlarged or reduced. Shown below are portions of map from this atlas. Note that all maps are in progressively larger scales.

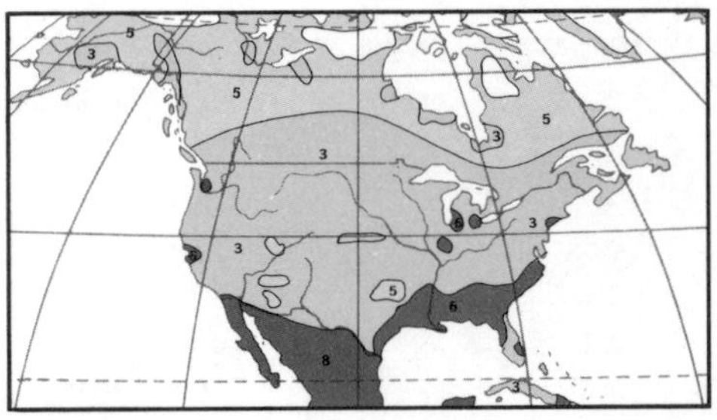

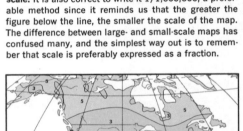

1 in. = 2257 mi. Equatorial Scale 1/143,000,000 1 cm. = 1430 km.

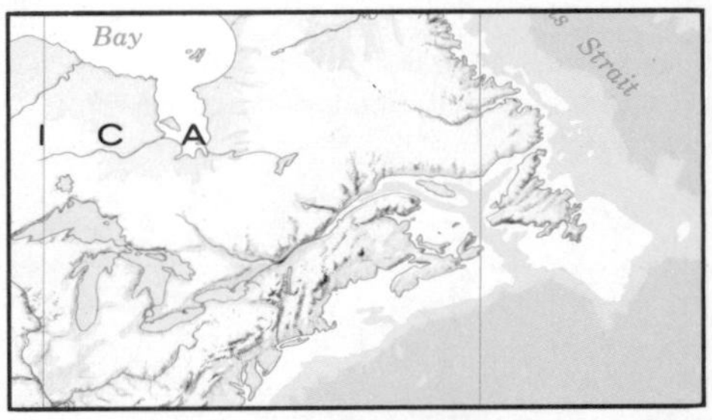

1 in. = 1394 mi. Equatorial Scale 1/88,300,000 1 cm. = 883 km.

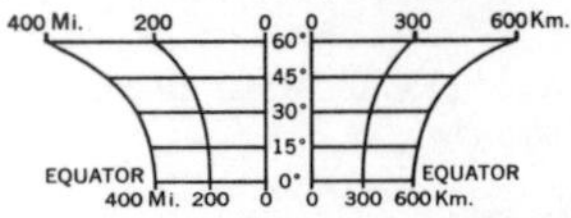

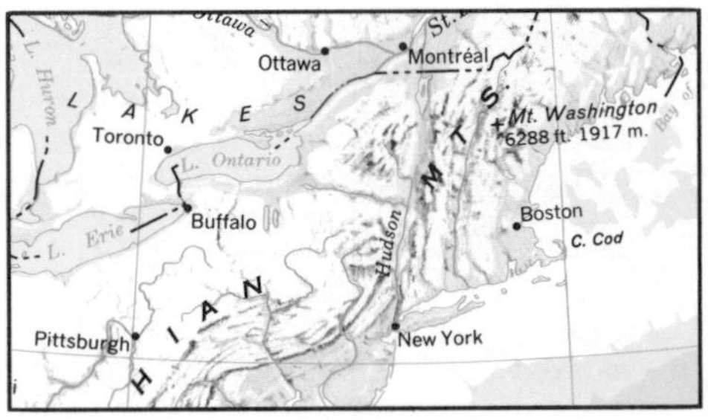

1 in. = 347 mi. 0 100 200
Scale 1/22,000,000
1 cm. = 220 km. 0 200 400

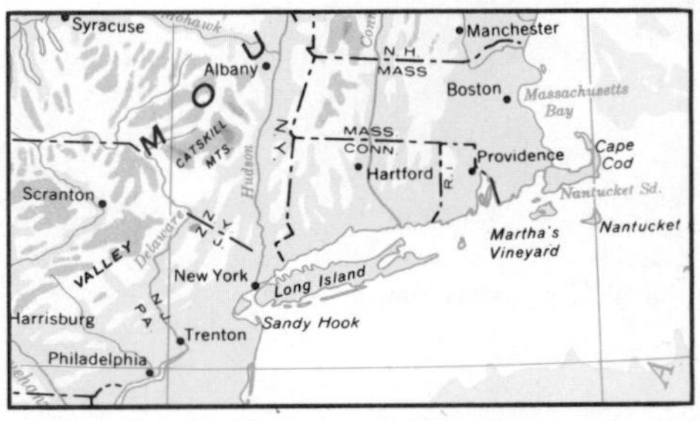

1 in. = 174 mi. 0 50 100
Scale 1/11,000,000
1 cm. = 110 km. 0 100 200

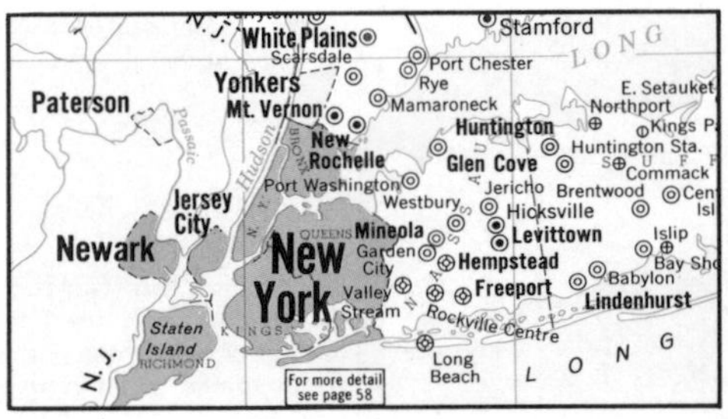

For more detail see page 58

1 in. = 28.9 mi. 0 10 20
Scale 1/1,830,000
1 cm. = 18.3 km. 0 10 20 30

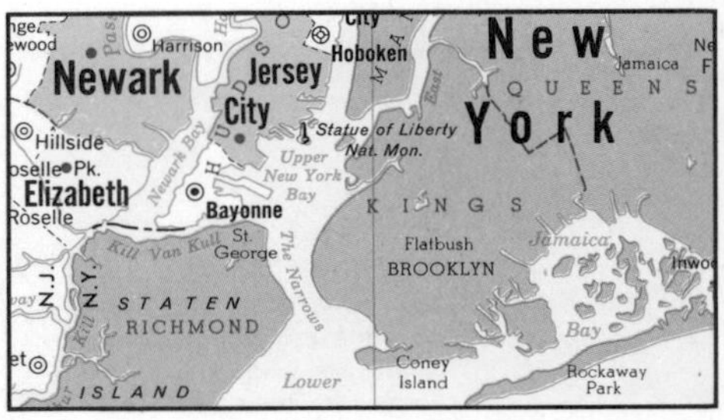

1 in. = 10.5 mi. 0 5
Scale 1/663,000
1 cm. = 6.6 km. 0 5 10

INTRODUCTION

At a time when the United States is increasingly involved with nations all over the world, when transportation and communication have been improved to a degree unimaginable only half a century ago, when an understanding of events at home and abroad is so vital to an intelligent appraisal of human relations at all levels, it becomes increasingly evident that the knowledge of "where places are" is fundamental. Just as we must have knowledge of words in order to speak, so we must know the location of places in order to begin to understand what is happening in the world. Just as a dictionary is basic in gaining a vocabulary, an atlas is an essential tool for beginning to understand the world in which we live and for acquiring geographic knowledge.

This is primarily a reference atlas, yet one which contains a well-balanced content of maps depicting political, cultural, economic, and physical patterns on the surface of the earth. The atlas represents an original compilation and design of maps created by cartographers of outstanding skill and experience. A new creation meant that there was no hindrance to fresh viewpoints and approaches concerning cartographic techniques and representation. Thus, it was possible to produce an atlas which in many ways is unique.

The basic organization is clear and simple. The 169 map pages are devoted first to a portrayal of world patterns, followed by a coverage of continental areas—North and South America, Europe, the Soviet Union, Asia, and Africa. New Zealand has been treated as part of Oceania, and separate maps have been provided for Australia, the Pacific and the Indian Oceans, the Atlantic Ocean, and the Polar Regions. Except for the World and North America maps the sequence of presentation is always parallel: first a map showing the physical features, then the political regional maps, and finally a series of thematic maps which depict selected patterns of man and his regional setting. The organization of the North America section has been designed so as to permit a more detailed presentation than is the case with other major land areas. Physical and cultural maps of the entire continent have been placed at the beginning of the section, and thematic maps for Canada and the United States at the end of each respective subdivision. Thus, each major division of this atlas is a self-contained unit which incorporates all data that have been provided; yet the sequential arrangement of maps and other illustrations enables the reader to use the atlas not only for quick reference but also for making easy comparisons among the major land areas of the world.

The 107 political maps contain a maximum number of place names without the sacrifice of clarity and legibility. This was accomplished by:

(1) a page size which provides a maximum of space for content; moreover, on political maps only areas of dense settlement were enlarged so as to be able to show the greatest possible number of settled places. By the same token, space was saved generally by not including sparsely settled regions in enlarged presentations;

(2) complete separation of political and relief maps of the same area in order to increase the clarity of each, yet

(3) retention of these maps on the same or adjacent pages in the atlas. Thus, one map does not obscure the other; nevertheless, political and physical information can be correlated rapidly and effectively, so that relationships are readily discernible and clearer than if the maps were superimposed upon each other;

(4) omission of detailed road and railroad information. Such data are subject to rapid change and obsolescence and are more readily available in accurate and up-to-date form from other sources. Of course, it is important to indicate general world-wide patterns of transportation. Hence comparative railroad and road densities are presented on separate thematic maps on page 19;

(5) a careful choice of type sizes and styles based on years of study and experience in legibility and emphasis. In general, the guiding principle has been the maintenance of a total balance in types of size and style, and at the same time the use of a sufficient variety to facilitate recognition of the features which have been portrayed. A larger range of type sizes and a greater boldness of type for important places have been employed than is usually the case in atlases. The style selected for place names throughout the atlas is sans-serif, a style which on maps is more legible and simultaneously more economic of space than other types. Other features are varied in type style in order to give them individuality and to make them easily recognizable. In general, upright styles were selected for states, place names, and other cultural information, while italics were used for physical features.

No attempt has been made to standardize scale, except for groups of thematic maps. Each map has been drawn at a scale which is commensurate with the amount of detail to be shown. Thus, highly populous and otherwise important regions have been enlarged and presented as insets on the same pages where the general map appears. Attention is thereby focused immediately upon the more significant sections of a country, such as the Central Industrial Region or the Central Scottish Lowland of the United Kingdom. This type of presentation takes the place of merely carving up land areas and enlarging all sections equally, regardless of their relative importance.

Portrayal of the physical earth has received special attention. There are 22 pages of full-color shaded relief maps with layer tints, most of them two-page spreads, of the main land areas of the world and of the major ocean floors. Names of physical features on these maps are generally limited to those of continental significance. Major ranges are named but the number of peak names and elevations has been kept to a minimum in order to preserve clarity. Similarly, only the major rivers have been identified and only the names of those cities included which were considered essential for orientation purposes.

In addition, physical maps depicting landform regions and distribution of temperature, precipitation, climate, and vegetation appear on facing pages for each continent and the Soviet Union. These are supplemented by climographs showing average monthly temperatures and precipitation for various types of climate which occur on each continent. Maps showing the distribution of population and of types of agriculture appear in conjunction with these physical maps on the same pages and facilitate correlation of some basic physical and human patterns.

Finally, 57 monochrome relief insets have been placed on political pages, covering the same subject areas. They are graphic, three-dimensional drawings without layer tints.

Thematic maps include a wide range of topical and special subject maps showing world, continental, and major regional distributions of physical and human phenomena. In a world which depends upon the interchange of raw materials and manufactured goods for an increase in the standard of living, it is important to show the nature and location of significant national resources. Moreover, numerous charts and graphs provide information concerning production of various products, country by country, both by quantity and percentage. The index is arranged in one simple alphabetical sequence for the entire world. It has more than 105,000 entries, making the atlas one of the most complete available in terms of place coverage. Population data are given in the index for all places in the United States which appear on maps, in accordance with the 1960 U.S. Census counts. For all other places with more than 1,000 population, the latest figures are given either from census data or from latest reliable estimates. Population totals are included for all other political entities which are shown in the atlas. Physical names in the index are distinguished from political names by the use of italic type.

The need for standardization of place names has been growing rapidly. At the same time the use of native forms of names has become increasingly an internationally accepted policy, as evidenced by the principles set forth by the U.S. Board on Geographic Names and the Permanent Committee on Geographical Names for British Official Use. The spelling of place names in this atlas is based entirely upon these principles. Anglicized versions are cross-referenced in the index and the better-known ones also appear on maps in parentheses. Likewise, names which have changed in time (such as Stalingrad to Volgograd, or Batavia to Djakarta) are listed and cross-referenced in the index.

For quick reference two important aids have been provided; inside the front cover there appears a series of aspects of the globe, which serve as a pictorial table of contents to continental, regional, and country maps. Also, after the Table of Contents there is an alphabetical listing with pagination of major countries, states, provinces, islands, and oceans.

In the compilation of this atlas, the most recent official government maps and documents have been used, including latest census materials and official estimates. Information was also obtained from yearbooks and statistical publications of learned societies and associations, and of business and trade associations.

GUIDO G. WEIGEND
Professor and Chairman, Department of Geography
Rutgers—The State University

LAND HEIGHTS

meters	feet
4000	13123
2000	6562
1000	3281
200	656

land below sea level

sea level

200	656
3000	9843
6000	19685

OCEAN DEPTHS

12A12

General Drafting Co., Inc.

EVIDENCES OF PRECAMBRIAN GLACIATION*
(more than 600,000,000 years ago)

*EXTENT OF GLACIATION INTO OCEANS UNKNOWN   ● = Age doubtful but presumed to be Precambrian

EVIDENCES OF PERMO-CARBONIFEROUS GLACIATION*
(230,000,000 to 345,000,000 years ago)

* GREEN AREAS INDICATE UNCERTAIN EVIDENCE REGARDING OCCURRENCE AND/OR AGE OF GLACIATION

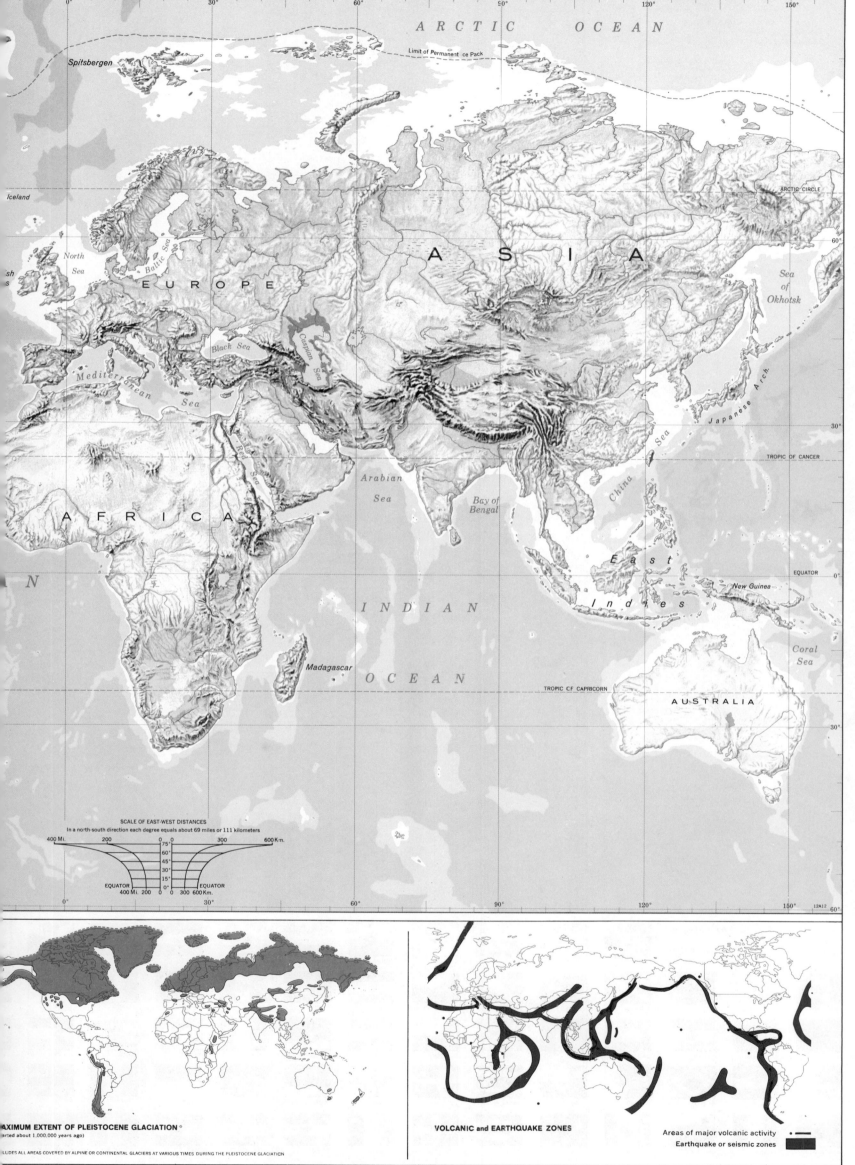

ARCTIC OCEAN

Spitsbergen

Limit of Permanent Ice Pack

Iceland

North
Sea

EUROPE

ASIA

Sea
of
Okhotsk

Baltic Sea

Black Sea

Caspian Sea

Mediterranean
Sea

Japanese Arch.

ARCTIC CIRCLE

Red Sea

TROPIC OF CANCER

AFRICA

Arabian
Sea

Bay of
Bengal

China
Sea

N

EQUATOR

INDIAN

New Guinea

East
Indies

Madagascar

OCEAN

Coral
Sea

TROPIC OF CAPRICORN

AUSTRALIA

SCALE OF EAST-WEST DISTANCES
In a north-south direction each degree equals about 69 miles or 111 kilometers

400 Mi.   200   300   600 K.m.
                        75°
                        60°
                        45°
                        30°
                        15°
           EQUATOR   0°   EQUATOR
           400 Mi. 200   0 0 300 600 K.m.

12A12

MAXIMUM EXTENT OF PLEISTOCENE GLACIATION
(started about 1,000,000 years ago)

INCLUDES ALL AREAS COVERED BY ALPINE OR CONTINENTAL GLACIERS AT VARIOUS TIMES DURING THE PLEISTOCENE GLACIATION

VOLCANIC and EARTHQUAKE ZONES

Areas of major volcanic activity

Earthquake or seismic zones

Equatorial scale 1/88,300,000   Miller Cylindrical Projection

General Drafting Co., Inc.

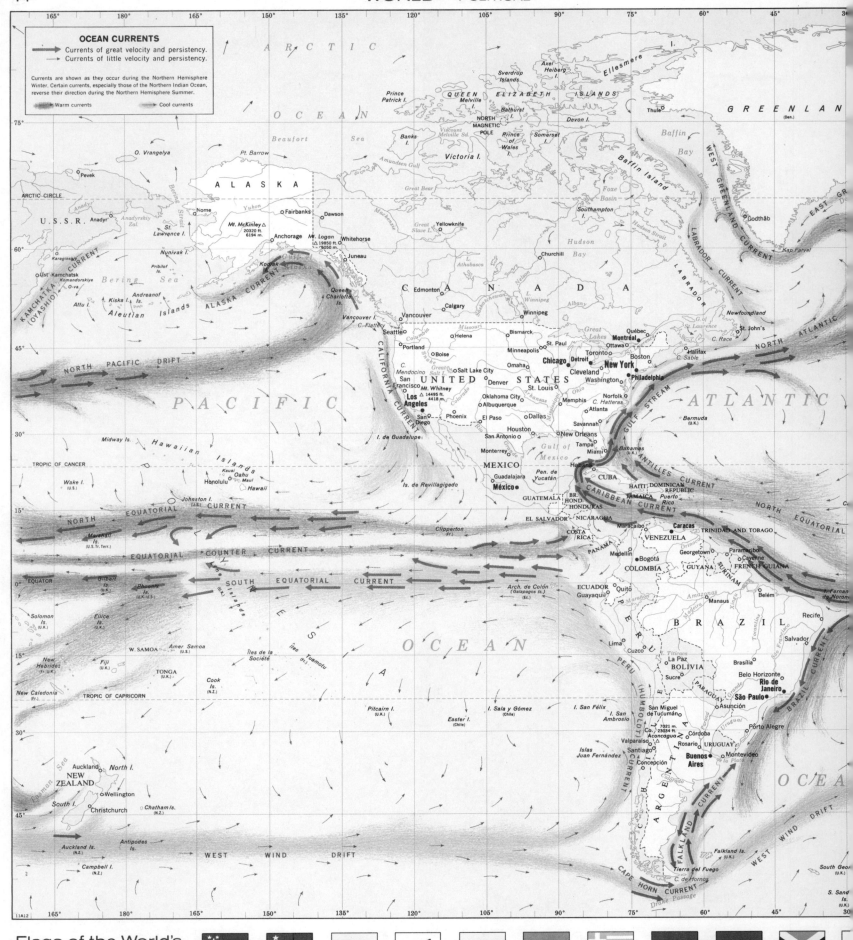

General Drafting Co., Inc.

Flags of the World's Sovereign Nations

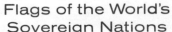
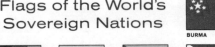

BURMA   CENTRAL AFRICAN REP.   COLOMBIA   CYPRUS   ECUADOR   GABON   GREECE   HUNGARY   IRAQ   JAMAICA   KO

AFGHANISTAN   ARGENTINA   BHUTAN   BURUNDI   CEYLON   CONGO   CZECHOSLOVAKIA   EL SALVADOR   GAMBIA   GUATEMALA   ICELAND   IRELAND   JAPAN   KU

ALBANIA   AUSTRALIA   BOLIVIA   CAMBODIA   CHAD   CONGO, D.R.   DAHOMEY   ETHIOPIA   GERMANY (EAST)   GUINEA   INDIA   ISRAEL   JORDAN   LA

ALGERIA   AUSTRIA   BRAZIL   CAMEROON   CHILE   COSTA RICA   DENMARK   FINLAND   GERMANY (WEST)   HAITI   INDONESIA   ITALY   KENYA   LE

ANDORRA   BELGIUM   BULGARIA   CANADA   CHINA   CUBA   DOMINICAN REP.   FRANCE   GHANA   HONDURAS   IRAN   IVORY COAST   KOREA (NORTH)   LIB

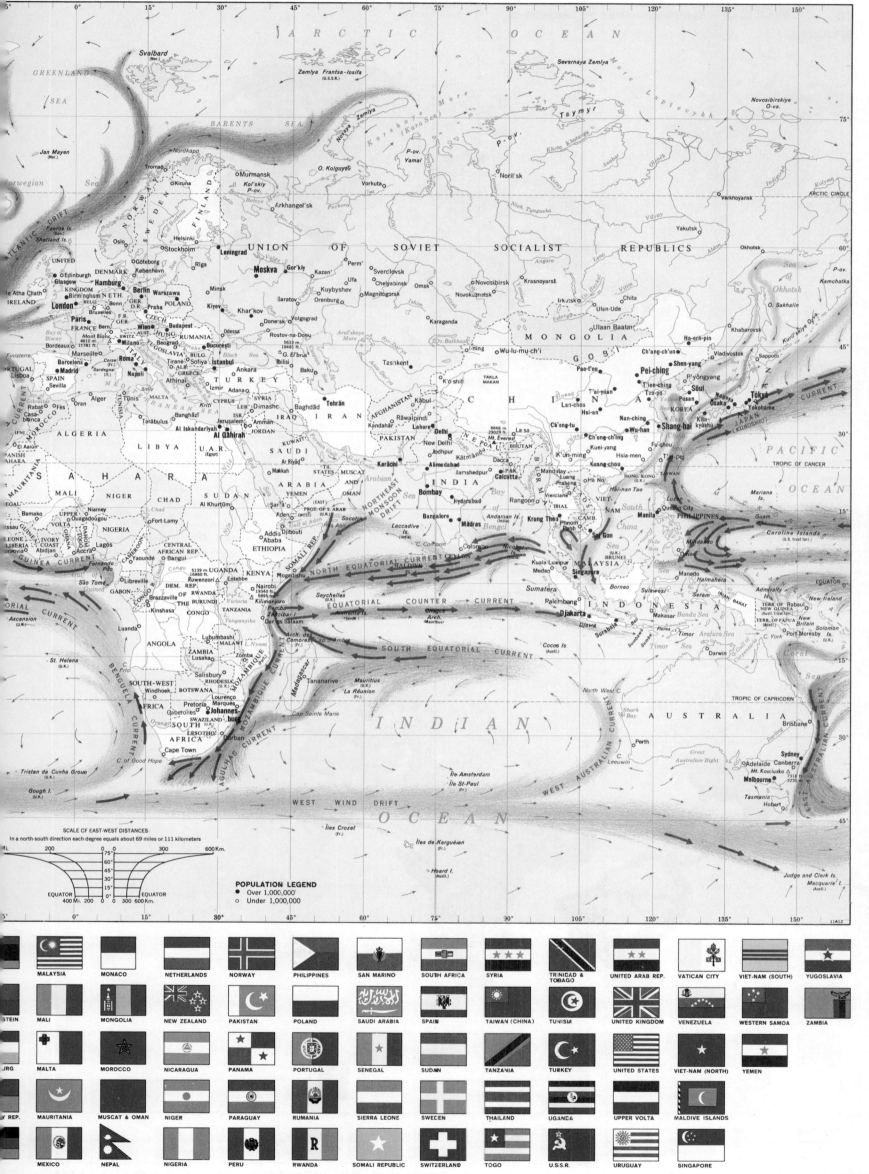

RELIGIONS

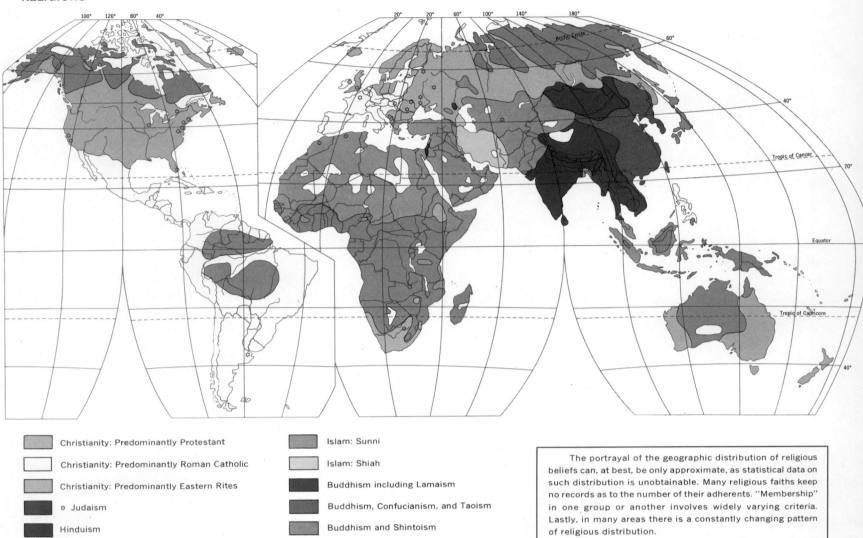

	Christianity: Predominantly Protestant		Islam: Sunni
	Christianity: Predominantly Roman Catholic		Islam: Shiah
	Christianity: Predominantly Eastern Rites		Buddhism including Lamaism
✿	Judaism		Buddhism, Confucianism, and Taoism
	Hinduism		Buddhism and Shintoism
	Unpopulated areas		Primitive religions

The portrayal of the geographic distribution of religious beliefs can, at best, be only approximate, as statistical data on such distribution is unobtainable. Many religious faiths keep no records as to the number of their adherents. "Membership" in one group or another involves widely varying criteria. Lastly, in many areas there is a constantly changing pattern of religious distribution.

RACES OF THE THE WORLD

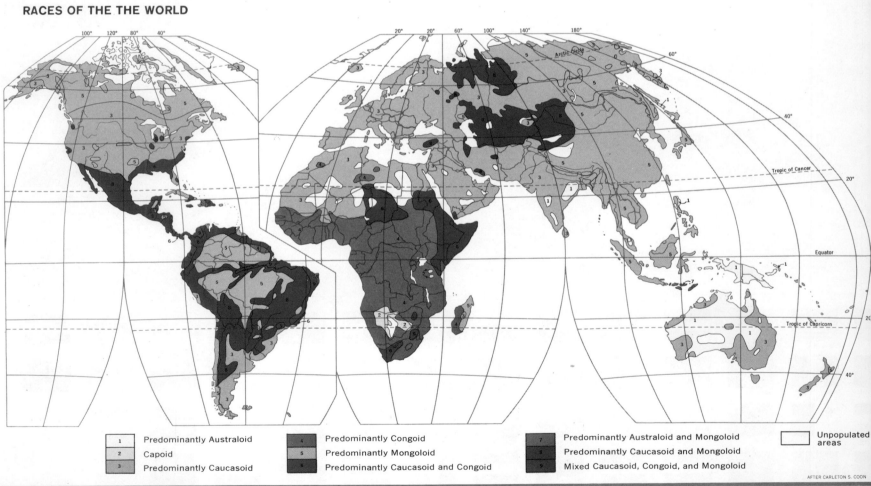

1	Predominantly Australoid	4	Predominantly Congoid	7	Predominantly Australoid and Mongoloid		Unpopulated areas
2	Capoid	5	Predominantly Mongoloid	8	Predominantly Caucasoid and Mongoloid		
3	Predominantly Caucasoid	6	Predominantly Caucasoid and Congoid	9	Mixed Caucasoid, Congoid, and Mongoloid		

AFTER CARLETON S. COON

PERCENTAGE OF WORLD RACES

PREDOMINANTLY CAUCASOID 55.2%	PREDOMINANTLY MONGOLOID 36.6%	PREDOMINANTLY CONGOID 6.6		

MIXED AND OTHERS 1.2%
INCLUDES .003% CAPOID
AUSTALOID 0.4

General Drafting Co., Inc.   1/143,000,000   Adapted from Aitoff's Interrupted Equal Area Projection

LANGUAGES

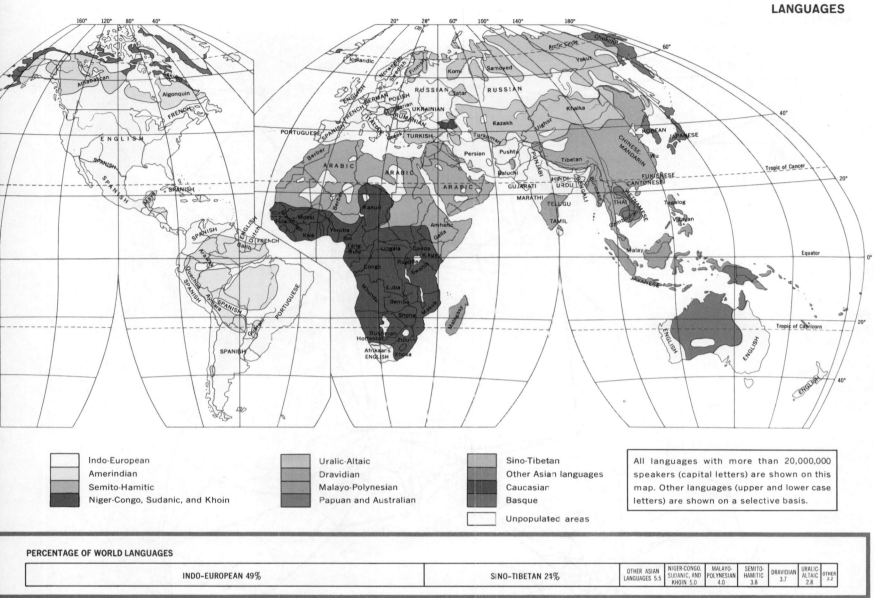

Indo-European	Uralic-Altaic	Sino-Tibetan
Amerindian	Dravidian	Other Asian languages
Semito-Hamitic	Malayo-Polynesian	Caucasian
Niger-Congo, Sudanic, and Khoin	Papuan and Australian	Basque
		Unpopulated areas

All languages with more than 20,000,000 speakers (capital letters) are shown on this map. Other languages (upper and lower case letters) are shown on a selective basis.

PERCENTAGE OF WORLD LANGUAGES

INDO-EUROPEAN 49%	SINO-TIBETAN 24%	OTHER ASIAN LANGUAGES 5.5	NIGER-CONGO, SUDANIC, AND KHOIN 5.0	MALAYO-POLYNESIAN 4.0	SEMITO-HAMITIC 3.8	DRAVIDIAN 3.7	URALIC ALTAIC 2.8	OTHER 2.2

POPULATION

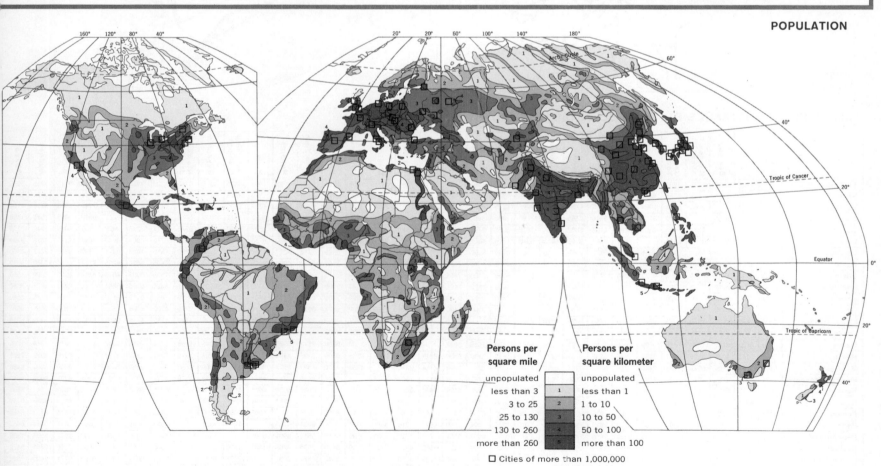

Persons per square mile	Persons per square kilometer
unpopulated	unpopulated
less than 3	less than 1
3 to 25	1 to 10
25 to 130	10 to 50
130 to 260	50 to 100
more than 260	more than 100

☐ Cities of more than 1,000,000

PERCENTAGE OF WORLD POPULATION (Total 1963 estimate — 3.2 billion)

													OCEANIA 0.5
CONTINENTS	ASIA* 56.3%					EUROPE* 13.8%		AMERICAS 13.8%		AFRICA 8.6%			
COUNTRIES	China 22.6%	India 14.3%	Indonesia 3.1	Pakistan 3.1	Japan 3.0	OTHER 10.2	F.R. GER. 1.7	U.K. 1.7	Italy 1.6	OTHER 8.8	U.S. 6.0%	Brazil 2.4	OTHER 5.4	U.S.S.R. 7.0%

*Excluding U.S.S.R.

General Drafting Co., Inc.

SHIPPING and AIR ROUTES

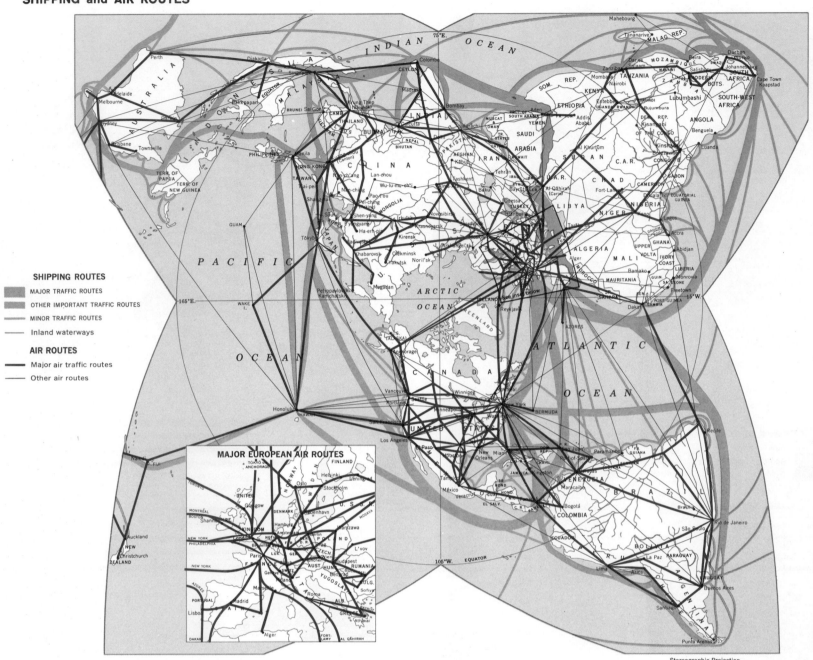

Stereographic Projection

GREAT CIRCLE DISTANCES BETWEEN SELECTED WORLD CENTERS (STATUTE MILES)

	Al Qāhirah (Cairo)	Berlin	Bombay	Buenos Aires	Cape Town	Caracas	Chicago	Dakar	Guam	Honolulu	İstanbul	Lima	Lisboa (Lisbon)	London	Manila	México	Montréal	Moskva (Moscow)	Nairobi	New York	Panamá	Paris	Pei-ching (Peking)	Reykjavík	Rio de Janeiro	Roma	San Francisco	Santiago	Seattle	Singapore	Sydney	Tōkyō
Al Qāhirah (Cairo)		1795	2698	7338	4500	6338	6130	3260	7083	8840	765	7650	2363	2175	5710	7688	5414	1805	2206	5600	7128	1995	4675	3270	6146	1325	7450	6970	6823	5137	8965	5950
Berlin	1795		3904	7411	5985	5247	4410	3115	7042	7305	1080	6800	1435	577	6130	6047	3725	1000	3975	3965	5902	540	4595	1480	6220	738	5655	7782	5045	6165	10000	5540
Bombay	2698	3904		9263	5115	9024	8056	5910	4758	8012	2992	10375	4981	4468	3191	9731	7509	3131	2819	7794	9832	4359	2965	5197	8335	3840	8394	9980	7744	2425	6316	4188
Buenos Aires	7338	7411	9263		4270	3168	5600	4340	10368	7549	7630	1950	5956	6919	11097	4595	5615	8375	6473	5300	3319	6891	11975	7098	1220	6924	6487	731	6915	9868	7335	11408
Cape Town	4500	5985	5115	4270		6365	8494	4105		11534	5220	6065	5325	6010	7486	8517	7931	6300	2548	7764	7025	5807	8050	7113	3770	5247	10247	4929	10209	6005	6840	9155
Caracas	6338	5247	9024	3168	6365		2501	3344	9725	6013	6048	1710	4041	4660	10620	2232	2449	6173	7200	2132	850	4736	8950	4285	2810	5270	3904	3045	4093	11375	9513	8799
Chicago	6130	4410	8056	5600	8494	2501		4530	7366	4245	5485	3785	3990	3960	8066	1685	752	4980	8025	713	2320	4140	6585	2950	5300	4815	1858	5311	1737	9371	9272	6300
Dakar	3260	3115	5910	4340	4105	3344	4530		10150	8780	3315	4475	1740	2720	8951	5358	3872	4050	3900	3810	4225	2615	7650	2950	3130	2625	6390	4830	6140	8275	10930	8650
Guam	7083	7042	4758	10368		9725	7366	10150		3801	6881	9650	8425	7454	1595	7533	7711	6100	7475	7958	9023	7549	2400	7025	11710	7549	5804	9818	5668	2923	3299	1564
Honolulu	8840	7305	8012	7549	11534	6013	4245	8780	3801		8109	5900	7820	7228	5300	3779	4910	7035	10700	4960	5246	7438	5069	7025	8285	8021	2395	6861	2678	6709	5073	3850
İstanbul	765	1080	2992	7630	5220	6048	5485	3315	6881	8109		7450	2012	1550	5664	7110	4790	1090	2965	5009	6750	1401	4381	2552	6389	855	6705	8143	6070	5375	9285	5560
Lima	7650	6800	10375	1950	6065	1710	3785	4475	9650	5900	7450		5600	6320	11100	2645	3980	7800	7825	3650	1490	6372	10350	5900	2345	6700	4400	1530	4965	11650	7955	9630
Lisboa (Lisbon)	2363	1435	4981	5956	5325	4041	3990	1740	8425	7820	2012	5600		985	7546	5390	3246	2427	4025	3364	4780	904	6007	1835	4796	1150	5666	6366	5197	7385	11302	6915
London	2175	577	4468	6919	6010	4660	3960	2720	7454	7228	1550	6320	985		6672	5550	3245	1550	4429	3465	5310	210	5051	1170	5766	896	5355	7252	4790	6745	10555	5940
Manila	5710	6130	3191	11097	7486	10620	8066	8951	1595	5300	5664	11100	7546	6672		8835	8186	5130	5850	8510	10283	5716	1771	6648	11259	6454	6965	10943	6641	1479	3944	1865
México	7688	6047	9731	4595	8517	2232	1685	5358	7533	3779	7110	2645	5390	5550	8835		2315	6663	9200	2090	1494	5716	6351	4621	4770	6454	1887	4197	2335	10318	8052	7021
Montréal	5414	3725	7509	5615	7931	2449	752	3872	7711	4910	4790	3980	3246	3245	8186	2315		4385	7300	330	2525	3420	6525	2400	5095	4070	2539	5456	2318	9200	9954	6455
Moskva (Moscow)	1805	1000	3131	8375	6300	6173	4980	4050	6100	7035	1090	7800	2427	1550	5130	6663	4385		3945	4665	6711	1544	3595	2050	7175	1471	5870	8781	5205	5235	9005	4650
Nairobi	2206	3975	2819	6473	2548	7200	8025	3900	7475	10700	2965	7825	4025	4429	5850	9200	7300	3945		7643	8050	4025	5718	5552	5552	4050	9602	7200	9000	4630	7542	6991
New York	5600	3965	7794	5300	7764	2132	713	3810	7958	4960	5009	3650	3364	3465	8510	2090	330	4665	7643		2211	3634	6841	2599	4820	4279	2571	5122	2408	9530	9933	6740
Panamá	7128	5902	9832	3319	7025	850	2320	4225	9023	5246	6750	1490	4780	5310	10283	1494	2525	6711	8050	2211		5397	8901	4700	3087	5903	3325	3000	3648	11675	8758	8429
Paris	1995	540	4359	6891	5807	4736	4140	2615	7549	7438	1401	6372	904	210	5716	5716	3420	1544	4025	3634	5397		5100	1391	5699	683	5577	7239	5000	6671	10544	6032
Pei-ching (Peking)	4675	4595	2965	11975	8050	8950	6585	7650	2400	5069	4381	10350	6007	5051	1771	6351	6525	3595	5718	6841	8901	5100		4900	10771	5050	5904	11850	5397	2777	5550	1309
Reykjavík	3270	1480	5197	7098	7113	4285	2950	3425	7025	7025	2552	5900	1835	1170	6648	4621	2400	2050	5552	2599	4700	1391	4900		5681	2045	4200	7250	3620	7166	10250	5475
Rio de Janeiro	6146	6220	8335	1220	3770	2810	5300	3130	11710	8285	6389	2345	4796	5766	11259	4770	5095	7175	5552	4820	3087	5699	10771	5681		5681	6621	1816	6890	9774	8400	11533
Roma	1325	738	3840	6924	5247	5270	4815	2625	7549	8021	855	6700	1150	896	6454	6454	4070	1471	4050	4279	5903	683	5050	2045	5681		6241	7391	5656	6231	10000	6120
San Francisco	7450	5655	8394	6487	10247	3904	1858	6390	5804	2395	6705	4400	5666	5355	6965	1887	2539	5870	9602	2571	3325	5577	5904	4200	6621	6241		5937	678	8444	7416	5135
Santiago	6970	7782	9980	731	4929	3045	5311	4830	9818	6861	8143	1530	6366	7252	10943	4197	5456	8781	7200	5122	3000	7239	11850	7250	1816	7391	5937		6445	10189	7046	10705
Seattle	6823	5045	7744	6915	10209	4093	1737	6140	5668	2678	6070	4965	5197	4790	6641	2335	2318	5205	9000	2408	3648	5000	5397	3620	6890	5656	678	6445		8068	8562	4785
Singapore	5137	6165	2425	9868	6005	11375	9371	8275	2923	6709	5375	11650	7385	6745	1479	10318	9200	5235	4630	9530	11675	6671	2777	7166	9774	6231	8444	10189	8068		3915	3305
Sydney	8965	10000	6316	7335	6840	9513	9272	10930	3299	5073	9285	7955	11302	10555	3944	8052	9954	9005	7542	9933	8758	10544	5550	10250	8400	10000	7416	7046	8562	3915		4860
Tōkyō	5950	5540	4188	11408	9155	8799	6300	8650	1564	3850	5560	9630	6915	5940	1865	7021	6455	4650	6991	6740	8429	6032	1309	5475	11533	6120	5135	10705	4785	3305	4860	

General Drafting Co., Inc.

RAILROADS

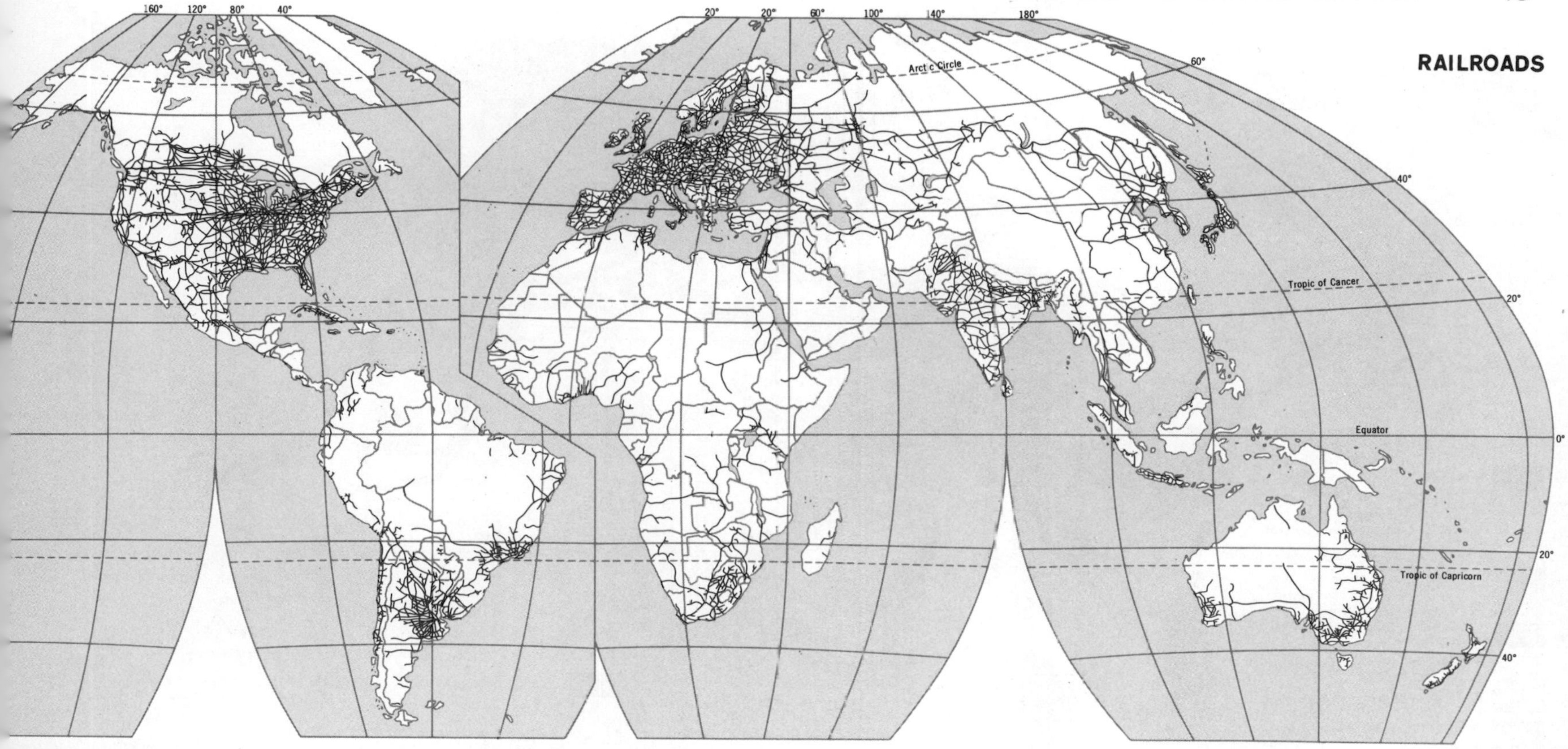

MAJOR RAILROAD CONCENTRATIONS*

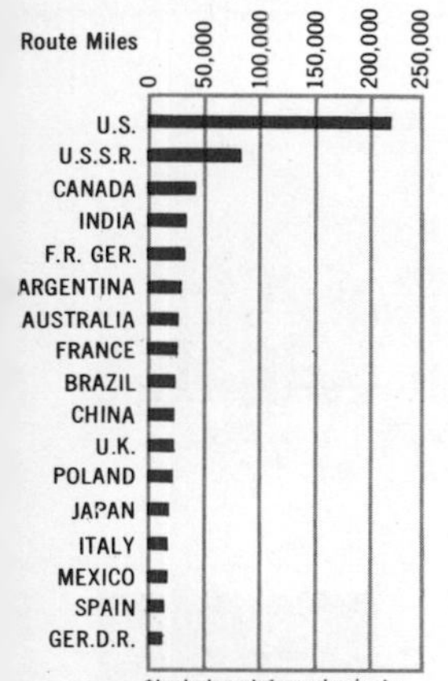

Route Miles — 0, 50,000, 100,000, 150,000, 200,000, 250,000

U.S.
U.S.S.R.
CANADA
INDIA
F.R. GER.
ARGENTINA
AUSTRALIA
FRANCE
BRAZIL
CHINA
U.K.
POLAND
JAPAN
ITALY
MEXICO
SPAIN
GER.D.R.

*Includes state and private
railroads of all gauges.

PRINCIPAL ROADS FOR SELECTED COUNTRIES*

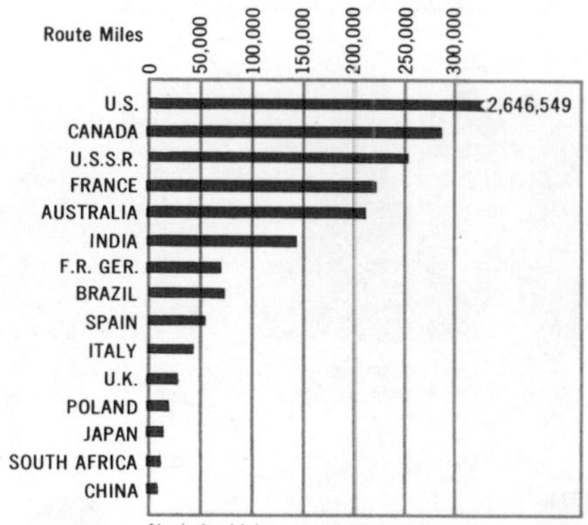

Route Miles — 0, 50,000, 100,000, 150,000, 200,000, 250,000, 300,000

U.S. 2,646,549
CANADA
U.S.S.R.
FRANCE
AUSTRALIA
INDIA
F.R. GER.
BRAZIL
SPAIN
ITALY
U.K.
POLAND
JAPAN
SOUTH AFRICA
CHINA

*Includes highways and other main roads.

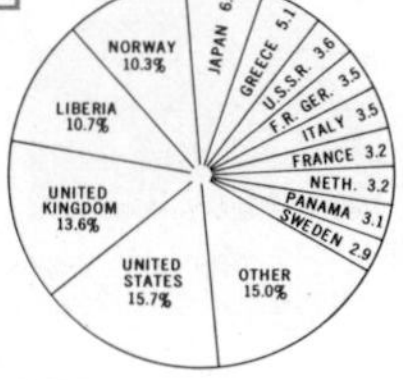

LEADING MERCHANT FLEETS*
(Percentage of deadweight tonnage)

1963 — 194,274,000 deadweight tons

*Includes oceangoing steam and motorships
of more than 1000 gross tons (including tankers).
Excludes ships operating exclusively on the
Great Lakes and inland waterways.

NORWAY 10.3%
LIBERIA 10.7%
UNITED KINGDOM 13.6%
UNITED STATES 15.7%
OTHER 15.0%
JAPAN 6.6
GREECE 5.7
U.S.S.R. 3.8
F.R. GER. 3.5
ITALY 3.5
FRANCE 3.2
NETH. 3.2
SWEDEN 2.8
PANAMA 3.1

AVERAGE POPULATION PER PASSENGER CAR

Countries having over 250,000 passenger cars in use.

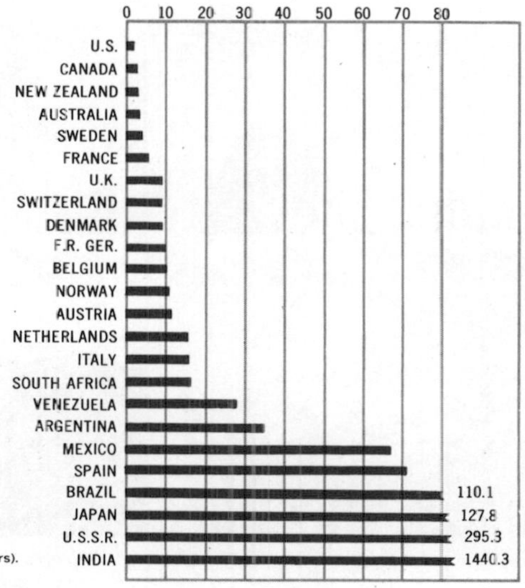

0, 10, 20, 30, 40, 50, 60, 70, 80

U.S.
CANADA
NEW ZEALAND
AUSTRALIA
SWEDEN
FRANCE
U.K.
SWITZERLAND
DENMARK
F.R. GER.
BELGIUM
NORWAY
AUSTRIA
NETHERLANDS
ITALY
SOUTH AFRICA
VENEZUELA
ARGENTINA
MEXICO
SPAIN
BRAZIL 110.1
JAPAN 127.8
U.S.S.R. 295.3
INDIA 1440.3

CARGO SHIPPING BY RAILROAD

In millions of short ton miles

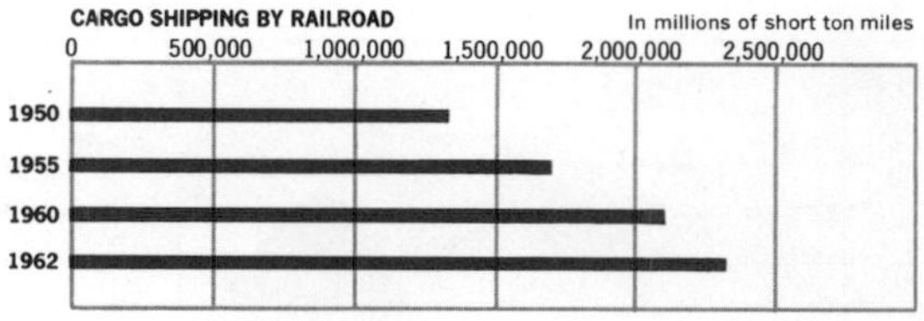

0, 500,000, 1,000,000, 1,500,000, 2,000,000, 2,500,000

1950
1955
1960
1962

INTERNATIONAL SEA-BORNE SHIPPING*

In millions of short tons loaded

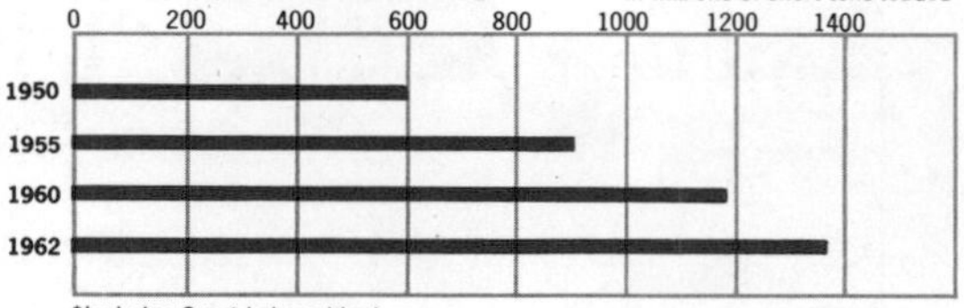

0, 200, 400, 600, 800, 1000, 1200, 1400

1950
1955
1960
1962

*Includes Great Lakes shipping.

CIVIL AIR FREIGHT AND MAIL TRAFFIC

In thousands of short ton miles

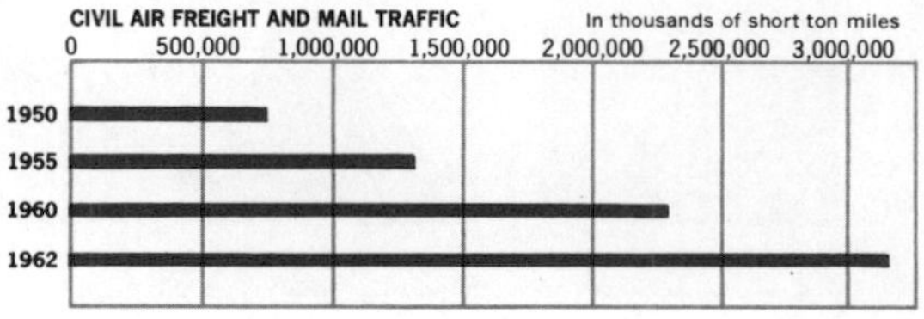

0, 500,000, 1,000,000, 1,500,000, 2,000,000, 2,500,000, 3,000,000

1950
1955
1960
1962

PRINCIPAL ROADS*

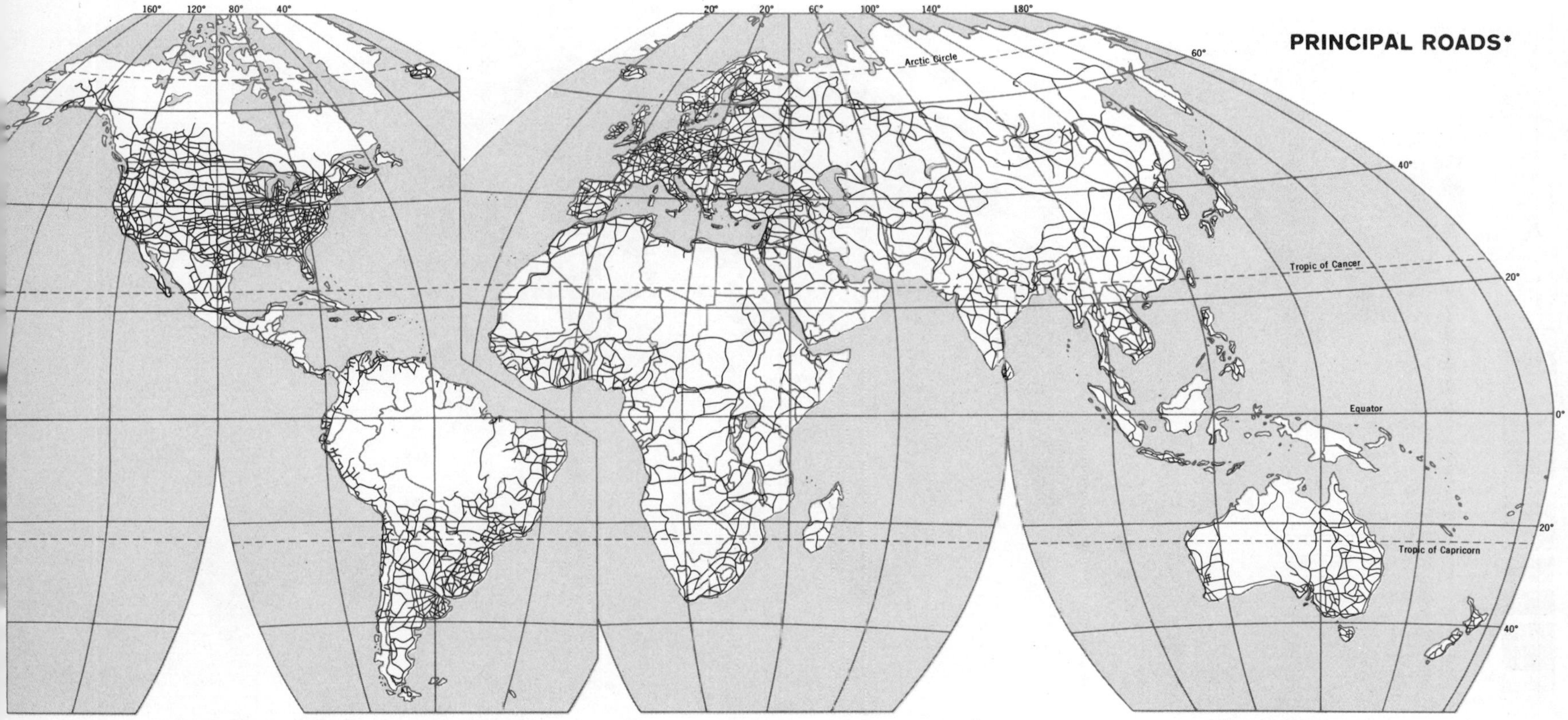

*In U.S., Canada, Western and Central Europe, and Southeastern Australia only
selected highways and other main roads are shown because of small scale.

Adapted from Aitoff's Interrupted Equal Area Projection   1/143,000,000   General Drafting Co., Inc.

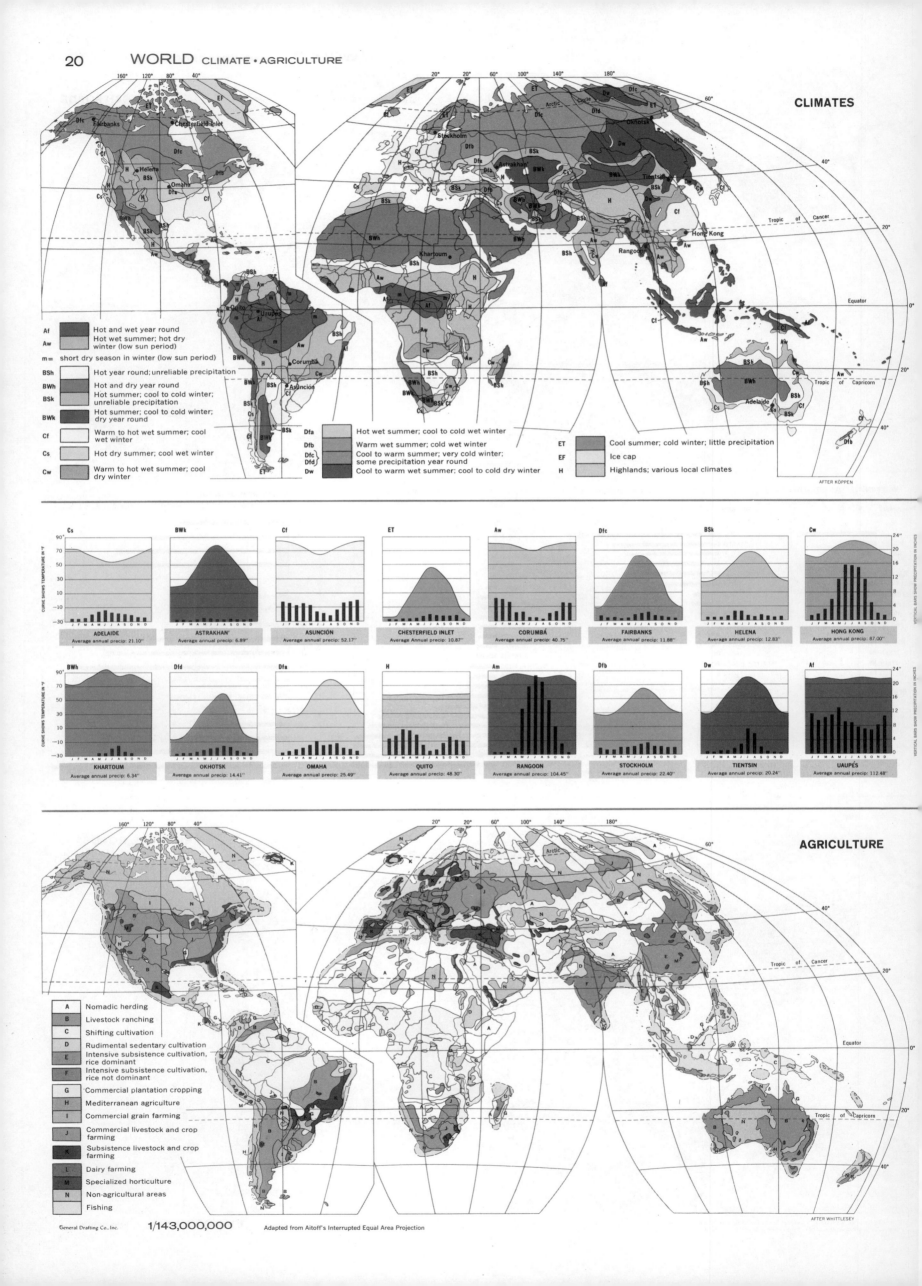

CLIMATES

Af — Hot and wet year round
Aw — Hot wet summer; hot dry winter (low sun period)
m = short dry season in winter (low sun period)
BSh — Hot year round; unreliable precipitation
BWh — Hot and dry year round
BSk — Hot summer; cool to cold winter; unreliable precipitation
BWk — Hot summer; cool to cold winter; dry year round
Cf — Warm to hot wet summer; cool wet winter
Cs — Hot dry summer; cool wet winter
Cw — Warm to hot wet summer; cool dry winter

Dfa — Hot wet summer; cool to cold wet winter
Dfb — Warm wet summer; cold wet winter
Dfc / Dfd — Cool to warm summer; very cold winter; some precipitation year round
Dw — Cool to warm wet summer; cool to cold dry winter

ET — Cool summer; cold winter; little precipitation
EF — Ice cap
H — Highlands; various local climates

AFTER KÖPPEN

CURVE SHOWS TEMPERATURE IN °F — VERTICAL BARS SHOW PRECIPITATION IN INCHES

Cs	BWk	Cf	ET	Aw	Dfc	BSk	Cw
ADELAIDE	ASTRAKHAN'	ASUNCIÓN	CHESTERFIELD INLET	CORUMBÁ	FAIRBANKS	HELENA	HONG KONG
Average annual precip: 21.10"	Average annual precip: 6.89"	Average annual precip: 52.17"	Average Annual precip: 10.87"	Average annual precip: 40.75"	Average annual precip: 11.88"	Average annual precip: 12.83"	Average annual precip: 87.00"

BWh	Dfd	Dfa	H	Am	Dfb	Dw	Af
KHARTOUM	OKHOTSK	OMAHA	QUITO	RANGOON	STOCKHOLM	TIENTSIN	UAUPÉS
Average annual precip: 6.34"	Average annual precip: 14.41"	Average annual precip: 25.49"	Average annual precip: 48.30"	Average annual precip: 104.45"	Average annual precip: 22.40"	Average annual precip: 20.24"	Average annual precip: 112.48"

AGRICULTURE

A — Nomadic herding
B — Livestock ranching
C — Shifting cultivation
D — Rudimental sedentary cultivation
E — Intensive subsistence cultivation, rice dominant
F — Intensive subsistence cultivation, rice not dominant
G — Commercial plantation cropping
H — Mediterranean agriculture
I — Commercial grain farming
J — Commercial livestock and crop farming
K — Subsistence livestock and crop farming
L — Dairy farming
M — Specialized horticulture
N — Non-agricultural areas
— Fishing

AFTER WHITTLESEY

General Drafting Co. Inc.   1/143,000,000   Adapted from Aitoff's Interrupted Equal Area Projection

AVERAGE ANNUAL PRECIPITATION

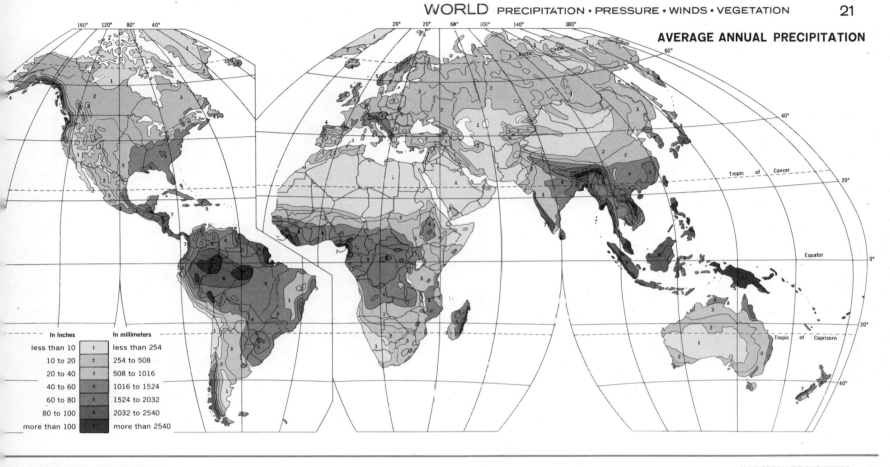

In Inches		In millimeters
less than 10	1	less than 254
10 to 20	2	254 to 508
20 to 40	3	508 to 1016
40 to 60	4	1016 to 1524
60 to 80	5	1524 to 2032
80 to 100	6	2032 to 2540
more than 100	7	more than 2540

JANUARY PRESSURE AND WINDS

JULY PRESSURE AND WINDS

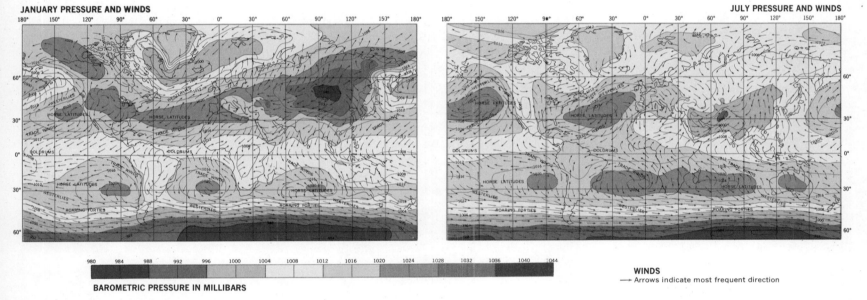

980 984 988 992 996 1000 1004 1008 1012 1016 1020 1024 1028 1032 1036 1040 1044

BAROMETRIC PRESSURE IN MILLIBARS

WINDS
→ Arrows indicate most frequent direction

VEGETATION

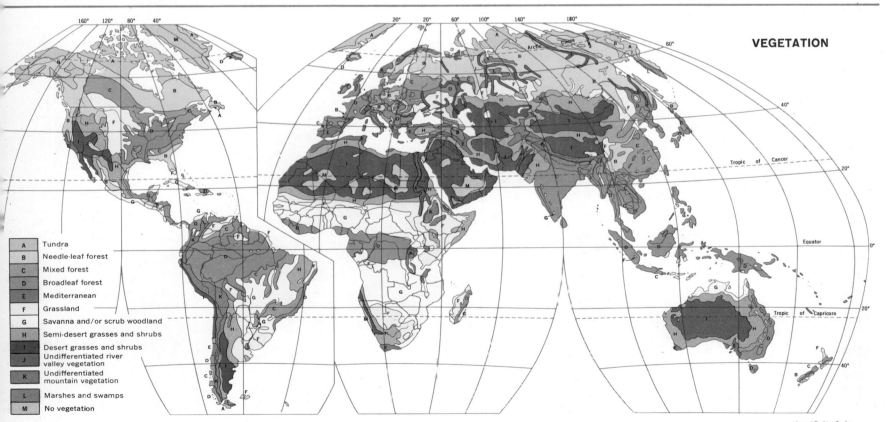

A	Tundra
B	Needle-leaf forest
C	Mixed forest
D	Broadleaf forest
E	Mediterranean
F	Grassland
G	Savanna and/or scrub woodland
H	Semi-desert grasses and shrubs
I	Desert grasses and shrubs
J	Undifferentiated river valley vegetation
K	Undifferentiated mountain vegetation
L	Marshes and swamps
M	No vegetation

General Drafting Co., Inc.

WHEAT and RICE

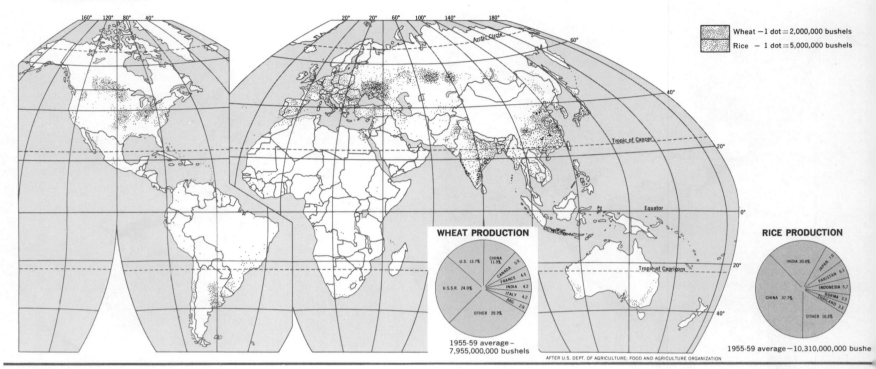

Wheat — 1 dot = 2,000,000 bushels
Rice — 1 dot = 5,000,000 bushels

WHEAT PRODUCTION

U.S. 13.7%
CHINA 11.3%
CANADA 5.9
FRANCE 4.5
INDIA 4.2
ITALY 4.2
U.S.S.R. 24.0%
ARG. 2.9
OTHER 29.3%

1955-59 average—
7,955,000,000 bushels

RICE PRODUCTION

INDIA 20.0%
JAPAN 7.0
PAKISTAN 6.1
INDONESIA 5.7
BURMA 3.9
CHINA 37.7%
THAILAND 3.3
OTHER 16.3%

1955-59 average—10,310,000,000 bushels

AFTER U.S. DEPT. OF AGRICULTURE; FOOD AND AGRICULTURE ORGANIZATION

BARLEY and SOYBEANS

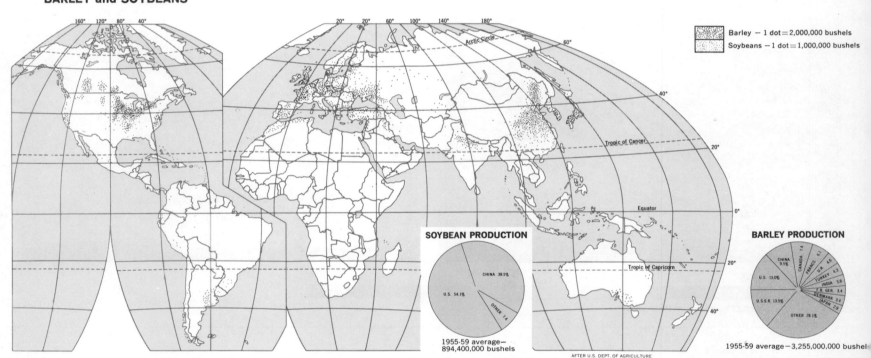

Barley — 1 dot = 2,000,000 bushels
Soybeans — 1 dot = 1,000,000 bushels

SOYBEAN PRODUCTION

CHINA 38.5%
U.S. 54.1%
OTHER 7.4

1955-59 average—
894,400,000 bushels

AFTER U.S. DEPT. OF AGRICULTURE

BARLEY PRODUCTION

CHINA 7.8
CANADA 6.1
FRANCE 4.9
U.K. 4.3
TURKEY 4.1
INDIA 3.9
U.S. 13.0%
W. GER. 3.4
DENMARK 3.4
JAPAN 2.8
U.S.S.R. 13.5%
OTHER 28.1%

1955-59 average—3,255,000,000 bushels

CORN, MILLET, and SORGHUM

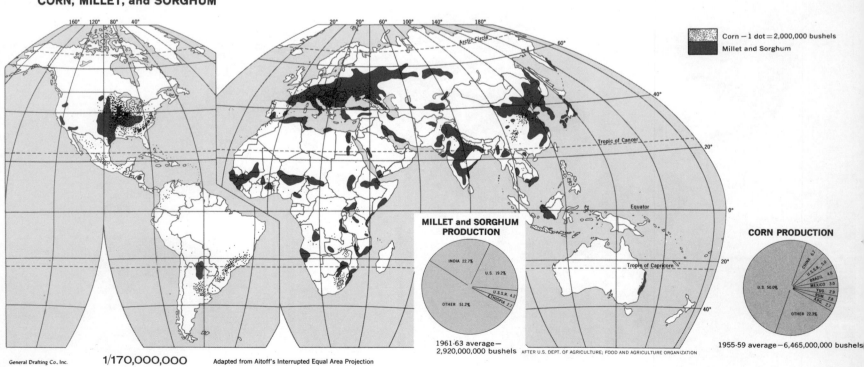

Corn — 1 dot = 2,000,000 bushels
Millet and Sorghum ■

MILLET and SORGHUM PRODUCTION

INDIA 22.7%
U.S. 19.2%
U.S.S.R. 4.2
OTHER 51.2%
ETHIOPIA 2.7

1961-63 average—
2,920,000,000 bushels

CORN PRODUCTION

CHINA 6.7
BRAZIL 5.0
MEXICO 3.0
YUG. 2.9
U.S. 50.0%
S. AFR. 2.8
ARG. 2.7
OTHER 22.9%

1955-59 average—6,465,000,000 bushels

AFTER U.S. DEPT. OF AGRICULTURE; FOOD AND AGRICULTURE ORGANIZATION

General Drafting Co., Inc.   1/170,000,000   Adapted from Aitoff's Interrupted Equal Area Projection

SHEEP

1 dot = 200,000 sheep

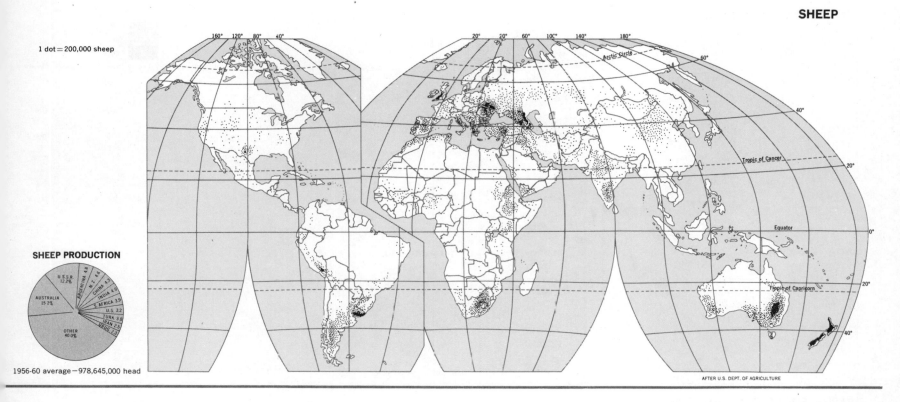

SHEEP PRODUCTION

U.S.S.R. 4.8
N.Z. 6.0
ARGENTINA 4.8
CHINA 6.3
INDIA 4.0
AUSTRALIA 15.2%
S. AFRICA 3.5
U.S. 3.2
TURK. 3.0
IRAN 2.5
URUG. 2.3
OTHER 40.0%

1956-60 average—978,645,000 head

AFTER U.S. DEPT. OF AGRICULTURE

HOGS

1 dot = 200,000 hogs

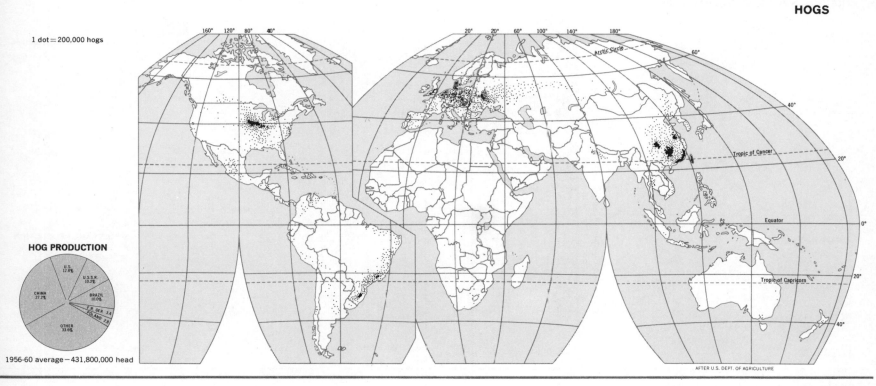

HOG PRODUCTION

U.S. 12.8%
U.S.S.R. 10.2%
CHINA 27.2%
BRAZIL 10.0%
F.R. GER. 3.4
POLAND 2.8
OTHER 33.6%

1956-60 average—431,800,000 head

AFTER U.S. DEPT. OF AGRICULTURE

CATTLE

1 dot = 200,000 cattle

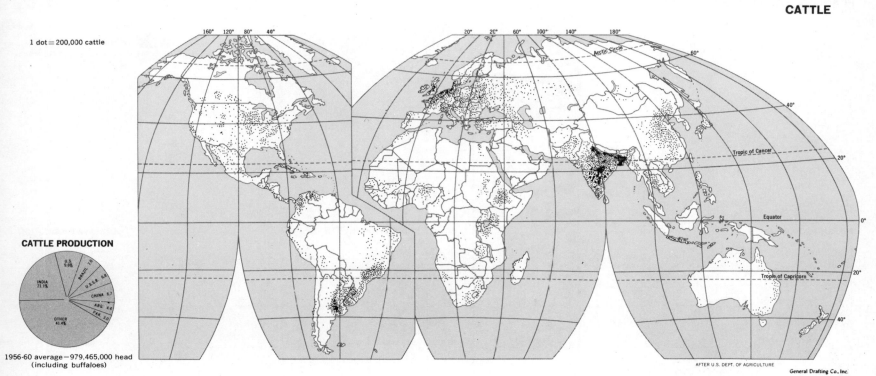

CATTLE PRODUCTION

U.S. 9.6%
BRAZIL 7.0
U.S.S.R. 6.6
INDIA 21.1%
CHINA 6.7
ARG. 4.4
PAK. 3.0
OTHER 41.4%

1956-60 average—979,465,000 head
(including buffaloes)

AFTER U.S. DEPT. OF AGRICULTURE

General Drafting Co., Inc.

COFFEE, TEA, CACAO, and RYE

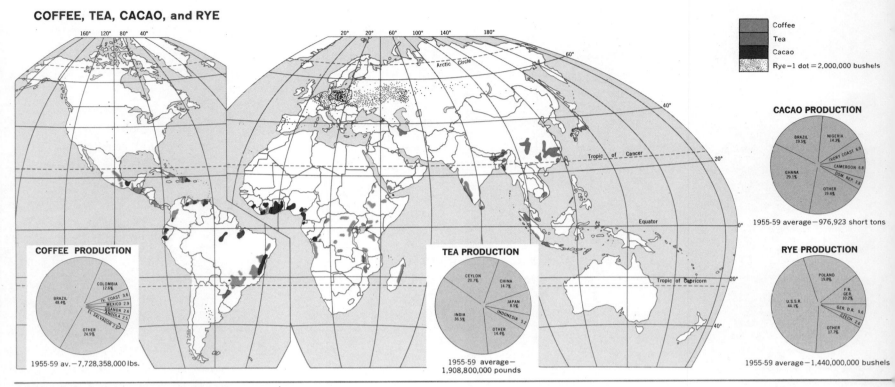

Coffee
Tea
Cacao
Rye—1 dot = 2,000,000 bushels

CACAO PRODUCTION

BRAZIL 19.5%
NIGERIA 14.7%
IVORY COAST 6.9
CAMEROON 6.8
GHANA 29.1%
DOM. REP. 3.6
OTHER 19.4%

1955-59 average—976,923 short tons

COFFEE PRODUCTION

COLOMBIA 12.6%
IV. COAST 3.6
MEXICO 2.9
UGANDA 2.6
BRAZIL 48.4%
ANGOLA 2.5
EL SALVADOR 2.7
OTHER 24.9%

1955-59 av.—7,728,358,000 lbs.

TEA PRODUCTION

CEYLON 20.7%
CHINA 14.7%
JAPAN 8.5%
INDIA 36.5%
INDONESIA 5.2
OTHER 14.4%

1955-59 average—
1,908,800,000 pounds

RYE PRODUCTION

POLAND 19.9%
F.R. GER. 10.7%
U.S.S.R. 44.1%
GER. D.R. 5.6
CZECH. 1.9
OTHER 17.7%

1955-59 average—1,440,000,000 bushels

GRAPES, SUGAR CANE, and SUGAR BEETS

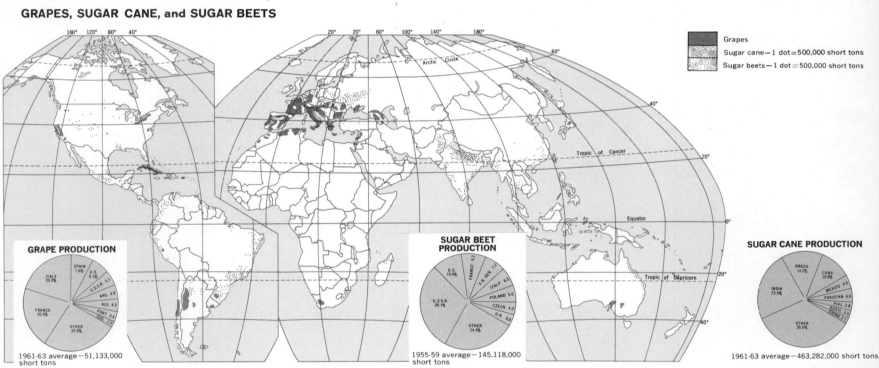

Grapes
Sugar cane—1 dot = 500,000 short tons
Sugar beets—1 dot = 500,000 short tons

GRAPE PRODUCTION

SPAIN 7.6%
U.S. 6.1%
ITALY 20.7%
U.S.S.R. 5.3
ARG. 4.8
ALG. 4.3
FRANCE 20.6%
PORT. 3.4
ROM. 2.0
OTHER 25.6%

1961-63 average—51,133,000
short tons

SUGAR BEET PRODUCTION

FRANCE 8.2
U.S. 10.0%
F.R. GER. 7.2
ITALY 6.1
U.S.S.R. 30.1%
POLAND 5.6
CZECH. 4.3
U.K. 3.9
OTHER 24.4%

1955-59 average—145,118,000
short tons

SUGAR CANE PRODUCTION

BRAZIL 14.7%
CUBA 10.8%
INDIA 23.4%
MEXICO 4.6
PAKISTAN 4.6
PHIL. 2.8
AUSTL. 2.0
OTHER 35.0%
CHINA 2.1

1961-63 average—463,282,000 short tons

PEANUTS, CASSAVA, and POTATOES

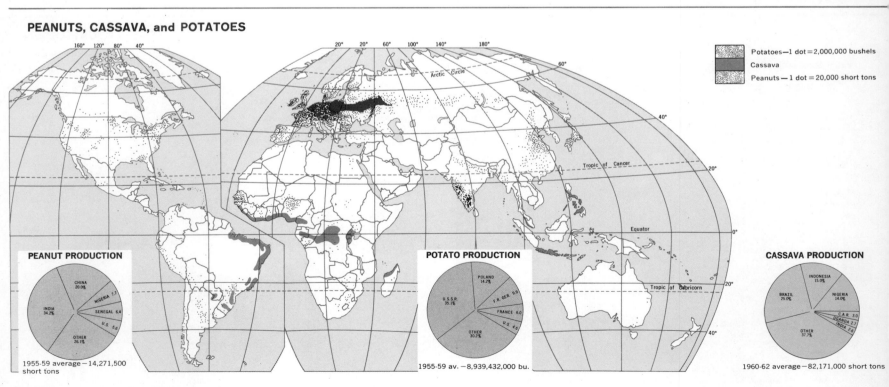

Potatoes—1 dot = 2,000,000 bushels
Cassava
Peanuts—1 dot = 20,000 short tons

PEANUT PRODUCTION

CHINA 20.0%
NIGERIA 7.7
INDIA 34.7%
SENEGAL 6.4
U.S. 5.0
OTHER 26.1%

1955-59 average—14,271,500
short tons

POTATO PRODUCTION

POLAND 14.7%
U.S.S.R. 35.1%
F.R. GER. 9.9
FRANCE 6.0
U.S. 4.6
OTHER 30.2%

1955-59 av.—8,939,432,000 bu.

CASSAVA PRODUCTION

INDONESIA 15.0%
NIGERIA 14.9%
BRAZIL 25.0%
C.A.R. 3.0
UGANDA 4.7
INDIA 2.6
OTHER 37.7%

1960-62 average—82,171,000 short tons

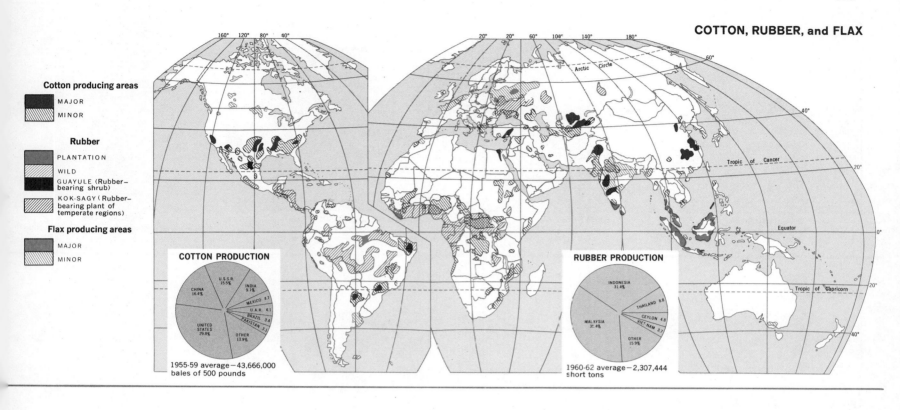

COTTON, RUBBER, and FLAX

Cotton producing areas
- MAJOR
- MINOR

Rubber
- PLANTATION
- WILD
- GUAYULE (Rubber–bearing shrub)
- KOK-SAGY (Rubber–bearing plant of temperate regions)

Flax producing areas
- MAJOR
- MINOR

COTTON PRODUCTION

CHINA 16.4%
U.S.S.R. 15.9%
INDIA 9.1%
MEXICO 8.7
U.A.R. 4.1
BRAZIL 3.4
PAKISTAN 3.1
UNITED STATES 29.8%
OTHER 13.9%

1955-59 average—43,666,000 bales of 500 pounds

RUBBER PRODUCTION

INDONESIA 31.4%
THAILAND 8.8
CEYLON 4.8
VIET-NAM 3.7
MALAYSIA 35.4%
OTHER 15.9%

1960-62 average—2,307,444 short tons

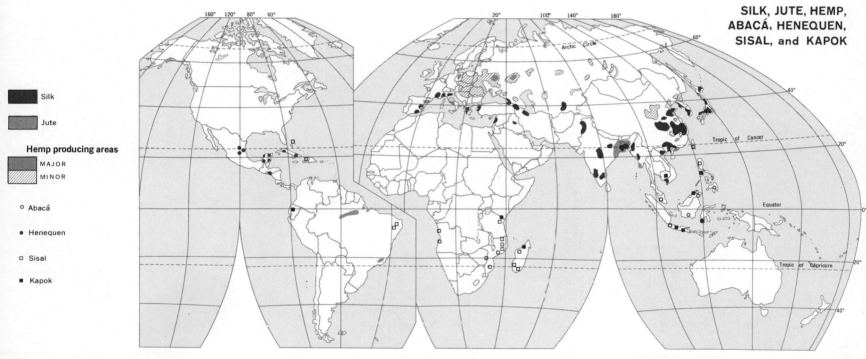

SILK, JUTE, HEMP, ABACÁ, HENEQUEN, SISAL, and KAPOK

- Silk
- Jute

Hemp producing areas
- MAJOR
- MINOR

- ○ Abacá
- ● Henequen
- □ Sisal
- ■ Kapok

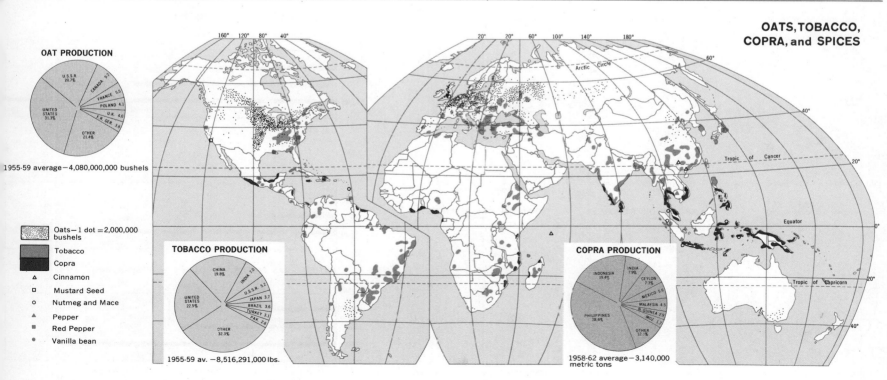

OATS, TOBACCO, COPRA, and SPICES

OAT PRODUCTION

U.S.S.R. 20.7%
CANADA 9.2
FRANCE 5.5
POLAND 4.1
U.K. 4.0
F.R. GER. 3.8
UNITED STATES 31.3%
OTHER 21.4%

1955-59 average—4,080,000,000 bushels

- Oats—1 dot = 2,000,000 bushels
- Tobacco
- Copra
- △ Cinnamon
- □ Mustard Seed
- ○ Nutmeg and Mace
- ▲ Pepper
- ■ Red Pepper
- ● Vanilla bean

TOBACCO PRODUCTION

CHINA 19.8%
INDIA 7.0
U.S.S.R. 5.5
JAPAN 3.7
BRAZIL 3.6
TURKEY 3.1
PAK. 2.8
UNITED STATES 22.5%
OTHER 32.3%

1955-59 av. — 8,516,291,000 lbs.

COPRA PRODUCTION

INDONESIA 19.8%
INDIA 7.9%
CEYLON 7.3%
MEXICO 5.5
MALAYSIA 4.5
N. GUINEA 2.0
MOZ. 1.2
PHILIPPINES 38.6%
OTHER 12.1%

1958-62 average—3,140,000 metric tons

General Drafting Co., Inc.

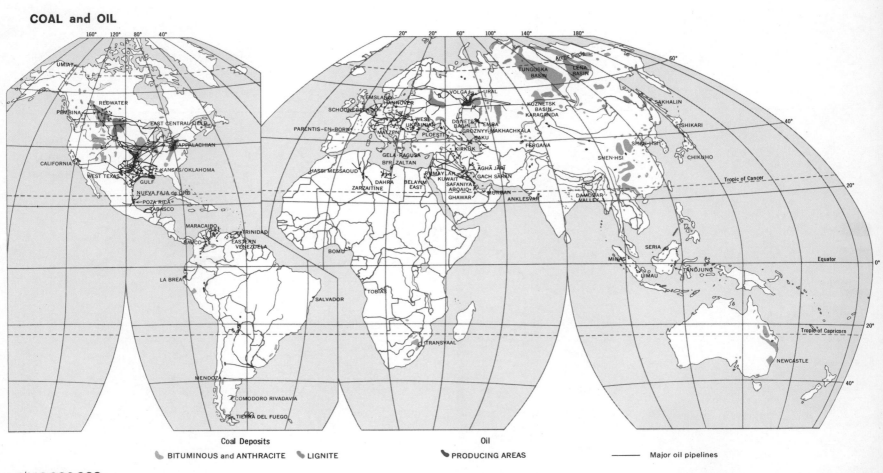

MARACAIBO BASIN
Oil producing areas

MIDDLE EAST
Oil producing areas

MIDLANDS, RUHR, SILESIAN AREAS
Coal deposits
Bituminous and anthracite   Lignite

DONETS BASIN
Coal producing centers   Limits of coal basin

COAL and OIL

Coal Deposits
BITUMINOUS and ANTHRACITE   LIGNITE

Oil
PRODUCING AREAS   Major oil pipelines

1/143,000,000

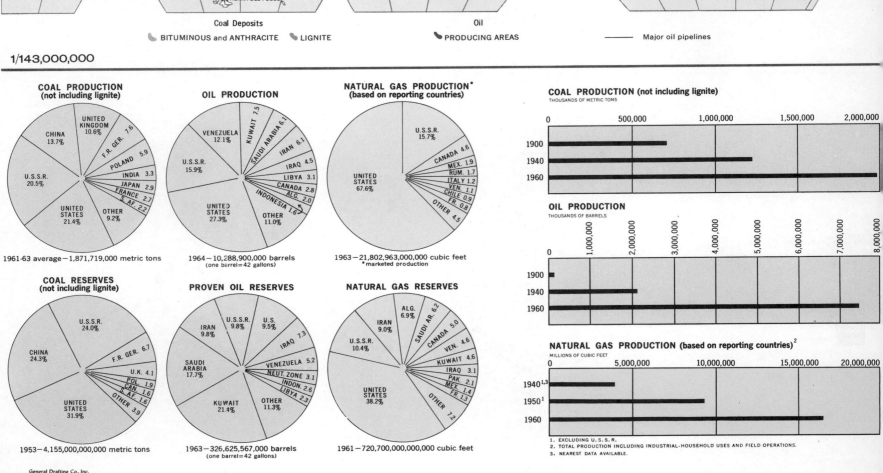

COAL PRODUCTION
(not including lignite)

CHINA 13.7%
UNITED KINGDOM 10.6%
F.R. GER. 7.6
POLAND 5.9
INDIA 3.3
JAPAN 2.9
FRANCE 2.7
S. AF. 2.2
U.S.S.R. 20.5%
UNITED STATES 21.4%
OTHER 9.2%

1961-63 average—1,871,719,000 metric tons

OIL PRODUCTION

KUWAIT 7.5
SAUDI ARABIA 6.1
IRAN 6.1
IRAQ 4.5
LIBYA 3.1
CANADA 2.8
ALG. 2.0
INDONESIA 1.6
VENEZUELA 12.1%
U.S.S.R. 15.9%
UNITED STATES 27.3%
OTHER 11.0%

1964—10,288,900,000 barrels
(one barrel=42 gallons)

NATURAL GAS PRODUCTION*
(based on reporting countries)

U.S.S.R. 15.7%
CANADA 4.6
MEX. 1.9
RUM. 1.7
ITALY 1.2
VEN. 1.1
CHILE 0.9
FR. 0.8
UNITED STATES 67.6%
OTHER 4.5

1963—21,802,963,000,000 cubic feet
*marketed production

COAL RESERVES
(not including lignite)

U.S.S.R. 24.0%
CHINA 24.3%
F.R. GER. 6.7
U.K. 4.1
POL. 1.9
CAN. 1.6
S. AF. 1.6
OTHER 3.9
UNITED STATES 31.9%

1953—4,155,000,000,000 metric tons

PROVEN OIL RESERVES

U.S.S.R. 9.8%
U.S. 9.5%
IRAQ 7.3
VENEZUELA 5.2
NEUT. ZONE 3.1
INDON. 2.6
LIBYA 2.3
IRAN 9.8%
SAUDI ARABIA 17.7%
KUWAIT 21.4%
OTHER 11.3%

1963—326,625,567,000 barrels
(one barrel=42 gallons)

NATURAL GAS RESERVES

ALG. 6.9%
SAUDI AR. 6.2
CANADA 5.0
VEN. 4.6
KUWAIT 4.6
IRAQ 3.1
PAK. 2.1
MEX. 1.4
FR. 1.3
IRAN 9.0%
U.S.S.R. 10.4%
UNITED STATES 38.2%
OTHER 7.2

1961—720,700,000,000,000 cubic feet

COAL PRODUCTION (not including lignite)
THOUSANDS OF METRIC TONS

0   500,000   1,000,000   1,500,000   2,000,000

1900
1940
1960

OIL PRODUCTION
THOUSANDS OF BARRELS

0   1,000,000   2,000,000   3,000,000   4,000,000   5,000,000   6,000,000   7,000,000   8,000,000

1900
1940
1960

NATURAL GAS PRODUCTION (based on reporting countries)[2]
MILLIONS OF CUBIC FEET

0   5,000,000   10,000,000   15,000,000   20,000,000

1940[1,3]
1950[1]
1960

1. EXCLUDING U.S.S.R.
2. TOTAL PRODUCTION INCLUDING INDUSTRIAL-HOUSEHOLD USES AND FIELD OPERATIONS.
3. NEAREST DATA AVAILABLE.

General Drafting Co. Inc.

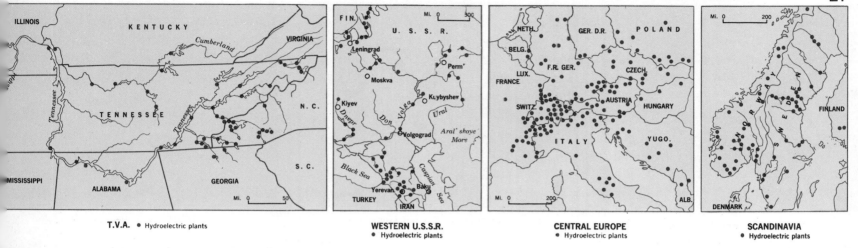

T.V.A.   • Hydroelectric plants

WESTERN U.S.S.R.
• Hydroelectric plants

CENTRAL EUROPE
• Hydroelectric plants

SCANDINAVIA
• Hydroelectric plants

NATURAL GAS, HYDROELECTRIC POWER, and NUCLEAR ENERGY SOURCES

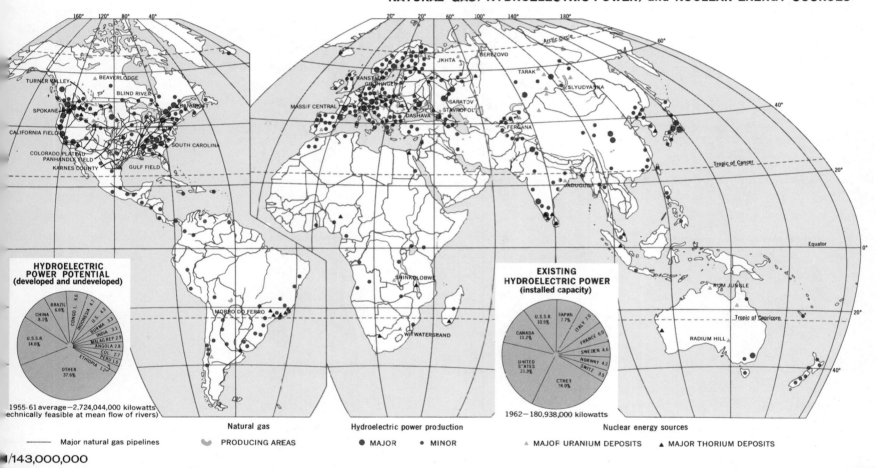

HYDROELECTRIC POWER POTENTIAL
(developed and undeveloped)

CHINA 8.1%
CONGO L. 6.6%
BRAZIL 6.6%
INDONESIA 4.1%
U.S. 4.3
BURMA 3.3
INDIA 3.1
U.S.S.R. 14.6%
MALAG.REP 2.9
ANGOLA 2.8
COL. 2.7
PERU 1.5
ETHIOPIA 1.2
OTHER 37.6%

1955-61 average—2,724,044,000 kilowatts
(technically feasible at mean flow of rivers)

EXISTING HYDROELECTRIC POWER
(installed capacity)

U.S.S.R. 10.5%
JAPAN 7.7%
ITALY 7.0
CANADA 11.2%
FRANCE 6.0
SWEDEN 4.6
NORWAY 4.2
SWITZ. 3.5
UNITED STATES 21.3%
OTHER 24.0%

1962—180,938,000 kilowatts

Natural gas   Hydroelectric power production   Nuclear energy sources

—— Major natural gas pipelines   ⌣ PRODUCING AREAS   ● MAJOR   • MINOR   ▲ MAJOR URANIUM DEPOSITS   ▲ MAJOR THORIUM DEPOSITS

1/143,000,000

NUCLEAR POWER

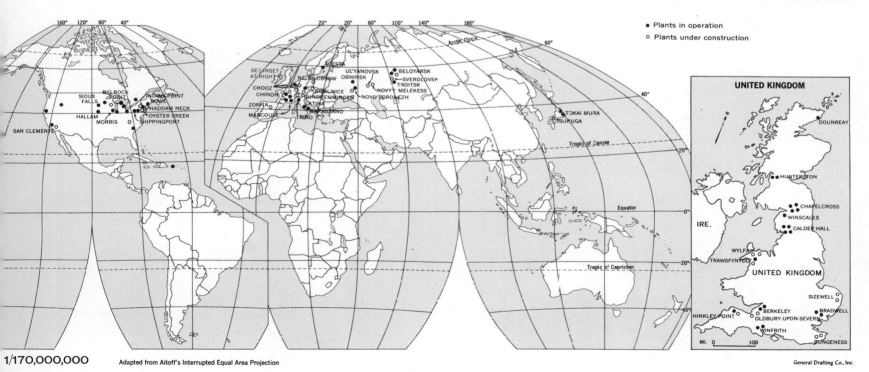

● Plants in operation
○ Plants under construction

UNITED KINGDOM

1/170,000,000   Adapted from Aitoff's Interrupted Equal Area Projection

General Drafting Co., Inc.

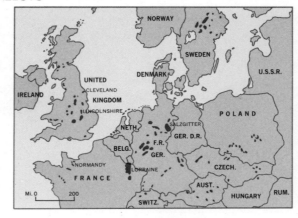

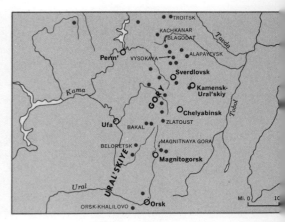

GREAT LAKES ◄ Iron ore deposits

WESTERN and CENTRAL EUROPE ◄ Iron ore deposits

URALS • Iron ore deposits

IRON ORE

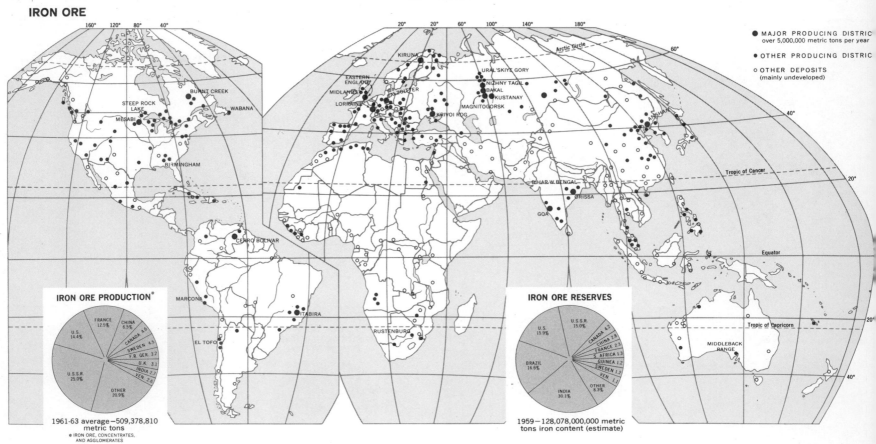

● MAJOR PRODUCING DISTRICT
over 5,000,000 metric tons per year

● OTHER PRODUCING DISTRICT

○ OTHER DEPOSITS
(mainly undeveloped)

IRON ORE PRODUCTION

FRANCE 12.5%
CHINA 6.5%
CANADA 4.6
SWEDEN 4.5
F.R.GER. 3.2
U.K. 3.1
INDIA 2.7
VEN. 2.6
U.S. 14.4%
U.S.S.R. 25.0%
OTHER 20.9%

1961-63 average—509,378,810 metric tons
* IRON ORE, CONCENTRATES, AND AGGLOMERATES

IRON ORE RESERVES

U.S. 15.9%
U.S.S.R. 15.0%
CANADA 4.2
CHINA 2.9
FRANCE 2.3
S. AFRICA 1.3
GUINEA 1.2
SWEDEN 1.2
VEN. 1.2
BRAZIL 16.9%
INDIA 30.1%
OTHER 8.3%

1959—128,078,000,000 metric tons iron content (estimate)

FERRO-ALLOYS

BORON PRODUCTION (Bolivia, Peru, and F. R. Ger. possess unexploited deposits of commercial value)

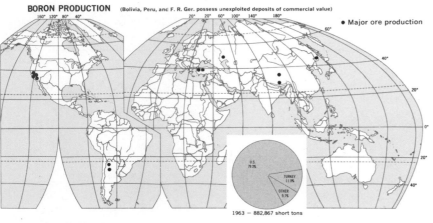

● Major ore production

U.S. 79.9%
TURKEY 11.0%
OTHER 9.7%

1963 — 882,867 short tons

CHROMIUM PRODUCTION

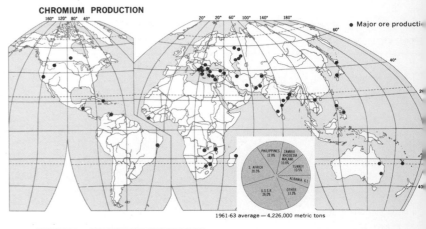

● Major ore production

PHILIPPINES 12.9%
ZAMBIA RHODESIA MALAWI 10.8%
TURKEY 10.5%
S. AFRICA 20.5%
ALBANIA 4.2
U.S.S.R. 26.9%
OTHER 13.9%

1961-63 average — 4,226,000 metric tons

NICKEL PRODUCTION

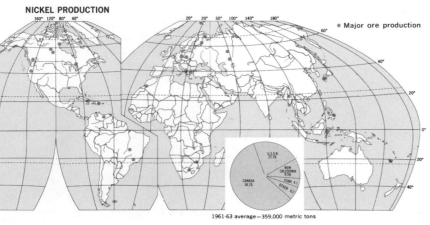

● Major ore production

U.S.S.R. 37.1%
NEW CALEDONIA
CUBA 4.1
CANADA 58.5%
OTHER 5.0

1961-63 average—359,000 metric tons

NIOBIUM and TANTALUM PRODUCTION

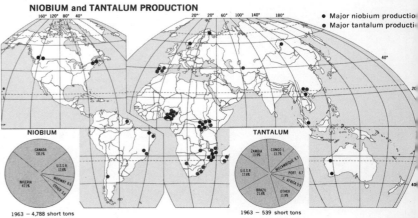

● Major niobium production
● Major tantalum production

NIOBIUM

CANADA 28.1%
U.S.S.R. 12.6%
NIGERIA 47.5%
NORWAY 4.4
OTHER 7.4

1963 — 4,788 short tons

TANTALUM

ZAMBIA 13.9%
CONGO L. 12.7%
MOZAMBIQUE 6.1
PORT. 6.7
U.S.S.R. 13.9%
BRAZIL 23.8%
OTHER 23.0%

1963 — 539 short tons

General Drafting Co., Inc.

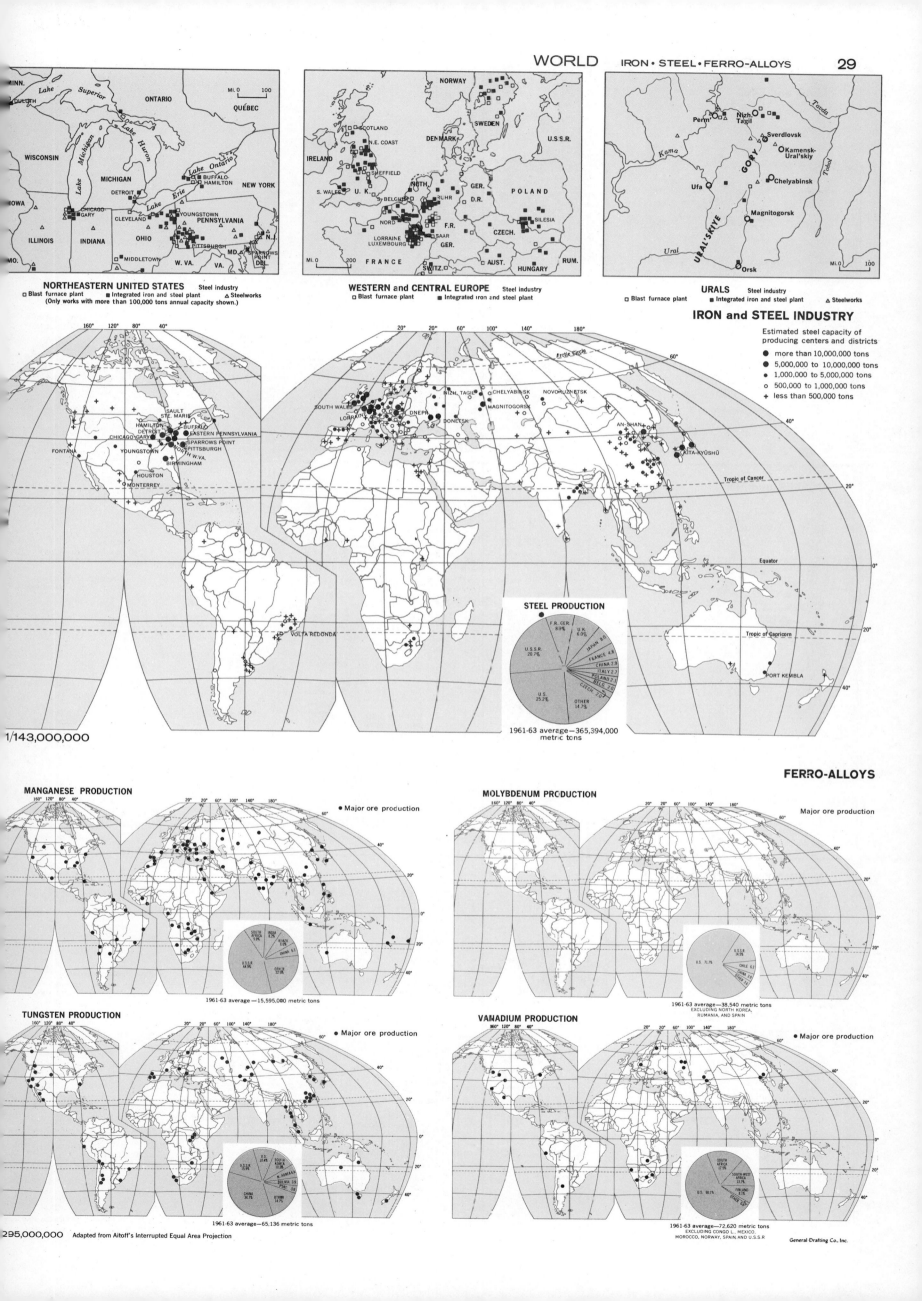

NORTHEASTERN UNITED STATES Steel industry
□ Blast furnace plant ■ Integrated iron and steel plant △ Steelworks
(Only works with more than 100,000 tons annual capacity shown.)

WESTERN and CENTRAL EUROPE Steel industry
□ Blast furnace plant ■ Integrated iron and steel plant

URALS Steel industry
□ Blast furnace plant ■ Integrated iron and steel plant △ Steelworks

IRON and STEEL INDUSTRY
Estimated steel capacity of producing centers and districts
● more than 10,000,000 tons
● 5,000,000 to 10,000,000 tons
● 1,000,000 to 5,000,000 tons
○ 500,000 to 1,000,000 tons
+ less than 500,000 tons

1/143,000,000

STEEL PRODUCTION
1961-63 average—365,394,000 metric tons

FERRO-ALLOYS

MANGANESE PRODUCTION
● Major ore production
1961-63 average—15,595,000 metric tons

MOLYBDENUM PRODUCTION
● Major ore production
1961-63 average—38,540 metric tons
EXCLUDING NORTH KOREA, RUMANIA, AND SPAIN

TUNGSTEN PRODUCTION
● Major ore production
1961-63 average—65,136 metric tons

VANADIUM PRODUCTION
● Major ore production
1961-63 average—72,620 metric tons
EXCLUDING CONGO L., MEXICO, MOROCCO, NORWAY, SPAIN, AND U.S.S.R.

295,000,000 Adapted from Aitoff's Interrupted Equal Area Projection

General Drafting Co., Inc.

LEAD and ZINC

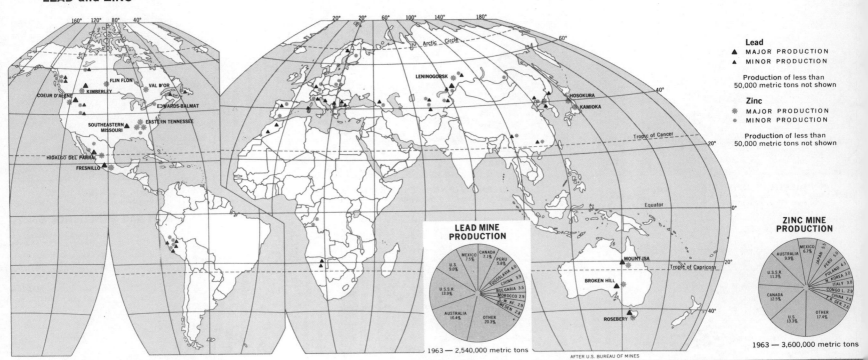

Lead
▲ MAJOR PRODUCTION
▲ MINOR PRODUCTION

Production of less than
50,000 metric tons not shown

Zinc
✳ MAJOR PRODUCTION
● MINOR PRODUCTION

Production of less than
50,000 metric tons not shown

LEAD MINE PRODUCTION

Mexico 7.5%
Canada 7.1%
Peru 5.8%
Yugoslavia 4.0%
China 3.9
Bulgaria 3.5
Morocco 2.9
Sweden 2.8
U.S. 9.0%
U.S.S.R. 13.9%
Australia 16.4%
Other 20.3%

1963 — 2,540,000 metric tons

ZINC MINE PRODUCTION

Australia 9.9%
Mexico 6.7%
Japan 5.5
Poland 4.3
N. Korea 3.0
Italy 3.0
Congo L. 2.9
China 2.9
F.R. Ger. 2.6
U.S.S.R. 11.5%
Canada 12.5%
U.S. 13.3%
Other 17.4%

1963 — 3,600,000 metric tons

AFTER U.S. BUREAU OF MINES

COPPER and TIN

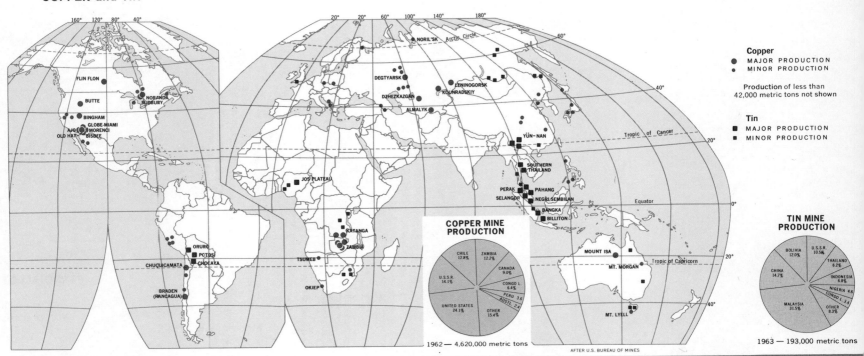

Copper
● MAJOR PRODUCTION
● MINOR PRODUCTION

Production of less than
42,000 metric tons not shown

Tin
■ MAJOR PRODUCTION
■ MINOR PRODUCTION

COPPER MINE PRODUCTION

Chile 12.8%
Zambia 12.2%
Canada 9.0%
Congo L. 6.4%
Peru 3.6
Austl. 2.4
U.S.S.R. 14.1%
United States 24.1%
Other 15.4%

1962 — 4,620,000 metric tons

TIN MINE PRODUCTION

Bolivia 12.0%
U.S.S.R. 10.5%
Thailand 8.2%
Indonesia 6.8%
Nigeria 4.6
Congo L. 3.6
China 14.7%
Malaysia 31.5%
Other 8.3%

1963 — 193,000 metric tons

AFTER U.S. BUREAU OF MINES

MERCURY and NATIVE SULFUR

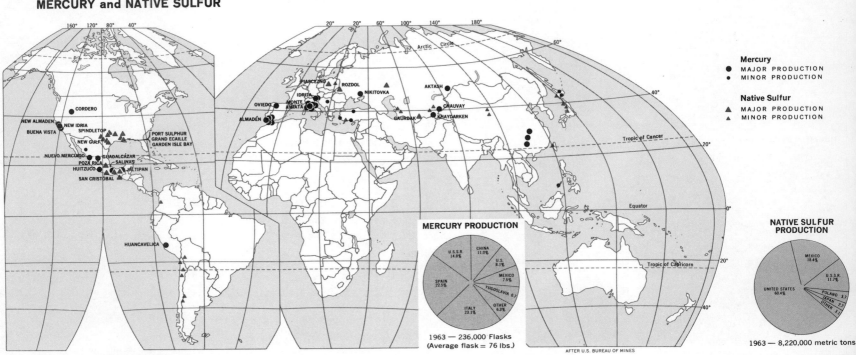

Mercury
● MAJOR PRODUCTION
● MINOR PRODUCTION

Native Sulfur
▲ MAJOR PRODUCTION
▲ MINOR PRODUCTION

MERCURY PRODUCTION

U.S.S.R. 14.8%
China 11.0%
U.S. 8.1%
Mexico 7.5%
Yugoslavia 6.7
Spain 22.5%
Italy 23.1%
Other 6.3%

1963 — 236,000 Flasks
(Average flask = 76 lbs.)

AFTER U.S. BUREAU OF MINES

NATIVE SULFUR PRODUCTION

Mexico 18.4%
U.S.S.R. 11.7%
Poland 3.7
Japan 2.7
Other
United States 60.4%

1963 — 8,220,000 metric tons

General Drafting Co., Inc.   1/170,000,000   Adapted from Aitoff's Interrupted Equal Area Projection

POTASH, PHOSPHATE, and NITRATE

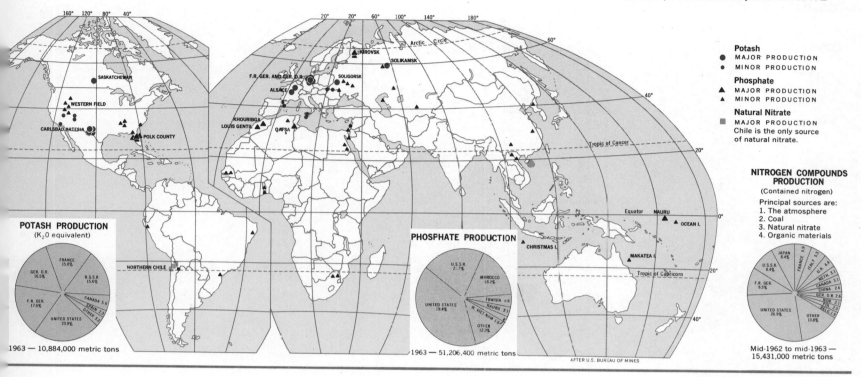

Potash
- ● MAJOR PRODUCTION
- • MINOR PRODUCTION

Phosphate
- ▲ MAJOR PRODUCTION
- ▲ MINOR PRODUCTION

Natural Nitrate
- ■ MAJOR PRODUCTION

Chile is the only source of natural nitrate.

NITROGEN COMPOUNDS PRODUCTION
(Contained nitrogen)

Principal sources are:
1. The atmosphere
2. Coal
3. Natural nitrate
4. Organic materials

Mid-1962 to mid-1963 — 15,431,000 metric tons

POTASH PRODUCTION
(K₂O equivalent)

1963 — 10,884,000 metric tons

PHOSPHATE PRODUCTION

1963 — 51,206,400 metric tons

AFTER U.S. BUREAU OF MINES

ASBESTOS and MICA

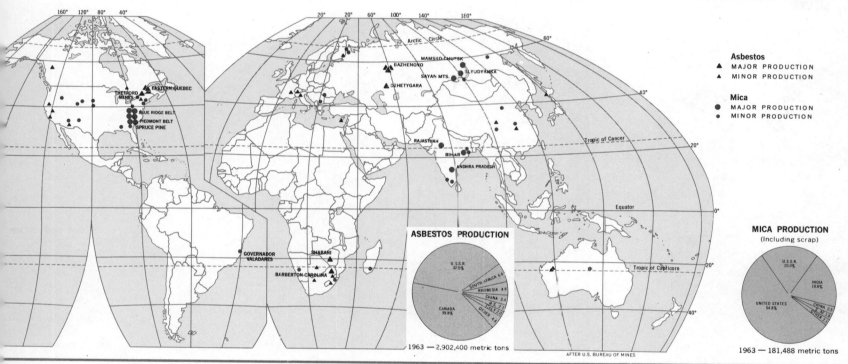

Asbestos
- ▲ MAJOR PRODUCTION
- ▲ MINOR PRODUCTION

Mica
- ● MAJOR PRODUCTION
- • MINOR PRODUCTION

ASBESTOS PRODUCTION

1963 — 2,902,400 metric tons

MICA PRODUCTION
(Including scrap)

1963 — 181,488 metric tons

AFTER U.S. BUREAU OF MINES

BAUXITE, TITANIUM, and MAGNESIUM

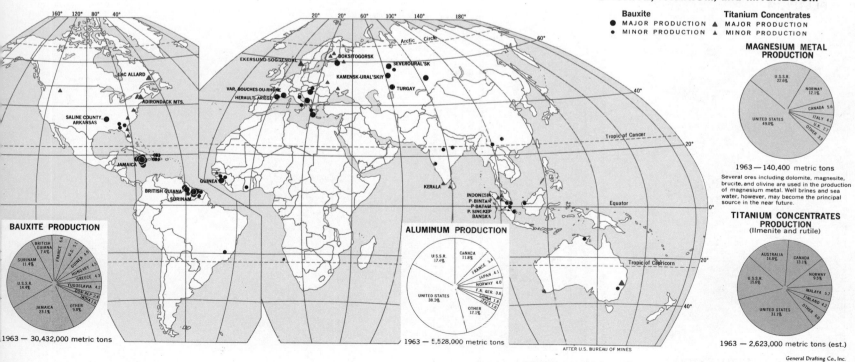

Bauxite
- ● MAJOR PRODUCTION
- • MINOR PRODUCTION

Titanium Concentrates
- ▲ MAJOR PRODUCTION
- ▲ MINOR PRODUCTION

MAGNESIUM METAL PRODUCTION

1963 — 140,400 metric tons

Several ores including dolomite, magnesite, brucite, and olivine are used in the production of magnesium metal. Well brines and sea water, however, may become the principal source in the near future.

TITANIUM CONCENTRATES PRODUCTION
(Ilmenite and rutile)

1963 — 2,623,000 metric tons (est.)

BAUXITE PRODUCTION

1963 — 30,432,000 metric tons

ALUMINUM PRODUCTION

1963 — 5,528,000 metric tons

AFTER U.S. BUREAU OF MINES

General Drafting Co., Inc.

GOLD

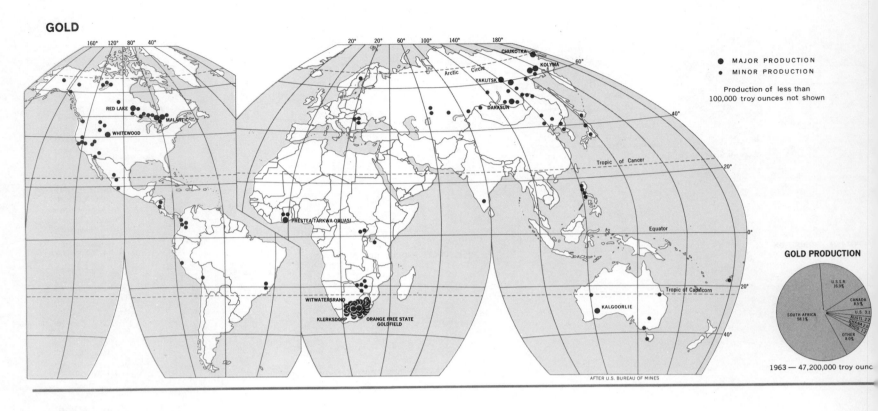

MAJOR PRODUCTION
MINOR PRODUCTION

Production of less than
100,000 troy ounces not shown

GOLD PRODUCTION

1963 — 47,200,000 troy ounces

AFTER U.S. BUREAU OF MINES

SILVER

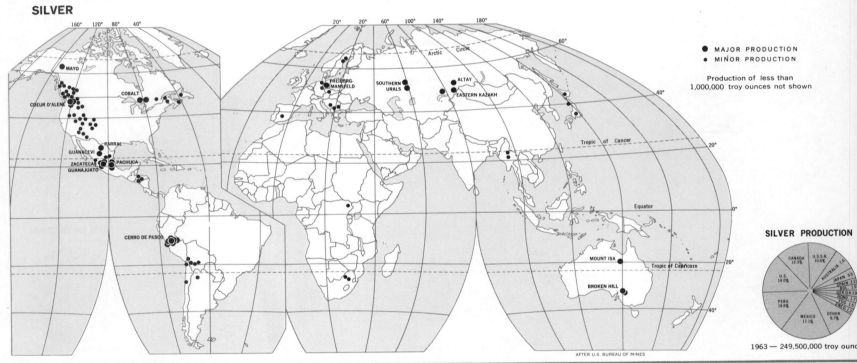

MAJOR PRODUCTION
MINOR PRODUCTION

Production of less than
1,000,000 troy ounces not shown

SILVER PRODUCTION

1963 — 249,500,000 troy ounces

AFTER U.S. BUREAU OF MINES

PLATINUM

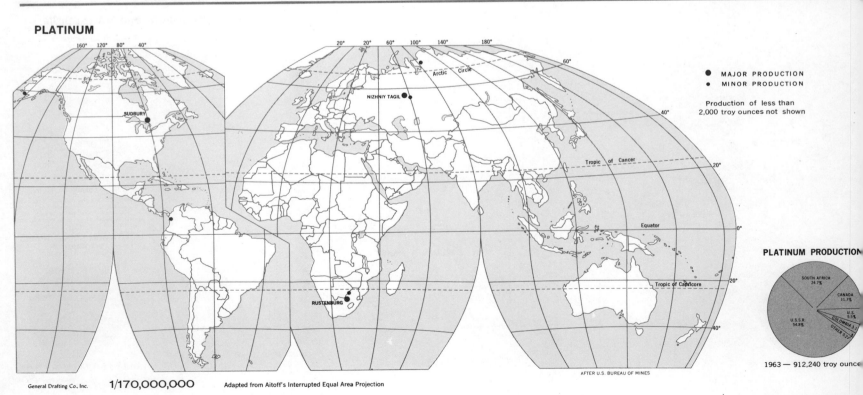

MAJOR PRODUCTION
MINOR PRODUCTION

Production of less than
2,000 troy ounces not shown

PLATINUM PRODUCTION

1963 — 912,240 troy ounces

General Drafting Co., Inc.   1/170,000,000   Adapted from Aitoff's Interrupted Equal Area Projection

AFTER U.S. BUREAU OF MINES

PRECIOUS GEMS

PRODUCING AREAS

- ▲ Diamonds
- ● Emeralds
- ■ Rubies
- ● Sapphires
- ★ Pearls

PRODUCTION OF GEM DIAMONDS

ANGOLA 11.5%
REP. OF THE CONGO 9.7%
SIERRA LEONE 8.4%
GHANA 8.2%
SOUTH-WEST AFRICA 16.4%
TANZANIA 4.2
U.S.S.R 3.7
LIBERIA** 3.7
SOUTH AFRICA 27.0%
OTHER 7.2%

1963 — 6,572,000 carats
*Estimate **Exports

PRODUCTION OF EMERALDS
Estimated

SOUTH AFRICA & RHODESIA 45%
COLOMBIA 50%
OTHER 5

PRODUCTION OF RUBIES

BURMA 70%
THAILAND 20%
CEYLON 5
OTHER 5

PRODUCTION OF SAPPHIRES

BURMA 15%
THAILAND 10%
KASHMIR 5
U.S 5
AUSTRALIA 30%
CEYLON 35%
OTHER 5

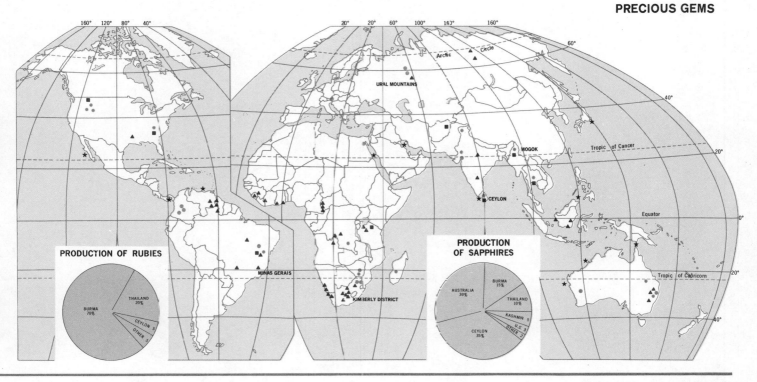

Arctic Circle
URAL MOUNTAINS
MOGOK
Tropic of Cancer
CEYLON
Equator
MINAS GERAIS
KIMBERLY DISTRICT
Tropic of Capricorn

SEMIPRECIOUS GEMS

PRODUCING AREAS

- □ Amber
- ★ Amethyst
- ▲ Aquamarine
- ◆ Garnet
- ● Jade
- ■ Lapis Lazuli
- ○ Opal
- + Topaz
- ★ Turquoise
- △ Zircon

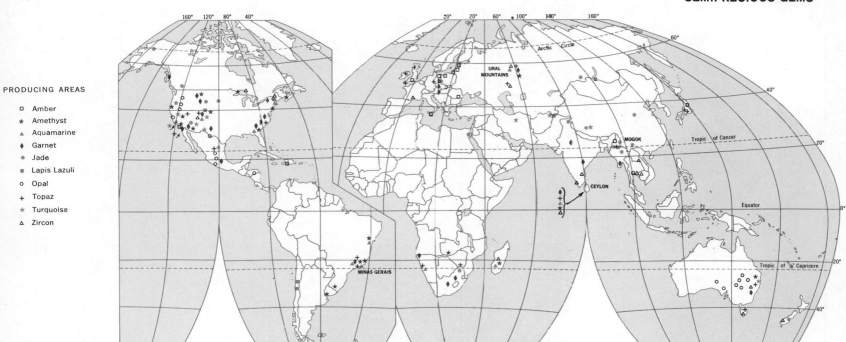

Arctic Circle
URAL MOUNTAINS
Tropic of Cancer
MOGOK
CEYLON
Equator
MINAS GERAIS
Tropic of Capricorn

RARE EARTHS

Bastnaesite
- ● MAJOR DEPOSITS
- • MINOR DEPOSITS

Thorite
- ◆ MAJOR DEPOSITS
- ◆ MINOR DEPOSITS

Monazite
- ▲ MAJOR DEPOSITS
- ▲ MINOR DEPOSITS

Euxenite
- ■ MAJOR DEPOSITS
- ■ MINOR DEPOSITS

Bastnaesite and Thorite each produce:

Cerium	Neodymium
Europium	Praseodymium
Lanthanum	Samarium

Monazite and Euxenite each produce:

Cerium	Neodymium
Erbium	Praseodymium
Europium	Samarium
Gadolininum	Terbium
Holmium	Thulium
Lanthanum	Ytterbium
Lutecium	Yttrium

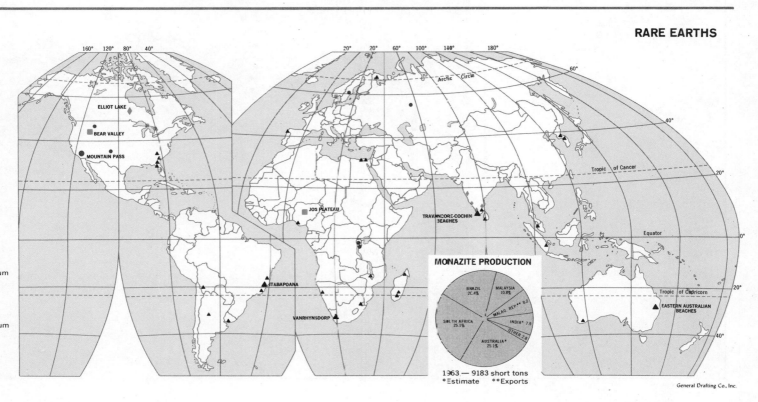

ELLIOT LAKE
BEAR VALLEY
Arctic Circle
MOUNTAIN PASS
Tropic of Cancer
JOS PLATEAU
TRAVANCORE-COCHIN BEACHES
Equator
ITABAPOANA
VANRHYNSDORP
Tropic of Capricorn
EASTERN AUSTRALIAN BEACHES

MONAZITE PRODUCTION

BRAZIL 20.4%
MALAYSIA 10.8%
MALAG. REP** 9.2
SOUTH AFRICA 25.1%
INDIA* 7.9
OTHER 2.8
AUSTRALIA* 25.1%

1963 — 9183 short tons
*Estimate **Exports

General Drafting Co., Inc.

1/22,000,000

1 in. = 347 mi.
1 cm. = 220 km.

LAND HEIGHTS

meters	feet
4000	13123
2000	6562
1000	3281
200	656
land below sea level
sea level
200	656
3000	9843
6000	19685

OCEAN DEPTHS

Azimuthal Equal
Area Projection

General Drafting Co., Inc.

LANDFORMS and PHYSICAL REGIONS

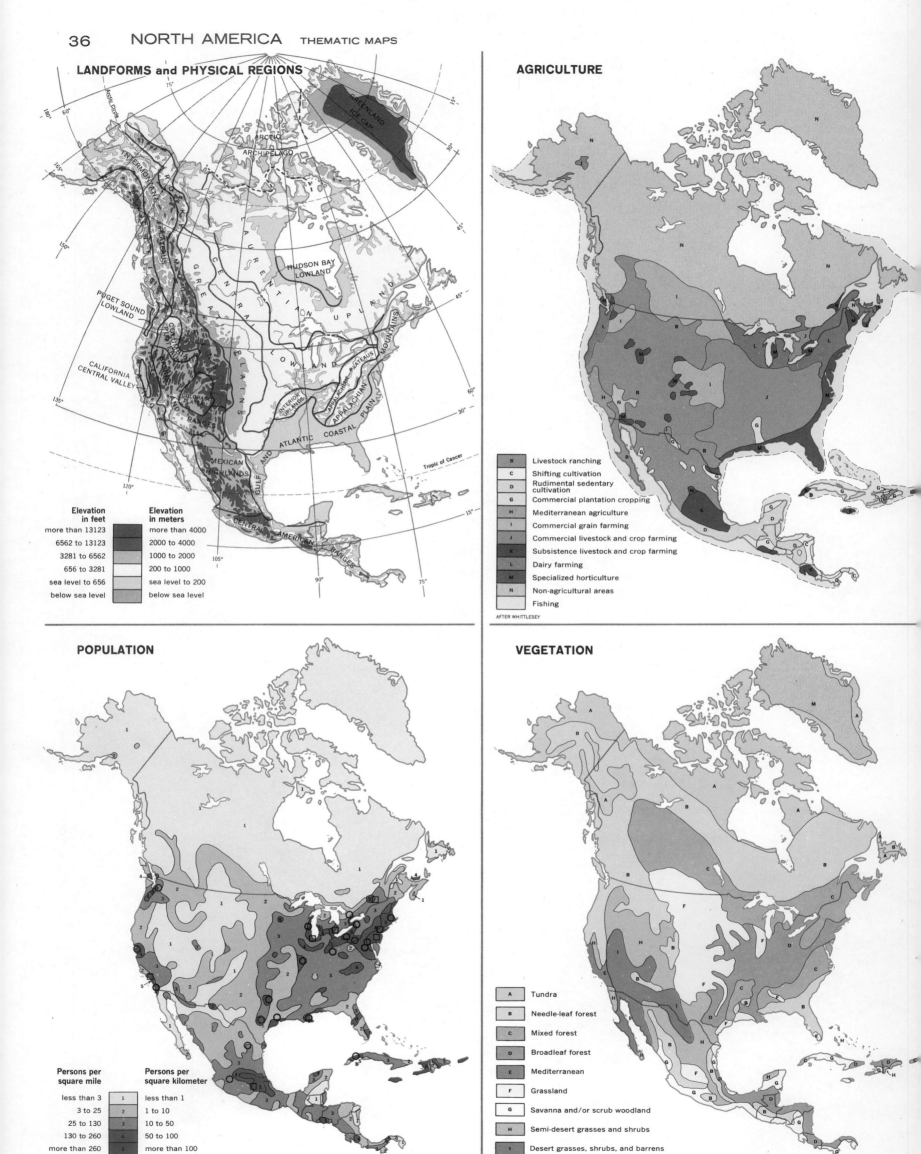

Elevation in feet
more than 13123
6562 to 13123
3281 to 6562
656 to 3281
sea level to 656
below sea level

Elevation in meters
more than 4000
2000 to 4000
1000 to 2000
200 to 1000
sea level to 200
below sea level

AGRICULTURE

B Livestock ranching
C Shifting cultivation
D Rudimental sedentary cultivation
G Commercial plantation cropping
H Mediterranean agriculture
I Commercial grain farming
J Commercial livestock and crop farming
K Subsistence livestock and crop farming
L Dairy farming
M Specialized horticulture
N Non-agricultural areas
Fishing

AFTER WHITTLESEY

POPULATION

Persons per square mile
less than 3
3 to 25
25 to 130
130 to 260
more than 260

Persons per square kilometer
less than 1
1 to 10
10 to 50
50 to 100
more than 100

○ Cities from 500,000 to 1,000,000
□ Cities of more than 1,000,000

General Drafting Co., Inc.   1/64,600,000   Azimuthal Equal Area Projection

VEGETATION

A Tundra
B Needle-leaf forest
C Mixed forest
D Broadleaf forest
E Mediterranean
F Grassland
G Savanna and/or scrub woodland
H Semi-desert grasses and shrubs
I Desert grasses, shrubs, and barrens
M No vegetation

AVERAGE ANNUAL PRECIPITATION

CLIMATES

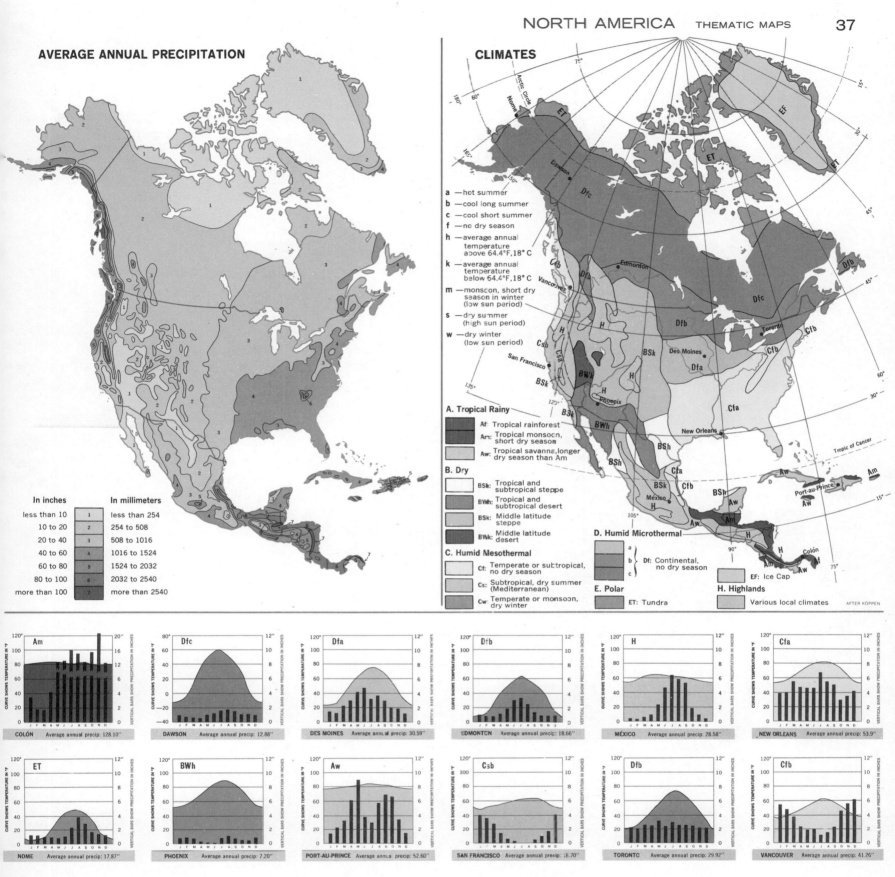

a —hot summer
b —cool long summer
c —cool short summer
f —no dry season
h —average annual
    temperature
    above 64.4°F,18° C
k —average annual
    temperature
    below 64.4°F,18° C
m —monsoon, short dry
    season in winter
    (low sun period)
s —dry summer
    (high sun period)
w —dry winter
    (low sun period)

A. Tropical Rainy
Af: Tropical rainforest
Am: Tropical monsoon,
    short dry season
Aw: Tropical savanne, longer
    dry season than Am

B. Dry
BSh: Tropical and
    subtropical steppe
BWh: Tropical and
    subtropical desert
BSk: Middle latitude
    steppe
BWk: Middle latitude
    desert

C. Humid Mesothermal
Cf: Temperate or subtropical,
    no dry season
Cs: Subtropical, dry summer
    (Mediterranean)
Cw: Temperate or monsoon,
    dry winter

D. Humid Microthermal
a
b   Df: Continental,
c   no dry season

E. Polar
ET: Tundra

EF: Ice Cap

H. Highlands
Various local climates

AFTER KÖPPEN

In inches		In millimeters
less than 10	1	less than 254
10 to 20	2	254 to 508
20 to 40	3	508 to 1016
40 to 60	4	1016 to 1524
60 to 80	5	1524 to 2032
80 to 100	6	2032 to 2540
more than 100	7	more than 2540

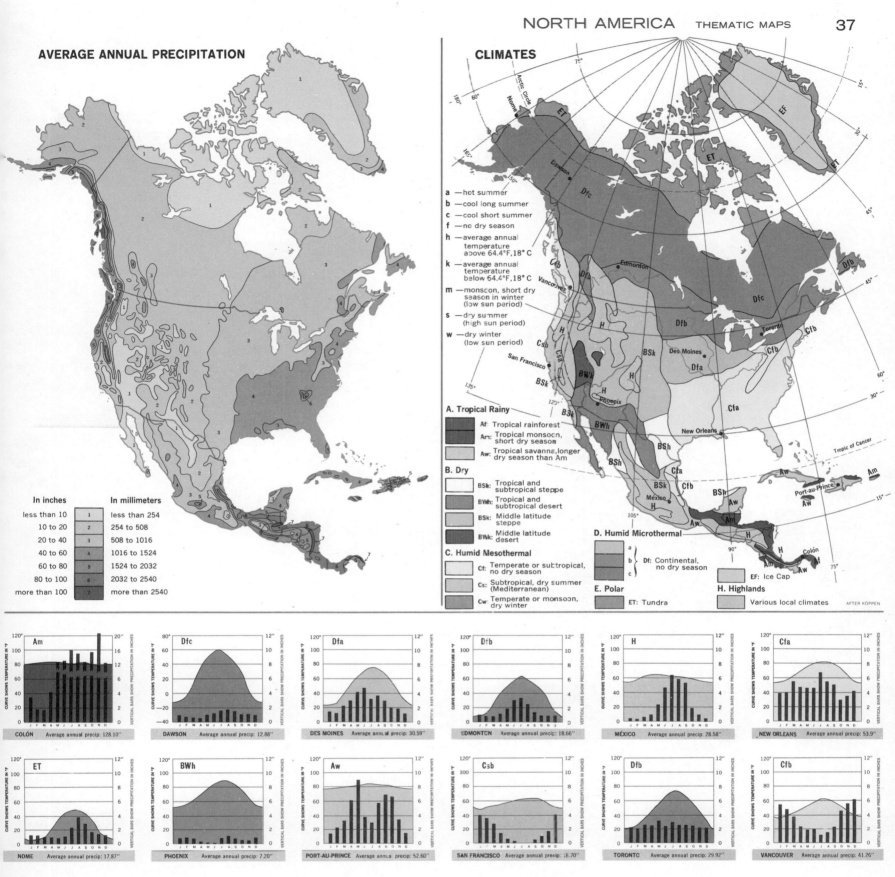

COLÓN Average annual precip: 128.10″
DAWSON Average annual precip: 12.88″
DES MOINES Average annual precip: 30.59″
EDMONTON Average annual precip: 18.66″
MÉXICO Average annual precip: 28.58″
NEW ORLEANS Average annual precip: 53.9″

NOME Average annual precip: 17.87″
PHOENIX Average annual precip: 7.20″
PORT-AU-PRINCE Average annual precip: 52.60″
SAN FRANCISCO Average annual precip: 18.70″
TORONTO Average annual precip: 29.92″
VANCOUVER Average annual precip: 41.26″

JANUARY AVERAGE TEMPERATURE
(Surface temperature)

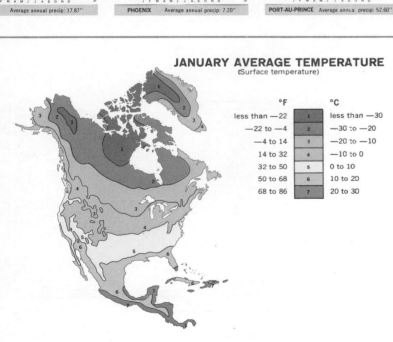

°F		°C
less than —22	1	less than —30
—22 to —4	2	—30 to —20
—4 to 14	3	—20 to —10
14 to 32	4	—10 to 0
32 to 50	5	0 to 10
50 to 68	6	10 to 20
68 to 86	7	20 to 30

JULY AVERAGE TEMPERATURE
(Surface temperature)

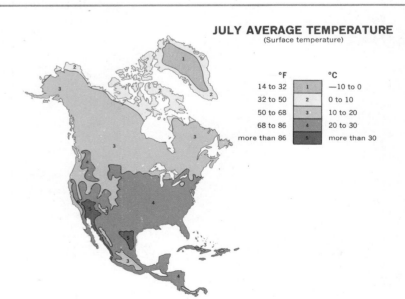

°F		°C
14 to 32	1	—10 to 0
32 to 50	2	0 to 10
50 to 68	3	10 to 20
68 to 86	4	20 to 30
more than 86	5	more than 30

General Drafting Co., Inc.

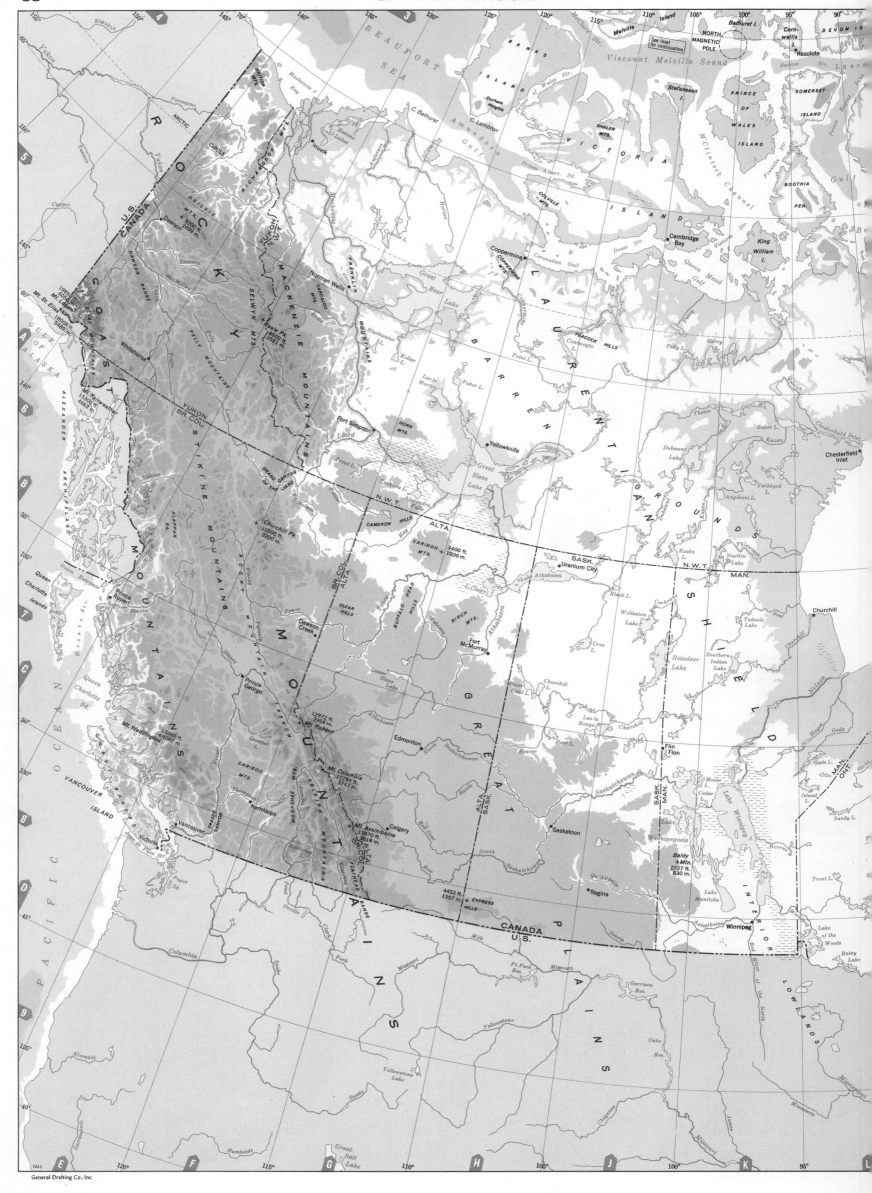

CANADA PHYSICAL

LAND HEIGHTS AND OCEAN DEPTHS

meters		feet
3000		9842
2000		6562
1000		3281
500		1640
200		656
sea level		sea level
		LAND BELOW SEA LEVEL
200		656
3000		9842
6000		19685

General Drafting Co., Inc.

1/12,100,000

1 in. = 191 mi.
1 cm. = 121 km.

0 50 100 150 200 250 300 350 400 Miles
0 100 200 300 400 500 600 Kilometers

Conformal
Conic Projection

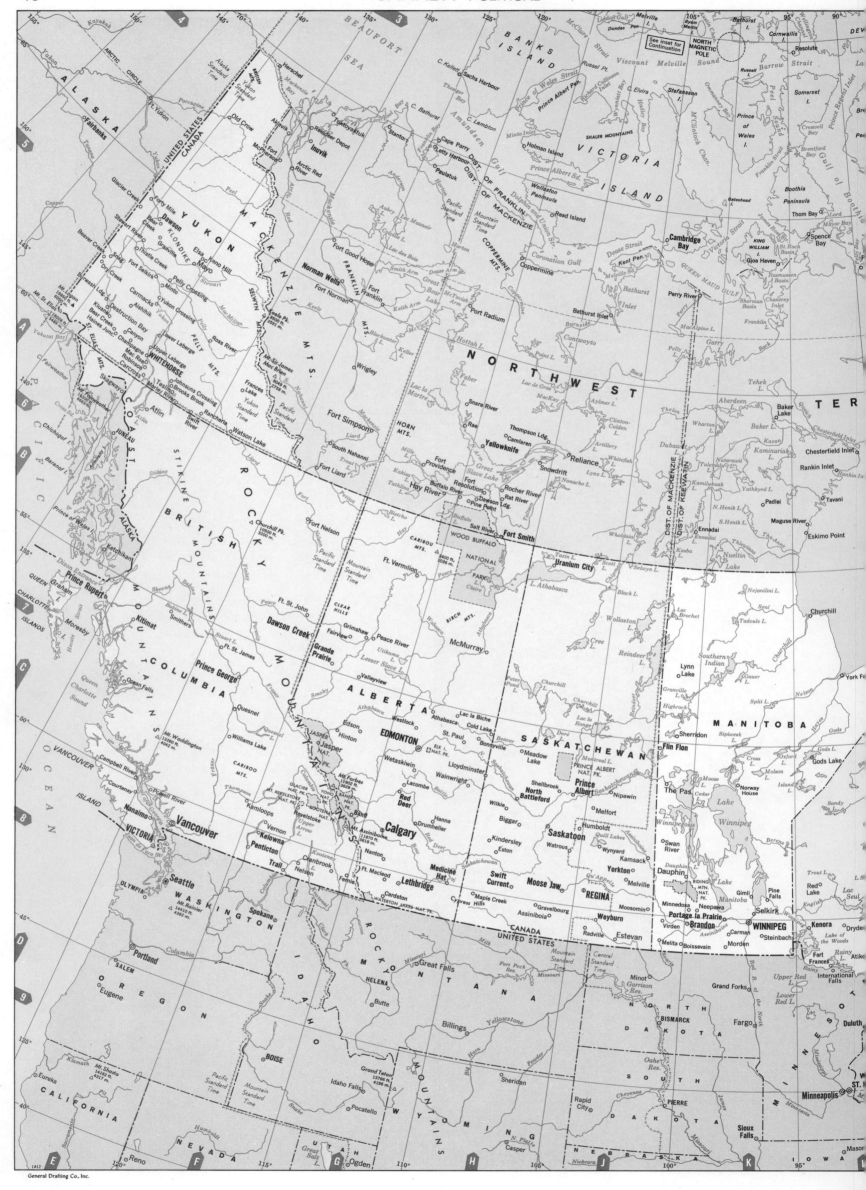

General Drafting Co., Inc.

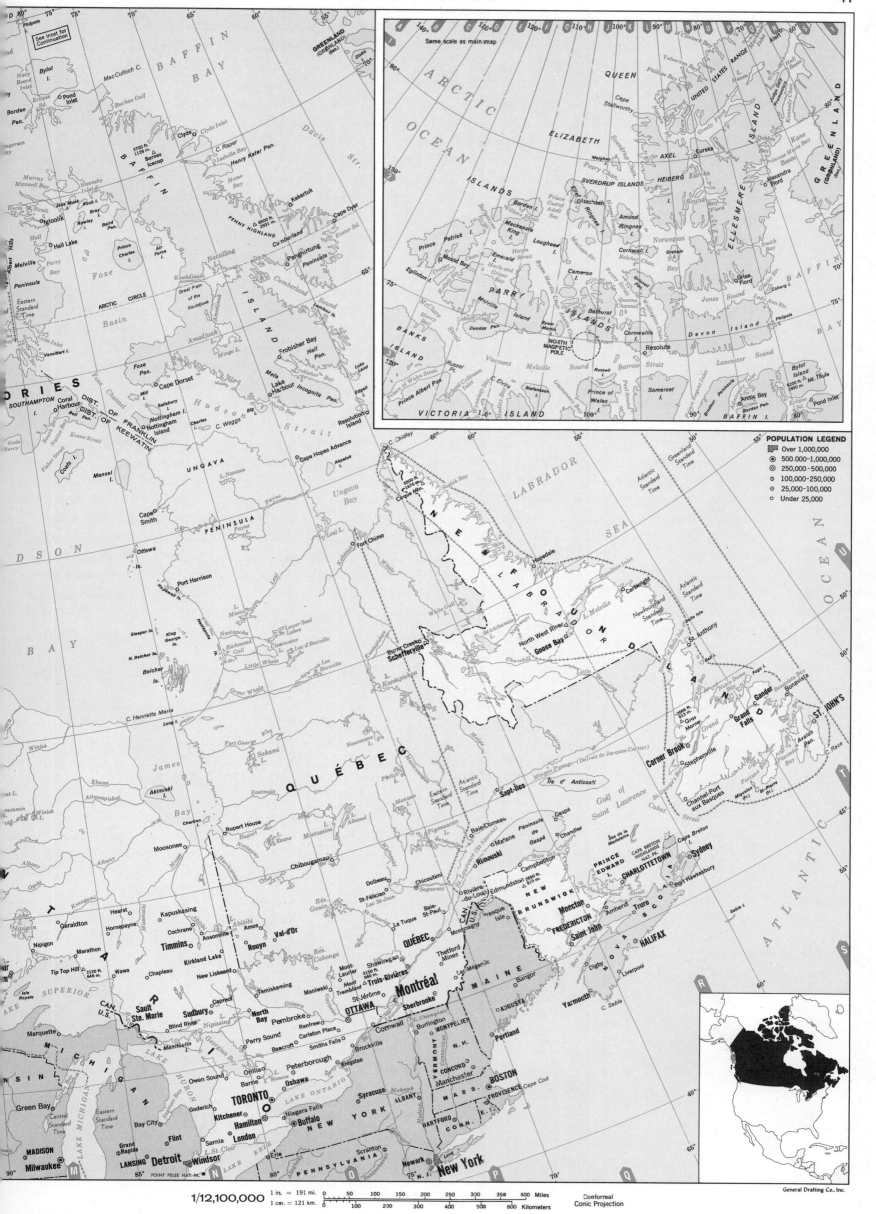

POPULATION LEGEND
- Over 1,000,000
- 500,000-1,000,000
- 250,000-500,000
- 100,000-250,000
- 25,000-100,000
- Under 25,000

1/12,100,000

1 in. = 191 mi.
1 cm. = 121 km.

0 50 100 150 200 250 300 350 400 Miles
0 100 200 300 400 500 600 Kilometers

Conformal
Conic Projection

General Drafting Co., Inc.

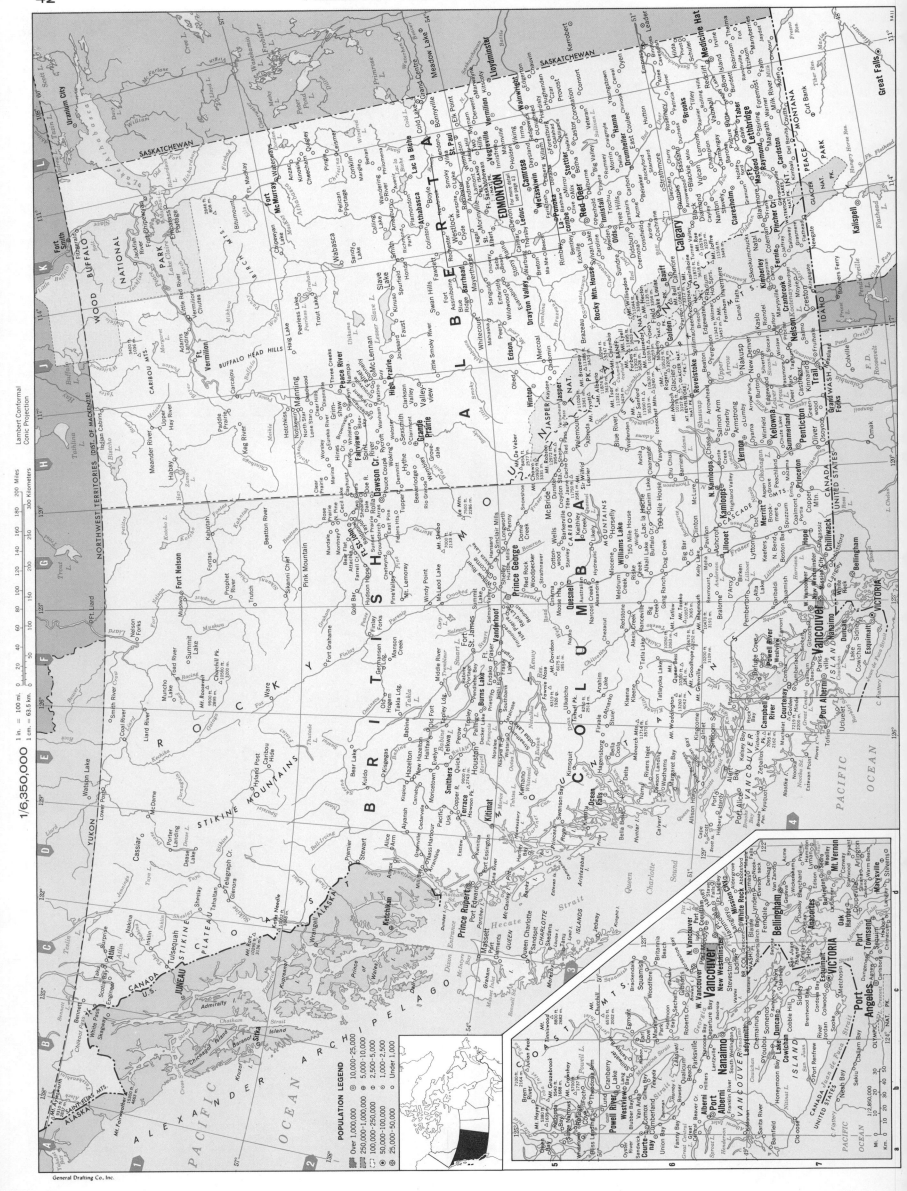

1/6,350,000   1 in. = 100 mi.
1 cm. = 63.5 km.

Lambert Conformal
Conic Projection

POPULATION LEGEND

General Drafting Co., Inc.

1/6,380,000 1 in. = 101 mi.
1 cm = 63.8 km.

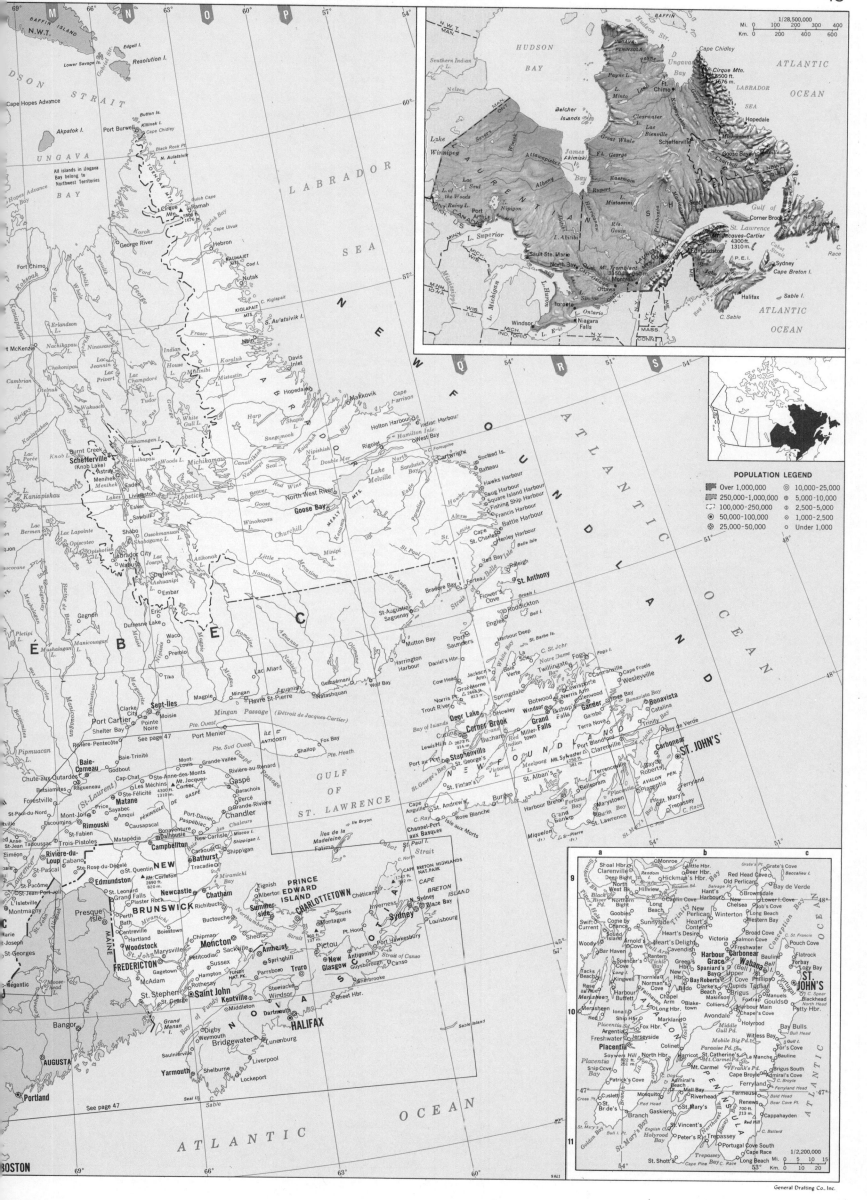

See page 47

See page 47

POPULATION LEGEND

Over 1,000,000	⊙ 10,000-25,000
250,000-1,000,000	⊕ 5,000-10,000
100,000-250,000	⊕ 2,500-5,000
⊙ 50,000-100,000	⊕ 1,000-2,500
⊛ 25,000-50,000	◦ Under 1,000

General Drafting Co., Inc.

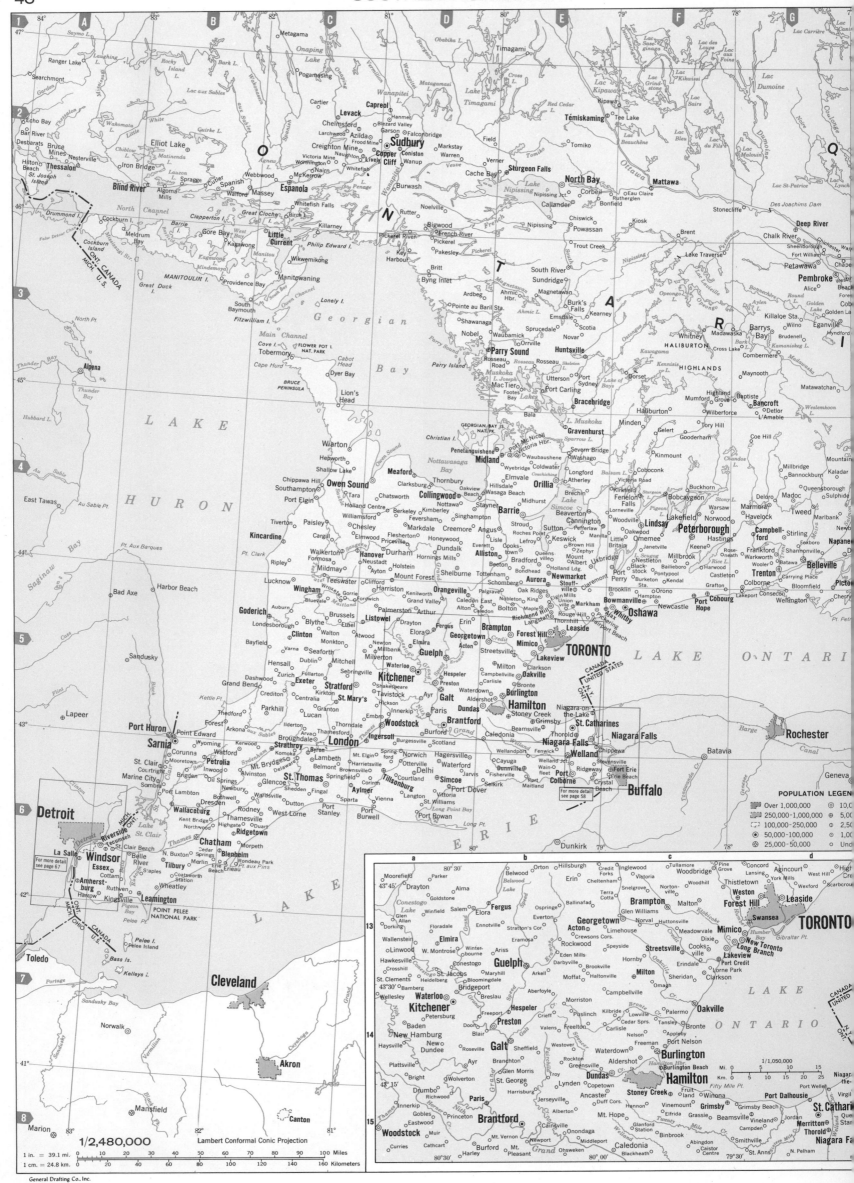

POPULATION LEGEND

Over 1,000,000   10,0
250,000–1,000,000   5,00
100,000–250,000   2,50
50,000–100,000   1,00
25,000–50,000   Und

1/2,480,000

1 in. = 39.1 mi.
1 cm. = 24.8 km.

0 10 20 30 40 50 60 70 80 90 100 Miles
0 20 40 60 80 100 120 140 160 Kilometers

Lambert Conformal Conic Projection

General Drafting Co., Inc.

1/1,050,000

Mi. 0 5 10 15
Km. 0 5 10 15 20 25

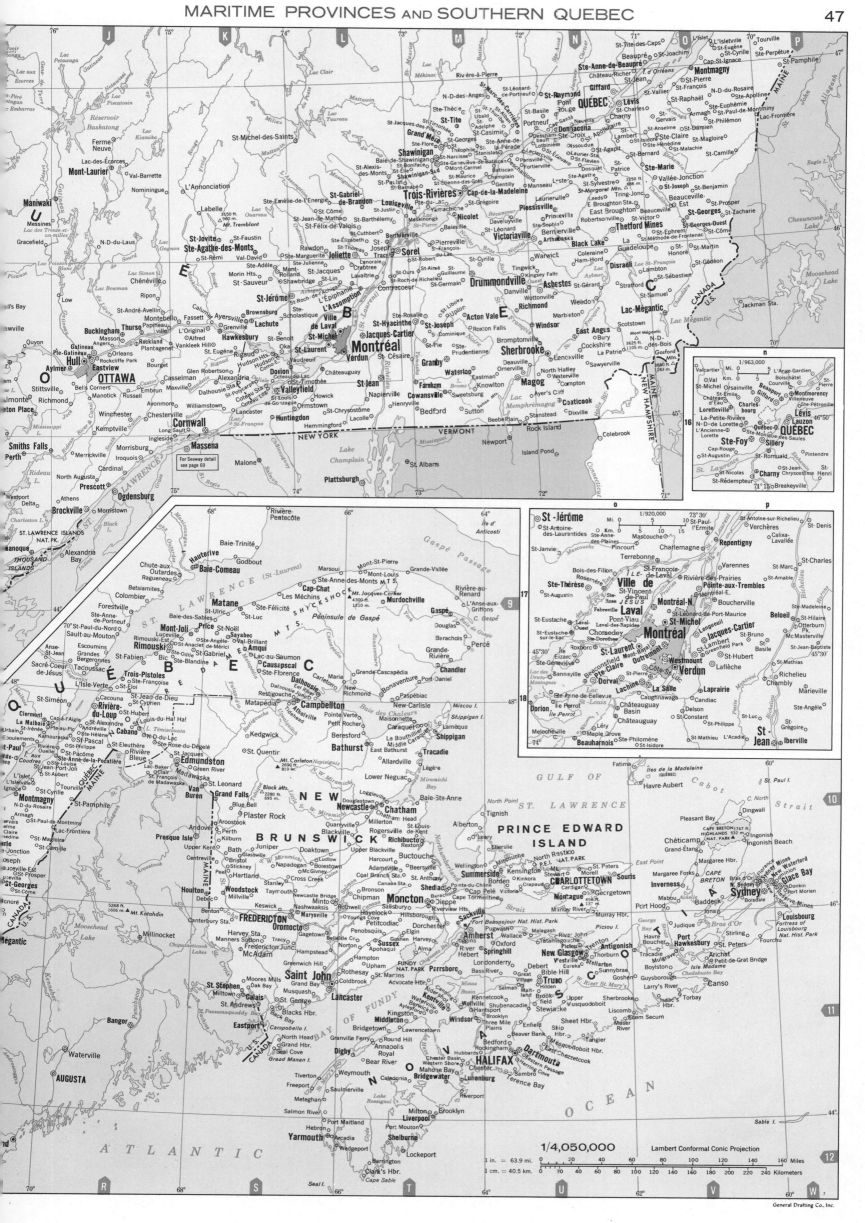

Maritime Provinces and Southern Quebec map. Includes Quebec, New Brunswick, Nova Scotia, and Prince Edward Island, with Ottawa, Montréal, Québec, Fredericton, Saint John, Halifax, Charlottetown, and Sydney.

Scale: 1/4,050,000 — Lambert Conformal Conic Projection
1 in. = 63.9 mi.   1 cm. = 40.5 km.

General Drafting Co., Inc.

IRON ORE, NICKEL, and ASBESTOS

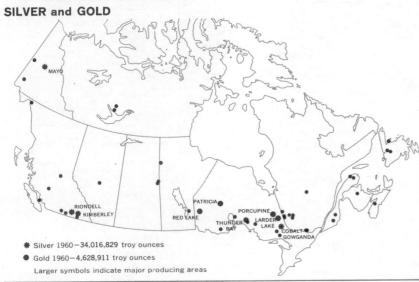

- ● Iron ore 1960—19,241,813 long tons
- ● Nickel 1960—214,506 short tons
- ▲ Asbestos 1960—1,118,456 short tons
Larger symbols indicate major producing areas

SILVER and GOLD

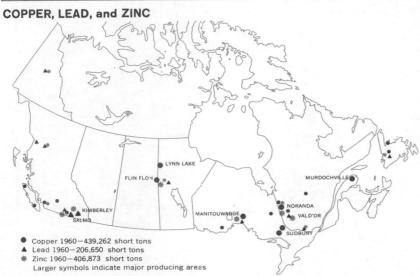

- ✳ Silver 1960—34,016,829 troy ounces
- ● Gold 1960—4,628,911 troy ounces
Larger symbols indicate major producing areas

COPPER, LEAD, and ZINC

- ● Copper 1960—439,262 short tons
- ▲ Lead 1960—206,650 short tons
- ✳ Zinc 1960—406,873 short tons
Larger symbols indicate major producing areas

COAL

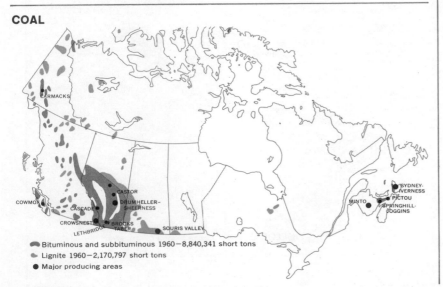

- ◗ Bituminous and subbituminous 1960—8,840,341 short tons
- ◗ Lignite 1960—2,170,797 short tons
- ● Major producing areas

General Drafting Co., Inc.   1/50,600,000   Lambert Conformal
Conic Projection

MAJOR OIL FIELDS, PIPELINES, and TAR SANDS

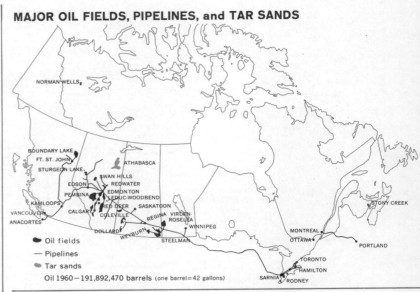

- ● Oil fields
- — Pipelines
- ● Tar sands
Oil 1960—191,892,470 barrels (one barrel = 42 gallons)

MAJOR NATURAL GAS FIELDS and PIPELINES

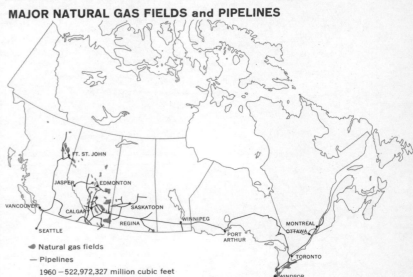

- ◥ Natural gas fields
- — Pipelines
1960—522,972,327 million cubic feet

HYDROELECTRIC POWER and URANIUM

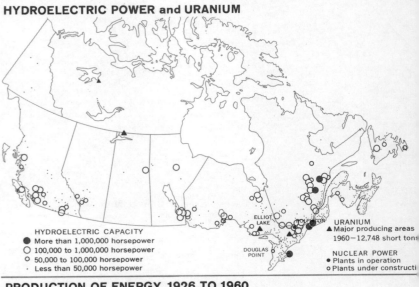

HYDROELECTRIC CAPACITY
- ● More than 1,000,000 horsepower
- ◯ 100,000 to 1,000,000 horsepower
- ○ 50,000 to 100,000 horsepower
- · Less than 50,000 horsepower

URANIUM
- ▲ Major producing areas
1960—12,748 short tons

NUCLEAR POWER
- ● Plants in operation
- ○ Plants under construction

PRODUCTION OF ENERGY 1926 TO 1960

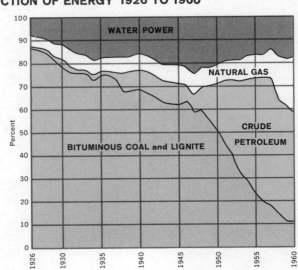

WATER POWER

NATURAL GAS

BITUMINOUS COAL and LIGNITE

CRUDE PETROLEUM

Percent

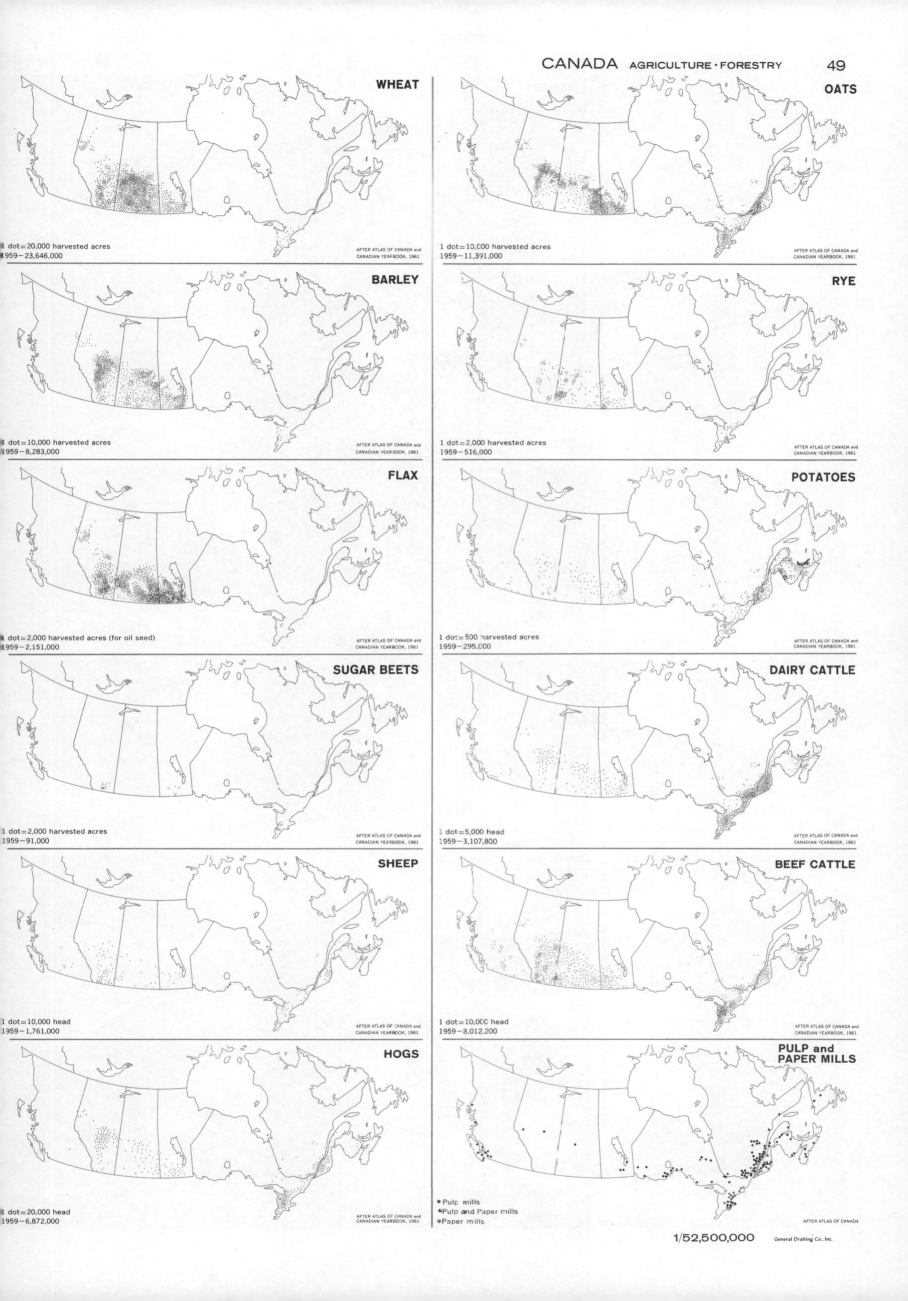

WHEAT

1 dot=20,000 harvested acres
1959—23,646,000

AFTER ATLAS OF CANADA and
CANADIAN YEARBOOK, 1961

OATS

1 dot=10,000 harvested acres
1959—11,391,000

AFTER ATLAS OF CANADA and
CANADIAN YEARBOOK, 1961

BARLEY

1 dot=10,000 harvested acres
1959—8,283,000

AFTER ATLAS OF CANADA and
CANADIAN YEARBOOK, 1961

RYE

1 dot=2,000 harvested acres
1959—516,000

AFTER ATLAS OF CANADA and
CANADIAN YEARBOOK, 1961

FLAX

1 dot=2,000 harvested acres (for oil seed)
1959—2,151,000

AFTER ATLAS OF CANADA and
CANADIAN YEARBOOK, 1961

POTATOES

1 dot=500 harvested acres
1959—295,000

AFTER ATLAS OF CANADA and
CANADIAN YEARBOOK, 1961

SUGAR BEETS

1 dot=2,000 harvested acres
1959—91,000

AFTER ATLAS OF CANADA and
CANADIAN YEARBOOK, 1961

DAIRY CATTLE

1 dot=5,000 head
1959—3,107,800

AFTER ATLAS OF CANADA and
CANADIAN YEARBOOK, 1961

SHEEP

1 dot=10,000 head
1959—1,761,000

AFTER ATLAS OF CANADA and
CANADIAN YEARBOOK, 1961

BEEF CATTLE

1 dot=10,000 head
1959—8,012,200

AFTER ATLAS OF CANADA and
CANADIAN YEARBOOK, 1961

HOGS

1 dot=20,000 head
1959—6,872,000

AFTER ATLAS OF CANADA and
CANADIAN YEARBOOK, 1961

**PULP and
PAPER MILLS**

• Pulp mills
• Pulp and Paper mills
• Paper mills

AFTER ATLAS OF CANADA

1/52,500,000   General Drafting Co., Inc.

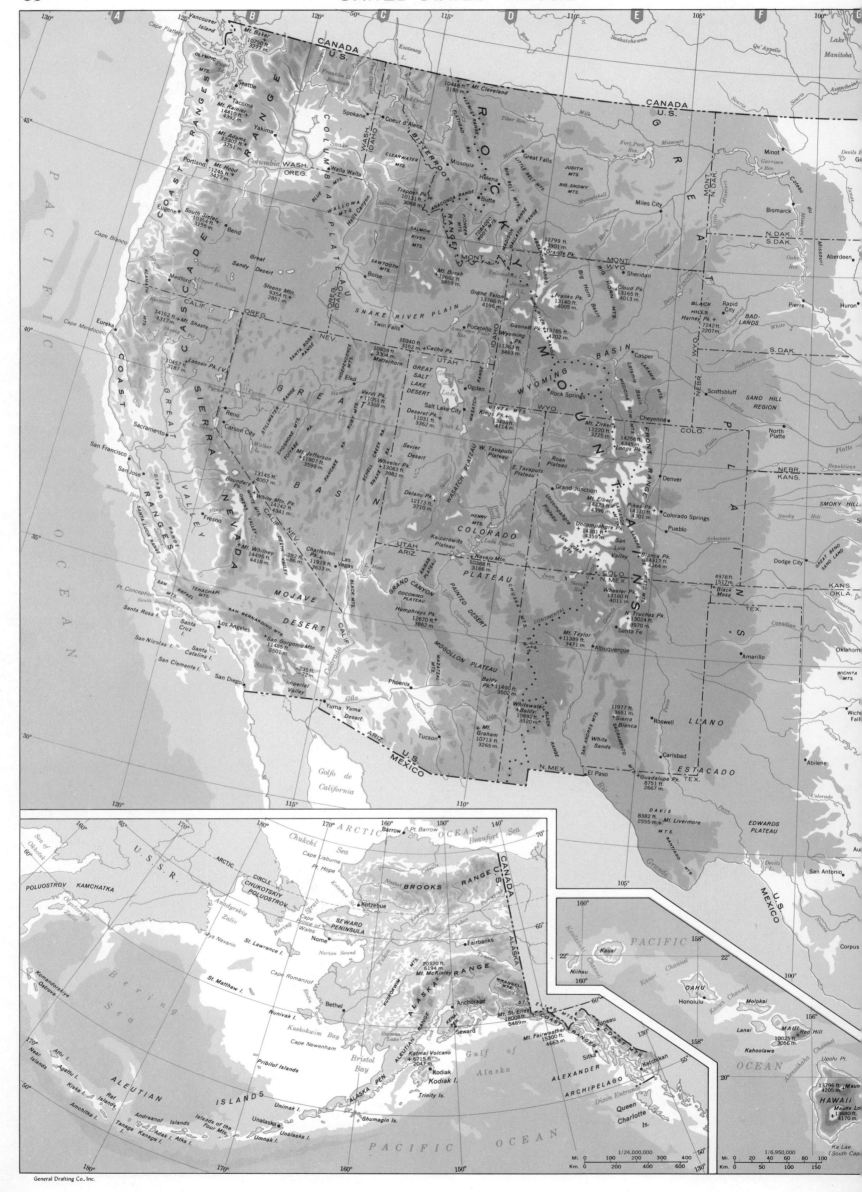

General Drafting Co., Inc.

1 in. = 174 mi.
1 cm. = 110 km.

0 50 100 150 200 250 300 350 400 450 500 Miles
0 100 200 300 400 500 600 700 800 Kilometers

Lambert Conformal
Conic Projection

General Drafting Co., Inc.

AND HEIGHTS
OCEAN DEPTHS

	feet
	9842
	6562
	3281
	1640
	656
	sea level
	LAND BELOW SEA LEVEL
	656
	9842
	19685

General Drafting Co., Inc.

POPULATION LEGEND
Over 1,000,000
500,000-1,000,000
250,000-500,000
100,000-250,000
25,000-100,000
Under 25,000

1/11,000,000

1 in. = 174 mi.
1 cm. = 110 km.

50 100 150 200 250 300 350 400 450 500 Miles
100 200 300 400 500 600 700 800 Kilometers

Lambert Conformal
Conic Projection

General Drafting Co., Inc.

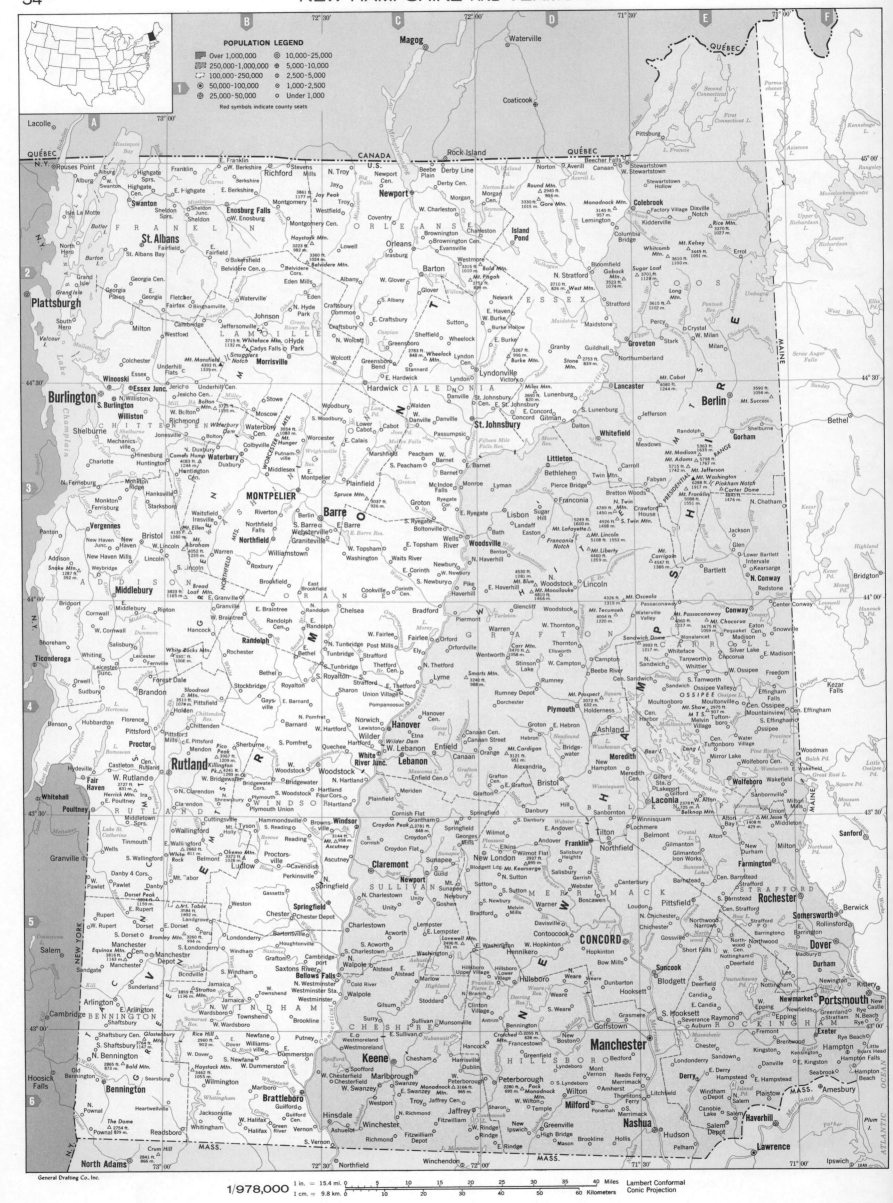

Over 1,000,000 ● 10,000-25,000
250,000-1,000,000 ⊕ 5,000-10,000
100,000-250,000 ⊙ 2,500-5,000
50,000-100,000 ○ 1,000-2,500
25,000-50,000 ○ Under 1,000

Red symbols indicate county seats

General Drafting Co., Inc.

1/978,000

1 in. = 15.4 mi.   0   5   10   15   20   25   30   35   40 Miles
1 cm. = 9.8 km.   0   10   20   30   40   50   60 Kilometers

Lambert Conformal
Conic Projection

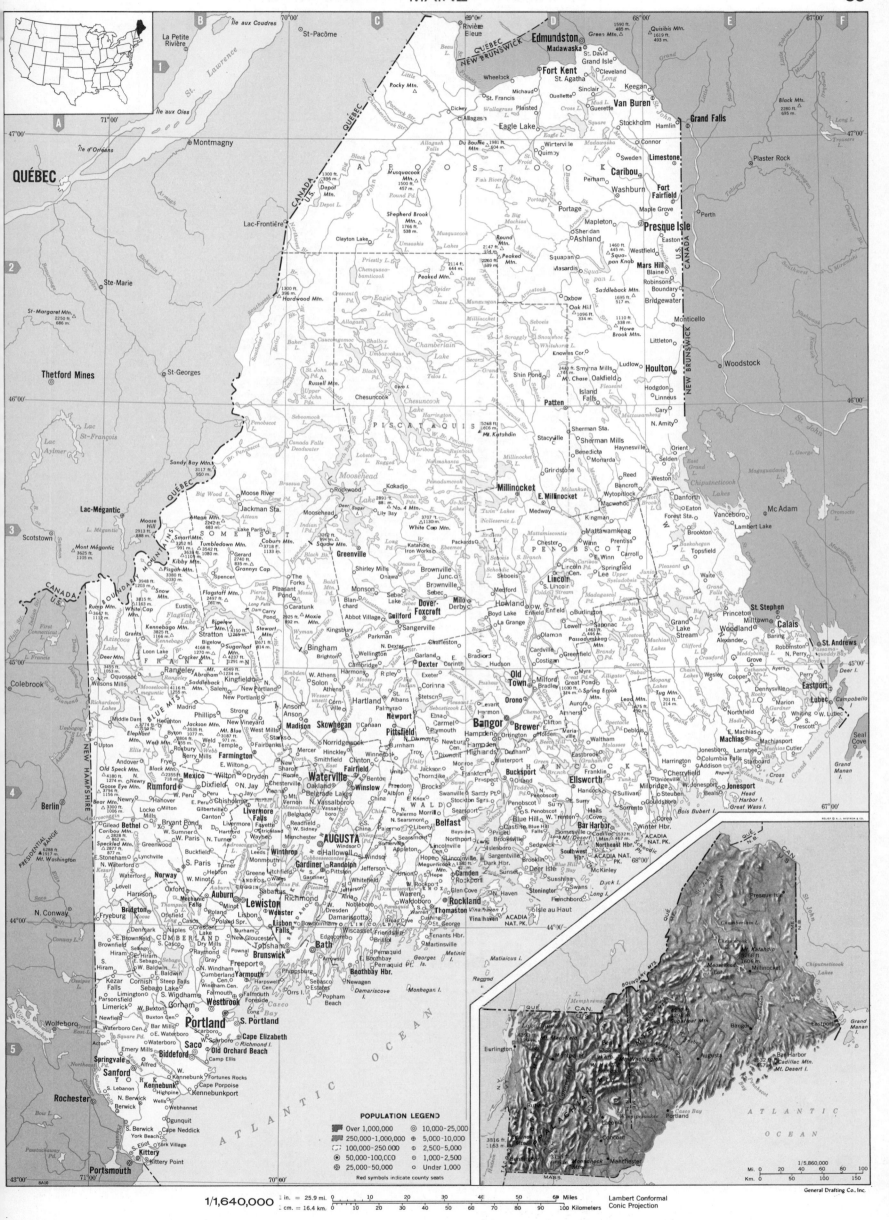

Atlantic Ocean

POPULATION LEGEND

Over 1,000,000	⊕ 10,000–25,000
250,000–1,000,000	⊕ 5,000–10,000
100,000–250,000	⊙ 2,500–5,000
⊚ 25,000–100,000	○ 1,000–2,500
⊙ 25,000–50,000	○ Under 1,000

Red symbols indicate county seats

1/1,640,000

1 in. = 25.9 mi.

1 cm. = 16.4 km.

Miles 0 10 20 30 40 50 60

Kilometers 0 10 20 30 40 50 60 70 80 90 100

Lambert Conformal
Conic Projection

General Drafting Co., Inc.

County government in Connecticut
was abolished by legislative act
October 1, 1960. However, counties
are shown since their names con-
tinue in common use.

General Drafting Co., Inc.

POPULATION LEGEND

Over 1,000,000	⊙	10,000–25,000
250,000–1,000,000	⊕	5,000–10,000
100,000–250,000	⊛	2,500–5,000
50,000–100,000	⊚	1,000–2,500
25,000–50,000	○	Under 1,000

Red symbols indicate county seats

1/733,000

| 1 in. = 11.6 mi. | 0 | 5 | 10 | 15 | 20 | 25 Miles |
| 1 cm. = 7.3 km. | 0 | 5 | 10 | 15 | 20 | 25 | 30 | 35 | 40 Kilometers |

Lambert Conformal
Conic Projection

General Drafting Co., Inc.

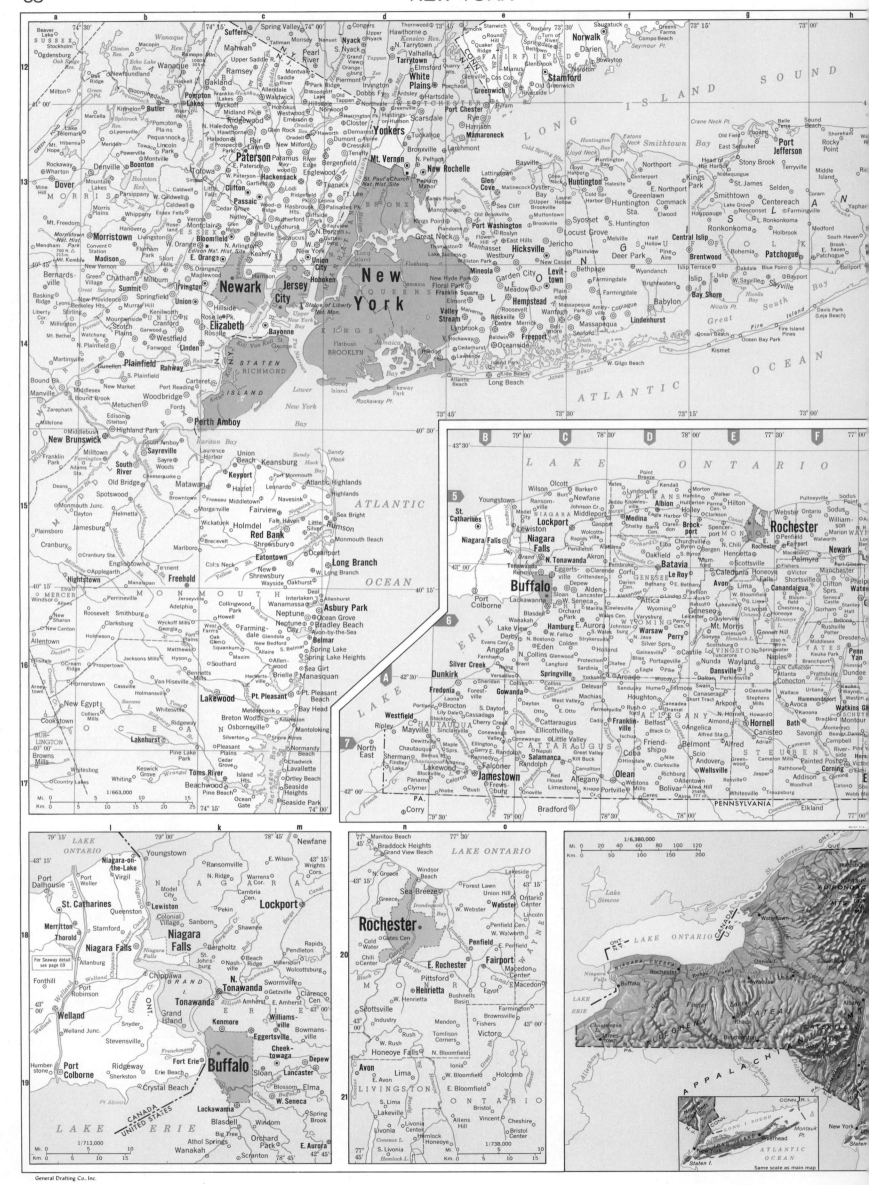

General Drafting Co., Inc.

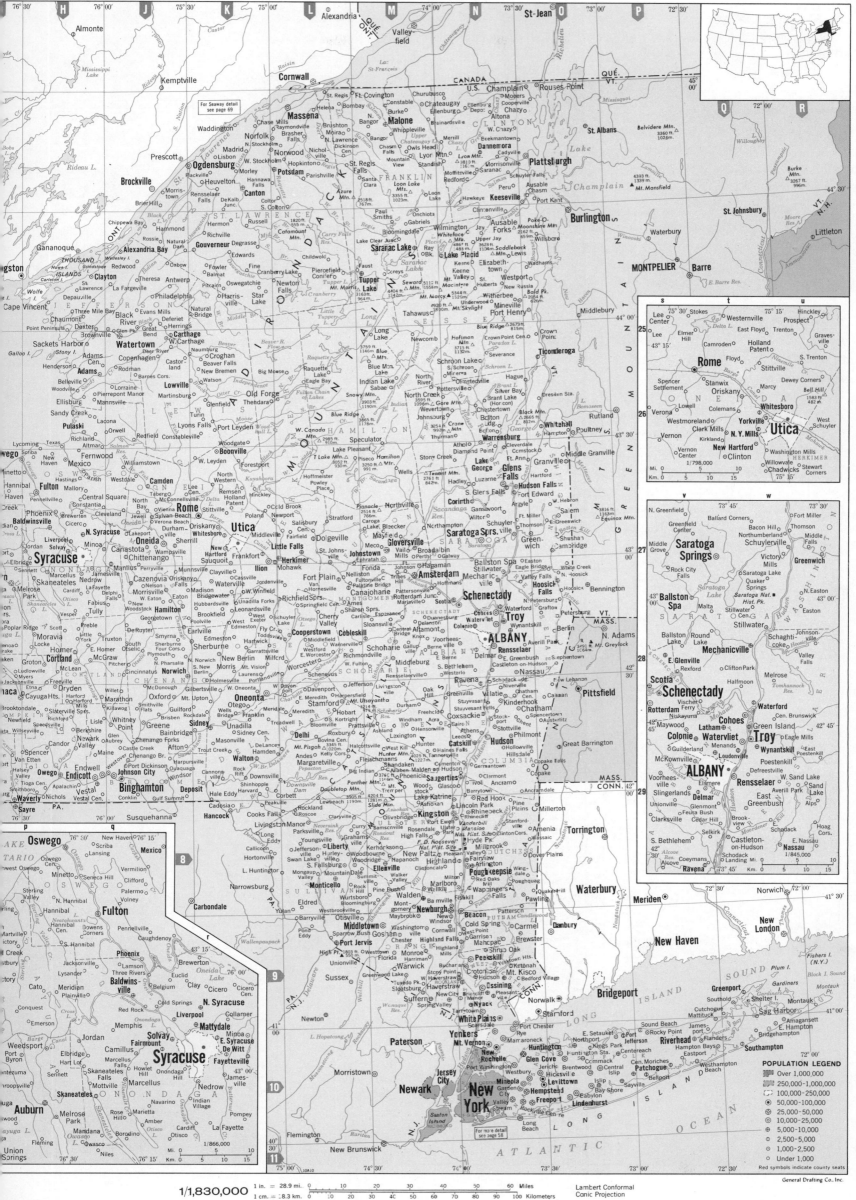

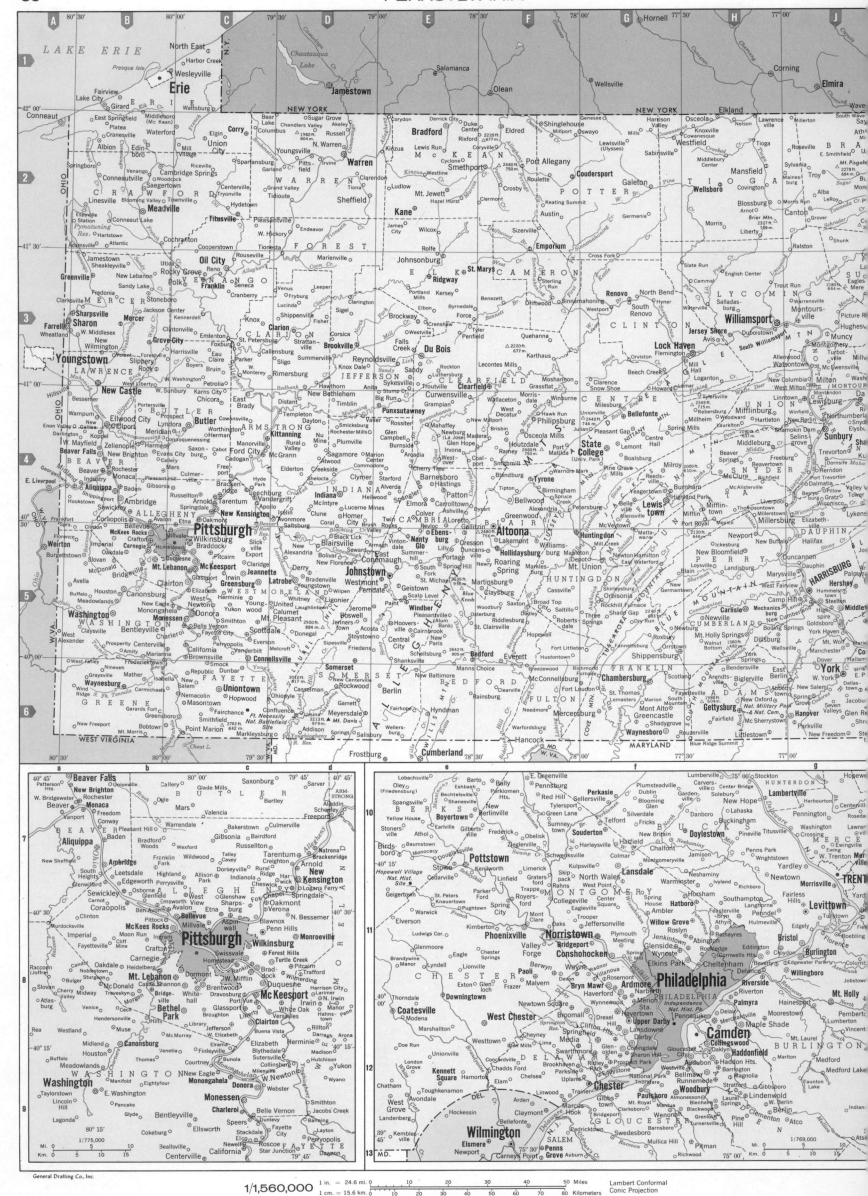

1/1,560,000

1 in. = 24.6 mi.
1 cm. = 15.6 km.

Lambert Conformal
Conic Projection

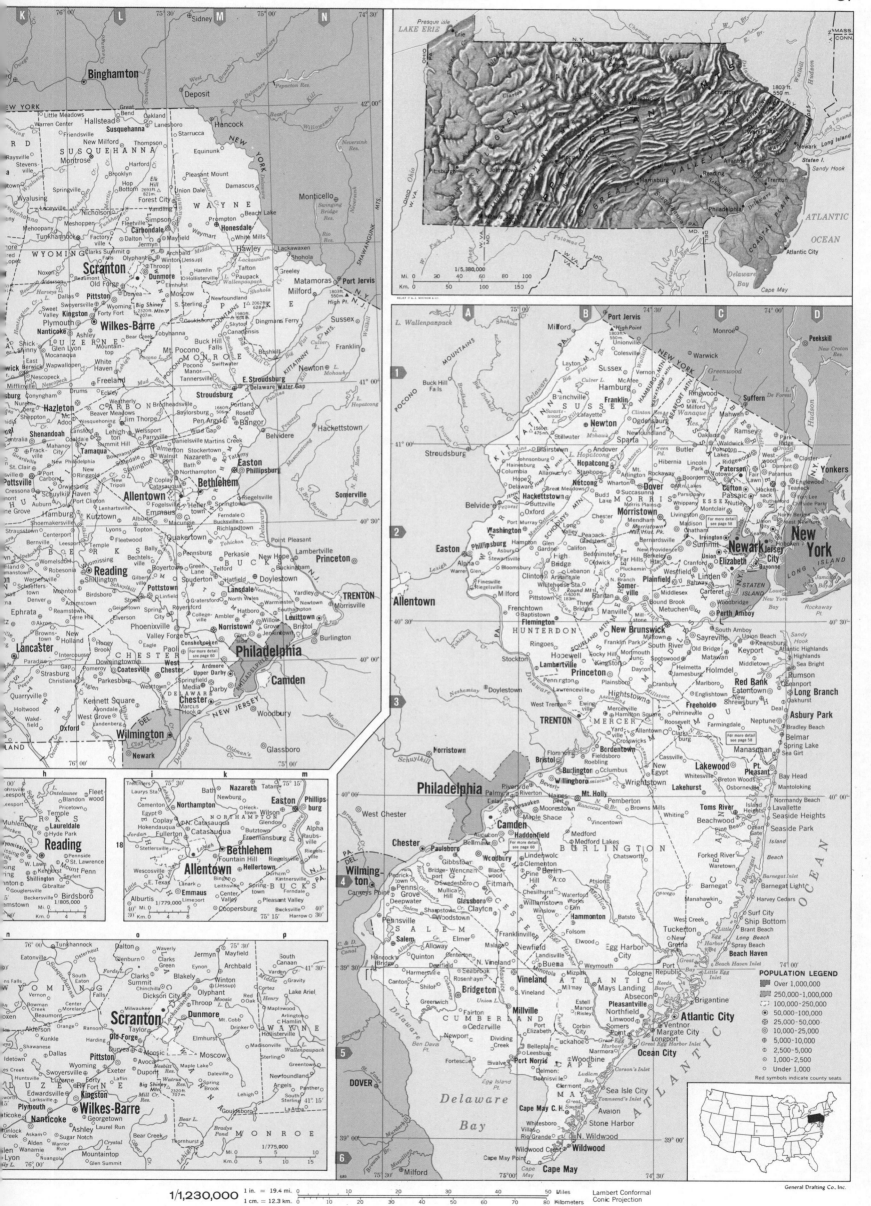

POPULATION LEGEND
- Over 1,000,000
- 250,000–1,000,000
- 100,000–250,000
- ◉ 50,000–100,000
- ⊙ 25,000–50,000
- ⊚ 10,000–25,000
- ⊕ 5,000–10,000
- ○ 2,500–5,000
- ○ 1,000–2,500
- · Under 1,000
- Red symbols indicate county seats

1/1,230,000

1 in. = 19.4 mi.
1 cm. = 12.3 km.

0 10 20 30 40 50 Miles
0 10 20 30 40 50 60 70 80 Kilometers

Lambert Conformal
Conic Projection

General Drafting Co., Inc.

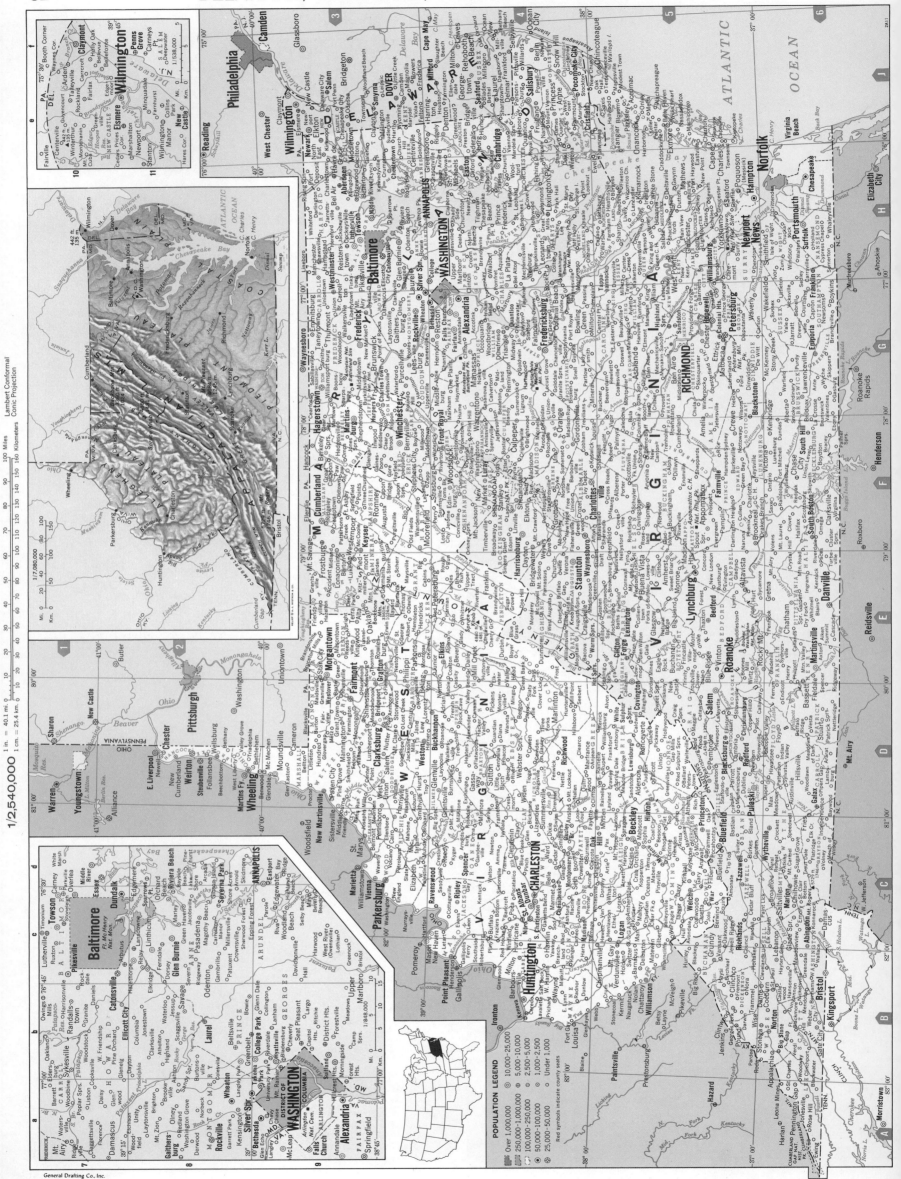

1/2,540,000

1 in. = 40.1 mi.
1 cm. = 25.4 km.

Lambert Conformal
Conic Projection

General Drafting Co., Inc.

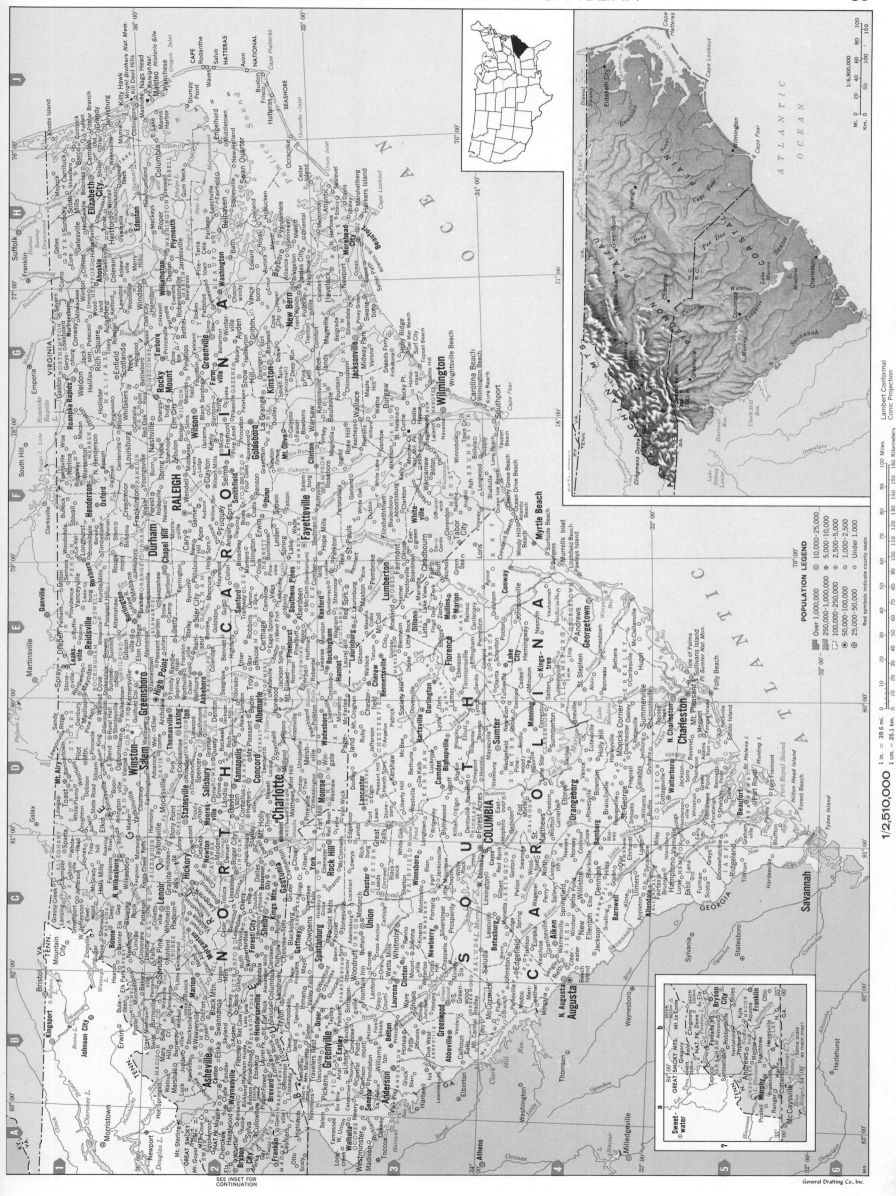

1/2,510,000

SEE INSET FOR
CONTINUATION

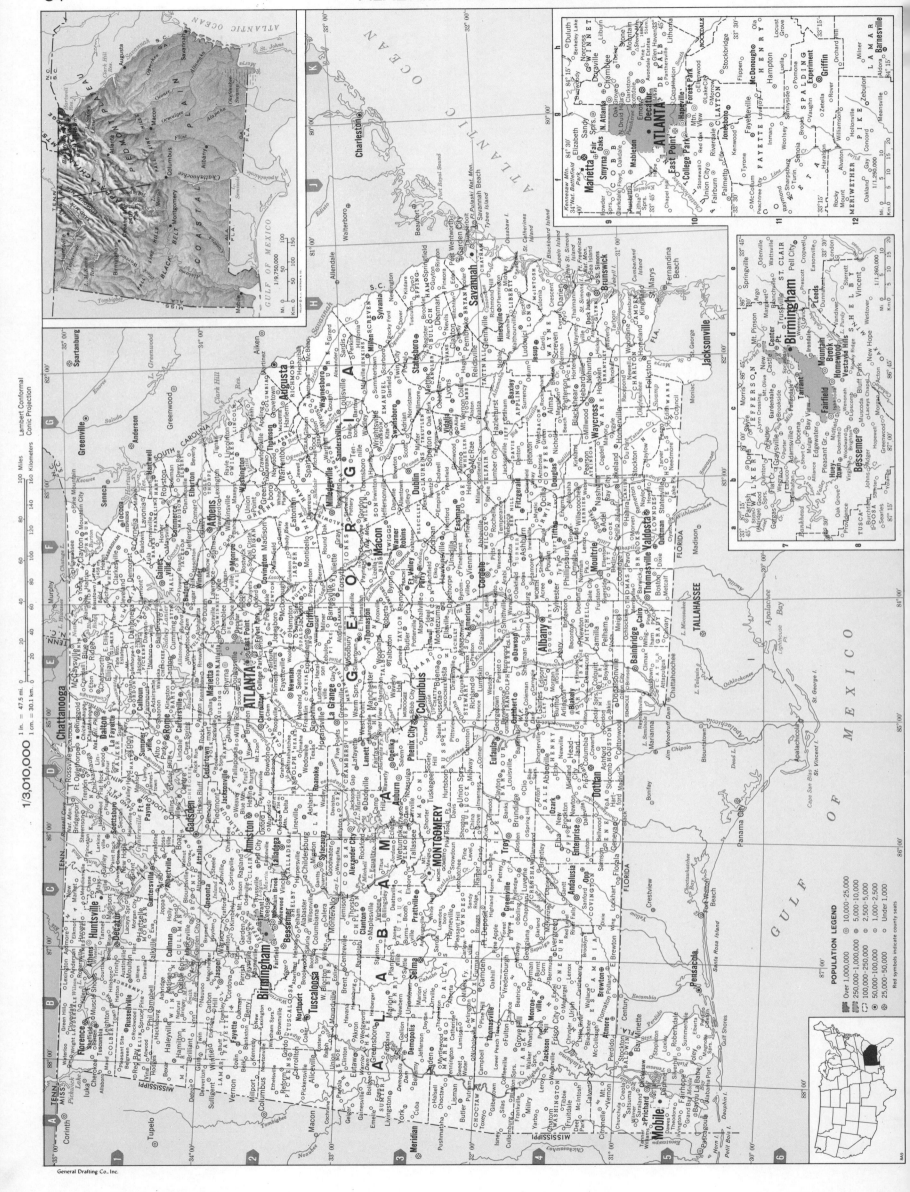

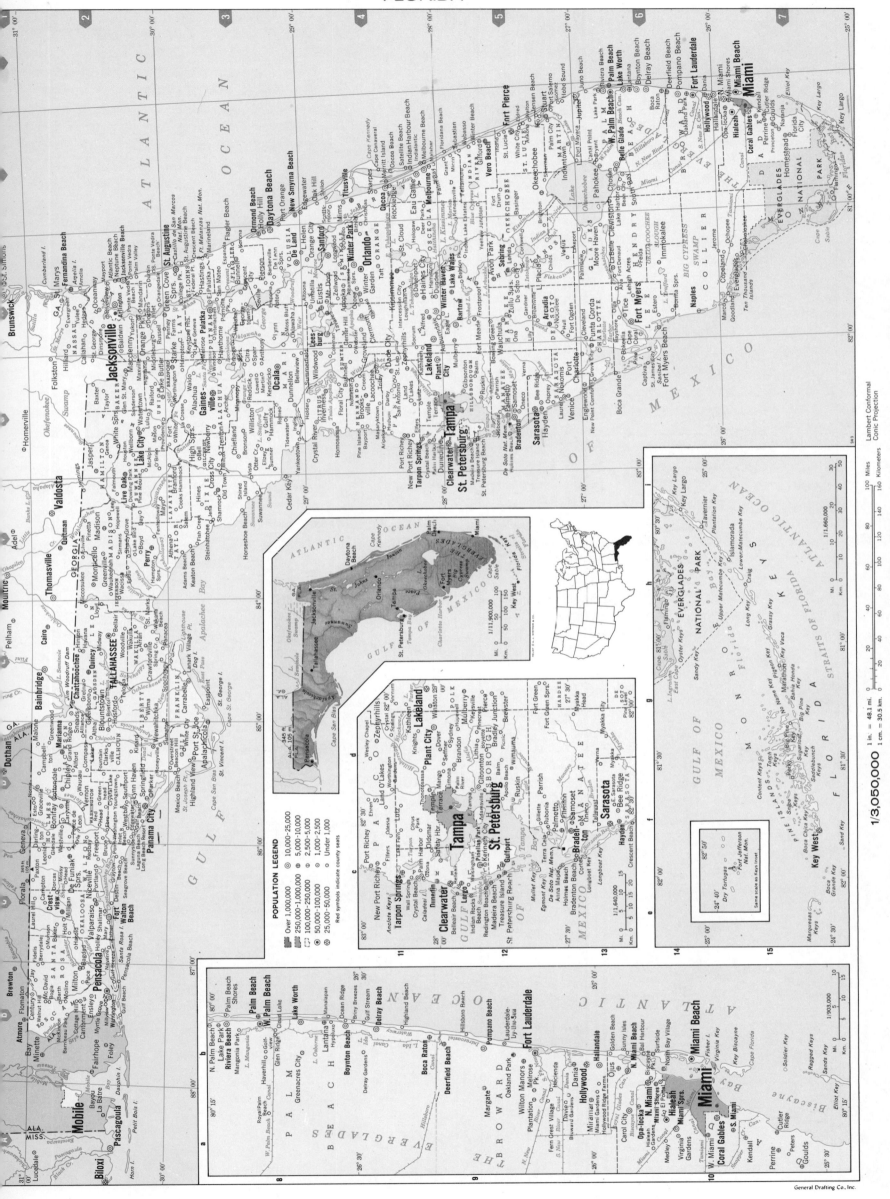

POPULATION LEGEND

Over 1,000,000
250,000–1,000,000
100,000–250,000
50,000–100,000
25,000–50,000

10,000–25,000
5,000–10,000
2,500–5,000
1,000–2,500
Under 1,000

Red symbols indicate county seats

1/3,050,000

1 in. = 48.1 mi.
1 cm. = 30.5 km.

Lambert Conformal
Conic Projection

General Drafting Co., Inc.

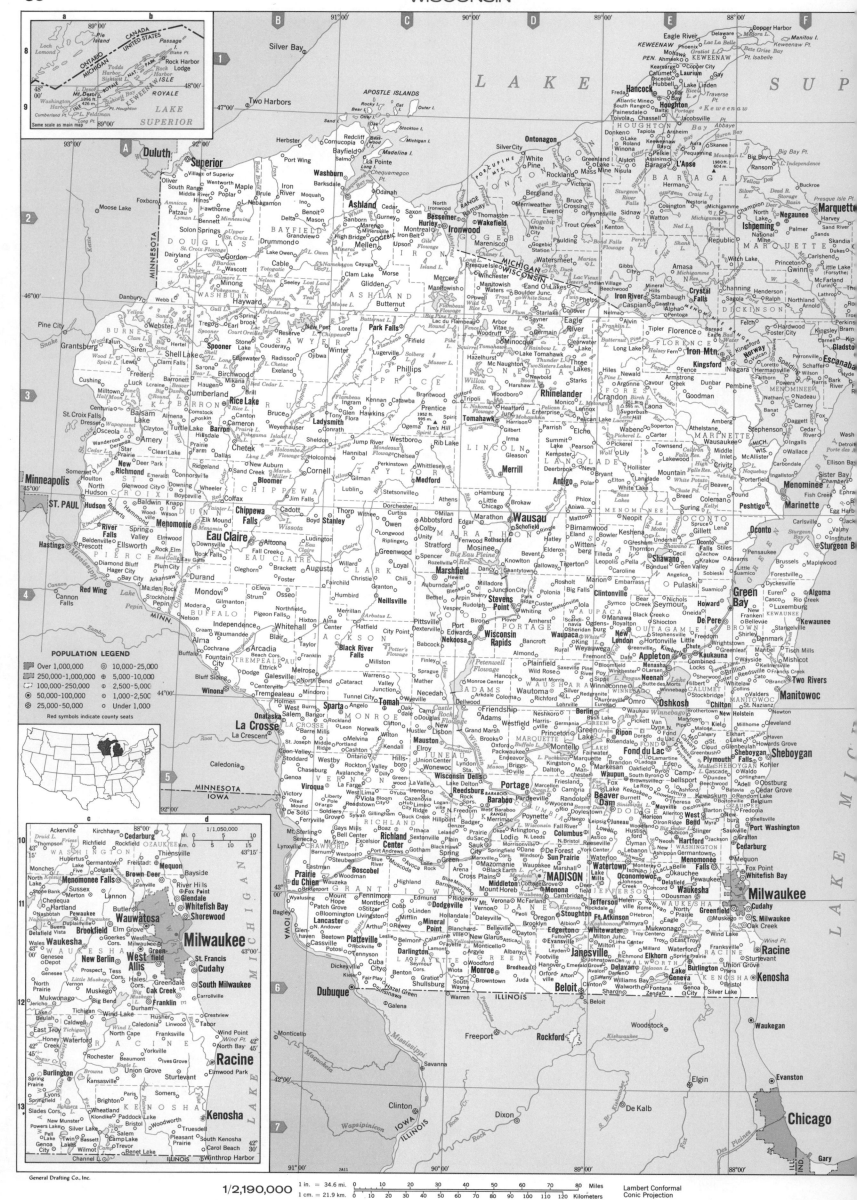

1/2,190,000

1 in. = 34.6 mi.

1 cm. = 21.9 km.

Lambert Conformal
Conic Projection

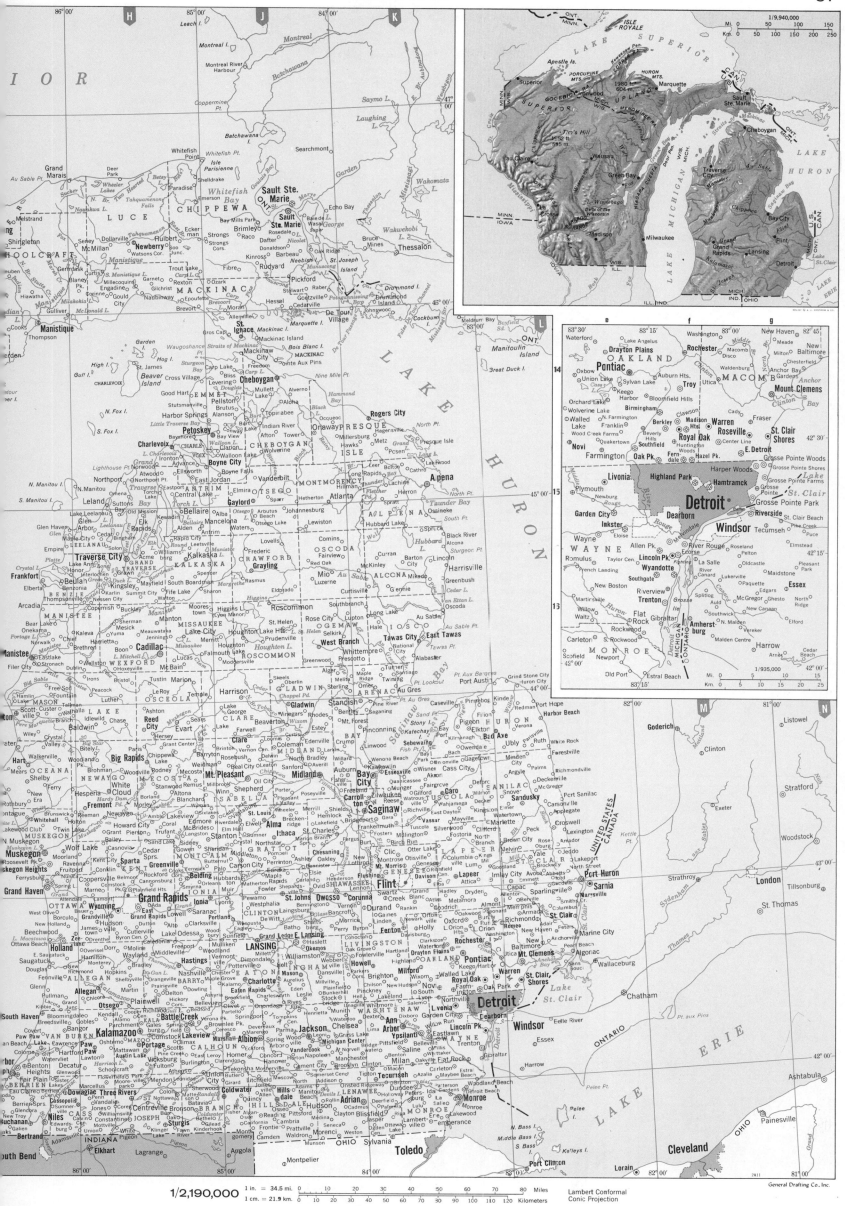

1 in. = 34.5 mi.
1 cm. = 21.9 km.

0 10 20 30 40 50 60 70 80 Miles
0 10 20 30 40 50 60 70 80 90 100 110 120 Kilometers

Lambert Conformal
Conic Projection

General Drafting Co. Inc.

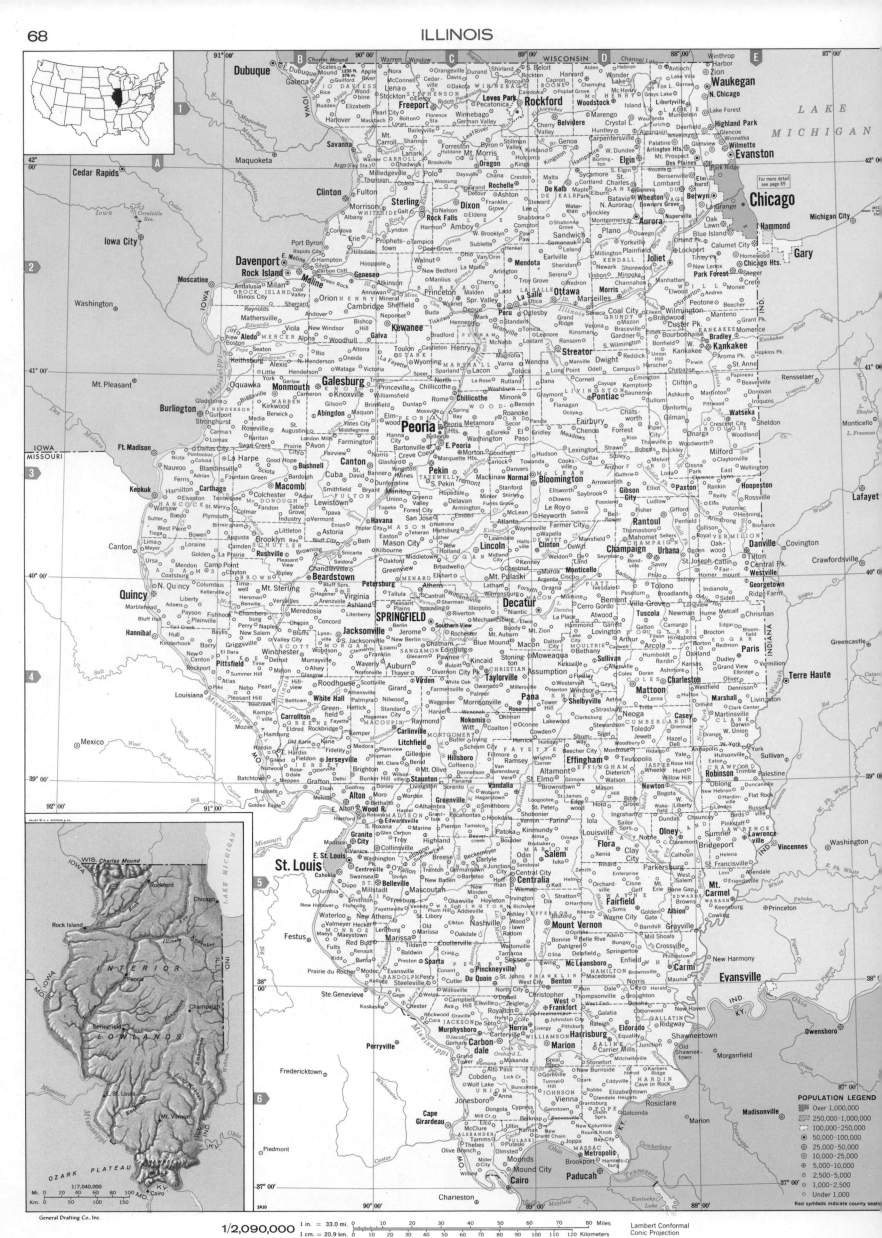

1/2,090,000

1 in. = 33.0 mi.

1 cm. = 20.9 km.

0 10 20 30 40 50 60 70 80 Miles

0 10 20 30 40 50 60 70 80 90 100 110 120 Kilometers

Lambert Conformal
Conic Projection

POPULATION LEGEND

- Over 1,000,000
- 250,000-1,000,000
- 100,000-250,000
- 50,000-100,000
- 25,000-50,000
- 10,000-25,000
- 5,000-10,000
- 2,500-5,000
- 1,000-2,500
- Under 1,000

Red symbols indicate county seats

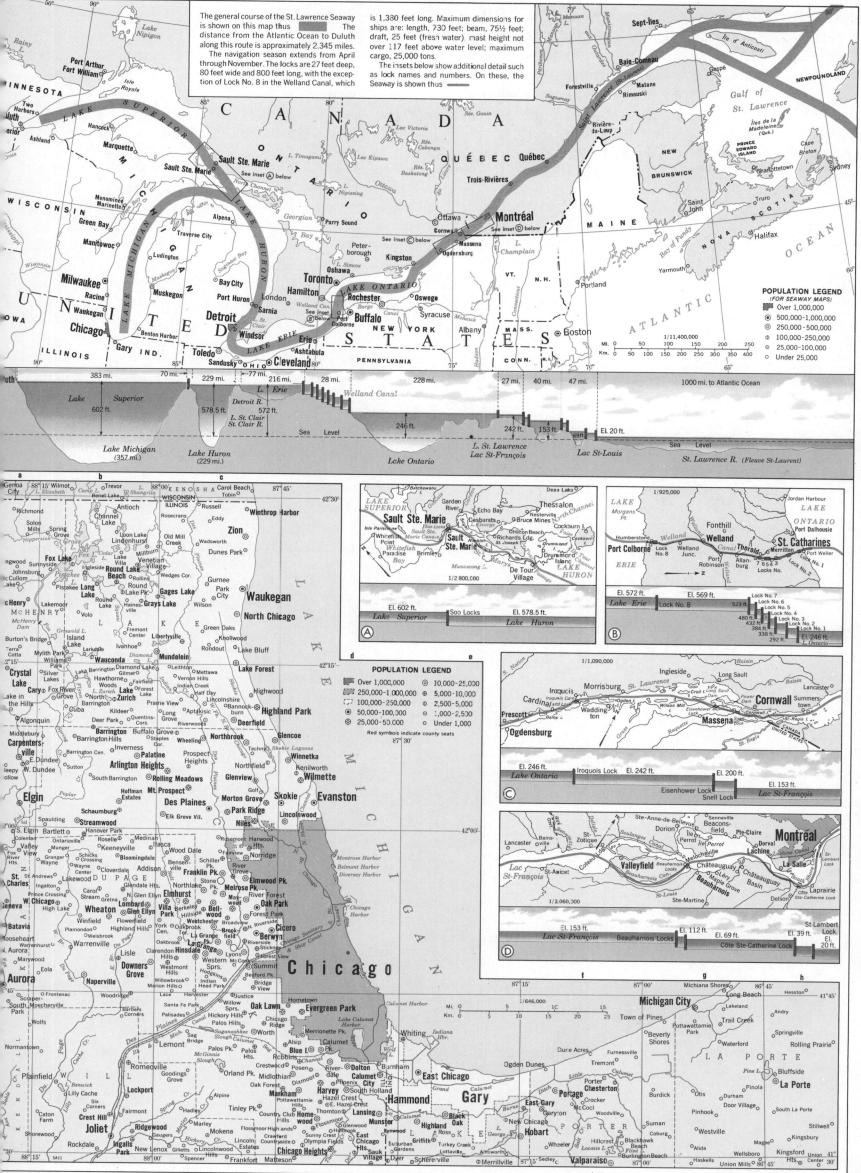

The general course of the St. Lawrence Seaway is shown on this map thus ▬ The distance from the Atlantic Ocean to Duluth along this route is approximately 2,345 miles.

The navigation season extends from April through November. The locks are 27 feet deep, 80 feet wide and 800 feet long, with the exception of Lock No. 8 in the Welland Canal, which is 1,330 feet long. Maximum dimensions for ships are: length, 730 feet; beam, 75½ feet; draft, 25 feet (fresh water); mast height not over 117 feet above water level; maximum cargo, 25,000 tons.

The insets below show additional detail such as lock names and numbers. On these, the Seaway is shown thus ▬

POPULATION LEGEND
(FOR SEAWAY MAPS)
- Over 1,000,000
- 500,000–1,000,000
- 250,000–500,000
- 100,000–250,000
- 25,000–100,000
- Under 25,000

POPULATION LEGEND
- Over 1,000,000
- 250,000–1,000,000
- 100,000–250,000
- 50,000–100,000
- 25,000–50,000
- 10,000–25,000
- 5,000–10,000
- 2,500–5,000
- 1,000–2,500
- Under 1,000

Red symbols indicate county seats

General Drafting Co. Inc.

1/2,810,000

Lambert Conformal
Conic Projection

General Drafting Co., Inc.

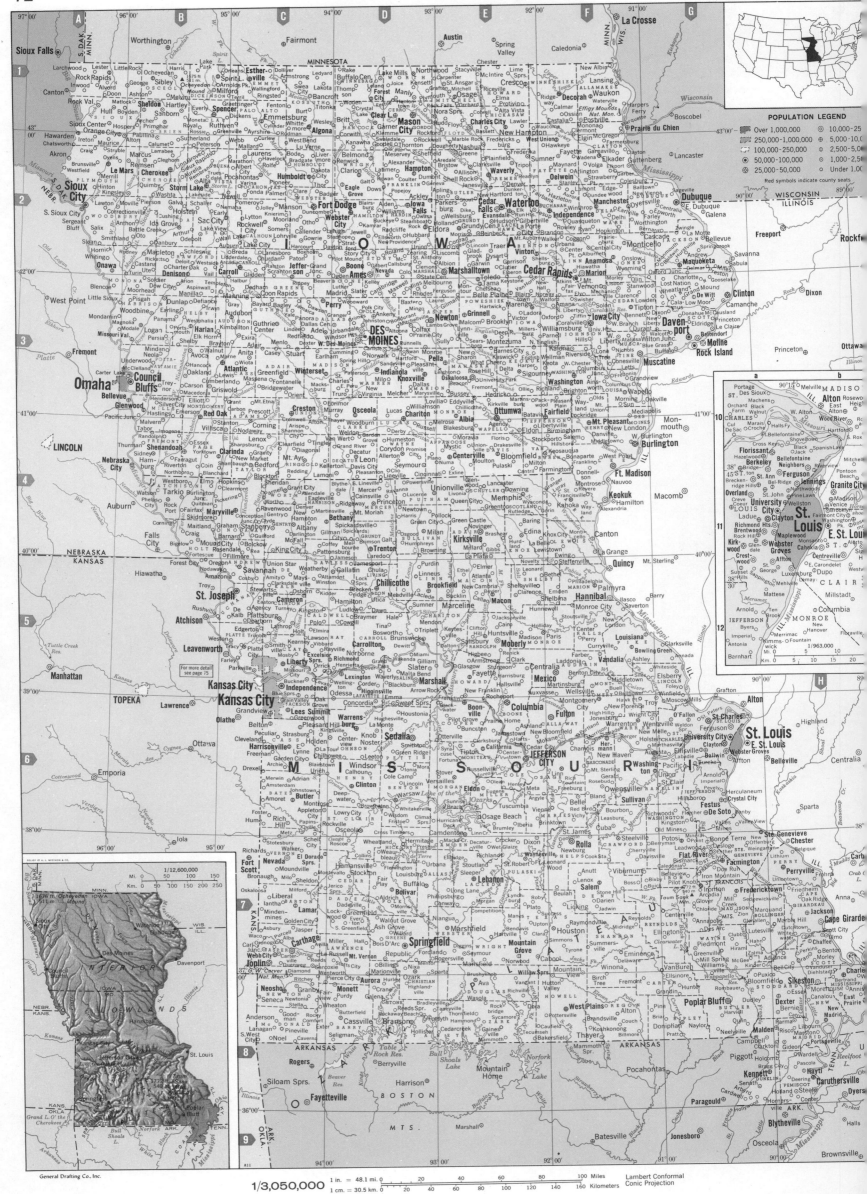

1/3,050,000   Lambert Conformal
                                Conic Projection

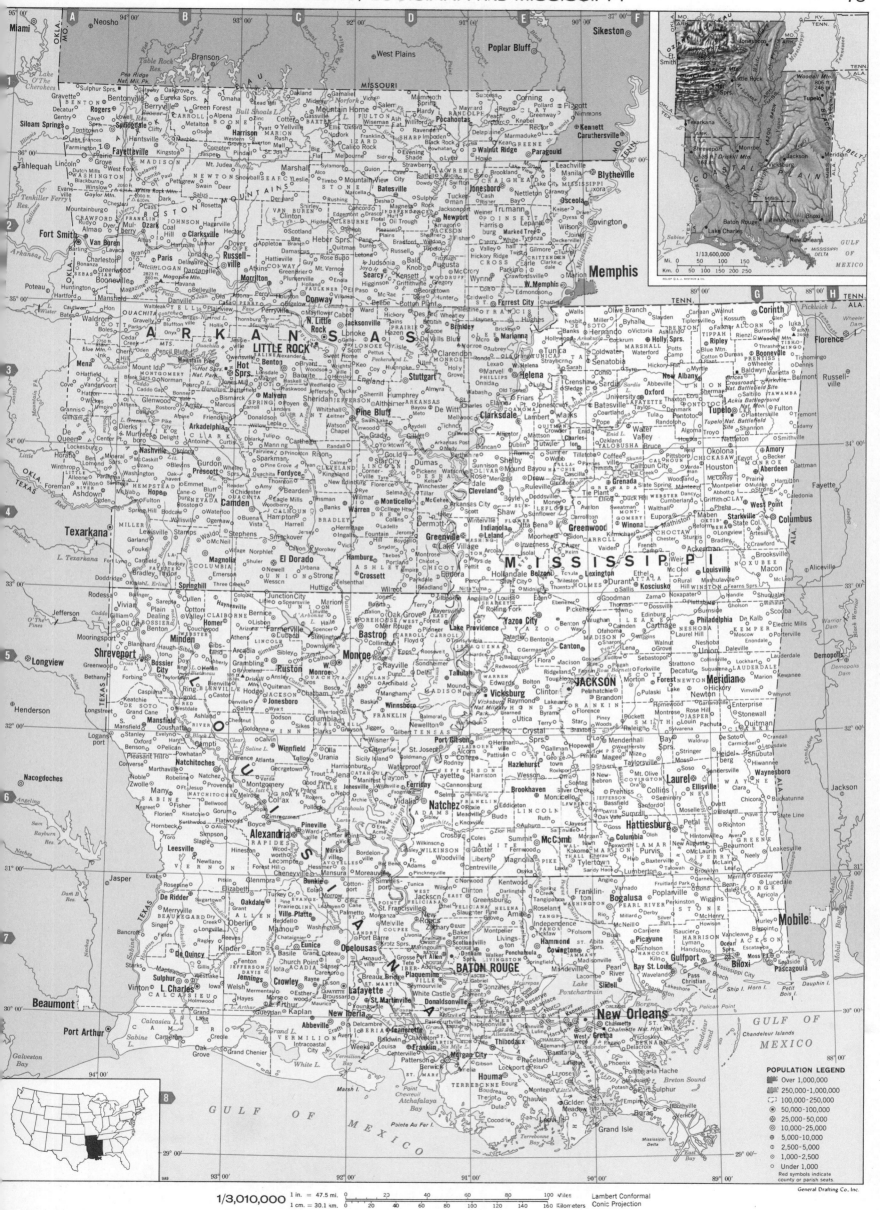

Population Legend

- ▪ Over 1,000,000
- ▣ 250,000–1,000,000
- ▭ 100,000–250,000
- ⊛ 50,000–100,000
- ⊕ 25,000–50,000
- ⊕ 10,000–25,000
- ⊕ 5,000–10,000
- ⊙ 2,500–5,000
- ○ 1,000–2,500
- ○ Under 1,000

Red symbols indicate county or parish seats.

1/3,010,000

1 in. = 47.5 mi.
1 cm. = 30.1 km.

0   20   40   60   80   100 Miles
0 20 40 60 80 100 120 140 160 Kilometers

Lambert Conformal
Conic Projection

General Drafting Co. Inc.

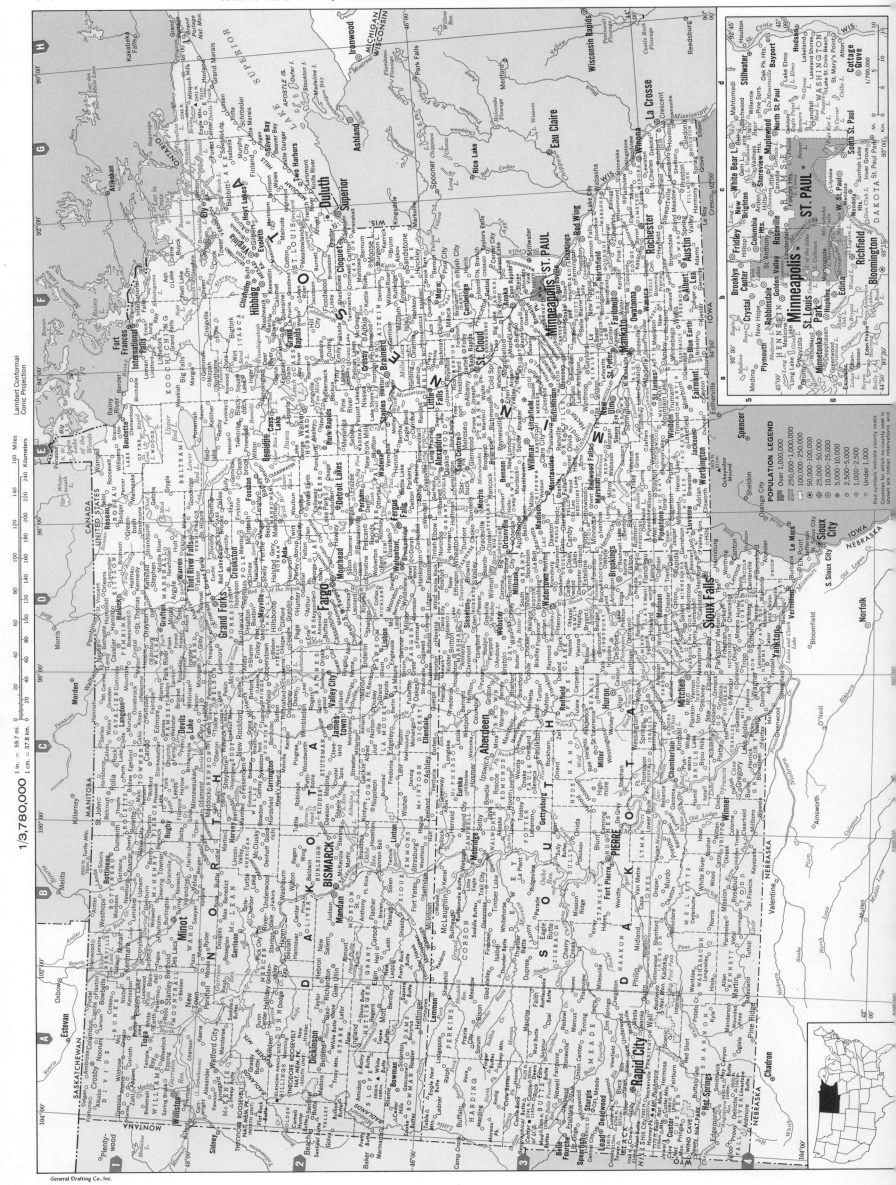

General Drafting Co., Inc.

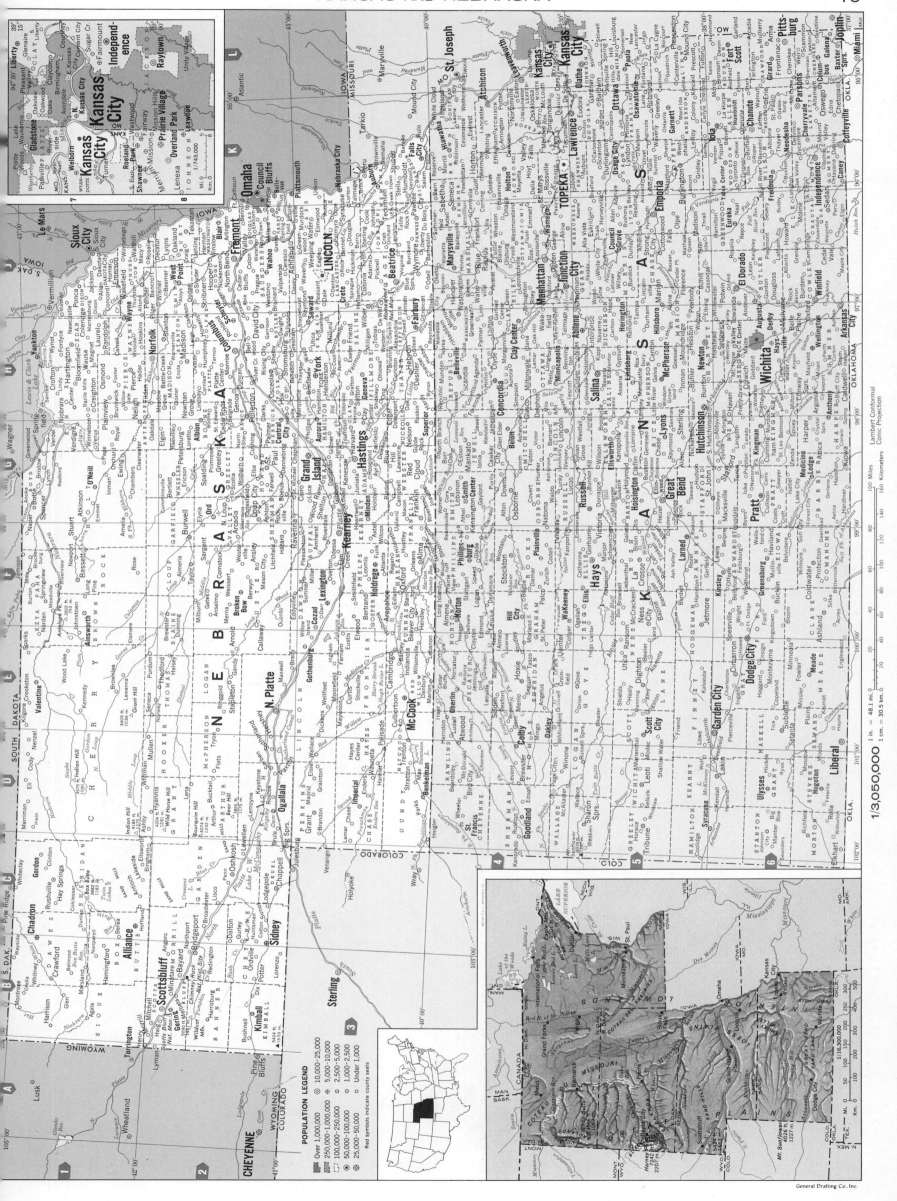

General Drafting Co., Inc.

1/3,050,000

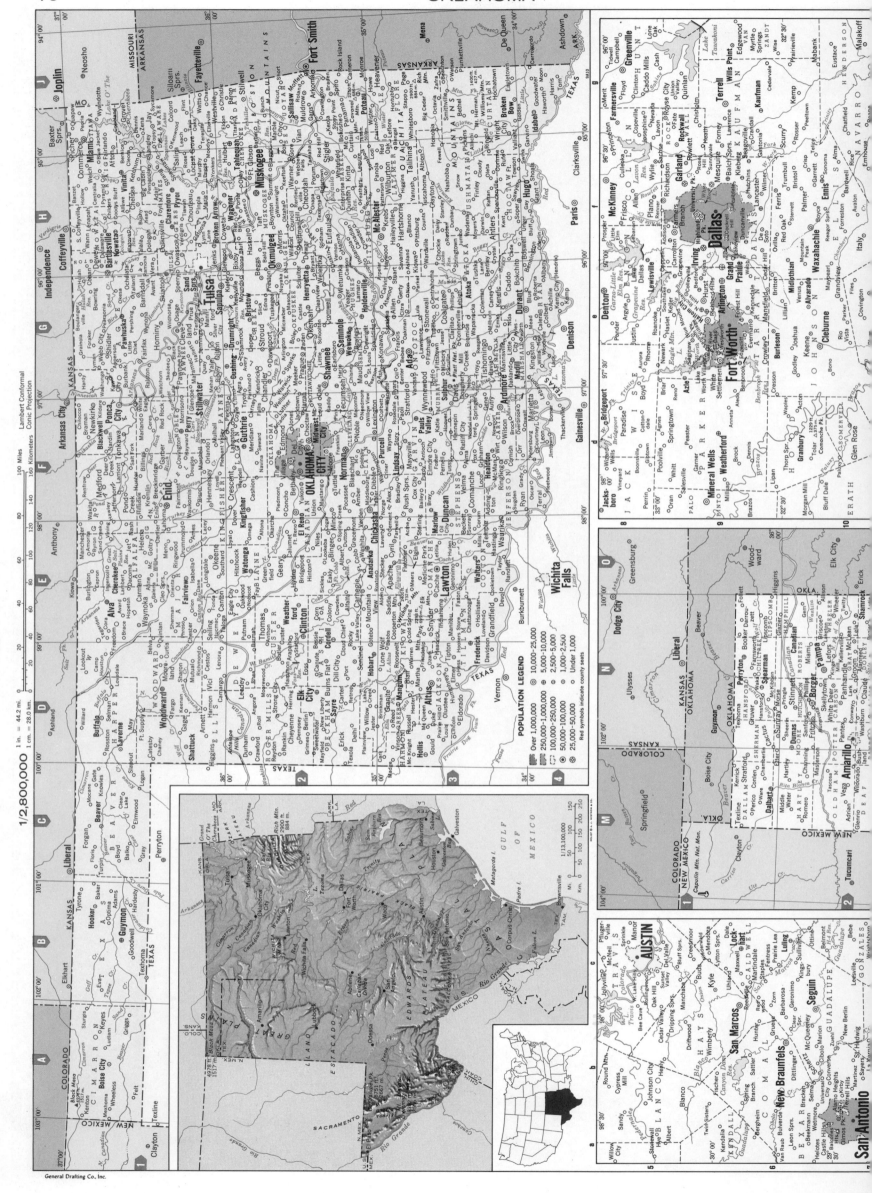

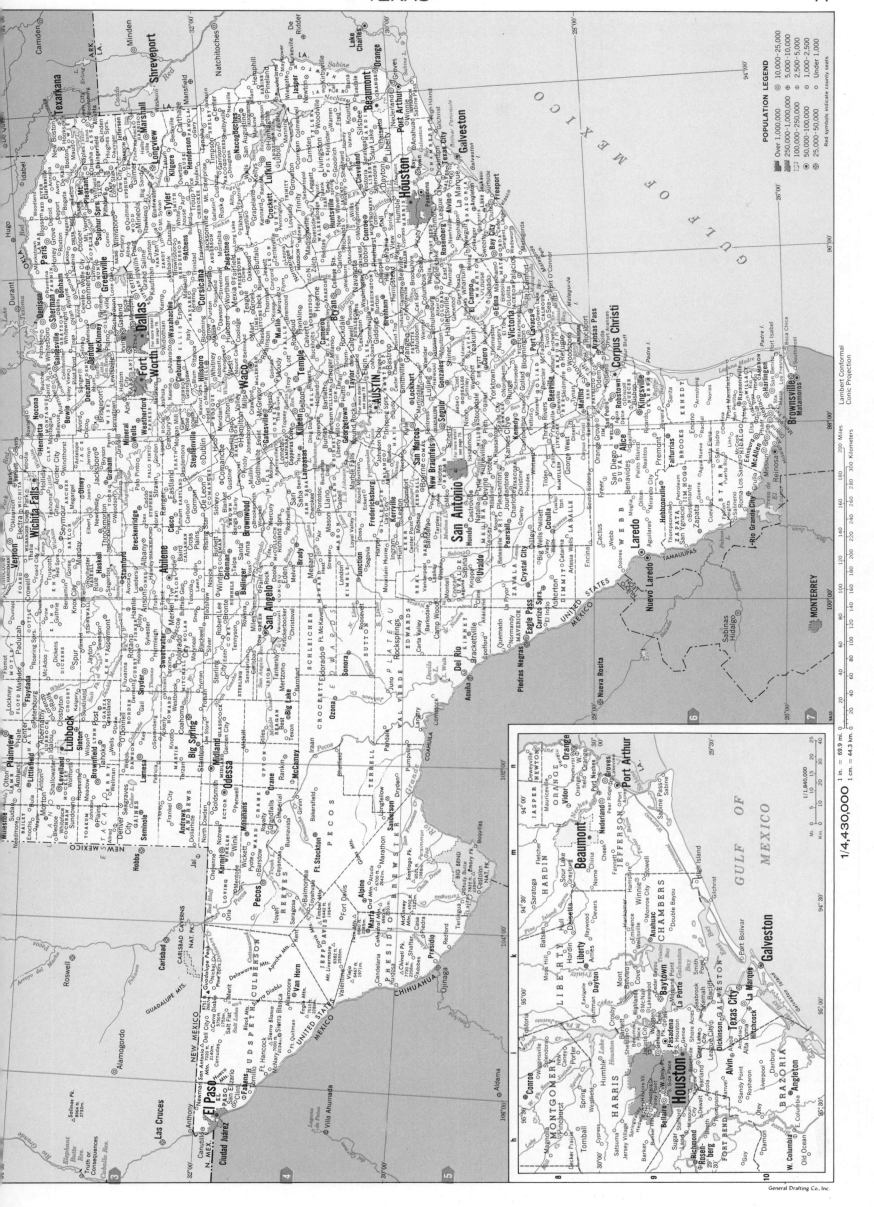

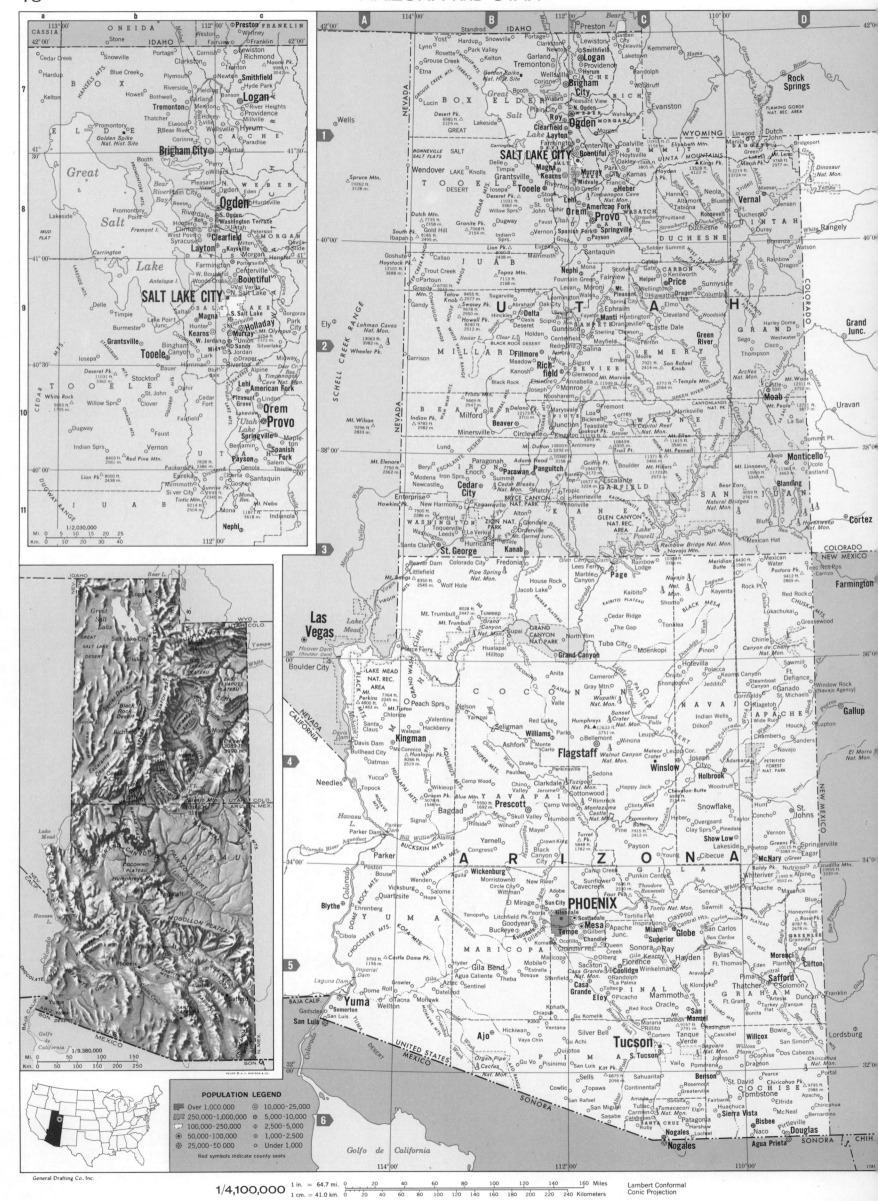

POPULATION LEGEND

Over 1,000,000	10,000–25,000
250,000–1,000,000	5,000–10,000
100,000–250,000	2,500–5,000
50,000–100,000	1,000–2,500
25,000–50,000	Under 1,000

Red symbols indicate county seats

1/4,100,000

1 in. = 64.7 mi.
1 cm. = 41.0 km.

Lambert Conformal
Conic Projection

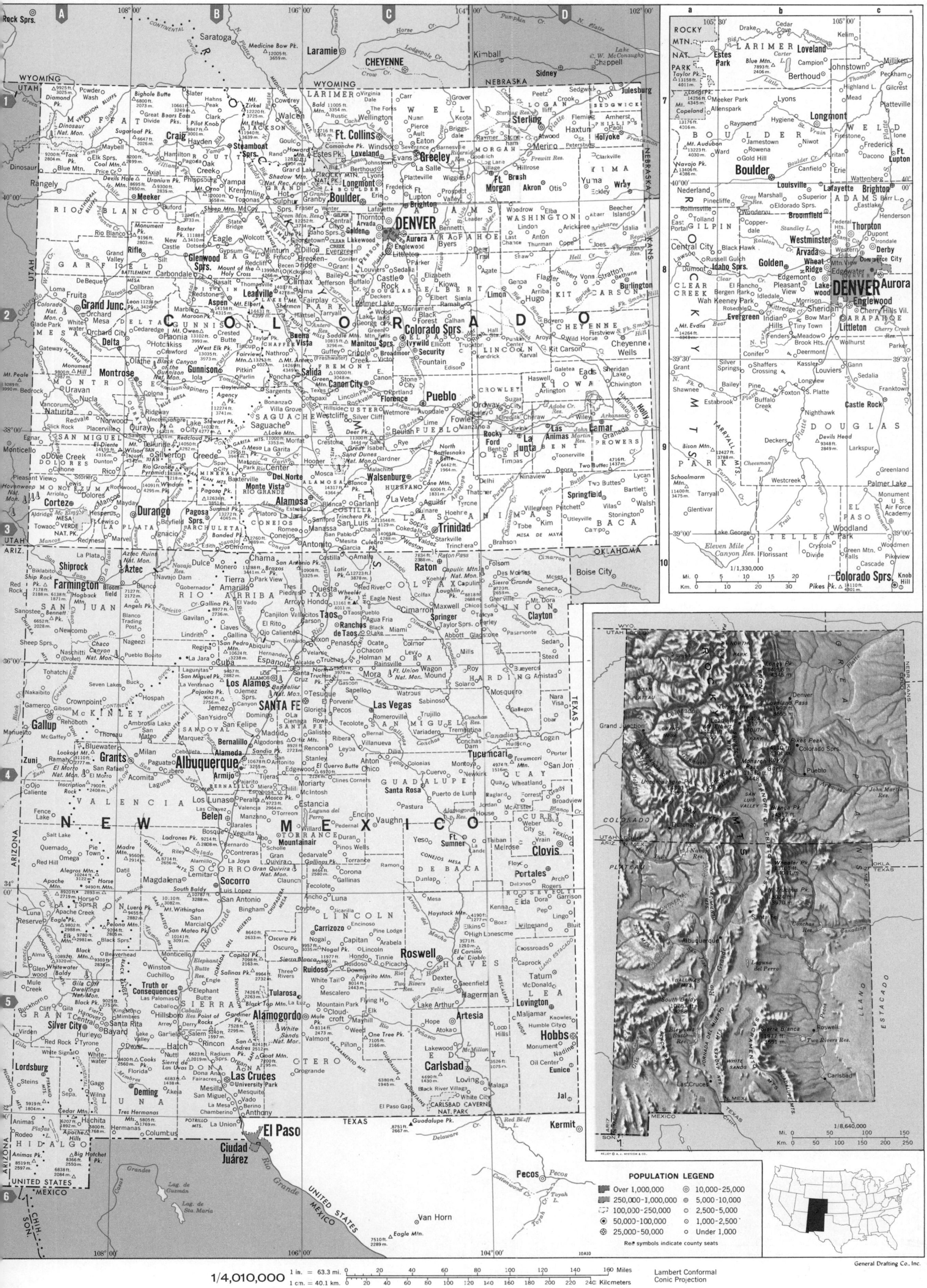
COLORADO
NEW MEXICO
DENVER
Albuquerque
SANTA FE
Colorado Sprs.
Pueblo
El Paso
Ciudad Juárez
ROCKY MTN. NAT. PARK
1/1,330,000
1/8,640,000
POPULATION LEGEND
Over 1,000,000
250,000-1,000,000
100,000-250,000
50,000-100,000
25,000-50,000
10,000-25,000
5,000-10,000
2,500-5,000
1,000-2,500
Under 1,000
Red symbols indicate county seats
General Drafting Co., Inc.

1/4,010,000 1 in. = 63.3 mi. 1 cm. = 40.1 km.

Miles 0 20 40 60 80 100 120 140 160

Kilometers 0 20 40 60 80 100 120 140 160 180 200 220 240

Lambert Conformal Conic Projection

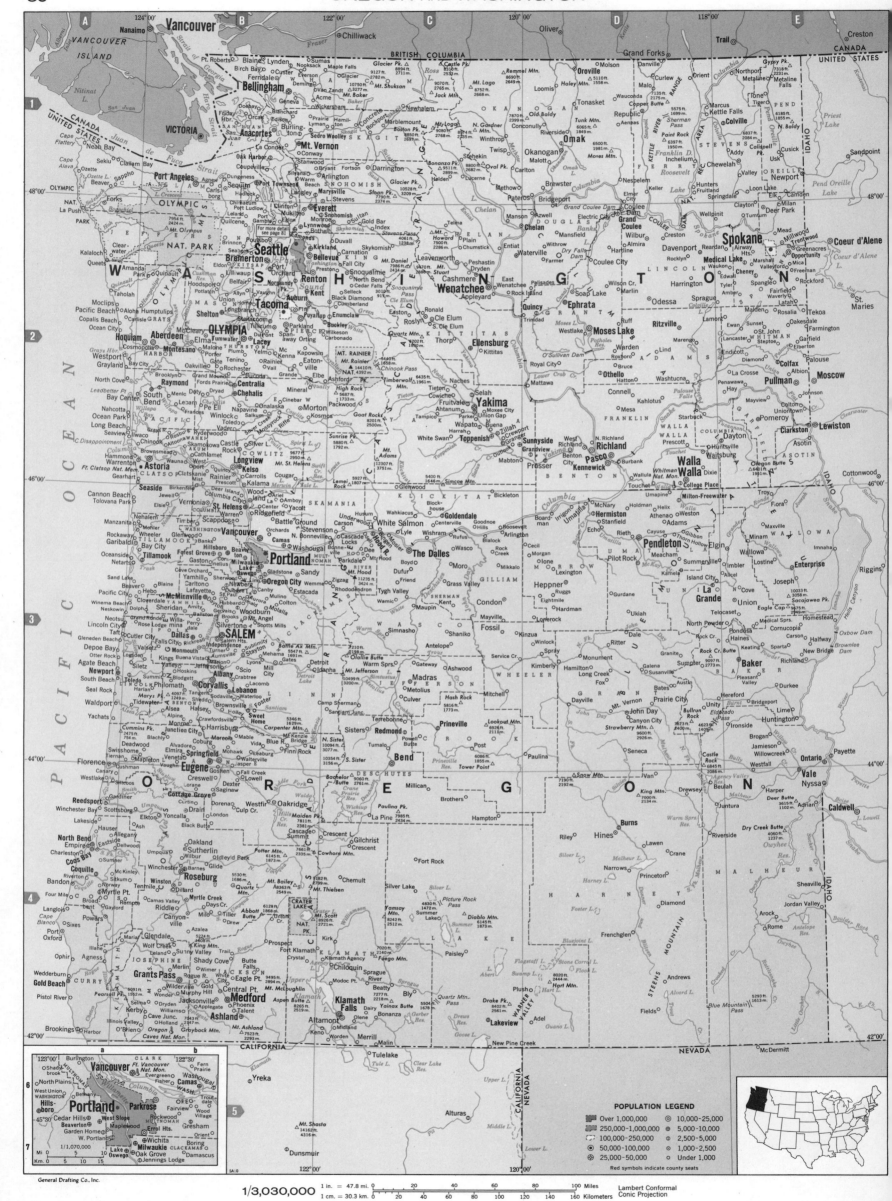

POPULATION LEGEND

■ Over 1,000,000		⊕ 10,000–25,000	
■ 250,000–1,000,000		⊕ 5,000–10,000	
▢ 100,000–250,000		⊕ 2,500–5,000	
◻ 50,000–100,000		⊕ 1,000–2,500	
⊙ 25,000–50,000		○ Under 1,000	

Red symbols indicate county seats

General Drafting Co., Inc.

1/3,030,000   1 in. = 47.8 mi.

1 cm. = 30.3 km.

Lambert Conformal
Conic Projection

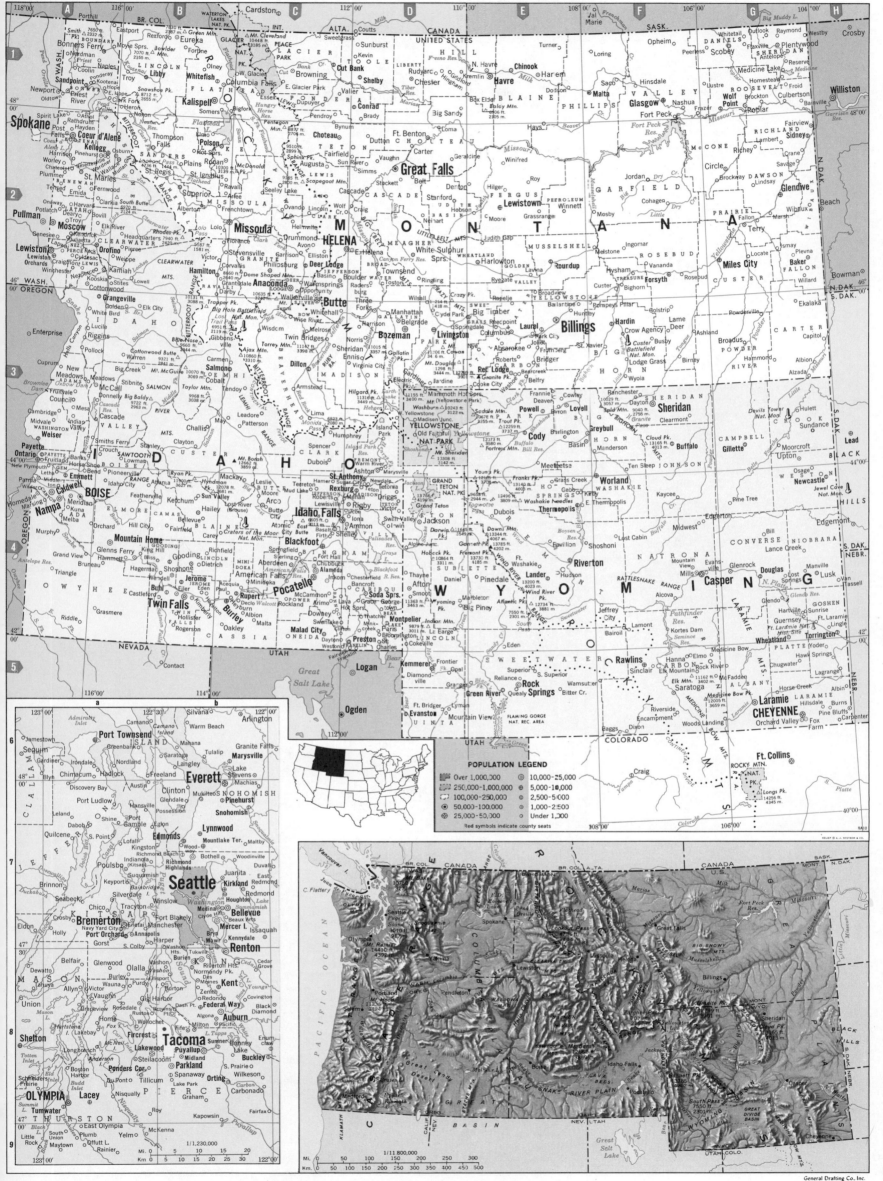

Population Legend

Over 1,000,000	10,000–25,000
250,000–1,000,000	5,000–10,000
100,000–250,000	2,500–5,000
50,000–100,000	1,000–2,500
25,000–50,000	Under 1,000

Red symbols indicate county seats

Lambert Conformal
Conic Projection

1/4,930,000

1 in. = 77.8 mi.
1 cm. = 49.3 km.

General Drafting Co., Inc.

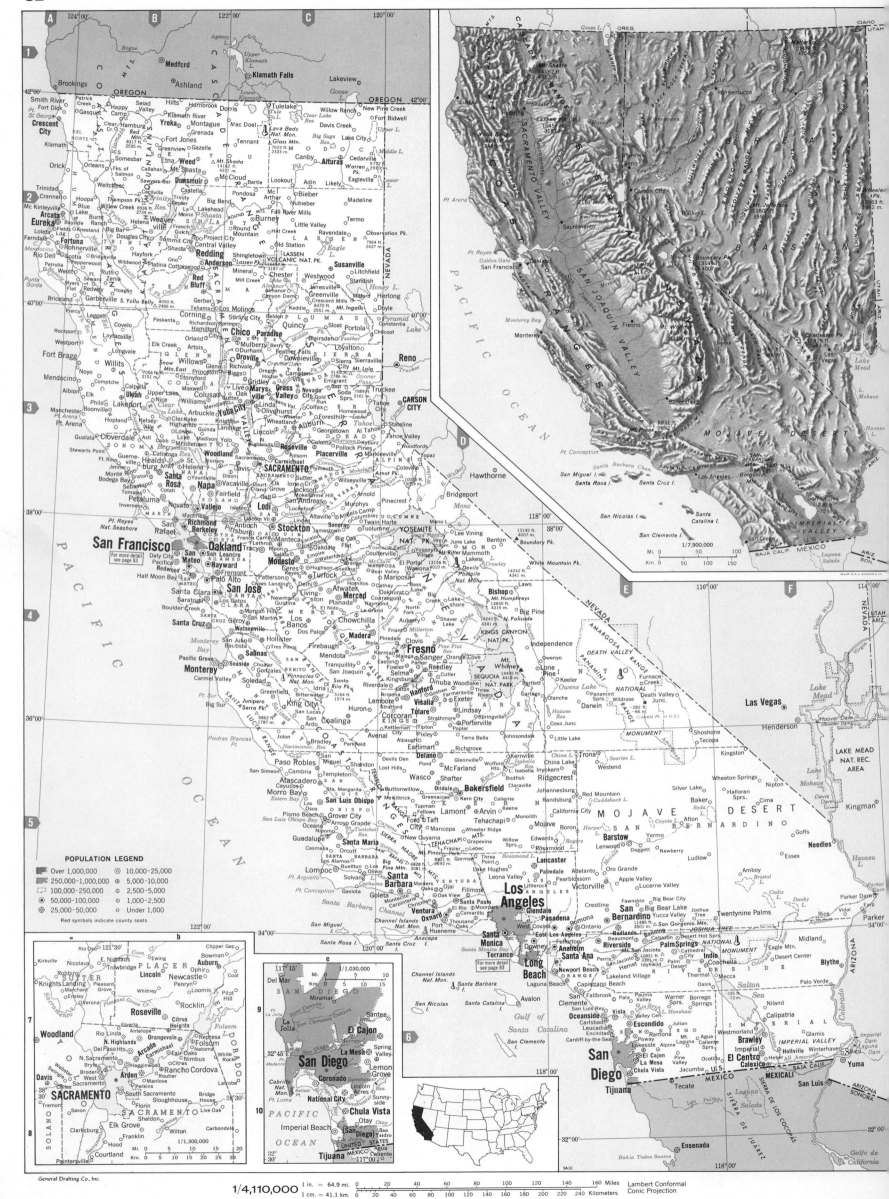

POPULATION LEGEND

Over 1,000,000	10,000-25,000
250,000-1,000,000	5,000-10,000
100,000-250,000	2,500-5,000
50,000-100,000	1,000-2,500
25,000-50,000	Under 1,000

Red symbols indicate county seats

General Drafting Co., Inc.

1/4,110,000

1 in. = 64.9 mi.
1 cm. = 41.1 km.

Lambert Conformal
Conic Projection

Kilometers from Wpg to Palm
                              Springs

3,336 ~~336~~ kms

Daytime travel 30 hrs
               32 hrs

To phoenix - 3023

→ Rinat
~~Niles~~
Niles city
Salt Lake City
Las Vegas

_____

Braendinton Florida
    3,361.7 km.   - 31 hrs

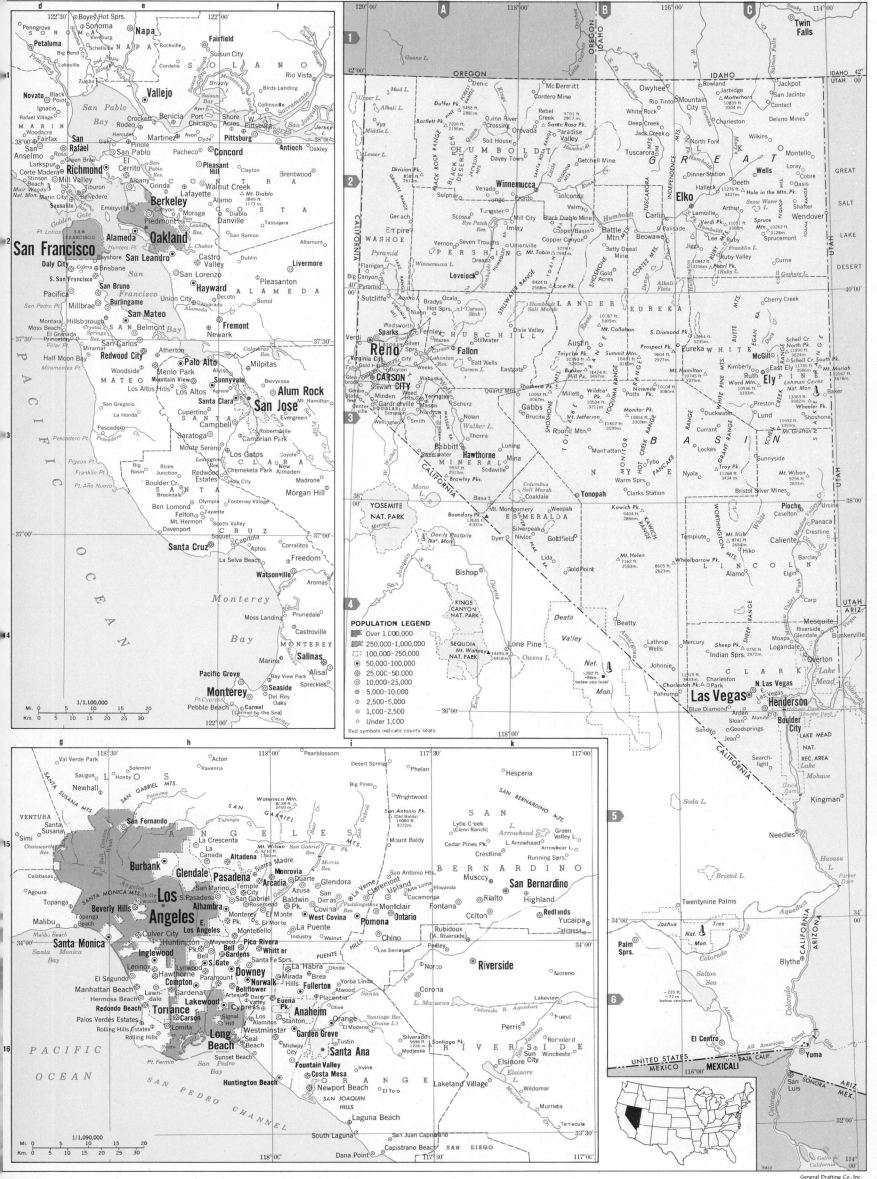

POPULATION LEGEND

- Over 1,000,000
- 250,000–1,000,000
- 100,000–250,000
- 50,000–100,000
- 25,000–50,000
- 10,000–25,000
- 5,000–10,000
- 2,500–5,000
- 1,000–2,500
- Under 1,000

Red symbols indicate county seats.

1/1,100,000

1/1,090,000

1/4,080,000

1 in. = 64.4 mi.
1 cm. = 40.8 km.

Lambert Conformal
Conic Projection

General Drafting Co. Inc.

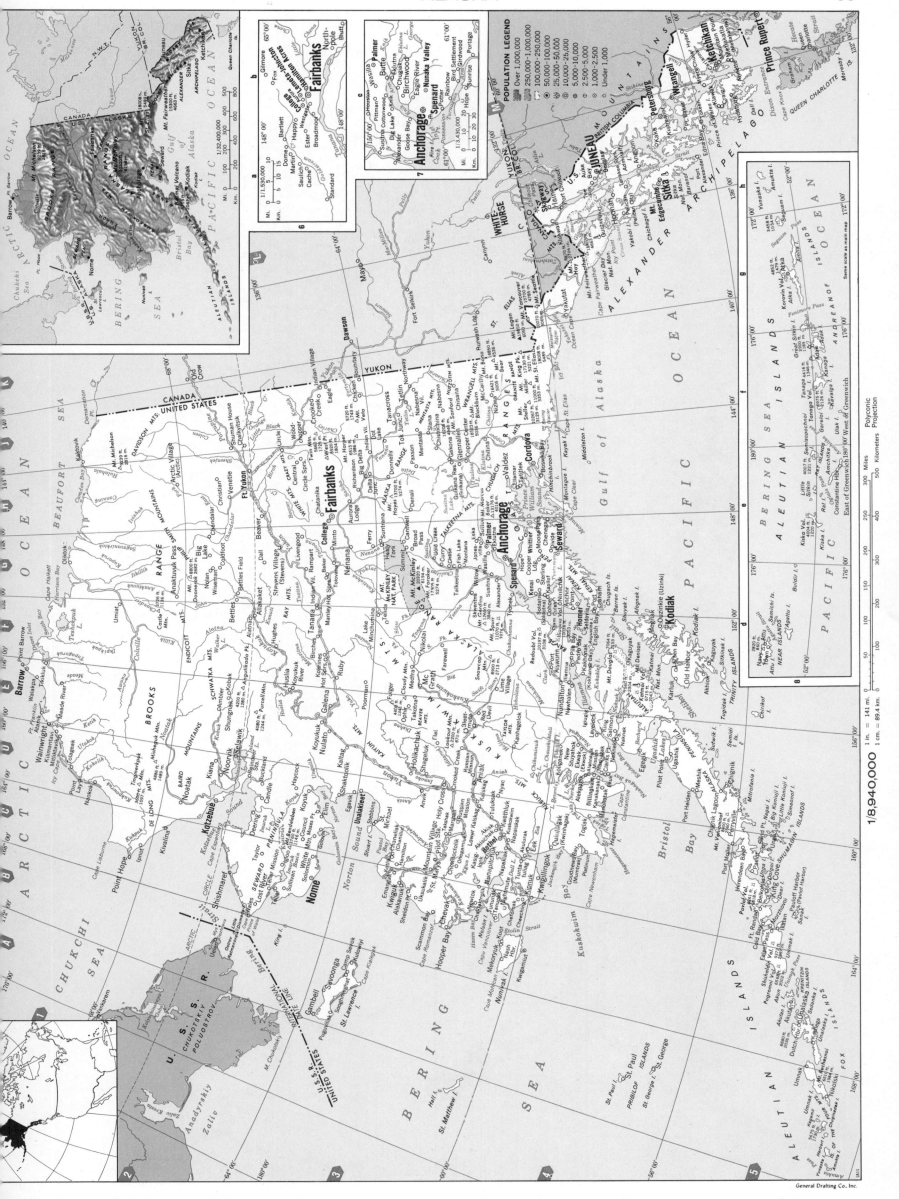

1/8,940,000

1 in. = 141 mi.
1 cm. = 89.4 km.

Polyconic
Projection

LEGEND

Cropland and pasture land

Cropland with woodland and grazing land

Grazing in forest, woodland and open woodland

Irrigated land (intensive agriculture)

Forest and woodland mostly ungrazed

Semi-arid and desert grasslands, grazed

Desert shrubland with minor grazing

Northern nonforested areas (includes tundra)

Alpine meadows and mountain peaks above timber line

Swamp and marshland ⎱
Permanent ice and snow ⎰ Unproductive

169 Urbanized areas
(See page 186 for key numbers)

FOREST—A stand of timber-producing trees. WOODLAND—Brush-covered land with smaller stands of trees than in forests. OPEN WOOD-LAND—Scattered tree stands not of commercial size. Principal use of this land is grazing.

URBANIZED AREAS—Approximately 96 million people (more than half the United States population) live within the urbanized areas shown on this map in red. These represent less than one per cent of the land area of the country and are defined by the Census Bureau as areas containing at least one central city of 50,000 or more as well as surrounding urban fringes that meet certain minimum standards of population density. The Urbanized Areas range in size from Tyler, Texas (51,739) to New York—Northeastern New Jersey (14,114,927). Sixteen urbanized areas had populations exceeding 1,000,000 in 1960. See page 186 for complete list and key numbers.

After F. J. Marschner, map titled "Major Land Uses in the United States." U. S. Dept. of Agriculture, Bureau of Agriculture Economics, 1950.

General Drafting Co., Inc.

1/10,800,000

1 in. = 170 mi.
1 cm. = 108 km.

0 50 100 150 200 250 300 350 400 450 500 Miles
0 100 200 300 400 500 600 700 800 Kilometers

Lambert Conformal Conic Projection

FRUIT TREES, VINEYARDS, and NUT TREES

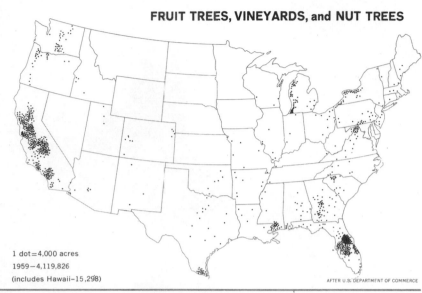

1 dot = 4,000 acres

1959 — 4,119,826

(includes Hawaii — 15,298)

AFTER U.S. DEPARTMENT OF COMMERCE

COTTON and TOBACCO

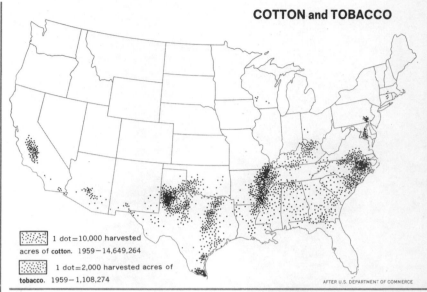

1 dot = 10,000 harvested acres of cotton. 1959 — 14,649,264

1 dot = 2,000 harvested acres of tobacco. 1959 — 1,108,274

AFTER U.S. DEPARTMENT OF COMMERCE

SUGAR CANE and SUGAR BEETS

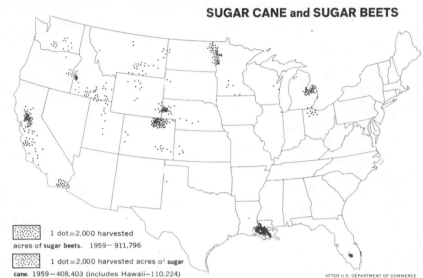

1 dot = 2,000 harvested acres of sugar beets. 1959 — 911,796

1 dot = 2,000 harvested acres of sugar cane. 1959 — 408,403 (includes Hawaii — 110,224)

AFTER U.S. DEPARTMENT OF COMMERCE

SOYBEANS and PEANUTS

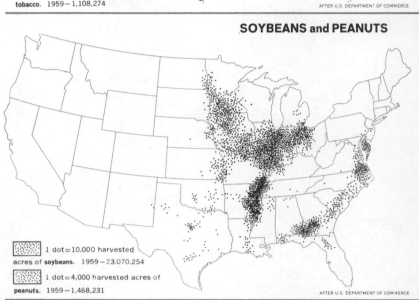

1 dot = 10,000 harvested acres of soybeans. 1959 — 23,070,254

1 dot = 4,000 harvested acres of peanuts. 1959 — 1,468,231

AFTER U.S. DEPARTMENT OF COMMERCE

HAWAII
LIVESTOCK, SUGAR CANE, PINEAPPLES, and VEGETABLES

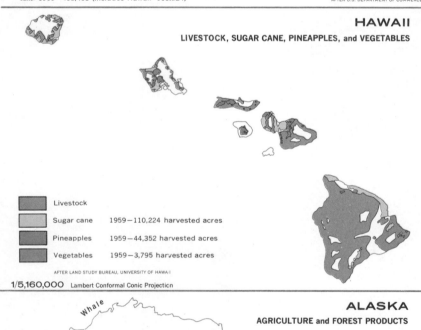

Livestock

Sugar cane   1959 — 110,224 harvested acres

Pineapples   1959 — 44,352 harvested acres

Vegetables   1959 — 3,795 harvested acres

AFTER LAND STUDY BUREAU, UNIVERSITY OF HAWAII

1/5,160,000   Lambert Conformal Conic Projection

ALASKA
AGRICULTURE and FOREST PRODUCTS

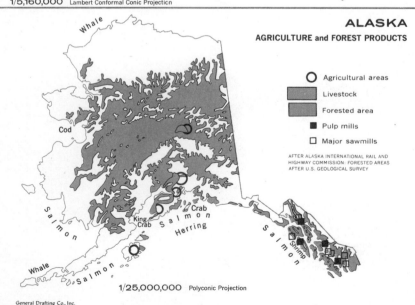

○ Agricultural areas

▨ Livestock

▨ Forested area

■ Pulp mills

□ Major sawmills

AFTER ALASKA INTERNATIONAL RAIL AND HIGHWAY COMMISSION: FORESTED AREAS
AFTER U.S. GEOLOGICAL SURVEY

1/25,000,000   Polyconic Projection

General Drafting Co., Inc.

AGRICULTURAL PRODUCTION

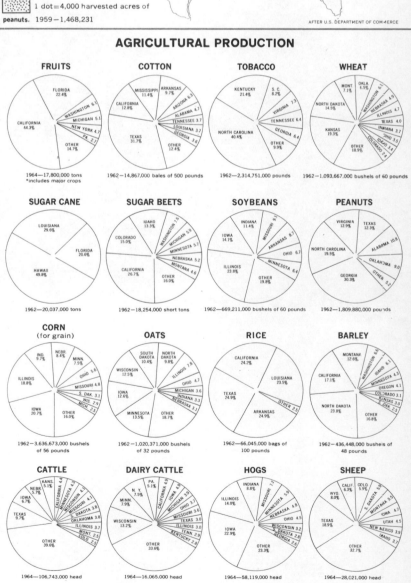

FRUITS
1964 — 17,800,000 tons
*includes major crops

COTTON
1962 — 14,867,000 bales of 500 pounds

TOBACCO
1962 — 2,314,751,000 pounds

WHEAT
1962 — 1,093,667,000 bushels of 60 pounds

SUGAR CANE
1962 — 20,037,000 tons

SUGAR BEETS
1962 — 18,254,000 short tons

SOYBEANS
1962 — 669,211,000 bushels of 60 pounds

PEANUTS
1962 — 1,809,880,000 pounds

CORN (for grain)
1962 — 3,636,673,000 bushels of 56 pounds

OATS
1962 — 1,020,371,000 bushels of 32 pounds

RICE
1962 — 66,045,000 bags of 100 pounds

BARLEY
1962 — 436,448,000 bushels of 48 pounds

CATTLE
1964 — 106,743,000 head

DAIRY CATTLE
1964 — 16,065,000 head

HOGS
1964 — 58,119,000 head

SHEEP
1964 — 28,021,000 head

AFTER U.S. DEPARTMENT OF AGRICULTURE

WHEAT

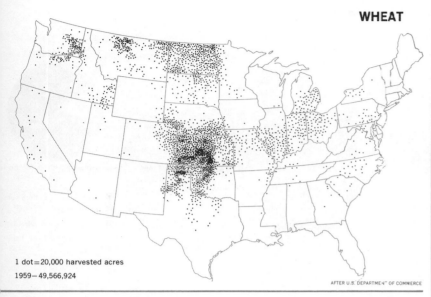

1 dot=20,000 harvested acres
1959—49,566,924

AFTER U.S. DEPARTMENT OF COMMERCE

CATTLE

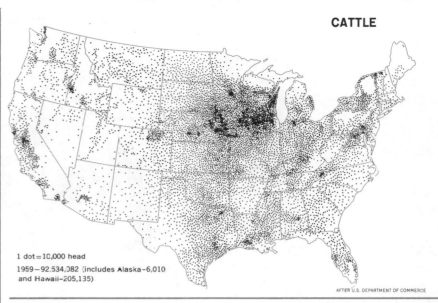

1 dot=10,000 head
1959—92,534,082 (includes Alaska-6,010
and Hawaii-205,135)

AFTER U.S. DEPARTMENT OF COMMERCE

CORN

1 dot=20,000 harvested acres
1959—79,616,031 (includes Hawaii-233)

AFTER U.S. DEPARTMENT OF COMMERCE

DAIRY CATTLE

1 dot=5,000 head
1959—16,522,026 includes Alaska-2,186
and Hawaii-14,100)

AFTER U.S. DEPARTMENT OF COMMERCE

OATS AND RICE

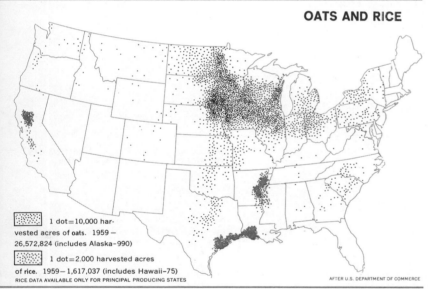

1 dot=10,000 har-
vested acres of oats. 1959—
26,572,824 (includes Alaska-990)

1 dot=2,000 harvested acres
of rice. 1959—1,617,037 (includes Hawaii-75)
RICE DATA AVAILABLE ONLY FOR PRINCIPAL PRODUCING STATES

AFTER U.S. DEPARTMENT OF COMMERCE

HOGS

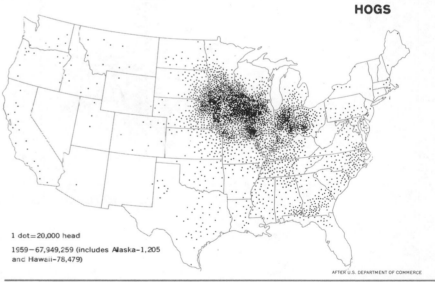

1 dot=20,000 head
1959—67,949,259 (includes Alaska-1,205
and Hawaii-78,479)

AFTER U.S. DEPARTMENT OF COMMERCE

BARLEY

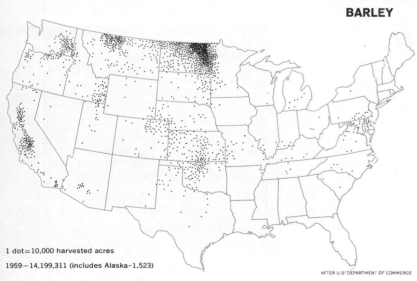

1 dot=10,000 harvested acres
1959—14,199,311 (includes Alaska-1,523)

AFTER U.S. DEPARTMENT OF COMMERCE

SHEEP

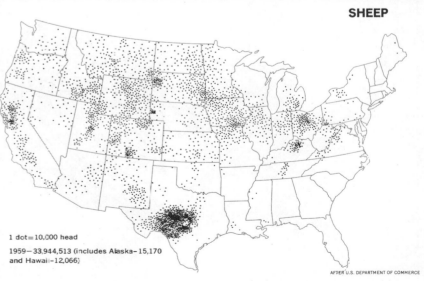

1 dot=10,000 head
1959—33,944,513 (includes Alaska-15,170
and Hawaii-12,066)

AFTER U.S. DEPARTMENT OF COMMERCE

Lambert Conformal Conic Projection   1/42,900,000   General Drafting Co., Inc.

COAL, URANIUM, and NUCLEAR POWER

COAL FIELDS
Anthracite
Bituminous and subbituminous
Lignite
URANIUM
Deposits
NUCLEAR POWER
• Plants in operation
○ Plants under construction

AFTER U.S. GEOLOGICAL SURVEY AND U.S. BUREAU OF MINES

COAL PRODUCTION

KENTUCKY 16.1%
ILLINOIS 11.1%
OHIO 8.2%
VIRGINIA 6.7
INDIANA 3.7
ALABAMA 3.7
PENNSYLVANIA 15.8%
WEST VIRGINIA 28.6%
OTHER 6.7%

1960 — 415,512,000 short tons
AFTER U.S. BUREAU OF MINES

COAL RESERVES

ILLINOIS 7.6%
WYO 6.2%
MONTANA 13.4%
NORTH DAKOTA 21.1%
KENTUCKY 4.0
OTHER 14.5%

1960 — 1,660,290,000,000 short tons
AFTER U.S. GEOLOGICAL SURVEY

■ Anthracite and bituminous
□ Bituminous
■ Bituminous and subbituminous
□ Subbituminous and lignite
■ Lignite
■ Mixed types

MAJOR OIL FIELDS and PIPELINES

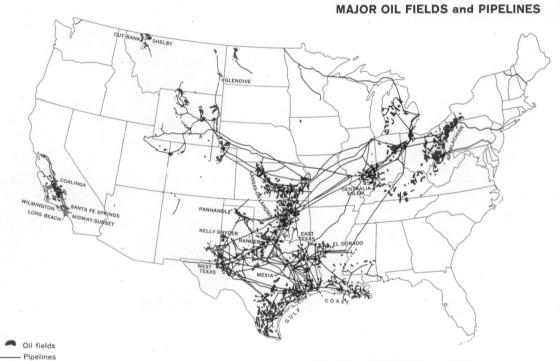

Oil fields
Pipelines

AFTER U.S. GEOLOGICAL SURVEY AND WORLD GEOGRAPHY OF PETROLEUM

OIL PRODUCTION

CALIFORNIA 11.8%
OKLAHOMA 7.0
KANSAS 4.4
WYOMING 5.3
NEW MEXICO 4.2
ILLINOIS 3.1
LOUISIANA 15.3%
TEXAS 36.2%
OTHER 12.2%

1960 — 2,574,933,000 barrels
(one barrel = 42 gallons)
AFTER U.S. BUREAU OF MINES

PROVEN OIL RESERVES

LOUISIANA 16.7%
CALIFORNIA 13.3%
OKLAHOMA 5.1
WYOMING 3.9
NEW MEXICO 3.1
KANSAS 2.6
TEXAS 46.1%
OTHER 9.2%

1964 — 30,990,510,000 barrels
(one barrel = 42 gallons)
AFTER U.S. BUREAU OF MINES

MAJOR NATURAL GAS FIELDS and PIPELINES

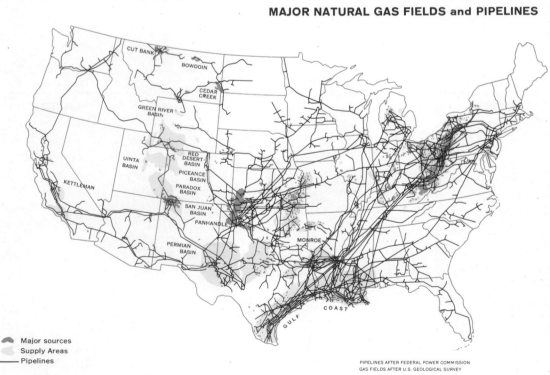

Major sources
Supply Areas
Pipelines

PIPELINES AFTER FEDERAL POWER COMMISSION
GAS FIELDS AFTER U.S. GEOLOGICAL SURVEY

NATURAL GAS PRODUCTION

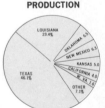

OKLAHOMA 6.0
NEW MEXICO 6.7
KANSAS 5.0
CALIFORNIA 4.0
W. VA. 1.8
LOUISIANA 23.4%
TEXAS 46.1%
OTHER 7.1%

1960 — 12,771,038 million cubic feet
AFTER U.S. BUREAU OF MINES

NATURAL GAS RESERVES

OKLA. 7.1%
KANSAS 6.7
NEW MEXICO 5.5
CALIFORNIA 3.2
LOUISIANA 28.1%
TEXAS 42.3%
OTHER 7.6%

1964 — 281,251,454 million cubic feet
AFTER U.S. BUREAU OF MINES

PRODUCTION OF ENERGY 1900 TO 1960

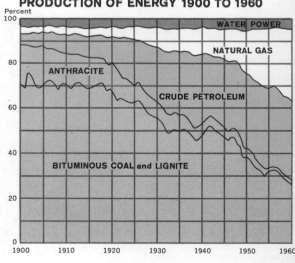

WATER POWER
NATURAL GAS
ANTHRACITE
CRUDE PETROLEUM
BITUMINOUS COAL and LIGNITE

AFTER U.S. BUREAU OF MINES

General Drafting Co. Inc.
1/33,800,000
Lambert Conformal Conic Projection

LEAD and ZINC

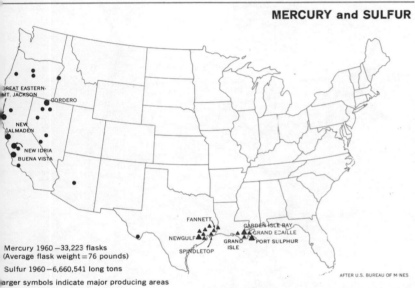

Lead 1960—246,669 short tons

Zinc 1960—435,427 short tons

Larger symbols indicate major producing areas

AFTER U.S. BUREAU OF MINES

IRON ORE

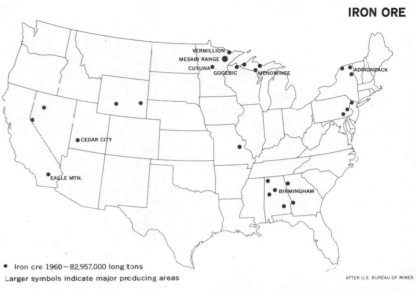

Iron ore 1960—82,957,000 long tons

Larger symbols indicate major producing areas

AFTER U.S. BUREAU OF MINES

MERCURY and SULFUR

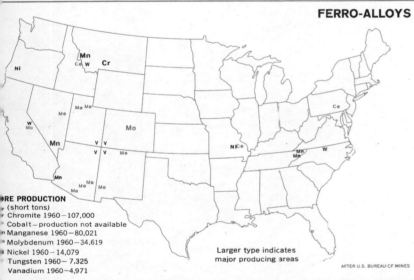

Mercury 1960—33,223 flasks
(Average flask weight = 76 pounds)

Sulfur 1960—6,660,541 long tons

Larger symbols indicate major producing areas

AFTER U.S. BUREAU OF MINES

POTASH, PHOSPHATE, BORON, and SYNTHETIC NITROGEN

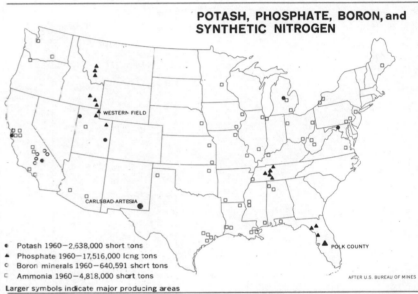

• Potash 1960—2,638,000 short tons

▲ Phosphate 1960—17,516,000 long tons

○ Boron minerals 1960—640,591 short tons

□ Ammonia 1960—4,818,000 short tons

Larger symbols indicate major producing areas

AFTER U.S. BUREAU OF MINES

FERRO-ALLOYS

ORE PRODUCTION
(short tons)
Chromite 1960—107,000
Cobalt—production not available
Manganese 1960—80,021
Molybdenum 1960—34,619
Nickel 1960—14,079
Tungsten 1960—7,325
Vanadium 1960—4,971

Larger type indicates major producing areas

AFTER U.S. BUREAU OF MINES

BAUXITE and MAGNESITE

• Bauxite mining
1960—1,998,000 long tons

▲ Magnesite 1960—499,000 short tons

● Manufacturing plants deriving magnesium compounds from sea water

Larger symbols indicate major producing areas

AFTER U.S. BUREAU OF MINES

SILVER and GOLD

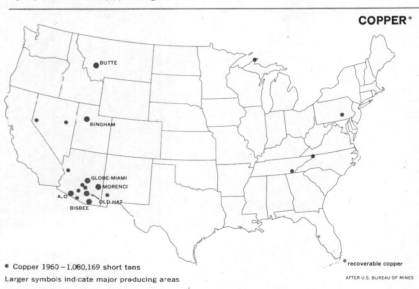

Silver 1960—30,766,327 troy ounces

Gold 1960—1,666,772 troy ounces

Larger symbols indicate major producing areas

AFTER U.S. BUREAU OF MINES

COPPER

Copper 1960—1,080,169 short tons

Larger symbols indicate major producing areas

AFTER U.S. BUREAU OF MINES

Lambert Conformal Conic Projection   1/45,000,000   General Drafting Co., Inc.

General Drafting Co., Inc.

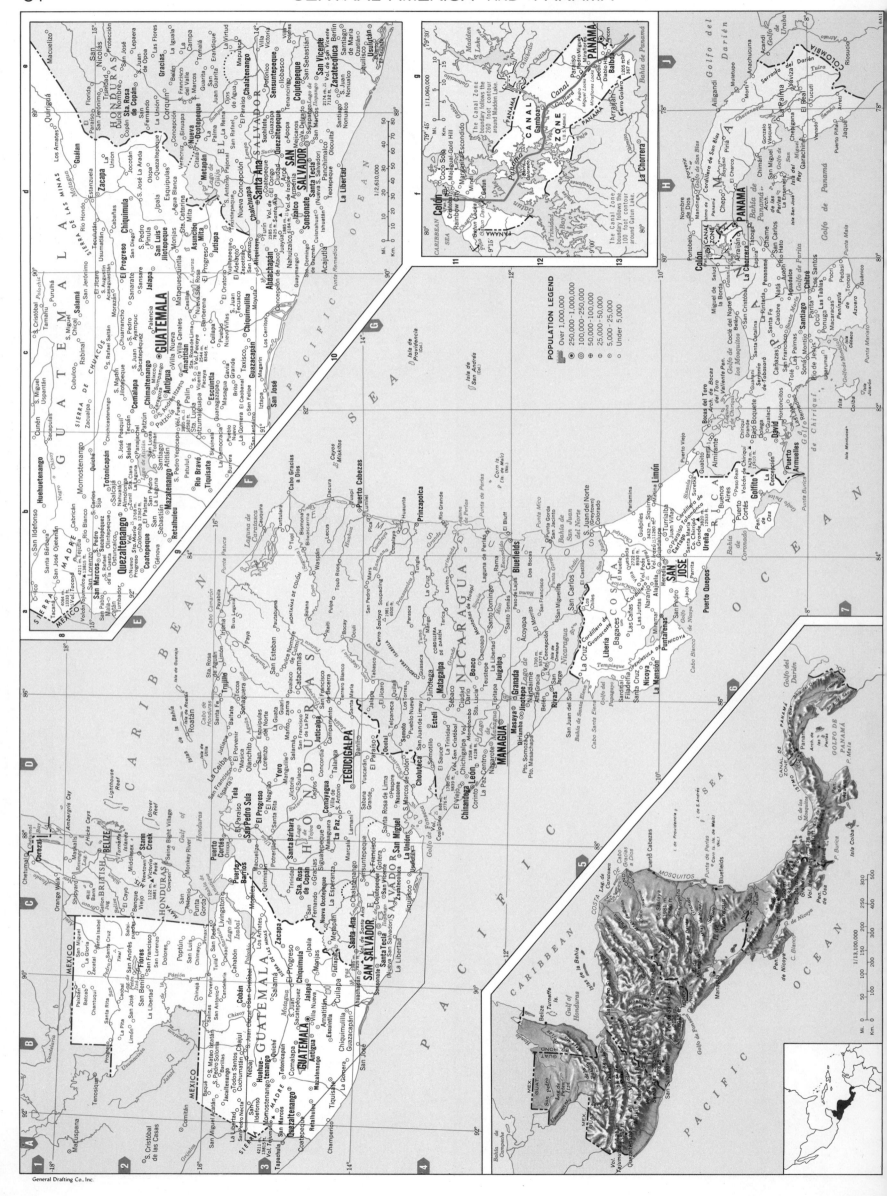

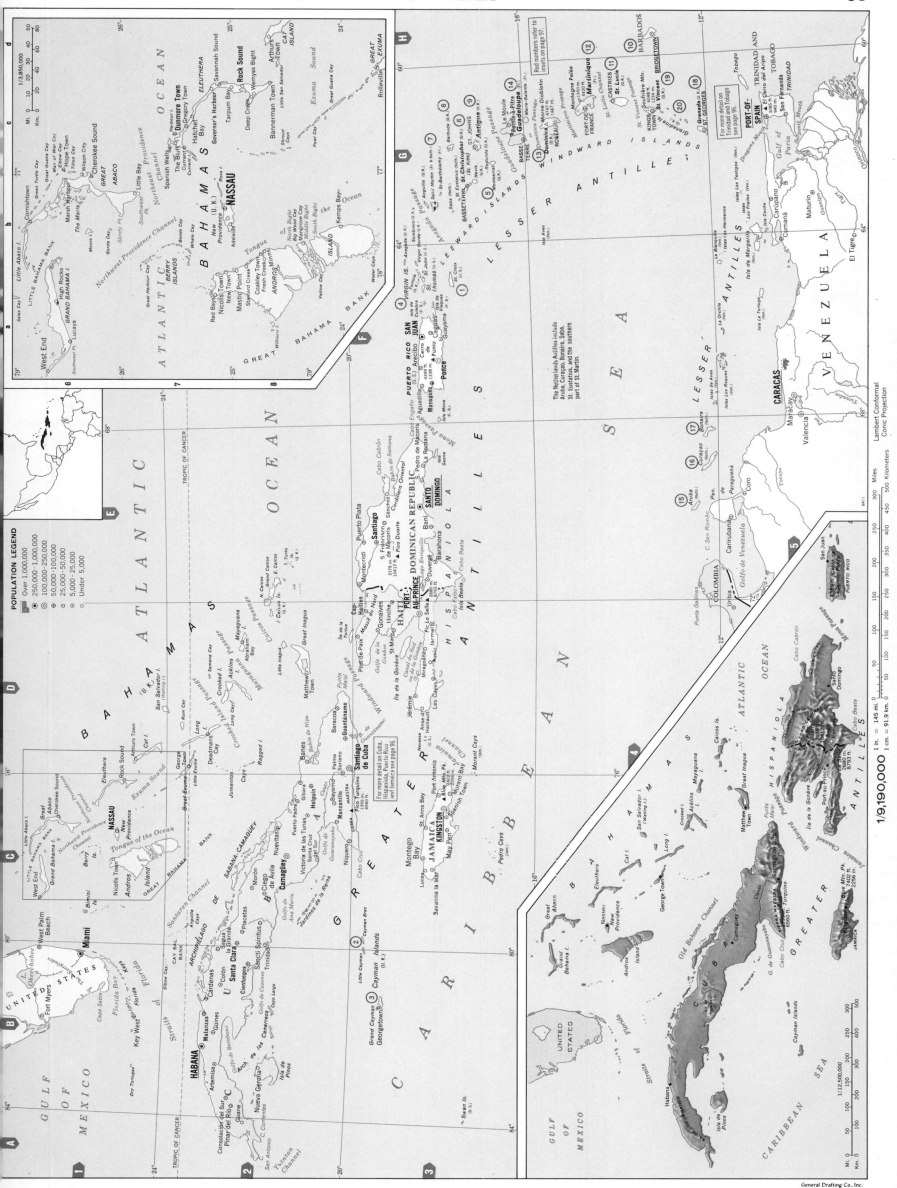

POPULATION LEGEND
- Over 1,000,000
- 250,000-1,000,000
- 100,000-250,000
- 50,000-100,000
- 25,000-50,000
- 5,000-25,000
- Under 5,000

1/9,190,000

Lambert Conformal
Conic Projection

General Drafting Co. Inc.

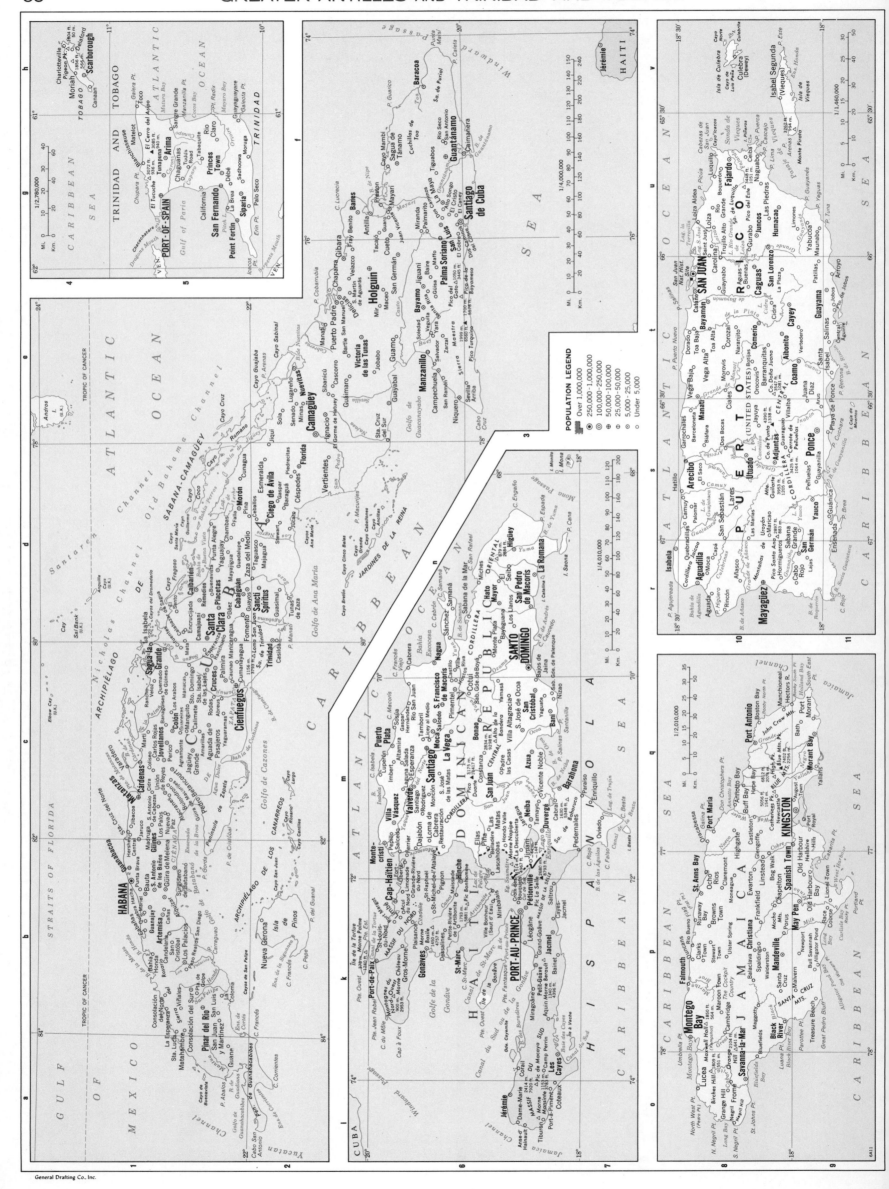

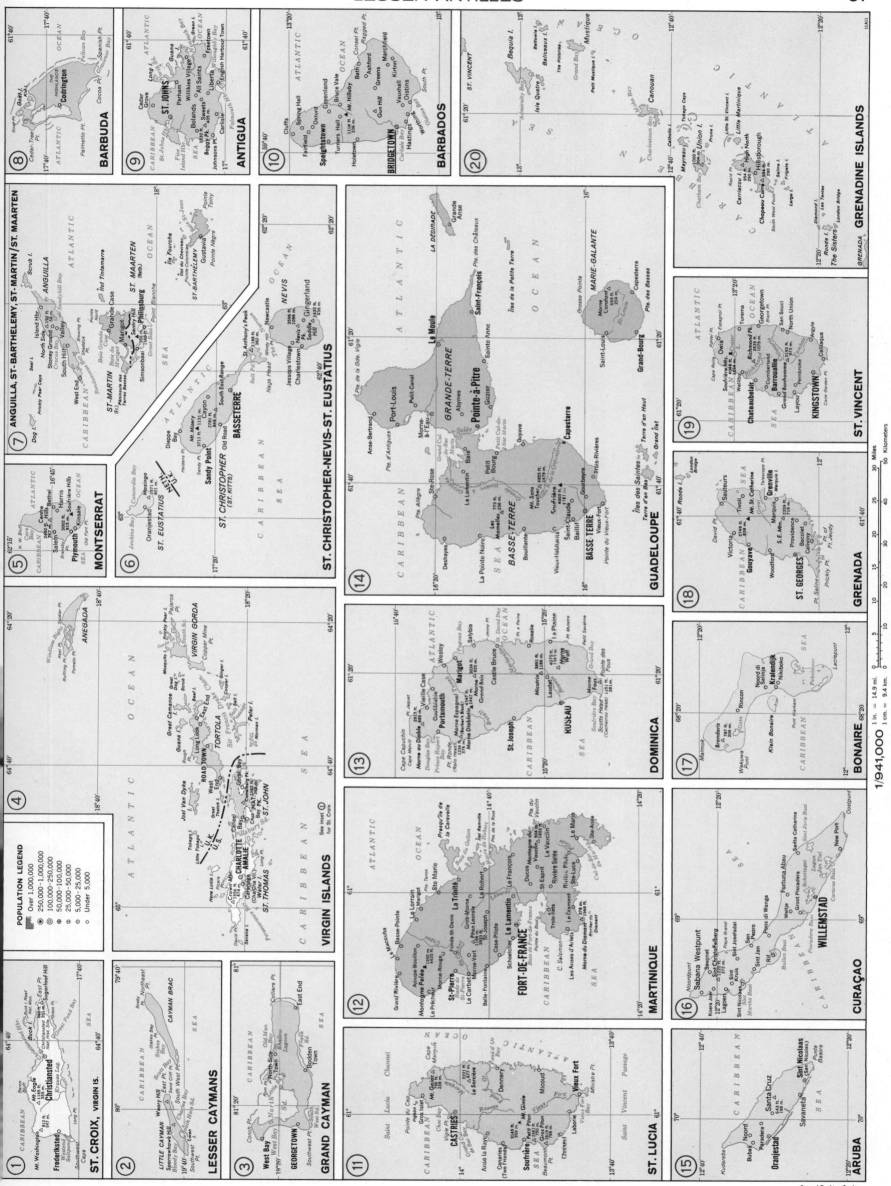

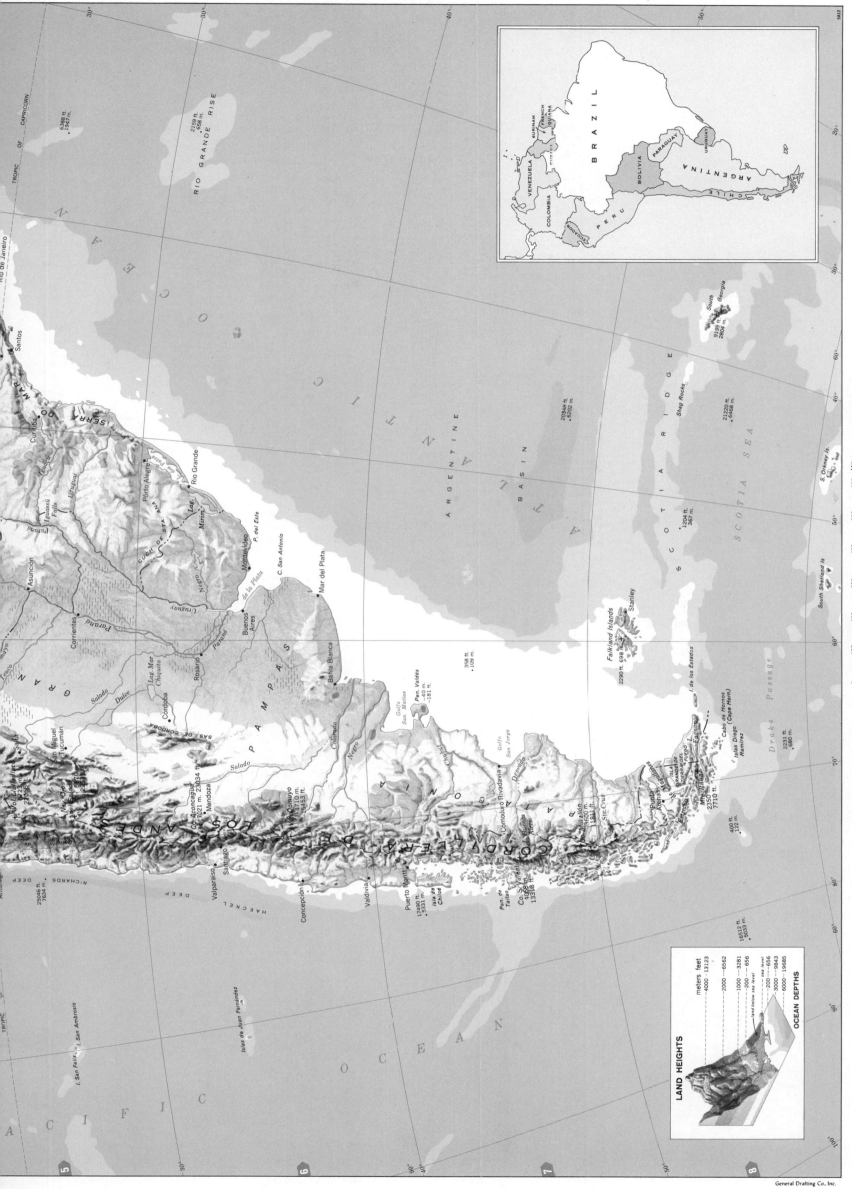

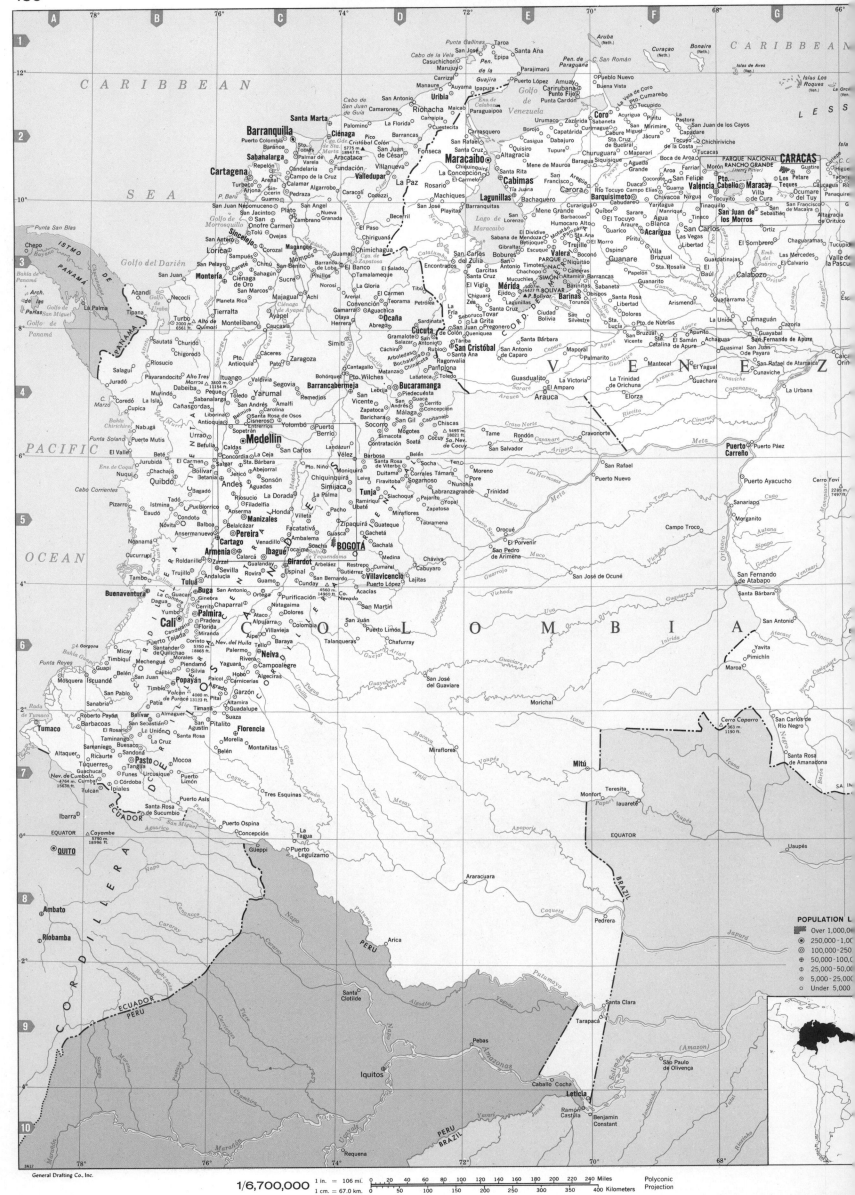

POPULATION L...
- Over 1,000,0...
- 250,000–1,00...
- 100,000–250...
- 50,000–100,0...
- 25,000–50,0...
- 5,000–25,000...
- Under 5,000...

General Drafting Co., Inc.

1/6,700,000

1 in. = 106 mi.
1 cm. = 67.0 km.

0 20 40 60 80 100 120 140 160 180 200 220 240 Miles
0 50 100 150 200 250 300 350 400 Kilometers

Polyconic
Projection

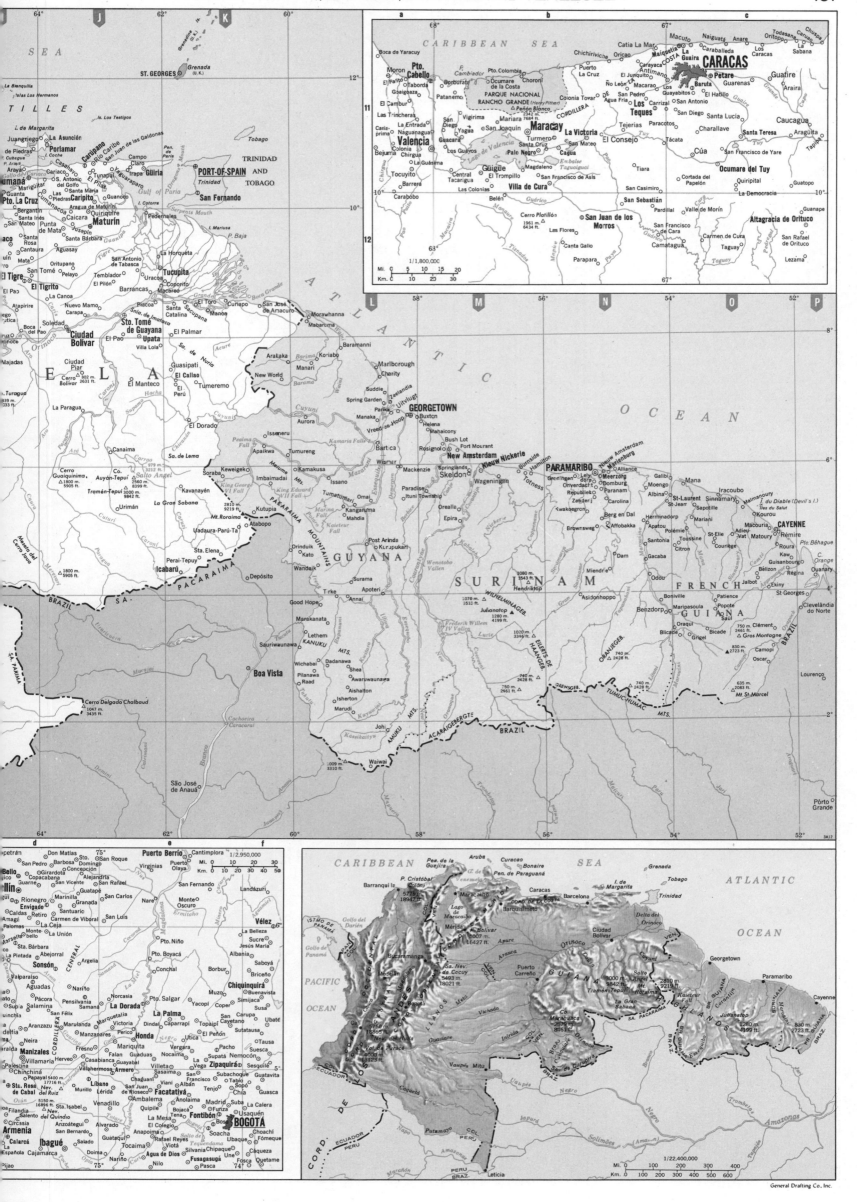

General Drafting Co., Inc.

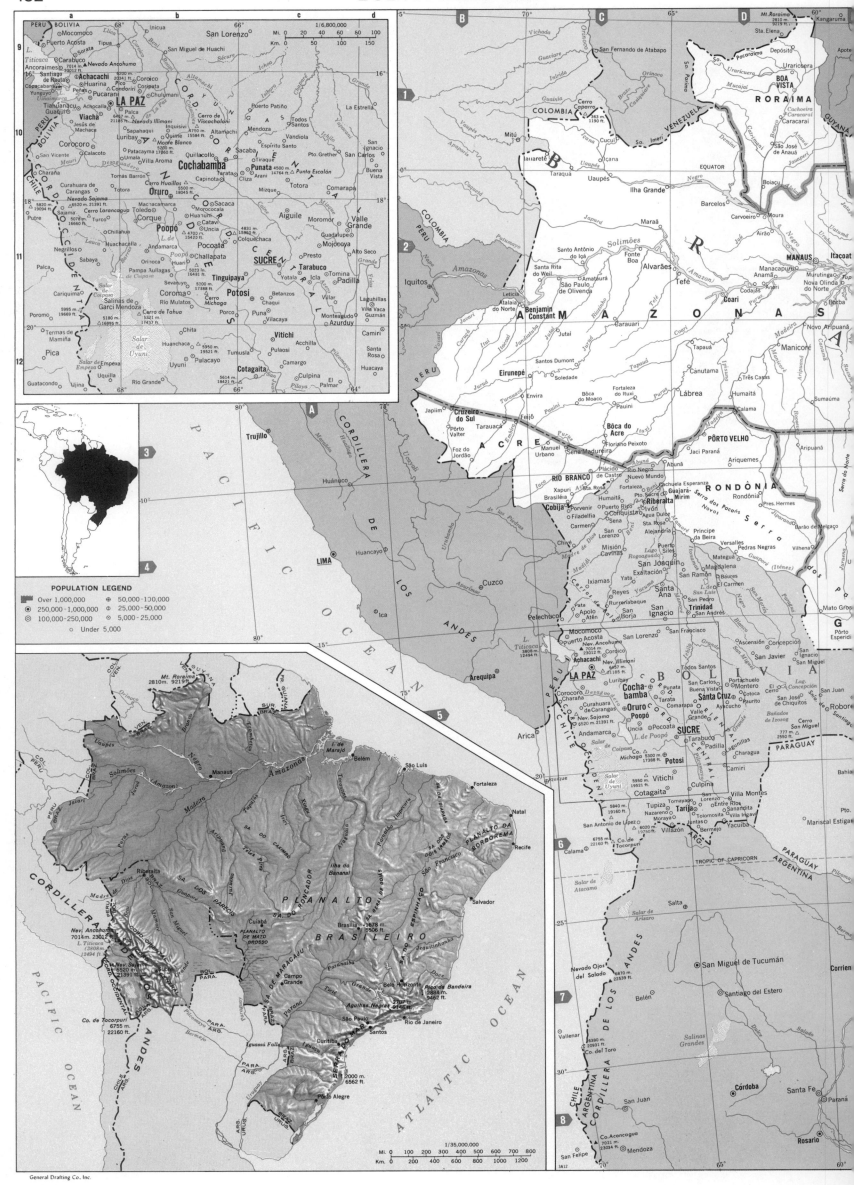

POPULATION LEGEND
- Over 1,000,000
- 250,000–1,000,000
- 100,000–250,000
- 50,000–100,000
- 25,000–50,000
- 5,000–25,000
- Under 5,000

General Drafting Co. Inc.

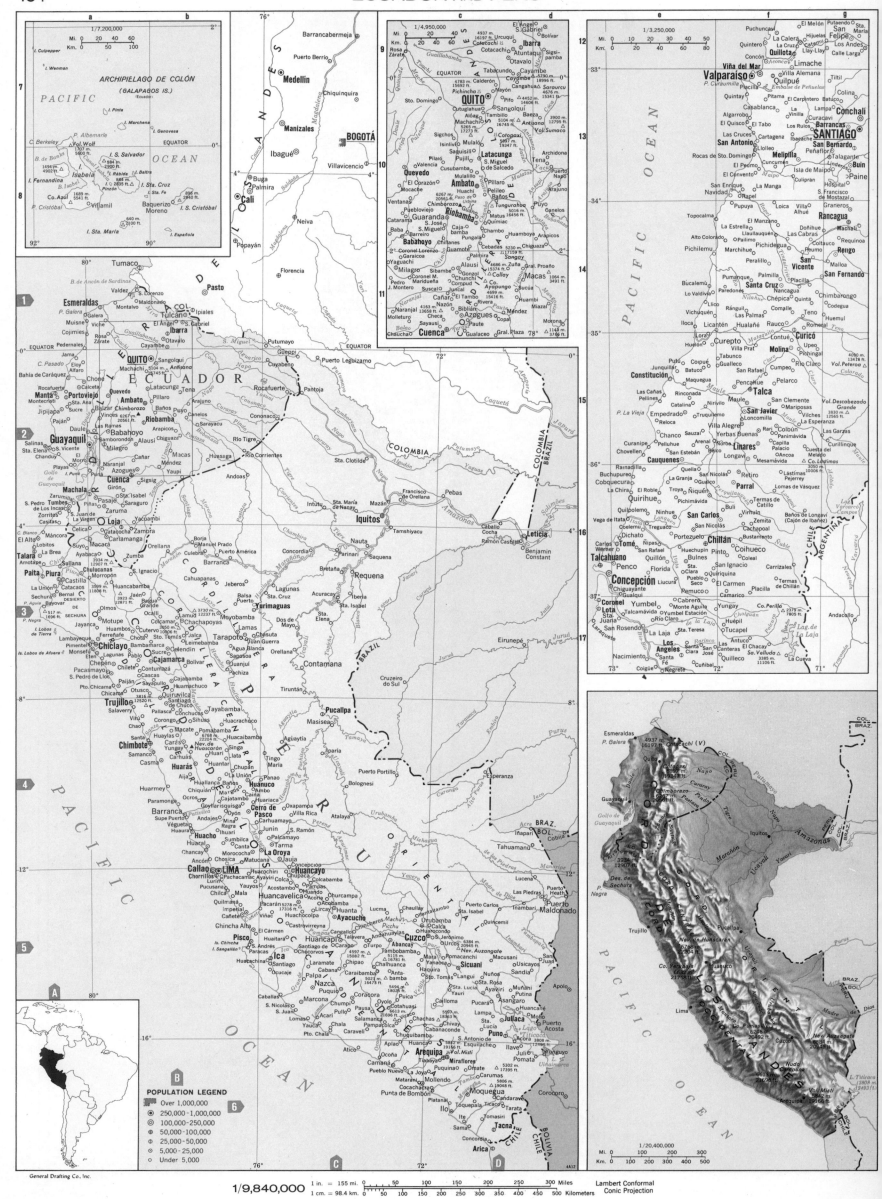

ARCHIPIELAGO DE COLÓN
(GALAPAGOS IS.)
(Ecuador)

PACIFIC

OCEAN

POPULATION LEGEND
- ⬤ Over 1,000,000
- ◉ 250,000–1,000,000
- ⊙ 100,000–250,000
- ⊕ 50,000–100,000
- ⊖ 25,000–50,000
- ○ 5,000–25,000
- ∘ Under 5,000

1/9,840,000
1 in. = 155 mi.
1 cm. = 98.4 km.

Lambert Conformal
Conic Projection

General Drafting Co., Inc.

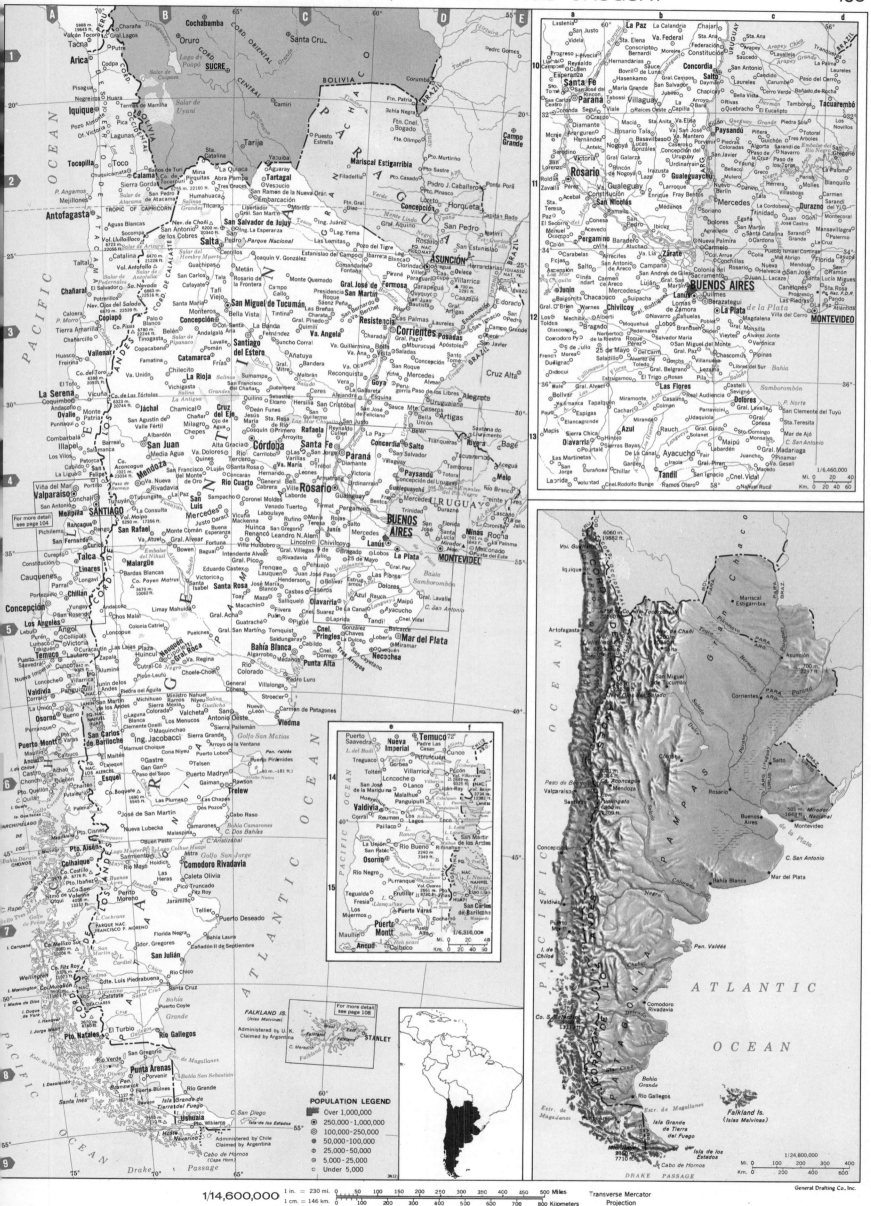

POPULATION LEGEND
- Over 1,000,000
- 250,000–1,000,000
- 100,000–250,000
- 50,000–100,000
- 25,000–50,000
- 5,000–25,000
- Under 5,000

1/14,600,000

1 in. = 230 mi.	0 50 100 150 200 250 300 350 400 450	500 Miles
1 cm. = 146 km.	0 100 200 300 400 500 600 700	800 Kilometers

Transverse Mercator Projection

General Drafting Co., Inc.

LANDFORMS and PHYSICAL REGIONS

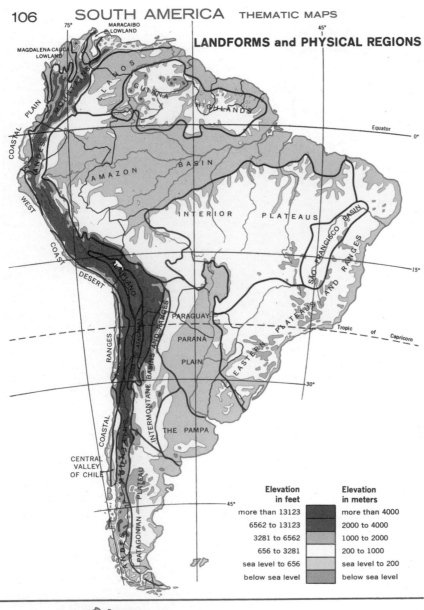

MARACAIBO LOWLAND
MAGDALENA-CAUCA LOWLAND
LLANOS
GUIANA HIGHLANDS
COASTAL PLAIN
ANDES MOUNTAINS
WEST COAST
AMAZON BASIN
Equator 0°
INTERIOR PLATEAUS
DESERT
SÃO FRANCISCO BASIN
15°
COASTAL RANGES
PUNA DE ATACAMA
ANDES MOUNTAINS AND RANGES
PARAGUAY
PARANÁ PLAIN
EASTERN PLATEAUS AND RANGES
Tropic of Capricorn
INTERMONTANE BASINS AND RANGES
THE PAMPA
30°
CENTRAL VALLEY OF CHILE
COASTAL MOUNTAINS
ANDES
PATAGONIAN PLATEAU
45°

Elevation in feet	Elevation in meters
more than 13123	more than 4000
6562 to 13123	2000 to 4000
3281 to 6562	1000 to 2000
656 to 3281	200 to 1000
sea level to 656	sea level to 200
below sea level	below sea level

AGRICULTURE

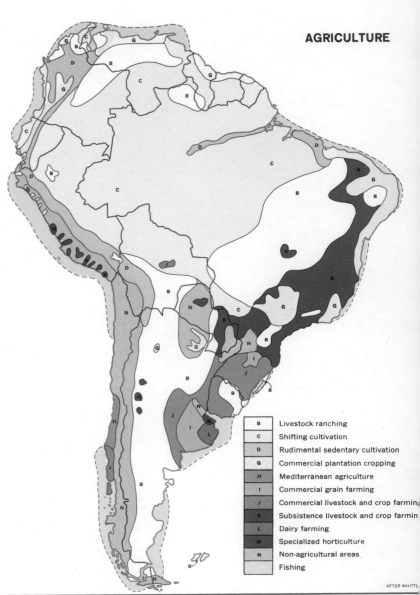

B	Livestock ranching
C	Shifting cultivation
D	Rudimental sedentary cultivation
G	Commercial plantation cropping
H	Mediterranean agriculture
I	Commercial grain farming
J	Commercial livestock and crop farming
K	Subsistence livestock and crop farming
L	Dairy farming
M	Specialized horticulture
N	Non-agricultural areas
	Fishing

AFTER WHITTL

POPULATION

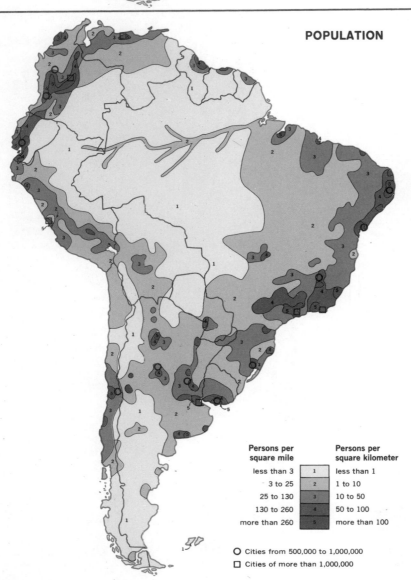

Persons per square mile	Persons per square kilometer
less than 3	less than 1
3 to 25	1 to 10
25 to 130	10 to 50
130 to 260	50 to 100
more than 260	more than 100

○ Cities from 500,000 to 1,000,000
□ Cities of more than 1,000,000

VEGETATION

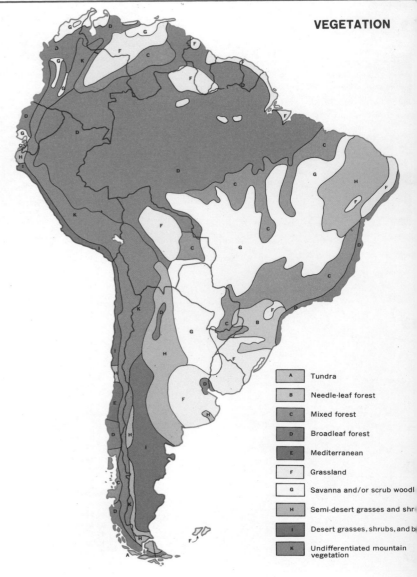

A	Tundra
B	Needle-leaf forest
C	Mixed forest
D	Broadleaf forest
E	Mediterranean
F	Grassland
G	Savanna and/or scrub woodl
H	Semi-desert grasses and shr
I	Desert grasses, shrubs, and b
K	Undifferentiated mountain vegetation

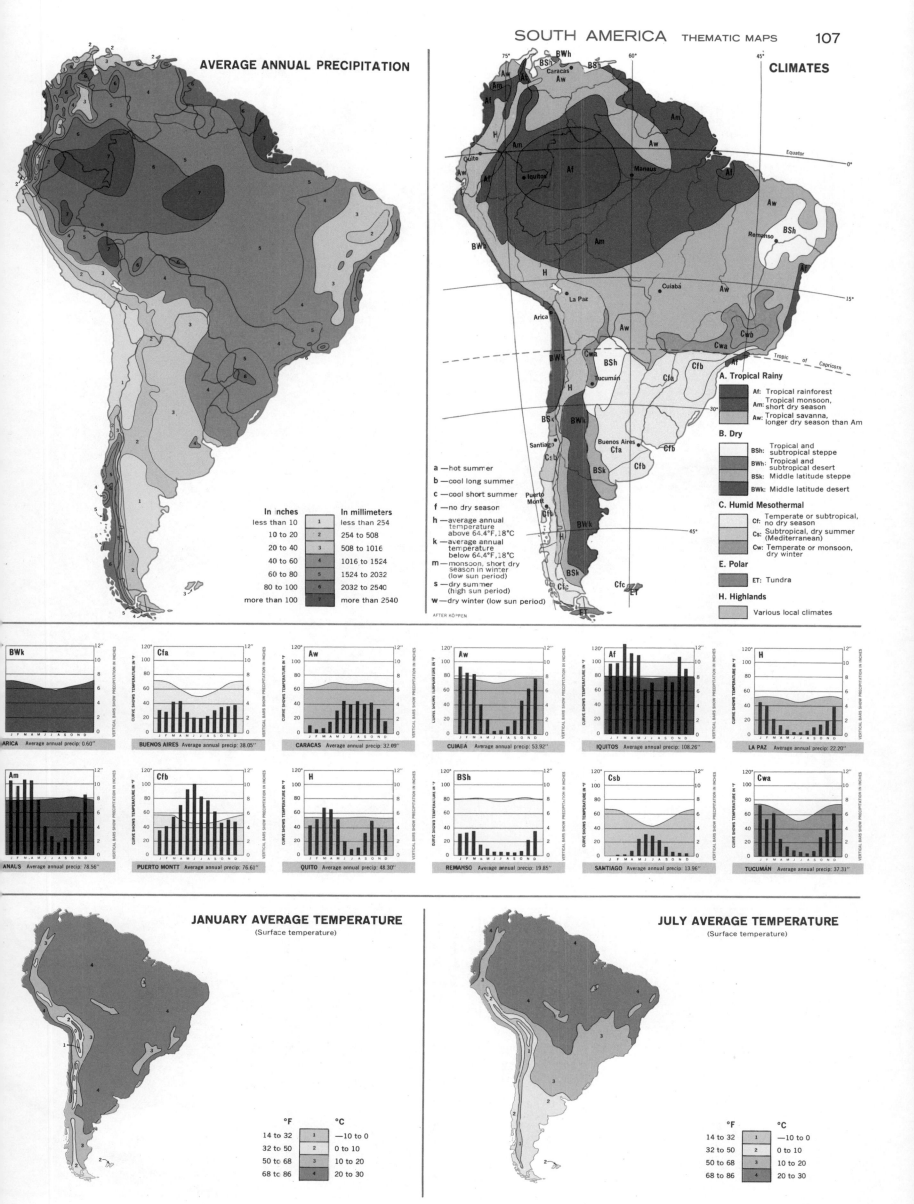

AVERAGE ANNUAL PRECIPITATION

CLIMATES

JANUARY AVERAGE TEMPERATURE
(Surface temperature)

JULY AVERAGE TEMPERATURE
(Surface temperature)

General Drafting Co. Inc.

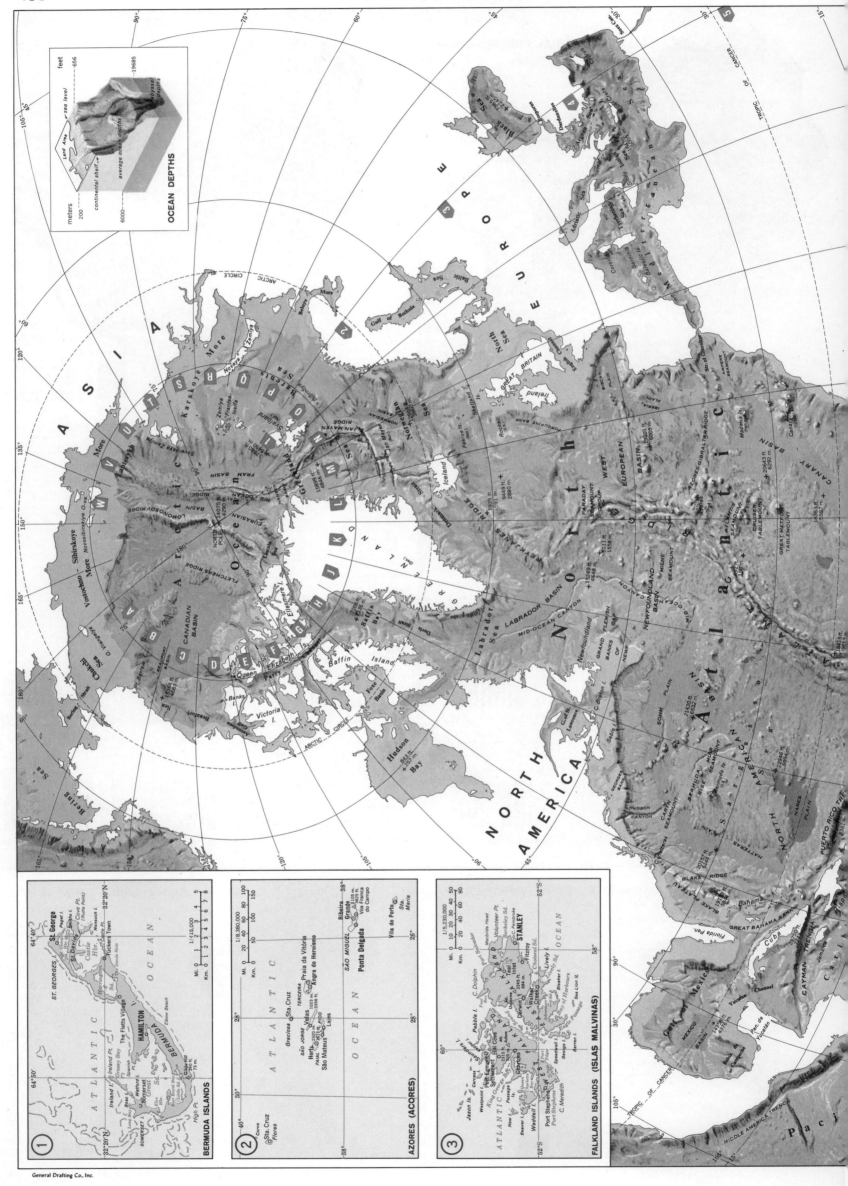

OCEAN DEPTHS

BERMUDA ISLANDS

AZORES (AÇORES)

FALKLAND ISLANDS (ISLAS MALVINAS)

General Drafting Co., Inc.

LAND HEIGHTS

meters	feet
4000	13123
2000	6562
1000	3281
200	656
land below sea level	
200	656
3000	9843
6000	19685

OCEAN DEPTHS

12A12

General Drafting Co., Inc.

1/14,800,000

1 in. = 234 mi.
1 cm. = 148 km.

0 50 100 150 200 250 300 350 400 450 500 Miles
0   100   200   300   400   500   600   700   800 Kilometers

Azimuthal
Equal Area Projection

LANGUAGES

INDO-EUROPEAN
GERMANIC
English
2 Frisian
3 Flemish and Dutch
4 German
5 Icelandic and Faroese
6 Norwegian
7 Swedish
8 Danish

ROMANCE
9 French
10 Spanish
11 Catalan
12 Portuguese and Galician
13 Italian
14 Sardinian
15 Rumanian
16 Rhaeto-Romanic

CELTIC
17 Irish and Scots Gaelic
18 Welsh
19 Breton

SLAVIC
20 Russian
21 Ukrainian
22 Byelorussian
23 Polish
24 Czech
25 Slovak
26 Lusatian (Wendish)
27 Serbo-Croatian
28 Slovenian
29 Macedonian
30 Bulgarian

BALTIC
31 Lithuanian
32 Latvian

GREEK
33 GREEK

ALBANIAN
34 ALBANIAN

URAL-ALTAIC
FINNIC
35 Finnish and Karelian
36 Estonian
37 Lapp
38 Vepse
39 Komi

UGRIC
40 Hungarian

SAMOYED

TURKIC
42 Turkish
43 Gaguz

44 **BASQUE**

Mi. 0   200

General Drafting Co., Inc.

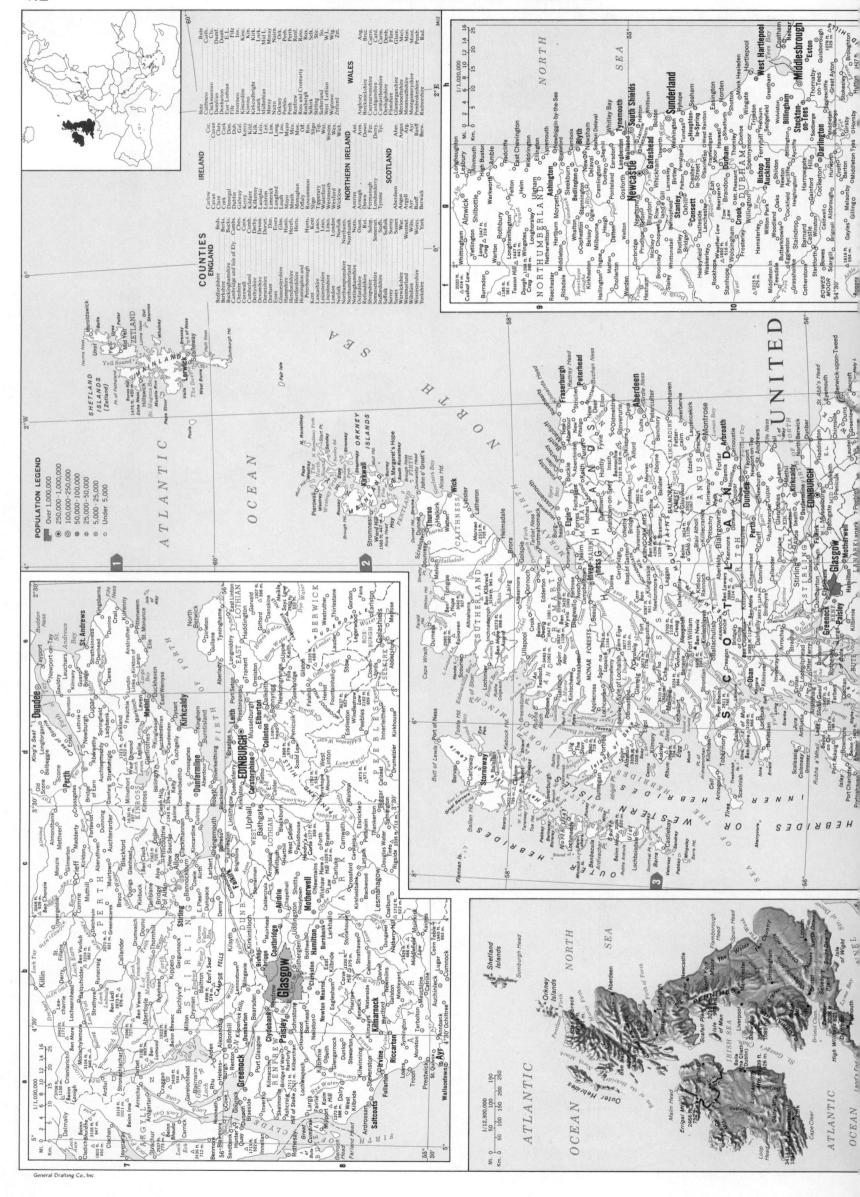

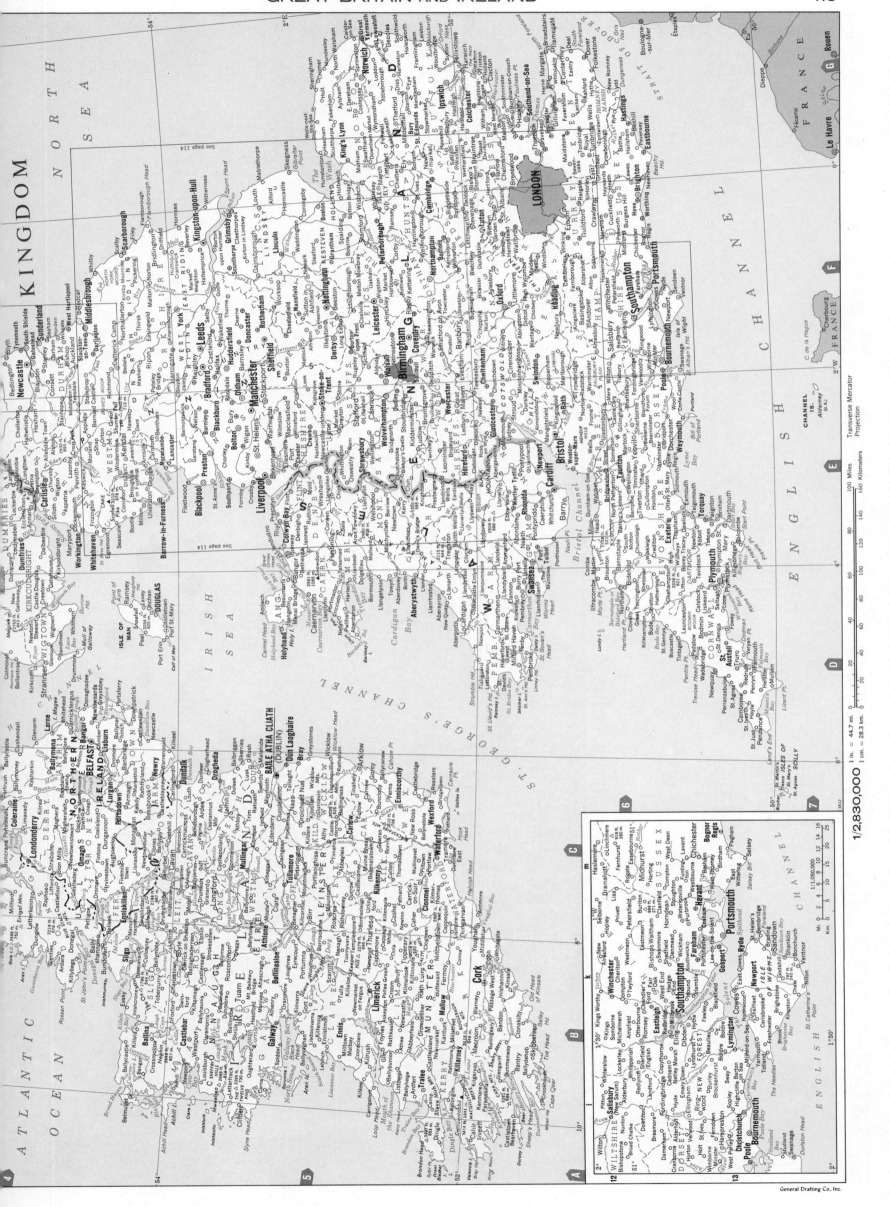

1/2,830,000

1 in. = 44.7 mi.
1 cm. = 28.3 km.

Transverse Mercator
Projection

General Drafting Co., Inc.

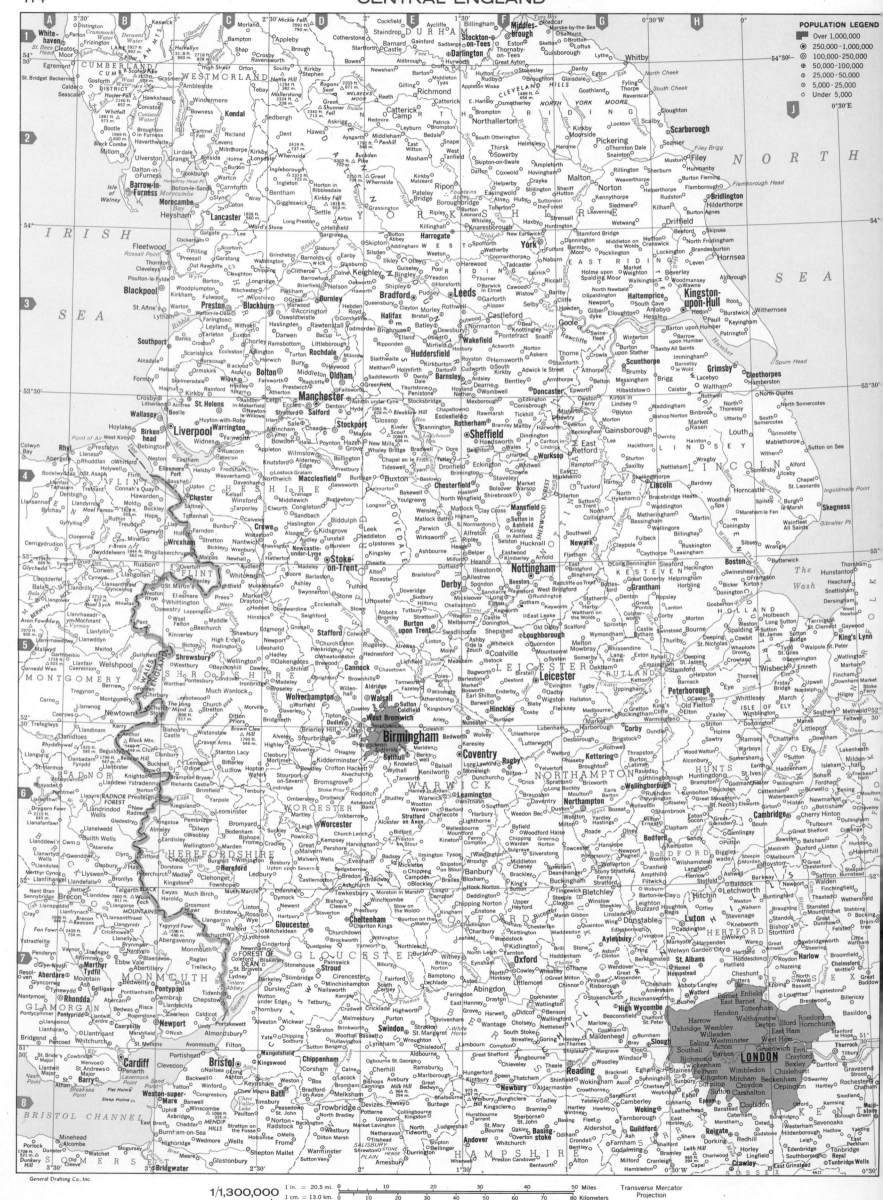

1/1,300,000

1 in. = 20.5 mi.
1 cm. = 13.0 km.

0 10 20 30 40 50 Miles

0 10 20 30 40 50 60 70 80 Kilometers

Transverse Mercator
Projection

General Drafting Co., Inc.

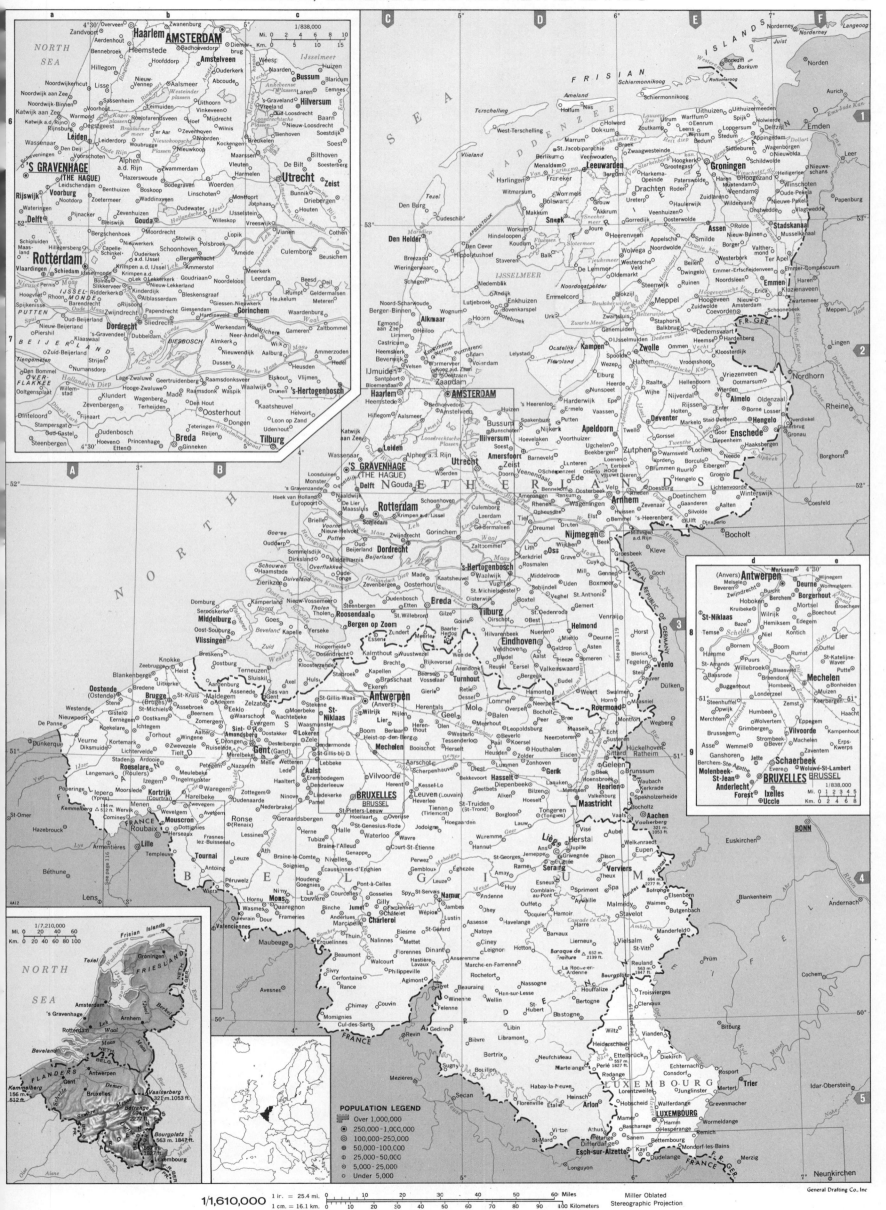

POPULATION LEGEND
- Over 1,000,000
- 250,000 - 1,000,000
- 100,000 - 250,000
- 50,000 - 100,000
- 25,000 - 50,000
- 5,000 - 25,000
- Under 5,000

1/1,610,000

1 in. = 25.4 mi.
1 cm. = 16.1 km.

Miles
Kilometers

Miller Oblated
Stereographic Projection

General Drafting Co., Inc.

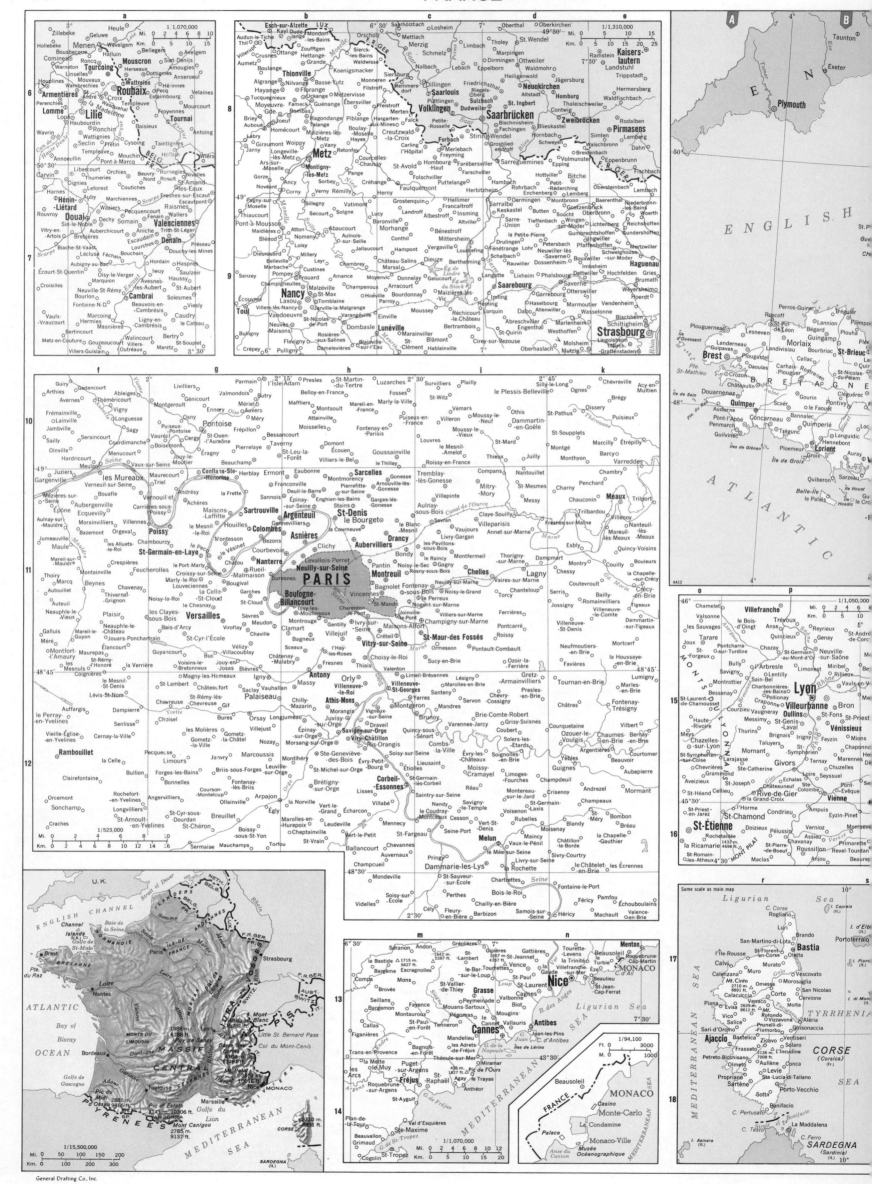

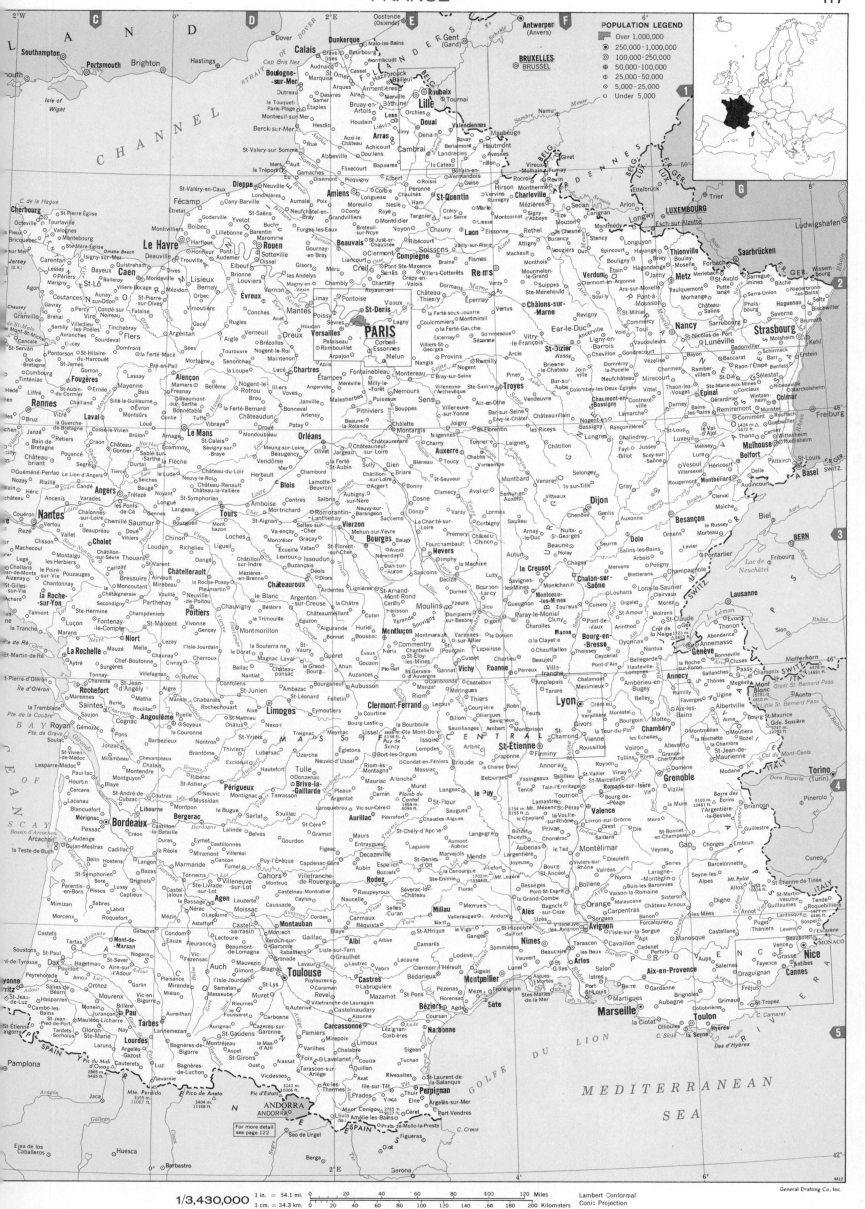

1/3,040,000

1 in. = 48.0 mi.
1 cm. = 30.4 km.

Conic Projection

1 in. = 19.6 mi.
1 cm. = 12.4 km.

Conic Projection

General Drafting Co., Inc.

50 Miles
80 Kilometers

POPULATION LEGEND

■   Over 1,000,000
◉   250,000 - 1,000,000
⊕   100,000 - 250,000
⊕   50,000 - 100,000
⊕   25,000 - 50,000
⊙   5,000 - 25,000
○   Under 5,000

ICELAND

REYKJAVIK

FAEROE IS. (FØROYAR) (Den.)

1/6,590,000

1 in. = 104 mi.
1 cm. = 65.9 km.

0 20 40 60 80 100 120 140 160 180 200 220 240 Miles
0 50 100 150 200 250 300 350 400 Kilometers

Conformal Conic Projection

General Drafting Co., Inc.

See page 121

1 in. = 32.0 mi.
1 cm. = 20.3 km.

Conformal Conic
Projection

General Drafting Co. Inc.

POPULATION LEGEND
- Over 1,000,000
- 250,000 - 1,000,000
- 100,000-250,000
- 50,000-100,000
- 25,000-50,000
- 5,000-25,000
- Under 5,000

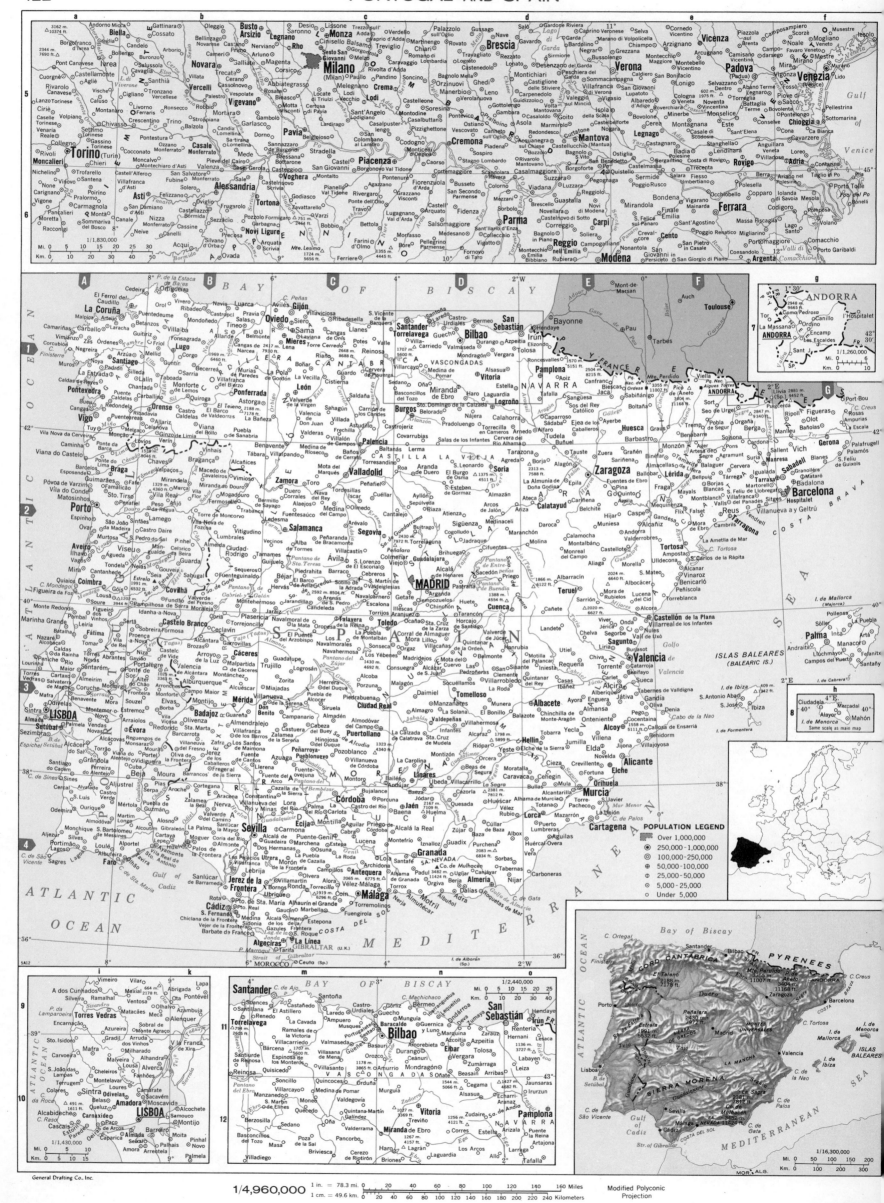

1/4,960,000

1 in. = 78.3 mi.
1 cm. = 49.6 km.

Modified Polyconic
Projection

General Drafting Co., Inc.

1/4,600,000

1 in. = 72.6 mi.
1 cm. = 46.0 km.

Lambert Conformal
Conic Projection

POPULATION LEGEND
- Over 1,000,000
- 250,000 - 1,000,000
- 100,000 - 250,000
- 50,000 - 100,000
- 25,000 - 50,000
- 5,000 - 25,000
- Under 5,000

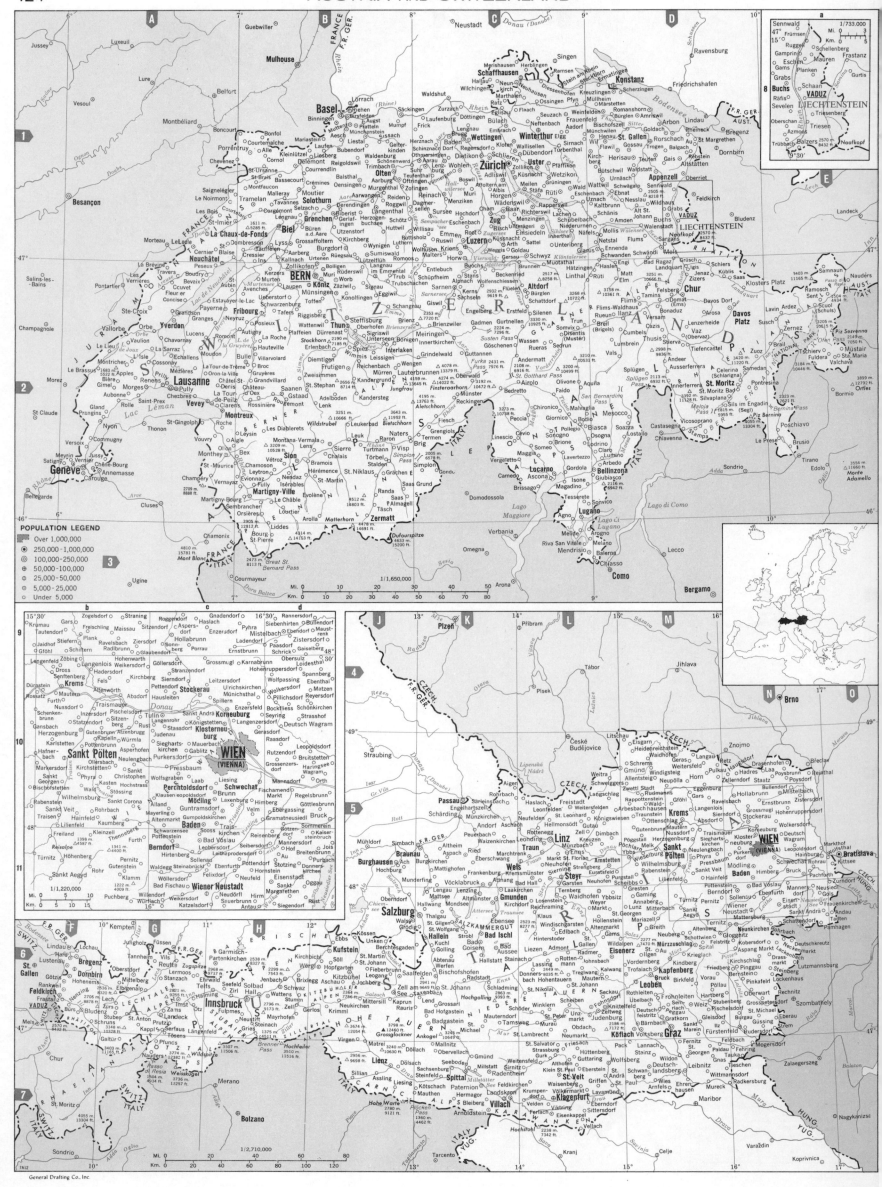

POPULATION LEGEND
● Over 1,000,000
◉ 250,000 - 1,000,000
⊕ 100,000 - 250,000
⊕ 50,000 - 100,000
⊙ 25,000 - 50,000
⊙ 5,000 - 25,000
○ Under 5,000

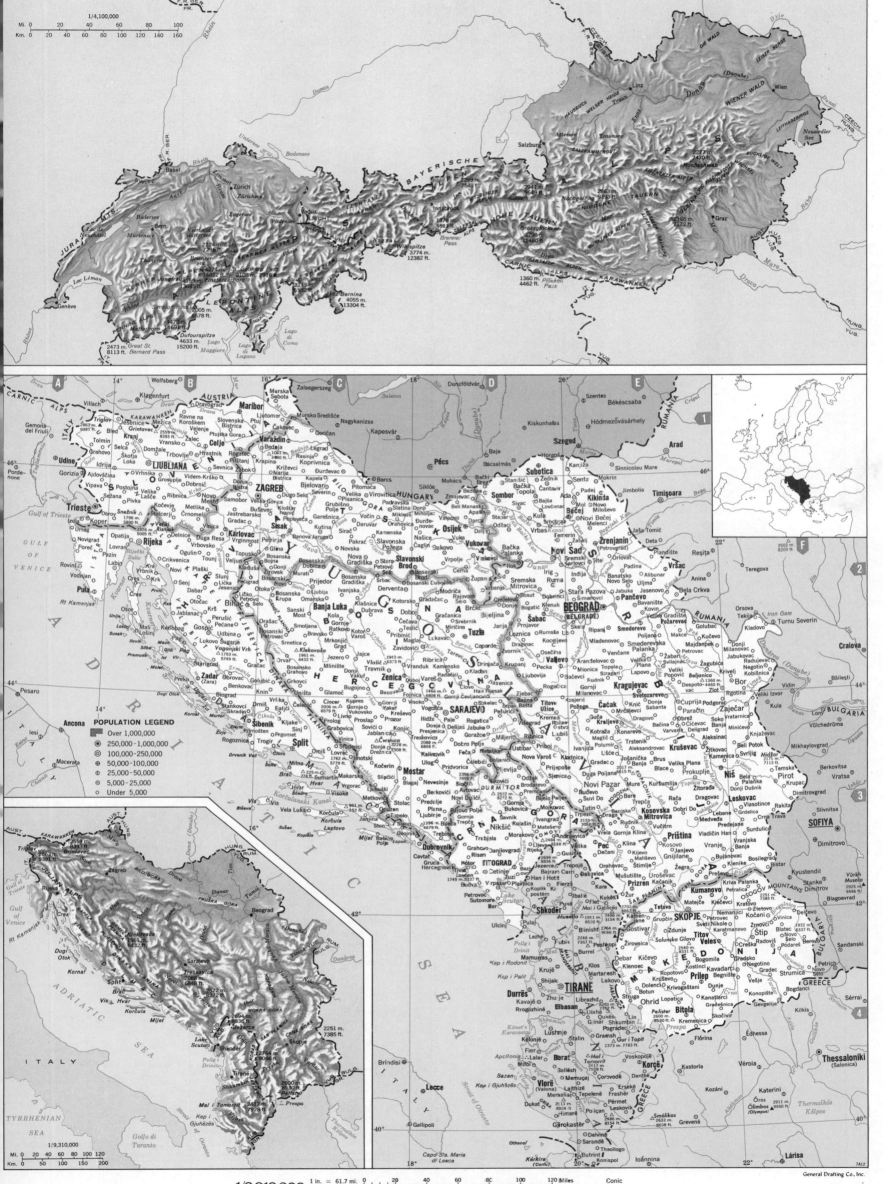

1/3,910,000

1 in. = 61.7 mi.

1 cm. = 39.1 km.

Conic Projection

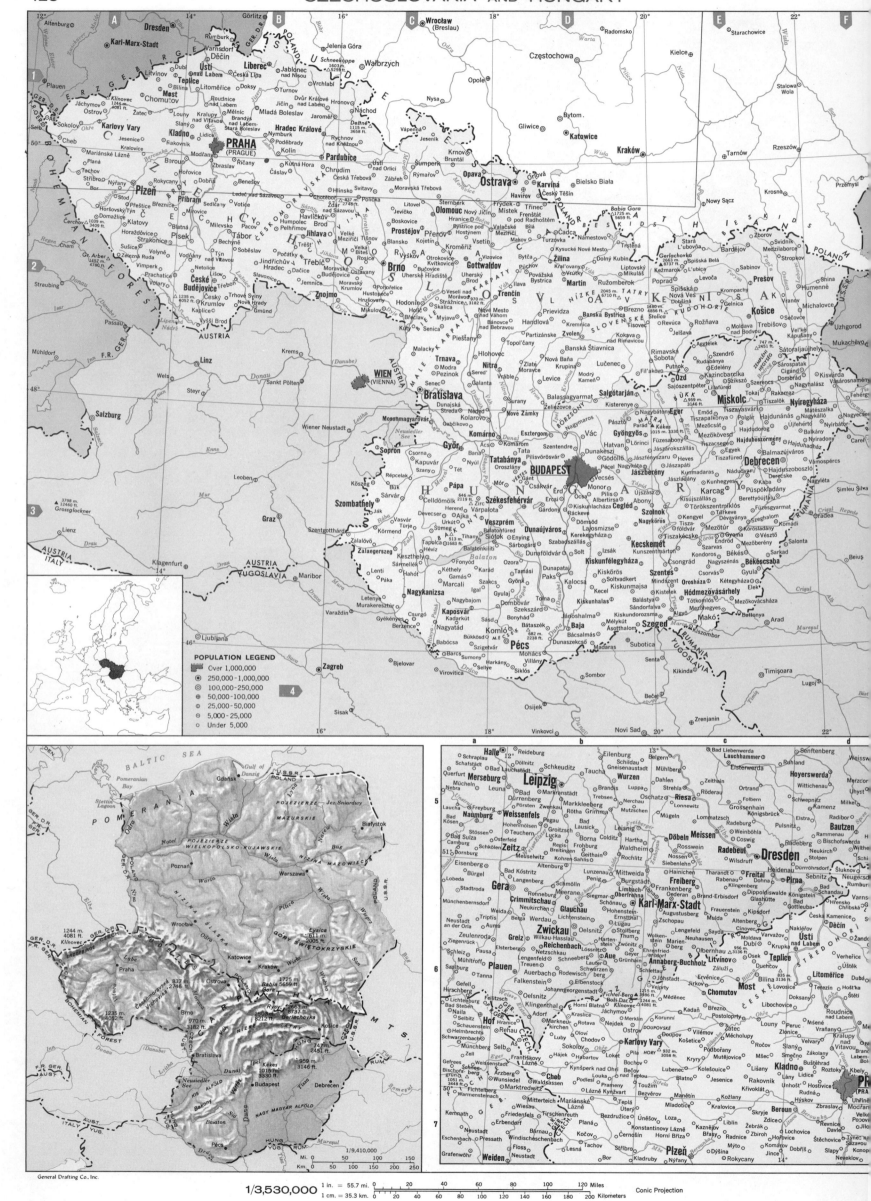

POPULATION LEGEND
■ Over 1,000,000
◎ 250,000–1,000,000
◉ 100,000–250,000
⊕ 50,000–100,000
⊕ 25,000–50,000
⊙ 5,000–25,000
○ Under 5,000

General Drafting Co., Inc.

1/9,410,000

1/3,530,000   1 in. = 55.7 mi.
1 cm. = 35.3 km.

Conic Projection

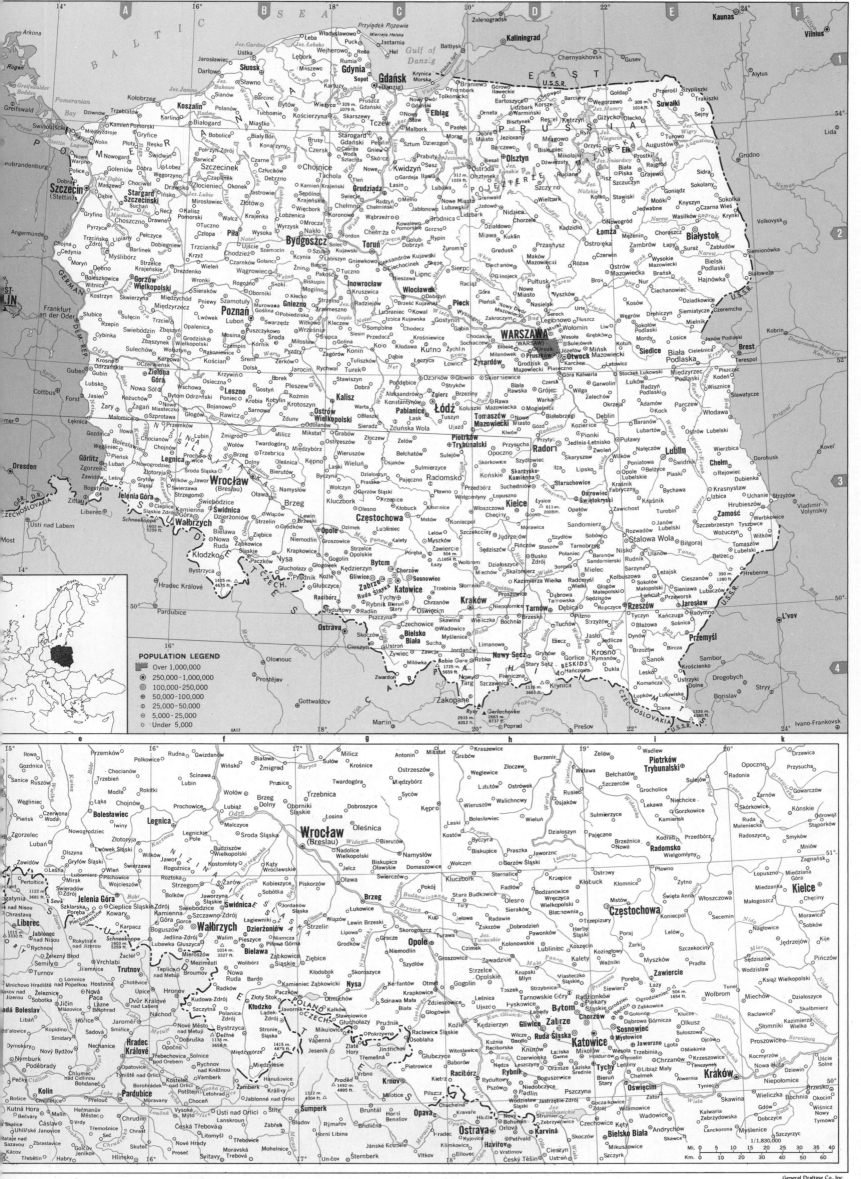

POPULATION LEGEND

Over 1,000,000
250,000 - 1,000,000
100,000 - 250,000
50,000 - 100,000
25,000 - 50,000
5,000 - 25,000
Under 5,000

1/3,590,000

1 in. = 56.7 mi.
1 cm. = 35.9 km.

120 Miles
200 Kilometers

Conic Projection

1/1,830,000

General Drafting Co., Inc.

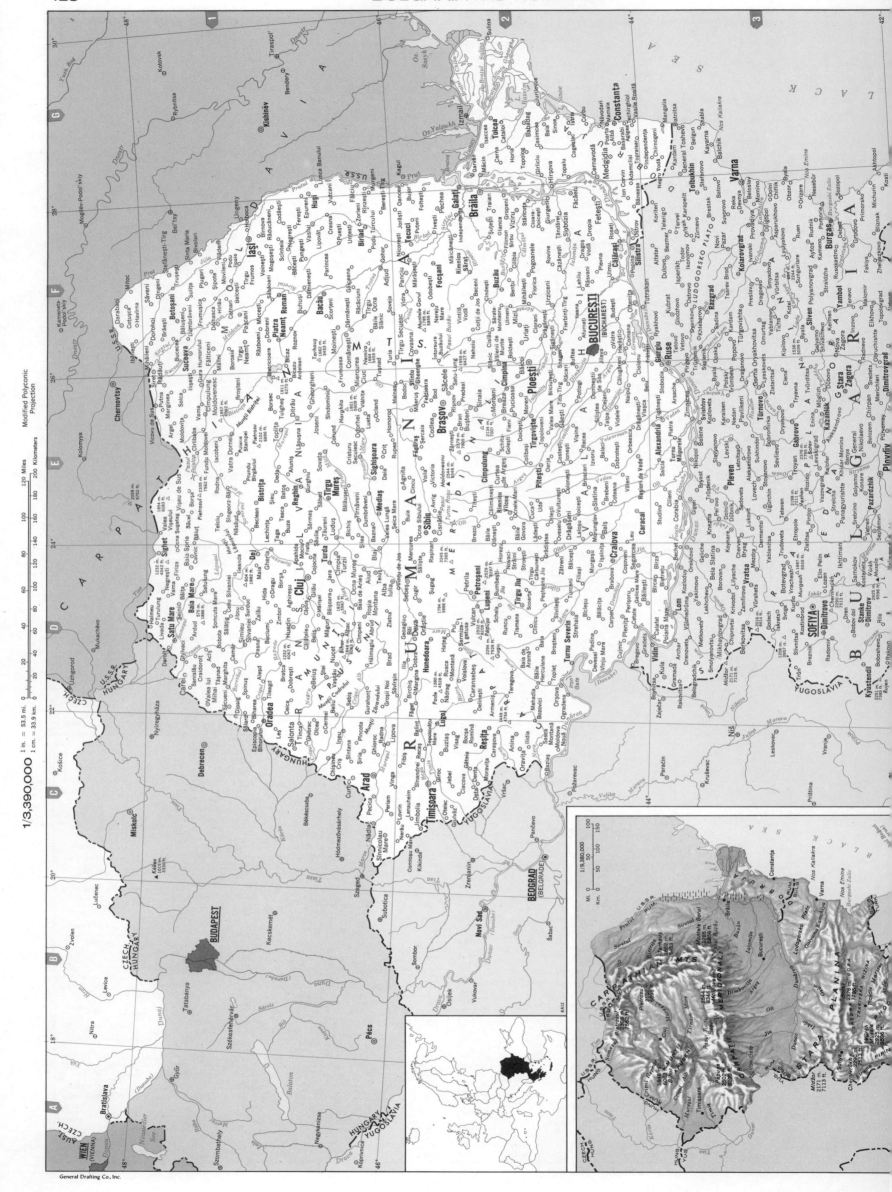

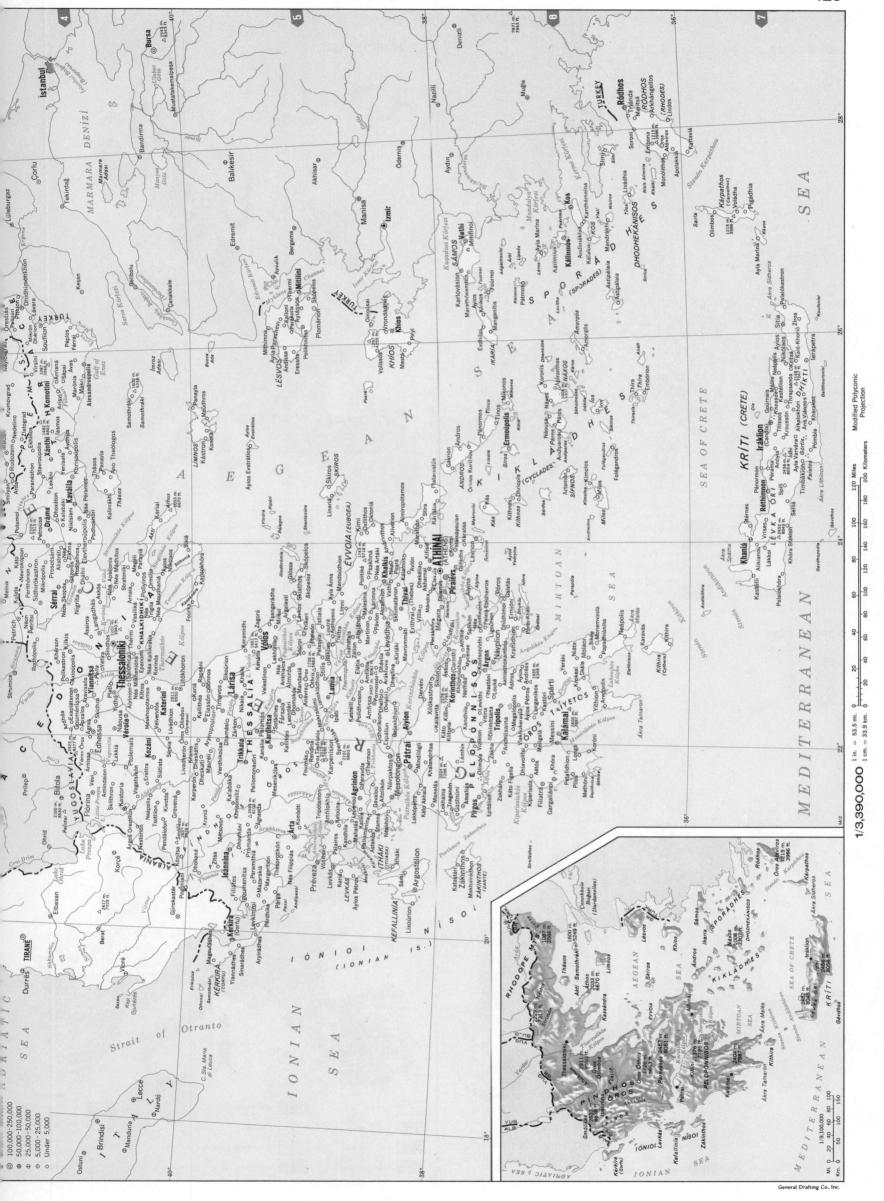

1/3,390,000   1 in. = 53.5 mi.
1 cm. = 33.9 km.

Modified Polyconic
Projection

General Drafting Co., Inc.

LANDFORMS and PHYSICAL REGIONS

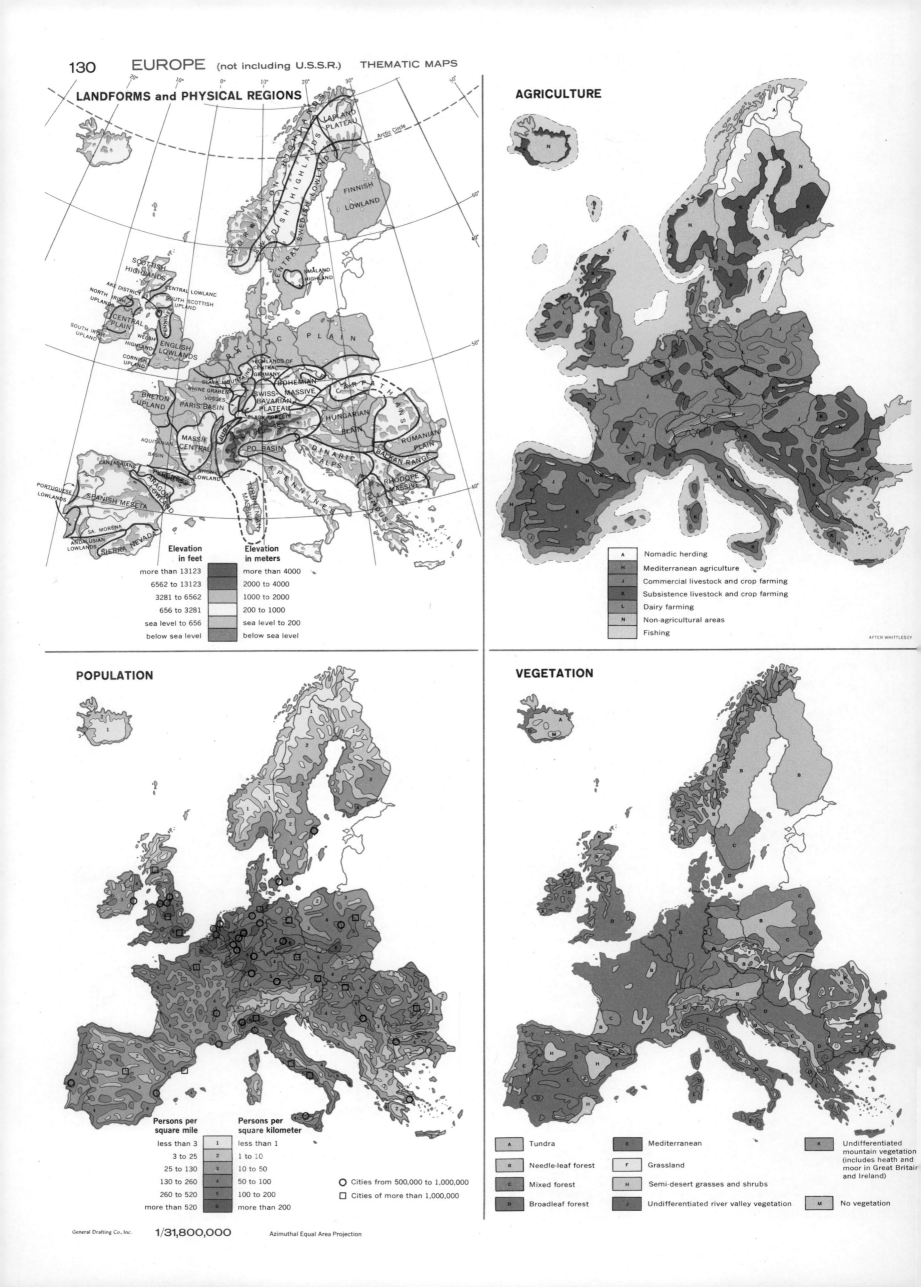

LAPLAND PLATEAU

Arctic Circle

FINNISH LOWLAND

SCOTTISH HIGHLANDS

LAKE DISTRICT

CENTRAL LOWLAND

NORTH IRISH UPLANDS

SOUTH SCOTTISH UPLAND

CENTRAL PLAIN

PENNINES

WELSH HIGHLAND

SOUTH IRISH UPLAND

ENGLISH LOWLANDS

CORNISH UPLAND

BALTIC PLAIN

HIGHLANDS OF CENTRAL GERMANY

BOHEMIAN MASSIVE

SLATE MOUNTAINS

BRETON UPLAND

RHINE GRABEN

VOSGES

SWISS-BAVARIAN PLATEAU

CARPATHIANS

PARIS BASIN

BLACK FOREST

HUNGARIAN PLAIN

RUMANIAN PLAIN

AQUITANIAN BASIN

MASSIF CENTRAL

JURA

PO BASIN

DINARIC ALPS

BALKAN RANGE

CANTABRIANS

RHONE LOWLAND

PYRENEES

ARAGON LOWLAND

APENNINES

RHODOPE MASSIVE

PINDUS

PORTUGUESE LOWLANDS

SPANISH MESETA

SA. MORENA

ANDALUSIAN LOWLANDS

SIERRA NEVADA

NORWEGIAN HIGHLANDS

SWEDISH HIGHLANDS

CENTRAL SWEDISH LOWLAND

SMÅLAND HIGHLAND

TYRRHENIAN MASSIVE

Elevation in feet		Elevation in meters
more than 13123		more than 4000
6562 to 13123		2000 to 4000
3281 to 6562		1000 to 2000
656 to 3281		200 to 1000
sea level to 656		sea level to 200
below sea level		below sea level

AGRICULTURE

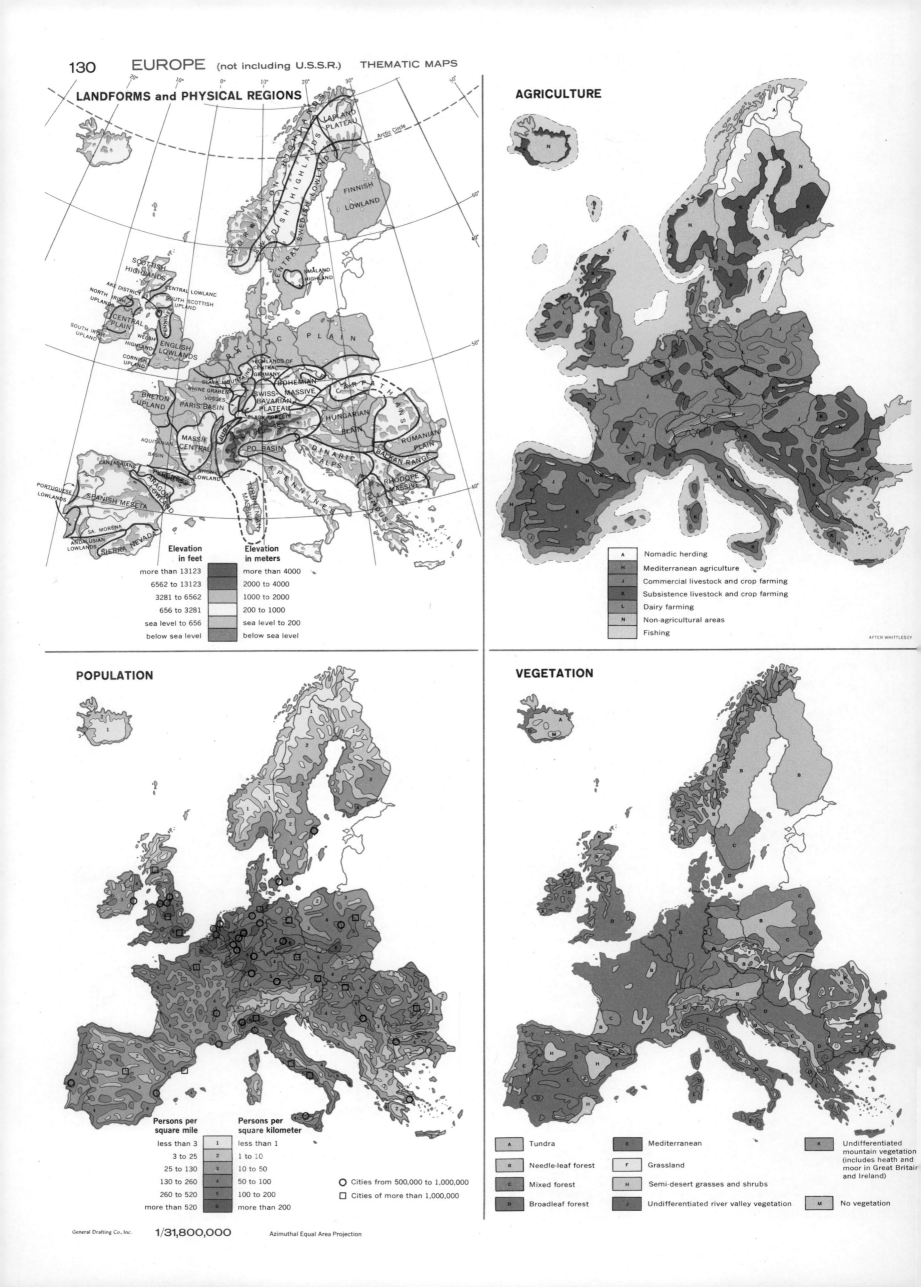

A	Nomadic herding
H	Mediterranean agriculture
J	Commercial livestock and crop farming
K	Subsistence livestock and crop farming
L	Dairy farming
N	Non-agricultural areas
	Fishing

AFTER WHITTLESEY

POPULATION

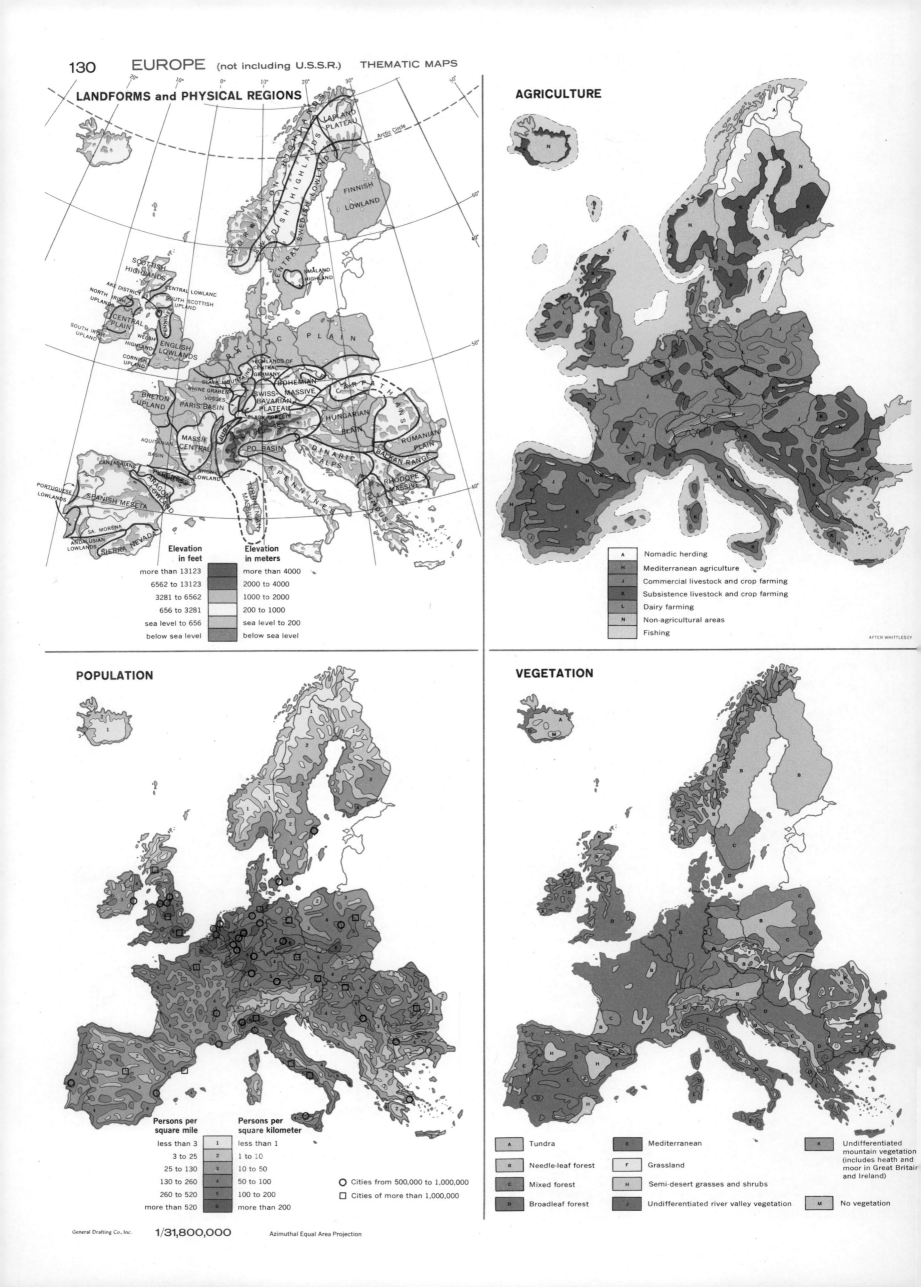

Persons per square mile		Persons per square kilometer
less than 3	1	less than 1
3 to 25	2	1 to 10
25 to 130	3	10 to 50
130 to 260	4	50 to 100
260 to 520	5	100 to 200
more than 520	6	more than 200

○ Cities from 500,000 to 1,000,000
□ Cities of more than 1,000,000

VEGETATION

A	Tundra	E	Mediterranean	K	Undifferentiated mountain vegetation (includes heath and moor in Great Britain and Ireland)
B	Needle-leaf forest	F	Grassland		
C	Mixed forest	H	Semi-desert grasses and shrubs		
D	Broadleaf forest	J	Undifferentiated river valley vegetation	M	No vegetation

AVERAGE ANNUAL PRECIPITATION

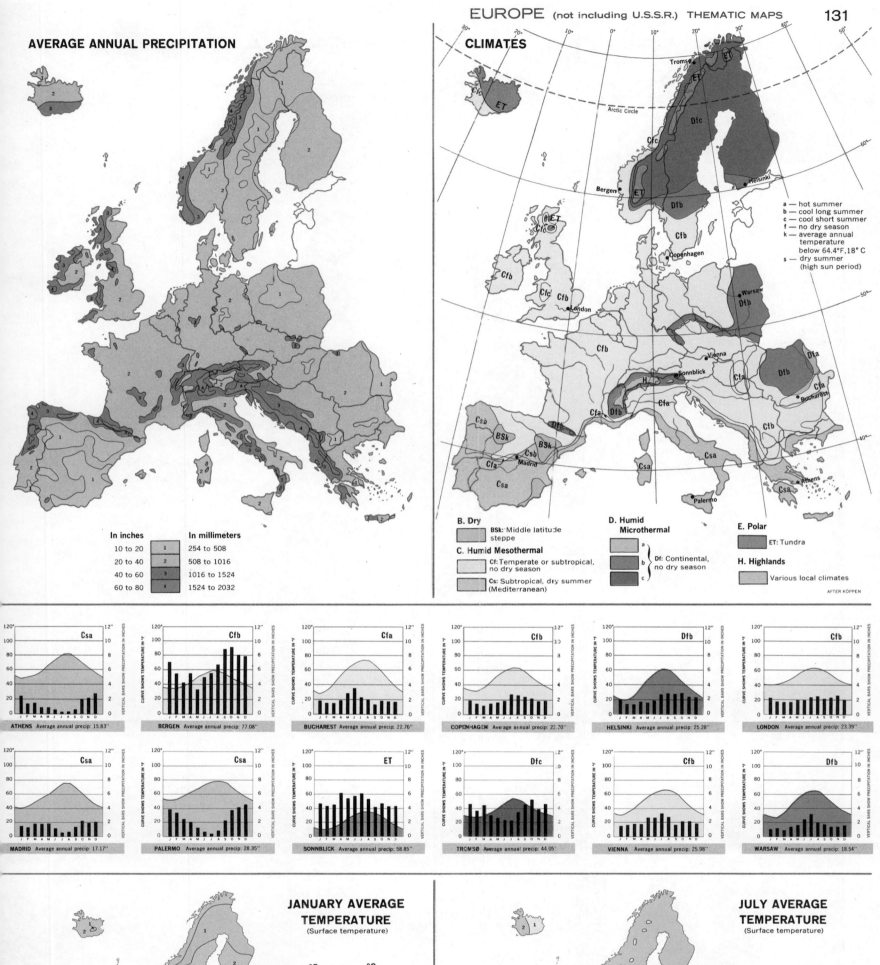

CLIMATES

a — hot summer
b — cool long summer
c — cool short summer
f — no dry season
k — average annual
temperature
below 64.4°F, 18° C
s — dry summer
(high sun period)

In inches

10 to 20	1
20 to 40	2
40 to 60	3
60 to 80	4

In millimeters

254 to 508
508 to 1016
1016 to 1524
1524 to 2032

B. Dry

BSk: Middle latitude steppe

C. Humid Mesothermal

Cf: Temperate or subtropical, no dry season

Cs: Subtropical, dry summer (Mediterranean)

D. Humid Microthermal

Df: Continental, no dry season
a
b
c

E. Polar

ET: Tundra

H. Highlands

Various local climates

AFTER KÖPPEN

ATHENS Average annual precip: 15.83″ Csa
BERGEN Average annual precip: 77.08″ Cfb
BUCHAREST Average annual precip: 22.76″ Cfa
COPENHAGEN Average annual precip: 25.70″ Cfb
HELSINKI Average annual precip: 25.28″ Dfb
LONDON Average annual precip: 23.39″ Cfb

MADRID Average annual precip: 17.17″ Csa
PALERMO Average annual precip: 28.35″ Csa
SONNBLICK Average annual precip: 58.85″ ET
TROMSØ Average annual precip: 44.05″ Dfc
VIENNA Average annual precip: 25.98″ Cfb
WARSAW Average annual precip: 18.54″ Dfb

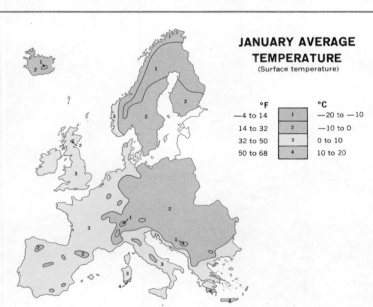

JANUARY AVERAGE TEMPERATURE
(Surface temperature)

°F		°C
—4 to 14	1	—20 to —10
14 to 32	2	—10 to 0
32 to 50	3	0 to 10
50 to 68	4	10 to 20

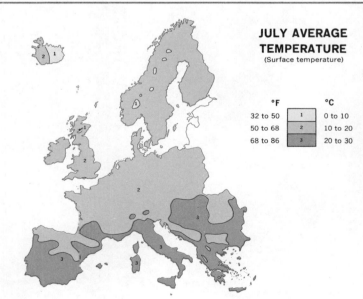

JULY AVERAGE TEMPERATURE
(Surface temperature)

°F		°C
32 to 50	1	0 to 10
50 to 68	2	10 to 20
68 to 86	3	20 to 30

General Drafting Co., Inc.

LAND HEIGHTS

	meters	feet
	4000	13123
	2000	6562
	1000	3281
	200	656
land below sea level		
	sea level	
	200	656
	2000	6562
	3000	9843
	6000	19685

OCEAN DEPTHS

General Drafting Co. Inc.

1/17,900,000

1 in. = 283 mi.
1 cm. = 179 km.

0 100 200 300 400 500 600 Miles

0 100 200 300 400 500 600 700 800 900 1000 Kilometers

Perspective Cylindrical
Projection

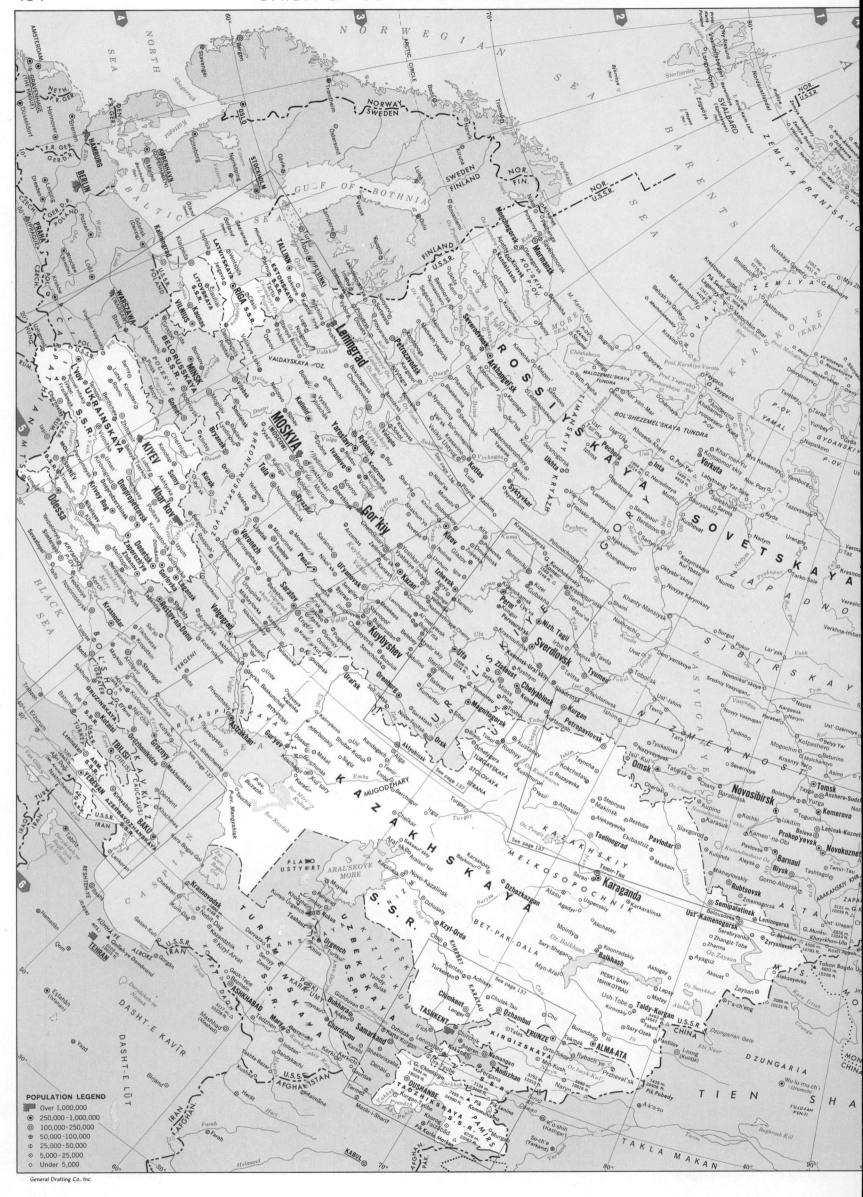

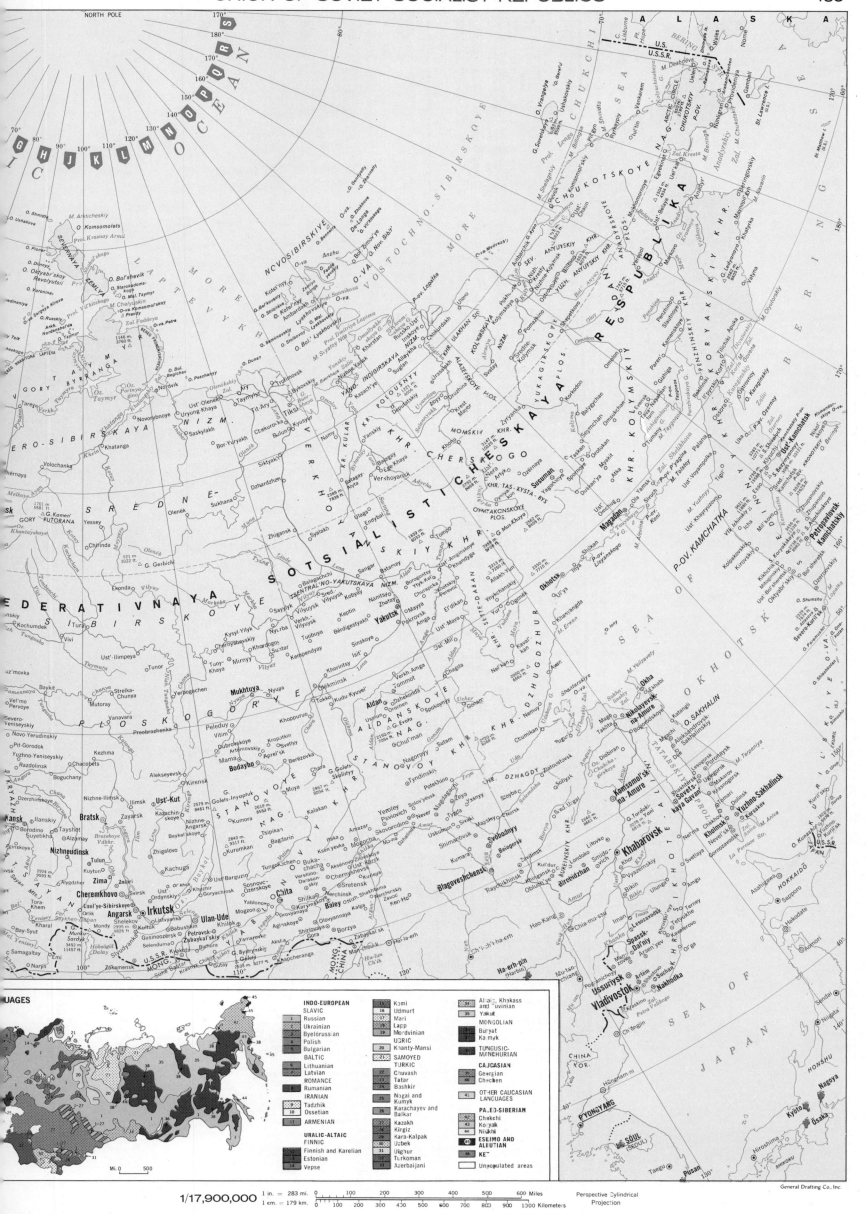

LANGUAGES

INDO-EUROPEAN
SLAVIC
2 Russian
Ukrainian
4 Byelorussian
Polish
Bulgarian
BALTIC
Lithuanian
Latvian
ROMANCE
Rumanian
IRANIAN
Tadzhik
10 Ossetian
13 Armenian

URALIC-ALTAIC
FINNIC
Finnish and Karelian
Estonian
Vepse

16 Komi
Udmurt
Mari
19 Lapp
Mordvinian
UGRIC
20 Khanty-Mansi
SAMOYED
TURKIC
Chuvash
Tatar
Bashkir
25 Nogai and Kumyk
Karachayev and Balkar
Kazakh
Kirgiz
Kara-Kalpak
Uzbek
31 Uighur
Turkoman
Azerbaijani

Altaic, Khakass and Tuvinian
35 Yakut
MONGOLIAN
Buryat
Kalmyk
TUNGUSIC-MANCHURIAN
CAUCASIAN
Georgian
Chechen
41 OTHER CAUCASIAN LANGUAGES
PALEO-SIBERIAN
Chukchi
43 Koryak
44 Nivkhi
ESKIMO AND ALEUTIAN
KET
Unpopulated areas

1/17,900,000

1 in. = 283 mi.
1 cm. = 179 km.

Mi. 0   100   200   300   400   500   600 Miles

0   100   200   300   400   500   600   700   800   900   1300 Kilometers

Perspective Cylindrical Projection

General Drafting Co. Inc.

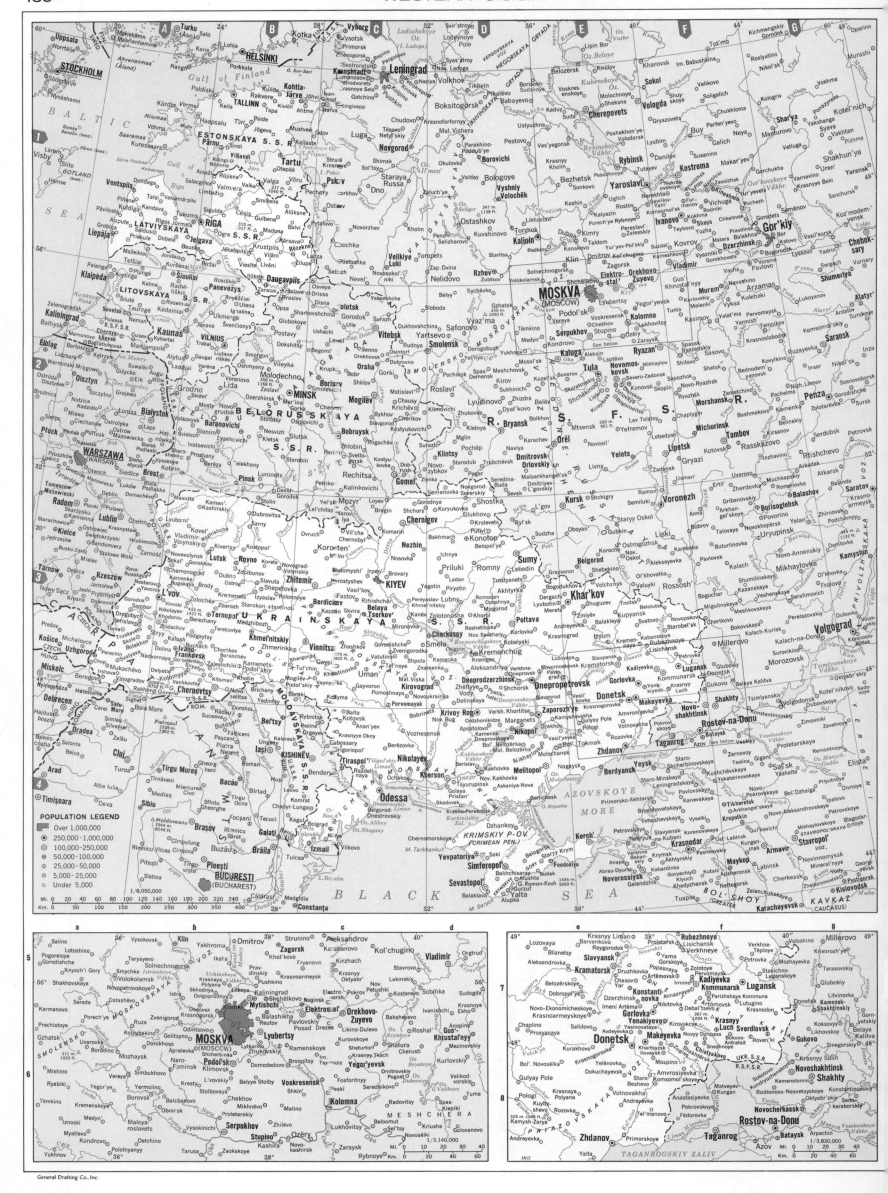

POPULATION LEGEND
- Over 1,000,000
- 250,000–1,000,000
- 100,000–250,000
- 50,000–100,000
- 25,000–50,000
- 5,000–25,000
- Under 5,000

General Drafting Co., Inc.

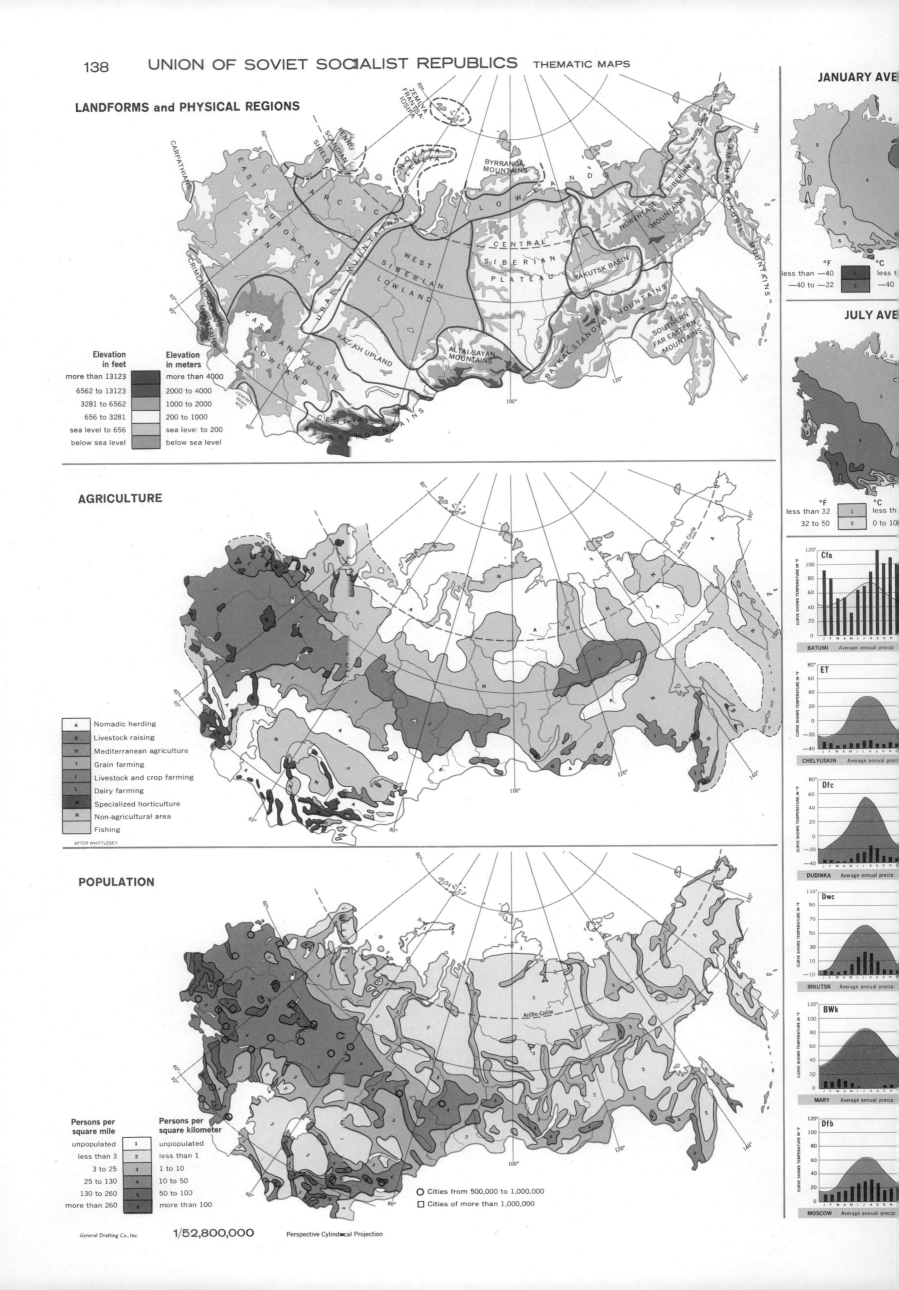

LANDFORMS and PHYSICAL REGIONS

CARPATHIANS
FENNO
SCANDIAN
SHIELD
ZEMLYA
FRANTSA
IOSIFA
NOVAYA
ZEMLYA
BYRRANGA
MOUNTAINS
ARCTIC
LOWLANDS
EAST EUROPEAN PLAIN
CRIMEAN
CAUCASUS
MOUNTAINS
URAL MOUNTAINS
WEST SIBERIAN LOWLAND
CENTRAL SIBERIAN PLATEAU
NORTHEAST SIBERIAN MOUNTAINS
KAMCHATKA-KURIL MOUNTAINS
YAKUTSK BASIN
CASPIAN LOWLAND
TURAN LOWLAND
KAZAKH UPLAND
ALTAI-SAYAN MOUNTAINS
BAYKAL-STANOVOY MOUNTAINS
SOUTHERN FAR EASTERN MOUNTAINS
CENTRAL ASIAN MOUNTAINS

Elevation in feet
more than 13123
6562 to 13123
3281 to 6562
656 to 3281
sea level to 656
below sea level

Elevation in meters
more than 4000
2000 to 4000
1000 to 2000
200 to 1000
sea level to 200
below sea level

AGRICULTURE

A	Nomadic herding
B	Livestock raising
H	Mediterranean agriculture
I	Grain farming
L	Livestock and crop farming
L	Dairy farming
M	Specialized horticulture
N	Non-agricultural area
	Fishing

AFTER WHITTLESEY

POPULATION

Persons per square mile
unpopulated
less than 3
3 to 25
25 to 130
130 to 260
more than 260

Persons per square kilometer
unpopulated
less than 1
1 to 10
10 to 50
50 to 100
more than 100

○ Cities from 500,000 to 1,000,000
□ Cities of more than 1,000,000

JANUARY AVE

°F
less than −40
−40 to −22

°C
less t
−40

JULY AVE

°F
less than 32
32 to 50

°C
less th
0 to 10

Cfa
BATUMI   Average annual precip.

ET
CHELYUSKIN   Average annual precip.

Dfc
DUDINKA   Average annual precip.

Dwc
IRKUTSK   Average annual precip.

BWk
MARY   Average annual precip.

Dfb
MOSCOW   Average annual precip.

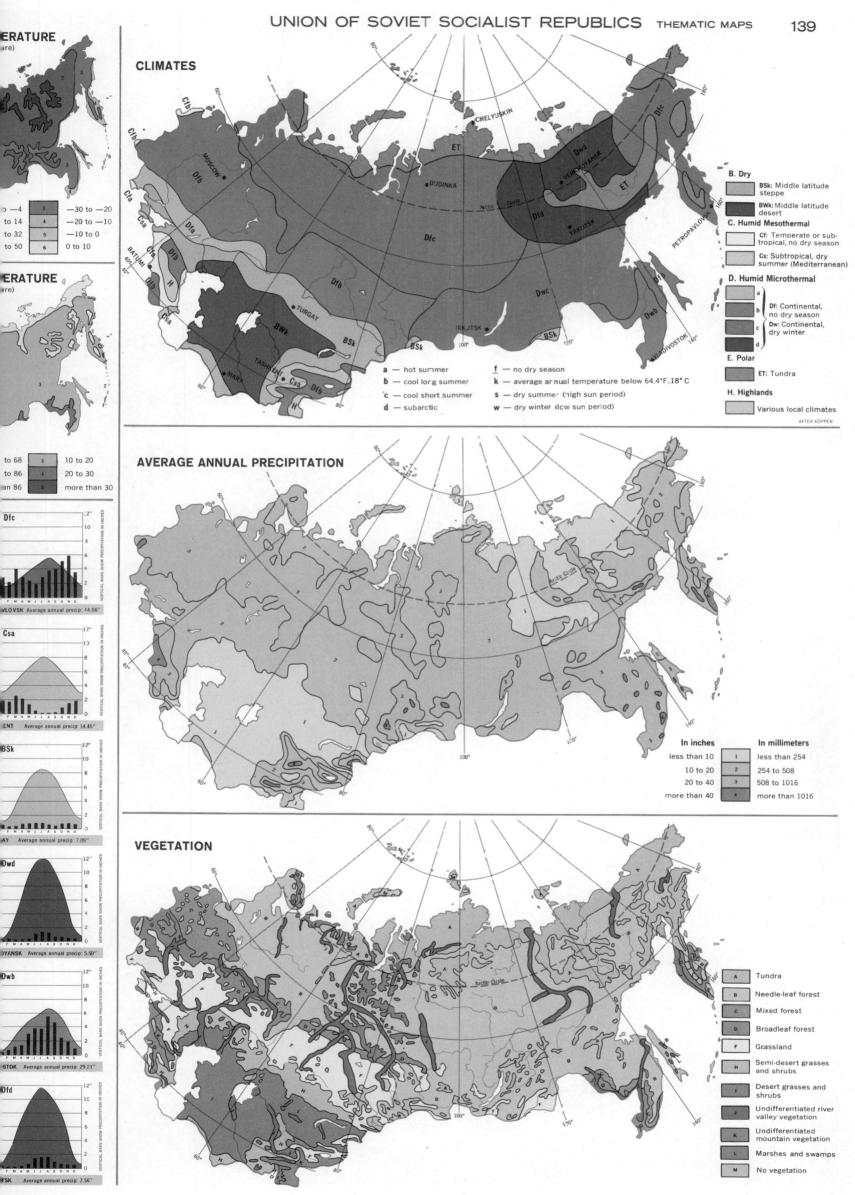

General Drafting Co., Inc.

LAND HEIGHTS

meters	feet
4000	13123
2000	6562
1000	3281
200	656
land below sea level	
sea level	
200	656
3000	9843
6000	19685

OCEAN DEPTHS

UNION OF SOVIET SOCIALIST REPUBLICS

General Drafting Co., Inc.

1/21,800,000

1 in. = 344 mi.	0 100 200 300 400 500 600 700 800 Miles
1 cm. = 218 km.	0 200 400 600 800 1000 1200 Kilometers

Conic Projection

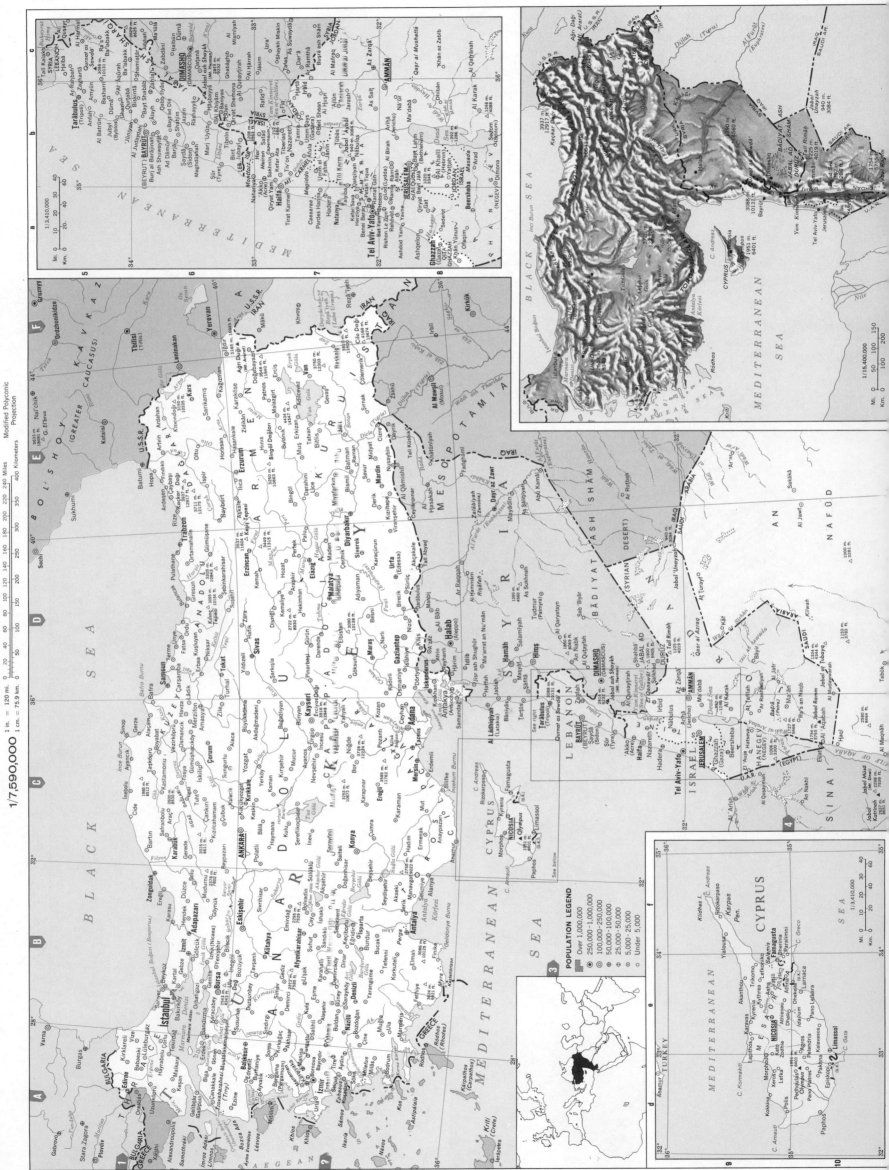

General Drafting Co., Inc.

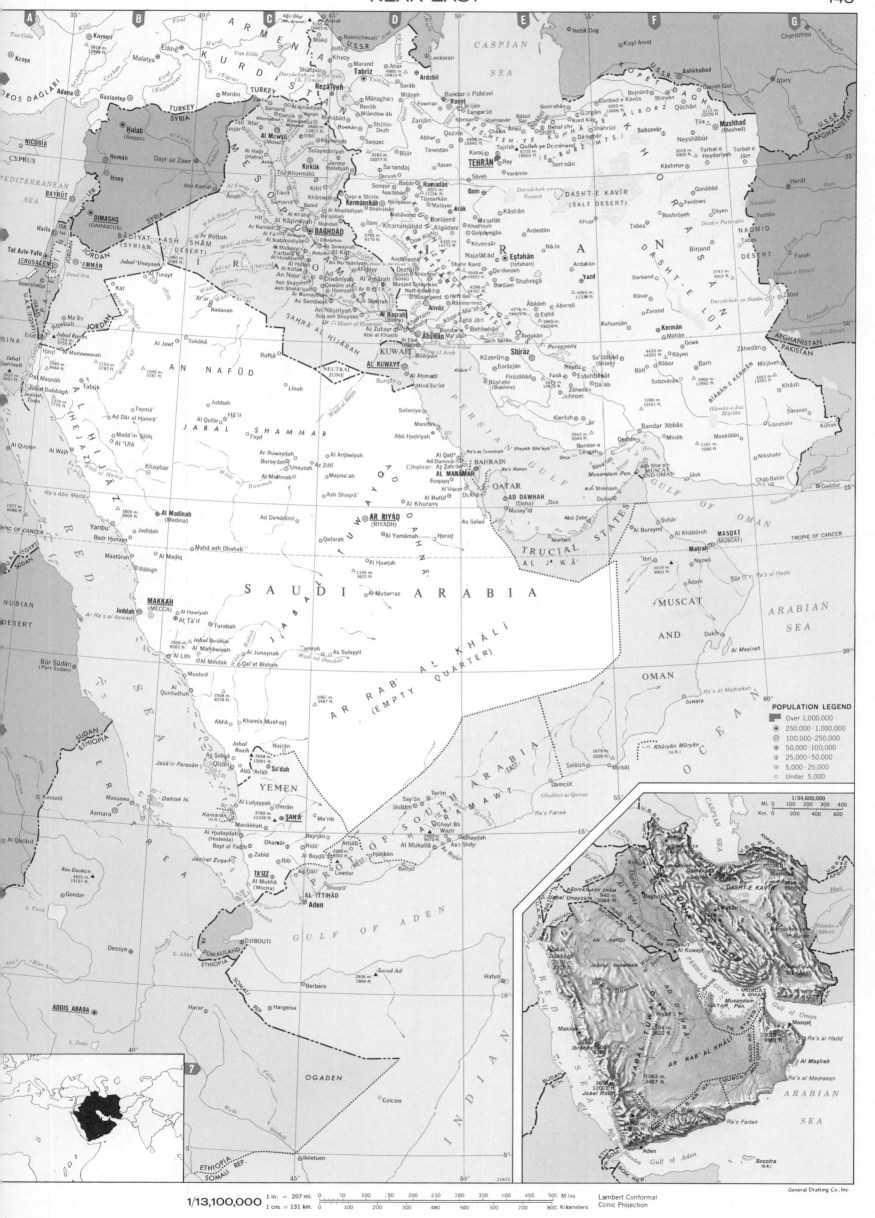

POPULATION LEGEND
- Over 1,000,000
- 250,000 - 1,000,000
- 100,000 - 250,000
- 50,000 - 100,000
- 25,000 - 50,000
- 5,000 - 25,000
- Under 5,000

1/13,100,000

1 in. = 207 mi.
1 cm. = 131 km.

Lambert Conformal
Conic Projection

General Drafting Co., Inc.

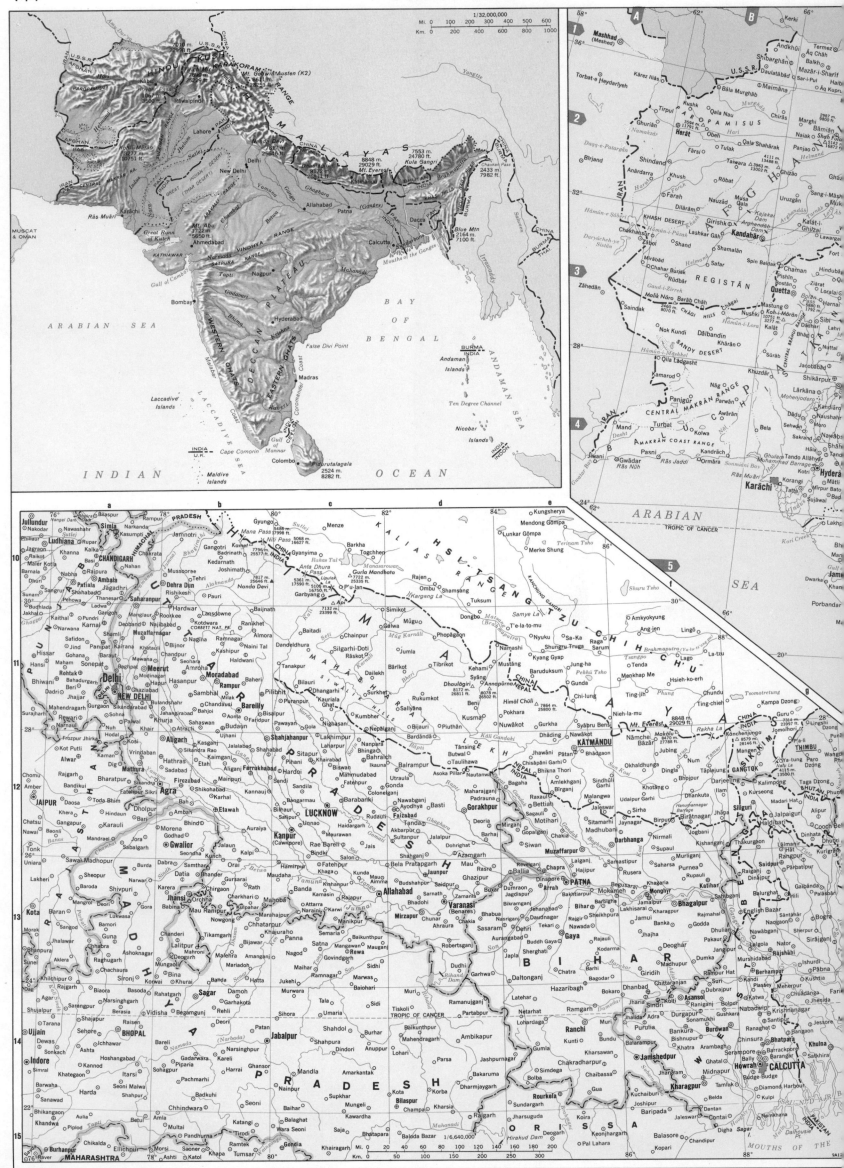

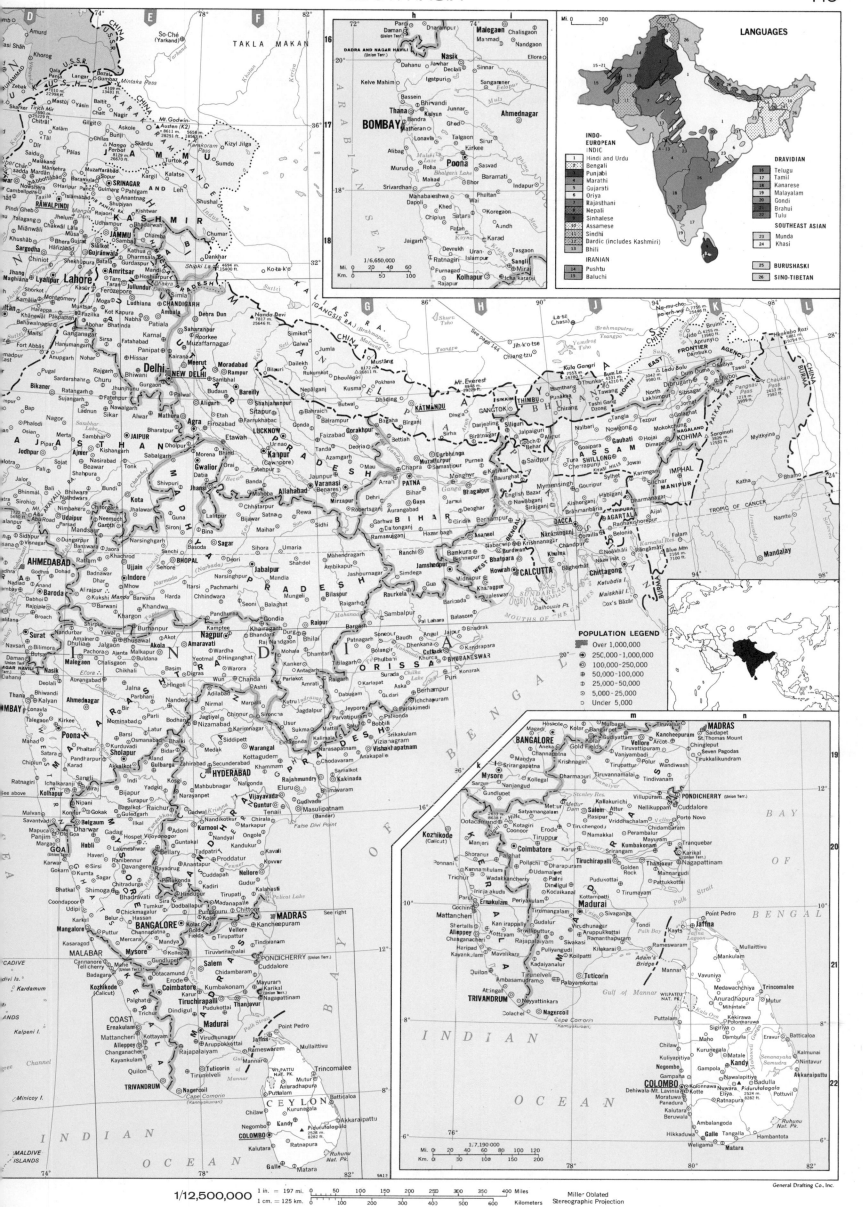

LANGUAGES

INDO-EUROPEAN
INDIC
1 Hindi and Urdu
2 Bengali
3 Punjabi
4 Marathi
6 Gujarati
7 Oriya
8 Rajasthani
9 Nepali
10 Sinhalese
11 Assamese
12 Sindhi
13 Dardic (includes Kashmiri)
Bhili

IRANIAN
14 Pushtu
15 Baluchi

DRAVIDIAN
16 Telugu
17 Tamil
18 Kanarese
19 Malayalam
20 Gondi
21 Brahui
22 Tulu

SOUTHEAST ASIAN
23 Munda
24 Khasi

25 BURUSHASKI

26 SINO-TIBETAN

POPULATION LEGEND
Over 1,000,000
250,000 – 1,000,000
100,000 – 250,000
50,000 – 100,000
25,000 – 50,000
5,000 – 25,000
Under 5,000

1/12,500,000
1 in. = 197 mi.
1 cm. = 125 km.
Miller Oblated
Stereographic Projection

General Drafting Co., Inc.

1/8,630,000

1 in. = 136 mi.
1 cm. = 86.3 km.

Miller Oblated
Stereographic Projection

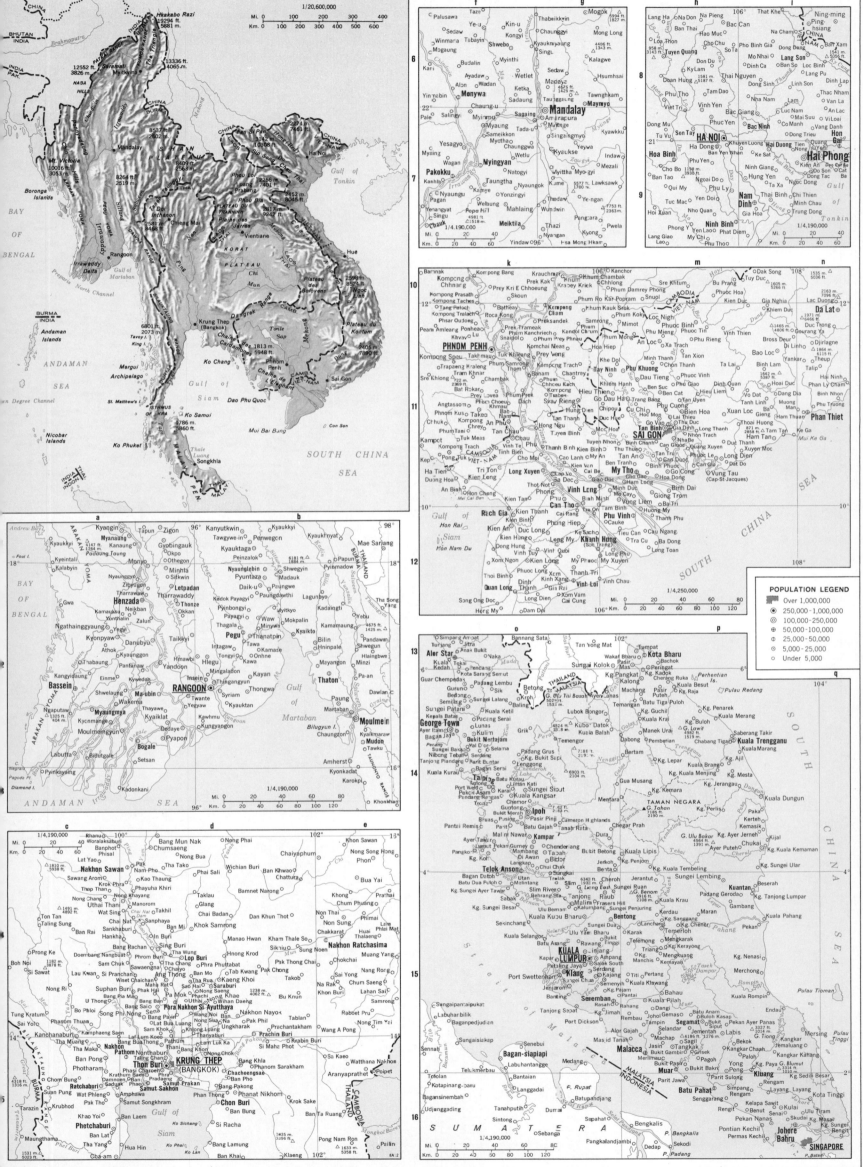

POPULATION LEGEND

- Over 1,000,000
- 250,000 - 1,000,000
- 100,000 - 250,000
- 50,000 - 100,000
- 25,000 - 50,000
- 5,000 - 25,000
- Under 5,000

General Drafting Co., Inc.

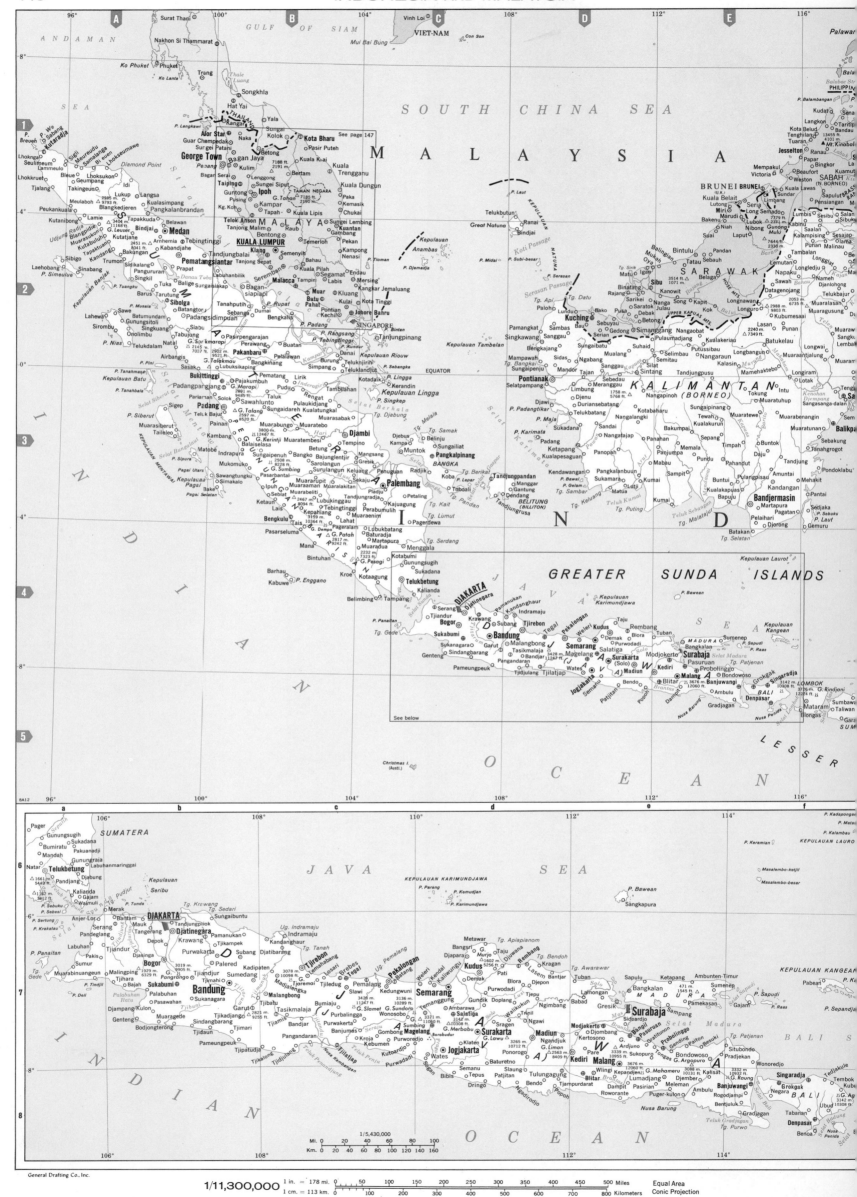

1/11,300,000   1 in. = 178 mi.   1 cm. = 113 km.   Equal Area   Conic Projection

General Drafting Co., Inc.

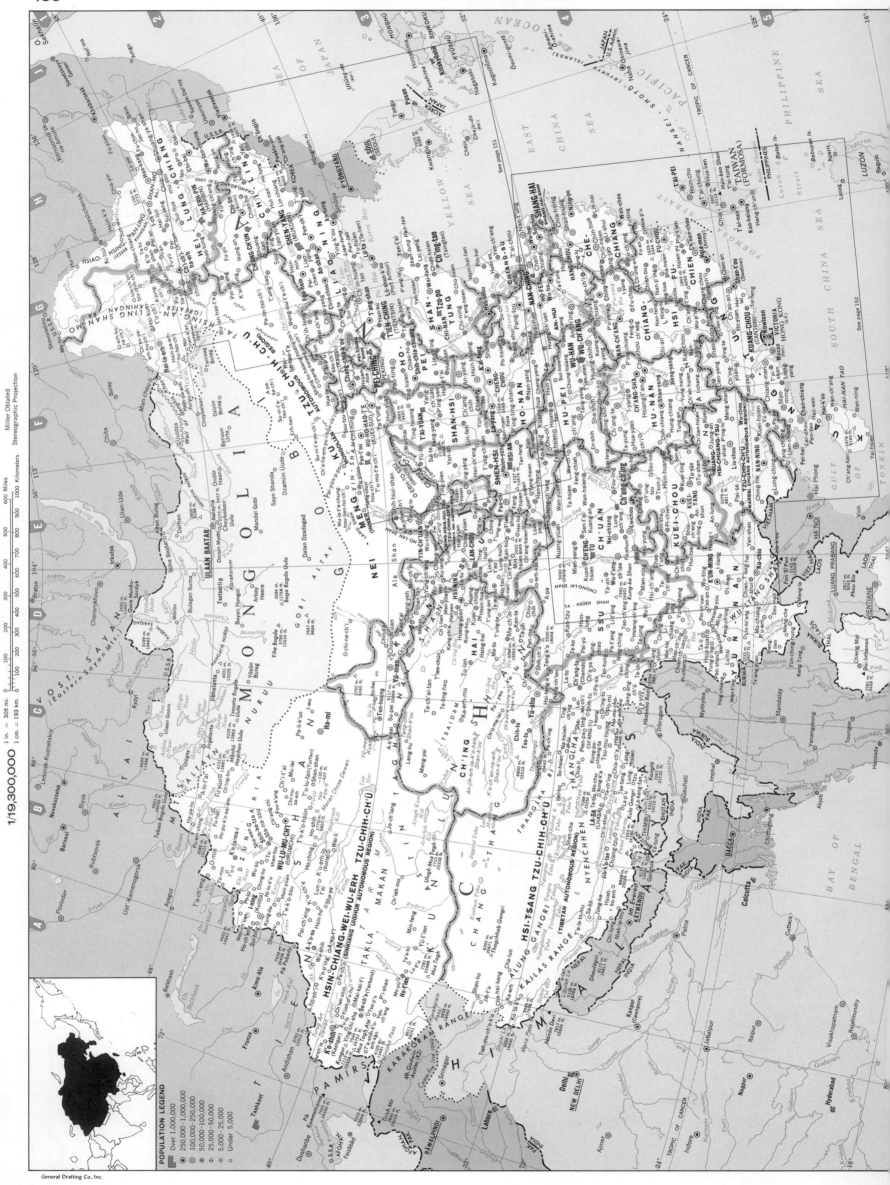

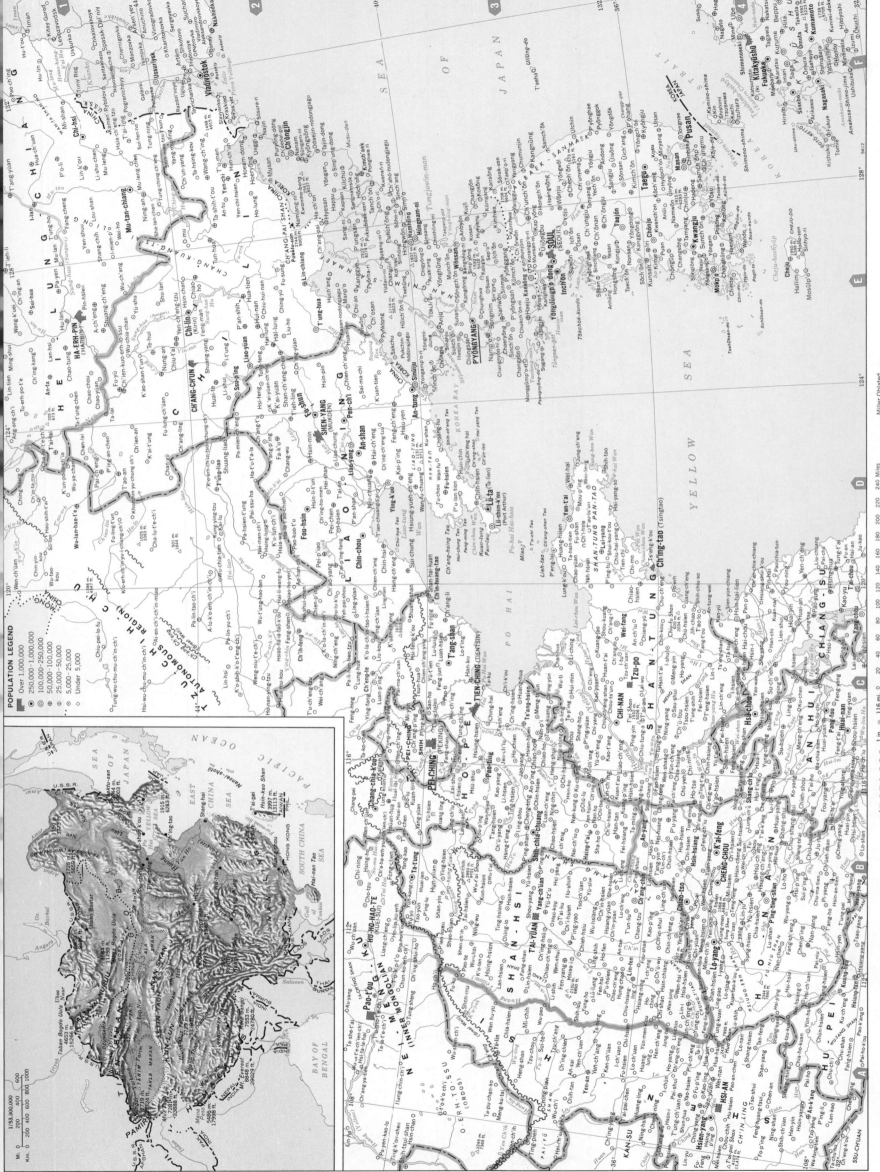

POPULATION LEGEND
◼ Over 1,000,000
◉ 250,000-1,000,000
⊕ 100,000-250,000
⊙ 50,000-100,000
◉ 25,000-50,000
⊕ 5,000-25,000
○ Under 5,000

1/7,350,000

1 in. = 116 mi.
1 cm. = 73.5 km.

Miller Oblated
Stereographic Projection

General Drafting Co., Inc.

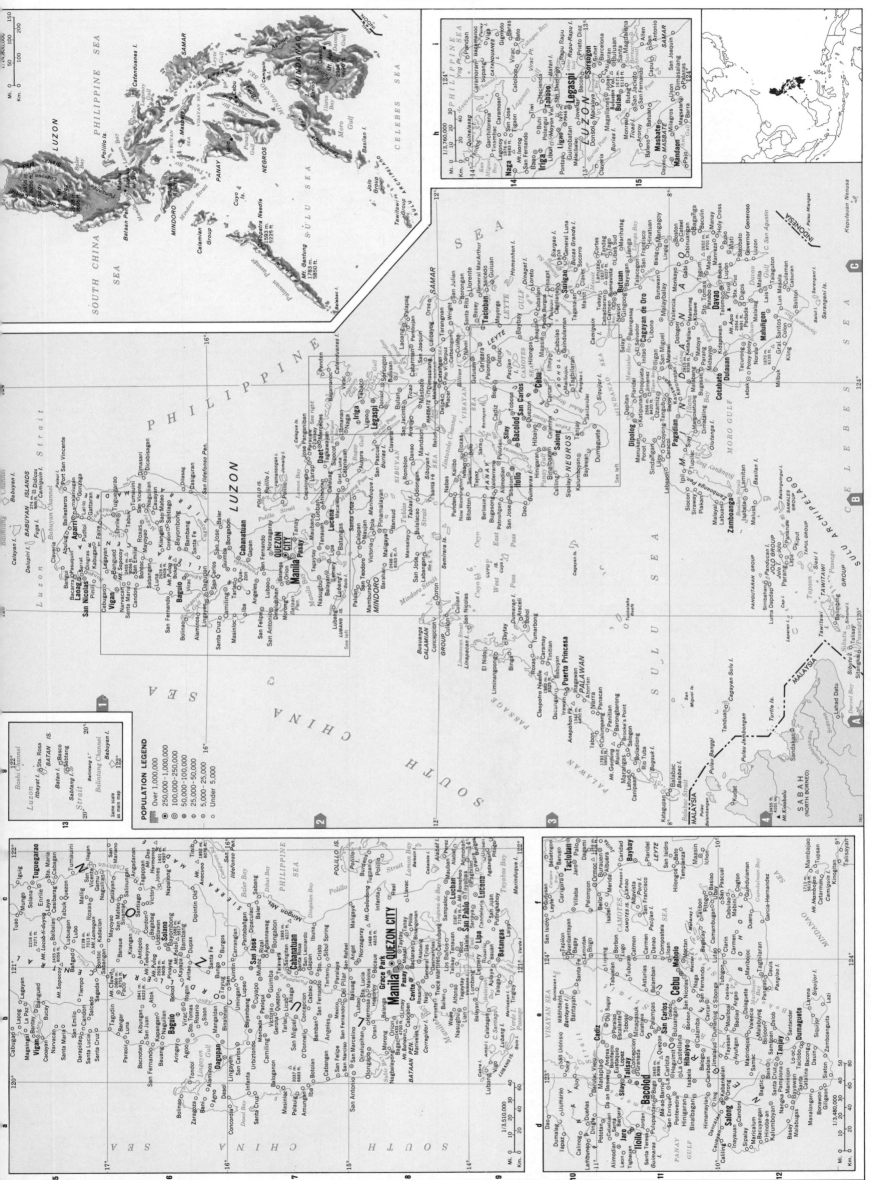

General Drafting Co., Inc.

1/7,350,000

1 in. = 116 mi.
1 cm. = 73.5 Km.

Polyconic
Projection

POPULATION LEGEND

Over 1,000,000
250,000–1,000,000
100,000–250,000
50,000–100,000
25,000–50,000
5,000–25,000
Under 5,000

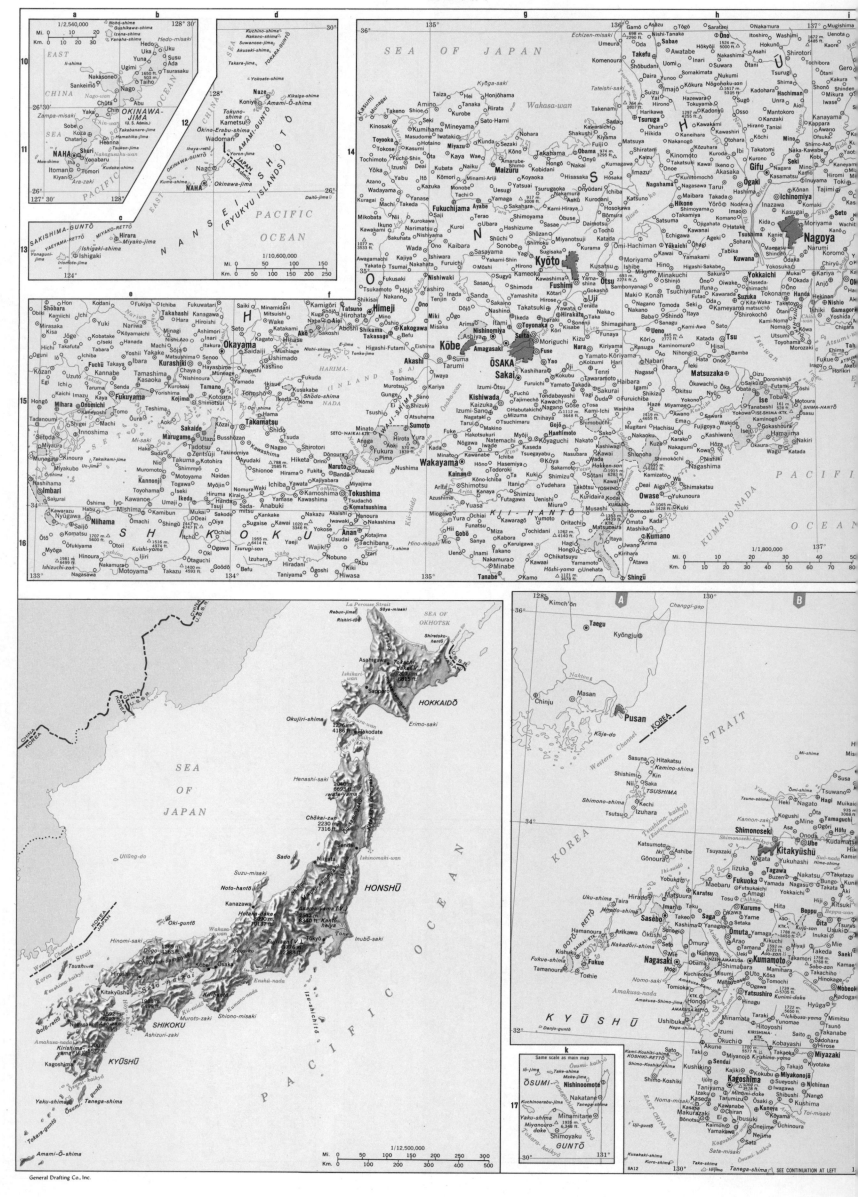

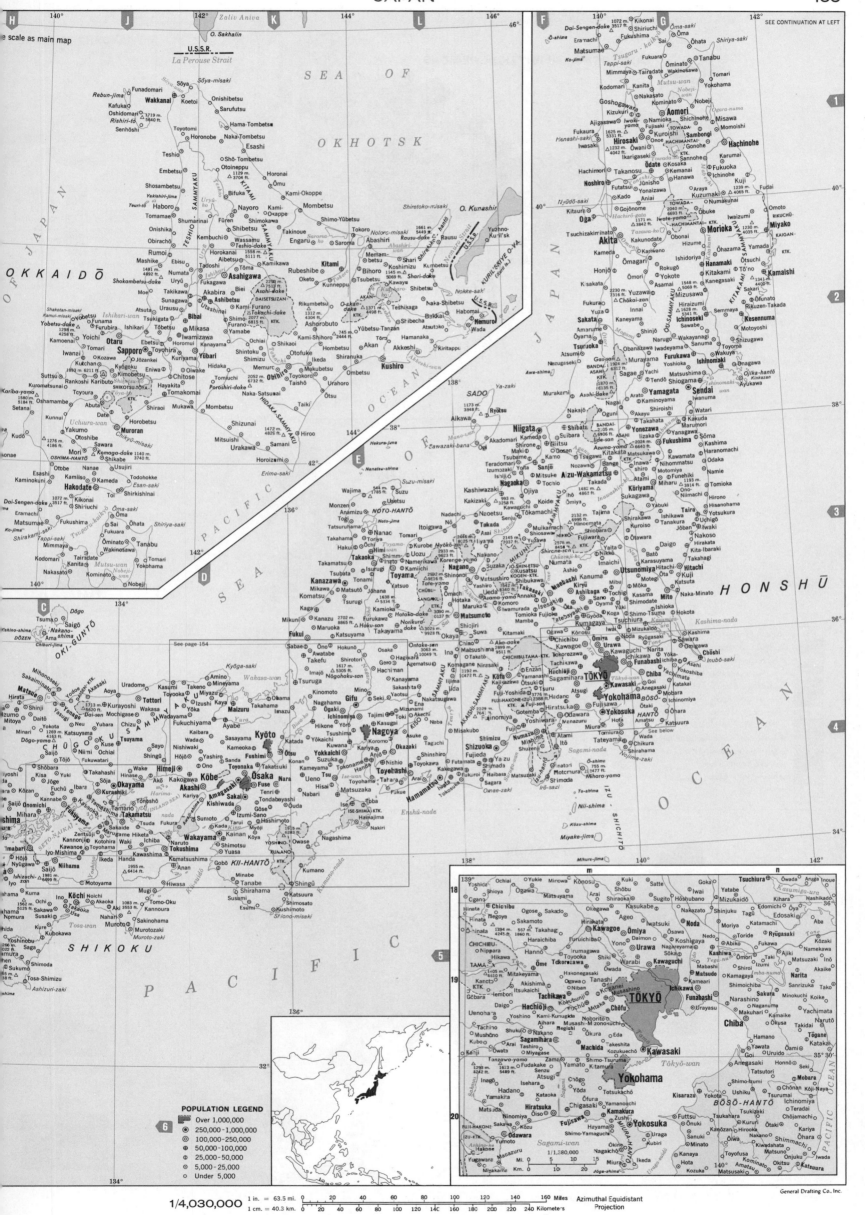

LANDFORMS and PHYSICAL REGIONS

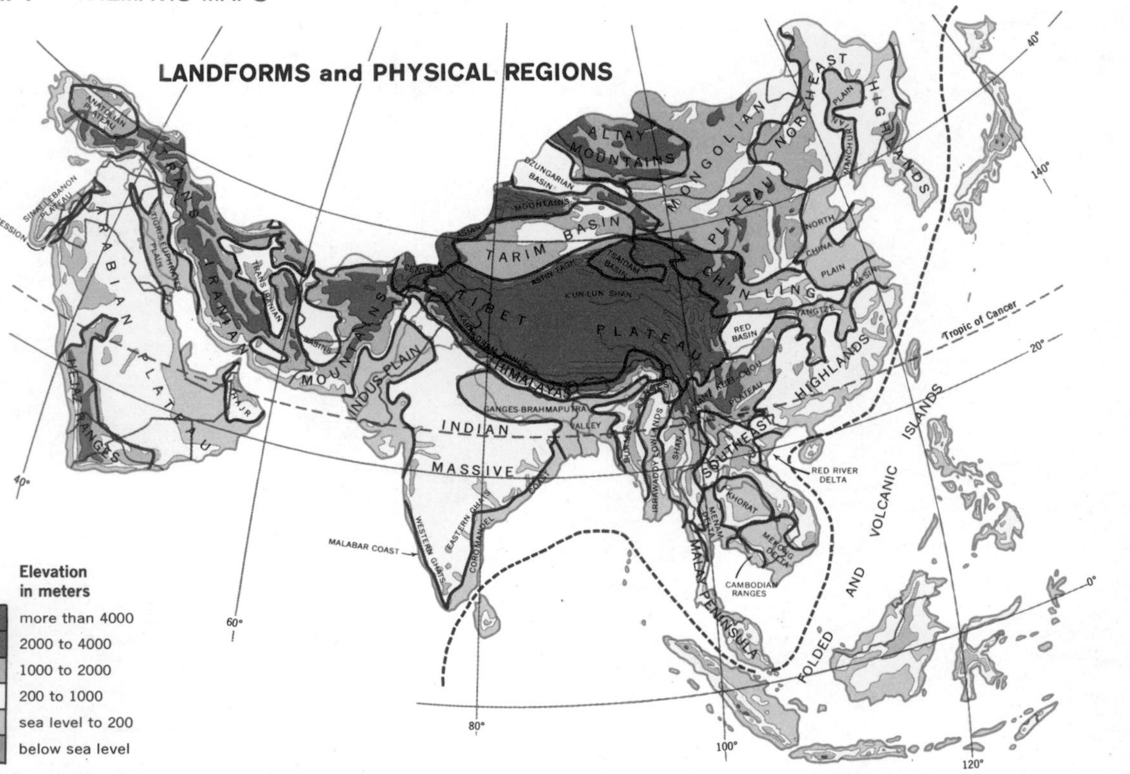

Elevation in feet

more than 13123
6562 to 13123
3281 to 6562
656 to 3281
sea level to 656
below sea level

Elevation in meters

more than 4000
2000 to 4000
1000 to 2000
200 to 1000
sea level to 200
below sea level

Tropic of Cancer

JANUARY AVERAGE T
(Surface temperature

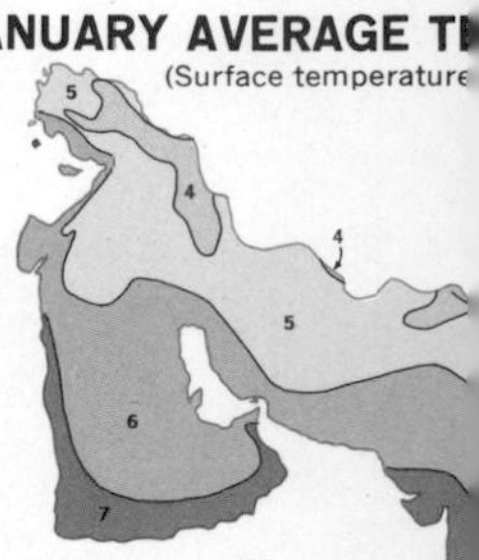

°F		°C
less than —22	1	less than —30
—22 to —4	2	—30 to —20
—4 to 14	3	—20 to —10
14 to 32	4	—10 to 0
32 to 50	5	0 to 10
50 to 68	6	10 to 20
68 to 86	7	20 to 30

JULY AVERAGE TE
(Surface temperature

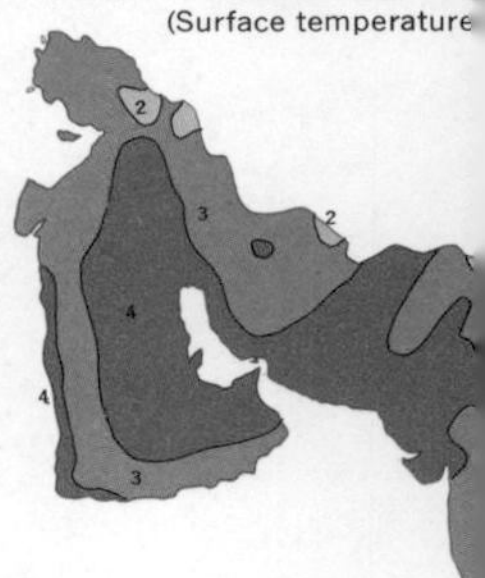

°F		°C
32 to 50	1	0 to 10
50 to 68	2	10 to 20
68 to 86	3	20 to 30
more than 86	4	more than 30

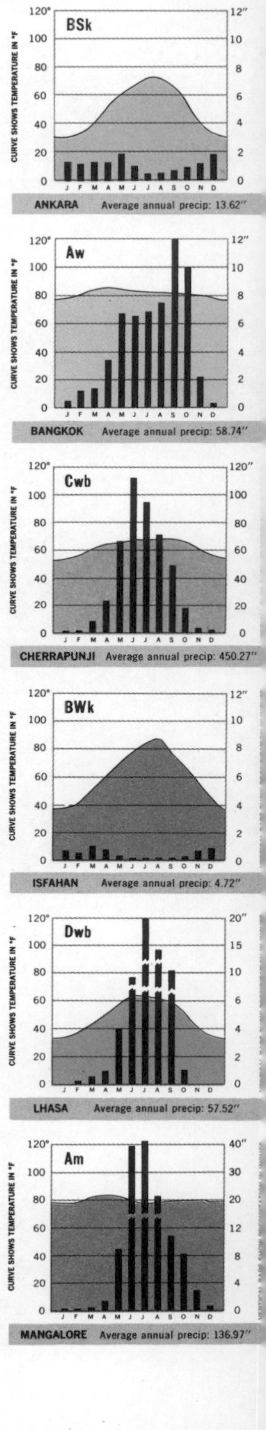

AGRICULTURE

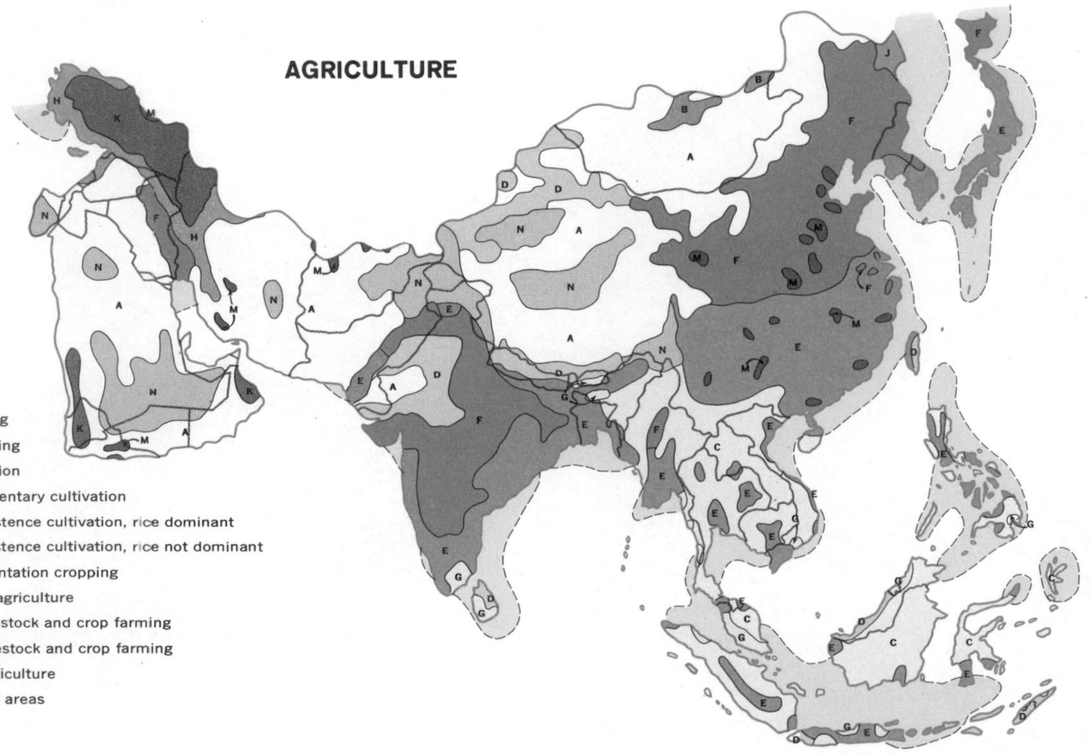

A	Nomadic herding
B	Livestock ranching
C	Shifting cultivation
D	Rudimental sedentary cultivation
E	Intensive subsistence cultivation, rice dominant
F	Intensive subsistence cultivation, rice not dominant
G	Commercial plantation cropping
H	Mediterranean agriculture
J	Commercial livestock and crop farming
K	Subsistence livestock and crop farming
M	Specialized horticulture
N	Non-agricultural areas
	Fishing

AFTER WHITTLESEY

ANKARA BSk Average annual precip: 13.62"

BANGKOK Aw Average annual precip: 58.74"

CHERRAPUNJI Cwb Average annual precip: 450.27"

ISFAHAN BWk Average annual precip: 4.72"

LHASA Dwb Average annual precip: 57.52"

MANGALORE Am Average annual precip: 136.97"

POPULATION

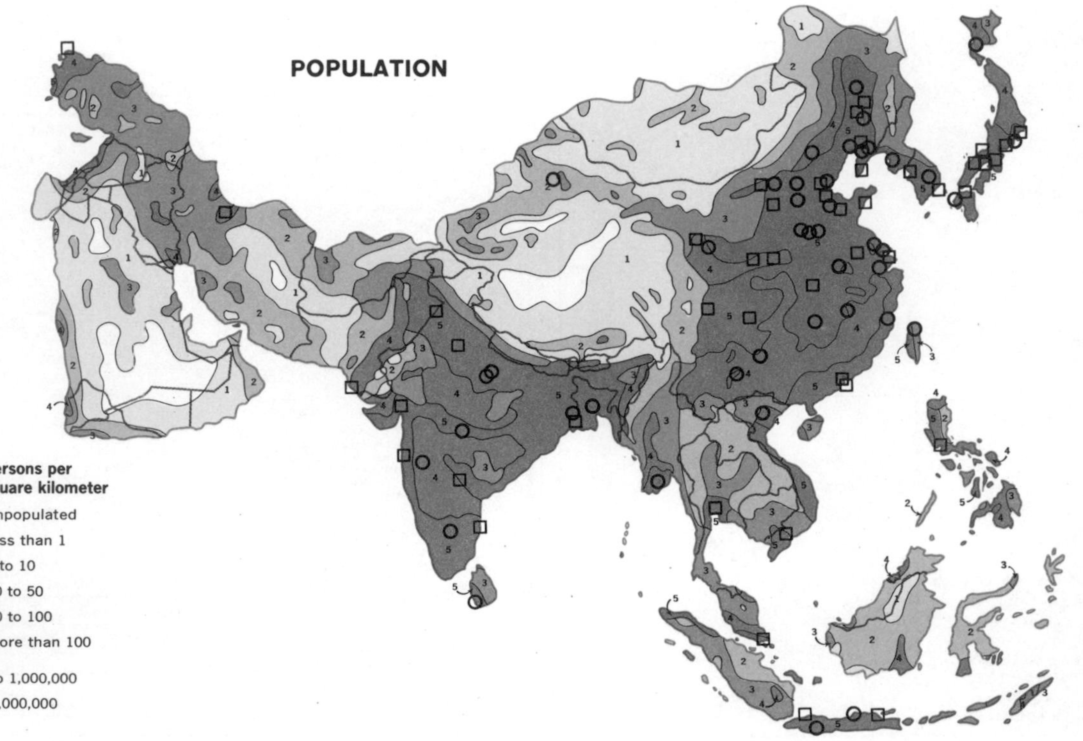

Persons per square mile

unpopulated
less than 3
3 to 25
25 to 130
130 to 260
more than 260

Persons per square kilometer

unpopulated
less than 1
1 to 10
10 to 50
50 to 100
more than 100

○ Cities from 500,000 to 1,000,000
□ Cities of more than 1,000,000

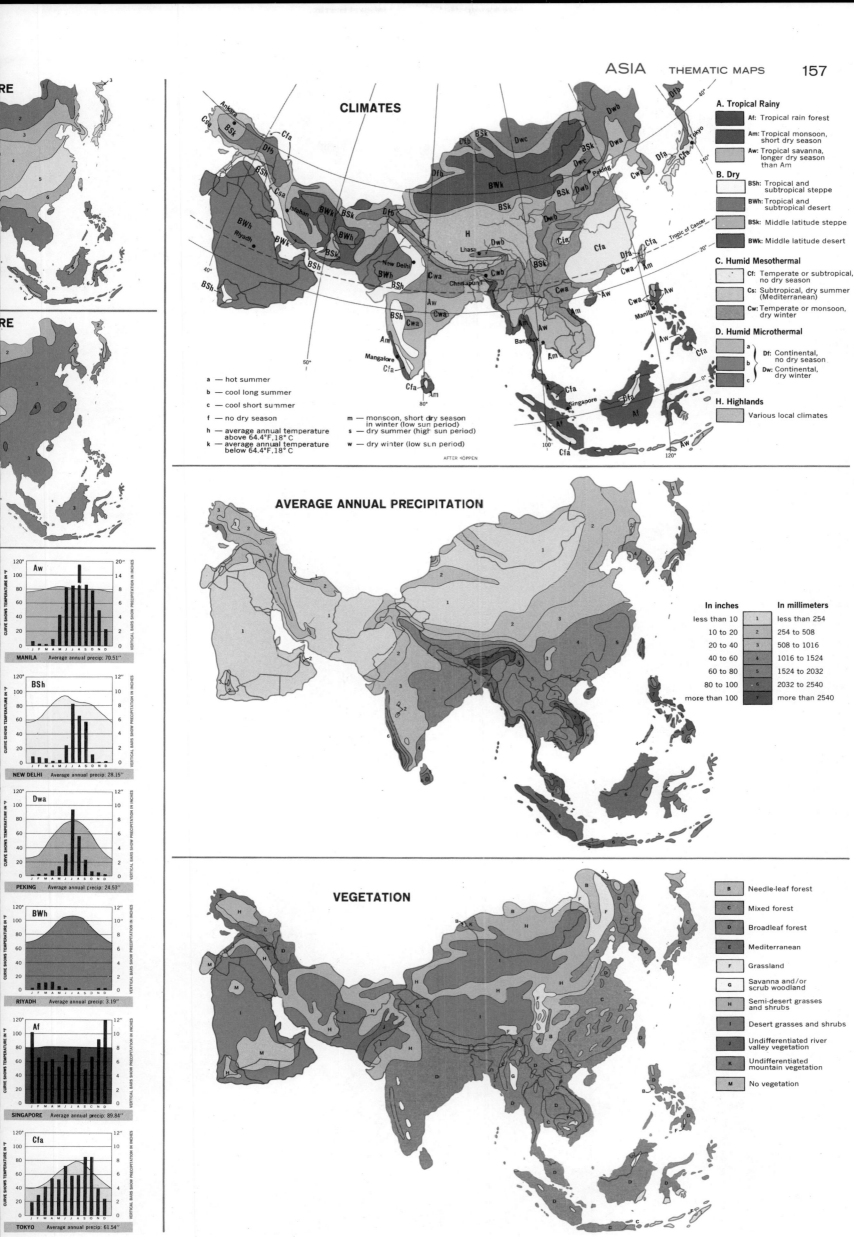

CLIMATES

A. Tropical Rainy
- Af: Tropical rain forest
- Am: Tropical monsoon, short dry season
- Aw: Tropical savanna, longer dry season than Am

B. Dry
- BSh: Tropical and subtropical steppe
- BWh: Tropical and subtropical desert
- BSk: Middle latitude steppe
- BWk: Middle latitude desert

C. Humid Mesothermal
- Cf: Temperate or subtropical, no dry season
- Cs: Subtropical, dry summer (Mediterranean)
- Cw: Temperate or monsoon, dry winter

D. Humid Microthermal
- Df: Continental, no dry season
- Dw: Continental, dry winter

H. Highlands
- Various local climates

a — hot summer
b — cool long summer
c — cool short summer
f — no dry season
h — average annual temperature above 64.4°F, 18° C
k — average annual temperature below 64.4°F, 18° C

m — monsoon, short dry season in winter (low sun period)
s — dry summer (high sun period)
w — dry winter (low sun period)

AFTER KÖPPEN

AVERAGE ANNUAL PRECIPITATION

In inches		In millimeters
less than 10	1	less than 254
10 to 20	2	254 to 508
20 to 40	3	508 to 1016
40 to 60	4	1016 to 1524
60 to 80	5	1524 to 2032
80 to 100	6	2032 to 2540
more than 100	7	more than 2540

VEGETATION

- B Needle-leaf forest
- C Mixed forest
- D Broadleaf forest
- E Mediterranean
- F Grassland
- G Savanna and/or scrub woodland
- H Semi-desert grasses and shrubs
- I Desert grasses and shrubs
- J Undifferentiated river valley vegetation
- K Undifferentiated mountain vegetation
- M No vegetation

Aw
MANILA Average annual precip: 70.51"

BSh
NEW DELHI Average annual precip: 28.15"

Dwa
PEKING Average annual precip: 24.53"

BWh
RIYADH Average annual precip: 3.19"

Af
SINGAPORE Average annual precip: 89.84"

Cfa
TOKYO Average annual precip: 61.54"

CURVE SHOWS TEMPERATURE IN °F
VERTICAL BARS SHOW PRECIPITATION IN INCHES

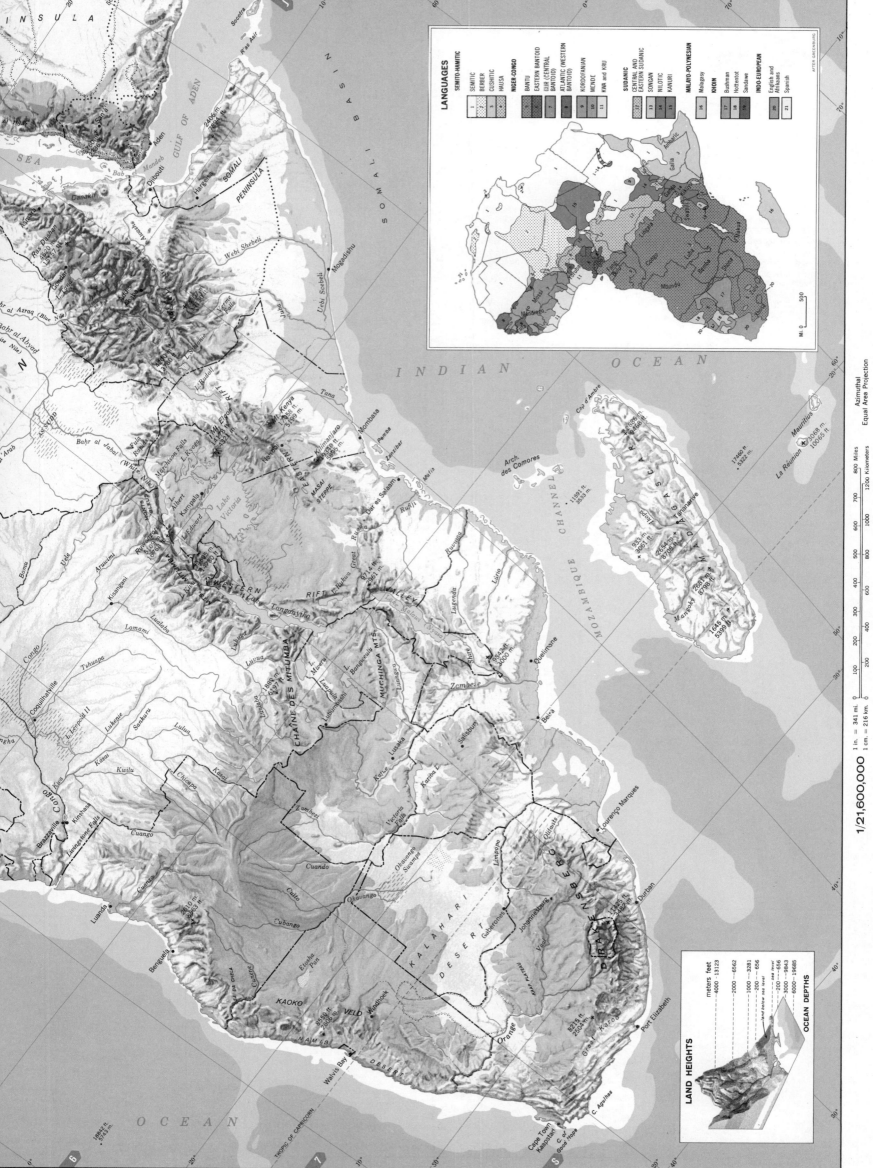

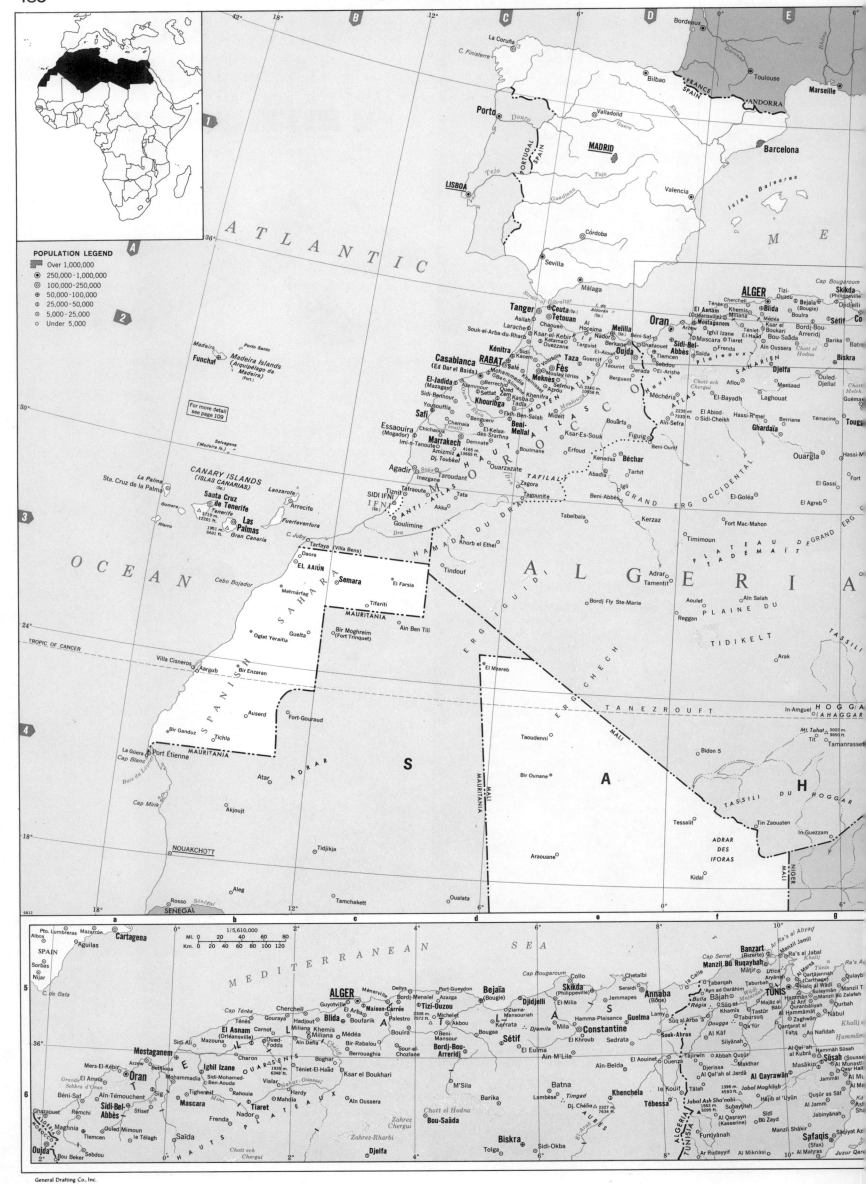

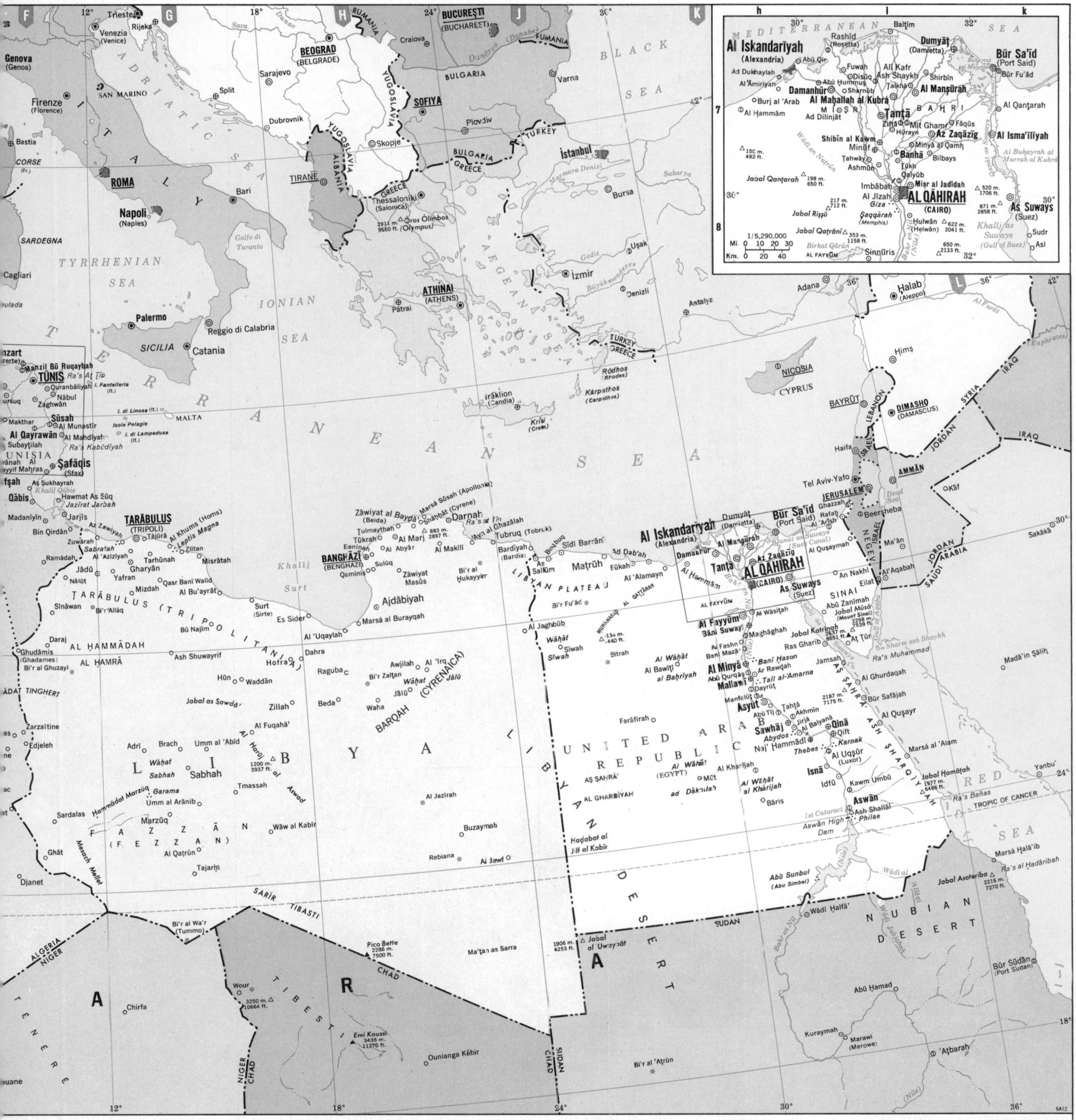

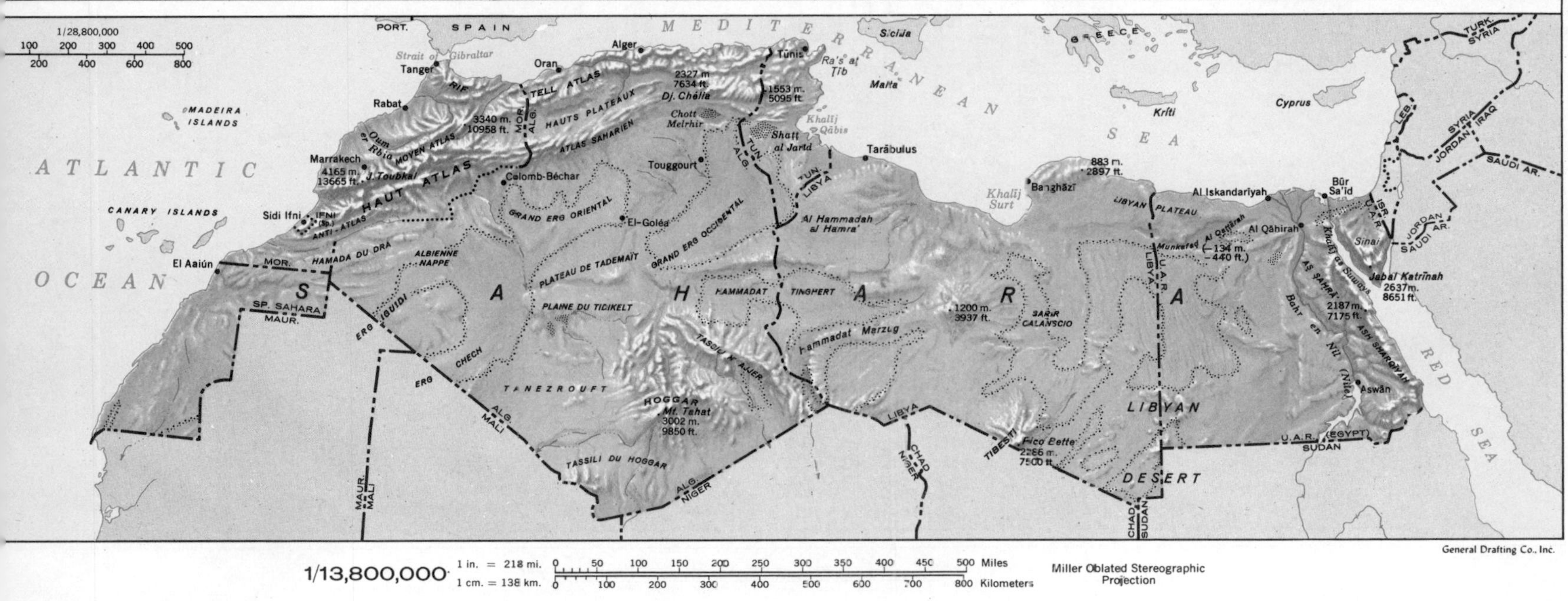

1/13,800,000 1 in. = 218 mi. 1 cm. = 138 km.

0 50 100 150 200 250 300 350 400 450 500 Miles
0 100 200 300 400 500 600 700 800 Kilometers

Miller Oblated Stereographic Projection

1/17,600,000

1 in. = 278 mi.
1 cm. = 176 km.

Miller Oblated
Stereographic Projection

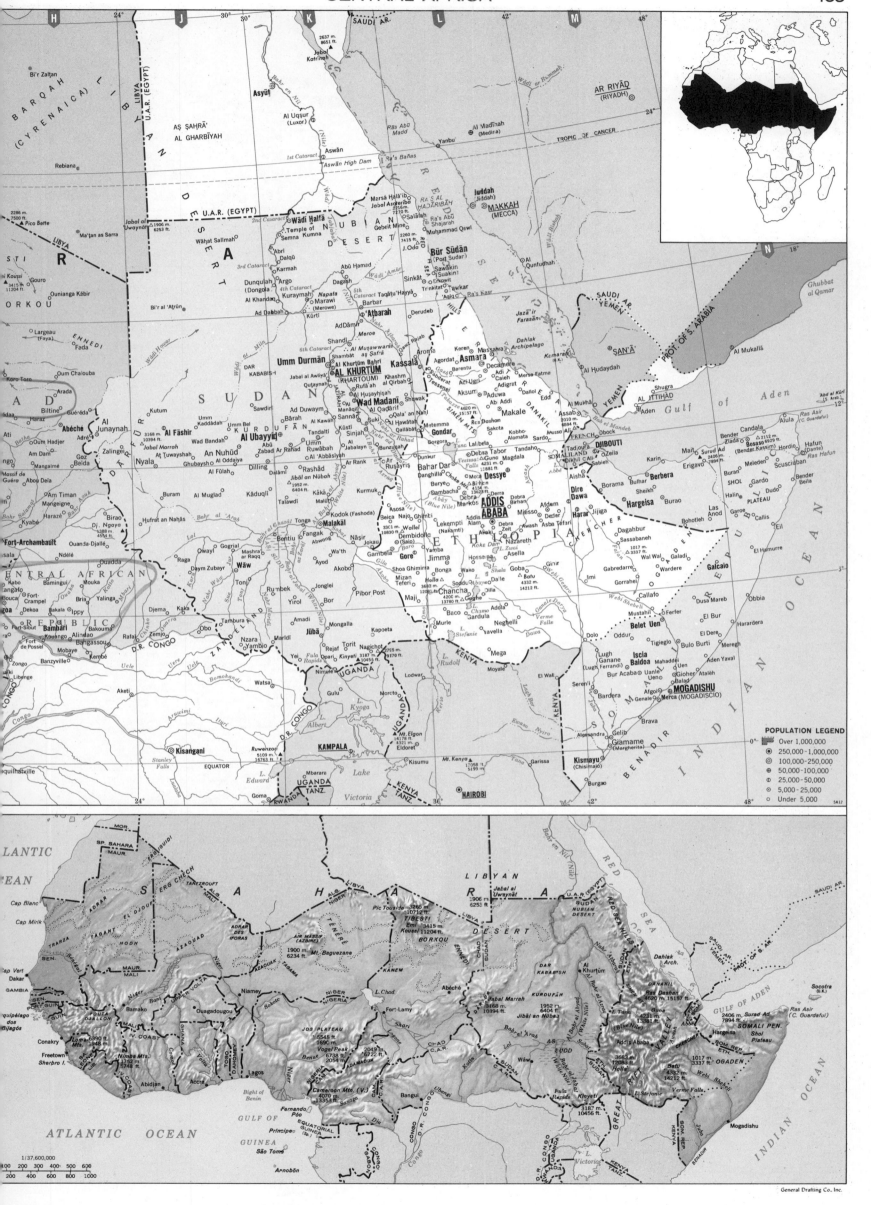

POPULATION LEGEND

- Over 1,000,000
- 250,000–1,000,000
- 100,000–250,000
- 50,000–100,000
- 25,000–50,000
- 5,000–25,000
- Under 5,000

1/37,600,000

100   200   300   400   500   600
200   400   600   800   1000

General Drafting Co., Inc.

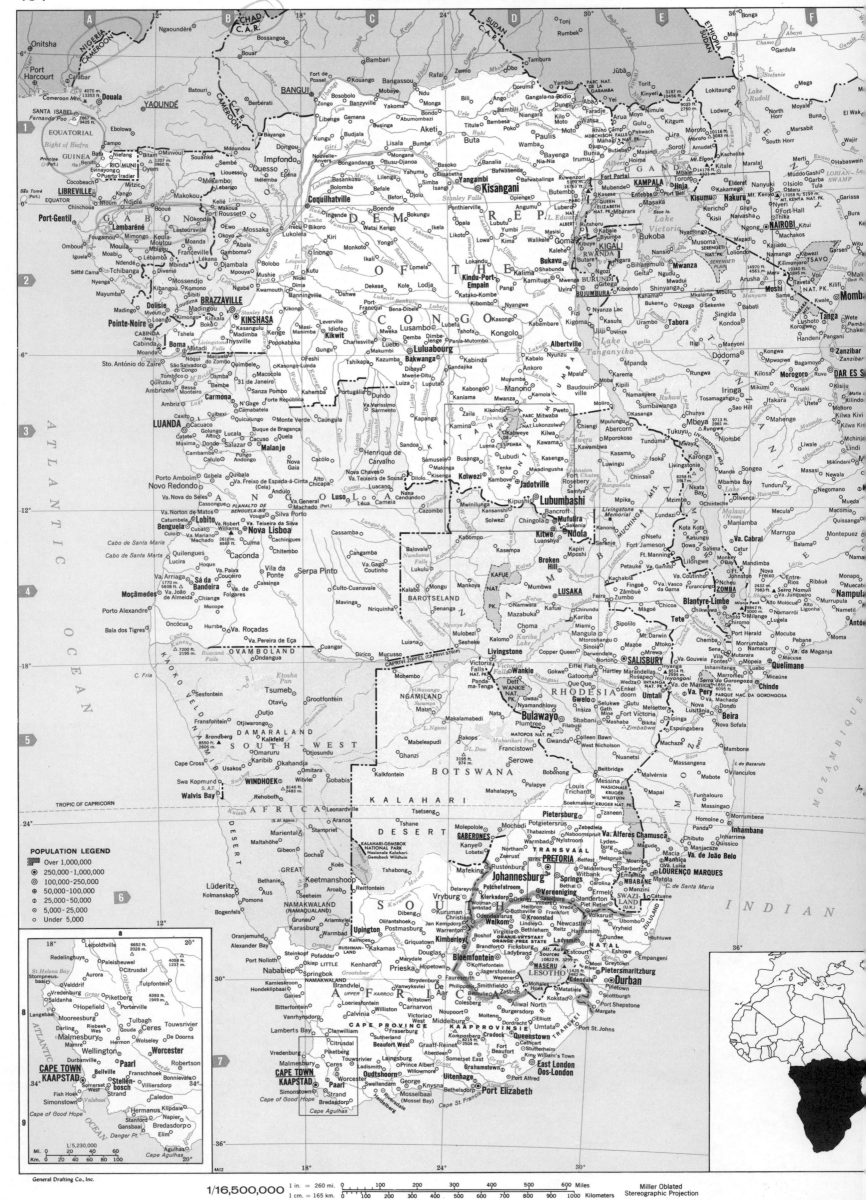

POPULATION LEGEND
▪ Over 1,000,000
◉ 250,000–1,000,000
⊕ 100,000–250,000
⊕ 50,000-100,000
⊕ 25,000–50,000
⊙ 5,000–25,000
○ Under 5,000

General Drafting Co., Inc.

1/16,500,000

1 in. = 260 mi.
1 cm. = 165 km.

0   100   200   300   400   500   600 Miles
0 100 200 300 400 500 600 700 800 900 1000 Kilometers

Miller Oblated
Stereographic Projection

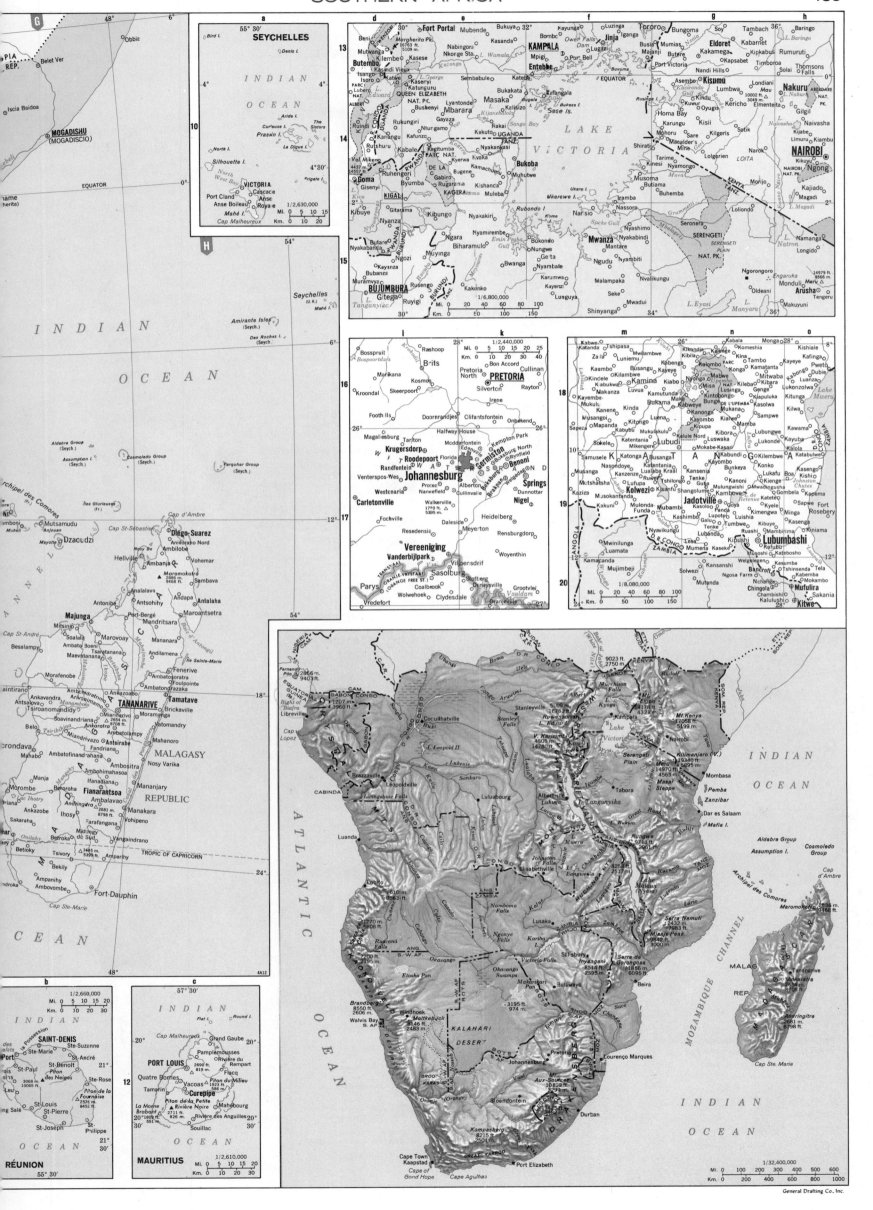

LANDFORMS and PHYSICAL REGIONS

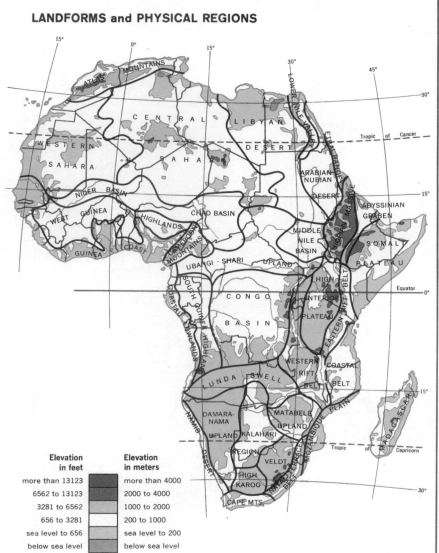

Elevation in feet	Elevation in meters
more than 13123	more than 4000
6562 to 13123	2000 to 4000
3281 to 6562	1000 to 2000
656 to 3281	200 to 1000
sea level to 656	sea level to 200
below sea level	below sea level

AGRICULTURE

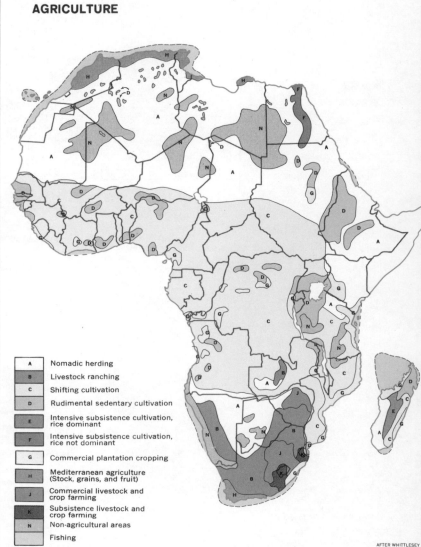

- A   Nomadic herding
- B   Livestock ranching
- C   Shifting cultivation
- D   Rudimental sedentary cultivation
- E   Intensive subsistence cultivation, rice dominant
- F   Intensive subsistence cultivation, rice not dominant
- G   Commercial plantation cropping
- H   Mediterranean agriculture (Stock, grains, and fruit)
- J   Commercial livestock and crop farming
- K   Subsistence livestock and crop farming
- N   Non-agricultural areas
-    Fishing

AFTER WHITTLESEY

POPULATION

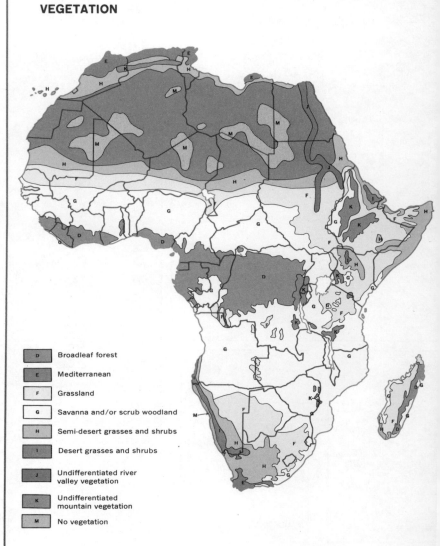

Persons per square mile	Persons per square kilometer
unpopulated	unpopulated
less than 3	less than 1
3 to 25	1 to 10
25 to 130	10 to 50
130 to 260	50 to 100
more than 260	more than 100

○ Cities from 500,000 to 1,000,000
□ Cities of more than 1,000,000

VEGETATION

- D   Broadleaf forest
- E   Mediterranean
- F   Grassland
- G   Savanna and/or scrub woodland
- H   Semi-desert grasses and shrubs
- I   Desert grasses and shrubs
- J   Undifferentiated river valley vegetation
- K   Undifferentiated mountain vegetation
- M   No vegetation

General Drafting Co., Inc.   1/69,000,000   Azimuthal Equal Area Projection

AVERAGE ANNUAL PRECIPITATION

In inches		In millimeters
less than 10	1	less than 254
10 to 20	2	254 to 508
20 to 40	3	508 to 1016
40 to 60	4	1016 to 1524
60 to 80	5	1524 to 2032
80 to 100	6	2032 to 2540
more than 100	7	more than 2540

CLIMATES

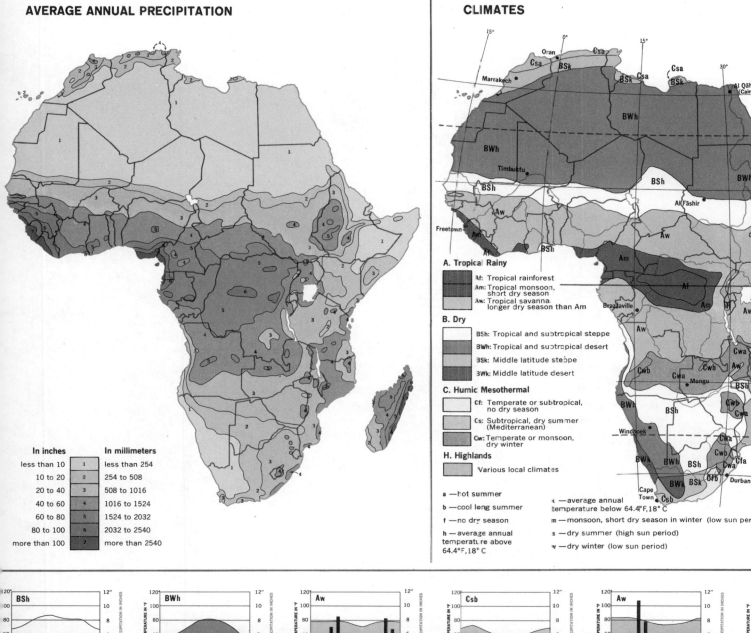

A. Tropical Rainy

Af: Tropical rainforest

Am: Tropical monsoon, short dry season

Aw: Tropical savanna longer dry season than Am

B. Dry

BSh: Tropical and subtropical steppe

BWh: Tropical and subtropical desert

BSk: Middle latitude steppe

BWk: Middle latitude desert

C. Humic Mesothermal

Cf: Temperate or subtropical, no dry season

Cs: Subtropical, dry summer (Mediterranean)

Cw: Temperate or monsoon, dry winter

H. Highlands

Various local climates

a — hot summer

b — cool long summer

f — no dry season

h — average annual temperature above 64.4° F, 18° C

k — average annual temperature below 64.4° F, 18° C

m — monsoon, short dry season in winter (low sun period)

s — dry summer (high sun period)

w — dry winter (low sun period)

AFTER KÖPPEN

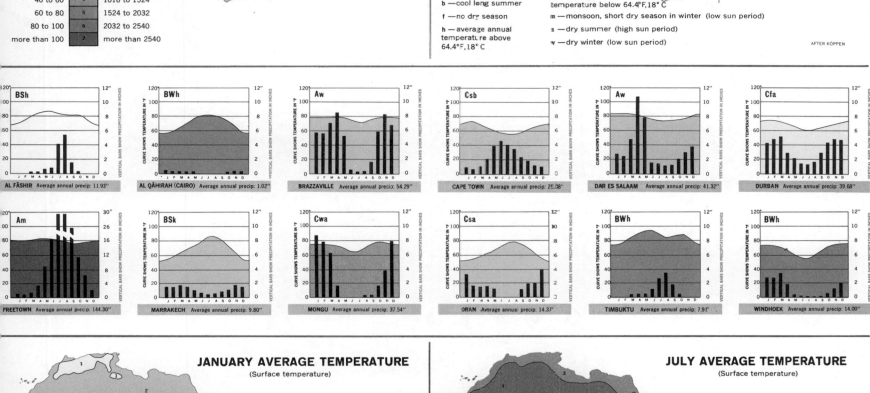

JANUARY AVERAGE TEMPERATURE
(Surface temperature)

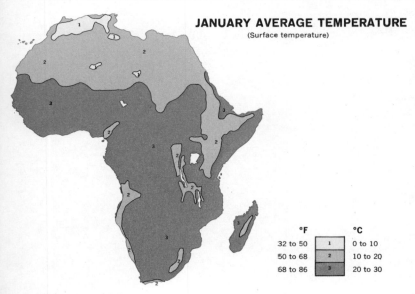

°F		°C
32 to 50	1	0 to 10
50 to 68	2	10 to 20
68 to 86	3	20 to 30

JULY AVERAGE TEMPERATURE
(Surface temperature)

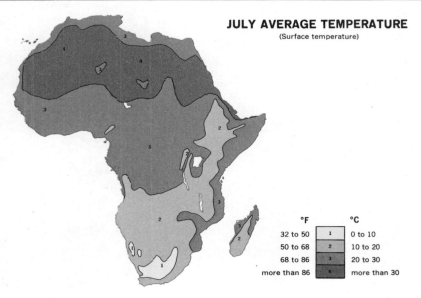

°F		°C
32 to 50	1	0 to 10
50 to 68	2	10 to 20
68 to 86	3	20 to 30
more than 86	4	more than 30

General Drafting Co., Inc.

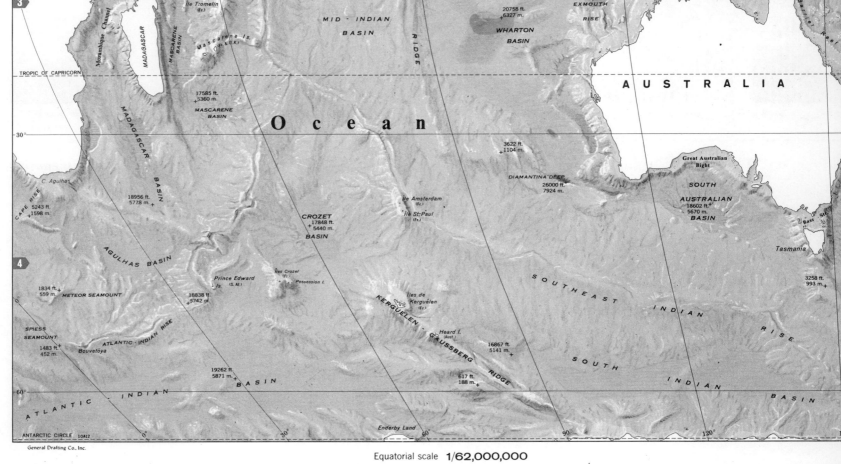

Equatorial scale 1/62,000,000

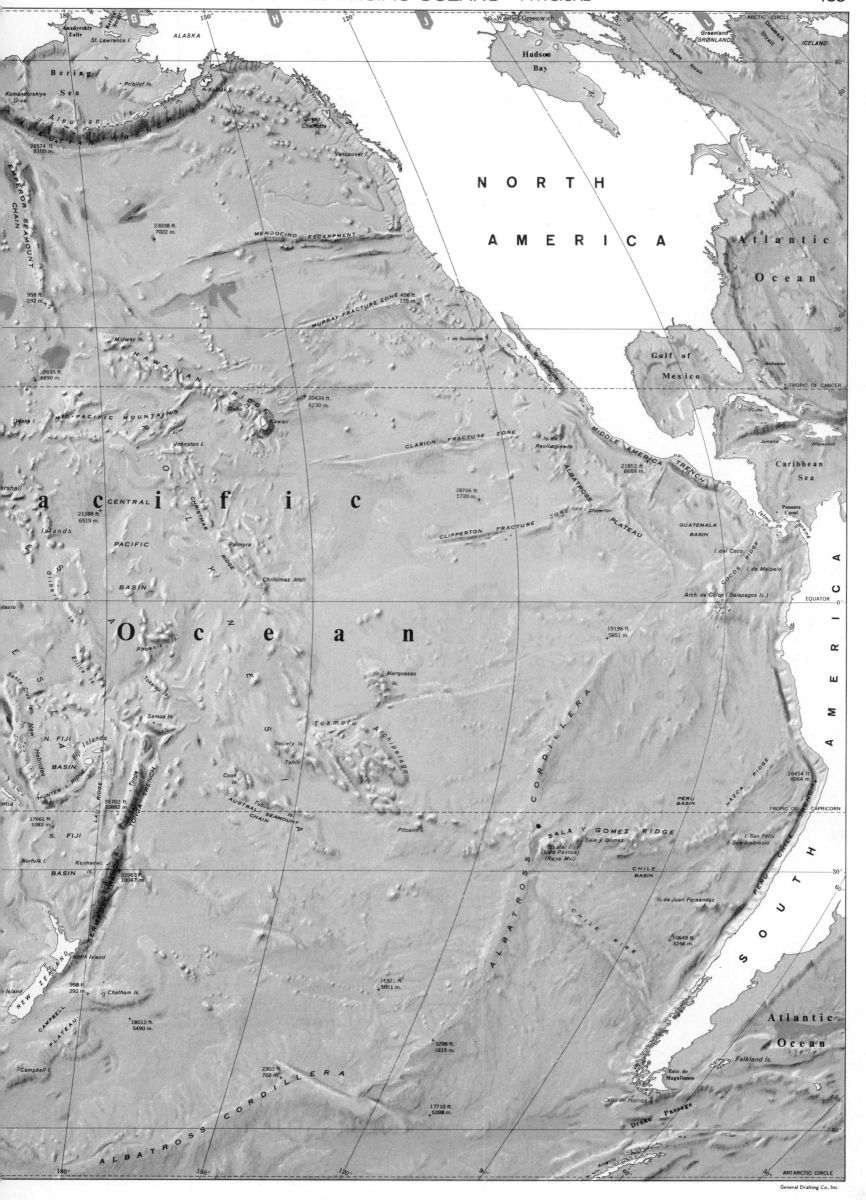

HUDSON BAY

Ungava Bay

CANADA

Anchorage

UNITED STATES
(ALASKA)

Bristol Bay

Afognak I.
Kodiak I.

Gulf of Alaska

Alaska Pen.

Juneau

Graham I.
Queen Charlotte Is.
Moresby I.

Vancouver I.

Vancouver

Seattle

Portland

Juan de Fuca Str.

Columbia

Edmonton

Calgary

Peace

L. Athabasca

Saskatchewan

Regina

L. Winnipegosis

L. Winnipeg

L. Manitoba

Winnipeg

L. Superior

James Bay

St. Lawrence

Québec

OTTAWA

Montréal

Toronto

L. Michigan

L. Huron

Detroit

Chicago

Omaha

Denver

Great Salt L.

San Francisco

Los Angeles

C. Mendocino

Colorado

UNITED STATES

Dallas

St. Louis

Ohio

L. Erie

Cleveland

L. Ontario

WASHINGTON

Philadelphia

Boston

C. Cod

New York

ATLANTIC

OCEAN

C. Hatteras

Atlanta

New Orleans

Houston

Rio Grande

I. de Guadalupe
(Mex.)

Pta. Eugenia

TROPIC OF CANCER

Monterrey

MEXICO

GULF OF MEXICO

Miami

Bahama Islands

Str. of Florida

C. Falso

Mazatlan

C. Corrientes

Guadalajara

Is. de Revillagigedo
(Mex.)

MEXICO

Bahía de Campeche

HABANA

CUBA

Yucatan Channel

JAMAICA

HAITI

DOMINICAN
REPUBLIC

SANTO
DOMINGO

Puerto Rico
(U.S.)

UNITED STATES
(HAWAI)

Nihoa

Niihau

Kauai

Oahu

Honolulu

Molokai

Lanai

Maui

Kahoolawe

Hilo

Hawaii

Islands

OCEAN

BRITISH
HONDURAS

GUATEMALA

HONDURAS

CARIBBEAN

SEA

EL SALVADOR

NICARAGUA

CARACAS

VENEZUELA

COSTA RICA

CANAL ZONE
(U.S.)

PANAMA

Clipperton
(Fr.)

I. del Coco
(C.R.)

I. de Malpelo
(Col.)

Medellín

Cali

BOGOTÁ

COLOMBIA

Kingman Reef (U.S.)

Palmyra (U.S.)

Washington I. (U.K.)

Fanning (U.K.)

41

40

Christmas Atoll
(U.K. & U.S. claim)

Jarvis I.
(U.S.)

Red numbers refer to insets
on pages 174-177

Malden I.
(U.K. & U.S. claim)

Starbuck I.

EQUATOR

P. Galera

QUITO

ECUADOR

Guayaquil

Arch. de Colón
(Galapagos Is.)
(Ec.)

G. de Guayaquil

P. Negra

BRAZIL

Penrhyn

Rakahanga

Manihiki

Vostok I.
(U.K. & U.S. claim)

Flint I.

Caroline

Islands

Eiao

Nuku Hiva

Ua Huka

Hiva Oa

Fatu Hiva

Îles Marquises
(Marquesas Is.)

PERU

COOK

Suvorov

Mataiva

Ahe

Napuka

Puka puka

Îles du
Désappointement

LIMA

ISLANDS
(N.Z.)

Palmerston

Aitutaki

Rarotonga

Mangaia

43

Bora-Bora

Moorea

Tahiti

Îles de la
Société
(Society Is.)

35

33

44

Niau

Kauehi

Anaa

Makemo

Marokau

Fangatau

Raroia

Fakahina

Tauere

Tatakoto

Hao

Îles Tuamotu

Îles Duc de
Gloucester

Ahunui

Groupe Actéon

Tematangi

I. de Malpelo

LA PAZ

BOLIVIA

Rurutu

Tubuai

FRENCH POLYNESIA
(Fr.)

42

Morane

Îles Gambier

TROPIC OF CAPRICORN

Raevavae

Îles Tubuai

Rapa

Îlots de Bass

Oeno
(U.K.)

Henderson I.
(U.K.)

Pitcairn I.
(U.K.)

Ducie
(U.K.)

45

I. Sala y Gómez
(Chile)

I. San Félix
(Chile)

I. San Ambrosio
(Chile)

San Miguel
de Tucumán

Easter I.
(I. de Pascua)
(Rapa Nui)
(Chile)

PACIFIC

OCEAN

Is. Juan
Fernández
(Chile)

Valparaíso

San Juan

SANTIAGO

Concepción

ARGENTINA

CHILE

I. de Chiloé

Pen. de Taitao

I. Wellington

SCALE OF EAST-WEST DISTANCES
In a north-south direction each degree equals about 69 miles or 111 kilometers

400 Mi.   200   300   600 Km.

60°
45°
30°
15°
EQUATOR   EQUATOR

400 Mi.   200   0   0   300   600 Km.

POPULATION LEGEND
● Over 1,000,000
○ Under 1,000,000

Punta Arenas

Str. de
Magallanes

I. Grande de
Tierra del Fuego

Equatorial scale 1/49,300,000   Miller Cylindrical Projection

General Drafting Co. Inc.

10A12

General Drafting Co., Inc.

1/13,100,000

1 in. = 207 mi.
1 cm. = 131 km.

Azimuthal Equidistant
Projection

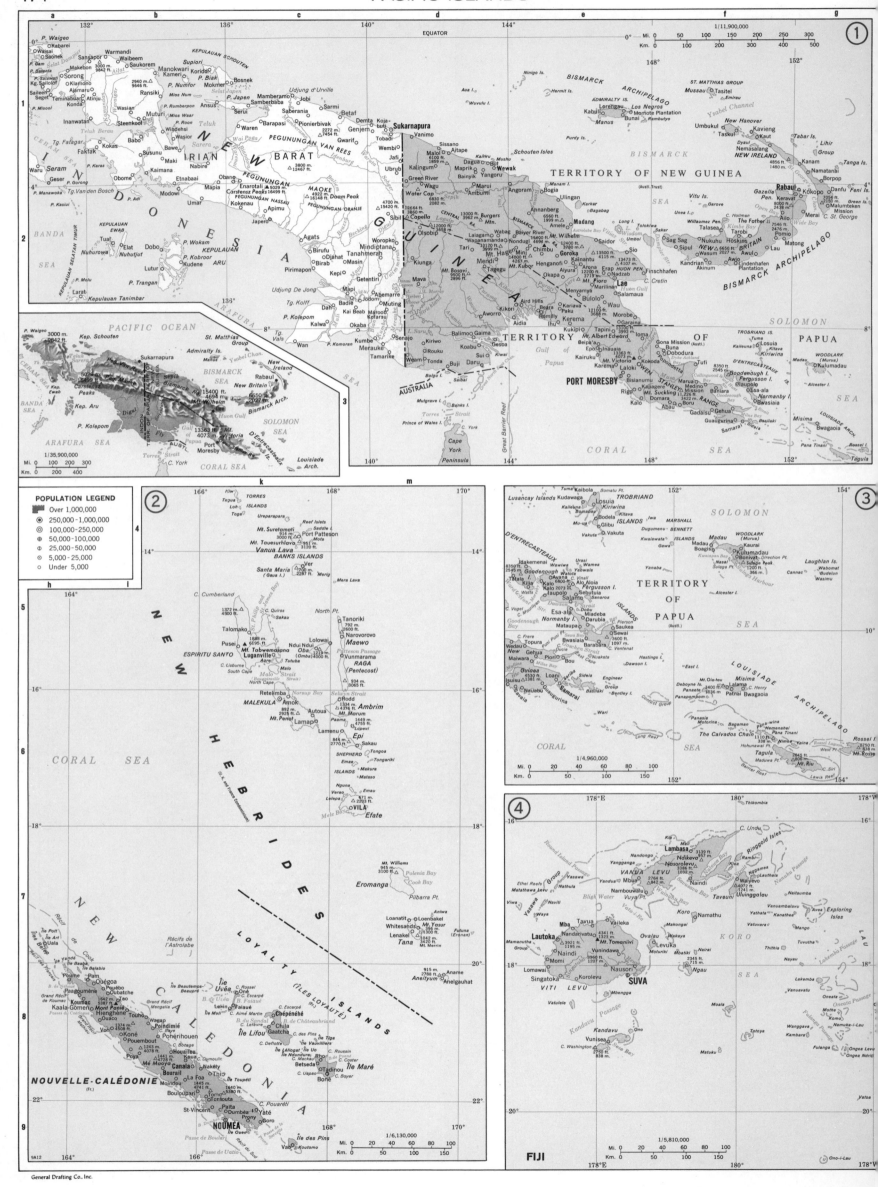

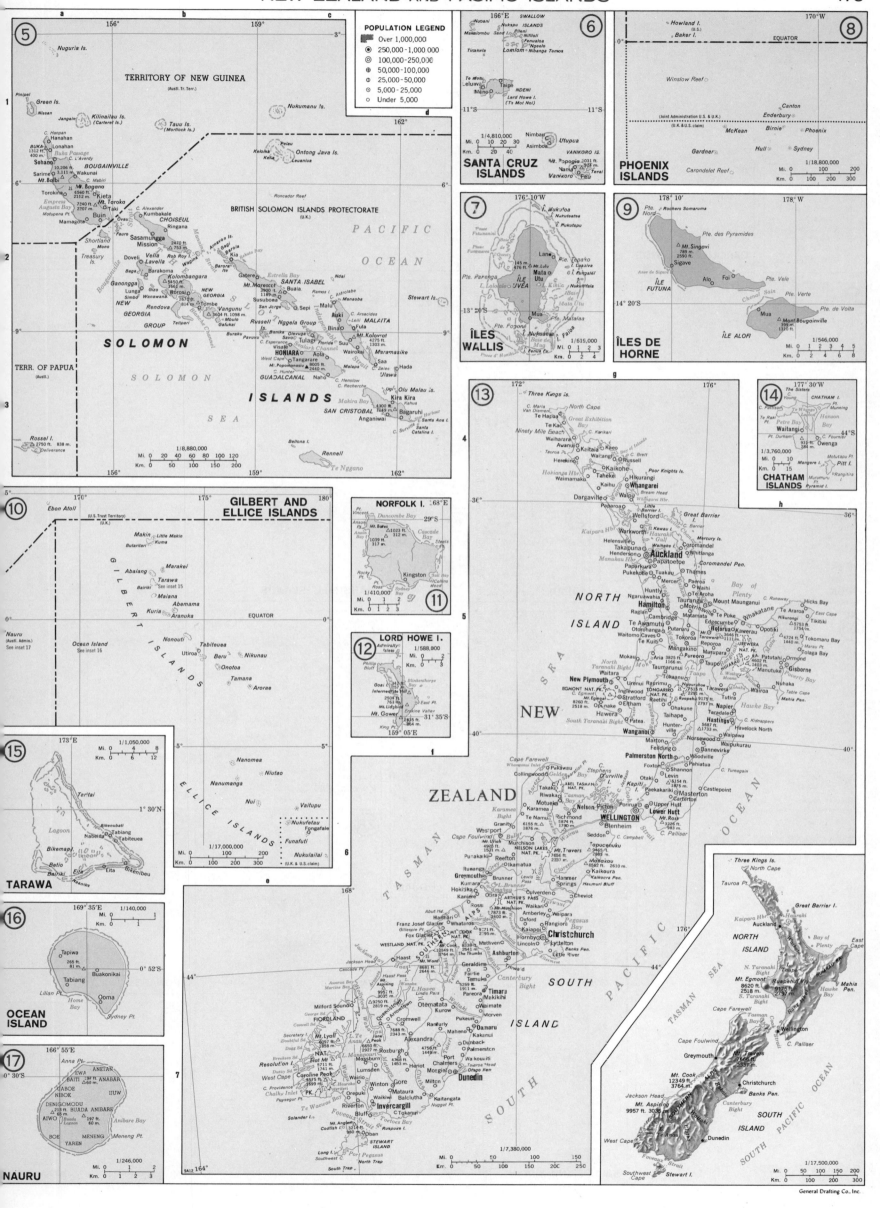

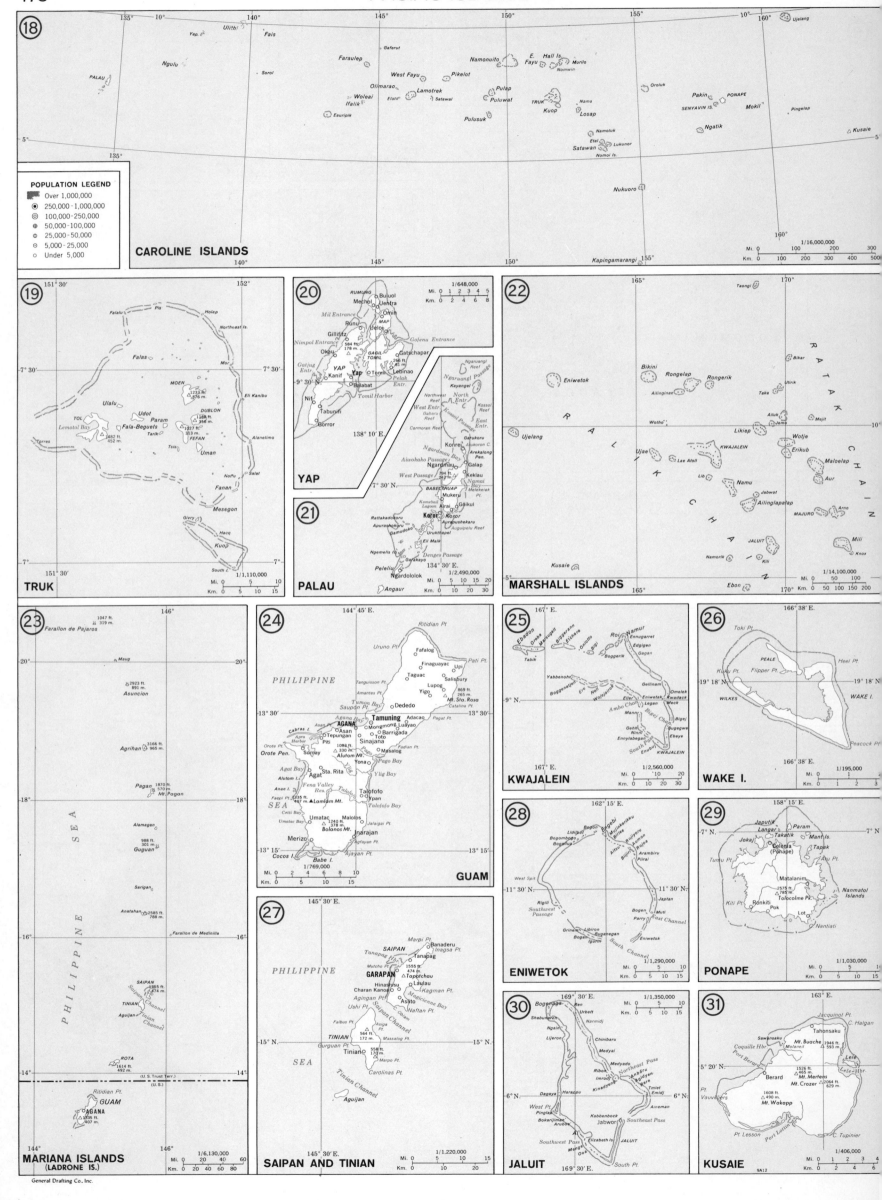

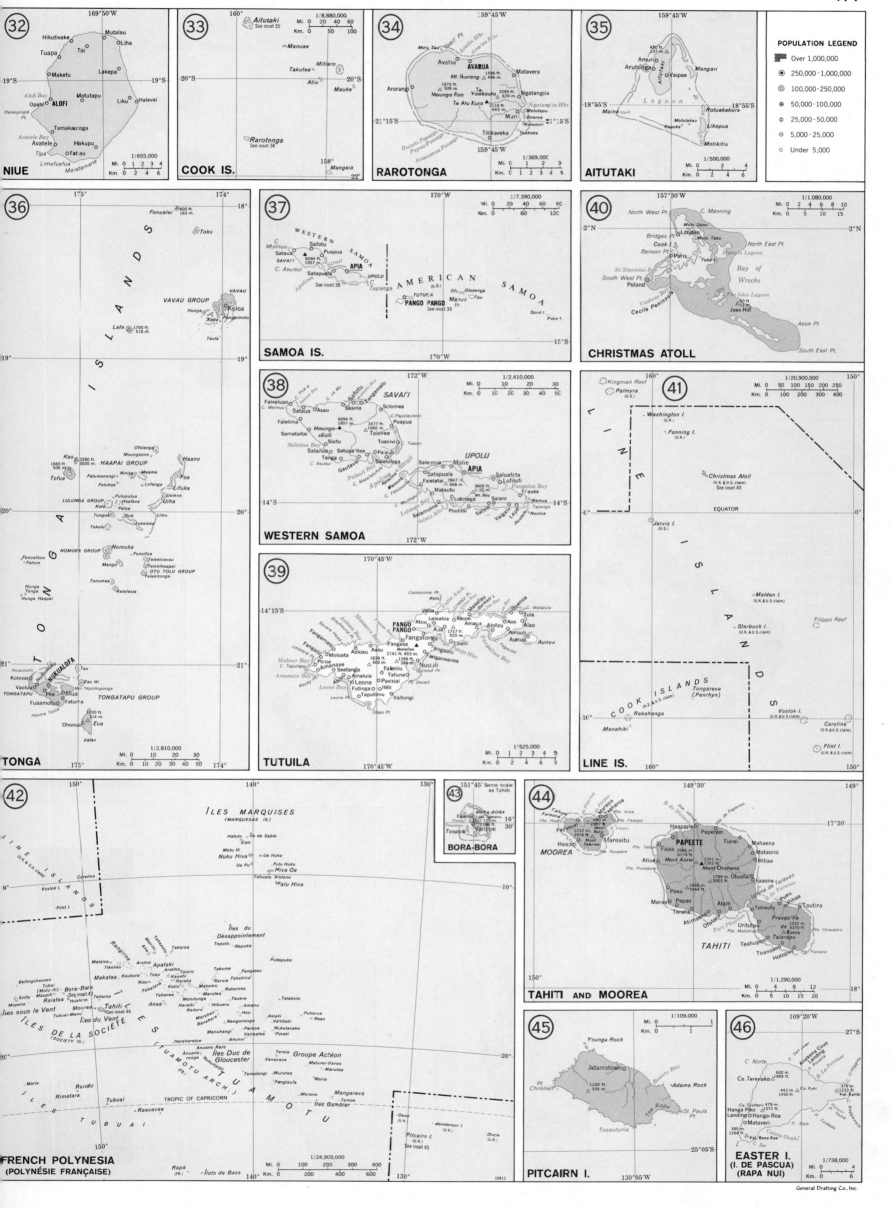

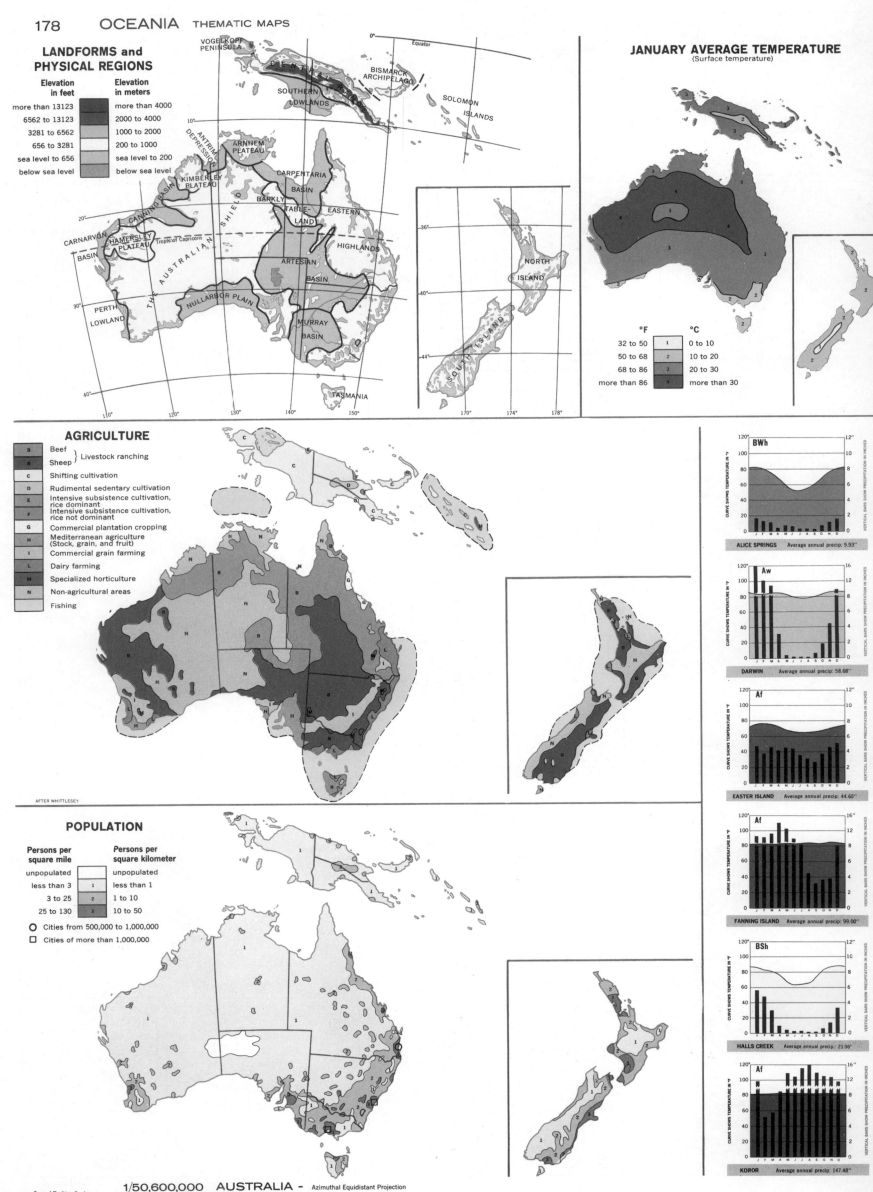

LANDFORMS and PHYSICAL REGIONS

Elevation in feet
- more than 13123
- 6562 to 13123
- 3281 to 6562
- 656 to 3281
- sea level to 656
- below sea level

Elevation in meters
- more than 4000
- 2000 to 4000
- 1000 to 2000
- 200 to 1000
- sea level to 200
- below sea level

VOGELKOFF PENINSULA
Equator
CENTRAL RANGE
SOUTHERN LOWLANDS
BISMARCK ARCHIPELAGO
SOLOMON ISLANDS
ANTRIM DEPRESSION
ARNHEM PLATEAU
KIMBERLEY PLATEAU
CARPENTARIA BASIN
CANNING BASIN
BARKLY
TABLE-LAND
EASTERN
THE AUSTRALIAN SHIELD
CARNARVON BASIN
HAMERSLEY PLATEAU
Tropic of Capricorn
ARTESIAN BASIN
HIGHLANDS
PERTH LOWLAND
NULLARBOR PLAIN
MURRAY BASIN
NORTH ISLAND
SOUTH ISLAND
TASMANIA

JANUARY AVERAGE TEMPERATURE
(Surface temperature)

°F		°C
32 to 50	1	0 to 10
50 to 68	2	10 to 20
68 to 86	3	20 to 30
more than 86	4	more than 30

AGRICULTURE

- B — Beef, Sheep — Livestock ranching
- R — Sheep
- C — Shifting cultivation
- D — Rudimental sedentary cultivation
- E — Intensive subsistence cultivation, rice dominant
- F — Intensive subsistence cultivation, rice not dominant
- G — Commercial plantation cropping
- H — Mediterranean agriculture (Stock, grain, and fruit)
- I — Commercial grain farming
- L — Dairy farming
- M — Specialized horticulture
- N — Non-agricultural areas
- Fishing

AFTER WHITTLESEY

BWh
ALICE SPRINGS   Average annual precip: 9.93"

Aw
DARWIN   Average annual precip: 58.68"

Af
EASTER ISLAND   Average annual precip: 44.65"

Af
FANNING ISLAND   Average annual precip: 99.00"

BSh
HALLS CREEK   Average annual precip: 21.06"

Af
KOROR   Average annual precip: 147.48"

POPULATION

Persons per square mile
- unpopulated
- less than 3
- 3 to 25
- 25 to 130

Persons per square kilometer
- unpopulated
- less than 1
- 1 to 10
- 10 to 50

○ Cities from 500,000 to 1,000,000
□ Cities of more than 1,000,000

General Drafting Co., Inc.

1/50,600,000 AUSTRALIA — Azimuthal Equidistant Projection
1/27,000,000 NEW ZEALAND — Lambert Conformal Conic Projection

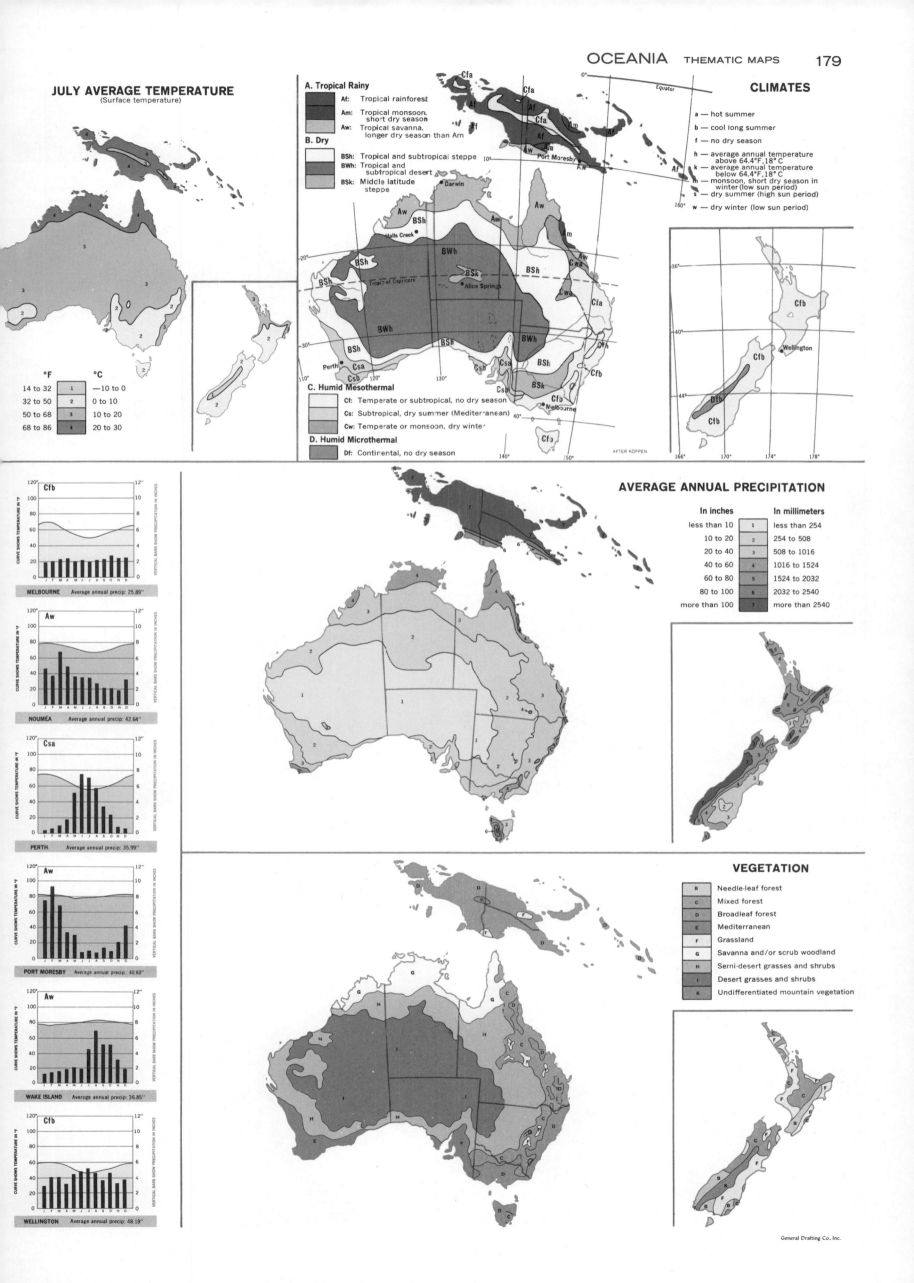

JULY AVERAGE TEMPERATURE
(Surface temperature)

°F		°C
14 to 32	1	—10 to 0
32 to 50	2	0 to 10
50 to 68	3	10 to 20
68 to 86	4	20 to 30

CLIMATES

A. Tropical Rainy
Af: Tropical rainforest
Am: Tropical monsoon, short dry season
Aw: Tropical savanna, longer dry season than Am

B. Dry
BSh: Tropical and subtropical steppe
BWh: Tropical and subtropical desert
BSk: Middle latitude steppe

C. Humid Mesothermal
Cf: Temperate or subtropical, no dry season
Cs: Subtropical, dry summer (Mediterranean)
Cw: Temperate or monsoon, dry winter

D. Humid Microthermal
Df: Continental, no dry season

a — hot summer
b — cool long summer
f — no dry season
h — average annual temperature above 64.4°F, 18° C
k — average annual temperature below 64.4°F, 18° C
m — monsoon, short dry season in winter (low sun period)
s — dry summer (high sun period)
w — dry winter (low sun period)

AFTER KÖPPEN

AVERAGE ANNUAL PRECIPITATION

In inches		In millimeters
less than 10	1	less than 254
10 to 20	2	254 to 508
20 to 40	3	508 to 1016
40 to 60	4	1016 to 1524
60 to 80	5	1524 to 2032
80 to 100	6	2032 to 2540
more than 100	7	more than 2540

VEGETATION

B	Needle-leaf forest
C	Mixed forest
D	Broadleaf forest
E	Mediterranean
F	Grassland
G	Savanna and/or scrub woodland
H	Semi-desert grasses and shrubs
I	Desert grasses and shrubs
K	Undifferentiated mountain vegetation

MELBOURNE   Average annual precip: 25.89"

NOUMÉA   Average annual precip: 42.64"

PERTH   Average annual precip: 35.99"

PORT MORESBY   Average annual precip: 40.83"

WAKE ISLAND   Average annual precip: 36.85"

WELLINGTON   Average annual precip: 48.19"

General Drafting Co., Inc.

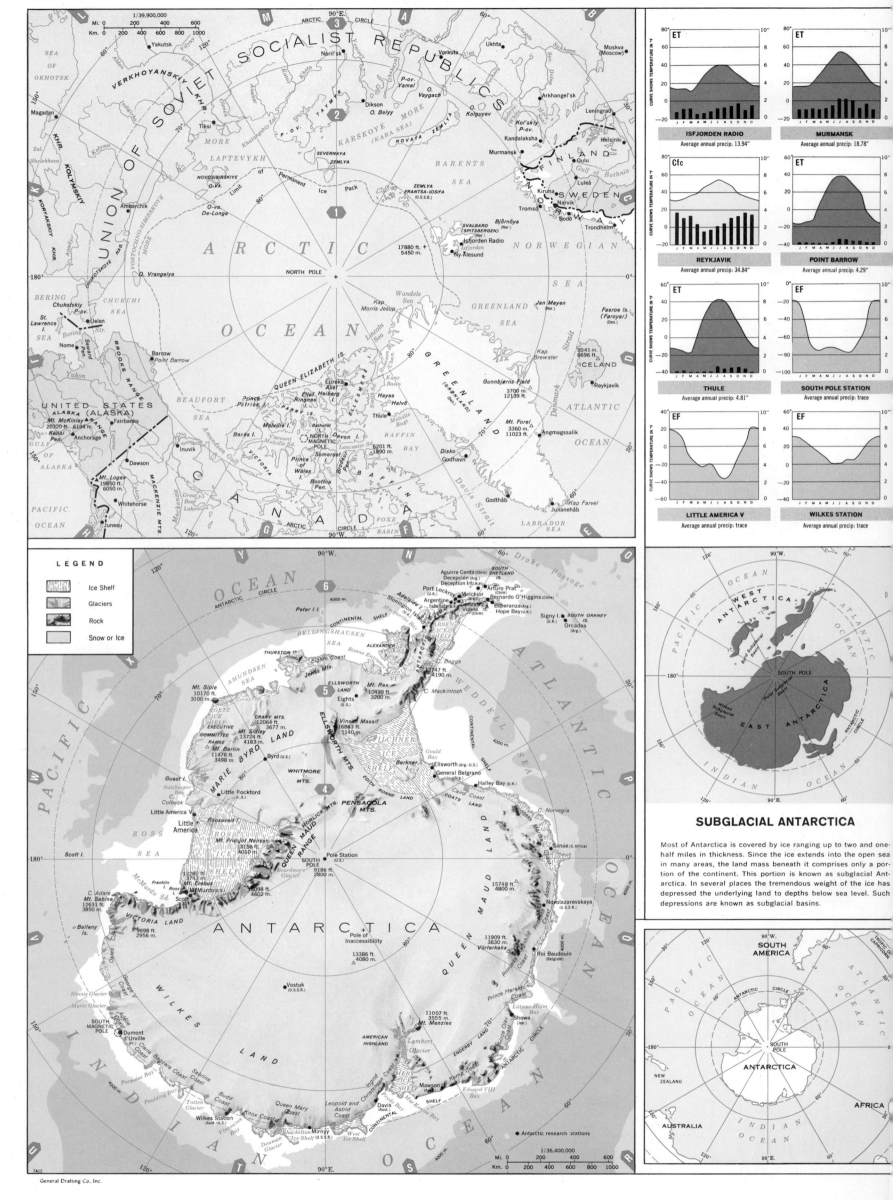

SUBGLACIAL ANTARCTICA

Most of Antarctica is covered by ice ranging up to two and one-half miles in thickness. Since the ice extends into the open sea in many areas, the land mass beneath it comprises only a portion of the continent. This portion is known as subglacial Antarctica. In several places the tremendous weight of the ice has depressed the underlying land to depths below sea level. Such depressions are known as subglacial basins.

LEGEND

Ice Shelf
Glaciers
Rock
Snow or Ice

General Drafting Co. Inc.

APPENDIX

COUNTRIES AND REGIONS OF THE WORLD

Country or Area	Capital; Largest City	Area in 1,000 sq. mi.	Pop. in 1,000's	Pop. per sq. mi.
Afghanistan	Kābul	251	15,352	61.2
Africa	----; Al Qāhirah (Cairo)	11,600	310,000	25.7
Alabama (U.S.)	Montgomery; Birmingham	51.6	3,486	67.6
Alaska (U.S.)	Juneau; Anchorage	586	267	0.46
Albania	Tiranë	11.1	1,865	168
Alberta (Can.)	Edmonton	255	1,451	5.69
Algeria	Alger	920	11,290	12.3
American Samoa (U.S.)	Pango Pango	0.08	21	263
Andaman & Nicobar Islands (Ind.)	Port Blair	3.22	64	19.9
Andhra Pradesh (Ind.)	Hyderabad	106	35,983	339
Andorra	Andorra	0.18	11	61.1
Angola (Port.)	Luanda	481	5,258	10.9
Antarctica	----	5,400	----	----
Argentina	Buenos Aires	1,072	22,691	21.2
Arizona (U.S.)	Phoenix	114	1,575	13.8
Arkansas (U.S.)	Little Rock	53.1	1,941	36.6
Armyanskaya S.S.R. (U.S.S.R.)	Yerevan	11.5	2,134	186
Asia	----; Tōkyō	16,900	1,875,000	111
Assam (Ind.)	Shillong	47.1	11,873	252
Australia	Canberra; Sidney	2,971	11,545	3.89
Australian Capital Territory (Austl.)	Canberra	0.91	96	106
Austria	Wien (Vienna)	32.4	7,273	224
Azerbaydzhanskaya S.S.R. (U.S.S.R.)	Baku	33.4	4,518	135
Baden-Württemberg (F.R.Ger.)	Stuttgart	13.8	8,257	598
Bahamas (U.K.)	Nassau	4.40	136	30.9
Bahrain	Al Manāmah	0.23	182	791
Barbados	Bridgetown	0.17	245	1,441
Bayern (F.R.Ger.)	München (Munich)	27.2	9,976	367
Belgium	Bruxelles (Brussels)	11.8	9,499	805
Belorusskaya S.S.R. (U.S.S.R.)	Minsk	80.1	8,633	108
Bermuda (U.K.)	Hamilton	0.02	50	2,500
Bhutan	Thimbu	19	750	39.5
Bihar (Ind.)	Patna	67.2	46,456	691
Bolivia	La Paz and Sucre; La Paz	424	3,748	8.84
Botswana	Gaberones; Serowe	222	543	2.45
Brazil	Brasília; São Paulo	3,287	84,679	25.8
Bremen (F.R.Ger.)	Bremen	0.16	733	4,581
British Columbia (Can.)	Victoria; Vancouver	366	1,789	4.89
British Honduras (U.K.)	Belize	8.87	109	12.3
British Solomon Is. Protectorate (U.K.)	Honiara	11.5	137	11.9
Brunei (U.K.)	Brunei	2.23	101	45.3
Bulgaria	Sofiya (Sofia)	42.8	8,230	192
Burma	Rangoon	262	24,732	94.4
Burundi	Bujumbura	10.7	2,800	262
California (U.S.)	Sacramento; Los Angeles	159	18,403	116
Cambodia	Phnom Penh	67	5,740	85.7
Cameroon	Yaoundé; Douala	184	5,229	28.4
Canada	Ottawa; Montréal	3,852	19,919	5.2
Canal Zone (U.S.)	Balboa Heights; Rainbow City	0.65	54	83.1
Cape Verde Islands (Port.)	Praia	1.56	219	140
Central African Republic	Bangui	242	1,352	5.55
Ceylon	Colombo	25.3	10,625	420
Chad	Fort-Lamy	495	3,300	6.67
Chile	Santiago	286	8,567	30.0
China	Pei-ching (Peking); Shang-hai	3,692	700,000	190
Colombia	Bogotá	440	17,485	39.7
Colorado (U.S.)	Denver	104	1,949	18.7
Comores, Arch. des (Fr.)	Dzaoudzi	0.84	212	252
Congo	Brazzaville	135	826	6.12
Congo, D.R. of the	Kinshasa	905	15,986	17.7
Connecticut (U.S.)	Hartford	5.01	2,830	565
Cook Islands (N.Z.)	Avarua	0.09	21	233
Costa Rica	San José	19.7	1,336	67.8
Cuba	Habana (Havana)	44.2	7,833	177
Cyprus	Nicosia	3.57	603	169
Czechoslovakia	Praha (Prague)	49.4	14,194	287
Dahomey	Porto Novo; Cotonou	44.7	2,300	51.5
Delaware (U.S.)	Dover; Wilmington	2.4	503	210
Denmark	København (Copenhagen)	16.6	4,758	287
District of Columbia (U.S.)	Washington	0.07	802	11,456
Dominican Republic	Santo Domingo	18.7	3,750	201
Ecuador	Quito; Guayaquil	106	4,476	42.2
El Salvador	San Salvador	8.24	2,928	355
England	London	50.3	45,070	896
Estonskaya S.S.R. (U.S.S.R.)	Tallinn	17.4	1,273	73.2
Ethiopia	Addis Ababa	455	23,000	50.5
Europe	----; London	3,810	595,000	156
Fiji (U.K.)	Suva	7.04	472	67.0
Finland	Helsinki	130	4,631	35.6
Florida (U.S.)	Tallahassee; Miami	58.6	5,796	98.9
France	Paris	213	49,157	231
French Guiana (Fr.)	Cayenne	35	36	1.03
French Polynesia (Fr.)	Papeete	1.45	85	58.6
French Somaliland (Fr.)	Djibouti	8.5	81	9.53
Gabon	Libreville	102	463	4.54
Gambia	Bathurst	4	315	78.8
Georgia (U.S.)	Atlanta	58.9	4,391	74.6
German D.R.	Ost-Berlin (East Berlin)	41.8	17,048	408
Germany, F.R. of	Bonn; West-Berlin	95.7	57,100	597
Ghana	Accra	92.1	7,740	84
Gibraltar (U.K.)	Gibraltar	0.0025	25	10,000
Gilbert and Ellice Is. (U.K.)	Tarawa	0.38	49	129
Greece	Athínai (Athens)	50.5	8,551	169
Greenland (Den.)	Godthab	840	40	0.05
Gruzinskaya S.S.R. (U.S.S.R.)	Tbilisi (Tiflis)	26.9	4,483	167
Guadeloupe (Fr.)	Basse-Terre	0.69	316	458
Guam (U.S.)	Agana; Tamuning	0.21	77	367
Guatemala	Guatemala	42	4,284	102
Guinea	Conakry	95	3,500	36.8
Gujarat (Ind.)	Ahmedabad	72.2	20,633	286
Guyana	Georgetown	83	647	7.80
Haiti	Port-au-Prince	10.7	4,485	419
Hamburg (F.R.Ger.)	Hamburg	0.29	1,857	6,403
Hawaii (U.S.)	Honolulu	6.42	710	111
Hessen (F.R.Ger.)	Wiesbaden; Frankfurt a. Main	8.14	5,087	625
Himachal Pradesh (Ind.)	Simla	10.9	1,351	124
Honduras	Tegucigalpa	43.2	2,363	54.7
Hong Kong (U.K.)	Victoria	0.4	3,836	9,590
Hungary	Budapest	35.9	10,179	284
Iceland	Reykjavik	39.8	192	4.82
Idaho (U.S.)	Boise	83.6	693	8.3
Illinois (U.S.)	Springfield; Chicago	56.4	10,641	189
India	New Delhi; Bombay	1,180	498,680	423
Indiana (U.S.)	Indianapolis	36.3	4,893	135
Indonesia	Djakarta	736	100,045	136
Iowa (U.S.)	Des Moines	56.3	2,758	49
Iran	Tehrān (Teheran)	636	23,428	36.8
Iraq	Baghdād	172	8,262	48.0
Ireland	Baile Atha Cliath (Dublin)	27.1	2,881	106
Israel	Jerusalem; Tel Aviv-Yafo	7.99	2,636	330
Italy	Roma (Rome)	116	51,784	446
Ivory Coast	Abidjan	125	3,750	30
Jamaica	Kingston	4.41	1,843	418
Japan	Tōkyō	148	98,275	664
Jordan	'Ammān	36.7	1,976	53.3
Kansas (U.S.)	Topeka; Wichita	82.3	2,248	27.3
Kazakhskaya S.S.R. (U.S.S.R.)	Alma-Ata	1,050	11,850	11.3
Kentucky (U.S.)	Frankfort; Louisville	40.4	3,173	73.5
Kenya	Nairobi	225	8,636	38.4
Kerala (Ind.)	Trivandrum	15	16,903	1,127
Kirgizskaya S.S.R. (U.S.S.R.)	Frunze	76.5	2,600	34
Korea	Sŏul (Seoul) and P'yŏngyang	85.2	40,477	475
Kuwait	Al Kuwayt	5.8	467	80.5
Laos	Luang Prabang and Vientiane; Vientiane	86	2,000	23.3
La Réunion (Fr.)	St-Denis	0.97	397	409
Latviyskaya S.S.R. (U.S.S.R.)	Rīga	25.6	2,200	85.9
Lebanon	Bayrūt (Beirut)	4	2,336	534
Lesotho	Maseru	11.7	859	73.4
Liberia	Monrovia	43	1,016	23.6
Libya	Tarābulus (Tripoli) and Banghāzī (Benghazi); Tarābulus	679	1,564	2.30
Liechtenstein	Vaduz	0.06	19	317
Litovskaya S.S.R. (U.S.S.R.)	Vilnius	25.2	2,950	117
Louisiana (U.S.)	Baton Rouge; New Orleans	48.5	3,560	73.4
Luxembourg	Luxembourg	1.0	333	333
Macao (Port.)	Macao	0.006	175	29,167
Madhya Pradesh (Ind.)	Bhopal; Indore	171	32,372	189
Madras (Ind.)	Madras	50.3	33,687	670
Maharashtra (Ind.)	Bombay	119	39,554	332
Maine (U.S.)	Augusta; Portland	33.2	986	29.7
Malagasy Republic	Tananarive	230	6,420	27.9
Malawi	Zomba; Blantyre-Limbe	36	3,753	104
Malaya (Malay.)	Kuala Lumpur	50.7	8,039	159
Malaysia	Kuala Lumpur	129	9,426	73.1
Maldive Islands	Malé	0.12	98	817
Mali	Bamako	465	4,654	10.0
Malta	Valletta	0.12	316	2,633
Manipur (Ind.)	Imphal	8.63	780	90.4
Manitoba (Can.)	Winnipeg	251	962	3.83
Martinique (Fr.)	Fort-de-France	0.42	321	764
Maryland (U.S.)	Annapolis; Baltimore	10.6	3,534	333
Massachusetts (U.S.)	Boston	8.26	5,361	649
Mauritania	Nouakchott; Kaédi	419	900	2.15
Mauritius (U.K.)	Port Louis	0.81	682	842
Mexico	México	760	44,145	58.1
Michigan (U.S.)	Lansing; Detroit	58.2	8,317	143
Minnesota (U.S.)	St. Paul; Minneapolis	84.1	3,562	42.4
Mississippi (U.S.)	Jackson	47.7	2,309	48.4
Missouri (U.S.)	Jefferson City; St. Louis	69.7	4,492	64.4
Moldavskaya S.S.R. (U.S.S.R.)	Kishinëv	13.3	3,300	248
Monaco	Monaco	0.0006	22	36,667
Mongolia	Ulaan Baatar	604	1,017	1.68
Montana (U.S.)	Helena; Great Falls	147	703	4.8
Morocco	Rabat; Casablanca	174	13,323	76.6
Mozambique (Port.)	Lourenço Marques	302	6,998	23.2
Muscat and Oman	Masqat (Muscat); Maṭraḥ	82	565	6.89
Mysore (Ind.)	Bangalore	74	23,587	319
Nagaland (Ind.)	Kohima	6.24	369	59.1
Nebraska (U.S.)	Lincoln; Omaha	77.2	1,459	18.9
Nepal	Kātmāndu	54.6	10,100	185
Netherlands	's Gravenhage (The Hague); Amsterdam	12	12,411	1,034
Nevada (U.S.)	Carson City; Las Vegas	111	434	3.9
New Brunswick (Can.)	Fredericton; Saint John	28.4	623	21.9
New Caledonia (Fr.)	Nouméa	8.55	87	10.2
Newfoundland (Can.)	St. John's	156	498	3.19
New Guinea, Terr. of (Austl.)	Port Moresby	93	1,576	16.9
New Hampshire (U.S.)	Concord; Manchester	9.3	673	72.4
New Hebrides (Fr.-U.K.)	Vila	5.7	68	11.9
New Jersey (U.S.)	Trenton; Newark	8.2	6,781	827
New Mexico (U.S.)	Santa Fe; Albuquerque	122	1,014	8.3
New South Wales (Austl.)	Sydney	309	4,235	13.7
New York (U.S.)	Albany; New York	49.5	18,106	365
New Zealand	Wellington; Auckland	104	2,677	25.7
Nicaragua	Managua	57.1	1,536	26.9
Niedersachsen (F.R.Ger.)	Hannover	18.6	6,855	368
Niger	Niamey	489	3,433	7.02
Nigeria	Lagos	357	55,670	156
Nordrhein-Westfalen (F.R.Ger.)	Düsseldorf; Köln (Cologne)	13.2	16,554	1,254
North America	----; New York	9,363	286,000	30.5
North Carolina (U.S.)	Raleigh; Charlotte	52.7	4,935	93.6
North Dakota (U.S.)	Bismarck; Fargo	70.7	652	9.2
North East Frontier Agency (Ind.)	Shillong	31.4	337	10.7
Northern Ireland (U.K.)	Belfast	5.46	1,469	269
Northern Terr. (Austl.)	Darwin	524	37	0.07
Northwest Terrs. (Can.)	Ottawa; Yellowknife	1,305	25	0.02
Norway	Oslo	125	3,738	29.9
Nova Scotia (Can.)	Halifax	21.4	761	35.6
Ohio (U.S.)	Columbus; Cleveland	41.2	10,241	249
Oklahoma (U.S.)	Oklahoma City	69.9	2,448	35.0
Ontario (Can.)	Toronto	413	6,731	16.3
Oregon (U.S.)	Salem; Portland	97	1,938	20.0
Orissa (Ind.)	Bhubaneswar; Cuttack	60.2	17,549	292
Pacific Is., Tr. Terr. of the (U.S.)	Garapan	0.70	92	131
Pakistan	Rawalpindi; Karāchi	365	105,044	288
Panama	Panamá	28.6	1,287	45.0
Papua (Austl.)	Port Moresby	90.5	573	6.3
Paraguay	Asunción	157	1,817	11.6
Pennsylvania (U.S.)	Harrisburg; Philadelphia	45.3	11,583	256
Peru	Lima	482	12,012	24.9
Philippines	Quezon City; Manila	116	33,477	289
Poland	Warszawa (Warsaw)	120	31,551	263
Portugal	Lisboa (Lisbon)	36	9,255	257
Portuguese Guinea (Port.)	Bissau	13.9	527	37.9
Portuguese Timor (Port.)	Dili	5.75	554	96.3
Prince Edward Island (Can.)	Charlottetown	2.18	108	49.5
Puerto Rico (U.S.)	San Juan	3.42	2,633	770
Qatar	Ad Dawhah (Doha)	4	71	17.8
Québec (Can.)	Québec; Montréal	595	5,657	9.49
Queensland (Austl.)	Brisbane	667	1,661	2.49
Rajasthan (Ind.)	Jaipur	132	20,155	153
Rheinland-Pfalz (F.R.Ger.)	Mainz; Ludwigshafen	7.65	3,545	463
Rhode Island (U.S.)	Providence	1.21	891	734
Rhodesia	Salisbury	150	3,618	24.1
Rossiyskaya S.F.S.R. (U.S.S.R.)	Moskva (Moscow)	6,590	125,800	19.1
Rumania	Bucureşti (Bucharest)	91.7	19,105	208
Rwanda	Kigali	10.2	3,018	296
Saarland (F.R.Ger.)	Saarbrücken	0.99	1,117	1,128
Sabah (Malay.)	Jesselton; Sandakan	29.4	549	18.7
St. Helena (U.K.)	Jamestown	0.05	5	100
San Marino	San Marino	0.024	17	708
Sarawak (Malay.)	Kuching	48.3	838	17.3
Saskatchewan (Can.)	Regina	252	951	3.77
Saudi Arabia	Ar Riyād (Riyadh) and Makkah (Mecca)	873	6,750	7.73
Schleswig-Holstein (F.R.Ger.)	Kiel	6.04	2,406	398
Scotland (U.K.)	Edinburgh; Glasgow	29.8	5,204	175
Senegal	Dakar	76.1	3,490	45.9
Seychelles (U.K.)	Victoria	0.16	48	300
Sierra Leone	Freetown	27.9	2,180	78.1
Sikkim (Ind.)	Gangtok	2.82	176	62.4
Singapore	Singapore	0.23	1,891	8,222
Somali Republic	Mogadishu	246	2,500	10.2
South Africa	Pretoria and Cape Town; Johannesburg	472	17,867	37.9
South America	----; Buenos Aires	6,870	162,000	23.6
South Arabia (U.K.)	Al Ittiḥād; Aden	112	1,099	9.81
South Australia (Austl.)	Adelaide	380	1,091	2.87
South Carolina (U.S.)	Columbia	31.1	2,550	82.0
South Dakota (U.S.)	Pierre; Sioux Falls	77	686	8.9
South-West Africa (S.Af.)	Windhoek	318	574	1.81
Spain	Madrid	195	31,871	163
Spanish Sahara (Sp.)	El Aaiun	103	48	0.46
Sudan	Al Khurtūm (Khartoum)	967	13,940	14.4
Surinam (Neth.)	Paramaribo	55	324	5.89
Swaziland (U.K.)	Mbabane	6.71	389	58.0
Sweden	Stockholm	174	7,773	44.7
Switzerland	Bern; Zürich	15.9	5,945	374
Syria	Dimashq (Damascus)	72	5,300	73.6
Tadzhikskaya S.S.R. (U.S.S.R.)	Dushanbe	55.2	2,432	44.1
Taiwan	T'ai-pei	13.9	12,791	920
Tanzania	Dar es Salaam	362	10,567	29.2
Tasmania (Austl.)	Hobart	26.2	371	14.2
Tennessee (U.S.)	Nashville; Memphis	42.2	3,850	91.2
Texas (U.S.)	Austin; Houston	267	10,591	41.0
Thailand	Krung Thep (Bangkok)	198	30,591	154
Togo	Lomé	21.9	1,682	76.8
Tonga (U.K.)	Nuku'alofa	0.27	74	274
Trinidad and Tobago	Port of Spain	1.98	975	492
Tripura (Ind.)	Agartala	4.04	1,142	283
Trucial States	----; Dubai	32.3	130	4.02
Tunisia	Tūnis	63	4,675	74.2
Turkey	Ankara; Īstanbul	296	31,391	106
Turkmenskaya S.S.R. (U.S.S.R.)	Ashkhabad	188	1,862	9.9
Uganda	Kampala	94	7,551	80.3
Ukrainskaya S.S.R. (U.S.S.R.)	Kiyev (Kiev)	232	45,516	196
Union of Soviet Socialist Republics	Moskva (Moscow)	8,650	233,200	27.0
United Arab Republic	Al Qāhirah (Cairo)	386	30,054	77.9
United Kingdom	London	94.5	54,436	576
United States	Washington; New York	3,615	197,967	54.8
Upper Volta	Ouagadougou	106	4,955	46.7
Uruguay	Montevideo	72.2	2,593	35.9
Utah (U.S.)	Salt Lake City	84.9	994	11.7
Uttar Pradesh (Ind.)	Lucknow; Kanpur	114	73,746	647
Uzbekskaya S.S.R. (U.S.S.R.)	Tashkent	172	10,130	58.9
Vatican City	Vatican City	0.0002	1.0	5,000
Venezuela	Caracas	352	9,030	25.7
Vermont (U.S.)	Montpelier; Burlington	9.61	404	42.0
Victoria (Austl.)	Melbourne	87.9	3,218	36.6
Viet-Nam	Sai Gon and Ha Noi	126	35,124	279
Virginia (U.S.)	Richmond; Norfolk	40.8	4,420	109
Wales (U.K.)	----; Cardiff	8.02	2,693	336
Washington (U.S.)	Olympia; Seattle	68.2	2,973	43.6
West Bengal (Ind.)	Calcutta	33.8	34,926	1,033
West-Berlin (F.R.Ger.)	West-Berlin	0.19	2,201	11,584
Western Australia (Austl.)	Perth	976	836	0.86
Western Samoa	Apia	1.13	130	115
West Virginia (U.S.)	Charleston; Huntington	24.3	1,815	74.7
Wisconsin (U.S.)	Madison; Milwaukee	56.2	4,140	73.7
Wyoming (U.S.)	Cheyenne	97.9	330	3.4
Yemen	Ṣan'ā' and Ta'izz	75.3	5,000	66.4
Yugoslavia	Beograd	98.7	19,742	200
Yukon (Can.)	Whitehorse	207	15	0.07
Zambia	Lusaka	290	3,409	11.8

184

THE WORLD • FACTS AND FIGURES

The Most Populous Countries

	Approx. Pop.
China	700,000,000
India	498,680,000
Union of Soviet Socialist Republics	233,200,000
United States	197,967,000
Pakistan	105,044,000
Indonesia	100,045,000
Japan	98,275,000
Brazil	84,679,000
Federal Republic of Germany	57,100,000
Nigeria	55,670,000
United Kingdom	54,436,000
Italy	51,784,000
France	49,157,000
Mexico	44,145,000
Korea	40,477,000
Viet-Nam	35,124,000
Philippines	33,477,000
Spain	31,871,000
Poland	31,551,000
Turkey	31,391,000
Thailand	30,591,000
United Arab Republic	30,054,000
Burma	24,732,000
Iran	23,428,000
Ethiopia	23,000,000

The Largest Countries

	Area in Sq. Mi.
Union of Soviet Socialist Republics	8,650,000
Canada	3,852,000
China	3,692,000
United States	3,615,000
Brazil	3,287,000
Australia	2,971,000
India	1,180,000
Argentina	1,072,000
Sudan	967,000
Algeria	920,000
D. R. Congo	905,000
Saudi Arabia	873,000
Mexico	760,000
Indonesia	736,000
Libya	679,000
Iran	636,000
Mongolia	604,000
Chad	495,000
Niger	489,000
Peru	482,000
South Africa	472,000

The Most Densely Populated Countries

	Pop. per Sq. Mi.
Monaco	36,667
Singapore	8,222
Vatican City	5,000
Malta	2,633
Barbados	1,441
Netherlands	1,034
Taiwan	920
Maldive Islands	817
Belgium	805
Bahrain	791
San Marino	708
Japan	664
Federal Republic of Germany	597
Lebanon	584
United Kingdom	576
Trinidad and Tobago	492
Korea	475
Italy	446
India	423
Ceylon	420
Haiti	419

The Largest Islands

	Area in Sq. Mi.
Greenland, North Atlantic	840,000
New Guinea, Southwest Pacific	317,000
Borneo, Southwest Pacific	287,000
Madagascar, Indian Ocean	228,000
Baffin, Canada	184,000
Sumatera, Indonesia	183,000
Honshū, Japan	89,000
Great Britain, Atlantic Ocean	87,000
Ellesmere, Canada	82,100
Victoria, Canada	81,900
Sulawesi, Indonesia	73,000
South (N.Z.), Pacific Ocean	58,100
Djawa, Indonesia	49,600
North (N.Z.), Pacific Ocean	44,300
Cuba, Caribbean Sea	44,200
Newfoundland, Canada	42,700
Luzon, Philippines	42,500
Iceland, North Atlantic	39,800
Mindanao, Philippines	37,400
Ireland, Atlantic Ocean	32,600
Hokkaidō, Japan	30,000
Hispaniola, Caribbean Sea	29,700
Sakhalin, Sea of Okhotsk	27,400
Tasmania, Australia	25,300
Ceylon, Indian Ocean	25,300
Banks, Canada	24,100
Devon, Canada	20,900
Tierra del Fuego, South Atlantic	18,600
Melville, Canada	16,200
Axel Heiberg, Canada	15,800
Southampton, Canada	15,700
Kyūshū, Japan	15,400

GENERAL INFORMATION

Dimensions and Movements

Equatorial diameter, 7,927 miles
Polar diameter, 7,900 miles
Mean diameter, 7,918 miles
Equatorial circumference, 24,902 miles
Polar circumference, 24,860 miles
Total area, 196,950,000 square miles
Land area, 57,800,000 square miles
Water area, 139,150,000 square miles
Revolution in orbit, 365¼ days
Rotation on its axis, 23 hours, 56 minutes, 4.09 seconds
Rotation speed, about 1,040 miles per hour

Elevations and Depths

Highest point, Mt. Everest, Asia, 29,028 feet
Lowest point, Dead Sea, Asia, 1,286 feet below sea level
Lowest ocean depth, Trieste Deep, Pacific Ocean, 35,800 feet below sea level

Temperature and Rainfall

Highest recorded temperature, 136° F. at Al Azīzīyah, Libya, September 13, 1922
Lowest recorded temperature, −126.9° F. at Vostok, Antarctica, August 24, 1960
Highest mean annual temperature, 88° F. at Lugh Ganane, Somali Republic
Lowest mean annual temperature, −67° F. at Vostok, Antarctica

Maximum 24-hour rainfall, 46 inches at Baguio, Luzon, Philippines, July 14–15, 1911
Maximum monthly rainfall, 366 inches at Cherrapunji, India, July, 1861

Population

Total estimated population, 3,200,000,000
Estimated population density, 55.7 per square mile

The Continents

	Area in Sq. Mi.	Population	Pop. per Sq. Mi.
Asia	16,900,000	1,875,000,000	111
Africa	11,600,000	310,000,000	26.7
North America	9,363,000	286,000,000	30.5
South America	6,870,000	162,000,000	23.6
Antarctica	5,400,000	---	---
Europe	3,810,000	595,000,000	156
Australia	2,971,000	11,545,000	3.9

		Highest Elevation in Ft.
Asia	Everest, China-Nepal	29,028
Africa	Kilimanjaro, Tanzania	19,340
North America	McKinley, Alaska	20,320
South America	Aconcagua, Argentina	23,034
Antarctica	Vinson Massif	16,863
Europe	El'brus, U.S.S.R.	18,481
Australia	Kosciusko, New South Wales	7,316

		Lowest Elevation in Ft.
Asia	Dead Sea, Israel-Jordan	−1,286
Africa	Munkhafad Al Qaṭṭārah, U.A.R.	−440
North America	Death Valley, California	−282
South America	Península Valdés, Argentina	−181
Antarctica	(Unknown)	
Europe	Caspian Sea, U.S.S.R.	−92
Australia	Lake Eyre, South Australia	−39

The Principal Mountains

NORTH AMERICA	Height in Ft.
McKinley, Alaska	20,320
Logan, Yukon	19,850
Orizaba, Mexico	18,701
St. Elias, Alaska-Yukon	18,008
Popocatépetl, Mexico	17,887
Ixtacihuatl, Mexico	17,342
Foraker, Alaska	17,305
Lucania, Yukon	17,150
King Pk., Alaska-B.C.	17,130
Blackburn, Alaska	16,523
Bona, Alaska	16,421
Sanford, Alaska	16,208
Vancouver, Alaska	15,700
Fairweather, Alaska-B.C.	15,300
Whitney, California	14,495
Elbert, Colorado	14,423
Rainier, Washington	14,410
Blanca Pk., Colorado	14,317
Uncompahgre Pk., Colorado	14,301
Evans, Colorado	14,264
Longs Pk., Colorado	14,256
Shasta, California	14,162
Pikes Pk., Colorado	14,110
Tajumulco, Guatemala	13,815
Mauna Kea, Hawaii	13,796
Gannett Pk., Wyoming	13,785
Grand Teton, Wyoming	13,766
Mauna Loa, Hawaii	13,680
Kings Pk., Utah	13,498
Waddington, Br. Columbia	13,260
Cloud Pk., Wyoming	13,165
Wheeler Pk., New Mexico	13,160
Boundary Pk., Nevada	13,145
Robson, Br. Columbia	12,972
Granite Pk., Montana	12,850

SOUTH AMERICA	Height in Ft.
Aconcagua, Argentina	23,034
Ancohuma, Bolivia	23,012
Ojos del Salado, Arg.-Chile	22,539
Pissis, Argentina	22,244
Huascarán, Peru	22,204
Tocorpuri, Bolivia-Chile	22,160
Llullaillaco, Arg.-Chile	22,056
Sajama, Bolivia	21,391
Antofalla, Arg.	21,228
Illimani, Bolivia	21,185
Auzangate, Peru	20,945
Chimborazo, Ecuador	20,561
Condoriri, Ecuador	20,341
Cotopaxi, Ecuador	19,347

EUROPE	Height in Ft.
El'brus, U.S.S.R.	18,481
Dykh Tau, U.S.S.R.	17,054
Kazbek, U.S.S.R.	16,558
Blanc, Mont, France	15,781
Dufourspitze, Switzerland	15,200
Matterhorn, Switzerland	14,691
Finsteraarhorn, Switzerland	14,022
Jungfrau, Switzerland	13,645
Viso, Italy	12,602
Grossglockner, Austria	12,460
Teide, Pico de, Canary Is.	12,200
Mulhacén, Spain	11,427
Aneto, Pico de, Spain	11,168
Perdido, Spain	11,007
Etna, Italy	10,705
Zugspitze, Germany	9,737
Coma Pedrosa, Andorra	9,665
Musala, Bulgaria	9,596

The Principal Mountains, con't.

Corno Grande, Italy	9,554
Ólimbos, Greece	9,550

ASIA	Height in Ft.
Everest, China-Nepal	29,028
Godwin Austen (K2), Pakistan	28,251
Kanchenjunga, India	28,146
Makālu, China-Nepal	27,788
Dhaulāgiri, Nepal	26,811
Nanga Parbat, Pakistan	26,670
Annapurna, Nepal	26,502
Nanda Devi, India	25,646
Kamet, India	25,577
Na-mu-cho-pa-erh-wa, China	25,446
Ulugh Muz, China	25,338
Gurla Mandhata, China	25,335
Tirich Mir, Pakistan	25,229
Kula Gangri, Bhutan-China	24,780
Kommunizma, Pik, U.S.S.R.	24,590
Muz Tagh, China	23,888
Lenina, Pik, U.S.S.R.	23,405
Api, Nepal	23,399
Karla Marksa, Pik, U.S.S.R.	22,067
Hkakabo Razi, Burma	19,294
Demāvand, Iran	18,373
Ağri Daği, Turkey	16,945
Taban Bogdo Uula, Mongolia	15,166
Kinabalu, Sabah	13,455
Hsin-kao, Taiwan	13,144
Erciyas Daği, Turkey	12,848
Kerintji, Indonesia	12,467
Fuji, Japan	12,388
Rindjani, Indonesia	12,224
Mahameru, Indonesia	12,060
Razih, Saudi Arabia	12,001
Munku-Sardyk, Mong.-USSR	11,457

AFRICA	Height in Ft.
Kilimanjaro, Tanzania	19,340
Kenya, Kenya	17,058
Ruwenzori, D.R. Congo-Uganda	16,763
Dashan, Ethiopia	15,157
Meru, Tanzania	14,970
Elgon, Uganda	14,178
Toubkal, Morocco	13,665
Cameroon, Cameroon	13,353
Emi Koussi, Chad	11,204
Aux Sources, South Africa	10,822

OCEANIA	Height in Ft.
Carstensz Pks., Irian Barat	16,499
Daam Peak, Irian Barat	16,148
Wilhelm, New Guinea	15,400
Kubor, New Guinea	14,300
Victoria, Papua	13,363
Albert Edward, Papua	13,100
Cook, New Zealand	12,349
Balbi, Bougainville	10,206
Ruapehu, New Zealand	9,175
Egmont, New Zealand	8,260

ANTARCTICA	Height in Ft.
Vinson Massif	16,863
Sidley	13,724
Fridtjof Nansen	13,156
Sabine	12,631

The Oceans and Large Seas

	Area in Sq. Mi.	Average Depth in Ft.	Greatest Depth in Ft.
Pacific Ocean	63,801,668	14,048	35,800
Atlantic Ocean	31,839,306	12,880	27,498
Indian Ocean	28,356,276	13,002	24,442
Arctic Ocean	5,440,197	3,953	17,880
Caribbean Sea	1,063,340	8,685	23,750
Mediterranean Sea	996,757	4,878	16,420
Bering Sea	875,753	4,714	13,422
Gulf of Mexico	595,760	4,961	14,358

The Principal Rivers

	Length in Mi.
Nile (Af.)	4,160
Amazon (S. Amer.)	3,900
Mississippi-Missouri (N. Amer.)	3,760
Ch'ang (Asia)	3,370
Huang (Asia)	2,870
Congo (Af.)	2,720
Amur (Asia)	2,700
Lena (Asia)	2,660
Mackenzie (N. Amer.)	2,640
Mekong (Asia)	2,600
Niger (Af.)	2,600
Paraná (S. Amer.)	2,580
Ob' (Asia)	2,500
Missouri (N. Amer.)	2,466
Yenisey (Asia)	2,410
Mississippi (N. Amer.)	2,350
Murray (Austl.)	2,310
Volga (Eur.)	2,290
Madeira (S. Amer.)	2,100
Yukon (N. Amer.)	2,000
Purus (S. Amer.)	1,950
St. Lawrence (N. Amer.)	1,900
Rio Grande (N. Amer.)	1,890
Irtysh (Asia)	1,840
Syr-Dar'ya (Asia)	1,810
Brahmaputra (Asia)	1,800
Indus (Asia)	1,800
São Francisco (S. Amer.)	1,800
Danube (Eur.)	1,750
Darling (Austl.)	1,725
Euphrates (Asia)	1,710
Tocantins (S. Amer.)	1,670
Zambezi (Af.)	1,630
Nelson (N. Amer.)	1,600
Orinoco (S. Amer.)	1,600
Salween (Asia)	1,600
Ural (Asia-Eur.)	1,570
Amu-Dar'ya (Asia)	1,550
Ganga (Asia)	1,550
Paraguay (S. Amer.)	1,530
Arkansas (N. Amer.)	1,450
Colorado (N. Amer.)	1,450
Dnepr (Eur.)	1,420
Negro (S. Amer.)	1,400
Hsi (Asia)	1,380
Angara (Asia)	1,350
Irrawaddy (Asia)	1,300
Orange (Af.)	1,300
Pilcomayo (S. Amer.)	1,300
Columbia (N. Amer.)	1,210
Don (Eur.)	1,210
Saskatchewan (N. Amer.)	1,210
Sungari (Asia)	1,170
Tigris (Asia)	1,160
Peace (N. Amer.)	1,150

The Largest Lakes

	Area in Sq. Mi.	Elevation above Sea Level in Ft.
Caspian Sea (Asia-Eur.)	153,000	−92
Superior (N. Amer.)	31,800	602
Victoria (Af.)	26,800	3,718
Aral'skoye More (Asia)	25,200	169
Huron (N. Amer.)	23,000	579
Michigan (N. Amer.)	22,400	579
Tanganyika (Af.)	12,700	2,534
Great Bear (N. Amer.)	12,200	450
Baykal (Asia)	12,000	1,490
Great Slave (N. Amer.)	11,100	500
Nyasa (Af.)	10,600	1,550
Erie (N. Amer.)	9,930	572
Winnipeg (N. Amer.)	9,320	713
Ontario (N. Amer.)	7,520	246
Ladozhskoye (Eur.)	6,970	40
Balkhash (Asia)	6,840	1,112
Chad (Af.)	6,300	790
Onezhskoye (Eur.)	3,780	108
Titicaca (S. Amer.)	3,200	12,494

The Outstanding Waterfalls

	Height in Ft.
Angel, Venezuela	3,281
Tugela, South Africa	3,110
Yosemite, U.S.	2,425
Cuquenán, Ven.-Guyana	2,000
Sutherland, New Zealand	1,904
Ribbon, U.S.	1,612
King George VI, Guyana	1,600
Gavarnie, Fr.	1,385
Takkakaw, Canada	1,248
Victoria, Rhodesia-Zambia	1,248
King Edward VIII, Guyana	850
Iguassú, Brazil-Argentina	230
Niagara, Canada-U.S.	167

THE WORLD'S LARGEST CITIES

THE FIRST FIFTY

1.	Tōkyō	Japan	9,683,802
2.	London	U.K.	8,171,902
3.	New York	U.S.	7,781,984
4.	Shang-hai	China	7,000,000
5.	Pei-ching (Peking)	China	6,800,000
6.	Moskva (Moscow)	U.S.S.R.	6,300,000
7.	Bombay	India	4,152,056
8.	Chicago	U.S.	3,550,404
9.	Al Qāhirah (Cairo)	U.A.R.	3,346,000
10.	México	Mexico	3,301,757
11.	Rio de Janeiro	Brazil	3,223,408
12.	São Paulo	Brazil	3,164,804
13.	Shen-yang (Mukden)	China	3,100,000
14.	Ōsaka	Japan	3,011,563
15.	Leningrad	U.S.S.R.	2,997,000
16.	Djakarta	Indonesia	2,973,052
17.	Buenos Aires	Argentina	2,966,816
18.	Calcutta	India	2,927,289
19.	T'ien-ching (Tientsin)	China	2,900,000
20.	Paris	France	2,811,171
21.	Ha-erh-pin (Harbin)	China	2,493,000
22.	Los Angeles	U.S.	2,479,015
23.	Sŏul (Seoul)	Korea	2,444,883
24.	Madrid	Spain	2,259,931
25.	West-Berlin	F.R.Ger.	2,223,777
26.	Ch'ung-ch'ing (Chungking)	China	2,200,000
27.	Kuang-chou (Canton)	China	2,160,000
28.	Delhi	India	2,061,758
29.	Philadelphia	U.S.	2,002,512
30.	Roma (Rome)	Italy	1,983,286
31.	Karāchi	Pakistan	1,912,598
32.	Sydney	Australia	1,863,161
33.	Budapest	Hungary	1,807,299
34.	Singapore	Singapore	1,780,000
35.	Hamburg	F.R.Ger.	1,751,289
36.	Madras	India	1,729,141
37.	Detroit	U.S.	1,670,144
38.	Wien (Vienna)	Austria	1,627,034
39.	Nagoya	Japan	1,591,935
40.	Barcelona	Spain	1,557,863
41.	Melbourne	Australia	1,524,111
42.	Al Iskandarīyah (Alexandria)	U.A.R.	1,513,000
43.	Tehrān (Teheran)	Iran	1,512,082
44.	Hsi-an (Sian)	China	1,500,000
45.	Pao-t'ou (Paotow)	China	1,500,000
46.	T'ai-yüan	China	1,500,000
47.	İstanbul	Turkey	1,493,910
48.	Milano (Milan)	Italy	1,471,471
49.	Nan-ching (Nanking)	China	1,419,000
50.	Sai Gon (Saigon)	Viet-Nam	1,400,000

NAME	COUNTRY	POPULATION
Accra	Ghana	491,060
Addis Ababa	Ethiopia	465,000
Adelaide	Australia	483,508
Agra	India	462,029
Ahmedabad	India	1,149,918
Alger (Algiers)	Algeria	722,066
Al Iskandarīyah (Alexandria)	U.A.R.	1,513,000
Allahabad	India	411,955
Alma-Ata	U.S.S.R.	508,000
Al Qāhirah (Cairo)	U.A.R.	3,346,000
Amagasaki	Japan	405,955
Amritsar	India	376,295
Amsterdam	Netherlands	840,100
An-shan	China	700,000
Astrakhan'	U.S.S.R.	313,000
Athínai (Athens)	Greece	627,564
Atlanta	U.S.	487,455
Baghdād	Iraq	355,958
Baile Atha Cliath (Dublin)	Ireland	548,483
Baku	U.S.S.R.	671,000
Baltimore	U.S.	939,024
Bandung	Indonesia	972,566
Bangalore	India	905,134
Barcelona	Spain	1,557,863
Bari	Italy	313,351
Barnaul	U.S.S.R.	338,000
Barranquilla	Colombia	452,140
Belém	Brazil	359,988
Belfast	U.K.	416,094
Belo Horizonte	Brazil	642,912
Beograd (Belgrade)	Yugoslavia	594,000
Birmingham	U.K.	1,105,651
Birmingham	U.S.	340,887
Bochum	F.R.Ger.	345,614
Bogotá	Colombia	1,329,230
Bologna	Italy	426,621
Bombay	India	4,152,056
Boston	U.S.	697,197
Bremen	F.R.Ger.	507,952
Brisbane	Australia	502,320
Bristol	U.K.	437,048
Brno	Czechoslovakia	323,309
Bucureşti (Bucharest)	Rumania	1,177,661
Budapest	Hungary	1,807,299
Buenos Aires	Argentina	2,966,816
Buffalo	U.S.	532,759
Calcutta	India	2,927,289
Cali	Colombia	590,770
Cape Town	South Africa	731,484
Caracas	Venezuela	1,038,622
Casablanca	Morocco	965,277
Catania	Italy	363,048
Chang-chia-k'ou (Kalgan)	China	630,000
Ch'ang-ch'un (Hsinking)	China	1,150,000
Ch'ang-sha	China	700,000
Chelyabinsk	U.S.S.R.	733,000
Cheng-chou	China	800,000
Ch'eng-tu	China	1,107,000
Chicago	U.S.	3,550,404
Ch'i-ch'i-ha-erh (Chichihar)	China	604,000
Chi-lin (Kirin)	China	568,000
Chi-nan (Tsinan)	China	860,000
Chin-chou	China	350,000
Ch'ing-tao (Tsingtao)	China	1,121,000
Chittagong	Pakistan	364,205
Ch'ung-ch'ing (Chungking)	China	2,200,000
Cincinnati	U.S.	502,550
Cleveland	U.S.	876,050
Colombo	Ceylon	510,947
Columbus	U.S.	471,316
Córdoba	Argentina	510,739
Curitiba	Brazil	344,560
Dacca	Pakistan	566,712
Dakar	Senegal	382,980
Dallas	U.S.	679,684
Delhi	India	2,061,758
Denver	U.S.	493,887
Detroit	U.S.	1,670,144
Dimashq (Damascus)	Syria	475,399
Djakarta	Indonesia	2,973,052
Dnepropetrovsk	U.S.S.R.	707,000
Donetsk	U.S.S.R.	749,000
Dortmund	F.R.Ger.	607,885
Dresden	Ger.D.R.	493,603
Duisburg	F.R.Ger.	476,523
Durban	South Africa	655,370
Düsseldorf	F.R.Ger.	654,850
Edinburgh	U.K.	468,378
Essen	F.R.Ger.	698,925
Firenze (Florence)	Italy	428,955
Fortaleza	Brazil	354,942
Fort Worth	U.S.	356,268
Fou-hsin	China	500,000
Frankfurt am Main	F.R.Ger.	623,172
Fu-chou (Foochow)	China	616,000
Fukuoka	Japan	672,122
Fu-shun	China	985,000
Gelsenkirchen	F.R.Ger.	374,697
Genova (Genoa)	Italy	758,491
Glasgow	U.K.	1,054,913
Gor'kiy	U.S.S.R.	1,003,000
Göteborg	Sweden	404,738
Guadalajara	Mexico	530,617
Guatemala	Guatemala	339,823
Guayaquil	Ecuador	506,037
Habana (Havana)	Cuba	785,455
Ha-erh-pin (Harbin)	China	2,493,000
Halab (Aleppo)	Syria	466,026
Hamamatsu	Japan	333,009
Hamburg	F.R.Ger.	1,751,289
Hang-chou	China	740,000
Hannover	F.R.Ger.	536,810
Ha Noi (Hanoi)	Viet-Nam	414,620
Helsinki	Finland	477,062
Himeji	Japan	328,689
Hiroshima	Japan	431,336
Ho-fei	China	500,000
Houston	U.S.	938,219
Howrah	India	512,598
Hsi-an (Sian)	China	1,500,000
Hsi-ning	China	325,220
Hu-ho-hao-t'e (Kuei-sui)	China	860,000
Hyderabad	India	1,118,553
Hyderābād	Pakistan	434,537
Ibadan	Nigeria	532,667
Inch'ŏn	Korea	402,009
Indianapolis	U.S.	476,258
Indore	India	394,941
Irkutsk	U.S.S.R.	380,000
İstanbul	Turkey	1,493,910
Ivanovo	U.S.S.R.	352,000
Izhevsk	U.S.S.R.	312,000
Jaipur	India	403,444
Jogjakarta	Indonesia	312,698
Johannesburg	South Africa	1,096,541
K'ai-feng	China	780,000
Kanpur (Cawnpore)	India	895,106
Kansas City	U.S.	475,539
Kao-hsuing	Taiwan	388,848
Karāchi	Pakistan	1,912,598
Karaganda	U.S.S.R.	441,000
Kawasaki	Japan	632,975
Kazan'	U.S.S.R.	693,000
Khabarovsk	U.S.S.R.	377,000
Khar'kov	U.S.S.R.	1,048,000
Kitakyūshū	Japan	1,000,000
Kiyev (Kiev)	U.S.S.R.	1,174,000
Kōbe	Japan	1,113,977
København (Copenhagen)	Denmark	721,381
Köln (Cologne)	F.R.Ger.	713,505
Kowloon	Hong Kong	726,976
Kraków (Cracow)	Poland	479,000
Krasnodar	U.S.S.R.	343,000
Krasnoyarsk	U.S.S.R.	468,000
Krivoy Rog	U.S.S.R.	436,000
Krung Thep (Bangkok)	Thailand	1,299,528
Kuala Lumpur	Malaysia	316,230
Kuang-chou (Canton)	China	2,160,000
Kuei-yang (Kweiyang)	China	600,000
Kumamoto	Japan	373,922
K'un-ming	China	880,000
Kuybyshev	U.S.S.R.	863,000
Kwangju	Korea	315,124
Kyōto	Japan	1,284,818
Lagos	Nigeria	358,860
Lahore	Pakistan	1,296,477
Lan-chou	China	1,200,000
Lanús	Argentina	381,561
La Paz	Bolivia	347,394
La Plata	Argentina	376,910
Leeds	U.K.	510,597
Leipzig	Ger.D.R.	598,632
Leningrad	U.S.S.R.	2,997,000
Léopoldville	Congo-L.	402,492
Lima	Peru	536,666
Lisboa (Lisbon)	Portugal	802,230
Liverpool	U.K.	747,490
Łódź	Poland	708,000
London	U.K.	8,171,902
Long Beach	U.S.	344,168
Los Angeles	U.S.	2,479,015
Louisville	U.S.	390,639
Lo-yang	China	600,000
Lucknow	India	595,440
Lü-ta (Port Arthur-Dairen)	China	770,000
L'vov	U.S.S.R.	436,000
Lyallpur	Pakistan	425,248
Lyon	France	535,784
Madras	India	1,729,141
Madrid	Spain	2,259,931
Madura (Madura)	India	424,810
Magnitogorsk	U.S.S.R.	328,000
Makasar	Indonesia	384,159
Makeyevka	U.S.S.R.	381,000
Malang	Indonesia	341,452
Manchester	U.K.	661,041
Manila	Philippines	1,138,611
Maracaibo	Venezuela	432,902
Marseille	France	783,738
Medan	Indonesia	479,098
Medellín	Colombia	690,710
Melbourne	Australia	1,524,111
Memphis	U.S.	497,524
México	Mexico	3,301,757
Milano (Milan)	Italy	1,471,471
Milwaukee	U.S.	741,324
Minneapolis	U.S.	482,872
Minsk	U.S.S.R.	599,000
Monterrey	Mexico	596,993
Montevideo	Uruguay	922,885
Montréal	Canada	1,155,178
Moskva (Moscow)	U.S.S.R.	6,300,000
Multān	Pakistan	358,201
München (Munich)	F.R.Ger.	962,860
Nagasaki	Japan	344,153
Nagoya	Japan	1,591,935
Nagpur	India	643,659
Nan-ch'ang	China	510,000
Nan-ching (Nanking)	China	1,419,000
Napoli (Naples)	Italy	1,150,393
Newark	U.S.	405,220
New Orleans	U.S.	627,525
New York	U.S.	7,781,984
Niigata	Japan	314,528
Nizhniy Tagil	U.S.S.R.	355,000
Nottingham	U.K.	311,899
Novokuznetsk	U.S.S.R.	405,000
Novosibirsk	U.S.S.R.	985,000
Nürnberg	F.R.Ger.	424,306
Oakland	U.S.	367,548
Odessa	U.S.S.R.	703,000
Oklahoma City	U.S.	324,253
Omsk	U.S.S.R.	650,000
Oran	Algeria	350,087
Ōsaka	Japan	3,011,563
Oslo	Norway	471,310
Ost-Berlin (East Berlin)	Ger.D.R.	1,071,775
Palembang	Indonesia	474,971
Palermo	Italy	591,041
Pang-fou	China	330,000
Pao-t'ou (Paotow)	China	1,500,000
Paris	France	2,811,171
Patna	India	363,700
Pei-ching (Peking)	China	6,800,000
Pen-ch'i	China	449,000
Perm'	U.S.S.R.	678,000
Philadelphia	U.S.	2,002,512
Phnom Penh	Cambodia	403,500
Phoenix	U.S.	439,170
Pittsburgh	U.S.	604,332
Poona	India	597,562
Portland	U.S.	372,676
Pôrto Alegre	Brazil	617,629
Poznań	Poland	408,000
Praha (Prague)	Czechoslovakia	1,003,341
Pretoria	South Africa	422,590
Pusan	Korea	1,162,614
P'yŏngyang	Korea	940,000
Quezon City	Philippines	397,990
Quito	Ecuador	348,151
Rangoon	Burma	737,079
Rāwalpindi	Pakistan	340,175
Recife	Brazil	788,569
Rīga	U.S.S.R.	620,000
Rio de Janeiro	Brazil	3,223,408
Rochester	U.S.	318,611
Roma (Rome)	Italy	1,983,286
Rosario	Argentina	604,084
Rostov-na-Donu	U.S.S.R.	662,000
Rotterdam	Netherlands	711,800
Sai Gon (Saigon)	Viet-Nam	1,400,000
St. Louis	U.S.	750,026
St. Paul	U.S.	313,411
Sakai	Japan	339,863
Salvador	Brazil	630,878
San Antonio	U.S.	587,718
San Diego	U.S.	573,224
San Francisco	U.S.	740,316
San Juan	Puerto Rico	432,377
Santiago	Chile	646,731
Santo Domingo	Dom. Rep.	367,053
São Paulo	Brazil	3,164,804
Sapporo	Japan	523,839
Saratov	U.S.S.R.	631,000
Seattle	U.S.	557,087
Semarang	Indonesia	503,153
Sendai	Japan	425,272
Sevilla	Spain	442,300
's Gravenhage (The Hague)	Netherlands	603,300
Shang-hai	China	7,000,000
Shan-t'ou	China	440,000
Sheffield	U.K.	493,954
Shen-yang (Mukden)	China	3,100,000
Shih-chia-chuang	China	503,000
Shizuoka	Japan	328,819
Sholapur	India	337,583
Singapore	Singapore	1,780,000
Sofiya (Sofia)	Bulgaria	592,845
Sŏul (Seoul)	Korea	2,444,883
Stockholm	Sweden	806,903
Stuttgart	F.R.Ger.	601,115
Su-chou (Soochow)	China	633,000
Surabaja	Indonesia	1,007,945
Surakarta	Indonesia	367,626
Sverdlovsk	U.S.S.R.	853,000
Sydney	Australia	1,863,161
Taegu	Korea	678,277
T'ai-pei	Taiwan	963,640
T'ai-yüan	China	1,500,000
Tallinn (Reval)	U.S.S.R.	320,000
T'ang-shan	China	788,000
Tashkent	U.S.S.R.	1,061,000
Tbilisi (Tiflis)	U.S.S.R.	724,000
Tehrān (Teheran)	Iran	1,512,082
Tel Aviv-Yafo	Israel	386,070
Thon Buri	Thailand	403,818
T'ien-ching (Tientsin)	China	2,900,000
Tōkyō	Japan	9,683,802
Toledo	U.S.	318,003
Torino (Turin)	Italy	946,029
Toronto	Canada	657,452
Toulouse	France	330,570
Tula	U.S.S.R.	351,000
Tūnis	Tunisia	410,000
Tzu-po (Poshan)	China	1,200,000
Ufa	U.S.S.R.	651,000
Valencia	Spain	505,066
Vancouver	Canada	376,808
Varanasi (Benaras)	India	471,258
Venezia (Venice)	Italy	345,537
Victoria	Hong Kong	674,962
Vladivostok	U.S.S.R.	317,000
Volgograd (Stalingrad)	U.S.S.R.	632,000
Voronezh	U.S.S.R.	496,000
Warszawa (Warsaw)	Poland	1,136,000
Washington	U.S.	763,956
West-Berlin	F.R.Ger.	2,223,777
Wien (Vienna)	Austria	1,627,034
Wrocław (Breslau)	Poland	429,000
Wu-hsi	China	613,000
Wu-hu	China	380,000
Wu-lu-mu-ch'i	China	700,000
Wuppertal	F.R.Ger.	406,225
Yaroslavl'	U.S.S.R.	433,000
Yerevan	U.S.S.R.	558,000
Yokohama	Japan	1,375,710
Yŏngdŭngp'o-dong	Korea	316,346
Zagreb	Yugoslavia	457,000
Zaporozh'ye	U.S.S.R.	475,000
Zaragoza	Spain	326,316
Zürich	Switzerland	440,170

URBANIZED AREAS OF THE UNITED STATES

(SEE LAND USE MAP, PAGES 86-87)

Key No.	Urbanized Area	Population
1	Abilene, Tex.	91,566
2	Akron, Ohio	458,253
3	Albany, Ga.	58,353
4	Albany-Schenectady-Troy, N.Y.	455,447
5	Albuquerque, N.Mex.	241,216
6	Allentown-Bethlehem, Pa.	256,016
7	Altoona, Pa.	83,058
8	Amarillo, Tex.	137,969
9	Ann Arbor, Mich.	115,282
10	Asheville, N.C.	68,592
11	Atlanta, Ga.	768,125
12	Atlantic City, N.J.	124,902
13	Augusta, Ga.-S.C.	123,698
14	Aurora, Ill.	85,522
15	Austin, Tex.	187,157
18	Bakersfield, Calif.	141,763
19	Baltimore, Md.	1,418,948
20	Baton Rouge, La.	193,485
21	Bay City, Mich.	72,763
22	Beaumont, Tex.	119,178
23	Billings, Mont.	60,712
24	Binghamton, N.Y.	158,141
25	Birmingham, Ala.	521,330
26	Boston, Mass.	2,413,236
27	Bridgeport, Conn.	366,654
28	Brockton, Mass.	111,315
29	Buffalo, N.Y.	1,054,370
32	Canton, Ohio	213,574
33	Cedar Rapids, Iowa	105,118
34	Champaign-Urbana, Ill.	78,014
35	Charleston, S.C.	160,113
36	Charleston, W.Va.	169,500
37	Charlotte, N.C.	209,551
38	Chattanooga, Tenn.-Ga.	205,143
39	Chicago-Northwestern Indiana, Ill.-Ind.	5,959,213
40	Cincinnati, Ohio-Ky.	993,568
41	Cleveland, Ohio	1,784,991
42	Colorado Springs, Colo.	100,220
43	Columbia, S.C.	162,601
44	Columbus, Ga.-Ala.	158,382
45	Columbus, Ohio	616,743
46	Corpus Christi, Tex.	177,380
49	Dallas, Tex.	932,349
50	Dayton, Ohio	501,664
51	Decatur, Ill.	89,516
52	Denver, Colo.	803,624
53	Des Moines, Iowa	241,115
54	Detroit, Mich.	3,537,709
55	Dubuque, Iowa-Ill.	59,447
56	Duluth-Superior, Minn.-Wis.	144,763
57	Durham, N.C.	84,642
60	El Paso, Tex.	277,128
61	Erie, Pa.	177,433
62	Eugene, Oreg.	95,686
63	Evansville, Ind.	143,660
66	Fall River, Mass.-R.I.	123,951
67	Fargo-Moorhead, N.Dak.-Minn.	72,730
68	Fitchburg-Leominster, Mass.	72,347
69	Flint, Mich.	277,786
70	Fort Lauderdale-Hollywood, Fla.	319,951
71	Fort Smith, Ark.-Okla.	61,640
72	Fort Wayne, Ind.	179,571
73	Fort Worth, Tex.	502,682
74	Fresno, Calif.	213,444
77	Gadsden, Ala.	68,944
78	Galveston-Texas City, Tex.	118,482
79	Grand Rapids, Mich.	294,230
80	Great Falls, Mont.	57,629
81	Green Bay, Wis.	97,162
82	Greensboro, N.C.	123,334
83	Greenville, S.C.	126,887
86	Hamilton, Ohio	89,778
87	Harlingen-San Benito, Tex.	61,658
88	Harrisburg, Pa.	209,501
89	Hartford, Conn.	381,619
90	High Point, N.C.	66,543
91	Honolulu, Hawaii	351,336
92	Houston, Tex.	1,139,678
93	Huntington-Ashland, W.Va.-Ky.-Ohio	165,732
94	Huntsville, Ala.	74,970
97	Indianapolis, Ind.	639,340
100	Jackson, Mich.	71,412
101	Jackson, Miss.	147,480
102	Jacksonville, Fla.	372,569
103	Johnstown, Pa.	96,474
104	Joliet, Ill.	116,585
107	Kalamazoo, Mich.	115,659
108	Kansas City, Mo.-Kans.	921,121
109	Kenosha, Wis.	72,852
110	Knoxville, Tenn.	172,734
113	Lake Charles, La.	89,115
114	Lancaster, Pa.	93,855
115	Lansing, Mich.	169,325
116	Laredo, Tex.	60,678
117	Las Vegas, Nev.	89,427
118	Lawrence-Haverhill, Mass.-N.H.	166,125
119	Lawton, Okla.	61,941
120	Lewiston-Auburn, Maine	65,253
121	Lexington, Ky.	111,940
122	Lima, Ohio	62,963
123	Lincoln, Nebr.	136,220
124	Little Rock-North Little Rock, Ark.	185,017
125	Lorain-Elyria, Ohio	142,860
126	Los Angeles-Long Beach, Calif.	6,488,791
127	Louisville, Ky.-Ind.	606,659
128	Lowell, Mass.	118,547
129	Lubbock, Tex.	129,289
130	Lynchburg, Va.	59,319
133	Macon, Ga.	114,161
134	Madison, Wis.	157,814
135	Manchester, N.H.	91,698
136	Memphis, Tenn.	544,505
137	Meriden, Conn.	51,850
138	Miami, Fla.	852,705
139	Midland, Tex.	63,274
140	Milwaukee, Wis.	1,149,997
141	Minneapolis-St. Paul, Minn.	1,377,143
142	Mobile, Ala.	268,139
143	Monroe, La.	80,546
144	Montgomery, Ala.	142,893
145	Muncie, Ind.	77,504
146	Muskegon-Muskegon Heights, Mich.	95,350
149	Nashville, Tenn.	346,729
150	New Bedford, Mass.	126,657
151	New Britain, Conn.	99,894
152	New Haven, Conn.	278,794
153	New Orleans, La.	845,237
154	Newport News-Hampton, Va.	208,874
155	New York-Northeastern, N.J.	14,114,927
156	Norfolk-Portsmouth, Va.	507,825
157	Norwalk, Conn.	82,270
160	Odessa, Tex.	84,285
161	Ogden, Utah	121,927
162	Oklahoma City, Okla.	429,188
163	Omaha, Nebr.-Iowa	389,881
164	Orlando, Fla.	200,995
167	Pensacola, Fla.	128,049
168	Peoria, Ill.	181,432
169	Philadelphia, Pa.-N.J.	3,635,228
170	Phoenix, Arizona	552,043
171	Pittsburgh, Pa.	1,804,400
172	Pittsfield, Mass.	62,306
173	Pomona-Ontario, Calif.	186,547
174	Port Arthur, Tex.	116,635
175	Portland, Maine	111,701
176	Portland, Oreg.-Wash.	651,685
177	Providence-Pawtucket, R.I., Mass.	659,542
178	Provo-Orem, Utah	60,795
179	Pueblo, Colo.	103,336
182	Racine, Wis.	95,862
183	Raleigh, N.C.	93,931
184	Reading, Pa.	160,297
185	Reno, Nev.	70,189
186	Richmond, Va.	333,438
187	Roanoke, Va.	124,752
188	Rochester, N.Y.	493,402
189	Rockford, Ill.	171,681
190	Rock Island-Moline-Davenport, Ill.-Iowa	227,176
193	Sacramento, Calif.	451,920
194	Saginaw, Mich.	129,215
195	St. Joseph, Mo.-Kans.	81,187
196	St. Louis, Mo.-Ill.	1,667,693
197	St. Petersburg, Fla.	324,842
198	Salt Lake City, Utah	348,661
199	San Angelo, Tex.	58,815
200	San Antonio, Tex.	641,965
201	San Bernardino-Riverside, Calif.	377,531
202	San Diego, Calif.	836,175
203	San Francisco-Oakland, Calif.	2,430,663
204	San Jose, Calif.	602,805
205	Santa Barbara, Calif.	72,740
206	Savannah, Ga.	169,887
207	Scranton, Pa.	210,676
208	Seattle, Wash.	864,109
209	Shreveport, La.	208,583
210	Sioux City, Iowa-Nebr.-S.Dak.	97,926
211	Sioux Falls, S.Dak.	66,582
212	South Bend, Ind.-Mich.	218,933
213	Spokane, Wash.	226,938
214	Springfield, Ill.	111,403
215	Springfield, Mo.	97,224
216	Springfield, Ohio	90,157
217	Springfield-Chicopee-Holyoke, Mass.-Conn.	449,777
218	Stamford, Conn.	166,990
219	Steubenville-Weirton, Ohio-W.Va.	81,613
220	Stockton, Calif.	141,604
221	Syracuse, N.Y.	333,286
224	Tacoma, Wash.	214,930
225	Tampa, Fla.	301,790
226	Terre Haute, Ind.	81,415
227	Texarkana, Tex.-Ark.	53,420
228	Toledo, Ohio	438,283
229	Topeka, Kans.	119,500
230	Trenton, N.J.-Pa.	242,401
231	Tucson, Ariz.	227,433
232	Tulsa, Okla.	298,922
233	Tuscaloosa, Ala.	76,815
234	Tyler, Tex.	51,739
237	Utica-Rome, N.Y.	187,779
240	Waco, Tex.	116,163
241	Washington, D.C., Md.-Va.	1,808,423
242	Waterbury, Conn.	141,626
243	Waterloo, Iowa	102,827
244	West Palm Beach, Fla.	172,835
245	Wheeling, W.Va.-Ohio	98,951
246	Wichita, Kans.	292,138
247	Wichita Falls, Tex.	102,104
248	Wilkes-Barre, Pa.	233,932
249	Wilmington, Del.-N.J.	283,667
250	Winston-Salem, N.C.	128,176
251	Worcester, Mass.	225,446
254	York, Pa.	100,872
255	Youngstown-Warren, Ohio	372,748

GLOSSARY OF GEOGRAPHICAL TERMS

ANTARCTIC CIRCLE A parallel of south latitude (66° 30′) south of which the sun does not set at the December solstice nor rise at the June solstice.

ARCTIC CIRCLE A parallel of north latitude (66° 30′) north of which the sun does not set at the June solstice nor rise at the December solstice.

ATOLL A chain of coral reefs or islets, roughly circular in shape, enclosing a lagoon.

BATHYMETRIC CHART A map illustrating submarine depths and relief of the sea floor by means of lines of equal depth below sea level.

BIGHT An open, shallow bay formed by a gentle indentation of a coastline.

BUTTE (U.S.) A loose term used in the western United States to designate conspicuous and frequently isolated hills and mountains.

CONTINENTAL DIVIDE (U.S.) The ridge of the Rocky Mountains which separates the rivers draining into the Pacific from those draining into the Atlantic.

CONTINENTAL SHELF The gently sloping sea bottom bordering a continental mass, the outer edge of which drops off rapidly to the deep ocean. It is conventionally considered to extend to depths of about 600 feet or 200 meters.

COULEE (U.S.) A ravine, gorge, or stream bed formed by an intermittent flow of water.

DEGREE A unit of measurement upon the earth's surface. On all meridians and on the Equator, one degree equals 1/360th of the earth's circumference, or about 69 statute miles.

DOLDRUMS A belt of variable light winds and calms, and associated low atmospheric pressure near the Equator; the doldrums are the convergence zone of the northeast and southeast trade wind belts.

DOWNS Unforested expanses of elevated land, especially in southern England and Australia.

EQUATOR The only parallel of latitude (0°) forming a great circle of the earth, equidistant from the poles and perpendicular to the earth's axis.

FIORD A long, narrow, steep-sided inlet of the sea, generally of glacial origin.

GREAT CIRCLE Any imaginary line on the earth's surface representing the intersection of the surface of the earth with a plane passing through the earth's center. Distances measured on great circles represent the shortest surface distance between two points.

HORSE LATITUDES Belts of variable winds and calms associated with high pressure near latitudes 32° N. and 30° S.; the trade winds are on equatorial margins and the westerly winds on the polar margins of the horse latitudes.

INTERNATIONAL DATE LINE A line from pole to pole, generally following the 180th meridian, at which the calendar day changes. As one crosses the line from west to east, the date changes to the previous day; in crossing from east to west, it changes to the following day.

KÖPPEN CLIMATIC CLASSIFICATION A classification devised in the early 20th century (over a period of several years) by a German climatologist, Wladimir Köppen; it is based on distributions of vegetation types and determined through an evaluation of temperature and precipitation data.

LATITUDE Angular distance in degrees, minutes, and seconds north or south from the Equator.

LONGITUDE Angular distance in degrees, minutes, and seconds east or west from a given meridian, which by international agreement is that of Greenwich, England (Prime Meridian).

MAGNETIC POLES Arctic and Antarctic locations at which the positive and negative fields of the earth's magnetism are centered.

MAP PROJECTION A systematic development of lines representing meridians and parallels on a plane surface, either for the whole earth or a portion of it. Projections are designed to have various characteristics and none will reproduce the earth's surface accurately in all respects.

An equidistant projection is one on which a measurement shown on the map from one point (the center of the projection) to any other point is the same as on a globe of the same scale.

An equal-area projection is one on which any region shown on the map has the same area as on a globe of the same scale. This characteristic cannot be achieved without considerable distortion of shapes.

A conformal projection is one on which the shape of any small region shown on the map has the same shape as on the globe.

MAP SCALE The ratio of distance on the map to distance on the earth; expressed as a representative fraction, 1/1,000,000; as a bar scale or graphic representation; or as a statement such as 1 inch equals 16 miles.

MERIDIAN A half great circle whose ends coincide with both poles.

MESA (U.S.) A large, steep-sided hill or mountain with a tabular or flat-topped surface.

MESOTHERMAL A climatic term which denotes moderate temperatures.

MICROTHERMAL A climatic term which denotes low temperatures.

MONSOON A type of wind system in which complete or nearly complete reversal of prevailing direction occurs from season to season, caused by periodic temperature and pressure variations.

POLE (geographic) A surface terminal of the earth's axis.

RARE EARTHS Rare earths are neither rare nor earths. They are metals used in the ceramic, nuclear, and refractory industries. Many are used in combination to produce special steels for jets and rockets. All are so chemically related, however, that they are not found except with each other.

ROARING FORTIES A particularly stormy portion of the westerly wind belt in the Southern Hemisphere between 40° and 50°S. where the absence of continental barriers results in consistently strong winds throughout the year.

SOLSTICE The point at which the sun is at its farthest north or south point from the Equator. On about June 22 (the summer solstice of the Northern Hemisphere) the sun is directly overhead at the Tropic of Cancer, and on about Dec. 22 (the winter solstice of the Northern Hemisphere) the sun is directly overhead at the Tropic of Capricorn.

STANDARD TIME ZONE Any one of 24 north-south belts of the earth's surface, each approximately 15° of longitude in width and representing a time change of one hour.

THEMATIC MAP A map depicting a particular subject.

TRADE WINDS Belts of winds which blow steadily from the northeast in the Northern Hemisphere and from the southeast in the Southern Hemisphere. The trades are located between about 5° and 30°; near the Equator they are separated by the doldrums and on the polar margins they border the horse latitudes.

TROPICS Parallels of latitude 23½° N (Tropic of Cancer) and 23½° S (Tropic of Capricorn) representing the parallels at which the sun is directly overhead on the solstices.

VOLCANO A rift or vent in the earth's crust from which molten or hot rock, steam, or ashes, etc. are ejected during periods of activity. A conical form composed of ejected material may be built up around the rift or vent.

WESTERLIES Mid-latitude wind belts between approximately 35° and 55° north and south of the Equator where storminess and winds from all directions are common, but where winds from a westerly direction are most frequent.

TABLE OF CONVERSIONS

1 meter	=	3.2808 feet	1 millibar	=	0.0295 inch
1 foot	=	0.3048 meter	1 inch	=	33.895 millibars
1 kilometer	=	0.6214 mile	1 short ton	=	2000 pounds
1 mile	=	1.609 kilometers	1 metric ton	=	2204.6 pounds
1 square kilometer	=	0.386 square mile	1 long ton	=	2240 pounds
1 square mile	=	2.589 square kilometers	1 troy ounce	=	1.097 ounces avoirdupois
1 millimeter	=	0.0394 inch	1 ounce avoirdupois	=	0.911 troy ounce
1 inch	=	25.4 millimeters			

To convert °F to °C, subtract 32 from °F, multiply by 5, and divide by 9.

To convert °C to °F, multiply °C by 9, divide by 5, and add 32.

TABLE OF FOREIGN GEOGRAPHICAL TERMS

A
-á	stream
-å	river
ab	water
adası	island
adrar	mountains
aigue	water
aiguille	peak
'aın	well
ákra	cape
alb	mountain
alpen	mountain
alpi	mountains
altiplanicie	plateau
altiplano	plateau
alto	height
-älv,-en	river
-anger	bay
áno	upper
anse	bay
archipel	archipelago
archipiélago	archipelago
arkhipelag	archipelago
arquipélago	archipelago
arrecife	reef
arroyo	watercourse

B
baai	bay
bab	strait
-bach	stream
bādiyat	desert
-baek	stream
baelt	strait
bahía	bay
bahr	river
baḥr	river
bãi	bay
baía	bay
baie	bay
baja	lower
ban	village
baraji	dam
basse	lower
-beek	stream
beinn,-e	mountain
ben	mountain
bereg	coast
-berg,-e	mountain
bĭābān	desert
bir	well
-bjerg	mountain
-bodden	bay
boğazı	strait
bolsón	basin
-bong	mountain
-bratul	river branch
brazo	channel, river branch
-bre,-en	glacier,-s
bredning	bay, lagoon
bucht	bay
-bugt	bay
buhyrat	lake, marsh
bukten	bay
bulu	mountain
burn	stream
burnu	cape
burun	cape

C
cabo	cape
cachoeira	rapids
caleta	bay, cove
cao nguyen	plateau
cap	cape
capo	cape
carse	plain
çayı	stream
cerro	mountain
cêrro	mountain
chaco	plain
chaîne	range
chang	mountain
chapada	plain
chien	island
ch'ih	lake
chott	salt lake
chou	island
chute	falls
ciénaga	swamp
cima	peak
col	pass
colonia	colony
cordilheira	range
cordillera	range
costa	coast
côte	coast
cu lao	island
cumbre	peak

D
dağ,-h,-ı	mountain
dagh	mountain
dağları	mountain, range
dak	stream
-dake	mountain
-dal	valley
dalay	lake
-dan	cape
danau	lake
daqq	salt flat
dar'ya	river
daryācheh	lake, marsh
dasht	desert, plain
dawan	pass
denizi	bay, sea
desierto	desert
dhíavlos	strait
dhiórix	canal
-diep	channel
-dijk	dike
distrito	district
djebel	mountain
-do	island
dolina	valley

E
eiland	island
-elv	river
embalse	reservoir
enseada	inlet
ensenada	inlet
erg	desert
estado	state
estrecho	strait
estuario	estuary
étang	lake, lagoon

F
-farvandet	channel
fiordo	fiord
firth	estuary
-fjället	mountains
-fjärden	fiord
-fjell,-et	mountains
fjorden	fiords
-fjördhur	fiord
fleuve	river
-flói	bay
fluss	river
foci	mouths
-foss	falls
foz	falls
fuente	spring

G
gangri	mountain
-gap	cape, point
-gat	channel, sound
gebergte	mountains
gebirge	mountains
ghats	range
giang	stream
gji	bay
gobi	desert
gol	stream
göl	lake
golfe	gulf
golfo	gulf
gölü	lake, swamp
gora	mountain
góra	mountain
gorki	hills
gory	mountains
góry	mountains
-got	point
gryada	ridge
guba	bay
gunong	mountain
-gunto	archipelago
gur	peak

H
hadabat	plateau
-haehyŏp	strait
-hafen	harbor
-haff	lagoon
hai	bay, lake
hai-hsia	strait
-hals	peninsula
-halvöya	peninsula
hamada,-h	desert
hammãdat	desert
hāmūn	lake bed
-hantō	peninsula
haute	upper
hawr	lake, marsh
head	point
heide	heath
-heiya	plain
-hnúkur	mountain
ho	canal, lake, river
hoek	cape
höhe	upper
-holm	island
hon	island
horí	mountains
-horn	cape
hory	mountains
hoved	headland
hsia	strait
hsü	island
hu	lake
huk	cape

I
île	island
ilha	island
inferiore	lower
insel,-n	island,-s
isla	island
isola	island
isole	islands
isthme	isthmus
istmo	isthmus

J
jabal	mountain
-järvi	lake
-jaur	lake
-javrre	lake
jazā'ir	island
jazīrat	island
jazireh	island
jezioro	lake
-jima	island
-joki	river
-jökull	glacier

K
kaap	cape
-kaikyō	channel, strait
kajse	mountains
kampong	village
kanaal	canal
kanal	canal
kanał	canal
kansallispuisto	national park
kap	cape
-kapp	cape
kas	island
káto	lower
kënet'	lagoon
kenohan	lake
kepulauan	archipelago
khālig	bay, gulf
khowr	gulf
khrebet	range
kiang	river
kill	channel, stream
-ko	inlet, island, lake
koh	island
kokoritsukōen	national park
kólpos	gulf
körfezi	bay, gulf
kosa	cape, spit
kotal	pass
kryazh	ridge
kuan	pass
kūh,-hā	mountain, range
kul	lake
kum	desert
-kundo	archipelago
kyle	strait

L
la	pass
lac	lake
lacul	lake
lago	lake
lagoa	lake
lagôa	lake
laguna	lagoon
-lampi	lake
-län	province
law	hill
liman	inlet
límni	lake
ling	mountain
llanos	plains
loch	lake
lough	lake

M
-maa	island
maenong	river
mal	mountain
-man	bay
mar	sea
meer	lake
melkosopochnik	plain
men	channel
mer	sea
meridionali	southern
meseta	plateau
-misaki	cape
mont	mount
montagne	mountain
montañas	mountains
monte	mount
more	sea
mui	cape, point
mull	promontory
munkhafad	depression
muntele	mountain
munţii	mountains
mys	cape, point

N
-nada	gulf, sea
nádrž	reservoir
naes	point
nagor'ye	plateau, range
nahr	river
-naikai	sea
nam	river
-nes	point
ness	point
nevado	mountain
nieder	lower
-niemi	cape, peninsula
nisoi	islands
nizhniy	lower
nizina	lowland, valley
nizmennost	lowland
noord	north
nord	north
norr-	north
nørre	north
nos	cape
nour	lake
-numa	lake
nuruu	range
nusa	island
nuur	lake

O
-ō	island
-ø	island
ober-	upper
odde	point
oost	east
óri	mountains
óros	mountain
öster-	eastern
østre	eastern
ostrov,-a	island,-s
ostrów	island
otok	island
over-	upper
över-	upper
oy	island
-öy,-a	island,-s
ozero	lake

P
-pää	mountain, point
palabuhan	bay
pampas	plains
pantano	reservoir
pan-tao	peninsula
páramo	plateau
parc	park
parco	park
parque	park
pasaje	passage
paso	pass
passo	pass
pasul	pass
pegunungan	mountains, range
pellg	bay, lagoon
p'enti	basin
pereval	pass
peski	desert
pic	peak
picco	peak
pik	peak
pizzo	peak
plaine	plain
planalto	plateau
planina	range
plassen	lakes
plato	plateau
ploskogor'ye	plateau
pointe	point
pojezierze	lakeland
poluostrov	peninsula
ponta	point
portezuelo	pass
porto	inlet, port
potamós	river
presa	dam
presqu'île	peninsula
proliv	strait
przylądek	cape
puerta	port
puerto	port
pulau	island
punta	point
puy	peak

Q
qolleh	mountain
quebrada	watercourse

R
rada	roadstead
-rak	strait
rann	swamp
ras	cape
ra's	cape
râul	river
ravnina	plain
récif,-e	reef
reka	river
represa	dam
reshteh	range
-rettō	island chain
rio	river
río	river
rivier	river
riviera	coast
rivière	river
rocca	rock
rt	cape, mountain

S
sabana	plain
sahara	desert
şahrā	desert
salar	salt flat
salina	salt flat
-salmi	strait
salto	falls
-sammyaku	range
-san	mountain
-sanmaek	range
sarīr	desert
sebkra	marsh; salt lake
see	lake
selat	strait
seno	bay
serra	mountain
serranía	range
serranía	range
-seto	strait
severnyy	northern
shan	island, mountain, range
shan-k'ou	pass
shatt	stream
-shima	island
-shotō	island chain
shott	salt lake
shui-tao	channel
sierra	range
silsilese	plateau, ridge
-sjö	lake
sø	lake
söder-	south
solonchak	salt lake
sommet	summit
søndre	south
song	river
sopka	volcano
sor	salt lake
-spitze	peak
sredniy	central
stenón	strait
step'	plain
strana	region
středohoří	mountains
strelka	spit
stretto	strait
-ström	stream
stung	stream
sü	river
-suidō	strait
-sund	sound
sungei	river

T
tagh	mountain
-tal	valley
tall	hill
talsperre	reservoir
tandjung	cape, point
tangi	point
tanjong	point
tao	island, peninsula, point
tasik	lake
taung	mountain
tell	hill
teluk	bay
tepesi	mountain
-thal	valley
thale	lake
tierra	land
-tind	peak
-tjåkko	mountain
-tō	island
tonle	lake, stream
torrente	stream
-träsk	swamp
tsho	lake
tsui	cape, point
tung	mountain
tunturi,-t	mountain
tzu-chih-ch'ü	autonomous region

U
udjung	cape
-ura	lake
uula	mountains

V
-vaara	mountain
vaart	canal
-våg	bay
val	valley
valea	valley
-vall	mountain
vallen	falls
vanua	land
-varre	mountain
väster-	west
-vatn	lake
-vatten	lake
vatu	island, reef
verkhne	upper
-vesi	bay, lake
vest	west
vestre	west
-vidda	plateau
-vig	bay, lake
-vik,-en	bay
-vik	bay
vodokhranilishche	reservoir
volcán	volcano
vostochno-	eastern
vozvyshennost'	highlands
vrchovina	highlands
vrh	mountain, summit
vrŭkh	mountain
vulkan	volcano
vŭrkh	mountain

W
wādī	water course
wāḥāt	oasis
-wald	forest
-wan	bay, gulf

Y
-yama	mountain
yoma	range
yuzhnyy	southern

Z
-zaki	cape, point
zalew	swamp
zaliv	bay, gulf, inlet
-zan	mountain
zapadnyy	western
zee	lake, sea
zemlya	land
zuid	south

ABBREVIATIONS

A

a. arroyo
Aber. Aberdeen
A.C.T. Australian Capital Territory
a.d. an der
admin. administration
Adm. Is. Admiralty Islands
Af. Africa, African
Afghan. Afghanistan
Ags. Aguascalientes
A-h. An-hui
aig. aiguille
Ala. Alabama
Alag. Alagoas
Alb. Albania
Alg. Algeria
Alta. Alberta
Amaz. Amazonas
Amer. American
Ang. Angola
Ant. Antarctic, Antarctica, Antrim
A.P. Andhra Pradesh
approx. approximate
arch. archipelago, archipiélago
Arg. Argentina
Ariz. Arizona
Ark. Arkansas
arkh. arkhipelag
Arm. Armyanskaya
arq. arquipélago
Atl. Oc. Atlantic Ocean
Aust. Austria
Austl. Australia, Australian
auton. autonomous
Az. Azerbaydzhanskaya

B

b. bach, bahía, baía, baie
Bad.-Württ. Baden-Württemberg
Bah. Is. Bahama Islands
Bahr. Bahrain
Barb. Barbados
Bay. Bayern
Bel. Belorusskaya
Belg. Belgium
Berm. Bermuda
B.-H. Bosna i Hercegovina
Bism.Arch. Bismarck Archipelago
Bol. Bolivia
bol'. bol'shoy
Bon. Bonaire
bor. borough
Bots. Botswana
Br. British
Braz. Brazil
Br. Col. British Columbia
Brem. Bremen
Br. Hond. British Honduras
Bulg. Bulgaria

C

c. cabo, cap, cape, capo
cach. cachoeira
Calif. California
Cam. Cameroon
Camb. Cambodia
Camp. Campeche
Can. Canada
can. canal
Can.Is. Canary Islands
cap. capital
C.A.R. Central African Republic
Car.Is. Caroline Islands
cem. cemetery
cen. center
cent. central
Cey. Ceylon
cga. ciénaga
c.h. court house
ch. church
Chag.Arch. Chagos Archipelago
chan. channel
Chan.Is. Channel Islands
chap. chapada
Ch-ch. Che-chiang
Ch-hai Ch'ing-hai
Ch-hsi Chiang-hsi
Chih. Chihuahua
Chis. Chiapas
Ch-l. Chi-lin
cm. centimeters
Cnel. Coronel
co. cerro, county
Coah. Coahuila
Col. Colombia
col. college, colonia
Colo. Colorado
comm. commune
Congo Congo, Republic of the
Conn. Connecticut
const. construction
cor.,-s. corner,-s
cord. cordilheira, cordillera
C.R. Costa Rica
cr. creek
Crna G. Crna Gora
ctry. country
Cur. Curaçao
Cyp. Cyprus
C.Z. Canal Zone
Czech. Czechoslovakia

D

Dahom. Dahomey
D.C. District of Columbia
Del. Delaware
Den. Denmark
D'Entre.Is. D'Entrecasteaux Islands
dep. depot
dept. department, departamento
des. desert, désert, desierto
D.F. Distrito Federal
Dgo. Durango
dist. district, distrito
div. division
dj. djebel
dom. dominion
Dom.Rep. Dominican Republic
D.R. Congo Democratic Republic of the Congo
Du. Dutch

E

E. Estonskaya
e. east, eastern
Ec. Ecuador
edo. estado
ég. étang
el. elevation
El Salv. El Salvador
Eng. England
ens. enseada, ensenada
entr. entrance
eo. estero
Equat.Guin. Equatorial Guinea
Esp.Sto. Espírito Santo
estuo. estuario
Eth. Ethiopia
Eur. Europe, European

F

F. Fahrenheit
Falk.Is. Falkland Islands
F-ch. Fu-chien
fdo. fiordo
Fern. Pc Fernando Po
Fin. Finland
fj. -fjärden, fjord
fk. fork
Fla. Florida
for. forest
Fr. France, French
F.R.Ger. Federal Republic of Germany
Fr. Guiana French Guiana
Fr. Poly. French Polynesia
Fr. Som French Somaliland
ft. feet, fort
ftn. fortin
fy. ferry

G

g. golfo, gora, góra, guba, gulf, gunong
Ga. Georgia
Galap. Is. Galápagos Islands
Gba. Guanabara
gde. grande
geb. gebergte, gebirge
geog. geographic
Ger. D.R. German Democratic Republic
Gib. Gibraltar
Gilb.Is. Gilbert Islands
gl. glacier
govt. government
Gr. Greece
gr. grosse, grove
Gral. General
Greenl. Greenland
Gro. Grenada
Gren.Is. Grenadine Islands
Gro. Guerrero
Gruz. Gruzinskaya
gt. great, groot
Gto. Guanajuato
Guad. Guadeloupe
Guadal. Guadalcanal
Guat. Guatemala
Guin. Guinea
Guj. Gujarat

H

Hamb. Hamburg
hbr. harbor, harbour
hd. head
Hess. Hessen
Hgo. Hidalgo
high. highlands
hist. historical
H.K. Hong Kong
H-l-ch. Hai-lung-chiang
Ho-n. Ho-nan
Hond. Honduras
Ho-p. Ho-pei
H.P. Himachal Pradesh
Hrva. Hrvatska
Hs-ch. Hsin-chiang-wei-wu-erh
Hs-ts. Hsi-tsang
hte. haute
hts. heights
Hu-n. Hu-nan
Hung. Hungary
Hu-p. Hu-pei

I

i. ilha, isla, island, isle, isola
ī. île
Ice. Iceland
Ill. Illinois
im. imeni
in. inches
incl. including, inclusive
Ind. Indiana
Ind.Oc. Indian Ocean
Indon. Indonesia
inf. inferiore
int. international
Ire. Ireland
is. islands, islas
īs. îles
Isr. Israel
It. Italy
Iv.Coast Ivory Coast

J

j. jabal
Jal. Jalisco
Jam. Jamaica
J. & K. Jammu and Kashmir
Jap. Japan
jez. jezero, jezioro
Jor. Jordan
jonc. jonction
junc. junction

K

k. kosa
kan. kanaal, kanal, kanal
Kans. Kansas
Kaz. Kazakhskaya
K-ch. Kuei-chou
kep. kepulauan
Ker. Kerala
Kerm.Is. Kermadec Islands
kg. kampong
khr. khrebet
K-hsi Kuang-hsi-chuang-tsu
Kir. Kirgizskaya
km. kilometers
Kor. Korea
K-su Kan-su
K-t. Kuang-tung
Ky. Kentucky

L

l. lac, lacul, lago, lagôa, lake, límni, loch, lough
La. Louisiana
Lac.Is. Laccadive Islands
Ladr.Is. Ladrone Islands
lag. laguna
Lat. Latviyskaya
lat. latitude
ldg. landing
Leb. Lebanon
Leew.Is. Leeward Islands
Li. Litovskaya
Lib. Liberia
Liecht. Liechtenstein
lit. little
L-n. Liao-ning
long. longitude
Loy.Is. Loyalty Islands
Lux. Luxembourg

M

m. meters, mys
Macq.Is. Macquarie Islands
Mad. Madras
Mah. Maharashtra
Mak. Makedonija
mal. malo, malyy
Malag.Rep. Malagasy Republic
Malay. Malaysia
Mald.Is. Maldive Islands
Man. Manitoba
mar. maritime
Mar.Is. Mariana Islands
Marq.Is. Marquesas Islands
Marsh.Is. Marshall Islands
Mart. Martinique
Mass. Massachusetts
Maur. Mauritania
Maurit. Mauritius
max. maximum
Md. Maryland
Me. Maine
mem. memorial
Mex. Mexico
Mhão. Maranhão
mi. miles
Mich. Michigan
Micho. Michoacán
mid. middle
mil. military
min. minimum
Minn. Minnesota
Miss. Mississippi
mñas. montañas
Mo. Missouri
Mo.Gro. Mato Grosso
Mol. Moldavskaya
Mon. Monaco
mon. monument
Mong. Mongolia
Mont. Montana
Mor. Morocco
Mors. Morelos
Moz. Mozambique
M.P. Madhya Pradesh
Ms.Gs. Minas Gerais
mt. mont, mount
mte. monte
mts. mountains
mun. municipal, municipio
Mys. Mysore

N

n. north, northern
nac. nacional
nag. nagor'ye
N.Amer. North America
nat. national
naut. nautical
Nay. Nayarit
N.B. New Brunswick
N.C. North Carolina
N.Caled. New Caledonia
N-D Notre-Dame
N.Dak. North Dakota
Ndrsachs. Niedersachsen
Nebr. Nebraska
Neth. Netherlands
Neth.Ant. Netherlands Antilles
Nev. Nevada
nev. nevado
New Br. New Britain
Newf. Newfoundland
New Ga. New Georgia
New Hebr. New Hebrides
N.H. New Hampshire
Nic. Nicaragua
Nic.Is. Nicobar Islands
N.Ire. Northern Ireland
nizh. nizhniy
N.J. New Jersey
N.L. Nuevo León
N.Mex. New Mexico
N-m-k. Nei-meng-ku
no. number
Nor. Norway
nov. novyy
nr. nørre
Nrh.-Wf. Nordrhein-Westfalen
N.S. Nova Scotia
N.S.W. New South Wales
N.Terr. Northern Territory
n.w. northwest, northwestern
N.W.T. Northwest Territories
N.Y. New York
N.Z. New Zealand

O

o. ostrov, ouest
Oax. Oaxaca
oc. ocean
O.Fr.St. Orange Free State
Okla. Oklahoma
Ont. Ontario
ør. østre
Oreg. Oregon
Ori. Orissa
o-va. ostrova
oz. ozero

P

p. picco, pico, pulau, punta, punto
Pa. Pennsylvania
Pac.Oc. Pacific Ocean
Pak. Pakistan
Pan. Panama
pan. pantano
par. parish
Para. Paraguay
P-ch. Pei-ching
Pbco. Pernambuco
pd. pond
pds. ponds
peg. pegunungan
P.E.I. Prince Edward Island
pen. peninsula, península
pén. péninsule
per. pereval
Pesc. Pescadores
Phil. Philippines
Pitc.I. Pitcairn Island
pje. pasaje
pk. park, peak
pl. place
plat. plateau
plo. portezuelo
plos. ploskogor'ye
p.o. post office
Pol. Poland
pop. population
Port. Portugal, Portuguese
Port.Guin. Portuguese Guinea
Port.Timor Portuguese Timor
p-ov. poluostrov
P.R. Puerto Rico
Prib.Is. Pribilov Islands
prol. proliv
prot. protectorate
Prot. of S.Ar. Protectorate of South Arabia
prov. province, provincial
pta. puerta
pte. pointe
Pue. Puebla
Pun. Punjab

Q

Qué. Québec
queb. quebrada
Qnsld. Queensland
Q.R. Quintana Roo
Qro. Querétaro

R

R. Russiskaya
r. rio, río, river, rivière
ra. range
Raj. Rajasthan
rav. ravine
R.Bnco. Rio Branco
R. de J. Rio de Janeiro
reg. region
rep. republic
res. reservoir
R.G. do N. Rio Grande do Norte
R.G. do S. Rio Grande do Sul
Rhod. Rhodesia
R.I. Rhode Island
Ronda. Rondônia
Rum. Rumania

S

S. San
s. sopka, south, southern, sungei, sur
sa. serra, sierra
Saar. Saarland
sab. sabana
S.Af. South Africa
Sakish Is. Sakishima Islands
Sa. Leone Sierra Leone
S.Amer. South America
Sask. Saskatchewan
Saudi Ar. Saudi Arabia
S.Austl. South Australia
S.C. South Carolina
S-ch. Ssu-ch'uan
Schl.-Hol. Schleswig-Holstein
Scot. Scotland
sd. sound, sund
S.Dak. South Dakota
s.e. southeast, southeastern
Sen. Senegal
sev. severnyy
Seych. Seychelles
Sgpe. Sergipe
sh. shire
Sh-ha. Shang-hai
shls. shoals
Sin. Sinaloa
S.L.P. San Luis Potosí
S.Mar. San Marino
Slvja. Slovenia
snía. serranía
Soc.Is. Society Islands
Sol.Is. Solomon Islands
Som.Rep. Somali Republic
Son. Sonora
S.Ork.Is. South Orkney Islands
S.P. São Paulo
Sp. Spain, Spanish
Spits. Spitsbergen
spr.,-s. spring,-s
sq. square
sr. sondre
Srba. Srbija
sred. sredniy
S.Sand.Is. South Sandwich Islands
S.Shet.Is. South Shetland Islands
S.F.S.R. Sovetskaya Federativnaya Sotsialisticheskaya Respublika
S.S.R. Sovetskaya Sotsialisticheskaya Respublika
St. Saint, Sankt, Sint
St- Saint
st. state
Sta. Santa
sta. station
Sta.Ctina. Santa Catarina
stby. storby
Ste- sainte
Stew.Is. Stewart Islands
Sto. Santo
str. strait, stretto
St.Vinc. St. Vincent
Sur. Surinam
s.w. southwest, southwestern
S.W.Af. South-West Africa
Swazi. Swaziland
Swed. Sweden
Switz. Switzerland
Syr. Syria

T

T. Tadzhikskaya
Tab. Tabasco
Tam. Tamaulipas
Tamb.Is. Tambelan Islands
Tanz. Tanzania
Tasm. Tasmania
temp. temperature
Tenn. Tennessee
ter. terrace
terr. territory
Tex. Texas
tg. tandjung
Thai. Thailand
tk. teluk
Tlax. Tlaxcala
Tob. Tobago
Treas.Is. Treasury Islands
Trin. Trinidad
Trip. Tripura
Trist. da Cunha Tristan da Cunha
Trobr.Is. Trobriand Islands
Tr. States Trucial States
tr.terr. trust territory
Tua.Is. Tuamotu Islands
Tun. Tunisia
Turk. Turkey, Turkmenskaya
Tvaal. Transvaal
twp. township

U

U.A.R. United Arab Republic
ug. udjung
Uga. Uganda
U.K. United Kingdom
Ukr. Ukrainskaya
U.N. United Nations
univ. university
U.P. Uttar Pradesh
Urug. Uruguay
U.S. United States
U.S.S.R. Union of Soviet Socialist Republics
Uzb. Uzbekskaya

V

v. volcán, volcano, von
Va. Virginia
va. vila, villa
val. vale, valle, vallée, valley
Vat. City Vatican City
vdkhr. vodkhranilischche
Ven. Venezuela
Ver.C. Veracruz
verkh. verkhne, verkhniy
V.I. Virgin Islands
Vict. Victoria
Viet. Viet-Nam
vil. village
vlk. vulkan
vol. volcán, volcano
Vol.Is. Volcano Islands
voz. vozyshennost'
vr. vestre
Vt. Vermont

W

w. west, western
Wash. Washington
W. Austl. Western Australia
W.B. West Bengal
W.I. West Indies
Wind.Is. Windward Islands
Wis. Wisconsin
W.Va. West Virginia
Wyo. Wyoming

Y

Y-n. Yün-nan
Yuc. Yucatán
Yug. Yugoslavia
yuzh. yuzhnyy

Z

Zac. Zacatecas
zal. zaliv
zap. zapadnyy

INDEX

CONTENT

The following index, containing some 105,000 entries, includes the names of all political entities, populated places, and physical and cultural features appearing on the map pages. A majority of the names are in the forms recommended by the United States Board on Geographic Names; others have been taken from official maps and statistics. In addition the index includes, by cross-reference, many alternate Anglicized forms and conventional historical equivalents.

RULES FOR ALPHABETIZING

A strict English order of the alphabet has been followed, disregarding accents, diacritical marks, and foreign alphabet characters.

Where abbreviations form parts of names they are alphabetized as if they were fully spelled out.

Where prepositions and/or articles form integral parts of a name, the name appears in its normal order, alphabetized to the preposition or article. For example: À la Truite, Aux Renards, La Guaira, The Dalles.

Names beginning with "Mc" or "Mac" are alphabetized without regard to the form of the prefix. For example: Macarthur, McArthur, MacKay, McKay, Mackenzie, McKenzie.

French and English names of saints are alphabetized to the Christian name, regardless of gender. For example: St-Basile, Ste-Béatrix, St. Bees, St. Catherine.

Names of river tributaries, such as North Fork or South Branch, are generally not indexed.
Where the name of a physical feature contains a generic, the specific portion of the name appears first. For example: Katahdin, Mt ; Mexico, Gulf of; May, C. (but "Cape May" as a town name).

When names recur in identical form, index priority is in alphabetical order by countries. Where locations are given by references to political subdivisions, the alphabetical order of the subdivisions within a country is followed.

FORM OF INDEX ENTRIES

All entry lines for political entities, populated places, and cultural features are set in upright type. All entry lines for physical features are set in italic type, except for the page numbers and index coordinates. If the nature of a feature cannot readily be recognized by its name, the name is followed by an abbreviation indicating its general category.

Latest available census figures or official population estimates are given. Figures followed by (*) represent official estimates; those followed by (T) are township populations. Except for the United States, populations have been omitted for places of under 1,000 population.

INDEX COORDINATES

The page number and map index coordinates are shown at the end of each entry. All features are indexed to the page upon which they are best portrayed. For easy reference, the page number is shown in bold type. Index coordinates having small letters are references to special maps of congested areas. Where a single number follows the page entry it refers to a special map bearing the number. A page number followed only by the symbol (·) refers to the relief map on that page.

SUPPLEMENTARY INDEX REFERENCE

In using the atlas, one will find indispensable the Table of Foreign Geographical Terms, on page 187, and the Table of Abbreviations, on page 188.

190 · Aach—Ahrensbök

A

Aach, F.R.Ger., 1,117 118 B5
Aachen, F.R.Ger., 152,075 118 A3
Aadorf, Switz., 2,258 124 C1
Aalborg, Den., 85,800 121 B3
Aalburg, Neth. 115 c7
Aalen, F.R.Ger., 29,360 118 B4
Aalsmeer, Neth., 12,700 115 C2
Aalst, Belg., 44,478 115 C4
Aalst, Neth., 4,400 115 D3
Aalten, Neth., 8,100 115 E3
Aalter, Belg., 7,555 115 B3
Äänekoski, Fin. 120 F3
Aar, r., F.R.Ger. 119 E4
Aarau, Switz., 17,045 124 C1
Aarberg, Switz., 2,355 124 B1
Aarburg, Switz., 5,303 124 B1
Aardenburg, Neth. 115 B3
Aare, r., Switz. 124 B2
Aargub, Sp. Sah. 160 B4
Aarschot, Belg., 11,923 115 C4
Aarwangen, Switz., 2,572 124 B1
Aasu, Tutuila 177 39
Aavasaksa, Fin. 120 F2
Aba, D.R.Congo, 3,715 164 E1
Aba, Jap., 3,555 155 n19
Aba, Nigeria, 66,455 162 F5
Abacaxis, r., Braz. 102 E3
Ābādān, Iran, 226,083 143 D2
Ābādeh, Iran, 8,192 143 E2
Abadla, Alg., 7,367 160 D2
Abaeté, Braz., 7,988 103 G5
Abaetetuba, Braz., 11,196 103 G2
Abaiang, atoll, Gilb. Is. 175 10
Abaji, Nigeria 162 g7
Abajo Pk., Utah 78 D3
Abakan, U.S.S.R., 62,000 134 J4
Abakan, r., U.S.S.R. 134 J4
Abakanskiy Khr., U.S.S.R. 134 H4
Abala, Congo 164 B2
Abalos, Punta, Cuba 96 a1
Abancay, Peru, 9,083 104 C5
Abano Terme, It., 10,385 122 e5
Abarqū, Iran, 6,268 143 E2
Abarr, Colo. 79 D2
Abashiri, Jap., 44,052 155 L7
Abashiri-wan, Jap. 155 L7
Abasolo, Mex. 93 F3
Abatskoye, U.S.S.R. 137 n11
Abau, Terr. Papua 174 f3
Abaucourt, Fr. 116 b9
Abāy, r., Eth. 163 L4
Abaya, L., Eth. 163 L4
Abaza, U.S.S.R., 11,500 134 J4
Abbah Quşūr, Tun., 4,102 160 f6
Abbaye, Pt., Mich. 66 E2
Abbé, L., Eth.-Fr. Som. 163 L4
Abbekås, Swed. 121 F5
Abbeville, Fr., 22,816 117 D1
Abbeville, Ala., 2,524 64 D4
Abbeville, Ga., 872 64 F3
Abbeville, La., 10,414 73 C8
Abbeville, Miss. 73 F3
Abbeville, co., S.C., 21,417 63 B3
Abbeville, S.C., 5,436 63 B3
Abbey, Sask., Can. 43 B5
Abbeycwmhir, U.K. 114 B6
Abbeyfeale, Ire. 113 B5
Abbeyleix, Ire. 113 C5
Abbiategrasso, It., 20,531 123 B2
Abbots Bromley, U.K., 1,188 114 E5
Abbotsford, Br. Col., Can. 42 G4
Abbotsford, U.K. 112 e8
Abbotsford, Wis., 1,171 66 C4
Abbots Langley, U.K., 18,157 114 H7
Abbott, Miss. 73 G4
Abbott, N. Mex. 79 C3
Abbott, Tex., 289 77 P4
Abbottābād, Pak., 31,036 145 D2
Abbott Butte, Oreg. 80 B4
Abbottsburg, N.C. 63 F3
Abbottsford, Mich. 67 L5
Abbottstown, Pa., 561 60 H6
Abbot Village, Me. 55 C3
Abbyville, Kans., 118 75 G6
Abcoude, Neth. 115 b6
'Abd al Kūrī, i., S. Arab. 163 N3
Abdulino, U.S.S.R., 28,000 134 E4
Abéché, Chad, 8,000* 163 H3
Abejorral, Col. 100 C5
Abel Tasman Nat. Pk., N.Z. 175 g6
Abemama, atoll, Gilb. Is. 175 10
Abemarre, Indon. 149 L4
Abengourou, Iv. Coast, 17,100 162 D4
Abenheim, F.R.Ger., 2,379 119 E5
Åbenrå, Den., 14,219 121 B5
Abensberg, F.R.Ger., 4,677 118 C4
Abeokuta, Nigeria, 97,963 162 E4
Aberayron, U.K., 1,209 113 D5
Abercarn, U.K., 19,224 114 B7
Aberchirder, U.K. 112 E3
Abercorn, Zamb., 1,652 164 E3
Aberdare, U.K., 39,155 113 E6
Aberdare Nat. Pk., Kenya 165 h14
Aberdaron, U.K., 1,161 113 D5
Aberdeen, Sask., Can. 43 C4
Aberdeen, H.K., 16,690 152 b6
Aberdeen, S.Af., 4,647 164 C7
Aberdeen, co., U.K., 298,503 112 E3
Aberdeen, U.K., 162,125 112 F3
Aberdeen, Idaho, 1,484 81 C4
Aberdeen, Ind. 70 D4
Aberdeen, Md., 9,679 62 H3
Aberdeen, Miss., 6,450 73 G4
Aberdeen, N.C., 1,531 63 E2
Aberdeen, Ohio, 774 70 F4
Aberdeen, S. Dak., 23,073 74 C3
Aberdeen, Wash., 18,741 80 B2
Aberdeen L., N.W.T., Can. 40 K5
Aberdour, U.K. 112 d7
Aberdovey, U.K., 1,112 113 D5
Aberedw, U.K. 114 B6
Aberfeldy, U.K., 1,469 112 D3
Aberfoyle, Ont., Can. 46 b14
Aberfoyle, U.K. 112 b7
Abergavenny, U.K., 9,624 113 E6
Abergele, U.K., 7,996 114 A4
Aberlady, U.K. 112 e7
Aberlour, U.K. 112 E3
Abernant, Ala. 64 B2
Abernathy, Tex., 2,491 77 N3
Abernethy, Sask., Can. 43 D5
Abernethy, U.K. 112 d7
Aberporth, U.K., 1,304 113 D5
Abertillery, U.K., 25,146 114 B7
Abert, L., Oreg. 80 C4
Aberuthven, U.K. 112 c7
Aberystwyth, U.K., 10,427 113 D5
Abhā, Saudi Ar. 143 C5
Abhar, Iran, 9,634 143 D1
Abi Addi, Eth. 163 L3
Abidjan, Iv. Coast, 212,000 162 D5
Abie, Nebr., 117 75 J2
Āb-i-Istāda, l., Afghan. 144 C2
Abiko, Jap., 24,918 155 n19
Abild, Den., 1,172 121 A6
Abild, Swed. 121 E4
Abilene, Kans., 6,746 75 H5
Abilene, Tex., 90,368 77 O3
Abingdon, Ont., Can. 46 c15
Abingdon, U.K., 14,287 113 F6
Abingdon, Ill., 3,469 68 B3
Abingdon, Md. 62 H3
Abingdon, Va., 4,758 62 C6
Abington (part of Pomfret), Conn. 56 H5
Abington, Mass., 10,607(T) 57 N4
Abington, Pa., 8,000* 60 f11
Abino, Pt., Ont., Can. 58 i19
Āb-i-Panja, r., Afghan-U.S.S.R. 134 F6
Abiquiu, N. Mex. 79 B3
Abisko, Swed. 120 D1
Abita Springs, La., 655 73 E7
Abitau, r., N.W.T.-Sask., Can. 43 B1
Abitibi, L., Ont.-Que., Can. 44 H5
Abitibi, r., Ont., Can. 44 G5
Ableiges, Fr. 116 f10
Ablis, Fr., 1.034 117 D2
Åbo = Turku
Abo, N. Mex. 79 B4
Abohar, India, 46,863 145 E3
Aboisso, Iv. Coast, 3,310 162 b9
Aboite, Ind. 70 D1
Abomey, Dahom., 23,311 162 E4
Abomey-Calavi, Dahom., 4,000 162 e8
Abondance, Fr., 1,273 117 G3
Abong Mbang, Cam., 2,000* 162 G5
Abonnema, Nigeria, 12,756 162 g9
Abony, Hung., 16,273 126 D3
Aborlan, Phil., 153 A3
Aboshi, Jap. 154 f15
Abosso, Ghana 162 c9
Abou Deïa, Chad 163 H4
Aboyne, U.K. 112 E3
Abra, r., Phil. 153 b5
Abraão, Braz., 1,255 103 d18
Abraham, Utah 78 B2
Abraham Bay, Bah. Is. 95 D2
Abraham Lincoln Nat. Hist. Site, Ky. 71 F4
Abraham, Mt., Me. 55 B4
Abraham, Mt., Vt. 54 B3
Abram, U.K., 6,017 114 C3
Abrams, Wis. 66 E4
Abrantes, Port., 8,172 122 A3
Abra Pampa, Arg., 2,566 105 B2
Abrau-Dyurso, U.S.S.R., 3,400 136 E4
Abrego, Col. 100 D3
Abreojos, P., Mex. 92 B2
Abreschviller, Fr., 1,512 116 d9
Abreus, Cuba, 1,682 96 c1
'Abrī, Sudan 163 K2
Abrigada, Port., 3,184 122 k9
Abrud, Rum., 4,411 128 D1
Absaroka Ra., Mont.-Wyo. 81 •
Absarokee, Mont. 81 E3
Absdorf, Aust., 1,351 124 M5
Absecon, N.J., 4,320 61 B5
Abtenau, Aust., 4,119 124 K6
Abu, Jap. 154 f16
Abu, Ryukyu Is. 154 b10
Abu, Mt., India 145 D4
Abū al Khaşīb, Iraq, 11,245 143 D2
Abū 'Arīsh, Saudi Ar. 143 C5
Abū Ḩadrīyah, Saudi Ar. 143 D3
Abū Ḩamad, Sudan 163 K2
Abū Ḩummuş, U.A.R. 161 i7
Abuja, Nigeria 162 F4
Abū Kamāl, Syr., 5,996 142 E3
Abukuma, r., Jap. 155 G3
Abulug, Phil., 1,920 153 B1
Abū Madd, Ra's, pt., Saudi Ar. 143 B4
Abumombazi, D.R.Congo 164 C1
Abunã, Braz. 102 C3
Abunã, r., Bol.-Braz. 102 C3
Abū Qīr, U.A.R. 161 i7
Abū Qurqāş, U.A.R. 161 K3
Abu Road, India, 17,728 145 D4
Abū Shajarah, Ra's, Sudan 163 L2
Abu Simbel = Abū Sunbul
Abū Sunbul, ruins, U.A.R. 161 K4
Abuta, Jap., 9,966 155 J8
Abut Head, N.Z. 175 f6
Abū Tīj, U.A.R. 161 K3
Abū Zabad, Sudan 163 J3
Abū Ẓaby, Tr. States 143 E4
Abū Zanīmah, U.A.R., 2,593 161 K3
Abwong, Sudan 163 K4
Aby, Swed. 120 d9
Aby, Lag., Iv. Coast 162 b9
Abyad, Ar Ra's al, Tun. 160 f5
Abydos, ruins, U.A.R. 161 K3
Abyssinia = Ethiopia
Abyy, U.S.S.R. 135 O3
Acacías, Col. 100 D6
Academy, S. Dak. 74 C4
Acadia, parish, La., 49,931 73 C7
Acadia Nat. Pk., Me. 55 D4
Acajete, Mex., 3,300 93 f10
Acajutla, El Salv., 3,659 94 d10
Acala, Mex., 4,577 93 G5
Acámbaro, Mex., 26,011 93 E4
Acambay, Mex., 1,570 93 e10
Acandí, Col. 100 B3
Acaponeta, Mex., 8,453 92 D3
Acaponeta, R. de, Mex. 92 D3
Acapulco, Mex., 48,846 93 E5
Acará, Braz., 1,385 103 G2
Acaraigebergte, Guyana 101 M7
Acaraú, Braz., 3,042 103 J2
Acari, Braz., 2,878 103 a14
Acarí, Peru, 1,430 104 C5
Acarigua, Ven., 31,737 100 F3
Acatepec, Mex. 93 f9
Acatic, Mex., 2,694 93 b9
Acatitlán, Méx., Mex., 1,303 93 d11
Acatitlán, Qro., Mex. 93 e8
Acatlán, Gro., Mex., 3,366 93 F5
Acatlán, Pue., Mex., 7,086 93 F4
Acatlipa, Mex., 2,507 93 e11
Acaxochitlán, Mex., 3,538 93 f9
Acayucan, Mex., 12,854 93 G5
Acchilla, Bol. 102 c12
Accident, Md., 237 62 E3
Accomac, Va., 414 62 J5
Accomack, co., Va., 30,635 62 J5
Accord (part of Norwell and Hingham), Mass. 57 N4
Accotink, Va. 62 G4
Accra, Ghana, 491,060 162 D5
Accrington, U.K., 40,987 114 D3
Acebal, Arg., 3,500* 105 a11
Aceguá, Urug. 105 E4
Acequia, Idaho, 107 81 C4
Acerra, It., 26,922 123 c10
Acevedo, Arg., 7,480 105 a11
Ach, Aust. 124 J5
Achacachi, Bol., 27,622 102 C5
Achaguas, Ven., 1,714 100 F4
Achao, Chile 105 A6
Achchik Köl, l., China 150 C3
Achen, r., Aust.-F.R.Ger. 124 J6
A-ch'eng, China 151 E1
Achères, Fr., 5,390 116 g11
Achern, F.R.Ger., 5,682 119 E7
Achí, Col. 100 C3
Achicourt, Fr., 5,190 117 E1
Achigan, r., Qué., Can. 47 L3
Achill, Ire. 113 B5
Achille, Okla., 294 76 G4
Achilles, Kans. 75 E4
Achilles, Va. 62 H5
Achill Head, Ire. 113 A5
Achill I., Ire. 113 A5
Achim, F.R.Ger., 7,705 118 B2
Achimota, Ghana 162 c9
Achinsk, U.S.S.R., 57,000 134 H4
Achiotepec, Mex., 1,728 93 f9
Achisay, U.S.S.R., 9,600 134 F5
Achi-Su, U.S.S.R. 137 c1
Achit, U.S.S.R. 137 i8
Achita Nuur, Mong. 150 C1
Achnasheen, U.K. 112 D3
Achocalla, Bol., 5,603 102 a10
A'Chralaig, mtn., U.K. 112 D3
Acı Göl, Turk. 142 B2
Acilia, It., 7,500* 123 a8
Acireale, It., 43,313 123 E6
Acîş, Rum. 128 D1
Ackerly, Tex. 77 N3
Ackerman, Miss., 1,382 73 F4
Ackerville, Wis. 66 c10
Ackia Battleground Nat. Mon., Miss. 73 G3
Ackley, Iowa, 1,731 72 D2
Acklins I., Bah. Is. 95 D2
Ackworth, U.K., 4,360 114 F3
Acme, Alta., Can. 42 K3
Acme, La. 73 D6
Acme, Mich. 67 H4
Acme, Okla. 76 E3
Acme, Wash. 80 B1
Acme, W.Va. 62 C4
Acoaxet (part of Westport), Mass. 57 M6
Acobamba, Peru, 2,070 104 C5
Acomita, N. Mex. 79 B4
Aconcagua, Co., Arg. 105 B4
Aconcagua, r., Chile 104 f12
Aconchi, Mex., 1,084 92 C2
Acopinalco, Mex., 1,254 93 f10
Acora, Peru, 1,105 104 D5
Açores = Azores
Acoria, Peru, 1,031 104 C5
Acorizal, Braz. 103 E5
Acosta, Pa. 60 D5
Acostambo, Peru, 1,358 104 C5
Acoyapa, Nic., 1,699 94 E5
Acquanegra sul Chiese, It., 4,119 122 d5
Acquaviva, S. Mar. 123 e11
Acqui, It., 18,395 123 B2
Acra, N.Y. 59 M7
Acraman, L., Austl. 172 E4
Acre, terr., Braz., 160,208 102 B3
Acre, Isr. = 'Akko
Acre, r., Braz. 102 C4
Acree, Ga. 64 F4
Acres, Kans. 75 F6
Acri, It., 22,303 123 F5
Ács, Hung., 8,508 126 C3
Actaeon, Mt., St. Helena 109 7
Actéon, Groupe, is., Tuam. Arch. 171 J6
Acteopan, Mex., 1,324 93 f11
Acton, Ont., Can., 4,120 46 D5
Acton, London, U.K. 114 H8
Acton, Ala. 64 c8
Acton, Calif. 83 h15
Acton, Me. 55 B5
Acton, Mass., 7,238(T) 57 L3
Acton, Tex. 76 d10
Acton Vale, Qué., Can., 3,940 47 M3
Actopan, Mex., 7,581 93 F4
Açu = Piranhas
Acuautla, Mex., 1,349 93 f10
Acuitzio, Mex., 3,436 93 c10
Acul du Nord, Haiti, 1,338 96 k6
Acultzingo, Mex., 1,742 93 F4
Acuña, Mex., 20,204 93 E2
Acuracay, Peru 104 C3
Acure, r., Ven. 101 K4
Acurigua, Ven. 100 F2
Acushnet, Mass., 5,755(T) 57 N6
Acushnet, r., Mass. 57 N6
Acutzilapan, Mex., 3,055 93 e10
Acworth, Ga., 2,359 64 E1
Acworth, N.H. 54 C5
Acy-en-Multien, Fr. 116 k10
Ada, Ghana 162 d9
Ada, Ryukyu Is. 154 b10
Ada, co., Idaho, 93,460 81 A4
Ada, Kans. 75 H4
Ada, Mich. 67 H6
Ada, Minn., 2,064 74 D2
Ada, Ohio, 3,918 70 F2
Ada, Okla., 14,347 76 G3
Ada, Yug., 10,000* 125 E2
Adacao, Guam 176 24
Adair, Ill. 68 B3
Adair, co., Iowa, 10,893 72 C3
Adair, Iowa, 742 72 C3
Adair, co., Ky., 14,699 71 F4
Adair, Mich. 67 L6
Adair, co., Mo., 20,105 72 E4
Adair, co., Okla., 13,112 76 J2
Adair, Okla., 434 76 H1
Adair, B. de, Mex. 92 B1
Adairsville, Ga., 1,026 64 E1
Adairville, Ky., 848 71 E5
Adaja, r., Sp. 122 C2
Adak, Alaska 85 f8
Adak I., Alaska 85 f8
Ådals-Liden, Swed. 120 D3
Adam, Muscat and Oman 143 F4
Adam, Mt., Falk. Is. 108 3
Adamana, Ariz. 78 C4
Adamantina, Braz., 18,164 103 F6
Adamaoua, reg., Cam. 162 G4
Adamclisi, Rum. 128 G2
Adamello, Monte, It. 123 C1
Adaminaby, Austl. 173 g11
Adamovka, U.S.S.R. 137 i9
Adamow, Pol. 127 E3
Adams, co., Colo., 120,296 79 C2
Adams, co., Idaho, 2,978 81 A3
Adams, co., Ill., 68,467 68 A3
Adams, Ill. 68 A4
Adams, co., Ind., 24,643 70 E2
Adams, co., Iowa, 7,468 72 C3
Adams, Kans. 75 H6
Adams, Mass., 11,949;12,391(T) 56 D2
Adams, Minn., 806 74 F4
Adams, co., Miss., 37,730 73 D6
Adams, co., Nebr., 28,944 75 G3
Adams, Nebr., 387 75 J3
Adams, N.Y., 1,914 59 H4
Adams, co., N. Dak., 4,449 74 A2
Adams, N. Dak., 360 74 C1
Adams, co., Ohio, 19,982 70 F4
Adams, Okla. 76 B1
Adams, Oreg., 192 80 D3
Adams, co., Pa., 51,906 60 H6
Adams, Tenn. 71 D5
Adams, co., Wash., 9,929 80 D2
Adams, co., Wis., 7,566 66 D4
Adams, Wis., 1,301 66 D5
Adams, Mt., N.H. 54 E3
Adams, Mt., Wash. 80 C2
Adams, r., Br. Col., Can. 42 H3
Adams Beach, Fla. 65 F3
Adam's Br., shoals, Cey.-India 145 m21
Adamsburg, S.C. 63 C3
Adams Center, N.Y. 59 H4
Adams City, Colo. 79 b8
Adams Head, pk., Utah 78 B3
Adams L., Br. Col., Can. 42 H3
Adams Landing, Alta., Can. 42 J1
Adams Mtn., Mass. 56 E2
Adams Nat. Hist. Site, Mass. 57 M3
Adams Rock, Pitc. I. 177 45
Adams Run, S.C. 63 D5
Adams Station, N.J. 58 a15
Adamston, N.J. 58 c16
Adamstown, Pitc. I. 177 45
Adamstown, Pa., 1,190 61 K5
Adamsville, N.B., Can. 47 T10
Adamsville, Ala., 2,095 64 B2
Adamsville, Fla. 65 d12
Adamsville, Mich. 67 G7
Adamsville, Ohio, 167 70 H2
Adamsville, Pa. 60 B2
Adamsville (part of Little Compton), R.I. 57 M6
Adamsville, Tenn., 1,046 71 C6
Adamsville, Tex. 77 O4
Adana, Turk., 230,024 142 C2
Adapazarı, Turk., 80,160 142 B1
Adare, C., Ant. 180 V5
Adavale, Austl. 173 F3
Adda, r., It. 123 B1
Aḑ Ḑab'ah, U.A.R., 10,222 161 J2
Ad Dabbah, Sudan 163 K2
Ad Dahnā', des., Saudi Ar. 143 D4
Aḑ Ḑāli', S. Ar. 143 D6
Ad Dāmir, Sudan, 5,458 163 K3
Ad Dammām, Saudi Ar. 143 E3
Ad Dāmūr, Leb., 5,922 142 b6
Ad Dār al Ḩamrā', Saudi Ar. 143 B3
Ad Darb, Saudi Ar. 163 M3
Ad Dawādimī, Saudi Ar. 143 C4
Ad Dawḩah, Qatar, 25,000* 143 E3
Addie, N.C. 63 A2
Addieville, Ill., 231 68 C5
Ad Dilinjāt, U.A.R. 161 i7
Addingham, U.K., 1,873 114 E3
Addington, Okla., 144 76 F3
Addis, La., 590 73 D7
Addis Ababa, Eth., 465,000* 163 L4
Addis Alam, Eth. 163 L4
Addison, Ala., 343 64 B1
Addison (part of Glastonbury), Conn. 56 F6
Addison, Ill., 16,997 69 b9
Addison, Me. 55 E4
Addison, Mich., 575 67 J6
Addison, N.Y., 2,185 58 F7
Addison, Ohio 70 G4
Addison, Pa., 222 60 D6
Addison, Tex., 308 76 f9
Addison, co., Vt., 20,076 54 A3
Addison, Vt. 54 A3
Ad Dīwānīyah, Iraq, 33,204 143 D2
Addor, N.C., 118 63 E2
Ad Dukhaylah, U.A.R. 161 h7
Ad Duwaym, Sudan, 12,319 163 K3
Addy, Wash. 80 E1
Addyston, Ohio, 1,376 71 g11
Adegem, Belg., 5,187 115 B3
Adel, Ga., 4,321 64 F4
Adel, Iowa, 2,060 72 C3
Adel, Oreg. 80 D4
Adelaide, Austl., 483,508 172 E5
Adelaide, Bah. Is. 95 b8
Adelaide I., Ant. 180 N6
Adelaide River, Austl. 172 D1
Adelanto, Calif. 82 E5
Adelboden, Switz., 2,881 124 B2
Adelie Coast, Ant. 180 U6
Adell, Wis., 398 66 F5
Adelphi, Ohio, 441 70 G3
Adelphia, N.J. 58 b16
Adelsheim, F.R.Ger., 2,659 119 G6
Adelsö, Swed. 120 e8
Aden, Alta., Can. 42 K4
Aden, S. Ar., 99,285 143 D6
Aden, Ill. 68 D5
Aden, G. of, Asia 143 D6
Adena, Ohio, 1,317 70 J2
Adenau, F.R.Ger., 2,895 118 A3
Adendorf, F.R.Ger., 3,188 119 b9
Aden Yaval, Som. Rep., 3,000* 163 M5
Adger, Ala. 64 B2
Adi, P., Indon. 149 K4
Adi Caieh, Eth. 163 L3
Adieu, C., Austl. 172 D5
Adieu-Vat, Fr. Guiana 101 O5
Adige, r., It. 123 C2
Adigrat, Eth. 163 L3
Adilabad, India, 20,970 145 F6
Adilcevaz, Turk., 4,614 142 E2
Adin, Calif. 82 C2
Adirondack Mts., N.Y. 59 K4
Adi Ugri, Eth., 4,600* 163 L3
Adıyaman, Turk., 17,021 142 D2
Adjai, r., India 144 f13
Adjohon, Dahom, 6,036 162 e8
Adjud, Rum., 6,119 128 F1
Adjuntas, P.R., 5,318 96 s10
Adler, U.S.S.R., 20,000 137 a1
Adlington, U.K., 4,281 114 C3
Adliswil, Switz., 9,078 124 C1
Admaston, Ont., Can. 46 H3
Admiral's Beach, Newf., Can. 45 b10
Admiral's Cove, Newf., Can. 45 c10
Admiralty Bay, Gren. Is. 97 20
Admiralty Gulf, Austl. 172 C2
Admiralty Inlet, N.W.T., Can. 40 M3
Admiralty Inlet, Wash. 81 a6
Admiralty I., Alaska 85 L4
Admiralty Is., Terr. New Guin. 170 D5
Admiralty Islets, Lord Howe I. 175 12
Admire, Kans., 149 75 J5
Admont, Aust., 3,056 124 L6
Ado, Nigeria, 28,589 162 e8
Adobe, Ariz. 78 B5
Adobe Cr. Res., Colo. 79 D2
Adobes, Tex. 77 L5
Ado Ekiti, Nigeria 162 f8
Adola, Eth. 163 L5
Adolphus, Ky. 71 E5
Adona, Ark., 153 73 C2
Adonara, P., Indon. 149 G4
Adoni, India, 69,951 145 E7
Adorf, Ger. D.R. 126 b6
A dos Cunhados, Port., 6,121 122 i9
Adour, r., Fr. 117 C5
Adra, India, 13,215 144 f14
Adra, Sp., 15,669 122 D4
Adrano, It., 30,004 123 E6
Adrar, Alg., 1,865 160 D3
Adrar, plat., Maur. 162 C2
Adrar des Iforas, plat., Mali 162 E2
Adré, Chad 163 H3
Adrī, Libya 161 G3
Adria, It., 27,889 123 D2
Adrian, Ga., 568 64 G3
Adrian, Ill. 68 A3
Adrian, Mich., 20,347 67 J7
Adrian, Minn., 1,215 74 E4
Adrian, Mo., 1,082 72 C6
Adrian, N.Y. 58 E7
Adrian, N. Dak. 74 C2
Adrian, Oreg. 80 E4
Adrian, Tex., 258 76 M2
Adrian, W.Va. 62 D4
Adriatic Sea, Eur. 110 E4
Aduwa, Eth. 163 L3
Advance, Mich. 67 H3
Advance, Mo., 692 72 H7
Advance, N.C., 197 63 D2
Adventure Sd., Falk. Is. 108 3
Advocate Harbour, N.S., Can. 47 T11
Adwick le Street, U.K., 18,212 114 F3
Adycha, r., U.S.S.R. 135 N3
Adzopé, Iv. Coast, 13,000 162 D4
Æbelø, i., Den. 121 C5
Aech'ang, N. Kor. 151 E3
Aegean Sea, Eur. 129 E5
Aeneas, Wash. 80 D1
Aeon Pt., Christmas Atoll 177 40
Aerdenhout, Neth., 4,900 115 b6
Ærø, i., Den. 121 C6
Ærøskøbing, Den., 1,273 121 C6
Aesch, Switz., 3,981 124 B1
Aetna, Ill. 68 D4
Aetna, Kans. 75 G6
Aetna, Tenn. 71 D6
Aëtós, Gr. 129 C6
Afam, Nigeria 162 F5
Afareaitu, Moorea 177 44
Afdem, Eth., 11,600* 163 L4
Affobakka, Sur. 101 N5
Affoltern am Albis, Switz., 4,904 124 C1
Affton, Mo. 72 G6
Afghanistan, ctry., 15,352,000* 144 B2
Afgoi, Som. Rep., 8,696* 163 M5
Åfjord, Nor. 120 B3
Aflou, Alg., 7,681 160 E2
Afognak, Alaska, 190 85 F4
Afognak I., Alaska 85 G4
Afono, Tutuila 177 39
Afono Bay, Tutuila 177 39
Afonso Bezerra, Braz., 2,057 103 a13
Afonso Cláudio, Braz., 2,823 103 f17
Afragola, It., 45,309 123 c10
Afram, r., Ghana 162 c8
Afrânio, Braz. 103 H3
'Afrīn, Syr., 5,379 142 D2
Afşin, Turk., 6,472 142 D2
Afsluitdijk, dam, Neth. 115 D2
Afton, Calif. 82 E5
Afton, Iowa, 773 72 C4
Afton, Mich. 67 J3
Afton, Minn., 158 74 d6
Afton, N.Y., 956 59 J7
Afton, Okla., 1,111 76 H1
Afton, Tenn. 71 J5
Afton, Va. 62 F4
Afton, Wis. 66 D6
Afton, Wyo., 1,337 81 D4
Afuá, Braz. 103 F2
Afula, Isr., 13,844 142 b7
Afumaţi, Rum. 128 F2
Afyonkarahisar, Turk., 38,392 142 B2
Agabama, r., Cuba 96 d2
Agadem, Niger 162 G3
Agadès, Niger, 6,235 162 F3
Agadir, Mor., 16,695 160 C2
Agadyr', U.S.S.R. 134 G5
Agaie, Nigeria 162 g7
Agana, Guam, 1,642 176 24
Agana Bay, Guam 176 24
Agano, r., Jap. 155 F3
Agapovka, U.S.S.R. 137 i9
Agar, India, 11,486 144 a14
Agar, S. Dak., 139 74 B3
Agartala, India, 54,878 145 J5
Agassiz, Br. Col., Can. 42 G4
Agat, Guam, 2,596 176 24
Agat Bay, Guam 176 24
Agate, Colo. 79 D2
Agate, Nebr. 75 B1
Agate Beach, Oreg. 80 A3
Agats, Indon. 149 L4
Agatti, i., India 145 D8
Agattu I., Alaska 85 d8
Agattu Str., Alaska 85 d8
Agawam, Mass., 15,718(T) 56 F4
Agawam, r., Mass. 57 O5
Agay, Fr. 116 m14
Agazzano, It., 2,716 122 c6
Agbaja, Nigeria 162 g8
Agbannawag, Phil., 3,434 153 c7
Agbor, Nigeria 162 g8
Agboville, Iv. Coast, 37,026 162 D5
Agdam, U.S.S.R., 16,000 137 c1
Agdangan, Phil., 2,611 153 c9
Agdash, U.S.S.R., 9,900 137 c1
Agde, Fr., 8,896 117 E5
Agege, Nigeria, 14,899 162 e8
Ageki, Jap. 154 h14
Agematsu, Jap., 9,540 155 E4
Agen, Fr., 35,150 117 D4
Agency, Iowa, 702 72 E4
Agency, Mo., 240 72 C5
Agency L., Oreg. 80 C4
Agency Pk., Colo. 79 B2
Agency Valley Res., Oreg. 80 D4
Agenda, Kans., 124 75 H4
Ageo, Jap., 38,889 155 m19
Ager, Sp., 1,105 122 F2
Agerbæk, Den. 121 A5
Agerskov, Den., 2,368 121 B5
Agersø, i., Den. 121 D5
Agfayan Pt., Guam 176 24
Agger, r., F.R.Ger. 119 C3
Aggtelek, Hung. 126 E2
Āghā Jārī, Iran, 24,195 143 E2
Aghireşu, Rum. 128 D1
Agidyen, i., Jaluit 176 30
Agigea, Rum. 128 G2
Agimont, Belg. 115 C4
Agincourt, Ont., Can., 1,738 46 d13
Agingan Pt., Saipan 176 27
Aginskoye, U.S.S.R. 135 J4
Aginskoye, U.S.S.R., 5,100 135 L4
Agliè, It., 2,378 122 a5
Agnanda, Gr. 129 C5
Agnes, Tex. 76 d9
Agness, Oreg. 80 B4
Agnew, Calif. 83 f13
Agnew, Wash. 80 B1
Agnew L., Ont., Can. 46 C2
Agnibilékrou, Iv. Coast, 5,030 162 D4
Agnita, Rum., 9,108 128 E2
Agno, Phil., 2,480 153 a6
Agno, Switz., 1,119 124 C2
Agno, r., Phil. 153 B1
Agnone, It., 9,077 123 E4
Agogna, r., It. 122 b5
Agogo, Ghana, 10,359 162 c8
Agon, Fr., 2,341 117 C2
Agona = Swedru
Agoo, Phil., 6,511 153 b6
Agordat, Eth. 163 L3
Agorou, Niger, 2,430 162 E3
Agosta, It., 1,710 123 b8
Agouna, Dahom. 162 d8
Agoura, Calif. 83 g15
Agout, r., Fr. 117 D5
Agra, India, 462,029 145 E4
Agra, Kans., 277 75 F4
Agra, Okla., 265 76 G2
Agraciada, Urug. 105 b11
Agrado, Col. 100 C6
Agramonte, Cuba, 2,948 96 c1
Agramunt, Sp., 3,282 122 F2
Ágras, Gr., 1,050 129 D4
Agreda, Sp., 3,624 122 D2
Agri, r., It. 123 F4
Agricola, Kans. 75 K5
Agricola, Miss. 73 G7
Ağrı Dağı, Turk. 142 E2
Agrigento, It., 46,258 123 D6
Agrihan, i., Mar. Is. 170 D3
Agrínion, Gr., 24,763 129 C5
Agropoli, It., 9,340 123 E4
Agros, Cyp., 1,464 142 e10
Agryz, U.S.S.R., 20,100 134 E4
Agua Blanca, Guat., 1,783 94 d9
Agua Blanca, Mex. 93 c11
Agua Blanca, Peru, 4,500 104 B3
Agua Blanca, Ven., 2,659 100 F3
Agua Blanca, r., Mex. 93 a8
Água Branca, Braz., 2,902 103 H3
Agua Caliente, Mex. 92 A1
Agua Caliente, Ariz. 78 B5
Agua Caliente Springs, Calif. 82 E6
Aguachica, Col. 100 D3
Água Clara, Braz. 103 F6
Aguada, P.R., 3,759 96 r10
Aguada de Pasajeros, Cuba, 5,112 96 c1
Aguada Grande, Ven., 1,668 100 F2
Aguadas, Col. 100 C5
Agua de Dios, Col. 101 e15
Aguadilla, P.R., 15,943 96 r10
Aguadilla, B. de, P.R. 96 r10
Agua Dulce, Bol. 102 C4
Aguadulce, Pan., 6,010 94 G6
Agua Dulce, Tex., 867 77 P6
Agua Dulce, r., Cuba 96 c1
Agua Fria, N. Mex. 79 C3
Agua Fría, Ven. 101 b11
Agua Fria, r., Ariz. 78 B5
Agualeguas, Mex., 2,423 93 F2
Aguamiel, r., Col. 101 f13
Aguán, r., Hond. 94 D3
Aguanish, Qué., Can. 45 O5
Agua Nueva, Tex. 77 O6
Aguanus, r., Qué., Can. 45 O4
Agua Prieta, Mex., 15,275 92 C1
Aguaray, Arg., 1,200* 105 C2
Aguarico, r., Ec. 104 B2
Aguaruto, Mex., 3,021 92 D3
Aguasay, Ven., 1,430 101 J3
Aguas Blancas, Chile 105 B2
Aguas Buenas, P.R., 2,470 96 t10
Aguascalientes, st., Mex., 243,363 92 E3
Aguascalientes, Mex., 126,222 92 E4
Aguaytia, Peru 104 C4
Aguaytia, r., Peru 104 C4
Águeda, Port., 8,345 122 A2
Aguia, P., Peru 104 A3
Aguijan, i., Mariana Is. 176 23
Aguila, Ariz. 78 B5
Aguilar, Sp., 16,409 122 C4
Aguilar, Colo., 777 79 C3
Aguilares, Tex. 77 O6
Aguilas, Sp., 15,250 122 E4
Aguilas, B. de las, Dom. Rep. 96 m7
Aguililla, Mex., 4,036 92 E4
Aguirre Cerda, Ant. 180 N6
Agujereada, P., P.R. 96 r10
Agul, r., U.S.S.R. 135 J4
Agulhas, S. Af. 164 a9
Agulhas, C., S. Af. 164 C7
Agulhas Basin, Indian Oc. 168 A4
Agulhas Negras, Braz., 11,636 103 d18
Agulhas Negras, pk., Braz. 103 d18
Agung, G., Indon. 148 f8
Agusan, r., Phil. 153 C3
Ahaggar = Hoggar
Ahalt, Turk., 1,651 137 b1
Ahar, Iran, 19,816 143 D1
Ahascragh, Ire. 113 B5
Ahaus, F.R.Ger., 8,809 118 A2
Ahe, i., Tuam. Arch. 171 J5
Ahlen, F.R.Ger., 36,270 118 A3
Ahmadpur East, Pak., 32,423 145 D3
Ahmedabad, India, 1,149,918 145 D5
Ahmednagar, India, 119,020 145 E6
Ahmeek, Mich., 265 66 E1
Ahmic Harbour, Ont., Can. 46 E3
Ahmic L., Ont., Can. 46 E3
Ahoada, Nigeria 162 g9
A-ho-ch'i, China 150 A2
Ahome, Mex., 2,905 92 C3
Ahome, P., Mex. 92 C3
Ahoskie, N.C., 4,583 63 H1
Ahr, r., F.R.Ger. 119 C3
Ahraura, India, 10,379 144 d13
Ahrensbök, F.R.Ger., 7,870 118 C1

Ahrensburg—Algyö · 191

Ahrensburg, F.R.Ger., 18,108 118 C2
Ahrensfelde, F.R.Ger. 119 b8
Ahrgebirge, mts., F.R.Ger. 119 B4
Ahrweiler, F.R.Ger., 8,247 118 A3
Ahse, r., F.R.Ger. 119 E1
Ahtanum, Wash. 80 C2
Ähtäri, Fin. 120 F3
Ahtme, U.S.S.R., 12,000 136 B1
Ahuacatlán, Nay., Mex., 5,004 92 D4
Ahuacatlán, S.L.P., Mex., 1,163 93 f8
Ahuachapán, El Salv., 13,298 94 B4
Ahualulco, Mex., 1,238 92 E3
Ahua Pt., Hawaii 84 c8
Ahuazotepec, Mex., 1,047 93 f9
Ahuisculco, Mex., 1,371 93 a9
Ahun, Fr., 1,693 117 E3
Ahunui, i., Tuam. Arch. 171 J6
Åhus, Swed. 121 G5
Ahvāz, Iran, 120,098 143 D2
Ahvenanmaa, is., Fin. 120 D3
Ai, i., Jaluit 176 30
Aibetsu, Jap., 9,834 155 K8
Aibonito, P.R., 5,477 96 t10
Aichach, F.R.Ger., 6,562 118 C4
Aid, Ohio 70 G4
Aidenbach, F.R.Ger., 2,056 118 D4
Aidia, Terr. Papua 174 e2
Aidlingen, F.R.Ger., 2,444 119 F7
Ai Duang, Thai. 146 C3
Aiea, Hawaii, 11,826 84 D2
Ai-en-ch'i-ch'in-miao, China 151 C1
Aifat, r., Indon. 149 K3
Aiga, Jap. 154 h15
Aigen, Aust., 1,939 124 K5
Aigle, Switz., 4,381 124 A2
Aigre, Fr., 1,264 117 D4
Aiguá, A. del, Urug. 105 E4
Aigues-Mortes, Fr., 4,203 117 F5
Aigues Tortes, Pq. Nac., Sp. 122 F1
Aigun = Ai-hui
Aigurande, Fr., 2,381 117 D3
Aihara, Jap. 155 m19
Ai-hui, China, 40,000* 150 G1
Aija, Peru, 1,592 104 B4
Aijal, India, 14,257 145 J5
Aikawa, Jap., 19,057 155 F2
Aiken, co., S.C., 81,038 63 C4
Aiken, S.C., 11,243 63 C4
Aiken Summit, Va. 62 E6
Ail, C.d', Fr. 116 n3
Ailey, Ga., 469 64 G3
Ailigandi, Pan., 1,353 94 J6
Ailinginae, atoll, Marsh. Is. 176 22
Ailinglapalap, atoll, Marsh. Is. 176 22
Ailo, Terr. New Guin. 174 f2
Ailuk, atoll, Marsh. Is. 176 22
Aime, Fr., 1,365 117 G4
Aimé Martin, C., Loy. Is. 174 k8
Aimere, Indon. 149 G5
Aimorés, Braz., 11,448 103 H5
Aimorés, Sa. dos, Braz. 98 E4
Ain, r., Fr. 117 F3
Aina Haina, Hawaii 84 d8
Ainaži, U.S.S.R., 2,100 136 A1
Aïn-Beïda, Alg., 26,976 160 F2
Aïn Ben Tili, Maur. 162 C1
Aïn Defla, Alg., 5,397 160 c5
Aineman, i., Jaluit 176 30
Aïn M'Lila, Alg., 11,787 160 e5
Aïn Oussera, Alg., 5,819 160 E2
Aïn Salah, Alg. 160 E3
Ainsdale, U.K., 4,324 114 B3
Aïn-Sefra, Alg., 7,068 160 D2
Ainslie, L., N.S., Can. 47 V10
Ainsworth, Ind. 69 e10
Ainsworth, Iowa, 371 72 F3
Ainsworth, Nebr., 1,982 75 E1
Aïn-Témouchent, Alg., 23,252 160 a6
Aintree, U.K., 2,884 114 C4
Aioi, Jap., 36,521 154 f15
Aioi, Jap. 154 h14
Aïoun el Atrouss, Maur., 3,044 162 C3
Aipe, Col. 100 C6
Aiquile, Bol., 8,865 102 c11
Air, Tex. 77 O4
Air, Pt. of, U.K. 114 B4
Airai, Palau 176 21
Airão, Braz. 102 D2
Airbangis, Indon. 148 A2
Aird Hills, Terr. Papua 174 e2
Airdrie, Alta., Can. 42 J3
Airdrie, U.K., 33,620 112 c8
Aire, Fr., 9,224 117 E1
Aire, r., Fr. 117 F2
Aire, r., U.K. 113 F5
Aire-sur-l'Adour, Fr., 6,109 117 C5
Air Force I., N.W.T., Can. 41 P4
Aïr Massif, Niger 162 F2
Airolo, Switz., 2,023 124 C2
Airth, U.K. 112 c7
Airton, U.K. 114 D2
Airvault, Fr., 2,075 117 C3
Airway Heights, Wash., 708 80 E2
Aisha, Eth., 11,000* 163 M4
Aishalton, Guyana 101 L6
Aishihik, Yukon, Can. 40 B5
Aishihik L., Yukon, Can. 85 K3
Aisne, r., Fr. 117 F2
Aitape, Terr. New Guin. 174 d1
Aitkin, co., Minn., 12,162 74 F2
Aitkin, Minn., 1,829 74 F2
Aitolikón, Gr., 3,459 129 C5
Aitsu, i., Eniwetok 176 28
Aitutaki, i., Cook Is. 171 H6
Aiud, Rum., 11,886 128 D1
Aiwo (dist.), Nauru 175 17
Aiwokako Passage, Palau 176 21
Aix, Ind. 70 B1
Aixe, Fr., 3,777 117 D4
Aix-en-Othe, Fr., 2,335 117 E2
Aix-en-Provence, Fr., 72,696 117 F5
Aix-la-Chapelle = Aachen
Aix-les-Bains, Fr., 18,270 117 G4
Aiyansh, Br. Col., Can. 42 E2
Aíyina, Gr., 4,989 129 D6
Aíyina, i., Gr. 129 D6
Aiyínion, Gr., 4,271 129 D4
Aiyion, Gr., 17,762 129 D5
Aiyura, Terr. New Guin. 174 e2
Aizenay, Fr., 4,077 117 C3
Aizpute, U.S.S.R., 4,200 136 A1
Aizu-Wakamatsu, Jap., 99,546 155 F3
Ajaccio, Fr., 42,282 116 r18
Ajacuba, Mex., 1,878 93 e9
Ajajú, r., Col. 100 D7
Ajalpan, Mex., 6,391 93 F4
Ajamaru, Indon. 149 K3
Ajana, Austl. 172 A4
Ajanta, India 145 E5
Ajasse, Nigeria 162 f7
Ajax, Ont., Can. 7,709 46 F5
Ajax Mtn., Idaho-Mont. 81 C3
Ajayan Pt., Guam 176 24
Ajdābiyah, Libya, 16,336 161 H2
Ajdovščina, Yug., 2,894 125 A2
Ajigasawa, Jap., 22,123 155 G1
Ajijic, Mex., 3,357 93 a9
Ajiki, Jap., 7,241 155 n19
Ajka, Hung., 15,375 126 C3
'Ajlūn, Jor., 5,390 142 b7
Ajmer, India, 231,240 145 E4
Ajo, Ariz., 7,049 78 B5
Ajo, C. de, Sp. 122 m11
Ajoe, Kep., Indon. 149 J2
Ajo Range, Ariz. 78 B5
Ajoupa-Bouillon, Mart. 97 12
Ajuchitlán, Mex., 3,170 93 E5
A-jung-ch'i, China 150 G1
Ajuy, Phil., 1,957 153 d10
Ak, r., Turk. 142 B2
Akabane, Jap. 154 i15
Akabira, Jap., 54,635 155 K8
Aka-dake, Jap. 155 F4
Akadomari, Jap., 5,982 155 F3
Akaike, Jap. 155 n19
Akaishi, Jap. 154 f16
Akaishi-sammyaku, mts., Jap. 155 F4
Akaki, Eth. 163 L4
Akakoa Pt., Hawaii 84 F3
Akalkot, India, 21,278 145 E6
Akan, Jap., 20,586 155 L8
Akan-ktk., Jap. 155 L8
Akanthou, Cyp, 1,761 142 e9
Akaoka, Jap., 5,532 155 C5
Akasaka, Jap., 11,227 154 h14
Akasaka, Jap. 154 i15
Akasaki, Jap., 11,525 155 C4
Akashi, Jap., 129,780 155 D4
Akaska, S. Dak., 90 74 B3
Äkäslompolo, Fin. 120 F2
Akavare, mt., Swed. 120 D2
Akayu, Jap., 13,865 155 G2
Akbaba Tepesi, Turk. 137 a2
Akbarpur, India, 9,563 144 d12
Akbeit, U.S.S.R. 137 n12
Akbou, Alg., 11,057 160 d5
Ak-Bulak, U.S.S.R., 13,600 137 h9
Akçakale, Turk., 3,939 142 D2
Akchatau, U.S.S.R. 134 G5
Akdağmadeni, Turk., 4,031 142 C2
Akechi, Jap., 6,210 155 E4
Akela, N. Mex. 79 B5
Akelamo, Indon. 149 J2
Akeley, Minn., 434 74 E2
Akeley, Pa. 60 D2
Aken, Ger.D.R., 12,675 118 D3
Åkersberga, Swed. 120 f8
Åkers krutbruk, Swed. 120 d8
Åkers styckebruk, Swed. 120 e8
Aketi, D.R.Congo, 15,038 164 C1
Akhalkalaki, U.S.S.R., 8,800 137 b1
Akhaltsikhe, U.S.S.R., 16,800 137 b1
Akharnaí, Gr., 11,290 129 D5
Akhelôos, r., Gr. 129 C5
Akhetaton = Tall al-'Amarna
Akhiok, Alaska, 84 85 F4
Akhisar, Turk., 40,013 142 A2
Akhladhókambos, Gr., 1,367 129 D6
Akhmīm, U.A.R. 161 K3
Akhtopol, Bulg., 1,038 128 G3
Akhtuba, r., U.S.S.R. 134 D5
Akhtubinsk, U.S.S.R., 16,400 134 D5
Akhtyrka, U.S.S.R., 31,500 134 C4
Akhtyrskiy, U.S.S.R., 16,000 136 E4
Aki, Jap., 16,492 154 B5
Aki, Jap., 30,370 155 C5
Akiachak, Alaska, 229 85 D3
Akiak, Alaska, 187 85 D3
Akiaki, i., Tuam. Arch. 177 42
Akimiski I., N.W.T., Can. 44 G4
Akin, Ill. 68 D6
Akinum, Terr. New Guin. 174 f2
Åkirkeby, Den., 1,461 121 G5
Akishima, Jap., 44,805 155 m19
Akita, Jap., 203,661 155 G2
Akjoujt, Maur., 2,360 162 B2
Akka, Mor. 160 C3
Akkajaure, l., Swed. 120 D2
Akkanburluk, r., U.S.S.R. 137 m11
Akkaraipattu, Cey. 145 F9
Akkarga, U.S.S.R. 137 k9
Akkeshi, Jap., 20,185 155 L8
Akkeshi-wan, Jap. 155 L8
'Akko, Isr., 25,222 142 C3
Akkrum, Neth. 115 D1
Aklavik, N.W.T., Can., 1,445 40 B4
Aklera, India 144 a13
Akō, Jap., 40,741 155 D4
Akobo, Sudan 163 K4
Akobo, r., Eth.-Sudan 163 K4
Akola, India, 115,760 145 E5
Akonolinga, Cam., 2,500* 162 G5
A-k'o-sai, China 150 C3
Akosombo, Ghana 162 c8
A-k'o-su, China 150 B2
Akot, India, 31,459 145 E5
Akpatok I., N.W.T., Can. 45 M1
Akraífnion, Gr., 1,316 129 D5
Akranes, Ice., 4,026 120 a6
Akron, Ala., 604 64 B3
Akron, Colo., 1,890 79 D1
Akron, Ind., 958 70 D1
Akron, Iowa, 1,351 72 A2
Akron, Kans. 75 J6
Akron, Mich., 503 67 K5
Akron, N.Y., 2,841 58 C5
Akron, Ohio, 290,351 70 H1
Akron, Pa., 2,167 61 K5
Akropong, Ghana 162 c9
Aksakovo, U.S.S.R., 3,600 137 h8
Aksaray, Turk., 20,046 142 C2
Aksay, r., U.S.S.R. 136 g8
Akşehir, Turk., 20,607 142 B2
Akşehir Gölü, Turk. 142 B2
Akseki, Turk., 2,745 142 B2
Aksënovo-Zilovskoye, U.S.S.R. 135 L4
Aksha, U.S.S.R. 135 L4
Ak su, r., China 150 A2
Aksu, r., Turk. 142 B2
Aksuat, U.S.S.R., 134 H5
Ak-Sug, r., U.S.S.R. 137 s12
Aksum, Eth., 12,200* 163 L3
Aktanysh, U.S.S.R. 137 h8
Aktasty, U.S.S.R. 137 k10
Aktau, U.S.S.R. 137 o12
Akti, pen., Gr. 129 E4
Aktogay, U.S.S.R. 134 G5
Aktyubinsk, U.S.S.R., 107,000 134 E4
Akulurak, Alaska 85 D3
Akune, Jap., 41,180 154 B6
Akun I., Alaska 85 C5
Akure, Nigeria, 45,069 162 E4
Akureyri, Ice., 9,152 120 a6
Akuse, Ghana, 3,027 162 c8
Akuseki-shima, Jap. 154 d12
Akutan, Alaska, 107 85 C5
Akutan I., Alaska 85 C5
Akutikha, U.S.S.R. 137 r11
Akwanga, Nigeria 162 F4
Akyab, Burma, 42,329 146 A2
Ak'yar, U.S.S.R. 137 i9
Ål, Nor. 120 B3
Alabama, st., U.S., 3,486,000* 64
Alabama, N.Y. 58 D5
Alabama, r., Ala. 64 B4
Alabama Port, Ala. 64 A5
Alabang, Phil., 5,007 153 c8
Alabaster, Ala., 1,623 64 C2
Alabaster, Mich. 67 K4
Alabat, Phil., 3,131 153 c8
Alabat I., Phil. 153 c8
Al 'Abbāsīyah, Sudan, 2,846 163 K3
Ålabodarna, Swed. 121 b7
Alabuga, r., U.S.S.R. 137 g4
Al Abyaḍ, Al Baḥr, Sudan 163 K4
Al Abyār, Libya 161 H2
Alaca, Turk., 7,180 142 C1
Alaçam, Turk., 6,853 142 C1
Alachua, co., Fla., 74,074 65 G3
Alachua, Fla., 1,974 65 G3
Alacrán, Arrecife, Mex. 93 H3
Alacranes, Cuba, 3,165 96 c1
Aladdin, Pa., 60 d7
Alaejos, Sp., 2,923 122 C2
Alafia, r., Fla. 65 d12
Alagir, U.S.S.R., 13,500 137 b1
Alagoa Grande, Braz., 12,115 103 b14
Alagoas, st., Braz., 1,271,062 103 J3
Alagoinhas, Braz., 38,246 103 J4
Alagón, Sp., 5,270 122 E2
Alahärmä, Fin. 120 E3
Al Aḥmadī, Kuwait, 7,280 143 D3
Al Aḥsā', reg., Saudi Ar. 140 C4
Alajärvi, Fin. 120 F3
Alajuela, C. R., 19,620 94 E5
Alakai Swamp, Hawaii 84 B1
Alakanuk, Alaska, 278 85 C3
Alaknanda, r., India 144 b10
Alakol', Oz., U.S.S.R. 134 H5
Alalakeiki Chan., Hawaii 84 E3
Alalaú, r., Braz. 102 D2
Al 'Alamayn, U.A.R. 161 J2
Al 'Amādīyah, Iraq, 3,356 143 C1
Alamagan, i., Mar. Is. 170 D3
Alamance, co., N.C., 85,674 63 E2
Alamance, N.C. 63 E1
Al 'Amārah, Iraq, 53,311 143 D2
Alameda, Sask., Can. 43 D5
Alameda, co., Calif., 908,209 82 C4
Alameda, Calif., 63,855 83 e12
Alameda, Idaho, 10,660 81 C4
Alameda (pt. of Albuquerque), N. Mex. 79 B4
Alameda Cr., Calif. 83 e12
Alamein = Al 'Alamayn
Alamillo, N. Mex. 79 B4
Alaminos, Phil., 3,740 153 A1
Al 'Āmirīyah, U.A.R. 161 h7
Alamito Cr., Tex. 77 L5
Alamitos, Sa. de los, Mex. 92 E2
Álamo, Mex., 6,375 93 F4
Alamo, Ariz. 78 B4
Alamo, Calif., 1,791 83 e12
Alamo, Ga., 822 64 G3
Alamo, Ind., 144 70 B3
Alamo, Mich. 67 H6
Alamo, Nev. 83 C4
Alamo, N. Dak., 182 74 A1
Alamo, Tenn., 1,665 71 B6
Alamo, Tex., 4,121 77 O6
Alamo, r., Calif. 82 F6
Alamogordo, N. Mex., 21,723 79 B5
Alamogordo Res., N. Mex. 79 C4
Alamo Heights, Tex., 7,552 76 b7
Álamos, Mex., 3,602 92 C2
Alamosa, co., Colo., 10,000 79 C3
Alamosa, Colo., 6,205 79 B3
Alamosa, r., N. Mex. 79 B5
Alamosa Cr., Colo. 79 B3
Alamota, Kans. 75 E5
Aland, India, 18,309 145 E6
Åland = Ahvenanmaa
Aland, r., Ger.D.R. 118 C2
Alanelimo, i., Truk 176 19
Alanreed, Tex. 76 N2
Alanson, Mich. 290 67 J3
Alanya, Turk., 10,133 142 B2
Alao, Tutuila 177 39
Alapa, Nigeria 162 f7
Alapaha, Ga., 631 64 F4
Alapaha, r., Ga. 64 F5
Alapayevsk, U.S.S.R., 45,100 137 k7
Al 'Aqabah, Jor., 8,908 142 C4
Al 'Āqūrah, Leb., 3,002 142 b5
Al 'Arīsh, U.A.R., 26,690 161 K2
Alarka, N.C. 63 A2
Al Arṭāwīyah, Saudi Ar. 143 D3
Alas, Selat, Indon. 148 F5
Alaşehir, Turk., 13,923 142 B2
Ala Shan, China 150 D3
A-la-shan-ch'i, China 150 E3
Alaska, st., U.S., 267,000* 85
Alaska, Gulf of, Alaska 85 H4
Alaska Pen., Alaska 85 E4
Alaska Range, Alaska 85 F3
Alassio, It., 10,491 123 B3
Alatna, Alaska 85 F2
Alatna, r., Alaska 85 F2
Alatri, It., 20,631 123 D4
Alatyr', U.S.S.R., 34,700 136 G2
Alatyr', r., U.S.S.R. 136 G2
Alausí, Ec., 6,659 104 B2
Alava, C., Wash. 80 A1
Alaverdi, U.S.S.R., 16,700 137 c1
Alavieska, Fin. 120 E2
Alavus, Fin. 120 E3
Alay, mts., U.S.S.R. 137 e5
'Ālayh, Leb., 6,127 142 b6
Alayor, Sp., 5,016 122 h8
Alayskiy Khr., U.S.S.R. 137 f4
Alazani, r., U.S.S.R. 137 c1
Alazeya, r., U.S.S.R. 135 P3
Alazeyskoye Plos., U.S.S.R. 135 O3
Al 'Azīzīyah, Libya 161 G2
Alb, r., F.R.Ger. 119 E7
Alba, It., 20,223 123 B2
Alba, Mich. 67 J4
Alba, Mo., 336 72 C7
Alba, Pa., 192 60 J2
Alba, Tex., 472 77 Q3
Al Bāb, Syr., 24,886 142 D2
Albac, Rum. 124 D1
Albacete, Sp., 74,417 122 E3
Alba de Tormes, Sp., 3,666 122 C2
Ålbæk, Den. 121 C3
Ålbæk Bugt, Den. 121 C3
Alba Iulia, Rum., 14,776 128 D1
Al Balyanā, U.A.R., 12,500 161 K3
Albán, Col. 101 e15
Alban, Fr. 117 E5
Albanel, L., Qué., Can. 44 K5
Albania, ctry., 1,865,000* 125
Albania, Col. 101 e14
Albano, Lago, It. 123 b8
Albano Laziale, It., 19,278 123 D4
Albany, Austl., 8,265 172 B5
Albany, Calif., 14,804 83 e12
Albany, Ga., 55,890 64 E4
Albany, Ill., 637 68 B2
Albany, Ind., 2,132 70 D2
Albany, Ky., 1,887 71 F5
Albany, Minn., 1,375 74 E3
Albany, Mo., 1,662 72 C4
Albany, co., N.Y., 272,926 59 M6
Albany, N.Y., 129,726 59 N6
Albany, Ohio, 629 70 G3
Albany, Okla. 76 G4
Albany, Oreg., 12,926 80 B3
Albany, Tex., 2,174 77 O3
Albany, Vt., 169 54 C2
Albany, Wis., 892 66 D6
Albany, co., Wyo., 21,290 81 G5
Albany, r., Ont., Can. 44 G4
Albardón, Arg., 19,921 105 B4
Albaredo d'Adige, It., 5,564 122 e5
Albarracín, Sp., 1,376 122 E2
Al Başrah, Iraq, 164,623 143 D2
Albatross Bay, Austl. 173 F1
Albatross Cordillera, Pac. Oc. 169 J4
Albatross Plateau, Pac. Oc. 169 J2
Al Batrūn, Leb., 3,884 142 b5
Al Bawīṭī, U.A.R. 161 J3
Al Bayḍā', Yemen, 25,000* 143 D6
Albay G., Phil. 153 C2
Albemarle, N.C., 12,261 63 D2
Albemarle, co., Va., 30,969 62 F4
Albemarle, P., Colón, Arch. de 104 a7
Albemarle Sd., N.C. 63 H1
Albenga, It., 14,805 123 B2
Alberche, r., Sp. 122 C2
Alberene, Va. 62 F5
Ålberga, Swed. 120 d9
Alberique, Sp., 7,945 122 E3
Alberni, Br. Col., Can., 4,544 42 b6
Alberni Inlet, Br. Col., Can. 42 b6
Albersdorf, F.R.Ger., 2,947 118 B1
Albersloh, F.R.Ger., 3,271 118 A3
Albersweiler, F.R.Ger., 2,557 119 E6
Albert, Fr., 10,423 117 E2
Albert, Kans., 221 75 F5
Albert, Okla. 76 E2
Albert, Tex. 77 O4
Albert, W.Va. 62 E3
Albert, Parc Nat., D.R.Congo 164 D2
Albert, L., Austl. 172 c8
Albert, L., D.R.Congo-Uganda 164 E1
Albert, L., S. Dak. 74 D3
Alberta, prov., Can., 1,451,000* 42
Alberta, Ala. 64 B3
Alberta, Va., 430 62 G6
Alberta, Mt., Alta., Can. 42 H3
Alberta Beach, Alta., Can. 43 a7
Albert City, Iowa, 722 72 C2
Albert Edward, Mt., Terr. Papua 174 e3
Alberti, Arg., 6,500* 105 a12
Albertirsa, Hung., 11,377 126 D3
Albert Kan., Belg. 115 D3
Albert Lea, Minn., 17,108 74 F4
Alberton, Ont., Can. 46 b15
Alberton, P.E.I., Can. 45 N6
Alberton, S.Af., 24,919 165 k17
Alberton, Mont., 356 81 B2
Albertville, D.R.Congo, 29,934 164 D2
Albertville, Fr., 12,657 117 G4
Albertville, Ala., 8,250 64 C1
Albestroff, Fr. 116 c9
Albi, Fr., 41,268 117 E5
Albia, Iowa, 4,582 72 E3
Albin, Wyo., 181 81 G5
Albina, Sur., 1,000* 101 N5
Albion, Calif. 82 B3
Albion, Idaho, 415 81 C4
Albion, Ill., 2,025 68 D5
Albion, Ind., 1,325 70 D1
Albion, Iowa, 538 72 E2
Albion, Me. 55 C4
Albion, Mich., 12,749 67 J6
Albion, Mont. 81 G3
Albion, Nebr., 1,982 75 G2
Albion, N.Y., 5,182 58 D5
Albion, Okla., 161 76 H3
Albion, Pa., 1,630 60 B2
Albion (part of Lincoln), R.I., 57 L5
Albion, Wash., 291 80 E2
Albion, Wis. 66 D6
Al Bīrah, Jor., 14,510 142 b8
Alblasserdam, Neth., 10,300 115 b7
Albocácer, Sp., 2,092 122 E2
Alborán, I. de, Sp. 122 D4
Ålborg Bugt, Den. 121 C4
Alborz, Reshteh-ye Kūhhā-ye, mts., Iran 143 E1
Albox, Sp., 9,049 122 D4
Albreda, Br. Co., Can. 42 H3
Albright, W.Va., 304 62 E3
Albrighton, U.K. 114 D5
Al Bu'ayrāt, Libya 161 G2
Albuera, Phil., 4,051 153 f11
Albufeira, Port., 8,416 122 A4
Albuñol, Sp., 7,199 122 D4
Albuquerque, N. Mex., 201,189 79 B4
Al Buraymī, Muscat and Oman 143 F4
Alburg, Vt., 426 54 A2
Alburnett, Iowa, 341 72 F2
Alburquerque, Sp., 10,054 122 B3
Alburtis, Pa., 1,086 61 L4
Albury, Austl., 16,726 173 G5
Alcabideche, Port., 12,725 122 i10
Alcácer do Sal, Port., 14,733 122 A3
Alcáçovas, Port., 4,314 122 A3
Alcalá, Col. 101 d15
Alcalá de Guadaira, Sp., 31,004 122 C4
Alcalá de Henares, Sp., 25,123 122 D2
Alcalá de los Gazules, Sp. 11,221 122 C4
Alcalá la Real, Sp., 23,314 122 D4
Alcalde, N. Mex. 79 B3
Alcamo, It., 44,016 123 D6
Alcanar, Sp., 6,944 122 F2
Alcañices, Sp., 1,549 122 B2
Alcañiz, Sp., 10,035 122 E2
Alcântara, Braz., 1,300 103 H2
Alcántara, Sp., 3,564 122 B3
Alcantarilla, Sp., 15,748 122 E4
Alcaraz, Sp., 4,771 122 D3
Alcázar de San Juan, Sp., 24,963 122 D3
Alcester, U.K., 2,924 114 E5
Alcester, S. Dak., 479 74 D4
Alcester I., Terr. Papua 174 g3
Alcira, Sp., 26,669 122 E3
Alco, Ark. 73 C2
Alco, La. 73 B6
Alcoa, Tenn., 6,395 71 H6
Alcoba, Sp., 1,964 122 C3
Alcobaça, Port., 5,166 122 A3
Alcocer, Mex. 93 d9
Alcochete, Port., 7,447 122 k10
Alcolu, S.C. 63 D4
Alcombe (part of Minehead), U.K., 2,122 114 B8
Alcomdale, Alta., Can. 43 a7
Alcona, co., Mich., 6,352 67 K4
Alcona, Mich. 67 K4
Alconbury, U.K. 114 H6
Alcora, Sp., 5,248 122 E2
Alcorn, co., Miss., 25,282 73 G3
Alcorn College, Miss. 73 D6
Alcoutim, Port., 2,605 122 B4
Alcova, Wyo. 81 F4
Alcove, N.Y. 59 v29
Alcove Res., N.Y. 59 v29
Alcovy, r., Ga. 64 F2
Alcoy, Sp., 51,096 122 E3
Alcudia, Sa. de, Sp. 122 C3
Alcuéscar, Sp., 4,075 122 B3
Aldabra Group, is., Ind. Oc. 165 G3
Aldama, Chih., Mex., 5,194 92 D2
Aldama, Méx., Mex., 2,189 93 e9
Aldama, Tam., Mex., 2,089 93 F3
Aldan, U.S.S.R., 12,100 135 M4
Aldan, r., U.S.S.R. 135 N3
Aldanskoye Nag., U.S.S.R. 135 M4
Aldbourne, U.K., 1,161 114 E8
Aldbrough, Dur., U.K. 114 E1
Aldbrough, York., U.K. 114 H3
Aldeburgh, U.K., 3,007 113 G5
Aldekerk, F.R.Ger., 2,717 119 A2
Alden, Ill. 68 D1
Alden, Iowa, 838 72 D2
Alden, Kans., 239 75 G5
Alden, Mich. 67 H4
Alden, N.Y., 2,694 58 C6
Alden, Okla. 76 E3
Alden, Pa. 61 n17
Aldenhoven, F.R.Ger., 5,193 119 A3
Aldenville (part of Chicopee), Mass. 56 F4
Alderbury, U.K., 1,038 113 i12
Aldergrove, Br. Col., Can. 42 d6
Alderholt, U.K. 113 i13
Alderley Edge, U.K., 3,618 114 D4
Aldermaston, U.K., 2,186 114 F8
Alderney, i., U.K. 113 E7
Aldershot, N.S., Can., 1,406 47 T11
Aldershot, Ont., Can., 2,459 46 D5
Aldershot, U.K., 31,225 113 F6
Alderson, Pa., 61 K3
Alderson, W.Va., 1,225 62 D5
Aldie, Va. 62 G4
Aldora, Ga., 535 64 E2
Aldorf, F.R.Ger., 2,144 119 H7
Aldrich, Mo., 181 72 D7
Aldridge, U.K., 50,981 113 F5
Aldridge = Stith
Aldridge, Colo. 79 A3
Aledo, Ill., 3,080 68 B2
Aledo, Tex. 76 d9
Aleg, Maur., 1,400 162 B3
Alegranza, I. de, Can. Is. 109 4
Alegre, Braz., 7,487 103 f17
Alegrete, Braz., 33,735 103 E7
Alegros Mtn., N. Mex. 79 A4
Alejandra, Arg., 5,500* 105 C3
Alejandría, Bol. 102 C4
Alejandría, Col. 101 d13
Aleknagik, Alaska 85 E4
Aleknagik Mission, Alaska, 50 85 E4
Aleksandriya, U.S.S.R., 57,000 136 D3
Aleksandrov, U.S.S.R., 36,600 136 c5
Aleksandrovac, Yug. 125 E3
Aleksandrovka, Ukr.S.S.R., U.S.S.R. 136 e7
Aleksandrovka, R.S.F.S.R., U.S.S.R. 137 h9
Aleksandrovo, Bulg., 3,086 128 E3
Aleksandrovo, Bulg., 2,807 128 E3
Aleksandrovsk, U.S.S.R., 17,900 137 i7
Aleksandrovsk-Sakhalinskiy, U.S.S.R., 23,000 135 O4
Aleksandrów, Pol., 11,377 127 C3
Aleksandrów Kujawski, Pol., 8,609 127 C2
Aleksandry, Zemlya, U.S.S.R. 134 C1
Alekseyevka, R.S.F.S.R., U.S.S.R., 18,900 136 E3
Alekseyevka, Kaz.S.S.R., U.S.S.R. 134 G4
Alekseyevka, Kaz.S.S.R., U.S.S.R. 134 H5
Alekseyevsk, U.S.S.R. 135 K4
Aleksin, U.S.S.R., 10,000 136 E2
Aleksinac, Yug., 6,788 125 E3
Alemán, Presa Miguel res., Mex. 93 F4
Além Paraíba, Braz., 18,399 103 e17
Alen, Nor. 120 B3
Alençon, Fr., 27,024 117 D2
Alenquer, Braz., 7,027 103 F2
Alenquer, Port., 8,273 122 k9
Alenuihaha Chan., Hawaii 84 E3
Alépé, Iv. Coast 162 b9
Aleppo = Ḥalab
Aléria, Fr., 1,176 116 r17
Alert, N.W.T., Can. 41 R1
Alert Bay, Br. Col., Can. 42 E4
Alès, Fr., 43,370 117 F4
Aleşd, Rum. 128 D1
Alessandra, Som. Rep. 163 M5
Alessandria, It., 89,234 123 B2
Alestrup, Den., 2,378 121 B4
Alesund, Nor., 18,908 120 A3
Aletschhorn, mtn. Switz. 124 C2
Aleutian Is., Alaska 85 B5
Aleutian Ra., Alaska 85 F4
Aleutian Trench, Pac. Oc. 169 F1
Alevina, M., U.S.S.R. 135 P4
Alewa Heights, Hawaii 84 c7
Alex, Okla., 545 76 F3
Alexander, Man., Can. 43 E5
Alexander, Alaska 85 G3
Alexander, Ark., 177 73 C3
Alexander, Ga. 64 G2
Alexander, co., Ill., 16,061 68 C6
Alexander, Iowa, 291 72 D2
Alexander, Kans., 153 75 F5
Alexander, Me. 55 E3
Alexander, N.Y., 335 58 D6
Alexander, co., N.C., 15,625 63 C2
Alexander, N.C. 63 B2
Alexander, N. Dak., 269 74 A2
Alexander, W.Va. 62 D4
Alexander, C., Sol. Is. 175 b2
Alexander Arch., Alaska 85 K4
Alexander Bay, S.Af., 2,066 164 B6
Alexander City, Ala., 13,140 64 C3
Alexander I., Ant. 109 G11
Alexander Mills, N.C., 947 63 B2
Alexandra, Austl., 1,712 173 e11
Alexandra, N.Z., 2,296 175 f7
Alexandra Falls, N.W.T., Can. 38 F5
Alexandra Fiord, N.W.T., Can. 41 P2
Alexandria, Austl. 172 E2
Alexandria, Br. Col., Can. 42 G3
Alexandria, Ont., Can., 2,560 47 K3
Alexandria, Rum., 19,294 128 E3
Alexandria = Al Iskandarīyah
Alexandria, U.K. 112 a7
Alexandria, Ind., 5,582 70 D2
Alexandria, Ky., 1,318 71 G3
Alexandria, La., 40,279 73 C6
Alexandria, Minn., 6,713 74 E3
Alexandria, Mo., 452 72 F4
Alexandria, Nebr., 257 75 H3
Alexandria, N.H. 54 D4
Alexandria, Ohio, 452 70 G2
Alexandria, Pa., 381 60 F4
Alexandria, S. Dak., 614 74 D4
Alexandria, Tenn., 599 71 E5
Alexandria, Va., 91,023 62 G4
Alexandria Bay, N.Y., 1,583 59 J3
Alexandrina, L., Austl. 172 c8
Alexandroúpolis, Gr., 18,712 129 E4
Alexis, Ill., 878 68 B2
Alexis, r., Newf., Can. 45 Q4
Alexis Creek, Br. Col., Can. 42 F3
Aley, r., U.S.S.R. 137 q11
Aleysk, U.S.S.R., 24,300 134 H4
Aleza Lake, Br. Col., Can. 42 G2
Alf, F.R.Ger., 1,421 119 C4
Alfalfa, co., Okla., 8,445 76 E1
Alfalfa, Okla. 76 E2
Al Fallūjah, Iraq, 20,009 143 C2
Alfaro, Sp., 8,570 122 E1
Al Fāshir, Sudan, 26,161 163 J3
Al Fashn, U.A.R. 161 K3
Alfatar, Bulg., 4,042 128 F3
Al Fāw, Iraq, 8,174 143 D2
Al Fayyūm, U.A.R., 102,000 161 K3
Alf-Bach, r., F.R.Ger. 119 B4
Alfeld, F.R.Ger., 13,053 118 B3
Alfenas, Braz., 16,051 103 G6
Alfiós, r., Gr. 129 C6
Alfonso, Phil., 3,461 153 b8
Alford, Eng., U.K., 2,139 113 G5
Alford, Scot., U.K. 112 E3
Alford, Fla., 380 65 D2
Alford, Ind. 70 B4
Alford, Mass., 256 (T) 56 C4
Alfordsville, Ind., 121 70 B4
Alfotbreen, ice cap, Nor. 120 A3
Alfred, Ont., Can., 1,188 47 K3
Alfred, Me. 55 B5
Alfred, N.Y., 2,807 58 E7
Alfred, N.Dak. 74 C2
Alfredo M. Terrazas, Mex., 2,797 93 f8
Alfred Station, N.Y. 58 E7
Alfreton, U.K., 22,999 113 F5
Alfta, Swed. 120 D3
Al Fūlah, Sudan 163 J4
Al Fuqahā', Libya 161 G3
Al Furāt, r., Asia 142 D3
Alga, U.S.S.R. 134 E5
Algansee, Mich. 67 J7
Algarrobo, Arg., 1,500* 105 C5
Algarrobo, Chile, 1,894 104 f13
Algarrobo, Col. 100 C2
Algeciras, Col. 100 C6
Algeciras, Sp., 66,317 122 C4
Alger, Alg., 722,066 160 E1
Alger, co., Mich., 9,250 67 G2
Alger, Mich. 67 J4
Alger, Ohio, 1,068 70 F2
Algeria, ctry., 11,290,000* 160 D3
Alghero, It., 26,698 123 B4
Al Ghurdaqah, U.A.R., 7,000 161 K3
Algiers = Alger
Algoa, Tex. 77 i10
Algoa Bay, S. Af. 164 D7
Algodón, r., Peru 104 C2
Algodones, N. Mex. 79 B4
Algoma, Miss. 73 F3
Algoma, Wis., 3,855 66 F4
Algoma Mills, Ont., Can. 46 B2
Algona, Iowa, 5,702 72 C1
Algona, Wash., 1,311 81 b8
Algonac, Mich., 3,190 67 L6
Algonquin, Ill., 2,692 68 D1
Algood, Tenn., 886 71 F5
Algorta, Urug., 1,000* 105 c11
Algrange, Fr., 9,163 116 b8
Algyő, Hung., 5,655 126 E3

192 · Al Ḩaḑr—Ambohidratrimo

Al Ḩaḑr, Iraq 143 C1
Alhama de Granada, Sp., 9,950 122 D4
Alhama de Murcia, Sp., 11,736 122 E4
Alhambra, Calif., 54,807 83 h15
Alhambra, Ill., 537 68 C5
Al Ḩammām, Syr. 142 D3
Al Ḩammāmāt, Tun., 7,088 160 g5
Al Ḩammān, U.A.R. 161 J2
Alhandra, Port., 5,506 122 i10
Al Harmal, Leb. 142 c5
Al Ḩārrah, Syr. 142 c6
Al Harūj al Aswad, hills, Libya 161 G3
Al Ḩasakah, Syr., 21,375 142 E2
Alhaurín el Grande, Sp., 11,525 122 C4
Al Ḩawātah, Sudan, 3,921 163 K3
Al Ḩawīyah, Saudi Ar. 143 C4
Al Ḩawṭah, Saudi Ar. 143 D4
Al Ḩayy, Iraq, 11,806 143 D2
Al Ḩijāz, reg., Saudi Ar. 143 B3
Al Ḩillah, Iraq, 54,095 143 C2
Al Hindīyah, Iraq, 12,839 143 C2
Al Hoceima, Mor., 11,262 160 D2
Al Ḩudaydah, Yemen, 25,000* 143 C6
Al Hufūf, Saudi Ar., 6,000* 143 D3
Al Ḩuṣayḩiṣah, Sudan, 6,601 163 K3
Al Ḩuṣn, Jor., 3,728 142 b7
Aliaga, Phil., 4,623 153 b7
Aliaga, Sp., 1,882 122 E2
Aliákmon, r., Gr. 129 C4
Aliança, Braz., 3,742 103 b14
Alia Pt., Hawaii 84 F4
Alibag, India, 9,909 145 h17
Ali-Bayramly, U.S.S.R., 14,200 137 d2
Alibey, Oz., U.S.S.R. 136 C4
Alibunar, Yug., 3,811 125 E2
Alicante, Sp., 121,527 122 E3
Alice, Ont., Can. 46 G3
Alice, N. Dak., 124 74 D2
Alice, Tex., 20,861 77 O6
Alice, Punta, It. 123 F5
Alice Arm, Br. Col., Can. 42 D2
Alicel, Oreg. 80 E3
Alice Springs, Austl., 2,785 172 E3
Alice Town = Hatchet Bay
Aliceville, Ala., 3,194 64 A2
Alichur, U.S.S.R. 137 g5
Alichur, r., U.S.S.R. 137 g5
Alicia, Ark., 236 73 D2
Alicudi, Isola, It. 123 E5
Alida, Sask., Can. 43 E5
Alida, Ind. 69 g10
Alida, Kans. 75 J4
Alife, It., 7,073 123 c9
Aliganj, India, 8,015 144 b12
Aligarh, India, 185,020 145 F4
Alīgūdarz, Iran, 9,592 143 D2
Alijó, Port., 3,316 122 B2
'Alī Kafr ash Shaykh, U.A.R., 31,343 161 i7
Alikchi, Okla. 76 H3
Alikianoú, Gr. 129 D7
Alima, r., Congo 164 B2
Alimnia, Nisis, i., Gr. 129 F6
Alimodian, Phil., 6,732 153 B3
Alindao, C.A.R., 8,032 163 H5
Alindau, Indon. 149 F3
Aline, Okla., 314 76 E1
Alingsås, Swed., 17,546 120 C4
Alipur, India, 28,927 145 H4
Aliquippa, Pa., 26,369 60 B4
Alirajpur, India, 10,161 145 E5
Al 'Irq, Libya 161 H3
Ali-Sabieh, Fr. Som. 163 M4
Alisal, Calif., 16,473 83 f14
Al Iskandarīyah, U.A.R., 1,513,000 161 J2
Al Isma'īlīyah, U.A.R., 111,000 161 k7
Alisos, R. de los, Mex. 92 C1
Alistráti, Gr., 3,536 129 D4
Al Ittiḩād, S. Ar. 143 D6
Alivérion, Gr., 3,523 129 E5
Aliwal North, S.Af., 10,706 164 D7
Alix, Alta., Can. 42 K3
Al Jabalayn, Sudan 163 K3
Al Jafr, Jor. 142 D4
Al Jaghbūb, Libya 161 J3
Al Jamm, Tun., 6,777 160 g6
Al Jawf, Libya 161 H3
Al Jawf, Saudi Ar. 143 B3
Al Jazīrah, Libya 161 H3
Al Jazīrah, area, Sudan 163 K3
Aljezur, Port., 5,333 122 A4
Al Jiwā', reg., Tr. States 143 E4
Al Jīzah, U.A.R., 245,000 161 i8
Al Judaydah, Leb. 142 b6
Al Junaynah, Saudi Ar. 143 C4
Al Junaynah, Sudan, 11,817 163 H3
Aljustrel, Port., 9,913 122 A4
Alkabo, N. Dak. 74 A1
Al Kāf, Tun., 14,743 160 f5
Alkali Flats, Nev. 83 B2
Alkali Lake, Br. Col., Can. 42 G3
Alkali L., Nev. 83 A2
Alkaline L., N. Dak. 74 C2
Al Karak, Jor., 7,422 142 C4
Al Kawah, Sudan 163 K3
Al Kāẓimīyah, Iraq, 126,443 143 C2
Alken, Belg., 6,583 115 D4
Al Khābūrah, Muscat and Oman 143 F4
Al Khalīl, Jor., 37,870 142 b8
Al Khāliṣ, Iraq, 5,512 143 C2
Al Khandaq, Sudan 163 J2
Al Khārījah, U.A.R., 28,249 161 J3
Al Khiyām, Leb., 5,750 142 b6
Al Khums, Libya 161 G2
Al Khurays, Saudi Ar. 143 D3
Al Khurṭūm, Sudan, 93,103 163 K3
Al Khurṭūm Baḩrī, Sudan, 39,090 163 K3
Alkmaar, Neth., 43,100 115 C2
Alkol, W.Va. 62 C4
Al Kūfah, Iraq, 21,880 143 C2
Al Kūt, Iraq, 26,524 143 D2
Al Kuwayt, Kuwait, 125,929 143 D3
Allaben, N.Y. 59 M7
Allada, Dahom. 162 e8
Al Lādhiqīyah, Syr., 61,535 142 C3
Allagash, Me. 55 D1
Allagash, r., Me. 55 C2
Allagash Falls, Me. 55 C2
Allagash L., Me. 55 C2
Allagen, F.R.Ger., 2,796 119 E2
Allahabad, India, 411,955 145 F4
Allaire, Fr., 2,103 117 B3
Allaire, N.J. 58 c16
Allakaket, Alaska, 115 85 F2
Allakh-Yun', U.S.S.R. 135 N3
Allamakee, co., Iowa, 15,982 72 F1
All American Can., Calif. 82 F6
Allamoore, Tex. 77 L4
Allamuchy, N.J., 61 B2
Allan, Sask., Can. 43 C4
Allanburg, Ont., Can. 58 i18
Allanche, Fr., 1,571 117 E4
Alland, Aust., 1,406 124 c10
Allande, Sp., 7,862 122 B1
Allanmyo, Burma, 15,560 146 A3
Allan Water, r., U.K. 112 c7
'Allāqī, Wādī al, Sudan-U.A.R. 161 K4
Allardt, Tenn. 71 G5
Allardville, N.B., Can. 47 T10
Allariz, Sp., 9,241 122 B1
Allatoona L., Ga. 64 E1
Allaykha, U.S.S.R. 135 O2
Alle, Switz., 1,471 124 B1
Alleene, Ark. 73 A4
Allegan, co., Mich., 57,729 67 H6
Allegan, Mich., 4,822 67 H6
Allegany, co., Md., 84,169 62 F3
Allegany, co., N.Y., 43,978 58 D7
Allegany, N.Y., 2,064 58 C7
Allegany, Oreg. 80 B4
Alleghany, co., N.C., 7,734 63 C1
Alleghany, co., Va., 12,128 62 D5
Alleghany, Va. 62 D5
Allegheny, co., Pa., 1,628,587 60 B4
Allegheny, r., N.Y.-Pa. 60 C3
Allegheny Mts., U.S. 53 K3
Allegheny Plateau, U.S. 51 K3
Allegre, Ky. 71 D5
Allègre, Pte., Guad. 97 14
Allemands, La., 1,167 73 E8
Allemands, L. des, La. 73 E8
Allen, Phil., 1,676 153 i15
Allen, co., Ind., 232,196 70 D2
Allen, co., Kans., 16,369 75 K6
Allen, Kans., 205 75 J5
Allen, co., Ky., 12,269 71 E5
Allen, Ky., 370 71 J4
Allen, parish, La., 19,867 73 C7
Allen, Mich., 325 67 J7
Allen, Nebr., 350 75 J1
Allen, co., Ohio, 103,691 70 E2
Allen, Okla., 1,005 76 G3
Allen, S. Dak. 74 B4
Allen, Tex., 659 76 f8
Allen, L., Ire. 113 B4
Allen, r., U.K. 113 i13
Allendale, Ill., 465 68 E5
Allendale, Ky. 71 F4
Allendale, Mich. 67 G6
Allendale, Mo., 136 72 C4
Allendale, N.J., 4,092 58 c12
Allendale, co., S.C., 11,362 63 C5
Allendale, S.C., 3,114 63 C4
Allendale Town, U.K. 113 E4
Allende, Coah., Mex., 9,938 93 E2
Allende, N.L., Mex., 6,491 93 E3
Allendorf, F.R.Ger., 6,198 118 B3
Allendorf, F.R.Ger., 1,340 119 E3
Allenhurst, Ga. 64 H4
Allenhurst, N.J., 795 58 d16
Allen Park, Mich., 37,052 67 e15
Allens, N.J. 58 a16
Allens Hill, N.Y. 58 n21
Allenspark, Colo. 79 a7
Allen Springs, Ky. 71 E5
Allensville, Ky., 286 71 D5
Allensville, Pa. 60 G4
Allenton, Mich. 67 L6
Allenton, R.I. 57 L6
Allenton, Wis. 66 E5
Allentown, Ga., 450 64 F3
Allentown, N.J., 1,393 61 B3
Allentown, N.Y. 58 D7
Allentown, Pa., 108,347 61 L4
Allentsteig, Aust., 1,774 124 M5
Allenville, Ill., 181 68 D4
Allenville, Mich. 67 J3
Allenwiller, Fr. 116 d9
Allenwood, N.J. 58 c16
Allenwood, Pa., 60 J3
Alleppey, India, 138,834 145 E8
Aller, r., F.R.Ger. 118 B2
Allerton, Ill., 282 68 E4
Allerton, Iowa, 692 72 D4
Allerton (part of Hull), Mass. 57 N3
Allerton, Pt., Mass. 57 N3
Allerum, Swed. 121 E4
Allestree, U.K., 7,298 114 F5
Allevard, Fr., 2,384 117 F4
Allgäuer Alpen, F.R.Ger. 118 C5
Alliance, Alta., Can. 42 K3
Alliance, Sur. 101 N5
Alliance, Ala. 64 b7
Alliance, Fla. 65 D2
Alliance, Nebr., 7,845 75 B1
Alliance, N.C. 63 H2
Alliance, Ohio, 28,362 70 H2
Allier, r., Fr. 117 E3
Alligator, Miss., 227 73 E3
Alligator, r., N.C. 63 H2
Alligator L., Me. 55 D4
Alligator Pond, Jam. 96 p9
Alligator Pond Bay, Jam. 96 p9
Allingåbro, Den. 121 C4
Allinge, Den., 2,114 121 G5
Allingtown (part of West Haven), Conn. 56 E7
Allipén, r., Chile 105 f14
Allison, Iowa, 952 72 E2
Allison, Kans. 75 E4
Allison, Tex. 76 N2
Allison Harbour, Br. Col., Can. 42 E3
Allison Park, Pa., 5,100* 60 c7
Alliston, Ont., Can., 2,821 46 D4
Al Līth, Saudi Ar. 143 C4
Allo, Sp., 1,441 122 n12
Alloa, U.K., 13,895 112 E3
Allons, Tenn. 71 F5
Allos, Fr. 117 G4
Alloway, U.K. 113 D4
Alloway, N.J., 61 A4
Alloway Cr., N.J. 61 A4
Allred, Tex. 77 M3
All Saints, Antigua, 2,077 97 9
Allsboro, Ala. 64 A1
Al Luḩayyah, Yemen 143 C5
Alluwe, Okla. 76 H1
Allyn, Wash. 80 B2
Alma, N.B., Can. 47 T11
Alma, Ont., Can. 46 b13
Alma, Qué., Can., 13,717 44 L5
Alma, Ark., 1,370 73 A2
Alma, Colo., 107 79 B2
Alma, Ga., 3,515 64 G4
Alma, Ill., 358 68 D5
Alma, Kans., 838 75 J4
Alma, Mich., 8,978 67 J5
Alma, Nebr., 1,342 75 F3
Alma, N. Mex. 79 A5
Alma, N.Y. 58 D7
Alma, Ohio 70 G3
Alma, Okla. 76 F3
Alma, Tex. 76 f10
Alma, Wis., 1,008 66 B4
Alma-Ata, U.S.S.R., 508,000 134 G5
Almacellas, Sp., 4,537 122 F2
Alma Center, Wis., 464 66 C4
Almada, Port., 31,523 122 A3
Almadén, Sp., 13,443 122 C3
Al Madīnah, Saudi Ar., 71,998 143 C4
Al Maḑīq, Saudi Ar., 1,163 143 C4
Al Mafraq, Jor., 9,499 142 c7
Almagro, Sp., 9,681 122 D3
Almaguer, Col. 100 B7
Al Maḩallah al Kubrá, U.A.R., 178,000 161 i7
Al Maḩāwiyah, Saudi Ar. 143 C4
Al Mahdīyah, Tun., 10,842 161 F2
Alma Hill, N.Y. 58 E7
Al Maḩmūdīyah, Iraq, 8,095 143 C2
Al Maḩras, Tun., 5,518 161 F2
Al Makīlī, Libya 161 H2
Almalyk, U.S.S.R., 50,000 137 f4
Al Manāmah, Bahr., 61,726* 143 D3
Al Manāqil, Sudan 163 K3
Almanor, Calif. 82 C2
Almanor, L., Calif. 82 C2
Almansa, Sp., 15,391 122 E3
Al Manṣūrah, U.A.R., 152,000 161 K2
Al Maqnāh, Saudi Ar. 143 B3
Al Marj, Libya, 9,982 161 H2
Al Marsá, Tun., 14,225 160 g5
Almas, P. das, Braz. 103 H4
Al Maṣīrah, i., Muscat and Oman 143 F4
Al Mawṣil, Iraq, 179,646 143 C1
Almazán, Sp., 3,958 122 D2
Almaznaya, U.S.S.R., 10,000 136 f7
Almeda, Tex. 77 i9
Almeida, Port., 1,585 122 B2
Almeirim, Braz., 2,082 103 F2
Almeirim, Port., 8,902 122 A3
Almejas, B., Mex. 92 C3
Almeley, U.K. 114 B6
Almelo, Neth., 47,100 115 E2
Almena, Kans., 555 75 F4
Almena, Wis., 398 66 A3
Almenara, Braz., 8,929 104 H5
Almendralejo, Sp., 20,884 122 B3
Almería, Sp., 86,808 122 D4
Almeria, Nebr. 75 F2
Almería, G. de, Sp. 122 D4
Al'met'yevsk, U.S.S.R., 56,000 134 E4
Älmhult, Swed. 120 C4
Al Midhnab, Saudi Ar. 143 C3
Al Miknāsī, Tun. 160 f6
Al Milḩ, Wādī, Sudan 163 J3
Al Mindak, Saudi Ar. 143 C4
Al Minyā, U.A.R., 94,000 161 K3
Al Miqdādīyah, Iraq, 7,626 143 D2
Almira, Wash., 414 80 D2
Almirante, Pan., 3,521 94 F6
Almiropótamos, Gr. 129 E5
Almirós, Gr., 6,010 129 D5
Al Mismīyah, Syr. 142 c6
Almkerk, Neth. 115 b7
Almodôvar, Port., 5,453 122 A4
Almodóvar del Campo, Sp., 15,618 122 C3
Almolonga, Guat., 4,114 94 b9
Almoloya, Mex., 1,387 93 f10
Almond, N.Y., 696 58 E7
Almond, N.C. 63 b7
Almond, Wis., 391 66 D4
Almond, r., U.K. 112 c7
Almondbank, U.K. 112 c7
Almondsbury, U.K., 4,144 113 E6
Almonesson, N.J., 1,600* 60 f12
Almont, Mich., 1,279 67 K6
Almont, N. Dak., 190 74 B2
Almonte, Ont., Can., 3,233 44 J6
Almonte, Sp., 11,538 122 B4
Almonte, r., Sp. 122 C3
Almora, India, 16,607 144 b11
Al Mubarraz, Saudi Ar. 143 D4
Al Mudawwarah, Jor. 142 D4
Al Mudawwarah, Saudi Ar. 143 B3
Al Muglad, Sudan, 3,735 163 J4
Al Mukallā, S. Ar., 35,000* 143 D6
Al Mukhā, Yemen 143 C6
Al Muknīn, Tun., 17,699 160 g6
Al Munastīr, Tun., 12,596 161 F2
Almuñécar, Sp., 14,603 122 D4
Al Muṣawwarāt aṣ Ṣafrā, ruins, Sudan 163 K3
Al Musayyib, Iraq, 12,179 143 C2
Almyra, Ark., 240 73 D3
Aln, r., U.K. 112 g9
Alna, Me. 55 C4
Alne, U.K. 114 F2
Alnmouth, U.K. 112 g9
Alnwick, U.K., 7,482 112 F4
Alo, Ìs. de Horne 175 9
Alóag, Ec. 104 c10
Alo Aloia, Terr. Papua 174 3
Al Oddaiya, Sudan 163 J3
Alofau, Tutuila 177 39
Alofi, Niue 177 32
Alofi Bay, Niue 177 32
Alofi, Î., Ìs. de Horne 175 9
Aloha, Mich. 67 J3
Aloha, Wash. 80 A2
Alon, Burma, 1,937 146 A2
Alonsa, Man., Can. 43 F5
Alonzo, Ky. 71 E5
Alor, P., Indon. 149 H5
Alora, Sp., 15,152 122 C4
Alor Gajah, Malay., 2,135 147 p15
Alor Star, Malay., 52,929 148 A1
Alorton, Ill., 3,282 72 b11
Alosno, Sp., 8,089 122 B4
Alost = Aalst
A-lo-t'ai, China 150 C2
Aloys, Nebr. 75 J2
Alpaugh, Calif. 82 D5
Alpen, F.R.Ger., 3,750 119 B1
Alpena, Ark., 283 73 B1
Alpena, co., Mich., 28,556 67 K4
Alpena, Mich., 14,682 67 K3
Alpena, S. Dak., 407 74 C3
Alpena, W.Va. 62 E4
Alpenrod, F.R.Ger., 1,040 119 D3
Alpha, Austl. 173 G3
Alpha, Ill., 637 68 B2
Alpha, Mich., 317 66 E2
Alpha, N.J., 2,406 61 A2
Alpha, Va. 62 F5
Alpharetta, Ga., 1,349 64 E1
Alphen a.d. Rijn, Neth., 19,300 115 C2
Alpine, Ariz. 78 D5
Alpine, Ark. 73 B3
Alpine, co., Calif., 397 82 D3
Alpine, Calif., 1,044 82 E6
Alpine, Ill. 69 c10
Alpine, N.J., 921 58 d13
Alpine, N.Y. 59 G7
Alpine, Oreg. 80 B3
Alpine, Tenn. 71 F5
Alpine, Tex., 4,740 77 M4
Alpine, Utah, 775 78 c10
Alpine Junction, Wyo. 81 D4
Alpirsbach, F.R.Ger., 3,785 118 B4
Alpnach, Switz., 3,211 124 C2
Alportel, Port., 9,058 122 B4
Alps, N.Y. 59 w29
Alps, mts., Eur. 110 D4
Alpujarra, Col. 100 C6
Al Qaḑārif, Sudan, 17,537 163 K3
Al Qāhirah, U.A.R., 3,346,000 161 K2
Al Qal'ah al Jardā, Tun. 160 f6
Al Qal'ah al Kubrá, Tun., 16,708 160 g6
Al Qāmishlī, Syr., 24,494 142 E2
Al Qanṭarah, U.A.R. 161 k7
Al Qaryatayn, Syr. 142 D3
Al Qasrayn, Tun., 2,705 160 f6
Al Qaṭīf, Saudi Ar., 5,000* 143 D3
Al Qaṭrānah, Jor. 142 c8
Al Qaṭrūn, Libya 161 G3
Al Qayrawān, Tun., 33,968 161 F2
Al Quds = Jerusalem
Al Qufār, Saudi Ar. 143 C3
Alquízar, Cuba, 7,111 96 b1
Al Qunayṭirah, Syr., 12,216 142 C3
Al Qunfudhah, Saudi Ar. 143 C5
Al Quṣaymah, U.A.R., 3,126 161 K2
Al Quṣayr, Syr. 142 c5
Al Quṣayr, U.A.R., 11,000 161 K3
Al Quṭayfah, Syr. 142 D3
Alresford, U.K., 2,232 114 E5
Als, Den., 2,493 121 C4
Als, i., Den. 121 B5
Alsace, reg., Fr. 117 G2
Alsager, U.K., 7,800 114 D4
Alsask, Sask., Can. 43 B4
Alsasua, Sp., 5,927 122 D1
Alsdorf, F.R.Ger., 28,051 118 A3
Alsea, Oreg. 80 B3
Alsea, r., Oreg. 80 B3
Alsek, r., Can.-U.S. 85 K3
Alsen, N. Dak., 228 74 C1
Alsenz, F.R.Ger., 1,864 119 D5
Alsenz, r., F.R.Ger. 119 D5
Alsey, Ill., 248 68 B4
Alsfeld, F.R.Ger., 9,164 118 B3
Alsheim, F.R.Ger., 2,357 119 E5
Alsip, Ill., 6,636 69 d10
Alsleben, Ger.D.R. 118 C3
Alsønderup, Den. 121 a7
Alstahaug, Nor. 120 B2
Alstead, N.H. 54 C5
Alster, r., F.R.Ger. 119 b8
Alston, U.K. 113 E4
Alston, Ga., 154 64 G3
Alston, Mich. 66 E2
Alta, Nor. 120 E1
Alta, Iowa, 1,393 72 B2
Altadena, Calif., 40,568 83 h15
Alta Gracia, Arg., 25,000* 105 B4
Alta Gracia, Nic., 1,602 94 E5
Altagracia, Ven., 14,000 100 E2
Altagracia de Orituco, Ven., 13,860 100 G3
Al Tahoe, Calif. 82 C3
Altai Mts., Asia 132 H4
Altair, Tex. 77 P5
Alta Lake, Br. Col., Can. 42 G4
Alta Loma, Calif. 83 i15
Alta Loma, Tex., 1,020 77 i10
Altamachi, Bol., 3,132 102 b10
Altamachi, r., Bol. 102 b10
Altamaha, r., Ga. 64 G4
Altamahaw, N.C. 63 E1
Altamira, Braz., 2,939 103 F2
Altamira, Col. 100 C6
Altamira, Dom. Rep., 1,336 96 m6
Altamira, Mex., 2,620 93 F3
Altamira, Ven. 100 E3
Altamont, Man., Can. 43 f10
Altamont, Calif. 83 f12
Altamont, Ill., 1,656 68 D4
Altamont, Kans., 672 75 K6
Altamont, Mo., 190 72 C5
Altamont, N.Y., 1,365 59 M6
Altamont, Oreg., 10,811 80 C4
Altamont, S. Dak., 77 74 D3
Altamont, Tenn., 552 71 F6
Altamont, Utah, 102 78 C1
Altamonte Springs, Fla., 1,212 65 H4
Altamura, It., 43,860 123 F4
Altamura, I., Mex. 92 C3
Altan Bulag, Mong. 150 E1
Altaquer, Col. 100 A7
Altar, Mex., 1,116 92 C1
Altar, r., Mex. 92 C1
Altar Wash, Ariz. 78 C6
Altassmore, U.K. 112 D3
Altata, Mex. 92 D3
Altavilla Irpina, It., 7,360 123 d9
Altaville, Calif. 82 C3
Altavista, Phil., 4,722 153 f11
Alta Vista, Iowa, 276 72 E1
Alta Vista, Kans., 400 75 J5
Altavista, Va., 3,299 62 E5
Altayn Nuruu, range, Mong. 150 C2
Altdorf, Switz., 7,477 124 C2
Alteelva, r., Nor. 120 E1
Altefjorden, Nor. 120 E1
Altena, F.R.Ger., 23,484 119 D2
Altenberg, Aust. 124 M6
Altenberg, Ger.D.R. 126 c6
Altenbögge-Bönen, F.R.Ger., 13,969 119 D1
Altenburg, Ger.D.R., 46,791 118 D3
Altendiez, F.R.Ger., 1,691 119 D4
Altendorf, F.R.Ger., 5,662 119 C2
Altengronau, F.R.Ger., 1,338 119 H4
Altenkirchen, F.R.Ger., 4,419 119 D3
Altenmarkt, Aust. 124 L6
Altenmarkt, Aust. 124 c10
Altensteig, F.R.Ger., 3,567 119 F7
Altentreptow, Ger.D.R. 118 D2
Altenwörth, Aust. 124 b10
Alte Oder, r., Ger.D.R. 118 E2
Alter do Chão, Port., 4,838 122 B3
Altha, Fla., 413 65 D2
Altheim, Aust., 4,281 124 K5
Altheim, F.R.Ger., 1,268 119 G5
Altheimer, Ark., 1,013 73 D3
Althofen, Aust., 3,231 124 L7
Althorpe, U.K., 1,067 114 G3
Altinho, Braz., 3,825 103 b15
Altkirch, Fr., 4,396 117 G3
Altlandsberg, Ger.D.R. 119 f10
Altlünen, F.R.Ger., 10,059 119 C1
Altmar, N.Y., 277 59 H4
Altmühl, r., F.R.Ger. 118 C4
Altmünster, Aust., 7,354 124 K6
Altnaharra, U.K. 112 D2
Alto, Ind. 70 C2
Alto, La. 73 D5
Alto, Mich. 67 H6
Alto, Tex., 869 77 Q4
Alto Araguaia, Braz., 2,077 103 F5
Alto Chicapa, Ang. 164 C3
Alto Colorado, Chile 104 e14
Alto Garças, Braz., 1,823 103 F5
Alto Ligonha, Moz. 164 F4
Alto Molócuè, Moz. 164 F4
Alton, Ont., Can. 46 D5
Alton, Hants., U.K., 9,159 113 F6
Alton, Staffs., U.K., 1,295 114 E5
Alton, Ill., 43,047 68 B5
Alton, Iowa, 1,048 72 B2
Alton, Kans., 299 75 G4
Alton, Ky. 71 F3
Alton, Mo., 677 72 F8
Alton, N.H. 54 E5
Alton, N.Y. 58 G5
Alton, Ohio 70 a7
Alton, R.I. 57 K7
Alton, Utah, 116 78 B3
Altona, Man., Can., 1,979 43 F5
Altona, Ill., 505 68 B2
Altona, Mich. 67 H5
Altona, Nebr. 75 J1
Altona, N.Y. 59 N2
Altona, Okla. 76 E2
Alton Bay, N.H. 54 E5
Altoona, Ala., 744 64 C1
Altoona, Fla. 65 H4
Altoona, Iowa, 1,458 72 D3
Altoona, Kans., 490 75 K6
Altoona, Pa., 69,407 60 F5
Altoona, Wash. 80 B2
Altoona, Wis., 2,114 66 B4
Alto Park, Ga., 2,526 64 D1
Alto Parnaíba, Braz., 1,167 103 G3
Alto Pass, Ill., 323 68 C6
Alto Purús, r., Peru 104 D4
Alto Seco, Bol., 3,429 102 d11
Alto Songo, Cuba, 2,197 96 f2
Altotonga, Mex., 5,408 93 F4
Altötting, F.R.Ger., 8,896 118 D4
Altrincham, U.K., 41,104 114 D4
Altruppin, Ger.D.R. 118 D2
Alt Sankt Johann, Switz., 1,351 124 D1
Altshausen, F.R.Ger., 3,210 118 B5
Altstadt, F.R.Ger., 1,316 116 d8
Altstätten, Switz., 8,751 124 D1
Altuda, Tex. 77 M4
Altura, Minn., 320 74 F3
Alturas, Calif., 2,819 82 C2
Altus, Ark., 392 73 B2
Altus, Okla., 21,225 76 D3
Altus, L., Okla. 76 D3
Altviller, Fr. 116 c9
Al Ubayyiḑ, Sudan, 52,372 163 J3
A-lu-k'o-erh-ch'in-ch'i, China 151 C2
Alūksne, U.S.S.R., 6,700 136 B1
Al 'Ulá, Saudi Ar., 3,835 143 B3
Alula, Som. Rep., 2,547* 163 N4
Alum Bank = Pleasantville
Alum Cr., Ohio 70 G2
Aluminé, Arg., 6,000* 105 A5
Alum Rock, Calif., 18,942 83 f13
Aluniș, Rum. 128 E1
Alunite, Nev. 83 C5
Alung Gangri, China 150 B3
Alupka, U.S.S.R., 6,700 136 D4
Al 'Uqaylah, Libya 161 H2
Al 'Uqayr, Saudi Ar. 143 D3
Al Uqṣur, U.A.R., 24,457 161 K3
Alushta, U.S.S.R., 12,200 136 D4
Alutom I., Guam 176 24
Alutom Mt., Guam 176 24
Alva, U.K., 3,957 112 c7
Alva, Fla. 65 H6
Alva, Ky. 71 H5
Alva, Okla., 6,258 76 E1
Alvadore, Oreg. 80 B3
Alvalade, Port., 3,292 122 A4
Alvarado, Col. 101 e15
Alvarado, Mex., 12,424 93 G4
Alvarado, Calif. 83 e12
Alvarado, Minn., 282 74 D1
Alvarado, Tex., 1,907 77 P3
Alvarães, Braz., 2,527 102 C2
Alvarez de Toledo, Arg. 105 b12
Álvarez Jonte, Arg., 1,428 105 c12
Alvaro Obregón, Mex. 93 H4
Álvaro Obregón, Presa, res., Mex. 92 C2
Alvaton, Ga., 24 64 f12
Alvdal, Nor. 120 B3
Älvdalen, Swed. 120 C3
Alvear, Arg., 10,500* 105 D3
Alvechurch, U.K., 4,578 114 D6
Alveley, U.K., 1,076 114 D6
Alvena, Sask., Can. 43 C4
Alverca, Port., 7,618 122 i10
Alverda, Pa., 60 E4
Alverno, Mich. 67 J3
Alveslohe, F.R.Ger., 1,670 119 a8
Alvesta, Swed. 120 C4
Alveston, U.K., 1,820 114 D7
Ålvik, Nor. 120 A3
Alvin, S.C. 63 E4
Alvin, Tex., 5,643 77 Q5
Alvin, Wis. 66 E3
Alvinópolis, Braz., 3,600 103 e17
Alvinston, Ont., Can. 46 C6
Alviso, Calif., 1,174 83 f13
Älvkarleby, Swed. 120 D3
Alvon, W.Va. 62 D5
Alvord, Iowa, 238 72 A1
Alvord, Tex., 694 77 P3
Alvord L., Oreg. 80 D4
Alvordton, Ohio, 388 70 E1
Älvsborg, Swed. 121 D3
Älvsbyn, Swed. 120 E2
Alvwood, Minn. 74 E2
Al Wajh, Saudi Ar. 143 B3
Alwar, India, 72,707 145 E4
Al Wāsiṭah, U.A.R., 11,000 161 K3
Alwernia, Pol. 127 i6
Al Yamāmah, Saudi Ar., 8,000* 143 D4
Alygdzher, U.S.S.R. 135 J4
Alyth, U.K., 1,862 112 E3
Alytus, U.S.S.R., 12,000 136 A2
Alz, r., F.R.Ger. 118 D4
Alzada, Mont. 81 G3
Alzamay, U.S.S.R., 11,800 135 J4
Alzette, r., Lux. 115 E5
Alzey, F.R.Ger., 11,515 118 A4
Alzonne, Fr., 1,275 117 E5
Ama, Jap., 6,678 155 C3
Amadeus, L., Austl. 172 D3
Amadi, Sudan 163 K5
Amadjuak, r., N.W.T., Can. 41 P4
Amadjuak L., N.W.T., Can. 41 P4
Amado, Ariz. 78 C6
Amador, co., Calif., 9,990 82 C3
Amador, Mich. 67 L5
Amadora, Port., 47,355 122 i10
Amagá, Col. 101 d13
Amagansett, N.Y., 1,095 59 Q10
Amagasaki, Jap., 405,955 155 D4
Amager, i., Den. 121 E5
Amagi, Jap., 45,988 154 B5
Amagon, Ark., 234 73 D2
Amahai, Indon. 149 J3
Amajac, Mex., 1,563 93 f9
Amajague, r., Mex. 93 e8
Amakusa-Kami-jima, Jap. 154 B5
Amakusa-nada, Jap. 154 A5
Amakusa-rettō, Jap. 154 B5
Amakusa-Shimo-jima, Jap. 154 A5
Åmål, Swed. 120 C4
Amalfi, Col. 100 C4
Amalfi, It., 6,803 123 d10
Amalia, N. Mex. 79 C3
Amaliás, Gr., 15,468 129 C6
Amalner, India, 46,963 145 E5
Amaluia, Tutuila 177 39
Amambaí, Braz., 2,601 103 E6
Amami-guntō, Jap. 154 d12
Amami-Ō-shima, Jap. 154 d12
Amana, Iowa 72 F3
Amanave, Tutuila 177 39
Amanave Bay, Tutuila 177 39
Amance, Fr. 116 b9
Amanda, Ohio, 732 70 G3
Amanda Park, Wash. 80 A2
Amanganj, India 144 b13
Amantea, It., 11,778 123 F5
Amantes Pt., Guam 176 24
Amanu, atoll, Tuam. Arch. 177 42
Amapá, terr., Braz., 68,889 103 F1
Amapá, Braz., 1,591 103 F1
Amarante, Braz., 3,199 103 H3
Amarante do Maranhão, Braz., 1,662 103 G3
Amaranth, Man., Can. 43 F5
Amarapura, Burma, 10,519 147 g7
Amaravati, India, 137,875 145 F5
Amargosa, r., Calif.-Nev. 82 E5
Amargosa Ra., Calif. 82 E4
Amarillas, Cuba, 1,935 96 c1
Amarillo, Tex., 137,969 76 M2
Amárinthos, Gr., 2,413 129 D5
Amarkantak, India 144 c14
Amarube-Shimo, Jap. 154 g14
Amarume, Jap., 22,996 155 F2
Amasa, Mich. 66 E2
Amasya, Turk., 28,188 142 C1
Amataurá, Braz. 102 C2
Amatique, B. de, Br. Hond.-Guat. 94 C3
Amatitán, Mex., 2,854 93 a9
Amatitlán, Guat., 8,538 94 B3
Amatlán de Cañas, Mex., 2,961 92 D4
Amatsu, Jap. 155 G4
Amaua, Tutuila 177 39
Amawalk Res., N.Y. 56 A7
Amay, Belg., 7,277 115 D4
Amayuca, Mex., 1,598 93 f11
Amazar, U.S.S.R. 135 M4
Amazon = Amazonas, r.
Amazon = Solimões
Amazonas, st., Braz., 721,215 102 B2
Amazonas, r., S.Amer. 98 D3
Amazonia, Mo., 326 72 B5
Ambah, India, 6,668 144 b12
Ambala, India, 105,543 145 E3
Ambalangoda, Cey., 10,554 145 n22
Ambalavao, Malag. Rep., 4,684 165 G5
Ambalema, Col. 100 C5
Ambam, Cam. 162 F5
Ambania, Malag. Rep., 4,264 165 H4
Ambarawa, Indon. 148 d7
Ambarchik, U.S.S.R. 135 Q3
Ambardakh, U.S.S.R. 135 N2
Ambasamudram, India, 22,447 145 k21
Ambato, Ec., 52,713 104 B2
Ambato Boeni, Malag. Rep., 2,916 165 G4
Ambatofinandrahana, Malag. Rep., 1,882 165 G5
Ambatolampy, Malag. Rep., 9,165 165 G5
Ambatondrazaka, Malag. Rep., 7,469 165 H4
Ambatosoratra, Malag. Rep., 1,876 165 H4
Ambazac, Fr., 3,655 117 D4
Amber, India, 6,932 144 a12
Amber, N.Y. 59 q24
Amber, Okla. 76 F2
Amber, Wash. 80 E2
Amberg, F.R.Ger., 41,574 118 C4
Amberg, Wis. 66 E3
Ambergris Cay, Br. Hond. 94 D2
Ambérieu-en-Bugey, Fr., 8,203 117 F4
Amberley, N.Z. 175 g6
Amberley, Ohio, 2,951 71 i10
Ambert, Fr., 7,600 117 E4
Ambia, Ind., 351 70 B2
Ambikapur, India, 15,240 145 G5
Ambil I., Phil. 153 b9
Ambilobe, Malag. Rep., 3,926 165 H4
Amble, U.K., 4,889 113 F4
Amble, Mich. 67 H5
Ambler, Alaska, 70 85 E2
Ambler, Pa., 6,765 61 M5
Ambleside, U.K., 2,392 114 C2
Amblève, Belg., 1,885 119 A4
Amblève, r., Belg. 115 E4
Ambo, Peru, 1,612 104 B4
Ambo Chan., Kwajalein 176 25
Ambohidratrimo, Malag. Rep., 1,965 165 G5

Ambohimahasoa—Antsalova · 193

Ambohimahasoa, Malag. Rep., 4,101 165 G5
Amboina=Ambon
Ambon, Indon., 56,037 149 J3
Amboise, Fr., 8,192 117 D3
Ambositra, Malag. Rep., 12,028 165 G5
Ambovombe, Malag. Rep., 2,034 165 G6
Amboy, Calif. 82 F5
Amboy, Ill., 2,067 68 C2
Amboy, Ind., 446 70 D2
Amboy, Minn., 629 74 E4
Amboy, Wash. 80 B3
Ambre, C.d', Malag. Rep. 165 H3
Ambridge, Pa., 13,865 60 B4
Ambrim, i., New Hebr. 174 m6
Ambriz, Ang. 164 B3
Ambrizete, Ang. 164 B3
Ambrose, Ga., 244 64 G4
Ambrose, N. Dak., 220 74 A1
Ambrosia Lake, N. Mex. 79 B4
Ambulu, Indon. 148 E5
Ambunten-Timur, Indon. 148 e7
Ambunti, Terr. New Guin. 174 d2
Amby, Austl. 173 G4
Amchitka I., Alaska 85 e8
Amchitka Pass, Alaska 85 e8
Am Dam, Chad 163 H3
Amden, Switz., 1,270 124 D1
Amderma, U.S.S.R., 2,200 134 F3
Amealco, Mex., 2,199 93 d9
Ameca, Mex., 17,396 92 E4
Ameca, r., Mex. 92 D4
Amecac, Mex., 1,427 93 f11
Amecameca, Mex., 12,271 93 F4
Ameide, Neth. 115 b7
Ameland, i., Neth. 115 D1
Amele, Terr. New Guin. 174 e2
Amelia, It., 11,705 123 D3
Amelia, Fla. 65 H2
Amelia, La. 73 D8
Amelia, Nebr. 75 F1
Amelia, Ohio. 913 70 E3
Amelia, co., Va., 7,815 62 F5
Amelia, Va. 62 F5
Amelia I., Fla. 65 H2
Amélie-les-Bains, Fr., 3,032 117 E5
Amenia, N.Y. 59 O8
Amenia, N. Dak., 117 74 D2
American, r., Calif. 82 C3
American Falls, Idaho, 2,602 81 C4
American Falls Res., Idaho 81 C4
American Fork, Utah, 6,373 78 C1
American Highland, Ant. 180 S5
American Samoa, Pac. Oc., 21,000* 170 G5
Americus, Ga., 13,472 64 E3
Americus, Ind. 70 C2
Americus, Kans., 300 75 J5
Amern, F.R.Ger., 5,824 119 A2
Amerongen, Neth., 3,000 115 D3
Amersfoort, Neth., 66,600 115 D2
Amersham, U.K., 14,612 114 G7
Amery, Wis., 1,769 66 A3
Amery Ice Shelf, Ant. 180 S5
Ames, Iowa, 27,003 72 D2
Ames, N.Y., 162 59 L6
Ames, Okla., 211 76 E1
Ames, Tex. 77 k8
Amesbury, Alta., Can. 42 K2
Amesbury, U.K., 5,511 113 F6
Amesbury, Mass., 9,625; 10,787(T) 57 N1
Amesville, Ohio, 255 70 H3
Amfíklia, Gr., 3,111 129 D5
Amfilokhía, Gr., 5,408 129 C5
Ámfissa, Gr., 6,076 129 D5
Amga, U.S.S.R. 135 N3
Amga, r., U.S.S.R. 135 N3
Amgu, U.S.S.R. 135 N5
Amgun', r., U.S.S.R. 135 N4
Amherst, Burma, 6,024 146 B3
Amherst, N.S., Can., 10,549 45 N6
Amherst, Colo. 79 D1
Amherst, Me. 55 D4
Amherst, Mass., 10,306; 13,718(T) 56 G3
Amherst, Nebr., 220 75 F3
Amherst, N.H. 54 D6
Amherst, N.Y. 58 k18
Amherst, Ohio, 6,750 70 G1
Amherst, S. Dak. 74 D3
Amherst, Tex., 883 77 M2
Amherst, co., Va., 22,953 62 E5
Amherst, Va., 1,200 62 E5
Amherst, Wis., 596 66 D4
Amherstburg, Ont., Can., 4,404 46 A6
Amherstdale, W.Va., 1,716 62 C5
Amherst I., Ont., Can. 46 H4
Amhurst, Mt., Austl. 172 C2
Amiata, Monte, It. 123 C3
Amidon, N. Dak., 84 74 A2
Amiens, Fr., 109,869 117 E2
Amik Gölü, Turk. 142 C2
Amíndaion, Gr., 3,861 129 C4
Amindivi Is., India 145 D8
Amino, Jap., 18,626 155 D4
Amirante Is., Ind. Oc. 165 H2
Amisk L., Sask., Can. 43 D3
Amissville, Va. 62 F4
Amistad, N. Mex. 79 D4
Amite, La., 3,316 73 E7
Amite, co., Miss., 15,573 73 E6
Amite, r., La. 73 E7
Amity, Ark., 543 73 B3
Amity, Ga. 64 G2
Amity, Mo., 111 72 C5
Amity, Ohio 70 a6
Amity, Oreg., 620 80 B3
Amity, Pa., 60 B5
Amityville, N.Y., 8,318 58 f14
Amizmiz, Mor., 4,036 160 C2
Amkyokyung, China 144 f11
Amla, India, 12,259 144 b15
Amlekhganj, Nepal 144 e12
Åmli, Nor. 120 B4
Amlia I., Alaska 85 g8
Amlin, Ohio 70 a6
Amlwch, U.K. 113 D5
Amma, W.Va. 62 C4
'Ammān, Jor., 244,221 142 D4
Ammanford, U.K., 6,267 113 E6
Ämmänsaari, Fin. 120 G2
Ammarfjället, mt., Swed. 120 C2
Ammersee, F.R.Ger. 118 C4
Ammerstol, Neth. 115 b7
Ammerzoden, Neth. 115 c7
Ammon, Idaho, 1,882 81 D4
Ammonoosuc, r., N.H. 54 D3
Amnat Charoen, Thai. 146 D4
Amnicon L., Wis. 66 A2
Amok, New Hebr. 174 k6
Āmol, Iran, 22,251 143 E1
Amolar, Braz. 102 E5
Amoles, Mex. 93 e8
Amonate, Va. 62 C5
Amora, Port., 7,361 122 i10
Amorbach, F.R.Ger., 3,878 119 G5
Amorebieta, Sp., 8,346 122 n11
Amoret, Mo., 261 72 C6
Amorgós, Gr. 129 E6
Amorgós, i., Gr. 129 F6
Amorita, Okla., 74 76 E1
Amory, Miss., 6,474 73 G4
Amos, Qué., Can., 6,006 44 H5
Amose, r., Den. 121 D5
Amotape, Peru, 3,500 104 A3
Amou, Fr., 1,400 117 C5
Amougies, Belg., 1,006 116 a6
Amouli, Tutuila 177 39
Amoy=Hsia-men
Amoy Bay=Hsia-men Wan
Ampana, Indon. 149 G3
Ampang, Malay., 9,741 147 o15
Ampanihy, Malag. Rep., 2,480 165 G6
Amparihy, Malag. Rep. 165 G5
Amparo, Braz., 14,382 103 c18
Amper, r., F.R.Ger. 118 C4
Ampere Seamount, Atl. Oc. 108 M4
Ampfield, U.K. 113 k12
Amphawa, Thai., 7,532 147 d5
Ampleforth, U.K. 114 F2
Amplepuis, Fr., 5,492 117 F4
Amposta, Sp., 12,507 122 F2
Ampthill, U.K., 3,852 114 G6
Ampuero, Sp., 3,581 122 m11
Ampuis, Fr., 1,545 116 p16
Ampurias, Sp. 122 G1
Amqui, Qué., Can., 3,544 45 M5
Amrati, India 145 F6
Amreli, India, 34,699 145 D5
Amriswil, Switz., 6,752 124 D1
Amritsar, India, 376,295 145 E3
Amroha, India, 68,965 144 b11
Amrum, i., F.R.Ger. 118 B1
Åmsele, Swed. 120 D2
Amstel, r., Neth. 115 C2
Amstelveen, Neth., 37,300 115 C2
Amsterdam, Neth., 840,100 115 D2
Amsterdam, Mo., 118 72 C6
Amsterdam, N.Y., 28,772 59 M6
Amsterdam, Ohio, 931 70 J2
Amsterdam, Île, Ind. Oc. 168 C4
Amsterdam-Rijn kan., Neth. 115 D2
Amstetten, Aust., 12,075 124 L5
Amston (part of Hebron), Conn. 56 G6
Am Timan, Chad, 1,600* 163 H4
Amuay, Ven. 100 E2
Amu-Dar'ya, r., U.S.S.R. 134 F5
Amudat, Uganda 164 E1
Amukta I., Alaska 85 B5
Amukta Pass, Alaska 85 B5
Amuku Mts., Guyana 101 L7
Amulree, U.K. 112 E3
Amund Ringnes I., N.W.T., Can. 41 K2
Amundsen G., N.W.T., Can. 40 E3
Amundsen Sea, Ant. 180 Y5
Amungan, Phil., 2,699 153 a7
Amungen, l., Swed. 120 D3
Amuntai, Indon. 148 E3
Amur=Hei-lung
Amur, r., U.S.S.R. 135 N4
'Amūr, Wādī, Sudan 163 K2
Amurang, Indon. 149 H2
Amurd, Afghan. 145 D1
Amuri, Aitutaki 177 35
Amurrio, Sp., 4,039 122 n11
Amvrakikós Kólpos, Gr. 129 C5
Amvrosiyevka, U.S.S.R., 20,000 136 E4
Amy, Ark. 73 C4
Amy, Kans. 75 E5
Amyl, r., U.S.S.R. 137 t11
Amyūn, Leb., 4,316 142 b5
An, Burma 146 A3
Anaa, i., Tuam. Arch. 171 J6
Anabar (dist.), Nauru 175 17
Anabar, r., U.S.S.R. 135 L2
Anabuki, Jap., 16,460 154 f15
Anabusko, r., Man., Can. 43 H2
Anacacho, Tex. 77 N5
Anacapa I., Calif. 82 D6
Anachucuna, Pan. 94 J6
Anaco, Ven., 22,733 101 H3
Anaconda, Mont., 12,054 81 C2
Anaconda Ra., Mont. 81·
Anacortes, Wash., 8,414 80 B1
Anacostia, r., D.C.-Md. 62 b9
Anacuao, Mt., Phil. 153 c6
Anadarko, Okla., 6,299 76 E2
Anadolu, reg., Turk. 142 B2
Anadyr', U.S.S.R., 4,600 135 R3
Anadyr', r., U.S.S.R. 135 R3
Anadyrskiy Zal., U.S.S.R. 135 S3
Anadyrskoye Plos., U.S.S.R. 135 R3
Anae I., Guam 176 24
Anáfi, i., Gr. 129 E6
Anaga, Jap. 154 f15
Anagni, It., 15,642 123 D4
'Ānah, Iraq, 11,070 143 C2
Anaheim, Calif., 104,184 82 E6
Anahim Lake, Br. Col., Can. 42 F3
Anaho I., Nev. 83 A3
Anahola, Hawaii 84 B1
Anáhuac, Mex., 5,973 93 E2
Anahuac, Tex., 1,985 77 Q5
Anahulu, r., Hawaii 84 b6
Anajás, Braz. 103 F2
Anakapalle, India, 46,402 145 G6
Anak Bukit, Malay., 1,606 147 o13
Anakena Cove Landing, Easter I. 177 46
Anakie, Austl. 173 G3
Anaktuvuk, r., Alaska 85 G1
Anaktuvuk Pass, Alaska 85 G1
Analalava, Malag. Rep., 1,925 165 H4
Anamã, Braz., 2,752 102 D2
Ana Maria, Cayos, Cuba 96 d2
Ana Maria, Golfo de, Cuba 96 d2
Anambas, Kep., Indon. 148 C2
Aname, New. Hebr. 174 m8
Anamizu, Jap., 19,182 155 E3
Anamoose, N. Dak., 503 74 B2
Anamosa, Iowa, 4,616 72 F2
Anamur, Turk., 6,579 142 C2
Anan, Jap. 155 D5
Anand, India, 40,458 145 D5
Anantapur, India, 52,280 145 E7
Anantnag, India, 21,807 145 E2
Anan'yev, U.S.S.R., 7,800 136 C4
Anapa, U.S.S.R., 17,600 136 E4
Anapoima, Col. 101 e15
Anápolis, Braz., 48,847 103 G5
Anapu, r., Braz. 103 F2
Anārdarra, Afghan. 144 A2
Anare, Ven. 101 c11
Anarjåkka, r., Nor. 120 F1
Anarjåkka, Nor.=Inarijoki, Fin.
Añasco, P.R., 2,068 96 r10
Añasco, B. de, P.R. 96 r10
Anastácio, Braz., 2,727 103 E6
Anastasiyevka, U.S.S.R. 136 f8
Anatahan, i., Mar. Is. 170 D3
Anatolia=Anadolu
Añatuya, Arg., 16,000* 105 C3
Anauá, r., Braz. 102 D1
Anávra, Gr., 1,043 129 D5
Anawalt, W.Va., 1,062 62 C5
Anaypazarı, Turk., 3,941 142 C2
An Binh, S. Viet. 147 k11
Anbōru, i., Jaluit 176 30
Anbyŏn, N. Kor. 151 E3
Ancaster, Ont., Can., 1,077 46 b15
Ancenis, Fr., 5,458 117 C3
Ancerville, Fr., 2,362 117 F2
Anchau, Nigeria 162 F4
An-ch'i, China 152 E2
An-ch'ing, China, 105,300* 150 F4
An-ch'iu, China 151 C3
Ancho, N. Mex. 79 C5
Anchor, U.K. 114 B6
Anchor, Ill., 194 68 D3
Anchorage, Alaska, 44,237 85 G3
Anchorage, Ky., 1,170 71 F3
Anchor Bay, Mich. 67 L6
Anchor Bay Gardens, Mich., 1,830 67 g14
Anchor Point, Alaska 85 G4
Anchorville, Mich. 67 L6
Anclitas, Cayo, Cuba 96 d2
Anclote Keys, Fla. 65 c11
Ancoa, Chile 104 f15
Ancohuma, Nev., Bol. 102 C5
Ancon, C.Z., 1,151 94 g13
Ancón, Peru, 3,607 104 B4
Ancona, It., 98,172 123 D3
Ancón de Sardinas, B. de, Ec. 104 B1
Ancoraimes, Bol., 18,245 102 a9
Ancram, N.Y. 59 N7
Ancramdale, N.Y. 59 N7
Ancroft, U.K. 112 F4
Ancud, Chile, 7,390 105 A6
Ancy, Fr., 1,164 116 b8
Andacollo, Arg. 105 A5
Andacollo, Chile, 5,381 105 A4
Andahuaylas, Peru, 4,551 104 C5
Andajes, Peru, 1,093 104 B4
Andalgalá, Arg., 7,000* 105 B3
Åndalsnes, Nor. 120 B3
Andalucía, Col. 100 B5
Andalucía, reg., Sp. 122 C4
Andalusia, Ala., 10,263 64 C4
Andalusia, Ill., 560 68 B2
Andalusia=Andalucía
Andaman Basin, Asia 141 H6
Andaman Is., India 146 A4
Andaman Sea, Asia 146 A4
Andamarca, Bol., 6,209 102 C5
Andamooka, Austl. 172 E4
Andapa, Malag. Rep., 3,037 165 H4
Andaraí, Braz., 2,510 103 H4
Andau, Aust., 3,011 124 O6
Andaung Pech, Camb. 146 D4
Ändebol, Swed. 120 d9
Andebu, Nor. 121 C1
Andeer, Switz. 124 D2
Andenes, Nor. 120 D1
Andenne, Belg., 7,834 115 D4
Anderlecht, Belg., 93,243 115 d9
Anderlues, Belg., 13,477 115 C4
Andermatt, Switz., 1,523 124 C2
Andernach, F.R.Ger., 19,025 118 A3
Anderson, Ala. 64 B1
Anderson, Calif., 4,492 82 B2
Anderson, Ind., 49,061 70 D2
Anderson, co., Kans., 9,035 75 K5
Anderson, co., Ky., 8,618 71 F4
Anderson, Mo., 992 72 C8
Anderson, co., S.C., 98,478 63 B3
Anderson, S.C., 41,316 63 B3
Anderson, co., Tenn., 60,032 71 G5
Anderson, co., Tex., 28,162 77 Q4
Anderson, Tex. 77 Q4
Anderson, r., N.W.T., Can. 40 D4
Anderson, Mt., Austl. 172 C2
Anderson I., Wash. 81 a8
Anderson L., Br. Col., Can. 42 G4
Anderson Lakes, Minn. 74 b6
Andersons Bay, Austl. 173 f13
Andersonville, Ga., 263 64 E3
Andes, Col. 100 C5
Andes, N.Y., 399 59 L7
Andes, Cord. de los, S. Amer. 98 B3
Andfjorden, chan., Nor. 120 D1
Andhra Pradesh, st., India, 35,983,447 145 F7
Andia, Sa. de, Sp. 122 n12
Andijk, Neth., 4,200 115 D2
Andikíthira, i., Gr. 129 D7
Andikíthiron Stenón, Gr. 129 D7
Andilamena, Malag. Rep., 2,155 165 H4
Andimákhia, Gr., 1,539 129 F6
Andīmeshk, Iran, 7,324 143 D2
Andímilos, i., Gr. 129 E6
Andíparos, Gr. 129 E6
Andíparos, i., Gr. 129 E6
Andípaxoi, i., Gr. 129 C5
Ándissa, Gr., 2,530 129 E5
Andizhan, U.S.S.R., 141,000 134 G5
Andkhūi, Afghan. 144 B1
Andoas, Peru 104 B2
Andoga, r., U.S.S.R. 136 E1
Andon, Fr. 116 m13
Andong, S. Kor., 53,685 151 F3
Andorf, Aust., 4,105 124 K5
Andorno Micca, It., 4,008 122 a5
Andorra, ctry., 11,000* 122
Andorra, Andorra, 3,434 122 F1
Andorra, Sp., 7,795 122 E2
Andover, N.B., Can. 47 S10
Andover, U.K., 16,985 113 F6
Andover, Conn., 1,771(T) 55 G6
Andover, Ill., 295 68 B2
Andover, Kans., 186 75 H6
Andover, Me. 55 B4
Andover, Mass., 15,878(T) 57 M2
Andover, N.H. 54 D5
Andover, N.J., 734 61 B2
Andover, N.Y., 1,247 58 E7
Andover, Ohio, 1,116 70 J1
Andover, S. Dak., 224 74 D3
Andöya, i., Nor. 120 C1
Andradas, Braz., 5,473 103 c18
Andradina, Braz., 20,485 103 F6
Andraitx, Sp. 122 G3
Andreafsky, r., Alaska 85 D3
Andrelândia, Braz., 4,617 103 d17
Andreanof Is., Alaska 85 g8
Andreas, C., Cyp. 142 C3
Andres, Ill. 68 E2
Andrés, B. de, Dom. Rep. 96 n6
Andres Bonifacio, Phil., 7,445 153 e11
Andrésy, Fr., 4,271 116 g11
Andréville, Qué., Can. 47 R10
Andrew, Alta., Can. 42 K3
Andrew, Iowa, 349 72 G2
Andrew, co., Mo., 11,062 72 C5
Andrew, Mt., Austl. 172 C5
Andrew Bay, Burma 147 a1
Andrew Johnson Nat. Mon., Tenn. 71 J5
Andrew L., Alta. Can. 43 B2
Andrews, Ind., 1,132 70 D2
Andrews, N.C., 1,404 63 b7
Andrews, Oreg. 80 D4
Andrews, S.C., 2,995 63 E4
Andrews, co., Tex., 13,450 77 M3
Andrews, Tex., 11,135 77 M3
Andreyevka, U.S.S.R. 136 E3
Andreyevka, U.S.S.R. 136 e8
Andrezel, Fr. 116 k12
Andria, It., 71,308 123 F4
Andrijevica, Yug. 125 D3
Andringitra, mts., Malag. Rep. 165 G5
Andritsaina, Gr., 1,391 129 D6
Androka, Malag. Rep. 165 G6
Ándros, Gr., 2,032 129 E6
Ándros, i., Gr. 129 E6
Androscoggin, co., Me., 86,312 55 B4
Androscoggin, r., Me.-N.H. 54 E3
Androscoggin L., Me. 55 B4
Andros I., Bah. Is. 95 C1
Andry, Ind. 69 h10
Andrychów, Pol., 8,914 127 i7
Andryushino, U.S.S.R. 137 k7
Andselva, Nor. 120 D1
Andújar, Sp., 32,185 122 D3
Andulo, Ang. 164 B3
Anduze, Fr., 3,066 117 E4
Anécho, Togo, 10,487 162 d8
Anegada, i., V.I. 97 4
Anegada Passage, W.I. 95 G3
Anegasaki, Jap., 11,323 155 G4
Aneityum, i., New Hebr. 174 m8
Anekal, India, 10,673 145 k19
Anelgauhat, New Hebr. 174 m8
Anepahan Pk., Phil. 153 A3
Aneroid, Sask., Can. 43 C5
Anet, Fr., 1,349 117 D2
Aneta, N. Dak., 451 74 D2
Anetan (dist.), Nauru 175 17
Aneto, P. de, Fr.-Sp. 122 F1
Anfah, Leb., 2,527 142 b5
An-fu, China 152 D2
Angadanan, Phil., 2,525 153 c6
Angahuán, Mex., 1,138 93 b10
Angamacutiro, Mex., 3,720 93 c9
Angamos, P., Chile 105 A2
Ang-ang-ch'i, China 151 E1
Angangueo, Mex., 7,394 93 d10
Anganiwai, Sol. Is. 175 c3
Angara, r., U.S.S.R. 135 K4
Angara Basin, Arctic Oc. 133 E1
Angarsk, U.S.S.R., 154,000 135 K4
Angaston, Austl., 1,839 172 c8
Angat, Phil., 5,033 153 c8
Angathonisi, i., Gr. 129 F6
Angaur, i., Palau 176 21
Ånge, Swed. 120 C3
Angel, Salto, Ven. 101 J5
Ángel de la Guarda, I., Mex. 92 B2
Angeles, Phil., 6,470 153 B2
Ängelholm, Swed. 120 C4
Angelica, N.Y., 898 58 E7
Angelica, Wis. 66 E4
Angelina, co., Tex., 39,814 77 Q4
Angelina, r., Tex. 77 Q4
Angelo, Wis. 66 C5
Angels, Pa., 61 p16
Angels Camp, Calif., 1,121 82 C3
Angelus, Kans. 75 E4
Angelus, S.C. 63 D3
Ångermanälven, r., Swed. 120 D3
Angermünde, Ger.D.R., 11,700 118 D2
Angers, Qué., Can. 47 J3
Angers, Fr., 122,269 117 C3
Angerville, Fr., 1,653 117 D2
Angervilliers, Fr. 116 g12
Anges, B. des, Fr. 116 n13
Angicos, Braz., 1,551 103 a13
Angie, La., 254 73 F7
Angier, N.C., 1,249 63 F2
Angikuni L., N.W.T., Can. 38 K5
Ang-jen, China 144 f11
Angkor Wat, ruins, Camb. 146 D4
Angledool, Austl. 173 G4
Anglem, Mt., N.Z. 175 e7
Anglesey, co., U.K., 51,705 113 D5
Angles Pk., N. Mex. 79 B3
Angleton, Tex., 7,312 77 Q5
Ango, D.R.Congo 164 D1
Angol, Chile, 18,637 105 A5
Angola (Port. Over. Terr.), 5,258,000* 164 B3
Angola, Ind., 4,746 70 E1
Angola, N.Y., 2,550 58 B6
Angola Basin, Atl. Oc. 108 N8
Angoon, Alaska, 395 85 L4
Angora, Nebr. 75 B2
Angora, Okla. 76 D2
Angoram, Terr. New Guin. 174 e2
Angostura Res., S. Dak. 74 A4
Angoulême, Fr., 51,223 117 C4
Angra do Heroísmo, Azores, 16,168 108 2
Angra dos Reis, Braz., 10,634 103 d18
Angren, U.S.S.R., 63,000 134 G5
Ängsö, Swed. 120 d8
Angtassom, Camb. 146 D5
Ang Thong, Thai., 6,454 147 d4
Anguilla, Miss., 580 73 E5
Anguilla, i., Lesser Ant. 97 7
Anguilla Cays, Bah. Is. 96 d1
Anguillara Sabazia, It., 3,311 123 a8
Anguillara Veneta, It., 6,430 122 e5
Angul, India, 15,738 145 G5
Angumu, D.R.Congo 164 D2
Angus, Ont., Can., 1,180 44 H7
Angus, co., U.K., 278,370 112 E3
Angusville, Man., Can. 43 E5
Angutikada Pk., Alaska 85 F2
Angwin, Calif. 82 B3
Anholt, i., Den. 121 D4
An-hsi, China 150 D2
An-hsiang, China 152 C1
An-hsien, China 152 B1
An-hua, China 152 C1
An-hui, prov., China, 33,560,000 150 F4
Anhŭng, S. Kor. 151 E3
Anhwei=An-hui
An-i, China 152 D1
Aniai, Jap., 11,004 155 G1
Aniak, Alaska, 308 85 E3
Aniak, r., Alaska 85 E3
Anibare (dist.), Nauru 175 17
Anibare Bay, Nauru 175 17
Aniche, Fr., 10,419 116 a7
Anié, Togo 162 d8
Aniene, r., It. 123 D4
Anikhovka, U.S.S.R. 137 k9
Animas, N. Mex. 79 A6
Animas, r., Colo. 79 B3
Animas Pk., N. Mex. 79 A6
Anina, Rum., 11,837 128 C2
Anita, Ariz. 78 B4
Anita, Iowa, 1,233 72 C3
Anita, Pa., 60 D3
Aniva, M., U.S.S.R. 135 O5
Aniva, Zal., U.S.S.R. 135 O5
Anivorano Nord, Malag. Rep., 1,424 165 H4
Aniwa, Wis., 247 66 D3
Aniwa, i., New Hebr. 174 m7
Anjar, India, 23,301 144 D5
'Anjarah, Jor., 3,163 142 b7
Anjean, W.Va. 62 D4
An-jen, China 152 D2
Anjer-Lor, Indon. 148 a7
An-jih-erh-la-k'o-hsia Shan-k'ou, China 150 C3
Anjō, Jap., 56,787 155 E4
Anjou, Fr. 116 p16
Anjouan, i., Arch. des Comores 165 G4
Anju, N. Kor. 151 E3
An-k'ang, China 150 E3
Ankara, Turk., 129,606 142 C2
Ankaratra, mts., Malag. Rep. 165 G5
Ankavandra, Malag. Rep., 1,215 165 G5
Ankazoabo, Malag. Rep., 2,318 165 G5
Ankazobe, Malag. Rep., 1,780 165 G5
Ankenes, Nor. 120 D1
Ankeny, Iowa, 5,910 72 D3
Anker, r., U.K. 114 E5
Ankerton, Alta., Can. 43 c8
Ankeveense Plassen, l., Neth. 115 c6
Anking=An-ch'ing
Anklam, Ger.D.R., 19,393 118 D2
Ankobra, r., Ghana 162 b9
Ankogel, mtn. Aust. 124 K6
Ankona, Fla. 65 J5
Ankoro, D.R.Congo 164 D3
Anlaby, U.K., 14,050 114 G3
An Lao, S. Viet., 2,160 146 E4
An Loc, S. Viet., 8,315 146 D5
Anlong Veng, Camb. 146 D4
An-lu, China 152 D1
An-lung, China 150 E4
Anmoore, W. Va., 1,050 62 D3
Ann, C., Mass. 57 O2
Anna, U.S.S.R. 136 F3
Anna, Ill., 4,280 68 C6
Anna, Ohio, 701 70 E2
Anna, Tex., 639 77 P3
Anna, N., r., Va. 62 G5
Anna, S., r., Va. 62 G5
Annaba, Alg., 135,150 160 F1
Annabella, Utah, 177 78 C2
Annaberg, Aust., 1,101 124 M6
Annaberg-Buchholz, Ger.D.R., 29,012 118 D3
An Nabk, Syr., 14,756 142 D3
Annaburg, Ger.D.R. 118 D3
Annada, Mo., 105 72 G5
An Nafīdah, Tun., 2,822 160 g5
An Nafūd, des., Saudi Ar. 143 C3
Annai, Guyana 101 L6
An Najaf, Iraq, 88,809 143 C2
Annaka, Jap., 42,808 155 F3
An Nakhl, U.A.R. 161 K3
Anna Maria, Fla., 690 65 c12
Annamitique, Chaîne, Laos-Viet-Nam 146 D3
Annan, U.K., 5,572 113 E4
Annanberg, Terr. New Guin. 174 e2
Annandale, Minn., 984 74 E3
Annandale, N.J., 61 B2
Annandale, Va. 62 G4
Anna Pt., Nauru 175 17
Annapolis, Ill. 68 E4
Annapolis, Md., 23,385 62 H4
Annapolis, Mo., 334 72 G7
Annapolis, Wash., 1,472 81 a7
Annapolis Royal, N.S., Can. 47 T11
Annapūrna, pk., Nepal 144 d11
Ann Arbor, Mich., 67,340 67 K6
An Nāṣirīyah, Iraq, 39,060 143 D2
Annawan, Ill., 701 68 B2
Annbank, U.K. 112 b8
Anne Arundel, co., Md., 206,634 62 H3
Annecy, Fr., 45,715 117 F4
Annelöv, Swed. 121 b7
Annemasse, Fr., 14,040 117 G3
Annenskoye, U.S.S.R. 137 i9
Anneta, Ky. 71 E4
Anneta, Tex. 76 d9
Annet-sur-Marne, Fr., 1,186 116 i11
Annette, Alaska, 337 85 L5
An Nhon, S. Viet., 3,002 146 E4
Annick Water, r., U.K. 112 a8
An-ning, r., China 152 A2
Annisquam (part of Gloucester), Mass. 57 O2
Anniston, Ala., 33,657 64 C2
Anniston, Mo., 307 72 H8
Annoeullin, Fr., 5,976 116 a6
Annona, Tex., 369 77 Q3
Annonay, Fr., 18,823 117 F4
Annot, Fr., 1,016 117 G4
Annotto Bay, Jam., 3,559 96 q8
Annotto Bay, Jam. 96 q8
An Nuhūd, Sudan, 16,498 163 J3
An Nu'mānīyah, Iraq, 10,004 143 D2
Annville, Ky. 71 H4
Annville, Pa., 4,264 60 J5
Annweiler, F.R.Ger., 5,127 119 D6
Anoka, co., Minn., 85,916 74 F3
Anoka, Minn., 10,562 74 F3
Anoka, Nebr., 32 75 G1
Anolaima, Col. 101 e15
Año Nuevo, Pt., Calif. 83 e13
Anopino, U.S.S.R. 136 d6
Anori, Braz., 1,232 102 D2
Áno Theólogos, Gr., 1,927 129 E4
Áno Viánnos, Gr., 1,820 129 E7
Anóyia, Gr., 2,461 129 E7
An Phu, S. Viet., 7,046 147 k11
An-p'ing, China 151 B3
Anrath, F.R.Ger., 7,588 119 A2
Anröchte, F.R.Ger., 3,729 119 E1
Ans, Belg., 16,836 115 D4
Ans, Den. 121 B4
Anṣāb, S. Ar. 143 D6
An-sai, China 151 A3
Ansbach, F.R.Ger., 33,237 118 C4
Anse, Fr., 2,290 116 p15
Anse-Bertrand, Guad., 1,147 97 14
Anse Boileau, Seych. 165 a10
Anse-d'Hainault, Haiti, 2,468 96 i6
Anse la Raye, St. Lucia, 2,048 97 11
Anselmo, Nebr., 269 75 F2
Anseremme, Belg., 1,420 115 C4
Anserma, Col. 100 C5
Ansermanuevo, Col. 100 B5
Anseroeul, Belg., 1,098 116 a6
Anse Royale, Seych. 165 a10
Anse-St-Jean, Qué., Can. 45 L5
An-shan, China, 700,000* 150 G2
An-shun, China 150 E4
Ansi=An-hsi
Ansley, La. 73 C5
Ansley, Nebr., 714 75 F2
Anson, Kans. 75 H6
Anson, Me. 55 C4
Anson, co., N.C., 24,962 63 D3
Anson, Tex., 2,890 77 N3
Anson Bay, Austl. 172 D1
Anson Bay, Norfolk I. 175 11
Ansongo, Mali 162 E3
Ansonia, Conn., 19,819 56 D7
Ansonia, Ohio, 1,002 70 E2
Anson Pt., Norfolk I. 175 11
Ansonville, Ont., Can., 3,080 44 H5
Ansonville, N.C., 558 63 D2
Ansted, W. Va., 1,511 62 C4
Anstruther, U.K. 112 e7
Ansupi, r., Ec. 104 d10
Ansus, Indon. 149 K3
An-ta, China 151 E1
Antabamba, Peru, 2,328 104 C5
Anta Dhura Pass, China-Nepal 144 c10
Antagarh, India 145 F5
Antakya, Turk., 45,848 142 C2
Antalaha, Malag. Rep., 12,064 165 H4
Antalya, Turk., 50,963 142 B2
Antalya Körfezi, Turk. 142 B2
Antarctic Pen., Ant. 180 N5
Antau, Aust. 124 c11
Ante, Va. 62 G6
An Teallach, mtn., U.K. 112 D3
Antelo, Arg., 1,600* 105 a11
Antelope, Calif. 82 b7
Antelope, Mont. 81 G1
Antelope, co., Nebr., 10,176 75 G1
Antelope, Oreg., 46 80 C3
Antelope, Tex. 77 O3
Antelope Hills, Okla. 76 D2
Antelope I., Utah 78 b9
Antelope Pk., Nebr. 75 F1
Antelope Res., Oreg. 80 E4
Anteojos, Mex. 93 e8
Antequera, Sp., 42,327 122 C4
Antero, Mt., Colo. 79 B2
Antero Res., Colo. 79 C2
Anthéor, Fr. 116 m14
Anthon, Iowa, 681 72 A2
Anthon, Okla. 76 E2
Anthony, Fla. 65 G3
Anthony, Kans., 2,744 75 H6
Anthony, N. Mex.-Tex. 79 B5
Anthony (part of Coventry), R.I. 57 K6
Anthony, Tex., 1,082 77 K3
Anthony, W. Va. 62 D5
Anthony Lagoon, Austl. 172 E2
Anti-Atlas, ra., Mor. 160 C3
Antibes, Fr., 35,976 117 G5
Antibes, C.d', Fr. 116 n13
Anticosti, Île d', Qué., Can. 45 N5
Antietam Nat. Battlefield Site, Md. 62 G3
Antigo, Wis., 9,691 66 D3
Antigonish, N.S., Can., 4,284 45 O6
Antigua, Guat., 14,634 94 B3
Antigua, i., Lesser Ant. 97 9
Antigues, Pte. d', Guad. 97 14
Antiguo Morelos, Mex. 93 F3
Anti-Lebanon=Sharqī, Al Jabal ash
Antilla, Cuba, 6,481 96 f2
Antímano, Ven. 101 b11
Antimony, Utah, 161 78 C2
Antioch, Turk.=Antakya
Antioch, Calif., 17,305 82 C4
Antioch, Ill., 2,778 68 D1
Antioch, Ind. 70 C2
Antioch, Nebr. 75 C1
Antioch, Ohio, 110 70 J3
Antioch, Okla. 76 F3
Antioquia, Col. 100 B4
Antipodes Is., N.Z. 170 F8
Antipolo, Phil., 2,496 153 c6
Antiquity, Ohio 70 H4
Antisana, r., Ec. 104 c10
Antisana, vol., Ec. 104 B2
Antler, N. Dak., 210 74 B1
Antler, r., Sask., Can. 43 D5
Antlers, Okla., 2,085 76 H3
Antofagasta, Chile, 87,860 105 A2
Antofalla, Salar de, Arg. 105 B3
Antofalla, Vol., Arg. 105 B3
Antoine, Ark., 163 73 B3
Antoing, Belg., 3,462 115 B4
Antón, Pan., 2,684 94 G6
Anton, Colo. 79 D2
Anton, Tex., 1,068 77 M3
Anton Chico, N. Mex. 79 C4
Antongil, B.d', Malag. Rep. 165 H4
Antonia, Mo. 72 a12
Antônia, Pico da, C. Verde Is. 109 5
Antonibe, Malag. Rep. 165 G4
Antonin, Pol. 127 g5
Antonina, Braz., 8,520 103 G7
Antonino, Kans. 75 F5
Antônio Carlos, Braz., 3,065 103 e17
Antônio Enes, Moz., 33,218 164 F4
Antônio Lemos, Braz. 103 F2
Antonito, Colo., 1,045 79 C3
Antony, Fr., 46,823 116 h12
Antostagan, L., Qué., Can. 47 H2
Antrim, co., U.K., 273,923 113 C4
Antrim, U.K., 1,448 113 C4
Antrim, co., Mich., 10,373 67 H3
Antrim, Mich. 67 H4
Antrim, N.H. 54 D5
Antrim, Ohio 70 H2
Antsalova, Malag. Rep., 1,683 165 G5

194 · An-tse—Arrecifes

An-tse, China 151 B3
Antsirabe, Malag. Rep., 23,129 165 G5
Antsohihy, Malag. Rep., 3,289 165 H4
An-t'u, China 151 F2
An Tuc, S. Viet., 1,616 146 E4
Antuco, Chile 104 f17
An-tung, China, 310,000* 150 G2
An-tung-wei, China 151 C4
Antweiler, F.R.Ger. 119 B4
Antwerp, Belg.=Antwerpen
Antwerp, N.Y., 881 59 J3
Antwerp, Ohio, 1,465 70 E1
Antwerpen, Belg., 261,666 115 C3
An Uaimh, Ire., 4,813 113 C5
Anuanrunga, i., Tuam. Arch. 177 42
Anuanu Raro, atoll, Tuam. Arch. 177 42
Anuchino, U.S.S.R. 151 F2
Anŭi, S. Kor. 151 E4
Anupgarh, India, 2,294 145 D3
Anuppur, India 144 c14
Anuradhapura, Cey., 18,390 145 F8
Anutiba, Braz. 103 f17
Anutt, Mo., 72 F7
Anuy, r., U.S.S.R. 137 r11
Anvers=Antwerpen
Anvik, Alaska, 120 85 D3
Anvik, r., Alaska 85 D3
Anxious Bay, Austl. 172 D5
Anyama, Iv. Coast, 8,000 162 b9
An-yang, China, 171,000* 150 F3
Anykščiai, U.S.S.R., 5,300 136 B2
Anyox, Br. Col., Can. 42 D2
An-yüan, China 150 F4
An-yüeh, China 152 B1
Anzá, Col. 101 d13
Anzac, Alta., Can. 42 K2
Anzhero Sudzhensk, U.S.S.R., 119,000 134 H4
Anzhu, O-va., U.S.S.R. 135 O2
Anzio, It., 16,242 123 D4
Anzoátegui, Col. 101 d15
Ao, Jap. 154 h15
Aoa, Tutuila 177 39
Aoa Bay, Tutuila 177 39
Aoga-shima, Japan 170 D2
Ao-han-ch'i, China 151 D2
Aoiz, Sp., 1,627 122 E1
Aoki, Jap. 154 e15
Aoki, Jap. 154 f15
Aola, Sol. Is. 175 c3
Aoloau, Tutuila 177 39
Aoloau Bay, Tutuila 177 39
Aomon, i., Eniwetok 176 28
Aomori, Jap., 202,211 155 G1
Aonae, Jap. 155 H8
Aonla, India, 17,613 144 b11
Aorai, Mt., Tahiti 177 44
Aore, i., New Hebr. 174 k5
Aorere, r., N.Z. 175 g6
Aosta, It., 30,354 123 A2
Aouk, Bahr, C.A.R.-Chad 163 H4
Aoulef, Alg. 160 E3
Aoya, Jap., 12,367 155 C4
A-pa, China 150 D3
Apa, r., Braz.-Para. 105 D2
Apache, co., Ariz., 30,438 78 D4
Apache, Ariz. 78 D6
Apache, Okla., 1,455 76 E3
Apache Creek, N. Mex. 79 A5
Apache Cr., N. Mex. 79 A5
Apache Hills, N. Mex. 79 A6
Apache Junction, Ariz. 78 C5
Apache Mtn., N. Mex. 79 A4
Apache Mts., Tex. 77 L4
Apahida, Rum. 128 D1
Apaikwa, Guyana 101 K4
A-pa-ka-ch'i, China 150 F2
Apalachee Bay, Fla. 65 E3
Apalachicola, Fla., 3,099 65 D3
Apalachicola, r., Fla. 65 D2
Apalachin, N.Y. 59 H7
Apam, Ghana 162 c9
Apan, Mex., 8,589 93 F4
Apapa, Nigeria 162 e8
Aparecida, Braz., 15,290 103 d18
Aparecida do Taboado, Braz., 2,913 103 F6
Aparri, Phil., 13,167 153 B1
Apaseo, Mex., 5,336 93 d9
Apaseo el Alto, Mex., 6,075 93 d9
Apataki, atoll, Tuam. Arch. 177 42
Apatin, Yug., 16,000* 125 D2
Apatity, U.S.S.R. 134 C3
Apatou, Fr. Guiana 101 N5
Apatzingán, Mex., 19,340 92 E4
Apaxco, Mex., 3,953 93 e10
Apaxtla, Mex., 3,459 93 E4
Apeldoorn, Neth., 79,100 115 D2
Apeldoornsch Kan., Neth. 115 E2
Apen, F.R.Ger., 7,705 118 A2
Apennines=Appennino
Apesco, Mex. 93 e9
Apex, Ky. 71 D4
Apex, N.C., 1,368 63 F2
Api, mtn., Nepal 144 c10
Api, Tg., Indon. 148 D2
Apia, W. Samoa, 21,699 177 37
Apiacá, Braz., 2,127 103 f17
Apiaí, Braz., 2,728 103 G6
Apiapianom, Tg., Indon. 148 d7
Apimu, Indon. 149 L4
Apíranthos, Gr., 1,393 129 E6
Apishapa, r., Colo. 79 C3
Apizaco, Mex., 15,622 93 f10
Aplao, Peru, 1,260 104 C6
Aplaya, Phil., 4,055 153 b9
Aplington, Iowa, 840 72 E2
Apodi, Braz., 2,512 103 J3
Apohaqui, N.B., Can. 47 T11
Apolakkiá, Gr. 129 F6
Apolda, Ger.D.R., 29,292 118 C3
Apolima, i., W. Samoa 177 38
Apolima Str., W. Samoa 177 37
Apollo, Pa., 2,694 60 C4
Apollo Bay, Austl. 173 F6
Apollo Beach, Fla. 65 d12
Apollonia=Marsá Sūsah
Apollonia, ruins, Alb. 125 D4
Apolo, Bol., 6,919 102 C4
Apo, Mt., Phil. 153 C4
Apopa, El Salv., 3,774 94 d10
Apopka, Fla., 3,578 65 H4
Apopka, L., Fla. 65 H4
Apoporis, r., Col. 100 E7
Aporé, r., Braz. 103 F5
Aporema, Braz. 103 F1
Apostle Is., Wis. 66 C1
Apóstoles, Arg., 8,500* 105 D3
Apostolovo, U.S.S.R., 12,500 136 D4
Apoten, Guyana 101 L5
Apozol, Mex., 1,855 93 a8
Appalachia, Va., 2,456 62 B6
Appalachian Mts., U.S. 53 K3
Appam, N. Dak. 74 A1
Appanoose, co., Iowa, 16,015 72 E4
Appelscha, Neth. 115 E2
Appen, F.R.Ger., 4,875 119 a8
Appennino, mtn. ra., Italy 110 E4
Appenweier, F.R.Ger., 2,184 119 E7
Appenzell, Switz., 5,082 124 D1
Apperson, Okla. 76 G1
Appingedam, Neth., 8,600 115 E1
Apple, r., Ill. 68 B1
Apple, r., Wis. 66 A3
Appleby, Ont., Can. 46 c14
Appleby, U.K., 1,751 113 E4
Apple Creek, Ohio, 722 70 H2
Apple Cr., Ill. 68 B4
Applecross, U.K. 112 D3
Applegarth, N.J. 58 b15
Applegate, Mich., 252 67 L5
Applegate, Oreg. 80 B4
Applegate, r., Oreg. 80 B4
Apple River, Ill., 477 68 B1
Apples, Switz. 124 A2
Appleton, U.K., 2,974 114 C4
Appleton, Ark. 73 C2
Appleton, Me. 55 C4
Appleton, Minn., 2,172 74 D3
Appleton, S.C. 63 C4
Appleton, Wis., 48,411 66 E4
Appleton City, Mo., 1,075 72 C6
Appleton Wiske, U.K. 114 F2
Apple Valley, Calif. 82 E5
Appleyard, Wash. 80 C2
Appling, co., Ga., 13,246 64 G4
Appling, Ga. 64 G2
Appomattox, co., Va., 9,148 62 F5
Appomattox,Va., 1,184 62 F5
Appomattox, r., Va. 62 F5
Appomattox C. H. Nat. Hist. Pk., Va. 62 F5
Apponagansett (part of Dartmouth), Mass. 57 M6
Approuague, r., Fr. Guiana 101 O5
Apra Hbr., Guam 176 24
Aprelevka, U.S.S.R. 136 b6
Aprel'sk, U.S.S.R. 135 L4
Apricena, It., 12,954 123 E4
Aprilia, It., 14,345 123 b8
Aprunyi, India 145 K3
Ápsalos, Gr., 1,491 129 D4
Apsheronsk, U.S.S.R., 24,800 136 E4
Apsheronskiy P-ov., U.S.S.R. 137 d1
Apsley Str., Austl. 172 D1
Apt, Fr., 7,812 117 F5
Aptakisic, Ill. 69 c8
Aptos, Calif. 83 f14
Apuane, Alpi, mts., It. 123 ·
Apua Pt., Hawaii 84 F4
Apucarana, Braz., 21,203 103 F6
Apuka, U.S.S.R. 135 Q3
Apurashokoru, i., Palau 176 21
Apure, r., Ven. 100 F4
Apurímac, r., Peru 104 C4
Apurito, Ven. 100 F4
Apuseni, Munții, Rum. 128 D1
Aqaba, Gulf of, Asia 142 C4
Āq Chāh, Afghan. 144 C1
'Aqīq, Sudan 163 L2
Āq Kupruk, Afghan. 144 A1
'Aqrah, Iraq, 6,092 143 C1
Aquarius Mts., Ariz. 78 B4
Aquarius Plat., Utah 78 ·
Aquasco, Md. 62 H4
Aquidauana, Braz., 11,997 103 E6
Aquidneck I., R.I. 57 L6
Aquila, Switz. 124 C2
Aquiles Serdán, Mex., 4,357 92 D2
Aquilla, Ohio, 459 70 H1
Aquin, Haiti, 2,880 96 k6
Aquone, N.C. 63 b7
Ara, r., Jap. 155 F4
Arab, Ala., 2,989 64 C1
'Arabah, Wādī al, Jor. 142 C4
Arabatskaya Strelka, U.S.S.R. 136 D4
'Arab, Baḥr al, Sudan 163 J4
Arab, Shatt al, r., Iraq-Saudi Ar. 143 D3
Arabela, N. Mex. 79 C5
Arabi, Ga., 303 64 F4
Arabian Basin, Ind. Oc. 168 C2
Arabian Pen., Asia 140 C4
Arabian Sea, Asia 140 E5
Araç, Turk., 2,302 142 C1
Aracaju, Braz., 112,516 103 J4
Aracataca, Col. 100 C2
Aracati, Braz., 11,016 103 J2
Araçatuba, Braz., 53,563 103 F6
Araceli, Phil, 1,325 153 B3
Aracena, Sp., 7,643 122 B4
Araçuaí, Braz., 6,763 103 H5
Araçuaí, r., Braz. 103 H5
'Arad, Isr. 142 b8
Arad, Rum., 106,460 128 C1
Arada, Chad 163 H3
Arafura Sea, Austl.-Indon. 149 K5
Arc, r., Fr. 117 G4
Aragarças, Braz., 2,311 103 F5
Aragats, G., U.S.S.R. 137 c1
Aragon, Ga., 1,023 64 E1
Aragón, reg., Sp. 122 E2
Aragón, r., Sp. 122 E1
Aragona, It., 15,496 123 D6
Araguacema, Braz., 1,745 103 G3
Araguaçu, Braz. 103 G4
Aragua de Barcelona, Ven., 6,830 101 H3
Aragua de Maturín, Ven., 2,658 101 J2
Araguaia, r., Braz. 103 F5
Araguaína, Braz., 2,382 103 G3
Araguari, Braz., 35,520 103 G5
Araguari, r., Braz. 103 F1
Araguari, r., Braz. 103 G5
Araguatins, Braz., 2,131 103 G3
Aragüita, Ven., 1,010 101 c11
Arai, Jap., 13,432 155 E4
Arai, Jap., 34,351 155 F3
Arai, Jap. 155 m18
Arai, Jap. 155 m20
Araira, Ven., 1,603 101 c11
Arajuno, Ec. 104 B2
Arajuno, r., Ec. 104 d10
Arak, Alg. 160 E3
Arāk, Iran, 58,998 143 D2
Arakaka, Guyana 101 K4
Arakamchechen, O., U.S.S.R. 135 S3
Arakan Yoma, Burma 146 A3
Arákhova, Gr., 3,056 129 D5
Árakhthos, r., Gr. 129 C5
Araks, Asia 142 F2
Aral'sk, U.S.S.R., 19,900 134 F5
Aral'skoye More, U.S.S.R. 134 E5
Aralsul'fat, U.S.S.R., 3,300 134 F5
Aramac, Austl. 173 F3
Arambagh, India, 16,551 144 f14
Aramberri, Mex., 1,310 93 E3
Arambiru, i., Eniwetok 176 28
Aramia, r., Terr. Papua 174 d2
Aranda de Duero, Sp., 13,454 122 D2
Arandas, Mex., 17,110 92 E4
Arandelovac, Yug., 5,752 125 E2
Aran Fawddwy, mtn., U.K. 113 E5
Aranguren, Arg., 1,550* 105 a11
Arani, Bol., 5,883 102 c10
Aran I., Ire. 113 B4
Aran Is., Ire. 113 B5
Aranjuez, Sp., 27,251 122 D2
Aranos, S.-W. Afr. 164 C6
Aransas, co., Tex., 7,006 77 P5
Aransas Pass, Tex., 6,956 77 P6
Aranuka, atoll, Gilb. Is. 175 10
Aranyaprathet, Thai., 11,078 146 C4
Aranzazu, Col. 101 d14
Aranzazú, Mex., 1,064 92 E3
Arao, Jap., 64,394 154 B5
Araouane, Mali 162 D2
Arapaho, Okla., 351 76 D2
Arapahoe, co., Colo., 113,426 79 C2
Arapahoe, Nebr., 1,084 75 F3
Arapahoe, N.C., 274 63 H2
Arapey, Urug. 105 c10
Arapey Chico, r., Urug. 105 c10
Arapey Grande, r., Urug. 105 c10
Arapiraca, Braz., 19,749 103 J3
Arapkir, Turk., 6,875 142 D2
Arapongas, Braz., 21,210 103 F6
Araquil, r., Sp. 122 E1
'Ar'ar, Saudi Ar. 143 C2
Araracuara, Col. 100 E8
Araranguá, Braz., 7,775 103 G7
Araraquara, Braz., 58,076 103 G6
Ararat, Austl., 7,414 173 F5
Ararat, U.S.S.R., 5,300 137 c2
Ararat, Va. 62 D6
Ararat, Mt.=Ağrı Dağı
Arari, Braz., 4,004 103 H2
Araripina, Braz., 4,712 103 H3
Araró, Mex., 1,616 93 d10
Araruama, Braz., 5,056 103 e18
Araruama, Lag. de, Braz. 103 e18
Araruna, Braz., 2,930 103 b14
'Ar'ar, Wādī, Iraq-Saudi Ar. 143 C2
Aras, r., Asia 142 E1
Aratika, atoll, Tuam. Arch. 177 42
Arato, Jap. 155 G2
Arauca, Col. 100 E4
Arauca, r., Col.-Ven. 100 F4
Araure, Ven., 11,331 100 F3
Aravaipa, Ariz. 78 C5
Aravalli Ra., India 145 D4
Aravissós, Gr., 1,691 129 D4
Arawata, r., N.Z. 175 f7
Araxá, Braz., 24,041 103 G5
Araya, Jap. 155 G1
Araya, Ven., 4,381 101 H2
Araya, P., Ven. 101 H2
Ara-zaki, Ryukyu Is. 154 a11
Arbay Heere, Mong. 150 D2
Arbedo, Switz., 1,467 124 D2
Arbeláez, Col. 100 C5
Arbesbach, Aust. 124 M5
Arboga, Swed. 120 C4
Arbois, Fr., 4,169 117 F3
Arboledas, Col. 100 D4
Arbon, Switz., 11,608 124 D1
Arbonne, Bayou d', La. 73 C5
Arborfield, Sask., Can. 43 D4
Arborg, Man., Can. 43 F5
Arborio, It., 1,361 122 b5
Arbor Vitae, Wis. 66 D3
Arbrå, Swed. 120 D3
Arbroath, U.K., 19,533 112 E3
Arbuckle, Calif. 82 B3
Arbuckle, L., Fla. 65 H5
Arbuckle Res., Okla. 76 G3
Arbus, It., 10,580 123 B5
Arbutus, Md. 62 c7
Arbutus Beach, Mich. 67 J4
Arbutus L., Wis. 66 C4
Arbyrd, Mo., 667 72 G8
Arcachon, Fr., 15,820 117 C4
Arcachon, Bassin d', Fr. 117 C4
Arcade, Calif. 82 b7
Arcade, N.Y., 1,930 58 D6
Arcadia, N.S., Can. 47 T12
Arcadia, Calif., 41,005 83 h15
Arcadia, Fla., 5,889 65 H5
Arcadia, Ind., 1,271 70 C2
Arcadia, Iowa, 437 72 B2
Arcadia, Kans., 507 75 L6
Arcadia, La., 2,547 73 C5
Arcadia, Mich. 67 G4
Arcadia, Mo., 489 72 G7
Arcadia, Nebr., 446 75 F2
Arcadia, Ohio, 610 70 F1
Arcadia, Okla. 76 F2
Arcadia, Pa., 60 E4
Arcadia (part of Richmond and Exeter), R.I. 57 K6
Arcadia, Tex. 77 i10
Arcadia, Wis., 2,084 66 B4
Arcanum, Ohio, 1,678 70 E2
Arcas, Cayos, Mex. 93 H4
Arcata, Calif., 5,235 82 A2
Arcelia, Mex., 8,526 93 E5
Arcen, Neth. 119 A2
Arch, N. Mex. 79 D4
Archangel=Arkhangel'sk
Archar, Bulg., 3,990 128 D3
Archbald, Pa., 5,471 61 L3
Archbold, Ohio, 2,348 70 E1
Archdale, N.C., 1,520 63 D2
Archer, Fla., 707 65 G3
Archer, Iowa, 209 72 B1
Archer, co., Tex., 6,110 77 O3
Archer, r., Austl. 173 F1
Archer Bay, Austl. 173 F1
Archer City, Tex., 1,974 77 O3
Archers Lodge, N.C. 63 F2
Archerwill, Sask., Can. 43 D4
Arches Nat. Mon., Utah 78 D2
Archibald, La. 73 D5
Archidona, Ec. 104 d10
Archidona, Sp., 11,594 122 C4
Archie, La. 73 D6
Archie, Mo., 348 72 C6
Archuleta, co., Colo., 2,629 79 B3
Arcis, Fr., 2,892 117 F2
Arco, Idaho, 1,562 81 C4
Arcola, Sask., Can. 43 D5
Arcola, Ill., 2,273 68 D4
Arcola, Ind. 70 D1
Arcola, Miss., 366 73 E4
Arcola, Tex. 77 i9
Arcos de Jalón, Sp., 2,969 122 D2
Arcot, India, 25,029 145 m19
Arcoverde, Braz., 18,008 103 J3
Arctic=Arctic Village
Arctic (part of W. Warwick), R.I. 57 K6
Arctic Bay, N.W.T., Can. 41 N3
Arctic Ocean 180
Arctic Red, r., N.W.T., Can. 40 C4
Arctic Red River, N.W.T., Can. 40 C4
Arctic Village, Alaska, 110 85 H1
Arcugnano, It., 5,100 122 e5
Ardlethan, Austl. 173 f10
Arda, Bulg. 129 E4
Arda, r., Bulg. 129 E4
Arda, r., It. 122 c6
Ardabīl, Iran, 65,742 143 D1
Ardahan, Turk., 7,191 142 E1
Ardakān, Iran, 8,490 143 E2
Årdal, Nor. 121 A2
Årdala, Swed. 120 d9
Årdalstangen, Nor. 120 A3
Ardara, Ire. 113 B4
Ardasa, Turk., 2,085 137 a1
Ardatov, U.S.S.R., 9,800 136 G2
Ardbeg, Ont., Can. 46 D3
Ardee, Ire., 2,719 113 C5
Arden, Man., Can. 43 E5
Arden, Ont., Can. 46 H4
Arden, Den., 1,365 121 B4
Arden, U.K. 112 a7
Arden, Calif. 82 b7
Arden, Del. 62 e10
Arden, Nev. 83 C5
Arden, N.C. 63 B2
Arden Hills, Minn., 3,930 74 c5
Ardennes, reg., Belg. 115 D4
Ardentes, Fr., 2,852 117 D3
Ardersier=Campbelltown
Ardeşen, Turk., 4,557 142 E1
Ardestān, Iran, 5,868 143 E2
Ardez, Switz. 124 E2
Ardfert, Ire. 113 B5
Ardgartan, U.K. 112 a7
Ardhéa, Gr., 3,222 129 D4
Ardino, Bulg., 2,558 129 E4
Ardivachar Pt., U.K. 112 C3
Ardjuno, G., Indon. 148 e7
Ardlui, U.K. 112 a7
Ardlussa, U.K. 112 D3
Ardmore, Ire. 113 C6
Ardmore, Ala., 439 64 C1
Ardmore, Okla., 20,184 76 F3
Ardmore, Pa., 15,175* 61 M6
Ardmore, S. Dak., 73 74 A4
Ardnamurchan, Pt. of, U.K. 112 C3
Ardoch, N. Dak., 106 74 D1
Ardooie, Belg., 7,106 115 B4
Ardrishaig, U.K. 112 D4
Ardrossan, Austl. 172 b8
Ardrossan, Alta., Can. 43 b7
Ardrossan, U.K., 9,574 112 a8
Ardsley, U.K., 11,278 114 F3
Ardsley, N.Y., 3,991 58 d12
Ardud, Rum. 128 D1
Åre, Swed. 120 C3
Areal, Braz., 2,389 103 e18
Arecibo, P.R., 28,828 96 s10
Aredale, Iowa, 153 72 E2
Areguá, Para., 3,672 105 D3
Aregüe, Ven., 1,056 100 E2
Areia, Braz., 5,934 103 b14
Areia Branca, Braz., 8,904 103 J2
Arekalong Pen., Palau 176 21
Aremark, Nor. 121 D1
Arena, Wis., 309 66 D5
Arena, Pt., Calif. 82 B3
Arenac, co., Mich., 9,860 67 K4
Arenal, Chile 104 e15
Arenal, Col. 100 C2
Arenal, Col. 100 D3
Arenal, Mex., 1,030 93 G5
Arenápolis, Braz., 1,500 103 E4
Arenas, Cayo, Mex. 93 H3
Arenas, P., Cuba 96 e2
Arenas, P., P.R. 96 u10
Arenas de San Pedro, Sp., 6,659 122 C2
Arendal, Nor., 11,395 120 B4
Arendonk, Belg., 8,670 115 D3
Arendsee, Ger.D.R., 118 C2
Arendtsville, Pa., 588 60 H6
Arenzville, Ill., 417 68 B4
Areópolis, Gr. 129 D6
Arequipa, Peru, 90,014 104 C6
Arês, Braz., 2,246 103 b14
Areuse, r., Switz. 124 A2
Arévalo, Sp., 5,208 122 C2
Arezzo, It., 73,176 123 C3
Argalastí, Gr., 1,864 129 D5
Arganda, Sp., 6,277 122 D2
Argao, Phil., 3,619 153 e12
Argayash, U.S.S.R. 137 k8
Argazi, Oz., U.S.S.R. 137 k8
Argel, Rum. 128 E1
Argelès-Gazost, Fr., 3,829 117 C5
Argelès-sur-Mer, Fr., 3,659 117 E5
Argelia, Col. 101 d14
Argens, r., Fr. 117 G5
Argent, Fr., 2,464 117 E3
Argenta, It., 30,506 123 C2
Argenta, Ill., 860 68 D4
Argentan, Fr., 13,411 117 D2
Argentat, Fr., 3,529 117 E4
Argentera, Punta, It., 123 A2
Argenteuil, Fr., 82,458 116 h11
Argenthal, F.R.Ger., 1,097 119 D5
Argentia, Newf., Can. 45 a10
Argentières, Fr. 116 k12
Argentina, ctry., 22,691,000* 105
Argentine Basin, Atl. Oc. 109 J9
Argentine Is., Ant. 180 N6
Argentino, L., Arg. 105 A8
Argenton-sur-Creuse, Fr., 6,906 117 D3
Argeş, r., Rum. 128 E2
Arghandāb, r., Afghan. 144 C2
Arghandāb Dam, Afghan. 144 B3
Argo, Sudan, 2,329 163 K2
Argo, Ala. 64 d7
Argo, Ill. 68 B1
Argolikós Kólpos, Gr. 129 D6
Argonia, Kans., 553 75 H6
Argonne, Wis. 66 E3
Argopuro, G., Indon. 148 e7
Árgos, Gr., 16,712 129 D6
Argos, Ind., 1,339 70 C1
Árgos Orestikón, Gr., 4,319 129 C4
Argostólion, Gr., 7,322 129 C5
Arguello, Pt., Calif. 82 C5
Arguin, C. d', Maur. 162 B2
Argun', r., China-U.S.S.R. 135 L4
Argun, r., U.S.S.R. 137 c1
Argungu, Nigeria 162 E3
Argusville, N. Dak., 118 74 D2
Argyle, Man., Can. 43 g9
Argyle, St. Vinc. 97 19
Argyle, Fla. 65 C2
Argyle, Ga., 225 64 G4
Argyle, Mich. 67 L5
Argyle, Minn., 789 74 D1
Argyle, Mo., 99 72 E6
Argyle, N.Y. 59 N5
Argyle, Tex. 76 e8
Argyle, Wis., 786 66 D6
Argyll, co., U.K., 59,345 112 D3
Argyrokastron=Gjirokastër
Århus, Den., 119,568 121 C4
Århus Bugt, Den. 121 C4
Aria, N.Z. 175 g5
Ariah Park, Austl. 173 f10
Ariakeno-umi, Jap. 154 B5
Ariake-wan, Jap. 154 B6
Arial, S.C. 63 B3
Ariamsvlei, S.-W. Afr. 164 C6
Ariano Irpino, It., 27,456 123 E4
Ariano nel Polesine, It., 10,259 122 f6
Ariari, r., Col. 100 D6
Aribinda, Upper Volta, 3,150 162 D3
Arica, Chile, 43,344 105 A1
Arica, Col. 100 D8
Arichat, N.S., Can. 47 V11
Arickaree, Colo. 79 D2
Arickaree, r., Colo. 79 D2
Aride I., Seych. 165 a10
Ariège, r., Fr. 117 D5
Ariel, Wash. 80 B3
Arieş, r., Rum. 128 D1
Ariguani, r., Col. 100 D3
Arīḥā, Jor., 10,166 142 C3
Arikawa, Jap., 13,202 154 A5
Arild, Swed. 121 E4
Arima, Jap. 154 g15
Arima, Jap. 154 h16
Arima, Trin. and Tob., 10,982 96 g5
Arimo, Idaho, 303 81 C4
Arinagour, U.K. 112 C3
Arinos, Braz. 103 G5
Arinos, r., Braz. 102 E4
Arinthod, Fr., 1,027 117 F3
Ario, Mex., 9,196 92 E4
Ario, Mex., 3,317 93 b9
Arion, Iowa, 201 72 B3
Aripao, Ven. 101 H4
Aripeka, Fla. 65 G4
Aripo, El Cerro del, Trin. and Tob. 96 g5
Ariporo, r., Col. 100 E4
Aripuanã, Braz. 102 D3
Aripuanã, r., Braz. 102 D3
Ariquemes, Braz. 102 D3
Arisaig, Sd. of, U.K. 112 D3
'Arīsh, Wādī al, U.A.R. 142 C4
Arismendi, Ven., 1,249 100 F3
Arispe, Iowa, 125 72 C4
Ariss, Ont., Can. 46 b13
Arista, Mex. 93 E3
Arista, W.Va. 62 C5
Aristazabal I., Br. Col., Can. 42 D3
Aristizábal, C., Arg. 105 B7
Arisvi, Gr., 1,364 129 E4
Arita, Jap., 29,373 154 g15
Arita, r., Jap. 154 g15
Aritao, Phil., 2,367 153 b6
Ariton, Ala., 687 64 D4
Arivonimamo, Malag. Rep., 6,712 165 G5
Ariza, Sp., 2,586 122 D2
Arizala, Sp. 122 o12
Arizaro, Salar de, Arg. 105 B2
Arizona, st., U.S., 1,575,000* 78
Arizona, La. 73 C5
Arizpe, Mex., 1,403 92 C1
Årjäng, Swed. 120 B4
Arjay, Ky. 71 H5
Arjeplog, Swed. 120 D2
Arjona, Col. 100 C2
Arkabutla Res., Miss. 73 E3
Arkadak, U.S.S.R., 16,000 136 F2
Arkadelphia, Ark., 8,069 73 B3
Arkaig, Loch, U.K. 112 D3
Arkalokhóri, Gr., 1,213 129 E7
Arkansas, st., U.S., 1,941,000* 73
Arkansas, co., Ark., 23,355 73 D3
Arkansas, r., U.S. 53 H3
Arkansas, Salt Fk. of, r., Kans.-Okla. 76 D1
Arkansas City, Ark., 783 73 D4
Arkansas City, Kans., 14,262 75 H6
Arkansas Post, Ark. 73 D3
Arkansaw, Wis. 66 A4
Arkdale, Wis. 66 D4
Arkell, Ont., Can. 46 b13
Arkhángellos, Gr., 2,918 129 G6
Arkhangel'sk, U.S.S.R., 271,000 134 D3
Arkhangel'skaya, U.S.S.R. 136 F4
Arkhangel'skoye, U.S.S.R. 136 F3
Arkhangel'skoye, U.S.S.R. 137 h8
Árki, i., Gr. 129 F6
Arkle Beck, r., U.K. 112 f11
Arklow, Ire., 5,292 113 C5
Arkoma, Okla., 1,862 76 J2
Arkona, Ont., Can. 46 C5
Arkona, c., Ger.D.R. 118 D1
Arkport, N.Y., 837 58 E7
Arkticheskiy, M., U.S.S.R. 135 J1
Arkticheskogo Instituta, O-va., U.S.S.R. 135 H2
Ärla, Swed. 120 d8
Arlanc, Fr., 2,543 117 E4
Arlanzón, r., Sp. 122 D1
Arlee, Mont. 81 C2
Arles, Fr., 42,353 117 F5
Arley, U.K., 3,396 114 E5
Arley, Ala. 64 B1
Arlington, Ala. 64 B3
Arlington, Colo. 79 D2
Arlington, Fla. 65 H2
Arlington, Ga., 1,462 64 E4
Arlington, Ill., 254 68 C2
Arlington, Iowa, 614 72 F2
Arlington, Kans., 466 75 G6
Arlington, Ky., 584 71 C5
Arlington, Mass., 49,953(T) 57 M3
Arlington, Minn., 1,601 74 E3
Arlington, Nebr., 740 75 J2
Arlington, N.Y., 8,317 59 N8
Arlington, N.C., 590 63 D1
Arlington, Ohio, 955 70 F2
Arlington, Okla. 76 G2
Arlington, Oreg., 643 80 C3
Arlington, Pa., 61 p16
Arlington, S. Dak., 996 74 D3
Arlington, Tenn., 620 71 B6
Arlington, Tex., 44,775 76 e9
Arlington, Vt., 1,111 54 A5
Arlington, co., Va., 163,401 62 G4
Arlington, Wash., 2,025 80 B1
Arlington, Wis., 349 66 D5
Arlington Heights, Ill., 27,878 68 D1
Arlington Nat. Cem., Va. 62 a9
Arlon, Belg., 13,117 115 D5
Arlöv, Swed. 121 c7
Arluno, It., 6,821 122 b5
Arm, Miss. 73 F6
Arma, Kans., 1,296 75 L6
Arma, r., Col. 101 d14
Armação dos Búzios, Braz., 1,068 103 f18
Armada, Mich., 1,111 67 L6
Armadale, Austl., 1,496 172 B5
Armadale, U.K., 6,193 112 c8
Armagh, Qué., Can. 47 O2
Armagh, co., U.K., 117,580 113 C4
Armagh, U.K., 9,982 113 C4
Armagh, Pa., 192 60 E5
Armagh, r., Qué., Can. 47 O2
Armançon, r., Fr. 117 F3
Armavir, U.S.S.R., 120,000 134 D5
Armena, Alta., Can. 43 b7
Armenia, Col. 100 C5
Armenia, Col. 101 d13
Armenia, El Salv., 6,820 94 d10
Armenia, reg., Turk.-U.S.S.R. 142 E2
Armenian S.S.R.=Armyanskaya S.S.R.
Armeniş, Rum. 128 D2
Armentières, Fr., 27,254 117 E1
Armeria, Mex., 4,852 92 D4
Armero, Col. 101 e15
Armidale, Austl., 8,661 173 G4
Armijo, N. Mex. 79 B4
Armington, Ill., 327 68 C3
Armona, Calif., 1,302 82 D4
Armonk, N.Y. 58 e12
Armour, S. Dak., 875 74 C4
Armstead, Mont. 81 C3
Armstrong, Arg., 8,500* 105 C4
Armstrong, Br. Col., Can., 1,252 42 H4
Armstrong, Ont., Can. 44 E5
Armstrong, Ill. 68 E3
Armstrong, Iowa, 958 72 C1
Armstrong, Mo., 387 72 E5
Armstrong, co., Pa., 79,524 60 D4
Armstrong, co., Tex., 1,966 76 N2
Armstrong, Tex. 77 P6
Armstrong Creek, Wis. 66 E3
Armthorpe, U.K., 6,321 114 F3
Armyanskaya S.S.R., U.S.S.R., 2,134,000* 134 D5
Arnage, Fr., 3,315 117 D3
Arnaía, Gr., 2,612 129 D4
Arnaud, Man., Can. 43 h10
Arnaudville, La., 1,184 73 D7
Arnauti, C., Cyp. 142 C3
Arnavon Is., Sol. Is. 175 b2
Arnay-le-Duc, Fr., 2,018 117 F3
Arneburg, Ger.D.R. 118 C2
Arnedo, Sp., 7,958 122 D1
Arnegard, N. Dak., 228 74 A2
Arner, Ont., Can. 67 g16
Arnett, Okla., 547 76 D1
Arnett, W.Va. 62 C5
Arneytown, N.J. 58 a16
Arnfels, Aust. 124 M7
Arnheim, Mich. 66 E2
Arnhem, Neth., 120,500 115 D3
Arnhem, C., Austl. 172 E1
Arnhemia, Indon. 148 A2
Arnhem Land, reg., Austl. 172 D1
Árnissa, Gr., 1,827 129 C4
Arno, atoll, Marsh. Is. 170 F4
Arnö, i., Swed. 120 e8
Arno, r., It. 123 C3
Arno Bay, Austl. 172 E5
Arnold, U.K., 26,829 114 F4
Arnold, Calif. 82 C3
Arnold, Kans. 75 E5
Arnold, Md. 62 d8
Arnold, Mich. 66 F2
Arnold, Minn. 74 F2
Arnold, Mo. 72 G6
Arnold, Nebr., 844 75 E2
Arnold, Pa., 9,437 60 C4
Arnoldsburg, W.Va. 62 C4
Arnold's Cove, Newf., Can. 45 b10
Arnolds Park, Iowa, 953 72 B1
Arnoldstein, Aust., 6,229 124 K7
Arnon, r., Fr. 117 E3
Arnot, Man., Can. 43 F3
Arnot, Pa. 60 H2
Arnot Pk., Calif. 82 D3
Arnouville-lès-Gonesse, Fr., 10,321 116 h11
Arnöya, i., Nor. 120 E1
Arnprior, Ont., Can., 5,384 44 J6
Arnsberg, F.R.Ger., 20,420 118 B3
Arnside, U.K., 1,381 113 E4
Arnstadt, Ger.D.R., 26,444 118 C3
Aro, r., Ven. 101 H4
Aroa, Ven., 3,930 100 F2
Aroab, S.-W. Afr. 164 C6
Aroa, Pte., Moorea 177 44
Aroche, Sp., 6,686 122 B4
Arock, Oreg. 80 E4
Aroda, Va. 62 F4
Arogno, Switz. 124 D3
Arolla, Switz. 124 B2
Arolsen, F.R.Ger., 5,854 118 B3
Aroma, Sudan, 3,451 163 L3
Aroma Park, Ill., 744 68 E2
Aromas, Calif. 83 f14
Aromashevo, U.S.S.R. 137 n11
Arona, It., 11,213 123 B2
Arona, Terr. New Guin. 174 e2
Arona, Pa., 467 60 d8
Aroostook, N.B., Can. 47 S10
Aroostook, co., Me., 106,064 55 D2
Aroostook, r., Me. 55 D2
Arorae, i., Gilb. Is. 175 10
Arorangi, Rarotonga 177 34
Aroroy, Phil., 2,277 153 B2
Arosa, Switz., 2,600 124 D2
Aroya, Colo. 79 D2
Arp, Tenn. 71 B6
Arp, Tex., 812 77 Q3
Arpa, r., Turk. 142 E1
Arpachin, U.S.S.R. 136 g8
Arpajon, Fr., 5,952 117 E2
Arpelar, Okla. 76 G3
Arpin, Wis. 66 D4
Arquata Scrivia, It., 5,081 122 b6
Arques, Fr., 7,224 117 E1
Ar Rab' al Khālī, des., Saudi Ar. 143 D5
Arracourt, Fr. 116 c9
Arrah, India, 76,766 145 G4
Ar Rahad, Sudan, 6,706 163 K3
Ar Rahbah, Leb., 3,109 142 b5
Arraial do Cabo, Braz., 5,930 103 f18
Arraias, Braz., 1,446 103 G4
Arraiján, Pan., 2,192 94 H6
Arraiolos, Port., 4,510 122 B3
Ar Ramādī, Iraq, 17,747 143 C2
Ar Ramthā, Jor., 10,791 142 c7
Arran, Fla. 65 E2
Arran, I. of, U.K. 112 D4
Arrandale, Br. Col., Can. 42 D2
Ar Rank, Sudan 163 K4
Ar Raqqah, Syr., 10,219 142 D2
Arras, Br. Col., Can. 42 G2
Arras, Fr., 45,643 117 E1
Ar Rashādīyah, Jor. 142 C4
Ar Rawḍah, U.A.R., 10,060 161 K3
Arrecife, Can. Is. 160 B3
Arrecifes, Arg. 105 b12

Arrentela—Auburn · 195

Arrentela, Port., 5,390 **122** i10
Arretí, Pan. **94** J7
Arrey, N. Mex. **79** B5
Arriaga, Mex., 11,601 **93** G5
Arrianá, Gr., 1,135 **129** E4
Arriba, Colo., 296 **79** D2
Arribas, Sp. **122** n11
Ar Rifā'ī, Iraq, 6,467 **143** D2
Arrilalah, Austl. **173** F3
Arrington, Kans. **75** K4
Arrington, Tenn. **71** E6
Arriola, Colo. **79** A3
Ar Riyād, Saudi Ar., 170,000* **143** D4
Ar Riyān, S. Ar. **143** D6
Arrochar, U.K. **112** D3
Arroio Grande, Braz., 5,623 **103** F8
Arronches, Port., 3,689 **122** B3
Arrone, r., It. **123** a8
Arrow, L., Ire. **113** B4
Arrow, r., U.K. **114** C6
Arrowbear Lake, Calif. **83** k15
Arrowhead, Br. Col., Can. **42** H4
Arrowhead, L., Calif. **83** k15
Arrow Park, Br. Col., Can. **42** H4
Arrow Rock, Mo., 245 **72** D5
Arrowsic, Me. **55** C5
Arrowsmith, Ill., 319 **68** D3
Arrowtown, N.Z. **175** f7
Arrowwood, Alta., Can. **42** K4
Arroyito, Arg., 5,000* **105** C4
Arroyo, P.R., 3,741 **96** t11
Arroyo Barú, Arg., 1,100* **105** b10
Arroyo de la Luz, Sp., 9,781 **122** B3
Arroyo de la Ventana, Arg. **105** B6
Arroyo Grande, Calif., 3,291 **82** C5
Arroyo Hondo, N. Mex. **79** B3
Arroyo Seco, Micho., Mex. **93** c10
Arroyo Seco, Qro., Mex. **93** e8
Arroyo Zarco, Mex., 1,472 **93** e9
Arruda dos Vinhos, Port., 3,960 **122** i10
Ar Rudayyif, Tun. **161** F2
Ar Rumaythah, Iraq, 7,598 **143** C2
Ar Ruşayriş, Sudan, 3,927 **163** K4
Ar Ruţbah, Iraq **143** C2
Ar Ruwayḑah, Saudi Ar. **143** C3
Års, Den., 4,249 **121** B4
Arsache, Rum. **128** E3
Arsacides, C., Sol. Is. **175** c2
Arsen'yev, U.S.S.R., 26,400 **135** N5
Arshaly, r., U.S.S.R. **137** n12
Ars-sur-Moselle, Fr., 5,193 **117** F2
Årstad, Swed. **121** E4
Art, Î., N. Caled. **174** h7
Árta, Gr., 16,899 **129** C5
Artá, Sp., 5,401 **122** G3
Artajona, Sp., 1,969 **122** o12
Artas, S. Dak., 87 **74** C3
Artashat, U.S.S.R., 6,300 **137** c2
Arteaga, Mex., 2,960 **92** E4
Arteijo, Sp., 10,887 **122** A1
Artel'nyy, U.S.S.R. **137** i7
Artëm, U.S.S.R., 60,000 **135** N5
Artemisa, Cuba, 17,461 **96** b1
Artemón, Gr. **129** E6
Artëmovsk, R.S.F.S.R., U.S.S.R., 12,800 **135** J4
Artëmovsk, Ukr.S.S.R., U.S.S.R., 18,000 **136** f7
Artëmovsk, Ukr.S.S.R., U.S.S.R., 64,000 **136** f7
Artëmovskiy, U.S.S.R. **135** L4
Artëmovskiy, U.S.S.R., 34,400 **137** k7
Artena, It., 7,977 **123** b8
Artenay, Fr., 1,357 **117** D2
Artern, Ger.D.R. **118** C3
Artesa de Segre, Sp., 2,931 **122** F2
Artesia, Ariz. **78** D5
Artesia, Calif., 9,993 **83** h16
Artesia, Miss., 469 **73** G4
Artesia, N. Mex., 12,000 **79** C5
Artesian, S. Dak., 330 **74** C4
Artesia Wells, Tex. **77** O5
Arth, Switz., 6,321 **124** C1
Arthabaska, Qué., Can., 2,953 **47** N2
Arthies, Fr. **116** f10
Arthur, Ont., Can., 1,178 **46** D5
Arthur, Ill., 2,120 **68** D4
Arthur, Iowa, 265 **72** B2
Arthur, co., Nebr., 680 **75** D2
Arthur, Nebr., 165 **75** D2
Arthur, Nev. **83** C2
Arthur, N. Dak., 325 **74** D2
Arthur, Tenn. **71** H5
Arthur, Wis. **66** C6
Arthur, r., Austl. **173** e13
Arthur, L., La. **73** C7
Arthur, Mt., Austl. **172** C2
Arthur Kill, N.Y. **58** c14
Arthur's Pass Nat. Pk., N.Z. **175** f6
Arthurs Town, Bah. Is. **95** D1
Arti, U.S.S.R. **137** i8
Artibonite, r., Haiti **96** k6
Artigas, Urug., 14,000* **105** D4
Artie, W. Va. **62** C5
Artik, U.S.S.R., 9,500 **137** c1
Artillery L., N.W.T., Can. **40** H5
Artlenburg, F.R.Ger., 1,170 **119** b9
Artois, Calif. **82** B3
Arturo Prat, Arg. **180** O6
Artvin', Turk., 7,908 **142** E1
Artyk, U.S.S.R. **135** O3
Aru, Kep., Indon. **149** K4
Arua, Uganda, 4,645 **164** E1
Aruanã, Braz., 2,405 **103** F4
Aruba, i., Lesser Ant. **97** 15
Aruboe, i., Jaluit **176** 30
Arucas, Can. Is. **109** 4
Aruga, Jap. **155** n18
Arukoron C., Palau **176** 21
Arun, r., Asia **145** H4
Arun, r., U.K. **113** F6
Århup, Den. **121** C5
Aru Pt., Ponape **176** 29
Aruppukkottai, India, 50,200 **145** F8
Arus, P.R. **96** s10
Arusha, Tanz., 10,038 **164** F2
Arut, r., Indon. **148** D3
Arutua, atoll, Tuam. Arch. **177** 42
Arutunga, Aitutaki **177** 35
Aruwimi, r., D.R.Congo **164** D1
Arva, Ont., Can. **46** C5
Arvada, Colo., 19,242 **79** C2
Arvagh, Ire. **113** C5
Arve, r., Fr. **117** G3
Arvida, Qué., Can., 14,309 **45** L5
Arvidsjaur, Swed. **120** D2
Arvika, Swed. **120** C4
Arvilla, Alta., Can. **43** b7
Arvilla, N. Dak. **74** D2
Arvin, Calif., 5,310 **82** D5
Arvonia, Kans. **75** K5
Arvonia, Va. **62** F5
Arwala, Indon. **149** H4
Ary, U.S.S.R. **135** M2
Aryānah, Tun., 16,341 **160** f5
Aryirádhes, Gr., 1,567 **129** B5
Aryiropoúlion, Gr., 2,132 **129** D5
Arys', U.S.S.R., 22,900 **137** e3
Arys', r., U.S.S.R. **137** f3
Arzamas, U.S.S.R., 39,600 **134** D4
Arzbach, F.R.Ger., 1,478 **119** D4
Arzberg, F.R.Ger., 6,702 **118** D3
Arzew, Alg., 11,507 **160** D2
Arzfeld, F.R.Ger. **119** A4
Arzignano, It., 16,883 **123** C2
Arzúa, Sp., 10,470 **122** A1
Aš, Czech., 10,273 **126** A1
Ås, Swed. **121** E3
Aså, Den. **121** C3
Asa, Jap., 19,466 **154** B4
Asaba, Nigeria, 20,169 **162** g8
Asadābād, Iran, 5,190 **143** D2
Asahi, Jap. **154** h14
Asahi, Jap., 30,076 **155** G4
Asahi, r., Jap. **154** e15
Asahi-dake, Jap. **155** F2
Asahi-dake, Jap. **155** K8
Asahigawa, Jap., 188,309 **155** K8
Asamai, Jap., 8,418 **155** G2
Asama-yama, Jap. **155** F3
Asan, Guam **176** 24
Asangaro, Peru, 5,412 **104** D5
Asan-man, S. Kor. **151** E3
Asan Pt., Guam **176** 24
Asansol, India, 103,405 **145** H5
Asau, W. Samoa **177** 38
Asba Tafari, Eth. **163** L4
Asbest, U.S.S.R., 65,000 **137** k7
Asbestos, Qué., Can., 10,923 **47** N3
Asbury, Mo., 186 **72** C7
Asbury, N.J. **61** A2
Asbury Grove, Mass. **57** N2
Asbury Park, N.J., 17,366 **61** D3
Ascension, i., Atl. Oc. **109** M7
Ascensión, Arg., 6,000* **105** a12
Ascensión, Bol., 3,174 **102** D5
Ascención, Mex., 1,959 **93** E3
Ascension, parish, La., 27,927 **73** E7
Ascensión, B. de la, Mex. **93** J4
Aschach, Aust., 2,035 **124** K5
Aschaffenburg, F.R.Ger., 51,998 **118** B4
Aschau, Aust. **124** J6
Ascheberg, F.R.Ger., 5,314 **119** D1
Aschendorf, F.R.Ger., 4,882 **118** A2
Aschersleben, Ger.D.R., 34,399 **118** C3
Ascoli Piceno, It., 49,625 **123** D3
Ascoli Satriano, It., 11,934 **123** E4
Ascona, Switz., 3,053 **124** C2
Ascot, U.K. **114** G8
Ascot, r., Qué., Can. **54** D1
Ascutney, Vt. **54** C5
Ascutney, Mt., Vt. **54** C5
Åseda, Swed. **120** C4
Åsele, Swed. **120** D2
Asella, Eth. **163** L4
Asembo, Kenya **165** g14
Asenovgrad, Bulg., 25,265 **128** E4
Åseral, Nor. **120** A4
Asferg, Den. **121** B4
Åsgårdstrand, Nor. **121** C1
Ash, U.K., 10,794 **114** G8
Ash, N.C. **63** F3
Ash, Oreg. **80** B4
Asha, Cyp., 2,119 **142** e9
Asha, U.S.S.R., 33,400 **137** i8
Ashausen, F.R.Ger., 1,320 **119** b9
Ashaway, R.I., 1,298 **57** J7
Ashbourne, U.K., 5,660 **114** E4
Ashburn, Ga., 3,291 **64** F4
Ashburnham, Mass., 2,758(T) **56** J2
Ashburton, N.Z., 11,602 **175** f6
Ashburton, r., Austl. **172** B3
Ashby, Mass., 1,883(T) **57** J2
Ashby, Minn., 426 **74** E2
Ashby, Nebr. **75** D1
Ashby de la Zouch, U.K., 13,594 **114** F5
Ashchisu, r., U.S.S.R. **137** o12
Ashchurch, U.K., 2,049 **114** D6
Ashcraig, U.K. **112** a8
Ash Cr., Utah **78** B3
Ashcroft, Br. Col., Can. **42** G4
Ashdad, Ont., Can. **46** H3
Ashdod Yam, Isr. **142** a8
Ashdown, Ark., 2,725 **73** A4
Ashe, co., N.C., 19,768 **63** C1
Asheboro, N.C., 9,449 **63** E2
Ashepoo, S.C. **63** D5
Ashepoo, r., S.C. **63** D5
Asher, Okla., 343 **76** G3
Ashern, Man., Can. **43** F4
Asherton, Tex., 1,890 **77** N5
Asherville, Kans. **75** G4
Asheville, N.C., 60,192 **63** B2
Asheweig, r., Ont., Can. **44** E4
Ashfield, Mass., 1,131(T) **56** E2
Ash Flat, Ark., 192 **73** D1
Ashford, Austl. **173** G4
Ashford, Barb. **97** 10
Ashford, U.K., 27,996 **113** G6
Ashford, Ala., 1,511 **64** D4
Ashford, Conn., 1,315(T) **56** H5
Ashford, N.C. **63** C2
Ashford, Wash. **80** C2
Ashford, W.Va. **62** C4
Ashford, Wis. **66** E5
Ashfork, Ariz. **78** B4
Ash Grove, Kans. **75** G4
Ash Grove, Mo., 886 **72** D7
Ashibe, Jap., 10,352 **154** A5
Ashibetsu, Jap., 67,137 **155** K8
Ashida, r., Jap. **154** e15
Ashikaga, Jap., 110,972 **155** F3
Ashimori, Jap., 2,776 **154** e15
Ashington, U.K., 27,294 **113** F4
Ashino-ko, Jap. **155** m20
Ashio, Jap., 16,608 **155** F3
Ashippun, Wis. **66** E5
Ashiya, Jap., 57,050 **154** g15
Ashizuri-zaki, Jap. **155** C5
Ashkhabad, U.S.S.R., 187,000 **134** E6
Ashkum, Ill., 601 **68** D3
Ash Lake, Minn. **74** F1
Ashland, Ala., 1,610 **64** D2
Ashland, Ill., 1,064 **68** B4
Ashland, Kans., 1,312 **75** F6
Ashland, Ky., 31,283 **71** J3
Ashland, La. **73** B5
Ashland, Me. **55** D2
Ashland, Mass., 7,779(T) **57** L3
Ashland, Miss., 309 **73** F3
Ashland, Mo., 495 **72** E6
Ashland, Mont. **81** F3
Ashland, Nebr., 1,989 **75** J2
Ashland, N.H., 1,237 **54** D4
Ashland, N.Y. **59** M7
Ashland, co., Ohio, 38,771 **70** G2
Ashland, Ohio, 17,419 **70** G2
Ashland, Okla., 87 **76** H3
Ashland, Oreg., 9,119 **80** B4
Ashland, Pa., 5,237 **61** K4
Ashland, Va., 2,773 **62** G5
Ashland, co., Wis., 17,375 **66** C2
Ashland, Wis., 10,132 **66** C2
Ashland, Mt., Oreg. **80** B4
Ashland City, Tenn., 1,400 **71** D5
Ashley, U.K., 1,149 **114** D5
Ashley, co., Ark., 24,220 **73** D4
Ashley, Ill., 662 **68** C5
Ashley, Ind., 721 **70** D1
Ashley, Mich., 448 **67** J5
Ashley, Mo. **72** F5
Ashley, N. Dak., 1,419 **74** C2
Ashley, Ohio, 907 **70** G2
Ashley, Pa., 4,258 **61** L3
Ashley, r., S.C. **63** D5
Ashley Cr., Utah **78** D1
Ashley Falls (part of Sheffield), Mass. **56** C4
Ashmore, Ill., 447 **68** D4
Ashmore Reef, Austl. **172** C1
Ashmūn, U.A.R. **161** i7
Ashokan, N.Y. **59** M8
Ashokan Res., N.Y. **59** M8
Ashoknagar, India, 14,440 **144** a13
Ashorobutu, Jap., 19,191 **155** K8
Ashqelon, Isr., 24,310 **142** a8
Ashridge, Ala. **64** B1
Ash Sha'am, Muscat and Oman **143** F3
Ash Shābbah, Tun., 9,309 **160** g6
Ash Shallāl, U.A.R. **161** K3
Ash Shāmīyah, Iraq, 9,381 **143** C2
Ash Shaqrā', Saudi Ar. **143** D3
Ash Shāriqah, Tr. States **143** E3
Ash Shaţrah, Iraq, 12,835 **143** D2
Ash Shiḩr, Saudi Ar., 8,000* **143** D6
Ash Shināfīyah, Iraq, 5,668 **143** C2
Ash Shuwayfāt, Leb., 6,781 **142** b6
Ash Shuwayrif, Libya **161** G3
Ashta, India, 8,981 **144** a14
Ashtabula, co., Ohio, 93,067 **70** J1
Ashtabula, Ohio, 24,559 **70** J1
Ashtabula, L., N. Dak. **74** D2
Ashti, India **144** b15
Ashti, India **145** F6
Ashton, Idaho, 1,242 **81** D3
Ashton, Ill., 1,024 **68** C2
Ashton, Iowa, 615 **72** B1
Ashton, Kans. **75** H6
Ashton, Md. **62** a8
Ashton, Mich. **67** H5
Ashton, Nebr., 320 **75** G2
Ashton (part of Cumberland), R.I. **57** L5
Ashton, S. Dak., 182 **74** C3
Ashton-in-Makerfield, U.K., 19,262 **114** C4
Ashton under Lyne, U.K., 50,165 **114** D4
Ashū, Jap. **154** g14
Ashuanipi L., Newf., Can. **45** N4
Ashuelot, N.H. **54** C6
Ashuelot, r., N.H. **54** C5
Ashuelot Pd., N.H. **54** C5
Ashur, ruins, Iraq **143** C1
Ash Valley, Kans. **75** F5
Ashville, Austl. **172** c8
Ashville, Ala., 973 **64** C2
Ashville, Fla. **65** F2
Ashville, Ohio, 1,639 **70** G3
Ashville, Pa., 422 **60** E4
Ashwell, U.K., 1,336 **114** H6
Ashwood, Oreg. **80** C3
'Āşī, r., Syr. **142** D3
Asi, r., Turk. **142** D2
Asia, Kep., Indon. **149** J2
Asid G., Phil. **153** B2
Asidonhoppo, Sur. **101** N6
Asiga Pt., Tinian **176** 27
Asige, Swed. **121** E4
Asilah, Mor., 10,839 **160** C2
Asili, Tutuila **177** 39
Asimboa, Sta. Cruz Is. **175** 6
Asinara, Isola, It., **123** B4
Asino, U.S.S.R., 21,100 **134** H4
Asir, Ras, Som. Rep. **163** N4
Ask, Swed. **121** c7
Aska, India, 9,024 **145** G6
Aşkale, Turk., 6,261 **142** E2
Askam, Pa. **61** o17
Askaniya-Nova, U.S.S.R., 3,900 **136** D4
Askarovo, U.S.S.R. **137** i9
Askeaton, Ire. **113** B5
Askern, U.K., 6,159 **114** F3
Askersund, Swed. **120** C4
Askewville, N.C., 195 **63** H1
Askim, Nor. **120** B4
Askino, U.S.S.R. **137** h8
Askival, mtn., U.K. **112** C3
Askiz, U.S.S.R. **137** s11
Askja, vol., Ice. **120** a6
Askol'd, O., U.S.S.R. **151** F2
Askole, Pak. **145** E2
Äsköping, Swed. **120** d8
Askós, Gr., 2,143 **129** D4
Askov, Minn., 331 **74** F2
Askrigg, U.K. **114** D2
Askum, Swed. **121** D2
Asl, U.A.R. **161** k8
Aslito, Saipan **176** 27
Asmara, Eth., 120,000* **163** L3
Asmundtorp, Swed. **121** c7
Asnæs, Den., 2,392 **121** D5
Åsnen, l., Swed. **120** C4
Asnières, Fr., 82,201 **116** h11
Asoka Pillar, Nepal **144** d12
Aso-ktk., Jap. **154** B5
Asola, It., 10,386 **122** d5
Asosa, Eth. **163** K4
Asoteriba, Jabal, Sudan **163** K2
Asotin, co., Wash., 12,909 **80** E2
Asotin, Wash., 745 **80** E2
Ásotthalom, Hung., 6,533 **126** D3
Aso-zan, vol., Jap. **154** B5
Asōzu, Jap. **154** h14
Aspach, Aust., 2,107 **124** K5
Aspang Markt, Aust., 2,352 **124** N6
Asparukhovo, Bulg., 2,284 **128** F3
Aspatria, U.K., 3,061 **113** E4
Aspen, Colo., 1,101 **79** B2
Aspen Butte, Oreg. **80** B4
Aspen Grove, Br. Col., Can. **42** G4
Aspen Hill, Tenn. **71** D6
Asperg, F.R.Ger., 7,390 **119** G7
Asperhofen, Aust. **124** b10
Aspermont, Tex., 1,286 **77** N3
Aspersdorf, Aust. **124** c9
Aspet, Fr., 1,315 **117** D5
Aspetuck (part of Easton), Conn. **56** C8
Äspinge, Swed. **121** F5
Aspinwall, Iowa, 95 **72** B3
Aspinwall, Pa., 3,727 **60** c8
Aspiring, Mt., N.Z. **175** f7
Aspö, Swed. **120** e8
Aspull, U.K., 6,753 **114** C3
Asquith, Sask., Can. **43** C4
Assa, r., U.S.S.R. **137** f3
Assab, Eth., 3,400* **163** M3
Assabet, r., Mass. **57** K3
Aş Şabyā, Saudi Ar. **143** C5
Assaikwatamo, r., Man., Can. **43** F3
Aş Şāliḩīyah, Syr. **142** E3
As Sallūm, U.A.R., 5,000 **161** J2
As Salţ, Jor., 16,177 **142** b7
As Salwá, Saudi Ar. **143** E4
Assam, st., India, 11,872,722 **145** J4
As Samāwah, Iraq, 26,838 **143** C2
Assamstadt, F.R.Ger., 1,491 **119** H6
Assaria, Kans., 322 **75** H5
Assateague I., U.S. **62** J4
Assawompset Pd., Mass. **57** N5
Asse, Belg., 11,898 **115** d9
Assebroek, Belg., 13,550 **115** B3
Assemini, It., 8,987 **123** B5
Assen, Neth., 26,400 **115** E2
Assenede, Belg., 5,400 **115** B3
Assens, Den. **121** B5
Assens, Den., 4,937 **121** C4
Assesse, Belg., 1,166 **115** D4
Assieu, Fr. **116** p16
Assiniboia, Sask., Can., 2,446 **43** C5
Assiniboine, r., Man., Can. **43** F5
Assiniboine, Mt., Alta.-Br. Col., Can. **42** J4
Assinica L., Qué., Can. **44** K5
Assinins, Mich. **66** E2
Assinippi (part of Hanover and Norwell), Mass. **57** N4
Ássiros, Gr., 1,776 **129** D4
Assis, Braz., 30,207 **103** F6
Assiscunk Cr., N.J. **61** B3
Assisi, It., 25,084 **123** D3
Asslar, F.R.Ger., 5,368 **118** B3
Assling, Aust., 1,968 **124** J7
Assonet, Mass. **57** M5
Ássos, Gr., 1,275 **129** D6
As Sudd, swamp, Sudan **163** J4
Aş Şukhayrah, Tun. **161** F2
As Sukhnah, Syr. **142** D3
As Sulayyil, Saudi Ar. **143** D4
Assumption, Ill., 1,439 **68** D4
Assumption, parish, La., 17,991 **73** D8
Assumption, Ohio **70** E1
Assumption I., Ind. Oc. **165** G3
Assunpink Cr., N.J. **61** B3
As Suwaydā', Syr., 15,954 **142** c7
Aş Şuwayrah, Iraq, 6,290 **143** D2
As Suways, U.A.R., 107,244 **161** K3
Assynt, Loch, U.K. **112** D2
Assyria, Mich. **67** H6
Astaffort, Fr., 1,822 **117** D4
Astakós, Gr., 3,465 **129** C5
Astara, U.S.S.R., 5,200 **137** d2
Asten, Neth., 5,400 **115** D3
Asti, It., 58,294 **123** B2
Asti, Calif. **82** B3
Astico, Wis. **66** E5
Astin Tagh, China **150** B3
Astipálaia, Gr., 1,205 **129** F6
Astipálaia, i., Gr. **129** F6
Astolfo Dutra, Braz., 3,681 **103** e17
Aston, U.K. **114** F7
Aston Clinton, U.K., 2,393 **114** G7
Astor, Fla. **65** H3
Astorga, Sp., 10,101 **122** B1
Astoria, Ill., 1,206 **68** B3
Astoria, Oreg., 11,239 **80** B2
Astra, Arg., 1,100* **105** B7
Astrakhan', U.S.S.R., 313,000 **134** D5
Astrakhan-Bazar, U.S.S.R., 8,800 **137** c2
Astray, Newf., Can. **45** M3
Astrolabe, C., Sol. Is. **175** c2
Astrolabe B., Terr. New Guin. **174** e2
Ástros, Gr., 1,978 **129** D6
Astudillo, Sp., 2,272 **122** C1
Asturias, Phil., 3,163 **153** e11
Asturias, reg., Sp. **122** B1
Astwood Bank, U.K. **114** E6
Asuisui, C., W. Samoa **177** 37
Asuke, Jap., 16,820 **155** E4
Asunción, Para., 281,007 **105** D3
Asuncion, i., Mar. Is. **170** D3
Asunción, E., Mex. **92** B2
Asunción, F. de la, Mex. **92** B1
Asunción Mita, Guat., 5,976 **94** d9
Aswad, Ar Ra's al, c., Saudi Ar. **143** B4
Aswān, U.A.R., 46,202 **161** K3
Aswān High Dam, U.A.R. **161** K4
Asyūţ, U.A.R., 122,000 **161** K3
Ata, i., Tonga **170** G6
Atabopo, Ven. **101** K5
Atacama, Des. de, Chile **105** A2
Atacama, Salar de, Chile **105** B2
Atacavi, r., Ven. **100** G6
Atacheo, Mex., 2,058 **93** b9
Ataco, Col. **100** C6
Atafu, i., Tokelau Is. **170** G5
Ataiti, Tahiti **177** 44
Atakpamé, Togo, 9,672 **162** E4
Atalaia do Norte, Braz. **102** B2
Atalándi, Gr., 4,552 **129** D5
Atalaya, Peru **104** C4
Atalèh, Som. Rep. **163** M5
Atalissa, Iowa, 212 **72** F3
Atambua, Indon. **149** H5
Atami, Jap., 52,163 **155** F4
Atami, Jap., 11,288 **155** G3
Atanik, Alaska **85** D1
Atapirire, Ven. **101** H3
Atar, Maur., 7,200 **162** B2
Atarjea, Mex. **93** e8
Atascadero, Calif., 5,983 **82** C5
Atascosa, co., Tex., 18,828 **77** O5
Atascosa, r., Tex. **77** O5
Atashika, Jap. **154** h16
Atasu, U.S.S.R., 12,200 **134** G5
Ataúro, I. de, Port. Timor **149** H5
Atáviros, Óros, Gr. **129** F6
Atawa, Jap., 4,666 **154** h16
Atbara = 'Aţbarah
'Aţbarah, Sudan, 36,293 **163** K3
'Aţbarah, Nahr, Eth.-Sudan **163** K3
Atbasar, U.S.S.R., 32,900 **134** F4
Atchafalaya, r., La. **73** D7
Atchafalaya Bay, La. **73** D8
Atchison, co., Kans., 20,898 **75** K4
Atchison, Kans., 12,529 **75** L4
Atchison, co., Mo., 9,213 **72** B4
Atco, N.J., 2,500* **61** B4
Ateburu, Ghana **162** c8
Ateca, Sp., 2,712 **122** E2
Atecoxco, Mex. **93** f9
Atecuario, Mex., 1,992 **93** b9
Atén, Bol., 2,732 **102** C4
Atenco, Mex., 7,235 **93** e10
Atenco, Mex., 1,650 **93** f10
Atengo, r., Mex. **92** D3
Atequiza, Mex., 1,489 **93** a9
Atessa, It., 10,230 **123** E3
Atezcatzinco, Mex., 1,053 **93** f10
Atglen, Pa., 721 **61** L6
Ath, Belg., 10,596 **115** B4
Athabasca, Alta., Can., 1,442 **42** K2
Athabasca, r., Alta., Can. **42** K2
Athabasca, L., Alta.-Sask., Can. **40** H6
Athalia, Ohio, 341 **70** C4
Athapapuskow L., Man., Can. **43** E3
Athboy, Ire. **113** C5
Athea, Ire. **113** B5
Athelstane, Wis. **66** E3
Athena, Fla. **65** F3
Athena, Oreg., 950 **80** D3
Athenry, Ire. **113** B5
Athens, Ont., Can. **47** J4
Athens, Gr. = Athínai
Athens, Ala., 13,652 **64** B1
Athens, Ark., 67 **73** B3
Athens, Ga., 31,355 **64** F2
Athens, Ill., 1,035 **68** C4
Athens, Ind. **70** C1
Athens, La., 406 **73** C5
Athens, Me. **55** C4
Athens, Mich., 966 **67** H6
Athens, N.Y., 1,754 **59** N7
Athens, co., Ohio, 46,998 **70** G3
Athens, Ohio, 16,470 **70** G3
Athens, Pa., 4,515 **60** J2
Athens, Tenn., 12,103 **71** G6
Athens, Tex., 7,086 **77** Q3
Athens, W. Va., 1,086 **62** D5
Athens, Wis., 770 **66** C3
Athensville, Ill. **68** B4
Atherley, Ont., Can. **46** E4
Atherstone, U.K., 5,825 **114** E5
Atherton, Austl., 2,527 **173** F2
Atherton, U.K., 19,755 **114** D3
Atherton, Calif., 7,717 **83** e13
Athiémé, Dahom., 1,781 **162** d8
Athienou, Cyp., 3,378 **142** e9
Athíkia, Gr., 1,477 **129** D6
Athínai, Gr., 627,564 **129** D5
Athis-Mons, Fr., 24,297 **116** h12
Athlone, Ire., 10,369 **113** B5
Athna, Cyp., 2,033 **142** e9
Athok, Burma, 4,770 **147** a2
Athol, Idaho, 214 **81** A2
Athol, Kans., 140 **75** G4
Athol, Mass., 10,161;11,637(T) **56** H2
Athol, N.Y. **59** N5
Athol, Pa., **60** e10
Athol, S. Dak. **74** C3
Athol Springs, N.Y. **58** k19
Atholton, Md. **62** b8
Atholville, N.B., Can., 2,275 **47** S10
Áthos, mt., Gr. **129** E4
Athus, Belg., 6,353 **115** D5
Athy, Ire., 3,948 **113** C5
Ati, Chad, 1,500* **163** H3
Atibaia, Braz., 8,957 **103** c18
Atico, Peru **104** C6
Atienza, Sp., 1,231 **122** D2
Atig, U.S.S.R. **137** i8
Atik, Man., Can. **43** E3
Atikameg, r., Ont., Can. **44** G4
Atikameg L., Man., Can. **43** E3
Atikokan, Ont., Can., 6,674 **44** D5
Atikonak L., Newf., Can. **45** N4
Atimaono, Tahiti **177** 44
Atimonan, Phil., 8,439 **153** B2
Atinju, Indon. **149** K3
Atiquizaya, El Salv., 6,338 **94** d10
Atitlán, L. de, Guat. **94** b9
Atiu, i., Cook Is. **177** 33
Atiue, Tahiti **177** 44
Atka, U.S.S.R. **135** P3
Atka, Alaska, 119 **85** g8
Atka I., Alaska **85** g8
Atkarsk, U.S.S.R., 26,100 **136** G3
Atkins, Ark., 1,391 **73** C2
Atkins, Iowa, 527 **72** F3
Atkins, Va. **62** C6
Atkinson, co., Ga., 6,188 **64** G4
Atkinson, Ga. **64** H4
Atkinson, Ill., 944 **68** C2
Atkinson, Nebr., 1,324 **75** G1
Atkinson, N.C., 302 **63** F3
Atlacomulco, Mex., 3,049 **93** e10
Atlán, Mex., 1,434 **93** e9
Atlanta, Ga., 487,455 **64** E2
Atlanta, Idaho **81** B4
Atlanta, Ill., 1,568 **68** C3
Atlanta, Ind., 602 **70** C2
Atlanta, Kans., 267 **75** J6
Atlanta, La. **73** C6
Atlanta, Mich. **67** J3
Atlanta, Mo., 386 **72** E5
Atlanta, Nebr., 107 **75** F3
Atlanta, N.Y. **58** F6
Atlanta, Tex., 4,076 **77** Q3
Atlantic, Iowa, 6,890 **72** C3
Atlantic, co., N.J., 160,880 **61** B5
Atlantic, N.C. **63** H3
Atlantic, Pa. **60** B2
Atlantic Beach, Fla., 3,125 **65** H2
Atlantic Beach, N.Y., 1,082 **58** e14
Atlantic Beach, N.C., 76 **63** H3
Atlantic Beach, S.C. **63** F4
Atlantic City, N.J., 59,544 **61** C5
Atlantic Highlands, N.J., 4,119 **61** D3
Atlantic-Indian Rise, Atl. Oc. **109** N10
Atlantic Mine, Mich. **66** E1
Atlantic Ocean **108–9**
Atlantic-Indian Basin, Atl. Oc.-Ind. Oc. **168** A4
Atlantic Pk., Wyo. **81** E4
Atlántida, Urug. **105** d12
Atlantis Seamount, Atl. Oc. **108** K4
Atlapulco, Mex., 5,555 **93** e10
Atlas, Ill. **68** B4
Atlas, Mich. **67** K6
Atlas, Haut, mts., Mor. **160** C2
Atlasburg, Pa. **60** a8
Atlasova, O., U.S.S.R. **135** P4
Atlas Saharien, ra., Af. **160** D2
Atlatlahuca, Mex., 2,501 **93** e10
Atlee, Alta., Can. **42** L4
Atlin, Br. Col., Can. **42** C1
Atlin L., Br. Col., Can. **42** C1
Atlixco, Mex., 30,433 **93** F4
Atmore, Ala., 8,173 **64** B4
Atnarko, Br. Col., Can. **42** F3
Atok, Phil., 2,326 **153** b6
Atoka, N. Mex. **79** C5
Atoka, co., Okla., 10,352 **76** G3
Atoka, Okla., 2,877 **76** G3
Atoka, Tenn., 357 **71** B6
Atoka Res., Okla. **76** H3
Atomic City, Idaho, 141 **81** C4
Atotonilco, Mex. **93** f9
Atotonilco, L. de, Mex. **93** a9
Atotonilco el Alto, Mex., 14,190 **93** b9
Atoyac, Gro., Mex., 6,514 **93** E5
Atoyac, Jal., Mex., 5,324 **93** a9
Atoyac, Oax., Mex., 1,722 **93** F5
Atoyac, r., Mex. **93** F5
Atrak, r., Iran **134** E6
Ätran, r., Swed. **120** C4
Atrato, r., Col. **100** B4
Atrauli, India, 17,936 **144** b11
Atri, It., 14,130 **123** D3
'Aţrūn, Bi'r al, Sudan **163** J2
Atsion, N.J. **61** B4
Atsugi, Jap., 46,239 **155** F4
Atsuhama, Jap. **154** f15
Atsumi, Jap., 23,007 **155** F2
Atsumi-hantō, Jap. **154** i15
Atsumi-wan, Jap. **154** i15
Atsuta, Jap., 6,476 **155** J8
Atsutoko, Jap. **155** L8
Attachie, Br. Col., Can. **42** G2
Aţ Ţafīlah, Jor., 4,506 **142** C4
Aţ Ţā'if, Saudi Ar., 53,953 **143** C4
Attainville, Fr. **116** h10
Attala, co., Miss., 21,335 **73** F4
Attalla, Ala., 8,257 **64** C1
Attapulgus, Ga., 567 **64** E5
Attarra, India **144** c13
Attawapiskat, Ont., Can. **44** G4
Attawapiskat, r., Ont., Can. **44** F4
Attawapiskat L., Ont., Can. **44** E4
Attawaugan, Conn. **56** J5
Attean L., Me. **55** B3
Attean Mtn., Me. **55** B3
Attendorn, F.R.Ger., 9,549 **118** A3
Attersee, Aust. **124** K6
Attica, Ind., 4,341 **70** B2
Attica, Kans., 845 **75** G6
Attica, Mich. **67** K5
Attica, N.Y., 2,758 **58** D6
Attica, Ohio, 965 **70** G1
Attica, Wis. **66** D6
Attigny, Fr., 1,525 **117** F2
Attikamagen L., Newf., Can. **45** M3
Attingal, India, 22,051 **145** k21
Attleboro, Mass., 27,118 **57** L5
Attleboro Falls (part of N. Attleboro), Mass. **57** L5
Attleborough, U.K., 3,027 **113** G5
Attnang, Aust., 7,529 **124** K5
Atton, Fr. **116** b9
Attopeu, Laos **146** D4
Attu, Alaska **85** d8
Attu I., Alaska **85** d8
Aţ Ţūr, U.A.R. **161** K3
Aţ Ţurayf, Saudi Ar. **143** B2
Aţ Ţuwayshah, Sudan **163** J3
Atucha, Arg., 2,000* **105** b11
Atuel, r., Arg. **105** B5
Atuntaqui, Ec., 8,874 **104** c9
Atur, India, 29,018 **145** m20
Atuu, Tutuila **177** 39
Åtvidaberg, Swed. **120** D4
Atwater, Calif., 11,105 **82** C4
Atwater, Minn., 899 **74** E3
Atwater, Ohio **70** H1
Atwood, Ont., Can. **46** D5
Atwood, Ala. **64** B1
Atwood, Calif. **83** i16
Atwood, Colo. **79** D1
Atwood, Ill., 1,258 **68** D4
Atwood, Kans., 1,906 **75** E4
Atwood, Mich. **67** H3
Atwood, Okla. **76** G3
Atwood, Pa., 131 **60** D4
Atwood, Tenn., 461 **71** C6
Atwood L., Ohio **70** H2
Atwoodville (part of Mansfield), Conn. **56** H5
Atzacualoya, Mex., 1,362 **93** f10
Atzcapotzalco, Mex., 49,617 **93** e10
Atzenbrugg, Aust., 1,401 **124** b10
Au, Aust. **124** d11
Au, Aust. **124** M6
Au, Switz., 3,688 **124** D1
Aua, Tutuila **177** 39
Aua I., Terr. New Guin. **174** d1
Auau Chan., Hawaii **84** E3
Aub, F.R.Ger., 1,443 **118** C4
Aubagne, Fr., 21,889 **117** F5
Aube, r., Fr. **117** F2
Aubel, Belg., 3,093 **115** D4
Aubenas, Fr., 10,569 **117** F4
Aubepierre, Fr. **116** k12
Auberchicourt, Fr., 5,085 **116** a7
Aubergenville, Fr., 2,729 **116** f11
Auberry, Calif. **82** D4
Aubervilliers, Fr., 70,836 **116** h11
Aubette, r., Fr. **116** f10
Aubigny, Man., Can. **43** g10
Aubigny-au-Bac, Fr., 1,055 **116** a7
Aubigny-sur-Nère, Fr., 4,712 **117** E3
Aubin, Fr., 7,918 **117** E4
Aubinadong, E. Br., r., Ont., Can. **67** K1
Aubonne, Switz., 1,766 **124** A2
Auboué, Fr., 5,088 **116** b8
Aubrey, Ark. **73** E3
Aubrey, Mt., Austl. **172** A4
Aubry L., N.W.T., Can. **40** D4
Auburn, Ont., Can. **46** C5
Auburn, Ala., 16,261 **64** D3
Auburn, Calif., 5,586 **82** C3
Auburn, Ill., 2,209 **68** C4
Auburn, Ind., 6,350 **70** D1
Auburn, Iowa, 367 **72** B2
Auburn, Kans. **75** K5
Auburn, Ky., 1,013 **71** E5
Auburn, Me., 24,449 **55** B4
Auburn, Mass., 14,147(T) **57** J4
Auburn, Mich., 1,497 **67** J5
Auburn, Miss. **73** E6
Auburn, Nebr., 3,229 **75** K3
Auburn, N.H. **54** E5
Auburn, N.J. **60** f13
Auburn, N.Y., 35,249 **59** G6
Auburn, N.C. **63** F2
Auburn, Pa., 936 **61** K4
Auburn (part of Cranston), R.I. **57** L5
Auburn, Wash., 11,933 **80** B2
Auburn, W.Va., 139 **62** D3
Auburndale, Fla., 5,595 **65** H4
Auburndale, Wis., 396 **66** C4
Auburn Heights, Mich. **67** f14
Auburn, L., Me. **55** B4

196 · Auburntown—Bagenkop

Auburntown, Tenn., 256 **71** E6
Aubusson, Fr., 6,279 **117** E4
Auby, Fr., 9,007 **116** a7
Auch, Fr., 20,834 **117** D5
Auchi, Nigeria **162** g8
Auchinleck, U.K. **112** b8
Auchterarder, U.K., 2,426 **112** E3
Auchterderran, U.K. **112** d7
Auchtermuchty, U.K., 1,354 **112** d7
Aucilla, r., Fla. **65** F2
Auckland, N.Z., 143,583 **175** g5
Auckland Is., N.Z. **170** F8
Aude, r., Fr. **117** E5
Auden, Ont., Can. **44** E5
Audenge, Fr., 2,001 **117** C4
Audierne, Fr., 3,913 **116** A3
Audincourt, Fr., 12,527 **117** G3
Audlem, U.K., 1,315 **114** C5
Audley, U.K., 5,006 **114** D4
Audrain, co., Mo., 26,079 **72** F5
Audruicq, Fr., 3,392 **117** D1
Audubon, co., Iowa, 10,919 **72** C3
Audubon, Iowa, 2,928 **72** C3
Audubon, Minn., 245 **74** E2
Audubon, N.J., 10,440 **61** A4
Audubon, Mt., Colo. **79** a7
Audun-le-Tiche, Fr., 8,522 **116** b8
Aue, Ger.D.R., 31,182 **118** D3
Aue, r., F.R.Ger. **118** B2
Aue, r., F.R.Ger. **119** a8
Auenheim, F.R.Ger., 1,888 **119** D7
Auerbach, F.R.Ger., 5,170 **118** C4
Auerbach, Ger.D.R., 19,396 **118** D3
Auffargis, Fr. **116** f12
Augathella, Austl. **173** G3
Aughnacloy, U.K. **113** C4
Aughwick Cr., Pa. **60** G5
Auglaize, co., Ohio, 36,147 **70** E2
Auglaize, r., Ohio **70** E1
Au Gres, Mich., 584 **67** K4
Au Gres, r., Mich. **67** K4
Au Gres, Pt., Mich. **67** K5
Augsburg, F.R.Ger., 200,236 **118** C4
Augst, Switz. **124** B1
Augulpelu Reef, Palau **176** 21
Augusta, Austl. **172** A5
Augusta, It., 26,610 **123** E6
Augusta, Ark., 2,624 **73** D2
Augusta, Ga., 70,626 **64** G2
Augusta, Ill., 915 **68** B3
Augusta, Kans., 6,434 **75** H6
Augusta, Ky., 1,458 **71** H3
Augusta, Me., 21,680 **55** C4
Augusta, Mo., 206 **72** F6
Augusta, Mont. **81** C2
Augusta, Ohio **70** J2
Augusta, Tex. **77** Q4
Augusta, co., Va., 37,363 **62** E4
Augusta, W.Va. **62** F3
Augusta, Wis., 1,338 **66** B4
Augusta Springs, Va. **62** E4
Augustenborg, Den., 1,926 **121** C6
Augustine I., Alaska **85** F4
Augustów, Pol., 13,266 **127** E2
August Town, Jam., 2,055 **96** q9
Augustowski, Kan., Pol. **127** E2
Augustus, Mt., Austl. **172** B3
Augustusberg, Ger.D.R. **126** c6
Auke Bay, Alaska **85** L4
Auki, Sol. Is. **175** c2
Aulander, N.C., 1,083 **63** G1
Auld, Ont., Can. **67** f16
Auld, L., Austl. **172** C3
Aulendorf, F.R.Ger., 4,660 **118** B5
Aulia, India **144** a15
Aullène, Fr., 2,084 **116** r18
Aulnay-sous-Bois, Fr., 47,686 **116** i11
Aulnay-sur-Mauldre, Fr. **116** f11
Aulne, Kans. **75** J5
Aulne, r., Fr. **116** B2
Aulneau Pen., Ont., Can. **74** E1
Aulnois-sur-Seille, Fr. **116** b9
Aulong, Malay., 5,499 **147** o14
Ault, Fr., 1,996 **117** D1
Ault, Colo., 799 **79** C1
Auma, Ger. D.R. **126** a6
Aumale, Fr., 3,002 **117** D2
Aumetz, Fr., 2,722 **116** b8
Aumont-Aubrac, Fr., 1,118 **117** E4
Aumsville, Oreg., 300 **80** B3
Aunay-sur-Odon, Fr., 3,219 **117** C2
Aundh, India **145** i18
Auning, Den., 1,672 **121** C4
Aunuu, Tutuila **177** 39
Aunuu, i, Tutuila **177** 39
Auob, r., S. Af.-S.-W. Af. **164** C6
Auponhia, Indon. **149** H3
Aups, Fr., 1,442 **117** G5
Aur, atoll, Marsh. Is. **176** 22
Aura, Mich. **66** E2
Auraiya, India, 17,463 **144** b12
Aurangabad, Bihar, India, 14,154 **145** G4
Aurangabad, Mah., India, 87,579 **145** E6
Aurapushekaru, i., Palau **176** 21
Auray, Fr., 8,354 **116** B3
Aurdal, Nor. **120** B3
Aure, r., Terr. New Guin. **174** e2
Aureilhan, Fr., 5,835 **117** D5
Aurelia, Iowa, 904 **72** B2
Aurelius, Mich. **67** J6
Aurès, mts., Alg. **160** e6
Aurich, F.R.Ger., 9,717 **118** A2
Aurignac, Fr., 1,203 **117** D5
Aurillac, Fr., 27,056 **117** E4
Aurora, Braz., 3,622 **103** J3
Aurora, Ont., Can., 8,735 **46** E4
Aurora, Guyana **101** L4
Aurora, Phil., 1,998 **153** B2
Aurora, S. Af. **164** a8
Aurora, Alaska, 293 **85** b6
Aurora, Colo., 48,548 **79** C2
Aurora, Ill., 63,715 **68** D2
Aurora, Ind., 4,119 **70** E3
Aurora, Iowa, 223 **72** F2
Aurora, Kans., 150 **75** H4
Aurora, Me. **55** D4
Aurora, Minn., 2,799 **74** F2
Aurora, Mo., 4,683 **72** D8
Aurora, Nebr., 2,576 **75** G3
Aurora, N.Y., 834 **59** G6
Aurora, N.C., 449 **63** H2
Aurora, Ohio, 4,049 **70** H1
Aurora, Oreg., 274 **80** B3
Aurora, co., S. Dak., 4,749 **74** C4
Aurora, S. Dak., 232 **74** D3
Aurora, Tex. **76** e8
Aurora, Utah, 465 **78** B2
Aurora Lodge, Alaska **85** H2
Auroraville, Wis. **66** E4
Aus, S.-W. Afr. **164** B6
Au Sable, Mich. **67** K4
Au Sable, r., Mich. **67** K4
Ausable, r., N.Y. **59** N3
Ausable Chasm, N.Y. **59** O2
Ausable Forks, N.Y., 2,026 **59** N3
Au Sable Pt., Mich. **67** G2
Au Sable Pt., Mich. **67** K4
Auserd, Sp. Sah. **160** B4
Ausserferrera, Switz. **124** D2
Austad, Nor. **121** A1
Austell, Ga., 1,867 **64** f9
Austerlitz, N.Y. **59** O7
Austin, Man., Can. **43** e10
Austin, Austl., 3,838 **70** D4
Austin, Ky. **71** F5
Austin, Minn., 27,908 **74** F4
Austin, Nev. **83** B3
Austin, N.C. **63** D1
Austin, Oreg. **80** D3
Austin, Pa., 721 **60** F2
Austin, co., Tex., 13,777 **77** P5
Austin, Tex., 186,545 **77** P4
Austin, Wash. **81** a7
Austin, L., Austl. **172** B4
Austinburg, Ohio **70** J1
Austin Chan., N.W.T., Can. **40** J3
Austin Lake, Mich., 3,520 **67** H6
Austin Str., Me. **55** C3
Austinville, Ala. **64** B1
Austinville, Va. **62** D6
Australia, ctry., 11,544,691 **172-3**
Australian, Br. Col., Can. **42** G3
Australian Alps, Austl. **173** f11
Australian Capital Terr., Austl., 95,913 **173** G5
Austral Seamount Chain, Pac. Oc. **169** G3
Austria, ctry., 7,273,000* **124**
Austvågöya, i., Nor. **120** C1
Austwell, Tex., 287 **77** P5
Autana, r., Ven. **100** G5
Autauga, co., Ala., 18,739 **64** C3
Autaugaville, Ala., 440 **64** C3
Auterive, Fr., 3,133 **117** D5
Auteuil, Fr. **116** f11
Authie, r., Fr. **117** D1
Autigny, Switz. **124** B2
Autlán, Mex., 17,069 **92** D4
Autopan, Mex., 5,688 **93** e10
Autoua, New Hebr. **174** k6
Autouillet, Fr. **116** f11
Au Train, Mich. **66** G2
Au Train Bay, Mich. **66** G2
Autryville, N.C., 192 **63** F3
Autun, Fr., 17,165 **117** F3
Auvernaux, Fr. **116** h12
Auvers, Fr., 3,772 **116** g10
Auvezère, r., Fr. **117** D4
Aux Barques, Pt., Mich. **67** K4
Aux Cayes=Les Cayes
Auxerre, Fr., 32,961 **117** E3
Auxi-le-Château, Fr., 3,143 **117** E1
Auxonne, Fr., 6,649 **117** F3
Auxvasse, Mo. 534 **72** E5
Auxvasse Cr., Mo. **72** F6
Auyama, Col. **100** D2
Auyán-Tepuí, Co., Ven. **101** J5
Auzances, Fr., 1,619 **117** E3
Auzangate, Nev., Peru **104** D5
Ava, Ill., 665 **68** C6
Ava, Mo., 1,581 **72** E8
Ava, Ohio **70** H3
Avaavaroa Passage, Rarotonga **177** 34
Avachinskaya, S., U.S.S.R. **135** P4
Avalanche, Wis. **66** C5
Avallon, Fr., 6,371 **117** E3
Avalon, Calif., 1,536 **82** D6
Avalon, Miss. **73** E4
Avalon, N.J., 695 **61** B5
Avalon, Pa., 6,859 **60** B4
Avalon, Tex. **76** f10
Avalon, Wis. **66** E6
Avalon Pen., Newf., Can. **45** R6
Avana, Terr. Papua **174** 3
Avanos, Turk., 5,651 **142** C2
Avant, Okla., 381 **76** G1
Avapicos, Ec. **104** B2
Avard, Okla., 56 **76** E1
Avaré, Braz., 20,334 **103** G6
Avarua, Rarotonga **177** 34
Avarua Hbr., Rarotonga **177** 34
Avas, Gr., 1,072 **129** E4
Avatele, Niue **177** 32
Avatele Bay, Niue **177** 32
Avatiu, Rarotonga **177** 34
Avatiu Hbr., Rarotonga **177** 34
Avdeyevka, U.S.S.R., 18,000 **136** e7
Ávdhira, Gr., 1,222 **129** E4
Avea, i., Fiji **174** 4
Avebury, U.K. **114** E8
Avedøre, Den. **121** a7
Aveiro, Port., 24,067 **122** A2
Aveizieux, Fr. **116** o15
Avelgem, Belg., 5,267 **115** B4
Avella, Pa., 1,310 **60** B5
Avellino, It., 41,861 **123** E4
Avenal, Calif., 3,147 **82** C5
Avenches, Switz., 1,776 **124** B2
Avenir, Alta., Can. **42** K2
Avera, Miss. **73** G6
Averill, Mich. **67** J5
Averill, Vt. **54** D2
Averill Park, N.Y. **59** O6
Avernes, Fr. **116** f10
Aversa, It., 38,158 **123** E4
Avery, co., N.C., 12,009 **63** C1
Avery, Ohio **70** G1
Avery, Okla. **76** G2
Avery, Tex., 343 **77** Q3
Avery Island, La. **73** C8
Aves, Is., Ven. **95** G4
Aves, Is. de, Ven. **100** G1
Avesnes, Fr., 6,716 **117** F1
Avesnes-les-Aubert, Fr., 4,426 **116** a7
Avesta, Swed. **120** D3
Aveyron, r., Fr. **117** D4
Avezzano, It., 28,970 **123** D3
Aviemore, U.K. **112** E3
Avigliano, It., 11,050 **123** E4
Avignon, Fr., 75,181 **117** F5
Ávila, Sp., 26,807 **122** C2
Avilés, Sp., 48,503 **122** C1
Avilla, Ind., 919 **70** D1
Avilla, Mo., 135 **72** C7
Avinger, Tex., 730 **77** Q3
Avis, Pa., 1,262 **60** H3
Avlón, Gr., 2,585 **129** D5
Avlum, Den., 2,811 **121** A4
Avoca, Austl., 1,025 **173** d11
Avoca, Iowa, 1,540 **72** B3
Avoca, Mich. **67** L5
Avoca, Nebr., 218 **75** J3
Avoca, N.Y., 1,086 **58** F7
Avoca, Pa., 3,562 **61** o16
Avoca, Tex. **77** O3
Avoca, Wis., 363 **66** C5
Avoca, r., Ire. **113** C5
Avoch, U.K. **112** D3
Avoid, Pt., Austl. **172** a8
Avola, Br. Col., Can. **42** H3
Avola, It., 26,510 **123** E6
Avon, Calif. **83** e11
Avon, Conn., 5,273(T) **56** E5
Avon, Ill., 996 **68** B3
Avon, Mass., 4,301(T) **57** M4
Avon, Mont. **81** C2
Avon, N.Y., 2,772 **58** E6
Avon, N.C. **63** J2
Avon, Ohio, 6,002 **70** c9
Avon, S. Dak., 637 **74** C4
Avon, r., W.L., U.K. **114** E7
Avon, r., Banff, U.K. **112** E3
Avon, r., Somerset, U.K. **113** E6
Avon, r., War., U.K. **113** F5
Avon-by-the-Sea, N.J., 1,707 **58** c16
Avondale, Newf., Can. **45** b10
Avondale, Ariz., 6,151 **78** B5
Avondale, Colo. **79** C2
Avondale, Mo., 663 **75** a7
Avondale, Pa., 1,016 **61** L6
Avondale (part of Westerly), R.I. **57** J7
Avondale, W. Va. **62** C5
Avondale Estates, Ga., 1,646 **64** h9
Avon Lake, Ohio, 9,403 **70** c8
Avonlea, Sask., Can. **43** C5
Avonmore, Ont., Can. **47** J3
Avonmore, Pa., 1,351 **60** D4
Avonmouth, U.K., 3,743 **114** C7
Avon Park, Fla., 6,073 **65** H5
Avon Water, r., U.K. **112** b8
Avord, Fr., 2,775 **117** E3
Avoyelles, parish, La., 37,606 **73** C6
Avranches, Fr., 10,127 **117** C2
Avrig, Rum. **128** E2
Avtovac, Yug. **125** D3
Awagamachi, Jap. **154** f14
Awaiara B., Terr. Papua **174** 3
A'waj, r., Syr. **142** c6
Awaji-shima, Jap. **155** D4
Awano, Jap. **154** h15
Awano, Jap. **154** i14
Awanui, N.Z. **175** g4
Awārān, Pak. **144** B4
Awarawar, Tg., Indon. **148** e7
Awarua Bay, N.Z. **175** e7
Awaruwaunawa, Guyana **101** L6
Awash, Eth. **163** L4
Awash, r., Eth. **163** L4
Awa-shima, Jap. **155** F2
Awaso, Ghana **162** b8
Awatabe, Jap., 11,645 **155** E4
A-wa-t'i, China **150** B2
Awe, Loch, U.K. **112** D3
Awio, Terr. New Guin. **174** f2
Awjilah, Libya **161** H3
Awka, Nigeria, 12,929 **162** g8
Aworro, Terr. Papua **174** d2
Awul, Terr. New Guin. **174** f2
Awuna, r., Alaska **85** E1
Axapusco, Mex., 1,027 **93** f10
Axat, Fr. **117** E5
Axbridge, U.K., 1,087 **114** C8
Axel, Neth., 5,800 **115** B3
Axel Heiberg I., N.W.T., Can. **41** L2
Axial, Colo. **79** B1
Axim, Ghana **162** b9
Axiós, r., Gr. **129** D4
Axioúpolis, Gr., 3,564 **129** D4
Ax-les-Thermes, Fr., 1,628 **117** D5
Axminster, U.K., 2,656 **113** E6
Axtell, Kans., 493 **75** J4
Axtell, Nebr., 477 **75** F3
Axton, Va. **62** E6
Axum=Aksum
Ay, Fr., 6,682 **117** F2
Ay, r., U.S.S.R. **137** i8
Ayabaca, Peru, 3,467 **104** A3
Ayabe, Jap., 51,258 **155** D4
Ayacucho, Arg., 18,000* **105** D5
Ayacucho, Bol., 4,480 **102** D5
Ayacucho, Peru, 21,454 **104** C5
Ayadaw, Burma, 2,444 **147** f6
Ayagh Kum Köl, China **150** C3
Ayaguz, U.S.S.R., 30,900 **134** H5
Ayamonte, Sp., 13,230 **122** B4
Ayan, U.S.S.R. **135** N4
Ayan, r., U.S.S.R. **135** J2
Ayancik, Turk., 3,607 **142** C1
Ayangba, Nigeria **162** g8
Ayapel, Col. **100** C3
Ayapel, Cga. de, Col. **100** C3
Ayapungo, Co., Ec. **104** c11
Ayarza, L., Guat. **94** d9
Ayat, r., U.S.S.R. **137** k9
Ayaviri, Peru, 7,516 **104** D5
Ayaviri, Peru., 1,096 **104** C5
'Aybāl, Jabal, Jor. **142** b7
Aycliffe, U.K., 1,478 **112** g10
Aydabul', U.S.S.R. **137** n11
Aydar, r., U.S.S.R. **136** E3
Ayden, N.C., 3,108 **63** G2
Aydın, Turk., 35,671 **142** A2
Aydlett, N.C. **63** J1
Aydyrlinskiy, U.S.S.R. **137** k9
Ayer, Mass., 3,323; 14,927(T) **57** K2
Ayerbe, Sp., 2,180 **122** E1
Ayer Itam, Malay., 22,369 **147** o14
Ayer Lanas, Malay., 1,041 **147** o14
Ayer Puteh, Malay. **147** p14
Ayers, Me. **55** E4
Ayer's Cliff, Qué., Can. **47** N3
Ayers Rock, mtn., Austl. **172** D3
Ayers Village (part of Haverhill), Mass. **57** M1
Ayersville, Qué., Can., 2,938 **47** K3
Ayer Tawar, Malay., 5,902 **147** o14
Aygues, r., Fr. **117** F4
Ayía Ánna, Gr., 1,408 **129** D5
Ayía Marína, Gr., 2,686 **129** F6
Ayía Marína, Gr. **129** F7
Ayía Paraskeví, Gr., 3,753 **129** F5
Ayiássos, Gr., 4,933 **129** F5
Ayía Varvára, Gr., 1,684 **129** E7
Áyion Óros=Áthos
Áyios Andréas, Gr., 1,165 **129** D6
Áyios Evstrátios, Gr., 1,061 **129** E5
Áyios Evstrátios, i., Gr. **129** E5
Áyios Kírikos, Gr. **129** F6
Áyios Nikólaos, Gr., 2,121 **129** D4
Áyios Nikólaos, Gr., 3,709 **129** E7
Áyios Pétros, Gr., 1,112 **129** C5
Áyios Pétros, Gr. **129** D6
Áyios Yeóryios, i., Gr. **129** D6
Ayke, Oz., U.S.S.R. **137** k10
Aylen L., Ont., Can. **46** G3
Aylesbury, U.K., 27,923 **113** F6
Aylesford, N.S., Can. **47** T11
Aylesworth, Okla. **76** G3
Aylesworth, Mt., Br. Col., Can. **42** A1
Aylett, Va. **62** G5
Ayllón, Sp., 1,291 **122** D2
Aylmer, Ont., Can., 4,591 **44** H7
Aylmer, Qué., Can., 6,229 **47** J3
Aylmer, L., Qué., Can. **47** N3
Aylmer L., N.W.T., Can. **40** H5
Aylsham, Sask., Can. **43** D4
Aylsham, U.K., 2,635 **113** G5
'Ayn ad Darāhim, Tun., 1,275 **160** f5
'Ayn al Ghazālah, Libya **161** H2
Ayni, U.S.S.R. **137** e4
Aynor, S.C., 635 **63** E4
Ayod, Sudan **163** K4
Ayodhya, India **144** d12
Ayo el Chico, Mex., 4,388 **93** b9
Ayon, O., U.S.S.R. **135** Q3
Ayora, Sp., 6,412 **122** E3
Ayotla, Mex., 4,654 **93** f10
Ayr, Austl., 7,082 **173** G2
Ayr, Ont., Can., 1,015 **46** D5
Ayr, co., U.K., 342,855 **113** D4
Ayr, U.K., 45,297 **112** D4
Ayr, Nebr., 111 **75** G3
Ayr, r., U.K. **112** b8
Ayre, Pt. of, U.K. **113** D4
Ayrshire, Iowa, 298 **72** C1
Aysary, U.S.S.R. **137** n11
Aysgarth, U.K. **114** D2
Ayton, Ont., Can. **46** D4
Aytos, Bulg., 13,914 **128** F3
Aytré, Fr., 5,302 **117** C3
Ayudaki, Jap. **154** f15
Ayukawa, Jap. **155** G2
Ayuñgon, Phil., 1,762 **153** e12
Ayutla, Gro., Mex., 2,688 **93** F5
Ayutla, Jal., Mex., 4,603 **92** D4
Ayutla, Qro., Mex. **93** e8
Aywalık, Turk., 16,057 **142** A2
Aywaille, Belg., 3,578 **115** D4
Azá, r., Ven. **101** J4
Azaguié, Iv. Coast, 2,300 **162** a9
Azaila, Sp. **122** E2
Azajo, Mex., 1,428 **93** c10
Azalea, Oreg. **80** B4
Azalia, Mich. **67** K6
Azambuja, Port., 3,814 **122** k9
Azamgarh, India, 32,391 **145** G4
Azano, Jap. **154** f14
Azaouad, reg., Mali **162** D3
Azaouak, des., Niger **162** E3
Azare, Nigeria, 12,128 **162** F4
A'zāz, Syr., 12,443 **142** D2
Azazga, Alg., 1,831 **160** d5
Azbine Massif=Aïr Massif
Azcoitia, Sp., 8,384 **122** n11
Azemmour, Mor., 12,449 **160** C2
Azerbaijan S.S.R.=Azerbaydzhanskaya S.S.R.
Azerbaydzhanskaya S.S.R., U.S.S.R., 4,518,000* **134** D5
Azergues, r., Fr. **116** p15
Azero, r., Bol. **102** c11
Azilda, Ont., Can., 2,256 **46** C2
Aziscoos L., Me. **55** B3
Azle, Tex., 2,969 **77** P3
Azmoos, Switz. **124** a8
Azogues, Ec., 8,236 **104** B2
Azolzintla, Mex. **93** f9
Azores (part of Port.), Atl. Oc., 327,480 **108** L4
Azores-Gibraltar Ridge, Atl. Oc. **108** L4
Azov, U.S.S.R., 37,400 **136** E4
Azovskoye More, U.S.S.R. **134** C5
Azoyú, Mex., 2,545 **93** F5
Azpeitia, Sp., 9,400 **122** D1
Azraq, Al Bahr al, Sudan **163** K4
Azrou, Mor., 14,143 **160** D2
Aztec, Ariz. **78** B5
Aztec, N. Mex., 4,137 **79** B3
Aztec Ruins Nat. Mon., N. Mex. **79** B3
Azua, Dom. Rep., 12,350 **96** m6
Azua de Compostela=Azua
Azuaga, Sp., 16,306 **122** C3
Azuero, Pen. de, Pan. **94** G7
Azufrado, r., Col. **101** d15
Azul, Arg., 28,236 **105** D5
Azul, r., Cent. Amer. **94** C2
Azul, A. del, Arg. **105** D5
Azul, Co., Colón, Arch. de **104** a8
Azules, r., Pan. **94** f12
Azuma-yama, Jap. **155** F3
Azurduy, Bol., 6,905 **102** c11
Azureira, Port., 2,682 **122** i9
Azure Mtn., N.Y. **59** L2
Azusa, Calif., 20,497 **83** i15
Azushima, Jap. **154** g15
Azwell, Wash. **80** D2
Az Zahrān, Saudi Ar. **143** D3
Az Zaqāzīq, U.A.R., 124,000 **161** K2
Az Zarqā', Jor., 96,055 **142** D3
Az Zāwiyah, Libya **161** G2
Az Zilfī, Saudi Ar. **143** D3
Az Zubayr, Iraq, 28,699 **143** D2

B

Ba, Song, r., S. Viet. **146** E4
Baa, Indon. **149** G5
Baaba, Î., N. Caled. **174** i8
Baao, Phil., 6,764 **153** h14
Baar, F.R.Ger. **119** C4
Baar, Switz., 9,114 **124** C1
Baarle-Hertog, Belg., 1,947 **115** C3
Baarn, Neth., 19,700 **115** c6
Baasrode, Belg., 6,848 **115** d8
Baba, Ec. **104** c10
Baba, Jap. **154** h15
Babad, Indon. **148** e7
Babadag, Rum., 5,549 **128** G2
Babaeski, Turk., 11,692 **142** A1
Babahoyo, Ec., 16,107 **104** B2
Babak, Phil., 2,121 **153** C4
Babar, Kep., Indon. **149** J4
Babar, P., Indon. **149** J5
Babati, Tanz. **164** E2
Babatngon, Phil., 3,344 **153** f10
Babayevo, U.S.S.R., 12,400 **136** D1
Babbitt, Minn., 2,587 **74** G2
Babbitt, Nev., 2,159 **83** A3
Babbs, Okla. **76** D3
Babcock, Wis. **66** C4
Babe I., Guam **176** 24
Bab el Mandeb, str., Af.-Asia **143** C5
Babelthuap, i., Palau **176** 21
Babenhausen, F.R.Ger., 3,438 **118** C4
Babia G., Czech. **127** C4
Babina, India **144** b13
Babinda, Austl., 1,641 **173** G2
Babine, Br. Col., Can. **42** E2
Babine, r., Br. Col., Can. **42** E2
Babine L., Br. Col., Can. **42** E2
Babine Portage, Br. Col., Can. **42** F2
Babino Polje, Yug. **125** C3
Babo, Indon. **149** K3
Babócsa, Hung., 2,456 **126** C3
Bābol, Iran, 36,194 **143** E1
Bābol Sar, Iran **143** E1
Baborów, Pol., 3,514 **127** h6
Baboua, C.A.R., 6,305 **162** G5
Babson Park, Fla. **65** H5
Babushkin, U.S.S.R., 8,100 **135** K4
Babuyan, Phil. **153** A3
Babuyan Chan., Phil. **153** B1
Babuyan I., Phil. **153** B1
Babuyan Is., Phil. **153** B1
Babylon, N.Y., 11,062 **59** O10
Babylon, ruins, Iraq **143** C2
Baca, co., Colo., 6,310 **79** D3
Bacabal, Braz., 15,531 **103** G2
Bacadéhuachi, Mex., 1,405 **92** C2
Bacalar, Mex. **93** H4
Bacanora, Mex. **92** C2
Bacarra, Phil., 7,268 **153** B1
Bacău, Rum., 54,138 **128** F1
Baccalieu I., Newf., Can. **45** c9
Bac Can, N. Viet. **146** D2
Baccarat, Fr., 6,164 **117** G2
Bacchus Marsh, Austl., 2,825 **173** e11
Băceşti, Rum. **128** F1
Bačevci, Yug. **125** E2
Bac Giang, N. Viet., 15,738 **146** D2
Bach, Mich. **67** K5
Bachaquero, Ven., 14,492 **100** E2
Bacharach, F.R.Ger., 1,997 **119** D4
Bachelor Bk., Mass. **56** F3
Bachelor Butte, Oreg. **80** C4
Bachok, Malay., 1,181 **147** p13
Bačina, Yug. **125** E3
Back, r., N.W.T., Can. **40** K4
Back, r., Md. **62** d7
Bačka Palanka, Yug., 16,000* **125** D2
Bačka Topola, Yug., 13,000* **125** D2
Back Bay, N.B., Can. **47** S11
Back Bay, Va. **62** J6
Backbone Mtn., Md. **62** E3
Backe, Swed. **120** D3
Bäckefors, Swed. **120** C4
Bački Breg, Yug., 2,218 **125** D2
Backnang, F.R.Ger., 21,687 **119** G7
Backstairs Passage, Austl. **172** b8
Backus, Minn., 317 **74** E2
Backwell, U.K., 3,185 **114** C8
Baclaran, Phil., 24,799 **153** c8
Bacliff, Tex., 1,707 **77** k9
Bac Nam, Camb. **147** k11
Bac Ninh, N. Viet., 22,520 **147** i8
Bacnotan, Phil., 1,139 **153** b6
Baco, Eth. **163** L5
Bacobampo, Mex., 4,848 **92** C2
Bacolet, Gren. **97** 18
Bacoli, It., 17,771 **123** c10
Bacolod, Phil., 88,854 **153** B3
Bacon, Phil., 3,271 **153** h14
Bacon, co., Ga., 8,359 **64** G4
Bacong, Phil., 1,671 **153** e12
Bacon Hill, N.Y. **59** w27
Baconton, Ga., 564 **64** E4
Bacova, Va. **62** E4
Bac Quang, N. Viet. **146** D2
Bácsalmás, Hung., 9,542 **126** D3
Baculin, Phil., 2,353 **153** C4
Bacungan, Phil. **153** A3
Bacup, U.K., 17,295 **114** D3
Bacuyangan, Phil., 2,096 **153** d12
Bad, r., S. Dak. **74** B3
Bad, r., Wis. **66** C2
Badagara, India, 43,908 **145** E8
Badagri, Nigeria **162** e8
Bad Aibling, F.R.Ger., 7,421 **118** D5
Badajoz, Sp., 96,317 **122** B3
Badalona, Sp., 92,257 **122** G2
Badanah, Saudi Ar. **143** C2
Bad Aussee, Aust., 5,156 **124** K6
Bad Axe, Mich., 2,998 **67** K5
Bad Berka, Ger.D.R. **118** C3
Bad Blankenburg, Ger.D.R., 10,126 **118** C3
Bad Bramstedt, F.R.Ger., 6,186 **118** C2
Baddeck, N.S., Can. **47** V10
Bad Doberan, Ger.D.R., 12,601 **118** C1
Bad Düben, Ger.D.R. **118** D3
Bad Dürkheim, F.R.Ger., 11,700 **118** B4
Bad Dürrenberg, Ger.D.R., 12,715 **118** D3
Badem, F.R.Ger. **119** B4
Bad Ems, F.R.Ger., 9,306 **119** D4
Baden, Aust., 22,000 **124** N5
Baden, Man., Can. **43** E4
Baden, Ont., Can., 1,000 **46** a14
Baden, Switz., 13,949 **124** C1
Baden, Pa., 6,109 **60** B4
Baden-Baden, F.R.Ger., 40,079 **118** B4
Badenweiler, F.R.Ger., 2,877 **118** A5
Baden-Württemberg, st., F.R.Ger., 8,257,000* **118** B4
Bad Fischau, Aust., 1,405 **124** c11
Bad Frankenhausen, Ger.D.R. **118** C3
Bad Freienwalde, Ger.D.R., 12,153 **118** D2
Bad Friedrichshall, F.R.Ger., 7,840 **119** G6
Badgastein, Aust., 5,736 **124** K6
Badger, Iowa, 340 **72** C2
Badger, Minn., 338 **74** E1
Badger, S. Dak., 117 **74** D3
Badger, Wis. **66** D5
Badger Cr., Colo. **79** D2
Bad Godesberg, F.R.Ger., 56,731 **118** A3
Bad Goisern, Aust., 6,032 **124** K6
Bad Gottleuba, Ger.D.R. **126** d6
Bad Hall, Aust., 3,691 **124** L5
Bad Harzburg, F.R.Ger., 11,353 **118** C3
Bad Hersfeld, F.R.Ger., 22,819 **118** B3
Badhoevedorp, Neth., 8,700 **115** C2
Bad Hofgastein, Aust., 4,688 **124** K6
Bad Homburg, F.R.Ger., 33,515 **118** B3
Bad Hönningen, F.R.Ger., 5,471 **118** A3
Badian, Phil., 2,192 **153** e12
Badia Polesine, It., 11,502 **122** e5
Badie, Indon. **149** L4
Badin, Pak., 6,387 **144** C4
Badin, N.C., 1,905 **63** D2
Badin L., N.C. **63** D2
Bad Ischl, Aust., 12,698 **124** K6
Bādiyat ash Shām, Asia **142** D3
Badjo, Indon. **149** G2
Bad Kissingen, F.R.Ger., 12,954 **118** B3
Bad König, F.R.Ger., 3,484 **119** F5
Bad Kösen, Ger.D.R. **126** a5
Bad Köstritz, Ger.D.R. **126** b6
Bad Kreuznach, F.R.Ger., 33,468 **118** A4
Bad Krozingen, F.R.Ger., 3,197 **118** A5
Badkuhi, India, 7,005 **144** b14
Badlands, N. Dak. **50** F2
Badlands Nat. Mon., S. Dak. **74** A4
Bad Lauchstädt, Ger.D.R. **126** a5
Bad Lausick, Ger.D.R. **118** D3
Bad Lauterberg, F.R.Ger., 10,171 **118** C3
Bad Liebenwerda, Ger.D.R. **126** c5
Bad Liebenzell, F.R.Ger., 2,306 **119** F7
Bad Lippspringe, F.R.Ger., 8,403 **118** B3
Bad Mergentheim, F.R.Ger., 10,919 **118** B4
Bad Münster am Stein, F.R.Ger., 2,053 **119** D5
Bad Nauheim, F.R.Ger., 13,062 **118** B3
Badnawar, India, 6,821 **145** E5
Bad Neuenahr, F.R.Ger., 7,455 **119** C3
Bad Neustadt, F.R.Ger., 8,332 **118** C3
Bad Oeynhausen, F.R.Ger., 13,100 **118** B2
Bad Oldesloe, F.R.Ger., 15,082 **118** C2
Ba Don, N. Viet. **146** D3
Ba Dong, S. Viet. **147** m12
Badonviller, Fr., 2,143 **117** G2
Bad Orb, F.R.Ger., 6,912 **118** B3
Bad Pyrmont, F.R.Ger., 14,471 **118** B2
Bad Ragaz, Switz., 2,699 **124** D2
Bad Rappenau, F.R.Ger., 3,529 **119** G6
Bad Reichenhall, F.R.Ger., 12,390 **118** D5
Badr Ḩunayn, Saudi Ar., 1,552 **143** B4
Badrinath, India **144** b10
Bad Sachsa, F.R.Ger., 5,339 **118** C3
Bad Salzig, F.R.Ger., 2,625 **119** D4
Bad Salzungen, Ger.D.R., 10,117 **118** C3
Bad Sassendorf, F.R.Ger., 2,945 **119** E1
Bad Schandau, Ger.D.R. **126** d6
Bad Schwalbach, F.R.Ger., 5,609 **119** E4
Bad Schwartau, F.R.Ger., 14,472 **119** c8
Bad Segeberg, F.R.Ger., 11,756 **119** b8
Badsey, U.K., 1,553 **114** E6
Bad Soden, F.R.Ger., 7,068 **119** E4
Bad Soden, F.R.Ger., 2,183 **119** G4
Bad Sooden-Allendorf, F.R.Ger., 6,381 **118** B3
Bad Steben, F.R.Ger., 2,053 **126** a6
Bad Sulza, Ger.D.R. **118** C3
Bad Sülze, Ger.D.R. **118** D1
Bad Tennstedt, Ger.D.R. **118** C3
Bad Tölz, F.R.Ger., 12,349 **118** C5
Badulla, Cey., 17,043 **145** n22
Badung, Selat, Indon. **148** f8
Bad Vilbel, F.R.Ger., 12,007 **119** F4
Bad Vöslau, Aust., 5,554 **124** N6
Bad Waldsee, F.R.Ger., 6,083 **118** B5
Bad Water L., Mich. **66** E3
Bad Wildungen, F.R.Ger., 11,120 **118** B3
Bad Wilsnack, Ger.D.R. **118** C2
Bad Wimpfen, F.R.Ger., 4,797 **119** G6
Baena, Sp., 21,976 **122** D4
Baependi, Braz., 5,109 **103** d17
Baerenthal, Fr. **116** e9
Baesweiler, F.R.Ger., 12,088 **118** A3
Báez, Cuba, 2,223 **96** d1
Baeza, Ec. **104** c10
Baeza, Sp., 15,461 **122** D4
Bafatá, Port. Guin., 3,570* **162** B3
Baffin Basin, Can. **39** R3
Baffin B., Can. **39** R3
Baffin Bay, Tex. **77** P6
Baffin I., N.W.T., Can. **41** P5
Bafia, Cam. **162** F5
Bafilo, Togo **162** d7
Bafing, r., Guin.-Mali **162** C3
Bafoulabé, Mali, 3,700 **162** C3
Bafoussam, Cam., 8,000* **162** F5
Bafra, Turk., 20,788 **142** D1
Bafra Burnu, Turk. **142** D1
Bāft, Iran, 3,861 **143** F3
Bafwabalinga, D.R.Congo **164** D1
Bafwasende, D.R.Congo **164** D1
Baga, i., Sol. Is. **175** b2
Bagabag, Phil., 2,734 **153** c6
Bagabag, i., Terr. New Guin. **174** e2
Baga Bogdo Uula, Mong. **150** D2
Bagac, Phil., 2,117 **153** b8
Bagacay, Phil., 1,767 **153** f11
Bagaces, C.R., 1,175 **94** E5
Bagadó, Col. **100** B5
Bagaha, India, 19,411 **145** G4
Bagalkot, India, 39,934 **145** E6
Bagaman, i., Terr. Papua **174** 3
Bagamanoc, Phil., 3,771 **153** C2
Bagamoyo, Tanz. **164** F3
Bagan, U.S.S.R. **137** p11
Bagana, Mt., Sol. Is. **175** a2
Bagan Datoh, Malay., 2,264 **147** o15
Bagañga, Phil., 5,019 **153** C4
Bagan Jaya, Malay., 42,506 **148** B1
Baganpedjudian, Indon. **147** o15
Bagan Serai, Malay., 5,386 **148** A1
Bagan-siapiapi, Indon. **148** B2
Bagansinembah, Indon. **147** o16
Bagaruhi, Sol. Is. **175** d3
Bagaryak, U.S.S.R. **137** k8
Bagay, Phil., 2,791 **153** f10
Bagdad, Iraq=Baghdād
Bagdad, Ariz., 1,462 **78** B4
Bagdad, Fla. **65** C2
Bagdad, Ky. **71** F3
Bagdarin, U.S.S.R. **135** L4
Bagé, Braz., 47,930 **103** F8
Bagenalstown=Muine Bheag
Bagenkop, Den. **121** C6

Baggs—Barada · 197

Baggs, Wyo., 199 81 F5
Baghdād, Iraq, 355,958 143 C2
Bāgherhāt, Pak., 16,398 145 H5
Bagheria, It., 34,299 123 D5
Bāghlān, Afghan., 38,000* 144 C1
Baghmati, r., India-Nepal 144 e12
Baghpat, India, 8,437 144 a11
Baghrash Köl, China 150 B2
Ba Gieng, S. Viet. 147 m11
Bagley, Iowa, 406 72 C3
Bagley, Minn., 1,385 74 E2
Bagley, Wis., 275 66 B6
Bagnacavallo, It., 17,429 123 D2
Bagnara Calabra, It., 14,289 123 E5
Bagnères-de-Bigorre, Fr., 11,254 117 D5
Bagnères-de-Luchon, Fr., 3,898 117 D5
Bagneux, Fr., 38,159 116 h11
Bagnolet, Fr., 31,577 116 h11
Bagnolo in Piano, It., 5,447 122 d6
Bagnolo Mella, It., 9,726 122 d5
Bagnolo San Vito, It., 6,619 122 d5
Bagnols-en-Fôret, Fr. 116 m13
Bagnols-sur-Cèze, Fr., 13,031 117 F4
Bago, Phil., 6,396 153 d11
Bagodar, India 144 e13
Bagot, Man., Can. 43 f10
Bagotville, Qué., Can., 5,515 45 L5
Bagrationovsk, U.S.S.R., 5,000 136 A2
Bagsværd, Den., 14,072 121 b7
Bagtic, Phil., 6,932 153 d12
Bagua Grande, Peru, 2,147 104 B3
Bagual, Arg. 105 B5
Baguezane, Mt., Niger 162 F3
Baguio, Phil., 27,251 153 B1
Bagworth, U.K., 1,869 114 F5
Bah, India, 5,641 144 b12
Bahadurgarh, India, 14,982 144 a11
Bahama, N.C. 63 F1
Bahama Islands, 136,368 95
Bahamas, is., N. Amer. 51 L5
Bahār, Iran, 9,615 143 D2
Bahar Dar, Eth., 7,400* 163 L4
Bahau, Malay., 5,399 148 B2
Bahau, r., Indon. 148 E2
Bahāwalnagar, Pak., 36,290 145 D3
Bahāwalpur, Pak., 84,377 145 D3
Baheesiuna, Indon. 149 G3
Baheri, India, 15,406 144 b11
Bahia, st., Braz., 5,990,605 103 G4
Bahía, Is. de la, Hond. 94 D2
Bahía Blanca, Arg., 118,315 105 C5
Bahía de Caráquez, Ec., 9,129 104 A2
Bahía Honda, Cuba, 3,042 96 b1
Bahia Honda Key, Fla. 65 g15
Bahía Laura, Arg. 105 B7
Bahía Negra, Para. 105 D2
Bahjoi, India, 8,083 144 b11
Bahoruco, Sierra de, Dom. Rep. 96 m6
Bahraich, India, 56,033 145 F4
Bahrain, ctry., 182,203 143 E3
Baḥr al Jabal, Sudan 163 K4
Baḥrīyah, Al Wāḥāt al, oasis, U.A.R. 161 J3
Bahusuai, Indon. 149 G3
Baia, Rum. 128 G2
Baia de Aramă, Rum. 128 D2
Baia de Arieş, Rum. 128 D1
Baía dos Tigres, Ang. 164 A4
Baia Mare, Rum., 35,920 128 D1
Baião, Braz., 2,265 103 G2
Baia-Sprie, Rum., 8,134 128 D1
Baïbokoum, Chad 162 G4
Bai Bung, Mui, pt., S. Viet. 146 D5
Băicoi, Rum., 8,287 128 E2
Baie-Comeau, Qué., Can., 7,805 45 M5
Baie-de-Shawinigan, Qué., Can., 1,076 47 L2
Baie-des-Sables, Qué., Can. 47 R9
Baie de Wasai, Mich. 67 J2
Baie-Mahault, Guad., 1,428 97 14
Baiersbronn, F.R.Ger., 8,408 118 B4
Baie-Ste-Anne, N.B., Can. 47 T10
Baie-St-Paul, Qué., Can., 4,604 45 L6
Baie-Trinité, Qué., Can. 45 M5
Baie Verte, Newf., Can. 45 Q5
Baieville, Qué., Can. 47 M2
Baigorrita, Arg., 2,052 105 a12
Baihar, India 144 c14
Baijnath, India 144 b11
Baikal, L.=Baykal, O.
Baikunthpur, India 144 c13
Baikunthpur, India, 3,262 144 d14
Baile Atha Cliath, Ire., 584,483 113 C5
Băile Govora, Rum., 1,590 128 E2
Băile Herculane, Rum., 1,656 128 D2
Bailen, Phil., 2,573 153 b8
Bailén, Sp., 11,245 122 D3
Băile Olăneşti, Rum., 3,836 128 E2
Băile Slănic, Rum., 3,082 128 F1
Băileşti, Rum., 15,932 128 D2
Bailey, Colo. 79 C2
Bailey, Mich. 67 H5
Bailey, N.C., 795 63 F2
Bailey, Okla. 76 F3
Bailey, co., Tex., 9,090 77 M3
Bailey, Mt., Oreg. 80 B4
Bailey Bk., Me. 55 B2
Baileys Harbor, Wis. 66 F3
Baileysville, W. Va. 62 C5
Baileyton, Tenn., 206 71 J5
Baileyville, Conn. 56 E6
Baileyville, Ill. 68 C1
Baileyville, Kans. 75 J4
Bailieboro, Ont., Can. 46 F4
Bailieborough, Ire. 113 C5
Bailique, Braz. 103 G1
Bailleul, Fr., 12,926 117 E1
Baillif, Guad., 1,215 97 14
Bailly-Romainvilliers, Fr. 116 k11
Bain, r., U.K. 114 H4
Bainbridge, Ga., 12,714 64 E5
Bainbridge, Ind., 603 70 C3
Bainbridge, N.Y., 1,712 59 J7
Bainbridge, Ohio, 1,001 70 F3
Bainbridge I., Wash. 81 a8
Bain-de-Bretagne, Fr., 4,084 117 C3
Bainet, Haiti, 1,039 96 k6
Baing, Indon. 149 G5
Bains-les-Bains, Fr., 1,696 117 G2
Bainsville, Ont., Can. 69 D
Bainville, Mont., 285 81 G1
Bainyik, Terr. New Guin. 174 d1
Baiohari, India 144 c13
Baird, Tex., 1,633 77 O3
Bairdford, Pa. 60 c7
Baird Mts., Alaska 85 D2
Baird Pen., N.W.T., Can. 41 O4
Baire, Cuba, 3,957 96 e2
Bairiki, i., Gilb. Is. 175 10
Bairiki, i., Tarawa 175 15
Bairnsdale, Austl., 5,718 173 G5
Bairoil, Wyo. 81 F4
Bais, Fr., 1,160 117 C2
Bais, Phil., 5,058 153 e12
Baïse, r., Fr. 117 D5
Baisieux, Fr., 2,879 116 a6
Băişoara, Rum. 128 D1
Băiţa, Rum. 128 D1
Baitadi, Nepal 144 c11
Bai Thuong, N. Viet. 146 D3
Baiti (dist.), Nauru 175 17
Băiuţ, Rum. 128 E1
Baixo Guandu, Braz., 6,975 103 H5
Baiyer River, Terr. New Guin. 174 e2
Baja, Hung., 30,355 126 D3
Baja California, st., Mex., 520,165 92 B1
Baja California Sur, terr., Mex., 81,594 92 B2
Bajah, Indon. 148 b7
Bājah, Tun., 22,668 161 F1
Baja, P., Easter I. 177 46
Baja, P., Mex. 92 A2
Baja, P., Ven. 101 K3
Bajina Bašta, Yug. 125 D3
Bajo Boquete, Pan., 2,611 94 F6
Bajor, Tg., Indon. 148 F3
Bajos de Jaina, Dom. Rep., 4,614 96 n6
Bajovo Polje, Yug. 125 D3
Bajram Curri, Alb., 1,650 125 D3
Bajša, Yug. 125 D2
Bajunglentjir, Indon. 148 B3
Bakal, U.S.S.R., 29,700 137 i8
Bakala, C.A.R., 3,500 163 H4
Bakaruma, India 144 d14
Bake, Indon. 148 B3
Bakel, Sen., 2,400 162 B3
Bakenu, Malay. 148 E1
Baker, Alaska 85 G2
Baker, Calif. 82 E5
Baker, co., Fla., 7,363 65 G2
Baker, Fla. 65 C2
Baker, co., Ga., 4,543 64 E4
Baker, La., 4,823 73 D7
Baker, Mont., 2,365 81 G2
Baker, Nev. 83 C3
Baker, Okla. 76 B1
Baker, co., Oreg., 17,295 80 E3
Baker, Oreg., 9,986 80 E3
Baker, Mt., Wash. 80 C1
Baker, r., Chile 105 A7
Baker, r., N.H. 54 D4
Baker Bk., Me. 55 C2
Bakerhill, Ala. 64 D4
Baker I., Pac. Oc. 170 G4
Baker Lake, N.W.T., Can. 40 K5
Baker L., N.W.T., Can. 40 K5
Baker L., Me. 55 C2
Baker L., Wash. 80 C1
Bakersfield, Calif., 56,848 82 D5
Bakersfield, Mo. 72 E8
Bakersfield, Tex. 77 M4
Bakersfield, Vt. 54 B2
Bakerstown, Pa. 60 c7
Bakersville (part of New Hartford), Conn. 56 D5
Bakersville, N.C., 393 63 B1
Bakewell, U.K., 3,606 114 E4
Bakhchisaray, U.S.S.R., 11,500 136 D4
Bakhmach, U.S.S.R., 12,900 136 D3
Bakhta, U.S.S.R. 137 t11
Bakhtīārī, reg., Iran 143 D2
Bakhtiarpur, India, 4,548 144 e13
Bakırköy, Turk., 75,386 142 B1
Bako, Malay., 1,298 148 D2
Bakony, mts., Hung. 126 C3
Bakony Patak, r., Hung. 126 C3
Bakouma, C.A.R. 163 H5
Bakov nad Jizerou, Czech. 127 e6
Bakoy, r., Guin.-Mali 162 C3
Baksa, r., U.S.S.R. 137 q11
Baksheyevo, U.S.S.R. 136 c6
Baku, U.S.S.R., 671,000 134 D5
Bakumpai, Indon. 148 E3
Bakungan, Indon. 148 A2
Bakwanga, D.R.Congo, 39,024 164 C3
Bala, Ont., Can. 46 E4
Bala, Rum. 128 D2
Bâlâ, Turk., 3,130 142 C2
Bala, U.K., 1,604 113 E5
Bala, Cerros de, Bol. 102 C4
Balabac, Phil., 1,094 153 A4
Balabac I., Phil. 153 A4
Balabac Str., Malay.-Phil. 153 A4
Ba'labakk, Leb., 10,831 142 c5
Balabanovo, U.S.S.R. 136 b6
Balabat, Yap 176 20
Balabio, Î., N. Caled. 174 i8
Balaci, Rum. 128 E2
Bălăciţa, Rum. 128 D2
Balaclava, Jam., 1,153 96 p8
Balad, Iraq, 9,316 143 C2
Balad, Som. Rep. 163 M5
Balagachchi, U.S.S.R. 135 M3
Balaghat, India, 18,990 145 F5
Balaguer, Sp., 8,342 122 F2
Balaiselasa, Indon. 148 B3
Balakhna, U.S.S.R., 56,000 136 F1
Balakhta, U.S.S.R. 137 s11
Balaklava, Austl., 1,195 172 c8
Balaklava, U.S.S.R., 7,100 136 D4
Balakleya, U.S.S.R., 17,200 136 E3
Balakovo, U.S.S.R., 36,400 134 D4
Bala L., U.K. 114 A5
Balallan, U.K. 112 C2
Balama, Moz. 164 F4
Balamban, Phil., 4,437 153 e11
Balambangan, P., Malay. 148 F1
Bāla Murghāb, Afghan. 144 B2
Balana, Nic. 94 E3
Balancán, Mex., 2,554 93 H5
Balanda, U.S.S.R. 136 G3
Balanga, Phil., 1,466 153 B2
Balanguingui I., Phil. 153 B4
Balao, r., Ec. 104 c11
Balarampur, India, 10,881 144 f14
Balashikha, U.S.S.R., 60,000 136 b6
Balashov, U.S.S.R., 67,000 134 D4
Balasore, India, 33,931 145 H5
Balassagyarmat, Hung., 12,457 125 D2
Balástya, Hung., 5,723 126 D3
Balaton, Minn., 723 74 D3
Balaton, l., Hung. 126 C3
Balatonfüred, Hung., 7,572 126 D3
Balatonkiliti, Hung., 3,088 126 C3
Bălăuşeri, Rum. 128 E1
Balayan, Phil., 5,693 153 B2
Balayan Bay, Phil. 153 b9
Balazote, Sp., 2,539 122 D3
Balbalan, Phil., 1,019 153 c5
Balbec, Ind. 70 D2
Balbeggie, U.K. 112 d7
Balbi, Mt., Sol. Is. 175 a1
Balboa, C.Z., 3,139 94 g13
Balboa, Col. 100 B5
Balbriggan, Ire., 2,935 113 C5
Balcarce, Arg., 18,500* 105 D5
Balcarres, Sask., Can. 43 D5
Bălceşti, Rum. 128 D2
Balchik, Bulg., 8,006 128 G3
Balch Pd., Me.-N.H. 54 F4
Balch Springs, Tex., 6,821 76 f9
Balclutha, N.Z., 3,935 175 f7
Balcones Esc., Tex. 76 ·
Balcones Heights, Tex., 950 76 a6
Bald Creek, N.C. 63 B2
Bald Eagle Cr., Pa. 60 G4
Bald Eagle Mtn., Pa. 60 G4
Bald Head, Austl. 172 B5
Bald Head, Newf., Can. 45 c11
Bald Hill, Okla. 76 H2
Bald Hill Cr., N. Dak. 74 C2
Bald Knob, Ark., 1,705 73 D2
Bald Knob, mtn., Va. 62 D5
Bald Mtn., Colo. 79 C1
Bald Mtn., Vt. 54 A6
Bald Mtn., Vt. 54 D2
Bald Mtn., Wyo. 81 F3
Bald Mtn. Pd., Me. 55 C3
Baldock, U.K., 6,764 113 F6
Baldock L., Man., Can. 43 F3
Baldonnel, Br. Col., Can. 42 G2
Bald Pk., N.Y. 59 O3
Baldringe, Swed. 121 F5
Baldur, Man., Can. 43 E5
Baldwin, co., Ala., 49,088 64 B5
Baldwin, Fla., 1,272 65 H2
Baldwin, co., Ga., 34,064 64 F2
Baldwin, Ga., 698 64 F1
Baldwin, Ill., 336 68 C5
Baldwin, Iowa, 228 72 G2
Baldwin, Kans., 1,877 75 K5
Baldwin, La., 1,548 73 D8
Baldwin, Mich., 835 67 H5
Baldwin, N.Y., 30,204 58 e14
Baldwin, N. Dak. 74 B2
Baldwin, Wis., 1,184 66 A4
Baldwin Park, Calif., 33,951 83 i15
Baldwinsville, N.Y., 5,985 59 H5
Baldwinville, Mass., 1,631 56 H2
Baldwyn, Miss., 2,023 73 G3
Baldy Mtn., Man., Can. 43 E4
Baldy Mtn., Mont. 81 E1
Baldy Pk., Ariz. 78 D5
Bâle=Basel
Baleares, Is., Sp. 122 F3
Balearic Is.=Baleares, Is.
Baleia, P. da, Braz. 103 J5
Balele, Phil., 2,192 153 c8
Balen, Belg., 12,940 115 D3
Baleno, Phil., 2,278 153 h15
Baler, Phil., 3,081 153 B2
Baler Bay, Phil. 153 c7
Balerna, Switz. 3,040 124 D3
Baleshare, i., U.K. 112 C3
Balesin I., Phil. 153 c8
Balestrand, Nor. 120 A3
Baley, U.S.S.R., 29,200 135 L4
Balfate, Hond. 94 D3
Balfour, Br. Col., Can. 42 J4
Balfour, N. Dak., 159 74 B2
Balfours, N.C., 3,805 63 E2
Balfron, U.K. 112 b7
Balgach, Switz., 3,170 124 D1
Balgonie, Sask., Can. 43 D5
Balḩāf, S. Ar. 143 D6
Bal Harbour, Fla., 727 65 b10
Bali, India, 9,855 145 D4
Bali, i., Indon. 148 E5
Bali, Selat, Indon. 148 f8
Baliceaux I., Gren. Is. 97 20
Baliem, r., Indon. 149 L4
Balige, Indon. 148 A2
Balıkesir, Turk., 61,012 142 A2
Balikpapan, Indon., 91,706 148 F3
Balimbing, Phil., 2,188 153 B4
Balimo, Terr. Papua 174 d3
Baling, Malay., 4,121 147 o14
Balingasag, Phil., 5,502 153 C3
Balingen, F.R.Ger., 10,831 118 B4
Balingian, Malay., 1,220 148 E2
Balinţ, Rum. 128 C2
Balintang Chan., Phil. 153 B1
Balintang I., Phil. 153 g13
Bali Sea, Indon. 148 f7
Baliton, Phil., 3,192 153 C4
Baliuag, Phil., 4,890 153 b8
Baljći, Yug. 125 C3
Balk, Neth. 115 D2
Balkan Pen., Eur. 110 F4
Balkány, Hung., 8,224 126 E3
Balkashino, U.S.S.R. 137 n11
Balkbrug, Neth. 115 E2
Balkh, Afghan. 144 C1
Balkh, U.S.S.R. 137 e5
Balkhash, U.S.S.R., 61,000 134 G5
Balkhash, Oz., U.S.S.R. 134 G4
Balko, Okla. 76 C1
Ball, Mt., Alta., Can. 42 J3
Ballachulish, U.K. 112 D3
Ballaghaderreen, Ire. 113 B5
Ballancourt, Fr., 2,825 116 h12
Ballantine, Mont. 81 E3
Ballantrae, U.K. 113 D4
Ballantyne Str., N.W.T., Can. 41 F2
Ballarat, Austl., 48,030 173 F5
Ballard, co., Ky., 8,291 71 B4
Ballard, W. Va. 62 D5
Ballard, C., Newf., Can. 45 c11
Ballard, L., Austl. 172 B4
Ballard Corners, N.Y. 59 v27
Ballardvale (part of Andover), Mass. 57 M2
Ballast Pt., Calif. 82 c10
Ballater, U.K., 1,132 112 E3
Ball Bay, Norfolk I. 175 1
Ballé, Mali, 2,933 162 C3
Ballenas, B. de, Mex. 92 B2
Ballenas, Can. de, Mex. 92 B2
Ballenstedt, Ger.D.R., 10,435 118 C3
Balleny Is., Ant. 180 V6
Balleroy, Fr. 117 C2
Ballerup, Den., 17,231 121 E5
Ballësh, Alb. 125 D4
Ballesteros, Phil., 3,408 153 B1
Ball Ground, Ga., 707 64 E1
Ballground, Miss. 73 E5
Ballia, India, 38,216 144 e13
Ballina, Austl., 3,558 173 F4
Ballina, Ire., 6,091 113 B4
Ballinafad, Ont., Can. 46 b13
Ballinasloe, Ire. 5,489 113 B5
Ballingeary, Ire. 113 B6
Ballinger, Tex., 5,043 77 O4
Ballingry, U.K. 112 d7
Ballinrobe, Ire. 113 B5
Ball Mountain Bk., Vt. 54 B5
Ballobar, Sp., 1,498 122 E2
Ball's Pyramid, i., Austl. 170 E7
Ballstad, Nor. 120 C1
Ballstädt, Ger.D.R. 118 C3
Ballston, Oreg. 80 B3
Ballston Lake, N.Y. 59 v28
Ballston Spa, N.Y., 4,991 59 N6
Balltown, Iowa, 43 72 F2
Ballwin, Mo., 5,710 72 G6
Bally, India, 101,159 144 g14
Bally, Pa., 1,033 61 L5
Ballybay, Ire. 113 C4
Ballybunion, Ire. 113 B5
Ballycanew, Ire. 113 C5
Ballycastle, Ire. 113 B4
Ballycastle, U.K., 2,643 113 C4
Ballyclare, U.K., 4,441 113 C4
Ballydehob, Ire. 113 B6
Ballyforan, Ire. 113 B5
Ballyhaunis, Ire. 113 B5
Ballyheige, Ire. 113 B5
Ballyjamesduff, Ire. 113 C5
Ballymena, U.K., 14,740 113 C4
Ballymoe, Ire. 113 B5
Ballymoney, U.K., 3,409 113 C4
Ballymore, Ire. 113 C5
Ballymote, Ire. 113 B4
Ballynabola, Ire. 113 C5
Ballynahinch, U.K., 2,038 113 D4
Ballyshannon, Ire., 2,434 113 B4
Ballyvaghan, Ire. 113 B5
Balm, Fla. 65 G5
Balmat, N.Y. 59 K3
Balmazújváros, Hung., 18,769 126 E3
Balmertown, Ont., Can. 44 C4
Balmoral, Man., Can. 43 g9
Balmoral, La. 73 D5
Balmoral Forest, U.K. 112 E3
Balmorhea, Tex., 604 77 M4
Balmville, N.Y., 1,538 59 M8
Baloda Bazar, India, 7,108 144 d15
Baloganon, Phil., 2,226 153 b7
Balogo, Phil., 8,875 153 e11
Balonne, r., Austl. 173 G4
Balotra, India, 12,110 145 D4
Balovale, Zamb. 164 C4
Balquhidder, U.K. 112 b7
Balrampur, India, 31,776 145 G4
Balranald, Austl., 1,273 173 c10
Balş, Rum., 6,956 128 E2
Balsall, U.K., 2,480 114 E6
Balsam, N.C. 63 A2
Balsam Lake, Wis., 541 66 A3
Balsam L., Ont., Can. 46 E4
Balsa Puerto, Peru 104 B3
Balsas, Braz., 4,690 103 G3
Balsas, r., Braz. 103 G3
Balsas, r., Mex. 92 E4
Balsfjord, Nor. 120 D1
Balsham, U.K. 114 J6
Bålsta, Swed. 120 e8
Balsthal, Switz., 5,735 124 B1
Balta, U.S.S.R., 18,000 136 C4
Balta, N. Dak., 165 74 B1
Balta, i., U.K. 112 F1
Baltanás, Sp., 2,710 122 C2
Baltic, Conn., 1,366 56 H6
Baltic, Mich. 66 E1
Baltic, Ohio, 537 70 H2
Baltic Sea, Eur. 110 E3
Balţīm, U.A.R. 161 i7
Baltimore, co., Md., 492,428 62 H3
Baltimore, Md., 939,024 62 H3
Baltimore, Ohio, 2,116 70 G3
Baltinglass, Ire. 113 C5
Baltit, Pak. 145 E1
Baltiysk, U.S.S.R., 17,300 136 A2
Baltra, I., Arch. de Colón 104 a8
Baluchistan, reg., Pak. 144 B4
Balud, Phil., 1,663 153 B2
Balui, r., Malay. 148 E2
Balurghat, India, 26,999 145 H4
Băluşeni, Rum. 128 F1
Balut I., Phil. 153 C4
Balvag, r., U.K. 112 a7
Balve, F.R.Ger., 3,166 119 D2
Balvi, U.S.S.R. 136 B1
Balygychan, U.S.S.R. 135 P3
Balyksa, U.S.S.R. 137 s11
Balzar, Ec., 6,517 104 B2
Balzers, Liech., 2,095 124 a8
Balzola, It., 2,361 122 b5
Bam, Iran, 15,737 143 F3
Bama, Nigeria 162 G4
Bamaji L., Ont., Can. 44 D4
Bamako, Mali, 127,000 162 C3
Bamba, Jap. 154 h15
Bamba, Mali 162 D3
Bambamarca, Peru, 4,265 104 B3
Bamban, Phil., 4,336 153 b7
Bambana, r., Nic. 94 E4
Bambang, Phil., 6,166 153 B1
Bambari, C.A.R., 20,749 163 H5
Bambaroo, Austl. 173 F2
Bamberg, Ont., Can. 46 a14
Bamberg, F.R.Ger., 75,116 118 C4
Bamberg, co., S.C., 16,274 63 C4
Bamberg, S.C., 3,081 63 D4
Bambesa, D.R.Congo 164 D1
Bambey, Sen., 5,998 162 B3
Bambili, D.R.Congo 164 D1
Bamble, Nor. 121 B1
Bamboi, Ghana 162 b7
Bambra, Austl. 173 e12
Bamenda, Cam. 162 F4
Bamfield, Br. Col., Can. 42 a7
Bāmiān, Afghan., 40,000* 144 C2
Bamingui, C.A.R. 163 H4
Bamnak, Camb. 147 k10
Bamnet Narong, Thai. 146 C4
Bamori, India 144 a13
Bampton, Devon., Eng., U.K., 1,517 113 E6
Bampton, Oxon., Eng., U.K., 1,427 114 E7
Bampton, Westmd., Eng., U.K. 114 C1
Bam Tsho, China 150 C4
Bana, Hung., 1,579 126 C3
Banaderu, Saipan 176 27
Bañado de Rocha, Urug. 105 c10
Banagher, Ire. 113 C5
Banagüises, Cuba, 1,245 96 c1
Banahao, Mt., Phil. 153 c8
Banalia, D.R.Congo 164 D1
Banam, Camb. 146 D5
Banamba, Mali, 7,100 162 C3
Banámichi, Mex., 1,082 92 C1
Bananal, Braz., 2,189 103 d18
Bananal, I. do, Braz. 103 F4
Banas, r., India 144 a12
Banās, Ra's, U.A.R. 161 L4
Banat, Mich. 66 F3
Banatsko Novo Selo, Yug., 6,378 125 E2
Banaue, Phil., 1,673 153 c6
Banavie, U.K. 112 D3
Banbridge, U.K., 6,115 113 C4
Ban Bung, Thai. 147 d5
Ban Bung Sai, Laos 146 D4
Banbury, U.K., 21,004 113 F5
Banchory, U.K., 1,918 112 E3
Bancroft, Ont., Can., 2,578 44 J6
Bancroft, Idaho, 416 81 D4
Bancroft, Iowa, 1,000 72 C1
Bancroft, La. 73 B7
Bancroft, Me. 55 D3
Bancroft (part of Becket), Mass. 56 D3
Bancroft, Mich., 536 67 J6
Bancroft, Nebr., 496 75 J1
Bancroft, S. Dak., 86 74 D3
Bancroft, W.Va. 52 C4
Bancroft, Wis. 66 D4
Bancroft, Zambia, 17,050 164 D4
Banda, M.P., India 144 b13
Banda, U.P., India, 37,744 145 F4
Banda, Kep., Indon. 149 J4
Bandai-Asahi-ktk., Jap. 155 F2
Bandak, l., Nor. 121 A1
Bandama, r., Iv. Coast 162 a9
Bandana, Ky. 71 B4
Bandar=Masulipatnam
Bandar 'Abbās, Iran, 17,710 143 F3
Bandar-e Lengeh, Iran, 4,920 143 E3
Bandar-e Ma'shūr, Iran, 15,694 143 D2
Bandar-e Pahlavī, Iran, 31,349 143 D1
Bandar Maharani=Muar
Bandar Penggaram=Batu Pahat
Banda Sea, Indon. 149 H4
Bandau, Malay. 148 F1
Banded Pk., Colo. 79 B3
Bandeira, P. da, Braz. 103 H6
Bandelier Nat. Mon., N. Mex. 79 B4
Bandera, Arg., 3,800* 105 C3
Bandera, co., Tex., 3,892 77 O5
Bandera, Tex. 77 O5
Bandera, Alto de la, mtn., Dom. Rep. 96 m6
Banderas, B. de, Mex. 92 D4
Bandholm, Den., 1,252 121 D6
Bandiagara, Mali, 4,506 162 D3
Bandikui, India, 10,638 144 a12
Bandirma, Turk., 28,858 142 B1
Bandjar, Indon. 148 D4
Bandjermasin, Indon., 214,096 148 E3
Bandō, Jap., 6,643 154 f15
Bandon, Ire., 3,821 113 B6
Ban Don, S. Viet. 146 D4
Ban Don=Surat Thani
Bandon, Ind. 70 C4
Bandon, Oreg., 1,653 80 A4
Ban Don, Ao, Thai. 146 B5
Bandon, r., Ire. 113 B6
Ban Done, Laos 146 D3
Bandra, India, 27,710 145 h17
Bandung, Indon., 972,566 148 C4
Băneasa, Rum. 128 F2
Banes, Cuba, 20,257 96 f2
Banff, Alta., Can., 2,518 42 J3
Banff, co., U.K., 46,400 112 E3
Banff, U.K., 3,329 112 E3
Banff Nat. Pk., Alta., Can. 42 J3
Banfora, Upper Volta, 4,912 162 D4
Bañgad, Phil., 1,556 153 c5
Bangalore, India, 905,134 145 E7
Bangaon, India 41,082 144 g14
Bangar, Phil., 2,209 153 b6
Bangarmau, India 144 c12
Bangarpet, India, 11,360 145 m19
Bangassou, C.A.R., 9,434 163 H5
Bang Ban, Thai. 147 d4
Bang Bua Thong, Thai., 5,287 147 d5
Bange, Jap., 25,358 155 F3
Bang Fai, r., Laos 146 D3
Banggai, Indon. 149 G3
Banggai, Kep., Indon. 149 G3
Banggi, P., Malay. 148 F1
Banghāzī, Libya, 69,718 161 H2
Bang Hieng, r., Laos 146 D3
Bangil, Indon. 148 e7
Bangka, i., Indon. 148 C3
Bangka, P., Indon. 149 H2
Bangka, Selat, Indon. 148 C3
Bangkai, Tg., Indon. 148 D2
Bangkalan, Indon. 148 E4
Bang Khla, Thai., 5,545 147 d5
Bang Khon, Thai. 147 d5
Bangkinang, Indon. 148 B2
Bangko, Indon. 148 B3
Bangkok=Krung Thep
Bangkulu, P., Indon. 149 G3
Bang Lamung, Thai. 146 C4
Bang Mun Nak, Thai., 8,965 146 C4
Bangor, Ire. 113 B4
Bangor, N. Ire., U.K., 23,865 113 D4
Bangor, Wales, U.K., 13,993 113 D5
Bangor, Me., 38,912 55 D4
Bangor, Mich., 2,109 67 G6
Bangor, N.Y. 59 M2
Bangor, Pa., 5,766 61 M4
Bangor, Wis., 928 66 B5
Bang Pa-in, Thai. 147 d4
Bang Pakong, Thai. 147 d5
Bang Pakong, r., Thai. 147 d5
Bang Pia Ma, Thai. 147 c4
Bang Rachan, Thai. 147 d4
Bangs, Ohio 70 G2
Bangs, Tex., 967 77 O4
Bang Sai, Thai. 147 d4
Bang Saphan, Thai. 146 B5
Bangs, Mt., Ariz. 78 B3
Bangsri, Indon. 148 d7
Bangued, Phil., 7,602 153 B1
Banguereau Bank, Can. 39 S9
Bangui, C.A.R., 79,637 163 G5
Bangui, Phil., 1,674 153 B1
Bangweulu, L. Zambia 164 E3
Banhā, U.A.R., 46,834 161 i7
Ban Hin Heup, Laos 146 C3
Baní, Dom. Rep., 14,472 96 m6
Bani, Phil., 3,121 153 a6
Bani, r., Mali 162 D3
Baniara, Terr. Papua 174 f3
Banī Ḩasan, ruins, U.A.R. 161 K3
Banika, i., Sol. Is. 175 c3
Banī Mazār, U.A.R. 161 K3
Banīnah, Libya 161 H2
Banister, r., Va. 62 E6
Banī Suwayf, U.A.R., 79,600 161 K3
Baniyas, Syr. 142 b6
Bāniyās, Syr., 7,164 142 C3
Banjak, Kep., Indon. 148 A2
Banja Luka, Yug., 51,000* 125 C2
Banjska, Yug. 125 E3
Banjumas, Indon. 148 c7
Banjuwangi, Indon. 148 E5
Bank, U.S.S.R., 7,200 137 d2
Banka, India, 12,494 144 f13
Ban Karai, N. Viet. 146 D3
Ban Kavak, Laos 146 D3
Ban Khai, Thai. 147 d5
Bankhead L., Ala. 64 a7
Ban Khwao, Thai. 147 d4
Banks, U.K., 2,062 114 C3
Banks, Ala., 201 64 D4
Banks, Ark., 233 73 C4
Banks, co., Ga., 6,497 64 F1
Banks, Idaho 81 A3
Banks, Miss. 73 E3
Banks, Oreg., 347 80 B3
Banks, B. de, Colón, Arch. de 104 a8
Banks I., Austl. 173 F1
Banks I., Br. Col., Can. 42 D3
Banks I., N.W.T., Can. 40 E3
Banks Is., New Hebr. 170 F5
Banks L., Ga. 64 F4
Banks L., Wash. 80 D2
Banks Pen., N.Z. 175 g6
Banks Str., Austl. 173 G6
Bankston, Ala. 64 B2
Bankura, India, 62,833 145 H5
Ban Laem, Thai. 147 d5
Ban Lat, Thai. 147 c5
Ban Lat Hane, Laos 146 C2
Banmauk, Burma 146 A1
Ban Me Thuot, S. Viet., 28,820 146 D4
Ban Mi, Thai., 4,092 147 d4
Ban Mo, Thai. 147 d4
Ban Muong, Laos 146 D3
Bann, r., U.K. 113 C4
Ban Na, Thai. 147 d4
Ban Na Khang, Laos 146 D3
Ban Na Le, Laos 146 C3
Bannalec, Fr., 5,561 116 B3
Ban Nam Bac, Laos 146 C2
Bannang Sata, Thai. 147 o13
Ban Na San, Thai., 8,983 146 B5
Banner, Ill., 247 68 C3
Banner, co., Nebr., 1,269 75 B2
Banner Elk, N.C., 564 63 C1
Bannerman Town, Bah. Is. 95 c8
Bannertown, N.C., 1,096 63 D1
Banning, Calif., 10,250 82 E6
Banning, Pa. 60 d9
Banningville, D.R.Congo 164 B2
Bannister, Mich. 67 J5
Bannock, co., Idaho, 49,342 81 C4
Bannockburn, Ont., Can. 46 G4
Bannockburn, U.K. 112 c7
Bannockburn, Ill., 466 69 c8
Bannu, Pak., 31,623 145 D2
Bañolas, Sp., 8,075 122 G1
Banon, Fr. 117 F4
Baños, Ec., 3,759 104 B2
Baños, Peru, 1,300 104 B4
Baños de Cerrato, Sp., 7,519 122 C2
Baños de Longaví, Chile 104 f16
Baños de Turi, Chile 105 B2
Banova Jaruga, Yug. 125 C2
Bánovce nad Bebravou, Czech. 126 D2
Ban Pak Neun, Laos 146 C3
Ban Phaeng, Thai. 146 D3
Ban Phaeo, Thai. 147 d5
Ban Pho, Thai. 147 d5
Banphot Phisal, Thai. 147 c4
Ban Pong, Thai., 16,032 147 c5
Ban Rai, Thai. 147 c4
Ban Se Mat, Camb. 146 D4
Banská Bystrica, Czech., 22,590 126 D2
Banská Štiavnica, Czech. 126 D2
Bansko, Bulg., 6,805 128 D4
Ban So, N. Viet. 147 i8
Ban Song Teu, Laos 146 C3
Ban Soukhouma, Laos 146 D4
Banstead, U.K., 41,559 114 H8
Bansud, Phil., 2,706 153 B2
Banswara, India, 19,566 145 E5
Bantaian, Indon. 147 o16
Bantam, Indon. 148 b7
Bantam, Conn., 833 56 D6
Bantam, W. Br., r., Conn. 56 D5
Bantam L., Conn. 56 D6
Ban Tao, N. Viet. 147 h9
Ban Ta Ruang, Thai. 147 e5
Bantay, Phil., 2,928 153 b5
Bantayan, Phil., 7,920 153 e10
Bantayan I., Phil. 153 B3
Ban Thai, N. Viet. 147 h8
Ban Thateng, Laos 146 D4
Banting, Malay., 3,072 147 o15
Bantjar, Indon. 148 d7
Bantry, Ire., 2,211 113 B6
Bantry, N. Dak., 66 74 B1
Bantry Bay, Ire. 113 B6
Ban Vang, Laos 146 C3
Banwell, U.K., 2,824 114 C8
Ban Xam, N. Viet. 147 i8
Ban Xien Kok, Laos 146 C2
Ban Yen Nhan, N. Viet. 147 h9
Banyo, Cam., 3,000* 162 G4
Banzare Coast, Ant. 180 U6
Banzart, Tun., 44,681 161 F1
Banzet, Okla. 76 H1
Banzyville, D.R.Congo 164 C1
Bao Ha, N. Viet. 146 D2
Bao Lac, N. Viet. 146 D2
Bao Loc, S. Viet., 7,231 146 D5
Baonli, India 144 a12
Baoro, C.A.R. 162 G5
Baoulé, r., Mali 162 C3
Bap, India 145 D4
Bapaume, Fr., 3,890 117 E1
Baptiste, Ont., Can. 46 G3
Baptistown, N.J. 61 B2
Bapuju, Indon. 148 E3
Ba'qūbah, Iraq, 18,547 143 D2
Baqué, Guat. 94 B3
Baquerizo Moreno, Colón, Arch. de 104 b8
Bar, Yug. 125 D3
Barabanki, India, 34,334 144 c12
Barabara, Terr. Papua 174 3
Barāb Chāh, Afghan. 144 B3
Barabinsk, U.S.S.R., 39,500 134 G4
Barabinskaya Step', U.S.S.R. 137 p11
Baraboo, Wis., 6,672 66 D5
Baraboo, r., Wis. 66 C5
Baraboo Ra., Wis. 66 D5
Baracaldo, Sp., 77,802 122 n11
Barachois, N.B., Can. 47 T10
Barachois, Qué., Can. 45 N5
Baracoa, Cuba, 11,459 96 f2
Barada, Nebr., 58 75 K3

198 · Baradá—Bayport

Baradá, r., Syr. **142** c6
Baradères, Baie des, Haiti **96** k6
Baradero, Arg., 12,000* **105** b11
Baradine, Austl. **173** G4
Baraga, co., Mich., 7,151 **66** E2
Baraga, Mich., 991 **66** E2
Baraguá, Cuba, 2,267 **96** d2
Baragua, Ven. **100** E2
Bārah, Sudan, 4,884 **163** K3
Barahan, Phil., 1,356 **153** B2
Barahona, Dom. Rep., 20,398 **96** m6
Barakar, r., India **144** e13
Barakkul', U.S.S.R. **137** m11
Barakoma, Sol. Is. **175** b2
Baralaba, Austl. **173** G3
Baralzon L., Man.-N.W.T., Can. **43** F1
Baram, r., Malay. **148** E2
Barama, r., Guyana **101** L4
Baramanni, Guyana **101** L4
Baramati, India, 21,118 **145** i17
Baramula, India, 19,854 **145** D2
Baran, India, 22,764 **144** a13
Baranchinskiy, U.S.S.R. **137** i7
Barangar, India, 107,837 **144** g14
Baranoa, Col. **100** C2
Baranof I., Alaska **85** L4
Baranovichi, U.S.S.R., 63,000 **134** B4
Baranów, Pol. **127** E3
Baranów Sandomierski, Pol., 1,220 **127** D3
Barão de Cocais, Braz., 7,223 **103** e17
Barão de Grajaú, Braz., 1,946 **103** H3
Barão de Melgaço, Braz. **102** D4
Barapasi, Indon. **149** L3
Baraque de Fraiture, mt., Belg. **115** D4
Baras, Phil., 1,356 **153** i14
Baratang I., India **146** A4
Barataria, La. **73** E8
Barataria Bay, La. **73** F8
Barat Daja, Kep., Indon. **149** H4
Barate, Indon. **149** G5
Baratta, Austl. **173** e10
Baraut, India, 22,818 **144** a11
Baraya, Col. **100** C6
Barbacena, Braz., 41,931 **103** H6
Barbacoas, Col. **100** B7
Barbacoas, Ven., 1,027 **100** E3
Barbados, ctry., Lesser Ant., 245,000* **97** 10
Barbar, Sudan, 10,978 **163** K2
Barbarosa, Tex. **76** c6
Barbastro, Sp., 10,227 **122** E1
Barbate de Franco, Sp., 18,411 **122** B4
Barbaza, Phil. **153** B3
Barbeau, Mich. **67** J2
Barber, co., Kans., 8,713 **75** G6
Barber, Okla. **76** J2
Barberena, Guat., 2,917 **94** c9
Barber's Block = Espagnol, Morne
Barbers Corners, Ill. **69** b10
Barbers Pt., Hawaii **84** C2
Barberton, S. Af., 11,016 **164** E6
Barberton, Ohio, 33,805 **70** H2
Barberville, Fla. **65** H3
Barbezieux, Fr., 4,895 **117** C4
Barbigha, India, 13,697 **144** e13
Barbizon, Fr., 1,066 **116** i12
Barbosa, Col. **100** D4
Barbosa, Col. **101** d13
Barbour, co., Ala., 24,700 **64** D4
Barbour, co., W. Va., 15,474 **62** D3
Barboursville, Va. **62** F4
Barboursville, W. Va., 2,331 **62** B4
Barbourville, Ky., 3,211 **71** H5
Barbuda, i., Lesser Ant. **97** 8
Barby, Ger.D.R. **118** C3
Barcaldine, Austl., 1,705 **173** F3
Barcarrota, Sp., 7,898 **122** B3
Barce = Al Marj
Barcellona Pozzo di Gotto, It., 32,176 **123** E5
Barcelona, Phil., 1,866 **153** i15
Barcelona, Sp., 1,557,863 **122** G2
Barcelona, Ven., 40,773 **101** H2
Barceloneta, P.R. **96** s10
Barcelonnette, Fr., 3,445 **117** G4
Barcelos, Braz., 1,094 **102** D2
Barcelos, Port., 5,420 **122** A2
Bárcena, Sp., 1,152 **122** m11
Barciany, Pol. **127** D1
Barcin, Pol., 2,409 **127** B2
Barcino, Pol. **127** B1
Barclay, Kans. **75** K5
Barclay, Nev. **83** C4
Barco, N.C. **63** H1
Barcoo = Coopers Cr.
Barcs, Hung., 7,294 **126** C4
Barcy, Fr. **116** k10
Barczewo, Pol., 4,862 **127** D2
Barda, Az. S.S.R., U.S.S.R., 12,700 **137** c1
Barda, R.S.F.S.R., U.S.S.R. **137** h8
Bardaï, Chad **163** G2
Bardāndā, Nepal **144** d12
Bardas Blancas, Arg. **105** B5
Bardějov, Czech., 9,768 **126** E2
Bardera, Som. Rep., 7,685 **163** M5
Bardia = Bardīyah
Bardīyah, Libya **161** J2
Bardney, U.K., 1,570 **114** H4
Bardo, Pol., 2,839 **127** f6
Bardolino, It., 4,305 **122** d5
Bardolph, Ill., 266 **68** B3
Bardon L., Wis. **66** B2
Bardowick, F.R.Ger., 3,539 **119** b9
Bardsey I., U.K. **113** D5
Bardsey Sd., U.K. **113** D5
Bardstown, Ky., 4,798 **71** F4
Bardu, Nor. **120** D1
Bardwell, Ky., 1,067 **71** B5
Bardwell, Tex., 220 **76** f10
Bare, Yug. **125** E3
Bareilly, India, 254,409 **145** F3
Bareli, India, 5,847 **144** b14
Barellan, Austl. **173** f10
Barendrecht, Neth., 3,800 **115** a7
Barentin, Fr., 8,693 **117** D2
Barents Depression **132** B2
Barentsöya, i., Nor. **134** B2
Barents Sea, Eur. **134** C2
Barentu, Eth. **163** L3
Barford, U.K. **114** E6
Bargarh, India, 15,375 **145** G5
Barge Can., N.Y. **59** K5
Bargème, Fr. **116** m13
Bargemon, Fr. **116** m13
Bargersville, Ind., 586 **70** C3
Bargfeld-Stegen, F.R.Ger., 1,117 **119** b8
Bargteheide, F.R.Ger., 5,683 **118** C2
Barhaj, India, 15,264 **144** d12
Barham, Austl. **173** F5
Bar Harbor, Me., 2,444 **55** D4
Barhau, Indon. **148** B4
Bar Haven, Newf., Can. **45** a10
Barhi, India **144** e13
Bari, India, 14,695 **144** a12
Bari, It., 313,351 **123** F4
Baria, r., Ven. **100** G7
Barichara, Col. **100** D4
Barika, Alg., 8,196 **160** E2
Bārīkot, Nepal **144** d11
Barillas, Guat. **94** B3
Barima, r., Guyana **101** L4
Barinas, Ven., 25,707 **100** E3
Baring, Me. **55** E3
Baring, Mo., 213 **72** E4
Baringo, Kenya **165** h13
Baringo, L., Kenya **165** h13
Barinitas, Ven., 5,245 **100** E3
Baripada, India, 20,301 **145** H5
Bārīs, U.A.R. **161** K3
Barisan, Pegunungan, Indon. **148** B3
Barito, r., Indon. **148** E3
Barium Springs, N.C. **63** D2
Barjā, Leb., 5,638 **142** b6
Barker, N.Y., 528 **58** C5
Barker, Tex. **77** h9
Barkerville, Br. Col., Can. **42** G3
Barkerville (part of Pittsfield), Mass. **56** C3
Barkha, China **144** c10
Barkhamsted, Conn., 1,370(T) **56** D5
Barkhamsted Res. Conn. **56** E5
Bārkhān, Pak. **144** C3
Bark L., Ont., Can. **46** B2
Bark L., Ont., Can. **46** G3
Barkley Sd., Br. Col., Can. **42** F4
Barkly Tableland, Austl. **172** E2
Bark River, Mich. **66** F3
Barksdale, Tex. **77** N5
Barksdale, Wis. **66** B2
Barkway, U.K. **114** H6
Barlaston, U.K., 2,041 **114** D5
Barlby, U.K., 3,206 **114** F3
Bar-le-Duc, Fr., 20,168 **117** F2
Barlee, L., Austl. **172** B4
Barlestone, U.K., 1,205 **114** F5
Barletta, It., 69,639 **123** F4
Barlinek, Pol., 6,407 **127** A2
Barling, Ark., 1,518 **73** A2
Barlow, Ky., 731 **71** B4
Barlow, N. Dak. **74** C2
Barlow, Ohio **70** H3
Barmby Moor, U.K. **114** G3
Barmedman, Austl. **173** f10
Barmer, India, 27,600 **145** D4
Barmera, Austl., 1,078 **172** E5
Bar Mills, Me. **55** B5
Barmouth, U.K., 2,309 **113** D5
Barmstedt, F.R.Ger., 7,834 **119** a8
Barnabus, W. Va. **62** B5
Barnack, U.K. **114** H5
Barnala, India, 21,354 **144** a10
Barnard, Kans., 205 **75** G4
Barnard, Mo., 237 **72** C4
Barnard, S. Dak. **74** C3
Barnard, Vt. **54** B4
Barnard Castle, U.K., 4,969 **113** E4
Barnardsville, N.C., 199 **63** B2
Bārnau, F.R.Ger., 2,012 **126** b7
Barnaul, U.S.S.R., 338,000 **134** H4
Bärnbach, Aust., 5,634 **124** M6
Barnegat, N.J. **61** C4
Barnegat Bay, N.J. **61** C4
Barnegat Inlet, N.J. **61** C4
Barnegat Light, N.J., 287 **61** C4
Barnes, London, U.K. **114** H8
Barnes, Kans., 247 **75** J4
Barnes, co., N. Dak., 16,719 **74** C2
Barnes, Oreg., 5,076 **80** B4
Barnesboro, Pa., 3,035 **60** E4
Barnes City, Iowa, 273 **72** E3
Barnes Corners, N.Y. **59** J4
Barnes Icecap, N.W.T., Can. **41** P3
Barneston, Nebr., 177 **75** J3
Barnesville, Colo. **79** C1
Barnesville, Ga., 4,919 **64** E2
Barnesville, Minn., 1,632 **74** D2
Barnesville, Ohio, 4,425 **70** H3
Barnet, London, U.K. **114** H7
Barnet, Vt. **54** C3
Barnetby le Wold, U.K., 1,279 **114** H3
Barnetts, Va. **62** G5
Barneveld, Neth., 7,500 **115** D2
Barneveld, Wis., 420 **66** D5
Barneville-sur-Mer, Fr., 1,166 **117** B2
Barney, N. Dak., 115 **74** D2
Barney Top, pk., Utah **78** C3
Barnhart, Mo. **72** a12
Barnhart, Tex. **77** N4
Barnhill, Ill. **68** D5
Barnoldswick, U.K., 10,267 **113** E5
Barnsboro, N.J., **60** f12
Barnsdall, Okla., 1,663 **76** G1
Barnsley, U.K., 74,650 **113** F5
Barnstable, co., Mass., 70,286 **57** O6
Barnstable, Mass., 13,465(T) **57** P6
Barnstaple, U.K., 15,944 **113** E6
Barnstaple or Bideford Bay, U.K. **113** D6
Barnstead, N.H. **54** E5
Barnum, Minn., 417 **74** F2
Barnum, Wis. **66** C5
Barnwell, co., S.C., 17,659 **63** C4
Barnwell, S.C., 4,568 **63** C4
Baro, Nigeria **162** F4
Baro, r., Eth. **163** K4
Baroda, Guj., India, 295,144 **145** D5
Baroda, M.P., India **144** a13
Baroda, Mich., 488 **67** G7
Barola, i., Sol. Is. **175** b2
Baron, Okla. **76** J2
Baron Bluff, St. Croix **97** 1
Barongbarong, Phil., 2,501 **153** A3
Barons, Alta., Can. **42** K4
Baronville, Fr. **116** c9
Barora Ite, i., Sol. Is. **175** b2
Barotac Viejo, Phil., 2,966 **153** d10
Barotseland, reg., Zambia **164** C4
Barouéli, Mali **162** C3
Baroy, Phil., 2,264 **153** B3
Barqah, prov. Libya, 291,236 **161** H3
Barquisimeto, Ven., 196,557 **100** F2
Barr, Fr., 4,406 **117** G2
Barra, Braz., 7,237 **103** H4
Barra, Phil., 1,794 **153** h15
Barra, i., U.K. **112** C3
Barra, Sd. of, U.K. **112** C3
Barraba, Austl., 1,521 **173** G4
Barrackpore, India, 63,778 **144** g14
Barraco, Sp., 2,452 **122** C2
Barra de Sta. Rosa, Braz., 2,094 **103** a14
Barra de São João, Braz., 1,763 **103** f18
Barra do Bugres, Braz. **103** E4
Barra do Corda, Braz., 3,723 **103** G3
Barra do Garças, Braz., 1,897 **103** F5
Barra do Piraí, Braz., 29,398 **103** e18
Barra Head, U.K. **112** C3
Barra Longa, Braz., 1,488 **103** e17
Barra Mansa, Braz., 47,398 **103** d18
Barranca, Peru **104** B3
Barranca, Peru, 10,912 **104** B4
Barrancabermeja, Col. **100** C4
Barranca Delucos, r., Mex. **93** d11
Barrancas, Chile, 13,787 **104** g13
Barrancas, Col. **100** D2
Barrancas, Ven., 3,119 **100** F3
Barrancas, Ven., 4,034 **101** J3
Barranco de Loba, Col. **100** C3
Barrancos, Port., 3,429 **122** B3
Barranquilla, Col., 452,140 **100** C2
Barranquitas, P.R., 4,684 **96** t10
Barranquitas, Ven. **100** E3
Barras, r., Bol. **102** b11
Barre, Mass., 1,065;3,479(T) **56** H3
Barre, Vt., 10,387 **54** C3
Barreal, Arg., 4,000* **105** A4
Barre Center, N.Y. **58** D5
Barre des Écrins, pk., Fr. **117** G4
Barreiras, Braz., 7,175 **103** G4
Barreirinhas, Braz., 2,184 **103** H2
Barreiro, Ec. **104** c10
Barreiro, Port., 23,433 **122** i10
Barreiros, Braz., 10,402 **103** K3
Barre Mills, Wis. **66** B5
Barren, co., Ky., 28,303 **71** F5
Barren, r., Ky. **71** E5
Barren I., Falk. Is. **108** 3
Barren I., India **146** A4
Barren Is., Alaska **85** G4
Barre Plains (part of Barre), Mass. **56** H3
Barrera, Ven. **101** a11
Barretos, Braz., 39,950 **103** G6
Barrett, Md. **62** a7
Barrett, Minn., 345 **74** E3
Barrett, Tex., 2,364 **77** i9
Barrhead, Alta., Can., 2,227 **42** J2
Barrhead, U.K., 14,422 **112** b8
Barrie, Ont., Can., 20,562 **44** H7
Barrie I., Ont., Can. **46** B3
Barrier, C., N.Z. **175** g5
Barrière, Br. Col., Can. **42** H3
Barrier Reef, Terr. Papua **174** 3
Barrigada, Guam, 1,729 **176** 24
Barrineau Park, Fla. **65** B2
Barrington, N.S., Can. **47** T12
Barrington, Ill., 5,434 **69** b8
Barrington, N.H. **54** E5
Barrington, N.J., 7,943 **60** f12
Barrington, R.I. 13,826 (T) **57** L6
Barrington Center, Ill. **69** b8
Barrington Hills, Ill., 1,726 **69** b8
Barrington L., Man., Can. **43** E2
Bar River, Ont., Can. **46** A2
Barr Lake, Colo. **79** c8
Barro Colorado I., C.Z. **94** f12
Barron, co., Wis., 34,270 **66** B3
Barron, Wis., 2,338 **66** B3
Barronett, Wis. **66** A3
Barroso, Braz., 5,973 **103** d17
Barroterán, Mex., 4,004 **92** E2
Barrouallie, St. Vinc., 2,578 **97** 19
Barrow, Alaska, 1,314 **85** E1
Barrow, co., Ga., 14,485 **64** F2
Barrow, Pt., Alaska **85** ·
Barrow, r., Ire. **113** C5
Barrow Creek, Austl. **172** E3
Barrowford, U.K., 4,766 **114** D3
Barrow-in-Furness, U.K., 64,824 **113** E4
Barrow I., Austl. **172** A3
Barrow Str., N.W.T., Can. **40** K3
Barrow upon Humber, U.K., 2,475 **114** H3
Barry, U.K., 42,084 **113** E6
Barry, Ill., 1,422 **68** A4
Barry, co., Mich., 31,738 **67** H6
Barry, co., Mo., 18,921 **72** D8
Barry, Tex., 178 **76** f10
Barrys Bay, Ont., Can., 1,422 **44** J6
Barryton, Mich., 418 **67** H5
Barrytown, N.Y. **59** N7
Barryville, N.Y. **59** L9
Barsebäckshamn, Swed. **121** b7
Barsi, India, 50,389 **145** E6
Barsinghausen, F.R.Ger., 10,639 **118** B2
Barssel, F.R.Ger., 7,214 **118** A2
Barstow, Calif., 11,644 **82** E5
Barstow, Tex., 707 **77** M4
Bar-sur-Aube, Fr., 4,898 **117** F2
Bar-sur-Seine, Fr., 2,763 **117** F2
Bartang, r., U.S.S.R. **137** f5
Bartelso, Ill., 370 **68** C5
Bartenstein, F.R.Ger., **119** H6
Barth, Ger.D.R., 12,210 **118** D1
Barth, Fla. **65** B2
Barthel, Sask., Can. **43** B4
Bartholomew, co., Ind., 48,198 **70** D3
Bartholomew, Bayou, Ark.-La. **73** D4
Bartica, Guyana **101** L4
Bartın, Turk., 11,655 **142** C1
Bartle, Cuba, 1,052 **96** e2
Bartle, Calif. **82** C2
Bartlesville, Okla., 27,893 **76** H1
Bartlett, Alaska **85** a6
Bartlett, Calif. **82** D4
Bartlett, Colo. **79** D3
Bartlett, Ill., 1,540 **69** b9
Bartlett, Nebr., 125 **75** G2
Bartlett, N.H. **54** E3
Bartlett, Ohio **70** H3
Bartlett, Tenn., 508 **71** B6
Bartlett, Tex., 1,540 **77** P4
Bartlett I., Tutuila **177** 39
Bartlett Pk., Nev. **83** A2
Bartletts Ferry L., Ala.-Ga. **64** D3
Bartley, Nebr., 309 **75** E3
Bartley, Pa., **60** c7
Barto, Pa., **60** e10
Barton, Lancs., Eng., U.K., 1,262 **114** C3
Barton, York., Eng., U.K. **112** g11
Barton, Ala. **64** B1
Barton, co., Kans., 32,368 **75** G5
Barton, Md., 731 **62** E3
Barton, co., Mo., 11,113 **72** C7
Barton, N. Dak., 80 **74** B1
Barton, Vt., 1,169 **54** C2
Barton, Wis., 1,569 **66** E5
Barton, r., Vt. **54** C2
Barton City, Mich. **67** K4
Bartonia, Ind. **70** E2
Barton-le-Clay, U.K., 2,755 **114** G7
Barton on Sea, U.K. **113** i13
Bartonsville, Vt. **54** B5
Barton upon Humber, U.K., 6,582 **113** F5
Bartonville, Ill., 7,253 **68** C3
Bartoszyce, Pol., 11,158 **127** D1
Bartow, Fla., 12,849 **65** H5
Bartow, co., Ga., 28,267 **64** E1
Bartow, Ga., 366 **64** G3
Barú, P., Col. **100** C2
Baruduksum, China **144** e11
Barueri, Braz., 13,821 **103** c18
Barugo, Phil., 4,081 **153** f10
Barumun, r., Indon. **147** o15
Barung, Nusa, Indon. **148** E5
Barus, Indon. **148** A2
Baruta, Ven., 41,949 **101** c11
Baruth, Ger.D.R. **118** D2
Baruun Urta, Mong. **150** F2
Barva, Swed. **120** d8
Barvas, U.K. **112** C2
Barvaux, Belg., 1,529 **115** D4
Barvenkovo, U.S.S.R., 13,400 **136** e7
Barwaha, India, 11,188 **145** E5
Barwani, India, 17,446 **145** E5
Barwell (part of Hinckley), U.K., 5,446 **114** F5
Barwice, Pol. **127** B2
Barwick, Ont., Can., **44** C5
Barwick, Ga., 400 **64** F5
Barwick in Elmet, U.K., 2,908 **114** F3
Barwon, r., Austl. **173** G4
Barycz, r., Pol. **127** B3
Bāsa'īdū, Iran **143** E3
Basalt, Colo., 213 **79** B2
Basalt, Idaho, 275 **81** C4
Basalt, Nev. **83** A3
Basankusu, D.R.Congo **164** C1
Basarabi, Rum. **128** G2
Basauri, Sp., 23,030 **122** m11
Basavilbaso, Arg., 12,000* **105** b11
Basay, Phil., 4,946 **153** d12
Basbeck, F.R.Ger., 2,592 **118** B2
Bascharage, Lux., 1,346 **115** E5
Baschurch, U.K., 1,508 **114** C5
Basco, Phil., **153** g13
Basco, Ill., 191 **68** A3
Basconcillos del Tozo, Sp., 1,258 **122** D1
Basconcobe, Mex., 1,151 **92** C2
Basedow, Ger.D.R. **118** D2
Basel, Switz., 206,746 **124** B1
Basento, r., It. **123** F4
Basey, Phil., 6,240 **153** C3
Basharrī, Leb., 6,192 **142** b5
Bashaw, Alta., Can. **42** K3
Bashi Chan., Phil.-Taiwan **150** G5
Bashkaus, r., U.S.S.R. **137** s12
Bashmakovo, U.S.S.R. **136** F2
Basi, India, 13,042 **144** a10
Basiao, Phil., 2,200 **153** f11
Basilaki, i., Terr. Papua **174** f3
Basilan I., Phil. **153** B4
Basilan Str., Phil. **153** B4
Basildon, U.K., 88,524 **113** G6
Basile, La., 1,932 **73** C7
Basile, Morne, Haiti **96** k6
Basim, India **145** E5
Basin, Mont. **81** C2
Basin, Wyo., 1,319 **81** E3
Basing, U.K., 2,964 **114** F8
Basinger, Fla. **65** J5
Basingstoke, U.K., 25,980 **113** F6
Baskahegan L., Me. **55** E3
Başkale, Turk., 2,463 **142** E2
Baskatong, Rés., Qué., Can. **44** J6
Baskerville, C., Austl. **172** B2
Baskin, La., 238 **73** D5
Basking Ridge, N.J., 2,438 **58** a14
Baslow, U.K. **114** E4
Basoda, India, 14,152 **145** E5
Basoko, D.R.Congo **164** C1
Basora, P., Aruba **97** 15
Basra = Al Başrah
Bass, Ind. **70** C1
Bass, Îlots de, Fr. Poly. **171** J6
Bassac, r., Camb. **147** k11
Bassano, Alta., Can. **42** K4
Bassano del Grappa, It., 29,721 **123** C2
Bassari, Togo, 10,012 **164** E4
Bassecourt, Switz., 2,284 **124** B1
Bassein, Burma, 77,905 **146** A3
Bassein, India, 22,598 **145** h17
Bassein, r., Burma **146** A3
Basse-Pointe, Mart., 1,010 **97** 12
Basses, Pte. des, Guad. **97** 14
Basse-Terre, Guad., 8,717 **97** 14
Basseterre, St. Christopher, 15,742 **97** 6
Basse-Terre, i., Guad. **97** 14
Bassett, Iowa, 130 **72** E1
Bassett, Kans., 67 **75** K6
Bassett, Nebr., 1,023 **75** F1
Bassett, Va., 3,148 **62** D6
Bassett, Wis. **66** c13
Basse-Yutz, Fr., 10,565 **116** b8
Bassfield, Miss., 295 **73** F6
Bassila, Dahom. **162** d7
Bassingham, U.K. **114** G4
Bass Is., Ohio **46** B7
Bass Lake, Calif. **82** D4
Bass L., Minn. **74** b5
Bass Lakes, Wis. **66** E3
Bass River, N.S., Can. **47** T11
Bass River (part of Yarmouth), Mass. **57** Q6
Bass Str., Austl. **173** F6
Bassum, F.R.Ger., 7,100 **118** B2
Basswood I., Wis. **66** C2
Basswood L., Can.-U.S. **74** F1
Båstad, Swed. **120** C4
Bastelica, Fr., 2,188 **116** r18
Basti, India **144** d12
Bastia, Fr., 50,881 **116** r17
Bastian, Va. **62** C5
Bastogne, Belg., 5,927 **115** D4
Bastrop, La., 15,193 **73** D5
Bastrop, co., Tex., 16,925 **77** P4
Bastrop, Tex., 3,001 **77** P4
Bastuträsk, Swed. **120** D2
Basutoland = Lesotho
Bata, Rio Muni, 3,548 **164** A1
Bataan, Mt., Phil. **153** b8
Bataan Pen., Phil. **153** B2
Batabanó, Golfo de, Cuba **96** b1
Batagay, U.S.S.R. **135** N3
Batagay-Alyta, U.S.S.R. **135** N3
Batagnaçu, Braz. **103** F6
Batak, Bulg., 10,372 **128** E4
Batakan, Indon. **148** E4
Batala, India, 51,300 **145** E3
Batalha, Port., 7,053 **122** A3
Bataly, r., Dominica **97** 13
Batam, Pulau, Indon. **147** p16
Batamay, U.S.S.R. **135** N3
Batamshinskiy, U.S.S.R. **137** i10
Batang, Indon. **148** c7
Batangafo, C.A.R., 8,468 **163** H4
Batangas, Phil., 14,182 **153** B2
Batangas Bay, Phil. **153** b9
Batangtoru, Indon. **148** A2
Batan I., Phil. **153** g13
Batan I., Phil. **153** i14
Batan Is., Phil. **153** g13
Batanta, P., Indon. **149** J3
Bátaszék, Hung., 7,378 **126** D3
Batatais, Braz., 15,266 **103** G6
Batavia, Indon. = Djakarta
Batavia, Ill., 7,496 **68** D2
Batavia, Iowa, 533 **72** E3
Batavia, Mich. **67** H7
Batavia, N.Y., 18,210 **58** D5
Batavia, Ohio, 1,729 **70** E3
Batavia, Wis. **66** F5
Batawa, Ont., Can. **46** G4
Bataysk, U.S.S.R., 70,000 **136** E4
Batcab, Guat. **94** B2
Bat Cave, N.C. **63** B2
Batchawana, r., Ont., Can. **67** J1
Batchawana I., Ont., Can. **67** J2
Batchawana Mtn., Ont., Can. **44** F6
Batchtown, Ill., 248 **68** B4
Batemans Bay, Austl. **173** h10
Bates, Ark., 106 **73** A3
Bates, co., Mo., 15,905 **72** C6
Bates, Oreg. **80** D3
Bates, Mt., Norfolk I. **175** 11
Batesburg, S.C., 3,806 **63** C4
Batesland, S. Dak. **74** B4
Batesville, Ark., 6,207 **73** D2
Batesville, Ind., 3,349 **70** D3
Batesville, Miss., 3,284 **73** F3
Batesville, Ohio, 160 **70** H3
Batesville, Tex. **77** O5
Batesville, Va. **62** F5
Bath, Barb. **97** 10
Bath, N.B., Can. **45** M6
Bath, Ont., Can. **46** H4
Bath, Jam., 1,803 **96** q9
Bath, U.K., 80,901 **113** E6
Bath, Ill., 398 **68** B3
Bath, co., Ky., 9,114 **71** H3
Bath, Me., 10,717 **55** C5
Bath, Mich. **67** J6
Bath, N.H. **54** D3
Bath, N.Y., 6,166 **58** F7
Bath, N.C., 346 **63** H2
Bath, Pa., 1,736 **61** M4
Bath, S.C., 1,419 **63** C4
Bath, co., Va., 5,335 **62** E4
Batha, r., Chad **163** H3
Batheay, Camb. **146** D4
Bathgate, U.K., 12,686 **112** E4
Bathgate, N. Dak., 175 **74** D1
Bathurst, Austl., 16,089 **173** G5
Bathurst, N.B., Can., 5,333 **45** N6
Bathurst, Gambia, 28,000* **162** B3
Bathurst, C., N.W.T., Can. **40** D3
Bathurst Inlet, N.W.T., Can. **40** H4
Bathurst Inlet, N.W.T., Can. **40** H4
Bathurst I., Austl. **172** D1
Bathurst I., N.W.T., Can. **41** J2
Batié, Upper Volta **162** D4
Bāṭin, Wādī al, Saudi Ar. **143** D3
Batiscan, Qué., Can. **47** M2
Batiscan, r., Qué., Can. **47** M1
Batjan, P., Indon. **149** H3
Batley, U.K., 39,390 **114** E3
Batlow, Austl., 1,114 **173** f10
Batman, Turk., 12,641 **142** E2
Batna, Alg., 18,114 **160** F1
Batō, Jap., 22,072 **155** G3
Bato, Phil., 3,918 **153** f11
Bato, Phil., 3,107 **153** i14
Ba To, S.Viet. **146** E4
Batobato, Phil., 3,170 **153** C4
Baton Rouge, La., 152,419 **73** D7
Batopilas, Mex. **92** D2
Batoş, Rum. **128** E1
Batouri, Cam. **162** G5
Batovo, Bulg. **128** F3
Baṭrā, ruins, Jor. **142** C4
Ba Tri, S. Viet., 3,271 **147** m11
Bat Rokar, Camb. **147** k11
Batson, Tex. **77** k8
Batsto, N.J., 60* **61** B4
Batsto, r., N.J. **61** B4
Battaglia Terme, It., 4,078 **122** e5
Battambang, Camb., 38,846 **146** C4
Batteau, Newf., Can. **45** Q4
Batten Kill, r., N.Y.-Vt. **59** O5
Batticaloa, Cey., 17,439 **145** F9
Battipaglia, It., 24,876 **123** E4
Battle, Brec., Eng., U.K. **114** B7
Battle, Sussex, Eng., U.K., 4,517 **113** G6
Battle, r., Alta.-Sask., Can. **40** G7
Battle Ax Mtn., Oreg. **80** B3
Battleboro, N.C., 364 **63** G1
Battle Creek, Iowa, 786 **72** B2
Battle Creek, Mich., 44,169 **67** H6
Battle Creek, Nebr., 587 **75** H2
Battlefields Mem. Nat. Mil. Pk., Va. **62** G4
Battleford, Sask., Can., 1,576 **43** B4
Battle Ground, Ind., 804 **70** C2
Battle Ground, Wash., 888 **80** B3
Battle Lake, Minn., 733 **74** E2
Battle Harbour, Newf., Can. **45** Q4
Battlement Mesa, Colo. **79** B1
Battle Mountain, Nev. **83** B2
Battleview, N. Dak. **74** A1
Battonya, Hung., 11,740 **126** E3
Battowia I., Gren. Is. **97** 20
Batu, Kep., Indon. **148** A3
Batu, pk., Eth. **163** L4
Batuan, Phil., 2,428 **153** h15
Batu Anam, Malay., 1,686 **147** p15
Batu Arang, Malay., 5,391 **147** o15
Batuc, Mex., 1,267 **92** C2
Batuco, Chile **104** e15
Batuco, Chile, 1,125 **104** g13
Batu Dua Puloh, Malay. **147** o15
Batu Gajah, Malay., 10,145 **147** o14
Batui, Indon. **149** G3
Batukelau, Indon. **148** E2
Batu Kurau, Malay., 1,258 **147** o14
Batumi, U.S.S.R., 87,000 **134** D5
Batumundam, Indon. **148** A2
Batu Pahat, Malay., 40,016 **148** B2
Batupandjang, Indon. **147** o16
Batuputih, Indon. **148** F2
Baturadja, Indon. **148** C4
Baturetno, Indon. **148** d7
Baturino, U.S.S.R. **134** H4
Baturité, Braz., 7,198 **103** J2
Batu Tiga Puloh, Malay. **147** p14
Bat Yam, Isr., 31,694 **142** a7
Bau, Malay., 1,203 **148** D2
Bauan, Phil., 2,737 **153** c9
Bauang, Phil., 3,956 **153** b6
Baubau, Indon. **149** G4
Bauchi, Nigeria, 15,725 **162** F4
Bauchi Plat. = Jos Plat.
Baudette, Minn., 1,597 **74** E1
Baudh, India, 6,088 **145** G5
Baudó, Col. **100** B5
Baudouinville, D.R.Congo **164** D3
Bauer, Mich. **67** H6
Bauer, Utah **78** b10
Baugé, Fr., 3,977 **117** C3
Baugy, Fr., 1,103 **117** E3
Baula, Indon. **149** G4
Bauline, Newf., Can. **45** c10
Baumholder, F.R.Ger., 4,496 **118** A4
Baumstown, Pa., **60** e10
Baun, Indon. **149** G5
Baures, Bol. **102** D4
Bauru, Braz., 85,237 **103** G6
Baús, Braz. **103** F5
Bausendorf, F.R.Ger., **119** B4
Bauska, U.S.S.R., 6,300 **136** A1
Bauta, Cuba, 11,518 **96** b1
Bautzen, Ger.D.R., 41,613 **118** E3
Bauxite, Ark. **73** C3
Bavanište, Yug., 6,053 **125** E2
Bavaria = Bayern
Bavaria, Kans. **75** H5
Bavarian Alps = Bayerische Alpen
Bavay, Fr., 3,355 **117** E1
Båven, l., Swed. **120** e8
Baviácora, Mex., 1,317 **92** C2
Bavispe, R. de, Mex. **92** C1
Bawal, P., Indon. **148** D3
Bawdwin, Burma **146** B2
Bawe, Indon. **149** K3
Bawean, P., Indon. **148** E4
Bawku, Ghana, 12,615 **162** D4
Bawlake, Burma **146** B3
Bawlf, Alta., Can. **43** c8
Bawtry, U.K., 1,346 **114** G4
Ba Xat, N.Viet. **146** C2
Baxley, Ga., 4,268 **64** G4
Baxter, co., Ark., 9,943 **73** C1
Baxter, Fla. **65** G2
Baxter, Iowa, 681 **72** D3
Baxter, Minn., 1,037 **74** E2
Baxter, Tenn., 853 **71** F5
Baxter, W.Va. **62** D3
Baxter Pk., Colo. **79** B2
Baxter Springs, Kans., 4,498 **75** L6
Baxterville, Colo. **79** B3
Baxterville, Miss. **73** F6
Baxthé, Mex. **93** e9
Bay, Ark., 627 **73** E2
Bay, co., Fla., 67,131 **65** D2
Bay, co., Mich., 107,042 **67** J5
Bay, Lag. de, Phil. **153** c8
Bayaguana, Dom. Rep., 1,848 **96** n6
Bayambang, Phil., 6,371 **153** b7
Bayamesa, Pico de la, Cuba **96** e3
Bayamo, Cuba, 20,178 **96** e2
Bayamón, P.R., 15,109 **96** t10
Bayamón, R. de, P.R. **96** t10
Bayan-Aul, U.S.S.R. **137** o12
Bayanga, C.A.R. **162** G5
Bayan Hongor, Mong. **150** D2
Bayano, r., Pan. **94** H6
Bayard, Iowa, 597 **72** C3
Bayard, Nebr., 1,519 **75** B2
Bayard, N. Mex., 2,327 **79** A5
Bayard, W.Va., 484 **62** E3
Bayawan, Phil., 6,204 **153** B3
Baybay, Phil., 10,021 **153** C3
Bayboro, N.C., 545 **63** H2
Bay Bulls, Newf., Can. **45** c10
Bayburt, Turk., 11,968 **142** E1
Bay Center, Wash. **80** A2
Baychunas, U.S.S.R., 2,400 **134** E5
Bay City, Ill. **68** D6
Bay City, Mich., 53,604 **67** K5
Bay City, Oreg., 996 **80** B3
Bay City, Tex., 11,656 **77** Q5
Bay City, Wash. **80** B2
Bay City, Wis., 327 **66** A4
Baydarag Gol, Mong. **150** D2
Baydaratskaya G., U.S.S.R. **134** F3
Bay de Verde, Newf., Can. **45** R5
Baydzhansay, U.S.S.R. **137** f3
Baye, C., N. Caled. **174** i8
Bayenga, D.R.Congo, 5,250* **164** D1
Bayerische Alpen, Aust.-F.R.Ger. **118** C5
Bayerische Alpen, Aust.-F.R.Ger. **124** H6
Bayerischer Wald, F.R.Ger. **118** D4
Bayern, st., F.R.Ger., 9,976,000* **118** C4
Bayeux, Fr., 10,641 **117** C2
Bayfield, Ont., Can. **46** C5
Bayfield, Colo., 322 **79** B3
Bayfield, co., Wis., 11,910 **66** B2
Bayfield, Wis., 969 **66** C2
Bayfield Sd., Ont., Can. **46** B3
Bay Fiord, N.W.T., Can. **41** N2
Bayḥān, Yemen **143** D6
Bay Head, N.J., 824 **61** C3
Bayındır, Turk., 11,343 **142** A2
Bāyir, Jor. **142** D4
Baykadam, U.S.S.R. **137** f3
Baykal, Oz., U.S.S.R. **135** K4
Baykal'skoye, U.S.S.R. **135** K4
Baykit, U.S.S.R. **135** J3
Baykonur, U.S.S.R. **134** F5
Baylis, Ill., 284 **68** B4
Baylor, co., Tex., 5,893 **77** O3
Baymak, U.S.S.R., 11,500 **137** i9
Bay Mills Park, Mich. **67** J2
Bay Minette, Ala., 5,197 **64** B5
Baynesville, Va. **62** G4
Bay of Islands, Newf., Can. **45** P5
Bay of Islands, N.Z. **175** g4
Bay of Pigs = Cochinos, B. de
Bayombong, Phil., 8,312 **153** B1
Bayon, Fr., 1,343 **117** G2
Bayonne, Fr., 41,149 **117** C5
Bayonne, N.J., 74,215 **61** C2
Bayou La Batre, Ala., 2,572 **64** A5
Bayou Meto, Ark. **73** D3
Bayovar, Peru **104** A3
Bay Park, Mich. **67** K5
Bayport, Fla. **65** G4
Bay Port, Mich. **67** K5
Bayport, Minn., 3,205 **74** d5
Bayport, N.Y. **58** g14

Bayrakkum—Belton Res. · 199

Bayrakkum, U.S.S.R. 137 e3
Bayram Ali, U.S.S.R., 27,300 134 F6
Bayreuth, F.R.Ger., 59,544 118 C4
Bay Ridge, Md. 62 d9
Bay Roberts, Newf., Can., 1,301 45 R6
Bayrût, Leb., 220,849 142 C3
Bay St. Louis, Miss., 5,073 73 F7
Bayshore, Calif. 83 e12
Bayshore, Fla. 65 H6
Bayshore, Mich. 67 H3
Bay Shore, N.Y. 59 O10
Bayside, Calif. 82 A2
Bayside, Me. 55 C4
Bayside, Wis., 3,181 66 d11
Bayside Beach, Md. 62 d8
Bay Springs, Miss., 1,544 73 F6
Baystonhill, U.K., 1,007 114 C5
Baysun, U.S.S.R. 137 e5
Bay-Syut, U.S.S.R. 135 J4
Bayt ad Dīn, Leb. 142 b6
Bayt al Faqīh, Yemen, 30,000* 143 C6
Bayt Jālā, Jor., 7,304 142 b8
Bayt Laḥm, Jor., 21,668 142 b8
Baytown, Tex., 28,159 77 Q5
Bayt Shabāb, Leb., 4,301 142 b6
Bayugan, Phil., 7,522 153 C3
Bay View, Ala., 1,081 64 c7
Bayview (part of Dartmouth), Mass. 57 N6
Bay View, Mich. 67 J3
Bay View, Ohio, 802 70 G1
Bay View Park, Calif. 83 f14
Bay Village, Ohio, 14,489 70 d9
Bayville, N.Y., 3,962 58 e13
Baywood, Va. 62 D6
Baza, Sp., 20,440 122 D4
Bazaar, Kans. 75 J5
Bazar-Dyuzi, G., U.S.S.R. 137 d1
Bazaruto, I. do, Moz. 164 E5
Bazas, Fr., 5,107 117 C4
Bazel, Belg., 4,160 115 d8
Bazemont, Fr. 116 f11
Bazhenovo, U.S.S.R. 137 k8
Baziaş, Rum. 128 C2
Bazile Mills, Nebr., 45 75 H1
Bazine, Kans., 429 75 F5
Bazna, Rum. 128 E1
Be, r., S. Viet. 146 D5
Beach, Ga., 53 64 G4
Beach, N. Dak., 1,460 74 A2
Beachburg, Ont., Can. 46 G3
Beach City, Ohio, 1,151 70 H2
Beach Corners, Wis. 66 B4
Beach Haven, N.J., 1,041 61 C4
Beach Haven Inlet, N.J. 61 C4
Beach Lake, Pa. 61 M2
Beach Pd., Conn.-R.I. 57 J6
Beachport, Austl. 172 E5
Beach Ridge, N.Y. 58 k18
Beachton, Okla. 76 J3
Beachwood, N.J., 2,765 61 C4
Beachwood, Ohio, 6,089 70 f8
Beachy Head, U.K. 113 G6
Beacon, Austl. 172 B4
Beacon, Iowa, 718 72 E3
Beacon, N.Y., 13,922 59 N9
Beacon Falls, Conn., 2,886(T) 56 D7
Beacon Hill, Fla. 65 D3
Beacon Hill, U.K. 114 B6
Beaconia, Man., Can. 43 h9
Beaconsfield, Austl., 2,629 173 f13
Beaconsfield, Qué., Can., 9,969 47 o18
Beaconsfield, U.K., 10,013 114 G7
Beadle, co., S. Dak., 21,682 74 C3
Beal, U.K. 114 F3
Beal, Ind. 70 B4
Beal City, Mich. 67 J5
Bealeton, Va. 62 G4
Beallsville, Ohio, 441 70 J3
Beallsville, Pa., 481 60 b9
Beals, Me. 55 E4
Beaman, Iowa, 247 72 E2
Beaminster, U.K., 2,000 113 E6
Beamsville, Ont., Can., 2,501 46 E5
Bean City, Fla. 65 J6
Bear, Mt., Alaska 85 J3
Bear, r., U.S. 52 D2
Bear, r., Me. 54 F2
Beara, Terr. Papua 174 e2
Bearcamp, r., N.H. 54 E4
Bear Cove Pt., Newf., Can. 45 c11
Bear Creek, Yukon, Can. 40 B5
Bearcreek, Mont., 61 81 E3
Bear Creek, Pa., 61 L3
Bear Creek, Wis., 455 66 E4
Bear Cr., Ont., Can. 46 B6
Bear Cr., Calif. 83 i15
Bear Cr., Colo. 79 b8
Bear Cr., Ill. 68 A3
Bear Cr., Pa., 61 o17
Bearden, Ark., 1,268 73 C4
Bearden, Tenn. 71 H6
Beardmore, Ont., Can., 1,043 44 E5
Beardmore Glacier, Ant. 180 V4
Beardsley, Kans. 75 D4
Beardsley, Minn., 410 74 D3
Beardstown, Ill., 6,294 68 B3
Beardstown, Ind. 70 C1
Bear Ears, pk., Utah 78 C3
Bear Flat, Br. Col., Can. 42 G2
Bearfort Mtn., N.J. 61 C1
Beargrass, N.C., 103 63 G2
Bear Hill, Nebr. 75 D2
Bear I., N.W.T., Can. 44 G3
Bear I., Ire. 113 B6
Bear I., N.H. 54 E4
Bear I., Wis. 66 C1
Bear Is. = Medvezh'i, O-va.
Bear Lake, Br. Col., Can. 42 E2
Bear Lake, co., Idaho, 7,148 81 D4
Bear Lake, Mich., 323 67 G4
Bear Lake, Pa., 260 60 C2
Bear L., Man., Can. 43 F3
Bear Lake, Pa., 61 o17
Bear L., Idaho-Utah 81 D5
Bear L., Wis. 66 B3
Bear Mtn., Conn. 56 C4
Bear Mtn., Me. 55 B4
Bear Mtn., S. Dak. 74 A4
Bearpark, U.K., 2,356 112 g10
Bear River, N.S., Can. 47 T11
Bear River, Utah, 447 78 b7
Bear River Bay, Utah 78 b8
Bearsden, U.K., 17,022 112 b8
Bears Ears Pks., Colo. 79 B1
Bear Valley, Calif. 82 C4
Beasain, Sp., 7,610 122 n11
Beas de Segura, Sp., 14,957 122 D3
Beata, C., Dom. Rep. 96 m7
Beata, Can. de la, Dom. Rep. 96 m7
Beata, I., Dom. Rep. 96 m7
Beaton, Br. Col., Can. 42 H4
Beatrice, Ala., 506 64 B4
Beatrice, Nebr., 12,132 75 J3
Beatrice, C., Austl. 172 E2
Beatton, r., Br. Col., Can. 42 G1
Beatton River, Br. Col., Can. 42 G1
Beatty, Nev. 83 B4
Beatty, Oreg. 80 C4
Beattyville, Ky., 1,048 71 H4
Beauchamp, Fr., 5,662 116 g10
Beaucaire, Fr., 11,211 117 F5
Beauceville, Qué., Can., 1,611 47 O2
Beauceville-Est, Qué., Can., 1,900 47 O2
Beauchêne, L., Qué., Can. 46 F2
Beaucoup Cr., Ill. 68 C5
Beaudesert, Austl., 2,388 173 H4
Beaudette, r., Ont., Can. 47 K3
Beaufort, Austl., 1,281 173 F5
Beaufort, Malay. 148 F1
Beaufort, co., N.C., 36,014 63 H2
Beaufort, N.C., 2,922 63 H3
Beaufort, co., S.C., 44,187 63 D5
Beaufort, S.C., 6,298 63 D5
Beaufort Basin, Arctic Oc. 108 B2
Beaufort Sea, Arctic Oc. 34 C2
Beaufort West, S. Af., 16,323 164 C7
Beaugency, Fr., 4,693 117 D3
Beauharnois, Qué., Can., 8,601 47 o18
Beauharnois Can., Qué., Can. 69 D
Beauharnois Locks, Qué., Can. 69 D
Beaujeu, Fr., 2,185 117 F3
Beau L., Can.-U.S. 55 C1
Beaulieu, Fr., 3,290 116 n13
Beaulieu, U.K., 1,165 113 i13
Beauly, U.K. 112 D3
Beauly, r., U.K. 112 D3
Beaumaris, U.K., 1,962 113 D5
Beaumont, Belg., 1,744 115 C4
Beaumont, Alta., Can. 43 b7
Beaumont, Calif., 4,288 82 E6
Beaumont, Miss., 926 73 G6
Beaumont, Pa., 61 L3
Beaumont, Tex., 119,175 77 Q4
Beaumont, Wis. 66 c13
Beaumont-de-Lomagne, Fr., 4,003 117 D5
Beaumont Place, Tex., 1,176 77 i9
Beaumont Pt., St. Lucia 97 11
Beaumont-sur-Sarthe, Fr., 1,966 117 D2
Beaune, Fr., 15,882 117 F3
Beaune-la-Rolande, Fr., 1,758 117 E2
Beauport, Qué., Can., 9,125 47 n16
Beaupré, Qué., Can., 2,557 47 N1
Beaupréau, Fr., 4,870 117 C3
Beauraing, Belg., 2,343 115 D4
Beauregard, parish, La., 19,191 73 B7
Beaurepaire, Fr., 3,294 116 p16
Beaurivage, r., Qué., Can. 55 A2
Beausejour, Man., Can., 1,762 43 F5
Beausoleil, Fr., 12,833 117 G5
Beautemps-Beaupre, I., Loy. Is. 174 i8
Beauvais, Fr., 36,533 117 E2
Beauval, Sask., Can. 43 C3
Beauvallon, Fr. 116 m14
Beauvoir, Fr. 116 k12
Beauvois-en-Cambrésis, Fr., 2,454 116 a7
Beaux Arts, Wash., 351 81 b7
Beaver, Man., Can. 43 f9
Beaver, Alaska, 101 85 G2
Beaver, Iowa, 115 72 C3
Beaver, Ohio, 341 70 G3
Beaver, co., Okla., 6,965 76 C1
Beaver, Okla., 2,087 76 C1
Beaver, Oreg. 80 B3
Beaver, co., Pa., 206,948 60 B4
Beaver, Pa., 6,160 60 B4
Beaver, co., Utah, 4,331 78 B2
Beaver, Utah, 1,548 78 B2
Beaver, Wash. 80 A1
Beaver, Wis. 66 E3
Beaver, r., Alta.-Sask., Can. 40 H7
Beaver, r., Br. Col.-Yukon, Can. 42 F1
Beaver, r., Newf., Can. 45 04
Beaver, r., Ont., Can. 44 E3
Beaver, r., Qué., Can. 44 H4
Beaver, r., N.Y. 59 K4
Beaver, r., Okla. 76 A1
Beaver, r., Pa. 60 B4
Beaver Bank, N.S., Can. 47 U11
Beaver Bay, Minn., 287 74 G2
Beaver Bk., Me. 55 D2
Beaver Bk., Mass. 57 N4
Beaver Bk., Mass.-N.H. 57 L1
Beaver City, Ind. 70 B2
Beaver City, Nebr., 818 75 F3
Beaver Creek, Br. Col., Can. 42 b6
Beaver Creek, Yukon, Can. 40 A5
Beavercreek, Ill. 68 C5
Beaver Cr., Alaska 85 H2
Beaver Cr., Kans. 75 D5
Beaver Cr., Kans.-Nebr. 75 D4
Beaver Cr., Mo. 72 E8
Beaver Cr., Mont. 81 E2
Beaver Cr., Mont.-N. Dak. 74 A2
Beaver Cr., N.Y. 58 o21
Beaver Cr., N. Dak. 74 B2
Beaver Cr., Okla. 76 E3
Beaver Dam, Ariz. 78 B3
Beaver Dam, Ind. 70 C1
Beaver Dam, Ky., 1,648 71 E4
Beaverdam, Ohio, 514 70 F2
Beaverdam, Va. 62 G5
Beaver Dam, Wis., 13,118 66 E5
Beaver Dam L., Wis. 66 A3
Beaver Dam L., Wis. 66 D5
Beaver Dams, N.Y. 58 F7
Beaver Falls, N.Y. 59 K4
Beaver Falls, Pa., 16,240 60 B4
Beaverhead, co., Mont., 7,194 81 C3
Beaverhead, N. Mex. 79 A5
Beaverhead, r., Mont. 81 C3
Beaverhill Cr., Alta., Can. 43 c7
Beaverhill L., Alta., Can. 43 c7
Beaver Hill L., Man., Can. 43 G3
Beaver I., Falk. Is. 108 3
Beaver I., Mich. 67 H3
Beaver Kill, r., N.Y. 61 N2
Beaver Lake, N.J. 58 a12
Beaver L., Minn. 74 c6
Beaverlick, Ky. 71 G3
Beaverlodge, Alta., Can. 42 H2
Beaver Meadows, Pa., 1,392 61 L4
Beaver Mts., Alaska 85 E3
Beaver Res., Ark. 73 B1
Beaver River Flow, N.Y. 59 K4
Beaver Run Reservoir, Pa. 60 C5
Beaver Springs, Pa. 60 H4
Beaverton, Ont., Can., 1,174 46 E4
Beaverton, Ala., 162 64 A2
Beaverton, Mich., 926 67 J5
Beaverton, Oreg., 5,937 80 B3
Beavertown, Pa., 738 60 H4
Beaverville, Ill., 430 68 E3
Beawar, India, 53,931 145 E4
Bebe, Tex. 77 P5
Bébédjia, Chad 162 G4
Bebedouro, Braz., 18,249 103 G6
Bebee, Okla. 76 G3
Bebington, U.K., 52,202 114 B4
Bebra, F.R.Ger., 7,473 118 B3
Becal, Mex., 4,036 93 H4
Bécancour, r., Qué., Can. 47 M2
Bécard, L., Qué., Can. 44 K1
Beccles, U.K., 7,332 113 G5
Bečej, Yug., 25,000* 125 E2
Beceni, Rum. 128 F2
Becerreá, Sp., 7,753 122 B1
Becerril, Col. 100 D3
Béchar, Alg., 16,650 160 D2
Becharof L., Alaska 85 E4
Bechem, Ghana 162 b8
Bechet, Rum. 128 D3
Bechtelsville, Pa., 625 61 L5
Bechuanaland = Botswana
Bechyně, Czech. 126 B2
Beckemeyer, Ill., 1,056 68 C5
Beckenham, London, U.K. 114 H8
Beckenried, Switz., 2,042 124 C2
Becker, co., Minn., 23,959 74 E2
Becker, Miss. 73 G4
Beckersville, Pa., 61 h14
Becket, Mass. 56 D3
Becket Center (part of Becket), Mass. 56 D3
Beckett, Okla. 76 E3
Beckham, co., Okla., 17,782 76 D2
Becking, r., Indon. 149 L4
Beckingham, U.K. 114 G4
Beckington, U.K. 114 D8
Beckley, W. Va., 18,642 62 C5
Beckum, F.R.Ger., 19,119 118 B3
Beckville, Tex., 632 77 Q3
Beckwith Cr., La. 73 B7
Beclean, Rum. 128 E1
Bečov nad Teplou, Czech. 126 b6
Bečva, r., Czech. 126 C2
Bečváry, Czech. 127 e7
Beda, Libya 161 H3
Bedale, U.K., 1,481 113 F4
Bédarieux, Fr., 7,800 117 E5
Bedburg, F.R.Ger., 8,923 118 A3
Bederkesa, F.R.Ger., 3,104 118 B2
Bedford, N.S., Can., 2,021 47 U11
Bedford, Qué., Can., 2,840 44 K6
Bedford, U.K., 63,334 113 F5
Bedford, Ind., 13,024 70 C4
Bedford, Iowa, 1,807 72 C4
Bedford, Ky., 717 71 F3
Bedford, Mass., 10,969(T) 57 L3
Bedford, Mich. 67 H6
Bedford, N.H. 54 D6
Bedford, Ohio, 15,223 70 e9
Bedford, co., Pa., 42,451 60 F6
Bedford, Pa., 3,696 60 F5
Bedford, co., Tenn., 23,150 71 E6
Bedford, Tex., 2,706 76 e9
Bedford, co., Va., 31,028 62 E5
Bedford, Va., 5,921 62 E5
Bedford Heights, Ohio, 5,275 70 f9
Bedford Park, Ill., 737 69 c9
Bedfordshire, co., U.K., 380,837 113 F5
Bedford Village, N.Y. 59 N9
Bedgerebong, Austl. 173 f9
Bedias, Tex. 77 Q4
Bedivere L., Ont., Can. 74 G1
Bedlington, U.K., 29,373 113 F4
Bedminster, N.J. 61 B2
Bednesti, Br. Col., Can. 42 F3
Bednja, Yug. 125 C1
Bednja, r., Yug. 125 C1
Bednodem'yanovsk, U.S.S.R., 7,000 136 F2
Bedong, Malay., 3,956 147 o14
Bedretto, Switz. 124 C2
Bedrock, Colo. 79 A2
Bedsted, Den. 121 A4
Bedum, Neth., 4,100 115 E1
Bedwas, U.K., 3,206 114 B7
Bedwellty, U.K., 27,308 114 B7
Bedworth, U.K., 32,501 114 E6
Będzin, Pol., 39,727 127 i6
Bee, co., Tex., 23,755 77 P5
Beebe, Ark., 1,697 73 D2
Beebe Plain, Qué., Can., 1,347 47 M3
Beebe Plain, Vt. 54 C2
Beebe River, N.H. 54 D4
Beebetown, Ohio 70 d9
Bee Branch, Ark., 63 73 C2
Bee Cave, Tex. 76 b5
Beech, r., N.H. 54 E4
Beechbottom, W. Va., 506 62 D2
Beech Creek, Ky. 71 D4
Beech Creek, Pa., 634 60 G3
Beech Cr., Pa. 60 G3
Beecher, Ill., 1,367 68 E2
Beecher City, Ill., 452 68 D4
Beecher Falls, Vt. 54 D1
Beecher Island, Colo. 79 D2
Beech Fork Chaplin, r., Ky. 71 F4
Beech Grove, Ind., 10,973 70 C3
Beech Grove, Ky., 159 71 D4
Beech Grove, Tenn. 71 E6
Beech Hill Pd., Me. 55 D4
Beech Island, S.C. 63 C4
Beechwood (part of Cohasset), Mass. 57 N4
Beechwood, Iron Co., Mich. 66 E2
Beechwood, Ottawa Co., Mich., 2,323 67 G5
Beechwood, Wis. 66 E5
Beechworth, Austl., 3,155 173 f11
Beechy, Sask., Can. 43 C5
Beecreek, Ill. 68 B4
Beef I., V.I. 97 4
Beeford, U.K. 114 H3
Beek, Neth., 3,300 115 D3
Beek, Neth., 5,000 115 D4
Beekbergen, Neth. 115 D2
Beekmann, Tex. 76 a6
Beekmantown, N.Y. 59 N2
Beeler, Kans. 75 E5
Beelitz, Ger.D.R. 118 D2
Beemer, Nebr., 667 75 J2
Beerfelden, F.R.Ger., 3,081 119 F5
Bee Ridge, Fla., 2,043 65 G5
Beernem, Belg., 5,730 115 B3
Beerse, Belg., 7,950 115 C3
Beersheba, Isr., 43,516 142 C4
Beersheba Springs, Tenn., 577 71 F6
Beersville, N.B., Can. 47 T10
Beesd, Neth. 115 c7
Beeskow, Ger.D.R. 118 E2
Bee Spring, Ky. 71 E4
Beeston, U.K., 20,487 113 F5
Beeton, Ont., Can. 46 E4
Beetown, Wis. 66 C6
Beeville, Tex., 13,811 77 P5
Befale, D.R.Congo 164 C1
Befandriana, Malag. Rep. 165 G5
Befori, D.R.Congo 164 C1
Befu, Jap. 154 f15
Befu, Jap. 154 f16
Bega, Austl., 3,518 173 G5
Bega, r., Rum. 128 C2
Begamganj, India, 10,029 144 b14
Bégard, Fr., 5,249 116 B2
Begejski Kan., Yug. 125 E2
Beggs, Okla., 1,114 76 G2
Begnište, Yug. 125 E4
Begoml', U.S.S.R. 136 C2
Begoro, Ghana 162 c8
Begovat, U.S.S.R., 40,000 137 f4
Beguildy, U.K. 114 B6
Begusarai, India, 27,346 144 f13
Béhague, Pte., Fr. Guiana 101 P5
Behan, Alta., Can. 42 K2
Behbehān, Iran, 29,886 143 E2
Behn, Mt., Austl. 172 D2
Beho, Belg., 1,131 119 A4
Behrang Station, Malay., 1,691 147 o15
Behshahr, Iran, 16,172 143 E1
Beiarn, Nor. 120 C2
Beica, Eth. 163 K4
Beida = Zāwiyat al Bayḍā'
Beighton, U.K., 23,056 114 F4
Beijerland, i., Neth. 115 C3
Beilen, Neth., 4,300 115 E2
Beilngries, F.R.Ger., 3,331 118 C4
Beinn a'Ghlò, mtn., U.K. 112 E3
Beinn an Oir, mtn., U.K. 112 C4
Beinn Bheigeir, mtn., U.K. 112 C4
Beinn Bheula, mtn., U.K. 112 a7
Beinn Bhreac, mtn., U.K. 112 a7
Beinn Bhuidhe, mtn., U.K. 112 a7
Beinn Dearg, mtn., U.K. 112 D3
Beinn Ime, mtn., U.K. 112 a7
Beinn Laoigh, U.K. 112 a7
Beinn Mhòr, mtn., U.K. 112 C3
Beipa'a, Terr. Papua 174 e3
Beira, Moz., 45,127 164 E5
Beirut = Bayrūt
Beiseker, Alta., Can. 42 K3
Beitbridge, Rhod. 164 E5
Beith, U.K. 112 a8
Beit Shean, Isr., 9,719 142 b7
Beiu, Rum. 128 E2
Beiuş, Rum., 6,467 128 D1
Beja, Port., 18,040 122 B3
Bejaïa, Alg., 57,572 160 E1
Béjar, Sp., 16,357 122 C2
Bejou, Minn., 164 74 D2
Bejuma, Ven., 7,037 101 a11
Békés, Hung., 21,699 126 E3
Békéscsaba, Hung., 49,488 126 E3
Bekily, Malag. Rep., 1,352 165 G6
Bekkai, Jap., 19,690 155 L8
Bekkevoort, Belg., 2,700 115 D4
Bekok, Malay., 2,953 147 p15
Bekwai, Ghana 162 c8
Bela, Pak., 3,139 144 C4
Bélâbre, Fr., 1,277 117 D3
Bela Crkva, Yug., 11,000* 125 E2
Belaga, Malay. 148 E2
Bel'agachskiy, U.S.S.R. 137 q12
Bel Air, Md., 4,300 62 H3
Belalcázar, Col. 100 C5
Bel Alton, Md. 62 H4
Belang, Indon. 149 H2
Bela Palanka, Yug., 3,168 125 F3
Bela Pratapgarh, India, 21,397 144 c13
Belapur, r., India 145 i17
Belas, Port., 7,509 122 i10
Bela Slatina, Bulg., 13,442 128 D3
Bela Vista, Braz., 8,878 103 E6
Belawan, Indon. 148 A2
Belaya, r., U.S.S.R. 135 R3
Belaya, r., U.S.S.R. 136 E4
Belaya, r., U.S.S.R. 137 h8
Belaya Kalitva, U.S.S.R., 23,100 136 F3
Belaya Tserkov', U.S.S.R., 76,000 134 C5
Belaya Zemlya, O-va., U.S.S.R. 134 E1
Belceşti, Rum. 128 F1
Bełchatów, Pol., 6,930 127 C3
Belcher, Ky. 71 J4
Belcher Chan., N.W.T., Can. 41 K2
Belcher Islands, N.W.T., Can. 44 H3
Belcher Is., N.W.T., Can. 44 H3
Belchertown, Mass., 5,186(T) 56 G3
Belchite, Sp., 2,650 122 E2
Belco, Chile 104 e15
Belcourt, N. Dak. 74 C1
Belcross, N.C. 63 H1
Belda, India 144 f14
Belden, Calif. 82 C3
Belden, N. Dak. 74 A1
Beldenville, Wis. 66 A4
Belding, Mich., 4,887 67 H5
Belebey, U.S.S.R., 28,500 134 E4
Belecke, F.R.Ger., 3,669 119 E2
Belém, Braz., 359,988 103 G2
Belén, Arg., 9,500* 105 B3
Belén, Col. 100 B6
Belén, Col. 100 C7
Belén, Col. 100 D4
Belén, Hond., 1,283 94 e9
Belén, Nic., 2,132 94 D5
Belén, Pan. 94 G6
Belen, N. Mex., 5,031 79 B4
Belén, Urug. 105 D4
Belén, Ven., 1,938 101 b12
Belén del Refugio, Mex., 1,359 93 b8
Belene, Bulg., 10,746 128 E3
Bélep, Îs., N. Caled. 170 E6
Belet Uen, Som. Rep., 11,615* 163 M5
Belëv, U.S.S.R., 17,000 136 D2
Belfair, Wash. 80 B2
Belfast, S. Af., 3,984 164 D6
Belfast, U.K., 416,094 113 C4
Belfast, Me., 6,140 55 C4
Belfast, N.Y. 58 D7
Belfast, Ohio 70 F3
Belfast, Tenn. 71 E6
Belfast L., U.K. 113 D4
Belfield, N. Dak., 1,064 74 A2
Belford, U.K. 112 E4
Belfort, Fr., 51,280 117 G3
Belfry, Ky. 71 J4
Belfry, Mont. 81 E3
Belgaum, India, 127,885 145 E7
Belgern, Ger.D.R. 126 c5
Belgian Congo = Congo, Democratic Republic of the
Belgioioso, It., 4,855 122 c5
Belgique, Mo., 61 72 H7
Belgium, ctry., 9,499,000* 115
Belgium, N.Y. 59 q23
Belgium, Wis., 643 66 F5
Belgorod, U.S.S.R., 81,000 134 C4
Belgorod-Dnestrovskiy, U.S.S.R., 26,000 136 C4
Belgrade, Me. 55 C4
Belgrade, Minn., 666 74 E3
Belgrade, Mont., 1,057 81 D3
Belgrade, Nebr., 224 75 H2
Belgrade, N.C. 63 G3
Belgrade, Yug. = Beograd
Belgrade Lakes, Me. 55 C4
Belgreen, Ala. 64 B1
Belgun, Bulg. 128 G3
Belhaven, N.C., 2,386 63 H2
Beli Drim, r., Yug. 125 E3
Beli Lom, r., Bulg. 128 F3
Beli Manastir, Yug. 125 D2
Belimbing, Indon. 148 C4
Belin, Fr., 1,714 117 C4
Belington, W. Va., 1,528 62 D3
Belinju, Indon. 148 C3
Belinskiy, U.S.S.R., 6,000 136 F2
Beli Potok, Yug., 2,082 125 F3
Beliş, Rum. 128 D1
Belitsa, Bulg., 3,281 128 D4
Belitung, i., Indon. 148 D3
Beliu, Rum. 128 D1
Belize, Br. Hond., 32,867 94 C2
Belize, r., Br. Hond.-Guat. 94 C2
Bélizon, Fr. Guiana 101 O5
Beljanica, mt., Yug. 125 E2
Belk, Ala. 64 B2
Belknap, Ill., 203 68 C6
Belknap, co., N.H., 28,912 54 D4
Belknap Mtn., N.H. 54 E4
Belkofski, Alaska, 57 85 D5
Bel'kovskiy, O., U.S.S.R. 135 N2
Bell, Calif., 19,450 83 h16
Bell, Fla., 134 65 G2
Bell, co., Ky., 35,336 71 H5
Bell, co., Tex., 94,097 77 P4
Bell, r., Qué., Can. 44 J5
Bella Bella, Br. Col., Can. 42 E3
Bellac, Fr., 5,131 117 D3
Bellaco, Urug. 105 c11
Bella Coola, Br. Col., Can. 42 E3
Belladère, Haiti, 1,342 96 m6
Bellair, Fla. 65 E2
Bellaire, Mich., 689 67 H4
Bellaire, Minn. 74 c5
Bellaire, Ohio, 11,502 70 J2
Bellaire, Tex., 19,872 77 h9
Bellaire, L., Mich. 67 H4
Bellamy, Ala. 64 A3
Bellamy, r., N.H. 54 E5
Bellarthur, N.C., 204 63 G2
Bellary, India, 85,673 145 E7
Bella Unión, Urug. 105 D4
Bella Vista, Arg., 20,000* 105 C3
Bella Vista, Arg., 17,300* 105 D3
Bella Vista, Urug. 105 c10
Bell Buckle, Tenn., 318 71 E6
Bell Center, Wis., 155 66 C5
Bell City, Mo., 409 72 H7
Belle, Mo., 1,016 72 F6
Belle, W. Va. 62 C4
Belle, r., Ont., Can. 46 B6
Belle, r., Mich. 67 L6
Belleair, Fla., 2,456 65 c12
Belleair Beach, Fla., 563 65 c12
Belle Center, Ohio, 949 70 F2
Belleek, U.K. 113 B4
Bellefont, Kans. 75 F6
Belle-Fontaine, Mart. 97 12
Bellefontaine, Ohio, 11,424 70 F2
Bellefontaine Neighbors, Mo., 13,650 72 b10
Bellefonte, Del., 1,536 62 f10
Bellefonte, Pa., 6,088 60 G4
Belle Fourche, S. Dak., 4,087 74 A3
Belle Fourche, r., S. Dak.-Wyo. 52 E2
Belle Fourche Res., S. Dak. 74 A3
Bellegarde, Fr., 6,716 117 F3
Bellegem, Belg., 3,224 116 a6
Belle Glade, Fla., 11,273 65 J6
Belle Haven, Va., 371 62 J5
Belle-Île, Fr. 116 B3
Belle I., Newf., Can. 45 Q4
Belle I., Mich. 67 g15
Belle Isle, Str. of, Newf., Can. 45 P4
Belleisle Creek, N.B., Can. 47 S11
Bellême, Fr., 1,841 117 D2
Belle Meade, Tenn., 3,082 71 D5
Belle Mina, Ala. 64 B1
Bellemont, Ariz. 78 C4
Belleoram, Newf., Can. 45 Q6
Belleplain, N.J., 61 B5
Belle Plaine, Iowa, 2,923 72 E3
Belle Plaine, Kans., 1,579 75 H6
Belle Plaine, Minn., 1,931 74 F3
Belle Rive, Ill., 303 68 D5
Belle River, Ont., Can., 1,840 46 B6
Belle Terre, N.Y., 295 58 g13
Belle Valley, Ohio 70 H3
Belle Vernon, Pa., 1,784 60 C5
Belleview, Fla., 864 65 G3
Belleview, Mo. 72 G7
Belleville, Ont., Can., 30,665 44 J7
Belleville, Fr., 1,281 116 b9
Belleville, Ark., 273 73 B2
Belleville, Ill., 37,264 68 C5
Belleville, Kans., 2,940 75 H4
Belleville, Mich., 1,921 67 K6
Belleville, N.J., 35,005 58 c13
Belleville, N.Y. 59 H4
Belleville, Pa., 1,539 60 G4
Belleville, R.I. 57 L6
Belleville, Wis., 844 66 D6
Bellevue, Del. 62 f10
Bellevue, Idaho, 384 81 B4
Bellevue, Ill., 1,561 68 C3
Bellevue, Iowa, 2,181 72 G2
Bellevue, Ky., 9,336 71 h11
Bellevue, Mich., 1,277 67 H6
Bellevue, Nebr., 8,831 75 K2
Bellevue, Ohio, 8,286 70 G1
Bellevue, Pa., 11,412 60 B5
Bellevue, Tex., 309 77 P3
Bellevue, Wash., 12,809 80 B2
Bellevue, Wis. 66 F4
Belley, Fr., 6,442 117 F4
Bellflower, Calif., 45,909 83 h16
Bellflower, Ill., 389 68 D3
Bellflower, Mo., 245 72 F5
Bell Gardens, Calif., 26,467 83 h16
Bellheim, F.R.Ger., 5,231 119 E6
Bell Hill, N.Y. 59 u26
Bellingen, Austl., 1,324 173 H4
Bellingham, Mass., 6,774(T) 57 L4
Bellingham, Minn., 327 74 D3
Bellingham, Wash., 34,688 80 B1
Bellingshausen, atoll, Soc. Is. 177 42
Bellingshausen Sea, Ant. 180 Y5
Bellinzago Novarese, It., 6,504 122 b5
Bellinzona, Switz., 13,435 124 D2
Bell-Irving, r., Br. Col., Can. 42 D2
Bellis, Alta., Can. 43 c6
Bell I. = Wabana
Bell I., Newf., Can. 45 c10
Bell I., Newf., Can. 45 Q5
Bell L., Ont., Can. 44 D5
Bellmawr, N.J., 11,853 61 A4
Bellmead, Tex., 5,127 77 P4
Bellmore, Ind. 70 B3
Bellmore, N.Y., 12,784 58 e14
Bello, Col. 101 d13
Bello, Phil., 4,462 153 f11
Bellona, N.Y. 58 F6
Bellona I., Sol. Is. 175 c3
Bellows Falls, Vt., 3,831 54 B5
Belloy-en-France, Fr., 1,045 116 h10
Bell Pen., N.W.T., Can. 41 N5
Bellport, N.Y., 2,774 59 P10
Bellpuig, Sp., 3,154 122 F2
Bells, Tenn., 1,232 71 B6
Bells, Tex., 707 77 P3
Bells Corners, Ont., Can., 1,900 47 J3
Bellsite, Man., Can. 43 E4
Bellton, W. Va. 62 D3
Belltown (part of Stamford), Conn. 56 B8
Belltown, Ill. 68 B4
Belluno, It., 30,896 123 D1
Bell Ville, Arg., 21,000* 105 C4
Bellville, S. Af., 27,386 164 a8
Bellville, Ohio, 1,621 70 G2
Bellville, Tex., 2,218 77 P5
Bellwood, Ala., 273 64 D4
Bellwood, Ill., 20,729 69 c9
Bellwood, La. 73 B6
Bellwood, Nebr., 361 75 H2
Bellwood, Pa., 2,330 60 F4
Belly, r., Alta., Can. 42 K4
Belmar, N.J., 5,190 61 D3
Belmira, Col. 100 C4
Belmond, Iowa, 2,506 72 D2
Belmont, Austl., 6,315 173 G5
Belmont, Man., Can. 43 E5
Belmont, Ont., Can. 46 C6
Belmont, Calif., 15,996 83 e12
Belmont, Kans. 75 G6
Belmont, Mass., 28,715 57 M3
Belmont, Mich. 67 H5
Belmont, Miss., 901 73 G3
Belmont, Nebr. 75 B1
Belmont, N.H. 54 E5
Belmont, N.Y., 1,146 58 E7
Belmont, N.C., 5,007 63 D2
Belmont, co., Ohio, 83,864 70 J2
Belmont, Ohio, 563 70 J2
Belmont, Tex. 76 c6
Belmont, Vt. 54 B5
Belmont, W. Va., 454 62 C3
Belmont, Wis., 616 66 C6
Belmonte, Braz., 7,897 103 J5
Belmonte, Sp., 6,162 122 B1
Belmonte, Sp., 3,780 122 D3
Belmont Hbr., Ill. 69 d9
Belmullet, Ire. 113 A4
Belo, Malag. Rep., 3,717 165 G5
Beloeil, Qué., Can., 6,128 47 p17
Belogorsk, R.S.F.S.R., U.S.S.R., 48,900 135 M4
Belogorsk, Ukr.S.S.R., U.S.S.R., 8,800 136 D4
Belogradchik, Bulg., 3,444 128 D3
Belo Horizonte, Braz., 642,912 103 H5
Beloit, Kans., 3,837 75 G4
Beloit, Ohio, 877 70 J2
Beloit, Wis., 32,846 66 D6
Belo Jardim, Braz., 11,091 103 a15
Belolutsk, U.S.S.R. 136 E3
Belomorsk, U.S.S.R., 13,600 134 C3
Belonia, India, 8,744 145 J5
Beloomut, U.S.S.R. 136 c6
Belopol'ye, U.S.S.R., 17,100 136 D3
Belorado, Sp., 2,741 122 D1
Beloretsk, U.S.S.R., 61,000 137 i9
Belorusskaya Gryada, U.S.S.R. 136 B2
Belorusskaya S.S.R., U.S.S.R., 8,633,000* 134 B4
Beloslav, Bulg., 5,653 128 F3
Belousovka, U.S.S.R., 14,300 134 H4
Belo Vale, Braz., 1,956 103 e17
Belovo, U.S.S.R., 115,000 134 H4
Beloye, Oz., U.S.S.R. 134 C3
Beloye, Oz., U.S.S.R. 134 s11
Beloye More, U.S.S.R. 134 C3
Belozem, Bulg., 5,031 128 E3
Belozërsk, U.S.S.R., 11,000 134 C3
Belozërskoye, U.S.S.R. 136 e7
Belper, U.K., 15,552 114 F4
Belpre, Kans., 211 75 F6
Belpre, Ohio, 5,418 70 H3
Bel-Ridge, Mo., 4,395 72 a11
Belsay, U.K. 112 g9
Belt, Mont., 757 81 D2
Beltana, Austl. 172 E4
Belterra, Braz., 5,347 103 F2
Belterwijde, l., Neth. 115 E2
Belton, U.K., 1,613 114 G3
Belton, Mo., 4,897 72 C6
Belton, S.C., 5,106 63 B3
Belton, Tex., 8,163 77 P4
Belton Res., Tex. 77 P4

200 · Beltrami—Bibb City

Beltrami, co., Minn., 23,425 **74** E1
Beltsville, Md. **62** b8
Bel'tsy, U.S.S.R., 72,000 **136** B4
Belturbet, Ire. **113** C4
Belukha, G., U.S.S.R. **134** H5
Belur, India **145** E7
Beluran, Malay. **148** F1
Belush'ya Guba, U.S.S.R. **134** D2
Belva, Okla. **76** D1
Belvedere, Calif., 2,148 **83** e12
Belvedere Marittimo, It., 10,378 **123** E5
Belvès, Fr., 1,927 **117** D4
Belvidere, Ill., 11,223 **68** D1
Belvidere, Kans., **75** F6
Belvidere, N.J., 2,636 **61** A2
Belvidere, N.C. **63** H1
Belvidere, S. Dak., 232 **74** B4
Belvidere Center, Vt. **54** B2
Belvidere Corners, Vt. **54** B2
Belvidere Mtn., Vt. **54** B2
Belwood, Ont., Can. **46** b13
Belwood, N.C. **63** C2
Belwood L., Ont., Can. **46** b13
Belyayevka, U.S.S.R. **137** h7
Belyayevka, U.S.S.R. **137** h9
Belyy, U.S.S.R., 4,100 **136** D2
Belyye Stolby, U.S.S.R. **136** b6
Belyy, O., U.S.S.R. **134** F2
Belyy Yar, U.S.S.R. **134** H4
Bełżec, Pol. **127** E3
Belzig, Ger.D.R. **118** D2
Belzoni, Miss., 4,142 **73** E4
Bełżyce, Pol., 4,868 **127** E3
Bembe, Ang. **164** B3
Bembézar, Pantano del, Sp. **122** C3
Bemboka, Austl. **173** g11
Bembridge, U.K., 2,429 **113** k13
Bement, Ill., 1,558 **68** D4
Bemidji, Minn., 9,958 **74** E2
Bemidji, L., Minn. **74** E2
Bemis, Tenn., 3,127 **71** C6
Bemmel, Neth., 3,200 **115** D3
Bemus Point, N.Y., 443 **58** B7
Bena, Minn., 286 **74** E2
Benāb, Iran, 14,396 **143** D1
Benabarre, Sp., 1,231 **122** F1
Bena-Dibele, D.R.Congo **164** C2
Benadir, coast, Som. Rep. **163** M6
Benalla, Austl., 6,045 **173** G5
Bénard, Man., Can. **43** g10
Benares = Varanasi
Benavente, Port., 6,223 **122** A3
Benavente, Sp., 11,080 **122** B2
Benavides, Tex., 2,459 **77** O6
Ben Avon, Pa., 2,553 **60** b7
Benbecula, i., U.K. **112** C3
Benbrook, Tex., 3,254 **76** d9
Benbrook Res., Tex. **76** d9
Ben Cat, S. Viet., 5,048 **147** m11
Benchley, Tex. **77** P4
Ben Chonzie, mtn., U.K. **112** c7
Ben Clach, mtn., U.K. **112** c7
Ben Cruachan, mtn., U.K. **112** D3
Bencubbin, Austl. **172** B4
Bend, Oreg., 11,936 **80** C3
Bend, Tex. **77** O4
Bendavis, Mo. **72** E7
Ben Davis Point, N.J. **61** A5
Bendeleben, Mt., Alaska **85** D2
Bender Beila, Som. Rep. **163** N4
Bender Kassim = Bosaso
Bendersville, Pa., 484 **60** H6
Bendery, U.S.S.R., 45,000 **136** C4
Bender Ziada, Som. Rep. **163** N4
Bendigo, Austl., 36,918 **173** F5
Bendo, Indon. **148** D5
Bendoc = Bendock
Bendock, Austl. **173** g11
Bendoh, Tg., Indon. **148** d7
Bendorf, F.R.Ger., 13,405 **118** A3
Benedict, Kans., 128 **75** K6
Benedict, Nebr., 170 **75** H2
Benedict, N. Dak., 129 **74** B2
Benedicta, Me. **55** D3
Benei Beraq, Isr. 46,984 **142** a7
Benemérita de San Cristóbal = San Cristóbal
Benešov, Czech., 9,131 **126** B2
Bénestroff, Fr. **116** c9
Benet Lake, Wis. **66** c13
Benevento, It., 55,161 **123** E4
Benevolence, Ga., 123 **64** E4
Benewah, co., Idaho, 6,036 **81** A2
Benezett, Pa. **60** F3
Benfeld, Fr., 3,453 **117** G2
Bengal, Okla. **76** H3
Bengal, Bay of, Asia **141** G5
Bengara, Indon. **148** F2
Benghazi = Banghāzī
Bengkajang, Indon. **148** D2
Bengkalis, Indon. **148** B2
Bengkalis, Pulau, Indon. **147** p16
Bengkulu, Indon., 25,330 **148** B3
Beng Lovea, Camb. **146** D4
Bengough, Sask., Can. **43** D5
Benguela, Ang., 15,399 **164** B4
Benguela-Bié, Planalto de, Ang. **164** B3
Benguerir, Mor., 4,325 **160** C2
Benham, Ky., 1,874 **71** H5
Benhams, Va. **62** B6
Ben Hill, co., Ga., 13,633 **64** F4
Ben Hope, mtn., U.K. **112** D2
Beni, D.R.Congo, 2,636 **165** d13
Beni, Nepal **144** d11
Beni, r., Bol. **102** C4
Beni-Abbès, Alg., 1,427 **160** D2
Benicarló, Sp., 10,627 **122** F2
Benicia, Calif., 6,070 **83** e11
Benidorm, Sp., 6,259 **122** E3
Benifayó, Sp., 8,095 **122** E3
Beni-Mansour, Alg., 1,419 **160** d5
Beni-Mellal, Mor., 28,933 **160** C2
Benin, r., Nigeria **162** f9
Benin, Bight of, Af. **162** E4
Benin City, Nigeria, 62,353 **162** E4
Beni-Ounif, Alg., 2,530 **160** D2
Béni-Saf, Alg., 17,521 **160** D2
Benito, Man., Can. **43** E4
Benito, Equat. Guin. **164** A1
Benito Juárez, Mex., 1,438 **93** f10
Benjamin, Tex., 338 **77** N3
Benjamin, Utah **78** c10
Benjamin Constant, Braz., 3,224 **102** C2
Benjamín Hill, Mex., 4,392 **92** C1
Benkelman, Nebr., 1,400 **75** D3
Ben Klibreck, mtn., U.K. **112** D2
Benkovac, Yug. **125** B2
Ben Lawers, mtn., U.K. **112** D3
Benld, Ill., 1,848 **68** C4
Ben Ledi, mtn., U.K. **112** b7
Ben Lomond, Ark., 157 **73** A4
Ben Lomond, Calif., 1,814 **83** e13
Ben Lomond, mtn., U.K. **112** a7
Ben Macdhui, mtn., U.K. **112** E3
Benmore, U.K. **112** a7
Ben More, mtn., U.K. **112** C3
Ben More, mtn., U.K. **112** D3
Ben More Assynt, mtn., U.K. **112** D2
Bennachie, mtn., U.K. **112** E3
Bennane Head, U.K. **113** D4
Benndale, Miss. **73** G7
Bennebroek, Neth., 3,300 **115** b6
Bennekom, Neth., 7,000 **115** D2
Bennet, Nebr., 381 **75** J3
Bennett, Br. Col., Can. **42** B1
Bennett, Colo., 287 **79** C2
Bennett, Iowa, 374 **72** F3
Bennett, N.C., 222 **63** E2
Bennett, co., S. Dak., 3,053 **74** B4
Bennett, Wis. **66** B2
Bennett, L., Austl. **172** D3
Bennetta, O., U.S.S.R. **135** O2
Bennett Branch, Pa. **60** F3
Bennett L., Br. Col.-Yukon, Can. **42** B1
Bennett Pk., N. Mex. **79** A3
Bennetts Corners, Ohio **70** d9
Bennetts Mills, N.J. **58** b16
Bennetts Point, S.C. **63** D5
Bennettsville, S.C., 6,963 **63** E3
Ben Nevis, mtn., U.K. **112** D3
Bennington, Kans., 535 **75** H4
Bennington, Mich. **67** J6
Bennington, Nebr., 341 **75** J2
Bennington, N.H. **54** D5
Bennington, Okla., 226 **76** G4
Bennington, co., Vt., 25,088 **54** A5
Bennington, Vt., 8,023 **54** A6
Benoa, Indon. **148** f8
Benoit, Wis. **66** B2
Benom, G., Malay. **147** p15
Benona, Mich. **67** G5
Benoni, S. Af., 135,467 **165** k17
Benque Viejo, Br. Hond., 1,607 **94** C2
Bensberg, F.R.Ger., 25,996 **118** A3
Bensenville, Ill., 12,212 **69** c9
Bensheim, F.R.Ger., 22,770 **118** B4
Ben-Slimane, Mor., 10,305 **160** C2
Benson, U.K., 2,624 **114** F7
Benson, Ariz., 2,494 **78** C6
Benson, Ill., 427 **68** C3
Benson, La. **73** B6
Benson, Minn., 3,678 **74** E3
Benson, N.C., 2,355 **63** F2
Benson, co., N. Dak., 9,435 **74** C2
Benson, Utah **78** c7
Benson, Vt. **54** A4
Benson Pt., Christmas Atoll **177** 40
Bens Run, W. Va. **62** C3
Ben Suc, S. Viet. **147** m11
Bent, co., Colo., 7,419 **79** D3
Benta, Malay., 2,365 **147** o14
Benteng, Indon. **149** G4
Bentham, U.K., 2,604 **113** E4
Bentheim, F.R.Ger., 6,673 **118** A2
Benthuizen, Neth. **115** b6
Bentinck I., Burma **146** B5
Bentiu, Sudan **163** K4
Bentjuluk, Indon. **148** f8
Bentley, Alta., Can. **42** J3
Bentley, Hants., Eng., U.K. **114** G8
Bentley, York., Eng., U.K., 16,120 **114** F3
Bentley, Kans., 204 **75** H6
Bentley, Mich. **67** J5
Bentley, N. Dak. **74** A2
Bentley, Okla. **76** G3
Bentley I., Terr. Papua **174** 3
Bento Gonçalves, Braz., 13,662 **103** F7
Benton, N.B., Can. **47** S11
Benton, co., Ark., 36,272 **73** A1
Benton, Ark., 10,399 **73** C3
Benton, Calif. **82** D4
Benton, Colo. **79** D3
Benton, Ill., 7,023 **68** D5
Benton, co., Ind., 11,912 **70** B2
Benton, co., Iowa, 23,422 **72** E2
Benton, Ky., 3,074 **71** C5
Benton, La., 1,336 **73** B5
Benton, Me. **55** C4
Benton, Mich. **67** K6
Benton, co., Minn., 17,287 **74** E3
Benton, co., Miss., 7,723 **73** F3
Benton, Miss. **73** E5
Benton, co., Mo., 8,737 **72** D6
Benton, Mo., 554 **72** H7
Benton, N.H. **54** D3
Benton, Ohio **70** F2
Benton, co., Oreg., 39,165 **80** B3
Benton, co., Tenn., 10,662 **71** C6
Benton, Tenn., 638 **71** G6
Benton, co., Wash., 62,070 **80** D2
Benton, Wis., 837 **66** C6
Benton City, Mo., 155 **72** F5
Benton City, Wash., 1,210 **80** D2
Bentong, Malay., 18,837 **148** B2
Benton Harbor, Mich., 19,136 **67** G6
Benton Heights, Mich., 6,112 **67** G6
Bentonia, Miss., 511 **73** E5
Benton Ridge, Ohio, 325 **70** F2
Bentonville, Ark., 3,649 **73** A1
Bentonville, Ohio **70** F4
Bentonville, Va. **62** F4
Bentleyville, Pa., 3,160 **60** B5
Ben Tranh, S. Viet., 2,255 **147** m11
Benţu, Rum. **128** F2
Bentworth, U.K. **114** F8
Benty, Guin. **162** B4
Benue, r., Cam.-Nigeria **162** F4
Benut, Malay., 2,216 **147** p16
Ben Venue, mtn., U.K. **112** b7
Benville, Ill. **68** B4
Ben Vorlich, mtn., U.K. **112** b7
Benwood, W. Va., 2,850 **62** D2
Ben Wyvis, mtn., U.K. **112** D3
Benzdorp, Sur. **101** N6
Benzie, co., Mich., 7,834 **67** G4
Benzonia, Mich., 407 **67** G4
Beo, Indon. **149** H1
Beograd, Yug., 594,000* **125** E2
Béoumi, Iv. Coast, 3,500 **162** C4
Beowawe, Nev. **83** B2
Beppu, Jap., 107,734 **154** B5
Beppu-wan, Jap. **154** B5
Bequia I., Gren. Is. **97** 20
Berard, Kusaie **176** 31
Berard, Port, Kusaie **176** 31
Berasia, India, 6,238 **144** a14
Berat, Alb., 20,450 **125** D4
Berau, Teluk, Indon. **149** K3
Berault, Morne, Haiti **96** k6
Berazategui, Arg. **105** b12
Berbera, Som. Rep., 20,000* **163** M4
Berbérati, C.A.R., 11,752 **162** G5
Berbice, r., Guyana **101** L5
Berchem, Belg., 47,548 **115** d8
Berchem-Ste-Agathe, Belg., 14,238 **115** d9
Berchogur, U.S.S.R. **134** E5
Berchtesgaden, F.R.Ger., 4,913 **118** D5
Berck-sur-Mer, Fr., 15,543 **117** D1
Berclair, Tex. **77** P5
Berd', r., U.S.S.R. **137** r11
Berda, r., U.S.S.R. **136** e8
Berdichev, U.S.S.R., 56,000 **134** B4
Berdigestyakh, U.S.S.R. **135** M3
Berdsk, U.S.S.R., 26,600 **137** q11
Berdyansk, U.S.S.R., 71,000 **134** C5
Berdyaush, U.S.S.R., 11,200 **137** i8
Berdyuzh'ye, U.S.S.R. **137** n11
Berea, Ky., 4,302 **71** G4
Berea, Nebr. **75** C1
Berea, N.C. **63** F1
Berea, Ohio, 16,592 **70** d9
Beregovo, U.S.S.R., 26,000 **136** A3
Berekum, Ghana, 11,531 **162** b8
Berens, r., Man.-Ont., Can. **44** C4
Berens I., Man., Can. **43** F4
Berens River, Man., Can. **43** F4
Beresford, Man., Can. **43** E5
Beresford, N.B., Can. **47** S10
Beresford, S. Dak., 1,794 **74** D4
Beresford Lake, Man., Can **43** g9
Bereşti-Tîrg, Rum. **128** F1
Beretău, r., Rum. **128** D1
Berettyóújfalu, Hung., 11,377 **126** E3
Berëza, U.S.S.R., 5,300 **136** B2
Berezhany, U.S.S.R., 9,300 **136** B3
Berezina, r., U.S.S.R. **134** B4
Berezniki, U.S.S.R., 117,000 **134** E4
Berëzovka, R.S.F.S.R., U.S.S.R. **134** E3
Berëzovka, R.S.F.S.R., U.S.S.R. **135** L4
Berëzovka, R.S.F.S.R., U.S.S.R. **137** i7
Berëzovka, Ukr. S.S.R., U.S.S.R. **136** C4
Berëzovo, U.S.S.R., 6,800 **134** F3
Berëzovskiy, U.S.S.R., 30,600 **137** k8
Berezovskoye, U.S.S.R. **137** s11
Berg, Nor. **121** D1
Berg, Swed. **120** C3
Berga, Ger.D.R. **126** b6
Berga, Sp., 9,822 **122** F1
Bergalia, Austl. **173** h10
Bergama, Turk., 21,797 **142** A2
Bergambacht, Neth. **115** b7
Bergamo, It., 113,489 **123** B2
Bergantín, Ven., 1,169 **101** H3
Bergantino, It., 3,447 **122** e5
Bergeijk, Neth. **115** D3
Bergen, F.R.Ger., 5,081 **118** B2
Bergen, Ger.D.R., 10,473 **118** D1
Bergen, Neth., **119** A1
Bergen, Nor., 115,845 **120** A3
Bergen, co., N.J., 780,255 **61** C1
Bergen, N.Y., 964 **58** E5
Bergen, N. Dak., 52 **74** B1
Bergen-Binnen, Neth., 6,900 **115** C2
Berg en Dal, Sur. **101** N5
Bergen-Enkheim, F.R.Ger., 9,145 **119** F4
Bergenfield, N.J., 27,203 **58** d13
Bergen op Zoom, Neth., 33,100 **115** C3
Bergen Park, Colo. **79** b8
Berger, Mo., 187 **72** F6
Bergerac, Fr., 25,971 **117** D4
Berghausen, F.R.Ger., 1,113 **119** E2
Bergheim, F.R.Ger., 7,799 **119** B3
Bergheim, Tex. **76** a6
Bergholtz, N.Y. **58** k18
Bergholtz Cr., N.Y. **58** k18
Bergholz, Ohio, 955 **70** J2
Bergisch Gladbach, F.R.Ger., 36,392 **119** C3
Bergkamen, F.R.Ger., 11,682 **119** D1
Bergland, Mich **66** D2
Bergnäs, Swed. **120** D2
Bergneustadt, F.R.Ger., 7,479 **119** D2
Bergoo, W. Va. **62** D4
Bergsche Maas, r., Neth. **115** c7
Bergschenhoek, Neth., 3,200 **115** b7
Bergsjö, Swed. **120** D3
Berguent, Mor. **160** D2
Bergum, Neth. **115** D1
Bergzabern, F.R.Ger., 4,301 **119** E6
Berhala, Selat, Indon. **148** C3
Berhampur, Ori., India, 76,931 **145** G6
Berhampur, W.B., India, 62,317 **145** H4
Beri, India, 10,840 **144** a11
Berikat, Tg., Indon. **148** C3
Berikul'skiy, U.S.S.R. **137** s11
Beringa, M., U.S.S.R. **135** S3
Beringa, O., U.S.S.R. **135** Q4
Bering Glacier, Alaska **85** J3
Beringovskiy, U.S.S.R., 2,600 **135** S3
Bering Sea, Asia-N. Amer. **169** F1
Berino, N. Mex. **79** B5
Berislav, U.S.S.R., 10,700 **136** D4
Berja, Sp., 12,732 **122** D4
Berk, F.R.Ger. **119** A4
Berkane, Mor., 20,496 **160** D2
Berkel, r., F.R.Ger.-Neth. **115** E2
Berkeley, Ont., Can. **46** D4
Berkeley, U.K. **114** D7
Berkeley, Calif., 111,268 **82** B4
Berkeley, Ill., 5,792 **69** c9
Berkeley, Mo., 18,676 **72** a10
Berkeley, R.I. **57** L5
Berkeley, co., S.C., 38,196 **63** E4
Berkeley, co., W. Va., 33,791 **62** F3
Berkeley, C., Colón, Arch, de **104** a7
Berkeley Heights, N.J., 8,721(T) **61** C2
Berkeley Lake, Ga., 94 **64** h9
Berkeley Sd., Falk. Is. **108** 3
Berkeley Springs, W. Va., 1,138 **62** F3
Berkenthin, F.R.Ger., 1,237 **119** c8
Berkhamsted, U.K., 13,051 **114** G7
Berkley, Mass., 1,609(T) **57** M5
Berkley, Mich., 23,275 **67** f14
Berkner I., Ant. **180** O5
Berkovići, Yug. **125** D3
Berkovitsa, Bulg., 9,229 **128** D3
Berks, co., Pa., 275,414 **61** L5
Berkshire, co., U.K., 504,154 **113** F6
Berkshire, co., Mass., 142,135 **56** C3
Berkshire (part of Lanesboro), Mass. **56** D2
Berkshire, N.Y. **59** H7
Berkshire, Vt. **54** B2
Berkshire Hills, Mass. **56** D4
Berkswell, U.K., 2,660 **114** E6
Berlaar, Belg., 8,873 **115** C3
Berlaimont, Fr., 3,980 **117** E1
Berleburg, F.R.Ger., 5,919 **118** B3
Berlevåg, Nor. **120** G1
Berlikum, Neth. **115** D1
Berlín, El Salv., 4,680 **94** e10
Berlin, F.R.Ger. = West Berlin
Berlin, Ger.D.R. = Ost-Berlin, Ger.D.R.
Berlin, Conn., 11,250(T) **56** E6
Berlin, Ga., 419 **64** F4
Berlin, Ill., 197 **68** C4
Berlin, Ky. **71** G3
Berlin, Md., 2,046 **62** J4
Berlin, Mass., 1,742(T) **57** K3
Berlin, N.H., 17,821 **54** E3
Berlin, N.J., 3,578 **61** B4
Berlin, N.Y. **59** O6
Berlin, N. Dak., 78 **74** C2
Berlin, Ohio **70** H2
Berlin, Okla. **76** D2
Berlin, Pa., 1,600 **60** E6
Berlin, Vt. **54** B3
Berlin, Wis., 4,838 **66** D5
Berlin, Mt., Ant. **180** X5
Berlin Heights, Ohio, 721 **70** G1
Berlin Res., Ohio **62** D2
Bermagui, Austl. **173** h11
Bermejillo, Mex., 3,900 **92** E3
Bermejo, Bol., 2,050 **102** D6
Bermejo, r., Arg. **105** D3
Bermejo, Paso de, Arg.-Chile **105** B4
Bermen, L., Qué., Can. **45** L4
Bermeo, Sp., 13,781 **122** D1
Bermillo de Sayago, Sp. **122** B2
Bermuda, Ala. **64** B4
Bermuda I., Berm. Is. **108** 1
Bermuda Is., Atl. Oc., 50,000* **108** H4
Bermuda Rise, Atl. Oc. **108** H4
Bern, Switz., 163,172 **124** B2
Bern, Kans., 206 **75** K4
Bernal, Mex., 1,331 **93** d9
Bernal, Peru, 1,319 **104** A3
Bernal, N. Mex. **79** C4
Bernalda, It., 10,825 **123** F4
Bernalillo, co., N. Mex., 262,199 **79** B4
Bernalillo, N. Mex., 2,574 **79** B4
Bernam, r., Malay. **147** o15
Bernard, Iowa, 173 **72** G2
Bernardino, Ariz. **78** D6
Bernardo, N. Mex. **79** B4
Bernardo O'Higgins, Ant. **180** O6
Bernardston, Mass., 1,370(T) **56** F2
Bernardsville, N.J., 5,515 **61** B2
Bernau, Ger.D.R., 13,638 **118** D2
Bernay, Fr., 10,112 **117** D2
Bernay-en-Brie, Fr. **116** k12
Bernburg, Ger.D.R., 44,482 **118** C3
Berndorf, Aust., 8,992 **124** M6
Berne, Switz. = Bern
Berne, Ind., 2,644 **70** E2
Berne, N.Y. **59** M6
Berner, Ga. **64** F2
Berner Alpen, Switz. **124** B2
Berneray, i., U.K. **112** C3
Bernice, La., 1,641 **73** C5
Bernice, Okla., 100 **76** H1
Bernie, Mo., 1,578 **72** H8
Bernier I., Austl. **172** A3
Bernierville, Qué., Can., 2,706 **47** N2
Bernina Pass, Switz. **124** E2
Bernina, Piz, mtn., Switz. **124** D2
Bernkastle-Kues, F.R.Ger., 5,726 **118** A4
Bernstein, Aust., 1,016 **124** N6
Bernville, Pa., 884 **61** K5
Beroroha, Malag. Rep., 1,300 **165** G5
Beroun, Czech., 15,946 **126** A2
Beroun, Minn. **74** F3
Berounka, r., Czech. **126** A2
Berovo, Yug., 4,176 **125** F4
Berra, It., 10,571 **122** e6
Berre, Fr., 10,335 **117** F5
Berrechid, Mor., 13,780 **160** C2
Berri, Austl., 1,470 **172** F5
Berriane, Alg., 4,759 **160** E2
Berridale, Austl. **173** g11
Berrien, co., Ga., 12,038 **64** F4
Berrien, co., Mich., 149,865 **67** G6
Berrien Center, Mich. **67** G7
Berrien Springs, Mich., 1,953 **67** G7
Berriew, U.K., 1,190 **113** E5
Berrigan, Austl. **173** e10
Berriozábal, Mex., 3,835 **93** G5
Berriwillock, Austl. **173** d10
Berrouaghia, Alg., 7,906 **160** c5
Berry, Austl., 1,349 **173** h10
Berry, Ala., 645 **64** B2
Berry, Ky., 279 **71** G3
Berry Creek, Calif. **82** C3
Berrydale, Fla. **65** C2
Berryessa, Calif. **83** f13
Berryessa Res., Calif. **82** B3
Berry Is., Bah. Is. **95** C1
Berryman, Mo. **72** F7
Berry Mills, Me. **55** B4
Berrysburg, Pa., 434 **60** J4
Berryville, Ark., 1,999 **73** B1
Berryville, Va., 1,645 **62** F3
Bertam, Malay., 1,420 **148** B1
Bertha, Minn., 562 **74** E2
Berthelming, Fr. **116** c9
Berthierville, Qué., Can., 3,662 **44** K6
Berthold, N. Dak., 431 **74** B1
Berthoud, Colo., 1,014 **79** C1
Bertie, co., N.C., 24,350 **63** G1
Bertincourt, Fr. **116** a7
Bertioga, Braz., 1,006 **103** c18
Bertogne, Belg. **115** D4
Bertolínia, Braz. **103** H3
Bertoua, Cam., 2,500* **162** G5
Bertram, Tex. **77** P4
Bertrambois, Fr. **116** c9
Bertrand, Mich., **67** G7
Bertrand, Mo., 465 **72** H8
Bertrand, Nebr., 691 **75** F3
Bertrix, Belg., 4,489 **115** D5
Bertry, Fr., 2,657 **116** a7
Bertwell, Sask., Can. **43** D4
Beru, i., Gilb. Is. **175** 10
Berumerfehn, F.R.Ger., 1,469 **118** A2
Beruwala, Cey., 12,498 **145** m22
Berville, Mich. **67** L6
Berwick, N.S., Can., 1,248 **47** T11
Berwick, co., U.K., 22,441 **112** E4
Berwick, Ill. **68** B3
Berwick, La., 3,880 **73** D8
Berwick, Me., 1,557 **55** B5
Berwick, N. Dak., 56 **74** B1
Berwick, Pa., 13,353 **61** K3
Berwick-upon-Tweed, U.K., 12,166 **112** F4
Berwind, W. Va. **62** C5
Berwyn, Alta., Can. **42** H2
Berwyn, Ill., 54,224 **68** E2
Berwyn, Nebr., 104 **75** F2
Berwyn, Pa., 5,050* **60** f11
Berwyn Mts., U.K. **114** A5
Beryl, Utah **78** B3
Berzence, Hung., 3,678 **126** C3
Berzosilla, Sp. **122** m12
Besalampy, Malag. Rep., 1,585 **165** G4
Besançon, Fr., 101,729 **117** G3
Besaya, r., Sp. **122** m11
Besbre, r., Fr. **117** E3
Beserah, Malay., 3,369 **147** p15
Besigheim, F.R.Ger., 5,935 **119** G6
Besikama, Indon. **149** H5
Beskids, mts., Czech.-Pol. **126** D2
Beslan, U.S.S.R. **137** c1
Besnard L., Sask., Can. **43** C3
Besni, Turk., 11,170 **142** D2
Besoco, W. Va. **62** C5
Bessa Monteiro, Ang. **164** B3
Bessancourt, Fr., 3,116 **116** g10
Bessbrook, U.K., 3,084 **113** C4
Bessèges, Fr., 5,720 **117** F4
Bessemer, Ala., 33,054 **64** C2
Bessemer, Mich., 3,304 **66** C2
Bessemer, Pa., 1,491 **60** B4
Bessemer City, N.C., 4,017 **63** C2
Bessenay, Fr., 1,306 **116** o15
Bessie, Okla., 226 **76** D2
Best, Neth., 3,000 **115** D3
Best, Tex. **77** N4
Bestobe, U.S.S.R., 12,600 **134** G4
Besuki, Indon. **148** e7
Betaf, Indon. **149** L3
Betania, Col. **100** B5
Betano, Port. Timor **149** H5
Betanzos, Bol. **102** c11
Betanzos, Sp., 10,223 **122** A1
Bétaré-Oya, Cam., 1,400* **162** G5
Beté, Col. **100** B4
Bete Grise Bay, Mich. **66** F1
Bétérou, Dahom. **162** e7
Bethal, S. Af., 11,952 **164** D6
Bethalto, Ill., 3,235 **68** C5
Bethanie, S.-W. Afr., 1,013 **164** B6
Bethany, Conn., 2,384(T) **56** E7
Bethany, Ill., 1,118 **68** D4
Bethany, La. **73** A5
Bethany, Mo., 2,771 **72** D4
Bethany, N.Y. **58** D6
Bethany, Okla., 12,342 **76** F2
Bethany, Oreg. **80** a6
Bethany, W. Va., 992 **62** D2
Bethany Beach, Del., 170 **62** J4
Bethayres, Pa., 2,600* **60** f11
Bethel, Montserrat **97** 5
Bethel, Alaska, 1,258 **85** D3
Bethel, Conn., 5,624; 8,200(T) **56** C7
Bethel, Del., 236 **62** J4
Bethel, Ind. **70** E3
Bethel, Ky. **71** H3
Bethel, Me., 1,117 **55** B4
Bethel, Mich. **67** H7
Bethel, Minn., 302 **74** F3
Bethel, Mo., 152 **72** F5
Bethel, N.C., 1,578 **63** G2
Bethel, Okla. **76** J3
Bethel, Ohio, 2,019 **70** E4
Bethel, Tenn. **71** D7
Bethel, Vt. **54** B4
Bethel, Wis. **66** C4
Bethel Park, Pa., 23,650 **60** b8
Bethelsdorp, S. Af., 16,457 **164** D7
Bethel Springs, Tenn., 533 **71** C6
Bethera, S.C. **63** E4
Bethesda, U.K., 4,159 **113** E5
Bethesda, Md., 56,527 **62** G4
Bethesda, Ohio, 1,178 **70** H2
Bethioua, Alg. **160** a6
Bethlehem, Jor. = Bayt Laḥm
Bethlehem, S. Af., 24,176 **164** D6
Bethlehem, Conn., 1,486(T) **56** D6
Bethlehem, Ind. **70** D4
Bethlehem, Ky. **71** F3
Bethlehem, N.H. **54** D3
Bethlehem, Pa., 75,408 **61** M4
Bethlehem, W. Va., 2,308 **62** D2
Bethpage, N.Y., 20,515 **58** f14
Bethpage, Tenn. **71** E5
Bethulie, S. Af., 3,488 **164** D7
Bethune, Sask., Can. **43** C5
Béthune, Fr., 24,655 **117** E1
Bethune, Colo. **79** D2
Bethune, S.C., 579 **63** D3
Béthune, r., Fr. **117** D2
Betijoque, Ven., 3,860 **100** E3
Betio, i., Tarawa **175** 15
Betioky, Malag. Rep., 1,492 **165** G5
Betong, Malay., 1,972 **148** D2
Betong, Thai., 12,052 **146** C6
Bet-Pak-Dala, des. steppe, U.S.S.R. **134** F5
Betroka, Malag. Rep., 2,611 **165** G5
Betseda, Loy. Is. **174** k8
Betsiamites, Qué., Can. **45** L5
Betsiamites, r., Qué., Can. **45** L5
Betsiboka, r., Malag. Rep. **165** G4
Betsie, r., Mich. **67** H4
Betsy, r., Mich. **67** H2
Betsy L., Mich. **67** H2
Betsy Layne, Ky. **71** J4
Bettembourg, Lux., 5,877 **115** E5
Bettendorf, Iowa, 11,534 **72** G3
Bettenfeld, F.R.Ger. **119** B4
Bette, Pico, Chad-Libya **161** H4
Betterton, Md., 328 **62** H3
Bettiah, India, 39,990 **145** G4
Bettingen, F.R.Ger., 1,197 **119** A5
Bettles, Alaska, 77 **85** F2
Bettles Field, Alaska **85** G2
Bettna, Swed. **120** d9
Bettola, It., 7,086 **122** c6
Bettsville, Ohio, 776 **70** F1
Betty Oneal Mine, Nev. **83** B2
Betul, India, 19,860 **144** a15
Betulia, Col. **100** B4
Betung, Indon. **148** B3
Betwa, r., India **145** F4
Betzdorf, F.R.Ger., 10,210 **118** A3
Beuel, F.R.Ger., 28,851 **118** A3
Beulah, Ark. **73** D3
Beulah, Colo. **79** C2
Beulah, Mich., 436 **67** G4
Beulah, Mo. **72** F7
Beulah, N. Dak., 1,318 **74** B2
Beulah, Oreg. **80** D4
Beulah, L., Wis. **66** E6
Beulahville, Va. **62** G5
Beulakerwijde, l., Neth. **115** D2
Beulaville, N.C., 1,062 **63** G3
Beusichem, Neth. **115** c7
Beuvry-Nord, Fr., 1,814 **116** a7
Bevaix, Switz., 1,407 **124** A2
Bevensen, F.R.Ger., 5,381 **118** C2
Bevent, Wis. **66** D4
Beveren, Belg., 14,656 **115** d8
Beverley, Austl. **172** B5
Beverley, U.K., 16,031 **113** F5
Beverley, L., Alaska **85** E4
Beverlo, Belg., 5,605 **115** D3
Beverly, Ga. **64** G1
Beverly, Kans., 199 **75** H4
Beverly, Ky. **71** H5
Beverly, Mass., 36,108 **57** N2
Beverly, N.J., 3,400 **61** B3
Beverly, Ohio, 1,194 **70** H3
Beverly, W. Va., 441 **62** E4
Beverly Beach, Md. **62** c9
Beverly Farms (part of Beverly), Mass. **57** N2
Beverly Hills, Calif., 30,817 **83** g15
Beverly Hills, Mich., 8,633 **67** f14
Beverly Shores, Ind., 733 **69** g10
Beverstedt, F.R.Ger., 1,859 **118** B2
Beverungen, F.R.Ger., 4,525 **118** B3
Beverwijk, Neth., 29,100 **115** C2
Bevier, Mo., 781 **72** E5
Bewdley, U.K., 5,033 **114** D6
Bex, Switz., 4,667 **124** B2
Bexar, Ala. **64** A1
Bexar, co., Tex., 687,151 **77** O5
Bexhill, U.K., 28,941 **113** G6
Bexley, London, U.K. **114** J8
Bexley, Miss. **73** G7
Bexley, Ohio, 14,319 **70** b7
Beya, U.S.S.R. **137** s11
Beykoz, Turk., 45,801 **142** B1
Beyla, Guin., 8,900 **162** C4
Beynes, Fr., 2,456 **116** f11
Beynost, Fr., 1,386 **116** q15
Beypazarı, Turk., 8,866 **142** C1
Beyrut = Bayrūt
Beyşehir, Turk., 5,853 **142** B2
Beyşehir Gölü, Turk. **142** B2
Bezdan, Yug., 6,681 **125** D2
Bezdružice, Czech. **126** b7
Bezhetsk, U.S.S.R., 25,200 **136** E1
Béziers, Fr., 75,541 **117** E5
Bezjovo, Yug. **125** D3
Bezmein, U.S.S.R., 3,900 **134** E6
Bezmer, Bulg., 2,470 **128** F3
Bezons, Fr., 22,258 **116** g11
Bezvěrov, Czech. **126** c6
Bezvodno, Bulg., 1,641 **129** E4
Bezymyannyy, S., U.S.S.R. **135** Q4
Bhabua, India, 9,890 **144** d13
Bhadarwah, India, 4,129 **145** E2
Bhādgaon, Nepal **144** e12
Bhadohi, India, 20,302 **144** d13
Bhadrak, India, 25,285 **145** H5
Bhadravati, India, 65,776 **145** E7
Bhāg, Pak., 4,316 **144** C3
Bhagalpur, India, 143,850 **145** H4
Bhagirathi, r., India **144** b10
Bhakkar, Pak., 21,749 **145** D3
Bhakra Dam, India **145** E3
Bhalgarh L., India **145** h17
Bhalki, India, 9,254 **145** E6
Bhamo, Burma, 9,817 **146** B1
Bhandara, India, 27,710 **145** F5
Bhander, India, 6,638 **144** b13
Bhanpura, India, 9,098 **144** a13
Bharatpur, India, 49,776 **145** E4
Bhatapara, India, 16,930 **144** c15
Bhatinda, India, 52,253 **145** E3
Bhatkal, India, 15,070 **145** E7
Bhatpara, India, 147,630 **145** H5
Bhavnagar, India, 171,039 **145** D5
Bhera, Pak., 17,992 **145** D2
Bheri, r., Nepal **144** d11
Bhikangaon, India, 4,350 **144** a15
Bhikna Thori, Nepal **144** e12
Bhilai, India, 86,116 **145** F5
Bhilwara, India, 43,499 **145** E4
Bhima, r., India **145** E6
Bhimavaram, India, 43,821 **145** F6
Bhind, India, 28,208 **145** F4
Bhinga, India, 8,979 **144** c12
Bhinmal, India, 11,832 **145** D4
Bhiwandi, India, 47,630 **145** D6
Bhiwani, India, 58,194 **145** E3
Bhojpur, Nepal **144** f12
Bhopal, India, 185,374 **145** E5
Bhor, India, 8,627 **145** h17
Bhubaneswar, India, 38,211 **145** H5
Bhuj, India, 38,953 **144** C5
Bhusawal, India, 73,994 **145** E5
Bhutan, ctry., 750,000* **145** H4
Bia, Phou, Laos **146** C3
Bia, r., Af. **162** b8
Biache-St-Vaast, Fr., 3,525 **116** a7
Biáfara, P.R. **96** s10
Biafra, Bight of, Af. **162** F5
Biak, P., Indon. **149** K3
Biała, Pol., 2,580 **127** g6
Biała, r., Pol. **127** D4
Biała Pista, Pol., 2,626 **127** E2
Biała Podlaska, Pol., 20,000* **127** E2
Biała Rawska, Pol., 2,032 **127** D3
Białława, Pol. **127** f5
Białobrzegi, Pol., 2,945 **127** D3
Białogard, Pol., 17,701 **127** B1
Białowieża, Pol. **127** F2
Biały Bór, Pol., 1,459 **127** B2
Białystok, Pol., 121,000* **127** E2
Bian, r., Indon. **149** L4
Biancavilla, It., 19,891 **123** E6
Biandora, r., Indon. **149** L3
Biaora, India, 10,133 **144** a14
Biaro, P., Indon. **149** H2
Biarritz, Fr., 25,514 **117** C5
Biasca, Switz., 3,349 **124** D2
Biau, Indon. **149** G2
Bibai, Jap., 87,345 **155** J8
Bibb, co., Ala., 14,357 **64** B2
Bibb, co., Ga., 141,249 **64** F3
Bibb City, Ga., 1,213 **64** E3

Bibbiano—Blagoveshchensk · 201

Bibbiano, It., 5,816 122 d6
Biberach, F.R.Ger., 18,216 118 B4
Biberach, F.R.Ger., 1,889 119 G6
Biberist, Switz., 7,188 124 B1
Bibiani, Ghana, 12,337 162 D4
Bibis, Indon. 148 d8
Bible Grove, Ill. 68 D5
Bible Hill, N.S., Can., 2,415 47 U11
Biblián, Ec., 1,825 104 c11
Biblis, F.R.Ger., 4,884 119 E5
Bibury, U.K. 114 E7
Bic, Qué., Can., 1,169 47 R9
Bicade, Fr. Guiana 101 O6
Bicas, Braz., 7,469 103 e17
Bicaz, Rum. 128 F1
Bicazu Ardelean, Rum. 128 E1
Bicester, U.K., 5,521 113 F6
Biche, L. la, Alta., Can. 42 K2
Bicheno, Austl. 173 g13
Bichiş, Rum. 128 E1
Bichura, U.S.S.R. 135 K4
Bicker, U.K. 114 H5
Bickerton I., Austl. 172 E1
Bickleton, Wash. 80 C3
Bickley, U.K. 114 C4
Bickmore, W. Va. 62 C4
Bicknell, Ind., 3,878 70 B4
Bicknell, Utah, 366 78 C2
Bîcleşu, Rum. 128 D2
Bicton, U.K. 114 C5
Bida, Nigeria 162 F4
Bidar, India, 32,420 145 E6
Bidasoa, r., Sp. 122 o11
Biddeford, Me., 19,255 55 B5
Biddulph, U.K., 14,060 114 D4
Bideford, U.K., 10,498 113 D6
Bidford, U.K., 2,136 114 E6
Bidon V, Alg. 160 E4
Bidor, Malay., 8,195 147 o14
Bidutgale, Burma 147 a2
Bie, Swed. 120 d8
Bieber, F.R.Ger., 1,711 119 G4
Bieber, Calif. 82 C2
Biebesheim, F.R.Ger., 4,531 119 F5
Biebrza, r., Pol. 127 E2
Biecz, Pol., 3,950 127 D4
Biedenkopf, F.R.Ger., 6,504 118 B3
Biederitz, Ger.D.R. 118 C2
Biei, Jap., 21,718 155 K8
Biel, Switz., 59,216 124 B1
Bielawa, Pol., 28,000* 127 B3
Bielefeld, F.R.Ger., 171,760 118 B2
Biele Karpaty, mts., Czech. 126 C2
Bielersee, Switz. 125 ·
Biella, It., 47,423 123 A2
Bielsko Biała, Pol., 76,000* 127 C4
Bielsk Podlaski, Pol., 9,575 127 E2
Biemenhorst, F.R.Ger., 2,068 119 B1
Bienfait, Sask., Can. 43 D5
Bien Hoa, S. Viet., 24,644 147 m11
Bienville, parish, La., 16,726 73 B5
Bienville, La., 305 73 B5
Bienville, L., Qué., Can. 44 K3
Bière, Switz., 1,166 124 A2
Biersted, Den., 1,746 121 B3
Bierun Stary, Pol., 5,145 127 C3
Bierutów, Pol., 3,887 127 B3
Biesal, Pol. 127 D2
Biesbosch, fenland, Neth. 115 b7
Biescas, Sp., 1,079 122 E1
Biesen-Berg, F.R.Ger. 119 D6
Biesme, Belg., 1,663 115 C4
Bietigheim, F.R.Ger., 4,035 119 E7
Bietigheim, F.R.Ger., 14,009 119 G7
Bietschhorn, mtn., Switz. 124 B2
Bièvre, Belg. 115 D5
Bièvres, Fr., 2,824 116 g11
Biferno, r., It. 123 E4
Bifuka, Jap., 14,046 155 K7
Big, r., Newf., Can. 45 P3
Big, r., Alaska 85 F3
Big, r., Mo. 72 G6
Biga, Turk., 10,831 142 A1
Big Baldy, mtn., Idaho 81 B3
Big Bar, Calif. 82 B2
Big Bar Creek, Br. Col., Can. 42 G3
Big Basin, Calif. 83 e13
Big Bay, Mich. 66 F2
Big Bay De Noc, Mich. 67 G3
Big Bay Pt., Mich. 66 F2
Big Bear City, Calif. 82 E5
Big Bear Cr., Tex. 76 e9
Big Bear Lake, Calif., 1,562 82 E5
Big Bell, Austl. 172 B4
Big Belt Mts., Mont. 81 D2
Big Bend, Shasta Co., Calif. 82 B2
Big Bend, Sonoma Co., Calif. 83 e11
Big Bend, La. 73 D6
Big Bend, Wis., 797 66 c12
Big Bend Nat. Pk., Tex. 77 M5
Big Black, r., Me. 55 C2
Big Black, r., Miss. 73 E5
Big Black Cr., Va. 62 E4
Big Black Mtn., Ky. 71 J5
Big Blue, r., Ind. 70 D3
Big Blue, r., Nebr. 75 J3
Big Bow, Kans. 75 D6
Bigbury Bay, U.K. 113 D6
Big Bushkill Cr., Pa. 61 M3
Big Cabin, Okla., 228 76 H1
Big Cane, La. 73 D7
Big Canyon, Nev. 83 A2
Big Cedar, Okla. 76 J3
Big Cedar L., Wis. 66 E5
Big Chino Wash, Ariz. 78 B4
Big Clifty, Ky. 71 E4
Big Creek, Br. Col., Can. 42 F3
Big Creek, Calif. 82 D4
Big Creek, Idaho 81 B3
Big Creek, Miss., 100 73 F4
Big Cr., Mo. 68 A5
Big Cr., Ohio 70 e9
Big Cypress Swamp, Fla. 65 H6
Big Darby Cr., Ohio 70 a6
Big Delta, Alaska 85 H2
Big Dry Cr., Mont. 81 F2
Big Eau Pleine Res., Wis. 66 D4
Big Eddy Settlement, Man., Can. 43 E4
Bigej, i., Kwajalein 176 25
Bigej Chan., Kwajalein 176 25
Big Elk Cr., Pa. 61 L6
Bigelow, Ark., 231 73 C2
Bigelow, Me. 55 B3
Bigelow, Mo., 100 72 B4
Bigelow Bk., Conn. 56 H5
Bigelow Mtn., Me. 55 B3
Big Falls, Minn., 526 74 E1
Big Falls, Wis., 119 66 D4
Big Falls, Vt. 54 C2
Big Flat, Ark., 217 73 C1
Big Flat Brook, N.J. 61 B1
Big Foot Pass, S. Dak. 74 B4
Bigfork, Minn., 464 74 F2
Bigfork, Mont. 81 C1
Big Fork, r., Minn. 74 F1
Biggar, Sask., Can., 2,662 43 C4
Biggar, U.K., 1,403 112 d8
Bigge, r., F.R.Ger. 119 D2
Biggerann, i., Kwajalein 176 25
Biggleswade, U.K., 8,050 113 F5
Big Graham Cr., Ind. 70 D4
Biggs, Calif., 831 82 C3
Biggsville, Ill., 345 68 B3
Big Hatchet Pk., N. Mex. 79 A6
Big Hay L., Alta., Can. 43 b7
Big Hole, r., Mont. 81 C3
Big Hole Battlefield Nat. Mon., Mont. 81 C3
Bighole Butte, Colo. 79 B1
Big Horn, co., Mont., 10,007 81 F3
Bighorn, Mont. 81 F2
Big Horn, co., Wyo., 11,898 81 F3
Bighorn, r., Mont.-Wyo. 81 E3
Bighorn Basin, U.S. 50 E2
Bighorn Mts., Wyo. 81 F3
Bigi, i., Kwajalein 176 25
Big Indian, N.Y. 59 L7
Big Indian Cr., Ga. 64 F3
Big Indian L., Me. 55 C4
Big Island, Va. 62 E5
Big I., N.W.T., Can. 41 P5
Big I., Ont., Can. 74 E1
Big Koniuji I., Alaska 85 E5
Big Lake, Alaska 85 c7
Big Lake, Alaska, 74 85 G2
Big Lake, Minn., 610 74 F3
Big Lake, Tex., 2,668 77 N4
Big L., Alta., Can. 43 b7
Big L., Me. 55 E3
Biglerville, Pa., 923 60 H6
Big Lost, r., Idaho 81 C4
Big Machias L., Me. 55 D2
Big Monon Cr., Ind. 68 E3
Big Moose, N.Y. 59 K4
Big Muddy, r., Ill. 68 C6
Big Muddy Cr., Colo. 79 B1
Big Muddy L., Sask., Can. 43 C5
Big Muskego L., Wis. 66 c12
Big Nemaha, r., Nebr. 75 J3
Bignona, Sen., 5,432 162 B3
Big Oak Flat, Calif. 82 C4
Big Pine, Calif. 82 D4
Big Pine Cr., Ind. 68 E3
Big Pine Key, Fla. 65 g15
Big Pine Key, Fla. 65 g15
Big Pine L., Minn. 74 E2
Big Pine L., Wis. 66 C3
Big Pine Mtn., Calif. 82 D5
Big Pines, Calif. 83 i15
Big Piney, Wyo., 663 81 E4
Bigpoint, Miss. 73 G7
Big Pd., Mass. 56 D4
Big Rapids, Mich., 8,686 67 H5
Big Rib, r., Wis. 66 C3
Big River, Sask., Can. 43 C4
Big Rock, Tenn. 71 D5
Big Rock, Va. 62 B5
Big Round L., Wis. 66 A3
Big Run, Pa., 857 60 E4
Big Run, r., Ohio 70 a7
Big Sable, r., Mich. 67 G4
Big Sable Pt., Mich. 67 G4
Big Sage Res., Calif. 82 C2
Big Sallisaw Cr., Okla. 76 J2
Big Salmon Ra., Yukon, Can. 85 L3
Big Sand L., Man., Can. 43 E2
Big Sand L., Wis. 66 A3
Big Sandy, Mont., 954 81 D1
Big Sandy, Tenn., 492 71 C5
Big Sandy, Tex., 848 77 Q3
Big Sandy, r., Ariz. 78 B4
Big Sandy, r., Ky.-W. Va. 62 B4
Big Sandy, r., Tenn. 71 C6
Big Sandy Cr., Colo. 79 D2
Big Sandy Cr., Nebr. 75 H3
Big Sandy L., Sask., Can. 43 D3
Big Satilla Cr., Ga. 64 G4
Bigsby I., Ont., Can. 74 E1
Big Shiney Mtn., Pa. 61 L3
Big Sioux, r., Iowa-S. Dak. 74 D3
Big Snowy Mts., U.S. 50 E1
Big Spring, Tex., 31,230 77 N3
Big Springs, Nebr., 506 75 D2
Big Springs, W. Va. 62 C4
Big Star L., Mich. 67 H5
Big Stone, co., Minn., 8,954 74 D3
Bigstone, r., Man., Can. 43 G3
Big Stone City, S. Dak., 718 74 D3
Big Stone Cr., Alta., Can. 43 b7
Big Stone Gap, Va., 4,688 62 B6
Bigstone L., Man., Can. 43 G4
Big Stone L., S. Dak. 74 D3
Big Sur, Calif. 82 C4
Big Swamp, r., N.C. 63 F3
Big Thompson, r., Colo. 79 C1
Big Timber, Mont., 1,660 81 E3
Big Tree, N.Y. 58 k19
Big Trout L., Ont., Can. 44 E4
Big Valley, Alta., Can. 42 K3
Big Walnut Cr., Ohio 70 b7
Big Walnut Cr., Rocky Fk., Ohio 70 b6
Big Wells, Tex., 801 77 O5
Bigwood, Ont., Can. 46 D2
Big Wood Cay, Bah. Is. 95 b8
Big Wood L., Me. 55 B3
Bihać, Yug., 16,000* 125 B2
Bihar, st., India, 46,455,610 145 G4
Bihar, India, 78,581 145 G4
Biharamulo, Tanz. 164 E2
Biharea, Rum. 128 D1
Bihor, mtn., Rum. 128 D1
Bihoro, Jap., 26,207 155 L8
Biijiri, i., Eniwetok 176 28
Bijagós, Arquipélago dos, Port. Guin. 162 B4
Bijapur, India, 78,854 145 E6
Bījār, Iran, 9,090 143 D1
Bijauri, Nepal 144 d11
Bijawar, India, 7,079 145 F4
Bijeljina, Yug., 18,000* 125 D2
Bijelo Polje, Yug., 4,029 125 D3
Bijnor, India, 33,821 144 b11
Bijou Cr., Colo. 79 C2
Bijou Hills, S. Dak. 74 C4
Bikampur, India 145 D4
Bikaner, India, 150,634 145 D3
Bikar, atoll, Marsh. Is. 176 22
Bikeman I., Tarawa 175 15
Bikenibeu, Tarawa 175 15
Bikenubati, i., Tarawa 175 15
Bikin, U.S.S.R., 20,400 135 N5
Bikin, r., U.S.S.R. 135 N5
Bikini, atoll, Marsh. Is. 170 F4
Bikita, Rhod. 164 E5
Biklabito, N. Mex. 79 A3
Bikoro, D.R.Congo 164 C2
Bikramganj, India, 5,681 144 e13
Bílá, Czech. 126 D2
Bila, r., Indon. 147 o15
Bilas = Bilwascarma
Bilaspur, H.P., India, 7,424 144 a10
Bilaspur, M.P., India, 86,706 145 G5
Bilatu, Indon. 149 G2
Bilauktaung Ra., Burma-Thai. 146 B4
Bilauri, Nepal 145 F3
Bilbao, Sp., 297,942 122 D1
Bilbays, U.A.R. 161 i7
Bilby, Alta., Can. 43 a7
Bilciureşti, Rum. 128 E2
Bildudalur, Ice. 120 a6
Bileća, Yug. 125 D3
Bilecik, Turk., 7,535 142 B1
Biłgoraj, Pol., 7,004 127 E3
Bilhaur, India 144 c12
Bili, D.R.Congo 164 D1
Bilibino, U.S.S.R. 135 Q3
Bilimora, India, 24,941 145 D5
Bilin, Burma, 5,267 146 B3
Bílina, Czech., 10,428 126 A1
Bílinc, r., Czech. 126 c6
Biliran I., Phil. 153 C3
Bill, Wyo. 81 G4
Bille, r., F.R.Ger. 119 b8
Billeberga, Swed. 121 c7
Billee, i., Eniwetok 176 28
Billerbeck, F.R.Ger., 4,425 118 A2
Billère, Fr., 7,469 117 C5
Billerica, Mass., 17,867(T) 57 L2
Billericay, U.K., 17,246 114 J7
Billigheim, F.R.Ger., 1,267 119 G6
Billingham, U.K., 32,130 112 h10
Billinghay, U.K., 1,634 114 H4
Billings, Mo., 602 72 D7
Billings, Mont., 52,851 81 E3
Billings, co., N. Dak., 1,513 74 A2
Billings, Okla., 510 76 F1
Billingsa, M., U.S.S.R. 135 R3
Billingsley, Ala., 179 64 C3
Billington Sea, l., Mass. 57 O5
Billiton = Belitung
Billmore, Mo. 72 F8
Bill of Portland, pt., U.K. 113 E6
Billom, Fr., 3,774 117 E4
Billund, Den. 121 B5
Bill Williams, r., Ariz. 78 B4
Bilma, Niger, 1,304 162 G2
Biloela, Austl., 1,399 173 G3
Bilo G., Yug. 125 C2
Bílovec, Czech. 127 h7
Biloxi, Miss., 44,053 73 G7
Bilthoven, Neth., 11,400 115 c6
Biltine, Chad 163 H3
Bilton, U.K., 6,619 114 F6
Bilugyun I., Burma 146 B3
Bilwascarma, Nic. 94 F3
Bilzen, Belg., 6,077 115 D4
Bima, Indon. 149 F5
Bimbéréké, Dahom., 2,543 162 E4
Bimberi Pk., Austl. 173 g10
Bimbila, Ghana 162 d7
Bimini Is., Bah. Is. 95 C1
Bina, India, 27,476 145 F4
Bina, Sol. Is. 175 c2
Binaija, G., Indon. 149 J3
Binalbagan, Phil., 13,545 153 B3
Binalonan, Phil., 4,227 153 b6
Binalong, Austl. 173 g10
Binangonan, Phil., 6,932 153 c8
Binasco, It., 3,970 122 c5
Binatang, Malay., 2,536 148 D2
Binbrook, Ont., Can. 46 c15
Binbrook, U.K. 114 H4
Binche, Belg., 10,273 115 C4
Bindjai, Indon., 45,235 148 A2
Bindjai, Indon. 148 D2
Bindki, India, 14,434 144 c12
Bindloss, Alta., Can. 42 L4
Bindslev, Den. 121 C3
Binéfar, Sp., 5,529 122 F2
Binford, N. Dak., 261 74 C2
Binga, Phil. 153 A3
Bingara, Austl., 1,465 173 G4
Bingen, F.R.Ger., 18,048 118 A4
Bingen, Pa. 61 k18
Bingen, Wash., 636 80 C3
Binger, Okla., 603 76 E2
Bingerville, Iv. Coast, 2,500 162 b9
Bingham, U.K., 2,457 114 G5
Bingham, co., Idaho, 28,218 81 C4
Bingham, Me., 1,180 55 C3
Bingham, Mich. 67 H4
Bingham, Nebr. 75 C1
Bingham, N. Mex. 79 B5
Bingham Canyon, Utah, 1,516 78 b9
Bingham Lake, Minn., 254 74 E4
Binghamton, N.Y., 75,941 59 J7
Binghamville, Vt. 54 B2
Bingkor, Malay. 148 F1
Bingley, U.K., 22,308 114 E3
Bingöl, Turk., 8,517 142 E2
Bingöl Dağları, Turk. 142 E2
Binh Chanh, S. Viet., 3,898 147 m11
Binh Dai, S. Viet., 16,829 147 m11
Binh Lam, S. Viet. 147 m11
Binh Minh, S. Viet., 7,399 147 k11
Binh Nhon, S. Viet. 147 n11
Binh Phuoc, S. Viet., 1,199 147 m11
Binh Son, S. Viet., 3,484 146 E4
Binnaway, Austl. 173 G4
Binningen, Switz., 11,765 124 B1
Bin Qirdān, Tun., 2,138 161 F2
Binscarth, Man., Can. 43 E5
Binsfeld, F.R.Ger., 1,093 119 B5
Bintan, P., Indon. 148 C2
Bintauna, Indon. 149 G2
Bint Jubayl, Leb., 5,831 142 b6
Bintuhan, Indon. 148 B4
Bintulu, Malay., 5,307 148 E2
Binz, Ger.D.R. 118 D1
Bio-Bio, r., Chile 104 e17
Bioč, mt., Yug. 125 D3
Biograd, Yug., 2,115 125 B3
Biola, Calif. 82 C4
Biörnöya, i., Nor. 108 O2
Biot, Fr., 2,648 116 n13
Bippus, Ind. 70 D2
Bir, India, 33,066 145 E6
Birab, Indon. 149 L4
Bi'r al Ghuzayl, Libya 161 F3
Bi'r al Ḩukayyim, Libya 161 H2
Bi'r 'Allāq, Libya 161 G2
Bi'r al Wa'r, Libya 161 G4
Birao, C.A.R., 8,006 163 H4
Birātnagar, Nepal, 33,293 145 H4
Bîrca, Rum. 128 D3
Birch, r., Alta., Can. 42 K1
Birch Bay, Wash. 80 B1
Birch Cr., Alaska 85 H2
Birchdale, Minn. 74 E1
Birches, Alaska 85 F2
Birches Hill, Jam. 96 o8
Birch Hills, Sask., Can. 43 C4
Birchiş, Rum. 128 D2
Birch Island, Ont., Can. 46 C2
Birch I., Man., Can. 43 E4
Birch L., Ont., Can. 44 D4
Birch L., Minn. 74 G2
Birch L., Wis. 66 E3
Birchleaf, Va. 62 B5
Birch Mts., Alta., Can. 42 K1
Birch River, Man., Can. 43 E4
Birch River, W. Va. 62 D4
Birch Run, Mich., 844 67 K5
Birch Str., Me. 55 D3
Birch Tree, Mo., 420 72 F8
Birchwood, Alaska, 534 85 c7
Birchwood, Minn., 598 74 d5
Birchwood, Wis., 433 66 B3
Bircza, Pol. 127 E4
Bird, Man., Can. 43 G3
Bird City, Kans., 678 75 D4
Bird Cr., Okla. 76 G1
Birdham, U.K., 1,198 113 m13
Bird Island, Minn., 1,384 74 E3
Bird I., Seych. 165 a10
Bird River, Man., Can. 43 G5
Birds, Ill., 235 68 E5
Birdsboro, Pa., 3,025 61 L5
Bird Settlement, Alaska, 25 85 c7
Birdseye, Ind., 366 70 C4
Birds Landing, Calif. 83 f11
Birdsville, Austl. 172 E3
Birdwood, Austl. 172 c8
Birecik, Turk., 13,123 142 D2
Bir el Ksaïb, Mali 162 D2
Bir Enzaran, Sp. Sah. 160 B4
Bireuen, Indon. 148 A1
Bi'r Fu'ād, Libya 161 J2
Bir Ganduz, Sp. Sah. 160 B4
Bīrganj, Nepal, 10,759 145 G4
Birgden, F.R.Ger., 2,072 119 A2
Birhan, pk., Eth. 163 L4
Birigui, Braz., 18,721 103 F6
Bīrjand, Iran, 13,934 143 F2
Birkeland, Nor. 121 A2
Birken, Br. Col., Can. 42 G4
Birkenau, F.R.Ger., 4,231 119 F5
Birkenes, Nor. 121 A2
Birkenfeld, Bad.-Württ., F.R.Ger., 5,422 119 F7
Birkenfeld, Rhein.-Pfalz, F.R.Ger., 4,765 118 A4
Birkenfeld, Oreg. 80 B3
Birkenhead, U.K., 141,683 113 E5
Birkenwerder, Ger.D.R. 119 e10
Birkerød, Den., 14,846 121 a7
Birkesdorf, F.R.Ger., 6,453 119 A3
Birkfeld, Aus., 1,563 124 M6
Birlad, Rum., 32,040 128 F1
Bîrlad, r., Rum. 128 F2
Birmingham, U.K., 1,105,651 113 F5
Birmingham, Ala., 340,887 64 B2
Birmingham, Ill. 68 B3
Birmingham, Iowa, 441 72 F4
Birmingham, Mich., 25,525 67 e14
Birmingham, Mo., 201 75 b7
Birmingham, Pa., 136 60 F4
Bir Moghreïn, Maur. 160 C3
Birnamwood, Wis., 568 66 D4
Birney, Mont. 81 F3
Birnie, atoll, Phoenix Is. 175 8
Birnin Kebbi, Nigeria 162 E3
Birni-N'Konni, Niger, 6,793 162 E3
Bîrnova, Rum. 128 F1
Birns Water, r., U.K. 112 e8
Birobidzhan, U.S.S.R., 41,000 135 N5
Biron, Wis., 726 66 D4
Bir Ounane, Mali 162 D2
Birpur, India, 8,061 144 f12
Birr, Ire., 3,322 113 C5
Bir-Rabalou, Alg., 1,423 160 c5
Birresborn, F.R.Ger., 1,422 119 B4
Birsfelden, Switz., 10,068 124 B1
Birsk, U.S.S.R., 28,000 137 h8
Birstall, Leics., Eng., U.K., 10,145 114 F5
Birstall, York., Eng., U.K., 6,702 114 E3
Birstein, F.R.Ger., 1,755 119 G4
Birtle, Man., Can. 43 E5
Birtley, U.K., 12,232 112 g10
Birufu, Indon. 149 L4
Biryuchiy, O., U.S.S.R. 136 D4
Biryusa, r., U.S.S.R. 135 J4
Bîrza, Rum. 128 D3
Biržai, U.S.S.R., 8,400 136 B1
Birzebbugia, Malta, 5,297 123 f12
Bisa, P., Indon. 149 H3
Bisalpur, India, 15,530 144 b11
Bisbee, Ariz., 9,914 78 D6
Bisbee, N. Dak., 388 74 C1
Biscay, Bay of, Fr.-Sp. 110 C4
Biscay Bay, Newf., Can. 45 b11
Biscayne, Key, Fla. 65 b10
Biscayne Bay, Fla. 65 b10
Biscayne Cr., Fla. 65 a10
Biscayne Park, Fla., 2,911 65 b10
Biscay Plain, Atl. Oc. 108 M3
Bisceglie, It., 41,966 123 F4
Bischheim, Fr., 12,400 116 e9
Bischmisheim, F.R.Ger., 5,474 116 d8
Bischofsgrün, F.R.Ger., 2,143 126 a6
Bischofshofen, Aust., 8,286 124 K6
Bischofstetten, Aust. 124 b10
Bischofswerda, Ger.D.R., 11,304 118 E3
Bischofszell, Switz., 3,811 124 D1
Bischwiller, Fr., 8,482 117 G2
Biscoe, Ark. 73 D3
Biscoe, N.C., 1,053 63 E2
Biscotasing, Ont., Can. 44 G6
Bisert', U.S.S.R. 137 i8
Biševo, i., Yug. 125 B3
Bīshah, Wādī, Saudi Ar. 143 C4
Bishnupur, India, 30,958 145 H5
Bishop, Calif., 2,875 82 D4
Bishop, Ga., 214 64 F2
Bishop, Tex., 3,722 77 P6
Bishop and Clerk Is., Austl. 170 E8
Bishop Auckland, U.K., 35,276 113 F4
Bishopbriggs, U.K. 112 b8
Bishop Hill, Ill., 164 68 B2
Bishop Norton, U.K. 114 H4
Bishops Cannings, U.K., 1,067 114 E8
Bishop's Castle, U.K., 1,228 113 E5
Bishop's Cleeve, U.K., 4,244 114 D7
Bishop's Falls, Newf., Can., 4,099 45 Q5
Bishops Frome, U.K. 114 C6
Bishop's Lydeard, U.K., 3,099 113 E6
Bishop's Stortford, U.K., 18,342 113 G6
Bishopstone, U.K. 113 i12
Bishops Waltham, U.K., 3,171 113 k13
Bishopville, S.C., 3,586 63 D3
Bisianumu, Terr. Papua 174 e3
Bisignano, It., 9,242 123 F5
Biskintā, Leb., 3,776 142 b6
Biskra, Alg., 55,073 160 E2
Biskupice, Pol. 127 h5
Biskupice Oławskie, Pol. 127 g5
Biskupiec, Pol., 5,550 127 D2
Biskupin, Pol. 127 B2
Bislich, F.R.Ger., 2,501 119 B1
Bislig, Phil., 1,968 153 C3
Bismarck, Ga. 64 E3
Bismarck, Ill. 68 E3
Bismarck, Mo., 1,237 72 G7
Bismarck, N. Dak., 27,670 74 B2
Bismarck, W. Va. 62 E3
Bismarck Arch., Terr. New Guin. 170 D5
Bismarck Ra., Terr. New Guin. 174 e2
Bismarck Sea 170 D5
Bismark, Ger.D.R. 118 C2
Bismil, Turk., 3,308 142 E2
Bismona, Nic. 94 F3
Bison, Kans., 291 75 F5
Bison, Okla. 76 F1
Bison, S. Dak., 457 74 A3
Bison Mtn., Colo. 79 a9
Bissau, Port. Guin. 162 B4
Bissen, Lux., 1,024 119 A5
Bissett, Man., Can. 43 G4
Bissingen, F.R.Ger., 5,840 119 G7
Bistar, Yug. 125 F3
Bistcho L., Alta., Can. 42 H1
Bistineau, L., La. 73 B5
Bistra, r., Rum. 128 D2
Bistreţu, Rum. 128 D3
Bistricioara, Rum. 128 F1
Bistriţa, Rum., 20,292 128 E1
Bistriţa, r., Rum. 128 E1
Bistriţei, Munţii, Rum. 128 E1
Biswan, India, 15,125 144 c12
Bisztynek, Pol., 1,916 127 D1
Bitadton, Phil., 1,748 153 B3
Bitam, Gabon 164 A1
Bitburg, F.R.Ger., 6,918 118 A4
Bitche, Fr., 6,806 117 G2
Bitely, Mich. 67 H5
Bithlo, Fla., 168 65 H4
Bitlis, Turk., 16,552 142 E2
Bitola, Yug., 49,000* 125 E4
Bitonto, It., 37,653 123 F4
Bitter Creek, Wyo. 81 E5
Bitterfeld, Ger.D.R., 31,687 118 D3
Bitterfontein, S. Af. 164 B7
Bitter L., S. Dak. 74 D3
Bitterley, U.K. 114 C6
Bittern Lake, Alta., Can. 43 c8
Bittern L., Alta., Can. 43 c7
Bitterroot Ra., Idaho-Mont. 81 B2
Bitterwater, Calif. 82 C4
Bitti, It., 6,206 123 B4
Bitumount, Alta., Can. 42 K1
Bitung, Indon. 149 H2
Bityug, r., U.S.S.R. 136 F3
Biu, Nigeria 162 G4
Bivalve, N.J. 61 A5
Bivolari, Rum. 128 F1
Biwabik, Minn., 1,836 74 F2
Biwa-ko, Jap. 155 E4
Bixby, Mo. 72 F7
Bixby, Okla., 1,711 76 H2
Biya, r., U.S.S.R. 134 H4
Biysk, U.S.S.R., 162,000 134 H4
Bizerte = Banzart
Bizhbulyak, U.S.S.R. 137 h9
Bjärred, Swed. 121 c7
Bjelovar, Yug., 13,000* 125 C2
Bjerringbro, Den., 5,554 121 B4
Björkfjället, mt., Swed. 120 D2
Björknäs, Swed. 120 f8
Björkvik, Swed. 120 d9
Björna, Swed. 120 D3
Björneborg = Pori
Björnlunda, Swed. 120 e8
Bjurholm, Swed. 120 D3
Blaasveld, Belg., 2,739 115 d8
Blabon, N. Dak. 74 D2
Blaby, U.K., 4,242 114 F5
Blace, Yug., 2,181 125 E3
Blachly, Oreg. 80 B3
Blachownia, Pol. 127 h6
Black, Ala., 133 64 D4
Black = Da
Black = Li-hsien
Black, r., Jam. 96 p8
Black, r., Alaska 85 J2
Black, r., Ariz. 78 D5
Black, r., Ark.-Mo. 73 D2
Black, r., La. 73 D6
Black, r., Mich. 66 C2
Black, r., Mich. 67 J3
Black, r., Mich. 67 L5
Black, r., Mo. 72 G7
Black, r., N.Y. 59 J3
Black, r., N.C. 63 F3
Black, r., Ohio 70 c9
Black, r., S.C. 63 E4
Black, r., Vt. 54 B5
Black, r., Vt. 54 C2
Black, r., Wash. 81 a8
Black, r., Wis. 66 C3
Blackall, Austl., 1,885 173 F3
Black Bear Cr., Okla. 76 F1
Blackbeard I., Ga. 64 H4
Black Belt, U.S. 51 J4
Blackberry, r., Conn. 56 C4
Black Birch L., Sask., Can. 43 C3
Black Bk., Me. 55 C3
Blackburn, Eng., U.K., 106,114 113 E5
Blackburn, Scot., U.K. 112 c8
Blackburn, Ark. 73 A2
Blackburn, Mo., 310 72 D5
Blackburn, Okla., 129 76 G1
Blackburn, Mt., Alaska 85 J3
Blackburn Village (part of Ashburnham), Mass. 56 J2
Black Butte, Oreg. 80 B4
Black Butte, N. Dak. 81 H2
Black Canyon City, Ariz. 78 B4
Black Canyon of the Gunnison Nat. Mon., Colo. 79 B2
Black Combe, mtn., U.K. 114 B2
Black Creek, N.Y. 58 D7
Black Creek, N.C., 310 63 G2
Black Creek, Wis., 707 66 E4
Black Cr., Ariz. 78 D4
Black Cr., Miss. 73 F6
Black Cr., N.Y. 58 n20
Black Cr., S.C. 63 E3
Black Cr., Vt. 54 B2
Black Diablo Mine, Nev. 83 B2
Black Diamond, Alta., Can., 1,022 42 J4
Black Diamond, Wash., 1,026 80 C2
Blackduck, Minn., 765 74 E2
Black Duck, r., Ont., Can. 44 E3
Black Earth, Wis., 784 66 D5
Blackey, Va. 62 B5
Blackfield, U.K. 113 k13
Blackfoot, Idaho, 7,378 81 C4
Blackfoot River Res., Idaho 81 D4
Blackford, U.K. 112 c7
Blackford, co., Ind., 14,792 70 D2
Black Forest, Colo. 79 C2
Black Forest = Schwarzwald
Blackfork, Ohio 70 G4
Black Hall (part of Old Lyme), Conn. 56 G7
Black Hawk, Colo., 171 79 b8
Blackhawk, Ind. 70 D3
Black Hawk, co., Iowa, 122,482 72 E2
Black Hawk, S. Dak. 74 A3
Black Hawk, Wis. 66 C5
Blackhawk Beach, Ind. 69 f10
Blackhead, Newf., Can. 45 c10
Black Head, Ire. 113 B5
Blackheath, Ont., Can. 46 c15
Black Hills, S. Dak. 74 A3
Blackie, Alta., Can. 42 K4
Blackinton (part of N. Adams), Mass. 56 D2
Black Jack, Mo. 72 b10
Black Lake, Qué., Can., 4,115 45 L6
Black Lake, N. Mex. 79 C3
Black L., Sask., Can. 43 C2
Black L., La. 73 B6
Black L., Mich. 67 J3
Black L., N.Y. 59 J3
Black L., Wash. 81 a8
Blackledge, r., Conn. 56 G6
Blacklick, Ohio 70 b6
Black Lick, Pa. 60 D5
Blacklick Cr., Ohio 70 b7
Blacklick Cr., Pa. 60 D5
Blacklog Cr., Pa. 60 G5
Black Mesa, Ariz. 78 C3
Black Mesa, Okla. 76 A1
Black Mountain, N.C., 1,313 63 B2
Black Mtn., U.K. 114 B6
Black Mtn., Me. 55 B4
Black Mtn., N. Mex. 79 A5
Black Mtn., N.Y. 59 O4
Black Mts., N.B., Can. 47 S10
Black Mts., U.K. 113 E6
Black Mts., Ariz. 78 A4
Black Mts., Tex. 77 L4
Blackness, U.K. 112 d7
Black Oak, Ind. 69 e10
Black Pk., N. Mex. 79 A5
Black Point, Calif. 83 d11
Black Point (part of E. Lyme), Conn. 56 H7
Black Pt., St. Vinc. 97 19
Black Pd., Me. 55 C2
Blackpool, U.K., 152,133 113 E5
Black Prairie, U.S. 50 G4
Black Ra., N. Mex. 79 B5
Black River, Jam., 3,077 96 p8
Black River, Mich. 67 K4
Black River, N.Y., 1,237 59 J3
Black River Bay, Jam. 96 p8
Black River Falls, Wis., 3,195 66 C4
Black River Pond, Newf., Can. 45 a9
Black River Village, N. Mex. 79 C5
Black Rock, Ark., 554 73 D1
Black Rock, Utah 78 B2
Black Rock Des., Nev. 83 A2
Black Rock Des., Utah 78 B2
Black Rock Pt., Newf., Can. 45 N1
Black Rock Ra., Nev. 83 A2
Blackrod, U.K., 3,609 114 C3
Blacksburg, S.C., 2,174 63 C2
Blacksburg, Va., 7,070 62 D5
Black Sea, Eur.-U.S.S.R. 111 G4
Blacks Harbour, N.B., Can., 1,546 47 S11
Blackshear, Ga., 2,482 64 G4
Blacksher, Ala. 64 B4
Blacksod Bay, Ire. 113 A4
Black Springs, Ark. 73 B3
Black Springs, N. Mex. 79 A5
Blackstairs Mts., Ire. 113 C5
Blackstock, Ont., Can. 46 F4
Blackstock, S.C. 63 C3
Blackstone, Mass., 5,130(T) 57 K4
Blackstone, Va., 3,659 62 G5
Blackstone, r., Mass. 57 K4
Black Str., Me. 55 C4
Blacksville, W. Va., 211 62 D3
Black Top Mtn., N. Mex. 79 B5
Blacktown, Austl., 25,417 173 G5
Blackville, N.B., Can. 47 S10
Blackville, S.C., 1,901 63 C4
Black Volta, r., Ghana-Upper Volta 162 D4
Black Walnut, Mo. 72 a10
Black Warrior, r., Ala. 64 B2
Blackwater, Mo., 284 72 E6
Blackwater, Va. 62 A6
Blackwater, r., Ire. 113 B5
Blackwater, r., U.K. 113 G6
Blackwater, r., Fla. 65 C2
Blackwater, r., Mo. 72 D6
Blackwater, r., N.H. 54 D5
Blackwater, r., Va. 62 E5
Blackwater, r., Va. 62 G5
Blackwater Cr., Fla. 65 d11
Blackwater L., N.W.T., Can. 40 E5
Blackwell, Okla., 9,588 76 F1
Blackwell, Tex., 314 77 N3
Blackwell Bk., Conn. 56 H5
Blackwood, U.K. 113 c8
Blackwood, N.J., 3,100* 61 A4
Bladel, Neth., 3,800 115 D3
Bladen, Nebr., 322 75 G3
Bladen, co., N.C., 28,881 63 F3
Bladen, Ohio 70 G4
Bladenboro, N.C., 774 63 F3
Bladensburg, Md., 3,103 62 b9
Bladensburg, Ohio 70 G2
Blades, Del., 729 62 J4
Bladon Springs, Ala. 64 A4
Blaenavon, U.K., 8,451 114 B7
Blagaj, Yug. 125 C3
Blagnac, Fr., 5,450 117 D5
Blagodarnoye, U.S.S.R. 136 F4
Blagodatnoye, U.S.S.R. 137 o12
Blagoevgrad, Bulg., 21,833 128 D3
Blagoveshchensk, U.S.S.R., 12,500 137 h8
Blagoveshchensk, U.S.S.R., 99,000 135 M4

202 · Blagoveshchenskiy Proliv—Bondhead

Blagoveshchenskiy Proliv, U.S.S.R. **133** O2
Blain, Fr., 6,650 **117** C3
Blain, Pa., 336 **60** H5
Blaine, co., Idaho, 4,598 **81** B4
Blaine, Ind. **70** D2
Blaine, Kans. **75** J4
Blaine, Ky. **71** J3
Blaine, Me. **55** E2
Blaine, Minn., 15,544 **74** F3
Blaine, co., Mont., 8,091 **81** E1
Blaine, co., Nebr., 1,016 **75** E2
Blaine, co., Okla., 12,077 **76** E2
Blaine, Oreg. **80** B3
Blaine, Wash., 1,735 **80** B1
Blaine Lake, Sask., Can. **43** C4
Blainville-sur-l'Eau, Fr., 4,321 **116** b9
Blair, Ont., Can. **46** b14
Blair, Nebr., 4,931 **75** J2
Blair, Okla., 893 **76** D3
Blair, co., Pa., 137,270 **60** F4
Blair, Wis., 909 **66** B4
Blair Athol, Austl. **173** G3
Blair Atholl, U.K. **112** E3
Blairgowrie, U.K., 5,168 **112** E3
Blairmore, Alta., Can., 1,938 **42** J4
Blairmore, U.K. **112** a7
Blairnairn, U.K. **112** a7
Blairs, Va. **62** E6
Blairsburg, Iowa, 287 **72** D2
Blairsden, Calif. **82** C3
Blairstown, Iowa, 583 **72** E3
Blairstown, Mo., 177 **72** C6
Blairstown, N.J., **61** B2
Blairsville, Ga., 437 **64** E1
Blairsville, Ind. **70** B4
Blairsville, Pa., 4,930 **60** D5
Blaisdell, N. Dak. **74** A1
Blaj, Rum., 8,731 **128** D1
Blakely, Ga., 5,190 **64** E4
Blakely, Pa., 6,374 **61** o16
Blakeney, U.K. **114** D7
Blake Plat., Atl. Oc. **108** G5
Blake Pt., Mich. **66** b8
Blake Ridge, Atl. Oc. **108** G4
Blakesburg, Iowa, 401 **72** E4
Blaketown, Newf., Can. **45** b10
Blalock, Oreg. **80** C3
Blâmont, Fr., 1,566 **116** c9
Blanc, C., Maur. **162** A2
Blanc, Mt., Fr.-It. **117** G4
Blanca, Colo., 233 **79** C3
Blanca, Sa., N. Mex. **79** B5
Blanca, Sa., Tex. **77** L4
Blancagrande, Arg. **105** a13
Blanca Pk., Colo. **79** C3
Blanchard, Iowa, 174 **72** B4
Blanchard, La. **73** B5
Blanchard, Me. **55** C3
Blanchard, Mich. **67** H5
Blanchard, Ohio **70** F2
Blanchard, Okla., 1,377 **76** F2
Blanchard, Wash. **80** B1
Blanchard, r., Ohio **70** F1
Blanchardville, Wis., 632 **66** D6
Blanche, L., Austl. **172** C3
Blanche, L., Austl. **172** E4
Blanche, Pt., St. Maarten **97** 7
Blanche Chan., Sol. Is. **175** b2
Blanchester, Ohio, 2,944 **70** F3
Blanchisseuse, Trin. and Tob. **96** g5
Blanco, N. Mex. **79** B3
Blanco, Okla. **76** H3
Blanco, co., Tex., 3,657 **77** O4
Blanco, Tex., 789 **77** O4
Blanco, r., Bol. **102** D5
Blanco, r., Peru **104** C3
Blanco, r., Tex. **77** O4
Blanco, C., C.R. **94** E6
Blanco, C., Peru **104** A3
Blanco, C., Oreg. **80** A4
Blanco, Mte., Bol. **102** b10
Blanco, Peñón, Ven. **101** b11
Blanco Cr., N. Mex.-Tex. **79** D4
Blanco Trading Post, N. Mex. **79** B3
Bland, Mo., 654 **72** F6
Bland, co., Va., 5,982 **62** C5
Bland, Va. **62** C5
Blandburg, Pa., **60** F4
Blandford, Mass. **56** E4
Blandford Forum, U.K., 3,566 **113** E6
Blanding, Utah, 1,805 **78** D3
Blandinsville, Ill., 853 **68** A3
Blandon, Pa., **61** h14
Blandy, Fr. **116** k12
Blanes, Sp., 9,492 **122** G2
Blane Water, r., U.K. **112** b7
Blaney Park, Mich. **67** H2
Blangkedjeren, Indon. **148** A1
Blangpidie, Indon. **148** A2
Blankenberge, Belg., 10,045 **115** A3
Blankenburg, Ger.D.R., 19,467 **118** C3
Blankenfelde, Ger.D.R. **119** e11
Blankenheim, F.R.Ger., 1,037 **119** B4
Blanket, Tex., 320 **77** O4
Blanquefort, Fr., 5,410 **117** C4
Blanquillo, Urug., 1000* **105** d11
Blansko, Czech., 9,390 **126** C2
Blantyre-Limbe, Malawi, 56,300* **164** E4
Blaricum, Neth., 6,200 **115** c6
Blarney, Ire. **113** B6
Blasdell, N.Y., 3,909 **58** C6
Błaszki, Pol., 2,856 **127** C3
Blatec, Yug., 3,241 **125** F4
Blatná, Czech. **126** B2
Blatnitsa, Bulg. **128** G3
Blatno, Czech. **126** c6
Blaubeuren, F.R.Ger., 7,503 **118** B4
Blåvands Huk, Den. **121** A5
Blavet, r., Fr. **116** B3
Blawnox, Pa., 2,085 **60** c8
Blaydon, U.K., 30,615 **113** F4
Blaye, Fr., 4,566 **117** C4
Blaye, Fr., 5,898 **117** E5
Blayney, Austl., 1,688 **173** g9
Blaze, Pt., Austl. **172** D1
Błażowa, Pol., 3,800 **127** E4
Bleaker I., Falk. Is. **108** 3
Bleaklow Hill, U.K. **114** E4
Bleckede, F.R.Ger., 3,780 **119** c9
Bleckley, co., Ga., 9,642 **64** F3
Bled, Yug. **125** A1
Blednaya, G., U.S.S.R. **134** F2
Bledsoe, co., Tenn., 7,811 **71** F6
Bledsoe, Tex. **77** M3
Bleecker, N.Y. **59** M5
Bleialf, F.R.Ger. **119** A4
Bleiberg, Aust., 3,954 **124** K7
Bleibuir, F.R.Ger., 1,496 **119** B3
Bleicherode, Ger.D.R. **118** C3
Bleidenstadt, F.R.Ger., 2,332 **119** E4
Bleiswijk, Neth., 3,000 **115** b6
Blencoe, Iowa, 286 **72** A3
Bléneau, Fr., 1,402 **117** E3
Blenheim, Ont., Can., 3,130 **44** G7
Blenheim, N.Z., 11,956 **175** g5
Blenheim, N.J., **60** f12
Blenheim, S.C., 185 **63** E3
Blenker, Wis. **66** D4
Blénod, Fr., 3,072 **116** b9
Blerick, Neth. **115** E3
Bleskensgraaf, Neth. **115** b7
Blessing, Tex. **77** P5
Bletchley, U.K., 17,095 **113** F6
Bletterans, Fr., 1,085 **117** F3
Bleu, L., Qué., Can. **46** F2
Bleue, Indon. **148** A1
Blevins, Ark., 198 **73** B4
Blewett Falls L., N.C. **63** E2
Blezard Valley, Ont., Can. **46** D2
Blicade, Fr. Guiana **101** N6
Blida, Alg., 73,618 **160** E1
Blies, r., F.R.Ger.-Fr. **116** d8
Blieskastel, F.R.Ger., 5,609 **116** d8
Bligh Water, Fiji **174** 4
Blind River, Ont., Can., 4,033 **44** G6
Blinisht, Alb. **125** E4
Blinkenthorpe Bay, Lord Howe I. **175** 12
Blinman, Austl. **172** E4
Bliss, Idaho, 91 **81** B4
Bliss, Mich. **67** J3
Bliss, N.Y. **58** D6
Blissfield, Mich., 2,653 **67** J7
Blissfield, Ohio **70** H2
Bliss Landing, Br. Col., Can. **42** a5
Blitar, Indon., 62,972 **148** E5
Blitchton, Ga. **64** H3
Blithe, r., U.K. **114** E5
Blitta, Togo **162** d7
Bliznak, Bulg. **128** F3
Bliznetsy, U.S.S.R. **136** e7
Blocher, Ind. **70** D4
Blocker, Okla. **76** H2
Blockhouse, Wash. **80** C3
Block Island (part of New Shoreham), R.I. **57** K8
Block I., R.I. **57** K8
Block I. Sd., R.I. **57** J8
Blockley, U.K., 2,395 **114** E6
Blockton, Iowa, 343 **72** C4
Blockville, N.Y. **58** A7
Blodgett, Miss. **73** G6
Blodgett, N.H., 1,489 **54** E5
Blodgett, Oreg. **80** B3
Blodgett Landing, N.H. **54** C5
Bloemendaal, Neth., 5,800 **115** C2
Bloemfontein, S. Af., 140,924 **164** D6
Blois, Fr., 36,426 **117** D3
Blokzijl, Neth. **115** E2
Blomberg, F.R.Ger., 6,907 **118** B3
Blönduós, Ice. **120** a6
Blongas, Indon. **148** F5
Błonie, Pol., 10,037 **127** D2
Bloodroot Mtn., Vt. **54** B4
Bloods Bk., N.H. **54** C4
Bloodvein, r., Man., Can. **43** G4
Bloody Bay, Lesser Caymans **97** 2
Bloody Foreland, Ire. **113** B4
Bloom, Kans. **75** F6
Bloomburg, Tex., 383 **77** R3
Bloom City, Wis. **66** C5
Bloomdale, Ohio, 669 **70** F1
Bloomer, Wis., 2,834 **66** B3
Bloomfield, Ont., Can. **46** G4
Bloomfield, Conn., 13,613(T) **56** E5
Bloomfield, Ill. **68** E4
Bloomfield, Ind., 2,224 **70** C3
Bloomfield, Iowa, 2,771 **72** E4
Bloomfield, Ky., 916 **71** F4
Bloomfield, Mo., 1,330 **72** G8
Bloomfield, Nebr., 1,349 **75** H1
Bloomfield, N.J., 51,867 **61** C2
Bloomfield, N. Mex., 1,292 **79** A3
Bloomfield, Ohio **70** H2
Bloomfield, Vt. **54** D2
Bloomfield, Wis. **66** E4
Bloomfield Hills, Mich., 2,378 **67** f14
Bloomingburg, N.Y., 303 **59** L8
Bloomingburg, Ohio, 719 **70** F3
Bloomingdale, Ont., Can. **46** b13
Bloomingdale, Ill., 1,262 **69** b9
Bloomingdale, Ind., 455 **70** B3
Bloomingdale, Mich., 471 **67** G6
Bloomingdale, N.J., 5,293 **58** b12
Bloomingdale, N.Y., 490 **59** M3
Blooming Glen, Pa., **60** f10
Blooming Grove, Tex., 725 **77** P3
Blooming Prairie, Minn., 1,778 **74** F4
Bloomington, Idaho, 254 **81** D4
Bloomington, Ill., 36,271 **68** D3
Bloomington, Ind., 31,357 **70** C3
Bloomington, Minn., 50,498 **74** b6
Bloomington, Nebr., 176 **75** F4
Bloomington, Tex., 1,756 **77** P5
Bloomington, Wis., 735 **66** C6
Blooming Valley, Pa., 296 **60** B2
Bloomsburg, Pa., 10,655 **61** K4
Bloomsbury, Austl. **173** G3
Bloomsbury, N.J., 838 **61** A2
Bloomville, N.Y. **59** L7
Bloomville, Ohio, 836 **70** F1
Blora, Indon. **148** D4
Blossburg, Pa., 1,956 **60** H2
Blossom, N.Y. **58** m19
Blossom, Tex., 545 **77** Q3
Blount, co., Ala., 25,449 **64** C1
Blount, co., Tenn., 57,525 **71** G6
Blountstown, Fla., 2,375 **65** D2
Blountsville, Ala., 672 **64** C1
Blountsville, Ind., 218 **70** D2
Blountville, Tenn. **71** J5
Blovstrød, Den., 2,182 **121** a7
Blowing Pt., Anguilla **97** 7
Blowing Rock, N.C., 711 **63** C1
Bloxham, U.K., 1,359 **113** F5
Bloxom, Va., 349 **62** J5
Blšanka, r., Czech. **126** c6
Blubber Bay, Br. Col., Can. **42** b6
Bludenz, Aust., 11,108 **124** F6
Bludov, Czech. **127** f7
Blue, Ariz. **78** D5
Blue, Okla. **76** G4
Blue, r., Ariz. **78** D5
Blue, r., Colo. **79** B2
Blue, r., Ind. **70** C4
Blue, r., Mo. **75** a8
Blue, r., Okla. **76** G3
Blue, Mt., Me. **55** B4
Blue, Mt., N.H. **54** D3
Blue Ash, Ohio, 8,341 **71** i10
Blue Bell, N.B., Can. **47** S10
Bluebell, Utah **78** C1
Blue Creek, Utah **78** b7
Blue Creek, W. Va. **62** C4
Blue Cr., Nebr. **75** C2
Blue Cypress L., Fla. **65** J5
Blue Diamond, Nev. **83** C4
Blue Earth, co., Minn., 44,385 **74** E3
Blue Earth, Minn., 4,200 **74** F4
Blue Earth, r., Minn. **74** E4
Bluefield, Va., 4,235 **62** C5
Bluefield, W. Va., 19,256 **62** C5
Bluefields, Jam. **96** p8
Bluefields, Nic., 10,844 **94** E5
Bluefields Bay, Jam. **96** o8
Blue Grass, Iowa, 568 **72** G3
Blue Grass, Va. **62** E4
Blue Grass Region, Ky. **51** K3
Blue Hill, Me. **55** D4
Blue Hill, Nebr., 723 **75** G3
Blue Hill Bay, Me. **55** D4
Blue Hill Falls, Me. **55** D4
Blue Hills (part of Bloomfield), Conn. **56** F5
Blue Island, Ill., 19,618 **68** E2
Blue Jacket, Okla., 245 **76** H1
Bluejoint L., Oreg. **80** D4
Blue Knob, mtn., Pa. **60** E5
Blue Lake, Calif., 1,234 **82** B2
Blue Mesa, Colo. **79** B2
Blue Mound, Ill., 1,038 **68** C4
Blue Mound, Tex., 1,253 **76** e9
Blue Mounds, Wis., 227 **66** D5
Blue Mountain, Ala., 446 **64** D2
Blue Mountain, Ark., 94 **73** B2
Blue Mountain, Colo. **79** A1
Blue Mountain, Miss., 741 **73** G3
Blue Mtn., India **145** J5
Blue Mtn., Ariz. **78** B4
Blue Mtn., Ark. **73** A3
Blue Mtn., Colo. **79** b7
Blue Mtn., N.Y. **59** M4
Blue Mtn., Pa. **60** G5
Blue Mountain Lake, N.Y. **59** M4
Blue Mtn. Pass, Oreg. **80** E4
Blue Mountain Peak, Jam. **96** q8
Blue Mts., Austl. **173** G5
Blue Mts., Jam. **96** q8
Blue Mts., Me. **55** B4
Blue Mts., Oreg.-Wash. **80** D3
Blue Mud Bay, Austl. **172** E1
Blue Nile = Abāy, Eth.
Blue Nile = Azraq, Ai Baḥral, Sudan
Blue Nose, mtn., Idaho **81** B3
Blue Point, N.Y. **58** g14
Blue Rapids, Kans., 1,426 **75** J4
Blue Ridge, Alta., Can. **42** J2
Blue Ridge, Ga., 1,406 **64** E1
Blue Ridge, Va. **62** E5
Blue Ridge, N.Y. **59** L4
Blue Ridge, N.Y. **59** N4
Blue Ridge, mtn. ra., U.S. **53** K3
Blue Ridge L., Ga. **64** E1
Blue Ridge Summit, Pa. **60** H6
Blue River, Br. Col., Can. **42** H3
Blue River, Oreg. **80** B3
Blue River, Wis., 356 **66** C5
Blue Rock, Ohio **70** H3
Bluesky, Alta., Can. **42** H2
Blue Springs, Ala., 94 **64** D4
Blue Springs, Mo., 2,555 **72** C5
Blue Springs, Nebr., 509 **75** J3
Blue Stack Mts., Ire. **113** B4
Bluestone Res., W. Va. **62** C5
Bluevale, Ont., Can. **46** C5
Bluewater, N. Mex. **79** A4
Bluff, N.Z., 3,042 **175** f7
Bluff, Ala. **64** B2
Bluff, Alaska **85** b6
Bluff, Okla. **76** H4
Bluff, Utah **78** D3
Bluff City, Ark. **73** B4
Bluff City, Ill. **68** B3
Bluff City, Kans., 152 **75** H6
Bluff City, Tenn., 948 **71** J5
Bluff Dale, Tex. **76** d10
Bluffdale, Utah **78** b10
Bluff Hall, Ill. **68** A4
Bluff Park, Ala. **64** c8
Bluffs, Ill., 779 **68** B4
Bluffside, Ind., 1,372 **69** h10
Bluff Siding, Wis. **66** B4
Bluff Springs, Ill. **68** B4
Bluff Springs, Tex. **76** c5
Bluffton, Alta., Can. **43** a8
Bluffton, Ark. **73** B3
Bluffton, Ga., 176 **64** E4
Bluffton, Ind., 6,238 **70** D2
Bluffton, Minn., 211 **74** E2
Bluffton, Ohio, 2,591 **70** F2
Bluffton, S.C., 356 **63** D5
Bluford, Ill., 388 **68** D5
Bluit, N. Mex. **79** D5
Blum, Tex., 315 **77** P3
Blumberg, F.R.Ger., 5,516 **118** B5
Blumberg, Ger.D.R. **119** f10
Blumenau, Braz., 46,591 **103** F7
Blumut, G., Malay. **147** p15
Blunt, S. Dak., 532 **74** B3
Bly, Oreg. **80** C4
Blyn, Wash. **81** a6
Blyth, U.K., 35,933 **113** F4
Blyth, r., U.K. **112** g9
Blythe, Ont., Can. **46** C5
Blythe, Calif., 6,023 **82** F6
Blythedale, Mo., 179 **72** D4
Blythedale, Pa., **60** c9
Blytheville, Ark., 25,883 **73** F2
Blythewood, S.C. **63** D3
Blyton, U.K. **114** G4
Bö, Nor. **120** B4
Bö, Nor. **120** C1
Bo, Sa. Leone **162** C4
Boa, D.R.Congo **165** o19
Boaco, Nic., 4,078 **94** E4
Boagis, Terr. Papua **174** 3
Boali, C.A.R. **163** G5
Boalsburg, Pa., **60** G4
Boano, P., Indon. **149** H3
Boardman, N.C. **63** E3
Boardman, r., Mich. **67** H4
Boat of Garten, U.K. **112** D3
Boatswainbird I., Ascencion **109** 6
Boa Vista, Braz., 10,180 **102** D1
Boa Vista, i, C. Verde Is. **109** 5
Boaz, Ala., 4,654 **64** C1
Boaz, N. Mex. **79** D5
Boaz, Wis., 117 **66** C5
Boaz I., Berm. Is. **108** 1
Bobbili, India, 25,592 **145** G6
Bobbio, It., 6,004 **122** c6
Bobcaygeon, Ont., Can., 1,186 **46** F4
Böblingen, F.R.Ger., 18,200 **118** B4
Bobdo Uula, mtn., China **132** H5
Bobo Dioulasso, Upper Volta, 50,000 **162** D4
Bobolice, Pol., 2,813 **127** B2
Bobonaza, r., Ec. **104** B2
Bobonong, Bots., 7,490 **164** D5
Boboshevo, Bulg., 3,093 **128** D3
Bobota, Rum. **128** D1
Bobr, U.S.S.R. **136** C2
Bóbr, r., Pol. **127** A3
Bobrinets, U.S.S.R., 11,500 **136** C4
Bobrov, U.S.S.R., 6,800 **136** F3
Bobruysk, U.S.S.R., 104,000 **134** B4
Bobs Cr., Pa. **60** E5
Bobs L., Ont., Can. **47** H4
Bobtown, Pa., 1,167 **60** B6
Bobures, Ven., 9,397 **100** E3
Boca Chica, Tex. **77** P7
Boca Chica Key, Fla. **65** f15
Boca de Aroa, Ven., 1,273 **100** F2
Boca del Pao, Ven. **101** H3
Boca del Río, Sin., Mex. **92** C3
Boca del Río, Ver. C., Mex., 2,660 **93** G4
Boca de Yaracuy, Ven. **101** a11
Bôca do Acre, Braz., 2,994 **102** C3
Bôca do Jari, Braz. **103** F2
Bôca do Moaco, Braz. **102** C3
Bocage, C., N. Caled. **174** i8
Boca Grande, Fla. **65** G6
Boca Grande, r., Ven. **101** K3
Boca Grande Key, Fla. **65** e15
Bocaiúva, Braz., 5,952 **103** H5
Bocanda, Iv. Coast, 1,724 **162** a8
Bocaneo, Mex., 1,134 **93** d10
Bocaranga, C.A.R. 4,000* **162** G4
Boca Raton, Fla., 6,961 **65** J6
Bocas del Toro, Pan., 2,459 **94** F6
Bocas del Toro, Arch. de, Pan. **94** G6
Bocaue, Phil., 2,391 **153** b8
Bocay, Nic. **94** E3
Bocay, r., Nic. **94** E4
Bochalema, Col. **100** D4
Bochil, Mex., 1,798 **93** G5
Bochnia, Pol., 11,814 **127** D4
Bocholt, Belg., 4,974 **115** D3
Bocholt, F.R.Ger., 43,568 **118** A3
Bocholtz, Neth., 3,100 **115** E4
Bochov, Czech. **126** b6
Bochum, F.R.Ger., 345,614 **118** A3
Bockenem, F.R.Ger., 4,067 **118** B2
Bockfliess, Aust., 1,301 **124** d10
Bockhorn, F.R.Ger., 7,089 **118** B2
Bocking, U.K., 7,433 **114** J7
Bockum-Hövel, F.R.Ger., 23,175 **119** D1
Boconó, Ven., 10,133 **100** E3
Bocşa Romînă, Rum. **128** C2
Bod, Rum. **128** E2
Boda, C.A.R., 2,840 **163** G5
Böda, Swed. **120** D4
Bodalla, Austl. **173** g11
Bodaybo, U.S.S.R., 17,500 **135** L4
Bodcau, Bayou, Ark.-La. **73** B4
Bodcaw, Ark. **73** B4
Bodden Town, Grand Cayman **97** 3
Bode, Iowa, 430 **72** C2
Bodega Bay, Calif. **82** B3
Bodegraven, Neth., 5,600 **115** b6
Bodela, Terr. Papua **174** 3
Bodelwyddan, U.K., 1,751 **114** A4
Boden, Swed. **120** E2
Bodenham, U.K. **114** C6
Bodenheim, F.R.Ger., 3,903 **119** E5
Bodenmais, F.R.Ger., 3,396 **118** D4
Bodensee, F.R.Ger.-Switz. **118** B5
Bodenteich, F.R.Ger., 2,201 **118** C2
Bode Sadu, Nigeria **162** f7
Bodfish, Calif. **82** D5
Bodhan, India, 30,929 **145** E6
Bodio, Switz., 1,276 **124** C2
Bodjongterong, Indon. **148** b7
Bodmin, U.K., 6,214 **113** D6
Bodmin Moor, U.K. **113** D6
Bodö, Nor., 12,495 **120** C2
Bodoc, Rum. **128** E2
Bodrog, r., Hung. **126** E2
Bodrum, Turk., 5,040 **142** A2
Bodzanowice, Pol. **127** h6
Boe (dist.), Nauru **175** 17
Boechout, Belg., 7,188 **115** e8
Boelus, Nebr. **75** G2
Boën, Fr., 3,463 **117** F4
Boende, D.R.Congo **164** C2
Boerne, Tex., 2,169 **77** O5
Boet, Thai. **146** B5
Boeuf, r., La. **73** D5
Boeuf, Bayou, La. **73** C6
Boffa, Guin., 10,000 **162** B4
Bogachiel, r., Wash. **80** A2
Bogale, Burma, 23,211 **146** A3
Bogale, r., Burma **147** a2
Bogallua, i., Eniwetok **176** 28
Bogalusa, La., 21,423 **73** F7
Bogan, i., Eniwetok **176** 28
Bogan, r., Austl. **173** G4
Bogandé, Upper Volta, 3,659 **162** E3
Bogan Gate, Austl. **173** f9
Bogangolo, C.A.R. **163** G5
Bogart, Ohio **70** G1
Bogata, Tex., 1,112 **77** Q3
Bogatić, Yug. **125** D2
Bogatynia, Pol., 7,851 **127** A3
Boğazlıyan, Turk., 7,179 **142** C2
Bogdanci, Yug., 2,951 **125** F4
Bogdanovich, U.S.S.R., 20,000 **137** k8
Bogdo Uula, mtn., China **132** H5
Bogembay, U.S.S.R. **137** n11
Bogen, F.R.Ger., 2,629 **118** D4
Bogen, i., Eniwetok **176** 28
Bogenaga, i., Jaluit **176** 30
Bogenfels, S.-W. Afr. **164** B6
Bogense, Den., 2,968 **121** C5
Boger City, N.C., 1,728 **63** C2
Boggabilla, Austl. **173** G4
Boggabri, Austl., 1,378 **173** G4
Boggenatjen, i., Kwajalein **176** 25
Boggeragh Mts., Ire. **113** B5
Boggerik, i., Kwajalein **176** 25
Boggs, C., Ant. **180** O5
Boggy Peak, Antigua **97** 9
Boghar, Alg., 1,215 **160** c6
Boghé, Maur., 5,900 **162** B3
Bogia, Terr. New Guin. **174** e2
Bogia, Fla. **65** B2
Bognor Regis, U.K., 28,064 **113** F6
Bogo, Phil., 6,786 **153** B3
Bogø, i., Den. **121** E6
Bogodukhov, U.S.S.R., 16,000 **136** D3
Bogombogo, i., Eniwetok **176** 28
Bogomila, Yug. **125** E4
Bogon, i., Eniwetok **176** 28
Bogong, Mt., Austl. **173** f11
Bogong Peaks, Austl. **173** g10
Bogor, Indon., 154,092 **148** C4
Bogoroditsk, U.S.S.R., 21,700 **136** E2
Bogorodsk, U.S.S.R., 25,800 **136** F1
Bogorodskoye, U.S.S.R. **135** O4
Bogotá, Col., 1,329,230 **100** D5
Bogota, Ill. **68** D5
Bogota, Tenn. **71** B5
Bogotá, r., Col. **101** e15
Bogotol, U.S.S.R., 28,800 **137** s11
Bogra, Pak., 33,784 **144** g13
Boguchany, U.S.S.R. **135** J4
Boguchar, U.S.S.R., 3,500 **136** F3
Bogue, Kans., 234 **75** F4
Bogue, N.C. **63** H3
Bogue Chitto, r., La. **73** E7
Bogue Homa Cr., Miss. **73** F6
Boguszów, Pol., 11,319 **127** f6
Boguszowice, Pol., 7,918 **127** h6
Bog Walk, Jam., 2,807 **96** p8
Bohain-en-Vermandois, Fr., 6,889 **117** E2
Bohdaneč, Czech. **127** e6
Bohemia, N.Y. **58** g13
Bohemia = Čechy
Bohemian Forest, Czech.-F.R.Ger. **118** D4
Bohicon, Dahom. **162** e8
Böhmer Wald = Bohemian Forest
Bohmte, F.R.Ger., 3,933 **118** B2
Bohners L., Wis. **66** c13
Boh Noi, Thai. **147** c4
Bohol, Phil. **153** A3
Bohol, i., Phil. **153** C3
Bohol Str., Phil. **153** B3
Bohórquez, Col. **100** C4
Bohotleh, Som. Rep. **163** M4
Boiaçu, Braz. **102** D2
Boicourt, Kans. **75** L5
Boiestown, N.B., Can. **45** M6
Boigu I., Austl. **174** d3
Boiling Springs, N.C., 1,311 **63** C2
Boiling Springs, Pa., 1,182 **60** H5
Bois, L. des, N.W.T., Can. **40** E4
Bois Blanc I., Mich. **67** J3
Bois Brule, r., Wis. **66** B2
Bois Bubert I., Me. **55** E4
Boischâtel, Qué., Can., 1,461 **47** n16
Boisdale, N.S., Can. **47** V10
Bois D'Arc, Mo. **72** D7
Bois-d'Arcy, Fr., 3,315 **116** g11
Bois-des-Filion, Qué., Can., 2,489 **47** o17
Bois de Sioux, r., Minn.-N. Dak. **74** D2
Boise, co., Idaho, 1,646 **81** B3
Boise, Idaho, 72,090 **81** A4
Boise, r., Idaho **81** B4
Boise City, Okla., 1,978 **76** A1
Boisemont, Fr. **116** g10
Bois-le-Roi, Fr., 3,020 **116** i12
Boissevain, Man., Can., 1,236 **43** E5
Boissy-sous-St-Yon, Fr. **116** g12
Boize, r., Ger.D.R. **119** c9
Boizenburg, Ger.D.R., 11,641 **118** C2
Bojacá, Col. **101** e15
Bojador, C., Sp. Sah. **160** B3
Bojanowo, Pol., 3,129 **127** B3
Bojnūrd, Iran, 19,253 **143** F1
Bokani, Nigeria **162** f7
Bokarijiman, i., Jaluit **176** 30
Bokaro, India, 5,406 **144** e14
Bokchito, Okla., 620 **76** G3
Boké, Guin., 25,000 **162** B4
Bokeelia, Fla. **65** G6
Boko, Congo **164** B2
Bokod, Phil., 3,080 **153** B1
Bokoro, Chad, 2,200* **163** G3
Bokoshe, Okla., 431 **76** J2
Bokovo-Antratsit, U.S.S.R., 24,000 **136** f7
Bokovskaya, U.S.S.R. **136** F3
Bokpyin, Burma **146** B5
Boksburg, S. Af., 70,939 **165** k17
Boksburg North, S. Af. **165** k17
Boksitogorsk, U.S.S.R., 20,900 **134** C4
Bokungu, D.R.Congo **164** C2
Bol, Chad **162** G3
Bolaang, Indon. **149** G3
Bolama, Port. Guin. **162** B4
Bolands, Antigua, 1,787 **97** 9
Bolangir, India, 18,663 **145** G5
Bolanos Mt., Guam **176** 24
Bolaños, R. de, Mex. **92** E4
Bolān Pass, Pak. **144** C3
Bolba, India **144** e14
Bolbec, Fr., 12,492 **117** D2
Bolckow, Mo., 232 **72** C4
Bolderslev, Den. **121** B6
Boldeşti, Rum. **128** F2
Boldon, U.K., 22,409 **112** h10
Boldre, U.K., 2,235 **113** i13
Bold Spring, Tenn. **71** D6
Bole, Ghana **162** D4
Bolekhov, U.S.S.R., 8,500 **136** A3
Boles, Ark. **73** A3
Bolesławiec, Pol., 23,000* **127** A3
Bolesławiec, Pol. **127** h5
Boleszkowice, Pol., 1,461 **127** A2
Boley, Okla., 573 **76** G2
Bolgatanga, Ghana, 5,523 **162** D4
Bolgrad, U.S.S.R., 13,900 **136** C4
Boliadiong, Phil., 1,386 **153** A3
Boliden, Swed. **120** E2
Boligee, Ala., 134 **64** A3
Bolinao, Phil., 2,600 **153** A1
Boling, Tex. **77** P5
Bolinger, La. **73** B5
Bolívar, Arg., 20,200* **105** C5
Bolívar, Col. **100** B5
Bolívar, Col. **100** B7
Bolívar, Ec. **104** d9
Bolívar, Peru **104** B3
Bolivar, co., Miss., 54,464 **73** E4
Bolivar, Mo., 3,512 **72** D7
Bolivar, N.Y., 1,405 **58** D7
Bolivar, Ohio, 932 **70** H2
Bolivar, Pa., 716 **60** D5
Bolivar, Tenn., 3,338 **71** B6
Bolívar, Co., Ven. **101** J4
Bolívar, Pico, Ven. **100** E3
Bolivar Pen., Tex. **77** Q5
Bolivia, ctry., 3,748,000* **102**
Bolivia, N.C., 201 **63** F3
Boljanići, Yug. **125** D3
Boljoon, Phil., 1,823 **153** e12
Bolkhov, U.S.S.R., 11,100 **136** D2
Bolków, Pol., 3,963 **127** f6
Bollendorf, F.R.Ger., 1,347 **118** A4
Bollène, Fr., 9,276 **117** F4
Bollengo, It., 2,072 **122** a5
Bolligen, Switz., 14,914 **124** B2
Bollin, r., U.K. **114** D4
Bolling, Ala. **64** C4
Bollinger, co., Mo., 9,167 **72** G7
Bollington, U.K., 5,642 **114** D4
Bollnäs, Swed. **120** D3
Bollon, Austl. **173** G4
Bolmen, l., Swed. **120** C4
Bolnes, Neth., 5,100 **115** b7
Bolo, Phil., 2,158 **153** B3
Bolobo, D.R.Congo **164** B2
Bologna, It., 426,621 **123** C2
Bolognesi, Peru **104** C4
Bologoye, U.S.S.R., 28,400 **134** C4
Bolomba, D.R.Congo **164** C1
Bolonchenticul, Mex., 1,540 **93** H4
Bolondron, Cuba, 3,444 **96** c1
Bolotnoye, U.S.S.R., 25,000 **134** H4
Bolovens, Plat. des, Laos **146** D4
Bolpur, India, 23,355 **144** f14
Bolsena, Lago di, It. **123** C3
Bol'shaya Belozërka, U.S.S.R. **136** D4
Bol'shaya Dzhalga, U.S.S.R. **136** F4
Bol'shaya Novosëlka, U.S.S.R. **136** e8
Bol'shaya Ob', r., U.S.S.R. **134** F3
Bol'shaya Rechka, r., U.S.S.R. **137** r11
Bol'shaya Sosnova, U.S.S.R. **137** h7
Bol'shaya Usa, U.S.S.R. **137** h8
Bol'sherech'ye, U.S.S.R. **137** o11
Bol'sheretsk, U.S.S.R. **135** P4
Bol'sheust'inskoye, U.S.S.R. **137** i8
Bol'shevik, O., U.S.S.R. **135** K2
Bol'shezemel'skaya Tundra, U.S.S.R. **134** E3
Bol'shoy Abakan, r., U.S.S.R. **137** s11
Bol'shoy Anyuy, r., U.S.S.R. **135** Q3
Bol'shoy Begichëv, O., U.S.S.R. **135** L2
Bol'shoye Zimov'ye, U.S.S.R. **135** O2
Bol'shoy Kavkaz, mts., U.S.S.R. **134** D5
Bol'shoy Lyakhovskiy, O., U.S.S.R. **135** N2
Bol'shoy Porog, U.S.S.R. **137** t11
Bol'shoy Pur, r., U.S.S.R. **134** G3
Bol'shoy Shatan, G., U.S.S.R. **137** i9
Bol'shoy Tokmak, U.S.S.R., 28,500 **136** D4
Bol'shoy Vagil'skiy Tuman, Oz., U.S.S.R. **137** k6
Bol'shoy Yenisey, r., U.S.S.R. **135** J4
Bolsover, U.K., 11,772 **114** F4
Bolsward, Neth., 8,000 **115** D1
Boltaña, Sp., 1,235 **122** E1
Bolt Head, U.K. **113** E6
Bolton, Ont., Can., 2,080 **46** E5
Bolton, U.K., 160,887 **113** E5
Bolton, Conn., 2,933(T) **56** G5
Bolton, Ill. **68** C1
Bolton, Kans. **75** K6
Bolton, Mass., 1,264(T) **57** K3
Bolton, Mich. **67** K3
Bolton, Miss., 797 **73** E5
Bolton, N.Y. **59** N4
Bolton, N.C., 617 **63** F3
Bolton, Vt. **54** B3
Bolton Abbey, U.K. **114** E3
Bolton Cr., Ont., Can. **59** G2
Bolton Landing, N.Y. **59** N4
Bolton-le-Sands, U.K., 1,937 **114** C2
Bolton Mtn., Vt. **54** B3
Bolton Notch (part of Bolton), Conn. **56** G5
Boltonville, Vt. **54** C3
Boltonville, Wis. **66** E5
Bolu, Turk., 13,743 **142** B1
Bolus Head, Ire. **113** A6
Bolvadin, Turk., 16,075 **142** B2
Bolzano, It., 84,794 **123** C1
Boma, D.R.Congo, 33,143 **164** B2
Boma, Tenn. **71** F5
Bomaderry, Austl., 1,465 **173** h10
Bomapau, i., Terr. Papua **174** 3
Bomar, Okla. **76** F4
Bomatu Pt., Terr. Papua **174** 3
Bombala, Austl., 1,258 **173** G5
Bombay, India, 4,152,056 **145** D6
Bombay, N.Y. **59** L2
Bombo, Uganda **165** f13
Bombon, Fr. **116** k12
Bom Conselho, Braz., 6,840 **103** J3
Bom Despacho, Braz., 13,568 **103** G5
Bomi Hills, Lib. **162** C4
Bom Jardim, Pbco., Braz., 3,138 **103** b14
Bom Jardim, R. de J., Braz., 1,894 **103** e18
Bom Jardim de Minas, Braz., 2,663 **103** d17
Bom Jesus, Braz., 1,431 **103** G3
Bom Jesus da Lapa, Braz., 6,107 **103** H4
Bom Jesus do Itabapoana, Braz., 7,203 **103** f17
Bömlo, i., Nor. **120** A4
Bomokandi, r., D.R.Congo **164** D1
Bomoseen, L., Vt. **54** A4
Bom Sucesso, Braz., 6,173 **103** d17
Bomu, r., C.A.R.-D.R.Congo **164** D1
Bōmura, Jap. **154** g14
Bona, Mt., Alaska **85** J3
Bon Accord, Alta., Can. **43** b7
Bon Accord, S. Af. **165** k16
Bonaduz, Switz., 1,093 **124** D2
Bon Air, Tenn. **71** F6
Bon Air, Va. **62** G5
Bonaire, i., Lesser Ant. **97** 17
Bonanza, Mex., 1,416 **92** E3
Bonanza, Ark., 247 **73** A2
Bonanza, Colo. **79** B2
Bonanza, Oreg., 297 **80** C4
Bonanza, Utah **78** D2
Bonanza Pk., Wash. **80** C1
Bonao, Dom. Rep., 12,951 **96** m6
Bonaparte, Iowa, 574 **72** F4
Bonaparte, r., Br. Col., Can. **42** G3
Bonaparte Arch., Austl. **172** C2
Bon Aqua, Tenn. **71** D6
Boñar, Sp., 5,105 **122** C1
Bonaventure, Qué., Can., 1,000 **45** M5
Bonaventure, r., Qué., Can. **47** T9
Bonavista, Newf., Can., 4,078 **45** R5
Bonavista Bay, Newf., Can. **45** R5
Bonawon, Phil., 4,197 **153** d12
Bonbon, Phil., 1,882 **153** e11
Bonchurch (part of Ventnor), U.K. **113** k13
Boncourt, Switz., 1,493 **124** A1
Bond, co., Ill., 14,060 **68** C5
Bond, Miss. **73** F7
Bondeno, It., 24,238 **123** C2
Bond Falls Flowage, Mich. **66** E2
Bondhead, Ont., Can. **46** E4

Bondo, D.R.Congo 164 C1
Bondorf, F.R.Ger., 2,263 119 F7
Bondoukou, Iv. Coast, 4,777 162 D4
Bondowoso, Indon. 148 E4
Bonds Cay, Bah. Is. 95 b7
Bondsville (part of Palmer and Belchertown), Mass. 56 G4
Bonduel, Wis., 876 66 E4
Bondurant, Iowa, 389 72 D3
Bondville, Ill. 68 D3
Bondville, Vt. 54 B5
Bondy, Fr., 38,054 116 h11
Bône, Alg.=Annaba
Bone, Indon. 149 G4
Boné, Loy. Is. 174 k8
Bone, Teluk, Indon. 149 G3
Bone Gap, Ill., 245 68 D5
Bone L., Wis. 66 A3
Bonelli, It. 122 f6
Bonerate, P., Indon. 149 G4
Bo'ness, U.K., 10,194 112 c7
Bonesteel, S. Dak., 452 74 C4
Bonetraill, N. Dak. 74 A1
Bonfield, Ont., Can. 44 H6
Bonfield, Ill., 178 68 D2
Bonfol, Switz. 124 B1
Bonga, Eth. 163 L4
Bonga, r., Phil. 153 B1
Bongabon, Phil., 8,358 153 B2
Bongandanga, D.R.Congo 164 C1
Bongka, Indon. 149 G3
Bongor, Chad, 4,000* 162 G4
Bongouanou, Iv. Coast, 5,050 162 D4
Bonham, Tex., 7,357 77 P3
Bonheiden, Belg., 6,144 115 e8
Bonhill, U.K. 112 a8
Bon Homme, co., S. Dak., 9,229 74 D4
Bonhomme, Pic, Haiti 96 k6
Bonifacio, Fr., 2,620 116 r18
Bonifacio, Strait of, It.-Fr. 123 B4
Bonifay, Fla., 2,222 65 D2
Bönigen, Switz., 1,833 124 B2
Bonin Is., Pac. Oc. 170 D3
Bonita, Ariz. 78 D5
Bonita, La., 574 73 D5
Bonita Springs, Fla. 65 H6
Bonito, Mo. Gro., Braz. 103 E6
Bonito, Pbco., Braz., 5,427 103 b15
Bonivat, Terr. Papua 174 3
Boniville, Fr. Guiana 101 N6
Bonlanden, F.R.Ger., 3,324 119 G7
Bonlee, N.C. 63 E2
Bonn, F.R.Ger., 136,031 118 A3
Bonnat, Fr., 1,580 117 D3
Bonndorf, F.R.Ger., 2,138 118 B5
Bonneau, S.C., 402 63 E4
Bonnechère, r., Ont., Can. 46 G3
Bonnelles, Fr. 116 g12
Bonner, co., Idaho, 15,587 81 A1
Bonnerdale, Ark. 73 B3
Bonners Ferry, Idaho, 1,921 81 A1
Bonner Springs, Kans., 3,171 75 K4
Bonnet, r., Ire. 113 B4
Bonnétable, Fr., 3,573 117 D2
Bonne Terre, Mo., 3,219 72 G7
Bonneval, Fr., 4,800 117 D2
Bonneville, Fr., 4,641 117 G3
Bonneville, co., Idaho, 46,906 81 D4
Bonneville, Oreg. 80 C3
Bonneville Salt Flats, Utah 78 B1
Bonney Lake, Wash., 645 81 b8
Bonnie, Ill., 215 68 D5
Bonnie Doon, Man., Can. 43 f9
Bonnievale, S. Af., 2,483 164 a8
Bonnieville, Ky., 376 71 F4
Bönnigheim, F.R.Ger., 4,033 119 G6
Bonny, Fr., 1,605 117 E3
Bonny, Nigeria 162 F5
Bonny Res., Colo. 79 D2
Bonnyrigg, U.K. 112 d8
Bonnyville, Alta., Can., 1,686 42 L2
Bono, It., 4,961 123 B4
Bono, Ark., 339 73 E2
Bono, Ind. 70 B3
Bono, Ohio 70 F1
Bono, Tex. 76 e10
Bonorva, It., 7,293 123 B4
Bōnotsu, Jap., 13,233 154 B6
Bonpas Cr., Ill. 68 E5
Bontang, Indon. 148 F2
Bonthain, Indon. 149 G4
Bonthe, Sa. Leone 162 B4
Bontoc, Phil., 3,241 153 B1
Bonyhád, Hung., 9,386 126 D3
Booborowie, Austl. 172 c7
Booby North Pt., Jam. 96 q8
Booby Pt., Lesser Caymans 97 2
Booby South Pt., Jam 96 q9
Boody, Ill. 68 C4
Booischot, Belg., 4,955 115 C3
Book Cliffs, Utah 78 •
Booker, Tex., 817 76 N1
Booker T. Washington Nat. Mon., Va. 62 E5
Bookham, Austl. 173 g10
Boolaboolka L., Austl. 173 d9
Booligal, Austl. 173 e9
Boom, Belg., 17,879 115 C3
Boomer, W. Va., 1,657 62 C4
Boom L., Wis. 66 D3
Boon, Mich. 67 H4
Boonah, Austl., 1,768 173 H4
Boone, co., Ark., 16,116 73 B1
Boone, Colo., 548 79 C2
Boone, co., Ill., 20,326 68 D1
Boone, co., Ind., 27,543 70 C2
Boone, co., Iowa, 28,037 72 D3
Boone, Iowa, 12,468 72 D2
Boone, co., Ky., 21,940 71 G3
Boone, Ky. 71 G4
Boone, co., Mo., 55,202 72 E6
Boone, co., Nebr., 9,134 75 G2
Boone, Nebr. 75 G2
Boone, N.C., 3,686 63 C1
Boone, co., W. Va., 28,764 62 C4
Boone, r., Iowa 72 D2
Boone L., Tenn. 71 J5
Boones Mill, Va., 371 62 E5
Booneville, Ark., 2,690 73 A2
Booneville, Ky., 143 71 H4
Booneville, Miss., 3,480 73 G3
Boonsboro, Md., 1,211 62 G3
Boonsville, Tex. 76 d8
Boonton, N.J., 7,981 61 C2
Boonton Res., N.J. 58 b13
Boonville, Calif. 82 B3
Boonville, Ind., 4,801 70 B4
Boonville, Mo., 7,090 72 E6
Boonville, N.Y., 2,403 59 K5
Boonville, N.C., 539 63 D1
Boopi, r., Bol. 102 b9
Boorithumble, Mt., Austl. 173 f9
Booroorban, Austl. 173 e10
Boorowa, Austl., 1,291 173 g10
Boot, Phil., 2,789 153 c8
Booth, Ala. 64 C3
Booth, Tex. 77 h9
Booth, Utah 78 B1
Boothbay Harbor, Me., 2,252 55 C5
Booth Corner, Pa. 62 e10
Boothia, G. of, N.W.T., Can. 40 L3
Boothia Pen., N.W.T., Can. 40 L3
Boothton, Ala. 64 B2
Boothville, La. 73 F8
Bootle, Cumb., Eng., U.K. 113 E4
Bootle, Lancs., Eng., U.K., 82,829 114 C4
Booué, Gabon 164 B2
Bopa, Dahom. 162 d8
Bo Phloi, Thai. 147 c4
Bopolu, Lib. 162 C4
Boppard, F.R.Ger., 8,175 118 A3
Boquerón, P.R. 96 u10
Boquerón, B. de, P.R. 96 r10
Boquete, Co., Arg. 105 A6
Boquillas, Tex. 77 M5
Bor, Czech. 126 A2
Bor, Sudan 163 K4
Bor, Swed. 120 C4
Bor, Turk., 13,253 142 C2
Bor, U.S.S.R., 52,000 136 G1
Bor, Yug., 18,000* 125 F2
Bora-Bora, i., Soc. Is. 171 H6
Borabu, Thai. 146 C4
Borah, Mt., Idaho 81 C3
Borama, Som. Rep., 4,000* 163 M4
Borås, Swed., 67,069 120 C4
Borāzjān, Iran, 10,233 143 E3
Borba, Braz., 1,304 102 E2
Borba, Port., 5,258 122 B3
Borbon, Phil., 2,482 153 f11
Borborema, Planalto da, Braz. 98 F3
Borbur, Col. 100 e14
Borburata, Ven. 101 b11
Borculo, Neth., 3,600 115 E2
Borculo, Mich. 67 G6
Borda, C., Austl. 172 b8
Borda da Mata, Braz., 3,318 103 c18
Bordeaux, Fr., 254,122 117 C4
Bordeaux, Tenn. 71 E5
Bordelonville, La. 73 D6
Borden, Austl. 172 B5
Borden, P.E.I., Can. 47 U10
Borden, Sask., Can. 43 C4
Borden, Ind. 70 D4
Borden, co., Tex., 1,076 77 N3
Borden I., N.W.T., Can. 41 G2
Borden Mtn., Mass. 56 D2
Borden Pen., N.W.T., Can. 41 N3
Borden Springs, Ala. 64 D2
Bordentown, N.J., 4,974 61 B3
Border, Minn. 74 E1
Bordertown, Austl., 1,315 172 E5
Bordesholm, F.R.Ger., 6,190 118 B1
Bordhoy, i., Faeroe Is. 120 c7
Bordighera, It., 10,561 123 A3
Bording, Den. 121 B4
Bordj-Bou-Arreridj, Alg., 35,238 160 E2
Bordj Fly Ste-Marie, Alg. 160 D3
Bordj-Menaïel, Alg., 12,517 160 c5
Bordulac, N. Dak. 74 C2
Bore, It., 2,101 122 c6
Boreas, r., N.Y. 59 M4
Borek, Pol., 1,882 127 B3
Boreray, i., U.K. 112 C3
Borgå, Fin., 11,849 120 F3
Borgarnes, Ice. 120 a6
Borgeby, Swed. 121 c7
Børgefjellet, mts., Nor. 120 C2
Borgentreich, F.R.Ger., 1,846 118 B3
Borger, Neth. 115 E2
Borger, Tex., 20,911 76 N2
Borgerhout, Belg., 50,645 115 d8
Borgholm, Swed. 120 D4
Borghorst, F.R.Ger., 15,162 118 A2
Borgloon, Belg., 3,471 115 D4
Borgne, L., La. 73 F7
Borgoforte, It., 4,820 122 d5
Borgofranco d'Ivrea, It., 2,965 122 a5
Borgo Maggiore, S. Mar., 2,500 123 e11
Borgomanero, It., 15,135 123 B2
Borgonovo Val Tidone, It., 7,006 122 c5
Borgo San Lorenzo, It., 15,241 123 C3
Borgosesia, It., 13,227 123 B2
Borgo Val di Taro, It., 10,200 123 B2
Borgsjö, Swed. 120 D3
Bori, Dahom. 162 e7
Borikhane, Laos 146 C3
Boring, Oreg. 80 b7
Borislav, U.S.S.R., 32,000 136 A3
Borisoglebsk, U.S.S.R., 56,000 134 D4
Borisov, U.S.S.R., 63,000 134 B4
Borisovka, U.S.S.R. 137 e3
Borisovo-Sudskoye, U.S.S.R. 136 D1
Borja, Peru 104 B3
Borja, Sp., 4,381 122 E2
Borjas Blancas, Sp., 5,082 122 F2
Bork, F.R.Ger., 5,772 119 C1
Borken, Hess., F.R.Ger., 4,098 118 B3
Borken, Nrh.-Wf., F.R.Ger., 10,630 118 A3
Børkop, Den. 121 B5
Borkou, reg., Chad 163 H2
Borkum, F.R.Ger., 5,199 118 A2
Borkum, i., F.R.Ger. 115 E1
Borland, Mich. 67 H5
Borlänge, Swed. 120 C3
Bormida, r., It. 123 B2
Bormio, It., 3,063 123 C1
Borna, Ger.D.R., 17,757 118 D3
Borne, Neth., 10,000 115 E2
Bornem, Belg., 9,686 115 d8
Borneo=Kalimantan
Bornheim, F.R.Ger., 11,663 118 A3
Bornholm, i., Den. 121 G5
Börnicke, Ger.D.R. 119 d10
Bornos, Sp., 8,697 122 C4
Bornova, Turk., 25,097 142 A2
Börnsen, F.R.Ger., 2,211 119 b9
Boroaia, Rum. 128 F1
Borobudur, ruins, Indon. 148 d7
Borodino, U.S.S.R., 10,000 135 J4
Borodino, U.S.S.R. 136 a6
Borodino, N.Y. 59 q24
Borogontsy, U.S.S.R. 135 N3
Boro Hörö Uula, China 132 H5
Borohrádek, Czech. 127 e6
Borojó, Ven. 100 E2
Boroko, Indon. 149 G2
Boromo, Upper Volta, 2,458 162 D4
Boron, Calif. 82 E5
Borongga Is., Burma 146 A3
Borongan, Phil., 3,970 153 C3
Boroughbridge, U.K., 1,847 114 E2
Borough Green, U.K., 2,826 114 J8
Borovan, Bulg., 5,647 128 D3
Borovichi, U.S.S.R., 48,000 134 C4
Borovlyanka, U.S.S.R. 137 r11
Borovoye, U.S.S.R., 4,600 137 n11
Borovsk, U.S.S.R., 10,900 136 b6
Borovsk, U.S.S.R., 34,900 137 h7
Borowa, Pol. 127 D3
Borpop, Terr. New Guin. 174 g1
Borrby, Swed. 120 C5
Borrego Springs, Calif. 82 E6
Borris, Ire. 113 C5
Borrisokane, Ire. 113 B5
Borrisoleigh, Ire. 113 C5
Borroloola, Austl. 172 E2
Börrstadt, F.R.Ger. 119 D5
Borşa, Rum. 128 D1
Borşa, Rum. 128 E1
Borsec, Rum., 2,318 128 E1
Borshchev, U.S.S.R., 5,100 136 B3
Borshchovochnyy Khr., U.S.S.R. 133 L4
Borstahusen, Swed. 121 b7
Borth, F.R.Ger., 3,215 119 B1
Borth, U.K. 113 D5
Bort-les-Orgues, Fr., 5,276 117 E4
Borton, Ill. 68 E4
Boru, Terr. Papua 174 f3
Borūjen, Iran, 7,460 143 E2
Borūjerd, Iran, 49,186 143 D2
Borup, Den. 121 E5
Borup, Minn., 145 74 D2
Bor-Yuryakh, U.S.S.R. 135 L2
Borzhomi, U.S.S.R., 15,400 137 b1
Börzsöny, mts., Hung. 126 D3
Borzya, U.S.S.R., 22,000 135 L4
Bosa, Col. 101 e15
Bosa, It., 8,771 123 B4
Bosanska Bojna, Yug. 125 C2
Bosanska Dubica, Yug., 4,963 125 C2
Bosanska Gradiška, Yug., 5,348 125 C2
Bosanska Krupa, Yug., 4,501 125 C2
Bosanski Brod, Yug., 5,328 125 D2
Bosanski Dubočac, Yug. 125 D2
Bosanski Novi, Yug., 4,884 125 C2
Bosanski Petrovac, Yug., 2,996 125 C2
Bosansko Grahovo, Yug. 125 C2
Bosarp, Swed. 121 b7
Bosaso, Som. Rep., 7,191 163 N4
Bosavi, Mt., Terr. Papua 174 d2
Bosbury, U.K. 114 D6
Boscastle, U.K. 113 D6
Boscawen, N.H. 54 D5
Bosco, La. 73 C5
Boscobel, Wis., 2,608 66 C5
Bosham, U.K., 3,147 113 m13
Boshof, S. Af., 2,865 164 D6
Boshrūyeh, Iran, 4,624 143 F2
Bošice, Czech. 127 e6
Bosilegrad, Yug. 125 F3
Boskoop, Neth., 9,400 115 b6
Boskovice, Czech. 126 C2
Bosna, r., Yug. 125 D2
Bosna i Hercegovina, st., Yug., 3,277,948 125 C2
Bosnek, Indon. 149 L3
Bosnia and Hercegovina=Bosna i Hercegovina
Bosobolo, D.R.Congo 164 C1
Bōsō-hantō, Jap. 155 G4
Bospoortdam, res., S. Af. 165 i16
Bosporus=İstanbul Boğazı, Turk.
Bosque, Ariz. 78 B5
Bosque, N. Mex. 79 B4
Bosque, co., Tex., 10,809 77 P4
Bosque, r., Tex. 77 P4
Boss, Mo. 72 F7
Bossangoa, C.A.R., 13,291 163 G4
Bossier, parish, La., 57,622 73 B5
Bossier City, La., 32,776 73 B5
Bosso, Niger 162 G3
Bosspruit, S. Af. 165 i16
Bostān, Pak. 144 C3
Boston, Phil., 2,131 153 C4
Boston, U.K., 24,915 113 F5
Boston, Ga. 1,357 64 F5
Boston, Ind., 240 70 E3
Boston, Ky. 71 F4
Boston, Mass., 697,197 57 M3
Boston, Ohio 70 e9
Boston, Tex. 77 Q3
Boston, Va. 62 F4
Boston Bar, Br. Col., Can. 42 G4
Boston Bay, Jam. 96 q8
Boston Bay, Mass. 57 N3
Boston Harbor, Wash. 81 a8
Boston Heights, Ohio, 831 70 f9
Boston Mts., Ark.-Okla. 53 H3
Boston Pk., Wash. 80 C1
Bostwick, Ga., 272 64 F2
Bosut, Yug. 125 D2
Bosut, r., Yug. 125 D2
Boswell, Ind., 957 70 B2
Boswell, Okla., 753 76 H4
Boswell, Pa., 1,508 60 D5
Boswell Bay, Alaska, 32 85 H3
Boswil, Switz., 1,663 124 C1
Bosworth, Mo., 465 72 D5
Botad, India, 26,168 145 D5
Botan, r., Turk. 142 E2
Botetourt, co., Va., 16,715 62 E5
Botev, mtn., Bulg. 128 E3
Botevgrad, Bulg., 8,646 128 D3
Botha, Alta., Can. 42 K3
Bothaville, S. Af., 5,364 164 D6
Bothell, Wash., 2,237 80 B2
Bothnia, G. of, Fin.-Swed. 120 E3
Bothwell, Austl. 173 f14
Bothwell, Ont., Can. 46 C6
Bothwell, U.K. 112 b8
Bothwell, Utah, 302 78 b7
Botijas, P.R. 96 t10
Botkins, Ohio, 854 70 E2
Botolan, Phil., 2,677 153 b7
Botoşani, Rum., 29,569 128 F1
Botrange, mt., Belg. 115 E4
Botsford (part of Newtown), Conn. 56 C7
Botswana, ctry., 543,105 164 C5
Botte Donato, mtn., It. 123 F5
Bottesford, U.K., 1,551 114 G5
Bottineau, co., N. Dak., 11,315 74 B1
Bottineau, N. Dak., 2,613 74 B1
Bottisham, U.K. 114 J6
Bottna, Swed. 121 D2
Bottrop, F.R.Ger., 104,816 119 B1
Botucatu, Braz., 33,878 103 G6
Botun, Yug. 125 E4
Botwood, Newf., Can., 3,648 45 Q5
Bou, Terr. Papua 174 3
Bouaflé, Iv. Coast 162 D4
Bouafle, Fr., 1,340 116 f11
Bouaké, Iv. Coast, 45,340 162 D4
Bouar, C.A.R., 25,032 162 G4
Bouârfa, Mor., 8,775 160 D2
Bou Beker, Mor. 160 a6
Boufarik, Alg., 21,901 160 c5
Bouca, C.A.R., 5,934 163 H4
Bouchain, Fr., 3,505 116 a7
Boucherville, Qué., Can., 7,253 47 p17
Bou Djéhiba, Mali 162 D2
Boudreaux, La. 73 E8
Boudry, Switz., 3,086 124 A2
Bougaa, Alg., 5,696 160 d5
Bougainville, i., Terr. New Guin. 170 E5
Bougainville, C., Austl. 172 C1
Bougainville, Mt., Is. de Horne 175 9
Bougainville Str.=Malo Str.
Bougainville Str., Sol. Is. 175 a2
Bougaroum, C., Alg. 160 E1
Bougie=Bejaïa
Bougival, Fr., 7,318 116 g11
Bougouni, Mali, 5,000 162 C4
Bouillante, Guad. 97 14
Bouillon, Belg., 3,088 115 D5
Bouïra, Alg., 16,379 160 E1
Boulange, Fr., 2,528 116 b8
Boulangerville, Okla. 76 G1
Boulari, Passe de, N. Caled. 174 k9
Boulay-Moselle, Fr., 3,036 117 G2
Boulder, co., Colo., 74,254 79 C1
Boulder, Colo., 37,718 79 C1
Boulder, Ill. 68 C5
Boulder, Mont., 1,394 81 D2
Boulder, Utah 78 C3
Boulder City, Nev., 4,059 83 C5
Boulder Creek, Calif., 1,306 82 B4
Boulder Cr., Colo. 79 b7
Boulder Dam=Hoover Dam
Boulder Junction, Wis. 66 D2
Boulder Rock Cr., Idaho-Wash. 80 E4
Bouleurs, Fr. 116 k11
Boulia, Austl. 172 E3
Bouligny, Fr., 5,374 117 F2
Boulmane, Mor. 160 D2
Boulogne-Billancourt, Fr., 107,074 116 h11
Boulogne-sur-Mer, Fr., 50,036 117 D1
Bouloupari, N. Caled. 174 i8
Boumba, r., Cam. 162 G5
Bouna, Iv. Coast, 3,410 162 D4
Boundary, Alaska 85 J2
Boundary, co., Idaho, 5,809 81 A1
Boundary, Me. 55 E2
Boundary Mts., Can.-U.S. 55 B3
Boundary Pk., Calif.-Nev. 52 C3
Bound Brook, N.J., 10,263 61 C2
Boundiali, Iv. Coast, 3,608 162 C4
Boun Neua, Burma 146 C2
Boun Tai, Burma 146 C2
Bountiful, Utah, 17,039 78 C1
Bounty Bay, Pitc. I. 177 45
Bounty Is., N.Z. 170 G8
Bouquet, r., N.Y. 59 O3
Bourail, N. Caled., 2,212 174 i8
Bourbeuse, r., Mo. 72 F6
Bourbon, Ind., 1,522 70 C1
Bourbon, co., Kans., 16,090 75 L6
Bourbon, co., Ky., 18,178 71 G3
Bourbon, Mo., 779 72 F6
Bourbon-Lancy, Fr., 6,171 117 E3
Bourbonnais, Ill., 3,336 68 D2
Bourbourg, Fr., 5,914 117 E1
Bourbriac, Fr., 3,049 116 B2
Bourdonnay, Fr. 116 e9
Bourem, Mali 162 D3
Bourg, La. 73 E8
Bourganeuf, Fr., 3,660 117 D4
Bourg-de-Péage, Fr., 6,201 117 F4
Bourg-en-Bresse, Fr., 35,640 117 F3
Bourges, Fr., 63,479 117 E3
Bourget, Ont., Can. 47 J3
Bourg-Lastic, Fr., 1,429 117 E4
Bourgogne, reg., Fr. 117 F3
Bourgoin, Fr., 9,754 117 F4
Bourgplatz, mt., Lux. 115 D4
Bourg-St-Andéol, Fr., 4,745 117 F4
Bourg-St-Maurice, Fr., 3,870 117 G4
Bourg-St-Pierre, Switz. 124 B3
Bourgueil, Fr., 3,141 117 D3
Bourke, Austl., 2,642 173 F4
Bourlon, Fr., 1,120 116 a7
Bourn, U.K. 114 H6
Bourne, U.K., 5,337 113 F5
Bourne, Mass., 14,011(T) 57 O6
Bournedale (part of Bourne), Mass. 57 O5
Bournemouth, U.K., 154,296 113 F6
Bourneville, Ohio 70 F3
Bourquim Hill, Nebr. 75 D2
Bourscheid, Lux. 119 A5
Bourton on the Water, U.K., 1,895 114 E7
Bou-Saâda, Alg., 21,059 160 E2
Bousbecque, Fr., 3,254 116 a6
Bouse, Ariz. 78 A5
Boussac, Fr., 1,519 117 E3
Boussé, Upper Volta, 2,915 162 D3
Bousso, Chad 162 G4
Bout, Pte. du, Mart. 97 12
Boutilimit, Maur., 1,503 162 B3
Bouvetøya, i., Atl. Oc. 109 N10
Bouxwiller, Fr., 2,754 116 d9
Bovenkarspel, Neth., 3,800 115 D2
Boves, It., 7,392 123 A2
Bovey, Minn., 1,086 74 F2
Bovey Tracey, U.K., 3,357 113 E6
Bovill, Idaho, 357 81 A2
Bovina, Tex., 1,029 77 M2
Bovina Center, N.Y. 59 L7
Bovolenta, It., 3,505 122 e5
Bovolone, It., 8,919 122 e5
Bovril, Arg., 5,500* 105 b10
Bow, r., Alta., Can. 42 J3
Bowbells, N. Dak., 683 74 A1
Bowden, Alta., Can. 42 J3
Bowdens, N.C., 300 63 F2
Bowdle, S. Dak., 673 74 C3
Bowdoinham, Me. 55 C4
Bowdon, U.K., 4,478 114 D4
Bowdon, Ga., 1,548 64 D2
Bowdon, N. Dak., 259 74 C2
Bowen, Arg., 7,900* 105 B5
Bowen, Austl., 3,571 173 G2
Bowen, Ill., 559 68 A3
Bowen, Mt., Austl. 173 G2
Bowen I., Br. Col., Can. 42 c6
Bowens Corners, N.Y. 59 q22
Bowers, Del., 324 62 J3
Bowerston, Ohio, 463 70 H2
Bowersville, Ohio, 327 70 F3
Bowes, U.K. 112 g10
Bowesmont, N. Dak. 74 D1
Bowes Moor, U.K. 113 E4
Bowie, Ariz. 78 D5
Bowie, Md., 1,072 62 H3
Bowie, co., Tex., 59,971 77 Q3
Bowie, Tex., 4,566 77 P3
Bowie Cr., Miss. 73 F6
Bow Island, Alta., Can., 1,070 42 K4
Bowkān, Iran, 5,307 143 D1
Bow L., N.H. 54 E5
Bowlder Mtn., Mont. 81 B1
Bowlegs, Okla. 76 G2
Bowler, Wis., 274 66 E4
Bowling Green, Fla., 1,171 65 G5
Bowling Green, Ind., 229 70 C3
Bowling Green, Ky., 28,338 71 E5
Bowling Green, Mo., 2,650 72 F5
Bowling Green, Ohio, 13,574 70 F1
Bowling Green, Va., 528 62 G4
Bowman, Calif. 82 b7
Bowman, Ga., 654 64 G1
Bowman, co., N. Dak., 4,154 74 A2
Bowman, N. Dak., 1,730 74 A2
Bowman, S.C., 1,106 63 D4
Bowman, L., Qué., Can. 47 J3
Bowman Creek, Pa. 61 o16
Bowman Cr., Pa. 61 K3
Bowmanstown, Pa., 888 61 L4
Bowmansville, N.Y. 58 m19
Bowmanville, Ont., Can., 7,338 44 H7
Bow Mar, Colo., 748 79 b8
Bow Mills, N.H. 54 D5
Bowmore, U.K. 112 C4
Bowness, U.K., 3,345 114 C2
Bowral, Austl., 3,926 173 h10
Bowraville, Austl., 1,047 173 H4
Bowring, Okla. 76 G1
Bowron, r., Br. Col., Can. 42 G3
Bowser, Br. Col., Can. 42 b6
Bowsman, Man., Can. 43 E4
Box, U.K., 4,209 114 D8
Box, Okla. 76 H2
Boxaxni, Mex. 93 e9
Boxaxní, Mex. 93 e9
Boxboro, Mass. 57 K3
Box Butte, co., Nebr., 11,688 75 B1
Box Butte, Nebr. 75 C1
Box Butte Cr., Nebr. 75 C1
Box Butte Res., Nebr. 75 B1
Box Elder, Mont. 81 E1
Box Elder, S. Dak. 74 A3
Box Elder, co., Utah, 25,061 78 B1
Boxford, Mass., 2,010(T) 57 M2
Boxholm, Swed. 120 C4
Boxholm, Iowa, 250 72 C2
Boxmeer, Neth., 6,100 115 D3
Boxtel, Neth., 13,900 115 D3
Boyabat, Turk., 8,345 142 C1
Boyce, La., 1,094 73 C6
Boyce, Tex. 76 f10
Boyce, Va., 384 62 F3
Boyceville, Wis., 660 66 A3
Boyd, Man., Can. 43 F3
Boyd, Fla. 65 F2
Boyd, co., Ky., 52,163 71 J3
Boyd, Minn., 419 74 D3
Boyd, co., Nebr., 4,513 75 G1
Boyd, Okla. 76 C1
Boyd, Oreg. 80 C3
Boyd, Tex., 581 76 d8
Boyd, Wis., 622 66 B4
Boydell, Ark. 73 D4
Boyden, Iowa, 562 72 A1
Boyden L., Me. 55 E3
Boyd Lake, Me. 55 D3
Boyd L., Qué., Can. 44 J4
Boyd L., Me. 55 D3
Boydton, Va., 449 62 F6
Boyer, W. Va. 62 E4
Boyer, r., Alta., Can. 42 J1
Boyer, r., Iowa 72 B3
Boyer, C., Loy. Is. 174 m8
Boyero, Colo. 79 D2
Boyers, Pa. 60 C3
Boyertown, Pa., 4,067 61 L5
Boyes Hot Springs, Calif. 83 e11
Boyette, Fla. 65 d12
Boykin, Ga., 601 64 E4
Boykin, S.C. 63 D3
Boykins, Va., 710 62 G6
Boyle, Alta., Can. 42 K2
Boyle, Ire., 1,835 113 B5
Boyle, co., Ky., 21,257 71 G4
Boyle, Miss., 848 73 E4
Boylston, N.S., Can. 47 V11
Boylston Center, Mass. 57 K3
Boyne, r., Man., Can. 43 f10
Boyne, r., Ire. 113 C5
Boyne City, Mich., 2,797 67 J3
Boyne Falls, Mich., 260 67 J3
Boynitsa, Bulg., 3,006 128 D3
Boynton, Okla., 604 76 H2
Boynton Beach, Fla., 10,467 65 K6
Boy River, Minn., 51 74 E2
Boysen Res., Wyo. 81 E4
Boys Town, Nebr., 997 75 J2
Bozal Gumbaz, Afghan. 145 E1
Bozca Ada, Turk. 142 A2
Bozdoğan, Turk., 5,787 142 B2
Bozeat, U.K., 1,082 114 G6
Bozel, Fr., 1,431 117 G4
Bozeman, Mont., 13,361 81 D3
Boži Dar, Czech. 126 b6
Bozouls, Fr., 1,616 117 E4
Bozoum, C.A.R., 4,872 162 G4
Bozovici, Rum. 128 D2
Bozshakul', U.S.S.R. 137 o12
Bozüyük, Turk., 9,197 142 B2
Bozzolo, It., 4,189 122 d5
Bra, It., 18,654 123 A2
Braassemer meer, Neth. 115 b6
Brabant L., Sask., Can. 43 D3
Brabova, Rum. 128 D2
Brabrand, Den., 5,699 121 C4
Brač, i., Yug. 125 C3
Bracciano, It., 8,425 123 a8
Bracciano, Lago di, It. 123 D3
Brace, Okla. 76 E1
Bracebridge, Ont., Can., 2,858 44 H6
Bracebridge Heath, U.K., 2,825 114 H4
Braceville, Ill., 558 68 D2
Bracey, Va. 62 F6
Brach, Libya 161 G3
Brachelen, F.R.Ger., 3,168 119 A2
Bracht, F.R.Ger., 4,631 119 A2
Bräcke, Swed. 120 C3
Bracken, Sask., Can. 43 B5
Bracken, Ind. 70 D2
Bracken, co., Ky., 7,422 71 G3
Bracken, Tex. 76 b6
Brackendale, Br. Col., Can. 42 c6
Brackenheim, F.R.Ger., 2,824 119 G6
Brackenridge, Pa., 5,697 60 C4
Brackett, Wis. 66 B4
Brackettville, Tex., 1,662 77 N5
Brackley, U.K., 3,208 113 F5
Bracknell, U.K., 20,378 114 G8
Brackwede, F.R.Ger., 25,023 118 B3
Braco, U.K. 112 c7
Brad, Rum., 9,963 128 D1
Bradano, r., It. 123 F4
Braddock, N. Dak., 141 74 B2
Braddock, Pa., 12,337 60 C5
Braddock Heights, N.Y. 58 n20
Braden, Okla. 76 J2
Braden, r., Fla. 65 d13
Bradenton, Fla., 19,380 65 G5
Bradenton Beach, Fla., 1,124 65 c13
Bradenville, Pa., 1,050* 60 D5
Bradevelt, N.J. 58 c15
Bradford, Ont., Can., 2,298 46 E4
Bradford, U.K., 295,768 113 F5
Bradford, Ark., 779 73 D2
Bradford, co., Fla., 12,446 65 G3
Bradford, Ill., 857 68 C2
Bradford, Kans. 75 K5
Bradford, Me. 55 D3
Bradford, N.H. 54 C5
Bradford, N.Y. 58 F7
Bradford, Ohio, 2,148 70 E2
Bradford, co., Pa., 54,925 61 K2
Bradford, Pa., 15,061 60 E2
Bradford (part of Westerly), R.I. 57 K7
Bradford, Tenn., 763 71 C5
Bradford, Vt., 760 54 C4
Bradford Mtn., Conn. 56 C5
Bradford-on-Avon, U.K., 5,760 114 D8
Bradfordsville, Ky., 387 71 F4
Bradford Woods, Pa., 866 60 b7
Bradgate, Iowa, 166 72 C2
Brading, U.K., 1,613 113 k13
Bradley, co., Ark., 14,029 73 C4
Bradley, Ark., 712 73 B4
Bradley, Calif. 82 C5
Bradley, Ill., 8,082 68 E2
Bradley, Me. 55 D4
Bradley, Mich. 67 H6
Bradley, Miss. 73 G4
Bradley, Okla., 294 76 F3
Bradley, S.C. 63 B3
Bradley, S. Dak., 188 74 D3
Bradley, co., Tenn., 38,324 71 G6
Bradley Beach, N.J., 4,204 61 D3
Bradley Junction, Fla., 1,035 65 d12
Bradleyville, Mo., 91 72 D8
Bradner, Ohio, 994 70 F1
Bradore Bay, Qué., Can. 45 P4
Bradshaw, Nebr., 306 75 H3
Bradshaw, Tex. 77 N3
Bradshaw, Port, Austl. 172 E1
Bradstreet (part of Hatfield), Mass. 56 F3
Bradwell, U.K., 1,368 114 E4
Brady, Mont. 81 D1
Brady, Nebr., 273 75 E2
Brady, Tex., 5,338 77 O4
Brady Cr., Tex. 77 O4
Bradys Hot Springs, Nev. 83 A3
Bradys Pond, Pa. 61 o17
Braehead, U.K. 112 c8
Braemar, U.K. 112 E3
Braeside, Ont., Can. 47 H3
Braeside, U.K. 112 a8
Brăeşti, Rum. 128 F1
Braga, Port., 34,085 122 A2
Bragado, Arg., 17,700* 105 C5
Bragança, Braz., 12,848 103 G2
Bragança, Port., 8,662 122 B2
Bragança Paulista, Braz., 27,328 103 c18
Bragg City, Mo., 274 72 G8
Braggs, Ala. 64 C3
Braggs, Okla., 279 76 H2
Braggville (part of Holliston), Mass. 57 L4
Bragin, U.S.S.R. 136 C3
Braham, Minn., 728 74 F3
Brāhmanbāria, Pak., 44,784 145 J4
Brahmani, r., India 144 e15
Brahmaputra, r., Asia 150 C4
Braid, r., U.K. 113 C4
Braidwood, Austl., 1,088 173 g10
Braidwood, Ill., 1,944 68 D2
Brail, Switz. 124 E2
Brăila, Rum., 102,500 128 F2
Brailes, U.K. 114 E6
Brailsford, U.K. 114 E5
Brainard, Nebr., 300 75 J2
Brainardsville, N.Y. 59 N2
Braine, Fr., 1,654 117 E2
Braine-l'Alleud, Belg., 13,428 115 C4
Braine-le-Comte, Belg., 10,760 115 B4
Brainerd, Minn., 12,898 74 F2
Braintree, U.K., 10,048 113 G6
Braintree, Mass., 31,069(T) 57 M4
Brake, F.R.Ger., 15,119 118 B2
Brakpan, S. Af., 78,778 165 k17
Braleys (part of New Bedford), Mass. 57 N6
Bralorne, Br. Col., Can. 42 F4
Braman, Okla., 336 76 F1
Bramanville (part of Millbury), Mass. 57 J4
Bramau, r., F.R.Ger. 119 a8
Bramley, Hants., Eng., U.K., 1,856 114 F8
Bramley, Surrey, Eng., U.K., 2,891 114 G8
Bramley, York., Eng., U.K., 3,726 114 F4
Bramminge, Den., 3,475 121 A5
Bramois, Switz. 124 B2
Brampton, Ont., Can., 18,323 44 H7
Brampton, Cumb., Eng., U.K., 3,130 113 E4
Brampton, Hunts., Eng., U.K., 3,068 114 H6
Brampton, Mich. 66 F3
Brampton, N. Dak. 74 D3
Brampton Bryan, U.K. 114 C6
Bramsche, F.R.Ger., 10,237 118 A2
Bramshott, U.K., 4,876 113 m12
Bramwell, W. Va., 1,195 62 C5
Bran, Rum. 128 E2

204 · Bran—Broughton

Bran, r., U.K. 112 D3
Branch, Newf., Can. 45 b11
Branch, Ark., 258 73 B2
Branch, co., Mich., 34,903 67 H7
Branch, Mich. 67 G5
Branch, Wis. 66 F4
Branch, r., Newf., Can. 45 a11
Branch Hill, Ohio 71 k10
Branch L., Me. 55 D4
Branchland, W. Va. 62 B4
Branchport, N.Y. 58 F6
Branchton, Ont., Can. 46 b14
Branchville, Ala. 64 e7
Branchville, N.J., 963 61 B1
Branchville, S.C., 1,182 63 D4
Branchville, Va., 158 62 G6
Branco, r., Braz. 102 D1
Brand, F.R.Ger., 8,668 119 A3
Brandaris, mtn., Bon. 97 17
Brandberg, mtn., S.-W. Afr. 164 B5
Brandbu, Nor. 120 B3
Brande, Den., 6,593 121 B5
Brandenburg, reg., Ger.D.R. 118 D2
Brandenburg, Ger.D.R., 86,722 118 D2
Brandenburg, Ky., 1,542 71 E4
Brand-Erbisdorf, Ger.D.R. 126 c6
Brandesburton, U.K., 1,044 114 H3
Brandfort, S. Af., 4,472 164 D6
Brandis, Ger.D.R. 126 b5
Brando, Fr., 1,066 116 r17
Brandon, Man., Can., 27,787 43 E5
Brandon, U.K. 112 g10
Brandon, Fla., 1,665 65 d12
Brandon, Iowa, 322 72 F2
Brandon, Miss., 2,139 73 F5
Brandon, Nebr. 75 D3
Brandon, S. Dak. 74 D4
Brandon, Tex., 121 76 e10
Brandon, Vt., 1,675 54 A4
Brandon, Va. 62 H5
Brandon, Wis., 758 66 E5
Brandon Bay, Ire. 113 A5
Brandon Head, Ire. 113 A5
Brandonville, W. Va., 109 62 E3
Brandsen, Arg. 105 b12
Brandstad, Swed. 121 F5
Brandsville, Mo., 128 72 F8
Brandt, S. Dak., 148 74 D3
Brandvlei, S. Af., 1,417 164 C7
Brandy, Va. 62 G4
Brandy Pd., Me. 55 D3
Brandýs nad Labem-Stará Boleslav, Czech., 13,243 126 B1
Brandywine, Md. 62 H4
Brandywine, W. Va. 62 E4
Brandywine Cr., Del.-Pa. 61 L6
Brandywine Manor, Pa. 60 e11
Branford, Conn., 2,371; 16,610(T) 56 E7
Branford, Fla., 663 65 F3
Braniewo, Pol., 9,050 127 D1
Bransby Point, Montserrat 97 5
Brańsk, Pol., 2,873 127 E2
Branson, Colo., 124 79 D3
Branson, Mo., 1,887 72 D8
Brant, Mich. 67 J5
Brant, N.Y. 58 B6
Brantas, r., Indon. 148 E5
Brant Beach, N.J., 61 C4
Brantford, Ont., Can., 54,458 44 H7
Brantford, N. Dak. 74 C2
Brant Lake, N.Y. 59 N4
Brant L., N.Y. 59 N4
Brantley, Ala., 1,014 64 C4
Brantley, co., Ga., 5,891 64 G4
Brantôme, Fr., 2,016 117 D4
Brant Rock (part of Marshfield), Mass. 57 O4
Brantwood, Wis. 66 C3
Bras d'Or, N.S., Can. 47 V10
Bras d'Or L., N.S., Can. 47 V11
Brashear, Mo., 309 72 E4
Brasher Falls, N.Y. 59 L2
Brasiléia, Braz., 1,852 102 C4
Brasileiro, Planalto, Braz. 98 D4
Brasília, D.F., Braz., 89,698 103 G5
Brasília, Ms. Gs., Braz., 3,182 103 H5
Brasília Legal, Braz. 103 E2
Braslav, U.S.S.R., 4,000 136 B2
Braşov, Rum., 123,834 128 E2
Brass, Nigeria 162 g9
Brasschaat, Belg., 22,114 115 C3
Brassey Ra., Malay. 148 F1
Brasstown, N.C. 63 a7
Brasstown Bald, mtn., Ga. 64 F1
Brassua L., Me. 55 C3
Břasy, Czech. 126 c7
Bratca, Rum. 128 D1
Bratenahl, Ohio, 1,332 70 e8
Brateş, L., Rum. 128 G2
Bratislava, Czech., 257,856 126 C2
Bratsk, U.S.S.R., 110,000 135 K4
Bratskoye Vdkhr., U.S.S.R. 135 K4
Brattleboro, Vt., 9,315 54 B6
Braubach, F.R.Ger., 3,818 119 D4
Braughing, U.K. 114 J7
Braunau, Aust., 14,442 124 J5
Braunfels, F.R.Ger., 3,545 119 E3
Braunlage, F.R.Ger., 5,969 118 C3
Braunschweig, F.R.Ger., 240,431 118 C2
Braunston, U.K., 1,198 114 F6
Braunton, U.K., 4,303 113 D6
Brauweiler, F.R.Ger., 5,648 119 B3
Brava, Som. Rep., 7,488 163 M5
Brava, i., C. Verde Is. 109 5
Brava, Costa, Sp. 122 G2
Bråviken, inlet, Swed. 120 d9
Bravo, r., Br. Hond.-Guat. 94 C2
Bravo del Norte=Rio Grande
Bravsko, Yug. 125 C2
Brawley, Calif., 12,703 82 F6
Brawley Pks., Nev. 83 A3
Brawly Wash, Ariz. 78 C5
Braxton, Miss., 191 73 E5
Braxton, co., W. Va., 15,152 62 D4
Bray, Ire., 12,403 113 C5
Bray, U.K., 4,858 114 G7
Bray, Okla. 76 F3
Bray Head, Ire. 113 A6
Bray I., N.W.T., Can. 41 O4
Braymer, Mo., 874 72 D5
Brays Mtn., Austl. 173 f9
Bray-sur-Seine, Fr., 1,822 117 E2
Brayton, Iowa, 225 72 B3
Braytonville (part of N. Adams), Mass. 56 D2
Brazeau, Alta., Can. 42 J3
Brazeau, r., Alta., Can. 42 J3
Brazeau, Mt., Alta., Can. 42 H3
Brazil, ctry., 84,679,000* 102-3
Brazil, Ind., 8,853 70 B3
Brazil Basin, Atl. Oc. 109 L7
Brazópolis, Braz., 4,446 103 d18
Brazoria, co., Tex., 76,204 77 Q5
Brazoria, Tex., 1,291 77 Q5
Brazos, co., Tex., 44,895 77 P4
Brazos, Tex. 76 d9
Brazos, r., Tex. 77 P3
Brazos, Double Mtn. Fk., r., Tex. 77 N3
Brazos Pk., N. Mex. 79 B3
Brazos, Salt Fk., r., Tex. 77 N3
Brazza, r., Indon. 149 L4
Brazzaville, Congo, 133,700 164 B2
Brčko, Yug., 19,000* 125 D2
Brda, r., Pol. 127 B2
Brdy, mts., Czech. 126 A2
Brea, Calif., 8,487 83 i16
Brea, P., P.R. 96 s11
Bread Loaf Mtn., Vt. 54 B3
Breakeyville, Qué., Can. 47 n16
Breaksea Pt., U.K. 114 B8
Breaksea Sd., N.Z. 175 e7
Bream Head, N.Z. 175 g4
Breamore, U.K. 113 i13
Breathitt, co., Ky., 15,490 71 H4
Bréau, Fr. 116 k12
Breaux Bridge, La., 3,303 73 D7
Breaza, Rum., 11,122 128 E2
Brebeni, Rum. 128 E2
Brebes, Indon. 148 c7
Brebières, Fr., 3,424 116 a7
Brechin, Ont., Can. 46 E4
Brechin, U.K., 7,114 112 E3
Brecht, Belg., 6,674 115 C3
Breckenridge, Colo., 393 79 C2
Breckenridge, Mich., 1,131 67 J5
Breckenridge, Minn., 4,335 74 D2
Breckenridge, Mo., 605 72 D5
Breckenridge, Tex., 6,273 77 O3
Breckenridge Hills, Mo., 6,299 72 a11
Breckerfeld, F.R.Ger., 5,782 119 C2
Breckinridge, co., Ky., 14,734 71 E4
Breckinridge, Okla., 42 76 F1
Brecknockshire, co., U.K., 55,185 113 E6
Brecksville, Ohio, 5,435 70 e9
Břeclav, Czech., 11,474 126 C2
Brecon, U.K., 5,766 113 E6
Brecon, Ohio 71 i10
Brecon Beacons, mtn., U.K. 114 B7
Breda, Neth., 102,400 115 C3
Breda, Iowa, 543 72 C2
Bredasdorp, S. Af., 4,686 164 C7
Bredbo, Austl. 173 g11
Bredbyn, Swed. 120 D3
Bredebro, Den. 121 A5
Bredenbury, Sask., Can. 43 D5
Bredene, Belg., 8,546 115 B3
Bredon, U.K., 1,028 114 D6
Bredstedt, F.R.Ger., 4,222 118 B1
Bredy, U.S.S.R., 13,000 134 F4
Bree, Belg., 6,823 115 D3
Breed, Wis. 66 E3
Breede, r., S. Af. 164 a8
Breeding, Ky. 71 F5
Breedsville, Mich., 245 67 G6
Breendonk, Belg., 3,010 115 d8
Breese, Ill., 2,461 68 C5
Breesport, N.Y. 59 G7
Breezand, Neth. 115 C2
Breezewood, Pa. 60 F6
Breezy Hill (part of Hanson), Mass. 57 N4
Brega, Marsa el=Burayqah, Marsá al
Bregalnica, r., Yug. 125 F4
Bregenz, Aust., 21,331 124 F6
Bregovo, Bulg., 4,976 128 D2
Brégy, Fr. 116 k10
Bréhal, Fr., 1,658 117 C2
Breidenbach, F.R.Ger., 1,869 119 F3
Breidenbach, Fr. 116 d8
Breidhafjördhur, bay, Ice. 120 a6
Breien, N. Dak. 74 B2
Breil, Switz., 1,272 124 D2
Breisach, F.R.Ger., 4,222 118 A4
Breitenbrunn, Aust., 1,208 124 d11
Breitscheid, F.R.Ger., 1,631 119 E3
Breitstetten, Aust. 124 d10
Brejning, Den., 2,242 121 B5
Brejo, Braz., 3,084 103 H2
Brejo da Madre de Deus, Braz., 2,995 103 a15
Brejo da Porta, Braz. 103 G3
Brejo Santo, Braz., 4,149 103 J3
Bremen, st., F.R.Ger., 733,000* 118 B2
Bremen, F.R.Ger., 507,952 118 B2
Bremen, Ala. 64 C2
Bremen, Ga., 3,132 64 D2
Bremen, Ind., 3,062 70 C1
Bremen, Kans. 75 J4
Bremen, Ohio, 1,417 70 G3
Bremer, co., Iowa, 21,108 72 E2
Bremerhaven, F.R.Ger., 130,492 118 B2
Bremerton, Wash., 28,922 80 B2
Bremervörde, F.R.Ger., 8,639 118 B2
Bremm, F.R.Ger., 1,069 119 C4
Bremo Bluff, Va. 62 F5
Bremond, Tex., 803 77 P4
Brem River, Br. Col., Can. 42 b5
Brems, Ind. 70 C1
Brenham, Tex., 7,740 77 P4
Brenner Pass, Aust.-It., 123 C1
Brent, Ont., Can. 46 F2
Brent, Ala., 1,879 64 B3
Brenta, r., It. 123 D2
Brentford, S. Dak., 96 74 C3
Brentford Bay, N.W.T., Can. 40 L3
Brenton Pt., R.I. 57 L7
Brentwood, U.K., 49,242 113 G6
Brentwood, Calif., 2,186 83 f12
Brentwood, Mo., 12,250 72 a11
Brentwood, N.H. 54 E6
Brentwood, N.Y., 15,387 59 O10
Brentwood, Ohio 71 h10
Brentwood, Pa., 13,706 60 c8
Brentwood, Tenn. 71 E5
Brentwood Bay, Br. Col., Can. 42 c7
Brentwood Lake, Ohio 70 c9
Breoenne, r., Fr. 116 p15
Brescello, It., 4,554 122 d6
Brescia, It., 164,575 123 C2
Breskens, Neth., 3,500 115 B3
Breslau, Ont., Can. 46 b14
Breslau, Pol.=Wrocław
Bresle, r., Fr. 117 D2
Bressana Bottarone, It., 3,220 122 c5
Bressanone, It., 13,956 123 C1
Bressay, i., U.K. 112 F1
Bressuire, Fr., 7,541 117 C3
Brest, Fr., 142,901 116 A2
Brest, U.S.S.R., 78,000 134 B4
Brestak, Bulg., 2,526 128 F3
Bretagne, reg., Fr. 116 B2
Bretaña, Peru 104 C3
Breteuil-sur-Noye, Fr., 2,748 117 E2
Brethren, Mich. 67 H4
Brétigny-sur-Orge, Fr., 7,153 116 h12
Breton, Alta., Can. 42 J3
Breton, Kans. 75 E4
Bretón, Cayo, Cuba 96 d2
Breton Sd., La. 73 F8
Breton Woods, N.J., 1,292 61 C3
Brettach, r., F.R.Ger. 119 G6
Brett, C., N.Z. 175 g4
Bretten, F.R.Ger., 9,543 118 B4
Bretton Woods, N.H. 54 D3
Breueh, P., Indon. 148 A1
Breuillet, Fr., 2,009 116 g12
Breukelen, Neth., 5,600 115 c6
Brevard, co., Fla., 111,435 65 J4
Brevard, N.C., 4,857 63 B2
Breves, Braz., 2,051 103 F2
Brevik, Nor. 121 B1
Brevoort L., Mich. 67 J2
Brevort, Mich. 67 H2
Brewarrina, Austl. 173 G4
Brewer, Me., 9,009 55 D4
Brewer Pd., Me. 55 D4
Brewerton, N.Y. 59 H5
Brewood, U.K., 3,576 114 D5
Brewster, Fla. 65 d12
Brewster, Kans., 317 75 D4
Brewster, Mass., 1,236(T) 57 Q5
Brewster, Minn., 500 74 E4
Brewster, Nebr., 44 75 E2
Brewster, N.Y., 1,714 59 N9
Brewster, Ohio, 2,025 70 H2
Brewster, co., Tex., 6,434 77 M4
Brewster, Wash., 940 80 D1
Brewton, Ala., 6,309 64 B4
Brewton, Ga. 64 G3
Brezhani, Bulg., 3,635 128 D4
Březnice, Czech. 126 A2
Breznik, Bulg., 3,448 128 D3
Březno, Czech. 126 c6
Brezno, Czech., 10,279 126 D2
Brezoi, Rum. 128 E2
Brézolles, Fr., 1,235 117 D2
Bria, C.A.R., 6,964 163 H4
Briançon, Fr., 10,105 117 G4
Briar, Mo. 72 F8
Briar, Tex. 76 d9
Briarcliff Manor, N.Y., 5,105 59 N9
Briar Creek, Pa., 399 61 K3
Briar Cr., Ga. 64 G2
Briare, Fr., 4,114 117 E3
Briartown, Okla. 76 H2
Bribbaree, Austl. 173 g10
Brice, Ohio 70 b7
Briceland, Calif. 82 A2
Bricelyn, Minn., 542 74 F4
Briceño, Col. 101 f14
Brices Crossroads Nat. Btfld. Site, Miss. 73 G3
Briceville, Tenn., 1,217 71 G5
Brichany, U.S.S.R. 136 B3
Brickaville, Malag. Rep., 1,952 165 H5
Brick Church, Tenn. 71 D6
Brickeys, Ark., 62 73 E3
Bricquebec, Fr., 3,138 117 C2
Bride, r., Ire. 113 B6
Bridgeboro, Ga. 64 E4
Bridgehampton, N.Y. 59 Q10
Bridge House, Calif. 82 b7
Bridgend, U.K., 15,174 114 A7
Bridge of Allan, U.K., 3,312 112 c7
Bridge of Earn, U.K. 112 d7
Bridge of Orchy, U.K. 112 D3
Bridge of Weir, U.K. 112 a8
Bridgeport, Ont., Can., 1,661 46 b14
Bridgeport, Ala., 2,906 64 D1
Bridgeport, Calif. 82 D3
Bridgeport, Conn., 156,748 56 C8
Bridgeport, Ill., 2,260 68 E5
Bridgeport, Mich., 1,326 67 J5
Bridgeport, Nebr., 1,645 75 C2
Bridgeport, N.J., 61 A4
Bridgeport, Ohio, 3,824 70 J2
Bridgeport, Okla., 139 76 E2
Bridgeport, Oreg. 80 E3
Bridgeport, Pa., 5,306 60 f11
Bridgeport, Tex., 3,218 77 P3
Bridgeport, Utah 78 D1
Bridgeport, Wash., 876 80 D1
Bridgeport, W. Va., 4,199 62 D3
Bridgeport, Wis. 66 C5
Bridgeport, L., Tex. 76 d8
Bridger, Mont., 824 81 E3
Bridges Pt., Christmas Atoll 177 40
Bridgeton, Ind. 70 B3
Bridgeton, Mo., 7,820 72 a10
Bridgeton, N.J., 20,966 61 A5
Bridgeton, N.C., 638 63 H2
Bridgetown, Austl., 1,777 172 B5
Bridgetown, Barb., 11,304 97 10
Bridgetown, N.S., Can., 1,020 47 T11
Bridgetown, Ire. 113 C5
Bridgetown, Ohio 71 g11
Bridgetown (part of Narragansett), R.I. 57 L7
Bridge View, Ill., 7,334 69 c9
Bridgeville, Calif. 82 B2
Bridgeville, Del., 1,469 62 J4
Bridgeville, Pa., 7,112 60 B5
Bridgewater, Austl., 1,252 172 c8
Bridgewater, N.S., Can., 4,399 45 N7
Bridgewater, Conn., 898(T) 56 C6
Bridgewater, Iowa, 225 72 C3
Bridgewater, Me. 55 E2
Bridgewater, Mass., 10,276(T) 57 N5
Bridgewater, Mich. 67 K6
Bridgewater, N.H. 54 D4
Bridgewater, N.Y., 373 59 K6
Bridgewater, S. Dak., 694 74 D4
Bridgewater, Vt. 54 B4
Bridgewater, Va., 1,815 62 E4
Bridgewater Corners, Vt. 54 B4
Bridgman, Mich., 1,454 67 G7
Bridgnorth, U.K., 7,552 113 E5
Bridgton, Me., 1,715 55 B4
Bridgwater, U.K., 25,600 113 E6
Břidličná, Czech. 127 g7
Bridlington, U.K., 26,023 113 F4
Bridport, Austl. 173 f13
Bridport, U.K., 6,530 113 E6
Bridport, Vt. 54 A4
Bridstow, U.K. 114 C7
Brie-Comte-Robert, Fr., 4,716 116 i12
Brielle, Neth., 4,100 115 C3
Brielle, N.J., 2,619 58 c16
Brienne-le-Château, Fr., 3,676 117 F2
Brienz, Switz., 2,864 124 B2
Brienzersee, Switz. 124 B2
Brienzwiler, Switz. 124 C2
Brierfield, U.K., 6,958 114 D3
Brier Hill, N.Y. 59 J2
Brierley Hill, U.K., 56,377 114 D6
Brier Mtn., Pa. 60 H2
Brieselang, Ger.D.R. 119 d10
Brieskow-Finkenheerd, Ger.D.R. 118 E2
Brietlingen, F.R.Ger., 1,062 119 b9
Briey, Fr., 5,396 117 G2
Brig, Switz., 4,647 124 C2
Brigantine, N.J., 4,201 61 C5
Brigden, Ont., Can. 46 B6
Brigels=Breil
Brigg, U.K., 4,912 114 H3
Briggs Corners (part of Attleboro), Mass. 57 L5
Briggsdale, Colo. 79 C1
Briggsdale, Ohio 70 a7
Briggsville, Ark. 73 B3
Briggsville, Mass. 56 D2
Briggsville, Wis. 66 D5
Brigham City, Utah, 11,728 78 C1
Brighouse, U.K., 30,783 114 E3
Brighstone, U.K. 113 k13
Brighstone Bay, U.K. 113 i13
Bright, Austl. 173 f11
Bright, Ont., Can. 46 a14
Brightlingsea, U.K., 4,801 113 G6
Brighton, U.K., 163,159 113 F6
Brighton, Ala., 2,884 64 b8
Brighton, Colo., 7,055 79 C2
Brighton, Fla. 65 H5
Brighton, Ill., 1,248 68 B4
Brighton, Iowa, 724 72 F3
Brighton, Me. 55 C3
Brighton, Md. 62 a8
Brighton, Mich., 2,282 67 K6
Brighton, Tenn., 652 71 B6
Brighton, Wis. 66 c13
Brightons, U.K. 112 c8
Brightshade, Ky. 71 H4
Brightview, Alta., Can. 43 b8
Brightwaters, N.Y., 3,193 58 f14
Brightwood, Va. 62 F4
Brignais, Fr., 3,119 116 p15
Brignall, U.K. 112 g10
Brignoles, Fr., 8,043 117 F5
Brigstock, U.K., 1,406 114 G6
Brigus, Newf., Can. 45 b10
Brigus South, Newf., Can. 45 c10
Brihuega, Sp., 2,287 122 D2
Briis-sous-Forges, Fr., 1,115 116 g12
Brill, U.K. 114 F7
Brill, Wis. 66 B3
Brilliant, Ala., 749 64 B1
Brilliant, Ohio, 2,174 70 J2
Brillion, Wis., 1,783 66 E4
Brilon, F.R.Ger., 11,248 118 B3
Brimfield, U.K. 114 C6
Brimfield, Ill., 656 68 B3
Brimfield, Mass., 1,414(T) 56 H4
Brimington, U.K., 8,163 114 E4
Brimley, Mich. 67 J2
Brimpton Lake, Austl. 172 a7
Brimson, Minn. 74 G2
Brimson, Mo., 107 72 D4
Brindisi, It., 68,555 123 G4
Brinkley, Ark., 4,636 73 D3
Brinkman, Okla., 14 76 D3
Brinktown, Mo. 72 F6
Brinkworth, U.K., 1,018 114 D7
Brinnon, Wash. 80 B2
Brinsmade, N. Dak., 110 74 C1
Brinson, Ga., 246 64 E5
Brinton, Mich. 67 J5
Briny Breezes, Fla. 65 b9
Brione, Switz. 124 C2
Briones, Sp., 1,417 122 n12
Brionne, Fr., 4,342 117 D2
Brioude, Fr., 6,928 117 E4
Brisbane, Austl., 502,320 173 H4
Brisbane, Calif. 83 e12
Brisben, N.Y. 59 J7
Brisbin, Pa., 398 60 F4
Brisco, Br. Col., Can. 42 J4
Briscoe, co., Tex., 3,577 77 N2
Briscoe, Tex. 76 N2
Brissago, Switz., 1,845 124 C2
Bristol, N.B., Can. 47 S10
Bristol, U.K., 437,048 113 E6
Bristol, Colo. 79 D2
Bristol, Conn., 45,499 56 E6
Bristol, Fla., 614 65 E2
Bristol, Ga., 162 64 G4
Bristol, Ind., 991 70 D1
Bristol, Me. 55 C5
Bristol, Md. 62 c9
Bristol, co., Mass., 398,488 57 L5
Bristol, Mich. 67 H4
Bristol, N.H. 54 D4
Bristol, N.Y. 58 o21
Bristol, Pa., 12,364 61 N5
Bristol, co., R.I., 37,146 57 L6
Bristol, R.I., 14,570(T) 57 L6
Bristol, S. Dak., 562 74 D3
Bristol, Tenn.-Va., 34,726 62 B6
Bristol, Tex. 76 f10
Bristol, Vt., 1,421 54 A3
Bristol, Wis. 66 F6
Bristol Bay, Alaska 85 D4
Bristol Center, N.Y. 58 o21
Bristol Chan., U.K. 113 E6
Bristol L., Calif. 82 F5
Bristolville, Ohio 70 J1
Bristol Silver Mines, Nev. 83 C3
Bristow, Ind. 70 C4
Bristow, Iowa, 268 72 E2
Bristow, Nebr., 153 75 E1
Bristow, Okla., 4,795 76 G2
Britannia Beach, Br. Col., Can. 42 c6
British Columbia, prov., Can., 1,789,000* 42
British Guiana=Guyana
British Honduras, Cent. Amer., 109,000* 94
British Mts., Can.-U.S. 40 A4
British Solomon Islands Prot., 137,000* 170 E5
Brito, Guat. 94 c9
Brits, S. Af., 9,393 164 D6
Britstown, S. Af., 2,834 164 C7
Britt, Ont., Can. 44 H6
Britt, Iowa, 2,042 72 D1
Brittany=Bretagne
Britton, Mich., 622 67 K7
Britton, S. Dak., 1,442 74 D3
Britton, Tex. 76 e9
Brive-la-Gaillarde, Fr., 43,683 117 D4
Briviesca, Sp., 3,779 122 m12
Brixham, U.K., 10,721 113 E6
Brixlegg, Aust., 2,328 124 H6
Brixworth, U.K., 1,578 114 G6
Brize Norton, U.K. 114 E7
Brlik, U.S.S.R. 137 g3
Brno, Czech., 323,309 126 C2
Bro, Swed. 121 D2
Bro, Swed. 120 e8
Broa, Ensenada de la, Cuba 96 c1
Broach, India, 73,639 145 D5
Broad, r., Man., Can. 43 G2
Broad, r., Ga. 64 F1
Broad, r., N.C.-S.C. 63 C3
Broad, r., S.C. 63 D5
Broadalbin, N.Y., 1,438 59 M5
Broad Arrow, Austl. 172 B4
Broadback, r., Qué., Can. 44 J4
Broad Bay, U.K. 112 C2
Broadbent, Oreg. 80 A4
Broad Brook, Conn., 1,389 56 F5
Broad Chalke, U.K. 113 i12
Broad Cove, Newf., Can. 45 b10
Broad Cove, Me. 55 C4
Broadford, Austl., 1,451 173 e11
Broadford, U.K. 112 D3
Broadford, Va. 62 C6
Broad Haven, inlet, Ire. 113 A4
Broadland, S. Dak., 33 74 C3
Broadlands, Ill., 344 68 D4
Broad Law, mtn., U.K. 112 E4
Broadman, Oreg., 153 80 D3
Broadmoor, Alaska 85 a6
Broadmoor, Colo. 79 C2
Broad Park, Ind. 70 C3
Broad Pass, Alaska 85 G3
Broad Sd., Austl. 173 G3
Broadstairs, U.K., 14,437 113 G6
Broad Top City, Pa., 334 60 F5
Broadus, Mont., 628 81 G3
Broadview, Sask., Can. 43 D5
Broadview, Ill., 8,588 69 c9
Broadview, Ind., 1,865 70 C3
Broadview, Mont., 160 81 E2
Broadview, N. Mex. 79 D4
Broadview Heights, Ohio, 6,209 70 H1
Broadwater, co., Mont., 2,804 81 D2
Broadwater, Nebr., 235 75 C2
Broadway, U.K., 2,564 114 E6
Broadway, N.C., 466 63 F2
Broadway, Va., 646 62 F4
Broadwell, Ill., 173 68 C3
Broadwell, Ky. 71 G3
Broager, Den., 3,799 121 B6
Broc, Switz., 1,653 124 B2
Brochet, Man., Can. 43 E2
Brochet, L., Man., Can. 43 E2
Brock, Sask., Can. 43 B4
Brock, Nebr., 213 75 K3
Brock, Okla. 76 F3
Brock, Tex. 76 d9
Brocken, pk., Ger.D.R. 118 C3
Brockenhurst, U.K., 2,661 113 i13
Brocket, N. Dak., 153 74 C1
Brockport, N.Y., 5,256 58 D5
Brocksburg, Nebr. 75 F1
Brockton, Mass., 72,813 57 M4
Brockton, Mont., 367 81 G1
Brockville, Ont., Can., 17,476 44 J7
Brockway, Conn. 56 G7
Brockway, Mich. 67 L5
Brockway, Mont. 81 G2
Brockway, Pa., 2,563 60 E3
Brockworth, U.K., 6,820 114 D7
Brocton, Ill., 380 68 E4
Brocton, N.Y., 1,416 58 B7
Brodarevo, Yug. 125 D3
Broderick, Calif. 82 a7
Brodeur Pen., N.W.T., Can. 40 M3
Brodhead, Ky., 762 71 G4
Brodhead, Wis., 2,444 66 D6
Brodhead Cr., Pa. 61 M3
Brodheadsville, Pa. 61 L4
Brodick, U.K. 112 D4
Brodie Mtn., Mass. 56 D2
Brodnax, Va., 561 62 F6
Brodnica, Pol., 14,444 127 C2
Brodokalmak, U.S.S.R. 137 k8
Brody, U.S.S.R., 12,200 136 B3
Broechem, Belg., 3,005 115 e8
Broek, Neth. 115 E1
Brogan, Oreg. 80 E3
Brohard, W. Va. 62 C3
Brohl, F.R.Ger., 2,142 119 C4
Brohman, Mich. 67 H5
Brok, Pol., 2,144 127 D2
Brok, r., Pol. 127 E2
Brokaw, Wis. 319 66 D3
Broken, r., Austl. 173 e11
Broken Arrow, Okla., 5,928 76 H1
Broken Bow, Nebr., 3,482 75 F2
Broken Bow, Okla., 2,087 76 J3
Brokenburg, Va. 62 G4
Brokenhead, Man., Can. 43 h9
Broken Hill, Austl., 31,351 173 F4
Broken Hill, Zamb., 30,100 164 D4
Brokenstraw Cr., Pa. 60 C2
Bröl-Bach, r., F.R.Ger. 119 C3
Brome, F.R.Ger., 1,783 118 C2
Brome, L., Qué., Can. 47 M3
Bromham, U.K., 1,524 114 D8
Bromhead, Sask., Can. 43 D5
Bromide, Okla., 264 76 G3
Bromley, Ky., 998 71 h11
Bromley Mtn., Vt. 54 A5
Bromley Tablemount, Atl. Oc. 109 K8
Brompton, U.K., 1,587 112 h11
Bromptonville, Qué., Can., 2,702 47 M3
Bromsgrove, U.K., 34,474 113 E5
Bromyard, U.K., 1,680 113 E5
Bron, Fr., 27,559 116 p15
Bronaugh, Mo., 173 72 C7
Brøndbyøster, Den., 11,719 121 a7
Brønderslev, Den., 9,454 121 C3
Bronllys, U.K. 114 B6
Bronnitsy, U.S.S.R., 10,000 136 c6
Brönnöysund, Nor., 1,855 120 B2
Bronson, N.B., Can. 47 T10
Bronson, Fla., 707 65 G3
Bronson, Kans., 354 75 L6
Bronson, Mich., 2,267 67 H7
Bronson, Tex. 77 Q4
Bronte, Austl., 1,832 173 f14
Bronte, Ont., Can., 2,024 46 E5
Bronte, It., 22,314 123 E6
Bronte, Tex., 999 77 N4
Bronte Cr., Ont., Can. 46 c14
Bronwood, Ga., 400 64 E4
Bronx, co., N.Y., 1,424,815 59 N10
Bronx, r., N.Y. 58 d13
Bronxville, N.Y., 6,744 58 d13
Brook, U.K. 113 k13
Brook, Ind., 845 70 B2
Brookdale, Calif. 83 e13
Brooke, co., W. Va., 28,940 62 D2
Brookeland, Tex. 77 R4
Brookesmith, Tex. 77 O4
Brooke's Point, Phil., 1,844 153 A3
Brookeville, Md., 140 62 a8
Brookfield, N.S., Can. 47 U11
Brookfield, Conn. 3,405(T) 56 C7
Brookfield, Ga. 64 F4
Brookfield, Ill., 20,429 69 c9
Brookfield, Mass., 1,751(T) 56 H4
Brookfield, Mich. 67 J6
Brookfield, Mo., 5,694 72 D5
Brookfield, N.Y. 59 K6
Brookfield, Ohio 70 J1
Brookfield, Vt. 54 B3
Brookfield, Wis., 19,812 66 c11
Brookfield Center (part of Brookfield), Conn. 56 C7
Brookford, N.C., 596 63 C2
Brookhaven, Miss., 9,885 73 E6
Brookhaven, N.Y. 58 h13
Brookhaven, Pa., 5,280 60 f12
Brookings, Oreg., 2,637 80 A4
Brookings, co., S. Dak., 20,046 74 D3
Brookings, S. Dak., 10,558 74 D3
Brookland, Ark., 301 73 E2
Brooklands, Man., Can., 4,302 43 g10
Brooklet, Ga., 557 64 H3
Brooklin, Ont., Can., 1,531 46 F5
Brooklin, Me. 55 D4
Brookline, Mass., 54,044(T) 57 M3
Brookline, N.H. 54 D6
Brookline, Vt. 54 B5
Brooklyn, N.S., Can. 47 T11
Brooklyn, N.S., Can. 47 U11
Brooklyn, Ala. 64 C4
Brooklyn, Conn., 3,312(T) 56 J5
Brooklyn, St. Clair Co., Ill., 1,922 72 b11
Brooklyn, Schuyler Co., Ill., 68 B3
Brooklyn, Ind., 866 70 C3
Brooklyn, Iowa, 1,415 72 E3
Brooklyn, Mich., 986 67 J6
Brooklyn, Miss. 73 F6
Brooklyn (Borough of N.Y.C.), N.Y. 58 d14
Brooklyn, Ohio, 10,733 70 d9
Brooklyn, Pa. 61 L2
Brooklyn, Wash. 80 B2
Brooklyn, Wis., 590 66 D6
Brooklyn Center, Minn., 30,108 74 b5
Brooklyn Heights, Ohio, 1,449 70 e9
Brooklyn Park, Minn., 10,197 74 F3
Brookmere, Br. Col., Can. 42 G4
Brookneal, Va., 1,070 62 F5
Brook Park, Minn., 108 74 F3
Brook Park, Ohio, 12,856 70 d9
Brookport, Ill., 1,154 68 D6
Brooks, Alta., Can., 2,789 42 K4
Brooks, co., Ga., 15,292 64 F5
Brooks, Ga., 158 64 g11
Brooks, Me. 55 C4
Brooks, Minn., 148 74 D2
Brooks, Oreg. 80 B3
Brooks, co., Tex., 8,609 77 O6
Brooks, Wis. 66 D5
Brooks Bay, Br. Col., Can. 42 E4
Brooks Brook, Yukon, Can. 40 C5
Brooksburg, Ind., 129 70 D4
Brooksby, Sask., Can. 43 D4
Brooksdale, N.C. 63 F1
Brookshire, Tex., 1,339 77 P5
Brookside, Ala., 999 64 c7
Brookside, Ohio 70 J1
Brookside, Tex., 560 77 i9
Brooks Pen., Br. Col., Can. 42 E4
Brooks Ra., Alaska 85 E1
Brookston, Ind., 1,202 70 B2
Brookston, Minn., 144 74 F2
Brooks Vale (part of Cheshire), Conn. 56 E7
Brooks Village (part of Templeton), Mass. 56 H2
Brooksville, Fla., 3,301 65 G4
Brooksville, Ky., 601 71 H3
Brooksville, Me. 55 D4
Brooksville, Miss., 857 73 G4
Brookton, Austl. 172 B5
Brookton, Me. 55 E3
Brooktondale, N.Y. 59 G7
Brookview, N.Y. 59 w29
Brookville, Ont., Can. 46 b13
Brookville, Ill. 68 C1
Brookville, Ind., 2,596 70 E3
Brookville, Kans., 246 75 G5
Brookville, N.Y., 2,601 58 e13
Brookville, Ohio, 3,184 70 E3
Brookville, Pa., 4,620 60 D3
Brookwood, Ala. 64 B2
Broom, Loch, U.K. 112 D3
Broomall, Pa., 19,722(T) 60 f12
Brooman, Austl. 173 h10
Broome, Austl., 1,095 172 C2
Broome, co., N.Y., 212,661 59 J7
Broomes Island, Md. 62 H4
Broomfield, U.K., 2,695 114 J7
Broomfield, Colo., 4,535 79 b8
Broomley, U.K., 1,837 112 f10
Broons, Fr., 2,625 117 B2
Brooten, Minn., 661 74 E3
Brora, U.K. 112 E2
Brora, r., U.K. 112 D2
Brørup, Den. 121 B5
Broscari, Rum. 128 E2
Broseley, U.K., 3,804 114 D5
Brosna, r., Ire. 113 C5
Bross Deur, S. Viet. 147 m11
Broşteni, Rum. 128 D2
Broşteni, Rum. 128 E1
Brothers, Oreg. 80 C4
Brothertown, Wis. 66 E5
Brotterode, Ger.D.R. 118 C3
Brotton, U.K., 4,636 114 G1
Brou, Fr., 3,280 117 D2
Brough, U.K. 114 D1
Broughdale, Ont., Can., 1,542 46 C5
Brough Head, U.K. 112 E2
Brough Ness, U.K. 112 E2
Broughton, Northants., Eng., U.K., 1,570 114 G6
Broughton, York., Eng., U.K. 114 F2
Broughton, Ill., 235 68 D6

Broughton—Burke Chan. · 205

Broughton, Kans. 75 J4
Broughton, Pa., 3,575* 60 c8
Broughton in Furness, U.K., 1,013 113 E4
Broula, Austl. 173 g9
Broumov, Czech. 127 f6
Broussard, La., 1,600 73 C7
Brovary, U.S.S.R., 22,000 136 C3
Brovès, Fr. 116 m13
Brovst, Den., 1,640 121 B3
Broward, co., Fla., 333,946 65 J6
Broward Gardens, Fla. 65 a9
Browerville, Minn., 744 74 E2
Browington, Mo. 72 D6
Brown, co., Ill., 6,210 68 B3
Brown, co., Ind., 7,024 70 C3
Brown, co., Kans., 13,229 75 K4
Brown, co., Minn., 27,676 74 E3
Brown, co., Nebr., 4,436 75 E1
Brown, co., Ohio, 25,178 70 F4
Brown, co., S. Dak. 34,106 74 C3
Brown, co., Tex., 24,728 77 O4
Brown, co., Wis., 125,082 66 F4
Brown City, Mich., 993 67 L5
Brown Clee Hill, U.K. 114 C6
Brown Deer, Wis., 11,280 66 c11
Brownell, Kans., 118 75 F5
Browney, r., U.K. 112 g10
Brownfield, Me. 55 B5
Brownfield, Tex., 10,286 77 M3
Brown Hill, Ont., Can. 46 E4
Brownhills, U.K., 26,392 114 D5
Browning, Ill., 300 68 B3
Browning, Mo., 412 72 D4
Browning, Mont., 2,011 81 C1
Brownington, Vt. 54 C2
Brownington Center. Vt. 54 C2
Brownlee, Nebr. 75 E1
Brownlee Dam, Idaho-Oreg. 81 A3
Brownlee Park., Mich., 3,307 67 H6
Browns, Ill., 251 68 D5
Browns, r., Vt. 54 A2
Brownsboro, Tex., 507 77 Q3
Browns Brook, Del. 61 A6
Brownsburg, Qué., Can., 3,579 47 K3
Brownsburg, Ind., 4,478 70 C3
Brownsburg, Va. 62 E5
Brownsdale, Newf., Can. 45 b9
Brownsdale, Minn., 622 74 F4
Browns L., Wis. 66 c13
Brownsmead, Oreg. 80 B2
Browns Mills, N.J., 61 B4
Browns Point, Wash. 81 b8
Browns Summit, N.C. 63 E1
Browns Town, Jam., 3,899 96 p8
Brownstown, Ill., 659 68 D5
Brownstown, Ind., 2,140 70 D4
Brownstown, Pa., 61 K5
Browns Valley, Calif. 82 C3
Browns Valley, Minn., 1,033 74 D3
Brownsville, Ont., Can. 46 C6
Brownsville, Ill. 68 D5
Brownsville, Ky., 473 71 E4
Brownsville, Minn., 382 74 G4
Brownsville, N.Y. 58 o20
Brownsville, Oreg., 875 80 B3
Brownsville, Pa., 6,055 60 C5
Brownsville, Tenn., 5,424 71 B6
Brownsville, Tex., 48,040 77 P7
Brownsville, Vt. 54 B5
Brownsville, Wis., 276 66 E5
Brownsweg, Sur. 101 N5
Brownton, Minn., 698 74 E3
Browntown, N.J. 58 b15
Browntown, Va. 62 F4
Browntown, Wis., 263 66 D6
Brownvale, Alta., Can. 42 H2
Brownville, Ala. 64 B2
Brownville, Fla. 65 H5
Brownville, Me. 55 C3
Brownville, Nebr., 243 75 K3
Brownville, N.Y., 1,082 59 H4
Brownville Junction, Me. 55 C3
Brownwood, Tex., 16,974 77 O4
Brownwood, L., Tex. 77 O4
Broxton, Ga., 907 64 G4
Broye, r., Switz. 124 A2
Broyle, C., Newf., Can. 45 c10
Brozas, Sp., 5,634 122 B3
Bruas, Malay., 3,705 147 o14
Bruay-en-Artois, Fr., 30,902 117 E1
Brubaker, Ill. 68 D5
Bruce, Alta., Can. 43 d7
Bruce, Fla. 65 C2
Bruce, Miss., 1,698 73 F3
Bruce, S. Dak., 272 74 D3
Bruce, Wash. 80 D2
Bruce, Wis., 815 66 B3
Bruce, Mt., Austl. 172 B3
Bruce Crossing, Mich. 66 D2
Bruce Mines, Ont., Can. 44 G6
Bruce Pen., Ont., Can. 44 G6
Bruceton, Tenn., 1,158 71 C5
Bruceton, W. Va., 209 62 E3
Bruce Vale, Barb. 97 10
Bruceville, Ind., 623 70 B4
Bruchsal, F.R.Ger., 19,476 118 B4
Brucite, Nev. 83 B3
Bruck, Aust., 16,101 124 M6
Bruck, Aust., 6,789 124 N5
Brück, Ger.D.R. 118 D2
Brücken, F.R.Ger., 2,279 119 C6
Brückenau, F.R.Ger., 5,733 118 B3
Bruckmühl, F.R.Ger., 7,084 118 C5
Brudenell, Ont., Can. 46 G3
Bruderheim, Alta., Can. 43 c7
Brue, r., U.K. 113 E6
Brüel, Ger.D.R. 118 C2
Bruff, Ire. 113 B5
Bruges = Brugge
Brugg, Switz., 6,683 124 C1
Brugge, Belg., 52,535 115 B3
Brühl, Bad.-Württ., F.R.Ger., 6,699 119 F6
Brühl, Nrh.-Wf., F.R.Ger., 32,342 118 A3
Bruin, Pa., 706 60 C3
Bruint, India 145 K3
Brule, Nebr., 370 75 D2
Brule, co., S. Dak., 6,319 74 C4
Brule, Wis. 66 B2
Brule, r., Mich.-Wis. 66 E3
Brule L., Minn. 74 G2
Brûlon, Fr., 1,206 117 C3
Brumadinho, Braz., 2,283 103 d17
Brumado, Braz., 7,054 103 H4
Brumath, Fr., 6,801 117 G2
Brumby (part of Scunthorpe), U.K., 10,659 114 G3
Brumley, Mo., 74 72 E6
Brummen, Neth., 4,200 115 E2
Brumunddal, Nor. 120 B3
Brundidge, Ala., 2,523 64 D4
Bruneau, Idaho 81 A4
Bruneau, W. Fk., Idaho-Nev. 83 C2
Brunei, Br. dependency, 101,000* 148 E1
Brunei, Brunei, 37,511 148 E1
Brünen, F.R.Ger., 2,515 119 B1
Brunette Downs, Austl. 172 E2
Brunflo, Swed. 120 C3
Brunico, It., 8,444 123 D1
Bruning, Nebr., 289 75 H3
Brunkeberg, Nor. 121 A1
Brunkild, Man., Can. 43 g10
Brunn, Aust., 5,786 124 c10
Brünn = Brno
Brunnen, Switz. 124 C2
Brunner, N.Z., 1,073 175 f6
Brunner, L., N.Z. 175 f6
Bruno, Sask., Can. 43 C4
Bruno, Minn., 116 74 F2
Brunoy, Fr., 15,247 116 i12
Bruns-Berg, F.R.Ger. 119 a9
Brunsbüttelkoog, F.R.Ger., 8,845 118 B2
Brunson, S.C., 603 63 C5
Brunssum, Neth., 21,400 115 E4
Brunsville, Iowa, 128 72 A2
Brunswick, F.R.Ger. = Braunschweig
Brunswick, Ga., 21,703 64 H4
Brunswick, Me., 9,444 55 B5
Brunswick, Md., 3,555 62 G3
Brunswick, Mich. 67 G5
Brunswick, Mo., 1,493 72 D5
Brunswick, Nebr., 254 75 H1
Brunswick, co., N.C., 20,278 63 F3
Brunswick, N.C., 169 63 F3
Brunswick, Ohio, 11,725 70 H1
Brunswick, Tenn. 71 B6
Brunswick, co., Va., 17,779 62 G6
Brunswick, Va. 62 F6
Brunswick Bay, Austl. 172 C2
Brunswick Junction, Austl., 1,154 172 A5
Brunswick, Pen., Chile 105 A8
Bruntál, Czech., 8,097 126 C1
Brunton, U.K. 112 d7
Brus, Yug. 125 E3
Brush, Colo., 3,621 79 D1
Brush Creek, Tenn. 71 F5
Brush Cr., Pa. 60 b7
Brush Cr., Pa. 60 F6
Brushton, N.Y., 553 59 L2
Brush Valley, Pa. 60 D4
Brushyknob, Mo. 72 E8
Brushy Run, W. Va. 62 E4
Brusio, Switz., 1,445 124 E2
Brus Laguna, Hond. 94 E3
Brussegem, Belg. 2,625 115 d9
Brussel(s) = Bruxelles
Brussels, Ont., Can. 46 C5
Brussels, Ill., 201 68 B5
Brussels, Wis. 66 F4
Brüssow, Ger.D.R. 118 E2
Brusy, Pol. 127 B2
Bruthen, Austl. 173 G5
Brutus, Mich. 67 J3
Bruxelles, Belg., 170,568 115 C4
Bruxelles, Man., Can. 43 e10
Bruz, Fr., 4,851 117 C2
Bruzual, Ven. 100 F4
Bryan, co., Ga., 6,226 64 H3
Bryan, Ohio, 7,361 70 E1
Bryan, co., Okla., 24,252 76 G4
Bryan, Tex., 27,542 77 P4
Bryan, Mt., Austl. 172 c7
Bryansk, U.S.S.R., 231,000 134 C4
Bryant, Ark., 737 73 C3
Bryant, Fla. 65 J6
Bryant, Ill., 346 68 B3
Bryant, Ind., 316 70 E2
Bryant, Okla., 72 76 G2
Bryant, S. Dak., 522 74 D3
Bryant, Wash. 80 B1
Bryant, Wis. 66 E3
Bryant Cr., Mo. 72 E8
Bryant L., Minn. 74 b6
Bryant Pond, Me. 55 B4
Bryantville (part of Hanson and Pembroke), Mass. 57 N4
Bryast, Bulg., 5,793 128 E3
Bryce Canyon Nat. Pk., Utah 78 B3
Bryceland, La., 89 73 C5
Bryher, i., U.K. 113 C7
Brylle, Den., 1,030 121 C5
Bryn Athyn, Pa., 1,057 60 f11
Brynica, r., Pol. 127 g6
Brynmawr, U.K., 6,482 114 B7
Bryn Mawr, Pa., 9,200* 61 f11
Bryn Mawr, Wash. 81 b7
Bryon, Île, Qué., Can. 45 O6
Bryrup, Den., 1,019 121 B4
Bryson, Qué., Can. 47 H3
Bryson, Tex., 545 77 O3
Bryson City, N.C., 1,084 63 A2
Bryson, L., Qué., Can. 46 H2
Bryte, Calif. 82 a7
Bryukhovetskaya, U.S.S.R. 136 E4
Brzeg, Pol., 24,000* 127 B3
Brzeg Dolny, Pol., 7,740 127 B3
Brześć Kujawski, Pol., 4,447 127 C2
Brzesko, Pol., 6,835 127 D4
Brzeziny, Pol., 7,538 127 C3
Brzeźnica Nowa, Pol. 127 i5
Brzozów, Pol., 4,148 127 E4
Buabuang, Indon. 149 G3
Buache, Mt., Kusaie 176 31
Buada (dist.), Nauru 175 17
Buada Lag., Nauru 175 17
Bua Kha, Thai. 146 C3
Buakonikai, Ocean I. 175 16
Buala, Sol. Is. 175 c2
Buapinang, Indon. 149 G4
Buaran, Indon. 148 B2
Bua Yai, Thai., 9,809 146 C4
Bubali, Aruba 97 15
Bubanza, Burundi 165 d15
Bubaque, Port. Guin. 162 B4
Bubendorf, Switz., 1,690 124 B1
Būbiyān, i., Kuwait 143 D3
Buc, Fr., 2,067 116 g11
Bucak, Turk., 8,786 142 B2
Bucalemu, Chile 104 e14
Bucaramanga, Col., 221,770 100 D4
Bucas Grande I., Phil. 153 C3
Bucay, Phil., 1,422 153 b5
Buccaneer Arch., Austl. 172 C2
Bucecea, Rum. 128 F1
Buch, F.R.Ger. 119 C4
Buchach, U.S.S.R., 8,100 136 B3
Buchan, Austl. 173 G5
Buchanan, Sask., Can. 43 D4
Buchanan, Lib. 162 C5
Buchanan, Ga., 753 64 D2
Buchanan, co., Iowa, 22,293 72 F2
Buchanan, Ky. 71 J3
Buchanan, Mich., 5,341 67 G7
Buchanan, co., Mo., 90,581 72 C5
Buchanan, N.Y., 2,019 59 M9
Buchanan, co., Va., 36,724 62 B5
Buchanan, Va., 1,349 62 E5
Buchanan Dam, Tex. 77 O4
Buchanan, L., Austl. 172 C3
Buchanan, L., Tex. 77 O4
Buchan G., N.W.T., Can. 41 P3
Buchan Ness, U.K. 112 F3
Buchans, Newf., Can., 2,413 45 P5
Bucharest = București
Buchau, F.R.Ger., 2,734 118 B4
Büchel, F.R.Ger. 119 C4
Buchen, F.R.Ger., 4,314 118 B4
Büchen, F.R.Ger., 3,346 119 c9
Büchenbronn, F.R.Ger., 3,119 119 F7
Buchholz, F.R.Ger., 6,957 118 B2
Buchloe, F.R.Ger., 5,385 118 C4
Buchlyvie, U.K. 112 b7
Buchs, Switz., 6,345 124 D1
Buchupureo, Chile 104 e16
Buchy, Fr., 1,019 117 D2
Buciumi, Rum. 128 D1
Buck, N. Mex. 79 B4
Buckatunna, Miss. 73 G6
Buck Creek, Wis. 66 C5
Buckden Pike, mtn., U.K. 114 D2
Bückeburg, F.R.Ger., 11,064 118 B2
Buckeye, Ariz., 2,518 78 B5
Buckeye, Iowa, 190 72 D2
Buckeye Lake, Ohio, 2,129 70 G3
Buckfield, Me. 55 B4
Buckhannon, W. Va., 6,386 62 D4
Buckhaven (incl. Methil), 21,104 112 e7
Buck Hill Falls, Pa. 61 M3
Buckholts, Tex. 77 P4
Buckhorn, Ont., Can. 46 F4
Buckhorn, Ky. 71 H4
Buckhorn, N. Mex. 79 A5
Buckie, U.K., 7,666 112 E3
Buckingham, Qué., Can., 7,353 44 J6
Buckingham, U.K., 4,379 113 F6
Buckingham (part of Glastonbury), Conn. 56 F6
Buckingham, Pa. 61 N5
Buckingham, co., Va., 10,877 62 F5
Buckingham, Va., 218 62 F5
Buckingham Bay, Austl. 172 E1
Buckinghamshire, co., U.K., 488,233 113 F6
Buck I., St. Croix 97 1
Buck Island Reef Nat. Mon., St. Croix 97 1
Buckland, Alaska, 87 85 D2
Buckland (part of Manchester), Conn. 56 F5
Buckland, Mass., 1,664(T) 56 E2
Buckleboo, Austl. 172 b7
Buckley, U.K., 7,659 114 B4
Buckley, Ill., 690 68 D3
Buckley, Mich., 247 67 H4
Buckley, Wash., 3,538 80 C2
Bucklige Welt, reg., Aust. 125
Bucklin, Kans., 752 75 F6
Bucklin, Mo., 639 72 E5
Buckman, Minn., 166 74 F3
Bucknell, U.K. 114 B6
Buckner, Mo., 1,198 72 C5
Buckner, Va. 62 G5
Buckow, Ger.D.R. 118 E2
Buckroe, Mich. 66 F2
Bucks, co., Pa., 308,567 61 M5
Buckskin Gulch, r., Utah 78 B3
Buckskin Mts., Ariz. 78 B4
Bucksport, Me., 2,327 55 D4
Bucksville, Pa. 61 M4
Bucktail, Nebr. 75 D2
Bucoda, Wash., 390 80 B2
Bučovice, Czech. 126 C2
Buctouche, N.B., Can., 1,537 45 N6
București, Rum., 1,177,661 128 F2
Bucyrus, N. Dak., 60 74 A2
Bucyrus, Ohio, 12,276 70 G2
Bud, Nor. 120 A3
Buda, Ill., 732 68 C2
Buda, Tex., 451 77 P4
Budalin, Burma 147 f6
Budapest, Hung., 1,807,299 126 D3
Budaun, India, 58,770 145 F3
Budd Coast, Ant. 180 T6
Buddha, Ind. 70 C4
Buddh Gaya, India, 6,299 144 e13
Budd Inlet, Wash. 81 a8
Budd Lake, N.J., 1,520 61 B2
Buddon Ness, U.K. 112 e7
Buddusò, It., 6,928 123 B4
Bude, U.K., 3,583 113 D6
Bude, Miss., 1,185 73 E6
Bude Bay, U.K. 113 D6
Budel, Neth. 115 D3
Budelun, i., Terr. Papua 174 3
Büderich, F.R.Ger., 4,237 119 B1
Büderich, F.R.Ger., 12,043 119 B2
Budești, Rum. 128 F2
Budevo, Yug. 125 E3
Budge-Budge, India, 39,824 144 g14
Búdhir, Ice. 120 b6
Budhlada, India, 8,620 144 a11
Budi, L. del, Chile 105 e14
Büdingen, F.R.Ger., 6,554 118 B3
Budjala, D.R.Congo 164 C1
Budkowiczanka, r., Pol. 127 g6
Budrio, It., 14,682 123 C2
Budshahpur, India, 7,280 144 d13
Budva, Yug. 125 D3
Budziszów Wielkopolski, Pol. 127 f5
Buea, Cam., 8,000* 162 F5
Buell, Mo., 53 72 F5
Buellton, Calif. 82 C5
Buena, N.J., 3,243 61 B4
Buena, Wash. 80 C2
Buena Esperanza, Arg., 1,100* 105 B4
Buena Park, Calif., 46,401 83 i16
Buenaventura, Col., 60,220 100 B6
Buenaventura, Mex., 2,780 92 C2
Buenaventura, B. de, Col. 98 B2
Buena Vista, Bol., 2,346 102 D5
Buenavista, Col. 101 f14
Buenavista, Cuba, 1,314 96 d1
Buenavista, Qro., Mex. 93 d9
Buenavista, S.L.P., Mex., 1,109 93 E3
Buenavista, Son., Mex. 92 C2
Buenavista, Phil., 5,770 153 C3
Buena Vista, Ark. 73 C4
Buena Vista, Colo., 1,806 79 B2
Buena Vista, Ga., 1,574 64 E3
Buena Vista, co., Iowa, 21,189 72 B2
Buena Vista, Ohio 70 F4
Buena Vista, Oreg. 80 B3
Buena Vista, Pa. 60 c8
Buena Vista, Tex. 77 M4
Buena Vista, Va., 6,300 62 E5
Buena Vista, Wis. 66 c11
Buena Vista, Ven. 100 F2
Buena Vista, Bahia de, Cuba 96 d1
Buenavista, Cayo de, Cuba 96 a1
Buendía, Pantano de, Sp. 122 D2
Bueno, r., Chile 105 e15
Buenos Aires, Arg., 2,966,816 105 D4
Buenos Aires, C.R. 94 F6
Buenos Aires, L., Arg.-Chile 105 A7
Buen Pasto, Arg. 105 B7
Buesaco, Col. 100 B7
Bueu, Sp., 10,317 122 A1
Buey, r., Cuba 96 e2
Bueyeros, N. Mex. 79 D4
Buffalo, Ind. 70 C2
Buffalo, Iowa, 1,088 72 G3
Buffalo, Kans., 422 75 K6
Buffalo, Ky. 71 D5
Buffalo, Minn., 2,322 74 F3
Buffalo, Mo., 1,477 72 D7
Buffalo, co., Nebr., 26,236 75 F3
Buffalo, N.Y., 532,759 58 C6
Buffalo, N. Dak., 234 74 D2
Buffalo, Okla., 1,618 76 D1
Buffalo, Pa. 60 B5
Buffalo, S.C., 1,209 63 C3
Buffalo, co., S. Dak., 1,547 74 C3
Buffalo, S. Dak., 652 74 A3
Buffalo, Tenn. 71 D6
Buffalo, Tex., 1,108 77 Q4
Buffalo, W. Va., 396 62 C4
Buffalo, co., Wis., 14,202 66 B4
Buffalo, Wis., 484 66 B4
Buffalo, Wyo., 2,907 81 F3
Buffalo, r., Alta., Can. 42 J1
Buffalo, r., Ark. 73 C2
Buffalo, r., Tenn. 71 D6
Buffalo Bill Res., Wyo. 81 E3
Buffalo Center, Alaska 85 H2
Buffalo Center, Iowa, 1,140 72 D1
Buffalo Creek, Br. Col., Can. 42 G3
Buffalo Creek, Colo. 79 C2
Buffalo Cr., N.Y. 58 m19
Buffalo Cr., Okla. 76 D1
Buffalo Cr., Pa.-W. Va. 60 B5
Buffalo Cr., Wyo. 81 F4
Buffalo Gap, S. Dak., 194 74 A4
Buffalo Gap, Tex., 316 77 N3
Buffalo Gap, Va. 62 E4
Buffalo Grove, Ill., 3,429 69 b8
Buffalo Head Hills, Alta., Can. 42 J1
Buffalo Lake, Minn., 707 74 E3
Buffalo L., N.W.T., Can. 40 G5
Buffalo L., Tex. 76 M2
Buffalo L., Wis. 66 D5
Buffalo Narrows, Sask., Can. 43 B3
Buffalo Ridge, Va. 62 D6
Buffalo River N.W.T., Can. 40 F5
Buff Bay, Jam., 2,821 96 q8
Buford, Alta., Can. 43 b7
Buford, Colo. 79 B2
Buford, Ga., 4,168 64 F1
Buford, N. Dak. 74 A1
Buford, Ohio 70 F3
Buford Dam, Ga. 64 E1
Buftea, Rum. 128 F2
Bug, r., Pol.-U.S.S.R. 110 F3
Buga, Col. 100 B6
Bugala I., Uganda 165 f14
Buganegan, i., Eniwetok 176 28
Bugasan, Phil., 5,433 153 B4
Bugasong, Phil., 3,325 153 B3
Bugene, Tanz. 165 e14
Buggenhout, Belg., 9,770 115 d8
Bugg Island L. = Kerr L.
Buggs Island L. = Kerr L.
Bughill, N.C. 63 F3
Bugio, i., Madeira Is. 109 4
Buglawton, U.K., 1,457 114 D4
Bugojno, Yug., 3,950 125 C2
Bugrino, U.S.S.R. 134 D3
Bugsuk I., Phil. 153 A3
Bugul'ma, U.S.S.R., 62,000 134 E4
Buguruslan, U.S.S.R., 41,500 134 E4
Buḩayrat Ḩimş, l., Syr. 142 c5
Buhemba, Tanz. 165 g14
Buhi, Phil., 1,987 153 h14
Bühl, F.R.Ger., 8,750 118 B4
Buhl, Idaho, 3,059 81 B4
Buhl, Minn., 1,526 74 F2
Buhler, Kans., 888 75 H5
Bühlertal, F.R.Ger., 6,885 119 E7
Buhuși, Rum., 12,382 128 F1
Buia, Rum. 128 E2
Buick, Mo. 72 F7
Buie, N.C. 63 E3
Buies Corner, N.C. 63 F2
Builth Wells, U.K., 1,604 113 E5
Buin, Chile, 5,269 104 g13
Buin, Sol. Is. 175 a2
Buir, F.R.Ger., 2,430 119 B3
Buis-les-Baronnies, Fr., 1,655 117 F4
Buitrago, Sp. 122 D2
Bujalance, Sp., 11,475 122 C4
Bujanovac, Yug., 3,681 125 E3
Buji, Terr. Papua 174 d3
Bujor, Rum. 128 F2
Bujumbura, Burundi 164 D2
Bük, Hung., 2,687 126 C3
Buka, i., Sol. Is. 175 a1
Bukachacha, U.S.S.R., 13,300 135 L4
Bukakata, Uganda 165 e14
Bukama, D.R.Congo 165 m18
Buka Passage, Sol. Is. 175 a1
Bukasa I., Uganda 165 f14
Bukavu, D.R.Congo, 60,575 164 D2
Bukden, U.K., 1,158 114 H6
Bukene, Tanz. 164 E2
Bukhara, U.S.S.R., 79,000 134 F6
Bukit Bakri, Malay., 3,968 147 p15
Bukit Betong, Malay. 147 o14
Bukit Gambir, Malay., 2,986 147 p15
Bukit Merah, Malay., 6,085 147 o14
Bukit Mertajam, Malay., 24,658 147 o14
Bukit Pasir, Malay., 2,795 147 p15
Bukit Siput, Malay. 2,156 147 p15
Bukittinggi, Indon., 51,456 148 A3
Bukit Tinggi, Malay., 1,075 147 o15
Bükk, mts., Hung. 126 E2
Bükkösd, Hung., 1,724 126 C3
Bu Knun, Thai. 147 d4
Bukoba, Tanz. 164 E2
Bukondo, Tanz. 165 f15
Bukowo, Jez., Pol. 127 B1
Bukuya, Uganda 165 e13
Bula, Indon. 149 J3
Bula, Tex. 77 M3
Bula, Va. 62 G5
Bülach, Switz., 8,188 124 C1
Buladean, N.C. 63 B1
Bulagan Suma, Mong. 150 D1
Bulalacao, Phil., 1,966 153 B2
Bulan, Phil., 16,042 153 B2
Bulan, Ky. 71 H4
Bulanash, U.S.S.R. 137 k7
Bulancak, Turk., 7,162 142 D1
Bulandshahr, India, 44,163 144 b11
Bulanık, Turk., 4,799 142 E2
Bulanovo, U.S.S.R. 137 h9
Bulawayo, Rhod., 195,000 164 D5
Bulayevo, U.S.S.R. 137 n11
Bulcher, Tex. 77 P3
Buldan, Turk., 10,431 142 B2
Buldana, India, 15,985 145 E5
Buldir I., Alaska 85 d8
Bulga, Austl. 173 h9
Bulgaria, ctry., 8,230,000* 128-9
Bulger, Pa. 60 a8
Bulhar, Som. Rep. 163 M4
Buli, Chile 104 f16
Buli, Teluk, Indon. 149 J2
Bulkley, r., Br. Col., Can. 42 E2
Bullard, Tex., 364 77 Q3
Bulla Régia, ruins, Tun. 160 f5
Bull Arm, Newf., Can. 45 b10
Bullas, Sp., 9,441 122 E3
Bull Bay, S.C. 63 E5
Bull Canyon Wash, Calif. 83 g15
Bull Cr., N.Y. 58 k18
Bulle, Switz., 5,983 124 B2
Bullen B., Cur. 97 16
Bullendorf, Aust. 124 N5
Buller, r., N.Z. 175 f6
Bullfinch, Austl. 172 B4
Bullhead, S. Dak. 74 B3
Bull Head, Newf., Can. 45 c10
Bullhead City, Ariz. 78 A4
Bulligny, Fr. 116 b9
Bullion, Fr. 116 f12
Bullion Butte, N. Dak. 74 A2
Bull I. Pt., Newf., Can. 45 a11
Bullitt, co., Ky., 15,726 71 F3
Bullittsville, Ky. 71 g11
Bulloch, co., Ga., 24,263 64 H3
Bullock, co., Ala., 13,462 64 D3
Bullock, N.C. 63 F1
Bulloo, r., Austl. 173 F4
Bullrun Rock, mtn., Oreg. 80 D3
Bull Savannah, Jam., 1,038 96 p9
Bulls Bridge (part of Kent), Conn. 56 C6
Bulls Gap, Tenn., 682 71 H5
Bull Shoals L., Ark.-Mo. 73 C1
Bulltofta, Swed. 121 c7
Bullumwaal, Austl. 173 f11
Bully, Fr., 1,039 116 p15
Bully Cr., Oreg. 80 E3
Bulnes, Chile, 5,831 104 e16
Bulo Burti, Som. Rep., 5,234 163 M5
Buloh Kasap, Malay., 2,964 147 p15
Buloke, L., Austl. 173 d11
Bulolo, Terr. New Guin., 2,460 174 e2
Bulpitt, Ill., 307 68 C4
Bulsar, India, 37,586 145 D5
Buluangan, Phil., 14,275 153 e11
Bulukumba, Indon. 149 G4
Bulun, U.S.S.R. 135 M2
Buluol, Yap 176 20
Bulusan, Phil., 5,394 153 C2
Bulusan Vol., Phil. 153 h15
Bulverde, Tex. 76 a6
Bulyea, Sask., Can. 43 D4
Bumba, D.R.Congo 164 C1
Bumbești-Jiu, Rum. 128 D2
Bumbulan, Indon. 149 G2
Bumhkang, Burma 146 B1
Bumiaju, Indon. 148 c7
Bumiratu, Indon. 148 a6
Bum La, pass, China-India 145 J3
Bumpus Mills, Tenn. 71 D5
Bumthang, Bhutan 145 J4
Buna, Kenya 164 F1
Buna, Terr. Papua 174 f3
Buna, Tex. 77 R4
Bunai, Terr. New Guin. 174 e1
Bu Najīm, Libya 161 G2
Bunavista, Tex. 76 N2
Bunawan, Phil., 2,415 153 C3
Bunbury, Austl., 9,869 172 A5
Bunbury, U.K. 114 C4
Bunceton, Mo., 468 72 E6
Bunch, Okla. 76 J2
Bunclody, Ire. 113 C5
Buncombe, Ill., 200 68 C6
Buncombe, co., N.C., 130,074 63 B2
Buncrana, Ire., 3,064 113 C4
Bundaberg, Austl., 19,951 173 H3
Bundanoon, Austl. 173 g10
Bundarra, Austl. 173 G4
Bünde, F.R.Ger., 10,314 118 B2
Bundenthal, F.R.Ger., 1,020 119 D6
Bundi, India, 26,478 145 E4
Bundicks Cr., La. 73 B7
Bundoran, Ire. 113 B4
Bundu, India, 9,285 144 e14
Bunessan, U.K. 112 C3
Bunga, Phil., 1,782 153 b6
Bungalaut, Selat, Indon. 148 A3
Bungay, U.K., 3,582 113 G5
Bungay, Ill. 68 D5
Bungendore, Austl. 173 g10
Bunge, Zemlya, U.S.S.R. 135 N2
Bung Kan, Thai. 146 C3
Bungku, Indon. 149 G3
Bungoma, Kenya 165 g13
Bungo-Takata, Jap., 28,280 154 B5
Bunia, D.R.Congo, 12,410 164 D1
Buninyong, Austl. 173 d11
Bunji, Pak. 145 E2
Bunkeflo, Swed. 121 b7
Bunker Hill, Ill., 1,524 68 B4
Bunker Hill, Ind., 1,049 70 C2
Bunker Hill, Kans., 200 75 G5
Bunkerhill, Mich. 67 J6
Bunker Hill, Tex., 2,216 77 h9
Bunker Hill Pk., Nev. 83 B3
Bunkerville, Nev. 83 C4
Bunkeya, D.R.Congo 165 n19
Bunkie, La., 5,188 73 C7
Bunn, N.C., 322 63 F2
Bunnell, Fla., 1,860 65 H3
Bunnik, Neth., 3,900 115 c6
Bünningstedt, F.R.Ger., 2,034 119 b8
Bunnlevel, N.C., 187 63 F2
Bunny Run, Mich., 1,058 67 K6
Bunola, Pa. 60 c9
Bunschoten, Neth. 115 D2
Buntharik, Thai. 146 D4
Buntingford, U.K., 1,559 114 J7
Buntok, Indon. 148 E3
Buntui, Indon. 148 E3
Buñuel, Sp., 2,777 122 E1
Bünyan, Turk., 7,388 142 C2
Bunzuqah, Sudan 163 K3
Buochs, Switz., 2,733 124 C2
Buol, Indon. 149 G2
Buon Ho, S. Viet. 146 E4
Buorkhaya, G., U.S.S.R. 135 N2
Buorkhaya, M., U.S.S.R. 135 N2
Bu Prang, S. Viet. 146 D4
Buqayq, Saudi Ar. 143 D3
Buqbuq, U.A.R. 161 J2
Bura, Kenya 164 F2
Bur Acaba, Som. Rep., 10,811* 163 M5
Buraku, i., Sol. Is. 175 b3
Buram, Sudan 163 J4
Buran, Som. Rep. 163 N4
Burannoye, U.S.S.R. 137 h9
Burao, Som. Rep., 10,000* 163 M4
Buras, La., 4,908 73 F8
Burauen, Phil., 8,677 153 f11
Buraydah, Saudi Ar. 143 C3
Burayevo, U.S.S.R. 137 h8
Burayqah, Marsá al, Libya 161 H2
Burbach, F.R.Ger., 2,208 119 E3
Burbage, Derby., Eng., U.K., 4,780 114 D4
Burbage (part of Hinckley), Leics., Eng., U.K., 9,308 114 F5
Burbage, Wilts., Eng., U.K. 114 E8
Burbank, Calif., 90,155 83 h15
Burbank, Okla., 238 76 G1
Burbank, S. Dak. 74 D4
Burbank, Wash. 80 D2
Burchard, Nebr., 132 75 J3
Burcher, Austl. 173 f9
Burchfield, Ala. 64 a8
Burcht, Belg., 6,667 115 d8
Burda, India 144 a13
Burdekin, r., Austl. 173 G2
Burden, Kans., 580 75 J6
Burdeos, Phil., 1,225 153 c8
Burdett, Alta., Can. 42 K4
Burdett, Kans. 75 F5
Burdick, Ind. 69 g10
Burdick, Kans. 75 J5
Burdur, Turk., 25,372 142 B2
Burdur Gölü, Turk. 142 B2
Burdwan, India, 108,224 145 H5
Burdwood Bank, Atl. Oc. 109 H10
Bure, r., U.K. 113 G5
Bureå, Swed. 120 E2
Bureau, co., Ill., 37,594 68 C2
Bureau Cr., Ill. 68 C2
Bureinskiy Khr., U.S.S.R. 135 N5
Büren, F.R.Ger., 5,897 118 B3
Büren an der Aare, Switz., 2,432 124 B1
Bures, Fr., 3,682 116 g12
Bureya, r., U.S.S.R. 135 N4
Burford, Ont., Can., 1,005 46 D5
Burford, U.K. 114 E7
Būr Fu'ād, U.A.R., 42,000 161 k7
Burg, F.R.Ger., 4,665 118 C1
Burg, Ger.D.R., 29,337 118 C2
Burg, Ger.D.R. 118 E3
Bur Gao, Som. Rep. 163 M6
Burgas, Bulg., 72,526 128 F3
Burgaski Zaliv, Bulg. 128 F3
Burgau, Aust., 1,143 124 N6
Burgau, F.R.Ger., 4,999 118 C4
Burgaw, N.C., 1,750 63 G3
Burgdorf, F.R.Ger., 11,119 118 C2
Burgdorf, Switz., 13,936 124 B1
Bürgel, Ger.D.R. 126 a6
Burgeo, Newf., Can., 1,444 45 P6
Burgersdorp, S. Af., 7,152 164 D7
Burgers Mtn., Terr. New Guin. 174 d2
Burgess, S.C. 63 F4
Burgess, Va. 62 H5
Burgess Hill, U.K., 13,997 113 F6
Burgessville, Ont., Can. 46 D5
Burgettstown, Pa., 2,383 60 A5
Burghausen, F.R.Ger., 11,726 118 D4
Burghclere, U.K., 1,121 114 F8
Burghead, U.K., 1,346 112 E3
Burghill, U.K., 1,552 114 C6
Burgh le Marsh, U.K., 1,190 114 J4
Burgin, Ky., 879 71 G4
Burgkirchen, Aust., 2,033 124 K5
Bürglen, Switz., 3,175 124 C2
Bürglen, Switz., 1,899 124 D1
Burglengenfeld, F.R.Ger., 7,447 118 D4
Burgoon, Ohio, 243 70 F1
Burgos, Phil., 1,735 153 c6
Burgos, Sp., 82,177 122 D1
Burgsinn, F.R.Ger., 2,777 118 B3
Burgsolms, F.R.Ger., 3,054 119 E3
Bürgstadt, F.R.Ger., 2,885 119 G5
Burgstädt, Ger.D.R., 17,343 126 b6
Burg Stargard, Ger.D.R. 118 D2
Burgsteinfurt, F.R.Ger., 12,143 118 A2
Burgundy = Bourgogne
Burhaniye, Turk., 10,281 142 A2
Burhanpur, India, 82,090 145 E5
Burhar, India, 6,481 144 c14
Burhi Gandak, r., India-Nepal 144 e12
Burias I., Phil. 153 B2
Burias Pass, Phil. 153 B2
Buribay, U.S.S.R. 137 i9
Burica, P., C.R.-Pan. 94 F6
Burie, Fr., 1,188 117 C4
Burien, Wash. 81 b8
Burin, Newf., Can., 1,128 45 Q6
Buri Ram, Thai., 12,579 146 C4
Buriti Alegre, Braz., 5,042 103 G5
Buriti Bravo, Braz., 1,910 103 H3
Buritis, Braz. 103 G5
Buriton, U.K. 113 m13
Burj al 'Arab, U.A.R. 161 h8
Burj al Barājinah, Leb., 6,579 142 b6
Burjasot, Sp., 17,624 122 E3
Burkburnett, Tex., 7,621 77 O2
Burke, co., Ga., 20,596 64 H2
Burke, N.Y., 273 59 M2
Burke, co., N.C., 52,701 63 C2
Burke, co., N. Dak., 5,886 74 A1
Burke, S. Dak., 811 74 C4
Burke Chan., Br. Col., Can. 42 E3

206 · Burke Hollow—Caliling

Burke Hollow, Vt. 54 D2
Burke Mtn., Vt. 54 D2
Burkes Garden, Va. 62 C5
Burkesville, Ky., 1,688 71 F5
Burketon Station, Ont., Can. 46 F4
Burketown, Austl. 172 E2
Burkett, Tex. 77 O4
Burkettsville, Ohio, 290 70 E2
Burkeville, Tex. 77 R4
Burkeville, Va., 705 62 F5
Burkittsville, Md., 208 62 G3
Burkley, Ky. 71 B5
Burk's Falls, Ont., Can. 44 H6
Burkville (part of Conway), Mass. 56 F3
Burla, r., U.S.S.R. 137 p11
Burleigh, co., N. Dak., 34,016 74 B2
Burleson, co., Tex., 11,177 77 P4
Burleson, Tex., 2,345 77 P3
Burley, U.K., 1,613 113 i13
Burley, Idaho, 7,508 81 C4
Burley, Wash. 81 a8
Burli, U.S.S.R. 137 k9
Burlingame, Calif., 24,036 83 e12
Burlingame, Kans., 1,151 75 K5
Burlington, Ont., Can., 46,636 44 H7
Burlington, Colo., 2,090 79 D2
Burlington, Conn., 2,790(T) 56 E5
Burlington, Ill., 360 68 D1
Burlington, Ind. 70 C2
Burlington, Iowa, 32,430 72 G4
Burlington, Kans., 2,113 75 K5
Burlington, Ky. 71 G2
Burlington, Me. 55 D3
Burlington, Mass., 12,852(T) 57 M2
Burlington, Mich., 366 67 H6
Burlington, co., N.J., 224,499 61 B4
Burlington, N.J., 12,687 61 B3
Burlington, N.C., 33,199 63 E1
Burlington, N. Dak., 262 74 B1
Burlington, Ohio 70 G4
Burlington, Okla., 174 76 E1
Burlington, Oreg. 80 a6
Burlington, Pa., 115 60 J2
Burlington, Vt., 35,531 54 A3
Burlington, Wash., 2,968 80 B1
Burlington, W. Va. 62 F3
Burlington, Wis., 5,856 66 E6
Burlington, Wyo. 81 E3
Burlington Beach, Ont., Can., 3,314 46 c14
Burlington Beach, Ind. 69 f10
Burlington Junction, Mo., 650 72 B4
Burma, ctry., 24,732,000* 146
Burmah, Okla. 76 D2
Burmester, Utah 78 b9
Burna, Ky. 71 C4
Burnbank, U.K. 112 b8
Burnet, co., Tex., 9,265 77 O4
Burnet, Tex., 2,214 77 O4
Burnett, Ind. 70 B3
Burnett, Minn. 74 F2
Burnett, co., Wis., 9,214 66 A3
Burnett, Wis. 66 E5
Burnettsville, Ind., 452 70 C2
Burney, Calif., 1,294 82 C2
Burnham, U.K., 16,143 114 G7
Burnham, Ill., 2,478 69 d10
Burnham, Me. 55 C4
Burnham, Pa., 2,755 60 G4
Burnham-on-Crouch, U.K., 4,167 113 G6
Burnham-on-Sea, U.K., 9,848 113 E6
Burnie, Austl., 11,193 173 F6
Burnley, U.K., 80,588 113 E5
Burnopfield, U.K., 4,404 112 g10
Burns, Kans., 314 75 J5
Burns, Oreg., 3,523 80 D4
Burns, Tenn., 386 71 D5
Burns, Wis. 66 B5
Burns, Wyo., 225 81 G5
Burns Ditch, Ind. 69 e10
Burns Flat, Okla., 2,280 76 D2
Burnshirt, r., Mass. 56 H3
Burnside, Sur. 101 M5
Burnside, Ky., 575 71 G5
Burnside, Pa., 307 60 E4
Burnside, r., N.W.T., Can. 40 G4
Burnside, Miss. 73 F5
Burns Lake, Br. Col., Can., 1,021 42 F2
Burns, Mt., Austl. 172 C2
Burnstad, N. Dak. 74 C2
Burnsville, Ala. 64 C3
Burnsville, Minn., 10,721 74 F3
Burnsville, Miss., 416 73 G3
Burnsville, N.C., 1,388 63 B2
Burnsville, W. Va., 728 62 D4
Burnt, r., Ont., Can. 46 F4
Burnt, r., Oreg. 80 E3
Burnt Corn, Ala. 64 B4
Burnt Creek, Qué., Can. 45 M3
Burntisland, U.K., 6,036 112 d7
Burnt Ranch, Calif. 82 B2
Burntside L., Minn. 74 F2
Burntwood, r., Man., Can. 43 E3
Burntwood L., Man., Can. 43 E3
Burnwell, W. Va. 62 C4
Buronzo, It., 1,424 122 b5
Burqān, Kuwait 143 D3
Burr, Nebr., 81 75 J3
Burra, Austl., 1,428 172 c7
Burradon, U.K. 112 f9
Burraga, Austl. 173 g9
Burray, i., U.K. 112 E2
Burrel, Alb., 2,950 125 E4
Burrera, Guat. 94 b9
Burrinjuck, Austl. 173 g10
Burrinjuck Res., Austl. 173 g10
Burr Oak, Kans., 473 75 G4
Burr Oak, Mich., 867 67 H7
Burro, Snias. del, Mex. 92 E2
Burrow Head, U.K. 113 D4
Burrows, Ind. 70 C2
Burrton, Kans., 774 75 H5
Burrville (part of Torrington), Conn. 56 D5
Burry Port, U.K., 5,865 113 D6
Bürs, Aust., 2,268 124 F6
Bursa, Turk., 153,574 142 B1
Būr Safājah, U.A.R., 11,000 161 K3
Būr Saʻīd, U.A.R., 244,000 161 K2
Burscheid, F.R.Ger., 12,362 119 C2
Burscough, U.K., 5,391 114 C3
Burslem, U.K., 7,904 114 D4
Bürstadt, F.R.Ger., 10,527 118 B4
Burstall, Sask., Can. 43 B5
Burstwick, U.K. 114 H3
Būr Sūdān, Sudan, 47,561 163 L2
Burt, Iowa, 620 72 C1
Burt, Mich. 67 K5
Burt, co., Nebr., 10,192 75 J2
Burt, N.Y. 58 C5
Burt Lake, Mich. 67 J3
Burt L., Mich. 67 J3
Burton, Br. Col., Can. 42 H4
Burton, U.K. 114 C2
Burton, Ky., 504 71 J4
Burton, Nebr., 17 75 F1
Burton, Ohio, 1,085 70 H1
Burton, Tex. 77 P4
Burton, Wash. 81 b8
Burton, W. Va. 62 D3
Burton Agnes, U.K. 114 H2
Burton Fleming, U.K. 114 H2
Burton I., Vt. 54 A2
Burton L., Ga. 64 F1
Burton Latimer, U.K., 4,402 114 G6
Burton Leonard, U.K. 114 F2
Burton's Bridge, Ill. 69 a7
Burtonsville, Md. 62 b8
Burton upon Stather, U.K., 1,398 114 G3
Burton upon Trent, U.K., 50,766 113 F5
Burträsk, Swed. 120 E2
Buru, i., Indon. 149 H3
Burullus, Buḥayrat al, U.A.R. 161 i7
Burunday, U.S.S.R., 6,300 134 G5
Burundi, ctry., 2,800,000* 164 D2
Burung, Indon. 148 B2
Burutu, Nigeria, 7,638 162 E5
Burwash, Ont., Can. 44 H6
Burwash Landing, Yukon, Can. 40 A5
Burwell, U.K., 2,734 114 J6
Burwell, Nebr., 1,425 75 F2
Bury, Qué., Can. 47 N3
Bury, U.K., 59,984 113 E5
Burye, Eth. 163 L4
Bury St. Edmunds, U.K., 21,179 113 G5
Burzenin, Pol. 127 h5
Burzet, Fr., 1,000 117 F4
Busanga, D.R.Congo 164 D3
Busangu, D.R.Congo 165 m18
Busby, Alta., Can. 43 b7
Busby, Kans. 75 J6
Busby, Mont. 81 F3
Buschhütten, F.R.Ger., 4,315 119 E3
Buševec, Yug. 125 B2
Bush, La. 73 F7
Būshehr, Iran, 18,412 143 E3
Bushell, Sask., Can. 43 B2
Bushenyi, Uganda 165 e14
Bushey, U.K., 20,666 114 H7
Bushimaie, r., D.R.Congo 164 C3
Bushire = Būshehr
Bushkill, Pa. 61 M3
Bush L., Minn. 74 b6
Bushland, Tex. 76 M2
Bush Lot, Guyana, 2,826 101 M4
Bushmanland, reg., S. Af. 164 C6
Bushmills, U.K. 113 C4
Bushnell, Fla., 644 65 G4
Bushnell, Ill., 3,710 68 B3
Bushnell, Nebr., 266 75 B2
Bushnell, S. Dak., 92 74 D3
Bushnells Basin, N.Y. 58 n20
Bushong, Kans., 51 75 J5
Bushton, Kans., 499 75 G5
Bushyhead, Okla. 76 H1
Busia, Uganda 165 f13
Busick, N.C. 63 B2
Businga, D.R.Congo 164 C1
Buskhyttan, Swed. 120 e9
Busko Zdrój, Pol., 7,753 127 D3
Buskul', U.S.S.R. 137 k9
Buso, Phil., 3,119 153 C4
Busovača, Yug. 125 C2
Buṣrá ash Shām, Syr. 142 c7
Bussa, Nigeria 162 E4
Busselton, Austl., 2,449 172 A5
Busseron Cr., Ind. 70 B3
Busseto, It., 8,597 122 d6
Bussey, Ark. 73 B4
Bussey, Iowa, 557 72 E3
Busseyville, Ky. 71 J3
Busshōzan, Jap., 5,738 154 e15
Bussolengo, It., 7,392 122 d5
Bussum, Neth., 47,500 115 D2
Bustamante, N.L., Mex., 3,115 93 E2
Bustamante, Tam., Mex., 1,114 93 F3
Bustamante, Tex. 77 O6
Bustamento, Chile 104 f16
Buštěhrad, Czech. 126 d6
Buşteni, Rum., 8,591 128 E2
Busti, N.Y. 58 B7
Bustillos, Lag., Mex. 92 D2
Busto Arsizio, It., 60,368 123 B2
Busuanga, i., Phil. 153 A2
Busu-Djanoa, D.R.Congo 164 C1
Büsum, F.R.Ger., 4,132 118 B1
But, Terr. New Guin. 174 d1
Buta, D.R.Congo, 10,845 164 D1
Butag, Phil., 2,185 153 h15
Butare, Rwanda 165 d15
Butaritari, i., Gilb. Is. 175 10
Bute, Austl. 172 c7
Bute, co., U.K., 15,129 112 D4
Bute Inlet, Br. Col., Can. 42 F4
Bute, I. of, U.K. 112 D4
Butembo, D.R.Congo, 9,980 164 D1
Butere, Kenya 165 g13
Butgenbach, Belg., 2,473 115 E4
Buthidaung, Burma, 3,193 146 A2
Butiaba, Uganda 164 E1
Butiama, Tanz. 165 f14
Butler, co., Ala., 24,560 64 C4
Butler, Ala., 1,765 64 A3
Butler, Ga., 1,346 64 E3
Butler, Ill., 249 68 C4
Butler, Ind., 2,176 70 E1
Butler, co., Iowa, 17,467 72 E2
Butler, co., Kans., 38,395 75 J6
Butler, co., Ky., 9,586 71 E4
Butler, Ky., 450 71 G3
Butler, Mich. 67 J6
Butler, co., Mo., 34,656 72 G8
Butler, Mo., 3,791 72 C6
Butler, co., Nebr., 10,312 75 H2
Butler, N.J., 5,414 61 C2
Butler, co., Ohio, 199,076 70 E3
Butler, Ohio, 976 70 G2
Butler, Okla., 351 76 D2
Butler, co., Pa., 114,639 60 C4
Butler, Pa., 20,975 60 C4
Butler, S. Dak., 62 74 D3
Butler, Wis., 2,274 66 c11
Butler I., Vt. 54 A2
Butlers Gorge, Austl. 173 f14
Butlers Pt., Mass. 57 O6
Butrint, Alb. 125 E4
Butry, Fr. 116 g10
Bütschwil, Switz., 3,414 124 D1
Butte, Alaska, 559 85 c7
Butte, co., Calif., 82,030 82 C3
Butte, co., Idaho, 3,498 81 C4
Butte, Mont., 27,877 81 C3
Butte, Nebr., 526 75 G1
Butte, N. Dak., 257 74 B2
Butte, co., S. Dak., 8,592 74 A3
Butte City, Idaho, 104 81 C4
Butte des Morts, Wis. 66 E4
Butte Falls, Oreg., 384 80 B4
Butte Mts., Nev. 83 C3
Butten, Fr. 116 d9
Butter Cr., Oreg. 80 D3
Butterfield, Ark. 73 C3
Butterfield, Mo., 125 72 D8
Butterknowle, U.K. 112 g10
Buttermilk, Kans. 75 F6
Buttermilk Pt., St. Helena 109 7
Butternut, Mich. 67 H5
Butternut, Wis., 499 66 C2
Butternut Cr., N.Y. 59 r24
Butternut L., Wis. 66 C3
Butternut L., Wis. 66 E3
Butterwick, U.K. 114 J5
Butterworth = Bagan Jaya
Buttevant, Ire. 113 B5
Büttgen, F.R.Ger., 6,891 119 B2
Buttisholz, Switz., 1,542 124 B1
Butt of Lewis, promontory, U.K. 112 C2
Button Bay, Man., Can. 43 G2
Button Is., N.W.T., Can. 45 N1
Buttonwillow, Calif. 82 D5
Butts, co., Ga., 8,976 64 F2
Buttstädt, Ger.D.R. 118 C3
Buttzville, N.J. 61 B2
Butuan, Phil., 25,354 153 C3
Butung, P., Indon. 149 G4
Buturlinovka, U.S.S.R., 13,000 136 F3
Butwal, Nepal 145 G4
Butzbach, F.R.Ger., 9,285 118 B3
Bützow, Ger.D.R., 10,934 118 D2
Butztown, Pa. 61 k18
Buu Son, S. Viet., 9,443 146 E5
Buvuma I., Uganda 165 f13
Buxar, India, 23,068 144 d13
Buxtehude, F.R.Ger., 13,587 118 B2
Buxton, Guyana, 3,812 101 M4
Buxton, U.K., 19,155 113 F5
Buxton, Kans. 75 K6
Buxton, N.C. 63 J2
Buxton, N. Dak., 321 74 D2
Buxton Center, Me. 55 B5
Buy, U.S.S.R., 27,000 134 D4
Buy, r., U.S.S.R. 137 h8
Buyck, Minn. 74 F1
Buynaksk, U.S.S.R., 35,000 137 c1
Buyr Nuur, China-Mong. 150 F2
Büyük, r., Turk. 137 b2
Büyükköhne, Turk., 4,664 142 C2
Büyükmenderes, r., Turk. 142 A2
Buza, Rum. 128 E1
Buzachi, P-ov., U.S.S.R. 134 E5
Buzançais, Fr., 4,800 117 D3
Buzancy, Fr. 117 F2
Buzău, Rum., 47,595 128 F2
Buzău, r., Rum. 128 F2
Buzău, Pasul, Rum. 128 F2
Buzaymah, Libya 161 H3
Buzdyak, U.S.S.R. 137 h8
Buzen, Jap., 34,818 154 B5
Buzha, r., U.S.S.R. 136 d6
Búzi, r., Moz. 164 E5
Buziaş, Rum., 5,140 128 C2
Búzios, C., Braz. 103 f18
Buzuluk, U.S.S.R., 57,000 134 E4
Buzuluk, r., U.S.S.R. 136 F3
Buzzards Bay, Mass., 2,170 57 O5
Buzzards Bay, Mass. 57 N6
Bwagaoia, Terr. Papua 174 g3
Bwanga, Tanz. 165 e15
Bwasiaia, Terr. Papua 174 f3
Byala, Bulg., 7,854 128 E3
Byala, Bulg., 2,324 128 F3
Byala, Bulg., 2,407 128 G3
Byam Martin Chan., N.W.T., Can. 41 H2
Byam Martin I., N.W.T., Can. 40 J2
Byars, Okla., 256 76 F3
Bybee, Va. 62 F5
Byblos = Jubyl
Bychawa, Pol., 2,742 127 E3
Byczyna, Pol., 2,111 127 C3
Bydgoszcz, Pol., 231,000* 127 B2
Byers, Colo. 79 C2
Byers, Kans., 52 75 G6
Byers, Mo. 72 a12
Byers, Tex., 497 77 O2
Byesville, Ohio, 2,447 70 H3
Byfield, U.K. 114 F6
Byfield (part of Newbury), Mass. 57 N1
Bygdeå, Swed. 120 E2
Bygland, Nor. 120 B4
Byglandsfjorden, l., Nor. 121 A2
Byhalia, Miss., 674 73 F3
Byhalia, Ohio 70 F2
Byk, r., U.S.S.R. 136 e7
Bykhov, U.S.S.R., 13,200 136 C2
Bykle, Nor. 120 A4
Bykovskiy, U.S.S.R. 135 N2
Bylas, Ariz. 78 C5
Bylchau, U.K. 114 A4
Bylderup, Den., 1,080 121 B6
Bylot I., N.W.T., Can. 41 O3
Byng Inlet, Ont., Can. 44 H6
Bynum, Mont. 81 C2
Bynum, N.C. 63 E2
Byram (part of Greenwich), Conn. 56 B9
Byram, Miss. 73 E5
Byram, r., Conn.-N.Y. 56 B8
Byrd, Ant. 180 Y4
Byrd, L., Qué., Can. 46 H1
Byrdstown, Tenn., 613 71 F5
Byrd Subglacial Basin 180 ·
Byrehope Mt., U.K. 112 d8
Byringe, Swed. 120 d8
Byrnedale, Pa. 60 E3
Byrock, Austl. 173 F4
Byromville, Ga., 349 64 F3
Byron, Ont., Can., 3,327 46 C6
Byron, Ga., 1,138 64 F3
Byron, Ill., 1,578 68 C1
Byron, Me. 55 B4
Byron, Mich., 542 67 J6
Byron, Minn., 1,209 74 F3
Byron, Nebr., 147 75 H3
Byron, N.Y. 58 D5
Byron, Okla., 82 76 E1
Byron, Wis. 66 E5
Byron, Wyo., 417 81 E3
Byron Center, Mich. 67 H6
Byrranga, Gory, U.S.S.R. 135 J2
Byrum, Den. 121 D3
Byske, Swed. 120 E2
Byskeälv, r., Swed. 120 D2
Bystřice, r., Czech. 127 e6
Bystřice pod Hostýnem, Czech. 126 C2
Bystrynskiy Golets, G., U.S.S.R. 135 L4
Bystrzyca, Pol., 7,669 127 B3
Bystrzyca, r., Pol. 127 f6
Bystryy Tanyp, r., U.S.S.R. 137 h8
Bytantay, r., U.S.S.R. 135 N3
Bytča, Czech. 126 D2
Bytom, Pol., 182,000* 127 C3
Bytom Odrzański, Pol., 2,255 127 A3
Bytów, Pol., 8,451 127 B1
Byumba, Rwanda 165 e14
Byxelkrok, Swed. 120 D4
Bzura, r., Pol. 127 C2

C

Ca, r., N. Viet. 146 D3
Caacupé, Para., 5,283 105 D3
Caazapá, Para., 3,772 105 D3
Cabadbaran, Phil., 5,954 153 C3
Cabagan, Phil., 1,808 153 c5
Cabaiguán, Cuba, 15,399 96 d1
Cabalete I., Phil. 153 c8
Cabalian, Phil., 4,475 153 C3
Caballas, Peru 104 C5
Caballerias, Mex. 93 a8
Caballo, N. Mex. 79 B5
Caballo Cocha, Peru 104 D2
Caballones, Cayo, Cuba 96 d2
Caballo Res., N. Mex. 79 B5
Caballos Mesteños, Llano de los, Mex. 92 D2
Cabana, Peru, 1,908 104 C5
Cabanaconde, Peru, 2,599 104 D5
Cabañas, Cuba, 2,528 96 b1
Cabañas, Guat. 94 d9
Cabanatuan, Phil., 22,621 153 B2
Cabangan, Phil., 2,319 153 b7
Cabano, Qué., Can., 2,654 45 M6
Cabarita, r., Jam. 96 o8
Cabarita Pt., Jam. 96 q9
Cabarrus, co., N.C., 68,137 63 D2
Cabatuan, Phil., 3,176 153 d11
Cabazon, Calif. 498 82 E6
Cabcaben, Phil., 3,544 153 b8
Cabedelo, Braz., 10,738 103 b14
Cabell, co., W. Va., 108,202 62 B4
Cabeza del Buey, Sp., 11,737 122 C3
Ca Bianca, It. 122 f5
Cabiao, Phil., 2,970 153 b7
Cabilao I., Phil. 153 e12
Cabildo, Arg., 4,400* 105 C5
Cabildo, Chile, 3,479 105 A4
Cabimas, Ven., 93,347 100 E2
Cabin Cr., Okla. 76 H1
Cabinda (enclave of Ang.) 164 A2
Cabinda, Ang. 164 A2
Cabins, W. Va. 62 E3
Cabinuangan, Phil., 2,953 153 C4
Cable, Wis., 262 66 B2
Cabo, Braz., 10,050 103 b15
Cabo Frio, Braz., 13,177 103 f18
Cabo Gracias a Dios, Nic., 1,764 94 F3
Cabonga, Rés., Qué., Can. 44 J6
Cabool, Mo., 1,284 72 E7
Caboolture, Austl., 1,533 173 H4
Cabo Raso, Arg. 105 C6
Caborca, Mex., 9,285 92 B1
Cabo Rojo, P.R., 3,086 96 r10
Cabot, Ark., 1,321 73 C3
Cabot, Pa. 60 C4
Cabot, Vt., 244 54 C3
Cabot, Mt., N.H. 54 E2
Cabot Head, Ont., Can. 46 C3
Cabot Str., Newf.-N.S., Can. 45 O6
Cabo Verde, Arq. de = Cape Verde Is.
Cabra, Sp., 20,739 122 C4
Cabra I., Phil. 153 b9
Cabral, Dom. Rep., 4,149 96 m6
Cabras I., Guam 176 24
Cabrera, Dom. Rep., 1,072 96 n6
Cabrera, I. de, Sp. 122 G3
Cabreras, r., Cuba 96 e2
Cabrero, Chile, 2,629 104 e17
Cabri, Sask., Can. 43 B5
Cabricán, Guat. 94 b8
Cabriel, r., Sp. 122 E3
Cabrillo Nat. Mon., Calif. 82 c10
Cabrón, Cabo, Dom. Rep. 96 n6
Cabudare, Ven., 4,327 100 F3
Cabugao, Phil., 4,434 153 B1
Cabugao Bay, Phil. 153 i14
Cabulao, Phil., 2,803 153 C3
Caburan, Phil. 153 C4
Cabure, Ven., 1,623 100 F2
Caburgua, L., Chile 105 f14
Cabuyaro, Col. 100 D5
Caçador, Braz., 10,480 103 F7
Cacahoatán, Mex. 93 G5
Cacahuatepec, Mex., 1,866 93 F5
Čačak, Yug., 27,000* 125 E3
Caçapava, Braz., 7,987 103 d18
Cacapon, r., W. Va. 62 F3
Cacequi, Braz., 8,458 103 F7
Cáceres, Braz., 8,246 102 E5
Cáceres, Col. 100 C4
Cáceres, Sp., 48,005 122 B3
Cachacrou Head = Scotts Head
Cachapoal, Chile 104 f16
Cachari, Arg., 9,800* 105 b13
Cache, Alaska 85 a6
Cache, Okla., 1,003 76 E3
Cache, co., Utah, 35,788 78 C1
Cache, r., Ark. 73 D2
Cache, r., Ill. 68 C6
Cache Bay, Ont., Can. 46 D2
Cache Cr., Okla. 76 E3
Cache la Poudre, r., Colo. 79 C1
Cache Pk., Idaho 50 D2
Cache Slough, Calif. 83 f11
Cachingues, Ang. 164 B4
Cáchira, Col. 100 D4
Cachoeira, Braz., 11,415 103 J4
Cachoeira do Arari, Braz., 2,532 103 G2
Cachoeira do Sul, Braz., 38,661 103 F7
Cachoeira Paulista, Braz., 10,366 103 d18
Cachoeiras de Macacu, Braz., 6,164 103 e18
Cachoeiro de Itapemirim, Braz., 39,470 103 H6
Cachuela Esperanza, Bol., 1,592 102 C4
Cachuma, L., Calif. 82 C5
Cacólo, Ang. 164 C3
Caconda, Ang. 164 B4
Cacouna, Qué., Can. 47 R10
Cactus, Sherman Co., Tex. 76 N1
Cactus, Webb Co., Tex. 77 O6
Cacuaco, Ang. 164 B3
Cacuso, Ang. 164 B3
Cadamy, Miss. 73 G3
Čadca, Czech., 11,172 126 D2
Caddington, U.K., 4,921 114 H7
Caddo, parish, La., 223,859 73 B5
Caddo, co., Okla., 28,621 76 E2
Caddo, Okla., 814 76 G3
Caddo, Tex. 77 O3
Caddo, r., Ark. 73 B3
Caddo Cr., Okla. 76 F3
Caddo Gap, Ark. 73 B3
Caddo L., La.-Tex. 73 A5
Caddo Mills, Tex., 732 76 g8
Cade, Okla. 76 H3
Cadenet, Fr., 2,409 117 F5
Cadereyta, N.L., Mex., 7,713 93 F3
Cadereyta, Qro., Mex., 1,635 93 e9
Cades, S.C. 63 E4
Cadibarrawirracanna, L., Austl. 172 D4
Cadillac, Sask., Can. 43 B5
Cadillac, Fr., 3,278 117 C4
Cadillac, Fla. 65 G3
Cadillac, Mich., 10,112 67 H4
Cadillac Mtn., Me. 55 D4
Cadiz, Phil., 15,514 153 B3
Cádiz, Sp., 117,871 122 B4
Cadiz, Ind., 198 70 D3
Cadiz, Ky., 1,980 71 D5
Cadiz, N.Y. 58 C7
Cadiz, Ohio, 3,259 70 H2
Cádiz, G. of, Port.-Sp. 122 B4
Cadiz L., Calif. 82 F5
Cadmus, Kans. 75 K5
Cadmus, Mich. 67 J7
Cadnam, U.K. 113 i13
Cadogan, Pa. 60 C4
Cadomin, Alta., Can. 42 H3
Cadosia, N.Y. 59 K8
Cadott, Wis., 881 66 B4
Cadwell, Ga., 360 64 G3
Cadwell, Ill. 68 D4
Cady, Mich. 67 g14
Cadys Falls, Vt. 54 B2
Cadyville, N.Y. 59 N2
Caen, Fr., 95,238 117 C2
Caerleon, U.K., 4,184 114 C7
Caernarvon, U.K., 9,055 113 D5
Caernarvon Bay, U.K. 113 D5
Caernarvonshire, co., U.K., 121,767 113 D5
Caerphilly, U.K., 35,997 113 E6
Caersws, U.K. 114 A5
Caesarea, ruins, Isr. 142 a7
Caeté, Braz., 10,840 103 e17
Caetité, Braz., 4,823 103 H4
Cafayate, Arg., 2,500* 105 B3
Cagayan, r., Phil. 153 B1
Cagayan de Oro, Phil., 23,707 153 C3
Cagayan Is., Phil. 153 B3
Cagayan Sulu I., Phil. 153 A4
Cagdianao, Phil., 1,639 153 C3
Cagliari, It., 171,946 123 B5
Čaglin, Yug. 125 D2
Cagnes, Fr., 15,401 116 n13
Cagua, Ven., 14,241 101 b11
Caguán, r., Col. 100 C7
Caguas, P.R., 32,015 96 t10
Cahaba, r., Ala. 64 B3
Cahabón, Guat. 94 C3
Caha Mts., Ire. 113 B6
Cahavieiras, Braz., 10,264 103 J5
Caher, Ire., 1,731 113 C5
Cahill Mtn., Pa. 60 J2
Cahirsiveen, Ire., 1,800 113 A6
Cahokia, Ill., 15,829 68 B5
Cahone, Colo. 79 A3
Cahore Pt., Ire. 113 C5
Cahors, Fr., 19,280 117 D4
Cahuapanas, Peru 104 B3
Caiapó, Sa. do, Braz. 103 F5
Caiapônia, Braz., 2,476 103 F5
Caiazzo, It., 6,177 123 c9
Cai Ban, Mui, pt., S. Viet. 147 k11
Caibarién, Cuba, 22,657 96 d1
Cai Bau, N. Viet. 146 D2
Cai Be, S. Viet. 147 k11
Caiçara, Braz., 2,153 103 b14
Caicara, Ven., 5,880 101 J3
Caicara de Orinoco, Ven., 3,082 100 G4
Caicedonia, Col. 101 d15
Caicó, Braz., 15,826 103 J3
Caicos Is., W.I. 95 D2
Caicos Passage, W.I. 95 D2
Cailloma, Peru 104 D5
Caimanera, Cuba, 5,647 96 f3
Caimito, r., Pan. 94 f13
Caina, Peru, 1,158 104 B4
Cain City, Tex. 77 O4
Cain Cr., S. Dak. 74 C3
Caine, r., Bol. 102 c11
Cains, r., N.B., Can. 47 S10
Cainsville, Ont., Can. 46 b15
Cainsville, Mo., 495 72 D4
Cai Nuoc, S. Viet., 1,058 146 D5
Cai Rang, S. Viet. 147 k12
Caird Coast, Ant. 180 P5
Cairnbrook, Pa., 1,100 60 E5
Cairngorm Mts., U.K. 112 E3
Cairns, Austl., 21,020 173 F2
Cairn Table, mtn., U.K. 112 b8
Cairo, U.A.R. = Al Qāhirah
Cairo, Ga., 7,427 64 E5
Cairo, Ill., 9,348 68 C6
Cairo, Kans. 75 G6
Cairo, Mo., 210 72 E5
Cairo, Nebr., 503 75 G3
Cairo, N.Y. 59 N7
Cairo, Allen Co., Ohio, 566 70 E2
Cairo, Stark Co., Ohio 70 H2
Cairo, W. Va., 418 62 C3
Cairo Montenotte, It., 14,003 123 B2
Caister-on-Sea, U.K., 4,104 113 G5
Caistor, U.K., 1,778 114 H3
Caistor Centre, Ont., Can. 46 c15
Caithness, co., U.K., 27,345 112 E2
Caivano, It., 22,938 123 c10
Cajabamba, Ec., 2,278 104 c10
Cajabamba, Peru, 5,253 104 B3
Caja de Muertos, I., P.R. 96 s11
Cajamarca, Col. 101 d15
Cajamarca, Peru, 23,008 104 B3
Cajatambo, Peru, 2,292 104 B4
Cajàzeiras, Braz., 15,884 103 J3
Cajibío, Col. 100 B6
Cajititlán, Mex., 1,607 93 a9
Cajón de Ibañez = Baños de Longaví
Čakovec, Yug., 7,684 125 C1
Cala, r., Sp. 122 B4
Calabacillas, Mex. 93 c8
Calabar, Nigeria, 53,711 162 F5
Calabasas, Ariz. 78 C6
Calabasas, Calif. 83 g15
Calabazar de Sagua, Cuba, 3,286 96 d1
Calabazas, Mex. 93 e8
Calabogie, Ont., Can. 46 H3
Calabozo, Ven., 15,282 100 G3
Calabozo, r., Mex. 93 f8
Calabozo, Ens. de, Ven. 100 E2
Calacoto, Bol. 102 a10
Calacuccia, Fr., 1,241 116 r17
Caladesi I., Fla. 65 c11
Calafat, Rum., 8,069 128 D3
Calafate, Arg. 105 A8
Calafquen, L., Chile 105 f14
Calagua Is., Phil. 153 B2
Calahoo, Alta., Can. 43 b7
Calahorra, Sp., 14,462 122 D1
Calais, Fr., 70,707 117 D1
Calais, Me., 4,223 55 E3
Calalaste, Cord. de, Arg. 105 B3
Calama, Braz. 102 D3
Calama, Chile, 26,166 105 B2
Calamar, Col. 100 C2
Calamba, Phil., 11,868 153 B3
Calamian Group, is., Phil. 153 A2
Calamine, Wis. 66 C6
Calamocha, Sp., 2,545 122 E2
Calamus, Iowa, 435 72 G3
Calamus, r., Nebr. 75 F1
Calangianus, It., 6,799 123 B4
Calapan, Phil., 4,180 153 B2
Calapooya, r., Oreg. 80 B3
Călăraşi, Rum., 25,555 128 F2
Calarcá, Col. 100 C5
Calatagan, Phil., 2,186 153 b9
Calatayud, Sp., 17,940 122 E2
Călăţele, Rum. 128 D1
Calatrava, Phil., 3,443 153 e11
Calau, Ger.D.R. 118 D3
Calauag, Phil., 3,981 153 B2
Calaveras, co., Calif., 10,289 82 C3
Calaveras, r., Calif. 82 C3
Calaveras Res., Calif. 83 f13
Calayan I., Phil 153 B1
Calbayog, Phil., 6,409 153 C2
Calbe, Ger.D.R., 16,613 118 C3
Calbuco, Chile, 2,532 105 A6
Calca, Peru, 3,434 104 D5
Calcasieu, parish, La., 145,475 73 B7
Calcasieu, r., La. 73 B7
Calcasieu L., La. 73 B8
Calceta, Ec., 5,108 104 A2
Calçoene, Braz. 103 F1
Calcutta, India, 2,927,289 145 H5
Calcutta, Ohio, 2,221 70 J2
Caldas, Braz., 3,958 103 c17
Caldas, Col. 100 C4
Caldas da Rainha, Port., 11,185 122 A3
Caldas de Reyes, Sp., 8,983 122 A1
Calder, Sask., Can. 43 E4
Calder, U.K. 114 A2
Caldera, Chile, 2,715 105 A3
Calderas, Ven. 100 E3
Caldercruix, U.K. 112 c8
Caldermill, U.K. 112 b8
Calderón, Ec. 104 c10
Caldicot, U.K., 3,351 114 C7
Caldiero, It., 3,168 122 e5
Caldron Falls Res., Wis. 66 E3
Caldwell, U.K. 112 g10
Caldwell, Ark. 73 E2
Caldwell, Idaho, 12,230 81 A4
Caldwell, Kans., 1,788 75 H6
Caldwell, co., Ky., 13,073 71 D4
Caldwell, parish, La., 9,004 73 C5
Caldwell, co., Mo., 8,830 72 C5
Caldwell, N.J., 6,942 58 b13
Caldwell, co., N.C., 49,552 63 C2
Caldwell, Ohio, 1,999 70 H3
Caldwell, co., Tex., 17,222 77 P5
Caldwell, Tex., 2,204 77 P4
Caldwell, W. Va. 62 D5
Caldwell, Wis. 66 c12
Caldy I., U.K. 113 D6
Caledon, Ont., Can. 46 D5
Caledon, S. Af., 4,323 164 a9
Caledon, Mt., Austl. 172 E1
Caledon East, Ont., Can. 46 D5
Caledonia, N.S., Can. 47 T11
Caledonia, Ont., Can., 2,182 46 E5
Caledonia, Ill. 68 D1
Caledonia, Mich., 739 67 H6
Caledonia, Minn., 2,563 74 G4
Caledonia, Mo., 119 72 G7
Caledonia, Miss., 289 73 G4
Caledonia, N.Y., 1,917 58 E6
Caledonia, Ohio, 673 70 F2
Caledonia, co., Vt., 22,786 54 C3
Caledonia, Va. 62 F5
Caledonia, Wis. 66 c12
Calen, Austl. 173 G3
Calenzana, Fr., 1,591 116 r17
Calera, Ala., 1,928 64 C2
Calera, Okla., 692 76 G4
Calera Victor Rosales, Mex., 5,439 92 E3
Caleta, Punta, Cuba 96 f2
Caleta Olivia, Arg., 6,000* 105 B7
Calexico, Calif., 7,992 82 F6
Calf of Man, i., U.K. 113 D4
Calgary, Alta., Can., 242,589 42 J4
Calhan, Colo., 347 79 C2
Calhau, C. Verde Is. 109 5
Calhoun, co., Ala., 95,878 64 D2
Calhoun, co., Ark., 5,991 73 C4
Calhoun, co., Fla., 7,422 65 D2
Calhoun, co., Ga., 7,341 64 E4
Calhoun, Ga., 3,587 64 E1
Calhoun, co., Ill., 5,933 68 B4
Calhoun, Ill., 188 68 D5
Calhoun, co., Iowa, 15,923 72 C2
Calhoun, Ky., 817 71 D4
Calhoun, La. 73 C5
Calhoun, co., Mich., 138,858 67 H6
Calhoun, co., Miss., 15,941 73 F4
Calhoun, Mo., 374 72 D6
Calhoun, co., S.C., 12,256 63 D4
Calhoun, Tenn. 71 G6
Calhoun, co., Tex., 16,592 77 P5
Calhoun, co., W. Va., 7,948 62 C4
Calhoun, L., Minn. 74 b6
Calhoun City, Miss., 1,714 73 F4
Calhoun Falls, S.C., 2,525 63 B3
Cali, Col., 590,770 100 B6
Calico Rock, Ark., 773 73 C1
Calicut = Kozhikode
Caliente, Calif. 82 D5
Caliente, Nev., 792 83 C4
Califon, N.J., 777 61 B2
California, Trin. and Tob., 2,350* 96 g5
California, st., U.S., 18,403,000* 82
California, Ky., 163 71 G3
California, Mich. 67 J7
California, Mo., 2,788 72 E6
California, Pa., 5,978 60 C5
California, G. de, Mex. 92 B1
California City, Calif. 82 E5
Caliling, Phil., 4,480 153 B3

Calima—Caprivi Zipfel · 207

Calima, r., Col. 100 B5
Călimăneşti, Rum., 6,651 128 E2
Calimaya, Mex., 3,639 93 e10
Calimesa, Calif. 83 k15
Calimete, Cuba, 2,260 96 c1
Calinog, Phil., 2,720 153 d10
Calio, N. Dak., 101 74 C1
Calion, Ark., 544 73 C4
Calipatria, Calif., 2,548 82 F6
Calispell Pk., Wash. 80 E1
Calistoga, Calif., 1,514 82 B3
Caliviny, Gren. 97 18
Calixa-Lavallée, Qué., Can. 47 p17
Calkiní, Mex., 5,462 93 H4
Call, Tex. 77 R4
Callabonna, L., Austl. 172 E4
Callac, Fr., 3,179 116 B2
Callafo, Eth. 163 M5
Callaghan, Va. 62 D5
Callahan, Calif. 82 B2
Callahan, Fla., 782 65 H2
Callahan, co., Tex., 7,929 77 O3
Callahan, Mt., Nev. 83 B3
Callahan Divide, Tex. 76 •
Callan, Ire. 113 C5
Callander, Ont., Can., 1,236 44 H6
Callander, U.K., 1,654 112 D3
Callands, Va. 62 E6
Callao, Peru, 161,286 104 B4
Callao, Mo., 329 72 E5
Callao, Utah 78 B2
Callao, Va. 62 H5
Callas, Fr. 116 m13
Callawadda, Austl. 173 d11
Callaway, Minn., 235 74 E2
Callaway, co., Mo., 23,858 72 F6
Callaway, Nebr., 603 75 E2
Callaway, Va. 62 D5
Calle, F.R.Ger., 4,345 119 E2
Calle Larga, Chile, 1,872 104 g12
Callender, Iowa, 358 72 C2
Callensburg, Pa., 280 60 C3
Callery, Pa., 419 60 B4
Calliaqua, St. Vinc. 97 19
Callicoon, N.Y. 59 K8
Calliham, Tex. 77 O5
Calling Lake, Alta., Can. 42 K2
Callis, Som. Rep. 163 N4
Callosa de Ensarriá, Sp., 4,617 122 E3
Calloway, co., Ky., 20,972 71 C5
Calmar, Alta., Can. 42 J3
Calmar, Iowa, 954 72 F1
Călmăţui, r., Rum. 128 F2
Calmbach, F.R.Ger., 4,004 119 F7
Calmeca, Mex., 1,636 93 f11
Calmer, Ark. 73 C4
Calnalí, Mex., 2,812 93 f9
Calne, U.K., 6,574 114 D8
Calobre, Pan. 94 G6
Calolbon, Phil., 3,826 153 h14
Caloola, Austl. 173 g9
Caloosahatchee, r., Fla. 65 H6
Calore, r., It. 123 d9
Calotmul, Mex., 1,518 93 H4
Calpella, Calif. 82 B3
Calpulalpan, Mex., 6,512 93 f10
Calstock, U.K., 3,884 113 D6
Caltagirone, It., 46,415 123 E6
Caltanissetta, It., 63,219 123 E6
Caltimacán, Mex., 1,162 93 e9
Călugăreni, Rum. 128 E2
Calulo, Ang. 164 B3
Calumet, Qué., Can. 47 K3
Calumet, Iowa, 225 72 B2
Calumet, Mich., 1,139 66 E1
Calumet, Minn., 799 74 F2
Calumet, Okla., 354 76 E2
Calumet, Pa., 1,241 60 D5
Calumet, co., Wis., 22,268 66 E4
Calumet City, Ill., 25,000 68 E2
Calumet Hbr., Ill. 69 d10
Calumet Park, Ill., 10,037 69 d10
Calumet Sag Chan., Ill. 69 c10
Calumpang, Phil., 153 A3
Caluso, It., 6,131 122 a5
Calvados, Chain, The, is., Terr. Papua 174 3
Calvary, Ga. 64 E5
Calvary, Wis. 66 E5
Calveley, U.K. 114 C4
Calvert, Ala. 64 A4
Calvert, co., Md., 15,826 62 H4
Calvert, Tex., 2,073 77 P4
Calvert City, Ky., 1,505 71 C5
Calvert I., Br. Col., Can. 42 E3
Calverton, Va. 62 G4
Calvertville, Ind. 70 C3
Calvi, Fr., 3,087 116 r17
Calvillo, Mex., 5,593 92 E4
Calvin, La., 232 73 C6
Calvin, N. Dak., 104 74 C1
Calvin, Okla., 331 76 G3
Calvin Center, Mich. 67 G7
Calvinia, S. Af., 5,189 164 C7
Calvi Risorta, It., 5,136 123 c9
Calvörde, Ger.D.R. 118 C2
Calw, F.R.Ger., 8,829 118 B4
Calypso, N.C., 633 63 F2
Calzeat, U.K. 112 d8
Cam, U.K., 4,874 114 D7
Cam, r., U.K. 114 J6
Camabatela, Ang. 164 B3
Camacho, Mex., 1,692 92 E3
Camaguán, Ven., 2,046 100 G3
Camagüey, Cuba, 110,388 96 e2
Camaiore, It., 26,065 123 C3
Camajuaní, Cuba, 12,574 96 d1
Camalaniugan, Phil., 1,828 153 B1
Camambugan, Phil., 4,158 153 f11
Camaná, Peru, 5,158 104 C6
Camanche, Iowa, 3,055 72 G3
Camanducaia, Braz., 2,226 103 c18
Camano, Wash. 81 a6
Camano I., Wash. 81 b6
Camapuã, Braz., 1,370 103 F5
Camaquã, Braz., 9,732 103 F8
Camaquã, r., Braz. 103 F8
Camăr, Rum. 128 D1
Camarat, C., Fr. 117 G5
Camarate, Port., 5,053 122 i10
Camarès, Fr., 1,288 117 E5
Camargo, Bol., 2,323 102 c12
Camargo, Chih., Mex., 18,850 92 D2
Camargo, Tam., Mex., 4,008 93 F2
Camargo, Ill., 276 68 D4
Camargo, Ky. 71 G3
Camargo, Okla., 254 76 D1
Camarico, Chile 104 f16
Camarillo, Calif., 2,359 82 D5
Camariñas, Sp., 6,269 122 A1
Camarón, Mex. 93 F2
Camarón, C., Hond. 94 E2
Camarones, Arg. 105 B6
Camarones, Col. 100 D2
Camarones, B., Arg. 105 C6
Camas, co., Idaho, 917 81 B4
Camas, Wash., 5,666 80 B3
Camas Valley, Oreg. 80 B4
Camatagua, Ven., 1,419 101 b12
Ca Mau = Quan Long
Cambambe, Ang. 164 B3
Cambay, India, 51,291 145 D5
Cambay, G. of, India 145 D5
Cambellpore, Pak., 19,041 145 D2
Camberg, F.R.Ger., 4,111 118 B3
Camberley, U.K., 28,552 113 F6
Cambiador, P., Ven. 101 b11
Cambodia, ctry., 5,740,115 146
Cambois, U.K. 112 g9
Cambo-les-Bains, Fr., 4,687 117 C5
Camborne, U.K., 14,125 113 D6
Cambrai, Fr., 35,373 117 E1
Cambria, Calif. 82 C5
Cambria, Ind. 70 C2
Cambria, Mich. 67 J7
Cambria, co., Pa., 203,283 60 E4
Cambria, Va., 722 62 D5
Cambria, Wis., 589 66 D5
Cambria Center, N.Y. 58 k18
Cambrian L., Qué., Can. 45 L3
Cambrian Mts., U.K. 113 E5
Cambrian Park, Calif. 83 f13
Cambridge, Jam., 1,433 96 p8
Cambridge, N.Z., 5,290 175 g5
Cambridge, U.K., 95,527 113 F5
Cambridge, Idaho, 473 81 A3
Cambridge, Ill., 1,665 68 B2
Cambridge, Iowa, 587 72 D3
Cambridge, Kans., 140 75 J6
Cambridge, Me. 55 C3
Cambridge, Md., 12,239 62 J4
Cambridge, Mass., 107,716 57 M3
Cambridge, Minn., 2,728 74 F3
Cambridge, Nebr., 1,090 75 E3
Cambridge, N.Y., 1,748 59 O5
Cambridge, Ohio, 14,562 70 H2
Cambridge, Vt., 217 54 B2
Cambridge, Wis., 605 66 D5
Cambridge and Isle of Ely, co., U.K., 190,384 113 G5
Cambridge Bay, N.W.T., Can. 40 J4
Cambridge City, Ind., 2,569 70 D3
Cambridgeport, Vt. 54 B5
Cambridge Res., Mass. 57 L3
Cambridge Springs, Pa., 2,031 60 C2
Cambrils, Sp., 4,761 122 F2
Cambuci, Braz., 2,423 103 f17
Cambuí, Braz., 3,556 103 d18
Cambuquira, Braz., 5,640 103 d17
Camburg, Ger.D.R. 126 a5
Camden, Austl., 4,847 173 h10
Camden, Ala., 1,121 64 B4
Camden, Ark., 15,823 73 B4
Camden, Del., 1,125 62 J3
Camden, co., Ga., 9,975 64 H5
Camden, Ill., 116 68 B3
Camden, Ind., 601 70 C2
Camden, Me., 3,523 55 C4
Camden, Mich. 434 67 J7
Camden, Miss. 73 F5
Camden, co., Mo., 9,116 72 E7
Camden, Mo., 310 72 D5
Camden, co., N.J., 392,035 61 A4
Camden, N.J., 117,159 61 A4
Camden, N.Y., 2,694 59 J5
Camden, co., N.C., 5,598 63 H1
Camden, N.C. 63 H1
Camden, Ohio, 1,308 70 E3
Camden, S.C., 6,842 63 D3
Camden, Tenn., 2,774 71 C5
Camden, Tex., 1,131 77 Q4
Camden, Wash. 80 E1
Camden Bay, Alaska 85 H1
Camden East, Ont., Can. 46 H4
Camden on Gauley, W. Va., 301 62 D4
Camdenton, Mo., 1,405 72 E6
Camedo, Switz. 124 C2
Cameia, Ang. 164 C3
Camelberg Pk., V.I. 97 4
Camelon, U.K. 112 c8
Camels Hump, Vt. 54 B3
Camels Hump Butte, N. Dak. 74 A2
Cameo, W. Va. 62 C4
Cameri, It., 6,661 122 b5
Cameron, Ariz. 78 C4
Cameron, Ill. 68 B3
Cameron, parish, La., 6,909 73 B8
Cameron, La. 73 B8
Cameron, Mo., 3,674 72 C5
Cameron, N.Y. 58 F7
Cameron, N.C., 298 63 E2
Cameron, Okla., 211 76 J2
Cameron, co., Pa., 7,586 60 F3
Cameron, S.C., 607 63 D4
Cameron, co., Tex., 151,098 77 P6
Cameron, Tex., 5,640 77 P4
Cameron, W. Va., 1,652 62 D3
Cameron, Wis., 982 66 B3
Cameron Burn, r., U.K. 112 e7
Cameron Falls, Ont., Can. 44 E5
Cameron Highlands, Malay. 147 o14
Cameron Hills, Alta., Can. 38 F6
Cameron I., N.W.T., Can. 41 J2
Cameron Mills, N.Y. 58 E7
Cameroon, ctry., 5,229,000* 162 F5
Cameroon Mtn., Cam. 162 F5
Cametá, Braz., 5,695 103 F2
Camiguin I., Phil. 153 B1
Camiguin I., Phil. 153 C3
Camiling, Phil., 9,799 153 B2
Camilla, Ga., 4,753 64 E4
Camillus, N.Y., 1,416 59 q23
Caminha, Port., 2,188 122 A2
Camiri, Bol., 6,499 102 D6
Camisano Vicentino, It., 5,952 122 e5
Cam Lam, S. Viet., 3,125 146 E5
Camlaren, N.W.T., Can. 40 G5
Cammack, Ind. 70 D2
Cammal, Pa. 60 H3
Camoapa, Nic., 1,738 94 E4
Camocim, Braz., 10,788 103 H2
Camooweal, Austl. 172 E2
Camopi, Fr. Guiana 101 O6
Camopi, r., Fr. Guiana 101 O6
Camorta I., India 146 A5
Camotes Is., Phil. 153 f11
Camotes Sea, Phil. 153 C3
Camp, Ire. 113 B5
Camp, co., Tex., 7,849 77 Q3
Campagna, It., 12,781 123 E4
Campaign, Tenn. 71 F6
Campamento, Hond., 1,859 94 D3
Campana, Arg., 19,000* 105 b12
Campana, I., Chile 105 A7
Campanario, Sp., 9,660 122 C3
Campanella, Punta, It. 123 c10
Campanha, Braz., 6,178 103 d17
Campania, I., Br. Col., Can. 42 D3
Campbell, Ala. 64 B4
Campbell, Calif., 11,863 83 e13
Campbell, co., Ky., 86,803 71 G3
Campbell, Minn., 365 74 D2
Campbell, Mo., 1,964 72 G8
Campbell, Nebr., 424 75 G3
Campbell, N.Y. 58 F7
Campbell, Ohio, 13,406 70 J1
Campbell, co., S. Dak., 3,531 74 B3
Campbell, co., Tenn., 27,936 71 G5
Campbell, Tex. 76 g8
Campbell, co., Va., 32,958 62 E5
Campbell, co., Wyo., 5,861 81 G3
Campbell, r., N.B., Can. 55 F1
Campbell, C., N.Z. 175 g6
Campbellford, Ont., Can., 3,411 46 G4
Campbell Hill, Ill., 263 68 C6
Campbell Hill, Ohio 70 F2
Campbell I., N.Z. 170 F8
Campbell Plateau, Pac. Oc. 169 F4
Campbell River, Br. Col., Can., 3,547 42 F4
Campbell's Bay, Qué., Can., 1,005 47 H3
Campbellsburg, Ind., 612 70 C4
Campbellsburg, Ky., 348 71 F3
Campbellsport, Wis., 1,472 66 E5
Campbellsville, Ky., 6,966 71 F4
Campbellsville, Tenn. 71 D6
Campbellton, N.B., Can., 9,662 45 M6
Campbellton, Fla., 309 65 D2
Campbellton, Tex., 271 77 O5
Campbell Town, Austl. 173 f13
Campbelltown, Austl., 9,690 173 h10
Campbelltown, Alta., Can. 43 b7
Campbelltown, U.K. 112 D3
Campbelltown, Pa., 1,061 60 J5
Campbellville, Ont., Can. 46 E5
Campbeltown, U.K., 6,525 113 D4
Camp Creek, Ariz. 78 C5
Camp Creek, W. Va. 62 C5
Camp Crook, S. Dak., 90 74 A3
Campden, Ont., Can. 46 d15
Camp Douglas, Wis., 489 66 C5
Campeche, st., Mex., 168,219 93 H4
Campeche, Mex., 44,426 93 H4
Campeche, B. de, Mex. 93 G4
Campechuela, Cuba, 5,536 96 e2
Camp Ellis, Me. 55 B5
Camperdown, Austl., 3,205 173 d12
Camperville, Man., Can. 43 E4
Campestre, Braz., 3,483 103 c17
Cam Pha, N. Viet., 32,228 146 D2
Camp Hill, Ala., 1,270 64 D3
Camp Hill, Pa., 8,559 60 H5
Camp Houston, Okla. 76 D1
Campillos, Sp., 8,791 122 C4
Campina Grande, Braz., 116,226 103 J3
Campinas, Braz., 179,797 103 c18
Campina Verde, Braz., 4,464 103 F5
Campion, Colo. 79 b7
Camp Lake, Wis. 66 c13
Camp Lake, Wis. 66 c13
Campli, It., 11,685 123 D3
Campo, Cam., 2,000* 162 F5
Campo, Colo., 235 79 D3
Campoalegre, Col. 100 C6
Campobasso, It., 32,559 123 E4
Campobello, S.C., 420 63 B2
Campobello I., N.B., Can. 47 S11
Campo Belo, Braz., 15,742 103 H6
Campo Claro, Ven., 1,563 101 J2
Campodarsego, It., 8,258 122 e5
Campo de Diauarum, Braz. 103 F4
Campo de la Cruz, Col. 100 C2
Campo Elías, Ven., 1,408 100 F2
Campogalliano, It., 5,722 122 c6
Campo Gallo, Arg., 1,950* 105 C3
Campo Grande, Arg., 8,000* 105 E3
Campo Grande, Braz., 64,477 103 F5
Campo Maior, Braz., 13,939 103 H2
Campo Maior, Port., 5,832 122 B3
Campo Mourão, Braz., 7,885 103 F6
Campos, Braz., 90,601 103 H6
Camposampiero, It., 6,685 122 e5
Campos Belos, Braz., 1,210 103 G4
Campos del Puerto, Sp., 6,820 122 G3
Campos do Jordão, Braz., 10,721 103 d18
Campos Sales, Braz., 3,390 103 H3
Campo Troco, Col. 100 F5
Camp-Perrin, Haiti, 1,561 96 k6
Camp Point, Ill., 1,092 68 A3
Camp Sevok, Alaska 85 B3
Camp Sherman, Oreg. 80 C3
Campsie Fells, mtn., U.K. 112 b7
Camp Springs, Md. 62 b9
Campti, La., 1,045 73 B6
Campton, Fla. 65 C2
Campton, Ky. 71 H4
Campton, N.H. 54 D4
Camptonville, Calif. 82 C3
Camptown, Pa. 61 K2
Campus, Ill., 165 68 D2
Campuzano, Mex. 93 c9
Camp Verde, Ariz. 78 B4
Campville (part of Harwinton), Conn. 56 D6
Camp Wood, Ariz. 78 B4
Camp Wood, Tex., 879 77 N5
Camroden, N.Y. 59 t25
Camrose, Alta., Can., 6,877 42 K3
Camsell Portage, Sask., Can. 43 B2
Camuy, P.R., 2,341 96 s10
Camuy, r., P.R. 96 s10
Cana, P., Dom. Rep. 96 n6
Canaan, Trin. and Tob. 96 h4
Canaan, Conn., 1,146 56 C4
Canaan, Ind. 70 D4
Canaan, Me. 55 C4
Canaan, Miss. 73 F3
Canaan, N.H. 54 C4
Canaan, N.Y. 59 O7
Canaan, Vt. 54 D2
Canaan, W. Va. 62 D4
Canaan, r., N.B., Can. 47 T10
Canaan Center, N.H. 54 C4
Canaan Station, N.B., Can. 47 T10
Canaan Street, N.H. 54 C4
Canaan Valley, Conn. 56 D4
Canada, ctry., 19,919,000* 40-1
Canada Falls Deadwater, l., Me. 55 C3
Canadensis, Pa. 61 M3
Canadian, co., Okla., 24,727 76 E2
Canadian, Okla., 255 76 H2
Canadian, Tex., 2,239 76 N2
Canadian, r., U.S. 52 F3
Canadian, Deep Fk., r., Okla. 76 G2
Canadian Basin, Arctic Oc. 108 C1
Cañadón 11 de Septiembre, Arg. 105 B7
Canadys, S.C. 63 D4
Canaguá, r., Ven. 100 E3
Canaima, Ven. 101 J4
Canairiktok, r., Newf., Can. 45 O3
Canajoharie, N.Y., 2,681 59 M6
Çanakkale, Turk., 19,484 142 A1
Çanakkale Boğazı, Turk. 142 A2
Canala, N. Caled., 2,816 174 i8
Canal du Sud ou de la Gonâve, Haiti 96 k6
Canale, It., 4,349 122 b6
Canalejas, Mex., 2,557 93 e10
Canal Flats, Br. Col., Can. 42 J4
Canal Fulton, Ohio, 1,555 70 H2
Canalou, Mo., 447 72 H8
Canal Point, Fla. 65 J6
Canal Winchester, Ohio, 1,976 70 b7
Canal Zone, Cent. Amer., 54,000* 94 H6
Canandaigua, N.Y., 10,058 58 F6
Canandaigua L., N.Y. 58 F6
Cananea, Mex., 19,895 92 C1
Cañar, Ec., 4,858 104 B2
Canard, r., Ont., Can. 67 f16
Canarias, Is. = Canary Is.
Canaries, St. Lucia, 1,675 97 11
Canarreos, Arch. de los, Cuba 96 b1
Canary, Oreg. 80 A4
Canary Basin, Atl. Oc. 108 L5
Canary Is., Atl. Oc., 944,488 108 L5
Cañas, Cuba, 1,789 96 b1
Canaseraga, N.Y., 730 58 E7
Cañasgordas, Col. 100 B4
Canastota, N.Y., 4,896 59 J5
Canatlán, Mex., 3,986 92 D3
Canaveral, C. = Kennedy, C.
Cañazas, Pan., 1,105 94 G6
Canbelego, Austl. 173 F4
Canberra, Austl., 28,277 173 G5
Canby, Calif. 82 C2
Canby, Minn., 2,146 74 D3
Canby, Oreg., 2,168 80 B3
Cancale, Fr., 5,236 117 C2
Cancello, It., 5,373 123 c9
Cancon, Fr., 1,227 117 D4
Cancún, P., Mex. 93 J4
Candala, Som. Rep., 2,452* 163 N4
Candarave, Peru 104 D6
Candé, Fr., 2,355 117 C3
Candeias, Braz., 12,500 103 J4
Candela, Mex., 2,243 93 E2
Candelaria, Col. 100 B6
Candelaria, Col. 100 C2
Candelaria, Cuba, 3,548 96 b1
Candelaria, Guat. 94 B3
Candelaria, Phil., 6,132 153 c9
Candelaria, Tex. 77 L4
Candelaria, r., Mex. 93 H4
Candeleda, Sp., 6,983 122 C2
Candelo, Austl. 173 g11
Candelo, It., 5,354 122 b5
Candia, Gr. = Iráklion
Candia, N.H. 54 E5
Candiac, Qué., Can., 1,033 47 p18
Candia Lomellina, It., 2,420 122 b5
Candido, Urug. 105 c10
Candle, Alaska, 103 85 D2
Candle L., Sask., Can. 43 C4
Candler, co., Ga., 6,672 64 G3
Candler, N.C. 63 B2
Candlewood L., Conn. 56 B6
Cando, Sask., Can. 43 B4
Cando, N. Dak., 1,566 74 C1
Candon, Phil., 4,203 153 B1
Candoni, Phil., 5,131 153 d12
Candor, N.Y., 956 59 H7
Candor, N.C., 593 63 E2
Candor, Pa. 60 a8
Can Duoc, S. Viet., 2,247 147 m11
Cane, r., N.C. 63 B2
Canea = Khaniá
Caneadea, N.Y. 58 D7
Cane Cr., Utah 78 D2
Caneel Bay, Virgin Is. 97 4
Cane Garden Pt., St. Vinc. 97 19
Canelli, It., 9,130 122 b6
Canelones, Urug., 10,000* 105 c12
Canelos, Ec. 104 B2
Cañete, Peru, 7,057 104 B5
Cañete, Sp., 1,398 122 E2
Cañete, r., Peru 104 B5
Cane Valley, Ky. 71 F4
Caney, Kans., 2,682 75 K6
Caney, Ky. 71 H4
Caney, Okla., 128 76 G3
Caney, r., Kan.-Okla. 76 H1
Caney Fk., r., Tenn. 71 F6
Caneyville, Ky., 278 71 E4
Canfield, Ark. 73 B4
Canfield, Colo. 79 b7
Canfield, Ohio, 3,252 70 J1
Canfranc, Sp., 1,035 122 E1
Cangahua, Ec. 104 c10
Cangallo, Peru, 1,579 104 C5
Cangamba, Ang. 164 C4
Cangas, Sp., 17,115 122 A1
Cangas de Narcea, Sp., 20,980 122 B1
Cangas de Onís, Sp., 10,261 122 C1
Can Gio, S. Viet., 3,507 147 m11
Can Giuoc, S. Viet., 3,140 147 m11
Canguaretama, Braz., 4,261 103 b14
Canhotinho, Braz., 3,557 103 a15
Canicattì, It., 32,722 123 D6
Canigou, Mt., Fr. 117 E5
Canillo, Andorra 122 g7
Canimina, L., Qué., Can. 46 G1
Canim Lake, Br. Col., Can. 42 G3
Canindé, Braz., 5,854 103 J2
Canindé, r., Braz. 103 H3
Canipaan, Phil., 153 A3
Canisteo, N.Y., 2,731 58 E7
Canisteo, r., N.Y. 58 E7
Canistota, S. Dak., 627 74 D4
Cañitas, Mex., 4,099 92 E3
Canjáyar, Sp., 2,399 122 D4
Canje, r., Guyana 101 M5
Canjilon, N. Mex. 79 B3
Çankırı, Turk., 20,009 142 C1
Canlubang, Phil., 11,404 153 c8
Canmore, Alta., Can., 1,379 42 J3
Canna, i., U.K. 112 C3
Cannac, i., Terr. Papua 174 3
Cannanore, India, 46,101 145 E8
Cannel City, Ky. 71 H4
Cannelton, Ind., 1,829 70 C5
Cannes, Fr., 59,173 117 G5
Canneto sull'Oglio, It., 5,202 122 d5
Canning, N.S., Can. 47 T11
Canning, S. Dak. 74 C3
Canning, r., Alaska 85 H1
Cannington, Ont., Can., 1,013 46 E4
Cannock, U.K., 42,186 113 E5
Cannon, co., Tenn., 8,537 71 E6
Cannon, r., Minn. 74 F3
Cannon Ball, N. Dak. 74 B2
Cannonball, r., N. Dak. 74 A2
Cannon Beach, Oreg., 495 80 A3
Cannondale (part of Wilton), Conn. 56 C8
Cannon Falls, Minn., 2,055 74 F3
Cannonsburg, Mich. 67 H5
Cannonsburg, Miss. 73 D6
Cannonsville, N.Y. 59 K7
Cannonville, Utah, 153 78 C3
Cann River, Austl. 173 g11
Canoas, Braz., 95,401 103 F8
Canoas, r., Braz. 103 F7
Canoas, P., Mex. 92 B2
Canobie Lake, N.H. 54 E6
Canoe, r., Br. Col., Can. 42 H3
Canoe, r., Mass. 57 M4
Canoe Lake, Sask., Can. 43 C3
Canoe L., Sask., Can. 43 B3
Canoga, N.Y. 59 p24
Canon, Ga., 626 64 F1
Canonbie, U.K. 113 E4
Canonchet (part of Hopkinton), R.I. 57 J7
Canon City, Colo., 8,973 79 C2
Canon Fiord, N.W.T., Can. 41 N1
Canonsburg, Pa., 11,877 60 B5
Canoochee, r., Ga. 64 H4
Canora, Sask., Can., 2,104 43 D4
Canosa di Puglia, It., 36,133 123 E4
Canot, r., Haiti 96 k6
Canouan, i., Gren. Is. 97 20
Canova, S. Dak., 247 74 D4
Canowindra, Austl., 1,913 173 G5
Cansahcab, Mex., 2,751 93 H4
Canso, N.S., Can., 1,141 45 O6
Canso, Str. of, N.S., Can. 45 O6
Canta, Peru, 2,313 104 B4
Cantabria, Mex., 2,570 93 c10
Cantábrica, Cord., Sp. 122 B1
Cantagallo, Col. 100 D4
Canta Gallo, Ven. 101 b12
Cantagalo, Braz., 3,479 103 e17
Cantalejo, Sp., 3,776 122 C2
Cantanhede, Port., 6,630 122 A2
Cantaura, Ven., 14,096 101 H3
Čantavir, Yug., 9,262 125 D2
Canterbury, U.K., 30,415 113 G6
Canterbury, Conn., 1,857(T) 56 J6
Canterbury, N.H. 54 D5
Canterbury Bight, N.Z. 175 f7
Canterbury Station, N.B., Can. 47 S11
Can Tho, S. Viet., 47,625 146 D5
Cantiles, Cayo, Cuba 96 c2
Cantimplora, Col. 101 e13
Canto do Buriti, Braz., 1,636 103 H3
Canton, China = Kuang-chou
Canton, Conn., 4,783(T) 56 E5
Canton, Ga., 2,411 64 E1
Canton, Ill., 13,588 68 B3
Canton, Ind. 70 D4
Canton, Kans., 784 75 H5
Canton, Ky. 71 D5
Canton, Me. 55 B4
Canton, Mass., 12,771(T) 57 M4
Canton, Miss., 9,707 73 E5
Canton, Mo., 2,562 72 F4
Canton, N.J. 61 A5
Canton, N.Y., 5,046 59 K2
Canton, N.C., 5,068 63 B2
Canton, Ohio, 113,631 70 H2
Canton, Okla., 1,216 76 E1
Canton, Pa., 2,102 60 J2
Canton, S. Dak., 2,511 74 D4
Canton, Tex., 1,114 77 Q3
Canton, Wis. 66 B3
Canton, atoll, Phoenix Is. 170 G5
Canton, Anse du, Mon. 116 n14
Canton Center (part of Canton), Conn. 56 E5
Cantonment, Fla., 2,499 65 B2
Canton Res., Okla. 76 E1
Cantrall, Ill., 115 68 C4
Cantril, Iowa, 299 72 E4
Cantù, It., 25,135 123 B2
Cantwell, Alaska 85 G3
Cañuelas, Arg., 6,592 105 b12
Canumã, r., Braz. 102 E3
Canutama, Braz. 102 D3
Canute, Okla., 370 76 D2
Canutillo, Mex., 1,252 92 D2
Canutillo, Tex., 1,377 77 K4
Canwood, Sask., Can. 43 C4
Cany-Barville, Fr., 1,648 117 D2
Canyon, Yukon, Can. 40 B5
Canyon, Calif. 83 e12
Canyon, co., Idaho, 57,662 81 A4
Canyon, N. Mex. 79 B4
Canyon, Tex., 5,864 76 N2
Canyon City, Oreg., 654 80 D3
Canyon Dam, Calif. 82 C2
Canyon Dam Res., Tex. 76 b6
Canyon de Chelly Nat. Mon., Ariz. 78 D3
Canyon Ferry Res., Mont. 81 D2
Canyonlands Nat. Pk., Utah 78 D2
Canyonville, Oreg., 1,089 80 B4
Caoayan, Phil., 2,029 153 b5
Caobal, Guat. 94 B2
Cao Bang, N. Viet. 146 D2
Cao Lanh, S. Viet. 147 k11
Caonillas, L., res., P.R. 96 s10
Caorso, It., 5,059 122 c5
Cap, Pte. du, St. Lucia 97 11
Capá, P.R. 96 r10
Capa, S. Dak. 74 B3
Capac, Mich., 1,235 67 L6
Capaccio, It., 10,921 123 E4
Capácuaro, Mex., 1,138 93 b10
Capadare, Ven. 100 F2
Cap-à-l'Aigle, Qué., Can. 47 Q10
Capalonga, Phil., 2,578 153 B2
Capanaparo, r., Ven. 100 G4
Capanema, Braz., 9,678 103 G2
Capannori, It., 40,823 123 C3
Capão Bonito, Braz., 6,829 103 G6
Caparde, Yug. 125 D2
Caparica, Port., 10,363 122 i10
Caparo, r., Trin. and Tob. 96 g5
Caparo, r., Ven. 100 E4
Caparrapí, Col. 101 e14
Caparro, Co., Col. 100 G7
Caparroso, Sp., 2,798 122 E1
Capatárida, Ven., 1,277 100 E2
Cap-Chat, Qué., Can., 2,012 45 M5
Cap-de-la-Madeleine, Qué., Can., 26,530 47 M2
Capdenac-Gare, Fr., 5,647 117 D4
Cape Anguille, Newf., Can. 45 P6
Cape Barren Island, Austl. 173 f13
Cape Barren I., Austl. 173 G6
Cape Basin, Atl. Oc. 109 N9
Cape Breton Highlands, N.S., Can. 39 R8
Cape Breton Highlands Nat. Pk., N.S., Can. 45 O6
Cape Breton I., N.S., Can. 45 P6
Cape Broyle, Newf., Can. 45 b10
Cape Canaveral = Cape Kennedy
Cape Charles, Va., 2,041 62 H5
Cape Coast, Ghana, 42,180 162 D5
Cape Cod Bay, Mass. 57 P5
Cape Cod Can., Mass. 57 P5
Cape Cod Nat. Seashore, Mass. 57 Q4
Cape Coral, Fla. 65 G6
Cape Cross, S.-W. Afr. 164 B5
Cape Dorset, N.W.T., Can. 41 O5
Cape Dyer, N.W.T., Can. 41 R4
Cape Elizabeth, Me. 55 B5
Cape Fear, r., N.C. 63 F3
Cape Freels, Newf., Can. 45 R5
Cape Girardeau, co., Mo., 42,020 72 H7
Cape Girardeau, Mo., 24,947 72 H7
Cape Hatteras Nat. Seashore Rec. Area, N.C. 63 J2
Cape Hopes Advance, Qué., Can. 45 L1
Cape Kennedy, Fla. 65 J4
Capel, U.K., 2,900 114 H8
Capella, Austl. 173 G3
Capella, pk., Terr. New Guin. 174 d2
Capelle-Schinkel, Neth., 3,900 115 b7
Cape May, co., N.J., 48,555 61 B5
Cape May, N.J., 4,477 61 B6
Cape May C.H., N.J., 1,749 61 B5
Cape May Point, N.J., 263 61 A6
Cape Neddick, Me. 55 B5
Cape Parry, N.W.T., Can. 40 E3
Cape Porpoise, Me. 55 B5
Cape Province = Kaapprovinsie
Cape Race, Newf., Can. 45 b11
Cape Rise, Atl. Oc. 109 O9
Capernaum, ruins, Isr. 142 b7
Cape St. Charles, Newf., Can. 45 Q4
Cape Scott, Br. Col., Can. 42 E4
Cape Smith, N.W.T., Can. 44 H1
Capesterre, Basse-Terre, Guad., 3,725 97 14
Capesterre, Marie-Galante, Guad. 97 14
Capesterre, Gde., R. de la, Guad. 97 14
Capetillo, Mex. 93 c8
Cape Tormentine, N.B., Can. 47 T10
Cape Town, S. Af., 731,484 164 B7
Cape Verde Basin, Atl. Oc. 109 L6
Cape Verde Is., Atl. Oc., 219,000* 109 L5
Cape Verde Terrace, Atl. Oc. 108 L5
Capeville, Va. 62 J5
Cape Vincent, N.Y., 770 59 H3
Cape York Pen., Austl. 173 F1
Cap-Haïtien, Haiti, 26,555 96 k6
Capheaton, U.K. 112 g9
Capilla de Guadalupe, Mex., 2,975 93 b9
Capilla Palacio, Chile 104 f15
Capim, r., Braz. 103 G2
Capinota, Bol., 6,077 102 b10
Capira, Pan., 1,067 94 G6
Cap I., Phil. 153 B4
Capistrano Beach, Calif., 2,026 82 E6
Capitan, N. Mex., 552 79 C5
Capitán Bado, Para. 105 D2
Capitanejo, Col. 100 D4
Capitol, Mont. 81 G3
Capitola, Calif., 2,021 83 f14
Capitol Heights, Md., 3,138 62 b9
Capitol Pk., N. Mex. 79 B5
Capitol Reef Nat. Mon., Utah 78 C2
Caplin Cove, Newf., Can. 45 b9
Capon Bridge, W. Va., 198 62 F3
Capon Springs, W. Va. 62 F3
Capot, r., Mart. 97 12
Capoterra, It., 6,321 123 B5
Cappadocia, reg., Turk. 142 C2
Cappagh White, Ire. 113 B5
Cappahayden, Newf., Can. 45 c11
Cappamore, Ire. 113 B5
Cap Pelé, N.B., Can. 47 T10
Cappoquin, Ire. 113 C5
Capraia, Isola, It. 123 B3
Capreol, Ont., Can., 2,937 44 H6
Capri, It., 7,332 123 c10
Capri, Isola di, It. 123 E4
Capricorn Chan., Austl. 173 G3
Caprino Veronese, It., 7,078 122 d5
Caprivi Strip = Caprivi Zipfel
Caprivi Zipfel, reg., S.-W. Af. 164 C5

Castlewellan—Chambly · 209

Castlewellan, U.K., 1,241 113 D4
Castlewood, S. Dak., 500 74 D3
Castlewood, Va. 62 B6
Castolon, Tex. 77 M5
Caston, Okla. 76 J3
Castor, Alta., Can., 1,019 42 K3
Castor, U.K. 114 H5
Castor, La., 142 73 B5
Castor, r., Ont., Can. 47 J3
Castor, r., Mo. 72 G7
Castor Bayou, La. 73 C5
Castorland, N.Y., 321 59 J4
Castres, Fr., 40,005 117 E5
Castricum, Neth., 11,600 115 C2
Castries, St. Lucia, 17,505 97 11
Castro, Braz., 9,249 103 G6
Castro, Chile, 7,001 105 A6
Castro, co., Tex., 8,923 77 M2
Castro Caldelas, Sp., 4,248 122 B1
Castro Daire, Port., 4,300 122 B2
Castro del Río, Sp., 11,842 122 C4
Castrojeriz, Sp., 1,838 122 C1
Castropol, Sp., 6,293 122 B1
Castrop-Rauxel, F.R.Ger., 83,376 119 C1
Castro-Urdiales, Sp., 11,988 122 D1
Castro Valley, Calif., 37,120 83 e12
Castro Verde, Port., 5,538 122 A4
Castroville, Tex., 1,508 77 O5
Castrovillari, It., 15,215 123 E5
Castroville, Calif., 2,838 83 f14
Castrovirreyna, Peru 104 C5
Castuera, Sp., 10,166 122 C3
Casuarina, Mt., Austl. 172 C2
Casuchichon, Col. 100 D1
Casupá, Urug., 2,000* 105 d12
Caswell, co., N.C., 19,912 63 E1
Caswell Sd., N.Z. 175 e7
Catacamas, Hond., 3,258 94 E3
Catacaos, Peru, 12,206 104 A3
Catacocha, Ec., 3,777 104 B3
Cataguases, Braz., 21,476 103 e17
Catahoula, parish, La., 11,421 73 D6
Catahoula L., La. 73 C6
Cataiñgan, Phil., 2,669 153 C3
Catalão, Braz., 11,471 103 G5
Catalina, Newf., Can., 1,110 45 R5
Catalina, Chile 104 e15
Catalina, Chile 105 B3
Catalina, I., Dom. Rep. 96 n6
Catalina Pt., Guam 176 24
Cataloi, Rum. 128 G2
Cataluña, reg., Sp. 122 F2
Catamarca, Arg., 49,322 105 B3
Catamount Mtn., N.Y. 59 L3
Catanauan, Phil., 3,994 153 B2
Catanduanes I., Phil. 153 C2
Catanduva, Braz., 37,307 103 G6
Catania, It., 363,048 123 E6
Cataño, P.R., 8,276 96 t10
Catanzaro, It., 72,012 123 F5
Cataract, Wis. 66 C4
Cataract Cr., Ariz. 78 B3
Cataract L., Ind. 68 E4
Catarama, Ec., 2,404 104 c10
Catarina, Tex., 160 77 O5
Catarman, Phil., 8,248 153 C2
Catarman, Phil., 2,757 153 f12
Catarroja, Sp., 11,680 122 E3
Catasauqua, Pa., 5,062 61 L4
Catatumbo, r., Col.-Ven. 100 D3
Catavi, Bol. 102 C5
Catawba, co., N.C., 73,191 63 C2
Catawba, N.C., 504 63 C2
Catawba, Va. 62 D5
Catawba, Wis., 230 66 C3
Catawba, r., N.C. 63 D2
Catawba L., N.C.-S.C. 63 D2
Catawissa, Pa., 1,824 61 K4
Catawissa Cr., Pa. 61 K4
Cat Ba, N. Viet. 147 i9
Cat Ba, Dao, i., N. Viet. 146 D2
Catbalogan, Phil., 14,274 153 C3
Cateechee, S.C. 63 B3
Cateel, Phil., 2,626 153 C4
Catemaco, Mex., 8,653 93 G4
Catemu, Chile, 1,498 104 f12
Catende, Braz., 9,428 103 b15
Caterham, U.K., 15,267 114 H8
Cates, Ind. 70 B2
Catesby, Okla. 76 D1
Catete, Ang. 164 B3
Catfish Cr., N.Y. 59 q22
Cathance L., Me. 55 E4
Catharine, Kans. 75 F5
Cathay, Calif. 82 D4
Cathay, N. Dak., 110 74 C2
Cathcart, Ont., Can. 46 a15
Cathcart, S. Af., 3,839 164 D7
Cathedral Bluffs, Colo. 79 A2
Cathedral City, Calif., 1,855 82 E6
Cathedral Mtn., Tex. 77 L4
Catherine, Ala. 64 B3
Catherines Peak, Jam. 96 q8
Cathlamet, Wash., 615 80 B2
Catholic I., Gren. Is. 97 20
Cathro, Mich. 67 K3
Catia La Mar, Ven. 101 b11
Catió, Port. Guin. 162 B4
Cat I., Bah. Is. 95 D1
Cat I., Miss. 73 F7
Cat I., Wis. 66 C1
Cat L., Ont., Can. 44 D4
Catlettsburg, Ky., 3,874 71 J3
Catlin, Ill., 1,263 68 E3
Catmon, Phil., 2,456 153 f11
Cato, Ind. 70 B4
Cato, N.Y., 476 59 p23
Cato, Wis. 66 F4
Catoche, C., Mex. 93 J4
Caton, U.K., 1,482 114 C2
Caton, N.Y. 58 F7
Caton Farm, Ill. 69 b10
Catonsville, Md., 37,372 62 H3
Catoosa, co., Ga., 21,101 64 D1
Catoosa, Okla., 638 76 H1
Catria, Monte, It. 123 D3
Catrimani, r., Braz. 102 D1
Catrine, U.K. 112 b8
Catron, Mo., 177 72 H8
Catron, co., N. Mex., 2,773 79 A5
Catskill, N.Y., 5,825 59 N7
Catskill Mts., N.Y. 59 L7
Cat Spring, Tex. 77 P5
Cattaraugus, co., N.Y., 80,187 58 C7
Cattaraugus, N.Y., 1,258 58 C7
Cattaraugus Cr., N.Y. 58 C7
Catterick, U.K., 2,011 114 E2
Catterick Camp, U.K. 113 F4
Cattolica, It., 12,047 123 D3
Catu, Braz., 8,883 103 J4
Catuane, Moz. 164 E6
Catumbela, Ang. 164 B4
Catur, Moz. 164 E4
Cau, r., N. Viet. 147 h8
Cauayan, Phil., 4,781 153 B1
Cauayan, Phil., 2,365 153 d11
Cauca, r., Col. 100 C4
Caucagua, Ven., 4,539 100 G2
Caucasia, Col. 100 C3
Caucasus=Kavkaz
Caucedo, C., Dom. Rep. 96 n6
Cauchon L., Man., Can. 43 F3
Caucomgomoc L., Me. 55 C2
Caudry, Fr., 13,292 116 a7
Caufield, Mo. 72 E8
Caughdenoy, N.Y. 59 q22
Caughnawaga, Qué., Can., 2,240 47 o18
Cau Ke, S. Viet., 2,160 147 m12
Caulnes, Fr., 1,822 117 B2
Caulonia, It., 12,568 123 F5
Caunao, Cuba, 3,403 96 c1
Cau Ngang, S. Viet., 1,838 146 D5
Caúngula, Ang. 164 C3
Cauquenes, Chile, 17,836 105 A5
Cauquira, Hond. 94 F3
Caura, r., Ven. 101 H4
Causapscal, Qué., Can., 3,390 45 M5
Caussade, Fr., 5,238 117 D4
Cauterets, Fr., 1,037 117 C5
Cauthron, Ark. 73 A3
Cauto, r., Cuba 96 e2
Cauvery, r., India 145 E8
Cauxithi, Mex. 93 e9
Cava de' Tirreni, It., 42,172 123 d10
Cávado, r., Port. 122 A2
Cavaglià, It., 2,980 122 b5
Cavaillon, Fr., 17,218 117 F5
Cavalcante, Braz. 103 G4
Cavaleiro, Braz., 35,216 103 b15
Cavalier, co., N. Dak., 10,064 74 C1
Cavalier, N. Dak., 1,423 74 D1
Cavally, r., Libya 162 C5
Cavan, co., Ire., 61,740 113 C5
Cavan, Ire., 4,277 113 C4
Cavanal Mtn., Okla. 76 J2
Cavarzere, It., 22,600 123 D2
Cave, It., 6,524 123 b8
Cave City, Ark., 540 73 D2
Cave City, Ky., 1,418 71 F4
Cavecreek, Ariz. 78 C5
Cave in Rock, Ill., 495 68 D6
Cave Junction, Oreg., 248 80 B4
Ca-Vel, N.C. 63 F1
Cavendish, Alta., Can. 42 L4
Cavendish, Newf., Can. 45 b10
Cavendish, Vt. 54 B5
Caverna, Mo. 72 C8
Cave Spring, Ga., 1,153 64 D1
Cave Springs, Ark., 281 73 A1
Cavett, Ohio 70 E2
Caviana, I., Braz. 103 G1
Cavite, Phil., 54,826 153 b8
Cavnic, Rum. 128 D1
Cavour, S. Dak., 140 74 C3
Cavour, Wis. 66 E3
Cavtat, Yug. 125 D3
Cawker City, Kans., 686 75 G4
Cawnpore=Kanpur
Cawood, U.K. 114 F3
Cawood, Ky. 71 H5
Caxambu, Braz., 10,491 103 d17
Caxias, Braz., 19,092 103 H2
Caxias do Sul, Braz., 60,607 103 F7
Caximbo, Sa. do, Braz. 103 E3
Caxito, Ang. 164 B3
Çay, Turk., 7,289 142 B2
Cayambe, Ec., 7,202 104 B1
Cayambe, mtn., Ec. 104 c10
Çaybaşı, Turk., 9,713 142 E1
Cayce, S.C., 8,517 63 C4
Cayenne, Fr. Guiana, 15,063* 101 O5
Cayes, Baie des, Haiti 96 k6
Cayes-Jacmel, Haiti, 1,043 96 k6
Cayey, P.R., 19,738 96 t10
Çaykara, Turk., 1,100 137 b1
Cayley, Alta., Can. 42 J4
Caylus, Fr., 1,662 117 D4
Cayman Brac, i., Lesser Caymans 97 2
Cayman Is., W.I. 95 B3
Cayman Trench, Caribbean Sea 108 G5
Cayo Mambí, Cuba, 1,553 96 f2
Cayon, St. Christopher, 1,524 97 6
Cay Sal Bank, Bah. Is. 96 d1
Caythorpe, U.K. 114 G4
Cayucos, Calif. 82 C5
Cayuga, Ont., Can. 46 E6
Cayuga, Ill. 68 D3
Cayuga, Ind., 904 70 B3
Cayuga, co., N.Y., 73,942 59 G5
Cayuga, N.Y., 621 59 G6
Cayuga, N. Dak., 195 74 D2
Cayuga, Tex. 77 P4
Cayuga, Wis. 66 C2
Cayuga Cr., N.Y. 58 k19
Cayuga Heights, N.Y., 2,788 59 H7
Cayuga L., N.Y. 59 G6
Cayuse, Oreg. 80 D3
Cayuta, N.Y. 59 G7
Cayuta Cr., N.Y. 59 G7
Cazalla de la Sierra, Sp., 10,109 122 C4
Căzănești, Rum. 128 F2
Cazenovia, N.Y., 2,584 59 J6
Cazenovia, Wis., 351 66 C5
Cazenovia Cr., N.Y. 58 k19
Cazeres-sur-Garonne, Fr., 3,114 117 D5
Cazis, Switz., 1,533 124 D2
Cazombo, Ang. 164 C4
Cazones, Golfo de, Cuba 96 c2
Cazorla, Sp., 12,232 122 D4
Ceananus Mór, Ire., 2,162 113 C5
Ceánuri, Sp., 2,352 122 n11
Ceará, st., Braz., 3,337,856 103 H3
Ceará-Mirim, Braz., 8,290 103 J3
Cearfoss, Md. 62 G3
Ceba, Sask., Can. 43 D4
Cébaco, I., Pan. 94 G7
Cebadas, Ec. 104 c10
Ceballos, Cuba, 1,405 96 d2
Ceballos, Mex., 2,508 92 D2
Cebolleta, N. Mex. 79 B4
Cebolleta Mts., N. Mex. 79 B4
Cebreros, Sp., 4,019 122 C2
Cebu, Phil., 56,158 153 C3
Cebu, i., Phil. 153 B3
Čečava, Yug., 2,781 125 C2
Ceccano, It., 18,766 123 D4
Čechy, reg., Czech. 126 B2
Cecil, Ga., 279 64 F4
Cecil, co., Md., 48,408 62 J3
Cecil, Ohio, 288 70 E1
Cecil, Oreg. 80 D3
Cecil, Pa. 60 b8
Cecil, Wis., 357 66 E4
Cecile Pen., Christmas Atoll 177 40
Cecilia, Mt., Austl. 172 B3
Cecil Lake, Br. Col., Can. 42 G2
Cecil Rhodes, Mt., Austl. 172 B3
Cecilton, Md., 596 62 J3
Cecilville, Calif. 82 B2
Cecina, It., 15,780 123 C3
Ceclavín, Sp., 4,719 122 B3
Cedar, co., Iowa, 17,791 72 F3
Cedar, Mich. 67 H4
Cedar, co., Mo., 9,185 72 D7
Cedar, co., Nebr., 13,368 75 H1
Cedar, Wis. 66 C2
Cedar, r., Iowa 72 F2
Cedar, r., Mich. 66 F3
Cedar, r., Mich. 67 J4
Cedar, r., Nebr. 75 G2
Cedar, r., N. Dak. 74 A2
Cedar, r., Wash. 81 b8
Cedar Bayou, Tex. 77 k9
Cedar Bayou, r., Tex. 77 k9
Cedar Beach, Ont., Can. 67 g16
Cedar Bluff, Ala., 687 64 D1
Cedar Bluff, Va., 995 62 C5
Cedar Bluff Res., Kans. 75 F5
Cedar Bluffs, Kans. 75 E4
Cedar Bluffs, Nebr., 585 75 J2
Cedar Breaks Nat. Mon., Utah 78 B3
Cedarburg, Wis., 5,191 66 F5
Cedar Bushes (part of Plymouth), Mass. 57 O5
Cedarbutte, S. Dak. 74 B4
Cedar City, Mo. 72 E6
Cedar City, Utah, 7,543 78 B3
Cedar Cove, Colo. 79 b7
Cedar Creek, Ark. 73 B3
Cedarcreek, Mo. 72 E8
Cedar Creek, Tex. 77 P4
Cedar Creek, Utah 78 a7
Cedar Cr., Colo. 79 D1
Cedar Cr., N.J. 61 C4
Cedaredge, Colo., 549 79 B2
Cedar Falls, Iowa, 26,016 72 E2
Cedar Falls, N.C. 63 E2
Cedar Falls, Wash. 80 C2
Cedar Fort, Utah 78 b10
Cedar Grove, Antigua 97 9
Cedar Grove, Essex Co., N.J., 14,603 58 c13
Cedar Grove, Ocean Co., N.J. 58 c17
Cedar Grove, Wash. 81 b8
Cedar Grove, W. Va., 1,569 62 C4
Cedar Grove, Wis., 1,175 66 F5
Cedar Hill, N.Y. 59 v29
Cedar Hill, Tenn. 71 E5
Cedar Hill, Tex., 1,848 76 e9
Cedar Hills, Oreg. 80 a6
Cedar Hills, N. Dak. 74 A2
Cedarhurst, N.Y., 6,954 58 e14
Cedar Island, N.C. 63 H2
Cedar Key, Fla., 668 65 F3
Cedar Lake, Ind., 5,766 70 B1
Cedar Lake, Mich. 67 J5
Cedar L., Man., Can. 43 E4
Cedar L., Ill. 69 b7
Cedar L., Mich. 67 K4
Cedar L., Minn. 74 b6
Cedar L., Tex. 77 M3
Cedar L., Wis. 66 A3
Cedar Lane, Tex. 77 P6
Cedar Mtn., N. Mex. 79 A5
Cedar Mts., Utah 78 B1
Cedar Pines Park, Calif. 83 k15
Cedar Point, Kans., 87 75 J5
Cedar Rapids, Iowa, 103,545 72 F2
Cedar Rapids, Nebr., 512 75 G2
Cedar Ridge, Ariz. 78 C3
Cedar River, Mich. 66 F3
Cedars, Del. 62 e11
Cedar Springs, Ont., Can. 46 B6
Cedar Springs, Ont., Can. 46 c14
Cedar Springs, Ga. 64 E4
Cedar Springs, Mich., 1,768 67 H5
Cedartown, Ga., 9,340 64 D2
Cedar-Tree Point, Barbuda 97 8
Cedarvale, Br. Col., Can. 42 E2
Cedar Vale, Kans., 859 75 J6
Cedarvale, N. Mex. 79 C4
Cedarvale, Tex. 76 g9
Cedar Valley, Tex. 76 b5
Cedarville, Calif. 82 C2
Cedarville, Ill., 570 68 C1
Cedarville (part of Plymouth), Mass. 57 O5
Cedarville, Mich. 67 J2
Cedarville, N.J., 1,095 61 A5
Cedarville, Ohio, 1,702 70 F3
Cedarville, Pa. 60 e11
Cedeira, Sp., 8,411 122 A1
Cedillos, Mex. 92 D1
Cedral, Mex., 4,221 93 E3
Cedro, Braz., 6,596 103 J3
Cedros, Hond., 1,841 94 D3
Cedros, I., Mex. 92 B2
Ceduna, Austl. 172 D5
Cedynia, Pol., 1,217 127 A2
Cefalù, It., 12,900 123 E5
Cegama, Sp., 2,043 122 n12
Cegléd, Hung., 37,943 126 D3
Ceglie Messapico, It., 23,947 123 F4
Cehegín, Sp., 15,928 122 E3
Cehu Silvaniei, Rum. 128 D1
Ceiba, P.R., 1,644 96 u10
Ceica, Rum. 128 D1
Cela=Vila Freixo de Espada-á-Cinta
Celano, It., 11,182 123 D3
Celanova, Sp., 8,127 122 B1
Celaya, Mex., 58,762 93 E4
Celebes=Sulawesi
Celebes Sea, Indon. 149 G2
Čelebić, Yug. 125 C3
Čelebići, Yug. 125 D3
Celendín, Peru, 5,801 104 B3
Celerina, Switz. 124 D2
Celeste, Tex., 538 77 P3
Celestine, Ind. 70 C4
Celica, Ec., 3,556 104 A3
Celina, Ohio, 7,659 70 E2
Celina, Tenn., 1,228 71 F5
Celina, Tex., 1,204 77 P3
Celje, Yug., 26,000* 125 B1
Celldömölk, Hung., 9,766 126 C3
Celle, F.R.Ger., 57,239 118 C2
Cellieu, Fr. 116 o15
Celorico da Beira, Port., 2,906 122 B2
Celoron, N.Y., 1,507 58 B7
Cély, Fr. 116 i12
Cement, Okla., 959 76 E3
Cement City, Mich., 471 67 J6
Cement City, Mo. 75 b7
Cementon, N.Y. 59 M7
Cementon, Pa., 1,900* 61 i18
Centenary, S.C. 63 E3
Centennial Wash, Ariz. 78 B5
Center, Colo., 1,600 79 B3
Center, Mo., 484 72 F5
Center, Nebr., 147 75 H1
Center, N. Dak., 476 74 B2
Center, Tex., 4,510 77 Q4
Center Barnstead, N.H. 54 E5
Center Bridge, Pa. 60 f10
Centerbrook (part of Essex), Conn. 56 G7
Center Brunswick, N.Y. 59 w28
Centerburg, Ohio, 963 70 G2
Center City, Minn., 293 74 F3
Center Conway, N.H. 54 E4
Center Cross, Va. 62 H5
Centerdale (part of N. Providence and Johnston), R.I. 57 K5
Centereach, N.Y., 8,524 59 O10
Center Effingham, N.H. 54 F4
Centerfield, Utah, 475 78 C2
Center Groton (part of Groton), Conn. 56 H7
Center Harbor, N.H. 54 E4
Center Hill, Fla., 529 65 H4
Center Hill L., Tenn. 71 F5
Center Line, Mich., 10,164 67 f14
Center Moreland, Pa. 61 o16
Center Moriches, N.Y., 2,521 59 P10
Center Ossipee, N.H. 54 E4
Center Point, Ala. 64 d7
Center Point, Ark., 136 73 A3
Centerpoint, Ind., 268 70 B3
Center Point, Iowa, 1,236 72 F2
Center Point, La. 73 C6
Center Point, Tex. 77 O5
Center Point, W. Va. 62 D3
Center Pd., Mass. 56 D3
Centerport, N.Y., 3,628 58 f13
Centerport, Pa., 208 61 K5
Center Rutland, Vt. 54 A4
Center Sandwich, N.H. 54 D4
Center Square, Pa. 60 f11
Center Strafford, N.H. 54 E5
Centerton, N.J. 61 A4
Centertown, Mo., 190 72 E6
Center Tuftonboro, N.H. 54 E4
Center Valley, Pa. 61 k18
Centerview, Mo., 208 72 D6
Centerville, Conn.=Hamden
Centerville, Del. 62 e10
Centerville, Ind., 2,378 70 D3
Centerville, Iowa, 6,629 72 E4
Centerville, Kans. 75 L5
Centerville, La. 73 D8
Centerville (part of Barnstable), Mass. 57 P6
Centerville (part of Beverly), Mass. 57 N2
Centerville (part of Uxbridge), Mass. 57 K4
Centerville, Mo., 163 72 G7
Centerville, N.J. 60 g10
Centerville, Nev. 83 A3
Centerville, N.C. 63 F1
Centerville, Crawford Co., Pa., 238 60 C2
Centerville, Washington Co., Pa., 5,088 60 B5
Centerville, S. Dak., 887 74 D4
Centerville, Tenn., 1,678 71 D6
Centerville, Tex., 836 77 Q4
Centerville, Utah, 2,361 78 C1
Centerville, Wash. 80 C3
Centerville, Wis. 66 B4
Centinela, Picacho del, Mex. 92 E2
Cento, It., 24,976 123 C2
Centrahoma, Okla., 148 76 G3
Central, Alaska 85 H2
Central, Ariz. 78 D5
Central, Ind. 70 C4
Central, N. Mex., 1,075 79 A5
Central, S.C., 1,473 63 B3
Central, Utah, 21 78 B3
Central, Cord., Bol. 102 C5
Central, Cord., Col. 100 B7
Central, Cord., C.R. 94 E5
Central, Cord., Dom. Rep. 96 m6
Central, Cord., Peru 104 B3
Central, Cord., Phil. 153 B1
Central, Cord., P.R. 96 s10
Central African Republic, ctry., 1,352,000* 163 H4
Central Aguirre, P.R., 1,689 96 t11
Central Brāhui Ra., Pak. 144 C3
Central Bridge, N.Y. 59 M6
Central Butte, Sask., Can. 43 C5
Central City, Colo., 250 79 C2
Central City, Ill., 1,422 68 C5
Central City, Iowa, 1,087 72 F2
Central City, Ky., 3,694 71 D4
Central City, Nebr., 2,406 75 G2
Central City, Pa., 1,604 60 E5
Central City, S. Dak., 784 74 A3
Central Falls, R.I., 19,858 57 L5
Centralhatchee, Ga., 174 64 D2
Central Heights, Ariz., 2,486 78 C5
Centralia, Ont., Can. 46 C5
Centralia, Ill., 13,904 68 C5
Centralia, Iowa, 85 72 G2
Centralia, Kans., 527 75 J4
Centralia, Mo., 3,200 72 E5
Centralia, Okla., 80 76 H1
Centralia, Pa., 1,435 61 K4
Centralia, Wash., 8,586 80 B2
Centralia, W. Va. 62 D4
Central Islip, N.Y. 59 O10
Central Lake, Mich., 692 67 H3
Central Makrān Ra., Pak. 144 B4
Central Pacific Basin, Pac. Oc. 169 G2
Central Park, Ill., 2,676 68 E3
Central Patricia, Ont., Can. 44 D4
Central Point, Oreg., 2,289 80 B4
Central Point, Va. 62 G5
Central Ra., Terr. New Guin. 174 d2
Central Square, N.Y., 935 59 H5
Central Tacarigua, Ven., 3,039 101 b11
Central Valley, Calif., 2,854 82 B2
Central Village (part of Westport), Mass. 57 M6
Centre, Ala., 2,392 64 D1
Centre, co., Pa., 78,580 60 G4
Centre Hall, Pa., 1,109 60 G4
Centre Hills, Montserrat 97 5
Centreville, N.B., Can. 45 M6
Centreville, Ala., 1,981 64 B3
Centreville, Ill., 12,769 68 B5
Centreville, Md., 1,863 62 H3
Centreville, Mich., 971 67 H7
Centreville, Miss., 1,229 73 D6
Centropolis, Kans. 75 K5
Centuria, Wis., 551 66 A3
Century, Fla., 2,046 65 B2
Century, W. Va. 62 D3
Cephalonia=Kefallinia
Ceram=Seram
Ceram Sea, Indon. 149 J3
Cerano, It., 5,893 122 b5
Cercal, Port., 6,487 122 A4
Čerčany, Czech. 126 d7
Čerchov, pk., Czech. 126 A2
Cerea, It., 12,093 122 e5
Cereal, Alta., Can. 42 L3
Ceredo, W. Va., 1,387 62 B4
Ceres, Arg., 12,000* 105 C3
Ceres, Braz., 6,895 103 G5
Ceres, S. Af., 6,173 164 C7
Ceres, U.K. 112 e7
Ceres, Calif., 4,406 82 C4
Ceres, N.Y. 58 D7
Ceres, Okla. 76 F1
Ceresco, Mich. 67 H6
Ceresco, Nebr., 429 75 J2
Céret, Fr., 5,618 117 E5
Cereté, Col. 100 C3
Cerezo de Riotirón, Sp., 1,525 122 m12
Cerfontaine, Belg., 1,825 115 C4
Cergy, Fr., 1,836 116 g10
Cerignola, It., 53,905 123 E4
Cérilly, Fr., 2,091 117 E3
Cerizay, Fr., 2,855 117 C3
Cermei, Rum. 128 C1
Çermik, Turk., 4,666 142 D2
Cerna, Rum. 128 G2
Cerna, Yug., 3,404 125 D2
Cerna, r., Rum. 128 D2
Cernavodă, Rum., 8,802 128 G2
Cernay, Fr., 8,322 117 G3
Cernay-la-Ville, Fr. 116 f12
Cernier, Switz., 1,545 124 A1
Černošín, Czech. 126 b7
Cerralvo, Mex., 4,057 93 F2
Cerralvo, I., Mex. 92 C3
Cerreto Sannita, It., 5,624 123 c9
Cerrigydrudion, U.K. 114 A4
Cerrillos, Arg., 3,950* 105 B3
Cerrito, Col. 100 B6
Cerrito, Col. 100 D4
Cerritos, Mex., 9,849 93 E3
Cerro Colorado, Mex., 1,295 93 f9
Cërro Corá, Braz., 1,152 103 a14
Cerro de Pasco, Peru, 5,720 104 B4
Cerro Gordo, Ill., 1,067 68 D4
Cerro Gordo, co., Iowa, 49,894 72 D1
Cerro Gordo, N.C., 306 63 F3
Cerrogordo, Okla. 76 J4
Cerro Jaua, Meseta del, mts., Ven. 101 H5
Cerro Verde, Urug. 105 c10
Certosa di Pavia, It., 2,991 122 c5
Cerulean, Ky., 206 71 D5
Cervati, Monte, It. 123 E4
Cervera, Sp., 5,330 122 F2
Cervera del Río Alhama, Sp., 5,860 122 D1
Cervera de Pisuerga, Sp., 2,096 122 C1
Cerveteri, It., 9,808 123 a8
Cervia, It., 18,339 123 D2
Cervialto, Monte, It. 123 E4
Cervinara, It., 12,006 123 d9
Cervione, Fr., 1,585 116 r17
Cervo, r., It. 122 b5
César, r., Col. 100 D2
Cesena, It., 78,031 123 D2
Cesenatico, It., 15,401 123 D2
Cēsis, U.S.S.R., 13,900 134 B4
Česká Kamenice, Czech. 126 d6
Česká Lípa, Czech., 14,388 126 B1
Česká Třebová, Czech., 13,575 126 C2
České Budějovice, Czech., 65,249 126 B2
České Středohoří, mts., Czech. 126 c6
Českomoravská Vrchovina, mts., Czech. 126 B2
Český Brod, Czech. 127 d6
Český Krumlov, Czech., 9,018 126 B2
Český Těšín, Czech., 15,778 126 D2
Česma, r., Yug. 125 C2
Céspedes, Cuba, 4,410 96 d2
Cessnock, Austl., 14,417 173 G5
Cessnock Water, r., U.K. 112 b8
Cesson, Fr., 1,073 116 i12
Cestos, Okla. 76 D1
Cetate, Rum. 128 D2
Cetina, r., Yug. 125 C3
Cetinje, Yug., 9,102 125 D3
Cetraro, It., 10,165 123 E5
Cetti Bay, Guam 176 24
Ceuta, Sp., 75,410 160 D2
Cévennes, mts., Fr. 116 ·
Cevio, Switz. 124 C2
Cevizlik, Turk., 1,808 137 a1
Ceyhan, Turk., 31,688 142 C2
Ceyhan, r., Turk. 142 D2
Ceylânpınar, Turk. 142 E2
Ceylon, Sask., Can. 43 D5
Ceylon, ctry., 10,624,507 145 F9
Ceylon, Minn., 554 74 E4
Ceyzériat, Fr., 1,219 117 F3
Chaac, Guat. 94 C3
Cha-am, Thai., 9,105 146 B4
Chabanais, Fr., 2,113 117 D4
Chabang Tiga, Malay., 1,709 147 p14
Chabjuwardoo Bay, Austl. 172 A3
Chablis, Fr., 1,887 117 E3
Chabot, L., Calif. 83 e12
Chacabuco, Arg., 16,045 105 a12
Chacachacare, i., Trin. and Tob. 96 g5
Chachajo, Col. 100 B5
Chachapoyas, Peru, 6,901 104 B3
Chachas, Peru, 1,357 104 C5
Chachaura, India 144 a13
Cha Cha Village=Carenage
Chachoengsao, Thai., 19,719 146 C4
Chachopo, Ven. 100 E3
Chaco, r., N. Mex. 79 A3
Chaco Canyon Nat. Mon., N. Mex. 79 A3
Chacon, N. Mex. 79 C3
Chacuaco Cr., Colo. 79 D3
Chad, ctry., 3,300,000 162 G3
Chad, L., Af. 162 G3
Chadan, U.S.S.R., 5,200 134 J4
Chadbourn, N.C., 2,323 63 F3
Chadds Ford, Pa. 60 e12
Chadlington, U.K. 114 F7
Chadobets, U.S.S.R. 135 J4
Chadron, Nebr., 5,079 75 C1
Chadwick, Ill., 602 68 C1
Chadwick, N.J. 58 c17
Chadwicks, N.Y. 59 u26
Chadyr-Lunga, U.S.S.R., 11,300 136 C4
Chaeryŏng, N. Kor. 151 E3
Chafee, N.Y. 58 D6
Chaffee, co., Colo., 8,298 79 B2
Chaffee, Mo., 2,862 72 H7
Chaffee, N. Dak. 74 D2
Chaffinville (part of Holden), Mass. 57 J3
Chafurray, Col. 100 D6
Chāgai, Pak. 144 B3
Chāgai Hills, Afghan. 144 B3
Chagda, U.S.S.R. 135 N4
Chaglinka, r., U.S.S.R. 137 n11
Chagny, Fr., 4,896 117 F3
Chagodoshcha, r., U.S.S.R. 136 D1
Chagos Arch., Ind. Oc. 168 C3
Chagres, r., C.Z. 94 f11
Chagres, r., Pan. 94 g11
Chagrin, r., Ohio 70 f9
Chagrin Falls, Ohio, 3,458 70 f9
Chaguanas, Trin. and Tob., 2,453* 96 g5
Chaguaní, Col. 101 e15
Chaguaramas, Ven., 1,363 100 G3
Ch'a-ha-erh-yu-i-ch'ien-ch'i, China 151 B2
Ch'a-ha-erh-yu-i-hou-ch'i, China 150 E2
Chahār Burjak, Afghan. 144 B3
Chāh Bahār, Iran, 1,800 143 G3
Ch'aho-nodongjagu, N. Kor. 151 F2
Cha-hsi-kang, China 150 B3
Chahuites, Mex., 3,325 93 G5
Chai Badan, Thai. 147 d4
Chaibassa, India, 22,019 144 e14
Chailland, Fr., 1,280 117 C2
Chailly-en-Bière, Fr., 1,097 116 i12
Chai Nat, Thai., 4,652 146 B4
Chai Nat Dam, Thai. 147 d4
Chain Lakes, Me. 55 E4
Chainpur, Nepal 144 c11
Chaitén, Chile 105 A6
Chaiya, Thai. 146 B5
Chaiyaphum, Thai., 9,633 146 C4
Chaiyo, Thai. 147 d4
Chajarí, Arg., 14,653 105 b10
Chajul, Guat., 3,492 94 B3
Chakachamna L., Alaska 85 F3
Chake Chake, Tanz., 7,167 164 F2
Chakhansūr, Afghan. 144 A3
Chakia, Bihar, India, 5,962 144 e12
Chakia, U.P., India 144 d13
Chakkarat, Thai. 147 e4
Chakonipau L., Qué., Can. 45 M3
Chakradharpur, India, 30,906 144 e14
Chakrata, India, 3,194 141 a10
Chakva, U.S.S.R., 6,100 137 b1
Chakwāl, Pak., 16,843 145 D2
Chala, Peru, 1,040 104 C5
Chalabre, Fr., 1,771 117 E5
Chalais, Fr., 1,764 117 C4
Chalais, Switz., 1,597 124 B2
Cha-lai-t'e-ch'i, China 151 D1
Chalamont, Fr., 1,184 117 F4
Chalatenango, El Salv., 5,183 94 C3
Chalchihuites, Mex., 3,951 92 D3
Chalchuapa, El Salv., 13,680 94 d9
Chalcidice=Khalkidhiki
Chalco, Mex., 7,546 93 F4
Chalé, Braz., 1,047 103 f17
Chale, U.K. 113 k13
Châlette, Fr., 9,531 117 E2
Chaleurs, B. des, Qué.-N.B., Can. 45 N6
Chalfont, Pa., 1,410 60 f10
Chalfont St. Peter, U.K., 12,460 114 G7
Chalhuanca, Peru, 2,436 104 C5
Chalindrey, Fr., 3,287 117 F3
Ch'a-ling, China 152 D2
Cha-ling Hu, China 150 D3
Chalisgaon, India, 34,280 145 E5
Chalk, Kans. 75 J5
Chalk, Tex. 77 N3
Chalk Draw, r., Tex. 77 M5
Chalki=Khálki
Chalk River, Ont., Can., 1,115 44 J6
Chalky Inlet, N.Z. 175 e7
Chalkyitsik, Alaska, 57 85 J2
Challans, Fr., 6,992 117 C3
Challapata, Bol., 11,008 102 b11
Challis, Idaho, 732 81 B3
Chama, Mex., 1,186 93 f8
Chalmers, Ind., 548 70 B2
Chalmette, La. 73 F8
Chalmette Nat. Hist. Pk., La. 73 F8
Chalonnes-sur-Loire, Fr., 4,058 117 C3
Châlons-sur-Marne, Fr., 45,348 117 F2
Chalon-sur-Saône, Fr., 45,993 117 F3
Chalt, Pak. 145 E1
Cha-lun, China 150 B3
Châlus, Fr., 2,121 117 D4
Chālūs, Iran, 9,758 143 E1
Cha-lu-t'e-ch'i, China 151 D1
Cham, F.R.Ger., 8,521 118 D4
Cham, Switz., 6,483 124 C1
Cham, Cu Lao, i., S. Viet. 146 E4
Chama, Colo. 79 C3
Chama, N. Mex. 79 B3
Chama, r., N. Mex. 79 B3
Chamácuaro, Mex., 1,533 93 d9
Chaman, Pak., 12,208 144 C3
Chamba, India, 8,609 145 E2
Chambak, Camb. 147 k11
Chambal, r., India 145 E4
Chambas, Cuba, 3,046 96 d1
Chamberino, N. Mex. 79 B5
Chamberlain, S. Dak., 2,598 74 C4
Chamberlain L., Me. 55 C2
Chamberlin, Tex. 76 M1
Chambers, co., Ala., 37,828 64 D3
Chambers, Ariz. 78 D4
Chambers, Nebr., 396 75 G1
Chambers, co., Tex., 10,379 77 Q5
Chambersburg, Ill. 68 B4
Chambersburg, Ind. 70 C4
Chambersburg, Ohio, 205 70 G4
Chambersburg, Pa., 17,670 60 G6
Chambers Cr., Tex. 76 f10
Chambers I., Wis. 66 F3
Chambéry, Fr., 47,447 117 F4
Chambeshi, r., Zambia 164 E3
Chambira, r., Peru 104 C3
Chambishi, Zambia 165 n20
Chamblee, Ga., 6,635 64 E2
Chambly, Qué., Can., 3,679 47 p18
Chambly, Fr., 5,403 117 E2

210 · Chambo—Cherokee

Chambo, Ec. 104 c10
Chambo, r., Ec. 104 c10
Chambord, Fr. 117 D3
Chambourcy, Fr., 2,068 116 f11
Chambrey, Fr. 116 b9
Chambry, Fr. 116 k11
Chamdo = Ch'ang-tu
Chame, Pan. 94 H6
Chamela, Mex. 92 D4
Chamelet, Fr. 116 o15
Chamical, Arg., 7,500* 105 B4
Chamnop, Camb. 146 C5
Chamo, L., Eth. 163 L5
Chamois, Mo., 658 72 F6
Chamonix, Fr., 7,966 117 G4
Chamoson, Switz., 2,088 124 B2
Champa, India, 16,258 144 d14
Champagne, Yukon, Can. 40 B5
Champagnole, Fr., 8,165 117 G3
Champagny Is., Austl. 172 C2
Champaign, co., Ill., 132,436 68 D3
Champaign, Ill., 49,583 68 D3
Champaign, co., Ohio, 29,714 70 F2
Champan, r., Mex. 93 H4
Champassak, Laos 146 D4
Champcueil, Fr. 116 h12
Champdeniers, Fr., 1,190 117 C3
Champdeuil, Fr. 116 k12
Champdoré, L., Qué., Can. 45 N3
Champeaux, Fr. 116 k12
Champenoux, Fr. 116 b9
Champerico, Guat., 1,467 94 A3
Champéry, Switz. 124 A2
Champigneulles, Fr., 5,854 116 b9
Champigny-sur-Marne, Fr., 57,925 116 i11
Champion, Alta., Can. 42 K4
Champion, Mich. 66 F2
Champlain, Qué., Can. 47 M2
Champlain, N.Y., 1,549 59 N2
Champlain, Va. 62 G4
Champlain, L., N.Y.-Vt. 59 O2
Champotón, Mex., 4,694 93 H4
Chan, Ko, Thai. 146 B5
Chana, Thai. 146 C6
Chana, Ill. 68 C2
Chañar, Arg., 1,500* 105 B4
Chañaral, Chile, 5,210 105 A3
Chañarcillo, Chile 105 A3
Chança, r., Port. 122 B4
Chancay, Peru, 5,794 104 B4
Chandos L., Ont., Can. 46 G4
Chance, Ala. 64 B4
Chance, Md. 62 H4
Chance, Okla. 76 J1
Chancellor, S. Dak., 214 74 D4
Chancellorsville, Va. 62 G4
Chancha, Eth. 163 L4
Chan-chiang, China, 170,000* 150 E5
Chanco, Chile, 1,966 104 e15
Chanda, India, 51,484 145 F6
Chandalar, Alaska 85 H2
Chandalar, r., Alaska 85 G2
Chandausi, India, 48,557 144 b11
Chandeleur Is., La. 73 G8
Chandeleur Sd., La. 73 F8
Chanderi, India, 8,268 144 b13
Chandigarh, India, 89,321 145 E3
Chandipur, India 144 f15
Chandler, Qué., Can., 3,378 45 N5
Chandler, Ariz., 12,181 78 C5
Chandler, Ind., 1,784 70 B4
Chandler, Okla., 2,524 76 G2
Chandler, Tex. 77 Q3
Chandler, r., Alaska 85 F1
Chandler Heights, Ariz. 78 C5
Chandler's Ford, U.K., 5,688 113 k13
Chandlers Valley, Pa. 60 D2
Chandlerville, Ill., 718 68 B3
Chandpur, India, 22,017 144 b11
Chāndpur, Pak., 34,837 145 J5
Chanduy, Ec. 104 A2
Chaneliak, Alaska, 93 85 D3
Chaney, Okla. 76 D1
Chaney L., Mich. 66 D2
Chang, r., China 152 D2
Ch'ang, r., China 150 F4
Ch'ang, r., China 152 C4
Ch'ang, r., China 152 E2
Chang, Ko, Thai. 146 C5
Changanacheri, India 42,376 145 E8
Changane, r., Moz. 164 E5
Ch'ang Ch'eng, China 150 E3
Ch'ang-chi, China 150 B2
Chang-chia-k'ou, China, 630,000* 150 F2
Ch'ang-chih, China, 180,000* 150 F3
Chang-chou, China 150 F4
Ch'ang-chou, China, 240,000* 152 F1
Ch'ang-ch'un, China, 1,150,000* 150 G2
Changgi-gap, S. Kor. 151 F3
Ch'ang-hai, China 151 D3
Ch'ang-hsing, China 152 E1
Ch'ang-hsing Tao, China 151 D3
Ch'ang-hua, China 152 E1
Chang-hua, Taiwan, 88,290 152 F2
Changhŭng, S. Kor., 26,844 151 E4
Ch'ang-i, China 151 C3
Changjin, N. Kor. 151 E2
Changjin, r., N. Kor. 151 E2
Changjŏn, N. Kor. 151 E3
Ch'ang-kan, China 150 E5
Ch'ang-kang, China 152 a6
Changkiakow = Chang-chia-k'ou
Chang-kuang-ts'ai Ling, China 150 G2
Ch'ang-li, China 151 C3
Ch'ang-ling, China 151 D1
Ch'ang-lo, F-ch., China 152 E2
Ch'ang-lo, Shant., China 151 C3
Chang-ming, China 152 B1
Ch'ang-ning, Hu-n., China 152 D2
Ch'ang-ning, S-ch., China 152 B1
Changnyŏn-ni, N. Kor. 151 E3
Ch'ang-pai, China 150 H2
Ch'ang-pai Shan, China 151 E2
Chang-pei, China 151 B2
Chang-p'ing, China 152 E2
Ch'ang-p'ing, China 151 C2
Ch'ang-p'u, China 152 E2
Ch'ang-sha, China, 700,000* 150 E4
Ch'ang-shan, China 152 E1
Ch'ang-shan Ch'ün-tao, China 151 D3
Ch'ang-shan Tao, China 151 D3
Ch'ang-shou, China 152 B1
Ch'ang-shu, China 152 F1
Ch'ang-shun, China 152 B2
Changsŏng, S. Kor., 24,868 151 E4
Ch'ang-t'ai, China 152 E2
Ch'ang-te, China, 100,000* 150 E4
Chang Thang, China 150 B3
Ch'ang-t'ing, China 154 F4
Ch'ang-tu, admin. div., China 150 C4
Ch'ang-tu, China, 60,000* 150 D4
Ch'ang-t'u, China 151 D2
Chang-tzu, China 151 B3
Chang-wu, China 151 D2
Ch'ang-wu, China 151 A4
Ch'ang-yang, China 152 C1
Ch'ang-ya-tien, China 151 A2
Chang-yeh, China 150 D3
Changyŏn, N. Kor. 151 E3
Ch'ang-yüan, China 151 B4
Chanhassen Minn., 244 74 a6
Chan-hua, China 151 C3
Chan-i, China 152 A2
Chañi, Nev. de, Arg. 105 B2
Chaniliut = Chaneliak
Chankiang = Chan-chiang
Channahon, Ill. 68 D2
Channapatna, India, 26,467 145 E7
Channel Is., U.K. 113 E7
Channel Islands Nat. Mon., Calif. 82 D6
Channel Lake, Ill., 1,969 68 D1
Channel-Port aux Basques, Newf., Can., 4,105 45 P6
Channing, Man., Can. 43 E3
Channing, Mich. 66 E2
Channing, Tex., 351 76 M2
Chantada, Sp., 14,116 112 A1
Chantelle, Fr. 1,147 117 E3
Chanteloup, Fr. 116 i11
Chanthaburi, Thai., 10,795 146 C4
Chantilly, Fr., 8,324 117 E2
Chantilly, Va. 62 G4
Chantonnay, Fr., 4,704 117 C3
Chantrey, Camb. 147 k11
Chantrey Inlet, N.W.T., Can. 40 K4
Chantuqui, Guat. 94 B2
Chanuman, Thai. 146 D3
Chanute, Kans., 10,849 75 K6
Chany, U.S.S.R., 8,900 134 G4
Chany, Oz., U.S.S.R. 134 G4
Chan-yü, China 151 D1
Chao, Peru 104 B4
Ch'ao, r., China 151 C2
Chao-an, China 150 F5
Ch'ao-an, China, 120,000* 150 F5
Chao-an Wan, China 152 E3
Chao-ch'eng, China 151 A3
Chao-chiao, China 152 A1
Chao-chou, China 151 E1
Chao-hsien, China 151 B3
Ch'ao-hsien, China 152 E1
Ch'ao Hu, China 152 E1
Chao-hua, China 152 B1
Chao Phraya, r., Thai. 146 C4
Chao-p'ing, China 152 C2
Chao-su, China 150 B2
Chao-tung, China 150 G2
Chao-t'ung, China 150 D4
Chaouen, Mor., 13,712 160 D2
Ch'ao-yang, K-t., China 152 E3
Ch'ao-yang, L-n., China 150 F2
Chao-yang Hu, China 151 C4
Chao-yüan, H-l-ch., China 151 E1
Chao-yüan, Shant., China 151 D3
Chapadinha, Braz., 3,698 103 H2
Chapais, Qué., Can., 2,363 44 K5
Chapala, Mex., 7,121 92 E4
Chapala, L. de, Mex. 92 E4
Chapantongo, Mex., 1,044 93 e9
Chaparé, r., Bol. 102 c10
Chaparra, Cuba, 5,604 96 e2
Chaparral, Col. 100 C6
Chapayevsk, U.S.S.R., 85,000 134 D4
Chapeau, Qué., Can. 46 G3
Chapeau Carré, mtn., Gren. Is. 97 20
Chapecó, Braz., 8,465 103 F7
Chapel Arm, Newf., Can. 45 b10
Chapel en le Frith, U.K., 6,460 114 E4
Chapelhall, U.K. 112 c8
Chapel Hill, Ga. 64 f10
Chapel Hill, N.C., 12,573 63 F2
Chapel Hill, Tenn., 630 71 E6
Chapel St. Leonards, U.K. 114 J4
Chapel's Cove, Newf., Can. 45 b10
Chapelton, Jam., 4,417 96 p8
Chapeltown, U.K., 3,724 114 E4
Chapicuy, Urug. 105 b10
Chapin, Ill., 477 68 B4
Chapin, S.C., 358 63 C3
Chapinville (part of Northboro), Mass. 57 K3
Chapleau, Ont., Can., 3,350 44 G6
Chapleau, r., Ont., Can. 44 G5
Chaplin, Sask., Can. 43 C5
Chaplin, Conn., 1,230(T) 56 H5
Chaplino, U.S.S.R. 136 e7
Chaplinville (part of Rowley), Mass. 57 N2
Chaplygin, U.S.S.R., 10,700 136 F2
Chapman, Ala., 617 64 C4
Chapman, Kans., 1,095 75 J5
Chapman, Nebr., 303 75 G2
Chapman Camp, Br. Col., Can. 42 J4
Chapmanville, W. Va., 1,241 62 B5
Chapo, L., Chile 105 e15
Chaponnay, Fr., 1,147 116 p15
Chappaquiddick I., Mass. 57 P7
Chappell, Nebr., 1,280 75 C2
Chappell Hill, Tex. 77 P4
Chappells, S.C., 128 63 C3
Chappel Pd., Mich 67 J4
Chapra, India, 75,580 145 G4
Chapulhuacán, Mex., 1,454 93 F4
Ch'a-pu-p'a-lung-la Shan-k'ou, China 150 C3
Chaput Hughes, Ont., Can., 1,144 44 H5
Chaqui, Bol. 102 c11
Chara, U.S.S.R. 135 L4
Chara, r., U.S.S.R. 135 L4
Charadai, Arg., 1,200* 105 D3
Charagua, Bol., 3,523 102 D5
Charallave, Ven., 3,976 101 c11
Charaña, Bol., 1,841 102 C5
Charan Kanoa, Saipan 176 27
Charapán, Mex., 2,657 93 b10
Charapitiro, Mex. 93 d10
Charata, Arg., 10,100* 105 C3
Charbonnières-les-Bains, Fr., 2,180 116 p15
Charcas, Mex., 9,058 92 E3
Charchan, r., China 150 B3
Charco, Tex. 77 P5
Charco Frio, Mex. 93 e9
Charcot I., Ant. 109 G11
Chard, U.K., 5,779 113 E6
Chardara, U.S.S.R. 137 e4
Chardon, Kans. 75 D4
Chardon, Ohio, 3,154 70 H1
Chardzhou, U.S.S.R., 95,000 134 F6
Charente, r., Fr. 117 C4
Charenton, La. 73 D8
Charenton-le-Pont, Fr., 22,957 116 h11
Chari, r., Chad 162 G4
Chārīkār, Afghan., 52,000* 144 C2
Chariton, Iowa, 5,042 72 D3
Chariton, co., Mo., 12,720 72 D5
Chariton, r., Iowa-Mo. 72 D4
Chariton, East Fork, r., Mo. 72 E5
Charity, Guyana 101 L4
Charkhari, India, 13,335 144 b13
Charlbury, U.K., 1,649 114 F7
Charlecote, U.K. 114 E6
Charlemagne, Qué., Can., 3,042 47 o17
Charlemont, Mass. 56 E2
Charleroi, Belg., 25,962 115 C4
Charleroi, Pa., 8,148 60 C5
Charles, co., Md., 32,572 62 G4
Charles, r., Mass. 57 M3
Charles, C., Va. 62 J5
Charles Bay, Lesser Caymans 97 2
Charlesbourg, Qué., Can., 14,308 47 n16
Charles City, Iowa, 10,419 72 E1
Charles City, co., Va., 5,492 62 G5
Charles City, Va. 62 G5
Charles I., N.W.T., Can. 41 P5
Charles Mix, co., S. Dak., 11,785 74 C4
Charles Mound, Ill. 68 B1
Charles Pt., Austl. 172 D1
Charleston, Ark., 1,036 73 A2
Charleston, Ill., 10,505 68 D4
Charleston, Kans. 75 E6
Charleston, Me. 55 C3
Charleston, Miss., 2,528 73 E3
Charleston, Mo., 5,911 72 H8
Charleston, Nev. 83 C2
Charleston, Oreg. 80 A4
Charleston, co., S.C., 216,382 63 D5
Charleston, S.C., 65,925 63 D5
Charleston, Tenn., 764 71 G6
Charleston, W. Va., 85,796 62 C4
Charleston L., Ont., Can. 47 H4
Charleston Park, Nev. 83 C4
Charleston Pk., Nev. 83 B4
Charlestown, Ire. 113 B5
Charlestown, Nevis, 1,852 97 6
Charlestown, Ind., 5,726 70 D4
Charlestown, Md., 711 62 H3
Charlestown, N.H., 1,173 54 C5
Charlestown, R.I., 2,586 (T) 57 K7
Charles Town, W. Va., 3,329 62 G3
Charlestown Bay, Gren. Is. 97 20
Charlestown Beach (part of Charlestown), R.I. 57 K7
Charlesville, D.R.Congo 164 C2
Charlesworth, Mich. 67 J6
Charleville, Austl., 4,573 173 F4
Charleville, Fr., 26,402 117 F2
Charleville, Ire. = Ráth Luirc
Charlevoix, co., Mich., 13,421 67 H3
Charlevoix, Mich., 2,751 67 H3
Charlevoix, L., Mich. 67 H3
Charley, r., Alaska 85 J2
Charlieu, Fr., 5,506 117 E3
Charlotte, co., Fla., 12,594 65 H6
Charlotte, Iowa, 417 72 G3
Charlotte, Mich., 7,657 67 J6
Charlotte, N.C., 201,564 63 D2
Charlotte, Tenn., 551 71 D5
Charlotte, Tex., 1,465 77 O5
Charlotte, Vt. 54 A3
Charlotte, co., Va., 13,368 62 F5
Charlotte Amalie, V.I., 12,880 97 4
Charlotte Court House, Va., 555 62 F5
Charlotte Cr., N.Y. 59 L7
Charlotte Hbr., Fla. 65 H6
Charlottenberg, Swed. 120 C4
Charlottesville, Va., 29,427 62 F4
Charlottetown, P.E.I., Can., 17,956 45 N6
Charlotteville, Trin. and Tob., 1,618* 96 h4
Charlson, N. Dak. 74 A1
Charlton, Austl., 1,408 173 F5
Charlton, co., Ga., 5,313 64 G5
Charlton, Mass., 3,685(T) 56 J4
Charlton City (part of Charlton), Mass. 56 H4
Charlton Depot, N.W.T., Can. 44 H4
Charlton Depot (part of Charlton), Mass. 56 J4
Charlton I., N.W.T., Can. 44 H4
Charlton Kings, U.K., 7,744 114 E7
Charlwood, U.K., 2,801 114 H8
Charmes, Fr., 5,380 117 G2
Charny, Qué., Can., 4,144 47 N2
Charny, Fr., 1,280 117 E3
Charny, Fr. 116 k11
Charo, Mex., 2,188 93 c10
Charolles, Fr., 3,771 117 F3
Charon, Alg., 1,714 160 b6
Charroux, Fr., 1,733 117 D3
Chārsadda, Pak., 37,396 145 D2
Charter Oak, Iowa, 665 72 B2
Charters Towers, Austl., 6,961 173 F3
Chartiers Cr., Pa. 60 B5
Chartley (part of Norton), Mass. 57 M5
Chartres, Falk. Is. 108 3
Chartres, Fr., 33,992 117 D2
Chartrettes, Fr., 1,065 116 i12
Charysh, r., U.S.S.R. 137 q12
Charyshskoye, U.S.S.R. 137 q12
Chascomús, Arg., 12,300* 105 c12
Chase, Br. Col., Can. 42 H4
Chase, Ala. 64 C1
Chase, Alaska 85 G3
Chase, co., Kans., 3,921 75 J5
Chase, Kans., 922 75 G5
Chase, Mich. 67 H5
Chase, co., Nebr., 4,317 75 D3
Chase, Nebr. 75 D3
Chase, Mt., Me. 55 D2
Chaseburg, Wis., 242 66 B5
Chase City, Va., 3,207 62 F6
Chase L., Me. 55 C2
Chase Mills, N.Y. 59 K2
Chase Pd., Me. 55 C2
Chasetown, U.K., 6,795 114 E5
Ch'a-shon, China 152 a5
Chaska, Minn., 2,501 74 F3
Chasm Falls, N.Y. 59 M2
Chasov Yar, U.S.S.R., 23,400 136 e7
Chassell, Mich. 66 E1
Chastyye, U.S.S.R. 137 h7
Chasuta, Peru, 2,101 104 B3
Chataignier, La. 73 C7
Chatan, Ryukyu Is. 154 a11
Chatanika, Alaska 85 H2
Chatcolet, Idaho, 101 81 A2
Château, Morne, Haiti 96 k6
Château-Arnoux, Fr., 5,785 117 F4
Chateaubelair, St. Vinc., 1,997 97 19
Châteaubriand, B. de, Loy. Is. 174 k8
Châteaubriant, Fr., 11,552 117 C3
Château-Chinon, Fr., 2,647 117 E3
Château-d'Eau, Qué., Can., 1,039 47 n16
Château-d'Oex, Switz., 3,378 124 B2
Château-du-Loir, Fr., 5,079 117 D3
Châteaudun, Fr., 12,469 117 D2
Châteaufort, Fr. 116 g12
Chateaugay, N.Y., 1,097 59 M2
Château-Gontier, Fr., 7,299 117 C3
Châteauguay, Qué., Can., 7,570 47 o18
Châteauguay, r., Qué., Can. 47 K4
Châteauguay Basin, Qué., Can., 7,373 47 o18
Château-la-Vallière, Fr., 1,434 117 D3
Châteaulin, Fr., 5,169 116 A2
Châteaumeillant, Fr., 2,678 117 D3
Châteauneuf, Fr. 116 p15
Châteauneuf-sur-Loire, Fr., 4,536 117 E3
Châteauponsac, Fr., 3,176 117 D3
Châteaurenard, Fr., 2,061 117 E3
Château-Renault, Fr., 4,238 117 D3
Château-Richer, Qué., Can., 1,422 47 N2
Châteauroux, Fr., 46,772 117 D3
Château-Salins, Fr., 2,398 117 G2
Château-Thierry, Fr., 10,619 117 E2
Châteauvillain, Fr., 1,162 117 F2
Châteaux, Pte. des, Guad. 97 14
Chatelain, L., Qué., Can. 44 K1
Châteldon, Fr., 1,213 117 E4
Châtelet, Belg., 15,528 115 C4
Châtellerault, Fr., 28,122 117 D3
Châtel-St-Denis, Switz., 2,666 124 A2
Châtenay-Malabry, Fr., 24,985 116 g11
Chater, r., U.K. 114 G5
Chatfield, Ark. 73 E2
Chatfield, Minn., 1,841 74 F4
Chatfield, Ohio, 263 70 G2
Chatfield, Tex. 76 g10
Chatham, N.B., Can., 6,823 45 N6
Chatham, Ont., Can., 27,447 44 G7
Chatham, U.K., 48,784 114 J8
Chatham, co., Ga., 188,299 64 H4
Chatham, Ill., 1,069 68 C4
Chatham, La., 758 73 C5
Chatham, Mass., 3,273(T) 57 R6
Chatham, Mich. 66 F2
Chatham, N.J., 9,517 61 C2
Chatham, N.Y., 2,426 59 N7
Chatham, co., N.C., 26,785 63 E2
Chatham, Pa. 60 e12
Chatham, Va., 1,822 62 E6
Chatham Bay, Gren. Is. 97 20
Chatham Center, N.Y. 59 N7
Chatham Head, N.B., Can., 1,246 47 T10
Chatham I., N.Z. 170 G7
Chatham Is., N.Z. 170 G7
Chatham Sd., Br. Col., Can. 42 D2
Chatham Str., Alaska 85 L4
Châtillon, Fr., 5,913 117 F3
Châtillon-la-Borde, Fr. 116 k12
Châtillon-sur-Indre, Fr., 3,539 117 D3
Châtillon-sur-Loire, Fr., 2,171 117 E3
Châtillon-sur-Sèvre, Fr., 1,299 117 C3
Chatkal, r., U.S.S.R. 137 f4
Chatkal'skiy Khr., U.S.S.R. 132 G5
Chatom, Ala., 993 64 A4
Chatou, Fr., 21,678 116 g11
Chatra, India, 12,507 144 e13
Châtres, Fr. 116 k12
Chatsu, India 144 a12
Chatsworth, Ont., Can. 46 D4
Chatsworth, Ga., 1,184 64 E1
Chatsworth, Ill., 1,330 68 D3
Chatsworth, Iowa, 84 72 A2
Chatsworth, N.J. 61 B4
Chatsworth Res., Calif. 83 g15
Chattahoochee, Fla., 9,699 65 E2
Chattahoochee, co., Ga., 13,011 64 E3
Chattahoochee, r., U.S. 64 D4
Chattanooga, Ohio 70 E2
Chattanooga, Okla., 356 76 E3
Chattanooga, Tenn., 130,009 71 F7
Chattaroy, W. Va. 62 B5
Chatteris, U.K., 5,491 113 G5
Chattooga, co., Ga., 19,954 64 D1
Chattooga, r., Ala.-Ga. 64 D1
Chattura, Thai. 147 d4
Chatuge L., Ga.-N.C. 64 F1
Cha-uat, Thai., 3,530 146 B5
Chaucha, Ec. 104 c11
Chauconin, Fr. 116 k11
Chaudes-Aigues, Fr., 1,331 117 E4
Chaudière, r., Qué., Can. 47 O3
Chauekuktuli, L., Alaska 85 E3
Chauffailles, Fr., 4,083 117 F3
Chauk, Burma, 24,466 146 A2
Chaukan Pass, Burma-India 146 B1
Chaullay, Peru 104 C5
Chaulnes, Fr., 1,500 117 E2
Chaumes-en-Brie, Fr., 1,729 116 k12
Chaumont, N.Y., 523 59 H3
Chaumont-en-Bassigny, Fr., 23,314 117 F2
Chaunay, Fr., 1,481 117 C3
Chauncey, Ill. 68 E5
Chauncey, Ohio, 996 70 G3
Chaunggwa, Burma 147 f7
Chaunggyi, Burma 147 g6
Chaung-u, Burma, 8,406 146 A2
Chaungwa, Burma 146 B1
Chaungzon, Burma, 3,581 147 b2
Chaunskaya G., U.S.S.R. 135 Q3
Chauny, Fr., 13,358 117 E2
Chau Phu, S. Viet., 9,095 147 k11
Chausey, Îls, Fr. 117 C2
Chausy, U.S.S.R., 6,300 136 C2
Chautauqua, co., Kans., 5,956 75 J6
Chautauqua, co., N.Y., 145,377 58 A7
Chautauqua, N.Y. 58 A7
Chautauqua L., N.Y. 58 A7
Chauvay, U.S.S.R., 2,000 137 g4
Chauvigny, Fr., 6,462 117 D3
Chauvin, Alta., Can. 42 L3
Chauvin, La. 73 E8
Chavanay, Fr., 1,645 116 p16
Chavenay, Fr. 116 f11
Chaves, Braz. 103 G2
Chaves, Port., 12,490 122 B2
Chaves, co., N. Mex., 57,649 79 C5
Chaville, Fr., 16,920 116 g11
Chavinda, Mex., 7,124 93 b10
Cháviva, Col. 100 D5
Chavornay, Switz., 1,414 124 A2
Ch'a-ya, China 150 D4
Chaya, Jap., 7,726 154 e15
Chaykovskiy, U.S.S.R., 11,000 137 h8
Ch'a-yü, China 150 D4
Chazay, Fr., 1,267 116 p15
Chazelles-sur-Lyon, Fr., 5,737 116 o15
Chazy, N.Y. 59 N2
Chazy L., N.Y. 59 N2
Cheadle, Ches., Eng., U.K., 45,599 114 D4
Cheadle, Staffs., Eng., U.K., 8,126 114 E4
Cheaha Mtn., Ala. 64 D2
Cheat, r., W. Va. 62 E3
Cheatham, co., Tenn., 9,428 71 D5
Cheat L., W. Va. 60 C6
Cheb, Czech., 21,380 126 A1
Chebanse, Ill., 995 68 D2
Chebarkul', U.S.S.R., 30,200 137 k8
Cheboksary, U.S.S.R., 123,000 135 D4
Cheboygan, co. Mich., 14,550 67 J3
Cheboygan, Mich., 5,859 67 J3
Checa, Ec. 104 c11
Chechen', O., U.S.S.R. 137 c1
Che-ch'eng, China 151 B4
Che-chiang, prov., China, 25,280,000 150 F4
Chech'ŏn, S. Kor., 38,924 151 F3
Chęciny, Pol., 3,072 127 D3
Checotah, Okla., 2,614 76 H2
Chedabucto Bay, N.S., Can. 47 V11
Cheddar, U.K., 2,845 114 C8
Cheddleton, U.K., 4,711 114 E4
Cheduba, Burma, 2,635 146 A3
Cheduba I., Burma 146 A3
Cheecham, Alta., Can. 42 K2
Cheeching, Alaska 85 C3
Cheek, Tex. 77 m9
Cheektowaga, N.Y., 65,128 58 m19
Cheepash, r., Ont., Can. 44 G5
Cheepie, Austl. 173 F4
Cheesequake, N.J. 58 b15
Cheesman L., Colo. 79 b9
Chef-Boutonne, Fr., 2,368 117 C3
Chefoo = Yen-t'ai
Chefornak, Alaska, 133 85 C3
Chegar Prah, Malay. 147 p14
Chegga, Alg. 162 C1
Chehalis, Wash., 5,199 80 B2
Chehalis, r., Wash. 80 B2
Cheju, S. Kor., 68,090 151 E4
Cheju-do, S. Kor. 151 E4
Cheju-haehyŏp, str., S. Kor. 151 E4
Chekhov, U.S.S.R., 8,500 135 O5
Chekhov, U.S.S.R., 14,000 136 E2
Chekiang = Che-chiang
Chekmagush, U.S.S.R. 137 h8
Chekurovka, U.S.S.R. 135 M2
Chelan, co., Wash., 40,744 80 C2
Chelan, Wash., 2,402 80 D2
Chelan, L., Wash. 80 C2
Cheleiros, Port., 1,361 122 i10
Cheleken, U.S.S.R., 12,000 134 E6
Chélia, Dj., Alg. 160 e6
Chéliff, r., Alg. 160 c5
Chelkar, U.S.S.R., 15,700 134 F5
Chellaston, U.K., 3,702 114 E5
Chelles, Fr., 28,453 116 i11
Chełm, Pol., 31,000* 127 E3
Chełmek, Pol., 5,161 127 i6
Chełmno, Pol., 15,732 127 C2
Chelmorton, U.K. 114 E4
Chelmsford, Ont., Can., 2,551 44 G6
Chelmsford, U.K., 49,908 113 G6
Chelmsford, Mass., 15,130(T) 57 L2
Chełmża, Pol., 13,372 127 C2
Chelsea, Iowa, 453 72 E3
Chelsea, Mass., 33,749 57 M3
Chelsea, Mich., 3,355 67 J6
Chelsea, Okla., 1,541 76 H1
Chelsea, Pa. 60 f12
Chelsea, S. Dak., 53 74 C3
Chelsea, Vt. 54 C4
Chelsea, Wis. 66 C3
Cheltenham, Ont., Can. 46 c13
Cheltenham, U.K., 72,154 113 F6
Cheltenham, Pa., 7,200* 60 f11
Chelva, Sp., 3,407 122 E3
Chelyabinsk, U.S.S.R., 733,000 134 F4
Chelyuskin, M., U.S.S.R. 135 K2
Chemaia, Mor., 2,319 160 C2
Chemainus, Br. Col., Can., 1,042 42 c7
Chemal, U.S.S.R. 137 r12
Chemax, Mex., 2,334 93 J4
Chemba, Moz. 164 E4
Chemeketa Park, Calif. 83 f13
Chemillé, Fr., 4,558 117 C3
Chemnitz = Karl-Marx-Stadt
Chemong, Sask., Can. 43 D4
Chemo Pd., Me. 55 D4
Chemor, Malay., 3,719 147 o14
Chemquasabamticook L., Me. 55 C2
Chemult, Oreg. 80 C4
Chemung, Ill. 68 D1
Chemung, co., N.Y., 98,706 58 G7
Chemung, r., N.Y. 58 F7
Chena, r., Alaska 85 b6
Chenab, r., Pak. 145 D3
Chenachane, Alg. 162 D1
Chen-an, China 151 A4
Chenango, co., N.Y., 43,243 59 J6
Chenango, r., N.Y. 59 J6
Chenango Bridge, N.Y. 59 J7
Chenango Forks, N.Y. 59 J7
Ch'en-ch'i, China 152 C1
Ch'en-chia-chiang, China 151 D4
Chen-chiang, China, 170,000* 150 F4
Chenderiang, Malay., 3,690 147 o14
Chenderoh L., Malay. 147 o14
Chêne-Bourg, Switz., 5,027 124 A2
Chenega, Alaska 85 G3
Chenequa, Wis., 445 66 c11
Chénéville, Qué., Can. 47 J3
Cheney, Kans., 1,101 75 H6
Cheney, Wash., 3,173 80 E2
Cheneyville, La., 1,037 73 C6
Chen-feng, China 152 B2
Cheng-an, China 150 E4
Ch'eng-ch'eng, China 151 A4
Ch'eng-chiang, China 152 A2
Cheng-chou, China, 800,000* 150 F3
Chengchow = Cheng-chou
Cheng-ho, China 152 E2
Cheng-hsiang-pai-ch'i, China 150 F2
Ch'eng-hsien, Ch-ch., China 152 F1
Ch'eng-hsien, K-su, China 150 E3
Ch'eng-hsi Hu, China 152 E1
Ch'eng-k'ou, China 152 C1
Ch'eng-kung, China 152 A2
Ch'eng-kung, Taiwan, 13,956 152 F3
Ch'eng-li, China 151 C3
Ch'eng-mai, China 152 C4
Cheng-ning, China 151 A4
Ch'eng-pu, China 152 C2
Ch'eng-ssu, China 152 F1
Ch'eng-te, China 150 F2
Cheng-ting, China 151 B3
Ch'eng-to, China 150 D3
Ch'eng-tu, China, 1,107,000* 150 E4
Ch'eng-tung Hu, China 152 E1
Ch'eng-wu, China 151 B4
Cheng-yang, China 150 F3
Cheng-yang-kuan, China 152 E1
Chen-hai, China 152 F1
Ch'en-hsien, China 150 F4
Chen-hsiung, China 152 B2
Chenkán, Mex. 93 H4
Chen-lai, China 151 D1
Chen-ning, China 152 B2
Chenoa, Ill., 1,523 68 D3
Chênove, Fr., 5,355 117 F3
Ch'en-pa-erh-hu-ch'i, China 150 F1
Chen-p'ing, Ho-n., China 151 B4
Chen-p'ing, Shen-hsi, China 151 A4
Chen-yüan, China 152 C2
Cheom Ksan, Camb. 146 D4
Chepachet, R.I. 57 K5
Chepachet, r., R.I. 57 K5
Chepelare, Bulg., 3,730 129 E4
Chepén, Peru, 16,464 104 B3
Chépénéhé, Loy. Is. 174 k8
Chepes, Arg. 105 B4
Chépica, Chile, 2,291 104 f14
Chepigana, Pan. 94 H6
Chepo, Pan., 1,664 94 H6
Chepstow, U.K., 6,091 114 C7
Cheptainville, Fr. 116 h12
Chequamegon Bay, Wis. 66 C2
Chequamegon Pt., Wis. 66 C2
Cher, r., Fr. 117 D3
Cherán, Mex., 5,644 93 b10
Cherang Ruka, Malay., 1,777 147 p14
Cheraw, Colo., 173 79 D2
Cheraw, Miss. 73 F6
Cheraw, S.C., 5,171 63 E3
Cherbourg, Fr., 40,018 117 C2
Cherchell, Alg., 10,943 160 E1
Cherchen = Ch'ieh-mo
Chercher, reg., Eth. 163 M4
Cherdyn', U.S.S.R., 7,400 137 h6
Cheremkhovo, U.S.S.R., 116,500 135 K4
Cheremukhovo, U.S.S.R. 137 i6
Cherepanovo, U.S.S.R., 20,400 137 q11
Cherepovets, U.S.S.R., 113,000 134 C4
Chergui, Chott ech, Alg. 160 E2
Chergui, Zahrez, salt flat, Alg. 160 c6
Cherhill, U.K., 2,620 113 F6
Cherikov, U.S.S.R., 4,600 136 C2
Cherkessk, U.S.S.R., 49,000 134 D5
Chermasan, r., U.S.S.R. 137 h8
Chermoz, U.S.S.R., 11,000 137 h7
Chernigovka, U.S.S.R. 151 F1
Cherni Lom, r., Bulg. 128 F3
Cheriton, U.K. 113 k12
Cheriton, Va., 761 62 J5
Cherkassy, U.S.S.R., 103,000 134 C5
Cherlak, U.S.S.R., 11,900 134 G4
Chërnaya, U.S.S.R. 134 E3
Chërnaya, r., U.S.S.R. 135 J2
Chernigov, U.S.S.R., 101,000 134 C4
Chernivrŭkh, mtn., Bulg. 128 D3
Chernobyl', U.S.S.R., 8,200 136 C3
Chernogorsk, U.S.S.R., 54,000 137 s11
Chernoistochinsk, U.S.S.R. 137 i7
Chernomorskoye, U.S.S.R. 136 C4
Chernovskoye, U.S.S.R. 137 h7
Chernovtsy, U.S.S.R., 147,000 134 B5
Chernoye, Oz., U.S.S.R. 137 m11
Chernushka, U.S.S.R. 137 h8
Chernyakhovsk, U.S.S.R., 29,100 136 A2
Chernyshevsk, U.S.S.R. 135 L4
Chernyshevskiy, U.S.S.R. 135 L3
Chernyy Mys, U.S.S.R. 137 q11
Chërnyy Otrog, U.S.S.R. 137 h9
Cheroh, Malay., 2,179 147 o15
Cherokee, co., Ala., 16,303 64 D1
Cherokee, Ala., 1,349 64 A1
Cherokee, co., Ga., 23,001 64 E1
Cherokee, co., Iowa, 18,598 72 B2
Cherokee, Iowa, 7,724 72 B2
Cherokee, co., Kans., 22,279 75 L6

Cherokee—Chiu-ling Shan · 211

Cherokee, Kans., 797 75 L6
Cherokee, co., N.C., 16,335 63 a7
Cherokee, N.C. 63 A2
Cherokee, co., Okla., 17,762 76 H2
Cherokee, Okla., 2,410 76 E1
Cherokee, co., S.C., 35,205 63 C2
Cherokee, co., Tex., 33,120 77 Q3
Cherokee, Tex. 77 O4
Cherokee Falls, S.C. 63 C2
Cherokee L., Tenn. 71 H5
Cherokee Sound, Bah. Is. 95 C1
Cherrapunji, India 145 J4
Cherry, Ill., 501 68 C2
Cherry, co., Nebr., 8,218 75 D1
Cherry, Tenn. 71 B6
Cherry Creek, Nev. 83 C3
Cherry Creek, N.Y., 649 58 B7
Cherry Creek, S. Dak. 74 B3
Cherry Cr., Ariz. 78 C5
Cherry Cr., Colo. 79 C2
Cherry Cr., N. Dak. 74 A2
Cherry Cr., S. Dak. 74 B3
Cherry Cr. Res., Colo. 79 c8
Cherryfield, Me. 55 E4
Cherry Grove, W. Va. 62 E4
Cherry Grove Beach, S.C., 208 63 F4
Cherry Hill, Ark. 73 B3
Cherry Hills Village, Colo., 1,931 79 c8
Cherry Hinton (part of Cambridge), U.K., 11,201 114 J6
Cherry I., Sta. Cruz Is. 170 F5
Cherry Tree, Pa., 469 60 E4
Cherryvale, Kans., 2,783 75 K6
Cherry Valley, Ont., Can. 46 G5
Cherry Valley, Ark., 455 73 E2
Cherry Valley, Ill., 875 68 D1
Cherry Valley (part of Leicester), Mass. 56 J4
Cherry Valley, N.Y., 668 59 L6
Cherry Valley, Pa. 60 a8
Cherryville, Mo., 39 72 F7
Cherryville, N.C., 3,607 63 C2
Cherskogo, Khr., U.S.S.R. 135 N3
Chertkovo, U.S.S.R., 9,300 134 D5
Chertsey, U.K., 40,390 114 G8
Cherul, r., Malay. 147 p14
Cherusti, U.S.S.R. 136 c6
Cherven', U.S.S.R., 8,000 136 C2
Cherven Bryag, Bulg., 9,518 128 D3
Chervonograd, U.S.S.R., 12,400 136 B3
Chesaning, Mich., 2,770 67 J5
Chesapeake, Ohio, 1,396 70 G4
Chesapeake, Va. 62 H6
Chesapeake, W. Va., 2,699 62 C4
Chesapeake and Delaware Canal, Del.-Md. 61 A4
Chesapeake Bay, Md.-Va. 62 H4
Chesapeake Beach, Md., 731 62 H4
Chesapeake City, Md., 1,104 62 J3
Chesham, U.K., 16,297 114 G7
Chesham, N.H. 54 C6
Cheshire, co., U.K., 1,367,860 113 E5
Cheshire, Conn., 4,072; 13,383(T) 56 E7
Cheshire, Mass., 1,078; 2,472(T) 56 D2
Cheshire, co., N.H., 43,342 54 C5
Cheshire, N.Y. 58 F6
Cheshire, Ohio, 369 70 G4
Cheshire Res., Mass. 56 D2
Chëshskaya G., U.S.S.R. 134 D3
Cheshunt, U.K., 35,371 114 H7
Chesilhurst, N.J., 384 61 B4
Chesley, Ont., Can., 1,691 44 G7
Chesma, U.S.S.R. 137 k9
Chesnee, S.C., 1,045 63 C2
Chesnokovka, U.S.S.R., 32,200 137 r11
Chessy, Fr. 116 k11
Chest Cr., Pa. 60 E4
Chester, N.S., Can. 47 T11
Chester, U.K., 59,283 113 E5
Chester, Ark., 99 73 A2
Chester, Calif., 1,553 82 C2
Chester, Conn., 1,414; 2,520(T) 56 G7
Chester, Ill., 5,300 68 C6
Chester, Ind. 70 E3
Chester, Iowa, 211 72 E1
Chester, Me. 55 D3
Chester, Mass., 1,155(T) 56 D3
Chester, Mich. 67 H6
Chester, Miss. 73 F4
Chester, Mont., 1,158 81 D1
Chester, Nebr., 480 75 H3
Chester, N.H. 54 E6
Chester, N.J., 1,074 61 B2
Chester, N.Y., 1,492 59 M9
Chester, Ohio 70 H3
Chester, Okla. 76 E1
Chester, co., Pa., 210,608 61 L5
Chester, Pa., 63,658 61 M6
Chester, co., S.C., 30,888 63 C3
Chester, S.C., 6,906 63 C3
Chester, S. Dak. 74 D4
Chester, co., Tenn., 9,569 71 C6
Chester, Vt., 923 54 B5
Chester, Va., 1,290 62 G5
Chester, W. Va., 3,787 62 D2
Chester, r., Md. 62 H3
Chester Basin, N.S., Can. 47 T11
Chester Center (part of Chester), Mass. 56 E3
Chester Depot, Vt. 54 B5
Chesterfield, U.K., 67,858 113 F5
Chesterfield, Idaho 81 D4
Chesterfield, Ind., 2,588 70 D2
Chesterfield, Mass. 56 E3
Chesterfield, Mich. 67 g14
Chesterfield, N.H. 54 C6
Chesterfield, co., S.C., 33,717 63 D3
Chesterfield, S.C., 1,532 63 D3
Chesterfield, co., Va., 71,197 62 G5
Chesterfield Court House, Va. 62 G5
Chesterfield Inlet, N.W.T., Can. 40 L5
Chesterfield Inlet, N.W.T., Can. 40 L5
Chesterhill, Ohio, 876 70 H3
Chesterland, Ohio 70 f8
Chester-le-Street, U.K., 18,948 112 g10
Chesters, U.K. 113 E4
Chester Springs, Pa. 60 e11
Chesterton, U.K. 114 F7
Chesterton, Ind., 4,335 70 C1
Chestertown, Md., 3,602 62 H3
Chestertown, N.Y. 59 N4
Chesterville, Ont., Can., 1,242 47 J3
Chesterville, Me. 55 B4
Chestnut, Ill. 68 C3
Chestnut, La. 73 C5
Chestnut Hill (part of Lebanon), Conn. 56 H6
Chestnut Hill, Tenn. 71 H6
Chesuncook, Me. 55 C2
Chesuncook L., Me. 55 C2
Cheswardine, U.K. 114 D5
Cheswick, Pa., 2,734 60 c7
Chetac, L., Wis. 66 B3
Chetaïbi, Alg., 1,077 160 e5
Chetco, r., Oreg. 80 A4
Chetek, Wis., 1,729 66 B3
Chéticamp, N.S., Can., 1,107 45 O6
Chetopa, Kans., 1,538 75 K6
Chetumal, Mex., 12,775 93 H4
Chetumal Bay, Br. Hond.-Mex. 93 H4
Chetwynd, Br. Col., Can., 1,020 42 G2
Cheung Sha Wan, H.K., 264,680 152 b6
Chevak, Alaska, 315 85 C3
Chevanceaux, Fr., 1,035 117 C4
Chevannes, Fr. 116 h12
Cheveley, U.K., 1,624 114 J6
Chevelon Butte, Ariz. 78 C4
Chevelon Cr., Ariz. 78 C4
Chevenez, Switz. 124 A1
Cheverly, Md., 5,223 62 b9
Chevillon, Fr., 1,094 117 F2
Cheviot, N.Z. 175 g6
Cheviot, Ohio, 10,701 71 h10
Cheviot, The, mtn., U.K. 112 E4
Cheviot Hills, U.K. 113 E4
Chevreau, Îlot du, i., St-Barthélemy 97 7
Chevreuil, Pt., La. 73 D8
Chevreuse, Fr., 2,766 116 g12
Chèvreville, Fr. 116 k10
Chevrières, Fr. 116 o15
Chevry-Cossigny, Fr. 116 i12
Chevy Chase, Md., 2,405 62 a9
Chewelah, Wash., 1,525 80 E1
Chew Magna, U.K., 1,038 114 C8
Chew Valley L., U.K. 114 C8
Chexbres, Switz., 1,449 124 A2
Cheyenne, co., Colo., 2,789 79 D2
Cheyenne, co., Kans., 4,708 75 D4
Cheyenne, co., Nebr., 14,828 75 B2
Cheyenne, Okla. 76 D2
Cheyenne, Tex. 77 M4
Cheyenne, Wyo., 43,505 81 G5
Cheyenne, r., U.S. 52 A2
Cheyenne Bottoms, l., Kans. 75 G5
Cheyenne Wells, Colo, 1,020 79 D2
Cheyne Bay, Austl. 172 B5
Cheyney, Pa. 60 e12
Chezacut, Br. Col., Can. 42 F3
Chhabra, India, 7,558 144 a13
Chhatarpur, India, 22,146 145 F4
Chhep, Camb. 146 D4
Chhindwara, India, 37,244 145 F5
Chhlong, Camb. 146 D4
Chhuk, Camb. 147 k11
Chi, r., Thai. 146 C4
Chia, Col. 101 e15
Chia-ch'a, China 150 C4
Chia-ho, China 152 D2
Chia-ho-kuan, China 151 A4
Chia-hsiang, China 151 C4
Chia-hsien, Ho-n., China 151 B4
Chia-hsien, Shen-hsi, China 151 A3
Chia-hsing, China, 132,000* 150 G4
Chia-i, Taiwan, 159,151 150 F5
Chia-li, China 150 C4
Chia-li, Taiwan, 37,542 152 E3
Chia-ling, r., China 150 E4
Chiampo, It., 7,530 122 e5
Chia-mu-ssu, China, 231,000* 150 H2
Chi-an, Ch-hsi, China 150 F4
Chi-an, Ch-l., China 151 E2
Chiang-an, China 152 B1
Chiang-ch'eng, China 152 A3
Chiang-ching, China 152 B1
Chiang Dao, Thai. 146 B3
Chiange, Ang. 164 B4
Chiang-hsi, prov., China, 18,610,000 150 F4
Chiang-hua, China 152 C2
Chiang Kham, Thai. 146 C3
Chiang Khong, Thai. 146 C2
Chiang-k'ou, China 152 E2
Chiang-ling, China 152 C1
Chiang-lo, China 152 E2
Chiang-men, China, 110,000* 150 E5
Chiang-p'u, China 152 E1
Chiang Rai, Thai., 11,659 146 C3
Chiang Saen, Thai. 146 B2
Chiang-shan, China 152 E1
Chiang-su, prov., China, 45,230,000 150 F3
Chiang-tzu, China 150 C4
Chiang-yin, China 151 F1
Chiang-yü, China 151 C3
Chiang-yung, China 152 C2
Chian Yai, Thai., 1,343 146 C5
Chiao, r., China 152 E2
Chiao-ch'eng, China 151 A3
Ch'iao'chia, China 150 D4
Chiao-chou Wan, China 151 D3
Chiao-ho, Ch-l., China 150 G2
Chiao-ho, Ho-P., China 151 C3
Chiao-hsien, China 150 G3
Chiao-lai, r., China 151 D2
Chiao-ling, China 152 E2
Chiao-liu, r., China 151 D1
Ch'i-ao Tao, China 152 a6
Chiao-tso, China, 300,000* 150 F3
Chiapa de Corzo, Mex., 6,972 93 G5
Chiapas, st., Mex., 1,210,870 93 G5
Chiapuk, Ariz. 78 B5
Chiari, It., 15,725 123 B2
Chia-shan, China 152 F1
Chiasso, Switz., 7,377 124 D3
Chia-ting, China 152 F1
Chiatura, U.S.S.R., 19,200 137 b1
Chiautempan, Mex., 8,937 93 f10
Chiautla, Mex., 3,957 93 F4
Chiavari, It., 23,312 123 B2
Chiavenna, It., 6,270 123 B1
Chia-yin, China, 3,100* 150 H1
Chia-yü, China 152 D1
Chiba, Jap., 241,615 155 G4
Chiblow L., Ont., Can. 46 A2
Chibcugamau, Qué., Can., 4,715 44 K5
Chiburi-jima, Jap. 155 C4
Chibuto, Moz. 164 E6
Chicago, Ill., 3,550,404 68 E2
Chicago, N. Br., r., Ill. 69 d9
Chicago, S. Br., r., Ill. 69 d9
Chicago, West Fk. N. Br., r., Ill. 69 c8
Chicago Hbr., Ill. 69 d9
Chicago Heights, Ill., 34,331 68 E2
Chicago Ridge, Ill., 5,748 69 c10
Chicago Sanitary and Ship Can., Ill. 69 d9
Chicama, Peru, 1,150 104 B3
Chicanán, r., Ven. 101 K4
Chicapa, r., Ang. 164 C3
Chichagof I., Alaska 85 K4
Chichaoua, Mor. 160 C2
Chichester, Qué., Can. 46 G2
Chichester, U.K., 20,124 113 F6
Chichester, N.H. 54 E5
Chi-ch'i, China 152 E1
Ch'i-chiang, China 152 B1
Chichibu, Jap., 59,796 155 F4
Chichibu-Tama-ktk., Jap. 155 F4
Chichicastenango, Guat., 2,141 94 c9
Chichigalpa, Nic., 6,825 94 D4
Ch'i-ch'i-ha-erh, China, 604,000* 150 G2
Chichiriviche, Ven., 2,564 100 F2
Chichiriviche, Ven. 101 b11
Chichi-shima, Bonin Is. 170 D3
Ch'i-ch'un, China 152 D1
Chickahominy, r., Va. 62 G5
Chickamauga, Ga., 1,824 64 D1
Chickamauga-Chattanooga Nat. Mil. Pk., Ga. 64 D1
Chickamauga L., Tenn. 71 F6
Chickasaw, Ala., 10,002 64 B5
Chickasaw, co., Iowa, 15,034 72 E1
Chickasaw, co., Miss., 16,891 73 G4
Chickasawhay, r., Miss. 73 G6
Chickasha, Okla., 14,866 76 E2
Chicken, Alaska 85 J2
Chicknagalur, India, 30,253 145 E7
Chickwolnepy Str., N.H. 54 E2
Chiclana de la Frontera, Sp., 21,524 122 B4
Chiclayo, Peru, 86,904 104 B3
Chico, Calif., 14,757 82 C3
Chico, N. Mex. 79 C3
Chico, Tex., 654 77 P3
Chico, Wash. 81 a7
Chico, r., Arg. 105 B6
Chico, r., Arg. 105 B7
Chico, r., Phil. 153 B1
Chico, r., N. Mex. 79 B4
Chicoa, Moz. 164 E4
Chiconamel, Mex., 1,264 93 f8
Chicontepec, Mex., 3,287 93 f9
Chicopee, Mass., 61,553 56 F4
Chicopee, r., Mass. 56 F4
Chicopee Falls (part of Chicopee), Mass. 56 F4
Chicora, Mich. 67 H6
Chicora, Miss. 73 G6
Chicora, Pa., 1,156 60 C4
Chicot, co., Ark., 18,990 73 D4
Chicot, Ark. 73 D4
Chicoutimi, Qué., Can., 30,549 45 L5
Chidambaram, India, 40,694 145 F8
Chidester, Ark., 348 73 C4
Chidley, C., N.W.T., Can. 45 N1
Chief, Mich. 67 G4
Chiefland, Fla., 1,459 65 G3
Chieh-hsiu, China 151 B3
Chieh-kou, China 151 C4
Ch'ieh-mo, China 150 B3
Ch'ieh-shih, China 150 A3
Chieh-shih Wan, China 152 D3
Chieh-shou, China 151 B4
Chieh-yang, China 152 D3
Chiemsee, F.R.Ger. 118 D5
Chien, r., China 152 E2
Ch'ien, r., China 151 C4
Ch'ien-an, China 151 D1
Chien-ch'ang, China 151 D2
Chien-ch'ang-ying, China 151 C2
Ch'ien-chiang, Hu-p., China 152 D1
Ch'ien-chiang, S-ch., China 152 C1
Chien-ch'uan, China 150 D4
Chiengi, Zamb. 164 D3
Chieng Mai, Thai., 65,736 146 B3
Chien-ho, China 152 C2
Ch'ien-hsi, China 152 B2
Chien-ko, China 152 B1
Ch'-ien-kuo-erh-lo-ssu, China 151 E1
Chien-li, China 150 F4
Ch'ien-nan, China 152 D2
Ch'ien-ning, China 152 A1
Chien-ning, China 152 E2
Chien-ou, China 150 F4
Chien-p'ing, China 151 C2
Ch'ien-shan, China 152 E1
Chien-shih, China 152 C1
Chien-shui, China 150 D5
Chien-te, China 152 E1
Chienti, r., It. 123 D3
Chien-wei, China 152 A1
Chien-yang, F-ch., China 152 E2
Chien-yang, S-ch., China 152 B1
Ch'ien-yang, China 152 C2
Chieri, It., 18,206 123 A2
Chiesanuova, S. Mar., 1,350 123 e11
Chiese, r., It. 122 d5
Chieti, It., 44,988 123 E3
Chietla, Mex., 4,651 93 F4
Chieveley, U.K., 2,032 114 F8
Chigara, Jap. 154 i15
Chigasaki, Jap., 68,054 155 m20
Chigirin, U.S.S.R., 8,800 136 D3
Chigmecatitlán, Mex., 1,907 93 f11
Chignahuapan, Mex., 3,081 93 f10
Chignecto Bay, N.S., Can. 47 T11
Chignik, Alaska 99 85 E4
Chignik Lagoon, Alaska, 108 85 E4
Chigorodó, Col. 100 B4
Chiguará, Ven., 1,316 100 E3
Chiguayante, Chile, 17,568 104 e16
Chiguaza, Ec. 104 B2
Chigyŏng, N. Kor. 151 E3
Chihaya, Jap. 154 g15
Chih-chiang, China 150 E4
Chih-chin, China 152 B2
Ch'ih-feng, China 150 F2
Chih-kou, China 151 C4
Chihli, G. of=Po Hai
Ch'ih-shui, China 152 B1
Ch'ih-shui, China 152 B2
Chi-hsi, China, 252,631 150 H2
Ch'i-hsia, China 151 D3
Chi-hsien, Ho-n., China 151 B4
Chi-hsien, Ho-p., China 151 B3
Chi-hsien, Shan-hsi, China 151 A3
Ch'i-hsien, Ho-n., China 151 B4
Ch'i-hsien, Shan-hsi, China 151 B3
Chih-tan, China 151 A3
Chih-te, China 152 E1
Chih-to, China 150 C3
Chihuahua, st., Mex., 1,226,793 93 D2
Chihuahua, Mex., 149,437 92 D2
Chiili, U.S.S.R. 134 F5
Chik, U.S.S.R. 137 q11
Chikalda, India, 1,338 144 a15
Chikaskia, r., Kans.-Okla. 76 F1
Chikatsuyu, Jap. 154 g15
Chikhali, India, 13,499 145 E5
Ch'i-k'ou, China 151 C3
Chikoy, r., U.S.S.R. 135 K4
Chikugo, r., Jap. 154 B5
Chikuma, r., Jap. 155 F3
Chikuminuk L., Alaska 85 E3
Chikura, Jap., 19,188 155 G4
Chikwawa, Malawi 164 E4
Chikyū-misaki, Jap. 155 J8
Chila, Loy. Is. 174 k8
Chila, Mex., 1,894 93 f9
Chilac, Mex., 6,131 93 F4
Chilapa, Mex., 7,105 93 F5
Chilas, Pak. 145 E2
Chilaw, Cey., 11,392 145 F9
Chilca, Peru, 2,415 104 B5
Chilcoot, Calif. 82 C3
Chilcotin, r., Br. Col., Can. 42 F3
Childers, Austl., 1,438 173 G3
Childers, Okla. 76 H1
Childersburg, Ala., 4,884 64 C2
Childress, co., Tex., 8,421 77 N2
Childress, Tex., 6,399 77 N2
Childs, Fla. 65 H5
Childwold, N.Y. 59 L3
Chile, ctry., 8,567,000* 105
Chile Basin, Pac. Oc. 169 J3
Chilecito, Arg., 6,500* 105 B3
Chile Rise, Pac. Oc. 169 J4
Chiles, Calif. 82 a7
Chilete, Peru, 1,106 104 B3
Chilhowee, Mo., 339 72 C6
Chilhowie, Va., 1 169 62 C6
Chili, Ind. 70 D2
Chili, Wis. 66 C4
Chilia, Braţul, Rum. 128 G2
Chilibre, r., Pan. 94 g12
Chilibrillo, r., Pan. 94 g12
Chili Center, N.Y. 58 n20
Ch'i-lien, China 150 D3
Ch'i-lien Shan, China 150 D3
Chilili, N. Mex. 79 B4
Chi-lin, prov., China, 12,550,000 150 G2
Chi-lin, China, 568,000* 150 G2
Chilka L., India 145 G6
Chilko, r., Br. Col., Can. 42 F3
Chilkoot Pass, Alaska-Br. Col. 85 L4
Chillagoe, Austl. 173 F2
Chillahua, Bol. 102 a11
Chillán, Chile, 65,112 105 A5
Chillanes, Ec. 104 c10
Chillar, Arg., 2,266 105 b13
Chillicothe, Ill. 3,054 68 C3
Chillicothe, Iowa, 148 72 E3
Chillicothe, Mo., 9,236 72 D5
Chillicothe, Ohio, 24,957 70 G3
Chillicothe, Tex., 1,161 77 O2
Chilliwack, Br. Col., Can., 7,883 42 G4
Chilly-Mazarin, Fr., 3,433 116 h12
Chilmark, Mass. 57 O7
Chilo, Ohio 70 E4
Chilocco, Okla. 76 F1
Chiloé, I. de, Chile 105 A5
Chiloquin, Oreg., 945 80 C4
Chilpancingo, Mex., 17,942 93 F5
Chilson, Mich. 67 K6
Chiltern Hills, U.K. 113 F6
Chilton, co., Ala., 25,693 64 C3
Chilton, Wis., 2,578 66 E4
Chiltonville (part of Plymouth), Mass. 57 O5
Chi-lung, China 150 B4
Chi-lung, Taiwan, 204,196 152 F2
Chimacum, Wash. 80 B2
Chimaltenango, Guat., 9,065 94 c9
Chimán, Pan. 94 H6
Chimay, Belg., 3,212 115 C4
Chimay, Guat. 94 C2
Chimbarongo, Chile, 3,982 104 g14
Chimbay, U.S.S.R., 13,400 134 E5
Chimbo, r., Ec. 104 c11
Chimborazo, mtn., Ec. 104 B2
Chimbote, Peru, 63,970 104 B4
Chimbu, Terr. New Guin. 174 e2
Ch'i-men, China 152 E1
Chimichagua, Col. 100 D3
Chimkent, U.S.S.R., 171,000 134 F5
Chimmenticook Str., Me. 55 C1
Chimney Rock, N.C. 63 B2
Chimney Rock Nat. Hist. Site, Nebr. 75 B2
Chi-mo, China 151 D3
Chimtorga, G., U.S.S.R. 134 F6
Chi-mu-sa-erh, China 150 C2
Chin, Ryukyu Is. 154 a11
Ch'in, r., China 151 B3
Ch'in, r., China 152 C3
Chin, r., China 152 D1
Chin, r., China 152 E2
China, ctry., 700,000,000* 150
China, Republic of=Taiwan
China, Mex., 2,496 93 F3
China, Ind. 70 D4
China, Me. 55 C4
China, Tex., 77 m9
Chinácota, Col. 100 D4
China Grove, Ala. 64 D3
China Grove, N.C., 1,500 63 D2
Chinajá, Guat. 94 B2
China Lake, Calif. 82 E5
China L., Calif. 82 E5
China L., Me. 55 C4
Chi-nan, China, 860,000* 150 F3
Chinandega, Nic., 18,222 94 D4
Chinati Mts., Tex. 76 •
Chinati Pk., Tex. 77 L5
Chinbyit, Burma 146 A2
Chincha, Is., Peru 104 B5
Chincha Alta, Peru, 19,614 104 B5
Chinchaga, r., Alta. Can. 42 H1
Chin-ch'eng, China 151 B4
Chincheros, Peru, 1,500 104 C5
Chin-ch'i, China 152 E2
Chin-chiang, China 152 E2
Chin-chieh-ling, China 152 a6
Chinchilla, Austl., 2,579 173 G4
Chinchilla, Pa., 1,130* 61 o16
Chinchilla de Monte-Aragón, Sp., 7,074 122 E3
Chinchiná, Col. 101 d15
Chinchón, Sp., 4,432 122 D2
Chinchorro, Banco, Mex. 93 J4
Chin-chou, China, 350,000* 150 F2
Chinchoua, Gabon 164 A2
Chin-chou Wan, China 151 D3
Ch'in-chou Wan, China 152 C3
Chinchow=Chin-chou
Chincoteague, Va., 2,131 62 J5
Chincoteague Bay, Md.-Va. 62 J4
Chinde, Moz., 25,924 164 F5
Chindiri, Ghana 162 c7
Chindo, S. Kor., 10,880 151 E4
Chin-do, S. Kor. 151 E4
Chindwin, r., Burma 146 A2
Ching, r., China 151 A4
Ch'ing, r., China 152 C1
Ching-an, China 152 D1
Ch'ing-an, China 151 E1
Ch'ing-chen, China 152 B2
Ch'ing-ch'eng-tzu, China 151 D2
Ching-chiang, China 152 F1
Ch'ing-chiang, China 152 D1
Ch'ing-chien, China 151 A3
Chinge-Kat, U.S.S.R. 137 s12
Ch'ing-feng, China 151 B4
Ch'ing-hai, prov., China, 2,050,000 150 C3
Ching-hai, China 151 C3
Ch'ing Hai, China 150 D3
Ching-hai Wan, China 151 D3
Ching-ho, China 150 B2
Ch'ing-ho, Ho-p., China 151 B3
Ch'ing-ho, Hs-ch., China 150 C2
Ch'ing-ho-men, China 151 D2
Ching-hsi, China 150 E5
Ching-hsien, A-h., China 152 E1
Ching-hsien, Hu-n., China 152 C2
Ch'ing-hsien, China 151 C3
Ching-hsing, China 151 D1
Ch'ing-hsü, China 151 A3
Ch'ing-i, r., China 152 A1
Ch'ing-kang, China 151 E1
Chingleput, India, 25,977 145 n19
Ch'ing-liu, China 152 E2
Ching-lo, China 151 B3
Ch'ing-lung, China 152 B2
Ching-men, China 152 D1
Ching-ning, Ch-ch., China 152 E2
Ching-ning, K-su, China 150 E3
Chingola, Zambia, 35,200* 164 D4
Ching-pien, China 151 A3
Ching-po Hu, China 151 F2
Ch'ing-p'u, China 152 F1
Ching-shan, China 152 D1
Ching Shan, China 152 C1
Ching-shih, China 150 E4
Ch'ing-shui, China 152 B2
Ch'ing-shui-ho, China 151 A3
Ch'ing-tao, China, 1,121,000* 150 G3
Ching-te, China 152 E1
Ching-te-chen, China, 300,000* 150 F4
Ching-t'ien, China 152 F1
Ch'ing-to, China 150 D4
Ch'ing-t'ung Gorge, China 150 E3
Ching-tzu-kuan, China 151 A4
Chinguetti, Maur., 2,400 162 C2
Ching-yang, China 151 A4
Ch'ing-yang, A-h., China 152 E1
Ch'ing-yang, K-su, China 150 E3
Ching-yen, China 152 B1
Ch'ing-yi, r., China 152 E1
Ching-yü, China 151 E2
Ching-yüan, China, 16,000* 150 E3
Ch'ing-yüan, Ch-ch., China 152 E2
Ch'ing-yüan, K-t., China 150 F5
Ch'ing-yüan, L-n., China 151 E2
Ch'ing-yün, China 151 C3
Chinhae, S. Kor., 67,412 151 F4
Chin Hills, Burma 146 A2
Chin-hsi, China 151 D2
Chin-hsiang, China 151 C4
Chin-hsien, Ch-hsi, China 152 D1
Chin-hsien, Ho-p., China 151 B3
Chin-hsien, L-n., China 151 D3
Ch'in-hsien, K-t., China 152 C3
Ch'in-hsien, Shan-hsi, China 151 B3
Chin-hsing Men, chan., China 152 a6
Chin-hua, China, 120,000* 150 G4
Ch'in-huang-tao, China, 210,000* 150 G3
Chinhŭng-ni, N. Kor. 151 E3
Chinibaru, i., Jaluit 176 30
Chi-ning, N-m-k., China 150 F2
Chi-ning, Shant., China 150 F3
Chiniot, Pak., 47,099 145 D3
Chinju, S. Kor., 86,867 151 E4
Chinko, r., C.A.R. 163 J5
Chin-k'uang, China 152 A1
Chinle, Ariz. 78 D3
Chinle Wash, Ariz. 78 D3
Ch'in Ling, China 151 A4
Chin-men Tao, Taiwan 152 E2
Chin-ning, China 152 A2
Chinnor, U.K., 1,751 114 G7
Chinnur, India, 9,645 145 F6
Chino, Jap., 36,007 155 F4
Chino, Calif., 10,305 83 i15
Chinon, Fr., 7,873 117 D3
Chinook, Alta., Can. 42 K3
Chinook, Mont., 2,326 81 E1
Chinook, Wash. 80 A2
Chinook Pass, Wash. 80 C2
Chino Valley, Ariz. 78 B4
Chin-p'ing, K-ch., China 152 C2
Chin-p'ing, Y-n., China 152 A3
Chinquapin, N.C. 63 G3
Chinsali, Zamb. 164 E3
Chin-sha, China 150 E4
Chin-sha, r., China 150 D4
Chin-shan, China 152 F1
Ch'in-shui, China 151 B4
Chinsura, India 144 g14
Chin-t'a, China 150 D2
Ch'in-ta-mu-i, China 151 D1
Chin-t'ang, China 152 B1
Chinteche, Malawi 164 E3
Chinú, Col. 100 C3
Chin-wan, Ryukyu Is. 154 a11
Chinwangtao=Ch'in-huang-tao
Ch'in-yang, China 151 B4
Chin-yin-kou, China 151 D1
Ch'in-yüan, China 151 B3
Chin-yün, China 152 F1
Chioggia, It., 48,542 123 D2
Chios=Khios
Chipao, Peru, 1,186 104 C5
Chipaque, Col. 101 e15
Chipewyan Lake, Alta., Can. 42 K2
Chipie, r., Ont., Can. 44 G4
Chipinga, Rhod. 164 E5
Chipley, Fla., 3,159 65 D2
Chiplun, India, 17,355 145 D6
Chipman, Alta., Can. 43 c7
Chipman, N.B., Can., 1,490 45 N6
Chipman, r., Sask., Can. 43 D2
Chipola, r., Fla. 65 D2
Chipou, Camb. 147 m11
Chippawa, Ont., Can., 3,238 46 F5
Chippawa Hill, Ont., Can. 46 C4
Chippawa Power Can., Ont., Can. 58 i18
Chippenham, U.K., 17,543 113 E6
Chippewa, co., Mich., 32,655 67 J2
Chippewa, co., Minn., 16,320 74 E3
Chippewa, co., Wis., 45,096 66 B3
Chippewa, r., Mich. 67 J5
Chippewa, r., Wis. 66 A4
Chippewa, L., Wis. 66 B3
Chippewa Bay, N.Y. 59 J3
Chippewa Falls, Wis., 11,708 66 B4
Chippewa Lake, Mich. 67 H5
Chipping, U.K. 114 C3
Chipping Campden, U.K., 1,951 114 E6
Chipping Norton, U.K., 4,245 113 F6
Chipping Sodbury, U.K., 1,104 114 D7
Chipping Warden, U.K. 114 F6
Chiprovtsi, Bulg., 3,517 128 D3
Chiputneticook Lakes, Can.-U.S. 55 E3
Chiquián, Peru, 3,345 104 B4
Chiquimula, Guat., 12,394 94 C3
Chiquimulilla, Guat., 5,377 94 B3
Chiquinquirá, Col. 100 C5
Chiquinquirá, Ven., 3,360 100 D2
Chira, r., Peru 104 A3
Chirala, India, 45,410 145 F7
Chiran, Jap., 24,134 154 B6
Chirang, Bhutan 145 J4
Chirās, Afghan. 144 B2
Chirbury, U.K. 114 B5
Chirchik, U.S.S.R., 76,000 134 G5
Chirchik, r., U.S.S.R. 137 f4
Chirfa, Niger 162 G2
Chirgaon, India, 7,514 144 b13
Chirgua, r., Ven. 100 G3
Chiricahua, Ariz. 78 D6
Chiricahua Mts., Ariz. 78 •
Chiricahua Nat. Mon., Ariz. 78 D5
Chiricahua Pk., Ariz. 78 D6
Chirichiri, B., Col. 100 B4
Chiriguaná, Col. 100 D3
Chirikof I., Alaska 85 F5
Chirinda, U.S.S.R. 135 K3
Chiriquí, G. de, Pan. 94 F7
Chiriquí, Lag. de, Pan. 94 F6
Chiriquí, Vol. de, Pan. 94 F6
Chiriquí Grande, Pan. 94 F6
Chirk, U.K., 3,652 113 E5
Chirnogeni, Rum. 128 G3
Chirnside, U.K. 112 E4
Chiromo, Malawi 164 E4
Chironico, Switz. 124 C2
Chirpan, Bulg., 15,432 128 E3
Chirripó, r., C.R. 94 F5
Chirripó Grande, Co., C.R. 94 F6
Chirundu, Rhod. 164 D4
Chiryū, Jap., 20,542 154 i14
Chisago, co., Minn., 13,419 74 F3
Chisana, Alaska 85 J3
Chisana, r., Alaska 85 J3
Chisāpāni Garhi, Nepal 144 e12
Chiscas, Col. 100 D4
Chiseldon, U.K., 2,598 114 E7
Chi-shan, China 151 A4
Ch'i-shan, Taiwan, 38,343 152 F3
Chishmy, U.S.S.R. 137 h8
Chisholm, Me., 1,193 55 B4
Chisholm, Minn., 7,144 74 F2
Chisholm, Tex. 76 g9
Chi-shou, China, 20,000* 152 C1
Chi-shui, China 152 D2
Chisimaio=Kismayu
Chişneu Criş, Rum. 128 C1
Chislehurst, London, U.K. 114 J8
Chisney, Okla. 76 G2
Chisos Mts., Tex. 76 •
Chistochina, Alaska, 28 85 H3
Chistoozërnoye, U.S.S.R. 137 o11
Chistopol', U.S.S.R., 55,000 134 E4
Chistyakovo, U.S.S.R., 90,000 136 f8
Chiswick, Ont., Can. 46 E2
Chita, Bol. 102 b12
Chita, U.S.S.R., 189,000 135 L4
Chita-hantō, Jap. 154 h15
Ch'i-t'ai, China 150 C2
Chita-wan, Jap. 154 h15
Chitek, r., Sask., Can. 43 C3
Chitembo, Ang. 164 B4
Chi Thien, N. Viet. 147 i9
Chitina, Alaska, 31 85 H3
Chitina, r., Alaska 85 J3
Chitorgarh, India, 16,888 145 E4
Chitose, Jap., 44,522 155 J8
Chitradurga, India, 33,336 145 E7
Chitrāl, Pak. 145 D2
Chitré, Pan., 9,120 94 G6
Chi-tse, China 151 B3
Chittagong, Pak., 364,205 145 J5
Chittaranjan, India, 28,957 144 f14
Chittenango, N.Y., 3,180 59 J5
Chittenden, co., Vt., 74,425 54 A3
Chittenden, Vt. 54 B4
Chittenden Res., Vt. 54 B4
Chittoor, India, 47,876 145 F7
Ch'i-tung, China 152 F1
Ch'i-tung, Hu-n., China 152 C2
Chiu-ch'ang-shan, China 151 C3
Chiu-chiang, China 150 F4
Chiu-chih, China 150 D3
Chiu-chou, r., China 152 C3
Chiu-ch'üan, China 150 D3
Chiu-fu Shan, China 151 C4
Chiu-hai-yang, China 151 D3
Chiu-hsiang-ch'eng, China 151 B4
Chiu-hsiang-ling, China 151 A3
Ch'iu-hsien, China 151 B3
Chiu-hui-nan, China 151 E2
Chiu-ling Shan, China 152 D1

212 · Chiu-lung—Clayton

Chiu-lung, China 152 A1
Chiu-lung, r., China 152 E2
Chiumbe, r., Ang. 164 C3
Ch'iung-chou Hai-hsia, China 152 C3
Chiung-lai, China 152 A1
Chiung-lai Shan, China 150 D4
Ch'iung-tung, China 152 C4
Ch'iu-pei, China 152 A2
Chiu-pei-lo-fu, China 151 C1
Chiu-shang-shui, China 151 B4
Chiu-t'ai, China 151 E1
Chiu-tung-a, China 151 C3
Chiva, Sp., 4,326 122 E3
Chivacoa, Ven., 10,474 100 F2
Chivasso, It., 14,914 123 A2
Chivay, Peru, 2,310 104 D5
Chivé, Bol. 102 C4
Chivilcoy, Arg., 47,043 105 C4
Chivington, Colo. 79 D2
Chixoy, r., Guat.-Mex. 94 B3
Chi-yang, China 151 C3
Ch'i-yang, China 152 D2
Chi-yüan, China 151 B4
Chizu, Jap., 14,643 155 D4
Chkalovsk, U.S.S.R., 11,500 136 F1
Chkalovskoye, U.S.S.R. 151 F1
Chloride, Ariz. 78 A4
Chloride, Mo. 72 G7
Chlumec nad Cidlinou, Czech. 127 e6
Choachí, Col. 101 f15
Chobe, r., Bots.-S.W.Af. 164 C5
Cho Bo, N. Viet. 147 h9
Choc Bay, St. Lucia 97 11
Choceň, Czech. 127 f6
Cho-chang, r., China 151 B3
Cho Chu, N. Viet. 147 h8
Chocianów, Pol., 3,600 127 A3
Chociwel, Pol., 2,090 127 A2
Chockie, Okla. 76 H3
Chocolate Mts., Ariz. 78 A5
Chocorua, N.H. 54 E4
Chocorua, Mt., N.H. 54 E4
Chocowinity, N.C., 580 63 G2
Choctaw, co., Ala., 17,870 64 A4
Choctaw, Ala. 64 A3
Choctaw, co., Miss., 8,423 73 F4
Choctaw, co., Okla., 15,637 76 H3
Choctaw, Okla., 623 76 F2
Choctawhatchee, r., Ala.-Fla. 64 D4
Choctawhatchee Bay, Fla. 65 C2
Chodaków, Pol., 5,161 127 D2
Chodavaram, India, 14,948 145 G6
Chodecz, Pol., 1,445 127 C2
Chodov, Czech. 126 b6
Chodro, U.S.S.R. 137 s12
Chodzież, Pol., 11,132 127 B2
Ch'oedal-gol, N. Kor. 151 F2
Choele-Choel, Arg., 2,000* 105 B5
Chōfu, Jap., 66,662 155 m19
Cho Gao, S. Viet., 1,777 147 m11
Chōgo, Jap. 155 m20
Choiceland, Sask., Can. 43 D4
Choisel, Fr. 116 g12
Choiseul, St. Lucia 97 11
Choiseul, i., Sol. Is. 170 E5
Choiseul Sd., Falk. Is. 108 3
Choisy-le-Roi, Fr., 41,269 116 h11
Choix, Mex., 1,500* 92 C2
Chójamachi, Jap. 155 n20
Chojna, Pol., 3,336 127 A2
Chojnice, Pol., 20,000* 127 B2
Chojnów, Pol., 8,656 127 A3
Chōkai-zan, mtn., Jap. 155 G2
Chokchai, Thai. 147 e4
Choke Mts., Eth. 163 L4
Chokio, Minn., 498 74 D3
Chokoloskee, Fla. 65 H7
Chokurdakh, U.S.S.R. 135 O2
Cholet, Fr., 37,557 117 C3
Cholguán, r., Chile 104 f17
Chollerton, U.K., 1,059 113 E4
Cholo, Malawi 164 E4
Ch'o-lo, r., China 151 D1
Cholsey, U.K., 3,107 113 F6
Cho-lu, China 151 B2
Cholula, Mex., 12,820 93 f10
Choluteca, Hond., 9,384 94 D4
Choluteca, r., Hond. 94 D4
Choma, Zamb., 2,240 164 D4
Chom Bung, Thai. 147 c5
Chomedey, Qué., Can. 47 o17
Chomérac, Fr., 1,748 117 F4
Cho Moi, S. Viet., 3,020 147 k11
Chom Thong, Thai. 146 B3
Chomu, India, 15,791 144 a12
Chomutov, Czech., 34,310 126 A1
Chona, r., U.S.S.R. 135 K3
Chōnan, Jap. 155 n20
Ch'ŏnan, S. Kor., 44,075 151 E3
Chon Buri, Thai., 32,498 146 C4
Chonchi, Chile, 1,453 105 A6
Chon Daen, Thai. 146 C3
Chone, Ec., 12,256 104 B2
Ch'ŏngch'ŏn, r., N. Kor. 151 E3
Ch'ŏngjin, N. Kor., 200,000* 151 F2
Chŏngju, N. Kor. 151 E3
Ch'ŏngju, S. Kor., 92,342 151 E3
Chong Kal, Camb. 146 C4
Chŏngŭp, S. Kor., 41,437 151 E4
Chŏnju, S. Kor., 188,726 151 E4
Chonos, Arch. de los, Chile 105 A6
Chon Thanh, S. Viet. 147 m11
Chontla, Mex., 1,198 93 f8
Chop, U.S.S.R., 5,000 136 A3
Chopin, La. 73 C6
Chopmist, R.I. 57 K5
Choptank, r., Md. 62 J4
Chopwell, U.K. 112 g10
Chorges, Fr., 1,141 117 G4
Ch'o-ri, N. Kor. 151 F2
Chorley, U.K., 31,262 113 E5
Choroní, Ven. 101 b11
Choroszcz, Pol., 2,028 127 E2
Chorrillos, Peru, 32,166 104 B5
Chortkov, U.S.S.R., 15,200 136 B3
Ch'ŏrwŏn, S. Kor., 4,706 151 E3
Chorzele, Pol., 2,141 127 D2
Chorzów, Pol., 147,000* 127 C3
Ch'osan, N. Kor. 151 E2
Chosen, Fla., 1,858 65 J6
Chōshi, Jap., 91,470 155 G4
Chosica, Peru 104 B4
Chos Malal, Agr., 3,500* 105 B5
Choszczno, Pol., 6,780 127 A2
Chota, Peru, 4,921 104 B3
Choteau, Mont., 1,966 81 C2
Chotěboř, Czech. 126 B2
Chotěvice, Czech. 127 e6
Cho-tzu, China 151 B2
Chou-chih, China 151 A4
Choudrant, La., 465 73 C5
Choum, Maur. 162 B2
Chou-ning, China 152 E2
Chou-shan, China 152 F1
Chou-shan Ch'ün-tao, China 152 F1
Chouteau, co., Mont., 7,348 81 D2
Chouteau, Okla., 958 76 H1
Chou-ts'un, China 151 C3
Chovellen, Chile 104 e15
Chowan, co., N.C., 11,729 63 H1
Chowan, r., N.C. 63 H1
Chowchilla, Calif., 4,525 82 C4
Chowhoctolik, Alaska 85 D3
Chown, Mt., Alta., Can. 42 H3
Choybalsan, Mong. 150 F2
Choybalsan Uula, Mong. 150 E2
Chrast, Czech. 127 e7
Chrastava, Czech. 127 e6
Chřibská, Czech. 126 d6
Chrisman, Calif., 3,923 82 D5
Chrisman, Ill., 1,221 68 E4
Chrisney, Ind., 380 70 C4
Christchurch, N.Z., 151,671 175 g6
Christchurch, U.K., 26,336 113 i13
Christchurch Bay, U.K. 113 i13
Christian, Alaska 85 H2
Christian, co., Ill., 37,207 68 C4
Christian, co., Ky., 56,904 71 D5
Christian, co., Mo., 12,359 72 D8
Christian, W. Va. 62 C5
Christian, Pt., Pitc. I. 177 45
Christiana, Jam., 4,404 96 p8
Christiana, S. Af., 5,848 164 D6
Christiana, Pa., 1,069 61 K6
Christiana, Tenn. 71 E6
Christian I., Ont., Can. 46 D4
Christiansburg, Ohio, 788 70 F2
Christiansburg, Va., 3,653 62 D5
Christiansfeld, Den. 121 B5
Christiansted, St. Croix, 5,137 97 1
Christiansted Harbor, St. Croix 97 1
Christiansted Nat. Hist. Site, St. Croix 97 1
Christie, Okla. 76 J2
Christie, Wis. 66 C4
Christie, Mt., Austl. 172 D4
Christina, r., Alta., Can. 42 K2
Christina, r., Del. 62 e11
Christina L., Br. Col., Can. 80 D1
Christine, N. Dak. 74 D2
Christine, Tex., 276 77 O5
Christmas, Fla. 65 J4
Christmas Atoll, Line Is. 171 H4
Christmas I., Ind. Oc. 170 B5
Christmas L., Minn. 74 a6
Christmas Ridge, Pac. Oc. 169 G2
Christopher, Ill., 2,854 68 D6
Christopher Lake, Sask., Can. 43 C4
Christoval, Tex. 77 N4
Chromo, Colo. 79 B3
Chrudim, Czech., 15,898 126 B2
Chrudimka, r., Czech. 127 e7
Chrysler, Ala. 64 B4
Chrzanów, Pol., 21,000* 127 C3
Chu, U.S.S.R. 134 G5
Ch'ü, r., S-ch., China 152 B1
Ch'ü, r., Hu-n., China 152 C2
Chu, r., N. Viet. 146 D3
Chu, r., U.S.S.R. 134 G5
Chuacús, Sa. de, Guat. 94 c8
Chuādānga, Pak., 11,625 144 g14
Chualar, Calif. 82 C4
Ch'üan, r., China 151 B4
Ch'üan-chiao, China 152 E1
Ch'üan-chou, China, 200,000* 150 F4
Chuang-ho, China 151 D3
Ch'üan-hsien, China 150 E4
Chuarrancho, Guat., 3,519 94 c9
Chubbuck, Idaho, 1,590 81 C4
Chūbu-Sangaku-ktk., Jap. 155 E3
Chubut, r., Arg. 105 B6
Chucándiro, Mex., 2,600 93 c10
Chuchelná, Czech. 127 h7
Chu-ch'eng, China 151 C4
Chu-chi, China 152 F1
Chu-ch'i, China 150 E3
Ch'ü-ch'i, China 152 A3
Ch'ü-ching, China 152 B2
Chu-chou, China, 250,000* 150 F4
Chu Chua, Br. Col., Can. 42 H3
Chuckatuck, Va. 62 H6
Chucunaque, r., Pan. 94 H6
Chudovo, U.S.S.R., 10,500 136 C1
Chudskoye Oz., U.S.S.R. 134 B4
Ch'üeh-shan, China 151 B4
Ch'ü-fou, China 151 C4
Chugach Is., Alaska 85 G4
Chugach Mts., Alaska 85 H3
Chugiak, Alaska, 51 85 c7
Chuginadak I., Alaska 85 B5
Chūgoku-sammyaku, mts., Jap. 155 C4
Chuguyev, U.S.S.R., 20,300 136 E3
Chugwater, Wyo., 287 81 G5
Chu-hai, China 152 a6
Chü-hsien, China 150 F3
Ch'ü-hsien, Ch-ch., China 150 F4
Ch'ü-hsien, S-ch., China 152 B1
Ch'u-hsien, China 152 E1
Ch'u-hsiung, China 152 A2
Chü-hua Tao, China 151 D2
Chui Chak, Malay., 2,663 147 o14
Chü-jung, China 152 E1
Chukai, Malay., 8,702 148 B1
Chukchagirskoye, Oz., U.S.S.R. 135 N4
Chukchi Sea, U.S.S.R.-U.S. 34 A2
Chukch'ŏn-ni, N. Kor. 151 E3
Chukfaktoolik, Alaska 85 C3
Chukhloma, U.S.S.R., 4,300 136 F1
Chukotskiy, M., U.S.S.R. 135 S3
Chukotskiy P-ov., U.S.S.R. 135 S3
Chukotskoye Nag., U.S.S.R. 135 R3
Chula, Ga. 64 F4
Chula, Mo., 285 72 D5
Chula, Va. 62 G5
Ch'ulak Akkan, r., China 150 C3
Chulak-Tau, U.S.S.R. 134 G5
Chula Vista, Calif., 42,034 82 E6
Chulitna, r., Alaska 85 G3
Chul'man, U.S.S.R., 8,000 135 M4
Chulmleigh, U.K. 113 E6
Chü-lu, China 151 B3
Chulucanas, Peru, 19,675 104 A3
Chu-lu-k'o, China 151 C2
Chulumani, Bol., 5,597 102 b10
Chu-lung, r., China 151 B3
Chuluuta, r., Mong. 150 D2
Chulym, U.S.S.R., 17,600 137 q11
Chulym, r., U.S.S.R. 134 J4
Chulym, r., U.S.S.R. 137 q11
Chulyshman, r., U.S.S.R. 137 s12
Chumaba, Mex. 93 H4
Ch'ü-ma-lai, China 150 C3
Chumar, India 145 F2
Chu-ma-tien, China 151 B4
Chumikan, U.S.S.R. 135 N4
Chumphae, Thai. 146 C3
Chumphon, Thai., 9,314 146 B5
Chum Phuang, Thai. 147 e4
Chumpi, Peru, 2,734 104 C5
Chumsaeng, Thai., 12,086 146 C4
Chum Saeng, Thai. 147 e4
Chumstick, Wash. 80 C2
Chumunjin, S. Kor., 30,421 151 F3
Chumysh, r., U.S.S.R. 137 r11
Chuna, r., U.S.S.R. 135 J4
Chu-nan, Taiwan, 29,950 152 F2
Chunar, India, 8,904 144 d13
Chunchi, Ec., 2,325 104 c11
Ch'unch'ŏn, S. Kor., 83,008 151 F3
Chunchula, Ala. 64 A5
Chundu, China 144 f11
Ch'ung-an, China 150 F4
Ch'ung-ch'ing, China, 2,200,000* 150 E4
Ch'ung-ch'ing, China 152 A1
Chung-hsiang, China 150 F4
Chung-hsien, China 152 B1
Chunghwa, N. Kor. 151 E3
Ch'ung-i, China 152 D2
Ch'ung-jen, China 152 E2
Ch'ungju, S. Kor., 68,624 151 E3
Chungking = Ch'ung-ch'ing
Chung-li, Taiwan, 63,941 152 F2
Ch'ung-ming, China 152 F1
Ch'ung-ming Tao, China 152 F1
Chung-mou, China 151 B4
Ch'ungmu, S. Kor., 47,757 151 F4
Chŭngsan, N. Kor. 151 E3
Chung-shan, China 152 D3
Ch'ung-te, China 152 F1
Chung-t'iao Shan, China 151 A4
Chung-tien, China 150 D4
Ch'ung-tso, China 152 B3
Chung-wei, China 150 E3
Ch'ung-yang, China 152 D1
Chung-yang Shan-mo, Taiwan 152 F3
Chün-hsien, Ho-n., China 151 B4
Chün-hsien, Hu-p., China 151 A4
Chun-ko-erh-ch'i, China 151 A2
Chunya, Tanz. 164 E3
Chunya, r., U.S.S.R. 135 K3
Ch'un-yang, China 151 F2
Ch'unyang, S. Kor. 151 F3
Chuong Nghia, S. Viet. 146 E4
Chupaca, Peru, 2,595 104 C5
Chupadera Mesa, N. Mex. 79 B5
Chupán, Peru, 1,400 104 B4
Chupara Point, Trin. and Tob. 96 g5
Chuquibamba, Peru, 3,049 104 C5
Chuquicamata, Chile, 24,798 105 B2
Chur, Switz., 24,825 124 D2
Churaki, U.S.S.R. 137 h7
Churapcha, U.S.S.R. 135 N3
Churayevo, U.S.S.R. 137 h8
Churcampa, Peru, 1,230 104 C5
Churchbridge, Sask., Can. 43 D5
Church Creek, Md., 146 62 H4
Churchdown, U.K., 7,075 113 E6
Church Eaton, U.K., 1,059 114 D5
Church Hill, Md., 263 62 J3
Church Hill, Tenn., 769 71 J5
Churchill, Man., Can. 43 G2
Churchill, co., Nev., 8,452 83 A3
Churchill, r., Man.-Sask., Can. 43 G2
Churchill, r., Newf., Can. 45 O4
Churchill, C., Man., Can. 43 H2
Churchill, Mt., Br. Col., Can. 42 c5
Churchill L., Sask., Can. 43 B3
Churchill Pk., Br. Col., Can. 42 F1
Church Lench, U.K. 114 D6
Church Point, La., 3,606 73 C7
Churchs Ferry, N. Dak., 161 74 C1
Churchstoke, U.K., 1,213 113 E5
Church Stretton, U.K., 2,707 114 C5
Churchton, Md. 62 H4
Churchville, N.Y., 1,003 58 D5
Churchville, Va. 62 E4
Churdan, Iowa, 586 72 C2
Churidó, Col. 100 B4
Churintzio, Mex., 2,965 93 b9
Churu, India, 41,727 145 E3
Churubusco, Ind., 1,284 70 D1
Churubusco, N.Y. 59 M2
Churuguara, Ven., 4,446 100 E2
Churumuco, Mex., 1,131 92 E4
Chu-shan, China 151 A4
Ch'ü-shui, China 150 C4
Chuska Mts., Ariz.-N. Mex. 78 D3
Chusovaya, r., U.S.S.R. 137 i7
Chusovoy, U.S.S.R., 63,000 137 i7
Chuspa, Ven. 101 c11
Chust, U.S.S.R., 15,500 137 f4
Chūta, Ryukyu Is. 154 a10
Chute-aux-Outardes, Qué., Can., 1,297 45 L5
Chute Lake, Br. Col., Can. 42 H4
Chute Pd., Wis. 66 E3
Ch'ü-wu, China 151 A4
Chuya, r., U.S.S.R. 137 r12
Ch'ü-yang, China 151 B3
Chü-yeh, China 151 D4
Chūzenji-ko, Jap. 155 F3
Chvaletice, Czech. 127 e6
Ciacova, Rum. 128 C2
Ciales, P.R., 3,275 96 t10
Cianorte, Braz., 8,480 103 F6
Cibecue, Ariz. 78 C4
Cibola, Ariz. 78 A5
Cibolo, Tex. 76 b6
Cibolo Cr., Tex. 76 b6
Cibuta, Co., Mex. 92 C1
Cicciano, It., 8,906 123 d10
Cicero, Ill., 69,130 68 E2
Cicero, Ind., 1,284 70 C2
Cicero, N.Y. 59 H5
Cicero Center, N.Y. 59 r23
Cićevac, Yug., 4,593 125 E3
Cide, Turk., 2,072 142 C1
Cidlina, r., Czech. 127 e6
Cidra, Cuba, 1,463 96 c1
Cidra, P.R., 3,191 96 t10
Cidra, L., P.R. 96 t10
Ciechanów, Pol., 20,000* 127 D2
Ciechanowiec, Pol., 3,277 127 E2
Ciechocinek, Pol., 6,152 127 C2
Ciego de Ávila, Cuba, 35,178 96 d2
Cieleśnica, Pol. 127 E2
Ciempozuelos, Sp., 9,042 122 D2
Ciénaga, Col. 100 C2
Ciénaga de Oro, Col. 100 C3
Cieneguilla, Mex. 93 e9
Cienfuegos, Cuba, 57,991 96 c1
Cienfuegos, Bahía de, Cuba 96 c2
Cieplice Śląskie Zdrój, Pol., 13,800 127 A3
Cieszanów, Pol., 1,278 127 E3
Cieszyn, Pol., 23,000* 127 C4
Cieza, Sp., 22,438 122 E3
Çiftlik, Turk., 3,900 137 a1
Cifuentes, Cuba, 2,298 96 d1
Cifuentes, Sp., 1,574 122 D2
Cigánd, Hung., 5,217 126 E2
Cigliano, It., 4,279 122 b5
Cihuatlán, Mex., 4,125 92 D4
Čikola, r., Yug. 125 C3
Çıldır Gölü, Turk. 142 E1
Cilibia, Rum. 128 F2
Cilicia, reg., Turk. 142 C2
Cilieni, Rum. 128 E3
Cîlnicu, Rum. 128 D2
Cilo Dağı, Turk. 142 F2
Cilycwm, U.K. 113 E5
Cima, Calif. 82 F5
Cimarron, Kans., 1,115 75 E6
Cimarron, N. Mex., 997 79 C3
Cimarron, co., Okla., 4,496 76 A1
Cimarron, r., U.S. 52 F3
Cimarron, r., N. Mex. 79 C3
Cimone, Monte, It. 123 C2
Cîmpeni, Rum. 128 D1
Cîmpia Turzii, Rum., 11,514 128 D1
Cîmpina, Rum., 18,680 128 E2
Cîmpulung, Rum., 18,880 128 E2
Cîmpulung Moldovenesc, Rum., 13,627 128 E1
Cinaruco, r., Ven. 100 F4
Cinca, r., Sp. 122 F1
Cincer, mt., Yug. 125 C3
Cincinnati, Ind. 70 C3
Cincinnati, Iowa, 583 72 D4
Cincinnati, Ohio, 502,550 70 E3
Cincinnatus, N.Y. 59 J6
Cinco Balas, Cayo, Cuba 96 d2
Cincu, Rum. 128 E2
Cinderford, U.K., 6,918 114 D7
Cîndeşti, Rum. 128 F2
Çine, Turk., 6,504 142 B2
Cinebar, Wash. 80 B2
Cinema, Br. Col., Can. 42 G3
Ciney, Belg., 6,787 115 D4
Cingoli, It., 14,076 123 D3
Cinisello Balsamo, It., 30,184 122 c5
Cínovec, Czech. 126 c6
Cintalapa, Mex., 7,879 93 G5
Cinto, Mt., Fr. 116 r17
Cioara-Doiceşti, Rum. 128 F2
Ciolanu, Rum. 128 E2
Ciorani, Rum. 128 F2
Čiovo, i., Yug. 125 C3
Cipolletti, Arg., 15,000* 105 B5
Circasia, Col. 101 d15
Circle, Alaska, 41 85 J2
Circle, Mont., 1,117 81 G2
Circle City, Ariz. 78 B5
Circle Springs, Alaska 85 H2
Circleville, Ohio, 11,059 70 G3
Circleville, Utah, 478 78 B2
Circleville, W. Va. 62 E4
Cirencester, U.K., 11,834 113 F6
Cirey-sur-Vezouze, Fr., 2,500 116 d9
Ciriè, It., 10,076 123 A2
Cîrlibaba, Rum. 128 E1
Cirò Marina, It., 9,303 123 F5
Cirque Mtn., Newf., Can. 45 N2
Cisa, Passo della, It. 123 C2
Cisco, Ill., 398 68 D3
Cisco, Tex., 4,499 77 O3
Cisco, Utah 78 D2
Cislău, Rum. 128 F2
Cisna, Pol. 127 E4
Cisnădie, Rum., 12,246 128 E2
Cisne, Ill., 615 68 D5
Cisne, Is. de = Swan Is.
Cisneros, Col. 100 C4
Cispus, r., Wash. 80 C2
Cissna Park, Ill., 803 68 E3
Cistern, Tex. 77 P5
Cisterna di Latina, It., 17,345 123 b8
Cistierna, Sp., 6,667 122 C1
Citadelle, site, Haiti 96 k6
Citalá, El Salv. 94 d9
Citala, Mex., 1,009 93 a9
Citlaltepec, Mex., 2,358 93 f8
Citlaltépetl, mtn., Mex. 93 F4
Citra, Fla. 65 G3
Citra, Okla. 76 G3
Citron, Fr. Guiana 101 O5
Citronelle, Ala., 1,918 64 A4
Citrus, Calif. 82 b7
Citrus, co., Fla., 9,268 65 G4
Citrusdal, S. Af., 1,643 164 C7
Citrus Heights, Calif. 82 b7
Citrus Park, Fla. 65 c11
Città di Castello, It., 38,232 123 D3
Cittanova, It., 14,233 123 F5
City Mills (part of Norfolk), Mass. 57 L4
City of Refuge Nat. Hist. Pk., Hawaii 84 E4
City Park, Ill., 1,133 68 C4
City Point, Wis. 66 C4
Ciudad Altamirano, Mex., 5,960 93 E4
Ciudad Arce, El Salv., 4,625 94 d10
Ciudad Bolívar, Ven., 56,032 101 J3
Ciudad Bolivia, Ven., 1,719 100 E3
Ciudad Cuauhtémoc, Mex. 93 H5
Ciudad Darío, Nic., 2,592 94 D4
Ciudad del Maíz, Mex., 4,767 93 F3
Ciudadela, Sp., 12,228 122 h8
Ciudad Guerrero, Mex., 2,719 92 D2
Ciudad Guzmán, Mex., 30,971 92 D4
Ciudad Hidalgo, Chis., Mex., 3,427 93 G5
Ciudad Hidalgo, Micho., Mex., 17,060 93 E4
Ciudad Juárez, Mex., 261,683 92 D1
Ciudad Madero, Mex., 53,526 93 F3
Ciudad Mante, Mex., 22,701 93 F3
Ciudad Miguel Alemán, Mex. 93 F2
Ciudad Obregón, Mex., 68,010 92 C2
Ciudad Piar, Ven., 4,593 101 J4
Ciudad Real, Sp., 37,081 122 C3
Ciudad-Rodrigo, Sp., 12,981 122 B2
Ciudad Serdán, Mex., 9,584 93 F4
Ciudad Trujillo = Santo Domingo
Ciudad Victoria, Mex., 50,727 93 F3
Cividale del Friuli, It., 11,096 123 D1
Civita Castellana, It., 13,420 123 D3
Civitavecchia, It., 38,408 123 C3
Civray, Fr., 3,026 117 D3
Çivril, Turk., 5,357 142 B2
Cizre, Turk., 6,656 142 E2
Clachan, U.K. 112 a7
Clachan, U.K. 112 D4
Clackamas, co., Oreg., 113,038 80 B3
Clackamas, r., Oreg. 80 B3
Clackmannan, co., U.K., 41,391 112 E3
Clackmannan, U.K. 112 c7
Clacton, U.K., 27,572 113 G6
Cladich, U.K. 112 a7
Claflin, Kans., 891 75 G5
Claggettsville, Md. 62 a7
Claiborne, parish, La., 19,407 73 B5
Claiborne, Md. 62 H4
Claiborne, co., Miss., 10,845 73 D6
Claiborne, co., Tenn., 19,067 71 H5
Clair, N.B., Can. 47 R10
Clair, L., Qué., Can. 47 L1
Claire, L., Alta., Can. 42 K1
Claire City, S. Dak., 86 74 D3
Clairefontaine, Fr. 116 f12
Clairmont, Alta., Can. 42 H2
Clairton, Pa., 18,389 60 C5
Clairvaux, Fr., 1,324 117 F3
Clallam, co., Wash., 30,022 80 B1
Clallam Bay, Wash. 80 A1
Clam, r., Mass. 56 D4
Clam, r., Mich. 67 H4
Clam, r., Wis. 66 A3
Clamart, Fr., 48,290 116 h11
Clamecy, Fr., 5,760 117 E3
Clam Falls, Wis. 66 A3
Clam Gulch, Alaska, 75 85 F3
Clam Lake, Wis. 66 C2
Clam L., Wis. 66 A3
Clan Alpine Mts., Nev. 82
Clandeboye, Man., Can. 43 h9
Clanfield, U.K., 1,464 113 m13
Clanton, Ala., 5,683 64 C3
Clanwilliam, S. Af., 2,214 164 C7
Clapham, U.K., 3,284 114 H6
Clapperton I., Ont., Can. 46 B2
Clara, Ire., 2,628 113 C5
Clara, Miss. 73 G6
Clara, Mo. 72 E7
Clara City, Minn., 1,358 74 E3
Clara I., Burma 146 B5
Claraville, Calif. 82 D5
Clare, N.S.W., Austl. 173 d9
Clare, S. Austl., Austl., 1,579 172 E5
Clare, co., Ire., 77,176 113 B5
Clare, Iowa, 245 72 C2
Clare, co., Mich., 11,647 67 J5
Clare, Mich., 2,442 67 J5
Clare, r., Ire. 113 B5
Clare I., Ire. 113 A5
Claremont, Ont., Can. 46 E4
Claremont, Jam., 1,417 96 p8
Claremont, Calif., 12,633 83 i15
Claremont, Ill., 223 68 D5
Claremont, N.H., 13,563 54 C5
Claremont, N.C., 728 63 C2
Claremont, S. Dak., 247 74 D3
Claremont, Va., 377 62 H5
Claremore, Okla., 6,639 76 H1
Claremorris, Ire., 1,512 113 B5
Clarence, Ill. 68 E3
Clarence, Iowa, 859 72 F3
Clarence, La., 286 73 C6
Clarence, Mo., 1,103 72 E5
Clarence, N.Y., 1,456 58 C6
Clarence, Pa. 60 G3
Clarence, r., N.Z. 175 g6
Clarence Center, N.Y. 58 m18
Clarence Str., Austl. 172 D1
Clarendon, Ark., 2,564 73 D3
Clarendon, Mich. 67 J6
Clarendon, N.Y. 58 D5
Clarendon, N.C. 63 F3
Clarendon, Pa., 825 60 D2
Clarendon, co., S.C., 29,490 63 D4
Clarendon, Tex., 2,172 76 N2
Clarendon, Vt. 54 B4
Clarendon, r., Vt. 54 A4
Clarendon Hills, Ill., 5,885 69 c9
Clarendon L., Ont., Can. 46 H4
Clarens, Switz. 124 A2
Clarenville, Newf., Can., 1,513 45 Q5
Claresholm, Alta., Can., 2,049 42 J4
Clareville, Tex. 77 P5
Claridge, Pa., 1,160* 60 C5
Clarie Coast, Ant. 180 U6
Clarin, Phil., 1,504 153 f12
Clarinda, Iowa, 4,903 72 C4
Clarington, Ohio, 394 70 J3
Clarington, Pa. 60 D3
Clarion, Iowa, 3,232 72 D2
Clarion, Mich. 67 J3
Clarion, co., Pa., 37,408 60 D3
Clarion, Pa., 4,958 60 D3
Clarion, r., Pa. 60 D3
Clarión, I., Mex. 92 b7
Clarion Fracture Zone, Pac. Oc. 169 H2
Clarissa, Minn., 569 74 E2
Clarita, Okla. 76 G3
Clark, co., Ark., 20,950 73 B3
Clark, Colo. 79 B1
Clark, co., Idaho, 915 81 C3
Clark, co., Ill., 16,546 68 E4
Clark, co., Ind., 62,795 70 D4
Clark, co., Kans., 3,396 75 F6
Clark, co., Ky., 21,075 71 G4
Clark, co., Mo., 8,725 72 F4
Clark, Mo., 260 72 E5
Clark, co., Nev., 127,016 83 C4
Clark, co., Ohio, 131,440 70 F3
Clark, Ohio 70 H2
Clark, co., S. Dak., 7,134 74 D3
Clark, S. Dak., 1,484 74 D3
Clark, co., Wash., 93,809 80 B3
Clark, co., Wis., 31,527 66 C4
Clark, L., Alaska 85 F3
Clark, Pt., Ont., Can. 46 C4
Clark Center, Ill. 68 E4
Clarkdale, Ariz., 1,095 78 B4
Clarkdale, Ga. 64 f9
Clarke, co., Ala., 25,738 64 B4
Clarke, co., Ga., 45,363 64 F2
Clarke, co., Iowa, 8,222 72 D4
Clarke, co., Miss., 16,493 73 G5
Clarke, co., Va., 7,942 62 F3
Clarke City, Qué., Can. 45 M5
Clarkedale, Ark. 73 E2
Clarke I., Austl. 173 f13
Clarke L., Sask., Can. 43 C3
Clarke's Beach, Newf., Can. 45 b10
Clarkesville, Ga., 1,352 64 F1
Clarkfield, Minn., 1,100 74 D3
Clark Fork, Idaho, 452 81 B1
Clark Fk., Idaho-Mont. 81 B2
Clark Fk., Mont.-Wyo. 81 E3
Clark Hill Res., Ga.-S.C. 63 B4
Clarkia, Idaho 81 A2
Clarke L., Mich. 66 D2
Clarkleigh, Man., Can. 43 g9
Clark Mills, N.Y., 1,148 59 t26
Clarkrange, Tenn. 71 G5
Clarks, La., 940 73 C5
Clarks, Nebr., 439 75 H2
Clarks, E. Fk., r., Ky. 71 C5
Clarksboro, N.J. 60 f12
Clarksburg, Ont., Can. 46 D4
Clarksburg, Calif. 82 a8
Clarksburg, Ill. 68 D4
Clarksburg, Md., 357 72 E6
Clarksburg, N.J. 61 C3
Clarksburg, Ohio, 438 70 F3
Clarksburg, W. Va., 28,112 62 D3
Clarks Corner (part of Hampton), Conn. 56 H5
Clarksdale, Miss., 21,105 73 E3
Clarksdale, Mo., 242 72 C5
Clarks Falls (part of N. Stonington), Conn. 57 J7
Clarks Green, Pa., 1,256 61 o15
Clark's Harbour, N.S., Can. 47 T12
Clarkson, Ont., Can., 1,450 46 E5
Clarkson, Ky., 645 71 E4
Clarkson, Nebr., 797 75 H2
Clarkson, N.Y. 58 E5
Clarkson, Mt., Austl. 172 C2
Clarkson Valley, Alta., Can. 42 H2
Clarks Point, Alaska, 138 85 E4
Clarks Station, Nev. 83 B3
Clarks Summit, Pa., 3,693 61 L3
Clarkston, U.K. 112 b8
Clarkston, Ga., 1,524 64 g9
Clarkston, Mich., 769 67 K6
Clarkston, Utah, 490 78 B1
Clarkston, Wash., 6,209 80 E2
Clarks Town, Jam., 1,543 96 p8
Clarksville, Ark., 3,919 73 B2
Clarksville (part of Stonington), Conn. 57 J7
Clarksville, Fla. 65 D2
Clarksville, Ind., 8,088 70 D4
Clarksville, Iowa, 1,328 72 E2
Clarksville, Md. 62 G3
Clarksville, Mich., 371 67 H6
Clarksville, Mo., 638 72 G5
Clarksville, N.Y. 59 v29
Clarksville, Ohio, 583 70 F3
Clarksville, Pa., 332 60 A3
Clarksville, Tenn., 22,021 71 D5
Clarksville, Tex., 3,851 77 Q3
Clarksville, Va., 1,530 62 F6
Clarkton, Mo., 1,049 72 G8
Clarkton, N.C., 662 63 F3
Clarkville, Colo. 79 D1
Claro, Switz. 124 D2
Claro, r., Braz. 103 F5
Claro, r., Chile 104 f15
Claro, r., Mex. 93 f8
Claryville, N.Y. 59 L8
Clatonia, Nebr., 203 75 J3
Clatskanie, Oreg., 797 80 B2
Clatsop, co., Oreg., 27,380 80 B2
Claud, N. Mex. 79 D4
Claude, Tex., 895 76 N2
Claudell, Kans. 75 G4
Cláudio, Braz., 3,743 103 d17
Claughton, U.K. 114 C3
Claunch, N. Mex. 79 B4
Clausen, F.R.Ger., 1,560 119 D6
Clausthal-Zellerfeld, F.R.Ger., 14,963 118 C3
Claver, Phil., 2,528 153 C3
Claveria, Phil., 3,175 153 B1
Claveria, Phil., 1,360 153 B2
Claverley, U.K., 1,304 114 D5
Clawit, Mt., Phil. 153 b6
Clawson, Mich., 14,795 67 f14
Clawson, Utah 78 C2
Claxton, Ga., 2,672 64 H3
Clay, co., Ala., 12,400 64 D2
Clay, co., Ark., 21,258 73 E1
Clay, co., Fla., 19,535 65 H3
Clay, co., Ga., 4,551 64 E4
Clay, co., Ill., 15,815 68 D5
Clay, co., Ind., 24,207 70 B3
Clay, co., Iowa, 18,504 72 B1
Clay, co., Kans., 10,675 75 H4
Clay, co., Ky., 20,748 71 H4
Clay, Ky., 1,343 71 D4
Clay, co., Minn., 39,080 74 D2
Clay, co., Miss., 18,933 73 G4
Clay, co., Mo., 87,474 72 C5
Clay, co., Nebr., 8,717 75 H3
Clay, N.Y. 59 r23
Clay, co., N.C., 5,526 63 b7
Clay, co., S. Dak., 10,810 74 D4
Clay, co., Tenn., 7,289 71 F5
Clay, co., Tex., 8,351 77 O3
Clay, co., W. Va., 11,942 62 C4
Clay, W. Va., 486 62 C4
Clay Center, Kans., 4,613 75 H4
Clay Center, Nebr., 792 75 H3
Clay Center, Ohio, 446 70 F1
Clay City, Ill., 1,144 68 D5
Clay City, Ind., 950 70 B3
Clay City, Ky., 764 71 G4
Claycomo, Mo., 1,423 75 b7
Clay Creek, S. Dak. 75 H1
Clay Cross, U.K., 9,163 114 F4
Claye-Souilly, Fr., 3,220 116 i11
Clayhurst, Br. Col., Can. 42 H2
Claymont, Del. 62 J3
Claypole, U.K. 114 G4
Claypool, Ariz., 2,505 78 C5
Claypool, Ind., 452 70 D1
Claysburg, Pa., 1,439 60 F5
Clay Springs, Ariz. 78 C4
Claysville, Pa., 1,063 60 B5
Clayton, U.K., 7,103 114 E3
Clayton, Ala., 1,313 64 D4
Clayton, Calif. 83 f12
Clayton, Del., 1,028 62 J3
Clayton, co., Ga., 46,365 64 E2
Clayton, Ga., 1,507 64 F1
Clayton, Idaho 81 B3
Clayton, Ill., 774 68 B3
Clayton, Ind., 653 70 C3
Clayton, co., Iowa, 21,962 72 F2
Clayton, Iowa, 130 72 F2

214 · Colombey—Corigliano Calabro

Colombey-les-Deux-Églises, Fr. 117 F2
Colombia, ctry., 17,484,508 100
Colombia, Col. 100 C6
Colombian Basin, Caribbean Sea 108 G6
Colombier, Qué., Can. 47 R9
Colombier, Pte., St-Barthélemy 97 7
Colombo, Cey., 510,947 145 F9
Colome, S. Dak., 398 74 C4
Colón, Arg., 15,000* 105 a11
Colón, Arg., 10,478 105 b11
Colón, Cuba, 15,755 96 c1
Colón, Mex., 2,716 93 F4
Colón, Pan., 59,598 94 G6
Colon, Phil., 2,610 153 C4
Colon, Mich., 1,055 67 H7
Colon, Nebr., 110 75 J2
Colon, N.C. 63 E2
Colón, Arch. de, Pac. Oc. 104 a7
Colón, Mñas. de, Hond. 94 E3
Colona, Colo. 79 B2
Colonarie, r., St. Vinc. 97 19
Colonelganj, India, 9,670 144 c12
Coloneşti, Rum. 128 E2
Colonia, Ponape 176 29
Colonia Arrue, Urug. 105 b12
Colonia Catriel, Arg., 1,000* 105 B5
Colonia Chirgua, Ven. 101 a11
Colonia del Sacramento, Urug., 10,000* 105 b12
Colonial Beach, Va., 1,769 62 G4
Colônia Leopoldina, Braz., 3,295 103 b15
Colonial Heights, Va., 9,587 62 G5
Colonial Village, N.Y. 58 k18
Colonia Ortega, Mex. 92 E3
Colonias, N. Mex. 79 C4
Colonia Sta. Ana, Arg., 12,000* 105 B3
Colonia Tovar, Ven. 101 b11
Colonie, N.Y., 6,992 59 N6
Colonsay, Sask., Can. 43 C4
Colonsay, i., U.K. 112 C3
Colony, Kans., 419 75 K5
Colony, Okla. 76 E2
Colorado, C. R. 94 F5
Colorado, st., U.S., 1,949,000* 79
Colorado, co., Tex., 18,463 77 P5
Colorado, r., Arg. 105 C5
Colorado, r., Chile 104 g15
Colorado, r., U.S. 52 D4
Colorado, r., Tex. 77 O4
Colorado, Beals Br., r., Tex. 77 N3
Colorado City, Ariz. 78 B3
Colorado City, Tex., 6,457 77 N3
Colorado Nat. Mon., Colo. 79 A2
Colorado Plateau, U.S. 52 D3
Colorado R. Aqueduct, Calif. 82 F6
Colorado Springs, Colo., 70,194 79 C2
Colorno, It., 7,317 122 d6
Colotlán, Mex., 6,281 92 E3
Colotlán, r., Mex. 92 E3
Colp, Ill., 201 68 C6
Colquechaca, Bol., 1,584 102 c11
Colquitt, co., Ga., 34,048 64 F4
Colquitt, Ga., 1,556 64 E4
Colquitt, La. 73 C5
Colrain, Mass., 1,426(T) 56 F2
Colsterworth, U.K. 114 G5
Colstrip, Mont. 81 F3
Colt, Ark., 394 73 E2
Coltauco, Chile, 1,096 104 f14
Colt Hill, U.K. 113 D4
Colţii de Jos, Rum. 128 F2
Colton, Calif., 18,666 83 k15
Colton, Md. 62 H4
Colton, Nebr. 75 C2
Colton, N.Y. 59 K2
Colton, Ohio 70 F1
Colton, Oreg. 80 B3
Colton, S. Dak., 593 74 D4
Colton, Wash., 253 80 E2
Colts Neck, N.J. 58 c15
Coltsville (part of Pittsfield), Mass. 56 D3
Columbia, Ala., 783 64 D4
Columbia, co., Ark., 26,400 73 B4
Columbia, Calif. 82 C3
Columbia, Conn., 2,163(T) 56 G6
Columbia, co., Fla., 20,077 65 G2
Columbia, co., Ga., 13,423 64 G2
Columbia, Ill., 3,174 68 B5
Columbia, Ky., 2,255 71 F4
Columbia, La., 1,021 73 C5
Columbia, Md. 62 b8
Columbia, Miss., 7,117 73 F6
Columbia, Mo., 36,650 72 E6
Columbia, N.J. 61 A2
Columbia, co., N.Y., 47,322 59 N7
Columbia, N.C., 1,099 63 H2
Columbia, co., Oreg., 22,379 80 B3
Columbia, co., Pa., 53,489 61 K3
Columbia, Pa., 12,075 60 J5
Columbia, S.C., 97,433 63 D4
Columbia, S. Dak., 272 74 C3
Columbia, Tenn., 17,624 71 D6
Columbia, Utah 78 C2
Columbia, Va., 86 62 F5
Columbia, co., Wash., 4,569 80 D2
Columbia, co., Wis., 36,708 66 D5
Columbia, r., Can.-U.S. 40 F8
Columbia, Mt., Alta., Can. 42 H3
Columbia, Sa., Mex. 92 B2
Columbia Bridge, N.H. 54 D2
Columbia City, Ind., 4,803 70 D1
Columbia City, Oreg., 423 80 B3
Columbia Falls, Me. 55 E4
Columbia Falls, Mont., 2,132 81 C1
Columbia Heights, Minn., 17,533 74 c5
Columbia Icefield, Alta.-Br. Col., Can. 42 H3
Columbiana, Ala., 2,264 64 C2
Columbiana, co., Ohio, 107,004 70 J2
Columbiana, Ohio, 4,164 70 J2
Columbia Plat., U.S. 50 C1
Columbia Seamount, Atl. Oc. 109 K8
Columbia Station, Ohio 70 c9
Columbiaville, Mich., 878 67 K5
Columbus, Ga., 116,779 64 E3
Columbus, Ill., 109 68 A4
Columbus, Ind., 20,778 70 C3
Columbus, Kans., 3,395 75 L6
Columbus, Ky., 357 71 B5
Columbus, Mich. 67 L6
Columbus, Miss., 24,771 73 G4
Columbus, Mont., 1,281 81 E3
Columbus, Nebr., 12,476 75 H2
Columbus, N.J. 61 B3
Columbus, N. Mex., 307 79 B6
Columbus, co., N.C., 48,973 63 F3
Columbus, N.C., 725 63 B2
Columbus, N. Dak., 672 74 A1
Columbus, Ohio, 471,316 70 F3
Columbus, Pa. 60 C2
Columbus, Tex., 3,656 77 P5
Columbus, Wis., 3,467 66 D5
Columbus City, Iowa, 327 72 F3
Columbus Grove, Ohio, 2,104 70 F2
Columbus Junction, Iowa, 1,016 72 F3
Columbus Salt Marsh, Nev. 83 B3
Colusa, co., Calif., 12,075 82 B3
Colusa, Calif., 3,518 82 B3
Colusa, Ill. 68 A3
Colver, Pa., 1,261 60 E4
Colville, Wash., 3,806 80 E1
Colville, r., Alaska 85 F1
Colville, r., Wash. 80 E1
Colville, L., Wash. 80 D2
Colville Chan., N.Z. 175 g5
Colville L., N.W.T., Can. 40 D4
Colville Mts., N.W.T., Can. 38 F4
Colwell, Iowa, 119 72 E1
Colwich, U.K., 1,657 114 D5
Colwich, Kans., 703 75 H6
Colwood, Br. Col., Can. 42 c7
Colwyn Bay, U.K., 23,201 113 E5
Comacchio, It., 16,883 123 D2
Comacchio, Valli di, lag., It. 123 D2
Comachuén, Mex., 1,178 93 b10
Comal, co., Tex., 19,844 77 O5
Comala, Mex., 4,943 92 D4
Comalapa, Guat., 9,265 94 B3
Comalcalco, Mex., 7,704 93 G4
Comalle, Chile 104 f14
Comana, Rum. 128 F2
Comanche, co., Kans., 3,271 75 F6
Comanche, co., Okla., 90,803 76 E3
Comanche, Okla., 2,082 76 F3
Comanche, co., Tex., 11,865 77 O3
Comanche, Tex., 3,415 77 O4
Comanche Cr., Tex. 77 M4
Comanche Pk., Colo. 79 C1
Comanche Pk., Tex. 76 d10
Comandante Fontana, Arg., 6,000* 105 C3
Comandante Luis Piedrabuena, Arg., 1,350* 105 A7
Comăneşti, Rum., 12,392 128 F1
Co Manh, N. Viet. 147 i8
Comanja, Mex., 1,049 93 c10
Comanjilla, Mex. 93 c8
Coma Pedrosa, pk., Andorra 122 g7
Comarapa, Bol., 4,597 102 C5
Comayagua, Hond., 7,300 94 D3
Comayagua, Mñas. de, Hond. 94 ·
Combahee, r., S.C. 63 D5
Combarbalá, Chile, 2,640 105 A4
Combe Martin, U.K., 2,228 113 D6
Comber, U.K., 3,980 113 D4
Combermere, Ont., Can. 46 G3
Combined Locks, Wis., 1,421 66 E4
Comblain-au-Pont, Belg., 3,471 115 D4
Combourg, Fr., 4,502 117 C2
Combronde, Fr., 1,559 117 E4
Combs, Ark. 73 B2
Combs-la-Ville, Fr., 4,692 116 i12
Come by Chance, Newf., Can. 45 a10
Comer, Ala. 64 D3
Comer, Ga., 882 64 F1
Comerío, P.R., 5,232 96 t10
Comet, Austl. 173 G3
Comfort, N.C. 63 G3
Comfort, Tex. 77 O5
Comfrey, Minn., 616 74 E3
Comilla, Pak., 54,504 145 J5
Comines, Belg., 8,449 115 A4
Comines, Fr., 9,040 116 a6
Comino, i., Malta 123 E6
Comins, Mich. 67 J4
Comiso, It., 25,407 123 E6
Comitán, Mex., 15,378 93 H5
Comloşu Mare, Rum. 128 C2
Commack, N.Y., 9,613 59 O10
Commander Is.=Komandorskiye O-va.
Commentry, Fr., 9,711 117 E3
Commerce, Ga., 3,551 64 F1
Commerce, Okla., 2,378 76 H1
Commerce, Tex., 5,789 77 P3
Commerce Town, Colo., 8,970 79 c8
Commercial Point, Ohio, 308 70 G3
Commercy, Fr., 7,918 117 F2
Committee Bay, N.W.T., Can. 40 M4
Commodore, Pa. 60 D4
Commonwealth Terr., Austl. 173 G5
Commugny, Switz. 124 A2
Como, It., 76,914 123 B2
Como, Miss., 789 73 F3
Como, N.C. 63 H1
Como, Tex., 300 77 Q3
Como, Lago di, It. 123 B2
Como, L., Minn. 74 c6
Comodoro Py, Arg., 2,857 105 a12
Comodoro Rivadavia, Arg., 39,867 105 B7
Comoé, r., Iv. Coast 162 D4
Como-Est, Qué., Can. 47 K3
Comondú, Mex. 92 B2
Comonfort, Mex., 8,575 93 d9
Comores, Arch. des, Ind. Oc., 212,000* 165 G3
Comorin, C., India 145 E9
Comoro Is=Comores, Arch. des
Comox, Br. Col., Can., 1,656 42 F4
Compans, Fr. 116 i11
Compass Lake, Fla. 65 D2
Compensating Res., Conn. 56 E5
Competition, Mo. 72 E7
Compiègne, Fr., 28,415 117 E2
Compo Beach (part of Westport), Conn. 56 C8
Compostela, Mex., 7,483 92 D4
Compostela, Phil., 2,290 153 f11
Comps, Fr. 116 m13
Comptche, Calif. 82 B3
Compton, Qué., Can. 47 N3
Compton, Berks., Eng., U.K., 1,114 114 F7
Compton, Hants., Eng., U.K., 1,273 113 k12
Compton, Sussex, Eng., U.K. 113 m13
Compton, Ark. 73 B1
Compton, Calif., 71,812 83 h16
Compton, Ill., 366 68 C2
Compud, Ec. 104 c11
Comrie, U.K. 112 D3
Comstock, Mich. 67 H6
Comstock, Minn., 138 74 D2
Comstock, Nebr., 235 75 F2
Comstock, N.Y. 59 N5
Comstock, Tex. 77 N5
Comstock, Wis. 66 B3
Comstock Park, Mich. 67 H5
Comté, r., Fr. Guiana 101 O5
Cona, It., 5,210 122 f5
Conakry, Guin., 120,000 162 B4
Conanicut I., R.I. 57 L6
Cona Niyeu, Arg. 105 B6
Conant, Ill. 68 C5
Conargo, Austl. 173 e10
Conasauga, r., Ga.-Tenn. 64 E1
Conca, Fr., 1,087 116 r18
Concan, Tex. 77 O5
Concarán, Arg., 2,295 105 B4
Concarneau, Fr., 16,271 116 A3
Conceição de Ipanema, Braz., 1,502 103 f17
Conceição de Macabu, Braz., 3,560 103 f18
Conceição do Araguaia, Braz., 2,332 103 F3
Conceição do Castelo, Braz. 103 f17
Concepción, Arg., 57,748 105 B3
Concepción, Arg., 6,000* 105 D3
Concepción, Bol., 5,653 102 D5
Concepción, Chile, 148,078 105 A5
Concepción, Col. 100 C7
Concepción, Col. 100 D4
Concepción, Col. 101 d13
Concepción, Hond. 94 d9
Concepción, Para., 20,642 105 D2
Concepción, Peru, 4,247 104 C4
Concepcion, Phil. 153 A2
Concepcion, Phil., 3,957 153 b7
Concepcion, Phil., 9,123 153 e11
Concepción, B., Mex. 92 B2
Concepción, Lag., Bol. 102 D5
Concepción, P., Mex. 92 C2
Concepción, R. de la, Mex. 92 B1
Concepción, Vol., Nic. 94 E5
Concepción de Ataco, El. Salv., 3,754 94 c10
Concepción de Buenos Aires, Mex., 3,831 93 a10
Concepción del Oro, Mex., 8,379 92 E3
Concepción del Uruguay, Arg., 38,500* 105 D4
Conception, Pt., Calif. 82 C5
Conception Bay, Newf., Can. 45 c10
Conception Junction, Mo., 253 72 C4
Conchal, Col. 101 e14
Conchalí, Chile, 150,462 105 A4
Conchas, r., N. Mex. 79 C4
Conchas Dam, N. Mex. 79 C4
Conchas Res., N. Mex. 79 C4
Conches, Fr., 3,028 117 D2
Conchillas, Urug., 2,000* 105 c12
Concho, Ariz. 78 D4
Concho, Okla. 76 F2
Concho, co., Tex., 3,672 77 O4
Concho, r., Tex. 77 N4
Conchos, r., Mex. 92 D2
Conch Pt., Grand Cayman 97 3
Conchucos, Peru, 2,259 104 B4
Concise, Switz. 124 A2
Concón, Chile, 5,381 104 f12
Conconully, Wash., 108 80 D1
Concord, Ont., Can., 1,061 46 d13
Concord, Ark. 73 D2
Concord, Calif., 36,208 83 f12
Concord, Ga., 333 64 g12
Concord, Ill., 210 68 B4
Concord, Ind. 70 C2
Concord, Mass., 3,188; 12,517(T) 57 L3
Concord, Mich., 990 67 J6
Concord, Nebr., 150 75 J1
Concord, N.H., 28,991 54 D5
Concord, N.C., 17,799 63 D2
Concord, Tex. 77 P4
Concord, Vt. 54 D3
Concord, Va. 62 E5
Concord, Wis. 66 E5
Concord, r., Mass. 57 L2
Concordia, Arg., 78,000* 105 D4
Concordia, Col. 100 C4
Concordia, Hond. 94 D3
Concordia, Mex., 4,099 92 D3
Concordia, Peru 104 C3
Concordia, Peru 104 D6
Concordia, Phil. 153 a7
Concordia, Kans., 7,022 75 H4
Concordia, Ky. 71 E3
Concordia, parish, La., 20,467 73 D6
Concordia, Mo., 1,471 72 D6
Concordia Bay, St. Eustatius 97 6
Concordville, Pa. 60 e12
Concrete, N. Dak. 74 C1
Concrete, Wash., 840 80 C1
Con Cuong, N. Viet. 146 D3
Condat-en-Féniers, Fr., 1,809 117 E4
Conde, Braz., 4,190 103 J4
Conde, S. Dak., 388 74 C3
Condé-sur-Noireau, Fr., 6,324 117 C2
Condit, Ohio 70 G2
Condobolin, Austl., 2,840 173 G5
Condom, Fr., 7,116 117 D5
Condon, Oreg., 1,149 80 C3
Condoriri, Pico, Bol. 102 b10
Condoto, Col. 100 B5
Condover, U.K., 4,140 114 C5
Condrieu, Fr., 3,015 116 p16
Coñecito, Mex. 93 e9
Conecuh, co., Ala., 17,762 64 B4
Conecuh, r., Ala.-Fla. 64 C4
Conegliano, It., 21,696 123 D2
Conejos, co., Colo., 8,428 79 B3
Conejos, Colo. 79 B3
Conejos, r., Colo. 79 B3
Conejos Mesa, N. Mex. 79 C4
Conemaugh, r., Pa. 60 D5
Cone Mtn., Colo. 79 C3
Conesa, Arg., 3,500* 105 a11
Conestee, S.C. 63 B3
Conestoga Cr., Pa. 61 K6
Conestogo, Ont., Can. 46 b13
Conestogo, r., Ont., Can. 46 D5
Conestogo L., Ont., Can. 46 a13
Conesus, N.Y. 58 E6
Conesus Cr., N.Y. 58 n21
Conesus L., N.Y. 58 E6
Conesville, Iowa, 248 72 F3
Conesville, Ohio, 451 70 H2
Conetoe, N.C., 147 63 G2
Conewago Cr., Pa. 60 J5
Conewango, N.Y. 58 C7
Conewango Cr., N.Y.-Pa. 60 D2
Conewango Valley, N.Y. 58 B7
Coney Island, (part of N.Y.C.), N.Y. 58 d14
Conflans-Ste-Honorine, Fr., 21,978 116 g11
Conflict Group, is., Terr. Papua 174 3
Confluence, Pa., 938 60 D6
Confolens, Fr., 3,074 117 D4
Confusion Ra., Utah 78 B2
Congamond (part of Southwick), Mass. 56 E4
Congamond Lakes, Conn.-Mass. 56 F4
Congaree, r., S.C. 63 D4
Conger, Minn., 215 74 F4
Congers, N.Y. 58 d12
Congleton, U.K., 16,802 113 E5
Congo, Democratic Republic of the, ctry., 15,986,000* 164 C2
Congo, Republic of the, ctry., 826,000* 164 B2
Congo, r., Af. 164 B2
Congo Canyon, Atl. Oc. 109 N7
Congonhas, Braz., 6,969 103 d17
Congresbury, U.K., 1,637 114 C8
Congress, Ariz. 78 B4
Congress, Ohio, 186 70 G2
Conicville, Va. 62 F4
Conifer, Colo. 79 C2
Conifer, N.Y. 59 L3
Coningsby, U.K., 2,629 113 F5
Conisbrough, U.K., 17,596 114 F4
Coniston, Ont., Can., 2,679 46 D2
Coniston, U.K., 1,100 113 E4
Coniston Water, l., U.K. 114 B2
Conjola, Austl. 173 h10
Conklin, Alta., Can. 42 K2
Conklin, Mich. 67 H5
Conklin, N.Y. 59 J7
Conkling, Ky. 71 H4
Conlen, Tex. 76 M1
Conlie, Fr., 1,515 117 D2
Conna, Ire. 113 B5
Connah's Quay, U.K., 8,375 114 B4
Connaught, Ont., Can. 44 G5
Connaught, prov., Ire., 446,221 113 B5
Connaughton, Mt., Austl. 172 C3
Conneaut, Ohio, 10,557 70 J1
Conneaut Cr., Pa. 60 B2
Conneaut Lake, Pa., 700 60 B2
Conneautville, Pa., 1,100 60 B2
Connecticut, st., U.S., 2,830,000* 56
Connecticut, r., U.S. 53 M2
Connell, Wash., 906 80 D2
Connellsville, Pa., 12,814 60 C5
Connersville, Ind., 17,698 70 D3
Connerville, Okla. 76 G3
Connetquot, r., N.Y. 58 g13
Conning Towers, Conn., 3,457 56 H7
Conn L., Ire. 113 B4
Connoquenessing, Pa., 513 60 C4
Connoquenessing Cr., Pa. 60 B4
Connor, Me. 55 E2
Connorsville, Wis. 66 A3
Conococheague Cr., Pa. 60 G6
Conodoguinet Cr., Pa. 60 H5
Conon, r., U.K. 112 D3
Cononaco, Ec. 104 B2
Cononaco, r., Ec. 104 B2
Conover, N.C., 2,281 63 C2
Conover, Wis. 66 D2
Conquest, Sask., Can. 43 C4
Conquest, N.Y. 59 p23
Conquista, Bol., 1,385 102 C4
Conrad, Iowa, 799 72 E2
Conrad, Mont., 2,665 81 D1
Conrath, Wis., 121 66 C3
Conroe, Tex., 9,192 77 Q4
Consandolo, It. 122 e6
Conscripto Bernardi, Arg., 4,500* 105 b10
Consdorf, Lux. 115 E5
Consecon, Ont., Can. 46 G5
Conselheiro Lafaiete, Braz., 29,208 103 H6
Conselheiro Paulino, Braz., 3,800 103 e18
Conselve, It., 7,630 122 e5
Conset Pt., Barb. 97 10
Consett, U.K., 38,927 113 F4
Conshohocken, Pa., 10,259 61 M5
Consolación del Norte, Cuba, 2,254 96 b1
Consolación del Sur, Cuba, 6,146 96 b1
Con Son, i., S. Viet. 146 D5
Consort, Alta., Can. 42 L3
Constable, N.Y. 59 M2
Constableville, N.Y., 439 59 J4
Constance, Ky. 71 h11
Constance, L.=Bodensee
Constant, Morne, Guad. 97 14
Constanţa, Rum., 99,676 128 G2
Constantia, Calif. 82 D3
Constantia, N.Y. 59 H5
Constantina, Sp., 13,488 122 C4
Constantine, Alg., 169,071 160 F1
Constantine, Mich., 1,710 67 H7
Constantine, C., Alaska 85 E4
Constantine Harbor, Alaska 85 e8
Constanza, Dom. Rep., 3,162 96 m6
Constitución, Chile, 9,536 105 A5
Constitución, Urug., 11,500* 105 b10
Constitution, Ga. 64 g10
Consuegra, Sp., 10,572 122 D3
Consul, Sask., Can. 43 B5
Contact, Nev. 83 C2
Contai, India, 22,094 144 f15
Contamana, Peru, 4,821 104 C3
Contarina, It., 10,284 122 f5
Contas, R. das, Braz. 103 J4
Content Keys, Fla. 65 f15
Contern, Lux. 119 A5
Conthil, Fr. 116 c9
Continental, Ariz. 78 C6
Continental, Ohio, 1,147 70 E1
Continental Divide, U.S. 50 E3
Contitlán, Mex. 93 a8
Contoocook, N.H. 54 D5
Contoocook, r., N.H. 54 D6
Contoocook L., N.H. 54 D6
Contoy, I., Mex. 93 J4
Contra Costa, co., Calif., 409,030 82 C4
Contratación, Col. 100 D4
Contrecoeur, Qué., Can., 1,975 47 L3
Contreras, N. Mex. 79 B4
Contres, Fr., 2,775 117 D3
Contrexéville, Fr., 2,864 117 F2
Contumazá, Peru, 2,600 104 B3
Contwoyto L., N.W.T., Can. 40 G4
Conty, Fr., 1,463 117 E2
Convención, Col. 100 D3
Convent, La. 73 E7
Convent Station, N.J. 58 b13
Conversano, It., 18,408 123 F4
Converse, Ind., 1,044 70 D2
Converse, La., 291 73 B6
Converse, Ohio 70 E2
Converse, Tex. 76 b6
Converse, co., Wyo., 6,366 81 G4
Convoy, Ohio, 976 70 E2
Conway, U.K., 11,183 113 E5
Conway, co., Ark., 15,430 73 C2
Conway, Ark., 12,500 77 C2
Conway, Mass. 56 F2
Conway, Mich. 67 J3
Conway, Mo., 500 72 E7
Conway, N.H., 1,143 54 E4
Conway, N.C., 662 63 G1
Conway, Pa., 1,926 60 b7
Conway, S.C., 8,563 63 E4
Conway, Tex. 76 N2
Conway, Wash. 80 B1
Conway, L., Ark. 73 C2
Conway Bay, U.K. 113 D5
Conway L., N.H. 54 E4
Conway Springs, Kans., 1,057 75 H6
Conyers, Ga., 2,881 64 F2
Conyngham, Pa., 1,163 61 K4
Coo, Cascade de, Belg. 115 D4
Coober Pedy, Austl. 172 E4
Cooch Behar, India, 41,922 145 H4
Coodys Bluff, Okla. 76 H1
Cook, Austl. 172 D4
Cook, co., Ga., 11,822 64 F4
Cook, co., Ill., 5,129,725 68 E2
Cook, Ind. 70 B1
Cook, co., Minn., 3,377 74 G2
Cook, Minn., 527 74 F2
Cook, Nebr., 313 75 J3
Cook, Mt., N.Z. 175 f6
Cook, Récif de, N. Caled. 174 h7
Cook B., New Hebr. 174 m7
Cooke, co., Tex., 22,560 77 P3
Cooke City, Mont. 81 E3
Cookeville, Tenn., 7,805 71 F5
Cookham, U.K., 5,481 114 G7
Cookietown, Okla. 76 E3
Cooking L., Alta., Can. 43 c7
Cook Inlet, Alaska 85 F4
Cook I., Christmas Atoll 177 40
Cook Is., Pac. Oc., 21,000* 171 H5
Cooks, Mich. 67 G3
Cooks Corners, Mich. 67 H5
Cooks Falls, N.Y. 59 K8
Cooks Hammock, Fla. 65 F3
Cookshire, Qué., Can., 1,392 47 N3
Cooks Pk., N. Mex. 79 B5
Cook Station, Mo. 72 F7
Cookstown, Ont., Can., 1,205 46 E4
Cookstown, U.K., 4,964 113 C4
Cookstown, N.J. 58 a16
Cook Str., N.Z. 175 g6
Cooksville, Ont., Can., 1,800 46 c13
Cooksville, Ill., 221 68 D3
Cooksville, Md. 62 a7
Cooktown, Austl. 173 F2
Cookville, Vt. 54 C3
Cool, Calif. 82 b7
Coolabah, Austl. 173 G4
Cooladdi, Austl. 173 F4
Coolah, Austl., 1,007 173 G4
Coolamon, Austl., 1,048 173 f10
Coolangatta, Austl., 2,343 173 H4
Cooleemee, N.C., 1,609 63 D2
Coolgardie, Austl. 172 B4
Coolidge, Ariz., 5,012 78 C5
Coolidge, Ga., 679 64 F4
Coolidge, Kans., 117 75 D5
Coolidge, Tex., 913 77 P4
Coolin, Idaho 81 A1
Coolville, Ohio, 443 70 H3
Cooma, Austl., 6,506 173 G5
Coomberdale, Austl. 172 A4
Coonabarabran, Austl., 2,210 173 G4
Coonamble, Austl., 2,910 173 G4
Coonana, Austl. 172 C4
Coon Cr., Calif. 82 b7
Coon Cr., Pa. 60 D3
Coondapoor, India, 17,538 145 D7
Coongoola, Austl. 173 G4
Coonoor, India, 30,690 145 k20
Coon Rapids, Iowa, 1,560 72 C3
Coon Rapids, Minn., 26,412 74 F3
Coon Valley, Wis., 536 66 B5
Cooper, Ky. 71 G5
Cooper, Me. 55 E4
Cooper, co., Mo., 15,448 72 E6
Cooper, Tex., 2,213 77 Q3
Cooper, r., S.C. 63 E4
Cooper, Mt., Austl. 172 a7
Cooper Center, Mich. 67 H6
Cooperdale, Ohio 70 H2
Cooper I., V.I. 97 4
Cooper Landing, Alaska, 88 85 G3
Coopersburg, Pa., 1,800 61 k18
Coopers Cr., Austl. 172 E4
Cooperstown, N.Y., 2,553 59 L6
Cooperstown, N. Dak., 1,424 74 D2
Cooperstown, Pa., 267 60 C2
Coopersville, Mich., 1,584 67 H5
Cooperton, Okla., 106 76 E3
Cooperville, N.Y. 59 N2
Coorabie, Austl. 172 D4
Cooraclare, Ire. 113 B5
Coorong, The, lagoon, Austl. 172 c8
Coorow, Austl. 172 A4
Cooroy, Austl., 1,069 173 H4
Coos, co., N.H., 37,140 54 E2
Coos, co., Oreg., 54,955 80 A4
Coos, South Fk., r., Oreg. 80 A4
Coosa, co., Ala., 10,726 64 C3
Coosa, r., Ala.-Ga. 64 C2
Coosawattee, r., Ga. 64 E1
Coosawhatchie, S.C. 63 C5
Coosawhatchie, r., S.C. 63 C5
Coos Bay, Oreg., 7,084 80 A4
Cootamundra, Austl., 5,760 173 G5
Cootehill, Ire., 1,540 113 C4
Cooter, Mo., 477 72 H8
Copacabana, Arg., 3,500* 105 B3
Copacabana, Bol., 13,848 102 a10
Copacabana, Col. 101 d13
Copake, N.Y. 59 N7
Copake Falls, N.Y. 59 O7
Copal, Ec. 104 c11
Copala, Mex., 3,375 93 F5
Copalis Beach, Wash. 80 A2
Copán, Hond., 1,378 94 d9
Copan, Okla., 617 76 G1
Copándaro, Mex., 2,611 93 c10
Copándaro, Mex. 93 d10
Copano Bay, Tex. 77 P5
Cope, Colo. 79 D2
Cope, S.C., 227 63 D4
Copeland, Fla. 65 H7
Copeland, Kans., 247 75 E6
Copeland, Okla. 76 J1
Copeland, Mt., Colo. 79 a7
Copemish, Mich., 232 67 H4
Copenhagen=København
Copenhagen, N.Y., 673 59 J4
Coper, Col. 101 e14
Copertino, It., 18,362 123 G4
Copetown, Ont., Can. 46 b15
Copeville, Tex. 76 g8
Copiague, N.Y., 14,081 58 f14
Copiah, co., Miss., 27,051 73 E6
Copiapó, Chile, 30,123 105 A3
Copiapó, r., Chile 105 A3
Coplay, Pa., 3,701 61 L4
Copley, Austl. 172 E4
Copmanthorpe, U.K. 114 F3
Coporito, Ven. 101 K3
Copparo, It., 23,464 123 C2
Coppell, Ont., Can. 44 F5
Coppell, Tex., 666 76 e9
Copename, r., Sur. 101 M5
Copper, r., Alaska 85 H3
Copperas Cove, Tex., 4,567 77 O4
Copper Basin, Nev. 83 B2
Copper Butte, Wash. 80 D1
Copper Canyon, Nev. 83 B2
Copper Center, Alaska, 151 85 H3
Copper City, Mich., 293 66 E1
Copper Cliff, Ont., Can., 3,580 46 D2
Copperdale, Colo. 79 b8
Copper Harbor, Mich. 66 F1
Copperhill, Tenn., 631 71 G6
Copper Hill, Va. 62 D5
Coppermine, N.W.T., Can. 40 G4
Coppermine, r., N.W.T., Can. 40 F4
Coppermine Mts., N.W.T., Can. 40 F4
Coppermine Pt., Ont., Can. 67 J1
Copper Mine Pt., V.I. 97 4
Copper Mountain, Br. Col., Can., 1,039 42 G4
Copper Queen, Rhod. 164 D4
Copper Ra., Mich. 67 ·
Copper River, Br. Col., Can. 42 E2
Copperton, Utah 78 b9
Copper Valley, Va. 62 D6
Copythorne, U.K., 2,644 113 i13
Coquet, r., U.K. 113 E4
Coquí, Ens. de, Col. 100 B5
Coquilhatville, D.R.Congo, 51,359 164 C1
Coquille, Oreg., 4,730 80 A4
Coquille, r., Oreg. 80 A4
Coquille Hbr., Kusaie 176 31
Coquimbo, Chile, 33,749 105 A4
Cora, Ill. 68 C6
Cora, Kans. 75 G4
Cora, Okla. 76 E1
Corabia, Rum., 11,502 128 E3
Coração de Jesus, Braz., 2,429 103 H5
Coracora, Peru, 6,500 104 C5
Corail, Haiti, 1,313 96 k6
Coral, Mich. 67 H5
Coral, Pa. 60 D4
Coral Bay, V.I. 97 4
Coral Gables, Fla., 34,793 65 J7
Coral Harbour, N.W.T., Can. 41 N5
Coral Sea 170 E5
Coralville, Iowa, 3,390 72 F3
Coralville Res., Iowa 72 F3
Coram, N.Y. 58 h13
Corangamite, L., Austl. 173 d12
Corantijn, r., Sur. 101 M5
Coraopolis, Pa., 9,643 60 B4
Corato, It., 42,576 123 F4
Corbeil, Ont., Can. 46 E2
Corbeil-Essonnes, Fr., 27,038 117 E2
Corbett, N.Y. 59 L7
Corbett, Okla. 76 F3
Corbett Nat. Pk., India 144 b11
Corbie, Fr., 4,772 117 E2
Corbigny, Fr., 2,243 117 E3
Corbin, Kans. 75 H6
Corbin, Ky., 7,119 71 G5
Corbin City, N.J., 271 61 B5
Corbridge, U.K., 2,434 112 g10
Corbu, Rum. 128 G2
Corby, Lincs., Eng., U.K. 114 H5
Corby, Northants., Eng., U.K., 35,938 113 F5
Corcieux, Fr., 1,450 117 G2
Corcoran, Calif., 4,976 82 D4
Corcovado, G., Chile 105 A6
Corcubión, Sp., 1,773 122 A1
Cordaville (part of Southboro), Mass. 57 K3
Cordeiro, Braz., 4,591 103 e18
Cordele, Ga., 10,609 64 F3
Cordelia, Calif. 83 e11
Cordell, Okla., 3,589 76 D2
Corder, Mo., 506 72 D5
Cordero Mine, Nev. 83 B2
Cordes, Fr., 1,201 117 D4
Cordesville, S.C. 63 E4
Córdoba, Arg., 510,739 105 C4
Córdoba, Col. 100 B7
Córdoba, Mex., 47,390 93 F4
Córdoba, Sp., 198,148 122 C4
Córdoba, Sas. de, Arg. 99 C6
Cordon, Phil., 2,971 153 B1
Cordova, Ala., 3,184 64 B2
Cordova, Alaska, 1,128 85 H3
Cordova, Ill., 502 68 B2
Cordova, Md. 62 H4
Cordova, N.C. 63 E3
Cordova, S.C., 209 63 C4
Cordova Bay, Br. Col., Can. 42 c7
Corea, Me. 55 E4
Coredó, Col. 100 B4
Coree South, Austl. 173 e10
Corey, Mich. 67 H7
Coreys, N.Y. 59 M3
Corfe Castle, U.K., 1,381 113 E6
Corfield, Austl. 173 F3
Corfu=Kérkira
Corfu, N.Y., 616 58 D6
Corgémont, Switz., 1,414 124 B1
Corgo, Sp., 7,399 122 B1
Cori, It., 9,450 123 b8
Coria, Sp., 8,204 122 B3
Coria del Río, Sp., 15,083 122 B4
Coricudgy, Mt., Austl. 173 h9
Corigliano Calabro, It., 25,632 123 F5

Corinna—Crnjelovo Donje · 215

Corinna, Me. 55 C4
Corinne, Mich 67 H2
Corinne, Okla. 76 H3
Corinne, Utah, 510 78 B1
Corinne, W. Va., 1,273 62 C5
Corinth, Ont., Can. 46 D6
Corinth, Gr. = Kórinthos
Corinth, Kans. 75 G4
Corinth, Ky., 238 71 G3
Corinth, Miss., 11,453 73 G3
Corinth, N.Y., 3,193 59 N5
Corinth, N. Dak. 74 A1
Corinth, G. of = Korinthiakos Kólpos
Corinth Can. = Korinthou, Dhiórix
Corinth Center, Vt. 54 C3
Corinto, Braz., 12,247 103 G5
Corinto, Col. 100 B6
Corinto, Nic., 6,567 94 D4
Coripata, Bol., 6,483 102 b10
Cork, co., Ire., 336,663 113 B6
Cork, Ire., 114,428 113 B6
Corleone, It., 15,686 123 D6
Çorlu, Turk., 21,956 142 A1
Cormoran Reef, Palau 176 21
Cormorant, Man., Can. 43 E3
Cormorant L., Man., Can. 43 E3
Corn, Okla., 317 76 E2
Cornedo Vicentino, It., 7,914 122 e5
Cornelia, Ga., 2,936 64 F1
Cornelio Procópio, Braz., 17,524 103 F6
Cornelius, N.C., 1,144 63 D2
Cornelius, Oreg., 1,146 80 B3
Cornell, Ill., 524 68 D3
Cornell, Mich. 66 F3
Cornell, Wis., 1,685 66 B3
Corner, Mo. 72 H8
Corner Brook, Newf., Can., 25,004 45 P5
Corner Inlet, Austl. 173 G6
Cornersville, Tenn., 314 71 E6
Cornerville, Ark. 73 D4
Cornfields, Ariz. 78 D4
Cornholme, U.K., 3,628 114 D3
Cornimont, Fr., 5,058 117 G3
Corning, Ark., 2,565 73 E1
Corning, Calif., 3,006 82 B3
Corning, Ind. 70 C4
Corning, Iowa, 2,041 72 C4
Corning, Kans., 240 75 J4
Corning, Ohio, 1,065 70 G3
Corning, Mo., 128 72 B4
Corning, N.Y., 17,085 58 F7
Cornish, Me. 55 B5
Cornish, Okla., 127 76 F3
Cornish, Utah, 157 78 b7
Cornish, Mt., Austl. 172 C3
Cornish Flat, N.H. 54 C4
Cornishtown, Bah. Is. 95 b6
Corn Is., Nic. 94 F4
Cornlea, Nebr., 44 75 H2
Corno Grande, mtn., It. 123 D3
Cornol, Switz. 124 B1
Cornucopia, Oreg. 80 E3
Cornucopia, Wis. 66 B2
Cornudas, Tex. 77 L4
Cornville, Me. 55 C4
Cornwall, Ont., Can., 42,355 44 K6
Cornwall, co., U.K., 342,301 113 D6
Cornwall, Conn., 1,051(T) 56 C5
Cornwall, N.Y., 2,785 59 M9
Cornwall, Pa., 1,934 61 K5
Cornwall, Vt. 54 A4
Cornwall, Va. 62 E5
Cornwall Bridge (part of Cornwall), Conn. 56 C5
Cornwall Hollow (part of Cornwall), Conn. 56 C5
Cornwallis I., N.W.T., Can. 40 K2
Cornwall I., N.W.T., Can. 41 K2
Cornwall I., Ont., Can. 69 C
Cornwell, Fla. 65 H5
Cornwell, S.C. 63 C3
Cornwells Heights, Pa., 10,200* 60 f11
Corny, Fr., 1,024 116 b8
Corny Pt., Austl. 172 b8
Coro, Ven., 44,757 100 F2
Coroa, Tope de, mtn., C. Verde Is. 109 5
Coroatá, Braz., 7,720 103 H2
Corocoro, Bol., 5,571 102 C5
Coroico, Bol., 9,638 102 C5
Coroico, r., Bol. 102 b9
Coroma, Bol., 4,369 102 b11
Coromandel, N.Z. 175 g5
Coromandel Coast, India 144
Coromandel Pen., N.Z. 175 h5
Coron, Phil., 3,888 153 B2
Corona, Calif., 13,336 83 i16
Corona, N. Mex., 420 79 C4
Corona, S. Dak., 150 74 D3
Coronach, Sask., Can. 43 C5
Coronado, Alta., Can. 43 b7
Coronado, Calif., 18,039 82 c10
Coronado, B. de, C.R. 94 F6
Coronation, Alta., Can. 42 K3
Coronation G., N.W.T., Can. 40 G4
Coronation Is., Austl. 172 C2
Coronda, Arg., 12,000* 105 a10
Coronel, Chile, 33,870 104 e17
Coronel Dorrego, Arg., 10,400* 105 C5
Coronel Fabriciano, Braz., 14,623 103 H5
Coronel Lorenzo Garaicoa, Ec. 104 c11
Coronel M. Maridueña, Ec. 104 c11
Coronel Moldes, Arg., 6,000* 105 C4
Coronel Pringles, Arg., 13,405 105 C5
Coronel Rodolfo Bunge, Arg. 105 b13
Coronel Suarez, Arg., 17,000* 105 C5
Coronel Vidal, Arg., 3,842 105 D5
Corongo, Peru, 2,431 104 C4
Coropuna, Nudo, Peru 104 ·
Çorovodë, Alb., 1,600 125 E4
Corowa, Austl., 3,045 173 f10
Corozal, Br. Hond., 3,171 94 C1
Corozal, Col. 100 C3
Corozal, P.R., 3,166 96 t10
Corpus Christi, Tex., 167,690 77 P6
Corpus Christi, L., Tex. 77 O5
Corque, Bol., 9,058 102 b11
Corquín, Hond., 3,507 94 e9
Corral, Chile, 3,740 105 A5
Corral de Almaguer, Sp., 8,261 122 D3
Corrales, Col. 100 D5
Corrales, Sp., 1,724 122 C2
Corralitos, Calif. 83 f14
Correctionville, Iowa, 912 72 A2
Correggio, It., 19,145 123 C2
Corregidor I., Phil. 153 b8
Corrente, Braz., 2,214 103 H4
Correntes, Braz., 4,845 103 a15
Correntina, Braz., 2,636 103 G4
Correo, N. Mex. 79 B4
Corres, Sp. 122 n12
Corrib, L., Ire. 113 B5
Corrientes, Arg., 113,000* 105 D3
Corrientes, r., Peru 104 C2
Corrientes, C., Col. 100 B5
Corrientes, C., Cuba 96 a2
Corrientes, C., Mex. 92 D4
Corrientes, Ensenada de, Cuba 96 a2
Corrigan, Tex., 986 77 Q4
Corrigin, Austl. 172 B5
Corry, Pa., 7,744 60 C2
Corryong, Austl. 173 f11
Corryton, Tenn. 71 H5
Corse, i., Fr. 116 r8
Corse, C., Fr. 116 r17
Corse Hill, U.K. 112 b8
Corsham, U.K., 9,309 114 D8
Corsica, Pa., 431 60 D3
Corsica, S. Dak., 479 74 C4
Corsica, Fr. = Corse
Corsicana, Tex., 20,344 77 P3
Corsico, It., 15,668 122 b5
Corson, co., S. Dak., 5,798 74 B3
Corson's Inlet, N.J. 61 B5
Corstorphine, U.K. 112 d8
Cortada del Papelón, Ven. 101 c11
Cortaro, Ariz. 78 C5
Cortazar, Mex., 17,884 93 d9
Corte, Fr., 5,491 116 r17
Cortegana, Sp., 8,344 122 B4
Corte Madera, Calif., 5,962 83 d12
Cortemaggiore, It., 6,167 122 c5
Cortes, Phil., 2,074 153 C3
Cortés, Ensenada de, Cuba 96 b1
Cortez, Colo., 6,764 79 A3
Cortez, Fla. 65 c13
Cortez, Pa. 61 p16
Cortez Mts., Nev. 83 B2
Cortijo, Mex., 1,753 93 e9
Cortina d'Ampezzo, It., 6,967 123 D1
Cortland, Ill., 461 68 D2
Cortland, co., N.Y., 41,113 59 H6
Cortland, N.Y., 19,181 59 H6
Cortland, Ohio, 1,957 70 J1
Cortona, It., 28,362 123 C3
Coruche, Port., 21,945 122 A3
Çoruh, r., Turk. 142 E1
Çorum, Turk., 34,629 142 C1
Corum, Okla. 76 E3
Corumbá, Braz., 36,744 102 E5
Corumbá, r., Braz. 103 G5
Corund, Rum. 128 E1
Corunna, Ont., Can., 1,381 46 B6
Corunna, Sp. = La Coruña
Corunna, Mich., 2,764 67 J6
Coruripe, Braz., 3,434 103 b16
Corvallis, Mont. 81 C2
Corvallis, Oreg., 20,669 80 B3
Corvette L., Qué., Can. 44 K4
Corvo, i., Azôres 108 2
Corwen, U.K., 2,048 113 E5
Corwin, Kans. 75 G6
Corwith, Iowa, 488 72 D1
Cory, Ind. 70 B3
Corydon, Ind., 2,701 70 C4
Corydon, Iowa, 1,687 72 D4
Corydon, Ky., 746 71 D4
Corydon, Pa. 60 E2
Coryell, co., Tex., 23,961 77 P4
Coryville, Pa. 60 F2
Cos = Kos
Cosalá, Mex., 1,400* 92 D3
Cosamaloapan, Mex., 16,499 93 F4
Cosby, U.K., 1,776 114 F5
Cosby, Mo., 119 72 C5
Cos Cob (part of Greenwich), Conn. 56 B8
Coscomatepec, Mex., 5,649 93 F4
Coseley, U.K., 39,557 114 D5
Cosenza, It., 74,249 123 F5
Cosham (part of Portsmouth), U.K., 13,706 113 k13
Coshocton, co., Ohio, 32,224 70 G2
Coshocton, Ohio, 13,106 70 H2
Cosigüina, Vol., Nic. 94 D4
Cosmoledo Group, is., Ind. Oc. 165 H3
Cosmopolis, Wash., 1,312 80 B2
Cosmos, Minn., 487 74 E3
Cosne, Fr., 9,010 117 E3
Coso Junction, Calif. 82 E4
Coşoveni, Rum. 128 D2
Cosquín, Arg., 17,746* 105 C4
Cossato, It., 11,323 123 B2
Cossatot, r., Ark. 73 A3
Cossayuna L., N.Y. 54 A5
Cossé-le-Vivien, Fr., 2,415 117 C3
Cossonay, Switz., 1,284 124 A2
Cost, Tex. 77 P5
Coste, Cord. de la, Ven. 101 b11
Costa di Rovigo, It., 3,782 122 e5
Costa Mesa, Calif., 37,550 83 i16
Costa Rica, ctry., 1,336,274 94 E5
Coster, C., Loy. Is. 174 m8
Costermansville = Bukavu
Costessey, U.K., 7,051 113 G5
Costeşti, Rum. 128 E2
Costigan, Me. 55 D3
Costigan L., Sask., Can. 43 C3
Costilla, co., Colo., 4,219 79 C3
Costilla, N. Mex. 79 C3
Cosumnes, r., Calif. 82 C3
Coswig (near Dessau), Ger.D.R., 13,710 118 D3
Coswig (near Dresden), Ger.D.R., 17,649 118 D3
Cotabato, Phil., 23,794 153 B4
Cotacachi, Ec., 4,265 104 c9
Cotacachi, mtn., Ec. 104 c9
Cotacajes, r., Bol. 102 b10
Cotagaita, Bol., 11,372 102 C6
Cotahuasi, Peru, 2,267 104 C5
Cotati, Calif., 1,852 82 B3
Coteana, Rum. 128 E2
Coteau, N. Dak. 74 A1
Coteau, The, hills, Sask., Can. 43 C4
Coteau des Prairies, Minn.-S. Dak. 75 ·
Coteau-du-Lac, Qué., Can. 47 K3
Coteau du Missouri, plat., N. Dak.-S. Dak. 75 ·
Coteau Landing, Qué., Can. 47 K3
Coteau Station, Qué., Can., 1,031 47 K3
Coteaux, Haiti, 3,146 96 i6
Cotentin, pen., Fr. 117 C2
Côte Ste-Catherine Lock, Qué., Can. 69 D
Côte-Saint-Luc, Qué., Can., 12,447 47 o18
Cotesfield, Nebr., 81 75 G2
Cothen, Neth. 115 c7
Cotherstone, U.K. 112 f10
Cotija, Mex., 8,006 92 E4
Cotnari, Rum. 128 F1
Cotoca, Bol., 3,633 102 D5
Cotonou, Dahom., 85,845 162 E4
Cotopaxi, Colo. 79 C2
Cotopaxi, mtn., Ec. 104 c10
Cotorra, I., Ven. 101 J2
Cotswold Hills, U.K. 113 E6
Cottage Grove, Minn., 10,949 74 d6
Cottage Grove, Oreg., 3,895 80 B4
Cottage Grove, Tenn., 130 71 C5
Cottage Grove, Wis., 1,195 66 D5
Cottage Hill, Fla. 65 B2
Cottageville, S.C., 520 63 D5
Cottageville, W. Va. 62 C4
Cottam, Ont., Can. 46 B6
Cottbus, Ger.D.R., 66,813 118 E3
Cottenham, U.K., 2,415 114 J6
Cotter, Ark., 683 73 C1
Cotteridge, U.K., 5,438 114 E6
Cottian Alps, mts., It.-Fr. 123 A2
Cottle, co., Tex., 4,207 77 N3
Cotton, Minn. 74 F2
Cotton, co., Okla., 8,031 76 E3
Cottondale, Fla., 849 65 D2
Cottondale, Tex. 76 d8
Cotton Plant, Ark., 1,704 73 D2
Cotton Plant, Miss. 73 G3
Cottonport, La., 1,581 73 C7
Cottonton, Ala. 64 D3
Cotton Valley, La., 1,145 73 B5
Cottonwood, Br. Col., Can. 42 G3
Cottonwood, Ala., 953 64 D4
Cottonwood, Alaska 85 c7
Cottonwood, Ariz., 1,879 78 C4
Cottonwood, Calif. 82 B2
Cottonwood, Idaho, 1,081 81 A2
Cottonwood, Ill. 68 D6
Cottonwood, co., Minn., 16,166 74 E4
Cottonwood, Minn., 717 74 E3
Cottonwood, S. Dak., 38 74 B4
Cottonwood, r., Kans. 75 J5
Cottonwood, r., Minn. 74 E3
Cottonwood Butte, Idaho 81 B3
Cottonwood Cr., Tex. 77 L4
Cottonwood Cr., Utah 78 D3
Cottonwood Cr., S. Fk., Calif. 82 B2
Cottonwood Falls, Kans., 971 75 J5
Cotuí, Dom. Rep., 4,706 96 m6
Cotuit (part of Barnstable), Mass. 57 P6
Cotulla, Tex., 3,960 77 O5
Coţuşca, Rum. 128 F1
Coubert, Fr., 1,055 116 i12
Coubre, Pte. de la, Fr. 117 C4
Couch, Mo. 72 F8
Couchiching, L., Ont., Can. 46 E4
Couchwood, La. 73 B5
Couderay, Wis., 113 66 B3
Coudersport, Pa., 2,889 60 G2
Coudres, Î. aux, Qué., Can. 47 Q10
Couedic, C. du, Austl. 172 b8
Couëron, Fr., 11,744 117 C3
Cougar, Wash. 80 B2
Couilly, Fr. 116 k11
Couiza, Fr., 1,126 117 E5
Coulee City, Wash., 654 80 D2
Coulee Dam, Wash., 1,344 80 D2
Coulee Dam Nat. Rec. Area, Wash. 80 D2
Coulibishie, Dominica 97 13
Coulommiers, Fr., 10,538 117 E2
Coulonge, r., Qué., Can. 44 J6
Coulonge Est, r., Qué., Can. 46 H2
Coulsdon, London, U.K. 114 H8
Coulta, Austl. 172 a8
Coulter, Iowa, 315 72 D2
Coulterville, Calif. 82 C4
Coulterville, Ill., 1,022 68 C5
Counce, Tenn. 71 C6
Council, Alaska 85 D2
Council, Ga. 64 G5
Council, Idaho, 827 81 A3
Council, Va. 62 B5
Council Bluffs, Iowa, 55,641 72 B3
Council Grove, Kans., 2,664 75 J5
Council Grove Res., Kan. 75 J5
Council Hill, Okla., 130 76 H2
Country Club Hills, Ill., 3,421 69 d10
Country Lakes, N.J. 58 a17
Counts, Okla. 76 H3
Coupar Angus, U.K., 2,049 112 E3
Coupeville, Wash., 740 80 B1
Coupland, Tex. 77 P4
Courantyne, r., Guyana-Sur. 101 L5
Courbevoie, Fr., 59,941 116 g11
Courcelles, Belg., 18,031 115 C4
Courcelles-Chaussy, Fr., 1,284 116 b8
Courdimanche, Fr. 116 f10
Courtiège, Fr. Guiana 101 O5
Courmayeur, It., 1,480 123 A2
Courpière, Fr., 3,826 117 E4
Courqetaine, Fr. 116 k12
Courrendlin, Switz., 2,418 124 B1
Coursan, Fr., 3,212 117 E5
Courson-Monteloup, Fr. 116 g12
Courtelary, Switz., 1330 124 A1
Courtemaîche, Switz. 124 B1
Courtenay, Br. Col., Can., 3,311 42 F4
Courtenay, N. Dak., 168 74 C2
Courtland, Ont., Can. 46 D6
Courtland, Ala., 495 64 B1
Courtland, Calif. 82 C3
Courtland, Kans., 384 75 H4
Courtland, Miss., 242 73 F3
Courtland, Va., 855 62 G6
Courtney, Mo. 75 b7
Courtney, N.C. 63 D1
Courtney, Okla. 76 F4
Courtney, Pa. 60 c9
Courtomer, Fr. 116 k12
Court Oreilles, L., Wis. 66 B3
Courtrai = Kortrijk
Courtright, Ont., Can. 46 B6
Court-St-Étienne, Belg., 5,184 115 C4
Courville, Qué., Can., 4,655 47 n16
Courzieu, Fr. 116 p15
Coushatta, La., 1,663 73 B5
Coutances, Fr., 9,236 117 C2
Coutevroult, Fr. 116 k11
Coutiches, Fr., 1,521 116 a7
Coutras, Fr., 6,038 117 C4
Coutts, Alta., Can. 42 K4
Couvet, Switz., 3,450 124 A2
Couvin, Belg., 3,626 115 C4
Covarrubias, Sp., 1,161 122 D1
Covasna, Rum., 7,290 128 F2
Cove, U.K. 112 a8
Cove, Ark., 320 73 A3
Cove, Ohio 70 G3
Cove, Oreg., 311 80 E3
Cove, Tex. 77 k9
Cove City, N.C., 551 63 G2
Cove Creek, N.C. 63 A2
Cove I., Ont., Can. 46 C3
Covelo, Calif. 82 B3
Cove Mtn., Pa. 60 G6
Cove Neck, N.Y., 299 58 e13
Coventry, U.K., 305,060 113 F5
Coventry, R.I. 15,432(T) 57 K6
Coventry, Vt. 54 C2
Cove Orchard, Oreg. 80 B3
Cove Point, Md. 62 H4
Cove Pt., Berm. Is. 108 1
Covert, Kans. 75 G4
Covert, Mich. 67 G6
Covesville, Va. 62 F5
Covilhã, Port., 23,595 122 B2
Covin, Ala. 64 B2
Covina, Calif., 20,124 83 i15
Covington, co., Ala., 35,631 64 C4
Covington, Ga., 8,167 64 F2
Covington, Ind., 2,759 70 B2
Covington, Ky., 60,376 71 G2
Covington, La., 6,754 73 E7
Covington, Mich. 66 E2
Covington, co., Miss., 13,637 73 F6
Covington, Ohio, 2,473 70 E2
Covington, Okla., 687 76 F1
Covington, Pa. 60 H2
Covington, Tenn., 5,298 71 B6
Covington, Tex. 76 e10
Covington, Va., 11,062 62 D5
Covington, Wash. 81 b8
Cowal, L., Austl. 173 f9
Cowan, Man., Can. 43 E4
Cowan, Ky. 71 H3
Cowan, Tenn., 1,979 71 E6
Cowan, r., Sask., Can. 43 C3
Cowan, L., Austl. 172 C4
Cowan, Mt., Mont. 81 D3
Cowanesque, Pa. 60 H2
Cowanesque, r., Pa. 60 H2
Cowansville, Que., Can., 7,015 47 M3
Cowansville, Pa. 60 C4
Coward, S.C., 552 63 E4
Cowarts, Ala. 64 D4
Cowbit, U.K. 114 H5
Cowbridge, U.K., 1,067 114 B8
Cow Cr., Wash. 80 D2
Cowden, Ill., 575 68 D4
Cowden, Okla. 76 E2
Cowdenbeath, U.K., 11,918 112 E3
Cowdrey, Colo. 79 B1
Cowell, Austl. 172 E5
Cowen, W. Va., 475 62 D4
Cowes, U.K., 16,992 113 F6
Cowesett (part of Warwick), R.I. 57 L6
Coweta, co., Ga., 28,893 64 E2
Coweta, Okla., 1,858 76 H2
Cowgill, Mo., 259 72 D5
Cow Head, Newf., Can. 45 P5
Cowhorn Mtn., Oreg. 80 C4
Cowichan L., Br. Col., Can. 42 F4
Cowiche, Wash. 80 C2
Cowie, U.K. 112 c7
Cowikee Creek, Ala. 64 D3
Cowlesville, N.Y. 58 D6
Cowley, U.K. 114 F7
Cowley, co., Kans., 37,861 75 J6
Cowley, Wyo., 459 81 E3
Cowlic, Ariz. 78 B6
Cowling, Ill. 68 E5
Cowlinge, U.K. 114 J6
Cowlington, Okla., 74 76 J2
Cowlitz, co., Wash., 57,801 80 B2
Cowlitz, r., Wash. 80 B2
Cowpen, Br. Hond. 94 C2
Cowpens, S.C., 2,038 63 C2
Cowra, Austl., 6,097 173 G5
Coxcatlán, Mex., 1,060 93 e8
Cox City, Okla. 76 F3
Coxhoe, U.K., 6,013 112 h10
Coxim, Braz., 1,371 103 F5
Coxsackie, N.Y., 2,849 59 N7
Cox's Bāzār, Pak., 8,427 145 J5
Coxwold, U.K. 114 F2
Coy, Ark. 73 D3
Coyame, Mex. 92 D2
Coyanosa, Tex. 77 M4
Coyle, Okla., 292 76 F2
Coyoacán, Mex., 46,031 93 e10
Coyote, Calif. 83 f13
Coyote, N. Mex. 79 B5
Coyote, r., Mex. 92 B1
Coyote Cr., Calif. 83 f13
Coyote L., Calif. 82 E5
Coyotepec, Mex., 4,471 93 e10
Coyote Wash, r., N. Mex. 79 A4
Coyotitán, Mex. 92 D3
Coyuca, Mex., 4,486 93 E5
Cozad, Nebr., 3,184 75 F3
Cozumel, Mex., 2,915 93 J4
Cozumel, I. de, Mex. 93 J4
Crab Orchard, Ky., 808 71 G4
Crab Orchard, Nebr., 103 75 J3
Crab Orchard, W. Va., 1,953 62 C5
Crab Orchard L., Ill. 68 C6
Crabtree, Qué., Can., 1,298 47 L3
Crabtree, Oreg. 80 B3
Craches, Fr. 116 f12
Craddockville, Va. 62 H5
Cradley, U.K., 1,119 114 D6
Cradock, S. Af., 19,476 164 D7
Crafton, Pa., 8,418 60 B5
Craftsbury, Vt. 54 C2
Craftsbury Common, Vt. 54 C2
Craggan, U.K. 112 a7
Craggy Pt., Tutuila 177 39
Crag Mtn., Mass. 56 G2
Craidorolţ, Rum. 128 D1
Craig, Alaska, 273 85 L5
Craig, Colo., 3,984 79 B1
Craig, Fla. 65 h15
Craig, Ill. 68 C5
Craig, Iowa, 117 72 A2
Craig, Mo., 488 72 B4
Craig, Mont. 81 D2
Craig, Nebr., 378 75 J2
Craig, co., Okla. 16,303 76 H1
Craig, co., Va., 3,356 62 D5
Craig Beach, Ohio, 1,139 70 J1
Craighead, co., Ark., 47,303 73 E2
Craig Healing Springs, Va. 62 D5
Craig L., Mich. 66 E2
Craigmont, Idaho, 703 81 A2
Craigmyle, Alta., Can. 42 K3
Craigsville, Va., 978 62 E4
Craigsville, W. Va. 62 D4
Craigville, Minn. 74 F2
Craik, Sask., Can. 43 C4
Crail, U.K., 1,065 112 E3
Crailsheim, F.R.Ger., 12,769 118 C4
Craiova, Rum., 96,897 128 D2
Cramerton, N.C., 3,123 63 C2
Cramlington, U.K. 112 g9
Cranage, U.K., 1,217 114 D4
Cranberry, Pa. 60 C3
Cranberry, r., W. Va. 62 D4
Cranberry Lake, Br. Col., Can., 1,346 42 b6
Cranberry Lake, N.Y. 59 K3
Cranberry L., N.Y. 59 L3
Cranberry Portage, Man., Can. 43 E3
Cranborne, U.K. 113 i13
Cranbrook, Austl. 173 g13
Cranbrook, Br. Col., Can., 5,445 42 J4
Cranbury, N.J., 1,038 61 C3
Cranbury Station, N.J. 58 b15
Crandall, Ga., 208 64 E1
Crandall, Ind., 156 70 C4
Crandall, Miss. 73 G6
Crandall, Tex., 640 76 g9
Crandon, Va. 62 D5
Crandon, Wis., 1,679 66 E3
Crane, Ind., 356 70 C4
Crane, Mo., 954 72 D8
Crane, Mont. 81 G2
Crane, Oreg. 80 D4
Crane, co., Tex., 4,699 77 M4
Crane, Tex., 3,796 77 M4
Crane Lake, Minn. 74 F1
Crane Mtn., N.Y. 59 N4
Crane Neck Pt., N.Y. 58 g13
Crane Prairie Res., Oreg. 80 C4
Cranesville, Pa., 575 60 B2
Cranfield, U.K., 2,501 114 G6
Cranfills Gap, Tex. 77 O4
Cranford, N.J., 26,424(T) 61 C2
Cranleigh, U.K., 6,016 114 G8
Crannell, Calif. 82 A2
Cranston, R.I., 66,766 57 L5
Craon, Fr., 4,256 117 C3
Crapaud, P.E.I., Can. 47 U10
Craponne, Fr., 2,859 116 p15
Craponne, Fr., 3,191 117 E4
Crary, N. Dak., 195 74 C1
Crary Mts., Ant. 180 Y5
Crasna, Rum. 128 D1
Crasna, Rum. 128 F1
Crasna, r., Rum. 128 D1
Crater L., St. Vinc. 97 19
Crater L., Oreg. 80 C4
Crater L. Nat. Pk., Oreg. 80 B4
Craters of the Moon Nat. Mon., Idaho 81 C4
Crateús, Braz., 14,572 103 H3
Crathie, U.K. 112 E3
Crati, r., It. 123 F5
Crato, Braz., 27,649 103 J3
Craven, co., N.C., 58,773 63 G2
Craven Arms, U.K. 114 C6
Cravonorte, Col. 100 E4
Cravo Norte, r., Col. 100 E4
Cravo Sur, r., Col. 100 E5
Crawford, U.K. 112 E4
Crawford, Ala. 64 D3
Crawford, co., Ark., 21,318 73 A2
Crawford, Colo., 147 79 B2
Crawford Co., Ga., 5,816 64 F3
Crawford, Ga., 541 64 F2
Crawford, co., Ill., 20,751 68 E4
Crawford, co., Ind., 8,379 70 C4
Crawford, co., Iowa, 18,569 72 B2
Crawford, co., Kans., 37,032 75 L6
Crawford, co., Mich., 4,971 67 J4
Crawford, Miss., 317 73 G4
Crawford, co., Mo., 12,647 72 F7
Crawford, Nebr., 1,588 75 B1
Crawford, co., Ohio, 46,775 70 G2
Crawford, Okla. 76 D2
Crawford, co., Pa., 77,956 60 B2
Crawford, Tex., 480 77 P4
Crawford, co., Wis., 16,351 66 C5
Crawford Countryside, Ill. 69 c10
Crawford House, N.H. 54 E3
Crawford L., Me. 55 E3
Crawfordsville, Ark., 744 73 E2
Crawfordsville, Ind., 14,231 70 C2
Crawfordsville, Oreg. 80 B3
Crawfordville, Fla. 65 E2
Crawfordville, Ga., 786 64 G2
Crawley, U.K., 53,768 113 F6
Crawley, W. Va. 62 D5
Crawshay, Mt., Br. Col., Can. 42 b5
Cray, U.K. 114 A7
Crayford, London, U.K. 114 J8
Crayke, U.K. 114 F2
Crazy Mts., Alaska 85 H2
Crazy Mts., Mont. 81 D2
Crazy Pk., Mont. 81 D2
Creagan, U.K. 112 D3
Creag Meagaidh, mtn., U.K. 112 D3
Creal Springs, Ill., 784 68 D6
Cream, Wis. 66 B4
Creamridge, N.J. 58 a16
Crécy-en-Brie, Fr., 1,028 116 k11
Crécy-sur-Serre, Fr., 1,691 117 E2
Credenhill, U.K., 2,481 114 C6
Credit, r., Ont., Can. 46 E5
Credit Forks, Ont., Can. 46 c13
Crediton, Ont., Can. 46 C5
Crediton, U.K., 4,427 113 E6
Cree, r., Sask., Can. 43 C2
Cree, r., U.K. 113 D4
Creede, Colo., 350 79 B3
Creedmoor, N.C., 1,330 63 F1
Creedmoor, Tex. 76 c5
Creek, co., Okla., 40,495 76 G2
Creekside, Pa., 482 60 D4
Cree Lake, Sask., Can. 43 C2
Cree L., Sask., Can. 43 C2
Creemore, Ont., Can. 46 D4
Cree River, Sask., Can. 43 C2
Creetown, U.K. 113 D4
Creggs, Ire. 113 B5
Creglingen, F.R.Ger., 1,807 118 B4
Créhange, Fr., 3,750 116 b8
Creighton, Sask., Can., 1,715 43 D3
Creighton, Nebr., 1,388 75 H1
Creighton, Pa., 2,900* 60 c7
Creighton, S. Dak. 74 A3
Creighton Mine, Ont., Can. 46 C2
Creil, Fr., 21,158 117 E2
Crema, It., 29,457 123 B2
Crémieu, Fr., 2,539 117 F4
Crémines, Switz. 124 B1
Cremona, Alta., Can. 42 J3
Cremona, It., 72,119 123 C2
Crenshaw, co., Ala., 14,909 64 C4
Crenshaw, Miss., 1,382 73 E3
Crenshaw, Pa. 60 E3
Creola, Ala. 64 A5
Creola, Ohio 70 G3
Creole, La. 73 B8
Créon, Fr., 1,324 117 C4
Crépey, Fr. 116 b9
Crépy-en-Valois, Fr., 7,417 117 E2
Cres, Yug. 125 B2
Cres, i., Yug. 125 B2
Cresaptown, Md., 1,680 62 F3
Cresbard, S. Dak., 229 74 C3
Crescent, Br. Col., Can. 42 d6
Crescent, Ga. 64 H4
Crescent, Ill., 393 68 E3
Crescent, Okla., 1,264 76 F2
Crescent, Oreg. 80 C4
Crescent Beach (part of E. Lyme), Conn. 56 H7
Crescent Beach, St. Johns Co., Fla. 65 H3
Crescent Beach, Sarasota Co., Fla. 65 c13
Crescent Beach (part of Mattapoisett), Mass. 57 N6
Crescent, Beach, S.C., 440 63 F4
Crescent City, Calif., 2,958 82 A2
Crescent City, Fla., 1,629 65 H3
Crescentino, It., 5,226 122 b5
Crescent Lake, Me. 55 B5
Crescent Lake, Oreg. 80 C4
Crescent L., Fla. 65 H3
Crescent L., Nebr. 75 C2
Crescent, L., Wash. 80 B1
Crescent Mills, Calif. 82 C2
Crescent Pd., Me. 55 C2
Cresciente, I., Mex. 92 C3
Cresco, Iowa, 3,809 72 E1
Creška, Yug. 125 F4
Crespières, Fr. 116 f11
Crespo, Arg., 10,000* 105 a11
Cressier, Switz., 1,200 124 B1
Cresskill, N.J., 7,290 58 d13
Cressmont, W. Va. 62 D4
Cresson, Pa., 2,659 60 E5
Cresson, Tex. 76 d9
Cressona, Pa. 1,854 61 K4
Cresswell, N.C., 402 63 H2
Crest, Fr., 6,793 117 F4
Crested Butte, Colo., 289 79 B2
Crest Hill, Ill., 5,887 69 b10
Crestline, Calif., 1,290 82 E5
Crestline, Kans. 75 L6
Crestline, Nev. 83 C4
Crestline, Ohio, 5,521 70 G2
Creston, Br. Col., Can., 2,403 42 J4
Creston, Ill., 454 68 C2
Creston, Iowa, 7,667 72 C3
Creston, Nebr., 177 75 H2
Creston, Ohio, 1,522 70 H2
Creston, S.C. 63 D4
Creston, Wash., 317 80 D2
Creston, W. Va. 62 C4
Crestone, Colo. 79 C3
Crestview, Fla., 7,467 65 C2
Crestview, Wis. 66 d12
Crestwood, Ill., 3,918 69 c10
Crestwood, Mo., 11,106 72 a11
Creswell, Oreg., 760 80 B4
Creswell Bay, N.W.T., Can. 40 L3
Crete, Ill., 3,463 68 E2
Crete, Nebr., 3,546 75 J3
Crete, N. Dak. 74 D2
Crete, Gr. = Kriti
Crete, Sea of, Gr. 129 E7
Créteil, Fr., 30,564 116 h11
Cretin, C., Terr. New Guin. 174 e2
Creus, C., Sp. 122 G1
Creuse, r., Fr. 117 D3
Creussen, F.R.Ger., 1,961 118 C4
Creutzwald-la-Croix, Fr., 13,683 116 c8
Crevalcore, It., 13,383 122 e6
Creve Coeur, Ill., 6,684 68 C3
Creve Coeur, Mo., 5,122 72 a11
Crevillente, Sp., 14,047 122 E3
Crewe, U.K., 53,394 113 E5
Crewe, Va., 2,012 62 F5
Crewkerne, U.K., 4,215 113 E6
Crewport, Wash. 80 C2
Crewsons Corners, Ont., Can. 46 b13
Crianlarich, U.K. 112 a7
Criccieth, U.K., 1,672 113 D5
Criciúma, Braz., 25,331 103 G7
Crick, U.K. 114 F6
Crickhowell, U.K., 1,367 114 B7
Cricklade, U.K., 1,945 114 E7
Cridersville, Ohio, 1,053 70 E2
Crieff, Ont., Can. 46 b14
Crieff, U.K., 5,773 112 E3
Criglersville, Va. 62 F4
Crikvenica, Yug., 3,590 125 B2
Crimean Pen. = Krymskiy P-ov.
Crimmitschau, Ger.D.R., 31,279 118 D3
Crinan, U.K. 112 D3
Criner, Okla. 76 F3
Cripple Creek, Colo., 614 79 C2
Crisenoy, Fr. 116 k12
Crisfield, Md., 3,540 62 J4
Crisp, co., Ga., 17,768 64 F4
Crisp, Tex. 76 f10
Cristalândia, Braz., 2,345 103 G4
Cristalina, Braz., 3,810 103 G5
Cristina, Braz., 2,696 103 d18
Cristino Castro, Braz. 103 H3
Cristobal, C.Z. 94 f11
Cristóbal, P., Arch. de Colón 104 a8
Cristóbal, Punta de, Cuba 96 b1
Cristóbal Colón, Pico, Col. 100 D2
Cristuru Secuiesc, Rum., 5,196 128 E1
Crişul Alb, r., Rum. 128 D1
Crişul Negru, r., Rum. 128 C1
Crişul Repede, r., Rum. 128 D1
Criţ, Rum. 128 E1
Crittenden, co., Ark., 47,564 73 E2
Crittenden, co., Ky., 8,648 71 C4
Crittenden, Ky., 287 71 G3
Crittenden, N.Y. 58 C6
Crittenden, Va. 62 H6
Crivitz, Ger.D.R. 118 C2
Crivitz, Wis. 66 E3
Crna, r., Yug. 125 E4
Crna Gora, st., Yug., 471,894 125 D3
Crna G., Yug. 125 E3
Crna Trava, Yug., 2,709 125 F3
Crni Drim, r., Yug. 125 E4
Crnjelovo Donje, Yug., 3,012 125 D2

216 · Črnomelj—Dālbandin

Črnomelj, Yug. 125 B2
Croatan, N.C. 63 G3
Croatia = Hrvatska
Crocker, Ind. 69 f10
Crocker, Mo., 821 72 E7
Crocker, S. Dak. 74 D3
Crocker Mtn., Me. 55 B3
Crockett, Calif. 83 e11
Crockett, Ky. 71 H4
Crockett, co., Tenn., 14,594 71 B6
Crockett, co., Tex., 4,209 77 N4
Crockett, Tex., 5,356 77 Q4
Crockett, Va. 62 C6
Crocodile = Krokodil
Crocus Bay, Anguilla 97 7
Croft, U.K. 112 g11
Croft, Kans. 75 G6
Crofton, Ky., 892 71 D4
Crofton, Nebr., 604 75 H1
Croghan, N.Y., 821 59 K4
Croik, U.K. 112 D3
Croil I., N.Y. 69 C
Croisilles, Fr. 116 a7
Croissy-sur-Seine, Fr., 5,926 116 g11
Croix, Fr., 20,156 116 a6
Croix, L. la., Can.-U.S. 44 D5
Croix-des-Bouquets, Haiti, 1,581 96 k6
Croker I., Austl. 172 D1
Cromarty, Man., Can. 43 G2
Cromarty, U.K. 112 E3
Crombach, Belg., 1,975 119 A4
Cromer, U.K., 4,892 113 G5
Cromers, Ohio 70 F1
Crompton (part of W. Warwick), R.I. 57 K6
Cromwell, N.Z. 175 f7
Cromwell, Conn., 2,889; 6,780(T) 56 F6
Cromwell, Ind., 451 70 D1
Cromwell, Iowa, 138 72 C3
Cromwell, Ky. 71 E4
Cromwell, Minn., 187 74 F2
Cromwell, Okla., 269 76 G2
Crondall, U.K., 2,503 114 G8
Crook (incl. Willington), U.K., 25,218 112 g10
Crook, Colo., 209 79 D1
Crook, co., Oreg., 9,430 80 C3
Crook, co., Wyo., 4,691 81 G3
Crooked, r., Br. Col., Can. 42 G2
Crooked, r., Me. 55 B4
Crooked, r., Oreg. 80 C3
Crooked Creek, Alaska, 92 85 E3
Crooked Creek, Alaska 85 J2
Crooked Cr., Oreg. 80 D4
Crooked Cr., Pa. 60 D4
Crooked Cr., Pa. 60 H2
Crooked I., Bah. Is. 95 D2
Crooked Island Passage, Bah. Is. 95 D2
Crooked L., Fla. 65 H5
Crookhaven, Ire. 113 B6
Crooks, S. Dak. 74 D4
Crooks Corner (part of Bellingham), Mass. 57 L4
Crookston, Minn., 8,546 74 D2
Crookston, Nebr., 139 75 E1
Crooks Tower, pk., S. Dak. 74 A3
Crooksville, Ohio, 2,958 70 G3
Crookwell, Austl., 1,957 173 G5
Croom, Ire. 113 B5
Croom, Fla. 65 G4
Croom, Md. 62 H4
Cropper, Ky. 71 F3
Cropwell, Ala. 64 e7
Crosby, U.K., 59,707 113 E5
Crosby, Minn., 2,629 74 F2
Crosby, Miss., 705 73 D6
Crosby, N. Dak., 1,759 74 A1
Crosby, Pa. 60 F2
Crosby, co., Tex., 10,347 77 N3
Crosby, Tex. 77 i9
Crosby, Wash. 81 a7
Crosby Ravensworth, U.K. 114 C1
Crosbyton, Tex., 2,088 77 N3
Cross, co., Ark., 19,551 73 E2
Cross Anchor, S.C. 63 C3
Cross City, Fla., 1,857 65 F3
Cross Creek, N.B., Can. 47 S10
Crossett, Ark., 5,370 73 D4
Cross Fell, mtn., U.K. 113 E4
Crossfield, Alta., Can. 42 J3
Crossford, U.K. 112 c8
Cross Fork, Pa. 60 G3
Crossgates, Fife, Scot., U.K. 112 d7
Crossgates, Perth, Scot., U.K. 112 d7
Crosshill, Ont., Can. 46 a13
Crosshill, U.K. 113 D4
Cross Hill, S.C., 441 63 C3
Cross I., Me. 55 E4
Cross Keys, Mo. 72 a10
Cross Lake, Man., Can. 43 F3
Cross Lake, Ont., Can. 46 F3
Cross Lake, Minn. 74 F2
Cross L., Man., Can. 43 F3
Cross L., Ont., Can. 46 E2
Cross L., Ont., Can. 46 H4
Cross L., La. 73 B5
Cross L., Me. 55 D1
Cross L., N.Y. 59 G5
Crossmolina, Ire. 113 B4
Crossnore, N.C., 277 63 C1
Cross Plains, Tenn. 71 E5
Cross Plains, Tex., 1,168 77 O3
Cross Plains, Wis., 1,066 66 D5
Cross Pt., Newf., Can. 45 a11
Cross River Res., N.Y. 56 B7
Crossroads, N. Mex. 79 D5
Cross Roads, Tex. 76 g10
Cross Roads, Va. 62 F5
Cross Sd., Alaska 85 K4
Cross Timbers, Mo., 186 72 D6
Cross Village, Mich. 67 H3
Crossville, Ala., 579 64 C1
Crossville, Ill., 874 68 D5
Crossville, Tenn., 4,668 71 G5
Crosswick Cr., N.J. 61 B3
Crosswicks, N.J. 61 B3
Croston, U.K., 2,005 114 C3
Croswell, Mich., 1,817 67 L5
Crotched Mtn., N.H. 54 D6
Crothersville, Ind., 1,449 70 D4
Croton = Hartford
Crotone, It., 40,455 123 F5
Croton-on-Hudson, N.Y., 6,812 59 N9
Crouch, Idaho, 89 81 B3
Crouse, N.C., 901 63 C2
Crow, r., Br. Col.-Yukon, Can. 42 F1
Crow, N. Fk., r., Minn. 74 E3
Crow Agency, Mont. 81 F3
Crowborough, U.K., 8,169 113 G6
Crow Buttes, S. Dak. 74 A3
Crow Cr., Colo.-Wyo. 79 C1
Crowder, Miss., 528 73 E3
Crowder, Okla., 254 76 H2
Crowell, Tex., 1,703 77 O3
Crowland, U.K., 2,879 114 H5
Crowle, U.K., 3,010 114 G3
Crowley, co., Colo., 3,978 79 D2
Crowley, Colo., 265 79 C2
Crowley, La., 15,617 73 C7
Crowley, Tex., 583 76 e9
Crowley, L., Calif. 82 D4
Crown City, Ohio, 323 70 G4
Crown King, Ariz. 78 B4
Crown Mtn., Virgin Is. 97 4
Crown Point, Ind., 8,443 70 B1
Crownpoint, N. Mex. 79 A4
Crown Point, N.Y. 59 O4
Crown Point Center, N.Y. 59 N4
Crownsville, Md. 62 c8
Crows Landing, Calif. 82 C4
Crow's Nest Butte, S. Dak. 74 A3
Crowthorne, U.K., 4,852 114 G8
Crow Wing, co., Minn., 32,134 74 E2
Crow Wing, r., Minn. 74 E2
Croydon, Austl. 173 F2
Croydon, London, U.K. 114 H8
Croydon, N.H. 54 C5
Croydon, Pa., 9,200* 60 g11
Croydon Flat, N.H. 54 C5
Croydon Pk., N.H. 54 C5
Croydon Station, Br. Col., Can. 42 G3
Crozer, Mt., Kusaie 176 31
Crozet, Va. 62 F4
Crozet, Îles, Ind. Oc. 168 B4
Crozet Basin, Ind. Oc. 168 C4
Crozier, Va. 62 G5
Crozier Chan., N.W.T., Can. 41 F2
Crozon, Fr., 6,919 116 A2
Cruces, Cuba, 11,000* 96 c1
Crudwell, U.K. 114 D7
Cruger, Miss., 362 73 E4
Cruiser Tablemount, Atl. Oc. 108 K4
Crum, W. Va. 62 B5
Crum Hill, Mass. 56 D2
Crummock Water, l., U.K. 114 B1
Crump, Mich. 67 J5
Crumpler, N.C. 63 C1
Crumpton, Md. 62 H3
Crumrod, Ark. 73 D3
Crusnes, Fr., 2,615 116 b8
Cruz, Cabo, Cuba 96 e3
Cruz, Cayo, Cuba 96 e1
Cruz Alta, Braz., 33,190 103 F7
Cruz Bay, V.I. 97 4
Cruz das Almas, Braz., 12,190 103 J4
Cruz de Elorza, Mex., 1,370 93 E3
Cruz del Eje, Arg., 25,800* 105 B4
Cruzeiro, Braz., 27,005 103 d18
Cruzeiro do Sul, Braz., 4,807 102 B3
Cruz Grande, Mex. 93 F5
Cruzília, Braz., 3,047 103 d17
Crystal, Mich. 67 J5
Crystal, Minn., 29,089 74 b5
Crystal, N.H. 54 E2
Crystal, N. Dak., 372 74 D1
Crystal, Okla. 76 H3
Crystal, Oreg. 80 B4
Crystal, r., Colo. 79 B2
Crystal Beach, Ont., Can., 1,881 46 E6
Crystal Beach, Fla. 65 G4
Crystal Brook, Austl., 1,001 172 E5
Crystal City, Man., Can. 43 e10
Crystal City, Mo., 3,678 72 G6
Crystal City, Tex., 9,101 77 O5
Crystal Falls, Mich., 2,203 66 E2
Crystal Hill, Va. 62 E6
Crystal Lake (part of Ellington), Conn. 56 G5
Crystal Lake, Fla. 65 D2
Crystal Lake, Ill., 10,211 68 D1
Crystal Lake, Iowa, 267 72 D1
Crystal L., Mich. 67 G4
Crystal L., N.H. 54 E5
Crystal Lake, Pa. 61 o17
Crystal L., Vt. 54 C2
Crystal Lakes, Ohio, 1,569 70 F3
Crystal River, Fla., 1,423 65 G4
Crystal Springs, Fla. 65 d11
Crystal Springs, Kans. 75 G6
Crystal Springs, Miss., 4,496 73 E5
Crystal Springs, N. Dak. 74 C2
Crystal Springs Res., Calif. 83 e12
Crystal Valley, Mich. 67 G5
Crystola, Colo. 79 b10
Csákvár, Hung., 5,139 126 D3
Csongrád, Hung., 20,690 126 E3
Csorna, Hung., 9,208 126 C3
Csorvás, Hung., 7,633 126 E3
Csurgó, Hung., 5,388 126 C3
Ctesiphon, ruins, Iraq 143 D2
Cúa, Ven., 5,544 101 c11
Cuajinicuilapa, Mex., 2,632 93 F5
Cualac, Mex., 1,568 93 F5
Cuamango, Mex., 1,229 93 e10
Cuanajo, Mex., 1,913 93 c10
Cuando, r., Ang. 164 C4
Cuangar, Ang. 164 C4
Cuango, r., Ang. 164 C3
Cuanza, r., Ang. 164 B3
Cuao, r., Ven. 100 G5
Cua Rao, N. Viet. 146 D3
Cuareim, r., Braz.-Urug. 103 E8
Cuarenta, Mex. 93 c8
Cuatrociénegas, Mex., 3931 92 E2
Cuauhtémoc, Chih., Mex., 14,639 92 D2
Cuauhtémoc, Colima, Mex., 3,765 92 E4
Cuautepec, Mex., 5,122 93 f9
Cuautitlán, Mex., 8,494 93 F4
Cuautla, Mex., 11,847 93 F4
Cuba, ctry., 7,833,000* 96
Cuba, Port., 4,212 122 B3
Cuba, Ala., 390 64 A3
Cuba, Ill. 68 B3
Cuba, N. Mex. 79 B3
Cuba, Ill., 1,380 68 B3
Cuba, Kans., 336 75 H4
Cuba, Mo., 1,672 72 F6
Cuba, N.Y., 1,949 58 D7
Cuba City, Wis., 1,673 66 C6
Cubagua, I., Ven. 101 H2
Cubal, Ang. 164 B4
Cubango, r., Ang. 164 B4
Cubatão, Braz., 18,885 103 c18
Cubero, N. Mex. 79 B4
Çubuk, Turk, 5,938 142 C1
Cubulco, Guat., 1,666 94 c8
Cuca, Rum. 128 E2
Cucalaya, Nic. 94 F4
Cucalaya, r., Nic. 94 F4
Cucamonga, Calif. 83 i15
Cucapás, Sa. de los, Mex. 82 F6
Cuchara, P., P.R. 96 s11
Cucharas, r., Colo. 79 C3
Cu Chi, S. Viet., 16,958 147 m11
Cuchillo, N. Mex. 79 B5
Cuchivero, r., Ven. 100 H4
Cuckfield, U.K., 20,134 113 F6
Cucuí, Braz. 102 C1
Cucurpe, Mex. 92 C1
Cucurrupí, Col. 100 B5
Cúcuta, Col. 100 D4
Cudahy, Wis., 17,975 66 F6
Cuddalore, India, 79,168 145 F8
Cuddapah, India, 49,027 145 F7
Cuddeback L., Calif. 82 E5
Cudworth, Sask., Can. 43 C4
Cudworth, U.K., 9,042 114 F3
Cue, Austl. 172 B4
Cuéllar, Sp., 6,693 122 C2
Cuemani, r., Col. 100 D7
Cuenca, Ec., 60,021 104 B2
Cuenca, Sp., 27,007 122 D2
Cuencamé de Ceniceros, Mex., 2,982 92 E3
Cuenca, Snia. de, Sp. 122 D2
Cuerámaro, Mex., 5,625 93 c9
Cuernavaca, Mex., 35,847 93 F4
Cuero, Tex., 7,338 77 P5
Cuervo, N. Mex. 79 C4
Cuesta del Melado, Chile 104 f15
Cuestecita, Col. 100 D2
Cueto, Cuba, 5,983 96 e2
Cuetzalá, Mex., 3,292 93 F4
Cuevas, Mex., 1,613 93 e10
Cuevitas, Tex. 77 O6
Cugir, Rum. 128 D2
Cuiabá, Braz., 43,112 103 E5
Cuiabá, r., Braz. 103 E5
Cuicatlán, Mex., 1,986 93 F5
Cuidado, P., Easter I. 177 46
Cuilapa, Guat., 3,948 94 B3
Cuilco, Guat. 94 a8
Cuileagh, mtn., Ire.-U.K. 113 C4
Cuilo, r., Ang. 164 C3
Cuima, Ang. 164 B4
Cuio, Ang. 164 B4
Cuisery, Fr., 1,444 117 F3
Cuisnahuat, El Salv., 1,308 94 d10
Cuité, Braz., 4,164 103 a14
Cuito, r., Ang. 164 C4
Cuito-Cuanavale, Ang. 164 C4
Cuitzeo, Mex., 4,485 93 c10
Cuitzeo, L. de, Mex. 93 c10
Cuitzeo de Hidalgo, Mex., 5,877 93 c9
Cuivre, N. Fk., r., Mo. 72 F5
Cuivre, W. Fk., r., Mo. 72 F5
Cujmir, Rum. 128 D2
Culaba, Phil., 3,463 153 C3
Culaman, Phil., 1,144 153 C4
Culan, Fr., 1,359 117 E3
Culberson, N.C. 63 a7
Culberson, co., Tex., 2,794 77 L4
Culbertson, Mont., 919 81 G1
Culbertson, Nebr., 803 75 E3
Culcairn, Austl., 1,093 173 f10
Culdesac, Idaho, 209 81 A2
Cul De Sac, Mo. 72 a10
Cul de Sac, plain, Haiti 96 k6
Cul-des-Sarts, Belg., 1,028 115 C5
Culebra, Peru 104 B3
Culebra, P.R. 96 v10
Culebra, Isla de, P.R. 96 v10
Culebra Pk., Colo. 79 C3
Culebrinas, r., P.R. 96 r10
Culebrita, I., P.R. 96 v10
Culemborg, Neth., 11,200 115 D3
Culiacán, Mex., 84,602 92 D3
Culion, Phil., 3,752 153 A3
Culion I., Phil. 153 B3
Culiprán, Chile 104 f13
Cúllar de Baza, Sp., 8,883 122 D4
Cullen, U.K., 1,327 112 E3
Cullen, La., 2,194 73 B5
Cullen, Va. 62 F5
Culleoka, Tenn. 71 D6
Culleoka, Tex. 76 f8
Cullin, L., Ire. 113 B5
Cullinan, S. Af., 4,211 165 k16
Cullinvaile, S. Af. 165 k17
Cullison, Kans., 129 75 G6
Cullman, co., Ala., 45,572 64 C1
Cullman, Ala., 10,883 64 C1
Cullom, Ill., 555 68 D3
Cullomburg, Ala. 64 A4
Cullompton, U.K., 3,415 113 E6
Cullowhee, N.C. 63 A2
Culmerville, Pa. 60 C4
Culp Creek, Oreg. 80 B4
Culpeper, co., Va., 15,088 62 F4
Culpeper, Va., 2,412 62 F4
Culpepper, I., Colón, Arch. de 104 a7
Culpina, Bol., 5,355 102 D6
Culross, U.K. 112 c7
Cults, U.K. 112 E3
Culuene, r., Braz. 103 F4
Culver, Ind., 1,558 70 C1
Culver, Kans., 200 75 H5
Culver, Oreg., 301 80 C3
Culver, Pt., Austl. 172 C5
Culver City, Calif., 32,163 83 h15
Culverden, N.Z. 175 g6
Culver Lake, N.J. 61 B1
Cumaná, Ven., 71,563 101 H2
Cumanacoa, Ven., 7,626 101 J2
Cumanayagua, Cuba, 4,679 96 c1
Cumaral, Col. 100 D5
Cumbal, Col. 100 B7
Cumbal, Nev. de, Col. 100 A7
Cumbels, Switz. 124 D2
Cumberland, Br. Col., Can., 1,256 42 F4
Cumberland, St. Vinc. 97 19
Cumberland, co., U.K., 294,162 113 E4
Cumberland, co., Ill., 9,936 68 D4
Cumberland, Ind., 872 70 D3
Cumberland, Iowa, 425 72 B3
Cumberland, co., Ky., 7,835 71 F5
Cumberland, Ky., 4,271 71 H4
Cumberland, co., Me., 182,751 55 B5
Cumberland, Md., 33,415 62 F3
Cumberland, Miss. 73 F4
Cumberland, co., N.C., 148,418 63 F2
Cumberland, N.C. 63 E2
Cumberland, co., N.J., 106,850 61 A5
Cumberland, Ohio, 493 70 H3
Cumberland, co., Pa., 124,816 60 H5
Cumberland, co., Tenn., 19,135 71 F6
Cumberland, co., Va., 6,360 62 F5
Cumberland, Va. 62 F5
Cumberland, Wash. 80 C2
Cumberland, Wis., 1,860 66 B3
Cumberland, r., Ky.-Tenn. 71 C5
Cumberland, Big S. Fk., r., Ky. 71 G5
Cumberland, C., New Hebr. 174 k5
Cumberland, L., Ky. 71 G5
Cumberland Center, Me. 55 B5
Cumberland City, Tenn., 314 71 D5
Cumberland Gap, Tenn., 291 71 H5
Cumberland Gap, U.S. 62 ·
Cumberland Gap Nat. Hist. Pk., U.S. 71 H5
Cumberland House, Sask., Can. 43 D4
Cumberland I., Ga. 64 H5
Cumberland L., Sask., Can. 43 D3
Cumberland Mts., U.S. 71 G5
Cumberland Pen., N.W.T., Can. 41 Q4
Cumberland Plat., Ky.-Tenn. 71 ·
Cumberland Pt., Mich. 66 a9
Cumberland Sd., N.W.T., Can. 41 Q4
Cumbrian Mts., U.K. 114 B2
Cumby, Tex., 447 77 P3
Cuminá, r., Braz. 103 E1
Cuming, co., Nebr., 12,435 75 J2
Cummaquid (part of Barnstable), Mass. 57 P6
Cumming, Ga., 1,561 64 E1
Cumming, Iowa, 148 72 D3
Cummings, S.C. 63 D5
Cummington, Mass. 56 E3
Cummins, Austl. 172 a8
Cummins Pk., Oreg. 80 B3
Cumminsville, Nebr. 75 G2
Cummock, Austl. 173 g9
Cumnock, U.K. 112 b8
Cumpas, Mex., 2,314 92 C2
Cumpeo, Chile, 1,006 104 f15
Çumra, Turk., 7,089 142 C2
Cumuato, Mex., 1,252 93 b9
Cunagua, Cuba, 1,879 96 d1
Cunani, Braz. 103 F1
Cunapo, r., Trin. and Tob. 96 g5
Cunaviche, Ven. 100 G4
Cunaviche, r., Ven. 100 G4
Cunco, Chile, 3,342 105 A5
Cuncumén, Chile 104 f13
Cunday, Col. 100 C5
Cunderdin, Austl. 172 B4
Cunén, Guat., 2,374 94 c8
Cunene, r., Ang. 164 B4
Cuneo, It., 44,926 123 A2
Cungena, Austl. 172 a7
Cunha, Braz., 2,693 103 d18
Cuñibal, Chile 104 e17
Cunnamulla, Austl., 1,955 173 G4
Cunningham, Kans., 618 75 G6
Cunningham, Ky. 71 C5
Cunucunuma, r., Ven. 100 H6
Čuokkarašša, mt., Nor. 120 F1
Cuorgnè, It., 7,903 122 a5
Cupar, Sask., Can. 43 D4
Cupar, U.K., 5,495 112 E3
Cupareo, Mex., 1,543 93 d9
Cupertino, Calif., 3,664 83 e13
Cupica, Col. 100 B4
Cupids, Newf., Can. 45 b10
Cúpira, Ven., 1,214 100 H2
Cupo, r., Ven. 101 c11
Ćuprija, Yug., 14,000* 125 E3
Cuprum, Idaho 81 A3
Cupsuptic, r., Me. 55 B3
Cúpula, P., Mex. 92 C3
Cuquío, Mex., 1,957 93 b9
Cura, r., Ven. 101 c12
Curaçá, Braz., 1,264 103 J3
Curaçao, i., Lesser Ant. 97 16
Curacautín, Chile, 9,601 105 A5
Curacaví, Chile, 4,116 104 f13
Curahuara de Carangas, Bol., 3,314 102 C5
Curanga, r., Peru 104 D4
Curanipe, Chile 104 e15
Curaray, r., Ec.-Peru 104 B2
Curarigua, Ven., 1,133 100 E3
Curaumilla, P., Chile 104 f13
Curdsville, Ky. 71 D4
Curepipe, Maurit., 22,000* 165 c12
Curepto, Chile, 1,699 105 A5
Curiapo, Ven. 101 K3
Curicó, Chile, 32,562 105 A4
Curiepe, Ven., 2,352 100 G2
Curieuse I., Seych. 165 a10
Curillinque, Chile 104 g15
Curimagua, Ven. 100 F2
Curimeo, Mex., 2,879 93 c9
Curinhuás, r., Nic. 94 E4
Curitiba, Braz., 344,560 103 F7
Curitibanos, Braz., 8,339 103 F7
Curlew, Iowa, 134 72 C2
Curlew, Wash. 80 D1
Curling, Newf., Can., 3,750 45 P5
Curone, r., It. 122 c6
Currais Novos, Braz., 7,782 103 a14
Curral Velho, C. Verde Is. 109 5
Curramulka, Austl. 172 b8
Curran, Mich. 67 K4
Currane, L., Ire. 113 A6
Currant, Nev. 83 C3
Current, Bah. Is. 95 c7
Current, r., Mo. 72 G8
Current I., Bah. Is. 95 c7
Currie, Austl. 173 F6
Currie, Minn., 438 74 E3
Currie, Nev. 83 C2
Currie, N.C. 63 F3
Curries, Ont., Can. 46 a15
Currituck, co., N.C., 6,610 63 J1
Currituck, N.C. 63 H1
Currituck Sd., N.C. 63 J1
Curry, Alaska 85 G3
Curry, co., N. Mex., 32,691 79 D4
Curry, N.Y. 59 L8
Curry, co., Oreg., 13,983 80 A4
Curryville, Mo., 287 72 F5
Curtatone, It., 8,108 122 d5
Curtea de Argeş, Rum., 10,764 128 E2
Curtici, Rum. 128 C1
Curtin, Oreg. 80 B4
Curtis, Ark. 73 B3
Curtis, Mackinac Co., Mich. 67 J5
Curtis, Midland Co., Mich. 67 H2
Curtis, Nebr., 868 75 E3
Curtis, Okla. 76 D1
Curtis Chan., Austl. 173 H3
Curtis I., Austl. 173 G3
Curtis I., N.Z. 170 G7
Curtiss, Wis., 147 66 C4
Curtisville, Mich. 67 K4
Curuá, r., Braz. 103 F3
Curuapanema, r., Braz. 103 E1
Curuçá, Braz., 3,871 103 G2
Curuçá, r., Braz. 102 B3
Curupira, Sa. de, Ven. 101
Cururupu, Braz., 4,822 103 H2
Curve, Tenn. 71 B6
Curvelo, Braz., 21,772 103 H5
Curwensville, Pa., 3,231 60 E4
Cusano Mutri, It., 5,432 123 c9
Cushat Law, mtn., U.K. 112 f9
Cushendall, U.K. 113 D4
Cushing, Iowa, 261 72 B2
Cushing, Me. 55 C4
Cushing, Nebr., 56 75 G2
Cushing, Okla., 8,619 76 G2
Cushing, Tex., 388 77 Q4
Cushing, Wis. 66 A3
Cushman (part of Amherst), Mass. 56 G3
Cushman, Oreg. 80 B4
Cusick, Wash., 299 80 E1
Cuslett, Newf., Can. 45 a11
Cusset, Fr., 11,784 117 E3
Cusseta, Ga., 768 64 E3
Cussewago Cr., Pa. 60 B2
Custar, Ohio, 246 70 F1
Custer, co., Colo., 1,305 79 C2
Custer, co., Idaho, 2,996 81 B3
Custer, Ky. 71 E4
Custer, Mich., 365 67 G5
Custer, co., Mont., 13,227 81 G2
Custer, Mont. 81 F2
Custer, co., Nebr., 16,517 75 F2
Custer, co., Okla., 21,040 76 D2
Custer, Okla., 448 76 E2
Custer, co., S. Dak., 4,906 74 A4
Custer, S. Dak., 2,105 74 A4
Custer, Wash. 80 B1
Custer, Wis. 66 D4
Custer Battlefield Nat. Mon., Mont. 81 F3
Custer Mtn., S. Dak. 74 A4
Custer Park, Ill. 68 D2
Custer Pk., S. Dak. 74 A3
Custines, Fr., 2,639 116 b9
Cusubamba, Ec. 104 c10
Cut Bank, Mont., 4,539 81 C1
Cut Bank Cr., Mont. 81 C1
Cut Bank Cr., N. Dak. 74 B1
Cutchogue, N.Y. 59 P9
Cutervo, Peru, 4,687 104 B3
Cuthbert, Ga., 4,300 64 E4
Cuthbert Pt., Austl. 172 E1
Cut Knife, Sask., Can. 43 B4
Cutler, Ont., Can. 46 B2
Cutler, Calif., 2,191 82 D4
Cutler, Ill., 445 68 C5
Cutler, Ind. 70 C2
Cutler, Me. 55 E4
Cutler, Ohio 70 H3
Cutler City, Oreg. 80 B3
Cutler Ridge, Fla., 7,005 65 J7
Cutlerville, Mich. 67 H6
Cut Off, La. 73 E8
Cutra, L., Ire. 113 B5
Cutral-Có, Arg., 16,000* 105 B5
Cutro, It., 12,121 123 F5
Cuttack, India, 146,303 145 G5
Cuttingsville, Vt. 54 B5
Cuttyhunk, Mass. 57 N7
Cuttyhunk I., Mass. 57 N7
Cutuglahua, Ec. 104 c10
Cuturi, r., Ven. 101 J5
Cutzamalá, r., Mex. 93 d11
Cutzio, Mex. 93 d11
Cuvier, C., Austl. 172 A3
Cuvo, r., Ang. 164 B3
Cuxhaven, F.R.Ger., 43,700 118 B2
Cuxpala, Mex. 93 a8
Cuyabeno, Ec. 104 C2
Cuyahoga, co., Ohio, 1,647,895 70 H1
Cuyahoga, r., Ohio 70 H1
Cuyahoga Falls, Ohio, 47,922 70 H1
Cuyama, r., Calif. 82 D5
Cuyapo, Phil., 7,617 153 b7
Cuyk, Neth., 5,600 115 D3
Cuylerville, N.Y. 58 E6
Cuyo East Pass, Phil. 153 B3
Cuyo I., Phil. 153 B3
Cuyo Is., Phil. 153 B3
Cuyo West Pass, Phil. 153 B3
Cuyuni, r., Guyana-Ven. 101 L4
Cuzco, Peru, 60,048 104 C5
Cuzco, Ind. 70 C4
Čvrsnica, mts., Yug. 125 C3
Cwmbran, U.K., 22,486 114 C7
C. W. McConaughy, L., Nebr. 75 C2
Cybinka, Pol., 2,421 127 A2
Cyclades = Kikládhes
Cyclone, Pa. 60 E2
Cygnet, Ohio, 593 70 F1
Cylinder, Iowa 161 72 C1
Cynthiana, Ind., 663 70 B4
Cynthiana, Ky., 5,641 71 G3
Cynthiana, Ohio 70 F3
Cynwyd, U.K. 114 B5
Cypress, Calif., 1,753 83 h16
Cypress, Ill., 264 68 C6
Cypress, Ind. 70 B5
Cypress, Tex. 77 Q5
Cypress, r., Man., Can. 43 f10
Cypress, Pt., Calif. 83 e14
Cypress Chapel, Va. 62 H2
Cypress Hills, Sask., Can. 43 B5
Cypress Mill, Tex. 76 b5
Cypress River, Man., Can. 43 f10
Cyprus, ctry., 603,000* 142 C3
Cyrenaica = Barqah
Cyrene = Shaḥḥāt
Cyril, Okla., 1,284 76 E3
Cyrn-y-Brain, mtn., U.K. 114 B4
Cysoing, Fr., 3,303 116 a6
Cythera = Kíthira
Czaplinek, Pol., 4,517 127 B2
Czar, Alta., Can. 42 L3
Czarna, r., Pol. 127 k5
Czarna Wieś, Pol., 4,593 127 E2
Czarna Woda, Pol., 1,460 127 C2
Czarne, Pol., 3,267 127 B2
Czarnków, Pol., 5,722 127 B2
Czechoslovakia, ctry., 14,194,000* 126
Czechowice, Pol., 23,000* 127 C4
Czempin, Pol., 3,258 127 B2
Czeremcha, Pol. 127 E2
Czerna Wielka, r., Pol. 127 e5
Czersk, Pol., 7,252 127 B2
Czersk, Pol. 127 D3
Czerwieńsk, Pol., 2,498 127 A2
Czerwin, Pol. 127 D2
Czerwionka, Pol., 8,924 127 h6
Czerwona Woda, Pol. 127 e5
Częstochowa, Pol., 164,000* 127 C3
Człopa, Pol., 1,807 127 B2
Człuchów, Pol., 5,944 127 B2

D

Da, China = Li-hsien
Da, r., N. Viet. 146 D2
Daaden, F.R.Ger., 2,879 119 D3
Daam Pk., Indon. 149 L4
Daanbantayan, Phil., 2,641 153 f10
Da-an Banwa, Phil., 11,702 153 d11
Dabajuro, Ven. 3,902 100 E2
Dabakala, Iv. Coast 162 a7
Dabar, Yug. 125 B2
Dabbāgh, Jabal, Saudi Ar. 143 B3
Dabeiba, Col. 100 B4
Dabhoi, India, 30,841 145 D5
Dąbie, Pol. 127 A2
Dąbie, Pol., 2,547 127 C2
Dąbie, Jez., Pol. 127 A2
Dabo, Fr., 3,037 116 d9
Dabob, Wash. 81 a7
Dabob Bay, Wash. 81 a7
Dabola, Guin., 5,000 162 C4
Dabong, Malay. 147 p14
Dabou, Iv. Coast, 4,500 162 a9
Daboya, Ghana 162 c7
Dabra, India, 12,661 144 b13
Dąbrowa Górnicza, Pol., 42,000* 127 i6
Dąbrowa Tarnowska, Pol., 4,880 127 D3
d'Abruzzo, Parco Naz., Italy 123 D4
Dabugam, India 145 G6
Dacca, Pak., 556,712 145 H5
Dachau, F.R.Ger., 25,592 118 C4
Dachi, Jap. 154 i14
Dačice, Czech. 126 B2
Dac Lac, Cao Nguyen, plat., S. Viet. 146 D4
Dacoma, Okla., 219 76 E1
Dacono, Colo., 302 79 c7
Dacura, Nic. 94 F3
Dacusville, S.C. 63 B3
Dadanawa, Guyana 101 L6
Dade, co., Fla., 935,047 65 J7
Dade, co., Ga., 8,666 64 D1
Dade, co., Mo., 7,577 72 D7
Dade City, Fla., 4,759 65 G4
Dadeville, Ala., 2,940 64 D3
Dadeville, Mo., 142 72 D7
Dādhar, Pak., 4,099 144 C3
Dadra-Nagar Havili, un. terr., India 145 D5
Dadri, India, 13,839 144 a11
Dādu, Pak., 19,142 144 C4
Daet, Phil., 19,726 153 B2
Dafter, Mich. 67 J2
Dagahbur, Eth. 163 M4
Dagami, Phil., 3,569 153 f10
Dagana, Sen., 4,156 162 B3
Dagash, Sudan 163 K2
Dagaya, i., Jaluit 176 30
Dagelet = Ullŭng-do
Dagestanskiye Ogni, U.S.S.R., 6,700 137 d1
Daggett, Calif. 82 E5
Daggett, co., Utah, 1,164 78 D1
Daggett, Mich., 296 66 F3
Dagg Sd., N.Z. 175 e7
Dagmersellen, Switz., 2,287 124 C1
Dagsboro, Del., 477 62 J4
Dagua, Col. 100 B6
Dagua, Terr. New Guin. 174 d1
Dagupan, Phil., 14,613 153 B1
Dah, Indon. 149 L4
Dahāna, Afghan. 144 C2
Dahanu, India, 9,648 145 D6
Dahl, F.R.Ger., 4,821 119 D2
Dahlak Arch., Eth. 163 L3
Dahlem, F.R.Ger., 1,242 119 B4
Dahlen, Ger.D.R. 126 c5
Dahlgren, Ill., 480 68 D5
Dahlhausen, Ger.D.R. 118 D2
Dahlonega, Ga., 2,604 64 E1
Dahme, Ger.D.R. 118 D3
Dahme, r., Ger.D.R. 118 D2
Dahn, F.R.Ger., 3,711 119 D6
Dahomey, ctry., 2,300,000* 162 E4
Dahra, Libya 161 H3
Dahūk, Iraq, 7,638 143 C1
Daia, Rum. 128 E1
Daigo, Jap., 43,124 155 G3
Daigo, Jap. 155 m19
Daik-u, Burma, 9,668 146 B3
d'Ail, C., Fr. 116 n13
Dailekh, Nepal 145 F3
Dailey, W. Va. 62 E4
Daimiel, Sp., 19,625 122 D3
Daimon, Jap. 155 m19
Daimotsu, Jap. 154 g14
Daingean, Ire. 113 C5
Daingerfield, Tex., 3,133 77 Q3
Daintree, Austl. 173 F2
Dairen = Lü-ta
Dairy, Oreg. 80 C4
Dairyland, Wis. 66 A2
Dairy Valley, Calif., 3,508 83 h16
Dai-sen, mtn., Jap. 155 C4
Dai-Sengen-dake, Jap. 155 H9
Daisen-ktk., Jap. 155 C4
Daisetsuzan-ktk., Jap. 155 K8
Daisetta, Tex., 1,500 77 Q4
Daisy, Ark. 86 73 B3
Daisy, Ga., 229 64 H3
Daisy, Md. 62 a7
Daisy, Okla. 76 H3
Daisy, Tenn., 1,508 71 F6
Daitō, Jap., 17,141 155 C4
Daitō-jima, Ryukyu Is. 154 d13
Dajabón, Dom. Rep., 3,230 96 m6
Dajarra, Austl. 172 E3
Daju, Indon. 148 E3
Daka, r., Ghana 162 c7
Dakar, Sen., 382,980 162 A3
Dākhilah, Al Wāḥāt ad, oasis, U.A.R. 161 J3
Dākhla Oasis = Dākhilah, Al Wāḥāt ad
Dakoro, Niger, 2,381 162 F3
Dakota, Ga. 64 F4
Dakota, Ill., 363 68 C1
Dakota, co., Minn., 78,303 74 F3
Dakota, Minn., 339 74 G4
Dakota, co., Nebr., 12,168 75 J1
Dakota City, Iowa, 706 72 C2
Dakota City, Nebr., 928 75 J1
Đakovica, Yug., 21,000* 125 E3
Đakovo, Yug., 12,000* 125 D2
Dak Song, S. Viet. 147 m10
Dak Sut, S. Viet. 146 D4
Dak To, S. Viet. 146 D4
Dalaba, Guin., 15,000 162 B4
Dalaguete, Phil., 3,115 153 e12
Dalälven, r., Swed. 120 D3
Dalaman, r., Turk. 142 B2
Dalāmī, Sudan 163 K4
Dalan Dzadagad, Mong. 150 E2
Dalark, Ark., 123 73 C3
Dalarö, Swed. 120 f8
Da Lat, S. Viet., 56,651 146 E5
Dālbandin, Pak., 1,724 144 B3

218 · Delaney—Dinar

Delaney, Ark. 73 B2
Delano, Calif., 11,913 82 D5
Delano, Minn., 1,612 74 F3
Delano Mines, Nev. 83 C2
Delano Pk., Utah 78 B2
Delanson, N.Y., 398 59 M6
Delaplaine, Ark., 186 73 E1
Delareyville, S. Af., 2,781 164 D6
Delaronde L., Sask., Can. 43 C3
Delavan, Ill., 1,377 68 C3
Delavan, Wis., 4,846 66 E6
Delavan L., Wis. 66 E6
Delaware, Ont., Can. 46 C6
Delaware, st., U.S., 503,000* 62
Delaware, Ark. 73 B2
Delaware, co., Ind., 110,938 70 D2
Delaware, co., Iowa, 18,483 72 F2
Delaware, Mich. 66 E1
Delaware, Mo. 72 F7
Delaware, N.J. 61 A2
Delaware, co., N.Y., 43,540 59 K7
Delaware, co., Ohio, 36,107 70 F2
Delaware, Ohio, 13,282 70 F2
Delaware, co., Okla., 13,198 76 J1
Delaware, Okla., 540 76 H1
Delaware, co., Pa., 553,154 61 M6
Delaware, r., U.S. 53 M2
Delaware Bay, Del.-N.J. 61 A5
Delaware City, Del., 1,658 62 J3
Delaware Cr., Tex. 77 L4
Delaware Mts., Tex. 77 L4
Delaware Res., Ohio 70 F2
Delaware Water Gap, Pa., 554 61 M4
Delaware Water Gap, N.J.-Pa. 61 ·
Delbarton, W. Va., 1,122 62 B5
Del Bonita, Alta., Can. 42 K4
Delbrück, F.R.Ger., 2,285 119 F1
Delburne, Alta., Can. 42 K3
Delcambre, La., 1,857 73 D8
Del Carril, Arg., 3,500* 105 b12
Delčevo, Yug., 3,033 125 F4
Del City, Okla., 12,934 76 F2
Delco, N.C., 466 63 F3
Delegate, Austl. 173 G5
De Lemmer, Neth., 4,400 115 D2
Delémont, Switz., 9,542 124 B1
De Leon, Tex., 2,022 77 O3
De Leon Springs, Fla. 65 H3
Delevan, N.Y., 777 58 C7
Delfina, Tex. 77 O6
Delft, Neth., 72,800 115 C2
Delfzijl, Neth., 13,900 115 E1
Delgado Chalbaud, Co., Braz.-Ven. 101 J6
Delger Mörön, r., Mong. 150 D1
Delhi, Ont., Can., 3,378 44 H7
Delhi, un. terr., India, 2,658,612 144 a11
Delhi, India, 2,061,758 145 E3
Delhi, Calif., 1,175 82 C4
Delhi, Colo. 79 D3
Delhi, Ill. 68 B4
Delhi, Iowa, 464 72 F2
Delhi, La., 2,514 73 D5
Delhi, N.Y., 2,664 59 L7
Delhi, Okla. 76 D2
Delia, Alta., Can. 42 K3
Delia, Kans., 163 75 K4
Delice, r., Turk. 142 C2
Delicias, Cuba, 5,849 96 e2
Delicias, Mex., 40,017 92 D2
De Lier, Neth., 3,400 115 C3
Delight, Ark., 446 73 B3
Deligrad, Yug. 125 E3
Delijaš, Yug. 125 D3
Delinești, Rum. 128 D2
Deli, P., Indon. 148 a7
Delisle, Sask., Can. 43 C4
Delisle, r., Ont., Can. 47 K3
Delitzsch, Ger.D.R., 22,892 118 D3
Deliverance, C., Rossel I. 175 a3
Dell (part of Heath), Mass. 56 E2
Dell City, Tex. 77 L4
Delle, Fr., 5,197 117 G3
Delle, Utah 78 B1
Dell Rapids, S. Dak., 1,863 74 D4
Dellrose, Tenn. 71 E6
Dellroy, Ohio, 391 70 H2
Dellvale, Kans. 75 F4
Dellwood, Oreg. 80 B4
Dellwood, Wis. 66 D4
Dellys, Alg., 7,506 160 c5
Del Mar., Calif., 3,124 82 c9
Delmar, Del.-Md., 2,225 62 J4
Delmar, Iowa, 556 72 G2
Delmar, N.Y. 59 N6
Del Mar Beach, N.C. 63 G3
Delmenhorst, F.R.Ger., 54,791 118 B2
Delmiro Gouveia, Braz., 6,147 103 J3
Delmont, N.J. 61 B5
Delmont, S. Dak., 363 74 C4
Delnice, Yug., 4,244 125 B2
Del Norte, co., Calif., 17,771 82 B2
Del Norte, Colo., 1,856 79 B3
Deloit, Iowa, 222 72 B2
Delong, Ind. 70 C1
De-Longa, O-va., U.S.S.R. 135 P2
De Long Mts., Alaska 85 D1
Deloraine, Austl., 1,772 173 F6
Deloraine, Man., Can. 43 E5
Delorme, L., Qué., Can. 45 L3
Deloro, Ont., Can. 46 C4
Del Paso Heights, Calif., 11,495 82 a7
Delphi=Dhelfoí
Delphi, Ind., 2,517 70 C2
Delphi Falls, N.Y. 59 J6
Delph or Old Bedford, r., U.K. 114 J6
Delphos, Kans., 619 75 H4
Delphos, N. Mex. 79 D4
Delphos, Ohio, 6,961 70 E2
Del Pilar, Phil., 5,152 153 b7
Delray Beach, 12,230 65 K6
Delray Gardens, Fla. 65 b9
Del Rey Oaks, Calif., 1,831 83 f14
Del Rio, Tex., 18,612 77 N5
Delson, Qué., Can., 1,847 47 o18
Delta, Br. Col., Can. 42 E3
Delta, Ont., Can. 47 H4
Delta, Ala. 64 D2
Delta, co., Colo., 15,602 79 B2
Delta, Colo., 3,832 79 A2
Delta, Iowa, 514 72 E3
Delta, La., 111 73 D5
Delta, co., Mich., 34,298 66 G3
Delta, Ohio, 2,376 70 F1
Delta, Pa., 822 61 K6
Delta, co., Tex., 5,860 77 Q3
Delta, Utah, 1,576 78 B2
Delta, Wis. 66 B2
Delta, r., Alaska 85 H3
Delta L., N.Y. 59 K5
Delta Station, Man., Can. 43 f9
Deltaville, Va. 62 H5
Delton, Mich. 67 H6
Delungra, Austl. 173 G4
Del Valle, Tex. 76 c5
Delvinë, Alb., 5,350 125 E4
Delwin, Mich. 67 J5
Delyatin, U.S.S.R., 7,400 136 B3
Dëma, r., U.S.S.R. 137 h9
Demak, Indon. 148 D4
Demarcation Pt., Alaska 85 J1
Demarest, N.J., 4,231 58 d13
Demay L., Alta., Can. 43 c7
Demba, D.R.Congo 164 C2
Dembidollo, Eth. 163 K4
Demer, r., Belg. 115 C3
Demerara, r., Guyana 101 L5
Deming, N. Mex., 6,764 79 B5
Deming, Wash. 80 B1
Demini, r., Braz. 102 D1
Demirci, Turk., 8,738 142 B2
Demirciköy, Turk., 3,604 142 B2
Demirköy, Turk., 2,348 128 F4
Demmin, Ger.D.R., 16,355 118 D2
Demmitt, Alta., Can. 42 H2
Demnate, Mor., 6,223 160 C2
Democrat, Tex. 77 O4
De Montreville, L., Minn. 74 d5
Demopolis, Ala., 7,377 64 B3
Demopolis Dam, Ala. 64 B3
Demorest, Ga., 1,029 64 F1
Demotte, Ind. 70 B1
Dempo, G., Indon. 148 B4
Dempsey, Okla. 76 D2
Dempster, S. Dak. 74 D3
Demta, Indon. 149 L3
Dem'yanovka, U.S.S.R. 137 m11
Dem'yanskoye, U.S.S.R. 134 G4
Denain, Fr., 29,467 117 E1
Denali, Alaska 85 H3
Denare Beach, Sask., Can. 43 D3
Denau, U.S.S.R., 17,100 134 F6
Denay Cr., Nev. 83 B2
Denbigh, U.K., 8,059 113 E5
Denbighshire, co., U.K., 174,151 113 E5
Den Bommel, Neth. 115 a7
Den Burg, Neth., 3,600 115 C1
Denby Dale, U.K., 9,304 114 E3
Dendang, Indon. 148 D3
Den Deijl, Neth. 115 a6
Dender, r., Belg. 115 B4
Denderleeuw, Belg., 8,704 115 C4
Dendermonde, Belg., 9,760 115 C3
Dendre=Dender
Dendron, Va., 403 62 H5
Deneysville, S. Af. 165 k17
Denezhkin Kamen', G., U.S.S.R. 137 i6
Denges Passage, Palau 176 21
Den Haag='s Gravenhage
Denham, Ind. 70 C1
Denham, Minn., 71 74 F2
Denham Sd., Austl. 172 A3
Denham Springs, La., 5,991 73 D7
Denhead, U.K. 112 e7
Den Helder, Neth., 43,500 115 C2
Denhoff, N. Dak. 74 B2
Den Hout, Neth. 115 b7
Denia, Sp., 12,185 122 F3
Denial Bay, Austl. 172 D5
Denigomodu (dist.), Nauru 175 17
Deniliquin, Austl., 4,704 173 F5
Denio, Nev. 83 A2
Denis I., Seych. 165 a10
Denison, Iowa, 4,930 72 B2
Denison, Kans., 184 75 K4
Denison, Tex., 22,748 77 P3
Denison, Mt., Alaska 85 F4
Denisovka, U.S.S.R. 137 k9
Denizli, Turk., 49,042 142 B2
Denklingen, F.R.Ger., 6,023 119 D3
Denman Gl., Ant. 180 T6
Denman I., Br. Col., Can. 42 b6
Denmark, ctry., 4,758,000* 121
Denmark, Austl., 1,113 172 B5
Denmark, Ga. 64 H3
Denmark, Kans. 75 G4
Denmark, Me. 55 B5
Denmark, Miss. 73 F3
Denmark, S.C., 3,221 63 C4
Denmark, Wis., 1,106 66 F4
Denmark Str., Eur. 108 L2
Denmead, U.K., 2,863 113 k13
Dennard, Ark. 73 C2
Dennery, St. Lucia, 1,889 97 11
Dennis, Kans. 75 K6
Dennis, Mass., 3,727(T) 57 Q6
Dennis, Miss. 73 G3
Dennis, Okla. 76 J1
Dennis, Tex. 76 d9
Dennison, Ill. 68 E4
Dennison, Ohio, 4,158 70 H2
Dennis Port, Mass., 1,271 57 Q6
Dennisville, N.J. 61 B5
Denny (incl. Dunipace), U.K., 7,761 112 c7
Dennysville, Me. 55 E4
Den Oever, Neth. 115 D2
Denpasar, Indon. 148 E5
Densmore, Kans. 75 F4
Dent, U.K. 113 E4
Dent, Minn., 176 74 E2
Dent, co., Mo., 10,445 72 F7
Dent, Ohio 71 g10
Denta, Rum. 128 C2
Denton, Lancs., Eng., U.K., 31,086 114 D4
Denton, Lincs., Eng., U.K. 114 G5
Denton, Ga., 255 64 G4
Denton, Ky. 71 J3
Denton, Md., 1,938 62 J4
Denton, Mont., 410 81 D2
Denton, Nebr., 94 75 J3
Denton, N.C., 852 63 D2
Denton, co., Tex., 47,432 77 P3
Denton, Tex., 26,844 77 P3
Denton Cr., Tex. 77 P3
D'Entrecasteaux Pt., Austl. 172 A5
D'Entrecasteaux Is., Terr. Papua 170 E5
Dentsville, S.C. 63 D3
Denver, co., Colo., 493,887 79 C2
Denver, Colo., 493,887 79 C2
Denver, Ind., 565 70 C2
Denver, Iowa, 1,046 72 E2
Denver, Mo., 116 72 C4
Denver, N.C., 113 63 C2
Denver, Pa., 1,875 61 K5
Denver City, Tex., 4,302 77 M3
Denville, N.J. 58 b13
Denzer, Wis. 66 D5
Denzil, Sask., Can. 43 B4
Deoband, India, 29,980 144 a11
Deogarh, India 6,839 144 e15
Deoghar, India, 30,813 145 H4
Deolali, India, 37,264 145 D6
Déols, Fr., 6,340 117 D3
Deora, Colo. 79 D3
Deori, M.P., India, 9,383 145 F5
Deori, Raj., India 144 a13
Deoria, India, 28,407 145 G4
De Panne, Belg., 5,989 115 A3
Departure Bay, Br. Col., Can., 1,235 42 c6
Depauville, N.Y. 59 H3
De Pere, Wis., 10,045 66 E4
Depew, N.Y., 13,580 58 C6
Depew, Okla., 686 76 G2
Depoe Bay, Oreg. 80 A3
Depok, Indon. 148 b7
Deport, Tex., 639 77 Q3
Deposit, N.Y., 2,025 59 J7
Depósito, Braz. 102 D1
Depot L., Me. 55 C2
Depot Mtn., Me. 55 C2
Depue, Ill., 1,920 68 C2
Deputatskiy, U.S.S.R. 135 O3
De Queen, Ark., 2,859 73 A3
De Quincy, La., 3,928 73 B7
Dera Ghāzi Khān, Pak., 47,105 145 D3
Dera Ismāīl Khān, Pak., 46,140 145 D3
Derbent, U.S.S.R., 50,000 134 D5
Derby, Austl. 172 C2
Derby, U.K., 132,408 113 F5
Derby, Colo., 10,124 79 c8
Derby, Conn., 12,132 56 D7
Derby, Ind. 70 C4
Derby, Iowa, 151 72 D4
Derby, Kans., 6,458 75 H6
Derby, Me. 55 C3
Derby, Miss. 73 F7
Derby, N.Y. 58 B6
Derby, Ohio 70 F3
Derby, Tex. 77 O5
Derby Center, Vt. 54 C2
Derby Line, Vt., 849 54 C2
Derbyshire, co., U.K., 877,620 113 F5
Derdingen, F.R.Ger., 2,930 119 F6
Derecske, Hung., 9,970 126 E3
Derendingen, Switz., 4,463 124 B1
Derg, r., U.K. 113 C4
Derg, L., Don., Ire. 113 C4
Derg, L. Tip., Ire. 113 B5
Dergachi, U.S.S.R., 20,300 136 D3
De Ridder, La., 7,188 73 B7
Derik, Turk., 5,705 142 E2
Derkul, r., U.S.S.R. 136 f7
Dermantsi, Bulg., 4,703 128 E3
Dermott, Ark., 3,665 73 D4
Dermott, Tex. 77 N3
Dérna=Darnah
Deronda, Wis. 66 A3
Derra, Eth. 163 L4
Derravaragh, L., Ire. 113 C5
Derrick City, Pa. 60 E2
Derry, U.K. 112 b7
Derry, N. Mex. 79 B5
Derry, Pa., 3,426 60 D5
Dersingham, U.K., 2,026 114 J5
Derudeb, Sudan 163 L3
De Ruyter, N.Y., 627 59 J6
Dervéni, Gr., 1,353 129 D5
Derventa, Yug., 8,820 125 C2
Derwent, Alta., Can. 42 L3
Derwent, r., Austl. 173 f14
Derwent, r., Northumb., U.K. 112 f10
Derwent, r., York., U.K. 113 F4
Derwent, r., Derby., U.K. 113 F5
Derwent Water, l., U.K. 114 B1
Derwood, Md. 62 a8
Derzhavinskoye, U.S.S.R. 137 m12
Desaguadero, r., Bol. 102 C5
Désappointement, Îs. du, Tuam. Arch. 171 J5
Des Arc, Ark., 1,482 73 D3
Des Arc, Mo., 275 72 G7
Desbarats, Ont., Can. 46 A2
Desborough, U.K., 4,553 114 G6
Descabezado Grande, Vol., Chile 104 g15
Deschaillons, Qué., Can. 47 M2
Deschambault, Qué., Can., 1,026 47 N2
Deschambault Lake, Sask., Can. 43 D3
Deschambault L., Sask., Can. 43 D3
Deschutes, co., Oreg., 23,100 80 C4
Deschutes, r., Oreg. 80 C3
Deschutes, r., Wash. 81 a8
Desdemona, Tex. 77 O3
Deseado, r., Arg. 105 B7
Desemboque, Mex. 92 B1
Desenzano del Garda, It., 13,920 122 d5
Deseret, Utah 78 B2
Deseret Pk., Utah 78 B1
Deseronto, Ont., Can., 1,797 44 J7
Désert, r., Qué., Can. 47 H2
Désert, L., Qué., Can. 47 H2
Deserta Grande, i., Madeira Is. 109 4
Desert Center, Calif. 82 F6
Desert Hot Springs, Calif., 1,472 82 E6
Desert Pk., Utah 78 B1
Desert Springs, Calif. 83 i15
Desford, U.K., 2,300 114 F5
Desha, co., Ark., 20,770 73 D4
Desha, Ark. 73 D2
Deshayes, Guad. 97 14
Deshler, Nebr., 956 75 H3
Deshler, Ohio, 1,824 70 E1
Desio, It., 21,024 122 c5
Des Joachims Dam, Ont.-Qué., Can. 46 G2
Des Lacs, N. Dak., 185 74 B1
Des Lacs, r., N. Dak. 74 B1
Desloge, Mo., 2,308 72 G7
De Smet, S. Dak., 1,324 74 D3
Des Moines, co., Iowa, 44,605 72 F4
Des Moines, Iowa, 208,982 72 D3
Des Moines, N. Mex., 207 79 D3
Des Moines, Wash., 1,987 81 b8
Des Moines, r., Iowa 72 E3
Desna, r., U.S.S.R. 134 C4
Desnățui, r., Rum. 128 D2
Desolación, I., Chile 105 A8
Desor, L., Mich. 66 a9
Desor, Mt., Mich. 66 a9
De Soto, co., Fla., 11,683 65 H5
De Soto, Ga., 282 64 F4
De Soto, Ill., 723 68 C6
De Soto, Kans., 1,271 75 K4
De Soto, parish, La., 24,248 73 B5
De Soto, co., Miss., 23,891 73 E3
De Soto, Miss. 73 G6
De Soto, Mo., 5,804 72 G6
De Soto, Tex., 1,969, 76 f9
De Soto, Wis., 357 66 B5
De Soto City, Fla., 245 65 H5
De Soto Nat. Mem., Fla. 65 G5
Des Plaines, Ill., 50,789 68 D1
Des Plaines, r., Ill.-Wis. 68 D2
Despotovac, Yug. 125 E2
Des Roches I., Ind. Oc. 165 H2
Dessalines, Haiti, 4,073 96 k6
Dessau, Ger.D.R., 93,459 118 D3
Dessel, Belg., 6,122 115 D3
Dessye, Eth., 56,400* 163 L4
Destelbergen, Belg., 6,117 115 B3
Destin, Fla. 65 C2
Deštné, pk., Czech. 126 C1
D'Estrees Bay, Austl. 172 b8
Destruction Bay, Yukon, Can. 40 B5
Desvres, Fr., 5,604 117 D1
Deta, Rum. 128 C2
Detchino, U.S.S.R. 136 b6
Detlor, Ont., Can. 46 G3
Detmold, F.R.Ger., 31,038 118 B3
Detour, Pt., Mich. 67 G3
Detour Passage, Mich. 67 K3
De Tour Village, Mich., 669 67 J3
Detrick, Va. 62 F4
Detroit, Ala., 113 64 A1
Detroit, Ill., 126 68 B4
Detroit, Mich., 1,670,144 67 K6
Detroit, Oreg., 206 80 B3
Detroit, Tex. 576 77 Q3
Detroit, r., Can.-U.S. 67 K6
Detroit Beach, Mich., 1,571 67 K7
Détroit de Jacques-Cartier=Mingan Passage
Detroit Harbor, Wis. 66 F3
Detroit L., Oreg. 80 B3
Detroit Lakes, Minn., 5,633 74 E2
Dett, Rhod. 164 D5
Dettifoss, falls, Ice. 120 b6
Dettingen, Bad.-Württ., F.R.Ger., 5,371 119 G7
Dettingen, Bay., F.R.Ger., 2,815 119 G4
Dettwiller, Fr., 2,558 116 d9
Det Udom, Thai. 146 D4
Deuel, co., Nebr., 3,125 75 C2
Deuel, co., S. Dak., 6,782 74 D3
Deuil-la-Barre, Fr., 13,681 116 h11
Deurne, Belg., 64,406 115 d8
Deurne, Neth., 8,200 115 D3
Deutschfeistritz, Aust., 3,445 124 M6
Deutschkreutz, Aust., 3,902 124 N6
Deutschlandsberg, Aust., 5,219 124 M7
Deutsch Wagram, Aust., 4,207 124 N5
Deux-Montagnes, L. des, Qué., Can. 47 o18
Deva, Rum., 16,879 128 D2
Deva, Sp., 4,041 122 n11
De Valls Bluff, Ark., 654 73 D3
Dévaványa, Hung., 12,731 126 E3
De Veber, Mt., Alta., Can. 42 H3
Devecser, Hung., 5,735 126 C3
Deventer, Neth., 55,700 115 E2
Devereaux, Mich. 67 J6
Devereux, Ga. 64 F3
Devers, Tex. 77 k8
Devesel, Rum. 128 D2
Deville, Alta., Can. 43 c7
Devils, r., Tex. 77 N4
Devil's Bridge, U.K. 113 E5
Devils Den, Calif. 82 D5
Devils Head, Colo. 79 b9
Devils Hole, The, bay, Berm. Is. 108 1
Devils Hole Mtn., Colo. 79 A1
Devil's I.=Diable, Î. du
Devils Lake, N. Dak., 6,299 74 C1
Devils L., Mich. 67 J7
Devils L., N. Dak. 74 C1
Devils L., Tex. 77 N5
Devils Postpile Nat. Mon., Calif. 82 D4
Devils Slide, Utah 78 c8
Devils Tower Nat. Mon., Wyo. 81 G3
Devils Track L., Minn. 74 G2
Devil's Water, r., U.K. 112 f10
Devin, Bulg., 3,581 129 E4
Devine, Tex., 2,522 77 O5
Devizes, U.K., 8,495 114 E8
Devlin, Ont., Can. 44 C5
Devol, Okla., 117 76 E3
Devoll, r., Alb. 125 E4
Devon, Alta., Can., 1,412 42 K3
Devon (part of Milford), Conn. 56 D8
Devon, Kans. 75 L6
Devon, Pa., 1,700* 60 f11
Devon, r., U.K. 112 c7
Devon, r., U.K. 114 G4
Devon I., N.W.T., Can. 41 M2
Devonport, Austl., 10,597 173 G6
Devonshire, co., U.K., 823,751 113 E6
Devrez, r., Turk. 142 C1
Devrukh, India 145 h18
Dew, Tex. 77 P4
Dewalt, Tex. 77 h9
Dewar, Okla., 817 76 H2
Dewas, India, 34,577 144 a14
Dewatto, Wash. 81 a8
Deweese, Nebr., 100 75 G3
Dewey, P.R.=Culebra
Dewey, co., Okla., 6,051 76 D2
Dewey, Okla., 3,994 76 H1
Dewey, co., S. Dak., 5,257 74 B3
Dewey, S. Dak. 74 A4
Dewey Corners, N.Y. 59 u26
Dewey Dam, Ky. 71 J4
Deweyville, Tex. 77 n8
De Witt, Ark., 3,019 73 D3
De Witt, co., Ill., 17,253 68 D3
De Witt, Ill., 245 68 D3
De Witt, Iowa, 3,224 72 G3
De Witt, Mich., 1,238 67 J6
Dewitt, Mo., 174 72 D5
De Witt, Nebr., 504 75 H3
De Witt, N.Y. 59 r23
De Witt, co., Tex., 20,683 77 P5
De Witt, Va. 62 G5
Dewittville, N.Y. 58 A7
Dewright, Okla. 76 G2
Dewsbury, U.K., 52,942 114 E3
Dewy Rose, Ga. 64 G1
Dexter, Ga., 359 64 F3
Dexter, Ind. 70 C4
Dexter, Iowa, 670 72 C3
Dexter, Ky., 250 71 C5
Dexter, Me., 2,720 55 C3
Dexter, Mich., 1,702 67 K6
Dexter, Mo., 5,519 72 H8
Dexter, N. Mex., 885 79 C5
Dexter, N.Y., 1,009 59 H3
Dexter, Ohio 70 G3
Dexter, Oreg. 80 B4
Dexter City, Ohio, 197 70 H3
Dexterville, Wis. 66 C4
Dey Dey, L., Austl. 172 D4
Deynau, U.S.S.R., 3,300 134 F6
Dezfūl, Iran, 52,121 143 D2
Dezhnëva, M., U.S.S.R. 135 S3
Dhāding, Nepal 145 G4
Dháfni, Gr., 1,084 129 D4
Dhahran=Az̧ Z̧ahrān
Dhali, Cyp., 2,375 142 e9
Dhamār, Yemen, 25,000* 143 C6
Dhamási, Gr., 1,379 129 D5
Dhamtari, India, 31,552 145 F5
Dhanbad, India, 57,352 144 f14
Dhangarhi, Nepal 144 c11
Dhankuta, Nepal 144 f12
Dhar, India, 28,325 145 E5
Dharampur, India, 9,780 145 h16
Dharapuram, India, 26,490 145 k20
Dharmanagar, India, 13,240 145 J4
Dharmapuri, India, 28,031 145 k19
Dharmjaygarh, India 144 d14
Dharmsala, India, 10,255 145 E2
Dharwar, India, 77,163 145 E7
Dhasan, r., India 144 b13
Dhaulāgiri, pk., Nepal 145 G3
Dhávlia, Gr., 2,111 129 D5
Dhekelia, Cyp. 142 e10
Dhekélia, Gr., 3,508 129 D5
Dhelfoí, Gr., 1,222 129 D5
Dhenkanal, India, 13,727 145 G5
Dhenoúsa, i., Gr. 129 E6
Dherinia, Cyp., 1,993 142 f9
Dhesfína, Gr., 2,416 129 D5
Dheskati, Gr., 4,714 129 C5
Dhiavolítsi, Gr., 1,306 129 C6
Dhībān, Jor. 142 b8
Dhídhimoi, Gr., 1,198 129 D6
Dhidhimótikhon, Gr., 7,287 129 F4
Dhíkti, mts., Gr. 129 E7
Dhimitsána, Gr., 1,300 129 D6
Dhodhekánisos, is., Gr. 129 F6
Dhodhóni, ruins, Gr. 129 C5
Dhokós, i., Gr. 129 D6
Dholianá, Gr., 1,059 129 C5
Dholpur, India, 27,412 145 E4
Dhomokós, Gr., 2,017 129 D5
Dhoraji, India, 48,951 144 C5
Dhoxáton, Gr., 4,402 129 E4
Dhrangadhra, India, 32,477 145 D5
Dhriopís, Gr., 1,128 129 E6
Dhubri, India, 28,355 144 g12
Dhulia, India, 98,893 145 E5
Dhulian, India, 17,220 144 f13
Dhuri, India, 18,435 144 a10
d'Hyères, Îs., Fr. 117 G5
Dia, i., Gr. 129 E7
Diable, Î. du, Fr. Guiana 101 O5
Diable, Morne au, Dominica 97 13
Diablo, Calif. 2,096 83 f12
Diablo, Co., Tex. 77 L4
Diablo, Mt., Calif. 83 f12
Diablo, Sa., Tex. 77 L4
Diablo Heights, C.Z., 1,075 94 g13
Diablo Mtn., Oreg. 80 C4
Diablo Ra., Calif. 82 C4
Diablotin, Morne, Dominica 97 13
Diafarabé, Mali, 5,500 162 D3
Diagonal, Iowa, 443 72 C4
Diamant, Morne du, Mart. 97 12
Diamant, Rocher du, Mart. 97 12
Diamante, Arg., 19,800* 105 C4
Diamantina, Braz., 14,252 103 H5
Diamantina, r., Austl. 172 F3
Diamantina, Chapada da, upland, Braz. 103 H4
Diamantina Deep, Pac. Oc. 168 D4
Diamantino, Braz. 103 E4
Diamond, Mo., 453 72 C7
Diamond, Oreg. 80 D4
Diamond, Wash. 80 E2
Diamond Bluff, Wis. 66 A4
Diamond Harbour, India, 10,135 144 g14
Diamond Head, Hawaii 84 D2
Diamond Hill, R.I. 57 L5
Diamond I., Burma 147 a3
Diamond I., Gren. Is. 97 20
Diamond Lake, Ill. 69 b8
Diamond L., Ill. 69 b7
Diamond Mts., Nev. 82 ·
Diamond Pk., Colo. 79 A1
Diamond Point, N.Y. 59 N5
Diamond Pt., Indon. 148 A1
Diamondville, Wyo., 398 81 D5
Diana, W. Va. 62 D4
Dianalund, Den. 121 D5
Diana Pk., St. Helena 109 7
Diangounté-Kamara, Mali, 6,000* 162 C3
Dianópolis, Braz., 2,145 103 G4
Diapaga, Upper Volta, 3,301 162 E4
Díaz Cutiérrez, Mex., 5,972 93 E3
Dibaya, D.R.Congo 164 C3
Dibble, Okla., 127 76 F2
Dibden, U.K., 9,803 113 k13
Dibeng, S. Af. 164 C6
d'Iberville, L., Qué., Can. 44 K3
Diboll, Tex., 2,506 77 Q4
Dibrell, Tenn. 71 F6
Dibrugarh, India, 58,480 145 K4
Dibut Bay, Phil. 153 c7
Dicabisagan, Phil., 1,302 153 B1
Dichato, Chile 104 e16
Dickens, Iowa, 241 72 C1
Dickens, Nebr., 25 75 E3
Dickens, co., Tex., 4,963 77 N3
Dickens, Tex., 302 77 N3
Dickenson, co., Va., 20,211 62 B5
Dickey, Me. 55 C1
Dickey, co., N. Dak., 8,147 74 C2
Dickey, N. Dak., 143 74 C2
Dickeyville, Wis., 671 66 C6
Dickinson, co., Iowa, 12,574 72 B1
Dickinson, co., Kans., 21,572 75 H5
Dickinson, co., Mich., 23,917 66 F2
Dickinson, N.Y. 59 L2
Dickinson, N. Dak., 9,971 74 A2
Dickinson, Tex., 4,715 77 Q5
Dickson, co., Tenn., 18,839 71 D5
Dickson, Tenn., 5,028 71 D5
Dickson City, Pa., 7,738 61 o16
Dicle, r., Turk. 142 E2
Dicoyong, Phil., 4,433 153 B3
Didbiran, U.S.S.R. 135 N4
Didcot, U.K., 11,212 113 F6
Didicas, vol., Phil. 153 B1
Didsbury, Alta., Can., 1,222 42 J3
Die, Fr., 3,870 117 F4
Diébougou, Upper Volta, 1,975 162 D4
Dieburg, F.R.Ger., 8,979 119 F5
Dieciocho de Julio, Urug. 105 E4
Dieciocho de Marzo, Mex., 10,650 93 F3
Diego Ramírez, I., Chile 99 C8
Diégo-Suarez, Malag. Rep., 29,887 165 H4
Diehlstadt, Mo., 141 72 H8
Diekirch, Lux., 4,397 115 E5
Diéma, Mali, 5,000* 162 C3
Diemel, r., F.R.Ger. 118 B3
Diemerbrug, Neth., 6,800 115 b6
Diémoz, Fr. 116 q15
Diemtigen, Switz., 1,934 124 B2
Dien Bien Phu, N. Viet. 146 C2
Dien Khanh, S. Viet., 4,508 146 E4
Diepenbeek, Belg., 9,450 115 D4
Diepenheim, Neth. 115 E2
Diepholz, F.R.Ger., 9,162 118 B2
Dieppe, N.B., Can., 3,999 47 T10
Dieppe, Fr., 30,327 117 D2
Dieppe Bay, St. Christopher 97 6
Dierdorf, F.R.Ger., 1,715 119 D3
Dieren, Neth., 8,500 115 E2
Dierks, Ark., 1,276 73 B3
Diesdorf, Ger.D.R. 118 C2
Diessen, F.R.Ger., 4,878 118 C5
Diessenhofen, Switz., 2,222 124 C1
Diest, Belg., 9,550 115 D4
Diestedde, F.R.Ger., 1,906 119 E1
Dieterich, Ill., 591 68 D4
Dietikon, Switz., 14,820 124 C1
Dietrich, Idaho, 118 81 B4
Dietzenbach, F.R.Ger., 5,359 119 F4
Dieu, Mui, pt., S. Viet. 146 E4
Dieulefit, Fr., 2,866 117 F4
Dieulouard, Fr., 4,854 116 b9
Dieuze, Fr., 3,779 116 c9
Die Wald, reg., Aust. 125 ·
Diez, F.R.Ger., 8,711 118 A3
Differdange, Lux., 17,637 115 D5
Difficult, Tenn. 71 F5
Dig, India, 17,668 144 a12
Digboi, India, 35,028 145 K4
Digby, N.S., Can., 2,206 45 N7
Digdeguash, r., N.B., Can. 55 E3
Diggins, Mo., 101 72 E7
Digha, India 144 f15
Dighton, Kans., 1,526 75 E5
Dighton, Mass., 3,769(T) 57 M5
Digne, Fr., 13,660 117 G4
Digoin, Fr., 8,647 117 E3
Digos, Phil., 8,725 153 C4
Digras, India, 15,525 145 E5
Digul, r., Indon. 149 L4
Dijlah, r., Iraq 143 C1
Dijle, r., Belg. 115 C4
Dijon, Fr., 141,104 117 F3
Dikanäs, Swed. 120 D2
Dike, Iowa, 630 72 E2
Dikhil, Fr. Som. 163 M4
Diklos-Mta, G., U.S.S.R. 137 c1
Diksmuide, Belg., 3,825 115 A3
Dikson, U.S.S.R. 134 G2
Dikwa, Nigeria 162 G3
Dilārām, Afghan. 144 B2
Dilasag, Phil., 153 B1
Dildo, Newf., Can. 45 b10
Dili, Port. Timor, 7,000* 149 H5
Dilia, N. Mex. 79 C4
Di Linh, S. Viet., 2,489 146 D5
Dilizhan, U.S.S.R., 11,600 137 c1
Dilkon, Ariz. 78 C4
Dill, r., F.R.Ger. 119 E3
Dilla, Eth. 163 L4
Dillard, Oreg. 80 B4
Dill City, Okla., 623 76 D2
Dillenburg, F.R.Ger., 10,331 118 B3
Dilley, Tex., 2,118 77 O5
Dilling, Sudan, 5,596 163 J4
Dillingen, Bay., F.R.Ger., 9,923 118 C4
Dillingen, Saar., F.R.Ger., 15,899 118 A4
Dillingham, Alaska, 424 85 E4
Dillingham Ranch, Hawaii 84 a6
Dillnäs, Swed. 120 e8
Dillon, Sask., Can. 43 B3
Dillon, Colo., 814 79 C2
Dillon, Mont., 3,690 81 C3
Dillon, co., S.C., 30,584 63 E3
Dillon, S.C., 6,173 63 E3
Dillon, r., Alta.-Sask., Can. 43 B3
Dillon Res., Ohio 70 G2
Dillonvale, Ohio, 1,232 70 J2
Dillsboro, Ind., 745 70 D3
Dillsburg, Pa., 1,322 60 H5
Dillwyn, Kans. 75 G6
Dillwyn, Va., 515 62 F5
Dilly, Wis. 66 C5
Dilolo, D.R.Congo 164 C3
Dilton Marsh, U.K., 1,339 114 D8
Dilworth, Minn., 2,102 74 D2
Dilwyn, U.K. 114 C6
Dima, D.R.Congo 164 B2
Dimapur, India, 5,753 145 J4
Dimasalang, Phil., 4,748 153 C2
Dimasari, Phil., 1,145 153 B1
Dimashq, Syr., 475,399 142 D3
Dimataling, Phil., 1,791 153 B4
Dimbach, Aust., 1,124 124 L5
Dimbelenge, D.R.Congo 164 C2
Dimbokro, Iv. Coast, 10,260 162 D4
Dimboola, Austl., 1,814 173 F5
Dimbovița, r., Rum. 128 E2
Dimitrovgrad, Bulg., 34,162 128 E3
Dimitrovgrad, Yug., 2,891 125 F3
Dimitrovo, Bulg., 59,930 128 D3
Dimmit, co., Tex., 10,095 77 O5
Dimmitt, Tex., 2,935 77 M2
Dimock, S. Dak. 74 C4
Dimona, Isr., 5,000 142 b8
Dimondale, Mich., 866 67 J6
Dinagat, Phil., 2,679 153 C3
Dinagat I., Phil. 153 C3
Dinagat Sd., Phil. 153 C3
Dinājpur, Pak., 37,711 144 g13
Dinalupihan, Phil., 4,978 153 B2
Dinan, Fr., 16,438 117 B2
Dinant, Belg., 6,276 115 C4
Dinant, Alta., Can. 43 c7
Dinapore, India, 58,539 144 e13
Dinar, Turk., 9,420 142 B2

Dinara Planina—Dråby · 219

Dinara Planina, Yug. 125 C2
Dinard, Fr., 9,432 117 B2
Dinaric Alps = Dinara Planina
Dindal, Col. 101 e14
Dindar, Nahr ad, Eth.-Sudan 163 K3
Dindigul, India, 92,947 145 E8
Dindori, India 144 c14
Dinero, Tex. 77 O5
Dingalan Bay, Phil. 153 c7
Ding Dong, Tex. 77 O4
Dingelstädt, Ger.D.R. 118 C3
Dingeni, Rum. 128 F1
Dingla, Nepal 145 H4
Dingle, Ire. 113 A5
Dingle, Phil., 1,521 153 d10
Dingle Bay, Ire. 113 A5
Dingley Dell (part of Brimfield), Mass. 56 H4
Dingmans Ferry, Pa. 61 N3
Dingo, Austl. 173 G3
Dingolfing, F.R.Ger., 9,027 118 D4
Dingras, Phil., 4,061 153 B1
Dingtuna, Swed. 120 d8
Dinguiraye, Guin., 3,000 162 C4
Dingwall, N.S., Can. 47 V10
Dingwall, U.K., 3,752 112 D3
Dinh, Mui, S. Viet. 146 E5
Dinhata, India, 11,306 144 g12
Dinh Ca, N. Viet. 147 i8
Dinh Lap, N. Viet. 147 i8
Dinh Quan, S. Viet., 1,024 146 D5
Dinh Thanh, S. Viet., 5,000 147 k12
Dinkelsbühl, F.R.Ger., 7,200 118 C4
Dinnebito Wash, Ariz. 78 C3
Dinner Station, Nev. 83 C2
Dinnington, U.K., 7,053 114 F4
Dinosaur, Colo., 318 79 A1
Dinosaur Nat. Mon., Colo.-Utah 79 A1
Dinslaken, F.R.Ger., 37,813 119 B1
Dinsmore, Sask., Can. 43 C4
Dinsmore, Fla. 65 H2
Dintel Mark, r., Neth. 115 a7
Dinteloord, Neth., 3,500 115 a7
Dinuba, Calif., 6,103 82 D4
Dinwiddie, co., Va., 22,183 62 G5
Dinwiddie, Va. 62 G5
Dinxperlo, Neth., 3,500 115 E3
Dioïla, Mali 162 C3
Diomede Is., U.S.S.R.-U.S. 135 S3
Dionísio, Braz., 2,322 103 e17
Diorbivol, Sen. 162 B3
Diors, Fr. 117 D3
Diosig, Rum. 128 D1
Diou, Fr., 1,515 117 E3
Diouloulou, Sen. 162 B3
Diourbel, Sen., 20,082 162 B3
Dipaculao, Phil., 2,216 153 c7
Dipintin Old, Phil., 1,216 153 c6
Diplo, Pak. 144 C4
Dipolog, Phil., 15,102 153 B3
Dipper L., Sask., Can. 43 C3
Dippoldiswalde, Ger.D.R. 118 D3
Dīr, Pak. 145 D2
Diré, Mali, 3,874 162 D3
Direction, C., Austl. 173 F1
Direction Pt., Terr. Papua 174 3
Dire Dawa, Eth., 32,300 163 M4
Diriamba, Nic., 11,484 94 D5
Dirico, Ang. 164 C4
Dirk Hartogs I., Austl. 172 A3
Dirksland, Neth. 115 C3
Dirleton, U.K. 112 e7
Dirmingen, F.R.Ger., 2,710 116 d8
Dirranbandi, Austl. 173 G4
Dirrung, Austl. 173 e9
Dirty Devil, r., Utah 78 C2
Disappointment, C., Wash. 80 A2
Disappointment, L., Austl. 172 B3
Disco, Mich. 67 f14
Discovery Bay, Wash. 81 a7
Discovery Tablemount, Atl. Oc. 109 N9
Disentis, Switz., 2,376 124 C2
Dishna, r., Alaska 85 E3
Dismal, r., Nebr. 75 E2
Dismal Swamp, N.C.-Va. 62 H6
Dismal Swamp Can., N.C.-Va. 63 H1
Disna, U.S.S.R., 2,300 136 C2
Dison, Belg., 9,324 115 D4
Disputanta, Va. 62 G5
Disraëli, Qué., Can., 3,047 47 N3
Disraeli Bay, N.W.T., Can. 41 O1
Diss, U.K., 3,681 113 G5
Distant, Pa. 60 D4
Distington, U.K., 2,493 114 B1
District Heights, Md., 7,524 62 b9
District of Columbia, U.S., 802,000* 62 G4
Distrito Federal, Braz., 141,742 103 G5
Distrito Federal, Mex., 4,870,876 93 F4
Disūq, U.A.R. 161 i7
Ditrău, Rum. 128 E1
Dittlinger, Tex. 76 b6
Ditton Priors, U.K. 114 C5
Ditzengen, F.R.Ger., 6,760 119 F7
Diu, India 145 D5
Divenié, Congo 164 B2
Divernon, Ill., 997 68 C4
Diversey Hbr., Ill. 69 d9
Diversion Chan., r., Mo. 72 H7
Dives, Fr., 6,521 117 D2
Dives, r., Fr. 117 C2
Divide, Alaska 85 G3
Divide, Colo. 79 b10
Divide, co., N. Dak., 5,566 74 A1
Dividend, Utah 78 b11
Dividing Creek, N.J. 61 A5
Divino, Braz., 2,716 103 e17
Divinópolis, Braz., 41,544 103 H6
Division Pk., Nev. 83 A2
Divnoye, U.S.S.R. 136 F4
Divoká Orlice, r., Czech. 127 f6
Divriği, Turk., 8,867 142 D2
Dix., Ill. 68 D5
Dix, Nebr., 420 75 B2
Dix, r., Ky. 71 G4
Dixboro, Mich. 67 K6
Dixfield, Me., 1,334 55 B4
Dixie, Ont., Can. 46 c13
Dixie, Ala. 64 C4
Dixie, Ark. 73 D2
Dixie, co., Fla., 4,479 65 F3
Dixie, Ga., 220 64 F5
Dixie, Wash. 80 D2
Dixie, W. Va. 62 C4
Dixie Valley, Nev. 83 B3
Dixmont, Me. 55 C4
Dixmoor, Ill., 3,076 69 d10
Dixon, Calif., 2,970 82 C3
Dixon, Ill., 19,565 68 C2
Dixon, Iowa, 280 72 G3
Dixon, Ky., 541 71 D4
Dixon, Mo., 1,473 72 E7
Dixon, co., Nebr., 8,106 75 J1
Dixon, Nebr., 139 75 J1
Dixon, N. Mex. 79 C3
Dixon, S. Dak. 74 C4
Dixon, Wyo., 108 81 F5
Dixon Entr., Can.-U.S. 42 C2
Dixon Springs, Ill. 68 D6
Dixon Springs, Tenn. 71 E5
Dixonville, Alta., Can. 42 H2
Dixville, Qué., Can. 47 N3
Dixville Notch, N.H. 54 E1
Diyālā, r., Iraq 143 D2
Diyarbakır, Turk., 80,645 142 D2
Dja, r., Cam. 162 G5
Djabung, Indon. 148 a6
Djabung, Tg., Indon. 148 C3
Djado, Plat. du, Niger 162 G2
Djahat, Indon. 149 L4
Djailolo, Indon. 149 H2
Djailolo = Halmahera
Djailolo, Selat, Indon. 149 J2
Djakarta, Indon., 2,973,052 148 C4
Djambala, Congo 164 B2
Djambi, Indon., 113,080 148 B3
Djampang-Kulon, Indon. 148 b7
Djanet, Alg. 161 F3
Djanlohong, Indon. 148 F2
Djapara, Indon. 148 d7
Djasinga, Indon. 148 b7
Djatibarang, Indon. 148 c7
Djatinegara, Indon. 148 C4
Djawa, i., Indon. 148 D4
Djawi, Indon. 148 D3
Djebel Toubkal, Mor. 160 C2
Djebus, Indon. 148 C3
Djédaa, Chad 163 H3
Djelfa, Alg., 27,067 160 E2
Djema, C.A.R. 163 J4
Djemadja, P., Indon. 148 C2
Djember, Indon. 148 e8
Djemila, ruins, Alg. 160 d5
Djempang, Kenohan, l., Indon. 148 F3
Djeneponto, Indon. 149 F4
Djenné, Mali, 6,345 162 D3
Djenu, Indon. 148 D3
Djepon, Indon. 148 d7
Djerissa, Tun. 160 f6
Djibo, Upper Volta, 3,097 162 D3
Djibouti, Fr. Som., 39,000 163 M4
Djidjelli, Alg., 26,570 160 E1
Djirlagne, S. Viet. 147 n11
Djolu, D.R.Congo 164 C1
Djombang, Indon. 148 e7
Djorong, Indon. 148 E3
Djouf, El, reg., Maur. 162 C2
Djougou, Dahom., 7,020 162 E4
Djoum, Cam. 162 G5
Djugu, D.R.Congo 164 E1
Djursholm, Swed. 120 f8
Djuwana, Indon. 148 d7
Dlinnyy, O., U.S.S.R. 135 H2
D'Lo, Miss., 428 73 F6
Dłubnia, r., Pol. 127 i6
Dmitriya Lapteva, Prol., U.S.S.R. 135 O2
Dmitriyev-L'govskiy, U.S.S.R., 8,500 136 D2
Dmitrov, U.S.S.R., 35,000 136 E1
Dmitrovskiy Pogost, U.S.S.R. 136 c6
Dmitrovsk-Orlovskiy, U.S.S.R., 5,500 136 D2
Dnepr, r., U.S.S.R. 134 C5
Dneprodzerzhinsk, U.S.S.R., 203,000 134 C5
Dnepropetrovsk, U.S.S.R., 707,000 134 C5
Dneprovsko-Bugskiy Kan., U.S.S.R. 136 B2
Dneprovskoye Vokhr., U.S.S.R. 136 D3
Dnestr, r., U.S.S.R. 134 B5
Dnestrovskiy Liman, estuary, U.S.S.R. 136 C4
Dno, U.S.S.R., 13,200 136 C1
Doaktown, N.B., Can. 47 S10
Doan Hung, N. Viet. 147 h8
Doba, Chad, 6,000*, 162 G4
Dobczyce, Pol., 2,914 127 k7
Dobbin, Tex. 77 Q4
Dobbin Bay, N.W.T., Can. 41 P2
Dobbs Ferry, N.Y., 10,076 58 d12
Dobbyn, Austl. 172 E2
Dobele, U.S.S.R., 6,300 136 A1
Döbeln, Ger.D.R., 28,904 118 D3
Döberitz, Ger.D.R. 119 e10
Doberlug-Kirchhain, Ger.D.R. 118 D3
Döbern, Ger.D.R. 118 E3
Dobiegniew, Pol., 2,825 127 A2
Dobo, Indon. 149 K4
Dobodura, Terr. Papua 174 f3
Doboj, Yug., 12,000* 125 C2
Doboj, Yug. 125 D2
Dobra, Pol., 1,940 127 A2
Dobra, Pol., 1,566 127 C3
Dobra, Rum. 128 D2
Dobre Miasto, Pol., 5,059 127 D2
Dobreni, Rum. 128 F1
Dobreşti, Rum. 128 D1
Dobri Do, Yug. 125 E3
Dobrinci, Yug. 125 D2
Dobříš Czech. 126 B2
Dobrnič, Yug. 125 B2
Dobrodzień, Pol., 3,925 127 h6
Dobromil', U.S.S.R., 5,000 136 A3
Dobromirka, Bulg., 2,784 128 E3
Dobro Polje, Yug. 125 D3
Dobropol'ye, U.S.S.R., 24,000 136 e7
Dobroszyce, Pol. 127 g5
Dobroteşti, Rum. 128 E2
Dobrovice, Czech. 127 d6
Dobruja, reg., Bulg.-Rum. 128 F3
Dobrush, U.S.S.R., 14,000 136 C2
Dobruška, Czech. 127 f6
Dobryanka, U.S.S.R., 14,500 137 h7
Dobrzyń, Pol., 2,176 127 C2
Dobšiná, Czech. 126 E2
Dobson, N.C., 684 63 D1
Dobu, i., Terr. Papua 174 3
Doce, r., Braz. 103 H5
Docena, Ala. 64 c7
Dochart, r., U.K. 112 b7
Dock Junction, Ga., 5,417 64 H4
Doctor Arroyo, Mex., 3,055 93 E3
Doctor González, Mex., 1,178 93 F3
Doctors Cr., N.J. 58 a16
Doctors Inlet, Fla. 65 H2
Dodballapur, India, 27,361 145 E7
Doddington, U.K., 1,325 114 H6
Doddridge, Ark. 73 A4
Doddridge, co., W. Va., 6,970 62 D3
Dodds, Alta., Can. 43 c7
Doddsville, Miss., 190 73 E4
Dodecanese = Dhodhekánisos
Dodge, co., Ga., 16,483 64 F3
Dodge (part of Charlton), Mass. 56 J4
Dodge, co., Minn., 13,259 74 F3
Dodge, co., Nebr., 32,471 75 J2
Dodge, Nebr., 649 75 J2
Dodge, N. Dak., 226 74 A2
Dodge, Tex. 77 Q4
Dodge, co., Wis., 63,170 66 E5
Dodge, Wis. 66 B4
Dodge Center, Minn., 1,441 74 F3
Dodge City, Kans., 13,520 75 E6
Dodge L., Sask., Can. 43 C2
Dodgeville (part of Attleboro), Mass. 57 L5
Dodgeville, Wis., 2,911 66 C6
Dodman Pt., U.K. 113 D6
Dodoma, Tanz., 13,435 164 E3
Dodowa, Ghana 162 d9
Dodsland, Sask., Can. 43 B4
Dodson, La., 512 73 C5
Dodson, Mont., 313 81 E1
Dodson, Tex., 308 76 N2
Doebay, Wash. 80 B1
Doe Hill, Va. 62 E4
Doembang Nangbuat, Thai. 147 c4
Doe River, Br. Col., Can. 42 H2
Doerun, Ga., 1,037 64 E4
Doe Run, Mo. 72 G7
Doe Run, Pa. 60 e12
Doesburg, Neth., 7,100 115 E2
Doetinchem, Neth., 18,200 115 E3
Dog, r., Vt. 54 B3
Dog, C., Newf., Can. 45 b10
Doğanhisar, Turk., 5,569 142 B2
Dog Creek, Br. Col., Can. 42 G3
Dogger Bank, North Sea 110 D3
Dog I., Lesser Ant. 97 7
Dog I., Fla. 65 E3
Dog L., Man., Can. 43 F5
Dog L., Ont., Can. 74 H1
Dōgo, i., Jap. 155 C3
Dogondoutchi, Niger, 6,426 162 E3
Dōgo-yama, Jap. 155 C4
Doğubayazıt, Turk., 6,772 142 E2
Dogwood, Ind. 70 C4
Doha = Ad Dawḥah
Dohad, India, 35,483 145 D5
Dohna, Ger.D.R. 126 c6
Dohrighat, India 144 d12
Doiceşti, Rum. 128 E2
Doima, Col. 101 d15
Dois Irmãoa, Sa. dos, Braz. 103 H3
Doizieux, Fr. 116 p16
Dōjō, Jap. 154 g15
Dokkum, Neth., 7,200 115 D1
Dokkumer Ee, can., Neth. 115 D1
Doksany, Czech. 126 d6
Dokshitsy, U.S.S.R. 136 B2
Doksy, Czech. 126 B1
Dokuchayevsk, U.S.S.R., 15,600 136 e8
Dolan, Austl. 173 F5
Dolbeau, Qué., Can., 5,979 44 K5
Dol-de-Bretagne, Fr., 5,077 117 C2
Dole, Fr., 25,863 117 F3
Dolega, Pan. 94 F6
Dolenci, Yug. 125 E4
d'Oléron, Î., Fr. 117 C4
Doles, Ga. 64 F4
Dolgellau, U.K., 2,267 113 D5
Dolgeville, N.Y., 3,058 59 L5
Dolgoi I., Alaska 85 D5
Dolgoprudnyy, U.S.S.R., 16,300 136 b6
Dolhasca, Rum. 128 F1
Doliánova, It., 6,404 123 B5
Dolina, U.S.S.R., 9,000 136 B3
Dolinsk, U.S.S.R., 14,500 135 O5
Dolinskaya, U.S.S.R., 14,300 136 D3
Dolisie, Congo, 18,000*, 164 B2
Döllach, Aust., 1,400 124 J7
Dollar, U.K. 112 c7
Dollar Bay, Mich. 66 E1
Dollarhide, Tex. 77 M3
Dollart, bay, F.R.Ger.-Neth. 115 F1
Dollarville, Mich. 67 H2
Dollendorf, F.R.Ger. 119 B4
Dollerup, Den., 1,343 121 B4
Döllnitz, Ger. D.R. 126 b5
Dollnstein, F.R.Ger., 1,305 118 C4
Dolni Chiflik, Bulg., 4,828 128 F3
Dolni Dŭbnik, Bulg., 6,794 128 E3
Dolný Kubín, Czech., 3,878 126 D2
Dolo, Eth. 163 M5
Dologon, Phil., 3,005 153 C4
Dolomite, Ala. 64 b8
Dolomitiche, Alpi, mts., It. 123 C1
Dolon, China = To-lun
Dolon', U.S.S.R. 137 p12
Dolores, Arg., 20,250* 105 D5
Dolores, Col. 100 C6
Dolores, Guat. 94 C2
Dolores, co., Colo., 2,196 79 A3
Dolores, Colo., 805 79 A3
Dolores, Tex. 77 O6
Dolores, Urug., 9,000* 105 b11
Dolores, Ven., 1,087 100 F3
Dolores, r., Colo.-Utah 79 A2
Dolores Hidalgo, Mex., 11,733 93 E4
Dolph, Oreg. 80 B3
Dolphin, C., Falk. Is. 108 3
Dolphin and Union Str., N.W.T., Can. 40 F4
Dölsach, Aust., 1,496 124 J7
Dolsk, Pol., 1,600 127 B2
Dolton, Ill., 18,746 69 d10
Domachëvo, U.S.S.R. 136 A3
Domagnano, S. Mar., 123 e11
Domain, Man., Can. 43 g10
Domara, Terr. Papua 174 f3
Domaszowice, Pol. 127 g5
Domat, Switz., 3,469 124 D2
Domažlice, Czech., 7,712 126 A2
Dombarovskiy, U.S.S.R., 10,600 137 i10
Dombås, Nor. 120 B3
Dombasle, Fr., 9,371 116 b9
Dombóvár, Hung., 15,355 126 D3
Dombrád, Hung., 6,871 126 E2
Dombresson, Switz., 1,040 124 B1
Domburg, Neth. 115 B3
Domburg, Sur. 1,215* 101 N5
Dome, Alaska 85 a6
Dome, Ariz. 78 A5
Dome, The, mtn., Vt. 54 A6
Dome Creek, Br. Col., Can. 42 G3
Domel I., Burma 146 B5
Domène, Fr., 4,372 117 F4
Dome Rock Mts., Ariz. 78 A5
Dome Shaped Mtn., Mont. 81 C2
Domett, C., Austl. 172 D2
Domfront, Fr., 3,982 117 C2
Domingo, N. Mex. 79 B4
Dominica, i., Lesser Ant. 97 13
Dominican Republic, ctry., 3,750,000* 96
Dominica Passage, W.I. 95 G4
Dominion, N.S., Can., 2,944 47 W10
Dominion City, Man., Can. 43 h10
Dömitz, Ger.D.R. 118 C2
Dommitzsch, Ger.D.R. 118 D3
Domneştii de Sus, Rum. 128 E2
Domodedovo, U.S.S.R., 27,000 136 b6
Domodossola, It., 15,993 123 B1
Domont, Fr., 5,855 116 h10
Dompago, Dahom. 162 d7
Dom Pedrito, Braz., 15,429 103 E8
Dom Pedro, Braz., 2,822 103 G2
Dompierre-sur-Besbre, Fr., 3,528 117 E3
Dompu, Indon. 148 F5
Domremy, Sask., Can. 43 C4
Domrémy-la-Pucelle, Fr. 117 F2
Dom Silvério, Braz., 2,809 103 e17
Dömsöd, Hung., 6,529 126 D3
Domusnovas, It., 6,218 123 B5
Domuyo, Vol., Arg. 99 C6
Domžale, Yug., 3,558 125 B1
Don, Mex. 92 C2
Don, r., U.S.S.R. 134 C4
Don, r., U.K. 112 E3
Dona Ana, co., N. Mex., 59,948 79 B5
Dona Ana, N. Mex. 79 B5
Donaghadee, U.K., 3,226 113 D4
Donahue, Iowa, 133 72 G3
Doña Juana, Co., P.R. 96 t10
Donald, Austl., 1,480 173 F5
Donald, Oreg., 201 80 B3
Donalda, Alta., Can. 42 K3
Donalds, S.C., 416 63 B3
Donaldson, Ark. 73 C3
Donaldson, Mich. 67 J2
Donaldson, Minn. 64 74 D1
Donaldsonville, La., 6,082 73 D7
Donalsonville, Ga., 2,621 64 E4
Donato Guerra, Mex., 1,296 92 D3
Donau, r., Aust.-F.R.Ger. 118 D4
Donaueschingen, F.R.Ger., 9,680 118 B5
Donauwörth, F.R.Ger., 9,426 118 C4
Donbass, reg., U.S.S.R. 134 C5
Don Benito, Sp. 25,248 122 C3
Doncaster, U.K., 86,402 113 F5
Don Christophers Point, Jam. 96 q8
Dondo, Ang. 164 B3
Dondo, Moz., 12,411 164 E5
Dondo, Teluk, Indon. 149 G2
Don Du, N. Viet. 147 h8
Donegal, co., Ire., 122,059 113 B4
Donegal, Ire. 113 B4
Donegal, Pa., 216 60 D5
Donegal Bay, Ire. 113 B4
Donelson, Tenn., 17,195 71 E5
Donetsk, R.S.F.S.R., U.S.S.R., 41,900 136 F3
Donetsk, Ukr.S.S.R., U.S.S.R., 749,000 134 C5
Donetskiy Kr., U.S.S.R. 136 e7
Dongara, Austl. 172 A4
Dongbo, China 144 d11
Dong Dang, N. Viet. 147 i8
Dongen, Neth., 12,300 115 b7
Donggala, Indon. 149 F3
Dong Hène, Laos 146 D3
Dong Hoi, N. Viet. 146 D3
Dong Hung, S. Viet. 147 k12
Dongkala, Indon. 149 G2
Dong Khe, N. Viet. 146 D2
Dong Mu, N. Viet. 147 h8
Dongola, Sudan = Dunqulah
Dongola, Ill., 757 68 C6
Dongou, Congo 164 B1
Dong Sinh, N. Viet. 147 i8
Dong Tac, N. Viet. 147 i9
Dong Trieu, N. Viet. 147 i8
Dongú, Mex., 1,029 93 e10
Dong Van, N. Viet. 146 D2
Dong Xuan, S. Viet., 2,258 146 E4
Donicá, Mex. 93 d9
Donie, Tex. 77 P4
Doñihue, Chile, 1,622 104 f14
Donington, U.K., 1,948 114 H5
Donington, C., Austl. 172 b8
Doniphan, co., Kans., 9,574 75 K4
Doniphan, Mo., 1,421 72 G8
Doniphan, Nebr., 390 75 G3
Donja Bistra, Yug. 125 B2
Donja Drežnica, Yug. 125 C3
Donja Presjenica, Yug. 125 D3
Donja Sabanta, Yug. 125 E3
Donjek, r., Yukon, Can. 85 K3
Donji Dušnik, Yug. 125 F3
Donji Miholjac, Yug. 125 D2
Donji Milanovac, Yug., 2,629 125 F2
Donji Vakuf, Yug., 2,583 125 C2
Donji Žirovac, Yug. 125 C2
Donken, Mich. 66 E2
Don Khi, Thai. 146 C3
Donkin, N.S., Can., 1,197 47 W10
Donley, co., Tex., 4,449 76 N2
Don Martín, Presa de, res., Mex. 93 E2
Don Matías, Col. 101 d13
Donna, Tex., 7,522 77 O6
Donnacona, Qué., Can., 4,719 47 N2
Donnelay, Fr. 116 c9
Donnellson, Ill., 292 68 C4
Donnellson, Iowa, 709 72 F4
Donnelly, Alta., Can. 42 J2
Donnelly, Alaska 85 H3
Donnelly, Idaho, 161 81 B3
Donnelly, Minn., 358 74 E3
Donner Pass, Calif. 82 C3
Donnersbach, Aust., 1,116 124 L6
Donners Berg, F.R.Ger. 119 D5
Donnerskirchen, Aust., 1,645 124 d11
Donner und Blitzen, r., Oreg. 80 D4
Donnybrook, Austl. 172 A5
Donnybrook, N. Dak., 196 74 B1
Donora, Pa., 11,131 60 C5
Dōnoura, Jap. 154 f15
Donovan, Ill., 320 68 E3
Don Pedro, Mex. 93 c8
Donskoy, U.S.S.R., 27,200 136 E2
Donsol, Phil., 5,509 153 B2
Donzenac, Fr., 2,059 117 D4
Donzy, Fr., 2,001 117 E3
Doole, Tex. 77 O4
Doolittle, Mo., 499 72 F7
Dooly, co., Ga., 11,474 64 F3
Doon, Ont., Can. 46 b14
Doon, Iowa, 436 72 A1
Doon, r., U.K. 113 D4
Doon, L., U.K. 113 D4
Doonerak, Mt., Alaska 85 G2
Door, co., Wis., 20,685 66 F4
Doorn, Neth., 6,800 115 D2
Doorn, r., S. Af. 164 a8
Doornrandjes, S. Af. 165 i16
Door Pen., Wis. 67 •
Door Village, Ind. 69 g10
Doplang, Indon. 148 d7
Dora, Ala., 1,776 64 B2
Dora, Mo. 72 E8
Dora, N. Mex. 79 D5
Dora Baltea, r., It. 123 A2
Dorado, P.R., 2,120 96 t10
Dora Lake, Minn. 74 F2
Doran, Ill. 68 D4
Doran, Minn. 136 74 D2
Dora Riparia, r., It. 123 A2
Doraville, Ga., 4,437 64 E2
Dorcas, Fla. 65 C2
Dorcheat Bayou, Ark.-La. 73 B4
Dorchester, N.B., Can., 1,779 47 T11
Dorchester, Dorset., Eng., U.K., 12,263 113 E6
Dorchester, Oxon., Eng., U.K., 1,775 114 F7
Dorchester, co., Md., 29,666 62 H4
Dorchester, Nebr., 460 75 H3
Dorchester, N.H. 54 D4
Dorchester, co., S.C., 24,383 63 D4
Dorchester, S.C. 63 D4
Dorchester, Wis., 504 66 C3
Dordogne, r., Fr. 117 D4
Dordrecht, Neth., 81,100 115 C3
Dordrecht, S. Af., 4,019 164 D7
Dore, U.K., 2,336 114 E4
Dore, r., Fr. 117 E4
Doré Lake, Sask., Can. 43 C3
Doré L., Sask., Can. 43 C3
Dorena, Oreg. 80 B4
Dorenlee, Alta., Can. 43 c8
Dores, U.K. 112 D3
Dores de Campos, Braz., 3,470 103 e17
Dorfen, F.R.Ger., 4,048 118 D4
Dorgali, It., 7,253 123 B4
Dori, Upper Volta, 3,385 162 D3
Dorintosh, Sask., Can. 43 B3
Dorion, Ont., Can. 44 E5
Dorion, Qué., Can., 4,899 47 K3
Dorking, Ont., Can. 46 a13
Dorking, U.K., 22,604 114 H8
Dorlar, F.R.Ger., 1,529 119 E2
Dormagen, F.R.Ger., 10,858 119 B2
Dormans, Fr., 2,250 117 E2
Dormont, Pa., 13,098 60 b8
Dornbirn, Aust., 28,033 124 F6
Dornburg, Ger. D.R. 126 a5
Dornes, Fr., 1,388 117 E3
Dorno, It., 4,120 122 b5
Dornoch, U.K. 112 D3
Dornoch Firth, U.K. 112 E3
Dornsife, Pa. 60 J4
Dorogobuzh, U.S.S.R., 5,800 136 D2
Dorohoi, Rum., 14,771 128 F1
Dorohusk, Pol. 127 E3
Dorokhovo, U.S.S.R. 136 b6
Dorolţ, Rum. 128 D1
Doronishijō, Jap. 154 h15
Dorotea, Swed. 120 D2
Dorothy, Minn. 74 D2
Dorothy, W. Va. 62 C5
Dorr, Mich. 67 H6
Dorrance, Kans., 331 75 G5
Dorre I., Austl. 172 A3
Dorrigo, Austl., 1,080 173 H4
Dorris, Calif., 973 82 B2
Dorset, Ont., Can. 46 F3
Dorset, Ohio 70 J1
Dorset, Vt. 54 A5
Dorset Pk., Vt. 54 A5
Dorsetshire, co., U.K., 313,460 113 E6
Dorsey, Ill. 68 C5
Dorsey, Md. 62 c8
Dorseyville, Pa. 60 c7
Dorsten, F.R.Ger., 32,527 119 C1
Dorstone, U.K. 114 C6
Dortmund, F.R.Ger., 607,885 118 A3
Dortmund-Ems-Kan., F.R.Ger. 118 A3
Dörtyol, Turk., 10,222 142 D2
Dorum, F.R.Ger., 3,098 118 B2
Doruma, D.R.Congo 164 D1
Dorval, Qué., Can., 18,014 47 o18
Dörzbach, F.R.Ger., 1,171 119 H6
Dos Bahias, C., Arg. 105 C6
Dos Bocas, Nic. 94 E5
Dos Bocas, P.R. 96 s10
Dos Cabezas, Ariz. 78 D5
Dos Caminos, Cuba, 2,004 96 f2
Dos Caminos del Cobre, Cuba, 2,278 96 e3
Dos de Mayo, Peru 104 C3
Dosewallips, r., Wash. 81 a7
Dos Hermanas, Sp., 27,696 122 C4
Dos Hermanos, Mt., Phil. 153 c6
Dösjebro, Swed. 121 c7
Do Son, N. Viet. 147 i9
Dos Palos, Calif., 2,028 82 C4
Dospat, Bulg., 1,884 129 E4
Dos Pozos, Arg. 105 B6
Dosquet, Qué., Can. 47 N2
Doss, Tex. 77 O4
Dosse, r., Ger.D.R. 118 D2
Dossenheim, Fr. 116 d9
Dosso, Niger, 2,516 162 E3
Dossor, U.S.S.R., 9,500 134 E5
Dossville, Miss. 73 F5
Doswell, Va. 62 G5
Dot, Br. Col., Can. 42 G4
Dothan, Ala., 31,440 64 D4
Dot Lake, Alaska 85 J3
Dotsero, Colo. 79 B2
Dottignies, Belg., 6,053 115 B4
Döttingen, Switz., 2,356 124 C1
Doty, Wash. 80 B2
Douai, Fr., 50,104 117 E1
Douala, Cam., 150,000* 162 F5
Douarnenez, Fr., 20,304 116 A2
Double Bayou, Tex. 77 k9
Double Mer, l., Newf., Can. 45 P3
Double Pk., Austl. 173 F5
Double Shoals, N.C. 63 C2
Double Springs, Ala., 811 64 B1
Double Springs, Tenn. 71 F5
Doubletop Mtn., N.Y. 59 L7
Doubrava, r., Czech. 127 e7
Doubs, r., Fr.-Switz. 117 G3
Doubtful I. Bay, Austl. 172 B5
Doubtful Sd., N.Z. 175 e7
Douchy-les-Mines, Fr., 5,242 116 a7
Doué, Fr., 3,914 117 C3
Douentza, Mali, 10,000 162 D3
d'Ouessant, Î., Fr. 116 A2
Dougga, ruins, Tun. 160 f5
Dough Crag, mtn., U.K. 112 f9
Dougherty, co., Ga., 75,680 64 E4
Dougherty, Iowa, 398 72 E2
Dougherty, Okla., 294 76 F3
Doughton, N.C. 63 D1
Douglas, Ont., Can. 46 H3
Douglas, Qué., Can. 47 T9
Douglas, S. Af., 3,974 164 C6
Douglas, I. of Man, U.K., 20,361 113 D4
Douglas, Scot., U.K. 112 D4
Douglas, Alaska, 1,042 85 L4
Douglas, Ariz., 11,925 78 D6
Douglas, co., Colo., 4,816 79 C2
Douglas, co., Ga., 16,741 64 E2
Douglas, Ga., 8,736 64 G4
Douglas, co., Ill., 19,243 68 D4
Douglas, co., Kans., 43,720 75 K5
Douglas, Mass., 2,559(T) 57 K4
Douglas, Mich., 602 67 G6
Douglas, co., Minn., 21,313 74 E3
Douglas, co., Mo., 9,653 72 E8
Douglas, co., Nebr., 343,490 75 J2
Douglas, Nebr., 197 75 J3
Douglas, co., Nev., 3,481 83 A3
Douglas, N. Dak., 210 74 B2
Douglas, Okla., 74 76 F1
Douglas, co., Oreg., 68,458 80 B4
Douglas, co., S. Dak., 5,113 74 C4
Douglas, co., Wash., 14,890 80 D2
Douglas, co., Wis., 45,008 66 A2
Douglas, Wyo., 2,822 81 G4
Douglas, Mt., Alaska 85 F4
Douglas, Mt., Mont. 81 D3
Douglas Bay, Dominica 97 13
Douglas City, Calif. 82 B2
Douglas L., Mich. 67 J3
Douglas L., Tenn. 71 H6
Douglass, Kans., 1,058 75 J6
Douglass, Tex. 77 Q4
Douglassville, Pa. 60 e10
Douglastown, N.B., Can. 47 T10
Douglasville, Ga., 4,462 64 E2
Douglas Water, U.K. 112 c8
Doullens, Fr., 7,008 117 E1
Doumé, Cam., 1,500* 162 G5
Douna, Mali 162 D3
Doune, U.K. 112 b7
Dounreay, U.K. 112 E2
Doupov, Czech. 126 c6
Doupovské Hory, Czech. 126 c6
Dour, Belg., 11,419 115 B4
Dourados, Braz., 10,757 103 E6
Douro, r., Port. 122 A2
Dousman, Wis., 410 66 E5
Dove, r., U.K. 114 G2
Dove Creek, Colo., 986 79 A3
Doveli, Sol. Is. 175 b2
Dover, Austl. 173 f14
Dover, U.K., 35,554 113 G6
Dover, Ark., 525 73 B2
Dover, Del., 7,250 62 J3
Dover, Fla. 65 d11
Dover, Ga. 64 H3
Dover, Kans. 75 K5
Dover, Ky., 718 71 H3
Dover, Mass., 2,846(T) 57 L4
Dover, Mo., 172 72 D5
Dover, N.H., 19,131 54 F5
Dover, N.J., 13,034 61 B2
Dover, N.C., 651 63 G2
Dover, Ohio, 11,300 70 H2
Dover, Okla. 76 E2
Dover, Pa., 975 60 J5
Dover, Tenn., 736 71 D5
Dover, Str. of, Eur. 110 D3
Dover-Foxcroft, Me., 2,481 55 C3
Doveridge, U.K. 114 E5
Dover Plains, N.Y. 59 N8
Dovesville, S.C. 63 D3
Dovol'noye, U.S.S.R. 137 p11
Dovre, Nor. 120 B3
Dow, L., Bots. 164 D5
Dowa, Malawi 164 E4
Dowagiac, Mich., 7,208 67 G7
Dowagiac, r., Mich. 67 G7
Dow City, Iowa, 531 72 B3
Dowdy, Ark. 73 D2
Dowell, Ill., 453 68 C6
Dowelltown, Tenn., 279 71 E6
Dowling, Mich. 67 H6
Dowling Park, Fla. 65 F2
Down, co., U.K., 267,013 113 C4
Downer, Minn. 74 D2
Downers Grove, Ill., 21,154 68 D2
Downey, Calif., 82,505 82 D6
Downey, Idaho, 726 81 C4
Downham, U.K., 1,800 114 J6
Downham Market, U.K., 2,835 113 G5
Downieville, Calif. 82 C3
Downing, Mo., 463 72 E4
Downing, Wis., 241 66 A3
Downingtown, Pa., 5,598 61 L5
Downpatrick, U.K., 4,219 113 D4
Downs, Ill., 497 68 D3
Downs, Kans., 1,206 75 G4
Downs Mtn., Wyo. 81 E4
Downsville, La. 73 C5
Downsville, N.Y. 59 K7
Downsville, Wis. 66 B4
Downsville Dam, N.Y. 59 L7
Downton, U.K., 1,796 113 i13
Dow Rūd, Iran, 7,088 143 D2
Dows, Iowa, 882 72 D2
Doxey, Mex., 1,441 93 e9
Doyle, Calif. 82 C2
Doylestown, Ohio, 1,873 70 H2
Doylestown, Pa., 5,917 61 M5
Doylestown, Wis., 249 66 D5
Doyleville, Colo. 79 B2
Doyline, La., 1,061 73 B5
Doyon, N. Dak. 74 C1
Dōzen, is., Jap. 155 C3
Dozier, Ala., 335 64 C4
Dozier, Tex. 76 N2
Dra, r., Alg.-Mor. 160 C3
Dra, Hamada du, Af. 160 C3
Drabenderhöhe, F.R.Ger., 8,573 119 C3
Dråby, Den. 121 C4

220 · Drac—Eagle Mills

Drac, r., Fr. 117 F4
Dracena, Braz., 15,997 103 F6
Drachenfels, pk., F.R.Ger. 119 E6
Drachten, Neth., 17,260 115 E1
Dracut, Mass., 13,674(T) 57 L2
Draga, Yug. 125 E3
Drăgănești, Rum. 128 F2
Drăgănești-Vlașca, Rum. 128 E2
Draganovo, Bulg., 4,304 128 E3
Drăgășani, Rum., 9,963 128 E2
Dragerton, Utah, 2,959 78 C2
Draginac, Yug. 125 D2
Dragoevo, Bulg., 2,539 128 F3
Dragon, Utah 78 D2
Dragons Mouth, Trin. and Tob.-Ven. 101 K2
Dragoon, Ariz. 78 D5
Dragør, Den., 4,243 121 E5
Dragoș Vodă, Rum. 128 F2
Dragovac, Yug. 125 E3
Dragovo, Yug. 125 E3
Dragsfjärd, Fin. 120 E3
Dragu, Rum. 128 D1
Draguignan, Fr., 16,083 117 G5
Drain, Oreg., 1,052 80 B4
Drake, Sask., Can. 43 C4
Drake, Ariz. 78 B4
Drake, Colo. 79 b7
Drake, N. Dak., 752 74 B2
Drake, S.C. 63 E3
Drakensberg, ra., S. Af. 164 D7
Drake Passage, Atl. Oc.-Pac. Oc. 99 C8
Drake Pk., Oreg. 80 C4
Drakesboro, Ky., 832 71 D4
Drakes Branch, Va., 759 62 F5
Drakesville, Iowa, 197 72 E4
Dráma, Gr., 32,195 129 E4
Drammen, Nor., 30,959 120 B4
Drancy, Fr., 65,940 116 h11
Dranesville, Ga. 64 E3
Dranesville, Va. 62 G3
Drangedal, Nor. 121 A1
Draper, N.C., 3,382 63 E1
Draper, S. Dak., 215 74 B4
Draper, Utah 78 C1
Draper, Va., 233 62 D6
Drasco, Ark. 73 D2
Drasenhofen, Aust. 124 N5
Drassmarkt, Aust., 1,029 124 N6
Drau, r., Aust. 124 L7
Dráva, r., Hung. 126 C4
Drava, r., Yug. 125 C1
Draveil, Fr., 18,906 116 h12
Dravograd, Yug. 125 B1
Dravosburg, Pa., 3,458 60 c8
Draw, Tex. 77 N3
Drawa, r., Pol. 127 A2
Drawno, Pol., 2,183 127 A2
Drawsko, Pol., 7,158 127 A2
Drayton, Ont., Can. 46 D5
Drayton, U.K., 1,916 114 F7
Drayton, N. Dak., 1,278 74 D1
Drayton Plains, Mich. 67 K6
Drayton Valley, Alta., Can., 3,771 42 J3
Drebkau, Ger.D.R. 118 E3
Dreiborn, F.R.Ger., 1,980 119 A3
Dreis, F.R.Ger., 1,122 119 B5
Dreis-Tiefenbach, F.R.Ger., 3,536 119 E3
Dren, Bulg., 2,691 128 D3
Drennen, W. Va. 62 D4
Drenovets, Bulg., 4,501 128 D3
Drensteinfurt, F.R.Ger., 2,683 119 D1
Drenthe, Mich. 67 H6
Drentsche Hoofdvaart, can., Neth. 115 E2
Dresden, Ont., Can., 2,286 44 G7
Dresden, Ger.D.R., 493,603 118 D3
Dresden, Kans., 134 75 E4
Dresden, N.Y., 437 58 F6
Dresden, N. Dak. 74 C1
Dresden, Ohio, 1,338 70 H2
Dresden, Tenn., 1,510 71 C5
Dresden Station, N.Y. 59 O4
Dresser, Wis., 498 66 A3
Dreumel, Neth. 115 D3
Dreux, Fr., 23,494 117 D2
Drew, co., Ark., 15,213 73 D4
Drew, Miss., 2,143 73 E4
Drew, Oreg. 80 B4
Drewryville, Va. 62 G6
Drewsey, Oreg., 39 80 D4
Drews Res., Oreg. 80 C4
Drexel, Mo., 651 72 C6
Drexel, N.C., 1,146 63 C2
Drexel Hill, Pa., 39,750* 60 f12
Drezdenko, Pol., 5,549 127 A2
Drezna, U.S.S.R., 11,500 136 c6
Driebergen, Neth., 12,900 115 c6
Driedmeat Cr., Alta., Can. 43 c8
Driedorf, F.R.Ger., 1,247 119 E3
Driffield, U.K., 6,892 113 F4
Driftless Area, unglaciated reg., Wis. 67 ·
Driftwood, Pa., 203 60 F3
Driftwood, Tex. 76 b5
Driftwood Branch, Pa. 60 F2
Driggs, Idaho, 824 81 D4
Drin, r., Alb. 125 D3
Drin, r., Alb. 125 E4
Drina, r., Yug. 125 D3
Dringo, Indon. 148 d8
Drinit, Pellg i, Alb. 125 D4
Drin i zi, r., Alb. 125 E4
Drinjača, Yug. 125 D2
Drinker, Pa. 61 p16
Dripping Springs, Tex. 77 P4
Driscoll, N. Dak. 74 B2
Driscoll, Tex., 669 77 P6
Driskill Mtn., La. 73 C5
Drissa, U.S.S.R., 3,000 136 C2
Driva, r., Nor. 120 B3
Driver, Ark. 73 E2
Drniš, Yug., 2,746 125 C3
Dröbak, Nor., 2,722 120 B4
Drochtersen, F.R.Ger., 5,584 118 B2
Drogheda, Ire., 17,008 113 C5
Drogobych, U.S.S.R., 42,000 136 A3
Drohiczyn, Pol., 1,399 127 E2
Droichead Nua, Ire., 4,157 113 C5
Droitwich, U.K., 7,975 113 E5
Drolet = Naschitti
Drolshagen, F.R.Ger., 2,466 119 D2
Dromahair, Ire. 113 B4
Dromana, Austl., 1,257 173 e12
Dromcolliher, Ire. 113 B5
Drôme, r., Fr. 117 F4
Dromedario, Cayos del, Cuba 96 d1
Dromore, U.K. 113 C4
Dronfield, U.K., 11,303 114 E4
Drongen, Belg., 7,497 115 B3
Dronne, r., Fr. 117 D4
Dronninglund, Den., 9,323 121 C3
Dropia, Rum. 128 F2
Dross, Aust. 124 b10
Droué, Fr., 1,022 117 D2
Drovyanaya, U.S.S.R. 134 F2
Drovyanaya, U.S.S.R. 135 L4
Druid, U.K. 114 B5
Druid L., Wis. 66 c10
Drulingen, Fr. 116 d9
Drumbo, Ont., Can. 46 a15
Drumelzier, U.K. 112 d8
Drumheller, Alta., Can., 2,821 42 K3
Drum Inlet, N.C. 63 H3
Drumlish, Ire. 113 C5
Drummond, Mont., 577 81 C2
Drummond, Okla., 281 76 E1
Drummond, Wis. 66 B2
Drummond, L., Va. 62 H6
Drummond, Mt., Austl. 172 E2
Drummond Island, Mich. 67 K2
Drummond I., Mich. 67 K2
Drummond Ra., Austl. 173 G3
Drummondville, Qué., Can., 27,493 44 K6
Drummore, U.K. 113 D4
Drumright, Okla., 4,190 76 G2
Drums, Pa. 61 L4
Drumshanbo, Ire. 113 C4
Drumvaich, U.K. 112 b7
Drunen, Neth., 4,800 115 c7
Drury (part of Florida), Mass. 56 E2
Drusenheim, Fr., 2,907 119 D7
Druten, Neth., 4,100 115 D3
Druzhina, U.S.S.R. 135 O3
Druzhkovka, U.S.S.R., 47,000 136 e7
Drvar, Yug., 2,493 125 C2
Drvenik Veli, i., Yug. 125 B3
Drwęca, r., Pol. 127 C2
Dry, r., N.H. 54 E3
Dryad, Wash. 80 B2
Dryanovo, Bulg., 5,401 128 E3
Dry Bk. Mass. 56 F2
Drybrough, Man., Can. 43 E3
Dry Creek, Yukon, Can. 40 A5
Dry Creek, La. 73 B7
Dry Cr., Ga. 64 E4
Dry Cr. Butte, Oreg. 80 E4
Dryden, Ont., Can., 5,376 44 D5
Dryden, Me. 55 B4
Dryden, Mich., 531 67 K6
Dryden, N.Y., 1,263 59 H7
Dryden, Oreg. 80 B4
Dryden, Tex. 77 M4
Dryden, Wash. 80 C2
Dry Falls Dam, Wash. 80 D2
Dry Fork, Va. 62 E6
Drygarn Fawr, mtn., U.K. 114 A6
Drylake, Newf., Can. 45 N4
Dry L., N. Dak. 74 C1
Drymen, U.K. 112 b7
Dry Mills, Me. 55 B5
Dry Prong, La., 360 73 C6
Dry Ridge, Ky., 802 71 G3
Dry Run, Pa. 60 G5
Drysdale, r., Austl. 172 C2
Dry Tortugas, is., Fla. 65 k16
Drzewica, Pol. 127 k5
Drzewiczka, r., Pol. 127 k5
Dschang, Cam., 6,000* 162 F5
Dsodse = Dzodze
Duaca, Ven., 6,400 100 F2
Duanesburg, N.Y. 59 M6
Duart, Ont., Can. 46 C6
Duarte, Mex., 1,546 93 c8
Duarte, Calif., 13,962 83 i15
Duarte, Pico, Dom. Rep. 96 m6
Dubá, Czech. 126 d6
Dubach, La., 1,013 73 C5
Dubai, Tr. States, 45,000* 143 E3
Dubawnt, r., N.W.T., Can. 40 J5
Dubawnt L., N.W.T., Can. 40 J5
Dubbeldam, Neth., 4,200 115 b7
Dubberly, La., 249 73 B5
Dubbo, Austl., 12,009 173 G5
Dübendorf, Switz., 11,784 124 C1
Dubenskiy, U.S.S.R. 137 h9
Dubí, Czech., 10,112 126 A1
Dubie, D.R.Congo 165 o18
Dubienka, Pol. 127 E3
Dublán, Mex., 1,346 92 D1
Dublin, Ont., Can. 46 C5
Dublin, co., Ire., 705,781 113 C5
Dublin = Baile Atha Cliath
Dublin, Calif. 83 f12
Dublin, Ga., 13,814 64 F3
Dublin, Ind., 1,021 70 D3
Dublin, Ky. 71 C5
Dublin, Mich. 67 G4
Dublin, Miss. 73 E3
Dublin, N.H. 54 C6
Dublin, N.C., 366 63 F3
Dublin, Pa., 517 60 f10
Dublin, Tex., 2,443 77 O3
Dublin, Va., 1,427 62 D5
Dublon, i., Truk 176 19
Dubna, U.S.S.R. 134 C4
Dubno, U.S.S.R., 18,500 136 B3
Dubois, Idaho, 447 81 C3
Dubois, co., Ind., 27,463 70 C4
Dubois, Ind. 70 C4
Du Bois, Nebr., 218 75 J3
Du Bois, Pa., 10,667 60 E3
Dubois, Wyo., 574 81 E4
Duboistown, Pa., 1,358 60 H3
Dubossary, U.S.S.R., 13,000 136 C4
Du Boullie Mtn., Me. 55 D2
Dubovka, U.S.S.R., 11,700 136 G3
Dŭbovo, Bulg., 2,652 128 E3
Dubovoye, Oz., U.S.S.R. 136 c6
Dubovskoye, U.S.S.R. 136 F4
Dubrajpur, India, 13,917 144 f14
Dubrava, Yug. 125 C2
Dubre, Ky. 71 F5
Dubréka, Guin., 2,000 162 B4
Dubrovitsa, U.S.S.R., 5,900 136 B3
Dubrovnik, Yug., 23,000* 125 D3
Dubrovno, U.S.S.R., 4,900 136 C2
Dubrovskoye, U.S.S.R. 135 L4
Dubuque, co., Iowa, 80,048 72 G2
Dubuque, Iowa, 56,606 72 G2
Duc de Gloucester, Îs., Fr. Poly. 171 J6
Ducey, Fr., 1,816 117 C2
Duchcov, Czech. 126 c6
Ducherow, Ger.D.R. 118 D2
Duchesne, co., Utah, 7,179 78 C1
Duchesne, Utah, 770 78 C1
Duchesne, r., Utah 78 C1
Duchess, Austl. 172 F3
Duchess, Alta., Can. 42 K4
Duc Hue, S. Viet. 147 m11
Ducie, i., Pac. Oc. 171 K6
Ducie C., Terr. Papua 174 3
Duck, r., Tenn. 71 D6
Duckabush, r., Wash. 81 a7
Duck Cr., Nev. 83 C3
Duck Hill, Miss., 674 73 F4
Duck I., Me. 55 D4
Duck Lake, Sask., Can. 43 C4
Duck L., Me. 55 D3
Duck L., Mich. 66 D2
Duck L., Mich. 67 H4
Duck Mtn., Man., Can. 43 E4
Ducktown, Tenn., 741 71 G6
Duckwater, Nev. 83 C3
Duc Lap, S. Viet. 146 D4
Duc Long, S. Viet., 20,768 146 D5
Ducos, Mart. 97 12
Duc Pho, S. Viet. 146 E4
Duc Thanh, S. Viet. 147 m11
Duc Trong, S. Viet. 147 n11
Duddon, r., U.K. 114 B2
Dudelange, Lux., 14,617 115 E5
Dudeldorf, F.R.Ger., 1,131 119 B5
Düdelsheim, F.R.Ger., 2,016 119 G4
Dudenhofen, F.R.Ger., 3,317 119 E6
Duderstadt, F.R.Ger., 10,559 118 C3
Dudhi, India 144 d13
Dudignac, Arg., 4,000* 105 a12
Dudinka, U.S.S.R., 16,400 135 H3
Dudley, Northumb., Eng., U.K. 112 g9
Dudley, Staffs., Eng., U.K., 61,748 113 E5
Dudley, Ga., 360 64 F3
Dudley, Ill. 68 E4
Dudley, Mass., 6,510(T) 56 J4
Dudley, Mo., 287 72 G8
Dudley, N.C., 158 63 G2
Dudley, Pa., 295 60 F5
Dudley, S.C. 63 D3
Dudo, Som. Rep. 163 N4
Dudváh, r., Czech. 126 C2
Dudweiler, F.R.Ger., 27,840 116 c8
Due, U.S.S.R., 3,500 135 O4
Duékoué, Iv. Coast, 5,026 162 C4
Dueñas, Phil., 2,052 153 d10
Dueodde, c., Den. 121 G6
Duenweg, Mo., 529 72 C7
Dueré, Braz. 103 G4
Duero, Phil., 1,231 153 f12
Duero, r., Sp. 122 D2
Due West, S.C., 1,166 63 B3
Duff Corners, Ont., Can. 46 c15
Duffel, Belg., 13,151 115 e8
Duffer Pk., Nev. 83 A2
Duffield, Alta., Can. 43 a7
Duffield, U.K., 3,375 114 E5
Dufftown, U.K., 1,555 112 E3
Duffy, Ohio 70 J3
Dufourspitze, mtn. Switz. 124 B3
Dufresne, Man., Can. 43 h10
Dufresne Lake, Qué., Can. 45 M4
Dufrost, Man., Can. 43 h10
Dufur, Oreg., 488 80 C3
Duga Poljana, Yug. 125 E3
Duga Resa, Yug., 3,773 125 B2
Dugger, Ind., 1,062 70 B3
Dugi, i., Yug. 125 B3
Dugo Selo, Yug., 2,074 125 C2
Dugumenu, i., Terr. Papua 174 3
Dugway, Utah 78 B1
Dugway Ra., Utah 78 a11
Duhamel, Alta., Can. 43 c8
Duich, Loch, U.K. 112 D3
Duisburg, F.R.Ger., 476,523 118 A3
Duisdorf, F.R.Ger., 7,738 119 B3
Duitama, Col. 100 D5
Duiveland, i., Neth. 115 B3
Dukat, Alb. 125 D4
Duke, Okla. 76 D3
Duke Center, Pa. 60 E2
Dukes, co., Mass., 5,829 57 O7
Dukes, Mich. 66 F2
Dukhān, Qatar 143 E3
Dukhovshchina, U.S.S.R., 3,300 136 C2
Duki, Pak. 144 C3
Dukla, Pol. 127 D4
Dukm, Muscat and Oman 143 F4
Dulac, La. 73 E8
Dulauan, Phil., 21,951 153 C4
Dulce, N. Mex. 79 B3
Dulce, r., Arg. 105 C3
Dulce, G., C.R. 94 F6
Dulce Nombre, Hond., 3,668 94 d9
Dulce Nombre de Culmí, Hond. 94 E3
Duleek, Ire. 113 C5
Dŭlgopol, Bulg., 5,204 128 F3
Dülken, F.R.Ger., 20,308 119 A2
Dullingham, U.K. 114 J6
Dülmen, F.R.Ger., 14,471 118 A3
Du Long, S. Viet. 146 E5
Dulovo, Bulg., 5,860 128 F3
Duluth, Ga., 1,483 64 E2
Duluth, Minn., 106,884 74 G2
Dūmā, Leb, 2,115 142 b5
Dūmā, Syr., 27,092 142 c6
Dumaguete, Phil., 10,528 153 B3
Dumai, Indon. 148 B2
Dumalag, Phil., 1,566 153 d10
Dumanjug, Phil., 2,014 153 e11
Dumaran I., Phil. 153 B3
Dumarao, Phil., 1,563 153 d10
Dumaring, Indon. 148 F2
Dumas, Ark., 3,540 73 D4
Dumas, Miss. 73 G3
Dumas, Tex., 8,477 76 N2
Dumbarton, U.K., 26,335 112 D4
Dumbéa, N. Caled. 174 k9
Dumbéa, B., N. Caled. 174 k9
Dumbleyung, Austl. 172 B5
Dumbrăveni, Rum., 5,367 128 E1
Dumbrăveni, Rum. 128 F1
Dum Duma, India, 8,192 145 K4
Dumfries, co., U.K., 88,423 113 E4
Dumfries, U.K., 27,275 113 E4
Dumfries, Va., 1,368 62 G4
Dumka, India, 18,720 144 f13
Dümmer, l., F.R.Ger. 118 B2
Dumoine, r., Qué., Can. 44 J6
Dumoine, L., Qué., Can. 44 J6
Dumont, Colo. 79 a8
Dumont, Iowa, 719 72 D2
Dumont, Minn., 226 74 D3
Dumont, N.J., 18,882 61 C2
Dumont d'Urville, Ant. 180 U6
Dumoulin, C., N. Caled. 174 k8
Dumraon, India, 19,662 144 e13
Dumyāṭ, U.A.R., 72,000 161 K2
Dun, Fr. 117 F2
Duna, r., Hung. 126 D3
Dunaföldvár, Hung., 11,251 126 D3
Dunaj, r., Czech. 126 D3
Dunajec, r., Pol. 127 D4
Dunajská Streda, Czech., 8,290 126 C2
Dunakeszi, Hung., 14,266 126 D3
Dunapataj, Hung., 5,658 126 D3
Dunărea, r., Rum. 128 F2
Dunaszekcső, Hung., 3,278 126 D3
Dunaújváros, Hung., 31,048 126 D3
Dunav, r., Bulg. 128 E3
Dunav, r., Yug. 125 D2
Dunay, U.S.S.R. 151 F2
Dunay, r., U.S.S.R. 128 G2
Dunay, O., U.S.S.R. 135 M2
Dunback, N.Z. 175 f7
Dunbar, U.K., 4,003 112 E3
Dunbar, Okla. 76 H3
Dunbar, Pa., 1,536 60 C6
Dunbar, S.C. 63 E3
Dunbar, W. Va., 11,006 62 C4
Dunbar, Wis. 66 E3
Dunbarton, co., U.K., 184,546 112 D3
Dunbarton, N.H. 54 D5
Dunblane, Sask., Can. 43 C4
Dunblane, U.K., 2,922 112 E3
Duncan, Br. Col., Can., 3,575 42 F4
Duncan, Ariz., 862 78 D5
Duncan, Miss., 465 73 E3
Duncan, Nebr., 294 75 H2
Duncan, N.C. 63 F2
Duncan, Okla., 20,009 76 F3
Duncan, S.C., 1,186 63 B3
Duncan Falls, Ohio 70 H3
Duncan L., Qué., Can. 44 J4
Duncannon, Pa., 1,800 60 J5
Duncans, Jam., 1,228 96 p8
Duncansby Head, U.K. 112 E2
Duncansville, Pa., 1,396 60 F5
Duncanville, Ill. 68 E5
Duncanville, Tex., 3,774 76 f9
Dunchurch, U.K., 1,608 114 F6
Duncombe, Iowa, 355 72 C2
Duncombe Bay, Norfolk I. 175 11
Dundaga, U.S.S.R., 3,200 136 A1
Dundalk, Ont., Can. 46 D4
Dundalk, Ire., 21,687 113 C5
Dundalk, Md., 82,428 62 c7
Dundalk Bay, Ire. 113 C5
Dundarrach, N.C., 109 63 E3
Dundas, Ont., Can., 12,750 46 D5
Dundas, Ill. 68 D5
Dundas, Ohio 70 G3
Dundas, Va. 62 F6
Dundas, L., Austl. 172 C5
Dundas I., Br. Col., Can. 42 D2
Dundas Pen., N.W.T., Can. 40 G3
Dundas Str., Austl. 172 D1
Dundee, S. Af., 10,943 164 E6
Dundee, U.K., 182,959 112 E3
Dundee, Fla., 1,554 65 H4
Dundee, Iowa, 185 72 F2
Dundee, Kans. 75 G5
Dundee, Ky. 71 E4
Dundee, Mich., 2,377 67 K7
Dundee, N.Y., 1,468 58 F6
Dundee, Oreg., 318 80 B3
Dundee, Wis. 66 E5
Dundo, Ang. 164 C3
Dundrum Bay, U.K. 113 D4
Dundurn, Sask., Can. 43 C4
Dundy, co., Nebr., 3,570 75 D3
Dune Acres, Ind., 238 69 f10
Dunedin, N.Z. 73,245 175 f7
Dunedin, Fla., 8,444 65 G4
Dunedoo, Austl. 173 G5
Dunellen, N.J., 6,840 58 b14
Dunes Park, Ill. 69 c7
Dunfermline, U.K., 47,159 112 E3
Dunfermline, Ill., 284 68 C3
Dung, r., S. Viet. 146 D5
Dungannon, U.K., 6,494 113 C4
Dungannon, Va., 444 62 B6
Dungarpur, India, 12,755 145 D5
Dungarvan, Ire., 5,394 113 C5
Dungavel, U.K. 112 b8
Dungeness, Wash. 80 B1
Dungeness, c., U.K. 113 G6
Dunglow, Ire. 113 B4
Dungog, Austl., 2,154 173 G5
Dungu, D.R.Congo 164 D1
Dungun, r., Malay. 147 p14
Dunino, U.K. 112 e7
Dunipace (incl. Denny), U.K., 7,761 112 D3
Dunje, Yug. 125 E4
Dunkeld, U.K. 112 E3
Dunker, Swed. 120 d8
Dunkerque, Fr., 28,388 117 E1
Dunkerton, Iowa, 507 72 E2
Dunkery Hill, U.K. 114 A8
Dunkirk, Ind., 3,117 70 D2
Dunkirk, N.Y., 18,205 58 B6
Dunkirk, Ohio, 1,006 70 F2
Dunklin, co., Mo., 39,139 72 G8
Dunkur, Eth. 163 L4
Dunkwa, Ghana, 12,839 162 D5
Dún Laoghaire, Ire., 64,855 113 D5
Dunlap, Ill., 564 68 C3
Dunlap, Ind., 1,935 70 D1
Dunlap, Iowa, 1,254 72 B3
Dunlap, Kans., 134 75 J5
Dunlap, Nebr. 75 C1
Dunlap, N. Mex. 79 C4
Dunlap, Tenn., 1,026 71 F6
Dunlap, Tex. 77 N2
Dunlavin, Ire. 113 C5
Dunleer, Ire. 113 C5
Dunlevy, Pa., 408 60 c9
Dunlop, U.K. 112 a8
Dunlow, W. Va. 62 B4
Dunmanus Bay, Ire. 113 A6
Dunmanway, Ire. 113 B6
Dunmor, Ky. 71 D4
Dunmore, Ire. 113 B5
Dunmore, Pa., 18,917 61 L3
Dunmore, W. Va. 62 E4
Dunmore, L., Vt. 54 A4
Dunmore East, Ire. 113 C5
Dunmore Town, Bah. Is. 95 c7
Dunn, Ind. 70 B2
Dunn, La. 73 D5
Dunn, N.C., 7,566 63 F2
Dunn, co., N. Dak., 6,350 74 A2
Dunn, co., Wis., 26,156 66 B4
Dunnavant, Ala. 64 c7
Dünn Bach, r., F.R.Ger. 119 C4
Dunn Center, N. Dak., 250 74 A2
Dunn Corner (part of Westerly), R.I. 57 K7
Dunnell, Minn., 260 74 E4
Dunnellon, Fla., 1,079 65 G3
Dunnet, U.K. 112 E2
Dunnet Head, U.K. 112 E2
Dunning, U.K. 112 c7
Dunning, Nebr., 210 75 E2
Dunning Cr., Pa. 60 E5
Dunnington, U.K. 114 G3
Dunnington, Ind. 70 B2
Dunnottar, Man., Can. 43 h9
Dunnottar, S. Af. 165 k17
Dunnsville, Va. 62 H5
Dunnville, Ont., Can., 5,119 46 E6
Dunnville, Ky. 71 G4
Dunolly, Austl. 173 d11
Dunoon, U.K., 9,211 112 D4
Duns, U.K., 1,838 112 E4
Dunqulah, Sudan, 3,350 163 J2
Dunscore, U.K. 113 E4
Dunseith, N. Dak., 1,017 74 B1
Dunsmuir, Calif., 2,873 82 B2
Dunstable, U.K., 25,645 113 F6
Dunstable, Mass. 57 L2
Dunster, Br. Col., Can. 42 G3
Dunster, U.K. 114 A8
Dun-sur-Auron, Fr., 4,100 117 E3
Dunton, Colo. 79 A3
Dunvegan, U.K. 112 C3
Dunvegan, Loch, U.K. 112 C3
Dunwoody, Ga. 64 g9
Duong Dong, S. Viet. 146 C5
Duong Hoa, S. Viet. 147 k11
Du Page, co., Ill., 313,459 68 D2
Du Page, r., Ill. 68 D2
Dupax, Phil., 3,361 153 c6
Duplainville, Wis. 66 c11
Duplin, co., N.C., 40,270 63 G3
Dupo, Ill., 2,937 68 B5
Dupont, Colo. 79 c8
Du Pont, Ga., 210 64 G5
Dupont, Pa., 3,669 61 o16
Du Pont, Wash., 354 80 B2
Dupree, S. Dak., 548 74 B3
Dupuyer, Mont. 81 C1
Duque de Bragança, Ang. 164 B3
Duque de Caxias, Braz., 173,007 103 e18
Duque de York, I., Chile 105 A8
Duquesne, Pa., 15,019 60 C5
Du Quoin, Ill., 6,558 68 C5
Dura, Malay. 147 o14
Durack Range, Austl. 172 C2
Duramana, Austl. 173 g9
Duran, N. Mex. 79 C4
Durance, r., Fr. 117 F5
Durand, Ill., 797 68 C1
Durand, Mich., 3,312 67 K6
Durand, Wis., 2,039 66 B4
Durango, st., Mex., 760,836 92 D3
Durango, Mex., 97,520 92 D3
Durango, Sp., 14,417 122 D1
Durango, Colo., 10,530 79 B3
Durañona, Arg. 105 a13
Durant, Iowa, 1,266 72 F3
Durant, Miss., 2,617 73 F4
Durant, Okla., 10,467 76 G3
Durants Neck, N.C. 63 H1
Duras, Fr., 1,303 117 D4
Durazno, Urug., 22,000* 105 D4
Duraznos, Mex. 93 f9
Durazzo = Durrës
Durban, Man., Can. 43 E4
Durban, S. Af., 655,370 164 E6
Durbanville, S. Af., 3,010 164 a8
Durbin, Fla. 65 H2
Durbin, W. Va., 431 62 E4
Đurđenovac, Yug., 2,759 125 D2
Đurđevac, Yug., 6,297 125 C1
Düren, F.R.Ger., 43,642 118 A3
Durg, India, 47,114 145 F5
Durgapur, India, 41,696 144 f14
Dürge Nuur, Mong. 150 C2
Durham, Ont., Can., 2,129 46 D4
Durham, co., U.K., 1,517,039 113 F4
Durham, U.K., 20,484 113 F4
Durham, Calif. 82 C3
Durham, Conn., 3,096(T) 56 F7
Durham, Ind. 69 g10
Durham, Kans., 183 75 H5
Durham, Me. 55 B5
Durham, N.H., 4,688 54 F5
Durham, N.Y. 59 M7
Durham, co., N.C., 111,995 63 F1
Durham, N.C., 78,302 63 F2
Durham, Okla. 76 D2
Durham, Pa. 61 k18
Durham, Wis. 66 c12
Durham, Pt., N.Z. 175 14
Durham Center (part of Durham), Conn. 56 F7
Durham Heights, N.W.T., Can. 38 E3
Durhamville, N.Y. 59 J5
Duriansebatang, Indon. 148 D3
Durkee, Oreg. 80 E3
Durlston Head, U.K. 113 i13
Durmersheim, F.R.Ger., 5,622 119 E7
Durmitor, mts., Yug. 125 D3
Durness, U.K. 112 D2
Dürnstein, Aust. 124 b10
Dürrenast, Switz. 124 B2
Durrës, Alb., 43,500 125 D4
Durrington, U.K., 4,737 114 E8
Dürröhrsdorf, Ger.D.R. 126 d5
Durrow, Ire. 113 C5
Dursey I., Ire. 113 A6
Dursley, U.K., 4,744 113 E6
Dursunbey, Turk., 5,927 142 B2
Durtal, Fr., 3,102 117 C3
Durup, Den. 121 B4
Durūz, Jabal ad, Syr. 142 D3
d'Urville, Udjung, Indon. 149 L3
D'Urville I., N.Z. 175 g6
Duryea, Pa., 5,626 61 L3
Dusa Mareb, Som. Rep. 163 M5
Dusey, r., Ont., Can. 44 E4
Dushanbe, U.S.S.R., 248,000 134 F6
Dushore, Pa., 731 61 K2
Duskan'ya, U.S.S.R. 135 O3
Dusky Sd., N.Z. 175 e7
Duson, La., 1,033 73 C7
Düsseldorf, F.R.Ger., 654,850 118 A3
Dussen, Neth. 115 b7
Dustin, Okla., 457 76 H2
Duston, U.K., 4,885 114 F6
Dutchess, co., N.Y., 176,008 59 N8
Dutch Guiana = Surinam
Dutch Harbor, Alaska 85 C5
Dutch John, Utah 78 D1
Dutch Mills, Ark. 73 A2
Dutch Mtn., Utah 78 B1
Dutchtown, Mo. 72 H7
Dutton, Ont., Can. 46 C6
Dutton, Mich. 67 H6
Dutton, Mont., 504 81 D2
Dutton, Okla. 76 E2
Dutton, Va. 62 H5
Dutton, Mt., Utah 78 B2
Duval, co., Fla., 455,411 65 H2
Duval, co., Tex., 13,398 77 O6
Duvall, Wash., 345 80 C2
Duvan, U.S.S.R. 137 i8
Duvannyy, U.S.S.R., 7,000 137 d2
Duveke, Swed. 121 c7
Duvergé, Dom. Rep., 6,701 96 m6
Duxbury, Mass., 1,069; 4,727(T) 57 O4
Duxbury, Vt. 54 B3
Duxbury Bay, Mass. 57 O4
Duxford, U.K., 1,398 114 J6
Düzce, Turk., 18,169 142 B1
Dvinskaya G., U.S.S.R. 134 C3
Dvůr Králové nad Labem, Czech., 15,010 126 B1
Dwarf, Ky. 71 H4
Dwarka, India, 14,314 144 C5
Dwight, Ill., 3,086 68 D2
Dwight (part of Belchertown), Mass. 56 G3
Dwight, Nebr., 209 75 H2
Dwight, N. Dak., 101 74 D2
Dwingelo, Neth. 115 E2
Dwyer, N. Mex. 79 B5
Dyankovo, Bulg., 3,772 128 F3
Dyat'kovo, U.S.S.R., 19,500 136 D2
Dyaul, i., Terr. New Guin. 174 f1
Dyberry Cr., Pa. 61 M2
Dybvad, Den. 121 C3
Dyce, Man., Can. 43 E3
Dyce, U.K. 112 E3
Dyckesville, Wis. 66 F4
Dyer, Ark., 450 73 A2
Dyer, Ind., 3,993 70 B1
Dyer, Ky. 71 E4
Dyer, Nev. 83 A4
Dyer, co., Tenn., 29,537 71 B5
Dyer, Tenn., 1,909 71 C5
Dyer Bay, Ont., Can. 46 C3
Dyersburg, Tenn., 12,499 71 B5
Dyersville, Iowa, 2,818 72 F2
Dyess, Ark., 409 73 E2
d'Yeu, Î., Fr. 116 B3
Dye Water, r., U.K. 112 e8
Dyje, r., Czech. 126 C2
Dyke, Va. 62 F4
Dyke Ackland B., Terr. Papua 174 f3
Dykehead, U.K. 112 b7
Dykh-Tau, G., U.S.S.R. 137 b1
Dyment, Ont., Can. 44 D5
Dymock, U.K., 1,212 113 E6
Dymokury, Czech. 127 e6
Dynów, Pol., 3,652 127 E4
Dypvåg, Nor. 121 B2
Dysart, Sask., Can. 43 D5
Dysart, U.K. 112 d7
Dysart, Iowa, 1,197 72 E2
Dysart, Pa. 60 F4
Dýšina, Czech. 126 c7
Dyul'tydag, G., U.S.S.R. 137 c1
Dyurtyuli, U.S.S.R. 137 h8
Dzabhan, r., Mong. 150 C2
Dzamiin, Üüde, Mong. 150 E2
Dzaoudzi, Arch. des Comores 165 G4
Dzerzhinsk, U.S.S.R., 176,000 134 D4
Dzerzhinskiy, U.S.S.R. 137 s11
Dzerzhinskoye, U.S.S.R. 135 J4
Dzhagdy, Khr., U.S.S.R. 135 N4
Dzhaksy, U.S.S.R. 137 m12
Dzhalal-Abad, U.S.S.R., 27,300 137 g4
Dzerzhinsk, Bel. S.S.R., U.S.S.R., 7,500 136 B2
Dzerzhinsk, Ukr. S.S.R., U.S.S.R., 45,000 136 e7
Dzhalinda, U.S.S.R. 135 M4
Dzhaltyr, U.S.S.R. 137 n12
Dzhambul, U.S.S.R., 131,000 134 G5
Dzhankoy, U.S.S.R., 30,500 136 D4
Dzhardzhan, U.S.S.R. 135 M3
Dzhar-Kurgan, U.S.S.R., 7,100 137 e5
Dzhekonda, U.S.S.R. 135 M4
Dzheksona, O., U.S.S.R. 134 E1
Dzhetygara, U.S.S.R., 14,800 134 F4
Dzhezkazgan, U.S.S.R., 29,100 134 F5
Dzhirgatal', U.S.S.R. 137 f4
Dzhizak, U.S.S.R., 15,000 134 F5
Dzhugdzhur, Khr., U.S.S.R. 135 N4
Dzhul'fa, U.S.S.R., 3,500 137 c2
Dzhungarskiy Alatau, Khr., U.S.S.R. 132 G5
Dzhusaly, U.S.S.R. 134 F5
Dziadkowice, Pol. 127 E2
Działdowo, Pol., 7,570 127 D2
Działoszyce, Pol., 1,821 127 D3
Działoszyn, Pol. 127 C3
Dzibalchén, Mex., 3,666 93 H4
Dzierzgoń, Pol., 2,875 127 C2
Dzierzoniów, Pol., 27,000* 127 B3
Dziewin, Pol. 127 k6
Dzilam de Bravo, Mex. 93 H4
Dziwnów, Pol., 1,330 127 A1
Dzodze, Ghana 162 d8
Dzungaria, reg., China 150 B2
Dzungarian Gate, China-U.S.S.R. 150 B2
Dzüün Bulag, Mong. 150 F2
Dzuun Modo, Mong. 150 E2
Dźwierzuty, Pol. 127 D2

E

Eabamet L., Ont., Can. 44 E4
Eads, Colo., 929 79 D2
Eads, Tenn. 71 B6
Eagar, Ariz., 1,172 78 D4
Eagle, Alaska, 92 85 J2
Eagle, co., Colo., 4,677 79 B2
Eagle, Colo., 546 79 B2
Eagle, Mich., 141 67 J6
Eagle, Nebr., 302 75 J3
Eagle, N.Y. 58 D6
Eagle, Pa. 61 L5
Eagle, Wis., 620 66 E6
Eagle, r., Newf., Can. 45 P4
Eagle, r., Colo. 79 B2
Eagle, Mt., St. Croix 97 1
Eagle Bay, N.Y. 59 L4
Eagle Bend, Minn., 611 74 E2
Eagle Bridge, N.Y. 59 N6
Eagle Butte, S. Dak., 495 74 B3
Eagle Cap, mtn., Oreg. 80 E3
Eagle City, Okla. 76 E2
Eagle Cr., Ariz. 78 D5
Eagle Cr., Ky. 71 G3
Eagle Grove, Iowa, 4,381 72 D2
Eagle Harbor, N.Y. 58 D5
Eagle Hill (part of Ipswich), Mass. 57 N2
Eagle Lake, Fla., 1,364 65 H5
Eagle Lake, Me. 55 D1
Eagle Lake, Tex., 3,565 77 P5
Eagle L., Ont., Can. 44 C5
Eagle L., Calif. 82 C2
Eagle L., Me. 55 C2
Eagle L., Me. 55 D1
Eagle L., Minn. 74 b5
Eagle L., Wis. 66 c13
Eagle Mills, Ark. 73 C4
Eagle Mills, N.Y. 59 w29

Eagle Mountain—Edwards · 221

Eagle Mountain, Calif. 82 F6
Eagle Mtn., Minn. 74 G2
Eagle Mtn., Tex. 77 L4
Eagle Mtn. L., Tex. 76 e9
Eagle Nest, N. Mex. 79 C3
Eagle Nest Butte, S. Dak. 74 A3
Eagle Pass, Tex., 12,094 77 N5
Eagle Passage, Falk. Is. 108 3
Eagle Pk., N. Mex. 79 A5
Eagle Point, Austl. 173 f12
Eagle Point, Oreg., 752 80 B4
Eagle Point L., Minn. 74 d6
Eagleport, Ohio 70 H3
Eagle River, Alaska 85 c7
Eagle River, Mich. 66 E1
Eagle River, Wis., 1,367 66 D3
Eagle Rock, Va. 62 E5
Eaglesham, Alta., Can. 42 H2
Eaglesham, U.K. 112 b8
Eagles Mere, Pa., 138 60 J3
Eagle Springs, N.C. 63 E2
Eagletown, Okla. 76 J3
Eagleville, Calif. 82 C2
Eagleville (part of Mansfield), Conn. 56 G5
Eagleville, Mo., 341 72 C4
Eagleville, Pa. 60 f11
Eakly, Okla., 217 76 E2
Ealing, London, U.K. 114 H7
Earby, U.K., 4,983 114 D3
Eardisley, U.K. 113 E5
Earith, U.K. 114 H6
Earl, Wis. 66 B3
Earl Cove, Br. Col., Can. 42 c6
Earle, Ark., 2,896 73 E2
Earl Grey, Sask., Can. 43 D5
Earlham, Iowa, 788 72 C3
Earlimart, Calif., 2,897 82 D5
Earling, Iowa, 431 72 B3
Earlington, Ky., 2,786 71 D4
Earl Park, Ind., 551 70 B2
Earls Barton, U.K., 2,699 114 G6
Earlsboro, Okla., 257 76 G2
Earl Shilton (part of Hinckley), U.K., 6,574 114 F5
Earl's Seat, mtn., U.K. 112 b7
Earlston, U.K. 112 e8
Earlton, Ont., Can. 44 H6
Earlton, Kans., 104 75 K6
Earlville, Ill., 1,420 68 D2
Earlville, Iowa, 668 72 F2
Earlville, N.Y., 1,004 59 K6
Earlville, Pa. 60 e10
Early, co., Ga., 13,151 64 E4
Early, Iowa, 824 72 B2
Early, Tex., 819 77 O4
Early Branch, S.C. 63 D5
Earn, r., U.K. 112 E3
Earn, Loch, U.K. 112 b7
Earp, Calif. 82 F5
Earsdon, U.K. 112 g9
Earth, Tex., 1,104 77 M2
Earthquake L., Mont. 81 D3
Easebourne, U.K., 2,023 113 m12
Easington, U.K., 11,462 112 h10
Easingwold, U.K., 2,686 113 F4
Easky, Ire. 113 B4
Easley, S.C., 8,283 63 B3
Easonville, Ala. 64 C2
East, r., N.Y. 58 d14
East Acton (part of Acton), Mass. 57 L3
East Alburg, Vt. 54 A2
East Alligator, r., Austl. 172 D1
East Alstead, N.H. 54 C5
East Alton, Ill., 7,630 68 B5
East Amherst, N.Y. 58 m18
East Andover, N.H. 54 D5
East Anglia, reg., U.K. 113 G5
East-Angus, Qué., Can., 4,709 47 N3
East Arcadia, N.C. 63 F3
East Arlington, Vt. 54 A5
East Aspetuck, r., Conn. 56 C6
East Aurora, N.Y., 6,791 58 C6
East Aux Sable Cr., Ill. 69 a10
East Avon, N.Y. 58 n21
East Baldwin, Me. 55 B5
East Barnard, Vt. 54 B4
East Barnet, London, U.K. 114 H7
East Barnet, Vt. 54 C3
East Barre, Vt. 54 C3
East Barre Res., Vt. 54 C3
East Barrington, N.H. 54 F5
East Bathurst, N.B., Can., 1,186 47 T10
East Baton Rouge, parish, La., 230,058 73 D7
East Bay, La. 73 F8
East Bay, r., N.Y.-Vt. 54 A4
East Bay, Tex. 77 k10
East Bend, N.C., 446 63 D1
East Berkshire, Vt. 54 B2
East Berlin = Ost-Berlin
East Berlin, Pa., 1,037 60 H6
East Bernard, Tex. 77 P5
East Berne, N.Y. 59 M6
East Bernstadt, Ky. 71 G4
East Berwick, Pa., 1,258 61 K3
East Bethany, N.Y. 58 D6
East Bethel, Vt. 54 B4
East Blackstone (part of Blackstone), Mass. 57 L4
East Bloomfield, N.Y., 488 58 F6
East Boldre, U.K. 113 k13
East Boothbay, Me. 55 C5
Eastbourne, U.K., 60,918 113 G6
East Brady, Pa., 1,282 60 C4
East Braintree (part of Braintree), Mass. 57 M4
East Braintree, Vt. 54 B4
East Brent, U.K. 114 B8
East Brewster (part of Brewster), Mass. 57 Q5
East Brewton, Ala., 2,511 64 C4
East Bridgewater, Mass., 6,139(T) 57 N4
East Bridgford, U.K. 114 G5
East Brimfield (part of Brimfield), Mass. 56 H4
Eastbrook, Me. 55 D4
East Brookfield, Mass., 1,150; 1,533(T) 56 H4
East Brookfield, Vt. 54 B3
East Brooklyn, Conn., 1,213 56 J5
East-Broughton, Qué., Can., 1,099 47 N2
East-Broughton-Station, Qué., Can., 1,136 47 N2
East Brownfield, Me. 55 B5
East Burke, Vt. 54 D2
East Butte, Idaho 81 C4
East Caicos, i., Caicos Is. 95 E2
East Calais, Vt. 54 C3
East Calder, U.K. 112 d8
East Canaan, Conn. 56 C4
East Candia, N.H. 54 E5
East Canon, Colo., 1,101 79 C2
East Canyon Cr., Utah 78 c9
East C., N.Z. 175 h5
East C., Terr. Papua 174 3
East C., Fla. 65 g14
East Carondelet, Ill., 463 72 b11
East Carroll, parish, La., 14,433 73 D5
East Carver (part of Carver), Mass. 57 O5
East Chan., Eniwetok 176 28
East Charleston, Vt. 54 C2
East Chevington, U.K., 3,626 113 F4
East Chezzetcook, N.S., Can. 47 U11
East Chicago, Ind., 57,669 70 B1
East Chicago Heights, Ill., 3,270 69 d10
East China Sea, Asia 141 L3
East Cleveland, Ohio, 37,991 70 e8
East Columbia, Tex. 77 h10
East Concord, Vt. 54 D3
East Conemaugh, Pa., 3,334 60 E5
East Corinth, Me. 55 C3
East Corinth, Vt. 54 C3
East Coulee, Alta., Can. 42 K3
East Cowes (part of Cowes), U.K., 2,194 113 k13
East Craftsbury, Vt. 54 C2
East Cr., Vt. 54 A4
East Dayton, Mich. 67 K5
East Deerfield (part of Deerfield), Mass. 56 F2
East Dennis (part of Dennis), Mass. 57 Q6
East Dereham, U.K., 7,199 113 G5
East Derry, N.H. 54 E6
East Detroit, Mich., 45,756 67 g15
East Dorset, Vt. 54 B5
East Douglas, Mass., 1,695 57 J4
East Dover, Vt. 54 B6
East Dubuque, Ill., 2,082 68 B1
East Dummerston, Vt. 54 B6
East Dundee, Ill., 2,221 69 b8
East Ellijay, Ga., 501 64 E1
East Elmira, N.Y. 59 G7
East Ely, Nev., 1,796 83 C3
Eastend, Sask., Can. 43 B5
East End, Grand Cayman 97 3
East End, V.I. 97 4
East Entr., Palau 176 21
Easter I., Pac. Oc. 171 L6
Eastern, r., Me. 55 C4
Eastern Chan. = Tsushima-kaikyō
Eastern Passage, N.S., Can. 47 U11
Eastern Point (part of Groton), Conn. 56 H7
Eastern Pt., Mass. 57 O2
Eastern Rift Valley, Afr. 159
Eastern Samoa = American Samoa
Eastern Sayan Mts. = Vostochnyy Sayan
East Fairfield, Vt. 54 B2
East Fairhaven (part of Fairhaven), Mass. 57 N6
East Falkland, i., Falkland Is. 108 3
East Falmouth, Mass., 1,655 57 O6
East Farms (part of Waterbury), Conn. 56 E6
East Fayu, atoll, Car. Is. 176 18
East Feliciana, parish, La., 20,198 73 D7
East Flat Rock, N.C. 63 B2
East Floyd, N.Y. 59 t25
Eastford, Conn., 746(T) 56 H5
East Foxboro (part of Foxboro), Mass. 57 M4
East Franklin, Vt. 54 B1
East Freetown, Mass. 57 N5
East Fultonham, Ohio 70 G3
East Gary, Ind., 9,309 70 B1
Eastgate, Nev. 83 A3
Eastgate, Tex. 77 k8
East Georgia, Vt. 54 A2
East Glacier Park, Mont. 81 C1
East Glenville, N.Y. 59 v28
East Gloucester (part of Gloucester), Mass. 57 O2
East Grafton, N.H. 54 D4
East Granby, Conn., 2,434(T) 56 E5
East Grand Forks, Minn., 6,998 74 D2
East Grand L., Me.-N.B. 55 E3
East Grand Rapids, Mich., 10,924 67 H6
East Granville, Vt. 54 B3
East Greenbush, N.Y., 1,325 59 N6
East Greenfield (part of Greenfield), Mass. 56 F2
East Greenville, Pa., 1,931 60 f10
East Greenwich, N.Y. 59 O5
East Greenwich, R.I., 6,100(T) 57 K6
East Grinstead, U.K., 15,448 113 G6
East Haddam, Conn., 3,637(T) 56 G7
East Ham, London, U.K. 114 J7
Eastham, U.K., 5,598 114 C4
Eastham, Mass., 1,200(T) 57 Q5
East Hampstead, N.H. 54 E6
East Hampton, Conn., 1,574; 5,403(T) 56 F6
Easthampton, Mass., 12,326(T) 56 F3
East Hampton, N.Y., 1,772 59 Q10
East Hanney, U.K. 114 E7
East Hardin, Ill. 68 B4
East Hardwick, Vt. 54 C2
East Harlsey, U.K. 114 F2
East Hartford, Conn., 43,977(T) 56 F5
East Hartland, Conn. 56 E5
East Harwich (part of Harwich and Chatham), Mass. 57 Q6
East Haven, Conn., 21,388(T) 56 E7
East Haven, Vt. 54 D2
East Haverhill, N.H. 54 D3
East Hazel Crest, Ill., 1,457 69 d10
East Hebron, N.H. 54 D4
East Helena, Mont., 1,490 81 D2
East Highgate, Vt. 54 B2
East Hills, N.Y., 7,184 58 e13
East Hiram, Me. 55 B5
East Holden, Me. 55 D4
East Holliston (part of Holliston), Mass. 57 L4
East Homer, N.Y. 59 H6
East Hope, Idaho, 154 81 A1
East Horsley, U.K., 3,466 114 H8
East I., Terr. Papua 174 3
East Islip, N.Y. 58 g14
East Jamaica, Vt. 54 B5
East Jan Mayen Ridge 108 N2
East Jordan, Mich., 1,919 67 H3
East Kansas City, Mo., 219 75 b7
East Kent (part of Kent), Conn. 56 C6
East Kilbride, 31,972 112 b8
East Killingly (part of Dayville), Conn. 57 J5
East Kingsford, Mich., 1,063 66 F3
East Kingston, N.H. 54 F6
East Knox, Me. 55 C4
Eastlake, Colo. 79 c8
Eastlake, Mich., 436 67 G4
East Lake, N.C. 63 J2
Eastlake, Ohio, 12,467 70 e8
East L., Me. 55 C4
Eastland, Tenn. 71 F6
Eastland, co., Tex., 19,526 77 O3
Eastland, Tex., 3,292 77 O3
Eastland, Utah 78 D3
East Lansing, Mich., 30,198 67 J6
East Las Vegas, Nev. 83 C4
East Laurinburg, N.C., 695 63 E3
Eastlawn, Mich., 17,652 67 K6
East Leake, U.K., 2,856 114 F5
East Lee (part of Lee), Mass. 56 D3
Eastleigh, U.K., 36,642 113 F6
East Lempster, N.H. 54 C5
East Leroy, Mich. 67 H6
East Leverett (part of Leverett), Mass. 56 G3
East Linton, U.K. 112 e8
East Litchfield (part of Litchfield), Conn. 56 D5
East Liverpool, Ohio, 22,306 70 J2
East Loch, Hawaii 84 c7
East Loch Roag, U.K. 112 C2
East London, S. Af., 114,584 164 D7
East Longmeadow, Mass., 10,294(T) 56 G4
East Long Pd., Vt. 54 C3
East Los Angeles, Calif. 82 D6
East Lothian, co., U.K., 52,653 112 E4
East Lyme = Flanders Village
East Lynn, Ill. 68 E3
East Lynn, W. Va. 62 B4
East Lynne, Mo., 243 72 C6
East Machias, Me. 55 E4
East Madison, N.H. 54 E4
Eastmain, r., Qué., Can. 44 J4
Eastman, Qué., Can. 47 M3
Eastman, Ga., 5,118 64 F3
Eastman, Wis., 348 66 C5
East Mansfield (part of Mansfield), Mass. 57 M4
East Markham, U.K. 114 G4
East Meadow, N.Y., 46,036 58 e14
Eastmeon, U.K., 1,438 113 k13
East Meredith, N.Y. 59 L7
East Middlebury, Vt. 54 A4
East Millbury (part of Millbury), Mass. 57 K4
East Millinocket, Me., 2,295 55 D3
East Moline, Ill., 16,732 68 B2
East Montpelier, Vt. 54 B3
East Nassau, N.Y. 59 w29
East Nicolaus, Calif. 82 a7
East Nishnabotna, r., Iowa 72 B4
East Nodaway, r., Iowa 72 C3
East Northfield (part of Northfield), Mass. 56 G2
East Northport, N.Y., 8,381 58 f13
East Norton (part of Norton), Mass. 57 M5
East Nueces, r., Tex. 77 N5
East Olympia, Wash. 81 a9
Easton, Calif. 82 D4
Easton, Conn., 3,407(T) 56 C8
Easton, Ill., 361 68 C3
Easton, Kans., 320 75 K4
Easton, Me. 55 E2
Easton, Md., 6,337 62 H4
Easton, Mass., 9,078(T) 57 M4
Easton, Mo., 198 72 C5
Easton, N.H. 54 D3
Easton, N.Y. 59 N6
Easton, Pa., 31,955 61 M4
Easton, Wash. 80 C2
Eastondale (part of Easton), Mass. 57 M4
Easton L., Conn. 56 C7
East Orange, N.J., 77,259 58 c13
East Orleans (part of Orleans), Mass. 57 R5
East Otis (part of Otis), Mass. 56 D4
East Otto, N.Y. 58 C7
Eastover, S.C., 713 63 D4
East Palatka, Fla., 1,133 65 H3
East Palestine, Ohio, 5,232 70 J2
East Pass, Fla. 65 E3
East Passage, R.I. 57 L7
East Patchogue, N.Y. 58 h13
East Paterson, N.J., 19,344 58 c13
East Pk., Austl. 173 e9
East Peckham, U.K., 2,006 114 J8
East Pembroke, N.Y. 58 D5
East Penfield, N.Y. 58 c20
East Peoria, Ill., 12,310 68 C3
East Pepperell (part of Pepperell), Mass. 57 K2
East Peru, Iowa, 173 72 D3
East Peru, Me. 55 B4
East Petersburg, Pa., 2,053 61 K5
East Pine, Br. Col., Can. 42 G2
East Pittsford, Vt. 54 B4
East Plean, U.K. 112 c7
East Plymouth (part of Plymouth), Conn. 56 D6
East Poestenkill, N.Y. 59 w29
Eastpoint, Fla. 65 E3
East Point, Ga., 35,633 64 E2
East Pt., P.E.I., Can. 47 V10
East Pt., Lesser Caymans 97 2
East Pt., Lord Howe I. 175 12
East Pt., St. Croix 97 1
East Pt., Mass. 57 N3
Eastport, Idaho 81 B1
Eastport, Me., 2,537 55 E4
Eastport, Md. 62 d9
Eastport, Mich. 67 H3
Eastport, N.Y. 59 P10
East Portal, Colo. 79 a8
East Poultney, Vt. 54 A4
East Prairie, Mo., 3,449 72 H8
East Princeton (part of Princeton), Mass. 57 J3
East Prospect, Pa., 623 60 J6
East Providence, R.I., 41,955 57 L5
East Prussia, reg., Pol. 127 D1
East Putnam (part of Putnam), Conn. 57 J5
East Rainelle, W. Va., 1,244 62 D5
E. Rainy Butte, N. Dak. 74 A2
East Randolph, N.Y., 594 58 B7
East Randolph, Vt. 54 B4
East Redmond, Wash., 203 81 b7
East Retford, U.K., 17,792 114 G4
East Riding (admin. part of Yorkshire), U.K., 527,292 113 F5
East Rindge, N.H. 54 D6
East River (part of Madison), Conn. 56 F7
East Rochester, N.Y., 8,152 58 E5
East Rockaway, N.Y., 10,721 58 e14
East Rupert, Vt. 54 A5
Eastry, U.K., 2,059 113 G6
East Ryegate, Vt. 54 C3
East St. Johnsbury, Vt. 54 D3
East St. Louis, Ill. 81,712 68 B5
East Sandwich (part of Sandwich), Mass. 57 P6
East Sarasota, Fla. 65 d13
East Saugatuck, Mich. 67 G6
East Schodack, N.Y. 59 w29
East Scotia Basin, Atl. Oc. 109 K10
East Sebago, Me. 55 B5
East Selkirk, Man., Can. 43 h9
East Setauket, N.Y., 1,127 59 O10
East Shoal L., Man., Can. 43 g9
Eastside, Miss., 4,518 73 G7
Eastside, Oreg., 1,380 80 A4
East Smithfield, Pa. 60 J2
East Sparta, Ohio, 961 70 H2
East Spring Cr., Colo. 79 D2
East Springfield, Pa., 511 60 B2
East Stoneham, Me. 55 B4
East Stroudsburg, Pa., 7,674 61 M3
East Sullivan, N.H. 54 C6
East Surry, Me. 55 D4
East Swanzey, N.H. 54 C6
East Syracuse, N.Y., 4,708 59 r23
East Tampa, Fla. 65 d12
East Taunton (part of Taunton), Mass. 57 M5
East Tavaputs Plat., Utah 78 D2
East Tawas, Mich., 2,462 67 K4
East Templeton (part of Templeton), Mass. 56 H2
East Texas, Pa. 61 i18
East Thermopolis, Wyo., 281 81 F4
East Thetford, Vt. 54 C4
East Thomaston, Ga., 2,237 64 E3
East Thompson (part of Thompson), Conn. 57 J5
East Tohopekaliga L., Fla. 65 H4
East Topsham, Vt. 54 C3
East Troy, Wis., 1,455 66 E6
East Trumbull, Ohio 70 H1
East Twin, r., Wis. 66 F4
East Unity, N.H. 54 C5
Eastview, Ont., Can., 23,764 47 J3
Eastview, Ky. 71 E4
East Village (part of Webster), Mass. 57 J4
Eastville, Va., 261 62 H5
East Wakefield, N.H. 54 F4
East Wallingford (part of Wallingford), Conn. 56 E7
East Wallingford, Vt. 54 B5
East Walpole (part of Walpole), Mass. 57 M4
East Wareham (part of Wareham), Mass. 57 O5
East Washington, N.H. 54 D5
East Washington, Pa., 2,483 60 b9
East Waterboro, Me. 55 B5
East Waterford, Pa. 60 G5
East Weare, N.H. 54 D5
East Wemyss, U.K. 112 d7
East Wenatchee, Wash., 383 80 C2
East Westmoreland, N.H. 54 C6
East Weymouth (part of Weymouth), Mass. 57 N4
East Whately (part of Whately), Mass. 56 F3
East Willington (part of Willington), Conn. 56 H5
East Wilson, N.Y. 58 k18
East Wilton, Me. 55 B4
East Windsor (part of Windsor), Mass. 56 D3
East Windsor Hill (part of S. Windsor), Conn. 56 F5
East Winn, Me. 55 D3
East Wittering, U.K., 1,850 113 m13
East Witton, U.K. 114 E2
Eastwood, Ont., Can. 46 a15
Eastwood, U.K., 10,607 114 F4
East Worcester, N.Y. 59 L6
Eaton, Colo., 1,267 79 C1
Eaton, Ill. 68 E4
Eaton, Me. 55 E3
Eaton, co., Mich., 49,684 67 J6
Eaton, N.Y. 59 J6
Eaton, Lorain Co., Ohio 70 c9
Eaton, Preble Co., Ohio, 5,034 70 E3
Eaton, r., Qué., Can. 54 E1
Eaton Center, N.H. 54 E4
Eatonia, Sask., Can. 43 B4
Eaton Rapids, Mich., 4,052 67 J6
Eatons Neck, N.Y. 58 f13
Eaton Socon, U.K., 3,264 114 H6
Eatonton, Ga., 3,612 64 F2
Eatontown, N.J., 10,334 61 C3
Eatonville, Pa. 61 n15
Eatonville, Wash. 896 80 B2
Eaubonne, Fr., 14,879 116 h11
Eau Claire, Ont., Can. 46 F2
Eau Claire, Mich., 562 67 G7
Eau Claire, Pa., 374 60 C3
Eau Claire, co., Wis., 58,300 66 B4
Eau Claire, Wis., 37,987 66 B4
Eau Claire, r., Wis. 66 D3
Eau Claire L., Wis. 66 B3
Eau Claire Cr., Wis. 66 C4
Eau Galle, Wis. 66 B4
Eau Galle, L., Wis. 66 A4
Eau Gallie, Fla., 12,300 65 J4
Eau Iki, i., Tonga 177 36
Eauripik, atoll, Car. Is. 170 D4
Eauripik Ridge, Pac. Oc. 168 E2
Eauze, Fr., 3,807 117 D5
Ebadon, i., Kwajalein 176 25
Ébano, Mex., 3,605 93 F3
Ebbe-Gebirge, mts., F.R.Ger. 119 D2
Ebberup, Den. 121 B5
Ebbs, Aust., 2,084 124 J6
Ebbw Vale, U.K., 28,627 113 E6
Ebeemee L., Me. 55 C3
Ebéjico, Col. 101 d13
Ebeltoft, Den., 2,227 121 C4
Ebendorf, Aust. 124 d9
Ebenezer, Miss. 73 E5
Ebenezer, Florence Co., S.C. 63 E3
Ebenezer, York Co., S.C. 63 C3
Ebenfurth, Aust., 2,345 124 N6
Ebensburg, Pa., 4,111 60 E5
Ebensee, Aust., 9,590 124 K6
Ebenthal, Aust. 124 d10
Eberau, Aust. 124 N6
Ebergach, F.R.Ger., 11,743 118 B4
Ebergassing, Aust. 1,711 124 d10
Eber Gölü, Turk. 142 B2
Ebermannstadt, F.R.Ger., 2,422 118 C4
Ebern, F.R.Ger., 2,812 118 C3
Eberndorf, Aust., 4,660 124 L7
Ebersbach, F.R.Ger., 8,278 119 G7
Ebersbach, Ger.D.R., 11,136 118 E3
Eberschwang, Aust., 3,186 124 K5
Eberstein, Aust., 1,886 124 L7
Ébersviller, Fr. 116 b8
Eberswalde, Ger.D.R., 32,012 118 D2
Ebetsu, Jap., 37,396 155 J8
Ebeye, i., Kwajalein 176 25
Ebeyty, Oz., U.S.S.R. 137 n11
Ebhausen, F.R.Ger., 1,527 119 F7
Ebingen, F.R.Ger., 19,570 118 B4
Ebi Nuur, l., Chinc 150 B2
Ebisu, Jap. 155 J8
Ebnat, Switz., 3,011 124 D1
Eboli, It., 25,115 123 E4
Ebolowa, Cam., 15,000* 162 F5
Ebon, atoll, Marsh. Is. 170 F4
Ebony, Va. 62 F6
Ebrach, F.R.Ger., 1,816 118 C4
Ebro, Fla. 65 D2
Ebro, r., Sp. 122 D1
Ebro, Pantano del, Sp. 122 m12
Ebstorf, F.R.Ger., 3,826 118 C2
Ecatepec, Mex., 4,632 93 f10
Écaussinnes-d'Enghien, Belg., 6,729 115 C4
Ecbatana = Hamadān
Ecclefechan, U.K. 113 E4
Eccles, U.K., 43,184 114 D4
Eccles, W. Va., 1,145 62 C5
Ecclesfield, U.K., 30,262 114 E4
Eccleshall, U.K., 4,232 114 D5
Eccleston, U.K., 2,022 114 C3
Echalas, Fr. 116 p15
Echallens, Switz. 1,428 124 A2
Écharcon, Fr. 116 h12
Echarri-Aranaz, Sp., 1,806 122 n12
Echeconnee Cr., Ga. 64 F3
Echigawa, Jap., 8,749 154 h14
Echizen-misaki, Jap. 154 g14
Echmiadzin, U.S.S.R., 19,800 137 b1
Echo, Ala. 64 D4
Echo, Minn., 459 74 E3
Echo, Oreg., 456 80 D3
Echo, L., Austl. 173 f14
Echo Bay, Ont., Can. 44 G6
Echoing, r., Man., Can. 43 H3
Echo Lake Res., N.J. 58 b12
Echols, co., Ga., 1,876 64 G5
Échouboulains, Fr. 116 k12
Echt, Neth., 4,500 115 D3
Echterdingen, F.R.Ger., 5,512 119 G7
Echternach, Lux., 3,389 115 E5
Echuca, Austl., 5,405 173 F5
Echzell, F.R.Ger., 2,278 119 F4
Ecija, Sp., 49,762 122 C4
Eck, Loch, U.K. 112 a7
Eckenhagen, F.R.Ger., 7,134 119 D3
Eckerman, Mich. 67 H2
Eckernförde, F.R.Ger., 20,027 118 B1
Eckers Berg, F.R.Ger. 119 G5
Eckert, Tex. 77 O4
Eckerty, Ind. 70 C4
Eckford, Mich. 67 J6
Eckington, U.K., 20,047 114 F4
Eckley, Colo., 207 79 D1
Eckley, Pa. 61 L4
Eckville, Alta., Can. 42 J3
Eclectic, Ala., 926 64 D3
Eclipse Sd., N.W.T., Can. 41 N3
Écommoy, Fr., 3,942 117 D3
Econfina, r., Fla. 65 F2
Economy, Ind., 280 70 D3
Écorces, L. aux, Qué., Can. 47 H1
Ecorse, Mich., 17,328 67 f16
Écouen, Fr., 3,191 116 h10
Écourt-St-Quentin, Fr., 1,485 116 a7
Écouvres, Fr., 4,596 116 b9
Ecquevilly, Fr., 2,109 116 f11
Ecru, Miss., 442 73 F3
Ector, co., Tex., 90,995 77 M4
Ecuador, ctry., 4,476,007 104
Ecuandureo, Mex., 4,481 93 b9
Écueillé, Fr., 1,568 117 D3
Ecum Secum, N.S., Can. 47 V11
Ed, Swed. 120 B4
Eda, Jap. 155 m19
Edam, Sask., Can. 43 B4
Edam, Neth., 4,000 115 D4
Eday, i., U.K. 112 E2
Edberg, Alta., Can. 42 K3
Edcouch, Tex., 2,814 77 P6
Edd, Eth. 163 L3
Ed Dar el Baida = Casablanca
Edderton, U.K. 112 D3
Eddiceton, Miss. 73 E6
Eddington, Pa., 2,000* 60 g11
Eddleston, U.K. 112 d8
Eddleston Water, r., U.K. 112 d8
Eddrachillis Bay, U.K. 112 D2
Eddy, Ill. 69 c7
Eddy, co., N. Mex., 50,783 79 C5
Eddy, co., N. Dak., 4,936 74 C2
Eddystone, Pa., 3,006 60 f12
Eddystone Pt., Austl. 173 g13
Eddyville, Ill., 125 68 D6
Eddyville, Iowa, 1,014 72 E3
Eddyville, Ky., 1,858 71 C4
Eddyville, Nebr., 119 75 F2
Ede, Neth., 28,100 115 D2
Ede, Nigeria, 51,977 162 f8
Edéa, Cam., 12,000* 162 F5
Edefors, Swed. 120 E2
Edegem, Belg., 11,349 115 d8
Edelény, Hung., 6,826 126 E2
Eden, Austl., 1,095 173 G5
Eden, Ariz. 78 D5
Eden, Ga. 64 H3
Eden, Idaho, 426 81 B4
Eden, Mich. 67 J6
Eden, Miss., 218 73 E5
Eden, N.Y., 2,366 58 C6
Eden, S. Dak., 136 74 D3
Eden, Tex., 1,486 77 O4
Eden, Utah 78 c8
Eden, Vt. 54 B2
Eden, Wis., 312 66 E5
Eden, Wyo. 81 E4
Eden, r., U.K. 113 E4
Eden, r., U.K. 112 e7
Edenbridge, U.K., 5,242 114 J8
Edendale, S. Af., 32,356 164 D6
Edenderry, Ire., 2,729 113 C5
Edenkoben, F.R.Ger., 5,968 119 E6
Eden Mills, Ont., Can. 46 b13
Eden Mills, Vt. 54 B2
Eden Prairie, Minn., 5,456 74 b6
Edenton, N.C., 4,458 63 H1
Edenvale, S. Af. 165 k17
Eden Valley, Minn., 793 74 E3
Edenville, Mich. 67 J5
Eder, r., F.R.Ger. 118 B3
Edesheim, F.R.Ger., 2,613 119 E6
Edessa = Urfa
Edewecht, F.R.Ger., 9,496 118 A2
Edgar, co., Ill., 22,550 68 E4
Edgar, Ill. 68 E4
Edgar, Nebr., 730 75 H3
Edgar, Wis., 803 66 D4
Edgar, Port, b., Falk. Is. 108 3
Edgard, La. 73 E7
Edgar Hoopes Res., Del. 62 e10
Edgars, Ont., Can. 67 g16
Edgartown, Mass., 1,181;1,474(T) 57 O7
Edgartown Great Pd., Mass. 57 O7
Edgecliff, Tex., 339 76 e9
Edgecomb, Me. 55 C5
Edgecombe, co., N.C., 54,226 63 G2
Edgecumbe, N.Z., 1,354 175 h5
Edgefield, co., S.C., 15,735 63 B4
Edgefield, S.C., 2,876 63 C4
Edgeley, N. Dak., 992 74 C2
Edgell I., N.W.T., Can. 41 R5
Edgely, Pa. 60 g11
Edgemere, Md. 62 c8
Edgemont, Ark. 73 C2
Edgemont, Colo. 79 b8
Edgemont, S. Dak., 1,772 74 A4
Edgemoor, Del. 62 e10
Edgemoor, S.C. 63 D3
Edgeöya, i., Nor. 134 B2
Edgerton, Alta., Can. 42 L3
Edgerton, Minn., 1,019 74 D4
Edgerton, Mo., 449 72 C5
Edgerton, Ohio, 1,566 70 E1
Edgerton, Wis., 4,000 66 D6
Edgerton, Wyo., 512 81 F4
Edgeville, Fla. 65 d13
Edgewater, Br. Col., Can. 42 J4
Edgewater, Ala. 64 b7
Edgewater, Colo., 4,314 79 b8
Edgewater, Fla., 2,051 65 J4
Edgewater, Md. 62 c9
Edgewater, Wis. 66 B3
Edgewater Gulf Beach, Fla., 70 65 D2
Edgewater Park, N.J., 2,866(T) 60 g11
Edgewater Park, Ohio 70 b7
Edgewood, Br. Col., Can. 42 H4
Edgewood, Ill., 515 68 D5
Edgewood, Ind., 2,119 70 D2
Edgewood, Iowa, 767 72 F2
Edgewood, Md., 1,670 62 H3
Edgewood, N. Mex. 79 B4
Edgewood, Tex., 887 76 g9
Edgeworth, Pa., 2,030 60 b7
Edgigen, i., Kwajalein 176 25
Edgmond, U.K., 1,239 114 D5
Édhessa, Gr., 15,534 129 C4
Edillilie, Austl. 172 a8
Edina, Minn., 28,501 74 b6
Edina, Mo., 1,457 72 E4
Edinboro, Pa., 1,703 60 B2
Edinburg, Ill., 1,003 68 C4
Edinburg, Ind., 3,664 70 C3
Edinburg, Miss. 73 F5
Edinburg, N. Dak., 330 74 D1
Edinburg, Tex., 18,706 77 O6
Edinburg, Va., 517 62 F4
Edinburgh, U.K., 468,378 112 E3
Edingen, F.R.Ger., 5,547 119 F6
Edirne, Turk., 31,865 142 A1
Edison, Colo. 79 C2
Edison, Ga., 1,232 64 E4
Edison, Nebr., 249 75 F3
Edison, N.J., 44,799(T) 58 b14
Edison, Ohio, 559 70 G2
Edison, Wash. 80 B1
Edison Nat. Hist. Site, N.J. 58 b13
Edisto, r., S.C. 63 D5
Edisto Island, S.C. 63 D5
Edith, Austl. 173 h9
Edith, Colo. 79 B3
Edith, Ga. 64 G5
Edith, Tex. 77 N4
Edithburgh, Austl. 172 b8
Edith Ronne Land, Ant. 180 O4
Edjeleh, Alg. 161 F3
Edlbach, Aust. 124 L6
Edlesborough, U.K., 1,334 114 G7
Edlington, U.K., 6,781 114 F4
Edmeston, N.Y. 59 K6
Edmond, Kans., 91 75 F4
Edmond, Okla., 8,577 76 F2
Edmonds, Wash., 8,016 80 B2
Edmondson, Ark., 288 73 E2
Edmonson, co., Ky., 8,085 71 E4
Edmonton, Alta., Can., 274,529 42 K3
Edmonton, Ky., 749 71 F5
Edmore, Mich., 1,234 67 H5
Edmore, N. Dak., 405 74 C1
Edmund, Wis. 66 C6
Edmunds, co., S. Dak., 6,079 74 C3
Edmundston, N.B., Can., 12,488 45 M6
Edna, Kans., 442 75 K6
Edna, Okla. 76 G2
Edna, Tex., 5,038 77 P5
Edna Bay, Alaska, 135 85 L4
Edo, r., Jap. 155 m19
Edolo, It., 4,512 123 C1
Edom, Va. 62 F4
Edomichi, Jap. 155 n19
Edon, Ohio, 757 70 E1
Edosaki, Jap., 13,724 155 n19
Edrans, Man., Can. 43 e9
Edremit, Turk., 22,246 142 A2
Edremit Körfezi, Turk. 142 A2
Edsbyn, Swed. 120 C3
Edson, Alta., Can., 3,108 42 J3
Edson, Nebr. 75 D4
Eduardo Castex, Arg., 7,271 105 B5
Edwall, Wash. 80 E2
Edward, N.C., 112 63 H2
Edward, L., D.R.Congo-Uganda 164 D2
Edward VIII Bay, Ant. 180 R6
Edwards, Calif. 82 D5
Edwards, co., Ill., 7,940 68 D5
Edwards, co., Kans., 5,118 75 F6
Edwards, Miss., 1,206 73 E5

222 · Edwards—Elsa

Edwards, N.Y., 658 59 K3
Edwards, co., Tex., 2,317 77 N5
Edwards, r., Ill. 68 B2
Edwardsburg, Mich., 902 67 G7
Edwards Plat., Tex. 77 N4
Edwardsport, Ind., 533 70 B4
Edwardsville, Ill., 9,996 68 C5
Edwardsville, Pa., 5,711 61 o16
Edwin, Man., Can. 43 f10
Edzell, U.K. 112 E3
Eek, Alaska, 200 85 D3
Eek, r., Alaska 85 D3
Eeklo, Belg., 18,129 115 B3
Eel, r., N.B., Can. 55 E3
Eel, r., Calif. 82 B3
Eel, r., Ind. 70 B3
Eel, r., Ind. 70 D2
Eel Pt., Mass. 57 Q7
Eel River, N.B., Can. 47 S9
Eem, r., Neth. 115 c6
Eemnes, Neth. 115 c6
Eems kan., Neth. 115 E1
Eenrum, Neth. 115 E1
Eerbeek, Neth., 3,200 115 D2
Eernegem, Belg., 5,831 115 A3
Eersel, Neth. 115 D3
Efate, i., New Hebr. 170 F6
Effie, Minn., 195 74 F2
Effigy Mounds Nat. Mon., Iowa 72 F1
Effingham, co., Ga., 10,144 64 H3
Effingham, co., Ill., 23,107 68 D4
Effingham, Ill., 8,172 68 D4
Effingham, Kans., 564 75 K4
Effingham, S.C. 63 E3
Effingham Falls, N.H. 54 E4
Effner, Ind. 70 B2
Ega, r., Sp. 122 n12
Egadi, Isole, It. 123 D6
Egan, S. Dak., 310 74 D3
Egaña, Urug. 105 c11
Egan Ra., Nev. 83 C3
Eganville, Ont., Can., 1,515 44 J6
Egavik, Alaska 85 D2
Egegik, Alaska, 150 85 E4
Ege-Khaya, U.S.S.R. 135 N3
Egeland, N. Dak., 190 74 C1
Egeln, Ger.D.R. 118 C3
Egelsbach, F.R.Ger., 5,520 119 F5
Egenolf L., Man., Can. 43 E2
Egens, Den. 121 C4
Eger, Hung., 35,375 126 E3
Eger, Czech.=Ohře
Eger, r., F.R.Ger. 126 b6
Eger, r., Hung. 126 E3
Egernsund, Den., 1,336 121 B6
Egersund, Nor., 3,932 120 A4
Eggebek, F.R.Ger., 1,676 118 B1
Eggenburg, Aust., 2,961 124 M5
Eggenfelden, F.R.Ger., 5,763 118 D4
Eggenstein, F.R.Ger., 3,610 119 E6
Eggertsville, N.Y., 44,807 58 C6
Eggesin, Ger.D.R. 118 D2
Egg Harbor, Wis. 66 F3
Egg Harbor City, N.J., 4,416 61 B4
Egg Island Point, N.J. 61 A5
Eggiwil, Switz., 2,591 124 B2
Egglescliffe, U.K., 1,695 112 h10
Eggleston, U.K. 112 g10
Eggleston, Va. 62 D5
Egham, U.K., 30,571 114 G8
Éghezée, Belg., 1,234 115 C4
Egi, Jap. 154 e15
Egiin, r., Mong. 150 D1
Egilsstadhir, Ice. 120 b6
Égletons, Fr., 4,601 117 E4
Eglinton I., N.W.T., Can. 41 E2
Eglisau, Switz., 1,911 124 C1
Eglon, Wash. 80 B2
Égly, Fr. 116 g12
Egmond aan Zee, Neth., 4,100 115 C2
Egmont, Br. Col., Can. 42 F4
Egmont, C., N.Z. 175 g5
Egmont, Mt., N.Z. 175 g5
Egmont Key, Fla. 65 c12
Egmont Nat. Pk., N.Z. 175 g6
Egnar, Colo. 79 A3
Egremont, Alta., Can. 43 b6
Egremont, U.K., 6,213 113 E4
Eğridir, Turk., 7,059 142 B2
Eğridir Gölü, Turk. 142 B2
Egton, U.K. 114 G2
Egtved, Den., 2,766 121 B5
Eguzon, Fr., 1,407 117 D3
Egvekinot, U.S.S.R. 135 R3
Egyek, Hung., 8,681 126 E3
Egypt=United Arab Republic
Egypt, Miss. 73 G4
Egypt, N.Y. 58 o20
Egypt, Pa., 1,550* 61 i18
Egypt, Lower=Mişr Baḥrī
Ehen, r., U.K. 114 B1
Ehima, Jap. 154 i15
Ehingen, F.R.Ger., 8,579 118 B4
Ehningen, F.R.Ger., 3,536 119 F7
Ehrang, F.R.Ger., 5,454 118 A4
Ehren, Fla. 65 d11
Ehrenberg, Ariz. 78 A5
Ehrenfriedersdorf, Ger.D.R. 126 c6
Ehrenhausen, Aust. 124 M7
Ehrhardt, S.C., 482 63 C4
Ehringshausen, F.R.Ger., 3,547 118 B3
Ehrwald, Aust., 1,943 124 G6
Ei, Jap., 28,524 154 B6
Ei, Jap. 154 f15
Eiao, i., Marq. Is. 171 J5
Eibar, Sp., 31,725 122 n11
Eibelshausen, F.R.Ger., 2,336 119 E3
Eibenstock, Ger.D.R. 126 b6
Eibergen, Neth., 4,600 115 E2
Eich, F.R.Ger., 2,202 119 E5
Eichelsdorf, F.R.Ger., 1,213 119 G4
Eichenzell, F.R.Ger., 1,446 119 H4
Eichstätt, F.R.Ger., 11,410 118 C4
Eichwalde, Ger.D.R. 119 f11
Eickelborn, F.R.Ger., 3,387 119 E1
Eidanger, Nor. 121 B1
Eide, Nor. 121 A2
Eidehamn, Nor. 121 A2
Eider, r., F.R.Ger. 118 B1
Eidfjord, Nor. 120 A3
Eidsvold, Austl. 173 G3
Eifel, highlands, F.R.Ger. 118 A3
Eiffel Flats, Rhod. 164 D5
Eigg, i., U.K. 112 C3
Eight Degree Channel, Asia 140 F6
Eightmile, Oreg. 80 D3
Eight Mile Bk., Conn. 56 D7
Eight Mile Bk., Conn. 56 G7
Eights, Ant. 180 N5
Eights Coast, Ant. 180 Y5
Eightyfour, Pa. 60 b9
Eighty Mile Beach, Austl. 172 B2
Eil, Som. Rep., 2,093* 163 N4
Eilat, Isr., 5,326 142 C4
Eildon Res., Austl. 173 f11
Eileen, Ill., 384 68 D2
Eilenburg, Ger.D.R., 19,371 118 D3
Eilendorf, F.R.Ger., 11,260 119 A3
Eilerts de Haangebergte, Sur. 101 M6
Eil, Loch, U.K. 112 D3
Eil Malk, i., Palau 176 21
Eina, Nor. 120 B3
Einasleigh, Austl. 173 F2
Einasleigh, r., Austl. 173 F2
Einbeck, F.R.Ger., 17,617 118 B3
Eindhoven, Neth., 162,700 115 D3
Einfeld, F.R.Ger., 5,683 118 C1
Einme, Burma 147 a2
Einsiedeln, Switz., 8,792 124 C1
Einville, Fr., 1,255 116 c9
Eire=Ireland
Eiríksjökull, Ice. 120 ·
Eirunepé, Braz., 3,023 102 B3
Eisden, Belg., 9,644 115 D3
Eisenach, Ger.D.R., 48,109 118 C3
Eisenberg, F.R.Ger., 5,072 119 E5
Eisenberg, Ger.D.R., 13,839 118 D3
Eisenerz, Aust., 12,413 124 L6
Eisenerzer Alpen, Aust. 125 ·
Eisenhower Lock, N.Y. 69 C
Eisenhüttenstadt, Ger.D.R., 24,372 118 E2
Eisenkappel, Aust., 1,443 124 L7
Eisenstadt, Aust., 7,158 124 N6
Eiserfeld, F.R.Ger., 9,282 119 E3
Eisgarn, Aust. 124 M5
Eishima, Jap. 154 f15
Eisleben, Ger.D.R., 34,507 118 C3
Eislingen, F.R.Ger., 14,564 118 B4
Eita, Tarawa 175 15
Eita, i., Tarawa 175 15
Eitorf, F.R.Ger., 12,031 118 A3
Eitzen, Minn., 181 74 G4
Ejby, Den. 121 B5
Ejea de los Caballeros, Sp., 10,988 122 E1
Ejer Bavnehøj, hill, Den. 121 B5
Ejido, Ven., 5,351 100 E3
Ejigbo, Nigeria, 18,387 162 f8
E-jima, Jap. 154 f15
Ejstrup, Den., 2,969 121 B5
Ejura, Ghana 162 c8
Ejutla, Mex., 4,288 93 F5
Ekalaka, Mont., 738 81 G3
Ekeby, Swed. 121 b7
Ekenäs, Fin., 5,517 120 E3
Ekeren, Belg., 19,907 115 C3
Ekerön, pt., Swed. 120 e8
Ekhabi, U.S.S.R., 4,500 135 O4
Ekhínos, Gr., 2,484 129 E4
Ekibastuz, U.S.S.R., 26,300 134 G4
Ekiny, Fr. Guiana 101 O5
Eklutna, Alaska, 50 85 G3
Eklutna L., Alaska 85 c7
Ekonda, U.S.S.R. 135 K3
Ekron, Ky., 205 71 E4
Ekshärad, Swed. 120 C3
Eksjö, Swed. 120 C4
Ekuk, Alaska, 40 85 E4
Ekwak, Alaska 85 E4
Ekwan, r., Ont., Can. 44 F4
Ekwok=Ekwak
Ela, Burma, 2,091 146 B3
Ela, N.C. 63 A2
El Aaiún, Sp. Sah. 160 B3
El Abiod-Sidi-Cheikh, Alg. 160 E2
El Adeb, Alg. 161 F3
El Adelanto, Guat., 1,798 94 d9
Elafónisos, i., Gr. 129 D6
El Agheila=Al 'Uqaylah
El Agreb, Alg. 160 E2
El Aguacate, Mex. 93 c10
Elaine, Ark., 898 73 E3
El-A'ïoun, Mor. 160 D2
El Álamo, Mex. 92 B1
El Alto, Peru, 8,217 104 A3
Elam, Pa. 60 e12
El Amparo, Ven., 1,093 100 E4
El Amria, Alg., 5,757 160 a6
Élancourt, Fr., 1,032 116 f11
Eland, Wis., 213 66 D4
El Ángel, Ec., 3,927 104 B1
El Aouinet, Alg., 1,957 160 e6
El-Arab, r., Alg. 160 e6
El Arba, Alg. 160 c5
El Arco, Mex. 92 B2
El Arenal, Mex., 3,258 93 a9
El Arish, Austl. 173 G2
El-Arisha, Alg. 160 D2
El Asnam, Alg., 38,607 160 E1
Elassón, Gr., 6,501 129 D5
El Astillero, Sp., 6,759 122 m11
Elat, Indon. 149 K4
Elátia, Gr., 1,750 129 D5
Elato, i., Car. Is. 176 18
El 'Auja, Isr. 142 C4
Elâzığ, Turk., 60,438 142 D2
El Azúcar, Presa de, res., Mex. 93 F2
Elba, Ala., 4,321 64 C4
Elba, Colo. 79 D2
Elba, Mich. 67 K5
Elba, Nebr., 184 75 G2
Elba, N.Y., 739 58 D5
Elba, Isola d', It. 123 B3
El Banco, Col. 100 D3
El Barco de Avila, Sp., 2,349 122 C2
El Barco de Valdeorras, Sp., 7,695 122 B1
El Barro, Mex., 1,055 92 E3
Elbasan, Alb., 32,400 125 D4
El Baúl, Ven., 1,522 100 F3
El-Bayadh, Alg., 15,932 160 E2
Elb-Bach, r., F.R.Ger. 119 D3
Elbe, Wash. 80 B2
Elbe, r., Eur. 118 B2
Elbe=Labe, Czech.
Elbe-Lübeck-Kanal, F.R.Ger. 119 c8
Elberfeld, Ind., 485 70 B4
Elberon, Iowa, 211 72 E2
Elbert, co., Colo., 3,708 79 C2
Elbert, Colo. 79 C2
Elbert, co., Ga., 17,835 64 G1
Elbert, Tex. 77 O3
Elbert, Mt., Colo. 79 B2
Elberta, Ala., 384 64 B5
Elberta, Mich., 552 67 G4
Elberta, Utah 78 c11
Elberton, U.K. 112 d8
Elberton, Ga., 7,107 64 F1
Elberton, Wash., 66 80 E2
Elbeuf, Fr., 19,182 117 D2
Elbigenalp, Aust. 124 G6
Elbing, Kans., 105 75 H5
Elbistan, Turk., 10,342 142 D2
Elbląg, Pol., 77,000* 127 C1
El Bluff, Nic. 94 F4
Elbon, Pa. 60 E3
El Bonillo, Sp., 5,286 122 D3
El Bosque, Mex., 1,415 93 G5
Elbow, Sask., Can. 43 C4
Elbow Beach, Berm. Is. 108 1
Elbow Cay, Bah. Is. 95 c6
Elbow Cay, W.I. 95 B2
Elbow Lake, Minn., 1,521 74 D3
Elbridge, Ill. 68 E4
Elbridge, N.Y., 828 59 G5
El'brus, G., U.S.S.R. 134 D5
El Bur, Som. Rep., 2,465* 163 M5
Elburg, Neth. 115 D2
El Burgo de Osma, Sp., 3,041 122 D2
Elburn, Ill., 960 68 D2
Elburz Mts.=Alborz, Reshteh-ye Kūhhā-ye
El Cajon, Calif., 37,618 82 E6
El Callao, Ven., 3,276 101 K4
El Calvario, Ven. 100 G3
El Cambur, Ven. 101 a11
El Camino del Diablo, mtn., N. Mex. 79 C5
El Campo, Tex., 7,700 77 P5
El Caney, Cuba, 2,009 96 f2
El Caobanal, Guat. 94 c9
El Carmelo, Ven., 1,890 100 D2
El Carmen, Bol., 1,605 102 D4
El Carmen, Chile, 2,263 104 f16
El Carmen, Col. 100 B5
El Carmen, Col. 100 D3
El Carmen, Mex. 92 C2
El Cármen, Peru, 1,080 104 C5
El Carpintero, Chile 104 f13
El Carrizal, Mex. 93 d9
El Castillo, Nic. 94 E5
El Cayo, Br. Hond., 1,890 94 C2
El Centro, Calif., 16,811 82 F6
El Cerrito, Calif., 25,437 83 e12
El Cerro, Bol., 102 D5
El Chacay, Chile 104 f17
El Chaparro, Ven. 101 H3
El Charco, Pan. 94 H6
Elche, Sp., 73,320 122 E3
Elche de la Sierra, Sp., 5,846 122 E3
Elcho, Wis. 66 D3
Elcho I., Austl. 172 E1
Elco, Ill. 68 C6
Elco, Pa., 521 60 c9
El Cobre, Cuba, 2,586 96 e2
El Colegio, Col. 101 e15
El Congo, El Salv., 3,060 94 d10
El Consejo, Ven., 4,799 101 b11
El Convento, Chile 104 f13
El Corazón, Ec., 1,120 104 c10
El Cristo, Cuba, 3,160 96 f2
El Cuervo Butte, N. Mex. 79 C4
Elda, Sp., 28,151 122 E3
El Dara, Ill., 98 68 B4
Elde, r., Ger.D.R. 118 C2
Eldena, Ger.D.R. 118 C2
Eldena, Ill. 68 C2
El Depósito, Mex., 2,131 93 d10
El Dere, Som. Rep. 163 M5
Elderon, Wis., 177 66 D4
Eldersburg, Md. 62 b7
Eldersfield, U.K. 114 D7
Elderton, Pa., 387 60 D4
El Diente, mt., Colo. 79 A3
El'dikan, U.S.S.R., 3,000 135 N3
Eld Inlet, Wash. 81 a8
El Dividive, Ven., 2,720 100 E3
Eldon, Iowa, 1,386 72 E4
Eldon, Mo., 3,158 72 E6
Eldon, Okla. 76 J2
Eldon, Wash. 80 B2
Eldora, Iowa, 3,225 72 D2
Eldorado, Arg., 22,307* 105 E3
Eldorado, Sask., Can. 43 B2
Eldorado, Mex. 92 D3
El Dorado, Ark., 25,292 73 C4
El Dorado, co., Calif., 29,390 82 C3
Eldorado, Ill., 3,573 68 D6
El Dorado, Kans., 12,523 75 J6
Eldorado, Mich. 67 J4
Eldorado, Nebr. 75 H3
Eldorado, N.C. 63 E2
Eldorado, Ohio, 449 70 E3
Eldorado, Okla., 708 76 D3
Eldorado, Tex., 1,815 77 N4
El Dorado, Wis. 66 E5
El Dorado, Ven., 2,016 101 K4
Eldorado Pass, Oreg. 80 D3
Eldorado Springs, Colo. 79 b8
El Dorado Springs, Mo., 2,864 72 C7
Eldoret, Kenya, 19,600* 164 E1
Eldred, Fla. 65 J5
Eldred, Ill., 302 68 B4
Eldred, N.Y. 59 L8
Eldred, Pa., 1,107 60 F2
Eldridge, Ala. 64 B2
Eldridge, Iowa, 583 72 G3
Eldridge, Mo. 72 E7
Eldridge, N. Dak. 74 C2
Eldsberga, Swed. 121 E4
Eleao, pk., Hawaii 84 c7
Electra, Tex., 4,759 77 O2
Electric City, Wash., 404 80 D2
Electric Mills, Miss. 73 G5
Electric Pk., Mont. 81 D3
Eleele, Hawaii, 617 84 B2
Elefante, Roca, Mex. 92 a6
Elek, Hung., 6,339 126 E3
Elekmonar, U.S.S.R. 137 r12
Elektrogorsk, U.S.S.R., 12,400 136 c6
Elektrostal', U.S.S.R., 102,000 134 C4
Elena, Bulg., 4,071 128 E3
Elena, Bulg., 1,598 128 E4
Elenore, Mt., Utah 78 A3
Elephant Butte, N. Mex. 79 B5
Elephant Butte Res., N. Mex. 79 B5
Elephant Mtn., Me. 55 B4
Eleroy, Ill. 68 C1
El Eucalipto, Urug. 105 c10
El Eulma, Alg., 10,542 160 d5
Eleusis=Elevsís
Eleuthera, i., Bah. Is. 95 C1
Eleva, Wis., 548 66 B4
Eleven Mile Canyon Res., Colo. 79 a10
Eleven Point, r., Ark.-Mo. 72 F8
Elevsís, Gr., 15,527 129 D5
Elevtheroúpolis, Gr., 5,448 129 D4
El Farisa, Sp. Sah. 160 C3
El Fâsher=Al Fāshir
El Ferrol del Caudillo, Sp., 74,799 122 A1
Elfers, Fla. 65 G4
Elford, Ont., Can. 67 g16
El Fresno, Mex., 1,057 93 d9
Elfrida, Ont., Can. 46 c15
Elfrida, Ariz. 78 D6
Elfros, Sask., Can. 43 D4
El Fuerte, Mex., 5,183 92 C2
El Gallego, Mex. 92 D2
El Gassi, Alg. 160 E2
Elgg, Switz., 2,643 124 C1
Elgin, Man., Can. 43 E5
Elgin, N.B., Can. 47 T11
Elgin, U.K., 11,971 112 E3
Elgin, Ariz. 78 C6
Elgin, Ill., 49,447 68 D1
Elgin, Iowa, 644 72 F2
Elgin, Kans., 148 75 J6
Elgin, Minn., 521 74 F3
Elgin, Nebr., 881 75 G2
Elgin, Nev. 83 C4
Elgin, N. Dak., 944 74 B2
Elgin, Ohio, 80 70 E2
Elgin, Okla., 540 76 E3
Elgin, Oreg., 1,315 80 D3
Elgin, Pa., 218 60 C2
Elgin, S.C., 329 63 D3
Elgin, Tex., 3,511 77 P4
Elgin Mills, Ont., Can. 46 E5
Elgol, U.K. 112 C3
El-Goléa, Alg., 7,452 160 E2
Elgon, Mt., Kenya-Uganda 164 E1
El Gorme de Hatuey, Cuba, 1,737 96 e2
El Granada, Calif. 83 d12
El Grullo, Mex., 9,028 92 D4
El Guayabo, Mex. 93 d10
El Hamurre, Som. Rep. 163 N4
El Hatillo, Ven. 101 c11
El Huisache, Mex. 93 c9
Eli, Nebr. 75 D1
Eliase, Indon. 149 J5
Elías Piña, Dom. Rep., 2,890 96 m6
Elida, N. Mex., 534 79 D5
Elida, Ohio, 1,215 70 E2
Elie, Man., Can. 43 g10
Elie, U.K. 112 e7
Eli Kanibu, i., Truk 176 19
Elila, r., D.R.Congo 164 D2
Elim, S. Af., 1,088 164 a9
Elim, Alaska, 145 85 D2
El Indio, Tex. 77 N5
Eling, U.K., 18,387 113 k13
Elin Pelin, Bulg., 4,002 128 D3
Elisabetha, Congo L. 164 C1
Élisabethville=Lubumbashi
Elista, U.S.S.R., 29,000 134 D5
Elizabeth, Austl., 10,000* 172 E5
Elizabeth, Colo., 326 79 C2
Elizabeth, Ga., 1,620 64 g9
Elizabeth, Ill., 729 68 B1
Elizabeth, Ind., 214 70 D4
Elizabeth, La., 1,030 73 C7
Elizabeth, Minn., 168 74 D2
Elizabeth, N.J., 107,698 61 C2
Elizabeth, Pa., 2,597 60 C5
Elizabeth, W. Va., 727 62 C3
Elizabeth, L., Wis. 69 b7
Elizabeth City, N.C., 14,062 63 H1
Elizabeth Is., Jaluit 176 30
Elizabeth Is., Mass. 57 N7
Elizabeth Mtn, Utah 78 C1
Elizabethton, Tenn., 10,896 71 J5
Elizabethtown, Ill., 524 68 D6
Elizabethtown, Ind., 417 70 D3
Elizabethtown, Ky., 9,641 71 E4
Elizabethtown, N.Y., 779 59 N3
Elizabethtown, N.C., 1,625 63 F3
Elizabethtown, Pa., 6,780 60 J5
Elizabethville, Pa., 1,455 60 J4
Elizaville, Ind. 70 C2
Elizondo, Sp. 122 E1
El-Jadida, Mor., 40,302 160 C2
El Jícaro, Guat., 2,028 94 c9
El Jícaro, Nic. 94 D4
El Junquito, Ven. 101 b11
Ełk, Pol., 22,000* 127 E2
Elk, Calif. 82 B3
Elk, co., Kans., 5,048 75 J6
Elk, N. Mex. 79 C5
Elk, co., Pa., 37,328 60 E3
Elk, Wash. 80 E1
Elk, r., Ala.-Tenn. 71 E6
Elk, r., Colo. 79 B1
Elk, r., Kans. 75 J6
Elk, r., Mich. 67 L5
Elk, r., W. Va. 62 C4
Elkader, Iowa, 1,526 72 F2
Elkader, Kans. 75 E5
Elk City, Idaho 81 B3
Elk City, Kans., 498 75 J6
Elk City, Okla., 8,196 76 D2
Elk Creek, Calif. 82 B3
Elk Creek, Nebr., 170 75 J3
Elk Creek, Va. 62 C6
Elk Cr., Pa. 60 B1
Elk Cr., S. Dak. 74 A3
El-Kelaa-des-Srarhna, Mor., 10,187 160 C2
Elkenroth, F.R.Ger., 1,163 119 D3
Elk Garden, Va. 62 C6
Elk Garden, W. Va., 329 62 E3
Elk Grove, Calif., 2,205 82 C3
Elk Grove Village, Ill., 13,155 69 c8
Elkhart, Ill., 418 68 C3
Elkhart, co., Ind., 106,790 70 D1
Elkhart, Ind., 40,274 70 D1
Elkhart, Kans., 1,780 75 D6
Elkhart, Tex., 780 77 Q4
Elkhart Lake, Wis., 651 66 F5
Elk Hill, Pa. 61 L2
Elkhorn, Man., Can. 43 E5
Elk Horn, Iowa, 679 72 B3
Elkhorn, Nebr., 749 75 J2
Elkhorn, Wis., 3,586 66 E6
Elkhorn, r., Nebr. 75 H1
Elkhorn City, Ky., 1,085 71 J4
Elkhorn Cr., Ill. 68 C2
Elkhorn Ranch Site, N. Dak. 74 A2
Elkhovo, Bulg., 10,325 128 F3
El Khroub, Alg., 4,801 160 e5
Elkin, N.C., 2,868 63 D1
Elkins, N.H. 54 D5
Elkins, N. Mex. 79 C5
Elkins, W. Va., 8,307 62 E4
Elkins Park, Pa., 12,200* 60 f11
Elkinsville, Ind. 70 C3
Elk I. Nat. Pk., Alta., Can. 42 K3
Elk Lake, Ont., Can. 44 H6
Elk L., Mich. 67 H4
Elkland, Pa., 2,189 60 H1
Elkmont, Ala., 169 64 C1
Elkmont, Tenn. 71 H6
Elk Mound, Wis., 379 66 B4
Elk Mountain, Wyo., 190 81 F5
Elk Mtn., N. Mex. 79 A5
Elk Mtn., Okla. 76 E3
Elk Mtn., Wyo. 81 F5
Elko, Ga., 165 64 F3
Elko, co., Nev., 12,011 83 C1
Elko, Nev., 6,298 83 C2
Elko, S.C., 194 63 C4
Elk Park, N.C., 460 63 B1
Elk Point, Alta., Can. 42 L3
Elk Point, S. Dak. 74 D4
Elkport, Iowa, 100 72 F2
Elk Rapids, Mich., 1,015 67 H4
Elkridge, Md. 62 b8
Elk River, Idaho, 382 81 A2
Elk River, Minn., 1,763 74 F3
Elk Run Heights, Iowa, 1,124 72 E2
Elk Springs, Colo. 79 A1
Elkton, Ill. 68 C5
Elkton, Ky., 1,448 71 D5
Elkton, Md., 5,989 62 J3
Elkton, Mich., 1,014 67 K5
Elkton, Oreg., 146 80 B4
Elkton, S. Dak., 621 74 D3
Elkton, Tenn., 199 71 E6
Elkton, Va., 1,506 62 F4
Elk Valley, Tenn. 71 G5
Elkville, Ill., 743 68 C6
Elkwater, W. Va. 62 D4
Ellamar, Alaska 85 H3
Elland, U.K., 18,353 114 E3
Ellaville, Ga., 905 64 E3
Ellef Ringnes I., N.W.T., Can. 41 J2
Elleker, Austl. 172 B5
Ellen, Mt., Utah 78 C2
Ellen, Mt., Vt. 54 B3
Ellenboro, N.C., 492 63 C2
Ellenboro, W. Va., 340 62 C3
Ellenburg, N.Y. 59 N2
Ellenburg Depot, N.Y. 59 N2
Ellendale, Del., 370 62 J4
Ellendale, N. Dak., 1,800 74 C2
Ellensburg, Wash., 8,625 80 C2
Ellenton, Fla. 65 d11
Ellenton, Ga., 385 64 F4
Ellenville, N.Y., 5,003 59 M8
Ellenwood, Ga. 64 g10
Eller, N.C. 63 D2
Eller, i., Kwajalein 176 25
Ellerbe, N.C., 843 63 E2
Ellerslie, Alta., Can. 43 b7
Ellerslie, P.E.I., Can. 47 U10
Ellerslie, Md. 62 F3
Ellerspring, pk., F.R.Ger. 119 D5
Ellerville, Okla. 76 J1
Ellesmere, U.K., 2,261 114 C5
Ellesmere, L., N.Z. 175 g6
Ellesmere I., N.W.T., Can. 41 N2
Ellesmere Port, U.K., 44,714 113 E5
Ellettsville, Ind., 1,222 70 C3
Ellice Is., Gilb. and Ellice Is. 170 F5
Ellichpur, India 144 a15
Ellicott, Colo. 79 C2
Ellicott City, Md. 62 H3
Ellicott Cr., N.Y. 58 k18
Ellicottville, N.Y., 1,150 58 C7
Ellijay, Ga., 1,320 64 E1
El Lindero, Mex. 93 f9
Ellingham, U.K. 113 i13
Ellington, U.K., 1,264 112 g9
Ellington, Conn., 5,580(T) 56 G5
Ellington, Mo., 812 72 G7
Ellington, N.Y. 58 B7
Ellinwood, Kans., 2,729 75 G5
Elliot, Ill., 343 68 D3
Elliot, S.C. 63 D3
Elliot Key, Fla. 65 J7
Elliot Knob, mtn., Va. 62 E4
Elliot Lake, Ont., Can., 9,950 44 G6
Elliott, Austl. 172 D2
Elliott, S. Af., 3,517 164 D7
Elliott (part of Pomfret), Conn. 56 H5
Elliott, Iowa, 459 72 B3
Elliott, co., Ky., 6,330 71 H3
Elliott, Miss. 73 F4
Elliott, N. Dak., 62 74 D2
Elliotville (part of Dayville), Conn. 57 J5
Ellis, Ark. 73 C1
Ellis, Ill. 68 E3
Ellis, co., Kans., 21,270 75 F5
Ellis, Kans., 2,218 75 F5
Ellis, co., Okla., 5,457 76 D1
Ellis, co., Tex., 43,395 77 P3
Ellis, r., Me. 55 B4
Ellis, r., N.H. 54 E3
Ellisburg, N.Y., 328 59 H4
Ellisdale, N.J. 58 a16
Ellison, Ind. 70 D1
Ellison Bay, Wis. 66 F3
Ellis Pd., Me. 55 B4
Ellisport, Wash. 81 a8
Elliston, Austl. 172 D5
Elliston, Mont. 81 C2
Elliston, Va. 62 D5
Ellisville (part of Plymouth), Mass. 57 O5
Ellisville, Miss., 4,592 73 F6
Ellisville, Mo., 2,732 72 G6
Ellithorpe (part of Stafford), Conn. 56 G5
El Llano, Mex., 1,279 93 e9
Ellon, U.K., 1,456 112 E3
Ellora, India 145 E5
Elloree, S.C., 1,031 63 D4
Elloughton, U.K., 3,174 114 G3
Ellport, Pa., 1,458 60 B4
Ells, r., Alta., Can. 42 K1
Ellsinore, Mo., 311 72 G8
Ellsworth, Ant. 180 O5
Ellsworth, Ill., 224 68 D3
Ellsworth, Iowa, 493 72 D2
Ellsworth, co., Kans., 7,677 75 G5
Ellsworth, Kans., 2,361 75 G5
Ellsworth, Me., 4,444 55 D4
Ellsworth, Mich., 386 67 H3
Ellsworth, Minn., 634 74 E4
Ellsworth, Nebr. 75 C1
Ellsworth, N.H. 54 D4
Ellsworth, Pa., 1,456 60 c9
Ellsworth, Wis., 1,701 66 A4
Ellsworth, L., Okla. 76 E3
Ellsworth Mts., Ant. 180 N5
Ellwangen, F.R.Ger., 11,298 118 C4
Ellwood City, Pa., 12,413 60 B4
Ellzey, Fla. 65 G3
Elm, F.R.Ger., 1,391 119 H4
Elm, Switz. 124 D2
Elm, U.K., 2,492 114 J5
Elm, N.J. 61 B4
Elm, r., S. Dak. 74 C3
Elma, Man., Can. 43 G5
Elma, Iowa, 706 72 E1
Elma, N.Y. 58 m19
Elma, Wash., 1,811 80 B2
Elmagonda, India 145 F6
El Maitén, Arg., 2,500* 105 A6
Elmalı, Turk., 7,800 142 B2
El Manteco, Ven. 101 J4
El Manzano, Chile, 1,073 104 f14
El Mármol, Mex. 92 B1
Elm City, N.C., 729 63 G2
Elm Creek, Man., Can. 43 F5
Elm Creek, Nebr., 778 75 F3
Elm Cr., S. Dak. 74 C3
El Melón, Chile, 4,211 104 f12
El Membrillo, Mex. 93 d8
Elmendorf, Tex. 76 b7
Elmenteita, Kenya 165 g14
Elmer, Mich. 67 L5
Elmer, Mo., 266 72 E5
Elmer, N.J., 1,505 61 A4
Elmer, Okla., 120 76 D3
Elmer City, Wash., 256 80 D1
Elmer Hill, N.Y. 59 t25
Elm Grove, Wis., 4,994 66 c11
Elm Hall, Mich. 67 J5
Elmhurst, Ill., 36,991 68 E2
Elmhurst, Pa. 61 L3
El-Milia, Alg., 8,611 160 e5
Elmina, Ghana 162 c9
Elmira, Ont., Can., 3,313 46 D5
Elmira, Mich. 67 J3
Elmira, Mo., 123 72 C5
Elmira, N.Y., 46,517 58 G7
Elmira, Ohio 70 E1
Elmira, Oreg. 80 B3
El Mirador, Mex., 1,232 93 f8
El Mirage, Ariz., 3,258 78 B5
Elmira Heights, N.Y., 5,157 58 G7
Elm L., S. Dak. 74 C3
Elmo, Mo., 213 72 B4
Elmo, Mont. 81 B2
Elmo, Utah, 175 78 C2
Elmo, Wyo., 91 81 F5
Elmo, L., Minn. 74 d6
Elmodel, Ga. 64 E4
El Modeno, Calif. 83 i16
Elmont, N.Y., 30,138 58 e14
Elmont, Va. 62 G5
El Monte, Calif., 13,163 83 h15
Elmora, Pa., 1,057 60 E4
Elmore, co., Ala., 30,524 64 C3
Elmore, Ala. 64 C3
Elmore, co., Idaho, 16,719 81 B4
Elmore, Minn., 1,078 74 E4
Elmore, Ohio, 1,302 70 F1
Elmore City, Okla., 982 76 F3
El Morrito, Nic. 94 E5
El Morro, Ec. 104 A2
El Morro, N. Mex. 79 A4
El Morro, Ven., 1,328 100 F3
El Morro Nat. Mon., N. Mex. 79 A4
Elmsford, N.Y., 3,795 58 d12
Elmshorn, F.R.Ger., 34,327 118 B2
Elm Springs, S. Dak. 74 A3
Elmstead, Ont., Can. 67 g15
Elmstein, F.R.Ger., 2,946 119 D6
El Muelle, C.R. 94 E5
Elmvale, Ont., Can. 46 E4
Elmwood, Ont., Can. 46 C4
Elmwood (part of W. Hartford), Conn. 56 E6
Elmwood, Ill., 1,882 68 C3
Elmwood (part of E. Bridgewater), Mass. 57 N4
Elmwood, Nebr., 481 75 J3
Elmwood, Okla. 76 C1
Elmwood, Tenn. 71 F5
Elmwood, Wis., 776 66 A4
Elmwood Park, Ill., 23,866 69 c9
Elmwood Park, Wis. 66 d13
Elmwood Place, Ohio, 3,813 71 h10
El Mzereb, Mali 162 C1
Elne, Fr., 5,744 117 E5
El Negrito, Hond., 1,391 94 D3
El Nido, Phil., 1,184 153 A3
El Nido, Calif. 82 C4
Elnora, Alta., Can. 42 K3
Elnora, Ind., 824 70 B4
El Obeid=Al Ubayyiḍ
Elói Mendes, Braz., 5,010 103 d17
Eloise, Mich. 67 e15
Elon College, N.C., 1,284 63 E1
Elora, Ont., Can., 1,481 46 D5
Elora, Tenn. 71 E6
El Oratorio, Guat., 1,740 94 c9
El Oro, Mex., 3,507 93 E4
Elorza, Ven., 2,219 100 F4
Elota, Mex., 1,203 92 D3
El-Oued, Alg., 13,001 160 F2
Eloxochitlán, Mex., 1,525 93 f9
Eloy, Ariz., 5,373 78 C5
Eloy Alfaro, Ec. 104 A2
El Palito, Ven. 101 a11
El Palmar, Bol. 102 c12
El Palmar, Guat., 1,359 94 b9
El Palmar, Ven., 1,959 101 K3
El Pao, Ven. 101 H3
El Pao, Ven., 2,112 101 J3
El Papayo, Mex., 1,186 93 E5
El Paraíso, El Salv., 1,008 94 d9
El Paraíso, Hond., 4,093 94 D3
El Paraíso, Hond., 3,756 94 D4
El Paraíso, Hond. 94 d8
El Paso, Col. 100 D3
El Paso, Ark. 73 C2
El Paso, co., Colo., 143,742 79 C2
El Paso, Ill., 1,964 68 C3
El Paso, co., Tex., 314,070 77 K4
El Paso, Tex., 276,687 77 K4
El Paso Gap, N. Mex. 79 C5
El Peñón, Col. 101 e14
El Perú, Ven. 101 K4
El Peumo, Chile 104 f13
Elphin, Ire. 113 B5
Elphinstone, Austl. 173 G3
Elphinstone, Man., Can. 43 E5
Elphinstone I., Burma 146 B4
El Pilar, Ven. 101 H3
El Pilar, Ven., 3,241 101 J2
El Pilón, Ven. 101 J3
El Portal, Calif. 82 D4
El Portal, Fla., 2,079 65 b10
El Porvenir, Col. 100 E5
El Porvenir, Hond., 1,488 94 D3
El Porvenir, Mex., 1,033 92 D1
El Porvenir, N. Mex. 79 C4
El Potosí, Mex., 1,178 93 E3
El Progreso, Guat., 3,190 94 C3
El Progreso, Guat., 3,475 94 d9
El Progreso, Hond., 12,970 94 D3
El Progreso, Mex., 1,011 93 d11
El Puente del Arzobispo, Sp., 2,040 122 C3
El Qanawât, ruins, Syr. 142 D3
El Quisco, Chile, 1,019 104 f13
Elrama, Pa. 60 c8
El Rancho, Colo. 79 b8
El Real, Pan., 1,071 94 J6
El Reno, Okla., 11,015 76 E2
El Rio, Calif., 6,966 82 D5
El Rito, N. Mex. 79 B3
El Roble, Chile 104 e16
El Roble, Mex., 2,507 92 D3
Elrosa, Minn., 205 74 E3
El Rosario, Col. 100 B7
Elrose, Sask., Can. 43 C4
Elroy, Wis., 1,505 66 C5
El Rucio, Mex., 1,051 92 E3
Elsa, Yukon, Can. 40 B5

Elsa, Tex., 3,847 **77** O6
El Saco, P.R. **96** s10
Elsah, Ill., 218 **68** B5
El Salado, Col. **100** D3
El Salto, Dgo., Mex., 6,540 **92** D3
El Salto, Jal., Mex., 5,926 **93** a9
El Salvador, ctry., 2,928,000* **94** C4
El Salvador, Chile **105** A3
El Salvador, Phil., 1,818 **153** C3
El Samán de Apure, Ven., 1,154 **100** F4
El Santo, Cuba, 2,219 **96** d1
Elsas, Ont., Can. **44** G5
El Sauce, Nic., 2,470 **94** D4
El Sauz, Mex., 1,395 **93** d9
El Sauzal, Mex., 2,538 **92** A1
Elsberry, Mo., 1,491 **72** G5
Elsdorf, F.R.Ger., 3,953 **119** B3
El Segundo, Calif., 14,219 **83** h16
El Seibo, Dom. Rep., 4,621 **96** n6
Elsenborn, Belg., 1,820 **115** E4
Elsenz, r., F.R.Ger. **119** F6
Elshout, Neth. **115** c7
Elsie, Mich., 933 **67** J5
Elsie, Nebr., 198 **75** D3
Elsie, Oreg. **80** B3
Elsinore, Calif., 2,432 **83** k16
Elsinore, Utah, 483 **78** B2
Elsinore L., Calif. **83** k16
El Sitio, Mex. **93** e9
Elsmere, Del., 7,319 **62** J3
Elsmere, Nebr. **75** E1
Elsmere, N.Y. **59** v29
Elsmore, Kans., 128 **75** K6
El Socorro, Arg., 3,360* **105** a11
El Socorro, Ven., 3,167 **100** H3
El Sombrero, Ven., 5,592 **100** G3
Elspe, F.R.Ger., 9,818 **118** B3
Elsrickle, U.K. **112** c8
Elst, Neth., 5,900 **115** D3
Elsterberg, Ger.D.R. **126** b6
Elsterwerda, Ger.D.R. **118** D3
Elstra, Ger.D.R. **126** d5
El Sueco, Mex. **92** D2
Elsworth, U.K. **114** H6
El Tabo, Chile **104** f13
El Tambo, Ec. **104** c11
El Teleno, mtn., Sp. **122** B1
Eltham, N.Z., 2,271 **175** g5
El Tigre, Ven., 41,550 **101** H3
El Tigrito, Ven. **101** H3
Eltmann, F.R.Ger., 3,214 **118** C4
El Tocuyo, Ven., 14,803 **100** F3
El Tofo, Chile, 1,175 **105** A3
El Tomaseño, Mex. **93** F3
Elton, U.K. **114** H5
Elton, La., 1,595 **73** C7
Elton, Wis. **66** E3
El Toro, Calif. **83** i16
El Toro, Tex. **77** P5
El Toro, Ven. **101** K3
El Trébol, Arg., 7,200* **105** C4
El Trigo, Arg., 1,550* **105** b12
El Triunfo, Mex. **92** C3
El Trompillo, Ven. **101** b11
El Tucuche, pk., Trin. and Tob. **96** g5
El Tuito, Mex. **92** D4
El Turbio, Arg. **105** A8
Eltville, F.R.Ger., 7,322 **119** E4
Eluru, India, 108,321 **145** F6
El Vado, N. Mex. **79** B3
El Valle, Col. **100** B4
Elvas, Port., 14,548 **122** B3
Elvaston, Ill., 232 **68** A3
Elven, Fr., 2,747 **116** B3
Elverson, Pa., 472 **61** L5
Elverta, Calif. **82** b7
Elverum, Nor. **120** B3
El Viejo, Nic., 7,216 **94** D4
El Vigía, Ven., 8,515 **100** E3
Elvins, Mo., 1,818 **72** G7
Elvira, C., N.W.T., Can. **40** H3
Elvo, r., It. **122** b5
El Wak, Kenya **164** F1
Elwell, Mich. **67** J5
Elwha, r., Wash. **80** B2
Elwin, Ill. **68** C4
Elwood, Ill., 746 **68** D2
Elwood, Ind., 11,793 **70** D2
Elwood, Kans., 1,191 **75** L4
Elwood, Nebr., 581 **75** E3
Elwood, N.J. **61** B4
Elwood, N.Y. **58** f13
Elwood, Utah, 345 **78** b7
Elworth, U.K., 2,571 **114** D4
Ely, U.K., 9,803 **113** G5
Ely, Iowa, 226 **72** F3
Ely, Minn., 5,438 **74** G2
Ely, Nev., 4,018 **83** C3
Ely, Vt. **54** C4
Ely, r., U.K. **114** B8
Ely, Isle of (part of Cambridgeshire), U.K., 89,180 **113** F5
El Yagual, Ven. **100** F4
Elyria, Nebr., 89 **75** G2
Elyria, Ohio, 43,782 **70** G1
Elysburg, Pa., 1,100 **60** J4
Elys Hbr., Berm. Is. **108** 1
Elz, F.R.Ger., 5,589 **119** E4
Elz, r., F.R.Ger. **118** A4
Elz Bach, r., F.R.Ger. **119** C4
Elze, F.R.Ger., 6,057 **118** B2
Ema, Jap. **154** h15
Emae, i., New Hebr. **174** m6
Emanuel, co., Ga., 17,815 **64** G3
Emau, i., New Hebr. **174** m6
Emba, U.S.S.R. **134** E5
Emba, r., U.S.S.R. **134** E5
Embar, Newf., Can. **45** N4
Embarcación, Arg., 10,000* **105** C2
Embarras, L., Qué., Can. **47** H2
Embarras Portage, Alta., Can. **42** K1
Embarrass, Wis., 306 **66** E4
Embarrass, r., Ill. **68** D5
Embden L., Me. **55** C4
Embetsu, Jap., 8,804 **155** J7
Embira, r., Braz. **102** B3
Émbona, Gr., 1,170 **129** F6
Embórion, Gr., 1,194 **129** E6
Embrach, Switz., 2,201 **124** C1
Embreeville, Tenn. **71** J5
Embro, Ont., Can. **46** D5
Embrun, Ont., Can., 1,112 **47** J3
Embrun, Fr., 4,285 **117** G4
Embudo, N. Mex. **79** B3
Emden, F.R.Ger., 42,858 **118** A2
Emden, Ill., 502 **68** C3
Emden, Mo. **72** F5
Emelle, Ala. **64** A3
Emerado, N. Dak., 1,406 **74** D2
Emerald, Austl., 1,633 **173** G3
Emerald, Wis. **66** A3
Emerald Grove, Wis. **66** D6
Emerald I., N.W.T., Can. **41** G2
Emeriau Pt., Austl. **172** B2
Emerson, Man., Can. **43** F5
Emerson, Ark., 350 **73** B4
Emerson, Iowa, 521 **72** B3
Emerson, Mich. **67** J2
Emerson, Nebr., 803 **75** J1
Emerson, N.J., 6,849 **58** c13
Emerson, N.Y. **59** p23
Emery, S. Dak., 502 **74** D4
Emery, co., Utah, 5,546 **78** C2
Emery, Utah, 326 **78** C2
Emery Down, U.K. **113** i13
Emery Mills, Me. **55** B5
Emeryville, Calif., 2,686 **83** e12
Emet, Okla. **76** G3
Emhouse, Tex., 170 **76** f10
Emi, U.S.S.R. **135** J4
Emida, Idaho **81** A2
Emidj, i., Jaluit **176** 30
Emigrant Gap, Calif. **82** C3
Emiliano Zapata, Hgo., Mex., 1,781 **93** e9
Emiliano Zapata, Hgo., Mex. **93** f10
Emiliano Zapata, Mors., Mex., 7,483 **93** e11
Emiliano Zapata, Tab., Mex., 3,751 **93** H5
Emily, Minn., 351 **74** F2
Emine, Nos, Bulg. **128** F3
Eminence, Ind. **70** C3
Eminence, Ky., 1,958 **71** F3
Eminence, Mo., 516 **72** F7
Eminence, Tex. **77** k9
Emington, Ill., 133 **68** D3
Emin Pasha G., Tanz. **165** e15
Emirau, i., Terr. New Guin. **174** f1
Emirdağ, Turk., 10,041 **142** B2
Emita, Austl. **173** f12
Emlembe, S. Af. **164** E6
Emlenton, Pa., 844 **60** C3
Emlichheim, F.R.Ger., 4,119 **118** A2
Emma, Ind. **70** D1
Emma, Mo., 202 **72** D5
Emmaboda, Swed. **120** C4
Emmaus, Pa., 10,262 **61** L4
Emme, r., Switz. **124** B2
Emmeloord, Neth., 7,300 **115** D2
Emmelshausen, F.R.Ger., 1,491 **119** C4
Emmen, Neth., 17,400 **115** E2
Emmen, Switz., 16,856 **124** C1
Emmendingen, F.R.Ger., 12,684 **118** A4
Emmeram, Kans. **75** F5
Emmer-Compascuum, Neth., 8,200 **115** F2
Emmer-Erfscheidenveen, Neth. **115** E2
Emmerich, F.R.Ger., 14,338 **118** A3
Emmet, Austl. **173** F3
Emmet, Ark., 474 **73** B4
Emmet, co., Iowa, 14,871 **72** C1
Emmet, co., Mich., 15,904 **67** J3
Emmet, Nebr., 66 **75** G1
Emmetsburg, Iowa, 3,887 **72** C1
Emmett, Idaho, 3,769 **81** A4
Emmett, Kans., 128 **75** J4
Emmett, Mich., 283 **67** L5
Emmitsburg, Md., 1,369 **62** G3
Emmons, co., N. Dak., 8,462 **74** B2
Emneth, U.K., 1,886 **114** J5
Emo, Ont., Can. **44** C5
Emőd, Hung., 5,250 **126** E3
Emory, Ga. **64** g9
Emory, Tex., 559 **77** Q3
Emory, Va. **62** C6
Emory, r., Tenn. **71** G5
Emory Pk., Tex. **77** M5
Empalme, Mex., 18,870 **92** C2
Empangeni, S. Af., 6,572 **164** E6
Empedrado, Chile, 8,769 **104** e15
Emperor Seamount Chain, Pac. Oc. **169** F1
Empexa, Bol. **102** a12
Empexa, Salar de, Bol. **102** a12
Empingham, U.K. **114** G5
Empire, Ark. **73** D4
Empire, Calif., 1,635 **82** C4
Empire, Ga. **64** F3
Empire, La. **73** F8
Empire, Mich., 448 **67** G4
Empire, Nev. **83** A2
Empire, Ohio, 551 **70** J2
Empire, Oreg., 3,781 **80** A4
Empoli, It., 34,989 **123** C3
Emporia, Fla. **65** H3
Emporia, Kans., 18,190 **75** J5
Emporia, Va., 5,535 **62** G6
Emporium, Pa., 3,397 **60** F2
Empress, Alta., Can. **42** L3
Empress Augusta Bay, Sol. Is. **175** a2
Empty Quarter=Ar Rab' al Khālī
Emrick, N. Dak. **74** C2
Ems=Domat
Ems, r., F.R.Ger. **118** A2
Emscher, can., F.R.Ger. **119** C1
Emsdale, Ont., Can. **46** E3
Emsdetten, F.R.Ger., 23,392 **118** A2
Ems-Jade Kan., F.R.Ger. **118** A2
Emstek, F.R.Ger., 6,505 **118** B2
Ems-Weser Kan., F.R.Ger. **118** B2
Emsworth, Pa., 3,341 **60** b7
Ena, Jap., 30,990 **155** E4
Enard Bay, U.K. **112** D2
Enarotali, Indon. **149** L3
Encamp, Andorra, 1,073 **122** g7
Encampment, Wyo., 333 **81** F5
Encarnação, Port., 3,192 **122** i9
Encarnación, Para., 18,783 **105** D3
Encarnación, r., Mex. **93** b8
Encarnación de Díaz, Mex., 8,638 **92** E4
Enchenberg, Fr., 1,255 **116** d8
Enchi, Ghana, 2,068 **162** b9
Encina, Tex. **77** O5
Encinillas, Lag. de, Mex. **92** D2
Encinitas, Calif., 2,786 **82** E6
Encino, N. Mex., 346 **79** C4
Encino, Tex. **77** O6
Encinoso, N. Mex. **79** C5
Enco, Chile **105** e14
Encontrados, Ven., 9,565 **100** D3
Encounter Bay, Austl. **172** c8
Encrucijada, Cuba, 4,791 **96** d1
Endako, Br. Col., Can. **42** F2
Endau, Malay., 2,675 **148** C2
Ende, Indon. **149** G5
Endeavor, Pa. **60** D2
Endeavor, Wis., 280 **66** D5
Endeavour, Sask., Can. **43** D4
Endeavour Str., Austl. **173** F1
Endelave, i., Den. **121** C5
Enderbury, atoll, Phoenix Is. **170** G5
Enderby, Br. Col., Can. **42** H4
Enderby, U.K., 4,024 **114** F5
Enderby Land, Ant. **180** R6
Endere, r., China **150** B3
Enderlin, N. Dak., 1,596 **74** D2
Enders, Nebr. **75** D3
Enders Res., Nebr. **75** D3
Endicott, Nebr., 166 **75** H3
Endicott, N.Y., 18,775 **59** H7
Endicott, Va. **62** D6
Endicott, Wash., 369 **80** E2
Endicott Mts., Alaska **85** F2
Endless L., Me. **55** D3
Endre, r., Fr. **116** m13
Endrick Water, r., U.K. **112** b7
Endrőd, Hung., 9,278 **126** E3
Endwell, N.Y. **59** H7
Endybal, U.S.S.R. **135** N3
Energy, Ill., 507 **68** D6
Enetai, Wash., 2,539 **81** a7
Enez, G. of, Gr. **129** E4
Enfield, N.S., Can. **47** U11
Enfield, London, U.K. **114** H7
Enfield, Conn., 31,464(T) **56** F5
Enfield, Ill., 791 **68** D5
Enfield, Me. **55** D3
Enfield, N.H., 1,121 **54** C4
Enfield, N.Y. **59** G7
Enfield, N.C., 2,978 **63** G1
Enfield Center, N.H. **54** C4
Engadine, Mich. **67** H2
Engaño, Cabo, Dom. Rep. **96** n6
Engaru, Jap., 19,177 **155** K7
Engaruka, ruins, Tanz. **165** h15
Engebi, i., Eniwetok **176** 28
Engelberg, Switz., 2,646 **124** C2
Engelhard, N.C. **63** J2
Engelhartszell, Aust., 1,243 **124** K5
Engel's, U.S.S.R., 102,000 **134** D4
Engelskirchen, F.R.Ger., 6,573 **119** C3
Engen, Br. Col., Can. **42** F3
Engenthal, Fr., 1,040 **116** d9
Enggano, P., Indon. **148** B4
Enghien-les-Bains, Fr., 12,504 **116** h11
Engi, Switz., 1,064 **124** D2
Engineer, Br. Col., Can. **42** C1
Engineer Group, is., Terr. Papua **174** 3
England, U.K., 45,070,000* **113** E5
England, Ark., 2,861 **73** D3
Engle, N. Mex. **79** B5
Englee, Newf., Can. **45** Q5
Englehart, Ont., Can., 1,763 **44** H6
Englevale, N. Dak. **74** D2
Englewood, Colo., 33,398 **79** C2
Englewood, Fla., 2,877 **65** G6
Englewood, Kans., 243 **75** E6
Englewood, N.J., 26,057 **61** D2
Englewood, Ohio, 1,515 **70** E3
Englewood, Tenn., 1,574 **71** G6
English, Ind., 698 **70** C4
English, r., Ont., Can. **44** C5
English, r., Iowa **72** E3
English Bay, Alaska **85** F4
English Bazar, India, 45,900 **145** H4
English Brook, Man., Can. **43** G4
English C., Newf., Can. **45** b11
English Center, Pa. **60** H3
English Chan., Eur. **110** C4
English Harbour Town, Antigua **97** 9
English Lake, Ind. **70** C1
Englishman Bay, Me. **55** E4
Englishtown, N.J., 1,143 **61** C3
Enguera, Sp., 5,144 **122** E3
Enid, Miss., 128 **73** E3
Enid, Okla., 38,859 **76** F1
Enid L., Miss. **73** F3
Enigma, Ga., 525 **64** F4
Enina, Bulg., 2,820 **128** E3
Enion, Ill. **68** B3
Enipévs, r., Gr. **129** D5
Eniwa, Jap., 26,642 **155** J8
Eniwetok, i., Kwajalein **176** 25
Eniwetok, atoll, Marsh. Is. **170** E4
Eniwetok, i., Eniwetok **176** 28
Enka, N.C. **63** B2
Enkeldoorn, Rhod. **164** E5
Enken, M., U.S.S.R. **135** O4
Enkenbach, F.R.Ger., 3,560 **119** D6
Enkhuizen, Neth., 10,100 **115** D2
Enköping, Swed., 13,233 **120** D4
Enloe, Tex., 150 **77** Q3
Enna, It., 29,730 **123** E6
Ennadai, N.W.T., Can. **40** J5
Ennadai L., N.W.T., Can. **40** J5
Ennedi, plat., Chad **163** H3
Ennell, L., Ire. **113** C5
Ennenda, Switz., 3,076 **124** D1
Ennepe, r., F.R.Ger. **119** C2
Ennepetal, F.R.Ger., 28,145 **119** C2
Ennery, Fr. **116** g10
Enngonia, Austl. **173** G4
Ennigerloh, F.R.Ger., 8,110 **118** A3
Enning, S. Dak. **74** A3
Enningdal, Nor. **121** D2
Ennis, Ire., 8,292 **113** B5
Ennis, Mont., 525 **81** D3
Ennis, Tex., 9,347 **77** P3
Enniscorthy, Ire., 6,422 **113** C5
Enniskillen, U.K., 7,438 **113** C4
Ennistimon, Ire. **113** B5
Ennotville, Ont., Can. **46** b13
Enns, Aust., 8,918 **124** L5
Enns, r., Aust. **124** L6
Ennugarret, i., Kwajalein **176** 25
Ennylabegan, i., Kwajalein **176** 25
Eno, Fin. **120** G3
Eno, r., N.C. **63** E1
Enoch, Utah **78** B3
Enochs, Tex. **77** M3
Enola, Ark. **73** C2
Enola, Nebr. **75** H2
Enondale, Miss. **73** G5
Enontekiö, Fin. **120** F1
Enon Valley, Pa., 455 **60** A4
Enonville, Va. **62** F5
Enoree, S.C. **63** C3
Enoree, r., S.C. **63** C3
Enos, Ind. **70** B1
Enosburg Falls, Vt., 1,321 **54** B2
En-p'ing, China **152** D3
Enrekang, Indon. **149** G3
Enrile, Phil., 5,570 **153** B1
Enrique, Arg. **105** b11
Enriquillo, Dom. Rep., 3,485 **96** m7
Enriquillo, Lago, Dom. Rep. **96** m6
Ensay, Austl. **173** f11
Enschede, Neth., 105,400 **115** E2
Ensenada, Mex., 42,770 **92** A1
Ensenada, P.R., 3,229 **96** s11
En-shih, China **150** E4
Enshū-nada, Jap. **155** E5
Ensign, Kans., 255 **75** E6
Ensign, Mich. **66** G3
Ensley, Calif. **82** a7
Ensley, Fla., 1,836 **65** B2
Enstaberga, Swed. **120** d9
Enstone, U.K. **114** F7
Entebbe, Uganda, 10,941 **164** E1
Enter, Neth., 3,400 **115** E2
Enterprise, Ont., Can. **46** H4
Enterprise, Ala., 11,410 **64** D4
Enterprise, Ill. **68** D5
Enterprise, Kans., 1,015 **75** H5
Enterprise, La. **73** D6
Enterprise, Miss., 532 **73** G5
Enterprise, Okla. **76** H2
Enterprise, Oreg., 1,932 **80** E3
Enterprise, Utah, 859 **78** B3
Enterprise, Wis. **66** D3
Entiat, Wash., 357 **80** C2
Entiat, r., Wash. **80** C2
Entlebuch, Switz., 3,318 **124** C2
Entraygues, Fr., 1,594 **117** E4
Entrepeñas, Pantano de, Sp. **122** D2
Entre Ríos, Bol., 1,109 **102** D6
Entre-Rios, Moz. **164** F4
Entre Rios de Minas, Braz., 2,521 **103** d17
Entrerríos, Col. **100** C4
Entringen, F.R.Ger., 1,483 **119** F7
Entwistle, Alta., Can. **42** J3
Enubuj, i., Kwajalein **176** 25
Enugu, Nigeria, 72,179 **162** F4
Enumclaw, Wash., 3,269 **80** C2
Envigado, Col. **101** d13
Enville, Tenn., 250 **71** C6
Envira, Braz. **102** C3
Enying, Hung., 6,417 **126** D3
Enz, r., F.R.Ger. **118** B4
Enza, Torrente, It. **123** C2
Enzan, Jap., 29,592 **155** F4
Enz-Bach, F.R.Ger. **119** A4
Enzersdorf, Aust. **124** c9
Enzersfeld, Aust. **124** c10
Eola, Ill. **69** b9
Eola, La. **73** C7
Eolie, Isole, It. **123** E5
Eoline, Ala. **64** B2
Epanomí, Gr., 4,639 **129** D4
Epazotes, Mex. **93** e8
Epe, F.R.Ger., 9,754 **118** A2
Epe, Neth., 5,500 **115** D2
Epe, Nigeria, 9,770 **162** f8
Epéna, Congo **164** B1
Épernay, Fr., 22,799 **117** E2
Epes, Ala., 337 **64** A3
Ephesus, ruins, Turk. **142** A2
Ephraim, Utah, 1,801 **78** C2
Ephraim, Wis., 221 **66** F3
Ephrata, Pa., 7,688 **61** K5
Ephrata, Wash., 6,548 **80** D2
Ephratah, N.Y. **59** M5
Epi, i., New Hebr. **174** m6
Epila, Sp., 5,072 **122** E2
Épinal, Fr., 34,806 **117** G2
Épinay-sur-Orge, Fr., 6,116 **116** h12
Épinay-sur-Seine, Fr., 34,234 **116** h11
Epipa, Col. **100** E1
Epira, Guyana **101** M5
Epirus=Ípiros
Episcopia Bihorului, Rum. **128** C1
Episkopi, Cyp., 2,001 **142** d10
Epitálion, Gr., 4,362 **129** C6
Epo, Terr. Papua **174** e3
Épône, Fr., 3,239 **116** f11
Epoufette, Mich. **67** H2
Eppegem, Belg., 3,500 **115** d9
Eppelborn, F.R.Ger., 4,802 **116** d8
Eppenbrunn, F.R.Ger., 1,299 **119** D6
Epping, Fr. **116** d8
Epping, U.K., 10,001 **114** J7
Epping, N.H. **54** E5
Epping, N. Dak., 151 **74** A1
Eppingen, F.R.Ger., 4,873 **119** F6
Epping Forest, Md. **62** c8
Epps, La., 411 **73** D5
Epsom, U.K., 47,769 **113** F6
Epsom, N.C. **63** F1
Epureni, Rum. **128** F1
Epworth, U.K., 1,975 **114** G3
Epworth, Iowa, 698 **72** G2
Eqlīd, Iran, 11,309 **143** E2
Equality, Ala. **64** C3
Equality, Ill., 665 **68** D6
Equatorial Guinea, Afr. **164** A1
Equatorial Mid-Ocean Canyon, Atl. Oc. **109** K7
Equinox Mtn., Vt. **54** A5
Equinunk, Pa. **61** M2
Éragny, Fr., 2,837 **116** g10
Eramachi, Jap. **155** H9
Eramosa, Ont., Can. **46** b13
Eramosa, r., Ont., Can. **46** D5
Erandique, Hond. **94** e9
Erap, Terr. New Guin. **174** e2
Erath, La., 2,019 **73** C8
Erath, co., Tex., 16,236 **77** O3
Eratíra, Gr., 2,459 **129** C4
Eravur, Cey. **145** n22
Erbaa, Turk., 10,765 **142** D1
Erbach, F.R.Ger., 1,746 **119** E4
Erbach, F.R.Ger., 5,360 **119** G5
Erbacon, W. Va. **62** D4
Erbendorf, F.R.Ger., 3,094 **126** b7
Erbeskopf, F.R.Ger. **119** C5
Erçek Gölü, Turk. **142** E2
Erciş, Turk., 9,930 **142** E2
Erciyas Dağı, Turk. **142** C2
Ercolano, ruins, It. **123** c10
Ercsi, Hung., 7,865 **126** D3
Érd, Hung., 23,177 **126** D3
Erda, F.R.Ger., 1,299 **119** F3
Erdek, Turk., 6,595 **142** A1
Erdemli, Turk., 8,124 **142** C2
Erding, F.R.Ger., 8,486 **118** C4
Erdre, r., Fr. **117** C3
Ere, i., Kwajalein **176** 25
Erebato, r., Ven. **101** H5
Erebus, Mt., Ant. **180** V5
Erechim, Braz., 24,941 **103** F7
Ereğli, Turk. **142** B1
Ereğli, Turk., 8,815 **142** C2
Erembodegem, Belg., 10,395 **115** C4
Eresma, r., Sp. **122** C2
Eressós, Gr., 2,675 **129** E5
Erfa, r., F.R.Ger. **119** G5
Erfde, F.R.Ger., 1,903 **118** B1
Erfenbach, F.R.Ger., 2,590 **119** D6
Erfoud, Mor., 4,491 **160** D2
Erft, r., F.R.Ger. **118** A3
Erfurt, Ger.D.R. 186,448 **118** C3
Ergani, Turk., 8,542 **142** D2
Erg Chech, des., Alg.-Mali **160** D4
Ergene, r., Turk. **142** A1
Ergenzingen, F.R.Ger., 1,532 **119** F7
Erg Iguidi, des., Alg.-Maur. **160** C3
Ergoldsbach, F.R.Ger., 3,478 **118** D4
Ergste, F.R.Ger., 3,012 **119** D2
Erh Chou, China **152** b6
Erh Hai, China **150** D4
Erh-lien, China **150** F2
Erh-lin, Taiwan, 45,473 **152** F3
Erh-t'ang, China **152** a6
Eriboll, Loch, U.K. **112** D2
Eric, Qué., Can. **45** N4
Erica, Neth., 3,700 **115** E2
Ericht, Loch, U.K. **112** D3
Erick, Okla., 1,342 **76** D2
Erickson, Man., Can. **43** E5
Ericsburg, Minn. **74** F1
Ericson, Nebr., 157 **75** G2
Eridu, Fla. **65** F2
Erie, Colo., 875 **79** C1
Erie, Ill., 1,215 **68** B2
Erie, Kans., 1,309 **75** K6
Erie, Mich. **67** K7
Erie, co., N.Y., 1,064,688 **58** C6
Erie, N. Dak. **74** D2
Erie, co., Ohio, 68,000 **70** G1
Erie, co., Pa., 250,682 **60** B1
Erie, Pa., 138,440 **60** B1
Erie, L., Can.-U.S. **53** K2
Erieau, Ont., Can. **46** C6
Erie Beach, Ont., Can. **46** C6
Erie Beach, Ont., Can. **46** F6
Erigavo, Som. Rep., 4,100* **163** M4
Erikoúsa, is., Gr. **129** B5
Eriksdale, Man., Can. **43** F5
Erikub, atoll, Marsh. Is. **176** 22
Erimo-saki, Jap. **155** K9
Erin, Ont., Can. **46** D5
Erin, N.Y. **59** G7
Erin, Tenn., 1,097 **71** D5
Erindale, Ont., Can. **46** c13
Erin Point, Trin. and Tob. **96** g5
Erinview, Man., Can. **43** g9
Eriskay, i., U.K. **112** C3
Erisort, Loch, U.K. **112** C2
Erith, London, U.K. **114** J8
Erithraí, Gr., 3,466 **129** D5
Eritrea, reg., Eth. **163** L3
Erkelenz, F.R.Ger., 9,831 **118** A3
Erkizan, Turk., 5,018 **142** E2
Erkner, Ger.D.R. **119** f11
Erkowit, Sudan **163** L2
Erkrath, F.R.Ger., 10,889 **119** B2
Erlandson L., Qué., Can. **45** M2
Erlangen, F.R.Ger., 60,378 **118** C4
Erlanger, Ky., 7,072 **71** G2
Erle, F.R.Ger., 1,292 **119** B1
Erlenbach, F.R.Ger., 4,061 **118** B4
Erlenbach, Switz., 1,471 **124** B2
Erlenbeck bei Marktheidenfeld, F.R.Ger., 1,195 **119** H5
Erling, L., Ark. **73** B4
Ermatingen, Switz., 1,857 **124** D1
Ermelo, Neth., 7,200 **115** D2
Ermelo, S. Af., 16,894 **164** E6
Ermenak, Turk., 7,536 **142** C2
Ermióni, Gr., 2,297 **129** D6
Ermitaño, r., Col. **101** e13
Ermont, Fr., 19,419 **116** g11
Ermoúpolis, Gr., 14,402 **129** E6
Erms, r., F.R.Ger. **119** G7
Ernakulam, India, 117,253 **145** E8
Erndtebrück, F.R.Ger., 3,901 **119** E3
Ernée, Fr., 5,126 **117** C2
Ernfold, Sask., Can. **43** C5
Ernstbrunn, Aust., 1,989 **124** N5
Ernul, N.C. **63** G2
Erode, India, 73,762 **145** E8
Eromanga, Austl. **173** F4
Eromanga, i., New Hebr. **170** F6
Eronan=Futuna
Erongarícuaro, Mex., 1,610 **93** c10
Eros, La., 176 **73** C5
Erp, F.R.Ger., 1,655 **119** B3
Erps-Kwerps, Belg. 3,351 **115** e9
Erquelinnes, Belg., 4,453 **115** C4
Erraid, i., U.K. **112** C3
Errigal Mtn., Ire. **113** B4
Erris, Br. Col., Can. **42** G4
Errol, U.K. **112** d7
Errol, N.H. **54** E2
Errol Heights, Oreg. **80** a7
Ersekë, Alb., 1,850 **125** E4
Erskine, Minn., 614 **74** E2
Erskine Val., Lord Howe I. **175** 12
Erstein, Fr., 6,204 **117** G2
Erstfeld, Switz., 4,126 **124** C2
Ertil', U.S.S.R. **136** F3
Ervália, Braz., 3,199 **103** e17
Ervěnice, Czech. **126** c6
Erving, Mass., 1,272(T) **56** G2
Ervy-le-Châtel, Fr., 1,204 **117** F2
Erwin, N.C., 3,183 **63** F2
Erwin, Tenn., 3,210 **71** J5
Erwin, W. Va. **62** E3
Erwinville, La. **73** D7
Erwitte, F.R.Ger., 4,025 **119** E1
Erzen, r., Alb. **125** D4
Erzgebirge, mts., Ger.D.R. **118** D3
Erzincan, Turk., 36,465 **142** D2
Erzurum, Turk., 91,196 **142** E2
Esa-ala, Terr. Papua **174** f3
Esan-saki, Jap. **155** J9
Esashi, Jap., 15,366 **155** H9
Esashi, Jap., 11,511 **155** K7
Esbjerg, Den., 55,171 **121** A5
Esbly, Fr., 2,452 **116** k11
Esbo=Espoo
Esbon, Kans., 237 **75** G4
Escada, Braz., 13,761 **103** b15
Escalante, Phil., 5,430 **153** e11
Escalante, Utah, 702 **78** C3
Escalante, r., Utah **78** C3
Escalante Des., Utah **78** B3
Escalón, Chih., Mex., 1,270 **92** D2
Escalón, Jal., Mex. **93** a8
Escalon, Calif., 1,763 **82** C4
Escalón, P., Bol. **102** c10
Escalona, Sp., 1,643 **122** C2
Escambia, co., Ala., 33,511 **64** B4
Escambia, co., Fla., 173,829 **65** B2
Escambia, r., Ala.-Fla. **65** C1
Escanaba, Mich., 15,391 **66** F3
Escanaba, r., Mich. **66** F2
Escarpé, C., Loy. Is. **174** k8
Escatawpa, Miss., 1,464 **73** G7
Escatawpa, r., Ala.-Miss. **73** G6
Escaudain, Fr., 11,705 **116** a7
Escaut, r., Fr. **117** E1
Escautpont, Fr., 5,953 **116** a7
Eschau, F.R.Ger., 1,428 **119** G5
Eschbach, F.R.Ger., 1,197 **119** E4
Eschede, F.R.Ger., 3,525 **118** C2
Eschen, Liecht., 1,576 **124** a8
Eschenbach, F.R.Ger., 3,137 **126** a7
Eschenbach, Switz., 2,866 **124** C1
Esch Kopf, F.R.Ger. **119** D6
Esch-sur-Alzette, Lux., 27,954 **115** D5
Eschwege, F.R.Ger., 23,011 **118** B3
Eschweiler, F.R.Ger., 37,866 **119** A3
Escobosa, N. Mex. **79** B4
Escocesa, B., Dom. Rep. **96** n6
Escoheag, R.I. **57** K6
Escondido, Calif., 16,377 **82** E6
Escondido, r., Nic. **94** E4
Escoumins, Qué., Can., 1,607 **45** L5
Escragnolles, Fr. **116** m13
Escravos, r., Nigeria **162** f9
Escrick, U.K. **114** F3
Escudilla Mtn., Ariz. **78** D5
Escuinapa, Mex., 9,875 **92** D3
Escuintla, Guat., 12,492 **94** B3
Escuintla, Mex., 3,468 **93** G5
Escuque, Ven., 3,177 **100** E3
Eséka, Cam. **162** F5
Esens, F.R.Ger., 4,273 **118** A2
Eşfahān, Iran, 254,708 **143** E2
Esh, U.K., 6,290 **112** g10
Esha Ness, U.K. **112** F1
Eshbach, Pa. **60** e10
Esher, U.K., 60,610 **114** H8
Eshowe, S. Af., 4,919 **164** E6
Esiama, Ghana **162** b9
Esino, r., It. **123** D3
Esk, r., Eng., U.K. **113** F4
Esk, r., Eng., U.K. **114** B2
Esk, r., Scot., U.K. **113** E4
Eska, Alaska, 53 **85** G3
Esker, Newf., Can. **45** M4
Eskilstrup, Den. **121** D6
Eskilstuna, Swed., 59,072 **120** D4
Eskimo Lakes, N.W.T., Can. **38** C4
Eskimo Point, N.W.T., Can. **40** L5
Eskişehir, Turk., 153,190 **142** B2
Eskridge, Kans., 519 **75** J5
Esla, r., Sp. **122** C1
Eslarn, F.R.Ger., 2,978 **118** D4
Eslohe, F.R.Ger., 3,745 **119** E2
Eslöv, Swed. **120** C5
Eşme, Turk., 4,925 **142** B2
Esmeralda, Cuba, 4,191 **96** d2
Esmeralda, co., Nev., 619 **83** B4
Esmeralda, Ven. **100** H6
Esmeraldas, Ec., 32,992 **104** A1
Esmond, N. Dak., 420 **74** C1
Esmond (part of Smithfield), R.I. **57** L5
Esnagami, r., Ont., Can. **44** F5
Esneux, Belg., 5,210 **115** D4
Espada, P., Dom. Rep. **96** n6
Espagnol, Morne, Dominica **97** 13
Espagnol Pt., St. Vinc. **97** 19
Espalion, Fr., 3,734 **117** E4
Espanola, Ont., Can., 5,308 **44** G6
Espanola, Fla. **65** H3
Espanola, N. Mex., 1,976 **79** B3
Española, I., Colón, Arch. de **104** b8
Esparta, Hond., 1,776 **94** D3
Espelkamp, F.R.Ger., 7,938 **118** B2
Espenberg, C., Alaska **85** C2
Espera Feliz, Braz., 2,788 **103** f17
Esperança, Braz., 9,105 **103** a14
Esperance, Austl. **172** C5
Esperance, N.Y., 314 **59** M6
Esperance, C., Sol. Is. **175** c3
Esperantina, Braz., 3,727 **103** H2
Esperanza, Ant. **180** O6
Esperanza, Arg., 20,000* **105** a10
Esperanza, Cuba, 4,712 **96** c1
Esperanza, Dom. Rep., 3,899 **96** m6
Esperanza, Mex. **93** G5
Esperanza, Peru **104** D4
Espergærde, Den. **121** a7
Espichel, C., Port. **122** A3
Espigas, Arg., 1,710* **105** a13
Espinal, Col. **100** C5
Espinhaço, Sa. do, Braz. **103** H5
Espinho, Port. 8,799 **122** A2
Espino, Ven. **100** H3
Espinosa de los Monteros, Sp., 3,062 **122** m11
Espírito Santo, st., Braz., 1,188,665 **103** H5
Espíritu Santo, Bol. **102** c10
Espíritu Santo, B. del, Mex. **93** J4
Espíritu Santo, i., New Hebr. **170** F5
Espiritu Santo, I. del, Mex. **92** C3
Espita, Mex., 5,089 **93** H4
Esplanada, Braz., 3,792 **103** J4
Espoo, Fin., 64,130 **120** F3
Esposende, Port., 1,751 **122** A2
Espungabera, Moz. **164** E5
Espy, Pa., 1,375 **61** K3
Espyville Station, Pa. **60** B2
Esqueda, Mex., 1,267 **92** C1
Esquel, Arg., 12,800* **105** A6
Esquimalt, Br. Col., Can., 10,174 **42** F4
Esquina, Arg., 11,200* **105** D3
Esquipulas, Guat., 3,959 **94** d9
Esquipulas del Norte, Hond., 1,428 **94** D3
Esrum Sø, Den. **121** a7
Essaouira, Mor., 26,392 **160** C2
Essen, Belg., 9,635 **115** C3
Essen, Ndrsachs., F.R.Ger., 7,049 **118** B2
Essen, Nrh.-Wf., F.R.Ger., 698,925 **118** A3
Essendon, Mt., Austl. **172** B3
Essequibo, r., Guyana **101** L5
Essex, Ont., Can., 3,384 **46** B6
Essex, co., U.K., 2,288,058 **113** G6
Essex, Calif. **82** F5
Essex, Conn., 1,470;4,057(T) **56** G7
Essex, Ill., 328 **68** D2
Essex, Iowa, 767 **72** B4
Essex, Md., 35,205 **62** c7
Essex, co., Mass., 568,831 **57** M2
Essex, Mass., 2,238(T) **57** N2
Essex, Mo., 511 **72** H8
Essex, Mont. **81** C1
Essex, co., N.J., 923,545 **61** C2
Essex, co., N.Y., 35,300 **59** N3
Essex, co., Vt., 6,083 **54** D2
Essex, Vt. **54** A2
Essex, co., Va., 6,690 **62** H5
Essex Fells, N.J., 2,174 **58** b13
Essex Junction, Vt., 5,340 **54** A3
Essexville, Mich., 4,590 **67** K5
Es Sider, Libya **161** G2
Esslingen, F.R.Ger., 76,996 **118** B4
Esso, U.S.S.R. **135** P4

224 · Est—Farrington

Est, Pointe, Haiti 96 k6
Estabrook, Colo. 79 a9
Estacada, Oreg., 957 80 B3
Estaca de Bares, P. de la, Sp. 122 B1
Estados, I. de los, Arg. 105 C8
Eşţahbānāt, Iran, 16,308 143 E3
Estaimbourg, Belg., 1,132 116 a6
Estância, Braz., 16,106 103 J4
Estancia, N. Mex., 797 79 C4
Estanislao del Campo, Arg., 5,000* 105 C3
Estanzuela, Guat., 2,728 94 d8
Estavayer-le-Lac, Switz., 2,583 124 A2
Estcourt, S. Af., 8,959 164 D6
Este, It., 16,255 123 C2
Este, r., F.R.Ger. 119 a9
Este, Pico del, P.R. 96 u10
Este, P., P.R. 96 v10
Este, P. del, Urug. 99 D6
Estelí, Nic., 7,394 94 D4
Estella, Sp., 8,236 122 D1
Estelline, S. Dak., 722 74 D3
Estelline, Tex., 346 77 N2
Estell Manor, N.J., 496 61 B5
Estepa, Sp., 9,476 122 C4
Estepona, Sp., 13,231 122 C4
Ester, Alaska, 81 85 a6
Esterhazy, Sask., Can., 1,109 43 E5
Esternay, Fr., 1,560 117 E2
Estero, Fla. 65 H6
Estero Bay, Calif. 82 C5
Esterwegen, F.R.Ger., 2,404 118 A2
Estes Park, Colo., 1,175 79 C1
Estevan, Sask., Can., 7,630 43 D5
Estevan Is., Br. Col., Can. 42 D3
Estevan Point, Br. Col., Can. 42 E4
Estey, Mich. 67 J5
Esther, Mo., 1,033 72 G7
Estherville, Iowa, 7,927 72 C1
Estherwood, La., 639 73 C7
Estill, co., Ky., 12,466 71 G4
Estill, S.C., 1,865 63 C5
Estipac, Mex., 3,219 93 a9
Esto, Fla., 148 65 D2
Esto, Ky. 71 F4
Eston, Sask., Can., 1,648 43 B4
Eston, U.K., 37,197 112 h10
Estonian S.S.R.=Estonskaya S.S.R.
Estonskaya S.S.R., U.S.S.R., 1,273,000* 134 B4
Estoril, Port., 11,193 122 i10
Estral Beach, Mich., 254 67 K6
Estrela, mt., Port. 122 B2
Estrela, Sa. da, Port. 122 B2
Estrêla do Norte, Braz., 1,359 103 G4
Estrella, Ariz. 78 B5
Estrella, Colo. 79 B3
Estrella, P., Mex. 92 B1
Estrella Bay, Sol. Is. 175 c2
Estremoz, Port., 10,122 122 B3
Estrugamou, Arg. 105 D5
Esumi, Jap., 2,832 155 D5
Esztergom, Hung., 23,065 126 D3
Etah, India, 24,719 145 F4
Étain, Fr., 3,764 117 F2
Etal, atoll, Car. Is. 176 18
Étalle, Belg., 1,107 115 D5
Étampes, Fr., 13,658 117 D2
Étang Salé, La Réunion, 1,846 165 b11
Étaples, Fr., 8,647 117 D1
Etawah, India, 69,681 145 F4
Etawney L., Man., Can. 43 F2
Etchara, i., Kwajalein 176 25
Etchemin, r., Qué., Can. 47 O2
Etchison, Md. 62 a8
Etchojoa, Mex., 4,075 92 C2
Etchoropo, Mex. 92 C2
Eten, Peru, 6,959 104 B3
Ethan, S. Dak., 297 74 C4
Ethel, Ont., Can. 46 C5
Ethel, Ind. 70 C4
Ethel, La. 73 D7
Ethel, Miss., 566 73 F4
Ethel, Mo., 149 72 E5
Ethel, W. Va. 62 C5
Ethel, Mt., Colo. 79 B1
Ethelbert, Man., Can. 43 E4
Ethel Reefs, Fiji 174 4
Ethelsville, Ala., 62 64 A2
Ether, N.C. 63 E2
Ethiopia, ctry., 23,000,000* 163 L4
Ethridge, Tenn. 71 D6
Étiolles, Fr. 116 h12
Etive, L., U.K. 112 D3
Etiwanda, Calif. 83 k15
Etla, Mex. 93 F5
Etlan, Va. 62 F4
Etna, Calif., 596 82 B2
Etna, Ind. 70 D1
Etna, Me. 55 C4
Etna, N.H. 54 C4
Etna, N.Y. 59 H7
Etna, Pa., 5,519 60 C4
Etna, Utah 78 B1
Etna, r., Nor. 120 B3
Etna, vol., It. 123 E6
Etnabaai, Indon. 149 K3
Etna Green, Ind., 483 70 C1
Etne, Nor. 120 A4
Etobicoke Cr., Ont., Can. 46 c13
Etolin Str., Alaska 85 C3
Eton, Austl. 173 G3
Eton, U.K., 3,894 114 G8
Eton, Ga., 275 64 E1
Etosha Pan, depression, S.-W. Af. 164 B5
Etowah, co., Ala., 96,980 64 C1
Etowah, N.C. 63 B2
Etowah, Tenn., 3,223 71 G6
Etowah, r., Ga. 64 E1
Etra, N.J. 58 a16
Étrépilly, Fr. 116 k10
Étretat, Fr., 1,565 117 D2
Etropole, Bulg., 5,008 128 E3
Etta, L., N. Dak. 74 C2
Ettelbrück, Lux., 5,101 115 D5
Etten, Neth., 6,900 115 C3
Etter, Tex. 76 M1
Ettlingen, F.R.Ger., 17,711 118 B4
Ettrick, Va., 2,998 62 G5
Ettrick, Wis., 479 66 B4
Etzatlán, Mex., 8,752 92 E4
Etzikom, Alta., Can. 42 L4
Eu, Fr., 7,512 117 D2
Eua, i., Tonga 177 36
Euabalong West, Austl. 173 f9
Eubank, Ky., 303 71 G4
Euboea=Évvoia
Eucla, Austl. 172 D4
Euclid, Minn. 74 D2
Euclid, N.Y. 59 r23
Euclid, Ohio, 62,998 70 H1
Euclides da Cunha, Braz., 4,516 103 J4
Eudora, Ark., 3,598 73 D4
Eudora, Kans., 1,526 75 K5
Eudunda, Austl. 172 c8
Eufaula, Ala., 8,357 64 D4
Eufaula, Okla., 2,382 76 H2
Eufaula Res., Okla. 76 H2
Eugene, Mo., 151 72 E6
Eugene, Oreg., 50,977 80 B4
Eugenia, P., Mex. 92 B2
Eugênio de Melo, Braz., 1,175 103 d18
Eugowra, Austl. 173 g9
Euless, Tex., 2,062 76 e9
Eulo, Austl. 173 F4
Eulonia, Ga. 64 H4
Eunice, La., 11,326 73 C7
Eunice, N. Mex., 3,531 79 D5
Eupen, Belg., 14,085 115 E4
Euphrates=Al Furāt, Iraq-Syr.
Euphrates=Firat, Turk.
Eupora, Miss., 1,468 73 F4
Eura, Fin. 120 E3
Eurasian Basin, Arctic Oc. 108 L1
Euratsfeld, Aust., 1,668 124 L5
Eure, N.C. 63 H1
Eure, r., Fr. 117 D2
Eureka, N.W.T., Can. 41 N1
Eureka, N.S., Can. 47 U11
Eureka, Calif., 28,137 82 A2
Eureka, Ill., 2,538 68 C3
Eureka, Kans., 4,055 75 J6
Eureka, Mich. 67 J5
Eureka, Mo., 1,134 72 G6
Eureka, Mont., 1,229 81 B1
Eureka, co., Nev., 767 83 B3
Eureka, Nev. 83 C3
Eureka, N.C., 246 63 G2
Eureka, S.C. 63 C4
Eureka, S.Dak., 1,555 74 C3
Eureka, Utah, 771 78 B2
Eureka, Wis. 66 E4
Eureka River, Alta., Can. 42 H2
Eureka Sd., N.W.T., Can. 41 M2
Eureka Springs, Ark., 1,437 73 B1
Euren, Wis. 66 F4
Europoort, Neth. 115 C3
Euskirchen, F.R.Ger., 18,379 118 A3
Eustace, Tex., 351 76 g10
Eustaquio Lopez, Phil., 15,640 153 e11
Eustis, Fla., 6,189 65 H4
Eustis, Me. 55 B3
Eustis, Nebr., 386 75 E3
Eutaw, Ala., 2,784 64 B3
Eutawville, S.C., 468 63 D4
Eutin, F.R.Ger., 16,860 118 C1
Eutingen, F.R.Ger., 5,839 119 F7
Eutsuk L., Br. Col., Can. 42 E3
Euxton, U.K., 3,310 114 C3
Eva, Ala. 64 C1
Eva, Okla. 76 B1
Evadale, Tex. 77 R4
Evangeline, parish, La., 31,639 73 C7
Evans, Colo., 1,453 79 C1
Evans, co., Ga., 6,952 64 H3
Evans, La. 73 B7
Evans, W. Va. 62 C4
Evans, L., Qué., Can. 44 J5
Evans, Mt., Colo. 79 a8
Evans, Mt., Mont. 81 C3
Evansburg, Alta., Can. 42 J3
Evans Center, N.Y. 58 B6
Evans City, Pa., 1,825 60 B4
Evans Cr., Nev. 83 B2
Evansdale, Iowa, 5,738 72 E2
Evans Falls, Pa. 61 n16
Evans Head, Austl., 1,057 173 H4
Evans Landing, Ind. 70 C4
Evans Mills, N.Y., 618 59 J3
Evans Str., N.W.T., Can. 41 N5
Evanston, Ill., 79,283 68 E1
Evanston, Ky. 71 H4
Evanston, Wyo., 4,901 81 D5
Evansville, Ark. 73 A2
Evansville, Ill., 829 68 C5
Evansville, Ind., 141,543 70 B5
Evansville, Minn., 411 74 E2
Evansville, Vt. 54 C2
Evansville, Wis., 2,858 66 D6
Evansville, Wyo., 678 81 F4
Evant, Tex. 77 O4
Evart, Mich., 1,775 67 H5
Evarts, Ky., 1,473 71 H5
Évaux, Fr., 1,873 117 E3
Évdhilos, Gr. 129 F6
Eveleth, Minn., 5,721 74 F2
Evelyn, Br. Col., Can. 42 E2
Evelyn, La. 73 B6
Evening Shade, Ark., 232 73 D1
Evenlode, r., U.K. 114 E7
Evensk, U.S.S.R. 135 P3
Evensville, Tenn. 71 F6
Everard, C., Austl. 173 g11
Everard, L., Austl. 172 D4
Evere, Belg., 20,766 115 d9
Everek, Turk., 13,680 142 C2
Everest, Kans., 348 75 K4
Everest, Mt., China-Nepal 145 H3
Everett, Ont., Can. 46 D4
Everett, Mass., 43,544 57 M3
Everett, Pa., 2,279 60 F5
Everett, Wash., 40,304 80 B2
Everett, Mt., Mass. 56 C4
Everett City, Ga. 64 H4
Everett Mts., N.W.T., Can. 39 Q5
Everetts, N.C., 225 63 G2
Evergem, Belg., 10,972 115 B3
Everglades, Fla., 552 65 H7
Everglades Nat. Pk., Fla. 65 F7
Everglades, The, Fla. 65 J6
Evergreen, Ala., 3,703 64 C4
Evergreen, Calif. 83 f13
Evergreen, Colo. 79 C2
Evergreen, Fla. 65 H2
Evergreen, N.C., 300 63 F3
Evergreen, Va. 62 F5
Evergreen, Wash. 80 a6
Evergreen Park, Ill., 25,284 69 d10
Everly, Iowa, 668 72 B1
Everman, Tex., 1,076 76 e9
Everöd, Swed. 121 G5
Everson, Pa., 1,304 60 C5
Everson, Wash., 431 80 B1
Everton, Ont., Can. 46 b13
Everton, U.K. 114 G4
Everton, Ark., 118 73 C1
Everton, Ind. 70 D3
Everton, Mo., 261 72 D7
Evesham, U.K., 12,608 113 F5
Evian, Fr., 5,200 117 G3
Evington (part of Leicester), U.K., 19,385 114 F5
Evington, Va. 62 E5
Evionnaz, Switz. 124 B2
Évisa, Fr. 116 r17
Evitts Cr., Pa. 60 E6
Evje, Nor. 120 B4
Evolène, Switz., 1,786 124 B2
Évora, Port., 34,145 122 B3
Evota, G., U.S.S.R. 135 M4
Evpálion, Gr., 1,009 129 D5
Évran, Fr., 1,617 117 B2
Évreux, Fr., 40,158 117 D2
Évron, Fr., 4,286 117 C2
Évros=Maritsa
Evrótas, r., Gr. 129 D6
Évry-les-Châteaux, Fr. 116 i12
Évry-Petit-Bourg, Fr., 5,086 116 h12
Évvoia, i., Gr. 129 D5
Ewa (dist.), Nauru 175 17
Ewa, Hawaii, 3,257 84 C2
Ewab, Kep., Indon. 149 K4
Ewa Beach, Hawaii, 2,459 84 b8
Ewan, Wash. 80 E2
Ewarton, Jam., 3,610 96 p8
Ewaso Ngiro, r., Kenya 165 h14
Ewell, Md. 62 H5
Ewen, Mich. 66 E2
Ewersbach, F.R.Ger., 2,845 119 E3
Ewing, Calif. 82 b7
Ewing, Ill., 250 68 D5
Ewing, Ky. 71 H3
Ewing, Mo., 324 72 F4
Ewing, Nebr., 583 75 G1
Ewing, N.J., 500* 60 g10
Ewing, Va. 62 A6
Ewingville, N.J. 61 B3
Ewo, Congo 164 B2
Ewyas Harold, U.K. 114 C7
Exaltación, Bol., 2,110 102 C4
Exaplátanon, Gr., 2,028 129 D4
Excel, Ala., 313 64 B4
Excelsior, Minn., 2,020 74 a6
Excelsior, Wis. 66 C5
Excelsior Springs, Mo., 6,473 72 C5
Exchange, W. Va. 62 D4
Excideuil, Fr., 1,811 117 D4
Exe, r., U.K. 116 B1
Executive Committee Ra., Ant. 180 X5
Exeland, Wis., 214 66 B3
Exeter, Ont., Can., 2,985 44 G7
Exeter, U.K., 80,321 113 E6
Exeter, Calif., 4,264 82 D4
Exeter (part of Lebanon), Conn. 56 H6
Exeter, Me. 55 C4
Exeter, Nebr., 745 75 H3
Exeter, N.H., 5,896 54 F6
Exeter, Pa., 4,747 61 o16
Exeter, R.I., 2,987 (T) 57 K6
Exeter, r., N.H. 54 F6
Exeter Sd., N.W.T., Can. 41 R4
Exira, Iowa, 1,111 72 C3
Exline, Iowa, 223 72 E4
Exmoor, plat., U.K. 113 E6
Exmore, Va., 1,566 62 J5
Exmouth, U.K., 19,753 113 E6
Exmouth Gulf, Austl. 172 A3
Exmouth Rise, Ind. Oc. 168 D3
Exning (part of Newmarket), U.K., 1,591 114 J6
Expedition Range, Austl. 173 G3
Experiment, Ga., 2,497 64 E2
Exploring Is., Fiji 174 4
Export, Pa., 1,518 60 C5
Exstew, Br. Col., Can. 42 D2
Exter, Mo., 294 72 C8
Exton, U.K. 114 G5
Exton, Pa. 60 e11
Extórax, r., Mex. 93 e8
Extrema, Braz., 1,685 103 c18
Extremadura, reg., Sp. 122 B3
Exuma Sound, Bah. Is. 95 C1
Eyam, U.K. 114 E4
Eyasi, L., Tanz. 164 E2
Eye, Northants., Eng., U.K., 2,364 114 H5
Eye, Suffolk, Eng., U.K., 1,583 113 G5
Eyebrow, Sask., Can. 43 C5
Eyemouth, U.K., 2,160 112 E4
Eye Pen., U.K. 112 C2
Eymet, Fr., 2,152 117 D4
Eymoutiers, Fr., 3,195 117 D4
Eynon, Pa. 61 o15
Eynsham, U.K., 2,628 114 F7
Eyota, Minn., 558 74 F3
Eyrarbakki, Ice. 120 a6
Eyre, Austl. 172 C5
Eyre, L., Austl. 172 E4
Eyrecourt, Ire. 113 B5
Eyre Pen., Austl. 172 a7
Eysturoy, i., Faeroe Is. 120 c7
Eyzin-Pinet, Fr., 1,013 116 p16
Èze, Fr., 1,592 116 n13
Ezequiel Montes, Mex., 1,732 93 d9
Ezine, Turk., 7,531 142 A2

F

Faaa, Tahiti 177 44
Faaone, Tahiti 177 44
Faaupo, Pte., Moorea 177 44
Fabens, Tex., 3,134 77 K4
Faber L., N.W.T., Can. 40 F5
Fabius, N.Y., 378 59 H6
Fåborg, Den., 5,135 121 C5
Fabreville, Qué., Can. 47 o17
Fabriano, It., 28,869 123 D3
Fabyan (part of Thompson), Conn. 56 J4
Fabyan, N.H. 54 E3
Făcăeni, Rum. 128 F2
Facatativá, Col. 100 C5
Fachi, Niger, 1,060 162 F2
Facpi Pt., Guam 176 24
Factory Village, N.H. 54 E2
Factoryville, Pa., 991 61 L2
Fada, Chad 163 H3
Fada Ngourma, Upper Volta, 4,655 162 E3
Faddeya, Zal., U.S.S.R. 135 L2
Faddeyevskiy, O., U.S.S.R. 135 O2
Faden, Newf., Can. 45 M3
Fadghāmī, Syr. 142 E3
Fadian Pt., Guam 176 24
Faenza, It., 50,832 123 C2
Faeroe Is., Den. 120 c7
Faetano, S. Mar., 1,150 123 e11
Fafa, Mali 162 E3
Fafalog, Guam 176 24
Fafan, r., Eth. 163 M4
Fafe, Port., 7,126 122 A2
Făgăraş, Rum., 17,256 128 E2
Fagasa Bay, Tutuila 177 39
Fagernes, Nor. 120 B3
Fagersta, Swed. 120 C4
Făget, Rum. 128 D2
Fagnano, L., Arg. 105 B8
Fagurhólsmyri, Ice. 120 b6
Faial, i., Azores 108 2
Faiaué, Is. Loy. Is. 174 k8
Faiaué, B., Loy. Is. 174 k8
Faibus Pt., Tinian 176 27
Faido, Switz., 1,441 124 C2
Failsworth, U.K., 19,805 114 D3
Faïoa, Î., Is. Wallis 175 7
Fair, Arg. 105 b13
Fairacres, N. Mex. 79 B5
Fairbank, Ariz. 78 C6
Fairbank, Iowa, 650 72 F2
Fairbanks, Alaska, 13,311 85 H2
Fairbanks, Ind. 70 B3
Fairbanks, Me. 55 B4
Fair Bluff, N.C., 1,030 63 E3
Fairborn, Ohio, 19,453 70 F3
Fairburn, Ga., 2,470 64 E2
Fairburn, S. Dak., 47 74 A4
Fairbury, Ill., 2,937 68 D3
Fairbury, Nebr., 5,572 75 H3
Fairchance, Pa., 2,120 60 C6
Fairchild, Wis., 596 66 C4
Fairchild Cr., Ont., Can. 46 b14
Fairdale, N. Dak., 126 74 C1
Faire, Phil., 2,520 153 B1
Fairfax, Ala., 3,107 64 D3
Fairfax, Calif., 5,813 83 d11
Fairfax, Del. 62 e10
Fairfax, Iowa, 528 72 F3
Fairfax, Minn., 1,489 74 E3
Fairfax, Mo., 736 72 B4
Fairfax, Hamilton Co., Ohio, 2,430 71 i11
Fairfax, Highland Co., Ohio 70 F3
Fairfax, Okla., 2,076 76 G1
Fairfax, S.C., 1,814 63 C5
Fairfax, S. Dak., 253 74 C4
Fairfax, co., Va., 275,002 62 G4
Fairfax, Va., 13,585 62 G4
Fairfax, Vt. 54 B2
Fairfax, Wash. 81 b8
Fairfield, Barb. 97 10
Fairfield, Ala., 15,816 64 B2
Fairfield, Calif., 14,968 82 C3
Fairfield, co., Conn., 653,589 56 C7
Fairfield, Conn., 46,183(T) 56 D8
Fairfield, Idaho, 474 81 B4
Fairfield, Lake Co., Ill. 69 b8
Fairfield, Wayne Co., Ill., 6,362 68 D5
Fairfield, Iowa, 8,054 72 F3
Fairfield, Ky., 290 71 F4
Fairfield, Me., 3,766 55 C4
Fairfield, Mont., 752 81 C2
Fairfield, Nebr., 495 75 G3
Fairfield, N.C. 63 H2
Fairfield, N.Y. 59 L5
Fairfield, co., Ohio, 63,912 70 G3
Fairfield, Ohio, 9,734 70 E3
Fairfield, Pa., 519 60 H6
Fairfield, co., S.C., 20,713 63 C3
Fairfield, Tex., 1,781 77 P4
Fairfield, Utah 78 b10
Fairfield, Va. 62 E5
Fairfield, Vt. 54 B2
Fairfield, Wash., 367 80 E2
Fairford, Man., Can. 43 F4
Fairford, U.K., 1,602 114 E7
Fairgrove, Mich., 609 67 K5
Fairhaven, Newf., Can. 45 b10
Fairhaven, Mass., 14,339(T) 57 N6
Fair Haven, N.J., 5,678 58 c15
Fair Haven, N.Y., 764 59 G5
Fair Haven, Vt. 54 A4
Fairhope, Ala., 4,858 64 A5
Fairhope, Pa. 60 E6
Fair I., U.K. 112 F2
Fairland, Ind. 70 D3
Fairland, Okla., 646 76 H1
Fairlawn, Mass.=Turnpike
Fair Lawn, N.J., 36,421 61 C2
Fairlee, Vt. 54 C4
Fairless Hills, Pa., 8,125* 60 g11
Fairlie, N.Z. 175 f7
Fairlie, U.K. 112 a8
Fairmont, Ill. 69 b10
Fairmont, Minn., 9,745 74 E4
Fairmont, Nebr., 829 75 H3
Fairmont, N.C., 2,286 63 E3
Fairmont, Okla., 115 76 F1
Fairmont, W. Va., 27,477 62 D3
Fairmont City, Ill., 2,688 72 b11
Fairmount, Ga., 619 64 E1
Fairmount, Ill., 725 68 E3
Fairmount, Ind., 3,080 70 D2
Fairmount, Md. 62 J4
Fairmount, Mo. 75 b7
Fairmount, N.Y. 59 q23
Fairmount, N. Dak., 503 74 D2
Fair Oak, U.K., 1,858 113 k13
Fair Oaks, Calif., 1,622 82 b7
Fair Oaks, Ga., 7,969 64 g9
Fair Oaks, Ind. 70 B1
Fair Plain, Mich., 7,998 67 G6
Fairplains, N.C. 63 C1
Fairplay, Colo., 404 79 C2
Fair Play, Mo., 335 72 D7
Fair Play, S.C. 63 B3
Fair Play, Wis. 66 C6
Fairpoint, S. Dak. 74 A3
Fairport, Kans., 75 F4
Fairport, Mich. 67 G3
Fairport, N.Y., 5,507 58 F5
Fairport, Ohio, 4,267 70 H1
Fairport Beach, Ont., Can. 46 E5
Fairton, N.J. 61 A5
Fairview, Alta., Can., 1,464 42 H2
Fairview, Ark. 73 C4
Fairview, Idaho 81 C4
Fairview, Cook Co., Ill. 69 c9
Fairview, Fulton Co., Ill., 544 68 B3
Fairview, Ind. 70 D4
Fairview (part of Chicopee), Mass. 56 F4
Fairview, Mich. 67 J4
Fairview, Mo., 249 72 C8
Fairview, Mont., 1,006 81 G2
Fairview, Bergen Co., N.J., 9,399 58 d13
Fairview, Monmouth Co., N.J. 58 c15
Fairview, N.Y., 8,626 59 N8
Fairview, Ohio, 166 70 H2
Fairview, Okla., 2,213 76 E1
Fairview, Oreg., 578 80 b6
Fairview, Pa., 1,399 60 B1
Fairview, Tenn., 1,017 71 D6
Fairview, Utah, 655 78 C2
Fairview, W. Va., 653 62 D3
Fairview Mtn., Colo. 79 B2
Fairview Park, Ind., 1,039 70 B3
Fairview Park, Ohio, 14,624 70 d9
Fairville, Pa. 62 e10
Fairwater, Wis., 330 66 E5
Fairway, Kans., 5,398 75 a7
Fairweather, C., Alaska 85 K4
Fairweather, Mt., Can.-U.S. 42 B1
Fais, i., Car. Is. 176 18
Faison, N.C., 666 63 F2
Faistos, ruins, Gr. 129 E7
Faith, Alta., Can. 42 K4
Faith, N.C., 494 63 D2
Faith, S. Dak., 591 74 A3
Faithorn, Mich. 66 F3
Faizābād, Afghan., 56,000 145 C1
Faizabad, India, 88,296 145 G4
Fajardo, P.R., 12,409 96 u10
Fajardo, r., P.R. 96 u10
Fajr, Wādī, Saudi Ar. 143 B3
Fakahina, i., Tuam. Arch. 171 J6
Fakaofu, i., Tokelau Is. 170 G5
Fakarava, atoll, Tuam. Arch. 177 42
Fakenham, U.K., 3,753 113 G5
Fakfak, Indon. 149 K3
Fakiya, Bulg., 1,658 128 F3
Fakse, Den., 3,577 121 E5
Fakse Bugt, Den. 121 E5
Fakse Ladeplads, Den. 121 E5
Fa-k'u, China 151 D2
Fala, U.K. 112 e8
Fala-beguets, i., Truk 176 19
Falahill, U.K. 112 d8
Falaise, Fr., 6,711 117 C2
Falalu, i., Truk 176 19
Falam, Burma 146 A2
Falan, Col. 101 e14
Falas, i., Truk 176 19
Fălciu, Rum. 128 F1
Falck, Fr., 2,792 116 c8
Falcon, N.C., 235 63 F2
Falcon, i., Tonga 177 36
Falconara Marittima, It., 16,065 123 D3
Falconbridge, Ont., Can., 1,138 44 H6
Falcon Dam, Mex.-U.S. 93 F2
Falcone, C. del, It. 123 A4
Falconer, N.Y., 3,343 58 B7
Falcon Heights, Minn., 5,927 74 c6
Falcon Heights, Tex. 77 O6
Falcon L., Mex.-U.S. 77 O6
Faléa, Mali, 2,100 162 C3
Falealupo, W. Samoa 177 38
Falémé, r., Mali-Sen. 162 C3
Falfurrias, Tex., 6,515 77 O6
Falher, Alta., Can. 42 H2
Falkenberg, Ger.D.R. 118 D3
Falkenberg, Swed. 120 B4
Falkensee, Ger.D.R., 30,845 118 D2
Falkenstein, Ger.D.R., 14,938 118 D3
Falkirk, U.K., 38,043 112 E4
Falkirk, N. Dak. 74 B2
Falkland, U.K., 1,032 112 d7
Falkland, N.C., 140 63 G2
Falkland Esc., Atl. Oc. 109 J10
Falkland Is., Atl. Oc., 2,140 150 C8
Falkland Rise, Atl. Oc. 109 J10
Falkland Sd., Falkland Is. 108 3
Falkland Trough, Atl. Oc. 109 J10
Falkner, Miss. 73 G3
Falköping, Swed. 120 C4
Falkville, Ala., 682 64 B1
Fall, r., Kans. 75 J6
Falla, Cuba, 1,876 96 d1
Fall Branch, Tenn. 71 J5
Fallbrook, Calif., 4,814 82 E6
Fall City, Wash. 80 C2
Fall Creek, Ill. 68 A4
Fall Creek, Oreg. 80 B4
Fall Creek, Wis., 710 66 B4
Fallersleben, F.R.Ger., 6,335 118 C2
Fällfors, Swed. 120 E2
Fallingbostel, F.R.Ger., 4,846 118 B2
Falling Spring, Va. 62 E5
Fallis, Okla., 42 76 F2
Fall Line Hills, Ala.-Ga. 64 ·
Fallon, Mont. 81 G2
Fallon, co., Mont., 3,997 81 G2
Fallon, Nev., 2,743 83 A3
Fall River, Kans., 226 75 K6
Fall River, Mass., 99,942 57 M6
Fall River, co., S. Dak., 10,688 74 A4
Fall River, Wis., 584 66 D5
Fall River Mills, Calif. 82 C2
Fall River Res., Kans. 75 J6
Falls, Pa. 61 L3
Falls, co., Tex., 21,263 77 P4
Falls, r., Mass. 56 F2
Fallsburg, Ky. 71 J3
Fallsburg, Ohio 70 G2
Falls Church, Va., 10,192 62 G4
Falls City, Nebr., 5,598 75 K3
Falls City, Oreg., 653 80 B3
Falls City, Tex., 462 77 P5
Falls Creek, Pa., 1,344 60 E3
Falls Village (part of Canaan), Conn. 56 C5
Falmouth, Jam., 3,727 96 p8
Falmouth, U.K., 17,621 113 D6
Falmouth, Fla. 65 F2
Falmouth, Ky., 2,568 71 G3
Falmouth, Me. 55 B5
Falmouth, Mass., 3,308; 13,037(T) 57 O6
Falmouth, Mich. 67 H4
Falmouth, Va., 1,478 62 G4
Falmouth Bay, U.K. 113 D6
Falmouth Foreside, Me., 1,062 55 B5
Falmouth Harbour, Antigua 97 9
Falmouth Heights (part of Falmouth), Mass. 57 O6
False, r., Qué., Can. 45 M2
False Detour Chan., Can.-U.S. 46 A3
False Divi Pt., India 145 F7
False Pass, Alaska, 41 85 C5
Falset, Sp., 2,484 122 F2
Falso, Cabo, Dom. Rep. 96 m7
Falso, C., Mex. 92 C3
Falster, i., Den. 121 E6
Falsterbo, Swed. 121 E5
Fălticeni, Rum., 13,305 128 F1
Falun, Swed., 18,813 120 D3
Falun, Wis. 66 A3
Famagusta, Cyp., 26,763 142 C3
Famalicão, Port., 3,530 122 A2
Famatina, Arg., 3,000* 105 B3
Fameck, Fr., 7,571 116 b8
Family L., Man., Can. 43 G4
Fanad Head, Ire. 113 C4
Fanan, i., Truk 176 19
Fan-ch'ang, China 152 E1
Fan-chih, China 151 B3
Fandon, Ill. 68 B3
Fandriana, Malag. Rep., 2,703 165 G5
Fan Fawr, mtn., U.K. 114 A7
Fang, Thai. 146 B3
Fang, r., China 151 C4
Fangaalu, Tutuila 177 39
Fangaitua Bay, Tutuila 177 39
Fangak, Sudan 163 K4
Fangalli, Tutuila 177 39
Fangaloa Bay, W. Samoa 177 38
Fangamalo, Tutuila 177 39
Fangamalo, W. Samoa 177 38
Fangatau, i., Tuam. Arch. 171 J6
Fangatonga, Tutuila, 1,344 177 39
Fang-cheng, China 151 F1
Fang-ch'eng, Ho-n., China 151 B4
Fang-ch'eng, K-t., China 150 E5
Fang-chia-chuang, China 152 a6
Fang-hsien, China 150 E3
Fang-shan, P-ch. Shih, China 151 C3
Fang-shan, Shan-hsi, China 151 A3
Fang-shen, China 151 C2
Fangtaufa, i., Tuam. Arch. 177 42
Fanhões, Port., 1,865 122 i10
Fan-hsien, China 151 B4
Fan i Madh, r., Alb. 125 D4
Fan Ling, H.K., 26,282 152 b6
Fannett, Tex. 77 m9
Fannettsburg, Pa. 60 G5
Fannin, co., Ga., 13,620 64 E1
Fannin, Miss. 73 E5
Fannin, co., Tex., 23,880 77 P3
Fanning, i., Line Is. 171 H4
Fanny Bay, Br. Col., Can. 42 a6
Fannystelle, Man., Can. 43 f10
Fano, It., 41,327 123 D3
Fanø, i., Den. 121 A5
Fanø Bugt, Den. 121 A5
Fans, U.K. 112 e8
Fan Si Pan, pk., N. Viet. 146 C2
Fantasque, Pointe, Haiti 96 k6
Fanwood, N.J., 7,963 58 b14
Fao=Al Fāw
Fāqūs, U.A.R. 161 i7
Faraday Seamount Group, Atl. Oc. 108 L3
Faradje, D.R.Congo 164 D1
Farafangana, Malag. Rep., 9,539 165 G5
Farāfirah, U.A.R. 161 J3
Farah, Afghan., 25,000* 144 B2
Farah, r., Afghan. 144 B2
Faraid Head, U.K. 112 D2
Faranah, Guin., 6,000 162 C4
Farasān, Jazā'ir, is., Saudi Ar. 143 C5
Faraulep, atoll, Car. Is. 176 18
Farber, Mo., 451 72 F5
Farciennes, Belg., 11,687 115 C4
Fareara, Pte., Tahiti 177 44
Farébersviller, Fr., 8,452 116 c8
Fareham, U.K., 58,308 113 F6
Fareone, i., Moorea 177 44
Farewell, Alaska 85 F3
Farewell, C., N.Z. 175 g6
Fargo, Ga. 64 G5
Fargo, N. Dak., 46,662 74 D2
Fargo, Okla., 291 76 D1
Fargo, Wis. 66 C5
Far Hills, N.J., 702 61 B2
Faribault, Minn., 16,926 74 F3
Faribault, co., Minn., 23,685 74 E4
Faridpur, India, 13,278 144 b11
Faridpur, Pak., 28,333 144 g14
Färila, Swed. 120 C3
Farim, Port. Guin. 162 B4
Farina, Ill., 692 68 D5
Faringdon, U.K. 114 E7
Farington, U.K., 4,054 114 C3
Farini d'Olmo, It., 5,477 122 c6
Färjestaden, Swed. 120 D4
Farkhar, Afghan. 145 C1
Farland Head, U.K. 112 a8
Farlane, Ont., Can. 44 C5
Farley, Iowa, 920 72 G2
Farley (part of Erving), Mass. 56 G2
Farley, Mo., 120 72 C5
Farley, N. Mex. 79 C3
Farlington, Kans. 75 L6
Farm, r., Conn. 56 E7
Farmer, Ohio 70 E1
Farmer, S. Dak., 95 74 D4
Farmer, Wash. 80 D2
Farmer City, Ill., 1,838 68 D3
Farmer I., N.W.T., Can. 44 H2
Farmers, Ky. 71 H3
Farmers Branch, Tex., 13,441 76 f9
Farmersburg, Ind., 1,027 70 B3
Farmersburg, Iowa, 250 72 F2
Farmersville, Calif., 3,101 82 D4
Farmersville, Ill., 495 68 C4
Farmersville, N.Y. 58 D7
Farmersville, Tex., 2,021 77 P3
Farmerville, La., 2,727 73 C5
Farmingdale, N.J., 959 61 C3
Farmingdale, N.Y., 6,128 58 f14
Farmington, Ark., 216 73 A1
Farmington, Conn., 10,813(T) 56 E6
Farmington, Del., 142 62 J4
Farmington, Ill., 2,831 68 B3
Farmington, Iowa, 902 72 F4
Farmington, Me., 2,749 55 B4
Farmington, Mich., 6,881 67 K6
Farmington, Minn., 2,300 74 F3
Farmington, Mo., 5,618 72 G7
Farmington, N.C. 63 D1
Farmington, N.H., 2,241 54 E5
Farmington, N. Mex., 23,786 79 A3
Farmington, N.Y. 58 o20
Farmington, Tenn. 71 E6
Farmington, Utah, 1,951 78 B1
Farmington, Wash., 176 80 E2
Farmington, W. Va., 709 62 D3
Farmington, r., Conn. 56 E5
Farmingville, N.Y., 2,134 58 g13
Farmland, Ind., 1,102 70 D2
Farmville, N.C., 3,997 63 G2
Farmville, Va., 4,293 62 F5
Farnam, Nebr., 258 75 E3
Farnams (part of Cheshire), Mass. 56 D2
Farnborough, U.K., 31,911 113 F6
Farndon, U.K., 1,010 114 C4
Farne Is., U.K. 112 F4
Farner, Tenn. 71 G6
Farnham, Qué., Can., 6,295 47 M3
Farnham, U.K., 26,934 114 G8
Farnham, N.Y., 422 58 B6
Farnham, Va. 62 H5
Farnham, Mt., Br. Col., Can. 42 J4
Farnhurst, Del. 62 e11
Farnsworth, Tex. 76 N1
Farnumsville, Mass., 1,041 57 K4
Farnworth, U.K. 114 D3
Farnworth, U.K., 27,474 114 C4
Faro, Braz., 1,434 103 E2
Faro, Port., 24,877 122 A4
Fåron, i., Swed. 120 D4
Faro, Punta del, It. 123 E5
Farquhar, C., Austl. 172 A3
Farquhar, Groupe, is., Ind. Oc. 165 H3
Farragut, Iowa, 495 72 B4
Farrell, Pa., 13,793 60 A3
Farrell Creek, Br. Col., Can. 42 G2
Farriar, Ven. 100 F2
Farrington, N.C. 63 E2

Farrington—Florida · 225

Farrington L., N.J. 58 b15
Farrukhabad, India, 87,793 145 F4
Fársala, Gr., 6,356 129 D5
Farschviller, Fr., 1,264 116 c8
Fārsi, Afghan. 144 B2
Farsø, Den., 2,696 121 B4
Farsund, Nor., 2,155 120 A4
Fartak, Ra's, pt., S. Ar. 143 E5
Farum, Den., 5,072 121 a7
Farview, Mt., Austl. 172 a7
Farwell, Mich., 737 67 J5
Farwell, Nebr. 75 G2
Farwell, Okla. 76 E3
Farwell, Tex., 1,009 77 M2
Fasā, Iran, 11,711 143 E3
Fasano, It., 28,595 123 F4
Fashoda = Kodok
Fassett, Qué., Can. 47 K3
Fastov, U.S.S.R., 29,300 136 C3
Fastrill, Tex. 77 Q4
Fatagar, Tg., Indon. 149 J3
Fatahabad, India, 12,461 145 E3
Fate, Tex., 191 76 g9
Fatehpur, Raj., India, 27,039 145 E4
Fatehpur, U.P., India 144 c12
Fatehpur, U.P., India, 28,323 145 F4
Fatehpur Sikri, India, 10,579 144 a12
Father, The, pk., Terr. New Guin. 174 f2
Fatiau, Niue 177 32
Fatima, Qué., Can., 1,061 45 O6
Fátima, Port., 5,852 122 A3
Fatsa, Turk., 6,847 142 D1
Fatu Hiva, i., Marq. Is. 171 J5
Fatu Huku, i., Marq. Is. 177 42
Fatuma, Tonga 177 36
Fatumanini, Passe, chan., Is. Wallis 175 7
Fatumanongi, i., Tonga 177 36
Fatuosofia, C., W. Samoa 177 38
Faulbach, F.R.Ger., 1,554 119 G5
Fauldhouse, U.K. 112 c8
Faulk, co., S. Dak., 4,397 74 C3
Faulkner, co., Ark., 24,303 73 C2
Faulkner, Md. 62 G4
Faulkton, S. Dak., 1,051 74 C3
Faulquemont, Fr., 5,128 117 G2
Fauquier, Ont., Can. 44 G5
Fauquier, co., Va., 24,066 62 G4
Fauresmith, S. Af., 2,171 164 D6
Fauro, i., Sol. Is. 175 b2
Fausing, Den. 121 C4
Fauske, Nor. 120 C2
Fausse Pointe, L., La. 73 D7
Faust, Alta., Can. 42 J2
Faust, N.Y. 59 M3
Faust, Utah 78 B1
Favara, It., 28,720 123 D6
Favaro Veneto, It. 122 f5
Faverges, Fr., 4,151 117 G4
Faversham, U.K., 12,984 113 G6
Favières, Fr. 116 k11
Fawcett, Alta., Can. 42 J2
Fawley, U.K., 7,685 113 k13
Fawn, r., Ont., Can. 44 E3
Fawnie Nose, mt., Br. Col., Can. 42 F3
Fawn River, Mich. 67 H7
Fawnskin, Calif. 82 E5
Faxaflói, bay, Ice. 120 a6
Faxälven, r., Swed. 120 C3
Faxon, Okla., 137 76 E3
Faxon, Tenn. 71 C5
Fay, Okla. 76 E2
Faya = Largeau
Fayd, Saudi Ar. 143 C3
Fayence, Fr., 1,435 117 G5
Fayette, co., Ala., 16,148 64 B2
Fayette, Ala., 4,227 64 B2
Fayette, co., Ga., 8,199 64 E2
Fayette, co., Ill., 21,946 68 C4
Fayette, Ill. 68 B4
Fayette, co., Ind., 24,454 70 D3
Fayette, co., Iowa, 28,581 72 F2
Fayette, Iowa, 1,597 72 F2
Fayette, co., Ky., 131,906 71 G3
Fayette, Me. 55 B4
Fayette, Mich. 67 G3
Fayette, Miss., 1,626 73 D6
Fayette, Mo., 3,294 72 E5
Fayette, N.Y. 58 G6
Fayette, co., Ohio, 24,775 70 F3
Fayette, Ohio, 1,090 70 E1
Fayette, co., Pa., 169,340 60 C6
Fayette, co., Tenn., 24,577 71 B6
Fayette, co., Tex., 20,384 77 P5
Fayette, Utah, 161 78 C2
Fayette, co., W. Va., 61,731 62 C4
Fayette, Wis. 66 D6
Fayette City, Pa., 1,159 60 C5
Fayetteville, Ark., 20,274 73 A1
Fayetteville, Ga., 1,389 64 E2
Fayetteville, Ill., 294 68 C5
Fayetteville, Ind. 70 C4
Fayetteville, N.Y., 4,311 59 r23
Fayetteville, N.C., 51,022 63 F2
Fayetteville, Ohio, 389 70 F3
Fayetteville, Allegheny Co., Pa. 60 a8
Fayetteville, Franklin Co., Pa. 60 H6
Fayetteville, Tenn., 6,804 71 E6
Fayetteville, Tex., 394 77 P5
Fayetteville, W. Va., 1,848 62 C4
Fayl-Billot, Fr., 1,463 117 F3
Fay Station = Argo
Fayville (part of Southboro), Mass. 57 L3
Faywood, N. Mex. 79 B5
Fayyūm, Al, oasis, U.A.R. 161 K3
Fazeley, U.K., 3,400 114 E5
Fazilka, India, 32,015 145 E3
Fazzān, prov. Libya, 59,315 161 G3
Feale, r., Ire. 113 B5
Fear, C., N.C. 63 G4
Fearns Springs, Miss. 73 G4
Feasterville, Pa., 6,100* 60 f11
Feather, r., Calif. 82 C3
Feather Falls, Calif. 82 C3
Featherston, Okla. 76 H2
Feathertop, Mt., Austl. 173 f11
Featherville, Idaho 81 B4
Fécamp, Fr., 19,851 117 D2
Féchain, Fr., 1,402 116 a7
Fechingen, F.R.Ger., 5,009 116 d8
Federación, Arg., 6,685 105 b10
Federal Dam, Minn., 185 74 E2
Federal Heights, Colo., 391 79 b8
Federal Point, Fla. 65 H3
Federalsburg, Md., 2,060 62 J4
Federal Way, Wash. 81 b8
Fedora, S. Dak. 74 D3
Fedorah, Alta., Can. 43 b7
Fëdorovka, U.S.S.R. 136 f8
Fedorovka, Kaz. S.S.R., U.S.S.R. 137 k9
Fedorovka, R.S.F.S.R., U.S.S.R. 137 h9
Feeding Hills (part of Agawam), Mass. 56 F4
Fefan, i., Truk 176 19
Fehérgyarmat, Hung., 6,036 126 F2
Fehmarn, i., F.R.Ger. 118 C1
Fehmarn Belt, str., Den.-F.R.Ger. 121 D6
Fehrbellin, Ger.D.R. 118 D2
Fehring, Aust., 1,449 124 N7
Feia, Lag., Braz. 103 f17
Fei-hsiang, China 151 B3
Fei-hsien, China 151 C4
Feijó, Braz., 1,628 102 B3
Feilding, N.Z., 8,172 175 g6
Feilitzsch, F.R.Ger., 1,210 126 a6
Feira, Zamb. 164 E4
Feira de Santana, Braz., 61,612 103 H4
Feira Grande, Braz., 1,480 103 a15
Feistritz, Aust. 124 M6
Felanitx, Sp., 11,797 122 G3
Felch, Mich. 66 F3
Felda, Fla. 65 H6
Feldbach, Aust., 3,683 124 M7
Feldberg, Ger.D.R. 118 D2
Feldberg, F.R.Ger. 118 B5
Feldioara, Rum. 128 E2
Feldkirch, Aust., 17,311 124 F6
Feldkirchen, Aust., 3,130 124 K7
Feldtman, L., Mich. 66 a9
Felenne, Belg. 115 C4
Felicity, Ohio, 878 70 E4
Felipe Carrillo Puerto, Mex. 93 H4
Felix, r., N. Mex. 79 C5
Felixdorf, Aust., 2,432 124 c11
Felixstowe, U.K., 17,296 113 G6
Felizzano, It., 2,241 122 b6
Fell, F.R.Ger., 1,695 119 B5
Fellbach, F.R.Ger., 23,445 119 G7
Fellers Heights, Br. Col., Can. 42 G2
Felletin, Fr., 3,118 117 E4
Fellows, Calif. 82 D5
Fellsburg, Kans., 75 F6
Fellsmere, Fla., 732 65 J5
Fels, Aust., 1,346 124 b10
Felsberg, Switz., 1,061 124 D2
Felsenthal, Ark. 73 C4
Felsted, U.K., 2,056 114 J7
Felt, Okla. 76 A1
Feltham, London, U.K. 114 H8
Felton, U.K. 112 g9
Felton, Calif., 1,380 83 e13
Felton, Del., 422 62 J3
Felton, Minn., 201 74 D2
Feltre, It., 22,042 123 C1
Feltwell, U.K., 3,192 113 G5
Femund, l., Nor. 120 C3
Fen, r., China 150 F3
Fenain, Fr., 5,253 116 a7
Fena Val. Res., Guam 176 24
Fence, Wis. 66 E3
Fence, r., Mich. 66 E2
Fence Lake, N. Mex. 79 A4
Fence L., Mich. 66 E2
Fence L., Wis. 66 D3
Fen Country, U.K. 114 H4
Fenders, Colo. 79 b8
Fenelon Falls, Ont., Can., 1,341 46 F4
Fenerive, Malag. Rep., 5,799 165 H4
Fénétrange, Fr., 1,206 116 d9
Feng-chen, China 151 B2
Feng-ch'eng, Ch-hsi, China, 30,000* 150 F4
Feng-ch'eng, L-n., China 151 D2
Feng-chieh, China 150 E4
Feng-ch'ing, China 150 D4
Feng-ch'iu, China 151 B4
Feng-ch'uan, China 152 C3
Feng-hsien, Chiang-su, China 151 C4
Feng-hsien, Sh-ha. Shih, China 152 F1
Feng-hsien, Shen-hsi, China, 30,000* 150 E3
Feng-hsin, China 152 D1
Feng-hua, China 152 F1
Feng-huang, China 152 C1
Feng-huang-tsui, China 151 A4
Feng-jun, China 151 C3
Feng-kang, China 152 B2
Feng-lin, Taiwan, 17,461 152 F3
Feng-ling-tu, China 151 A4
Feng-man, China 151 E2
Feng-ming Tao, China 151 D3
Feng-ning, China 151 C2
Feng-shan, China 152 B2
Feng-shun, China 152 E2
Feng-t'ai, China 151 C4
Feng-tu, China 152 B1
Feng-yang, China 151 C4
Feng-yüan, Taiwan, 61,177 152 F2
Fenholloway, Fla. 65 F2
Fenholloway, r., Fla. 65 F2
Fen-hsi, China 151 A3
Fen-i, China 152 D2
Feni Is., Terr. New Guin. 174 g2
Fenimore Pass, Alaska 85 g8
Fennimore, Wis., 1,747 66 C6
Fennville, Mich., 705 67 G6
Fenny Compton, U.K. 114 F6
Fenny Stratford, U.K. 114 G6
Fen-shui, China 152 E1
Fenton, Iowa, 440 72 C1
Fenton, La., 429 73 C7
Fenton, Mich., 6,142 67 K6
Fentress, co., Tenn., 13,288 71 G5
Fentress, Tex. 77 P5
Fenua Fu, Î., Is. Wallis 175 7
Fenualoa, i., Swallow Is. 175 6
Fenwick, Ont., Can. 46 E5
Fenwick, U.K. 112 b8
Fenwick, Conn., 36 56 G7
Fenwick, Mich. 67 H5
Fenwick, W. Va. 62 D4
Fenwood, Wis., 147 66 D4
Fen-yang, China 150 E3
Feodosiya, U.S.S.R., 50,100 134 C5
Ferdinand, Ind., 1,427 70 B4
Ferdows, Iran, 6,834 143 F2
Ferentino, It., 16,680 123 D4
Fereşti, Rum. 128 F1
Ferfer, Som. Rep. 163 M5
Fergana, U.S.S.R., 87,000 134 G5
Fergus, Ont., Can., 3,798 46 D5
Fergus, Mich. 67 J5
Fergus, co., Mont., 14,018 81 E2
Fergus Falls, Minn., 13,733 74 E2
Ferguson, Br. Col., Can. 42 H4
Ferguson, Iowa, 186 72 E3
Ferguson, Ky., 468 71 G4
Ferguson, Mo., 22,149 72 G6
Ferguson, N.C. 63 C1
Fergusson I., Terr. Papua 174 f3
Féricy, Fr. 116 k12
Ferintosh, Alta., Can. 42 K3
Ferkéssédougou, Iv. Coast, 7,496 162 C4
Ferlach, Aust., 5,668 124 L7
Fermanagh, co., U.K., 51,613 113 C4
Ferme-Neuve, Qué., Can., 1,929 47 J2
Fermeuse, Newf., Can. 45 b11
Fermin, Pt., Calif. 83 h16
Fermo, It., 29,199 123 D3
Fermoselle, Sp., 3,885 122 B2
Fermoy, Ire., 3,674 113 B5
Fern, Wis. 66 E3
Fernald, Ohio 71 g10
Fernández, Arg., 8,000* 105 C3
Fernandina, I., Colón, Arch. de 104 a8
Fernandina Beach, Fla., 7,276 65 H2
Fernando de Noronha, i, Braz. 98 F3
Fernando Póo, prov., Equatorial Guinea 164 A1
Ferncliff, Va. 62 F5
Fern Crest Village, Fla., 93 65 a9
Ferndale, Calif., 1,371 82 A2
Ferndale, Md. 62 c8
Ferndale, Mich., 31,347 67 f15
Ferndale, Bucks Co., Pa. 61 M4
Ferndale, Cambria Co., Pa., 2,717 60 D5
Ferndale, Wash., 1,442 80 B1
Ferndown, U.K. 113 i13
Ferney, S. Dak. 74 C3
Fernhurst, U.K., 2,549 113 m12
Fernie, Br. Col., Can., 2,588 42 J4
Fernitz, Aust., 1,456 124 M7
Fernley, Nev. 83 A3
Fern Prairie, Wash. 80 b6
Ferns, Ire. 113 C5
Fernville, Vt. 54 A4
Fernwood, Idaho 81 A2
Fernwood, Miss. 73 E6
Fernwood, N.Y. 59 H5
Ferozepore, India, 93,387 145 E3
Férrai, Gr., 4,600 129 F4
Ferrara, It., 148,861 123 C2
Ferreira do Alentejo, Port., 8,108 122 A3
Ferreira Gomes, Braz. 103 F1
Ferreñafe, Peru, 12,158 104 B3
Ferriday, La., 4,563 73 D6
Ferrier, Haiti, 1,530 96 m6
Ferriere, It., 5,722 122 c6
Ferrières, Fr. 116 i11
Ferring, Den. 121 A4
Ferris, Ill., 208 68 A3
Ferris, Tex., 1,807 76 f9
Ferrisburg, Vt. 54 A3
Ferro, C., It. 123 B4
Ferro, Can. Is. = Hierro
Ferron, Utah, 386 78 C2
Ferron Cr., Utah 78 C2
Ferrum, Va. 62 D6
Ferry, Alaska 85 G2
Ferry, Mich. 67 G5
Ferry, co., Wash., 3,889 80 D1
Ferryhill, U.K., 10,892 112 g10
Ferryland, Newf., Can. 45 R6
Ferryland Head, Newf., Can. 45 c10
Ferrysburg, Mich., 2,590 67 G5
Ferryville, Wis., 194 66 B5
Fershampenuaz, U.S.S.R. 137 k9
Fertile, Iowa, 386 72 D1
Fertile, Minn, 968 74 D2
Fès, Mor., 216,133 160 D2
Feshi, D.R.Congo 164 C3
Fessenden, N. Dak., 920 74 C2
Festus, Mo., 7,021 72 G6
Feterita, Kans. 75 D6
Feteşti, Rum., 15,383 128 F2
Fethaland, Pt of, U.K. 112 F1
Fethard, Ire. 113 C5
Fethiye, Turk., 7,652 142 B2
Fetlar, i., U.K. 112 F1
Fetoa, i., Tonga 177 36
Fettercairn, U.K. 112 E3
Feucherolles, Fr., 1,288 116 f11
Feucht, F.R.Ger., 6,120 118 C4
Feuchtwangen, F.R.Ger., 3,985 118 C4
Feura Bush, N.Y. 59 v29
Feurs, Fr., 6,252 117 F4
Feversham, Ont., Can. 46 D4
Fewell, Okla. 76 H3
Feyzin, Fr., 3,363 116 p15
Fezzan = Fazzān
Ffestiniog, U.K., 6,708 113 E5
Fianarantsoa, Malag. Rep., 36,189 165 G5
Fianga, Chad, 5,000* 162 G4
Fiat, Ind. 70 D2
Fibiş, Rum. 128 C2
Fibre, Mich. 67 J2
Fichtelberg, F.R.Ger., 2,594 126 a7
Fichtel-Berg, Ger.D.R. 118 D3
Fichtelgebirge, mts., F.R.Ger. 118 C4
Ficksburg, S. Af., 7,778 164 D6
Fidelis, Fla. 65 C2
Fidelity, Ill., 125 68 B4
Fidenza, It., 20,499 123 B2
Fieberbrunn, Aust., 3,014 124 J6
Field, Br. Col., Can. 42 J3
Field, Ont., Can. 46 D2
Fieldale, Va., 1,499 62 D6
Fielding, Utah, 270 78 b7
Fieldon, Ill., 239 68 B4
Fields, La. 73 B7
Fields, Ohio 70 c9
Fields, Oreg. 80 D4
Fieldsboro, N.J., 583 61 B3
Fields Landing, Calif. 82 A2
Fieni, Rum. 128 E2
Fier, Alb., 16,200* 125 D4
Fierbinţi-Tîrg, Rum. 128 F2
Fierro, N. Mex. 79 A5
Fiery Cr., Austl. 173 d11
Fierzë, Alb. 125 D3
Fiesch, Switz. 124 C2
Fiesso Umbertiano, It., 5,239 122 e6
Fife, co., U.K., 320,541 112 E3
Fife, Ga. 64 f10
Fife, Tex. 77 O4
Fife, Wash., 1,463 80 B2
Fife Lake, Mich., 218 67 H4
Fife Ness, U.K. 112 E3
Fifield, Wis. 66 C3
Fifteen Mile Falls Res., N.H.-Vt. 54 D3
Fifth Cataract, Sudan 163 K2
Fifty Lakes, Minn., 143 74 E2
Fifty Mile Pt., Ont., Can. 46 c15
Figanières, Fr. 116 m13
Figari, C., It. 123 B4
Figeac, Fr., 9,108 117 D4
Fighting I., Ont., Can. 67 f16
Figueira da Foz, Port., 10,568 122 A2
Figueiró dos Vinhos, Port., 5,781 122 A3
Figueras, Sp., 17,548 122 G1
Figuig, Mor., 12,108 160 D2
Fiji, Pac. Oc., 472,000* 170 F5
Fijnaart, Neth. 115 a7
Filabusi, Rhod. 164 D5
Filadelfia, Bol., 1,123 102 C4
Filadélfia, Braz., 1,067 103 G3
Filadelfia, Col. 100 C5
Filadelfia, C.R., 1,574 94 E5
Filadelfia, It., 10,359 123 F5
Filadelfia, Para. 105 C2
Fil'akovo, Czech. 126 D2
Filandia, Col. 101 d15
Filbert, S.C. 63 C2
Filbert, W. Va. 62 C5
Filchner Ice Shelf, Ant. 180 N5
Filer, Idaho, 1,249 81 B4
Filer City, Mich. 67 G4
Files, Tex. 76 e10
Filey, U.K., 4,703 113 F4
Filey Brigg, pen., U.K. 114 H2
Filiaşi, Rum. 128 D2
Filiátes, Gr., 3,065 129 C5
Filiatrá, Gr., 6,753 129 C6
Filicudi, I., It. 123 E5
Filimon Sîrbu, Rum. 128 F2
Filingué, Niger, 5,215 162 E3
Filion, Mich. 67 K5
Filiourí, r., Gr. 129 E4
Filippo Reef, Pac. Oc. 177 41
Filipstad, Swed. 120 C4
Fillmore, Sask., Can. 43 D5
Fillmore, Calif., 4,808 82 D5
Fillmore, Ill., 360 68 C4
Fillmore, Ind. 70 C3
Fillmore, co., Minn., 23,768 74 F4
Fillmore, Mo., 254 72 C4
Fillmore, co., Nebr., 9,425 75 H3
Fillmore, N.Y., 522 58 D7
Fillmore, N. Dak. 74 C1
Fillmore, Utah, 1,602 78 B2
Fils, r., F.R.Ger. 119 H7
Fils, L. du, Qué., Can. 46 F2
Filson, Ill. 68 D4
Filstroff, Fr. 116 b8
Filton, U.K., 12,297 114 C7
Filyos, r., Turk. 142 C1
Fimi, r., D.R.Congo 164 B2
Finaguayac, Guam 176 24
Finale Emilia, It., 16,592 123 C2
Finale Ligure, It., 12,027 123 B2
Fincastle, Va., 403 62 E5
Fincham, U.K. 114 J5
Finchingfield, U.K., 1,130 114 J7
Finchville, Ky. 71 F3
Findhorn, r., U.K. 112 E3
Fındıklı, Turk., 3,720 142 E1
Findlay, Ill., 759 68 D4
Findlay, Ohio, 30,344 70 F1
Findley Lake, N.Y. 58 A7
Findochty, U.K., 1,331 112 E3
Fine, N.Y. 59 K3
Finesville, N.J. 61 A2
Fingal, Austl. 173 g13
Fingal, Ont., Can. 46 C6
Fingal, N. Dak., 190 74 D2
Finger, Tenn. 71 C6
Finger Buttes, S. Dak. 74 A3
Finger L., Ont., Can. 44 C4
Finger Lakes, N.Y. 58
Fingoè, Moz. 164 E4
Finike, Turk., 2,942 142 B2
Finisterre, C., Sp. 122 A1
Finke, Austl. 172 E3
Finke, r., Austl. 172 D3
Finksburg, Md. 62 H3
Finland, ctry., 4,631,000* 120
Finland, Minn. 74 G2
Finland, G. of, Eur. 110 F3
Finlay, r., Br. Col., Can. 42 F2
Finlay Forks, Br. Col., Can. 42 F2
Finlayson, Minn., 213 74 F2
Finley, Austl., 1,294 173 F5
Finley, N. Dak., 808 74 D2
Finley, Okla. 76 H3
Finley, Tenn. 71 B5
Finley, Wis. 66 C4
Finleyville, Pa., 582 60 c9
Finmoore, Br. Col., Can. 42 F3
Finney, co., Kans., 16,093 75 E5
Finniss, Austl. 172 c8
Finnmarksvidda, uplands, Nor. 120 E1
Finn Rock, Oreg. 80 B3
Finschhafen, Terr. New Guin. 174 f2
Finspång, Swed. 120 D4
Finsteraarhorn, mtn. Switz. 124 C2
Finsterwalde, Ger.D.R., 20,658 118 D3
Finström, Fin. 120 E3
Fintona, U.K., 1,266 113 C4
Fiordland Nat. Pk., N.Z. 175 e7
Fiorentino, S. Mar., 1,100 123 e11
Fiorenzuola d'Arda, It., 12,890 122 c6
Fīq, Syr., 2,129 142 b7
Firat, r., Turk. 142 D2
Firavitoba, Col. 100 D5
Fircrest, Wash., 3,565 81 a8
Firdale, Man., Can. 43 e9
Firebag, r., Alta., Can. 42 L1
Firebaugh, Calif., 2,070 82 C4
Fire I., Alaska 85 c7
Fire I., N.Y. 58 g14
Fire Island Pines, N.Y. 58 g14
Firenze, It., 428,955 123 C3
Firesteel, S. Dak. 74 B3
Firesteel, r., Mich. 66 D2
Firestone, Colo., 276 79 b7
Firiza, Rum. 128 D1
Firmat, Arg., 8,000* 105 C4
Firminópolis, Braz., 3,259 103 F5
Firminy, Fr., 26,065 117 F4
Firozabad, India, 98,611 145 F4
Firozpur Jhirka, India, 5,775 144 a12
First Broad, r., N.C. 71 K6
First Cataract, U.A.R. 161 K3
First Connecticut L., N.H. 54 E1
Firstview, Colo. 79 D2
Firth, Idaho, 322 81 C4
Firth, Nebr., 277 75 J3
Firth, r., Yukon, Can. 85 J1
Fīrūzābād, Iran, 5,747 143 E3
Firvale, Br. Col., Can. 42 E3
Fisao, Togo, 1,238 162 e7
Fischamend Markt, Aust., 2,913 124 d10
Fischbach, F.R.Ger., 1,295 119 D6
Fischbacher Alpen, Aust. 125
Fischer, Tex. 77 O4
Fish, r., Ala. 64 B5
Fish, r., Me. 55 D2
Fishburn, U.K., 2,324 112 h10
Fish Creek, Fla. 65 F3
Fish Creek, Wis. 66 F3
Fish Cr., E. Br., N.Y. 59 J4
Fish Cr., W. Br., N.Y. 59 J5
Fisheating Cr., Fla. 65 H5
Fisher, Ark., 303 73 D2
Fisher, Ill., 1,155 68 D3
Fisher, La. 73 B6
Fisher, Mich. 67 J7
Fisher, Minn., 326 74 D2
Fisher, Pa. 60 D3
Fisher, co., Tex., 7,865 77 N3
Fisher, Wash. 80 a6
Fisher Branch, Man., Can. 43 F4
Fisher I., Fla. 65 b10
Fishers, N.Y. 58 F5
Fishers I., N.Y. 59 R9
Fisher Str., N.W.T., Can. 41 N5
Fishersville, Va. 62 F4
Fisherville, Ont., Can. 46 E6
Fisherville, Mass., 1,663 57 K4
Fisherville, Mich. 67 J5
Fishguard, U.K., 2,790 113 D6
Fish Hoek, S. Af. 164 a9
Fishhook, Ill. 68 B4
Fishing Creek, Md. 62 H4
Fishing Cr., Pa. 60 H3
Fishing Cr., Pa. 61 K3
Fishing L., Man., Can. 43 G4
Fishing Ship Harbour, Newf., Can. 45 Q4
Fishkill, N.Y., 997 59 N8
Fishkill Cr., N.Y. 59 N8
Fish Lake, Alaska 85 G3
Fish Pt., Mich. 67 K5
Fish River L., Me. 55 D2
Fiskdale (part of Sturbridge), Mass. 56 H4
Fiskeville, R.I. 57 K6
Fismes, Fr., 3,545 117 E2
Fitchburg, Mass., 43,021 57 J2
Fitchville, Conn. 56 H6
Fito, Mt., W. Samoa 177 38
Fitri, L., Chad 163 H3
Fittja, Swed. 120 e8
Fittstown, Okla. 76 G3
Fitzgerald, Alta., Can. 42 K1
Fitzgerald, Ga., 8,781 64 F4
Fitzhugh, Ark. 73 D2
Fitzhugh, Okla. 76 G3
Fitz Roy, Arg. 105 B7
Fitzroy, Falk Is. 108 3
Fitzroy, r., Austl. 172 C2
Fitzroy, r., Austl. 173 G3
Fitz Roy, Co., Arg.-Chile 105 A7
Fitzroy Crossing, Austl. 172 C2
Fitzwilliam, N.H. 54 C6
Fitzwilliam Depot, N.H. 54 C6
Fitzwilliam I., Ont., Can. 44 G6
Fiume = Rijeka
Fiume, G. of = Riječki Zaliv
Fiumicino, It., 7,500* 123 a8
Fiura, C. Verde Is. 109 5
Five Island Harbour, Antigua 97 9
Five Mile, r., Conn. 57 J5
Five Mile Cr., Ala. 64 c7
Fivemiletown, U.K. 113 C4
Five Points, Ala., 285 64 D2
Fivizzano, It., 14,297 123 C2
Fizi, D.R.Congo 164 D2
Fjære, Nor. 121 A2
Fjällbacka, Swed. 121 D2
Fjellerup, Den. 121 C4
Fjerritslev, Den., 2,540 121 B3
Fkih-Ben-Salah, Mor., 13,484 160 C2
Flaach, Switz. 124 C1
Flackville, N.Y. 59 K2
Flacq, Maurit. 165 c12
Fladså, r., Den. 121 B5
Flagler, Colo., 693 79 D2
Flagler, co., Fla., 4,566 65 H3
Flagler Beach, Fla., 970 65 H3
Flag Point, Jam. 96 p8
Flagstaff, Ariz., 18,214 78 C4
Flagstaff Hill, St. Helena 109 7
Flagstaff L., Me. 55 B3
Flagstaff L., Oreg. 80 D4
Flagstaff Mtn., Me. 55 B3
Flaherty, Ky. 71 E4
Flambeau, r., Wis. 66 B3
Flambeau, L., Wis. 66 C3
Flambeau Flowage, Wis. 66 C2
Flamborough, U.K., 1,706 113 F4
Flamborough Head, pen., U.K. 113 G4
Flaming Gorge Nat. Rec. Area, Wyom. 81 E5
Flaming Gorge Res., Utah-Wyo. 81 E5
Flamingo, Fla. 65 J7
Flanagan, Ill., 841 68 D3
Flanagan, r., Ont., Can. 44 C4
Flanders, Ont., Can. 44 D5
Flanders, N.Y., 1,248 59 P10
Flanders, reg., Belg.-Fr. 115 A4
Flanders Village (part of E. Lymetown), Conn. 56 H7
Flandreau, S. Dak., 2,129 74 D3
Flanigan, Nev. 83 A2
Flannagan Res., Va. 62 B5
Flannan Is., U.K. 112 C2
Flasher, N. Dak., 515 74 B2
Flat, Alaska, 27 85 E3
Flat, r., Mich. 67 H5
Flat, r., N.C. 63 E1
Flatbush (part of N.Y.C.), N.Y. 58 d14
Flat Creek, Ala. 64 b7
Flat Creek, Tenn. 71 E6
Flat Cr., Mo. 73 B1
Flateyri, Ice. 120 a6
Flathead, Br. Col., Can. 42 J4
Flathead, co., Mont., 32,965 81 B1
Flathead, r., Can.-U.S. 81 B1
Flathead L., Mont. 81 B2
Flathead Ra., Can.-U.S. 50 D1
Flat Holm, i., U.K. 114 B8
Flat I., Maurit. 165 c12
Flat Mt., N.Z. 175 e7
Flatonia, Tex., 1,009 77 P5
Flat Point = Flag Point
Flatridge, Va. 62 C6
Flat River, Mo., 4,515 72 G7
Flatrock, Newf., Can. 45 c10
Flat Rock, Ala. 64 D1
Flat Rock, Ill., 497 68 E5
Flat Rock, Mich., 4,696 67 K6
Flat Rock, N.C. 63 B2
Flat Rock, Ohio 70 G1
Flat Rock, r., Ind. 70 D3
Flat Rock Butte, N. Dak. 74 A2
Flats, Nebr. 75 D2
Flattery, C., Austl. 173 F2
Flattery, C., Wash. 80 A1
Flattop, Ala. 64 c7
Flat Top, W. Va. 62 C5
Flatwoods, La. 73 B6
Flat Woods, Tenn. 71 D6
Flatwoods, W. Va., 248 62 D4
Flåvatnet, l., Nor. 121 A1
Flavigny, Fr., 1,435 116 b9
Flawil, Switz., 7,256 124 D1
Flaxton, N. Dak., 375 74 A1
Flaxville, Mont., 262 81 G1
Fleckney, U.K., 1,495 114 F5
Fleet, U.K., 12,893 114 G8
Fleeton, Va. 62 H5
Fleetville, Pa. 61 L2
Fleetwood, U.K., 27,760 113 E5
Fleetwood, N.C. 63 C1
Fleetwood, Okla. 76 F4
Fleetwood, Pa., 2,647 61 L5
Flehingen, F.R.Ger., 2,535 119 F6
Flein, F.R.Ger., 2,551 119 G6
Fleischmanns, N.Y., 450 59 M7
Flejsborg, Den. 121 B4
Flekkefjord, Nor., 3,135 120 A4
Fleming, Colo., 384 79 D1
Fleming, co., Ky., 10,890 71 H3
Fleming, Ky., 670 71 J4
Fleming, N.Y. 59 p24
Flemingsburg, Ky., 2,067 71 H3
Flemington, Ga., 149 64 H4
Flemington, Mo., 142 72 D7
Flemington, N.J., 3,232 61 B2
Flemington, Pa., 1,608 60 G3
Flemington, W. Va., 489 62 D3
Flemish Cap, Atl. Oc. 108 J3
Flen, Swed. 120 D4
Flensburg, F.R.Ger., 93,046 118 B1
Flers, Fr., 15,631 117 C2
Flesherton, Ont., Can. 46 D4
Flet, Alb. 125 E3
Fletcher, Mo. 72 G6
Fletcher, N.C. 63 B2
Fletcher, Ohio, 569 70 E2
Fletcher, Okla., 884 76 E3
Fletcher, Tex. 77 m8
Fletcher, Vt. 54 B2
Fletcher Pd., Mich. 67 K3
Fletchers Ridge, Arctic Oc. 108 E1
Fleurance, Fr., 4,310 117 D5
Fleurier, Switz., 3,814 124 A2
Fleury-en-Bière, Fr. 116 i12
Flieden, F.R.Ger., 3,187 118 B3
Flims, Switz., 1,444 124 D2
Flims-Waldhaus, Switz. 124 D2
Flinders, r., Austl. 173 F2
Flinders Bay, Austl. 172 A5
Flinders I., S. Austl., Austl. 172 D5
Flinders I., Tasm., Austl. 173 G6
Flinders Range, Austl. 172 E4
Flin Flon, Man., Can., 10,992 43 E3
Flint, U.K., 13,707 113 E5
Flint, Ala., 432 64 B1
Flint, Mich., 196,940 67 K5
Flint, Okla. 76 J1
Flint, r., Ala.-Tenn. 64 C1
Flint, r., Ga. 64 E2
Flint, r., Mich. 67 K5
Flintham, U.K., 1,208 114 G4
Flint Hill, Va. 62 F4
Flint Hills, Kans. 75
Flint I., Line Is. 171 H5
Flint L., Ind. 69 f10
Flintshire, co., U.K., 150,082 113 E5
Flippen, Ga. 64 g11
Flipper Pt., Wake I. 176 26
Flitwick, U.K., 3,604 114 G6
Flix, Sp., 5,418 122 F2
Flixecourt, Fr., 3,325 117 E1
Flize, Fr., 1,200 117 F2
Floda, Swed. 120 C3
Floda, Swed. 120 d8
Flöha, Ger.D.R. 126 c6
Flomaton, Ala., 1,454 64 B4
Flomot, Tex. 77 N2
Floodwood, Minn., 677 74 F2
Flookburgh, U.K., 1,619 114 C2
Flook L., Oreg. 80 D4
Flora, Ind., 1,742 70 C2
Flora, Ill., 5,331 68 D5
Flora, Miss., 743 73 E5
Flora, Oreg. 80 E3
Florac, Fr., 1,648 117 E4
Floradale, Ont., Can. 46 a13
Floral, Ark. 73 D2
Florala, Ala., 3,011 64 C4
Floral City, Fla. 65 G4
Floral Park, N.Y., 17,499 58 d14
Florange, Fr., 14,270 116 b8
Florânia, Braz., 1,346 103 J3
Floraville, Ill. 68 B5
Florence, N.S., Can., 1,941 47 V10
Florence, Italy = Firenze
Florence, Ala., 31,649 64 B1
Florence, Ariz., 2,143 78 C5
Florence, Ark. 73 D4
Florence, Colo., 2,821 79 C2
Florence, Ga. 64 E3
Florence, Ind. 70 D4
Florence, Kans., 853 75 J5
Florence, Ky., 5,837 71 G3
Florence, Md. 62 a7
Florence (part of Northampton), Mass. 56 F3
Florence, Miss., 360 73 E5
Florence, Mont. 81 C2
Florence, N.J., 4,215 61 B3
Florence, Oreg., 1,642 80 A4
Florence, Pa. 60 B5
Florence, co., S.C., 84,438 63 E4
Florence, S.C., 24,722 63 E3
Florence, S. Dak., 216 74 D3
Florence, Tex., 610 77 O4
Florence, Vt. 54 A4
Florence, co., Wis., 3,437 66 E3
Florence, Wis. 66 E3
Florence Station, Ill. 68 C1
Florencia, Col. 100 C7
Florennes, Belg., 3,761 115 C4
Florensac, Fr., 2,893 117 E5
Florenville, Belg., 2,187 115 D5
Flores, Guat., 1,999 94 C2
Flores, i., Azores 108 2
Flores, i., Indon. 149 G5
Flores I., Br. Col., Can. 42 E4
Flores Sea, Indon. 149 G4
Floresta, Braz., 2,377 103 J3
Floresville, Tex., 2,126 77 O5
Florey, Tex. 77 M3
Florham Park, N.J., 7,222 58 b13
Floriano, Braz., 16,063 103 H3
Floriano Peixoto, Braz. 102 C3
Florianópolis, Braz., 74,323 103 G7
Florica, Rum. 128 F2
Florida, Chile, 1,102 104 e16
Florida, Col. 100 B6
Florida, Cuba, 21,159 96 d2
Florida, Hond., 1,779 94 e8
Florida, S. Af. 165 i17
Florida, st., U.S., 5,796,000* 65
Florida, Mass., 569(T) 56 D2
Florida, N. Mex. 79 B5
Florida, N.Y., 1,550 59 M9

228 · Gachetá—General Piran

Gachetá, Col. 100 D5
Gach Sārān, Iran 143 E2
Gackle, N. Dak., 523 74 C2
Gadag, India, 76,614 145 E7
Gadaisu, Terr. Papua 174 f3
Gadancourt, Fr. 116 f10
Gadara=Umm Qays
Gadarwara, India, 14,696 144 b14
Gäddede, Swed. 120 C2
Gaddy, Okla. 76 F2
Gadebusch, Ger.D.R. 118 C2
Gadmen, Switz. 124 C2
Gadsden, Ala., 58,088 64 D1
Gadsden, Ariz. 78 A5
Gadsden, co., Fla., 41,989 65 E2
Gadsden, S.C. 63 D4
Gadsden, Tenn., 222 71 C6
Gadwal, India, 16,375 145 E6
Găeşti, Rum., 7,179 128 E2
Gaeta, It., 19,625 123 D4
Gaeta, Golfo di, It. 123 D4
Gaferut, i., Car. Is. 176 18
Gaffney, S.C., 10,435 63 C2
Gag, P., Indon. 149 J3
Gagan, i., Kwajalein 176 25
Gage, co., Nebr., 26,818 75 J3
Gage, N. Mex. 79 A5
Gage, Okla., 482 76 D1
Gages Lake, Ill., 3,395 69 c7
Gagetown, N.B., Can. 45 M6
Gagetown, Mich., 376 67 K5
Gaggenau, F.R.Ger., 10,290 118 B4
Gagi, i., Sol. Is. 175 b2
Gagil-Tomil, i., Yap 176 20
Gagnoa, Iv. Coast, 9,120 162 D4
Gagnon, Qué., Can. 45 M4
Gagnon, L., Qué., Can. 47 J2
Gagny, Fr., 29,004 116 i11
Gagra, U.S.S.R., 14,000 137 b1
Gahanna, Ohio, 2,717 70 G2
Gahlen, F.R.Ger., 2,023 119 B1
Gaiac, Mt., St. Lucia 97 11
Gaibānda, Pak., 17,738 144 g13
Găiceana, Rum. 128 F1
Gaïdhouronísi, i., Gr. 129 E7
Gail, Tex. 77 N3
Gaildorf, F.R.Ger., 4,264 119 H7
Gailenkirchen, F.R.Ger., 1,506 119 H6
Gaillac, Fr., 9,058 117 D5
Gaillard, L., Conn. 56 F7
Gaillard Cut, C.Z. 94 g12
Gailtaler Alpen, Aust. 125 ·
Gaima, Terr. Papua 174 d3
Gaiman, Arg., 5,500* 105 B6
Gaines, Mich., 387 67 K6
Gaines, co., Tex., 12,267 77 M3
Gainesboro, Tenn., 1,021 71 F5
Gainesboro, Va. 62 F3
Gainesville, Ala., 214 64 A3
Gainesville, Fla., 29,701 65 G3
Gainesville, Ga., 16,523 64 F1
Gainesville, Mo., 266 72 E8
Gainesville, N.Y., 369 58 D6
Gainesville, Tex., 13,083 77 P3
Gainford, U.K. 114 E1
Gainsborough, U.K., 17,278 113 F5
Gairdner, L., Austl. 172 E4
Gairloch, U.K. 112 D3
Gairloch, U.K. 112 D3
Gais, Switz., 2,488 124 D1
Gaiselberg, Aust. 124 d9
Gaithersburg, Md., 3,847 62 G3
Gajam, Indon. 148 a6
Gajam, Indon. 148 f7
Gakona, Alaska, 33 85 H3
Gala, Va. 62 E5
Galadang, Mt., Phil. 153 c8
Galadi, Eth. 163 M4
Galahad, Alta., Can. 42 K3
Galana, r., Kenya 164 F2
Galanta, Czech., 7,199 126 C2
Galap, Palau 176 21
Galapagos Is.=Colón, Arch. de
Galargambone, Austl. 173 G4
Galas, r., Malay. 147 p14
Galashiels, U.K., 12,374 112 E4
Galatás, Gr., 1,542 129 D6
Galaţi, Rum., 95,646 128 F2
Galatia, Ill., 830 68 D6
Galatia, Kans., 73 75 F5
Galatina, It., 25,190 123 G4
Galatone, It., 14,385 123 F4
Gala Water, r., U.K. 112 e8
Galax, Va., 5,254 62 D6
Galaxídhion, Gr., 1,535 129 D5
Galcaio, Som. Rep., 9,292* 163 M4
Galdhöpiggen, mt., Nor. 120 B3
Gale, r., N.H. 54 D3
Galeana, Mex., 3,127 93 F3
Galela, Indon. 149 H2
Galena, Alaska, 261 85 E2
Galena, Ill., 4,410 68 B1
Galena, Ind. 70 C4
Galena, Kans., 3,827 75 L6
Galena, Md., 299 62 J3
Galena, Mo., 389 72 D8
Galena, Okla. 76 E1
Galena, Oreg. 80 D3
Galena r., Ill. 68 B1
Galena Park, Tex., 10,852 77 i9
Galĕnki, U.S.S.R. 151 F1
Galeota Point, Trin. and Tob. 96 h5
Galera, Ec. 104 B1
Galera, Co., C.Z. 94 g13
Galera, P., Ec. 104 A1
Galera Point, Trin. and Tob. 96 h5
Galesburg, Ill., 37,243 68 B3
Galesburg, Kans., 128 75 K6
Galesburg, Mich., 1,410 67 H6
Gales Ferry (part of Ledyard), Conn. 56 H7
Galesville, Md. 62 H4
Galesville, Wis., 1,199 66 B4
Galetea, Colo. 79 D2
Galeton, Pa., 1,646 60 G2
Galets, Pte. des, La Réunion 165 b11
Galgate, U.K. 114 C3
Gali, U.S.S.R., 10,000 137 b1
Galiano I., Br. Col., Can. 42 c7
Galibi, Sur. 101 N5
Galicea Mare, Rum. 128 D2
Galich, U.S.S.R., 16,100 136 F1
Galiche, Bulg., 5,179 128 D3
Galicia, reg., Sp. 122 A1
Galien, Mich., 750 67 G7
Galilee (part of Narragansett), R.I. 57 L7
Galilee, Sea of=Kinneret, Yam
Galina Point, Jam. 96 q8
Galion, La. 73 D5
Galion, Ohio, 12,650 70 G2
Galion, B. du, Mart. 97 12
Galisteo, N. Mex. 79 C4
Galiuro Mts., Ariz. 78 C5
Gallan Head, U.K. 112 C2
Gallarate, It., 33,447 123 B2
Gällared, Swed. 121 E3
Gallatin, co., Ill., 7,638 68 D6
Gallatin, co., Ky., 3,867 71 G3
Gallatin, Mo., 1,658 72 D5
Gallatin, co., Mont., 26,045 81 D3
Gallatin, Tenn., 7,901 71 E5
Gallatin, Tex. 77 Q4
Gallatin, r., Mont.-Wyo. 81 D3
Gallatin Pk., Mont. 81 D3
Gallatin Ra., Mont. 50 D1
Galle, Cey., 55,848 145 F9
Gállego, r., Sp. 122 E1
Gallegos, N. Mex. 79 D4
Gallegos, r., Arg. 105 A8
Galley Head, Ire. 113 B6
Gallia, co., Ohio, 26,120 70 G4
Galliate, It., 12,215 122 b5
Gallikós, r., Gr. 129 D4
Gallina, N. Mex. 79 B3
Gallina Pk., N. Mex. 79 B3
Gallinas, N. Mex. 79 C4
Gallinas, P., Col. 100 D1
Gallinas, r., N. Mex. 79 C4
Gallinas Mts., N. Mex. 79 B4
Gallinas Pk., N. Mex. 79 C4
Gallion, Ala. 64 B3
Gallipoli, It., 16,954 123 F4
Gallipoli, Turk.=Gelibolu
Gallipolis, Ohio, 8,775 70 G4
Gallipolis Ferry, W. Va. 62 B4
Gallitzin, Pa., 2,783 60 E4
Gällivare, Swed. 120 E2
Gallman, Miss., 100 73 E6
Gallon Jug, Br. Hond. 94 C2
Galloo I., N.Y. 59 G4
Galloway, Br. Col., Can. 42 J4
Galloway, Ark. 73 C3
Galloway, Ohio 70 a7
Galloway, Wis. 66 D4
Galluis, Fr. 116 f11
Gallup, N. Mex., 14,089 79 A4
Gallupville, N.Y. 59 M6
Gallya, O., U.S.S.R. 134 F1
Gälöfjärden, bay, Swed. 120 e9
Galop I., N.Y. 69 C
Galston, U.K., 4,023 112 b8
Galt, Ont., Can., 27,494 44 H7
Galt, Calif., 1,868 82 C3
Galt, Ill. 68 C2
Galt, Iowa, 75 72 D2
Galt, Mo., 373 72 D4
Galt Cr., Ont., Can. 46 b14
Galten, Den. 121 B4
Galten, bay, Swed. 120 d8
Galton, Ill. 68 D4
Galtür, Aust. 124 G7
Galty Mts., Ire. 113 B5
Galu, D.R.Congo 165 n19
Galva, Ill., 3,060 68 B2
Galva, Iowa, 469 72 B2
Galva, Kans., 442 75 H5
Galveston, Ind., 1,111 70 C2
Galveston, co., Tex., 140,364 77 Q5
Galveston, Tex., 67,175 77 Q5
Galveston Bay, Tex. 77 Q5
Galveston I., Tex. 77 Q5
Galwa, Nepal 145 F3
Galway, co., Ire., 155,553 113 B5
Galway, Ire., 21,366 113 B5
Galway, N.Y., 309 59 M5
Galway Bay, Ire. 113 B5
Gam, P., Indon. 149 J3
Gam, r., China-N. Viet. 146 D2
Gamaches, Fr., 3,353 117 D1
Gamagori, Jap., 55,926 154 i15
Gamaliel, Ark. 73 C1
Gamaliel, Ky., 868 71 F5
Gamarra, Col. 100 D3
Gamás, Hung., 2,265 126 C3
Gambach, Bay., F.R.Ger., 1,013 119 H5
Gambach, Hess., F.R.Ger., 2,212 119 F4
Gambaga, Ghana, 1,949 162 D4
Gambang, Malay., 2,571 148 B2
Gambara, It., 4,757 122 d5
Gambela, Eth., 10,500* 163 K4
Gambell, Alaska, 358 85 B3
Gambia, ctry., 315,486 162 B3
Gambia, r., Af. 162 B3
Gambier, Ohio, 1,148 70 G2
Gambier, Is., Fr. Poly. 171 K6
Gambier I., Br. Col., Can. 42 c6
Gambier Is., Austl. 172 b8
Gambo, Newf., Can. 45 Q5
Gamboa, C.Z., 3,489 94 g12
Gambolò, It., 6,871 122 b5
Gamboma, Congo 164 B2
Gambrills, Md. 62 c8
Gambsheim, Fr., 2,834 119 D7
Gambuta, G., Indon. 149 G2
Gameleira, Braz., 5,078 103 b15
Gamerco, N. Mex. 79 A4
Gameren, Neth. 115 c7
Gaming, Aust., 4,220 124 M6
Gamkonora, G., Indon. 149 ·
Gamlakarleby=Kokkola
Gamleby, Swed. 120 D4
Gamlingay, U.K., 1,622 114 H6
Gamō, Jap. 154 h14
Gampaha, Cey., 7,496 145 m22
Gampola, Cey., 10,773 145 n22
Gamprin, Liecht. 124 a8
Gams, Aust. 124 L6
Gams, Switz., 1,984 124 a8
Gamu, Phil., 3,363 153 c5
Gamudoko, i., Palau 176 21
Ganado, Ariz. 78 D4
Ganado, Tex., 1,626 77 P5
Ganale Dorya, r., Eth. 163 L5
Gananoque, Ont., Can., 5,060 44 J7
Gand=Gent
Gandajika, D.R.Congo 164 D3
Gander, Newf., Can., 5,654 45 Q5
Gandesa, Sp., 2,778 122 F2
Gandía, Sp., 20,340 122 E3
Gandrup, Den. 121 C3
Gandy, Nebr., 41 75 E2
Gandy, Utah 78 B2
Ganedidalem, Indon. 149 J3
Ganga, r., India 145 H4
Gangala-na-Bodio, D.R.Congo 164 D1
Gan Gan, Arg., 3,500* 105 B6
Ganganagar, India, 63,854 145 D3
Gangapur, India, 22,591 144 a12
Gangaw, Burma, 3,800 146 A2
Gangelt, F.R.Ger., 3,843 119 A3
Ganges, Fr., 4,953 117 E5
Ganges=Ganga
Ganges, Mouths of the, India 145 H5
Gangoh, India, 18,886 144 a11
Gangotri, India 144 b10
Gang Ranch, Br. Col., Can. 42 G3
Gangtok, Sikkim, 6,848 145 H4
Ganløse, Den., 1,245 121 a7
Gann, Colo. 79 c9
Gannat, Fr., 5,756 117 E3
Gannett Hill, N.Y. 58 E6
Gannett Pk., Wyo. 81 E4
Ganntown, Ill. 68 D6
Gannvalley, S. Dak. 74 C3
Ganongga, i., Sol. Is. 175 b2
Gans, Okla., 234 76 J2
Gansbaai, S. Af., 1,215 164 a9
Gansbach, Aust. 124 b10
Gansevoort, N.Y. 59 N5
Ganshoren, Belg., 13,203 115 d9
Gánt, Hung., 1,216 126 D3
Ganta, Lib. 162 C4
Gantt, Ala. 64 C4
Gantts Quarry, Ala., 238 64 C2
Gantung, Indon. 148 D3
Gantung, Mt., Phil. 153 A3
Gao, Mali, 12,839 162 E3
Gaoua, Upper Volta, 5,864 162 D4
Gaoual, Guin., 4,000 162 B4
Gap, Fr., 21,935 117 F4
Gap, Pa. 61 K6
Gapan, Phil., 6,741 153 B2
Gap Mills, W. Va. 62 D5
Gara, L., Ire. 113 B5
Garachiné, Pan., 1,326 94 H6
Garah, Austl. 173 G4
Garaina, Terr. New Guin. 174 e2
Garakayo, i., Palau 176 21
Garama, Libya 161 G3
Garamba, Parc Nat. de la, D.R.Congo 164 E1
Garanhuns, Braz., 34,050 103 J3
Garantah, Indon. 148 F5
Garapan, Saipan 176 27
Garards Fort, Pa. 60 B6
Garbagna, It., 1,019 122 b6
Garba Tula, Kenya 164 F1
Garber, Iowa 148 72 F2
Garber, Okla., 905 76 F1
Garberville, Calif. 82 B2
Garbyang, India 144 C10
Garça, Braz., 18,155 103 G6
Garches, Fr., 13,676 116 g11
Garchitorena, Phil., 2,050 153 h14
Garcia, Colo. 79 C3
García de la Cadena, Mex., 1,759 93 a8
Garcia-Hernandez, Phil., 2,197 153 f12
Garcitas, Ven., 1,224 100 E3
Gard, r., Fr. 117 F5
Garda, It., 2,574 122 d5
Garda, Lago di, It. 123 C2
Gardanne, Fr., 11,311 117 F5
Gardeja, Pol. 127 C2
Gardelegen, Ger.D.R., 12,434 118 C2
Garden, co., Nebr., 3,472 75 C2
Garden, Mich., 380 67 G3
Garden, r., Ont., Can. 46 A2
Gardena, Calif., 35,943 83 h16
Gardena, N. Dak., 113 74 B1
Garden City, Ala., 536 64 C1
Garden City, Ga., 5,451 64 H3
Garden City, Kans., 11,811 75 E6
Garden City, Mich., 38,017 67 K6
Garden City, Mo., 600 72 C6
Garden City, N.Y., 23,948 59 N10
Garden City, S. Dak., 226 74 D3
Garden City, Tex. 77 N4
Garden City, Utah, 168 78 C1
Gardendale, Ala., 4,712 64 C2
Garden Grove, Calif., 84,238 83 i16
Garden Grove, Iowa, 335 72 D4
Garden Home, Oreg. 80 a7
Garden I., Mich. 67 H3
Garden River, Ont., Can. 44 G6
Gardenton, Man., Can. 43 h10
Gardenville, Pa. 60 f10
Gardey, Arg. 105 b13
Gardez, Afghan., 46,000* 144 C2
Gardi, Ga. 64 H4
Gardiner, Me., 6,897 55 C4
Gardiner, Mont. 81 D3
Gardiner, Oreg. 80 A4
Gardiner, Wash. 81 a6
Gardiner Pk., N. Mex. 79 B5
Gardiners Bay, N.Y. 59 Q9
Gardiners I., N.Y. 59 Q9
Gardner, Colo. 79 C3
Gardner, Fla. 65 H5
Gardner, Ill., 1,041 68 D2
Gardner, Kans., 1,619 75 K5
Gardner, Mass., 19,038 56 J2
Gardner, N. Dak., 107 74 D2
Gardner, atoll, Phoenix Is. 170 G5
Gardner Can., Br. Col., Can. 42 E3
Gardner L., Conn. 56 G6
Gardner L., Me. 55 E4
Gardner Pinnacles, is., Hawaii 84 f9
Gardnerville, Nev. 83 A3
Gardno, Jez., Pol. 127 B1
Gardo, Som. Rep., 4,697* 163 N4
Gardone Riviera, It., 2,745 122 d5
Gárdony, Hung., 5,113 126 D3
Gardula, Eth. 163 L5
Gare Loch, U.K. 112 D3
Garelochhead, U.K. 112 a7
Gareloi I., Alaska 85 f8
Garešnica, Yug., 2,326 125 C2
Garfield, co., Colo., 12,017 79 A2
Garfield, Ga., 225 64 G3
Garfield, Kans., 278 75 F5
Garfield, Minn., 240 74 E3
Garfield, co., Mont., 1,981 81 F2
Garfield, co., Nebr., 2,699 75 F2
Garfield, N. Mex. 79 B5
Garfield, N.J., 29,253 58 c13
Garfield, co., Okla., 52,975 76 F1
Garfield, co., Utah, 3,577 78 C3
Garfield, co., Wash., 2,976 80 E2
Garfield, Wash., 607 80 E2
Garfield, Mass. 56 D4
Garfield Center, Kans. 75 H4
Garfield Heights, Ohio, 38,455 70 e9
Garforth, U.K., 14,641 114 F3
Gargaliánoi, Gr., 6,637 129 C6
Gargenville, Fr., 3,134 116 f11
Garges-lès-Gonesse, Fr., 10,398 116 h11
Gargnäs, Swed. 120 D2
Gargrave, U.K., 1,417 114 D3
Gargunnock, U.K. 112 b7
Garhakota, India, 11,341 144 b14
Garhwa, India, 11,656 145 G4
Gari, U.S.S.R. 137 k7
Garibaldi, Br. Col., Can. 42 G4
Garibaldi, Oreg., 1,163 80 A3
Garies, S. Afr., 1,103 164 B7
Garissa, Kenya 164 F2
Garland, Ala. 64 C4
Garland, co., Ark., 46,697 73 B3
Garland, Ark., 377 73 B4
Garland, Kans. 75 L6
Garland, Me. 55 C3
Garland, N.C., 642 63 F3
Garland, Pa. 60 C2
Garland, Tenn., 168 71 B6
Garland, Tex., 38,501 77 P3
Garland, Utah, 1,119 78 B1
Garlandville, Miss. 73 F5
Garlasco, It., 8,869 122 b5
Garlin, Fr. 117 C5
Garm, U.S.S.R. 137 f4
Garmisch-Partenkirchen, F.R.Ger., 23,938 118 C5
Garmo, Pik, U.S.S.R. 137 f5
Garnavillo, Iowa, 662 72 F2
Garner, Iowa, 1,990 72 D1
Garner, N.C., 3,451 63 F2
Garner, Tex. 76 d9
Garnet, Mich. 67 H2
Garnett, Kans., 3,034 75 K5
Garnoch, r., U.K. 112 a8
Garoe, Som. Rep., 3,790* 163 N4
Garonne, r., Fr. 117 D4
Garoth, India, 6,571 145 E4
Garoua, Cam., 13,000 162 G4
Garoua Boulaï, Cam., 3,000* 162 G5
Garove, i., Terr. New Guin. 174 f2
Garrard, co., Ky., 9,747 71 G4
Garrattsville, N.Y. 59 K6
Garrebourg, Fr. 116 d9
Garrel, F.R.Ger., 6,114 118 B2
Garretson, S. Dak., 850 74 D4
Garrett, Ill., 249 68 D4
Garrett, Ind., 4,364 70 D1
Garrett, Ky. 71 J4
Garrett, co., Md., 20,420 62 E3
Garrett, Pa., 617 60 D6
Garrett, Tex., 167 76 f10
Garrett Park, Md., 965 62 a8
Garretts Bend, W. Va. 62 C4
Garrettsville, Ohio, 1,662 70 H1
Garrick, Sask., Can. 43 D4
Garrison, Iowa, 421 72 E2
Garrison, Ky. 71 H3
Garrison, Minn., 118 74 F2
Garrison, Mont. 81 C2
Garrison, Nebr., 82 75 H2
Garrison, N. Mex. 79 D5
Garrison, N.Y. 59 N9
Garrison, N. Dak., 1,794 74 B2
Garrison, Tex., 951 55 Q4
Garrison, Utah 78 B2
Garrison Res., N. Dak. 74 A2
Garrochales, P.R. 96 s10
Garroch Head, U.K. 112 a8
Garrovillas, Sp., 5,764 122 B3
Garry, r., U.K. 112 D3
Garry Bay, N.W.T., Can. 41 M4
Garry L., N.W.T., Can. 40 J4
Gars, Aust., 1,529 124 M5
Garsen, Kenya 164 F2
Garske, N. Dak. 74 C1
Garson, Man., Can. 43 h9
Garson, Ont., Can., 3,786 46 D2
Garstang, U.K., 1,439 113 E5
Garstedt, F.R.Ger., 9,236 119 a8
Garsten, Aust., 5,333 124 L5
Gartempe, r., Fr. 117 D3
Garthbeibio, U.K. 114 A5
Gartok=Ko-ta-k'o
Gartow, F.R.Ger., 1,409 118 C2
Gartz, Ger.D.R. 118 E2
Garukoru, i., Palau 176 21
Garut, Indon. 148 C4
Garvald, U.K. 112 e8
Garvăn, Rum. 128 G2
Garvin, co., Okla., 28,290 76 F3
Garvin, Okla., 109 76 H4
Garwin, Iowa, 546 72 E2
Garwolin, Pol., 6,723 127 D3
Garwood, N.J., 5,426 58 b14
Garwood, Tex. 77 P5
Gary, Ind., 178,320 70 B1
Gary, Minn., 262 74 D2
Gary, S. Dak., 471 74 D3
Gary, Tex. 77 Q3
Gary, W. Va., 1,393 62 C5
Garysburg, N.C., 181 63 G1
Garyton, Ind. 69 f10
Garyville, La., 2,389 73 E7
Garz, Ger.D.R. 118 D1
Garza, co., Tex., 6,611 77 N3
Garza-Little Elm Res., Tex. 77 P3
Garzan=Zok
Garzón, Col. 100 C6
Gasan-Kuli, U.S.S.R., 2,800 134 E6
Gasburg, Va. 62 G6
Gas City, Ind., 4,469 70 D2
Gascogne, reg., Fr. 117 C5
Gascogne, G. de, Fr. 116 ·
Gascon, N. Mex. 79 C4
Gasconade, co., Mo., 12,195 72 F6
Gasconade, Mo., 333 72 F6
Gasconade, r., Mo. 72 E7
Gascony=Gascogne
Gascoyne, N. Dak., 50 74 A2
Gascoyne, r., Austl. 172 A3
Gash, r., Eth. 163 L3
Gashua, Nigeria 162 F3
Gaskiers, Newf., Can. 45 b11
Gaspar, Cuba, 1,740 96 d2
Gaspar, Selat-Selat, Indon. 148 C3
Gaspar Hernández, Dom. Rep., 1,327 96 m6
Gaspé, Qué., Can., 2,524 45 N5
Gaspé, B. de, Qué., Can. 47 T9
Gaspé, C., Qué., Can. 47 T9
Gaspé, Pén. de, Qué., Can. 45 M5
Gaspé Passage, Qué., Can. 45 N5
Gasport, N.Y. 58 C5
Gasquet, Calif. 82 B2
Gas-san, Jap. 155 F2
Gassaway, W. Va., 1,223 62 D4
Gassetts, Vt. 54 B5
Gassino Torinese, It., 5,497 122 a5
Gassville, Ark., 233 73 C1
Gaston, Ind., 801 70 D2
Gaston, co., N.C., 127,074 63 C2
Gaston, N.C., 1,214 63 G1
Gaston, Oreg., 320 80 B3
Gaston, S.C. 63 C4
Gastonia, N.C., 37,276 63 C2
Gastonia, Tex. 76 g9
Gastoúni, Gr., 4,360 129 C6
Gastre, Arg., 3,900* 105 B6
Gata, C., Cyp. 142 e10
Gata, C. de, Sp. 122 D4
Gata, Sa. de, Sp. 122 B2
Gataga, r., Br. Col., Can. 42 E1
Gătaia, Rum. 128 C2
Gatchel, Ind. 70 C4
Gatchina, U.S.S.R., 33,300 134 B4
Gate, Okla., 130 76 C1
Gate, Wash. 80 B2
Gate City, Va., 2,142 62 B6
Gatehouse, U.K. 113 D4
Gatere, Sol. Is. 175 b2
Gates, Nebr. 75 F2
Gates, co., N.C., 9,254 63 H1
Gates, N.C. 63 H1
Gates, Oreg., 189 80 B3
Gates, Tenn., 291 71 B6
Gates Center, N.Y. 58 n20
Gateshead, U.K., 103,232 113 F4
Gateshead I., N.W.T., Can. 40 K3
Gates Mills, Ohio, 1,588 70 f8
Gatesville, N.C., 460 63 H1
Gatesville, Tex., 4,626 77 O4
Gateway, Ark., 63 73 B1
Gateway, Colo. 79 A2
Gateway, Oreg. 80 C3
Gath Mine, Rhod. 164 E5
Gatineau, Qué., Can., 12,963 47 J3
Gatineau, r., Qué., Can. 44 J6
Gatjug Entr., Yap 176 20
Gatlinburg, Tenn., 1,764 71 H6
Gato, Pico del, Cuba 96 e2
Gatooma, Rhod., 10,400 164 D5
Gatschapar, Yap 176 20
Gattaran, Phil., 1,926 153 B1
Gattières, Fr. 116 n13
Gattinara, It., 7,768 122 b5
Gattman, Miss., 145 73 G4
Gatton, Austl., 2,163 173 H4
Gatukai, i., Sol. Is. 175 b2
Gatun, C.Z. 94 f11
Gatún, r., Pan. 94 g11
Gatuncillo, r., Pan. 94 g11
Gatun Dam, C.Z. 94 f11
Gatun L., C.Z.-Pan. 94 G6
Gatun Locks, C.Z. 94 f11
Gatzke, Minn. 74 E1
Gaua I.=Sta. Maria
Gaucín, Sp., 3,689 122 C4
Gaud-i-Zirreh, salt flat, Afghan. 144 B3
Gauer L., Man., Can. 43 F2
Gaugers, Ill. 69 c10
Gauhati, India, 100,707 145 J4
Gauja, r., U.S.S.R. 136 B1
Gauldry, U.K. 112 e7
Gauley, r., W. Va. 62 D4
Gauley Bridge, W. Va. 62 C4
Gaurdak, U.S.S.R., 4,200 134 F6
Gausta, mt., Nor. 120 B4
Gautavai, W. Samoa 177 38
Gavaloú, Gr., 1,624 129 C5
Gavardo, It., 8,064 122 d5
Gavarnie, Fr. 117 D5
Gavdhopoúla, i., Gr. 129 D7
Gávdhos, i., Gr. 129 E7
Gave de Pau, r., Fr. 117 C5
Gavia Grande, Guat. 94 c9
Gavião, Port., 2,801 122 B3
Gavilan, N. Mex. 79 B3
Gavins Pt. Dam, Nebr.-S. Dak. 75 H1
Gaviota, Calif. 82 D5
Gävle, Swed., 54,768 120 D3
Gavorrano, It., 15,832 123 C3
Gavray, Fr., 1,180 117 C2
Gavrilov-Yam, U.S.S.R., 20,100 136 F1
Gávrion, Gr. 129 E6
Gawa, i., Terr. Papua 174 3
Gawai, Burma 146 B1
Gawler, Austl., 5,117 172 E5
Gawler Ranges, Austl. 172 a7
Gawsworth, U.K., 1,093 114 D4
Gay, U.S.S.R. 137 i9
Gay, Ga., 194 64 E2
Gay, Mich. 66 E1
Gay, N.C. 63 A2
Gay, Okla. 76 H4
Gay, W. Va. 62 C4
Gaya, India, 151,105 145 G4
Gaya, Niger, 3,507 162 E3
Gayaza, Uganda 165 e14
Gaychur, r., U.S.S.R. 136 e8
Gay Head, Mass., 103(T) 57 N7
Gayles, U.K. 112 g11
Gaylord, Kans., 239 75 G4
Gaylord, Mich., 2,568 67 J3
Gaylord, Minn., 1,631 74 E3
Gaylord, Oreg. 80 A4
Gaylordsville (part of New Milford), Conn. 56 B6
Gaylor Mtn., Ark. 73 A2
Gayndah, Austl., 1,644 173 G3
Gayny, U.S.S.R. 137 h6
Gays, Ill., 263 68 D4
Gaysin, U.S.S.R., 17,500 136 C3
Gays Mills, Wis., 634 66 C5
Gaysville, Vt. 54 B4
Gayville, S. Dak., 261 74 D4
Gayvoron, U.S.S.R., 12,800 136 C3
Gaywood (part of King's Lynn), U.K., 7,507 114 J5
Gaza=Ghazzah
Gaza Strip=Ghazzah, Qiṭā'
Gazelle, Calif. 82 B2
Gazelle Pen., Terr. New Guin. 174 f2
Gaziantep, Turk., 125,498 142 D2
Gázoros, Gr., 2,587 129 D4
Gbarnga, Lib. 162 C4
Gboko, Nigeria 162 F4
Gdańsk, Pol., 286,000* 127 C1
Gdov, U.S.S.R., 3,600 136 B1
Gdów, Pol. 127 k7
Gdynia, Pol., 148,000* 127 C1
Gearhart, Oreg., 725 80 A2
Geary, co., Kans., 28,779 75 J5
Geary, Okla., 1,416 76 E2
Geauga, co., Ohio, 47,573 70 H1
Geauga Lake, Ohio 70 H1
Gebe, P., Indon. 149 J3
Gebeit Mine, Sudan 163 K2
Gebo, Wyo. 81 E4
Gebze, Turk., 7,867 142 B1
Geddes, S. Dak., 380 74 C4
Gede, Tg., Indon. 148 C4
Gedern, F.R.Ger., 2,973 118 B3
Gedinne, Belg. 115 C5
Gedi Ruins, Kenya 164 F2
Gediz, Turk., 7,308 142 B2
Gediz, r., Turk. 142 B2
Gedong, Malay., 1,779 148 D2
Gedser, Den. 121 D6
Gedser Odde, Den. 121 E6
Gedsted, Den., 1,276 121 B4
Geel, Belg., 25,727 115 C3
Geelong City, Austl., 20,034 173 F6
Geelvink Chan., Austl. 172 A4
Geer, r., Belg. 115 D4
Geertruidenberg, Neth., 4,200 115 b7
Geesthacht, F.R.Ger., 19,530 118 C2
Geetbets, Belg., 3,113 115 D4
Geeveston, Austl. 173 f14
Gefell, Ger.D.R. 126 a6
Geff, Ill. 68 D5
Gefrees, F.R.Ger., 2,922 126 a6
Geharty, Mt., Austl. 172 b7
Gehh, i., Kwajalein 176 25
Gehua, Terr. Papua 174 f3
Geidam, Nigeria 162 F3
Geiger, Ala., 104 64 A3
Geigertown, Pa. 61 L5
Geikie, r., Sask., Can. 43 D2
Geilenkirchen, F.R.Ger., 7,830 119 A3
Geilo, Nor. 120 B3
Geiranger, Nor. 120 A3
Geiselhöring, F.R.Ger., 2,996 118 D4
Geisenfeld, F.R.Ger., 2,844 118 C4
Geisenhausen, F.R.Ger., 2,678 118 D4
Geisenheim, F.R.Ger., 7,172 119 D4
Geislingen, F.R.Ger., 23,843 118 B4
Geispolsheim, Fr., 3,672 119 D7
Geistown, Pa., 3,186 60 E5
Geist Res., Ind. 70 D3
Geita, Tanz. 164 E2
Geithain, Ger.D.R. 126 b5
Gela, It., 52,542 123 E6
Gelam, P., Indon. 148 D3
Gelantipy, Austl. 173 f11
Geldermalsen, Neth., 5,400 115 D3
Geldern, F.R.Ger., 9,642 119 A1
Geldrop, Neth., 12,700 115 D3
Geleen, Neth., 30,400 115 D4
Gelendzhik, U.S.S.R., 14,200 136 E4
Gelert, Ont., Can. 46 F4
Gelib, Som. Rep., 10,510* 163 M5
Gelibolu, Turk., 12,956 142 A1
Gelidonya Burnu, pt., Turk. 142 B2
Geliting, Indon. 149 G5
Gelligaer, U.K., 34,656 114 B7
Gellinam, i., Kwajalein 176 25
Gelnhausen, F.R.Ger., 7,979 118 B3
Gelnica, Czech. 126 E2
Gels, r., Den. 121 B5
Gelsenkirchen, F.R.Ger., 374,697 118 A3
Gelsted, Den., 2,365 121 B5
Gelterkinden, Switz., 3,870 124 B1
Gelting, F.R.Ger., 1,667 118 B1
Gelucourt, Fr. 116 c9
Geluwe, Belg., 6,047 116 a6
Gem, co., Idaho, 9,127 81 A4
Gem, Kans., 116 75 E4
Gem, Tex. 76 N2
Gem, W. Va. 62 D4
Gemas, Malay., 4,841 147 p15
Gembloux, Belg., 5,858 115 C4
Gemena, D.R.Congo 164 C1
Gemert, Neth., 8,200 115 D3
Gem Lake, Minn., 305 74 c5
Gemlik, Turk., 12,731 142 B1
Gemmell, Minn. 74 E2
Gemmrigheim, F.R.Ger., 2,330 119 G6
Gemona del Friuli, It., 12,671 123 D1
Gémozac, Fr., 2,194 117 C4
Gemünd, F.R.Ger., 3,569 118 A3
Gemünden, Bay., F.R.Ger., 3,649 119 H4
Gemünden, Hess., F.R.Ger., 2,379 118 B3
Gemünden, Rhein.-Pfalz, F.R.Ger., 1,071 119 C5
Gemuru, Indon. 148 F3
Genale, Som. Rep. 163 M5
Genappe, Belg., 1,801 115 C4
Genarp, Swed. 121 F5
Genay, Fr., 1,458 116 p15
Genazzano, It., 5,280 123 b8
Gençay, Fr., 1,076 117 D3
Gending, Indon. 148 e7
Gene Autry, Okla., 110 76 F3
Genemuiden, Neth., 4,200 115 D2
General Acha, Arg., 6,000* 105 B5
General Alvear, Arg., 3,229 105 a13
General Alvear, Arg., 10,364 105 B4
General Aquino, Para. 105 D2
General Artigas, Para., 3,233 105 D3
General Belgrano, Ant. 180 O5
General Belgrano, Arg., 7,700* 105 b12
General Bravo, Mex., 1,717 93 F3
General Cabrera, Arg., 4,200* 105 C4
General Campos, Arg., 6,000* 105 b10
General Cepeda, Mex., 3,832 92 E3
General Conesa, Arg., 2,500* 105 C5
General Conesa, Arg. 105 c13
General Galarza, Arg., 3,700* 105 b11
General Guido, Arg., 4,093 105 b13
General Jesús Agustín Castro, Mex., 2,901 92 E3
General José de San Martín, Arg., 70,000* 105 C3
General Lagos, Chile 105 B1
General Lavalle, Arg., 2,107 105 D5
General Luna, Phil., 2,072 153 B2
General Luna, Phil., 3,473 153 C3
General MacArthur, Phil., 2,835 153 C3
General Madariaga, Arg., 9,500* 105 c13
General Mansilla, Arg., 4,019* 105 c12
General Mitre, Arg., 3,400* 105 C3
General Nikolaevo, Bulg., 11,948 128 E3
General O'Brien, Arg., 2,845 105 a12
General Paz, Arg., 4,500* 105 D3
General Paz, Arg., 8,738 105 D5
General Pedro Antonio Santos, Mex., 1,673 93 f8
General Pico, Arg., 25,176* 105 C5
General Pinedo, Arg., 6,500* 105 C3
General Piran, Arg., 2,011 105 b13

General Plaza—Glenrothes · 229

General Plaza, Ec. 104 c11
General Proaño, Ec., 104 c11
General Roca, Arg., 28,000* 105 B5
General Rodríguez, Arg., 18,621 105 b12
General San Martín, Arg., 5,500* 105 C5
General San Martín, Arg., 49,053 105 b12
General Santos, Phil., 13,529 153 C4
General Terán, Mex., 3,739 93 F3
General Toshevo, Bulg., 5,999 128 G3
General Treviño, Mex., 1,500 93 F2
General Trías, Mex. 92 D2
General Trias, Phil., 6,011 153 c8
General Vicente Guerrero, Mex., 6,086 92 E3
General Villegas, Arg., 9,500* 105 C5
Genesee, Idaho, 535 81 A2
Genesee, co., Mich., 374,313 67 K5
Genesee, Mich. 67 K5
Genesee, co., N.Y., 53,994 58 D6
Genesee, Pa. 60 G2
Genesee, Wis. 66 c12
Genesee, r., N.Y.-Pa. 58 E6
Genesee Depot, Wis. 66 c12
Geneseo, Ill., 5,169 68 B2
Geneseo, Kans., 558 75 G5
Geneseo, N.Y., 3,284 58 E6
Geneva, Switz.=Genève
Geneva, co., Ala., 22,310 64 D4
Geneva, Ala., 3,840 64 D4
Geneva, Ga., 261 64 E3
Geneva, Ill., 7,646 68 D2
Geneva, Ind., 1,053 70 D2
Geneva, Iowa, 219 72 D2
Geneva, Kans. 75 K5
Geneva, Ky. 71 D4
Geneva, Minn., 347 74 F4
Geneva, Nebr., 2,352 75 H3
Geneva, N.Y., 17,286 58 G6
Geneva, Ohio, 5,677 70 J1
Geneva, Wash. 80 B1
Geneva, L., Wis. 66 E6
Geneva, L. of=Léman, L.
Geneva-on-the-Lake, Ohio, 631 70 H1
Genève, Switz., 176,183 124 A2
Genge, D.R.Congo 165 n18
Gengenbach, F.R.Ger., 5,402 118 A4
Genghis Khan, Wall of, Asia 150 F1
Genichesk, U.S.S.R., 14,300 136 D4
Génicourt, Fr. 116 g10
Genil, r., Sp. 122 C4
Genjem, Indon. 149 L3
Genk, Belg., 46,554 115 D4
Genlis, Fr., 2,264 117 F3
Gennep, Neth., 4,500 115 D3
Gennes, Fr., 1,457 117 C3
Gennevilliers, Fr., 42,611 116 h11
Genoa, Austl. 173 g11
Genoa, It.=Genova
Genoa, Colo., 185 79 D2
Genoa, Fla. 65 G2
Genoa, Ill., 2,862 68 D1
Genoa, Nebr., 1,009 75 H2
Genoa, Nev. 83 A3
Genoa, N.Y. 59 G6
Genoa, Ohio, 1,957 70 F1
Genoa, Tex. 77 i9
Genoa, Wis., 325 66 B5
Genoa City, Wis., 1,005 66 E6
Genola, Minn., 108 74 E3
Genola, Utah, 380 78 c10
Génova, Guat., 1,769 94 b9
Genova, It., 758,491 123 B2
Genova, Golfo di, It. 123 B2
Genovesa, I., Colón, Arch. de 104 b7
Genriyetty, O., U.S.S.R. 135 P2
Gens-de-Terre, r., Qué., Can. 47 H1
Gent, Belg., 160,669 115 B3
Genteng, Indon. 148 C4
Genthin, Ger.D.R., 15,197 118 D2
Gentilly, Qué., Can. 47 M2
Gentilly, Fr., 19,211 116 h11
Gentilly, Minn. 74 D2
Gentofte, Den., 88,308 121 E5
Gentry, Ark., 686 73 A1
Gentry, co., Mo., 8,793 72 C4
Gentry, Mo., 98 72 C4
Gentryville, Ind., 297 70 B4
Genzano di Roma, It., 12,211 123 b8
Geoagiu Băi, Rum. 128 D2
Geographe Bay, Austl. 172 A5
Geographe Chan., Austl. 172 A3
Geographical Center of U.S., S. Dak. 74 A3
Geokchay, U.S.S.R., 17,000 137 c1
Geok-Tepe, U.S.S.R., 4,900 134 E6
Georga, Zemlya, U.S.S.R. 134 D1
George, S. Af., 14,505 164 C7
George, Iowa, 1,200 72 B1
George, co., Miss., 11,098 73 G7
George, r., Qué., Can. 45 N2
George, L., Austl. 173 g10
George, L., N.B., Can. 55 E3
George, L., Uganda 165 e14
George, L., Alaska 85 c7
George, L., Fla. 65 H3
George, L., Ind. 69 e10
George, L., Mich. 67 J2
George, L., N.Y. 59 N4
George Bay, N.S., Can. 47 V11
George V Coast, Ant. 180 U6
George Gills Range, Austl. 172 D3
George I., Falk. Is. 108 3
George River, Qué., Can. 45 N2
Georges Bank, Atl. Oc. 108 H4
Georges Fork, Va. 62 B5
Georges Is., Me. 55 C5
George VI Sound, Ant. 180 N5
Georges Mills, N.H. 54 C5
George Sd., N.Z. 175 e7
Georgesville, Ohio 70 a7
Georgetown, Ascension 109 6
Georgetown, Qnsld., Austl. 1,868 173 F2
Georgetown, Tasm., Austl. 173 f13
George Town, Bah. Is. 95 D2
Georgetown, Ont., Can., 10,150 46 D5
Georgetown, P.E.I., Can. 47 U10
Georgetown, Gambia 162 B3
Georgetown, Grand Cayman, 2,558 97 3
Georgetown, Guyana, 162,000* 101 M4
George Town, Malay., 234,930 148 A1
Georgetown, St. Vinc., 1,212 97 19
Georgetown, Ark. 73 D2
Georgetown, Calif. 82 C3
Georgetown, Colo., 307 79 B2
Georgetown (part of Redding, Wilton, Weston), Conn. 56 C7
Georgetown, Del., 1,765 62 J4
Georgetown, Fla. 65 H3
Georgetown, Ga., 554 64 E4
Georgetown, Idaho, 551 81 D4
Georgetown, Ill., 3,544 68 E4
Georgetown, Ky., 6,986 71 G3
Georgetown, La., 321 73 C6
Georgetown, Mass., 3,755(T) 57 M2
Georgetown, Minn., 178 74 D2
Georgetown, Miss., 285 73 E6
Georgetown, N.Y. 59 J6
Georgetown, Ohio, 2,674 70 E4
Georgetown, Beaver Co., Pa., 246 60 A4
Georgetown, Luzerne Co., Pa., 2,275* 61 o17
Georgetown, co., S.C., 34,798 63 E4
Georgetown, S.C., 12,261 63 E4
Georgetown, Tex., 5,218 77 O4
George Washington Carver Nat. Mon., Mo. 72 C7
George West, Tex., 1,878 77 O5
Georgia, st., U.S., 4,391,000* 64
Georgia, Ind. 70 C4
Georgia, N.J. 58 b16
Georgia, Str. of, Br. Col., Can. 42 b6
Georgia Center, Vt. 54 A2
Georgiana, Ala., 2,093 64 C4
Georgian Bay, Ont., Can. 44 G6
Georgian Bay Is. Nat. Pk., Ont., Can. 46 D4
Georgian S.S.R.=Gruzinskaya S.S.R.
Georgia Plains, Vt. 54 A2
Georgiaville (part of Smithfield), R.I. 57 K5
Georgina, r., Austl. 172 E3
Georgiyevsk, U.S.S.R., 35,200 136 F4
Gera, Ger.D.R., 101,373 118 D3
Gera, Mich. 67 K5
Gera, r., Ger.D.R. 118 C3
Geraardsbergen, Belg., 10,004 115 B4
Gerabronn, F.R.Ger., 2,202 118 B4
Geral, Sa., Braz. 103 G7
Gerald, Mo., 474 72 F6
Geral'd, O., U.S.S.R. 135 S2
Geral de Goiás, Sa., Braz. 103 G4
Geraldine, N.Z., 1,831 175 f7
Geraldine, Ala., 340 64 C1
Geraldine, Mont., 364 81 D2
Geraldton, Austl., 8,309 172 A4
Geraldton, Ont., Can., 3,267 44 E5
Gerard, Me. 55 B3
Gérardmer, Fr., 9,626 117 G2
Geras, Aust. 124 M5
Gerasdorf, Aust., 3,524 124 c10
Gerāsh, Iran, 6,062 143 E3
Gerber, Calif. 82 B2
Gerber Res., Oreg. 80 C4
Gerbichi, G., U.S.S.R. 135 K3
Gerbstedt, Ger.D.R. 118 C3
Gerdine, Mt., Alaska 85 F3
Gerede, Turk., 5,357 142 C1
Gering, Nebr., 4,585 75 B2
Gerlach, Nev. 83 A2
Gerlachovka, pk., Czech. 126 E2
Gerlachsheim, F.R.Ger., 1,560 119 H5
Gerlafingen, Switz., 4,413 124 B1
Gerlane, Kans. 75 G6
Gerlaw, Ill. 68 B3
Gerlingen, F.R.Ger., 8,507 119 G7
Gerlos, Aust. 124 J6
German Democratic Republic, ctry., 17,048,000* 118
Germania, Miss. 73 E5
Germania, Pa. 60 G2
Germania, Wis. 66 D5
Germansen Landing, Br. Col., Can. 42 F2
Germanton, N.C., 162 63 D1
Germantown, Ill., 983 68 C5
Germantown, N.Y. 59 N7
Germantown, Ohio, 3,399 70 E3
Germantown, Tenn., 1,104 71 B6
Germantown, Wis., 622 66 E5
German Valley, Ill., 224 68 C1
Germany, Federal Republic of, ctry., 57,100,000* 118-9
Germersheim, F.R.Ger., 5,785 119 E6
Germfask, Mich. 67 H2
Germī, Iran 137 c2
Germiston, S. Af., 204,605 165 k17
Gernsbach, F.R.Ger., 5,821 119 E7
Gernsheim, F.R.Ger., 6,723 119 F5
Gero, Jap., 16,163 155 E4
Gero I., Me. 55 C2
Gerolstein, F.R.Ger., 3,408 118 A3
Gerolzhofen, F.R.Ger., 5,067 118 C4
Gerona, Phil., 3,151 153 b7
Gerona, Sp., 32,784 122 G2
Geronimo, Okla., 199 76 E3
Geronimo, Tex. 76 c6
Gerrish, N.H. 54 D5
Gerry, N.Y. 58 B7
Gers, r., Fr. 117 D5
Gersau, Switz., 1,754 124 C1
Gersfeld, F.R.Ger., 2,281 119 H4
Gersprenz, r., F.R.Ger. 119 F5
Gersthofen, F.R.Ger., 8,931 118 C4
Gerty, Okla., 135 76 G3
Gervais, Oreg., 438 80 B3
Gervais L., Minn. 74 c5
Géryville=El-Bayadh
Gerze, Turk., 4,668 142 C1
Gesäter, Swed. 121 D2
Gescher, F.R.Ger., 5,423 118 A3
Geseke, F.R.Ger., 10,951 118 B3
Geser, Indon. 149 J3
Gesoa, Terr. Papua 174 d3
Gesten, Den., 1,428 121 B5
Gestro, Webi, Eth. 163 L4
Getafe, Sp., 21,895 122 D2
Getchell Mine, Nev. 83 B2
Getentiri, Indon. 149 L4
Gethsémani, Qué., Can. 45 O5
Getinge, Swed. 121 E4
Gettorf, F.R.Ger., 3,458 118 B1
Gettysburg, Pa., 7,960 60 H6
Gettysburg, S. Dak., 1,950 74 C3
Gettysburg Nat. Mil. Pk. Cem., Pa. 60 H6
Getz Ice Shelf, Ant. 180 X5
Getzville, N.Y. 58 k18
Geumpang, Indon. 148 A1
Gevaş, Turk., 3,575 142 E2
Gevelsberg, F.R.Ger., 30,571 119 C2
Gevgelija, Yug., 5,777 125 F4
Gex, Fr., 2,475 117 G3
Geyer, Ger.D.R. 126 b6
Geyers-Kopf, F.R.Ger. 118 B4
Gezira=Al Jazīrah
Gföhl, Aust., 1,448 124 M5
Ghabāghib, Syr. 142 c6
Ghadames=Ghudāmis
Ghaggar, r., India 144 a11
Ghaghara, r., India 144 d12
Ghana, ctry., 7,740,000* 162 D4
Ghansor, India 144 b14
Ghantiai, India 145 D4
Ghanzi, Bots. 164 C5
Gharbīyah, Aş Şaḥrā, U.A.R. 161 J3
Ghardaïa, Alg., 14,046 160 E2
Gharyān, Libya 161 G2
Ghāt, Libya 161 F3
Ghatal, India 21,062 144 f14
Ghats, Eastern, ra., India 145 F7
Ghaydah, S. Ar. 143 E6
Ghayl Bā Wazīr, S. Ar. 143 D5
Ghazāl, Bahr al, Sudan 163 J4
Ghazal, Bahr el, Chad 162 G3
Ghazaouet, Alg., 12,625 160 D2
Ghaziabad, India, 70,438 144 a11
Ghazipur, India, 37,147 144 d13
Ghazīr, Leb., 3,578 142 b5
Ghazni, Afghan., 19,000* 144 C2
Ghazzah 161 K2
Ghazzah, Qiţā', reg. 142 A8
Ghedi, It., 11,091 122 d5
Gheen, Minn. 74 F2
Ghent, Belg.=Gent
Ghent, Ky., 342 71 F3
Ghent, Minn., 326 74 E3
Ghent, N.Y. 59 N7
Gheorgheni, Rum., 11,969 128 E1
Gherla, Rum., 7,617 128 D1
Ghesto, Ont., Can. 67 g16
Ghilvaci, Rum. 128 D1
Ghimbi, Eth. 163 K4
Ghiorac, Rum. 128 C1
Ghioroc, Rum. 128 C1
Ghisonaccia, Fr., 1,577 116 r17
Ghizão, Afghan. 144 C2
Ghod, India 145 h17
Ghod, r., India 145 i17
Gholson, Miss. 73 G5
Ghorband, Afghan. 144 C2
Ghubaysh, Sudan 163 J3
Ghudāf, Wādī al, Iraq 143 C2
Ghudāmis, Libya 161 F2
Ghulam Muhammad Bge., Pak. 144 C4
Ghuriān, Afghan. 144 A2
Gia Dinh, S. Viet., 25,500 147 m11
Gia Hoa, N. Viet. 147 i9
Giamame, Som. Rep., 21,073 163 M5
Gia Nghia, S. Viet., 1,705 147 m10
Giant, Calif. 83 e11
Giant Hill, Nebr. 75 E1
Giao Duc, S. Viet. 147 k11
Gia Rai, S. Viet. 147 k12
Gibara, Cuba, 8,144 96 e2
Gibbon, Minn., 896 74 E3
Gibbon, Nebr., 1,083 75 G3
Gibbon, Oreg. 80 D3
Gibbons Station, Alta., Can. 43 b7
Gibbonsville, Idaho 81 B3
Gibbs, Mo., 158 72 E4
Gibbsboro, N.J., 2,141 60 g12
Gibbs City, Mich. 66 E2
Gibbs Hill, Berm. Is. 108 1
Gibbstown, N.J., 2,820 61 A4
Gibeon, S.-W. Afr. 164 B6
Gibraleón, Sp., 8,865 122 B4
Gibraltar, U.K., 25,000* 122 C4
Gibraltar, Mich., 2,196 67 K6
Gibraltar, Pa. 61 h14
Gibraltar, Ven. 100 E3
Gibraltar Pt., Ont., Can. 46 d13
Gibraltar Pt., U.K. 113 G5
Gibsland, La., 1,150 73 B5
Gibson, Ga., 479 64 G2
Gibson, co., Ind., 29,949 70 B4
Gibson, La. 73 E8
Gibson, N. Mex. 79 A4
Gibson, N.C., 501 63 E3
Gibson, co., Tenn., 44,699 71 B5
Gibson, Tenn., 297 71 C6
Gibsonburg, Ohio, 2,540 70 F1
Gibson City, Ill., 3,453 68 D3
Gibson Desert, Austl. 172 C3
Gibsonia, Pa., 1,150 60 B4
Gibson Island, Md. 62 c8
Gibsons, Br. Col., Can., 1,011 42 F4
Gibsonton, Fla., 1,673 65 G5
Gibsonville, N.C., 1,784 63 E1
Gibtown, Tex. 76 d8
Giddings, Tex., 2,821 77 P4
Gideå, Swed. 120 D3
Gideon, Mo., 1,411 72 H8
Gien, Fr., 10,254 117 E3
Giengen, F.R.Ger., 8,116 118 C4
Gier, r., Fr. 116 p15
Gierle, Belg., 2,452 115 C3
Giessen, F.R.Ger., 58,178 118 B3
Giessendam, Neth., 3,900 115 b7
Giessen-Nieuwkerk, Neth. 115 b7
Gif, Fr., 4,064 116 g12
Giffard, Qué., Can., 10,082 45 L6
Gifford, U.K. 112 e8
Gifford, Fla., 3,509 65 J5
Gifford, Ill., 609 68 D3
Gifford, Ind. 70 B1
Gifhorn, F.R.Ger., 14,251 118 C2
Gifu, Jap., 304,492 155 E4
Gigant, U.S.S.R., 11,300 136 F4
Giganta, Co. Mex. 92 C2
Giganta, Sa. de la, Mex. 92 C3
Gigen, Bulg., 5,874 128 E3
Giggleswick, U.K. 114 D2
Gigha, Sd. of, U.K. 112 D4
Gigha I., U.K. 112 D4
Gig Harbor, Wash., 1,094 81 a8
Giglio, Isola del, It. 123 C3
Gigmoto, Phil., 2,189 153 i14
Gignac, Fr., 2,594 117 E5
Gihon, r., Vt. 54 B2
Gijón, Sp., 124,714 122 C1
Gila, co., Ariz., 25,745 78 C5
Gila, N. Mex. 79 A5
Gila, r., Eth. 163 K4
Gila, r., Ariz.-N. Mex. 52 D4
Gila Bend, Ariz., 1,813 78 B5
Gila Cliff Dwellings Nat. Mon., N. Mex. 79 A5
Gila Mts., Ariz. 78 D5
Gilău, Rum. 128 D1
Gilberdyke, U.K., 1,129 114 G3
Gilbert, Ariz., 1,833 78 C5
Gilbert, Iowa, 318 72 D2
Gilbert, La., 472 73 D5
Gilbert, Minn., 2,591 74 F2
Gilbert, S.C., 171 63 C4
Gilbert, W. Va., 874 62 C5
Gilbert, Wis. 66 D3
Gilbert, r., Austl. 173 F2
Gilbert and Ellice Is., Pac. Oc., 48,780 170 F5
Gilbert Is., Gilb. and Ellice Is. 170 F4
Gilbertown, Ala., 270 64 A4
Gilbert Plains, Man., Can. 43 E4
Gilbert River, Austl. 173 F2
Gilbertsville, N.Y., 522 59 K7
Gilbertsville, Pa. 61 L5
Gilbertville, Iowa, 533 72 E2
Gilbertville, Me. 55 B4
Gilbertville, Mass., 1,202 56 H3
Gilby, N. Dak., 281 74 D1
Gilchrist, co., Fla., 2,868 65 G3
Gilchrist, Mich. 67 H2
Gilchrist, Oreg. 80 C4
Gilchrist, Tex. 77 Q5
Gilcrest, Colo., 357 79 c7
Gildersleeve (part of Portland), Conn. 56 F6
Gildford, Mont. 81 D1
Gilead (part of Hebron), Conn. 56 G6
Gilead, Ill. 68 B4
Gilead, Me. 55 B4
Gilead, Mich. 67 H7
Gilead, Nebr., 79 75 H3
Gile Flowage, Wis. 66 C2
Giles, co., Tenn., 22,410 71 D6
Giles, co., Va., 17,219 62 D5
Gilford, Mich. 67 K5
Gilford, N.H. 54 E4
Gilford Station, N.H. 54 E4
Gilgandra, Austl., 2,032 173 G4
Gilgil, Kenya 164 F2
Gilgit, Pak. 145 D2
Giligaon, Phil., 1,751 153 d12
Gil I., Br. Col., Can. 42 D3
Gilkey, N.C. 63 B2
Gill, Mass., 1,203(T) 56 F2
Gill, L., Ire. 113 B4
Gillam, Man., Can. 43 G3
Gilleleje, Den., 2,512 121 E4
Gillenfeld, F.R.Ger., 1,057 119 B4
Gilles, L., Austl. 172 E5
Gillespie, Ill., 3,569 68 C4
Gillespie, co., Tex., 10,048 77 O4
Gillespie Pt., N.Z. 175 f6
Gillett, Ark., 1,184 74 D3
Gillett, Tex. 77 P5
Gillett, Wis., 1,374 66 E4
Gillette, Fla. 65 c12
Gillette, Wyo., 3,580 81 G3
Gilletts, Ill. 69 c10
Gillham, Ark., 177 73 A3
Gilliam, La. 73 B5
Gilliam, Mo., 249 72 D5
Gilliam, co., Oreg., 3,069 80 C3
Gilliat, Austl. 173 F3
Gillies Bay, Br. Col., Can. 42 b6
Gillifitz, Yap 176 20
Gilling, U.K. 112 g11
Gillingham, Dorset, U.K., 3,619 113 E6
Gillingham, Kent, U.K., 72,910 113 G6
Gillingham, Wis. 66 C5
Gillis, La. 73 B7
Gill Pt., St. Helena 109 7
Gills Rock, Wis. 66 C4
Gilly, Belg., 25,116 115 C4
Gilman, Ill., 1,704 68 D3
Gilman, Iowa, 491 72 E3
Gilman, Vt. 54 D3
Gilman, Wis., 379 66 C3
Gilman City, Mo., 379 72 D4
Gilmanton, N.H. 54 E5
Gilmanton, Wis. 66 B4
Gilmanton Iron Works, N.H. 54 E5
Gilmer, co., Ga., 8,922 64 E1
Gilmer, Ill. 69 b8
Gilmer, Tex., 4,312 77 Q3
Gilmer, co., W. Va., 8,050 62 D4
Gilmerton, U.K. 112 c7
Gilmore, Alaska 85 b6
Gilmore, Ark., 438 73 E2
Gilmore, Ill. 68 D4
Gilmore L., Wis. 66 B2
Gilort, r., Rum. 128 D2
Gilpin, co., Colo., 685 79 C2
Gilroy, Calif., 7,348 82 C4
Gilson, Ill. 68 B3
Gilston, U.K. 112 e8
Gilsum, N.H. 54 C5
Giltner, Nebr., 293 75 G3
Gilze, Neth., 4,400 115 C3
Gimborn, F.R.Ger., 6,372 119 C2
Gimbsheim, F.R.Ger., 3,319 119 E5
Gimel, Switz., 1,091 124 A2
Gimie, Mt., St. Lucia 97 11
Gimli, Man., Can., 1,766 43 F5
Gimont, Fr., 2,650 117 D5
Gindie, Austl. 173 G3
Ginebra, Col. 100 B6
Ginger I., V.I. 97 4
Gingerland, Nevis, 3,071 97 6
Gingin, Austl. 172 A4
Gin Gin, Austl. 173 G3
Gingoog, Phil., 9,152 153 C3
Gingoog Bay, Phil. 153 C3
Gings, Ind. 70 D3
Ginir, Eth. 163 L4
Ginneken, Neth. 115 b7
Ginosa, It., 17,758 123 F4
Ginsheim-Gustavsburg, F.R.Ger., 10,265 119 E5
Ginzo de Limia, Sp., 9,680 122 B1
Gioher, Som. Rep. 163 M5
Gioia del Colle, It., 28,335 123 F4
Gioia Tauro, It., 15,271 123 E5
Giong Trom, S. Viet., 9,745 147 m11
Giornico, Switz., 1,063 124 C2
Gipières, Fr. 116 m13
Gippsland, reg., Austl. 173 f12
Girard, Ga. 64 H2
Girard, Ill., 1,734 68 C4
Girard, Kans., 2,350 75 L6
Girard, Mich. 67 J6
Girard, Ohio, 12,997 70 J1
Girard, Pa., 2,451 60 B1
Girard, Tex. 77 N3
Girardot, Col. 100 C5
Girardota, Col. 101 d13
Girardville, Pa., 2,958 61 K4
Giraumont, Fr., 2,064 116 b8
Girdle Ness, U.K. 112 F3
Girdler, Ky. 71 H5
Girdletree, Md. 62 J4
Girdwood, Alaska, 63 85 c7
Giresun, Turk., 19,946 142 D1
Giri, r., D.R.Congo 164 C1
Giridih, India, 35,881 145 H4
Girilambone, Austl. 173 G4
Girishk, Afghan., 27,000* 144 B3
Gîrliciu, Rum. 128 G2
Giroc, Rum. 128 C2
Girón, Ec., 1,912 104 B2
Gironde, estuary, Fr. 117 C4
Giroux, Man., Can. 43 h10
Girouxville, Alta., Can. 42 H2
Girsby, U.K. 112 h11
Girton, U.K., 3,115 114 J6
Giru, Austl. 173 G2
Girvan, U.K., 6,159 113 D4
Girvin, Tex. 77 M4
Gisborne, N.Z., 21,769 175 h5
Gisburn, U.K. 114 D3
Giscome, Br. Col., Can. 42 G2
Gisenyi, Rwanda 165 d14
Gislaved, Swed. 120 C4
Gisors, Fr., 6,734 117 D2
Gistel, Belg., 5,706 115 A3
Giswil, Switz., 2,656 124 C2
Gitarama, Rwanda 165 d15
Gitega, Burundi 165 d15
Giuba=Juba
Giubiasco, Switz., 4,281 124 D2
Giugliano in Campania, It., 29,871 123 c10
Giulianova, It., 14,841 123 E3
Giulvăz, Rum. 128 C2
Giurgeni, Rum. 128 F2
Giurgiu, Rum., 32,613 128 F3
Give, Den., 3,841 121 B5
Givet, Fr., 7,925 117 F1
Givhans, S.C. 63 D4
Givors, Fr., 7,066 117 F4
Givry, i., Truk 176 19
Gîza=Al Jīzah
Giza, ruins, U.A.R. 161 i8
Gizhduvan, U.S.S.R., 11,000 134 F5
Gizhiga, U.S.S.R. 135 Q3
Gizhiginskaya G., U.S.S.R. 135 P3
Gizo, i., Sol. Is. 175 b2
Giżycko, Pol., 14,549 127 D1
Gjalicës, Mal i, Alb. 125 E3
Gjedved, Den. 121 B5
Gjerstad, Nor. 121 A2
Gjinar, Alb. 125 E4
Gjirokastër, Alb., 14,100 125 D4
Gjoa Haven, N.W.T., Can. 40 K4
Gjöv, r., Nor. 121 A2
Gjövdal, Nor. 121 A2
Gjövik, Nor., 7,733 120 B3
Gjuhëzës, Kep i, Alb. 125 D4
Glace, W. Va. 62 D5
Glace Bay, N.S., Can., 23,653 45 P6
Glacier, Br. Col., Can. 42 H3
Glacier, co., Mont., 11,565 81 C1
Glacier, Wash. 80 C1
Glacier Bay, Alaska 85 K4
Glacier Bay Nat. Mon., Alaska 85 K4
Glacier Creek, Yukon, Can. 40 A5
Glacier Nat. Pk., Br. Col., Can. 42 H3
Glacier Nat. Pk., Mont. 81 B1
Glacier Pk., Wash. 80 C1
Glacier Str., N.W.T., Can. 41 O2
Gladbeck, F.R.Ger., 79,158 119 B1
Gladbrook, Iowa, 949 72 E2
Glade, Kans., 133 75 F4
Gladehill, Va. 62 E6
Glade Mills, Pa. 60 c7
Gladenbach, F.R.Ger., 3,161 119 F3
Glade Park, Colo. 79 A2
Glades, co., Fla., 2,950 65 H6
Glade Spring, Va., 1,407 62 C6
Gladestry, U.K. 114 B6
Gladewater, Tex., 5,742 77 Q3
Gladsakse, Den., 64,693 121 a7
Gladstone, Qnsld., Austl., 6,944 173 G3
Gladstone, S. Austl., Austl. 172 E5
Gladstone, Tasm., Austl. 173 g13
Gladstone, Man., Can., 1,838 43 F5
Gladstone, Ill., 356 68 B3
Gladstone, Mich., 5,267 66 F3
Gladstone, Mo., 14,502 75 a7
Gladstone, N. Mex. 79 C3
Gladstone, N. Dak., 185 74 A2
Gladstone, Oreg., 3,854 80 B3
Gladstone, Va. 62 F5
Glad Valley, S. Dak. 74 A3
Gladwin, co., Mich., 10,769 67 J4
Gladwin, Mich., 2,226 67 J5
Glady, W. Va. 62 E4
Gladys, Va. 62 E5
Glaisdale, U.K. 114 G2
Glåma, r., Nor. 120 B3
Glamis, U.K. 112 E3
Glamis, Calif. 82 F6
Glamoč, Yug. 125 C2
Glamorganshire, co., U.K., 1,229,728 113 E6
Glamsbjerg, Den. 121 C5
Glan, r., F.R.Ger. 119 D5
Gland, Switz., 1,545 124 A2
Glandorf, Ohio, 747 70 E1
Glanerbrug, Neth., 7,500 115 F2
Glanford Station, Ont., Can. 46 c15
Glang, Thai. 147 d4
Glarner Alpen, Switz. 124 C2
Glarus, Switz., 5,852 124 C1
Glasbury, U.K. 114 B6
Glasco, Kans., 812 75 H4
Glasco, N.Y. 59 M7
Glascock, co., Ga., 2,672 64 G2
Glasford, Ill., 1,012 68 C3
Glasgow, U.K., 1,054,913 112 D4
Glasgow, Ill., 166 68 B4
Glasgow, Ky., 10,069 71 F4
Glasgow, Mo., 1,200 72 E5
Glasgow, Mont., 6,398 81 F1
Glasgow, Va., 1,091 62 E5
Glasgow, W. Va., 914 62 C4
Glashütte, Ger.D.R. 118 D3
Glaslyn, Sask., Can. 43 B4
Glas Maol, mtn., U.K. 122 E3
Glass, Va. 62 H5
Glassboro, N.J., 10,253 61 A4
Glasscock, co., Tex., 1,118 77 N4
Glass Mtn., Calif. 82 C2
Glass Mts., Tex. 77 M4
Glassport, Pa., 8,418 60 C5
Glassville, N.B., Can. 47 S10
Glastenbury Mtn., Vt. 54 A6
Glastonbury, U.K., 5,602 113 E6
Glastonbury, Conn., 14,497(T) 56 F6
Glaubendorf, Aust. 124 b9
Glauchau, Ger.D.R., 33,653 118 D3
Glavacioc, r., Rum. 128 E2
Glavan, Bulg., 2,533 128 F3
Glazier, Tex. 76 N1
Glazov, U.S.S.R., 61,000 134 E4
Gleason, Tenn., 900 71 C5
Gleason, Wis. 66 D3
Gleasondale (part of Stow), Mass. 57 K3
Gleason L., Minn. 74 b6
Gleichen, Alta., Can. 42 K4
Gleinalpe, Aust. 125 ·
Gleisdorf, Aust., 4,400 124 M6
Glen, Nebr. 75 B1
Glen, N.H. 54 E3
Glen, Miss. 73 G3
Glen, W. Va. 62 C4
Glen, r., U.K. 114 H5
Glenaire, Mo., 341 75 b7
Glen Allan, Ont., Can. 46 a13
Glenallen, Mo., 113 72 G7
Glen Allen, Va. 62 G5
Glen Alpine, N.C., 734 63 C2
Glénan, Îs. de, Fr. 116 A3
Glen Arbor, Mich. 67 H4
Glenarm, U.K. 113 D4
Glenarm, Ill. 68 C4
Glen Artney, U.K. 112 b7
Glen Aubrey, N.Y. 59 J7
Glenavon, Sask., Can. 43 D5
Glenbarr, U.K. 112 D4
Glenbeulah, Wis., 428 66 F5
Glenboro, Man., Can. 43 E5
Glenbrook (part of Stamford), Conn. 56 B8
Glenbrook, Nev. 83 A3
Glenburn, N. Dak., 363 74 B1
Glenburn, Pa. 61 o15
Glen Burnie, Md. 62 H3
Glen Campbell, Pa., 400 60 E4
Glen Canyon Dam, Ariz. 78 C3
Glen Canyon Nat. Rec. Area, Utah 78 C3
Glen Carbon, Ill., 1,241 68 C5
Glencliff, N.H. 54 D4
Glencoe, Ont., Can., 1,146 46 C6
Glencoe, Ala., 2,592 64 D2
Glencoe, Ill., 10,472 68 E1
Glencoe, Ky. 71 G3
Glencoe, Minn., 3,216 74 E3
Glencoe, Okla., 284 76 F1
Glen Cove, Me. 55 C4
Glen Cove, N.Y., 23,817 59 N10
Glencross, S. Dak. 74 B3
Glendale, Ariz., 30,760 78 B5
Glendale, Calif., 119,442 82 D5
Glendale, Fla. 65 C2
Glendale, Ind. 70 B4
Glendale, Kans. 75 H5
Glendale (part of Stockbridge), Mass. 56 C3
Glendale, Minn. 74 F1
Glendale, Mo., 7,048 72 a11
Glendale, Nev. 83 C4
Glendale, Ohio, 2,823 71 i10
Glendale, Oreg., 748 80 B4
Glendale, R.I. 57 K5
Glendale, Utah, 223 78 B3
Glendale, Wash. 81 b7
Glendale, W. Va., 1,905 62 D3
Glendale, Wis., 10,432 66 d11
Glendale Hts., DuPage Co., Ill., 7,419 69 b9
Glendale Hts., Pope Co., Ill., 173 68 D6
Glen Dean, Ky. 71 E4
Glendive, Mont., 7,058 81 G2
Glendo, Wyo., 292 81 G4
Glendola, N.J. 58 c16
Glendon, Alta., Can. 42 K2
Glendon, Pa., 555 61 k18
Glendora, Calif., 20,752 83 i15
Glendora, Mich. 67 G7
Glendora, Miss., 147 73 E4
Glendo Res., Wyo. 81 G4
Glen Easton, W. Va. 62 D3
Glen Echo, Md., 310 62 a9
Gleneden Beach, Oreg. 80 A3
Glen Elder, Kans., 444 75 G4
Glenelg, U.K. 112 D3
Glenelg, Md. 62 b7
Glenella, Man., Can. 43 F5
Glenelly, r., U.K. 113 C4
Glen Ellyn, Ill., 15,972 69 b9
Glen Falloch, U.K. 112 a7
Glen Falls, N.Y., 18,580 59 N5
Glenfarg, U.K. 112 d7
Glenfield, N.Y. 59 K4
Glenfield, Pa., 741 60 b7
Glenfield, N. Dak., 129 74 C2
Glen Flora, Tex. 77 P5
Glen Flora, Wis., 75 66 C3
Glenford, Ohio, 190 70 G3
Glen Gardner, N.J., 787 61 B2
Glengariff, Ire. 113 B6
Glengarnock, U.K. 112 a8
Glengary, W. Va. 62 F3
Glengoffe, Jam. 96 q8
Glenham, S. Dak., 171 74 B3
Glen Haven, Ga., 4,050 64 h10
Glen Haven, Mich. 67 G4
Glenhaven, Wis. 66 B6
Glenhayes, W. Va. 62 B4
Glenhead, U.K. 112 c7
Glen Hope, Pa., 169 60 E4
Glen Innes, Austl., 5,842 173 H4
Glen L., Mich. 67 G4
Glen Lednock, U.K. 112 b7
Glenloch, Pa. 60 e11
Glenluce, U.K. 113 D4
Glen Lyon, Pa., 4,173 61 K3
Glen Mills, Pa. 60 e12
Glenmont, N.Y. 59 v29
Glenmont, Ohio, 283 70 G2
Glenmoore, Pa. 60 e11
Glenmora, La., 1,447 73 C7
Glenmorgan, Austl. 173 G4
Glen Morris, Ont., Can. 46 b14
Glenn, co., Calif., 17,245 82 B3
Glenn, Calif. 82 B3
Glenn, Mich. 67 G6
Glennallen, Alaska, 169 85 H3
Glenn Dale, Md. 62 b9
Glennie, Mich. 67 K4
Glenn Ranch=Lytle Creek
Glenns Ferry, Idaho, 1,374 81 B4
Glenn Springs, S.C. 63 C3
Glennville, Calif. 82 D5
Glennville, Ga., 2,791 64 H4
Glen Ogle, U.K. 112 b7
Glenolden, Pa., 7,249 60 f12
Glenora, Br. Col., Can. 42 D1
Glen Park, N.Y., 561 59 J3
Glenpool, Okla., 353 76 H2
Glen Ridge, Fla., 226 65 b8
Glen Ridge, N.J., 8,322 58 c13
Glenrio, Tex. 76 M2
Glen Robertson, Ont., Can. 47 K3
Glen Rock, N.J., 12,896 58 c13
Glen Rock, Pa., 1,546 60 J6
Glen Rock, R.I. 57 K6
Glenrock, Wyo., 1,584 81 G4
Glen Rose, Tex., 1,422 77 P3
Glenrothes, U.K. 112 E3

Glen St. Mary, Fla., 329 65 G2
Glenshaw, Pa. 60 c7
Glenside, Pa., 22,600* 61 M5
Glen Summit, Pa. 61 o17
Glenties, Ire. 113 B4
Glen Turret, U.K. 112 c7
Glen Ullin, N. Dak., 1,210 74 A2
Glenview, Ill., 18,132 68 E1
Glenville (part of Greenwich),
  Conn. 56 B8
Glenville, Minn., 643 74 F4
Glenville, N.C. 63 A2
Glenville, W. Va., 1,828 62 D4
Glen Water, r., U.K. 112 b8
Glenwillard, Pa., 1,150* 60 a7
Glen Williams, Ont., Can. 46 c13
Glenwillow, Ohio, 359 70 f9
Glen Wilton, Va. 62 E5
Glenwood, Newf., Can., 1,130
  45 Q5
Glenwood, Ala., 416 64 C4
Glenwood, Ark., 1,145 73 B3
Glenwood, Ga., 682 64 G3
Glenwood, Hawaii 84 F4
Glenwood, Ill., 882 69 d10
Glenwood, Iowa, 4,783 72 B3
Glenwood, Md. 62 a7
Glenwood, Mich. 67 G6
Glenwood, Minn., 2,631 74 E3
Glenwood, Mo., 242 72 E4
Glenwood, N. Mex. 79 A5
Glenwood, N.Y. 58 C6
Glenwood, Oreg. 80 B3
Glenwood, Utah, 277 78 C2
Glenwood, Kitsap Co., Wash.
  81 a8
Glenwood, Klickitat Co., Wash.
  80 C2
Glenwood, W. Va. 62 B4
Glenwood City, Wis., 835 66 A3
Glenwood Springs, 3,637
  79 B2
Glenwoodville, Alta., Can. 42 K4
Glezen, Ind. 70 B4
Glibu, Terr. Papua 174 3
Glidden, Iowa, 993 72 C2
Glidden, Wis. 66 C2
Glide, Oreg. 80 B4
Glienicke, Ger.D.R. 118 D2
Glienicke, Ger.D.R. 119 e10
Glifádha, Gr., 12,361 129 D6
Glin, Ire. 113 B5
Glina, Yug. 125 C2
Glina, r., Yug. 125 B2
Glinde, F.R.Ger., 5,744 119 b8
Glindow, Ger.D.R. 119 d11
Glinojeck, Pol. 127 D2
Gliwice, Pol., 135,000* 127 C3
Gliwicki, Kan., Pol. 127 h6
Globe, Ariz., 6,217 78 C5
Glodzhovo, Bulg., 4,680 128 F3
Gloggnitz, Aust., 7,225 124 N6
Głogów, Pol., 7,945 127 B3
Głogówek, Pol., 5,134 127 B3
Głogów Małopolski, Pol., 2,106
  127 D3
Glomfjord, Nor. 120 D2
Glommersträsk, Swed. 120 E2
Glonn, F.R.Ger., 2,721 118 C4
Glorieta, N. Mex. 79 C4
Glorieuses, Îs., Ind. Oc. 165 G3
Glóssa, Gr., 1,456 129 D5
Glossop, U.K., 17,430 114 E4
Gloster, Miss., 1,369 73 E6
Glostrup, Den., 21,845 121 a7
Gloucester, Austl., 1,894 173 H5
Gloucester, U.K., 69,773 113 E6
Gloucester, Mass., 25,789 57 O2
Gloucester, co., N.J., 134,840
  61 A4
Gloucester, co., Va., 11,919 62 H5
Gloucester, Va. 62 H5
Gloucester City, N.J., 15,511
  60 f12
Gloucester Point, Va. 62 H5
Gloucestershire, co., U.K.,
  1,001,706 113 E6
Glouster, Ohio, 2,255 70 G3
Glover, Mo. 72 G7
Glover, Vt., 230 54 C2
Glover Cr., Okla. 76 J3
Glovergap, W. Va. 62 D3
Glover Reef, Br. Hond. 94 D2
Gloversville, N.Y., 21,741 59 M5
Głowno, Pol., 11,154 127 C3
Głubczyce, Pol., 8,905 127 B3
Glubokaya, r., U.S.S.R. 136 g7
Glubokaya, r., U.S.S.R. 136 F3
Glubokoye, U.S.S.R., 7,000
  136 B2
Głuchołazy, Pol., 10,599 127 B3
Gluck, S.C. 63 B3
Glücksburg, F.R.Ger., 4,592
  118 B1
Glückstadt, F.R.Ger., 11,699
  118 B2
Glukhov, U.S.S.R., 21,000 136 D3
Glumslöv, Swed. 121 b7
Glusburn, U.K., 2,706 114 D3
Głuszyca, Pol., 6,471 127 f6
Glychedd, mtn., U.K. 114 A5
Glyde, Pa. 60 b9
Glyncorrwg, U.K., 9,368 114 A7
Glyndon, Minn., 489 74 D2
Glyngøre, Den., 1,020 121 A4
Glynn, co., Ga., 41,954 64 H4
Glyn Neath, U.K. 114 A7
Gmünd, Aust., 2,192 124 K7
Gmünd, Aust., 6,549 124 M5
Gmunden, Aust., 12,473 124 K6
Gnadendorf, Aust. 124 c9
Gnadenhutten, Ohio, 1,257
  70 H2
Gnarp, Swed. 120 D3
Gnarrenburg, F.R.Ger., 2,051
  118 B2
Gnas, Aust. 124 M7
Gnesta, Swed. 120 e8
Gniben, pt., Den. 121 D4
Gniew, Pol., 3,879 127 C2

Gniewkowo, Pol., 4,575 127 C2
Gniezno, Pol., 44,000* 127 B2
Gnjilane, Yug., 13,000* 125 E3
Gnoien, Ger.D.R. 118 D2
Gnosall, U.K., 2,098 114 D5
Gnowangerup, Austl. 172 B5
Goa, un. terr., India 145 D7
Goaigoaza, Ven. 101 a11
Goalpara, India, 13,692 145 J4
Goaso, Ghana 162 b8
Goat Fell, mtn., U.K. 112 D4
Goathland, U.K. 114 G2
Goat Island, Barbuda 97 8
Goat I., Lord Howe I. 175 12
Goat Mtn., N. Mex. 79 B5
Goat Rocks, mtn., Wash. 80 C2
Goba, Eth. 163 L4
Gobabis, S.-W. Afr., 4,316
  164 C5
Goback Mtn., N.H. 54 D2
Gôbara, Jap. 155 m19
Gobernador, N. Mex. 79 B3
Gobernador Gregores, Arg.
  105 B7
Gobi, des., China-Mong. 150 E2
Gobi Altay, ra., Mong. 150 D2
Gobles, Ont., Can. 46 a15
Gobles, Mich., 816 67 H6
Goboô, Jap., 30,700 155 D5
Goch, F.R.Ger., 13,864 118 A3
Gochas, S.-W. Afr. 164 C6
Gochsheim, F.R.Ger., 3,655
  118 C3
Go Cong, S. Viet., 16,660
  147 m11
Goczałkowice Zdrój, Pol. 127 i7
Goczałkowickie, Jez., Pol. 127 h7
Godairi, India 145 G6
Godalming, U.K., 15,780 113 F6
Go Dau Ha, S. Viet., 10,725
  147 m11
Godavari, r., India 145 F6
Godbout, Qué., Can. 45 M5
Godda, India, 7,500 144 f13
Goddard, Kans., 533 75 H6
Goddelau, F.R.Ger., 4,009
  119 F5
Godech, Bulg., 2,915 128 D3
Goderich, Ont., Can., 6,267
  44 G7
Goderville, Fr., 1,611 117 D2
Godfrey, Ga., 181 64 F2
Godfrey, Ill., 1,231 68 B5
Godhra, India, 52,167 145 D5
Godiasco, It., 2,538 122 c6
Godley, Tex., 401 76 n10
Godmanchester, U.K., 2,502
  114 H6
Gödöllö, Hung., 17,740 126 D3
Gods, r., Man., Can. 43 G3
Godshill, U.K. 113 k13
Gods Lake, Man., Can. 43 G3
Gods L., Man., Can. 43 G3
Gods Lake Narrows, Man., Can.
  43 G3
Gods Mercy, Bay of, N.W.T.,
  Can. 41 M5
Godstone, U.K., 5,510 114 H8
Godwin, N.C., 149 63 F2
Godwin-Austen, Mt., Pak. 145 E1
Goehner, Nebr., 106 75 H3
Goéland, L. au, Qué., Can. 44 J5
Goeree, i., Neth. 115 B3
Goerkes Corners, Wis. 66 c11
Goes, Neth., 14,900 115 B3
Goessel, Kans., 327 75 H5
Goetzenbruck, Fr., 1,890 116 d9
Goetzville, Mich. 67 J2
Gofenu Entr., Yap 176 20
Goff, Kans., 259 75 K4
Goff Cr., Okla. 76 B1
Goffs, Calif. 82 F5
Goffstown, N.H., 1,052 54 D5
Goffton, Tenn. 71 F5
Gogama, Ont., Can. 44 M8
Gogebic, co., Mich., 24,370 66 D2
Gogebic, L., Mich. 66 D2
Gogebic Ra., Mich.-Wis. 66 C2
Gogebic Station, Mich. 66 D2
Göggingen, F.R.Ger., 12,615
  118 C4
Gogolin, Pol., 5,398 127 C3
Gogrial, Sudan 163 J4
Gohad, India, 10,289 144 b12
Gohana, India, 11,076 144 a11
Gohfeld, F.R.Ger., 14,187 118 B2
Gohor, Rum. 128 F1
Göhren, Ger.D.R. 118 D1
Goi, Jap., 17,955 155 G4
Goiana, Braz., 19,026 103 b14
Goiânia, Braz., 132,577 103 G5
Goianinha, Braz., 2,716 103 b14
Goiás, st., Braz., 1,954,862 103 F5
Goiás, Braz., 7,121 103 G5
Goikul, Palau 176 21
Goil, Loch, U.K. 112 a7
Goirle, Neth., 8,300 115 C3
Góis, Port., 3,081 122 A2
Goitacazes, Braz., 2,214 103 f17
Goito, It., 9,354 122 d5
Gojô, Jap., 32,805 154 g15
Gojnome, Jap., 19,700 155 G2
Gök, r., Turk. 142 C1
Goka, Jap. 155 m18
Gokak, India, 21,854 145 E6
Gokarn, India, 9,175 145 D7
Gokase, r., Jap. 155 k14
Gokashô, Jap. 154 g15
Gokashoura, Jap. 154 h15
Göksu, r., Turk. 142 C2
Göksun, Turk., 3,703 142 D2
Gokwe, Rhod. 164 D5
Gol, Nor. 120 B3
Gola, India 144 c11
Golaghat, India, 14,699 145 K4
Gola I., Ire. 113 B4
Gołańcz, Pol. 127 B2
Golaya Pristan', U.S.S.R., 11,000
  136 D4
Gol'chikha, U.S.S.R. 134 H2
Golconda, Ill., 864 68 D6

Golconda, Nev. 83 B2
Gölcük, Turk., 19,114 142 B1
Golčův Jeníkov, Czech. 127 e7
Goldach, Switz., 6,233 124 D1
Gold Acres, Nev. 83 B2
Gold Bar, Br. Col., Can. 42 F2
Gold Bar, Wash., 315 80 C2
Gold Beach, Oreg., 1,765 80 A4
Goldberg, Ger.D.R. 118 C2
Gold Coast=Ghana
Gold Creek, Alaska 85 G3
Golddale, Va. 62 G4
Golddust, Tenn. 71 B6
Golden, Br. Col., Can., 1,742
  42 J3
Golden, Colo., 7,118 79 C2
Golden, Idaho 81 B3
Golden, Ill., 491 68 A3
Golden, Okla. 76 J4
Golden Bay, Newf., Can. 45 L4
Golden Bay, N.Z. 175 g6
Golden Beach, Fla., 413 65 b10
Golden City, Mo., 714 72 C7
Goldendale, Wash., 2,536 80 C3
Golden Eagle, Ill. 68 B5
Golden Gate, Ill., 156 68 D5
Golden Gate, str., Calif. 83 d12
Golden Hinde, mtn., Br. Col.,
  Can. 42 F4
Golden Lake, Ont., Can. 46 G3
Golden L., Ont., Can. 46 G3
Golden Meadow, La., 3,097
  73 E8
Golden Pond, Ky. 71 D5
Golden Prairie, Sask., Can. 43 B5
Golden Rock, India, 43,120
  145 m20
Golden Spike Nat. Hist. Site,
  Utah 78 B1
Golden Valley, Minn., 14,559
  74 b5
Golden Valley, co., Mont., 1,203
  81 E2
Golden Valley, co., N. Dak.,
  3,100 74 A2
Goldenvalley, N. Dak., 286
  74 A2
Goldfield, Nev. 83 B4
Goldfields, Sask., Can. 43 B2
Gold Hill, Colo. 79 b7
Gold Hill, N.C. 63 A3
Gold Hill, Oreg., 608 80 B4
Gold Hill, Utah 78 B1
Goldman, La. 73 D6
Goldonna, La., 292 73 C5
Gold Point, Nev. 83 B4
Gold Rock, N.C. 63 G1
Gold Run, Calif. 82 C3
Goldsand L., Man., Can. 43 E2
Goldsboro, Md., 204 62 J3
Goldsboro, N.C., 28,873 63 F2
Goldsboro, Pa., 542 60 J5
Goldsby, Okla. 76 J2
Goldsmith, Tex., 670 77 M4
Goldston, N.C., 374 63 E2
Goldthwaite, Tex., 1,383 77 O4
Goldvein, Va. 62 G4
Goleniów, Pol., 9,497 127 A2
Goleta, Calif. 82 D5
Golets-Inyaptuk, G., U.S.S.R.
  135 L4
Golets-Skalistyy, G., U.S.S.R.
  135 L4
Golf, Ill., 409 69 c8
Golfito, C.R., 6,859 94 F6
Golf Manor, Ohio, 4,648 71 h10
Golfview, Fla., 131 65 b8
Goliad, co., Tex., 5,429 77 P5
Goliad, Tex., 1,782 77 P5
Golina, Pol., 1,917 127 C2
Golinda, Tex. 77 P4
Golitsyno, U.S.S.R. 136 b6
Göllersdorf, Aust., 1,016 124 c10
Göllheim, F.R.Ger., 1,875 119 E5
Golling, Aust., 2,831 124 K6
Golo, r., Fr. 116 r17
Golo I., Phil. 153 B2
Golok, r., Malay.-Thai. 147 o14
Gołonóg, Pol., 11,430 127 i6
Golovanovo, U.S.S.R. 136 d6
Golovin, Alaska 85 D2
Golovnin Bay, Alaska 85 D2
Golpāyegān, Iran, 12,400 143 E2
Gols, Aust., 3,100 124 N6
Golspie, U.K. 112 E3
Golssen, Ger.D.R. 118 D3
Goltry, Okla., 313 76 E1
Golubac, Yug. 125 E2
Golub-Dobrzyń, Pol., 6,568
  127 C2
Golubić, Yug., 2,405 125 C2
Golungo Alto, Ang. 164 B3
Golva, N. Dak., 162 74 A2
Golyama Kamchiya, r., Bulg.
  128 F3
Golyamo Konare, Bulg., 7,564
  128 E3
Golyamo Shivachevo, Bulg.,
  3,625 128 F3
Goma, Congo L., 14,115 164 D2
Gomati, r., India 144 c12
Gombe, Nigeria 162 F4
Gombela, D.R.Congo 165 n19
Gombong, Indon. 148 c7
Gomel', U.S.S.R., 184,000 134 B4
Gomera, i., Can. Is. 109 4
Gometz-la-Châtel, Fr. 116 g12
Gometz-la-Ville, Fr. 116 g12
Gomez, Fla. 65 J5
Gómez Farias, Chih., Mex.,
  2,514 92 D2
Gómez Farías, Coah., Mex.
  93 E3
Gómez Palacio, Mex., 60,765
  92 D3

Gomīshān, Iran, 5,168 143 E1
Gommern, Ger.D.R. 118 C2
Gonābād, Iran, 7,555 143 F2
Gonaïves, Haiti, 14,829 96 k6
Gonam, U.S.S.R. 135 N4
Gona Mission, Terr. Papua
  174 f3
Gonâve, Golfe de la, Haiti 96 k6
Gonâve, Île de la, Haiti 96 k6
Gonbad-e Kāvūs, Iran, 18,347
  143 F1
Gonda, India, 43,496 145 F4
Gondal, India, 45,069 144 D5
Gondar, Eth., 14,200 163 L3
Gondia, India, 56,320 145 F5
Gondo, Switz. 124 C2
Gondrecourt, Fr., 1,088 117 F2
Gonen, Turk., 10,848 142 A1
Gonesse, Fr., 8,541 116 h11
Gongola, r., Nigeria 162 F4
Gongolgon, Austl. 173 G4
Goñi, Urug., 1,000* 105 c11
Goniądz, Pol., 2,497 127 E2
Gónnos, Gr., 2,971 129 D5
Gonnosfanadiga, It., 7,877 123 B5
Gonô, r., Jap. 155 D4
Gonohe, Jap., 20,919 155 G1
Gonor, Man., Can. 43 g9
Gônoura, Jap., 19,612 154 A5
Gonvick, Minn., 363 74 B2
Gonzaga, Phil., 3,075 153 B1
Gonzales, Calif., 2,138 82 C4
Gonzales, La., 3,252 73 k7
Gonzales, co., Tex., 17,845 77 P5
Gonzales, Tex., 5,829 77 P5
González, Mex., 3,270 93 F3
González Chaves, Arg., 8,000*
  105 D5
Gonzalez Videla, Ant. 180 N6
Gonzalo Vásquez, Pan. 94 H6
Gonzol, Ec. 104 c11
Goobies, Newf., Can. 45 L4
Goochland, co., Va., 9,206 62 F5
Goochland, Va. 62 G5
Goodell, Iowa, 231 72 D2
Goodells, Mich. 67 L6
Goodenough, B., Terr. Papua
  174 f3
Goodenough I., Terr. Papua
  174 f3
Gooderham, Ont., Can. 46 F4
Gooderve, Sask., Can. 43 D4
Goodfield, Ill., 286 68 C3
Good Hart, Mich. 67 H3
Good Hope, Guyana 101 L6
Good Hope, Ill., 394 68 B3
Good Hope, Ohio 70 F3
Goodhope, W. Va. 62 D3
Good Hope, C. of, S. Af. 164 B7
Goodhue, co., Minn., 33,035
  74 F3
Goodhue, Minn., 566 74 F3
Goodie Water, r., U.K. 112 b7
Gooding, co., Idaho, 9,544 81 B4
Gooding, Idaho, 2,750 81 B4
Goodings Grove, Ill. 69 c10
Goodland, co., Idaho 81 B4
Goodland, Ind., 1,202 70 B2
Goodland, Kans., 4,459 75 D4
Goodland, Mich. 67 K5
Goodland, Minn. 74 F2
Goodlett, Tex. 77 O2
Goodlettsville, Tenn., 3,163
  71 E5
Goodman, Miss., 932 73 F5
Goodman, Mo., 540 72 C8
Goodman, Wis. 66 E3
Goodnews Bay, Alaska 85 D4
Goodnight, Tex. 76 N2
Goodnoe Hills, Wash. 80 C3
Goodoô, Jap. 154 e16
Goodrich, Colo. 79 C1
Goodrich, Kans. 75 L5
Goodrich, Mich., 701 67 K6
Goodrich, N. Dak., 392 74 B2
Goodrich, Tex. 77 O4
Goodridge, Minn., 134 74 E1
Goodsoil, Sask., Can. 43 D1
Good Springs, Ala. 64 b7
Goodsprings, Nev. 83 C5
Good Thunder, Minn., 468
  74 F3
Goodview, Minn., 1,348 74 G3
Goodwater, Ala., 2,023 64 C2
Goodwater, Okla. 76 J4
Goodwell, Okla., 771 76 B1
Goodwin, S. Dak., 134 74 D3
Goodyear, Ariz., 1,654 78 B5
Goodyear, Conn.=Rogers
Goole, U.K., 18,875 113 F5
Goolgowi, Austl. 173 e9
Gooloogong, Austl. 173 g9
Goomalling, Austl. 172 B4
Goondiwindi, Austl., 2,950
  173 G4
Goor, Neth., 7,500 115 D2
Goose, r., Newf., Can. 45 O4
Goose, r., N. Dak. 74 D2
Goose Bay, Alaska 85 C2
Goose Creek, S.C., 830 63 D5
Goose Cr., Nebr. 75 L1
Goose Eye Mtn., Me. 55 B4
Gooselake, Iowa, 191 72 G3
Goose L., Man., Can. 43 C4
Goose L., Calif.-Oreg. 80 C5
Goose L., Minn. 74 d6
Goose Pd., N.H. 54 C4
Gooserock, Ky. 71 H4
Gopalganj, India, 14,090 144 e12
Goplo, Jez., Pol. 127 C2
Göppingen, F.R.Ger., 46,391
  118 B4
Gora, India 144 a13

Góra, Pol. 127 D2
Góra Kalwaria, Pol., 6,970
  127 D3
Gorakhpur, India, 180,255
  145 G4
Goražde, Yug., 4,485 125 D3
Gorbea, Chile, 3,016 105 e14
Gorce, Pol., 4,441 127 f6
Gorchs, Arg., 2,200* 105 b12
Gorchukha, U.S.S.R. 136 F1
Gorda, Punta, Cuba 96 b1
Gorda, P., Calif. 82 A2
Gorda Cay, Bah. Is. 95 b6
Gorda Sd., V.I. 97 4
Gørding, Den. 121 A5
Gordino, U.S.S.R. 137 h7
Gordo, Ala., 1,714 64 B2
Gordola, Switz., 1,794 124 C2
Gordon, Man., Can. 43 g9
Gordon, U.K. 112 e8
Gordon, Ala., 222 64 D4
Gordon, co., Ga., 19,228 64 E1
Gordon, Ga., 1,793 64 F3
Gordon, Kans. 75 J6
Gordon, Nebr., 2,223 75 C1
Gordon, Pa., 888 61 K4
Gordon, Tex., 349 77 O3
Gordon, Wis. 66 B2
Gordon, r., Austl. 173 e14
Gordon Cr., Nebr. 75 D1
Gordon L., Alta., Can. 42 L2
Gordonsburg, Tenn. 71 D6
Gordonsville, Va., 1,109 62 F4
Gordonvale, Austl., 1,989 173 G2
Goré, Chad. 162 G4
Gore, Eth. 163 K4
Gore, N.Z., 7,270 175 f7
Gore, Okla., 334 76 H2
Gore, Va. 62 F3
Gore Bay, Ont., Can. 44 G6
Gorebridge, U.K. 112 d8
Goree, Tex., 543 77 O3
Gore Mtn., Vt. 54 D2
Gore Ra., Colo. 79 B2
Goreville, Ill., 625 68 D6
Gorey, Ire., 2,816 113 C5
Gorgān, Iran, 28,380 143 E1
Gorgas, Ala. 64 a7
Gorgona, I., Col. 100 A6
Gorgonzola, It., 8,564 122 c5
Gorgora, Eth. 163 L3
Gorgorza, Utah 78 c9
Gorham, Ill., 378 68 C6
Gorham, Kans., 429 75 F5
Gorham, Me., 2,322 55 B5
Gorham, N.H., 1,945 54 E3
Gorham, N.Y. 58 F4
Gori, U.S.S.R., 35,200 137 c1
Gori, r., Kenya 165 g14
Goričan, Yug., 4,266 125 C1
Gorin, Mo. 72 F4
Gorinchem, Neth., 20,500 115 C3
Goring, U.K., 2,157 114 F7
Goris, U.S.S.R., 10,400 137 c2
Gorizia, It., 42,456 123 D2
Gorki, U.S.S.R., 14,600 136 C2
Gor'kiy, U.S.S.R., 1,003,000
  134 D4
Gor'kovskoye Vdkhr., U.S.S.R.
  136 F1
Gor'koye, Oz., U.S.S.R. 137 q11
Gørlev, Den., 2,086 121 D5
Gorlice, Pol., 10,433 127 D4
Görlitz, Ger.D.R., 89,909 118 E3
Görlíz, Sp., 1,922 122 n11
Gørløse, Den. 121 a7
Gorlovka, U.S.S.R., 307,000
  134 C5
Gorman, Calif. 82 D5
Gorman, Tex., 1,142 77 O3
Gormania, W. Va. 62 E3
Gorna Oryakhovitsa, Bulg.,
  18,863 128 E3
Gornja Bukovica, Yug., 2,036
  125 D3
Gornja Klina, Yug. 125 E3
Gornja Trepča, Yug. 125 D3
Gornje Ratkovo, Yug. 125 C2
Gornje Vukovsko, Yug. 125 C2
Gornji Cevljanovići, Yug. 125 D2
Gornji Milanovac, Yug., 3,402
  125 E2
Gornji Vakuf, Yug. 125 C3
Górno, Pol. 127 D3
Gorno-Altaysk, U.S.S.R., 29,000
  134 H4
Gornozavodsk, U.S.S.R., 10,800
  135 O5
Gornyak, U.S.S.R. 137 q12
Gornyatskiy, U.S.S.R., 16,000
  136 g7
Gornyy, U.S.S.R., 7,300 134 D4
Goro, N. Caled. 174 k9
Gorodënka, U.S.S.R., 7,000
  136 B3
Gorodets, U.S.S.R., 26,400
  136 F1
Gorodishche, R.S.F.S.R.,
  U.S.S.R., 6,100 136 G2
Gorodishche, Ukr.S.S.R.,
  U.S.S.R., 16,000 136 C4
Gorodnya, U.S.S.R., 8,600 136 C3
Gorodok, Bel.S.S.R., U.S.S.R.,
  7,700 136 C2
Gorodok, Ukr.S.S.R., U.S.S.R.,
  10,000 136 A3
Goroka, Terr. New Guin., 3,250
  174 e2
Goroke, Austl. 172 F5
Gorokhov, U.S.S.R., 4,400
  136 B3
Gorokhovets, U.S.S.R., 8,900
  136 F1
Gorong, P., Indon. 149 J3
Gorongosa, Parque Nac. da, Moz.
  164 E5
Gorongosa, Sa. da, Moz. 164 E5
Gorontalo, Indon., 71,378 149 G2
Górowo Iławeckie, Pol., 2,669
  127 D1
Gorrahei, Eth. 163 M4

Gourock, U.K., 9,609 112 a8
Goussainville, Fr., 13,028 116 h10
Gouvêa, Braz., 3,055 103 H5
Gouverneur, N.Y., 4,946 59 K3
Gouyave, Gren., 2,256 97 18
Gouzeaucourt, Fr., 1,263 116 a7
Gouzon, Fr., 1,447 117 E3
Govan, Sask., Can. 43 G4
Govan, S.C., 138 63 C4
Go Vap, S. Viet., 26,624 147 n11
Gove, Kans., 4,107 75 E5
Gove, Kans., 228 75 E5
Govena, M., U.S.S.R. 135 Q4
Govenor Generoso, Phil., 1,744
  153 C4
Governor's Harbour, Bah. Is.
  95 c7
Govindgarh, India 144 c13
Gowanda, N.Y., 3,352 58 B7
Gowarczów, Pol. 127 k5
Gowen, Mich. 67 H5
Gower, Mt., Lord Howe I. 175 12
Gowganda, Ont., Can. 44 G6
Gowk, Ire, 6,285 143 F3
Gowna, L., Ire. 113 C5
Gowran, Ire. 113 C5
Gowrie, Iowa, 1,127 72 C2
Goya, Arg., 45,000* 105 D3
Goya, D.R.Congo 165 n19
Goyave, Guad. 97 14
Goyder, L., Austl. 172 C4
Goyllarisquisga, Peru, 4,251
  104 B4
Göynük, Turk., 2,017 142 B1
Goz Beïda, Chad, 2,000* 163 H3
Gózd, Pol. 127 D3
Gozdnica, Pol., 2,998 127 A3
Gozier, Guad., 1,304 97 14
Gozo, i., Malta 123 b8
Graaff-Reinet, S. Af., 16,703
  164 C7
Graben, F.R.Ger., 3,461 119 E6
Grabill, Ind., 495 70 E1
Grabovica, Yug., 2,508 125 D3
Grabow, Ger.D.R. 118 C2
Grabów, Pol., 1,635 127 C3
Grabs, Switz., 4,218 124 D1
Gračac, Yug., 2,308 125 B2
Gračanica, Yug., 6,102 125 D2
Graçay, Fr., 1,889 117 D3
Grace, Idaho, 725 81 D4
Grace, Mt., Mass. 56 G2
Grace City, N. Dak. 74 C2
Gracefield, Qué., Can. 44 J6
Gracemont, Okla., 376 76 E2
Grace Park, Phil., 71,425 153 b8
Graceton, Minn. 74 E1
Graceville, Fla., 2,307 65 D2
Graceville, Minn., 823 74 D3
Gracey, Ky. 71 D5
Grächen, Switz. 124 B2
Gracias, Hond., 2,039 94 C3
Gracias a Dios, C., Hond.-Nic.
  94 ·
Graciosa, i., Azores 108 2
Graciosa, i., Can. Is. 109 4
Gracze, Pol. 127 g6
Gradac, Hrva., Yug. 125 B2
Gradac, Srba., Yug. 125 E3
Gradačac, Yug., 4,602 125 D2
Gradaús, Braz. 103 F3
Gradaús, Sa. dos, Braz. 103 F3
Gradec, Yug., 2,012 125 F4
Gradešnica, Yug. 125 E4
Gradets, Bulg., 4,060 128 D2
Gradil, Port. 122 i10
Gradişte, Rum. 128 D2
Gradjagan, Indon. 148 E5
Gradjagan, Teluk, Indon. 148 f8
Gradsko, Yug. 125 E4
Grady, Ala. 64 C3
Grady, Ark., 622 73 D3
Grady, co., Ga., 18,015 64 E5
Grady, N. Mex., 100 79 D4
Grady, co., Okla., 29,590 76 F3
Grady, Okla. 76 F3
Gradyville, Ky. 71 F4
Grædstrup, Den. 121 B5
Graettinger, Iowa, 879 72 C1
Grafenau, F.R.Ger., 2,371
  118 D4
Gräfenhainichen, Ger.D.R.
  118 D3
Grafenwöhr, F.R.Ger., 5,266
  118 C4
Graford, Tex., 448 77 O3
Grafton, Austl., 9,759 173 H4
Grafton, co., N.H., 54,914 54 C4
Grafton, Ill., 1,084 68 B4
Grafton, Iowa, 273 72 E1
Grafton, Mass., 10,627(T) 57 K4
Grafton, co., N.H., 48,857 54 D4
Grafton, Nebr., 176 75 H3
Grafton, N.H. 54 D4
Grafton, N.Y. 59 O6
Grafton, N. Dak., 5,885 74 D1
Grafton, Ohio, 1,683 70 G1
Grafton, Va. 62 H5
Grafton, W. Va., 5,791 62 D3
Grafton, Wis., 3,748 66 F5
Grafton, co., Austl. 173 G2
Grafton, Mt., Nev. 83 C3
Grafton Center, N.H. 54 D4
Grafton Park, N.J. 60 c9
Graglia, It., 2,010 122 a5
Gragnano, It., 22,145 123 D3
Graham, Ont., Can. 44 D5
Graham, Ala. 64 D2
Graham, co., Ariz., 14,045 78 D5
Graham, Ga., 130 64 G4
Graham, co., Kans., 5,586 75 F4
Graham, Mo., 215 72 C4
Graham, co., N.C., 6,432 63 b7
Graham, N.C., 7,723 63 E1
Graham, Okla. 76 F3
Graham, Tex., 8,505 77 O3

Graham—Green Sea · 231

Graham, Wash. 81 b8
Graham, r., Br. Col., Can. 42 F2
Graham, Mt., Ariz. 50 E4
Graham I., Br. Col., Can. 42 C3
Graham I., N.W.T., Can. 41 L2
Graham L., Alta., Can. 42 J2
Graham L., Me. 55 D4
Grahamstown, S. Af., 32,195 164 D7
Grahamsville, N.Y. 59 L8
Grahamville, S.C. 63 D5
Grahn, Ky. 71 H3
Grahovo, Crna G., Yug. 125 D3
Grahovo, Slvja., Yug. 125 A1
Graian Alps, mts., It.-Fr. 123 A2
Grainfield, Kans., 389 75 E4
Grainger, N.C., 188 63 G2
Grainger, co., Tenn., 12,506 71 H5
Grainola, Okla., 67 76 G1
Grainton, Nebr., 35 75 D3
Grain Valley, Mo., 552 72 C6
Grajaú, Braz., 2,539 103 G3
Grajaú, r., Braz. 103 G2
Grajewo, Pol., 8,576 127 E2
Gram, Den., 3,388 121 B5
Gramada, Bulg., 4,817 128 D3
Gramalote, Col. 100 D4
Gramat, Fr., 3,253 117 D4
Gramatneusiedl, Aust., 2,058 124 d10
Grambling, La., 3,144 73 C5
Gramercy, La., 2,094 73 E7
Grammond, Fr. 116 o15
Grampian, Pa., 529 60 E4
Grampian Mts., U.K. 112 D3
Gramsh, Alb., 1,750 125 E4
Gran, r., Sur. 101 N6
Granada, Col. 101 d13
Granada, Nic., 30,158 94 E5
Granada, Phil., 8,563 153 e11
Granada, Sp., 157,178 122 D4
Granada, Colo., 593 79 D3
Granada, Minn., 418 74 E4
Granados, Mex., 1,124 92 C2
Granard, Ire. 113 C5
Granbury, Tex., 2,227 77 O3
Granby, Qué., Can., 30,852 44 K6
Granby, Colo., 503 79 C1
Granby, Conn., 4,968(T) 56 E5
Granby, Mass., 4,221(T) 56 G4
Granby, Mo., 1,808 72 C8
Granby, Vt. 54 D2
Granby, r., Br. Col., Can. 42 H4
Granby, L., Colo. 79 C1
Gran Canaria, i., Can. Is. 109 4
Gran Chaco, S. Amer. 99 C5
Grand, co., Colo., 3,557 79 B1
Grand, co., Utah, 6,345 78 D2
Grand, r., N.B., Can. 55 E1
Grand, r., Ont., Can. 46 D5
Grand, r., Mich. 67 G5
Grand, r., Mo. 72 D5
Grand, r., Ohio 70 J1
Grand, r., Okla. 76 H1
Grand, r., S. Dak. 74 B3
Grand Bahama I., Bah. Is. 95 C1
Grand Bank, Newf., Can., 2,675 45 Q6
Grand Banks of Newfoundland, Atl. Oc. 108 J3
Grand Bassam, Iv. Coast, 12,330 162 D5
Grand Bay, N.B., Can. 47 S11
Grand Bay, Ala. 64 A5
Grand Bay, Dominica 97 13
Grand Bay, Gren. Is. 97 20
Grand Beach, Man., Can. 43 F5
Grand Bend, Ont., Can. 46 C5
Grand Blanc, Mich., 1,565 67 K6
Grand Bois, Morne, Dominica 97 13
Grand Bonhomme, mtn., St. Vinc. 97 19
Grand-Bourg, Guad., 2,019 97 14
Grand Caicos, i., Caicos Is. 95 E2
Grand Calumet, r., Ill.-Ind. 69 e10
Grand Can., China = Yün Ho
Grand Can., Ire. 113 B5
Grand Cane, La., 322 73 B5
Grand Canyon, Ariz. 78 C3
Grand Canyon Nat. Mon., Ariz. 78 B3
Grand Canyon Nat. Pk., Ariz. 78 B3
Grand Canyon of Pa. 61 ·
Grand Canyon of the Liard, Br. Col., Can. 38 D6
Grand Cayman, i., Lesser Ant. 97 3
Grand Centre, Alta., Can., 1,443 42 L2
Grand Cess, Lib. 162 C5
Grand Chenier, La. 73 C8
Grand Coteau, La., 1,165 73 C7
Grand Coulee, Wash., 1,058 80 D2
Grand Coulee Dam, Wash. 80 D2
Grand Cul de Sac Bay, St. Lucia 97 11
Grand Cul-de-Sac Marin, bay, Guad. 97 14
Grand Detour, Ill. 68 C2
Grande, F.R.Ger. 119 b8
Grande, B., Arg. 105 B8
Grande, Cayo, Cuba 96 d2
Grande, I., Braz. 103 d18
Grande, Sa., N. Mex. 79 D3
Grande, r., Bol. 102 D5
Grande, r., Braz. 103 F5
Grande, r., Braz. 103 H4
Grande, r., Jam. 96 q8
Grande, r., Nic. 94 E4
Grande, r., Peru 104 C5
Grande, r., Ven. 101 c11
Grande, r., Ven. 101 K3
Grande Anse, Guad. 97 14
Grande-Cascapédia, Qué., Can. 47 T9
Grande Case, St-Martin 97 7
Grande Case, B., St-Martin 97 7
Grande Cayemite, i., Haiti 96 k6
Grande-Chartreuse, Fr. 117 F4
Grande Comore, i., Arch. des Comores 165 G3
Grande de Añasco, r., P.R. 96 r10
Grande de Arecibo, r., P.R. 96 s10
Grande de Loíza, r., P.R. 96 u10
Grande de Manatí, r., P.R. 96 t10
Grande de Sta. Marta, Cga., Col. 100 C2
Grande de Santiago, r., Mex. 92 D4
Grand Erg Occidental, des., Alg. 160 D2
Grand Erg Oriental, des., Alg. 160 E3
Grandeeville, W. Va. 62 C4
Grande Leyre, r., Fr. 117 C4
Grande Prairie, Alta., Can., 8,231 42 H2
Grande-Rivière, Qué., Can., 1,141 45 N5
Grande-Rivière-du-Nord, Haiti, 2,931 96 k6
Grande Ronde, r., Oreg.-Wash. 80 E3
Grande Sassière, mtn., Fr. 117 G4
Grandes, Salinas, Arg. 105 B2
Grandes, Salinas, Arg. 105 B3
Grandes Bergeronnes, Qué., Can. 47 f12
Grande Sebkra d'Oran, salt lake, Alg. 160 a6
Gran Desierto, Mex. 92 B1
Grand-Étang, N.S., Can. 47 V10
Grande-Terre, i., Guad. 97 14
Grande-Vallée, Qué., Can. 45 N5
Grande Vigie, Pte. de la, Guad. 97 14
Grand Falls, N.B., Can., 3,913 45 M6
Grand Falls, Newf., Can., 6,606 45 Q5
Grand Falls, Minn. 74 F1
Grandfalls, Tex., 1,012 77 M4
Grand Falls, Ariz. 78 C4
Grand Falls L., Me. 55 E3
Grandfield, Okla., 1,606 76 E3
Grand Forks, Br. Col., Can., 2,307 42 H4
Grand Forks, co., N. Dak., 48,677 74 D1
Grand Forks, N. Dak., 34,451 74 D2
Grand Gaube, Maurit. 165 c12
Grand-Goâve, Haiti, 2,022 96 k6
Grand Harbour, N.B., Can. 47 S11
Grand Haven, Mich., 11,066 67 G5
Grand Îlet, Guad. 97 14
Grandin, Mo., 259 72 G8
Grandin, N. Dak., 147 74 D2
Grand Island, Nebr., 25,742 75 G3
Grand Island, N.Y. 58 k19
Grand I., Mich. 67 G2
Grand I., N.Y. 58 C5
Grand Isle, La., 2,074 73 F8
Grand Isle, Me. 55 D1
Grand Isle, co., Vt., 2,927 54 A2
Grand Isle, Vt. 54 A2
Grand Isle, Vt. 54 A2
Grand Junction, Colo., 18,694 79 A2
Grand Junction, Iowa, 949 72 C2
Grand Junction, Mich. 67 G6
Grand Junction, Tenn., 446 71 B6
Grand Lahou, Iv. Coast, 2,716 162 a9
Grand Lake, Colo., 170 79 B1
Grand Lake, La. 73 B7
Grand L., Newf., Can. 45 P5
Grand L., La. 73 C8
Grand L., La. 73 D8
Grand L., Me. 55 D2
Grand L., Me. 55 E3
Grand L., Mich. 67 K3
Grand L., Ohio 70 E2
Grand Lake Stream, Me. 55 E3
Grand Ledge, Mich., 5,165 67 J6
Grand Manan Chan., Me. 55 E4
Grand Manan I., N.B., Can. 45 M7
Grand Marais, Mich. 67 G2
Grand Marais, Minn., 1,301 74 G2
Grand Marsh, Wis. 66 D5
Grand Meadow, Minn., 837 74 F4
Grand'Mère, Qué., Can., 15,365 44 K6
Grand Mesa, Colo. 79 B2
Grand Mesa, Colo. 79 ·
Grand Morin, r., Fr. 116 k11
Grand Mound, Iowa, 565 72 G3
Grand Mound, Wash. 80 B2
Grândola, Port., 12,028 122 A3
Grand Pass, Mo., 120 72 D5
Grand Popo, Dahom. 162 E4
Grand Portage, Minn. 74 H1
Grand Portage Nat. Mon., Minn. 74 H2
Grand Prairie, Tex., 30,386 76 e9
Grand Rapids, Man., Can. 43 F4
Grand Rapids, Mich., 177,313 67 H6
Grand Rapids, Minn., 7,265 74 F2
Grand Rapids, N. Dak. 74 C2
Grand Rapids, Ohio, 670 70 F1
Grand Ridge, Fla., 415 65 D2
Grand Ridge, Ill., 659 68 D2
Grand River, Iowa, 284 72 D4
Grand River, Ohio, 477 70 f8
Grand Rivers, Ky., 378 71 C5
Grand' Rivière, Mart., 1,128 97 12
Grand Rivière à Goyaves, Guad. 97 14
Grand Ronde, Oreg. 80 B3
Grand Saline, Tex., 2,006 77 P3
Grandson, Switz., 2,091 124 A2
Grand Teton, mtn., Wyo. 81 D4
Grand Teton Nat. Pk., Wyo. 81 D4
Grand Tower, Ill., 847 68 C6
Grand Traverse, co., Mich., 33,490 67 H4
Grand Traverse Bay, Mich. 67 H3
Grand Valley, Ont., Can. 46 D5
Grand Valley, Colo., 245 79 A2
Grand Valley, Pa. 60 D2
Grandview, Man., Can., 1,025 43 E4
Grand View, Idaho 81 A4
Grand View, Ill. 68 E4
Grandview, Ind., 599 70 B5
Grandview, Iowa, 300 72 F3
Grandview, Mo., 6,027 72 C6
Grand View, N.Y., 330 58 d12
Grandview, Ohio 70 H3
Grandview, Tex., 961 77 P3
Grandview, Wash., 3,366 80 D2
Grandview, Wis. 66 B2
Grand View Beach, N.Y. 58 n20
Grandview Heights, Ohio, 8,270 70 F3
Grandvillard, Switz. 124 B2
Grandville, Mich., 7,975 67 H6
Grandvilliers, Fr., 2,215 117 E2
Grand Wash Cliffs, Ariz. 78 B4
Grandy, N.C. 63 J1
Grane, Nor. 120 C2
Grañén, Sp., 2,246 122 E2
Graneros, Chile, 5,644 104 g14
Grange, U.K., 3,113 113 E4
Grange City, Ky. 71 H3
Grange Hill, Jam., 1,407 96 o8
Grangemouth, U.K., 18,860 112 c7
Grangenal, Mex., 1,202 93 E3
Granger, Ill. 69 b9
Granger, Ind. 70 C1
Granger, Iowa, 468 72 D3
Granger, Mo., 146 72 F4
Granger, Tex., 1,339 77 P4
Granger, Wash., 1,424 80 C2
Granger, Wyo., 159 81 D5
Granges, Switz. 124 A2
Grängesberg, Swed. 120 C3
Grangeville, Idaho, 3,642 81 B3
Granite, Md. 62 b7
Granite, co., Mont., 3,014 81 C2
Granite, Okla., 952 76 D3
Granite, Oreg., 3 80 D3
Granite City, Ill., 40,073 68 B5
Granite Falls, Minn., 2,728 74 E3
Granite Falls, N.C., 2,644 63 C2
Granite Falls, Wash., 599 81 b6
Granite Mtn., Utah 78 B2
Granite Pass, Wyo. 81 F3
Granite Pk., Mont. 81 E3
Granite Pk., Utah 78 B1
Granite Quarry, N.C., 1,059 63 D2
Granite Range, Alaska 85 J3
Granite Ra., Nev. 83 A2
Granite Springs, Va. 62 G4
Graniteville (part of Westford), Mass. 57 L2
Graniteville, S.C., 1,017 63 C4
Graniteville, Vt. 54 B3
Granity, N.Z. 175 f6
Granja, Braz., 5,074 103 H2
Gran Morelos, Mex., 1,323 92 D2
Gränna, Swed. 120 C4
Grannis, Ark., 185 73 A3
Grannys Cap, Me. 55 B3
Granollérs, Sp., 20,194 122 G2
Gran Paradiso, mtn., It. 123 A2
Gran Quivira, N. Mex. 79 B4
Gran Quivira Nat. Mon., N. Mex. 79 B4
Gransee, Ger.D.R. 118 D2
Grant, Ala., 274 64 C1
Grant, Colo. 79 C2
Grant, Fla. 65 J5
Grant, co., Ind., 75,741 70 D2
Grant, Iowa, 180 72 C3
Grant, co., Kans., 5,269 75 D6
Grant, co., Ky., 9,489 71 G3
Grant, parish, La., 13,330 73 C6
Grant, La. 73 C7
Grant, Mich., 732 67 H5
Grant, co., Minn., 8,870 74 D3
Grant, co., Nebr., 1,009 75 D2
Grant, Nebr., 1,166 75 D3
Grant, co., N. Mex., 18,700 79 A5
Grant, co., N. Dak., 6,248 74 B2
Grant, Ohio 70 F2
Grant, co., Okla., 8,140 76 F1
Grant, Okla., 286 76 H4
Grant, co., Oreg., 7,726 80 D3
Grant, co., S. Dak., 9,913 74 D3
Grant, co., Wash., 46,477 80 D2
Grant, co., W. Va., 8,304 62 E3
Grant, co., Wis., 44,419 66 C5
Grant Center, Mich. 67 H5
Grant City, Mo., 1,061 72 C4
Grantfork, Ill., 134 68 C5
Grantham, U.K., 25,048 113 F5
Grantham, N.H. 54 C5
Grantham, N.C. 63 F2
Granton, Ont., Can. 46 C5
Granton, U.K. 112 d8
Granton, Wis., 278 66 C4
Grantown-on-Spey, U.K., 1,581 112 E3
Grant Park, Ill., 757 68 E2
Grant Ra., Nev. 83 C3
Grants, Me. 55 B3
Grants, N. Mex., 10,274 79 A4
Grantsburg, Ill. 68 D6
Grantsburg, Wis., 900 66 A3
Grantsdale, Mont. 81 C2
Grants Pass, Oreg., 10,118 80 B4
Grantsville, Md., 446 62 E3
Grantsville, Utah, 2,166 78 B1
Grantsville, W. Va., 866 62 C4
Grant Town, W. Va., 1,105 62 D3
Grantville, Ga. 1,158 64 E2
Granum, Alta., Can. 42 K4
Granville, Yukon, Can. 40 B5
Granville, Fr., 11,482 117 C2
Granville, Ariz. 78 D5
Granville, Ill., 1,048 68 C2
Granville, Mass., 874(T) 56 E4
Granville, N.Y., 2,715 59 O5
Granville, co., N.C., 33,110 63 F1
Granville, N. Dak., 400 74 B1
Granville, Ohio, 2,868 70 G2
Granville, Vt. 54 B4
Granville, W. Va., 806 62 D3
Granville, Wis. 66 c11
Granville Center (part of Granville), Mass. 56 E4
Granville Ferry, N.S., Can. 47 T11
Granville L., Man., Can. 43 E3
Grapeland, Tex., 1,113 77 Q4
Grapeview, Wash. 81 a8
Grapevine, Calif. 82 D5
Grapevine, Tex., 2,821 76 e9
Grapevine Res., Tex. 76 e8
Gras, L. de, N.W.T., Can. 40 G5
Grasmere, Br. Col., Can. 42 J4
Grasmere, U.K., 1,043 114 B2
Grasmere, Idaho 81 B4
Grasmere, N.H. 54 D5
Gräsö, i., Swed. 120 D3
Grasonville, Md. 62 H4
Grass, r., Man., Can. 43 F3
Grass, r., N.Y. 59 K2
Grass Creek, Ind. 70 C2
Grass Creek, Wyo. 81 E4
Grasse, Fr., 27,226 117 G5
Grassflat, Pa. 60 F3
Grassholme, U.K. 112 f10
Grassie, Ont., Can. 46 c15
Grassington, U.K., 1,151 114 E2
Grass Lake, Mich., 1,037 67 J6
Grass L., Ill. 69 b7
Grassland, Tex. 77 N3
Grass Patch, Austl. 172 B5
Grass Pt., St. Croix 97 1
Grassrange, Mont., 222 81 E2
Grass Valley, Calif., 4,876 82 C3
Grass Valley, Oreg., 234 80 C3
Grassy, Austl. 173 F6
Grassy Bay, Berm. Is. 108 1
Grassy Butte, N. Dak. 74 A2
Grassy Creek, Ky. 71 H4
Grassy Creek, N.C. 63 C1
Grassy Key, Fla. 65 h15
Grassy Lake, Alta., Can. 42 K4
Gråsten, Den. 121 B6
Gratangen, Nor. 120 D1
Gratersford, Pa. 61 M5
Grate's Cove, Newf., Can. 45 c9
Grate's Pt., Newf., Can. 45 b9
Gratiot, co., Mich., 37,012 67 J5
Gratiot, Ohio, 222 70 G3
Gratiot, Wis., 294 66 C6
Gratiot L., Mich. 66 E1
Gratitunon, Indon. 148 e7
Gratkorn, Aust., 5,258 124 M6
Graton, Calif., 1,055 82 B3
Gratz, Ky., 140 71 G3
Gratz, Pa., 704 60 J4
Graulhet, Fr., 10,155 117 E5
Graus, Sp., 3,012 122 F1
Gravatá, Braz., 15,550 103 b15
Grave, Neth., 4,300 115 D3
Grave, Pte. de, Fr. 117 C4
Gravelbourg, Sask., Can., 1,490 43 C5
Gravelines, Fr., 7,731 117 D1
Gravelly, Ark. 73 B3
Gravenhurst, Ont., Can., 3,038 44 H7
Gravenor Bay, Berbuda 97 8
Graves, co., Ky., 30,021 71 C5
Gravesend, U.K., 51,389 113 G6
Gravesville, N.Y. 59 u25
Gravette, Ark., 855 73 A1
Gravina di Puglia, It., 34,424 123 F4
Gravity, Iowa, 275 72 C4
Gravity, Pa. 61 p16
Grawn, Mich. 67 H4
Gray, Fr., 8,150 117 F3
Gray, Ga., 1,320 64 F2
Gray, Iowa, 152 72 C3
Gray, co., Kans., 4,380 75 E6
Gray, Me. 55 B5
Gray, Okla. 76 C1
Gray, co., Tex., 31,535 76 N2
Grayback Mtn., Oreg. 80 B4
Grayburg, Tex. 77 m8
Gray Court, S.C., 473 63 B3
Grayland, Wash. 80 A2
Grayling, Mich., 2,015 67 J4
Graymont, Ill. 68 D3
Gray Mountain, Ariz. 78 C4
Grays, S.C. 63 C5
Grays Harbor, co., Wash., 54,465 80 B2
Grays Hbr., Wash. 80 A2
Grays Lake, Ill., 3,762 68 D1
Grays L., Idaho 81 D4
Grayson, Sask., Can. 43 D5
Grayson, co., Ky., 15,834 71 E4
Grayson, Ky., 1,692 71 H3
Grayson, La., 428 73 C5
Grayson, co., Tex., 73,043 77 P3
Grayson, co., Va., 17,390 62 C6
Grays River, Wash. 80 B2
Graysville, Man., Can. 43 f10
Graysville, Ala., 2,870 64 B2
Graysville, Ind. 70 B3
Graysville, Ohio, 127 70 H3
Graysville, Pa. 60 B6
Graysville, Tenn., 838 71 F6
Grayton, Md. 62 G4
Grayton Beach, Fla. 65 C2
Grayville, Ill., 2,280 68 D5
Grayvoron, U.S.S.R., 4,700 136 D3
Graz, Aust., 237,041 124 M6
Grazebrook, Mt., Br. Col. Can. 42 b5
Grazzanise, It., 6,932 123 c9
Grazzano Visconti, It. 122 c6
Grdelica, Yug. 125 F3
Greaca, L., Rum. 128 F2
Greasewood, Ariz. 78 D3
Great, r., Gren. 97 18
Great, r., Jam. 96 p8
Great Abaco, i., Bah. Is. 95 C1
Great Amwell, U.K., 2,396 114 J7
Great Artesian Basin, Austl. 173 ·
Great Atlas = Haut Atlas
Great Australian Bight, Austl. 172 D5
Great Averill L., Vt. 54 D2
Great Ayton, U.K., 3,451 112 h10
Great Baddow, U.K., 9,647 114 J7
Great Bahama Bank, Atl. Oc. 108 G5
Great Barrier I., N.Z. 175 g5
Great Barrier Reef, Austl. 173 F1
Great Barrington, Mass., 2,943; 6,624(T) 56 C4
Great Basin, U.S. 81 ·
Great Basin, Nev. 83 C2
Great Bay, N.H. 54 F5
Great Bay, N.J. 61 C4
Great Bear L., N.W.T., Can. 40 E4
Great Bedwyn, U.K. 114 E8
Great Bend, Kans., 16,670 75 G5
Great Bend, N.Y. 59 J3
Great Bend, N. Dak., 164 74 D2
Great Bend, Pa., 777 61 L2
Great Bend Sand Land, Kans. 50 G3
Great Berg, r., S. Af. 164 a8
Great Bernera, i., U.K. 112 C2
Great Bitter L. = Al Buḥayrah al Murrah al Kubrá
Great Blasket I., Ire. 113 A5
Great Britain, i., U.K. 112-3
Great Bk., Mass. 56 F4
Great Bk., N.Y. 58 o21
Great Cacapon, W. Va. 62 F3
Great Camanoe I., V.I. 97 4
Great Central, Br. Col., Can. 42 a6
Great Central L., Br. Col., Can. 42 F4
Great Chazy, r., N.Y. 59 N2
Great Chesterford, U.K. 114 J6
Great Cloche I., Ont., Can. 46 B2
Great Coco I., Burma 146 A4
Great Coharie Cr., N.C. 63 F2
Great Cumbrae I., U.K. 112 a8
Great Divide, Colo. 79 B1
Great Divide Basin, Wyo. 81 ·
Great Dog I., V.I. 97 4
Great Duck I., Ont., Can. 46 B3
Great Dunmow, U.K., 3,827 113 G6
Great East L., Me.-N.H. 55 A5
Great Egg Harbor, r., N.J. 61 B4
Great Egg Harbor, N.J. 61 B5
Great Egg Harbor Inlet, N.J. 61 C5
Greater Antilles, W.I. 95 G3
Greater Caucasus = Bol'shoy Kavkaz
Greater Khingan Ra. = Ta-hsing-an-ling Shan-mo
Greaterville, Ariz. 78 C6
Great Exhibition Bay, N.Z. 175 g4
Great Exuma, i., Bah. Is. 95 C2
Great Falls, Mont., 55,357 81 D2
Great Falls, S.C., 3,030 63 D3
Great Falls L., Tenn. 71 F6
Great Fish, r., S. Af. 164 D7
Great Gandak, r., India 145 G4
Great Gonerby, U.K., 1,128 114 G5
Great Gransden, U.K. 114 H6
Great Guana Cay, Bah. Is. 95 b6
Great Guana Cay, Bah. Is. 95 c8
Greatham, U.K., 1,457 112 h10
Great Harbour Cay, Bah. Is. 95 a7
Great Harwood, U.K., 10,718 114 D3
Great Inagua, i., Bah. Is. 95 D2
Great Indian Des., India 144 ·
Great L., Austl. 173 f13
Great Lakes, N. Amer. 35 F5
Great Malvern, U.K., 24,373 113 E5
Great Meadows, N.J. 61 B2
Great Meteor Tablemount, Atl. Oc. 180 K5
Great Miami, r., Ohio 70 E3
Great Mills, Md. 62 H4
Great Milton, U.K. 114 F7
Great Missenden, U.K., 5,737 114 G7
Great Namakwaland, reg., S.-W. Af. 164 B6
Great Natuna, i., Indon. 148 C2
Great Neck, N.Y., 10,171 58 d13
Great Nicobar, i., India 146 A6
Great North East Chan., Austl.-Terr. Papua 174 d3
Great Ormes Head, pt., U.K. 113 E5
Great Peconic Bay, N.Y. 56 G9
Great Pedro Bluff, pt., Jam. 96 p9
Great Plain of the Koukdjuak, N.W.T., Can. 41 P4
Great Plains, U.S. 50 E1
Great Pt., Mass. 57 Q7
Great Pond, Me. 55 D4
Great Pd., Me. 55 D4
Great Pond Bay, St. Croix 97 1
Great Ponton, U.K. 114 G5
Great Quittacas Pd., Mass. 57 N5
Great Rann of Kutch, salt waste, India 144 C4
Great Ruaha, r., Tanz. 164 E3
Great St. Bernard Pass, It.-Switz. 124 B3
Great Salt L., Utah 78 B1
Great Salt Lake Des., Utah 78 B1
Great Salt Plains Res., Okla. 76 E1
Great Sand Dunes Nat. Mon., Colo. 79 C3
Great Sandy Desert, Austl. 172 C3
Great Sandy Des., U.S. 50 D2
Great Sandy I. = Fraser I.
Great Shefford, U.K. 114 F8
Great Shelford, U.K., 3,761 114 J6
Great Shunner Fell, mtn., U.K. 113 E4
Great Sitkin I., Alaska 85 f8
Great Slave L., N.W.T., Can. 40 G4
Great Smoky Mts., N.C.-Tenn. 63 ·
Great Smoky Mts. Nat. Pk., N.C.-Tenn. 71 H6
Great Sound, Berm. Is. 108 1
Great Sound, N.J. 61 B5
Great South Bay, N.Y. 58 g14
Great Staughton, U.K. 114 H6
Great Swamp, N.J. 58 b14
Great Tenasserim, r., Burma 146 B4
Great Thatch I., V.I. 97 4
Great Torrington, U.K., 2,920 113 D6
Great Valley, N.Y. 58 C7
Great Valley, U.S. 50 B3
Great Valley, U.S. 51 K3
Great Victoria Desert, Austl. 172 C4
Great Village, N.S., Can. 47 U11
Great Wall = Ch'ang Ch'eng
Great Wass I., Me. 55 E4
Great West Chan. = Ta-hsi Shui-tao
Great Whale, r., Qué., Can. 44 J3
Great Whale River, Qué., Can. 44 H3
Great Whernside, mtn., U.K. 114 E2
Great Works, r., Me. 54 F5
Great Works Str., Me. 55 D4
Great Yarmouth, U.K., 52,970 113 G5
Great Zab = Zap
Grebenau, F.R.Ger. 118 B3
Grebenhain, F.R.Ger., 1,086 119 G4
Grebbestad, Swed. 121 D2
Grebków, Pol. 127 D2
Greco, Urug. 105 c11
Greco, C., Cyp. 142 f10
Gredos, Sa. de, Sp. 122 C2
Greece, ctry., 8,551,000* 129
Greece, N.Y. 58 n20
Greeley, Colo., 26,314 79 C1
Greeley, co., Kans., 2,087 75 D5
Greeley, Kans., 415 75 K5
Greeley, co., Nebr., 4,595 75 G2
Greeley, Nebr., 656 75 G2
Greeley, Pa. 61 N3
Greeleyville, S.C., 504 63 E4
Greely Fiord, N.W.T., Can. 41 N1
Greem-Bell', O., U.S.S.R. 134 F1
Green, Kans., 190 75 J4
Green, co., Ky., 11,249 71 F4
Green, co., Wis., 25,851 66 D6
Green, r., Ill. 68 C2
Green, r., Ky. 71 D4
Green, r., Mass.-Vt. 56 F2
Green, r., Utah 78 D2
Green, r., Wash. 80 B2
Green, r., Wash. 80 C2
Green, r., Wyo. 81 D4
Green, W. Br., r., Mass. 56 C2
Greenacres, Calif. 82 D5
Greenacres, Wash., 2,074 80 E2
Greenacres City, Fla., 1,026 65 b8
Greenback, Tenn., 285 71 G6
Greenbank, Wash. 81 a6
Green Bank, W. Va. 62 D4
Green Bay, Va. 62 F5
Green Bay, Wis., 62,888 66 F4
Green Bay, Mich.-Wis. 66 F4
Greenbelt, Md., 7,479 62 b8
Greenbo L., Ky. 71 H3
Green Brae, Calif. 83 e12
Greenbrier, Ark., 401 73 C2
Greenbrier, Ind. 70 C4
Greenbrier, Tenn., 1,238 71 E5
Greenbrier, co., W. Va., 34,446 62 D4
Greenbrier, r., W. Va. 62 D4
Green Bk., N.J. 58 b14
Greenbush (part of Scituate), Mass. 57 O4
Greenbush, Mich. 67 K4
Greenbush, Minn., 706 74 D1
Greenbush, Wis. 66 E5
Green Camp, Ohio, 492 70 F2
Green C., Austl. 173 h11
Greencastle, Ind., 8,506 70 C3
Green Castle, Mo., 250 72 E4
Greencastle, Pa., 2,988 60 G6
Green City, Mo., 628 72 D4
Green Cove Springs, Fla., 4,233 65 H3
Greendale, Ind., 2,861 70 D3
Greendale (part of Worcester), Mass. 57 J3
Greendale, Va. 62 B6
Greendale, Wis., 6,843 66 d12
Greene, co., Ala., 13,600 64 A3
Greene, co., Ark., 25,198 73 E1
Greene, co., Ga., 11,193 64 F2
Greene, co., Ill., 17,460 68 B4
Greene, co., Ind., 26,327 70 B3
Greene, co., Iowa, 14,379 72 C3
Greene, Iowa, 1,427 72 E2
Greene, Me. 55 B4
Greene, co., Miss., 8,366 73 G6
Greene, co., Mo., 126,276 72 D7
Greene, co., N.Y., 31,372 59 M7
Greene, N.Y., 2,051 59 J7
Greene, co., N.C., 16,741 63 G2
Greene, co., Ohio, 94,642 70 F3
Greene, co., Pa., 39,424 60 B6
Greene (part of Coventry), R.I. 57 K6
Greene, co., Tenn., 42,163 71 J5
Greene, co., Va., 4,715 62 F4
Greene I., Ont., Can. 67 K3
Greeneville, Tenn., 11,759 71 H5
Greenfield, U.K., 1,210 114 C4
Greenfield, Calif., 1,680 82 C4
Greenfield, Ill., 1,064 68 B4
Greenfield, Ind., 9,049 70 D3
Greenfield, Iowa, 2,243 72 C3
Greenfield, Me. 55 D3
Greenfield, Mass., 14,389; 17,690(T) 56 F2
Greenfield, Mo., 1,172 72 D7
Greenfield, N.H. 54 D6
Greenfield, N. Mex. 79 C5
Greenfield, Ohio, 5,422 70 F3
Greenfield, Okla., 128 76 E2
Greenfield, Tenn., 1,779 71 C5
Greenfield, Va. 62 F5
Greenfield, Wis., 17,636 66 E6
Greenfield Center, N.Y. 59 v27
Greenfield Hill (part of Fairfield), Conn. 56 C8
Greenfield Park, Qué., Can., 7,684 47 p17
Green Forest, Ark., 1,038 73 B1
Green Harbor (part of Marshfield), Mass. 57 O4
Green Haven, Md., 1,302 62 c8
Greenhead, Fla. 65 D2
Green Head, Austl. 172 A4
Green Hill, Ala. 64 B1
Green Hill, R.I. 57 K7
Greenhills, Ohio, 5,407 71 h10
Green Island, N.Y., 3,533 59 w29
Green I., Antigua 97 9
Green Is., Sol. Is. 175 a1
Green Is., Terr. New Guin. 174 g2
Green Lake, Sask., Can. 43 C3
Green Lake, Tex. 77 P5
Green Lake, co., Wis., 15,418 66 E5
Green Lake, Wis., 953 66 D5
Green L., Me. 55 D4
Green L., Mich. 67 H4
Green L., Minn. 74 E3
Green L., Wis. 66 E5
Green Lakes, Utah 78 D1
Greenland, Barb. 97 10
Greenland, N. Amer., 40,000* 34 H2
Greenland, Colo. 79 c9
Greenland, Mich. 66 D2
Greenland, N.H. 54 F5
Greenland, Ohio 70 F3
Greenland Sea 108 M1
Green Lane, Pa., 582 61 M5
Greenlaw, U.K. 112 E4
Greenlawn, N.Y., 5,422 58 f13
Greenleaf, Kans., 562 75 H4
Greenleaf, Wis. 66 E4
Greenlee, co., Ariz., 11,509 78 D5
Green Mountain, N.C. 63 B2
Green Mtn., N.B., Can. 55 D1
Green Mtn., Colo. 79 C2
Green Mtn., Mont. 81 B1
Green Mountain Falls, Colo., 179 79 C2
Green Mtn. Res., Colo. 79 B2
Green Mts., Vt. 54 A6
Green Oaks, Ill. 69 c7
Greenock, Austl. 172 c8
Greenock, U.K., 74,578 112 D4
Greenock, Md. 62 c9
Greenough, r., Austl. 172 A4
Green Pond, S.C. 63 D5
Green Pond, N.J. 61 C2
Green Pond Mtn., N.J. 58 a13
Greenport, N.Y., 2,608 59 Q9
Green Ridge, Mo., 375 72 D6
Green River, N.B., Can., 1,359 47 R10
Green River, Terr. New Guin. 174 d1
Green River, Utah, 1,075 78 C2
Green River, Vt. 54 B6
Green River, Wyo., 3,497 81 E5
Green River Des., Utah 78 C2
Green River Res., Vt. 54 B2
Green Rock, Ill., 2,677 68 B2
Greens, Barb. 97 10
Greensboro, Ala., 3,081 64 B3
Greensboro, Fla., 709 65 E2
Greensboro, Ga., 2,773 64 F2
Greensboro, Md., 1,160 62 H4
Greensboro, N.C., 119,574 63 D1
Greensboro, Pa., 505 60 B6
Greensboro, Vt. 54 C2
Greensboro Bend, Vt. 54 C2
Greensburg, Ind., 6,605 70 D3
Greensburg, Kans., 1,988 75 F6
Greensburg, Ky., 2,334 71 F4
Greensburg, La., 512 73 E7
Greensburg, Pa., 17,383 60 C5
Greenscares, U.K. 112 b7
Green Sea, S.C. 63 E3

232 · Green Farms—Guledgarh

Greens Farms (part of Westport), Conn. 56 C8
Green's Harbour, Newf., Can. 45 b10
Greens Norton, U.K. 114 F6
Greens Pk., Ariz. 78 D4
Green Springs, Ohio, 1,262 70 G1
Greenstone Pt., U.K. 112 D3
Greensville, Ont., Can. 46 b14
Greensville, co., Va., 16,155 62 G6
Greentop, Mo., 311 72 E4
Greentown, Ind., 1,266 70 D2
Greentown, Pa. 61 p16
Green Turtle Cay, Bah. Is. 95 b6
Greenup, Ill., 1,477 68 D4
Greenup, co., Ky., 29,238 71 H3
Greenup, Ky., 1,240 71 J3
Green Valley, Ill., 522 68 C3
Green Valley, Wis. 66 E4
Green Valley Lake, Calif. 83 k15
Greenview, Calif. 82 B2
Greenview, Ill., 796 68 C3
Green Village, N.J. 58 b14
Greenville, Br. Col., Can. 42 D2
Greenville, Lib., 3,583 162 C5
Greenville, Ala., 6,894 64 C4
Greenville, Calif., 1,140 82 C2
Greenville, Del. 62 e10
Greenville, Fla., 1,318 65 F2
Greenville, Ga., 726 64 E2
Greenville, Ill., 4,569 68 C5
Greenville, Ind., 453 70 C4
Greenville, Iowa, 173 72 B1
Greenville, Ky., 3,198 71 D4
Greenville, Me., 1,893 55 C3
Greenville, Mich., 7,440 67 H5
Greenville, Miss., 41,502 73 D4
Greenville, Mo., 282 72 G7
Greenville, N.H., 1,251 54 D6
Greenville, Greene Co., N.Y. 59 N7
Greenville, Westchester Co., N.Y. 58 d13
Greenville, N.C., 22,860 63 G2
Greenville, Ohio, 10,585 70 E2
Greenville, Pa., 8,765 60 B3
Greenville (part of Smithfield), R.I. 57 K5
Greenville, co., S.C., 209,776 63 B3
Greenville, S.C., 66,188 63 B3
Greenville, Tex., 19,087 77 P3
Greenville, Va. 62 E4
Greenville, W. Va. 62 D5
Greenville, Wis. 66 E4
Greenwater L., Ont., Can. 74 G1
Greenway, Man., Can. 43 e10
Greenway, Ark., 179 73 E1
Greenway, S. Dak. 74 C3
Greenwich, London, U.K. 114 H8
Greenwich, Conn., 53,793(T) 56 B8
Greenwich, N.J. 61 A5
Greenwich, N.Y., 2,263 59 N5
Greenwich, Ohio, 1,371 70 G1
Greenwich Hill, N.B., Can. 47 S11
Greenwood, Br. Col., Can. 42 H4
Greenwood, Ala. 64 b8
Greenwood, Ark., 1,558 73 A2
Greenwood, Del., 768 62 J4
Greenwood, Fla. 65 D2
Greenwood, Ind., 7,169 70 C3
Greenwood, co., Kans., 11,253 75 J6
Greenwood, Warren Co., Ky. 71 E5
Greenwood, McCreary Co., Ky. 71 G5
Greenwood, La. 73 A5
Greenwood, Me. 55 B4
Greenwood, Mich. 67 J4
Greenwood, Minn. 74 a6
Greenwood, Miss., 20,436 73 E4
Greenwood, Mo., 488 72 C6
Greenwood, Nebr., 403 75 J3
Greenwood, N.Y. 58 E7
Greenwood, Pa., 1,575* 60 F4
Greenwood (part of Warwick), R.I. 57 L6
Greenwood, co., S.C., 44,346 63 B3
Greenwood, S.C., 16,644 63 B3
Greenwood, S. Dak. 74 C4
Greenwood, Va. 62 F4
Greenwood, Clark Co., Wis., 1,041 66 C4
Greenwood, Vernon Co., Wis. 66 C5
Greenwood, L., S.C. 63 B3
Greenwood Lake, N.Y., 1,236 59 M9
Greenwood Lake, N.J.-N.Y. 61 C1
Greer, Ariz. 78 D4
Greer, Ohio 70 G2
Greer, co., Okla., 8,877 76 D3
Greer, S.C., 8,967 63 B3
Greer, W. Va. 62 E3
Greeson, L., Ark. 73 B3
Gregg, co., Tex., 69,436 77 Q3
Gregory, Ark. 73 D2
Gregory, co., S. Dak., 7,399 74 C4
Gregory, S. Dak., 1,478 74 C4
Gregory, Tex., 1,970 77 P6
Gregory, L., Austl. 172 B3
Gregory, L., Austl. 172 E4
Gregory Bald, mtn., N.C.-Tenn. 63 b7
Gregory Range, Austl. 173 F2
Gregory Town, Bah. Is. 95 c7
Greiffenberg, Ger.D.R. 118 D2
Greifswald, Ger.D.R., 46,728 118 D1
Greifswalder B., Ger.D.R. 118 D1
Greipstad, Nor. 121 A2
Greith, Aust. 124 M6
Greiz, Ger.D.R., 39,097 118 D3
Gremikha, U.S.S.R. 134 C3
Gremyachinsk, U.S.S.R., 36,000 137 i7
Grenå, Den., 9,088 121 C4
Grenada, Calif. 82 B2
Grenada, co., Miss., 18,409 73 F4
Grenada, Miss., 7,914 73 F4
Grenada, i., Lesser Ant. 97 18
Grenada L., Miss. 73 F4
Grenade, Fr., 3,394 117 D5
Grenadine Is., Lesser Ant. 97 20
Grenchen, Switz., 18,000 124 B1
Grenen, spit, Den. 121 C3
Grenfell, Austl., 2,584 173 G5
Grenfell, Sask., Can., 1,226 43 D5
Grengiols, Switz. 124 C2
Grenloch, N.J. 60 f12
Grenoble, Fr., 162,764 117 F4
Grenola, Kans., 349 75 J6
Grenora, N. Dak., 448 74 A1
Grensgebergte, Sur. 101 N6
Grenville, Qué., Can., 1,300 47 K3
Grenville, Gren., 1,817 97 18
Grenville, N. Mex., 55 79 D3
Grenville, S. Dak., 151 74 D3
Grenville, Mt., Br. Col., Can. 42 F3
Gréolières, Fr. 116 m13
Gresham, Nebr., 239 75 H2
Gresham, Oreg., 3,944 80 b7
Gresham, S.C. 63 E4
Gresham, Wis. 66 E4
Gresik, Indon. 148 C3
Gresik, Indon. 148 e7
Gressenich, F.R.Ger., 7,700 119 A3
Gressvik, Nor. 121 C1
Gresten, Aust., 1,463 124 M6
Gretna, Man., Can. 43 F5
Gretna, U.K. 113 E4
Gretna, Fla., 647 65 E2
Gretna, Ill. 69 b9
Gretna, La., 21,967 73 F8
Gretna, Nebr., 745 75 J2
Gretna, Va., 900 62 E6
Gretton, U.K. 114 G5
Gretz-Armainvilliers, Fr., 3,119 116 i12
Greussen, Ger.D.R. 118 C3
Greve, Den., 2,587 121 a7
Grevelingen, estuary, Neth. 115 C3
Greven, F.R.Ger., 20,894 118 A2
Grevená, Gr., 6,892 129 C4
Grevenbroich, F.R.Ger., 19,012 119 B2
Grevenmacher, Lux., 2,722 115 E5
Grevesmühlen, Ger.D.R., 11,109 118 C2
Grey, C., Austl. 172 E1
Grey, r., N.Z. 175 f6
Greyabbey, U.K. 113 D4
Greybull, Wyo., 2,286 81 F3
Grey Eagle, Minn., 372 74 E3
Greyhound, Selat, Indon. 149 H3
Greyhound Pt., Tutuila 177 39
Greylock, Mt., Mass. 56 D2
Greymouth, N.Z., 8,881 175 f6
Grey Ra., Austl. 173 F4
Greystone (part of N. Providence), R.I. 57 L5
Greystones, Ire., 3,565 113 D5
Greytown, Nic.=San Juan del Norte
Greytown, S. Af., 7,737 164 E6
Grezzana, It., 6,485 122 e5
Griba, mts., Alb. 125 D4
Gribanovskiy, U.S.S.R. 136 F3
Gridley, Calif., 3,343 82 C3
Gridley, Ill., 889 68 D3
Gridley, Kans., 321 75 K5
Gries, Aust., 1,267 124 H6
Gries, Fr., 1,908 116 e9
Griesbach, F.R.Ger., 2,349 118 D4
Griesheim, F.R.Ger., 12,484 119 E5
Griffen, Aust., 3,014 124 L7
Griffin, Ga., 21,735 64 E2
Griffin, Ind., 212 70 B4
Griffin Point, pk., Utah 78 C3
Griffith, Austl., 6,608 173 F5
Griffith, Ind., 12,810 70 B1
Griffith, Miss. 73 G4
Griffithville, Ark., 172 73 D2
Grifton, N.C., 1,816 63 G2
Grigel, Fr. Guiana 101 O6
Griggs, co., N. Dak., 5,023 74 C2
Griggs, Okla. 76 A1
Griggsville, Ill., 1,240 68 B4
Grignols, Fr., 1,333 117 C4
Grigoriopol', U.S.S.R., 8,000 136 C4
Grigston, Kans. 75 E5
Grijalva, r., Mex. 93 G5
Grik, Malay., 3,394 147 o14
Grillby, Swed. 120 e8
Grim, C., Austl. 173 F6
Grimaud, Fr., 1,378 117 G5
Grimbergen, Belg., 8,871 115 d9
Grimes, Iowa, 697 72 D3
Grimes, Okla. 76 D2
Grimes, co., Tex., 12,709 77 Q4
Grimesland, N.C., 362 63 G2
Grimeton, Swed. 121 E3
Grimma, Ger.D.R., 16,113 118 D3
Grimmen, Ger.D.R. 118 D1
Grimoldby, U.K. 114 J4
Grimsby, Ont., Can., 5,039 46 E5
Grimsby, U.K., 96,712 113 F5
Grimsby Beach, Ont., Can. 46 d15
Grimsey, i., Ice. 120 a6
Grimshaw, Alta., Can., 1,059 42 H2
Grimsley, Tenn. 71 G5
Grimstad, Nor., 2,285 120 B4
Grindavík, Ice. 120 a6
Grindelwald, Switz., 3,244 124 C2
Grindleton, U.K. 114 D3
Grindsted, Den., 7,385 121 A5
Grindstone, Me. 55 D3
Grindstone, L., Qué., Can. 46 F2
Grind Stone City, Mich. 67 L4
Grindstone I., N.Y. 59 H3
Grindstone L., Wis. 66 B3
Grinem, i., Eniwetok 176 28
Grinnell, Iowa, 7,367 72 E3
Grinnell, Kans., 396 75 E4
Grinnell Pen., N.W.T., Can. 41 K2
Grintavec, mt., Yug. 125 B1
Grinton, U.K. 112 g11
Griquatown, S. Af., 2,524 164 C6
Grise Fiord, N.W.T., Can. 41 N2
Grisek, Malay., 2,257 147 p15
Gris Nez, C., Fr. 117 D1
Grisslehamn, Swed. 120 D3
Griswold, Iowa, 1,207 72 B3
Griswold L., Ill. 69 b7
Griswold Pt., Conn. 56 G7
Griswoldville (part of Colrain), Mass. 56 F2
Grisy-Suisnes, Fr., 1,074 116 i12
Grivegnée, Belg., 22,482 115 D4
Grizzly I., Calif. 83 e11
Grkovci, Yug. 125 C2
Grmeč Planina, Yug. 125 C2
Groais I., Newf., Can. 45 Q4
Grobiņa, U.S.S.R., 4,300 136 A1
Grocholice, Pol. 127 i5
Grödig, Aust., 3,365 124 J6
Grodków, Pol., 4,032 127 B3
Grodno, U.S.S.R., 81,000 134 B4
Grodziec, Pol., 10,522 127 i6
Grodzisk Mazowiecki, Pol., 18,892 127 D2
Grodzisk Wielkopolski, Pol., 7,736 127 B2
Groenlo, Neth., 5,200 115 E2
Groesbeck, Ohio 71 h10
Groesbeck, Tex., 2,498 77 P4
Groesbeek, Neth., 4,100 115 D3
Grogan, Austl. 173 f10
Groitzsch, Ger.D.R. 126 b5
Groix, Fr., 3,525 116 B3
Groix, Î. de, Fr. 116 B3
Grójec, Pol., 8,593 127 D3
Grokgak, Indon. 148 E5
Grömitz, F.R.Ger., 3,273 118 C1
Gronau, Ndrsachs., F.R.Ger., 5,260 118 B2
Gronau, Nrh.-Wf., F.R.Ger., 24,789 118 A2
Grong, Nor. 120 C2
Grønholt, Den. 121 a7
Groningen, Neth., 141,500 115 E1
Groningen, Sur. 101 N5
Grønland, N. Amer.=Greenland
Gronlid, Sask., Can. 43 D4
Groom, Tex., 679 76 N2
Groom Pk., Ariz. 78 B4
Groot, r., S. Af. 164 C7
Groot Baai, St. Maarten 97 7
Grootebroek, Neth., 3,000 115 D2
Groote Eylandt, Austl. 172 E1
Grootegast, Neth. 115 E1
Grootfontein, S.-W. Afr., 3,722 164 C5
Groot Piscadera, Cur. 97 16
Grootvlei, S. Af. 165 k17
Grootvloer, l., S. Af. 164 C6
Gropeni, Rum. 128 F2
Grosbliederstroff, Fr., 3,108 116 d8
Gros Cap, Mich. 67 J3
Groşii Noi, Rum. 128 D1
Gros Islet, St. Lucia, 1,016 97 11
Grosmont Fawr, U.K. 114 C7
Gros Montagne, Fr. Guiana 101 O6
Gros-Morne, Haiti, 2,451 96 k6
Gros-Morne, Mart. 97 12
Gros Morne, Newf., Can. 45 P5
Gros Piton, mtn., St. Lucia 97 11
Grossaffoltern, Switz., 2,063 124 B1
Grossarl, Aust., 2,566 124 K6
Grossauheim, F.R.Ger., 10,345 119 G4
Grossbeeren, Ger.D.R. 119 e11
Gross Bieberau, F.R.Ger., 3,053 119 F5
Grossbottwar, F.R.Ger., 3,127 119 G6
Grossbreitenbach, Ger.D.R. 118 C3
Grosse Isle, Man., Can. 43 g9
Grosse I., Mich. 67 f16
Grossen Buseck, F.R.Ger., 3,348 119 F3
Grossenhain, Ger.D.R., 19,514 118 D3
Grossenlinden, F.R.Ger., 4,010 119 F3
Grossenlüder, F.R.Ger., 3,037 119 H3
Grossensee, F.R.Ger., 1,047 119 b8
Grossenzersdorf, Aust., 2,406 124 d10
Grosse Pointe, Mich., 6,631 67 g15
Grosse Pte., Guad. 97 14
Grosse Pointe Farms, Mich., 12,172 67 g15
Grosse Pointe Park, Mich., 15,457 67 g15
Grosse Pointe Shores, Mich., 2,301 67 g15
Grosse Pointe Woods, Mich., 18,580 67 g15
Grosser Arber, mt., F.R.Ger. 118 D4
Grosser Feldberg, F.R.Ger. 119 E4
Grosser Plöner See, F.R.Ger. 118 C1
Grosse Tete, La., 768 73 D7
Grosseto, It., 49,371 123 C3
Grossgartach, F.R.Ger., 3,657 119 G6
Gross-Gerau, F.R.Ger., 10,616 119 E5
Grossglockner, mtn. Aust. 124 J6
Gross Grönau, F.R.Ger., 1,532 119 c8
Grosshahnberg, F.R.Ger. 119 E7
Grosshansdorf, F.R.Ger., 5,040 119 b8
Grossheubach, F.R.Ger., 3,088 119 G5
Grosskarben, F.R.Ger., 2,705 119 F4
Grossmugl, Aust. 124 N5
Grossostheim, F.R.Ger., 6,127 119 G5
Grosspetersdorf, Aust., 2,045 124 N6
Grossräschen, Ger.D.R., 12,129 118 D3
Gross Reken, F.R.Ger., 5,994 119 C1
Gross Res., Colo. 79 b8
Grossrinderfeld, F.R.Ger., 1,196 119 H5
Gross Rohrheim, F.R.Ger., 3,048 119 F5
Grossschönau, Ger.D.R. 118 E3
Gross Umstadt, F.R.Ger., 6,079 119 F5
Gross-Zimmern, F.R.Ger., 6,423 119 F5
Grostenquin, Fr. 116 c9
Grosuplje, Yug. 125 B2
Groszowice, Pol., 3,349 127 C3
Groton, Conn., 10,111;29,937(T) 56 H7
Groton, Mass., 1,178;3,904(T) 57 K2
Groton, N.H. 54 D4
Groton, N.Y., 2,123 59 H6
Groton, S. Dak., 1,063 74 C3
Groton, Vt., 387 54 C3
Groton, L., Vt. 54 C3
Grottaferrata, It., 7,878 123 b8
Grottaglie, It., 22,329 123 F4
Grottoes, Va., 969 62 F4
Grötzingen, F.R.Ger., 5,653 119 F6
Groundbirch, Br. Col., Can. 42 G2
Grouse=Lost River, Idaho
Grouse Creek, Utah 78 B1
Grouse Creek Mts., Utah 78 B1
Grouw, Neth., 3,200 115 D1
Grove, U.K., 1,845 114 F7
Grove, Me. 55 E3
Grove Beach (part of Westbrook), Conn. 56 G7
Grove City, Fla. 65 G6
Grove City, Ohio, 8,107 70 F3
Grove City, Pa., 8,368 60 B3
Grovedale, Alta., Can. 42 H2
Grove Hill, Ala., 1,834 64 B4
Groveland, Fla., 1,747 65 G4
Groveland, Ind. 70 C3
Groveland, Kans. 75 H5
Groveland, Mass., 3,297(T) 57 M1
Groveport, Ohio, 2,043 70 b7
Grover, Colo., 133 79 C1
Grover, N.C., 538 63 C2
Grover, Okla. 76 J1
Grover, Pa. 60 J2
Grover, Utah 78 C2
Grover City, Calif., 5,210 82 C5
Grover Hill, Ohio, 547 70 E1
Grovertown, Ind. 70 C1
Groves, Tex., 17,304 77 R5
Groveton, N.H., 2,004 54 E2
Groveton, Tex., 1,148 77 Q4
Grovetown, Ga., 1,396 64 G2
Grow, Tex. 77 N3
Growler, Ariz. 78 B5
Growler Wash, Ariz. 78 B5
Groznyy, U.S.S.R., 270,000 134 D5
Grubbenvorst, Neth. 119 A2
Grubišno Polje, Yug., 2,591 125 C2
Gruda, Yug. 125 D3
Grudovo, Bulg., 7,680 128 F3
Grudusk, Pol. 127 D2
Grudziądz, Pol., 65,000* 127 C2
Gruene, Tex. 76 b6
Gruinard Bay, U.K. 112 D3
Grulla, Tex., 1,436 77 O6
Grummetti, r., Tanz. 165 g15
Grums, Swed. 120 C4
Grünau, S.-W. Afr. 164 B6
Grunberg, F.R.Ger., 3,711 119 G3
Grundy, co., Ill., 22,350 68 D2
Grundy, co., Iowa, 14,132 72 E2
Grundy, co., Mo., 12,220 72 D4
Grundy, co., Tenn., 11,512 71 F6
Grundy, Va., 2,287 62 B5
Grundy Center, Iowa, 2,403 72 E2
Grünhain, Ger.D.R. 126 b6
Grunheide, Ger.D.R. 119 f11
Grüningen, Switz., 1,649 124 C1
Grünsfeld, F.R.Ger., 1,914 119 H5
Grunstadt, F.R.Ger., 7,099 119 E5
Grunthal, Man., Can. 43 h10
Grunwald, Pol. 127 D2
Grupčin, Yug. 125 E4
Grüsch, Switz. 124 D2
Gruver, Tex., 1,030 76 N1
Gruyère, L. de la, Switz. 124 B2
Gruyères, Switz., 1,349 124 B2
Gruzinskaya S.S.R., U.S.S.R., 4,483,000* 134 D5
Gryazi, U.S.S.R., 33,500 136 F2
Gryazovets, U.S.S.R., 9,100 136 F1
Grybów, Pol., 3,087 127 D4
Gryfice, Pol., 10,949 127 A2
Gryfino, Pol., 5,020 127 A2
Gryfów Śląski, Pol., 5,835 127 A3
Grygla, Minn., 192 74 E1
Gschwend, F.R.Ger., 1,853 119 H7
Gstaad, Switz. 124 B2
Gua, India, 8,633 145 G5
Guabito, Pan. 94 F6
Guaca, Col. 100 D4
Guacanayabo, Golfo de, Cuba 96 e2
Guacara, Ven., 11,141 101 b11
Guacarí, Col. 100 B6
Guachara, Ven. 100 F4
Gu Achi, Ariz. 78 C5
Guachipas, Arg., 1,500* 105 B3
Guachucal, Col. 100 B7
Guaçuí, Braz., 7,724 103 f17
Guadalajara, Mex., 580,617 92 E4
Guadalajara, Sp., 21,230 122 D2
Guadalcanal, i., Sol. Is. 170 E5
Guadalcázar, Mex., 1,170 93 E3
Guadalimar, r., Sp. 122 D3
Guadalope, r., Sp. 122 E2
Guadalquivir, r., Sp. 122 C4
Guadalupe, Bol., 5,149 102 c11
Guadalupe, Col. 100 C6
Guadalupe, C.R., 21,413 94 F5
Guadalupe, Cuba, 1,098 96 d1
Guadalupe, Gto., Mex. 93 d8
Guadalupe, N.L., Mex., 26,830 93 F3
Guadalupe, Zac., Mex., 7,846 92 E3
Guadalupe, Sp., 4,079 122 C3
Guadalupe, Calif., 2,614 82 C5
Guadalupe, co., N. Mex., 5,610 79 C4
Guadalupe, co., Tex., 29,017 77 P5
Guadalupe, r., Calif. 83 f13
Guadalupe, r., Tex. 77 O5
Guadalupe, I. de, Mex. 92 a6
Guadalupe Bravos, Mex., 1,864 92 D1
Guadalupe Mts., N. Mex. 79 C5
Guadalupe Pk., Tex. 77 L4
Guadalupe Victoria, Mex., 6,597 92 D3
Guadarrama, Ven. 100 G3
Guadarrama, Sa. de, Sp. 122 D2
Guadeloupe, i., Lesser Ant., 316,000* 97 14
Guadeloupe Passage, W.I. 95 G3
Guadiana, Bahia de, Cuba 96 a1
Guadiana, r., Port. 122 B4
Guadiana, r., Sp. 122 C3
Guadiana Menor, r., Sp. 122 D4
Guadiato, r., Sp. 122 C3
Guadix, Sp., 24,704 122 D4
Guaduas, Col. 101 e14
Guafo, I., Chile 105 A6
Guaíba, Braz., 7,375 103 F8
Guaico, Chile 104 e16
Guaillabamba, r., Ec. 104 B1
Guáimaro, Cuba, 4,503 96 e2
Guainia, r., Col.-Ven. 100 E6
Guaiquinima, Co., Ven. 101 J5
Guaíra, Braz., 5,196 103 F6
Guaire, r., Ven. 101 c11
Guaitecas, Is., Chile 105 A6
Guajaba, Cayo, Cuba 96 e2
Guajará-Mirim, Braz., 7,115 102 D4
Guajataca, L. de, res., P.R. 96 s10
Guajataca, r., P.R. 96 s10
Guajillo, Tex. 77 O6
Guajira, Pen. de la, Col. 100 E1
Gualaca, Pan., 1,380 94 F6
Gualaceo, Ec., 3,070 104 c11
Gualaco, Hond., 1,894 94 E3
Gualala, Calif. 82 B3
Guálan, Guat., 4,141 94 d8
Gualanday, Col. 100 C5
Gualdo Tadino, It., 13,971 123 D3
Gualeguay, Arg., 30,000* 105 C4
Gualeguay, r., Arg. 105 b10
Gualeguaychú, Arg., 50,000* 105 D4
Guali, r., Col. 101 e14
Gualicho, Salina, Arg. 105 B6
Guallatiri, Vol., Chile 105 •
Gualleco, Chile 104 f15
Gualqui, Chile, 3,491 104 e16
Guam, Pac. Oc., 77,000* 170 D4
Guamá, Braz., 2,470 103 G2
Guama, Ven., 3,422 100 F2
Guamal, Col. 100 C3
Guamo, Col. 100 C2
Guamo, Col. 100 C5
Guamo, Cuba, 2,507 96 e2
Guamote, Ec., 2,657 104 c10
Guamúchil, Mex., 5,865 92 C3
Gua Musang, Malay., 2,324 147 p14
Guanabacoa, Cuba, 32,490 96 b1
Guanabara, st., Braz., 3,307,163 103 H6
Guanacaste, Cord. de, C.R. 94 E5
Guanaceví, Mex., 1,148 92 D3
Guanagazapa, Guat. 94 c9
Guanahacabibes, Golfo de, Cuba 96 a1
Guanahacabibes, Pen. de, Cuba 96 a2
Guana Island, Antigua 97 9
Guana I., V.I. 97 4
Guanaja, I. de, Hond. 94 E2
Guanajay, Cuba, 12,908 96 b1
Guanajibo, r., P.R. 96 r10
Guanajuato, st., Mex., 1,735,490 92 E4
Guanajuato, Mex., 28,135 92 E4
Guanal, Punta del, Cuba 96 b2
Guanambi, Braz., 5,268 103 H4
Guanape, Ven. 100 H3
Guanape, Ven. 101 c12
Guanare, Ven., 16,935 100 F3
Guanare, r., Ven. 100 F3
Guanarito, Ven., 1,047 100 F3
Guane, Cuba, 4,070 96 a1
Guánica, P.R., 4,100 96 s11
Guánico, Pan. 94 G7
Guanipa, r., Ven. 101 J3
Guano, Ec., 4,847 104 c10
Guanoco, Ven. 101 J2
Guano L., Oreg. 80 D4
Guanta, Ven., 8,211 101 H2
Guantánamo, Cuba, 64,671 96 f2
Guantánamo, Bahia de, Cuba 96 f3
Guantánamo, r., Cuba 96 f2
Guapi, Col. 100 B6
Guapi, B., Col. 100 A6
Guápiles, C.R. 94 F5
Guaporé, Braz., 6,405 103 F7
Guaporé, r., Bol.-Braz. 102 D4
Guaqui, Bol., 14,204 102 a10
Guarabira, Braz., 15,848 103 J3
Guaraciaba, Braz., 1,561 103 e17
Guaraguao, P.R. 96 s10
Guaranda, Ec., 9,598 104 c10
Guarani, Braz., 2,708 103 e17
Guarani, Pan. 94 G6
Guarapuava, Braz., 13,546 103 F7
Guaratinguetá, Braz., 38,293 103 H6
Guar Chempedak, Malay., 5,246 148 A1
Guarda, Port., 12,787 122 B2
Guardafui, C.=Asir, Ras
Guardatinajas, Ven. 100 F3
Guard Bridge, U.K. 112 e7
Guardiagrele, It., 12,143 123 E3
Guardian, W. Va. 62 D4
Guardia Sanframondi, It., 6,854 123 c9
Guardo, Sp., 7,531 122 C1
Guareiras, Cuba, 1,122 96 c1
Guareña, Sp., 9,742 122 B3
Guarenas, Ven., 13,779 101 c11
Guarico, Ven., 2,729 100 F3
Guárico, Embalse del, Ven. 100 G3
Guarico, Punta, Cuba 96 f2
Guárico, r., Ven. 100 G3
Guarino, r., Col. 101 d14
Guarita, Hond., 1,458 94 e9
Guaritico, r., Ven. 100 F4
Guarne, Col. 101 d13
Guaro, Cuba, 1,362 96 f2
Guarrojo, r., Col. 100 E5
Guarulhos, Braz., 77,980 103 c18
Guarumal, Pan. 94 G7
Guarus, Braz., 21,492 103 f17
Guasaca, Nic. 94 E4
Guasave, Mex., 17,398 92 C3
Guasca, Col. 100 C5
Guasdualito, Ven., 4,580 100 E4
Guasimal, Cuba, 1,752 96 d2
Guasimal, Ven. 100 G4
Guasipati, Ven., 3,382 101 K4
Guastalla, It., 13,845 122 d6
Guatacondo, Chile 102 a12
Guatapé, Col. 101 d13
Guataquí, Col. 101 e15
Guatavita, Col. 101 f14
Guatemala, ctry., 4,284,473 94 B3
Guatemala, Guat., 389,823 94 B3
Guatemala Basin, Pac. Oc. 169 J2
Guateque, Col. 100 D5
Guática, Col. 101 d14
Guatire, Ven., 10,979 100 G2
Guatopo, Ven. 101 c11
Guatraché, Arg., 2,500* 105 C5
Guaugurina, Terr. Papua 174 f3
Guaviare, r., Col. 100 E6
Guaxupé, Braz., 14,168 103 G6
Guayabal, Col. 101 e14
Guayabal, Cuba, 5,889 96 e2
Guayabal, Ven. 100 G4
Guayabero, r., Col. 100 D6
Guayaguayare, Trin. and Tob. 96 h5
Guayama, P.R., 19,183 96 t10
Guayanés, P., P.R. 96 u10
Guayanés, r., P.R. 96 u10
Guayanilla, P.R., 3,067 96 s10
Guayanilla, Bahia de, P.R. 96 s11
Guayape, r., Hond. 94 D3
Guayapo, r., Ven. 100 G5
Guayaquil, Ec., 506,037 104 A2
Guayaquil, G. de, Ec. 104 A2
Guayas, r., Col. 100 C7
Guaymango, El Salv. 94 d10
Guaymas, Mex., 34,845 92 C2
Guaynabo, P.R., 3,343 96 t10
Guayos, Cuba, 5,509 96 d1
Guazacapán, Guat., 4,995 94 B3
Guazapa, El Salv., 1,996 94 d10
Guba, D.R.Congo 165 n19
Gubakha, U.S.S.R., 93,000 134 E4
Gubat, Phil., 8,392 153 i15
Gubbio, It., 34,606 123 D3
Guben, Ger.D.R., 22,548 118 E3
Guber, r., Pol. 127 D1
Gubin, Pol., 10,739 127 A3
Gubio, Nigeria 162 G3
Gubkin, U.S.S.R., 21,300 136 E3
Guča, Yug., 2,060 125 E3
Gudalur, India, 24,635 145 k21
Gudauta, U.S.S.R., 12,800 137 b1
Guddu Barrage, Pak. 144 C3
Gudenå, r., Den. 121 B4
Gudermes, U.S.S.R., 19,300 137 c1
Gudivada, India, 44,801 145 F6
Gudiyatam, India, 50,384 145 m19
Gudow, F.R.Ger., 1,558 119 c8
Gudur, India, 25,618 145 F7
Guebwiller, Fr., 10,864 117 G3
Guecho, Sp., 22,951 122 D1
Guejar, r., Col. 100 D6
Guékédou, Guin., 1,360 162 C4
Guelma, Alg., 33,312 160 F1
Guelph, Ont., Can., 39,336 44 H7
Guelph, N. Dak. 74 C2
Guelta, Sp. Sah. 160 B3
Guelta Zemmur=Guelta
Guémar, Alg., 6,461 160 F2
Guéméné-Penfao, Fr., 5,189 117 C3
Güémez, Mex. 93 F3
Guénange, Fr., 8,471 116 b8
Güeñes, Sp., 5,083 122 m11
Güeppi, Peru 104 C2
Guer, Fr., 6,683 117 B3
Guéra, Massif de, Cam. 163 H4
Guérande, Fr., 6,688 116 B3
Guercif, Mor., 5,579 160 D2
Guéréda, Chad 163 H3
Guéret, Fr., 12,577 117 D3
Guerette, Me. 55 D1
Guérin-Kouka, Togo, 7,043 162 d7
Guerneville, Calif. 82 B3
Guernica y Luno, Sp., 7,847 122 n11
Guernsey, co., Ohio, 38,579 70 H2
Guernsey, Ohio 70 H2
Guernsey, Wyo., 800 81 G4
Guernsey, i., U.K. 116 B2
Guerra, Tex. 77 O6
Guerrero, st., Mex., 1,186,716 93 E5
Guerrero, Coah., Mex., 1,171 93 E2
Guerrero, Tam., Mex., 3,409 93 F2
Guest I., Ant. 180 W5
Gueugnon, Fr., 8,374 117 F3
Gueydan, La., 2,156 73 C7
Guffey, Colo. 79 C2
Gugegwe, i., Kwajalein 176 25
Gughe, pk., Eth. 163 L4
Gugu, mtn., Rum. 128 D2
Guguan, i., Mariana Is. 176 23
Guia Lopes da Laguna, Braz., 1,368 103 E6
Guiana Basin, Atl. Oc. 109 J6
Guiana Highlands, S. Amer. 98 C2
Guichen, Fr., 2,869 117 C3
Guichón, Urug., 2,500* 105 c11
Guider, Cam., 4,500* 162 G4
Guide Rock, Nebr., 441 75 G3
Guidizzolo, It., 3,926 122 d5
Guidonia, It., 19,359 123 D3
Guiglo, Iv. Coast, 2,872 162 C4
Guignes, Fr., 1,049 116 k12
Güigüe, Ven., 8,614 101 b11
Guijá=Vila Alferes Chamusca
Güija, L. de, El Salv. 94 d9
Guijuelo, Sp., 3,463 122 C2
Guilarte, Mte., P.R. 96 s10
Guild, N.H. 54 C5
Guilderland, N.Y. 59 v29
Guildford, U.K., 53,976 113 F6
Guildhall, Vt. 54 D2
Guilford, Conn., 2,420;7,913(T) 56 F7
Guilford, Ill. 68 B1
Guilford, Me., 1,372 55 C3
Guilford, Mo., 125 72 C4
Guilford, N.Y. 59 J7
Guilford, co., N.C., 246,520 63 E1
Guilford, Vt. 54 B6
Guilford Center, Vt. 54 B6
Guilford College, N.C. 63 D1
Guillaumes, Fr. 117 G4
Guillermo, Cayo, Cuba 96 d1
Guillestre, Fr., 1,505 117 G4
Guilsfield, U.K. 114 B5
Guilvinec, Fr., 5,037 116 A3
Guímar, Can. Is. 109 4
Guimarães, Braz., 1,512 103 G2
Guimarães, Port., 11,909 122 A2
Guimaras I., Phil. 153 B3
Guimaras Str., Phil. 153 B3
Guimba, Phil., 8,280 153 B2
Guin, Ala., 1,462 64 B2
Guinda, Calif. 82 B3
Guindulaman, Phil., 2,952 153 C3
Guindulman B., Phil. 153 f12
Guinea, ctry., 3,500,000* 162 B4
Guinea, Va. 62 G4
Guinea, G. of, Af. 162 E5
Guinea Basin, Atl. Oc. 109 M6
Guinea Rise, Atl. Oc. 109 M7
Güines, Cuba, 29,226 96 b1
Guingamp, Fr., 10,571 116 B2
Guinobatan, Phil., 7,935 153 h14
Guintacan I., Phil. 153 e10
Guion, Ark., 222 73 D2
Guipavas, Fr., 6,746 116 A2
Güira de Macurijes, Cuba, 1,187 96 c1
Güira de Melena, Cuba, 13,715 96 b1
Guiratinga, Braz., 4,203 103 F5
Güiria, Ven., 10,724 101 J2
Guiry, Fr. 116 f10
Güisa, Cuba, 2,357 96 e2
Guisanbourg, Fr. Guiana 101 O5
Guisborough, U.K., 12,079 112 h10
Guise, Fr., 6,447 117 E2
Guiseley, U.K., 7,552 114 E3
Guitiriz, Sp., 10,406 122 A1
Guiuan, Phil., 5,865 153 C3
Gujan-Mestras, Fr., 5,694 117 C4
Gujarat, st., India, 20,633,350 144 C5
Gujrānwāla, Pak., 196,154 145 E2
Gujrāt, Pak., 59,608 145 D2
Gu Komelik, Ariz. 78 C5
Gukovo, U.S.S.R., 58,000 136 F3
Gulbarga, India, 97,069 145 E6
Gulbene, U.S.S.R., 7,200 136 B1
Gulch C., Newf., Can. 45 N2
Guldborg, Den. 121 D6
Guldenbach, r., F.R.Ger. 119 D5
Guledgarh, India 145 E6

Gulf—Hamont · 233

Gulf, co., Fla., 9,937 65 D3
Gulf, N.C. 63 E2
Gulf Beach, Fla. 65 B2
Gulf Breeze, Fla. 65 B2
Gulf Hammock, Fla. 65 G3
Gulfport, Fla., 9,730 65 c12
Gulfport, Ill., 214 68 A3
Gulfport, Miss., 30,204 73 F7
Gulf Shores, Ala., 356 64 B5
Gulf Stream, Fla., 176 65 b9
Gulf Summit, N.Y. 59 J7
Gulgong, Austl., 1,473 173 G5
Gulistan, U.S.S.R., 12,900 137 e4
Gulkana Reservation, Alaska 85 H3
Gul'kevichi, U.S.S.R. 136 F4
Gull, r., Ont., Can. 46 F4
Gullane, U.K. 112 e7
Gullfoss, falls, Ice. 120 a6
Gullholmen, Swed. 121 D2
Gull I., Newf., Can. 45 c10
Gull I., Mich. 67 H3
Gulliver, Mich. 67 G2
Gulliver L., Ont., Can. 74 G1
Gull Lake, Sask., Can., 1,004 43 B5
Gull L., Mich. 67 H6
Gull L., Minn. 74 E2
Gull Lake, Wis. 66 B3
Gully, Minn., 168 74 E2
Gulmarg, India 145 E2
Gulnare, Colo. 79 C3
Güls, F.R.Ger., 3,669 119 D4
Gulstav, headland, Den. 121 C6
Gulu, Uganda, 4,770 164 E1
Gulvain, mtn., U.K. 112 D3
Gulyay Pole, U.S.S.R., 17,300 136 E4
Gülzow, F.R.Ger., 1,207 119 c9
Guma=P'i-shan
Gumbrechtshoffen, Fr., 1,091 116 d9
Gumel, Nigeria 162 F3
Gümgüm, Turk., 2,040 137 b2
Gumla, India, 10,710 144 e14
Gumlu, Austl. 173 G2
Gummersbach, F.R.Ger., 31,219 118 A3
Gum Neck, N.C. 63 H2
Gumpoldskirchen, Aust., 2,918 124 c10
Gum Spring, Va. 62 G5
Gümüşane, Turk., 5,373 142 D1
Gümüşhacıköy, Turk., 9,426 142 C1
Guna, India, 31,031 145 E4
Guna, pk., Eth. 163 L4
Gunbower, Austl. 173 d10
Gun Club L., Minn. 74 c6
Gunda, China 144 e11
Gundagai, Austl., 2,127 173 G5
Gundelsheim, F.R.Ger., 2,968 119 G6
Gundershoffen, Fr., 1,691 116 e9
Gundik, Indon. 148 e7
Gundlupet, India, 11,732 145 E8
Güney, Turk., 7,046 142 B2
Gunflint L., Can.-U.S. 74 G1
Gunge, Jap. 154 f15
Gungu, D.R.Congo 164 C2
Gun Hill, Barb. 97 10
Gunib, U.S.S.R. 137 c1
Gunisao, r., Man., Can. 43 F4
Gunisao L., Man., Can. 43 F4
Gun L., Mich. 67 H6
Gunn, Alta., Can. 43 a7
Gunnar, Sask., Can. 43 B2
Gunnedah, Austl., 5,129 173 G4
Gunnison, co., Colo., 5,477 79 B2
Gunnison, Colo., 3,477 79 B2
Gunnison, Miss., 448 73 E4
Gunnison, Utah, 1,059 78 C2
Gunnison, r., Colo. 79 A2
Gunt, r., U.S.S.R. 137 g5
Guntakal, India, 48,083 145 E7
Guntersblum, F.R.Ger., 3,048 119 E5
Guntersville, Ala., 6,592 64 C1
Guntersville L., Ala. 64 C1
Guntín, Sp., 6,243 122 B1
Gunton, Man., Can. 43 g9
Guntong, Malay., 15,094 148 B1
Guntramsdorf, Aust., 5,895 124 c10
Guntur, India, 187,122 145 F6
Gunungapi, P., Indon. 149 H4
Gunungraja, Indon. 148 a6
Gunungsitoli, Indon. 148 A2
Gunungsugih, Indon. 148 C4
Günz, r., F.R.Ger. 118 C4
Günzburg, F.R.Ger., 11,353 118 C4
Gunzenhausen, F.R.Ger., 8,817 118 C4
Gurabo, P.R., 3,957 96 u10
Gurahonţ, Rum. 128 D1
Gura Humorului, Rum., 7,216 128 F1
Gurara, r., Nigeria 162 g7
Gurdane, Oreg. 80 D3
Gurdaspur, India, 27,665 145 E3
Gurdon, Ark., 2,166 73 B4
Gurdzhaani, U.S.S.R., 7,700 137 c1
Gurgaon, India, 37,868 145 E3
Gurghiu, Rum. 128 E1
Gurguan Pt., Tinian 176 27
Gurgueia, r., Braz. 103 H3
Gurk, Aust., 1,018 124 L7
Gurkha, Nepal 144 e11
Gurktaler Alpen, Aust. 125 •
Gurla Mandhata, mts., China 144 c10
Gurley, Ala., 706 64 C1
Gurley, Nebr., 329 75 C2
Gurnee, Ill., 1,831 68 E1
Gurnet Pt., Mass. 57 O4
Gurney, Wis. 66 C2
Gursarai, India, 6,504 144 b13
Gurtis, Aust. 124 a8
Gurtnellen, Switz., 1,048 124 C2
Guru, China 144 g11
Gurun, Malay., 4,346 147 o14
Gürün, Turk., 5,650 142 D2
Gurupá, Braz. 103 F2
Gurupi, Braz., 4,148 103 G4
Gurupi, r., Braz. 103 G2
Gur'yev, U.S.S.R., 86,000 134 E5
Gur'yevsk, U.S.S.R., 28,800 137 r11
Gurzuf, U.S.S.R., 5,900 136 D4
Gus', r., U.S.S.R. 136 d6
Gusau, Nigeria, 47,036 162 F3
Gusev, U.S.S.R., 14,300 136 A2
Gushikawa-shima, Ryukyu Is. 154 b10
Gushkara, India, 7,017 144 f14
Gusinje, Yug., 2,555 125 D3
Gusinoozërsk, U.S.S.R., 11,000 135 K4
Gus'-Khrustal'nyy, U.S.S.R., 58,000 136 F2
Guspini, It., 13,107 123 B5
Gussago, It., 8,383 122 d5
Güssing, Aust., 2,707 124 N6
Gustavia, St-Barthélemy 97 7
Gustavo A. Madero, Mex., 60,239 93 e10
Gustavsberg, Swed. 120 f8
Gustavus, Alaska 85 K4
Güster, F.R.Ger. 119 c8
Gustine, Calif., 2,300 82 C4
Gustine, Tex., 380 77 O4
Gustorf, F.R.Ger., 4,748 119 B2
Güstrow, Ger.D.R., 37,967 118 D2
Gutau, Aust., 2,292 124 L5
Gutay, U.S.S.R. 135 K5
Gutenberg, Arg. 105 C3
Gutenbrunn, Aust. 124 M5
Gutenbrunn, Aust. 124 b10
Gutenstein, Aust., 1,778 124 b11
Gütersloh, F.R.Ger., 48,326 118 B3
Gutha, Austl. 172 B4
Guthrie, Ill. 68 D3
Guthrie, Ind. 70 C4
Guthrie, co., Iowa, 13,607 72 C3
Guthrie, Ky., 1,211 71 D5
Guthrie, Okla., 9,502 76 F2
Guthrie, Tex. 77 N3
Guthrie Center, Iowa, 2,071 72 C3
Gutiérrez, Col. 100 D5
Gutiérrez Zamora, Mex., 6,444 93 F4
Guttannen, Switz. 124 C2
Guttaring, Aust., 2,093 124 L7
Guttenberg, Iowa, 2,087 72 F2
Guttenberg, N.J., 5,118 58 d13
Gutu, Rhod. 164 E5
Gutusan, Phil., 6,552 153 C3
Gützkow, Ger.D.R. 118 D2
Gu Vo, Ariz. 78 B5
Guy, Alta., Can. 42 J2
Guy, Ark. 73 C2
Guy, Tex. 77 h10
Guyana, ctry., 647,000* 101 L5
Guyancourt, Fr., 1,243 116 g11
Guyandot, r., W. Va. 62 B4
Guyencourt, Del. 62 e10
Guymon, Okla., 5,768 76 B1
Guyot, Mt., N.C.-Tenn. 71 H6
Guyotville, Alg., 8,186 160 c5
Guyra, Austl., 1,557 173 G4
Guysborough, N.S., Can. 45 O6
Guyton, Ga. 64 H3
Guzmán, Lag. de, Mex. 92 D1
Gvarv, Nor. 121 B1
Gwa, Burma 147 a2
Gwaai, Rhod. 164 D5
Gwadabawa, Nigeria 162 E3
Gwādar, Pak., 8,146 144 B4
Gwalia, Austl. 172 B4
Gwalior, India, 300,587 145 F4
Gwanda, Rhod., 1,130 164 D5
Gwarif, Indon. 149 L3
Gwatar Bay, Iran-Pak. 144 A4
Gwda, r., Pol. 127 B2
Gweebarra Bay, Ire. 113 B4
Gwelo, Rhod., 32,400 164 D5
Gwenddwr, U.K. 114 B6
Gwersyllt, U.K., 6,603 114 B4
Gwinn, Mich., 1,009 66 F2
Gwinner, N. Dak., 242 74 D2
Gwinnett, co., Ga., 43,541 64 E2
Gwizdanów, Pol. 127 f5
Gwyddelwern, U.K. 114 B4
Gwynn, Va. 62 H5
Gwynne, Alta., Can. 43 b8
Gy, Fr., 1,160 117 F3
Gyaing, r., Burma 147 b2
Gyamysh, G., U.S.S.R. 137 c1
Gyangtse=Chiang-tzu
Gyanyima, China 144 c10
Gyda, U.S.S.R. 134 G2
Gydan=Kolymskiy, Khr.
Gydanskaya G., U.S.S.R. 134 G2
Gydanskiy P-ov., U.S.S.R. 134 G2
Gyékényes, Hung., 2,007 126 C3
Gyffylliog, U.K. 114 B4
Gympie, Austl., 9,964 173 H4
Gyobingauk, Burma, 9,922 146 A3
Gyōda, Jap., 54,746 155 F3
Gyoma, Hung., 11,374 126 E3
Gyöngyös, Hung., 28,668 126 D3
Gyönk, Hung., 2,699 126 D3
Győr, Hung., 70,812 126 C3
Gypsum, Colo., 358 79 B2
Gypsum, Kans., 593 75 H5
Gypsumville, Man., Can. 43 E4
Gypsy Pk., Wash. 80 E1
Gyula, Hung., 24,609 126 E3
Gyulaj, Hung., 2,267 126 D3
Gyungo, China 144 b10
Gzhatsk, U.S.S.R., 10,500 136 D2

H

Haacht, Belg., 3,863 115 e9
Haafeva, i., Tonga 177 36
Haakon, co., S. Dak., 3,303 74 B3
Haaksbergen, Neth., 7,800 115 E2
Haaltert, Belg., 6,569 115 B4
Haamstede, Neth. 115 B3
Haan, F.R.Ger., 16,090 119 C2
Haano, i., Tonga 177 36
Haapai Group, is., Tonga 170 G6
Haapajärvi, Fin. 120 F3
Haapape, Tahiti 177 44
Haapavesi, Fin. 120 F2
Haapiti, Moorea 177 44
Haapsalu, U.S.S.R., 9,100 136 A1
Haar, F.R.Ger., 9,270 118 C4
Haardtkopf, F.R.Ger. 119 C5
Haarlem, Neth., 166,800 115 C2
Haast, N.Z. 175 f6
Haast, r., N.Z. 175 f6
Haast Pass, N.Z. 175 f7
Hab, r., Pak. 144 C4
Habana, Cuba, 785,455 96 b1
Habartov, Czech. 126 b6
Habaswein, Kenya 164 F1
Habay, Alta., Can. 42 H1
Habay-la-Neuve, Belg., 2,179 115 D5
Ḥabbān, S. Ar. 143 D6
Habersham, co., Ga., 18,116 64 F1
Ha-besor, wadi, Isr. 142 a8
Habiganj, Pak., 12,097 145 J4
Hablainville, Fr. 116 c9
Habomai, Jap., 5,205 155 L8
Haboro, Jap., 24,270 155 J7
Habry, Czech. 127 e7
Habu, Jap. 154 e16
Habutakichō, Jap. 154 g15
Hacha, r., Ven. 101 J4
Hachenburg, F.R.Ger., 2,915 119 D3
Hachijō-jima, Japan 170 D2
Hachiman, Jap., 22,029 155 E4
Hachimori, Jap., 8,120 155 F1
Hachinohe, Jap., 174,348 155 G1
Hachiōji, Jap., 158,443 155 F4
Hachirō-gata, Jap. 155 G2
Hachisu, Jap. 154 h15
Hachita, N. Mex. 79 A6
Ha-ch'on, N. Kor. 151 F2
Hacienda, Phil., 2,276 153 h14
Hacienda, Fla., 125 65 b9
Hackberry, Ariz. 78 B4
Hackensack, Minn., 204 74 E2
Hackensack, N.J., 30,521 61 C2
Hackensack, r., N.J.-N.Y. 58 c13
Hacker Valley, W. Va. 62 D4
Hackettstown, N.J., 5,276 61 B2
Hackleburg, Ala., 527 64 B1
Hackney, Kans. 75 J6
Hackney, Ohio 70 H3
Hackthorn, U.K. 114 G4
Ha Coi, N. Viet. 146 D2
Hacq, i., Truk 176 19
Hada, Sol. Is. 175 d3
Hadamar, F.R.Ger., 6,007 118 B3
Hadano, Jap., 39,602 155 F4
Hadar, Nebr., 100 75 H1
Ḥadāribah, Ra's al, Sudan 163 L2
Ḥadd, Ra's al, c., Muscat and Oman 143 G4
Haddam, Conn., 3,466(T) 56 F7
Haddam, Kans., 311 75 H4
Haddam Neck (part of Haddam), Conn. 56 F6
Haddenham, Bucks., Eng., U.K., 2,240 114 F7
Haddenham, Cambs., Eng., U.K., 1,701 114 J6
Haddington, U.K., 5,506 112 E4
Haddonfield, N.J., 13,201 61 B4
Haddon Heights, N.J., 9,260 60 f12
Hadejia, Nigeria 162 F3
Hadera, Isr., 25,638 142 C3
Hadersdorf, Aust. 124 b10
Haderslev, Den., 19,735 121 B5
Hadım, Turk., 3,501 142 C2
Hadjout, Alg., 14,936 160 c5
Hadleigh, U.K., 3,463 113 G5
Hadley, U.K., 5,088 114 D5
Hadley, Ill. 69 c10
Hadley, Ky. 71 E4
Hadley, Mass., 3,099(T) 56 F3
Hadley, Mich. 67 K6
Hadley, N.Y. 59 N5
Hadley Bay, N.W.T., Can. 40 H3
Hadley L., Me. 55 E4
Hadlock, Wash. 80 B1
Hadlow, U.K., 2,305 114 J8
Hadlyme, Conn. 56 G7
Ha Dong, N. Viet., 25,001 147 h9
Hadong, S. Kor., 19,275 151 E4
Ḥaḍramawt, reg., S. Ar. 143 D5
Hadres, Aust., 1,057 124 N5
Hadsten, Den. 121 C4
Hadsund, Den., 7,074 121 C4
Haeckel Deep, Pac. Oc. 99 B6
Hægeland, Nor. 121 A2
Haeju, N. Kor. 151 E3
Haeju-man, N. Kor. 151 E3
Haena, Hawaii 84 B1
Haenam, S. Kor., 20,479 151 E4
Ha-erh-pin, China, 2,493,000* 150 G2
Hafenlohr, F.R.Ger., 1,116 119 H5
Ḥaffah, Syr., 4,215 142 D3
Haffen-Mehr, F.R.Ger., 3,197 119 A2
Hafford, Sask., Can. 43 C4
Hafik, Turk., 2,501 142 D2
Hāfizābād, Pak., 34,576 145 D2
Hafnarfjördhur, Ice., 7,490 120 a6
Hafnerbach, Aust. 124 b10
Haft Gel, Iran, 7,693 143 D2
Hafun, Som. Rep. 163 N4
Hafun, Ras, Som. Rep. 163 N4
Hagaman, Ill. 68 B4
Hagaman, N.Y., 1,292 59 M6
Hagan, Ga., 552 64 G3
Hagansport, Tex. 77 Q3
Hagari, r., India 145 E7
Hagarstown, Ill. 68 C5
Hagarville, Ark. 73 B2
Hage, F.R.Ger., 2,418 118 A2
Hagedis, P., Indon. 149 G4
Hagemeister I., Alaska 85 D4
Hagemeister Str., Alaska 85 D4
Hagen, F.R.Ger., 177,896 118 A3
Hagener, Ill. 68 B4
Hagenow, Ger.D.R., 10,294 118 C2
Hagensborg, Br. Col., Can. 42 E3
Hagensville, Mich. 67 K3
Hager City, Wis. 66 A4
Hagerman, Idaho, 430 81 B4
Hagerman, N. Mex., 1,144 79 C5
Hagerstown, Ind., 1,730 70 D3
Hagerstown, Md., 36,660 62 G3
Hagersville, Ont., Can., 2,040 46 D6
Hagetmau, Fr., 3,387 117 C5
Hagfors, Swed. 120 C3
Haggard, Kans. 75 E6
Hagginwood, Calif., 11,469 82 b7
Hagi, Jap., 56,831 154 B4
Hagi, Jap. 154 g16
Ha Giang, N. Viet. 146 D2
Hagiwara, Jap., 6,667 155 E4
Hagley, U.K., 2,519 114 D6
Hagondange, Fr., 10,098 117 F2
Hagonoy, Phil., 1,946 153 b8
Hagood, S.C. 63 D3
Hague, Sask., Can. 43 C4
Hague, N.Y. 59 N4
Hague, N. Dak., 197 74 C2
Hague, C. de la, Fr. 117 C2
Haguenau, Fr., 21,841 117 G2
Haguimit, Phil., 8,528 153 e11
Haha-jima, Bonin Is. 170 D3
Hahira, Ga., 1,297 64 F5
Hahn, Mo. 72 G7
Hahns Peak, Colo. 79 B1
Hahnstätten, F.R.Ger., 1,846 119 D4
Hahnstown, Pa. 60 d8
Hahnville, La., 1,297 73 E8
Hahót, Hung., 2,528 126 C3
Hai, r., China 151 C3
Hai-an, China 151 D4
Haibak, Afghan. 144 C1
Haibara, Jap., 25,079 155 F4
Haibara, Jap., 13,047 154 h15
Hai-ch'eng, F-ch., China 152 E2
Hai-ch'eng, L-n, China 151 D2
Hai-chou, China 151 C4
Haidargarh, India 144 c12
Hai Duong, N. Viet., 24,752 146 D2
Haifa, Isr., 183,021 142 C3
Hai-feng, China 152 D3
Haig, Nebr. 75 B2
Haiger, F.R.Ger., 3,884 119 E3
Haight, Alta., Can. 43 c7
Haig Lake, Alta., Can. 42 J2
Haigler, Nebr., 268 75 D4
Hai-k'ang, China 152 C3
Hai-k'ou, China, 120,000* 150 E5
Haiku, Hawaii, 422 84 E3
Ḥā'il, Saudi Ar., 5,000* 143 C3
Hai-la-erh, China, 129,000* 150 F1
Hai-la-erh, r., China 150 G1
Hai Lang, S. Viet., 5,060 146 D3
Hailar=Hai-la-erh
Haile, La. 73 C5
Hailey, Idaho, 1,185 81 B4
Haileybury, Ont., Can., 2,583 44 H6
Haileyville, Okla., 922 76 H3
Hai-ling Tao, China 152 D3
Hai-li-wang-fu, China 151 C2
Hailsham, U.K., 5,955 113 G6
Hai-lun, China 150 G2
Hai-lung, China 151 E2
Hailuoto, Fin. 120 F2
Hai-men, Ch-ch., China 152 F1
Hai-men, Chiang-su, China 152 F1
Haiming, Aust., 2,439 124 G6
Haina, Hawaii 84 F3
Hainan Str.=Ch'iung-chou Hai-hsia
Hai-nan Tao, China 150 E5
Hainburg, Aust., 6,440 124 N5
Haines, Alaska, 392 85 L4
Haines, Oreg., 331 80 E3
Hainesburg, N.J. 61 A2
Haines City, Fla., 9,135 64 H4
Haines Falls, N.Y. 59 M7
Haines Junction, Yukon, Can. 40 B5
Hainesport, N.J., 2,100* 61 B4
Hainesville, Ill., 132 69 b7
Hainfeld, Aust., 3,875 124 M5
Hainichen, Ger. D.R., 11,188 126 c6
Hai-ning, China 152 F1
Hai Ninh, S. Viet., 1,957 147 m11
Hainstadt, F.R.Ger., 1,418 119 G5
Hainton, U.K. 114 H4
Hai Phong, N. Viet., 182,496 146 D2
Hairlaw, U.K. 112 b8
Hairy Hill, Alta., Can. 42 K3
Hai-t'an Tao, China 152 F2
Haiterbach, F.R.Ger., 1,809 119 F7
Haiti, ctry., 4,485,000* 96
Haiwee Res., Calif. 82 E4
Hai-yang-so, China 151 D3
Hai-yang Tao, China 151 D3
Hai-yen, Ch-hai, China 150 D3
Hai-yen, Ch-ch., China 152 F1
Hai-yüan, China 150 E3
Haja, Indon. 149 J3
Hajdúböszörmény, Hung., 32,214 126 E3
Hajdudorog, Hung., 11,009 126 E3
Hajduhadház, Hung., 13,092 126 E3
Hajdunánás, Hung., 18,413 126 E3
Hajduszoboszló, Hung., 19,661 126 E3
Hájek, Czech. 126 b6
Ḥājib al 'Uyūn, Tun., 1,902 160 f6
Hajipur, India, 34,044 144 e13
Hajnówka, Pol., 11,824 127 E2
Hajo-do, S. Kor. 151 E4
Haka, Burma 146 A2
Hakalau, Hawaii, 650 84 F4
Hakkas, Swed. 120 E2
Hakken-san, mtn., Jap. 154 g15
Hako, Jap. 154 e15
Hakodate, Jap., 243,012 155 J9
Hakone, Jap. 155 m20
Hakonegasaki, Jap. 155 m19
Hakotsukuri, Jap. 154 g15
Hakui, Jap., 29,556 155 E3
Hakupu, Niue 177 32
Haku-san, mtn., Jap. 155 E3
Hāla, Pak. 11,956 144 C4
Ḥalab, Syr., 466,026 142 D2
Ḥalabjah, Iraq, 7,393 143 D1
Halachó, Mex., 4,019 93 H4
Halalii L., Hawaii 84 A2
Halangingie Pt., Niue 177 32
Ha-la-t'ao-chieh, China 151 D2
Halaula, Hawaii 84 F3
Halavai, Niue 177 32
Halawa, Hawaii 84 E2
Halawa, C., Hawaii 84 E2
Halawa Bay, Hawaii 84 E2
Halawa Heights, Hawaii, 2,045* 84 c7
Ḥalbā, Leb., 3,165 142 c5
Halberstadt, Ger.D.R., 44,894 118 C3
Halbstadt, Man., Can. 43 g10
Ḥalbūn, Syr. 142 c6
Halbur, Iowa, 214 72 C3
Halcottsville, N.Y. 59 L7
Hald, Den. 121 B4
Haldane, Ill. 68 C1
Haldeman, Ky. 71 H3
Halden, Nor., 9,979 120 B4
Haldensleben, Ger.D.R., 21,281 118 C2
Haldibari, India, 4,371 144 g12
Haldwani, India, 38,032 144 b11
Hale, Arg., 2,000* 105 a13
Hale, U.K., 14,800 114 D4
Hale, co., Ala., 19,537 64 B3
Hale, Mich. 67 K4
Hale, Mo., 504 72 D5
Hale, co., Tex., 36,798 77 N3
Hale, Mt., Austl. 172 B4
Hale, r., Austl. 172 E3
Haleakala Crater, Hawaii 84 E3
Haleakala Nat. Pk., Hawaii 84 E3
Hale Center, Tex., 2,196 77 N2
Haledon, N.J., 6,161 58 c13
Hale Eddy, N.Y. 59 K7
Haleiwa, Hawaii, 2,504 84 C2
Hales Bar L., Tenn. 71 F6
Hales Corners, Wis., 5,549 66 c12
Halesite, N.Y., 2,857 58 f13
Halesowen, U.K., 44,160 114 E6
Halesworth, U.K., 2,253 113 G5
Halethorpe, Md. 62 b8
Haley, Ont., Can. 46 H3
Haley Mtn., Wash. 80 D1
Haleyville, Ala., 3,740 64 B1
Half Assini, Ghana 162 b9
Half Day, Ill. 69 c8
Half Hollow, N.Y. 58 f13
Halfmoon, N.Y. 59 w28
Halfmoon Bay, Br. Col., Can. 42 c6
Half Moon Bay, Calif., 1,957 82 B4
Half Moon L., Wis. 66 A3
Halfway, Oreg., 505 80 E3
Halfway House, S. Af. 165 i17
Halfway Pond (part of Plymouth), Mass. 57 O5
Halgan, C., Kusaie 176 31
Halhaiin, r., Mong. 150 F2
Haliburton, Ont., Can. 44 H6
Haliburton Highlands, Ont., Can. 46 F3
Halifax, Austl. 173 G2
Halifax, Br. Col., Can. 42 E2
Halifax, N.S., Can., 90,072 45 N7
Halifax, U.K., 96,073 113 F5
Halifax, Mass., 1,599 57 N5
Halifax, co., N.C., 58,956 63 G1
Halifax, N.C., 370 63 G1
Halifax, Pa., 824 60 J5
Halifax, Vt. 54 B5
Halifax, co., Va., 33,637 62 E6
Halifax, Va., 795 62 F6
Halifax Bay, Austl. 173 G2
Halin, Som. Rep. 163 N4
Halkett, C., Alaska 85 G1
Halkirk, Alta., Can. 42 K3
Halkirk, U.K. 112 E2
Hall, co., Ga., 49,739 64 F1
Hall, Ind. 70 C3
Hall, Md. 62 c9
Hall, Mo. 72 D7
Hall, co., Nebr., 35,757 75 G3
Hall, N.Y. 58 F6
Hall, co., Tex., 7,322 77 N2
Halladale, r., U.K. 112 E2
Hallam, Nebr., 264 75 J3
Hallam, Pa., 1,234 60 J5
Hallandale, Fla., 10,483 65 J7
Halla-san, S. Kor. 151 E4
Hallaton, U.K. 114 G5
Hallau, Switz., 1,966 124 C1
Hall Basin, N.W.T., Can. 41 R1
Hällberga, Swed. 120 d8
Hällbybrunn, Swed. 120 d8
Halle, Belg., 18,354 115 C4
Halle, F.R.Ger., 5,378 118 B2
Halle, Ger.D.R., 277,855 118 C3
Halleck, Nev. 83 C2
Hällefors, Swed. 120 C4
Hälleforsnäs, Swed. 120 d8
Hallein, Aust., 13,326 124 K6
Hallenberg, F.R.Ger., 2,248 119 F2
Hallett, Austl. 172 c7
Hallett, Okla., 132 76 G1
Hallettsville, Tex., 2,808 77 P5
Halley, Ark., 213 73 D4
Halley Bay, Ant. 180 P5
Halliday, N. Dak., 509 74 A2
Hallim, S. Kor., 20,571 151 E4
Hallingdalselvi, r., Nor. 120 B3
Hallington, U.K. 112 f9
Hall I., Alaska 85 A3
Hall Is., Car. Is. 170 E4
Hall Lake, N.W.T., Can. 41 N4
Hall L., N.W.T., Can. 41 N4
Hällnäs, Swed. 120 D2
Hallock, Minn., 1,527 74 D1
Halloran Springs, Calif. 82 F5
Hallowell, Me., 3,169 55 C4
Hall Pen., N.W.T., Can. 41 Q5
Halls, Tenn., 1,890 71 B6
Hallsberg, Swed. 120 C4
Hallsboro, N.C. 63 F3
Halls Cove, Me. 55 D4
Halls Creek, Austl. 172 C2
Halls Ferry, Mo. 72 a10
Halls Mills, N.C. 63 C1
Halls Str., Can.-U.S. 54 E1
Halls Summit, Kans. 75 K5
Hällsta, Swed. 120 d8
Hallstadt, F.R.Ger., 4,839 118 C4
Hallstahammar, Swed. 120 d8
Hall Station, Colo. 79 D2
Hallstatt, Aust., 1,409 124 K6
Hallstead, Pa., 1,580 61 L2
Hallsville, Ill. 68 C3
Hallsville, Mo., 363 72 E5
Hallsville, Tex., 684 77 Q3
Halluin, Fr., 14,138 116 a6
Hallwang, Aust., 1,787 124 K6
Hallwilersee, Switz. 124 C1
Hallwood, Va., 269 62 J5
Halma, Minn., 115 74 D1
Hălmagiu, Rum. 128 D1
Halmahera, i., Indon. 149 J2
Halmahera Sea, Indon. 149 J2
Halmeu, Rum. 128 D1
Halmstad, Swed., 39,032 120 C4
Halmstad, Swed. 121 c7
Ḥalq al Wādī, Tun., 26,323 160 g5
Hals, Den. 121 C3
Halsall, U.K., 2,048 114 B3
Halsell, Ala. 64 A3
Halsey, Nebr., 111 75 E2
Halsey, Oreg., 404 80 B3
Halsey L., Wis. 66 E3
Halsey Valley, N.Y. 59 G7
Hälsingborg, Swed., 76,574 120 C4
Halsskov, Den. 121 D5
Halstad, Minn., 639 74 D2
Halstead, U.K., 6,463 113 G6
Halstead, Kans., 1,598 75 H6
Halstenbek, F.R.Ger., 6,822 119 a8
Haltemprice, U.K., 42,386 113 F5
Haltern, F.R.Ger., 13,994 118 A3
Haltiatunturi, mt., Fin. 120 E1
Haltom City, Tex., 23,133 77 P3
Haltonville, Ont., Can. 46 b13
Haltwhistle, U.K., 3,745 113 E4
Halver, F.R.Ger., 12,907 119 D2
Halvesbostel, F.R.Ger. 119 a9
Halvrimmen, Den. 121 B3
Ham, Fr., 4,314 117 E2
Hama, Jap. 154 f15
Hamada, Jap., 46,626 154 B4
Hamadān, Iran, 99,909 143 D2
Ḥamāh, Syr., 107,859 142 D3
Hamahika-jima, Ryukyu Is. 154 b11
Hamajima, Jap., 7,450 155 E4
Hamamatsu, Jap., 333,009 155 E4
Hamanaka, Jap., 11,563 155 L8
Hamano, Jap. 155 n19
Hamanoura, Jap., 4,025 154 A5
Hamar, Nor., 13,280 120 B3
Hamaröy, Nor. 120 C1
Ḥamāṭah, Jabal, U.A.R. 161 K3
Hama-Tombetsu, Jap., 8,231 155 K7
Hambach, F.R.Ger., 3,731 119 E6
Hambach, Fr., 1,703 116 d8
Hambantota, Cey., 4,299 145 n22
Hamberg, N. Dak., 64 74 C2
Hamble, U.K., 3,001 113 k13
Hambledon, U.K., 1,486 114 G8
Hamblen, co., Tenn., 33,092 71 H5
Hambleton, W. Va., 275 62 E3
Hamburg, st., F.R.Ger., 1,857,000* 118 C2
Hamburg, F.R.Ger., 1,857,000* 118 C2
Hamburg, Ark., 2,904 73 D4
Hamburg, Calif. 82 B2
Hamburg, Conn. 56 G7
Hamburg, Ill., 264 68 B4
Hamburg, Ind. 70 D3
Hamburg, Iowa, 1,647 72 B4
Hamburg, Miss. 73 D6
Hamburg, N.J., 1,532 61 B1
Hamburg, N.Y., 9,145 58 C6
Hamburg, Pa., 3,747 61 K4
Hamburg, Wis. 66 D3
Hamburg Mtn., N.J. 61 B1
Ḥamḍ, Wādī al, Saudi Ar. 143 B3
Hamden, Conn., 41,056(T) 56 E7
Hamden, N.Y. 59 K7
Hamden, Ohio, 1,035 70 G3
Hämeenkyrö, Fin. 120 E3
Hämeenlinna, Fin., 29,159 120 E3
Hamel, Ill., 362 68 C5
Hamelin=Hameln
Hamelin Pool, Austl. 172 A4
Hameln, F.R.Ger., 50,418 118 B2
Hamer, Idaho, 144 81 C4
Hamer, Ohio 70 E1
Hamer, S.C. 63 E3
Hamersley Range, Austl. 172 B3
Hamersville, Ohio, 524 70 F4
Hamfelde, F.R.Ger. 119 b8
Ham-Hord, Qué., Can. 47 N3
Hamhŭng, N. Kor., 150,000* 151 E3
Ha-mi, China, 100,000* 150 C2
Hamill, S. Dak. 74 C4
Hamilton, Austl., 8,507 172 F5
Hamilton, Berm. Is., 2,942 108 1
Hamilton, Ont., Can., 270,801 44 H7
Hamilton, N.Z., 42,212 175 g5
Hamilton, Sur. 101 M5
Hamilton, U.K., 41,928 112 D4
Hamilton, co., Ala., 1,934 64 B1
Hamilton, Alaska, 35 85 D3
Hamilton, Colo. 79 B1
Hamilton, co., Fla., 7,705 65 G2
Hamilton, Ga., 396 64 E3
Hamilton, co., Ill., 10,010 68 D5
Hamilton, Ill., 2,228 68 A3
Hamilton, co., Ind., 40,132 70 C2
Hamilton, Ind., 380 70 E1
Hamilton, co., Iowa, 20,032 72 D2
Hamilton, co., Kans., 3,144 75 D5
Hamilton, Kans., 400 75 J6
Hamilton, Mich. 67 H6
Hamilton, Miss. 73 G4
Hamilton, Mo., 1,701 72 D5
Hamilton, Mont., 2,475 81 B2
Hamilton, co., Nebr., 8,714 75 G3
Hamilton, co., N.Y., 4,267 59 L4
Hamilton, N.Y., 3,348 59 J6
Hamilton, N.C., 565 63 G2
Hamilton, N. Dak., 217 74 D1
Hamilton, co., Ohio, 864,121 70 E3
Hamilton, Ohio, 72,354 70 E3
Hamilton, Oreg. 80 D3
Hamilton, co., Tenn., 237,905 71 F6
Hamilton, co., Tex., 8,488 77 O4
Hamilton, Tex., 3,106 77 O4
Hamilton, Va., 403 62 G3
Hamilton, Wash., 271 80 C1
Hamilton, L., Ark. 73 B3
Hamilton, Mt., Nev. 83 C3
Hamilton Acres, Alaska, 2,162 85 b6
Hamilton City, Calif. 82 B3
Hamilton Hbr., Ont., Can. 46 c14
Hamilton Inlet, Newf., Can. 45 P3
Hamilton Mtn., N.Y. 59 M5
Hamilton Res., Mass. 56 H4
Hamilton Square, N.J., 6,000* 61 B3
Hamina, Fin., 9,781 120 F3
Hamiota, Man., Can. 43 E5
Ḥāmir, Wādī, Iraq-Saudi Ar. 143 C2
Hamirpur, India, 10,921 144 c13
Hamlet, Ind., 688 70 C1
Hamlet, Nebr., 113 75 D3
Hamlet, N.C., 4,460 63 E3
Hamletsburg, Ill., 107 68 D6
Hamlin, Me. 55 E1
Hamlin, N.Y. 58 D5
Hamlin, Pa. 61 M3
Hamlin, co., S. Dak., 6,303 74 D3
Hamlin, Tex., 3,791 77 N3
Hamlin, W. Va., 850 62 B4
Hamlin Lake, Mich. 67 G4
Ham Long, S. Viet., 5,299 147 m11
Hamm, Nrh.-Wf., F.R.Ger., 10,383 118 A3
Hamm, Nrh.-Wf., F.R.Ger., 66,327 118 A3
Hamm, Rheinland-Pfalz, F.R.Ger., 1,754 119 D3
Hamm, Lux., 1,304 115 E5
Ḥammām al Anf, Tun., 22,060 160 g5
Ḥammāmāt, Khalīj al, Tun. 160 g5
Ḥammām Sūsah, Tun., 9,044 160 g6
Hamma-Plaisance, Alg., 2,480 160 e5
Ḥammār, Hawr al, l., Iraq 143 D2
Hammarö, Swed. 120 C4
Hamme, Belg., 16,805 115 d8
Hammel, Den., 2,832 121 B4
Hammelburg, F.R.Ger., 5,137 118 B3
Hammerdal, Swed. 120 C3
Hammeren, pen., Den. 121 G5
Hammerfest, Nor., 5,652 120 F1
Hammerum, Den. 121 A4
Hammett, Idaho 81 B4
Hamminkeln, F.R.Ger., 3,005 119 B1
Hammon, Okla., 656 76 D2
Hammonasset, r., Conn. 56 F7
Hammonasset Pt., Conn. 56 F8
Hammond, Austl. 172 c7
Hammond, Ill., 471 68 D4
Hammond, Ind., 111,698 70 B1
Hammond, Kans. 75 L6
Hammond, La., 10,563 73 E7
Hammond, Minn., 205 74 F3
Hammond, Mo. 72 E8
Hammond, Mont. 81 G3
Hammond, N.Y., 314 59 J3
Hammond, Oreg., 480 80 A2
Hammond, W. Va. 62 D3
Hammond, Wis., 645 66 A4
Hammond Bay, Mich. 67 J3
Hammondsport, N.Y., 1,176 58 F7
Hammondsville, Vt. 54 B5
Hammonton, N.J., 9,854 61 B4
Hamoir, Belg., 1,301 115 D4
Hamont, Belg., 5,778 115 D3

Hamorton, Pa. 60 e12
Hampden, Me. 55 D4
Hampden, co., Mass., 429,353 56 E4
Hampden, Mass., 2,345(T) 56 G4
Hampden, N. Dak., 71 74 C1
Hampden Highlands, Me., 1,030 55 D4
Hampden Sydney, Va. 62 F5
Hampont, Fr. 116 c9
Hampreston, U.K., 6,534 113 i13
Hampshire, co., U.K., 1,197,170 113 F6
Hampshire, Ill., 1,309 68 D1
Hampshire, co., Mass., 103,229 56 E3
Hampshire, Tenn. 71 D6
Hampshire, co., W. Va., 11,705 62 F3
Hampstead, N.B., Can. 47 S11
Hampstead, Md., 696 62 H3
Hampstead, N.H. 54 E6
Hampstead, N.C. 63 G3
Hampton, N.B., Can. 47 S11
Hampton, Ont., Can. 46 F5
Hampton, Ark., 1,011 73 C4
Hampton, Conn., 934(T) 56 H5
Hampton, Fla., 340 65 G3
Hampton, Ga., 1,253 64 E2
Hampton, Ill., 742 68 B2
Hampton, Iowa, 4,501 72 D2
Hampton, Ky. 71 C4
Hampton, Minn., 305 74 F3
Hampton, Nebr., 331 75 H3
Hampton, N.H., 3,281 54 F6
Hampton, N.J., 1,135 61 B2
Hampton, N.Y. 59 O4
Hampton, Oreg. 80 C4
Hampton, co., S.C., 17,425 63 C5
Hampton, S.C., 2,486 63 C5
Hampton, Tenn., 1,048 71 J5
Hampton, Va., 89,258 62 H5
Hampton Bays, N.Y., 1,431 59 P10
Hampton Beach, N.H. 54 F6
Hampton Falls, N.H. 54 F6
Hampton Harbour, Austl. 172 A3
Hampton Springs, Fla. 65 F2
Hamra, Swed. 120 C3
Ḥamra', Al Ḥammādah al, Libya 161 F2
Hamrun, Malta, 16,895 123 f12
Hamshire, Tex. 77 m9
Hamsterley, U.K. 112 g10
Ham Tan, S. Viet. 146 D5
Ham Thuon, S. Viet. 147 m11
Hamtramck, Mich., 34,137 67 f15
Hāmūn-e Sāberī, l., Afghan.-Iran 144 A3
Hāmūn-i-Lora, salt marsh, Pak. 144 B3
Hāmūn-i-Māshkel, salt marsh, Pak. 144 B3
Hāmūn-i-Pūzak, l., Afghan. 144 B3
Han, n., Hu.p.—Shen-hsi, China 150 F4
Han, r., K-t., China 152 E2
Han, r., S. Kor. 151 E3
Hana, Hawaii, 435 84 F3
Hanada, Jap. 154 e15
Hanahan, Sol. Is. 175 a1
Hanalei, Hawaii, 370 84 B1
Hanalei, r., Hawaii 84 B1
Hanalei Bay, Hawaii 84 B1
Hanamaki, Jap., 62,385 155 G2
Hanamaulu, Hawaii, 977 84 B1
Hanapepe, Hawaii, 1,383 84 B2
Hanapepe, r., Hawaii 84 B2
Hanau, F.R.Ger., 42,774 118 B3
Hanauma Bay, Hawaii 84 d8
Hanawa, Jap., 20,826 155 G1
Hanceville, Br. Col., Can. 42 F3
Hanceville, Ala., 1,174 64 C1
Han-ch'eng, China 150 E3
Han-chi, China 151 C4
Han-chiang, China 152 E2
Han-chung, China 150 E3
Hancock, co., Ga., 9,979 64 F2
Hancock, co., Ill., 24,574 68 A3
Hancock, co., Ind., 26,665 70 D3
Hancock, co., Iowa, 14,604 72 D1
Hancock, Iowa, 252 72 B3
Hancock, co., Ky., 5,330 71 E4
Hancock, co., Me., 32,293 55 D4
Hancock, Me. 55 D4
Hancock, Md., 2,004 62 F3
Hancock, Mass., 455(T) 56 C2
Hancock, Mich., 5,022 66 E1
Hancock, co., Minn., 942 74 E3
Hancock, co., Miss., 14,039 73 F7
Hancock, N.H. 54 C6
Hancock, N.Y., 1,830 59 K8
Hancock, co., Ohio, 53,686 70 F1
Hancock, co., Tenn., 7,757 71 H5
Hancock, Vt. 54 B4
Hancock, co., W. Va., 39,615 62 D2
Hancock, Wis., 367 66 D4
Hancock Pd., Me. 54 F4
Hancock's Bridge, N.J. 61 A4
Hańczowa, Pol. 127 D4
Hand, co., S. Dak., 6,712 74 C3
Handa, Jap., 8,016 155 D5
Handa, Jap.,'71,380 155 E4
Handa I., U.K. 112 D2
Handen, Swed. 120 f8
Handle, Miss. 73 C6
Handlová, Czech., 16,367 126 D2
Handsboro, Miss., 1,577 73 f7
Handsworth, U.K., 36,122 114 F4
Hanegev, reg., Isr. 142 C4
Hanemachi, Jap. 154 i15
Haney, Br. Col., Can., 1,538 42 d6
Hanford, Calif., 10,133 82 D4
Hanga Roa, Easter I. 177 46
Hanga-Roa, Easter I. 177 46
Hangayn Nuruu, Mong. 150 D2
Hang-chin-ch'i, China 151 A2

Hang-chin-hou-ch'i, China 150 E2
Hang-chou, China, 740,000* 150 F4
Hang-chou Wan, China 152 F1
Hangchow=Hang-chou
Hangō, Fin., 8,157 120 E4
Hänigsen, F.R.Ger., 4,315 118 C2
Han i Hotit, Alb. 125 D3
Hankamer, Tex. 77 k9
Hankha, Thai. 147 c4
Hankinson, Miss. 73 D5
Hankinson, N. Dak., 1,285 74 D2
Hanko=Hangō
Han-k'ou, China 152 D1
Hanksville, Utah 78 C2
Hanksville, Vt. 54 A3
Han-ku, China 150 F3
Hanley, Sask., Can. 43 C4
Hanlontown, Iowa, 193 72 D1
Hanmer, Ont., Can., 1,575 46 D2
Hanmer Springs, N.Z. 175 g6
Hann, Mt., Austl. 172 C2
Hanna, Alta., Can., 2,563 42 K3
Hanna, Ind. 70 C1
Hanna, La. 73 B6
Hanna, Okla., 233 76 H2
Hanna, Utah 78 C1
Hanna, Wyo., 625 81 F5
Hanna City, Ill., 1,056 68 C3
Hannaford, N. Dak., 277 74 C2
Hannah, N. Dak., 253 74 C1
Hannah Bay, Ont., Can. 44 H4
Hannawa Falls, N.Y. 59 K2
Hannibal, Mo., 20,028 72 F5
Hannibal, N.Y., 611 59 G5
Hannibal, Ohio 70 J3
Hannibal, Wis. 66 C3
Hannibal Center, N.Y. 59 p22
Hannō, Jap., 44,153 155 m19
Hannon, Ont., Can. 46 c15
Hannover, F.R.Ger., 536,810 118 B2
Hannover, N. Dak. 74 B2
Hannut, Belg., 2,695 115 D4
Ha Noi, N. Viet., 414,620 146 D2
Hanoura, Jap., 8,050 154 f16
Hanover, Ont., Can., 4,335 46 D4
Hanover=Hannover
Hanover, F.R.Ger.=Hannover
Hanover, Conn. 56 H6
Hanover, Ill., 1,396 68 B1
Hanover, Ind., 1,170 70 D4
Hanover, Kans., 773 75 J4
Hanover, Me. 55 B4
Hanover, Mass., 5,923(T) 57 N4
Hanover, Mich., 449 67 J6
Hanover, N.H., 5,649 54 C4
Hanover, N.J. 58 b13
Hanover, N. Mex. 79 A5
Hanover, Ohio, 267 70 G2
Hanover, Pa., 15,538 60 J6
Hanover, co., Va., 27,550 62 G5
Hanover, Va. 62 G5
Hanover, Wis. 66 D6
Hanover Center, N.H. 54 C4
Hanover Park, Ill., 6,620 69 b9
Hanoverton, Ohio, 442 70 J2
Hanpan, C., Sol. Is. 175 a1
Han Pijesak, Yug. 125 D2
Hansard, Br. Col., Can. 42 G2
Hansboro, N. Dak., 143 74 C1
Hansels Mts., Utah 78 b7
Hansen, Nebr. 75 G3
Hansford, co., Tex., 6,208 76 N1
Hansford, Tex. 76 N1
Han-shou, China 152 C1
Hansi, India, 33,712 144 a11
Hanslope, U.K., 1,032 114 G6
Hanson, Ky., 376 71 D4
Hanson, Mass., 4,370(T) 57 N4
Hanson, co., S. Dak., 4,584 74 D4
Hanson Bay, N.Z. 175 14
Hansonville, Va. 62 B6
Hansted, Den. 121 A4
Hanstedt, F.R.Ger., 1,490 119 b9
Hanston, Kans., 279 75 F5
Han-sur-Lesse, Belg. 115 D4
Hanston, Wash. 81 a7
Han-tan, China 150 F3
Hant's Harbour, Newf., Can. 45 b9
Hantsport, N.S., Can., 1,345 47 T11
Hanumangarh, India, 17,909 145 D3
Hanumannagar Bge., Nepal 144 f12
Hanušovice, Czech. 127 f6
Hanwood, Austl. 173 e10
Han-yang, China 152 D1
Han-yin, China 151 A4
Han-yüan, China 152 A1
Hao, i., Tuam. Arch. 171 J6
Hao-ch'ing, China 150 D4
Hao-feng, China 152 C1
Hao-kang, China, 200,000* 150 D1
Hao Muc, N. Viet. 147 h8
Hao-pi, China 150 E3
Hao-shih-t'ai, China 151 D1
Ha-pa-ho, China 150 B1
Haparanda, Swed. 120 E2
Hapeville, Ga., 10,082 64 g10
Hapo, Indon. 149 J2
Happy, Alaska 85 a6
Happy, Tex., 624 76 M2
Happy Camp, Calif. 82 B2
Happy Jack, Ariz. 78 C4
Hapsu, N. Kor. 151 F2
Hapur, India, 55,248 144 a11
Haql, Saudi Ar. 143 B3
Haquira, Peru, 2,300 104 C5
Ḥaraḍ, Saudi Ar. 143 D4
Hara, r., Mong. 150 E1
Hāraḍ, Saudi Ar. 143 D4
Hārād, Swed. 120 d8
Harads, Swed. 120 D2
Harahan, La., 9,275 73 E8
Haraichiba, Jap. 155 m19

Haraiki, atoll, Tuam. Arch. 177 42
Haralson, co., Ga., 14,543 64 D2
Haralson, Ga., 141 64 E2
Haranomachi, Jap., 41,006 155 G3
Hara Nuur, Mong. 150 C1
Harappa, Pak. 145 D3
Harappu, i., Jaluit 176 30
Harar, Eth., 42,700* 163 M4
Harardera, Som. Rep. 163 N5
Hara Usa, l., Mong. 150 C1
Harbel, Lib. 162 C4
Harbin=Ha-erh-pin
Harboøre, Den., 2,065 121 A4
Harbor, Oreg. 80 A4
Harbor Beach, Mich., 2,282 67 L5
Harbor Creek, Pa. 60 C1
Harbor Springs, Mich., 1,433 67 H3
Harborton, Va. 62 J5
Harbour Breton, Newf., Can., 1,071 45 Q6
Harbour Buffett, Newf., Can. 45 a10
Harbour Deep, Newf., Can. 45 Q5
Harbour Grace, Newf., Can., 2,604 45 b10
Harbour I., Bah. Is. 95 c7
Harbour Main, Newf., Can. 45 b10
Harbours, B. of, Falk. Is. 108 3
Harbourton, N.J. 60 g10
Harbury, U.K., 1,316 114 F6
Hárby, Den. 121 C5
Harby, Leics., Eng., U.K. 114 G5
Harby, Notts., Eng., U.K. 114 G5
Harcourt, N.B., Can. 47 T10
Harcourt, Iowa, 268 72 C2
Harcuvar Mts., Ariz. 78 B3
Hard, Aust., 6,653 124 F6
Harda, India, 22,279 145 E5
Hardal Saridag, mt., Mong. 150 D1
Hardangerfjorden, Nor. 120 A3
Hardee, co., Fla., 12,370 65 H5
Hardee, Miss. 73 E5
Hardeeville, S.C., 700 63 C5
Hardegsen, F.R.Ger., 2,568 118 B3
Hardeman, co., Tenn., 21,517 71 B6
Hardeman, co., Tex., 8,275 77 O2
Hardenberg, Neth., 3,100 115 E2
Harderwijk, Neth., 13,900 115 D2
Hardesty, Okla., 187 76 B1
Hardheim, F.R.Ger., 3,663 119 G5
Hardin, co., Ill., 5,879 68 D6
Hardin, Ill., 356 68 B4
Hardin, co., Iowa, 22,533 72 D2
Hardin, co., Ky., 67,789 71 E4
Hardin, Ky., 458 71 C5
Hardin, co., Ohio, 29,633 70 F2
Hardin, co., Tenn., 17,397 71 C6
Hardin, co., Tex., 24,629 77 Q4
Hardin, Tex. 77 k8
Harding, part of (Medfield), Mass. 57 L4
Harding, Minn. 74 E2
Harding, co., N. Mex., 1,874 79 D4
Harding, Pa. 61 o16
Harding, co., S. Dak., 2,371 74 A3
Harding, S. Dak. 74 A3
Hardinsburg, Ind., 218 70 C4
Hardinsburg, Ky., 1,377 71 E4
Hardinville, Ill. 68 E5
Hardinxveld, Neth., 8,400 115 b7
Hardisty, Alta., Can. 42 K3
Hard Knott Pass, U.K. 114 B2
Hardman, Oreg., 30 80 D3
Hardoi, India, 36,725 144 c12
Hardricourt, Fr., 1,402 116 f10
Hardtner, Kans., 372 75 E5
Hardup, Utah 78 B1
Hardwar, India, 58,513 144 b11
Hardwick, Mass., 2,340(T) 56 H3
Hardwick, Vt., 1,521 54 C3
Hardwood, Mich. 66 F3
Hardwood Mtn., Me. 55 B2
Hardy, Alg., 1,132 160 c6
Hardy, Ark., 555 73 D1
Hardy, Ky. 71 J4
Hardy, Nebr., 285 75 H3
Hardy, Okla., 6 76 G1
Hardy, co., W. Va., 9,308 62 F3
Hardy Dam Pd., Mich. 67 H5
Hare Bay, Newf., Can., 1,195 45 R5
Hare Fiord, N.W.T., Can. 41 M1
Hare Hill, U.K. 112 c8
Harelbeke, Belg., 15,794 115 B4
Haren, F.R.Ger., 5,733 118 A2
Haren, Neth., 9,600 115 E1
Hares Corner, Del. 62 e11
Hareskov, Den. 121 a7
Harewood, U.K., 1,126 114 F3
Harfleur, Fr., 10,514 117 D2
Harford, co., Md., 76,722 62 H3
Harford, N.Y. 59 H7
Harford, Pa. 61 L2
Harford Mills, N.Y. 59 H7
Harg, Swed. 120 d9
Hargarten-aux-Mines, Fr., 1,008 116 c8
Hargeisa, Som. Rep., 40,000* 163 M4
Harghita, mtn., Rum. 128 E1
Hari, Jap. 154 g15
Hari, r., Afghan. 144 B2
Hari, r., Indon. 148 B3
Haricha, Hamada el, Mali 162 D2
Harihari, N.Z. 175 f6
Harikawa, Jap. 154 h14
Hārim, Syr., 6,503 142 D2
Harima-nada, Jap. 155 D4

Haringsee, Aust. 124 d10
Haringvliet, r., Neth. 115 C3
Haripad, India, 20,378 145 k21
Harīpur, Pak., 10,217 145 D2
Harjo, Okla. 76 G2
Harkány, Hung., 1,628 126 D4
Harkema-Opeinde, Neth. 115 E1
Harkers Island, N.C., 1,362 63 H3
Harlan, Ind. 70 E1
Harlan, Iowa, 4,350 72 B3
Harlan, co., Ky., 51,107 71 H5
Harlan, Ky., 4,177 71 H5
Harlan, co., Nebr., 5,081 75 D4
Harlan, Oreg. 80 B3
Harlan County Res., Nebr. 75 F3
Harlech, U.K. 113 D5
Harlem, Ga., 1,423 64 G2
Harlem, Mont., 1,267 81 E1
Harlem, r., N.Y. 58 e13
Harleston, U.K. 113 G5
Harley, Ont., Can. 46 b15
Harley Dome, Utah 78 D2
Harleysville, Pa. 60 f10
Harleyville, S.C., 561 63 D4
Harlingen, Neth., 11,800 115 D1
Harlingen, Tex., 41,207 77 P6
Harlow, U.K., 53,680 113 G6
Harlow, N. Dak. 74 C1
Harlowton, Mont., 1,734 81 E2
Harman, W. Va., 128 62 E4
Harmelen, Neth. 115 b6
Harmersville, N.J. 61 A5
Harmon, Ill., 214 68 C2
Harmon, co., Okla., 5,852 76 D3
Harmon, Okla. 76 D1
Harmony, Ill. 68 b5
Harmony, Ind. 70 B3
Harmony, Me. 55 C4
Harmony, Minn., 1,214 74 F4
Harmony, N.C., 322 63 D2
Harmony, Pa., 1,142 60 B4
Harmony, R.I. 57 K5
Harnai, Pak., 1,940 144 C3
Harndrup, Den. 121 C5
Harned, Ky. 71 E4
Harnes, Fr., 14,625 116 a7
Harnett, co., N.C., 48,236 63 F2
Harney, co., Oreg., 6,744 80 D4
Harney L., Oreg. 80 D4
Harney Pk., S. Dak. 74 A4
Härnösand, Swed., 17,163 120 D3
Haro, Sp., 8,554 122 D1
Harold, Fla. 65 C2
Harold, Ky. 71 J4
Haroldswick, U.K. 112 F1
Harome, U.K. 114 G2
Haro Str., Can.-U.S. 42 c7
Harpenden, U.K., 18,307 114 H7
Harper, Lib. 162 C5
Harper, Iowa, 177 72 E3
Harper, co., Kans., 9,541 75 G6
Harper, Kans., 1,899 75 G6
Harper, co., Okla., 5,956 76 D1
Harper, Oreg. 80 E4
Harper, Wash. 81 b7
Harper, W. Va. 62 C5
Harper, Mt., Alaska 85 H2
Harper L., Calif. 82 E5
Harpers Ferry, Iowa, 211 72 F1
Harpers Ferry, W. Va., 572 62 G3
Harpersfield, N.Y. 59 L7
Harpersville, Ala., 667 64 C2
Harpersville, Ala. 64 C2
Harpster, Ohio, 302 70 F2
Harpswell Center, Me. 55 D3
Harpursville, N.Y. 59 J7
Harrah, Okla., 934 76 F2
Harrah, Wash., 284 80 C2
Harrai, India 144 b14
Harre, Belg. 115 D4
Harrell, Ark., 267 73 C4
Harrells, N.C., 259 63 F3
Harrellsville, N.C., 171 63 H1
Harricanaw, r., Ont.-Qué., Can. 44 H5
Harricot, Newf., Can. 45 b10
Harriet, L., Minn. 74 b6
Harrietsville, Ont., Can. 46 D6
Harrietta, Mich., 119 67 H4
Harrietville, Austl. 173 f11
Harriman, r., N.Y. 752 59 M9
Harriman, Tenn., 5,931 71 G6
Harrington, Del., 2,495 62 J4
Harrington, Me. 55 E4
Harrington, S. Dak. 74 B4
Harrington, Wash., 575 80 D2
Harrington Harbour, Qué., Can. 45 P5
Harrington L., Me. 55 C3
Harrington Park, N.J. 58 d13
Harrington Sd., Berm. Is. 108 1
Harris, Sask., Can. 43 C4
Harris, Montserrat, 704 97 5
Harris, co., Ga., 11,167 64 E3
Harris, Iowa, 258 72 B1
Harris, Kans., 36 75 K5
Harris, Mich. 66 F3
Harris, Minn., 552 74 F3
Harris, Mo. 171 72 D4
Harris, Okla. 76 J4
Harris (part of Coventry), R.I. 57 K6
Harris, co., Tex., 1,243,158 77 Q5
Harris, L., Austl. 172 E4
Harris, Sd. of, U.K. 112 C3
Harris Bluff, Austl. 172 b7
Harrisburg, co., Can. 46 b15
Harrisburg, Ala. 64 B3
Harrisburg, Ark., 1,481 73 E2
Harrisburg, Ill., 9,171 68 D6
Harrisburg, Ind. 70 D3

Harrisburg, Mo., 124 72 E5
Harrisburg, Nebr. 75 B2
Harrisburg, Ohio, 359 70 F3
Harrisburg, Oreg., 939 80 B3
Harrisburg, Pa., 79,697 60 J5
Harrisburg, S. Dak., 313 74 D4
Harrismith, S. Af., 13,753 164 D6
Harrison, Ark., 6,580 73 B1
Harrison, Ga., 209 64 G3
Harrison, co., Ind., 19,207 70 C4
Harrison, co., Iowa, 17,600 72 B3
Harrison, co., Ky., 13,704 71 G3
Harrison, Idaho, 249 81 A2
Harrison, Me. 55 B4
Harrison, Mich., 1,072 67 J4
Harrison, co., Miss., 119,489 73 F7
Harrison, co., Mo., 11,603 72 C4
Harrison, Mont. 81 D3
Harrison, Nebr., 448 75 B1
Harrison, N.J., 11,743 58 c14
Harrison, N.Y. 58 e13
Harrison, co., Ohio, 17,995 70 H2
Harrison, Ohio, 3,878 70 B3
Harrison, S. Dak. 74 C4
Harrison, co., Tex., 45,594 77 Q3
Harrison, co., W. Va., 77,856 62 D3
Harrison, Wis. 66 D3
Harrison, C., Newf., Can. 45 P3
Harrison Bay, Alaska 85 G1
Harrisonburg, La., 594 73 C6
Harrisonburg, Va., 11,916 62 E4
Harrison City, Pa. 60 d8
Harrison L., Mich. 67 H6
Harrison Valley, Pa. 60 G2
Harrisonville, Md. 62 b7
Harrisonville, Mo., 3,510 72 C6
Harrisonville, Ohio 70 G3
Harriston, Ont., Can., 1,610 46 D5
Harriston, Miss. 73 E6
Harrisville, Md. 62 b7
Harrisville, Mich., 487 67 K4
Harrisville, N.H. 54 C6
Harrisville, N.Y., 842 59 K3
Harrisville, Pa., 896 60 C3
Harrisville, R.I., 1,024 57 K5
Harrisville, W. Va., 1,428 62 C3
Harrisville, Wis. 66 D5
Harrodsburg, Ind. 70 C3
Harrodsburg, Ky., 6,061 71 G4
Harrogate, U.K., 56,332 113 F4
Harrogate, Tenn. 71 H5
Harrold, S. Dak., 255 74 C3
Harrold, Tex., 557 77 O2
Harrow, Ont., Can., 1,779 46 A6
Harrow, London, U.K. 114 H7
Harrow, Pa. 61 m18
Harrowgate Hill, U.K. 112 g10
Harrowgate Hill, U.K. 112 g10
Harry Strunk L., Nebr. 75 E3
Harsefeld, F.R.Ger., 3,877 118 B2
Harshaw, Ariz. 78 C6
Harshaw, Wis. 66 D3
Harsjit, r., Turk. 142 D1
Härslöv, Swed. 121 E5
Harsprånget, falls, Swed. 120 D2
Harstad, Nor., 4,024 120 D1
Harszberode, Ger.D.R. 118 C3
Hasankale, Turk., 8,023 142 E2
Hasanpur, India, 17,731 144 b11
Ḥāṣbayyā, Leb., 5,163 142 b6
Haselünne, F.R.Ger., 4,489 118 A2
Haselbourg, Fr. 116 d9
Hasle, Den., 1,487 121 G5
Haslemere, U.K., 12,523 113 F6
Haslet, Texas 76 c9
Haslett, Mich. 67 J6
Haslev, Den., 6,496 121 E5
Haslingden, U.K., 14,370 114 D3
Haslington, U.K., 3,223 114 D4
Hasparren, Fr., 5,506 117 C5
Haspres, Fr., 2,962 116 a7
Hassan, India, 32,172 145 E7
Hassayampa, r., Ariz. 78 B4
Hassela, Swed. 120 D3
Hassell, N.C., 147 63 H2
Hasselt, Belg., 35,019 115 D4
Hassfurt, F.R.Ger., 6,481 118 C3
Hassi-Messaoud, Alg. 160 F2
Hassi-R'mel, Alg. 160 F2
Hassleben, Ger.D.R. 118 D2
Hassloch, F.R.Ger., 13,762 119 E6
Hassmersheim, F.R.Ger., 2,564 119 G6
Hastière-Lavaux, Belg., 1,011 115 C4

Hartman, Colo., 164 79 D2
Hartney, Man., Can. 43 E5
Hartola, Fin. 120 F3
Hartpury, U.K. 114 D7
Hartsburg, Ill., 300 68 C3
Hartsburg, Mo., 158 72 E6
Hartsdale, N.Y. 58 d12
Hartsel, Colo. 79 B2
Hartselle, Ala., 5,000 64 C1
Hartshorne, Okla., 1,903 76 H3
Hartsgrove, Ohio 70 H1
Hartstene I., Wash. 81 a8
Hartsville (part of New Marlboro), Mass. 57 L4
Hartsville, S.C., 6,392 63 D3
Hartsville, Tenn., 1,712 71 E5
Hartville, Mo., 486 72 E7
Hartville, Ohio, 1,353 70 H2
Hartville, Wyo., 177 81 G4
Hartwell, Ga., 4,599 64 G1
Hartwell Res., Ga.-S.C. 63 A3
Hartwick, Iowa, 126 72 E3
Hartwick, N.Y. 59 K6
Hartwood, Va. 62 G4
Harty, Ont., Can. 44 G3
Hartz, r., Afghan. 144 A2
Haruka, Jap. 154 h15
Harut, r., Afghan. 144 A2
Harvard, Idaho 81 A2
Harvard, Ill., 5,019 68 D1
Harvard, Mass., 2,563(T) 57 K2
Harvard, Nebr., 1,261 75 G3
Harvard, N.Y. 59 K7
Harvel, Ill., 285 68 C4
Harvest, Ala. 64 B1
Harvester, Ill., 299 69 c10
Harvey, Austl., 1,625 172 B5
Harvey, N.B., Can. 47 T11
Harvey, N. Dak., 2,365 74 B2
Harvey, co., Kans., 25,865 75 H5
Harvey, Mich. 66 F2
Harvey, N. Dak., 2,365 74 B2
Harvey Cedars, N.J., 134 61 C4
Harveysburg, Ohio, 510 70 F3
Harveys Lake, Pa. 61 K13
Harvey Station, N.B., Can. 47 S11
Harveyville, Kans., 204 75 J5
Harvieston, U.K. 112 h10
Harvington, U.K. 114 D6
Harwell, U.K., 2,214 114 F7
Harwich, U.K., 13,699 113 G6
Harwich Port (part of Harwich), Mass. 57 Q6
Harwick, Pa., 1,520* 60 c7
Harwinton, Conn., 3,344(T) 56 D5
Harwood, Ont., Can. 46 F4
Harwood, Md. 62 c9
Harwood, Tex., 132 77 P5
Harwood Heights, Ill., 5,688 69 c9
Harworth, U.K., 8,289 114 F4
Harz, mts., F.R.Ger. 118 C3
Harzgerode, Ger.D.R. 118 C3
Hasankale, Turk., 8,023 142 E2
Hasanpur, India, 17,731 144 b11
Ḥāṣbayyā, Leb., 5,163 142 b6
Hasbrouck Heights, N.J., 13,046 58 c13
Hase, r., F.R.Ger. 118 A2
Hasedashimachi, Jap. 154 h15
Haselbourg, Fr. 116 d9
Haselünne, F.R.Ger., 4,489 118 A2
Hasemiya, Jap. 155 g15
Hasenkamp, Arg., 4,000* 105 b10
Hashihama, Jap. 154 e15
Hashimoto, Jap., 32,013 155 D4
Hashizume, Jap. 154 g14
Hashima, Jap., 41,438 154 h14
Hash Rock, mtn., Oreg. 80 C3
Hashima, Jap. 154 h14
Hasi-Messaoud=Hassi-Messaoud
Haskell, co., Kans., 2,990 75 E6
Haskell, Ark., 215 73 C3
Haskell, co., Okla., 9,121 76 H2
Haskell, Okla., 1,887 76 H2
Haskell, co., Tex., 11,174 77 O3
Haskell, N.J. 58 b12
Haskell, Ind. 69 g10
Haskell Hill, Mass. 57 b6
Haskins, Ohio, 521 70 F1
Haslach, Aust., 2,569 124 L5
Haslach, Aust. 124 c9
Haslach, F.R.Ger., 4,772 118 A4
Hasland (part of Chesterfield), U.K., 4,413 114 F4
Hasle, Den., 1,487 121 G5
Haslemere, U.K., 12,523 113 F6
Haslen, Switz. 124 D2
Haslet, Texas 76 c9
Haslett, Mich. 67 J6
Haslev, Den., 6,496 121 E5
Hauvieste, Qué., Can., 5,837 47 R9
Haute-Rivoire, Fr., 1,168 116 o15
Hautes Fagnes, upland, Belg. 115 E4
Hauteville, Switz. 124 B2
Hauteville-Lompnès, Fr., 5,710 117 F3
Hautmont, Fr., 18,632 117 F1
Hauts Plateaux, Alg. 160 D2
Hauula, Hawaii, 806 84 D2
Hauzenberg, F.R.Ger., 2,526 118 D4
Havana=Habana
Havana, Ala. 64 B3
Havana, Ark., 277 73 B2
Havana, Fla., 2,090 65 E2
Havana, Ill., 4,363 68 C3
Havana, Kans., 162 75 K6
Havana, N. Dak., 206 74 D3
Havana, Ohio 70 G1

Hastings, U.K., 66,478 113 G6
Hastings, Fla., 617 65 H3
Hastings, Iowa, 260 72 B3
Hastings, Mich., 6,375 67 H6
Hastings, Minn., 10,588 74 F3
Hastings, Nebr., 21,412 75 G3
Hastings, N.Y. 59 H5
Hastings, N. Dak. 74 C2
Hastings, Okla., 200 76 E3
Hastings, Pa., 1,751 60 E4
Hastings I., Terr. Papua 174 3
Hastings-on-Hudson, N.Y., 8,979 58 d13
Hasvik, Nor. 120 E1
Haswell, U.K., 6,160 112 h10
Haswell, Colo., 169 79 D2
Hata, Jap. 154 h15
Hatake, Jap. 154 h15
Hatboro, Pa., 7,315 61 M5
Hatch, N. Mex., 888 79 B5
Hatch, Utah, 198 78 B3
Hatches Creek, Austl. 172 E4
Hatchet Bay, Bah. Is. 95 c7
Hatchet L., Sask., Can. 43 D2
Hatchie, r., Tenn. 71 B6
Hatchineha, L., Fla. 65 H4
Hatchville (part of Falmouth), Mass. 57 O6
Hat Cr., Nebr.-S. Dak. 75 B1
Haṭeg, Rum., 3,853 128 D2
Hatfield, U.K., 21,019 114 H7
Hatfield, Ark., 337 73 A3
Hatfield, Ind. 70 B5
Hatfield, Mass., 1,330;2,350(T) 56 F3
Hatfield, Pa., 1,941 61 M5
Hatfield, Wis. 66 C4
Hatherleigh, U.K. 113 D6
Hatherton, U.K. 114 D4
Hathras, India, 64,045 144 b12
Ha Tien, S. Viet., 6,027 146 D5
Hatillo, P.R., 2,582 96 s10
Ha Tinh, N. Viet. 146 D3
Hatley, Wis., 306 66 D4
Hato Mayor, Dom. Rep., 5,775 96 n6
Hatra=Al Ḥaḍr
Hatseva, Isr. 142 C4
Hatsukaichi, Jap., 5,119 155 C4
Hatta, India, 9,114 144 b13
Hattem, Neth., 7,100 115 E2
Hatten, F.R.Ger., 6,633 118 B2
Hatten, Fr., 1,404 119 E7
Hatteras, N.C. 63 J2
Hatteras, c., N.C. 63 J2
Hatteras Plain, Atl. Oc. 108 H5
Hattersheim, F.R.Ger., 5,687 119 E4
Hattertown (part of Newtown), Conn. 56 C7
Hattfjelldal, Nor. 120 C2
Hattiesburg, Miss., 34,989 73 F6
Hattieville, Ark. 73 C2
Hatting, Den., 1,305 121 B5
Hattingen, F.R.Ger., 24,837 119 C2
Hatton, Ala. 64 B1
Hatton, Ark. 73 A3
Hatton, N. Dak., 856 74 D2
Hatton, Wash., 65 80 D2
Hattstedt, F.R.Ger., 1,156 118 B1
Ha-t'u-t'a-la, China 151 D2
Hatutu, i., Marq. Is. 177 42
Hatvan, Hung., 19,952 126 D3
Hat Yai, Thai., 35,504 146 C6
Hatzfeld, F.R.Ger., 1,519 119 E3
Hätzingen, Switz. 124 C2
Hau, F.R.Ger., 6,540 119 A1
Haubourdin, Fr., 13,235 116 a6
Haubstadt, Ind., 1,029 70 B4
Hau Duc, S. Viet. 146 E4
Hauenstein, F.R.Ger., 3,913 119 D6
Haugen, Wis., 265 66 B3
Haugesund, Nor., 27,101 120 A4
Haughton, La., 611 73 B5
Hau Giang, r., S. Viet. 146 D5
Haugsdorf, Aust., 1,293 124 N5
Hau Hoi Wan=Deep Bay
Haukipudas, Fin. 120 F2
Haukivesi, l., Fin. 120 G3
Haulerwijk, Neth. 115 E1
Haultain, r., Sask., Can. 43 C3
Haumuri Bluff, N.Z. 175 g6
Haunstetten, F.R.Ger., 13,222 118 C4
Hauppauge, N.Y. 58 g13
Hauraki G., N.Z. 175 g5
Hauroko, L., N.Z. 175 e7
Hauru, Pte., Moorea 177 44
Hauser, Oreg. 80 A4
Hausleiten, Aust. 124 c10
Hausruck, mts., Aust. 125 —
Haussy, Fr., 2,011 116 a7
Haut Atlas, ra., Mor. 160 C2
Haute Deûle, Can. de la, Fr. 116 a6
Hautefort, Fr., 1,002 117 D4
Havant (includes Waterlooville), U.K., 74,552 113 m13

Havasu—Herstedvester · 235

Havasu L., Ariz.-Calif. 78 A4
Havdhem, Swed. 120 D4
Havel, r., Ger.D.R. 118 D2
Havelange, Belg., 1,529 115 D4
Havelberg, Ger.D.R. 118 D2
Havelländischer Kan., Ger.D.R. 118 D2
Havelock, N.B., Can. 47 T10
Havelock, Ont., Can., 1,211 44 J7
Havelock, Iowa, 289 72 C2
Havelock, N.C., 2,433 63 G3
Havelock I., India 146 A5
Havelock North, N.Z., 3,622 175 h5
Haven, Kans., 982 75 H6
Haven, Wis. 66 F5
Havensville, Kans., 166 75 K4
Haven, The, chan., U.K. 114 J5
Haverford, Pa., 5,400* 60 f11
Haverfordwest, U.K., 8,892 113 D6
Haverhill, U.K., 5,445 113 G5
Haverhill, Fla., 442 65 b8
Haverhill, Mass., 46,346 57 M1
Haverhill, N.H. 54 C3
Haverhill, Ohio 70 G4
Haveri, India, 21,043 145 E7
Häverödal, Swed. 120 D4
Haverslev, Den. 121 B4
Haverstraw, N.Y., 5,771 59 M9
Haverthwaite, U.K. 114 B2
Havertown, Pa., 36,000* 60 f12
Haviland, Kans., 725 75 F6
Havîrna, Rum. 128 F1
Havířov, Czech., 53,525 126 D2
Havlíčkův Brod, Czech., 16,607 126 B2
Havndal, Den. 121 C4
Havre, Mont., 10,740 81 E1
Havre-Aubert, Qué., Can. 47 V10
Havre Boucher, N.S., Can. 47 V11
Havre de Grace, Md., 8,510 62 H3
Havre St-Pierre, Qué., Can., 2,407 45 N5
Havza, Turk., 9,463 142 C1
Haw, r., N.C. 63 E1
Hawaii, st., U.S., 710,000* 84
Hawaii, co., Hawaii, 61,332 84 E4
Hawaii, i., Hawaii 84 F4
Hawaiian Is., Pac. Oc. 170 G3
Hawaiian Ridge, Pac. Oc. 169 G2
Hawaii Volcanoes Nat. Pk., Hawaii 84 F4
Hawarden, Sask., Can. 43 C4
Hawarden, U.K., 16,575 114 B4
Hawarden, Iowa, 2,544 72 A2
Hawea, L., N.Z. 175 f7
Hawera, N.Z., 7,542 175 g5
Hawes, U.K., 1,137 113 E4
Hawesville, Ky., 882 71 E4
Hawes Water, l., U.K. 114 C1
Hawi, Hawaii, 985 84 F3
Hawick, U.K., 16,204 113 E4
Hawke, r., Newf., Can. 45 Q4
Hawke Bay, N.Z. 175 h5
Hawker, Austl. 172 E4
Hawkesbury, Ont., Can., 8,577 44 K6
Hawkesbury I., Br. Col., Can. 42 E3
Hawkesville, Ont., Can. 46 a13
Hawkeye, Iowa, 516 72 F2
Hawkeye, N.Y. 59 N2
Hawkins, co., Tenn., 30,468 71 H5
Hawkins, Tex., 868 77 Q3
Hawkins, Wis., 402 66 C3
Hawkins Pk., Utah 78 A3
Hawkinsville, Ga., 3,967 64 F3
Hawk Junction, Ont., Can. 44 F5
Hawk Lake, Ont., Can. 44 C5
Hawk Point, Mo., 270 72 F6
Hawk Run, Pa. 60 F4
Hawks, Mich. 67 K3
Hawks Harbour, Newf., Can. 45 Q4
Hawkshead, U.K. 114 B2
Hawk's Nest, mtn., N. Dak. 74 C2
Hawk Springs, Wyo. 81 G5
Hawley, U.K., 3,757 114 G8
Hawley, Mass., 251(T) 56 E2
Hawley, Minn., 1,270 74 D2
Hawley, Okla. 76 F1
Hawley, Pa., 1,433 61 M3
Hawley, Tex. 77 O3
Hawleyville (part of Newtown), Conn. 56 C7
Ḥawmat as Sūq, Tun., 4,179 161 F2
Hawng Luk, Burma 146 C2
Haworth, U.K., 3,382 114 D3
Haworth, N.J., 3,215 58 d13
Haworth, Okla., 351 76 J4
Ḥawrān, Wādī, Iraq 143 C2
Haw River, N.C., 1,410 63 E1
Hawthorn, Pa., 612 60 D3
Hawthorne, Calif., 33,035 83 h16
Hawthorne, Fla., 1,167 65 G3
Hawthorne, Nev., 2,838 83 A3
Hawthorne, N.J., 17,735 58 c13
Hawthorne, N.Y. 58 d12
Hawthorne, Wis. 66 B2
Hawthorne Woods, Ill., 239 69 b8
Haxby, U.K., 2,407 114 F2
Haxtun, Colo., 990 79 D1
Hay, Austl., 3,009 173 F5
Hay, U.K., 1,327 113 E5
Hay, Wash. 80 E2
Hay, C., Austl. 172 D2
Hay, Mt., Can.-U.S. 85 K4
Hay, r., Austl. 172 E3
Hay, r., Alta.-Br. Col., Can. 42 H1
Hay, r., Wis. 66 A3
Hayakita, Jap., 7,497 155 J8
Hayama, Jap., 15,229 155 m20
Hayange, Fr., 11,009 117 F2
Hayashima, Jap., 9,137 154 e15
Hay Canyon Butte, S. Dak. 74 A4
Haycock, Alaska 85 D2
Haydān, Wādī al, Jor. 142 b8
Hayden, Ala., 187 64 C2
Hayden, Ariz., 1,760 78 C5
Hayden, Colo., 764 79 B1
Hayden, Fla., 5,471 65 G5
Hayden, Idaho, 901 81 A2
Hayden Pk., Utah 78 C1
Hayden Row (part of Hopkinton), Mass. 57 L4
Haydenville (part of Williamsburg), Mass. 56 F3
Hayes, Fr. 116 b8
Hayes, La. 73 C7
Hayes, co., Nebr., 1,919 75 D3
Hayes, S. Dak. 74 B3
Hayes, Mt., Br. Col., Can. 42 b5
Hayes, Mt., Alaska 85 H3
Hayes, r., Man., Can. 43 G3
Hayes Center, Nebr., 283 75 D3
Hayes I., Burma 146 B5
Hayesville, N.C., 428 63 b7
Hayfield, Minn., 889 74 F4
Hayfield, Va. 62 F3
Hayfork, Calif. 82 B2
Hay Lakes, Alta., Can. 43 c7
Hayle, U.K., 4,830 113 D6
Haylow, Ga. 64 G5
Haymana, Turk., 4,585 142 C2
Haymarket, Va., 257 62 G4
Hayne, Kans. 75 E6
Haynes, Ark. 73 E3
Haynes, N. Dak., 111 74 A3
Haynesville, La., 3,031 73 B5
Haynesville, Me. 55 D3
Hayneville, Ala. 64 C3
Hayrabolu, Turk., 8,589 142 A1
Hay River, N.W.T., Can. 40 F5
Hays, Kans., 11,947 75 F5
Hays, Mont. 81 E2
Hays, co., Tex., 19,934 77 O4
Haysi, Va., 485 62 B5
Hay Springs, Nebr., 823 75 C1
Haystack Mtn., N. Mex. 79 C5
Haystack Mtn., Vt. 54 B2
Haystack Mtn., Vt. 54 B6
Haystack Pk., Utah 78 A2
Haysville, Ont., Can. 46 a14
Haysville, Ind. 70 B4
Haysville, Kans., 5,836 75 H6
Hayters Gap, Va. 62 B6
Hayti, Mo., 3,737 72 H8
Hayti, S. Dak., 425 74 D3
Hayward, Calif., 72,700 82 C4
Hayward, Okla. 76 F1
Hayward, Wis., 1,540 66 B2
Haywards Heath, U.K., 14,373 113 F6
Haywood, Man., Can. 43 f10
Haywood, Ky. 71 F5
Haywood, co., N.C., 39,711 63 A2
Haywood, N.C., 713 63 E2
Haywood, Okla. 76 H3
Haywood, co., Tenn., 23,393 71 B6
Hayyā, Taqāṭu, Sudan 163 K2
Hazard, Ky., 5,958 71 H4
Hazard, Nebr., 104 75 F2
Hazardville (part of Enfield), Conn. 56 F4
Hazar Gölü, Turk. 142 D2
Hazaribagh, India, 40,958 145 G5
Haze, Jap. 154 h15
Hazebrouck, Fr., 18,126 117 E1
Hazel, Ky., 342 71 C5
Hazel, S. Dak., 128 74 D3
Hazel Crest, Ill., 6,205 69 d10
Hazel Dell, Ill. 68 D4
Hazel Green, Wis., 807 66 C6
Hazel Grove, U.K., 30,399 114 D4
Hazel Hurst, Pa. 60 E2
Hazelhurst, Wis. 66 D3
Hazel Park, Mich., 25,631 67 f15
Hazelton, Br. Col., Can. 42 E2
Hazelton, Idaho, 433 81 B4
Hazelton, Kans., 246 75 G6
Hazelton, N. Dak., 451 74 B2
Hazelton, W. Va. 62 E3
Hazelwood, Mo., 6,045 72 a10
Hazelwood, N.C., 1,925 63 A2
Hazen, Ark., 1,456 73 D3
Hazen, Nev. 83 A3
Hazen, N. Dak., 1,222 74 B2
Hazen, L., N.W.T., Can. 41 P1
Hazen Bay, Alaska 85 C3
Hazen Str., N.W.T., Can. 41 G2
Hazerswoude, Neth. 115 b6
Hazewara, Jap. 154 h14
Hazlehurst, Ga., 3,699 64 G4
Hazlehurst, Miss., 3,400 73 E6
Hazlet, Sask., Can. 43 B5
Hazlet, N.J. 58 c15
Hazleton, Iowa, 665 72 F2
Hazleton, Pa., 32,056 61 K4
Hazlett, L., Austl. 172 D3
Heacham, U.K., 2,680 113 G5
Headford, Ire. 113 B5
Head Harbor I., Me. 55 E4
Headingley, Man., Can. 43 g10
Headland, Ala., 2,650 64 D4
Headlee, Ind. 70 C2
Head of the Harbor, N.Y., 524 58 g13
Headquarters, Idaho 81 B2
Headrick, Okla., 152 76 D3
Heafford Junction, Wis. 66 D3
Heage (part of Ripley), U.K., 2,007 114 E4
Healdsburg, Calif., 4,816 82 B3
Healdton, Okla., 2,898 76 F3
Healesville, Austl., 2,707 173 e11
Healeyfield, U.K., 1,084 112 g10
Healing Springs, Va. 62 E5
Healy, Kans. 75 E5
Healy Fork, Alaska 85 G3
Heanna, Ryukyu Is. 154 a11
Heanor, U.K., 23,870 113 F5
Heard, co., Ga., 5,333 64 D2
Heard I., Ind. Oc. 168 C4
Heards, Va. 62 F5
Hearne, Tex., 5,072 77 P4
Hearst, Ont., Can., 2,254 44 G5
Heart, r., N. Dak. 74 A2
Heart Butte Dam, N. Dak. 74 B2
Heart's Content, Newf., Can. 45 b10
Heart's Delight, Newf., Can. 45 b10
Heart's Desire, Newf., Can. 45 b10
Heartwell, Nebr., 113 75 G3
Heartwellville, Vt. 54 A6
Heaslip, Ont., Can. 44 H6
Heaters, W. Va. 62 D4
Heath, Mass., 304(T) 56 E2
Heath, Ohio, 6,066 70 G2
Heath, Tex. 76 g9
Heath, Pte., Qué., Can. 45 O5
Heathcote, Austl., 1,273 173 e11
Heath Springs, S.C., 832 63 D3
Heathsville, Va. 62 H5
Heaton, N.C. 63 B1
Heavener, Okla., 1,891 76 J3
Hebardville, Ga., 2,758 64 G4
Hebbardsville, Ky. 71 D4
Hebbronville, Tex., 3,987 77 O6
Hebburn, U.K., 15,042 112 h10
Hebden Royd, U.K., 9,409 114 D3
Heber, Ariz. 78 C4
Heber, Calif. 82 F6
Heber, Utah, 2,936 78 C1
Heber Springs, Ark., 2,265 73 C2
Hebgen L., Mont. 81 D3
Hebo, Oreg. 80 B3
Hebrides or Western Is., U.K. 112 C3
Hebrides, Sea of the, U.K. 112 C3
Hebron, Newf., Can. 45 O2
Hebron, N.S., Can. 47 S12
Hebron, Jordan = Al Khalīl
Hebron, Conn., 1,819(T) 56 G6
Hebron, Ill., 701 68 D1
Hebron, Ind., 1,401 70 B1
Hebron, Me. 55 B4
Hebron, Md., 754 62 J4
Hebron, Nebr., 1,920 75 H3
Hebron, N.H. 54 D4
Hebron, N. Dak., 1,340 74 B2
Hebron, Ohio, 1,260 70 G3
Hebron, Va. 62 G5
Hebron, Wis. 66 E6
Hebronville (part of Attleboro), Mass. 57 L5
Hecate Str., Br. Col., Can. 42 D3
Hecelchakán, Mex., 3,879 93 H4
Hechingen, F.R.Ger., 9,630 118 B4
Hechtsheim, F.R.Ger., 5,431 119 E5
Hecker, Ill., 313 68 B5
Heckington, U.K., 1,691 114 H5
Hecktown, Pa. 61 k18
Hecla, S. Dak., 444 74 C3
Hecla and Griper Bay, N.W.T., Can. 41 G2
Hector, Ark. 73 B2
Hector, Minn., 1,297 74 E3
Hector, Mt., Alta., Can. 42 J3
Hectors River, Jam. 96 q8
Hédé, Fr. 117 C2
Hede, Swed. 120 C3
Hedehusene, Den. 121 E5
Hedekas, Swed. 121 D2
Hedel, Neth. 115 c7
Hedemora, Swed. 120 D3
Hedensted, Den., 2,649 121 B5
Hedesunda, Swed. 120 D3
Hedge End, U.K., 4,464 113 k13
Hedges, Fla. 65 H2
Hedgesville, W. Va., 342 62 F3
Hedley, Tex., 494 76 N2
Hednesford, U.K., 12,485 114 E5
Hedo, Ryukyu Is. 154 b10
Hedo-misaki, Ryukyu Is. 154 b10
Hedon, U.K., 2,345 114 H3
Hedrick, Iowa, 762 72 E3
Hedrum, Nor. 121 C1
Hedwig, Tex., 1,182 77 h9
Heeia, Hawaii 84 d7
Heel Pt., Wake I. 176 26
Heemse, Neth. 115 E2
Heemskerk, Neth., 12,000 115 C2
Heemstede, Neth., 23,300 115 C2
Heerde, Neth., 3,700 115 D2
Heerenveen, Neth., 10,500 115 E2
Heeren-Werve, F.R.Ger., 7,929 119 D1
Heerlen, Neth., 49,100 115 D4
Heessen, F.R.Ger., 15,644 118 A3
Heeze, Neth., 3,500 115 D3
Heflin, Ala., 2,400 64 D2
Heflin, La., 289 73 B5
Hegins, Pa. 60 J4
Hei, Jap. 154 g14
Heiberger, Ala. 64 B3
Hei-ch'eng-ch'a, China 151 A3
Heide, F.R.Ger., 20,036 118 B1
Heidelberg, Ont., Can. 46 a13
Heidelberg, F.R.Ger., 121,910 118 B4
Heidelberg, Cape, S. Af., 3,711 164 C7
Heidelberg, Tvaal., S. Af., 9,292 165 k17
Heidelberg, Ky. 71 H4
Heidelberg, Miss., 1,049 73 G6
Heidelberg, Pa., 2,118 60 b8
Heiden, F.R.Ger., 4,201 119 B1
Heidenau, F.R.Ger., 1,454 119 a9
Heidenau, Ger.D.R., 19,386 118 D3
Heidenheim, F.R.Ger., 45,742 118 C4
Heidenreichstein, Aust., 3,647 124 M5
Heiderscheid, Lux. 115 D5
Heighington, U.K., 1,267 112 g10
Heigun-jima, Jap. 154 C5
Hei-ho, China 150 C4
Heikendorf, F.R.Ger., 5,735 118 C1
Heil, N. Dak. 74 B2
Heilbron, S. Af., 7,182 164 D6
Heilbronn, F.R.Ger., 79,458 118 B4
Heiligenhafen, F.R.Ger., 8,136 118 C1
Heiligenhaus, F.R.Ger., 17,709 119 B2
Heiligenstadt, Ger.D.R., 12,500 118 C3
Heiligenwald, F.R.Ger., 5,991 116 d8
Heiligerlee, Neth. 115 F1
Heiloo, Neth., 10,600 115 C2
Hei-lung = Amur
Hei-lung, r., China-U.S.S.R. 150 H1
Hei-lung-chiang, prov., China, 14,860,000 150 G2
Heilungkiang = Hei-lung-chiang
Heilwood, Pa. 60 D4
Heimbach, Nrh.-Wf., F.R.Ger., 2,034 119 B3
Heimbach, Rhein.-Pfalz, F.R.Ger., 1,572 119 C5
Heimdal, N. Dak. 74 C2
Heinävesi, Fin. 120 G3
Heinerscheid, Lux. 119 A4
Heining, F.R.Ger., 4,700 118 D4
Heinola, Fin., 10,995 120 F3
Heinsch, Belg., 2,587 115 D5
Heirnkut, Burma 146 A1
Hei-shan, China 151 D2
Hei-shui, China 152 A1
Hei-shui-chen, China 151 C2
Heist, Belg., 8,159 115 B3
Heist-op-den-Berg, Belg., 12,518 115 C3
Heizer, Kans. 75 G5
Hejaz = Al Ḥijāz
Hejninge, Den. 121 D5
Hejnsvig, Den. 121 A5
Heki, Jap., 7,900 154 B4
Hekimhan, Turk., 3,546 142 D2
Hekinan, Jap., 50,116 154 i15
Hekla, vol., Ice. 120 a6
Hekura-jima, Jap. 155 E3
Hel, Pol., 2,265 127 C1
Helagsfjället, mt., Swed. 120 C3
Helden, F.R.Ger., 3,254 119 D2
Helden, Neth. 119 A2
Heldens Point, St. Christopher 97 6
Helemano Str., Hawaii 84 b6
Helen, Ga., 227 64 F1
Helen, Mt., Nev. 83 B4
Helena, Guyana 101 M4
Helena, Ala., 523 64 C2
Helena, Ark., 11,500 73 E3
Helena, Calif. 82 B2
Helena, Ga., 1,290 64 F3
Helena, Ill. 68 E5
Helena, Mont., 20,227 81 C2
Helena, N.Y. 59 L2
Helena, Okla., 580 76 E1
Helen I., Caroline Is. 149 J2
Helensburgh, U.K., 9,605 112 a7
Helensville, N.Z., 1,214 175 g5
Helenville, Wis. 66 E6
Helgesta, Swed. 120 c8
Helgoland, i., F.R.Ger. 118 A1
Helgoländer B., F.R.Ger. 118 B2
Heliopolis = Miṣr al Jadīdah
Helix, Oreg., 148 80 D3
Hell, Mich. 67 J6
Hella, Ice. 120 a6
Hellbranch, r., Ohio 70 a7
Hell Cr., Colo. 79 D2
Hellebæk, Den., 2,378 121 E4
Hellendoorn, Neth. 115 E2
Hellenthal, F.R.Ger., 4,485 119 A4
Hellertown, Pa., 6,716 61 M4
Hellevad, Den. 121 C3
Hellier, Ky., 104 71 J4
Hellifield, U.K., 1,045 114 D2
Hellimer, Fr. 116 c9
Hellín, Sp., 27,242 122 E3
Helli Ness, U.K. 112 F1
Hellmonsödt, Aust., 1,064 124 L5
Hells Canyon, Idaho-Oreg. 81 A3
Hellshire Hills, Jam. 96 q9
Hellville, Malag. Rep., 7,497 165 G4
Helm, U.K. 112 g9
Helm, Ill. 68 D5
Helmand, r., Afghan. 144 B3
Helmbrechts, F.R.Ger., 8,377 118 C3
Helme, r., Ger.D.R. 118 C3
Helmetta, N.J., 779 61 C3
Helmond, Neth., 41,600 115 D3
Helmsburg, Ind. 70 C3
Helmsdale, U.K. 112 E2
Helmsdale, r., U.K. 112 E2
Helmsley, U.K., 1,324 114 F2
Helmstadt, F.R.Ger., 1,526 119 H5
Helmstedt, F.R.Ger., 28,780 118 C2
Helmville, Mont. 81 C2
Helotes, Tex. 77 O5
Helper, Utah, 2,459 78 C2
Helperby, U.K. 114 F2
Helperthorpe, U.K. 114 H2
Helpringham, U.K. 114 H5
Helpston, U.K. 114 H5
Helsby, U.K., 2,739 114 C4
Helsinge, Den. 121 a7
Helsingfors = Helsinki
Helsingør, Den., 26,658 121 E4
Helsinki, Fin., 477,062 120 F3
Helska, Mierzeja, pen., Pol. 127 C1
Helston, Man., Can. 43 e9
Helston, U.K., 7,086 113 D6
Helton, Ky. 71 H5
Heltonville, Ind. 70 C4
Helvecia, Arg., 7,245 105 a10
Helvellyn, mtn., U.K. 114 C1
Helvick Head, Ire. 113 C5
Helvoirt, Neth. 115 c7
Helwân = Ḥulwān
Hem, Nor. 121 C1
Hemau, F.R.Ger., 2,770 118 C4
Hembori, Jap. 155 m19
Hemel Hempstead, U.K., 55,270 113 F6
Hemenahei, i., Terr. Papua 174 3
Hemer, F.R.Ger., 21,753 119 D2
Hemet, Calif., 5,416 82 E6
Hemfosa, Swed. 120 e8
Hemiksem, Belg., 9,765 115 d8
Héming, Fr. 116 d9
Hemingford, Nebr., 904 75 B1
Hemingway, S.C., 951 63 E4
Hemlock, Ind. 70 D2
Hemlock, Mich. 67 J5
Hemlock, N.Y. 58 n21
Hemlock L., N.Y. 58 E6
Hemmerde, F.R.Ger., 2,053 119 D1
Hemmersdorf, F.R.Ger., 1,815 116 c8
Hemmet, Den. 121 A5
Hemmingford, Qué., Can. 47 L3
Hemne, Nor. 120 B3
Hemnesberget, Nor. 120 C2
Hemphill, co., Tex., 3,185 76 N2
Hemphill, Tex., 913 77 R4
Hempstead, co., Ark., 19,661 73 B4
Hempstead, N.Y., 34,641 59 N10
Hempstead, Tex., 1,505 77 P4
Hempstead Hbr., N.Y. 58 e13
Hemsbach, F.R.Ger., 4,523 119 F5
Hemse, Swed. 120 D4
Hemsworth, U.K., 14,401 114 F3
Henashi-saki, Jap. 155 F1
Henau, Switz., 7,828 124 D1
Hendaye, Fr., 7,936 117 C5
Hendek, Turk., 9,871 142 B1
Henderson, Arg., 13,500* 105 C5
Henderson, N.Z., 3,959 175 g5
Henderson, Colo. 79 c8
Henderson, co., Ill., 8,237 68 B3
Henderson, Ill., 212 68 B2
Henderson, Iowa, 191 72 B3
Henderson, co., Ky., 33,519 71 D4
Henderson, Ky., 16,892 71 D4
Henderson, Dickinson Co., Mich. 66 F2
Henderson, Shiawassee Co., Mich. 67 J5
Henderson, Nebr., 730 75 H3
Henderson, Nev., 12,525 83 C4
Henderson, N.Y. 59 H4
Henderson, co., N.C., 36,163 63 B2
Henderson, N.C., 12,740 63 F1
Henderson, co., Tenn., 15,115 71 C6
Henderson, Tenn., 2,691 71 C6
Henderson, co., Tex., 21,786 77 Q3
Henderson, Tex., 9,666 77 Q3
Henderson, W. Va., 601 62 B4
Henderson Cr., Ill. 68 B2
Henderson I., Pac. Oc. 171 K6
Henderson L., Br. Col., Can. 42 a6
Hendersonville, N.C., 5,911 63 B2
Hendersonville, Pa. 60 b8
Hendersonville, S.C. 63 D5
Hendersonville, Tenn. 71 E5
Hendley, Nebr., 79 75 F3
Hendon, London, U.K. 114 H7
Hendricks, co., Ind., 40,896 70 C3
Hendricks, Ky. 71 H4
Hendricks, Minn., 797 74 D3
Hendricks, W. Va., 407 62 E3
Hendriktop, mtn., Sur. 101 M5
Hendrix = Kemp City
Hendrum, Minn., 305 74 D2
Hendry, co., Fla., 8,119 65 H6
Hendry's Corse, mtn., U.K. 112 c8
Henefer, Utah, 408 78 c8
Henganofi, Terr. New Guin. 174 e2
Heng-ch'un, Taiwan, 23,486 150 F5
Hengelo, Neth., 58,000 115 E2
Hengelo, Neth. 115 E2
Heng-feng, China 152 E1
Heng-hsien, China 152 C3
Heng-kang, China 152 b6
Heng-shan, Hu-n., China 152 D2
Heng-shan, Shen-hsi, China 151 A3
Heng Shan, China 152 D2
Heng-shih-chi, China 152 a6
Heng-shui, China 151 C3
Heng-yang, China, 210,000* 150 F4
Hénin-Liétard, Fr., 25,660 116 a7
Henkel, Ill. 68 C2
Henlawson, W. Va., 1,670 62 C5
Henley, Mo., 73 72 E6
Henley Harbour, Newf., Can. 45 Q4
Henley in Arden, U.K., 1,691 114 E6
Henley-on-Thames, U.K., 9,144 114 G7
Henlopen, C., Del. 62 J4
Henlow, U.K., 3,682 114 H6
Henly, Tex. 76 b5
Henne, Den., 1,159 121 A5
Hennebont, Fr., 11,899 116 B3
Hennef, F.R.Ger., 12,175 119 C3
Hennen, F.R.Ger., 4,181 119 D2
Hennepin, Ill., 391 68 C2
Hennepin, co., Minn., 842,854 74 F3
Hennepin, Okla. 76 F3
Hennessey, Okla., 1,228 76 F1
Hennigsdorf, Ger.D.R., 19,042 118 D2
Henniker, N.H. 54 D5
Henning, Ill., 271 68 E3
Henning, Minn., 980 74 E2
Henning, Tenn., 466 71 B6
Henrico, co., Va., 117,339 62 G5
Henrietta, Mich. 67 J6
Henrietta, Mo., 497 72 D5
Henrietta, N.Y. 58 E5
Henrietta, Tex., 3,062 77 O3
Henrietta Maria, C., Ont., Can. 44 G3
Henrieville, Utah, 152 78 C3
Henrique de Carvalho, Ang. 164 C3
Henry, co., Ala., 15,286 64 D4
Henry, co., Ga., 17,619 64 E2
Henry, co., Ill., 49,317 68 B2
Henry, Ill., 2,278 68 C2
Henry, co., Ind., 48,899 70 D3
Henry, co., Iowa, 18,187 72 F4
Henry, co., Ky., 10,987 71 F3
Henry, co., Mo., 19,226 72 D6
Henry, Nebr., 138 75 B1
Henry, co., Ohio, 25,392 70 E1
Henry, S. Dak., 276 74 D3
Henry, co., Tenn., 22,275 71 C5
Henry, co., Va., 40,335 62 E6
Henry, Va. 62 E6
Henry, C., Terr. Papua 174 3
Henry, C., Va. 62 J6
Henryetta, Okla., 6,551 76 G2
Henry Kater Pen., N.W.T., Can. 41 Q4
Henry Lake, Pa. 61 p16
Henry Lawrence I., India 146 A4
Henry Mts., Utah 78 C2
Henry Pittier = Rancho Grande, Pq. Nac.
Henrys Fork, r., Idaho 81 D3
Henryville, Qué., Can. 47 L3
Henryville, Ind. 70 D4
Hensall, Ont., Can. 46 C5
Henshaw, L., Calif. 82 E6
Hensley, Ark. 73 C3
Henslow, C., Sol. Is. 175 c3
Hensonville, N.Y. 59 M7
Henstedt, F.R.Ger., 2,702 119 b8
Henteyn Nuruu, Mong. 150 E1
Henton, Ill. 68 D4
Henty, Austl., 1,073 173 f10
Henzada, Burma, 61,972 146 A3
Hepburn, Sask., Can. 43 C4
Hephzibah, Ga., 676 64 G2
Heppendorf, F.R.Ger., 5,747 119 B3
Heppenheim, F.R.Ger., 13,332 119 F5
Heppner, Oreg., 1,661 80 D3
Hepworth, Ont., Can. 46 C4
Herald, Ill. 68 D6
Herăşti, Rum. 128 F2
Herāt, Afghan., 62,000* 144 B2
Hérault, r., Fr. 117 E5
Herbault, Fr., 1,052 117 D3
Herbede, F.R.Ger., 11,488 119 C2
Herbern, F.R.Ger., 4,199 119 D1
Herbert, Sask., Can., 1,019 43 C5
Herbert, Mt., Austl. 172 D2
Herbert Hoover, L., Indon.-Terr. Papua 174 d2
Herbert I., Alaska 85 B5
Herberton, Austl., 1,101 173 F2
Herbertsville, N.J. 58 c16
Herbignac, Fr., 3,037 116 B3
Herbitzheim, Fr., 1,739 116 c8
Herb Lake, Man., Can. 43 E3
Herblay, Fr., 10,220 116 g11
Herblingen, Switz., 1,935 124 C1
Herbolzheim, F.R.Ger., 4,221 118 A4
Herborg, Den. 121 A4
Herborn, F.R.Ger., 9,668 118 B3
Herbornseelbach, F.R.Ger., 2,487 119 E3
Herbstein, F.R.Ger., 1,793 119 G3
Herbster, Wis. 66 B2
Herby Śląski, Pol. 127 h6
Hercegnovi, Yug. 125 D3
Hercegovina = Bosna i Hercegovina
Herchen, F.R.Ger., 4,891 119 C3
Herchmer, Man., Can. 43 G2
Herculaneum, It. = Ercolano
Herculaneum, Mo., 1,767 72 G6
Hercules, Alta., Can. 43 b7
Hercules, Calif., 310 83 e11
Herdecke, F.R.Ger., 15,995 119 C2
Herdman Seamount, Atl. Oc. 109 M10
Herdorf, F.R.Ger., 7,148 119 D3
Heredia, C.R., 19,249 94 E6
Hereford, U.K., 40,434 113 E5
Hereford, Md. 62 H3
Hereford, Oreg. 80 E3
Hereford, Tex., 7,652 76 M2
Herefordshire, co., U.K., 130,928 113 E5
Herefoss, Nor. 121 A2
Hereheretue, atoll, Tuam. Arch. 177 42
Herekino, N.Z. 175 g4
Hereleng, r., China-Mong. 150 E2
Herémence, Switz., 1,868 124 B2
Herend, Hung., 2,120 126 C3
Herendeen Bay, Alaska 85 D5
Herent, Belg., 8,658 115 C4
Herentals, Belg., 17,280 115 C3
Herenthout, Belg., 5,803 115 C3
Herfølge, Den., 3,663 121 E5
Herford, F.R.Ger., 53,889 118 B2
Héric, Fr., 2,624 117 C3
Héricourt, Fr., 7,175 117 G3
Héricy, Fr., 1,398 116 k12
Heringen, F.R.Ger., 4,743 118 C3
Heringen, Ger.D.R. 118 C3
Heringsdorf, Ger.D.R. 118 D2
Herington, Kans., 3,702 75 H5
Hérinnes, Belg., 1,490 116 a6
Heriot, N.Z. 175 f7
Heriot, U.K. 112 d8
Herisau, Switz., 14,361 124 D1
Hérisson, Fr., 1,170 117 E3
Herkimer, co., N.Y., 66,370 59 L5
Herkimer, N.Y., 9,396 59 L5
Herlev, Den., 21,358 121 a7
Herlikofen, F.R.Ger., 2,894 119 H7
Herlong, Calif. 82 C2
Hermagor, Aust., 2,778 124 K7
Herman, Mich. 66 E2
Herman, Minn., 764 74 D3
Herman, Nebr., 335 75 J2
Herman, Pa. 60 C4
Hermanas, Mex. 92 E2
Hermanas, N. Mex. 79 B6
Herma Ness, U.K. 112 F1
Hermann, Mo., 2,536 72 F6
Hermannsburg, Austl. 172 D3
Hermannsburg, F.R.Ger., 4,758 118 C2
Hermansville, Mich. 66 F3
Hermanus, S. Af., 4,586 164 a9
Heřmanův Městec, Czech. 127 e7
Hermanville, Miss. 73 E6
Hermersberg, F.R.Ger., 1,671 119 D6
Hermeskeil, F.R.Ger., 4,076 119 B5
Hermidale, Austl. 173 G4
Hermies, Fr., 1,360 116 a7
Herminadorp, Sur. 101 N5
Herminie, Pa., 1,571 60 C5
Hermiston, Oreg., 4,402 80 D3
Hermitage, Ark., 379 73 C4
Hermitage, Mo., 328 72 D7
Hermit Is., Terr. New Guin. 174 e1
Hermleigh, Tex. 77 N3
Hermon, S. Af. 164 a8
Hermon, Me. 55 D4
Hermon, N.Y., 612 59 K3
Hermon, Mt. = Shaykh, Jabal ash
Hermosa, Phil., 4,465 153 b8
Hermosa, S. Dak., 126 74 A4
Hermosa, Cāno de la, r., Col. 100 E5
Hermosa Beach, Calif., 16,115 83 g16
Hermosillo, Baja Calif., Mex., 1,144 92 B1
Hermosillo, Son., Mex., 96,122 92 C2
Hernandarias, Arg., 4,900* 105 b10
Hernandarias, Para., 1,129 105 D3
Hernández, Arg., 2,228 105 a11
Hernández, Mex., 2,088 92 E3
Hernandez, N. Mex. 79 B3
Hernando, Arg., 3,000* 105 C4
Hernando, co., Fla., 11,205 65 G4
Hernando, Miss., 1,898 73 F3
Hernani, Sp., 13,080 122 o11
Herndon, Kans., 339 75 E4
Herndon, Ky. 71 D5
Herndon, Pa., 622 60 J4
Herndon, Va., 1,960 62 G4
Herndon, W. Va. 62 C5
Herne, Belg., 3,429 115 C4
Herne, F.R.Ger., 115,365 118 A3
Herne Bay, U.K., 21,291 113 G6
Herning, Den., 24,790 121 A4
Herny, Fr. 116 c8
Herod, Ill. 68 D6
Heron, Mont. 81 B1
Heron Bay, Ont., Can. 44 F5
Heron Lake, Minn., 852 74 E4
Heröya, Nor. 121 B1
Herre, Nor. 121 B1
Herreid, S. Dak., 767 74 B3
Herrenalb, F.R.Ger., 2,396 119 E7
Herrenberg, F.R.Ger., 7,448 118 B4
Herrera, Urug. 105 c11
Herrera del Duque, Sp., 6,254 122 C3
Herrero, P., Mex. 93 J4
Herrick, Ill., 440 68 C4
Herrick, S. Dak., 160 74 C4
Herrick Mtn., Vt. 54 A4
Herriman, Utah 78 b10
Herrin, Ill., 9,474 68 C6
Herring, Okla. 76 D2
Herring Cove, N.S., Can., 1,368 47 U11
Herringen, F.R.Ger., 15,272 119 D1
Herrings, N.Y., 171 59 J3
Herriot, Man., Can. 43 E3
Herrlisheim, Fr., 2,461 119 D7
Herrljunga, Swed. 120 C4
Herron, Mich. 67 K3
Herrsching, F.R.Ger., 3,844 118 C5
Hersbruck, F.R.Ger., 8,349 118 C4
Herschbach, F.R.Ger., 1,648 119 D3
Herschel, Sask., Can. 43 B4
Herschel, Yukon, Can. 40 B4
Herschel I., Yukon, Can. 85 K1
Herscher, Ill., 658 68 D2
Herschweiler-Pettersheim, F.R.Ger., 1,314 119 C6
Herseaux, Belg., 7,194 115 B4
Herselt, Belg., 6,752 115 C3
Hersey, Mich., 246 67 H5
Hersheid, F.R.Ger., 4,567 119 D2
Hershey, Nebr., 504 75 E2
Hershey, Pa., 6,851 60 J5
Hershey Central, Cuba, 1,428 96 b1
Hersilia, Arg., 3,050* 105 C4
Hersman, Ill. 68 B4
Herstal, Belg., 29,658 115 D4
Herstedøster, Den. 121 a7
Herstedvester, Den., 2,957 121 a7

236 · Hertel—Holland

Hertel, Wis. 66 A3
Herten, F.R.Ger., 48,854 119 C1
Hertford, U.K., 15,737 113 G6
Hertford, co., N.C., 22,718 63 G1
Hertford, N.C., 2,068 63 H1
Hertfordshire, co., U.K., 832,901 113 F6
Hervás, Sp., 4,352 122 C2
Herveo, Col. 101 d14
Hervey Bay, Austl. 173 H3
Herxheim, F.R.Ger., 6,174 118 B4
Herzberg, F.R.Ger., 10,696 118 C3
Herzberg, Ger.D.R. 118 D3
Herzfeld, F.R.Ger., 2,433 119 E1
Herzliya, Isr., 26,934 142 a7
Herznach, Switz. 124 C1
Herzogenaurach, F.R.Ger., 8,323 118 C4
Herzogenbuchsee, Switz., 4,641 124 B1
Herzogenburg, Aust., 5,156 124 M5
Hesdin, Fr., 3,598 117 D1
Hesler, Ky. 71 G3
Hespeler, Ont., Can., 4,504 46 D5
Hesperange, Lux. 115 E5
Hesperia, Calif. 83 k15
Hesperia, Mich., 822 67 H5
Hesperus, Colo. 79 A3
Hess, Okla. 76 D3
Hessel, Mich. 67 J2
Hesselager, Den., 1,716 121 C5
Hesselø, i., Den. 121 D4
Hessen, st., F.R.Ger., 5,087,000* 118 B3
Hessisch Lichtenau, F.R.Ger., 5,751 118 B3
Hessle (part of Haltemprice), U.K., 13,891 114 G3
Hessmer, La., 433 73 C6
Hesston, Ind. 69 h9
Hesston, Kans., 1,103 75 H5
Hester, Okla., 22 76 D3
Hetherton, Mich. 67 J3
Hetland, S. Dak., 107 74 D3
Hettange-Grande, Fr., 5,082 116 b8
Hettick, Ill., 253 68 B4
Hettingen, F.R.Ger., 1,836 119 G5
Hettinger, co., N. Dak., 6,317 74 A2
Hettinger, N. Dak., 1,769 74 A2
Hettstedt, Ger.D.R., 16,977 118 C3
Hetzerath, F.R.Ger., 1,323 119 B5
Heugh, U.K. 112 g9
Heukelum, Neth. 115 c7
Heule, Belg., 8,964 116 a6
Heure, Eau d', r., Belg. 115 C4
Heusden, Belg., 5,527 115 D3
Heusden, Neth. 115 c7
Heuvelton, N.Y., 810 59 K2
Heverlee, Belg., 15,353 115 C4
Heves, Hung., 11,578 126 E3
Hévíz, Hung., 3,076 126 C3
Hewett, W. Va. 62 C5
Hewitt, Wis. 66 C4
Hewlett, Va. 62 G5
Hexham, U.K., 9,897 113 E4
Hext, Tex. 77 O4
Heyburn, Idaho, 829 81 C4
Heyburn Res., Okla. 76 G2
Heyrieux, Fr., 1,529 116 q15
Heysham (incl. Morecambe), U.K., 40,950 114 B2
Heywood, Austl. 172 F6
Heywood, U.K., 24,053 114 D3
Heyworth, Ill., 1,196 68 D3
H-4 Res., Tex. 76 c7
Hialeah, Fla., 66,972 65 J7
Hialeah Gardens, Fla., 172 65 a10
Hiawassee, Ga., 455 64 F1
Hiawatha, Iowa, 1,336 72 F2
Hiawatha, Kans., 3,391 75 K4
Hiawatha, Mich. 67 G2
Hiawatha, Utah, 439 78 C2
Hibaiyo, Phil., 17,287 153 B3
Hibaldstow, U.K., 1,142 114 G3
Hibbard, Ind. 70 C1
Hibbing, Minn., 17,731 74 F2
Hibbs, Pt., Austl. 173 e14
Hibernia, N.J. 61 C2
Hibernia Reef, Austl. 172 C1
Hichi, Jap. 154 e15
Hickiwan, Ariz. 78 B5
Hickman, co., Ky., 6,747 71 B5
Hickman, Ky., 1,537 71 B5
Hickman, Nebr., 288 75 J3
Hickman, co., Tenn., 11,862 71 D6
Hickman's Harbour, Newf., Can. 45 b9
Hickok, Kans. 75 D6
Hickory, Ky., 170 71 C5
Hickory, Miss., 539 73 G5
Hickory, co., Mo., 4,516 72 D7
Hickory, N.C., 19,328 63 C2
Hickory, Okla., 112 76 G3
Hickory Corners, Mich. 67 H6
Hickory Cr., Ill. 69 c10
Hickory Flat, Miss., 344 73 F3
Hickory Grove, S.C., 287 63 C3
Hickory Hills, Ill., 6,946 69 c10
Hickory Plains, Ark. 73 D3
Hickory Ridge, Ark., 364 73 E2
Hickory Valley, Tenn., 179 71 B6
Hickox, Ga., 71 64 H4
Hicks Bay, N.Z. 175 h5
Hicks Cays, Br. Hond. 94 D2
Hickson, Ont., Can. 46 D5
Hickson L., Sask., Can. 43 D3
Hicksville (part of Dartmouth), Mass. 57 M6
Hicksville, N.Y., 50,405 59 O10
Hicksville, Ohio, 3,116 70 E1
Hico, Tex., 1,020 77 O4
Hida, Rum. 128 D1
Hida, r., Jap. 154 i14
Hidaka, Jap., 4,352 155 K8
Hidaka-sammyaku, mts., Jap. 155 K8
Hidalgo, st., Mex., 994,598 93 F4
Hidalgo, N.L., Mex., 3,438 93 E3
Hidalgo, Tam., Mex., 3,394 93 F3
Hidalgo, Ill., 126 68 D4
Hidalgo, co., N. Mex., 4,961 79 A6
Hidalgo, co., Tex., 180,904 77 O6
Hidalgo, Tex., 1,078 77 O6
Hidalgo, Presa, res., Mex. 92 C2
Hidalgo del Parral, Mex., 41,461 92 D2
Hidalgotitlán, Mex., 1,467 93 G5
Hiddenite, N.C. 63 C2
Hidden Timber, S. Dak. 74 B4
Hienghène, N. Caled., 1,940 174 i8
Hiep Duc, S. Viet. 146 D4
Hierro, i., Can. Is. 109 4
Hieu Liem, S. Viet. 147 m11
Hieu Thien, S. Viet., 10,158 146 D5
Higashi-Futami, Jap. 154 f15
Higashi-Sakabe, Jap. 154 h14
Higbee, Mo., 646 72 E5
Higden, Ark., 40 73 C2
Higganum (part of Haddam), Conn. 56 F7
Higgins, Okla. 76 H3
Higgins, Tex., 711 76 O1
Higgins Lake, Mich. 67 J4
Higgins L., Mich. 67 J4
Higginson, Ark., 183 73 D2
Higginsport, Ohio, 412 70 F4
Higginsville, Mo., 4,003 72 D5
Higham, U.K., 4,333 114 F4
High Atlas = Haut Atlas
High Bluff, Man., Can. 43 f9
Highbridge (part of Burnham-on-Sea), U.K., 3,845 114 C8
High Bridge, N.H. 54 D6
High Bridge, N.J., 2,148 61 B2
High Bridge, Wis. 66 C2
High Buston, U.K. 112 g9
Highcliffe (part of Christchurch), U.K., 5,190 113 i13
High Ercall, U.K., 1,482 114 C5
High Falls, N.Y. 59 M8
Highfalls, N.C. 63 E2
High Falls Res., Wis. 66 E3
Highgate, Ont., Can. 46 C6
Highgate, Jam., 3,626 96 q8
Highgate Center, Vt. 54 A2
Highgate Springs, Vt. 54 A2
High Hill, Mo., 173 72 F6
High Hill, r., Man., Can. 43 G3
High Island, Tex. 77 Q5
High I., Mich. 67 H3
High Lake, Ill. 69 b9
Highland, Calif. 83 k15
Highland, Fla. 65 G2
Highland, Ill., 4,943 68 C5
Highland, Ind., 16,284 70 B1
Highland, Kans., 755 75 K4
Highland, Md. 62 b8
Highland, Mich. 67 K6
Highland, Minn. 74 G2
Highland, N.Y., 2,931 59 M8
Highland, co., Ohio, 29,716 70 F3
Highland, Pa., 2,000* 60 b7
Highland, co., Va., 3,221 62 E4
Highland, Wis., 741 66 C5
Highland Beach, Fla., 65 65 b9
Highland Beach, Md., 5 62 c9
Highland Creek, Ont., Can., 2,400 46 d13
Highland Falls, N.Y., 4,469 59 M9
Highland Grove, Ont., Can. 46 F3
Highland Heights, Ohio, 2,929 70 f8
Highland Hills, Ill. 69 b9
Highland Home, Ala. 64 C4
Highland Lake, Colo. 79 c7
Highland L., Conn. 56 D5
Highland L., Me. 54 F3
Highland L., N.H. 54 C5
Highland Mills, N.Y. 59 M9
Highland Park, Ill., 25,532 68 E1
Highland Park, Mich., 38,063 67 f15
Highland Park, N.J., 11,049 58 b15
Highland Park, Pa., 1,534 60 G4
Highland Park, Tex., 10,411 76 f9
Highlands, co., Fla., 21,338 65 H5
Highlands, N.J., 3,536 61 D3
Highlands, N.C., 592 63 A2
Highlands, Tex., 4,336 77 i9
Highlands, Scot., U.K. 110 C3
Highlands, The, Barbuda 97 8
Highland Springs, Va. 62 G5
Highland Valley, Br. Col., Can. 42 G4
Highland View, Fla. 65 D3
Highlandville, Mo., 84 72 D8
Highley, U.K., 2,145 114 D6
High Lonesome, N. Mex. 79 C5
Highmore, S. Dak., 1,078 74 C3
High North, pk., Gren. Is. 97 20
High Peak, Jam. 96 q8
Highpine, Me. 55 B5
High Point, N.C., 62,063 63 E2
High Pt., Berm. Is. 108 1
High Point, mtn., N.J. 61 B1
High Prairie, Alta., Can., 1,718 42 H2
Highridge, Alta., Can. 43 a6
High Ridge (part of Stamford), Conn. 56 B8
High Rock, Man., Can. 43 E3
High Rock, mtn., Wash. 80 C2
High Rock L., Man., Can. 43 E3
Highrock L., Sask., Can. 43 C2
High Rock L., N.C. 63 D2
High Rocks, Bah. Is. 95 a6
High Shoals, N.C. 63 C2
Highspire, Pa., 2,999 60 J5
High Springs, Fla., 2,329 65 G3
High Street, mtn., U.K. 114 C2
Hightstown, N.J., 4,317 61 B3
High Willhays, mtn., U.K. 113 E6
Highwood, Ill., 4,499 68 E1
Highworth, U.K., 3,451 114 E7
High Wycombe, U.K., 49,981 113 F6
Higuera de Zaragoza, Mex., 3,260 92 C2
Higuerillas, Mex. 93 e9
Higüero, P., P.R. 96 r10
Higüerote, Ven., 2,880 100 G2
Higüey, Dom. Rep., 10,084 96 n6
Hii, Jap. 154 g16
Hiiumaa, i., U.S.S.R. 134 B4
Híjar, Sp., 3,093 122 E2
Ḩijārah, Şaḩrā'al, Iraq 143 C2
Ḩijāz, Jabal al, Saudi Ar., 140 C5
Hiji, Jap., 22,688 154 B5
Hijuelas, Chile 104 f12
Hikari, Jap., 37,615 154 B5
Hikawa, Jap. 155 m19
Hiketa, Jap., 12,829 155 D4
Hikida, Jap. 154 h14
Hikkaduwa, Cey. 145 m22
Hiko, Nev. 83 C4
Hikone, Jap., 60,864 155 E4
Hikueru, atoll, Tuam. Arch. 177 42
Hikurangi, N.Z. 175 g4
Hikurangi, pk., N.Z. 175 h5
Hikutivake, Niue 177 32
Hilbert, Wis., 736 66 E4
Hilchenbach, F.R.Ger., 4,145 119 E2
Hilda, Alta., Can. 42 L4
Hilda, S.C., 259 63 C4
Hildburghausen, Ger.D.R. 118 C3
Hildebran, N.C., 518 63 C2
Hilden, N.S., Can. 47 U11
Hilden, F.R.Ger., 33,274 119 B2
Hildenborough, U.K., 5,012 114 J8
Hilderthorpe, U.K., 3,745 114 H2
Hildesheim, F.R.Ger., 84,695 118 C2
Hildreth, Nebr., 305 75 F3
Hilea, Hawaii 84 F4
Hiles, Wis. 66 D3
Hilgard Pk., Mont. 81 D3
Hilgay, U.K., 1,343 114 J5
Hilger, Mont. 81 E2
Hili, India, 6,032 144 g13
Hill, Ill. 68 D5
Hill, co., Mont., 18,653 81 D1
Hill, N.H. 54 D4
Hill, co., Tex., 23,650 77 P3
Hill, Va. 62 B6
Hillaby, Mt., Barb. 97 10
Hill Bank, Br. Hond. 94 C2
Hill City, Idaho 81 B4
Hill City, Kans., 2,421 75 F4
Hill City, Minn., 429 74 F2
Hill City, S. Dak., 419 74 A4
Hill Cove, Falk. Is. 108 3
Hill Cr., Utah 78 D2
Hillcrest, Ind. 69 f10
Hillcrest Heights, Md., 15,295 62 a9
Hillegersberg, Neth. 115 a7
Hillegom, Neth., 10,500 115 C2
Hillerød, Den., 11,605 121 E5
Hillers, Mt., Utah 78 C3
Hillesheim, F.R.Ger., 1,493 118 A3
Hillham, Ind. 70 C4
Hilliard, Alta., Can. 43 c7
Hilliard, Fla., 1,075 65 G2
Hilliard, Ohio, 5,633 70 a6
Hilliers, Br. Col., Can. 42 b6
Hillister, Tex. 77 Q4
Hillman, Mich., 445 67 J3
Hillman, Minn., 80 74 F2
Hill of Stake, U.K. 112 a8
Hillpoint, Wis. 66 C5
Hillrose, Colo., 157 79 D1
Hills, Iowa, 310 72 F3
Hills, Minn., 516 74 D4
Hills, Pa., 1,048 60 b8
Hillsboro, Ala., 218 64 B1
Hillsboro, Ill., 4,232 68 C4
Hillsboro, Ind., 517 70 B2
Hillsboro, Iowa, 218 72 F4
Hillsboro, Kans., 2,441 75 H5
Hillsboro, Mo., 457 72 G6
Hillsboro, co., N.H., 178,161 54 D6
Hillsboro, N.H., 1,645 54 D5
Hillsboro, N. Mex. 79 B5
Hillsboro, N.C., 1,349 63 E1
Hillsboro, N. Dak., 1,278 74 D2
Hillsboro, Ohio, 5,474 70 F3
Hillsboro, Oreg., 8,232 80 B3
Hillsboro, Tex., 7,402 77 P3
Hillsboro, W. Va., 210 62 D4
Hillsboro, Wis., 1,366 66 C5
Hillsboro Beach, Fla., 437 65 b9
Hillsboro Can., Fla. 65 J6
Hillsboro Lower Village, N.H. 54 D5
Hillsborough, N.B., Can. 47 T11
Hillsborough, Gren. Is. 97 20
Hillsborough, Calif., 7,554 83 e12
Hillsborough, co., Fla., 397,788 65 G5
Hillsborough, N.C., 1,349 63 E1
Hillsborough, r., Fla. 65 G4
Hillsboro Upper Village, N.H. 54 C5
Hillsburgh, Ont., Can. 46 b13
Hills Cr. Res., Oreg. 80 B4
Hillsdale, Ont., Can. 46 E4
Hillsdale, Ill., 490 68 B2
Hillsdale, Ind. 70 B3
Hillsdale, Kans. 75 L5
Hillsdale, co., Mich., 34,742 67 J7
Hillsdale, Mich., 7,629 67 J7
Hillsdale, N.J., 8,734 58 c13
Hillsdale, N.Y. 59 N7
Hillsdale, Okla., 60 76 F1
Hillsdale, Wis. 66 B3
Hillsdale, Wyo. 81 G5
Hillsgrove (part of Warwick), R.I. 57 L6
Hillside, Ariz. 78 B4
Hillside, Colo. 79 C2
Hillside, Ill., 7,794 69 c9
Hillside, N.J., 22,304 58 c14
Hillsport, Ont., Can. 44 F5
Hillston, Austl., 1,019 173 F5
Hillsview, S. Dak., 44 74 C3
Hillsville (part of Spencer), Mass. 56 H3
Hillsville, Pa. 60 A4
Hillsville, Va., 905 62 D6
Hillswick, U.K. 112 F1
Hilltonia, Ga., 353 64 H3
Hilltop, Ky. 71 H3
Hilltop, Minn., 607 74 b5
Hillview, Newf., Can. 45 b9
Hillview, Ill., 305 68 B4
Hilo, Hawaii, 25,966 84 F4
Hilo Bay, Hawaii 84 F4
Hilongos, Phil., 3,169 153 C3
Hilpoltstein, F.R.Ger., 3,554 118 C4
Hilshire Village, Tex., 543 77 i9
Hilton, U.K. 114 E5
Hilton, Ga. 64 E4
Hilton, N.Y., 1,334 58 E5
Hilton Beach, Ont., Can. 46 A2
Hilton Head I., S.C. 63 D5
Hiltrup, F.R.Ger., 8,343 118 A3
Hilts, Calif. 82 B2
Hilvarenbeek, Neth., 3,600 115 D3
Hilversum, Neth., 98,600 115 D2
Himachal Pradesh, un. terr., India, 1,351,144 145 E3
Himalayas, ra., Asia 140 G3
Himāl Chūli, pk., Nepal 144 e11
Himamaylan, Phil., 5,195 153 d11
Himarë, Alb. 125 D4
Himberg, Aust., 3,210 124 N5
Himeji, Jap., 328,689 155 D4
Hime-shima, Jap. 154 B5
Himi, Jap., 65,962 155 E3
Himlerville, Ky. 71 J4
Himrod, N.Y. 58 F6
Ḩimş, Syr., 152,077 142 D3
Hinagu, Jap. 154 B5
Hinase, Jap., 12,610 155 D4
Hinashisu, Saipan 176 27
Hinata, Jap. 155 m19
Hinatuan, Phil., 3,233 153 C3
Hinche, Haiti, 5,847 96 m6
Hinchinbrook I., Alaska 85 H3
Hinckley, U.K., 41,608 113 F5
Hinckley, Ill., 940 68 D2
Hinckley, Me. 55 C4
Hinckley, Minn., 851 74 F2
Hinckley, N.Y. 59 K5
Hinckley, Ohio 70 d9
Hinckley, Utah, 397 78 B2
Hindaun, India, 20,237 144 a12
Hindelang, F.R.Ger., 4,617 118 C5
Hindeloopen, Neth. 115 D2
Hindes, Tex. 77 O5
Hindley, U.K., 19,395 114 C3
Hindman, Ky., 793 71 J4
Hinds, co., Miss., 187,045 73 E5
Hindsboro, Ill., 376 68 D4
Hindubāgh, Pak., 2,217 144 C3
Hindu Kush, ra., Afghan.-Pak. 145 C2
Hindupur, India, 32,445 145 E7
Hines, Fla. 65 F3
Hines, Oreg., 1,207 80 D4
Hines, Wis. 66 B2
Hinesburg, Vt. 54 A3
Hines Creek, Alta., Can. 42 H2
Hineston, La. 73 C6
Hinesville, Ga., 3,174 64 H4
Hingan = An-k'ang
Hinganghat, India, 36,890 145 F5
Hingham, Mass., 15,378(T) 57 N4
Hingham, Mont., 254 81 D1
Hingham, Wis. 66 F5
Hingham Bay, Mass. 57 N3
Hingham Center (part of Hingham), Mass. 57 N4
Hingoli, India, 23,407 145 E6
Hinigaran, Phil., 10,231 153 B3
Hınıs, Turk., 4,016 142 E2
Hinnerup, Den. 121 C4
Hinnöya, i., Nor. 120 C1
Hino, Jap., 24,652 154 h14
Hinoba-an, Phil., 2,919 153 d12
Hinoemata, Jap. 155 F3
Hinojo, Arg., 4,000* 105 a13
Hinojosa del Duque, Sp., 14,767 122 C3
Hinokage, Jap., 14,480 154 B5
Hino-misaki, Jap. 154 f16
Hinomi-saki, Jap. 155 C4
Hinoura, Jap. 154 e16
Hinsdale, co., Colo., 208 79 B3
Hinsdale, Ill., 12,859 69 c9
Hinsdale, Mass., 1,414(T) 56 D3
Hinsdale, N.H., 1,235 54 C6
Hinsdale, Mont. 81 F1
Hinsdale, N.Y. 58 D7
Hinson, Fla. 65 E2
Hinstock, U.K. 114 C5
Hinterstoder, Aust., 1,023 124 L6
Hinton, Alta., Can., 3,416 42 H3
Hinton, Iowa, 403 72 A2
Hinton, Okla., 907 76 E2
Hinton, W. Va., 5,197 62 D5
Hintonville, Miss. 73 F6
Hippolytushoef, Neth., 3,100 115 D2
Hiradani, Jap. 154 f16
Hirado, Jap., 43,302 154 A5
Hirado-shima, Jap. 154 A5
Hiraizumi, Jap., 11,124 155 G2
Hirakata, Jap., 80,312 154 g15
Hirakata, Jap., 3,534 155 G3
Hirakata, Jap. 155 m19
Hirakud Dam, India 144 e15
Hiram, Me. 55 B5
Hiram, Mo. 72 G7
Hiram, Ohio, 1,011 70 H1
Hirama, Jap. 154 f15
Hirano, Jap. 154 h14
Hirara, Ryukyu Is., 33,250 154 c13
Hirata, Jap. 154 g14
Hirata, Jap., 34,799 155 C4
Hiratsuka, Jap., 108,279 155 F4
Hirfanli Barajı, Turk. 142 C2
Hirgis Nuur, Mong. 150 C1
Hîrlău, Rum. 128 F1
Hirm, Aust. 124 c11
Hirohata, Jap. 154 f15
Hiroishi, Jap. 154 e15
Hiromi, Jap. 154 i14
Hirono, Jap. 154 g14
Hirono, Jap. 154 h14
Hirono, Jap., 6,532 155 G3
Hiroo, Jap., 11,469 155 K8
Hirooka, Jap. 155 n20
Hirosaki, Jap., 152,132 155 G1
Hirose, Jap., 10,337 154 B5
Hirose, Jap. 154 g15
Hiroshima, Jap., 431,336 155 C4
Hirota, Jap. 154 f15
Hirsau, F.R.Ger., 1,610 119 F7
Hirschaid, F.R.Ger., 3,008 118 C4
Hirschau, F.R.Ger., 4,441 118 D4
Hirschberg, F.R.Ger., 1,502 119 E2
Hirschberg, Ger.D.R. 118 C3
Hirschhorn, F.R.Ger., 3,048 119 F6
Hirson, Fr., 12,104 117 F2
Hîrşova, Rum., 4,761 128 G2
Hirtenberg, Aust., 2,130 124 c11
Hirtshals, Den. 121 B3
Hiruma, Jap. 154 e15
Hirzenhain, F.R.Ger., 1,272 119 G4
Hisai, Jap., 28,848 155 E4
Hisanohama, Jap., 6,197 155 G3
Hisasaka, Jap. 154 g14
Hiseville, Ky. 71 F4
Hisle, S. Dak. 74 B4
Hispaniola, i., W.I. 95 E3
His-po, r., China 151 C2
Hissar, India, 60,222 145 E3
Histon, U.K., 3,258 114 J6
Hīt, Iraq, 6,808 143 C2
Hita, Jap., 68,437 154 B5
Hitachi, Jap., 161,226 155 G3
Hitachi-Ōta, Jap., 38,541 155 G3
Hitakatsu, Jap. 154 A4
Hitchcock, co., Nebr., 4,829 75 D3
Hitchcock, Okla., 134 76 E2
Hitchcock, S. Dak., 193 74 C3
Hitchcock, Tex., 5,216 77 i10
Hitchin, U.K., 24,254 114 H7
Hitchins, Ky. 71 J3
Hitdorf, F.R.Ger., 3,833 119 B2
Hitiaa, Tahiti 177 44
Hitoyoshi, Jap., 47,259 154 B5
Hitra, Nor. 120 B3
Hitra, i., Nor. 120 B3
Hitterdal, Minn., 235 74 D2
Hittfeld, F.R.Ger., 2,202 119 a9
Hitzacker, F.R.Ger., 3,507 118 C2
Hiva Oa, i., Marq., Is. 171 J5
Hiw, i., New Hebr. 174 k4
Hiwannee, Miss. 73 G6
Hiwasa, Jap., 5,927 155 D5
Hiwassee, Va. 62 D6
Hiwassee, L., N.C. 63 a7
Hiwassee, r., U.S. 71 G6
Hixton, Wis., 310 66 B4
Hiyane, Jap. 155 E4
Hjälmaren, l., Swed. 120 D4
Hjärnarp, Swed. 121 E4
Hjelm, i., Den. 121 C4
Hjerm, Den., 1,482 121 A4
Hjerting, Den. 121 A5
Hjo, Swed. 120 C4
Hjordkær, Den. 121 B5
Hjørring, Den., 15,038 121 C3
Hjort Basin, Pac. Oc. 169 F4
Hka, r., Burma 146 B2
Hkakabo Razi, pk., Burma 146 B1
Hlaingbwe, Burma 147 b2
Hlegu, Burma, 6,778 147 b2
Hlinsko, Czech. 126 C2
Hlohovec, Czech., 12,263 126 C2
Hlučín, Czech. 127 h7
Hluhluwe, S. Af. 164 E6
Hmawbi, Burma, 5,370 147 a2
Hnausa, Man., Can. 43 F5
Hninpale, Burma, 2,327 147 b2
Hnong Krod, Thai. 147 d4
Ho, Ghana, 14,497 162 E4
Hoa Binh, N. Viet. 146 D2
Hoa Da, S. Viet., 5,335 146 E5
Hoa Dong, S. Viet., 6,477 147 m11
Hoag Corners, N.Y. 59 w29
Hoagland, Ind. 70 E2
Hoaglin, Calif. 82 B2
Hoa Hiep, S. Viet. 147 m11
Hoai Duc, S. Viet., 1,454 147 m11
Hoai Nhon, S. Viet., 11,096 146 E4
Hoback Pk., Wyo. 81 D4
Hobart, Austl., 54,887 173 G6
Hobart, Ind., 18,680 70 B1
Hobart, N.Y., 585 59 L7
Hobart, Okla., 5,132 76 D2
Hobbema, Alta., Can. 43 b8
Hobbs, N. Mex., 26,275 79 D5
Hobbs, Tex. 77 N3
Hobbsville, N.C. 63 H1
Hobdo, r., Mong. 150 C1
Hobe Sound, Fla. 65 J5
Hobgood, N.C., 630 63 G1
Hobo, Col. 100 C6
Hoboken, Belg., 30,305 115 d8
Hoboken, Ga., 552 64 G4
Hoboken, N.J., 48,441 61 C2
Hobro, Den., 8,208 121 B4
Hobscheid, Lux. 115 D5
Hōbsögöl Dalay, Mong. 150 D1
Hobson, Mont., 207 81 D2
Hobucken, N.C. 63 H2
Ho-chang, China 152 B2
Hochatown, Okla. 76 J3
Hochburg, Aust., 2,316 124 J5
Hochdahl, F.R.Ger., 5,008 119 B2
Hochdorf, Switz., 4,452 124 C1
Ho-ch'eng, China 150 A2
Hochfeiler, mtn. Aust.-It. 124 H7
Hochfeld, Man., Can. 43 g10
Hochfelden, Fr., 2,755 116 e9
Hochgolling, mtn. Aust. 124 K6
Hochheim, Tex. 77 P5
Hochheim am Main, F.R.Ger., 6,555 119 E4
Ho-chiang, China 152 B1
Ho-chien, China 151 C3
Ho-ch'ih, China 152 B2
Ho-ching, Hs-ch., China 150 B2
Ho-ching, Shan-hsi, China 151 A4
Ho-ch'iu, China 152 D1
Hochkirch, Ger.D.R. 126 d5
Hochneukirch, F.R.Ger., 6,201 119 A2
Höch'ŏn, N. Kor. 151 F2
Hochschwab, pk., Aust. 125 ·
Hochspeyer, F.R.Ger., 3,838 119 D6
Höchst, F.R.Ger. 119 F5
Höchstadt, F.R.Ger., 4,024 118 C4
Hochstrass, Aust. 124 b10
Hochstuhl, mtn. Aust.-Yug. 124 L7
Ho-ch'uan, China 151 A3
Ho-ch'uan, China 152 B1
Hockanum, r., Conn. 56 F5
Hockenheim, F.R.Ger., 12,198 119 F6
Hockessin, Del. 60 e12
Hocking, co., Ohio, 20,168 70 G3
Hocking, r., Ohio 70 G3
Hockingport, Ohio 70 H3
Hockley, U.K., 7,790 113 G6
Hockley, co., Tex., 22,340 77 M3
Hoc Mon, S. Viet., 13,730 147 m11
Hoctún, Mex., 3,421 93 H4
Hodal, India, 10,558 144 a12
Hoddesdon, U.K., 17,908 114 H7
Hodeida = Al Ḩudaydah
Hodgdon, Me. 55 E2
Hodge, La., 878 73 C5
Hodgeman, co., Kans., 3,115 75 E6
Hodgenville, Ky., 1,985 71 F4
Hodges, Ala., 194 64 A1
Hodges, S.C., 209 63 B3
Hodgesville, W. Va. 62 D3
Hodgeville, Sask., Can. 43 C5
Hodgkins, Ill., 1,126 69 c9
Hodgson, Man., Can. 43 F4
Hodh, reg., Maur. 162 C3
Hódmezővásárhely, Hung., 53,505 126 E3
Hodna, Chott el, Alg. 160 E2
Hodnet, U.K., 1,578 114 C5
Hodonín, Czech., 17,964 126 C2
Hoeam-dong, N. Kor. 151 F2
Hoea Mill, Hawaii 84 F3
Hoëdic, Î., Fr. 116 B3
Hoef, Neth. 115 b6
Hoegaarden, Belg., 4,707 115 C4
Hoehne, Colo. 79 C3
Hoeilaart, Belg., 6,569 115 C4
Hoek van Holland, Neth., 5,000 115 B3
Hoengsŏng, S. Kor., 14,932 151 F3
Hoensbroek, Neth., 16,300 115 D4
Hoerdt, Fr., 3,560 116 e9
Hoeryŏng, N. Kor. 151 F2
Hoeselt, Belg., 4,743 115 D4
Hoevelaken, Neth. 115 D2
Hoeven, Neth. 115 b7
Hoéville, Fr. 116 b9
Hoeyang, N. Kor. 151 E3
Hof, Aust., 1,081 124 d11
Hof, F.R.Ger., 56,653 118 C3
Ho-fei, China, 500,000* 150 F4
Ho-fen, China 151 A3
Hoffland, Nebr. 75 C1
Hoffman, Ill., 235 68 C5
Hoffman, Minn., 605 74 E3
Hoffman, N.C., 344 63 E2
Hoffman, Okla., 248 76 H2
Hoffman Estates, Ill., 15,896 69 b8
Hoffman Mtn., N.Y. 59 N4
Hoffmans, N.Y. 59 M6
Hoffmeister, N.Y. 59 L5
Hofgeismar, F.R.Ger., 8,747 118 B3
Hofheim, Bay., F.R.Ger., 1,723 118 C3
Hofheim, Hess., F.R.Ger., 11,970 119 E4
Hofheim, Hess., F.R.Ger., 4,203 119 E5
Höfn, Ice. 120 b6
Hofors, Swed. 120 D3
Hofra, Libya 161 G3
Hofsjökull, ice cap, Ice. 120 a6
Hōfu, Jap., 94,513 154 B4
Höganäs, Swed. 121 E4
Hogansville, Ga., 3,658 64 D2
Hogarth, Mt., Austl. 172 E3
Hogback Mtn., N. Mex. 79 A3
Hogdal, Swed. 121 D1
Hoge Veluwe, nat. pk., Neth. 115 D2
Hoggar, mtn., Alg. 160 E4
Hog I., Mich. 67 H3
Hogup Mts., Utah 78 B1
Hoh, r., Wash. 80 A2
Hohe Acht, mt., F.R.Ger. 118 A3
Hohegrass, pk., F.R.Ger. 118 B3
Höhenberg, Aust. 124 b11
Hohenecken, F.R.Ger., 2,485 119 D6
Hohenems, Aust., 9,175 124 F6
Hohenfelde, F.R.Ger., 1,046 119 a8
Hohenlimburg, F.R.Ger., 25,607 118 A3
Hohenmölsen, Ger.D.R. 126 b5
Hohen Neuendorf, Ger.D.R., 10,927 119 e10
Hohenruppersdorf, Aust., 1,117 124 N5
Hohenstein-Ernstthal, Ger.D.R., 16,913 126 b6
Hohentauern, Aust. 124 L6
Hohenwald, Tenn., 2,194 71 D6
Hohenwarth, Aust. 124 b9
Hohenwestedt, F.R.Ger., 4,040 118 B1
Hoher Fläming, highlands, Ger.D.R. 118 D2
Hohe Tauern, mts. Aust. 124 J6
Hohe Warte, mtn. Aust.-It. 124 J7
Hohloh, pk., F.R.Ger. 119 E7
Hohoe, Ghana, 9,527 162 d8
Hohokus, N.J., 3,988 58 c13
Hohokus Bk., N.J. 58 c12
Hoholitna, r., Alaska 85 F3
Höhr-Grenzhausen, F.R.Ger., 7,946 119 D4
Ho-hsi, China 152 A2
Ho-hsien, A-h., China 152 E1
Ho-hsien, K-hsi, China 152 C2
Ho Hu, China 152 E1
Hohunawai Pt., Terr. Papua 174 3
Hoi An, S. Viet., 16,605 146 E4
Hoima, Uganda 164 E1
Hoisdorf, F.R.Ger., 2,279 119 b8
Hoisington, Kans., 4,248 75 G5
Hoi Xuan, N. Viet. 147 h9
Hojai, India, 12,857 145 J4
Højby, Den., 3,375 121 D5
Højen, Den. 121 B5
Højer, Den., 1,400 121 A6
Hōjō, Jap., 29,160 155 C5
Hōjō, Jap., 23,470 155 D4
Højslev, Den. 121 B4
Hoke, co., N.C., 16,356 63 E2
Hokendauqua, Pa., 1,420* 61 i18
Hokes Bluff, Ala., 1,619 64 D1
Hokianga Hbr., N.Z. 175 g4
Hokitika, N.Z., 3,007 175 f6
Hokkaidō, i., Jap. 155 H8
Hököpinge, Swed. 121 F5
Hokota, Jap., 29,720 155 G3
Ho-k'ou, China 150 E5
Hokunō, Jap., 2,891 155 E4
Hōkyōji, Jap. 154 h14
Holabird, S. Dak. 74 C3
Ho-lan Shan, China 150 E3
Holap, i., Truk 176 19
Holbæk, Den., 15,475 121 D5
Holbeach, U.K., 6,620 113 G5
Holberg, Br. Col., Can. 42 E4
Holboca, Rum. 128 F1
Holbrook, Austl., 1,210 173 G5
Holbrook, Ariz., 3,438 78 C4
Holbrook, Ill. 69 d10
Holbrook, Mass., 10,104(T) 57 N4
Holbrook, Nebr., 354 75 F3
Holbrook, N.Y., 3,441 58 g13
Holcomb, Ill. 68 C1
Holcomb, Kans. 75 E5
Holcomb, Mo., 436 72 G8
Holcomb, N.Y., 460 58 o21
Holcombe, U.K. 114 C8
Holcombe, Wis. 66 B3
Holcombe Flowage, Wis. 66 B3
Holden, Alta., Can. 42 K3
Holden, Mass., 1,704;10,117(T) 56 J3
Holden, Mo., 1,951 72 C6
Holden, Utah, 388 78 B2
Holden, Vt. 54 B4
Holden, Wash. 80 C1
Holden, W. Va., 1,900 62 B5
Holdenville, Okla., 5,712 76 G2
Holder, Fla. 65 G4
Holderness, N.H. 54 D4
Holdfast, Sask., Can. 43 C5
Holdich, Arg. 105 B7
Holdingford, Minn., 526 74 E3
Holdman, Oreg. 80 D3
Holdrege, Nebr., 5,226 75 F3
Hołdunów, Pol., 5,793 127 i6
Holeby, Den., 1,357 121 D6
Hole in the Mtn. Pk., Nev. 83 C2
Holetown, Barb. 97 10
Holgate, Ohio, 1,374 70 E1
Holguín, Cuba, 57,573 96 e2
Holič, Czech. 126 C2
Holikachuk, Alaska, 122 85 E3
Ho-lin-ko-erh, China 151 B2
Holitna, r., Alaska 85 E3
Ho-liu-chi, China 151 C4
Holla, pk., Eth. 163 L4
Hollabrunn, Aust., 5,827 124 N5
Holladay, Tenn. 71 C6
Holladay, Utah 78 c9
Hollain, Belg., 1,355 116 a6
Holland, Man., Can. 43 e10
Holland = Netherlands
Holland (admin. part of Lincolnshire), U.K., 103,327 113 F5
Holland, U.K. 113 G6
Holland, Ark. 73 C2
Holland, Ind., 661 70 B4
Holland, Iowa, 264 72 E2
Holland, Ky. 71 E5
Holland, Mass., 561(T) 56 H4

Holland—Hsien-ning · 237

Holland, Mich., 24,777 67 G6
Holland, Minn., 264 74 D3
Holland, Mo., 405 72 H8
Holland, N.Y. 58 C6
Holland, Ohio, 924 70 F1
Holland, Oreg. 80 B4
Holland, Tex., 653 77 P4
Holland, Va., 338 62 H6
Holland, Mt., Austl. 172 E5
Hollandale, Minn., 363 74 F4
Hollandale, Miss., 2,646 73 E4
Hollandale, Wis., 275 66 D6
Holland Bay, Jam. 96 q9
Holland Centre, Ont., Can. 46 C4
Hollandia = Sukarnapura
Holland Landing, Ont., Can. 46 E4
Holland Patent, N.Y., 538 59 K5
Holland Pd., Vt. 54 D2
Hollandsch Diep, estuary, Neth. 115 C3
Hollandsche IJssel, r., Neth. 115 b6
Hollebeke, Belg. 116 a6
Hollenstedt, F.R.Ger., 1,475 119 a9
Hollenstein, Aust., 2,159 124 L6
Hollerath, F.R.Ger., 1,593 119 A4
Holley, Fla. 65 C2
Holley, N.Y., 1,788 58 D5
Holley, Oreg. 80 B3
Holliday, Ill. 68 D4
Holliday, Mo., 181 72 E5
Holliday, Tex., 1,139 77 O3
Hollidaysburg, Pa., 6,475 60 F5
Hollis, Ark. 73 B3
Hollis, Kans. 75 H4
Hollis, N.H. 54 D6
Hollis, Okla., 3,006 76 D3
Hollis School, Ala. 64 D2
Hollister, Calif., 6,071 82 C4
Hollister, Idaho, 60 81 B4
Hollister, Mo., 600 72 D8
Hollister, N.C. 63 G1
Hollister, Okla., 156 76 E3
Hollister, Wis. 66 E3
Hollisterville, Pa. 61 M3
Holliston, Mass., 2,447;6,222(T) 57 L4
Hollman, C., Terr. New Guin. 174 f2
Hollonville, Ga. 64 g12
Hollow, Okla. 76 H1
Holloway, Mich. 67 K7
Holloway, Minn., 242 74 E3
Holloway, Ohio, 541 70 H2
Hollowville, N.Y. 59 N7
Hollum, Neth. 115 D1
Holly, Colo., 1,108 79 D2
Holly, Mich., 3,269 67 K6
Holly, Wash. 81 a7
Hollyford, r., N.Z. 175 f7
Holly Grove, Ark., 672 73 D3
Holly Hill, Fla., 4,182 65 J3
Holly Hill, S.C., 1,235 63 D4
Holly Oak, Del. 62 f10
Holly Pond, Ala., 193 64 C1
Holly Ridge, N.C., 731 63 G3
Holly Springs, Miss., 5,621 73 F3
Holly Springs, N.C., 588 63 F2
Hollywood, Ala., 246 64 D1
Hollywood, Calif. 83 h15
Hollywood, Fla., 35,237 65 J6
Hollywood, Md. 62 H4
Hollywood, Miss. 73 E3
Hollywood, Mo., 104 72 G8
Hollywood, W. Va. 62 D5
Hollywood Ridge Farms, Fla., 108 65 a10
Holman, N. Mex. 79 C3
Holman Island, N.W.T., Can. 40 F3
Holmansville, N.J. 58 b16
Hólmavík, Ice. 120 a6
Holmdel, N.J. 61 C3
Holme, Hunts., Eng., U.K. 114 H6
Holme, Westmd., Eng., U.K. 114 C2
Holmen, Wis., 635 66 B5
Holmes, co., Fla., 10,844 65 D2
Holmes, co., Miss., 27,096 73 E4
Holmes, co., Ohio, 21,591 70 G2
Holmes Beach, Fla., 1,143 65 G5
Holmes Cr., Fla. 65 D2
Holmeson, N.J. 58 b16
Holmesville, N.Y. 59 K6
Holmesville, Ohio, 422 70 H2
Holme upon Spalding Moor, U.K., 1,711 114 G3
Holmfirth, U.K., 18,391 114 E3
Holmsund, Swed. 120 E3
Holmwood, La. 73 B7
Hölö, Swed. 120 e8
Ho-lo, r., China 151 D1
Holohit, P., Mex. 93 H4
Holon, Isr., 48,970 142 a8
Holopaw, Fla. 65 H4
Holroyd, r., Austl. 173 F2
Holstebro, Den., 18,563 121 A4
Holsted, Den., 2,604 121 A5
Holsted Station, Den. 121 A5
Holstein, Ont., Can. 46 D4
Holstein, Iowa, 1,413 72 B2
Holstein, Mo. 72 F6
Holstein, Nebr., 205 75 G3
Holston, r., Tenn. 71 H5
Holston, Mid. Fk., r., Tenn.-Va. 62 B6
Holston, North Fk., r., Va. 62 B6
Holt, Nor. 121 A2
Holt, Dorset., Eng., U.K., 1,066 113 i13
Holt, Norfolk, Eng., U.K., 2,061 113 G5
Holt, Denb., Wales, U.K., 1,038 114 C4
Holt, Fla. 65 C2
Holt, Mich., 4,818 67 J6
Holt, Minn., 114 74 D1
Holt, co., Mo., 7,885 72 B4
Holt, Mo., 281 72 C5
Holt, co., Nebr., 13,722 75 G1
Holte, Den. 121 a7
Holten, Neth. 115 E2
Holtland, Tenn. 71 E6
Holton, Kans., 3,028 75 K4
Holton, Mich. 67 G5
Holton Harbour, Newf., Can. 45 P3
Holtville, Calif., 3,080 82 F6
Holtwood, Pa. 61 K6
Holualoa, Hawaii, 704 84 F4
Ho-lung, China 150 H2
Holwerd, Neth. 115 D1
Holwierde, Neth. 115 E1
Holy City, Calif. 83 f13
Holy Cross, Phil., 2,581 153 C4
Holy Cross, Alaska, 256 85 D3
Holy Cross, Mt. of the, Colo. 79 B2
Holyhead, U.K., 10,412 113 D5
Holyhead Bay, U.K. 113 D5
Holy I., Eng., U.K. 112 F4
Holy I., Scot., U.K. 112 D4
Holy I., Wales, U.K. 113 D5
Holy Loch, U.K. 112 a8
Holyoke, Colo., 1,555 79 D1
Holyoke, Mass., 52,689 56 F4
Holyrood, Newf., Can. 45 b10
Holyrood, Kans., 737 75 G5
Holyrood Bay, Newf., Can. 45 b11
Holytown, U.K. 112 c8
Holywell, U.K., 8,477 114 B4
Holzgerlingen, F.R.Ger., 4,379 119 F7
Holzhausen, F.R.Ger., 1,522 119 E3
Holzheim, F.R.Ger., 5,943 119 B2
Holzminden, F.R.Ger., 22,372 118 B3
Holzwickede, F.R.Ger., 9,494 119 D2
Homa Bay, Kenya 165 g14
Homalin, Burma 146 A1
Hombeek, Belg., 3,295 115 d8
Homberg, Hess., F.R.Ger., 5,884 118 B3
Homberg, Nrh.-Wf., F.R.Ger., 33,855 119 B2
Hombetsu, Jap., 17,014 155 K8
Hombori, Mali, 3,600 162 D3
Hombourg-Haut, Fr., 10,111 116 c8
Hombre Muerto, Salar del, Arg. 105 B3
Homburg, F.R.Ger., 25,521 118 A4
Home, Kans. 75 J4
Home, Wash. 80 B2
Home Bay, N.W.T., Can. 41 Q4
Home Bay, Ocean I. 175 16
Homécourt, Fr., 10,159 116 b8
Homedale, Idaho, 1,381 81 A4
Homedale, Ohio 70 a6
Home Hill, Austl., 2,793 173 G2
Homeland, Ga., 508 64 H5
Homer, Alaska, 1,247 85 F4
Homer, Ga., 612 64 F1
Homer, Ill., 1,276 68 E3
Homer, La., 4,665 73 B5
Homer, Mich., 1,629 67 J6
Homer, Nebr., 370 75 J1
Homer, N.Y., 3,622 59 H6
Homer, Ohio 70 G2
Homer City, Pa., 2,471 60 D4
Homer Cr., Ont., Can. 46 a15
Homerville, Ga., 2,634 64 G4
Homestead, Austl. 173 F3
Homestead, Fla., 9,152 65 J7
Homestead, Mont. 81 G1
Homestead, Oreg. 80 E3
Homestead, Pa., 7,502 60 C5
Homestead, Tenn. 71 F6
Homestead Nat. Mon., Nebr. 75 J3
Hometown, Ill., 7,479 69 d10
Homewood, Ala., 20,289 64 C2
Homewood, Calif. 82 C3
Homewood, Ill., 13,371 68 E2
Homewood, Miss. 73 F5
Hominy, Okla., 2,866 76 G1
Hominy Cr., Okla. 76 G1
Homochitto, r., Miss. 73 D6
Homonhon I., Phil. 153 C3
Homorod, Rum. 128 E1
Homosassa, Fla. 65 G4
Homs = Al Khums
Hon, Jap. 154 e15
Hon, Ark. 73 A3
Hon, Cu Lao, S. Viet. 146 E5
Honaker, Va., 851 62 B5
Ho-nan, prov., China, 48,670,000 150 F3
Ho-nan, China 150 D3
Ho-nan, China 152 b5
Ho-nan-ying-tzu, China 151 C2
Honaunau, Hawaii 84 F4
Honby, Calif. 83 h15
Hon Chong, S. Viet. 146 D5
Honda, Col. 100 C5
Honda, Bahía, Cuba 96 b1
Honda, Ens., P.R. 96 v10
Hondeklipbaai, S. Af. 164 B7
Hondo, Alta., Can. 42 J2
Hondo, Jap., 41,893 154 B5
Hondo, N. Mex. 79 C5
Hondo, Tex., 4,992 77 O5
Hondo, r., Br. Hond.-Mex. 94 C1
Hondo, r., Cuba 96 b1
Hondo, r., N. Mex. 79 C5
Hondo Valle, Dom. Rep. 96 m6
Honduras, ctry., 2,363,000* 94 D3
Honduras, C. de, Hond. 94 D2
Honduras, G. of, Cent. Amer. 94 D2
Honea Path, S.C., 3,453 63 B3
Hønefoss, Nor., 4,263 120 B3
Honeoye, N.Y. 58 F6
Honeoye Cr., N.Y. 58 n21
Honeoye Falls, N.Y., 2,143 58 E6
Honeoye L., N.Y. 58 F6
Honesdale, Pa., 5,569 61 M2
Honey Brook, Pa., 1,023 61 L5
Honey Creek, Wis. 66 c12
Honey Cr., Wis. 66 c12
Honey Grove, Tex., 2,071 77 Q3
Honey Island, Tex. 77 Q4
Honey L., Calif. 82 C2
Honeymoon, Ariz. 78 D5
Honeymoon Bay, Br. Col., Can. 42 b7
Honeyville, Fla. 65 D2
Honeyville, Utah, 646 78 b7
Honeywood, Ont., Can. 46 D4
Honfleur, Fr., 9,132 117 D2
Høng, Den. 121 D5
Hong, r., N. Viet. 146 D2
Hong = *Yüan*
Hon Gai, N. Viet., 35,412 146 D2
Hongch'ŏn, S. Kor., 19,966 151 F3
Hong Kong, Br. col., 3,836,000* 150 F5
Hong Kong, i., H.K. 152 b6
Hong My, S. Viet. 147 k12
Hong Ngu, S. Viet. 147 k11
Hongō, Jap., 10,445 154 e15
Hongō, Jap. 154 g14
Hongsŏng, S. Kor., 20,395 151 E3
Hongū, Jap. 154 g16
Hongwŏn, N. Kor. 151 E2
Honiara, Sol. Is. 175 c3
Honikulu, Passe d', str., Îs. Wallis 175 7
Honiton, U.K., 4,718 113 E6
Honjō, Jap., 38,738 155 F2
Honjōhama, Jap. 154 g14
Honnef, F.R.Ger., 14,533 118 A3
Hönningen, F.R.Ger. 119 C4
Honningsvåg, Nor. 120 F1
Honnō, Jap., 7,774 155 n20
Hōno, Jap. 154 g15
Honobia, Okla. 76 J3
Honohina, Hawaii 84 F4
Honoipu Landing, Hawaii 84 F3
Honokaa, Hawaii, 1,247 84 F3
Honokahua, Hawaii, 354 84 E2
Honokohau, Hawaii 84 E4
Honolulu, co., Hawaii, 500,409 84 C2
Honolulu, Hawaii, 294,194 84 D2
Honolulu District, Hawaii, 294,194 84 d8
Honolulu Hbr., Hawaii 84 c8
Honomalino Camp, Hawaii 84 F4
Honomu, Hawaii, 663 84 F4
Honor, Mich., 278 67 G4
Honouliuli, Hawaii 84 b7
Honrubia, Sp., 2,254 122 D3
Honshū, i., Jap. 155 G3
Hontheim, F.R.Ger. 119 C4
Hontubby, Okla. 76 J3
Honuapo, Hawaii 84 F4
Hood, Calif. 82 b8
Hood, co., Tex., 5,443 77 P3
Hood, Mt., Oreg. 80 C3
Hood Can., Wash. 81 a7
Hood Pt., Austl. 172 B5
Hood River, co., Oreg., 13,395 80 C3
Hood River, Oreg., 3,657 80 C3
Hoodsport, Wash. 80 B2
Hoofddorp, Neth., 4,800 115 b6
Hooge, i., F.R.Ger. 118 B1
Hoogerheide, Neth. 115 C3
Hoogeveen, Neth., 14,400 115 E2
Hoogeveensche Vaart, can., Neth. 115 E2
Hoogezand, Neth., 17,400 115 E1
Hooge-Zwaluwe, Neth. 115 b7
Hooghly, r., India 144 f15
Hoogkerk, Neth., 3,300 115 E1
Hoogvliet, Neth. 115 a7
Hookdale, Ill. 68 C5
Hookena, Hawaii 84 F4
Hooker, co., Nebr., 1,130 75 D2
Hooker, Okla., 1,684 76 B1
Hookers Store, Okla. 76 E3
Hookerton, N.C., 358 63 G2
Hook Head, Ire. 113 C5
Hook Norton, U.K., 1,198 114 F6
Hooks, Tex., 2,048 77 Q3
Hooksett, N.H. 54 D5
Hookstown, Pa., 295 60 B4
Hoolehua, Hawaii, 990 84 D2
Hoonah, Alaska, 686 85 K4
Hoopa, Calif. 82 B2
Hooper, Colo., 58 79 C3
Hooper, Nebr., 832 75 J2
Hooper, Utah 78 b8
Hooper Bay, Alaska, 460 85 C3
Hoopeston, Ill., 6,606 68 E3
Hoople, N. Dak., 334 74 D1
Hooppole, Ill., 227 68 B2
Höör, Swed. 121 F5
Hoorn, Neth., 15,800 115 D2
Hoosac Ra., Mass.-Vt. 56 D2
Hoosac Tunnel (part of Florida), Mass. 56 E2
Hoosic, r., U.S. 59 O6
Hoosick, N.Y. 59 O6
Hoosick Falls, N.Y., 4,023 59 O6
Hoosierville, Ind. 70 B3
Hooven, Ohio 71 g10
Hoover, Okla. 76 F3
Hoover, S. Dak. 74 A3
Hoover Dam, Ariz.-Nev. 78 A3
Hoover Res., Ohio 70 G2
Hoovers, Ind. 70 C2
Hooversville, Pa., 1,120 60 E5
Hop, r., Conn. 56 G6
Hopa, Turk., 4,881 142 E1
Hopatcong, N.J., 3,391 61 B2
Hopatcong, L., N.J. 61 B2
Hop Bottom, Pa., 381 61 L2
Hop Bk., Mass. 56 D4
Hope, Br. Col., Can., 2,682 42 G4
Hope, U.K., 5,241 114 B4
Hope, Alaska, 44 85 G3
Hope, Ariz. 78 B5
Hope, Ark., 8,399 73 B4
Hope, Idaho, 96 81 A1
Hope, Ind., 1,489 70 D3
Hope, Kans., 463 75 H5
Hope, Me. 55 C4
Hope, N.J. 61 A2
Hope, N. Mex., 108 79 C5
Hope, N. Dak., 390 74 D2
Hope, R.I. 57 K6
Hope Bay, Ant. 180 O6
Hope Bay, Jam. 96 q8
Hopedale, Newf., Can. 45 O3
Hopedale, Ill., 737 68 C3
Hopedale, Mass., 2,904; 3,987(T) 57 K4
Hopedale, Ohio, 932 70 J2
Hopefield, S. Af., 2,106 164 a8
Hopeh = Ho-pei
Ho-pei, prov., China, 43,730,000 150 F3
Hopelchén, Mex., 3,006 93 H4
Hopeman, U.K. 112 E3
Hope Mills, N.C., 1,109 63 F3
Hopen, i., Nor. 134 B2
Hopes Advance Bay, Qué., Can. 45 L2
Hopes Water, r., U.K. 112 e8
Hopeton, Okla. 76 E1
Hopetoun, N.S.W., Austl. 173 F5
Hopetoun, W. Austl., Austl. 172 B5
Hope Town, Bah. Is. 95 c6
Hopetown, S. Af., 2,631 164 C6
Hope Valley (part of Hopkinton), R.I. 57 J6
Hopeville, Conn. 56 J6
Hopewell, Ala. 64 c8
Hopewell, Hillsborough Co., Fla. 65 d12
Hopewell, Madison Co., Fla. 65 F2
Hopewell, Miss. 73 E6
Hopewell, N.J., 1,928 61 B3
Hopewell, Pa., 301 60 F5
Hopewell, Va., 17,895 62 G5
Hopewell Is., N.W.T., Can. 44 H2
Hopewell Village Nat. Hist. Site, Pa. 60 e11
Hopfgarten, Aust., 4,166 124 J6
Höpfingen, F.R.Ger., 2,148 119 G5
Hopin, Burma 146 B1
Ho-p'ing, China 152 D2
Hopkins, co., Ky., 38,458 71 D4
Hopkins, Mich., 556 67 H6
Hopkins, Minn., 11,370 74 b6
Hopkins, Mo., 710 72 C4
Hopkins, S.C. 63 D4
Hopkins, co., Tex., 18,594 77 Q3
Hopkins L., Austl. 172 D3
Hopkins Park, Ill. 68 E2
Hopkinsville, Ky., 19,465 71 D5
Hopkinton, Iowa, 768 72 F2
Hopkinton, Mass., 2,754; 4,932(T) 57 K4
Hopkinton, N.H. 54 D5
Hopkinton, N.Y. 59 L2
Hopkinton, R.I., 4,174(T) 57 J7
Hopland, Calif. 82 B3
Hopohoponga, Mui, pt., Tonga 177 36
Hoppstädten, F.R.Ger., 1,900 119 C5
Hop River (part of Columbia), Conn. 56 G6
Hopton Wafers, U.K. 114 C6
Ho-p'u, China 152 C3
Ho-pu-k'o-sai-erh, China 150 B2
Hopwood, Pa., 1,615 60 C6
Hoque, Ang. 164 B4
Hoquiam, Wash., 10,762 80 A2
Horace, Kans., 195 75 D5
Horace, N. Dak., 178 74 D2
Horasan, Turk., 4,594 142 E1
Horatio, Ark., 722 73 A4
Horatio, S.C. 63 D3
Horaždóvice, Czech. 126 A2
Horbelev, Den., 1,524 121 E6
Horbling, U.K. 114 H5
Horbury, U.K., 8,642 114 E3
Hörby, Swed. 121 F5
Horcajo de Santiago, Sp., 3,914 122 D3
Horconcitos, Pan., 1,079 94 F6
Hord, Ill. 68 D5
Hordain, Fr., 1,210 116 a7
Horden, U.K., 15,202 113 F4
Hordio, Som. Rep. 163 N4
Hordville, Nebr., 128 75 H2
Horezu, Rum. 128 D2
Horgen, Switz., 13,482 124 C1
Horgoš, Yug., 7,768 125 D1
Horia, Rum. 128 G2
Hořice, Czech. 127 e6
Horicon, N.Y. = Brant Lake
Horicon, Wis., 2,996 66 E5
Horikiri, Jap. 154 i15
Horley, U.K., 16,052 113 F6
Horlick Mts., Ant. 180 Y4
Hormigueros, P.R., 1,647 96 r10
Hormuz, Str. of, Asia 143 F3
Horn, Aust., 4,704 124 M5
Horn, Neth. 115 D3
Horn, C., Chile = Hornos, C. de
Horn, c., Ice. 120 a6
Hornavan, L., Swed. 120 D2
Hornbach, F.R.Ger., 1,599 119 C6
Hornbæk, Den., 3,030 121 E4
Hornbeak, Tenn., 307 71 B5
Hornbeck, La., 374 73 B6
Hornbrook, Calif. 82 B2
Hornby, Ont., Can. 46 c13
Hornby, N.Z., 5,660 175 g6
Hornby, U.K. 112 h11
Hornby I., Br. Col., Can. 42 b6
Horncastle, U.K., 3,771 113 G5
Hornchurch, London, U.K. 114 J7
Horndean, U.K., 5,555 113 k13
Horne, Den. 121 C5
Horne, Îs. de, Wallis and Futuna 170 G5
Hörnefors, Swed. 120 D3
Hornell, N.Y., 13,907 58 E7
Hornepayne, Ont., Can., 1,692 44 F5
Horner, W. Va. 62 D3
Hornerstown, N.J. 58 b16
Hornersville, Mo., 752 72 G8
Horní Benešov, Czech. 127 g7
Horní Blatná, Czech. 126 b6
Horní Bříza, Czech. 126 c7
Hornick, Iowa, 275 72 A2
Horní Libina, Czech. 127 g7
Hornings Mills, Ont., Can. 46 D4
Horn I., Miss. 73 G7
Hornitos, Calif., 73 82 C4
Horn Mts., N.W.T., Can. 40 F5
Hornnes, Nor. 121 A2
Hornos, C. de, Chile 105 B9
Hornsby, Tenn., 228 71 C6
Hornsea, U.K., 5,955 113 F5
Hornslet, Den., 2,758 121 C4
Hornstein, Aust., 2,381 124 c11
Hornu, Belg., 11,245 115 B4
Horobetsu, Jap., 29,100 155 J8
Horoizumi, Jap., 9,267 155 K8
Horokanai, Jap., 12,107 155 K8
Horomui, Jap., 7,844 155 J8
Horonai, Jap. 155 K7
Horonobe, Jap., 7,182 155 J7
Hořovice, Czech. 126 B2
Horqueta, Para., 4,573 105 D2
Horrem, F.R.Ger., 7,201 119 B3
Horry, co., S.C., 68,247 63 E4
Horse Cave, Ky., 1,780 71 F4
Horse Creek, Wyo. 81 G5
Horse Cr., Mo. 72 C7
Horsefly, Br. Col., Can. 42 G3
Horsehead L., N. Dak. 74 C2
Horseheads, N.Y., 7,207 58 G7
Horse Mtn., N. Mex. 79 A4
Horseneck Beach (part of Westport), Mass. 57 M7
Horseneck Bk., Conn. 58 e12
Horsens, Den., 37,261 121 B5
Horse Shoe, N.C. 63 B2
Horseshoe Bay, Br. Col., Can. 42 c6
Horseshoe Beach, Fla. 65 F3
Horse Shoe Bend, Idaho, 480 81 A4
Horseshoe L., Ill. 72 b11
Horse Springs, N. Mex. 79 A5
Horsforth, U.K., 15,351 114 E3
Horsham, Austl., 7,767 173 F5
Horsham, U.K., 21,198 113 F6
Horsham, Pa., 3,700* 60 f11
Hørsholm, Den., 12,401 121 b7
Horslunde, Den., 1,914 121 D6
Horšovský Týn, Czech. 126 A2
Horst, F.R.Ger., 4,078 119 a8
Horst, Neth. 115 E3
Horta, Azores, 7,489 108 2
Horten, Nor., 13,289 120 B4
Hortense, Ga. 64 G4
Hortlax, Swed. 120 E2
Horton, U.K. 113 i13
Horton, Kans., 2,361 75 K4
Horton, Mich. 67 J6
Horton, r., N.W.T., Can. 40 E4
Hortonia, L., Vt. 54 A4
Horton in Ribblesdale, U.K. 114 D2
Horton L., N.W.T., Can. 40 E4
Hortonville, Ind. 70 C2
Hortonville (part of Swansea), Mass. 57 M5
Hortonville, N.Y. 59 K8
Hortonville, Wis., 1,366 66 E4
Hørve, Den., 1,767 121 D5
Horw, Switz., 7,638 124 C1
Horwich, U.K., 16,067 114 C3
Hōsaka, Jap. 154 g14
Hösbach, F.R.Ger., 5,501 118 B3
Hoschton, Ga., 370 64 F1
Hose Mts., Malay. 148 E2
Hosenfeld, F.R.Ger. 119 H3
Hosford, Fla. 65 E2
Ho-shan, China 152 E1
Hoshangabad, India, 19,284 144 a14
Hoshiarpur, India, 50,739 145 E3
Ho-shih, China 150 B2
Hōshi-yama, Jap. 154 g16
Hōshubano, Jap. 155 m18
Ho-shun, China 151 B3
Hosingen, Lux. 119 A4
Hoskins, Terr. New Guin. 174 f2
Hoskins (part of Simsbury), Conn. 56 E5
Hoskins, Nebr., 179 75 H1
Hoskins, Oreg. 80 B3
Hoskote, India, 9,132 145 k19
Hosmer, S. Dak., 433 74 C3
Hosokawa, Jap. 154 g15
Hospah, N. Mex. 79 B4
Hospers, Iowa, 600 72 A1
Hospet, India, 53,242 145 E7
Hospital, Chile 104 g13
Hospitalet, Sp., 122,813 122 G2
Hosseina, Eth. 163 L4
Hoste, I., Chile 105 B9
Hostens, Fr., 1,190 117 C4
Hostinné, Czech. 127 e6
Hostivice, Czech. 126 d6
Hošťka, Czech. 126 d6
Hostos, Dom. Rep. 96 m6
Hot, Thai. 146 B3
Hota, Jap. 155 F4
Hotagen, Swed. 120 C3
Hotaino, Jap. 154 f14
Hotaka, Jap., 20,378 155 E3
Hotaka-dake, Jap. 155 E3
Hot Brook L., Me. 55 E3
Hotchkiss, Alta., Can. 42 H1
Hotchkiss, Colo., 626 79 B2
Hotchkissville (part of Woodbury), Conn. 56 D6
Hot Cr. Ra., Nev. 83 B3
Hötensleben, Ger.D.R. 118 C2
Hotevilla, Ariz. 78 C4
Ho-t'ien, China 150 A3
Hoting, Swed. 120 D2
Hotopuu, Tahiti 177 44
Ho-tse, China 151 B4
Ho-tso, China 150 D3
Hot Spring, co., Ark., 21,893 73 C3
Hot Springs, Alaska 85 F2
Hot Springs, Ark., 28,337 73 C3
Hot Springs, Mont., 585 81 B2
Hot Springs, N.C., 723 63 B2
Hot Springs, S. Dak., 4,943 74 A4
Hot Springs, Va. 62 E4
Hot Springs, co., Wyo., 6,365 81 E4
Hot Springs Nat. Pk., Ark. 73 B3
Hot Sulphur Springs, Colo., 237 79 B1
Hottah L., N.W.T., Can. 40 F4
Hotton, Belg., 1,724 115 D4
Hottviller, Fr. 116 d8
Houaïlou, N. Caled., 2,241 174 i8
Houat, Î., Fr. 116 B3
Houck, Ariz. 78 D4
Houdain, Fr., 8,869 117 E1
Houdan, Fr., 2,358 117 D2
Houdeng-Goegnies, Belg., 9,109 115 C4
Houei Sai, Laos 146 C2
Houffalize, Belg., 1,254 115 D4
Houghton, Me. 55 B4
Houghton, co., Mich., 35,654 66 E2
Houghton, Mich., 3,393 66 E1
Houghton, N.Y. 58 D7
Houghton, S. Dak. 74 C3
Houghton, Wash., 2,426 81 b7
Houghton, Pt., Mich. 66 b9
Houghton Lake, Mich. 67 J4
Houghton L., Mich. 67 J4
Houghton Lake Heights, Mich., 1,195 67 J4
Houghton-le-Spring, U.K., 31,049 112 h10
Houghton Regis, U.K., 7,293 114 H7
Houghtonville, Vt. 54 B5
Houilles, Fr., 26,491 116 g11
Houlka, Miss., 547 73 F3
Houlton, Me., 5,976 55 E2
Houlton, Wis. 66 A3
Hou-lung, Taiwan, 38,116 152 F2
Houma, La., 29,772 73 E8
Hound, U.K., 4,992 113 k13
Houndé, Upper Volta, 1,138 162 D4
Houplines, Fr., 5,934 116 a6
Hourn, Loch, U.K. 112 D3
Hourtin, Fr., 4,390 117 C4
Housatonic, Mass., 1,370 56 C3
Housatonic, r., Conn.-Mass. 56 D7
House, N. Mex. 79 C4
House Ra., Utah 78 B2
House Rock, Ariz. 78 B3
Houston, Br. Col., Can. 42 E2
Houston, co., Ala., 50,718 64 D4
Houston, Alaska 85 c7
Houston, Ark., 206 73 C2
Houston, Del., 421 62 J4
Houston, Fla. 65 G2
Houston, co., Ga., 39,154 64 F3
Houston, Ind. 70 C3
Houston, co., Minn., 16,588 74 G4
Houston, Minn., 1,082 74 G4
Houston, Miss., 2,577 73 G4
Houston, Mo., 1,660 72 F7
Houston, Pa., 1,865 60 B5
Houston, co., Tenn., 4,794 71 D5
Houston, co., Tex., 19,376 77 Q4
Houston, Tex., 938,219 77 Q5
Houston, L., Tex. 77 Q5
Houston, r., La. 73 B7
Houstonia, Mo., 261 72 D6
Houten, Neth. 115 c6
Houthalen, Belg., 10,548 115 D3
Houtman Rocks, Austl. 172 A4
Houtzdale, Pa., 1,239 60 F4
Hövåg, Nor. 121 A2
Hove, Den. 121 A4
Hove, U.K., 72,973 113 F6
Hovedgård, Den. 121 C5
Hoven, S. Dak., 568 74 C3
Hovenweep Nat. Mon., Colo.-Utah 78 D3
Hovey, Ind. 70 B5
Hovingham, U.K. 114 F2
Hovland, Minn. 74 G2
Howar, Wādī, Sudan 163 J3
Howard, Austl., 1,053 173 H3
Howard, co., Ark., 10,878 73 A3
Howard, co., Ind., 69,509 70 C2
Howard, co., Iowa, 12,734 72 E1
Howard, Kans., 1,017 75 J6
Howard, co., Md., 36,152 62 G3
Howard, co., Mo., 10,859 72 E5
Howard, co., Nebr., 6,541 75 G2
Howard, N.Y. 58 E7
Howard, Pa., 770 60 G3
Howard, S. Dak., 1,208 74 D3
Howard, co., Tex., 40,139 77 N3
Howard, Wis., 3,485 66 E4
Howard, Mt., Wash. 80 C2
Howard City, Mich., 1,004 67 H5
Howard Lake, Minn., 1,007 74 E3
Howard Mtn., Colo. 79 B1
Howards Grove, Wis. 66 F5
Howden, U.K., 2,282 114 G3
Howe, Ind. 70 D1
Howe, Nebr. 75 K3
Howe, Okla., 390 76 J3
Howe, C., Austl. 173 G5
Howe Brook Mtn., Me. 55 D2
Howe I., Ont., Can. 59 H3
Howell, Ga., 141 64 F5
Howell, Kans. 75 E6
Howell, Mich., 4,861 67 J6
Howell, co., Mo., 22,027 72 F8
Howell, N.J. 58 c16
Howell, Utah, 188 78 b7
Howell Pk., Utah 78 B2
Howells, Nebr., 694 75 H2
Howes, S. Dak. 74 A3
Howick, Qué., Can. 47 L3
Howison, Miss. 73 F7
Howitt, L., Austl. 172 E4
Howland, Me., 1,313 55 D3
Howland I., Pac. Oc. 170 G4
Howlet Hill, N.Y. 59 q23
Howley, Newf., Can. 45 Q5
Howrah, India, 512,598 145 H5
Howson Pk., Br. Col., Can. 42 E2
Howwood, U.K. 112 a8
Hoxeyville, Mich. 67 H4
Hoxie, Ark., 1,886 73 E1
Hoxie, Kans., 1,289 75 E4
Hoxsie (part of Warwick), R.I. 57 L6
Höxter, F.R.Ger., 14,356 118 B3
Hoy, i., U.K. 112 E2
Hoya, F.R.Ger., 4,286 118 B2
Ho-yang, Shant., China 151 C4
Ho-yang, Shen-hsi, China 151 A4
Höyanger, Nor. 120 A3
Hoyerswerda, Ger.D.R., 24,549 118 E3
Höyjord, Nor. 121 C1
Hoylake, U.K., 32,268 114 B4
Höylandet, Nor. 120 B2
Hoyland Nether, U.K., 15,707 114 E3
Hoyleton, Ill., 475 68 C5
Hōyo-kaikyō, Jap. 154 B5
Hoyran Gölü, Turk. 142 B2
Hoyt, Kans., 283 75 K4
Hoyt, r., Camb.-S. Viet. 147 m10
Höytiäinen, l., Fin. 120 G3
Hoyt Lakes, Minn., 3,186 74 G2
Hoytsville, Utah 78 C1
Ho-yüan, China 150 F5
Hōza, Jap. 154 h15
Hozat, Turk., 3,626 142 D2
Hradec, Czech. 127 g7
Hradec Králové, Czech., 57,221 126 B1
Hrádek nad Nisou, Czech. 127 d6
Hranice, Czech. 126 b6
Hranice, Czech., 11,339 126 C2
Hrastnik, Yug., 5,161 125 B1
Hrebenne, Pol. 127 E3
Hřensko, Czech. 126 d6
Hron, r., Czech. 126 D2
Hronov, Czech., 10,082 126 C1
Hrubieszów, Pol., 11,972 127 E3
Hrušovany, Czech. 126 C2
Hrvatska, st., Yug., 4,159,696 125 B2
Hsa Mong Hkam, Burma 147 g7
Hsenwi, Burma 146 B2
Hsi, r., China 150 F5
Hsia-ch'eng-tzu, China 151 F1
Hsia-chiang, China 152 D2
Hsia-ch'uan Shan, China 152 D3
Hsia-hsien, China 151 A4
Hsia-i, China 151 C4
Hsia-kuan, China 150 D4
Hsia-men, China, 308,000* 150 F4
Hsia-men Wan, China-Taiwan 152 E2
Hsi-an, China, 1,500,000* 150 E3
Hsiang, r., China 150 F4
Hsiang-ch'eng, Ho-n., China 151 B4
Hsiang-ch'eng, S-ch., China 150 D4
Hsiang-fan, China, 90,000* 150 E3
Hsiang-hsiang, China 152 D2
Hsiang-ning, China 151 A4
Hsiang-shan, China 152 F1
Hsiang-shui-k'ou, China 151 C4
Hsiang-t'an, China, 260,000* 150 E4
Hsiang-yang, China 152 D1
Hsiang-yin, China 152 D1
Hsiang-yüan, China 151 B3
Hsiang-yün, China 150 D4
Hsiao, r., China 152 C2
Hsiao-ch'ing, r., China 151 C3
Hsiao-feng, China 152 E1
Hsiao-ha-la-tao-k'ou, China 151 C2
Hsiao-ho-yen, China 151 C2
Hsiao-hsien, China 151 C4
Hsiao-hsing-an-ling Shan-mo, China 150 G1
Hsiao-hsing-k'ai Hu, China 151 F1
Hsiao-huang-pu, China 152 a6
Hsiao-hung-t'ou Hsü, Taiwan 152 F3
Hsiao-i, China 151 A3
Hsiao-kan, China 152 D1
Hsiao-lan, China 152 a6
Hsiao-shan, China 152 F1
Hsiao-t'o, China 152 a6
Hsiao-wan Shan, China 152 a7
Hsia-p'u, China 150 G4
Hsia-ts'un, China 152 a6
Hsia-wa, China 151 D2
Hsi-ch'ang, China 150 D4
Hsi-ch'ou, China 152 B3
Hsi-ch'uan, China 151 A4
Hsi-chung Tao, China 151 D3
Hsieh-ch'u, r., China 152 A1
Hsieh-ko-erh, China 150 B4
Hsien-chü, China 152 F1
Hsien-feng, China 152 C1
Hsien-hsien, China 151 C3
Hsien-ning, China 152 D1

Iberia—Iona Island · 239

Iberia, Mo., 694 72 E6
Iberia, Ohio 70 G2
Iberian Pen., Eur. 110 C4
Iberia Plain, Atl. Oc. 108 M4
Iberville, Qué., Can., 7,449 47 p18
Iberville, parish, La., 29,939 73 D7
Ibex, Tex. 77 O3
Ibi, Jap., 15,311 154 h14
Ibi, Nigeria 162 F4
Ibi, r., Jap. 154 h14
Ibiapaba, Sa. da, Braz. 103 H2
Ibicaraí, Braz., 13,155 103 H4
Ibicuí, r., Braz. 103 E7
Ibicuy, Arg., 2,500* 105 b11
Ibipetuba, Braz., 2,288 103 H4
Ibiúna, Braz., 3,010 103 c18
Ibiza, Sp., 11,259 122 F3
Ibiza, I. de, Sp. 122 F3
Ibo, Moz., 4,366 164 F4
Ibotirama, Braz., 2,556 103 H4
Ibrāhīm, Jabal, Saudi Ar. 143 C4
'Ibrī, Muscat and Oman 143 F4
Ibstock, U.K., 4,954 114 F5
Ibuna, Phil., 153 c7
Ibusuki, Jap., 33,623 154 Bb
Ica, Peru, 38,347 104 C5
Ica, r., Peru 104 C5
Icabarú, Ven. 101 J5
Icacos, Cayo, P.R. 96 u10
Icacos Point, Trin. and Tob. 96 g5
Içana, Braz. 102 C1
Içana, r., Braz. 102 C1
Iceland, ctry., 192,000* 120
Iceland-Faeroes Rise, Atl. Oc. 110 B2
Ice Mtn., Br. Col., Can. 42 G2
Icha, U.S.S.R. 135 P4
Icha, r., U.S.S.R. 137 p11
Ichalkaranji, India, 50,978 145 D6
I-ch'ang, China, 110,000* 150 E4
I-chang, China 150 F4
Ichawaynochaway Cr., Ga. 64 E4
Ichchapuram, India, 12,961 145 G6
I-ch'eng, Hu-p., China 152 D1
I-ch'eng, Shan-hsi, China 151 A4
I-cheng, China 152 E1
Ichhawar, India, 5,136 144 a14
Ichi, Jap. 154 e15
Ichi, r., Jap. 154 f14
Ichiba, Jap., 16,384 155 D4
Ichiba, Jap. 154 e15
Ichiba, Jap. 154 g14
Ichiba, Jap. 154 g15
Ichibusa-yama, Jap. 154 B5
Ichikawa, Jap., 157,301 155 G4
Ichilo, r., Bol. 102 D5
Ichinohe, Jap., 5,953 155 G1
Ichinomiya, Jap., 182,984 155 E4
Ichinomiya, Jap., 11,387 155 G4
Ichinoseki, Jap., 57,585 155 G2
Ichinskiy, Vlk., U.S.S.R. 135 P4
Ichnya, U.S.S.R., 13,000 136 D3
Ichoa, r., Bol. 102 c9
Ich'ŏn, N. Kor. 151 E3
Ichon, Phil., 2,595 153 f11
Ich'ŏn, S. Kor., 17,041 151 E3
Ichtegem, Belg., 5,726 115 B3
I-ch'uan, Ho-n., China 151 B4
I-ch'uan, Shen-hsi, China 151 A3
I-ch'un, Ch-hsi, China 152 D2
I-ch'un, H-l-ch., China, 248,000* 150 G2
I-chün, China 151 A4
Ickesburg, Pa. 60 H5
Icla, Bol., 6,289 102 c11
Iconoclast Mtn., Br. Col., Can. 42 H3
Icoraci, Braz., 11,512 103 G2
Icy Bay, Alaska 85 J4
Icy C., Alaska 85 D1
Icy Pt., Alaska 85 K4
Icy Str., Alaska 85 L4
Ida, co., Iowa, 10,269 72 B2
Ida, Mich. 67 K7
Ida, Va. 62 F4
Ida, L., Fla. 65 b9
Idabel, Okla., 4,967 76 J4
Ida Grove, Iowa, 2,265 72 B2
Idah, Nigeria 162 g8
Idaho, st., U.S., 693,000* 81
Idaho, co., Idaho, 13,542 81 B3
Idaho, Ohio 70 F3
Idaho City, Idaho, 188 81 B4
Idaho Falls, Idaho, 33,161 81 C4
Idaho Springs, Colo., 1,480 79 C2
Idakemenai, Terr. Papua 174 3
Idalia, Colo. 79 D2
Idalium, ruins, Cyp. 142 e10
Idalou, Tex., 1,274 77 N3
Idana, Kans. 75 H4
Idanha, Oreg., 295 80 C3
Idanha-a-Nova, Port., 4,567 122 B3
Idapa, r.=Siapo
Idar-Oberstein, F.R.Ger., 28,399 118 A4
Idawgaw, Nigeria 162 e8
Idd, Nor. 121 D1
Ideal, Ga., 432 64 E3
Ideal, S. Dak. 74 B4
Idenburg, r., Indon. 174 c1
Ideriin, r., Mong. 150 D1
Idetown, Pa. 61 n16
Idfū, U.A.R., 8,630 161 K3
Ídhi, mt., Gr. 129 E7
Ídhra, i., Gr. 129 D6
Idi, Indon. 148 A1
Idiofa, D.R.Congo 164 C2
Iditarod, r., Alaska 85 E3
Idle, r., U.K. 114 G4
Idledale, Colo. 79 b8
Idlewild, Mich. 67 H5
Idleyld Park, Oreg. 80 B4
Idlib, Syr., 36,726 142 D3
Idom, Den. 121 A4
Idre, Swed. 120 C3
Idria, Calif. 82 C4
Idrigill Pt., U.K. 112 C3
Idrija, Yug., 5,013 125 A1
Idrinskoye, U.S.S.R. 137 t11
Idstein, F.R.Ger., 7,454 118 B3
Idyllwild, Calif. 82 E6
Ieki, Jap. 154 h15
Ieper, Belg., 17,952 115 A4
Ierápetra, Gr., 6,488 129 E7
Iesi, It., 35,612 123 D3
Iesolo, It., 15,727 123 D2
Ifakara, Tanz. 164 F3
Ifalik, atoll, Car. Is. 176 18
Ifanadiana, Malag. Rep. 165 G5
Ife, Nigeria, 128,516 162 E4
I-feng, China 152 D1
Iferouane, Niger, 7,153 162 F2
Iffezheim, F.R.Ger., 2,789 119 E7
Ifni (part of Sp.), Af., 49,889 160 C3
Ifon, Nigeria, 15,901 162 f8
Ifuna, Jap. 154 h15
Igal, Hung., 2,041 126 C3
Igami, Jap. 154 h15
Igan, Malay., 1,187 148 D2
Iganga, Uganda, 3,146 165 f13
Igarapé-Miri, Braz., 2,591 103 G2
Igarassu, Braz., 9,206 103 b14
Igarka, U.S.S.R., 14,300 134 H3
Igatimi, Para. 105 D2
Igatpuri, India, 15,003 145 h17
Igbara-Oke, Nigeria, 12,313 162 f8
Igbo-Ora, Nigeria 162 e8
Iğdır, Turk., 12,658 142 F2
Igel, F.R.Ger. 118 A4
Igersheim, F.R.Ger., 1,764 119 H5
Iggelheim, F.R.Ger., 4,215 119 E6
Iggesund, Swed. 120 D3
Ighil Izane, Alg., 32,889 160 E2
Ightfield, U.K. 114 C5
Igis, Switz., 3,902 124 D2
Igiugig, Alaska 85 E4
Iglesias, It., 29,765 123 B5
Igli, Alg., 1,938 160 D2
Iglino, U.S.S.R. 137 h8
Igloo, Alaska 85 C2
Igloo, S. Dak. 74 A4
Igloolik, N.W.T., Can. 41 N4
Ignace, Ont., Can. 44 D5
Ignacio, Cuba, 7,021 96 e2
Ignacio, Calif. 83 d11
Ignacio, Colo., 609 79 B3
Ignacio Zaragoza, Mex., 1,504 92 C2
Ignalina, U.S.S.R., 2,500 136 B2
Igny, Fr., 6,278 116 g12
Igombe, r., Tanz. 164 E2
Igoumenítsa, Gr., 3,235 129 C5
Igra, U.S.S.R., 9,800 134 E4
Iguaçu, r., Braz. 103 F7
Iguala, Mex., 28,814 93 F4
Igualada, Sp., 19,866 122 F2
Iguana, r., Ven. 100 H3
Iguape, Braz., 5,465 103 G6
Iguassú Falls, Arg.-Braz. 103 F7
Iguassú Nat. Pk., Arg.-Braz. 105 E3
Iguatemi, Braz. 103 E6
Iguatu, Braz., 16,540 103 J3
Iguéla, Gabon 164 A2
Iguig, Phil., 1,554 153 c5
Igurin, i., Eniwetok 176 28
Iha, Ryukyu Is. 154 a11
Ihema, L., Rwanda-Tanz. 165 e14
Iheya-rettō, Ryukyu Is. 154 c12
Ihlen, Minn., 111 74 D4
Ihō, Jap. 155 F3
I Ho, Ho-n., China 151 B4
I Ho, Shant., China 151 C4
Ihosy, Malag. Rep., 3,438 165 G5
Ihotry, L., Malag. Rep. 165 G5
I-hsien, Ho-p, China 151 B3
I-hsien, Shant., China 151 C4
I-hsien, L-n., China 151 D2
I-hsien, A-h., China 152 B1
I-hsing, China 152 E1
Ihu, Terr. Papua 174 e2
I-huang, China 152 E2
Ihuari, Peru 104 B4
Ihuatzio, Mex., 1,419 93 c10
Ii, Fin. 120 F2
Iida, Jap., 67,555 155 E4
Iide-san, mtn., Jap. 155 F3
Iijärvi, l., Fin. 120 G1
Iijima, Jap., 8,189 155 E4
Iijoki, r., Fin. 120 F2
Iisalmi, Fin., 5,998 120 F3
Ii-shima, Ryukyu Is. 154 a10
Iiyama, Jap., 37,592 155 F3
Iizaka, Jap., 26,089 155 G3
Iizuka, Jap., 60,431 154 B5
Ijebu-Ode, Nigeria, 31,967 162 E4
Ijiri, Jap. 154 e16
IJmuiden, Neth., 37,200 115 C2
IJssel, r., Neth. 115 E2
IJsselmeer, Neth. 115 D2
IJsselmonde, Neth. 115 b7
IJsselmonde, i., Neth. 115 a7
IJsselmuiden, Neth. 115 E2
IJsselstein, Neth., 5,700 115 b6
Ijuí, Braz., 19,671 103 F7
Ijūin, Jap., 14,658 154 B6
Ijuw (dist.), Nauru 175 17
IJzer, r., Belg. 115 A4
Ikali, Congo L. 164 C2
Ikamatua, N.Z. 175 f6
Ikare, Nigeria, 29,277 162 f8
Ikaría, i., Gr. 129 E6
Ikarigaseki, Jap., 5,571 155 G1
Ikast, Den., 7,973 121 B4
Ikatan, Alaska 85 D5
Ikauna, India 144 c12
Ikeda, Jap., 28,403 155 C5
Ikeda, Jap., 9,963 154 f15
Ikeda, Jap., 17,049 155 K8
Ikeda, Jap. 155 m20
Ikeda, Jap., 59,688 154 g15
Ikela, D.R.Congo 164 C2
Ikélemba, Congo 164 B1
Ikene, Nigeria 162 e8
Ikeno, Jap. 154 h14
Ikerre, Nigeria 162 f8
Ikhtiman, Bulg., 9,063 128 D3
Iki, i., Jap. 154 A5
Ikirun, Nigeria, 30,166 162 f8
Ikisue, Jap. 154 f15
Iki-suidō, Jap. 154 A5
Ikom, Nigeria, 8,117 162 F4
Ikopa, r., Malag. Rep. 165 G4
Ikorodu, Nigeria, 10,461 162 e8
Ikoyi, Nigeria 162 f7
Ikpikpuk, r., Alaska 85 F1
Iksha, U.S.S.R. 136 b5
I-kung, China 150 C4
Ikuno, Jap. 154 f14
Ikurangi, Mt., Rarotonga 177 34
Ilagan, Phil., 1,186 153 c5
Īlām, Iran, 8,346 143 D2
Ilam, Nepal 144 f12
Ilamatlán, Mex., 1,228 93 f9
I-lan, China 150 H2
I-lan, Taiwan, 53,672 152 F2
Ilanskiy, U.S.S.R., 26,900 135 J4
Ilanz, Switz., 1,843 124 D2
Ilaro, Nigeria, 14,384 162 e8
Ilasco, Mo. 72 F5
Ilava, Czech. 126 D2
Ilave, Peru, 4,795 104 D6
Iława, Pol., 10,443 127 C2
Ilderton, Ont., Can. 46 C5
Ile-à-la-Crosse, Sask., Can. 43 B3
Ileana, Rum. 128 F2
Ileanda, Rum. 128 D1
Île Bizard, Qué., Can., 1,350 47 o18
Île-de-France, reg., Fr. 116 •
Île Europa, Ind. Oc. 164 F5
Île-Jésus, Qué., Can. 47 L3
Ilek, r., U.S.S.R. 134 E4
Île Perrot, Qué., Can., 3,050 47 o18
Ilero, Nigeria, 12,995 162 e7
Ilesha, Nigeria 162 e7
Ilesha, Nigeria, 83,239 162 f8
Ilford, Man., Can. 43 G3
Ilford, London, U.K. 114 J7
Ilfracombe, Austl. 173 F3
Ilfracombe, U.K., 8,696 113 D6
Ilgaz, Turk., 2,219 142 C1
Ilgaz Dağları, Turk. 142 C1
Ilhabela, Braz., 1,506 103 d18
Ilha Grande, Braz. 102 C2
Ilha Grande, B. da, Braz. 103 d18
Ílhavo, Port., 12,646 122 A2
Ilhéu Branco, i., C. Verde Is. 109 5
Ilhéu Raso, i., C. Verde Is. 109 5
Ilhéus, Braz., 45,712 103 J4
Ilhéus Seivagens, i., Atl. Oc. 160 B2
Ili, U.S.S.R., 14,100 134 G5
Ili, r., U.S.S.R. 134 G5
Ilia, Rum. 128 D2
Iliamna, Alaska 85 F4
Iliamna L., Alaska 85 E4
Iliamna Volcano, Alaska 85 F3
I-liang, China 150 D4
I-liang, China 152 B2
Ilica, Turk. 142 E2
Il'ich, U.S.S.R., 22,900 134 F5
Ilidia, Rum. 128 C2
Ilidža, Yug., 2,199 125 D3
Iliff, Colo., 204 79 D1
Iligan, Phil., 14,281 153 C3
Iligan Bay, Phil. 153 B3
Ilili, Tutuila 177 39
Ilim, r., U.S.S.R. 135 K4
Ilimsk, U.S.S.R. 135 K4
Ilin I., Phil. 153 B2
Il'inskoye, U.S.S.R. 137 h7
Iliodhrómia, i., Gr. 129 D5
Ilion, N.Y., 10,199 59 K6
Ilio Pt., Hawaii 84 D2
Ilişeşti, Rum. 128 E1
Ilkal, India, 24,222 145 E7
Ilkeston, U.K., 34,672 113 F5
Ilkley, U.K., 18,519 113 F5
Ill, r., Aust. 124 F6
Ill, r., Fr. 119 D7
Illahe, Oreg. 80 A4
Illana Bay, Phil. 153 B4
Illapel, Chile, 10,395 105 A4
Illbillee, Mt., Austl. 172 D4
Illéla, Niger, 6,712 162 E3
Iller, r., F.R.Ger. 118 C5
Illertissen, F.R.Ger., 5,749 118 C4
Illescas, Sp., 2,560 122 D2
Ille-sur-Têt, Fr., 5,074 117 E5
Illgen, Minn. 74 G2
Illiers, Fr., 3,250 117 D2
Illimani, Nev., Bol. 102 C5
Illingen, F.R.Ger., 3,416 119 F7
Illinois, st., U.S., 10,641,000* 68
Illinois, r., Ark.-Okla. 76 J1
Illinois, r., Ill. 68 D3
Illinois, r., Oreg. 80 A4
Illinois and Michigan Can., Ill. 68 D2
Illinois and Mississippi Can., Ill. 68 C2
Illinois City, Ill. 68 B2
Illinois Valley, Oreg. 80 B4
Illiopolis, Ill., 995 68 C4
Illiwa, r., Guyana 101 L6
Illkirch-Graffenstaden, Fr., 9,607 116 e9
Ilmenau, r., F.R.Ger. 118 C2
Illmo, Mo., 1,174 72 H7
Illushi, Nigeria 162 g8
Ilm, r., Ger.D.R. 118 C3
Ilmajoki, Fin. 120 E3
Il'men', Oz., U.S.S.R. 134 B4
Ilmenau, Ger.D.R., 17,738 118 C3
Ilmenau-Kanal, F.R.Ger. 119 b9
Ilmington, U.K. 114 E6
Ilminster, U.K., 2,799 113 E6
Ilo, Peru, 10,172 104 D6
Ilobasco, El Salv., 4,797 94 e10
Iloca, Chile 104 e14
Ilog, Phil., 3,327 153 d11
Iloilo, Phil., 56,649 153 B3
Ilok, Yug., 5,696 125 D2
Ilomantsi, Fin. 120 G3
Ilopango, L. de, El Salv. 94 C4
Ilorin, Nigeria, 47,963 162 E4
Ilova, r., Yug. 125 C2
Ilovaysk, U.S.S.R., 20,900 136 e8
Ilovik, i., Yug. 125 B2
Ilovlya, r., U.S.S.R. 136 G3
Ilowa, Pol., 3,490 127 A3
Il'pyrskiy, U.S.S.R. 135 Q3
Ilsfeld, F.R.Ger., 2,308 119 G6
Ilshofen, F.R.Ger., 1,134 118 B4
Ilūkste, U.S.S.R., 2,600 136 B1
I-lung, China 152 B1
Ilwaco, Wash., 518 80 A2
Ilwaki, Indon. 149 H4
Ilz, Aust., 1,130 124 M6
Iłża, Pol., 3,742 127 D3
Imabari, Jap., 100,082 155 C4
Imaichi, Jap., 42,476 155 F3
Imajō, Jap., 3,724 155 E4
Iman, U.S.S.R., 25,400 135 N5
Iman, r., U.S.S.R. 135 N5
Imanburluk, r., U.S.S.R. 137 m11
Imandra, Oz., U.S.S.R. 134 C3
Imao, Jap. 154 h14
Imari, Jap., 78,397 154 A5
Imataca, Srra. de, Ven. 101 J3
Imatra, Fin., 34,363 120 G3
Imazu, Jap. 154 e15
Imazu, Jap., 11,682 155 D4
Imbābah, U.A.R., 136,000 161 i7
Imbaimadai, Guyana 101 K5
Imba-numa, l., Jap. 155 n19
Imbert, Dom. Rep., 2,325 96 m6
Imbituba, Braz., 6,638 103 G7
Imbler, Oreg., 137 80 E3
Imboden, Ark., 400 73 D1
Imbsheim, Fr. 116 d9
I-men, China 150 D4
Imeni Artema, U.S.S.R. 17,300 136 e7
Imeni Babushkina, U.S.S.R. 136 F1
Imeni 26 Bakinskikh Komissarov, U.S.S.R., 5,800 137 d2
Imeni Kirova, U.S.S.R. 137 e5
Imeni Tsyurupy, U.S.S.R. 136 c6
Imeri, Sa., Ven. 102 C1
Imi, Eth. 163 M4
Imielin, Pol., 6,206 127 i6
I-mien-p'o, China 151 F1
Imi-n-Tanoute, Mor. 160 C2
Imlay, Nev. 83 A2
Imlay City, Mich., 1,968 67 K5
Imling, Fr. 116 d9
Immenstadt, F.R.Ger., 9,585 118 C5
Immingham, U.K., 4,208 114 H3
Immokalee, Fla., 3,224 65 H6
Imnaha, Oreg. 80 E3
Imnaha, r., Oreg. 80 E3
Imogene, Iowa, 264 72 B4
Imola, It., 50,748 123 C2
Imotski, Yug., 3,591 125 C3
Imperatriz, Braz., 9,004 103 G3
Imperia, It., 33,815 123 A3
Imperial, Sask., Can. 43 C4
Imperial, Peru, 6,439 104 B5
Imperial, co., Calif., 72,105 82 F6
Imperial, Calif., 2,658 82 F6
Imperial, Mo. 72 G6
Imperial, Nebr., 1,423 75 D3
Imperial, Pa., 1,592 60 B5
Imperial, Tex. 77 M4
Imperial Beach, Calif., 17,773 82 c10
Imperial Dam, Ariz.-Calif. 78 A5
Imperial Valley, Calif. 82 F6
Impfondo, Congo 164 B1
Imphal, India, 67,717 145 J4
Imphy, Fr., 3,086 117 E3
Imrodj, i., Jaluit 176 30
İmroz Adası, Turk. 142 A1
Imst, Aust., 3,082 124 G6
Imuris, Mex., 1,004 92 C1
Imuruk Basin, Alaska 85 C2
Imuruk L., Alaska 85 D2
Ina, Dahom. 162 e7
Ina, Jap., 46,179 155 E4
Ina, Ill., 332 68 D5
Ina, r., Pol. 127 A2
Inabón, r., P.R. 96 s10
Inada, Jap. 154 g15
Inagawan, Phil., 2,081 153 A3
Inagō, Jap. 155 m20
Inagsa Pt., Saipan 176 27
Inambari, Peru 104 D5
Inambari, r., Peru 104 D5
Inamenas, Alg. 161 F3
In-Amguel, Alg. 160 E4
Inami, Jap., 3,726 154 g16
Inanwatan, Indon. 149 J3
Iñapari, Peru 104 D4
Inarajan, Guam 176 24
Inari, Fin. 120 F1
Inari, Jap. 154 e15
Inari, Jap. 154 h14
Inari, l., Fin. 120 F1
Inarijoki, r., Fin. 120 F1
Inarijoki, Fin.=Anarjåkka, Nor.
Inatori, Jap., 7,990 155 F4
Inauaia, Terr. Papua 174 e3
Inavale, Nebr. 75 G3
Inawashiro, Jap., 27,522 155 G3
Inawashiro-ko, Jap. 155 F3
Inayauan, Phil., 3,241 153 d12
In-Azaoua, Niger 162 F2
Inazawa, Jap., 46,871 154 h14
In Buri, Thai. 147 d4
Inca, Sp., 13,816 122 G3
İnce Burun, Turk. 142 C1
İncekum Burnu, Turk. 142 C2
İncesu, Turk., 5,885 142 C2
Inchelium, Wash. 80 D1
Inchnadamph, U.K. 112 D2
Inch'ŏn, S. Kor., 402,009 151 E3
Indaiatuba, Braz., 13,507 103 c18
Indalsälven, r., Swed. 120 D3
Indaparapeo, Mex., 3,383 93 d10
Indapur, India, 5,756 145 i17
Indaw, Burma, 2,138 146 B1
Indaw, Burma 147 g7
Indawgyi L., Burma 146 B1
Inde, r., F.R.Ger. 119 A3
Independence, co., Ark., 20,048 73 D2
Independence, Calif. 82 D4
Independence, Ind. 70 B2
Independence, Iowa, 5,498 72 F2
Independence, Kans., 11,222 75 K6
Independence, Ky., 309 71 G3
Independence, La., 1,941 73 E7
Independence, Minn., 1,446 74 F3
Independence, Mo., 62,328 72 C5
Independence, Ohio, 6,868 70 H1
Independence, Oreg., 1,930 80 B3
Independence, Va., 679 62 C6
Independence, Wis., 954 66 B4
Independence, L., Mich. 66 F2
Independence, r., N.Y. 59 K4
Independence Mts., Nev. 83 B2
Independence Nat. Hist. Pk., Pa. 60 f12
Independenţa, Rum. 128 F2
Independenţa, Rum. 128 G3
Inderagiri, r., Indon. 148 B3
Inderborskiy, U.S.S.R., 5,400 134 E5
Index, Va. 62 G4
Index, Wash., 158 80 C2
Indi, India, 10,616 145 E6
India, ctry., 498,680,000* 144-5
Indiahoma, Okla., 378 76 E3
Indialantic, Fla., 1,653 65 J4
Indian, r., Fla. 65 J4
Indian, r., Mich. 67 G2
Indian, r., N.Y. 59 J3
Indian, r., N.Y. 59 M4
Indiana, st., U.S., 4,893,000* 70
Indiana, co., Pa., 75,366 60 D4
Indiana, Pa., 13,005 60 D4
Indiana Hbr., Ind. 69 e10
Indianapolis, Ind., 476,258 70 C3
Indian Cabins, Alta., Can. 42 H1
Indian Creek, Ill., 239 69 c8
Indian Cr., Ill. 69 c8
Indian Cr., S. Dak. 74 A3
Indian Cr., Utah 78 D2
Indian Harbour, Newf., Can. 45 P3
Indian Harbour Beach, Fla. 65 J4
Indian Head, Sask., Can., 1,721 43 D5
Indian Head, Md., 780 62 G4
Indian Head Park, Ill., 385 69 c9
Indian Hill, Ohio, 4,526 71 k10
Indian Hill, Nebr. 75 D1
Indian Hills, Colo. 79 b8
Indian House L., Qué., Can. 45 N3
Indian Lake, N.Y. 59 M4
Indian L., Mich. 67 G2
Indian L., N.Y. 59 M4
Indian L., Ohio 70 F2
Indian Lake Estates, Fla. 65 H5
Indian Mills, N.J., 60 g12
Indian Mound, Tenn. 71 D5
Indian Mtn., Wyo. 81 D4
Indian Ocean 168
Indianola, Il., 295 68 E4
Indianola, Iowa, 7,062 72 D3
Indianola, Miss., 6,714 73 E4
Indianola, Nebr., 754 75 E3
Indianola, Okla., 234 76 H2
Indianola, Pa. 60 c7
Indianola, Utah 78 c11
Indianola, Wash. 81 a7
Indian Orchard (part of Springfield), Mass. 56 F4
Indian Pk., Utah 78 B2
Indian Pd., Me. 55 C3
Indian Prairie Can., Fla. 65 H5
Indian River, co., Fla., 25,309 65 J5
Indian River, Mich. 67 J3
Indian Rocks Beach, Fla., 1,940 65 c12
Indian Springs, Ind. 70 C4
Indian Springs, Nev. 83 C4
Indian Springs, Utah 78 B1
Indian Str., N.H. 54 E1
Indiantown, Fla., 1,411 65 J5
Indian Trail, N.C., 364 63 D2
Indian Valley, Idaho 81 A3
Indian Valley, Va. 62 D6
Indian Village, Alaska 85 G2
Indian Village, Alaska 85 H2
Indian Village, Alaska 85 J2
Indian Village, Mich. 66 D2
Indian Village, N.Y. 59 r24
Indian Wells, Ariz. 78 C4
Indiga, U.S.S.R. 134 D3
Indigirka, r., U.S.S.R. 135 O2
Indija, Yug., 8,566 125 E2
Indio, Calif., 9,745 82 E6
Indio, r., Nic. 94 E5
Indispensable Str., Sol. Is. 175 c2
Indonesia, ctry., 100,045,000* 148-9
Indore, India, 394,941 145 E5
Indramaju, Indon. 148 D4
Indramaju, Udjung, Indon. 148 c7
Indrapura, Indon. 148 B3
Indravati, r., India 145 F6
Indre, r., Fr. 117 D3
Indre Söndeled, Nor. 121 B2
Indrio, Fla. 65 J5
Indus, r., Asia 145 D2
Industry, Calif., 778 83 i15
Industry, Ill., 514 68 B3
Industry, N.Y. 58 n20
Industry, Pa., 2,338 60 B4
Industry, Tex. 77 P5
İnebolu, Turk., 5,886 142 C1
İnegöl, Turk., 25,227 142 B1
In Ekker, Alg. 162 E1
Inés Indart, Arg., 4,000* 105 a12
Ineu, Rum. 128 C1
İnevi, Turk., 5,764 142 C2
Inez, Ky., 566 71 J4
Inezgane, Mor., 6,917 160 C2
In-Ezzane, Alg. 162 F2
Infanta, Phil., 3,302 153 c8
Infanta, Phil., 1,323 153 a7
Infantes, Sp., 9,909 122 D3
Ingá, Braz., 6,383 103 b14
In Gall, Niger, 1,555 162 F3
Ingalls, Ark. 73 C4
Ingalls, Ind., 873 70 D3
Ingalls, Kans., 174 75 E6
Ingalls, Mich. 66 F3
Ingalls, Mt., Calif. 82 C2
Ingalls Park, Ill. 69 b10
Ingallston, Mich. 66 F3
Ingalton, Ill. 69 b9
Ingarö, Swed. 120 f8
Ingatestone, U.K. 114 J7
Ingelfingen, F.R.Ger., 2,253 119 H6
Ingelheim, F.R.Ger., 14,831 119 E5
Ingelmunster, Belg., 9,502 115 B4
Ingende, D.R.Congo 164 C2
Ingeniero Jacobacci, Arg., 6,300* 105 B6
Ingeniero Juárez, Arg., 3,500* 105 C2
Ingeniero La Esperanza, Arg., 4,500* 105 C2
Inger, Minn. 74 E2
Ingersoll, Ont., Can., 6,774 46 D5
Ingersoll, Okla., 30 76 E1
Ingham, Austl., 3,943 173 F2
Ingham, co., Mich., 211,296 67 J6
Ingham, Nebr. 75 E3
Ingleborough, mtn., U.K. 114 D2
Inglefield, Ind. 70 B4
Ingleside, Ont., Can. 47 J4
Ingleside, Ill. 69 b7
Ingleside (part of Holyoke), Mass. 56 F4
Ingleside, Tex., 3,022 77 P6
Ingleton, U.K., 1,892 114 D2
Inglewood, Qnsld., Austl., 1,026 173 G4
Inglewood, Vict., Austl. 173 e11
Inglewood, Ont., Can. 46 c13
Inglewood, N.Z., 1,901 175 g5
Inglewood, Calif., 63,390 83 h16
Inglis, Man., Can. 43 E5
Inglis, Fla., 250 65 G3
Ingoda, r., U.S.S.R. 135 L4
Ingoe, U.K. 112 g9
Ingold, N.C. 63 F3
Ingoldmells Pt., U.K. 114 J4
Ingolf, Ont., Can. 44 C5
Ingolstadt, F.R.Ger., 46,726 118 C4
Ingomar, Mont. 81 F2
Ingonish, N.S., Can. 47 V10
Ingonish Beach, N.S., Can. 47 V10
Ingraham, Ill. 68 D5
Ingraham, L., Fla. 65 g14
Ingram, Pa., 4,730 60 b8
Ingram, Tex. 77 O4
Ingram, Va. 62 E6
Ingram, Wis., 99 66 C3
Ingrid Christensen Coast, Ant. 180 S6
In-Guezzam, Alg. 160 E4
Ingul, r., U.S.S.R. 136 D4
Ingulets, r., U.S.S.R. 136 D4
Inguri, r., U.S.S.R. 137 b1
Ingwiller, Fr., 3,074 116 e9
Inhambane, Moz., 21,992 164 E6
Inhambupe, Braz., 3,811 103 J4
Inhamitanga, Moz. 164 E5
Inharrime, Moz. 164 E6
Inhuma, Braz., 1,323 103 H3
Inhumas, Braz., 8,298 103 F5
Inicua, Bol. 102 b9
Iniesta, Sp., 4,694 122 E3
I-ning, K-hsi, China 152 C2
I-ning, Hs-ch., China 150 B2
Inirida, r., Col. 100 F6
Inishannon, Ire. 113 B6
Inishbofin, i., Ire. 113 A5
Inishcrone, Ire. 113 B4
Inishmurray, i., Ire. 113 B4
Inishowen Head, Ire. 113 C4
Inishturk, i., Ire. 113 A5
Initao, Phil., 3,258 153 C3
Injune, Austl. 173 G3
Ink, Ark. 73 A3
Inkberrow, U.K., 1,375 114 D6
Inklin, Br. Col., Can. 42 C1
Inklin, r., Br. Col., Can. 42 C1
Inkom, Idaho, 528 81 C4
Inkster, Mich., 39,097 67 e15
Inkster, N. Dak., 282 74 D1
Inland, Alta., Can. 43 c7
Inland L., Ala. 64 C2
Inland L., Alaska 85 E2
Inland Sea=Seto-naikai
Inle L., Burma 146 B2
Inlet Beach, Fla. 65 D2
Inman, Ga. 64 g11
Inman, Kans., 729 75 H5
Inman, Nebr., 192 75 G1
Inman, S.C., 1,714 63 B2
Inn, r., F.R.Ger. 118 D4
Innai, Jap. 155 G2
Innellan, U.K. 112 a8
Innerferrera, Switz. 124 D2
Inner Hebrides, i. group, U.K. 112 C3
Innerkip, Ont., Can. 46 D5
Innerleithen, U.K., 2,299 112 E4
Inner Mongolia=Nei-meng-ku Tzu-chih-ch'ü
Inner Mongolian Autonomous Region=Nei-meng-ku Tzu-chih-ch'ü
Inner Sd., U.K. 112 D3
Innerste, r., F.R.Ger. 118 C3
Innerthal, Switz. 124 C1
Innertkirchen, Switz., 1,230 124 C2
Innfield, Ire. 113 C5
Innisfail, Austl., 6,649 173 G2
Innisfail, Alta., Can., 2,233 42 K3
Innisfree, Alta., Can. 42 K3
Innoko, r., Alaska 85 E3
Innoshima, Jap., 41,502 154 e15
Innsbruck, Aust., 100,699 124 H6
Ino, Jap., 21,846 155 C5
Inō, Jap. 155 n19
Ino, Wis. 66 B2
Inocência, Braz. 103 F5
Inola, Okla., 584 76 H1
Inongo, D.R.Congo 164 C2
Inoue, Jap. 155 n18
Inowrocław, Pol., 47,000* 127 C2
Inquisivi, Bol. 102 b10
Ins, Switz., 2,486 124 B1
Insar, U.S.S.R., 5,800 136 G2
Insar, r., U.S.S.R. 136 G2
Insch, U.K. 112 E3
Inscription, C., Austl. 172 A3
Inscription Rock, mtn., N. Mex. 79 A4
Insein, Burma, 27,030 147 a2
Insiza, Rhod. 164 D5
Ińsko, Pol., 1,499 127 A2
Insming, Fr. 116 c9
Inspiration, Ariz. 78 C5
Institute, Wis. 66 F4
Insu, Ghana 162 c9
Insula L., Minn. 74 G2
Inta, U.S.S.R., 45,000 134 F3
Intagaw, Burma, 2,234 147 b2
Intendente Alvear, Arg., 3,200* 105 C5
Intercession City, Fla. 65 H4
Intercourse, Pa. 61 K5
Interior, S. Dak., 179 74 A4
Interior Lowlands, Can.-U.S. 51 G1
Interlachen, Fla., 349 65 H3
Interlaken, Switz., 4,738 124 B2
Interlaken (part of Stockbridge), Mass. 56 C3
Interlaken, N.J., 1,168 58 c16
Interlaken, N.Y., 780 59 G6
Interlochen, Mich. 67 H4
Intermediate Hill, Lord Howe I. 175 12
International Falls, Minn., 6,778 74 F1
International Peace Pk., Can.-U.S. 42 K4
Intervale, N.H. 54 E3
Interview I., India 146 A4
Inthanon, Doi, pk., Thai. 146 B3
Întorsura Buzăului, Rum. 128 F2
Intracoastal City, La. 73 C8
Intracoastal Waterway, Fla. 65 b9
Intu, Indon. 148 E3
Intutu, Peru 104 C2
Inubō-saki, Jap. 155 G4
Inukai, Jap., 10,005 154 B5
Inuvik, N.W.T., Can. 40 C4
Inuyama, Jap., 38,202 154 h14
In'va, r., U.S.S.R. 137 h7
Inveralocky, Austl. 173 g10
Inveraray, U.K. 112 D3
Inverbervie, U.K. 112 E3
Invercargill, N.Z., 35,605 175 f7
Inverell, Austl., 7,514 173 G4
Invergeldie, U.K. 112 b7
Invergordon, U.K., 1,640 112 D3
Inver Grove, Minn., 713 74 c6
Inverkeithing, U.K., 4,069 112 d7
Inverkip, U.K. 112 a8
Inverloch, Austl. 173 e12
Invermay, Sask., Can. 43 D4
Invermere, Br. Col., Can. 42 J4
Inverness, N.S., Can., 2,066 45 O6
Inverness, co., U.K., 83,425 112 D3
Inverness, U.K., 29,773 112 D3
Inverness, Ala. 64 D3
Inverness, Calif. 82 B3
Inverness, Fla., 1,878 65 G4
Inverness, Ill. 69 b8
Inverness, Miss., 1,039 73 E4
Inverurie, U.K., 5,152 112 E3
Investigator Group, is., Austl. 172 D5
Investigator Str., Austl. 172 E5
Inwood, Man., Can. 43 g9
Inwood, Ont., Can. 46 B6
Inwood, Iowa, 638 72 A1
Inwood, N.Y., 10,362 58 d14
Inwood, W. Va. 62 F3
Inya, U.S.S.R. 135 O4
Inya, r., U.S.S.R. 137 r11
Inyanga, Rhod. 164 E5
Inyangani, pk., Rhod. 164 E5
Inyo, co., Calif., 11,684 82 E4
Inyokern, Calif. 82 E5
Inyo Mts., Calif. 82 •
Inza, U.S.S.R., 18,600 136 G2
Inzer, r., U.S.S.R. 137 h8
Inzersdorf, Aust. 124 b10
Inzhavino, U.S.S.R. 136 F2
Inzovo, Bulg., 2,671 128 F3
Iō, Jap. 154 e15
Ioánnina, Gr., 34,997 129 C5
Ioco, Br. Col., Can. 42 d6
Iō-jima, Jap. 154 k17
Iō-jima, Vol. Is. 170 D3
Iola, Colo. 79 B2
Iola, Ill., 155 68 D5
Iola, Kans., 6,885 75 K6
Iola, Wis., 831 66 D4
Iolanda di Savoia, It., 8,203 122 f6
Iolotan', U.S.S.R., 9,000 134 F6
Ioma, Terr. Papua 174 e3
Iona, N.S., Can. 47 V11
Iona, Idaho, 702 81 D4
Iona, Ind. 70 B4
Iona, Minn., 328 74 E4
Iona, S. Dak. 74 C4
Iona, i., U.K. 112 C3
Iona Island, Newf., Can. 45 a10

240 · Ion Corvin—Jais

Ion Corvin, Rum. 128 F2
Ione, Calif., 1,118 82 C3
Ione, Colo. 79 c7
Ione, Oreg., 350 80 D3
Ione, Wash., 648 80 E1
Ioneşti, Rum. 128 E2
Ionia, Kans. 75 G4
Ionia, co., Mich., 43,132 67 H5
Ionia, Mich., 6,754 67 H6
Ionia, Mo., 114 72 D6
Ionia, N.Y. 58 n21
Ionian Is. = Iònioi Nisoi
Ionian Sea, Eur. 110 E5
Iònioi Nisoi, is., Gr. 129 B5
Iony, O., U.S.S.R. 135 O4
Iori, r., U.S.S.R. 137 c1
Íos, Gr., 1,231 129 E6
Íos, i., Gr. 129 E6
Iosco, co., Mich., 16,505 67 K4
Iosepa, Utah 78 B1
Iota, La., 1,245 73 C7
Iowa, st., U.S., 2,758,000* 72
Iowa, co., Iowa, 16,396 72 E3
Iowa, La., 1,857 73 B7
Iowa, co., Wis., 19,631 66 C5
Iowa, r., Iowa 72 E3
Iowa City, Iowa, 33,443 72 F3
Iowa Falls, Iowa, 5,565 72 D2
Iowa Park, Tex., 3,295 77 O3
Ipala, Guat., 2,942 94 C3
Ipameri, Braz., 8,987 103 G5
Ipanema, Braz., 4,572 103 f17
Ipapure, Col. 100 E2
Iparía, Peru 104 C4
Ipáti, Gr. 129 D5
Ipatovo, U.S.S.R. 136 F4
Ipava, Ill., 623 68 B3
Ipel, r., Czech.-Hung. 126 D3
Ipiales, Col. 100 B7
Ipiaú, Braz., 13,164 103 J4
Ipil, Phil., 3,473 153 B4
I-pin, China, 150,000* 150 D4
Ipiros, reg., Gr. 129 C5
Ipixuna, r., Braz. 102 D3
Ipnot, Alaska 85 C1
Ipoh, Malay., 125,776 148 B1
Ipojuca, r., Braz. 103 b15
Iporá, Braz., 4,120 103 F5
Ippy, C.A.R., 9,077 163 H4
Ipstones, U.K., 1,634 114 E4
Ipswich, Austl., 38,953 173 H4
Ipswich, U.K., 117,395 113 G5
Ipswich, Mass., 4,617; 8,544(T) 57 N2
Ipswich, S. Dak., 1,131 74 C3
Ipswich, r., Mass. 57 M2
Ipswich Bay, Mass. 57 O2
Ipu, Braz., 7,724 103 H2
Ipuh, Indon. 148 B3
Iput', r., U.S.S.R. 136 D2
Iquique, Chile, 50,655 105 A2
Iquitos, Peru, 55,696 104 C2
Ira, Vt. 54 A4
Iraan, Tex., 1,255 77 N4
Iracoubo, Fr. Guiana 101 O5
Irago, Jap. 154 h15
Irago-suidō, Jap. 154 h15
Iraí, Braz., 4,351 103 F7
Iràklia, i., Gr. 129 E6
Iráklion, Gr., 63,458 129 E7
Iramba, Tanz. 165 f14
Iran, ctry., 23,428,000* 143 D2
Iranian Plat., Asia 140 D3
Īrānshahr, Iran, 3,618 143 G3
Iraola, Arg., 1,613 105 b13
Irapa, Ven., 4,517 101 J2
Irapuato, Mex., 83,505 92 E4
Irapuato, r., Mex. 93 c9
Iraq, ctry., 8,261,527 143 C2
Irasburg, Vt. 54 C2
Irasville, Vt. 54 B3
Irati, Braz., 12,764 103 F7
Irawan, Phil., 3,163 153 A3
Irazú, Vol., C.R. 94 F5
Irazusta, Arg., 1,800* 105 b11
Irbid, Jor., 44,688 142 C3
Irbīl, Iraq, 34,751 143 C1
Irbit, U.S.S.R., 45,000 134 F4
Irebu, D.R.Congo 164 B2
Irecê, Braz., 3,855 103 H4
Iredell, co., N.C., 62,526 63 D2
Iredell, Tex., 366 77 P3
Ireland, ctry., 2,880,752 113
Ireland I., Berm. Is. 108 1
Ireland Pt., Berm. Is. 108 1
Iremel', G., U.S.S.R. 137 i8
Iren', r., U.S.S.R. 137 h7
Irendyk, Khr., U.S.S.R. 137 i9
Irene, S. Af., 1,259 165 k16
Irene, S. Dak., 399 74 D4
Ireng, r., Braz.-Guyana 101 L5
Ireton, Iowa, 510 72 A2
Irgiz, U.S.S.R. 134 F5
Irgiz, r., U.S.S.R. 137 k10
Iri, S. Kor., 65,726 151 E4
Irian Barat, reg., Indon. 149 K3
Irig, Yug., 4,211 125 D2
Iriga, Phil., 27,469 153 B2
Irigny, Fr., 3,368 116 p15
Iriklinskiy, U.S.S.R. 137 i9
Iriklinskoye Vdkhr., U.S.S.R. 137 i9
Iringa, Tanz., 9,587 164 E3
Irinjalakuda, India, 22,335 145 k20
Iriomote-jima, Ryukyu Is. 154 c13
Irion, co., Tex., 1,183 77 N4
Iriona, Hond., 3,785 94 E3
Iriri, r., Braz. 103 F2
Irish, Mt., Nev. 83 C4
Irish Sea, Ire.-U.K. 113 D5
Irkutsk, U.S.S.R., 380,000 135 K4
Irlam, U.K., 15,365 114 D4
Irma, Alta., Can. 42 K3
Irma, Wis. 66 D3
Irmino, U.S.S.R., 22,900 136 f7
Irmo, S.C., 359 63 C3
Iron, co., Mich., 17,184 66 E2
Iron, co., Mo., 8,041 72 G7
Iron, co., Utah, 10,795 78 B3
Iron, co., Wis., 7,830 66 C2
Iron, r., Mich. 66 D2
Iron, r., Wis. 66 B2
Iron Belt, Wis. 66 C2
Iron Bridge, Ont., Can. 46 A2
Ironbridge, U.K., 1,806 114 C5
Iron City, Ga., 298 64 E4
Iron City, Tenn. 71 D6
Irondale, Ala., 3,501 64 d7
Irondale, Colo. 79 c8
Irondale, Ohio, 705 70 J2
Irondale, Wash. 81 a6
Irondequoit, r., N.Y. 58 n20
Irondequoit Bay, N.Y. 58 n20
Iron Gate, Va., 716 62 E5
Iron Gate, gorge, Rum.-Yug. 128 D2
Iron Knob, Austl. 172 E5
Iron Mountain, Mich., 9,299 66 E3
Iron Mountain, Mo. 72 G7
Iron Ridge, Wis., 419 66 E5
Iron River, Mich., 3,754 66 E2
Iron River, Wis. 66 B2
Irons, Mich. 67 H4
Ironside, Oreg. 80 E3
Iron Springs, Utah 78 B3
Ironton, Mich. 67 H3
Ironton, Minn., 724 74 E2
Ironton, Mo., 1,310 72 G7
Ironton, Ohio, 15,745 70 G4
Ironton, Wis., 167 66 C5
Ironwood, Mich., 10,265 66 C2
Iroquois, Ont., Can., 1,027 47 J4
Iroquois, co., Ill., 33,562 68 E3
Iroquois, Ill., 231 68 E3
Iroquois, S. Dak., 385 74 D3
Iroquois, r., Ill.-Ind. 70 B2
Iroquois Dam and Lock, N.Y. 69 C
Iroquois Falls, Ont., Can., 1,657 44 H5
Irō-saki, Jap. 155 F4
Irpen', U.S.S.R., 18,700 136 C3
Irrawaddy, r., Burma 146 A3
Irrawaddy Delta, Burma 147 •
Irrel, F.R.Ger. 119 A5
Irrigon, Oreg., 232 80 D3
Irsch, F.R.Ger., 1,293 119 B5
Irshava, U.S.S.R., 4,800 136 A3
Irsta, Swed. 120 d8
Irt, r., U.K. 114 B2
Irthlingborough, U.K., 5,125 114 G6
Irtyash, Oz., U.S.S.R. 137 k8
Irtysh, U.S.S.R. 137 o11
Irtysh, r., U.S.S.R. 134 G4
Irumagawa, Jap. 155 m19
Irumu, D.R.Congo 164 D1
Irún, Sp., 29,814 122 E1
Irurzun, Sp. 122 o12
Irvine, Alta., Can. 42 L4
Irvine, U.K., 16,910 112 D4
Irvine, Calif. 83 i16
Irvine, Ky., 2,955 71 H4
Irvine, Pa. 60 D2
Irvine, r., U.K. 112 a8
Irvine L. = Santiago Res.
Irvinestown, U.K. 113 C4
Irving, Ill., 570 68 C4
Irving, N.Y. 58 B6
Irving, Tex., 45,985 77 P3
Irvington, Ala. 64 A5
Irvington, Ill., 387 68 C5
Irvington, Ky., 1,190 71 E4
Irvington, N.J., 59,379 61 C2
Irvington, N.Y., 5,494 58 d12
Irvington, Va., 570 62 H5
Irvona, Pa., 781 60 E4
Irwin, co., Ga., 9,211 64 F4
Irwin, Idaho, 330 81 D4
Irwin, Ill., 92 68 E2
Irwin, Iowa, 425 72 B3
Irwin, Nebr. 75 D1
Irwin, Pa., 4,270 60 C5
Irwinton, Ga., 673 64 F3
Irwinville, Ga. 64 F4
Is, U.S.S.R. 137 i7
Isa, Nigeria, 12,636 162 F3
Isaac's Harbour, N.S., Can. 47 V11
Isabel, Phil., 4,715 153 f11
Isabel, Kans., 181 75 G6
Isabel, S. Dak., 488 74 B3
Isabel, B., Colòn, Arch. de 104 a8
Isabela, P.R., 7,302 96 r10
Isabela, Phil., 11,715 153 B4
Isabela, Phil., 6,052 153 f11
Isabela, B., Dom. Rep. 96 m6
Isabela, C., Dom. Rep. 96 m6
Isabela, Can., Colòn, Arch. de 104 a8
Isabela, I., Colón, Arch. de 104 a8
Isabella, co., Mich., 35,348 67 J5
Isabella, Mich. 67 G3
Isabella, Minn. 74 G2
Isabella, Okla. 76 E1
Isabella, Pa. 60 B6
Isabella, Tenn. 71 G6
Isabella, Cord., Nic. 94 E4
Isabella Bay, N.W.T., Can. 41 Q4
Isabella Res., Calif. 82 D5
Isabelle, Pt., Mich. 66 F1
Isabel Segunda, P.R., 2,487 96 v10
Isábena, r., Sp. 122 F1
Isaccea, Rum., 5,203 128 G2
Isachsen, N.W.T., Can. 41 J2
Ísafjördhur, Ice., 2,685 120 a6
Isahaya, Jap., 64,506 154 B5
Işalniţa, Rum. 128 D2
Isangi, D.R.Congo 164 C1
Isango-Isoro, Congo L. 165 d14
Isanlu Makutu, Nigeria 162 f7
Isanti, co., Minn., 13,530 74 F3
Isanti, Minn., 521 74 F3
Isar, r., F.R.Ger. 118 C4
Isarog, Mt., Phil. 153 h14
Iscar, Sp., 5,133 122 C2
Ischia, It., 12,136 123 c10
Ischia, Isola d', It., 132 D4
Ischua, N.Y. 58 D7
Ischua Cr., N.Y. 58 D7
Iscia Baidoa, Som. Rep., 17,960* 163 M5
Iscuandé, Col. 100 B6
Ise, Jap., 99,026 155 E4
Isefjord, bays, Den. 121 D5
Isehara, Jap., 26,984 155 m20
Iseji, Jap. 154 h15
Iseki, Jap. 154 e15
Iselin, Pa., 60 D4
Isenach, r., F.R.Ger. 119 E6
Isérables, Switz., 1,157 124 B2
Isère, r., Fr. 117 F4
Iserlohn, F.R.Ger., 50,912 118 A3
Isernia, It., 13,071 123 E4
Isesaki, Jap., 84,250 155 F3
Ise-Shima-ktk., Jap. 155 E4
Iset', r., U.S.S.R. 134 F4
Ise-wan, Jap. 155 E4
Iseyin, Nigeria, 57,629 162 e8
Isfahan = Eşfahān
Isfara, U.S.S.R., 13,600 137 f4
Isfjorden, Nor. 134 A2
İshaklı, Turk., 5,001 142 B2
I-shan, China 150 E4
Isherton, Guyana 101 L6
Ishibe, Jap., 4,491 154 h14
Ishidoriya, Jap., 17,021 155 G2
Ishigaki, Ryukyu Is., 40,632 154 c13
Ishigaki-shima, Ryukyu Is. 154 c13
Ishiji, Jap., 2,967 155 F3
Ishikari, Jap., 10,129 155 J8
Ishikari, r., Jap. 155 K8
Ishikari-wan, Jap. 155 J8
Ishikawa, Jap., 25,117 155 G3
Ishiki, Jap., 23,842 154 i15
Ishim, U.S.S.R., 47,800 134 F4
Ishim, r., U.S.S.R. 134 F4
I-shima, Jap. 154 f16
Ishimbay, U.S.S.R., 46,600 137 h9
Ishimskaya Step', U.S.S.R. 137 n11
Ishinomaki, Jap., 83,947 155 G2
Ishinomaki-wan, Jap. 155 G2
Ishioka, Jap., 34,758 155 G3
Ishiwara, Jap. 154 g14
Ishizuchi-zan, mtn., Jap. 155 C5
Ishkooda, Ala. 64 c8
Ishøj, Den., 1,726 121 a7
Ishpeming, Mich., 8,857 66 F2
Ishuatán, El Salv., 1,351 94 d10
I-shui, China 151 C4
Ishurdi, Pak., 11,566 144 g13
Isiboro, r., Bol. 102 c10
Isigny-sur-Mer, Fr., 3,267 117 C2
Isil'-Kul', U.S.S.R., 23,100 134 G4
Isinliví, Ec. 104 c10
Isiolo, Kenya 164 F1
Isisford, Austl. 173 F3
Isit', U.S.S.R. 135 M3
İskenderun, Turk., 63,736 142 D2
İskenderun Körfezi, Turk. 142 C2
Iski-Angor, Kan., U.S.S.R. 137 e4
İskilip, Turk., 12,285 142 C1
Iskitim, U.S.S.R., 34,300 134 H4
Iskra, Bulg., 4,161 128 E4
Iskrets, Bulg., 2,664 128 D3
Iskŭr, r., Bulg. 128 D3
Iskut, r., Br. Col., Can. 42 D2
Isla de Maipo, Chile, 2,981 104 f13
Islâhiye, Turk., 11,975 142 D2
Islāmābād, Pak. 145 D2
Islamorada, Fla. 65 h15
Island, Ky., 462 71 D4
Island, co., Wash., 19,638 80 B1
Island Beach, N.J. 61 C4
Island City, Oreg., 158 80 D3
Island Falls, Ont., Can. 44 G5
Island Falls, Sask., Can. 43 D3
Island Falls, Me. 55 D2
Island Harbour, Anguilla 97 7
Island Heights, N.J., 1,150 61 C4
Island Lake, Ill., 1,639 68 D1
Island L., Wis. 66 B3
Island L., Wis. 66 C2
Island L., Man., Can. 43 G4
Island L., Minn. 74 E2
Island Park, Idaho, 53 81 D3
Island Park, N.Y., 3,846 58 e14
Island Park, R.I., 1,147 57 L6
Island Park Res., Idaho 81 D3
Island Pond, Vt., 1,319 54 D2
Island Pd., N.H. 54 E6
Islandton, S.C. 63 C4
Islay, i., U.K. 112 C4
Isle, Minn., 529 74 F2
Isle, r., Fr. 117 D4
Isle au Haut, Me. 55 D4
Isle aux Morts, Newf., Can. 45 P6
Isleham, U.K., 1,392 114 J6
Isle La Motte, Vt. 54 A2
Isle of Man, U.K., 55,253 113 D4
Isle of Palms, S.C., 1,186 63 E5
Isle of Wight, co., Va., 17,164 62 H6
Isle of Wight, Va. 62 H6
Isle Pierre, Br. Col., Can. 42 F3
Isle Royale, Mich. 66 b8
Isle Royale Nat. Pk., Mich. 66 a9
Islesboro, Me. 55 D4
Isles Lagoon, The, Christmas Atoll 177 40
Isleton, Calif., 1,039 82 C3
Islington (part of Westwood), Mass. 57 M4
Islip, N.Y. 59 O10
Islip Terrace, N.Y. 58 g14
Ismalia = Al Ismā'īlīyah
Ismaning, F.R.Ger., 5,288 118 C4
Ismay, Mont., 59 81 G2
İsmetpaşa, Turk., 6,315 142 D2
Isnā, U.A.R., 7,764 161 K3
Isney, Ala. 64 A4
Isny, F.R.Ger., 6,018 118 B5
Isojoki, Fin. 120 E3
Isoka, Zamb. 164 E3
Isola, Miss., 532 73 E4
Isola della Scala, It., 10,363 122 d5
Isone, Switz. 124 C2
Isparta, Turk., 36,201 142 B2
Isperikh, Bulg., 6,759 128 F3
İspir, Turk., 2,015 142 E1
Israel, ctry., 2,636,000* 142 C4
Israel, r., N.H. 54 D3
Issano, Guyana 101 L5
Issaquah, Wash., 1,870 81 b7
Issaquena, co., Miss., 3,576 73 E5
Isselburg, F.R.Ger., 2,523 119 A1
Isseneru, Guyana 101 K4
Issia, Iv. Coast, 2,060 162 C4
Issoire, Fr., 11,628 117 E4
Issoudun, Qué., Can. 47 N2
Issoudun, Fr., 14,483 117 D3
Issum, F.R.Ger., 4,617 119 A1
Is-sur-Tille, Fr., 2,568 117 F3
Issyk-Kul', Oz., U.S.S.R. 134 G5
Issy-les-Moulineaux, Fr., 53,298 116 h11
Ist, i., Yug. 125 B2
İstanbul, Turk., 1,493,910 142 B1
İstanbul Boğazı, Turk. 142 B1
Istiaia, Gr., 3,882 129 D5
Istmina, Col. 100 B5
Istmo de Ofqui, Chile 105 A7
Istokpoga, L., Fla. 65 H5
Istra, U.S.S.R., 5,900 136 b6
Istra, pen., Yug. 125 A2
Istra, r., U.S.S.R. 136 b6
Istres, Fr., 10,526 117 F5
Istria, Rum. 128 G2
Istria = Istra
Istrinskoye Vdkhr., U.S.S.R. 136 b5
Isuisu, Terr. Papua 174 3
Isurugi, Jap., 26,679 155 E3
Isyangulovo, U.S.S.R. 137 h9
Itabaiana, Paraíba, Braz., 11,847 103 b14
Itabaiana, Sgpe., Braz., 11,050 103 J4
Itabapoana, Braz., 1,529 103 f17
Itabapoana, r., Braz. 103 f17
Itaberaba, Braz., 8,555 103 H4
Itabira, Braz., 15,539 103 H5
Itabirito, Braz., 10,511 103 e17
Itabuna, Braz., 54,268 103 H4
Itacaiunas, r., Braz. 103 F3
Itacoai, r., Braz. 102 B3
Itacoatiara, Braz., 8,818 102 E2
Itaguaí, Braz., 4,396 103 e18
Itaguara, Braz., 2,466 103 d17
Itagüí, Col. 101 d13
Itaim, r., Braz. 103 d18
Itaituba, Braz., 1,187 103 E2
Itajaí, Braz., 38,889 103 G7
Itajubá, Braz., 31,262 103 G6
Itaka, U.S.S.R. 135 L4
Itakura, Jap. 154 e15
Itala = Atalèh
Italia, Mte., Chile 105 •
Italva, Braz., 3,191 103 f17
Italy, ctry., 51,784,000* 123
Italy, Tex., 1,183 77 P3
Itamaraté, Braz. 103 G2
Itambacuri, Braz., 5,478 103 H5
Itambé, Braz., 7,361 103 H5
Itami, Jap., 86,455 154 g15
Itanhém, Braz., 4,250 103 H5
Itani, Jap. 154 g15
Itaocara, Braz., 2,073 103 e17
Itapaci, Braz., 2,625 103 G4
Itapebi, Braz., 2,596 103 J5
Itapecuru, r., Braz. 103 H3
Itapecuru-Mirim, Braz., 3,385 103 H2
Itaperuna, Braz., 18,095 103 f17
Itapetinga, Braz., 17,646 103 H5
Itapetininga, Braz., 29,468 103 G6
Itapeva, Braz., 13,510 103 G6
Itapicuru, r., Braz. 103 J4
Itapipoca, Braz., 7,186 103 J2
Itapira, Braz., 16,859 103 c18
Itapiúna, Braz., 1,307 103 J2
Itaporã, Goiás, Braz. 103 G3
Itaporã, Mo. Gro., Braz., 2,422 103 F6
Itaporanga, Braz., 5,328 103 J3
Itaqui, Braz., 13,223 103 E7
Itarsi, India, 33,611 145 E5
Itasca, Ill., 3,564 69 c9
Itasca, co., Minn., 38,006 74 F2
Itasca, Tex., 1,383 77 P3
Itasca, L., Minn. 74 E2
Itata, r., Chile 104 e16
Itatiba, Braz., 12,336 103 c18
Itatuba, Braz., 2,255 103 b14
Itatupã, Braz. 103 F2
Itaúna, Braz., 22,319 103 H5
Itawamba, co., Miss., 15,080 73 G3
Itaya, Jap. 154 g16
Itaya, Jap. 154 h15
Itbayat I., Phil. 153 g13
Itchen, r., U.K. 113 k12
Itchū, Jap. 154 e16
Ite, Peru 104 D6
Iténez = Guaporé
Ithaca, Mich., 2,611 67 J5
Ithaca, N.Y., 28,799 59 G7
Ithaca, Wis. 66 C5
Ithaca, Gr. = Ithàki
Itháki, Gr., 2,632 129 C5
Itháki, i., Gr. 129 C5
Itigi, Tanz. 164 E2
Itimbiri, r., D.R.Congo 164 C1
Itiquira, Braz. 103 F5
Itiquira, r., Braz. 103 E5
Itkillik, r., Alaska 85 G1
Itō, Jap. 154 f14
Itō, Jap., 54,564 155 F4
Itogon, Phil., 7,466 153 b6
Itoigawa, Jap., 41,910 155 E3
Itoman, Ryukyu Is., 35,049 154 a11
Itonamas, r., Bol. 102 D4
Itoshiro, Jap. 154 h14
Itsukaichi, Jap., 15,094 155 m19
Itta Bena, Miss., 1,914 73 E4
Ittiri, It., 9,256 123 B4
Itu, Braz., 23,435 103 c18
I-tu, Hu-p., China 152 C1
I-tu, Shant., China 151 C3
Ituango, Col. 100 C4
Ituberá, Braz., 4,097 103 J4
Itui, r., Braz. 102 B3
Ituiutaba, Braz., 29,724 103 F5
Itumbiara, Braz., 12,575 103 F5
Itumirim, Braz., 1,525 103 d17
Ituna, Sask., Can. 43 D4
I-t'ung, China 151 E2
I-t'ung, r., China 151 E1
Ituni Township, Guyana 101 L5
Itupiranga, Braz., 1,098 103 F3
Ituri, r., D.R.Congo 164 D1
Iturup, O., U.S.S.R. 135 O5
Ituxi, r., Braz. 102 C3
Itzehoe, F.R.Ger., 34,257 118 B2
Itztacoyotla, Mex., 1,181 93 f9
Iuka, Ill., 378 68 D5
Iuka, Kans., 225 75 G6
Iuka, Ky. 71 C4
Iuka, Miss., 2,010 73 G3
Iul'tin, U.S.S.R. 135 S3
Iúna, Braz., 1,951 103 f17
Iva, S.C., 1,357 63 B3
Ivaí, r., Braz. 103 F6
Ivalo, Fin. 120 F1
Ivalojoki, r., Fin. 120 F1
Ivan, Ark. 73 C4
Ivan-Gorod, U.S.S.R., 14,500 136 C1
Ivangrad, Yug., 4,513 125 D3
Ivanhoe, N.S.W., Austl. 173 F5
Ivanhoe, W. Austl. Austl. 172 D2
Ivanhoe, Ill. 69 b7
Ivanhoe, Minn., 719 74 D3
Ivanhoe, N.C. 63 F3
Ivanhoe, r., Ont., Can. 44 G5
Ivanishchi, U.S.S.R. 136 d6
Ivanjica, Yug. 125 E3
Ivanjska, Yug., 4,598 125 C2
Ivano-Frankovsk, U.S.S.R., 72,000 134 B5
Ivanovka, U.S.S.R. 151 F1
Ivanovo, U.S.S.R., 352,000 134 C4
Ivanski, Bulg., 2,943 128 F3
Ivatsevichi, U.S.S.R., 5,000 136 B2
Ivaylovgrad, Bulg., 2,907 129 E4
Ivdel', U.S.S.R., 22,000 134 F3
Iveland, Nor. 121 A2
Ivesdale, Ill., 360 68 D4
Ives Grove, Wis. 66 d13
Iveşti, Rum. 128 F2
Ivigtut, Greenl. 34 H3
Ivindo, r., Gabon 164 B1
Ivinghoe, U.K. 114 G7
Ivisan, Phil., 1,789 153 B3
Ivishak, r., Alaska 85 H1
Ivón, Bol., 1,047 102 C4
Ivor, Va., 398 62 H6
Ivory Coast, ctry., 3,750,000* 162 C4
Ivoryton (part of Essex), Conn. 56 G7
Ivrea, It., 21,379 123 A2
Ivry-sur-Seine, Fr., 53,646 116 h11
Ivugivik, Qué., Can. 44 J1
Ivydale, W. Va. 62 C4
Ivy Depot, Va. 62 F4
Ivyland, Pa., 425 60 f11
Ivyton, Ky. 71 J4
Ivywild, Colo., 11,065 79 C2
Iwa, i., Terr. Papua 174 3
Iwada, Jap. 155 n20
Iwade, Jap., 4,479 154 g15
Iwadeyama, Jap., 21,995 155 G2
Iwagawa, Jap. 154 B6
Iwai, Jap., 35,154 155 F3
Iwaizumi, Jap., 7,371 155 G2
Iwaki, Jap., 58,080 155 G3
Iwaki-yama, Jap. 155 G1
Iwakuni, Jap., 100,346 154 B4
Iwamizawa, Jap., 60,650 155 J8
Iwamurada, Jap. 155 F3
Iwanai, Jap., 25,093 155 J8
Iwanuma, Jap., 26,452 155 G2
Iwasaki, Jap., 7,030 155 G1
Iwase, Jap. 154 i14
Iwata, Jap., 57,380 155 E4
Iwataki, Jap., 6,022 154 g14
Iwate-yama, Jap. 155 G2
Iwatsuki, Jap., 35,169 155 m19
Iwawaki, Jap. 154 f16
Iwaya, Jap. 154 g15
Iwiny, Pol. 127 e5
Iwo, Nigeria, 116,007 162 E4
Iwo-jima = Iō-jima
I-wu, Ch-ch., China 152 E1
I-wu, Hs-ch., China 150 C2
Iwuy, Fr., 3,579 116 a7
Ixcatlán, Mex., 1,681 93 f8
Ixelles, Belg., 93,930 115 d9
Ixhuatlán, Mex., 1,317 93 f9
Ixiamas, Bol. 102 C4
Ixmiquilpan, Mex., 1,739 93 e9
Ixonia, Wis. 66 E5
Ixtacihuatl, mtn., Mex. 93 f10
Ixtapa, Mex. 92 D4
Ixtapan, r., Mex. 93 d11
Ixtapan de la Sal, Mex., 3,578 93 E4
Ixtenco, Mex., 5,666 93 f10
Ixtepec, Mex., 12,083 93 G5
Ixtlahuaca, Mex., 1,550 93 e10
Ixtlahuacán, Mex., 1,187 92 E4
Ixtlahuacán, r., Mex. 93 a9
Ixtlahuacán del Río, Mex., 1,125 93 a9
Ixtlán, Mex., 5,150 93 b9
Ixtlán de Juárez, Mex., 1,108 93 F5
Ixtlán del Río, Mex., 8,282 92 D4
I-yang, Ch-hsi, China 150 F4
I-yang, Ho-n., China 151 A4
I-yang, Ho-n., China 151 B4
I-yang, Hu-n., China 150 E4
Iyo, Jap., 30,047 155 C5
Iyo-Mishima, Jap., 39,947 155 C4
Iyo-nada, Jap. 154 C5
Iž, i., Yug. 125 B2
Izabal, L. de, Guat. 94 C3
Izaku, Jap. 154 B6
Izalco, El Salv., 9,150 94 d10
Izalco, Vol. de, El Salv. 94 d10
Izamal, Mex., 8,675 93 H4
Izard, co., Ark., 6,766 73 D1
Izari, Jap. 154 f16
Izberbash, U.S.S.R., 11,000 137 d1
Izbica, Pol. 127 E3
Izbica Kujawska, Pol., 3,269 127 C2
Izegem, Belg., 17,089 115 B4
Izena-shima, Ryukyu Is. 154 b10
Izhevsk, U.S.S.R., 312,000 134 E4
Izhma, U.S.S.R. 134 E3
Izmail, U.S.S.R., 52,000 134 B5
İzmir, Turk., 301,434 142 A2
İzmir Körfezi, Turk. 142 A2
İzmit, Turk., 73,705 142 B1
Iznalloz, Sp., 7,964 122 D4
İznik, Turk., 6,304 142 B1
İznik Gölü, Turk. 142 B1
Iznoski, U.S.S.R. 136 a6
Izola, Yug., 6,008 125 A2
Izozog, Bañados de, Bol. 102 D5
Izra', Syr., 2,728 142 c7
Izsák, Hung., 8,613 126 D3
Iztapa, Guat. 94 c10
Izu-hantō, Jap. 155 F4
Izuhara, Jap., 23,472 154 A4
Izuhara, Jap. 154 f16
Izumi, Jap., 45,241 154 B5
Izumi, Jap. 155 n19
Izumi-Ōtsu, Jap., 42,304 154 g15
Izumi-Sano, Jap., 56,827 155 D4
Izumo, Jap., 69,219 155 C4
Izumozaki, Jap., 5,756 155 F3
Izumrud, U.S.S.R. 137 k7
Izushi, Jap., 5,262 155 D4
Izu-shichitō, is., Jap. 155 F4
Izvestiy Tsik, O., U.S.S.R. 135 H2
Izvoru, Rum. 128 E2
Izyaslav, U.S.S.R., 11,500 136 B3
Izyum, U.S.S.R., 36,600 134 C5

J

Jabal, Bahr al, Sudan 163 K4
Jabal al Awliyā', Sudan 163 K3
Jabalón, r., Sp. 122 D3
Jabalpur, India, 295,375 145 F5
Jabal Shammar, reg., Saudi Ar. 143 C3
Jabal-us-Sirāj, Afghan. 144 C2
Jabeso, Ghana 162 b8
Jabinyānah, Tun., 3,871 160 g6
Jabish Bk., Mass. 56 G3
Jabjabah, Wādī, Sudan-U.A.R. 163 K2
Jablah, Syr., 13,866 142 D3
Jablanac, Yug. 125 B2
Jablanica, Yug., 2,196 125 C3
Jablanica, mts., Alb. 125 E4
Jablanica, r., Yug. 125 E3
Jablonec nad Nisou, Czech., 27,533 126 B1
Jablonné nad Orlicí, Czech. 127 f6
Jablonné v Podještědí, Czech. 126 d6
Jabłonowo, Pol., 3,345 127 C2
Jaboatão, Braz., 33,963 103 b15
Jaboticabal, Braz., 20,231 103 G6
Jabuka, B.-H., Yug. 125 D3
Jabuka, Srba., Yug. 125 E2
Jabukovac, Yug., 4,592 125 F2
Jabwor, Jaluit 176 30
Jabwot, i., Marsh. Is. 176 22
Jaca, Sp., 9,856 122 E1
Jacala, Mex., 1,612 93 F4
Jacaltenango, Guat., 4,172 94 B3
Jacaré, r., Braz. 103 d17
Jacareí, Braz., 28,131 103 d18
Jacarèzinho, Braz., 14,813 103 G6
Jáchal, Arg. 105 B4
Jáchymov, Czech. 126 A1
Jacinto City, Tex., 9,547 77 i9
Jaci Paraná, Braz. 102 D3
Jack, co., Tex., 7,418 77 O3
Jack Creek, Nev. 83 B2
Jackfish, Ont., Can. 44 F5
Jackfish, r., Alta., Can. 42 K1
Jackfish River, Alta., Can. 42 K1
Jackman Station, Me. 55 B3
Jack Mtn., Wash. 80 C1
Jackpot, Nev. 83 C2
Jacksboro, Tenn. 71 G5
Jacksboro, Tex., 3,816 77 O3
Jacks Creek, Tenn. 71 C6
Jacks Cr., Pa. 60 H4
Jacks Fk., r., Mo. 72 F7
Jacksmith Bay, Alaska 85 D4
Jackson, co., Ala., 36,681 64 C1
Jackson, Ala., 4,959 64 B4
Jackson, co., Ark., 22,843 73 D2
Jackson, Calif., 1,852 82 C3
Jackson, co., Colo., 1,758 79 B1
Jackson, co., Fla., 36,208 65 D2
Jackson, co., Ga., 18,499 64 F1
Jackson, Ga., 2,545 64 E2
Jackson, co., Ill., 42,151 68 C6
Jackson, co., Ind., 30,556 70 C4
Jackson, co., Iowa, 20,754 72 G2
Jackson, co., Kans., 10,309 75 K4
Jackson, co., Ky., 10,677 71 H4
Jackson, Ky., 1,852 71 H4
Jackson, parish, La., 15,828 73 C5
Jackson, La., 1,824 73 D7
Jackson, Me. 55 C4
Jackson, co., Mich., 131,994 67 J6
Jackson, Mich., 50,720 67 J6
Jackson, co., Minn., 15,501 74 E4
Jackson, Minn., 3,370 74 E4
Jackson, co., Miss., 55,522 73 G7
Jackson, Miss., 144,422 73 E5
Jackson, co., Mo., 622,732 72 C6
Jackson, Mo., 5,070 72 H7
Jackson, Nebr., 224 75 J1
Jackson, N.H. 54 E3
Jackson, co., N.C., 17,780 63 A2
Jackson, N.C., 765 63 G1
Jackson, co., Ohio, 29,372 70 G4
Jackson, Ohio, 6,980 70 G3
Jackson, co., Okla., 29,736 76 D3
Jackson, co., Oreg., 73,962 80 B4
Jackson, S.C., 1,746 63 C4
Jackson, co., S. Dak., 1,985 74 B4
Jackson, co., Tenn., 9,233 71 F5
Jackson, Tenn., 33,849 71 C6
Jackson, co., Tex., 14,040 77 P5
Jackson, co., W. Va., 18,541 62 C4
Jackson, co., Wis., 15,151 66 C4
Jackson, Wis., 458 66 E5
Jackson, Wyo., 1,437 81 D4
Jackson, C., N.Z. 175 g6
Jackson, r., Va. 62 E4
Jackson Bay, N.Z. 175 f6
Jacksonboro, S.C. 63 D5
Jackson Center, Ohio, 980 70 F2
Jackson Center, Pa., 640 60 B3
Jackson Head, N.Z. 175 f6
Jackson Hill, N.C. 63 D2
Jackson L., Ga. 64 F2
Jackson L., Wyo. 81 D4
Jackson Mtn., Me. 55 B4
Jackson Mts., Nev. 83 A2
Jacksonport, Ark., 271 73 D2
Jacksonport, Wis. 66 F4
Jackson's Arm, Newf., Can 45 P5
Jacksons Gap, Ala. 64 D3
Jacksons Mill, W. Va. 62 D3
Jacksons Mills, N.J. 58 b16
Jackson Springs, N.C., 244 63 E2
Jacksonville, Ala., 5,678 64 D2
Jacksonville, Ark., 14,488 73 C3
Jacksonville, Fla., 201,030 65 H2
Jacksonville, Ga., 236 64 G4
Jacksonville, Ill., 21,690 68 B4
Jacksonville, Md. 62 H3
Jacksonville, Mo., 153 72 E5
Jacksonville, Onondaga Co., N.Y. 59 q23
Jacksonville, Tompkins Co., N.Y. 59 G6
Jacksonville, N.C., 13,491 63 G3
Jacksonville, Adams Co., Ohio 70 F4
Jacksonville, Athens Co., Ohio, 580 70 G3
Jacksonville, Oreg., 1,172 80 B4
Jacksonville, Tex., 9,590 77 Q4
Jacksonville, Vt., 240 54 B6
Jacksonville Beach, Fla., 12,049 65 H2
Jacktown, Okla. 76 F2
Jacmel, Haiti, 9,397 96 k6
Jaco, C.R. 94 E6
Jacob, Ill. 68 C6
Jacobabad, Pak., 35,278 144 C3
Jacobina, Braz., 12,373 103 H4
Jacob Lake, Ariz. 78 B3
Jacobs Creek, Pa. 60 d9
Jacobson, Minn. 74 F2
Jacobsville, Md. 62 c8
Jacobsville, Mich. 66 E1
Jacobus, Pa., 968 60 J6
Jacona, Mex., 13,373 93 b10
Jacques-Cartier, Qué., Can., 40,157 47 L3
Jacques-Cartier, Mt., Qué., Can. 45 N5
Jacques-Cartier, r., Qué., Can. 47 N2
Jacquinot Pt., Kusaie 176 31
Jacuí, r., Braz. 103 F7
Jacuípe, r., Braz. 103 H4
Jacumba, Calif. 82 E6
Jacupiranga, Braz., 2,144 103 G6
Jácura, Ven. 100 F2
Jacutinga, Braz., 3,699 103 c18
Jadar, r., Yug. 125 D2
Jaddi, Rās, Pak. 144 B4
Jadebusen, bay, F.R.Ger. 118 B2
Jadīdah, Saudi Ar. 143 B4
Jadotville, D.R.Congo, 80,075 164 D3
Jadraque, Sp., 1,934 122 D2
Jādū, Libya 161 F2
Jadwin, Mo. 72 F7
Jaén, Peru, 2,107 104 B3
Jaén, Sp., 64,917 122 D4
Jaffa, C., Austl. 172 E5
Jaffna, Cey., 77,181 145 F8
Jaffna Lag., Cey. 145 n21
Jaffray, Br. Col., Can. 42 J4
Jaffrey, N.H., 1,648 54 C6
Jaffrey Center, N.H. 54 C6
Jafi, Indon. 149 L3
Jagadhri, India, 32,637 144 a10
Jagdalpur, India, 20,412 145 F6
Jagdispur, India, 11,840 144 e13
Jägersburg, F.R.Ger., 2,634 119 C6
Jagersfontein, S.Af., 3,885 164 D6
Jagraon, India, 29,617 144 a10
Jagst, r., F.R.Ger. 118 B4
Jagtiyal, India, 20,941 145 F6
Jaguarão, Braz., 12,336 103 F8
Jaguarão, r., Braz. 103 F8
Jaguariaíva, Braz., 6,465 103 G6
Jaguaribe, Braz., 3,635 103 J3
Jaguaribe, r., Braz. 103 J3
Jagüey Grande, Cuba, 5,244 96 c1
Jahangirabad, India, 17,149 144 b11
Jahrom, Iran, 29,169 143 E3
Jaicoa, Cord., P.R. 96 r10
Jaidhof, Aust. 124 b9
Jaigarh, India 145 h18
Jaipur, India, 403,444 145 E4
Jais, India, 9,906 144 c12

Jaisalmer—Jordan Valley · 241

Jaisalmer, India, 8,352 145 D4
Jajce, Yug., 5,557 125 C2
Jajpur, India, 13,802 145 H5
Ják, Hung., 2,722 126 C3
Jakarta = Djakarta
Jakhal, India, 3,138 144 a11
Jakin, Ga., 176 64 E4
Jakobstad, Fin., 14,718 120 E3
Jal, N. Mex., 3,051 79 D5
Jala, Mex., 3,803 92 D4
Jalaigai Pt., Guam 176 24
Jalālābād, Afghan., 44,000 145 C2
Jalalabad, India, 8,575 144 b12
Jalalpur, India, 11,241 144 d12
Jalán, r., Hond. 94 D3
Jalapa, Guat., 9,245 94 B3
Jalapa, Mex., 66,317 93 F4
Jalapa, Nic. 94 D4
Jalasjärvi, Fin. 120 E3
Jalaun, India, 14,101 144 b12
Jalbot, Fr. Guiana 101 O5
Jalca, Peru, 1,395 104 B3
Jalcocotán, Mex., 2,737 92 D4
Jaleswar, India, 10,202 145 H5
Jaleswar, Nepal 144 e12
Jalgaon, India, 80,351 145 E5
Jalingo, Nigeria 162 F4
Jalisco, st., Mex., 2,443,261 92 D4
Jalisco, Mex., 4,189 92 D4
Jallaucourt, Fr. 116 b9
Jalna, India, 67,158 145 E6
Jalón, r., Sp. 122 E2
Jalor, India, 12,882 145 D4
Jalostotitlán, Mex., 13,540 93 b8
Jalostotitlán, r., Mex. 93 b8
Jalpa, Tab., Mex., 5,186 93 G4
Jalpa, Zac., Mex., 6,204 92 E4
Jalpaiguri, India, 48,738 145 H4
Jalpan, Mex., 1,009 93 F4
Jalpan, r., Mex. 93 e8
Jaltenango, Mex., 1,875 93 G5
Jáltipan, Mex., 4,905 93 G4
Jaltocán, Mex., 3,243 93 f8
Jālū, Libya 161 H3
Jālū, Wāḥat, oasis, Libya 161 H3
Jaluit, atoll, Marsh. Is. 170 F4
Jaluit, i., Jaluit 176 30
Jama, Ec. 104 A2
Jamaica, ctry., 1,843,000* 96
Jamaica, Iowa, 256 72 C3
Jamaica, (part of N.Y.C.), N.Y. 58 d14
Jamaica, Vt. 54 B5
Jamaica Bay, N.Y. 58 d14
Jamaica Channel, W.I. 95 D3
Jamalpur, India, 57,039 144 f13
Jamālpur, Pak., 37,988 144 g13
Jamanxim, r., Braz. 103 E3
Jamas, Indon. 149 L3
Jamay, Mex., 8,459 93 b9
Jambes, Belg., 12,128 115 C4
Jamboree, Ky. 71 J4
Jambville, Fr. 116 f10
Jamdena, P., Indon. 149 K4
James, Md. 62 H4
James, r., Mo. 72 D8
James, r., N. Dak.-S. Dak. 74 C3
James, r., Va. 62 G5
James, L., Ind. 70 D1
James, L., N.C. 63 C2
Jamesburg, N.J., 2,853 61 C3
James City, N.C., 1,474 63 H2
James City, Pa. 60 E2
James City, co., Va., 11,539 62 H5
Jameson, Mo., 177 72 D4
Jamesport, Mo., 622 72 D5
Jamesport, N.Y. 59 P10
James Ross Str., N.W.T., Can. 40 K4
Jamestown, Austl., 1,489 172 c7
Jamestown, St. Helena, 1,550 109 7
Jamestown, Ala. 64 D1
Jamestown, Calif. 82 C4
Jamestown, Colo., 107 79 b7
Jamestown, Ind., 827 70 C3
Jamestown, Kans., 422 75 G4
Jamestown, Ky., 792 71 F5
Jamestown, Mich. 67 H6
Jamestown, Mo., 216 72 E6
Jamestown, N.Y., 41,818 58 B7
Jamestown, N.C., 1,247 63 E2
Jamestown, N. Dak., 15,163 74 C2
Jamestown, Ohio, 1,730 70 F3
Jamestown, Pa., 897 60 B3
Jamestown, R.I., 1,843; 2,267(T) 57 L6
Jamestown, S.C., 184 63 E4
Jamestown, Tenn., 1,727 71 G5
Jamestown, Wash. 81 a6
Jamestown Nat. Hist. Site, Va. 62 H5
Jamesville, N.Y. 59 H6
Jamesville, N.C., 538 63 H2
Jamieson, Austl. 173 f11
Jamieson, Oreg. 80 E3
Jamiltepec, Mex., 3,737 93 F5
Jamison, Nebr. 75 F1
Jamison, Pa. 60 f10
Jammāl, Tun., 11,200 160 g6
Jammerbugt, Den. 121 B3
Jammu, India, 102,738 145 E2
Jammu and Kashmir, reg., India-Pak., 3,560,000* 145 E2
Jamnagar, India, 139,652 144 C5
Jamno, Jez., Pol. 127 A1
Jamnotri, India 144 b10
Jāmpur, Pak., 3,161 145 D3
Jämsä, Fin. 120 F3
Jamsah, U.A.R. 161 K3
Jamshedpur, India, 291,791 145 G5
Jamui, India, 24,213 145 H4
Jamuna, r., India-Pak. 145 J4
Janakkala, Fin. 120 F3
Janaúba, Braz., 5,055 103 H5
Janda, Lag. de la, Sp. 122 C4
Jandaia, Braz., 5,814 103 F5
Jandelsbrunn, F.R.Ger., 1,511 118 D4
Jandiatuba, r., Braz. 102 B3
Jandowae, Austl., 1,028 173 G4
Jane Lew, W. Va., 426 62 D3
Jane Pk., N.Z. 175 f7
Janesville, Calif. 82 C2
Janesville, Iowa, 648 72 E2
Janesville, Minn., 1,426 74 F3
Janesville, Wis., 35,164 66 D6
Janetville, Ont., Can. 46 F4
Jangain, i., Sol. Is. 175 a1
Jangipur, India, 24,201 144 f13
Janīn, Jor., 14,402 142 b7
Janja, Yug., 6,108 125 D2
Janjevo, Yug., 3,420 125 E3
Janjina, Yug. 125 C3
Jan Kempdorp, S. Af., 1,944 164 C6
Jan Mayen, i., Atl. Oc. 108 M2
Jánoshalma, Hung., 13,189 126 D3
Janów Lubelski, Pol., 4,615 127 E3
Janów Podlaski, Pol. 127 E2
Jansen, Sask., Can. 43 D4
Jansen, Nebr., 204 75 H3
Jánské Koupele, Czech. 127 g7
Jan Tiel, Lagun, Cur. 97 16
Januária, Braz., 9,741 103 H5
Janville, Fr., 1,392 117 D2
Janvry, Fr. 116 g12
Janzé, Fr., 4,276 117 C3
Jao-ho, China, 4,000* 150 H2
Jao-p'ing, China 152 E3
Jaora, India, 31,140 145 E5
Jao-yang, China 151 B3
Japan, ctry., 98,274,961 154-5
Japan, Sea of, Asia 170 C2
Japan Basin, Asia 141 M2
Japan Trench, Pac. Oc. 168 E1
Japen, P., Indon. 149 L3
Japen, Selat, Indon. 149 L3
Japero, Indon. 149 L4
Japiim, Braz. 102 B3
Japla, India 144 e13
Japtan, i., Eniwetok 176 28
Japurá, r., Braz. 102 C2
Japutik, i., Ponape 176 29
Jaqué, Pan., 1,195 94 H7
Jaquet, Point, Dominica 97 13
Jarābulus, Syr., 8,477 142 D2
Jarácuaro, Mex. 93 c10
Jaraguá, Braz., 3,813 103 G5
Jaragua, Dom. Rep., 3,828 96 m6
Jaraiz, Sp., 8,130 122 C2
Jaral, Mex., 7,040 93 c9
Jarales, N. Mex. 79 B4
Jaramillo, Arg. 105 B7
Jarandilla, Sp., 3,626 122 C2
Jarash, Jor., 3,796 142 b7
Jarbah, Jazīrat, i., Tun. 161 F2
Jarbridge, Nev. 83 C2
Jardim, Braz., 3,824 103 E6
Jardim do Seridó, Braz., 2,734 103 a14
Jardín, Col. 101 d14
Jardine, Mont. 81 D3
Jardines de la Reina, arch., Cuba 96 d2
Järflotta, i., Swed. 120 e9
Jargeau, Fr., 2,846 117 E3
Jari, r., Braz. 103 F1
Jarīd, Shaṭṭ al, Tun. 161 F2
Jaripitio, Mex., 1,639 93 c9
Jarjīs, Tun., 10,829 161 F2
Jarmen, Ger.D.R. 118 D2
Jarmo, ruins, Iraq 143 D1
Järna, Swed. 120 e8
Jarny, Fr., 9,323 117 F2
Jaro, Panay, Phil., 27,148 153 d11
Jaro, Leyte, Phil., 7,243 153 f10
Jarocin, Pol., 15,569 127 B2
Jaroměř, Czech., 12,359 126 B1
Jarosław, Pol., 26,000* 127 E3
Jarosławiec, Pol. 127 B1
Järpen, Swed. 120 C3
Jarratt, Va., 608 62 G6
Jarres, Plaine des, Laos 146 C3
Jarrettsville, Md. 62 H3
Jarrow, U.K., 28,752 112 h10
Jaruco, Cuba, 5,291 96 c1
Järvenpää, Fin. 120 F3
Jarville-la-Malgrange, Fr., 7,343 116 b9
Jarvis, Ont., Can. 46 D6
Jarvisburg, N.C. 63 J1
Jarvis I., Line Is. 171 H5
Järvsö, Swed. 120 C3
Jaša Tomić, Yug., 4,569 125 E2
Jasenovo, Yug., 2,159 125 E2
Jashpurnagar, India, 5,765 145 G5
Jasień, Pol., 3,309 127 A3
Jāsim, Syr. 142 c7
Jasin, Malay., 3,063 147 p15
Jāsk, Iran, 1,078 143 F3
Jasło, Pol., 10,162 127 D4
Jason Is., Falk. Is. 108 3
Jasonville, Ind., 2,436 70 B3
Jasper, Alta., Can., 2,105 42 H3
Jasper, Ala., 10,799 64 B2
Jasper, Ark. 73 B1
Jasper, Fla., 2,103 65 G2
Jasper, co., Ga., 6,135 64 F2
Jasper, Ga., 1,036 64 E1
Jasper, co., Ill., 11,346 68 D4
Jasper, co., Ind., 18,842 70 B2
Jasper, Ind., 6,737 70 C4
Jasper, co., Iowa, 35,282 72 D3
Jasper, Mich. 67 K7
Jasper, Minn., 850 74 D4
Jasper, co., Miss., 16,909 73 F5
Jasper, co., Mo., 78,863 72 C7
Jasper, Mo., 746 72 C7
Jasper, N.Y. 58 E7
Jasper, N.C. 63 G2
Jasper, Oreg. 80 B3
Jasper, co., S.C., 12,237 63 C5
Jasper, Tenn., 1,450 71 F6
Jasper, co., Tex., 22,100 77 R4
Jasper, Tex., 4,889 77 R4
Jasper Nat. Pk., Alta., Can. 42 H3
Jastarnia, Pol., 3,739 127 C1
Jastrebarsko, Yug., 2,434 125 B2
Jastrowie, Pol., 5,249 127 B2
Jastrzębie-Zdrój, Pol., 2,536 127 h7
Jászapáti, Hung., 10,869 126 E3
Jászárokszállás, Hung., 11,124 126 E3
Jászberény, Hung., 30,211 126 D3
Jászfényszaru, Hung., 7,566 126 D3
Jászladány, Hung., 8,844 126 E3
Jataí, Braz., 14,022 103 F5
Jatapu, r., Braz. 102 E2
Jatate, r., Mex. 93 H5
Játiva, Sp., 19,896 122 E3
Jatún Yacu, r., Ec. 104 c10
Jaú, Braz., 31,229 103 G6
Jaú, r., Braz. 102 D2
Jauaperi, r., Braz. 102 D1
Jauja, Peru, 12,673 104 C4
Jaumave, Mex., 1,883 93 F3
Jaunpur, India, 61,851 145 G4
Jaunsaras, Sp. 122 o12
Java, S. Dak., 406 74 C3
Java = Djawa
Java Head = Gede, Tandjung
Javari, r., Braz. 102 B2
Java Sea, Indon. 148 D4
Java Trench, Ind. Oc. 168 D3
Jävenitz, Ger.D.R. 118 C2
Javorník, Czech. 127 f6
Jawhar, India, 4,732 145 h17
Jawor, Pol., 12,914 127 B3
Jaworzno, Pol. 127 h5
Jaworzno, Pol., 53,000* 127 i6
Jaworzyna Śląska, Pol., 4,560 127 f6
Jay, Fla., 672 65 B2
Jay, co., Ind., 22,572 70 E2
Jay, Me. 55 B4
Jay, N.Y. 59 N3
Jay, Okla., 1,120 76 J1
Jay, Vt. 54 C2
Jayanca, Peru, 4,016 104 A3
Jaydot, Alta., Can. 42 L4
Jayess, Miss. 73 E6
Jaynagar, India, 7,904 144 f12
Jay Pk., Vt. 54 B2
Jayton, Tex., 649 77 N3
Jayuya, P.R., 2,344 96 s10
Jaz Mūrīān, Hāmūn-e, Iran 143 F3
Jazzīn, Leb., 4,842 142 b6
Jean, Nev. 83 C5
Jean, Tex. 77 O3
Jeanerette, La., 5,568 73 D8
Jeannette, Pa., 16,565 60 C5
Jeannin, L., Qué., Can. 45 M3
Jean-Père, L., Qué., Can. 47 H2
Jean Rabel, Pointe, Haiti 96 k6
Jebba, Nigeria 162 E4
Jebel, Rum. 128 C2
Jeberos, Peru, 1,878 104 B3
Jebjerg, Den., 1,005 121 B4
Jedburg, S.C. 63 D4
Jedburgh, U.K., 3,647 112 E4
Jedda = Juddah
Jeddito, Ariz. 78 C4
Jeddo, Mich. 67 L5
Jeddo, N.Y. 58 D5
Jedlicze, Pol., 3,138 127 D4
Jedlina-Zdrój, Pol., 6,110 127 f6
Jedlnia-Letnisko, Pol., 3,012 127 D3
Jędrzejów, Pol., 11,918 127 D3
Jedwabne, Pol., 1,874 127 E2
Jedway, Br. Col., Can. 42 D3
Jeetze, r., F.R.Ger.-Ger.D.R. 118 C2
Jeff Davis, co., Ga., 8,914 64 G4
Jeff Davis, co., Tex., 1,582 77 L4
Jeffers, Minn., 489 74 E3
Jefferson, co., Ala., 634,864 64 C2
Jefferson, Ala. 64 B3
Jefferson, co., Ark., 81,373 73 C3
Jefferson, Ark. 73 C3
Jefferson, co., Colo., 127,520 79 C2
Jefferson, Colo. 79 C2
Jefferson, co., Fla., 9,543 65 F2
Jefferson, co., Ga., 17,468 64 G2
Jefferson, Ga., 1,746 64 F1
Jefferson, co., Idaho, 11,672 81 C4
Jefferson, co., Ill., 32,315 68 D5
Jefferson, co., Ind., 24,061 70 D4
Jefferson, Ind. 70 C2
Jefferson, co., Iowa, 15,818 72 E4
Jefferson, Iowa, 4,570 72 C2
Jefferson, co., Kans., 11,252 75 K4
Jefferson, co., Ky., 610,947 71 F3
Jefferson, parish, La., 208,769 73 E8
Jefferson, Me. 55 C4
Jefferson, co., Miss., 10,142 73 D6
Jefferson, co., Mo., 66,377 72 G6
Jefferson, co., Mont., 4,297 81 C2
Jefferson, co., Nebr., 11,620 75 H3
Jefferson, N.H. 54 E3
Jefferson, co., N.Y., 87,835 59 H3
Jefferson, N.Y. 59 L7
Jefferson, N.C., 841 63 C1
Jefferson, co., Ohio, 99,201 70 J2
Jefferson, Ohio, 2,116 70 J1
Jefferson, co., Okla., 8,192 76 F3
Jefferson, Okla., 119 76 F1
Jefferson, co., Oreg., 7,130 80 C3
Jefferson, Oreg., 716 80 B3
Jefferson, co., Pa., 46,792 60 D3
Jefferson, S.C., 493 63 D3
Jefferson, S. Dak., 443 74 D4
Jefferson, co., Tenn., 21,493 71 H5
Jefferson, co., Tex., 245,659 77 Q5
Jefferson, Tex., 3,082 77 Q3
Jefferson, co., Wash., 9,639 80 B2
Jefferson, co., W. Va., 18,665 62 G3
Jefferson, co., Wis., 50,094 66 E5
Jefferson, Wis., 4,548 66 E6
Jefferson, r., Mont. 81 C3
Jefferson, Mt., Nev. 83 B3
Jefferson, Mt., N.H. 54 E3
Jefferson, Mt., Oreg. 80 C3
Jefferson City, Mo., 28,228 72 E6
Jefferson City, Tenn., 4,550 71 H5
Jefferson Davis, parish, La., 29,825 73 C7
Jefferson Davis, co., Miss., 13,540 73 F6
Jefferson Heights, La., 19,353 73 E7
Jeffersonton, Va. 62 F4
Jeffersontown, Ky., 5,055 71 F3
Jeffersonville, Ga., 1,013 64 F3
Jeffersonville, Ind., 19,522 70 D4
Jeffersonville, Ky. 71 H4
Jeffersonville, N.Y., 434 59 L8
Jeffersonville, Ohio, 897 70 F3
Jeffersonville, Pa., 3,000* 60 f11
Jeffersonville, Vt., 346 54 B2
Jeffrey City, Wyo. 81 F4
Jega, Nigeria, 12,737 162 E3
Jehanabad, India, 23,209 144 e13
Jehol = Ch'eng-te
Jēkabpils, U.S.S.R., 7,400 136 B1
Jekyll I., Ga. 64 H4
Jelcz, Pol. 127 g5
Jelenia Góra, Pol., 50,000* 127 A3
Jelgava, U.S.S.R., 36,300 134 B4
Jellico, Tenn., 2,210 71 G5
Jelling, Den., 2,433 121 B5
Jelloway, Ohio 70 G2
Jelowa, Pol. 127 h6
Jelšava, Czech. 126 E2
Jelstrup, Den. 121 B3
Jemaa, Nigeria 162 F4
Jembongan, P., Malay. 148 F1
Jementah, Malay., 4,294 147 p15
Jemeppe, Belg., 13,348 115 D4
Jemez, N. Mex. 79 B4
Jemez Springs, N. Mex. 79 B4
Jemison, Ala., 977 64 C3
Jemmapes, Alg., 9,476 160 e5
Jemnice, Czech 126 B2
Jemo, i., Marsh. Is. 176 22
Jena, Ger.D.R., 81,190 118 C3
Jena, Fla. 65 F3
Jena, La., 2,098 73 C6
Jenaz, Switz., 1,143 124 D2
Jenbach, Aust., 5,476 124 H6
Jen-ch'iu, China 151 C3
Jenera, Ohio, 272 70 F2
Jen-hsien, China 151 B3
Jen-hua, China 152 D2
Jen-huai, China 152 B2
Jenjarom, Malay., 5,785 147 o15
Jenkins, co., Ga., 9,148 64 H3
Jenkins, Ky., 3,202 71 J4
Jenkins, Minn., 144 74 E2
Jenkins Bay, St Eustatius 97 6
Jenkinsville, S.C. 63 C3
Jenkintown, Pa., 5,017 61 M5
Jenks, Okla., 1,734 76 H1
Jenner, Alta., Can. 42 K4
Jenner, Calif. 82 B3
Jennerstown, Pa., 422 60 D5
Jennings, Fla., 516 65 F2
Jennings, co., Ind., 17,267 70 D3
Jennings, Kans., 292 75 E4
Jennings, La., 11,887 73 C7
Jennings, Mich. 67 H4
Jennings, Mo., 19,965 72 b11
Jennings, Okla., 306 76 G1
Jennings, r., Br. Col., Can. 42 D1
Jennings Lodge, Oreg. 80 a7
Jenny Jump Mts., N.J. 61 B2
Jenny Point, Dominica 97 13
Jensen, Utah 78 D1
Jensen Beach, Fla. 65 J5
Jens Munk I., N.W.T., Can. 41 O4
Jequié, Braz., 2,097 103 e17
Jequié, Braz., 40,158 103 J4
Jequitinhonha, Braz., 5,410 103 H5
Jequitinhonha, r., Braz. 103 H5
Jérada, Mor., 18,872 160 D2
Jerantut, Malay., 3,266 147 p15
Jerauld, co., S. Dak., 4,048 74 C3
Jerécuaro, Mex., 3,906 93 d9
Jeremey's, r., Conn. 56 G6
Jérémie, Haiti, 12,012 96 i6
Jeremoabo, Braz., 3,117 103 J4
Jeremy Pt., Mass. 57 Q5
Jerez de García Salinas, Mex., 14,948 92 E3
Jerez de la Frontera, Sp., 130,900 122 B4
Jerez de los Caballeros, Sp., 19,268 122 B3
Jérica, Sp., 2,399 122 E3
Jericho, Austl. 173 G3
Jericho, Jordan = Arīḥā
Jericho, N.Y., 10,795 59 N10
Jericho, Vt. 54 B3
Jericho, Wis. 66 c12
Jericho Center, Vt. 54 B3
Jerichow, Ger.D.R. 118 D2
Jericó, Col. 100 C5
Jerico Springs, Mo., 179 72 D7
Jerilderie, Austl. 173 e10
Jerimoth Hill, R.I. 57 L5
Jerkoh, Malay., 1,159 147 o14
Jermyn, Pa., 2,568 61 L2
Jermyn, Tex. 77 O3
Jerome, Ariz., 243 78 B4
Jerome, Ark., 76 73 D4
Jerome, Fla. 65 H6
Jerome, co., Idaho, 11,712 81 B4
Jerome, Idaho, 4,761 81 B4
Jerome, Ill., 1,666 68 C4
Jerome, Pa., 1,241 60 D5
Jerome, Va., 62 F4
Jeromesville, Ohio, 540 70 G2
Jerônimo Monteiro, Braz., 2,074 103 f17
Jerry City, Ohio 386 70 F1
Jerryville, W. Va. 62 D4
Jersey, Ark. 73 C4
Jersey, co., Ill., 17,023 68 B4
Jersey, i., U.K. 117 C2
Jersey City, N.J., 276,101 61 C2
Jersey I., Calif. 83 f11
Jersey Shore, Pa., 5,613 60 H3
Jerseyside, Newf., Can. 45 b10
Jersey Village, Tex., 493 77 h9
Jerseyville, Ont., Can. 46 b15
Jerseyville, Ill., 7,420 68 B4
Jerseyville, N.J. 58 b16
Jerumenha, Braz., 1,473 103 H3
Jerusalem, Isr.-Jor., 227,922 142 C4
Jerusalem, Oh o, 317 70 H3
Jerusalem, R.I. 57 K7
Jervis Bay, Austl. 173 h10
Jervis Inlet, Br. Col., Can. 42 c5
Jesenice, Czech. 126 A1
Jesenice, Yug., 16,000 125 B1
Jeseník, Czech 126 C1
Jessamine, co., Ky., 13,625 71 G4
Jesse, Okla. 76 G3
Jesse, Mt., N.H. 54 E3
Jesselton, Malay., 21,497 148 E1
Jessen, Ger.D.R. 118 D3
Jessie, N. Dak. 74 C2
Jessieville, Ark 73 B3
Jessnitz, Ger.D.R., 10,309 118 C3
Jessops Village, Nevis 97 6
Jessore, Pak., 45,365 144 g14
Jessup, Md. 62 b8
Jessup, Pa. = Winton
Jesteburg, F.R.Ger., 2,175 119 a9
Ještěd, pk., Czech. 127 d6
Jester, Okla. 76 D2
Jesup, Ga., 7,304 64 H4
Jesup, Iowa, 1,488 72 F2
Jesús Carranza, Mex., 2,088 93 G5
Jesús de Machaca, Bol. 102 a10
Jesús María, Arg., 14,000* 105 C4
Jesús María, Col. 101 f14
Jesús María, Mex., 1,466 93 b9
Jet, Okla., 339 76 E1
Jetait, Man., Can. 43 E3
Jetersville, Va. 62 F5
Jetmore, Kans., 1,028 75 F5
Jetpur, India, 31,185 144 D5
Jette, Belg., 32,453 115 d9
Jever, F.R.Ger. 9,853 118 A2
Jevíčko, Czech. 126 C2
Jevnaker, Nor. 121 C1
Jewel Cave Nat. Mon., S. Dak. 74 A4
Jewell, Ga. 64 G2
Jewell, Iowa, 1,113 72 D2
Jewell, co., Kans., 7,217 75 G4
Jewell, Kans., 582 75 G4
Jewell, N.Y. 59 J5
Jewell, Oreg. 80 B3
Jewell Ridge, Va. 62 C5
Jewett, Ill., 238 68 D4
Jewett, Ohio, 925 70 H2
Jewett, Tex., 445 77 P4
Jewett City, Conn., 3,608 56 H6
Jeypore, India, 25,291 145 G6
Jezerce mt., Alb. 125 D3
Jezero, Yug. 125 C2
Jeziorak, Jez., Pol. 127 C2
Jeziorany, Pol., 2,893 127 D2
Jhajha, India, 14,150 144 f13
Jhajjar, India, 14,234 144 a11
Jhalawar, India, 14,543 145 E4
Jhalida, India, 9,692 144 f14
Jhang Maghiāna, Pak., 94,971 145 D3
Jhansi, India, 140,217 145 F4
Jhāpa, Nepal 144 f12
Jhargram, India, 13,965 144 f14
Jharia, India, 33,683 144 f14
Jharsuguda, India, 19,227 144 e15
Jhawāni, Nepal 144 e12
Jhelum, Pak., 52,585 145 D2
Jhelum, r., Pak. 145 D3
Jhenida, Pak., 5,055 144 g14
Jhunjhunu, India, 24,962 145 E3
Jibacoa, Cuba, 1,134 96 c1
Jibhalanta, Mong. 150 C2
Jibou, Rum. 128 D1
Jibuti = Djibouti
Jicarilla, N. Mex. 79 C5
Jicarón, I., Pan. 94 G7
Jičín, Czech., 11,961 126 B1
Jidda = Juddah
Jido, India 145 K3
Jiesjav'ri, l., Nor. 120 F1
Jigger, La. 73 D5
Jiggitai Tsho, China 150 B3
Jiggs, Nev. 83 C2
Jiguaní, Cuba, 6,940 96 e2
Jigüero, P. = Higüero, P.
Jigüey, Bahia, Cuba 96 d1
Jih-chao, China 151 C4
Jih-k'o-tse, China, 20,000* 150 B4
Jihlava, Czech., 36,487 126 B2
Jihlava, r., Czech. 126 B2
Jih-t'u, China 150 A3
Jijiga, Eth. 163 M4
Jijona, Sp., 6,383 122 E3
Jilava, Rum. 128 F2
Jilemnice, Czech. 127 e6
Jilf al Kabīr, Haḍabat al, upland, U.A.R. 161 J3
Jiliapan, Mex. 93 e9
Jilotepec, Mex., 2,689 93 e10
Jilotzingo, Mex. 1,953 93 e10
Jilové, Czech. 126 d7
Jimalalud, Phil., 2,126 153 e11
Jimaní, Dom. Rep., 1,503 96 m6
Jimbolia, Rum., 11,281 128 C2
Jimena de la Frontera, Sp., 11,056 122 C4
Jiménez, Chih., Mex., 14,922 92 D2
Jiménez, Coah., Mex. 93 E2
Jiménez, Tam., Mex., 1,353 93 F3
Jimenez, Phil., 2,025 153 B3
Jim Falls, Wis. 66 B3
Jim Hogg, co., Tex., 5,022 77 O6
Jimma, Eth., 8,500* 163 L4
Jim Thorpe, Pa. 5,945 61 L4
Jimtown, Okla. 76 F4
Jim Wells, co., Tex., 34,548 77 O6
Jim Woodruff Dam, Fla.-Ga. 64 D5
Jince, Czech. 126 c7
Jind, India, 24,216 144 a11
Jindabyne, Austl. 173 g11
Jindřichov, Czech. 127 g6
Jindřichův Hradec, Czech., 10,312 126 B2
Jingo, Kans. 75 L5
Jinja, Uganda, 29,741 164 E1
Jinjang, Malay., 16,685 147 o15
Jinotega, Nic., 4,932 94 E4
Jinotepe, Nic., 14,193 94 D5
Jintotolo Chan., Phil. 153 B3
Jiparaná, r., Braz. 102 D4
Jipijapa, Ec., 13,401 104 A2
Jiquí, Cuba, 1,135 96 e2
Jiquilisco, El Salv., 4,416 94 C4
Jiquilpan, Mex., 12,013 93 b10
Jiquipilco, Mex., 6,377 93 e10
Jirgalanta, Mong., 6,000* 150 C2
Jirjā, U.A.R., 19,000 161 K3
Jirkov, Czech. 126 c6
Jisr ash Shughūr, Syr., 12,371 142 D3
Jitra, Malay., 3,260 147 o13
Jiu, r., Rum. 128 D2
Jīwani, Pak., 2,856 144 A4
Jizera, r., Czech. 126 B1
Joaçaba, Braz., 7,921 103 F7
Joachimsthal, Ger.D.R. 118 D2
Joaíma, Braz., 4,122 103 H5
Joanna, S.C., 1,831 63 C3
João Monlevade, Braz., 27,042 103 e17
João Pessoa, Braz., 135,820 103 K3
João Pinheiro, Braz., 3,433 103 G5
Joaquin, Tex., 528 77 R4
Joaquín V. González, Arg., 5,000* 105 C3
Joatinga, C., Braz. 103 d18
Job, W. Va. 62 E4
Jobabo, Cuba, 3,246 96 e2
Jōban, Jap., 44,041 155 G3
Jobi, Indon. 149 L3
Jobos, P.R. 96 t11
Job's Cove, Newf., Can. 45 c10
Jobstown, N.J. 60 g11
Jochberg, Aust., 1,350 124 J6
Jo-ch'iang, China 150 C3
Jock, r., Ont., Can. 47 J3
Jockgrim, F.R.Ger., 2,977 119 E6
Jocotán, Guat., 1,659 94 d9
Jocotepec, Mex., 8,015 92 E4
Jocotitlán, Mex., 4,922 93 e10
Jocutla, Mex., 1,380 93 F5
Jódar, Sp., 14,424 122 D4
Jo Daviess, co., Ill., 21,821 68 B1
Jodhpur, India, 224,760 145 D4
Jodoigne, Belg., 4,145 115 C4
Jodom, Indon. 149 L4
Joensuu, Fin., 29,541 120 G3
Jo-erh-kai, China 150 D3
Joes, Colo. 79 D2
Joes Bk., Vt. 54 C3
Joes Hill, Christmas Atoll 177 40
Joes Pd., Vt. 54 C3
Joeuf, Fr., 12,591 116 b8
Joffre, Pa. = Raccoon
Joffre, Mt., Br. Col., Can. 42 J4
Jōga-shima, Jap. 155 m20
Jogbani, India, 8,852 144 f12
Jōge, Jap., 10,693 155 C4
Jōgeva, U.S.S.R., 2,500 136 B1
Joggins, N.S., Can. 47 T11
Jogjakarta, Indon., 312,698 148 D5
Jōhana, Jap., 13,820 155 E3
Johanna, Austl. 173 d12
Johannesburg, S. Af., 1,096,541 164 D6
Johannesburg, Calif. 82 E5
Johannesburg, Mich. 67 J4
Johanngeorgenstadt, Ger.D.R., 10,646 118 D3
Jōhen, Jap., 8,199 155 C5
Johi, Guyana 101 L7
John, r., Alaska 85 F2
John Crow Mts., Jam. 96 q8
John Day, Oreg., 1,520 80 D3
John Day, r., Oreg. 80 C3
John Martin Res., Colo. 79 D2
Johnnie, Nev. 83 B4
John O'Groat's, U.K. 112 E2
John Redmond Res., Kans. 75 K5
Johns, Ala. 64 b8
Johns, r., N.H. 54 D3
Johnsbach, Aust. 124 L6
Johnsburg, Ill. 69 a7
Johnsburg, N.Y. 59 M4
Johnson, Ariz. 78 C5
Johnson, co., Ark., 12,421 73 B2
Johnson, co., Ga., 8,048 64 G3
Johnson, co., Ill., 6,928 68 D6
Johnson, co., Ind., 43,704 70 C3
Johnson, co., Iowa, 53,663 72 F3
Johnson, co., Kans., 143,792 75 L5
Johnson, co., Ky., 19,748 71 J4
Johnson, co., Mo., 28,981 72 D6
Johnson, co., Nebr., 6,281 75 J3
Johnson, Nebr., 304 75 J3
Johnson, co., Tenn., 10,765 71 K5
Johnson, co., Tex., 34,720 77 P3
Johnson, Tex. 77 M3
Johnson, Vt., 941 54 B2
Johnson, Wash. 80 E2
Johnson, co., Wyo., 5,475 81 F3
Johnsonburg, N.J. 61 B2
Johnsonburg, N.Y. 58 D6
Johnsonburg, Pa., 4,966 60 E3
Johnson City, Kans., 860 75 D6
Johnson City, N.Y., 19,118 59 J7
Johnson City, Tenn., 31,187 71 J5
Johnson City, Tex., 611 77 O4
Johnson Creek, N.Y. 58 C5
Johnson Creek, Wis., 686 66 E5
Johnson Cr., Ariz.-Utah 78 B3
Johnson Cr., Tex. 77 N4
Johnsondale, Calif. 82 D5
Johnson Res., Nebr. 75 F3
Johnsons Crossing, Yukon, Can. 40 C5
Johnsons Point, Antigua 97 9
Johnsonville, N.Y. 59 w28
Johnsonville, S.C., 882 63 E4
Johnston, Iowa 72 D3
Johnston, co., N.C., 62,936 63 F2
Johnston, co., Okla., 8,517 76 G3
Johnston, S.C., 2,119 63 C4
Johnston, Chutes, D.R.Congo-Zambia 164 D3
Johnston City, Ill., 3,891 68 D6
Johnstone, U.K., 18,369 112 b8
Johnston I., Pac. Oc. 170 G3
Johnston Lakes, The, Austl. 172 B4
Johnstown, Colo., 976 79 C1
Johnstown, Mo., 27 72 C6
Johnstown, Nebr., 81 75 F1
Johnstown, N.Y., 10,390 59 M5
Johnstown, Ohio, 2,881 70 G2
Johnstown, Pa., 53,949 60 D5
Johnstown Center, Wis. 66 E6
Johnswood, Mich. 67 K3
Johol, Malay., 1,451 147 p15
Johore, r., Malay. 147 p16
Johore Bahru, Malay., 75,080 148 C2
Jöhstadt, Ger.D.R. 126 c6
Jõhvi, U.S.S.R., 10,500 136 B1
Joice, Iowa, 231 72 D1
Joigny, Fr., 8,137 117 E2
Joiner, Ark., 748 73 E2
Joinville, Braz., 44,255 103 G7
Joinville, Fr., 4,324 117 F2
Joinville-le-Pont, Fr., 18,183 116 h11
Jois, Aust., 1,295 124 d11
Jojutla, Mex., 11,489 93 F4
Jokaj, i., Ponape 176 29
Jokau, Sudan 163 K4
Jokkmokk, Swed. 120 D2
Jökulsá á Brú, r., Ice. 120 b6
Jökulsá á Fjöllum, r., Ice. 120 a6
Jolfā, Iran, 5,970 143 D1
Joliet, Ill., 66,780 68 D2
Joliet, Mont., 452 81 E3
Joliette, Qué., Can., 17,710 44 K6
Jöllenbeck, F.R.Ger., 9,015 118 B2
Jolley, Iowa, 120 72 C2
Jolly, Ohio 70 H3
Jollyville, Tex. 76 c5
Jolo, Phil., 3,464 153 B4
Jolo, W. Va. 62 C5
Jolo Group, is., Phil. 153 B4
Jolo I., Phil. 153 B4
Jolon, Calif. 82 C5
Jomalig I., Phil. 153 B2
Jo-Mary Lakes, Me. 55 C3
Jomolhari, mtn., Bhutan-China 144 g12
Jonacapa, Mex., 1,247 93 e9
Jönåker, Swed. 120 d9
Jonava, U.S.S.R., 5,000 136 B2
Jones, Phil., 2,396 153 c6
Jones, Ala. 64 C3
Jones Co., Ga., 8,468 64 F3
Jones, co., Iowa, 20,693 72 F2
Jones, La. 73 D5
Jones, Mich. 67 H7
Jones, co., Miss., 59,542 73 F6
Jones, co., N.C., 11,005 63 G2
Jones, Okla., 794 76 F2
Jones, co., S. Dak., 2,066 74 B3
Jones, co., Tex., 19,299 77 O3
Jones, C., Qué., Can. 44 H3
Jones Beach, N.Y. 58 e14
Jonesboro, Ark., 21,418 73 E2
Jonesboro, Ga., 3,014 64 E2
Jonesboro, Ill., 1,636 68 C6
Jonesboro, Ind., 2,260 70 D2
Jonesboro, La., 3,848 73 C5
Jonesboro, Me. 55 E4
Jonesboro, Tenn., 1,148 71 J5
Jonesboro, Tex. 77 O4
Jonesburg, Mo., 415 72 F6
Jones Mill, Ark. 73 B3
Jones Mts., Ant. 180 Y5
Jonesport, Me. 55 E4
Jones Sd., N.W.T., Can. 41 M2
Jones Springs, W. Va. 62 F3
Jonestown, Md. 62 b8
Jonestown, Miss., 889 73 E3
Jonestown, Pa., 813 60 J5
Jonesville, Alaska 85 G3
Jonesville, Ind., 196 70 C3
Jonesville, La., 2,347 73 D6
Jonesville, Mich., 1,896 67 J7
Jonesville, N.C., 1,895 63 D1
Jonesville, S.C., 1,439 63 C3
Jonesville, Vt. 54 B3
Jonesville, Va., 711 62 A6
Jonglei, Sudan 163 K4
Joniškis, U.S.S.R., 5,900 136 A1
Jönköping, Swed., 50,652 120 C4
Jonquière, Qué., Can., 28,192 45 L5
Jonuta, Mex., 1,482 93 G4
Jonzac, Fr., 4,053 117 C4
Joplin, Mo., 38,958 72 C7
Joppa, Ala. 64 C1
Joppa, Ill., 578 68 D6
Jora, India, 6,320 144 a12
Jorăşti, Rum. 128 F2
Jordan, ctry., 1,976,000* 142 D4
Jordan, Ont., Can. 46 d15
Jordan, Phil., 1,607 153 d11
Jordan, Minn., 1,479 74 F3
Jordan, Mont., 557 81 F2
Jordan, N. Mex. 79 C4
Jordan, N.Y., 1,390 59 H5
Jordan, r., Asia 142 C3
Jordan, r., Utah 78 C1
Jordan, L., Ala. 64 C3
Jordan Cr., Pa. 61 i18
Jordan Harbour, Ont., Can. 69 B
Jordan Mines, Va. 62 D5
Jordanów, Pol., 3,059 127 C4
Jordanów Śląska, Pol. 127 f6
Jordan Valley, Oreg., 204 80 E4

242 · Jordanville—Kamo

Jordanville, N.Y. 59 K6
Jorge Montt, I., Chile 105 A8
Jorhat, India, 24,953 145 K4
Jork, F.R.Ger., 2,317 118 B2
Jörlanda, Swed. 121 D3
Jörn, Swed. 120 E2
Jornada del Muerto, mts., N. Mex. 79 B5
Jos, Nigeria, 45,076 162 F4
Jošanička Banja, Yug. 125 E3
José de San Martín, Arg., 2,100* 105 B6
José María Blanco, Arg., 5,500* 105 C5
Joseni, Rum. 128 E1
Jose Panganiban, Phil., 5,291 153 B2
José Pedro, r., Braz. 103 f17
Joseph, Oreg., 788 80 E3
Joseph, Utah, 117 78 B2
Joseph, L., Newf., Can. 45 N4
Joseph, L., Ont., Can. 46 E3
Joseph Bonaparte Gulf, Austl. 172 D1
Joseph City, Ariz. 78 C4
Joseph Cr., Oreg.-Wash. 80 E3
Josephine, co., Oreg., 29,917 80 B4
Josephine, Tex., 296 76 g8
Josephs Mills, W. Va. 62 C3
Joshimath, India 144 b10
Jō-Shin-Etsu-Kogen-ktk., Jap. 155 F3
Joshipur, India 144 f14
Joshua, Tex., 764 77 P3
Joshua Tree, Calif. 82 E5
Joshua Tree Nat. Mon., Calif. 82 E5
Jos Plat., Nigeria 162 F4
Jossigny, Fr. 116 k11
Jostedalsbreen, ice cap, Nor. 120 A3
Jost Van Dyke I., V.I. 97 4
Jotunheimen, mts., Nor. 120 A3
Jouars-Ponchartrain, Fr., 1,753 116 f11
Jourdanton, Tex., 1,504 77 O5
Joure, Neth., 5,500 115 D2
Joussard, Alta., Can. 42 J2
Joutseno, Fin. 120 G3
Joux, Fr. 116 o15
Joux, L. de, Switz. 124 A2
Jouy-en-Josas, Fr., 4,366 116 g11
Jouy-le-Moutier, Fr. 116 g10
Jovellanos, Cuba, 10,444 96 c1
Jovellar, Phil., 2,279 153 h14
Jowai, India, 6,197 145 J4
Joy, Ark. 73 D2
Joy, Ill., 503 68 B2
Joya, Lag. de la, Mex. 93 G5
Joyeuse, Fr., 1,294 117 F4
Joynes, N.C. 63 C1
Jōzankei, Jap. 155 J8
Józefów, Pol., 14,344 127 D2
Ju, r., Ho-n., China 150 F3
Ju, r., Ch-hsi, China 152 E2
Juab, co., Utah, 4,597 78 B2
Juan, G., Fr. 116 n13
Juanacatlán, Salto, Mex. 93 a9
Juana Díaz, P.R., 4,618 96 t10
Juan Aldama, Mex., 7,672 92 E3
Juancho, Arg., 1,500* 105 c13
Juan de Fuca Strait, Can.-U.S. 52 B1
Juan Fernández, Is., Chile 171 N7
Juangriego, Ven., 4,545 101 H2
Juan Guerra, Peru, 1,749 104 B3
Juanita, N. Dak. 74 C2
Juanita, Wash. 81 b7
Juan José Castro, Urug. 105 c11
Juan José Paso, Arg., 6,000* 105 C5
Juanjui, Peru, 5,190 104 B3
Juan-les-Pins, Fr. 116 n13
Juan L. Lacaze, Urug., 5,000* 105 c12
Juan Vicente, Cuba, 1,392 96 f2
Juan Viñas, C.R., 1,072 94 F6
Juárez, Chis., Mex., 1,587 93 G5
Juárez, Coah., Mex., 1,198 93 E2
Juárez, Sa. de, Mex. 92 B1
Juaso, Ghana 162 c8
Juayúa, El Salv., 3,807 94 d10
Juàzeiro, Braz., 21,196 103 H3
Juàzeiro do Norte, Braz., 53,421 103 J3
Jūbā, Sudan, 10,660 163 K5
Juba, r., Som. 163 M5
Juban, Phil., 1,728 153 h15
Jubbah, Saudi Ar. 143 C3
Jubbah, Syr. 142 c6
Jubilee L., Austl. 172 C4
Jubileo, Arg., 2,500* 105 b10
Jubing, Nepal 144 f12
Juby, C., Mor. 160 B3
Jubyl, Leb., 3,930 142 b5
Júcar, r., Sp. 122 D2
Juçara, Braz., 2,174 103 F5
Júcaro, Cuba, 1,411 96 d2
Jucás, Braz., 1,585 103 J3
Jüchen, F.R.Ger., 5,851 119 B2
Ju-ch'eng, China 152 D2
Juchipila, Mex., 3,459 92 E4
Juchipila, r., Mex. 93 a8
Juchitán, Mex., 20,031 93 G5
Juchitepec, Mex., 4,509 93 f10
Juchitlán, Mex., 3,091 92 D4
Jud, N. Dak., 156 74 C2
Juda, Wis. 66 D6
Judaea, reg., Isr.-Jor. 142 a8
Juddah, Saudi Ar., 147,859 143 B4
Judds Bridge (part of Roxbury), Conn. 56 C6
Judenau, Aust. 124 c10
Judenburg, Aust., 9,848 124 L6
Judge and Clerk Is., Austl. 170 E8
Judge Daly Promontory, N.W.T., Can. 41 Q1
Judique, N.S., Can. 47 V11
Judith, r., Mont. 81 E2
Judith Basin, co., Mont., 3,085 81 D2
Judith Gap, Mont., 185 81 E2
Judith Mts., Mont. 50 E1
Judson, Ind., 80 70 B3
Judson, N. Dak. 74 B2
Judson, W. Va. 62 D5
Judsonia, Ark., 1,470 73 D2
Judyville, Ind. 70 B2
Jugiong, Austl. 173 g10
Jugoslavia=Yugoslavia
Jui-an, China 152 F2
Jui-chin, China 150 F4
Jui-fang, Taiwan, 53,853 152 F2
Juigalpa, Nic., 4,821 94 E4
Juilly, Fr., 1,401 116 i10
Juist, F.R.Ger., 1,534 118 A2
Juiz de Fora, Braz., 124,979 103 H6
Ju-kao, China 151 D4
Jukehi, India 144 c13
Jukkasjärvi, Swed. 120 E2
Julesburg, Colo., 1,840 79 D1
Juli, Peru, 3,816 104 D6
Juliaca, Peru, 20,786 104 D5
Julia Creek, Austl. 173 F3
Juliaetta, Idaho, 368 81 A2
Julian, Calif. 82 E6
Julian, N.C. 63 E2
Julian, Pa. 60 G4
Juliana kan., Neth. 115 D3
Julian Alps, Yug. 125 B2
Julianatop, mtn., Sur. 101 M6
Julian Pk., Br. Col., Can. 42 b5
Jülich, F.R.Ger., 12,566 118 A3
Juliette, Ga. 64 F2
Julimes, Mex., 1,209 92 D2
Julita, Phil., 2,599 153 f11
Jullundur, India, 222,569 145 E3
Jumbo, Ohio 70 F2
Jumbo, Okla. 76 H3
Jumeauville, Fr. 116 f11
Jumentos Cays, Bah. Is. 95 C2
Jumet, Belg., 29,365 115 C4
Jumilla, Sp., 21,590 122 E3
Jumla, Nepal 145 G3
Jumna=Yamuna
Jump, r., Wis. 66 C3
Jump River, Wis. 66 C3
Junagadh, India, 74,298 144 C5
Ju-nan, China 151 B4
Juncal, Ec. 104 c11
Juncos, P.R., 6,247 96 u10
Junction, Ill., 238 68 D6
Junction, Tex., 2,441 77 O4
Junction, Utah, 219 78 B2
Junction City, Ark.-La., 1,388 73 C5
Junction City, Ill., 315 68 C5
Junction City, Kans., 18,700 75 J4
Junction City, Ky., 1,047 71 G4
Junction City, Ohio, 763 70 G3
Junction City, Oreg., 1,614 80 B3
Junction City, Wis., 381 66 D4
Jundah, Austl. 173 F3
Jundiaí, Braz., 79,536 103 c18
Juneau, Alaska, 6,797 85 L4
Juneau, co., Wis., 17,490 66 C5
Juneau, Wis., 1,718 66 E5
Junee, Austl., 4,064 173 G5
June Lake, Calif. 82 D4
Jung, r., China 152 C2
Jung-an, China 150 E4
Jungapeo, Mex., 3,400 93 d10
Jung-ch'eng, China 151 D3
Jung-ch'i-hsü, China 152 a6
Jung-ching, China 152 A1
Jungersen Bay, N.W.T., Can. 41 N3
Jungfeng=Hsüan-wei
Jungfrau, mtn. Switz. 124 B2
Jung-ha, China 150 B4
Jung-ho, China 151 A4
Jungholz, Aust. 124 G6
Jung-hsien, K-hsi, China 152 C3
Jung-hsien, S-ch., China 152 B1
Junglinster, Lux. 115 E5
Jungo, Nev. 83 A2
Juniata, Kans. 75 G5
Juniata, Nebr., 422 75 G3
Juniata, co., Pa., 15,874 60 H4
Juniata, r., Pa. 60 H4
Junín, Arg., 53,715 105 C4
Junín, Peru, 5,105 104 C4
Junín de los Andes, Arg., 2,500* 105 A5
Junior, W. Va., 552 62 E4
Junior L., Me. 55 E3
Juniper, N.B., Can. 47 S10
Juniper Mts., Ariz. 78 B4
Junipero Serra Pk., Calif. 82 C4
Jūnisho, Jap. 155 G1
'Jūniyah, Leb., 12,000 142 b5
Jünkerath, F.R.Ger., 1,728 118 A3
Junnar, India, 12,141 145 h17
Juno, Tex. 77 N4
Juno Beach, Fla., 249 65 K6
Junosuando, Swed. 120 E2
Junquillar, Chile 104 e15
Junsele, Swed. 120 D3
Juntas, Bol., 2,067 102 D6
Juntura, Oreg., 98 80 E4
Juojärvi, l., Fin. 120 G3
Juoksengi, Swed. 120 E2
Jupille, Belg., 10,210 115 D4
Jupiter, Fla., 1,058 65 J6
Jupiter, N.C., 174 63 B2
Juquiá, Braz., 2,573 103 G6
Jur, r., Sudan 163 J4
Jura, i., U.K. 112 D3
Jura, Sd. of, U.K. 112 D4
Juradó, Col. 100 B4
Jura Mts. Fr.-Switz. 124 A2
Jurançon, Fr., 6,581 117 C5
Júrica, Mex. 93 d9
Jurilovca, Rum. 128 G2
Juruá, r., Braz. 102 C3
Jurubidá, Col. 100 B5
Juruena, r., Braz. 102 E4
Juruti, Braz., 1,868 103 E2
Jurva, Fin. 120 E3
Jusepín, Ven., 2,369 101 J3
Jussey, Fr., 2,474 117 F3
Jussy, Switz. 124 A2
Justice, Ill., 5,252 69 c10
Justin, Tex., 622 76 e8
Justo Daract, Arg., 7,800* 105 B4
Justöy, Nor. 121 A2
Jutaí, Braz. 102 C3
Jutaí, r., Braz. 102 C3
Jüterbog, Ger.D.R., 13,518 118 D3
Juti, Braz. 103 E6
Jutiapa, Guat., 7,485 94 C3
Jutiapa, Hond., 1,045 94 D3
Juticalpa, Hond., 4,331 94 D3
Jutland=Jylland
Jutphaas, Neth. 115 c6
Juuka, Fin. 120 G3
Juva, Fin. 120 G3
Juventino Rosas, Mex., 11,720 93 d9
Juvisy-sur-Orge, Fr., 11,814 116 h12
Juvre, Den. 121 A5
Juwara, Muscat and Oman 143 F5
Ju-yüan, China 152 D2
Juziers, Fr., 1,557 116 f11
Južna Morava, r., Yug. 125 E3
Jyderup, Den., 2,552 121 D5
Jylland, reg., Den. 121 B5
Jyväskylä, Fin., 43,638 120 F3

K

Kaaawa, Hawaii, 581 84 c6
Kaaihue, Hawaii 84 F3
Kaala, Mt., Hawaii 84 C2
Kaala-Gomen, N. Caled. 174 h8
Kaalualu, Hawaii 84 F4
Kaapprovinsie, prov., S. Af. 164 D7
Kaapstad=Cape Town
Kaaresuvanto, Fin. 120 E1
Kaatsheuvel, Neth., 8,700 115 C3
Kaba, Hung., 6,939 126 E3
Kabaena, P., Indon. 149 G4
Kabala, D.R.Congo 165 n18
Kabala, Sa. Leone 162 C4
Kabale, Uganda, 10,919 164 E2
Kabalebo, r., Sur. 101 M5
Kabalo, D.R.Congo 164 D3
Kabambare, D.R.Congo 164 D2
Kabandjahe, Indon. 148 A2
Kabankalan, Phil., 8,856 153 d12
Kabanskoye, U.S.S.R. 136 E3
Kabara, Mali, 2,000* 162 D3
Kabardinka, U.S.S.R., 3,000 136 E4
Kabarei, Indon. 149 J3
Kabarnet, Kenya 165 g13
Kabba, Nigeria 162 F4
Kabbenbock, i., Jaluit 176 30
Kabe, Jap., 17,691 155 C4
Kabelvåg, Nor. 120 C1
Kabemba, D.R.Congo 165 o20
Kabenga, D.R.Congo 165 m18
Kabetogama L., Minn. 74 F1
Kabinakagami, r., Ont., Can. 44 F5
Kabinakagami L., Ont., Can. 44 F5
Kabinda, D.R.Congo 164 D3
Kabinu, Indon. 148 E2
Kabo, C.A.R. 163 H4
Kabompo, Zambia 164 D4
Kabompo, r., Zambia 164 C4
Kabongo, D.R.Congo 164 D3
Kabongo, D.R.Congo 165 o18
Kabora, Jap. 154 g16
Kabosa L., Burma 146 B4
Kabou, Togo 162 d7
Kabubu, D.R.Congo 165 m18
Kabūdīyah, Ra's, Tun. 161 F2
Kabugao, Phil., 153 B1
Kābul, Afghan., 224,000* 144 C2
Kābul, r., Afghan. 145 C2
Kabuli, Terr. New Guin. 174 e1
Kabundi, D.R.Congo 165 n19
Kaburuang, P., Indon. 149 H2
Kabuwe, Indon. 148 B4
Kabwe-Katanda, D.R.Congo 165 m18
Kabweye, D.R.Congo 164 D3
Kačanik, Yug., 2,430 125 E3
Kachalola, Zambia 164 E4
Kacheliba, Kenya 164 E1
Kachiry, U.S.S.R. 137 p11
Kachkanar, G., U.S.S.R. 137 i7
Kachuga, U.S.S.R., 8,800 135 K4
Kaçkar Dağı, Turk. 142 E1
Kácov, Czech. 127 e7
Kaczawa, r., Pol. 127 A3
Kada, Jap. 154 h16
Kada, Jap., 6,113 155 D4
Kadaclan, Phil., 1,592 153 c5
Kadaingti, Burma 147 b2
Kadaiyanalur, India, 41,249 145 k21
Kadaň, Czech. 126 c6
Kadañgilan, Phil., 4,197 153 C4
Kadapongan, P., Indon. 148 f6
Kadarkút, Hung., 2,970 126 C3
Kade, Ghana 162 c8
Kadina, Austl., 1,808 172 b8
Kadin Bilin, r., Burma 146 B3
Kadiolo, Mali 162 D4
Kadipaten, Indon. 148 b7
Kadiri, India 145 F7
Kadirli, Turk., 11,074 142 D2
Kadiyevka, U.S.S.R., 191,000 134 C5
Kado, Jap. 155 G1
Kadogawa, Jap., 15,764 154 B5
Kadohara, Jap. 154 h14
Kadoka, S. Dak., 840 74 B4
Kadok Payagyi, Burma, 1,260 147 b2
Kadonkani, Burma 147 a3
Kadonyū, Jap. 154 h14
Kaduna, Nigeria, 45,389 162 F4
Kaduna, r., Nigeria 162 F4
Kadungle, Austl. 173 f9
Kāduqlī, Sudan, 4,716 163 J4
Kaduy, U.S.S.R. 136 E1
Kadzharan, U.S.S.R., 15,000 137 c2
Kadzidło, Pol. 127 D2
Kaédi, Maur., 9,100 162 B3
Kaélé, Cam. 162 G4
Kaelepulu Pd., Hawaii 84 d7
Kaena Pt., Lanai, Hawaii 84 C2
Kaena Pt., Oahu, Hawaii 84 D3
Kaeng Khoi, Thai., 6,771 146 C4
Kaeo, N.Z. 175 g4
Kærby, Den. 121 C4
Ka-erh, China 150 B3
Ka-erh-mu, China 150 C3
Kaesŏng, N. Kor., 139,900* 151 E3
Kāf, Saudi Ar. 143 B2
Kafan, U.S.S.R., 19,100 137 c2
Kafanchan, Nigeria 162 F4
Kafinga, D.R.Congo 164 o18
Kafirnigan, r., U.S.S.R. 137 e5
Kafubu, D.R.Congo 165 n19
Kafue, Zambia, 2,462 164 D4
Kafue, r., Zambia 164 D4
Kafue Nat. Pk., Zambia 164 D4
Kafuka, Jap. 155 J7
Kafunzo, Uganda 165 e14
Kaga, Jap., 54,548 155 E3
Kagamil I., Alaska 85 B5
Kagan, U.S.S.R., 21,100 134 F6
Kagato, Jap. 154 f15
Kagawong, Ont., Can. 46 B3
Kagawong L., Ont., Can. 46 B3
Kagera, r., Af. 165 e14
Kagera, Parc Nat. de la, Rwanda 165 e14
Kågeröd, Swed. 121 c7
Kagerplassen, l., Neth. 115 b6
Kagitumba, Rwanda 165 e14
Kağızman, Turk., 7,190 142 E1
Kagman Pt., Saipan 176 27
Kagoshima, Jap., 296,003 154 B6
Kagoshima-wan, Jap. 154 B6
Kagul, U.S.S.R., 16,200 136 C4
Kaguyak, Alaska 85 F4
Kahakuloa, Hawaii 84 E3
Kahala, Hawaii 84 d8
Kahaluu, Hawaii, 1,125 84 c7
Kahama, Tanz. 164 E2
Kahana, Hawaii 84 D2
Kahana Bay, Hawaii 84 c6
Kahemba, D.R.Congo 164 C3
Kahl, r., F.R.Ger. 119 G4
Kahla, Ger.D.R. 118 C3
Kahl am Main, F.R.Ger., 5,570 119 G4
Kahler Asten Berg, F.R.Ger. 119 E2
Kahlotus, Wash., 131 80 D2
Kahntah, Br. Col., Can. 42 G1
Kahntah, r., Br. Col., Can. 42 G1
Kahoka, Mo., 2,160 72 F4
Kahoolawe, i., Hawaii 84 E3
Kahua, Hawaii 84 F3
Kahua, pt., Sol. Is. 175 d3
Kahuku, Hawaii, 1,238 84 D2
Kahuku Pt., Hawaii 84 D2
Kahului, Hawaii, 4,223 84 E3
Kahului Bay, Hawaii 84 E3
Kaiaka Bay, Hawaii 84 b6
Kaiama, Nigeria 162 E4
Kaiapoi, N.Z., 3,110 175 g6
Kaiashk, r., Ont., Can. 44 E5
Kaibab Plat., Ariz. 78 B3
Kaibara, Jap., 8,162 155 D4
Kai Beab, Indon. 149 L4
Kaibito, Ariz. 78 C3
Kaibito Plat., Ariz. 78 C3
Kaibola, Terr. Papua 174 3
Kaichi, Jap. 154 e15
K'ai-chien, China 152 C3
Kaieteur Fall, Guyana 101 L5
K'ai-feng, China, 780,000* 150 F3
K'ai-hsien, China 152 C1
Kaihu, N.Z. 175 g4
K'ai-hua, China 152 E1
Kaikohe, N.Z., 2,732 175 g4
Kaikoura, N.Z., 1,328 175 g6
Kaikoura Pen., N.Z. 175 g6
Kailas Ra., China 164 B4
Kaileuna, i., Terr. Papua 174 f3
Kailio Pt., Hawaii 84 E3
K'ai-lu, China 151 D2
Kailua, Hawaii Co., Hawaii 84 E4
Kailua, Honolulu Co., Hawaii, 18,170* 84 D2
Kailua, Maui Co., Hawaii 84 E3
Kailua Bay, Hawaii 84 d7
Kaimana, Indon. 149 K3
Kaimes, U.K. 112 b8
Kaimganj, India, 13,053 144 b12
Kaim Hill, U.K. 112 a8
Kaimon, Jap., 11,859 154 B6
Kaimu, Hawaii 84 G4
Kainaliu, Hawaii, 549 84 F4
Kainan, Jap., 52,532 155 D4
Kainantu, Terr. New Guin. 174 e2
Kaipara Har., N.Z. 175 g5
Kaiparowits Plat., Utah 78 C3
Kai-p'ing, China 151 D2
K'ai-p'ing, China 152 D3
Kaipokok, r., Newf., Can. 45 O3
Kairana, India, 26,454 145 E3
Kairiru, i., Terr. New Guin. 174 d1
Kairuku, Terr. Papua 174 e3
Kaisersbach, F.R.Ger., 1,804 119 H7
Kaisersesch, F.R.Ger., 1,715 119 C4
Kaiserslautern, F.R.Ger., 84,145 118 A4
Kaisersteinbruch, Aust. 124 d11
Kaiserstuhl, pk., F.R.Ger. 118 A4
Kait, Tg., Indon. 148 C3
Kaitaia, N.Z., 2,706 175 g4
Kai Tak, H.K., 250,808 152 b6
Kaitangata, N.Z., 1,249 175 f7
Kaithal, India, 34,890 144 a11
K'ai-t'ung, China 150 G2
Kaiwi Chan., Hawaii 84 D2
K'ai-yang, China 152 B2
K'ai-yüan, L-n., China 151 E2
K'ai-yüan, Y-n., China 152 A3
K'ai-yüan-ch'eng, China 151 E2
Kaiyuh Mts., Alaska 85 E3
Kaizu, Jap. 154 h14
Kaizuka, Jap., 61,067 154 g15
Kaja, Indon. 148 F2
Kajaani, Fin., 14,705 120 G2
Kajabbi, Austl. 172 E3
Kajakai Dam, Afghan. 144 B2
Kajan, r., Indon. 148 F2
Kajang, Malay., 9,630 147 o15
Kajiado, Kenya 164 F2
Kajikazawa, Jap., 7,757 155 F4
Kajiki, Jap., 19,791 154 B6
Kajino, Jap. 154 i15
Kajiya, Jap. 154 f14
Kajiyabara, Jap. 154 f15
Kajoa, P., Indon. 149 H2
Kajuagung, Indon. 148 C3
Kaka, C.A.R. 163 J4
Kākā, Sudan, 163 K4
Kaka, Ariz. 78 B5
Kakabeka Falls, Ont., Can. 44 D5
Kakabia, P., Indon. 149 G4
Kakagi L., Ont., Can. 74 F1
Kakali, Indon. 149 F3
Kakamas, S. Af. 164 C6
Kakamega, Kenya 164 E1
Kakanui, N.Z. 175 f7
Kaka Pt., Hawaii 84 E3
Kakata, Lib. 162 C4
Kake, Jap., 7,888 155 C4
Kake, Alaska 85 L4
Kakegawa, Jap., 59,762 155 E4
Kakhonak, Alaska 85 F4
Kakhovka, U.S.S.R., 19,100 136 D4
Kakhovskoye Vdkhr., U.S.S.R. 136 D4
Kakinada, India, 122,865 145 G6
Kakisa L., N.W.T., Can. 40 F5
Kakizaki, Jap., 16,562 155 F3
Kako, r., Jap. 154 f15
Kakogawa, Jap., 89,539 155 D4
Kakonko, Tanz. 165 e15
Kakpin, Iv. Coast 162 b7
Kaktovik, Alaska 85 J1
Kakuda, Jap., 36,508 155 G3
Kakuni, D.R.Congo 165 m19
Kakunodate, Jap., 17,862 155 G2
Kakura, Jap. 154 i14
Kakuto, Uganda 165 e14
Kalabahi, Indon. 149 H5
Kalabáka, Gr., 4,640 129 C5
Kalabáki, Gr., 3,199 129 E4
Kalabo, Zambia 164 C4
Kalabyin, Burma 147 a2
Kalach, U.S.S.R., 16,900 136 F3
Kalachinsk, U.S.S.R., 19,000 137 o11
Kalach-Kurlak, U.S.S.R. 136 F3
Kalach-na-Donu, U.S.S.R., 16,700 136 F3
Kaladan, r., Burma 146 A2
Kaladar, Ont., Can. 46 G4
Kalae, Hawaii 84 E2
Ka Lae, c., Hawaii 84 F4
Kalagwe, Burma 147 g6
Kalahari Des., Bots. 164 C5
Kalahari-Gemsbock Nat. Pk., S. Af. 164 C6
Kalahasti, India, 26,460 145 F7
Kalaheo, Hawaii, 1,185 84 B2
Kalai-Khumb, U.S.S.R. 137 f5
Kalaipaloa Pt., Hawaii 84 c6
Kalajoki, Fin. 120 E2
Kalajoki, r., Fin. 120 F3
Kalakan, U.S.S.R. 135 L4
Kalaloch, Wash. 80 A2
Kalām, Pak. 145 D2
Kalama, Wash., 1,088 80 B2
Kalámai, Gr., 38,211 129 D6
Kalamazoo, co., Mich., 169,712 67 H6
Kalamazoo, Mich., 82,089 67 H6
Kalamazoo, r., Mich. 67 H6
Kalambau, P., Indon. 148 f6
Kalamo, Mich. 67 J6
Kálamos, Gr., 1,192 129 D5
Kálamos, i., Gr. 129 C5
Kalampising, Indon. 148 F2
Kalan, Turk., 3,775 137 a2
Kalangala, Uganda 165 f14
Kalannie, Austl. 172 B4
Kalao, P., Indon. 149 G4
Kalaotoa, P., Indon. 149 G4
Kala Oya, r., Cey. 145 n21
Kalapana, Hawaii 84 G4
Kalarash, U.S.S.R., 5,700 136 B4
Kalasin, Indon. 148 E2
Kalasin, Thai., 11,043 146 C3
Kalāt, Pak., 5,321 144 C3
Kalāt-i-Ghilzai, Afghan. 144 C2
Kalatse, India 145 E2
Kalau, i., Tonga 177 36
Kalaupapa, Hawaii 84 D2
Kalavasos, Cyp., 1,227 142 e10
Kalávrita, Gr., 2,039 129 D5
Kalaw, Burma, 3,621 146 B2
Kalawao, co., Hawaii, 279 84 E2
Kalawao, Hawaii 84 E2
Kalbe, Ger.D.R. 118 C2
Kaldenkirchen, F.R.Ger., 7,652 119 A2
Kaldi Daği, Turkey 111 G5
Kalecik, Turk., 4,113 142 C1
Kalegauk I., Burma 146 B4
Kalehe, D.R.Congo 164 D2
Kaleida, Man., Can. 43 f9
Kalemyo, Burma, 2,609 146 A2
Kalenge, D.R.Congo 165 n18
Kalety, Pol., 6,602 127 C3
Kaleva, Mich., 348 67 H4
Kalewa, Burma, 2,263 146 A2
Kalga, U.S.S.R. 135 L4
Kalgan=Chang-chia-k'ou
Kalgary, Tex. 77 N3
Kalgoorlie, Austl., 22,837 172 B4
Kali, r., India-Nepal 145 F3
Kaliakra, Nos, Bulg. 128 G3
Kalianda, Indon. 148 C4
Kalibek, Oz., U.S.S.R. 137 n11
Kalibo, Phil., 6,025 153 B3
Kalida, Ohio, 705 70 E2
Kāli Gandak, r., Nepal 144 d12
Kalihi, Hawaii 84 c8
Kalihi Str., Hawaii 84 c7
Kalihiwai Bay, Hawaii 84 B1
Kalima, D.R.Congo, 6,396 164 D2
Kalimala, India 145 F6
Kalimantan, i., Indon. 148 E3
Kálimnos, Gr., 10,211 129 F6
Kálimnos, i., Gr. 129 F6
Kalimpong, India, 25,105 144 g12
Kalingum, Terr. New Guin. 174 d1
Kalinin, U.S.S.R., 279,000 134 C4
Kaliningrad, U.S.S.R., 226,000 134 A4
Kaliningrad, U.S.S.R., 74,000 136 b6
Kalinino, U.S.S.R. 137 h7
Kalinkovichi, U.S.S.R., 16,000 136 C2
Kalinovik, Yug. 125 D3
Kalirrákhi, Gr., 1,429 129 E4
Kalisat, Indon. 148 e8
Kali Sindh, r., India 144 a14
Kalisizo, Uganda 165 e14
Kalispell, Mont., 10,151 81 B1
Kalisz, Pol., 70,000* 127 C3
Kalisz Pomorski, Pol., 2,572 127 C2
Kalitva, r., U.S.S.R. 136 F3
Kalívia, Gr., 1,297 129 C5
Kaliwungu, Indon. 148 d7
Kalix, Swed. 120 E2
Kalixälv, r., Swed. 120 E2
Kalka, India, 18,068 144 a10
Kalkar, F.R.Ger., 2,392 119 A1
Kalkaska, co., Mich., 4,382 67 H4
Kalkaska, Mich., 1,321 67 H4
Kalkfeld, S.-W. Afr. 164 B5
Kalkfontein, Bots., 1,470 164 C5
Kalków, Pol. 127 g6
Kall, F.R.Ger., 2,567 119 B3
Kallakurichi, India, 13,312 145 m20
Kallaste, U.S.S.R., 1,700 136 B1
Kallavesi, l., Fin. 120 F3
Kallhäll, Swed. 120 e8
Kallifóni, Gr., 1,601 129 C5
Kallithéa, Gr. 129 D5
Kallnach, Switz., 1,316 124 B1
Kalloní, Gr., 2,043 129 F5
Kållsjö, Swed. 121 E3
Kallsjön, l., Swed. 120 C3
Kållvik, Swed. 120 e9
Kalmakkol', Oz., U.S.S.R. 137 m11
Kalmar, Swed., 30,839 120 C4
Kalmarsund, Swed. 120 D4
Kalmit, pk., F.R.Ger. 119 E6
Kal'mius, r., U.S.S.R. 136 E4
Kalmthout, Belg., 10,643 115 C3
Kalmunai, Cey. 145 n22
Kalmykovo, U.S.S.R. 134 E5
Kalo, Terr. Papua 174 e3
Kalocsa, Hung., 13,663 126 D3
Kalofer, Bulg., 4,854 128 E3
Kalohi Chan., Hawaii 84 D3
Kalo Kalo, Terr. Papua 174 f3
Kaló-Khorió, Gr., 1,933 129 E7
Kalola, D.R.Congo 165 o18
Kaloli Pt., Hawaii 84 G4
Kalombo, D.R.Congo 165 n18
Kalomo, Zambia 164 D4
Kalona, Iowa, 1,235 72 F3
Kalopa Gulch, r., Hawaii 84 F4
Kalpeni I., India 145 D8
Kalpi, India, 17,278 144 b12
Kalskag, Alaska, 147 85 D3
Kalsoy, i., Faeroe Is. 120 c7
Kaltag, Alaska, 165 85 E2
Kaltan, U.S.S.R. 137 r11
Kaltasy, U.S.S.R. 137 h8
Kaltbrunn, Switz., 2,527 124 D1
Kaltenkirchen, F.R.Ger., 4,640 119 b8
Kalterherberg, F.R.Ger., 2,176 119 A3
Kaluaaha, Hawaii 84 E2
Kaluanui Str., Hawaii 84 c6
Kaluga, U.S.S.R., 145,000 134 C4
Kalule Nord, D.R.Congo 165 n18
Kalulushi, Zambia, 3,337 165 n20
Kalumboyan, Phil., 7,748 153 B3
Kalumpang, Malay., 3,359 147 o15
Kalundborg, Den., 9,763 121 C5
Kalush, U.S.S.R., 12,800 136 B3
Kalutara, Cey., 20,323 145 F9
Kalvesta, Kans. 75 E5
Kalvträsk, Swed. 120 D2
Kalwa, Indon. 149 L4
Kalwang, Aust., 1,617 124 L6
Kalwaria Zebrzydowska, Pol., 3,787 127 i7
Kal'ya, U.S.S.R. 137 k6
Kalyan, India, 73,482 145 D6
Kalyazin, U.S.S.R., 10,900 136 E1
Kam, Alb. 125 E3
Kama, Burma, 3,523 146 A3
Kama, U.S.S.R. 137 k6
Kama, r., U.S.S.R. 134 E4
Kamachumu, Tanz. 165 e14
Kamae, Jap., 17,012 154 B5
Kamagaya, Jap. 155 n19
Kamaike, Jap. 155 n19
Kamaiki Pt., Hawaii 84 E3
Kamaing, Burma 146 B1
Kamaishi, Jap., 87,511 155 G2
Kamakoa Gulch, r., Hawaii 84 F4
Kamakou, pk., Hawaii 84 E2
Kamakura, Jap., 98,617 155 m20
Kamakusa, Guyana 101 L5
Kamalasai, Thai. 146 C3
Kamālia, Pak., 35,248 145 D3
Kamalino, Hawaii 84 A2
Kamalo, Hawaii 84 E2
Kamamaung, Burma 147 b2
Kaman, India, 12,140 144 a12
Kaman, Turk., 8,896 142 C2
Kamananui Str., Hawaii 84 b6
Kamaniskeg L., Ont., Can. 46 G3
Kamapanda, Zambia 165 m20
Kamarah, Austl. 173 f10
Kamarān, i., Red Sea 143 C5
Kamaria Falls, Guyana 101 L4
Kamarod, Pak. 144 B4
Kamas, Utah, 749 78 C1
Kamase, Burma, 2,300 147 b2
Kamashi, U.S.S.R. 137 e5
Kamasin, India 144 c13
Kamatanta, D.R.Congo 165 n18
Kamauksu, Burma 147 a2
Kamba, Nigeria 162 E4
Kambang, Indon. 148 B3
Kambangan, Nusa, Indon. 148 c7
Kambara, i., Fiji 174 4
Kambarka, U.S.S.R., 13,400 137 h8
Kambove, D.R.Congo 164 D3
Kamchatka, P-ov., U.S.S.R. 135 P4
Kamchatka, r., U.S.S.R. 135 P4
Kamchatskiy, P-ov., U.S.S.R. 135 Q4
Kameari, Jap. 155 m19
Kameda, Jap. 155 F2
Kameda, Jap., 19,716 155 F3
Kameda, Jap., 14,600 155 J9
Kamela, Oreg. 80 D3
Kamen, F.R.Ger., 18,328 118 A3
Kamen', G., U.S.S.R. 135 J3
Kamenets-Podol'skiy, U.S.S.R., 38,200 136 B3
Kamenica, Yug., 2,006 125 E3
Kamenjak, Rt, c., Yug. 125 A2
Kamenjane, Yug., 2,014 125 E4
Kamenka, U.S.S.R. 134 D3
Kamenka, U.S.S.R., 7,000 136 E3
Kamenka, U.S.S.R., 27,000 136 F2
Kamenka, Ukr.S.S.R., U.S.S.R., 11,600 136 D3
Kamenka-Bugskaya, U.S.S.R., 7,800 136 B3
Kamenka-Dneprovskaya, U.S.S.R., 13,600 136 D4
Kamen'-Kashirskiy, U.S.S.R., 5,300 136 B3
Kamen'-na-Obi, U.S.S.R., 30,100 134 H4
Kameno, Bulg., 4,672 128 F3
Kamenolomni, U.S.S.R. 136 f8
Kamen'-Rybolov, U.S.S.R. 151 F1
Kamenska, Yug. 125 C2
Kamensko, Yug. 125 D2
Kamenskoye, U.S.S.R. 135 Q3
Kamensk-Shakhtinskiy, U.S.S.R., 60,000 136 g7
Kamensk-Ural'skiy, U.S.S.R., 151,000 134 F4
Kamenz, Ger.D.R., 14,888 118 E3
Kameoka, Jap., 30,049 155 D4
Kameri, Indon. 149 K3
Kameshkovo, U.S.S.R., 11,700 136 F1
Kamet, mtn., China-India 144 b10
Kametsu, Jap., 12,201 154 d12
Kameyama, Jap., 30,950 155 E4
Kamiah, Idaho, 1,245 81 B2
Kami-Awa, Jap. 154 h15
Kamibun, Jap. 154 e16
Kamidoai, Jap. 154 i14
Kamieniec Ząbkowicki, Pol., 4,275 127 f6
Kamień Krajeński, Pol., 1,596 127 B2
Kamienna, r., Pol. 127 D3
Kamienna Góra, Pol., 15,952 127 B3
Kamień Pomorski, Pol., 4,355 127 A2
Kamiensk, Pol. 127 i5
Kamieskroon, S. Af. 164 B7
Kami-Furano, Jap., 16,918 155 K8
Kamigōri, Jap., 19,000 154 f15
Kami-Hiraya, Jap. 154 g14
Kamiichi, Jap. 154 e15
Kamiichi, Jap., 25,278 155 E3
Kami-Ichi, Jap., 3,463 154 g15
Kamiiso, Jap., 24,674 155 J9
Kamikawa, Jap., 13,391 155 K8
Kami-Koshiki-shima, Jap. 154 A6
Kami-Kunigida, Jap. 155 m19
Kamiloloa, Hawaii 84 E2
Kamilukuak L., N.W.T., Can. 40 J5
Kaministikwia, Ont., Can. 44 D5
Kaminogō, Jap. 154 h15
Kaminokuni, Jap., 14,317 155 H9
Kami-Noma, Jap. 154 h15
Kaminomura, Jap. 154 h15
Kaminoseki, Jap., 9,677 154 B5
Kamino-shima, Jap. 154 A4
Kaminoyama, Jap., 40,383 155 G2
Kaminuriak L., N.W.T., Can. 40 K5
Kamioka, Jap., 27,603 155 E3
Kami-Okoppe, Jap. 155 K7
Kami-Shihoro, Jap., 13,608 155 K8
Kamituga, D.R.Congo, 5,140 164 D2
Kamizato, Jap. 154 h15
Kamloops, Br. Col., Can., 9,725 42 G4
Kammuri-yama, Jap. 154 C4
Kamo, Jap. 154 g16
Kamo, Jap., 39,292 155 F3

Kamo, U.S.S.R., 8,800 137 c1
Kamoenai, Jap., 3,877 155 J8
Kamohio Bay, Hawaii 84 E3
Kamola, D.R.Congo 164 D3
Kamooloa, Hawaii 84 b6
Kamoshima, Jap., 24,119 154 f15
Kamouraska, Qué., Can. 47 Q10
Kampa, Indon. 148 C3
Kampa Dzong, China 144 g11
Kampala, Uganda, 46,735 164 E1
Kampar, Malay., 24,611 148 B1
Kampar, r., Indon. 148 B2
Kampen, Neth., 25,600 115 D2
Kampenhout, Belg., 4,027 115 e9
Kamperland, Neth. 115 B3
Kampeska, L., S. Dak. 74 D3
Kamphaeng Phet, Thai., 7,137 146 B3
Kamphaeng Saen, Thai. 147 c4
Kamp-Lintfort, F.R.Ger., 31,878 119 B2
Kampong Ajil, Malay. 147 p14
Kampong Ayer Jerneh, Malay., 1,064 147 p14
Kampong Bukit Sapi, Malay., 1,822 147 o14
Kampong Buloh, Malay. 147 p14
Kampong Chenor, Malay., 1,085 147 p15
Kampong Guchil, Malay., 3,170 147 p14
Kampong Jerangau, Malay. 147 p14
Kampong Jimah, Malay., 4,477 147 o15
Kampong Kadok, Malay., 7,208 147 p14
Kampong Kemara, Malay. 147 p14
Kampong Kerayong, Malay. 147 p15
Kampong Koh, Malay., 6,114 148 B1
Kampong Kuala Kemaman, Malay., 2,183 147 p14
Kampong Kuala Menjing, Malay. 147 p14
Kampong Kuala Tembeling, Malay. 147 p14
Kampong Lepar, Malay. 147 p14
Kampong Manchis, Malay., 1,121 147 p15
Kampong Mesta, Malay. 147 p14
Kampong Nenasi, Malay., 1,070 148 B2
Kampong Pajam, Malay., 1,339 147 o15
Kampong Pangkat Kalong, Malay., 11,248 147 p14
Kampong Paya, Malay., 2,134 147 p15
Kampong Penarek, Malay. 147 p14
Kampong Penjom, Malay. 147 p14
Kampong Perlis, Malay. 147 p14
Kampong Raja, Malay., 1,807 147 p14
Kampong Sanggang, Malay. 147 p15
Kampong Sedili Besar, Malay., 2,724 147 p16
Kampong Sungei Ayer Tawar, Malay. 147 o15
Kampong Sungei Besar, Malay., 1,285 147 o15
Kampong Sungei Rengit, Malay., 2,310 147 q16
Kampong Sungei Ular, Malay. 147 p14
Kampong Tanjong Lumpar, Malay., 1,669 147 p15
Kampot, Camb., 12,558 146 D5
Kampsville, Ill., 453 68 B4
Kamptee, India, 40,859 145 F5
Kampti, Upper Volta 162 D4
Kampungbaru, Indon. 149 G2
Kampung Sailolof, Indon. 149 J3
Kamrar, Iowa, 268 72 D2
Kamrau, Teluk, Indon. 149 K3
Kamsack, Sask., Can., 2,941 43 E4
Kamskiy, U.S.S.R. 137 h6
Kamskoye Vdkhr., U.S.S.R. 137 h7
Kamuchawie L., Man.-Sask., Can. 43 D3
Kamuela, Hawaii, 657 84 F4
Kamui-misaki, Jap. 155 J8
Kamundan, r., Indon. 149 K3
Kamutunda, D.R.Congo 165 m18
Kamye, Burma 147 f7
Kamyshevakha, U.S.S.R. 136 D4
Kamyshin, U.S.S.R., 62,000 134 D4
Kamyshlov, U.S.S.R., 30,100 137 k8
Kamyshnyy, U.S.S.R. 137 k9
Kamysh-Zarya, U.S.S.R. 136 e8
Kan, r., Ch-hsi., China 150 F4
Kan, r., N-m-k., China 150 G1
Kan, r., U.S.S.R. 135 J4
Kanaaupscow, Qué., Can. 44 J3
Kanaaupscow, r., Qué., Can. 44 J3
Kanab, Utah, 1,645 78 B3
Kanab Cr., Ariz.-Utah 78 B3
Kanabec, co., Minn., 9,007 74 F2
Kanaga I., Alaska 85 f8
Kanagawa, Jap. 154 e15
Kanaio, Hawaii 84 E3
Kanakanak, Alaska 85 D4
Kanália, Gr., 1,579 129 C5
Kanália, Gr., 1,733 129 D5
Kanam, Terr. New Guin. 174 g1
Kanapou Bay, Hawaii 84 E3
Kanarraville, Utah, 236 78 B3
Kanash, U.S.S.R., 33,000 134 D4
Kanathea, i., Fiji 174 4
Kanatlarci, Yug., 2,655 125 E4
Kanauga, Ohio 70 G4
Kanaung, Burma, 4,134 147 a1
Kanawha, Iowa, 735 72 D2
Kanawha, co., W. Va., 252,925 62 C4
Kanawha, r., W. Va. 62 B4
Kanaya, Jap. 154 g15
Kanaya, Jap. 155 m20
Kanayama, Jap., 13,035 155 E4
Kanayama, Jap. 155 K8
Kanazawa, Jap., 298,972 155 E3
Kanazu, Jap., 17,276 155 E3
Kanbalu, Burma, 3,281 146 A2
Kanchanaburi, Thai., 12,957 146 B4
Kancheepuram, India, 92,714 145 F7
Kānchenjunga, mtn., India 144 g12
Kanchor, Camb. 147 m10
Kan-chou, China 150 F4
Kanchow = Chang-yen
Kan-ch'üan, China 151 A3
Kanchung Gangri, mts., China 144 e10
Kańczuga, Pol., 1,696 127 E4
Kandagach, U.S.S.R., 8,400 134 E5
Kandahār, Afghan., 115,000* 144 B3
Kandalaksha, U.S.S.R., 36,000 134 C3
Kandang, Indon. 148 A2
Kandangan, Indon. 148 E3
Kandanghaur, Indon. 148 D4
Kandava, U.S.S.R., 5,000 136 A1
Kandavu, i., Fiji 174 4
Kandavu Passage, Fiji 174 4
Kandé, Togo 162 d7
Kandel, F.R.Ger., 5,394 118 B4
Kandergrund, Switz. 124 B2
Kandersteg, Switz. 124 B2
Kandhíla, Gr., 1,572 129 C5
Kandhíla, Gr., 1,598 129 D6
Kandhkot, Pak., 12,253 144 C3
Kandi, Dahom., 5,050 162 E4
Kandi, India, 19,780 144 g14
Kandiāro, Pak., 4,852 144 C4
Kandik, r., Alaska 85 J2
Kandiyohi, co., Minn., 29,987 74 E3
Kando, Jap. 154 i14
Kandos, Austl., 1,728 173 h9
Kandrian, Terr. New Guin. 174 f2
Kandukur, India, 12,436 145 F7
Kandy, Cey., 57,200 145 F9
Kane, co., Ill., 208,246 68 D2
Kane, Ill., 469 68 B4
Kane, Pa., 5,380 60 E2
Kane, co., Utah, 2,667 78 C3
Kane Basin, N.W.T., Can. 41 Q2
Kanegasaki, Jap., 17,112 155 G2
Kaneihara, Jap. 154 h14
Kaneilio Pt., Hawaii 84 a7
Kanem, reg., Chad 162 G3
Kanene, D.R.Congo 165 m18
Kaneohe, Hawaii, 14,414 84 D2
Kaneohe Bay Hawaii 84 D2
Kanëv, U.S.S.R., 7,300 136 C3
Kanevskaya, U.S.S.R. 136 E4
Kaneyama, Jap., 10,284 155 G2
Kaneyama, Jap. 154 i14
Kaneyoshi, Jap. 154 e15
Kangaba, Mali 162 C4
Kangar, Malay., 6,065 148 B1
Kangara, Niger 162 F3
Kangaroo I., Austl. 172 E5
Kangaruma, Guyana 101 L5
Kangasala, Fin. 120 F3
Kangasniemi, Fin. 120 F3
Kangāvar, Iran, 6,251 143 D2
Kang-ch'a, China 150 D3
Kangdong, N. Kor. 151 E3
Kangean, Kep., Indon. 148 E4
Kangean, P., Indon. 148 f7
Kanggye, N. Kor. 151 E2
Kanggyŏng, S. Kor., 24,554 151 E3
Kanghwa, S. Kor. 151 E3
Kangkar Chaah, Malay., 4,747 147 p15
Kangkar Jemaluang, Malay., 2,981 148 C2
Kangkar Kahang, Malay., 2,467 147 p15
Kangkar Masai, Malay., 1,393 147 p16
Kangnŭng, S. Kor., 58,703 151 F3
Kango, Gabon 164 A1
Kang Pabong, Laos 146 D4
K'ang-ping, China 151 D2
Kang-shan, Taiwan, 45,581 152 F3
K'ang'ting, China 152 A1
Kangtö, mtn., China 150 C4
Kangyidaung, Burma, 2,641 147 a2
Kanhla, Burma 147 f7
Kanhsien = Kan-chou
Kani, Burma, 2,602 146 A2
Kaniama, D.R.Congo 164 D3
Kaniapiskau, L., Qué., Can. 45 L3
Kaniapiskau, r., Qué., Can. 45 L2
Kanibadam, U.S.S.R., 17,500 137 f4
Kanie, Jap., 15,294 154 h14
Kaniere, N.Z. 175 f6
Kanif, Yap 176 20
Kanin, P-ov., U.S.S.R. 134 D3
Kanin Nos, M., U.S.S.R. 134 D3
Kanioumé, Mali 162 D3
Kânireş, Turk. 137 b2
Kanita, Jap., 7,304 155 G1
Kaniva, Austl. 172 F5
Kanji, Jap. 155 m19
Kanjirappally, India, 19,038 145 k21
Kanjiža, Yug., 10,000* 125 E1
Kankaanpää, Fin. 120 E3
Kankake, Jap. 154 f16
Kankakee, co., Ill., 92,063 68 E2
Kankakee, Ill., 27,666 68 E2
Kankakee, r., Ill. 68 D2
Kankakee R. Ditch, Ill.-Ind. 70 B1
Kankan, Guin., 50,000 162 C4
Kanker, India, 6,487 145 F5
Kankossa, Maur., 1,100 162 C3
Kan-ku, China 150 E3
Kannabe, Jap., 24,259 155 C4
Kan-nan, China 150 G1
Kannapolis, N.C., 34,647 63 D2
Kannauj, India, 24,646 144 b12
Kanniyakumari = Comorin, C.
Kannod, India, 6,540 144 a14
Kannonji, Jap., 46,731 155 C4
Kanaon-zaki, Jap. 154 B4
Kannoura, Jap., 4,061 155 D5
Kannus, Fin. 120 E3
Kanō, Jap. 154 i14
Kano, Nigeria, 152,302 162 F3
Kanona, Kans. 75 E4
Kanona, N.Y. 58 F7
Kanona, Zambia 164 E4
Kanonga, D.R.Congo 165 n18
Kanoni, D.R.Congo 165 n19
Kanopolis, Kans. 75 G5
Kanopolis Res., Kans. 75 G5
Kanorado, Kans., 245 75 C4
Kanosh, Utah, 499 78 B2
Kanoto, Jap. 155 m19
Kanowit, Malay., 1,555 148 E2
Kanoya, Jap., 72,498 154 B6
Kanōzan, Jap. 155 m20
Kan-pa, r., China 152 B2
Kanpur, India, 895,106 145 F4
Kanrāch, Pak. 144 B4
Kansanchi, Zambia 164 D4
Kansas, st., U.S., 2,248,000* 75
Kansas, Ill., 815 68 D4
Kansas, r., Kans. 75 K4
Kansas City, Kans., 121,901 75 L4
Kansas City, Mo., 475,539 72 C6
Kansasville, Wis. 66 c13
Kansenia, D.R.Congo 165 n19
Kansk, U.S.S.R., 88,000 135 J4
Kansŏng, S. Kor., 7,876 151 F3
Kan-su, prov., China, 12,800,000 150 D3
Kant, U.S.S.R., 15,600 137 g3
Kantang, Thai., 5,090 146 B6
Kantchari, Upper Volta 162 E3
Kan-te, China 150 D3
Kantegir, r., U.S.S.R. 137 s11
Kantharalak, Thai. 146 D4
Kantishna, r., Alaska 85 G2
Kantō-heiya, plain, Jap. 154 ·
Kantunil, Mex., 1,577 93 H4
Kanturk, Ire., 2,005 113 B5
Kan-tzu, China, 7,000* 150 D4
Kanuchuan L., Ont., Can. 44 E4
Kanuku Mts., Guyana 101 L6
Kanuma, Jap., 77,927 155 F3
Kanungu, Uganda 165 d14
Kanuti, r., Alaska 85 F2
Kanye, Bots., 34,045 164 D6
Kan-yü, China 151 C4
Kanyutkwin, Burma, 5,580 147 b1
Kanzaki, Jap. 154 h14
Kanzenze, D.R.Congo 165 m19
Kao, i., Tonga 177 36
Kao-an, China 152 D1
Kaohikaipu I., Hawaii 84 e8
Kao-hsien, China 152 B1
Kao-hsiung, Taiwan, 388,848 150 F5
Kaoko Veld, reg., S.-W. Af. 164 B5
Kaolack, Sen., 46,886 162 B3
Kao-lan, China 152 a7
Kao-lan Shan, China 152 a7
Kao-ling, China 151 A4
Kao-ming, China 152 D3
Kao-p'ing, China 151 B4
Kaore, Jap. 154 i14
K'ao-shan-t'un, China 151 E1
Kao-shun, China 152 E1
Kao-t'ai, China 150 D3
Kao-t'ang, China 151 C3
Kao Thaung, Thai. 147 d4
Kao-yang, China 151 B3
Kao-yao, China, 70,000* 150 E5
Kao-yu, China 151 C4
Kao-yüan, China 151 C3
Kao-yu Hu, China 151 C4
Kapa, i., Tonga 177 36
Kapaa, Hawaii, 3,439 84 B1
Kapaau = Kohala
Kapagere, Terr. Papua 174 e3
Kapahulu, Hawaii 84 d8
Kapanga, D.R.Congo 164 C3
Kapangan, Phil., 2,351 153 b6
Kapapa I., Hawaii 84 d7
Kapar, Malay., 5,637 147 o15
Kapela, Yug. 125 C2
Kapela, mts., Yug. 125 B2
Kapelle, Neth., 3,200 115 B3
Kapellen, Belg, 11,133 115 C3
Kapellen, F.R.Ger., 3,651 119 A1
Kapelln, Aust. 124 b10
Kapema, D.R.Congo 165 o19
Kapfenberg, Aust., 23,868 124 M6
Kapikotongwa, r., Ont., Can. 44 E5
Kapingamarangi, atoll, Car. Is. 170 E4
Kapingamarangi Rise, Pac. Oc. 168 E2
Kapiri Mposhi, Zambia 164 D4
Kapiskau, r., Ont., Can. 44 F4
Kapit, Malay., 1,834 148 E2
Kapiti I., N.Z. 175 g6
Kaplan, La., 5,267 73 C7
Kaplice, Czech. 126 B2
Kapoeta, Sudan 163 K5
Kapoho Pt., Hawaii 84 d7
Kapong, Thai. 146 B5
Kapos, r., Hung. 126 C3
Kaposvár, Hung., 43,458 126 C3
Kapowsin, Wash. 80 B2
Kappara, Jap. 154 i14
Kappeln, F.R.Ger., 4,766 118 B1
Kappl, Aust., 1,972 124 G6
Kaprun, Aust., 2,162 124 J6
Kapsabet, Kenya 165 g13
Kapsan, N. Kor. 151 F2
Kapsokhóra, Gr. 129 D5
Kapuas, r., Indon. 148 D2
Kapuas, r., Indon. 148 E3
Kapulena, Hawaii 84 F3
Kapunda, Austl. 1,185 172 E5
Kapuskas = Marijampolė
Kapuskasing, Ont., Can., 6,697 44 G5
Kapuskasing, r., Ont., Can. 44 G5
Kapustin Yar, U.S.S.R. 134 D5
Kapuvár, Hung., 10,902 126 C3
Kap'yŏng, S. Kor., 18,377 151 E3
Kara, U.S.S.R. 134 F3
Kara, r., Turk. 137 b2
Karabalty, U.S.S.R., 10,700 137 g3
Karabanovo, U.S.S.R., 18,100 136 c5
Karabash, U.S.S.R., 24,900 137 i8
Kara-Bogaz-Gol, U.S.S.R. 134 E5
Kara-Bogaz-Gol, Zal., U.S.S.R. 134 E5
Karabük, Turk., 31,483 142 C1
Karacabey, Turk., 15,985 142 B1
Karachayevsk, U.S.S.R., 75,000 136 F4
Karachev, U.S.S.R., 11,000 136 D2
Karāchi, Pak., 1,912,598 144 C4
Karaçürun, Turk., 2,300 142 D2
Karád, Hung., 3,451 126 C3
Karad, India, 33,772 145 E6
Karaganda, U.S.S.R., 441,000 134 G5
Karagay, U.S.S.R. 137 h7
Karaginskiy, O., U.S.S.R. 135 Q4
Karaginskiy Zal., U.S.S.R. 135 Q4
Karagosh, G., U.S.S.R. 137 s12
Karahalli, Turk., 4,758 142 B2
Karai, Malay., 2,293 147 o14
Karaidel'skiy, U.S.S.R. 137 h8
Kara Irtish, r., China 150 B2
Karaisen, Bulg., 3,655 128 E3
Karaj, Iran, 14,526 143 E1
Karak, Malay., 2,854 147 p15
Karak Kash = Mo-yü
Karakelong, P., Indon. 149 H1
Karako, Jap. 154 h15
Karakoram Pass, India-Pak. 145 F2
Karakoram Ra., India-Pak. 145 E1
Karakorum, ruins, Mong. 150 D2
Karaköse, Turk., 19,786 142 E2
Kara-Kul', Oz., U.S.S.R. 137 g4
Karakuldzha, r., U.S.S.R. 137 g4
Karakul'skoye, U.S.S.R. 137 k8
Karakumskiy Kan., U.S.S.R. 134 F6
Karakumy, Peski, U.S.S.R. 134 F6
Karama, r., Indon. 149 F3
Karaman, Turk., 21,660 142 C2
Karamea, N.Z. 175 g6
Karamea Bight, N.Z. 175 f6
Karapelit, Bulg., 2,033 128 F3
Karapınar, Turk., 10,770 142 C2
Karas, P., Indon. 149 K3
Karaš, r., Yug. 125 E2
Karasburg, S.-W. Afr., 2,233 164 B6
Kara Sea = Karskoye More
Karashoky, U.S.S.R. 137 o12
Karašjåkka, r., Nor. 120 F1
Karasjok, Nor. 120 F1
Karasor, Oz., U.S.S.R. 137 n11
Karasu, Turk., 5,681 142 B1
Karasu, U.S.S.R. 137 k9
Karasu, r., U.S.S.R. 137 o11
Karasuk, U.S.S.R. 20,000 134 G4
Karasuk, r., U.S.S.R. 137 p11
Karasuyama, Jap., 24,729 155 G3
Karatalyayat, r., U.S.S.R. 137 k9
Karatau, Khr., Kaz.S.S.R., U.S.S.R. 134 F5
Karatau, Khr., R.S.F.S.R., U.S.S.R. 137 i8
Karathuri, Burma 146 B5
Karatmanovo, Yug. 125 E4
Karaton, U.S.S.R., 4,200 134 E5
Karatsu, Jap., 77,825 154 B5
Karaul, U.S.S.R. 134 H2
Karauli, India, 23,696 144 a12
Karavas, Cyp., 2,340 142 e9
Karavás, Gr. 129 D6
Karavastas, Kënet' e, Alb. 125 D4
Karawanken, mts., Aust. 124 L7
Karbalā', Iraq, 60,804 143 C2
Karbers Ridge, Ill. 68 D6
Karcag, Hung., 26,098 126 E3
Karczew, Pol., 6,212 127 D2
Kardam, Bulg., 2,585 128 F3
Kardam, Bulg., 2,198 128 G3
Kardamum, i., India 145 D8
Karden, F.R.Ger. 118 A3
Kardhámaina, Gr., 1,229 129 F6
Kardhítsa, Gr., 23,708 129 D5
Kärdla, U.S.S.R., 2,700 136 A1
Kareli, India, 8,603 144 b14
Karema, Tanz. 164 E3
Karema, Terr. Papua 174 e3
Karera, India, 5,025 144 b13
Kārez Iliās, Afghan. 144 A2
Kargala, U.S.S.R. 137 h9
Kargang La, China-Nepal 144 d10
Kargasok, U.S.S.R. 134 H4
Kargat, U.S.S.R. 137 q11
Kargat, r., U.S.S.R. 137 q11
Kargil, India 145 E2
Kargopol', U.S.S.R., 8,600 134 C3
Kargowa, Pol., 2,414 127 A2
Karhal, India, 7,512 144 b12
Karhula, Fin., 22,693 120 F3
Kariá, Gr., 1,739 129 C5
Kariá, Gr., 1,230 129 D5
Kariai, Gr. 129 E4
Kariava, Terr. Papua 174 e2
Kariba, Rhod. 164 D4
Kariba L., Zambia 164 D4
Kariba-yama, Jap. 155 H8
Karibib, S.-W. Afr., 1,395 164 B5
Kaributo, Jap., 8,435 155 J8
Karigasniemi, Fin. 120 F1
Karikal, India 22,252 145 F8
Karikari, C., N.Z. 175 g5
Karima = Kureymah
Karimata, P., Indon. 148 D3
Karimata, Selat, Indon. 148 D3
Karimganj, India, 28,683 145 J4
Karimnagar, India, 31,554 145 F6
Karimundjawa, Kep., Indon. 148 D4
Karimundjawa, P., Indon. 148 d6
Karin, Som. Rep. 163 M4
Käringön, Swed. 121 D2
Karis, Fin. 120 E3
Karise, Den., 1,558 121 E5
Káristos, Gr., 3,335 129 E5
Kariwano, Jap. 155 G2
Kariya, Jap., 6,386 155 D4
Kariya, Jap., 59,245 155 E4
Kariya, Jap. 155 n20
Karjaa = Karis
Karkala, India 15,535 145 E7
Karkar, i., Terr. New Guin. 174 e2
Karkaralinsk, U.S.S.R., 6,900 134 G5
Karkheh, r., Iran 143 D2
Karkinitskiy Zal., U.S.S.R. 136 D4
Karkuidighin = Sapone
Karla-Aleksandra, O., U.S.S.R. 134 D1
Karla Marksa, Pik, U.S.S.R. 134 G6
Karlapat, India 145 G6
Karlburg, F.R.Ger., 1,492 119 H5
Karlby, Den. 121 C4
Karlebo, Den., 3,243 121 a7
Karlin, Mich. 67 H4
Karlino, Pol., 2,894 127 A1
Karl-Marx-Stadt, Ger.D.R., 286,329 118 D3
Karlovac, Yug. 34,000* 125 B2
Karlovásion, Gr., 5,308 129 F6
Karlovka, U.S.S.R., 14,500 136 D3
Karlovy Vary, Czech., 46,877 126 A1
Karlshamn, Swed. 120 C4
Karlskoga, Swed. 120 C4
Karlskrona, Swed., 32,977 120 C4
Karlsruhe, F.R.Ger., 222,237 118 B4
Karlsruhe, N. Dak., 221 74 B1
Karlstad, Swed., 43,064 120 C4
Karlstad, Minn., 720 74 D1
Karlstadt, F.R.Ger., 5,767 118 B4
Karlstetten, Aust., 1,160 124 b10
Karluk, Alaska, 129 85 F4
Karmah, Sudan 163 K2
Karmanovo, U.S.S.R. 136 a6
Karnabrunn, Aust. 124 c10
Karnack, Tex. 77 Q3
Karnaful Res., India 146 A2
Karnaful Res., Pak. 145 J5
Karnak, Ill., 667 68 C6
Karnak, ruins, U.A.R. 161 K3
Karnal, India, 72,109 145 E3
Karnali, r., China-Nepal 144 c11
Karnes, co., Tex., 14,995 77 P5
Karnes City, Tex., 2,693 77 O5
Karns City, Pa. 404 60 C4
Karokpi, Burma 147 b3
Karonga, Malawi 164 E3
Karoonda, Austl. 172 c8
Karomatan, Phil., 1,310 153 B4
Káros, i., Gr. 129 E6
Karosa, Indon. 149 F3
Karpacz, Pol., 4,022 127 e6
Karpas Pen., Cyp. 142 f9
Kárpathos, i., Gr. 129 F7
Karpáthou, Stenón, Gr. 129 F7
Karpenísion, Gr., 3,523 129 C5
Karperón, Gr. 129 C5
Karpinsk, U.S.S.R., 50,000 137 i7
Karpogory, U.S.S.R. 134 D3
Karpuninskiy, U.S.S.R. 137 k7
Karrebæksminde Bugt, Den. 121 D5
Karrkila, Fin. 120 F3
Karroo, Upper, plat., S. Af. 164 C7
Kars, Turk., 32,046 142 E1
Karsakpay, U.S.S.R., 10,000 134 F5
Kärsämäki, Fin. 120 F3
Kārsava, U.S.S.R., 4,000 136 B1
Karshi, U.S.S.R., 19,700 134 F6
Karşıyaka, Turk., 69,489 142 A2
Karskiye Vorota, Prol., U.S.S.R. 134 E2
Karskoye More, U.S.S.R. 134 F2
Karstädt, Ger.D.R. 118 C2
Karstula, Fin. 120 F3
Kartal, Turk., 10,790 142 B1
Kartaly, U.S.S.R., 33,900 137 k9
Karthaus, Pa. 60 F3
Karttula, Fin. 120 F3
Kartuzy, Pol., 7,760 127 C1
Karuigawa, Jap. 154 g16
Karumai, Jap., 17,553 155 G1
Karumwa, Tanz. 165 f15
Kārūn, r., Iran 143 D2
Karungu, Kenya 165 g14
Karunki, Fin. 120 F2
Karup, Den. 121 B4
Karur, India, 50,564 145 E8
Karval, Colo. 79 D2
Karvia, Fin. 120 E3
Karviná, Czech., 53,729 126 D2
Karwar, India, 23,906 145 D7
Karwi, India 144 c13
Karymskoye, U.S.S.R., 10,400 135 L4
Kås, Den. 121 B3
Kasai, r., Ang.-D.R.Congo 164 C2
Kasama, Zambia, 2,400 164 E3
Kasamatsu, Jap., 19,065 154 h14
Kasanda, Uganda 165 e13
Kasanga, Tanz. 164 E3
Kasangulu, D.R.Congo 164 B2
Kasan-nodongjagu, N. Kor. 151 E2
Kasaoka, Jap., 68,987 155 C4
Kasaragod, India, 27,635 145 E7
Kasasa, Jap., 11,820 154 B6
Kasawara, Jap. 154 i14
Kasba L., N.W.T., Can. 40 J5
Kasba-Tadla, Mor., 11,733 160 C2
Kaseda, Jap., 34,608 154 B6
Kaseda, Jap. 154 g15
Kaseke, D.R.Congo 165 n19
Kasempa, Zambia 164 D4
Kasengo, D.R.Congo 165 o19
Kasenyi, Uganda 165 e14
Kasese, Uganda 164 E1
Kasganj, India, 37,559 144 b12
Kashabowie, Ont., Can. 44 D5
Kāshān, Iran, 45,955 143 E2
Kashega, Alaska 85 C5
Kashegelok, Alaska 85 E3
Kashgar = K'o-shih
Kashgar, r., China 150 A3
Kashihara, Jap., 35,645 154 g15
Kashima, Jap., 39,392 154 A5
Kashima, Jap., 18,048 155 G3
Kashima, Jap., 16,407 155 G4
Kashima-nada, Jap. 155 G3
Kashimbo, D.R.Congo 165 n19
Kashin, U.S.S.R., 16,300 136 E1
Kashino, Jap. 154 f15
Kashipur, India, 24,258 144 b11
Kashira, U.S.S.R., 21,000 136 b6
Kashiwa, Jap., 63,745 155 m19
Kashiwagi, Jap. 154 g15
Kashiwano, Jap. 154 h15
Kashiwazaki, Jap., 74,139 155 F3
Kashka-Dar'ya, r., U.S.S.R. 137 e4
Kāshmar, Iran, 13,299 143 F1
Kashmir = Jammu and Kashmir
Kashmor, Pak. 144 C3
Kashum Tsho, China 150 B3
Kashunuk, r., Alaska 85 C3
Kasiglook, Alaska, 244 85 D3
Kasilof, Alaska, 89 85 G3
Kasimov, U.S.S.R., 30,000 136 F2
Kasindi Vieux, Congo L. 165 d13
Kasiruta, P., Indon. 149 H3
Kasiui, P., Indon. 149 J4
Kaskaskia, Ill. 68 B6
Kaskaskia, r., Ill. 68 C5
Kaskattama, r., Man., Can. 43 H3
Kaskinen = Kaskö
Kaskö, Fin., 1,482 120 E3
Kas Kong, Camb. 146 C5
Kasli, U.S.S.R., 21,800 137 k8
Kaslo, Br. Col., Can. 42 J4
Kasmere L., Man., Can. 43 E2
Kas Moul, Camb. 146 C5
Kasolo, D.R.Congo 165 n19
Kasolwa, D.R.Congo 165 n18
Kasongo, D.R.Congo 164 D2
Kasongo-Lunda, D.R.Congo 164 C3
Kásos, i., Gr. 129 F7
Kasota, Minn., 649 74 F3
Kaspi, U.S.S.R., 9,200 137 c1
Kaspiysk, U.S.S.R., 25,300 137 c1
Kaspiyskiy, U.S.S.R. 134 D5
Kasr, Ra's, Sudan 163 L2
Kassalā, Sudan, 40,612 163 K3
Kassándra, pen., Gr. 129 D4
Kassel, F.R.Ger., 191,935 118 B3
Kasserine = Al Qasrayn
Kassikaityu, r., Guyana 101 L7
Kassler, Colo. 79 b9
Kasson, Ind. 70 B4
Kasson, Minn., 1,732 74 F3
Kastamonu, Turk., 19,450 142 C1
Kastanéai, Gr., 2,072 129 F4
Kastellaun, F.R.Ger., 2,012 118 A3
Kastélli, Gr. 129 D5
Kastélli, Gr., 2,071 129 D7
Kastéllion, Gr., 1,351 129 E7
Kastellórizon, I., Gr. 142 B2
Kasten, Aust. 124 b10
Kastl, F.R.Ger., 1,216 118 C4
Kastóri, Gr., 1,332 129 D6
Kastoria, Gr., 10,162 129 C4
Kástron, Gr., 3,460 129 E5
Kastrup, Den., 20,305 121 b7
Kasuga, Jap. 154 h15
Kasugai, Jap., 77,174 155 E4
Kasukabe, Jap., 34,280 155 m19
Kasulu, Tanz. 164 E2
Kasumba, Congo L. 165 n20
Kasumi, Jap. 154 f14
Kasumi, Jap., 17,356 155 D4
Kasumiga-ura, Jap. 155 G3
Kasumkent, U.S.S.R. 137 c1
Kasumpti, India 144 a10
Kasungu, Malawi 164 E4
Kasūr, Pak., 74,546 145 E3
Katabulwe, Congo L. 165 o19
Katada, Jap. 154 h15
Katada, Jap., 16,877 155 D4
Katagum, Nigeria 162 F3
Katagupan, Phil., 153 A3
Katahdin Iron Works, Me. 55 C3
Katahdin, Mt., Me. 55 D3
Katakai, Jap. 155 G4
Katakami, Jap. 154 f15
Katako-Kombe, Congo L. 164 D2
Katamachi, Jap. 155 n19
Katanga, r., U.S.S.R. 135 K4
Katanga, Congo L. 164 D3
Katangi, India, 7,205 144 b15
Katangli, U.S.S.R., 2,600 135 O4
Katanning, Austl., 2,864 172 B5
Kataoka, Jap. 155 m20
Katastári, Gr., 1,324 129 C6
Katav-Ivanovsk, U.S.S.R., 20,600 137 i8
Kataysk, U.S.S.R., 11,800 137 k8
Katcha, Nigeria 162 g7
Katchall I., India 146 A6
Katebe, Uganda 165 e14
Katebosho, D.R.Congo 165 n19
Katechay I., Mich. 67 K5
Katentania, D.R.Congo 165 m18
Katentania, D.R.Congo 165 m19
Katerini, Gr., 28,046 129 D4
Kates Needle, pk., Br. Col., Can. 42 D1
Katete, D.R.Congo 165 n19
Katha, Burma, 7,714 146 B1
Katherine, Austl. 172 D2
Kathiawar, pen., India 144 ·
Kathleen, Fla. 65 G4
Kathleen, Ga. 64 F3
Kathua, India, 9,647 145 E2
Kati, Mali, 32,000 162 C3
Katie, Okla. 76 F3
Katihar, India, 59,344 145 H4
Katiki, Vol., Easter I. 177 46
Katiola, Iv. Coast, 7,778 162 D4
Katipunan, Phil., 3,846 153 B3
Katiu, atoll, Tuam. Arch. 177 42
Katla, vol., Ice. 120 a6
Katmai Nat. Mon., Alaska 85 F4
Katmai Vol., Alaska 85 F4
Kātmāndu, Nepal, 122,507 145 G4
Kato, Guyana 101 L5
Káto Akhaïa, Gr., 2,987 129 C5
Káto Figalía, Gr., 1,669 129 C6
Káto Klitoría, Gr., 1,183 129 D6
Katol, India, 14,581 144 b15
Katonah, N.Y. 59 N9
Káto Nevrokópion, Gr., 2,994 129 D4
Katonga, D.R.Congo 165 m19
Katonga, r., Uganda 165 e13
Katoomba, Austl., 6,975 173 g9
Katoúna, Gr., 2,910 129 C5
Katowice, Pol., 269,000* 127 C3
Kato Zodhia, Cyp., 2,143 142 d9
Katrime, Man., Can. 43 f9
Katrīnah, Jabal, U.A.R. 161 K3
Katrine, Loch, U.K. 112 D3
Katrineholm, Swed. 120 D4
Katsbakhskiy, U.S.S.R. 137 i9
Katsina, Nigeria 162 F3
Katsina Ala, Nigeria 162 F4
Katsumoto, Jap., 10,960 154 A5
Katsuno, Jap. 154 h14
Katsuta, Jap., 43,286 155 G3
Katsuura, Jap. 155 E5
Katsuura, Jap., 31,141 155 G4
Katsuyama, Jap., 15,477 155 C4
Katsuyama, Jap., 36,531 155 E3
Katta-Kurgan, U.S.S.R., 34,100 134 F6
Kattavia, Gr. 129 F7
Kattawagami, r., Ont., Can. 44 H5
Kattegat, str., Den.-Swed. 120 B4
Katun', r., U.S.S.R. 134 H4
Katunguru, Uganda 165 e14
Katupa, Indon. 148 F5
Katwa, India, 20,621 144 g14
Katwe, Uganda 165 d14
Katwijk aan Zee, Neth., 17,100 115 C2
Katwijk a.d. Rijn, Neth., 4,900 115 a6
Katy, Tex., 1,569 77 Q5
Kąty Wrocławskie, Pol., 3,355 127 f5
Katzelsdorf, Aust., 1,343 124 c11
Katzenbuckel, mt., F.R.Ger. 119 G6
Katzenelnbogen, F.R.Ger., 1,367 119 D4
Katzenfurt, F.R.Ger., 1,688 119 E3
Kau, Teluk, Indon. 149 H2
Kauai, co., Hawaii, 28,176 84 B2
Kauai, i., Hawaii 84 B1
Kauai Chan., Hawaii 84 C2
Kauaopuu, pk., Hawaii 84 b7
Kaub, F.R.Ger., 2,346 119 D4
Kau Des., Hawaii 84 F4
Kauehi, i., Tuam. Arch. 171 J6
Kaueleau, Hawaii 84 F4
Kaufbeuren, F.R.Ger., 29,443 118 C5
Kaufman, co., Tex., 29,931 77 P3
Kaufman, Tex., 3,087 77 P3
Kauhajoki, Fin. 120 E3
Kauhava, Fin. 120 E3
Kaukauna, Wis., 10,096 66 E4
Kaukonahua Str., Hawaii 84 b6
Kaukura, atoll, Tuam. Arch. 177 42
Kaula, i., Hawaii 84 g9
Kaulakahi Chan., Hawaii 84 B1
Kaumajet Mts., Newf., Can. 45 O2
Kaumakani, Hawaii, 921 84 B2
Kaumalapau, Hawaii 84 D3
Kaumberg, Aust. 124 b10
Kaumbo, Congo L. 165 m18
Kaunakakai, Hawaii, 740 84 D2
Kauna Pt., Hawaii 84 F4
Kaunas, U.S.S.R., 232,000 134 B4
Kaunisvaara, Swed. 120 E2
Kaupo, Hawaii 84 E3
Kaupuni Str., Hawaii 84 a7
Kaurai, Terr. Papua 174 3
Kaura Namoda, Nigeria 162 F3
Kauriala Ghat, India 144 c11
Kauswagan, Phil., 4,502 153 B4
Kaut, Terr. New Guin. 174 f1
Kautokeino, Nor. 120 E1
Kau-ye Kyun, i., Burma 146 B5
Kavadarci, Yug., 11,000* 125 E4
Kavajë, Alb., 16,400 125 D4

244 · Kavalerovo—Khenifra

Kavalerovo, U.S.S.R., 11,900 135 N5
Kavalga I., Alaska 85 f8
Kavali, India, 20,544 145 F7
Kaval'-kan, U.S.S.R. 135 N4
Kávalla, Gr., 44,517 129 E4
Kavanagh, Alta., Can. 43 b7
Kavanayén, Ven. 101 K5
Kavarna, Bulg., 7,053 128 G3
Kavieng, Terr. New Guin. 174 f1
Kavir, Dasht-e, Iran 143 E2
Kavirondo G., Kenya 165 g14
Kävlinge, Swed. 121 F5
Kaw, Fr. Guiana 101 O5
Kawa, Burma, 2,336 147 b2
Kawaai, Jap. 154 g16
Kawachi-Nagano, Jap., 34,399 154 g15
Kawagama L., Ont., Can. 46 F3
Kawagoe, Jap., 107,523 155 F4
Kawaguchi, Jap., 8,628 155 F3
Kawaguchi, Jap., 170,066 155 F4
Kawai, Jap. 154 f16
Kawai, Jap. 154 g15
Kawai, Jap. 154 h14
Kawaihae, Hawaii 84 F3
Kawaihae Bay, Hawaii 84 F3
Kawaihoa Pt., Hawaii 84 A2
Kawaikini Pk., Hawaii 84 B1
Kawailoa Beach, Hawaii 84 b6
Kawailoa Camp, Hawaii 84 b6
Kawakami, Jap. 154 f14
Kawakami, Jap. 154 h14
Kawama, D.R.Congo 164 D3
Kawamata, Jap. 154 i14
Kawamata, Jap., 25,983 155 G3
Kawambwa, Zambia 164 D3
Kawanabe, Jap., 21,119 154 B6
Kawanabe, Jap. 154 g15
Kawanai, Jap. 154 h14
Kawanoe, Jap., 36,068 155 C4
Kawarada, Jap. 154 h15
Kawaragō, Jap. 154 g16
Kawaraichi, Jap. 154 g14
Kawarazu, Jap. 154 e16
Kawardha, India, 10,117 144 c15
Kawasaki, Jap., 632,975 155 F4
Kawashima, Jap. 154 f15
Kawashima, Jap. 154 g15
Kawashima, Jap., 9,264 155 D4
Kawashiri, Jap. 154 h14
Kawau I., N.Z. 175 g5
Kawayu, Jap. 155 L8
Kaw City, Okla., 457 76 G1
Kawela, Hawaii 84 C2
Kawene, Ont., Can. 44 D5
Kaweonui Pt., Hawaii 84 B1
Kawerau, N.Z., 4,491 175 h5
Kawhmu, Burma 147 b2
Kawich Pk., Nev. 83 B4
Kawich Ra., Nev. 83 B4
Kawkareik, Burma, 6,575 146 B3
Kawkawlin, Mich. 67 K5
Kawlin, Burma, 3,766 146 A2
Kawludo, Burma 146 B3
Kawn Umbū, U.A.R. 161 K3
Kay, co., Okla., 51,042 76 F1
Kaya, Jap. 154 e15
Kaya, Jap., 10,127 155 D4
Kaya, Upper Volta, 10,280 162 D3
Kayak I., Alaska 85 H4
Kayan, Burma, 10,955 146 B3
Kayankulam, India, 44,571 145 E8
Kayanza, Burundi 165 d15
Kayapa, Phil., 3,656 153 b6
Kaycee, Wyo., 284 81 F4
Kaydak, Sor, U.S.S.R. 134 E5
Kaydee, Alta., Can. 42 H3
Kayembe-Mukulu, D.R.Congo 165 m18
Kayenta, Ariz. 78 C3
Kayenzi, Tanz. 165 f15
Kayes, Mali, 35,000 162 C3
Kayeye, D.R.Congo 165 m18
Kayeye, D.R.Congo 165 o18
Kayl, Lux., 6,505 115 E5
Kayombo, D.R.Congo 165 n18
Kayombo, D.R.Congo 165 n19
Kayrakty, r., U.S.S.R. 137 n11
Kayrakumskoye Vdkhr., U.S.S.R. 137 f4
Kayseri, Turk., 102,795 142 C2
Kaysville, Utah, 3,608 78 c8
Kayts, Cey. 145 m21
Kayuba, D.R.Congo 165 o18
Kayunga, Uganda 165 f13
Kazachinskoye, U.S.S.R. 135 K4
Kazach'ye, U.S.S.R. 135 N2
Kazakh, U.S.S.R., 9,200 137 c1
Kazakh S.S.R. = Kazakhskaya S.S.R.
Kazakhskaya S.S.R., U.S.S.R., 11,850,000* 134 E5
Kazakhskiy Melkosopochnik, U.S.S.R. 134 F4
Kazalinsk, U.S.S.R., 7,700 134 F5
Kazan', U.S.S.R., 693,000 134 E4
Kazan, r., N.W.T., Can. 40 K5
Kazandzhik, U.S.S.R., 8,000 134 E6
Kazan L., Sask., Can. 43 B3
Kazanlŭk, Bulg., 30,934 128 E3
Kazan-rettō = Volcano Is.
Kazanskaya, U.S.S.R. 136 F3
Kazatin, U.S.S.R., 21,700 136 C3
Kazbek, G., U.S.S.R. 137 c1
Kazënnyy Torets, r., U.S.S.R. 136 e7
Kāzerūn, Iran, 30,641 143 E3
Kazhim, U.S.S.R. 134 E3
Kazi-Magomed, U.S.S.R., 11,400 137 d1
Kazimierza Wielka, Pol., 4,211 127 D3
Kazincbarcika, Hung., 15,285 126 E2
Kaziza, D.R.Congo 165 m19
Kaznějov, Czech. 126 c7
Kazuka, Jap. 154 f14
Kazumba, D.R.Congo 164 C3
Kazymskaya Kul'tbaza, U.S.S.R. 134 F3
Kazyr, r., U.S.S.R. 137 t11
Kbely, Czech. 126 d6
Kcynia, Pol., 4,600 127 B2
Kéa, Gr., 1,788 129 E6
Kéa, i., Gr. 129 E6
Keaau, Hawaii = Olaa
Keaau, Hawaii Co., Hawaii 84 G4
Keaau, Honolulu Co., Hawaii 84 a6
Keady, U.K., 1,638 113 C4
Keahole Pt., Hawaii 84 E4
Kealaikahiki Chan., Hawaii 84 E3
Kealaikahiki Pt., Hawaii 84 E3
Kealakekua, Hawaii, 579 84 E4
Kealakekua Bay, Hawaii 84 E4
Kealia, Hawaii Co., Hawaii 84 F4
Kealia, Kauai Co., Hawaii 84 B1
Keams Canyon, Ariz. 78 C4
Keamuku, Hawaii 84 F4
Keanae, Hawaii 84 E3
Keanakolu, Hawaii 84 F4
Keansburg, N.J., 6,854 61 C3
Kearney, Ont., Can. 44 H6
Kearney, Mo., 678 72 C5
Kearney, co., Nebr., 6,580 75 F3
Kearney, Nebr., 14,210 75 F3
Kearns, Ont., Can. 44 H5
Kearns, Utah, 17,172 78 B1
Kearny, Ariz., 1,739 78 C5
Kearny, co., Kans., 3,108 75 D5
Kearny, N.J., 37,472 61 C2
Kearsarge, Mich. 66 E1
Kearsarge, N.H. 54 E3
Kearsarge, Mt., N.H. 54 D5
Keatchie, La., 345 73 B5
Keating, Oreg. 80 E3
Keating Summit, Pa. 60 F2
Keaton, Ky. 71 H3
Keaton Beach, Fla. 65 F3
Keauhou, Hawaii 84 E4
Keaukaha, Hawaii, 2,550* 84 G4
Keawakapu, Hawaii 84 E3
Keawanui Bay, Hawaii 84 A2
Kébémer, Sen., 3,513 162 B3
Kebezen', U.S.S.R. 137 r12
Kebnekaise, mt., Swed. 120 D2
Kebock Head, U.K. 112 C2
Kebumen, Indon. 148 c7
Kecel, Hung., 10,607 126 D3
Kechi, Jap. 154 A4
Kechika, r., Br. Col., Can. 42 E1
Keçiborlu, Turk., 4,911 142 B2
Kecskemét, Hung., 66,819 126 D3
Kedainiai, U.S.S.R., 10,600 136 A2
Kedarnath, India 144 b10
Keddie, Calif. 82 C2
Kedgwick, N.B., Can., 1,095 47 S10
Kêdia d'Idjil, hills, Maur. 162 B2
Kediri, Indon., 158,918 148 E4
Kédougou, Sen., 1,938 162 B3
Kedungwuni, Indon. 148 c7
Kędzierzyn, Pol., 20,000* 127 C3
Keech Pd., R. I. 57 K5
Keefers, Br. Col., Can. 42 G4
Keefton, Okla. 76 H2
Keegan, Me. 55 D1
Keego Harbor, Mich., 2,761 67 K6
Keehi Lagoon, Hawaii 84 c8
Keele, r., N.W.T., Can. 40 D5
Keele Pk., Yukon, Can. 40 D5
Keeler, Calif. 82 E4
Keeley L., Sask., Can. 43 B3
Keelinawi, Hawaii 84 A2
Keeling, Tenn. 71 B6
Keeling Is. = Cocos Is.
Keel Pt., V.I. 97 4
Keelung = Chi-lung
Keenan, Okla. 76 D1
Keene, Ont., Can. 46 F4
Keene, Calif. 82 D5
Keene, Kans. 75 J5
Keene, Ky. 71 G4
Keene, N.Y. 59 N3
Keene, N. Dak. 74 A2
Keene, N.H., 17,562 54 C6
Keene, Ohio 70 H2
Keene, Tex., 1,532 77 P3
Keenes, Ill., 114 68 D5
Keene Valley, N.Y. 59 N3
Keeneyville, Ill. 69 b9
Keensburg, Ill., 263 68 E5
Keeper Hill, Ire. 113 B5
Keerbergen, Belg., 4,993 115 e9
Keeseville, N.Y., 2,213 59 N2
Keesus, L., Wis. 66 c11
Keetmanshoop, S.-W. Afr., 7,989 164 C6
Keewatin, Dist. of, N.W.T., Can. 40 J5
Keewatin, Ont., Can., 2,175 44 C5
Keewatin, Minn., 1,651 74 F2
Kefallinia, i., Gr. 129 C5
Kéfalos, Gr., 1,818 129 F6
Kefannanu, Indon. 149 H5
Kefar Ata, Isr., 14,255 142 b7
Kefar Sava, Isr., 17,861 142 a7
Keflavik, Ice., 4,819 120 a6
Ke Ga, S. Viet. 147 n11
Ke Ga, Mui, pt., S. Viet. 147 n11
Keg Cr., Iowa 72 B3
Kegonsa, L., Wis. 66 D6
Keg River, Alta., Can. 42 H1
Kegworth, U.K., 2,645 114 F5
Kehamí, Nepal 144 d11
Kehl, F.R.Ger., 11,360 118 A4
Kehoe, Ky. 71 H3
Kehrig, F.R.Ger. 119 C4
Ke-hsi Mansam, Burma 146 B2
Keighley, U.K., 55,852 113 F5
Keighley, Kans. 75 J6
Keila, U.S.S.R., 3,000 136 B1
Keila, i., Sol. Is. 175 c1
Keilor, Austl., 10,681 173 F5
Keimoes, S. Af., 2,995 164 C6
Keirn, Miss. 73 E4
Keiser, Ark., 516 73 E2
Keita, Niger, 5,000* 162 E3
Keitele, l., Fin. 121 ·
Keith, Austl. 172 F5
Keith, U.K., 4,208 112 E3
Keith, co., Nebr., 7,958 75 D2
Keith Arm, N.W.T., Can. 40 E4
Keithley Creek, Br. Col., Can. 42 G3
Keithsburg, Ill., 963 68 B2
Kekaha, Hawaii, 2,082 84 B2
Kekertuk, N.W.T., Can. 41 R4
Kékes, mt., Hung. 126 E3
Kekirawa, Cey. 145 n21
Keklau, Palau 176 21
Kekoskee, Wis., 247 66 E5
Kelai, r., Indon. 148 F2
Kelang, P., Indon. 149 J3
Kelapa Sawit, Malay., 2,888 147 p16
Kelberg, F.R.Ger. 119 B4
Kelbra, Ger.D.R. 118 C3
Keldron, S. Dak. 74 B3
Kelefesia, i., Tonga 177 36
Kelford, N.C., 362 63 G1
Kelheim, F.R.Ger., 11,969 118 C4
Kelim, Colo. 79 b7
Kelkheim, F.R.Ger., 8,590 119 E4
Kelkit, r., Turk. 142 D1
Kell, F.R.Ger., 1,557 119 B5
Kell, Ill., 194 68 D5
Kellé, Congo 164 B1
Keller, Tex., 827 76 e9
Keller, Va., 263 62 J5
Keller, Wash. 80 D1
Kellerberrin, Austl., 1,145 172 B4
Keller L., N.W.T., Can. 40 E5
Kellerton, Iowa, 341 72 C4
Kellerville, Ill. 68 A4
Kellerville, Tex. 76 N2
Kellett, C., N.W.T., Can. 40 D3
Kellett Str., N.W.T., Can. 41 F2
Kelley, Iowa, 239 72 D3
Kelleys I., Ohio 70 G1
Kelliher, Sask., Can. 43 D4
Kelliher, Minn., 297 74 E2
Kellinghusen, F.R.Ger., 7,145 118 B2
Kellnersville, Wis. 66 F4
Kellogg, Idaho, 5,061 81 A2
Kellogg, Ill. 68 C5
Kellogg, Minn., 446 74 F3
Kells = Ceanannus Mór
Kelly, N.C. 63 F3
Kelly Corners, N.Y. 59 L7
Kelly Lake, Br. Col., Can. 42 G3
Kelly L., Wis. 66 E3
Kellyton, Ala. 64 D2
Kellyville, Okla., 501 76 G2
Kelmé, U.S.S.R., 5,100 136 A2
Kélo, Chad, 4,000* 162 G4
Keloma, i., Sol. Is. 175 c1
Kelowna, Br. Col., Can., 12,926 42 H4
Kelsall, U.K., 1,030 114 C4
Kelsey, Alta., Can. 43 c8
Kelsey, Mt., N.H. 54 E2
Kelsey Bay, Br. Col., Can. 42 E4
Kelseyville, Calif. 82 B3
Kelso, U.K., 3,964 112 E4
Kelso, Ark., 95 73 D4
Kelso, Tenn. 71 E6
Kelso, Wash., 8,379 80 B2
Kelsterbach, F.R.Ger., 9,679 119 F4
Kelton, Utah 78 B1
Kelty, U.K. 112 d7
Keltys, Tex., 1,056 77 Q4
Keluang, Indon. 148 B3
Keluang, Tg., Indon. 148 D3
Kelve Mahim, India 145 h17
Kelvin, r., U.K. 112 b8
Kelvington, Sask., Can. 43 D4
Kelwood, Man., Can. 43 E5
Kem', U.S.S.R., 17,000 134 C3
Kema, r., U.S.S.R. 136 E1
Ké-Macina, Mali, 1,706 162 D3
Kemah, Turk., 2,911 142 D2
Kemah, Tex. 77 k9
Kemaliye, Turk., 2,642 142 D2
Kemanai, Jap. 155 G1
Kemano, Br. Col., Can. 42 E3
Kemasik, Malay., 1,708 148 B1
Kemayan, Malay. 147 p15
Kembani, Indon. 149 G3
Kembé, C.A.R., 1,341 163 H5
Kemble, U.K. 114 D7
Kemble, Mt., N.J. 58 a13
Kemblesville, Pa. 60 e12
Kembuchi, Jap., 9,334 155 K7
Kemchik, r., U.S.S.R. 137 s12
Kemerovo, U.S.S.R., 298,000 134 H4
Kemi, Fin., 29,376 120 F2
Kemijärvi, Fin. 120 F2
Kemijärvi, l., Fin. 120 F2
Kemijoki, r., Fin. 120 F2
Kemmelberg, hill, Belg. 115 A4
Kemmerer, Wyo., 2,028 81 D5
Kemnath, F.R.Ger., 3,040 118 C4
Kemoo Camp, Hawaii 84 b6
Kemp, Okla. 153 76 G4
Kemp, Tex., 816 77 P3
Kemp, L., Tex. 77 O3
Kemp City, Okla., 142 76 G4
Kemp Coast, Ant. 180 R6
Kempen, F.R.Ger., 12,179 119 A2
Kempendyay, U.S.S.R. 135 L3
Kempenich, F.R.Ger., 1,088 119 C4
Kemper, Ill. 68 B4
Kemper, co., Miss., 12,277 73 G5
Kempfeld, F.R.Ger. 119 C5
Kemps Bay, Bah. Is. 95 b8
Kempsey, Austl., 7,489 173 H4
Kempsey, U.K., 1,559 114 D6
Kempshot = Maxwell Hall
Kempster, Wis. 66 D3
Kempston, U.K., 9,190 113 F5
Kempt, L., Qué., Can. 44 K6
Kempten, F.R.Ger., 41,394 118 C5
Kempton, Ill., 252 68 D3
Kempton, Ind., 480 70 C2
Kempton Park, S. Af., 17,719 165 k17
Kemptville, Ont., Can., 1,926 47 J3
Kemsing, U.K., 3,907 114 J8
Kemudjan, P., Indon. 148 d6
Ken, r., China 150 G1
Ken, r., India 145 F4
Kenadsa, Alg., 1,936 160 D2
Kenai, Alaska, 778 85 G3
Kenai Mts., Alaska 85 G4
Kenai Pen., Alaska 85 G4
Kenamu, r., Newf., Can. 45 O4
Kenansville, Fla. 65 J5
Kenansville, N.C., 724 63 G3
Kenaston, Sask., Can. 43 C4
Kenaston, N. Dak. 74 A1
Kenbridge, Va., 1,188 62 F6
Kendal, Ont., Can. 46 F4
Kendal, Indon. 148 d7
Kendal, U.K., 18,595 113 E4
Kendalia, Tex. 76 a6
Kendall, Austl. 173 H4
Kendall, Fla. 65 J7
Kendall, co., Ill., 17,540 68 D2
Kendall, Kans. 75 D6
Kendall, Mich. 67 H6
Kendall, N.Y. 58 D5
Kendall, co., Tex., 5,889 77 O5
Kendall, Wis., 528 66 C5
Kendallville, Ind., 6,765 70 D1
Kendari, Indon. 149 G3
Kendawangan, Indon. 148 D3
Kendenup, Austl. 172 B5
Kendrapara, India, 15,830 145 H5
Kendrick, Colo. 79 D2
Kendrick, Fla. 65 G3
Kendrick, Idaho, 443 81 A2
Kendrick, Okla., 155 76 G2
Kenduskeag Str., Me. 55 C4
Kenedy, co., Tex., 884 77 P6
Kenedy, Tex., 4,301 77 O5
Kenefic, Okla., 125 76 G3
Kenel, S. Dak. 74 B3
Kenema, Sa. Leone 162 C4
Kenesaw, Nebr., 546 75 G3
Keng Hkam, Burma 146 B2
Keng Kok, Laos 146 D3
Keng Lon, Burma 146 B2
Keng Tung, Burma, 5,508 146 B2
Kengyel, Hung., 5,183 126 E3
Kenhardt, S. Af., 2,832 164 C6
Kenhorst, Pa., 2,815 61 h14
Kéniéba, Mali, 1,689 162 C3
Kenilworth, Ont., Can. 46 D5
Kenilworth, U.K., 14,427 114 E6
Kenilworth, Ill., 2,959 69 d8
Kenilworth, N.J., 8,379 58 b14
Kenilworth, Pa. 60 e11
Kenilworth, Utah 78 C2
Kénitra, Mor., 86,775 160 C2
Kenly, N.C., 1,147 63 F2
Kenmare, Ire. 113 B6
Kenmare, N. Dak., 1,696 74 B1
Kenmare, r., Ire. 113 B6
Kenmore, U.K. 112 E3
Kenmore, N.Y., 21,261 58 C6
Kenna, N. Mex. 79 D5
Kennan, Wis., 162 66 C3
Kennard, Tex. 77 Q4
Kennebago, r., Me. 55 B3
Kennebago L., Me. 55 B3
Kennebago Mtn., Me. 55 B3
Kennebec, co., Me., 89,150 55 C4
Kennebec, S. Dak., 372 74 B4
Kennebec, r., Me. 55 C4
Kennebunk, Me., 2,804 55 B5
Kennebunk, r., Me. 55 B5
Kennebunkport, Me. 55 B5
Kennedale, Tex., 1,521 76 e9
Kennedy, Sask., Can. 43 D5
Kennedy, Ala., 379 64 B2
Kennedy, Minn., 458 74 D1
Kennedy, Nebr. 75 E1
Kennedy, N.Y. 58 B7
Kennedy, C., Fla. 65 J4
Kennedy Chan., N.W.T., Can. 41 Q1
Kennedyville, Md. 62 H3
Kenner, La., 17,037 73 E7
Kennerdell, Pa. 60 C3
Kennesaw, Ga., 1,507 64 E1
Kennesaw Mtn. Nat. Btfld. Pk., Ga. 64 f9
Kennetcook, N.S., Can. 47 T11
Kenneth City, Fla., 2,114 65 c12
Kennett, Mo., 9,098 72 G8
Kennett Square, 4,355 61 L6
Kennewick, Wash., 14,244 80 D2
Kenney, Ill., 400 68 C3
Kennisis L., Ont., Can. 46 F3
Kennydale, Wash. 81 b7
Kenny Res., Br. Col., Can. 42 F3
Kennythorpe, U.K. 114 G2
Keno, Oreg. 80 C4
Kenogami, r., Ont., Can. 44 F5
Keno Hill, Yukon, Can. 40 C5
Kenora, Ont., Can., 10,707 44 C5
Kenosha, co., Wis., 100,615 66 E6
Kenosha, Wis., 67,899 66 F6
Kenova, W. Va., 4,577 62 B4
Kensal, N. Dak., 334 74 C2
Kensett, Ark., 905 73 D2
Kensett, Iowa, 409 72 D1
Kensico Res., N.Y. 58 d12
Kensington, P.E.I., Can. 47 U10
Kensington (part of Berlin), Conn. 56 E6
Kensington, Kans., 619 75 G4
Kensington, Md., 2,175 62 a8
Kensington, Minn., 324 74 E3
Kensington, N.H. 54 F6
Kent, co., U.K., 1,701,851 113 G6
Kent, Conn., 1,686(T) 56 C6
Kent, co., Del., 65,651 62 J3
Kent, co., Md., 15,481 62 H3
Kent, co., Mich., 363,187 67 H5
Kent, Minn., 134 74 D2
Kent, Ohio, 17,836 70 H1
Kent, Okla. 76 H3
Kent, Oreg. 80 C3
Kent, co., R.I., 112,619 57 K6
Kent, co., Tex., 1,727 77 N3
Kent, Tex. 77 L4
Kent, Wash., 9,017 80 B2
Kent, r., U.K. 114 C2
Kentau, U.S.S.R., 38,100 134 F5
Kent Bridge, Ont., Can. 46 B6
Kent City, Mich., 617 67 H5
Kent Furnace (part of Kent), Conn. 56 B6
Kent Group, is., Austl. 173 f12
Kentland, Ind., 1,783 70 B2
Kenton, co., Ky., 120,700 71 G2
Kenton, Mich. 66 E2
Kenton, Ohio, 8,747 70 F2
Kenton, Okla. 76 A1
Kenton, Tenn., 1,095 71 C5
Kent Pen., N.W.T., Can. 40 H4
Kentuck, Va. 62 E6
Kentuck, W. Va. 62 C4
Kentucky, st., U.S., 3,173,000* 71
Kentucky, r., Ky. 71 F3
Kentucky L., Ky.-Tenn. 71 C5
Kentville, N.S., Can., 4,430 45 N6
Kentwood, La., 2,607 73 E7
Kenville, Man., Can. 43 E4
Kenwood, Ga. 64 g10
Kenwood (part of Dracut), Mass. 57 L2
Kenwood, Okla. 76 J1
Kenya, ctry., 8,636,263 164 F1
Kenya, Mt., Kenya 164 F2
Kenyon, Minn., 1,624 74 F3
Kenyon (part of Charlestown), R.I. 57 K7
Kenyonville (part of Woodstock), Conn. 56 H5
Kenzingen, F.R.Ger., 4,649 118 A4
Keo, Ark., 237 73 D3
Keokea, Hawaii Co., Hawaii 84 F4
Keokea, Maui Co., Hawaii, 436 84 E3
Keokuk, co., Iowa, 15,492 72 E3
Keokuk, Iowa, 16,316 72 F4
Keolu Hills, Hawaii, 4,075* 84 d7
Keomuku, Hawaii 84 E3
Keonjhargarh, India, 12,624 144 e15
Keosauqua, Iowa, 1,023 72 F4
Keota, Colo., 13 79 C1
Keota, Iowa, 1,096 72 F3
Keota, Okla., 579 76 J2
Keowee, r., S.C. 63 B3
Kep, Camb. 147 k11
Kepahiang, Indon. 148 B3
Kepala Batas, Malay., 2,941 147 o14
Kepandjen, Indon. 148 e8
Kepi, Indon. 149 L4
Kępno, Pol., 9,150 127 B3
Keppel B., Austl. 173 G3
Keppel I., Falk. Is. 108 3
Keptin, U.S.S.R. 135 M3
Kepuhi, Hawaii 84 D2
Kepuhi Pt., Hawaii 84 a7
Kerala, st., India, 16,903,715 145 E8
Keramian, P., Indon. 148 f6
Keramídhi, Gr. 129 D5
Kerandin, Indon. 148 C3
Kerang, Austl., 3,227 173 e10
Keratéa, Gr., 4,857 129 E6
Kerava, Fin. 120 F3
Keravat, Terr. New Guin. 174 f2
Kerby, Oreg. 80 B4
Kerch', U.S.S.R., 104,000 134 C5
Kerchenskiy Prol., U.S.S.R. 136 E4
Kerchevskiy, U.S.S.R., 4,100 137 h7
Kerdau, Malay. 147 p15
Kerekegyháza, Hung., 6,183 126 D3
Kerema, Terr. Papua 174 e2
Keren, Eth., 9,500* 163 L3
Kerens, Tex., 1,123 77 P3
Kerens, W. Va. 62 E3
Keresley, U.K., 3,115 114 F6
Kerfantów, Pol. 127 g6
Kerguélen, Îs. de, Ind. Oc. 168 C4
Kerguelen-Gaussberg Ridge, Ind. Oc. 168 C4
Kerhonkson, N.Y. 59 M8
Kericho, Kenya 164 E2
Kerintji, G., Indon. 148 B3
Kerio, r., Kenya 164 F1
Keriya, China = Yü-t'ien
Keriya, r., China 150 B3
Kerkdriel, Neth., 3,100 115 D3
Kerkhoven, Minn., 645 74 E3
Kerki, U.S.S.R., 11,500 134 F6
Kerkichi, U.S.S.R., 3,300 134 F6
Kérkira, Gr., 26,991 129 C5
Kérkira, i., Gr. 129 B5
Kerkrade, Neth., 10,300 115 E4
Kermadec Is., N.Z. 170 G6
Kermadec Trench, Pac. Oc. 169 G4
Kermān, Iran, 62,157 143 F2
Kerman, Calif., 2,545 82 D4
Kermān, Bīābān-e, des., Iran 143 F3
Kermānshāh, Iran, 125,439 143 D2
Kerme Körfezi, Turk. 142 A2
Kermen, Bulg., 2,984 128 F3
Kermit, Tex., 10,465 77 M4
Kermit, W. Va., 743 62 B5
Kern, co., Calif., 291,984 82 D5
Kern, r., Calif. 82 D5
Kern City, Calif. 82 D5
Kernersville, N.C., 2,942 63 D1
Kerns, Switz. 3,553 124 C2
Kernville, Calif. 82 D5
Kérouané, Guin., 3,000 162 C4
Kerr, co., Tex., 16,800 77 O5
Kerrara, i., U.K. 112 D3
Kerrata, Alg., 1,996 160 d5
Kerrick, Minn., 110 74 F2
Kerrick, Tex. 76 M1
Kerrobert, Sask., Can., 1,205 43 B4
Kerrville, Tenn. 71 B6
Kerrville, Tex., 8,901 77 O4
Kerry, co., Ire., 122,072 113 B5
Kerry, U.K., 1,397 113 E5
Kerry Head, Ire. 113 A5
Kersbrook, Austl. 172 c8
Kersey, Pa. 60 E3
Kershaw, co., S.C., 33,585 63 D3
Kershaw, S.C., 1,567 63 D3
Kerteh, Malay., 1,534 147 p14
Kerteminde, Den., 4,024 121 C5
Kertosono, Indon. 148 e7
Kerulen = Hereleng
Kerwood, Ont., Can. 46 C6
Kerzaz, Alg., 3,697 160 D3
Kerzers, Switz., 2,228 124 B2
Kerzhenets, r., U.S.S.R. 136 G1
Ke Sach, S. Viet. 147 k12
Kesagami L., Ont., Can. 44 H5
Keşan, Turk., 15,062 142 A1
Ke Sat, N. Viet. 147 i9
Kesennuma, Jap., 57,016 155 G2
Keshena, Wis. 66 E4
Keşiş Tepesi, Turk. 142 D2
Keskastel, Fr., 1,506 116 d9
Keskin, Turk., 6,478 142 C2
Kessel-Lo, Belg., 18,429 115 C4
Kesteven (admin. part of Lincolnshire), U.K., 134,842 113 F5
Kestilä, Fin. 120 F2
Keswick, N.B., Can. 47 S10
Keswick, Ont., Can. 46 E4
Keswick, U.K., 4,752 113 E4
Keswick, Iowa, 265 72 E3
Keswick, Va. 62 F4
Keswick, r., N.B., Can. 55 E2
Keswick Grove, N.J. 58 b17
Keszthely, Hung., 18,454 126 C3
Ket', r., U.S.S.R. 134 H4
Keta, Ghana, 16,724 162 d9
Keta, Oz., U.S.S.R. 135 H3
Ketama, Mor. 160 D2
Ketapang, Indon. 148 D3
Ketapang, Indon. 148 e7
Ketaun, Indon. 148 B3
Ketchikan, Alaska, 6,483 85 M5
Ketchum, Idaho, 746 81 B4
Ketchum, Okla., 255 76 H1
Kétegyháza, Hung., 5,094 126 E3
Kete Krachi, Ghani, 2,022 162 D4
Kéthely, Hung., 3,620 126 C3
Ketik, r., Alaska 85 E1
Ketka, Burma 147 b2
Ketman', Krh., Asia 132 H5
Kétou, Dahom., 6,814 162 E4
Kętrzyn, Pol., 15,769 127 D1
Kettering, U.K., 38,659 113 F5
Kettering, Ohio, 54,462 70 E3
Kettle, r., Can.-U.S. 42 H4
Kettle, r., Man., Can. 43 J3
Kettle, r., Minn. 74 F2
Kettle Cr., Pa. 60 G3
Kettle Falls, Wash., 905 80 E1
Kettleman City, Calif. 82 D4
Kettle Pt., Ont., Can. 46 B5
Kettle River, Minn., 234 74 F2
Kettle River Ra., Canada-U.S. 80 D1
Ketton, U.K., 1,142 114 G5
Kettwig, F.R.Ger., 16,812 119 B2
Kęty, Pol., 9,217 127 i7
Ketzin, Ger.D.R. 119 d11
Keuka, N.Y. 58 F7
Keuka L., N.Y. 58 F6
Keuka Park, N.Y. 58 F6
Keuruu, Fin. 120 F3
Keuruunselkä, l., Fin. 120 F3
Kevelaer, F.R.Ger., 11,146 118 A3
Kevin, Mont., 375 81 D1
Kewadin, Mich. 67 H4
Kewanee, Ill., 16,324 68 C2
Kewanee, Miss. 73 G5
Kewanna, Ind., 683 70 C1
Kewaskum, Wis., 1,572 66 E5
Kewaunee, co., Wis., 18,282 66 F4
Kewaunee, Wis., 2,772 66 F4
Keweenaw, co., Mich., 2,417 66 E1
Keweenaw Bay, Mich. 66 E2
Keweenaw Bay, Mich. 66 E1
Keweenaw Pen., U.S. 53 J1
Keweenaw Pt., Mich. 66 F1
Keweigek, Guyana 101 K5
Key, Tex. 77 N3
Keya Paha, co., Nebr., 1,672 75 F1
Keyapaha, S. Dak. 74 B4
Keya Paha, r., S. Dak. 74 B4
Keyes, Man., Can. 43 e9
Keyes, Calif., 1,546 82 C4
Keyes, Okla., 627 76 A1
Key Harbour, Ont., Can. 46 D3
Keyingham, U.K. 114 H3
Key Largo, Fla. 65 J7
Keynsham, U.K., 15,152 114 C8
Keyport, N.J., 6,440 61 C3
Keyport, Wash. 81 a7
Keyser, W. Va., 6,192 62 F3
Keystone, Ind. 70 D2
Keystone, Iowa, 522 72 E3
Keystone, Nebr. 75 D2
Keystone, W. Va., 1,457 62 C5
Keystone Heights, Fla., 655 65 H3
Keystone Res., Okla. 76 G1
Keysville, Fla. 65 d12
Keysville, Va., 733 62 F5
Keytesville, Mo., 644 72 E5
Key West, Fla., 33,956 65 f15
Keyworth, U.K., 2,652 114 F5
Kezar, r., Me. 54 F3
Kezar Falls, Me. 55 B5
Kezar L., Me. 55 B4
Kezar Pd., Me. 54 F3
Kezhma, U.S.S.R. 135 K4
Kežmarok, Czech. 126 E2
Kgun L., Alaska 85 D3
Khabarovo, U.S.S.R. 134 F3
Khabarovsk, U.S.S.R., 377,000 135 N5
Khabary, U.S.S.R. 137 p11
Khābūr, r., Syr. 142 E3
Khachmas, U.S.S.R., 17,200 134 D5
Khachrod, India, 14,793 145 E5
Khadyzhensk, U.S.S.R., 19,500 136 E4
Khaga, India 144 c13
Khagaria, India, 13,731 144 f13
Khair, India 144 a11
Khairabad, India, 14,687 144 c12
Khairagarh, India, 6,576 145 F5
Khaipur, Pak., 34,144 144 C4
Khajuraho, India 144 b13
Khalandritsa, Gr., 1,286 129 C5
Khalik Tau, China 132 H5
Khálki, Gr., 1,777 129 D5
Khálki, i., Gr. 129 F6
Khalkidhikí, pen., Gr. 129 D4
Khalkís, Gr., 24,745 129 D5
Khal'mer-Yu, U.S.S.R., 7,400 134 F3
Khalturin, U.S.S.R., 9,200 134 D4
Khambhaliya, India, 20,064 144 C5
Khamīs Mushayṭ, Saudi Ar. 143 C5
Kham Keut, Laos 146 D3
Khammam, India, 35,888 145 F6
Kham Thale So, Thai. 147 d4
Khan, r., Laos 146 C3
Khānaqīn, Iraq, 19,312 143 C2
Khān az Zabīb, Jor. 142 c8
Khandwa, India, 63,505 145 E5
Khandyga, U.S.S.R. 135 N3
Khānewāl, Pak., 49,093 145 D3
Khangokurt, U.S.S.R. 134 F3
Khanh Duong, S. Viet. 146 E4
Khanh Hung, S. Viet., 39,689 146 D5
Khaniá, Gr., 38,467 129 D7
Khanka, L., China-U.S.S.R. 135 N5
Khanlar, U.S.S.R., 11,500 137 c1
Khanna, India, 24,416 144 a10
Khānpur, Pak., 31,465 145 D3
Khantayskoye, Oz., U.S.S.R. 135 J3
Khanty-Mansiysk, U.S.S.R., 22,000 134 F3
Khanyangda, U.S.S.R. 135 O4
Khān Yūnus, U.A.R. 142 a8
Khao Yoi, Thai. 147 c5
Khapa, India, 9,536 144 b15
Khapcheranga, U.S.S.R., 7,100 135 L5
Kharagpur, Bihar, India, 9,825 144 f13
Kharagpur, W.B., India, 147,253 145 H5
Khárakas, Gr., 1,142 129 E7
Kharal, U.S.S.R. 135 J4
Khārān, Pak., 2,692 144 B3
Khargon, India, 30,652 145 E5
Khārijah, Al Wāḥāt al, oasis, U.A.R. 161 K3
Kharitona Laptëva, Bereg, U.S.S.R. 135 H2
Kharitonovka, U.S.S.R. 151 F2
Khārk, i., Iran 143 D3
Khar'kov, U.S.S.R., 1,048,000 134 C5
Kharmanli, Bulg., 12,553 128 E4
Kharovsk, U.S.S.R., 11,300 134 D4
Kharsawan, India, 4,012 144 e14
Kharsia, India, 7,737 144 d14
Khartaum, U.S.S.R. 135 O2
Khartoum = Al Khurṭūm
Khartoum North = Al Khurṭūm Baḥrī
Khartsyzsk, U.S.S.R., 33,000 136 e8
Khasavyurt, U.S.S.R., 34,700 137 c1
Khāsh, Iran, 7,439 143 G3
Khash, r., Afghan. 144 B3
Khash Des., Afghan. 144 A3
Khashm al Qirbah, Sudan 163 K3
Khashuri, U.S.S.R., 18,700 137 b1
Khasi Hills, India 145 J4
Khaskovo, Bulg., 38,812 128 E4
Khatanga, U.S.S.R. 135 K2
Khatanga, r., U.S.S.R. 135 K2
Khatangskiy Zal., U.S.S.R. 135 K2
Khatauli, India, 17,898 144 a11
Khategaon, India, 5,573 144 a14
Khatra, India, 6,757 144 f14
Khātūnīyah, Syr. 142 E2
Khatyrka, U.S.S.R. 135 R3
Khaudag, U.S.S.R. 137 e5
Khawsa, Burma 146 B4
Khaybar, Saudi Ar., 6,300* 143 B3
Khaydarken, U.S.S.R., 6,800 137 f4
Khe Bo, N. Viet. 146 D3
Khed, India, 7,315 145 h18
Khe Dol, S. Viet. 147 m11
Khemarak Phouminville; Camb. 146 C5
Khemarat, Thai. 146 D4
Khemis Miliana, Alg., 21,349 160 E1
Khemisset, Mor., 13,695 160 D2
Khenchela, Alg., 25,009 160 e6
Khenifra, Mor., 18,503 160 D2

Khera—Kismayu · 245

Khera, India 144 a12
Khérson, Gr., 1,803 129 D4
Kherson, U.S.S.R., 174,000 134 C5
Kheta, r., U.S.S.R. 135 K2
Khiem Duc, S. Viet. 147 m11
Khiem Hanh, S. Viet. 147 m11
Khilchipur, India, 6,970 144 a13
Khiliomódhion, Gr., 1,534 129 D6
Khilok, U.S.S.R., 29,500 135 K4
Khilok, r., U.S.S.R. 135 K4
Khimki, U.S.S.R., 43,100 136 b6
Khingansk, U.S.S.R., 4,300 135 M5
Khíos, Gr., 24,053 129 F5
Khíos, i., Gr. 129 E5
Khisar-Momina Banya, Bulg., 5,713 128 E3
Khiva, U.S.S.R., 15,400 134 F5
Khlebarovo, Bulg., 5,604 128 F3
Khlong Khlung, Thai. 146 B3
Khlong Luang, Thai. 147 d4
Khlung, Thai., 5,072 146 C4
Khmel'nitskiy, U.S.S.R., 67,000 134 B5
Khoai, Hon, S. Viet. 146 D5
Khodorov, U.S.S.R., 8,800 136 B3
Khodzhent, U.S.S.R., 14,900 137 f4
Khodzheyli, U.S.S.R., 28,100 134 E5
Khok Samrong, Thai., 6,087 146 C4
Kholm, U.S.S.R. 136 C1
Kholmogory, U.S.S.R. 134 D3
Kholmsk, U.S.S.R., 35,700 135 O5
Khomeyn, Iran, 8,397 143 E2
Khon Buri, Thai. 147 e4
Khong, Laos 146 D4
Khong, Thai. 146 C4
Khong = Mekong
Khong Sédone, Laos 146 D4
Khon Kaen, Thai., 19,548 146 C3
Khonkhan, Burma 147 b3
Khon Sawan, Thai. 147 e4
Khonu, U.S.S.R. 135 O3
Khopër, r., U.S.S.R. 134 D4
Khoppuruo, U.S.S.R. 135 L4
Khor, U.S.S.R. 135 N5
Khor, r., U.S.S.R. 135 N5
Khóra, Gr., 3,752 129 C6
Khorāsān, reg., Iran 143 F2
Khóra Sfakíon, Gr. 129 D7
Khorat = Nakhon Ratchasima
Khorb el Ethel, Alg. 160 C3
Khordogoy, U.S.S.R. 135 L3
Khor-e-Ma'shur, Iran 143 D2
Khorintsy, U.S.S.R. 135 M3
Khorog, U.S.S.R., 9,000 134 G6
Khorol, U.S.S.R., 12,200 136 D3
Khorramābād, Iran, 38,676 143 D2
Khorramshahr, Iran, 43,850 143 D2
Khorsabad, ruins, Iraq 143 C1
Khoseda-Khard, U.S.S.R. 134 E3
Khotan = Ho-t'ien
Khotan, r., China 150 B3
Khotāng, Nepal 144 f12
Khotin, U.S.S.R., 10,200 136 B3
Khot'kovo, U.S.S.R., 14,400 136 c5
Khouribga, Mor., 40,838 160 C2
Khrisomiliá, Gr., 1,101 129 C5
Khrisoúpolis, Gr., 5,779 129 E4
Khristinovka, U.S.S.R., 8,400 136 C3
Khromskaya G., U.S.S.R. 135 O2
Khrom-Tau, U.S.S.R., 5,700 137 i10
Khrustal'nyy, U.S.S.R. 135 N5
Khudat, U.S.S.R., 7,100 137 d1
Khukhan, Thai. 146 D4
Khulna, Pak., 127,970 145 H5
Khum Chambak, Camb. 147 k10
Khum Kauk Srok, Camb. 147 m11
Khum Krabey Kriek, Camb. 147 k10
Khurai, India, 15,316 144 b13
Khurasan = Khorāsān
Khurda, India, 12,497 145 G5
Khurja, India, 41,491 144 a11
Khūryān Mūryān, is., Ind. Oc. 143 F5
Khush, Afghan. 144 B2
Khushāb, Pak., 24,851 145 D2
Khuyen Luong, N. Viet. 147 h9
Khuzdār, Pak. 144 B4
Khuzhir, U.S.S.R. 135 K4
Khvalynsk, U.S.S.R., 17,200 134 D4
Khvav, Camb. 147 k11
Khvonsār, Iran, 10,669 143 E2
Khvor, Iran, 2,307 143 E2
Khvoy, Iran, 34,491 143 D1
Khyber Pass, Afghan.-Pak. 145 D2
Kia, Sol. Is. 175 b2
Kia, i., Fiji 174 4
Kiabo, D.R.Congo 165 m18
Kiabukwa, D.R.Congo 165 m18
Kiah, Austl. 173 g11
Kialegak, C., Alaska 85 B3
Kialwe, D.R.Congo 165 n18
Kiama, Austl., 2,400 173 h10
Kiambu, Kenya 165 h14
Kiamichi, r., Okla. 76 H3
Kiamika, L., Qué., Can. 47 J2
Kiamusze = Chia-mu-ssu
Kiana, Alaska, 253 85 D2
Kiangan, Phil., 3,019 153 B1
Kiangsi = Chiang-hsi
Kiangsu = Chiang-su
Kiantajärvi, l., Fin. 120 G2
Kiapuluka, D.R.Congo 165 n18
Kibæk, Den. 121 A4
Kibangou, Congo 164 B2
Kibara, D.R.Congo 165 n18
Kibawe, Phil., 2,655 153 C4
Kibbie, Mich. 67 G6
Kibby Mtn., Me. 55 B3
Kibi, Ghana 162 c8
Kibila, D.R.Congo 165 n18
Kiblah, Ark. 73 B4
Kibombo, D.R.Congo 164 D2
Kibondo, Tanz. 164 E2
Kibora, D.R.Congo 165 n18
Kibungan, Phil., 1,610 153 b6
Kibungo, Rwanda 165 e15
Kibuye, D.R.Congo 165 n19
Kibuye, Rwanda 164 D2
Kibwezi, Kenya 164 F2
Kičevo, Yug., 10,000* 125 E4
Kichmengskiy Gorodok, U.S.S.R. 136 G1
Kickapoo, r., Wis. 66 C5
Kickapoo Cr., Ill. 68 C3
Kida, Jap. 154 h14
Kidal, Mali 162 E2
Kidapawan, Phil., 5,727 153 C4
Kidd, Ill. 68 B5
Kidder, Mo., 224 72 C5
Kidder, co., N. Dak., 5,386 74 C2
Kidder, S. Dak. 74 D3
Kidderminster, U.K., 40,822 113 E5
Kidderville, N.H. 54 E2
Kid I., Barbuda 97 8
Kidlington, U.K., 8,514 114 F7
Kidnappers, C., N.Z. 175 h5
Kidsgrove, U.K., 19,726 113 E5
Kidston, Austl. 173 F2
Kidwelly, U.K., 2,879 113 D6
Kiečevci, Yug. 125 E3
Kiedrich, F.R.Ger., 3,203 119 E4
Kief, N. Dak., 97 74 B2
Kiefer, Okla., 489 76 G2
Kiefersfelden, F.R.Ger., 4,319 118 D5
Kiekie, Hawaii 84 A2
Kiel, F.R.Ger., 256,727 118 C1
Kiel, Wis., 2,524 66 E5
Kiel Bay, Den.-F.R.Ger. 121 C6
Kielce, Pol., 89,000* 127 D3
Kielder, U.K. 113 E4
Kieler, Wis. 66 C6
Kien An, N. Viet. 147 i9
Kien An, S. Viet., 14,492 147 k12
Kien Binh, S. Viet., 2,602 147 k11
Kien Binh, S. Viet., 2,790 147 k12
Kien Duc, S. Viet. 147 m10
Kienge, D.R.Congo 165 n19
Kien Hung, S. Viet. 147 k12
Kien Long, S. Viet., 10,018 146 D5
Kien Tan, S. Viet., 3,517 147 k11
Kien Thanh, S. Viet., 13,953 147 k12
Kien Van, S. Viet. 147 k11
Kierspe, F.R.Ger., 9,733 119 D2
Kiester, Minn., 741 74 F4
Kieta, Sol. Is. 175 a2
Kietrz, Pol., 4,663 127 g6
Kiev = Kiyev
Kiffa, Maur., 1,506 162 C3
Kifisiá, Gr., 14,193 129 D5
Kifissós Voiotikós, r., Gr. 129 D5
Kifrī, Iraq, 5,775 143 C2
Kigali, Rwanda 164 E2
Kiglapait, C., Newf., Can. 45 O2
Kiglapait Mts., Newf., Can. 45 O2
Kigoma, Tanz. 164 D2
Kihara, Jap. 155 n18
Kihei, Hawaii, 938 84 E3
Kiholo Bay, Hawaii 84 F4
Kii-hantō, Jap. 155 D5
Kii Landing, Hawaii 84 A2
Kiiminki, Fin. 120 F2
Kii-suidō, Jap. 155 D5
Kijabe, Kenya 165 h14
Kijal, Malay., 1,740 147 p14
Kijanebalola, L., Uganda 165 e14
Kije, Pol. 127 k6
Kijevo, Yug. 125 E3
Kikaiga-shima, Jap. 154 d12
Kikepa Pt., Hawaii 84 A1
Kikhchik, U.S.S.R., 2,600 135 P4
Kiki, Jap. 154 f16
Kikila, L., Îs. Wallis 175 7
Kikinda, Yug., 31,000* 125 E2
Kikkerteluk, r., Qué., Can. 44 J2
Kikládhes, is., Gr. 129 E6
Kikoa Pt., Hawaii 84 E3
Kikonai, Jap., 12,926 155 J9
Kikondja, D.R.Congo 164 D3
Kikongo, D.R.Congo 164 B2
Kikori, Terr. Papua 174 d2
Kikori, r., Terr. Papua 174 d2
Kikuchi, Jap., 34,363 154 B5
Kikuyu, Kenya 165 h14
Kikwissi, L., Qué., Can. 46 F2
Kikwit, D.R.Congo, 16,101 164 C2
Kil, Nor. 121 B2
Kil, r., Neth. 115 b7
Kilakarai, India, 16,860 145 m21
Kilambwe, D.R.Congo 165 m18
Kilauea, Hawaii, 665 84 B1
Kilauea Crater, Hawaii 84 F4
Kilauea Pt., Hawaii 84 B1
Kilbarchan, U.K. 112 a8
Kilbeggan, Ire. 113 C5
Kilbirnie, U.K. 112 D4
Kilbourne, Ill., 352 68 C3
Kilbourne, La., 227 73 D5
Kilbourne, Ohio 70 F2
Kilbrannan Sd., U.K. 112 D4
Kilbride, Ont., Can. 46 c14
Kilbuck Mts., Alaska 85 E3
Kilburn, N.B., Can. 47 S10
Kilchoan, U.K. 112 C3
Kilchu, N. Kor. 151 F2
Kilcormac, Ire. 113 C5
Kilcoy, Austl. 173 H4
Kilcullen, Ire. 113 C5
Kildare, co., Ire., 65,915 113 C5
Kildare, Ire., 2,617 113 C5
Kildare, Ga. 64 H3
Kildare, Okla., 124 76 F1
Kildebrønde, Den., 1,894 121 a7
Kildeer, Ill., 173 69 b8
Kildonan, Br. Col., Can. 42 b7
Kileba, D.R.Congo 165 n18
Kilembe, Uganda 165 d13
Kilembwe, D.R.Congo 165 n19
Kilfenora, Ire. 113 B5
Kilfinnane, Ire. 113 B5
Kilgarvan, Ire. 113 B6
Kilgore, Nebr., 157 75 E1
Kilgore, Tex., 10,092 77 Q3
Kilgoris, Kenya 165 g14
Kilham, U.K. 114 H2
Kili, i., Marsh. Is. 176 22
Kilia, Terr. Papua 174 3
Kilibo, Dahom. 162 e7
Kilifi, Kenya 164 F2
Kilimanjaro, mtn., Tanz. 164 F2
Kilimantavi, Alaska 85 D1
Kilinailau Is., Terr. New Guin. 175 a1
Kılınç Tepesi, Turk. 142 D1
Kilindoni, Tanz. 164 F3
Kilingi-Nõmme, U.S.S.R., 2,100 136 B1
Kilis, Turk., 33,289 142 D2
Kiliya, U.S.S.R., 19,700 136 C4
Kilkee, Ire., 1,565 113 B5
Kilkeel, U.K., 2,490 113 D4
Kilkenny, co., Ire., 64,089 113 C5
Kilkenny, Ire., 12,328 113 C5
Kilkerran, Austl. 172 E5
Kilkhampton, U.K. 113 D6
Kilkís, Gr., 10,963 129 D4
Killala, Ire. 113 B4
Killala Bay, Ire. 113 B4
Killaloe, Ire. 113 B5
Killaloe Station, Ont., Can. 45 G3
Killaly, Sask., Can. 43 D5
Killam, Alta., Can. 42 K3
Killarney, Man., Can., 1,687 43 E5
Killarney, Ont., Can. 46 C2
Killarney, Ire., 6,464 113 B5
Killashandra, Ire. 113 C4
Killawog, N.Y. 59 J7
Kill Buck, N.Y. 58 C7
Killbuck, Ohio, 865 70 H2
Killbuck Cr., Ohio 70 G2
Killdeer, N. Dak., 765 74 A2
Killdeer Mts., N. Dak. 74 A2
Kill Devil Hills, N.C., 268 63 J1
Killean, U.K. 112 D4
Killeen, Tex., 23,377 77 P4
Killen, Ala., 620 64 B1
Killenaule, Ire. 113 C5
Killian, S.C. 63 D3
Killiecrankie, U.K. 112 E3
Killik, r., Alaska 85 F1
Killin, U.K. 112 D3
Killinek I., N.W.T., Can. 45 N1
Killinghall, U.K., 2,206 114 E2
Killingly = Dayville, Conn.
Killington Pk., Vt. 54 B4
Killingworth, Conn., 1,098(T) 56 F7
Killini, mt., Gr. 129 D6
Killorglin, Ire. 113 B5
Kill Van Kull, str., N.J.-N.Y. 58 c14
Killybegs, Ire. 113 B4
Kilmacolm, U.K. 112 a8
Kilmacthomas, Ire. 113 C5
Kilmallock, Ire. 113 B5
Kilmanagh, Mich. 67 K5
Kilmany, U.K. 112 e7
Kilmarnock, U.K., 47,509 112 D4
Kilmarnock, Va., 927 62 H5
Kilmaurs, U.K. 112 b8
Kilmichael, Miss., 532 73 F4
Kilmory, U.K. 112 C3
Kiln, Miss. 73 F7
Kilninver, U.K. 112 D3
Kilombero, r., Tanz. 164 F3
Kilo Moto, D.R.Congo 164 D1
Kilosa, Tanz. 164 F3
Kilpatrick Hills, U.K. 112 b8
Kilrea, U.K. 113 C4
Kilrenny (incl. Anstruther), U.K., 2,888 112 e7
Kilrush, Ire., 3,000 113 B5
Kilsyth, U.K., 9,831 112 E4
Kiltamagh, Ire. 113 B5
Kilubi, r., D.R.Congo 165 m18
Kilwa, D.R.Congo 164 D3
Kilwah, ruins, Jor. 142 D4
Kilwa Kisiwanu, Tanz. 164 F3
Kilwa Kivinje, Tanz. 164 F3
Kilwinning, U.K., 7,287 112 a8
Kim, Colo. 79 D3
Kima, D.R.Congo 164 D2
Kimasozero, U.S.S.R. 134 C3
Kimba, Austl. 172 b7
Kimball, Alta., Can. 42 K4
Kimball, co., Nebr., 7,975 75 B2
Kimball, Nebr., 4,384 75 B2
Kimball, S. Dak., 912 74 C4
Kimball, W. Va., 1,175 62 C5
Kimballton, Iowa, 380 72 C3
Kimbe B., Terr. New Guin. 174 f2
Kimberley, Br. Col., Can., 5,887 42 J4
Kimberley, Ont., Can. 46 D4
Kimberley, S. Af., 77,180 164 D6
Kimberley, U.K., 4,642 144 F4
Kimberley Plateau, Austl. 172 C2
Kimberly, Ala., 763 64 C2
Kimberly, Idaho, 1,298 81 B4
Kimberly, Nev. 83 C3
Kimberly, Oreg. 80 D3
Kimberly, Wis. 66 E4
Kimberton, Pa. 60 e11
Kimble, co., Tex., 3,943 77 O4
Kimbolton, U.K. 114 H6
Kimch'aek, N. Kor. 151 F2
Kimch'ŏn, S. Kor., 51,150 151 F3
Kimengwa, D.R.Congo 165 n19
Kimhwa, N. Kor. 151 E3
Kimi, Gr., 3,252 129 E5
Kimje, S. Kor., 30,087 151 E4
Kimmswick, Mo., 303 72 a12
Kimobetsu, Jap., 7,487 155 J8
Kímolos, Gr., 1,412 129 E6
Kímolos, i., Gr. 129 E6
Kimongo, Congo 164 B2
Kimovsk, U.S.S.R., 54,300 136 E2
Kimry, U.S.S.R., 41,300 136 E1
Kimsquit, Br. Col., Can. 42 E3
Kin, Jap. 154 A4
Kina, D.R.Congo 165 n18
Kinabalu, Mt., Malay. 148 F1
Kinabatangan, r., Malay. 148 F1
Kinadyeng, i., Jaluit 176 30
Kinard, Fla. 65 D2
Kinards, S.C. 63 C3
Kinbuck, U.K. 112 c7
Kinburnskaya K., U.S.S.R. 136 C4
Kincaid, Sask., Can. 43 C5
Kincaid, Ill., 1,544 68 C4
Kincaid, Kans., 220 75 K5
Kincardine, Ont., Can., 2,807 44 G7
Kincardine, co., U.K., 48,810 112 E3
Kincardine, U.K. 112 c7
Kinchafoonee Cr., Ga. 64 E4
Kinda, D.R.Congo 165 m18
Kindberg, Aust., 5,766 124 M6
Kinde, Mich., 624 67 L5
Kindele, D.R.Congo 165 m18
Kinder, La., 2,299 73 C7
Kinder, Mo. 72 G7
Kinderdijk, Neth., 4,700 115 b7
Kinderhook, Ill., 276 68 A4
Kinderhook, Mich. 67 H7
Kinderhook, N.Y., 1,078 59 N7
Kinderhook Cr., N.Y. 56 B3
Kinder Scout, mtn., U.K. 114 E4
Kindersley, Sask., Can., 2,910 43 B4
Kindia, Guin., 13,096 162 B4
Kindred, N. Dak., 580 74 D2
Kindu, Kenya 165 g14
Kindu-Port-Empain, D.R.Congo, 19,385 164 D2
Kineshma, U.S.S.R., 90,000 134 D4
Kinesi, Tanz. 165 f14
Kineton, U.K., 1,223 113 F5
King, Ont., Can., 1,864 46 E5
King, N.C. 63 D1
King, co., Tex., 640 77 N3
King, co., Wash., 935,014 80 C2
King, Wis. 66 D4
King and Queen, co., Va., 5,889 62 G5
King and Queen Court House, Va. 62 H5
Kingaroy, Austl., 4,464 173 G4
King City, Calif., 2,937 82 C4
King City, Mo., 1,009 72 C4
Kingcome Inlet, Br. Col., Can. 42 E3
King Cove, Alaska, 290 85 D5
King Edward VII Fall, Guyana 101 K5
Kingfield, Me. 55 B4
Kingfisher, co., Okla., 10,635 76 E1
Kingfisher, Okla., 3,249 76 E2
King George, co., Va., 7,243 62 G4
King George, Va. 62 G4
King George I., Falk. Is. 108 3
King George Is., N.W.T., Can. 44 H2
King George VI Fall, Guyana 101 K5
Kingham, U.K. 114 E7
King Hill, Idaho 81 B4
Kinghorn, U.K. 112 d7
Kingisepp, R.S.F.S.R., U.S.S.R., 8,000 136 C1
Kingisepp, E.S.S.R., = Kuressaare
King I., Austl. 173 F6
King I., Burma 146 B4
King I., Br. Col., Can. 42 E3
King I., Alaska 85 B2
Kinglassie, U.K. 112 d7
King Leopold Ranges, Austl. 172 C2
Kingman, Alta., Can. 43 c7
Kingman, Ariz., 6,021 78 B4
Kingman, Ind., 461 70 B3
Kingman, co., Kans., 9,958 75 G6
Kingman, Kans., 3,582 75 G6
Kingman, Me. 55 D3
Kingman Reef, Line Is. 171 H4
King Mtn., Oreg. 80 B4
King Mtn., Oreg. 80 D4
Kingoonya, Austl. 172 E4
King Pk., Alaska 85 J3
King Pt., Lord Howe I. 175 12
Kings, co., Calif., 49,954 82 D4
Kings, Ill. 68 C1
Kings, co., N.Y., 2,627,319 59 M10
Kings, r., Ark. 73 B1
Kings, r., Calif. 82 D4
Kings, r., Nev. 83 A2
King Salmon, Alaska, 227 85 E4
Kingsbarns, U.K. 112 e7
Kingsbridge, U.K., 3,287 113 E6
Kingsburg, Calif., 3,093 82 D4
Kingsbury, U.K., 4,494 114 E5
Kingsbury, Ind., 281 70 C1
Kingsbury, Me. 55 C3
Kingsbury, co., S. Dak., 9,227 74 D3
Kingsbury, Tex. 76 c6
Kingsbury Str., Me. 55 C3
Kings Canyon Nat. Pk., Calif. 82 D4
Kingsclere, U.K., 3,320 113 F6
King's Cliffe, U.K., 1,010 114 G5
Kingscote, Austl. 172 E5
Kings Creek, N.C. 63 C1
Kings Creek, S.C. 63 C2
Kingsdale, Minn. 74 F2
Kingsdown, Kans. 75 F6
Kingsey Falls, Qué., Can. 47 N3
Kingsford, Mich., 5,084 66 E3
Kingsford Heights, Ind., 1,276 70 C1
Kingsgate, Br. Col., Can. 42 J4
Kingsland, U.K. 114 C6
Kingsland, Ark., 249 73 C4
Kingsland, Ga., 1,536 64 H5
Kingsley, U.K., 2,442 114 E4
Kingsley, Iowa, 1,044 72 A2
Kingsley, Delta Co., Mich. 67 H4
Kingsley, Grand Traverse Co., Mich., 586 66 F3
Kingsley Dam, Nebr. 75 D2
Kingsley Res. = C. W. McConaughy, L.
King's Lynn, U.K., 27,536 113 G5
Kings Mill, Mich. 67 K5
Kings Mill, Tex. 76 N2
Kings Mountain, Ky. 71 G4
Kings Mountain, N.C., 8,008 63 C2
King Sd., Austl. 172 C2
Kings Park, N.Y., 4,949 59 O10
Kings Point, N.Y., 5,410 58 d13
King's Seat, mtn., U.K. 112 d7
Kings Somborne, U.K., 1,269 113 k12
King's Sutton, U.K., 1,550 114 F6
Kingston, Austl. 172 F5
Kingston, N.S., Can., 1,434 47 T11
Kingston, Ont., Can., 52,105 44 J7
Kingston, Jam., 123,403 96 q8
Kingston, Norfolk I. 175 11
Kingston, Hants., Eng., U.K. 113 k13
Kingston, Herefs., Eng., U.K. 114 C6
Kingston, London, U.K. 114 H8
Kingston, Ark. 73 B1
Kingston, Calif. 82 F5
Kingston, Ga., 695 64 E1
Kingston, Ill., 405 68 D1
Kingston, Ind. 70 D3
Kingston, Ky. 71 G4
Kingston, Mass., 1,301; 4,302(T) 57 O5
Kingston, Mich., 456 67 K5
Kingston, Caldwell Co., Mo., 311 72 C5
Kingston, Washington Co., Mo. 72 G6
Kingston, N.H. 54 E6
Kingston, N.J. 61 B3
Kingston, N. Mex. 79 B5
Kingston, N.Y., 29,260 59 M8
Kingston, Ohio, 1,066 70 F3
Kingston, Okla., 639 76 G4
Kingston, Pa., 20,261 61 L3
Kingston, R.I., 2,616 57 K7
Kingston, Tenn., 2,010 71 G6
Kingston, Utah, 143 78 B2
Kingston, Wash. 81 a7
Kingston, W. Va. 62 C5
Kingston, Wis., 343 66 D5
Kingstone, U.K. 114 C6
Kingston Harbour, Jam. 96 q9
Kingston Mines, Ill., 375 68 C3
Kingston-upon-Hull, U.K., 303,261 113 F5
Kingstown, St. Vinc., 15,981 97 19
Kingstree, S.C., 3,847 63 E4
Kings Valley, Oreg. 80 B3
Kingsville, Ont., Can., 3,041 44 G7
Kingsville, Mo., 225 72 D6
Kingsville, Ohio 70 J1
Kingsville, Tex., 25,297 77 P6
Kingswood, U.K., 25,417 113 E6
Kings Worthy, U.K., 2,113 113 k12
Kingussie, U.K., 1,079 112 D3
Kingwell, Newf., Can. 45 a10
King William, co., Va., 7,563 62 G5
King William, Va. 62 G5
King William I., N.W.T., Can. 40 K4
King William's Town, S. Af., 14,646 164 D7
Kingwood, W. Va., 2,530 62 E3
Kiniama, D.R.Congo 165 o19
Kinistino, Sask., Can. 43 D4
Kinkala, Congo 164 B2
Kinkazan, i., Japan 155 G2
Kinkora, P.E.I., Can. 47 U10
Kinlochewe, U.K. 112 D3
Kinlochleven, U.K. 112 D3
Kinloch Rannoch, U.K. 112 D3
Kinmount, Ont., Can. 46 F4
Kinmundy, Ill., 813 68 D5
Kinna, Swed. 120 C4
Kinnaird, Br. Col., Can., 2,092 42 H4
Kinnairds Head, U.K. 112 F3
Kinnegad, Ire. 113 C5
Kinnelon, N.J., 4,431 58 b13
Kinneret, Yam, l., Isr. 142 C3
Kinnerley, U.K. 114 C5
Kinney, co., Tex., 2,452 77 N5
Kinnickinnic, r., Wis. 66 A4
Kinniconick, Ky. 71 H3
Kino, Mex. 92 B2
Kino, r., Jap. 155 D4
Kinogitan, Phil., 2,202 153 f12
Kinomoto, Jap., 12,629 155 E4
Kinoosao, Sask., Can. 43 E2
Kinosaki, Jap., 5,922 154 f14
Kinosis, Alta., Can. 42 K2
Kinoura, Jap. 154 e15
Kinross, co., U.K., 6,704 112 E3
Kinross, U.K., 2,365 112 d7
Kinross, Mich. 67 J2
Kinsale, Ire., 1,808 113 B6
Kinsale, Montserrat 97 5
Kinsale, Va. 62 H4
Kinshasa, D.R.Congo, 402,492* 164 B2
Kinsley, Kans., 2,263 75 F6
Kinsman, Ill., 134 68 D2
Kinsman, Ohio 70 J1
Kinston, Ala., 470 64 C4
Kinston, N.C., 24,819 63 G2
Kinta, Okla., 233 76 H2
Kinta, r., Malay. 147 o14
Kintampo, Ghana 162 c7
Kintbury, U.K., 1,864 114 F8
Kintnersville, Pa. 61 m18
Kintobongo-Bunge, D.R.Congo 165 n18
Kintore, U.K. 112 E3
Kintyre, N. Dak. 74 C2
Kintyre, i., U.K. 112 D4
Kin-u, Burma, 3,222 146 A2
Kinuso, Alta., Can. 42 J2
Kinvarra, Ire. 113 B5
Kinyeti, pk., Sudan 163 K5
Kinzig, r., Hess., F.R.Ger. 118 B3
Kinzig, r., Württ., F.R.Ger. 118 B4
Kinzua, Oreg. 80 D3
Kinzua, Pa. 60 E2
Kinzua Cr., Pa. 60 E2
Kioa, i., Fiji 174 4
Kioga, Lake = Kyoga, Lake
Kiosk, Ont., Can. 46 F2
Kiowa, co., Colo., 2,425 79 D2
Kiowa, Colo., 195 79 C2
Kiowa, co., Kans., 4,626 75 F6
Kiowa, Kans., 1,674 75 G6
Kiowa, co., Okla., 14,825 76 D3
Kiowa, Okla., 607 76 G3
Kiowa Cr., Colo. 79 C2
Kiowa Cr., Okla.-Tex. 76 C1
Kipahulu, Hawaii 84 E3
Kipapa Str., Hawaii 84 b7
Kiparissía, Gr., 4,602 129 C6
Kiparissiakós Kólpos, Gr. 129 C6
Kipawa, Qué., Can. 46 E2
Kipawa, L., Qué., Can. 44 H6
Kipili, Tanz. 164 E3
Kipilovo, Bulg., 1,660 128 F3
Kipini, Kenya 164 F2
Kipkabus, Kenya 165 g13
Kipling, Sask., Can. 43 D5
Kipling, Mich. 66 F3
Kipling, N.C. 63 E2
Kipnuk, Alaska, 221 85 D3
Kipp, Kans. 75 H5
Kippax, U.K., 4,984 114 F3
Kippen, U.K. 112 b7
Kipsdorf, Ger.D.R. 126 c6
Kiptopeke, Va. 62 J5
Kipupa, D.R.Congo 165 n18
Kipushi, D.R.Congo, 22,602 164 D3
Kiput, Phil., 3,013 153 B4
Kir, Alb. 125 D3
Kirai, Jap. 154 f15
Kira Kira, Sol. Is. 175 c3
Kirby, Tex., 680 76 b7
Kirby, Wyo., 82 81 E4
Kirbyville, Tex., 1,660 77 R4
Kirchberg, Aust. 124 b10
Kirchberg, F.R.Ger., 2,200 119 C5
Kirchberg, Switz., 3,304 124 B1
Kirchberg, Switz., 5,554 124 D1
Kirchbichl, Aust., 4,062 124 H6
Kirchdorf, Aust., 2,961 124 K6
Kirchen, F.R.Ger., 7,007 119 D3
Kirchhain, F.R.Ger., 4,789 118 B3
Kirchhayn, Wis. 66 c10
Kirchheim, F.R.Ger., 22,224 118 B4
Kirchheim, F.R.Ger., 3,319 119 G6
Kirchheimbolanden, F.R.Ger., 5,112 118 A4
Kirchhellen, F.R.Ger., 8,880 119 B1
Kirchhundem, F.R.Ger., 10,298 118 B3
Kirchschlag, Aust., 1,328 124 N6
Kirchstetten, Aust. 124 b10
Kirchveischede, F.R.Ger., 2,237 119 D2
Kirchzell, F.R.Ger., 1,396 119 G5
Kirenga, r., U.S.S.R. 135 K4
Kirensk, U.S.S.R., 14,400 135 K4
Kireyevsk, U.S.S.R., 20,000 136 E2
Kirgiz-Miyaki, U.S.S.R. 137 h9
Kirgizskaya S.S.R., U.S.S.R., 2,600,000* 134 G5
Kirgizskiy Khr., U.S.S.R. 137 g3
Kirgiz S.S.R. = Kirgizskaya S.S.R.
Kiri, D.R.Congo 164 C2
Kiriáki, Gr., 2,123 129 D5
Kirihara, Jap. 154 h16
Kırıkhan, Turk., 15,014 142 C2
Kırıkkale, Turk., 42,838 142 C2
Kirillov, U.S.S.R., 6,100 136 E1
Kirin = Chi-lin
Kirishima-ktk., Jap. 154 B5
Kirishima-yama, Jap. 154 B6
Kiritappu, Jap. 155 L8
Kiriwina, i., Terr. Papua 174 f3
Kiriwo, Terr. Papua 174 d3
Kiriyama, Jap. 154 g15
Kirk, Oreg. 80 C4
Kırkağaç, Turk., 11,337 142 A2
Kirkburton, U.K., 18,066 114 E3
Kirkby, U.K., 52,207 113 E5
Kirkby Fell, mtn., U.K. 114 D2
Kirkby in Ashfield, U.K., 21,686 114 F4
Kirkby Lonsdale, U.K., 1,240 114 C2
Kirkby Malzeard, U.K. 114 E2
Kirkby Moorside, U.K., 1,883 113 F4
Kirkby Stephen, U.K., 1,718 114 D2
Kirkcaldy, U.K. 112 E3
Kirkcolm, U.K. 113 D4
Kirkconnel, U.K. 113 E4
Kirkcudbright, co., U.K., 28,877 113 D4
Kirkcudbright, U.K., 2,448 113 E4
Kirkee, India, 58,496 145 D6
Kirke-Hvalsø, Den. 121 D5
Kirkenes, Nor. 120 G1
Kirkfield, Ont., Can. 46 F4
Kirkfieldbank, U.K. 112 c8
Kirkfield Park, Man., Can. 43 g10
Kirkham, U.K., 4,760 114 C3
Kirkheaton, U.K. 112 f9
Kirkhouse, U.K. 112 d8
Kirkintilloch, U.K., 18,257 112 b8
Kirkjubæjarklaustur, Ice. 120 a6
Kirkland, Ga. 64 G4
Kirkland, Ill., 928 68 D1
Kirkland, N.Y. 59 t26
Kirkland, Tex. 77 N2
Kirkland, Wash., 6,025 80 B2
Kirkland Lake, Ont., Can., 15,366 44 H5
Kirklareli, Turk., 20,246 142 A1
Kirklin, Ind., 767 70 C2
Kirkliston, U.K. 112 d8
Kirkoswald, U.K. 113 D4
Kirksville, Ill. 68 D4
Kirksville, Mo., 13,123 72 E4
Kirkton, Ont., Can. 46 C5
Kirkton, U.K. 112 c7
Kirkton of Largo, U.K. 112 e7
Kirkūk, Iraq, 120,593 143 C1
Kirkville, Calif. 82 a7
Kirkville, Iowa, 203 72 E3
Kirkville, Miss. 73 G3
Kirkwall, U.K., 4,315 112 E2
Kirkwood, Del. 62 J3
Kirkwood, Ill., 771 68 B3
Kirkwood, Mo., 29,421 72 a11
Kirley, S. Dak. 74 B3
Kirmasti, r., Turk. 142 B2
Kirn, F.R.Ger., 9,526 118 A4
Kirov, U.S.S.R., 269,000 134 E4
Kirov, U.S.S.R., 16,800 136 D2
Kirovabad, Az.S.S.R., U.S.S.R., 123,000 134 D5
Kirovabad, T.S.S.R., U.S.S.R., 5,100 137 f5
Kirovakan, U.S.S.R., 57,000 137 c1
Kirovgrad, U.S.S.R., 22,700 137 k7
Kirovograd, U.S.S.R., 134,000 134 C5
Kirovsk, U.S.S.R., 38,400 134 C3
Kirovsk, U.S.S.R., 10,900 136 C1
Kirovskiy, Kaz.S.S.R., U.S.S.R. 134 G5
Kirovskiy, R.S.F.S.R., U.S.S.R., 3,900 135 P4
Kirovskoye, U.S.S.R., 16,300 136 f7
Kirrberg, F.R.Ger., 2,164 119 C6
Kirriemuir, U.K., 3,485 112 E3
Kirrlach, F.R.Ger., 6,513 118 B4
Kirs, U.S.S.R., 10,700 134 E4
Kirsanov, U.S.S.R., 15,000 136 F2
Kırşehir, Turk., 20,229 142 C2
Kirtland, Ohio 70 f8
Kirtland Hills, Ohio, 292 70 f8
Kirtlington, U.K. 114 F7
Kirton, Barb. 97 10
Kirton, U.K., 3,265 114 H5
Kirton in Lindsey, U.K., 2,553 113 F5
Kiruna, Swed. 120 D2
Kirwin, Kans., 356 75 F4
Kirwin Res., Kans. 75 F4
Kiryū, Jap., 123,010 155 F3
Kirzhach, U.S.S.R., 18,200 136 c5
Kisa, Jap., 9,524 155 C4
Kisabe, Jap. 154 g15
Kisakata, Jap., 14,966 155 F2
Kisaki, Tanz. 164 F3
Kis Alföld, plain, Hung. 126 ·
Kisanfu, D.R.Congo 165 m19
Kisangani, D.R.Congo, 126,533 164 D1
Kisar, P., Indon. 149 H4
Kisarazu, Jap., 52,689 155 m20
Kisatchie, La. 73 B6
Kisbey, Sask., Can. 43 D5
Kisdorf, F.R.Ger., 1,629 119 a8
Kiselëvsk, U.S.S.R., 141,000 137 r11
Kisenga, D.R.Congo 164 C3
Kisgegas, Br. Col., Can. 42 E2
Kishanda, Tanz. 165 e14
Kishanganj, India, 27,002 144 f12
Kishangarh, India, 25,244 145 E4
Kishanpur, India 144 c13
Kishi, D.R.Congo 165 o19
Kishi, Nigeria, 9,079 162 e7
Kishiale, D.R.Congo 165 o18
Kishikaroy, Oz., U.S.S.R. 137 n11
Kishinëv, U.S.S.R., 236,000 134 B5
Kishiwada, Jap., 120,265 155 D4
Kishorganj, Pak., 24,031 145 J4
Kishtwar, India, 4,140 145 E2
Kishuku, Jap., 9,978 154 A5
Kishwaukee, r., Ill. 68 D1
Kisii, Kenya 164 E2
Kisiju, Tanz. 164 F3
Kısırındağı, Turk. 142 E1
Kiska I., Alaska 85 e8
Kiska Vol., Alaska 85 e8
Kiskittogisu L., Man., Can. 43 F3
Kiskitto L., Man., Can. 43 F3
Kiskőrös, Hung., 13,173 126 D3
Kiskundorozsma, Hung., 8,705 126 D3
Kiskunfélegyháza, Hung., 33,187 126 D3
Kiskunhalas, Hung., 26,461 126 D3
Kiskunlacháza, Hung., 8,109 126 D3
Kiskunmajsa, Hung., 13,013 126 D3
Kislovodsk, U.S.S.R., 82,000 134 D5
Kismayu, Som. Rep., 11,838* 163 L6

246 · Kismet—Körlach

Kismet, Kans., 150 75 E6
Kismet, N.Y. 58 g14
Kiso, r., Jap. 154 h14
Kiso-sammyaku, mts., Jap. 155 E4
Kispiox, Br. Col., Can. 42 E2
Kisseraing I., Burma 146 B5
Kissidougou, Guin., 12,000 162 C4
Kissimmee, Fla., 6,845 65 H4
Kissimmee, L., Fla. 65 H5
Kissimmee, r., Fla. 65 H5
Kississing, Man., Can. 43 E3
Kississing L., Man., Can. 43 E3
Kist, F.R.Ger., 1,342 119 H5
Kistelek, Hung., 8,955 126 E3
Kisterenye, Hung., 6,594 126 D2
Kistigan L., Man., Can. 43 H3
Kistler, W. Va., 1,084 62 C5
Kisújszállás, Hung., 13,790 126 E3
Kisumu, Kenya, 23,200 164 E2
Kisvárda, Hung., 13,284 126 F2
Kiszombor, Hung., 5,117 126 E3
Kita, Mali, 5,230 162 C3
Kitab, U.S.S.R., 8,400 137 e4
Kita-Daitō-jima, Ryukyu Is. 170 C3
Kita-Ibaraki, Jap., 60,567 155 G3
Kita-iō-jima, Vol. Is. 170 D3
Kitakami, Jap., 42,979 155 G2
Kitakami, r., Jap. 155 G2
Kitakami-sammyaku, mts., Jap. 155 G2
Kitakata, Jap., 42,388 155 F3
Kitakyūshū, Jap., 1,000,000 154 B5
Kitale, Kenya 164 E1
Kitamaki, Jap., 5,223 155 F3
Kitami, Jap., 66,932 155 K8
Kitami-sammyaku, mts., Jap. 155 K7
Kitamura, Jap. 155 m20
Kitaura, Jap. 155 F2
Kitava, i., Terr. Papua 174 f3
Kita-Wakamatsuchō, Jap. 154 h15
Kitayama, r., Jap. 154 h15
Kitay-Gorod, U.S.S.R. 151 F1
Kit Carson, co., Colo., 6,957 79 D2
Kit Carson, Colo., 356 79 D2
Kitchell, Ind. 70 E3
Kitchener, Ont., Can., 73,811 44 H7
Kitchigama, r., Qué., Can. 44 H5
Kite, Ga., 424 64 G3
Kitee, Fin. 120 G3
Kitgum, Uganda, 1,615 164 E1
Kíthira, Gr. 129 D6
Kíthira, i., Gr. 129 D6
Kithíron, Stenón, Gr. 129 D7
Kíthnos, Gr. 129 E6
Kíthnos, i., Gr. 129 E6
Kitimat, Br. Col., Can., 8,000 42 E2
Kitinen, r., Fin. 120 F2
Kiti Pt., Ponape 176 29
Kitongo, D.R.Congo 165 m18
Kítros, Gr., 2,220 129 D4
Kitsap, co., Wash., 84,176 80 B2
Kitsap=Indianola, Wash.
Kitscoty, Alta., Can. 42 L3
Kitsman', U.S.S.R., 6,000 136 B3
Kitsuki, Jap., 27,753 154 B5
Kittanning, Pa., 6,793 60 D4
Kittatinny Mts., N.J. 61 B1
Kittery, Me., 8,051 55 B5
Kittery Point, Me., 1,259 55 B5
Kittilä, Fin. 120 F2
Kittitas, co., Wash., 20,467 80 C2
Kittitas, Wash., 536 80 C2
Kitt Pk., Ariz. 78 C5
Kittredge, Colo. 79 b8
Kittrell, N.C. 63 F1
Kittsee, Aust., 2,309 124 O5
Kittson, co., Minn., 8,343 74 D1
Kittville (part of Grafton), Mass. 57 K4
Kitty Hawk, N.C. 63 J1
Kitui, Kenya 164 F2
Kitunga, D.R.Congo 165 o18
Kitwe, Zambia, 80,500* 164 D4
Kitzbühel, Aust., 7,743 124 J6
Kitzbühler Alpen, Aust. 124 J6
Kitzingen, F.R.Ger., 17,215 118 B4
Kitzmiller, Md., 535 62 E3
Kiuchüan=Chiu-ch'üan
Kiunga, Terr. Papua 174 d2
Kiuruvesi, Fin. 120 F3
Kiutaköngäs, rapids, Fin. 120 G2
Kivalina, Alaska, 142 85 C2
Kivertsy, U.S.S.R., 10,000 136 B3
Kivik, Swed. 120 C5
Kiviõli, U.S.S.R., 10,400 136 B1
Kivotós, Gr. 129 C4
Kivu, prov., Congo L. 165 d14
Kivu, L., Congo L.-Rwanda 165 d14
Kiwadahata, Jap. 155 n20
Kiwai, i., Terr. Papua 174 d3
Kiya, r., U.S.S.R. 137 r11
Kiyama, Jap. 154 g14
Kiyan, Ryukyu Is. 154 a11
Kiyev, U.S.S.R., 1,174,000 134 C4
Kiyevka, U.S.S.R. 137 n12
Kiyma, U.S.S.R. 137 m12
Kiyotake, Jap., 11,569 154 B6
Kizel, U.S.S.R., 61,000 134 E4
Kızıl, r., Turk. 142 C1
Kızılcahamam, Turk., 4,133 142 C1
Kizil'skoye, U.S.S.R. 137 i9
Kızıltepe, Turk., 6,418 142 E2
Kizir, r., U.S.S.R. 137 t11
Kizlyar, U.S.S.R., 24,900 134 D5
Kizu, Jap., 11,058 154 g15
Kizu, r., Jap. 154 g15
Kizukuri, Jap., 28,649 155 G1
Kizyl-Arvat, U.S.S.R., 14,300 134 E6
Kizyl Jilga, India 145 F2
Kjellerup, Den., 3,010 121 B4
Kjölen Mts., Nor. 121 ·
Kjöllefjord, Nor. 120 F1
Klaaswaal, Neth. 115 a7
Kladanj, Yug., 2,410 125 D2
Klädesholmen, Swed. 121 D3
Kladnica, Yug. 125 E3
Kladno, Czech., 51,698 126 A1
Kladovo, Yug., 2,336 125 F2
Kladruby, Czech. 126 c7
Kladuša, Yug. 125 B2
Klaeng, Thai. 147 d5
Klafeld, F.R.Ger., 13,058 118 A3
Klagenfurt, Aust., 69,193 124 L7
Klagetoh, Ariz. 78 D4
Klaipėda, U.S.S.R., 100,000 134 B4
Klaksvík, Faeroe Is. 120 c7
Klamath, Calif. 82 A2
Klamath, co., Oreg., 47,475 80 C4
Klamath, r., Calif.-Oreg. 82 B2
Klamath Agency, Oreg. 80 C4
Klamath Falls, Oreg., 16,949 80 C4
Klamath Mts., Calif.-Oreg. 50 B2
Klamath River, Calif. 82 B2
Klamm, Aust. 124 b11
Klamono, Indon. 149 J3
Klang, Malay., 75,649 148 B2
Klappan Ra., Br. Col., Can. 38 D6
Klarälven, r., Swed. 120 C4
Klašnice, Yug. 125 C2
Klaten, Indon. 148 d7
Klatovy, Czech., 14,273 126 A2
Klaus, Aust., 1,356 124 L6
Klausenleopoldsdorf, Aust., 1,139 124 c10
Klawak, Alaska, 251 85 L5
Klazienaveen, Neth., 8,400 115 F2
Kleberg, co., Tex., 30,052 77 P6
Kleberg, Tex., 3,572 76 f9
Klecko, Pol., 1,770 127 B2
Kleczew, Pol., 2,196 127 C2
Kleena Kleene, Br. Col., Can. 42 F3
Klein Bonaire, i., Bon. 97 17
Klein Emme, r., Switz. 124 B2
Kleinlützel, Switz., 1,269 124 B1
Kleinmachnow, Ger.D.R., 15,647 119 e11
Klein Offenseth, F.R.Ger., 1,536 119 a8
Kleinrinderfeld, F.R.Ger., 1,569 119 H5
Klein Sankt Paul, Aust., 2,205 124 L7
Kleinzell, Aust., 1,050 124 b11
Klekovača, mt., Yug. 125 C2
Klemme, Iowa, 615 72 D1
Klemtu, Br. Col., Can. 42 E3
Klenak, Yug., 2,180 125 D2
Klenike, Yug. 125 F3
Klenoec, Yug. 125 E4
Klerksdorp, S. Af., 43,067 164 D6
Kletnya, U.S.S.R. 136 D2
Kletsk, U.S.S.R., 3,800 136 B2
Kleve, F.R.Ger., 20,114 118 A3
Klickitat, co., Wash., 13,455 80 C3
Klickitat, r., Wash. 80 C2
Klidhes I., Cyp. 142 f9
Klim, Den. 121 B3
Klimkovice, Czech. 127 h7
Klimovichi, U.S.S.R., 11,600 136 D2
Klimovsk, U.S.S.R., 29,400 136 b6
Klin, U.S.S.R., 57,000 136 E1
Klina, Yug. 125 E3
Klinaklini, r., Br. Col., Can. 42 F3
Kline, S.C., 213 63 C4
Kling, Phil., 2,408 153 C4
Klingenberg, Ger.D.R. 126 c6
Klingenmünster, F.R.Ger., 3,013 119 D6
Klingenthal, Ger.D.R., 15,497 118 D3
Klinger Lake, Mich. 67 H7
Klínovec, pk., Czech. 126 A1
Klintehamn, Swed. 120 D4
Klintsy, U.S.S.R., 42,000 134 C4
Klipdale, S. Af. 164 a9
Kliplev, Den. 121 B6
Klitmøller, Den. 121 A3
Klitten, Ger.D.R. 126 d5
Klitten, Ger.D.R. 127 d5
Kljake, Yug. 125 C3
Kłobuck, Pol., 8,272 127 C3
Klockestrand, Swed. 120 D3
Kłodawa, Pol., 5,746 127 C2
Kłodobok, Pol. 127 g6
Kłodzko, Pol., 23,000* 127 B3
Klomnice, Pol. 127 C3
Klondike, Wis. 66 c13
Klondike, r., Yukon, Can. 85 K3
Klondyke, Ariz. 78 C5
Klöntalersee, Switz. 124 C1
Kloosterdijk, Neth. 115 E2
Kloosterzande, Neth. 115 C3
Klos, Alb. 125 E4
Kloštar Ivanić, Yug. 125 C2
Klosterneuburg, Aust., 23,037 124 N5
Klosters Platz, Switz., 3,181 124 D2
Kloten, Switz., 8,446 124 C1
Kloten, N. Dak. 74 C2
Klotten, F.R.Ger., 1,841 119 C4
Klötze, Ger.D.R. 118 C2
Klotz L., Qué., Can. 44 K1
Klotzville, La. 73 D7
Klouto, Togo 162 d8
Kluane, Yukon, Can. 40 B5
Kluane L., Yukon, Can. 85 K3
Kluang, Malay., 31,183 148 B2
Kluczbork, Pol., 13,328 127 C3
Klucze, Pol. 127 i6
Klukwan, Alaska 85 K4
Klundert, Neth., 3,600 115 b7
Klutina L., Alaska 85 H3
Klütz, Ger.D.R. 118 C2
Klwów, Pol. 127 D3
Klyaz'ma, r., U.S.S.R. 136 E2
Klyuchevskaya Sopka, U.S.S.R. 133 Q4
Klyuchi, U.S.S.R., 7,200 135 Q4
Klyuchi, U.S.S.R. 137 i8
Klyuchi, U.S.S.R. 137 p11
Knaben, Nor. 120 A4
Knabstrup, Dem. 121 D5
Knapp, Wis., 374 66 A4
Knapp Creek, N.Y. 58 C7
Knaresborough, U.K., 9,311 113 F4
Knauertown, Pa. 60 e11
Knebel, Den. 121 C4
Knebworth, U.K., 3,024 114 H7
Knee L., Man., Can. 43 G3
Knee L., Sask., Can. 43 C3
Kneeland, Calif. 82 B2
Knellsville, Wis. 66 F5
Knesebeck, F.R.Ger., 2,521 118 C2
Knezha, Bulg., 13,804 128 E3
Knić, Yug., 2,197 125 E3
Knickerbocker, Tex. 77 N4
Knierim, Iowa, 153 72 C2
Knife, r., N. Dak. 74 A2
Knife River, Minn. 74 G2
Knifley, Ky. 71 F4
Knight Inlet, Br. Col., Can. 42 F4
Knighton, U.K., 2,782 113 E5
Knights, Fla. 65 d11
Knights Landing, Calif. 82 C3
Knightstown, Ind., 2,496 70 D3
Knightsville, Ind., 722 70 B3
Knightville Res., Mass. 56 E3
Knik, Alaska 85 c7
Knik, r., Alaska 85 c7
Knik Arm, Alaska 85 c7
Kniman, Ind. 70 B1
Knin, Yug., 3,543 125 C2
Knippa, Tex. 77 O5
Knittelfeld, Aust., 14,261 124 L6
Knittlingen, F.R.Ger., 3,723 119 F6
Knivsta, Swed. 120 D4
Knjaževac, Yug., 5,906 125 F3
Knobel, Ark., 339 73 E1
Knob Hill, Colo. 79 c10
Knob Noster, Mo., 2,292 72 D6
Knokke, Belg., 13,085 115 B3
Knolls, Utah 78 B1
Knollwood (part of Old Saybrook), Conn. 56 G7
Knollwood, Ill. 69 c7
Knossós, ruins, Gr. 129 E7
Knott, co., Ky., 17,362 71 H4
Knott, Tex. 77 N3
Knottingley, U.K., 11,153 114 F3
Knotts Island, N.C. 63 J1
Knottsville, Ky. 71 D4
Knowle, U.K., 4,636 114 E6
Knowles, N. Mex. 79 D5
Knowles, Okla., 62 76 C1
Knowles, Wis. 66 E5
Knowles Corner, Me. 55 D2
Knowles Cr., Ga. 64 f9
Knowlesville, N.Y. 58 D5
Knowlton, Qué., Can., 1,352 47 M3
Knowlton, Wis. 66 D4
Knox, co., Ill., 61,280 68 B3
Knox, co., Ind., 41,561 70 B4
Knox, Ind., 3,458 70 C1
Knox, co., Ky., 25,258 71 H5
Knox, co., Me., 28,575 55 C4
Knox, co., Mo., 6,558 72 E4
Knox, co., Nebr., 13,300 75 H1
Knox, N.Y. 59 M6
Knox, N. Dak., 122 74 C1
Knox, co., Ohio, 38,808 70 G2
Knox, Pa., 1,247 60 C3
Knox, co., Tenn., 250,523 71 G6
Knox, co., Tex., 7,857 77 O3
Knox, atoll, Marsh. Is. 176 22
Knox, C., Br. Col. 85 L5
Knox City, Mo., 330 72 F4
Knox City, Tex., 1,805 77 N3
Knox Coast, Ant. 180 T6
Knox Dale, Pa. 60 D3
Knoxville, Ga. 64 E3
Knoxville, Ill., 2,560 68 B3
Knoxville, Iowa, 7,817 72 D3
Knoxville, Miss. 73 D6
Knoxville, Pa., 694 60 H2
Knoxville, Tenn., 111,827 71 H6
Knurów, Pol., 14,140 127 h6
Knutsford, U.K., 9,389 114 D4
Knyazh'i Gory, U.S.S.R. 136 a5
Knysna, S. Af., 11,085 164 C7
Knyszyn, Pol., 2,300 127 E2
Ko, r., China 151 C4
Koabu, Terr. Papua 174 d3
Koa Mill, Hawaii 84 F4
Koba, Indon. 148 C3
Kobatake, Jap. 154 e15
Kobayashi, Jap., 43,894 154 B5
Kobbo-Alomata, Eth. 163 L3
Kobdo=Jirgalanta
Kōbe, Jap., 1,113,977 155 D4
Kobelyaki, U.S.S.R., 9,500 136 D3
Kobenhavn, Den., 721,381 121 E5
Kobersdorf, Aust., 1,063 124 N6
Kobi, Indon. 149 J3
Kobi, Jap. 154 i14
Kobidani, Jap. 154 g14
Kobierzyce, Pol. 127 f6
Kobišnica, Yug., 2,935 125 F2
Koblenz, F.R.Ger., 84,275 118 A3
Kobrin, U.S.S.R., 13,700 136 A2
Kobroor, P., Indon. 149 K4
Kobuk, Alaska, 54 85 E2
Kobuk, r., Alaska 85 E2
Kobuleti, U.S.S.R., 12,400 137 b1
Kobyay, U.S.S.R. 135 M3
Kobylin, Pol., 2,617 127 B3
Koca, r., Turk. 142 A2
Kočani, Yug., 11,000* 125 F4
Koceljevo, Yug., 2,010 125 D2
Kočerin, Yug., 2,111 125 C3
Kočevje, Yug., 4,447 125 B2
Kōch'ang, S. Kor., 31,895 151 F4
Kochechum, r., U.S.S.R. 135 J3
Kochenëvo, U.S.S.R. 137 q11
K'o-ch'en-na-erh Shan-k'ou, China 150 C3
Kocher, r., F.R.Ger. 119 G6
Kochevo, U.S.S.R. 137 h7
Kōchi, Jap. 154 h14
Kōchi, Jap., 196,288 155 C5
Koch I., N.W.T., Can. 41 O4
Ko-chiu, China, 180,000* 150 D5
Kochki, U.S.S.R. 134 H4
Kochugaon, India 144 g12
Kochumdek, U.S.S.R. 135 J3
Kock, Pol., 2,409 127 E3
Kockengen, Neth. 115 b6
Kocmyrzów, Pol. 127 k6
Kočov, Czech. 126 b7
Kodai, Jap. 154 g15
Kodaikanal, India, 12,860 145 k20
Kodal, Nor. 121 C1
Kodani, Jap. 154 e15
Kodarma, India 144 e13
Kodeń, Pol. 127 E3
Kodiak, Alaska, 2,628 85 F4
Kodiak I., Alaska 85 F4
Kodinar, India, 11,426 144 D5
Kodok, Sudan 163 K4
Kodomari, Jap., 5,948 155 G1
Kodrab, Pol. 127 i5
Kodyma, U.S.S.R., 6,800 136 C3
Koehler, N. Mex. 79 C3
Koekelare, Belg., 6,353 115 A3
Koele, Hawaii 84 E3
Koenigsmacker, Fr., 1,531 116 b8
Koera Joer, Cur. 97 16
K'o-erh-ch'in-tso-i-chung-ch'i, China 151 D2
K'o-erh-ch'in-yu-i-chung-ch'i, China 151 D1
Koersel, Belg., 8,927 115 D3
Koës, S.-W. Afr. 164 C6
Koetoi, Jap. 155 J7
Kofa Mts., Ariz. 78 B5
Koffiefontein, S. Af., 2,985 164 D6
Kofiau, P., Indon. 149 J3
Koforidua, Ghana, 28,261 162 D4
Kōfu, Jap., 160,963 155 F4
Koga, Jap., 42,474 155 F3
Kogaluk, r., Qué., Can. 44 J2
Koganei, Jap., 45,734 155 m19
Køge, Den. 12,294 121 E5
Køge Bugt, Den. 121 E5
Kōgūm-do, S. Kor. 151 E4
Kogushi, Jap., 5,525 154 B4
Kogushi, Jap. 154 f15
Kohala, Hawaii 84 F3
Kohala Mts., Hawaii 84 F3
Kohāt, Pak., 49,854 145 D2
Kohatk, Ariz. 78 B5
Kohelepelepe, pk., Hawaii 84 d8
Koh-i-Kwāja Muhammad, mts., Afghan. 145 D1
Kohima, India, 7,246 145 K4
Koh-i-Mārān, pk., Pak. 144 C3
Kohler, Wis., 1,524 66 F5
Kohlscheid, F.R.Ger., 14,421 119 A3
Kohlsville, Wis. 66 E5
Kohren-Sahlis, Ger. D.R. 126 b5
Kohtla-Järve, U.S.S.R., 58,000 134 B4
Kohŭng, S. Kor., 15,567 151 E4
Koide, Jap., 14,105 155 F3
Koike, Jap. 155 n19
Koilpatti, India, 33,305 145 m21
Koira, India 144 e15
Koizumi, Jap. 154 g15
Kojabuti, Indon. 149 L3
Köje-do, S. Kor. 151 F4
Kojetín, Czech. 126 C2
Kojima, Jap., 75,256 154 e15
Ko-jima, Jap. 155 H9
Kōji-naya, Jap. 155 n20
Kojŏ, N. Kor. 151 F3
Kok, Malay. 148 E2
Kok, r., Burma-Thai. 146 B3
Koka Dam, Eth. 163 L4
Kokadjo, Me. 55 C3
Kokand, U.S.S.R., 113,000 134 G5
Kokas, Indon. 149 K3
Kokava nad Rimavicou, Czech. 126 D2
Kokcha, r., Afghan. 145 C1
Kokchetav, U.S.S.R., 59,000 134 F4
Kokemäki, Fin. 120 E3
Kokenau, Indon. 149 L4
Ko Kha, Thai. 146 B3
Kokhanok Bay=Kakhonak
Kokhma, U.S.S.R., 21,000 136 F1
Kokkina, Cyp. 142 d9
Kokkola, Fin., 16,190 120 E3
Koko, Nigeria 162 E5
Koko Crater, Hawaii 84 d8
Kokoda, Terr. Papua 174 e3
Koko Head, Hawaii 84 D2
Kokokahi, Hawaii 84 d7
Kokolik, r., Alaska 85 D1
Kokomo, Ind., 47,197 70 C2
Kokomo, Miss. 73 E6
Koko Nor=Ch'ing Hai
Kokonselkä, l., Fin. 120 G3
Kokopo, Terr. New Guin. 174 g2
Kokosing, r., Ohio 70 G2
Kokrines, Alaska 85 F2
Koksan, N. Kor. 151 E3
Kökse Dağı, Turk. 137 b2
Kokshaal-Tau, Khr., U.S.S.R. 132 G5
Kök Shal Tau, mts., China 134 G5
Koksoak, r., Qué., Can. 45 L2
Koksovyy, U.S.S.R., 14,000 136 g7
Kokstad, S. Af., 7,984 164 D7
Kokubu, Jap., 35,480 154 B6
Kokubu, Jap., 8,957 154 g15
Kokubunji, Jap., 39,098 155 m19
Kōkura, Jap. 154 h14
Kok-Yangak, U.S.S.R., 17,400 137 g4
Kola, Yug., 2,506 125 C2
Kola, r., U.S.S.R. 134 C3
K'o-la-ch'in-ch'i, China 151 C2
K'o-la-ch'in-tso-i-hsien, China 151 C2
Kolahun, Lib. 162 C4
Kolaka, Indon. 149 G4
K'o-la-ma-i, China, 50,000* 150 B2
K'o-lan, China 151 A3
Kolar, India, 32,387 145 F7
Kolar Gold Fields, India, 146,811 145 E7
Kolari, Fin. 120 F2
Kolarovgrad, Bulg., 41,546 128 F3
Kolárovo, Czech., 10,248 126 C3
Kolašin, Yug. 125 D3
Kolbäck, Swed. 120 d8
Kolbano, Indon. 149 H5
Kolbio, Kenya 164 F2
Kolbuszowa, Pol., 2,310 127 D3
Kol'chugino, U.S.S.R., 38,400 136 E1
Kolda, Sen., 5,300 162 B3
Kolding, Den., 35,101 121 B5
Kole, D.R.Congo 164 C2
Kolekole Pass, Hawaii 84 b7
Kölen=Kjölen
Kolepom, P., Indon. 149 L4
Kolešovice, Czech. 126 c6
Koleul, U.S.S.R. 137 r11
Kolff, Tg., Indon. 149 L4
Kolguyev, O., U.S.S.R. 134 D3
Kolhapur, India, 187,442 145 D6
Koliganek, Alaska, 100 85 E4
Kolín, Czech., 23,137 126 B1
Kolind, Den., 1,075 121 C4
Kølkær, Den. 121 B4
Kolkasrags, pt., U.S.S.R. 136 A1
Kölleda, Ger.D.R. 118 C3
Kollegal, India, 22,663 145 E7
Kollund, Den. 121 B6
Kolmanskop, S.-W. Afr. 164 B6
Köln, F.R.Ger., 713,505 118 A3
Kolno, Pol., 4,388 127 D2
Koło, Pol., 10,685 127 C2
Koloa, Tonga 2,873 177 36
Koloa, Hawaii, 1,426 84 B2
Kołobrzeg, Pol., 13,169 127 A1
Kologriv, U.S.S.R., 4,600 136 G1
Kolokani, Mali, 2,250 162 C3
Koloksha, r., U.S.S.R. 136 d5
Kolombangara, i., Sol. Is. 175 b2
Kolomna, U.S.S.R., 124,000 134 C4
Kolomyya, U.S.S.R., 31,300 136 B3
Kolonjë, Alb. 125 D4
Kolonnawa, Cey., 21,384 145 n22
Kolono, Indon. 149 G4
Kolonodale, Indon. 149 G3
Kolonowskie, Pol., 3,222 127 h6
Kolosovka, U.S.S.R. 137 o11
Kolovai, Tonga 177 36
Kolovrat, Mt., Sol. Is. 175 c3
Kolpakovskiy, U.S.S.R. 135 P4
Kolpashevo, U.S.S.R., 22,600 134 H4
Kolpino, U.S.S.R., 34,700 136 C1
Kol'skiy P-ov., U.S.S.R. 134 C3
Kolu, Khr., U.S.S.R. 137 h9
Kolubara, r., Yug. 125 E2
Koluszki, Pol., 7,107 127 C3
Koluton, U.S.S.R. 137 n12
Koluton, r., U.S.S.R. 137 n12
Kolva, r., U.S.S.R. 137 h6
Kolvereid, Nor. 120 B2
Kølvrå, Den. 121 B4
Kolwa, Pak. 144 B4
Kolwezi, D.R.Congo, 45,192 164 D3
Kolyma, r., U.S.S.R. 135 P3
Kolymskaya, U.S.S.R. 135 P3
Kolymskaya Nizm., U.S.S.R. 135 P3
Kolymskiy, Khr., U.S.S.R. 135 P3
Kolyubakino, U.S.S.R. 136 b6
Kolyuchinskaya G., U.S.S.R. 135 S3
Kolyvan', U.S.S.R., 6,600 137 q11
Kolyvan', U.S.S.R. 137 q12
Koma, Burma 146 B4
Komádi, Hung., 9,862 126 E3
Komaga-dake, Jap. 155 J8
Komagane, Jap., 27,579 155 E4
Komaki, Jap., 38,531 154 h14
Komańcza, Pol. 127 E4
Komandorskiye O-va., U.S.S.R. 135 Q4
Komano, Jap. 154 h14
Komarin, U.S.S.R. 136 C3
Komarno, Man., Can. 43 g9
Komárno, Czech., 24,975 126 C3
Komárom, Hung., 9,862 126 D3
Komárov, Czech. 126 c7
Komatke, Ariz. 78 B5
Komatsu, Jap., 10,470 154 e16
Komatsu, Jap., 89,085 155 E3
Komatsushima, Jap., 39,884 155 D4
Kombot, Indon. 149 H2
Kombóti, Gr., 2,277 129 C5
Komchai Meas, Camb. 147 k11
Komebail Lag., Palau 176 21
Kome I., Tanz. 165 f15
Komenoura, Jap. 154 g14
Komeshia, D.R.Congo 165 n18
Kominato, Jap. 155 G1
Kominato, Jap. 155 n20
Komló, Hung., 24,850 126 D3
Kommern, F.R.Ger., 2,404 119 B3
Kommunar, U.S.S.R., 6,900 137 s11
Kommunarsk, U.S.S.R., 107,000 136 E3
Kommunizma, Pik, U.S.S.R. 134 G6
Komo, i., Fiji 174 4
Komodo, P., Indon. 149 F5
Komoé=Comoé
Komoka, Ont., Can. 46 C6
Komono, Congo 164 B2
Komoran, P., Indon. 149 L5
Kōmori, Jap. 154 g14
Komoro, Jap., 39,283 155 F3
Komotiní, Gr., 28,335 129 E4
Komovi, mts., Yug. 125 D3
Kompasberg, mtn., S. Af. 164 D7
Kompong Bang, Camb. 147 k10
Kompong Cham, Camb., 28,534 146 D5
Kompong Chhnang, Camb., 12,847 146 D4
Kompong Chikreng, Camb. 146 D4
Kompong Chrey, Camb. 147 k11
Kompong Kleang, Camb. 146 D4
Kompong Prasath, Camb. 147 k10
Kompong Som, Camb. 146 C5
Kompong Som, B. de, Camb. 146 C5
Kompong Speu, Camb., 7,453 146 D5
Kompong Taches, Camb. 147 k10
Kompong Thom, Camb., 9,682 146 D4
Kompong Trabek, Camb. 147 k11
Kompong Trach, Camb., 5,608 146 D5
Kompong Trach, Camb. 147 k11
Kompong Tralach, Camb. 146 D5
Komrat, U.S.S.R., 14,300 136 C4
Komsomolets, U.S.S.R. 137 k9
Komsomolets, O., U.S.S.R. 135 K1
Komsomol'sk, U.S.S.R., 11,200 136 F1
Komsomol'skiy, U.S.S.R., 18,800 134 F3
Komsomol'skiy, U.S.S.R. 135 R3
Komsomol'sk-na-Amure, U.S.S.R., 189,000 135 N4
Komsomol'skoye, U.S.S.R., 13,800 136 f8
Komsomol'skoy Pravdy, O-va., U.S.S.R. 135 K2
Komungla, Austl. 173 g10
Komyshlyayat, r., U.S.S.R. 137 k9
Kona, Mali, 2,000 162 D3
Konakovo, U.S.S.R., 13,700 136 E1
Kōnan, Jap., 49,278 154 h14
Konan, Jap., 11,495 155 E4
Konarak, India 145 H6
Konarevo, Yug. 125 E3
Konarzyny, Pol. 127 B2
Konawa, Okla., 1,555 76 G3
Konda, Indon. 149 K3
Konda, r., U.S.S.R. 134 F4
Kondiá, Gr., 1,127 129 E5
Kondiaronk, L., Qué., Can. 46 H2
Kondinin, Austl. 172 B5
Kondoa, Tanz. 164 E2
Kondoma, r., U.S.S.R. 137 r11
Kondopoga, U.S.S.R., 16,000 134 C3
Kondoros, Hung., 7,454 126 E3
Kondrovo, U.S.S.R., 12,800 136 E2
Koné, N. Caled., 2,037 174 i8
Kong, Iv. Coast, 2,500* 162 D4
Kong, r., Camb.-Laos 146 D4
Kong, Koh, i., Camb. 146 C5
Konga, D.R.Congo 165 n18
Konga, Swed. 121 c7
Kongerslev, Den. 121 C4
Kongju, S. Kor., 27,071 151 E3
Kong Karls Land, is., Nor. 134 B2
Konglu, Burma 146 B1
Kongmoon=Chiang-men
Kongolo, D.R.Congo, 10,434 164 D2
Kongsberg, Nor., 9,589 120 B4
Kongsvinger, Nor., 2,286 120 C3
Kongwa, Tanz. 164 F3
Kongyi, Burma 147 f6
Koni, P-ov., U.S.S.R. 135 P4
Koniecpol, Pol., 2,478 127 C3
Königsbach, F.R.Ger., 3,744 119 F7
Königsberg, F.R.Ger., 1,609 118 C3
Königsberg, U.S.S.R.=Kaliningrad
Königsberg, F.R.Ger. 118 A4
Königsbrück, Ger.D.R. 118 D3
Königshofen, F.R.Ger., 1,591 119 H5
Königssee, F.R.Ger. 118 D5
Königstein, F.R.Ger., 6,143 119 E4
Königstein, Ger.D.R. 118 D3
Königstetten, Aust., 1,084 124 c10
Königswiesen, Aust., 2,707 124 L5
Königswinter, F.R.Ger., 6,878 119 C3
Königs Wusterhausen, Ger.D.R. 118 D2
Konin, Pol., 16,653 127 C2
Konispol, Alb. 125 E4
Kónitsa, Gr., 3,485 129 C4
Koniya, Jap., 11,910 154 d12
Köniz, Switz., 27,243 124 B2
Konjic, Yug., 4,272 125 C3
Konka, r., U.S.S.R. 136 E4
Könkämäälv, r., Swed. 120 E1
Könkämäälv=Könkämäeno
Könkämäeno, r., Fin. 120 E1
Könkämäeno=Könkämäälv
Konkapot (part of New Marlborough), Mass. 56 C4
Konko, D.R.Congo 165 n19
Konnarock, Va. 62 C6
Konnevesi, l., Fin. 120 F3
Konnur, India, 20,795 145 E6
Kōno, Jap. 154 g14
Kōno-Ichiba, Jap. 154 g15
Konolfingen, Switz., 3,964 124 B2
Konongo, Ghana, 10,062 162 D4
Konopiště, Czech. 126 d7
Konopište, Yug. 125 F4
Konosha, U.S.S.R., 13,800 134 C3
Kōnosu, Jap., 31,868 155 F3
Konotop, U.S.S.R., 56,000 134 C4
Konrei, Palau 176 21
Końskie, Pol., 9,219 127 D3
Konstantinovka, U.S.S.R., 93,000 136 e7
Konstantinovskiy, U.S.S.R., 11,000 136 F4
Konstantinovy Lázně, Czech. 126 c7
Konstantynów, Pol., 10,216 127 C3
Konstanz, F.R.Ger., 48,918 118 B5
Kontagora, Nigeria 163 E4
Kontich, Belg., 10,442 115 d8
Kontiolahti, Fin. 120 G3
Kontum, S. Viet., 8,757 146 D4
Kontum, Plat. du, S. Viet. 146 D4
Konya, Turk., 122,704 142 C2
Konz, F.R.Ger., 7,142 118 A4
Konzhakovskiy Kamen', G., U.S.S.R. 134 E3
Koochiching, co., Minn., 18,190 74 E1
Koog a.d. Zaan, Neth., 7,400 115 C2
Kookynie, Austl. 172 B4
Koolau Range, Hawaii 84 c6
Kooloonong, Austl. 173 d10
Koorawatha, Austl. 173 g10
Koosharem, Utah 148 78 B2
Kooskia, Idaho, 801 81 A2
Koostatak, Man., Can. 43 F4
Koot, Alaska 85 C3
Kootenai, co., Idaho, 29,556 81 A2
Kootenai, Idaho, 180 81 A1
Kootenai, r., Can.-U.S. 81 B1
Kootenay, r., Br. Col., Can. 42 H4
Kootenay L., Br. Col., Can. 42 J4
Kootenay Nat. Pk., Br. Col. 42 J4
Kopaonik, mts., Yug. 125 E3
Kopari, India 144 f13
Kópasker, Ice. 120 a6
Koper, Yug., 10,000* 125 A2
Kopervik, Nor., 1,836 120 A4
Kopet Dagh, Iran-U.S.S.R. 143 F1
Kopeysk, U.S.S.R., 168,000 134 F4
Ko-pi, r., China 152 B2
Kopidlno, Czech. 127 e6
K'o-p'ing, China 150 A2
Köping, Swed. 120 C4
Köpingebro, Swed. 121 G5
Kopište, i., Yug. 125 C3
Kopka, r., Ont., Can. 44 E5
Koplik i poshtëm, Alb. 125 D3
Koppang, Nor. 120 B3
Kopparberg, Swed. 120 C4
Koppel, Pa., 1,389 60 B4
Koppel, Tex. 76 d10
Köppern, F.R.Ger., 3,573 119 F4
Kopperston, W. Va. 62 C5
Koprivnica, Yug., 12,000* 125 C1
Koptelovo, U.S.S.R. 137 k7
Korab, mts., Yug. 125 E4
Koraluk, r., Newf., Can. 45 O3
Korana, r., Yug. 125 B2
Korangi, Pak. 144 C4
Korangp'o-ri, S. Kor. 151 E3
Korat Plat., Thai. 146 C3
Korba, India, 12,424 144 d14
Korbach, F.R.Ger., 13,530 118 B3
Korçë, Alb., 41,200 125 E4
Korčula, Yug., 2,414 125 C3
Korčula, i., Yug. 125 C3
Korčulanski Kan., Yug. 125 C3
Kord Kūy, Iran, 9,855 143 E1
Kordel, F.R.Ger., 2,023 119 B5
Kordofan=Kurdufān
Kordon, U.S.S.R. 137 i7
Korea, reg., Asia, 40,477,000* 151
Korea Bay, China-Korea 150 G3
Korea Str., Jap.-Kor. 154 A5
Koregaon, India 145 i18
Korenge-yama, Jap. 155 E3
Korenovskaya, U.S.S.R. 136 E4
Korets, U.S.S.R., 3,400 136 B3
Korf, U.S.S.R., 2,100 135 Q3
Korfa, Zal., U.S.S.R. 135 Q4
Korgen, Nor. 120 C2
Korhogo, Iv. Coast, 14,150 162 D4
Kōri, Jap. 154 g15
Kōri, Jap. 154 h15
Koriabo, Guyana 101 L4
Kori Cr., India 144 C5
Korido, Indon. 149 K3
Korienze, Mali, 3,000 162 D3
Korinós, Gr., 2,861 129 D4
Korinthiakós Kólpos, Gr. 129 D5
Kórinthos, Gr., 15,892 129 D6
Korinthou, Dhiórix, can., Gr. 129 D6
Koriten, Bulg. 128 F3
Kōriyama, Jap., 102,636 155 G3
Korkino, U.S.S.R., 87,000 137 k8
Korkodon, U.S.S.R. 135 P3
Korkuteli, Turk., 5,076 142 B2
Korla=K'u-erh-lo
Körlach, Aust., 12,363 124 L6

248 · Kung—Laguna Yema

Kung, r., China 152 D2
Kungälv, Swed. 120 B4
Kung-an, China 152 C1
Kung-ch'eng, China 152 C2
Kung-chiao, China 150 D4
Kunges, r., China 150 B2
Kungey-Alatau, Khr., U.S.S.R. 132 G5
Kunghit I., Br. Col., Can. 42 D3
Kung-ho, China 150 D3
Kung-hsien, China 151 B4
Kung-ka Shan, China 150 D4
Kung-liu, China 150 B2
Kung-pu-chiang-ta, China 150 C4
Kungrad, U.S.S.R., 9,800 134 E5
Kungsbacka, Swed. 120 B4
Kung-shan, China 150 D4
Kungsherya, China 144 e10
Kungsör, Swed. 120 d8
Kungu, D.R.Congo 164 C1
Kungur, U.S.S.R., 66,000 134 E4
Kungur, mtn., China 150 A3
Kungyangon, Burma, 4,972 147 b2
Kung-ying-tzu, China 151 D2
Kunhegyes, Hung., 10,970 126 E3
Kunia Camp, Hawaii 84 b7
Kunimi-dake, Jap. 154 B5
Kunisaki, Jap., 26,341 154 B5
Kunitomochō, Jap. 154 h14
Kunkle, Pa. 61 o16
Kunlong, Burma 146 B2
K'un-lun Shan, China 150 B3
Kunmadaras, Hung., 8,486 126 E3
K'un-ming, China, 880,000* 150 D4
Kunnamkulam, India, 16,268 145 k20
Kunneppu, Jap., 10,903 155 K8
Kunnui, Jap. 155 J8
Kunoy, i., Faeroe Is. 120 c7
K'un-po-la-ch'ia, China 151 D1
Kunsan, S. Kor., 90,481 151 E4
Kunszentmárton, Hung., 10,775 126 D3
Kunta-ur, Gambia 162 B3
Kunti, India, 8,156 144 e14
Kunya-Urgench, U.S.S.R., 9,000 134 E5
Künzell, F.R.Ger., 2,889 119 H3
Künzelsau, F.R.Ger., 7,259 118 B4
Kuo-hsien, China 151 B3
Kuop, atoll, Car. Is. 176 18
Kuopio, Fin., 47,598 120 G3
Kup, Pol. 127 g6
Ku-pa, China 152 a6
Kupa, r., Yug. 125 B2
Kupaahu, Hawaii 84 F4
Kupang, Indon. 149 G5
Kuparuk, r., Alaska 85 G1
Kupferzell, F.R.Ger., 1,465 119 H6
Kupino, U.S.S.R., 23,200 134 G4
Kuppenheim, F.R.Ger., 3,910 119 E7
Kupreanof I., Alaska 85 L4
Kupres, Yug. 125 C3
Kupyansk, U.S.S.R., 24,800 136 E3
Kura, r., U.S.S.R. 134 D5
Kuragai, Jap. 154 f14
Kurakhovo, U.S.S.R., 10,700 136 e8
Kurama, Jap. 154 g14
Kurashassay, U.S.S.R. 137 h10
Kurashiki, Jap., 125,097 155 C4
Kuraymah, Sudan, 5,989 163 K2
Kurayoshi, Jap., 51,528 155 C4
Kurdistan, reg., Asia 142 E2
Kurdufān, reg., Sudan 163 J3
Kurduwadi, India, 13,816 145 E6
Kŭrdzhali, Bulg., 20,955 129 E4
Kure, Jap., 210,032 155 C4
Kure, Jap., 7,121 155 C5
Kure Beach, N.C., 293 63 G4
Kure I., Hawaii 84 f9
Kuressaare, U.S.S.R., 9,700 136 A1
Kureyka, U.S.S.R. 134 H3
Kureyka, r., U.S.S.R. 135 J3
Kurgal'dzhin, Oz., U.S.S.R. 137 n12
Kurgal'dzhino, U.S.S.R. 137 n12
Kurgan, U.S.S.R., 164,000 134 F4
Kurganinsk, U.S.S.R. 136 F4
Kurgan-Tyube, U.S.S.R., 23,600 134 F6
Kuria, i., Gilb. Is. 175 10
Kuria Muria Is.=Khūryān Mūryān
Kuridaira, Jap. 154 g15
Kurīgrām, Pak., 8,703 144 g13
Kurikka, Fin. 120 E3
Kuril Is.=Kuril'skiye O-va.
Kuril Trench, Pac. Oc. 168 E1
Kurilo, Bulg., 3,823 128 D3
Kuril'sk, U.S.S.R., 1,500 135 O5
Kuril'skiye O-va., U.S.S.R. 135 O5
Kurinskaya K., U.S.S.R. 137 d2
Kuřívody, Czech. 127 d6
Kuriyama, Jap., 23,003 155 J8
Kurleya, U.S.S.R. 135 L4
Kurlovskiy, U.S.S.R., 9,500 136 F2
Kurmuk, Sudan, 1,647 163 K4
Kurnool, India, 100,815 145 F7
Kurobe, Jap. 154 g14
Kurobe, Jap., 31,216 155 E3
Kuroda, Jap. 154 h14
Kurodani, Jap. 154 g14
Kuroi, Jap. 154 g14
Kuroishi, Jap., 41,033 155 G1
Kuroiso, Jap., 30,413 155 G3
Kurokawa, Jap. 154 f14
Kuromatsunai, Jap. 155 J8
Kurono, Jap. 154 h14
Kurosaki, Jap. 154 e15
Kuro-shima, Jap. 154 A6
Kurovskoye, U.S.S.R., 16,800 136 c6
Kurow, N.Z. 175 f7
Kurri Kurri, Austl., 4,702 173 h9
Kuršėnai, U.S.S.R., 9,100 136 A1
Kurseong, India, 13,410 144 g12
Kursk, U.S.S.R., 222,000 134 C4
Kurskaya K., U.S.S.R. 136 A2
Kuršumlija, Yug., 2,649 125 E3
Kurtamysh, U.S.S.R., 12,300 134 F4
Kürten, F.R.Ger., 3,769 119 C2
Kurthwood, La. 73 B6
Kūrtī, Sudan 163 K3
Kurtistown, Hawaii, 1,025 84 F4
Kuru, r., Sudan 163 J4
Kuruman, S. Af., 6,386 164 C6
Kuruman, r., S. Af. 164 C6
Kurumdy, G., U.S.S.R. 137 g4
Kurume, Jap., 155,041 154 B5
Kurumkan, U.S.S.R. 135 L4
Kurunegala, Cey., 17,505 145 F9
Kurupukari, Guyana 101 L5
Kururi, Jap. 155 n20
Kusa, U.S.S.R., 21,800 137 i8
Kuşadasi, Turk. 142 A2
Kuşadasi Körfezi, Turk. 129 F6
Kusaie, i., Car. Is. 170 E4
Kusakabe, Jap. 154 f15
Kusakaki-shima, Jap. 154 A6
Kusakan, U.S.S.R. 137 k9
Kusary, U.S.S.R., 7,300 137 d1
Kusatsu, Jap., 35,022 154 g14
Kusatsu, Jap., 7,776 155 F3
Kusawa L., Yukon, Can. 85 K3
Kuse, Jap., 12,702 155 C4
Kusel, F.R.Ger., 5,268 118 A4
Kusem, U.S.S.R. 137 i9
Ku-shan, China 151 D3
Kushchëvskaya, U.S.S.R. 136 E4
Kushëvat, U.S.S.R. 134 F3
Kushida, r., Jap. 154 h15
Ku-shih, China 152 D1
Kushikino, Jap., 33,104 154 B6
Kushima, Jap., 42,305 154 B6
Kushimoto, Jap., 22,000 155 D5
Kushiro, Jap., 150,624 155 L8
Kushiro, r., Jap. 155 L8
Kushk, Afghan. 144 B2
Kushka, U.S.S.R., 4,500 134 F6
Kushmurun, U.S.S.R. 134 F4
Kushmurun, Oz., U.S.S.R. 134 F4
Kushnarënkovo, U.S.S.R. 137 h8
Kushtia, Pak., 24,952 144 g14
Kushva, U.S.S.R., 46,200 137 i7
Kuskokwim, Alaska 85 D3
Kuskokwim, r., Alaska 85 F3
Kuskokwim Bay, Alaska 85 C4
Kuskokwim Mts., Alaska 85 E3
Kuşluyan, Turk., 4,936 142 D1
Kusma, Nepal, 1,817 145 G3
Küsnacht, Switz., 11,984 124 C1
Küssnacht, Switz., 6,287 124 C1
Kustanay, U.S.S.R., 98,000 134 F4
Küstenkanal, F.R.Ger. 118 A2
Kūstī, Sudan, 22,688 163 K3
Kut, Ko, Thai. 146 C5
Kuta, Nigeria 162 F4
Kutabuluh, Indon. 148 A2
Kütahya, Turk., 39,851 142 B2
Kutais, U.S.S.R., 3,200 136 E4
Kutaisi, U.S.S.R., 137,000 134 D5
Kutami, Jap., 3,767 154 i14
Kutanibong, Indon. 148 A2
Kutaradja, Indon., 40,067 148 A1
Kutatjane, Indon. 148 A2
Kutch, G. of, India 144 C5
Kutchan, Jap., 18,195 155 J8
Kutcharo-ko, Jap. 155 L8
Ku-t'ien, China 152 E2
Kutina, Yug., 5,222 125 C2
Kutkai, Burma 146 B2
Kutná Hora, Czech., 16,740 126 B2
Kutno, Pol., 26,000* 127 C2
Kutoardjo, Indon. 148 c7
Kutru, India 145 F6
Kuttawa, Ky., 635 71 C4
Kutu, D.R.Congo 164 C2
Kutubidia I., Pak. 145 J5
Kutum, Sudan 163 J3
Kutupia, Guyana 101 K5
Kúty, Czech. 126 C2
Kutztown, Pa., 3,312 61 L4
Kuusamo, Fin. 120 G2
Kuusankoski, Fin., 22,090 120 F3
Kuvandyk, U.S.S.R., 21,400 137 i9
Kuvasay, U.S.S.R., 10,800 137 g4
Kuvshinovo, U.S.S.R., 13,300 136 D1
Kuwabara, Jap. 154 i14
Kuwait, ctry., 467,339 143 D3
Kuwana, Jap., 69,391 155 E4
Kuwur, Kenya 165 g14
Kuyahoora L., N.Y. 59 K5
Ku-yang, China 151 A2
Kuybyshev, U.S.S.R., 863,000 134 E4
Kuybyshev, U.S.S.R., 30,000 137 p11
Kuybyshevo, U.S.S.R. 136 e8
Kuybyshevskiy, U.S.S.R. 137 e5
Kuybyshevskoye Vdkhr., U.S.S.R. 134 D4
Kuyeda, U.S.S.R. 137 h8
K'u-yeh, r., China 151 A3
Kŭysanjaq, Iraq, 8,347 143 D1
Kuytun, U.S.S.R. 135 K4
Ku-yüan, China 150 E3
Kuyuwini, r., Guyana 101 L6
Kuzey Anadolu Dağlari, Turk. 142 C1
Kuzitrin, r., Alaska 85 D2
Kuz'movka, U.S.S.R. 135 J3
Kuznetsk, U.S.S.R., 62,000 134 D4
Kuznetskiy Alatau, Khr., U.S.S.R. 137 s11
Kuznetsova, U.S.S.R. 137 k7
Kuźnia Raciborska, Pol., 3,084 127 h6
Kuzomen', U.S.S.R. 134 C3
Kuzu, Jap. 154 h15
Kuzumaki, Jap., 15,558 155 G1
Kværfjord, Nor. 120 C1
Kvænangen, fj., Nor. 120 E1
Kværndrup, Den., 1,975 121 C5
Kvaløy, i., Nor. 120 D1
Kvalsund, Nor. 120 F1
Kvam, Nor. 120 B3
Kvarkeno, U.S.S.R. 137 i9
Kvarner, g., Yug. 125 B2
Kvarnerić, chan., Yug. 125 B2
Kvarsebo, Swed. 120 d9
Kvelde, Nor. 121 C1
Kvichak Bay, Alaska 85 E4
Kvigtinden, mt., Nor. 120 C2
Kvikne, Nor. 120 B3
Kville, Swed. 121 D2
Kvinesdal, Nor. 120 A4
Kvistofta, Swed. 121 b7
Kviteseid, Nor. 121 A1
Kvitöya, i., Nor. 134 B1
Kvols, Den. 121 B4
Kwa, r., D.R.Congo 164 B2
Kwadack, i., Kwajalein 176 25
Kwaiapan B., Terr. Papua 174 3
Kwaiawata, i., Terr. Papua 174 3
Kwajalein, atoll, Marsh. Is. 170 F4
Kwajalein, i., Kwajalein 176 25
Kwakoegron, Sur. 101 N5
Kwale, Kenya 164 F2
Kwale, Nigeria 162 g9
Kwamouth, D.R.Congo 164 B2
Kwanch'on, S. Kor. 151 E4
Kwando, r., Zambia 164 C4
Kwangju, S. Kor., 315,124 151 E4
Kwango, r., D.R.Congo 164 B2
Kwangsi Chuang Autonomous Reg.=Kuang-hsi-chuang-tsu Tzu-chih-ch'ü
Kwangtung=Kuang-tung
Kwanmo-bong, mtn., N. Kor. 151 F2
Kwansŏ-ri, N. Kor. 151 F2
Kwataboahegan, r., ont., Can. 44 G4
Kweichow=Kuei-chou
Kweilin=Kuei-lin
Kweiyang=Kuei-yang, K-ch., China
Kwenge, r., D.R.Congo 164 C3
Kwethluk, Alaska, 325 85 D3
Kwidzyń, Pol., 20,000* 127 C2
Kwigamiut, Alaska 85 C4
Kwigillingok, Alaska, 344 85 D4
Kwiguk, Alaska, 358 85 C3
Kwilu, r., Afr. 164 C2
Kwinhagak=Quinhagak
Kwinitsa, Br. Col., Can. 42 D2
Kwisa, r., Pol. 127 A3
Kwitaro, r., Guyana 101 L6
Kyabé, Chad, 3,000* 163 H4
Kyabram, Austl., 3,335 173 e11
Kyaiklat, Burma, 15,781 146 A3
Kyaikmaraw, Burma 147 b2
Kyaikto, Burma, 13,154 146 B3
Kyaka, Tanz., 165 e14
Kyakhta, U.S.S.R., 10,300 135 K4
Kyancutta, Austl. 172 a7
Kyang Gyap, China 144 e11
Kyangin, Burma, 6,073 147 a1
Ky Anh, N. Viet. 146 D3
Kyaring Tsho, China 150 C4
Kyaukhnyat, Burma 147 b1
Kyaukkyi, Burma 147 a1
Kyaukkyi, Burma, 1,474 147 b1
Kyaukme, Burma 146 B2
Kyaukmyaung, Burma 147 g6
Kyaukpadaung, Burma, 5,474 147 A2
Kyaukpyu, Burma, 7,335 146 A3
Kyaukse, Burma, 8,659 146 B2
Kyauktaga, Burma, 5,916 147 b1
Kyauktan, Burma, 3,812 147 b2
Kyaunggon, Burma, 4,395 147 a2
Kyawkku, Burma 147 g7
Kybartai, U.S.S.R., 6,200 136 A2
Kyburz, Calif. 82 C3
Ky Cung, r., N. Viet. 147 i8
Kyeamba, Austl. 173 f10
Kyebogyi, Burma 146 B3
Kyeikdon, Burma 146 B3
Kyeintali, Burma 147 a1
Kyela, D.R.Congo 165 n19
Kyerwa, Tanz. 165 e14
Kyger, W. Va. 62 C4
Kyidaunggan, Burma, 3,896 146 A3
Kyjovice, Czech. 127 h7
Ky Lam, N. Viet. 147 h8
Kyle, Sask., Can. 43 C5
Kyle, N.C. 63 b7
Kyle, S. Dak. 74 A4
Kyle, Tex., 1,023 77 P5
Kyle of Lochalsh, U.K. 112 D3
Kyll, r., F.R.Ger. 118 A3
Kyllburg, F.R.Ger., 1,220 119 B4
Kyn, U.S.S.R. 137 i7
Kyneton, Austl., 3,232 173 e11
Kynšperk nad Ohří, Czech. 126 b6
Kynuna, Austl. 173 F3
Kyoga, L., Uganda 164 E1
Kyōga-saki, Jap. 155 D4
Kyogle, Austl., 2,929 173 H4
Kyōgoku, Jap., 7,533 155 J8
Kyong, Burma 147 g7
Kyŏngju, S. Kor., 76,032 151 F4
Kyŏngsŏng, N. Kor. 151 F2
Kyonkadat, Burma 147 b3
Kyonmange, Burma, 9,272 147 a2
Kyonpyaw, Burma, 5,389 147 a2
Kyōto, Jap., 1,284,818 155 D4
Kype Water, r., U.K. 112 b8
Kyrenia, Cyp., 3,680 142 C3
Kyritz, Ger.D.R. 118 D2
Kyrönjoki, r., Fin. 120 E3
Kyshtym, U.S.S.R., 34,300 134 F4
Kysucké Nové Mesto, Czech. 126 D2
Kysyl-Yllyk, U.S.S.R. 135 L3
Kythrea, Cyp., 3,068 142 e9
Kytlym, U.S.S.R. 137 i7
Kyuquot, Br. Col., Can. 42 E4
Kyurdamir, U.S.S.R., 10,500 137 d1
Kyūshū, i., Jap. 154 A5
Kyustendil, Bulg., 25,025 128 D3
Kyusyur, U.S.S.R. 135 M2
Kywedon, Burma 147 a2
Kyyjärvi, Fin. 120 F3
Kyzas, U.S.S.R. 137 s11
Kyzyl, U.S.S.R., 38,000 135 J4
Kyzylkak, Oz., U.S.S.R. 137 o11
Kyzyl-Kiya, U.S.S.R., 30,200 137 g4
Kyzyl-Kum, Peski, U.S.S.R. 134 F5
Kyzyl-Mazhalyk, U.S.S.R. 137 s12
Kyzyl-Su, r., U.S.S.R. 137 g4
Kyzyltas, U.S.S.R. 137 o12
Kyzyl-Tayga, G., U.S.S.R. 134 J4
Kzyl-Orda, U.S.S.R., 71,000 134 F5
Kzyl-Tu, U.S.S.R. 137 o11

L

Laa, Aust., 4,910 124 N5
Laab, Aust. 124 c10
Laage, Ger.D.R. 118 D2
Laakirchen, Aust., 6,731 124 K6
La Aldea, Mex., 2,947 93 c9
La Almunia de Doña Godina, Sp., 4,337 122 E2
La Ametlla de Mar, Sp., 2,954 122 F2
La Angostura, Presa de, res., Mex. 92 C1
La Anna, Pa. 61 p17
La Antigua, Salina, Arg. 105 B3
La Arena, Mex. 93 e8
La Ascensión, Mex., 2,807 92 C1
Laasphe, F.R.Ger., 5,300 118 B3
La Asunción, Ven., 5,541 101 J2
Laau Pt., Hawaii 84 D2
La Aurora, Mex., 1,599 93 a9
Lab, r., Yug. 125 E3
Laba, r., U.S.S.R. 136 F4
Labadie, Mo. 72 G6
Labadieville, La. 73 E8
Labala, Indon. 149 G5
La Banda, Arg., 18,283 105 C3
La Bañeza, Sp., 8,325 122 B1
Labangan, Phil., 1,461 153 B2
La Barca, Mex., 16,330 93 b9
Labardén, Arg., 1,823 105 c13
La Barge, Wyo. 81 D4
La Barra de Navidad, Mex. 92 D4
Labason, Phil., 2,465 153 B3
la Bastide, Fr. 116 m13
Labateca, Col. 100 D4
la Baule-Escoublac, Fr., 13,225 116 B3
Labayen, Sp. 122 o11
Labdah=Leptis Magna
Labé, Guin., 15,000 162 B4
Labe, r., Czech. 126 B1
Łabędy, Pol., 13,742 127 h6
Labelle, Qué., Can., 1,210 44 K6
LaBelle, Fla., 1,262 65 H6
La Belle, Mo., 866 72 E4
La Belle, L., Mich. 66 E1
La Belleza, Col. 101 e14
Laberge, L., Yukon, Can. 85 K3
Labette, co., Kans., 26,805 75 K6
Labin, Yug., 5,879 125 B2
Labinsk, U.S.S.R., 41,900 136 F4
Labis, Malay., 6,720 148 B2
Łabiszyn, Pol., 2,794 127 C2
La Blanquilla, i., Ven. 101 H2
La Bolt, S. Dak., 125 74 D3
Laborde, Arg., 5,000* 105 C4
Laborec, r., Czech. 126 E2
Laborie, St. Lucia, 1,608 97 11
Laboulaye, Arg., 15,000* 105 C4
la Bourboule, Fr., 2,424 117 E4
Labrador, reg., Newf., Can. 45 O3
Labrador Basin, Atl. Oc. 108 J3
Labrador City, Newf. Can. 45 M4
Labrador Sea, Can. 108 J3
Labranzagrande, Col. 100 D5
Lábrea, Braz., 2,080 102 D3
La Brea, Peru, 7,299 104 A3
La Brea, Trin. and Tob., 2,000* 96 g5
La Brévine, Switz. 124 A2
Labrit, Fr. 117 C4
La Broquerie, Man., Can. 43 h10
Labruguière, Fr., 4,838 117 E5
Labry, Fr., 1,419 116 b8
Labuan, Phil., 2,295 153 B4
Labuco, Ala. 64 b7
Labuha, Indon. 149 H3
Labuhan, Indon. 148 a7
Labuhanbilik, Indon. 148 B2
Labuhanmaringgai, Indon. 148 a6
Labuhantangge, Indon. 147 o15
Labuk, r., Malay. 148 F1
Labuk Bay, Malay. 148 F1
Labutta, Burma, 12,843 146 A3
Labytnangi, U.S.S.R., 5,200 134 F3
Lac, inlet, Bon. 97 17
Lacadena, Sask., Can. 43 B5
L'Acadie, Qué., Can. 47 p18
La Calandria, Arg., 5,100* 105 b10
La Calera, Chile, 18,134 104 f12
La Calera, Col. 101 f15
Lac Allard, Qué., Can. 45 N5
la Calle, Alg., 3,731 160 f5
La Calle, Mex., 1,222 93 c9
La Calzada de Calatrava, Sp., 8,513 122 D3
La Campa, Hond., 2,389 94 e9
La Cañada, Mex., 2,692 93 d9
La Canada, Calif., 18,338 83 h15
Lacanau, Fr., 1,956 117 C4
La Canoa, Ven. 101 J3
la Canourgue, Fr., 1,245 117 E4
La Cantera, Mex., 1,012 93 b10
Lacantum, r., Mex. 93 H5
La Capilla, Arg., 2,800* 105 b10
Lácar, L., Arg. 105 f15
La Carlota, Phil., 15,286 153 e11
La Carlota, Sp., 10,611 122 C4
Lacarne, Ohio 70 F1
La Carolina, Sp., 12,854 122 D3
La Castellana, Phil., 14,011 153 e11
Lacaune, Fr., 3,139 117 E5
Lac-au-Saumon, Qué., Can., 1,522 47 S9
La Cavada, Sp. 122 m11
Lac-Baker, N.B., Can. 47 R10
Laccadive Is., India 145 D8
Laccadive Sea, Asia 144 ·
Lac-des-Écorces, Qué., Can. 47 J2
Lac du Bonnet, Man., Can. 43 F5
Lac du Flambeau, Wis. 66 C3
Lac Duong, S. Viet., 1,271 147 n10
Lace, Ill. 69 c10
Laceby, U.K., 1,369 114 H3
Lac Édouard, Qué., Can. 44 K6
La Ceiba, Hond., 24,315 94 D3
La Ceja, Col. 100 C4
La Ceja, Mex. 93 a8
la Celle, Fr. 116 f12
la Celle-St-Cloud, Fr., 20,284 116 g11
La Center, Ky., 882 71 B4
La Center, Wash., 244 80 B3
Lacepede Bay, Austl. 172 E5
Lacey, Okla. 76 E1
Lacey, Wash., 6,630 80 B2
Laceys Chapel, Ala. 64 c8
Lacey Spring, Va. 62 F4
Laceys Spring, Ala. 64 C1
Laceyville, Pa., 468 61 K2
Lac-Frontière, Qué., Can. 47 P2
la Chaise Dieu, Fr. 117 E4
la Chambre, Fr. 117 G4
la Chapelle-Gauthier, Fr. 116 k12
la Chapelle-sur-Crécy, Fr. 116 k11
La Charité-sur-Loire, Fr., 5,836 117 E3
la Châtaigneraie, Fr., 2,056 117 C3
la Châtre, Fr., 4,529 117 E3
La Chaux-de-Fonds, Switz., 38,906 124 A1
Lachen, Switz., 3,913 124 C1
Lachin, U.S.S.R., 2,400 137 c2
Lachine, Qué., Can., 37,691 47 o18
Lachine, Mich. 67 K3
Lachine Can., Qué., Can. 69 D
La Chira, Chile 104 e16
Lachlan, r., Austl. 173 F5
La Chorrera, Pan., 13,696 94 G6
Lachute, Qué., Can., 7,468 47 K3
La Cienega, N. Mex. 79 B4
la Ciotat, Fr., 18,827 117 F5
Lackawanna, N.Y., 29,564 58 C6
Lackawanna, co., Pa., 234,531 61 L3
Lackawanna, r., Pa. 61 M2
Lackawaxen, Pa. 61 N3
Lackawaxen, r., Pa. 61 M3
Lackenbach, Aust. 1,244 124 N6
Lac La Belle, Wis., 276 66 E5
Lac la Biche, Alta., Can., 1,261 42 B4
Lac la Hache, Br. Col., Can. 42 G3
la Clayette, Fr., 2,255 117 F3
Laclede, co., Mo., 18,991 72 E7
Laclede, Mo., 428 72 D5
Lac-Mégantic, Qué., Can., 6,938 45 L6
Lacob-ti-duyog, Mt., Phil. 153 c5
Lacock, U.K., 1,363 114 D8
Lacolle, Qué., Can., 1,191 47 L3
La Coloma, Cuba, 1,907 96 b1
La Colorada, Mex. 92 C2
Lacomb, Oreg. 80 B3
Lacombe, Alta., Can., 2,942 42 K3
Lacombe, La. 73 E7
Lacon, Ill., 2,175 68 C2
Lacona, N.Y., 556 59 H4
La Concepcion, Pan., 6,532 94 F6
La Concepción, Ven., 9,449 100 D2
La Concordia, Mex., 1,880 93 G5
La Condamine, Mon., 9,565 116 n14
Laconia, N.H., 15,288 54 E4
La Conner, Wash., 638 80 B1
La Consulta, Arg., 7,000* 105 B4
Lacoochee, Fla., 1,523 65 G4
La Cordobesa, Urug. 105 c11
La Coronilla, Urug. 105 E4
La Coruña, Sp., 177,502 122 A1
Lacota, Mich. 67 G6
la Courneuve, Fr., 25,802 116 h11
la Couronne, Fr., 5,537 117 D4
la Courtine, Fr., 1,268 117 E4
Lac Qui Parle, co., Minn., 13,330 74 D3
Lacrepunt, pt., Bon. 97 17
La Crescent, Minn., 2,624 74 G4
La Crescenta, Calif. 83 h15
Lacroix, Piton, Mart. 97 12
La Crosse, Fla., 165 65 G3
La Crosse, Ind., 632 70 C1
La Crosse, Kans., 1,767 75 F5
La Crosse, Va., 726 62 F6
La Crosse, Wash., 463 80 E2
La Crosse, co., Wis., 72,465 66 B5
La Crosse, Wis., 47,575 66 B5
La Cruz, Chile, 3,000 104 f12
La Cruz, Col. 100 B7
La Cruz, C.R. 94 E5
La Cruz, Chih., Mex., 1,072 92 D2
La Cruz, Sin., Mex., 2,740 92 D3
La Cruz, Nic. 94 E4
La Cruz, Urug. 105 c11
Lac Thien, S. Viet., 1,502 146 E4
La Cuchilla, Mex. 92 E3
La Cueva, Chile 104 f17
La Cumbre, Col. 100 B6
Lacy, Ind. 70 C4
La Cygne, Kans., 810 75 L5
Ladan, U.S.S.R., 5,300 136 D3
Ladd, Ill., 1,255 68 C2
Laddonia, Mo., 671 72 F5
La De, Mex., 1,046 93 d9
Lądek-Zdrój, Pol., 5,264 127 f6
Ladelle, Ark., 23 73 D4
La Democracia, Guat., 1,483 94 b9
La Democracia, Ven. 101 c12
Ladenburg, F.R.Ger., 7,781 119 F6
Ladendorf, Aust., 1,249 124 c9
La Descubierta, Dom. Rep., 1,809 96 m6
La Désirade, i., Guad. 97 14
Lădeşti, Rum. 128 E2
La Digue I., Seych. 165 a10
Lâdik, Turk., 5,522 142 D1
Ladismith, S. Af., 2,332 164 C7
Ladner, Br. Col., Can., 2,000 42 c6
Ladner, S. Dak. 74 A3
Ladnun, India, 23,825 145 E4
Ladoga, Ind., 974 70 C3
Ladoga, Wis. 66 E5
Ladoga, L.=Ladozhskoye Oz.
Ladonia, Tex., 890 77 Q3
Ladora, Iowa, 307 72 E3
La Dorada, Col. 100 C5
Ladozhskoye Oz., U.S.S.R. 134 C3
Ladrone Is.=Mariana Is.
Ladrones Pk., N. Mex. 79 B4
Ladu Balu, mtn., India 145 J4
Ladue, Mo., 9,466 72 a11
La Dulce, Arg., 3,800* 105 D5
Ladwa, India, 8,273 144 a11
Lady Ann Str., N.W.T., Can. 41 N2
Ladybank, U.K., 1,207 112 d7
Ladybrand, S. Af., 7,045 164 D6
Ladyhower Res., U.K. 114 E4
Ladysmith, Br. Col., Can., 2,082 42 b7
Ladysmith, S. Af., 22,997 164 D6
Ladysmith, Va. 62 G4
Ladysmith, Wis., 3,584 66 B3
Ladyzhenka, U.S.S.R. 137 n12
Lae, Terr. New Guin., 8,600 174 e2
Lae, atoll, Marsh. Is. 176 22
Laea, Indon. 149 G4
Laehobang, Indon. 148 A2
Laem Ngop, Thai. 146 C4
La Encantada, Co. de, Mex. 92 B1
La Ensenada, Pan. 94 H6
La Entrada, Ven. 101 a11
Lae o Ka Oio, c., Hawaii 84 d6
Lærdalsöyri, Nor. 120 A3
La Escala, Sp., 2,451 122 G1
Læsø, i., Den. 121 D3
La Española, Col. 101 d15
La Esperanza, Chile 104 f15
La Esperanza, Cuba, 1,867 96 b1
La Esperanza, Hond., 2,498 94 C3
La Esperanza, Mex. 93 H4
La Estancia, Mex., 1,149 93 d9
Læsten, Den. 121 B4
La Estrada, Sp., 28,716 122 A1
La Estrella, Bol. 102 c10
La Estrella, Chile, 4,085 104 f14
La Farge, Wis., 833 66 C5
La Fargeville, N.Y. 59 J3
Lafayette, Ala., 2,605 64 D3
Lafayette, co., Ark., 11,030 73 B4
Lafayette, Calif., 7,114 83 e12
Lafayette, Colo., 2,612 79 C2
Lafayette, co., Fla., 2,889 65 F3
La Fayette, Ga., 5,588 64 D1
La Fayette, Ill., 269 68 C2
Lafayette, Ind., 42,330 70 C2
La Fayette, Ky., 196 71 D5
Lafayette, parish, La., 84,656 73 C7
Lafayette, La., 50,312 73 D7
Lafayette, Minn., 516 74 E3
Lafayette, co., Miss., 21,355 73 F3
Lafayette, co., Mo., 25,274 72 D5
Lafayette, N.J. 61 B1
La Fayette, N.Y. 59 H6
Lafayette, Madison Co., Ohio 70 F3
Lafayette, Medina Co., Ohio 70 G1
Lafayette, Oreg., 553 80 B3
Lafayette, R.I. 57 K6
Lafayette, Tenn., 1,590 71 F5
Lafayette, Va. 62 D5
Lafayette, co., Wis., 18,142 66 C6
Lafayette, Mt., N.H. 54 D3
La Feria, Tex., 3,047 77 P6
la Ferté-Bernard, Fr., 6,235 117 D2
la Ferté-Gaucher, Fr., 2,585 117 E2
la Ferté-Macé, Fr., 6,334 117 C2
la Ferté-St-Auban, Fr., 4,400 117 E3
la Ferté-sous-Jouarre, Fr., 5,490 117 E2
Lafferty, Ohio 70 H2
Lafia, Nigeria, 11,137 162 F4
Lafiagi, Nigeria 162 f7
Lafitte, La. 73 E8
Laflamme, r., Qué., Can. 44 J5
Laflèche, Qué., Can., 10,868 47 p18
Lafleche, Sask., Can. 43 C5
la Flèche, Fr., 12,941 117 D3
Laflin, Pa., 235 61 o16
La Florida, Col. 100 D2
La Florida, Mex. 93 H4
Lafnitz, r., Aust. 124 N6
La Foa, N. Caled. 174 i8
La Follette, Tenn., 6,204 71 G5
La Fontaine, Ind., 779 70 D2
Lafourche, parish, La., 55,381 73 E8
Lafourche, Bayou, La. 73 C5
Lafourche, Bayou, La. 73 E8
La France, S.C. 63 B3
la Frette, Fr., 2,840 116 g11
La Fria, Ven., 4,765 100 D3
Laful, India 146 A6
la Gacilly, Fr., 1,142 117 B3
Lagaip, r., Terr. New Guin. 174 d2
La Gallareta, Arg., 9,000* 105 C3
Lagan, r., Swed. 120 C4
Lagan, r., U.K. 113 C4
La Garita, Colo. 79 B3
La Garita Cr., Colo. 79 B3
La Garita Mts., Colo. 79 B3
Lagarto, Braz., 7,092 103 J4
la Gaude, Fr., 1,072 116 n13
Lagayan, Phil. 153 B1
Lage, F.R.Ger., 11,710 118 B2
Lågen, r., Nor. 120 B3
Lägerdorf, F.R.Ger., 4,117 119 a8
Lagernyy, U.S.S.R. 134 E2
Lage-Zwaluwe, Neth. 115 b7
Lagg, U.K. 112 D4
Laggan, Austl. 173 g10
Laggan, U.K. 112 D3
Laggan, Loch, U.K. 112 D3
Lagh Bor, wadi, Kenya 164 F1
Laghouat, Alg., 11,058 160 E2
Łagiewniki, Pol. 127 f6
La Gloria, Col. 100 D3
La Gloria, Guat. 94 C2
Lagna, r., S. Viet. 147 m11
Lagny, Fr., 12,459 117 E2
Lago, China 144 f11
Lago, Mt., Wash. 80 C1
Lagoa, Port., 5,915 122 A4
Lagoa dos Gatos, Braz., 3,177 103 a15
Lagoa Dourada, Braz., 1,898 103 d17
Lagoa Vermelha, Braz., 8,623 103 F7
Lago da Pedra, Braz., 1,723 103 G2
Lagodekhi, U.S.S.R., 7,000 137 c1
Lagoen, Cur. 97 16
La Gomera, Guat. 94 B3
Lagonda, Pa. 60 a9
Lagonegro, It., 6,519 123 E4
Lagonoy, Phil., 3,672 153 h14
Lagonoy G., Phil. 153 B2
Lagos, Nigeria, 358,860 162 E4
Lagos, Port., 10,008 122 A4
Lago Santo, It. 122 f6
Lagos de Moreno, Mex., 23,298 92 E4
Lagrán, Sp. 122 n12
la Grand-Croix, Fr., 5,040 116 p15
La Grande, Oreg., 9,014 80 D3
La Grande, Wash. 80 B2
la Grande-Combe, Fr., 14,458 117 F4
La Grange, Ark. 73 E3
La Grange, Calif. 82 C4
La Grange, Ga., 23,632 64 E2
La Grange, Ill., 15,285 68 E2
Lagrange, co., Ind., 17,380 70 D1
Lagrange, Ind., 1,990 70 D1
La Grange, Ky., 2,168 71 F3
La Grange, Me. 55 E3
La Grange, Mo., 1,347 72 F4
La Grange, N.C., 2,133 63 G2
Lagrange, Ohio, 1,007 70 G1
La Grange, Tex., 3,623 77 P5
Lagrange, Wyo., 176 81 G5
La Grange Bay, Austl. 172 B2
La Grange Park, Ill., 13,793 69 C9
La Granja, Chile 104 e16
La Gran Sab., Ven. 101 K5
La Grita, Ven., 7,255 100 E3
Lagro, Ind. 70 D2
La Guadeloupe, Qué., Can., 1,714 47 N3
La Guaira, Ven., 20,681 101 c11
Laguardia, Sp., 2,095 122 D1
La Guásima, Ven. 101 a11
La Guata, Hond., 1,161 94 D3
La Güera, Sp. Sah. 160 B4
la Guerche-de-Bretagne, Fr., 3,219 117 C3
Laguiole, Fr., 1,269 117 E4
Laguna, Braz., 17,451 103 G7
Laguna, N. Mex. 79 B4
Laguna, Tex. 77 O5
Laguna Beach, Calif., 9,288 82 D6
Laguna Beach, Fla. 65 C2
Laguna Blanca, Arg., 5,000* 105 D3
Laguna Blanca, Arg. 105 B6
Laguna Cr., Ariz. 78 C3
Laguna Dam, Ariz.-Calif. 78 A5
Laguna de Perlas, Nic. 94 E4
Laguna Larga, Mex., 1,043 93 c9
Lagunas, Chile 105 B2
Lagunas, Peru, 2,351 104 B3
Lagunas, Peru, 3,690 104 C3
Laguna Salada, Dom. Rep., 2,000 96 m6
Laguna Yema, Arg., 1,500* 105 C2

Lędziny—L'Hospitalet · 251

Lędziny, Pol., 5,802 127 i6
Lee, U.K. 114 C3
Lee, co., Ark., 21,001 73 E3
Lee, co., Ala., 49,754 64 D3
Lee, co., Fla., 54,539 65 H6
Lee, Fla., 243 65 F2
Lee, co., Ga., 6,204 64 E4
Lee, co., Ill., 38,749 68 C2
Lee, Ill., 228 68 C2
Lee, Ind. 70 C2
Lee, co., Iowa, 44,207 72 F4
Lee, co., Ky., 7,420 71 H4
Lee, Me. 55 D3
Lee, Mass., 3,078; 5,271(T) 56 D3
Lee, co., Miss., 40,589 73 G3
Lee, Nev. 83 C2
Lee, N.H. 54 E5
Lee, N.Y. 59 s25
Lee, co., N.C., 26,561 63 E2
Lee, co., S.C., 21,832 63 D3
Lee, co., Tex., 8,949 77 P4
Lee, co., Va., 25,824 62 A6
Lee, r., Ire. 113 B6
Leebotwood, U.K. 114 C5
Lee Center, N.Y. 59 K5
Leechburg, Pa., 3,545 60 C4
Leech L., Minn. 74 E2
Leechville, N.C. 63 H2
Leedey, Okla., 451 76 D2
Leeds, Qué., Can. 47 N2
Leeds, U.K., 510,597 113 F5
Leeds, Ala., 6,162 64 C2
Leeds, Me. 55 B4
Leeds (part of Northampton), Mass. 56 F3
Leeds, N.Y. 59 N7
Leeds, N. Dak., 797 74 C1
Leeds, S.C. 63 C3
Leeds, Utah, 109 78 B3
Leek, U.K., 19,173 113 F5
Leelanau, co., Mich., 9,321 67 H4
Leelanau, L., Mich. 67 H4
Leens, Neth. 115 E1
Lee-on-the-Solent, U.K., 4,361 113 k13
Leeper, Pa. 60 D3
Leer, F.R.Ger., 21,158 118 A2
Leer, Mich. 67 K3
Leerdam, Neth., 10,200 115 D3
Leesburg, Fla., 11,172 65 H4
Leesburg, Ga., 774 64 E4
Leesburg, Ind., 427 70 D1
Leesburg, N.J. 61 B5
Leesburg, Ohio, 932 70 F3
Leesburg, Va., 2,869 62 G3
Lees Creek, Ohio 70 F3
Lees Ferry, Ariz. 78 C3
Leesport, Pa., 1,138 61 K5
Lees Summit, Mo., 8,267 72 C6
Leeste, F.R.Ger., 6,515 118 B2
Lee Store, Tex. 77 N3
Leesville, Ind. 70 C4
Leesville, La., 4,689 73 B6
Leesville, S.C., 1,619 63 C4
Leesville, Tex. 76 c7
Leesville L., Ohio 70 H2
Leetes Island (part of Guilford), Conn. 56 F7
Leeton, Austl., 5,148 173 F5
Leeton, Mo., 371 72 D6
Leetonia, Ohio, 2,543 70 J2
Leetsdale, Pa., 2,153 60 b7
Leetsville, Mich. 67 H4
Leeuwarden, Neth., 78,400 115 D1
Leeuwin, C., Austl. 172 A5
Leeville, La. 73 E8
Lee Vining, Calif. 82 D4
Leeward Is., Lesser Antilles 95 G3
Leezen, F.R.Ger., 1,123 119 b8
Lefa, r., U.S.S.R. 151 F1
Lefanga Bay, W. Samoa 177 38
le Fauët, Fr., 3,232 116 B2
Lefèvre, C., Loy. Is. 174 k8
Leffingwell, Conn. 56 H6
Léfini, r., Congo 164 B2
Lefka, Cyp., 3,462 142 d9
Lefkoniko, Cyp., 2,579 142 e9
Leflore, co., Miss., 47,142 73 E4
Le Flore, co., Okla., 29,106 76 J3
Leflore, Okla. 76 J3
Lefor, N. Dak. 74 A2
Leforest, Fr., 7,380 116 a7
Lefors, Tex., 864 76 N2
le Fousseret, Fr., 1,437 117 D5
Le François, Mart., 2,189 97 12
Lefroy, Ont., Can. 46 E4
Lefroy, L., Austl. 172 B4
Legal, Alta., Can. 42 K3
Legan, i., Kwajalein 176 25
Legaspi, Phil., 60,593 153 B2
Legé, Fr., 3,649 117 C3
Légère, N.B., Can. 47 T10
Legerwood, U.K. 112 e8
Legge Pk., Austl. 173 f13
Legges Tor = Legge Pk.
Leggett, Calif. 82 B3
Leggett, Tex. 77 Q4
Leghorn = Livorno
Legion, Tex., 1,691 77 O4
Legion L., Minn. 74 b6
Legionowo, Pol., 20,000* 127 D2
Legnano, It., 40,798 123 B2
Legnago, It., 25,000 123 C2
Legnaro, It., 5,052 122 e5
Legnica, Pol., 64,000* 127 A3
Legnickie Pole, Pol. 127 f5
Legrad, Yug., 2,586 125 C1
Le Grand, Calif. 82 C4
le Grand-Bourg, Fr., 2,115 117 D3
Leh, India, 3,720 145 E2
Le Havre, Fr., 184,133 117 C2
Lehi, Utah, 4,377 78 C1
Lehigh, Iowa, 846 72 D2
Lehigh, Kans., 178 75 H5
Lehigh, Okla., 296 76 G3
Lehigh, co., Pa., 227,536 61 L4
Lehigh, Pa. 61 p16
Lehigh, r., Pa. 61 L4
Lehigh Acres, Fla. 65 H6
Lehighton, Pa., 6,318 61 L4
Lehinch, Ire. 113 B5
Lehliu, Rum. 128 F2
Lehman Caves Nat. Mon., Nev. 83 C3
Lehmen, F.R.Ger. 119 C4
Lehnin, Ger.D.R. 118 D2
Lehr, N. Dak., 381 74 C2
Lehrberg, F.R.Ger., 1,636 118 C4
Lehua I., Hawaii 84 A1
Lehua Landing, Hawaii 84 A1
Lei, r., China 152 D2
Leiah, Pak., 19,608 145 D3
Leibnitz, Aust., 6,354 124 M7
Leicester, U.K., 273,470 113 F5
Leicester, Mass., 1,750; 8,177(T) 56 J4
Leicester, N.Y., 365 58 D6
Leicester, Vt. 54 A4
Leicester Junction, Vt. 54 A4
Leicestershire, co., U.K., 682,568 113 F5
Leichhardt, r., Austl. 172 E2
Leichlingen, F.R.Ger., 12,841 119 C2
Lei-chou Chiang, China 152 C3
Lei-chou Pan-tao, China 150 E5
Leiden, Neth., 96,600 115 C2
Leiderdorp, Neth., 4,200 115 b6
Leidschendam, Neth., 13,400 115 a6
Leie, r., Belg.-Fr. 116 a6
Leigh, Kent, Eng., U.K., 1,582 114 J8
Leigh, Lancs., Eng., U.K., 46,153 114 D4
Leigh, Worcs., Eng., U.K., 1,113 114 D6
Leigh, Nebr., 502 75 H2
Leigh Creek, Austl. 172 E4
Leighton, Ala., 1,158 64 B1
Leighton, Iowa, 167 72 E3
Leighton Buzzard, U.K., 11,745 114 G7
Leignon, Belg., 1,519 115 D4
Leikanger, Nor. 120 A3
Leiktho, Burma 146 B3
Leili, i., Sol. Is. 175 c2
Leimbach, Ger.D.R. 118 C3
Leimebamba, Peru, 1,008 104 B3
Leimen, F.R.Ger., 6,554 119 F6
Leimuiden, Neth. 115 b6
Leine, r., F.R.Ger. 118 B3
Leinster, prov., Ire., 1,388,942 113 C5
Leintwardine, U.K. 114 C6
Leipoldtville, S. Af. 164 a8
Leipsic, Del., 281 62 J3
Leipsic, Ohio, 1,802 70 F1
Leipsig, Wis. 66 E5
Leipzig, Sask., Can. 43 B4
Leipzig, Ger.D.R., 589,632 118 D3
Leiria, Port., 7,477 122 A3
Leirvik, Nor. 120 A4
Leiser Berge, Aust. 125 ·
Lei-shan, China 152 C2
Leisler, Mt., Austl. 172 D3
Leismer, Alta., Can. 42 L2
Leisnig, Ger.D.R. 118 D3
Leissigen, Switz. 124 B2
Leiston, U.K., 4,121 113 G5
Leitchfield, Ky., 2,982 71 E4
Leith (part of Edinburgh), U.K. 112 d8
Leith, N. Dak., 100 74 B2
Leitha, r., Aust. 124 N6
Leithagebirge, Aust. 125 ·
Leithaprodersdorf, Aust. 124 c11
Leith Hill, U.K. 114 H8
Leithsville, Pa. 61 k18
Leithton, Ill. 69 c8
Leitrim, co., Ire., 37,056 113 C5
Leitrim, Ire. 113 B4
Lei-tung, China 152 C3
Leitzerdorf, Aust. 124 c10
Leiva, Col. 100 D5
Lei-wu-ch'i, China 150 D4
Lei-yang, China 152 D2
Leiza, Sp., 1,564 122 o11
Leja Beach = Davis Park
Lek, r., Neth. 115 C3
Leka, i., Nor. 120 B2
Lékana, Congo 164 B2
Lekáni, Gr. 129 E4
Lekawa, Pol. 127 i5
Lekeleka, i., Tonga 177 36
Lekempti, Eth. 163 L4
Lekhainá, Gr., 3,120 129 C6
Lekhchevo, Bulg., 4,042 128 D3
Lekhónia, Gr., 1,186 129 D5
Lekin, Loy. Is. 174 k8
Lekkerkerk, Neth., 3,600 115 b7
Łęknica, Pol., 2,086 127 A3
le Kouif, Alg., 6,821 160 f6
Leksands-Noret, Swed. 120 C3
Leksula, Indon. 149 H3
Leksvik, Nor. 120 B3
Lela, Okla. 76 G1
Lela, Tex. 76 N2
Le Lamentin, Guad. 97 14
Le Lamentin, Mart., 3,930 97 12
Leland, Ill., 642 68 D2
Leland, Iowa, 209 72 D1
Leland, Mich. 67 H3
Leland, Miss., 6,295 73 E4
Leland, N.C. 63 F3
Leland, Oreg. 80 B4
Leland, Wash. 80 B2
Leland, Wis. 66 C5
Lel'chitsy, U.S.S.R. 136 C3
Lele, i., Kusaie 176 31
Lele Hbr., Kusaie 176 31
Leleiwi Pt., Hawaii 84 G4
Lelepa, i., New Hebr. 174 m6
l'Éléphant, Chaîne de, Camb. 146 C5
Leleque, Arg. 105 A6
Lelia Lake, Tex. 76 N2
Le Lieu, Switz. 124 A2
Léliogat, I., Loy. Is. 174 k8
Le Lion-d'Angers, Fr., 2,226 117 C3
Leloaloa, Tutuila 177 39
Le Locle, Switz., 13,762 124 A1
Le Lorrain, Mart., 1,498 97 12
Lelów, Pol. 127 C3
le Lude, Fr., 3,392 117 D3
Leluova, Sta. Cruz. Is. 175 6
Lelydorp, Sur. 101 N5
Lelystad, Neth. 115 D2
Lem, Den. 121 A4
Lema, Sa. de, Ven. 101 K4
Lema Chan., China-H.K. 152 b6
Le Macouba, Mart. 97 12
Lemahabang, Indon. 148 c7
Léman, L., Fr.-Switz. 124 A2
Le Mans, Fr., 136,083 117 D3
Le Marin, Mart., 1,815 97 12
Le Mars, Iowa, 6,767 72 A2
le Mas-d'Azil, Fr., 1,643 117 D5
Lemasters, Pa. 60 G6
Lemay, Mo. = Luxemburg
Lembach, Fr., 1,602 116 e8
Lembak, Indon. 148 F2
Lembeck, F.R.Ger., 3,173 119 C1
Lemberg, Sask., Can. 43 D5
Lemberg, F.R.Ger., 3,598 119 D6
Lemberg, Fr., 1,608 116 d8
le Mée-sur-Seine, Fr., 1,391 116 i12
Lemei Rock, mtn., Wash. 80 C2
Lemert, Ohio 70 F2
Lemery, Phil., 8,617 153 B2
le Mesnil-Amelot, Fr. 116 i10
le Mesnil-le-Roi, Fr., 5,120 116 g11
le Mesnil-St-Denis, Fr. 116 f12
Lemeta-Johnston, Alaska, 1,227 85 b6
Lemgo, F.R.Ger., 21,046 118 B2
Lemhi, co., Idaho, 5,816 81 B3
Lemhi Ra., Idaho 81 C3
Lemieux Is., N.W.T., Can. 41 R5
Lemington, Vt. 54 D2
Lemitar, N. Mex. 79 B4
Lemme, r., It. 122 b6
Lemmenjoen Kansallispuisto, Fin. 120 F1
Lemmon, S. Dak., 2,412 74 A3
Lemmon, Mt., Ariz. 78 C5
Lemnos = Límnos
Lemon Fair, r., Vt. 54 A4
Lemon Grove, Calif., 19,348 82 c10
Lemon Springs, N.C. 63 E2
Lemont, Ill., 3,397 69 c10
Lemont, Pa., 1,153 60 G4
le Mont-Dore, Fr., 2,256 117 E4
le Mont-St-Michel, Fr. 117 C2
Lemonweir, r., Wis. 66 D5
Lemoore, Calif., 2,561 82 D4
Le Morne Brabant, mtn., Maurit. 165 c12
Lemotol Bay, Truk 176 19
Le Moule, Guad., 5,784 97 14
Le Moyen, La. 73 C7
Lemoyne, Nebr. 75 D2
Lemoyne, Pa., 4,662 60 J5
Lempa, r., Cent. Amer. 94 C3
Lempäälä, Fin. 120 E3
Lempdes, Fr., 1,937 117 E4
Lempster, N.H. 54 C5
Lemro, r., Burma 146 A2
Lemtybozh, U.S.S.R. 134 E3
Le Mu, C., W. Samoa 177 38
Lemutan, Indon. 148 E2
le Muy, Fr., 3,128 116 m14
Lemvig, Den., 5,783 121 A4
Lena, Sp., 16,457 122 C1
Lena, Ill., 1,552 68 C1
Lena, Miss., 307 73 F5
Lena, Nebr. 75 D2
Lena, Ohio 70 E2
Lena, S.C. 63 C5
Lena, Wis., 506 66 E4
Lena, Mt., Utah 78 D1
Lena, r., U.S.S.R. 135 M2
Lenakel, New Hebr. 174 m7
Lenapah, Okla., 322 76 H1
Lenauheim, Rum. 128 C2
Lenawee, co., Mich., 77,789 67 J7
Lençóis, Braz., 2,843 103 H4
Lend, Aust., 2,173 124 K6
Lendinara, It., 15,437 123 C2
Lendringsen, F.R.Ger., 9,389 119 D2
Lendum, Den., 1,324 121 C3
Lenexa, Kans., 2,487 75 a8
Lengau, Aust., 3,561 124 K6
Lengby, Minn., 181 74 E2
Lengefeld, Ger.D.R. 126 c6
Lengenfeld, Aust., 1,073 124 b10
Lengenfeld, Ger.D.R. 126 b6
Lenger, U.S.S.R., 23,000 134 F5
Lengerich, F.R.Ger., 20,055 118 A2
Lenggong, Malay., 4,075 148 B1
Lenggries, F.R.Ger., 6,701 118 C5
Leng-hu, China 150 C3
Lengnau, Switz., 3,524 124 B1
Lengnau, Switz., 1,356 124 C1
Leng-shui-t'an, China 152 C2
Lenham, U.K., 2,487 113 G6
Lenhartsville, Pa., 209 61 L4
Lenina, Kan. im., U.S.S.R. 137 c1
Lenina, Pik, U.S.S.R. 134 G6
Leninabad, U.S.S.R., 83,000 134 F5
Leninakan, U.S.S.R., 113,000 134 D5
Leningrad, U.S.S.R., 2,997,000 134 C4
Leningradskaya, U.S.S.R. 136 E4
Leninogorsk, Kaz. S.S.R., U.S.S.R., 68,000 134 H4
Leninogorsk, R.S.F.S.R., U.S.S.R., 39,400 134 E4
Leninsk, U.S.S.R., 20,400 137 g4
Leninsk-Kuznetskiy, U.S.S.R., 138,000 134 H4
Lenk, Switz., 1,900 124 B2
Lenkoran', U.S.S.R., 25,000 134 D6
Lennartsfors, Swed. 121 D1
Lenne, r., F.R.Ger. 118 A3
Lennegebirge, mts., F.R.Ger. 119 D2
Lennon, Mich. 67 J5
Lennox, Calif., 31,224 83 h16
Lennox, S. Dak., 1,353 74 D4
Lennox, Wis. 66 D3
Lennoxtown, U.K. 112 b8
Lennoxville, Qué., Can., 3,592 47 N3
Leno, It., 10,270 122 d5
Lenoir, co., N.C., 55,276 63 G2
Lenoir, N.C., 10,257 63 C2
Lenoir City, Tenn., 4,979 71 G6
Le Noirmont, Switz., 1,559 124 A1
Lenora, Kans., 512 75 F4
Lenora, Okla. 76 D1
Lenore L., Sask., Can. 43 D4
Lenox, Ala. 64 B4
Lenox, Ga., 802 64 F4
Lenox, Iowa, 1,178 72 C4
Lenox, Mass., 1,713; 4,253(T) 56 C3
Lenox, Mo. 72 F7
Lenoxdale (part of Lenox), Mass. 56 D3
Lens, Fr., 42,733 117 E1
Lens, Switz., 1,743 124 B2
Lensahn, F.R.Ger., 4,081 118 C1
Lentföhrden, F.R.Ger. 119 a8
Lenti, Hung., 2,847 126 C3
Lentilly, Fr., 1,296 116 p15
Lentini, It., 32,345 123 E6
Lenton, U.K. 114 H5
Lentua, l., Fin. 120 G2
Lenvik, Nor. 120 D1
Lenwood, Calif., 2,407 82 E5
Lenzburg, Switz., 6,378 124 C1
Lenzburg, Ill., 420 68 C5
Lenzen, Ger.D.R. 118 C2
Lenzerheide, Switz. 124 D2
Lenzing, Aust., 5,362 124 K6
Léo, Upper Volta, 2,084 162 D4
Leoben, Aust., 36,313 124 M6
Leobersdorf, Aust., 3,406 124 c11
Léogâne, Haiti, 3,922 96 k6
Leogang, Aust., 2,202 124 J6
Leola, Ark., 321 73 C3
Leola, S. Dak., 833 74 C3
Leoma, Tenn. 71 D6
Leominster, U.K., 6,405 113 E5
Leominster, Mass., 27,929 57 J2
León, Mex., 209,469 92 E4
León, Nic., 46,321 94 D4
Leon, Phil., 3,103 153 d11
León, Sp., 73,483 122 C1
Leon, co., Fla., 74,225 65 E2
Leon, Iowa, 2,004 72 D4
Leon, Kans., 541 75 J6
Leon, N.Y. 58 B7
Leon, Okla., 109 76 F4
Leon, co., Tex., 9,951 77 Q4
Leon, W. Va., 236 62 C4
Leon, Wis. 66 C5
León, reg., Sp. 122 C2
Leon, r., Tex. 77 O3
Leona, Kans., 110 75 K4
Leona, Tex. 77 Q4
Leona, r., Tex. 77 O5
Leona Mines, Va. 62 A6
Leonard, Mich., 359 67 K6
Leonard, Mo., 142 72 E5
Leonard, N. Dak., 232 74 D2
Leonard, Tex., 1,117 77 P3
Leonardo, N.J. 58 c15
Leonardsville, N.Y. 59 K6
Leonardtown, Md., 1,281 62 H4
Leonardville, S.-W. Afr. 164 C5
Leonardville, Kans., 378 75 J4
Leona Valley, Calif. 82 D5
Leona Vicario, Mex. 93 J4
Leonberg, F.R.Ger., 16,132 118 B4
Leondári, Gr., 1,645 129 D5
Leonding, Aust., 11,178 124 L5
Leone, Tutuila, 1,192 177 39
Leone Bay, Tutuila 177 39
Leone Pt., Tutuila 177 39
Leones, Arg., 8,126 105 C4
Leonfelden, Aust., 2,547 124 L5
Leonforte, It., 18,750 123 E6
Leongatha, Austl., 2,304 173 e12
Leoni, Mich. 67 J6
Leonia, Fla. 65 C2
Leonia, N.J., 8,384 58 c13
Leonidas, Mich. 67 H6
Leonora, Austl. 172 B4
Leonore, Ill., 195 68 D2
Leon Pk., Colo. 79 B2
Leon Springs, Tex. 76 a6
Leopard Pt., Tutuila 177 39
Leopold and Astrid Coast, Ant. 180 S6
Léopold II, L., D.R.Congo 164 B2
Leopoldina, Braz., 17,726 103 e17
Leopoldsburg, Belg., 8,788 115 D3
Leopoldsdorf, Aust., 1,715 124 N5
Léopoldville = Kinshasa
Leopolis, Wis. 66 E4
Leoti, Kans. 75 D5
Leoville, Sask., Can. 43 C4
Leoville, Kans. 75 E4
Leovo, U.S.S.R., 6,000 136 C4
Lepa, W. Samoa 177 38
Lepaera, Hond., 1,068 94 e9
le Palais, Fr., 2,734 116 B3
Lepanto, Ark., 1,585 73 E2
Lepar, r., Malay. 147 p15
Lepar, P., Indon. 148 C3
le Passage, Fr., 5,669 117 D4
Lepe, Sp., 10,038 122 B4
le Pecq, Fr., 10,859 116 g11
Lepel', U.S.S.R., 9,700 136 C2
Lepenac, r., Yug. 125 E3
Lepenoú, Gr., 1,856 129 C5
le Perray-en-Yvelines, Fr., 1,916 116 f12
le Perreux, Fr., 27,900 116 i11
L'Épiphanie, Qué., Can. 2,640 47 L3
le Plessis-Belleville, Fr., 1,016 116 i10
le Poiré-sur-Vie, Fr., 3,546 117 C3
Lepontine Alps, mts., It.-Switz., 123 B1
le Port, La Réunion, 13,281 165 b11
le Port-Marly, Fr., 3,650 116 g11
Leppävirta, Fin. 120 F3
Le Prêcheur, Mart. 97 12
Le Prese, Switz. 124 D2
Lepsy, U.S.S.R., 7,400 134 G5
Leptis Magna, ruins, Libya 161 G2
le Puy, Fr., 28,007 117 E4
Lequeitio, Sp., 5,011 122 n11
Lequire, Okla. 76 H2
Lerado, Kans. 75 G6
le Raincy, Fr., 15,267 116 i11
Le Raysville, Pa., 371 61 K2
Lerbjerg, Den. 121 B4
Lercara Friddi, It., 14,350 123 D6
Lerdal, Swed. 121 D2
Lerdo, Mex., 17,537 92 E3
Léré, Chad, 2,300*, 162 G4
Lérida, Col. 101 e15
Lérida, Sp., 63,850 122 F2
Lérins, Îs. de, Fr. 116 n13
Lerma, Mex., 3,175 93 H4
Lerma, Sp., 2,605 122 D2
Lerma, r., Mex. 92 E4
Lermoos, Aust. 124 G6
Lerna, Ill., 296 68 D4
Le Robert, Mart., 1,622 97 12
Léros, i., Gr. 129 F6
Leroux Wash, Ariz. 78 C4
Leroy, Sask., Can. 43 D4
Leroy, Ala. 64 A4
Le Roy, Ill., 2,088 68 D3
Leroy, Ind. 70 B1
Le Roy, Kans. 601 75 K5
Le Roy, Mich. 267 67 H4
Le Roy, Minn., 971 74 F4
Le Roy, N.Y., 4,662 58 D6
Leroy, N. Dak. 74 D1
Le Roy, Pa. 60 J2
Le Roy, Wis. 66 E5
le Russey, Fr., 1,646 117 G3
Lerwick, U.K., 5,906 112 F1
Léry, Qué., Can., 1,929 47 o18
Leş, Rum. 128 C1
Lesa, D.R.Congo 165 n19
Les Abymes, Guad. 97 14
Lesaca, Sp., 2,294 122 o11
les Adrets-de-Fréjus, Fr. 116 m13
les Alluets-le-Roi, Fr. 116 f11
les Andelys, Fr., 6,640 117 D2
Les Anses d'Arlet, Mart. 97 12
les Arcs, Fr., 3 152 116 m14
les Baux, Fr. 117 F5
Les Bois, Switz., 1,098 124 A1
Lesbos = Lésvos
Lesbury, U.K., 1,033 112 g9
l'Escarène, Fr., 1,218 117 G5
Les Cayes, Haiti, 12,621 96 k6
les Clayes-sous-Bois, Fr., 6,079 116 g11
Les Diablerets, Switz. 124 B2
Les Eboulements, Qué., Can. 47 Q10
les Échelles, Fr., 1,238 117 F4
les Écrennes, Fr. 116 k12
Les Escaldes, Andorra, 2,840 122 g7
les Herbiers, Fr., 5,232 117 C3
Leshukonskoye, U.S.S.R. 134 D3
Lésigny, Fr. 116 i12
Lesima, Mte., It. 122 c6
Lesja, Nor. 120 B3
Lesko, Pol., 2,171 127 E4
Leskovac, Yug., 34,000* 125 F3
Leskovik, Alb., 1,500 125 E4
Leslie, U.K., 3,421 112 d7
Leslie, Ark., 505 73 C2
Leslie, Ga., 494 64 E4
Leslie, Idaho 81 C4
Leslie, co., Ky., 10,941 71 H4
Leslie, Mich., 1,807 67 J6
Leslie, S.C. 63 D3
Leslie, Wis. 66 C6
Lesmahagow, U.K. 112 E4
Les Mamelles, mts., Guad. 97 14
Les Méchins, Qué., Can., 1,455 45 M5
les Mées, Fr., 2,399 117 G4
les Mesnuls, Fr. 116 f11
les Molières, Fr. 116 g12
les Mureaux, Fr., 19,087 116 f11
Lesná, Czech. 126 b7
Leśna, Pol., 4,201 127 A3
Lesneven, Fr., 3,997 116 A2
Leśnica, Pol., 2.481 127 h5
Lesnoy, U.S.S.R. 134 C3
Lesogorsk, U.S.S.R., 3,600 135 O5
Lesotho, ctry., 859,000* 164 D6
Lesovo, Bulg., 2,725 128 F4
Lesozavodsk, U.S.S.R., 32 100 135 N5
Lesparre-Medoc, Fr., 3,512 117 C4
les Pavillons-sous-Bois, Fr., 19,022 116 i11
L'Esperance Rock, N.Z. 170 G7
les Pieux, Fr., 1,136 117 C2
les Ponts-de-Cé, Fr., 6,066 117 C3
les Riceys, Fr., 1,565 117 F3
les Sables-d'Olonne, Fr., 19,256 117 C3
les Sauvages, Fr. 116 o15
Lessay, Fr., 1,326 117 C2
Lessebo, Swed. 120 C4
Lesser Antilles, is., W.I. 95 G4
Lesser Caymans, is., Lesser Ant. 97 2
Lesser Khingan Ra. = Hsiao-hsing-an-ling Shan-mo
Lesser Slave L., Alta., Can. 42 J2
Lesser Sunda Is., Indon. 149 G5
Lessines, Belg., 9,438 115 B4
Lessley, Miss. 73 D6
Lesson, Pt., Kusaie 176 31
l'Est, L. de, Qué., Can. 55 C1
Les Tantes, is., Gren.-Is. 97 20
Lester, Iowa, 239 72 A1
Lester Manor, Va. 62 G5
Lesterville, S. Dak., 173 74 D4
Lestijoki, r., Fin. 120 F3
Lestock, Sask., Can. 43 D4
Le Sueur, co., Minn., 19,906 74 F3
Le Sueur, Minn., 3,310 74 F3
Les Verrières, Switz., 1,084 124 A2
Lésvos, i., Gr. 129 E5
Leszczyny, Pol., 5,447 127 h6
Leszno, Pol., 29,000* 127 B3
Letart, W. Va. 62 B4
Letart Falls, Ohio 70 G4
Letcher, co., Ky., 30,102 71 J4
Letcher, S. Dak., 296 74 C4
Letchworth, U.K., 25,511 113 F6
le Teil, Fr., 8,344 117 F4
Letellier, Man., Can. 43 g10
Letenye, Hung., 4,509 126 C3
Letha, Idaho 81 A4
Le Thanh, S. Viet., 2,452 146 D4
Lethbridge, Alta., Can., 35,068 42 K4
Lethem, Guyana 101 L6
le Thillay, Fr., 2,186 116 h10
Le Thuy, N. Viet. 146 D3
Leticia, Col. 100 E10
Letitia, Okla. 76 E3
Letmathe, F.R.Ger., 12,842 119 D2
Letnitsa, Bulg., 5,183 128 E3
Letohatchee, Ala. 64 C3
Letohrad, Czech. 127 f6
Letona, Ark., 141 73 D2
le Touquet-Paris-Plage, Fr., 4,064 117 D1
Letpadan, Burma, 15,896 146 A3
le Trayas, Fr. 116 m14
le Tréport, Fr., 6,136 117 D1
Letterfrack, Ire. 113 B5
Letterkenny, Ire., 4,178 113 B4
Letterston, U.K. 113 D6
Letts, Iowa, 392 72 F3
Letty Harbour, N.W.T., Can. 40 E4
Leu, Rum. 128 E2
Léua, Ang. 164 C3
Leuaniua, i., Sol. Is. 175 c1
Leucadia, Calif., 5,665 82 E6
Leuchars, U.K. 112 e7
Leudeville, Fr. 116 h12
Leuk, Switz., 2,546 124 B2
Leukerbad, Switz. 124 B2
Leun, F.R.Ger., 1,858 119 E3
Leuna, Ger.D.R., 12,965 126 a5
Leupp, Ariz. 78 C4
Leupp Corner, Ariz. 78 C4
Leuser, G., Indon. 148 A2
Leutkirch, F.R.Ger., 6,328 118 B5
Leuven, Belg., 34,215 115 C4
Leuville-sur-Orge, Fr., 1,198 116 g12
Leuze, Belg., 6,987 115 B4
Leuze, Belg., 1,415 115 C4
Levack, Ont., Can., 3,148 44 G6
Levádhia, Gr., 12,609 129 D5
le Val-d'Ajol, Fr., 6,224 117 G3
Levallois-Perret, Fr., 61,962 116 h11
Levan, Utah, 421 78 C2
Levang, Nor. 121 B2
Levanger, Nor., 1,714 120 B3
Levanna, Ohio 70 F4
Levant, Kans. 75 D4
Levant, Me. 55 D4
Levanto, It., 6,130 123 B2
Levasy, Mo., 140 72 C5
Le Vauclin, Mart., 2,172 97 12
Levee, Ky. 71 G4
Levelland, Tex., 10,153 77 M3
Levelock, Alaska, 88 85 E4
Leven, Eng., U.K. 114 H3
Leven, Scot., U.K., 8,872 112 E3
Leven, r., Eng., U.K. 112 h11
Leven, r., Scot., U.K. 112 d7
Leven, Loch, Inv., U.K. 112 D3
Leven, Loch, Kin., U.K. 112 d7
Levens, Fr., 1,223 117 G5
Levens, U.K. 113 E4
Leveque, C., Austl. 172 C2
Leverburgh, U.K. 112 C3
Leverett, Mass., 914(T) 56 G3
Levering, Mich. 67 J3
Leverington, U.K., 2,920 114 J5
Leverkusen, F.R.Ger., 78,042 118 A3
Leverville, D.R.Congo 164 C2
le Vésinet, Fr., 18,493 116 g11
Levice, Czech., 13,770 126 D2
Levídhi, Gr., 2,156 129 D6
Levie, Fr., 3,422 116 r18
Levier, Fr., 1,446 117 G3
le Vigan, Fr., 4,312 117 E5
Levin, N.Z., 7,934 175 g6
Lévis, Qué., Can., 14,871 47 N2
Levisa Fk., r., Ky. 71 J4
Lévis-St-Nom, Fr. 116 f12
Levitha, i., Gr. 129 F6
Levittown, N.J. = Willingboro
Levittown, N.Y., 65,276 59 O10
Levittown, Pa., 61,000* 60 N5
Lévka Óri, Gr. 129 E7
Levkás, Gr., 6,552 129 C5
Levkás, i., Gr. 129 C5
Levkímmi, Gr., 2,366 129 C5
Levoča, Czech. 126 E2
Lévrier, B. du, Maur. 160 B4
Levroux, Fr., 3,229 117 D3
Levski, Bulg., 8,025 128 E3
Levskigrad, Bulg., 12,663 128 E3
Lev Tolstoy, U.S.S.R., 8,100 136 E2
Levuka, Fiji 174 4
Levy, co., Fla., 10,364 65 G3
Levy, N. Mex. 79 C3
Lewanna, Nebr. 75 E1
Lewarae, N.C., 425 63 E3
Lewbeach, N.Y. 59 L8
Lewe, Burma, 5,830 146 A3
Lewellen, Nebr., 411 75 C2
Lewes, U.K., 13,645 113 G6
Lewes, Del., 3,025 62 J4
Lewin Brzeski, Pol., 2,914 127 B3
Lewis, Colo. 79 A3
Lewis, co., Idaho, 4,423 81 A2
Lewis, Iowa, 501 72 B3
Lewis, Kans., 486 75 F6
Lewis, co., Ky., 13,115 71 H3
Lewis, co., Mo., 10,984 72 F4
Lewis, co., N.Y., 23,249 59 J4
Lewis, N.Y. 59 N3
Lewis, co., Tenn., 6,269 71 D6
Lewis, co., Wash., 41,858 80 B2
Lewis, co., W. Va., 19,711 62 D3
Lewis, Wis. 66 A3
Lewis, I. of, U.K. 112 C2
Lewis, r., Wash. 80 C2
Lewis and Clark, co., Mont., 28,006 81 C2
Lewis and Clark L., Nebr.-S. Dak. 75 H1
Lewisburg, Ohio, 1,415 70 E3
Lewisburg, Pa., 5,523 60 J4
Lewisburg, Tenn., 6,338 71 E6
Lewisburg, W. Va., 2,259 62 D5
Lewis Cr., Vt. 54 A3
Lewis Cr., Pond Br., Vt. 54 A3
Lewis Hills, Newf., Can. 45 P5
Lewis Pass, N.Z. 175 g6
Lewisport, Ky., 610 71 D4
Lewisporte, Newf., Can., 2,677 45 Q5
Lewis Ra., Mont. 81 C1
Lewis Run, Pa., 714 60 E2
Lewiston, Idaho, 12,691 81 A2
Lewiston, Ind. 70 C1
Lewiston, Me., 40,804 55 B4
Lewiston, Mich. 67 J4
Lewiston, Minn., 890 74 G4
Lewiston, Nebr., 77 75 J3
Lewiston, N.Y., 3,320 58 C5
Lewiston, N.C., 360 63 G1
Lewiston, Utah, 1,336 78 C1
Lewiston, Vt. 54 C4
Lewiston Orchards, Idaho, 9,680 81 A2
Lewistown, Ill., 2,603 68 B3
Lewistown, Mo., 454 72 F4
Lewistown, Mont., 7,408 81 E2
Lewistown, Pa., 12,640 60 G4
Lewisville, Ark., 1,373 73 B4
Lewisville, Idaho, 385 81 C4
Lewisville, Henry Co., Ind., 592 70 D3
Lewisville, Morgan Co., Ind. 70 C3
Lewisville, Ohio, 193 70 H3
Lewisville, Pa., 590 60 G2
Lewisville, Tex., 3,956 77 P3
Lexa, Ark. 73 E3
Lexie, Miss. 73 E6
Lexington, Ala., 315 64 B1
Lexington, Ga., 376 64 F2
Lexington, Ill., 1,244 68 D3
Lexington, Ind. 70 D4
Lexington, Ky., 62,810 71 G3
Lexington, Mass., 27,691(T) 57 L3
Lexington, Mich., 722 67 L5
Lexington, Miss., 2,839 73 F4
Lexington, Mo., 5,140 72 D5
Lexington, Nebr., 5,572 75 F3
Lexington, N.Y. 59 M7
Lexington, N.C., 16,093 63 D2
Lexington, Ohio, 1,311 70 G2
Lexington, Okla., 1,216 76 F2
Lexington, Oreg., 240 80 D3
Lexington, co., S.C., 60,726 63 C4
Lexington, S.C., 1,127 63 C4
Lexington, Tenn., 3,943 71 C6
Lexington, Tex., 711 77 P4
Lexington, Va., 7,537 62 E5
Lexington Park, Md., 7,039 62 H4
Lexington Res., Calif. 83 e13
Lexton, Austl. 173 d11
Leyba, N. Mex. 79 C4
Leyburn, U.K., 1,357 114 E2
Leyden, Mass., 343(T) 56 F2
Leyden, Wis. 66 D6
Leyland, U.K., 19,241 114 C3
Leyr, Fr. 116 b9
Leysin, Switz., 2,241 124 B2
Leyte, Phil., 2,161 153 f10
Leyte, i., Phil. 153 C3
Leyte G., Phil. 153 C3
Leyton, London, U.K. 114 H7
Leytron, Switz., 1,732 124 B2
Leżajsk, Pol., 5,438 127 E3
Lezama, Arg. 105 b12
Lezama, Ven. 101 c12
Lézarde, r., Mart. 97 12
Lezay, Fr., 2,144 117 D3
Lezhë, Alb., 2,650 125 D4
Lézignan-Corbières, Fr., 7,120 117 E5
Lezoux, Fr., 3,510 117 E4
Lgota, Pol. 127 i6
L'gov, U.S.S.R., 21,800 136 D3
Lhasa = La-sa
l'Haÿ-les-Roses, Fr., 17,969 116 h11
Lhokkruet, Indon. 148 A1
Lhoknga, Indon. 148 A1
Lhokseumawe, Indon. 148 A1
Lhoksukon, Indon. 148 A1
L'Hôpital, Fr., 5,925 116 c8
l'Horme, Fr., 4,342 116 p16
l'Hospitalet, Fr. 122 g7

Li, r., China 152 C1
Li, r., China 152 B3
Lian, Phil., 4,102 153 b8
Liancourt, Fr., 4,850 117 E2
Lianga, Phil., 5,772 153 C3
Lianga Bay, Phil. 153 C3
Liang-ch'eng, N-m-k., China 151 A2
Liang-ch'eng, Shant., China 151 C4
Liangchow = Wu-wei
Liang East, G., Malay. 147 o15
Liang-p'ing, China 152 B1
Liang-yang, China 150 F5
Lianokládhion, Gr., 1,247 129 D5
Liao, r., China 150 G2
Liao-ch'eng, China 151 C3
Liao-chung, China 151 D2
Liao-ning, prov., China, 24,090,000 150 G2
Liao-pu, China 152 a6
Liao-tung Pan-tao, China 150 G3
Liao-tung Wan, China 150 G2
Liao-yang, China 150 G2
Liao-yüan, China, 176,600* 150 G2
Liard, r., N.W.T., Can. 40 E5
Liard River, Br. Col., Can. 42 E1
Lib, i., Marsh. Is. 176 22
Libagon, Phil., 1,983 153 C3
Libáň, Czech. 127 e6
Líbano, Col. 101 d15
Libas Sud, Phil., 1,170 153 C3
Libau, Man., Can. 43 h9
Libby, Minn. 74 F2
Libby, Mont., 2,828 81 B1
Libenge, D.R.Congo 164 C1
Liberal, Kans., 13,813 75 D6
Liberal, Mo., 612 72 C7
Libercourt, Fr., 10,523 116 a7
Liberdade, r., Braz. 103 F4
Liberec, Czech., 67,180 126 B1
Liberia, ctry., 1,016,443 162 C4
Liberia, C.R., 6,087 94 E5
Liberta, Antigua, 1,988 97 9
Libertad, Ven., 1,006 100 F3
Libertad, Ven., 1,171 100 F3
Libertador General San Martín, Arg., 8,000* 105 C2
Liberty, co., Fla., 3,138 65 E2
Liberty, co., Ga., 14,487 64 H4
Liberty, Ill., 118 68 A4
Liberty, Ind., 1,745 70 E3
Liberty, Ky., 1,578 71 F4
Liberty, Me. 55 C4
Liberty, Miss., 642 73 E6
Liberty, Mo., 8,909 72 C5
Liberty, co., Mont., 2,624 81 D1
Liberty, Nebr., 174 75 J3
Liberty, N.Y., 4,704 59 L8
Liberty, N.C., 1,438 63 E2
Liberty, Allegheny Co., Pa., 60 c8
Liberty, Tioga co., Pa., 60 H2
Liberty (part of Exeter), R.I. 57 K6
Liberty, S.C., 2,657 63 B3
Liberty, co., Tex., 31,595 77 Q4
Liberty, Tex., 6,127 77 Q4
Liberty, Mt., N.H. 54 D3
Liberty Center, Ohio, 867 70 E1
Liberty Corner, N.J. 58 a14
Liberty Hill (part of Lebanon), Conn. 56 H6
Liberty Hill, S.C. 63 D3
Liberty Hill, Tex. 77 O4
Liberty Pole, Wis. 66 C5
Libertytown, Md. 62 G3
Libertyville, Ill., 8,560 68 D1
Libertyville, Iowa, 368 72 F4
Libiąż Mały, Pol., 7,655 127 i6
Libin, Belg., 1,102 115 D5
Libiron, i., Eniwetok 176 28
Liblar, F.R.Ger., 6,117 119 B3
Liblin, Czech. 126 c7
Libmanan, Phil., 5,291 153 B2
Libochovice, Czech. 126 c6
Libon, Phil., 4,449 153 h14
Libona, Phil., 3,087 153 C3
Libong, Ko, Thai. 146 B6
Liborina, Col. 100 B4
Libourne, Fr., 21,399 117 C4
Libramont, Belg., 2,429 115 D5
Library, Pa., 3,100* 60 b8
Librazhd, Alb., 1,100 125 E4
Libres, Mex., 2,447 93 F4
Libres del Sur, Arg. 105 c12
Libreville, Gabon 164 A1
Libya, ctry., 1,564,369 161 G3
Libyan Desert, Af. 161 J3
Libyan Plateau, Libya-U.A.R. 161 J2
Licab, Phil., 2,204 153 b7
Licán-Ray, Chile 105 e14
Licantén, Chile, 1,368 104 e14
Licata, It., 41,173 123 D6
Lice, Turk., 6,720 142 E2
Licey al Medio, Dom. Rep., 2,043 96 m6
Lich, F.R.Ger., 4,961 118 B3
Li-ch'eng, China 151 B3
Lichfield, U.K., 14,077 113 F5
Li-chiang, China 150 D4
Li-ching, China 151 C3
Lichtenau, Bad.-Württ., F.R.Ger., 1,321 119 E7
Lichtenau, Nrh.-Wf., F.R.Ger., 1,514 118 B3
Lichtenberg, Fr. 116 e9
Lichtenburg, F.R.Ger., 1,256 126 a6
Lichtenfels, F.R.Ger., 10,403 118 C3
Lichtenstein, Ger.D.R., 13,243 126 b6
Lichtenvoorde, Neth., 5,000 115 E2
Lichtervelde, Belg., 6,846 115 B3
Li-ch'uan, Ch-hsi, China 152 E2
Li-ch'uan, Hu-p., China 152 C1
Lička Jesenica, Yug. 125 B2
Lick Creek, Ill. 68 C6
Licking, Mo., 954 72 F7
Licking, co., Ohio, 90,242 70 G2
Licking, r., Ky. 71 G3
Licking Cr., Pa. 60 F6
Ličko Petrovo Selo, Yug. 125 B2
Licosa, Punta, It. 123 E4
Lid, Swed. 120 d9
Lida, U.S.S.R., 28,500 134 B4
Lida, Nev. 83 B4
Lidderdale, Iowa, 201 72 C2
Liddes, Switz. 124 B3
Liddon G., N.W.T., Can. 40 G3
Liden, Swed. 120 D3
Lidgbird, Mt., Lord Howe I. 175 12
Lidgerwood, N. Dak., 1,081 74 D2
Lidhoríkion, Gr., 1,302 129 D5
Lidice, Czech. 126 B1
Lidilbut, i., Eniwetok 176 28
Lidingö, Swed. 120 f8
Lidköping, Swed. 120 C4
Lido, It. 122 f5
Lido Beach, N.Y. 58 e14
Lido di Roma, It., 15,000* 123 a8
Lidzbark, Pol., 4,133 127 C2
Lidzbark Warmiński, Pol., 10,521 127 D1
Liebenau, F.R.Ger., 2,540 118 B2
Liebenthal, Kans., 191 75 F5
Liebenwalde, Ger.D.R. 118 D2
Lieberhausen, F.R.Ger., 4,253 119 D2
Lieberose, Ger.D.R. 118 E3
Liechtenstein, ctry., 19,000* 124 D1
Liedekerke, Belg., 9,423 115 C4
Liège, Belg., 156,599 115 D4
Lieksa, Fin. 120 G3
Lien, r., China 152 C3
Lien-ch'eng, China 152 E2
Lien-chiang, F-ch., China 152 E2
Lien-chiang, K-t., China 150 E5
Lien-hua, China 152 D2
Lien-nan, China 152 D2
Lien-p'ing, China 150 F4
Lien-shan, China 152 C2
Lien-shui, China 151 C4
Lien-yang, China 150 F4
Lien-yüan, China 152 C2
Lien-yün-chiang, China 151 C4
Lienz, Aust., 11,115 124 J7
Liepāja, U.S.S.R., 76,000 134 B4
Lier, Belg., 29,092 115 C3
Lierneux, Belg., 2,943 115 D4
Liesberg, Switz., 1,129 124 B1
Liesborn, F.R.Ger., 4,985 119 E1
Lieser Bach, r., F.R.Ger. 119 B4
Liesing, Aust. 124 c10
Liesing, Aust. 124 J7
Liesse, Fr., 1,677 117 E2
Liestal, Switz., 10,262 124 B1
Lieusaint, Fr. 116 i12
Liévin, Fr., 35,127 117 E1
Lièvre, R. du, Qué., Can. 44 J6
Liezen, Aust., 5,432 124 L6
Lifford, Ire. 113 C4
Liffré, Fr., 2,641 117 C2
Lifou, Î., Loy. Is. 174 k8
Lifton, U.K. 113 D6
Lifuka, i., Tonga 177 36
Ligao, Phil., 10,547 153 B2
Lightfoot, Va. 62 H5
Lighthorne, U.K. 114 F6
Lighthouse Pt., Fla. 65 E3
Lighthouse Pt., Mich. 67 H3
Lighthouse Reef, Br. Hond. 94 D2
Lignières, Fr. 117 E3
Lignite, N. Dak., 355 74 A1
Lignum, Va. 62 G4
Ligny-en-Barrois, Fr., 5,522 117 F2
Ligny-en-Cambrésis, Fr., 2,112 116 a7
Ligonier, Ind., 2,595 70 D1
Ligonier, Pa., 2,276 60 D5
Ligoúrion, Gr. 129 D6
Ligueil, Fr., 2,133 117 D3
Ligurian Sea, It., 123 B3
Liha, Niue 177 32
Lihir Group, is., Terr. New Guin. 174 g1
Li-hsien, Ho-p., China 151 B3
Li-hsien, Hu-n., China 152 D1
Li-hsien, S-ch., China 152 A1
Li-hsien, r., China 150 D5
Lihue, Hawaii, 3,908 84 B2
Lijeron, i., Jaluit 176 30
Lijeva Rijeka, Yug. 125 D3
Likely, Br. Col., Can. 42 G3
Likely, Calif. 82 C2
Likhoslavl', U.S.S.R., 10,000 136 D1
Likhovskoy, U.S.S.R., 16,600 136 g7
Likiep, atoll, Marsh. Is. 176 22
Likino-Dulevo, U.S.S.R., 24,600 136 c6
Likitobi, Indon. 149 H3
Likopua, i., Aitutaki 177 35
Likoto, D.R.Congo 164 D2
Likouala, r., Congo 164 B1
Liku, Niue 177 32
Likupang, Indon. 149 H2
Lilbourn, Mo., 1,216 72 H8
Lilburn, Ga., 753 64 h9
Lilenga, D.R.Congo 164 C1
l'Île-Rousse, Fr., 1,867 116 r17
Lilesville, N.C., 635 63 D3
Lilian Pt., Ocean I. 175 16
Lilienfeld, Aust., 3,304 124 M5
Li-ling, China 152 D2
Lilla Edet, Swed. 120 C4
Lillafüred, Hung. 126 E2
Lille, Fr., 199,033 117 E1
Lille Bælt, Den. 121 B5
Lillebonne, Fr., 7,870 117 D2
Lillehammer, Nor., 6,138 120 B3
Lillerød, Den., 3,815 121 a7
Lillesand, Nor., 1,041 120 B4
Lilleshall, U.K., 8,857 113 E5
Lilleström, Nor. 120 B4
Lillhärdal, Swed. 120 C3
Lillian, Tex. 76 e10
Lillie, La. 73 C5
Lillington, N.C., 1,242 63 F2
Lillinonah, L., Conn. 56 C6
Lillis, Kans. 75 J4
Lilliwaup, Wash. 80 B2
Lillkyrka, Swed. 120 e8
Lillo, Sp., 4,024 122 D3
Lillooet, Br. Col., Can., 1,313 42 G4
Lillooet, r., Br. Col., Can. 42 G4
Lillooet L., Br. Col., Can. 42 G4
Lilly, Fla. 65 H5
Lilly, Pa., 1,642 60 E5
Lilly Cache, Ill. 69 b10
Lilly Cache Cr., Ill. 69 b10
Liloan, Phil., 2,812 153 f11
Lilongwe, Malawi 164 E4
Liloy, Phil., 4,141 153 B3
Lily, Ky. 71 G4
Lily, S. Dak., 119 74 D3
Lily, Wis. 66 E3
Lilyache, Bulg., 2,596 128 D3
Lily Bay, Me. 55 C3
Lilydale, Austl. 173 e11
Lilydale, Minn., 116 74 c6
Lily Dale, N.Y. 58 B7
Lily Lake, Pa. 61 n17
Lim, r., Yug. 125 D3
Lima, Austl. 173 f11
Lima, Peru, 536,666 104 B5
Lima, Swed. 120 C3
Lima, Ill., 160 68 A3
Lima, Mich. 67 K6
Lima, Mont., 397 81 C3
Lima, N.Y., 1,366 58 E6
Lima, Ohio, 51,037 70 E2
Lima, Pa. 60 f12
Lima, P., P.R. 96 u10
Lima, r., Port. 122 A2
Lima Center, Wis. 66 E6
Limache, Chile, 14,488 104 f12
Li-ma Ch'ün-tao, arch., China 152 b7
Lima Duarte, Braz., 3,554 103 e17
Limafuafua, pt., Niue 177 32
Liman, G., Indon. 148 d7
Liman Kati, Malay., 2,132 147 o14
Limanowa, Pol., 4,914 127 D4
Limassol, Cyp., 36,536 142 C3
Limavady, U.K., 4,324 113 C4
Limay, Fr., 5,082 117 D2
Limay, Phil., 1,950 153 b8
Limay, r., Arg. 105 A6
Limay Mahuida, Arg., 1,900* 105 B5
Limbach, Bad.-Württ., F.R.Ger., 1,151 119 G6
Limbach, Saar., F.R.Ger., 2,205 116 c8
Limbach-Oberfrohna, Ger.D.R., 26,381 118 D3
Limbang, Malay., 1,961 148 E1
Limbaži, U.S.S.R., 6,000 136 B1
Limbé, Haiti, 3,488 96 k6
Limbourg, Belg., 3,941 119 A3
Limbung, Indon. 148 D3
Limburg, F.R.Ger., 15,535 118 B3
Limburgerhof, F.R.Ger., 5,079 119 E6
Lime, Colo. 79 C2
Lime, Oreg. 80 E3
Limehouse, Ont., Can. 46 c13
Limeil-Brévannes, Fr., 8,696 116 i12
Limeira, Braz., 45,256 103 G6
Limeport, Pa. 61 k18
Limerick, Sask., Can. 43 C5
Limerick, co., Ire., 137,881 113 B5
Limerick, Ire., 51,666 113 B5
Limerick, Me. 55 B5
Limerick, Pa. 60 e11
Lime Ridge, Wis., 152 66 C5
Lime Rock (part of Salisbury), Conn. 56 C5
Lime Springs, Iowa, 581 72 E1
Limestone, co., Ala., 36,513 64 C1
Limestone, Me., 1,772 55 E2
Limestone, N.Y., 539 58 C7
Limestone, co., Tex., 20,413 77 P4
Limestone, r., Man., Can. 43 G3
Limestone Butte, S. Dak. 74 A4
Lime Village, Alaska 85 F3
Limfjorden, chan., Den. 121 B4
Limhamn, Swed. 121 b7
Liminangoong, Phil., 1,253 153 A3
Limingen, l., Nor. 120 C2
Limington, Me. 55 B5
Liminka, Fin. 120 F2
Limmat, r., Switz. 125 ·
Limmen, Neth., 3,100 115 C2
Limmen Bight, Austl. 172 E2
Límni, Gr., 2,394 129 D5
Límnos, i., Gr. 129 E5
Limoeiro, Braz., 21,252 103 b14
Limoeiro do Norte, Braz., 5,705 103 J3
Limoges, Fr., 120,596 117 D4
Limoges-Fourches, Fr. 116 i12
Limón, C.R., 19,432 94 F5
Limón, Guat. 94 B3
Limón, Hond. 94 E3
Limon, Colo., 1,811 79 D2
Limona, Fla. 65 d12
Limonade, Haiti, 1,313 96 k6
Limones, P.R. 96 u10
Limonest, Fr., 1,658 116 p15
Limours, Fr., 2,048 116 g12
Limoux, Fr., 10,115 117 E5
Limousin, Monts du, Fr. 116 ·
Limpopo, r., Af. 164 D5
Limu, i., Tonga 177 36
Li-mu Ling, China 152 C4
Limuru, Kenya 165 h14
Lin, Alb. 125 E4
Lin, r., China 152 D2
Līnah, Saudi Ar. 143 C3
Lin-an, China 152 E1
Linapacan I., Phil. 153 A3
Linapacan Str., Phil. 153 A3
Linares, Chile, 27,568 105 A5
Linares, Mex., 13,318 93 F3
Linares, Sp., 60,068 122 D3
Linariá, Gr. 129 E5
Lin-ch'eng, Ho-p., China 151 B3
Lin-ch'eng, Shant., China 151 C4
Lin-ch'i, China 151 B4
Lin-chiang, China 150 G2
Lin-chin, China 151 A4
Lin-ch'ing, China 150 F3
Linchmere, U.K., 1,526 113 m12
Lincoln, Arg., 17,070* 105 C4
Lincoln, N.Z., 1,181 175 g6
Lincoln, U.K., 77,077 113 F5
Lincoln, co., Ark., 14,447 73 D4
Lincoln, Ark., 820 73 A2
Lincoln, Calif., 3,197 82 C3
Lincoln, co., Colo., 5,310 79 D2
Lincoln, co., Ga., 5,906 64 G2
Lincoln, co., Idaho, 3,686 81 B4
Lincoln, Ill., 16,890 68 C3
Lincoln, Ind. 70 C2
Lincoln, Iowa, 183 72 E2
Lincoln, co., Kans., 5,556 75 G4
Lincoln, Kans., 1,717 75 G4
Lincoln, co., Ky., 16,503 71 G4
Lincoln, parish, La., 28,535 73 C5
Lincoln, co., Me., 18,497 55 B4
Lincoln, Me., 3,616 55 D3
Lincoln, Mass., 5,613(T) 57 L3
Lincoln, Mich., 441 67 K4
Lincoln, co., Minn., 9,651 74 D3
Lincoln, co., Miss., 26,759 73 E6
Lincoln, co., Mo., 14,783 72 G5
Lincoln, Mo., 446 72 D6
Lincoln, co., Mont., 12,537 81 B1
Lincoln, Mont. 81 C2
Lincoln, co., Nebr., 28,491 75 E3
Lincoln, Nebr., 128,521 75 J3
Lincoln, co., Nev., 2,431 83 C4
Lincoln, N.H. 54 D3
Lincoln, co., N. Mex., 7,744 79 C5
Lincoln, N. Mex. 79 C5
Lincoln, N.Y. 58 o20
Lincoln, co., N.C., 28,814 63 C2
Lincoln, co., Okla., 18,783 76 G2
Lincoln, Okla. 76 D3
Lincoln, co., Oreg., 24,635 80 B3
Lincoln, co., S. Dak., 12,371 74 D4
Lincoln, co., Tenn., 23,829 71 E6
Lincoln, Vt. 54 A3
Lincoln, co., Wash., 10,919 80 D2
Lincoln, co., W. Va., 20,267 62 B4
Lincoln, co., Wis., 22,338 66 D3
Lincoln, co., Wyo., 9,018 81 D4
Lincoln, Mt., N.H. 54 D3
Lincoln Acres, Calif. 82 c10
Lincoln Center, Me. 55 D3
Lincoln City, Oreg. 80 A3
Lincoln Cr., Nebr. 75 H3
Lincoln Estates, Ill. 69 c10
Lincoln Heights, Hamilton co., Ohio, 71 i10
Lincoln Heights, Richland co., Ohio, 8,004 70 G2
Lincoln Hill, Pa. 60 a9
Lincoln Park, Colo., 2,085 79 C2
Lincoln Park, Mich., 53,933 67 K6
Lincoln Park, N.J., 6,048 61 C2
Lincoln Park, N.Y., 2,707 59 N8
Lincolnshire, co., U.K., 743,596 113 F5
Lincolnshire, Ill., 1,390 69 c8
Lincolnton, Ga., 1,450 64 G2
Lincolnton, N.C., 5,699 63 C2
Lincoln Valley, N. Dak. 74 B2
Lincoln Village, Calif. 82 C3
Lincolnville, Kans., 244 75 J5
Lincolnville, Me. 55 C4
Lincolnville, S.C., 420 63 D4
Lincolnville Center, Me. 55 C4
Lincolnwood, Ill., 11,744 69 d8
Lincolnwood Hills, Ill. 69 c10
L'Incudine, mtn., Fr. 116 r18
Lind, Wash., 697 80 D2
Linda, Calif., 6,129 82 C3
Lindale, U.K. 114 C2
Lindale, Ga., 2,635 64 D1
Lindale, Tex., 1,285 77 Q3
Lindau, F.R.Ger., 21,763 118 B5
Lindbrook, Alta., Can. 43 c7
Linde, r., U.S.S.R. 135 M3
Lindelfels, F.R.Ger., 1,968 119 F5
Linden, Ala., 2,516 64 B3
Linden, Calif. 82 C3
Linden, Ind., 619 70 C2
Linden, Iowa, 258 72 C3
Linden, Mich., 1,146 67 K6
Linden, N.J., 39,931 61 C2
Linden, N.Y. 58 D6
Linden, N.C., 157 63 F2
Linden, Tenn., 1,086 71 D6
Linden, Tex., 1,832 77 Q3
Linden, Wis., 418 66 C6
Lindenhafen Plantation, Terr. New Guin. 174 f2
Lindenhurst, Ill., 1,259 69 b7
Lindenhurst, N.Y., 20,905 59 O10
Lindenwold, N.J., 7,335 61 B4
Linderöd, Swed. 121 F5
Linderos, Chile, 1,401 104 g13
Lindesberg, Swed. 120 C4
Lindesnes, c., Nor. 120 A4
Lindford, Minn. 74 F1
Lindholm, F.R.Ger., 1,316 118 B1
Lindholmen, Swed. 120 f8
Lindi, Tanz., 10,315 164 F3
Lindi, r., D.R.Congo 164 D1
Lindis Pass, N.Z. 175 f7
Lindlar, F.R.Ger., 10,397 119 C2
Lindley, S. Af., 2,612 164 D6
Lindon, Colo. 79 D2
Lindon, Utah, 1,150 78 c10
Líndos, Gr. 129 G6
Lindow, Ger.D.R. 118 D2
Lindre, Ég. de, Fr. 116 c9
Lindridge, U.K. 114 D6
Lindrith, N. Mex. 79 B3
Lindsay, Ont., Can., 11,240 44 H7
Lindsay, Calif., 5,397 82 D4
Lindsay, Mont. 81 G2
Lindsay, Nebr., 218 75 H2
Lindsay, Okla., 4,258 76 F3
Lindsay, Tex., 236 77 P3
Lindsborg, Kans., 2,609 75 H5
Lindsey (admin. part of Lincolnshire), 505,427 113 F5
Lindsey, Ohio, 581 70 F1
Lindy, Nebr. 75 H1
Lineboro, Md. 62 H3
Line Cr., Ga. 64 f11
Line Is., Pac. Oc. 171 H4
Linescio, Switz. 124 C2
Linesville, Pa., 1,255 60 B2
Lineville, Ala., 1,612 64 D2
Lineville, Iowa, 452 72 D4
Lin-fen, China 150 E3
Linfield, Pa. 61 L5
Ling, r., China 152 F1
Lingayen, Phil., 8,221 153 B1
Lingayen G., Phil. 153 B1
Lingbo, Swed. 120 D3
Ling-ch'iu, China 151 B3
Ling-ch'uan, K-hsi, China 152 C2
Ling-ch'uan, Shan-hsi, China 151 B4
Linge, r., Neth. 115 D3
Lingen, F.R.Ger., 22,763 118 A2
Lingfield, U.K., 6,871 114 H8
Lingga, Kep., Indon. 148 C3
Lingga, P., Indon. 148 C3
Ling-hsien, China 152 D2
Lingig, Phil., 1,566 153 C3
Lingle, Wyo., 437 81 G4
Ling-ling, China 152 C2
Ling-lo, China 152 B2
Ling-nan, China 151 C2
Lingō, China 144 f11
Lingo, N. Mex. 79 D5
Lingolsheim, Fr., 7,738 116 e9
Ling-pao, China 151 A4
Ling-pi, China 151 C4
Ling-shan, China 152 C3
Lingshi Dzong, Bhutan 144 g12
Ling-shih, China 151 A3
Ling-shou, China 151 B3
Ling-shui, China 152 C4
Linguère, Sen., 2,516 162 B3
Ling-yüan, China 151 C2
Linh, Ngoc, pk., S. Viet. 146 D4
Lin-hai, China 150 G4
Linhares, Braz., 5,751 103 J5
Linh Cam, N. Viet. 146 D3
Lin-ho, China 151 A2
Linhouse Water, r., U.K. 112 d8
Lin-hsi, China 151 C2
Lin-hsia, China 150 D3
Lin-hsiang, China 152 D1
Lin-hsien, Ho-n., China 151 B4
Lin-hsien, Shan-hsi, China 151 A3
Linh Son, N. Viet. 147 i8
Lin-i, Shan-hsi, China 151 A4
Lin-i, Shant., China 151 C4
Lin-ju, China 151 B4
Lin-kao, China 152 C4
Linkenheim, F.R.Ger., 3,476 119 E6
Linköping, Swed., 65,237 120 C4
Lin-k'ou, China 151 F1
Linkville, Ind. 70 C1
Lin-li, China 152 C1
Linlithgow, U.K., 4,327 112 c8
Linn, Ill. 68 E5
Linn, co., Iowa, 136,899 72 F2
Linn, co., Kans., 8,274 75 L5
Linn, Kans., 466 75 H4
Linn, co., Mo., 16,815 72 D5
Linn, Mo., 1,050 72 F6
Linn, co., Oreg., 58,867 80 B3
Linn, Tex. 77 O6
Linnaeus, Mt., Utah 78 D3
Linn Creek, Mo., 174 72 E6
Linndale, Ohio, 381 70 d9
Linneus, Me. 55 E2
Linneus, Mo., 471 72 D5
Linney Head, U.K. 113 D6
Linn Grove, Ind. 70 E2
Linn Grove, Iowa, 330 72 B2
Linnhe, Loch, U.K. 112 D3
Linnich, F.R.Ger., 3,603 119 A3
Linnsburg, Ind. 70 C2
Linntown, Pa., 1,628 60 H4
Linosa, Isola di, It. 123 D7
Lin-pien, Taiwan 152 F3
Lins, Braz., 32,204 103 G6
Linschoten, Neth. 115 b6
Linselles, Fr., 5,572 116 a6
Linsia = Lin-hsia
Linslade, U.K., 4,139 114 G7
Linstead, Jam., 3,781 96 p8
Lin-t'an, China 150 D3
Lin-t'ao, China 150 D3
Linté, Cam. 162 F5
Linthal, Switz., 2,645 124 C2
Linthicum, Md. 62 c8
Lin-tien, China 151 E1
Lintlaw, Sask., Can. 43 D4
Linton, Cambs., Eng., U.K., 1,982 114 J6
Linton, Derby., Eng., U.K., 1,958 114 E5
Linton, Herefs., Eng., U.K. 114 C7
Linton, Ind., 5,736 70 B3
Linton, Ky. 71 D5
Linton, N. Dak., 1,826 74 B2
Lintorf, F.R.Ger., 7,240 119 B2
Lin-ts'ang, China 150 D5
Linville, La. 73 C5
Linville, N.C. 63 C1
Linville, Va. 62 F4
Linville, r., N.C. 71 K6
Linville Falls, N.C. 63 C2
Linwood, Ont., Can. 46 a13
Linwood, Ala. 64 D4
Linwood, Ark. 73 D3
Linwood, Ga., 760 64 D1
Linwood (part of Northbridge and Uxbridge), Mass 57 K4
Linwood, Mich. 67 K5
Linwood, N.J., 3,847 61 B5
Linwood, N.C. 63 D2
Linwood, Pa., 4,500* 60 f12
Linwood, Utah 78 D1
Linwood, Wis. 66 d12
Lin-wu, China 152 D2
Lin-ying, China 151 B4
Lin-yu, China 151 A4
Linz, Aust., 196,206 124 L5
Linz, F.R.Ger., 6,169 119 C3
Lion, G. du, Fr. 117 E5
Lionel Town, Jam., 2,664 96 p9
Lion Pk., Utah 78 B2
Lion's Head, Ont., Can. 44 G6
Lionville, Pa. 60 e11
Lioppa, Indon. 149 H4
Liouesso, Congo B. 164 B1
Lipa, Phil., 12,521 153 B2
Lipan, Tex., 309 77 O3
Lipari, Isola, It. 123 E5
Lipenská Nádrž, res., Czech. 126 A2
Liperi, Fin. 120 G3
Lipetsk, U.S.S.R., 183,000 134 C4
Lipiany, Pol., 4,389 127 A2
Lipin Bor, U.S.S.R. 136 E1
Li-p'ing, China 150 E4
Lipki, U.S.S.R., 19,500 136 E2
Lipno, Pol., 10,202 127 C2
Li-po, China 150 E4
Lipova, Rum., 10,064 128 C1
Lipovăţ, Rum. 128 F1
Lipowa, Pol. 127 g6
Lippborg, F.R.Ger., 2,701 119 E1
Lippe, r., F.R.Ger. 118 A3
Lipperode, F.R.Ger., 2,194 119 E1
Lippstadt, F.R.Ger., 34,414 118 B3
Lipscomb, Ala., 2,811 64 c8
Lipscomb, co., Tex., 3,406 76 N1
Lipscomb, Tex. 76 N1
Lipsko, Pol., 2,090 127 D3
Lipsós, i., Gr. 129 F6
Lipton, Sask., Can. 43 D5
Liptovský Mikuláš, Czech., 12,553 126 D2
Liptrap, C., Austl. 173 e12
Li-p'u, China 152 C2
Lipulek La, China-India 150 B4
Lira, Uganda, 2,929 164 E1
Lircay, Peru, 2,019 104 C5
Liria, Sp., 9,723 122 E3
Lirik, Indon. 148 B3
Lisabata, Indon. 149 J3
Lisala, D.R.Congo 164 C1
Lišany, Czech. 126 c6
Lisboa, Port., 802,230 122 A3
Lisbon, Port. = Lisboa
Lisbon, Ill., 234 68 D2
Lisbon, Ind. 70 D1
Lisbon, Iowa, 1,227 72 F3
Lisbon, La., 229 73 C5
Lisbon, Me., 1,542 55 B4
Lisbon, Md. 62 a7
Lisbon, N.H., 1,220 54 D3
Lisbon, N.Y. 59 K2
Lisbon, N. Dak., 2,093 74 D2
Lisbon, Ohio, 3,579 70 J2
Lisbon Falls, Me., 2,640 55 B4
Lisburn, U.K., 17,691 113 D4
Lisburne, C., New Hebr. 174 k5
Lisburne, C., Alaska 85 C1
Liscannor B., Ire. 113 B5
Lisco, Nebr. 75 C2
Liscomb, N.S., Can. 47 U11
Liscomb, Iowa, 295 72 E2
Lisdoonvarna, Ire. 113 B5
Li-shih, China 151 A3
Li-shu-chen, China 151 F1
Li-shui, Ch-ch., China 150 G4
Li-shui, Chiang-su, China 152 E1
Li-shui, Ch-l., China 151 E2
Lisianski I., Hawaii 84 f9
Lisichansk, U.S.S.R., 37,800 136 E3
Lisieux, Fr., 22,472 117 D2
Liskeard, U.K., 4,492 113 D6
Liski, U.S.S.R., 35,000 136 E3
Lisle, Ont., Can. 46 E4
L'Isle, Switz. 124 A2
Lisle, Ill., 5,037 69 b9
Lisle, N.Y., 335 59 H7
l'Isle-Adam, Fr., 5,915 116 g10
l'Isle-Jourdain, Fr., 1,251 117 D3
l'Isle-Jourdain, Fr., 3,683 117 D5
l'Isle-sur-la-Sorgue, Fr., 9,199 117 F5
Lisle-sur-Tarn, Fr., 3,308 117 D5
L'Islet, Qué., Can. 47 O1
L'Isletville, Qué., Can., 1,135 45 L6
L'Isle-Verte, Qué., Can., 1,485 47 R9
Lisman, Ala., 909 64 A3
Lismore, Austl., 17,372 173 H4
Lismore, Ire. 113 C5
Lismore I., U.K. 112 D3
Lisnaskea, U.K. 113 C4
Lišov, Czech. 126 B2
Liss, U.K., 3,283 113 m12
Lisse, Neth., 10,900 115 b6
Lisses, Fr. 116 h12
Lissone, It., 22,867 122 c5
List, F.R.Ger., 2,582 118 B1
Lister, r., F.R.Ger. 119 D2
Listowel, Ont., Can., 3,951 46 D5
Listowel, Ire., 3,144 113 B5
Listvyanka, U.S.S.R., 2,700 135 K4
Liswarta, r., Pol. 127 h5
Lisyanskogo, P-ov., U.S.S.R. 135 O4
Lit, Swed. 120 C3
Li-t'ang, K-hsi, China 152 C3
Li-t'ang, S-ch., China 150 D4
Li-t'ang, r., China 152 A2
Līţānī, r., Leb. 142 C3
Litani, r., Sur. 101 N6
Litava, r., Czech. 126 d7
Litchfield, Calif. 82 C2
Litchfield, co., Conn., 119,856 56 C5
Litchfield, Conn., 1,363; 6,264(T) 56 D5
Litchfield, Ill., 7,330 68 C4
Litchfield, Me. 55 B4
Litchfield, Mich., 993 67 J6
Litchfield, Minn., 5,078 74 E3
Litchfield, Nebr., 264 75 F2
Litchfield, N.H. 54 E6
Litchfield, Ohio 70 H1
Litchfield Beach, S.C. 63 E4
Litchfield Park, Ariz. 78 B5
Litchville, N. Dak., 345 74 C2
Literberry, Ill. 68 B4
Lith, Neth. 115 D3
Litherland, U.K., 24,872 114 B4
Lithgow, Austl., 15,128 173 g9
Lithia, Fla. 65 d12
Lithia (part of Goshen), Mass. 56 E3
Lithia Springs, Ga. 64 f9
Lithinon, Ákra, Gr. 129 E7
Lithium, Mo., 54 72 H7
Lithonia, Ga., 1,667 64 E2
Lithuanian S.S.R. = Litovskaya S.S.R.
Lititz, Pa., 5,987 61 K5
Litke, Proliv, U.S.S.R. 133 Q4
Litókhoron, Gr., 5,032 129 D4
Litoměřice, Czech., 16,938 126 B1
Litomyšl, Czech. 127 f7
Litovel, Czech. 126 C2
Litovko, U.S.S.R., 8,400 135 N5
Litovskaya S.S.R., U.S.S.R., 2,950,000* 134 B4
Litschau, Aust., 1,735 124 L5
Little, Okla. 76 G2
Little, r., N.B., Can. 55 E1
Little, r., Ala. 64 D1
Little, r., Ark.-Okla. 73 A4
Little, r., Conn. 56 H6
Little, r., Ga. 64 F4
Little, r., Ga. 64 G2
Little, r., Ky. 71 D5
Little, r., Me. 54 F5
Little, r., Mass. 56 E4
Little, r., Mo. 72 H8
Little, r., N.C. 63 E2
Little, r., Okla. 76 F2
Little, r., Okla. 76 J4
Little, r., Tex. 77 P4
Little, r., Va. 62 D6
Little Abaco I., Bah. Is. 95 C1
Little Abitibi, r., Ont., Can. 44 G5
Little America, Ant. 180 W5
Little Andaman, i., India 146 A5
Little Auglaize, r., Ohio 70 E2
Little Bahama Bank, Bah. Is. 95 C1
Little Barrier I., N.Z. 175 g5
Little Bay, Bah. Is. 95 b7
Little Bay de Noc, Mich. 66 G3
Little Belt Mts., Mont. 81 D2
Little Big Horn, r., Mont.-Wyo. 81 F3
Little Birch, W. Va. 62 D4
Little Black, r., Alaska 85 J2
Little Black, r., Me. 55 C1
Little Blue, r., Kans.-Nebr. 75 H3
Little Boars Head, N.H. 54 F6
Littleborough, U.K., 10,514 114 D3
Little Bow, r., Alta., Can. 42 K4
Little Britain, Ont., Can. 46 F4
Little Buffalo, r., Alta.-N.W.T. 42 K1
Little Cahaba, r., Ala. 64 d7
Little Calumet, r., Ill.-Ind. 69 e10
Little Canada, Minn., 3,512 74 c5
Little Cayman, i., Lesser Caymans 97 2
Little Cedar, r., Mich. 66 F3
Little Chena, r., Alaska 85 b6
Little Chicago, Wis. 66 D3
Little Chief, Okla. 76 G1
Little Churchill, r., Man., Can. 43 G2
Little Chute, Wis., 5,099 66 E4
Little City (part of Haddam), Conn. 56 F7
Little City, Okla., 102 76 G3
Little Coal, r., W. Va. 62 C4
Little Colorado, r., Ariz. 78 C4
Little Compton, R.I., 1,702(T) 57 M6
Little Cottonwood, r., Minn. 74 E3
Little Creek, Del., 306 62 J3
Little Current, Ont., Can., 1,479 44 G6
Little Current, r., Ont., Can. 44 F5
Little Diomede I., Alaska 85 B2
Little Dry Cr., Mont. 81 F2
Little Eagle, S. Dak. 74 B3
Little Egg Harbor, N.J. 61 C4
Little Egg Inlet, N.J. 61 C5
Little Elm, Tex. 76 f8
Little Exuma, i., Bah. Is. 95 C2
Little Falls, Minn., 7,551 74 E3
Little Falls, N.J., 9,730(T) 58 c13
Little Falls, N.Y., 8,935 59 L5
Littlefield, Ariz. 78 B3
Littlefield, Tex., 7,236 77 M3
Littlefork, Minn., 805 74 F1
Little Fork, r., Minn. 74 F1
Little Grand Rapids, Man., Can. 43 G4

254 · Longueuil—Lumpkin

Longueuil, Qué., Can., 24,131 47 p17
Longuro, Indon. 148 E2
Longuyon, Fr., 8,341 117 F2
Longvale, Calif. 82 B3
Long Valley, N.J., 1,220 61 B2
Longvalley, S. Dak. 74 B4
Longview, Colo. 79 b9
Longview, Ill., 270 68 D4
Longview, Miss. 73 G4
Longview, N.C., 2,997 63 C2
Longview, Tex., 40,050 77 Q3
Longview, Wash., 23,349 80 B2
Longville, La. 73 B7
Longville, Minn., 159 74 E2
Longvilliers, Fr. 116 f12
Longwai, Indon. 148 F2
Longwood, Fla., 1,689 65 H4
Longwood, N.C. 63 F3
Longwood, Wis. 66 C4
Longworth, Br. Col., Can. 42 G3
Longwy, Fr., 22,214 117 F2
Long Xuyen, S. Viet., 25,665 146 D5
Longyearbyen, Nor. 134 A2
Lonigo, It., 12,172 122 e5
Lo-ning, China 151 A4
Löningen, F.R.Ger., 9,154 118 A2
Lonja, r., Yug. 125 C2
Lonkin, Burma 146 B1
Lonnewitz, Ger.D.R. 126 c5
Lonoke, co., Ark., 24,551 73 D3
Lonoke, Ark., 2,856 73 C3
Lonquen, r., Chile 104 e16
Lonsdale, Ark., 95 73 C3
Lons-le-Saunier, Fr., 18,757 117 F3
Lontué, Chile, 1,115 104 f15
Lo-oc, Phil., 2,093 153 e12
Looe, U.K., 3,883 113 D6
Loogootee, Ill. 68 D5
Loogootee, Ind., 2,858 70 B4
Lookeba, Okla., 158 76 E2
Looking Glass, r., Mich. 67 J6
Lookout, Calif. 82 C2
Lookout, Okla. 76 D1
Lookout, W. Va. 62 C4
Lookout, C., Ont., Can. 44 G3
Lookout, C., N.C. 63 H3
Lookout, Pt., Mich. 67 K4
Lookout Mountain, Tenn., 1,817 71 F7
Lookout Mtn., Ala.-Ga.-Tenn. 64 D1
Lookout Mtn., Alaska 85 E3
Lookout Mtn., N. Dak. 74 C2
Lookout Mtn., N. Mex. 79 A4
Lookout Mtn., Oreg. 80 C3
Lookout Pass, Idaho-Mont. 81 B2
Lookout Pk., Utah 78 C2
Looma, Alta., Can. 43 b7
Loomis, Calif. 82 b7
Loomis, Mich. 67 J5
Loomis, Nebr., 299 75 F3
Loomis, Wash. 80 D1
Loomis L., Ind. 69 f10
Loon, r., Man., Can. 43 E3
Loon Lake, Sask., Can. 43 B4
Loon Lake, Ill. 69 b7
Loon Lake, Me. 55 B3
Loon Lake, N.Y. 59 M2
Loon Lake, Wash. 80 E1
Loon L., Me. 55 C2
Loon Lake Mts., N.Y. 59 M2
Loon op Zand, Neth., 3,000 115 c7
Loon Straits, Man., Can. 43 F4
Loop Head, Ire. 113 A5
Loorana, Austl. 173 d12
Loos, Fr., 18,885 116 a6
Loosdrechtsche Plassen, l., Neth. 115 C2
Loosduinen, Neth. 115 C2
Lopatica, Yug. 125 E4
Lopatin, U.S.S.R. 137 c1
Lopatka, M., U.S.S.R. 135 P4
Lopatka, P-ov., U.S.S.R. 135 P2
Lop Buri, Thai., 21,232 146 C4
Lo-pei, China, 4,000* 150 H2
Lopevi, i., New Hebr. 174 m6
Lopez, Pa. 61 K3
Lopik, Neth. 115 b7
Lo-p'ing, Ch-hsi, China 152 E1
Lo-p'ing, Y-n., China 152 B2
Lop Nor, China 150 C2
Lopori, r., D.R.Congo 164 C1
Loppa, Nor. 120 E1
Loppersum, Neth. 115 E1
Loppington, U.K. 114 C5
Lo-p'u, China 150 B3
Lopud, i., Yug. 125 C3
Łopuszno, Pol. 127 D3
Lora, Chile 104 e15
Lora, r., Afghan. 144 C2
Lora del Río, Sp., 20,914 122 C4
Lorado, W. Va. 62 C5
Lorain, co., Ohio, 217,500 70 G1
Lorain, Ohio, 68,932 70 G1
Loraine, Ill., 303 68 A3
Loraine, N. Dak., 54 74 B1
Loraine, Tex., 837 77 N3
Loraine, Wis. 66 A3
Loralai, Pak., 5,519 144 C3
Loran, Ill. 68 C1
Lorane, Ind. 70 D1
Lorane, Oreg. 80 B4
Loray, Nev. 83 C2
Loray, N.C. 63 C2
Lorca, Sp., 58,641 122 E4
Lorch, Bad.-Württ., F.R.Ger., 5,463 119 H7
Lorch, Hess., F.R.Ger., 2,916 118 A3
Lord Howe I., Austl. 170 E7
Lord Howe I., Sta. Cruz Is. 175 6
Lord Howe Rise, Pac. Oc. 169 F3
Lord Loughborough I., Burma 146 B5
Lord Mayor Bay, N.W.T., Can. 40 L4
Lordsburg, N. Mex., 3,436 79 A5
Lordship (part of Stratford), Conn. 56 D8
Loreburn, Sask., Can. 43 C4
Lore City, Ohio, 458 70 H3
Lorena, Braz., 26,068 103 d18
Lorengau, Terr. New Guin. 174 e1
Lorentz, W. Va. 62 D3
Lorentzweiler, Lux. 115 E5
Lorenzo, Nebr. 75 B2
Lorenzo, Tex., 1,188 77 N3
Loreo, It., 5,339 122 f5
Loreto, Braz. 103 G3
Loreto, It., 8,862 123 D3
Loreto, Baja Calif., Mex., 1,409 92 C2
Loreto, Zac., Mex., 4,969 92 E3
Loreto, Para., 1,315 105 D2
Loreto, Phil., 2,466 153 C3
Loretta, Wis. 66 C3
Lorette, Man., Can. 43 h10
Loretteville, Qué., Can., 6,420 47 n16
Loretto, Ky. 71 F4
Loretto, Mich. 66 F3
Loretto, Nebr. 75 G2
Loretto, Pa., 1,338 60 E4
Loretto, Tenn., 929 71 D6
Lorian Swamp, Kenya 164 F1
Lorica, Col. 100 C3
Lorida, Fla. 65 H5
Lorient, Fr., 63,924 116 B3
L'Orignal, Ont., Can., 1,154 47 K3
Lorimor, Iowa, 460 72 D3
Lőrinci, Hung., 11,172 126 D3
Loring, Mont. 81 F1
Loris, S.C., 1,702 63 F3
Lormes, Fr., 1,691 117 E3
Lorn, Firth of, U.K. 112 D3
Lorne, Austl. 173 e12
Lorne Park, Ont., Can. 46 c13
Lorneville, Ont., Can. 46 F4
Lorquin, Fr., 2,201 116 d9
Lörrach, F.R.Ger., 27,378 118 A5
Lorraine, reg., Fr. 117 F2
Lorraine, Kans., 157 75 G5
Lorraine, N.Y. 59 J4
Lorsch, F.R.Ger., 8,352 119 F5
Lorscheid, F.R.Ger. 119 C3
Lorton, Nebr., 58 75 K3
Los, Swed. 120 C3
Los Alamitos, Calif., 8,197 83 h16
Los Alamos, Calif. 82 C5
Los Alamos, co., N. Mex., 13,037 79 B4
Los Alamos, N. Mex., 12,584 79 B4
Los Alerces, Pq. Nac., Arg. 105 A6
Los Altos, Calif., 19,696 83 e13
Los Altos Hills, Calif., 3,412 83 e13
Los Amates, Guat., 1,016 94 C3
Los Andes, Chile, 20,448 104 g12
Los Angeles, Chile, 35,511 105 A5
Los Angeles, co., Calif., 6,038,771 82 D5
Los Angeles, Calif., 2,479,015 82 D5
Los Angeles, r., Calif. 83 g15
Losantville, Ind., 868 70 D2
Losap, atoll, Car. Is. 176 18
Los Arabos, Cuba, 1,690 96 c1
Los Arcos, Sp., 1,901 122 n12
Losari, Indon. 148 c7
Los Baños, Phil. 153 c8
Los Banos, Calif., 5,272 82 C4
Los Caracas, Ven. 101 c11
Los Cerritos, Guat. 94 c10
Los Chiles, C.R. 94 E5
Los Colorines, Mex., 4,362 93 d10
Losenstein, Aust., 1,709 124 L6
Los Fresnos, Tex., 1,289 77 P6
Los Gatos, Calif., 9,036 82 C4
Los Glaciares, Pq. Nac., Arg. 105 A8
Los Guayabitos, Ven. 101 c11
Los Guayos, Ven. 101 H2
Lo-shan, Ho-n., China 152 D1
Lo-shan, S-ch., China 152 A1
Losheim, F.R.Ger., 3,485 116 c8
Los Hermanos, Is., Ven. 101 H2
Los Herreras, Mex., 1,846 93 F3
Los Huesos, A. de, Arg. 105 b13
Łosice, Pol., 3,290 127 E2
Łosina, Pol. 127 g5
Lošinj, i., Yug. 125 B2
Los Lagos, Chile, 3,897 105 e14
Los Llanos, Dom. Rep., 1,009 96 n6
Los Lunas, N. Mex., 1,186 79 B4
Los Menucos, Arg., 1,200* 105 B6
Los Mochis, Mex., 37,682 92 C3
Los Molinos, Calif. 82 C2
Los Muermos, Chile, 1,616 105 e15
Los Navalmorales, Sp., 4,686 122 C3
Los Negros, i., Terr. New Guin. 174 e1
Los Negros, r., Cuba 96 d2
Løsning, Den., 1,703 121 B5
Los Novillos, Urug. 105 d11
Los Olivos, Calif. 82 C5
Los Osos, Calif. 82 C5
Los Palacios, Cuba, 5,250 96 b1
Los Palacios, r., Cuba 96 b1
Los Palacios y Villafranca, Sp., 12,524 122 B4
Los Palos, Cuba, 4,042 96 c1
Los Pechos, mtn., Can. Is. 109 4
Los Pinos, r., Colo. 79 B3
Los Reyes, Méx., Mex., 2,077 93 e10
Los Reyes, Micho., Mex., 9,777 93 b10
Los Roques, Is., Ven. 100 G2
Los Rulos, Chile 104 f13
Los Santos, Pan., 3,165 94 G7
Los Santos de Maimona, Sp., 9,565 122 B3
Losser, Neth., 6,600 115 E2
Los Serranos, Calif. 83 i16
Lossiemouth, U.K. 112 E3
Lössnitz, Ger.D.R. 126 b6
Lost, r., W. Va. 62 F4
Lostallo, Switz. 124 D2
Lostant, Ill., 460 68 D2
Lost Cabin, Wyo., 47 81 F4
Lost Chance Cr., Utah 78 C2
Lost City, W. Va. 62 F4
Lost Creek, Ky. 71 H4
Lost Creek, W. Va., 678 62 D3
Lost Cr., Ala. 64 a7
Los Teques, Ven., 34,874 100 G2
Los Testigos, Is., Ven. 101 J2
Lost Hills, Calif. 82 D5
Lostine, Oreg., 240 80 E3
Lost L., Minn. 74 E1
Lost Land L., Wis. 66 B2
Lost Nation, Iowa, 567 72 G3
Lostock Gralam, U.K., 1,522 114 D4
Los Toldos, Arg., 12,650* 105 a12
Los Torres, Nic. 94 E4
Lost River, Alaska 85 C2
Lost River, Idaho, 58 81 C4
Lost Springs, Wyo., 5 81 G4
Lost Trail Pass, Idaho-Mont. 81 B3
Lostwood, N. Dak. 74 A1
Losuia, Terr. Papua 174 f3
Los Vilos, Chile, 3,027 105 A4
Los Yébenes, Sp., 6,830 122 C3
Lot, Ponape 176 29
Löt, Swed. 120 e8
Lot, r., Fr. 117 D4
Lota, Chile, 27,739 104 e17
Lotak, Indon. 148 F3
Lotbinière, Qué., Can. 47 N2
Lothian, Md. 62 c9
Lo-tien, China 152 B2
Lo-t'ien, China 152 D1
Lo-ting, China 152 C3
Lo-t'ing, China 151 C3
Lotofaga, W. Samoa 177 38
Lotoshino, U.S.S.R. 136 a5
Lott, Tex., 924 77 P4
Lottaville, Ind. 69 e10
Lottin, Port, Kusaie 176 31
Lottsburg, Va. 62 H5
Lotts Cr., Ga. 64 H3
Lo-tu, China 150 D3
Lo-tung, China 152 C4
Lo-tung, Taiwan, 34,990 152 F2
Lotus L., Minn. 74 a6
Lo-tz'u, China 152 A2
Loučná, r., Czech. 127 f7
Loudéac, Fr., 6,582 116 B2
Loudima, Congo 164 B2
Loudon, N.H. 54 D5
Loudon, Ohio 70 F3
Loudon, co., Tenn., 23,757 71 G6
Loudon, Tenn., 3,812 71 G6
Loudonville, N.Y. 59 v29
Loudonville, Ohio, 2,611 70 G2
Loudoun, co., Va., 24,549 62 G3
Loudrefing, Fr. 116 c9
Loudun, Fr., 6,004 117 C3
Loudville (part of Westhampton and Northampton), Mass. 56 F3
Loué, Fr., 1,765 117 C2
Louga, Sen., 15,446 162 B3
Loughborough, U.K., 38,638 113 F5
Loughborough L., Ont., Can. 47 H4
Lougheed, Alta., Can. 42 K3
Lougheed I., N.W.T., Can. 41 H2
Loughman, Fla. 65 H4
Loughrea, Ire., 2,834 113 B5
Loughton, U.K., 33,864 114 J7
Louhans, Fr., 4,398 117 F3
Louin, Miss., 389 73 F5
Louis, Okla. 76 D3
Louisa, co., Iowa, 10,290 72 F3
Louisa, Ky., 2,071 71 J3
Louisa, La. 73 D8
Louisa, co., Va., 12,959 62 F5
Louisa, Va., 576 62 F4
Louisburg, N.S., Can., 1,417 45 P6
Louisburg, Kans., 862 75 L5
Louisburg, Mo. 72 D7
Louisburg, N.C., 2,862 63 F1
Louisburgh, Ire. 113 B5
Louise, Miss., 481 73 E5
Louise, Tex. 77 P5
Louise I., Br. Col., Can. 42 D3
Louiseville, Qué., Can., 4,110 47 L2
Louisiade Arch., Terr. Papua 170 E5
Louisiana, st., U.S., 3,560,000* 73
Louisiana, Mo., 4,286 72 F5
Louis Trichardt, S. Af., 9,703 164 D5
Louisville, Ala., 890 64 D4
Louisville, Colo., 2,073 79 b8
Louisville, Ga., 2,413 64 G3
Louisville, Ill., 906 68 D5
Louisville, Kans., 204 75 J4
Louisville, Ky., 390,639 71 E3
Louisville, Miss., 5,066 73 G4
Louisville, Nebr., 1,194 75 J2
Louisville, Ohio, 5,116 70 H2
Louka, Czech. 126 b6
Louká, Gr., 1,186 129 D6
Loulé, Port., 16,152 122 A4
Louny, Czech., 12,123 126 A1
Loup, co., Nebr., 1,097 75 F2
Loup, r., Fr. 116 n13
Loup, r., Nebr. 75 H2
Loup, R. du, Qué., Can. 47 L2
Loup City, Nebr., 1,415 75 G2
Loups, L. des, Qué., Can. 46 F1
Lourches, Fr., 5,743 116 a7
l'Ourcq, Can. de, Fr. 116 i11
Lourdes, Fr., 16,376 117 C5
Lourenço, Braz. 103 F1
Lourenço Marques, Moz., 78,530 164 E6
Loures, Port., 7,623 122 i10
Loures, R. de, Port. 122 i10
Lourinhã, Port., 8,677 122 A3
l'Ours, Pic de, Fr. 116 m14
Lourtier, Switz. 124 B2
Lousã, Port., 8,191 122 A2
Lousa, Port., 2,439 122 i10
Lou-shan, China 151 F1
Louth, Austl. 173 F4
Louth, co., Ire., 69,194 113 C5
Louth, Ire. 113 C5
Louth, U.K., 11,564 113 G5
Louth Bay, Austl. 172 b8
Loutrá Aidhipsoú, Gr., 1,859 129 D5
Loutráki, Gr., 4,987 129 D6
Lou-ts'un, China 152 a6
Louvain=Leuven
Louvale, Ga. 64 E3
Louveciennes, Fr., 4,262 116 g11
Louviers, Fr., 13,668 117 D2
Louviers, Colo. 79 C2
Louvres, Fr., 2,394 116 i10
Lo Valdivia, Chile 104 e14
Lövånger, Swed. 120 E2
Lovat', r., U.S.S.R. 136 C1
Lovćen, mt., Yug. 125 D3
Lovćenac, Yug. 125 D2
Love, Sask., Can. 43 D4
Love, co., Okla., 5,862 76 F4
Lovea, Camb. 146 C4
Lovech, Bulg., 17,901 128 E3
Lovedale, Okla. 76 D1
Lovejoy, Ga., 191 64 g11
Lovelace, Tex. 76 e10
Lovelady, Tex., 466 77 Q4
Loveland, Colo., 9,734 79 C1
Loveland, Ohio, 5,008 70 E3
Loveland, Okla., 90 76 E3
Loveland Pass, Colo. 79 ·
Lovell, Me. 55 B4
Lovell, Ohio 70 F2
Lovell, Okla., 27 76 F1
Lovell, Wyo., 2,451 81 E3
Lovells, Mich. 67 J4
Lovelock, Nev., 1,948 83 A2
Lövenich, F.R.Ger., 3,147 119 A2
Lövenich, F.R.Ger., 17,063 119 B3
Lovering, L., Qué., Can. 54 C1
Loves Park, Ill., 10,880 68 C1
Lövestad, Swed. 121 F5
Lovettsville, Va., 217 62 G3
Lovewell, Kans. 75 H4
Lovewell Mtn., N.H. 54 C5
Lovewell Pd., Me. 54 F4
Lovewell Res., Kans. 75 G4
Lovick, Ala. 64 d7
Lovilia, Iowa, 630 72 D3
Loving, N. Mex., 1,646 79 C5
Loving, co., Tex., 226 77 M4
Lovingston, Va. 62 F5
Lovington, Ill., 1,200 68 D4
Lovington, N. Mex., 9,660 79 D5
Lovios, Sp., 5,064 122 A2
Lovisa, Fin., 6,564 120 F3
Lovns Bredning, Den. 121 B4
Lovosice, Czech. 126 c6
Lovran, Yug., 2,419 125 B2
Lovreć, Yug. 125 C3
Lovrin, Rum. 128 C2
Low, Qué., Can. 47 J3
Lowa, D.R.Congo 164 D2
Lowa, r., D.R.Congo 164 D2
Low Bush River, Ont., Can. 44 H5
Lowden, Iowa, 641 72 F3
Lowe, Kans. 75 E5
Lowe Farm, Man., Can. 43 g10
Lowell, Ark., 277 73 A1
Lowell, Fla. 65 G3
Lowell, Idaho 81 B2
Lowell, Ind., 2,270 70 B1
Lowell, Me. 55 D3
Lowell, Mass., 92,107 57 L2
Lowell, Mich., 2,545 67 H6
Lowell, Nebr. 75 G3
Lowell, N.Y. 59 t26
Lowell, N.C., 2,784 63 C2
Lowell, Ohio, 783 70 H3
Lowell, Oreg., 503 80 B4
Lowell, Vt. 54 C2
Lowell, Wis., 341 66 E5
Lowell, L., Idaho 80 E4
Lowellville, Ohio, 2,055 70 J1
Löwenstein, F.R.Ger., 1,526 119 G6
Lower Arrow L., Br. Col., Can. 42 H4
Lower Bartlett, N.H. 54 E3
Lower Brule, S. Dak. 74 C3
Lower Cabot, Vt. 54 C3
Lower Crab Cr., Wash. 80 D2
Lower Hutt, N.Z., 53,044 175 g6
Lower Island Cove., Newf., Can. 45 c10
Lower Kalskag, Alaska, 122 85 D3
Lower Klamath L., Calif. 82 C1
Lower Laberge, Yukon, Can. 40 C5
Lower Lake, Calif. 82 B3
Lower L., Calif. 82 C2
Lower Lough Erne, U.K. 113 C4
Lower Matecumbe Key, Fla. 65 h15
Lower Neguac, N.B., Can. 47 T10
Lower N.Y. Bay 58 c14
Lower Paia, Hawaii, 925 84 E3
Lower Peach Tree, Ala. 64 B4
Lower Post, Br. Col., Can. 42 E1
Lower Red L., Minn. 74 E1
Lower Rice L., Minn. 74 E2
Lower Richardson L., Me. 54 F2
Lower Sabao L., Me. 55 D3
Lower Savage Is., N.W.T., Can. 45 M1
Lower Saxony=Niedersachsen
Lower Seal Lakes, Qué., Can. 44 K3
Lower Sysladobsis L., Me. 55 D3
Lower Village, Hawaii 84 b7
Lowes, Ky. 71 C5
Lowestoft, U.K., 45,730 113 G5
Lowesville, Va. 62 E5
Lowgap, N.C. 63 D1
Lowick, U.K. 112 E4
Łowicz, Pol., 17,638 127 C2
Low L., Qué., Can. 44 J4
Lowland, N.C. 63 H2
Lowman, Idaho 81 B3
Lowmansville, Ky. 71 J4
Low Moor, Iowa, 343 72 G3
Lowmoor, Va. 62 E5
Lowndes, co., Ala., 15,417 64 C3
Lowndes, co., Ga., 49,270 64 F5
Lowndes, co., Miss., 46,639 73 G4
Lowndesboro, Ala. 64 C3
Lowndesville, S.C., 274 63 B3
Low Rocky Pt., Austl. 173 e14
Lowry, S. Dak., 44 74 C3
Lowry City, Mo., 437 72 D6
Lowrys, S.C., 298 63 C3
Lowther, Ont., Can. 44 G5
Lowther, r., U.K. 114 C1
Lowville, Ont., Can. 46 c14
Lowville, N.Y., 3,616 59 J4
Loxley, Ala., 831 64 B5
Loxton, Austl., 2,321 172 F5
Loyal, Okla., 87 76 E2
Loyal, Wis., 1,146 66 C4
Loyalhanna Cr., Pa. 60 D5
Loyall, Ky., 1,260 71 H5
Loyalsock Cr., Pa. 60 J3
Loyalton, Calif., 936 82 C3
Loyalton, S. Dak., 34 74 C3
Loyalty Is., N. Caled. 170 F6
Loyal Valley, Tex. 77 O4
Lo-yang, China, 600,000* 150 E3
Loyauté, Is.=Loyalty Is.
Lo-yeh, China 152 B3
Loyev, U.S.S.R. 136 C3
Loysville, Pa. 60 H5
Lo-yüan, China 152 E2
Loza, Czech. 126 c7
Lozen, Bulg., 4,958 128 D3
Lozère, Mt., Fr. 117 E4
Loznica, Yug., 11,000* 125 D2
Lozovaya, U.S.S.R., 25,400 136 D3
Loz'va, r., U.S.S.R. 137 k7
Lu, r., China 151 B4
Lua, r., D.R.Congo 164 C1
Luabo, Moz. 164 F5
Luacano, Ang. 164 C3
Luachimo, r., Ang. 164 C3
Lualaba, r., D.R.Congo 164 D2
Lualaba Kraal, D.R.Congo 165 m19
Luama, r., D.R.Congo 164 D2
Luamata, Zambia 165 m19
Luan, r., China 150 F2
Luana Point, Jam. 96 o8
Luan-ch'eng, China 151 B3
Luanda, Ang., 189,590 164 B3
Luang, Thale, Thai. 146 C6
Luang Prabang, Laos 146 C3
Luangue, r., Ang. 164 C3
Luangwa, r., Zambia 164 E4
Luan-hsien, China 151 C3
Luaniva, Î., Îs. Wallis 175 7
Luan-p'ing, China 151 C2
Luanshya, Zamb. 164 D4
Luanza, D.R.Congo 165 o18
Luapula, r., D.R.Congo-Zambia 164 D3
Luarca, Sp., 25,211 122 B1
Luayao, Guam 176 24
Lubaczów, Pol., 5,327 127 E3
Lubań, Pol., 14,352 127 A3
Lubanda, D.R.Congo 165 n19
Lubang, Phil., 3,493 153 A2
Lubang I., Phil. 153 B2
Lubang Is., Phil. 153 A2
Lubao, Phil., 3,364 153 B2
Lubartów, Pol., 6,927 127 E3
Lubawa, Pol., 4,951 127 C2
Lubawka, Pol., 5,482 127 f6
Lübbecke, F.R.Ger., 10,131 118 B2
Lübben, Ger.D.R. 118 D3
Lübbenau, Ger.D.R., 11,976 118 D3
Lubbock, co., Tex., 156,271 77 N3
Lubbock, Tex., 128,691 77 N3
Lubec, Me., 1,289 55 E4
Lübeck, F.R.Ger., 229,554 118 C2
Lübecker B., F.R.Ger. 118 C1
Lubefu, D.R.Congo 164 D2
Lubefu, r., D.R.Congo 164 C2
Lubenec, Czech. 126 c6
Lubenham, U.K. 114 F6
Lubero, D.R.Congo 164 D2
Lubersac, Fr., 2,513 117 D4
Lubiąż, Pol. 127 f5
L'ubica, Czech. 126 E2
Lubie, Jez., Pol. 127 B2
Lubilash, r., D.R.Congo 164 D3
Lubin, Pol., 4,868 127 B3
Lublin, Pol., 181,000* 127 E3
Lublin, Wis., 160 66 C3
Lubliniec, Pol., 14,382 127 C3
Lubnaig, Loch, U.K. 112 b7
Lubny, U.S.S.R., 29,100 134 C4
Lubo, Phil., 1,286 153 c5
Lubok Bongor, Malay. 147 o14
Lubok Nibong, Malay., 2,405 148 E1
Lubomierz, Pol., 1,417 127 e6
Luboń, Pol., 13,950 127 B2
Lubraniec, Pol., 2,659 127 C2
Lubsko, Pol., 10,843 127 A3
Lübtheen, Ger.D.R. 118 C2
Lubuagan, Phil., 1,127 153 c5
Lubudi, D.R.Congo, 5,915 164 D3
Lubudi, r., D.R.Congo 165 m19
Lubukbatang, Indon. 148 C4
Lubukinggau, Indon. 148 B3
Lubuksikaping, Indon. 148 B2
Lubumbashi, D.R.Congo, 183,711 164 D3
Lubungwe, D.R.Congo 165 n18
Lubutu, D.R.Congo 164 D2
Luby, Czech. 126 b6
Lubz, Ger.D.R. 118 C2
Lucala, Ang. 164 B3
Lucama, N.C., 498 63 F2
Lucan, Ont., Can. 46 C5
Lucania, Mt., Yukon, Can. 85 K3
Lucas, co., Iowa, 10,923 72 D4
Lucas, Iowa, 357 72 D3
Lucas, Kans., 559 75 G4
Lucas, Ky. 71 F5
Lucas, Mich. 67 H4
Lucas, co., Ohio, 456,931 70 F1
Lucas Gonzáles, Arg., 5,118 105 b11
Lucasville, Ohio, 1,277 70 G4
Luc Au Chu, N. Viet. 146 D2
Lucaya, Bah. Is. 95 a6
Lucban, Phil., 14,292 153 B2
Lucca, It., 87,804 123 C3
Lucé, Fr., 6,714 117 D2
Luce, co., Mich., 7,827 67 H2
Luce, Nebr. 75 G3
Lucea, Jam., 2,803 96 o8
Luce Bay, U.K. 113 D4
Lucedale, Miss., 1,977 73 G7
Lucena, Peru 104 D5
Lucena, Phil., 24,955 153 B2
Lucena, Sp., 28,287 122 C4
Lucena del Cid, Sp., 2,877 122 E2
Lučenec, Czech., 16,805 126 D2
Lucens, Switz., 1,620 124 A2
Lucera, It., 28,667 123 E4
Lucerne, Switz.=Luzern
Lucerne, Kans. 75 E4
Lucerne, Mo., 157 72 D4
Lucerne, Wash. 80 C1
Lucerne, L., Wis. 66 E3
Lucerne, L. of=Vierwaldstättersee
Lucerne Mines, Pa., 1,524 60 D4
Lucerne Valley, Calif. 82 E5
Luceville, Qué., Can., 1,403 47 R9
Lu-chai, China 152 C2
Lu-ch'eng, China 151 B3
Lu-ch'i, China 150 E4
Lu-chiang, China 152 E1
Lu-chiang, Taiwan, 54,549 152 F2
Lu-chou, China, 160,000* 150 E4
Lüchow F.R.Ger., 6,088 118 C2
Lu-ch'uan, K-hsi, China 152 C3
Lu-ch'üan, Y-n., China 152 A2
Lucie, r., Sur. 101 M6
Lucile, Idaho 81 A3
Lucin, Utah 78 B1
Lucinda, Pa. 60 D3
Lucindale, Austl. 172 E5
Lucipara, Kep., Indon. 149 H4
Lucira, Ang. 164 B4
Luck, N.C. 63 B2
Luck, Wis., 853 66 A3
Lucka, Ger.D.R. 126 b5
Luckau, Ger.D.R. 118 D3
Luckenwalde, Ger.D.R., 28,610 118 D2
Luckey, Ohio, 946 70 F1
Lucknow, Ont., Can., 1,000 44 G7
Lucknow, India, 595,440 145 F4
Lucknow, S.C. 63 D3
Lucky Lake, Sask., Can. 43 C5
Lucma, Peru 104 C5
Luc Nam, N. Viet. 147 i8
Luçon, Fr., 8,332 117 C3
Lucrecia, Cabo, Cuba 96 f2
Lucy, Fr. 116 b9
Luda Kamchiya, r., Bulg. 128 F3
Ludden, N. Dak., 59 74 C2
Ludell, Kans. 75 E4
Lüdenscheid, F.R.Ger., 55,278 118 A3
Lüderitz, S.W. Afr., 3,604 164 B6
Ludgershall, U.K., 2,457 114 E8
Ludgo, Swed. 120 e9
Ludhiana, India, 244,032 145 E3
Lüdinghausen, F.R.Ger., 8,712 119 D1
Ludington, Mich., 9,421 67 G5
Ludington, Wis. 66 B4
Ludlam, Okla. 76 A1
Ludlam Bay, N.J. 61 B5
Ludlow, N.B., Can. 47 S10
Ludlow, U.K., 6,796 113 E5
Ludlow, Calif. 82 E5
Ludlow, Ill., 460 68 D3
Ludlow, Ky., 6,233 71 h11
Ludlow, Me. 55 D2
Ludlow, Mass., 13,805(T) 56 G4
Ludlow, Miss. 73 F5
Ludlow, Mo., 235 72 D5
Ludlow, Pa. 60 E2
Ludlow, Vt., 1,658 54 B5
Ludlow Center (part of Ludlow), Mass. 56 G4
Ludlowville, N.Y. 59 H6
Ludogorsko Plato, Bulg. 128 F3
Ludowici, Ga., 1,578 64 H4
Luduş, Rum. 128 E1
Ludvika, Swed. 120 C3
Ludwigsburg, F.R.Ger., 69,535 118 B4
Ludwigs Corner, Pa. 60 e11
Ludwigsfelde, Ger.D.R., 10,579 118 D2
Ludwigshafen, F.R.Ger., 147,557 118 B4
Ludwigs Kan., F.R.Ger. 118 C4
Ludwigslust, Ger.D.R., 12,002 118 C2
Ludza, U.S.S.R., 6,200 136 B1
Luebo, D.R.Congo 164 C2
Lueders, Tex., 654 77 O3
Lüeh-yang, China 150 E3
Luella, Ga. 64 h11
Luembe, r., Ang.-D.R.Congo 164 C3
Luena, D.R.Congo 164 D3
Luena, r., Zambia 164 C4
Luenha, r., Moz. 164 E4
Luera Pk., N. Mex. 79 B5
Lueta, Rum. 128 E1
Lu-feng, K-t., China 150 F5
Lu-feng, Y-n., China 152 A2
Lufilufi, W. Samoa 177 38
Lufira, r., D.R.Congo 164 D3
Lufkin, Tex., 17,641 77 Q4
Lufupa, D.R.Congo 165 m19
Luga, U.S.S.R., 26,500 134 B4
Luga, r., U.S.S.R. 136 C1
Lugagnano Val d'Arda, It., 5,515 122 c6
Lugano, Switz., 19,758 124 C2
Lugano, L. di, It.-Switz. 124 D3
Lugansk, U.S.S.R., 300,000 134 C5
Luganville, New Hebr. 174 k5
Lugar, U.K. 112 b8
Lugareño, Cuba, 3,135 96 e2
Lugau, Ger.D.R., 10,612 126 b6
Lugazi, Uganda 165 f13
Lugela, Moz. 164 F4
Lugenda, r., Moz. 164 F4
Lugerville, Wis. 66 C3
Lugg, r., U.K. 114 C6
Lugh Ferrandi=Lugh Ganane
Lugh Ganane, Som. Rep., 3,478 163 M5
Lugnaquillia Mtn., Ire. 113 C5
Lugo, It., 33,733 123 C2
Lugo, Phil., 2,357 153 f11
Lugo, Sp., 58,264 122 B1
Lugoff, S.C. 63 D3
Lugoj, Rum., 30,252 128 C2
Lugovoy, U.S.S.R. 137 g3
Luhe, r., F.R.Ger. 119 b9
Lu-ho, China 152 A1
Lu-hsi, China 150 D4
Lu-hsi, China 152 A2
Luhsien=Lu-chou
Lu-i, China 151 B4
Luiana, Ang. 164 C4
Luik=Liège
Luilaka, r., D.R.Congo 164 C2
Luing, i., U.K. 112 D3
Luino, It., 10,919 123 B1
Luís Domingues, Braz., 1,917 103 G2
Luís Gomes, Braz., 1,480 103 J3
Luishia, D.R.Congo 165 n19
Luis Lopez, N. Mex. 79 B4
Luis Moya, Mex., 1,891 92 E3
Luis Peña, Cayo de, P.R. 96 v10
Luiza, D.R.Congo 164 C3
Luján, Arg., 3,500* 105 B4
Luján, Arg., 25,800* 105 b12
Lukachukai, Ariz. 78 D3
Lukafu, D.R.Congo 165 n19
Lukavac, Yug., 5,321 125 D2
Luke, Md., 587 62 E3
Lukenie, r., D.R.Congo 164 C2
Lukerville, Ont., Can. 67 f16
Lukhovitsy, U.S.S.R., 9,400 136 E2
Lukolela, Congo 164 B2
Lukonde, D.R.Congo 165 n18
Lukonzolwa, D.R.Congo 164 D3
Lukovit, Bulg., 8,795 128 E3
Lukovo, Yug. 125 E4
Lukovo Šugarje, Yug. 125 B2
Łuków, Pol., 10,657 127 E3
Łukowice, Pol. 127 g6
Lukoyanov, U.S.S.R., 6,200 136 G2
Lukserfjell, Nor. 121 B1
Lukuga, r., D.R.Congo 164 D2
Lukulu, Zamb. 164 C4
Lukunor, atoll, Car. Is. 176 18
Lukup, Indon. 148 A1
Lukwasa, India 144 a13
Lula, Ga., 557 64 F1
Lula, Miss., 484 73 E3
Lula, Okla. 76 G3
Luleå, Swed., 30,614 120 E2
Luleälv, r., Swed. 120 E2
Lüleburgaz, Turk., 22,332 142 A1
Lü-liang, Shan-hsi, China 151 A3
Lu-liang, Y-n., China 152 A2
Lu-liang Shan, China 151 A3
Luling, La., 2,122 73 E8
Luling, Tex., 4,412 77 P5
Lulonga, r., D.R.Congo 164 C1
Lulu, Fla. 65 G2
Lulu, Mich. 67 K7
Lulu, Mt., Îs. Wallis 175 7
Lulua, r., D.R.Congo 164 C3
Luluabourg, D.R.Congo, 115,049 164 C2
Lu-lung, China 151 C3
Lulunga Group, is., Tonga 177 36
Lum, Mich. 67 K5
Lumaco, Chile 105 A5
Luma Dapdap, Phil., 1,688 153 B4
Lumadjang, Indon. 148 e8
Lumbang, Phil., 4,092 153 b9
Lumber, r., N.C. 63 E3
Lumber Bridge, N.C., 100 63 E3
Lumber City, Ga., 1,360 64 G4
Lumberport, W. Va., 1,031 62 D3
Lumberton, Miss., 2,108 73 F6
Lumberton, N.J. 60 g12
Lumberton, N.C., 15,305 63 E3
Lumberville, Pa. 60 f10
Lumbis, Indon. 148 F1
Lumbrales, Sp., 3,720 122 B2
Lumbrein, Switz. 124 D2
Lumbwa, Kenya 165 g14
Lumby, Br. Col., Can. 42 H4
Lumigny, Fr. 116 k12
Luminárias, Braz., 1,192 103 d17
Lumino, Switz. 124 D2
Lumlel, Nic. 94 F4
Lummen, Belg., 6,166 115 D4
Lumpkin, co., Ga., 7,241 64 E1
Lumpkin, Ga., 1,348 64 E3

Lumsden—McTavish · 255

Lumsden, N.Z. 175 f7
Lumu, Indon. 149 F3
Lumut, Malay., 2,947 147 o14
Lumut, Tg., Indon. 148 C3
Luna, Phil., 2,840 153 B1
Luna, co., N. Mex., 9,839 79 B5
Luna, Catron Co., N. Mex. 79 A5
Luna, Lincoln Co., N. Mex. 79 C5
Lu-nan, China 152 A2
Lunan Bay, U.K. 112 E3
Lunas, Malay., 2,925 147 o14
Lunca Banului, Rum. 128 G1
Lund, Br. Col., Can. 42 b6
Lund, Swed., 40,380 120 C5
Lund, Nev. 83 C3
Lund, Utah 78 B2
Lundar, Man., Can. 43 F5
Lundazi, Zamb. 164 E4
Lundby, Den. 121 D5
Lunde, Nor. 121 B1
Lunderskov, Den. 121 B5
Lundi, r., Rhod. 164 E5
Lundin Links, U.K. 112 e7
Lundtofte, Den., 12,964 121 b7
Lundu, Malay. 148 D2
Lundy I., U.K. 113 D6
Lune, r., U.K. 113 E4
Lüneburg, F.R.Ger., 56,845 118 C2
Lüneburger Heide, heath, F.R. Ger. 118 B2
Lunel, Fr., 9,100 117 E5
Lünen, F.R.Ger., 68,371 118 A3
Lunenburg, N.S., Can., 3,012 45 N7
Lunenburg, Mass., 6,334(T) 57 K2
Lunenburg, Vt. 54 D3
Lunenburg, co., Va., 12,523 62 F5
Lunenburg, Va. 62 F6
Lunéville, Fr., 24,463 117 G2
Lung, r., China 152 C2
Lunga, Sol. Is. 175 b2
Lunga, r., Zambia 164 D4
Lung-an, China 152 B3
Lung-ch'ang, China 150 E4
Lung-ch'i = Chang-chou
Lung-chiang, China, 100,000* 150 G2
Lung-ching, China 150 E5
Lung-ch'ü, China 151 B4
Lung-ch'üan, Ch-ch., China 152 E1
Lung-ch'uan, K-t., China 152 D2
Lung-hsi, China 150 D3
Lung-hua, Ho-p., China 151 C2
Lung-hua, K-t., China 152 a6
Lung-hui, China 152 C2
Lung-kang, China 152 b6
Lungki = Chang-chou
Lung-k'ou, China 151 C3
Lung-kuan, China 151 B2
Lung-li, China 152 B2
Lung-lin, China 152 B2
Lung-men, Ho-n., China 151 B4
Lung-men, K-t., China 152 D3
Lung-nan, China 152 D2
Lung-shan, China 152 C1
Lung-sheng, China 152 C2
Lung-te, China 150 E3
Lung-tzu, China 150 C4
Lungué-Bungo, r., Ang. 164 C4
Lunguya, Tanz. 165 f15
Lung-wu, China 152 A3
Lung-yen, China 152 E2
Lung-yu, China 152 E1
Luni, r., India 145 D4
Luniemu, D.R.Congo 165 m18
Luninets, U.S.S.R., 10,300 136 B2
Luning, Nev. 83 A3
Lunkar Gömpa, China 144 e10
Lun Masala, Phil., 3,989 153 C4
Lunna Ness, U.K. 112 F1
Lunsemfwa, r., Zambia 164 D4
Lun-t'ai, China 150 B2
Lunteren, Neth., 3,700 115 D2
Lunz, Aust., 2,352 124 M6
Lunzenau, Ger.D.R. 126 b6
Lupa, r., Tanz. 164 E3
Lupao, Phil., 4,195 153 b7
Lupar, r., Malay. 148 D2
Łupawa, r., Pol. 127 B1
Lupeni, Rum., 21,188 128 D2
Luperón, Dom. Rep., 1,548 96 m6
Łupków, Pol. 127 E4
Lupog, Guam 176 24
Lupon, Phil., 4,356 153 C4
Lupoto, D.R.Congo 165 n19
Luppa, Ger.D.R. 126 b5
Lupton, Ariz. 78 D4
Lupton, Mich. 67 J4
Luputa, D.R.Congo 164 C3
Lup'ya, r., U.S.S.R. 137 h6
Luquillo, P.R., 2,107 96 u10
Luquillo, Sa. de, P.R. 96 u10
Lur, Swed. 121 D2
Luray, Kans., 328 75 G4
Luray, Mo., 154 72 F4
Luray, S.C., 102 63 C5
Luray, Tenn. 71 C6
Luray, Va., 3,014 62 F4
Lure, Fr., 7,924 117 G3
Lurgan, U.K., 17,873 113 C4
Luri, Fr. 116 r17
Luribay, Bol., 5,755 102 C5
Lurín, Peru, 2,714 104 B5
Lúrio, Moz. 164 F4
Lúrio, r., Moz. 164 F4
Lusaka, Zamb., 83,200 164 D4
Lusambo, D.R.Congo, 9,395 164 C2
Lusancay Is., Terr. Papua 174 3
Luseland, Sask., Can. 43 B4
Lu-shan, Ho-n., China 151 B4
Lu-shan, K-ch., China 152 B2
Lu-shan, S-ch., China 152 A1
Lu Shan, China 152 D1
Lu-shih, China 151 A4
Lushnje, Alb., 14,000* 125 D4
Lushoto, Tanz. 164 F2
Lü-shun-k'ou, China 150 G3
Lusi, r., Indon. 148 d7
Lusinga, D.R.Congo 165 n18
Lusk, Ire. 113 C5
Lusk, Wyo., 1,890 81 G4
Luso, Ang. 164 C3
Lustenau, Aust., 12,554 124 F6
Lustin, Belg., 1,417 115 C4
Lustre, Mont. 81 G1
Luswaka, D.R.Congo 165 n18
Lūt, Dasht-e, Iran 143 F2
Lü-ta, China, 770,000* 150 G3
Lutao, Phil., 1,553 153 f11
Lü Tao, Taiwan 152 F3
Lutcher, La., 3,274 73 E7
Lutesville, Mo., 658 72 G7
Luther, Ill. 68 C3
Luther, Iowa, 147 72 D3
Luther, Mich., 325 67 H4
Luther, Okla., 517 76 F2
Luthern, Switz., 1,801 124 B1
Luthersburg, Pa. 60 E3
Luthersville, Ga., 282 64 E2
Lutherville, Md., 12,265 62 H3
Luthrie, U.K. 112 d7
Lutie, Tex. 76 N2
Lu-tien, China 152 A2
Lu-ting, China 152 A1
Lutjebroek, Neth. 115 D2
Lütjenburg, F.R.Ger., 4,038 118 C1
Lutji, Indon. 148 D3
Luton, U.K., 131,583 113 F6
Lutong, Malay., 3,039 148 E1
Lutowiska, Pol. 127 E4
Lutsen, Minn. 74 G2
Lutsk, U.S.S.R., 63,000 134 B4
Lutterworth, U.K., 3,729 114 F6
Luttrell, Tenn. 71 H5
Lutts, Tenn. 71 D6
Lutugino, U.S.S.R., 11,300 136 f7
Lutur, Indon. 149 K4
Lututów, Pol. 127 h5
Lutz, Fla. 65 G4
Lützelflüh, Switz., 3,960 124 B1
Lutzmannsburg, Aust. 124 N6
Lützow-Holm B., Ant. 180 R6
Luverne, Ala., 2,238 64 C4
Lu Verne, Iowa, 468 72 C2
Luverne, Minn., 4,249 74 D4
Luverne, N. Dak., 109 74 D2
Luvua, D.R.Congo 165 m18
Luvua, r., D.R.Congo 164 D3
Luwingu, Zamb. 164 E3
Luwuk, Indon. 149 G3
Luxembourg, ctry., 333,000* 115
Luxembourg, Lux., 71,653 115 E5
Luxemburg, Mo. 72 a11
Luxemburg, Wis., 730 66 F4
Luxeuil, Fr., 9,015 117 G3
Luxey, Fr. 117 C4
Luxor = Al Uqşur
Luxora, Ark., 1,236 73 F2
Luy, r., Fr. 117 C5
Luyang, Phil., 1,022 153 e11
Luz, Fr., 1,249 117 D5
Luza, U.S.S.R., 13,300 134 D3
Luzarches, Fr., 1,781 116 h10
Luzern, Switz., 67,433 124 C1
Luzerne, Mich. 67 J4
Luzerne, N.Y. 59 N5
Luzerne, co., Pa., 346,972 61 K3
Luzerne, Pa., 5,118 61 o16
Luzha, r., U.S.S.R. 136 a6
Luziânia, Braz., 4,849 103 G5
Lužické Hory, Czech. 126 d6
Luzilândia, Braz., 3,434 103 H2
Luzinga, Uganda 165 f13
Lužnice, r., Czech. 126 B2
Luzon, Phil., 1,512 153 C4
Luzon, i., Phil. 153 B2
Luzon Str., Phil. 153 B1
Luzy, Fr., 2,527 117 E3
Luzzara, It., 8,802 122 d6
Luzzi, It., 10,008 123 F5
L'vov, U.S.S.R., 436,000 134 B5
L'vovskiy, U.S.S.R. 136 b6
Lwówek, Pol., 2,379 127 B2
Lwówek Śląski, Pol., 5,460 127 e5
Lyakhovichi, U.S.S.R., 3,400 136 B2
Lyakhovskiye O., U.S.S.R. 135 N2
Lyall, Mt., N.Z. 175 e7
Lyallpur, Pak., 425,248 145 D3
Lyal'-Mikar, U.S.S.R. 137 e5
Lyalya, r., U.S.S.R. 137 k7
Lyantonde, Uganda 165 e14
Lyaskovets, Bulg., 6,405 128 E3
Lybster, U.K. 112 E2
Lycan, Colo. 79 D3
Lychen, Ger.D.R. 118 D2
Lycksele, Swed. 120 D2
Lycoming, N.Y. 59 H4
Lycoming, co., Pa., 109,367 60 H3
Lycoming Cr., Pa. 60 H3
Lydbrook, U.K., 2,465 114 C7
Lydd, U.K., 2,698 113 G6
Lydda = Lod
Lyddal, Man., Can. 43 F3
Lydenburg, S. Af., 7,393 164 E6
Lydia, S.C. 63 D3
Lydick, Ind., 1,217 70 C1
Lydney, U.K., 5,041 113 E6
Lyell, Mt., Alta.-Br. Col., Can. 42 J3
Lyell I., Br. Col., Can. 42 D3
Lyerly, Ga., 409 64 D1
Lyford, Ind. 70 B3
Lyford, Tex., 1,554 77 P6
Lykens, Pa., 2,527 60 J4
Lyle, Kans. 75 E4
Lyle, Wash. 80 C3
Lyles, Tenn. 71 D6
Lyman, Miss. 73 F7
Lyman, Nebr., 626 75 A2
Lyman, N.H. 54 D3
Lyman, Okla. 76 G1
Lyman, S.C., 1,261 63 B3
Lyman, co., S. Dak., 4,428 74 B3
Lyman, S. Dak. 74 C4
Lyman, Wash., 400 80 B1
Lyman, Wyo., 425 81 D5
Lyman L., Wis. 66 A2
Lyme, N.H. 54 C4
Lyme Bay, U.K. 113 E6
Lyme Regis, U.K., 3,526 113 E6
Lymington, U.K., 28,721 113 F6
Lymington, r., U.K. 113 i13
Lymm, U.K., 7,330 114 D4
Łyna, r., Pol. 127 D1
Lynbrook, N.Y., 19,881 58 e14
Lynch, Ky., 3,810 71 J5
Lynch, Md. 62 H3
Lynch, Nebr., 409 75 G1
Lynch, Va. 62 E5
Lynch, L., Qué., Can. 46 G2
Lynchburg, Mo. 72 E7
Lynchburg, Ohio, 1,022 70 F3
Lynchburg, S.C., 544 63 D3
Lynchburg, Tenn., 396 71 E6
Lynchburg, Va., 54,790 62 E5
Lynches, r., S.C. 63 D3
Lynchville, Me. 55 B4
Lynd, Minn., 259 74 E3
Lyndeboro, N.H. 54 D6
Lyndell, Pa. 60 e11
Lynden, Ont., Can. 46 b15
Lynden, Wash., 2,542 80 B1
Lyndhurst, Austl. 172 E4
Lyndhurst, U.K., 2,931 113 i13
Lyndhurst, N.J., 21,867 58 c13
Lyndhurst, Ohio, 16,805 70 H1
Lyndon, Ill., 677 68 C2
Lyndon, Kans., 953 75 K5
Lyndon, Vt. 54 C2
Lyndon B. Johnson L., Tex. 77 O4
Lyndon Center, Vt., 274 54 C2
Lyndon Station, Wis., 335 66 D5
Lyndonville, N.Y., 755 58 D5
Lyndonville, Vt., 1,477 54 D2
Lyndora, Pa., 3,232 60 C4
Lyneham, U.K., 3,688 114 E7
Lynemouth, U.K., 2,897 112 g9
Lyne Water, r., U.K. 112 d8
Lyngdal, Nor. 120 A4
Lynge, Den. 121 a7
Lyngseidet, Nor. 120 E1
Lyngsjö, Swed. 121 G5
Lynn, Ala., 531 64 B1
Lynn, Ark., 263 73 D1
Lynn, Fla. 65 H3
Lynn, Ind., 1,260 70 E2
Lynn, Ky. 71 J3
Lynn, Mass., 94,478 57 N3
Lynn, co., Tex., 10,914 77 N3
Lynn, Utah 78 B1
Lynn Crossing, Ala. 64 c7
Lynndyl, Utah, 145 78 B2
Lynnfield, Mass., 8,398(T) 57 M2
Lynnfield Center (part of Lynnfield), Mass. 57 M2
Lynn Gardens, Tenn., 5,261 71 J5
Lynn Grove, Ky. 71 C5
Lynn Haven, Fla., 3,078 65 D2
Lynn Lake, Man., Can., 1,218 43 E3
Lynn Lane, Okla. 76 H1
Lynnville, Ill., 97 68 B4
Lynnville, Ind., 409 70 B4
Lynnville, Iowa, 411 72 E3
Lynnville, Ky. 71 C5
Lynnville, Tenn., 362 71 E6
Lynnwood, Wash., 7,207 80 B2
Lynton, U.K., 1,918 113 E6
Lynwood, Calif., 31,614 83 h16
Lynwood, Ill., 255 69 d10
Lynx, Ohio 70 F4
Lynx L., N.W.T., Can. 40 H5
Lynxville, Wis., 183 66 B5
Lyø, i., Den. 121 C5
Lyon, Fr., 535,784 117 F4
Lyon, co., Iowa, 14,468 72 A1
Lyon, co., Kans., 26,928 75 J5
Lyon, co., Ky., 5,924 71 C4
Lyon, co., Minn., 22,655 74 E3
Lyon, co., Nev., 6,143 83 A3
Lyon Inlet, N.W.T., Can. 41 N4
Lyon Manor = Higgins Lake
Lyon Mountain, N.Y. 59 M2
Lyon Mtn., N.Y. 59 N2
Lyonnais, Monts du, Fr. 116 o15
Lyons, Colo., 706 79 C1
Lyons, Ga., 3,219 64 G3
Lyons, Ill., 10,891 69 c9
Lyons, Ind., 651 70 B4
Lyons, Kans., 4,592 75 G5
Lyons, Mich., 687 67 J6
Lyons, N.J. 58 a14
Lyons, N.Y., 4,673 58 G5
Lyons, Ohio, 590 70 E1
Lyons, Nebr., 974 75 J2
Lyons, Oreg., 463 80 B3
Lyons, Pa., 571 61 L5
Lyons, Tex. 77 P4
Lyons, Wis. 56 c13
Lyons Falls, N.Y., 887 59 K4
Lyonsville (part of Colrain), Mass. 56 F2
Lyonsville, N.J. 58 b13
Lysander, N.Y. 59 p23
Lysekil, Swed. 120 B4
Lysi, Cyp., 3,545 142 e9
Łysica, pk., Pol. 127 D3
Lyskovo, U.S.S.R., 16,800 136 G2
Lyss, Switz., 5,616 124 B1
Lyster, Qué., Can. 47 N2
Lys'va, U.S.S.R., 76,000 134 E4
Lytham, U.K. 114 B3
Lythe, U.K. 114 G1
Lytkarino, U.S.S.R., 20,000 136 b6
Lytle, Tex., 798 77 O5
Lytle Creek, Calif. 83 k15
Lyttelton, N.Z., 3,400 175 g6
Lytton, Br. Col., Can. 42 G4
Lytton, Iowa, 376 72 C2
Lytton Springs, Tex. 76 c6
Lyubertsy, U.S.S.R., 100,000 136 E2
Lyubim, U.S.S.R., 7,600 136 F1
Lyubimets, Bulg., 7,646 128 F4
Lyubinskiy, U.S.S.R., 8,500 137 n11
Lyuboml', U.S.S.R., 7,000 136 B3
Lyubotin, U.S.S.R., 31,100 136 D3
Lyudinovo, U.S.S.R., 26,400 134 C4
Lyulyakovo, Bulg., 2,569 128 F3

M

Ma, r., Laos-Viet. 146 D2
Maalaea, Hawaii 84 E3
Maalaea Bay, Hawaii 84 E3
Ma'ān, Jor., 6,543 142 C4
Ma-an-shan, China 152 E1
Ma-ao Barrio, Phil., 9,363 153 d11
Maarianhamina = Mariehamn
Ma'arrat an Nu'mān, Syr., 17,113 142 D3
Maarssen, Neth., 8,800 115 b6
Maas, r., Neth. 115 D3
Maaseik, Belg., 7,944 115 D3
Maashees, Neth. 119 A1
Maasin, Phil., 7,339 153 C3
Maasland, Neth. 115 a7
Maasniel, Neth. 115 E3
Maassluis, Neth., 11,300 115 C3
Maastricht, Neth., 81,600 115 D4
Mabana, Wash. 81 b6
Mabank, Tex., 944 77 P3
Mabaruma, Guyana 101 L3
Mabashi, Jap. 155 m19
Mabau, Indon. 148 E3
Mabechi, r., Jap. 155 G1
Mabein, Burma 146 B2
Mabeleapudi, Bots., 1,414 164 C5
Maben, Miss., 596 73 F4
Maben, W. Va. 62 C5
Mabie, W. Va. 62 D4
Mabini, Phil., 1,743 153 f12
Mabiri, C., Sol. Is. 175 a1
Mable, Oreg. 80 B3
Mablethorpe, U.K., 3,611 113 G5
Mableton, Ga., 7,127 64 f9
Mabolo, Phil., 24,081 153 e11
Mabote, Moz. 164 E5
Mabou, N.S., Can. 47 V10
Mabscott, W. Va., 1,591 62 C5
Mabton, Wash., 958 80 C2
Mabwe, D.R.Congo 165 n18
Macachín, Arg., 3,000* 105 C5
McAdam, N.B., Can., 2,570 45 M6
McAdoo, Pa., 3,560 61 K4
McAdoo, Tex. 77 N3
Macaé, Braz., 19,830 103 f18
McAfee, N.J. 61 B1
Macaíba, Braz., 7,472 103 b13
Macaira, r., Ven. 101 b12
Macajalar Bay, Phil. 153 C3
Macalaya, Phil., 1,706 153 h15
Macalder's Mine, Kenya 165 g14
Macalelon, Phil., 2,854 153 B2
McAlester, Okla., 17,419 76 H3
McAlister, N. Mex. 79 D4
Macalister, r., Austl. 173 f11
McAlisterville, Pa. 60 H4
McAllaster, Kans. 75 D4
McAllen, Tex., 32,728 77 O6
McAllister, Wis. 66 F3
McAlpin, Fla. 65 G2
MacAlpine L., N.W.T., Can. 40 J4
Macao, Port. col., 175,000* 150 F5
Macapá, Braz., 27,585 103 F1
Macará, Ec., 5,088 104 B3
Macaracas, Pan. 94 G7
Macarani, Braz., 3,991 103 H5
Macarao, Ven. 101 b11
Macareo, Ven. 101 K3
McArthur, Calif. 82 C2
McArthur, Ohio, 1,529 70 G3
McArthur, r., Austl. 172 E2
McArthur, Port, Austl. 172 E2
Macas, Ec., 1,342 104 B2
Macatawa, L., Mich. 67 G6
Macate, Peru, 3,316 104 B4
Macaúbas, Braz., 2,504 103 H4
Macauley I., N.Z. 170 G7
Macaya, Pic de, Haiti 96 k6
Macaya, r., Col. 100 D7
McBain, Mich., 551 67 H4
McBean, Ga. 64 H2
McBee, S.C., 512 63 D3
McBride, Br. Col., Can. 42 G3
MacBride Head, Falk. Is. 108 3
McBrides, Mich., 265 67 H5
McCain, N.C. 63 E2
McCall, Idaho, 1,423 81 B3
McCallsburg, Iowa, 272 72 D2
McCamey, Tex., 3,375 77 M4
McCammon, Idaho, 557 81 C4
Maccarese, It., 7,500* 123 a8
McCarthy, Alaska 85 J3
McCaskell, Ark., 62 73 B4
McCauley I., Br. Col., Can. 42 D3
McCausland, Iowa, 173 72 G3
McCaysville, Ga., 1,871 64 E1
McClain, co., Okla., 12,740 76 F2
McCleary, Wash., 1,115 80 B2
McClelland, Iowa, 150 72 B3
McClellanville, S.C., 354 63 E4
Macclenny, Fla., 2,671 65 G2
Macclesfield, U.K., 37,578 113 E5
Macclesfield, N.C., 473 63 G2
Machico, Madeira Is., 11,608 109 4
M'Clintock, Man., Can. 43 G2
M'Clintock Bay, N.W.T., Can. 41 N1
M'Clintock Chan., N.W.T., Can. 40 J3
McCloud, Calif., 2,140 82 B2
McClure, Ill. 68 C6
McClure, Ohio, 651 70 F1
McClure, Pa., 1,001 60 H4
McClure, L., Calif. 82 C4
McClure Str., N.W.T., Can. 40 F3
McClusky, N. Dak., 751 74 B2
McCoin, Tenn. 71 F5
McColl, S.C., 2,479 63 E3
McCollum, Ga. 64 f11
McComas, W. Va. 62 C5
McComb, Miss., 12,020 73 E6
McComb, Ohio, 1,176 70 F1
McCondy, Miss. 73 G4
McCone, co., Mont., 3,321 81 G2
McConnell, Ill. 68 C1
McConnells, S.C., 266 63 C3
McConnellsburg, Pa., 1,245 60 F6
McConnelsville, N.Y. 59 J5
McConnelsville, Ohio, 2,257 70 H3
McConnico, Ariz. 78 B4
McCook, Ill., 441 69 c9
McCook, Nebr., 8,301 75 E3
McCook, co., S. Dak., 8,268 74 D4
McCook, Tex. 77 O6
McCool, Ind. 69 f10
McCool, Miss., 211 73 F4
McCoole, Md. 62 F3
McCool Junction, Nebr., 246 75 H3
McCormick, co., S.C., 8,629 63 B4
McCormick, S.C., 1,998 63 B4
McCoy, Colo. 79 B2
McCoysburg, Ind. 70 C2
McCracken, Kans., 406 75 F5
McCracken, co., Ky., 57,306 71 C4
McCreary, Man., Can. 43 E5
McCreary, co., Ky., 12,463 71 G5
McCrory, Ark., 1,053 73 D2
MacCulloch C., N.W.T., Can. 41 P3
McCullom Lake, Ill., 759 69 a7
McCullough, Ala. 64 B4
McCullough, co., Tex., 8,815 77 O4
McCune, Kans., 433 75 K6
McCurtain, co., Okla., 25,851 76 J3
McCurtain, Okla., 528 76 H2
McDade, Tex. 77 P4
McDame, Br. Col., Can. 42 E1
McDavid, Fla. 65 B2
McDermitt, Nev. 83 B2
McDermott, Ohio 70 F4
Macdiarmid, Ont., Can. 44 E5
MacDoel, Calif. 82 C2
Macdonald, Man., Can. 43 f9
McDonald, Kans., 323 75 D4
McDonald, co., Mo., 11,798 72 C8
McDonald, N. Mex. 79 D5
McDonald, Ohio, 2,727 70 J1
McDonald, Pa., 3,141 60 B5
Macdonald, L., Austl. 172 C3
McDonald L., Mich. 67 H2
McDonald Pk., Mont. 81 C2
Macdonnell Ranges, Austl. 172 D3
McDonough, Ga., 2,224 64 E2
McDonough, co., Ill., 28,928 68 B3
McDonough, N.Y. 59 J7
McDowell, co., N.C., 26,742 63 B2
McDowell, Va. 127 62 E4
McDowell, co., W. Va., 71,359 62 C5
MacDowell L., Ont., Can. 44 D4
Macduff, U.K., 3,479 112 E3
McDuffie, co., Ga., 12,627 64 G2
Macedo, Arg. 105 c13
Macedo de Cavaleiros, Port., 3,167 122 B2
Macedon, N.Y. 645 58 F5
Macedon Center, N.Y. 58 o20
Macedonia, Ill. 96 68 D5
Macedonia, Iowa, 290 72 B3
Macedonia, Yug. = Makedonija
Macedonia, reg., Gr.-Yug. 129 D4
Maceió, Braz., 153,305 103 J3
McElmo Cr., Colo. 79 A3
Macenta, Guin., 10,000 162 C4
Maceo, Cuba, 11,433 96 e2
Macerata, It., 36,633 123 D3
McEwen, Tenn., 979 71 D5
McEwensville, Pa., 795 60 J3
McFadden, Wyo. 81 G5
McFaddin, Tex. 77 P5
McFall, Mo., 206 72 C4
McFarlan, N.C., 161 63 D3
Macfarlan, W. Va. 62 C3
McFarland, Calif., 3,686 82 D5
McFarland, Mich. 66 F2
McFarland, Wis., 1,272 66 D6
Macfarlane, L., Austl. 172 E5
McFarlane, r., Sask., Can. 43 C2
McGaffey, N. Mex. 79 A4
McGee, Mo. 72 G7
McGehee, Ark., 4,448 73 D4
McGill, Nev., 2,195 83 C3
Macgillycuddy's Reeks, mts. ra., Ire. 113 B6
McGinnis Slough, Ill. 69 c10
McGivney, N.B., Can. 47 S10
McGrady, N.C. 63 C1
McGrann, Pa. 60 D4
McGrath, Alaska, 241 85 F3
McGrath, Minn., 96 74 F2
McGraw, N.Y., 1,276 59 H6
MacGregor, Man., Can. 43 f10
McGregor, Ont., Can. 67 g16
McGregor, Iowa, 1,040 72 F2
McGregor, Mich. 67 L5
McGregor, Minn., 283 74 F2
McGregor, N. Dak. 74 A1
McGregor, Tex., 4,642 77 P4
McGuffey, Ohio, 647 70 F2
McGuire, Mt., Idaho 81 B3
Machacamarca, Bol., 4,224 102 b11
Machachi, Ec., 3,822 104 B2
Machado, Braz., 8,373 103 d17
Machakos, Kenya 164 F2
Machala, Ec., 29,714 104 A2
Machalí, Chile, 3,008 104 g14
Machang, Malay., 2,098 147 p13
Machap, Malay., 1,922 147 p15
Machattie, L., Austl. 172 E3
Machault, Fr. 116 k12
Machault, Fr. 117 F2
Machaze, Moz. 164 E5
Mache, r., Ec. 104 c9
Machecoul, Fr., 4,091 117 C3
Machelen, Belg., 6,806 115 d9
Ma-ch'eng, China 150 F4
McHenry, co., Ill., 84,210 68 D1
McHenry, Ill., 3,336 68 D1
McHenry, Ky., 446 71 D4
McHenry, Miss. 73 F7
McHenry, co., N. Dak., 11,099 74 B1
McHenry, N. Dak., 155 74 C2
McHenry Dam, Ill. 69 a7
Machens, Mo. 72 a10
Machi, Jap. 154 e15
Machi, Jap. 154 f14
Ma-chiang, China 152 B2
Machias, Me., 1,523 55 E4
Machias, N.Y. 58 C7
Machias, Wash. 81 b7
Machias, r., Aroostook Co., Me. 55 D2
Machias, r., Washington Co., Me. 55 E4
Machias Bay, Me. 55 E4
Machias Lakes, Me. 55 E3
Machiasport, Me. 55 E4
Ma-chia-tien, China 151 C4
Machichaco, C., Sp. 122 n11
Machichi, r., Man., Can. 43 H3
Machida, Jap., 71,269 155 m19
Ma-ch'in, China 150 D3
Machipongo, Va. 62 J5
Machiques, Ven., 13,685 100 D2
Macho, A. del, N. Mex. 79 C5
Ma-ch'ü, China 150 D3
Machu Picchu, ruins, Peru 104 C5
Machynlleth, U.K., 1,904 113 E5
Maciá, Arg., 3,500* 105 b11
Macia, Moz., 16,018 164 E6
Măcin, Rum., 6,533 128 G2
Macina = Ké-Macina
McIndoe Falls, Vt. 54 C3
McIntire, Iowa, 270 72 E1
McIntosh, Ala. 64 A4
McIntosh, co., Ga., 6,364 64 H4
McIntosh, Minn., 785 74 D2
McIntosh, N. Mex. 79 C4
McIntosh, co., N. Dak., 6,702 74 C2
McIntosh, co., Okla., 12,371 76 H2
McIntosh, S. Dak., 568 74 B3
McIntosh L., Sask., Can. 43 D3
McIntyre, Pa. 60 D4
MacIntyre, Mt., N.Y. 59 N3
McIntyre Bay, Br. Col., Can. 42 C2
Mack, Ohio 71 g11
Mackau, C., Loy. Is. 174 k8
Mackay, Austl., 14,762 173 G3
Mackay, Idaho, 652 81 C4
Mackay, L., Austl. 172 D3
MacKay, r., Alta., Can. 42 K2
McKay Cr., Oreg. 80 D3
MacKay L., N.W.T., Can. 40 G5
McKean, co., Pa., 54,517 60 E2
McKean, Pa. = Middleboro
McKean, atoll, Phoenix Is. 170 G5
McKee, Ky., 234 71 G4
McKee Cr., Ill. 68 B4
McKeesport, Pa., 45,489 60 C5
McKees Rocks, Pa., 13,185 60 B5
McKenna, Wash. 80 B2
McKenney, Va., 519 62 G6
Mackenzie, Dist. of, N.W.T., Can. 40 F4
MacKenzie, Ont., Can. 44 E5
Mackenzie, Guyana 101 L5
McKenzie, Ala., 558 64 C4
McKenzie, co., N. Dak., 7,296 74 A2
McKenzie, N. Dak. 74 B2
McKenzie, Tenn., 3,780 71 C5
Mackenzie, r., Austl. 173 G3
Mackenzie, r., Can. 40 D4
McKenzie, r., Oreg. 80 B3
Mackenzie Bay, Ant. 180 S6
Mackenzie Bay, N.W.T.-Yukon, Can. 40 B4
McKenzie Bridge, Oreg. 80 B3
McKenzie Island, Ont., Can. 44 C4
Mackenzie King I., N.W.T., Can. 41 G2
McKenzie L., Wis. 66 A3
Mackenzie Mts., N.W.T., Can. 40 C4
McKerrow, Ont., Can. 46 C2
Mackeys, N.C. 63 H2
McKibben, Tex. 76 N1
Mackinac, co., Mich., 10,853 67 J2
Mackinac, Straits of, Mich. 67 J3
Mackinac Island, Mich., 942 67 J3
Mackinac I., Mich. 67 J3
Mackinaw, Ill., 1,163 68 C3
Mackinaw, r., Ill. 68 C3
Mackinaw City, Mich., 934 67 J3
McKinlay, Austl. 173 F3
McKinley, Ind. 70 C4
McKinley, Me. 55 D4
McKinley, Mich. 67 K4
McKinley, co., N. Mex., 37,209 79 A4
McKinley, Oreg. 80 B4
McKinley, Mt., Alaska 85 G3
McKinleyville, Calif. 82 A2
McKinney, Tex., 13,763 77 P3
McKinney, L., Kans. 75 D5
McKinney Mtn., Tex. 77 M5
McKinnon, Fla. 65 B2
MacKintosh, C., Ant. 180 O5
McKittrick, Calif. 82 D5
Macklin, Sask., Can. 43 B4
McKnight, Okla. 76 D3
McKownville, N.Y. 59 v29
Macksburg, Iowa, 174 72 C3
Macksburg, Ohio, 314 70 H3
Macks Creek, Mo., 123 72 E7
Macksville, Austl., 2,007 173 H4
Macksville, Kans., 546 75 G6
Mackville, Ky. 71 F4
McLain, Miss. 73 G6
Maclaralin, r., Dominica 97 13
Maclas, Fr., 1,013 116 p16
McLaughlin, S. Dak., 983 74 B3
McLaurin, Miss. 73 F6
Maclean, Austl., 1,698 173 H4
McLean, co., Ill., 83,877 68 D3
McLean, Ill., 758 68 C3
McLean, co., Ky., 9,355 71 D4
McLean, N.Y. 59 H6
McLean, co., N. Dak., 14,030 74 B2
McLean, Tex., 1,330 76 N2
McLean, Va. 62 a9
McLeansboro, Ill., 2,951 68 D5
Maclean Str., N.W.T., Can. 41 J2
McLennan, Alta., Can., 1,045 42 J2
McLennan, co., Tex., 150,091 77 P4
McLeod, co., Minn., 24,401 74 E3
McLeod, Miss. 73 G4
McLeod, N. Dak. 74 D2
McLeod, r., Alta., Can. 42 J3
McLeod Lake, Br. Col., Can. 42 G2
McLoud, Okla., 837 76 F2
McLoughlin, Mt., Oreg. 80 B4
McLouth, Kans., 494 75 K4
McLure, Br. Col., Can. 42 G3
McMan, Okla. 76 F3
McMasterville, Qué., Can., 2,055 47 p17
McMechen, W. Va., 2,999 62 D3
McMillan, Mich. 67 H2
McMillan, L., N. Mex. 79 C5
MacMillan, r., Yukon, Can. 40 C5
McMinn, co., Tenn., 33,662 71 G6
McMinnville, Oreg., 7,656 80 B3
McMinnville, Tenn., 9,013 71 F6
McMullen, co., Tex., 1,116 77 O5
McMurdo, Ant. 180 V5
McMurdo Sd., Ant. 180 V5
McMurray, Pa. 60 b8
McNab, Ark., 142 73 B4
McNabb, Ill., 176 68 C2
McNair, Tex., 1,880 77 k9
McNairy, co., Tenn., 18,085 71 C6
McNairy, Tenn. 71 C6
McNary, Ariz., 1,608 78 D4
McNary, Oreg. 80 D3
McNary, Tex. 77 L4
McNaughton, Wis. 66 D3
McNeal, Ariz. 78 D6
McNeil, Ark., 746 73 B4
McNeil, Tex. 76 c5
McNeil I., Wash. 81 a8
McNeill, Miss. 73 F7
Maco, Phil., 5,241 153 C4
Macocola, Ang. 164 B3
Macomb, Ill., 12,135 68 B3
Macomb, co., Mich., 405,804 67 K6
Macomb, Mich. 67 g14
Macomb, Okla., 76 76 F2
Macomer, It., 8,277 123 B4
Macomia, Moz. 164 F4
Macon, Fr., 27,669 117 F3
Macon, co., Ala., 26,717 64 D3
Macon, co., Ga., 13,170 64 E3
Macon, Ga., 122,876 64 F3
Macon, co., Ill., 118,257 68 D4
Macon, Ill., 1,229 68 C4
Macon, Mich. 67 K6
Macon, Miss., 2,432 73 G4
Macon, co., Mo., 16,473 72 E5
Macon, Mo., 4,547 72 E5
Macon, Nebr. 75 G3
Macon, co., N.C., 14,935 63 A2
Macon, N.C., 187 63 F1
Macon, co., Tenn., 12,197 71 E5
Maconí, Mex. 93 e9
Macopin, N.J. 58 b12
Macorís, C., Dom. Rep. 96 m6
Macoun L., Sask., Can. 43 D3
Macoupin, co., Ill., 43,524 68 C4
Macoupin Cr., Ill. 68 C4
Macouria, Fr. Guiana 101 O5
McPherson, co., Kans., 24,285 75 H5
McPherson, Kans., 9,996 75 H5
McPherson, co., Nebr., 735 75 D2
McPherson, co., S. Dak., 5,821 74 C3
McQuady, Ky. 71 E4
Macquarie, r., N.S.W., Austl. 173 G5
Macquarie, r., Tasm., Austl. 173 f13
Macquarie Harbour, Austl. 173 e14
Macquarie I., Austl. 170 E8
McQueen, Okla. 76 D3
McQueeney, Tex. 76 b6
McRae, Yukon, Can. 40 B5
McRae, Ark., 428 73 D2
McRae, Ga., 2,738 64 G3
McRoberts, Ky., 1,363 71 J4
Macroom, Ire., 2,277 113 B6
McSherrystown, Pa., 2,839 60 H6
Mactan, Phil., 5,518 153 f11
Mactan, I., Phil. 153 e11
McTavish, Man., Can. 43 g10
McTavish Arm, N.W.T., Can. 40 F4

256 · McTavish—Malvern

McTavish L., Sask., Can. 43 D3
MacTier, Ont., Can. 46 E3
Macuco, Brazil, 1,515 103 e18
Macuelizo, Hond., 1,299 94 C3
Macune, Tex. 77 Q4
Macungie, Pa., 1,266 61 L4
Macurijes, Punta, Cuba 96 d2
Macusani, Peru, 1,619 104 D5
Macuse, Moz. 164 F4
Macuspana, Mex., 6,709 93 G5
Macuto, Ven., 6,982 101 c11
McVeigh, Ky. 71 J4
McVeytown, Pa., 488 60 G4
McVicar Arm, N.W.T., Can. 40 E5
McVille, N. Dak., 551 74 C2
Macwahoc, Me. 55 D3
McWillie, Okla. 76 E1
Macy, Ind., 328 70 C2
Macy, Nebr. 75 J1
Mad, r., Calif. 82 B2
Mad, r., Conn. 56 D6
Mad, r., N.H. 54 D4
Mad, r., Ohio 70 F2
Mad, r., Vt. 54 B3
Ma'dabā, Jor., 11,224 142 C4
Madagascal Pd., Me. 55 D3
Madagascar=Malagasy Republic
Madagascar, i. 165 g5
Madagascar Basin, Ind. Oc. 168 B3
Madā'in Şāliḩ, Saudi Ar., 1,779 143 B3
Madame, I., N.S., Can. 47 V11
Madan, Bulg., 5,849 129 E4
Madanapalle, India, 24,386 145 F7
Madang, Terr. New Guin. 174 e2
Madanīyīn, Tun., 5,350 161 F2
Madaoua, Niger, 2,479 162 F3
Madaras, Hung., 5,187 126 D3
Madari Hat, India 144 g12
Mādārīpur, Pak., 25,328 144 g14
Madarounfa, Niger, 1,778 162 F3
Madau, Terr. Papua 174 3
Madau, i., Terr. Papua 174 g3
Madauk, Burma, 4,593 147 b2
Madawaska, Ont., Can. 46 F3
Madawaska, Me., 4,035 55 D1
Madawaska, r., Ont., Can. 46 G3
Madawaska L., Me. 55 D2
Madaya, Burma, 3,929 146 B2
Madbury, N.H. 54 F5
Maddaket (part of Nantucket), Mass. 57 Q7
Maddaloni, It., 30,963 123 E4
Madden L., C.Z.-Pan. 94 g11
Madderty, U.K. 112 c7
Maddock, N. Dak., 740 74 C2
Made, Neth., 6,200 115 C3
Madeira, Ohio, 6,744 71 i10
Madeira, i, Madeira Is. 109 4
Madeira, r., Braz. 102 D3
Madeira, Arquipélago da=Madeira Is.
Madeira Beach, Fla., 3,943 65 G5
Madeira Is., Atl. Oc., 282,678 108 L4
Madeira Park, Br. Col., Can. 42 c6
Mädelegabel, mt., F.R.Ger. 118 C5
Madeleine, Îles de la, Qué., Can. 45 O6
Madeley, Salop., Eng., U.K. 7,768 114 D5
Madeley, Staffs., Eng., U.K., 2,844 114 D5
Madelia, Minn., 2,190 74 E3
Madeline, Calif. 82 C2
Madeline I., Wis. 66 C2
Maden, Turk., 8,011 142 D2
Madera, Mex., 7,327 92 C2
Madera, co., Calif., 40,468 82 D4
Madera, Calif., 14,430 82 C4
Madera, Pa. 60 F4
Madge, Okla. 76 C3
Madhubani, India, 28,229 144 e12
Madhumati, r., Pak. 144 g14
Madhupur, India, 19,519 144 f13
Madhya Pradesh, st., India, 32,372,408 145 E4
Madidi, r., Bol. 102 C4
Madill, Okla., 3,084 76 G3
Madimba, D.R.Congo 164 B2
Madingo, Congo 164 A2
Madingou, Congo 164 B2
Madison, co., Ala., 117,348 64 C1
Madison, Ala., 1,435 64 C1
Madison, co., Ark., 9,068 73 B2
Madison, Calif. 82 B3
Madison, Conn., 1,416;4,567(T) 56 F7
Madison, co., Fla., 14,154 65 F2
Madison, Fla., 3,239 65 F2
Madison, co., Ga., 11,246 64 F1
Madison, Ga., 2,680 64 F2
Madison, co., Idaho, 9,417 81 D4
Madison, co., Ill., 224,689 68 C5
Madison, Ill., 6,861 68 B5
Madison, co., Ind., 125,819 70 D2
Madison, Ind., 10,488 70 D4
Madison, co., Iowa, 12,295 72 C3
Madison, Kans., 1,105 75 J5
Madison, co., Ky., 33,482 71 G4
Madison, parish, La., 16,444 73 D5
Madison, Me., 2,761 55 C4
Madison, Md. 62 H4
Madison, Minn., 2,380 74 D3
Madison, co., Miss., 32,904 73 F5
Madison, Miss., 703 73 E5
Madison, co., Mo., 9,366 72 G7
Madison, Mo., 528 72 E5
Madison, co., Mont., 5,211 81 C3
Madison, co., Nebr., 25,145 75 H2
Madison, Nebr., 1,513 75 H2
Madison, N.H. 54 E4
Madison, N.J., 15,122 61 C2
Madison, co., N.Y., 54,635 59 J5
Madison, N.Y., 327 59 K6
Madison, co., N.C., 17,217 63 B2
Madison, N.C., 1,912 63 D1
Madison, co., Ohio, 26,454 70 F3
Madison, Ohio, 1,347 70 J1
Madison, Pa., 399 60 d9
Madison, S.C. 63 A3
Madison, S. Dak., 5,420 74 D4
Madison, co., Tenn., 60,655 71 C6
Madison, Tenn., 13,583 71 E5
Madison, co., Tex., 6,749 77 Q4
Madison, co., Va., 8,187 62 F4
Madison, Va., 301 62 F4
Madison, W. Va., 2,215 62 C4
Madison, Wis., 126,706 66 D5
Madison, r., Mont. 81 D3
Madison, Mt., N.H. 54 E3
Madison Heights, Mich., 33,343 67 f14
Madison Heights, Va. 62 E5
Madison Junction, Wyo. 81 D3
Madison-on-the-Lake, Ohio 70 H1
Madison Ra., Mont. 50 D1
Madison Run, Va. 62 F4
Madisonville, Ky., 13,110 71 D4
Madisonville, La., 860 73 E7
Madisonville, Pa. 61 p16
Madisonville, Tenn., 1,812 71 G6
Madisonville, Tex., 2,324 77 Q4
Madiun, Indon., 123,373 148 D4
Madjalengka, Indon. 148 c7
Madjene, Indon. 149 F3
Madley, U.K. 114 C6
Madley, Mt., Austl. 172 C3
Madoc, Ont., Can., 1,308 44 J7
Madona, U.S.S.R., 5,700 136 B1
Madrakah, Ra's al, pt., Muscat and Oman 143 F5
Madras, st., India, 33,686,953 145 F8
Madras, India, 1,729,141 145 F7
Madras, Oreg., 1,515 80 C3
Madre, Lag., Mex. 93 F3
Madre, Lag., Tex. 77 P6
Madre, Sa., Guat.-Mex. 93 G5
Madre, Sa., Phil. 153 B1
Madre de Deus de Minas, Braz., 1,224 103 d17
Madre de Dios, I., Chile 105 A8
Madre de Dios, r., Bol.-Peru 102 C4
Madre de Dios, r., Peru 104 D5
Madre del Sur, Sa., Mex. 92 E4
Madre Mtn., N. Mex. 79 B4
Madre Occidental, Sa., Mex. 92 D2
Madre Oriental, Sa., Mex. 92 E2
Madrid, Col. 101 e15
Madrid, Sp., 2,259,931 122 D2
Madrid, Ala., 245 64 D4
Madrid, Iowa, 2,286 72 D3
Madrid, Ky. 71 E4
Madrid, Me. 55 B4
Madrid, Nebr., 271 75 D3
Madrid, N. Mex. 79 B4
Madrid, N.Y. 59 K2
Madridejos, Phil., 2,901 153 e10
Madridejos, Phil., 1,791 153 e12
Madridejos, Sp., 9,795 122 D3
Madrone, Calif. 83 f13
Madruga, Cuba, 4,377 96 c1
Madsen, Ont., Can. 44 C5
Madura, i., Indon. 148 E4
Madura, Selat, Indon. 148 E4
Madurai, India, 424,810 145 F8
Maduwa Pt., Terr. Papua 174 3
Maebaru, Jap., 32,410 154 B5
Maebashi, Jap., 181,937 155 F3
Maegasu-Shinden, Jap. 154 h14
Mae Hongson, Thai., 3,445 146 B3
Mae Klong, r., Thai. 147 c4
Mae Ramat, Thai. 146 B3
Ma-erh-k'ang, China 152 A1
Mae Rim, Thai. 146 B3
Măeruş, Rum. 128 E2
Mae Sai, Thai. 146 B2
Mae Sariang, Thai. 146 B3
Maeser, Utah, 929 78 D1
Maeshiba, Jap. 154 i15
Mae-shima, Ryukyu Is. 154 a11
Mae Sot, Thai., 10,359 146 B3
Maestra, Sierra, Cuba 96 e2
Mae Suai, Thai. 146 B3
Mae Taeng, Thai. 146 B3
Maevatanana, Malag. Rep., 2,897 165 G4
Maewo, i., New Hebr. 174 m5
Maeys, Ill. 68 B5
Maeystown, Ill., 158 68 B5
Mafeking, Man., Can. 43 E4
Mafeking, Bech., 8,279 164 D6
Maffliers, Fr. 116 h10
Maffo, Cuba, 2,304 96 e2
Maffra, Austl., 3,161 173 f11
Mafia I., Tanz. 164 F3
Ma-fou, China 152 D1
Mafra, Braz., 12,981 103 G7
Mafra, Port., 7,032 122 A3
Magadan, U.S.S.R., 65,000 135 O4
Magadi, India, 11,154 145 k19
Magadi, Kenya 164 E2
Magadi, L., Kenya 165 h15
Magadino, Switz. 124 C2
Magaguadavic, r., N.B., Can. 55 F3
Magaguadavic L., N.B., Can. 55 E3
Magalhães de Almeida, Braz., 2,122 103 H2
Magaliesburg, S. Af. 165 i17
Magallanes, Phil., 6,002 153 h15
Magallanes, Estr. de, Arg.-Chile 105 A8
Magalta, Burma 146 B1
Magangué, Col. 100 C3
Magaria, Niger, 2,526 162 F3
Magarin, Guat. 94 c10
Magat, r., Phil. 153 B1
Magazine, Ark., 463 73 B2
Magazine Mtn., Ark. 73 B2
Magburaka, Sa. Leone 162 C4
Magdagachi, U.S.S.R. 135 M4
Magdala, Eth. 163 L4
Magdalena, Arg., 9,200* 105 c12
Magdalena, Bol., 3,252 102 D4
Magdalena, Mex., 9,413 92 C1
Magdalena, N. Mex., 1,211 79 B4
Magdalena, B., Mex. 92 C3
Magdalena, I., Chile 105 A6
Magdalena, Llano de la, Mex. 92 C3
Magdalena, r., Col. 100 C3
Magdalena, r., Mex. 92 C1
Magdalena Tequisistlán, Mex., 1,822 93 F5
Magdaleno, Ven., 3,745 101 b11
Magdeburg, Ger.D.R., 261,594 118 C2
Magé, Braz., 10,712 103 e18
Magee, Ind. 69 g10
Magee, Miss., 2,917 73 F6
Magee, I., U.K. 113 D4
Magelang, Indon., 96,454 148 D4
Magenta, It., 17,420 122 b5
Magenta, L., Austl. 172 B5
Magerøy, i., Nor. 120 F1
Maggia, Switz. 124 C2
Maggia, r., Switz. 124 C2
Maggie, N.C. 63 A2
Maggie, Va. 62 D5
Maggiorasca, Monte, It. 123 B2
Maggiore, L. It. 123 B1
Maggotty, Jam. 96 p8
Maghāghah, U.A.R. 161 K3
Maghama, Maur., 2,800 162 B3
Maghdūshah, Leb., 2,337 142 b6
Maghera, U.K., 1,613 113 C4
Magherafelt, U.K., 2,460 113 C4
Maghīlah, Jabal, Tun. 160 f6
Maghnia, Alg., 18,300 160 a6
Maghull, U.K., 10,883 114 B3
Magicienne Bay, Saipan 176 27
Magione, It., 11,493 123 D3
Magistral, Mex., 2,341 92 D2
Maglaj, Yug., 2,498 125 C2
Magleby, Den. 121 D5
Maglehem, Swed. 121 G5
Maglič, Yug. 125 E3
Maglie, It., 13,156 123 G4
Magna, Utah, 6,442 78 B1
Magnac-Laval, Fr., 2,799 117 D3
Magness, Ark., 140 73 D2
Magnet, Man., Can. 43 E4
Magnet, Ark. 73 C3
Magnet, Nebr., 116 75 H1
Magnetawan, Ont., Can. 44 H6
Magnetawan, r., Ont., Can. 46 E3
Magnetic I., Austl. 173 G2
Magnitka, U.S.S.R., 15,500 137 i8
Magnitnaya, G., U.S.S.R. 137 i9
Magnitogorsk, U.S.S.R., 328,000 134 E4
Magnolia, Ark., 10,651 73 B4
Magnolia, Del., 310 62 J3
Magnolia, Ill., 245 68 C2
Magnolia, Iowa, 215 72 B3
Magnolia, Ky. 71 F4
Magnolia, La. 73 F8
Magnolia (part of Gloucester), Mass. 57 O2
Magnolia, Miss., 2,083 73 E6
Magnolia, N.J., 4,199 60 f12
Magnolia, N.C., 629 63 F3
Magnolia, Ohio, 1,596 70 H2
Magnolia, Tex. 77 h8
Magnolia Springs, Ala. 64 B5
Magny-en-Vexin, Fr., 2,565 117 D2
Magny-les-Hameaux, Fr., 1,267 116 g12
Mago, U.S.S.R., 5,500 135 N4
Màgoé, Moz. 164 E4
Magoffin, co., Ky., 11,156 71 H4
Magog, Qué., Can., 12,983 44 K6
Magog, L., Qué., Can. 54 C1
Magothy, r., Md. 62 c8
Magothy Beach, Md. 62 c8
Magouládhes, Gr. 129 B5
Magpie, Qué., Can. 45 N5
Magpie, r., Qué., Can. 45 N4
Magrath, Alta., Can., 1,324 42 K4
Magsalañgi, Phil., 1,530 153 h15
Magsingal, Phil., 3,849 153 b5
Magstadt, F.R.Ger., 4,319 119 F7
Maguarinho, C., Braz. 103 G1
Magude, Moz. 164 E6
Māguri, Rum. 128 D1
Maguse River, N.W.T., Can. 40 K5
Magwe, Burma, 13,270 146 A2
Mahābād, Iran, 20,332 143 D1
Mahabaleshwa, India 145 h18
Mahābhārat Lekh, ra., Nepal 144 c11
Mahabo, Malag, Rep., 2,115 165 G5
Mahad, India, 11,803 145 D6
Mahaddei Uen, Som. Rep. 163 M5
Mahaena, Tahiti 177 44
Mahaffey, Pa., 582 60 E4
Mahagi, D.R.Congo 164 E1
Mahaicony, Guyana 101 M4
Mahajamba, r., Malag. Rep. 165 H4
Mahakam, r., Indon. 148 E2
Mahalapye, Bots., 13,199 164 D5
Mahalás, Gr., 2,275 129 C5
Maḩallāt, Iran, 10,575 143 E2
Maham, India, 9,300 144 a11
Mahameru, G., Indon. 148 e8
Māhān, Iran, 6,239 143 F2
Mahanadi, r., India 145 G5
Mahanay I., Phil. 153 f11
Mahanoy City, Pa., 8,536 61 K4
Mahanoy Cr., Pa. 60 J4
Maharajganj, India 144 d12
Maharashtra, st., India, 39,553,718 145 E6
Maha Rat, Thai. 147 d4
Maha Sarakham, Thai., 15,680 146 C3
Mahaska, Alta., Can. 42 J3
Mahaska, co., Iowa, 23,602 72 E3
Mahaska, Kans., 160 75 H4
Mahavavy, r., Malag. Rep. 165 G4
Mahaweli Ganga, r., Cey. 145 n22
Mahaxay, Laos 146 D3
Mahbubnagar, India, 35,588 145 F6
Mahd adh Dhahab, Saudi Ar. 143 C4
Mahdia, Alg. b6
Mahdia, Guyana 101 L5
Mahe, India, 7,951 145 E8
Mahébourg, Maurit. 165 c12
Mahé I., Seych. 165 H2
Mahendragarh, M.P., India, 9,807 145 G5
Mahendragarh, Pun., India, 9,071 144 a11
Mahenge, Tanz. 164 F3
Maheno, N.Z. 175 f7
Mahi, r., India 145 D5
Mahia Pen., N.Z. 175 h5
Mahkeenac, L., Mass. 56 C3
Mahlaing, Burma, 6,604 147 f7
Mahmudabad, India, 10,193 144 c12
Mahnomen, co., Minn., 6,341 74 E2
Mahnomen, Minn., 1,462 74 D2
Maho, Cey. 145 n22
Mahoba, India, 24,878 145 F4
Mahomet, Ill., 1,367 68 D3
Mahón, Sp., 16,619 122 h8
Mahone, W. Va. 62 C3
Mahone Bay, N.S., Can., 1,097 47 T11
Mahoning, co., Ohio, 300,480 70 J2
Mahoning, r., Pa. 60 B3
Mahoning Cr., Pa. 60 D4
Mahopac, N.Y., 1,337 59 N9
Mahopac L., N.Y. 56 A7
Mahroni, India 144 b13
Mahtomedi, Minn., 2,127 74 d5
Mahtowa, Minn. 74 F2
Mahukona, Hawaii 84 F3
Mahuva, India, 32,732 145 D5
Mahwah, N.J., 3,300* 61 C1
Maia, Rum. 128 D1
Maiana, atoll, Gilb. Is. 175 10
Maibara, Jap. 154 h14
Măicăneşti, Rum. 128 F2
Maicao, Col. 100 D2
Maîche, Fr., 3,534 117 G3
Maicuru, r., Braz. 103 F2
Maiden, N.C., 2,039 63 C2
Maiden Cr., Pa. 61 L4
Maidenhead, U.K., 35,411 113 F6
Maiden Pk., Oreg. 80 B4
Maiden Rock, Wis., 189 66 A4
Maidières, Fr. 116 b9
Maidstone, Ont., Can. 67 g16
Maidstone, Sask., Can. 43 B4
Maidstone, U.K., 59,790 113 G6
Maidstone, Vt. 54 D2
Maidstone L., Vt. 54 D2
Maidsville, W. Va. 62 D3
Maiduguri, Nigeria 162 G4
Maigue, r., Ire. 113 B5
Maihar, India, 12,115 145 F4
Maihue, L., Chile 105 f15
Mai-kai-t'i, China 150 A3
Maikammer, F.R.Ger., 3,942 119 E6
Maili, Hawaii, 2,400* 84 a7
Maili Pt., Hawaii 84 a7
Mailsi, Pak., 13,617 145 D3
Maimāna, Afghan., 49,000* 144 B2
Main, r., F.R.Ger. 118 B3
Main, r., U.K. 113 C4
Maina, i., Aitutaki 177 35
Mainburg, F.R.Ger., 5,277 118 C4
Main Chan., Ont., Can. 46 C3
Maincy, Fr., 1,457 116 i12
Maine, st., U.S., 986,000* 55
Maine, N.Y. 59 H7
Mainesburg, Pa. 60 J2
Maïné-Soroa, Niger, 1,489 162 F3
Maingkwan, Burma 146 B1
Mainit, Phil., 1,689 153 A3
Mainit, Phil., 4,482 153 C3
Mainit, L., Phil. 153 C3
Mainland, i., Ork., U.K. 112 E2
Mainland, i., Zet., U.K. 112 F1
Mainpuri, India, 33,610 144 b12
Main Str., Me. 55 C3
Maintenon, Fr., 3,071 117 D2
Maintirano, Malag. Rep., 3,146 165 G5
Mainz, F.R.Ger., 115,812 118 B4
Maio, i., C. Verde Is. 109 5
Maipo, r., Chile 104 f13
Maipo, Vol., Arg.-Chile 105 B4
Maipú, Arg., 10,000* 105 D5
Maiquetía, Ven., 76,157 101 b11
Maisí, Punta, Cuba 96 f2
Maiskhāl I., Pak. 145 J5
Maison Carrée, Alg., 41,200 160 c5
Maisonnette, N.B., Can. 47 T10
Maisons-Alfort, Fr., 51,689 116 h11
Maisons-Laffitte, Fr., 19,385 116 g11
Maïssade, Haiti, 1,318 96 k6
Maissau, Aust. 124 b9
Mai Suu, N. Viet. 147 i8
Mait, Som. Rep. 163 M4
Maitland, N.S.W., Austl., 21,331 173 G5
Maitland, S. Austl., Austl. 172 b8
Maitland, N.S., Can. 47 U11
Maitland, Mo., 427 72 B4
Maitland, L., Austl. 172 B4
Maitland, r., Ont., Can. 46 C5
Maiwara, Terr. Papua 174 3
Maíz, Is. de=Corn Is.
Maize, Kans., 623 75 H6
Maizières-lès-Metz, Fr., 8,817 116 b8
Maizières-lès-Vic, Fr. 116 c9
Maizuru, Jap., 99,615 155 D4
Maja, P., Indon. 148 D3
Majagua, Cuba, 2,289 96 d2
Majagual, Col. 100 C3
Majagual-Gold Hill, C.Z. 94 f11
Majanji, Uganda 165 f13
Majardah, Wādī, Alg.-Tun. 160 f5
Majāz al Bāb, Tun., 4,068 160 f5
Majdanpek, Yug., 2,244 125 E2
Majenica, Ind. 70 D2
Majestic, Ky. 71 J4
Maji, Eth. 163 K4
Majma'ah, Saudi Ar. 143 D3
Major, co., Okla., 7,808 76 E1
Majorca=Mallorca, I. de
Maju, P., Indon. 149 H2
Majunga, Malag, Rep., 34,119 165 G4
Majuro, atoll, Marsh. Is. 170 F4
Mak, Nebr. 75 D3
Maka, D.R.Congo 165 m18
Makaha, Hawaii, 2,745* 84 C2
Makaha Pt., Hawaii 84 B1
Makaha Str., Hawaii 84 a7
Makahoa Pt., Hawaii 84 c5
Makahuena Pt., Hawaii 84 B2
Makalamabedi, Bots., 1,318 164 D5
Makalawena, Hawaii 84 E4
Makale, Eth., 8,800* 163 L3
Makaleha Str., Hawaii 84 b6
Makalii Pt., Hawaii 84 c6
Makalombu, i., Sol. Is. 175 6
Makālu, mtn., China-Nepal 144 f12
Makanalua Pen., Hawaii 84 D2
Makanda, Ill., 168 68 C6
Makanza, D.R.Congo 165 m18
Makapala, Hawaii, 353 84 F3
Makapuu Pt., Hawaii 84 D2
Makarikari Pan, Bots. 164 D5
Makaroff, Man., Can. 43 E4
Makarov, U.S.S.R., 13,900 135 O5
Makarska, Yug., 2,547 125 C3
Makar'yev, U.S.S.R., 10,400 136 F1
Makasar, Indon., 384,159 149 F4
Makassar=Makasar
Makassar Str., Indon. 148 F3
Makat, U.S.S.R., 5,900 134 E5
Makatea, i., Tuam. Arch. 177 42
Makati, Phil., 12,869 153 c8
Makawao, Hawaii, 977 84 E3
Makaweli=Kaumakani
Makaweli, r., Hawaii 84 B1
Makce, Yug. 123 E2
Makebon, Indon. 149 J3
Makedonija, st., Yug., 1,406,003 125 E4
Makefu, Niue 177 32
Make-jima, Jap. 154 k17
Makemo, i., Tuam. Arch. 171 J6
Makena, Hawaii 84 E3
Makeni, Sa. Leone 162 C4
Makeyevka, U.S.S.R., 381,000 136 E4
Makhachkala, U.S.S.R., 129,000 134 D5
Makhariádhon, Gr., 1,163 129 C6
Makharadze, U.S.S.R., 19,000 137 b1
Makhedonia=Macedonia, Gr.-Yug.
Makhnëvo, U.S.S.R. 137 k7
Maki, Indon. 149 K3
Maki, Jap. 154 h15
Maki, Jap., 28,035 155 F3
Makian, P., Indon. 149 H2
Makikihi, N.Z. 175 f7
Makin, atoll, Gilb. Is. 170 F4
Makinen, Minn. 74 F2
Makino, Jap. 154 g15
Makinsk, U.S.S.R., 23,000 134 G4
Makinson, Newf., Can. 45 b10
Makira Bay, Sol. Is. 175 c3
Makkah, Saudi Ar., 150,000* 143 B4
Mak-Klintoka, O., U.S.S.R. 134 E2
Makkovik, Newf., Can. 45 P3
Makkum, Neth. 115 D1
Makó, Hung., 29,935 126 E3
Makokou, Gabon 164 B1
Makongai, i., Fiji 174 4
Makoop L., Ont., Can. 44 D4
Makoti, N. Dak., 224 74 B2
Makoua, Congo 164 B2
Makov, Czech. 126 D2
Maków Mazowiecki, Pol., 4,594 127 D2
Makrakómi, Gr., 1,875 129 D5
Makrān Coast Ra., Pak. 144 B4
Mákri, Gr. 129 E4
Makronisi, i., Gr. 129 E6
Makthar, Tun., 4,000 161 F2
Mākū, Iran, 5,306 143 D1
Makua, Hawaii 84 a6
Ma-kuan, China 152 B3
Makubetsu, Jap., 18,264 155 K8
Makuhari, Jap. 155 n19
Makumbi, D.R.Congo 164 C2
Makura, i., New Hebr. 174 m6
Makurazaki, Jap., 33,511 154 B6
Makurdi, Nigeria, 19,554 162 F4
Makushino, U.S.S.R., 13,700 137 m11
Makuu, Hawaii 84 G4
Makuyuni, Tanz. 165 h15
Mala, Peru, 2,656 104 B5
Mala, P., Pan. 94 H7
Malabang, Phil., 7,884 153 C4
Malabar, Fla. 65 J4
Malabar Coast, India 145 E7
Mal Abrigo, Urug. 105 c12
Malabugas, Phil., 1,926 153 d12
Malabuyog, Phil., 1,834 153 e12
Malacatán, Guat., 3,205 94 a9
Malacbalac, Phil., 5,637 153 h14
Malacca, Malay., 69,851 148 B2
Malacca, Str. of, Indon.-Malay. 148 B2
Malachi, Ont., Can. 44 C5
Malachite, Colo. 79 C3
Malacky, Czech. 126 C2
Malad, r., Utah-Idaho 78 B1
Malad City, Idaho, 2,274 81 C4
Malaekahana Str., Hawaii 84 c6
Málaga, Col. 100 D4
Málaga, Sp., 301,048 122 C4
Malaga, Calif. 82 D4
Malaga, N.J. 61 A4
Malaga, N. Mex. 79 C5
Malagash, N.S., Can. 47 U11
Malagasy Republic, ctry., 6,420,000* 165 H5
Malagón, Sp., 11,208 122 D3
Malahide, Ire., 2,490 113 C5
Malaita, i., Sol. Is. 170 E5
Malakāl, Sudan, 9,680 163 K4
Malākand, Pak. 145 D2
Malakoff, Tex., 1,657 77 P3
Malalag, Phil., 5,242 153 C4
Malalhue, Chile, 1,425 105 e14
Malamala, Indon. 149 G3
Malampaka, Tanz. 165 f15
Malang, Indon., 341,452 148 E4
Malangbong, Indon. 148 D4
Malangwa, Nepal 144 e12
Malanje, Ang., 12,815 164 B3
Malanville, Dahom., 1,700 162 E4
Malapa, i., Sol. Is. 175 c3
Mała Panew, r., Pol. 127 C3
Mälaren, l., Swed. 120 d8
Malargüe, Arg., 23,500* 105 B5
Malartic, Qué., Can., 6,892 44 H5
Malaspina, Arg. 105 B6
Malaspina Glacier, Alaska 85 J4
Malaspina Str., Br. Col., Can. 42 b6
Malatajur, Tg., Indon. 148 E3
Malåträsk, Swed. 120 D2
Malatya, Turk., 84,162 142 D2
Malaucène, Fr., 1,780 117 F4
Malawi, ctry., 3,753,000* 164 E4
Malawi, L., Afr. 164 E4
Malaya, F. of (part of Malay.), 8,039,000* 148 B2
Malaya Belozërka, U.S.S.R. 136 D4
Malayal, Phil., 2,130 153 B4
Malaya Ob', chan., U.S.S.R. 134 F3
Malaya Vishera, U.S.S.R., 14,400 136 D1
Malaya Viska, U.S.S.R., 11,300 136 C3
Malaybalay, Phil., 7,624 153 C3
Malāyer, Iran, 21,105 143 D2
Malay Pen., Asia 141 J6
Malaysia, ctry., 9,426,000* 148
Malazgirt, Turk., 5,056 142 E2
Malbaie, r., Qué., Can. 47 Q10
Malberg, F.R.Ger. 119 B4
Malbon, Austl. 172 F3
Malbork, Pol., 25,000* 127 C1
Malborn, F.R.Ger., 1,315 119 B5
Malbrán, Arg., 1,600* 105 C3
Malbug, Phil., 2,068 153 B2
Malchin, Ger.D.R. 118 D2
Malchow, Ger.D.R. 118 D2
Malcom, Iowa, 416 72 E3
Malczyce, Pol., 2,844 127 f5
Maldegem, Belg., 13,366 115 B3
Malden, Ill., 258 68 C2
Malden, Ind. 70 C1
Malden, Mass., 57,676 57 M3
Malden, Mo., 5,007 72 G8
Malden, Wash., 292 80 E2
Malden Centre, Ont., Can. 67 f16
Malden I., Line Is. 171 H5
Malden-on-Hudson, N.Y. 59 M7
Maldive Is., ctry., 97,743 140 F6
Maldon, U.K., 10,509 113 G6
Maldonado, Ec. 104 B1
Maldonado, Urug. 105 E4
Malėa, Ákra, Gr. 129 D6
Malegaon, India, 121,408 145 E5
Malehra, India 144 b13
Male Karpaty, mts., Czech. 126 C2
Malekula, i., New Hebr. 170 F6
Maler Kotla, India, 39,543 144 a10
Malesherbes, Fr., 2,610 117 E2
Malesína, Gr., 3,133 129 D5
Malesus, Tenn. 71 C6
Malevo, Bulg., 1,696 128 E4
Malgobek, U.S.S.R., 29,500 137 c1
Malheur, co., Oreg., 22,764 80 E4
Malheur, r., Oreg. 80 E4
Malheur, L., Oreg. 80 D4
Malheureux, C., Maurit. 165 c11
Malheureux, C., Seych. 165 a10
Mali, ctry., 4,654,000* 162 D3
Mali, Guin., 3,000 162 B4
Mali, i., Fiji 174 4
Mali, r., Burma 146 B1
Mali Bački Kan., Yug. 125 D2
Malibu, Calif. 83 g15
Malibu Beach, Calif. 83 g15
Malie, W. Samoa, 1,006 177 38
Maligaya, Phil., 5,764 153 B2
Maligaya, Phil., 1,001 153 c8
Malik, Indon. 149 G3
Malik Nāro, mtn., Afghan.-Pak. 144 B3
Malili, Indon. 149 G3
Mali Lošinj, Yug., 3,247 125 B2
Malim Nawar, Malay., 5,716 147 o14
Malín, Czech. 127 e7
Malin, U.S.S.R., 11,000 136 C3
Malin, Oreg., 568 80 C4
Malinaltepec, Mex., 3,211 93 F5
Malinau, Indon. 148 F2
Malindi, Kenya 164 F2
Malingping, Indon. 148 b7
Malin Head, Ire. 113 C4
Mălini, Rum. 128 F1
Malino, U.S.S.R. 136 c6
Malinta, Ohio, 339 70 F1
Ma-li-p'o, China 152 B3
Mališevo, Yug. 125 E3
Malita, Phil., 5,947 153 C4
Maljamar, N. Mex. 79 D5
Malka, r., U.S.S.R. 137 b1
Malkapur, India, 29,687 145 E5
Malkara, Turk., 9,338 142 A1
Malko Tŭrnovo, Bulg., 3,744 128 F4
Mallacoota, Austl. 173 G5
Mallaig, U.K. 112 D3
Mallala, Austl. 172 c8
Mallard, Iowa, 431 72 C2
Mallawī, U.A.R., 52,000 161 K3
Mall Bay, Newf., Can. 45 b10
Malleray, Switz., 1,838 124 B1
Mallersdorf, F.R.Ger., 2,219 118 D4
Mallerstang, mtn., U.K. 114 D2
Malletts Bay, Vt. 54 A2
Mállia, Gr., 1,465 129 E7
Mallig, Phil., 1,328 153 c5
Malling, Den., 2,043 121 C4
Mallnitz, Aust., 1,063 124 K7
Malloa, Chile 104 g14
Mallorca, I. de, Sp. 122 G2
Mallory, N.Y. 59 H5
Mallory, W. Va., 1,133 62 C5
Mallow, Ire., 5,729 113 B5
Mallwyd, U.K. 113 E5
Malmanoury, Fr. Guiana 101 O5
Malmberget, Swed. 120 E2
Malmédy, Belg., 6,028 115 D4
Malmesbury, S. Af., 8,206 164 B7
Malmesbury, U.K., 2,610 114 D7
Malmköping, Swed. 120 d8
Malmö, Swed., 229,388 120 C5
Malmok, c., Bon. 97 17
Malmön, Swed. 121 D2
Malnaş, Rum. 128 E1
Malo, Wash. 80 D1
Malo, i., New Hebr. 174 k5
Maloarkhangel'sk, U.S.S.R., 2,500 136 D2
Maloca, Braz. 103 E1
Maloelap, atoll, Marsh. Is. 170 F4
Małogoszcz, Pol. 127 k6
Maloja Pass, Switz. 124 D2
Malol, Terr. New Guin. 174 d1
Malo-les-Bains, Fr., 14,628 117 E1
Malolos, Guam 176 24
Malolos, Phil., 2,240 153 b8
Malomice, Pol., 2,873 127 A3
Malomir, Bulg., 3,352 128 F3
Malone, Fla., 661 65 D2
Malone, N.Y., 8,737 59 M2
Malone, Tex., 240 77 P4
Malone, Wash. 80 B2
Malone, Wis. 66 E5
Malonga, D.R.Congo 164 C3
Malonton, Man., Can. 43 g9
Malorita, U.S.S.R. 136 B3
Maloshuyka, U.S.S.R. 134 C3
Malo Str., New Hebr. 174 k5
Malott, Wash. 80 D1
Malo-Uchalinskiy, U.S.S.R. 137 i8
Malouin, L., Qué., Can. 46 G2
Måløv, Den., 2,351 121 a7
Maloyaroslavets, U.S.S.R., 18,900 136 b6
Malozemel'skaya Tundra, U.S.S.R. 134 D3
Malpartida de Cáceres, Sp., 5,751 122 B3
Malpas, U.K., 1,219 114 C4
Malpelo, I. de, Col. 171 N4
Malpica, Sp., 7,827 122 A1
Malsch, F.R.Ger., 6,996 118 B4
Målselv, Nor. 120 D1
Malta, ctry., 316,000* 123 E7
Malta, Idaho 81 C4
Malta, Ill., 782 68 D2
Malta, Mont., 2,239 81 F1
Malta, N.Y. 59 v28
Malta, Ohio, 983 70 H3
Malta, i., Malta 123 E7
Malta Bend, Mo., 338 72 D5
Maltahöhe, S.-W. Afr., 1,044 164 B6
Maltby, U.K., 13,691 114 F4
Maltby, Wash. 81 b7
Malters, Switz., 4,579 124 C1
Malton, Ont., Can., 1,923 46 c13
Malton, U.K., 4,197 113 F4
Malu, Sol. Is. 175 c2
Maluku, is., Indon. 149 H3
Ma'lūlā, Syr. 142 c6
Malumteken Mission, Terr. New Guin. 174 g2
Ma-lung, China 152 A2
Malung, Swed. 120 C3
Malungon, Phil., 17,961 153 C4
Maluso, Phil., 3,646 153 B4
Malūţ, Sudan 163 K4
Malvaglia, Switz., 1,120 124 C2
Malvan, India, 17,828 145 D6
Malveira, Port., 2,097 122 i10
Malvern, Jam., 1,090 96 p9
Malvern, Ark., 9,566 73 C3

Malvern—Maria · 257

Malvern, Iowa, 1,193 72 B4
Malvern, Ohio, 1,320 70 H2
Malvern, Pa., 2,268 60 f11
Malverne, N.Y., 9,968 58 e14
Malvérnia, Moz. 164 E5
Malvern Wells, U.K., 2,133 114 D6
Malvinas, Is.=Falkland Is.
Malwa Plat., India 140 F4
Malygina, Prol., U.S.S.R. 134 F2
Malyye Chany, Oz., U.S.S.R. 137 p11
Malyye Karmakuly, U.S.S.R. 134 D2
Malyy Kavkaz, mts., U.S.S.R. 137 b1
Malyy Lyakhovskiy, O., U.S.S.R. 135 N2
Malyy Taymyr, O., U.S.S.R. 135 K2
Malyy Yenisey, r., U.S.S.R. 135 J4
Malzéville, Fr., 7,572 116 b9
Mama, U.S.S.R., 5,000 135 L4
Mamagota, Sol. Is. 175 a2
Mamahatun, Turk. 137 b2
Mamaia, Rum. 128 G2
Mamala Bay, Hawaii 84 c8
Mamanguape, Braz., 8,512 103 b14
Mamanguape, r., Braz. 103 b14
Mamanutha Group, is., Fiji 174 4
Mamaroneck, N.Y., 17,673 59 N10
Mamatla, Mex. 93 e11
Mamawi L., Alta., Can. 42 K1
Mamba, D.R.Congo 165 n18
Mamba, Jap., 6,635 155 F3
Mambajao, Phil., 3,880 153 f12
Mambang Di Awan, Malay., 6,191 147 o14
Mambare, r., Terr. Papua 174 e3
Mamberamo, Indon. 149 L3
Mamberamo, r., Indon. 149 L3
Mambirima, D.R.Congo 165 n19
Mambojao, Mt., Phil. 153 f12
Mambone, Moz. 164 E5
Mamburao, Phil., 2,519 153 B2
Mamehaktebo, Indon. 148 E2
Ma-Me-O Beach, Alta., Can. 42 J3
Mamer, Lux., 1,644 115 D5
Mamers, Fr., 5,295 117 D2
Mamers, N.C. 63 E2
Mamfe, Cam. 162 F5
Mamie, N.C. 63 J1
Mamihara, Jap., 3,446 154 B5
Mamithi, Mex. 93 e9
Mamlyutka, U.S.S.R. 137 n11
Mammoth, Ariz., 1,913 78 C5
Mammoth, Mo. 72 E8
Mammoth Cave Nat. Pk., Ky. 71 E4
Mammoth Hot Springs, Wyo. 81 D3
Mammoth Lakes, Calif. 82 D4
Mammoth Spring, Ark., 825 73 D1
Mammouth, Utah 78 B2
Mamonovo, U.S.S.R., 5,500 136 A2
Mamontovo, U.S.S.R. 137 q11
Mamoré, r., Bol. 102 D4
Mamou, Guin., 15,000 162 C4
Mamou, La., 2,928 73 C7
Mamozekel, r., N.B., Can. 55 E1
Mampawah, Indon. 148 D2
Mampong, Ghana 162 c8
Mamre, S. Af., 2,355 164 a8
Mamry, Jez., Pol. 127 D1
Mamudju, Indon. 149 F3
Mamuel Choique, Arg. 105 B6
Mamurras, Alb. 125 D4
Mamyt, U.S.S.R. 137 i10
Man, Iv. Coast, 12,147 162 C4
Man, W. Va., 1,486 62 C5
Man, r., Col. 100 C4
Man, r., India 145 i18
Mana, Fr. Guiana 101 O5
Mana, Indon. 148 B4
Mana, Hawaii 84 B1
Mana, r., Fr. Guiana 101 O5
Mana, r., U.S.S.R. 137 t11
Manacacías, r., Col. 100 D6
Manacapuru, Braz., 2,584 102 D2
Manacas, Cuba, 2,515 96 c1
Manacor, Sp., 19,224 122 G3
Manado, Indon., 129,912 149 H2
Managua, Nic., 183,783 94 D4
Managua, L. de, Nic. 94 D4
Manahawkin, N.J. 61 C4
Manaka, Guyana 101 L4
Manakara, Malag. Rep., 11,787 165 H5
Manakau, pk., N.Z. 175 g6
Manākhah, Yemen, 12,000* 143 C5
Manakin-Sabot, Va. 62 G5
Manalapan, Fla., 62 65 b8
Manalapan, N.J. 58 b15
Manalapan Bk., N.J. 58 b15
Manalongan, Phil., 2,505 153 d12
Manambolo, r., Malag. Rep. 165 G5
Manam I., Terr. New Guin. 174 e2
Manana I., Hawaii 84 e7
Manan Chose Dawar, pass, China 150 C2
Mananjary, Malag. Rep., 15,583 165 H5
Manaoba, i., Sol. Is. 175 c2
Manao Hwan, Thai. 147 d4
Mana Pass, China-India 150 A4
Manapiare, r., Ven. 100 G5
Manapire, r., Ven. 100 G3
Manapla, Phil., 8,044 153 e11
Manapouri, L., N.Z. 175 f7
Manari, Guyana 101 L4
Manas, G., U.S.S.R. 137 f3
Manas, r., China 150 B2
Manasarowar, l., China 150 B4
Manasquan, N.J., 4,022 61 C3
Manasquan, r., N.J. 58 c16
Manassa, Colo., 831 79 C3
Manassas, Va., 3,555 62 G4
Manassas Nat. Battlefield Pk., Va. 62 G4
Ma-na-ssu, China 150 B2
Manatang, Indon. 149 H5
Manatawny Cr., Pa. 60 e10
Manatee, co., Fla., 69,168 65 G5
Manatee, r., Fla. 65 G5
Manatí, Cuba, 2,318 96 e2
Manatí, P.R., 9,682 96 s10
Manatí, Punta, Cuba 96 d2
Manaure, Col. 100 D2
Manaure, r., Ven. 101 b12
Manaus, Braz., 154,040 102 D2
Manavgat, Turk., 3,184 142 B2
Manawa, Wis., 1,037 66 E4
Manawan L., Alta., Can. 43 b7
Manawatu, r., N.Z. 175 g6
Manawoka, P., Indon. 149 J4
Manay, Phil., 3,053 153 C4
Manazuru, Jap., 9,141 155 F4
Manbij, Syr., 12,650 142 D2
Mancelona, Mich., 1,141 67 J4
Manchaca, Tex. 76 c5
Manchaug Pd., Mass. 57 J4
Manchester, U.K., 661,041 113 E5
Manchester, Ala. 64 B2
Manchester, Calif. 82 B3
Manchester, Conn., 42,102(T) 56 F5
Manchester, Ga., 4,115 64 E3
Manchester, Iowa, 4,402 72 F2
Manchester, Kans., 153 75 H4
Manchester, Ky., 1,868 71 H4
Manchester, Me. 55 C4
Manchester, Md., 1,108 62 H3
Manchester, Mass., 3,932(T) 57 O2
Manchester, Mich., 1,568 67 J6
Manchester, N.H., 88,282 54 D6
Manchester, N.Y., 1,344 58 F6
Manchester, Okla., 162 76 E1
Manchester, Pa., 1,454 60 J5
Manchester, Adams Co., Ohio, 2,172 70 F4
Manchester, Summit Co., Ohio 70 H2
Manchester, Tenn., 3,930 71 E6
Manchester, Vt., 403 54 A5
Manchester, Wash. 81 a7
Manchester, Wis. 66 D5
Manchester Center, Vt. 54 A5
Manchester Depot, Vt., 1,387 54 A5
Manchioneal, Jam. 96 q8
Man-chou-li, China, 30,000* 150 F1
Máncora, Peru, 3,912 104 A3
Mancos, Colo., 832 79 A3
Mancos, r., Colo. 79 A3
Mand, Pak. 144 B4
Mand, r., Iran 143 E3
Manda, Tanz. 164 E3
Mandah, Indon. 148 a6
Mandal, Nor., 5,158 120 A4
Mandalay, Burma, 185,867 146 B2
Mandal Gobi, Mong. 150 E2
Mandalī, Iraq, 9,775 143 D2
Mandalya Körfezi, Turk. 129 F6
Mandan, N. Dak., 10,525 74 B2
Mandana, N.Y. 59 q24
Mandaon, Phil., 11,419 153 B2
Mandaree, N. Dak. 74 A2
Mandarin, Fla. 65 H2
Mandasiá, Gr. 129 D5
Mandeb, Bab el, str., Af.-Asia 143 C5
Mandelieu, Fr., 4,082 116 m13
Mandera, Kenya 164 F1
Manderfeld, Belg., 1,276 115 E4
Manderscheid, F.R.Ger., 1,051 119 B4
Manderson, S. Dak. 74 A4
Manderson, Wyo., 167 81 F3
Mandeville, Jam., 8,416 96 p8
Mandeville, La., 1,740 73 E7
Mandi, India, 13,034 145 E3
Mandiana, Guin. 162 C4
Mandimba, Moz. 164 F4
Mandinga, Pan. 94 H6
Mandioli, P., Indon. 149 H3
Mandla, India, 19,416 145 F5
Mandor, Indon. 148 D2
Mandoúdhion, Gr., 2,801 129 D5
Mándra, Gr., 4,636 129 D5
Mandrael, India 144 a12
Mandrákhi, Gr., 1,098 129 F6
Mandres, Fr., 1,403 116 i12
Mandritsara, Malag. Rep., 3,758 165 H4
Mandsaur, India, 41,876 145 E4
Mandu, ruins, India 145 E5
Mandurah, Austl., 1,623 172 A5
Manduria, It., 27,059 123 F4
Mandvi, India, 26,609 144 C5
Mandya, India, 33,347 145 E7
Manea, U.K., 1,393 114 J6
Manek Urai, Malay., 1,350 147 p14
Manerbio, It., 10,622 123 B2
Manes, Mo. 72 E7
Manětín, Czech. 126 c6
Manfalūṭ, U.A.R., 29,000 161 K3
Manfred, N. Dak. 74 C2
Manfredonia, It., 37,723 123 F4
Manfredonia, Golfo di, It. 123 F4
Manga, Braz., 2,000 103 H4
Mangabeiras, Chapada das, upland, Braz. 103 G3
Mangagoy, Phil., 5,501 153 C3
Mangaia, i., Cook Is. 171 H6
Mangakino, N.Z., 5,025 175 g5
Mangaldan, Phil., 3,768 153 b6
Mangalia, Rum., 4,792 128 G3
Mangalmé, Chad 163 H3
Mangalore, India, 142,669 145 E7
Manganítis, Gr. 129 F6
Mangaratiba, Braz., 2,741 103 d18
Mangareva, i., Is. Gambier 177 42
Mangari, i., Aitutaki 177 35
Mangawan, India 144 c13
Mangeigne, Chad 163 H4
Mangen, Sikkim 144 g12
Mangere I., N.Z. 175 14
Manggar, Indon. 148 D3
Mangham, La., 521 73 D5
Mangkalihat, Tg., Indon. 149 F2
Mangla Dam, Pak. 145 D2
Manglaur, India, 15,206 144 a11
Mango, Nic. 94 E4
Mango, Fla. 65 d11
Mango, i., Fiji 174 4
Mango, i., Tonga 177 36
Mangohick, Va. 62 G5
Mangoky, r., Malag. Rep. 165 G5
Mangole, P., Indon. 149 H3
Mangonia, L., Fla. 65 b8
Mangonia Park, Fla., 594 65 b8
Mangosiza, r., Ec. 104 d11
Mangotsfield, U.K., 24,154 113 E6
Mangrol, Guj., India, 21,089 144 C5
Mangrol, Raj., India 144 a13
Mangrove Cay, Bah. Is. 95 b8
Mangsang, Indon. 148 C3
Mangualde, Port., 6,972 122 B2
Mangueira, Lag., Braz. 103 F8
Manguito, Cuba, 2,569 96 c1
Mangula, Rhod., 6,620 164 D4
Mangulile, Hond., 1,561 94 D3
Mangum, Okla., 3,950 76 D3
Mang-yai, China 150 C3
Mangyshlak, P-ov., U.S.S.R. 134 E5
Manhan, r., Mass. 56 F4
Manhasset, N.Y. 58 e13
Manhattan, Ill., 1,117 68 D2
Manhattan, Kans., 22,993 75 J4
Manhattan, Mont., 889 81 D3
Manhattan, Nev. 83 B3
Manhattan, (Borough of N.Y.C.), N.Y. 58 d14
Manhattan Beach, Calif., 33,934 83 g16
Manhiça, Moz., 39,501 164 E6
Manhuaçu, Braz., 10,546 103 f17
Manhumirim, Braz., 9,477 103 e17
Maniago, It. 8,168 123 D1
Maniamba, Moz. 164 E4
Manicaragua, Cuba, 3,993 96 d1
Manicoré, Braz., 2,268 102 D3
Manicoré, r., Braz. 102 D3
Manicouagan, r., Qué., Can. 45 M5
Manicouagan L., Qué., Can. 45 M4
Manifah, Saudi Ar. 143 D3
Manifest, La. 73 D6
Manifold, Pa. 60 b9
Manigotagan, Man., Can. 43 F4
Manigotagan, r., Man., Can. 43 G5
Manihi, atol', Tuam. Arch. 177 42
Manihiki, i., Cook Is. 171 H5
Manikpur, India, 5,408 144 c13
Manila, Phil., 1,138,611 153 B2
Manila, Ark., 1,753 73 E2
Manila, Utah 329 78 D1
Manila Bay, Phil. 153 B2
Manildra, Austl. 173 g9
Manilla, Austl., 1,972 173 G4
Manilla, Ont., Can. 46 E4
Manilla, Ind. 70 D3
Manilla, Iowa, 939 72 B3
Manimbaja, Tg., Indon. 149 F3
Maninijon, Phil., 1,980 153 d12
Manipa, P., Indon. 149 J3
Manipa, Selat, Indon. 149 H3
Manipur, un. terr., India, 780,037 145 J4
Manipur, r., Burma 146 A2
Manisa, Turk., 59,223 142 A2
Manistee, co., Mich., 19,042 67 G4
Manistee, Mich., 8,324 67 G4
Manistee, r., Mich. 67 H4
Manistee L., Mich. 67 J4
Manistique, Mich., 4,875 67 G3
Manistique, r., Mich. 67 G2
Manistique L., Mich. 67 H2
Manito, Ill., 1,093 68 C3
Manitoba, prov., Can., 962,000* 43
Manitoba, L., Man., Can. 43 F5
Manitou, Man., Can. 43 f10
Manitou, Okla., 269 76 E3
Manitou Beach, Mich., 1,544 67 J7
Manitou Beach, N.Y. 58 n20
Manitou I., Mich. 66 F1
Manitou L., Ont., Can. 46 C3
Manitou Lakes, Ont., Can. 44 D5
Manitoulin I., Ont., Can. 44 G6
Manitou Springs, Colo., 3,626 79 C2
Manitouwadge, Ont., Can. 44 F5
Manitowaning, Ont., Can. 46 C3
Manitowish, Wis. 66 C2
Manitowish Waters, Wis. 66 D2
Manitowoc, co., Wis., 75,215 66 F4
Manitowoc, Wis., 32,275 66 F4
Manitsauá-Missu, r., Braz. 103 F4
Maniwaki, Qué., Can., 6,171 44 J6
Manizales, Col., 176,080 100 C5
Manja, Malag. Rep., 3,870 165 G5
Manjacaze, Moz. 164 E6
Manjeri, India, 12,276 145 k20
Manjimup, Austl., 2,223 172 B5
Mankato, Kans., 1,231 75 G4
Mankato, Minn., 28,454 74 F3
Mankono, Iv. Coast, 6,717 162 C4
Mankota, Sask., Can. 43 C5
Mankoya, Zambia 164 D4
Mankulam, Cey. 145 n21
Manley Hot Springs, Alaska, 72 85 F2
Manlius, Ill., 374 68 C2
Manlius, N.Y., 2,781 59 J6
Manlleu, Sp., 9,410 122 G1
Manlove, Calif. 82 b7
Manly, Austl., 32,473 173 G5
Manly, Iowa, 1,425 72 D1
Manly, N.C., 239 63 E2
Manmad, India, 31,551 145 i16
Mann, i., Kwajalein 176 25
Mannar, Cey. 145 F8
Mannar, G. of, Cey.-India 145 F8
Mannargudi, India, 33,558 145 m20
Mannersdorf, Aust., 3,903 124 N6
Manners Sutton, N. B., Can. 47 S11
Mannford, Okla., 358 76 G1
Mannheim, F.R.Ger., 287,210 118 B4
Manning, Alta., Can. 42 H2
Manning, Ark. 73 C3
Manning, Iowa, 1,676 72 C3
Manning, Kans. 75 E5
Manning, N. Dak. 74 A2
Manning, S.C., 3,917 63 D4
Manning, Tex. 77 Q4
Manning, C., Christmas Atoll 177 40
Manning Str., Sol. Is. 175 b2
Mannington, W. Va., 2,996 62 D3
Manns Choice, Pa., 351 60 E6
Mannsdorf, Aust. 124 d10
Manns Harbor, N.C. 63 J2
Mannsville, N.Y., 446 59 J4
Mannsville, Okla., 297 76 G3
Mannu, r., It. 123 B5
Mannum, Austl., 1,817 172 c8
Mannus, Austl. 173 g10
Mannville, Alta., Can. 42 K3
Mano, Sta. Cruz Is. 175 6
Manø, i., Den. 121 A5
Manoa, Ven. 101 K3
Manoa, r., Hawaii 84 d8
Man of War Cay, Bah. Is. 95 c6
Manokotak, Alaska, 149 85 E4
Manokwari, Indon. 149 K3
Manola, Alta., Can. 43 a6
Manolás, Gr. 129 C5
Manomet (part of Plymouth), Mass. 57 O5
Manono, D.R.Congo, 12,234 164 D3
Manono, i., W. Samoa 177 38
Manor, Sask., Can. 43 E5
Manor, Ga. 64 G4
Manor, Pa., 1,136 60 d8
Manor, Tex., 756 76 c5
Manora, Burma 146 B5
Manor Hamilton, Ire. 113 B4
Manorhaven, N.Y., 3,566 58 d13
Manorom, Thai. 147 d4
Manorville, Pa., 557 60 C4
Manosque, Fr., 10,507 117 F5
Manotick, Ont., Can. 47 J3
Mano-wan, Jap. 155 F3
Manp'o, N. Kor. 151 E2
Manquin, Va. 62 G5
Manresa, Sp., 52,216 122 F2
Manreza, Phil., 3,958 153 C4
Manrique, Ven. 100 F3
Mansalay, Phil., 4,395 153 B2
Mansavillagra, Urug. 105 d11
Manseau, Qué., Can. 47 N2
Mānsehra, Pak., 11,848 145 D2
Mansel I., N.W.T., Can. 44 H1
Mansfield, Austl., 1,861 173 G5
Mansfield, U.K., 53,218 113 F5
Mansfield, Ark., 881 73 A2
Mansfield, Conn., 14,638(T) 56 H5
Mansfield, Ga., 394 64 F2
Mansfield, Ill., 743 68 D3
Mansfield, Ind. 70 B3
Mansfield, La., 5,839 73 B5
Mansfield, Mass., 4,674;7,773(T) 57 L4
Mansfield, Mo., 949 72 E7
Mansfield, Ohio, 47,325 70 G2
Mansfield, Pa., 2,678 60 H2
Mansfield, S. Dak. 74 C3
Mansfield, Tenn. 71 C5
Mansfield, Tex., 1,375 76 e9
Mansfield, Wash., 335 80 D2
Mansfield, Mt., Vt. 54 B2
Mansfield Center (part of Mansfield), Conn. 56 H5
Mansinte, Morne, Haiti 96 i6
Mansle, Fr., 1,348 117 D4
Manso, r., Arg.-Chile 105 f15
Manso, r., Braz. 103 F4
Mansôa, Port. Guin., 1,311* 162 B3
Manson, Ind. 70 C2
Manson, Iowa, 1,789 72 C2
Manson, Wash. 80 C2
Manson Creek, Br. Col., Can. 42 F2
Mansura, La., 1,579 73 C6
Manta, Ec., 33,222 104 A2
Mantador, N. Dak., 98 74 D2
Mantare, Tanz. 165 f15
Mantaro, r., Peru 104 B4
Manteca, Calif., 8,242 82 C4
Mantecal, Ven. 100 F4
Mantee, Miss., 166 73 F4
Manteno, Ill., 2,225 68 E2
Manteo, N.C., 587 63 J2
Manter, Kans., 183 75 D6
Mantes, Fr., 19,227 117 D2
Manti, Utah, 1,739 78 C2
Mantiqueira, Sa. da, Braz. 103 G6
Mant Is., Ponape 176 29
Manto, Hond., 1,796 94 D3
Mantokoro, Jap. 154 h14
Mantoloking, N.J., 160 61 C3
Manton, Mich., 1,050 67 H4
Mantorville, Minn., 498 74 F3
Mantova, It., 60,331 123 C2
Mäntsälä, Fin. 120 F3
Mänttä, Fin. 120 F3
Mantua, It.=Mantova
Mantua, N.J., 1,550* 60 f12
Mantua, Ohio, 1,194 70 H1
Mantua, Utah, 275 78 c7
Mantuc, r., Cuba 96 a1
Manturovo, U.S.S.R., 16,400 136 G1
Mäntyharju, Fin. 120 F3
Manuae, atoll, Cook Is. 177 33
Manua Is., Amer. Samoa 177 37
Manuan, r., Qué., Can. 45 L5
Manuan L., Qué., Can. 45 L5
Manuel, Mex., 2,716 93 F3
Manuel Avila Camacho, Presa, res., Mex. 93 f11
Manuel Benavides, Mex. 92 E2
Manuel Doblado, Mex., 4,770 93 c9
Manuelito, N. Mex. 79 A4
Manuel Luis, Recife, Braz. 103 H2
Manuel Ocampo, Arg., 2,014 105 a11
Manuel Prado, Peru 104 B3
Manuels, Newf., Can. 45 c10
Manuel Urbano, Braz. 102 C3
Manuhangi, atoll, Tuam. Arch. 177 42
Manui, P., Indon. 149 G3
Manuk, P., Indon. 149 J4
Manukan, Phil., 3,513 153 B3
Manukau Hbr., N.Z. 175 g5
Manulu Lag., Christmas Atoll 177 40
Manuripe, r., Bol.-Peru 104 D4
Manus, i., Terr. New Guin. 170 D5
Manutuke, N.Z. 175 h5
Manvel, N. Dak., 313 74 D1
Manvel, Tex. 77 i10
Manville, Ill. 68 D2
Manville, N.J., 10,995 61 B2
Manville, R.I. 57 L5
Manville, Wyo., 124 81 G4
Many, La., 3,164 73 B6
Manyara, L., Tanz. 164 F2
Manyas Gölü, Turk. 142 A1
Manyberries, Alta., Can. 42 L4
Manych, r., U.S.S.R. 136 g8
Manych-Gudilo, Oz., U.S.S.R. 136 F4
Manyoni, Tanz. 164 E2
Manzanares, Col. 101 d14
Manzanares, Mex. 93 d8
Manzanares, Sp., 17,847 122 D3
Manzanedo, Sp. 122 m12
Manzanilla Point, Trin. and Tob. 96 h5
Manzanillo, Cuba, 42,252 96 e2
Manzanillo, Mex., 16,591 92 D4
Manzanita, Oreg., 363 80 A3
Manzano, N. Mex. 79 B4
Manzanola, Colo., 562 79 C2
Manzanos, Mex. 93 d8
Manzat, Fr., 1,499 117 E4
Manzilah, Buhayrat al, L., U.A.R. 161 k7
Manzil Bū Ruqaybah, Tun., 34,732 161 F1
Manzil Bū Zalafah, Tun., 7,615 160 g5
Manzil Jamīl, Tun., 7,558 160 g5
Manzil Shākir, Tun. 160 g6
Manzil Tamīm, Tun., 11,350 160 g5
Manzini, Swaz. 164 E6
Manzovka, U.S.S.R., 9,000 135 N5
Mao, Chad 162 G3
Maoke, Pegunungan, Indon. 149 L3
Mao-ming, China 150 E5
Mao-pi T'ou, Taiwan 152 F3
Mao-wen, China 152 A1
Maoya, Mé, pk., N. Caled. 174 i8
Map, i., Yap 176 20
Mapai, Moz. 164 E5
Mapanda, D.R.Congo 165 m18
Maparari, Ven., 1,364 100 F2
Mapastepec, Mex., 4,664 93 G5
Mapi, Indon. 149 L4
Mapi, r., Indon. 149 L4
Mapia, Indon. 149 K3
Mapia, Kep., Indon. 149 K2
Ma-pien, China 152 A1
Mapimí, Mex., 2,998 92 D3
Mapimí, Bolsón de, des., Mex. 92
Mapire, Ven. 101 H4
Mapire, r., Ven. 101 b12
Mapis, Arg. 105 a13
Maple, Ont., Can., 1,174 46 E5
Maple, Tex. 77 M3
Maple, Wis. 66 B2
Maple, r., Iowa 72 B2
Maple, r., Mich. 67 J5
Maple, r., N. Dak. 74 C2
Maple, r., N. Dak. 74 D2
Maple City, Kans. 75 J6
Maple City, Mich. 67 H4
Maple Creek, Sask., Can., 2,243 43 B5
Maple Falls, Wash. 80 C1
Maple Grove, Qué., Can., 1,382 47 o18
Maple Grove, Me. 55 E2
Maple Grove, Mich. 67 H6
Maple Grove, Minn., 3,653 74 F3
Maple Heights, Ohio, 31,667 70 e9
Maple Hill, N.C. 63 G3
Maple Lake, Minn., 1,018 74 F3
Maple Lake, Pa. 61 o16
Maple Park, Ill., 592 68 D2
Maple Rapids, Mich., 683 67 J5
Maple Ridge, Mich. 67 K4
Maples, Ind. 70 E1
Maple Shade, N.J., 12,947(T) 61 B4
Maple Springs, N.Y. 58 B7
Maplesville, Ala., 679 64 C3
Mapleton, Iowa, 1,686 72 B2
Mapleton, Me. 55 D2
Mapleton, Minn., 1,107 74 F4
Mapleton, N. Dak., 180 74 D2
Mapleton, Oreg. 80 B3
Mapleton, Utah, 1,516 78 c10
Mapleton Depot, Pa., 666 60 G5
Mapleville, R.I. 57 K5
Maplewood, La., 2,432 73 B7
Maplewood, Minn., 18,519 74 c5
Maplewood, Mo., 12,552 72 a11
Maplewood, N.J., 23,977 58 b14
Maplewood, Oreg. 80 a7
Maplewood, Pa. 61 p16
Maplewood, Wis. 66 F4
Maporal, Ven. 100 E4
Mappsville, Va. 62 J5
Maprik, Terr. New Guin. 174 d1
Mapuca, India 145 D7
Mapuera, r., Braz. 102 E1
Mapulaca, Hond. 94 e9
Maqueda Chan., Phil. 153 h14
Maquegua, Chile 104 e15
Maquela do Zombo, Ang. 164 B3
Maquinchao, Arg., 1,600* 105 B6
Maquoketa, Iowa, 5,909 72 G2
Maquoketa, r., Iowa 72 F2
Maquon, Ill., 386 68 B3
Mar, Sa. do, Braz. 99 E5
Mara, Indon. 148 F2
Mara, Indon. 149 G4
Mara, Peru, 1,930 104 D5
Maraã, Braz. 102 C2
Maraa, Tahiti 177 44
Marabá, Braz., 8,533 103 G3
Maracá, I. de, Braz. 103 G1
Maracaibo, Ven., 432,902 100 D2
Maracaibo, L. de, Ven. 100 E3
Maracaju, Braz., 1,848 103 E6
Maracaju, Sa. de, Braz. 103 E6
Maracanã, Braz., 3,903 103 G2
Maracás, Braz., 1,828 103 H4
Maracay, Ven., 134,123 100 G2
Maradi, Niger, 11,653 162 F3
Marāgheh, Iran, 36,551 143 D1
Maragogipe, Braz., 12,575 103 J4
Marahajpur, India, 11,762 144 b13
Marahuaca, Co., Ven. 100 H6
Marainviller, Fr. 116 c9
Marais Croche, Mo. 72 a10
Marais des Cygnes, r., Kans.-Mo. 75 K5
Marajó, I. de, Braz. 103 F2
Marakanata, Guyana 101 L6
Marakei, atoll, Gilb. Is. 175 10
Maralal, Kenya 164 F1
Maralinga, Austl. 172 D4
Maramag, Phil., 2,077 153 C4
Maramasike, i., Sol. Is. 175 c3
Marambaia, Restinga da, i., Braz. 103 e18
Maramec, Okla., 169 76 G1
Marampa, Sa. Leone 162 B4
Maran, Malay. 147 p15
Marana, Ariz. 78 C5
Maranboy, Austl. 172 D2
Maranchón, Sp. 122 D2
Marand, Iran, 13,822 143 D1
Marandellas, Rhod., 3,600 164 E5
Marangas, Phil., 2,695 153 A3
Maranguape, Braz., 8,715 103 J2
Maranhão, st., Braz., 2,492,139 103 G3
Marano, Torrente, It. 123 e11
Marano di Volpolicella, It., 2,809 122 d5
Marañón, r., Peru 104 C3
Marans, Fr., 3,836 117 C3
Marapi, G., Indon. 148 B3
Maraş, Turk., 54,646 142 D2
Mărăşeşti, Rum., 5,604 128 F2
Maratea, It., 5,114 123 E5
Marathókambos, Gr., 2,333 129 F6
Marathon, Ont., Can., 2,568 44 F5
Marathón, Gr., 2,167 129 E5
Marathon, Fla. 65 g15
Marathon, Iowa, 516 72 C2
Marathon, N.Y., 1,079 59 J7
Marathon, Tex. 77 M4
Marathon, co., Wis., 88,874 66 D4
Marathon, Wis., 1,022 66 D4
Marau Pt., N.Z. 175 h5
Maravatío, Mex., 5,182 93 d10
Marav L., Pak. 144 C3
Marawi, Phil., 7,787 153 C4
Marawī, Sudan, 1,620 163 K2
Marbach, F.R.Ger., 6,839 119 G7
Marbache, Fr., 1,632 116 b9
Marbeck, F.R.Ger., 1,840 119 B1
Marbella, Sp., 12,069 122 C4
Marble, Ark. 73 B1
Marble, Colo., 5 79 B2
Marble, Minn., 879 74 F2
Marble, N.C. 63 b7
Marble Bar, Austl. 172 B3
Marble Canyon, Ariz. 78 C3
Marble City, Okla., 271 76 J2
Marble Cliff, Ohio, 622 70 a7
Marbledale (part of Washington), Conn. 56 C6
Marble Falls, Tex., 2,161 77 O4
Marblehead, Ill. 68 A4
Marblehead, Mass., 18,521(T) 57 N3
Marblehead, Ohio, 858 70 G1
Marble Hill, Mo., 497 72 H7
Marblemount, Wash. 80 C1
Marble Rock, Iowa, 442 72 E2
Marbleton, Qué., Can. 47 N3
Marbleton, Wyo., 189 81 E4
Marburg, F.R.Ger., 39,566 118 B3
Marbury, Md. 62 G4
Marcal, r., Hung. 126 C3
Marcala, Hond., 2,457 94 C3
Marcali, Hung., 7,871 126 C3
Marcelin, Sask., Can. 43 C4
Marceline, Mo., 2,872 72 E5
Marcella, Ark. 73 C2
Marcella, N.J. 58 b13
Marcellon, Wis. 66 D5
Marcellus, Mich., 1,073 67 H6
Marcellus, N.Y., 1,697 59 H6
Marcellus Falls, N.Y. 59 q23
March, U.K., 13,144 113 G5
Marchant, Calif. 82 a7
Marche-en-Famenne, Belg., 4,239 115 D4
Marchena, Sp., 20,600 122 C4
Marchena, I., Colón, Arch. de 104 a7
Marchfield, Barb. 97 10
Marchiennes, Fr., 3,417 116 a7
Marchihue, Chile 104 f14
Mar Chiquita, Lag., Arg. 105 a12
Mar Chiquita, Lag., Arg. 105 C4
Marchtrenk, Aust., 6,869 124 K5
Marcianise, It., 24,249 123 c9
Marcilly, Fr. 116 k10
Marcinelle, Belg., 24,930 115 C4
Marckolsheim, Fr., 4,653 117 G2
Marco, Fla. 65 H7
Marco, Ind. 70 B4
Marcoing, Fr., 2,165 116 a7
Marcola, Oreg. 80 B3
Marcona, Peru, 6,652 104 C5
Marcounda, C.A.R. 163 G4
Marcoussis, Fr., 2,188 116 g12
Marcq, Fr. 116 f11
Marcus, Ark. 73 B3
Marcus, Iowa, 1,307 72 B2
Marcus, S. Dak. 74 A3
Marcus, Wash., 126 80 E1
Marcus Baker, Mt., Alaska 85 H3
Marcus Hook, Pa., 3,299 61 M6
Marcus I.=Minami-tori-shima
Marcy, N.Y. 59 t26
Marcy, Mt., N.Y. 59 M3
Mardān, Pak., 77,932 145 D2
Mar de Ajó, Arg., 1,000* 105 c13
Mar de Espanha, Braz., 3,661 103 e17
Mardela Springs, Md., 380 62 J4
Mar del Plata, Arg., 160,000* 105 D5
Marden, U.K. 114 C6
Mardin, Turk., 27,390 142 E2
Maré, I., Loy. Is. 174 m8
Mare, Rîul, Rum. 128 D2
Marecchia, r., It. 123 D3
Marechal Deodoro, Braz., 5,296 103 b15
Maree, Loch, U.K. 112 D3
Mareeba, Austl., 3,369 173 F2
Mareham le Fen, U.K. 114 H4
Mareil-en-France, Fr. 116 h10
Mareil-le-Guyon, Fr. 116 f11
Mareil-sur-Mauldre, Fr. 116 f11
Marengo, co., Ala., 27,098 64 B3
Marengo, Ill., 3,568 68 D1
Marengo, Ind., 803 70 C4
Marengo, Iowa, 2,264 72 E3
Marengo, Mich. 67 J6
Marengo, Ohio, 321 70 G2
Marengo, Wash. 80 D2
Marengo, Wis. 66 C2
Marengo, r., Wis. 66 B2
Marenisco, Mich. 66 D2
Marennes, Fr. 116 p15
Marennes, Fr., 4,389 117 C4
Marepa, Moorea 177 44
Marescot, Mt., Sol. Is. 175 c2
Marest, L., Qué., Can. 44 J3
Maretz, Fr., 1,816 116 a7
Mareuil-lès-Meaux, Fr. 116 k11
Marfa, Tex., 2,799 77 M4
Marfrance, W. Va. 62 D4
Marganets, U.S.S.R., 35,500 136 D4
Margao, India 145 D7
Margaree Forks, N.S., Can. 47 V10
Margaree Harbour, N.S., Can. 47 V10
Margaret, Ala., 715 64 d7
Margaret Bay, Br. Col., Can. 42 E3
Margaret L., Alta., Can. 42 J1
Margaret River, Austl., 1,008 172 A5
Margaretville, N.Y., 833 59 L7
Margarita, I. de, Ven. 101 H2
Margarita-Escondido, C.Z., 1,364 94 f11
Margaritas, Mex. 93 b9
Margarítion, Gr. 129 C5
Margate, S. Af., 2,895 164 E7
Margate, U.K., 45,739 113 G6
Margate, Fla., 2,646 65 b9
Margate City, N.J., 9,474 61 C5
Margelan, U.S.S.R., 73,000 137 f4
Margherita=Giamame
Margherita Pk., D.R.Congo-Uganda 165 e13
Marghi, Afghan. 144 C2
Marghita, Rum. 128 D1
Margie, Alta., Can. 42 K2
Margie, Minn. 74 E1
Margina, Rum. 128 D2
Marginea, Rum. 128 E1
Margo, Sask., Can. 43 D4
Margos, Peru, 1,179 104 B4
Margosatubig, Phil., 4,457 153 B4
Margrethe, L., Mich. 67 J4
Marguerite, r., Qué., Can. 45 M5
Marguerite B., Ant. 180 N6
Marham, U.K., 3,021 113 G5
Mari, Braz., 8,242 103 b14
Maria, Qué., Can. 47 S9

258 · Maria—Mati

Maria, atoll, Tuam. Arch. 177 42
Maria, atoll, Îs. Tubuai 177 42
María Cleofas, I., Mex. 92 D4
Mariadoh, India 144 b13
Mariager, Den., 1,483 121 C4
Mariager Fjord, bay, Den. 121 C4
María Grande, Arg., 3,058 105 b10
Maria I., Austl. 173 g14
Maria I., Austl. 172 E2
Marial, Oreg. 80 B4
María Madre, I., Mex. 92 D4
María Magdalena, I., Mex. 92 D4
Marian, L., Fla. 65 J5
Mariana, Braz., 6,378 103 e17
Mariana Basin, Pac. Oc. 168 F2
Mariana Is., Tr. Terr. Pac. Is. 170 D3
Mariana Trench, Pac. Oc. 168 E2
Mariani, Fr. Guiana 101 O5
Marianna, Ark., 5,134 73 E3
Marianna, Fla., 7,152 65 D2
Marianna, Pa., 1,088 60 B5
Mariannelund, Swed. 120 C4
Mariánské Lázně, Czech., 16,456 126 A2
Mariapolis, Man., Can. 43 f10
Mariara, Ven., 7,372 101 b11
Marias, r., Mont. 81 D1
Mariastein, Switz. 124 B1
María Teresa, Arg., 5,500* 105 C4
Mariato, P., Pan. 94 G7
Maria van Diemen, C., N.Z. 175 g4
Mariaville, Me. 55 D4
Mariaville, N.Y. 59 M6
Mariazell, Aust., 2,188 124 M6
Ma'rib, Yemen 143 D5
Mariba, Ky. 71 H4
Maribel, Wis. 66 F4
Maribo, Den., 5,235 121 D6
Maribojoc, Phil., 1,560 153 C3
Maribojoc B., Phil. 153 e12
Maribor, Yug., 85,000* 125 B1
Maricaban I., Phil. 153 b9
Maricalum, Phil., 2,685 153 d12
Maricao, P.R., 1,475 96 s10
Maricopa, co., Ariz., 663,510 78 B5
Maricopa, Ariz. 78 B5
Maricopa, Calif., 648 82 D5
Marīdī, Sudan 163 J5
Marīdī, Nahr, Sudan 163 J4
Marie Byrd Land, Ant. 180 X5
Mariefred, Swed. 120 e8
Marie-Galante, i., Guad. 97 14
Mariehamn, Fin., 6,688 120 E3
Marieholm, Swed. 121 c7
Mariel, Cuba, 4,511 96 b1
Mariemont, Ohio, 4,120 71 i11
Marienbaum, F.R.Ger., 2,741 119 A1
Marienberg, F.R.Ger., 1,946 119 E3
Marienberg, Ger.D.R. 126 c6
Marienberghausen, F.R.Ger., 4,339 119 D3
Marienburg, Sur., 3,760* 101 N5
Marienheide, F.R.Ger., 7,407 119 D2
Marienthal, S.-W. Afr., 3,456 164 B6
Marienthal, Kans. 75 D5
Marienville, Pa. 60 D3
Maries, co., Mo., 7,282 72 F6
Maries, r., Mo. 72 F6
Mariestad, Swed. 120 C4
Marietta, Ga., 25,565 64 E2
Marietta, Ind. 70 D3
Marietta, Kans. 75 J4
Marietta, Minn., 327 74 D3
Marietta, Miss. 73 G3
Marietta, N.Y. 59 q24
Marietta, N.C., 239 63 E3
Marietta, Ohio, 16,847 70 H3
Marietta, Okla., 1,933 76 F4
Marietta, Pa., 2,385 60 J5
Marietta, S.C. 63 B2
Marieville, Qué., Can., 3,704 47 p18
Marigny, Fr., 1,125 117 C2
Marigot, Dominica, 2,792 97 13
Marigot, Mart. 97 12
Marigot, St-Martin 97 7
Marigot, B. du, St-Martin 97 7
Marigüitar, Ven., 4,250 101 H2
Marihatag, Phil., 4,091 153 C3
Mariinsk, U.S.S.R., 40,800 137 r11
Marija Bistrica, Yug. 125 C1
Marijampolė, U.S.S.R., 19,600 136 A2
Marikana, S. Af., 1,995 165 i16
Marília, Braz., 51,789 103 F6
Marilianan, Terr. New Guin. 174 e2
Marilla, N.Y. 58 C6
Marin, co., Calif., 146,820 82 B3
Marin, Cul-de-Sac du, bay, Mart. 97 12
Marina, Alta., Can. 42 H2
Marina, Calif., 3,310 83 f14
Marina Fall, Guyana 101 L5
Mar'ina Gorka, U.S.S.R., 9,200 136 B2
Marin City, Calif. 83 d12
Marinduque I., Phil. 153 B2
Marine, Ill., 813 68 C5
Marine City, Mich., 4,404 67 L6
Marineland, Fla., 9 65 H3
Marinette, co., Wis., 34,660 66 E3
Marinette, Wis., 13,329 66 F3
Maringá, Braz., 42,228 103 F6
Maringa, r., D.R.Congo 164 C1
Maringouin, La., 1,168 73 D7
Maringues, Fr., 2,318 117 E4
Marinha Grande, Port., 15,699 122 A3
Marinilla, Col. 101 d13
Marino, It., 26,109 123 b8
Marion, co., Ala., 21,837 64 B1
Marion, Ala., 3,807 64 B3
Marion, co., Ark., 6,041 73 C1
Marion, Ark., 881 73 E2
Marion (part of Southington), Conn. 56 E6
Marion, co., Fla., 51,616 65 G3
Marion, co., Ga., 5,477 64 E3
Marion, co., Ill., 39,349 68 D5
Marion, Ill., 11,274 68 D6
Marion, co., Ind., 697,567 70 C3
Marion, Ind., 37,854 70 D2
Marion, co., Iowa, 25,886 72 D3
Marion, Iowa, 10,882 72 F2
Marion, co., Kans., 15,143 75 H5
Marion, Kans., 2,169 75 J5
Marion, co., Ky., 16,887 71 F4
Marion, Ky., 2,468 71 C4
Marion, La., 685 73 C5
Marion, Me. 55 E4
Marion, Md. 62 J4
Marion, Mass., 1,160;2,881(T) 57 N6
Marion, Mich., 898 67 H4
Marion, co., Miss., 23,293 73 F6
Marion, Miss. 73 G5
Marion, co., Mo., 29,522 72 F5
Marion, Nebr. 75 E3
Marion, N.Y. 58 F5
Marion, N.C., 3,345 63 B2
Marion, N. Dak., 309 74 C2
Marion, co., Ohio, 60,221 70 F2
Marion, Ohio, 37,079 70 F2
Marion, co., Oreg., 120,888 80 B3
Marion, Oreg. 80 B3
Marion, Pa. 60 G6
Marion, co., S.C., 32,014 63 E3
Marion, S.C., 7,174 63 E3
Marion, S. Dak., 843 74 D4
Marion, co., Tenn., 21,036 71 F6
Marion, co., Tex., 8,049 77 Q3
Marion, Tex., 557 76 b6
Marion, Va., 8,385 62 C6
Marion, co., W. Va., 63,717 62 D3
Marion, Wis., 1,200 66 E4
Marion, L., S.C. 63 D4
Marion, Mt., Austl. 172 B4
Marion Center, Pa., 407 60 D4
Marion Hills, Ill. 69 c9
Marion Junction, Ala. 64 B3
Marion L., Mich. 66 D2
Marion Springs, Mich. 67 J5
Marionville, Mo., 1,251 72 D7
Maripa, Ven. 101 H4
Maripasoula, Fr. Guiana 101 O6
Mariposa, co., Calif., 5,064 82 C4
Mariposa, Calif. 82 D4
Mariposas, Chile, 1,336 104 f15
Mariquita, Col. 101 e14
Marisa, Indon. 149 G2
Mariscal Estigarribia, Para., 3,684 105 C2
Mărişel, Rum. 128 D1
Marissa, Ill., 1,722 68 C5
Maritime Alps, mts., Fr.-It. 123 A2
Maritsa, Bulg., 7,155 128 E3
Maritsá, Gr., 1,003 129 G6
Maritsa, r., Eur. 129 F4
Mariusa, Is., Ven. 101 K3
Mariveles, Phil., 2,292 153 b8
Marj 'Uyūn, Leb. 142 b6
Mark, Ill., 445 68 C2
Markala, Mali 162 D3
Markapur, India, 16,665 145 F7
Markaryd, Swed. 120 C4
Markdale, Ont., Can., 1,079 44 H7
Marked Tree, Ark., 3,216 73 E2
Markelo, Neth. 115 E2
Markersdorf, Aust. 124 b10
Markesan, Wis., 1,060 66 E5
Market Bosworth, U.K., 1,253 114 F5
Market Drayton, U.K., 5,859 113 E5
Market Harborough, U.K., 11,535 113 F5
Markethill, U.K. 113 C4
Market Lavington, U.K., 1,148 114 E8
Market Rasen, U.K., 2,267 114 H4
Market Warsop, U.K., 11,606 114 F4
Market Weighton, U.K., 2,185 113 F5
Markgröningen, F.R.Ger., 5,910 119 G7
Markha, r., U.S.S.R. 135 L3
Markham, Ont., Can., 4,244 46 E5
Markham, Ill., 11,704 69 d10
Markham, Minn. 74 F2
Markham, Tex. 77 P5
Markham, Va. 62 G4
Markham Inlet, N.W.T., Can. 41 Q1
Marki, Pol., 11,235 127 D2
Markinch, U.K., 2,446 112 d7
Märkisch Buchholz, Ger.D.R. 118 D2
Markkleeberg, Ger.D.R., 20,545 118 D3
Markland, Newf., Can. 45 b10
Markland, Ind. 70 D4
Markle, Ind., 789 70 D2
Markleeville, Calif. 82 C3
Markleysburg, Pa., 197 60 F5
Markleville, Ind., 402 70 D3
Markleysburg, Pa., 345 60 C6
Markneukirchen, Ger.D.R. 118 D3
Markópoulon, Gr., 5,046 129 E6
Markovo, U.S.S.R. 135 R3
Markoye, Upper Volta 162 D3
Markranstädt, Ger.D.R., 10,252 126 b5
Marks, U.S.S.R., 13,100 134 D4
Marks, Miss., 2,572 73 E3
Markstay, Ont., Can. 46 D2
Marksville, La., 4,257 73 C6
Marktheidenfeld, F.R.Ger., 4,430 118 B4
Marktl, Aust. 124 O5
Marktoberdorf, F.R.Ger., 6,611 118 C5
Marktredwitz, F.R.Ger., 15,647 118 D4
Markt Sankt Florian, Aust., 3,709 124 L5
Markt Schwaben, F.R.Ger., 4,890 118 C4
Markville, Minn. 74 F2
Markyate, U.K., 2,242 114 H7
Marl, F.R.Ger., 64,228 119 C1
Marland, Okla., 191 76 F1
Marlbank, Ont., Can. 46 G4
Marlboro, N.J. 61 C3
Marlboro, N.Y., 1,733 59 M8
Marlboro, co., S.C., 28,529 63 E3
Marlboro, Vt. 54 B6
Marlborough, Austl. 173 G3
Marlborough, Guyana 101 L4
Marlborough, U.K., 4,852 113 F6
Marlborough, Conn., 1,961(T) 56 F6
Marlborough, Mass., 18,819 57 K3
Marlborough, N.H., 1,097 54 C6
Marle, Fr., 3,023 117 E2
Marlenheim, Fr., 1,528 116 d9
Marler, N.C. 63 D1
Marles-en-Brie, Fr. 116 k12
Marlette, Mich., 1,640 67 K5
Marley, Ill. 69 c10
Marley, Md. 62 c8
Marley Cr., Ill. 69 c10
Marlin, Tex., 6,918 77 P4
Marlin, Wash. 80 D2
Marlinton, W. Va., 1,586 62 D4
Marlo, Austl. 173 g11
Marlow, U.K., 8,724 114 G7
Marlow, N.H. 54 C5
Marlow, Okla., 4,027 76 E3
Marlowe, W. Va. 62 G3
Marls, The, shls., Bah. Is. 95 b6
Marlton, N.J. 60 g12
Marly-la-Ville, Fr., 1,466 116 h10
Marly-le-Roi, Fr., 10,409 116 g11
Marmaduke, Ark., 657 73 E1
Marmande, Fr., 14,004 117 D4
Marmara, Sea of = Marmara Denizi
Marmara Adası, Turk. 142 B1
Marmara Denizi, Turk. 142 A1
Marmaris, Turk., 3,398 142 B2
Marmarth, N. Dak., 319 74 A2
Marmato, Col. 101 d14
Marmet, W. Va., 2,500 62 C4
Marmion L., Ont., Can. 74 G1
Marmirolo, It., 6,955 122 d5
Marmolada, Monte, It. 123 D1
Marmora, Ont., Can., 1,348 46 G4
Marmora, N.J. 61 B5
Marmoutier, Fr., 1,686 116 d9
Marne, F.R.Ger., 5,230 118 B2
Marne, Iowa, 205 72 C3
Marne, Mich. 67 H5
Marne, r., Fr. 117 E2
Maroa, Ill., 1,235 68 D3
Maroa, Ven. 100 G6
Marokau, i., Tuam. Arch. 171 J6
Marolles-en-Brie, Fr. 116 i12
Marolles-en-Hurepoix, Fr., 1,401 116 h12
Maromas (part of Middletown), Conn. 56 F6
Maromme, Fr., 8,212 117 D2
Maromokotro, mtn., Malag. Rep. 165 H4
Maroni = Marouini, Fr. Guiana
Maroni = Marowijne, Sur.
Marónia, Gr. 129 E4
Maroob Kofarau, Indon. 149 L4
Maroon Pk., Colo. 79 B2
Maroon Town, Jam., 1,350 96 p8
Maro Reef, Hawaii 84 f9
Maros, Indon. 149 F4
Maros, r., Hung. 126 E3
Maroua, Cam., 20,000* 162 G4
Marouini, r., Fr. Guiana 101 O6
Marovoay, Malag. Rep., 13,960 165 G4
Marowijne, r., Sur. 101 N5
Marpalli, India 145 F6
Marpingen, F.R.Ger., 3,936 116 d8
Marpi Pt., Saipan 176 27
Marple, U.K., 16,812 114 D4
Marpo Pt., Tinian 176 27
Marquand, Mo., 392 72 G7
Marque, r., Fr. 116 a6
Marquesas Is. = Marquises, Îs.
Marquesas Keys, Fla. 65 e15
Marquetalia, Col. 101 e14
Marquette, Man., Can. 43 g9
Marquette, Iowa, 572 72 F1
Marquette, Kans., 607 75 H5
Marquette, co., Mich., 56,154 66 F2
Marquette, Mich., 19,824 66 F2
Marquette, Nebr., 210 75 H3
Marquette, co., Wis., 8,516 66 D5
Marquette, Wis., 162 66 D5
Marquette Heights, Ill., 2,517 68 C3
Marquette I., Mich. 67 J3
Marquez, N. Mex. 79 B4
Marquez, Tex., 194 77 P4
Marquina, Sp., 3,868 122 n11
Marquion, Fr. 116 a7
Marquis, Gren. 97 18
Marquis, C., St. Lucia 97 11
Marquis, r., St. Lucia 97 11
Marquise, Fr., 4,880 117 D1
Marquises, Îs., Fr. Poly. 171 J5
Marquis I., Gren. 97 18
Marr, Ohio 70 H3
Marrah, Jabal, Sudan 163 J3
Marrakech, Mor., 243,134 160 C2
Marree, Austl. 172 E4
Marromeu, Moz. 164 E5
Marroqui, P., Sp. 122 C4
Marrum, Neth. 115 D1
Marrupa, Moz. 164 F4
Mars, Nic. 94 E4
Mars, Pa., 1,522 60 C4
Marsá al 'Alam, U.A.R. 161 K3
Marsabit, Kenya 164 F1
Marsá Ḩalā'ib, Sudan 163 K2
Marsal, Fr. 116 c9
Marsala, It., 81,318 123 D6
Marsá Sūsah, Libya 161 H2
Marsciano, It., 17,899 123 D3
Marsden, Sask., Can. 43 B4
Marsdiep, str., Neth. 115 C2
Marseille, Fr., 783,738 117 F5
Marseilles, Ill., 4,347 68 D2
Marsella, Col. 101 d14
Marsella, Col. 101 d15
Marsfjället, mt., Swed. 120 C2
Marsh, Mont. 81 G2
Marshall, Sask., Can. 43 B4
Marshall, Lib. 162 C4
Marshall, co., Ala., 48,018 64 C1
Marshall, Alaska, 166 85 D3
Marshall, Ark., 1,095 73 C2
Marshall, Colo. 79 b8
Marshall, co., Ill., 13,334 68 C2
Marshall, Ill., 3,270 68 E4
Marshall, co., Ind., 32,443 70 C1
Marshall, co., Iowa, 37,984 72 D2
Marshall, co., Kans., 15,598 75 J4
Marshall, co., Ky., 16,736 71 C5
Marshall, Mich., 6,736 67 J6
Marshall, co., Minn., 14,262 74 D1
Marshall, Minn., 6,681 74 E3
Marshall, co., Miss., 24,503 73 F3
Marshall, Mo., 11,142 72 D5
Marshall, N.C., 926 63 B2
Marshall, co., Okla., 7,263 76 G3
Marshall, Okla., 363 76 F1
Marshall, co., S. Dak., 6,663 74 D3
Marshall, co., Tenn., 16,859 71 E6
Marshall, Tex., 23,846 77 Q3
Marshall, Wash. 80 E2
Marshall, co., W. Va., 38,041 62 D3
Marshall, Wis., 736 66 D5
Marshall Bennett Is., Terr. Papua 174 3
Marshallberg, N.C. 63 H3
Marshall Is., Tr. Terr. Pac. Is. 170 F4
Marshallton, Del. 62 e11
Marshallton, Pa. 60 e12
Marshalltown, Iowa, 22,521 72 E2
Marshallville, Ga., 1,308 64 E3
Marsh Cr., Mich. 67 e16
Marshepaug, r., Conn. 56 C5
Marshfield, U.K. 114 B7
Marshfield, Ind. 70 B2
Marshfield, Mass., 6,748(T) 57 N4
Marshfield, Mo., 2,221 72 E7
Marshfield, Vt. 54 C3
Marshfield, Wis., 14,153 66 C4
Marshfield Center (part of Marshfield), Mass. 57 O4
Marshfield Hills (part of Marshfield), Mass. 57 O4
Marsh Gibbon, U.K. 114 F7
Marsh Harbour, Bah. Is. 95 b6
Mars Hill, Ind. 70 C3
Mars Hill, Me., 1,458 55 E2
Mars Hill, N.C., 1,574 63 B2
Marsh I., La. 73 C8
Marsh L., Yukon, Can. 85 L3
Marsh-Miller L., Wis. 66 B3
Marsh Pk, Utah 78 D1
Marsh Str., Me. 55 C4
Marshville, N.C., 1,360 63 D2
Marsico Nuovo, It., 10,218 123 E4
Marsing, Idaho, 555 81 A4
Marske-by-the-Sea, U.K., 6,791 114 G1
Marsland, Nebr. 75 D1
Marsoui, Qué., Can. 47 S9
Märsta, Swed. 120 e8
Marstal, Den., 1,986 121 C6
Märstetten, Switz. 124 D1
Marston, Mo., 631 72 H8
Marston, N.C. 63 E3
Marstons Mills (part of Barnstable), Mass. 57 P6
Marstrand, Swed. 121 D3
Marsugalt, i., Kwajalein 176 25
Mart, Tex., 2,197 77 P4
Marta, r., It. 123 C3
Martaban, Burma, 5,639 147 b2
Martaban, G. of, Burma 146 B3
Martanesh, Alb. 125 E4
Martapura, Indon. 148 C4
Martapura, Indon. 148 E3
Martel, Ohio 70 G2
Martelange, Belg., 1,593 115 D5
Martha, Okla., 243 76 D3
Martha Brae, r., Jam. 96 p8
Marthalen, Switz., 1,252 124 C1
Marthasville, Mo., 339 72 F6
Martha's Vineyard, i., Mass. 57 O7
Marthaville, La., 181 73 B6
Martí, Cuba, 2,605 96 c1
Martigny-Bourg, Switz., 2,354 124 A2
Martigny-Ville, Switz., 5,239 124 B2
Martigues, Fr., 21,526 117 F5
Martim Longo, Port., 2,441 122 B4
Martin, Czech., 26,758 126 D2
Martin, U.K. 114 H4
Martin, Alaska 85 a6
Martin, co., Fla., 16,932 65 J5
Martin, Fla. 65 G3
Martin, Ga., 209 64 F1
Martin, co., Ind., 10,608 70 C4
Martin, co., Ky., 10,201 71 J4
Martin, Ky., 992 71 J4
Martin, Mich., 483 67 H6
Martin, co., Minn., 26,986 74 E4
Martin, co., N.C., 27,139 63 G2
Martin, N. Dak., 146 74 B2
Martin, S. Dak., 1,184 74 B4
Martin, Tenn., 4,750 71 C5
Martin, co., Tex., 5,068 77 M3
Martin, L., Ala. 64 D3
Martina Franca, It., 37,798 123 F4
Martin Cr., Pa. 61 L2
Martindale, Tex. 77 P5
Martinengo, It., 5,778 122 c5
Martinez, Calif., 9,604 82 B3
Martinez, Ga. 64 H2
Martinez, Tex. 76 b7
Martinez de la Torre, Mex., 14,461 93 F4
Martinique, i., Lesser Ant., 321,000* 97 12
Martinique Passage, W.I. 95 G4
Martínon, Gr., 2,271 129 D5
Martins Bay, N.Z. 175 e7
Martinsburg, Iowa, 172 72 E3
Martinsburg, Mo., 330 72 F5
Martinsburg, Nebr., 68 75 H1
Martinsburg, N.Y. 59 J4
Martinsburg, Ohio, 228 70 G2
Martinsburg, Pa., 1,772 60 F5
Martinsburg, W. Va., 15,179 62 F3
Martins Creek, Pa. 61 M4
Martins Ferry, Ohio, 11,919 70 J2
Martinsville, Ill., 1,351 68 E4
Martinsville, Ind., 7,525 70 C3
Martinsville, Me. 55 C5
Martinsville, Mich. 67 e16
Martinsville, Mo., 79 72 C4
Martinsville, N.J. 58 a14
Martinsville, Va., 18,798 62 E6
Martinton, Ill., 314 68 E3
Martin Vaz, i., Atl. Oc. 109 L8
Martley, U.K. 114 D6
Martock, U.K., 2,230 113 E6
Marton, N.Z., 4,319 175 g6
Martorell, Sp., 7,926 122 F2
Martre, L. la, N.W.T., Can. 40 F5
Martuk, U.S.S.R. 137 h10
Martville, N.Y. 59 p22
Marty, S. Dak. 74 C4
Martz, Ind. 70 B3
Marua, Terr. Papua 174 f3
Marudi, Guyana 101 L6
Marudi, Malay., 2,663 148 E1
Marugame, Jap., 61,403 155 C4
Marui, Terr. New Guin. 174 d2
Marujuy, Col. 100 D1
Maruko, Jap., 26,176 155 F3
Marulanda, Col. 101 d14
Mårum, Den., 1,029 121 a7
Marum, Mt., New Hebr. 174 m6
Marumori, Jap., 28,943 155 G3
Maruoka, Jap., 23,021 155 E3
Marutea, atoll, Tuam. Arch. 177 42
Maruyama, r., Jap. 154 f14
Marvejols, Fr., 4,384 117 E4
Marvel, Colo. 79 A3
Marvell, Ark., 1,690 73 E3
Marvel Loch, Austl. 172 B4
Marvin Cr., Pa. 60 E2
Marvine, Mt., Utah 78 C2
Marwas, India 144 c13
Marwayne, Alta., Can. 42 L3
Marxville, Wis. 66 D5
Mary, U.S.S.R., 51,000 134 F6
Mar'yanovka, U.S.S.R. 137 n11
Maryborough, Queensland, Austl., 17,952 173 H3
Maryborough, Vict., Austl., 6,827 173 d11
Maryborough, Ire. = Portlaoighise
Marydale, S. Af. 164 C6
Marydel, Md., 130 62 J3
Mary Esther, Fla., 780 65 C2
Mar'yevka, U.S.S.R. 137 m11
Maryfield, Sask., Can. 43 E5
Maryhill, Ont., Can. 46 b13
Maryland, st., U.S., 3,534,000* 62
Maryneal, Tex. 77 N3
Maryport, U.K., 12,334 113 E4
Mary's, r., Ill. 68 C6
Mary's, r., Nev. 83 C2
Marys Pk., Oreg. 80 B3
Marystown, Newf., Can., 1,668 45 Q6
Marysvale, Utah, 354 78 B2
Marysville, Austl. 173 e11
Marysville, Br. Col., Can., 1,044 42 J4
Marysville, N.B., Can., 3,210 45 M6
Marysville, Calif., 9,553 82 C3
Marysville, Idaho, 201 81 D3
Marysville, Ind. 70 D4
Marysville, Iowa, 113 72 D3
Marysville, Kans., 4,143 75 J4
Marysville, Mich., 4,065 67 L6
Marysville, Ohio, 4,952 70 F2
Marysville, Pa., 2,580 60 H5
Marysville, Wash., 3,117 80 B1
Marytown, Wis. 66 E5
Maryville, Mo., 7,807 72 B4
Maryville, Tenn., 10,348 71 G6
Marywood, Ill. 69 a9
Marzo, C., Col. 100 B4
Marzūq, Libya 161 G3
Marzūq, Ḩammādat, Libya 161 G3
Mas, r., Indon. 148 e7
Masa, Sp. 122 m12
Masada, ruins, Isr. 142 b8
Masagua, Guat. 94 c9
Masaguara, Hond., 1,004 94 C3
Masaka, Uganda, 4,782 164 E2
Masākin, Tun., 26,142 160 g6
Masalembo-besar, i., Indon. 148 f6
Masalembo-ketjil, i., Indon. 148 f6
Masally, U.S.S.R., 6,700 137 d2
Masalog, Guam 176 24
Masamba, Indon. 149 F3
Masan, S. Kor., 157,547 151 F4
Masardis, Me. 55 D2
Masaryktown, Fla. 65 G4
Masasi, Tanz. 164 F3
Masaya, Nic., 28,208 94 D5
Masbate, Phil., 11,647 153 B2
Masbate, i., Phil. 153 B2
Mascara, Alg., 44,839 160 E2
Mascardi, L., Arg. 105 f15
Mascarene Basin, Ind. Oc. 168 B3
Mascarene Is., Ind. Oc. 168 B3
Maschen, F.R.Ger., 2,353 119 b9
Mascoma, r., N.H. 54 C4
Mascoma L., N.H. 54 C4
Mascot, Tenn. 71 H5
Mascota, Mex., 5,214 92 D4
Mascouche, Qué., Can., 1,152 47 o17
Mascouche, r., Qué., Can. 47 o17
Mascoutah, Ill., 3,625 68 C5
Masefau, Tutuila 177 39
Masefau Bay, Tutuila 177 39
Masein, Burma 146 A2
Maseru, Lesotho, 5,739 164 D6
Mashaba, Rhod. 164 E5
Masham, U.K. 113 F4
Ma-shan, China 152 C3
Mashapaug (part of Union), Conn. 56 H4
Mashapaug Pd., Conn. 56 H4
Mashhad, Iran, 241,989 143 G1
Mashike, Jap., 16,768 155 J8
Mashita, r., Jap. 154 i14
Mashoes, N.C. 63 J2
Mashpee, Mass., 867(T) 57 P6
Mashra'ar Raqq, Sudan 163 J4
Mashtagi, U.S.S.R., 16,500 137 d1
Mashulaville, Miss. 73 G4
Masica, Hond., 2,136 94 D3
Masīlah, Wādī, S. Ar. 143 E5
Masi-Manimba, D.R.Congo 164 B2
Masimbu, Indon. 149 F3
Masin, Indon. 149 L4
Masindi, Uganda 164 E1
Masinloc, Phil., 3,851 153 A2
Masisea, Peru, 1,520 104 C4
Masisi, D.R.Congo 164 D2
Masjed Soleymān, Iran, 44,651 143 D2
Masjid Tanah, Malay., 1,150 147 o15
Mask, L., Ire. 113 B5
Maskalls, Br. Hond. 94 C2
Maskell, Nebr., 54 75 J1
Maskinongé, Qué., Can. 47 M2
Maskinongé, r., Qué., Can. 47 K3
Maskūtān, Iran, 1,051 143 F3
Maslovo, U.S.S.R. 137 k6
Masnières, Fr., 2,399 116 a7
Mason, Fla. 65 G2
Mason, co., Ill., 15,193 68 C3
Mason, Ill., 332 68 D5
Mason, co., Ky., 18,454 71 H3
Mason, Ky. 71 G3
Mason, co., Mich., 21,929 67 G4
Mason, Mich., 4,522 67 J6
Mason, Nev. 83 A3
Mason, N.H. 54 D6
Mason, Ohio, 4,727 70 E3
Mason, Okla. 76 G2
Mason, Tenn., 407 71 B6
Mason, co., Tex., 3,780 77 O4
Mason, Tex., 1,910 77 O4
Mason, co., Wash., 16,251 80 B2
Mason, co., W. Va., 24,459 62 B4
Mason, W. Va., 1,005 62 B4
Mason, Wis., 100 66 B2
Mason, L., Austl. 172 B4
Mason, L., Wis. 66 D5
Mason City, Ill., 2,160 68 C3
Mason City, Iowa, 30,642 72 D1
Mason City, Nebr., 277 75 F2
Masonic Park, Colo. 79 B3
Mason L., Wash. 81 a8
Masons Cross, N.C. 63 E3
Masontown, Pa., 4,730 60 C6
Masontown, W. Va., 841 62 E3
Masonville, N.Y. 59 K7
Masqaṭ, Muscat and Oman, 6,655* 143 F4
Mass, Mich. 66 D2
Massa, It., 56,011 123 C2
Massabesic L., N.H. 54 E6
Massac, co., Ill., 14,341 68 D6
Massachusetts, st., U.S., 5,361,000* 56-7
Massachusetts Bay, Mass. 57 O3
Massacre, r., Haiti-Dom. Rep. 96 m6
Massacre Bay, Tutuila 177 39
Massa Fiscaglia, It., 6,808 122 e6
Massafra, It., 19,733 123 F4
Massaguet, Chad 162 G3
Massakory, Chad, 1,400* 162 G3
Massalog Pt., Tinian 176 27
Massalubrense, It., 9,373 123 c10
Massa Marittima, It., 16,710 123 C3
Massangena, Moz. 164 E5
Massapê, Braz., 4,760 103 H2
Massapequa, N.Y., 32,900 58 f14
Massapequa Park, N.Y., 19,904 58 f14
Massat, Fr. 117 D5
Massava, U.S.S.R. 137 k6
Massawa, Eth., 15,800* 163 L3
Massawippi, L., Qué., Can. 54 D1
Massbach, Ill. 68 B1
Massen, F.R.Ger., 8,132 119 D1
Massena, Iowa, 456 72 C3
Massena, N.Y., 15,478 59 L2
Massenya, Chad, 1,700* 162 G4
Masset Inlet, Br. Col., Can. 42 C3
Massett, Br. Col., Can. 42 D3
Masseube, Fr., 1,350 112 D5
Massey, Ont., Can., 1,292 44 G6
Massiac, Fr., 1,973 117 E4
Massif Central, upland, Fr. 117 E4
Massillon, Ohio, 31,236 70 H2
Massinga, Moz. 164 E5
Massiv Këksu, mt., U.S.S.R. 137 f4
Masson, Qué., Can., 1,915 47 J3
Massy, Fr., 19,355 116 h12
Mastershausen, F.R.Ger. 119 C4
Masterson, Tex. 76 M2
Masterton, N.Z., 15,128 175 g6
Mastic Beach, N.Y., 3,035 58 h13
Mastic Point, Bah. Is. 95 a8
Mastigouche, r., Qué., Can. 47 L2
Mastūj, Pak. 145 D1
Mastung, Pak., 5,962 144 C3
Mastūrah, Saudi Ar. 143 B4
Masuda, Jap., 56,053 154 B4
Masudome, Jap. 154 f14
Masulipatnam, India, 101,417 145 F6
Masuria = Mazury
Masury, Ohio, 2,512 70 J1
Maşyāf, Syr., 6,375 142 D3
Maszewo, Pol., 2,967 127 A2
Maszewo, Pol. 127 B1
Mat, r., Alb. 125 D4
Mata, Cuba, 1,349 96 c1
Mata, Ven. 101 H3
Matacães, Port., 1,526 122 i9
Matachewan, Ont., Can. 44 G6
Matáchic, Mex., 1,176 92 D2
Matadi, D.R.Congo, 60,295 164 B2
Matador, Tex., 1,217 77 N2
Matafao, pk., Tutuila 177 39
Matafotufotu, C., W. Samoa 177 38
Matagalpa, Nic., 13,919 94 E4
Matagamasi L., Ont., Can. 46 D2
Matagorda, co., Tex., 25,744 77 P5
Matagorda, Tex. 77 Q5
Matagorda Bay, Tex. 77 P5
Matagorda I., Tex. 77 P5
Matagorda Pen., Tex. 77 P5
Matahambre, Cuba, 4,569 96 a1
Matahiae, Pte., Tahiti 177 44
Ma-t'ai-an, Taiwan 152 F3
Mataiva, i., Tuam. Arch. 171 J5
Matalaa, Pte., Îs. Wallis 175 7
Matalanim, Ponape 176 29
Matale, Cey., 17,244 145 n22
Matam, Sen., 4,509 162 B3
Matamata, N.Z., 3,298 175 g5
Matameye, Niger 162 F3
Matamoras, Pa., 2,087 61 N3
Matamoros, Camp., Mex. 93 H4
Matamoros, Coah., Mex., 13,572 92 E3
Matamoros, Pue., Mex., 16,175 93 F4
Matamoros, Tam., Mex., 93,334 93 F3
Ma'ṭan as Sarra, Libya 161 H4
Matandu, r., Tanz. 164 F3
Matane, Qué., Can., 8,883 45 M5
Matanza, Col. 100 D4
Matanzas, Cuba, 63,916 96 c1
Matanzas, Puerto de, Cuba 96 c1
Mataorio, Tahiti 177 44
Mata Ortiz, Mex., 1,721 92 C1
Matapédia, Qué., Can., 1,100 45 M5
Matapédia, r., Qué., Can. 47 S9
Mataquescuintla, Guat., 3,085 94 c9
Mataquito, r., Chile 104 f15
Matara, Cey., 27,641 145 F9
Mataram, Indon. 148 F5
Matarani, Peru 104 C6
Mataranka, Austl. 172 D2
Mataró, Sp., 41,128 122 G2
Matasiri, P., Indon. 148 f6
Mataso, i., New Hebr. 174 m6
Matatamane, pt., Niue 177 32
Matathawa Levu, i., Fiji 174 4
Matatiele, S. Af., 3,237 164 D7
Matatula, C., Tutuila 177 39
Mataupa, Terr. Papua 174 3
Mataura, N.Z., 2,085 175 f7
Mataura, r., N.Z. 175 f7
Mata Utu, Îs. Wallis 175 7
Matautu, W. Samoa 177 38
Mata Utu, B. de, Îs. Wallis 175 7
Matautu Bay, W. Samoa 177 38
Matavai, B. de, Tahiti 177 44
Matavera, Rarotonga 177 34
Mataveri, Easter I. 177 46
Matawan, N.J., 5,097 61 C3
Matawatchan, Ont., Can. 46 G3
Matay, U.S.S.R. 134 G5
Matchaponix Bk., N.J. 58 b15
Mateguá, Bol. 102 D4
Matehuala, Mex., 19,738 93 E3
Mateira, Braz., 2,358 103 F5
Matejče, Yug., 2,637 125 E3
Matelot, Trin. and Tob. 96 g5
Matera, It., 37,466 123 F4
Mateševo, Yug. 125 D3
Mátészalka, Hung., 11,249 126 F3
Matewan, W. Va., 896 62 B5
Matfen, U.K. 112 f9
Matfield Green, Kans., 95 75 J5
Matha, Fr., 2,322 117 C4
Mather, Man., Can. 43 e10
Mather, Pa., 1,033 60 B6
Mather, Wis. 66 C4
Matheran, India 145 h17
Mathersville, Ill., 612 68 B2
Matherton, Mich. 67 J5
Matheson, Ont., Can. 44 H5
Matheson Island, Man., Can. 43 F4
Mathews, co., Va., 7,121 62 H5
Mathews, Va. 62 H5
Mathews, L., Calif. 83 k16
Mathieu, Grand Récif, N. Caled. 174 i8
Mathis, Tex., 6,075 77 P5
Mathiston, Miss., 597 73 F4
Mathoura, Austl. 173 e10
Mathura, India, 116,959 145 E4
Mati, Phil., 7,870 153 C4

Matias—Menai · 259

Matias Barbosa, Braz., 4,129 103 e17
Matías Romero, Mex., 10,240 93 G5
Matina, C.R. 94 F5
Matinecock, N.Y., 824 58 e13
Matinenda L., Ont., Can. 46 B2
Matinicus I., Me. 55 D5
Matipó, Braz., 3,558 103 e17
Mâţir, Tun., 14,641 160 f5
Matla, r., India 144 g15
Mātli, Pak., 10,496 144 C4
Matlock, U.K., 18,505 113 F5
Matlock, Iowa, 103 72 A1
Matlock Bath, (part of Matlock), U.K., 1,385 114 E4
Ma-to, China 150 D3
Matoaca, Va. 62 G5
Matoaka, W. Va. 62 C5
Matobe, Indon. 148 A3
Matochkin Shar, U.S.S.R. 134 E2
Matochkin Shar, Prol., U.S.S.R. 134 E2
Mato Grosso, st., Braz., 910,262 102 E4
Mato Grosso, Braz. 102 E4
Mato Grosso, Planalto de, Braz. 98 D4
Matola, Moz., 19,373 164 E6
Matong, Austl. 173 f10
Matong, Terr. New Guin. 174 f2
Matopos Nat. Pk., Rhod. 164 D5
Matosinhos, Port., 24,804 122 A2
Ma-tou, Taiwan, 44,206 152 F3
Matoury, Fr. Guiana 101 O5
Mato Verde, Braz. 103 F4
Matoya, Phil., 5,129 153 C4
Mátra, mts., Hung. 126 D3
Maţraḩ, Muscat and Oman, 14,190* 143 F4
Matre, Nor. 120 A3
Matrei, Aust., 3,430 124 J7
Matriz de Camaragibe, Braz., 4,556 103 b15
Maţrūh, U.A.R., 30,000* 161 J2
Matsang, r., China 150 B4
Matsu = Ma-tsu Shan
Matsubase, Jap., 19,091 154 B5
Matsuda, Jap., 10,389 155 m20
Matsudo, Jap., 86,372 155 m19
Matsue, Jap., 106,476 155 C4
Matsukawa, Jap., 15,434 155 G3
Matsumae, Jap., 20,072 155 H9
Matsumoto, Jap., 148,710 155 F3
Matsuno, Jap. 155 n20
Matsuoaira, Jap. 154 g16
Matsusaki, Jap. 155 n20
Ma-tsu Shan, Taiwan 152 F2
Matsushima, Jap. 154 e15
Matsushima, Jap. 155 F4
Matsushima, Jap., 15,687 155 G2
Matsushiro, Jap., 22,912 155 F3
Matsutō, Jap., 28,885 155 E3
Matsuura, Jap., 41,113 154 A5
Matsuya, Jap. 154 h14
Matsuyama, Jap., 238,604 155 C5
Matsuyama, Jap. 155 m18
Matsuzaka, Jap., 98,441 155 E4
Matsuzaki, Jap., 8,576 155 F4
Matsuzaki, Jap. 155 n19
Matt, Switz. 124 D2
Mattabesset, r., Conn. 56 F6
Mattagami, r., Ont., Can. 44 G5
Mattagami Heights, Ont., Can., 1,423 44 G5
Mattagami L., Qué., Can. 44 J5
Mattamiscontis L., Me. 55 D3
Mattamuskeet L., N.C. 63 H2
Mattancheri, India, 83,896 145 E8
Mattapoisett, Mass., 1,640; 3,117(T) 57 N6
Mattapoisett, r., Mass. 57 N6
Mattaponi, r., Va. 62 G4
Mattawa, Ont., Can., 3,225 44 H6
Mattawa, Wash., 394 80 D2
Mattawamkeag, Me. 55 D3
Mattawamkeag, r., Me. 55 D3
Mattawamkeag L., Me. 55 D3
Mattawan, Mich. 67 H6
Mattawana, Pa. 60 G5
Mattawin, r., Qué., Can. 47 L2
Matterhorn, mtn. It.-Switz. 124 B2
Matterhorn, pk., Nev. 83 C2
Mattersburg, Aust., 4,266 124 N6
Mattese, Mo. 72 a12
Matteson, Ill., 3,225 69 d10
Matteson, Mich. 67 H7
Matthew, i., N. Caled. 170 F6
Matthews, Ga., 106 64 G2
Matthews, Ind., 627 70 D2
Matthews, N.J. 58 b16
Matthews, N.C., 609 63 D2
Matthew Town, Bah. Is. 95 D2
Mattice, Ont., Can. 44 G5
Mattighofen, Aust., 19 124 K5
Mattili, India 145 G6
Mattituck, N.Y., 1,274 59 P9
Mattole, r., Calif. 82 A2
Mattoon, Ill., 19,088 68 D4
Mattoon, Wis., 435 66 D4
Mattsee, Aust., 1,553 124 K6
Mattson, Miss. 73 E3
Mattydale, N.Y. 59 r23
Matu, Malay., 1,370 148 D2
Matua, Indon. 148 D3
Matucana, Peru, 2,950 104 B4
Matuku, i., Fiji 174 4
Matunuck, R.I. 57 K7
Matura Bay, Trin. and Tob. 96 h5
Maturei-Vavao, atoll, Tuam. Arch. 177 42
Maturín, Ven., 53,445 101 J3
Matus, Ec. 104 c10
Matveyev-Kurgan, U.S.S.R. 136 f8
Matzaco, Mex., 1,103 93 f11
Matzen, Aust., 1,464 124 d10
Mau, India 145 G4
Mau, mtn., Kenya 165 g14
Mau Aimma, India, 6,385 144 c13
Mauban, Phil., 6,293 153 B2
Maubeuge, Fr., 27,287 117 F1
Ma-ubin, Burma, 23,362 146 A3
Mauchamps, Fr. 116 g12
Mauchline, U.K. 112 b8
Mauckport, Ind., 107 70 C4
Maud, Ala. 64 A1
Maud, Okla., 1,137 76 G2
Maud, Tex., 951 77 Q3
Maudaha, India 144 c13
Maude, Austl. 173 e10
Maud Seamount, Atl. Oc. 109 N11
Mauerbach, Aust., 1,366 124 c10
Maués, r., Braz. 102 E2
Maug, is., Mariana Is. 176 23
Mauganj, India 144 c13
Maughold Head, U.K. 113 D4
Maui, co., Hawaii, 42,576 84 D3
Maui, i., Hawaii 84 E3
Mauk, Indon. 148 b7
Mauke, i., Cook Is. 177 33
Maulbronn, F.R.Ger., 2,424 119 F7
Mauldin, S.C., 2,577 63 B3
Mauldre, r., Fr. 116 f11
Maule, Chile 104 f15
Maule, Fr., 2,963 116 f11
Maule, r., Chile 104 e15
Mauléon-Licharre, Fr., 5,048 117 C5
Maullín, Chile, 1,789 105 A6
Maumee, Ohio, 12,063 70 F1
Maumee, r., Ind.-Ohio 70 E1
Maumelle, L., Ark. 73 C3
Maumere, Indon. 149 G5
Maun, Bots., 4,591 164 C5
Maun, i., Yug. 125 B2
Maun, r., U.K. 114 F4
Maunabo, P.R., 1,027 96 u10
Mauna Kea, mtn., Hawaii 84 F4
Maunaloa, Hawaii, 789 84 D2
Mauna Loa, mtn., Hawaii 84 F4
Maunalua Bay, Hawaii 84 D2
Maunawai, Hawaii 84 C2
Maunawili Str., Hawaii 84 d7
Maunga Roa, pk., Rarotonga 177 34
Maungaisilisili, pk., W. Samoa 177 38
Maungdaw, Burma, 3,846 146 A2
Maungthama, Burma 147 c5
Maunie, Ill., 363 68 D5
Maunoir, L., N.W.T., Can. 40 E4
Maupin, Oreg., 381 80 C3
Maupiti, i., Soc. Is. 177 42
Mau Ranipur, India, 20,224 144 b13
Maurawan, India 144 c12
Maurecourt, Fr., 1,729 116 g11
Mauren, Liecht., 1,525 124 a8
Maurepas, Fr. 116 f11
Maurepas, L., La. 73 E7
Mauri, r., Bol. 102 a10
Mauriac, Fr., 3,939 117 E4
Maurice, Iowa, 237 72 A2
Maurice, La., 411 73 C7
Maurice, L., Austl. 172 D4
Maurice, r., N.J. 61 A5
Mauriceville, Tex. 77 n8
Maurine, S. Dak. 74 A3
Mauritania, ctry., 900,000* 162 C2
Mauritius, i., Ind. Oc., 681,619 165 c12
Mauron, Fr., 3,370 117 B2
Maurs, Fr., 2,631 117 E4
Maury, N.C., 285 63 G2
Maury, co., Tenn., 41,699 71 D6
Maury City, Tenn., 624 71 B6
Mauston, Wis., 3,531 66 C5
Maustrenk, Aust. 124 d9
Mautern, Aust., 2,357 124 L6
Mautern, Aust., 1,714 124 M5
Mauterndorf, Aust., 1,606 124 K6
Mauthen, Aust. 124 K7
Mauvezin, Fr., 1,866 117 D5
Mauzé, Fr., 1,961 117 C3
Mava, Terr. Papua 174 d2
Mavaca, r., Ven. 101 H6
Mavelikara, India, 18,974 145 k21
Maverick, Ariz. 78 D5
Maverick, co., Tex., 14,508 77 N5
Mavie, Minn. 74 E1
Mavinga, Ang. 164 C4
Mavréli, Gr., 1,055 129 C5
Mavrommáti, Gr., 2,059 129 D5
Mawana, India, 20,677 144 a11
Mawchi, Burma 146 B3
Mawhun, Burma 146 B1
Mawjib, Wādī al, Jor. 142 b8
Mawlaik, Burma, 3,042 146 A2
Mawson, Ant. 180 S6
Max, Ind. 70 C2
Max, N. Dak., 410 74 B2
Maxbass, N. Dak., 218 74 B1
Maxcanú, Mex., 5,127 93 H4
Maxeys, Ga., 149 64 F2
Maxhütte-Haidhof, F.R.Ger., 5,663 118 D4
Maxial, Port., 4,216 122 i9
Maxim, N.J. 58 c16
Maximiliansau, F.R.Ger., 3,140 119 E6
Maximo, Ohio 70 H2
Max Meadows, Va. 62 D6
Maxton, N.C., 1,755 63 E3
Maxville, Ont., Can. 47 K3
Maxville, Fla. 65 G2
Maxville, Oreg. 80 E3
Maxwell, Calif. 82 B3
Maxwell, Iowa, 773 72 D3
Maxwell, Nebr., 324 75 E2
Maxwell, N. Mex., 392 79 C3
Maxwell, Tex. 76 c6
Maxwell Hall, hill, Jam. 96 p8
Maxwelton, Austl. 173 F3
May, Idaho 81 B3
May, Okla., 114 76 D1
May, C., N.J. 61 B6
May, I. of, U.K. 112 E3
Maya, Mesa de, Colo. 79 D3
Maya, r., U.S.S.R. 135 N4
Mayādīn, Syr., 10,322 142 E3
Mayaguana I., Bah. Is. 95 D2
Mayaguana Passage, Bah. Is. 95 D2
Mayagüez, P.R., 50,147 96 r10
Mayajigua, Cuba, 2,950 96 d1
Mayals, Sp., 1,647 122 F2
Maya Mts., Br. Hond. 94 C2
Ma-yang, China 152 C2
Mayangon, Burma 147 b2
Mayari, Cuba, 6,386 96 f2
Mayari, r., Cuba 96 f2
Mayaro Bay, Trin. and Tob. 96 h5
Maybee, Mich., 459 67 K6
Maybell, Colo. 79 A1
Maybole, U.K., 4,677 113 D4
Maybrook, N.Y., 1,348 59 M9
Maycoba, Mex. 92 C2
Mayday, Colo. 79 A3
Mayen, F.R.Ger., 16,169 118 A3
Mayenne, Fr., 11,163 117 C2
Mayenne, r., Fr. 117 C2
Mayer, Ariz. 78 B4
Mayerling, Aust. 124 c10
Mayersville, Miss. 73 D5
Mayerthorpe, Alta., Can. 42 J2
Mayes, co., Okla., 20,073 76 H1
Mayesville, S.C., 750 63 D4
Mayetta, Kans., 218 75 K4
Mayfield, Kans., 119 75 H6
Mayfield, Ky., 10,762 71 C5
Mayfield, Mich. 67 H4
Mayfield, N.Y., 818 59 M5
Mayfield, Ohio, 1,977 70 f8
Mayfield, Okla. 76 D2
Mayfield, Pa., 1,996 61 M2
Mayfield, Utah, 329 78 C2
Mayfield Cr., Ky. 71 C5
Mayfield Heights, Ohio, 13,478 70 f8
Mayflower, Ark., 355 73 C3
Mayflower, Tex. 77 R4
Mayhill, N. Mex. 79 C5
Maykain, U.S.S.R., 8,600 134 G4
Maykop, U.S.S.R., 88,000 134 D5
Maykor, U.S.S.R., 6,200 137 h7
Mayland, Tenn. 71 F5
Mayli-Say, U.S.S.R., 24,700 137 g4
Maymo, Burma, 22,287 146 B2
Maymont, Sask., Can. 43 B4
Mayn, r., U.S.S.R. 135 R3
Maynard, Ark., 201 73 D1
Maynard, Iowa, 515 72 F2
Maynard, Mass., 7,695(T) 57 L3
Maynardville, Tenn., 620 71 H5
Maynooth, Ont., Can. 44 H6
Maynooth, Ire., 1,722 113 C5
Maynopil'gyn, U.S.S.R. 135 R3
Mayo, Yukon, Can. 40 B5
Mayo, co., Ire., 133,052 113 B5
Mayo, Fla., 687 65 F2
Mayo, Md. 62 c9
Mayo, S.C. 63 C2
Mayo, r., Arg. 105 A7
Mayo, r., Mex. 92 C2
Mayo, r., Peru 104 B3
Mayodan, N.C., 2,366 63 E1
Mayo Darlé, Cam. 162 F4
Mayon Vol., Phil. 153 h14
Mayorga, Phil., 1,853 153 C3
Mayotte, i., Arch. des Comores 165 G4
Mayoyao, Phil., 3,051 153 B1
Maypearl, Tex. 359 76 e10
May Pen, Jam., 14,085 96 p9
Mayport, Fla. 65 H2
Mayreau, i., Gren. Is. 97 20
Mayrhofen, Aust., 2,522 124 H6
Mayskiy, U.S.S.R. 135 M4
Mayskoye, U.S.S.R. 137 p12
Mays Landing, N.J., 1,404 61 B5
Mays Lick, Ky. 71 H3
Maysville, Ala. 64 C1
Maysville, Ga., 553 64 F1
Maysville, Ky., 8,484 71 H3
Maysville, Mo., 942 72 C5
Maysville, N.C., 892 63 G3
Maysville, Okla., 1,530 76 F3
Maysville, W. Va. 62 E3
Maytown, Wash. 81 a9
Mayumba, Gabon 164 A2
Mayuram, India, 51,393 145 F8
Mayview, Wash. 80 E2
Mayville, Mich., 896 67 K5
Mayville, N.Y., 1,619 58 A7
Mayville, N. Dak., 2,168 74 D2
Mayville, Oreg. 80 C3
Mayville, Wis., 3,607 66 E5
Maywood, Calif., 14,588 83 h16
Maywood, Ill., 27,330 69 c9
Maywood, Nebr., 337 75 E3
Maywood, N.J., 11,460 58 c13
Maywood, N.Y. 59 v28
Mayya, U.S.S.R. 135 N3
Maza, Arg., 5,000* 105 C5
Mazabuka, Zambia, 1,930 164 D4
Mazagan = El-Jadida
Mazagão, Braz. 103 F2
Mazagão Velho, Braz. 103 F2
Mazama, Br. Col., Can. 42 G4
Mazamet, Fr., 17,891 117 E5
Mazán, Peru 104 C2
Mazapil, Mex., 1,742 92 E3
Mazara del Vallo, It., 37,229 123 D6
Mazarakiá, Gr. 129 C5
Mazār-i-Sharif, Afghan., 40,000* 144 C1
Mazarrón, Sp., 9,865 122 E4
Mazaruni, r., Guyana 101 L5
Mazatenango, Guat., 15,306 94 B3
Mazatlán, Mex., 74,934 92 D3
Mazatzal Mts., Ariz. 50 D4
Mažeikiai, U.S.S.R., 8,000 136 A1
Mazie, Okla. 76 H1
Mazinga, pk., St. Eustatius 97 6
Mazoe, Rhod. 164 E4
Mazoe, r., Moz.-Rhod. 164 E4
Mazomanie, Wis., 1,069 66 D5
Mazon, Ill., 683 68 D2
Mazouna, Alg., 3,906 160 b5
Mazul'skiy, U.S.S.R. 137 s11
Mczury, reg., Pol. 127 D2
Mazzarino, It., 19,073 123 E6
Mba, Fiji 174 4
Mbabane, Swazi., 8,400 164 E6
Mbahiakro, Iv. Coast 162 a8
Mbaïki, C.A.R., 8,958 163 H5
Mbalageti, r., Tanz. 165 g15
Mbalmayo, Cam., 5,500* 162 F5
Mbamba Bay, Tanz. 164 E3
Mbarara, Uganda, 3,844 164 E2
Mbari, r., C.A.R. 163 H4
Mbatiki, i., Fiji 174 4
Mbengga, i., Fiji 174 4
Mbeya; Tanz., 6,932 164 E3
Mbigou, Gabon 164 B2
Mbinda, Congo B. 164 B2
Mbokou, Congo L. 164 D1
M'Bour, Sen., 9,812 162 B3
M'Bout, Maur., 3,100 162 B3
M'Bridge, r., Ang. 164 B3
Mbua, Fiji 174 4
Mbulo, i., Sol. Is. 175 b2
Mbulu, Tanz. 164 E2
Mburucuyá, Arg., 7,000* 105 D3
Mbwenkuru, r., Tanz. 164 F3
Mchinja, Tanz. 164 F3
Mdina, Malta 123 f12
Me, Hon, N. Viet. 146 D3
Meacham, Oreg. 80 D3
Meacham, Sask., Can. 43 C4
Mead, Colo., 192 79 c7
Mead, Okla. 76 G4
Mead, Wash. 80 E2
Mead, L., Ariz.-Nev. 78 A3
Meade, co., Kans., 5,505 75 E6
Meade, Kans., 2,019 75 E6
Meade, co., Ky., 18,938 71 E4
Meade, Mich. 67 g14
Meade, Ohio 70 G3
Meade, co., S. Dak., 12,044 74 A3
Meade, r., Alaska 85 E1
Meade River, Alaska 85 E1
Meadow, S. Dak. 74 A3
Meadow, Tex., 484 77 M3
Meadow, Utah, 244 78 B2
Meadow, r., W. Va. 62 D4
Meadow Bridge, W. Va., 426 62 D5
Meadowbrook, W. Va. 62 D3
Meadow Brook Heights, Colo. 79 b8
Meadow Grove, Nebr., 430 75 H2
Meadow Lake, Sask., Can., 2,705 43 B3
Meadowlands, Minn., 176 74 F2
Meadowlands, Pa., 1,967 60 B5
Meadow Portage, Man., Can. 43 E4
Meadows, Austl. 172 c8
Meadows, Man., Can. 43 g9
Meadows, Idaho 81 A3
Meadows, Ill. 68 D3
Meadows, Md. 62 b9
Meadows, N.H. 54 E3
Meadows of Dan, Va. 62 D6
Meadowvale, Ont., Can. 46 c13
Meadow Val. Cr., Nev. 83 C4
Meadow Val. Wash, Nev. 83 C4
Meadowview, Va. 62 B6
Meadville, Miss., 611 73 D6
Meadville, Mo., 447 72 D5
Meadville, Nebr. 75 F1
Meadville, Pa., 16,671 60 B2
Meaford, Ont., Can., 3,777 44 H7
Meagher, co., Mont., 2,616 81 D2
Mealy Mts., Newf., Can. 45 O4
Meama, i., Tonga 177 36
Meandarra, Austl. 173 G4
Meander River, Alta., Can. 42 H1
Meansville, Ga. 335 64 g12
Meare, U.K. 114 C8
Mearim, r., Braz. 103 H2
Mearns, Alta., Can. 43 b7
Mears, Mich. 67 G5
Mease, r., U.K. 114 E5
Measham, U.K., 2,728 114 E5
Meath, co., Ire., 66,762 113 C5
Meath Park, Sask., Can. 43 C4
Meauwataka, Mich. 67 H4
Meaux, Fr., 23,305 117 E2
Mebane, N.C., 2,364 63 E1
Meca, Port., 2,168 122 i9
Mecatán, Mex., 2,501 92 D4
Mecca, Saudi Ar. = Makkah
Mecca, Calif. 82 F6
Mecca, Ind. 70 B3
Mechanic Falls, Me., 1,992 55 B4
Mechanicsburg, Ill., 438 68 C4
Mechanicsburg, Ohio, 1,810 70 F2
Mechanicsburg, Pa., 8,123 60 H5
Mechanicsburg, Va. 62 D5
Mechanicsville (part of Thompson), Conn. 56 J5
Mechanicsville, Iowa, 1,010 72 F3
Mechanicsville, Md. 62 H4
Mechanicsville, Vt. 54 A3
Mechanicsville, Va. 62 G5
Mechanicville, N.Y., 6,831 59 N6
Mechelen, Belg., 63,678 115 C3
Mechengue, Col 100 B6
Méchéria, Alg., 10,460 160 D2
Mechernich, F.R.Ger., 5,937 118 A3
Mechita, Arg., 6,000* 105 a12
Mechol, Yap 176 20
Měcholupy, Czech. 126 c6
Meck, i., Kwajalein 176 25
Meckelfeld, F.R.Ger., 2,707 119 a9
Meckenheim, F.R.Ger., 2,891 119 C3
Mecklenburg, reg., Ger.D.R. 118 D2
Mecklenburg, co., N.C., 272,111 63 D2
Mecklenburg, co., Va., 31,428 62 F6
Mecklenburger B., F.R.Ger. 118 C1
Meckling, S. Dak., 93 74 D4
Meco, N.Y. 59 M5
Mecosta, co., Mich., 21,051 67 H5
Mecosta, Mich., 303 67 H5
Mecsek, mts., Hung. 126 D3
Mecúfi, Moz. 164 F4
Mecula, Moz. 164 F4
Medak, India, 15,891 145 F6
Medan, Indon. 479,098 148 A2
Medang, Indon. 147 o15
Médanos, Arg., 6,663 105 C5
Médanos, Arg., 1,600* 105 b11
Medanos, Pt., Calif. 82 c10
Medaryville, Ind., 758 70 C1
Medawachchiya, Cey. 145 n21
Medbourne, U.K. 114 G5
Meddybemps L., Me. 55 E3
Mede, It., 7,018 122 b5
Médéa, Alg., 13,348 160 E1
Medebach, F.R.Ger., 3,092 118 B3
Medeiros Neto, Braz., 5,177 103 J5
Medellín, Col., 690,710 100 C4
Medemblik, Neth., 4,800 115 D2
Mědĕnec, Czech. 126 c6
Mederdra, Maur., 1,400 162 B3
Medesano, It., 7,661 122 d6
Medfield, Mass., 2,424;6,021(T) 57 L4
Medford, Me. 55 D3
Medford, Mass., 64,971 57 M3
Medford, N.J., 1,480 61 B4
Medford, N.Y. 58 h13
Medford, Okla., 1,223 76 F1
Medford, Oreg., 24,425 80 B4
Medford, Wis., 3,260 66 C3
Medford Lakes, N.J., 2,876 61 B4
Medfra, Alaska 85 F3
Medgidia, Rum., 17,943 128 G2
Media, Ill., 165 68 B3
Media, Pa., 5,803 61 M6
Media Agua, Arg., 12,800* 105 B4
Mediapolis, Iowa, 1,040 72 F3
Mediaş, Rum., 32,498 128 E1
Medical Lake, Wash., 4,765 80 E2
Medical Springs, Oreg. 80 E3
Medicine Bow, Wyo., 392 81 F5
Medicine Bow Mts., Colo.-Wyo. 81 F5
Medicine Bow Pk., Wyo. 81 F5
Medicine Bow Ra., Colo. 79 B1
Medicine Cr., Mo. 72 D5
Medicine Cr., Nebr. 75 E3
Medicine Cr., S. Dak. 74 B4
Medicine Hat, Alta., Can., 23,414 42 L4
Medicine Lake, Minn., 323 74 b6
Medicine Lake, Mont., 452 81 G1
Medicine L., Minn. 74 b5
Medicine L., Mont. 81 G1
Medicine Lodge, Kans., 3,072 75 G6
Medicine Lodge, r., Kans.-Okla. 75 G6
Medicine Park, Okla. 76 E3
Medina, Col. 100 D5
Medina, Saudi Ar. = Al Madīnah
Medina, Mich. 67 J7
Medina, Minn., 1,472 74 a5
Medina, N.Y., 6,681 58 D5
Medina, N. Dak., 545 74 C2
Medina, co., Ohio, 65,315 70 G1
Medina, Ohio, 8,235 70 H1
Medina, Tenn., 722 71 C6
Medina, co., Tex., 18,904 77 O5
Medina, Tex. 77 O5
Medina, Wash., 2,285 81 b7
Medina, r., Tex. 77 O5
Medinaceli, Sp. 122 D2
Medina del Campo, Sp., 14,327 122 C2
Medina de Pomar, Sp., 2,878 122 D1
Medina de Ríoseco, Sp., 5,011 122 C2
Medinah, Ill. 69 b9
Medina L., Minn. 74 a5
Medina L., Tex. 77 O5
Medina Sidonia, Sp., 16,190 122 C4
Medinilla, Farallon de, i., Mariana Is. 176 23
Medino Mission, Terr. Papua 174 f3
Medio, A. del, Arg. 105 a11
Mediterranean Sea, 110 C5
Medley, Fla., 112 65 a10
Mednogorsk, U.S.S.R., 36,300 137 i9
Medomac, r., Me. 55 C4
Medora, Ill., 447 68 B4
Medora, Ind. 70 C4
Medora, Kans. 75 H5
Medora, N. Dak., 133 74 A2
Medora L., Mich. 66 F1
Medstead, Sask. Can. 43 C4
Medveđa, Yug. 125 E3
Medveditsa, r., U.S.S.R. 136 E1
Medveditsa, r., U.S.S.R. 136 F3
Medvezh'i, O-va, U.S.S.R. 135 Q2
Medvezh'yegorsk, U.S.S.R., 13,300 134 C3
Medway, Me. 55 D3
Medway, Mass., 1,602;5,168(T) 57 L4
Medyado, i., Jaluit 176 30
Medyai, i., Jaluit 176 30
Medyn', U.S.S.R., 6,000 136 D2
Medzilaborce, Czech. 126 E2
Medzhibozh, U.S.S.R., 3,000 136 B3
Meekatharra, Austl. 172 B4
Meeker, Colo., 1,655 79 B1
Meeker, co., Minn., 18,887 74 E3
Meeker, Ohio 70 F2
Meeker, Okla., 664 76 G2
Meeker Park, Colo. 79 a7
Meelpaeg L., Newf., Can. 45 Q5
Meerane, Ger.D.R., 24,520 118 D3
Meerholz, F.R.Ger., 2,247 119 G4
Meerhout, Belg., 7,768 115 D3
Meerkerk, Neth. 115 c7
Meerle, Belg., 2,607 115 C3
Meerlo, Neth. 119 A1
Meers, Okla. 76 E3
Meerssen, Neth., 5,400 115 D4
Meerut, India, 200,740 145 E3
Meerzorg, Sur., 4,537* 101 N5
Meeteetse, Wyo., 514 81 E3
Mega, Eth. 163 L5
Megáli Panayiá, Gr., 2,477 129 D4
Megalópolis, Gr., 2,235 129 D6
Meganisi i., Gr. 129 C5
Megansett (part of Falmouth), Mass. 57 O6
Mégantic, L., Qué., Can. 47 O3
Mégantic, Mt., Qué., Can. 47 N3
Mégara, Gr., 15,450 129 D5
Megargel, Ala. 64 B4
Megargel, Tex., 417 77 O3
Mégdhova, r., Gr. 129 C5
Megève, Fr., 4,874 117 G4
Meggett, S.C., 188 63 D5
Megiddo, ruins, Isr. 142 b7
Megorskaya Gryada, U.S.S.R. 136 D1
Megunticook Mtn., Me. 55 C4
Mehadia, Rum. 128 D2
Mehaigne, r., Belg. 115 C4
Mehakit, Indon. 148 F3
Mehama, Oreg. 80 B3
Mehan, Okla. 76 G1
Meherpur, Pak., 8,147 144 g14
Meherrin, r., Va. 62 F6
Mehetia, i., Soc. Is. 177 42
Mehlville, Mo. 72 a12
Mehoopany, Pa. 61 K2
Mehren, F.R.Ger. 119 B4
Mehsana, India, 32,577 145 D5
Mehun-sur-Yèvre, Fr., 5,700 117 E3
Mei, r., China 152 E2
Mei-chou Wan, China 152 E2
Meifod, U.K. 114 B5
Meiganga, Cam., 2,000* 162 G4
Meighen I., N.W.T., Can. 41 J1
Meigs, Ga., 1,236 64 E4
Meigs, co., Ohio, 22,159 70 G3
Meigs, co., Tenn., 5,160 71 G6
Mei-hsien, Shen-hsi, China 151 A4
Mei-hsien, K-t., China 152 D2
Meikle, r., Alta., Can. 42 H1
Meikle Says Law, mtn., U.K. 112 e8
Meiktila, Burma, 25,180 146 A2
Mei-ku, China 152 A1
Meilen, Switz., 8,203 124 C1
Mei-ling Kuan, China 152 D2
Meiners Oaks, Calif., 3,513 82 D5
Meinerzhagen, F.R.Ger., 8,700 119 D2
Meiningen, Ger.D.R., 23,748 118 C3
Meiningen, Switz., 3,749 124 C2
Mei-nung, Taiwan, 44,061 152 F3
Meisenheim, F.R.Ger., 2,760 119 D5
Mei-shan, China 152 B1
Meissen, Ger.D.R., 48,214 118 D3
Mei-t'an, China 152 B2
Meitingen, F.R.Ger., 2,799 118 C4
Mejicanos, El Salv., 15,031 94 d10
Mejillones, Chile, 3,363 105 A2
Mejit, i., Marsh. Is. 176 22
Mékambo, Gabon 164 B1
Mekhtar, Pak. 144 C3
Mékinac, L., Qué., Can. 47 M1
Meknès, Mor., 175,943 160 D2
Mekong, r., Asia 141 H4
Mekoryuk, Alaska, 242 85 C3
Melado, r., Chile 104 g16
Melala, Tg., Indon. 148 C3
Melanesia, reg., New Guin.-Pac. Oc. 170 D5
Melano, Switz. 124 D3
Melba, Idaho, 197 81 A4
Melbecks Moor, U.K. 114 D2
Melbeta, Nebr., 118 75 B2
Melbourn, U.K., 1,832 114 J6
Melbourne, Austl., 1,524,111 173 F5
Melbourne, U.K., 3,640 114 E5
Melbourne, Ark., 839 73 C1
Melbourne, Fla., 11,982 65 J4
Melbourne, Iowa, 517 72 D3
Melbourne, Mo., 70 72 D4
Melbourne Beach, Fla., 1,004 65 J4
Melcher, Iowa, 867 72 D3
Melchior, Ant. 180 N6
Melchor, I., Chile 105 A7
Melchor Ocampo, Mex. 92 E4
Melcroft, Pa. 60 D5
Meldorf, F.R.Ger., 8,282 118 B1
Meldreth, U.K. 114 J6
Meldrum Bay, Ont., Can. 46 A3
Meldrum Creek, Br. Col., Can. 42 G3
Mele B., New Hebr. 174 m6
Meleden, Som. Rep. 163 N4
Melegnano, It., 12,551 122 c5
Melekeiok Pt., Palau 176 21
Melekess, U.S.S.R., 54,000 134 E4
Melekhina, U.S.S.R. 137 h7
Meleman, Indon. 148 e8
Melenci, Yug., 8,363 125 E2
Melenki, U.S.S.R., 17,500 136 F2
Meleuz, U.S.S.R., 16,900 137 h9
Melfa, Va., 409 62 J5
Melfi, Chad, 1,200* 163 H4
Melfi, It., 19,287 123 E4
Melfort, Sask., Can., 3,946 43 D4
Melgaço, Port., 1,369 122 A1
Melick, Neth. 119 A2
Melide, Switz., 1,046 124 C3
Meligalá, Gr., 1,960 129 C6
Melilla, Af., 78,788 160 D2
Melipilla, Chile, 15,593 105 A4
Mélisey, Fr., 1,750 117 G3
Melissa, Tex., 405 77 P3
Melita, Man., Can., 1,016 43 E5
Melita, Mich. 67 J4
Melitopol', U.S.S.R., 102,000 134 C5
Melk, Aust., 3,534 124 M5
Melkoye, Oz., U.S.S.R. 135 J3
Melksham, U.K., 8,351 114 D8
Melle, Belg., 8,298 115 B4
Melle, F.R.Ger., 9,215 118 B2
Melle, Fr., 3,915 117 C3
Mellen, Wis., 1,182 66 C2
Mellerud, Swed. 120 C4
Mellette, co., S. Dak., 2,664 74 B4
Mellette, S. Dak., 208 74 C3
Mellid, Sp., 8,659 122 B1
Mellizo Sur, Co., Chile 105 A7
Mello, r., It. 122 d5
Mellösa, Swed. 120 d8
Mellott, Ind., 312 70 B2
Mellrichstadt, F.R.Ger., 3,750 118 C3
Mells, U.K. 114 D8
Mellwood, Ark. 73 D3
Melmore, Ohio 70 F1
Melnik, Bulg. 129 D4
Mělník, Czech., 13,540 126 B1
Mełno, Pol. 127 C2
Melo, Urug., 30,000* 105 E4
Melocheville, Qué., Can., 1,666 47 o18
Melolo, Indon. 149 G5
Melouprey, Camb. 146 D4
Melozitna, r., Alaska 85 F2
Melrhir, Chott, Alg. 160 F2
Melrose, N.S.W., Austl. 173 f9
Melrose, S. Austl., Austl. 172 E5
Melrose, U.K., 2,133 112 E4
Melrose, Conn. 56 F5
Melrose, Fla. 65 G3
Melrose, Iowa, 214 72 E4
Melrose, La. 73 C6
Melrose, Mass., 29,619 57 M3
Melrose, Minn., 2,135 74 E3
Melrose, Mont. 81 C3
Melrose, N. Mex., 698 79 D4
Melrose, N.Y. 59 w28
Melrose, Ohio, 260 70 E1
Melrose, Wis., 516 66 B4
Melrose Park, Fla. 65 b9
Melrose Park, Ill., 22,291 69 c9
Melrose Park, N.Y., 2,058 59 H6
Melrude, Minn. 74 F2
Mels, Switz., 5,254 124 D1
Melsele, Belg., 6,280 115 d8
Melsetter, Rhod. 164 E5
Melsonby, U.K. 112 g11
Melstone, Mont., 266 81 F2
Melstrand, Mich. 67 G2
Melsungen, F.R.Ger., 7,927 118 B3
Meltham, U.K., 5,413 114 E3
Melton Mowbray, U.K., 15,914 113 F5
Melun, Fr., 28,796 117 E2
Melvern, Kans., 376 75 K5
Melvich, U.K. 112 D2
Melvill, Cape = Capuchin, Cape
Melville, Sask., Can., 5,136 43 D5
Melville, Ill. 68 B5
Melville, La., 1,939 73 D7
Melville, N.Y. 58 f13
Melville, N. Dak. 74 C2
Melville (part of Portsmouth), R.I. 57 L6
Melville, C., Austl. 173 F2
Melville, L., Newf., Can. 45 P4
Melville Bay, Austl. 172 E1
Melville I., Austl. 172 D1
Melville I., N.W.T., Can. 41 G2
Melville Pen., N.W.T., Can. 41 N4
Melville Sd., N.W.T., Can. 40 H4
Melvin, Ill., 559 68 D3
Melvin, Iowa, 364 72 B1
Melvin, Ky. 71 J4
Melvin, Mich., 196 67 L5
Melvin, Tex., 401 77 O4
Melvin, L., Ire.-U.K. 113 B4
Melvin, r., Alta., Can. 42 H1
Melvina, Wis., 111 66 C5
Melvindale, Mich., 13,089 67 f15
Melvin Mills, N.H. 54 D5
Melvin Village, N.H. 54 E4
Mélykút, Hung., 8,198 126 D3
Melzo, It., 11,912 122 c5
Memala, Indon. 148 E3
Memaliaj, Alb., 3,500 125 D4
Memambetsu, Jap., 10,506 155 L8
Memel = Klaipėda
Mēmele, r., U.S.S.R. 136 B1
Memmingen, F.R.Ger., 28,161 118 B5
Mempakul, Malay. 148 E1
Memphis, U.A.R. = Şaqqārah
Memphis, Ind. 70 D4
Memphis, Mich., 996 67 L6
Memphis, Mo., 2,106 72 E4
Memphis, N.Y. 59 q23
Memphis, Tenn., 497,524 71 A6
Memphis, Tex., 3,332 76 N2
Memphrémagog, L., Qué., Can. 47 M3
Memuçaj, Alb. 125 D4
Memuro, Jap., 17,131 155 K8
Mena, Ark., 4,388 73 A3
Menahga, Minn., 799 74 E2
Menai Bridge, U.K., 2,335 113 D5

260 · Menaik—Midville

Menaik, Alta., Can. 43 b8
Menai Str., U.K. 113 D5
Ménaka, Mali, 1,300 162 E3
Menaldum, Neth. 115 D1
Menan, Idaho, 496 81 D4
Menands, N.Y., 2,919 59 v29
Menanga, Indon. 149 H3
Menard, co., Ill., 9,248 68 C3
Menard, co., Tex., 2,964 77 O4
Menard, Tex., 1,914 77 O4
Menasha, Wis., 14,647 66 E4
Mendawai, r., Indon. 148 E3
Mende, Fr., 10,061 117 E4
Menden, F.R.Ger., 25,752 118 A3
Menden, F.R.Ger., 5,351 119 C3
Mendenhall, Miss., 1,946 73 F6
Mendes, Braz., 7,047 103 e18
Mendesh, U.S.S.R. 137 m12
Méndez, Ec. 104 B2
Méndez, Mex. 93 F3
Mendham, Sask., Can. 43 B5
Mendham, N.J., 2,371 61 B2
Mendi, Terr. Papua 174 d2
Mendip Hills, U.K. 113 E6
Mendlesham, U.K. 113 G5
Mendocino, co., Calif., 51,059 82 B3
Mendocino, Calif. 82 B3
Mendocino, C., Calif. 82 A2
Mendocino Escarpment, Pac. Oc. 169 H1
Mendon, Ill., 784 68 A3
Mendon, Mass., 2,068(T) 57 K4
Mendon, Mich., 867 67 H6
Mendon, Mo., 287 72 D5
Mendon, N.Y. 58 n20
Mendon, Ohio, 663 70 E2
Mendon, Utah, 345 78 b7
Mendon, Vt. 54 B4
Mendong Gömpa, China 144 e10
Mendota, Calif., 3,086 82 C4
Mendota, Ill., 6,154 68 C2
Mendota, Minn., 259 74 c6
Mendota, Va. 62 B6
Mendota, L., Wis. 66 D5
Mendota Heights, Minn., 5,028 74 c6
Mendoza, Arg., 109,149 105 B4
Mendoza, Bol. 102 c10
Mendoza, Mex., 1,055 93 c9
Mendoza, Tex. 76 c5
Mendoza, Urug. 105 c12
Mendrisio, Switz., 5,109 124 C3
Mene de Mauroa, Ven., 3,606 100 E2
Mene Grande, Ven., 12,992 100 E3
Menemen, Turk., 15,118 142 A2
Menemsha (part of Chilmark), Mass. 57 N7
Menen, Belg., 21,979 115 B4
Meneng (dist.), Nauru 175 17
Meneng Pt., Nauru 175 17
Ménerville, Alg., 8,209 160 c5
Mengalia, Grand Récif, N. Caled. 174 i8
Meng-che, China 150 D5
Meng-ch'eng, China 151 C4
Menge, i., Jaluit 176 30
Mengen, F.R.Ger., 4,490 118 B4
Menggala, Indon. 148 C4
Meng-hsien, China 151 B4
Mengkarak, Malay., 1,155 147 p15
Mengkuang, Malay., 1,085 147 p15
Meng-ku-tai, China 151 A3
Meng-la, China 150 D5
Meng-lien, China 150 D5
Meng-shan, China 150 E4
Meng Shan, China 151 C4
Meng-ts'un, China 151 C3
Meng-tzu, China 152 A3
Meng-yin, China 151 C4
Menifee, co., Ky., 4,276 71 H4
Menihek, Newf., Can. 45 M3
Menihek Lakes, Newf., Can. 45 M3
Menindee, Austl. 173 F5
Meningie, Austl. 172 E5
Menkhap Me, China 144 f11
Menlo, Ga., 466 64 D1
Menlo, Iowa, 421 72 C3
Menlo, Kans., 99 75 E4
Menlo, Wash. 80 B2
Menlo Park, Calif., 26,957 83 e13
Mennecy, Fr., 2,164 116 h12
Menno, S. Dak., 837 74 D4
Meno, Okla., 118 76 E1
Menomin, L., Wis. 66 B4
Menominee, co., Mich., 24,685 66 F3
Menominee, Mich., 11,289 66 F3
Menominee, r., Mich.-Wis. 66 F3
Menominee Ra., Mich. 66 E3
Menomonee, r., Wis. 66 c11
Menomonee Falls, Wis., 18,276 66 E5
Menomonie, Wis., 8,624 66 A4
Menor, Mar, Sp. 122 E4
Menorca, I. de, Sp. 122 h8
Mens, Fr., 1,143 117 F4
Mentana, It., 9,916 123 b8
Mentara, Malay. 147 o14
Mentasta, Alaska, 40 85 H3
Mentasta Mts., Alaska 85 J3
Mentawai, Kep., Indon. 148 A3
Mentawai, Selat, Indon. 148 A3
Menteith, L. of, U.K. 112 b7
Menton, Fr., 20,069 116 n13
Mentone, Ind., 813 70 D1
Mentone, Tex. 77 M4
Mentor, Kans. 75 H5
Mentor, Minn., 281 74 D2
Mentor, Mo. 72 D7
Mentor, Ohio, 4,354 70 H1
Mentor-on-the-Lake, Ohio, 3,290 70 H1
Menucourt, Fr. 116 f10
Menunketesuck, r., Conn. 56 F7
Menyamaya, Terr. New Guin. 174 e2
Men-yüan, China 150 D3
Menze, China 144 c10
Menzelen, F.R.Ger., 2,564 119 A1
Menzies, Austl. 172 B4
Menzies, Mt., Ant. 180 R5
Menziken, Switz., 4,060 124 C1
Menzingen, Switz., 3,340 124 C1
Meon, r., U.K. 113 k13
Meoqui, Mex., 10,298 92 D2
Meota, Sask., Can. 43 B4
Meppel, Neth., 16,900 115 E2
Meppen, F.R.Ger., 13,349 118 A2
Meppen, Ill. 68 B4
Mequinenza, Sp., 6,378 122 F2
Mequon, Wis., 8,543 66 F5
Mer, Fr., 3,477 117 D3
Merai, Terr. New Guin. 174 g2
Merak, Indon. 148 b6
Mera Lava, i., New Hebr. 174 m5
Meramangye, L., Austl. 172 D4
Meramec, r., Mo. 72 F6
Meranggau, Indon. 148 D3
Merano, It., 29,852 123 C1
Merasheen, Newf., Can. 45 a10
Merasheen I., Newf., Can. 45 a10
Merauke, Indon. 149 L5
Merauke, r., Indon. 149 L5
Merbabu, G., Indon. 148 d7
Merca, Som. Rep., 20,620* 163 M5
Mercadal, Sp., 2,821 122 h8
Mercara, India, 14,453 145 E7
Merced, co., Calif., 90,446 82 C4
Merced, Calif., 20,068 82 C4
Merced, r., Calif. 82 C4
Mercedes, Arg., 36,500* 105 B4
Mercedes, Arg., 17,490* 105 D3
Mercedes, Arg., 43,275 105 D4
Mercedes, Phil., 5,081 153 B2
Mercedes, Tex., 10,943 77 O7
Mercedes, Urug., 25,000* 105 D4
Mercer, N.Z. 175 g5
Mercer, co., Ill., 17,149 68 B2
Mercer, co., Ky., 14,596 71 G4
Mercer, Me. 55 C4
Mercer, co., Mo., 5,750 72 D4
Mercer, Mo., 368 72 D4
Mercer, co., N.J., 266,392 61 B3
Mercer, co., N. Dak., 6,805 74 B2
Mercer, N. Dak., 154 74 B2
Mercer, co., Ohio, 32,559 70 E2
Mercer, Ohio 70 E2
Mercer, co., Pa., 127,519 60 B3
Mercer, Pa., 2,800 60 B3
Mercer, Tenn. 71 B6
Mercer, co., W. Va., 68,206 62 C5
Mercer, Wis. 66 C2
Mercer Island, Wash. 81 b7
Mercersburg, Pa., 1,759 60 F6
Mercerville, N.J., 9,100* 61 B3
Mercês, Braz., 2,897 103 e17
Merchantville, N.J., 4,075 61 f12
Merchong, Malay. 147 p15
Merchtem, Belg., 7,944 115 d9
Mercoal, Alta., Can. 42 J3
Mercurea, Rum. 128 D2
Mercury, Nev. 83 C4
Mercury, Tex. 77 O4
Mercury Is., N.Z. 175 h5
Mercy Bay, N.W.T., Can. 41 F3
Méré, Fr. 116 f11
Mere, U.K., 1,920 113 E6
Meredith, N.H. 54 D4
Meredith, N.Y. 59 L7
Meredith, C., Falkland Is. 108 3
Meredith, L., Colo. 79 D2
Meredith Center, N.H. 54 D4
Meredosia, Ill., 1,034 68 B4
Merefa, U.S.S.R., 26,200 136 D3
Meregh, Som. Rep. 163 M5
Merelbeke, Belg., 12,365 115 B3
Merevari, r., Ven. 101 J5
Méréville, Fr., 1,908 117 E2
Mergui, Burma, 33,697 146 B4
Mergui Arch., Burma 146 B5
Meriç, r., Turk. 129 F4
Meriç=Maritsa
Merichleri, Bulg., 4,413 128 E3
Mérida, Mex., 170,513 93 H4
Merida, Phil., 4,014 153 f11
Mérida, Sp., 34,297 122 B3
Mérida, Ven., 40,404 100 E3
Mérida, Cord. de, Ven. 100 E3
Meridale, N.Y. 59 K7
Meriden, U.K., 1,758 114 E6
Meriden, Conn., 51,850 56 E6
Meriden, Kans., 402 75 K4
Meriden, N.H. 54 C4
Meriden, N.J. 58 b13
Meridian, Calif. 82 B3
Meridian, Idaho, 2,081 81 A4
Meridian, Miss., 49,374 73 G5
Meridian, N.Y., 379 59 G5
Meridian, Okla., 160 76 F2
Meridian, Pa., 1,649 60 B4
Meridian, Tex., 993 77 P4
Meridian Butte, Ariz. 78 C3
Meridianville, Ala. 64 C1
Mériel, Fr., 2,028 116 g10
Merig, i., New Hebr. 174 k5
Mérignac, Fr., 33,910 117 C4
Merigold, Miss., 602 73 E4
Merikarvia, Fin. 120 E3
Merinda, Austl. 173 G3
Mering, F.R.Ger., 6,090 118 C4
Merino, Colo., 268 79 D1
Merino, Mass., 3,099 56 J4
Merionethshire, co., U.K., 38,310 113 E5
Merion Station, Pa., 5,550* 60 f12
Merir, i., Car. Is. 170 C4
Merishausen, Switz. 124 C1
Merit, Hudspeth Co., Tex. 77 L4
Merit, Hunt Co., Tex. 76 g8
Meriwether, co., Ga., 19,756 64 E2
Meriwether, S.C. 63 B4
Meriwether Lewis Nat. Pk., Tenn. 71 D6
Merizo, Guam 176 24
Merke, U.S.S.R. 137 g3
Merkel, Tex., 2,312 77 N3
Merke Shung, China 144 e10
Merklín, Czech. 126 b6
Merksem, Belg., 33,674 115 d8
Merkstein, F.R.Ger., 14,297 119 A3
Merl, F.R.Ger., 1,743 119 C4
Merlebach, Fr., 8,715 117 G2
Merlimau, Malay., 1,647 147 p15
Merlin, Ont., Can. 46 B6
Merlin, Oreg. 80 B4
Mermentau, La., 716 73 C7
Mern, Den., 1,269 121 E5
Merna, Nebr., 349 75 F2
Meroe, ruins, Sudan 163 K3
Merom, Ind., 352 70 B3
Merowe=Marawī, Sudan
Merredin, Austl., 2,342 172 B4
Merriam, Ind. 70 D1
Merriam, Kans., 5,084 75 a7
Merrick, co., Nebr., 8,363 75 G2
Merrick, N.Y., 18,789 58 e14
Merrick, mtn., U.K. 113 D4
Merrick Bk., Conn. 56 H6
Merrickville, Ont., Can. 47 J4
Merricourt, N. Dak., 66 74 C2
Merrill, Iowa, 645 72 A2
Merrill, Mich., 963 67 J5
Merrill, Miss. 73 G7
Merrill, N.Y. 59 N2
Merrill, Oreg., 804 80 C4
Merrill, Wis., 9,451 66 D3
Merrillan, Wis., 591 66 C4
Merrillville, Ga., 111 64 E5
Merrillville, Ind. 70 B1
Merrimac, Ill. 72 a12
Merrimac, Ky. 71 F4
Merrimac, Mass., 3,261(T) 57 M1
Merrimac, Wis., 297 66 D5
Merrimack, co., N.H., 67,785 54 D5
Merrimack, N.H. 54 D6
Merrimack, r., Mass.-N.H. 54 D5
Merriman, Nebr., 285 75 D1
Merrimbula, Austl. 173 G5
Merrimon, N.C. 63 H3
Merrin, Mt., New Hebr. 174 m7
Merrionette Park, Ill., 2,354 69 d10
Merritt, Br. Col., Can., 2,930 42 G4
Merritt, Mich. 67 H4
Merritt, N.C. 63 H2
Merritt Island, Fla., 3,554 65 J4
Merritton, Ont., Can., 5,404 46 d15
Merriwa, Austl. 173 G5
Merriweather, Mich. 66 D2
Mer Rouge, La., 853 73 D5
Merrow (part of Mansfield), Conn. 56 G5
Merryall (part of New Milford), Conn. 56 C6
Merry Hill, N.C. 63 H1
Merrymeeting L., N.H. 54 E4
Merryville, La., 1,232 73 B7
Mers, Fr., 3,834 117 D1
Mersa Fatma, Eth. 163 L3
Mersch, Lux., 1,514 119 A5
Merseburg, Ger.D.R., 47,199 118 C3
Mers-El-Kébir, Alg., 4,687 160 a6
Mersey, r., Austl. 173 f13
Mersey, r., U.K. 113 E5
Mershon, Ga. 64 G4
Mersin, Turk., 68,574 142 C2
Mersing, Malay., 7,229 148 C2
Merstham, U.K., 3,568 114 H8
Merta, India, 13,083 145 D4
Merten, Fr., 1,133 116 c8
Mertens, Tex., 104 76 f10
Mertens, Mt., Kusaie 176 31
Mertert, Lux. 115 E5
Merthyr Cynog, U.K. 114 A6
Merthyr Tydfil, U.K., 59,039 113 E6
Merti, Kenya 164 F1
Mertingen, F.R.Ger., 2,147 118 C4
Mértola, Port., 5,682 122 B4
Merton, Austl. 173 e11
Merton, Wis., 407 66 c11
Mërtvyy Kultuk, Sor, U.S.S.R. 134 E5
Mertz Gl., Ant. 180 U6
Mertzon, Tex., 584 77 N4
Mertzwiller, Fr., 2,692 116 e9
Méru, Fr., 5,479 117 E2
Meru, Kenya 164 F1
Meru, mtn., Tanz. 164 F2
Merume Mts., Guyana 101 K5
Merutai, Malay. 148 F1
Mervans, Fr., 1,608 117 F3
Merville, Fr., 8,378 117 E1
Mervin, Sask., Can. 43 B4
Merwede kan., Neth. 115 C3
Merwin, Mo., 76 72 C6
Merwin, L., Wash. 80 B2
Merxheim, F.R.Ger., 1,388 119 D5
Méry, Fr., 3,286 116 g10
Merzdorf, Ger.D.R. 126 d5
Merzenich, F.R.Ger., 3,061 119 B3
Merzifon, Turk., 22,173 142 C1
Merzig, F.R.Ger., 11,493 118 A4
Mesa, Ariz., 50,529 78 C5
Mesa, co., Colo., 50,715 79 A2
Mesa, Idaho 81 A3
Mesa, N. Mex. 79 C5
Mesa, Wash., 263 80 D2
Mesabi Ra., Minn. 74 F2
Mesach Mellet, hills, Libya 161 F3
Mesagne, It., 26,030 123 F4
Mesamávida, Chile 104 f15
Mesaoria, reg., Cyp. 142 e9
Mesa Pk., Colo. 79 B3
Mesa Verde Nat. Pk., Colo. 79 A3
Mesay, r., Col. 100 D7
Mescalero, N. Mex. 79 C5
Mescalero Ridge, N. Mex. 79 D5
Meschede, F.R.Ger., 10,862 118 B3
Mesegon, i., Truk 176 19
Mesenikólas, Gr., 1,018 129 C5
Meservey, Iowa, 331 72 D2
Meshchera, reg., U.S.S.R. 136 c6
Meshchovsk, U.S.S.R., 5,000 136 D2
Meshed=Mashhad
Meshik, Alaska 85 E4
Meshkovskaya, U.S.S.R. 136 F3
Meshoppen, Pa., 470 61 L2
Meshoppen Cr., Pa. 61 L2
Mesic, N.C. 63 H2
Mesick, Mich., 304 67 H4
Mesilla, N. Mex., 1,264 79 B5
Mesita, Colo. 79 C3
Mesocco, Switz., 1,324 124 D2
Mesola, It., 14,988 122 f6
Mesolóngion, Gr., 11,266 129 C5
Mesopotamia, reg., Iraq-Syr. 142 E2
Mesoraca, It., 8,916 123 F5
Mesquite, Nev. 83 C4
Mesquite, N. Mex. 79 B5
Mesquite, Tex., 27,526 77 P3
Messaad, Alg. 160 E2
Messalonskee L., Me. 55 C4
Messick=Poquoson
Messimy, Fr., 1,023 116 p15
Messina, It., 248,523 123 E5
Messina, S. Af., 10,225 164 E5
Messina, Stretto di, It. 123 E6
Messines, Qué., Can. 44 J6
Messingham, U.K., 1,436 114 G3
Messíni, Gr., 8,249 129 D6
Messiniakós Kólpos, Gr. 129 D6
Messkirch, F.R.Ger., 3,438 118 B4
Messy, Fr. 116 i11
Mestá, Gr. 129 E5
Mesta, r., Bulg. 129 D4
Mestre, It., 25,000* 123 D2
Meta, Mo., 360 72 E6
Meta, r., Col.-Ven. 100 F4
Metagama, Ont., Can. 44 G6
Meta Incognita Pen., N.W.T., Can. 41 Q5
Metaline, Wash., 299 80 E1
Metaline Falls, Wash., 469 80 E1
Metaljka, Yug. 125 D3
Metalton, Ark. 73 B1
Metamora, Ill., 1,808 68 C3
Metamora, Ind. 70 D3
Metamora, Mich., 452 67 K6
Metamora, Ohio, 598 70 E1
Metán, Arg., 15,000* 105 C3
Metapán, El Salv., 4,073 94 C3
Metaponto, It. 123 F4
Metauro, r., It. 123 D3
Metawar, Indon. 148 d7
Metcalf, Ariz. 78 D5
Metcalf, Ga., 241 64 F5
Metcalf, Ill., 278 68 E4
Metcalf (part of Holliston), Mass. 57 L4
Metcalfe, co., Ky., 8,367 71 F5
Metchosin, Br. Col., Can. 42 c7
Metedeconk, N.J. 58 c16
Metedeconk, North Branch, r., N.J. 61 C3
Meteghan, N.S., Can. 47 S11
Metemma, Eth. 163 L3
Meteor Crater, Ariz. 78 C4
Meteor Seamount, Atl. Oc. 109 N10
Metepec, Méx., Mex., 6,613 93 e10
Metepec, Pue., Mex., 1,296 93 f10
Meteren, Neth. 115 c7
Metheringham, U.K., 1,679 114 G4
Methil (incl. Buckhaven), 21,104 112 E3
Methóni, Gr., 1,484 129 C6
Methow, Wash. 80 C1
Methow, r., Wash. 80 C1
Methuen, Mass., 28,114(T) 57 M2
Methven, N.Z. 175 f6
Methven, U.K. 112 c7
Methwold, U.K., 1,560 114 J5
Methy L., Sask., Can. 43 B3
Metinic I., Me. 55 C5
Metkovets, Bulg., 5,166 128 D3
Metković, Yug., 3,606 125 C3
Metlakatla, Alaska, 798 85 M5
Metlika, Yug. 125 B2
Metmárfag, Sp. Sah. 160 B3
Metolius, Oreg., 270 80 C3
Metolius, r., Oreg. 80 C3
Metonga, L., Wis. 66 D3
Metropolis, Ill., 7,339 68 D6
Métsovon, Gr., 2,976 129 C5
Mettawa, Ill., 126 69 c8
Mettawee, N.Y.-Vt. 54 A5
Mettendorf, F.R.Ger., 1,126 119 A5
Metter, Ga., 2,362 64 G3
Mettet, Belg., 3,150 115 C4
Mettlach, F.R.Ger., 4,428 118 A4
Mettmann, F.R.Ger., 21,338 119 B2
Mettur, India, 27,698 145 k20
Mettur Dam, India 145 k20
Metuchen, N.J., 14,041 61 C2
Metuje, r., Czech. 127 f6
Metung, Austl. 173 g11
Metz, Fr., 109,678 117 G2
Metz, Ind. 70 E1
Metz, Mich. 67 K3
Metz, Mo., 137 72 C6
Metz, W. Va. 62 D3
Metz-en-Couture, Fr. 116 a7
Metzervisse, Fr., 1,009 116 b8
Metzingen, F.R.Ger., 11,062 119 G7
Metzquititlán, Mex., 1,404 93 f9
Metztitlán, Mex., 1,496 93 F4
Meudon, Fr., 35,824 116 g11
Meulaboh, Indon. 148 A1
Meulan, Fr., 4,451 116 f10
Meulebeke, Belg., 10,522 115 B4
Meung-sur-Loire, Fr., 3,851 117 D3
Meureudu, Indon. 148 A1
Meurthe, r., Fr. 116 c9
Meuse, r., Eur. 110 D4
Meuselwitz, Ger.D.R., 10,501 118 D3
Mexborough, U.K., 17,095 114 F4
Mexcala, Mex., 1,035 93 F5
Mexhoma, Okla. 76 A1
Mexia, Tex., 6,121 77 P4
Mexiana, I., Braz. 103 G1
Mexicalcingo, Mex., 2,736 93 e10
Mexicali, Mex., 172,554 92 B1
Mexicana, Altiplanicie, Mex. 92 ·
Mexican Hat, Utah 78 D3
Mexican Water, Ariz. 78 D3
Mexicanos, Lag. de los, Mex. 92 D2
Mexico, ctry., 44,145,000* 92-93
México, st., Mex., 1,897,851 93 F4
México, Mex., 3,301,757 93 F4
Mexico, Phil., 2,174 153 b7
Mexico, Ky. 71 C4
Mexico, Me., 3,951 55 B4
Mexico, Mo., 12,889 72 E5
Mexico, N.Y., 1,465 59 H5
Mexico, Ohio 70 F2
Mexico, Pa. 60 H4
Mexico, Gulf of, N. Amer. 35 E7
Mexico Basin, Mexico, G. of 108 F5
Mexico Beach, Fla. 65 D3
Meximieux, Fr., 2,540 117 F4
Mexticacán, Mex., 2,949 93 b8
Meyenburg, Ger.D.R. 118 D2
Meyer, Ill. 68 A3
Meyersdale, Pa., 2,901 60 D6
Meyerton, S. Af., 7,781 165 k17
Meymac, Fr., 2,649 117 E4
Meyrin, Switz., 3,215 124 A2
Meyrueis, Fr., 1,198 117 E4
Meys, Fr. 116 o15
Meyzieux, Fr., 4,506 116 q15
Mezali, Burma 147 g7
Mezcala, Mex., 1,482 93 a9
Mezdra, Bulg., 6,487 128 D3
Mèze, Fr., 4,546 117 E5
Mezen', U.S.S.R., 4,100 134 D3
Mezen', r., U.S.S.R. 134 D3
Mézenc, Mt., Fr. 117 F4
Mężenin, Pol. 127 E2
Mezhdurechensk, U.S.S.R., 62,000 137 s11
Mezhdusharskiy, O., U.S.S.R. 134 D2
Mežica, Yug. 125 B1
Mézidon, Fr., 3,335 117 D2
Mezieres, Man., Can. 43 f10
Mézières, Fr., 12,435 117 F2
Mézières, Switz. 124 A2
Mézières-en-Brenne, Fr., 1,312 117 D3
Mézières-sur-Seine, Fr., 1,617 116 f11
Mezimĕstí, Czech. 127 f6
Mézin, Fr., 2,211 117 D4
Mezinovskiy, U.S.S.R., 6,000 136 d6
Mezőberény, Hung., 13,126 126 E3
Mezőcsát, Hung., 6,570 126 E3
Mezőhegyes, Hung., 9,146 126 E3
Mezőkovácsháza, Hung., 6,246 126 E3
Mezőkövesd, Hung., 18,640 126 E3
Mezőtúr, Hung., 23,632 126 E3
Mezquital, r., Mex. 92 D3
Mezzani, It., 3,290 122 d6
Mgachi, U.S.S.R., 6,600 135 O4
Mglin, U.S.S.R., 5,400 136 D2
Mhow, India, 48,032 145 E5
Mi, r., China 151 C3
Miadeba, Terr. Papua 174 3
Miahuatlán, Mex., 7,420 93 F5
Miajadas, Sp., 8,632 122 C3
Miami, Man., Can. 43 f10
Miami, Rhod. 164 D4
Miami, Ariz., 3,350 78 C5
Miami, Fla., 291,688 65 J7
Miami, co., Ind., 38,000 70 C2
Miami, co., Kans., 19,884 75 L5
Miami, Mo., 156 72 D5
Miami, N. Mex. 79 C3
Miami, co., Ohio, 72,901 70 E2
Miami, Okla., 12,869 76 J1
Miami, Tex., 656 76 N2
Miami, r., Fla. 65 b10
Miami, r., Ohio 70 E3
Miami Beach, Fla., 63,145 65 J7
Miami Can., Fla. 65 J6
Miami Gardens, Fla. 65 a9
Miamisburg, Ohio, 9,893 70 E3
Miami Shores, Fla., 8,865 65 J7
Miami Springs, Fla., 11,229 65 a10
Miamitown, Ohio 71 g10
Mīāndow āb, Iran, 14,796 143 D1
Miandrivazo, Malag. Rep., 1,456 165 G5
Mīāneh, Iran, 21,100 143 D1
Miangas, P., Indon. 149 H1
Mianus (part of Greenwich), Conn. 56 B8
Mianus, r., Conn. 56 B8
Miānwāli, Pak., 31,398 145 D2
Miao-li, Taiwan, 42,510 152 F2
Miao Lieh-tao, China 151 D3
Miarinarivo, Malag. Rep., 2,258 165 G5
Miass, U.S.S.R., 107,000 134 F4
Miass, r., U.S.S.R. 137 k8
Miasteczko Śląskie, Pol., 3,241 127 h6
Miastko, Pol., 4,600* 127 B1
Miazal, Ec. 104 d11
Mibu, Jap., 25,282 155 F3
Mica, Wash. 80 E2
Micanopy, Fla., 658 65 G3
Micaúne, Moz. 164 F5
Micaville, N.C. 63 B2
Micawber, Okla. 76 G2
Micay, Col. 100 B6
Micco, Fla. 65 J5
Miccosukee, Fla. 65 F2
Michaga, Co., Bol. 102 C5
Michalovce, Czech., 16,480 126 F2
Michaud, Me. 55 D1
Michel, Sask., Can. 43 B3
Michelbach, F.R.Ger., 1,477 119 E4
Michelet, Alg. 160 d5
Michelfeld, F.R.Ger., 1,451 119 H6
Michelmersh, U.K. 113 k12
Michelson, Mt., Alaska 85 J1
Michelstadt, F.R.Ger., 6,153 118 B4
Miches, Dom. Rep., 3,110 96 n6
Michiana, Mich., 135 67 G7
Michiana Shores, Ind., 229 69 g9
Michie, Tenn. 71 C6
Michigamme, Mich. 66 E2
Michigamme, L., Mich. 66 E2
Michigamme, r., Mich. 66 E2
Michigamme Res., Mich. 66 E2
Michigan, st., U.S., 8,317,000* 66–7
Michigan, N. Dak., 451 74 C1
Michigan, r., Colo. 79 B1
Michigan, L., U.S. 53 J2
Michigan Center, Mich., 4,611 67 J6
Michigan City, Ind., 36,653 70 C1
Michigan I., Wis. 66 C2
Michigantown, Ind., 513 70 C2
Mi-chih, China 151 A3
Michihuao, Arg. 105 B6
Michikamau L., Newf., Can. 45 N3
Michipicoten Harbour, Ont., Can. 44 F6
Michipicoten I., Ont., Can. 44 F6
Michoacán, st., Mex., 1,851,876 92 E4
Michoacanejo, Mex., 1,057 93 b8
Michurin, Bulg., 2,783 128 F3
Michurinsk, U.S.S.R., 84,000 134 D4
Mickle Fell, mtn., U.K. 114 D1
Mickleover, U.K., 9,709 114 E5
Mickleton, U.K. 114 E6
Mickley, U.K., 1,862 112 g10
Mico, Tex. 77 O5
Mico, P., Nic. 94 F5
Mico, r., Nic. 94 E4
Micotrin, mtn., Dominica 97 13
Micoud, St. Lucia, 2,091 97 11
Micro, N.C., 350 63 F2
Micronesia, reg., Pac. Oc. 170 D4
Midai, P., Indon. 148 C2
Midale, Sask., Can. 43 D5
Mid-Atlantic Ridge, Atl. Oc. 108 J5
Middelburg, Neth., 22,400 115 B3
Middelburg, Cape, S. Af., 8,711 164 D7
Middelburg, Tvaal., S. Af., 12,907 164 D6
Middelfart, Den., 8,801 121 B5
Middelharnis, Neth., 4,900 115 C3
Middelrode, Neth. 115 D3
Middle, r., Iowa 72 D3
Middle America Trench, Pac. Oc. 169 J2
Middle Andaman, i., India 146 A4
Middle Atlas=Moyen Atlas
Middleback, Mt., Austl. 172 b7
Middle Bass I., Ohio 70 G1
Middle Bight, Bah. Is. 95 b8
Middleboro, Mass., 6,003; 11,065(T) 57 N5
Middleboro, Pa., 442 60 B2
Middlebourne, W. Va., 711 62 C3
Middlebrook, Va. 62 E4
Middleburg, Fla. 65 H2
Middleburg, N.Y., 1,317 59 M6
Middleburg, Ohio 70 F2
Middleburg, Okla. 76 F2
Middleburg, Pa., 1,366 60 H4
Middleburg, Va., 761 62 G4
Middleburgh Heights, Ohio, 7,282 70 d9
Middlebury, Conn., 4,785(T) 56 D6
Middlebury, Ill., 216 69 a8
Middlebury, Ind., 917 70 D1
Middlebury, Vt., 3,688 54 A3
Middlebury, r., Vt. 54 A4
Middlebury Center, Pa. 60 H2
Middlebush, N.J. 58 a15
Middle Caraquet, N.B., Can. 47 T10
Middle Concho, r., Tex. 77 N4
Middle Cr., Pa. 60 H4
Middle Cr., Pa. 61 M3
Middle Dam, Me. 55 B4
Middle Falls, N.Y. 59 w27
Middlefield, N.Y. 59 L6
Middlefield, Ohio, 1,467 70 H1
Middlefield Center, Conn. 56 F6
Middlefield Law, mtn., U.K. 112 b8
Middle Granville, N.Y. 59 O5
Middlegrove, Ill. 68 B3
Middle Grove, N.Y. 59 v27
Middle Gull Pond, Newf., Can. 45 b10
Middle Haddam (part of E. Hampton), Conn. 56 F6
Middleham, U.K. 114 E2
Middle Inlet, Wis. 66 E3
Middle Island, N.Y. 58 h13
Middle I., Austl. 172 C5
Middle Island Cr., W. Va. 62 D3
Middle L., Calif. 82 C2
Middle Loch, Hawaii 84 c7
Middle Loup, r., Nebr. 75 F2
Middle Moaula Camp, Hawaii 84 F4
Middle Pk., basin, Colo. 79 ·
Middle Point, Ohio, 571 70 E2
Middleport, Ont., Can. 46 b15
Middleport, N.Y., 1,882 58 C5
Middleport, Ohio, 3,373 70 G3
Middle Raccoon, r., Iowa 72 C3
Middle Ridge, Wis. 66 C5
Middle River, Br. Col., Can. 42 F2
Middle River, Md., 10,825 62 H3
Middle River, Minn., 414 74 D1
Middle River, Wis. 66 A2
Middlesboro, Ky., 12,607 71 H5
Middlesbrough, U.K., 157,395 113 F4
Middlesex, Br. Hond. 94 C2
Middlesex, co., Conn., 88,865 56 F7
Middlesex, co., Mass., 1,238,742 57 L2
Middlesex, co., N.J., 433,856 61 C3
Middlesex, N.J., 10,520 61 C2
Middlesex, N.Y. 58 F6
Middlesex, N.C., 588 63 F2
Middlesex, Vt. 54 B3
Middlesex, co., Va., 6,319 62 H5
Middleton, N.S., Can., 1,884 45 N7
Middleton, Ire., 3,145 113 B6
Middleton, Lancs., Eng., U.K., 56,674 114 D3
Middleton, Northumb., Eng., U.K. 112 g9
Middleton, Idaho, 541 81 A4
Middleton, Mass., 3,718(T) 57 M2
Middleton, Mich. 67 J5
Middleton, N.H. 54 E5
Middleton, Tenn., 461 71 C6
Middleton, Wis., 4,410 66 D5
Middleton Cheney, U.K., 1,784 114 F6
Middleton in Teesdale, U.K., 1,603 113 E4
Middleton I., Alaska 85 H4
Middleton on the Wolds, U.K. 114 G3
Middleton St. George, U.K., 2,618 112 h10
Middleton Tyas, U.K. 112 g11
Middletown, Calif. 82 B3
Middletown, Conn., 33,250 56 F6
Middletown, Del., 2,191 62 J3
Middletown, Ill., 543 68 C3
Middletown, Ind., 2,033 70 D2
Middletown, Iowa, 245 72 F4
Middletown, Jefferson Co., Ky., 2,764 71 F3
Middletown, Simpson Co., Ky. 71 E5
Middletown, Md., 1,036 62 G3
Middletown, Mo., 199 72 F5
Middletown, N.J., 3,550* 61 C3
Middletown, N.Y., 23,475 59 L9
Middletown, N.C. 63 J2
Middletown, Ohio, 42,115 70 E3
Middletown, Pa., 11,182 60 J5
Middletown, R.I., 12,675(T) 57 L6
Middletown, Va., 378 62 F3
Middletown Springs, Vt. 54 A5
Middleville, Mich., 1,196 67 H6
Middleville, N.Y., 648 59 K5
Middle Water, Tex. 76 M2
Middleway, W. Va. 62 F3
Middlewich, U.K., 6,833 114 D4
Middleyard, U.K. 112 b8
Midelt, Mor., 6,504 160 D2
Midfield, Ala., 3,556 64 c8
Midhurst, Ont., Can. 46 E4
Midhurst, U.K., 1,880 113 F6
Midi d'Ossau, Pic du, Fr. 117 C5
Mid-Indian Basin, Ind. Oc. 168 C3
Midkiff, Tex. 77 N4
Midkiff, W. Va. 62 B4
Midland, Ont., Can., 8,464 44 H7
Midland, Calif. 82 F6
Midland, Md., 737 62 E3
Midland, co., Mich., 51,450 67 J5
Midland, Mich., 27,779 67 J5
Midland, N.C. 63 D2
Midland, Oreg. 80 C4
Midland, Beaver Co., Pa., 6,425 60 B4
Midland, Washington Co., Pa., 1,317 60 a8
Midland, S. Dak., 401 74 B3
Midland, co., Tex., 67,717 77 M4
Midland, Tex., 62,625 77 N4
Midland, Va. 62 G4
Midland, Wash. 81 b8
Midland City, Ala., 854 64 D4
Midland City, Ill. 68 C3
Midland Park, N.J., 7,543 58 c13
Midlothian, co., U.K., 580,332 112 E4
Midlothian, Ill., 11,789 69 c10
Midlothian, Tex., 1,521 77 P3
Midlothian, Va. 62 G5
Midnapur, India, 59,532 145 H5
Midnight, Miss. 73 E4
Mid-Ocean Canyon, Atl. Oc. 108 J3
Mid-Ocean Ridge, Arctic Oc. 108 M1
Midongy du Sud, Malag. Rep. 165 G5
Midouze, r., Fr. 117 C5
Mid-Pacific Mountains, Pac. Oc. 169 F2
Midridge, Mo. 72 F7
Midsayap, Phil., 6,789 153 C4
Midvale, Idaho, 211 81 A3
Midvale, Ohio, 683 70 H2
Midvale, Utah, 5,802 78 C1
Midville, Ga., 676 64 G3

Midway—Misquamicut · 261

Midway, Bullock Co., Ala., 594 64 D3
Midway, Monroe Co., Ala. 64 C4
Midway, Ark. 73 C1
Midway, Fla. 65 E2
Midway, Ga., 240 64 H4
Midway, Ky., 1,044 71 G3
Midway, Pa., 1,012 60 a8
Midway, S.C. 63 D4
Midway, Tex. 77 Q4
Midway, Utah, 713 78 c9
Midway City, Calif. 83 i16
Midway Island, Va. 62 G4
Midway Is., Hawaii 84 f9
Midway Park, N.C., 4,164 63 G3
Midwest, Wyo. 81 F4
Midwest City, Okla., 36,058 76 F2
Midyat, Turk., 9,580 142 E2
Mid Yell, U.K. 112 F1
Midžor, mt., Yug. 125 F3
Mie, Jap., 6,813 154 A5
Mie, Jap., 21,330 154 B5
Miechów, Pol., 6,868 127 D3
Miedwie, Jez., Pol. 127 A2
Miedzanka, Pol. 127 k6
Miedziana Góra, Pol. 127 k6
Międzybórz, Pol., 1,039 127 B3
Międzychód, Pol., 6,788 127 A2
Międzygórze, Pol. 127 f6
Międzylesie, Pol., 1,941 127 f6
Międzyrzec Podlaski, Pol., 10,636 127 E3
Międzyrzecz, Pol., 10,161 127 A2
Międzyzdroje, Pol., 3,797 127 A2
Miehlen, F.R.Ger., 1,448 119 D4
Miekinia, Pol. 127 i6
Miélan, Fr., 1,214 117 D5
Mielec, Pol., 22,000* 127 D3
Mielnik, Pol. 127 E2
Mien-ch'ih, China 151 B4
Mien-chu, China 152 A1
Miendrie, Sur. 101 N5
Mien-hsien, China 150 E3
Mien-ning, China 150 D4
Mien-yang, Hu-p., China 152 D1
Mien-yang, S-ch., China 150 D4
Mier, Mex., 4,120 93 F2
Miera, N. Mex. 79 B4
Miercurea Ciuc, Rum., 11,996 128 E1
Mieres, Sp., 70,871 122 C1
Mierlo, Neth., 3,700 115 D3
Mieroszów, Pol., 5,207 127 f6
Mier y Noriega, Mex., 1,018 93 E3
Mierzawa, r., Pol. 127 k6
Miesau, F.R.Ger., 3,029 119 C6
Miesbach, F.R.Ger., 5,141 118 C5
Miesso, Eth., 10,400 163 L4
Mifflin, Ind. 70 C4
Mifflin, co., Pa., 44,348 60 G4
Mifflin, Pa., 745 60 H4
Mifflin, Wis. 66 C6
Mifflinburg, Pa., 2,476 60 H4
Mifflintown, Pa., 887 60 H4
Mifflinville, Ohio 70 b6
Mifflinville, Pa., 1,027 61 K3
Mifol, Alb. 125 D4
Migennes, Fr., 6,546 117 E3
Migliarino, It., 9,744 122 e6
Mignon, Ala., 2,271 64 C2
Miguel Alemán, Presa, res., Mex. 93 F4
Miguel Auza, Mex., 7,140 92 E3
Miguel Calmon, Braz., 4,822 103 H4
Miguel de la Borda, Pan. 94 G6
Migues, Urug., 2,000* 105 d12
Migulinskaya, U.S.S.R. 136 F3
Migyaunglaung, Burma 146 B4
Mihăileni, Rum. 128 F1
Mihăileşti, Rum. 128 F2
Mihara, Jap., 80,395 155 C4
Mihara-yama, Jap. 155 F4
Miharu, Jap., 22,119 155 G3
Mihintale, Cey. 145 n21
Mihonoseki, Jap., 10,690 155 C4
Mi-hsien, China 151 B4
Mijares, r., Sp. 122 E2
Mijdrecht, Neth., 4,000 115 b6
Mikado, Mich. 67 K4
Mikame, Jap., 15,146 155 C5
Mikana, Wis. 66 B3
Mikasa, Jap., 56,196 155 J8
Mikawa, Jap., 11,166 155 E3
Mikengere, D.R.Congo 165 m18
Mikeno, Volcan, D.R.Congo 165 d14
Mikha Tskhakaya, U.S.S.R., 17,900 137 b1
Mikhaylov, U.S.S.R., 6,500 136 E2
Mikhaylovgrad, Bulg., 15,122 128 D3
Mikhaylovka, Kaz. S.S.R., U.S.S.R. 137 o11
Mikhaylovka, R.S.F.S.R., U.S.S.R., 34,600 134 D4
Mikhaylovka, Ukr. S.S.R., U.S.S.R. 136 D4
Mikhaylovskiy, U.S.S.R., 7,200 134 H4
Mikhaylovskiy, U.S.S.R. 137 i8
Mikhaylovskoye, U.S.S.R. 136 F4
Mikhnëvo, U.S.S.R. 136 b6
Miki, Jap., 38,264 154 g15
Mikindani, Tanz., 4,807 164 F3
Mikkalo, Oreg. 80 C3
Mikkeli, Fin., 21,074 120 F3
Mikkwa, r., Alta., Can. 42 J1
Mikleuš, Yug. 125 C2
Mikobata, Jap. 154 f14
Mikołajki, Pol., 2,843 127 D2
Mikołów, Pol., 17,091 127 h6
Mikonos, Gr. 129 E6
Mikonos, i., Gr. 129 E6
Mikrón Dhérion, Gr. 129 F4
Mikrópolis, Gr., 2,228 129 D4
Mikstat, Pol., 1,410 127 B3
Mikulov, Czech. 126 C2
Mikulovice, Czech. 127 g6
Mikumi, Tanz. 164 F3
Mikumo, Jap. 154 h15
Mikun', U.S.S.R., 11,300 134 E3
Mikuni, Jap., 22,530 155 E3
Mikuni-sammyaku, mts., Jap. 155 F3
Mikura, Jap. 154 i14
Mikura-jima, Jap. 155 F5
Mikuszowice, Pol. 127 i7
Mila, Alg., 12,670 160 e5
Milaca, Minn., 1,821 74 F3
Milagro, Arg., 10,000* 105 B4
Milagro, Ec., 27,327 104 B2
Milagros, Phil., 2,112 153 h15
Milak, India 144 b11
Milakokia L., Mich. 67 H2
Milam, co., Tex., 22,263 77 P4
Milam, Tex. 77 R4
Milan, It.=Milano
Milan, Ga., 786 64 F3
Milan, Ill., 3,065 68 B2
Milan, Ind., 1,174 70 D3
Milan, Kans., 144 75 H6
Milan, Mich., 3,616 67 K6
Milan, Minn., 482 74 E3
Milan, Mo., 1,670 72 D4
Milan, N.H. 54 E2
Milan, N. Mex., 2,658 79 B4
Milan, Ohio, 1,309 70 G1
Milan, Pa. 60 J2
Milan, Tenn., 5,208 71 C6
Milan, Wash. 80 E2
Milan, Wis. 66 C4
Milange, Moz. 164 F4
Milano, It., 1,471,471 123 B2
Milano, Tex. 77 P4
Milanówek, Pol., 14,421 127 D2
Milâs, Turk., 11,670 142 A2
Milazzo, It., 23,390 123 E5
Milbank, S. Dak., 3,500 74 D3
Milberger, Kans. 75 G5
Milbourne, U.K. 112 g9
Milbridge, Me. 55 E4
Milbuk, Phil., 2,046 153 C4
Milburn, Nebr. 75 F2
Milburn, Okla., 228 76 G3
Milden, Sask., Can. 43 C4
Mildenhall, U.K., 7,132 113 G5
Mildmay, Ont., Can. 46 C4
Mildred, Sask., Can. 43 C4
Mildred, Kans., 60 75 K5
Mildred, Pa. 61 K3
Mildura, Austl., 10,972 173 F5
Miléai, Gr., 1,065 129 D5
Mil Entr., Yap 176 20
Miles, Austl., 1,193 173 G4
Miles, Iowa, 376 72 G2
Miles, Tex., 626 77 N4
Miles, r., Mass. 57 N2
Milesburg, Pa., 1,158 60 G4
Miles City, Mont., 9,665 81 G2
Miles Mtn., Vt. 54 D3
Mileston, Miss. 73 E4
Milestone, Sask., Can. 43 D5
Milesville, N.C. 63 E1
Milesville, Pa. 60 c9
Milesville, S. Dak. 74 B3
Miletto, Monte, It. 123 E4
Miletus, ruins, Turk. 142 A2
Milevsko, Czech. 126 B2
Miley, S.C. 63 D5
Milford, (part of Belper), U.K. 114 E4
Milford, U.K., 2,869 114 G8
Milford, Calif. 82 C2
Milford, Conn., 41,662 56 D8
Milford, Del., 5,795 62 J4
Milford, Ill., 1,699 68 E3
Milford, Decatur Co., Ind., 1,167 70 D3
Milford, Kosciusko Co., Ind., 197 70 D1
Milford, Iowa, 1,476 72 B1
Milford, Kans., 318 75 J4
Milford, Me. 55 D4
Milford, Mass., 13,722;15,749(T) 57 K4
Milford, Mich., 4,323 67 K6
Milford, Mo. 72 C7
Milford, Nebr., 1,462 75 H3
Milford, N.H., 3,916 54 D6
Milford, N.J., 1,114 61 A2
Milford, N.Y., 548 59 K6
Milford, Ohio, 4,131 70 E3
Milford, Pa., 1,198 61 N3
Milford, Tex., 590 76 f10
Milford, Utah, 1,471 78 B2
Milford, Va. 62 G4
Milford Center, Ohio, 794 70 F2
Milford Haven, U.K., 12,802 113 D6
Milford-on-Sea (part of Lymington), U.K., 2,819 113 i13
Milford Res., Kans. 75 J4
Milford Sound, N.Z. 175 e7
Milharado, Port., 4,603 122 i10
Mili, atoll, Marsh. Is. 170 F4
Miliana, Alg., 7,425 160 c5
Milicz, Pol., 5,800 127 B3
Milieu, Piton du, pk., Maurit. 165 c12
Milieu, R. du., Qué., Can. 47 K2
Milijeno, Yug. 125 D3
Milk, r., Can.-U.S. 81 E1
Milk, r., Jam. 96 p9
Milkel, Ger.D.R. 126 d5
Milk Hill, U.K. 114 E8
Mil'kovo, U.S.S.R. 135 P4
Milk River, Alta., Can. 42 K4
Mill, Neth. 115 D3
Mill, r., Conn. 56 C8
Mill, r., Mass. 56 F3
Mill, r., Mass. 57 K4
Mill, r., Vt. 54 B5
Milladore, Wis. 66 D4
Millard, Miss. 73 F7
Millard, Mo. 72 E4
Millard, Nebr., 1,014 75 J2
Millard, co., Utah, 7,886 78 B2
Millard, Wis. 66 E6
Millarton, N. Dak. 74 C2
Millau, Fr., 22,174 117 E4
Milla - l, Pan. 94 F6
Millbank, Ont., Can. 46 D5
Mill Bay, Br. Col., Can. 42 D2
Millboro, S. Dak. 74 C4
Millboro Spring, Va. 62 E5
Millbrae, Calif., 15,873 83 e12
Millbridge, Ont., Can. 46 G4
Millbrook, Ont., Can. 46 F4
Millbrook (part of Southampton), U.K., 11,591 113 k13
Millbrook, Mich. 67 H5
Millbrook, N.Y., 1,717 59 N8
Mill Bk., Vt. 54 B3
Mill Bk., Vt. 54 B5
Millburn, Ill. 69 b7
Millburn, N.J., 18,799 58 b14
Millbury, Mass., 9,623(T) 57 K4
Mill City, Nev. 83 B2
Mill City, Oreg., 1,289 80 B3
Mill Creek, Calif. 82 C2
Mill Creek, Ill., 102 68 C6
Mill Creek, Mo. 72 G7
Mill Creek, Okla., 289 76 G3
Mill Creek, Pa., 400 60 G5
Mill Creek, W. Va., 817 62 E4
Mill Cr., Ind. 70 C3
Mill Cr., Mich. 67 L5
Mill Cr., Ohio 71 h11
Mill Cr., Pa. 60 E3
Mill Cr., Pa. 60 f10
Mill Cr., Tex. 77 h8
Mill Creek Res., Pa. 61 o16
Milldale (part of Southington), Conn. 56 E6
Millecoquins, Mich. 67 H2
Milledgeville, Ga., 11,117 64 F2
Milledgeville, Ill., 1,208 68 C2
Milledgeville, Tenn. 71 C6
Mille Îles, R. des, Qué., Can. 47 o17
Mille Lacs, co., Minn., 14,560 74 F2
Mille Lacs, Lac des, Ont., Can. 44 D5
Mille Lacs L., Minn. 74 F2
Millen, Ga., 3,633 64 H3
Miller, co., Ark., 31,686 73 B4
Miller, co., Ga., 6,908 64 E4
Miller, Miss. 73 F3
Miller, co., Mo., 13,800 72 E6
Miller, Mo., 601 72 D7
Miller, Nebr., 137 75 F3
Miller, Ohio 70 G4
Miller, S. Dak., 2,081 74 C3
Miller, Mt., Alaska 85 J3
Miller Bk., Vt. 54 B3
Miller City, Ill. 68 C6
Millerovo, U.S.S.R., 33,000 136 F3
Millers, r., Mass. 56 G2
Millersburg, Ind., 489 70 D1
Millersburg, Iowa, 186 72 E3
Millersburg, Ky., 913 71 G3
Millersburg, Mich., 280 67 K3
Millersburg, Ohio, 3,101 70 G2
Millersburg, Pa., 2,984 60 H4
Millers Falls, Mass., 1,199 56 G2
Millers Ferry, Ala. 64 B3
Millersport, N.Y. 58 m18
Millersport, Ohio, 752 70 G3
Millers Tavern, Va. 62 G5
Millerstown, Pa., 675 60 H4
Millersville, Ill. 68 C4
Millersville, Md. 62 c8
Millersville, Ohio 70 F1
Millersville, Pa., 3,883 61 K5
Millerton, N.B., Can. 47 T10
Millerton, N.Y., 1,027 59 O8
Millerton, Pa. 60 J2
Millerton L., Calif. 82 D4
Millertown, Newf., Can. 45 Q5
Millery, Fr. 116 b9
Millet, Alta., Can. 43 b7
Millett, Mich. 67 J6
Millett, Nev. 83 B3
Millett, Tex. 77 O5
Millford, Ire. 113 C4
Mill Fork, Utah 78 C2
Mill Hall, Pa., 1,891 60 H3
Millheim, Pa., 780 60 H4
Millhome, Wis. 66 F5
Millhousen, Ind., 212 70 D3
Millican, Oreg. 80 C4
Millicent, Austl., 2,251 172 E5
Milligan, Fla. 65 C2
Milligan, Nebr., 323 75 H3
Milliken, Colo., 630 79 c7
Millingen, F.R.Ger., 1,900 119 A1
Millingen a.d. Rijn, Neth., 3,600 115 E3
Millington (part of E. Haddam), Conn. 56 G7
Millington, Ill., 309 68 D2
Millington, Md., 408 62 J3
Millington, Mich., 1,159 67 K5
Millington, N.J., 1,182 58 a14
Millington, Tenn., 6,059 71 B6
Millinocket, Me., 7,318 55 D3
Millinocket L., Me. 55 D2
Millinocket L., Me. 55 D3
Millis, Mass., 4,374(T) 57 L4
Mill I., N.W.T., Can. 41 O5
Millmerran, Austl. 173 G4
Millom, U.K., 7,116 113 E4
Mill Plain (part of Danbury), Conn. 56 B7
Mill Point, W. Va. 62 D4
Millport, U.K., 1,592 112 a8
Millport, Ala., 943 64 A2
Millport, N.Y., 425 58 G7
Millport, Pa. 60 F2
Mill River (part of New Marlboro), Mass. 56 C4
Mill River (part of Deerfield), Mass. 56 F3
Millry, Ala., 645 64 A4
Mills, co., Iowa, 13,050 72 B3
Mills, Nebr. 75 F1
Mills, N. Mex. 79 C3
Mills, Okla. 76 E3
Mills, Pa. 60 G2
Mills, co., Tex., 4,467 77 O4
Mills, Wyo., 1,477 81 F4
Millsap, Tex. 76 d9
Millsboro, Del., 536 62 J4
Mill Shoals, Ill., 322 68 D5
Mills L., N.W.T., Can. 40 F5
Mill Spring, Mo., 226 72 G7
Millstadt, Ill., 1,830 68 B5
Millstatt, Aus., 1,243 124 K7
Millstätter See, Aust. 124 K7
Millston, Wis. 66 C4
Millstone, N.J., 409 61 B2
Millstone, W. Va. 62 C4
Millstone, r., N.J. 61 C3
Millstreet, Ire. 113 B5
Milltown, N.B., Can., 1,870 47 S11
Milltown, Ind., 793 70 C4
Milltown, N.J., 5,435 61 C3
Milltown, Wis., 608 66 A3
Milltown Malbay, Ire. 113 B5
Millvale, Pa., 6,624 60 C5
Mill Valley, Calif., 10,411 83 d12
Millview, Fla. 65 B2
Mill Village, Pa., 336 60 C2
Millville, N.B., Can. 47 S10
Millville, Del., 231 62 J4
Millville, Mass., 1,141;1,567(T) 57 K4
Millville, Mich. 67 J6
Millville, N.J., 19,096 61 B5
Millville, Ohio, 676 70 E3
Millville, Pa., 952 60 J3
Millville, Utah, 364 78 c7
Millwood, Ga. 64 G4
Millwood, Ohio 70 G2
Millwood, Va. 62 F3
Millwood, Wash., 1,776 80 E2
Milly-la-Forêt, Fr., 3,040 117 E2
Milmay, N.J. 61 B5
Milmine, Ill. 68 D4
Milna, Yug. 125 C3
Milnathort, U.K. 112 d7
Milne B., Terr. Papua 174 f3
Milne Edwards Deep, Pac. Oc. 98 A3
Milner, Ga., 305 64 E2
Milnesand, N. Mex. 79 D5
Milne Seamount, Atl. Oc. 108 K4
Milngavie, U.K., 8,894 112 b8
Milnor, N. Dak., 658 74 D2
Milnrow, U.K., 7,819 114 D3
Milnthorpe, U.K., 1,390 114 C2
Milo, Alta., Can. 42 K4
Mi-lo, China 152 A2
Milo, Iowa, 458 72 D3
Milo, Kans. 75 H4
Milo, Me., 1,802 55 C3
Milo, Mo., 108 72 C7
Milo, Oreg. 80 B4
Milo, r., Guin. 162 C4
Milolii, Hawaii 84 F4
Milos, Gr. 129 E6
Milos, i., Gr. 129 E6
Milosław, Pol., 2,807 127 B2
Milotice, Czech. 127 g5
Milovice, Czech. 127 e6
Milówka, Pol. 127 C4
Milpa Alta, Mex., 5,299 93 e10
Milparinka, Austl. 173 F4
Milpillas, Jal. Mex., 1,248 93 b9
Milpillas, Zac., Mex. 93 a8
Milpitas, Calif., 6,572 83 f13
Milroy, Ind. 70 D3
Milroy, Minn., 268 74 E3
Milroy, Pa., 1,666 60 G4
Milt, r., Mass. 56 E3
Miltenberg, F.R.Ger., 8,034 118 B4
Milton, N.S., Can., 2,021 47 T11
Milton, Ont., Can., 5,583 46 E5
Milton, N.Z., 1,922 175 f7
Milton, Northants., Eng., U.K. 114 G6
Milton, Stir., Scot., U.K. 112 b7
Milton (part of Litchfield), Conn. 56 D5
Milton, Del., 1,617 62 J4
Milton, Fla., 4,108 65 B2
Milton, Ill., 309 68 B4
Milton, Ohio Co., Ind. 70 E4
Milton, Wayne Co., Ind., 700 70 D3
Milton, Iowa, 609 72 E4
Milton, Kans. 75 H6
Milton, Ky., 365 71 F3
Milton, Me. 55 B4
Milton, Mass., 26,375(T) 57 M3
Milton, Mich. 67 g14
Milton, N.H. 54 E5
Milton, N.J. 58 a12
Milton, N.Y. 59 M8
Milton, N.C., 235 63 E1
Milton, N. Dak., 264 74 D1
Milton, Pa., 7,972 60 J3
Milton, Tenn. 71 E6
Milton, Utah 78 c8
Milton, Vt., 817 54 A2
Milton, Wash., 2,218 81 b8
Milton, W. Va., 1,714 62 B4
Milton, Wis., 1,671 66 E6
Milton Ernest, U.K. 114 G6
Milton-Freewater, Oreg., 4,110 80 D3
Milton Junction, Wis., 1,433 66 E6
Milton L., Ohio 62 D1
Milton Mills, N.H. 54 E4
Miltonvale, Kans., 814 75 H4
Milverton, Ont., Can., 1,099 46 D5
Milwaukee, N.C., 311 63 G1
Milwaukee, Pa. 61 o16
Milwaukee, co., Wis., 1,036,041 66 F5
Milwaukee, Wis., 741,324 66 F5
Milwaukie, Oreg., 9,099 80 B3
Mimbres, N. Mex. 79 B5
Mimbres, r., N. Mex. 79 B5
Mimico, Ont. Can., 17,878 46 E5
Mimitsu, Jap. 154 B5
Mimizan, Fr. 4,958 117 C4
Mimmaya, Jap., 5,647 155 G1
Mimongo, Gabon 164 A2
Mimoso do Sul, Braz., 5,278 103 f17
Mimot, Camb. 147 m11
Mims, Fla., 1,307 65 J4
Min, r., China 150 D4
Min, r., China 150 F4
Mina, Nev. 83 A3
Mina, S. Dak. 74 C3
Mina, r., Alg. 160 b6
Mīnāb, Iran, 4,228 143 F3
Minabe, Jap., 9,368 155 D5
Minagi, Jap. 154 e15
Minahasa, pen., Indon. 149 H2
Minahico, Ont., Can. 44 C5
Minaki, Ont., Can. 44 C5
Minakuchi, Jap., 22,837 154 h15
Minam, Oreg. 80 E3
Minamata, Jap., 48,342 154 B5
Minami-Ariji, Jap. 154 g14
Minami-dake, Jap. 154 B6
Minamidani, Jap. 154 f14
Minami-iō-jima, Vol. Is. 170 D3
Minamitane, Jap., 12,157 154 k17
Minami-tori-shima, Pac. Oc. 170 E3
Minapasuk, Phil., 10,497 153 e11
Mina Pirquitas, Arg., 2,000* 105 B2
Mina Ragra, Peru 104 B4
Minari, Jap. 155 C4
Minas, Cuba, 5,827 96 e2
Minas, Urug., 30,000* 105 E4
Minas, Sa. de las, Guat. 94 C3
Minas Basin, N.S., Can. 47 T11
Minas Gerais, st., Braz., 9,798,880 103 G5
Mīnā' Su'ūd, Saudi Ar. 143 D3
Minatare, Nebr., 894 75 B2
Minatitlán, Mex., 34,980 93 G5
Minato, Jap. 154 f15
Minato, Jap. 154 g15
Minato, Jap. 155 m20
Minbu, Burma, 9,096 146 A2
Minbya, Burma, 5,815 146 A2
Min-ch'in, China 150 D3
Min-ch'ing, China 152 E2
Minchinhampton, U.K., 4,318 113 E6
Mincio, r., It. 123 C2
Minco, Okla., 1,021 76 E2
Mindanao, i., Phil. 153 B4
Mindanao Sea, Phil. 153 B3
Mindanao Trench, Pac. Oc. 141 L5
Mindat Sakan, Burma 146 A2
Mindelheim, F.R.Ger., 8,058 118 C4
Mindelo, C. Verde Is. 109 5
Mindemoya L., Ont., Can. 46 B3
Minden, Ont., Can. 46 F4
Minden, F.R.Ger., 45,725 118 B2
Minden, Iowa, 355 72 B3
Minden, La., 12,785 73 B5
Minden, Nebr., 2,383 75 G3
Minden, Nev. 83 A3
Minden, Tex. 77 Q3
Minden, W. Va., 1,114 62 C5
Minden City, Mich., 369 67 L5
Mindenmines, Mo., 356 72 C7
Mindi, C.Z. 94 f11
Mindiólgi, Gr., 1,006 129 C5
Mindiptana, Indon. 149 L4
Mindon, Burma 146 A3
Mindoro, Wis. 66 B4
Mindoro, i., Phil. 153 B2
Mindoro Str., Phil. 153 B2
Mindszent, Hung., 9,191 126 E3
Minduri, Braz., 1,644 103 d17
Mine, Jap., 39,704 154 B4
Mine Centre, Ont., Can. 44 D5
Minehead, U.K., 7,671 113 E6
Mine Hill, N.J. 58 a13
Mineiros, Braz., 5,105 103 F5
Mineola, N.Y., 20,519 59 N10
Mineola, Tex., 3,810 77 Q3
Miner, co., S. Dak., 5,398 74 D3
Minera, U.K., 1,226 114 B4
Mineral, Calif. 82 C2
Mineral, co., Colo., 424 79 B3
Mineral, Ill., 330 68 C2
Mineral, co., Mont., 3,037 81 B2
Mineral, co., Nev., 6,329 83 A3
Mineral, Tex. 77 P5
Mineral, Va., 366 62 G4
Mineral, Wash. 80 B2
Mineral, co., W. Va., 22,354 62 E3
Mineral City, Ind. 70 C4
Mineral City, Ohio, 917 70 H2
Mineral del Monte, Mex., 10,090 93 f9
Mineral Hills, Mich., 311 66 E2
Mineral L., Wis. 66 C2
Mineral Mts., Utah 78 B2
Mineral'nyye Vody, U.S.S.R., 40,000 136 F4
Mineral Point, Mo., 332 72 G7
Mineral Point, Wis., 2,385 66 C6
Mineral Springs, Ark., 616 73 A4
Mineral Wells, Tex., 11,053 77 O3
Minerbe, It., 4,797 122 e5
Minero, r., Col. 101 e13
Minersville, Pa., 6,606 61 K4
Minersville, Utah, 580 78 B2
Minersville, Wis. 66 C2
Minerva, N.Y. 59 N4
Minerva, Ohio, 3,833 70 H2
Minerva Park, Ohio, 1,169 70 b6
Minervino Murge, It., 20,666 123 E4
Minetto, N.Y. 59 G5
Mineville, N.Y., 1,181 59 N3
Mineyama, Jap., 14,412 155 D4
Min-feng, China 150 B3
Minford, Ohio 70 G4
Minga, D.R.Congo 165 o19
Mingaladon, Burma 147 b2
Mingan, Qué., Can. 45 N5
Mingan, r., Qué., Can. 45 N5
Mingan Mts., Phil. 153 c7
Mingan Passage, Qué., Can. 45 N5
Ming-chiang, China 152 D1
Mingechaur, U.S.S.R., 33,000 137 c1
Mingechaurskoye Vdkhr., U.S.S.R. 137 c1
Mingenew, Austl. 172 A4
Mingin, Burma, 1,833 146 A2
Mingo, Iowa, 260 72 D3
Mingo, Kans. 75 E4
Mingo, Ohio 70 F2
Mingo, co., W. Va., 39,742 62 B5
Mingo, W. Va. 62 D4
Mingo Junction, Ohio, 4,987 70 J2
Mingo L., N.W.T., Can. 41 P5
Mingolsheim, F.R.Ger., 3,294 119 F6
Ming-shui, China 151 E1
Mingulay, i., U.K. 112 C3
Minh Chau, N. Viet. 147 i9
Minh Duc, S. Viet., 5,161 147 m11
Minhla, Burma, 6,470 146 A3
Minhla, Burma, 4,721 146 A3
Minho, r., Jam. 96 p9
Min-hou, China 152 E2
Min-hsien, China 150 D3
Minh Thanh, S. Viet. 147 m11
Minićevo, Yug. 125 F3
Minicoy I., India 145 D8
Minidoka, co., Idaho, 14,394 81 C4
Minidoka, Idaho 154 81 C4
Minier, Ill., 847 68 C3
Minigwal, L., Austl. 172 C4
Minija, r., U.S.S.R. 136 A2
Miniota, Man., Can. 43 E5
Minipi L., Newf., Can. 45 O4
Miniss L., Ont., Can. 44 D5
Ministik L., Alta., Can. 43 c7
Ministre Pt., St. Lucia 97 11
Ministro Ramos Mexía, Arg. 105 B6
Minitonas, Man., Can. 43 E4
Minj, Terr. New Guin. 174 e2
Minkcreek, Idaho, 109 81 D4
Min-Kush, U.S.S.R. 134 G5
Minlaton, Austl. 172 E5
Min-lo, China 150 D3
Minna, Nigeria, 14,987 162 F4
Minneapolis, Kans., 2,024 75 H4
Minneapolis, Minn., 482,872 74 F3
Minneapolis, N.C. 63 B1
Minnedosa, Man., Can., 2,196 43 E5
Minnehaha, co., S. Dak., 86,575 74 D4
Minnehaha Cr., Minn. 74 b6
Minnehaha Falls, Minn. 74 c6
Minneiska, Minn., 110 74 G3
Minneola, Kans., 679 75 E6
Minneota, Minn., 1,297 74 D3
Minnesota, st., U.S., 3,562,000* 74
Minnesota, r., Minn. 74 E3
Minnesuing L., Wis. 66 B2
Minnetonka, Minn., 25,037 74 a6
Minnetonka, L., Minn. 74 a6
Minnewaska, L., Minn. 74 E3
Minnewaukan, N. Dak., 420 74 C1
Minnie Moud Cr., Utah 78 C2
Minnipa, Austl. 172 E5
Minnora, W. Va. 62 C4
Minns, Bah. Is. 95 b8
Mino, Jap. 154 f15
Mino, Jap., 28,937 155 E4
Miño, r., Port.-Sp. 122 A1
Minoa, N.Y., 1,838 59 H5
Minocqua, Wis. 66 D3
Mino-Kamo, Jap., 31,132 154 h14
Minokuchi, Jap. 155 n19
Minong, Wis., 348 66 B2
Minonk, Ill., 2,001 68 C3
Minooka, Ill., 539 68 D2
Minorca=Menorca, I. de
Minor Hill, Tenn. 71 D6
Minorsville, Ky. 71 G3
Minot, Me. 55 B4
Minot (part of Scituate), Mass. 57 O4
Minot, N. Dak., 30,604 74 B1
Minotola, N.J. 61 B5
Minowa, Jap. 155 m18
Minquadale, Del. 62 e11
Minsk, U.S.S.R., 599,000 134 B4
Mińsk Mazowiecki, Pol., 20,000* 127 D2
Minster, Ohio, 2,193 70 E2
Mintaka Pass, China-Pak. 150 A3
Minter, Ga., 147 64 G3
Mint Hill, N.C. 63 D2
Mintlaw, U.K. 112 F3
Minto, Man., Can. 43 E5
Minto, N.B., Can., 1,549 47 S10
Minto, Yukon, Can. 40 B5
Minto, Alaska, 161 85 G2
Minto, N. Dak., 642 74 D1
Minto, L., Qué., Can. 44 K2
Minto Inlet, N.W.T., Can. 40 F3
Minton, Sask., Can. 43 D5
Minturn, Colo., 662 79 B2
Minturno, It., 15,629 123 D4
Minūf, U.A.R. 161 i7
Minusinsk, U.S.S.R., 38,300 135 J4
Minvoul, Gabon 164 B1
Minyā al Qamḥ, U.A.R. 161 i7
Minya Konka=Kung-ka Shan
Min'yar, U.S.S.R., 15,400 137 i8
Minywa, Burma 146 A2
Minywa, Burma, 4,107 147 b2
Minzi, Burma 147 b2
Mio, Jap. 154 g16
Mio, Mich. 67 J4
Miocene, Br. Col., Can. 42 G3
Miogawa, Jap. 154 g16
Mionica, Yug., 3,804 125 E2
Mions, Fr., 1,867 116 p15
Miquelon, i., N. Amer. 45 Q6
Miquelon Lakes, Alta., Can. 43 c7
Miquihuana, Mex., 1,777 93 F3
Mir, Cuba 96 e2
Mira, It., 27,247 123 D2
Mira, Port., 13,384 122 A2
Mira, r., Ec. 104 B1
Mīrābād, Afghan. 144 A3
Mirabella Eclano, It., 10,394 123 E4
Miracema, Braz., 9,810 103 e17
Miracema do Norte, Braz., 3,145 103 G3
Mirada Hills, Calif., 22,444 83 i16
Mirador Nac., pk., Urug. 105 D4
Miradouro, Braz., 2,475 103 e17
Miraflores, C.Z. 94 g12
Miraflores, Col. 100 D5
Miraflores, Col. 100 D7
Miraflores, Peru, 51,851 104 D6
Miraflores Locks, C.Z. 94 g12
Miragoâne, Haiti, 2,711 96 k6
Miraí, Braz., 4,181 103 e17
Miraj, India, 53,345 145 E6
Miramar, Arg., 8,350* 105 D5
Miramar, C.R., 1,122 94 E5
Miramar, Fr. 116 m14
Miramar, San Diego Co., Calif. 82 c9
Miramar, San Mateo Co., Calif. 83 e13
Miramar, Fla. 65 b9
Mirambeau, Fr., 1,553 117 C4
Miramichi, r., N.B., Can. 45 M6
Miramichi Bay, N.B., Can. 45 N6
Miramont, Fr., 3,110 117 D4
Miramonte, Arg. 105 b13
Miramontes Pt., Calif. 83 d13
Miranda, Arg., 1,600* 105 b13
Miranda, Braz., 2,075 103 E6
Miranda, Col. 100 B6
Miranda, Cuba, 2,186 96 f2
Miranda, r., Braz. 103 E5
Miranda de Ebro, Sp., 27,881 122 D1
Miranda do Douro, Port., 5,867 122 B2
Mirande, Fr., 3,830 117 D5
Mirandela, Port., 5,979 122 B2
Mirando City, Tex. 77 O6
Mirandola, It., 23,361 123 C2
Mirano, It., 18,859 123 C2
Mirasaka, Jap., 6,368 154 e15
Mir-Bashir, U.S.S.R., 6,000 137 c1
Mirbāṭ, Muscat and Oman 143 F5
Mirceşti, Rum. 128 F1
Mirebalais, Haiti, 1,995 96 k6
Mirebeau, Fr., 2,220 117 C3
Mirecourt, Fr., 9,117 117 F2
Mirepoix, Fr., 3,322 117 D5
Mirfield, U.K., 12,289 114 E3
Mirganj, India, 9,392 144 e12
Mirgorod, U.S.S.R., 25,000 136 D3
Miri, Malay., 13,183 148 E1
Miriam Vale, Austl. 173 G3
Miribel, Fr., 4,751 116 p15
Miričina, Yug. 125 D2
Mirik, C., Maur. 162 B2
Mirim, Lag., Braz. 103 F8
Mirimire, Ven., 2,018 100 F2
Mīrjāveh, Iran 143 G3
Mirnyy, Ant. 180 T6
Mirnyy, U.S.S.R., 6,200 135 L3
Mirond L., Sask., Can. 43 D3
Mironovka, U.S.S.R., 10,000 136 C3
Mirosławiec, Pol., 2,132 127 B2
Mirovice, Czech. 126 B2
Mirow, Ger.D.R. 118 D2
Mīrpur Batoro, Pak., 3,015 144 C4
Mīrpur Khās, Pak., 60,861 144 C4
Mirror, Alta., Can. 42 K3
Mirror Lake, N.H. 54 E4
Mirs B., H.K. 152 b6
Mirsk, Pol., 3,269 127 e6
Mirtoan Sea, Gr. 129 D6
Mirtöön Pélagos=Mirtoan Sea
Miryang, S. Kor., 36,021 151 F4
Mirzaani, U.S.S.R. 137 c1
Mirzapur, India, 100,097 145 G4
Misa, D.R.Congo 165 n18
Misahöhé, Togo 162 d8
Misaka, Jap. 154 g15
Misaki, Jap., 21,784 154 C5
Mi-saki, Jap. 154 e15
Misakubo, Jap., 10,947 155 E4
Misantla, Mex., 9,078 93 F4
Misawa, Jap., 36,570 155 G1
Misburg, F.R.Ger., 12,395 118 B2
Miscouche, P.E.I., Can. 47 U10
Miscou I., N.B., Can. 45 N6
Misery, Mount, St. Christopher 97 6
Mishagua, r., Peru 104 C4
Mishamattawa, r., Ont., Can. 44 F3
Mi-shan, China, 30,000* 150 H2
Mishaum Pt., Mass. 57 N6
Mishawaka, Ind., 33,361 70 C1
Misheguk Mtn., Alaska 85 D1
Mishicot, Wis., 762 66 F4
Mishima, Jap., 62,495 155 F4
Mi-shima, Jap. 154 B4
Mishino, U.S.S.R. 136 a6
Mishkino, U.S.S.R. 137 h8
Misima, i., Terr. Papua 174 g3
Misión Cavinas, Bol., 1,371 102 C4
Miskitos, Cayos, Nic. 94 F3
Miskolc, Hung., 143,364 126 E2
Misool, P., Indon. 149 J3
Mispillion, r., Del. 61 A6
Misquah Hills, Minn. 74 G2
Misquamicut (part of Westerly), R.I. 57 J7

262 · Mişr al Jadīdah—Monte Aguila

Mişr al Jadīdah, U.A.R. 161 i7
Misrātah, Libya 161 G2
Mişr Baḩrī, reg., U.A.R. 161 i7
Missanabie, Ont., Can. 44 G5
Missaukee, co., Mich., 6,784 67 H4
Missaukee, L., Mich. 67 H4
Missinaibi, r., Ont., Can. 44 G5
Mission, Kans., 4,626 75 a7
Mission, S. Dak., 611 74 B4
Mission, Tex., 14,081 77 O6
Mission City, Br. Col., Can., 3,193 42 G4
Mission Hill, S. Dak., 165 74 D4
Mission Hills, Kans., 3,621 75 a7
Mission Ridge, S. Dak. 74 B3
Missisicabi, r., Ont.-Qué., Can. 44 H4
Missisquoi, r., Vt. 54 B2
Missisquoi Bay, Can.-U.S. 54 A1
Mississagi, r., Ont., Can. 46 A2
Mississagi Str., Ont., Can. 46 A3
Mississinewa, r., Ind. 70 D2
Mississippi, st., U.S., 2,309,000* 73
Mississippi, co., Ark., 70,174 73 E2
Mississippi, co., Mo., 20,695 72 H8
Mississippi, r., Ont., Can. 47 H4
Mississippi, r., U.S. 53 H4
Mississippi City, Miss., 4,169 73 G7
Mississippi Delta, La. 73 F8
Mississippi L., Ont., Can. 47 H3
Missler, Kans. 75 E6
Missoula, co., Mont., 44,663 81 C2
Missoula, Mont., 27,090 81 C2
Missouri, st., U.S., 4,492,000 72
Missouri, r., U.S. 53 G2
Missouri, Coteau du, N. Dak.-S. Dak. 50 F1
Missouri City, Mo., 404 72 C5
Missouri City, Tex., 604 77 h9
Missouri Coteau, hills, Sask., Can. 43 D5
Missouri Valley, Iowa, 3,567 72 A3
Mist, Oreg. 80 B2
Mistassibi, r., Qué., Can. 44 K5
Mistassini, Qué., Can., 3,349 44 K5
Mistassini, L., Qué., Can. 44 K5
Mistassini, r., Qué., Can. 44 K5
Mistastin L., Newf., Can. 45 N3
Mistatim, Sask., Can. 43 D4
Misteguay Cr., Mich. 67 K5
Mistelbach, Aust., 5,433 124 N5
Misterton, U.K., 1,529 114 G4
Misti, Vol., Peru 104 D6
Mistigokan, r., Man., Can. 43 H3
Mistinibi L., Qué., Can. 45 N3
Miston, Tenn. 71 B5
Mistrato, Col. 101 d14
Mistretta, It., 10,516 123 E6
Misumi, Jap., 18,415 154 B5
Misumi, Jap., 14,971 155 B4
Misurata=Misrātah
Mita, P. de, Mex. 92 D4
Mitaka, Jap., 98,038 155 m19
Mitakeyama, Jap. 155 m19
Mitcham, London, U.K. 114 H8
Mitcheldean, U.K., 1,931 114 D7
Mitchell, Austl., 1,407 173 G4
Mitchell, Ont., Can., 2,226 46 C5
Mitchell, co., Ga., 19,652 64 E4
Mitchell, Ga., 184 64 G2
Mitchell, Ind., 3,552 70 C4
Mitchell, Ill. 72 b10
Mitchell, co., Iowa, 14,043 72 E1
Mitchell, Iowa, 237 72 E1
Mitchell, co., Kans., 8,866 75 G4
Mitchell, Nebr., 1,920 75 B2
Mitchell, co., N.C., 13,906 63 B1
Mitchell, Oreg., 236 80 D3
Mitchell, S. Dak., 12,555 74 C4
Mitchell, co., Tex., 11,255 77 N3
Mitchell, r., Austl. 173 F2
Mitchell, r., Austl. 173 f11
Mitchell, L., Mich. 67 H4
Mitchell, Mt., N.C. 63 B2
Mitchell L., Ala. 64 C3
Mitchell L., Tex. 76 a7
Mitchells, Va. 62 F4
Mitchellsville, Ill. 68 D6
Mitchellville, Iowa, 957 72 D3
Mitchelstown, Ire., 2,674 113 B5
Mīt Ghamr, U.A.R. 161 i7
Mithimna, Gr., 1,828 129 F5
Mitiaro, i., Cook Is. 177 33
Mitilíni, Gr., 25,758 129 F5
Mitilini Str., Gr.-Turk. 142 A2
Mitilinoí, Gr., 3,346 129 F6
Mitla, Mex., 3,651 93 F5
Mitliktavik, Alaska 85 D1
Mito, Jap., 139,389 155 G3
Mitoc, Rum. 128 F1
Mitoginskiy, U.S.S.R. 135 P4
Mitoya, Jap., 12,893 155 C4
Mitre I., Sta. Cruz Is. 170 F5
Mitrofania I., Alaska 85 E5
Mitry-Mory, Fr., 11,428 116 i11
Mitsinjo, Malag. Rep. 165 G4
Mitsuishi, Jap. 154 f15
Mitsuishi, Jap., 11,479 155 K8
Mitsuke, Jap., 40,443 155 F3
Mitsukue, Jap., 5,282 154 C5
Mittagong, Austl., 2,372 173 h10
Mittelberg, Aust., 3,524 124 G6
Mittelberg, F.R.Ger., 2,678 118 C5
Mittelsinn, F.R.Ger., 1,029 119 H4
Mittenwald, F.R.Ger., 6,664 118 C5
Mitterbach, Aust. 124 M6
Mittersheim, Fr. 116 c9
Mittersill, Aust., 3,481 124 J6
Mitterteich, F.R.Ger. 6,623 126 b7
Mittweida, Ger.D.R., 20,877 118 D3
Mi-tu, China 150 D4
Mitú, Col. 100 E7
Mitumba, Monts, D.R.Congo 164 D3
Mitwaba, D.R.Congo 164 D3
Mitzic, Gabon 164 A1
Miura, Jap. 154 g15
Miura, Jap., 39,811 155 F4
Miura-hantō, Jap. 155 m20
Mius, r., U.S.S.R. 136 f7
Miusskiy, Liman, estuary, U.S.S.R. 136 f8
Mixco, Guat., 5,669 94 c9
Mixquiahuala, Mex., 7,184 93 e9
Mixtepec, Mex., 1,844 93 F5
Mixville (part of Cheshire), Conn. 56 E6
Miya, r., Jap. 154 h15
Miyafarkın, Turk., 6,505 142 E2
Miyagase, Jap. 155 m19
Miyāh, Wādī al, Saudi Ar. 163 M1
Miyaji, Jap. 154 B5
Miyajima, Jap. 154 f15
Miyakama, Jap. 155 m20
Miyake-jima, Jap. 155 F4
Miyako, Jap., 55,385 155 G2
Miyako-jima, Ryukyu Is. 154 c13
Miyakonojō, Jap., 92,230 154 B6
Miyako-rettō, Ryukyu Is. 154 c13
Miyakubo, Jap. 154 e15
Miyamae, Jap. 154 h15
Miyanojō, Jap., 27,835 154 B6
Miyanotsuji, Jap. 154 g14
Miyanoura-dake, Jap. 154 k17
Miyaura, Jap. 154 e15
Miyazaki, Jap., 158,328 154 B6
Miyazu, Jap., 33,897 155 D4
Miyoshi, Jap., 42,163 155 C4
Mi-yün, China 151 C2
Miza, Jap. 154 g16
Mizan Teferi, Eth. 163 K4
Mizano, Jap. 154 i14
Mizdah, Libya 161 G2
Mize, Ky. 71 H4
Mize, Miss., 371 73 F6
Mizen Head, Ire. 113 B6
Mizil, Rum., 7,460 128 F2
Mizpah, Minn., 140 74 E2
Mizpah, N.J. 61 B5
Mizque, Bol. 102 c10
Mizque, r., Bol. 102 c11
Mizukaidō, Jap., 37,577 155 G3
Mizuma, Jap. 154 g15
Mizunami, Jap., 36,905 155 E4
Mizusawa, Jap., 44,187 155 G2
Mjölby, Swed. 120 C4
Mjösa, l., Nor. 120 B3
Mkalama, Tanz. 164 E2
Mladá Boleslav, Czech., 26.569 126 B1
Mladenovac, Yug., 11,000* 125 E2
Mladotice, Czech. 126 c7
Mlanje Pk., Malawi 164 E4
Mlava, r., Yug. 125 E2
Mława, Pol., 15,394 127 D2
Mlázovice, Czech. 127 e6
Mlinište, Yug. 125 C2
Mljet, i., Yug. 125 C3
Mnichovo Hradiště, Czech. 127 e6
Mniów, Pol. 127 k5
Mo, Nor., 8,113 120 C2
Mo, Swed. 121 D2
Moa, P., Indon. 149 J5
Moab, Utah, 4,682 78 D2
Moabi, Gabon 164 A2
Moak Lake, Man., Can. 43 F3
Moala, i., Fiji 174 4
Moalboal, Phil., 2,172 153 e12
Moamba, Moz. 164 E6
Moanalua Str., Hawaii 84 c7
Moanda, D.R.Congo 164 A2
Moanda, Gabon 164 B2
Moapa, Nev. 83 C4
Moate, Ire., 1,340 113 C5
Moba, D.R.Congo 164 E3
Mobara, Jap., 39,378 155 G4
Mobaye, C.A.R., 3,667 163 H5
Moberly, Br. Col., Can. 42 H3
Moberly, Mo., 13,170 72 E5
Mobile, co., Ala., 314,301 64 A5
Mobile, Ala., 202,779 64 A5.
Mobile, Ariz. 78 B5
Mobile, r., Ala. 64 B5
Mobile Bay, Ala. 64 A5
Mobile Big Pond, Newf., Can. 45 b10
Mobridge, S. Dak., 4,391 74 B3
Moca, Dom. Rep., 13,829 96 m6
Moca, P.R., 1,938 96 r10
Mocache, Ec. 104 c10
Mocajuba, Braz., 1,352 103 G2
Moçambique, terr.=Mozambique
Moçambique, Moz., 12,493 164 F4
Moçâmedes, Ang., 7,185 164 A4
Mocanaqua, Pa., 1,104 60 K3
Mocane, Okla. 76 C1
Mocapra, r., Ven. 100 G3
Mo Cay, S. Viet., 2,778 147 m11
Moc Chau, N. Viet. 146 D2
Mocha=Al Mukhā
Mo-chiang, China 150 D5
Mochigase, Jap., 6,493 155 D4
Moc Hoa, S. Viet., 5,926 147 m11
Mocho Mts., Jam. 96 p8
Mochudi, Bots., 10,384 164 D6
Mo-chu-kung-k'a, China 150 C4
Mocímboa da Praia, Moz., 28,342 164 F3
Mociu, Rum. 128 D1
Möckmühl, F.R.Ger., 2,750 118 B4
Mocksville, N.C., 2,379 63 D2
Moclips, Wash. 80 A2
Mocoa, Col. 100 B7
Mocomoco, Bol., 13,294 102 C5
Mocorito, Mex., 4,223 92 D3
Moctezuma, Chih., Mex. 92 D1
Moctezuma, S.L.P., Mex., 1,333 92 E3
Moctezuma, Son., Mex., 2,151 92 C2
Moctezuma, r., Mex. 92 C2
Moctezuma, r., Mex. 93 f8
Mocuba, Moz. 164 F4
Mocuzari, Presa, res., Mex. 92 C2
Modale, Iowa, 276 72 B3
Modane, Fr., 5,137 117 G4
Modau, r., F.R.Ger. 119 F5
Modder, r., S. Af. 164 D6
Modderfontein, S. Af., 7,578 165 i17
Moddersville, Mich. 67 J4
Model City, N.Y. 58 C5
Modena, It., 130,910 123 C2
Modena, Pa., 859 60 e12
Modena, Utah 78 B3
Modena, Wis. 66 B4
Moder, r., Fr. 119 D7
Modesto, Calif., 36,585 82 C4
Modest Town, Va. 62 J5
Modica, It., 44,642 123 E6
Modinagar, India, 24,266 144 a11
Modjeska, Calif. 83 i16
Modjokerto, Indon., 51,732 148 E4
Modła, Pol. 127 e5
Mödling, Aust., 17,339 124 N5
Modoc, co., Calif., 8,308 82 C2
Modoc, Ill. 68 B5
Modoc, Ind., 238 70 D2
Modoc, Kans. 75 D5
Modoc, S.C. 63 B4
Modoc Point, Oreg. 80 C4
Modowi, Indon. 149 K4
Modra, Czech. 126 C2
Modřany, Czech., 9,622 126 B1
Modriča, Yug., 3,620 125 D2
Modrý Kameň, Czech. 126 D2
Moe, Austl., 8,770 173 f12
Moe, Jap. 155 J8
Moeda, Braz., 1,307 103 d17
Moel Famau, mtn., U.K. 114 B4
Moel Sych, mtn., U.K. 114 B5
Moen, i., Truk 176 19
Moengo, Sur., 2,500* 101 N5
Moenkopi, Ariz. 78 C3
Moerbeke, Belg., 5,243 115 C3
Moers, F.R.Ger., 42,561 119 B2
Moesa, r., Switz. 124 D2
Moese, F.R.Ger., 1,973 119 E1
Moffat, Ont., Can. 46 b13
Moffat, U.K., 1,917 113 E4
Moffat, co., Colo., 7,061 79 A1
Moffat, Colo., 104 79 B3
Moffett, Okla., 357 76 J2
Moffit, N. Dak. 74 B2
Moffitsville, N.Y. 59 N2
Moga, India, 47,779 145 E3
Mogadiscio=Mogadishu
Mogadishu, Som. Rep., 98,683 163 M5
Mogador=Essaouira
Mogadore, Ohio, 3,851 70 H1
Mogadouro, Port., 2,090 122 B2
Mogami, r., Jap. 155 G2
Mogaung, Burma, 2,940 146 B1
Mogaung, Burma 147 f6
Møgeltønder, Den., 1,230 121 A6
Mogersdorf, Aust. 124 N7
Mogi, Jap., 14,020 154 A5
Mogi das Cruzes, Braz., 63,748 103 c18
Mogielnica, Pol., 3,414 127 D3
Mogi-Guaçu, Braz., 13,143 103 c18
Mogilëv, U.S.S.R., 134,000 134 C4
Mogilëv-Podol'skiy, U.S.S.R., 20,000 136 C3
Mogilno, Pol., 6,691 127 B2
Mogi-Mirim, Braz., 18,345 103 c18
Mogincual, Moz. 164 F4
Moglia, Tex. 77 O6
Mogliano Veneto, It., 16,820 122 f5
Mogo, Austl. 173 h10
Mogocha, U.S.S.R., 14,700 135 L4
Mogochin, U.S.S.R. 134 H4
Mogok, Burma, 8,369 146 B2
Mogollon Mts., N. Mex. 79 A5
Mogollon Plat., Ariz. 50 D4
Mogoşeşti, Rum. 128 F1
Mogotes, Col. 100 D4
Moguer, Sp., 7,222 122 B4
Mogumber, Austl. 172 A4
Mogutovskiy, U.S.S.R. 137 i9
Mogzon, U.S.S.R., 8,200 135 L4
Moha, Br. Col., Can. 42 G4
Moha Bay, Gren. Is. 97 20
Mohács, Hung., 18,045 126 D4
Mohaka, r., N.Z. 175 h5
Mohala, India 145 F5
Mohales Hoek, Lesotho 164 D7
Mohall, N. Dak., 1,204 74 B1
Mohammadia, Alg., 11,817 160 b6
Mohammedia, Mor., 35,010 160 C2
Mohave, co., Ariz., 7,736 78 B4
Mohave, L., Ariz.-Nev. 78 A4
Mohave Mts., Ariz.-Calif. 78 A4
Mohawk, Ariz. 78 B5
Mohawk, Mich. 66 E1
Mohawk, N.Y., 3,533 59 L6
Mohawk, Oreg. 80 B3
Mohawk, Lake, N.J. 61 B1
Mohawk, r., N.H. 54 E2
Mohawk, r., N.Y. 59 M6
Mohawk Mts., Ariz. 78 B5
Mohawksin, L., Wis. 66 D3
Mohegan (part of Montville), Conn. 56 H7
Mohéli, i., Arch. des Comores 165 G4
Mohelnice, Czech. 127 d6
Mohelnice, Czech. 127 f7
Mohembo, Bots. 164 C5
Mohenjodero, ruins, Pak. 144 C4
Mohican, C., Alaska 85 B3
Mohican, r., Ohio 70 G2
Mohican, Black Fk., r., Ohio 70 G2
Mohill, Ire. 113 C5
Mohler, Oreg. 80 B3
Möhne, r., F.R.Ger. 119 F2
Möhnetalsperre, res., F.R.Ger. 119 E1
Mohnton, Pa., 2,223 61 K5
Mo-ho, China 150 G1
Moho, Peru, 1,378 104 D5
Mohoro, Tanz. 164 F3
Mohoru, Kenya 165 g14
Mohrsville, Pa. 61 h14
Moindou, N. Caled. 174 i8
Moineşti, Rum., 12,934 128 F1
Mointy, U.S.S.R., 5,200 134 G5
Moira, Austl. 173 e10
Moira, U.K. 114 E5
Moira, N.Y. 59 L2
Moira, r., Ont., Can. 46 G4
Moirons, Fr., 1,647 117 F3
Moisenay, Fr. 116 i12
Moisie, Qué., Can. 45 N5
Moisie, r., Qué., Can. 45 M4
Moissac, Fr., 10,591 117 D4
Moïssala, Chad, 3,000* 163 H4
Moisselles, Fr. 116 h10
Moissy-Cramayel, Fr., 2,060 116 i12
Moïta, Fr. 116 r17
Moita, Port., 9,504 122 k10
Mojave, Calif., 1,845 82 D5
Mojave, r., Calif. 82 E5
Mojave Des., Calif. 82 E5
Mojkovac, Yug. 125 D3
Mojocoya, Bol., 5,197 102 c11
Moju, r., Braz. 103 G2
Mōka, Jap., 39,440 155 G3
Mokabe-Kasiri, D.R.Congo 165 n18
Mokambo, D.R.Congo 165 o20
Mokameh, India, 35,743 144 e13
Mokane, Mo., 419 72 F6
Mokapu Pen., Hawaii 84 D2
Mokapu Pt., Hawaii 84 d7
Mokau, N.Z. 175 g5
Mokau, r., N.Z. 175 g5
Mokelumne, N. Fk., r., Calif. 82 C3
Mokelumne Hill, Calif. 82 C3
Mokena, Ill., 1,332 69 c10
Mokhatra, India 145 D4
Mokil, atoll, Car. Is. 176 18
Mokio Pt., Hawaii 84 D2
Mokmer, Indon. 149 K3
Mokokchung, India, 6,158 145 J4
Mokolii I., Hawaii 84 d6
Mokolo, Cam., 3,000* 162 G4
Mokpalin, Burma, 3,317 147 b2
Mokp'o, S. Kor., 129,667 151 E4
Mokra G., Yug. 125 E3
Mokrin, Yug., 7,984 125 E2
Moksha, r., U.S.S.R. 136 F2
Moku, Hawaii 84 E2
Mokuauia I., Hawaii 84 c5
Mokuaweoweo Crater, Hawaii 84 F4
Mokuleia, Hawaii 84 a6
Mokulua Is., Hawaii 84 d7
Moku Manu, is., Hawaii 84 d7
Mol, Belg., 23,260 115 D3
Mol, Yug., 8,181 125 E2
Mola di Bari, It., 23,131 123 F4
Molalla, Oreg., 1,501 80 B3
Moland, Nor. 121 A1
Molaneil, i., Kusaie 176 31
Molango, Mex., 1,577 93 F4
Molanosa, Sask., Can. 43 C3
Moláoi, Gr., 2,526 129 D6
Molasses Pd., Me. 55 D4
Molat, i., Yug. 125 B2
Molchanovo, U.S.S.R. 134 H4
Mold, U.K., 6,894 113 E5
Moldau=Vltava
Moldava, Czech. 126 c6
Moldava nad Bodvou, Czech. 126 E2
Moldavia, reg., Rum.-U.S.S.R. 128 F1
Moldavian S.S.R.=Moldavskaya S.S.R.
Moldavskaya S.S.R., U.S.S.R., 3,300,000* 134 B5
Molde, Nor., 7,977 120 A3
Moldova, reg.=Moldavia
Moldova, r., Rum. 128 F1
Moldova Nouă, Rum., 3,582 128 C2
Moldoveanu, mtn., Rum. 128 E2
Moldoviţa, Rum. 128 E1
Møldrup, Den. 121 B4
Môle, Cap du, Haiti 96 k6
Mole, r., U.K. 114 H8
Molenbeek, r., Belg. 115 d9
Molenbeek-St-Jean, Belg., 63,492 115 d9
Molepolole, Bots., 29,625 164 D6
Molfetta, It., 60,316 123 F4
Molii Pd., Hawaii 84 c6
Molina, Chile, 7,621 104 f15
Molina, Sp., 3,181 122 E2
Moline, Ill., 42,705 68 B2
Moline, Kans., 698 75 J6
Moline, Mich. 67 H6
Moline, Tex. 77 O4
Molino, Fla. 65 B2
Moliro, D.R.Congo 164 E3
Mölle, Swed. 121 E4
Mollendo, Peru, 13,574 104 D6
Molles, Urug., 1,000* 105 c11
Molleturo, Ec. 104 c11
Mollis, Switz., 2,303 124 D1
Mölln, F.R.Ger., 13,716 118 C2
Mollys Falls Pd., Vt. 54 C3
Mölnbo, Swed. 120 e8
Mölndal, Swed. 120 C4
Mölntorp, Swed. 120 d8
Moloata, Tutuila 177 39
Moloch, Mt., Br. Col., Can. 42 H3
Molochansk, U.S.S.R., 11,000 136 D4
Molochnoye, U.S.S.R., 4,400 136 E1
Molochnoye, Oz., U.S.S.R. 136 D4
Molodechno, U.S.S.R., 29,000 136 B2
Molodo, Mali, 1,283 162 C3
Mologa, r., U.S.S.R. 136 D1
Molokai, i., Hawaii 84 D2
Moloma, r., U.S.S.R. 136 G1
Molong, Austl., 1,791 173 g9
Molopo, r., S. Af. 164 C6
Moloundou, Cam. 162 G5
Molsheim, Fr., 5,197 117 G2
Molson, Wash. 80 D1
Molson L., Man., Can. 43 F3
Molteno, S. Af., 4,377 164 D7
Molu, P., Indon. 149 J4
Moluccas=Maluku
Molucca Sea, Indon. 149 H3
Molunkus L., Me. 55 D3
Molunkus Str., Me. 55 D3
Molus, Ky. 71 H5
Moma, Moz. 164 F4
Momauquin (part of East Haven), Conn. 56 E8
Mombaça, Braz., 3,251 103 J3
Mombasa, Kenya, 116,000* 164 F2
Mombetsu, Jap., 40,281 155 K7
Mombetsu, Jap., 17,599 155 K8
Momboyo, r., D.R.Congo 164 C2
Mömbris, F.R.Ger., 3,758 119 G4
Momchilgrad, Bulg., 4,324 129 E4
Momence, Ill., 2,949 68 E2
Momi, Fiji 174 4
Momignies, Belg., 2,185 115 C4
Mominabad, India, 17,443 145 E6
Momino, Bulg., 2,771 128 F3
Mömlingen, F.R.Ger., 3,281 119 G5
Momoishi, Jap., 9,445 155 G1
Momostenango, Guat., 6,272 94 B3
Momote Plantation, Terr. New Guin. 174 e1
Momotombo, Vol., Nic. 94 D4
Momozaki, Jap. 154 h16
Mompog Pass, Phil. 153 B2
Mompós, Col. 100 C3
Momskiy Khr., U.S.S.R. 135 O3
Møn, i., Den. 121 E6
Mon, r., Burma 146 A2
Mona, Utah, 347 78 C2
Mona, Isla, P.R. 96 n6
Monaca, Pa., 8,394 60 B4
Monach, Sd. of, U.K. 112 C3
Monach Is., U.K. 112 C3
Monachylemore, U.K. 112 a7
Monaco, ctry., 21,783 117 G5
Monaco-Ville, Mon., 1,819 116 n14
Monadhliath Mts., U.K. 112 D3
Monadnock Mtn., N.H. 54 C6
Monadnock Mtn., Vt. 54 D2
Monaghan, co., Ire., 52,064 113 C4
Monaghan, Ire., 5,126 113 C4
Monahans, Tex., 8,567 77 M4
Monango, N. Dak., 133 74 C2
Mona Passage, W.I. 95 E3
Monapo, Moz. 164 F4
Monarch, S.C., 1,990 63 C3
Monarch Mtn., Br. Col., Can. 42 E3
Monarch Pass, Colo. 79 ·
Monarda, Me. 55 D3
Mona Res., Utah 78 c11
Monar Forests, U.K. 112 D3
Monashee Mts., Br. Col., Can. 38 F7
Moncada, Phil., 3,952 153 b7
Moncalieri, It., 32,876 123 A2
Moncalvo, It., 3,973 122 b5
Monção, Port., 2,510 122 A2
Monchegorsk, U.S.S.R., 45,500 134 C3
Mönchen-Gladbach, F.R.Ger., 146,490 118 A3
Monches, Wis. 66 c11
Monchique, Port., 9,371 122 A4
Monción, Dom. Rep., 1,137 96 m6
Moncks Corner, S.C., 2,030 63 D4
Monclova, Mex., 43,333 92 E2
Moncoutant, Fr., 2,538 117 C3
Moncton, N.B., Can., 42,874 45 N6
Moncure, N.C. 63 E2
Mondamin, Iowa, 436 72 A3
Mondeaux Flowage, Wis. 66 C3
Mondego, C., Port. 122 A2
Mondego, r., Port. 122 A2
Mondeodo, Indon. 149 G3
Mondeville, Fr. 116 h12
Mondeville, Fr., 9,081 117 C2
Mondoñedo, Sp., 8,010 122 B1
Mondorf-les-Bains, Lux., 1,179 115 E5
Mondoubleau, Fr., 1,519 117 D3
Mondovi, It., 20,709 123 A2
Mondovi, Wis., 2,320 66 B4
Mondragón, Sp., 14,148 122 D1
Mondragone, It., 18,116 123 c9
Mondrain I., Austl. 172 B5
Mondsee, Aust., 2,047 124 K6
Monduli, Tanz. 165 h15
Mondy, U.S.S.R. 135 K4
Moneague, Jam. 96 p8
Monee, Ill., 646 68 E2
Monein, Fr., 3,563 117 C5
Monemvasía, Gr. 129 D6
Moneo, Sp. 122 m12
Monero, N. Mex. 79 B3
Monessen, Pa., 18,424 60 C5
Monet, Qué., Can. 44 J5
Moneta, Iowa, 76 72 B1
Monett, Mo., 5,359 72 D8
Monetta, S.C. 63 C4
Monette, Ark., 981 73 E2
Money, Miss. 73 E4
Moneymore, U.K. 113 C4
Monfalcone, It., 27,300 123 D2
Monfort, Col. 100 E7
Monforte, Port., 1,469 122 B3
Monforte de Lemos, Sp., 20,741 122 B1
Monfort Heights, Ohio 71 h10
Mong, Camb. 146 C4
Monga, D.R.Congo 165 o18
Mongala, r., D.R.Congo 164 C1
Mongalla, Sudan 163 K5
Mongana, D.R.Congo 164 C1
Mongaup Valley, N.Y. 59 L8
Mong Cai, N. Viet. 146 D2
Monger, L., Austl. 172 B4
Monggŭmp'o-ri, N. Kor. 151 E3
Mong Hpayak, Burma 146 B2
Mong Hsat, Burma 146 B2
Mong Hsu, Burma 146 B2
Monghyr, India, 89,768 145 H4
Mongkol Borey, r., Camb. 147 e5
Mong Kung, Burma 146 B2
Mong Kyawt, Burma 146 B3
Mong Long, Burma 147 g6
Mong Mit, Burma 146 B2
Mongmong, Guam, 2,285 176 24
Mong Nai, Burma 146 B2
Mong Nawng, Burma 146 B2
Mongo, Chad, 3,000* 163 H3
Mongo, Ind. 70 D1
Mongolia, ctry., 1,017,100 150
Mongolian People's Republic=Mongolia
Mongonu, Nigeria 162 G3
Mongoumba, C.A.R. 164 B1
Mong Pai, Burma 146 B2
Mong Pan, Burma 146 B2
Mong Ping, Burma 146 B2
Mongu, Zambia 164 C4
Mong Yai, Burma 146 B2
Mong Yang, Burma 146 B2
Mong Yawng, Burma 146 C2
Mo Nhai, N. Viet. 147 i8
Monhegan I., Me. 55 C5
Monheim, F.R.Ger., 8,192 119 B2
Mönhö Hayrhan Uula, Mong. 150 C2
Moniac, Ga. 64 G5
Moniaive, U.K. 113 D4
Monico, Wis. 66 D3
Monida Pass, Idaho-Mont. 81 C3
Monifieth, U.K., 3,475 112 E3
Moniquirá, Col. 100 D5
Moniteau, co., Mo., 10,500 72 E6
Monito, I., P.R. 96 n6
Monitor Pk., Nev. 83 B3
Monitor Ra., Nev. 83 B3
Monivea, Ire. 113 B5
Monjas, Guat., 2,847 94 C3
Monje, Arg., 3,100* 105 a11
Monkayo, Phil., 3,679 153 C4
Monkey Bay, Malawi 164 E4
Monkey River, Br. Hond. 94 C2
Monk Hesleden, U.K., 8,780 112 h10
Mońki, Pol. 127 E2
Monkoto, D.R.Congo 164 C2
Monkstown, Tex. 77 Q3
Monkton, Ont., Can. 46 C5
Monkton, U.K. 112 a8
Monkton, Vt. 54 A3
Monkton Ridge, Vt. 54 A3
Monmouth, U.K., 5,504 113 E6
Monmouth, Ill., 10,372 68 B3
Monmouth, Ind. 70 E2
Monmouth, Iowa, 291 72 G2
Monmouth, Me. 55 B4
Monmouth, co., N.J., 334,401 61 C3
Monmouth, Oreg., 2,229 80 B3
Monmouth, Mt., Br. Col., Can. 42 F3
Monmouth Beach, N.J., 1,363 58 d15
Monmouth Junction, N.J. 61 B3
Monmouthshire, co., U.K., 444,658 113 E6
Monneren, Fr. 116 b8
Monnett, Ohio 70 G2
Mono, co., Calif., 2,213 82 D4
Mono, i., Sol. Is. 175 a2
Mono, r., Togo 162 E4
Monobe, Jap. 154 g14
Monocacy, Pa. 60 e10
Mono Lake, Calif. 82 D3
Mono L., Calif. 82 D3
Monolith, Calif. 82 D5
Monólithos, Gr. 129 F6
Monomonac, L., Mass.-N.H. 56 J2
Monomoy I., Mass. 57 R6
Monomoy Pt., Mass. 57 Q6
Monon, Ind., 1,417 70 C2
Monona, co., Iowa, 13,916 72 B3
Monona, Iowa, 1,346 72 F1
Monona, Wis., 8,178 66 D5
Monongah, W. Va., 1,321 62 D3
Monongahela, Pa., 8,388 60 B5
Monongahela, r., Pa.-W. Va. 62 E2
Monongalia, co., W. Va., 55,617 62 D3
Monopoli, It., 36,935 123 F4
Monor, Hung., 14,830 126 D3
Monowi, Nebr., 40 75 G1
Monreal, F.R.Ger. 119 C4
Monreal, Phil., 1,826 153 h15
Monreal del Campo, Sp., 3,051 122 E2
Monreale, It., 23,945 123 D5
Monroe, Newf., Can. 45 b9
Monroe, co., Ala., 22,372 64 B4
Monroe, co., Ark., 17,327 73 D3
Monroe, Ark. 73 D3
Monroe, Conn., 6,402(T) 56 D7
Monroe, co., Fla., 47,921 65 H7
Monroe, co., Ga., 10,495 64 F2
Monroe, Ga., 6,826 64 F2
Monroe, co., Ill., 15,507 68 B5
Monroe, co., Ind., 59,225 70 C3
Monroe, Ind., 499 70 E2
Monroe, co., Iowa, 10,463 72 E3
Monroe, Iowa, 1,366 72 D3
Monroe, co., Ky., 11,799 71 F5
Monroe, La., 52,219 73 C5
Monroe, Me. 55 C4
Monroe, co., Mich., 101,120 67 K7
Monroe, Mich., 22,968 67 K7
Monroe, co., Miss., 33,953 73 G4
Monroe, co., Mo., 10,688 72 E5
Monroe, Nebr., 261 75 H2
Monroe, N.H. 54 C3
Monroe, co., N.Y., 586,387 58 E5
Monroe, N.Y., 3,323 59 M9
Monroe, N.C., 10,882 63 D3
Monroe, co., Ohio, 15,268 70 H3
Monroe, Okla. 76 J2
Monroe, Oreg., 374 80 B3
Monroe, co., Pa., 39,567 61 M3
Monroe, co., Tenn., 23,316 71 G6
Monroe, Utah, 955 78 C2
Monroe, Va. 62 E5
Monroe, Wash., 1,901 80 B2
Monroe, co., W. Va., 11,584 62 D5
Monroe, co., Wis., 31,241 66 C5
Monroe, Wis., 8,050 66 D6
Monroe, L., Fla. 65 H4
Monroe Bridge, Mass. 56 E2
Monroe Center, Ohio 70 J1
Monroe Center, Wis. 66 D4
Monroe City, Ind., 505 70 B4
Monroe City, Mo., 2,337 72 F5
Monroe City, Tex. 77 k9
Monroe Res., Ind. 70 C3
Monroeton, Pa. 60 J2
Monroeville, Ala., 3,632 64 B4
Monroeville, Ind., 1,294 70 E2
Monroeville, Ohio, 1,371 70 G1
Monroeville, Pa., 22,446 60 d8
Monrovia, Lib., 80,000 162 C4
Monrovia, Calif., 27,079 83 i15
Mons, Belg., 26,206 115 B4
Mons, Fr. 116 m13
Monsalvo, Arg. 105 c13
Monsanto, Ill., 324 72 b11
Monschau, F.R.Ger., 2,432 119 A3
Monse, Indon. 149 G4
Monsefú, Peru, 11,284 104 A3
Monselice, It., 16,663 123 C2
Monserrate, I., Mex. 92 C3
Monsey, N.Y. 58 c12
Møns Klint, bluff, Den. 121 E6
Monson, Me. 55 C3
Monson, Mass., 2,413;6,712(T) 56 G4
Monster, Neth., 7,700 115 C2
Mönsterås, Swed. 120 C4
Montà, It., 3,338 122 a6
Montabaur, F.R.Ger., 5,789 119 D4
Montagnana, It., 11,565 122 e5
Montague, P.E.I., Can., 1,100 45 O6
Montague, Calif., 782 82 B2
Montague, Mass., 7,836(T) 56 F2
Montague, Mich., 2,366 67 G5
Montague, co., Tex., 14,893 77 P3
Montague, Tex. 77 P3
Montague, I., Mex. 92 B1
Montague I., Alaska 85 H4
Montague Sd., Austl. 172 C2
Montague Str., Alaska 85 G4
Montaigu, Fr., 2,568 117 C3
Montainville, Fr. 116 f11
Montalba, Tex. 77 Q4
Montalbán, Sp., 2,766 122 E2
Montalbano Ionico, It., 15,790 123 F4
Montalto, It., 1,726 122 c6
Mont Alto, Pa., 1,039 60 G6
Montalto, mtn., It. 123 F5
Montalto Uffugo, It., 10,789 123 E5
Montalvo, Ec. 104 B1
Montana, st., U.S., 703,000* 81
Montana, Alaska, 39 85 G3
Montanaro, It., 4,249 122 a5
Montana-Vermala, Switz., 1,543 124 B2
Montánchez, Sp., 4,190 122 B3
Montandon, Pa. 60 J4
Montañitas, Col. 100 C7
Montara, Calif. 83 d12
Montargil, Port., 6,357 122 A3
Montargis, Fr., 17,645 117 E3
Montauban, Fr., 43,401 117 D4
Montauk, N.Y. 59 Q9
Montauk Pt., N.Y. 59 R9
Montauroux, Fr. 116 m13
Montbard, Fr., 6,407 117 F3
Montbazon, Fr., 1,622 117 D3
Montbéliard, Fr., 23,374 117 G3
Mont Belvieu, Tex. 77 k9
Montblanch, Sp., 4,545 122 F2
Montbrison, Fr., 9,548 117 F4
Montbronn, Fr., 1,649 116 d9
Montcalm, co., Mich., 35,795 67 H5
Montcalm, Lac, China 150 C3
Mont-Carmel, Qué., Can. 47 M2
Montceau-les-Mines, Fr., 29,364 117 F3
Mont-Cenis, Col du, Fr. 117 G4
Montchanin, Fr., 6,405 117 F3
Montchanin, Del. 62 e10
Montclair, Calif., 13,546 83 i15
Montclair, N.J., 43,129 61 C2
Mont Clare, Pa., 1,124 60 f11
Montcornet, Fr., 1,439 117 F2
Montcuq, Fr., 1,261 117 D4
Mont-de-Marsan, Fr., 23,254 117 C5
Montdidier, Fr., 5,778 117 E2
Monteagle, Tenn. 71 F6
Monteagudo, Bol., 4,229 102 c11
Monte Aguila, Chile, 2,166 104 e17

Monte Alegre—Mosquitos · 263

Monte Alegre, Braz., 3,911 103 F2
Monte Alegre do Piauí, Braz., 2,574 103 G3
Monte Azul, Braz., 4,860 103 H4
Montebello, Qué., Can., 1,494 47 J3
Montebello, Col. 101 d14
Montebello, Calif., 32,097 83 h15
Monte Bello Is., Austl. 172 A3
Montebello Vicentino, It., 5,145 122 e5
Montebelluna, It., 18,529 123 D2
Montebourg, Fr., 2,049 117 C2
Monte-Carlo, Mon., 9,038 116 n14
Monte Carlo, Ariz. 78 B4
Monte Carmelo, Braz., 10,016 103 G5
Monte Caseros, Arg., 17,200* 105 D4
Montecatini Terme, It., 17,345 123 C3
Montecchio Emilia, It., 5,854 122 d6
Montecchio Maggiore, It., 11,700 122 e5
Montech, Fr., 2,486 117 D5
Montechiaro d'Asti, It., 1,393 122 b5
Montecito, Calif. 82 D5
Monte Comán, Arg., 9,000* 105 B4
Montecoral, Urug. 105 d11
Montecorvino Rovella, It., 12,578 123 E4
Monte Creek, Br. Col., Can. 42 H4
Montecristi, Dom. Rep., 5,912 96 m6
Montecristi, Ec., 4,488 104 A2
Montecristo, Isola di, It. 123 C3
Monte Escobedo, Mex., 1,487 92 E3
Montefiascone, It., 12,195 123 C3
Montefrío, Sp., 13,874 122 D4
Monte Giardino, S. Mar. 123 e11
Montego Bay, Jam., 23,610 96 p8
Montego Bay, Jam. 96 o8
Montegut, La. 73 E8
Montehermoso, Sp., 6,006 122 B2
Monteiro, Braz., 6,028 103 J3
Montelavar, Port., 6,279 122 i10
Montelíbano, Col. 100 C3
Montélimar, Fr., 21,642 117 F4
Monte Lindo, r., Para. 105 D2
Montell, Tex. 77 O5
Montello, Nev. 83 C2
Montello, Wis., 1,021 66 D5
Montelongo, Mex. 93 d8
Montemorelos, Mex., 11,525 93 F3
Montemor-o-Novo, Port., 13,115 122 A3
Montendre, Fr., 2,781 117 C4
Montenegro, Col. 101 d15
Montenegro, Mex. 93 d9
Montenegro, Yug.=Crna Gora
Montenegro=Crna Gora
Monte Oscuro, Col. 101 e13
Monte Patria, Chile 105 A4
Monte Plata, Dom. Rep., 2,202 96 n6
Montepuez, Moz. 164 F4
Montepulciano, It., 16,513 123 C3
Monte Quemado, Arg., 4,500* 105 C3
Montereau, Fr., 14,121 117 E2
Montereau-sur-le-Jard, Fr. 116 i12
Monte Redondo, Port., 5,811 122 A3
Monterey, co., Calif., 198,351 82 C4
Monterey, Calif., 22,618 82 B4
Monterey, Ind., 278 70 C1
Monterey, Mass., 480(T) 56 D4
Monterey, Mich. 67 H6
Monterey, N.Y. 58 F7
Monterey, Tenn., 2,069 71 F5
Monterey, Va., 270 62 E4
Monterey, Wis. 66 E5
Monterey Bay, Calif. 82 B4
Monterey Park, Calif., 37,821 83 h15
Montería, Col. 100 B3
Monte Rio, Calif. 82 B3
Montero, Bol., 9,667 102 D5
Monteros, Arg., 15,000* 105 B3
Monterotondo, It., 14,617 123 a8
Monterrey, Mex., 596,993 93 E3
Monterville, W. Va. 62 D4
Montesano, Wash., 2,486 80 B2
Monte Sant'Angelo, It., 23,547 123 F4
Montesarchio, It., 11,811 123 d9
Montes Claros, Braz., 40,545 103 H5
Monte Sereno, Calif., 1,506 83 e13
Monte Sião, Braz., 1,794 103 c18
Montesson, Fr., 7,430 116 g11
Montevallo, Ala., 2,755 64 C2
Montevallo, Mo., 50 72 C7
Montevarchi, It., 19,592 123 C3
Monte Verde, Ang. 164 B3
Montevideo, Minn., 5,693 74 E3
Montevideo, Urug., 922,885 105 D5
Monte Vista, Colo., 3,385 79 B3
Montezuma, co., Colo., 14,024 79 A3
Montezuma, Ga., 3,744 64 E3
Montezuma, Ind., 1,231 70 B3
Montezuma, Iowa, 1,416 72 E3
Montezuma, Kans., 543 75 E6
Montezuma, N.Y. 59 p24
Montezuma Castle Nat. Mon., Ariz. 78 C4
Montezuma Cr., Utah 78 D3
Montezuma Slough, Calif. 83 f11
Montfaucon, Switz. 124 B1
Montfermeil, Fr., 12,143 116 i11
Montfoort, Neth. 115 b6
Montfort, Neth. 115 E3
Montfort, Wis., 538 66 C6
Montfort, ruins, Isr. 142 b6
Montfort-l'Amaury, Fr., 2,051 116 f11
Montgé, Fr. 116 k10
Montgeron, Fr., 15,730 116 h12
Montgeroult, Fr. 116 g10
Montgomery, Pak., 75,180 145 D3
Montgomery, U.K. 114 B5
Montgomery, co., Ala., 169,210 64 C3
Montgomery, Ala., 134,393 64 C3
Montgomery, co., Ark., 5,370 73 B3
Montgomery, co., Ga., 6,284 64 G3
Montgomery, co., Ill., 31,244 68 C4
Montgomery, Ill., 2,744 68 D2
Montgomery, co., Ind., 32,089 70 C2
Montgomery, co., Iowa, 14,467 72 B3
Montgomery, co., Kans., 45,007 75 K6
Montgomery, co., Ky., 13,461 71 H3
Montgomery, La., 866 73 C6
Montgomery, co., Md., 340,928 62 G3
Montgomery, Mass., 333(T) 56 E4
Montgomery, Mich., 362 67 J7
Montgomery, Minn., 2,118 74 F3
Montgomery, co., Miss., 13,320 73 F4
Montgomery, co., Mo., 11,097 72 F5
Montgomery, co., N.Y., 57,240 59 L6
Montgomery, N.Y., 1,312 59 M8
Montgomery, co., N.C., 18,408 63 E2
Montgomery, co., Ohio, 527,080 70 E3
Montgomery, Ohio, 3,075 71 i10
Montgomery, co., Pa., 516,682 61 M5
Montgomery, Pa., 2,150 60 J3
Montgomery, co., Tenn., 55,645 71 D5
Montgomery, co., Tex., 26,839 77 Q4
Montgomery, Tex. 77 Q4
Montgomery, Vt. 54 B2
Montgomery, co., Va., 32,923 62 D5
Montgomery, W. Va., 3,000 62 C4
Montgomery Center, Vt. 54 B2
Montgomery City, Mo., 1,918 72 F6
Montgomeryshire, co., U.K., 44,165 113 E5
Montgomeryville, Pa. 60 f10
Montguyon, Fr., 1,737 117 C4
Monthermé, Fr., 3,682 117 F2
Monthey, Switz., 6,834 124 A2
Monthois, Fr. 117 F2
Monthyon, Fr. 116 k10
Monticelli d'Ongina, It., 6,733 122 c5
Monticello, Ark., 5,031 73 D4
Monticello, Fla., 2,490 65 F2
Monticello, Ga., 1,931 64 F2
Monticello, Ill., 3,219 68 D3
Monticello, Ind., 4,035 70 C2
Monticello, Iowa, 3,190 72 F2
Monticello, Ky., 2,940 71 G5
Monticello, Me. 55 E2
Monticello, Minn., 1,477 74 E3
Monticello, Miss., 1,432 73 E6
Monticello, Mo., 159 72 F4
Monticello, N. Mex. 79 B5
Monticello, N.Y., 5,222 59 L8
Monticello, S.C. 63 C3
Monticello, Utah, 1,845 78 D3
Monticello, Wis., 789 66 D6
Montichiari, It., 13,432 122 d5
Mont Ida, Kans. 75 K5
Montignac, Fr., 2,809 117 D4
Montigny-lès-Metz, Fr., 24,156 116 b8
Montijo, Pan. 94 G6
Montijo, Port., 21,947 122 k10
Montijo, Sp., 14,961 122 B3
Montijo, G. de, Pan. 94 G7
Montilla, Sp., 23,896 122 C4
Montivilliers, Fr., 8,581 117 C2
Montizón, Sp., 3,349 122 D3
Mont-Joli, Qué., Can., 6,045 45 M5
Mont-Laurier, Qué., Can., 5,830 44 J6
Montlhéry, Fr., 3,682 116 h12
Mont-Louis, Qué., Can. 45 N5
Montluçon, Fr., 58,855 117 E3
Montluel, Fr., 2,823 116 q15
Montmagny, Qué., Can., 6,723 45 L6
Montmarault, Fr., 1,409 117 E3
Montmartre, Sask., Can. 43 D5
Montmédy, Fr., 3,093 117 F2
Montmélian, Fr., 1,583 117 G4
Montmirail, Fr., 2,382 117 E2
Montmorency, Qué., Can., 5,956 47 n16
Montmorency, Fr., 16,682 116 h11
Montmorency, co., Mich., 4,424 67 J3
Montmorillon, Fr., 6,345 117 D3
Montney, Br. Col., Can. 42 G2
Monto, Austl., 1,702 173 G3
Montodine, It., 2,184 122 c5
Montoro, Sp., 14,950 122 C3
Montour, Iowa, 452 72 E3
Montour, co., Pa., 16,730 60 J3
Montour Falls, N.Y., 1,533 58 F7
Montoursville, Pa., 5,211 60 J3
Montowese (part of North Haven), Conn. 56 E7
Montoya, N. Mex. 79 C4
Montpelier, Idaho, 3,146 81 D4
Montpelier, Ind., 1,954 70 D2
Montpelier, La., 197 73 E7
Montpelier, Miss. 73 G4
Montpelier, N. Dak., 97 74 C2
Montpelier, Ohio, 4,131 70 E1
Montpelier, Vt., 8,782 54 B3
Montpelier, Va. 62 G5
Montpellier, Fr., 123,367 117 E5
Montpon, Fr., 3,220 117 D4
Montréal, Qué., Can., 1,155,178 44 K6
Montreal, Wis., 1,361 66 C2
Montreal, r., Ont., Can. 67 J1
Montreal, r., Mich.-Wis. 66 C2
Montréal-Est, Qué., Can., 5,793 47 p17
Montreal I., Ont., Can. 67 J1
Montreal Lake, Sask., Can. 43 C3
Montreal L., Sask., Can. 43 C3
Montréal-Nord, Qué., Can., 47,359 47 o17
Montreal River Harbour, Ont., Can. 67 J1
Montréjeau, Fr., 3,421 117 D5
Montrésor, Fr. 117 D3
Montreuil, Fr., 92,316 116 h11
Montreuil-sur-Mer, Fr., 3,399 117 D1
Montreux, Switz., 18,478 124 A2
Montrichard, Fr., 3,020 117 D3
Montricher, Switz. 124 A2
Montrock, Ont., Can. 44 G5
Mont-Rolland, Qué., Can., 1,300 47 K3
Montrose, U.K., 10,702 112 E3
Montrose, Ark., 399 73 D4
Montrose, co., Colo., 18,286 79 A2
Montrose, Colo., 5,044 79 A2
Montrose, Ill., 320 68 D4
Montrose, Iowa, 632 72 F4
Montrose, Mich., 1,466 67 K5
Montrose, Miss., 169 73 F5
Montrose, Mo., 526 72 C6
Montrose, Nebr. 75 B1
Montrose, Pa., 2,363 61 L2
Montrose, S. Dak., 430 74 D4
Montrose, W. Va., 114 62 E3
Montrose Hbr., Ill. 69 d9
Montross, Va., 394 62 H4
Montrottier, Fr., 1,086 116 p15
Montrouge, Fr., 45,324 116 h11
Mont-Royal, Qué., Can., 22,521 47 o18
Montry, Fr., 1,025 116 k11
Mont-St-Pierre, Qué., Can. 47 T9
Montserrat, i., Lesser Ant. 97 5
Montseveroux, Fr. 116 q16
Montsoult, Fr., 1,548 116 h10
Montsûrs, Fr., 1,534 117 C2
Montuosa, I., Pan. 94 F7
Montvale, N.J., 3,699 58 c12
Montvale, Va. 62 E5
Mont Vernon, N.H. 54 D6
Montville, Conn., 1,060;7,759(T) 56 H7
Montville (part of Sandisfield), Mass. 56 D4
Montville, N.J. 58 b13
Monument, Colo., 204 79 C2
Monument, Kans. 75 E4
Monument, N. Mex. 79 D5
Monument, Oreg., 214 80 D3
Monument Beach (part of Bourne), Mass. 57 O6
Monument Cr., Colo. 79 c10
Monument Hill, Colo. 79 A2
Monument Pk., Colo. 79 B2
Monyo, Burma, 5,126 146 A3
Monywa, Burma, 26,172 146 A2
Monza, It., 79,023 123 B2
Monzen, Jap., 14,299 155 E3
Monzie, U.K. 112 c7
Monzón, Sp., 9,020 122 F2
Moodus (part of E. Haddam), Conn., 1,103 56 G6
Moodus Res., Conn. 56 G6
Moody, co., S. Dak., 8,810 74 D3
Moody, Tex., 1,074 77 P4
Moody Corner (part of S. Hadley and Granby), Mass. 56 F3
Moodys, Okla. 76 H1
Mooers, N.Y., 543 59 N2
Mooetong, Indon. 149 G2
Mooi River, S. Af. 164 E6
Mooleyville, Ky. 71 E3
Moon, Okla. 76 J4
Moonbeam, Ont., Can. 44 G5
Moonda L., Austl. 172 F3
Moon Run, Pa. 60 b8
Moonta, Austl., 1,220 172 b8
Moora, Austl. 172 B4
Moorcroft, Wyo., 826 81 G3
Moordener Kill, r., N.Y. 59 w29
Moordrecht, Neth. 115 b7
Moore, Idaho, 358 81 C4
Moore, Mont., 216 81 E2
Moore, co., N.C., 36,733 63 E2
Moore, Okla., 1,783 76 F2
Moore, co., Tenn., 3,454 71 E6
Moore, co., Tex., 14,773 76 N2
Moore, Tex. 77 O5
Moore, Utah 78 C2
Moore, L., Austl. 172 B4
Moorea, i., Soc. Is. 171 H6
Mooreesburg, S. Af., 3,840 164 a8
Moorefield, Ont., Can. 46 a13
Moorefield, Nebr., 55 75 E3
Moorefield, r., W. Va. 62 E4
Moore Haven, Fla., 790 65 H6
Mooreland, Ind., 477 70 D3
Mooreland, Okla., 871 76 D1
Moorepark, Mich. 67 H6
Moore Res., N.H.-Vt. 54 D3
Mooresburg, Tenn. 71 H5
Moores Corner (part of Leverett), Mass. 56 G3
Moores Corners (part of Sterling), Mass. 57 J3
Moores Creek Nat. Mil. Pk., N.C. 63 F3
Moores Mills, N.B., Can. 47 S11
Moorestown, Mich. 67 H4
Moorestown, N.J., 12,497(T) 61 B4
Mooresville, Ind., 3,856 70 C3
Mooresville, N.C., 6,918 63 D2
Mooreton, N. Dak., 164 74 D2
Mooretown, Ont., Can. 46 B6
Moorewood, Okla. 76 D2
Moorfoot Hills, U.K. 112 d8
Moorhead, Iowa, 313 72 B3
Moorhead, Minn., 26,964 74 D2
Moorhead, Miss., 1,754 73 E4
Mooringsport, La., 864 73 A5
Moorland, Iowa, 281 72 C2
Moorland, Mich. 67 G5
Mooroopna, Austl., 1,796 173 e11
Moorpark, Calif., 2,902 82 D5
Moors I., Bah. Is. 95 b6
Moorslede, Belg., 6,578 115 B4
Moos-Berg, F.R.Ger. 118 B3
Moosburg, F.R.Ger., 9,214 118 D4
Moose, r., Ont., Can. 44 G5
Moose, r., N.Y. 59 K4
Moose, r., Vt. 54 D2
Moose Bk., Mass. 56 H3
Moose Factory, Ont., Can. 44 H4
Moosehead, Me. 55 C3
Moosehead L., Me. 55 C3
Mooseheart, Ill. 69 a9
Moose Heights, Br. Col., Can. 42 F3
Moose Hill, Can.-U.S. 55 B3
Moosehorn, Man., Can. 43 F4
Moose Jaw, Sask., Can., 33,065 43 C5
Moose Jaw Cr., Sask., Can. 43 C5
Moose Lake, Minn., 1,514 74 F2
Moose L., Man., Can. 43 E4
Moose L., Wis. 66 C2
Mooseleuk Str., Me. 55 D2
Mooselookmeguntic L., Me. 55 B4
Moose Mtn., Sask., Can. 43 D5
Moose Mountain Cr., Sask., Can. 43 D5
Moose Pass, Alaska, 136 85 G3
Moose Pd., Me. 55 B4
Moose Pd., Me. 55 C4
Moose River, Me. 55 B3
Moosic, Pa., 4,243 61 o16
Moosic Lake, Pa. 61 o16
Moosilauke, Mt., N.H. 54 D3
Moosomin, Sask., Can., 1,767 43 E5
Moosonee, Ont., Can. 44 H4
Moosup, Conn., 2,760 56 J6
Moosup, r., Conn.-R.I. 57 J6
Mopang Lakes, Me. 55 E4
Mopang Str., Me. 55 E4
Mopeia, Moz. 164 E4
Mopelia, atoll, Soc. Is. 171 42
Mopti, Mali, 18,000 162 D3
Moquah, Wis. 66 B2
Moquegua, Peru, 7,697 104 D6
Moquegua, r., Peru 104 D6
Moquehuá, Arg., 1,277 105 b12
Mór, Hung., 11,482 126 D3
Mor, i., Truk 176 19
Mora, Cam., 3,000* 162 G4
Mora, Port., 3,686 122 A3
Mora, Sp., 10,557 122 D3
Mora, Swed. 120 C3
Mora, Minn., 2,329 74 F3
Mora, Mo. 72 D6
Mora, co., N. Mex., 6,028 79 C3
Mora, N. Mex. 79 C4
Mora, r., N. Mex. 79 C4
Morača, r., Yug. 125 D3
Moradabad, India, 180,100 145 F3
Mora de Ebro, Sp., 3,756 122 F2
Mora de Rubielos, Sp., 2,068 122 E2
Morafenobe, Malag. Rep. 165 G4
Morag, Pol., 7,980 127 C2
Moraga, Calif. 83 e12
Morago, Austl. 173 e10
Morainvilliers, Fr. 116 f11
Morak, India 144 a13
Morakovo, Yug. 125 D3
Moraleja, Sp., 8,248 122 B2
Morales, Col. 100 B6
Morales, Guat., 3,202 94 C3
Morales, Tex. 77 P5
Moramanga, Malag. Rep., 5,687 165 H5
Moran, Kans., 549 75 K6
Moran, Mich. 67 J2
Moran, Tex., 392 77 O3
Morane, i., Tuam. Arch. 171 J6
Morangis, Fr., 5,298 116 h12
Morant Bay, Jam., 5,054 96 q9
Morant Cays, Jam. 95 D3
Morar, Loch, U.K. 112 D3
Mörarp, Swed. 121 E4
Moratalla, Sp., 14,029 122 D3
Moratuwa, Cey., 60,215 145 m22
Morava, reg., Czech. 126 C2
Morava, r., Czech. 126 C2
Moravany, Czech. 127 f6
Moravia, Iowa, 621 72 E4
Moravia, N.Y., 1,575 59 H6
Moravia, reg.=Morava
Moravian Falls, N.C. 63 C1
Moravica, r., Yug. 125 E3
Moravice, r., Czech. 126 C2
Moraviţa, Rum. 128 C2
Moravská Třebová, Czech. 126 C2
Moravské Budějovice, Czech. 126 B2
Moravský Krumlov, Czech. 126 C2
Morawa, Austl. 172 B4
Morawhanna, Guyana 101 L3
Morawica, Pol. 127 D3
Moray, co., U.K., 49,156 112 E3
Moraya, Bol., 2,068 102 C6
Moray Firth, U.K. 112 E3
Morazán, Guat., 1,611 94 c9
Morbach, F.R.Ger., 2,253 118 A4
Mörbylånga, Swed. 120 D4
Morcenx, Fr., 4,166 117 C4
Morcone, It., 9,002 123 d9
Mordelles, Fr., 2,279 117 B2
Morden, Man., Can., 2,729 43 F5
Mordy, Pol., 1,461 127 E2
Morea, Arg., 1,000* 105 a12
Moreau, r., S. Dak. 74 B3
Moreau Pk., S. Dak. 74 A3
Moreauville, La., 815 73 D6
Morecambe (incl. Heysham), U.K., 40,950 113 E4
Morecambe Bay, U.K. 113 E4
Moree, Austl., 5,502 173 G4
Morehead, Ky., 4,170 71 H3
Morehead City, N.C., 5,583 63 H3
Morehouse, parish, La., 33,709 73 D5
Morehouse, Mo., 1,417 72 H8
Moreira, Arg. 105 b10
Moreland, Ga., 329 64 E2
Moreland, Ky. 71 G4
Morelia, Col. 100 C7
Morelia, Mex., 100,258 92 E4
Morell, P.E.I., Can. 47 U10
Morella, Austl. 173 F3
Morella, Sp., 4,132 122 E2
Morelos, st., Mex., 386,264 93 F4
Morelos, Méx., Mex., 2,836 93 e10
Morelos, Micho., Mex., 1,173 93 c10
Morelos Dam, Mex.-U.S. 92 B1
Morena, India, 28,337 145 F4
Morena, Sa., Sp. 122 B4
Morenci, Ariz., 2,431 78 D5
Morenci, Mich., 2,053 67 J7
Moreni, Rum., 11,687 128 E2
Moreno, Col. 100 E5
Moreno, Calif. 83 k16
Moresby I., Br. Col., Can. 42 C3
Moresby Str., Terr. Papua 174 3
Morestel, Fr., 1,492 117 F4
Moreton Bay, Austl. 173 H4
Moreton in Marsh, U.K., 1,935 114 E7
Moreton I., Austl. 173 H4
Moretta, It., 3,082 122 a6
Moreuil, Fr., 3,609 117 E2
Morey, L., Vt. 54 C4
Morez, Fr., 6,101 117 F3
Morfasso, It., 4,553 122 c6
Mörfelden, F.R.Ger., 8,606 119 F5
Morgam-Viibus, mt., Fin. 120 F1
Morgan, Austl. 172 E5
Morgan, co., Ala., 60,454 74 C1
Morgan, Ala. 64 c8
Morgan, co., Colo., 21,192 79 D1
Morgan, co., Ga., 10,280 64 F2
Morgan, Ga., 293 64 E4
Morgan, co., Ill., 36,571 68 B4
Morgan, co., Ind., 33,875 70 C3
Morgan, co., Ky., 11,056 71 H4
Morgan, Minn., 975 74 E3
Morgan, co., Mo., 9,476 72 E6
Morgan, Mo., 69 72 E7
Morgan, co., Ohio, 12,747 70 H3
Morgan, Oreg. 80 D3
Morgan, Pa. 60 b8
Morgan, co., Tenn., 14,304 71 G5
Morgan, Tex., 381 77 P3
Morgan, co., Utah, 2,837 78 C1
Morgan, Utah 78 C1
Morgan, Vt. 54 C2
Morgan, co., W. Va., 8,376 62 F3
Morgana, S.C. 63 B4
Morgan Center, Vt. 54 D2
Morgan City, Ala. 64 C1
Morgan City, La., 13,540 73 D8
Morganfield, Ky., 3,741 71 D4
Morgan Hill, Calif., 3,151 82 C4
Morganito, Ven. 100 G5
Morgan Mill, Tex. 77 C3
Morgans Point, Tex., 560 77 k9
Morgans Pt., Ont., Can. 69 B
Morgan Springs, Tenn. 71 F6
Morganton, N.C., 9,186 63 C2
Morgantown, Ind., 971 70 C3
Morgantown, Ky., 1,318 71 E4
Morgantown, Miss. 73 E6
Morgantown, W. Va., 22,487 62 E3
Morganville, Kans., 226 75 H4
Morganville, N.J. 58 c15
Morganza, La., 937 73 D7
Morges, Switz., 8,420 124 A2
Morhange, Fr., 4,367 117 G2
Mori, Jap., 22,076 155 J8
Moriah, Trin. and Tob., 2,538* 96 h4
Moriah, N.C. 63 F1
Moriah, Mt., Nev. 83 C3
Moriarty, N. Mex., 720 79 C4
Morice, r., Br. Col., Can. 42 E2
Morice L., Br. Col., Can. 42 E3
Moricetown, Br. Col., Can. 42 E2
Morichal, Col. 100 E6
Moriguchi, Jap., 102,295 154 g15
Morijo, Kenya 165 g14
Morillo, Arg., 1,800* 105 C2
Morin Heights, Qué., Can. 47 K3
Morinville, Alta., Can. 42 K3
Morioka, Jap., 157,441 155 G2
Morisset, Austl. 173 h9
Moriston, r., U.K. 112 D3
Moriya, Jap., 12,095 155 n19
Moriyama, Jap., 24,403 154 h14
Moriyama, Jap., 58,798 154 i14
Mörkö, Swed. 120 e9
Morkoka, r., U.S.S.R. 135 L3
Mørkøv, Den., 1,572 121 D5
Morlaix, Fr., 20,248 116 B2
Morland, U.K. 113 E4
Morland, Kans., 317 75 E4
Morley, U.K., 40,322 114 E3
Morley, Iowa, 124 72 F3
Morley, Mich., 445 67 H5
Morley, Mo., 472 72 H7
Morley, N.Y. 59 K2
Morley, Tenn. 71 G5
Morley River, Yukon, Can. 40 C5
Mormant, Fr., 1,308 116 k12
Mormon Ra., Nev. 82 ·
Mornant, Fr., 2,262 116 p15
Morne-à-l'Eau, Guad., 2,469 97 14
Morne-Rouge, Mart. 97 12
Morne-Vert, Mart. 97 12
Morningside, Md., 1,708 62 b9
Morningside, Minn., 1,981 74 b6
Morningside Park, Conn., 3,181 56 H7
Morning Sun, Iowa, 875 72 F3
Mornington, Austl., 3,589 173 e12
Mornington, I., Chile 105 A7
Mornington I., Austl. 172 E2
Morno, Ghana 162 c7
Mórnos, r., Gr. 129 D5
Moro, Pak., 10,019 144 C4
Moro, Ark., 182 73 E3
Moro, Ill. 68 C5
Moro, Oreg., 327 80 C3
Morobay, Ark. 73 C4
Morobe, Terr. New Guin. 174 e2
Morocco, ctry., 13,323,000* 160 C2
Morocco, Ind., 1,341 70 B2
Morococala, Bol., 3,907 102 b11
Morococha, Peru, 6,472 104 B4
Moro Cr., Ark. 73 C4
Moroeni, Rum. 128 E2
Morogoro, Tanz., 14,507 164 F3
Moro G., Phil. 153 B4
Moroleón, Mex., 17,955 92 E4
Morombe, Malag. Rep., 5,419 165 G5
Moromoro, Bol., 5,130 102 c11
Morón, Cuba, 18,629 96 d1
Mörön, Mong. 150 D1
Morón, Ven., 5,174 100 F2
Morona, Ec. 104 d11
Morona, r., Peru 104 B2
Morondava, Malag. Rep., 10,725 165 G5
Morón de la Frontera, Sp., 35,248 122 C4
Morong, Phil., 3,055 153 B2
Moroni, Arch. des Comores, 6,545 165 G3
Moroni, Utah, 879 78 C2
Morosaglia, Fr., 1,222 116 r17
Morotai, i., Indon. 149 J2
Morotai, Selat, Indon. 149 J2
Moroto, Uganda 164 E1
Moroto, mtn., Uganda 164 E1
Morovis, P.R., 2,428 96 t10
Morowali, Indon. 149 G3
Morozaki, Jap., 7,148 154 h15
Morozkovo, U.S.S.R. 137 k7
Morozovsk, U.S.S.R., 27,000 134 D5
Morpará, Braz., 1,708 103 H4
Morpeth, Ont., Can. 46 C6
Morpeth, U.K., 12,430 113 F4
Morphou, Cyp., 6,097 142 C3
Morral, Ohio, 493 70 F2
Morrice, Mich., 530 67 J6
Morrill, Kans., 299 75 K4
Morrill, Me. 55 C4
Morrill, co., Nebr., 7,057 75 B2
Morrill, Nebr., 884 75 B2
Morrilton, Ark., 5,997 73 C2
Morrin, Alta., Can. 42 K3
Morrinhos, Braz., 9,879 103 G5
Morrinsville, N.Z., 1,257 175 g5
Morris, Man., Can., 1,330 43 F5
Morris, Ala., 638 64 c7
Morris, Conn., 1,190(T) 56 D6
Morris, Ill., 7,935 68 D2
Morris, Ind. 70 D3
Morris, co., Kans., 7,392 75 J5
Morris, Minn., 4,199 74 E3
Morris, co., N.J., 261,620 61 B2
Morris, N.Y., 677 59 K6
Morris, Okla., 982 76 H2
Morris, Pa. 60 H2
Morris, co., Tex., 12,576 77 Q3
Morris, r., Man., Can. 43 g10
Morris, Mt., N.Y. 59 L3
Morrisburg, Ont., Can., 1,799 47 J4
Morrisdale, Pa. 60 F4
Morrison, Colo., 426 79 b8
Morrison, Ill., 4,159 68 B2
Morrison, Iowa, 139 72 E2
Morrison, co., Minn., 26,641 74 E2
Morrison, Mo., 232 72 F6
Morrison, Okla., 256 76 F1
Morrison, Tenn., 294 71 F6
Morrisonville, Ill., 1,129 68 C4
Morrisonville, N.Y. 59 N2
Morrisonville, Wis. 66 D5
Morris Plains, N.J., 4,703 61 B2
Morris Res., Calif. 83 i15
Morris Run, Pa. 60 J2
Morriston, Ont., Can. 46 b14
Morristown, Ariz. 78 B5
Morristown, Ind., 704 70 D3
Morristown, N.J., 17,712 61 B2
Morristown, N.Y., 541 59 J2
Morristown, S. Dak., 219 74 B3
Morristown, Tenn., 21,267 71 H5
Morristown Nat. Hist. Pk., N.J. 61 B2
Morrisville, Mo., 228 72 D7
Morrisville, N.Y., 1,304 59 J6
Morrisville, N.C., 222 63 F2
Morrisville, Pa., 7,790 61 N5
Morrisville, Vt., 2,047 54 B2
Morro, P., Chile 105 A3
Morro Bay, Calif., 3,692 82 C5
Morropón, Peru, 4,798 104 B3
Morrosquillo, G. de, Col. 100 C3
Morrow, Ga., 580 64 g10
Morrow, La. 73 C7
Morrow, co., Ohio, 19,405 70 G2
Morrow, Ohio, 1,477 70 E3
Morrow, co., Oreg., 4,871 80 D3
Morrowville, Kans., 195 75 H4
Morrumbala, Moz. 164 E4
Morrumbene, Moz. 164 E5
Mors, i., Den. 121 A4
Morsang-sur-Orge, Fr., 8,666 116 h12
Morsbach, F.R.Ger., 6,732 119 D3
Mörsch, F.R.Ger., 5,074 119 E7
Morse, Sask., Can. 43 C5
Morse, La., 682 73 C7
Morse, Tex. 76 N1
Morse, Wis. 66 C2
Morse Village (part of New Salem), Mass. 56 G2
Morshansk, U.S.S.R., 42,000 134 D4
Morsi, India, 11,946 144 b15
Mortagne, Fr., 4,468 117 D2
Mortara, It., 14,252 122 b5
Mortcerf, Fr. 116 k11
Morteau, Fr., 5,419 117 G3
Morte Pt., U.K. 113 D6
Mortes, R. das, Mo. Gro., Braz.=Manso
Mortes, R. das, Ms. Gs., Braz. 103 d17
Mortí, Pan. 94 J6
Mortlach, Sask., Can. 43 C5
Mortlake, Austl., 1,048 173 d11
Mortlock Is.=Tauu Is.
Morton, U.K. 114 G4
Morton, U.K. 114 H5
Morton, Ill., 5,325 68 C3
Morton, co., Kans., 3,354 75 D6
Morton, Miss., 2,260 73 F5
Morton, N.Y. 58 E5
Morton, co., N. Dak., 20,992 74 B2
Morton, Tex., 2,731 77 M3
Morton, Wash., 1,183 80 B2
Morton Grove, Ill., 25,154 69 c8
Mortons Gap, Ky., 1,308 71 D4
Mortsel, Belg., 23,332 115 d8
Moruga, Trin. and Tob. 96 g5
Morundah, Austl. 173 e10
Morunglav, Rum. 128 E2
Moruya, Austl., 1,145 173 G5
Morvan, ra., Fr. 116 ·
Morven, Austl. 173 G4
Morven, N.Z. 175 f7
Morven, Ga., 476 64 F5
Morven, N.C., 518 63 D3
Morven, mtn. U.K. 112 E2
Morven, mtn., U.K. 112 E3
Morvi, India, 50,192 145 D5
Morville, U.K. 114 C5
Morwell, Austl., 9,040 173 G6
Moryakovskiy Zaton, U.S.S.R., 6,200 137 r11
Moryń, Pol., 1,014 127 A2
Morzhovoi, Alaska 85 D5
Mosal'sk, U.S.S.R., 3,900 136 D2
Mosbach, F.R.Ger., 10,047 118 B4
Mosby, Nor. 121 A2
Mosby, Mo., 293 72 C5
Mosby, Mont. 81 F2
Mosca, Colo. 79 C3
Mosca Pk., N. Mex. 79 B4
Moscavide, Port., 22,065 122 i10
Moscow, U.S.S.R.=Moskva
Moscow, Idaho, 11,183 81 A2
Moscow, Ind. 70 D3
Moscow, Kans., 211 75 D6
Moscow, Ky. 71 B5
Moscow, Mich. 67 J6
Moscow, Miss. 73 G5
Moscow, Ohio, 438 70 E4
Moscow, Pa., 1,212 61 M3
Moscow, Tenn., 368 71 B6
Moscow, Vt. 54 B3
Moscow Mills, Mo., 360 72 G6
Mosel, r., F.R.Ger. 118 A3
Moselle, Miss. 73 F6
Moselle, F.R.Ger.=Mosel
Moselle, r., Fr. 117 G2
Moser River, N.S., Can. 47 U11
Moses, N. Mex. 79 D3
Moses Lake, Wash., 11,299 80 D2
Moses L., Wash. 80 D2
Moses Mtn., Wash. 80 D1
Moses Point, Alaska 85 D2
Mosgiel, N.Z., 6,456 175 f7
Moshannon, Pa. 60 F3
Moshannon Cr., Pa. 60 F4
Mosher, S. Dak. 74 B4
Mosherville, Mich. 67 J6
Mōshi, Jap. 154 g14
Moshi, Tanz., 13,726 164 F2
Mosier, Oreg., 252 80 C3
Mosina, Pol., 6,928 127 B2
Mosinee, Wis., 2,067 66 D4
Mosjöen, Nor., 4,730 120 C2
Moskenesöya, i., Nor. 120 C2
Moskhopótamos, Gr. 129 D4
Moskosel, Swed. 120 D2
Moskovskiy, U.S.S.R., 9,400 137 f4
Moskva, U.S.S.R., 6,300,000 134 C4
Moskva, r., U.S.S.R. 136 D2
Moskvy, Kan. im., U.S.S.R. 136 b5
Mosonmagyaróvár, Hung., 21,199 126 C3
Mospino, U.S.S.R., 20,000 136 f8
Mosqueiro, Braz., 7,216 103 G2
Mosquera, Col. 100 A6
Mosquero, N. Mex., 310 79 D4
Mosquito, Newf., Can. 45 b11
Mosquito Coast=Mosquitos, Costa de
Mosquito I., V.I. 97 4
Mosquito Res., Ohio 70 J1
Mosquitos, Costa de, Hond.-Nic. 94 E3
Mosquitos, G. de los, Pan. 94 G6

264 · Moss—Münster

Moss, Nor., 20,461 120 B4
Moss, Miss. 73 F6
Moss, Tenn. 71 F5
Mossaka, Congo 164 B2
Mossamedes=Moçâmedes
Mossbank, Sask., Can. 43 C5
Moss Beach, Calif. 83 d12
Moss Bluff, Fla. 65 H3
Mossburn, N.Z. 175 f7
Mosselbaai, S. Af., 12,178 164 C7
Mossel Bay=Mosselbaai
Mossendjo, Congo 164 B2
Mossgiel, Austl. 173 e9
Moss Hill, Tex. 77 k8
Mössingen, F.R.Ger., 5,794 118 B4
Moss Landing, Calif. 83 f14
Mossman, Austl., 1,461 173 F2
Mossoró, Braz., 38,833 103 J3
Moss Point, Miss., 6,631 73 G7
Mossuril, Moz. 164 F4
Moss Vale, Austl., 2,748 173 g10
Mossville, Ill. 68 C3
Mossy Head, Fla. 65 C2
Mossyrock, Wash., 344 80 B2
Most, Czech., 45,417 126 A1
Mostaganem, Alg., 64,786 160 E2
Mostar, Yug., 49,000* 125 C3
Mostardas, Braz. 103 F8
Mosty, U.S.S.R., 8,300 136 B2
Mosul=Al Mawşil
Mosŭlp'o, S. Kor., 20,625 151 E4
Mota, Eth. 163 L4
Mota, i., New Hebr. 174 k4
Mota del Cuervo, Sp., 5,403 122 D3
Mota del Marqués, Sp., 1,080 122 C2
Motagua, r., Guat.-Hond. 94 B3
Motala, Swed., 27,148 120 C4
Motane, i., Marq. Is. 177 42
Motatán, Ven., 4,358 100 E3
Motegi, Jap., 28,952 155 G3
Mothe, i., Fiji 174 4
Mothern, Fr., 1,505 119 E7
Motherwell (incl. Wishaw), 72,799 112 E4
Motihari, India, 32,620 144 e12
Motikitiu, i., Aitutaki 177 35
Motilla del Palancar, Sp., 4,398 122 E3
Motley, Minn., 430 74 E2
Motley, co., Tex., 2,870 77 N2
Moto, D.R.Congo 164 D1
Motomiya, Jap., 18,227 155 G3
Motomura, Jap., 12,434 155 F4
Motorina, i., Terr. Papua 174 3
Motoura, Jap. 154 h15
Motoyama, Jap. 154 e15
Motoyama, Jap., 10,238 155 C5
Motoyoshi, Jap., 15,792 155 G2
Motozintla de Mendoza, Mex., 4,084 93 H5
Motril, Sp., 24,734 122 D4
Motru, r., Rum. 128 D2
Mott, N. Dak., 1,463 74 A2
Motta Visconti, It., 4,229 122 c5
Mottville, Mich. 67 H7
Mottville, N.Y. 59 q24
Motu, r., N.Z. 175 h5
Motueka, N.Z., 3,310 175 g6
Motueka, r., N.Z. 175 g6
Motu Iti, i., Marq. Is. 177 42
Motu-Iti, Soc. Is.=Tubai
Motul, Mex., 9,965 93 H4
Motulakau, i., Aitutaki 177 35
Motupe, Peru, 5,854 104 B3
Motupena Pt., Sol. Is. 175 a2
Moturiki, i., Fiji 174 4
Motu Tabu, i., Christmas Atoll 177 40
Motutapu, Niue 177 32
Motutapu, i., Rarotonga 177 34
Motutapu Pt., N.Z. 175 14
Motu Tou, i., Rarotonga 177 34
Motutunga, atoll, Tuam. Arch. 177 42
Mouans-Sartoux, Fr., 2,098 116 m13
Mouchin, Fr., 1,058 116 a6
Moúdhros, Gr., 1,236 129 E5
Moudjéria, Maur., 2,100 162 B3
Moudon, Switz., 2,806 124 A2
Mougins, Fr., 5,274 116 n13
Mouila, Gabon 164 A2
Mouka, C.A.R. 163 H4
Moulamein, Austl. 173 F5
Moulapamok, Laos 146 D4
Moulay Idriss, Mor. 160 D2
Mould Bay, N.W.T., Can. 41 F2
Moulins, Fr., 25,671 117 E3
Moulmein, Burma, 102,777 146 B3
Moulmeingyun, Burma, 16,464 146 A3
Moulouya, r., Mor. 160 D2
Moulton, Northants., Eng., U.K., 3,424 114 G6
Moulton, Suffolk, Eng., U.K. 114 J6
Moulton, Ala., 1,716 64 B1
Moulton, Iowa, 773 72 E4
Moulton, Tex., 646 77 P5
Moultonboro, N.H. 54 E4
Moultonboro Bay, N.H. 54 E4
Moultonville, N.H. 54 E4
Moultrie, Ga., 15,764 64 F4
Moultrie, co., Ill., 13,635 68 D4
Moultrie, L., S.C. 63 D4
Mound, La., 107 73 D5
Mound Bayou, Miss., 1,354 73 E4
Mound City, Ill., 1,669 68 C6
Mound City, Kans., 661 75 L5
Mound City, Mo., 1,249 72 B4
Mound City, S. Dak., 144 74 C3
Mound City Group Nat. Mon., Ohio 70 G3
Moundou, Chad, 25,000* 162 G4
Moundridge, Kans., 1,214 75 H5
Mounds, Ill., 1,835 68 C6
Mounds, Okla., 674 76 G2
Mounds View, Minn., 6,416 74 F3
Moundsville, W. Va., 15,163 62 D3
Mound Valley, Kans., 481 75 K6
Moundville, Ala., 922 64 B2
Moundville, Mo., 136 72 C7
Moungaone, i., Tonga 177 36
Mountain, N. Dak., 218 74 C1
Mountain, W. Va. 62 C3
Mountain, Wis., 420 66 E3
Mountainair, N. Mex., 1,605 79 B4
Mountain Ash, U.K., 29,575 114 B7
Mountain Brook, Ala., 12,680 64 C2
Mountainburg, Ark., 402 73 A2
Mountain City, Ga., 550 64 F1
Mountain City, Nev. 83 C2
Mountain City, Tenn., 1,379 71 K5
Mountain Cr., Pa. 60 H5
Mountain Dale, N.Y. 59 L8
Mountain Fork, r., Okla. 76 J3
Mountain Grove, Ont., Can. 46 G4
Mountain Grove, Mo., 3,176 72 E7
Mountain Grove, Va. 62 E4
Mountain Home, Ark., 3,258 73 C1
Mountain Home, Idaho, 10,075 81 B4
Mountain Home, N.C. 63 B2
Mountain Home, Tex. 77 O4
Mountain Iron, Minn., 1,808 74 F2
Mountain Island L., N.C. 63 D2
Mountain Lake, Minn., 1,943 74 E4
Mountain L., Mich. 66 E2
Mountain Lake Park, Md., 975 62 E3
Mountain Lakes, N.J., 4,037 61 C2
Mountain Park, N. Mex. 79 C5
Mountain Park, Okla., 403 76 E3
Mountain Peak, Tex. 76 f10
Mountain Pine, Ark., 1,279 73 B3
Mountain Point, Alaska, 372 85 M5
Mountain Road, Va. 62 E6
Mountainside, N.J., 6,325 58 b14
Mountaintop, Pa. 61 L3
Mountain Valley, Va. 62 E6
Mountain View, Ark., 983 73 C2
Mountain View, Calif., 30,889 83 e13
Mountain View, Colo., 826 79 b8
Mountain View, Ga., 2,025 64 g10
Mountain View, Hawaii, 566 84 F4
Mountain View, Mo., 1,252 72 F7
Mountainview, N.H.=Center Ossipee
Mountain View, N.Y. 59 M2
Mountain View, Okla., 864 76 E2
Mountain View, Natrona Co., Wyo., 1,721 81 F4
Mountain View, Uinta Co., Wyo. 81 D5
Mountain Village, Alaska 85 D3
Mount Airy, Md., 1,352 62 G3
Mount Airy, N.C., 7,055 63 D1
Mount Airy, Va. 62 E6
Mount Albert, Ont., Can. 46 E4
Mount Angel, Oreg., 1,428 80 B3
Mount Arlington, N.J., 1,246 61 B2
Mount Auburn, Ill., 502 68 C4
Mount Auburn, Iowa, 186 72 E2
Mount Ayr, Ind., 186 70 B2
Mount Ayr, Iowa, 1,738 72 C4
Mount Baldy, Calif. 83 i15
Mount Barker, S. Austl., Austl., 1,621 172 c8
Mount Barker, W. Austl., Austl., 1,242 172 B5
Mount Beauty, Austl., 1,782 173 G5
Mount Bellew Bridge, Ire. 113 B5
Mount Bethel, N.J. 58 a14
Mount Brydges, Ont., Can., 1,036 46 C6
Mt. Buffalo Nat. Pk., Austl. 173 f11
Mount Calm, Tex., 379 77 P4
Mount Calvary, Wis. 66 E5
Mount Carmel, Newf., Can. 45 b10
Mount Carmel (part of Hamden), Conn. 56 E7
Mount Carmel, Ill., 8,594 68 E5
Mount Carmel, Ky. 71 H3
Mount Carmel, N. Dak. 74 C1
Mount Carmel, Ohio 71 i11
Mount Carmel, Pa., 10,760 61 K4
Mount Carmel, S.C., 109 63 B3
Mount Carmel, Va. 62 C6
Mount Carmel Junc., Utah 78 B3
Mount Carmel Pond, Newf., Can. 45 b10
Mount Carroll, Ill., 2,056 68 C1
Mount Clare, Ill., 320 68 C4
Mount Clare, W. Va. 62 D3
Mount Clemens, Mich., 21,016 67 L6
Mount Cobb, Pa. 61 o16
Mt. Cook Nat. Pk., N.Z. 175 f6
Mount Coolon, Austl. 173 G3
Mount Crawford, Va., 247 62 F4
Mount Croghan, S.C., 145 63 D3
Mount Cuba, Del. 62 e10
Mount Darwin, Rhod. 164 E4
Mount Desert I., Me. 55 D4
Mount Dora, Fla., 3,756 65 H4
Mount Dora, N. Mex. 79 D3
Mount Edgecumbe, Alaska, 1,884 85 K4
Mount Elgin, Ont., Can. 46 D6
Mount Emu Cr., Austl. 173 d11
Mount Enterprise, Tex. 77 Q4
Mount Erie, Ill., 134 68 D5
Mount Etna, Ind., 192 70 D2
Mount Etna, Iowa 72 C3
Mount Forest, Ont., Can., 2,604 46 D4
Mount Forest, Mich. 67 J5
Mount Freedom, N.J., 1,328 58 a13
Mount Gambier, Austl., 10,331 172 E5
Mount Gay, W. Va., 3,386 62 B5
Mount Gilead, N.C., 1,229 63 E2
Mount Gilead, Ohio, 2,788 70 G2
Mount Gretna, Pa., 93 61 K5
Mount Hagen, Terr. New Guin., 1,837 174 d2
Mount Hamilton, Calif. 83 f13
Mount Healthy, Ohio, 6,553 71 h10
Mount Herman, Okla. 76 J3
Mount Hermon, Calif. 83 e13
Mount Hermon, Ky. 71 F5
Mount Hermon (part of Gill and Northfield), Mass. 56 G2
Mount Holly, N.J., 13,271(T) 61 B3
Mount Holly, N.C., 4,037 63 D2
Mount Holly, Vt. 54 B5
Mount Holly, Va. 62 H4
Mount Holly Springs, Pa., 1,840 60 H5
Mount Hood, Oreg. 80 C3
Mount Hope, Austl. 173 F5
Mount Hope, Ont., Can. 46 c15
Mount Hope, Kans., 539 75 H6
Mount Hope, N.J. 58 a13
Mount Hope, W. Va., 2,000 62 C5
Mount Hope, Wis., 218 66 C6
Mount Hope, r., Conn. 56 H5
Mount Hope Bay, Mass.-R.I. 57 M6
Mount Horeb, Wis., 1,991 66 D5
Mount Ida, Austl. 172 B4
Mount Ida, Ark., 564 73 B3
Mount Isa, Austl., 7,433 172 E3
Mount Jackson, Va., 722 62 F4
Mount Jewett, Pa., 1,226 60 E2
Mount Joy, Pa., 3,292 60 J5
Mount Judea, Ark. 73 B2
Mt. Kenya Nat. Pk., Kenya 164 F2
Mount Kisco, N.Y., 6,805 59 N9
Mount Laguna, Calif. 82 E6
Mountlake Terrace, Wash., 9,122 81 b7
Mount Laurel, N.J. 60 g12
Mount Laurel, Va. 62 F6
Mount Lebanon, Pa., 35,361(T) 60 C5
Mount Lemoray, Br. Col., Can. 42 G2
Mount Liberty, Ohio 70 G2
Mount Lookout, W. Va. 62 D4
Mount McKinley Nat. Pk., Alaska 85 G3
Mount Magnet, Austl. 172 B4
Mount Maunganui, N.Z., 5,091 175 h5
Mount Meigs, Ala. 64 C3
Mountmellick, Ire., 2,677 113 C5
Mount Montgomery, Nev. 83 A4
Mount Morgan, Austl., 4,152 173 G3
Mount Moriah, Mo., 225 72 D4
Mount Morris, Ill., 3,075 68 C1
Mount Morris, Mich., 3,484 67 K5
Mount Morris, N.Y., 3,250 58 E6
Mount Morris, Pa. 60 B6
Mount Morris, Wis. 66 D4
Mountnorris Bay, Austl. 172 D1
Mount Olive, Ala. 64 c7
Mount Olive, Ill., 2,295 68 C4
Mount Olive, Miss., 841 73 F6
Mount Olive, N.C., 4,673 63 F2
Mount Olivet, Ky., 386 71 G3
Mount Orab, Ohio, 1,058 70 F3
Mount Penn, Pa., 3,574 61 h14
Mount Pinson, Ala., 1,121 64 C2
Mount Pleasant, Ont., Can. 46 b15
Mount Pleasant, U.K. 112 g10
Mount Pleasant, Iowa, 7,339 72 F4
Mount Pleasant, Mich., 14,875 67 J5
Mount Pleasant, N.C., 1,041 63 D2
Mount Pleasant, Hocking Co.-Vinton Co., Ohio 70 G3
Mount Pleasant, Jefferson Co., Ohio, 656 70 J2
Mount Pleasant, Pa., 6,107 60 D5
Mount Pleasant, S.C., 5,116 63 D5
Mount Pleasant, Tenn., 2,921 71 D6
Mount Pleasant, Tex., 8,027 77 Q3
Mount Pleasant, Utah, 1,572 78 C2
Mount Pocono, Pa., 935 61 M3
Mount Prospect, Ill., 30,202 68 D1
Mount Pulaski, Ill., 1,689 68 C3
Mountrail, co., N. Dak., 10,077 74 A1
Mount Rainier, Md., 9,855 62 a9
Mount Rainier Nat. Pk., Wash. 80 C2
Mountrath, Ire. 113 C5
Mount Revelstoke Nat. Pk., Br. Col., Can. 42 H3
Mount Royal, N.J. 60 f12
Mt. Rushmore Nat. Mem., S. Dak. 74 A4
Mount St. Joseph, Ohio 71 h11
Mount Savage, Md., 1,639 62 E3
Mount's Bay, U.K. 113 D6
Mount Shasta, Calif., 1,936 82 B2
Mount Sidney, Va. 62 F4
Mount Solon, Va. 62 E4
Mountsorrel, U.K., 4,032 114 F5
Mount Sterling, Ill., 2,262 68 B4
Mount Sterling, Ky., 5,370 71 H3
Mount Sterling, Mo. 72 F6
Mount Sterling, N.C. 63 A2
Mount Sterling, Ohio, 1,338 70 F3
Mount Sterling, Wis. 66 B5
Mount Stewart, P.E.I., Can. 47 U10
Mount Storm, W. Va. 62 E3
Mount Sunapee, N.H. 54 C5
Mount Surprise, Austl. 173 F2
Mount Sylvan, Tex. 77 Q3
Mount Tabor, Vt. 54 E5
Mount Tom (part of Easthampton), Mass. 56 F3
Mount Tremper, N.Y. 59 M7
Mount Trumbull, Ariz. 78 B3
Mount Union, Iowa, 176 72 F3
Mount Union, Pa., 4,091 60 G5
Mount Upton, N.Y. 59 K7
Mount Vernon, Ont., Can. 46 b15
Mount Vernon, Ala., 553 64 A4
Mount Vernon, Ark. 73 C2
Mount Vernon, Ga., 1,166 64 G3
Mount Vernon, Ill., 15,566 68 D5
Mount Vernon, Ind., 5,970 70 B5
Mount Vernon, Iowa, 2,593 72 F3
Mount Vernon, Ky., 1,177 71 G4
Mount Vernon, Me. 55 C4
Mount Vernon, Md. 62 J4
Mount Vernon, Mo., 2,381 72 D7
Mount Vernon, N.Y., 76,010 59 N10
Mount Vernon, Ohio, 13,284 70 G2
Mount Vernon, Oreg., 502 80 D3
Mount Vernon, S. Dak., 379 74 C4
Mount Vernon, Tenn. 71 G6
Mount Vernon, Tex., 1,338 77 Q3
Mount Vernon, Wash., 7,921 80 B1
Mount Vernon, Wis. 66 D6
Mount Victory, Ky. 71 G4
Mount Victory, Ohio, 598 70 F2
Mountville, S.C. 63 C3
Mount Vision, N.Y. 59 K6
Mount Washington, Ky., 1,173 71 F3
Mount Washington, Mass., 34(T) 56 C4
Mount Wolf, Pa., 1,514 60 J5
Mount Zion, Ga., 211 64 D2
Mount Zion, Ill., 925 68 D4
Mount Zion, Md. 62 a8
Mount Zion, W. Va. 62 C4
Mount Zion, Wis. 66 C5
Mou-p'ing, China 151 D3
Moura, Braz. 102 D2
Moura, Port., 12,126 122 B3
Mourão, Port., 3,074 122 B3
Mourcourt, Belg. 116 a6
Mourdiah, Mali, 1,686 162 C3
Mourenx, Fr., 8,660 117 C5
Mourilyan, Austl. 173 G2
Mourilyan, C., Terr. Papua 174 3
Mourmelon-le-Grand, Fr., 5,582 117 F2
Mousam, r., Me. 55 B5
Mousam Pd., Me. 54 F4
Mouscron, Belg., 36,647 115 B4
Mousie, Ky. 71 H4
Moussey, Fr., 1,051 116 c9
Moussoro, Chad, 5,000* 162 G3
Moussy-le-Neuf, Fr. 116 i10
Moussy-le-Vieux, Fr. 116 i10
Mouth of Wilson, Va. 62 C6
Moutier, Switz., 7,472 124 B1
Moûtiers, Fr., 4,141 117 G4
Mou-ting, China 152 A2
Mouvaux, Fr., 11,140 116 a6
Mouzon, Fr., 2,582 117 F2
Mouzon, S.C. 63 E4
Movas, Mex. 92 C2
Movileni, Rum. 128 F1
Moville, Ire. 113 C4
Moville, Iowa, 1,156 72 B2
Mowbray, Man., Can. 43 f10
Moweaqua, Ill., 1,614 68 D4
Mower, co., Minn., 48,498 74 F4
Mowming=Mao-ming
Moxee City, Wash., 499 80 C2
Moxie, L., Me. 55 C3
Moxie Mtn., Me. 55 C3
Moya, Mex., 1,003 93 c8
Moyahua, Mex., 1,787 92 E4
Moyale, Kenya 164 F1
Moyamba, Sa. Leone 162 B4
Mo-yang, r., China 152 C3
Moyen Atlas, ra., Mor. 160 D2
Moyenvic, Fr. 116 b9
Moyers, Okla. 76 H3
Moyeuvre-Grande, Fr., 15,146 116 b8
Moyhu, Austl. 173 f11
Moyie, Br. Col., Can. 42 J4
Moyie, r., Br. Col., Can. 42 J4
Moyie Springs, Idaho, 196 81 B1
Moyo, Uganda 164 E1
Moyobamba, Peru, 8,308 104 B3
Moyock, N.C. 63 H1
Moyowosi, r., Tanz. 165 e15
Moyto, Chad 162 G3
Mo-yü, China 150 A3
Moyuta, Guat., 2,414 94 c9
Moyyero, r., U.S.S.R. 135 K3
Mozambique, Port. Overseas Terr., 6,998,000* 164 E5
Mozambique Chan., Af. 164 F5
Mozdok, U.S.S.R., 24,500 137 c1
Mozhayevka, U.S.S.R. 136 f7
Mozhaysk, U.S.S.R., 12,600 136 b6
Mozhga, U.S.S.R., 30,000 134 E4
Mozier, Ill. 68 B4
Mozo, Burma 146 A2
Mozyr', U.S.S.R., 30,000 134 B4
Mpala, D.R.Congo 164 D3
Mpanda, Tanz. 164 E3
Mpésikion, Límni=Vólvi, Límni
M'pésoba, Mali 162 D3
Mpigi, Uganda 165 f13
Mpika, Zambia 164 E3
Mporokoso, Zambia 164 E3
Mpouya, Congo B. 164 B2
Mpraeso, Ghana 162 c8
Mpulungu, Zambia 164 E3
Mpwapwa, Tanz. 164 F3
Mrągowo, Pol., 10,261 127 D2
Mrakovo, U.S.S.R. 137 h9
Mras-Su, r., U.S.S.R. 137 s11
Mrčajevci, Yug., 2,858 125 E3
Mrewa, Rhod. 164 E4
Mrkonjić Grad, Yug., 2,479 125 C2
Mrocza, Pol., 2,861 127 B2
Mšec, Czech. 126 c6
Mšené, Czech. 126 d6
Mšeno, Czech. 126 d6
M'Sila, Alg., 17,521 160 d6
Msta, r., U.S.S.R. 136 D1
Mstera, U.S.S.R., 6,500 136 F1
Mstislavl', U.S.S.R., 8,400 136 C2
Mstów, Pol. 127 C3
Mtoko, Rhod. 164 E4
Mtoroshangu, Rhod. 164 D4
Mtsensk, U.S.S.R., 14,100 136 E2
Mtskheta, U.S.S.R., 7,100 137 c1
Mtwara, Tanz., 10,459 164 F3
Mu, r., Burma 146 A2
Mua, Îs. de Horne 175 9
Mua, Tonga, 2,560 177 36
Mua, Îs. Wallis 175 7
Mua, B. de, Îs. Wallis 175 7
Mualang, Indon. 148 D2
Muang Yang, Thai. 147 e4
Muar, Malay., 39,050 148 B2
Muar, r., Malay. 147 p15
Muaraaman, Indon. 148 B3
Muaraantjalung, Indon. 148 F2
Muarabelti, Indon. 148 B3
Muarabenangin, Indon. 148 E3
Muarabinuangeun, Indon. 148 a7
Muarabungo, Indon. 148 B3
Muaradua, Indon. 148 C4
Muaraenim, Indon. 148 C3
Muaragede, Indon. 148 b7
Muaragusung, Indon. 148 F2
Muaralakitan, Indon. 148 B3
Muaralasan, Indon. 148 F2
Muaramawai, Indon. 148 F2
Muararupit, Indon. 148 B3
Muarasabak, Indon. 148 B3
Muarasiberut, Indon. 148 A3
Muarasukon, Indon. 148 A2
Muaratebo, Indon. 148 B3
Muaratembesi, Indon. 148 B3
Muaratewe, Indon. 148 E3
Muaratuhup, Indon. 148 E3
Muaratunan, Indon. 148 F3
Muarawahau, Indon. 148 F2
Muāri, Rās, Pak. 144 B4
Mubambi, D.R.Congo 165 m19
Mubende, Uganda 164 E1
Mubi, Nigeria 162 G4
Mucajaí, r., Braz. 102 D1
Much, F.R.Ger., 6,618 119 C3
Muchalat, Br. Col., Can. 42 E4
Much Birch, U.K. 114 C7
Mücheln, Ger.D.R., 13,227 118 C3
Muchinga Mts., Zambia 164 E4
Muchkapskiy, U.S.S.R. 136 F3
Much Marcle, U.K. 114 C7
Much Wenlock, U.K., 2,351 114 C5
Muck, i., U.K. 112 C3
Muckadilla, Austl. 173 G4
Muckalee Cr., Ga. 64 E4
Muckle Roe, i., U.K. 112 F1
Mucklestone, U.K. 114 C5
Muco, r., Col. 100 E5
Mucope, Ang. 164 B4
Mucuchies, Ven. 100 E3
Mucur, Turk., 5,301 142 C2
Mucuri, r., Braz. 103 H5
Mucusso, Ang. 164 C4
Mud, r., Ky. 71 E4
Muda, r., Malay. 147 o13
Mudau, F.R.Ger., 1,653 119 G5
Mud Butte, S. Dak. 74 A3
Mud Buttes, S. Dak. 74 A3
Mud Cr., N.Y. 58 o21
Mud Cr., Okla. 76 F3
Mud Cr., S. Dak. 74 C3
Muddo Gashi, Kenya 164 F1
Muddus Nat. Pk., Swed. 120 D2
Muddy, r., Conn. 56 E7
Muddy Boggy Cr., Okla. 76 G3
Muddy Bk., Mass. 56 H3
Muddy Cr., Ill. 68 D5
Muddy Cr., Mo. 72 D6
Muddy Cr., Ohio 71 g11
Muddy Cr., Utah 78 C2
Mud Flat, Utah 78 a8
Mudgee, Austl., 5,294 173 G5
Mudjatik, r., Sask., Can. 43 C3
Mud Lake, Idaho, 187 81 C4
Mud L., Me. 55 D1
Mud L., Minn. 74 d6
Mud L., Minn. 74 E1
Mud L., Nev. 83 A2
Mudon, Burma, 20,123 146 B3
Mud Run, r., Pa. 61 L3
Mudurnu, Turk., 3,500 142 B1
Muecate, Moz. 164 F4
Mueda, Moz. 164 F3
Muenster, Tex., 1,190 77 P3
Muéo, N. Caled. 174 i8
Muerto, Mar, Mex. 93 G5
Mu-fou Shan, China 152 D1
Mufulira, Zambia, 56,600* 164 D4
Mügeln, Ger.D.R. 126 c5
Muggensturm, F.R.Ger., 3,482 119 E7
Muggia, It., 12,717 123 D2
Mugi, Jap., 10,568 155 D5
Mugishima, Jap. 154 i14
Mugitani, Jap. 154 h15
Mūg Karnāli, r., Nepal 144 d11
Muğla, Turk., 14,053 142 B2
Müglizh, Bulg., 3,550 128 E3
Mugodzhary, Gory, U.S.S.R. 134 E5
Mugu, Nepal 144 d11
Mugur-Aksy, U.S.S.R. 137 s12
Muhammad, Ra's, U.A.R. 161 K3
Muḥammad Qawl, Sudan 163 L2
Mühlacker, F.R.Ger., 10,810 119 F7
Mühl-Bach, r., F.R.Ger. 119 D4
Mühlberg, Ger.D.R. 126 c5
Mühldorf, F.R.Ger., 10,541 118 D4
Muhlenberg, Ky., 27,791 71 D4
Muhlenberg, Pa., 1,050* 61 h14
Mühlhausen, Ger.D.R., 45,154 118 C3
Mühlheim, F.R.Ger., 15,188 119 F4
Mühltroff, Ger.D.R. 126 a6
Muhos, Fin. 120 F2
Muhu, i., U.S.S.R. 136 A1
Muhutwe, Tanz. 165 e14
Muikaichi, Jap., 7,946 154 B4
Muikamachi, Jap., 10,504 155 F3
Muine Bheag, Ire., 1,984 113 C5
Muir, Man., Can. 43 f9
Muir, Ont., Can. 46 a15
Muir, Mich., 610 67 J5
Muir Glacier, Alaska 85 K4
Muirhead, U.K. 112 b8
Muirkirk, U.K. 112 D4
Muir Seamount, Atl. Oc. 108 H4
Muirtown, U.K. 112 c7
Muir Woods Nat. Mon., Calif. 83 d12
Muisne, Ec., 2,794 104 A1
Muizen, Belg., 4,419 115 e8
Mujeres, I., Mex. 93 J4
Mujimbeji, Zambia 165 m20
Mujinkarikku, i., Eniwetok 176 28
Mukachëvo, U.S.S.R., 44,000 136 A3
Mukah, Malay., 1,423 148 D2
Mukai, Jap. 154 e16
Mukai, Jap. 154 h15
Mukaihara, Jap., 8,612 155 C4
Mukalik, r., Qué., Can. 45 M2
Mukana, D.R.Congo 165 n18
Mukawa, Jap., 9,720 155 J8
Mukdahan, Thai. 146 D3
Mukden=Shen-yang
Mukeru, Palau 176 21
Mukhomornoye, U.S.S.R. 135 R3
Mukhtuya, U.S.S.R., 11,000 135 L3
Mukilteo, Wash., 1,128 80 B2
Mukinbudin, Austl. 172 B4
Muko, r., Jap. 154 g15
Mukomuko, Indon. 148 B3
Muko-shima, Bonin Is. 170 D3
Muksu, r., U.S.S.R. 137 f4
Muktsar, India, 30,765 145 E3
Mukulakulu, D.R.Congo 165 m18
Mukur, Afghan. 144 C2
Mukutawa, r., Man., Can. 43 F4
Mukwonago, Wis., 1,877 66 E6
Mula, Sp., 14,721 122 E3
Mula, r., India 145 i17
Mulalillo, Ec. 104 c10
Mulaló, Ec. 104 c10
Mu-lan, China 151 F1
Mulata, Bahía de la, Cuba 96 b1
Mulatos, r., Ec. 104 c10
Mulatre, Point, Dominica 97 13
Mulatupo, Pan. 94 J6
Mulbagal, India, 11,977 145 m19
Mulberry, Ark., 934 73 B2
Mulberry, Calif., 2,643 82 C3
Mulberry, Fla., 2,922 65 G5
Mulberry, Ind., 1,062 70 C2
Mulberry, Kans., 642 75 L6
Mulberry, r., Ark. 73 A2
Mulberry Cr., Ga. 64 E3
Mulberry Fork, r., Ala. 64 C1
Mulchatna, r., Alaska 85 F3
Mulda, Ger.D.R. 126 c6
Mulde, r., Ger.D.R. 118 D3
Muldon, Miss. 73 G4
Muldoon, Tex. 77 P5
Muldraugh, Ky., 1,743 71 F4
Muldrow, Okla., 1,137 76 J2
Muleba, Tanz. 165 e14
Mule Creek, N. Mex. 79 A5
Mu-lei, China 150 C2
Mulejé, Mex. 92 B2
Mu-leng, China 151 F1
Mu-leng, r., China 150 H2
Mu-leng-chen, China 151 F1
Mule Pk., N. Mex. 79 C5
Mulero, Urug. 105 c11
Muleshoe, Tex., 3,871 77 M2
Mulga, Ala., 482 64 b7
Mulgrave, N.S., Can., 1,129 47 V11
Mulgrave I., Austl. 173 F1
Mulhacén, Co., de, Sp. 122 D4
Mulhall, Okla., 253 76 F1
Mülheim, Nrh.-Wf., F.R.Ger., 169,306 119 B2
Mülheim, Rhein.-Pfalz, F.R.Ger., 5,799 119 D4
Mulhouse, Fr., 110,735 117 G3
Mu-li, China 150 D4
Muli, I., Loy. Is. 174 k8
Muli, r., Indon. 149 L4
Mulino, Oreg. 80 B3
Mulinuu, C., W. Samoa 177 37
Mulitapu'ili, C., W. Samoa 177 38
Mull, Ark. 73 C1
Mull, I. of, U.K. 112 D3
Mull, Sd. of, U.K. 112 D3
Mullaittivu, Cey. 145 F8
Mullan, Idaho, 1,477 81 B2
Mullen, Nebr., 811 75 D1
Mullens, W. Va., 3,544 62 C5
Mullet Key, Fla. 65 c12
Mullet L., Wis. 66 E5
Mullett Lake, Mich. 67 J3
Mullett L., Mich. 67 J3
Mullewa, Austl. 172 A4
Mull Head, Mainland, U.K. 112 E2
Mull Head, Papa Westray, i., U.K. 112 E2
Müllheim, F.R.Ger., 6,027 118 A5
Müllheim, Switz., 1,475 124 D1
Mullica, r., N.J. 61 B4
Mullica Hill, N.J. 61 A4
Mulliken, Mich. 484 67 J6
Mullin, Tex., 219 77 O4
Mullinavat, Ire. 113 C5
Mullingar, Ire., 7,488 113 C5
Mullins, S.C., 6,229 63 E3
Mullins Hbr., Terr. Papua 174 3
Mullinville, Kans., 385 75 F6
Mullion, U.K., 1,166 113 D6
Mull of Galloway, pt., U.K. 113 D4
Mull of Kintyre, pt., U.K. 113 D4
Mull of Oa, U.K. 112 C4
Mullumbimby, Austl., 2,017 173 H4
Mulobezi, Zambia 164 D4
Mulonda-Funda, D.R.Congo 165 m19
Mulshi L., India 145 h17
Multai, India, 8,232 144 b15
Multān, Pak., 358,201 145 D3
Multnomah, co., Oreg., 522,813 80 B3
Mulu, G., Malay. 148 E2
Mulungwishi, D.R.Congo 165 n19
Mulvane, Kans., 2,981 75 H6
Mulvihill, Man., Can. 43 F5
Mumbwa, Zambia 164 D4
Mumena, D.R.Congo 165 n19
Mumford, Ont., Can. 46 F3
Mumford, N.Y. 58 E5
Mumias, Kenya 165 g13
Mümling, r., F.R.Ger. 119 F5
Mumpf, Switz. 124 B1
Mumtrak=Goodnews Bay
Mun, r., Thai. 146 D4
Muna, Mex., 4,443 93 H4
Muna, r., U.S.S.R. 135 L3
Muna, P., Indon. 149 G4
Munagai, Jap. 154 f14
Munagata, Jap. 154 e15
Muñani, Peru, 1,124 104 D5
Münchberg, F.R.Ger., 10,323 118 C3
Müncheberg, Ger.D.R. 118 E2
München, F.R.Ger., 962,860 118 C4
Münchenbernsdorf, Ger.D.R. 126 a6
Münchenstein, Switz., 10,345 124 B1
Muncho Lake, Br. Col., Can. 42 F1
Munch'ŏn, Japan 151 E3
Münchwilen, Switz., 2,919 124 D1
Muncie, Ind., 68,603 70 D2
Muncy, Pa., 2,830 60 J3
Muncy Cr., Pa., 60 J3
Muncy Valley, Pa. 60 J3
Mundale (part of Westfield), Mass. 56 E4
Mundare, Alta., Can. 43 c7
Munday, Tex., 1,978 77 O3
Munday, W. Va. 62 C3
Mundelein, Ill., 10,526 68 D1
Münden, F.R.Ger., 20,555 118 B3
Munden, Kans., 177 75 H4
Munderfing, Aust., 2,175 124 J5
Mundesley, U.K., 1,558 113 G5
Mundubbera, Austl. 173 G3
Mundybash, U.S.S.R., 11,900 137 r11
Muneage, Jap. 154 e15
Munella, mt., Alb. 125 D4
Munera, Sp., 5,931 122 D3
Munford, Ala. 64 D2
Munford, Tenn., 1,014 71 B6
Munfordville, Ky., 1,157 71 E4
Mungallala, Austl. 173 G4
Mungaoli, India, 8,168 144 b13
Mungeli, India, 12,431 145 F5
Munger, Ill. 69 b9
Munger, Mich. 67 K5
Mungindi, Austl. 173 G4
Mungo, Phil., 2,638 153 c5
Munguía, Sp., 5,780 122 n11
Munich, F.R.Ger.=München
Munich, N. Dak., 213 74 C1
Münichsthal, Aust. 124 c10
Muniesa, Sp., 1,672 122 E2
Munising, Mich., 4,228 67 G2
Munith, Mich. 67 J6
Muniz Freire, Braz., 1,857 103 f17
Munjor, Kans. 75 F5
Munk, Man., Can. 43 G3
Munkarp, Swed. 121 F5
Munkedal, Swed. 120 B4
Munkfors, Swed. 120 C4
Munk's Corners, Ohio 70 b7
Munku-Khayrkhan-Ula, G., U.S.S.R. 134 H4
Munku-Sardyk, G., Mong.-U.S.S.R. 135 J4
Münnerstadt, F.R.Ger., 4,080 118 C3
Munning, Pt., N.Z. 175 14
Munnsville, N.Y., 391 59 J6
Muñoz, Mex., 1,053 93 f10
Muñoz, Phil., 5,213 153 b7
Munroe L., Man., Can. 43 F2
Munsan-ni, S. Kor. 151 E3
Münsingen, Switz., 6,051 124 B2
Munson, Fla. 65 C2
Munson, Mich. 67 J7
Munsön, pt., Swed. 120 e8
Munsonville, N.H. 54 C5
Munster, Fr. 5,078 117 G2
Münster, Hess., F.R.Ger., 5,297 119 F5

Munster—Nanakuli · 265

Munster, Ndrsachs., F.R.Ger., 8,594 118 C2
Münster, Nrh.-Wf., F.R.Ger., 155,241 118 A3
Munster, prov., Ire., 877,238 113 B5
Münster, Switz. 124 C2
Munster, Ind., 10,313 70 B1
Münstereifel, F.R.Ger., 3,911 119 B3
Münstermaifeld, F.R.Ger., 1,694 119 C4
Munsungan L., Me. 55 D2
Muntadgin, Austl. 172 B4
Munte, Indon. 149 F2
Muntendam, Neth., 3,000 115 E1
Muntok, Indon. 148 C3
Munuscong, r., Mich. 67 J2
Munuscong L., Mich. 67 J2
Münzbach, Aust., 1,353 124 L5
Münzkirchen, Aust., 1,972 124 K5
Munzur, r., Turk. 142 D2
Muong Beng, Laos 146 C2
Muong Boum, N. Viet. 146 C2
Muong Et, Laos 146 C2
Muong Hiem, Laos 146 C2
Muong Hung, N. Viet. 146 C2
Muong Hun Xiêng Hun, Laos 146 C2
Muong Khoua, Laos 146 C2
Muong Ki, Laos 146 C3
Muong La, Laos 146 C2
Muong Luong Namtha, Laos 146 C2
Muong Man, S. Viet. 147 m11
Muong Ngoi, Laos 146 C2
Muong Nhie, N. Viet. 146 C2
Muong Nông, Laos 146 D3
Muong Ou Tay, Laos 146 C2
Muong Pa, Laos 146 C3
Muong Pao, Laos 146 D2
Muong Phalane, Laos 146 D3
Muong Phieng, Laos 146 C3
Muong Phine, Laos 146 D3
Muong Sai, Laos 146 C2
Muong Sen, N. Viet. 146 D3
Muong Sing, Laos 146 C2
Muong Son, Laos 146 C2
Muong Song Khone, Laos 146 D3
Muong Soui, Laos 146 C3
Muong Wapi, Laos 146 D4
Muong You, Laos 146 C3
Muonio, Fin. 120 F2
Muonioälv, Fin. = Muoniojoki
Muonioälv, r., Swed. 120 E2
Muoniojoki, r., Fin. 120 E2
Muoniojoki, Swed. = Muonioälv
Muotathal, Switz., 2,592 124 C2
Mu-pien, China 152 B3
Muqui, Braz., 4,262 103 f17
Mur, r., Aust. 124 K6
Mura, r., Yug. 125 C1
Muradiye, Turk., 2,281 137 b2
Murakami, Jap., 32,878 155 F2
Murakeresztúr, Hung., 2,379 126 C3
Murallón, Co., Arg.-Chile 105 A7
Muramvya, Burundi 165 d15
Murano, It. 122 f5
Murashi, U.S.S.R., 14,200 134 D4
Murat, Fr., 2,844 117 E4
Murat, r., Turk. 142 D2
Murati, Yug. 125 C2
Muratkovo, U.S.S.R. 137 k7
Murato, Fr., 1,031 116 r17
Murau, Aust., 2,755 124 L6
Murayama, Jap., 39,057 155 G2
Murban, Tr. States 143 E4
Murça, Port., 1,789 122 B2
Murchison, Austl. 173 e11
Murchison, N.Z. 175 g6
Murchison, Mt., N.Z. 175 f6
Murchison, r., Austl. 172 A4
Murchison Falls Nat. Pk., Uganda 164 E1
Murcia, Sp., 249,738 122 E4
Murcia, reg., Sp. 122 D3
Murdale, Br. Col., Can. 42 G2
Murderkill, r., Del. 61 A5
Murdo, S. Dak., 783 74 B4
Murdochville, Qué., Can., 2,891 47 T9
Murdock, Kans. 75 G6
Murdock, Minn., 381 74 E3
Murdock, Nebr., 247 75 J3
Murdocksville, Pa. 60 a8
Mure, Yug. 125 E3
Mureck, Aust., 1,890 124 M7
Mureşul, r., Rum. 128 C1
Muret, Fr., 6,777 117 D5
Murfreesboro, Ark., 1,096 73 B3
Murfreesboro, N.C., 2,643 63 G1
Murfreesboro, Tenn., 18,991 71 E6
Murg, r., F.R.Ger. 119 E7
Murgab, U.S.S.R., 134 G6
Murgab, r., U.S.S.R. 134 F6
Murgab, r., U.S.S.R. 137 g5
Murgash, mtn., Bulg. 128 D3
Murgaşu, Rum. 128 D1
Murgeni, Rum. 128 G1
Murgenthal, Switz., 2,758 124 B1
Murghāb, r., Afghan. 144 B2
Murgon, Austl., 1,710 173 G4
Murguía, Sp. 122 D1
Murgul, U.S.S.R. 137 b1
Muri, Bihar, India, 4,654 144 e14
Muri, M.P., India 144 d14
Muri, Rarotonga 177 34
Muri, Switz., 7,855 124 B2
Muri, Switz., 3,957 124 C1
Muriaé, Braz., 22,571 103 e17
Muriaé, r., Braz. 103 e17
Murias de Paredes, Sp., 2,318 122 B1
Murillo, Ont., Can. 44 E5
Murillo, Col. 101 d15
Murilo, atoll, Car. Is. 176 18
Murindó, Col. 100 B4
Müritz, Ger.D.R. 118 D1
Müritz See, Ger.D.R. 118 D2
Murjo, G., Indon. 148 d7
Murle, Eth. 163 L5
Murliganj, India, 9,848 144 f13
Murmansk, U.S.S.R., 237,000 134 C3
Murmansk Rise, Barents Sea 132 C2
Murnau, F.R.Ger., 5,516 118 C5
Muro, Fr. 116 r17
Murochō, Jap. 154 i15
Murom, U.S.S.R., 81,000 134 D4
Muromoto, Jap. 154 e15
Muromtsevo, U.S.S.R. 137 o11
Muroran, Jap., 145,679 155 J8
Muros, Sp., 10,029 122 A1
Muroto, Jap., 30,498 155 C5
Murotozaki, Jap., 8,027 155 D5
Muroto-zaki, Jap. 155 D5
Murotsu, Jap. 154 f15
Murowana Goślina, Pol., 3,212 127 B2
Murphy, Idaho 81 A4
Murphy, N.C., 2,235 63 a7
Murphy, Okla. 76 H1
Murphy, Oreg. 80 B4
Murphy City, Minn. 74 G2
Murphys, Calif. 82 C3
Murphysboro, Ill., 8,673 68 C6
Murr, r., F.R.Ger. 119 G7
Murrah al Kubrá, Al Buḩayrah al, l, U.A.R. 161 k7
Murray, co., Ga., 10,447 64 E1
Murray, Ind. 70 D2
Murray, Iowa, 613 72 D3
Murray, Ky., 9,303 71 C5
Murray, co., Minn., 14,743 74 E4
Murray, co., Okla., 10,622 76 F3
Murray, Utah, 16,806 78 C1
Murray, r., Br. Col., Can. 42 G2
Murray, L., Terr. Papua 174 d2
Murray, L., Calif. 82 c9
Murray, L., Okla. 76 F3
Murray, L., S.C. 63 C3
Murray Bridge, Austl., 4,362 172 c8
Murray City, Ohio, 717 70 G3
Murray Fracture Zone, Pac. Oc. 169 H1
Murray Harbour, P.E.I., Can. 47 U11
Murray Hill, N.J. 58 b14
Murray Maxwell Bay, N.W.T., Can. 41 N3
Murray River, P.E.I., Can. 47 U10
Murraysville, W. Va. 62 C3
Murrayville, Ill., 448 68 B4
Murrells Inlet, S.C. 63 F4
Mürren, Switz. 124 B2
Murrhardt, F.R.Ger., 8,106 118 B4
Murri, r., Col. 100 B4
Murrieta, Calif. 83 k16
Murrieta Cr., Calif. 83 k16
Murrumbidgee, r., Austl. 173 F5
Murrumburrah, Austl., 2,727 173 G5
Murrupula, Moz. 164 F4
Murrurundi, Austl., 1,106 173 G4
Murshidabad, India, 16,990 144 g13
Murska Sobota, Yug., 5,346 125 C1
Mursko Središće, Yug., 2,241 125 C1
Murten, Switz., 3,330 124 B2
Murtensee, Switz. 124 B2
Murter, i., Yug. 125 B3
Murtosa, Port., 5,779 122 A2
Murua = Woodlark
Murud, India, 10,055 145 h17
Murumuru Pt., N.Z. 175 14
Murung, r., Indon. 148 E2
Murupara, N.Z., 1,571 175 h5
Mururoa, atoll, Tuam. Arch 177 42
Murutinga, Braz., 1,604 102 E2
Murwara, India 144 c14
Murwillumbah, Austl., 6,748 173 H4
Mürz, r., Aust. 124 M6
Mürzzuschlag, Aust., 11,565 124 M6
Muş, Turk., 12,015 142 E2
Mūsā, Jabal, U.A.R. 161 K3
Mūsā, Khowr-e, inlet, Iran 143 D3
Musa, r., Terr. Papua 174 f3
Muša, r., U.S.S.R. 136 B1
Musala, P., Indon. 148 A2
Musala, Vŭrkh, mtn., Bulg. 128 D3
Musan, N. Kor. 151 F2
Musandam Pen., Muscat and Oman 143 F3
Musanga, D.R.Congo 165 m19
Musangoi, D.R.Congo 165 m18
Musa Qala, Afghan. 144 B2
Musashi, Jap. 154 g15
Musashi-Mizonokuchi, Jap. 155 m19
Musashino, Jap., 120,337 155 m19
Musay'id, Qatar 143 E4
Muscat = Masqaṭ
Muscat and Oman, ctry., 565,000* 143 F4
Muscatatuck, r., Ind. 70 C4
Muscatine, co., Iowa, 33,840 72 F3
Muscatine, Iowa, 20,997 72 G3
Muscle Shoals, Ala., 4,084 64 B1
Muscoda, Ala. 64 c8
Muscoda, Wis., 927 66 C5
Muscogee, co., Ga., 158,623 64 E3
Musconetcong, r., N.J. 61 B2
Muscoot Res., N.Y. 56 B7
Muscoy, Calif. 83 k15
Mu-Se, Burma 146 B2
Muse, Pa., 1,386 60 b8
Musestre, It. 122 f5
Musgrave Ranges, Austl. 172 D4
Mushalagan, r., Qué., Can. 45 L4
Mushalagan L., Qué., Can. 45 L4
Mushiage, Jap. 154 f15
Mushie, D.R.Congo 164 B2
Mushōno, Jap. 155 m19
Mushrif, Saudi Ar. 143 C5
Mushu, i., Terr. New Guin. 174 d1
Musi, r., Indon. 148 B3
Muskeget Chan., Mass. 57 P7
Muskeget I., Mass. 57 P7
Muskeg L., Ont., Can. 74 G1
Muskego, Wis., 10,497 66 E6
Muskegon, co., Mich., 149,943 67 G5
Muskegon, Mich., 46,485 67 G5
Muskegon, r., Mich. 67 H5
Muskegon Heights, Mich., 19,552 67 G5
Muskegon L., Mich. 67 G5
Mus-Khaya, G., U.S.S.R. 135 O3
Muskingum, co., Ohio, 79,159 70 H3
Muskingum, r., Ohio 70 H3
Muskö, Swed. 120 f8
Muskogee, co., Okla., 61,866 76 H2
Muskogee, Okla., 38,059 76 H2
Muskoka, L., Ont., Can. 46 E4
Muskoka Lakes, Ont., Can. 46 E3
Muskwa, Br. Col., Can. 42 F1
Muskwa, r., Br. Col., Can. 42 F1
Muslyumovo, U.S.S.R. 137 k8
Musokantanda, Congo L. 165 m19
Musoma, Tanz. 164 E2
Musoshi, Congo L. 165 n19
Musquacook Lakes, Me. 55 C2
Musquacook Mtn., Me. 55 C2
Musquash, N.B., Can. 47 S11
Musques, Sp., 4,761 122 m11
Musquodoboit Harbour, N.S., Can. 47 U11
Musra Ali, mtn., Eth. 163 L3
Mussau, i., Terr. New Guin. 174 f1
Musselburgh, U.K., 17,273 112 E4
Mussel Cr., Mo. 72 E5
Musselkanaal, Neth. 115 F2
Musselshell, co., Mont., 4,888 81 E2
Musselshell, r., Mont. 81 F2
Musser L., Wis. 66 C3
Mussidan, Fr., 3,138 117 D4
Mussomeli, It., 15,754 123 D6
Mussoorie, India, 9,849 144 b10
Mussum, F.R.Ger., 1,974 119 B1
Mustafakemalpaşa, Turk., 20,874 142 A1
Mustahil, Eth. 163 M5
Müstair, Switz. 124 E2
Mustang, Nepal 145 G3
Mustang, Okla., 198 76 F2
Mustér = Disentis
Musters, L., Arg. 105 A7
Mustique, i., Gren. Is. 97 20
Muston, U.K. 114 H2
Mustvee, U.S.S.R., 2,300 136 B1
Musu-dan, N. Kor. 151 F2
Mušutište, Yug., 2,541 125 E3
Muswellbrook, Austl., 5,635 173 G5
Mut, Turk., 4,594 142 C2
Mūt, U.A.R. 161 J3
Mutá, P. do, Braz. 103 J4
Mutalau, Niue 177 32
Mu-tan, r., China 150 H2
Mu-tan-chiang, China, 250,000* 150 H2
Mutanda, Zambia 165 n20
Mutankiang = Mu-tan-chiang
Mutarara, Moz. 164 E4
Mutcho Pt., Saipan 176 27
Mutějovice, Czech. 126 c6
Muthill, U.K. 112 c7
Muti, i., Eniwetok 176 28
Muting, Indon. 149 L4
Mutnaya, U.S.S.R. 137 h7
Mutoray, U.S.S.R. 135 K3
Mutsamudu, Arch. des Comores, 4,819 165 G4
Mutscheid, F.R.Ger., 1,404 118 A3
Mutshatsha, D.R.Congo 165 m19
Mutsu-wan, Jap. 155 G1
Muttaburra, Austl. 173 F3
Muttenz, Switz., 11,963 124 B1
Mutterstadt, F.R.Ger., 7,935 119 E6
Mutton Bay, Qué., Can. 45 P5
Muttontown, N.Y., 1,265 58 e13
Mutual, Ohio, 163 70 F2
Mutual, Okla., 84 76 D1
Mutum, Mc. Gro., Braz., 3,212 103 F5
Mutum, Ms. Gs., Braz., 3,318 103 f17
Mutur, Cey. 145 F8
Muturi, Indon. 149 K3
Mutwanga, D.R.Congo 165 d13
Mutzig, Fr., 4,187 116 d9
Mutzschen, Ger.D.R. 126 b5
Mu-ua, i., Terr. Papua 174 3
Muxima, Ang. 164 B3
Muya, U.S.S.R. 135 L4
Muyinga, Burundi 165 e15
Muynak, U.S.S.R., 10,400 134 E5
Muyumba, D.R.Congo 164 D3
Muyun-Kum, Peski, U.S.S.R. 137 f3
Muzaffarābād, Pak. 145 E2
Muzaffarnagar, India, 87,622 145 F3
Muzaffarpur, India, 109,048 145 G4
Muzhi, U.S.S.R. 134 F3
Muzillac, Fr., 2,189 116 B3
Muzo, Col. 101 e14
Múzquiz, Mex., 12,659 92 E2
Muz Tagh, China 150 B3
Muz Tagh Ata, China 150 A3
Mvouti, Congo 164 A2
Mwadingusha, D.R.Congo 164 D3
Mwadui, Tanz. 164 E2
Mwanza, D.R.Congo 164 D3
Mwanza, Tanz., 19,877 164 E2
Mwaya, Tanz. 164 E3
Mweelrea, mtn., Ire. 113 A5
Mweka, D.R.Congo 164 C2
Mwene Ditu, D.R.Congo 164 C3
Mwenga, D.R.Congo 164 D2
Mweru, L., D.R.Congo-Zambia 164 D3
Mwilambwe, D.R.Congo 165 m18
Mwinilunga, Zambia 164 D3
Myaing, Burma, 1,999 147 f7
Myakit, U.S.S.R. 135 P3
Myakka, Fla. 65 d13
Myakka, r., Fla. 65 G5
Myakka City, Fla. 65 d13
Myakka Head, Fla. 65 d13
My An, S. Viet. 147 k11
Myanaung, Burma, 11,155 146 A3
Myatlevo, U.S.S.R. 136 a6
Myaung, Burma, 6,867 146 A2
Myaungmya, Burma, 24,532 146 A3
Myawadi, Burma 146 B3
Mycenae, Gr. 129 D6
My Chi, N. Viet. 147 h9
Myddle, U.K. 114 C5
Myebon, Burma, 3,492 146 A2
Myers, N.Y. 59 G6
Myers Chuck, Alaska 85 M5
Myers Flat, Calif. 82 B2
Myerstown, Pa., 3,268 61 K5
Myingyan, Burma, 36,536 146 A2
Myinmu, Burma, 7,081 147 f7
Myinthi, Burma 147 f6
Myitkyina, Burma, 12,833 146 B1
Myitkyo, Burma 147 b2
Myitmaka, r., Burma 147 a2
Myitnge, Burma, 3,888 147 g7
Myitnge, r., Burma 146 B2
Myitta, Burma 146 B4
Myittha, Burma 147 g7
Myittha, r., Burma 146 A2
Myjava, Czech. 126 C2
Mykines, i., Faeroe Is. 120 c7
Mykland, Nor. 121 A2
Mylith Park, Ill. 69 b7
Mylo, N. Dak., 103 74 C1
Mymensingh, Pak., 53,256 145 H4
Mynämäki, Fin. 120 E3
Myn-Aral, U.S.S.R. 134 G5
Mynzhilgi, G., U.S.S.R. 137 e3
Myōga, Jap. 154 e16
Myo-gyi, Burma 147 g7
Myohaung, Burma, 6,556 146 A2
Myohla, Burma, 3,333 146 A3
Myōji, Jap., 7,051 155 D4
Myōjin, Jap. 154 e15
Myōkō-zan, Jap. 155 E3
Myotha, Burma 147 f7
My Phuoc, S. Viet. 147 k12
Myra, Me. 55 D4
Myra, Wis. 66 E5
Myra, ruins, Turk. 142 B2
Mýrdalsjökull, ice cap, Ice. 120 a6
Myricks (part of Berkley), Mass. 57 M5
Myrnam, Alta., Can. 42 K3
Myrtle, Man., Can. 43 g10
Myrtle, Miss., 313 73 F3
Myrtle Beach, S.C., 7,834 63 F4
Myrtle Creek, Oreg., 2,231 80 B4
Myrtle Grove, Fla. 65 B2
Myrtle Point, Oreg., 2,886 80 A4
Myrtle Springs, Tex. 76 g9
Myrtlewood, Ala., 403 64 B3
Mysen, Nor. 120 B4
Mysingen, bay, Swed. 120 f9
Mys Kamennyy, U.S.S.R. 134 G3
Myski, U.S.S.R., 32,200 137 r11
Myślenice, Pol., 8,327 127 C4
Myślibórz, Pol., 7,470 127 A2
Mysłowice, Pol., 40,000* 127 i6
Mysore, st., India, 23,586,772 145 E7
Mysore, India, 253,865 145 E7
Mystic, Conn., 2,536 56 J7
Mystic, Ga., 274 64 F4
Mystic, Iowa, 761 72 E4
Mystic Grove (part of Charlton), Mass. 56 H4
Mys-Vkhodnoy, U.S.S.R. 135 H2
Mysy, U.S.S.R. 137 h6
Mys Zhelaniya, U.S.S.R. 134 F2
Myszków, Pol., 13,466 127 C3
My Tho, S. Viet., 51,713 146 D5
Mytilene = Mitilíni
Mytilene Chan., Gr.-Turk. 129 F5
Mytishchi, U.S.S.R., 104,000 136 b6
Myto, Czech. 126 c7
Myton, Utah, 329 78 D1
My Xuyen, S. Viet., 12,135 147 m12
Mže, r., Czech. 126 c7
Mzimba, Malawi 164 E3

N

Naab, r., F.R.Ger. 118 C4
Naafkoph, mtn., Liecht. 124 D1
Naaldwijk, Neth., 8,700 115 C3
Naalehu, Hawaii, 952 84 F4
Naanika, i., Tarawa 175 15
Naarden, Neth. 115 c6
Naas, Ire., 3,915 113 C5
Naba, Jap. 154 f15
Nababiep, S. Af., 6,418 164 B6
Nabadwip, India, 72,861 145 H5
Nabari, Jap., 33,904 155 E4
Nabas, Phil., 1,650 153 B3
Nabb, Ind. 70 D4
Nabberu, L., Austl. 172 B3
Nabburg, F.R.Ger., 3,966 118 D4
Nabeina, Tarawa 175 15
Naberezhnyye Chelny, U.S.S.R., 25,000 134 E4
Nabesna, Alaska 85 J3
Nabesna Village, Alaska 85 J3
Nabha, India, 30,603 145 E3
Nabingora, Uganda 165 e13
Nabire, Indon. 149 K3
Nabisipi, r., Qué., Can. 45 O5
Nabnasset, Mass., 1,381 57 L2
Naboomspruit, S. Af., 3,036 164 D6
Nabugá, Col. 100 B4
Nābul, Tun., 14,047 161 F1
Nābulus, Jor., 45,773 142 C3
Naburn, U.K. 114 F3
Nacala, Moz. 164 F4
Nacaome, Hond., 4,737 94 D4
Na Cham, N. Viet. 147 i8
Naches, Wash. 680 80 C2
Naches, r., Wash. 80 C2
Na-ch'i, China 152 B1
Nachikapau L., Qué., Can. 45 M3
Náchod, Czech., 18,593 126 C1
Na-chou, China 152 a6
Nacimiento, Chile, 3,823 104 e17
Nacimiento Mts., N. Mex. 79
Nacimiento Res., Calif. 82 C5
Nacka, Swed. 120 f8
Nackara, Austl. 172 c7
Naco, Mex., 2,364 92 C1
Naco, Ariz. 78 D6
Nacogdoches, co., Tex., 28,046 77 Q4
Nacogdoches, Tex., 12,674 77 Q4
Nacozari, r., Mex. 92 C1
Nacozari Viejo, Mex. 92 C1
Nadachi, Jap., 3,899 155 E3
Nadeau, Mich. 66 F3
Nadiad, India, 78,952 145 D5
Nadina River, Br. Col., Can. 42 E3
Nadine, N. Mex. 79 D5
Nădlac, Rum. 128 C1
Nadolice Wielkopolski, Pol. 127 g5
Na Don, N. Viet. 147 h8
Nador, Alg. 160 b6
Nador, Mor., 17,583 160 D2
Nădrag, Rum. 128 D2
Nádudvar, Hung., 10,380 126 E3
Nadur, Malta, 4,136 123 f12
Nadvornaya, U.S.S.R., 9,500 136 A3
Nady, Ark. 73 D3
Nadym, U.S.S.R. 134 G3
Nadym, r., U.S.S.R. 134 G3
Nadzab, Terr. New Guin. 174 e2
Nærbö, Nor. 120 A4
Nærum, Den. 121 a7
Næstved, Den. 19,617 121 D5
Nafada, Nigeria 162 F4
Näfels, Switz., 3,617 124 C1
Naftah, Alg. 160 F2
Naftah, Tun., 14,584 160 F2
Naftan Pt., Saipan 176 27
Naft-e Safīd, Iran, 6,183 143 D2
Nāg, Pak. 144 B4
Naga, Indon. 149 F5
Naga, Luzon, Phil., 13,554 153 B2
Naga, Cebu, Phil., 4,646 153 e11
Nagahama, Jap., 18,246 155 C5
Nagahama, Jap., 47,700 155 E4
Naga Hills, Burma-India 146 A1
Nagai, Jap., 36,211 155 F2
Nagaichō, Jap. 155 m20
Nagai I., Alaska 85 E5
Nagaland, st., India, 369,200 145 K4
Nagambie, Austl. 173 e11
Nagano, Jap. 154 h15
Nagano, Jap., 160,522 155 E3
Naganuma, Jap. 155 n19
Nagao, Jap., 9,419 154 f15
Nagaoka, Jap. 148,254 155 F3
Nagapattinam, India, 59,063 145 F8
Nagara, Jap. 154 h14
Nagara, r., Jap. 155 E4
Nagareyama, Jap., 19,077 155 m19
Nagarote, Nic. 5,619 94 D4
Nagasaki, Jap., 344,153 154 A5
Nagasawa, Jap. 154 e16
Nagasawa, Jap. 154 h14
Nagase, Jap. 154 h15
Nagashima, Jap., 15,649 155 E4
Naga-shima, Jap. 154 B5
Nagasu, Jap., 20,341 154 B5
Nagatani, Jap. 154 g15
Nagato, Jap., 30,903 154 B4
Nagawicka L., Wis. 66 c11
Nagbalayong, Phil., 1,529 153 b8
Nageezi, N. Mex. 79 B3
Nagercoil, India, 106,207 145 E8
Nagichot, Sudan 163 K5
Nagina, India, 30,427 144 b11
Nagir, Pak. 145 E1
Nagisa, Jap. 154 i14
Nagłowice, Pol. 127 k6
Nago, Ryukyu Is., 19,198 154 c12
Nagod, India, 5,846 144 c13
Nagold, F.R.Ger., 7,369 118 B4
Nagold, r., F.R.Ger. 119 F7
Nagor, India, 24,296 145 D4
Nagornyy, U.S.S.R. 135 M4
Nago-wan, Ryukyu Is. 154 a10
Nagoya, Jap., 1,591,935 155 E4
Nagpur, India, 643,659 145 F5
Nags Head, N.C. 63 J2
Nags Head, cliff, St. Christopher, 97 6
Nagua, Dom. Rep., 9,337 96 n6
Naguabo, P.R. 3,396 96 u10
Naguanagua, Ven. 101 a11
Naguilian, Phil., 4,827 153 B1
Naguilian, Phil., 2,056 153 b6
Nagyatád, Hung., 8,801 126 C3
Nagybajom, Hung., 4,983 126 C3
Nagybátony, Hung., 7,211 126 D3
Nagyecsed, Hung., 8,363 126 F3
Nagyhalász, Hung., 6,658 126 E2
Nagykálló, Hung., 11,843 126 E3
Nagykanizsa, Hung., 34,222 126 C3
Nagykáta, Hung., 11,929 126 D3
Nagykőrös, Hung., 25,861 126 D3
Nagyléta, Hung., 6,904 126 F3
Nagy Magyar Alföld, plain, Hung. 126 ·
Nagymaros, Hung., 5,173 126 D3
Nagyszénás, Hung., 7,442 126 E3
Naha, Ryukyu Is., 251,661 154 c12
Nahan, India, 12,439 144 a10
Nahant, Mass., 3,960(T) 57 N3
Nahant Bay, Mass. 57 N3
Nahari, Jap., 7,293 155 C5
Nahariya, Isr., 14,574 142 a7
Nahar-Ouassel, r., Alg. 160 c6
Nahāvand, Iran, 20,972 143 D2
Nahbollenbach, F.R.Ger., 2,243 119 C5
Nahcotta, Wash. 80 A2
Nahe, r., F.R.Ger. 118 A4
Nahiku, Hawaii 84 E3
Nahma, Mich. 67 G3
Nahmakanta L., Me. 55 C3
Naho, Sol. Is. 175 c3
Na-hsüeh-pi-ju, China 150 C4
Nahualá, Guat., 1,148 94 b9
Nahuatzen, Mex., 3,976 93 c10
Nahuel Huapi, L., Arg. 105 f15
Nahuel Huapi, Pq. Nac., Arg. 105 A6
Nahuel Niyeu, Arg. 105 B6
Nahuel Rucá, Arg. 105 c13
Nahuizalco, El Salv., 4,261 94 d10
Nahunta, Ga., 952 64 G4
Naiak, Afghan. 144 C2
Naic, Phil., 4,253 153 b8
Naica, Mex. 92 D2
Naicam, Sask., Can. 43 D4
Naiden, Jap. 154 e15
Naiguatá, Ven., 6,833 101 c11
Naikliu, Indon. 149 G5
Naiku, Jap. 154 g14
Naila, F.R.Ger., 6,436 118 C3
Nailsea, U.K., 4,173 114 C8
Nailsworth, U.K., 3,634 114 D7
Nai-man-ch'i, China 151 D2
Nain, Newf., Can. 45 O3
Nā'īn, Iran, 4,681 143 E2
Naindi, Fiji 174 4
Naini Tal, India, 16,080 144 b11
Nainpur, India, 13,728 144 c14
Naipu, Rum. 128 E2
Nairai, i., Fiji 174 4
Nairn, Ont., Can. 46 C2
Nairn, co., U.K., 8,421 112 E3
Nairn, U.K., 4,899 112 E3
Nairn, r., U.K. 112 D3
Nairobi, Kenya, 297,000* 164 F2
Nairobi Nat. Pk., Kenya 165 h14
Naitaumba, i., Fiji 174 4
Naivasha, Kenya 164 E2
Naivasha, L., Kenya 165 h14
Najafābād, Iran, 30,422 143 E2
Najasa, r., Cuba 96 e2
Nájera, Sp., 4,014 122 D1
Naj' Ḩammādī, U.A.R., 7,900* 161 K3
Najibabad, India, 34,310 144 a11
Najin, N. Kor. 151 F2
Najo, Eth. 163 K4
Najrān, Saudi Ar. 143 C5
Naju, S. Kor., 25,262 151 E4
Naka, Jap. 154 g15
Naka, Malay., 1,454 148 B1
Naka, r., Jap. 154 f16
Naka, r., Jap. 155 G3
Nakadōri-shima, Jap. 154 A5
Nakagumi, Jap. 154 h15
Nakagusuku-wan, Ryukyu Is. 154 a11
Nakahata, Jap. 154 f14
Nakai, Jap. 154 g14
Nakaibito, N. Mex. 79 A4
Nakajō, Jap., 12,786 155 F2
Naka-Kawabe, Jap., 8,977 154 h14
Nakalele Pt., Hawaii 84 E2
Naka-Minato, Jap., 34,522 155 G3
Nakamti = Lekempti
Nakamura, Jap., 38,951 155 C5
Nakamura, Jap. 154 e16
Nakamura, Jap. 154 g16
Nakamura, Jap. 154 h14
Nakano, Jap. 154 f15
Nakano, Jap. 154 h15
Nakano, Jap. 155 n20
Nakano, Jap. 155 m19
Nakano, Jap., 37,035 155 F3
Nakanogō, Jap. 154 h14
Nakano-shima, Jap. 154 d12
Nakano-shima, Jap. 155 C3
Nakaoku, Jap. 154 h15
Nakasato, Jap., 16,693 155 G1
Naka-Satsunai, Jap., 5,148 155 K8
Naka-Shibetsu, Jap., 13,566 155 L8
Nakashima, Jap. 154 f16
Nakashima, Jap. 154 h14
Nakasone, Ryukyu Is. 154 a10
Nakatane, Jap., 18,670 154 k17
Nakato, Jap. 154 g15
Naka-Tombetsu, Jap., 7,366 155 K7
Nakatsu, Jap., 61,667 154 B5
Nakatsugawa, Jap., 47,492 155 E4
Nakazato, Jap. 155 m19
Nakazu, Jap. 154 f16
Nakéty, N. Caled. 174 k8
Nakhichevan', U.S.S.R., 27,000 134 D6
Nakhodka, U.S.S.R., 71,000 135 N5
Nakhon Nayok, Thai., 8,029 146 C4
Nakhon Pathom, Thai., 28,425 146 B4
Nakhon Phanom, Thai., 15,725 146 D3
Nakhon Ratchasima, Thai., 42,218 146 C4
Nakhon Sawan, Thai., 34,947 146 B4
Nakhon Si Thammarat, Thai., 25,919 146 C5
Nakhon Thai, Thai. 146 C3
Nakhrachi, U.S.S.R. 134 F4
Nakina, Br. Col., Can. 42 C1
Nakina, Ont., Can. 44 F5
Nakina, N.C. 63 F3
Nakina, r., Br. Col., Can. 42 C1
Nakiri, Jap. 155 E4
Nakléřov, Czech. 126 d6
Nakło, Pol., 13,540 127 B2
Naknek, Alaska, 249 85 E4
Naknek L., Alaska 85 F4
Nakodar, India, 14,452 144 a10
Nakoso, Jap., 48,117 155 G3
Nakskov, Den., 16,639 121 D6
Naktong, r., S. Kor. 151 F4
Nakuru, Kenya, 37,900* 164 E2
Nakuru, L., Kenya 165 h14
Nakusp, Br. Col., Can. 42 H4
Nāl, r., Pak. 144 B4
Nalayha, Mong. 150 E2
Nalbach, F.R.Ger., 3,167 116 c8
Nalbari, India, 9,285 145 J4
Nal'chik, U.S.S.R., 98,000 134 D5
Nałęczów, Pol., 3,850 127 E3
Nalgonda, India, 24,383 145 F6
Nalinnes, Belg., 3,130 115 C4
Nallen, W. Va. 62 D4
Nālūt, Libya 161 F2
Nam, r., N. Kor. 151 E3
Nama, Sta. Cruz Is. 175 6
Nama, i., Car. Is. 176 18
Namacurra, Moz. 164 F4
Namai Bay, Palau 176 21
Namak, Daryacheh-ye, Iran 143 E2
Namakan L., Ont., Can. 74 F1
Namakkal, India, 19,935 145 m20
Namakzār, salt pan, Afghan.-Iran 143 G2
Namanga, Kenya 164 F2
Namangan, U.S.S.R., 134,000 134 G5
Namanyere, Tanz. 164 E3
Namao, Alta., Can. 43 b7
Namapa, Moz. 164 F4
Namaqualand = Great Namakwaland and Little Namakwaland
Namarrói, Moz. 164 F4
Namashi, Nepal 144 e11
Namatanai, Terr. New Guin. 174 g1
Namathu, Fiji 174 4
Namboma Falls, Zambia 164 C4
Nambour, Austl., 4,678 173 H4
Nambouwalu, Fiji 174 4
Nambucca Heads, Austl., 1,998 173 H4
Nam Can, S. Viet., 3,417 146 D5
Namcha Barwa = Na-mu-cho-pa-erh-wa
Nāmche Bāzār, Nepal 144 f12
Nam Dinh, N. Viet., 86,132 146 D2
Nam Du, Hon, S. Viet. 147 k12
Nameh, Indon. 148 F2
Namekagon, r., Wis. 66 B3
Namekagon L., Wis. 66 B2
Namekawa, Jap. 155 n19
Namepi Cr., Alta., Can. 43 b6
Namerikawa, Jap., 31,392 155 E3
Náměstovo, Czech. 126 D2
Nametil, Moz. 164 F4
Namhkam, Burma 146 B2
Nam-hoi = Fo-shan
Namib Des., S.-W. Af. 164 B5
Namie, Jap., 14,085 155 G3
Namioka, Jap., 24,129 155 G1
Namiquipa, Mex. 92 D2
Namjang-ni, N. Kor. 151 F2
Namkhana, India 144 g15
Namlea, Indon. 149 H3
Namoluk, atoll, Car. Is. 176 18
Namonuito, atoll, Car. Is. 176 18
Namorik, atoll, Marsh. Is. 176 22
Nampa, Alta., Can. 42 J2
Nampa, Idaho, 18,013 81 A4
Nam Phong, Thai. 146 C3
Namp'o, N. Kor. 151 E3
Nampō-shotō, Japan 170 D2
Nampula, Moz. 164 F4
Namsen, r., Nor. 120 C2
Nam Shan, China 150 D3
Namsos, Nor., 5,291 120 B2
Nam Tsho, China 150 C4
Namtsy, U.S.S.R. 135 M3
Namtu, Burma, 12,780 146 B2
Nam-tu, r., China 152 C4
Namu, r., Br. Col., Can. 42 E3
Namu, atoll, Marsh. Is. 176 22
Namua, i., W. Samoa 177 38
Na-mu-cho-pa-erh-wa, mtn., China 150 C4
Namuka-i-Lau, i., Fiji 174 4
Namuli, Sa., Moz. 164 F4
Namur, Belg., 33,062 115 C4
Namur, i., Kwajalein 176 25
Namwala, Zamb. 164 D4
Namwŏn, S. Kor., 39,362 151 E4
Namy, U.S.S.R. 135 N3
Namysłów, Pol., 8,012 127 B3
Nan, Thai., 13,802 146 C3
Nan, r., Thai. 146 C3
Nanacamilpa, Mex., 5,283 93 f10
Nana Candundo, Ang. 164 C3
Nanae, Jap., 18,076 155 J9
Nanaimo, Br. Col., Can., 13,551 42 F4
Nanaimo, r., Br. Col., Can. 42 b6
Nanakuli, Hawaii, 2,745 84 C2

266 · Nanam—Nerchau

Nanam, N. Kor. 151 F2
Nan-an, China 152 E2
Nanango, Austl., 1,353 173 H4
Nan-ao, China 152 E3
Nanao, Jap., 50,121 155 E3
Nanatsu-shima, Jap. 155 E3
Nancagua, Chile, 1,961 104 f14
Nance, co., Nebr., 5,635 75 G2
Nancefield, S. Af. 165 i17
Nan-chang, China 152 C1
Nan-ch'ang, China, 510,000* 150 F4
Nan-chao, China 151 B4
Nan-ch'eng, China 152 E2
Nan-ch'i, China 152 B1
Nan-chiang, China 152 B1
Nan-chi Lieh-tao, China 152 F2
Nan-ching, Chiang-su, China, 1,419,000* 150 F3
Nan-ching, F-ch., China 152 E2
Nanchititla, Mex. 93 d11
Nan-ch'uan, China 152 B1
Nan-ch'ung, China 152 B1
Nancowry I., India 146 A6
Nancy, Fr., 133,532 117 G2
Nancy Flowage, L., Wis. 66 A2
Nanda Devi, pk., India 145 F3
Nandaime, Nic., 6,256 94 E5
Nandarivatu, Fiji 174 4
Nanded, India, 81,087 145 E6
Nandgaon, India, 13,026 145 i16
Nandi, Fiji 174 4
Nandi Hills, Kenya 165 g13
Nandikotkur, India, 12,130 145 F7
Nandongo, i., Fiji 174 4
Nandurbar, India, 41,055 145 D5
Nandy, Fr. 116 i12
Nandyal, India, 42,927 145 F7
Nan-feng, China 150 F4
Nanga-Eboko, Cam., 3,000* 162 G5
Nanga Julau, Malay. 148 E2
Nangalangki, Indon. 148 D3
Nangal Dam, India 144 a10
Nangaobat, Indon. 148 E2
Nanga Parbat, mtn., Pak. 145 E2
Nangapinoh, Indon. 148 E3
Nangaraun, Indon. 148 E2
Nangatajap, Indon. 148 D3
Nang-ch'ien, China 150 D3
Nangin, Burma 146 B5
Nangis, Fr., 3,761 117 E2
Nangka, Phil., 3,040 153 d12
Nangnim-sanmaek, N. Kor. 151 E2
Nangō, Jap., 12,908 154 B6
Nang Rong, Thai. 146 C4
Nan-hai = Fo-shan
Nan-ho, China 151 B3
Nan-hsien, China 152 D1
Nan-hsiung, China 150 F4
Nan-hui, China 152 F1
Nan-i Hu, China 152 E1
Nanjangud, India, 17,599 145 k19
Nan-k'ang, China 152 D2
Nanking = Nan-ching
Nan-kung, China 151 B3
Nan-lang, China 152 a6
Nan-ling, China 152 E1
Nan Ling, China 150 F4
Nanmatol Is., Ponape 176 29
Nan-ming, r., China 152 B2
Nan-ning, China, 250,000* 150 E5
Nannup, Austl. 172 A5
Na Noi, Thai. 146 C3
Nanomea, i., Ellice Is. 170 F5
Nanoose Bay, Br. Col., Can. 42 b6
Nan-p'an, r., China 150 E4
Nanpara, India, 14,576 144 c12
Nan-p'i, China 151 C3
Nan-p'ing, China 150 F4
Nan-pu, China 152 B1
Nansei-shotō, Jap. and U.S. Admin. 154 c13
Nansemond, co., Va., 31,366 62 H6
Nansen Basin, Arctic Oc. 108 M1
Nansen Sd., N.W.T., Can. 41 L1
Nansio, Tanz. 164 E2
Nanson, N. Dak. 74 C1
Nant, Fr., 1,057 117 E4
Nantahala, N.C. 63 b7
Nantahala, r., N.C. 63 b7
Nantahala L., N.C. 63 b7
Nantais, L., Qué., Can. 44 K1
Nan-tan, China 152 B2
Nantasket Beach (part of Hull), Mass. 57 N3
Nanterre, Fr., 83,528 116 g11
Nantes, Fr., 246,227 117 C3
Nanteuil-lès-Meaux, Fr., 2,181 116 k11
Nantiat, Fr., 1,418 117 D3
Nantiati, C., Ponape 176 29
Nanticoke, Md. 62 J4
Nanticoke, Pa., 15,601 61 K3
Nanticoke, r., Del.-Md. 62 J4
Nantmel, U.K. 114 A6
Nanton, Alta., Can., 1,048 42 J4
Nan-t'ou, Taiwan, 52,079 152 F3
Nantouillet, Fr. 116 i11
Nantua, Fr., 3,647 117 F3
Nantucket, co., Mass., 3,559 57 Q7
Nantucket, Mass., 2,804; 3,559(T) 57 Q7
Nantucket Hbr., Mass. 57 Q7
Nantucket I., Mass. 57 Q8
Nantucket Sd., Mass. 57 P6
Nan-t'ung, China 150 G3
Nantwich, U.K., 10,454 113 E5
Nantyglo, U.K., 10,959 114 B7
Nanty Glo, Pa., 4,608 60 E5
Nantymoel, U.K., 3,412 114 A7
Nanualele Pt., Hawaii 84 F3
Nanuet, N.Y. 58 c12
Nanuku Passage, Fiji 174 4
Nanumanga, i., Ellice Is. 175 10
Nanuque, Braz., 18,073 103 H5
Nan-wan Res., China 152 D1
Nan-yang, China 150 F3
Nanyuki, Kenya 164 F1
Nao, C. de la, Sp. 122 F3
Nao Chou, China 152 C3
Naococane L., Qué., Can. 45 L4
Naoetsu, Jap., 43,304 155 F3
Naogaon, Pak., 20,276 144 g13
Naokok, Alaska 85 D1
Naomid Des., Afghan.-Iran 143 G2
Naomi Pk., Utah 78 c7
Náousa, Gr., 15,492 129 D4
Náousa, Gr., 1,219 129 E6
Napa, co., Calif., 65,890 82 B3
Napa, Calif., 22,170 82 B3
Napa, r., Calif. 83 e11
Napadogan, N.B., Can. 47 S10
Napaiskak, Alaska, 154 85 D3
Napakiak, Alaska, 190 85 D3
Napaku, Indon. 148 E2
Napaliong, Phil., 1,011 153 c6
Napalkovo, U.S.S.R. 134 G2
Napan, Indon. 149 K3
Napanee, Ont., Can., 4,500 44 J7
Napanoch, N.Y. 59 M8
Napas, U.S.S.R. 134 H4
Napata, ruins, Sudan 163 K2
Napatree Pt., R.I. 56 J7
Napavine, Wash., 314 80 B2
Napé, Laos 146 D3
Naper, Nebr., 198 75 F1
Naperville, Ill., 12,933 68 D2
Na Pieng, N. Viet. 147 h8
Napier, N.Z., 24,579 175 h5
Napier, S. Af., 1,523 164 a9
Napier, Tenn. 71 D6
Napier, Mt., Austl. 172 D2
Napier Broome Bay, Austl. 172 C1
Napierville, Qué., Can., 1,768 47 L3
Napipe, Morne, Haiti 96 m6
Naples, It. = Napoli
Naples, Fla., 4,655 65 H6
Naples, Idaho 81 A1
Naples, Ill., 92 68 B4
Naples, Me. 55 B5
Naples, N.Y., 1,237 58 E6
Naples, S. Dak., 36 74 D3
Naples, Tex., 1,692 77 Q3
Napo, r., Ec.-Peru 104 C2
Napoleon, Ind., 290 70 D3
Napoleon, Mich. 67 J6
Napoleon, N. Dak., 1,078 74 C2
Napoleon, Ohio, 6,739 70 E1
Napoleonville, La., 1,148 73 E8
Napoli, It., 1,150,393 123 E4
Napoli, N.Y. 58 C7
Napoli, Golfo di, It. 123 c10
Naponee, Nebr., 206 75 F3
Napoopoo, Hawaii 84 F4
Napoule, G. de la, Fr. 116 m13
Nappanee, Ind., 3,895 70 D1
Napuka, i., Tuam. Arch. 171 J5
Nara, Jap., 134,577 155 D4
Nara, Mali, 2,206 162 C3
Nara, r., Pak. 144
Nara, r., U.S.S.R. 136 b6
Naracoorte, Austl., 3,329 172 F5
Naradhan, Austl. 173 f9
Naraini, India 144 c13
Na Rak, Thai. 147 a6
Naranja, Fla., 2,509 65 J7
Naranjal, Ec., 2,919 104 B2
Naranjal, r., Ec. 104 c11
Naranjito, P.R., 2,719 96 t10
Naranjo, C.R., 2,387 94 E5
Narasapatnam, India, 22,768 145 G6
Narashino, Jap., 42,167 155 n19
Narathiwat, Thai., 17,613 146 C6
Nara Visa, N. Mex. 79 D4
Nārāyanganj, Pak., 162,056 145 H5
Narayanpet, India, 20,504 145 E6
Narbada = Narmada
Narberth, Pa., 5,109 60 f11
Narbonne, Fr., 35,899 117 E5
Narcea, r., Sp. 122 B1
Narcondam I., India 146 A4
Narcosli Creek, Br. Col., Can. 42 F3
Nardin, Okla., 142 76 F1
Nardò, It., 29,087 123 F4
Nare, Col. 101 e13
Narembeen, Austl. 172 B5
Nares Plain, Atl. Oc. 108 H5
Narew, r., Pol. 127 D2
Narimatsu, Jap. 154 f14
Nariño, Col. 101 d14
Nariño, Col. 101 e15
Narita, Jap., 43,149 155 G4
Nariwa, Jap., 11,729 154 e15
Nariwa, r., Jap. 154 e15
Narka, Kans., 166 75 H4
Narkanda, India 144 a10
Narlı, Turk. 142 D2
Narmada, r., India 145 E5
Narmidj, i., Jaluit 176 30
Narnaul, India, 23,959 144 a11
Narni, It., 21,658 123 D3
Naro, It., 15,728 123 D6
Naroch', Oz., U.S.S.R. 136 B2
Narodnaya, G., U.S.S.R. 134 F3
Naro-Fominsk, U.S.S.R., 36,000 136 b6
Narok, Kenya 165 g14
Narooma, Austl., 1,142 173 G5
Narovlya, U.S.S.R. 136 C3
Narovorovo, New Hebr. 174 m5
Närpes, Fin. 120 E3
Närpiö = Närpes
Narra, Phil., 3,000 153 A3
Narrabri, Austl., 3,722 173 G4
Narragansett, R.I. 1,741; 3,444(T) 57 L7
Narragansett Bay, R.I. 57 L6
Narragansett Pier = Narragansett
Narraguagus, r., Me. 55 E4
Narrandera, Austl., 4,418 173 F5
Narrogin, Austl., 3,768 172 B5
Narromine, Austl., 1,975 173 G5
Narrows, Oreg. 80 D4
Narrows, Va., 2,508 62 D5
Narrows, The, chan., St. Christopher-Nevis 97 6
Narrowsburg, N.Y. 59 K8
Narsinghgarh, India, 11,558 145 E5
Narsinghpur, India 145 F5
Narugo, Jap., 16,719 155 G2
Narumi, Jap., 31,519 154 h14
Naruna, Va. 62 F5
Naruto, Jap., 48,828 155 D4
Narutō, Jap., 21,298 155 n19
Naruto-kaikyō, Jap. 154 f15
Narva, U.S.S.R., 27,600 136 C1
Narvacan, Phil., 2,900 153 B1
Narvik, Nor., 13,046 120 D1
Narwana, India, 14,037 144 a11
Narwar, India 144 a13
Nar'yan-Mar, U.S.S.R., 13,200 134 E3
Narym, U.S.S.R. 134 H4
Naryn, Kir. S.S.R., U.S.S.R., 16,000 134 G5
Naryn, R.S.F.S.R., U.S.S.R. 135 J4
Naryn, r., U.S.S.R. 134 G5
Nasai, i., Terr. Papua 174 3
Năsăud, Rum., 5,725 128 E1
Naschitti, N. Mex. 79 A3
Naseby, U.K. 114 G6
Nash, U.K., 1,756 114 C7
Nash, co., N.C., 61,002 63 G1
Nash, Okla., 230 76 E1
Nashawena I., Mass. 57 N7
Nash Harbor, Alaska 85 C3
Nashino, Jap. 154 g15
Nash L., Me. 55 E3
Nashoba, Okla. 76 H3
Nashotah, Wis., 321 66 c11
Nash Pt., U.K. 113 E6
Nashport, Ohio 70 G2
Nash Str., N.H. 54 E2
Nashua, Iowa, 1,737 72 E2
Nashua, Mont., 796 81 F1
Nashua, N.H., 39,096 54 D6
Nashua, r., Mass.-N.H. 57 K2
Näshulta, Swed. 120 d8
Nashville, Ark., 3,579 73 B4
Nashville, Ga., 4,070 64 F4
Nashville, Ill., 2,606 68 C5
Nashville, Ind. 70 C3
Nashville, Mich., 1,525 67 H6
Nashville, N.Y. 58 k18
Nashville, N.C., 1,423 63 F2
Nashville, Ohio, 234 70 G2
Nashville, Tenn., 170,874 71 E5
Nashville Basin, Tenn. 51 J3
Nashwaak, r., N.B., Can. 55 E2
Nashwaaksis, N.B., Can., 2,193 47 S10
Nashwauk, Minn., 1,712 74 F2
Našice, Yug., 3,383 125 D2
Nasielsk, Pol., 5,014 127 D2
Näsijärvi, l., Fin. 120 E3
Nasik, India, 131,103 145 D5
Näsinge, Swed. 121 D1
Nasionale Kalahari-Gemsbock Wildtuin = Kalahari-Gemsbock Nat. Pk.
Nasionale Kruger Wildtuin = Kruger Nat. Pk.
Nasipit, Phil., 7,531 153 C3
Nāşir, Sudan 163 K4
Nasirabad, India, 24,148 145 E4
Naskaupi, r., Newf., Can. 45 O3
Naslednitskiy, U.S.S.R. 137 k9
Nasondoye, D.R.Congo 165 m19
Nasonville, R.I. 57 K5
Nasorolevu, pk., Fiji 174 4
Nasriganj, India, 8,920 144 d13
Nass, r., Br. Col., Can. 42 E2
Nassau, Bah. Is. 95 C1
Nassau, F.R.Ger., 2,959 119 D4
Nassau, co., Fla., 17,189 65 H2
Nassau, co., N.Y., 1,300,171 59 N10
Nassau, N.Y., 1,248 59 N6
Nassau, Pegunungan, Indon. 149 L4
Nassau I., Cook Is. 171 H5
Nassawadox, Va., 650 62 J5
Nass Harbour, Br. Col., Can. 42 D2
Nässjö, Swed. 120 C4
Nassogne, Belg., 1,018 115 D4
Nassoro, Tanz. 165 f15
Nastapoka, r., Qué., Can. 44 J3
Nastapoka Is., N.W.T., Can. 44 J2
Nastätten, F.R.Ger., 2,456 118 A3
Nasubara, Jap. 154 g15
Nasugbu, Phil., 8,468 153 B2
Nata, Bots., 1,009 164 D5
Na-ta, China 152 C4
Natá, Pan., 2,319 94 G6
Natagaima, Col. 100 C6
Natal, Braz., 154,276 103 J3
Natal, Br. Col., Can. 42 J4
Natal, Indon. 148 A2
Natal, prov., S. Af. 164 E6
Natalbany, r., La. 73 E7
Natalia, Tex., 1,154 77 O5
Natalkuz L., Br. Col., Can. 42 F3
Natanes Plat., Ariz. 78 C5
Natanya, Isr., 41,217 142 a7
Natar, Indon. 148 a6
Natashquan, Qué., Can. 45 O5
Natashquan, r., Newf., Can. 45 O4
Natchaug, r., Conn. 56 H5
Natchez, La. 73 B6
Natchez, Miss., 23,791 73 D6
Natchitoches, parish, La., 35,653 73 B6
Natchitoches, La., 13,924 73 B6
Natemachi, Jap. 154 g15
Naters, Switz., 3,797 124 B2
Natewa Bay, Fiji 174 4
Nathan, Mich. 66 F3
Na Thawi, Thai. 146 C6
Nathdwara, India, 13,890 145 D4
Nathrop, Colo. 79 B2
Nathula, i., Fiji 174 4
Natick, Mass., 28,831(T) 57 L3
Natick (part of West Warwick), R.I. 57 L6
National City, Calif., 32,771 82 c10
National City, Mich. 67 K4
National Mine, Mich. 66 F2
National Park, N.J., 3,380 60 f12
Natitingou, Dahom., 2,251 162 E4
Native Bay, N.W.T., Can. 41 N5
Natividad, I., Mex. 92 B2
Natividade, Braz., 1,243 103 G4
Natkyizin, Burma 146 B4
Natland, U.K. 114 C2
Natogyi, Burma, 4,086 147 f7
Natoma, Calif. 82 b7
Natoma, Kans., 775 75 G4
Nator, Pak., 13,317 144 g13
Nátora, Mex. 92 C2
Natoye, Belg., 1,195 115 D4
Natron, L., Tanz. 165 h15
Natrona, Ill. 68 C3
Natrona, Kans. 75 G6
Natrona, Pa., 5,000* 60 d7
Natrona, co., Wyo., 49,623 81 F4
Naţrūn, Wādī an, U.A.R. 161 i7
Nattalin, Burma, 8,927 146 A3
Nättarö, i., Swed. 120 f9
Nattavaara, Swed. 120 E2
Natu La, China-Nepal 144 g12
Natuna, Kep., Indon. 148 D2
Natural Bridge, Ala. 64 B1
Natural Bridge, N.Y. 59 K3
Natural Bridge, Va. 62 E5
Natural Bridges Nat. Mon., Utah 78 D3
Natural Dam, N.Y. 59 J3
Naturaliste, C., Austl. 172 A5
Naturaliste Chan., Austl. 172 A3
Naturita, Colo., 979 79 A2
Nauabu, Terr. Papua 174 3
Naubinway, Mich. 67 H2
Naucalpan, Mex., 10,372 93 e10
Naucelle, Fr., 2,317 117 E4
Nauders, Aust., 1,146 124 G7
Nauen, Ger.D.R., 12,336 118 D2
Naugatuck, Conn., 19,511 56 D7
Naugatuck, W. Va. 62 B5
Naugatuck, r., Conn. 56 D7
Naughton, Ont., Can. 46 C2
Nauheim, F.R.Ger., 4,637 119 E5
Naujan, Phil., 2,244 153 B2
Naumburg, Ger.D.R., 37,377 118 C3
Naumburg, N.Y. 59 K4
Naungpale, Burma 146 B3
Nā'ūr, Jor., 2,382 142 b8
Naurod, F.R.Ger., 1,725 119 E4
Nauru, Pac. Oc., 4,849 170 F4
Nauset Heights (part of Orleans), Mass. 57 R5
Naushahro Fīroz, Pak., 4,615 144 C4
Naushon I., Mass. 57 O7
Nausori, Fiji 174 4
Nauta, Peru, 1,878 104 C3
Nautanwa, India 144 d12
Nautla, Mex., 1,437 93 F4
Nauvoo, Ala., 318 64 B2
Nauvoo, Ill., 1,039 68 A3
Nauzād, Afghan. 144 B2
Nava, Mex., 3,118 93 E2
Nava del Rey, Sp., 3,860 122 C2
Navahermosa, Sp., 4,761 122 C3
Navajo, co., Ariz., 37,994 78 C4
Navajo, Ariz. 78 D4
Navajo, r., Colo. 79 B3
Navajo Agency = Window Rock
Navajo Dam, N. Mex. 79 B3
Navajo Mtn., Utah 78 C3
Navajo Nat. Mon., Ariz. 78 C3
Navajo Pk., Colo. 79 a7
Navajo Res., Colo.-N. Mex. 79 B3
Naval, Phil., 4,409 153 C3
Navalcarnero, Sp., 4,681 122 C2
Navalmoral de la Mata, Sp., 9,073 122 C3
Navan = An Uaimh
Navarin, M., U.S.S.R. 135 S3
Navarino, N.Y. 59 q24
Navarino, I., Chile 105 B9
Navarra, reg., Sp. 122 E1
Navarre, Austl. 173 d11
Navarre, Sp. = Navarra
Navarre, Fla. 65 C2
Navarre, Kans. 75 H5
Navarre, Ohio, 1,698 70 H2
Navarro, Arg., 6,890* 105 b12
Navarro, co., Tex., 34,423 77 P3
Navashino, U.S.S.R., 12,400 136 F2
Navasota, Tex., 4,937 77 Q4
Navasota, r., Tex. 77 P4
Navassa, N.C. 63 F3
Navassa Island, W.I. 95 D3
Nave, It., 6,425 122 d5
Nävekvarn, Swed. 120 d9
Naver, r., U.K. 112 D2
Naverstad, Swed. 121 D2
Navesink, N.J. 58 c15
Navesink, r., N.J. 58 c15
Navia, Sp., 8,150 122 B1
Navia, r., Sp. 122 B1
Navidad, Chile 104 f13
Navidad, r., Tex. 77 P5
Navina, Okla., 11 76 F2
Navirai, Braz. 103 F6
Naviti, i., Fiji 174 4
Navlya, U.S.S.R., 7,000 136 D2
Năvodari, Rum. 128 G2
Navojoa, Mex., 30,762 92 C2
Navolato, Mex., 6,000* 92 D3
Navoloki, U.S.S.R., 13,700 136 F1
Návpaktos, Gr., 7,080 129 C5
Návplion, Gr., 8,918 129 D6
Navrongo, Ghana 162 D4
Navsari, India, 53,600 145 D5
Navy Board Inlet, N.W.T., Can. 41 N3
Navy Town, Alaska 85 d8
Navy Yard City, Wash., 3,341 81 a7
Nawabganj, India, 7,198 144 d12
Nawābganj, Pak., 29,725 145 H4
Nawābshāh, Pak., 45,651 144 C4
Nawada, India, 17,468 144 e13
Nawai, India, 8,317 144 a12
Nawākot, Nepal 144 e12
Nawakwa L., Mich. 67 H2
Nawalapitiya, Cey., 9,862 145 n22
Nawalgarh, India, 24,911 145 E4
Nawashahr, India, 14,097 144 a10
Nawiliwili Bay, Hawaii 84 B2
Nawng Hpa, Burma 146 B2
Náxos, Gr., 2,458 129 E6
Náxos, i., Gr. 129 E6
Nay, Fr., 3,857 117 C5
Nayakhan, U.S.S.R. 135 P3
Nayarit, st., Mex., 389,929 92 D3
Nayau, i., Fiji 174 4
Naylor, Ga., 272 64 F5
Naylor, Mo., 499 72 G8
Nayón, Ec. 104 c10
Nayoro, Jap., 33,339 155 K7
Na-yung, China 152 B2
Nazaré, Braz., 14,644 103 J4
Nazaré, Port., 9,189 122 A3
Nazaré da Mata, Braz., 9,246 103 b14
Nazareno, Bol., 1,730 102 C6
Nazareth, Belg., 4,551 115 B4
Nazareth, Eth., 7,700* 163 L4
Nazareth, Isr., 25,047 142 C3
Nazareth, Pa., 6,209 61 M4
Nazareth, Tex. 77 M2
Nazarovo, U.S.S.R., 36,300 134 H4
Nazas, Mex., 2,738 92 D3
Nazas, r., Mex. 92 D3
Nazca, Peru, 13,556 104 C5
Nazca Ridge, Pac. Oc. 169 K3
Naze, Jap., 42,539 154 d12
Nazeing, U.K., 3,880 114 J7
Nazilli, Turk., 36,601 142 B2
Nāzir Hāt, Pak. 145 J5
Naziya, U.S.S.R., 11,700 136 C1
Nazko, Br. Col., Can. 42 F3
Nazón, Ec. 104 c11
Nazwá, Muscat and Oman 143 F4
Nazyvayevsk, U.S.S.R., 16,400 134 G4
Nchanga, Zambia 165 n20
Ncheu, Malawi 164 E4
Ndai, i., Sol. Is. 175 c2
N'Dali, Dahom. 162 e7
Ndélé, C.A.R., 2,847, 163 H4
Ndendé, Gabon 164 A2
Ndeni, i., Sta. Cruz Is. 175 6
Ndikeva, pk., Fiji 174 4
Ndikiniméki, Cam., 2,500* 162 F5
Ndjolé, Gabon 164 A1
Ndola, Zamb., 91,000 164 D4
Ndouci, Iv. Coast 162 a9
Ndu, D.R.Congo 164 C1
Ndui Ndui, New. Hebr. 174 K5
Ndundure, Î., Loy. Is. 174 k8
Nea, r., Nor. 120 B3
Néa Ankhíalos, Gr., 3,224 129 D5
Néa Apollonía, Gr., 1,570 129 D4
Néa Artáki, Gr., 3,173 129 D5
Néa Epídhavros, Gr., 1,246 129 D6
Néa Filippiás, Gr. 129 C5
Neagh, L., U.K. 113 C4
Neah Bay, Wash. 80 A1
Neajlov, r., Rum. 128 E2
Néa Kallikrátia, Gr., 1,943 129 D4
Neal, Kans. 75 J6
Neale, L., Austl. 172 D3
Néa Mádhitos, Gr., 1,521 129 D4
Néa Mikhanióna, Gr., 3,059 129 D4
Néa Moudhaniá, Gr., 2,600 129 D4
Néa Péramos, Gr., 1,244 129 E4
Neápolis, Gr., 1,838 129 C4
Neápolis, Gr., 2,464 129 D6
Neápolis, Gr., 2,955 129 E7
Néa Psará, Gr., 1,891 129 D5
Near Is., Alaska 85 d8
Nearman, Kans. 75 a7
Neatahwanta, L., N.Y. 59 q22
Neath, U.K., 30,935 113 E6
Néa Tríglia, Gr., 1,864 129 D4
Neauphle-le-Château, Fr., 1,317 116 f11
Neauphle-le-Vieux, Fr. 116 f11
Néa Víssi, Gr., 2,831 129 F4
Neavitt, Md. 62 H4
Néa Zíkhna, Gr., 3,942 129 D4
Neba, Jap., 3,282 155 E4
Nebaj, Guat., 4,810 94 B3
Nebish, Minn. 74 E2
Nebit-Dag, U.S.S.R., 32,900 134 E6
Nebo, Ill., 441 68 B4
Nebo, La. 73 C6
Nebo, N.C. 63 C2
Nebo, Okla. 76 G3
Nebo, Mt., Utah 78 c11
Nebra, Ger.D.R. 126 a5
Nebraska, st., U.S., 1,459,000* 75
Nebraska City, Nebr., 7,252 75 K3
Nebužely, Czech. 126 d6
Necedah, Wis., 691 66 C4
Nechanice, Czech. 127 e6
Neche, N. Dak., 545 74 D1
Neches, r., Tex. 77 Q4
Nechí, r., Col. 100 C4
Neckar, r., F.R.Ger. 118 B4
Neckarelz, F.R.Ger., 3,226 119 G6
Neckargemünd, F.R.Ger., 6,726 119 F6
Neckargerach, F.R.Ger., 1,638 119 G6
Neckarsteinach, F.R.Ger., 2,693 119 F6
Neckarsulm, F.R.Ger., 14,150 118 B4
Neckartenzlingen, F.R.Ger., 2,529 119 G7
Neckenmarkt, Aust., 1,735 124 N6
Necker I., Hawaii 84 g9
Necochea, Arg., 58,172 105 D5
Necocli, Col. 100 B3
Nedan, Bulg., 2,925 128 E3
Neded, Czech. 126 C3
Nedelino, Bulg., 3,646 129 E4
Nederbrakel, Belg., 6,453 115 B4
Nederby, Den. 121 B4
Nederland, Colo., 272 79 a8
Nederland, Tex., 12,036 77 Q5
Ned L., Mich. 66 E2
Nedlitz, Ger.D.R. 118 D2
Nedluk L., Qué., Can. 44 K2
Nedo, Jap. 155 m19
Nedrow, N.Y. 59 H6
Nedstrand, Nor. 120 A4
Nędza, Pol. 127 h6
Neeb, Sask., Can. 43 B3
Neebish I., Mich. 67 J2
Neede, Neth., 5,200 115 E2
Needham, Mass., 25,793(T) 57 M3
Needles, Calif., 4,590 82 F5
Needles, The, pt., U.K. 113 i13
Needmore, Ga. 64 G5
Needmore, Ind. 70 C4
Needmore, Okla. 76 F2
Needmore, Pa. 60 F6
Needmore, Tex. 77 M2
Needville, Tex., 861 77 Q5
Neely, Miss. 73 G6
Neelyville, Mo., 385 72 G8
Neemuch, India, 36,287 145 E4
Neenah, Wis., 18,057 66 E4
Neepawa, Man., Can., 3,127 43 E5
Neer, Neth. 119 A2
Neer-Andel, Neth. 115 c7
Neeroeteren, Belg., 5,355 115 D3
Neerpelt, Belg., 7,072 115 D3
Neeses, S.C., 347 63 C4
Neetze, F.R.Ger., 1,583 119 c9
Neetze, r., F.R.Ger. 119 c9
Neetze-Kanal, F.R.Ger. 119 b9
Neffsville, Pa. 61 K5
Neftegorsk, U.S.S.R., 8,800 136 E4
Neftekamsk, U.S.S.R. 137 h8
Neftenbach, Switz., 2,042 124 C1
Nefyn, U.K., 2,164 113 D5
Negara, Indon. 148 f8
Negaunee, Mich., 6,126 66 F2
Negev = Hanegev
Neghelli, Eth. 163 L5
Negishi, Jap. 155 m19
Negley, Ohio 70 J2
Negomano, Moz. 164 F3
Negombo, Cey., 38,628 145 F9
Negotin, Yug., 6,982 125 F2
Negotino, Yug., 2,820 125 F4
Negoya, Jap. 155 m19
Negra, P., Peru 104 A3
Negrais, C., Burma 147 a3
Negrar, It., 8,458 122 d5
Nègre, Pte., St-Barthélemy 97 7
Negreet, La. 73 B6
Negreira, Sp., 8,538 122 A1
Negreiros, Chile 105 A1
Negreşti, Rum. 128 D1
Negreşti, Rum. 128 F1
Negrete, Chile, 2,435 104 e17
Negril, Jam., 1,101 96 o8
Negril Hill, Jam. 96 o8
Negrillos, Bol. 102 a11
Negrito Cr., N. Mex. 79 A5
Negro, r., Arg. 105 B5
Negro, r., Bol. 102 D4
Negro, r., Mo. Go., Braz. 103 E5
Negro, r., Amaz., Braz. 102 D2
Negro, r., Col. 101 e14
Negro, r., Jam. 96 q9
Negro, r., Para. 105 D2
Negro, r., Urug. 105 c11
Negro, r., Ven. 100 D3
Negro o Chixoy, r., Guat. 94 b8
Negros, i., Phil. 153 B3
Negru Vodă, Rum. 128 G3
Nehalem, Oreg., 233 80 B3
Nehalem, r., Oreg. 80 B3
Neheim-Hüsten, F.R.Ger., 32,012 119 E2
Nehoiu, Rum. 128 F2
Néhoué, B. de, N. Caled. 174 h8
Neiba, Dom. Rep., 7,322 96 m6
Neiba, B. de, Dom. Rep. 96 m6
Nei-chiang, China, 190,000* 150 E4
Nei-ch'iu, China 151 B3
Neige, Crêt de la, ridge, Fr. 117 F3
Neiges, Piton des, La Réunion 165 b11
Neihart, Mont., 150 81 D2
Nei-hsiang, China 151 A4
Nei-huang, China 151 B4
Neikban, Burma, 1,898 147 a2
Neilburg, Sask., Can. 43 B4
Nei-ling-ting, i., China 152 a6
Neillsville, Wis., 2,728 66 C4
Neilston, U.K. 112 a8
Nei-meng-ku Tz-chih-ch'ü, a. reg., China, 9,200,000 150 E2
Neira, Col. 101 d14
Neisse, r., Ger.D.R. 118 E3
Neiva, Col. 100 C6
Neive, It., 3,044 122 b6
Nejanilini L., Man., Can. 43 F2
Nejapa, Mex., 1,051 93 G5
Nejdek, Czech. 126 b6
Nejime, Jap., 13,589 154 B6
Nekoma, Kans. 75 F5
Nekoma, N. Dak., 143 74 C1
Nekoosa, Wis., 2,515 66 D4
Nekrasovskoye, U.S.S.R., 3,000 136 F1
Neksø, Den., 3,220 121 G5
Nelas, Port., 3,431 122 B2
Nelia, Austl. 173 F3
Nelidovo, U.S.S.R., 26,500 134 C4
Neligh, Nebr., 1,776 75 H1
Nel'kan, U.S.S.R. 135 N4
Nell, i., Kwajalein 176 25
Nellikuppam, India, 22,168 145 m20
Nellingen, F.R.Ger., 1,225 119 H7
Nelliston, N.Y., 729 59 L6
Nellore, India, 106,776 145 F7
Nellysford, Va. 62 F5
Nel'ma, U.S.S.R., 1,800 135 N5
Nelma, Wis. 66 E2
Nelson, Br. Col., Can., 6,873 42 H4
Nelson, Ont., Can. 46 c14
Nelson, N.Z., 23,971 175 g6
Nelson, U.K., 31,950 113 E5
Nelson, Ariz. 78 B4
Nelson, Ga., 658 64 E1
Nelson, Ill., 283 68 C2
Nelson, co., Ky., 22,168 71 F4
Nelson, Nebr., 695 75 G3
Nelson, N.Y. 59 J6
Nelson, co., N. Dak., 7,034 74 C2
Nelson, Pa. 60 H2
Nelson, co., Va., 12,752 62 F5
Nelson, Wis. 66 B4
Nelson, r., Man., Can. 43 G3
Nelson, C., Austl. 172 F6
Nelson Forks, Br. Col., Can. 42 F1
Nelson House, Man., Can. 43 F3
Nelson I., Br. Col., Can. 42 b6
Nelson I., Alaska 85 C3
Nelson L., Man., Can. 43 E3
Nelson L., Wis. 66 B2
Nelson Lakes Nat. Pk., N.Z. 175 g6
Nelsonville, Ohio, 4,834 70 G3
Nelsonville, Wis., 170 66 D4
Nelspruit, S. Af., 15,344 164 E6
Néma, Maur., 2,946 162 C3
Nemacolin, Pa., 1,404 60 C6
Nemaha, Iowa, 151 72 B2
Nemaha, co., Kans., 12,897 75 J4
Nemaha, co., Nebr., 9,099 75 K3
Nemaha, Nebr., 232 75 K3
Neman, U.S.S.R., 9,500 136 A2
Neman, r., U.S.S.R. 134 B4
Nemanjici, Yug. 125 E4
Nemasalang, Terr. New Guin. 174 f1
Nemasket (part of Middleboro), Mass. 57 N5
Nemasket, r., Mass. 57 N5
Neméa, Gr., 4,720 129 D6
Nemegos, Ont., Can. 44 G6
Nemira, mtn., Rum. 128 F1
Nemiscau, r., Qué., Can. 44 J4
Nemocón, Col. 101 e14
Nemours, Fr., 6,402 117 E2
Nemuro, Jap., 42,740 155 L8
Nemuro Str., Jap. 155 L8
Nemuy, U.S.S.R. 135 N4
Nen, r., China 150 G2
Nenagh, Ire., 4,568 113 B5
Nenana, Alaska, 286 85 G2
Nenana, r., Alaska 85 G2
Nen-chiang, China 150 G1
Nendaz, Switz., 3,838 124 B2
Nene, r., U.K. 113 F5
Nenggiri, r., Malay. 147 o14
Nengonengo, atoll, Tuam. Arch. 177 42
Nenusa, Kep., Indon. 149 H1
Nenzel, Nebr., 43 75 D1
Nenzing, Aust., 3,470 124 F6
Neo, r., Jap. 154 h14
Neodesha, Kans., 3,594 75 K6
Neoga, Ill., 1,145 68 D4
Neokhóri, Gr., 3,191 129 C5
Neola, Iowa, 870 72 B3
Neola, Utah 78 C1
Neon, Ky., 766 71 J4
Néon Petrítsi, Gr., 3,474 129 D4
Neopit, Wis., 1,359 66 E4
Neópolis, Braz., 7,356 103 a16
Neosho, co., Kans., 19,455 75 K6
Neosho, Mo., 7,452 72 C8
Neosho, Wis., 345 66 E5
Neosho, r., Kans.-Okla. 75 K6
Néos Skopós, Gr., 3,150 129 D4
Neoskweskau, Qué., Can. 44 K4
Neotsu, Oreg. 80 A3
Nepal, ctry., 10,100,000* 145 G3
Nepālganj, Nepal, 15,817 145 F3
Nepaug (part of New Hartford), Conn. 56 E5
Nepaug Res., Conn. 56 E5
Nephi, Utah, 2,566 78 C2
Nephin, mtn., Ire. 113 B4
Nepisiguit, r., N.B., Can. 47 S10
Nepomuceno, Braz., 5,598 103 d17
Neponset, Ill., 495 68 C2
Neponset, r., Mass. 57 M4
Neptune, N.J., 16,175* 61 C3
Neptune, Ohio 70 E2
Neptune, Tenn. 71 D5
Neptune Beach, Fla., 2,868 65 H2
Neptune City, N.J., 4,013 58 c16
Neptune Is., Austl. 172 b8
Ner, r., Pol. 127 C2
Nera, r., It. 123 D3
Nera, r., Rum. 128 C2
Nérac, Fr., 6,677 117 D4
Nerău, Rum. 128 C1
Nerchau, Ger.D.R. 126 b5

Nerchinsk—Newton · 267

Nerchinsk, U.S.S.R., 13,500 135 L4
Nerchinskiy Zavod, U.S.S.R. 135 M4
Nerdva, U.S.S.R. 137 h7
Nereju Mare, Rum. 128 F2
Nerekhta, U.S.S.R., 22,300 136 E1
Neretva, r., Yug. 125 C3
Néris, Fr., 3,117 117 E3
Nerja, Sp., 7,032 122 D4
Nerka, L., Alaska 85 E4
Nérondes, Fr., 1,513 117 E3
Neroth, F.R.Ger. 119 B4
Nerstrand, Minn., 584 74 F3
Nerva, Sp., 12,686 122 B4
Nerviano, It., 10,839 122 b5
Nervión, r., Sp. 122 n11
Nes, Neth. 115 D1
Nes, Nor. 120 B3
Nesbit, Miss. 73 E3
Nesbitt Res., Pa. 61 o16
Nesbyen, Nor. 120 B3
Nesconset, N.Y., 1,964 58 g13
Nescopeck, Pa., 1,934 61 K3
Nescopeck Cr., Pa. 61 K3
Nesebür, Bulg. 128 F3
Neshaminy, Pa. 60 f11
Neshaminy Cr., Pa. 61 M5
Neshannock Cr., Pa. 60 B3
Neshkoro, Wis., 368 66 D5
Neshoba, co., Miss., 20,927 73 F5
Neshoba, Miss. 73 F5
Neshobe, r., Vt. 54 A4
Neskaupstadhur, Ice., 1,457 120 b6
Neskowin, Oreg. 80 A3
Nesle, Fr., 2,417 117 E2
Nesmith, S.C. 63 E4
Nesna, Nor. 120 C2
Nespelem, Wash., 358 80 D1
Nesquehoning, Pa., 2,714 61 L4
Ness, co., Kans., 5,470 75 E5
Ness, Loch, U.K. 112 D3
Ness City, Kans., 1,653 75 F5
Nesseby, Nor. 120 G1
Nessen City, Mich. 67 H4
Nesslau, Switz., 2,002 124 D1
Nestáni, Gr., 1,651 129 D6
Nestawkanow, r., Qué., Can. 44 K5
Nesterov, U.S.S.R., 7,500 136 A3
Nesterville, Ont., Can. 46 A2
Nestleton, Ont., Can. 46 F4
Neston, U.K., 11,836 114 B4
Nestoria, Mich. 66 E2
Nestórion, Gr. 129 C4
Nestorville, W. Va. 62 E3
Néstos, r., Gr. 129 E4
Nesttun, Nor. 120 A3
Nesvatn. l., Nor. 121 A1
Nesvizh, U.S.S.R., 5,500 136 B2
Net, r., Mich. 66 E2
Netarhat, India, 2,085 144 e14
Netarts, Oreg. 80 A3
Netcong, N.J., 2,765 61 B2
Nete, r., Belg. 115 e8
Netheravon, U.K., 1,075 114 E8
Nethercote, Austl. 173 g11
Netherhill, Sask., Can. 43 B4
Netherlands, ctry., 12,411,000* 115
Netherlands Antilles, is., W.I. 95 F4
Netherwitton, U.K. 112 g9
Nethy Bridge, U.K. 112 E3
Netley, Man., Can. 43 g9
Netley Marsh, U.K., 2,618 113 i13
Netolice, Czech. 126 B2
Netstal, Switz., 2,925 124 D1
Nettebach, r., F.R.Ger. 119 C4
Nettie, W. Va. 62 D4
Nettilling L., N.W.T., Can. 41 P4
Nett Lake, Minn. 74 F1
Nett L., Minn. 74 F1
Nettlebed, U.K. 114 F7
Nettleham, U.K., 1,940 114 H4
Nettle Hill, U.K. 114 D2
Nettleridge, Va. 62 D6
Nettleton (part of Jonesboro), Ark. 73 E2
Nettleton, Miss., 1,389 73 G3
Nettuno, It., 18,178 123 D4
Netzschkau, Ger.D.R. 126 b6
Neu, Jap., 5,967 155 C4
Neubeckum, F.R.Ger., 8,190 119 E1
Neuberg, Aust., 2,411 124 M6
Neubrandenburg, Ger.D.R., 33,369 118 D2
Neubrunn, F.R.Ger., 1,511 119 H5
Neuburg, Bay., F.R.Ger., 14,592 118 C4
Neuburg, Bad.-Württ., F.R.Ger., 2,122 119 E7
Neuchâtel, Switz., 33,430 124 A1
Neuchâtel, L. de, Switz. 124 A2
Neudenau, F.R.Ger., 1,788 119 G6
Neudorf, Sask., Can. 43 D5
Neudorf, F.R.Ger., 3,291 119 F6
Neudörfl, Aust., 2,485 124 c11
Neuenbürg, F.R.Ger., 3,817 119 F7
Neuendettelsau, F.R.Ger., 4,560 118 C4
Neuenhagen, Ger.D.R., 13,363 118 D2
Neuenhaus, F.R.Ger., 2,772 118 A2
Neuenrade, F.R.Ger., 4,811 119 D2
Neuerburg, F.R.Ger., 1,674 118 A3
Neufchâteau, Belg., 2,702 115 D5
Neufchâteau, Fr., 5,175 117 F2
Neufchâtel-en-Bray, Fr., 5,861 117 D2
Neufeld, Aust., 2,425 124 c11
Neufelden, Aust., 1,033 124 L5
Neufmoutiers-en-Brie, Fr. 116 k11
Neugersdorf, Ger.D.R., 12,344 118 E3
Neuhaus, F.R.Ger., 9,318 118 B3
Neuhaus, Ger.D.R. 118 C3
Neuhausen, Ger.D.R. 126 c6
Neuhausen, Switz., 10,280 124 C1
Neuhof, F.R.Ger., 4,081 119 H4
Neuhofen, (near Wels), Aust., 3,145 124 L5
Neuhofen, Aust., 1,248 124 L5
Neuilly-sur-Marne, Fr., 15,144 116 i11
Neuilly-sur-Seine, Fr., 73,315 116 h11
Neu-Isenburg, F.R.Ger., 22,089 118 B3
Neukalen, Ger.D.R. 118 D2
Neukirch, Ger.D.R. 126 d5
Neukirchen, Aust., 1,933 124 J6
Neukirchen, F.R.Ger., 2,619 118 B3
Neukirchen, Ger.D.R. 126 b6
Neukirchen-Vluyn, F.R.Ger., 18,676 119 B2
Neukloster, Ger.D.R. 118 C2
Neulengbach, Aust., 2,074 124 M5
Neumagen, F.R.Ger., 1,867 119 B5
Neumarkt, Aust., 1,880 124 L6
Neumarkt, F.R.Ger., 14,074 118 C4
Neumarkt-Sankt Veit, F.R.Ger., 3,426 118 D4
Neumünster, F.R.Ger., 72,134 118 C1
Neunkirch, Switz., 1,208 124 C1
Neunkirchen, Aust., 10,032 124 N6
Neunkirchen, F.R.Ger., 44,935 118 A4
Neupokoyeva, O., U.S.S.R. 134 G2
Neupölla, Aust. 124 M5
Neuquén, Arg., 14,299 105 B5
Neuquén, r., Arg. 104 g16
Neureut, F.R.Ger., 9,937 119 E6
Neuruppin, Ger.D.R., 22,040 118 D2
Neuse, N.C. 63 F2
Neuse, r., N.C. 63 H3
Neusiedl, Aust., 3,825 124 N6
Neusiedler See, Aust. 124 N6
Neuss, F.R.Ger., 79,903 118 A3
Neustadt, Ont., Can. 46 D4
Neustadt, Bad.-Württ., F.R.Ger., 6,592 118 B5
Neustadt, Bay., F.R.Ger., 13,018 118 C3
Neustadt, Bay., F.R.Ger., 8,847 118 C4
Neustadt, Bay., F.R.Ger., 3,402 118 C4
Neustadt, Bay., F.R.Ger., 5,314 118 D4
Neustadt, Bay., F.R.Ger. 126 a7
Neustadt, Hess., F.R.Ger., 4,468 118 B3
Neustadt, Rhein.-Pfalz, F.R.Ger., 1,431 119 C3
Neustadt, Schl.-Hol., F.R.Ger., 13,186 118 C1
Neustadt am Rübenberge, F.R.Ger., 8,262 118 B2
Neustadt an der Orla, Ger.D.R., 10,556 118 C3
Neustadt an der Weinstrasse, F.R.Ger., 30,457 118 A4
Neustadt-Glewe, Ger.D.R. 118 C2
Neustift, Aust., 2,191 124 H6
Neustrelitz, Ger.D.R., 27,959 118 D2
Neutla, Mex., 2,198 93 d9
Neutraubling, F.R.Ger., 2,509 118 D4
Neu-Ulm, F.R.Ger., 20,566 118 C4
Neuves-Maisons, Fr., 6,459 116 b9
Neuvic, Fr., 2,727 117 D4
Neuvic-d'Ussel, Fr., 2,436 117 D4
Neuville, Qué., Can. 47 N2
Neuville, Fr., 6,723 117 D2
Neuville, Tex. 77 Q4
Neuville-de-Poitou, Fr., 3,051 117 D3
Neuville-St-Rémy, Fr., 2,846 116 a7
Neuville-sur-Saône, Fr., 5,107 116 p15
Neuvy-le-Roi, Fr., 1,206 117 D3
Neuvy-sur-Barangeon, Fr., 1,227 117 E3
Neuwerk, i., F.R.Ger. 118 B2
Neuwied, F.R.Ger., 25,920 118 A3
Neuwildflecken, F.R.Ger., 2,143 119 H4
Neuwiller-lès-Saverne, Fr., 1,213 116 d9
Neuzauche, Ger.D.R. 118 E3
Neva, Wis. 66 D3
Neva, r., U.S.S.R. 136 C1
Nevada, st., U.S., 434,000* 83
Nevada, co., Ark., 10,700 73 B4
Nevada, co., Calif., 20,911 82 C3
Nevada, Iowa, 4,227 72 D2
Nevada, Mo., 10,518 72 C7
Nevada, Ohio, 919 70 F2
Nevada, Tex. 76 g8
Nevado, Co., Col. 100 D6
Nevada, Sa., Arg.-Chile 105 B3
Nevada, Sa., Sp. 122 D4
Nevada City, Calif., 2,353 82 C3
Nev. de Cocuy, Sa., Col. 100 D4
Nevatovice, Czech. 126 d6
Neveklov, Czech. 126 d7
Nevel', U.S.S.R., 15,000 136 C1
Nevel'sk, U.S.S.R., 19,900 135 O5
Never, U.S.S.R., 6,500 135 M4
Nevers, Fr., 41,051 117 E3
Neversink, r., N.Y. 61 N2
Neversink Res., N.Y. 59 L8
Nevesinje, Yug. 125 D3
Nevėžis, r., U.S.S.R. 136 A2
Neviges, F.R.Ger., 16,853 119 C2
Neville, Ohio, 164 70 E4
Nevils, Ga. 64 H3
Nevinnomyssk, U.S.S.R., 39,800 136 F4
Nevis, Minn., 344 74 E2
Nevis, i., Lesser Ant. 97 6
Nevis Peak, Nevis 97 6
Nevşehir, Turk., 18,808 142 C2
Nev'yansk, U.S.S.R., 30,500 137 k7
New, r., Guyana-Sur. 101 M6
New, r., Br. Hond. 94 C2
New, r., U.S. 53 K3
New, r., Calif. 82 E6
New, r., Fla. 65 E2
New, r., Fla. 65 G3
New, r., N.C. 63 G3
New, r., S.C. 63 C5
New, r., Tenn. 71 G5
New, S. Fk., r., Fla. 65 b9
New Aberdour, U.K. 112 E3
Newagen, Me. 55 C5
Newala, Tanz. 164 F3
New Albany, Ind., 37,812 70 D4
New Albany, Miss., 5,151 73 F3
New Albany, Ohio, 307 70 G2
New Albany, Pa., 359 61 K2
New Albin, Iowa, 643 72 F1
Newald, Wis. 66 E3
New Alexandria, Pa., 685 60 D5
New Almaden, Calif. 83 f13
New Almelo, Kans. 75 E4
New Alresford, U.K., 2,159 113 k12
New Amsterdam, Guyana, 14,046 101 M4
New Amsterdam, Ind., 43 70 C4
Newark, U.K., 24,651 113 F5
Newark, Calif., 9,884 83 e12
Newark, Del., 11,404 62 J3
Newark, Ill., 489 68 D2
Newark, Ind. 70 C3
Newark, Md. 62 J4
Newark, Mich. 67 K6
Newark, N.J., 405,220 61 C2
Newark, N.Y., 12,868 58 F5
Newark, Ohio, 41,790 70 G2
Newark, S. Dak., 39 74 D3
Newark, Tex., 392 76 e9
Newark, Vt. 54 D2
Newark Bay, N.J. 58 C14
Newark Valley, N.Y., 1,234 59 H7
New Ashford, Mass., 165(T) 56 D2
New Athens, Ill., 1,923 68 B5
New Auburn, Wis., 383 66 B3
New Augusta, Miss., 275 73 F6
Newaygo, co., Mich., 24,160 67 H5
Newaygo, Mich., 1,447 67 H5
New Baden, Ill., 1,464 68 C5
New Baltimore, Mich., 3,159 67 L6
New Baltimore, Ohio 71 h10
New Baltimore, Pa., 263 60 E6
New Bavaria, Ohio, 153 70 E1
New Bedford, Ill., 166 68 C2
New Bedford, Mass., 102,477 57 N6
New Bedford, N.J. 58 c16
Newberg, Oreg., 4,204 80 B3
New Berlin, Ill., 627 68 C4
New Berlin, N.Y., 1,262 59 K6
New Berlin, Pa., 654 60 J4
New Berlin, Tex. 76 b7
New Berlin, Wis., 15,788 66 c12
New Berlinville, Pa., 1,151 60 e10
Newbern, Ala., 316 64 B3
Newbern, Ind. 70 D3
New Bern, N.C., 15,717 63 G2
Newbern, Tenn., 1,695 71 B5
Newbern, Va. 62 D5
Newberry, Calif. 82 E5
Newberry, Fla., 1,105 65 G3
Newberry, Ind., 256 70 C4
Newberry, Mich., 2,612 67 H2
Newberry, co., S.C., 29,416 63 C3
Newberry, S.C., 8,208 63 C3
New Bethlehem, Pa., 1,599 60 D4
Newbiggin-by-the Sea, U.K., 10,066 112 h9
New Bloomfield, Mo., 359 72 E6
New Bloomfield, Pa., 1,025* 60 H5
Newbold, Wis. 66 D3
New Boston, Ill., 726 68 B2
New Boston (part of Sandisfield), Mass. 56 D4
New Boston, Mich. 67 e16
New Boston, N.H. 54 D6
New Boston, Ohio, 3,984 70 G4
New Boston, Tex., 2,773 77 Q3
New Braintree, Mass., 509(T) 56 H3
New Braunfels, Tex., 15,631 77 O5
New Bremen, N.Y. 59 K4
New Bremen, Ohio, 1,972 70 E2
New Bridge, Oreg. 80 E3
New Brighton, Minn., 10,890 74 c5
New Brighton, Pa., 8,397 60 B4
New Britain, Conn., 82,201 56 F6
New Britain, Pa., 1,109 60 f10
New Britain, i., Terr. New Guin. 170 E5
New Brockton, Ala., 1,093 64 D4
Newbrook, Alta., Can. 42 K2
New Brunswick, prov., Can., 623,000* 45 M6
New Brunswick, N.J., 40,139 61 B3
New Buffalo, Mich., 2,128 67 G7
New Buffalo, Pa., 153 60 H5
Newburg, Md. 62 H4
Newburg, Mich. 67 e15
Newburg, Mo., 884 72 F7
Newburg, N. Dak., 158 74 B1
Newburg, Clearfield Co., Pa., 150 60 E4
Newburg, Cumberland Co., Pa., 283 60 G5
Newburg, Northampton Co., Pa. 61 k18
Newburg, W. Va., 494 62 E3
Newburg, Wis. 66 E5
Newburg Center, Me. 55 C4
Newburgh, Ont., Can. 46 G4
Newburgh, U.K., 2,079 112 E3
Newburgh, Ind., 1,450 70 B5
Newburgh, N.Y., 30,979 59 M8
Newburgh Heights, Ohio, 3,512 70 e9
New Burlington, Ohio 71 h10
Newburn, U.K., 27,379 112 g10
New Burnside, Ill., 227 68 D6
Newbury, Ont., Can. 46 C6
Newbury, U.K., 20,397 113 F6
Newbury, Mass., 2,519(T) 57 N1
Newbury, N.H. 54 C5
Newbury, Vt. 54 C3
Newburyport, Mass., 14,004 57 N1
New Bussa, Nigeria 162 f7
New Caledonia, Pac. Oc., 86,519 170 E6
New Cambria, Mo., 270 72 E5
New Canaan, Ont., Can. 67 g16
New Canaan, Conn., 13,466(T) 56 C8
New Caney, Tex. 77 i8
New Canton, Ill., 449 68 A4
New Canton, N.J. 58 a16
New Canton, Va. 62 F5
New-Carlisle, Qué., Can., 1,333 45 N6
New Carlisle, Ind., 1,376 70 C1
New Carlisle, Ohio, 4,107 70 F3
New Cassel, N.Y. 58 e13
New Castile = Castilla la Nueva
Newcastle, Austl., 178,144 173 H5
Newcastle, N.B., Can., 5,179 45 M6
Newcastle, Ont., Can., 1,270 46 F5
Newcastle, Ire., 2,640 113 B5
Newcastle, Jam. 96 q8
Newcastle, Nevis 97 6
Newcastle, S. Af., 17,418 164 D6
Newcastle, U.K., 3,722 113 D4
Newcastle, U.K., 269,389 113 F4
New Castle, Ala. 64 d7
Newcastle, Calif. 82 b7
New Castle, Colo., 447 79 B2
New Castle, co., Del., 307,446 62 J3
New Castle, Del., 4,469 62 J3
New Castle, Ind., 20,349 70 D3
New Castle, Ky., 699 71 F3
Newcastle, Nebr., 357 75 H1
New Castle, N.H. 54 F5
Newcastle, Ohio 70 G2
New Castle, Pa., 44,790 60 B4
Newcastle, Tex., 617 77 O3
Newcastle, Utah 78 B3
New Castle, Va., 200 62 D5
Newcastle, Wyo., 4,345 81 G4
Newcastle Bay, Austl. 173 F1
Newcastle Bridge, N.B., Can. 47 S10
Newcastle Emlyn, U.K. 113 D5
Newcastleton, U.K. 113 E4
Newcastle-under-Lyme, U.K., 76,443 113 E5
Newcastle Waters, Austl. 172 D2
New Centerville, Pa., 198 60 D6
New Chelsea, Newf., Can. 45 b9
New Chicago, Ind., 2,312 69 f10
New Church, Va. 62 J5
New City, N.Y. 59 M9
New Columbia, Ill. 68 D6
New Columbia, Pa. 60 J3
New Columbus, Pa., 144 61 K3
Newcomb, N. Mex. 79 A3
Newcomb, N.Y. 59 M4
Newcomb, Tenn. 71 G5
Newcomerstown, Ohio, 4,273 70 H2
New Concord, Ohio, 2,127 70 H3
New Croton Res., N.Y. 56 B8
New Cumberland, Pa., 9,257 60 J5
New Cumberland, W. Va., 2,076 62 D2
New Cuyama, Calif. 82 D5
Newdale, Man., Can. 43 E5
Newdale, Idaho, 272 81 D4
New Deer, U.K. 112 E3
Newdegate, Austl. 172 B5
New Delaval, U.K. 112 g9
New Delhi, India, 261,545 145 E3
New Denver, Br. Col., Can. 42 H4
New Dundee, Ont., Can. 46 a14
New Durham, N.H. 54 E5
New Eagle, Pa., 2,670 60 B5
New Earswick, U.K., 2,001 114 F3
New Edinburg, Ark. 73 C4
New Effington, S. Dak., 280 74 D3
New Egypt, N.J., 1,737 61 C3
Newell, Ark. 73 C4
Newell, Ga. 64 G5
Newell, Iowa, 893 72 C2
Newell, N.C. 63 D2
Newell, Pa., 746 60 c9
Newell, S. Dak., 797 74 A3
Newell, W. Va., 1,842 62 D2
New Ellenton, S.C., 2,309 63 C4
Newellton, La., 1,453 73 D5
New England, N. Dak., 1,095 74 A2
New England, W. Va. 62 C3
New England Ra., Austl. 173 G4
Newenham, C., Alaska 85 D4
Newent, U.K., 3,167 113 E6
New Era, La. 73 D6
New Era, Mich., 403 67 G5
New Fairfield, Conn., 3,355 56 B7
Newfane, N.Y., 1,423 58 C5
Newfane, Vt., 146 54 B6
Newfield (part of Middletown), Conn. 56 F6
Newfield, Me. 55 B5
Newfield, N.J., 1,299 61 B4
Newfield, N.Y. 59 G7
Newfields, N.H. 54 E5
New Florence, Mo., 616 72 F6
New Florence, Pa., 953 60 D5
Newfolden, Minn., 370 74 D1
Newfound L., N.H. 54 D4
Newfoundland, prov., Can., 498,000* 45 P3
Newfoundland, N.J. 61 B1
Newfoundland, N.C. 63 H2
Newfoundland, Pa. 61 M3
Newfoundland Basin, Atl. Oc. 109 K4
New Franken, Wis. 66 F4
New Franklin, Mo., 1,096 72 E5
New Freedom, Pa., 1,395 60 J6
New Freeport, Pa. 60 B6
New Galilee, Pa., 593 60 B4
New Galloway, U.K. 113 D4
Newgate, Br. Col., Can. 42 J4
New Georgia, i., Sol. Is. 175 b2
New Georgia Group, is., Sol. Is. 170 E5
New Germantown, Pa. 60 G5
New Glarus, Wis., 1,468 66 D6
New Glasgow, N.S., Can., 9,564 45 O6
New Gloucester, Me. 55 B5
New Goshen, Ind. 70 B3
New Grand Chain, Ill., 282 68 D6
New Gretna, N.J. 61 C4
New Guinea, Terr. of, 1,576,000* 170 D5
New Guinea, i. 170 D5
Newgulf, Tex., 1,419 77 Q5
Newhalem, Wash. 80 B1
Newhalen, Alaska, 110 85 F4
Newhall, U.K. 114 C4
Newhall, Calif., 4,705 83 g15
Newhall, Iowa, 495 72 F3
New Hamburg, Ont., Can., 2,155 46 a14
New Hampshire, st., U.S., 673,000* 54
New Hampton, Iowa, 3,456 72 E1
New Hampton, Mo., 289 72 C4
New Hampton, N.H. 54 D4
New Hanover, Ill. 68 B5
New Hanover, co., N.C., 71,742 63 G3
New Hanover, i., Terr. New Guin. 174 f1
New Harbour, Newf., Can. 45 b10
New Harmony, Ind., 1,121 70 B4
New Harmony, Utah, 105 78 B3
New Hartford, Conn., 1,034; 3,033(T) 56 D5
New Hartford, Iowa, 649 72 E2
New Hartford, N.Y., 2,468 59 K5
Newhaven, U.K., 8,419 113 G6
New Haven, co., Conn., 660,315 56 D7
New Haven, Conn., 152,048 56 E7
New Haven, Ill., 642 68 D6
New Haven, Ind., 3,396 70 D2
New Haven, Ky., 1,009 71 F4
New Haven, Mich., 1,198 67 L6
New Haven, Mo., 1,223 72 F6
New Haven, N.Y. 59 H5
New Haven, Ohio 71 g10
New Haven, Vt. 54 A3
New Haven, W. Va., 1,314 62 B4
New Haven, r., Vt. 54 A3
New Haven Junction, Vt. 54 A3
New Haven Mills, Vt. 54 A3
New Hazelton, Br. Col., Can. 42 E2
New Hebrides, Pac. Oc., 68,000* 170 F6
New Hebron, Ill. 68 E5
Newhebron, Miss., 271 73 F6
New Hill, N.C. 63 E2
New Holland, Ill., 314 68 C3
New Holland, Mich. 67 G6
New Holland, N.C. 63 H2
New Holland, Ohio, 798 70 F3
New Holland, Pa., 3,425 61 K5
New Holland, S. Dak. 74 C4
New Holstein, Wis., 2,401 66 E5
New Hope, Madison co., Ala., 1,046 64 C1
New Hope, Shelby Co., Ala. 64 d8
New Hope, Ga. 64 f10
New Hope, Minn., 11,620 74 b5
New Hope, Ohio 70 E3
New Hope, Pa., 958 61 M5
New Hope, Va. 62 F4
New Hradec, N. Dak. 74 A2
New Hudson, Mich. 67 K6
New Hyde Park, N.Y., 10,808 58 d14
New Iberia, La., 29,062 73 C7
Newington, Conn., 17,654(T) 56 F6
Newington, Ga., 399 64 H3
Newington, N.H. 54 F5
Newinn, Ire. 113 C5
New Ipswich, N.H. 54 D6
New Ireland, i., Terr. New Guin. 170 E5
New I., Falk. Is. 108 3
New Jersey, st., U.S., 6,781,000* 61
New Johnsonville, Tenn., 559 71 D5
New Kensington, Pa., 23,485 60 C4
New Kent, co., Va., 4,504 62 G5
New Kent, Va. 62 H5
Newkirk, N. Mex. 79 C4
Newkirk, Okla., 2,092 76 F1
New Knoxville, Ohio, 792 70 E2
New L., N.C. 63 H2
New Lancaster, Kans. 75 L5
Newland, Ind. 70 C1
Newland, N.C., 564 63 C1
New Lebanon, N.Y. 59 O7
New Lebanon, Ohio, 1,459 70 E3
New Lebanon, Pa., 166 60 B3
New Leipzig, N. Dak., 390 74 B2
New Lenox, Ill., 1,750 68 E2
New Lenox (part of Lenox), Mass. 56 C3
New Lexington, Ala. 64 B2
New Lexington, Ohio, 4,514 70 G3
New Liberty, Iowa, 145 72 G3
New Liberty, Okla. 76 D2
New Lisbon, Wis., 1,337 66 C5
New Liskeard, Ont., Can., 4,727 44 H6
Newllano, La., 264 73 B6
New London, co., Conn., 185,745 56 H6
New London, Conn., 34,182 56 H7
New London, Iowa, 1,694 72 F4
New London, Minn., 721 74 E3
New London, Mo., 875 72 F5
New London, N.H., 1,007 54 D5
New London, N.C., 223 63 D2
New London, Ohio, 2,392 70 G1
New London, Va. 62 E5
New London, Wis., 5,288 66 E4
New Lothrop, Mich., 510 67 J5
New Madison, Ohio, 910 70 E3
New Madrid, co., Mo., 31,350 72 H8
New Madrid, Mo., 2,867 72 H8
Newmains, U.K. 112 c8
Newman, Calif., 2,558 82 C4
Newman, Ill., 1,097 68 D4
Newman, Tex. 77 K4
Newman Grove, Nebr., 880 75 H2
Newmanstown, Pa., 1,459 61 K5
Newmarket, Ont., Can., 8,794 44 H7
Newmarket, Ire. 113 B5
Newmarket, U.K., 11,227 113 G5
New Market, Ala. 64 C1
New Market, Ind., 578 70 C3
New Market, Iowa, 506 72 C4
New Market, Md., 358 62 G3
Newmarket, N.H., 2,745 54 E5
New Market, N.J. 58 b14
New Market, Tenn. 71 H5
New Market, Va., 783 62 F4
Newmarket on Fergus, Ire. 113 B5
New Marlboro, Mass., 1,083(T) 56 D4
New Marshfield, Ohio 70 G3
New Martinsville, W. Va., 5,607 62 C3
New Matamoras, Ohio, 925 70 H3
New Meadows, Idaho, 647 81 A3
New Melle, Mo. 72 F6
New Mexico, st., U.S., 1,014,000* 79
New Miami, Ohio, 2,360 70 E3
New Middleton, Tenn. 71 E5
New Middletown, Ind., 132 70 C4
New Middletown, Ohio, 500 70 J2
New Milford, Conn., 3,023; 8,318(T) 56 C6
New Milford, N.J., 18,810 58 c13
New Milford, Pa., 1,129 61 L2
New Millport, Pa. 60 F4
New Mills, U.K., 8,514 114 E4
Newmilns, U.K. 112 b8
New Minden, Ill., 166 68 C5
New Munster, Wis. 66 c13
Newnan, Ga., 12,169 64 E2
Newnans L., Fla. 65 G3
Newnham, U.K., 1,118 114 C7
New Norcia, Austl. 172 B4
New Norfolk, Austl., 4,756 173 f14
New Norway, Alta., Can. 43 b8
New Offenburg, Mo. 72 G7
New Orleans, La., 627,525 73 F7
New Oxford, Pa., 1,407 60 H6
New Palestine, Ind., 725 70 D3
New Paltz, N.Y., 3,041 59 M8
New Paris, Ind. 70 D1
New Paris, Pa., 232 60 E5
New Pekin, Ind., 661 70 D4
New Perlican, Newf., Can. 45 b10
New Philadelphia, Ohio, 14,241 70 H2
New Philadelphia, Pa., 1,702 61 K4
New Pine Creek, Calif. 82 C2
New Pine Creek, Oreg. 80 C4
New Pitsligo, U.K. 112 E3
New Plymouth, N.Z. 29,368 175 g5
New Plymouth, Idaho, 940 81 A4
New Plymouth, Ohio 70 G3
New Point, Ind., 319 70 D3
New Point, Va. 62 H5
New Point Comfort, Fla. 65 G6
Newport, Ont., Can. 46 b15
New Port, Cur. 97 16
Newport, Ire. 113 B5
Newport, Jam. 96 p9
Newport, Essex, Eng., U.K., 1,154 114 J7
Newport, Hants., Eng., U.K., 19,479 113 F6
Newport, Mon., Wales, U.K., 108,101 113 E6
Newport, Pemb., Wales, U.K., 1,180 113 D6
Newport, Salop., Eng., U.K., 4,369 114 D5
Newport, York., Eng., U.K. 114 G3
Newport, Ark., 7,007 73 D2
Newport, Del., 1,239 62 J3
Newport, Ind., 627 70 B3
Newport, Ky., 30,070 71 G2
Newport, Me., 1,589 55 C4
Newport, Mich. 67 e16
Newport, Nebr., 162 75 F1
Newport, N.H., 3,222 54 C5
Newport, N.J. 61 A5
Newport, N.Y., 827 59 L5
Newport, N.C., 861 63 H3
Newport, Ohio 70 H3
Newport, Okla. 76 F3
Newport, Oreg., 5,344 80 A3
Newport, Pa., 1,861 60 H5
Newport, co., R.I., 81,891 57 L6
Newport, R.I., 47,049 57 L7
Newport, Tenn., 6,448 71 H6
Newport, Vt., 5,019 54 C2
Newport, Va. 62 D5
Newport, Wash., 1,513 80 E1
Newport Beach, Calif., 26,564 82 E6
Newport Center, Vt. 54 C2
New Portland, Me. 55 B4
Newport News, Va., 113,662 62 H5
Newport-on-Tay, U.K., 3,326 112 E3
Newport Pagnell, U.K., 4,743 114 G6
New Port Richey, Fla., 3,520 65 G4
New Post, Wis. 66 B3
New Prague, Minn., 2,533 74 F3
New Preston (part of Washington), Conn. 56 C6
New Prospect, S.C. 63 B2
New Providence, Iowa, 206 72 D2
New Providence, N.J., 10,243 61 C2
New Providence, Tenn., 4,451 71 D5
New Providence, i., Bah. Is. 95 C1
New Quay, Card., Wales, U.K. 113 D5
New Radnor, U.K. 114 B6
New Richland, Minn., 1,046 74 F4
New Richmond, Qué., Can. 47 T9
New Richmond, Mich. 67 G6
New Richmond, Ohio, 2,834 70 E4
New Richmond, Wis., 3,316 66 A3
New Riegel, Ohio, 349 70 F1
New Ringgold, Pa., 314 61 L4
New River, Ariz. 78 B5
New Roads, La., 3,965 73 D7
New Rochelle, N.Y., 76,812 59 N10
New Rockford, N. Dak., 2,177 74 C2
Newquay, Corn., Eng., U.K., 11,881 113 D6
New Rome, Ohio, 94 70 a7
New Romney, U.K., 2,555 113 G6
New Ross, Ire., 4,643 113 C5
New Ross, Ind., 332 70 C3
New Russia, N.Y. 59 N3
Newry, U.K., 12,450 113 C4
Newry, Me. 55 B4
Newry, Pa., 432 60 F5
Newry, S.C. 63 B3
New Salem, Ill., 172 68 B4
New Salem, Ind. 70 D3
New Salem, Mass., 397(T) 56 G2
New Salem, N. Dak., 986 74 B2
New Salem, Fayette Co., Pa. 60 C6
New Salem, York Co., Pa., 350 60 J6
New Sarepta, Alta., Can. 43 b7
New Sarpy, La., 1,259 73 E7
New Sarum = Salisbury, U.K.
New Sauchie, U.K. 112 c7
Newsham, Northumb., Eng., U.K. 112 h9
Newsham, York., Eng., U.K. 114 E2
New Sharon, Iowa, 1,063 72 E3
New Sharon, Me. 55 C4
New Sharon, N.J. 58 a16
New Sheffield, Pa. 60 a7
New Shoreham, R.I., 486(T) 57 K8
New Shrewsbury, N.J., 7,313 61 C3
New Siberian Is. = Novosibirskiye O-va.
New Smyrna Beach, Fla., 8,781 65 J3
Newsoms, Va., 423 62 G6
New South Wales, st., Austl., 4,235,030 173 F5
New Straitsville, Ohio, 1,019 70 G3
New Stuyahok, Alaska, 145 85 E4
New Tazewell, Tenn., 768 71 H5
New Territories = Hong Kong
Newtok, Alaska, 129 85 C3
Newton, Ont., Can. 46 D5
Newton, Ala., 958 64 D4
Newton, co., Ark., 5,963 73 B2
Newton, co., Ga., 20,999 64 F2
Newton, Ga., 529 64 E4
Newton, Ill., 2,901 68 D5
Newton, co., Ind., 11,502 70 B2
Newton, Iowa, 15,381 72 E3
Newton, Kans., 14,877 75 H5

Nora—Norwalk · 269

Nora, Va. 62 B5
Nørager, Den. 121 B4
Norala, Phil., 3,213 153 C4
Noralee, Br. Col., Can. 42 E2
Noranda, Qué., Can., 11,304 44 H5
Norashen, U.S.S.R., 1,300 137 c2
Nora Springs, Iowa, 1,275 72 E1
Norbeck, Md. 62 a8
Norberg, Swed. 120 D3
Norberto de la Riestra, Arg., 6,089 105 a12
Norborne, Mo., 965 72 D5
Norcasia, Col. 101 c14
Norcatur, Kans., 302 75 E4
Norco, Calif., 4,964 83 i16
Norco, La., 4,682 73 E7
Norcross, Ga., 1,605 64 g9
Norcross, Minn., 153 74 D3
Nord, Massif du, Haiti 96 k6
Nord, Pte., Îs. de Horne 175 9
Nord, Pte., St-Martin 97 7
Nordaustlandet, i., Nor. 134 B2
Nordborg, Den., 2,563 121 B5
Nordbruk, O., U.S.S.R. 134 D2
Nordby, Den. 121 A5
Nordby, Den. 121 C5
Nordelph, U.K. 114 J5
Norden, F.R.Ger., 16,423 118 A2
Norden, Nebr. 75 F1
Nordenham, F.R.Ger., 25,927 118 B2
Nordenshel'da, Arkh., U.S.S.R. 135 J2
Norderney, F.R.Ger., 6,721 118 A2
Norderney, i., F.R.Ger. 115 F1
Nordfjordeid, Nor. 120 A3
Nordfold, Nor. 120 C2
Nord-Fröya, Nor. 120 B3
Nordhalben, F.R.Ger., 2,610 118 C3
Nordhausen, Ger.D.R., 39,768 118 C3
Nordheim, Tex., 407 77 P5
Nordhorn, F.R.Ger., 37,360 118 A2
Nordhoyar, is., Faeroe Is. 120 c7
Nordkapp, Nor. 120 F1
Nordkirchen, F.R.Ger., 2,331 119 D1
Nordkynhalvöya, pen., Nor. 120 G1
Nordland, Wash. 81 a6
Nördlingen, F.R.Ger., 13,829 118 C4
Nordmaling, Swed. 120 E3
Nordman, Idaho 81 A1
Nordmöre, reg., Nor. 120 A3
Nord-Ostsee-Kan., F.R.Ger. 118 B1
Nord-Ouest, Montagnes du, Haiti 96 k6
Nordreisa, Nor. 120 E1
Nordrhein-Westfalen, st., F.R.Ger., 16,554,000* 118 A3
Nordstrand, i., F.R.Ger. 118 B1
Nordvik, U.S.S.R. 135 L2
Nordwalde, F.R.Ger., 6,332 118 A2
Nordyke, Nev. 83 A3
Nore, Nor. 120 B3
Nore, r., Ire. 113 C5
Norembega, Ont., Can. 44 H5
Norfolk, co., U.K., 561,071 113 G5
Norfolk, Conn., 1,827(T) 56 D5
Norfolk, co., Mass., 510,256 57 L4
Norfolk, Mass., 3,471(T) 57 L4
Norfolk, Nebr., 13,640 75 H1
Norfolk, N.Y., 1,353 59 K2
Norfolk, Va., 304,869 62 H6
Norfolk I., Pac. Oc. 170 F6
Norfork, Ark., 283 73 C1
Norfork L., Ark. 73 C1
Norge, Okla. 76 F3
Norheimsund, Nor. 120 A3
Noria, Co., Mex. 92 D1
Norias, Tex. 77 P6
Norikura-dake, Jap. 155 E3
Noril'sk, U.S.S.R., 109,000 135 H3
Norlina, N.C., 927 63 F1
Norma, Alta., Can. 43 c7
Norma, It., 3,568 123 b8
Normal, Ill., 13,357 68 C3
Norman, Ark., 482 73 B3
Norman, Ind. 70 C4
Norman, co., Minn., 11,253 74 D2
Norman, N.C., 220 63 E2
Norman, Okla., 33,412 76 F2
Norman, r., Austl. 173 F2
Norman, L., N.C. 63 C2
Normanby, r., Austl. 173 F2
Normanby I., Terr. Papua 174 f3
Normandie, reg., Fr. 117 C2
Normandin, Qué., Can., 1,785 44 K5
Normandy, Fr.=Normandie
Normandy, Tex. 77 N5
Normandy Beach, N.J. 61 C4
Normandy Park, Wash., 3,224 80 B2
Normangee, Tex., 718 77 Q4
Norman I., V.I. 97 4
Norman Park, Ga., 891 64 F4
Norman's Cove., Newf., Can. 45 b10
Normans Kill, r., N.Y. 59 v29
Normanton, Austl. 173 F2
Normanton, U.K., 18,307 114 F3
Normantown, Ill. 69 a10
Norman Wells, N.W.T., Can. 40 D4
Noroa, Chile 104 f15
Norogachic, Mex., 1,003 92 D2
Norosí, Col. 100 C3
Noroton (part of Darien), Conn. 56 C8
Noroton, r., Conn. 58 e12
Norphlet, Ark., 459 73 C4
Norquay, Sask., Can. 43 E4
Norra Storfjället, mts., Swed. 120 C2
Nørra Yngern, l., Swed. 120 e8
Nørre Åby, Den. 121 B5
Nørre Aggersund, Den. 121 B3
Nørre Alslev, Den., 1,546 121 D6
Nørre Balling, Den. 121 A4
Nørre Nebel, Den., 1,275 121 A5
Nørre Saltum, Den. 121 B3
Nørresundby, Den., 10,456 121 B3
Nørre Vorupør, Den. 121 A4
Norrfjärden, Swed. 120 E2
Norrfors, Swed. 120 D3
Norridge, Ill., 14,087 69 c9
Norridgewock, Me. 55 C4
Norris, Ill., 307 68 B3
Norris, Mont. 81 D3
Norris, S.C., 594 63 B3
Norris, S. Dak. 74 B4
Norris, Tenn., 1,389 71 G5
Norris Arm, Newf., Can., 1,226 45 Q5
Norris City, Ill., 1,243 68 D6
Norris L., Tenn. 71 H5
Norris Point, Newf., Can. 45 P5
Norristown, Ga. 64 G3
Norristown, Pa., 38,925 61 M5
Norrköping, Swed., 90,955 120 D4
Norrland, reg., Swed. 120 D2
Norrtälje, Swed. 120 D4
Norrvidinge, Swed. 121 E5
Norseman, Austl., 2,539 172 B5
Norsewood, N.Z. 175 h5
Norsjå, l., Nor. 121 B1
Norsjö, Swed. 120 D2
Norsk, U.S.S.R. 135 N4
Norsup B., New Hebr. 174 k6
Norte, C., Easter I. 177 46
Norte, Cayo, P.R. 96 v10
Norte, P., Arg. 105 c13
Norte, Sa. do, Braz. 102 E4
Nortelândia, Braz., 3,134 103 E4
North, S.C., 1,047 63 C4
North, C., N.S., Can. 45 O6
North, r., Newf., Can. 45 P4
North, r., Mass. 56 F2
North, r., Mass. 57 N4
North, r., N.H. 54 E5
North, r., N.C. 63 J1
North, r., Wash. 80 B2
North, r., W. Va. 62 F3
North Abington (part of Abington), Mass. 57 N4
North Acton (part of Acton), Mass. 57 L2
North Adams, Mass., 19,905 56 D2
North Adams, Mich., 494 67 J7
North Agawam (part of Agawam), Mass. 56 F4
Northallerton, U.K., 6,726 113 F4
Northam, Austl., 5,725 172 B4
Northam, S. Af. 164 D6
Northam, U.K., 6,572 113 D6
North American Basin, Atl. Oc. 108 H5
North Amherst, Mass., 1,009 56 F3
North Amity, Me. 55 E3
Northampton, Austl. 172 A4
Northampton, U.K., 105,421 113 F5
Northampton, Mass., 30,058 56 F3
Northampton, N.Y. 59 M5
Northampton, co., N.C., 26,811 63 G1
Northampton, co., Pa., 201,412 61 M4
Northampton, Pa., 8,866 61 M4
Northampton, co., Va., 16,966 62 J5
Northamptonshire, co., U.K., 398,005 113 F5
North Andaman, i., India 146 A4
North Andover, Mass., 10,908(T) 57 M2
North Andover, Wis. 66 C6
North Anson, Me. 55 C4
North Arlington, N.J., 17,477 58 c13
North Arm, N.W.T., Can. 40 G5
North Ashburnham (part of Ashburnham), Mass. 56 J2
North Ashford (part of Eastford), Conn. 56 H5
North Atlanta, Ga., 12,661 64 E2
North Attleboro, Mass., 14,777(T) 57 L5
North Augusta, Ont., Can. 47 J4
North Augusta, S.C., 10,348 63 B4
North Aulatsivik I., Newf., Can. 45 N2
North Aurora, Ill., 3,488 68 D2
North Baldy, mtn., Wash. 80 E1
North Baltimore, Ohio, 3,011 70 F1
North Bangor, N.Y. 59 M2
North Barrington, Ill., 282 69 b8
North Bass I., Ohio 70 G1
North Battleford, Sask., Can., 11,081 43 C4
North Bay, Ont., Can., 22,914 44 H6
North Bay, N.Y. 59 J5
North Bay, Wis., 264 66 d12
North Bay, N.W.T., Can. 41 Q5
North Bay, Me. 55 C3
North B., Wis. 66 G3
North Bay Village, Fla., 2,006 65 b10
North Beach, Md., 606 62 H4
North Belcher Is., N.W.T., Can. 44 H3
North Bellingham (part of Bellingham), Mass. 57 L4
North Bend, Br. Col., Can. 42 G4
North Bend, Nebr., 1,174 75 J2
North Bend, Ohio, 622 71 g11
North Bend, Oreg., 7,512 80 A4
North Bend, Pa. 60 G3
North Bend, Wash., 945 80 C2
North Bend, Wis. 66 B4
North Bennington, Vt., 1,437 54 A6
North Bergen, N.J., 42,387(T) 61 D2
North Bernardston (part of Bernardston), Mass. 56 F2
North Berwick, U.K., 4,161 112 E3
North Berwick, Me., 1,295 55 B5
North Bessemer, Pa., 2,000* 60 d8
North Beverly (part of Beverly), Mass. 57 N2
North Bight, Bah. Is. 95 b8
North Billerica (part of Billerica), Mass. 57 L2
North Bloomfield (part of Bloomfield), Conn. 56 F5
North Bloomfield, N.Y. 58 n21
North Bonneville, Wash., 494 80 B3
North Borneo=Sabah
Northboro, Iowa, 135 72 B4
Northboro, Mass., 6,687(T) 57 K3
North Boston, N.Y. 58 C6
North Bradley, U.K. 114 D8
North Bradley, Mich. 67 J5
North Branch, Ont., Can. 44 C5
North Branch, Kans. 75 G4
North Branch, Mich., 901 67 K5
North Branch, Minn., 949 74 F3
North Branch, N.H. 54 C5
North Branch, N.J. 61 B2
North Branford, Conn., 6,771(T) 56 F7
Northbridge, Mass., 10,800(T) 57 K4
Northbridge Center (part of Northbridge), Mass. 57 K4
North Bristol, Wis. 66 D5
Northbrook, Ill., 11,635 69 c8
North Brookfield, Mass., 3,616(T) 56 H3
North Bruny, i., Austl. 173 f14
North Buxton, Ont., Can. 46 B6
North Caicos, i., Caicos Is. 95 E2
North Caldwell, N.J., 4,163 58 b13
North Canadian, r., Okla. 76 E2
North Canton (part of Canton), Conn. 56 E5
North Canton, Ohio, 7,727 70 H2
North Cape, Wis. 66 c12
North C., New Hebr. 174 k5
North C., N.Z. 175 g4
North C., Nor.=Nordkapp
North Caribou L., Ont., Can. 44 D4
North Carolina, st., U.S., 4,935,000* 63
North Carver (part of Carver), Mass. 57 N5
North Catasauqua, Pa., 2,805 61 k18
North Chan., Ont., Can. 46 A2
North Chan., U.K. 113 D4
North Charleston, S.C. 63 D5
North Charlestown, N.H. 54 C5
North Chatham (part of Chatham), Mass. 57 R6
North Chatham, N.H. 54 E3
North Cheek, pt., U.K. 114 H2
North Chelmsford (part of Chelmsford), Mass. 57 L2
North Chester (part of Chester), Mass. 56 E3
North Chicago, Ill., 20,517 68 E1
North Chichester, N.H. 54 E5
North Chili, N.Y. 58 E5
North Chillicothe, Ill., 2,259 68 C3
North City, Ill., 362 68 C6
North Clarendon, Vt. 54 B4
Northcliffe, Austl. 172 B5
North Coates, U.K. 114 J4
North Cohasset (part of Cohasset), Mass. 57 N3
North Cohocton, N.Y. 58 F6
North College Hill, Ohio, 12,035 71 h10
North Collingham, U.K., 1,149 114 G4
North Collins, N.Y., 1,574 58 C6
North Concho, r., Tex. 77 N4
North Conway, N.H., 1,104 54 E3
North Cove, Wash. 80 A2
North Cowden, Tex. 77 M3
North Creek, N.Y. 59 M4
North Dakota, st., U.S., 652,000* 74
North Danville, Vt. 54 C3
North Dartmouth (part of Dartmouth), Mass. 57 N6
North Dexter, Me. 55 C3
North Dighton, Mass., 1,167 57 M5
North Dixmont, Me. 55 C4
North Downs, reg., U.K. 112
North Druid Hills, Ga. 64 g9
North Duxbury (part of Duxbury), Mass. 57 O4
North Duxbury, Vt. 54 B3
North East, Md., 1,628 62 J3
North East, Pa., 4,217 60 C1
North East Cape Fear, r., N.C. 63 G3
North East Frontier Agency, un. terr., India, 336,558 145 J3
North Eastham (part of Eastham), Mass. 57 R5
Northeast Harbor, Me. 55 D4
Northeast Is., Truk 176 19
Northeast Mistassibi, r., Qué., Can. 44 L5
North Easton (part of Easton), Mass. 57 M4
North Easton, N.Y. 59 w27
Northeast Pass, Jaluit 176 30
North East Pt., Christmas Atoll 177 40
Northeast Pt., Lesser Caymans 97 2
Northeast Pd., Me.-N.H. 54 F5
Northeast Providence Channel, Bah. Is. 95 C1
North Edisto, r., S.C. 63 C4
North Egremont, Mass. 56 C4
Northeim, F.R.Ger., 19,050 118 C3
North English, Iowa, 1,004 72 E3
North Enid, Okla., 286 76 F1
North Entr., Palau 176 21
Northern Bright, Newf., Can. 45 a10
Northern Indian L., Man., Can. 43 F2
Northern Ireland, U.K., 1,469,000* 113 C4
Northern Rhodesia=Zambia
Northern Terr., Austl., 37,166 172 D2
North Esk, r., U.K. 112 d8
North Esk, r., U.K. 112 E3
North Fabius, r., Mo. 72 F4
North Fairfield, Ohio, 547 70 G1
North Falmouth (part of Falmouth), Mass. 57 O6
North Farmington, Mich. 67 e14
North Ferrisburg, Vt. 54 A3
Northfield (part of Litchfield), Conn. 56 D6
Northfield, Ill., 4,005 69 c8
Northfield, Me. 55 E4
Northfield, Mass., 2,320(T) 56 G2
Northfield, Minn., 8,707 74 F3
Northfield, N.H., 1,243 54 D5
Northfield, N.J., 5,849 61 B5
Northfield, Ohio, 1,055 70 e9
Northfield, Vt., 2,159 54 B3
Northfield, Wis. 66 B4
Northfield Falls, Vt. 54 B3
Northfield Farms (part of Northfield), Mass. 56 G2
Northfield Mts., Vt. 54 B3
North Fiji Basin, Pac. Oc. 169 F3
North Fond du Lac, Wis., 2,549 66 E5
Northford (part of N. Branford), Conn. 56 E7
North Foreland, c., U.K. 113 G6
North Fork, Calif. 82 D4
North Fork, Nev. 83 C2
North Fox I., Mich. 67 H3
North Freedom, Wis., 579 66 D5
North French, r., Ont., Can. 44 G5
North Frodingham, U.K. 114 H3
North Gardner Mtn., Wash. 80 C1
North Glen Ellyn, Ill. 69 b9
North Grafton (part of Grafton), Mass. 57 K4
North Granby (part of Granby), Conn. 56 E5
North Greece, N.Y. 58 n20
North Greenfield, N.Y. 59 v27
North Grosvenor Dale, Conn., 1,874 56 J5
North Guilford (part of Guilford), Conn. 56 F7
North Hadley (part of Hadley), Mass. 56 F3
North Halawa Str., Hawaii 84 c7
North Haledon, N.J., 6,026 58 c13
North Hampton, Ohio, 495 70 E2
North Hannibal, N.Y. 59 p22
North Hanover (part of Hanover), Mass. 57 N4
North Harbour, Newf., Can. 45 b10
North Harlowe, N.C. 63 H3
North Hartland, Vt. 54 C4
North Harwich (part of Harwich), Mass. 57 Q6
North Hatfield (part of Hatfield), Mass. 56 F3
North Hatley, Qué., Can. 47 N3
North Haven, Conn., 15,935(T) 56 E7
North Haven, Me. 55 D4
North Haverhill, N.H. 54 C3
North Havre, Mont., 1,168 81 E1
North Head, N.B., Can. 47 S11
North Head, Newf., Can. 45 c10
North Heath (part of Heath), Mass. 56 E2
North Henderson, Ill., 210 68 B2
North Henderson, N.C., 1,995 63 F1
North Henik L., N.W.T., Can. 40 K5
North Hero, Vt. 54 A2
North Highlands, Calif., 21,271 82 C3
North Hinksey, U.K., 4,452 114 F7
North Hoosick, N.Y. 59 O6
North Hornell, N.Y., 917 58 E7
North Horr, Kenya 164 F1
North Hudson, Wis., 1,019 66 A3
North Hyde Park, Vt. 54 B2
North Hykeham, U.K., 5,308 114 G4
North Ironwood, Mich. 66 C2
North Irwin, Pa., 1,143 60 d8
North I., N.Z. 175 g5
North I., Seych. 165 a10
North Java, N.Y. 58 D6
North Jay, Me. 55 B4
North Judson, Ind., 1,942 70 C1
North Kamloops, Br. Col., Can., 6,406 42 G4
North Kansas City, Mo., 5,657 75 a7
North Kent (part of Kent), Conn. 56 C5
North Kingsville, Ohio, 1,854 70 J1
North Knife, r., Man., Can. 43 F2
North Knife L., Man., Can. 43 F2
North Korea, ctry., 12,100,000* 151
Northlake, Ill., 12,318 69 c9
North Lake, Mich. 66 F2
North Lake, Wis. 66 c11
North L., Me. 55 C4
North Lakhimpur, India, 6,576 145 J4
Northland, Mich. 66 F2
North Land=Severnaya Zemlya
North Las Vegas, Nev., 18,422 83 C4
North Lawrence, N.Y. 59 L2
Northleach, U.K. 114 E7
North Leeds, Wis. 66 D5
North Leigh, U.K., 1,197 114 F7
North Leominster (part of Leominster), Mass. 57 K2
North Leverett (part of Leverett), Mass. 56 G2
North Lewisburg, Ohio, 879 70 F2
North Liberty, Ind., 1,241 70 C1
North Liberty, Iowa, 334 72 F3
North Little Rock, Ark., 50,032 73 C3
North Llano, r., Tex. 77 N4
North Loup, Nebr., 453 75 G2
North Loup, r., Nebr. 75 F2
North Lyme Center, Conn. 56 G7
North Madison (part of Madison), Conn. 56 F7
North Magnetic Pole 180 G2
North Malden, Ont., Can. 67 f16
North Manchester, Ind., 4,377 70 D1
North Manitou, Mich. 67 H3
North Manitou I., Mich. 67 G3
North Mankato, Minn., 5,927 74 E3
North Marshfield (part of Marshfield), Mass. 57 N4
North Medwin, r., U.K. 112 c8
North Miami, Fla., 28,708 65 J7
North Miami Beach, Fla., 21,405 65 b10
North Middleboro (part of Middleboro), Mass. 57 N5
North Middletown, Ky., 291 71 G3
North Minch, str., U.K. 112 C3
North Monson (part of Monson), Mass. 56 G4
North Muskegon, Mich., 3,855 67 G5
North Nashua, r., Mass. 57 K2
North Negril Pt., Jam. 96 o8
North Newbald, U.K. 114 G3
North New Portland, Me. 55 B4
North New River Can., Fla. 65 J6
North New Salem (part of New Salem), Mass. 56 G2
North Norwich, N.Y. 59 K6
North Ogden, Utah, 2,621 78 C1
North Olmsted, Ohio, 16,290 70 G1
Northome, Minn., 291 74 E2
North Orange (part of Orange), Mass. 56 G2
North Palermo, Me. 55 C4
North Palisade, mt., Calif. 82 D4
North Palm Beach, Fla. 65 b8
North Pk., basin, Colo. 79
North Pelham, Ont., Can. 46 d15
North Pelham, N.Y., 5,326 58 d13
North Penobscot, Me. 55 D4
North Perry, Me. 55 E3
North Perry, Ohio, 658 70 H1
North Petersburg, N.Y. 59 O6
North Petherton, U.K., 3,769 113 E6
North Pharsalia, N.Y. 59 J6
North Pine, Br. Col., Can. 42 G2
North Plain (part of E. Haddam), Conn. 56 G7
North Plainfield, N.J., 16,993 58 b14
North Plains, Oreg. 80 a5
North Platte, Nebr., 17,184 75 E2
North Platte, r., U.S. 52 F2
North Pleasanton, Tex., 1,018 77 O5
North Plymouth, Mass., 3,467 57 O5
North Point, H.K., 132,994 152 b6
North Pt., Ascension 109 6
North Pt., P.E.I., Can. 47 U10
North Pt., New Hebr. 174 k5
North Pt., Mich. 67 K3
North Pole, Alaska, 615 85 b6
North Pole 180 K1
North Pomfret, Vt. 54 B4
North Pd., Mass. 57 K4
Northport, Ala., 5,245 64 B2
Northport, Me. 55 C4
Northport, Mich., 530 67 H3
Northport, Nebr. 75 C2
Northport, N.Y., 5,972 59 O10
Northport, Wash., 482 80 E1
North Portal, Sask., Can. 43 D5
Northport Point, Mich. 67 H3
North Powder, Oreg., 399 80 D3
North Pownal, Vt. 54 A6
North Prairie, Wis., 489 66 E6
North Providence, R.I., 18,220(T) 57 L5
North Quincy, Ill., 2,256 68 A4
North Randolph, Vt. 54 B4
North Rattlesnake Butte, Colo. 79 C3
North Reading, Mass., 8,331(T) 57 M2
North Rehoboth (part of Rehoboth), Mass. 57 M5
North Richland, Wash. 80 D2
North Richland Hills, Tex., 8,662 76 e9
North Richmond, N.H. 54 C6
North Richview, Ill. 68 C5
North Ridge, Ont., Can. 67 g16
North Ridge, N.Y. 58 k18
North Ridgeville, Ohio, 8,057 70 c9
North Riding (admin. part of Yorkshire), U.K., 554,102 113 F4
North Rim, Ariz. 78 C3
North River, Man., Can. 43 G2
North River, N.Y. 59 M4
North Riverside, Ill., 7,989 69 c9
North Ronaldsay, i., U.K. 112 E2
North Ronaldsay Firth, U.K. 112 E2
North Rose, N.Y. 58 G5
North Royalton, Ohio, 9,290 70 d9
North Rustico, P.E.I., Can. 47 U10
North Rutland (part of Rutland), Mass. 56 J3
North Sacramento, Calif., 12,922 82 a7
North St. Paul, Minn., 10,521 74 d5
North Salem, Ind., 626 70 C3
North Salem, N.H. 54 E6
North Salem, Ohio 70 H2
North Salt Lake, Utah, 1,655 78 c9
North Sandwich, N.H. 54 E4
North Saskatchewan, r., Alta., Can. 42 J3
North Scituate, Mass., 3,421 57 N4
North Scituate, R.I. 57 K5
North Sea, Eur. 110 D3
North Seal, r., Man., Can. 43 E2
North Searsmont, Me. 55 C4
North Sentinel I., India 146 A5
North Shoal L., Man., Can. 43 g9
North Shore Chan., Ill. 69 d8
North Shrewsbury, Vt. 54 B4
North Side, mtn., Anguilla 97 7
North Side Town, Grand Cayman 97 3
North Sioux City, S. Dak., 736 74 D4
North Sister, mtn., Oreg. 80 C3
North Somercotes, U.K., 1,132 114 J4
North Somers (part of Somers), Conn. 56 G4
North Sd., Antigua 97 9
North Sd., Grand Cayman 97 3
North Sd., Ire. 113 B5
North Sd., The, U.K. 112 E2
North Spencer (part of Spencer), Mass. 56 H3
North Spirit L., Ont., Can. 44 D4
North Springfield, Vt. 54 C5
North Stamford (part of Stamford), Conn. 56 B8
North Star, Alta., Can. 42 H2
Northstar, Mich. 67 J5
North Star, Nebr. 75 G2
North Stockholm, N.Y. 59 K2
North Stonington, Conn., 1,982(T) 56 J7
North Stratford, N.H. 54 D2
North Street, Mich. 67 L5
North Sunderland, U.K., 1,580 112 F4
North Sutton, N.H. 54 D5
North Sydney, N.S., Can., 8,493 45 O6
North Syracuse, N.Y., 7,412 59 H5
North Taranaki Bight, N.Z. 175 g5
North Tarrytown, N.Y., 8,818 58 d12
North Tewksbury (part of Tewksbury), Mass. 57 M2
North Thames, r., Ont., Can. 67 M5
North Thetford, Vt. 54 C4
North Thompson, r., Br. Col., Can. 42 G3
North Thoresby, U.K. 114 H4
North Tidworth, U.K., 2,824 114 E8
North Tisbury, Mass. 57 O7
North Tiverton (part of Tiverton), R.I. 57 M6
North Toe, r., N.C. 63 B2
North Tonawanda, N.Y., 34,753 58 C5
North Trap, i., N.Z. 175 f7
North Troy, Vt., 961 54 C2
North Truchas Pk., N. Mex. 79 C4
North Truro (part of Truro), Mass. 57 Q4
North Tunbridge, Vt. 54 C4
North Turkey Cr., Colo. 79 b8
North Turner, Me. 55 B4
North Twin I., N.W.T., Can. 44 H4
North Twin L., Wis. 66 D2
North Twin Mtn., N.H. 54 D3
North Uist, i., U.K. 112 C3
Northumberland, co., U.K., 818,988 113 E4
Northumberland, N.H. 54 D2
Northumberland, N.Y. 59 w27
Northumberland, co., Pa., 104,138 60 J4
Northumberland, Pa., 4,156 60 J4
Northumberland, co., Va., 10,185 62 H5
Northumberland, C., Austl. 172 E6
Northumberland Is., Austl. 173 G3
Northumberland Str., Can. 45 N6
North Umpqua, r., Oreg. 80 B4
North Union, St. Vinc. 97 19
Northup, Ohio 70 G4
North Uxbridge, Mass., 1,882 57 K4
Northvale, N.J., 2,892 58 d13
North Vancouver, Br. Col., Can., 23,964 42 d6
North Vassalboro, Me. 55 C4
North Vernon, Ind., 4,062 70 D3
North Victory, N.Y. 59 p22
North Viet-Nam, ctry., 17,000,000* 146 D3
North Village (part of Lancaster), Mass. 57 K3
Northville (part of New Milford), Conn. 56 C6
Northville (part of East Bridgewater), Mass. 57 N4
Northville, Mich., 3,967 67 K6
Northville, N.Y., 1,156 59 M5
Northville, S. Dak., 153 74 C3
North Vineland, N.J. 61 A4
North Wales, Pa., 3,673 61 M5
North Walpole, N.H. 54 C5
North Walsham, U.K., 5,014 113 G5
North Wardsboro, Vt. 54 B5
North Warren, Pa., 1,458 60 D2
North Washington, Pa. 60 C3
North Waterford, Me. 55 B4
Northway, Alaska, 196 85 J3
North Weald Bassett, U.K., 3,957 114 J7
North Weare, N.H. 54 D5
North Webster, Ind., 494 70 D1
North West Arm, Newf., Can. 45 b9
North West Bay, Seych. 165 a10
Northwest Bluff, Montserrat 97 5
North West Brook, Newf., Can. 45 a9
Northwest Brook, Newf., Can. 45 b11
North West C., Austl. 172 A3
North Westchester (part of Colchester), Conn. 56 G6
North Western, N.Y. 59 K5
North Westminster, Vt., 368 54 B5
Northwest Miramichi, r., N.B., Can. 47 S10
North West Pt., Christmas Atoll 177 40
North West Pt., Jam. 96 o8
North Westport (part of Westport), Mass. 57 M6
Northwest Providence Channel, Bah. Is. 95 C1
Northwest Reef, Palau 176 21
North West River, Newf., Can. 45 O4
Northwest Territories, Can., 25,000* 40 F5
Northwich, U.K., 19,374 114 D4
North Wilbraham (part of Wilbraham), Mass. 56 G4
North Wildwood, N.J., 3,598 61 B5
North Wilkesboro, N.C., 4,197 63 C1
North Williston, Vt. 54 A3
North Windham (part of Windham), Conn. 56 H6
North Windham, Me. 55 B5
North Wingfield, U.K., 8,012 114 E4
North Wolcott, Vt. 54 C2
Northwood, Ont., Can. 46 B6
Northwood (part of Cowes), U.K., 2,906 113 k13
Northwood, Iowa, 1,768 72 D1
Northwood, N.H. 54 E5
Northwood, N. Dak., 1,195 74 D2
Northwood Center, N.H. 54 E5
Northwood L., N.H. 54 E5
Northwood Narrows, N.H. 54 E5
Northwoods, Mo., 4,701 72 b11
North Woodstock (part of Woodstock), Conn. 56 H5
North Woodstock, N.H. 54 D3
North York Moors, U.K. 113 F4
North Zulch, Tex. 77 P4
Norton, N.B., Can. 47 T11
Norton, Rhod., 1,480 164 E4
Norton, Rad., Wales, U.K. 114 B6
Norton, York., Eng., U.K., 1,858 114 F3
Norton, York., Eng., U.K., 4,770 113 F4
Norton, co., Kans., 8,035 75 F4
Norton, Kans., 3,345 75 F4
Norton, Mass., 6,818(T) 57 M5
Norton, Vt. 54 D2
Norton, Va., 5,013 62 B6
Norton, W. Va. 62 D4
Norton Bay, Alaska 85 D2
Norton L., Vt. 54 D2
Norton-Radstock, U.K., 12,793 113 E6
Norton Res., Mass. 57 M4
Norton Sd., Alaska 85 C3
Nortonsville, Va. 62 F4
Nortonville, Ont., Can. 46 c13
Nortonville, Ill. 68 B4
Nortonville, Kans., 595 75 K4
Nortonville, Ky., 755 71 D4
Nortonville, N. Dak. 74 C2
Nortorf, F.R.Ger., 5,695 118 B1
Norval, Ont., Can. 46 c13
Norvegia, C., Ant. 108 P5
Norvell, Mich. 67 J6
Norwalk, Calif., 88,739 83 h16
Norwalk, Conn., 67,775 56 C8
Norwalk, Iowa, 1,328 72 D3
Norwalk, Mich. 67 G4
Norwalk, Ohio, 12,900 70 G1
Norwalk, Wis., 484 66 C5

270 · Norwalk—Oberschan

Norwalk, r., Conn. 56 C8
Norway, ctry., 3,738,000* 120
Norway, Ind. 70 C2
Norway, Iowa, 516 72 F3
Norway, Me., 2,654 55 B4
Norway, Mich., 3,171 66 F3
Norway, Nebr. 75 E2
Norway, Oreg. 80 A4
Norway, S.C., 525 63 C4
Norway House, Man., Can. 43 F4
Norwegian Basin, North Sea 108 M2
Norwegian Bay, N.W.T., Can. 41 L2
Norwegian Sea, 108 M2
Norwell, Mass., 5,207(T) 57 N4
Norwich, Ont., Can., 1,678 46 D6
Norwich, U.K., 120,096 113 G5
Norwich, Conn., 38,506 56 H6
Norwich, Kans., 430 75 H6
Norwich (part of Huntington), Mass. 56 E3
Norwich, N.Y., 9,175 59 J6
Norwich, N. Dak. 74 B1
Norwich, Ohio, 193 70 H3
Norwich, Vt. 54 C4
Norwichtown (part of Norwich), Conn. 56 H6
Norwood, Ont., Can., 1,060 44 J7
Norwood, Colo., 443 79 A2
Norwood, Ga., 294 64 G2
Norwood, La., 427 73 D7
Norwood, Mass., 24,898(T) 57 M4
Norwood, Mich. 67 H3
Norwood, Mo., 263 72 E7
Norwood, N.J., 2,852 58 d13
Norwood, N.Y., 2,200 59 L2
Norwood, N.C., 1,844 63 D2
Norwood, Ohio, 34,580 70 E3
Norwood, Va. 62 F5
Norzagaray, Phil., 5,080 153 B2
Noshiro, Jap., 63,002 155 F1
Nosova, U.S.S.R. 137 k7
Nosovka, U.S.S.R. 136 C3
Noss, I. of, U.K. 112 F1
Nossen, Ger.D.R. 126 c5
Noss Head, U.K. 112 E2
Nossi-Bé=Nosy Be
Nossob, r., S. Af. 164 C6
Nosy Be, i., Malag. Rep. 165 H4
Nosy Varika, Malag. Rep. 165 H5
Notasulga, Ala., 884 64 D3
Notawissi, r., Qué., Can. 47 J1
Noteć, r., Pol. 127 B2
Notikewin, Alta., Can. 42 H2
Notikewin, r., Alta., Can. 42 H2
Noto, It., 27,254 123 E6
Notodden, Nor., 7,396 120 B4
Noto-hantō, Jap. 155 E3
Noto-jima, Jap. 155 E3
Notoro-misaki, Jap. 155 L7
Notre Dame B., Newf., Can. 45 Q5
Notre-Dame-de-Lorette, Qué., Can., 3,961 44 K5
Notre-Dame-de-Lorette, Qué., Can., 3,956 47 n16
Notre Dame de Lourdes, Man., Can. 43 F5
Notre-Dame-des-Anges, Qué., Can. 47 M2
Notre-Dame-des-Bois, Qué., Can. 47 O3
Notre-Dame-du-Lac, Qué., Can., 1,680 47 R10
Notre-Dame-du-Laus, Qué., Can. 47 J2
Notre-Dame-du-Rosaire, Qué., Can. 47 O2
Notre-Dame Mts., Qué., Can. 47 R10
Notress, Tex. 77 M4
Nottawa, Ont., Can. 46 D4
Nottawa, Mich. 67 H7
Nottawasaga B., Ont., Can. 46 D4
Nottaway, r., Qué., Can. 44 H4
Nottely L., Ga. 64 E1
Nottingham, U.K., 311,899 113 F5
Nottingham, N.H. 54 E5
Nottingham Island, N.W.T., Can. 40 O5
Nottingham I., N.W.T., Can. 41 O5
Nottinghamshire, co., U.K., 902,988 113 F5
Nottoway, co., Va., 15,141 62 F5
Nottoway, Va. 62 F5
Nottoway, r., Va. 62 F5
Nottu, i., Truk 176 19
Nouakchott, Maur., 5,700 162 B2
Nouatta, Togo 162 d8
Nough, Tenn. 71 J6
Nouméa, N. Caled., 22,235 174 k9
Nouna, Upper Volta, 4,915 162 D3
Noupoort, S. Af., 6,322 164 D7
Nouvelle-Anvers, D.R.Congo 164 C1
Nouvelle-Calédonie, i., N. Caled. 174 h8
Nova, Ohio 70 G1
Nova Andradina, Braz. 103 F6
Novabad, U.S.S.R. 137 f4
Nová Baňa, Czech. 126 D2
Nova Chaves, Ang. 164 C3
Novaci-Străini, Rum. 128 D2
Nova Cruz, Braz., 6,780 103 J3
Nova Era, Braz., 7,326 103 e17
Nova Freixo, Moz. 164 F4
Nova Friburgo, Braz., 49,901 103 e18
Nova Gaia, Ang. 164 B3
Nova Gradiška, Yug., 7,548 125 C2
Nova Iguaçu, Braz., 134,708 103 e18
Nova Lamego, Port. Guin. 162 B3
Nova Lima, Braz., 21,135 103 e17
Nova Lisboa, Ang. 164 B4
Nova Lusitânia, Moz. 164 E5
Nova Mambone=Mambone
Nova Olinda do Norte, Braz., 2,701 102 E2
Nová Paca, Czech. 127 e6
Novar, Ont., Can. 46 E3
Novara, It., 83,231 123 B2
Nova Russas, Braz., 4,666 103 H2
Nova Sagres, Port. Timor 149 H5
Nova Scotia, prov., Can., 761,000* 45 N7
Nova Sofala, Moz. 164 E5
Novato, Calif., 17,881 82 B3
Nova Varoš, Yug., 2,179 125 D3
Nova Venécia, Braz., 4,567 103 H5
Novaya Kakhovka, U.S.S.R., 19,900 136 D4
Novaya Kazanka, U.S.S.R. 134 D5
Novaya Ladoga, U.S.S.R., 7,900 136 D1
Novaya Lyalya, U.S.S.R., 17,700 137 k7
Novaya Sibir', O., U.S.S.R. 135 P2
Novaya Zemlya, U.S.S.R. 134 E2
Novaya Zemlya Trench, 132 E2
Nova Zagora, Bulg., 14,892 128 F3
Novéant, Fr., 1,416 116 b8
Nové Hrady, Czech. 126 B2
Nové Hrady, Czech. 127 f7
Novelda, Sp., 12,911 122 E3
Novellara, It., 10,671 122 d6
Novelty, Mo., 176 72 E5
Novelty, Ohio 70 f8
Nové Město nad Metují, Czech. 127 f6
Nové Mesto nad Váhom, Czech., 12,309 126 C2
Noventa Vicentina, It., 6,580 122 e5
Nové Zámky, Czech., 21,874 126 D3
Novgorod, U.S.S.R., 68,000 134 B4
Novgorod-Severskiy, U.S.S.R., 12,200 136 D2
Novi, Mich., 6,390 67 K6
Novi, Yug. 125 B2
Novi Bečej, Yug., 16,000* 125 E2
Novice, Tex., 227 77 O3
Novi di Modena, It., 10,108 122 d6
Novi Dulići, Yug. 125 D3
Novigrad, Yug. 125 A2
Novi Ligure, It., 25,017 123 B2
Novinger, Mo., 621 72 E4
Novi Pazar, Bulg., 9,139 128 F3
Novi Pazar, Yug., 21,000* 125 E3
Novi Sad, Yug., 111,000* 125 D2
Nóvita, Col. 100 B5
Nôvo Acôrdo, Braz. 103 G4
Novo-Aleksandrovskaya, U.S.S.R. 136 F4
Novo-Annenskiy, U.S.S.R., 18,700 136 F3
Novo Aripuanã, Braz., 1,116 102 E3
Novobelokatay, U.S.S.R. 137 i8
Novocherkassk, U.S.S.R., 96,000 136 f8
Novo-Ekonomicheskoye, U.S.S.R., 36,200 136 e7
Novograd-Volynskiy, U.S.S.R., 27,500 136 B3
Novogrudok, U.S.S.R., 12,600 136 B2
Novo il'inskiy, U.S.S.R. 137 h7
Novokashirsk, U.S.S.R., 9,400 136 c6
Novo-Kazalinsk, U.S.S.R. 134 F5
Novokhopërsk, U.S.S.R., 8,900 136 F3
Novokuznetsk, U.S.S.R., 405,000 134 H4
Novolazarevskaya, Ant. 180 Q6
Novo Mesto, Yug., 5,134 125 B2
Novo Miloševo, Yug., 9,356 125 E2
Novomoskovsk, R.S.F.S.R., U.S.S.R., 112,000 134 C4
Novomoskovsk, Ukr. S.S.R., U.S.S.R., 44,200 136 D3
Novonikol'skoye, U.S.S.R. 134 G4
Novo-Orsk, U.S.S.R. 137 i9
Novo-Pashiyskiy, U.S.S.R., 10,100 137 i7
Novopetrovskoye, U.S.S.R. 136 b6
Novopokrovka, U.S.S.R. 137 m11
Novo-Pokrovskaya, U.S.S.R. 136 F4
Novopskov, U.S.S.R. 136 E3
Novo Redondo, Ang. 164 B3
Novorossiysk, U.S.S.R., 101,000 134 C5
Novo-Ryazhsk, U.S.S.R., 6,600 136 F2
Novorybnoye, U.S.S.R. 135 K2
Novorzhev, U.S.S.R., 2,800 136 C1
Novoselishche, U.S.S.R. 151 F1
Novoselitsa, U.S.S.R., 11,500 136 B3
Novosëlki, U.S.S.R. 136 c6
Novo Selo, Yug. 125 F4
Novoselovo, U.S.S.R. 137 s11
Novoshakhtinsk, U.S.S.R., 108,000 136 E4
Novosibirsk, U.S.S.R., 985,000 134 H4
Novosibirskiye O-va., U.S.S.R. 135 N2
Novosibirskoye Vdkhr., U.S.S.R. 134 G4
Novosil', U.S.S.R., 2,400 136 E2
Novosokol'niki, U.S.S.R., 9,500 136 C1
Novo-Troitsk, U.S.S.R., 64,000 134 E4
Novoukrainka, U.S.S.R., 16,000 136 C3
Novoural'sk, U.S.S.R. 137 h9
Novouzensk, U.S.S.R., 12,800 134 D4
Novo-Varshavka, U.S.S.R. 137 o11
Novovolynsk, U.S.S.R., 23,800 136 B3
Novo-Yerudinskiy, U.S.S.R. 135 J4
Novozybkov, U.S.S.R., 24,700 136 D2
Novska, Yug. 125 C2
Nový Bohumín, Czech., 11,851 127 h7
Nový Bydžov, Czech. 127 e6
Nový Jičín, Czech., 16,976 126 C2
Novyy Afon, U.S.S.R., 3,500 137 b1
Novyy Bug, U.S.S.R., 15,300 136 D4
Novyy Donbass, U.S.S.R., 16,300 136 f7
Novyye Karymkary, U.S.S.R. 134 F3
Novyye Petushki, U.S.S.R. 136 c6
Novyye Senzhary, U.S.S.R., 4,700 136 D3
Novyy Oskol, U.S.S.R., 12,900 136 E3
Novyy Port, U.S.S.R. 134 G3
Novyy Vasyugan, U.S.S.R. 134 G4
Nowa Ruda, Pol., 17,819 127 B3
Nowa Sól, Pol., 25,000* 127 A3
Nowata, co., Okla., 10,848 76 H1
Nowata, Okla., 4,163 76 H1
Nowe, Pol., 4,666 127 C2
Nowe Miasteczko, Pol., 2,388 127 A3
Nowe Miasto, Pol. 127 D2
Nowe Miasto, Pol., 3,327 127 D3
Nowe Miasto Lubawskie, Pol., 5,634 127 C2
Nowe Warpno, Pol. 127 A2
Nowgong, Assam, India, 38,600 145 J4
Nowgong, M.P., India, 8,604 144 b13
Nowitna, r., Alaska 85 F2
Nowlin, S. Dak. 74 B3
Nowogard, Pol., 6,374 127 A2
Nowogród, Pol., 1,609 127 E2
Nowogrodziec, Pol., 1,180 127 A3
Nowra, Austl., 5,981 173 G5
Nowshera, Pak., 43,757 145 D2
Nowy Dwór Gdański, Pol., 4,953 127 C1
Nowy Dwór Mazowiecki, Pol., 7,752 127 D2
Nowy Sącz, Pol., 34,000* 127 D4
Nowy Staw, Pol., 4,045 127 C1
Nowy Targ, Pol., 15,742 127 C4
Noxapater, Miss., 549 73 F5
Noxen, Pa. 61 K3
Noxon, Mont. 81 B2
Noxon Res., Mont. 81 B2
Noxubee, co., Miss., 16,826 73 G4
Noxubee, r., Miss. 73 G4
Noya, Sp., 12,241 122 A1
Noyant, Fr., 1,632 117 C3
Noyo, Calif. 82 B3
Noyon, Fr., 9,548 117 E2
Nozawa, Jap. 155 F3
Nozay, Fr. 116 g12
Nozay, Fr., 3,387 117 C3
Nriquinha, Ang. 164 C4
Nsawam, Ghana, 20,312 162 c9
Nsefu, Zamb. 164 E4
Nsukka, Nigeria, 16,875 162 F4
Nsuta, Ghana 162 b9
Ntoum, Gabon 164 A1
Ntungamo, Uganda 165 e14
Nu=Salween
Nuakata, i., Terr. Papua 174 3
Nuanetsi, Rhod. 164 E5
Nuangola, Pa., 346 61 o17
Nūbah, Jibāl an, Sudan 163 K4
Nubanusit L., N.H. 54 C6
Nubeena, Austl. 173 f14
Nubian Desert, Sudan-U.A.R. 163 K2
Nubieber, Calif. 82 C2
Ñuble, r., Chile 104 f16
Nucet, Rum. 9,879 128 D1
Nuckolls, co., Nebr., 8,217 75 G3
Nucla, Colo., 906 79 A2
Nueces, co., Tex., 221,573 77 P6
Nueces, r., Tex. 77 P6
Nueltin L., Man.-N.W.T., Can. 43 E1
Nuenen, Neth., 3,800 115 D3
Nueva Concepción, El Salv., 2,632 94 d9
Nueva Gerona, Cuba, 3,203 96 b2
Nueva Granada, Col. 100 C3
Nueva Helvecia, Urug., 7,000* 105 c12
Nueva Imperial, Chile, 6,442 105 A5
Nueva Italia, Mex., 8,913 92 E4
Nueva Lubecka, Arg. 105 B6
Nueva Ocotepeque, Hond., 5,746 94 C3
Nueva Palmira, Urug., 5,000* 105 b11
Nueva Paz, Cuba, 4,032 96 c1
Nueva Rosita, Mex., 32,294 92 E2
Nueva San Salvador=Sta. Tecla
Nueva Sta. Rosa, Guat., 2,075 94 c9
9 de Julio, Arg., 17,469 105 C5
Nuevitas, Cuba, 12,390 96 e2
Nuevitas, Bahía de, Cuba 96 e2
Nuevo, Calif. 83 k16
Nuevo, r., Jam. 96 q8
Nuevo, Cayo, Mex. 93 H4
Nuevo, G., Arg. 105 C6
Nuevo Berlín, Urug., 1,500* 105 c11
Nuevo Casas Grandes, Mex., 11,735 92 D1
Nuevo Ideal, Mex., 3,726 92 D3
Nuevo Laredo, Mex., 93,787 93 F2
Nuevo León, Arg. 105 C6
Nuevo León, st., Mex., 1,078,848 93 E2
Nuevo Mamo, Ven. 101 J3
Nuevo Mundo, Bol. 102 C4
Nuevo Progreso, Guat. 94 b9
Nuevo Urecho, Mex., 1,021 93 c10
Nuevo Valle, Mex., 1,061 93 c8
Nugget Pt., N.Z. 175 f7
Nuguria Is., Terr. New Guin. 175 a1
Nugush, r., U.S.S.R. 137 h9
Nuh, India, 3,772 144 a11
Nuh, Rās, Pak. 144 B4
Nuhaka, N.Z. 175 h5
Nuhurowa, i., Indon. 149 K4
Nuhutjut, i., Indon. 149 K4
Nui, i., Ellice Is. 175 10
Nuits-St-Georges, Fr., 3,979 117 F3
Nukapu, i., Swallow Is. 175 6
Nukey Bluff, mtn., Austl. 172 E5
Nukha, U.S.S.R., 34,300 137 c1
Nukuaéta, Î., Îs. Wallis 175 7
Nukualofa, Tonga, 9,202 177 36
Nukufetau, atoll, Ellice Is. 175 10
Nukuhifala, Î., Îs. Wallis 175 7
Nuku Hiva, i., Marq. Is. 171 J5
Nukuhu, Terr. New Guin. 174 f2
Nukulailai, atoll, Ellice Is. 170 F5
Nukuloa, Î., Îs. Wallis 175 7
Nukumanu Is., Sol. Is. 175 c1
Nukumi, Jap. 154 h14
Nukunono, atoll, Tokelau Is. 170 G5
Nukunuku, Tonga 177 36
Nukuoro, atoll, Car. Is. 170 E4
Nukus, U.S.S.R., 42,000 134 F5
Nukutapu, Î., Îs. Wallis 175 7
Nukutavake, i., Tuam. Arch. 177 42
Nukuteatea, Î., Îs. Wallis 175 7
Nukutipipi, atoll, Tuam. Arch. 177 42
Nulato, Alaska, 283 85 E2
Nules, Sp., 8,460 122 E3
Nulhegan, r., Vt. 54 D2
Nulhegan, Black Br., r., Vt. 54 D2
Nullagine, Austl. 172 B3
Nullarbor Plain, Austl. 172 C4
Nulltown, Ind. 70 D3
Num, Nepal 144 f12
Num, Mios, i., Indon. 149 K3
Numa, Iowa, 202 72 E4
Numakunai, Jap. 155 G2
Numan, Nigeria 162 G4
Numansdorp, Neth. 115 a7
Numata, Jap., 42,919 155 F3
Numata, Jap., 19,362 155 J8
Numazu, Jap., 142,609 155 F4
No. 4 Mtn., Me. 55 C3
Nümbrecht, F.R.Ger., 5,073 119 D3
Numfor, P., Indon. 149 K3
Numidia, Pa. 61 K4
Nu Mine, Pa. 60 D4
Numto, U.S.S.R. 134 G3
Numurkah, Austl., 2,195 173 e11
Nunaka Valley, Alaska, 1,442 85 c7
Nunapitchuk, Alaska, 327 85 D3
Nunchía, Col. 100 D5
Nunda, N.Y., 1,224 58 E6
Nunda, S. Dak., 106 74 D3
Nuneaton, U.K., 56,598 113 F5
Nung-an, China 150 G2
Nungwe, Tanz. 165 f15
Nunica, Mich. 67 G5
Nunivak I., Alaska 85 B3
Nunkiang=Nen-chiang
Nunligran, U.S.S.R. 135 S3
Nunn, Colo., 228 79 C1
Nunnelly, Tenn. 71 D6
Nuñoa, Peru, 2,142 104 D5
Nunspeet, Neth., 7,100 115 D2
Nunton, U.K. 113 i12
Nuoro, It., 22,019 123 B4
Nupani, i., Sol. Is. 175 6
Nuquí, Col. 100 B5
Nur, Pol. 127 E2
Nura, r., U.S.S.R. 134 G4
Nurakita, i., Ellice Is. 170 G5
Nuratau, Khr., U.S.S.R. 137 e4
Nure, r., It. 122 c6
Nurek, U.S.S.R., 7,000 137 f5
Nuremberg, F.R.Ger.=Nürnberg
Nuremberg, Pa. 61 K4
Nuri, Mex. 92 C2
Nuria, Sa. de, Ven. 101 K4
Nurío, Mex., 1,028 93 b10
Nurmes, Fin. 120 G3
Nürnberg, F.R.Ger., 424,306 118 C4
Nursery, Tex. 77 P5
Nürtingen, F.R.Ger., 18,556 118 B4
Nurzec, r., Pol. 127 E2
Nus, r., Col. 101 e13
Nusaybin, Turk., 5,008 142 E2
Nushagak, Alaska 85 E4
Nushagak, r., Alaska 85 E4
Nushagak Bay, Alaska 85 E4
Nushima, Jap. 154 f15
Nushki, Pak., 3,153 144 B3
Nussdorf, Aust., 1,103 124 M5
Nusse, F.R.Ger. 119 c8
Nussloch, F.R.Ger., 5,722 119 F6
Nutak, Newf., Can. 45 O2
Nutarawit L., N.W.T., Can. 40 K5
Nutberry Hill, U.K. 112 b8
Nuthe, r., Ger.D.R. 118 D2
Nutley, N.J., 29,513 61 C2
Nut Plains (part of Guilford), Conn. 56 F7
Nutrioso, Ariz. 78 D5
Nutt, N. Mex. 79 B5
Nuttal, Pak. 144 C3
Nutter Fort, W. Va., 2,440 62 D3
Nutwood, Ill. 68 B4
Nützen, F.R.Ger., 1,049 119 a8
Nutzotin Mts., Alaska 85 J3
Nuuanu Str., Hawaii 84 c8
Nuulua, i., W. Samoa 177 38
Nuupere, Pte., Moorea 177 44
Nuutele, i., W. Samoa 177 38
Nuuuli, Tutuila, 1,137 177 39
Nuwākot, Nepal 144 e11
Nuwara Eliya, Cey., 14,405 145 n22
Nuyaka, Okla. 76 G2
Nuyts Arch., Austl. 172 D5
Nyac, Alaska, 54 85 E3
Nyack, N.Y., 6,062 59 N9
Nyah, Austl. 173 d10
Nyah West, Austl. 173 f5
Nyakabanda, Rwanda 165 d15
Nyakabindi, Tanz. 165 f15
Nyakakiri, Tanz. 165 e15
Nyakanyasi, Tanz. 165 e14
Nyaksimvol', U.S.S.R. 134 F3
Nyala, Sudan, 12,278 163 J3
Nyala, Nev. 83 C3
Ny-Ålesund, Nor. 134 A2
Nyalikungu, Tanz. 165 f15
Nyamandhlovu, Rhod. 164 D5
Nyambale, Tanz. 165 f15
Nyambiti, Tanz. 165 f15
Nyamirembe, Tanz. 165 e15
Nyandoma, U.S.S.R., 21,700 134 D3
Nyanga, Gabon 164 A2
Nyanga, L., Austl. 172 C4
Nyanga, r., Congo B.-Gabon 164 A2
Nyangan, Burma 147 g7
Nyangwe, D.R.Congo 164 D2
Nyanza, Rwanda 165 d15
Nyanza Lac, Burundi 164 E2
Nyasa, L.=Malawi, L.
Nyasaland=Malawi
Nyashimo, Tanz. 165 f15
Nyaungbintha, Burma, 1,692 146 B3
Nyaunggyo, Burma 147 a2
Nyaunglebin, Burma, 12,155 146 B3
Nyaungok, Burma 147 f7
Nyaungu, Burma, 9,416 146 A2
Nyavikungu, D.R.Congo 165 m19
Nyawarongo, r., Rwanda 165 d15
Nyazepetrovsk, U.S.S.R., 22,500 137 i8
Nyborg, Den., 11,667 121 C5
Nybro, Swed. 120 D4
Nyda, U.S.S.R. 134 G3
Nye, Mont. 81 E3
Nye, co., Nev., 4,374 83 B3
Nyenchhen Thanglha, mts., China 150 C4
Nyeri, Kenya 164 F2
Nyinahin=Yenahin
Nyíradony, Hung., 7,342 126 E3
Nyírbátor, Hung., 10,639 126 F3
Nyíregyháza, Hung., 56,875 126 E3
Nykarleby, Fin., 1,055 120 E3
Nykøbing, Den., 9,326 121 A4
Nykøbing, Den., 4,803 121 D5
Nykøbing, Den., 17,850 121 D6
Nyköping, Swed., 24,250 120 D4
Nykvarn, Swed. 120 e8
Nylarsker, Den., 1,011 121 G5
Nylstroom, S. Af., 6,662 164 D6
Nymagee, Austl. 173 F5
Nymburk, Czech., 12,529 126 B1
Nynäshamn, Swed. 120 D4
Nyngan, Austl., 2,257 173 G4
Nyon, Switz., 7,643 124 A2
Nyonga, D.R.Congo 165 n18
Nyons, Fr., 4,479 117 F4
Nýřany, Czech. 126 A2
Nyrob, U.S.S.R. 137 h6
Nysa, Pol., 23,000* 127 B3
Nysa Kłodzka, r., Pol. 127 g6
Nyssa, Oreg., 2,611 80 E4
Nystad=Uusikaupunki
Nysted, Den., 1,328 121 D6
Nytva, U.S.S.R., 19,200 137 h7
Nyū, Jap. 154 h15
Nyūdō-saki, Jap. 155 F1
Nyūgawa, Jap., 26,290 155 C5
Nyuku, China 144 e11
Nyúl, Hung., 3,641 126 C3
Nyunzu, D.R.Congo 164 D3
Nyurba, U.S.S.R. 135 L3
Nyuvchim, U.S.S.R. 134 E3
Nyuya, U.S.S.R. 135 L3
Nyuya, r., U.S.S.R. 135 L3
Nzara, Sudan, 2,971 163 J5
Nzega, Tanz. 164 E2
N'zérékoré, Guin., 8,500 162 C4
Nzi, r., Iv. Coast 162 a8
Nzoia, r., Kenya 165 g13

O

Oacoma, S. Dak., 312 74 C4
Oadby, U.K., 12,256 114 F5
Oahe Res., N. Dak.-S. Dak. 74 B3
Oahu, i., Hawaii 84 C2
Oak, Nebr., 125 75 H3
O-akan-dake, Jap. 155 L8
Oak Bay, N.B., Can. 47 S11
Oak Bluffs, Mass., 1,027;1,419(T) 57 O7
Oakboro, N.C., 581 63 D2
Oakbrook, Ill., 1,644 69 c9
Oakbrook Terrace, Ill., 1,121 69 c9
Oakburn, Man., Can. 43 E5
Oak City, N.C., 574 63 G2
Oak City, Utah, 312 78 B2
Oak Creek, Colo., 666 79 B1
Oak Creek, Wis., 11,548 66 F6
Oak Cr., S. Dak. 74 B3
Oakdale, Calif., 4,980 82 C4
Oakdale (part of Montville), Conn. 56 H7
Oakdale, Ga. 64 f9
Oakdale, Ill. 68 C5
Oakdale, La., 6,618 73 C7
Oakdale (part of W. Boylston), Mass. 57 J3
Oakdale, Minn. 74 d6
Oakdale, Nebr., 397 75 G1
Oakdale, N.Y. 58 g14
Oakdale, Pa., 1,695 60 B5
Oakdale, Tenn., 470 71 G6
Oakdale, Wis. 66 C5
Oakengates, U.K., 12,163 114 D5
Oakes, N. Dak., 1,650 74 C2
Oakesdale, Wash., 474 80 E2
Oakey, Austl., 1,641 173 G4
Oakfield, Ga., 141 64 F4
Oakfield, Me. 55 D2
Oakfield, N.Y., 2,070 58 D5
Oakfield, Wis., 772 66 E5
Oakford, Ill., 301 68 C3
Oak Forest, Ill., 7,952 69 c10
Oak Glen, N.J. 58 c16
Oak Grove, Ala. 64 b8
Oakgrove, Ark., 151 73 B1
Oak Grove, Ga., 3,525 64 g9
Oak Grove, Cameron Parish, La. 73 B8
Oak Grove, West Carroll Parish, La., 1,797 73 D5
Oak Grove, Mich. 67 J6
Oak Grove, Mo., 1,100 72 C6
Oak Grove, Oreg. 80 a7
Oak Grove, Va. 62 G4
Oak Hall, Va. 62 J5
Oakham, U.K., 4,089 113 F5
Oakham, Mass., 524(T) 56 H3
Oakharbor, Ohio, 2,903 70 F1
Oak Harbor, Wash., 3,942 80 B1
Oakhaven, Ark., 87 73 B4
Oakhill, Ala., 116 64 B4
Oak Hill, Fla., 758 65 J4
Oak Hill, Kans., 69 75 H4
Oak Hill, N.Y. 59 M7
Oak Hill, Ohio, 1,748 70 G4
Oak Hill, Tex. 76 c5
Oak Hill, W. Va., 4,711 62 C4
Oak Hill, Me. 55 D2
Oakhurst, Calif. 82 D4
Oakhurst, N.J., 4,374 61 D3
Oak I., Wis. 66 C2
Oak Lake, Man., Can. 43 E5
Oakland, Man., Can. 43 f9
Oakland, Ark. 73 C1
Oakland, Calif., 367,548 82 C4
Oakland, Fla., 821 65 H4
Oakland, Ga. 64 f12
Oakland, Ill., 939 68 E4
Oakland, Iowa, 1,340 72 B3
Oakland, Ky., 148 71 E4
Oakland, Me., 1,880 55 C4
Oakland, Md., 1,977 62 E3
Oakland (part of Taunton), Mass. 57 M5
Oakland, co., Mich., 690,259 67 K6
Oakland, Miss., 488 73 F3
Oakland, Nebr., 1,429 75 J2
Oakland, N.J., 9,446 61 C1
Oakland, Okla., 288 76 G3
Oakland, Oreg., 856 80 B4
Oakland, Pa., 889 61 L2
Oakland, R.I. 57 K5
Oakland, Tenn., 306 71 B6
Oakland Beach (part of Warwick), R.I. 57 L6
Oakland City, Ind., 3,016 70 B4
Oaklandon, Ind. 70 D3
Oakland Park, Fla., 5,331 65 J6
Oaklands, Austl. 173 e10
Oak Lawn, Ill., 27,471 68 E2
Oak Lawn (part of Cranston), R.I. 57 K5
Oakley, Fife, U.K. 112 c7
Oakley, Hants., U.K. 114 F8
Oakley, Calif. 83 f12
Oakley, Idaho, 613 81 C4
Oakley, Kans., 2,190 75 E4
Oakley, Mich., 417 67 J5
Oakley, S.C. 63 D4
Oakley, Utah, 247 78 C1
Oaklyn, N.J., 4,778 60 f12
Oakman, Ala., 849 64 B2
Oakman, Ga., 156 64 E1
Oakman, Okla. 76 G3
Oakmont, Pa., 7,504 60 C4
Oak Mtn., Ala. 64 d8
Oak Orchard, Del. 62 J4
Oak Orchard Cr., N.Y. 58 D5
Oak Park, Ga., 302 64 G3
Oak Park, Ill., 61,093 68 E2
Oak Park, Mich., 36,632 67 K6
Oak Park Heights, Minn. 74 d5
Oak Point, Man., Can. 43 g9
Oak Ridge, La., 287 73 D5
Oak Ridge, Mich. 67 J2
Oak Ridge, Mo., 175 72 H7
Oak Ridge, N.J. 58 b12
Oakridge, Oreg., 1,973 80 B4
Oak Ridge, Tenn., 27,169 71 G5
Oak Ridge Res., N.J. 58 a12
Oak Ridges, Ont., Can., 1,593 46 E5
Oaks, U.K. 112 g10
Oaks, Mo., 159 75 a7
Oaks, Pa. 60 f11
Oaktown, Ind., 798 70 B4
Oak Vale, Miss., 99 73 F6
Oakvale, W. Va., 267 62 C5
Oak Valley, Kans. 75 K6
Oak View, Calif., 2,448 82 D5
Oakview, Mo., 543 75 a7
Oakview Beach, Ont., Can. 46 D4
Oakville, Man., Can. 43 f10
Oakville, Ont., Can., 10,043 46 E5
Oakville (part of Watertown), Conn. 56 D6
Oakville, Iowa, 346 72 G3
Oakville, Mich. 67 K6
Oakville, Tex. 77 P5
Oakville, Wash., 377 80 B2
Oakville Cr., Ont., Can. 46 c13
Oakway, S.C. 63 A3
Oakwood, Ont., Can. 46 F4
Oakwood, Ill., 861 68 E3
Oakwood, Mich. 67 K6
Oakwood, Mo., 159 75 a7
Oakwood, N.Y. 59 p24
Oakwood, Cuyahoga Co., Ohio, 3,283 70 f9
Oakwood, Montgomery Co., Ohio, 10,493 70 E3
Oakwood, Paulding Co., Ohio, 686 70 E1
Oakwood, Okla., 122 76 E2
Oakwood, Tex., 716 77 P4
Oakwood, Va. 62 C5
Oakworth, U.K., 5,428 114 D3
Oamaru, N.Z., 12,429 175 f7
Ōami, Jap. 155 n19
Oancea, Rum. 128 F2
Oarja, Rum. 128 E2
Oark, Ark. 73 B2
Ōasa, Jap., 6,903 155 C4
Oasis, Calif. 82 E6
Oasis, Nev. 83 C2
Oasis, Utah 78 B2
Oates Coast, Ant. 180 V5
Oatlands, Austl. 173 G6
Oatman, Ariz. 78 A4
Oats, S.C. 63 D3
Oaxaca, st., Mex., 1,727,266 93 F5
Oaxaca, Mex., 72,313 93 F5
Ob', U.S.S.R. 137 q11
Ob', r., U.S.S.R. 134 F3
Oba, Ont., Can. 44 F5
Oba, i., New Hebr. 174 k5
Obabika L., Ont., Can. 46 D1
Obama, Jap., 17,945 154 B5
Obama, Jap., 36,236 155 D4
Oban, N.Z. 175 f7
Oban, U.K., 6,659 112 D3
Obanazawa, Jap., 33,277 155 G2
Obano, Indon. 149 L3
Obar, N. Mex. 79 D4
Obata, Jap., 11,040 154 h15
Obbia, Som. Rep., 2,102* 163 N5
Obdach, Aust., 1,087 124 L6
Obed, Alta., Can. 42 H3
Obed, r., Tenn. 71 G5
Obeh, Afghan. 144 B2
Obelisk, Pa. 60 f10
Oberá, Arg., 12,000* 105 E3
Oberachern, F.R.Ger., 2,869 119 E7
Oberaden, F.R.Ger., 9,052 119 D1
Oberammergau, F.R.Ger., 4,546 118 C5
Oberbach, F.R.Ger., 1,012 119 H4
Oberbronn, Fr., 1,342 116 e9
Oberbruch, F.R.Ger., 4,835 119 A2
Oberdreis, F.R.Ger. 119 D3
Ober Engadin, val., Switz. 124 D2
Oberhaslach, Fr., 1,004 116 d9
Oberhausen, Bad.-Württ., F.R.Ger., 5,429 119 F6
Oberhausen, Nrh.-Wf., F.R.Ger., 241,570 119 B2
Oberhof, Ger.D.R. 118 C3
Oberhofen, Switz., 1,605 124 B2
Oberhoffen-sur-Moder, Fr., 2,248 119 D7
Oberkassel, F.R.Ger., 5,515 119 C3
Oberkessach, F.R.Ger., 1,007 119 G6
Oberkirch, F.R.Ger., 7,524 118 A4
Oberkirchen, Nrh.-Wf., F.R.Ger., 3,103 119 E2
Oberkirchen, Sarr., F.R.Ger., 2,030 116 d8
Oberkochen, F.R.Ger., 6,366 118 C4
Oberlahnstein, F.R.Ger., 11,924 118 A3
Oberlin, Kans., 2,337 75 E4
Oberlin, La., 1,794 73 C7
Oberlin, Mich. 67 J4
Oberlin, Ohio, 8,198 70 G1
Oberlin, Okla. 76 H4
Obermörlen, F.R.Ger., 3,178 119 F4
Obernburg, F.R.Ger., 3,406 119 G5
Oberndorf, Aust., 3,083 124 J6
Oberndorf, Bad.-Württ., F.R.Ger., 7,020 118 B4
Oberndorf, Hess., F.R.Ger., 1,039 119 G4
Oberon, Austl., 1,354 173 g9
Oberon, N. Dak., 248 74 C2
Oberpleis, F.R.Ger., 6,321 119 C3
Ober Ramstadt, F.R.Ger., 7,565 119 F5
Oberriet, Switz., 5,498 124 D1
Oberroden, F.R.Ger., 5,146 119 F5
Oberrot, F.R.Ger., 1,720 119 H6
Oberschan, Switz. 124 a8

Oberschefflenz—Olofström · 271

Oberschefflenz, F.R.Ger., 1,269 119 G6
Oberscheld, F.R.Ger., 2,262 119 E3
Oberschleissheim, F.R.Ger., 4,363 118 C4
Oberseebach, Fr., 1,353 119 D7
Oberseeman, F.R.Ger., 1,390 119 G4
Obersinn, F.R.Ger., 1,185 119 H4
Oberstdorf, F.R.Ger., 7,815 118 C5
Obersteinbach, Fr. 116 e8
Obersuhl, F.R.Ger., 3,284 118 B3
Obersulz, Aust. 124 d10
Oberthal, F.R.Ger., 2,814 116 d8
Oberursel, F.R.Ger., 19,186 119 F4
Obervaz=Vaz
Obervellach, Aust., 2,371 124 K7
Oberwald, Switz. 124 C2
Oberwart, Aust., 4,734 124 N6
Oberwesel, F.R.Ger., 3,787 118 A3
Obetz, Ohio, 1,984 70 G3
Obey, E. Fk., r., Tenn. 71 F5
Obi, i., Indon. 149 H3
Obi, Selat, Indon. 149 H3
Obiam, C., Saipan 176 27
Óbidos, Braz., 5,901 103 E2
Obihiro, Jap., 100,915 155 K8
Obikhingou, r., U.S.S.R. 137 f5
Obiki, Jap. 154 e15
Obion, co., Tenn., 26,957 71 B5
Obion, Tenn., 1,097 71 B5
Obion, r., Tenn. 71 B5
Obirachō, Jap., 10,142 155 J7
Obispos, Ven. 100 E3
Oblong, Ill., 1,817 68 E5
Obluch'ye, U.S.S.R., 15,300 135 M5
Obninsk, U.S.S.R., 16,300 136 b6
Obo, C.A.R., 2,141 163 J5
Obock, Fr. Som. 163 M3
Obolo, Nigeria, 13,650 162 F4
Obome, Indon. 149 K3
Obonai, Jap., 6,661 155 G2
Oborniki, Pol., 7,825 127 B2
Oborniki Śląskie, Pol., 5,694 127 f5
Oboyan', U.S.S.R., 10,200 136 E3
Obra, r., Pol. 127 A2
Obrajuelo, Mex., 1,092 93 d9
Obrež, Yug., 4,020 125 E3
O'Brien, Fla. 65 G2
O'Brien, co., Iowa, 18,840 72 B1
O'Brien, Oreg. 80 B4
O'Brien, Tex., 287 77 N3
Obrigheim, F.R.Ger., 2,150 119 G6
Obrov, Yug. 125 A2
Obrovac, Yug. 125 B2
Obruchishte, Bulg., 2,962 128 F3
Observation Pk., Calif. 82 C2
Obskaya G., U.S.S.R. 134 G3
Obuasi, Ghana, 22,948 162 D4
Ōbuke, Jap., 6,757 155 G2
Ōbuse, Jap. 154 g14
Obva, r., U.S.S.R. 137 h7
Obzor, Bulg., 1,520 128 F3
Ocala, Fla., 13,598 65 G3
Ocala, Nev. 83 A3
Ocalli, Peru, 1,234 104 B3
Ocamo, r., Ven. 101 H6
Ocampo, Coah., Mex., 1,299 92 E2
Ocampo, Tam., Mex., 3,348 93 F3
Ocaña, Col. 100 D3
Ocaña, Sp., 6,686 122 D3
Ocate, N. Mex. 79 C3
Occhiobello, It., 5,532 122 e6
Occidental, Cord., Bol.-Chile 102 C5
Occidental, Cord., Col. 100 B6
Occidental, Cord., Peru 104 B3
Occoquan, Va., 301 62 G4
Occum (part of norwich), Conn. 56 H6
Ocean, co., N.J., 108,241 61 C4
Ocean, N.C. 63 H3
Oceana, co., Mich., 16,547 67 G5
Oceana, W. Va., 1,303 62 C5
Ocean Bay Park, N.Y. 58 g14
Ocean Beach (part of New London), Conn. 56 H7
Ocean Beach, N.Y., 111 58 g14
Ocean Bluff (part of Marshfield), Mass. 57 O4
Ocean C., Alaska 85 J4
Ocean City, Md., 983 62 J4
Ocean City, N.J., 7,618 61 B5
Ocean City, Wash. 80 A2
Ocean Drive Beach, S.C., 313 63 F4
Ocean Falls, Br. Col., Can., 2,832 42 E3
Ocean Gate, N.J., 706 61 C4
Ocean Grove (part of Swansea), Mass. 57 M6
Ocean Grove, N.J. 58 d16
Ocean I., Pac. Oc. 170 F5
Ocean Isle Beach, N.C., 5 63 F4
Oceanlake, Oreg., 1,342 80 A3
Oceano, Calif., 1,317 82 C5
Ocean Park, Wash. 80 A2
Oceanport, N.J., 4,937 61 D3
Ocean Ridge, Fla., 209 65 b8
Oceanside, Calif., 24,971 82 E6
Oceanside, N.Y., 30,448 58 e14
Oceanside, Oreg. 80 A3
Ocean Springs, Miss., 5,025 73 G7
Ocean View, Del., 422 62 J4
Oceanway, Fla., 1,271 65 H2
Oceola, Ohio 70 F2
Ochakov, U.S.S.R., 8,400 136 C4
Ochamchire, U.S.S.R., 16,500 137 b1
Ochelata, Okla., 312 76 G1
O-ch'eng, China 152 D1
Ocher, U.S.S.R., 19,800 137 h7
Ocheyedan, Iowa, 662 72 B1
Ocheyedan, r., Iowa-Minn. 72 B1
Ocheyedan Mound, Iowa 72 B1
Ochi, Jap., 12,587 155 C5
Ōchi, Jap., 6,493 155 E3
Ochiai, Jap. 154 e16
Ochiai, Jap. 154 g16
Ochiai, Jap. 154 i14
Ochiai, Jap., 22,884 155 C4
Ochiai, Jap. 155 K8
Ochiai, Jap. 155 m18
Ochiltree, co., Tex., 9,380 76 N1
O-chi-na, r., China 150 D2
O-chi-na-ch'i, China 150 D2
Ochlocknee, Ga., 502 64 E5
Ochlockonee, r., Fla.-Ga. 64 E5
Ochopee, Fla. 65 H7
Ocho Rios, Jam., 4,570 96 p8
Ochre River, Man., Can. 43 E5
Ochsenfurt, F.R.Ger., 7,077 118 B4
Ochsenhausen, F.R.Ger., 3,276 118 C4
Ochtendung, F.R.Ger., 3,708 119 C4
Ochtrup, F.R.Ger., 12,797 118 A2
Ocilla, Ga., 3,217 64 F4
Ockelbo, Swed. 120 D3
Öckerö, Swed. 121 D3
Ockley, Ind. 70 C2
Ocland, Rum. 128 E1
Ocmulgee, r., Ga. 64 F3
Ocmulgee Nat. Mon., Ga. 64 F3
Ocna Mureş, Rum., 10,701 128 D1
Ocna Sibiului, Rum. 128 E2
Ocna Şugatag, Rum. 128 E1
Ocnele Mari, Rum., 4,420 128 E2
Ocoa, B. de, Dom. Rep. 96 m6
Ocoa, r., Dom. Rep. 96 m6
Ocoee, Fla., 2,628 65 H4
Ocoee, Tenn. 71 G6
Ocoña, Peru, 1,199 104 C6
Ocoña, r., Peru 104 C6
Oconee, co., Ga., 6,304 64 F2
Oconee, Ill., 257 68 C4
Oconee, co., S.C., 40,204 63 A3
Oconee, r., Ga. 64 G3
Oconomowoc, Wis., 6,682 66 E5
Oconto, Nebr., 219 75 F2
Oconto, co., Wis., 25,110 66 E4
Oconto, Wis., 4,805 66 F4
Oconto, r., Wis. 66 E4
Oconto Falls, Wis., 2,331 66 E4
Ocosingo, Mex., 1,271 93 H5
Ocotal, Nic., 3,521 94 D4
Ocotepec, Mex., 1,068 93 d11
Ocotillo, Ariz. 78 C5
Ocotillo, Calif. 82 E6
Ocotlán, Jal., Mex., 25,435 92 E4
Ocotlán, Oax., Mex., 5,287 93 F5
Ocoya, Ill. 68 D3
Ocozocoautla de Espinosa, Mex., 6,442 93 G5
Ocqueoc, Mich. 67 J3
Ocquier, Belg. 115 D4
Ocracoke, N.C. 63 H2
Ocracoke Inlet, N.C. 63 J2
Ocros, Peru, 1,204 104 B4
Ócsa, Hung., 7,356 126 D3
Octavia, Nebr., 94 75 J2
Octavia, Okla. 76 J3
Octeville, Fr., 6,247 117 C2
Octoraro Cr., Pa. 61 K6
Ocú, Pan., 1,617 94 G7
Ocucaje, Peru 104 C5
Ocuituco, Mex., 1,769 93 f11
Oculi, Nic. 94 E3
Ocumare de la Costa, Ven., 1,186 101 b11
Ocumare del Tuy, Ven., 14,019 100 G2
Ocumicho, Mex., 1,295 93 b10
Ocussi, enclave of Port. Timor 149 H5
Oda, Ghana, 19,752 162 D5
Oda, Jap. 154 h14
Oda, Jap. 154 h15
Ōda, Jap., 40,196 155 C4
Oda, Jabal, Sudan 163 L2
Ōdaejin-nodongjagu, N. Kor. 151 F2
Ōdaka, Jap., 10,297 154 h14
Odaka, Jap., 19,264 155 G3
Odanah, Wis. 66 C2
Ōdate, Jap., 57,775 155 G1
Odawara, Jap., 121,813 155 F4
O'Day, Man., Can. 43 G2
Odda, Nor. 120 A3
Odder, Den., 6,953 121 C5
Oddur, Som. Rep., 2,290* 163 M5
Odebolt, Iowa, 1,331 72 B2
Ödeborg, Swed. 121 D2
Odei, r., Man., Can. 43 F3
Odell, Ill., 936 68 D2
Odell, Ind. 70 B2
Odell, Nebr., 358 75 J3
Odell, Oreg. 80 C3
Odell, Tex., 131 77 O2
Odem, Tex., 2,088 77 P6
Odemira, Port., 7,727 122 A4
Ödemiş, Turk., 28,525 142 B2
Oden, Ark., 90 73 B3
Odenbach, F.R.Ger., 1,131 119 D5
Odendaalsrus, S. Af., 15,047 164 D6
Odenheim, F.R.Ger., 3,165 119 F6
Odense, Den., 111,145 121 C5
Odense, r., Den. 121 C5
Odense Fjord, bay, Den. 121 C5
Odenthal, F.R.Ger., 6,868 119 C2
Odenton, Md., 1,914 62 H3
Odenville, Ala., 300 64 C2
Odenwald, reg., F.R.Ger. 118 B4
Oder, r., Ger.D.R.-Pol. 127 A2
Oder, Czech.-Pol.=Odra
Oderberg, Ger.D.R. 118 E2
Oder-Havel-Kan., Ger.D.R. 118 D2
Odernheim, F.R.Ger., 1,915 119 D5
Oder-Spree-Kan., Ger.D.R. 118 E2
Oderzo, It., 12,521 123 D2
Odessa, Ont., Can. 46 H4
Odessa, Sask., Can. 43 D5
Odessa, U.S.S.R., 703,000 134 C5
Odessa, Del., 526 62 J3
Odessa, Fla. 65 c11
Odessa, Minn., 234 74 D3
Odessa, Mo., 2,034 72 D5
Odessa, Nebr. 75 F3
Odessa, N.Y., 573 58 G7
Odessa, Tex., 80,338 77 M4
Odessa, Wash., 1,231 80 D2
Odesskoye, U.S.S.R. 137 o11
Odiel, r., Sp. 122 B4
Odienné, Iv. Coast, 4,000 162 C4
Odiham, U.K., 3,416 114 F8
Odin, Ill., 1,242 68 C5
Odintsovo, U.S.S.R., 20,300 136 b6
Odiongan, Phil., 2,409 153 B2
Odivelas, Port., 27,423 122 A3
Odobeşti, Rum., 4,977 128 F2
Odolanów, Pol., 2,855 127 B3
Odon, Ind., 1,192 70 B4
O'Donnell, Phil., 4,701 153 b7
O'Donnell, Tex., 1,356 77 N3
Odorhei, Rum., 14,162 128 E1
Odou, Fr. Guiana 101 N5
Odra=Oder, Ger.D.R.
Odra, r., Czech.-Pol. 126 C2
Odrowąż, Pol. 127 k5
Odum, Ga., 404 64 G4
Odumasi, Ghana 162 d7
Odžaci, Yug., 7,266 125 D2
Odžak, Yug., 4,305 125 D3
Oebisfelde, Ger.D.R. 118 C2
Oedeme, F.R.Ger., 1,163 119 b9
Oederan, Ger.D.R. 126 c6
Oegstgeest, Neth., 12,100 115 b6
Oeiras, Braz., 6,098 103 H3
Oeiras, Port., 6,857 122 i10
Oelde, F.R.Ger., 12,430 118 B3
Oelrichs, S. Dak., 132 74 A4
Oelsnitz, Ger.D.R., 18,485 118 D3
Oelsnitz, Ger.D.R., 16,389 126 b6
Oelwein, Iowa, 8,282 72 F2
Oeno, i., Pac. Oc. 171 K6
Oensingen, Switz., 2,907 124 B1
Oer-Erkenschwick, F.R.Ger., 21,700 119 C1
O-erh-ku-na-ch'i, China 150 G1
O-erh-to-ssu, China 150 E3
Oermingen, Fr., 1,561 116 d9
Oeventrop, F.R.Ger., 5,166 119 E2
Ofahoma, Miss. 73 F5
O'Fallon, Ill., 4,018 68 C5
O'Fallon, Mo., 3,770 72 G6
Ofaqim, Isr. 142 a8
Ofen Pass, Switz. 124 E2
Offa, Nigeria, 24,181 162 f7
Offaly, co., Ire., 51,970 113 C5
Offenbach, Hess., F.R.Ger., 104,283 118 B3
Offenbach, Rheinland-Pfalz, F.R.Ger., 3,015 119 E6
Offenburg, F.R.Ger., 26,742 118 B4
Offerle, Kans., 208 75 F6
Offerman, Ga. 64 G4
Offley, U.K., 1,310 114 H7
Offutt Lake, Wash. 81 a9
Oficina Victoria, Chile, 4,943 105 A2
Ofolanga, i., Tonga 177 36
Ofsuka, Jap. 154 i14
Oftringen, Switz., 7,731 124 B1
Ofu, i., Amer. Samoa 177 37
Ōfukiyama, Jap. 154 e16
Ōfuna, Jap. 155 m20
Ōfunato, Jap., 35,946 155 G2
Oga, Jap., 48,563 155 F2
Ogaden, plat., Eth. 163 M4
Ōgaki, Jap., 102,478 155 E4
Ogallah, Kans. 75 F5
Ogallala, Nebr., 4,250 75 D2
Ogano, Jap., 8,598 155 m18
Ogara-numa, l., Jap. 155 G1
Ogasawara-guntō=Bonin Is.
Ogawa, Jap., 5,241 154 B5
Ogawa, Jap. 154 e16
Ogawa, Jap., 24,769 155 F3
Ogawa, Jap. 155 m19
Ogbomosho, Nigeria, 161,861 162 E4
Ogbourne St. George, U.K. 114 E8
Ogburntown, N.C. 63 D1
Ogden, Ark., 282 73 A4
Ogden, Ill., 515 68 D3
Ogden, Iowa, 1,525 72 D2
Ogden, Kans., 1,780 75 J4
Ogden, Utah, 70,197 78 C1
Ogden Center, Mich. 67 K7
Ogden Dunes, Ind., 947 69 f10
Ogden I., N.Y. 69 C
Ogdensburg, N.J., 1,212 61 B1
Ogdensburg, N.Y., 16,122 59 K2
Ogdensburg, Wis., 181 66 D4
Ogeechee, r., Ga. 64 G2
Ogema, Sask., Can. 43 C5
Ogema, Minn., 224 74 E2
Ogema, Wis. 66 C3
Ogemaw, Ark. 73 B4
Ogemaw, co., Mich., 9,680 67 J4
Oggau, Aust., 1,763 124 d11
Ogi, Jap., 6,447 155 F3
Ogilvie, Austl. 172 A4
Ogilvie, Minn., 376 74 F3
Ogilvie Mts., Yukon, Can. 38 B4
Ogilville, Ind. 70 C3
Ogi-shima, Jap. 154 f15
Oglala, S. Dak. 74 A4
Oglala Pass, Alaska 85 e8
Oglat Yeraifia, Sp. Sah. 160 B3
Ogle, U.K. 112 g9
Ogle, co., Ill., 38,106 68 C1
Ogle, Pa. 60 b7
Oglesby, Ill., 4,215 68 D2
Oglesby, Tex., 414 77 P4
Oglethorpe, co., Ga., 7,926 64 F2
Oglethorpe, Ga., 1,169 64 F3
Oglethorpe, Mt., Ga. 64 E1
Oglio, r., It. 123 C2
Ogmore, Austl. 173 G3
Ognes, Fr. 116 k10
Ognon, r., Fr. 117 F3
Ōgo, Jap. 154 g15
Ogoja, Nigeria 162 F4
Ogoki, r., Ont., Can. 44 E5
Ogoki L., Ont., Can. 44 F5
Ogoki Res., Ont., Can. 44 E5
Ogoněk, U.S.S.R. 135 N4
Ogooué, r., Gabon 164 A2
Ogōri, Jap., 15,369 154 B4
Ogose, Jap., 10,157 155 m19
Ōgoshi, Jap. 154 f16
Ogosta, r., Bulg. 128 D3
Ogou, r., Togo 162 d7
Ogradena, Rum. 128 D2
Ogre, U.S.S.R., 7,500 136 B1
Ogrodzieniec, Pol., 3,992 127 i6
Ogulin, Yug. 125 B2
Ogun, r., Nigeria 162 e8
Oguni, Jap. 154 e15
Oguni, Jap., 15,142 155 F2
Ogunquit, Me. 55 B5
Ogurugu, Nigeria 162 g8
Oguta, Nigeria, 16,975 162 g9
Ogwashi Uku, Nigeria, 18,573 162 g8
Ōhagi, Jap. 154 h14
Ohakune, N.Z., 1,542 175 g5
Ohanet, Alg. 161 F3
Ōhara, Jap. 154 h14
Ōhara, Jap. 154 h15
Ōhara, Jap., 23,926 155 G4
Ōhata, Jap., 13,172 155 G1
Ohatchee, Ala., 437 64 C2
Ohaton, Alta., Can. 43 c8
Ōhazama, Jap., 11,204 155 G2
Ohey, Belg., 1,090 115 D4
O'Higgins, C., Easter I. 177 46
Ō-hinata, Jap. 155 m19
Ohio, st., U.S., 10,241,000* 70
Ohio, Ill., 489 68 C2
Ohio, co., Ind., 4,165 70 E4
Ohio, co., Ky., 17,725 71 E4
Ohio, co., W. Va., 68,437 62 D2
Ohio, r., U.S. 53 J3
Ohio City, Ohio, 851 70 E2
Ohiopyle, Pa., 287 60 D6
Ohiowa, Nebr., 195 75 H3
Ohlman, Ill., 215 68 C4
Ohogamiut, Alaska 85 D3
Ohonua, Tonga 177 36
Ohoopee, r., Ga. 64 G3
Ohře, r., Czech. 126 A1
Ohrid, Yug., 17,000* 125 E4
Ohrid, L., Alb.-Yug. 125 E4
Öhringen, F.R.Ger., 8,341 118 B4
Ohsweken, Ont., Can. 46 b15
Ōi, Jap. 154 h15
Oiapoque, Braz. 103 F1
Oiapoque, r., Braz. 103 F1
Oia-tau, Mt., Terr. Papua 174 3
Oies, Î. aux, Qué., Can. 55 B1
Oignies, Fr., 11,345 116 a7
Oil Center, N. Mex. 79 D5
Oil Center, Okla. 76 G3
Oil City, La., 1,430 73 B5
Oil City, Mich. 67 J5
Oil City, Okla. 76 E3
Oil City, Pa., 17,692 60 C3
Oil Cr., Pa. 60 C2
Oildale, Calif. 82 D5
Oilfield, Ill. 68 E4
Oil Hill, Kans. 75 J6
Oil Springs, Ont., Can. 46 B6
Oilton, Okla., 1,100 76 G1
Oilton, Tex. 77 O6
Oil Trough, Ark., 237 73 D2
Oilville, Va. 62 G5
Oinoúsai, Gr., 1,561 129 F5
Oinville, Fr. 116 f10
Oio Str., Hawaii 84 c5
Oirschot, Neth., 4,000 115 D3
Oise, r., Fr. 117 E2
Oisemont, Fr., 1,039 117 D2
Ōiso, Jap., 22,278 155 m20
Oissel, Fr., 10,147 117 D2
Oissery, Fr. 116 k10
Oisterwijk, Neth., 9,600 115 D3
Oistins, Barb. 97 10
Oistins Bay, Barb. 97 10
Oisy-le-Verger, Fr., 1,353 116 a7
Ōita, Jap., 124,807 154 B5
Ōiwa, Jap. 155 n20
Oiwake, Jap. 154 h15
Oiwake, Jap. 154 i14
Oiwake, Jap., 6,533 155 J8
Oiya, Jap. 154 e16
Oizu, Jap. 154 h15
Ojai, Calif., 4,495 82 D5
Ojców, Pol. 127 i6
Ōji, Jap., 9,507 154 g15
Ojibwa, Wis. 66 B3
Ojigahata, Jap. 154 h14
Ojika-hantō, Jap. 155 G2
Ojinaga, Mex., 8,384 92 D2
Ojiya, Jap., 49,445 155 F3
Ojocaliente, Mex., 6,642 92 E3
Ojo Caliente, Taos Co., N. Mex. 79 B3
Ojo Caliente, Valencia Co., N. Mex. 79 A4
Ojo de Agua, Arg. 105 B4
Ojo de Agua, Mex. 93 d9
Ojo de Agua de Peturo, Mex. 93 c11
Ojo de Liebre, Lag., Mex. 92 B2
Ojos de Agua, El Salv., 1,029 94 e9
Ojos del Salado, Nev., Arg.-Chile 105 B3
Ojuelos de Jalisco, Mex., 4,747 92 E4
Ojus, Fla. 65 b10
Oka, Qué., Can., 1,243 47 K3
Ōka, Jap. 154 h15
Oka, r., U.S.S.R. 134 C4
Oka, r., U.S.S.R. 135 K4
Okaba, Indon. 149 L4
Okada, Jap. 154 h15
Okahandja, S.-W. Afr., 2,962 164 B5
Okaka, Nigeria 162 e7
Okaloosa, co., Fla., 61,175 65 C2
Okanagan L., Br. Col., Can. 42 H4
Okano, r., Gabon 164 A1
Okanogan, co., Wash., 25,520 80 C1
Okanogan, Wash., 2,001 80 D1
Okanogan, r., Can.-U.S. 80 D1
Okapa, Terr. New Guin. 174 e2
Okapilco Cr., Ga. 64 F5
Okarche, Okla. 584 76 E2
Okaton, S. Dak. 74 B4
Okau, Yap 176 20
Okauchee, Wis., 1,879 66 E5
Ōkaura, Jap. 154 h15
Okavango, r., S.-W. Afr. 164 C4
Okavango Swamps, Bots. 164 C5
Ōkawa, Jap., 50,351 154 B5
Ōkawachi, Jap. 154 h15
Okawville, Ill., 931 68 C5
Okay, Okla., 419 76 H2
Okaya, Jap., 52,256 155 E3
Okayama, Jap., 260,773 155 D4
Okazaki, Jap. 154 f15
Okazaki, Jap., 166,095 155 E4
O'Kean, Ark., 137 73 E1
Okeana, Ohio 70 E3
Okee, Wis. 66 D5
Okeechobee, co., Fla., 6,424 65 H5
Okeechobee, Fla., 2,947 65 J5
Okeechobee, L., Fla. 65 J6
Okeene, Okla., 1,164 76 E1
Okefenokee Swamp, Fla.-Ga. 64 G5
Okegawa, Jap., 21,309 155 m19
Okehampton, U.K., 3,854 113 D6
Okemah, Okla., 2,836 76 G2
Okemo Mtn., Vt. 54 B5
Okemos, Mich., 1,010 67 J6
Okene, Nigeria, 38,144 162 g8
Oker, r., F.R.Ger. 118 C2
Okesa, Okla. 76 G1
Oketo, Jap., 12,671 155 K8
Oketo, Kans., 128 75 J4
Okfuskee, co., Okla., 11,706 76 G2
Okha, U.S.S.R., 27,600 135 O4
Okhaldhunga, Nepal 144 f12
Okhansk, U.S.S.R., 8,000 137 h7
Okhotsk, U.S.S.R., 8,500 135 O4
Okhotsk, Sea of, U.S.S.R. 135 O4
Okhotsk Basin 133 O4
Okhotskiy Perevoz, U.S.S.R. 135 N3
Oki, Jap. 154 e16
Okiep, S. Af., 2,967 164 C6
Oki-guntō, Jap. 155 C3
Okinawa-guntō, Ryukyu Is. 154 c12
Okinawa-jima, Ryukyu Is. 154 d12
Ōkine, Jap. 155 m20
Okino-Daitō-jima, Ryukyu Is. 170 C3
Ōkino-Erabu-shima, Jap. 154 d12
Okino-shima, Jap. 155 C5
Okitipupa, Nigeria, 12,408 162 f8
Okitsu, Jap. 154 h15
Okitsu, Jap. 155 n20
Okkan, Burma 147 a2
Oklahoma, st., U.S., 2,448,000* 76
Oklahoma, co., Okla., 439,506 76 F2
Oklahoma City, Okla., 324,253 76 F2
Oklaunion, Tex., 138 77 O2
Oklawaha, Fla. 65 H3
Oklawaha, r., Fla. 65 H3
Oklee, Minn., 529 74 E2
Okloacoochee Slough, Fla. 65 H6
Okmulgee, co., Okla., 36,945 76 G2
Okmulgee, Okla., 15,951 76 H2
Okobojo, S. Dak. 74 B3
Okobojo Cr., S. Dak. 74 E3
Okocim, Pol. 127 k7
Okolona, Ark., 344 73 B4
Okolona, Ky. 71 F3
Okolona, Miss., 2,622 73 G4
Okome, Swed. 121 E3
Okondja, Gabon 164 B2
Okonek, Pol., 3,092 127 B2
Okoppe, Jap., 9,327 155 K7
Okotoks, Alta., Can., 1,026 42 K4
Okoyo, Congo 164 B2
Okpara, r., Dahom.-Nigeria 162 e7
Okpo, Burma, 4,390 147 a1
Okreek, S. Dak. 74 B4
Okrzeja, Pol. 127 D3
Oksbøl, Den., 1,261 121 A5
Oksby, Den. 121 A5
Oksino, U.S.S.R. 134 E3
Okstindane, mt., Nor. 120 C2
Oksu, r., U.S.S.R. 137 g5
Oktaha, Okla., 99 76 H2
Oktemberyan, U.S.S.R., 15,000 137 b1
Oktibbeha, co., Miss., 26,175 73 G4
Oktoniá, Gr., 1,367 129 E5
Oktwin, Burma, 3,706 146 B3
Oktyabr', U.S.S.R., 6,500 137 e5
Oktyabr'skiy, Kaz.S.S.R., U.S.S.R. 137 k9
Oktyabr'skiy, R.S.F.S.R., U.S.S.R., 68,000 134 E4
Oktyabr'skiy, R.S.F.S.R., U.S.S.R., 5,500 135 P4
Oktyabr'skiy, R.S.F.S.R., U.S.S.R. 136 F4
Oktyabr'skiy, R.S.F.S.R., U.S.S.R. 136 g8
Oktyabr'skiy, R.S.F.S.R., U.S.S.R. 137 h8
Oktyabr'skiy, Uzb.S.S.R., U.S.S.R., 6,800 137 e4
Oktyabr'skoye, U.S.S.R. 137 h9
Oktyabr'skoye, U.S.S.R. 137 k8
Oktyabr'skoy Revolyutsii, O., U.S.S.R. 135 J2
Ōkuchi, Jap., 41,899 154 B5
Okujiri-shima, Jap. 155 H8
Okulovka, U.S.S.R., 6,400 136 D1
O-kung-ling, China 152 b6
Ōkura, Jap. 155 m19
Ōkusa, Jap. 155 n19
Ōkushi, Jap., 5,640 154 A5
Okuta, Nigeria 162 e7
Ola, U.S.S.R. 135 P4
Ola, Ark., 805 73 B2
Ola, Ga. 64 G4
Olaa, Hawaii, 1,334 84 F4
Ólafsfjördhur, Ice. 120 a6
Ólafsvík, Ice. 120 a6
Olalla, Wash. 81 a8
Olallie Butte, Oreg. 80 C3
Olamon, Me. 55 D3
Olancha, Calif. 82 E4
Olanchito, Hond., 4,622 94 D3
Öland, i., Swed. 120 D4
Olanta, S.C., 568 63 E4
Olar, S.C., 467 63 C4
Olary, Austl. 172 E5
Olascoaga, Arg., 2,200* 105 a12
Olathe, Colo., 773 79 B2
Olathe, Kans., 10,987 75 L5
Olavarría, Arg., 42,900* 105 C5
Oława, Pol., 10,876 127 B3
Olawa, r., Pol. 127 B3
Olaya Herrera, Col. 100 D3
Olberg, Ariz. 78 C5
Olbernhau, Ger.D.R., 14,318 118 D3
Olbia, It., 18,762 123 B4
Ølby, Den. 121 A4
Olcea, Rum. 128 C1
Olching, F.R.Ger., 5,084 118 C4
Olcott, Ky. 71 H5
Olcott, N.Y., 1,215 58 C5
Old Bahama Chan., Cuba, 96 d1
Old Baldy, Calif.=San Antonio Pk.
Old Baldy, mtn., Wash. 80 D1
Old Bath, Ind. 70 E3
Old Bedford=Delph or Old Bedford
Old Bennington, Vt., 205 54 A6
Old Brahmaputra, r., India-Pak. 144 g13
Old Bridge, N.J., 6,100* 61 C3
Old Brookville, N.Y., 1,126 58 e13
Oldbury, U.K., 53,935 114 D6
Old Castile=Castilla la Vieja
Oldcastle, Ont., Can. 67 g16
Old Cleeve, U.K., 1,429 114 B8
Old Crow, Yukon, Can. 40 B4
Old Crow, r., Yukon, Can. 85 K1
Old Dalby, U.K. 114 F5
Oldeani, Tanz. 165 g15
Oldemarkt, Neth. 115 D2
Oldenburg, Ndrsachs., F.R.Ger., 119,644 118 B2
Oldenburg, Schl.-Hol., F.R.Ger., 8,278 118 C1
Oldenburg, Ind., 694 70 D3
Oldenstadt, F.R.Ger., 1,358 118 C2
Oldenzaal, Neth., 17,400 115 E2
Olenegorsk, U.S.S.R., 12,100 134 C3
Old Factory, Qué., Can. 44 H4
Old Factory, r., Qué., Can. 44 H4
Old Faithful, Wyo. 81 D3
Old Field, N.Y., 373 58 g13
Old Fields, W. Va. 62 F3
Old Fletton, U.K., 11,677 114 H5
Old Forge, N.Y. 59 K4
Old Forge, Pa., 8,928 61 L3
Old Fort, Br. Col., Can. 42 E2
Old Fort, N.C., 787 63 B2
Old Fort, r., Alta., Can. 42 L1
Old Fort Point, Montserrat 97 5
Old Goa, India 145 E7
Old Greenwich (part of Greenwich), Conn. 56 B8
Oldham, U.K., 115,426 113 E5
Oldham, co., Ky., 13,388 71 F3
Oldham, S. Dak., 291 74 D3
Oldham, co., Tex., 1,928 76 M2
Oldhams, Va. 62 H4
Old Harbor, Alaska, 193 85 F4
Old Harbour, Jam., 4,192 96 p9
Old Harbour Bay, Jam., 3,409 96 p9
Old Head of Kinsale, Ire. 113 B6
Old Hickory, Tenn. 71 E5
Old Hickory L., Tenn. 71 E5
Old Hogem, Br. Col., Can. 42 F2
Old Kane, Ill. 68 B4
Old Kildonan, Man., Can. 43 g9
Old Lodge Cr., S. Dak. 74 C4
Old Logan Cr., Nebr. 75 J1
Old Lyme, Conn., 3,068(T) 56 G7
Oldman, r., Alta., Can. 42 J4
Old Man Bay, Grand Cayman 97 3
Oldman's Cr., N.J. 61 A4
Old Marissa, Ill., 217 68 C5
Oldmeldrum, U.K., 1,083 112 E3
Old Mill Creek, Ill., 149 69 c7
Old Mines, Mo. 72 G6
Old Mission, Mich. 67 H4
Old Mystic (part of Groton and Stonington), Conn. 56 J7
Old Ocean, Tex. 77 h10
Old Orchard Beach, Me., 4,431 55 B5
Old Perlican, Newf., Can. 45 b9
Old Port, Mich. 67 e16
Old Road, St. Christopher, 1,206 97 6
Olds, Alta., Can., 2,394 42 J3
Olds, Iowa, 189 72 F3
Old Sagay, Phil., 5,620 153 e11
Old Saybrook, Conn., 1,671; 5,274(T) 56 G7
Old Scone, U.K. 112 d7
Old Shawneetown, Ill., 433 68 D6
Oldsmar, Fla., 878 65 c11
Old Speck Mtn., Me. 55 B4
Old Station, Calif. 82 C2
Old Str., Me. 55 E4
Old Tappan, N.J., 2,330 58 d12
Old Town, Ark. 73 E3
Old Town, Fla. 65 F3
Oldtown, Idaho, 211 81 A1
Old Town, Me., 8,626 55 D4
Oldtown, Md. 62 F3
Old Trap, N.C. 63 J1
Oldwick, N.J. 61 B2
Old Wives L., Sask., Can. 43 C5
Old Womans Point, Jam. 96 p9
Olean, Ind. 70 D4
Olean, Mo., 135 72 E6
Olean, N.Y., 21,868 58 D7
O'Leary, P.E.I., Can. 47 T10
Olecko, Pol., 6,747 127 E1
Oleggio, It., 9,036 122 b5
Olëkma, r., U.S.S.R. 135 M4
Olëkminsk, U.S.S.R., 7,900 135 M3
Olekminskiy Stanovik, U.S.S.R. 133 L4
Olen, Belg., 6,803 115 C3
Olene, Oreg. 80 C4
Olenëk, U.S.S.R. 135 L3
Olenëk, r., U.S.S.R. 135 M2
Olenëkskiy Zal., U.S.S.R. 135 M2
Oleniy, O., U.S.S.R. 134 G2
Olentangy, r., Ohio 70 G2
Olenty, r., U.S.S.R. 137 o12
Oléron, Î. d', Fr. 117 C4
Oleśnica, Pol., 16,481 127 B3
Olesno, Pol., 7,388 127 C3
Oleta, Okla. 76 H3
Oletta, Fr., 1,037 116 r17
Olevano Romano, It., 6,255 123 b8
Olevuga, i., Sol. Is. 175 c3
Oley, Pa. 60 e10
Olfen, F.R.Ger., 3,543 119 C1
Ol'ga, U.S.S.R., 3,400 135 N5
Olga, Fla. 65 H6
Olga, Mt., Austl. 172 D3
Ølgod, Den. 121 A5
Olhalvo, Port., 2,200 122 i9
Olhão, Port., 12,654 122 B4
Olib, i., Yug. 125 B2
Oliden, Arg. 105 b12
Oliena, It., 6,915 123 B4
Olifants, r., S. Af. 164 a8
Olifantsfontein, S. Af. 165 k16
Olifantshoek, S. Af. 164 C6
Oliktok, Alaska 85 G1
Olimarao, i., Car. Is. 176 18
Olimbia, ruins, Gr. 129 C6
Ólimbos, Gr. 129 F7
Ólimbos, Óros, Gr. 129 D4
Olin, Iowa, 703 72 F3
Olinalá, Mex., 3,097 93 F5
Olinda, Braz., 100,545 103 K3
Olinda, Calif. 83 i16
O-ling Hu, China 150 D3
Olintepeque, Guat., 2,000 94 b9
Oliva, Sp., 14,579 122 E3
Oliva de la Frontera, Sp., 11,314 122 B3
Olive, Calif. 83 i16
Olive Branch, Ill. 68 C6
Olive Branch, Miss., 642 73 F3
Olivebridge, N.Y. 59 M8
Olive Hill, Ky., 1,398 71 H3
Olivehill, Tenn. 71 D6
Olivehurst, Calif., 4,835 82 C3
Oliveira, Braz., 12,919 103 d17
Olivença, Moz. 164 E3
Olivenza, Sp., 12,956 122 B3
Oliver, Br. Col., Can., 1,724 42 H4
Oliver, Ill. 68 E4
Oliver, co., N. Dak., 2,610 74 B2
Oliver, Wis., 222 66 A2
Oliver L., Sask., Can. 43 D3
Oliver Springs, Tenn., 1,163 71 G5
Olivet, Fr., 7,592 117 D3
Olivet, Kans., 116 75 K5
Olivet, Mich., 1,185 67 J6
Olivet, S. Dak., 135 74 D4
Olivia, Minn., 2,355 74 E3
Olivia, N.C. 63 E2
Olivone, Switz. 124 C2
Ol'khon, O., U.S.S.R. 135 K4
Ol'khovatka, U.S.S.R., 4,700 136 E3
Ol'khovka, U.S.S.R. 136 G3
Olkusz, Pol., 12,126 127 i6
Olla, La., 1,246 73 C6
Ollainville, Fr., 1,232 116 g12
Ollantaitambo, Peru 104 C5
Ollersbach, Aust. 124 b10
Ollerton, U.K., 5,529 114 G4
Ollerup, Den., 1,153 121 C5
Ollie, Iowa, 291 72 E3
Olliergues, Fr., 1,432 117 E4
Ollioules, Fr., 6,964 117 F5
Ollon, Switz., 4,126 124 A2
Olmedo, Sp., 3,681 122 C2
Olmeto, Fr., 1,276 116 r18
Ölmevalla, Swed. 121 E3
Olmos, Peru, 3,610 104 B3
Olmos Park, Tex., 2,457 76 a7
Olmstead, Ky. 71 D5
Olmsted, Ill., 475 68 C6
Olmsted, co., Minn., 65,532 74 F3
Olmsted Falls, Ohio, 2,144 70 d9
Olmstedville, N.Y. 59 N4
Olney, U.K., 2,384 114 G6
Olney, Ill., 8,780 68 D5
Olney, Md. 62 G3
Olney, Mont. 81 B1
Olney, Tex., 3,872 77 O3
Olocuilta, El Salv., 2,782 94 d10
Olofström, Swed. 120 C4

272 · Ölögey—Osen

Ölögey, Mong. 150 C1
Oloh, Miss. 73 F6
Oloibiri, Nigeria 162 g9
Olomana Pk., Hawaii 84 d7
Olomane, r., Qué., Can. 45 O5
Olomouc, Czech., 72,348 126 C2
Olonets, U.S.S.R., 5,000 134 C3
Olongapo, Phil., 5,034 153 b8
Olopa, Guat., 1,303 94 d9
Oloron-Ste-Marie, Fr., 13,598 117 C5
Olosega, i., Amer. Samoa 177 37
Olot, Sp., 17,185 122 G1
Olovi, Czech. 126 b6
Olovo, Yug. 125 D2
Olovyannaya, U.S.S.R. 135 L4
Olowalu, Hawaii 84 E3
Oloy, r., U.S.S.R. 135 Q3
Olpe, F.R.Ger., 11,202 118 A3
Olpe, Kans., 722 75 J5
Olsberg, F.R.Ger., 2,979 119 F2
Olsburg, Kans., 137 75 J4
Olše, r., Czech. 127 h7
Olsobip, Terr. Papua 174 d2
Olsztyn, Pol., 68,000* 127 D2
Olsztynek, Pol., 3,773 127 D2
Olszyna, Pol., 2,875 127 e5
Olt, r., Rum. 128 E2
Olten, Switz., 20,044 124 B1
Oltenița, Rum., 14,111 128 F2
Olteț, r., Rum. 128 D2
Olton, Tex., 1,917 77 M2
Oltu, Turk., 4,352 142 E1
Oltu, r., Turk. 142 E1
O-luan Pi, c., Taiwan 152 F3
Olu Malau Is., Sol. Is. 175 d3
O-lun-ch'un-tzu-chih-ch'i, China 150 G1
Olustee, Okla., 463 76 D3
Olutanga I., Phil. 153 B4
Olvera, Sp., 10,982 122 C4
Olympia, Calif. 83 e13
Olympia, Ky. 71 H3
Olympia, Wash., 18,273 80 B2
Olympia Fields, Ill., 2,578 69 d10
Olympic Mts., Wash. 80 B2
Olympic Nat. Pk., Wash. 80 B2
Olympus, mt., Cyp. 142 C3
Olympus, Gr.=Olimbos, Óros
Olympus, Mt., Utah 78 c9
Olympus, Mt., Wash. 80 B2
Olyphant, Pa., 5,864 61 L3
Olyutorskiy, M., U.S.S.R. 135 R4
Olyutorskiy Zal., U.S.S.R. 135 Q3
Olzheim, F.R.Ger. 119 B4
Om', r., U.S.S.R. 134 G4
Ōma, Jap., 7,835 155 G1
Oma, Miss. 73 E6
Ōmachi, Jap. 154 e16
Ōmachi, Jap., 35,151 155 E3
Omae-zaki, Jap. 155 F4
Ōmagari, Jap., 41,090 155 G2
Omagh, Ont., Can. 46 c14
Omagh, U.K., 8,109 113 C4
Omaha, Ala. 64 D2
Omaha, Ark., 195 73 B1
Omaha, Ga., 174 64 E3
Omaha, Ill., 312 68 D6
Omaha, Nebr., 301,598 75 K2
Omaha, Tex., 854 77 Q3
Omaha Beach, Fr. 117 C2
Omai, Guyana 101 L5
Omak, Wash., 4,068 80 D1
Omak L., Wash. 80 D1
Oman, G. of, Asia 143 F3
Oman L., Sask., Can. 43 C2
Omarska, Yug. 125 C2
Omaruru, S.-W. Afr., 2,689 164 B5
Ōma-saki, Jap. 155 G1
Ōmata, Jap. 154 h16
Omate, Peru, 1,008 104 D6
Omba=Oba
Ombersley, U.K., 2,130 114 D6
Ombetsu, Jap., 9,900 155 L8
Omboué, Gabon 164 A2
Ombrone, r., It. 123 C3
Ombu, China 144 d10
Omdurman=Umm Durmān
Ōme, Jap., 56,896 155 m19
Omega, Ga., 940 64 F4
Omega, Ill. 68 D5
Omega, Ind. 70 D2
Omega, La. 73 D6
Omega, N. Mex. 79 A4
Omega, Ohio 70 G3
Omega, Okla. 76 E2
Omega, Va. 62 F6
Omegna, It., 13,493 123 B2
O-mei, China 152 A1
Omelek, i., Kwajalein 176 25
Omemee, Ont., Can. 46 F4
Omena, Mich. 67 H3
Omeo, Austl. 173 G5
Omer, Mich., 322 67 K4
Omerville, Qué., Can., 1,089 47 M3
Omessa, Fr. 116 r17
Ometepe, I. de, Nic. 94 E5
Ometepec, Mex., 4,990 93 F5
Omigawa, Jap., 22,638 155 G4
Ōmi-Hachiman, Jap., 44,545 154 h14
O-min, China 150 B2
Omin, Yap 176 20
Ōminato, Jap., 14,861 155 G1
Omineca, r., Br. Col., Can 42 F2
Omiš, Yug. 125 C3
Ōmi-shima, Jap. 154 B4
Omitara, S.-W. Afr. 164 C5
Omitlán, Mex., 1,231 93 f9
Ōmiya, Jap. 155 F3
Ōmiya, Jap., 169,996 155 F4
Omkoi, Thai. 146 B3
Ommanney Bay, N.W.T., Can. 40 J3
Omme, r., Den. 121 B5
Ommel, Den. 121 C6
Ommen, Neth., 3,400 115 E2
Omø, i., Den. 121 D5
Omo, r., Eth. 163 K5
Omoa, Hond. 94 C3
Omoko, Nigeria, 12,242 162 g9
Omolon, U.S.S.R. 135 P3
Omolon, r., U.S.S.R. 135 Q3
Omoloy, r., U.S.S.R. 135 N2
Omono, r., Jap. 155 G2
Ōmori, Jap., 7,907 155 G2
Ōmori, Jap. 155 n19
Omoto, Jap., 3,635 155 G2
Ompah, Ont., Can. 46 H3
Ompompanoosuc, r., Vt. 54 C4
Omps, W. Va. 62 F3
Omro, Wis., 1,991 66 E4
Omsk, U.S.S.R., 650,000 134 G4
Omsukchan, U.S.S.R. 135 P3
O-mu, China 151 F2
Ōmu, Jap., 10,453 155 K7
Ōmu Aran, Nigeria 162 f7
Omulew, r., Pol. 127 D2
Omullyakhskaya G., U.S.S.R. 135 O2
Ōmura, Jap., 59,498 154 B5
Omuramba, wadi, S.-W. Af. 164 C5
Omurtag, Bulg., 6,127 128 F3
Ōmuta, Jap., 205,766 154 B5
Omutninsk, U.S.S.R., 23,000 134 E4
Oña, Sp., 1,493 122 D1
Ona, Fla., 134 65 H5
Ona, r., U.S.S.R. 137 s11
Onaga, Kans., 850 75 J4
Onagawa, Jap., 18,002 155 G2
Onaka, S. Dak., 85 74 C3
Onalaska, Wash. 80 B2
Onalaska, Wis., 3,161 66 B5
Onaman L., Ont., Can. 44 E5
Onamia, Minn., 645 74 F2
Onancock, Va., 1,759 62 J5
Onapa, Okla. 76 H2
Onaping, r., Ont., Can. 46 C2
Onaping L., Ont., Can. 46 C1
Onaqui Mts., Utah 78 b10
Onarga, Ill., 1,397 68 E3
Oñate, Sp., 8,432 122 n11
Onawa, Iowa, 3,176 72 A2
Onawa, Me. 55 C3
Onawa L., Me. 55 C3
Onaway, Idaho, 191 81 A2
Onaway, Mich., 1,388 67 J3
Onbekend, S. Af. 165 k16
Onchan, U.K., 3,362 113 D4
Onchiota, N.Y. 59 M3
Oncócua, Ang. 164 B4
Onda, Sp., 12,414 122 E3
Ondangua, S.-W. Afr. 164 B4
Ondárroa, Sp., 7,462 122 n11
Ondava, r., Czech. 126 E2
Ondo, Jap., 18,413 155 C4
Ondo, Nigeria, 42,030 162 f8
Ondolean, Indon. 149 G3
Öndör Haan, Mong. 150 E2
Öndverdharnes, pt., Ice. 120 a6
Oné, Loy. Is. 174 k8
Oneata, i., Fiji 174 4
Oneata Passage, Fiji 174 4
Oneco, Conn. 57 J6
Oneco, Fla., 1,530 65 G5
Onefour, Alta., Can. 42 L4
Onega, U.S.S.R., 21,300 134 C3
Onega, r., U.S.S.R. 134 C3
100 Mile House, Br. Col., Can. 42 G3
150 Mile House, Br. Col., Can. 42 G3
Oneida, Ark. 73 E3
Oneida, co., Idaho, 3,603 81 C4
Oneida, Ill., 672 68 B2
Oneida, Ky. 71 H4
Oneida, co., N.Y., 264,401 59 J5
Oneida, N.Y., 11,677 59 J5
Oneida, Tenn., 2,480 71 G5
Oneida, co., Wis., 22,112 66 D3
Oneida, Wis. 66 E4
Oneida, r., N.Y. 59 q23
Oneida L., N.Y. 59 J5
O'Neill, Nebr., 3,181 75 G1
Ōnejime, Jap., 14,949 154 B6
Onekama, Mich., 469 67 G4
Onekotan, O., U.S.S.R. 135 P5
Onenoa, Tutuila 177 39
Oneonta, Ala., 4,136 64 C2
Oneonta, N.Y., 13,412 59 K7
Oneroa, i., Rarotonga 177 34
One Tree Pk., N. Mex. 79 C5
Oneula Beach, Hawaii 84 b8
Onezhskaya G., U.S.S.R. 134 C3
Onezhskoye Oz., U.S.S.R. 134 C3
Ong, Nebr., 128 75 H3
Ongea Levu, i., Fiji 174 4
Ongea Ndriti, i., Fiji 174 4
Ongjin, N. Kor. 151 E3
Ongole, India, 35,804 145 F7
Onguday, U.S.S.R. 137 r12
Onhne, Burma, 3,746 147 b2
Oni, U.S.S.R., 4,300 137 b1
Onida, S. Dak., 843 74 B3
Onilahy, r., Malag. Rep. 165 G5
Onion Cr., Tex. 76 c5
Onion Lake, Sask., Can. 43 B4
Oniotto, i., Kwajalein 176 25
Onishibetsu, Jap. 155 K7
Onishika, Jap., 4,808 155 J7
Onitsha, Nigeria, 88,459 162 F4
Onjuku, Jap., 9,753 155 n20
Onley, Va., 415 62 J5
Only, Tenn. 71 D6
Onny, r., U.K. 114 C6
Ono, Jap., 2,191 154 g14
Ōno, Jap. 154 h15
Ōno, Jap., 35,232 155 D4
Ōno, Jap., 44,666 155 E4
Ono, Calif. 82 B2
Ono, i., Fiji 174 4
Onoda, Jap., 55,192 154 B4
Onoe, Jap. 154 h14
Onoe, Jap. 154 h15
Onoe, Jap., 14,998 155 G1
Ono-i-Lau, i., Fiji 174 4
Onolimbu, Indon. 148 A2
Onomea, Hawaii 84 F4
Onomichi, Jap., 91,003 155 C4
Onon, r., Mong.-U.S.S.R. 135 L4
Onondaga, Ont., Can. 46 b15
Onondaga, Mich. 67 J6
Onondaga, co., N.Y., 423,028 59 H6
Onondaga Cr., N.Y. 59 r24
Onondaga Hill, N.Y. 59 r24
Onondaga L., N.Y. 59 q23
Ono-Niimachi, Jap., 17,620 155 G3
Onota L., Mass. 56 C3
Onotoa, atoll, Gilb. Is. 170 F5
Onoville, N.Y. 58 C7
Onoway, Alta., Can. 42 J3
Onsala, Swed. 121 D3
Onset, Mass., 1,714 57 O6
Onslow, Austl. 172 A3
Onslow, Iowa, 269 72 F2
Onslow, co., N.C., 82,706 63 G3
Onsöy, Nor. 121 C1
Onsted, Mich., 526 67 J7
Onstwedde, Neth. 115 E1
Ontake-san, mtn., Jap. 155 E4
Ontario, prov., Can., 6,731,000* 44 D5
Ontario, Calif., 46,617 82 E5
Ontario, co., N.Y., 68,070 58 E6
Ontario, N.Y. 58 F5
Ontario, Ohio, 3,049 70 G2
Ontario, Oreg., 5,101 80 E3
Ontario, Va. 62 F6
Ontario, Wis., 448 66 C5
Ontario, L., Can.-U.S. 53 L2
Ontario Center, N.Y. 58 o20
Ontarioville, Ill. 69 b9
Ontelaunee, L., Pa. 61 h14
Onteniente, Sp., 18,787 122 E3
Ontonagon, co., Mich., 10,584 67 D2
Ontonagon, Mich., 2,358 66 D2
Ontonagon, r., Mich. 66 D2
Ontong Java Is., Sol. Is. 175 c1
Ōnuki, Jap. 155 m20
Onverdacht, Sur., 1,200* 101 N5
Onward, Ind., 153 70 C2
Onyū, Jap. 154 g14
Onyūdani, Jap. 154 g14
Onyx, Ark. 73 B3
Ooa, i., Jaluit 176 30
Oodnadatta, Austl. 172 E4
Ookala, Hawaii, 562 84 F3
Oola, Ire. 113 B5
Ooldea, Austl. 172 D4
Oolitic, Ind., 1,140 70 C4
Oologah, Okla., 299 76 H1
Oologah Res., Okla. 76 H1
Ooltewah, Tenn. 71 F6
Ooltgensplaat, Neth. 115 a7
Ooma, Ocean I. 175 16
Oona River, Br. Col., Can. 42 D3
Ooraminna, Mt., Austl. 172 E3
Oorindi, Austl. 173 F3
Oosendrecht, Neth., 3,000 115 C3
Oos-London=East London
Oostakker, Belg., 8,028 115 B3
Oostanaula, r., Ga. 64 D1
Oostburg, Neth., 3,700 115 B3
Oostburg, Wis., 1,065 66 F5
Oostelijk-Flevoland, lowland, Neth. 115 D2
Oostende, Belg., 54,653 115 A3
Oosterbeek, Neth., 13,100 115 D3
Oosterhout, Neth., 17,800 115 C3
Ooster Schelde, chan., Neth. 115 B3
Oosterwolde, Neth. 115 E1
Oostkamp, Belg., 7,974 115 B3
Oostpunt, pt., Cur. 97 16
Oost-Souburg, Neth., 5,800 115 B3
Oostzaan, Neth., 5,300 115 C2
Ootacamund, India, 50,140 145 E8
Ootmarsum, Neth. 115 E2
Ootsa Lake, Br. Col., Can. 42 E3
Ootsa L., Br. Col., Can. 42 E3
Opaeula Camp, Hawaii 84 b6
Opaeula Str., Hawaii 84 b6
Opahi, Niue 177 32
Opaka, Bulg., 4,669 128 F3
Opal, Alta., Can. 43 b7
Opal, S. Dak. 74 A3
Opal, Wyo., 55 81 D5
Opala, D.R.Congo 164 D2
Opalenica, Pol., 5,165 127 B2
Opa-locka, Fla., 9,810 65 J7
Opari, Sudan 163 K5
Oparino, U.S.S.R. 136 G1
Opasatika, Ont., Can. 44 G5
Opataca L., Qué., Can. 44 K5
Opatija, Yug., 6,830 125 B2
Opatovice, Czech. 127 e6
Opatów, Pol., 5,419 127 D3
Opava, Czech., 44,216 126 C2
Opava, r., Czech. 127 g6
Opavice, r., Czech. 127 g6
Opazatika, r., Ont., Can. 44 G5
Opdyke, Ill. 68 D5
Opelika, Ala., 15,678 64 D3
Opelousas, La., 17,417 73 C7
Open B., Terr. New Guin. 174 f2
Opeongo, r., Ont., Can. 46 F3
Opeongo L., Ont., Can. 46 F3
Opequon, Va. 62 F3
Opheim, Mont., 457 81 F1
Opheusden, Neth., 3,000 115 D3
Ophir, Alaska 85 E3
Ophir, Calif. 82 b7
Ophir, Oreg. 80 A4
Ophir, Utah, 36 78 B1
Opia, r., Col. 101 d15
O-pien, China 152 A1
Opienge, D.R.Congo 164 D1
Opihikao, Hawaii 84 G4
Opinaca, r., Qué., Can. 44 J4
Opinaca L., Qué., Can. 44 J4
Opiscoteo L., Qué., Can. 45 M4
Opiskotish L., Qué., Can. 45 M4
Opladen, F.R.Ger., 29,457 118 A3
Oplin, Tex. 77 O3
Opobo, Nigeria, 8,499 162 F5
Opochka, U.S.S.R., 10,800 136 C1
Opočno, Czech. 127 f6
Opoczno, Pol., 9,444 127 D3
Opodepe, Mex., 1,050 92 C2
Opole, Pol., 61,000* 127 C3
Opole Lubelskie, Pol., 3,456 127 E3
Opopeo, Mex., 3,191 93 c10
Oporto=Porto
Oposhnya, U.S.S.R., 7,000 136 D3
Opotiki, N.Z., 2,582 175 h5
Opp, Ala., 5,535 64 C4
Oppdal, Nor. 120 B3
Oppenau, F.R.Ger., 2,962 119 E7
Oppenheim, F.R.Ger., 5,373 118 B4
Opportunity, Mont. 81 C2
Opportunity, Wash., 12,465 80 E2
Opsa, U.S.S.R. 136 B2
Optima, Okla., 64 76 B1
Opunake, N.Z., 1,595 175 g5
Oputo, Mex., 1,961 92 C1
Opuzen, Yug. 125 C3
Opwijk, Belg., 9,017 115 d9
O Pyam, Camb. 146 C5
Oquawka, Ill., 1,090 68 B3
Oquirrh Mts., Utah 78 b10
Oquossoc, Me. 55 B4
Or', r., U.S.S.R. 137 i10
Ora, Ind. 70 C1
Ora, Miss. 73 F6
Ora, S.C. 63 C3
Oracabessa, Jam., 1,313 96 q8
Oracle, Ariz. 78 C5
Oradea, Rum., 98,950 128 C1
Oradell, N.J., 7,487 58 c13
Oradell Res., N.J. 61 C2
Orahovac, Yug. 125 E3
Orahovica, Yug., 3,003 125 C2
Orai, India, 29,587 145 F4
Oraibi, Ariz. 78 C4
Oramel, N.Y. 58 D7
Oran, Alg., 350,087 160 D2
Oran, Mo., 1,090 72 H7
Oran, Tex. 76 d9
Orange, Austl., 18,247 173 G5
Orange, Fr., 21,450 117 F4
Orange, co., Calif., 703,925 82 E6
Orange, Calif., 67,206 83 i16
Orange, Conn., 8,547(T) 56 D7
Orange, co., Fla., 263,540 65 H4
Orange, Ill. 68 E4
Orange, co., Ind., 16,877 70 C4
Orange, Ind. 70 D3
Orange, Mass., 3,689;6,154(T) 56 G2
Orange, N.H. 54 D4
Orange, co., N.Y., 183,734 59 M9
Orange, co., N.C., 42,970 63 E1
Orange, Ohio, 2,006 70 e9
Orange, Pa. 61 o16
Orange, co., Tex., 60,357 77 R4
Orange, Tex., 25,605 77 R4
Orange, co., Va., 12,900 62 F4
Orange, Va., 2,955 62 F4
Orange, co., Vt., 16,014 54 B3
Orange, r., S. Af.-S. W. Afr. 164 C6
Orange, C., Braz. 103 F1
Orangeburg, N.Y. 58 d12
Orangeburg, S.C., 13,852 63 D4
Orangeburg, co., S.C., 68,559 63 D4
Orange City, Fla., 1,598 65 H4
Orange City, Iowa, 2,707 72 A1
Orange Cliffs, Utah 78 C2
Orange Cove, Calif., 2,885 82 D4
Orange Cr., Alaska 85 J2
Orangedale, Fla. 65 H2
Orangefield, Tex. 77 n8
Orange Free State=Oranje-Vrystaat
Orange Grove, Tex., 1,109 77 O6
Orange Hill, Jam. 96 o8
Orange L., Fla. 65 G3
Orange Park, Fla., 2,624 65 H2
Orange Springs, Fla. 65 G3
Orangevale, Calif. 82 b7
Orangeville, Ont., Can., 4,513 44 H7
Orangeville, Ill., 491 68 C1
Orangeville, Mich. 67 H6
Orangeville, Ohio, 397 70 J1
Orangeville, Utah, 571 78 C2
Orange Walk, Br. Hond., 2,157 94 C1
Orani, Phil., 2,499 153 b8
Oranienbaum, Ger.D.R. 118 D3
Oranienburg, Ger.D.R., 21,104 118 D2
Oranje, r., S. Af. 164 C6
Oranje, Pegunungan, Indon. 149 L4
Oranjegebergte, Sur. 101 N6
Oranje kan., Neth. 115 E2
Oranjemund, S.-W. Afr. 164 B6
Oranjestad, Aruba, 15,398 97 15
Oranjestad, St. Eustatius 97 6
Oranjeville, S. Af. 165 k17
Oranje-Vrystaat, prov., S. Af. 164 D6
Oranmore, Ire. 113 B5
Orantjugur, L., Austl. 172 C3
Oraqui, Fr. Guiana 101 O6
Oras, Phil., 4,863 153 C2
Orašac, Yug., 2,182 125 C2
Orăștie, Rum., 10,488 128 D2
Oraville, Ill. 68 C6
Oravița, Rum., 8,175 128 C2
Orb, r., Fr. 117 E5
Orbe, Switz., 3,824 124 A2
Orbe, r., Switz. 124 A2
Orbeasca, Rum. 128 E2
Orbec, Fr., 3,153 117 D2
Orbetello, It., 18,005 123 C3
Órbigo, r., Sp. 122 C1
Orbisonia, Pa., 643 60 G5
Orbost, Austl., 2,214 173 G5
Orcadas, Ant. 180 O6
Orcas, Wash. 80 B1
Orcemont, Fr. 116 f12
Orcera, Sp., 3,393 122 D3
Orchard, Idaho 81 B4
Orchard, Iowa, 116 72 E1
Orchard, Nebr., 421 75 G1
Orchard Beach, Md., 1,691 62 c8
Orchard City, Colo., 1,021 79 A2
Orchard Farm, Mo. 72 a10
Orchard Grove, Ind. 70 B1
Orchard Hill, Ga., 105 64 h12
Orchard Lake, Mich., 1,127 67 e14
Orchard L., Minn. 74 F2
Orchard Mesa, Colo., 4,956 79 A2
Orchard Park, N.Y., 3,278 58 C6
Orchards, Wash. 80 B3
Orchard Valley, Wyo., 1,449 81 G5
Orchardville, Ill. 68 D5
Orchha, India 144 b13
Orchies, Fr., 5,886 117 E1
Orco, Torrente, It. 123 A2
Orcutt, Calif., 1,414 82 C5
Orcuttsville (part of Stafford), Conn. 56 G5
Ord, Nebr., 2,413 75 G2
Ord, r., Austl. 172 D2
Ord, Mt., Austl. 172 C2
Ördenes, Sp., 11,770 122 A1
Orderville, Utah, 398 78 B3
Ordesa, Pq. Nac. de, Sp. 122 E1
Ordino, Andorra 122 g7
Ord Mtn., Tex. 77 M4
Ordoqui, Arg., 1,700* 105 a12
Ordos=O-erh-to-ssu
Ord River, Austl. 172 D2
Ordu, Turk., 20,171 142 D1
Ordubad, U.S.S.R., 7,500 137 c2
Orduña, Sp., 3,697 122 m12
Ordville, Nebr. 75 B2
Ordway, Colo., 1,254 79 D2
Ordynskoye, U.S.S.R. 137 q11
Ordzhonikidze, R.S.F.S.R., U.S.S.R., 175,000 134 D5
Ordzhonikidze, Ukr.S.S.R., U.S.S.R., 17,500 136 D4
Ordzhonikidze, Uzb.S.S.R., U.S.S.R., 14,800 137 f4
Ordzhonikidzeabad, U.S.S.R., 11,100 137 f5
Ore, Swed. 120 C3
Orealla, Guyana 101 M5
Oreana, Ill., 464 68 D4
Oreana, Nev. 83 A2
Oreba, i., Kwajalein 176 25
Örebro, Swed., 75,434 120 C4
Ore City, Tex., 819 77 Q3
Oregon, st., U.S., 1,938,000* 80
Oregon, Ill., 3,732 68 C1
Oregon, co., Mo., 9,845 72 F8
Oregon, Mo., 887 72 B5
Oregon, Ohio, 13,319 70 F1
Oregon, Wis., 1,701 66 D6
Oregon Butte, Wash. 80 E2
Oregon Caves Nat. Mon., Oreg. 80 B4
Oregon City, Oreg., 7,996 80 B3
Oregon House, Calif. 82 C3
Oregon Inlet, N.C. 63 J2
Öregrund, Swed. 120 D3
Ore Hill (part of Salisbury), Conn. 56 C5
Orekhov, U.S.S.R., 12,000 136 D4
Orekhovo, Bulg., 8,179 128 D3
Orekhovo-Zuyevo, U.S.S.R., 112,000 136 E1
Orekhovsk, U.S.S.R., 4,000 136 C2
Orël, U.S.S.R., 167,000 134 C4
Orel', r., U.S.S.R. 136 D3
Orella, Nebr. 75 B1
Orellana, Peru 104 B3
Orellana, Peru 104 C3
Orem, Utah, 18,394 78 C1
Orenburg, U.S.S.R., 282,000 134 E4
Orenhofen, F.R.Ger., 1,235 119 B5
Orense, Sp., 64,153 122 B1
Orepuki, N.Z. 175 e7
Orestiás, Gr., 10,281 129 F4
Øresund=Sound, The
Öresund=Sound, The
Oreti, r., N.Z. 175 f7
Orford, N.H. 54 C4
Orford Ness, U.K. 113 G5
Orfordville, N.H. 54 C4
Orfordville, Wis., 665 66 D6
Organ, N. Mex. 79 B5
Orgañá, Sp., 1,171 122 F1
Organitos, Mex. 93 e8
Órganos, Sa. de los, Cuba 95 ·
Organ Pipe Cactus Nat. Mon., Ariz. 78 B5
Orgaz, Sp., 3,502 122 D3
Orge, r., Fr. 116 h12
Orgelet, Fr., 1,528 117 F3
Orgeval, Fr., 1,948 116 f11
Orgeyev, U.S.S.R., 14,400 136 C4
Orgiva, Sp., 6,586 122 D4
Orgtrud, U.S.S.R. 136 d5
Orhangazi, Turk., 7,215 142 B1
Orhon, r., Mong. 150 D1
Oricao, Ven. 101 b11
Orick, Calif. 82 A2
Orient, Iowa, 341 72 C3
Orient, Me. 55 E3
Orient, Ohio, 310 70 F3
Orient, Oreg. 80 b7
Orient, S. Dak., 133 74 C3
Orient, Wash. 80 D1
Orienta, Okla. 76 E1
Oriental, N.C., 522 63 H2
Oriental, Cord., Bol. 102 C5
Oriental, Cord., Col. 100 C6
Oriental, Cord., Dom. Rep. 96 n6
Oriental, Cord., Peru 104 B3
Orient Bay, Ont., Can. 44 E5
Orient Pt., N.Y. 56 G8
Orihuela, Sp., 44,830 122 E3
Orillia, Ont., Can., 14,606 44 H7
Orinda, Calif., 4,712 83 e12
Orinduik, Guyana 101 L5
Orino, Jap. 154 f15
Orinoca, Bol. 102 b11
Orinoco, r., Ven. 101 J4
Orinoco, Delta del, Ven. 101 ·
Orion, Phil., 7,663 153 B2
Orion, Ala. 64 D4
Orion, Ill., 1,269 68 B2
Orion, Kans. 75 E5
Orion, Okla. 76 E1
Oriska, N. Dak., 148 74 D2
Oriskany, N.Y., 1,580 59 K5
Oriskany, Va. 62 D5
Oriskany Falls, N.Y., 972 59 J6
Orissa, st., India, 17,548,846 145 G5
Oristano, It., 23,540 123 B5
Oritachi, Jap. 154 g16
Oritopo, Ven. 101 c11
Orituco, r., Ven. 100 G3
Oritupano, Ven. 101 J3
Orivesi, Fin. 120 F3
Orivesi, l., Fin. 120 G3
Oriximiná, Braz., 3,974 103 E2
Orizaba, Mex., 69,672 93 F4
Orizaba, P. de=Citlaltépetl
Orizabita, Mex., 1,573 93 e9
Orizare, Bulg., 1,428 128 F3
Orizatlán, Mex., 1,781 93 f8
Örja, Swed. 121 b7
Örje, Nor. 121 D1
Orkanger, Nor. 120 B3
Örkelljunga, Swed. 120 C4
Orkla, r., Nor. 120 B3
Orkney, Sask., Can. 43 C5
Orkney, S. Af., 22,350 164 D6
Orkney, co., U.K., 18,743 112 E2
Orkney Is., U.K. 112 E2
Orkney Springs, Va. 62 F4
Orla, Tex. 77 M4
Orla, r., Pol. 127 B3
Orland, Calif., 2,534 82 B3
Orland, Ind., 424 70 D1
Orland, Me. 55 D4
Orlando, Fla., 88,135 65 H4
Orlando, Okla., 194 76 F1
Orland Park, Ill., 2,592 68 D2
Orleans, Ont., Can., 1,005 47 J3
Orléans, Fr., 88,105 117 D3
Orleans, Calif. 82 B2
Orleans, Ind., 1,659 70 C4
Orleans, Iowa, 280 72 B1
Orleans, parish, La., 627,525 73 F7
Orleans, Mass., 2,342(T) 57 Q5
Orleans, Mich. 67 H5
Orleans, Minn. 74 D1
Orleans, Nebr., 608 75 F3
Orleans, co., N.Y., 34,159 58 D5
Orleans, co., Vt., 20,143 54 C2
Orleans, Vt., 1,240 54 C2
Orléans, Î. d', Qué., Can. 47 O2
Orléansville=El Asnam
Orlești, Rum. 128 E2
Orlice, r., Czech. 127 f6
Orlik, U.S.S.R. 135 K4
Orlinda, Tenn. 71 E5
Orljava, r., Yug. 125 C2
Orlová, Czech., 23,731 126 D2
Orlovat, Yug., 2,318 125 E2
Orly, Fr., 18,469 116 h12
Orlyak, Bulg., 3,225 128 F3
Orma, W. Va. 62 C4
Ormāra, Pak. 144 B4
Ormesson, Fr. 116 i11
Ormília, Gr., 2,558 129 D4
Ormiston, U.K. 112 e8
Ormoc, Phil., 9,377 153 C3
Ormond, N.Z. 175 h5
Ormond Beach, Fla., 8,658 65 H3
Órmos Korthíou, Gr. 129 E6
Ormsby, co., Nev., 8,063 83 A3
Ormskirk, U.K., 21,815 114 C3
Ormstown, Qué., Can., 1,492 47 L3
Ornans, Fr., 3,731 117 F3
Orne, r., Fr. 117 C2
Orneta, Pol., 7,107 127 D1
Ornö, Swed. 120 f8
Orno, Mt., Colo. 79 B1
Örnsköldsvik, Swed. 120 D3
Oro, R. del, Mex. 92 D3
Orobie, Alpi, mts., It. 123 B1
Orochen, U.S.S.R. 135 M4
Orocovis, P.R., 3,005 96 t10
Orocué, Col. 100 E5
Orofino, Idaho, 2,471 81 A2
Oro Grande, Calif. 82 E5
Orogrande, N. Mex. 79 B5
Orohena, Mt., Tahiti 177 44
Orol, Sp., 4,410 122 B1
Oroluk, atoll, Car. Is. 176 18
Oromocto, N.B., Can., 11,781 47 S11
Oromocto L., N.B., Can. 55 F3
Orong, Phil., 7,300 153 d12
Oron-la-Ville, Switz. 124 A2
Orono, Ont., Can. 46 F5
Orono, Me., 3,234 55 D4
Orono, Minn., 5,643 74 a6
Oronogo, Mo., 513 72 C7
Oronoque, r., Guyana 101 M6
Oronsay, i., U.K. 112 C3
Orontes=Asi
Oropesa, Sp., 4,548 122 C3
Oroquieta, Phil., 5,331 153 B3
Orós, Braz., 4,928 103 J3
Orosháza, Hung., 32,086 126 E3
Oroshi, Jap. 154 i14
Oroszlány, Hung., 13,074 126 D3
Orote Pen., Guam 176 24
Orote Pt., Guam 176 24
Orotukan, U.S.S.R. 135 P3
Orovada, Nev. 83 B2
Oroville, Calif., 6,115 82 C3
Oroville, Wash., 1,437 80 D1
Oroville Dam, Calif. 82 C3
Oroz, Mex. 92 C2
Orozco, Sp., 2,545 122 m11
Orpington, London, U.K. 114 J8
Orr, Minn., 361 74 F1
Orr, Okla. 76 F3
Orrefors, Swed. 120 C4
Orrick, Mo. 800 72 C5
Orrin, N. Dak. 74 B1
Orrington, Me. 55 D4
Orroroo, Austl. 172 c7
Orrs Island, Me. 55 C5
Orrstown, Pa., 318 60 G5
Orrum, N.C., 139 63 F3
Orrville, Ont., Can. 46 E3
Orrville, Ala., 422 64 B3
Orrville, Ohio, 6,511 70 H2
Orsa, Swed. 120 C3
Orsainville, Qué., Can., 4,216 47 n16
Orsay, Fr., 9,353 116 g12
Orscholz, F.R.Ger., 2,589 116 b8
Orsha, U.S.S.R., 71,000 136 C2
Orsières, Switz., 2,281 124 B2
Orsk, U.S.S.R., 195,000 134 E4
Orşova, Rum., 6,527 128 D2
Ørsta, Nor. 120 A3
Ørsted, Den. 121 C4
Ortamahalle, Turk., 5,429 142 D1
Orta Nova, It., 15,239 123 E4
Ortega, Col. 100 C6
Ortega, Mex. 93 d8
Ortegal, C., Sp. 122 ·
Ortenberg, F.R.Ger., 1,611 119 G4
Orth, Aust., 1,522 124 d10
Orthez, Fr., 8,829 117 C5
Ortigueira, Sp., 20,391 122 B1
Orting, Wash., 1,520 80 B2
Ortiz, Mex. 92 C2
Ortiz, Ky. 71 D4
Ortiz, Ven., 1,317 100 G3
Ortiz Mts., N. Mex. 79 B4
Ortles, mtn., It. 123 C1
Ortley, S. Dak., 127 74 D3
Ortley Beach, N.J. 58 c17
Örtofta, Swed. 121 c7
Ortoire, r., Trin. and Tob. 96 g5
Orton, Ont., Can. 46 b13
Orton, U.K. 113 E4
Ortona, It., 23,063 123 E3
Ortonville, Mich., 771 67 K6
Ortonville, Minn., 2,674 74 D3
Orto-Tokoy, U.S.S.R., 1,100 134 G5
Ortrand, Ger.D.R. 118 D3
Örträsk, Swed. 120 D2
Örtze, r., F.R.Ger. 118 C2
Ørum, Den. 121 C4
Orune, It., 5,969 123 B4
Oruro, Bol., 81,553 102 C5
Orust, i., Swed. 121 D2
Orvieto, It., 25,168 123 C3
Orviston, Pa. 60 G3
Orwell, N.Y. 59 J4
Orwell, Ohio, 819 70 J1
Orwell, Vt. 54 A4
Orwell, r., U.K. 113 G5
Orwigsburg, Pa., 2,131 61 K4
Orysa, Tenn. 71 B6
Orzesze, Pol., 6,518 127 h6
Orzinuovi, It., 10,585 122 c5
Orzyc, r., Pol. 127 D2
Orzysz, Pol., 3,967 127 D2
Os, Nor. 120 A3
Os, Nor. 120 B3
Osa, U.S.S.R., 12,700 137 h7
Osa, Pen. de, C.R. 94 F6
Osage, Ark. 73 B1
Osage, Iowa, 3,753 72 E1
Osage, co., Kans., 12,886 75 K5
Osage, Minn. 74 E2
Osage, co., Mo., 10,867 72 F6
Osage, co., Okla., 32,441 76 G1
Osage, Okla., 220 76 G1
Osage, Wyo. 81 G4
Osage, r., Mo. 72 E6
Osage Beach, Mo., 741 72 E6
Osage City, Kans., 2,213 75 K5
Osage Fork, r., Mo. 72 E7
Ōsaka, Jap., 3,011,563 155 D4
Osaka, Jap., 6,477 155 E4
Osakarovka, U.S.S.R. 137 o12
Ōsaka-wan, Jap. 154 g15
Ōsaki, Jap., 24,760 154 B6
Osakis, Minn., 1,396 74 E3
Osan, S. Kor., 18,036 151 E3
Ōsasu, Jap. 154 h15
Ōsawa, Jap. 155 m19
Osawatomie, Kans., 4,622 75 K5
Osborn, Mo., 274 72 C5
Osborne, co., Kans., 7,506 75 G4
Osborne, Kans., 2,049 75 G4
Osborne, Pa., 609 60 b7
Osborne, L., Fla. 65 b8
Osborneville, N.J. 61 C3
Osburg, F.R.Ger., 1,264 119 B5
Osburn, Idaho, 1,788 81 B2
Osby, Swed. 120 C4
Oscar, Fr. Guiana 101 O6
Oscar, Okla. 76 F4
Osceola, Ark., 6,189 73 E2
Osceola, co., Fla., 19,029 65 H4
Osceola, Ind., 1,350 70 C1
Osceola, co., Iowa, 10,064 72 B1
Osceola, Iowa, 3,350 72 D3
Osceola, co., Mich., 13,595 67 H4
Osceola, Mich. 66 E1
Osceola, Mo., 1,066 72 D6
Osceola, Nebr., 1,013 75 H2
Osceola, Pa. 60 H2
Osceola, Tex. 76 e10
Osceola, Wis., 942 66 A3
Osceola, Mt., N.H. 54 E3
Osceola Mills, Pa., 1,777 60 F4
Oschatz, Ger.D.R., 15,507 118 D3
Oschersleben, Ger.D.R., 19,069 118 C2
Oscoda, co., Mich., 3,447 67 J4
Oscoda, Mich. 67 K4
Oscura Pk., N. Mex. 79 B5
Oscuro, N. Mex. 79 B5
Osečina, Yug., 2,147 125 D2
Osek, Czech. 126 c6
Osen, Nor. 120 B2

Osëtr—Pagan · 273

Osëtr, r., U.S.S.R. 136 c6
Osgood, Ind., 1,434 70 D3
Osgood, Mo., 135 72 D4
Osgood, Ohio, 241 70 E2
Osgood Mts., Nev. 83 B2
Osh, U.S.S.R., 79,000 137 g4
Osha, r., U.S.S.R. 137 o11
Oshamambe, Jap., 14,667 155 J8
O-shan, China 152 A2
Oshawa, Ont., Can., 61,887 44 H7
Oshidomari, Jap. 155 J7
Ōshima, Jap. 154 e15
Ō-shima, Jap. 154 e15
Ō-shima, Jap. 155 F4
Ō-shima, Jap. 155 H9
Oshima-hantō, Jap. 155 J8
Ōshio, Jap., 6,870 154 f15
Oshkosh, Nebr., 1,025 75 C2
Oshkosh, Wis., 45,110 66 E4
Oshmyany, U.S.S.R., 7,700 136 B2
Oshogbo, Nigeria, 142,385 162 E4
Oshtemo, Mich. 67 H6
Oshwe, D.R.Congo 164 C2
Osian, India 145 D4
Osieczna, Pol., 1,501 127 B3
Osierfield, Ga., 82 64 F4
Osijek, Yug., 72,000* 125 D2
Osimo, It., 23,540 123 D3
Osinniki, U.S.S.R., 71,000 137 r11
Osintorf, U.S.S.R., 4,200 136 C2
Osipovichi, U.S.S.R., 15,800 136 B2
Osjaków, Pol. 127 C3
Oskaloosa, Iowa, 11,053 72 E3
Oskaloosa, Kans., 807 75 K4
Oskaloosa, Mo. 72 C7
Oskarshamn, Swed., 12,862 120 C4
Oskarström, Swed. 120 C4
Oskelaneo, Qué., Can. 44 K5
Oskol, r., U.S.S.R. 136 E3
Oslavany, Czech. 126 C2
Osler, Sask., Can. 43 C4
Oslo, Nor., 471,310 120 B3
Oslo, Minn., 372 74 D1
Oslob, Phil., 2,812 153 e12
Oslofjorden, Nor. 121 C1
Oslyanka, G., U.S.S.R. 137 i7
Osmanabad, India, 18,868 145 E6
Osmancık, Turk., 6,780 142 C1
Osmaniye, Turk., 29,291 142 D2
Ösmo, Swed. 120 e9
Osmond, Nebr., 719 75 H1
Osmotherley, U.K. 112 h11
Osnabrock, N. Dak., 289 74 C1
Osnabrück, F.R.Ger., 127,658 118 B2
Osnaburgh House, Ont., Can. 44 E4
Osny, Fr., 2,937 116 g10
Osoblaha, Czech. 127 g6
Osobłoga, r., Pol. 127 g6
Osogna, Switz. 124 D2
Osogov Mts., Bulg.-Yug. 125 F3
Osojnik, Yug. 125 C3
Osor, Yug. 125 B2
Osorno, Chile, 55,091 105 A6
Osorno, Vol., Chile 105 e15
Osoyoos, Br. Col. Can. 42 H4
Ospino, Ven., 1,541 100 F3
Osprey, Fla. 65 G5
Ospringe, Ont., Can. 46 b13
Oss, Neth., 25,000 115 D3
Ossa, Mt., Austl. 173 G6
Ossabaw I., Ga. 64 J4
Osse, r., Nigeria 162 f8
Össeby-Garn, Swed. 120 f8
Osseo, Mich. 67 J7
Osseo, Minn., 2,726 74 F3
Osseo, Wis., 1,144 66 B4
Ossett, U.K., 14,729 114 E3
Ossian, Ind., 1,108 70 D2
Ossian, Iowa, 827 72 F1
Ossineke, Mich. 67 K4
Ossingen, Switz. 124 C1
Ossining, N.Y., 18,662 59 N9
Ossipee, N.H. 54 E4
Ossipee, r., Me.-N.H. 54 F4
Ossipee L., N.H. 54 E4
Ossipee Mts., N.H. 54 E4
Ossipee Valley, N.H. 54 E4
Osso, Jap. 154 h14
Ossokmanuan L., Newf., Can. 45 N4
Ossora, U.S.S.R. 135 Q4
Ostaboningue, L., Qué., Can. 46 F1
Ostashëvo, U.S.S.R. 136 a6
Ostashkov, U.S.S.R., 19,500 136 D1
Ost-Berlin, Ger.D.R., 1,071,775 118 D2
Østbirk, Den., 1,873 121 B5
Oste, r., F.R.Ger. 118 B2
Osted, Den., 1,438 121 E5
Ostend (e) = Oostende
Osterburg, Ger.D.R. 118 C2
Osterburg, Pa. 60 F5
Osterburken, F.R.Ger., 2,487 119 G6
Österdalälven, r., Swed. 120 C3
Osterfeld, Ger.D.R. 126 a5
Österhaninge, Swed. 120 f8
Osterhofen, F.R.Ger., 2,614 118 D4
Osterholz-Scharmbeck, F.R.Ger., 12,791 118 B2
Øster Hornum, Den., 1,937 121 B4
Osterhout, Pa. 61 o15
Øster Hurup, Den. 121 C4
Østerild, Den. 121 A3
Østerlars, Den. 121 G5
Osterode, F.R.Ger., 15,469 118 C3
Östersund, Swed., 24,866 120 C3
Osterville, Mass., 1,094 57 P6
Østervrå, Den. 121 C3
Osterwieck, Ger.D.R. 118 C3
Östhammar, Swed. 120 D3
Osthofen, F.R.Ger., 5,029 118 B4
Ostia, ruins, It. 123 a8
Ostiano, It., 3,600 122 d5
Ostiglia, It., 9,288 122 e5
Östmark, Swed. 120 C3
Östraby, Swed. 121 F5
Östra Husby, Swed. 120 d9
Östra Karup, Swed. 121 E4
Ostrander, Ohio, 438 70 F2
Östra Sallerup, Swed. 121 F5
Ostrava, Czech., 264,278 126 D2
Östrich, F.R.Ger., 9,723 119 D2
Östringen, F.R.Ger., 4,636 119 F6
Ostróda, Pol., 16,942 127 D2
Ostrog, U.S.S.R., 8,400 136 B3
Ostrogozhsk, U.S.S.R., 28,400 134 C4
Ostrołeka, Pol., 13,698 127 D2
Ostrov, Czech., 17,022 126 A1
Ostrov, Rum. 128 F2
Ostrov, U.S.S.R., 17,600 134 B4
Ostrovnoy, U.S.S.R. 135 Q4
Ostrovnoye, U.S.S.R. 135 Q3
Ostrovo, Bulg., 3,550 128 F3
Ostrówek, Pol. 127 h5
Ostrowiec Świętokryski, Pol., 38,000* 127 D3
Ostrów Lubelski, Pol., 2,577 127 E3
Ostrów Mazowiecka, Pol., 12,541 127 E2
Ostrów Wielkopolski, Pol., 42,000* 127 B3
Ostrowy, Pol. 127 i6
Ostrzeszów, Pol., 7,213 127 C3
Ostuncalco, Guat., 4,486 94 b9
Ostuni, It., 32,002 123 F4
O'Sullivan Dam, Wash. 80 D2
Osum, r., Alb. 125 E4
Osŭm, r., Bulg. 128 E3
Ōsumi-guntō, Jap. 154 k17
Ōsumi-kaikyō, Jap. 154 B6
Osuna, Sp., 20,775 122 C4
Osvaldo Cruz, Braz., 15,745 103 F6
Osveya, U.S.S.R. 135 C2
Oswaldtwistle, U.K., 11,915 114 D3
Oswalt, Okla. 76 F3
Oswayo, Pa., 162 60 G2
Oswayo Cr., Pa. 60 F2
Oswegatchie, N.Y. 59 K3
Oswegatchie, r., N.Y. 59 K3
Oswego, Ill., 1,510 68 D2
Oswego, Kans., 2,027 75 K6
Oswego, co., N.Y., 86,118 59 H5
Oswego, N.Y., 22,155 59 G5
Oswego, S.C. 63 D3
Oswego, r., N.J. 61 C4
Oswego, r., N.Y. 59 H5
Oswego Center, N.Y. 59 p22
Oswestry, U.K., 11,215 113 E5
Oświęcim, Pol., 31,000* 127 C3
Osyka, Miss., 712 73 E6
Ōta, Jap. 154 B4
Ōta, Jap. 154 f14
Ōta, Jap., 62,600 155 F3
Ota, Port., 1,390 122 k9
Ota, r., Port. 122 i9
Otago Pen., N.Z. 175 f7
Ōtaguchi, Jap. 154 e16
Ōtake, Jap., 34,546 154 C4
Ōtaki, Jap. 155 G4
Otaki, N.Z., 2,973 175 g6
Ōtani, Jap. 154 h14
Ōtani, Jap. 154 h15
Ōtani, Jap. 154 i14
Otanmäki, Fin. 120 F2
Otar, U.S.S.R. 137 g3
Otaru, Jap., 198,511 155 J8
Otasawian, r., Ont., Can. 44 F5
Otates, Mex., 1,070 93 c9
Otava, r., Czech. 124 K4
Otavalo, Ec., 7,292 104 B1
Otavi, S.-W. Afr., 1,303 164 B5
Ōtawara, Jap., 42,111 155 G3
Otay, Calif. 82 c10
Otay, r., Calif. 82 c10
Oteen, N.C. 63 B2
Otego, N.Y., 875 59 K7
Otelec, Rum. 128 C2
Otelnuk L., Qué., Can. 45 M3
Otematata, N.Z., 2,838 175 f7
Otepää, U.S.S.R., 2,200 136 B1
Otero, co., Colo., 24,128 79 D3
Otero, co., N. Mex., 36,976 79 C5
Oteros, r., Mex. 92 C2
Otey, Tex. 77 h10
Otford, U.K., 3,179 114 J8
Othegon, Burma, 2,989 147 a1
Othello, Wash., 2,669 80 D2
Othis, Fr. 116 i10
Othmarsingen, Switz., 1,362 124 C1
Otho, Iowa, 593 72 C2
Othonoi, i., Gr. 129 B5
Óthris, Óros, Gr. 129 D5
Oti, Indon. 149 F3
Oti, r., Af. 162 E4
Otinapa, Mex., 1,785 92 D3
Otira, N.Z. 175 f6
Otis, Colo., 568 79 D1
Otis, Ind. 69 g10
Otis, Kans., 362 75 G5
Otis, Mass., 473(T) 56 D4
Otisco, Ind. 70 D4
Otisco, N.Y. 59 r24
Otisco L., N.Y. 59 H6
Otisfield, Me. 55 B4
Otisheim, F.R.Ger., 3,187 119 F7
Otish Mts., Qué., Can. 45 L4
Otis Res., Mass. 56 D4
Otisville, Mich., 701 67 K5
Otisville, N.Y., 896 59 L9
Otjiwarongo, S.-W. Afr., 6,162 164 B5
Otjosundu, S.-W. Afr. 164 C5
Otley, U.K., 11,930 114 E3
Otmęt, Pol., 3,884 127 g6
Otmuchów, Pol., 3,215 127 g6
Ōtō, Jap. 154 e16
Oto, Iowa, 221 72 B2
Otobe, Jap., 9,117 155 J9
Otočac, Yug., 3,055 125 B2
Otoe, co., Nebr., 16,503 75 J3
Otoe, Nebr., 225 75 J3
Otofuke, Jap., 23,850 155 K8
Otohara, Jap. 154 h14
Otoii, Jap. 154 e16
Otoineppu, Jap. 155 K7
Otoka, Yug., 2,125 125 C2
O-t'o-k'o-ch'i, China 151 A3
Ōtori, r., Jap. 155 F2
Otorohanga, N.Z., 2,002 175 g5
Otoshibe, Jap., 5,258 155 J8
Otoskwin, r., Ont., Can. 44 E4
Otosquen, Sask., Can. 43 D4
Otra, r., Nor. 120 A4
Otranto, It., 4,065 123 G4
Otranto, Str. of, Alb.-It. 129 B4
Otrokovice-Kvítkovice, Czech., 10,904 126 C2
Otsego, co., Mich., 7,545 67 J3
Otsego, Mich., 4,142 67 H6
Otsego, co., N.Y., 51,942 59 K6
Otsego, Ohio 70 H2
Otsego, Wis. 66 D5
Otsego Lake, Mich. 67 J4
Otsego L., Mich. 67 J4
Otsego L., N.Y. 59 L6
Otselic, r., N.Y. 59 J6
Ōtsu, Jap., 113,547 155 D4
Ōtsu, Jap. 155 K8
Ōtsuchi, Jap., 20,004 155 G2
Ōtsuki, Jap., 39,783 155 F4
Otta, Nigeria 162 e8
Otta, Nor. 120 B3
Ottange, Fr., 3,563 116 b8
Ottauquechee, r., Vt. 54 B4
Ottaviano, It., 16,187 123 d10
Ottawa, Ont., Can., 258,492 44 J6
Ottawa, Ill., 19,408 68 D2
Ottawa, co., Kans., 6,779 75 H4
Ottawa, Kans., 10,673 75 K5
Ottawa, co., Mich., 98,719 67 G6
Ottawa, co., Ohio, 35,323 70 F1
Ottawa, Ohio, 3,245 70 F1
Ottawa, co., Okla., 28,301 76 J1
Ottawa, r., Ont.-Qué., Can. 44 J6
Ottawa Beach, Mich. 67 G6
Ottawa Hills, Ohio, 3,870 70 F1
Ottawa Is., N.W.T., Can. 44 H2
Ottawa Lake, Mich. 67 K7
Ottenby, Swed. 120 D4
Ottenhöfen, F.R.Ger., 2,495 119 E7
Ottenschlag, Aust. 124 M5
Otter, r., Mass. 56 H2
Otter, r., Mich. 66 E2
Otterbach, F.R.Ger., 3,008 119 D6
Otter-Bach, r., F.R.Ger. 119 E6
Otterbein, Ind., 788 70 B2
Otterberg, F.R.Ger., 3,836 119 D5
Otterbourne, U.K. 113 k13
Otterburne, Man., Can. 43 h10
Otterburn Park, Qué., Can., 2,627 47 p17
Otter Creek, Fla. 65 G3
Otter Cr., N.Y. 59 K4
Otter Cr., Utah 78 C2
Otter Cr., Vt. 54 B5
Otter Ferry, U.K. 112 D3
Otter I., Wis. 66 C2
Otter Lake, Mich., 562 67 K5
Otter L., Sask., Can. 43 D3
Otterlo, Neth. 115 D2
Otterndorf, F.R.Ger., 6,695 118 B2
Otter River (part of Templeton), Mass. 56 H2
Otter Rock, Oreg. 80 A3
Ottersweier, F.R.Ger., 3,275 119 E7
Otterswiller, Fr. 116 d9
Otter Tail, co., Minn., 48,960 74 D2
Ottertail, Minn. 74 E2
Otter Tail, r., Minn. 74 D2
Otter Tail L., Minn. 74 E2
Otterup, Den., 2,138 121 C5
Otterville, Ont., Can. 46 D6
Otterville, Ill., 140 68 B4
Otterville, Mo., 416 72 E6
Ottery Saint Mary, U.K., 4,121 113 E6
Ottine, Tex. 76 c6
Öttingen, F.R.Ger., 3,813 118 C4
Otto, N.Y. 58 C7
Otto, N.C. 63 A2
Ottobeuren, F.R.Ger., 4,413 118 C5
Otto Fiord, N.W.T., Can. 41 M1
Ottoman, Va. 62 H5
Ottoville, Ohio, 793 70 E2
Ottumwa, Iowa, 33,871 72 E3
Ottweiler, F.R.Ger., 8,760 118 A4
Otukamamoan L., Ont., Can. 74 F1
Otumba, Mex., 1,701 93 f10
Otún, r., Col. 101 d15
Otuofai, Tahiti 177 44
Oturkpo, Nigeria 162 F4
Otusco, Peru, 4,516 104 B3
Otutara, Tahiti 177 44
Otu Tolu Group, is., Tonga 177 36
Otway, N.C. 63 H3
Otway, Ohio, 235 70 F4
Otway, C., Austl. 173 d12
Otway, Seno, Chile 105 A8
Otwell, Ind. 70 B4
Otwock, Pol., 36,000* 127 D2
Ötz, Aust. 124 G6
Ötztal Alps, Aust.-It. 124 G7
Ou, r., China 152 F1
Ou, r., Laos 146 C2
Oua, i., Tonga 177 36
Ouachita, co., Ark., 31,641 73 C4
Ouachita, Ark. 73 C4
Ouachita, parish, La., 101,663 73 C5
Ouachita, L., Ark. 73 B3
Ouachita, r., Ark.-La. 73 C5
Ouachita Mts., Ark.-Okla. 53 H4
Ouaco, N. Caled. 174 i8
Ouadda, C.A.R., 3,143 163 H4
Ouagadougou, Upper Volta, 63,000 162 D3
Ouahigouya, Upper Volta, 1,924 162 D3
Oualata, Maur., 1,285 162 C3
Ouaka, r., C.A.R. 163 H4
Ouallan, Niger 162 E3
Ouallene, Alg. 162 E1
Ouanary, Fr. Guiana 101 P5
Ouanda-Djallé, C.A.R. 163 H4
Ouango-Fitini, Iv. Coast 162 a7
Ouanne, r., Fr. 117 E3
Ouaquaga, N.Y. 59 J7
Ouareau, L., Qué., Can. 47 K2
Ouareau, r., Qué., Can. 47 L2
Ouargla, Alg., 6,456 160 E2
Ouarra, r., C.A.R. 163 J5
Ouarsenis, mts., Alg. 160 b6
Ouarzazate, Mor., 4,200 160 C2
Oubatche, N. Caled. 174 i8
Ōuda, Jap., 12,155 155 E4
Oud-Beijerland, Neth., 6,800 115 C3
Ouddorp, Neth., 3,100 115 B3
Oude IJssel, r., Neth. 115 E3
Oude Maas, r., Neth. 115 C3
Oudenaarde, Belg., 6,668 115 B4
Oudenbosch, Neth., 7,400 115 C3
Oude-Pekela, Neth., 6,600 115 F1
Oude Rijn, r., Neth. 115 C2
Ouderkerk, Neth., 3,200 115 b6
Ouderkerk a.d. IJssel, Neth., 4,000 115 b7
Oudeschild, Neth. 115 C1
Oude-Tonge, Neth. 115 C3
Oudewater, Neth., 4,100 115 b6
Oud-Gastel, Neth., 4,300 115 a7
Oud-Loosdrecht, Neth. 115 c6
Oudon, r., Fr. 117 C3
Oudtshoorn, S. Af., 22,186 164 C7
Oued-Fodda, Alg., 7,058 160 b5
Oued-Zem, Mor., 18,640 160 C2
Ouégoa, N. Caled., 1,199 174 i8
Ouellé, Iv. Coast 162 a8
Ouellette, Me. 55 D1
Ouémé, r., Dahom. 162 E4
Ouen, Î., N. Caled. 174 k9
Ouenza, Alg., 6,469 161 F1
Ouesso, Congo 164 B1
Ouest, B. de l', Îs. Wallis 175 7
Ouest, Pte., Qué., Can. 45 N5
Ouest, Pte., Haiti 96 k6
Ouezzane, Mor., 26,203 160 C2
Ouffet, Belg., 1,579 115 D4
Oughterard, Ire. 113 B5
Ougrée, Belg., 21,263 115 D4
Ouidah, Dahom., 18,910 162 d8
Ouistreham, Fr., 4,797 117 C2
Oujda, Mor., 128,645 160 D2
Oulainen, Fin. 120 F2
Oulangan Kansallispuisto, Fin. 120 G2
Ouled-Djellal, Alg., 8,602 160 E2
Ouled Mimoun, Alg., 5,973 160 a6
Oullins, Fr., 24,788 116 p15
Oulu, Fin., 63,607 120 F2
Oulujärvi, l., Fin. 120 F2
Oulujoki, r., Fin. 120 F2
Oum Chalouba, Chad 163 H3
Oum er Rbia, r., Mor. 160 C2
Oum Hadjer, Chad 163 H3
Ounasjoki, r., Fin. 120 F2
Oundle, U.K., 2,547 114 G6
Ou Neua, Laos 146 C2
Ounianga Kébir, Chad 163 H2
Our, r., F.R.Ger. 118 A3
Ōura, Jap. 154 e15
Ouray, co., Colo., 1,601 79 B2
Ouray, Colo., 785 79 B2
Ouray, Utah 78 D1
Ourém, Braz., 2,004 103 G2
Ourinhos, Braz., 25,717 103 G6
Ourique, Port., 6,189 122 A4
Ournie, Austl. 173 f11
Ouro Branco, Braz., 2,010 103 e17
Ouro Fino, Braz., 8,044 103 c18
Ouro Prêto, Braz., 14,722 103 H6
Ourthe, r., Belg. 115 D4
Ōu-sammyaku, mts., Jap. 155 G2
Ouse, Austl. 173 f14
Ouse, r., U.K. 113 F5
Ouse, r., U.K. 113 G5
Oust, Fr. 117 D5
Outagamie, co., Wis., 101,794 66 E4
Outardes, R. aux, Qué., Can. 45 L4
Outer Hebrides, i. group, U.K. 112 C3
Outer I., Wis. 66 C1
Outing, Minn. 74 F2
Outjo, S.-W. Afr., 2,943 164 B5
Outlook, Sask., Can., 1,335 43 C4
Outlook, Mont., 226 81 G1
Outlook, Wash. 80 C2
Outokumpu, Fin. 120 G3
Out Rawcliffe, U.K. 114 C3
Outreau, Fr., 13,548 117 D1
Outremont, Qué., Can., 30,036 47 o18
Out Skerries, is., U.K. 112 F1
Outwood, U.K., 6,730 114 F3
Ouyen, Austl., 1,426 173 F5
Ouzinkie, Alaska 85 G4
Ovada, It., 9,549 122 b6
Ovahi, Caleta, Easter I. 177 46
Ovalau, i., Fiji 174 4
Ovalle, Chile, 25,282 105 A4
Oval Pk., Wash. 80 C1
Ovamboland, reg., S.-W. Afr. 164 B4
Ovando, Mont. 81 C2
Ovar, Port. 14,128 122 A2
Ovau, i., Sol. Is. 175 b2
Ovauaara, Pte., Tahiti 177 44
Ovejas, Col. 100 C3
Ovens, r., Austl. 173 f11
Overall, Va. 62 F4
Overath, F.R.Ger., 10,473 119 C3
Overbrook, Okla. 76 F3
Overdinkel, Neth., 3,100 115 F2
Överenhörna, Swed. 120 e8
Overflakkee, i., Neth. 115 C3
Overflowing, r., Man.-Sask., Can. 43 E4
Overflowing River, Man., Can. 43 E4
Overgaard, Ariz. 78 C4
Overhalla, Nor. 120 B2
Overijse, Belg., 11,428 115 C4
Overijsselsche Kan., Neth. 115 E2
Overisel, Mich. 67 H6
Over Jerstal, Den. 121 B5
Överkalix, Swed. 120 E2
Overland, Mo., 22,763 72 a11
Overland Park, Kans., 21,110 75 a8
Overlea, Md., 10,795 62 c7
Overly, N. Dak., 65 74 B1
Overpelt, Belg., 8,276 115 D3
Overstreet, Fla. 65 D3
Overton, Hants., U.K., 2,936 114 F8
Overton, Denb., U.K., 1,035 113 E5
Overton, Nebr., 523 75 F3
Overton, Nev. 83 C4
Overton, co., Tenn., 14,561 71 F5
Overton, Tex., 1,950 77 Q3
Övertorneå, Swed. 120 E2
Överum, Swed. 120 C4
Overveen, Neth., 4,700 115 b6
Oveselu, Rum. 128 E2
Ovett, Miss., 290 73 G6
Ovid, Colo., 571 79 D1
Ovid, Mich., 1,505 67 J5
Ovid, N.Y., 789 58 G6
Oviedo, Dom. Rep., 1,493 96 m7
Oviedo, Para., 8,298 105 D3
Oviedo, Sp., 127,058 122 C1
Oviedo, Fla., 1,926 65 H4
Oviglio, It., 1,734 122 b6
Ovilla, Tenn. 71 D6
Ovilla, Tex. 76 f9
Övre-Årdal, Nor. 120 B3
Övrebö, Nor. 121 A2
Ovruch, U.S.S.R., 11,400 136 C3
Ovtrup, Den. 121 A5
Ōwada, Jap. 155 m19
Ōwada, Jap. 155 n18
Owaneco, Ill., 290 68 C4
Ōwani, Jap., 17,347 155 G1
Owanka, S. Dak. 74 A3
Owasa, Iowa, 104 72 D2
Owasco, N.Y. 59 q24
Owasco L., N.Y. 59 G6
Owase, Jap., 34,534 155 E4
Owasso, Okla., 2,032 76 H1
Owasso, L., Minn. 74 a6
Ōwata, Jap. 155 m19
Owatonna, Minn., 13,409 74 F3
Owego, N.Y., 5,417 59 H7
Owego Cr., N.Y. 59 H7
Owel, L., Ire. 113 C5
Owen, F.R.Ger., 2,299 119 G7
Owen, co., Ind., 11,400 70 C3
Owen, co., Ky., 8,237 71 G3
Owen, Wis., 1,098 66 C4
Owen, L., Wis. 66 B2
Owen, Mt., Colo. 79 B2
Owen Bay, Br. Col., Can. 42 a5
Owen Chan., Ont., Can. 46 C3
Owendale, Mich., 298 67 K5
Owen Falls Dam, Uganda 165 f13
Owenga, N.Z. 175 14
Oweniny, r., Ire. 113 B4
Owen I., Lesser Caymans 97 2
Owens, Va. 62 G4
Owens, r., Calif. 82 D4
Owensboro, Ky., 42,471 71 D4
Owensburg, Ind. 70 C4
Owens Cross Roads, Ala. 64 C1
Owens L., Calif. 82 E4
Owen Sound, Ont., Can., 17,046 44 G7
Owen Sd., Ont., Can. 46 D4
Owen Stanley Ra., Terr. Papua 174 e3
Owens Val., U.S. 50 C3
Owensville, Ark. 73 C3
Owensville, Ind., 1,121 70 B4
Owensville, Md. = West River
Owensville, Mo., 2,379 72 F6
Owenton, Ky., 1,376 71 G3
Owenyo, Calif. 82 E4
Owerri, Nigeria, 9,500* 162 F5
Owia, St. Vinc. 97 19
Owings Mills, Md., 3,810 62 b7
Owingsville, Ky., 1,040 71 H3
Owl, r., Man., Can. 43 G2
Owl Kill, r., N.Y. 54 A6
Owls Head, N.Y. 59 M2
Owmby, U.K. 114 H4
Owo, Nigeria, 35,568 162 f8
Owosso, Mich., 17,006 67 J6
Owsley, co., Ky., 5,369 71 H4
Owston Ferry, U.K., 1,066 114 G4
Owyhee, co., Idaho, 6,375 81 A4
Owyhee, Nev. 83 B2
Owyhee, r., Oreg. 80 E4
Owyhee Res., Oreg. 80 E4
Oxapampa, Peru, 2,536 104 C4
Oxbow, Sask., Can., 1,340 43 D5
Oxbow, Me. 55 D2
Oxbow, Mich. 67 e14
Oxbow, N.Y. 59 J3
Oxbow Dam, Idaho-Oreg. 81 A3
Ox Cr., N. Dak. 74 C1
Oxdrift, Ont., Can. 44 C5
Oxelösund, Swed. 120 D4
Oxford, Barb. 97 10
Oxford, N.S., Can., 1,465 47 U11
Oxford, N.Z. 175 g6
Oxford, U.K., 106,291 113 F6
Oxford, Ala., 3,603 64 D2
Oxford, Ark., 191 73 C1
Oxford, Conn., 3,292(T) 56 D7
Oxford, Ga., 1,047 64 F2
Oxford, Ind., 1,108 70 B2
Oxford, Iowa, 633 72 F3
Oxford, Kans., 989 75 H6
Oxford, La. 73 B6
Oxford, co., Me., 44,345 55 B4
Oxford, Me. 55 B4
Oxford, Md., 852 62 H4
Oxford, Mass., 6,985;9,282(T) 56 J4
Oxford, Mich., 2,357 67 K6
Oxford, Miss., 5,283 73 F3
Oxford, Nebr., 1,090 75 F3
Oxford, N.J. 61 B2
Oxford, N.Y., 1,871 59 J7
Oxford, N.C., 6,978 63 F1
Oxford, Ohio, 7,828 70 E3
Oxford, Pa., 3,376 61 K6
Oxford, Wis., 548 66 D5
Oxford House, Man., Can. 43 G3
Oxford Junction, Iowa, 725 72 G2
Oxford L., Man., Can. 43 G3
Oxfordshire, co., U.K., 309,452 113 F6
Oxhill, U.K. 112 g10
Oxie, Swed. 121 c7
Oxílithos, Gr., 1,393 129 E5
Oxkutzcab, Mex., 6,249 93 H4
Oxley, Austl. 173 e10
Ox Mts., The, Ire. 113 B4
Oxnard, Calif., 58,259 82 D5
Oxted, U.K., 8,094 114 H8
Oxtongue, r., Ont., Can. 46 F3
Oxtotilpan, Mex., 1,204 93 d10
Ōya, Jap. 155 n19
Oya, Malay., 1,115 148 D2
Oya, r., U.S.S.R. 137 t11
Oyama, Br. Col., Can. 42 H4
Ōyama, Jap., 13,163 155 F2
Oyama, Jap., 34,973 155 F3
Oyan, r., Nigeria 162 e8
Oyapock, r., Fr. Guiana 101 O6
Oyem, Gabon 164 A1
Oyen, Alta., Can. 42 L3
Oyens, Iowa, 114 72 A2
Öyestad, Nor. 121 A2
Oykel, r., U.K. 112 D3
Öymark, Nor. 121 D1
Oymyakon, U.S.S.R. 135 O3
Oymyakonskoye Plos., U.S.S.R. 135 O3
Oyo, Nigeria, 83,674 162 e8
Ōyodo, r., Jap. 154 B6
Oyolo, Peru, 2,127 104 C5
Oyón, Peru, 2,179 104 B4
Oyonnax, Fr., 15,189 117 F3
Oyster Bay, N.Y., 58 e13
Oyster Bay, Austl. 173 g14
Oyster Harbors (part of Barnstable), Mass. 57 P6
Oyster Keys, Fla. 65 g14
Oyster River, Br. Col., Can. 42 a6
Oytal, U.S.S.R. 137 g3
Oyugis, Kenya 165 g14
Ozama, r., Dom. Rep. 96 n6
Ozamiz, Phil., 8,664 153 B3
Ozan, Ark., 95 73 B4
Ozark, Ala., 9,534 64 D4
Ozark, Ark., 1,965 73 B2
Ozark, Ill. 68 D6
Ozark, Mich. 67 J2
Ozark, co., Mo., 6,744 72 E8
Ozark, Mo., 1,536 72 D8
Ozark, Okla. 76 D3
Ozark Mts., Ark. 73 B2
Ozark Plat., U.S. 51 H3
Ozarks, L. of the, Mo. 72 E6
Ozatlán, El Salv., 2,807 94 e10
Ozaukee, co., Wis., 38,441 66 F5
Ózd, Hung., 34,155 126 E2
Ozërnaya, U.S.S.R. 135 O3
Ozernovskiy, U.S.S.R., 5,500 135 P4
Ozernoy, P-ov., U.S.S.R. 135 Q4
Ozernoy, Zal., U.S.S.R. 135 Q4
Ozëry, U.S.S.R., 24,800 136 E2
Ozette, Wash. 80 A1
Ozette L., Wash. 80 A1
Ozhiski L., Ont., Can. 44 E4
Ozieri, It., 12,106 123 B4
Ozimek, Pol., 3,395 127 C3
Ozinki, U.S.S.R., 8,800 134 D4
Ozoir-la-Ferrière, Fr., 3,026 116 i11
Ozona, Fla. 65 c11
Ozona, Tex., 3,361 77 N4
Ozone, Tenn. 71 G6
Ozora, Hung., 3,573 126 D3
Ozorków, Pol., 15,582 127 C3
Ozouer-le-Voulgis, Fr., 1,019 116 k12
Ōzu, Jap., 43,583 155 C5
Ozumba, Mex., 5,289 93 f10
Ozzano Monferrato, It., 2,382 122 b5

P

Paagoumène, N. Caled. 174 i8
Paal, Belg., 5,427 115 D3
Paama, i., New Hebr. 174 m6
Pa-an, Burma, 4,139 147 b2
Paan, China = Pa-t'ang
Paar, r., F.R.Ger. 118 C4
Paarl, S. Af., 38,059 164 C7
Paasdorf, Aust. 124 d9
Paauhau, Hawaii 84 F3
Paauilo, Hawaii, 1,059 84 F3
Paavola, Fin. 120 F2
Pabbay, i., U.K. 112 C3
Pabean, Indon. 148 f7
Pabianice, Pol., 56,000* 127 C3
Pābna, Pak., 40,792 144 g13
Pacaás Novos, Sa. dos, Braz. 102 D4
Pacaraima, Sa., Braz. 102 D1
Pacarán, Peru 104 C5
Pacasmayo, Peru, 11,890 104 A3
Pacaya, Vol., Guat. 94 c9
Pace, Fla. 65 B2
Paces, Va. 62 E6
Pachacamac, Peru, 1,456 104 B5
Pachaug, Conn. 56 J6
Pachaug Pd., Conn. 56 J6
Pacheco, Calif., 1,518 83 e12
Pachelma, U.S.S.R., 10,900 136 F2
Pachfurth, Aust. 124 N5
Pa-ch'ing, China 150 C3
Pachino, It., 25,916 123 E6
Pachitea, r., Peru 104 C4
Pachiza, Peru, 1,300 104 B3
Pachmarhi, India, 6,142 145 F5
Pacho, Col. 100 C5
Pachora, India, 18,338 145 E5
Pa-ch'u, China 150 A3
Pachuca, Mex., 64,564 93 F4
Pa-chung, China 152 B1
Pachuta, Miss., 271 73 F5
Pacific, Br. Col., Can. 42 E2
Pacific, Mo., 2,795 72 G6
Pacific, co., Wash., 14,674 80 B2
Pacific, Wash., 1,577 81 b8
Pacifica, Calif., 20,995 82 B4
Pacific Beach, Wash. 80 A2
Pacific City, Oreg. 80 A3
Pacific Grove, Calif., 12,121 82 B4
Pacific Islands, Tr. Terr. of the, Pac. Oc., 92,000* 170 D4
Pacific Junction, Iowa, 560 72 A3
Pacific Ocean 168-9
Pacijan I., Phil. 153 C3
Pack, Aust. 124 L7
Packard Pk., Utah 78 b10
Packards, Me. 55 C3
Pack Monadnock Mtn., N.H. 54 D6
Packwaukee, Wis. 66 D5
Packwood, Iowa, 215 72 E3
Packwood, Wash. 80 C2
Paco, Phil., 5,475 153 b6
Paço de Arcos, Port., 8,413 122 i10
Pacoima Cr., Calif. 83 h15
Pacolet, S.C., 1,252 63 C3
Pacolet, r., S.C. 63 B2
Pacolet Mills, S.C., 1,476 63 C3
Pácora, Col. 101 d14
Pacov, Czech. 126 B2
Pactolus, N.C., 211 63 G2
Pacula, Mex. 93 e8
Paczków, Pol., 6,207 127 B3
Padada, Phil., 4,420 153 C4
Padanaram = South Dartmouth
Padang, Indon., 143,699 148 A3
Padang, Indon. 148 D3
Padang, Indon. 149 G4
Padang, P., Indon. 148 B2
Padang Geroda, Malay. 147 p15
Padang Grus, Malay., 1,620 147 o14
Padang Lembu, Malay., 1,388 147 o14
Padangpangjang, Indon., 25,521 148 A3
Pandang Rengas, Malay., 2,170 147 o14
Padang Serai, Malay., 2,587 147 o14
Padangsidimpuan, Indon. 148 A2
Padangtikar, P., Indon. 148 D3
Padasjoki, Fin. 120 F3
Padaung, Burma, 3,430 146 A3
Padaung Taung, Burma 147 a1
Padborg, Den. 121 B6
Paddle Prairie, Alta., Can. 42 H1
Paddock Lake, Wis. 66 c13
Paddockwood, Sask., Can. 43 C4
Pade, mtn., Rum. 128 D2
Padej, Yug., 4,610 125 E2
Paden, Okla., 417 76 G2
Paden City, W. Va., 3,137 62 D3
Paderborn, F.R.Ger., 47,343 118 B3
Padiham, U.K., 9,893 114 D3
Padilla, Bol., 9,436 102 D5
Padilla, Mex., 2,898 93 F3
Padina, Rum. 128 D2
Padina, Yug., 5,654 125 E2
Padjelanta Nat. Pk., Swed. 120 D2
Padlei, N.W.T., Can. 40 K5
Padma, r., Pak. 144 g14
Padova, It., 194,706 123 C2
Padrauna, India, 13,906 144 d12
Padre Burgos, Phil., 2,093 153 C3
Padre Burgos, Phil., 2,346 153 c9
Padre I., Tex. 77 P6
Padre Las Casas, Chile 105 e14
Padre las Casas, Dom. Rep., 3,026 96 m6
Padre Paraíso, Braz., 2,830 103 H5
Padrón, Sp., 8,170 122 A1
Padstow, U.K., 2,675 113 D6
Padua = Padova
Paducah, Ky., 34,479 71 C4
Paducah, Tex., 2,392 77 N2
Padul, Sp., 6,956 122 D4
Paea, Tahiti 177 44
Paekakariki, N.Z., 1,682 175 g6
Paektu-san, mtn., China-N. Kor. 151 F2
Paengnyŏng-do, S. Kor. 151 E3
Paeroa, N.Z., 2,894 175 g5
Paestum, ruins, It. 123 E4
Pag, Yug., 2,798 125 B2
Pag, i., Yug. 125 B2
Paga, Indon. 149 G5
Pagadian, Phil., 17,865 153 B4
Pagai, Kep., Indon. 148 A3
Pagai Selatan, i., Indon. 148 A3
Pagai Utara, i., Indon. 148 A3
Pagan, Burma, 2,825 147 f7
Pagan, i., Mar. Is. 170 D3
Pagan, Mt., Mariana Is. 176 23

274 · Pagani—Parkdale

Pagani, It., 26,785 123 d10
Pagasitikós Kólpos, Gr. 129 D5
Pagatan, Indon. 148 E3
Pagat Pt., Guam 176 24
Pagbilao, Phil., 8,367 153 c9
Page, Ariz., 2,960 78 C3
Page, co., Iowa, 21,023 72 B4
Page, Nebr., 230 75 G1
Page, N. Dak., 432 74 D2
Page, Okla. 76 J3
Page, co., Va., 15,572 62 F4
Page City, Kans., 2,687 75 D4
Pageland, S.C., 2,020 63 D3
Pager, Indon. 148 a6
Pageralam, Indon. 148 B4
Pagerdewa, Indon. 148 C3
Paget I., Berm. Is. 108 1
Pagham, U.K., 1,772 113 m13
Pagny-sur-Moselle, Fr., 3,301 116 b9
Pago, r., Guam 176 24
Pago Bay, Guam 176 24
Pagoda, Colo. 79 B1
Pagoda Pt., Burma 147 a3
Pagoh, Malay., 2,007 147 p15
Pagosa Pk., Colo. 79 B3
Pagosa Springs, Colo., 1,374 79 B3
Pagoua Bay, Dominica 97 13
Paguate, N. Mex. 79 B4
Pahala, Hawaii, 1,392 84 F4
Pahandut, Indon. 148 E3
Pahang, r., Malay. 147 p15
Pahiatua, N.Z., 2,578 175 h6
Pahlgam, India, 1,920 145 E2
Pahoa, Hawaii, 1,046 84 G4
Pahokee, Fla., 4,709 65 J6
Pahranagat Ra., Nev. 82 •
Pahrump, Nev. 83 B4
Pa-hsien, China 152 B1
Pa-hsien-t'ung, China 151 D2
Pahuatlán, Mex., 3,286 93 f9
Pai, Thai. 146 B3
Pai, r., China 150 F2
Pai, r., China 151 B4
Paia, Hawaii, 2,149 84 E3
Pai-ch'eng, Ch-1., China 150 G2
Pai-ch'eng, Hs.-ch., China 150 B2
Pai-chü, China 151 D4
Pai-ch'üan, China 150 G2
Paicol, Col. 100 C6
Paide, U.S.S.R., 6,000 135 B1
Pai-erh Hu = Buyr Nuur
Paige, Tex. 77 P4
Paignton, U.K., 30,292 113 E6
Pai-ho, China 151 A4
Pai-ho, Taiwan, 35,742 152 F3
Pai-ho-k'ou, China 152 C1
Pai Hu, China 152 E1
Pai-hua-tung, China 152 b6
Paiján, Peru, 5,883 104 B3
Päijänne, r., Fin. 120 F3
Pai-li, i., China 152 a7
Pailimo, Chile 104 f14
Pailin, Camb. 146 C4
Paillaco, Chile, 3,539 105 e15
Pailolo Chan., Hawaii 84 E2
Pai-ma-ch'uan, China 151 C2
Paimpol, Fr., 8,044 116 B2
Paimún, L., Arg. 105 f14
Painan, Indon. 148 B3
Paincourtville, La. 73 D8
Paine, Chile, 2,720 104 g13
Painesdale, Mich. 66 E1
Painesville, Ohio, 16,116 70 H1
Pai-niu, China 151 B4
Painswick, U.K., 2,844 114 D7
Paint, Pa., 1,275 60 E5
Paint, r., Mich. 66 E2
Paint Cr., Ohio 70 F3
Painted Desert, Ariz. 78 C4
Painted Post, N.Y., 2,570 58 F7
Painter, Va., 349 62 J5
Paintersville, Calif. 82 a8
Paint L., Man., Can. 43 F3
Paint Lick, Va. 62 C6
Paint Rock, Ala., 264 64 C1
Paint Rock, Tex. 77 O4
Paint Rock, mtn., Wash. 80 D1
Paint Rock, r., Ala.-Tenn. 64 C1
Paintsville, Ky., 4,025 71 J4
Pai-se, China 150 E4
Pai-sha, China 152 C4
Pai-shui, China 151 A4
Paisley, Ont., Can. 46 C4
Paisley, U.K., 95,753 112 D4
Paisley, Oreg., 219 80 C4
Paisley, Mt., Austl. 172 E4
Pai-ssu-ha, China 151 D2
Paistunturit, mts., Fin. 120 F1
Païta, N. Caled., 1,397 174 k9
Paita, Perú, 33,076 104 A3
Paito, r., Ven. 101 a12
Paiton, Indon. 148 e7
Pai-t'ou Shan = Paektu-san
Paixbán, Guat. 94 B2
Pai-yin, China, 50,000* 150 D3
Pai-yü, China 150 D4
Pai-yün-o-po, China, 12,000* 150 E2
Pai-yü Shan, China 151 A3
Paja, r., Pan. 94 f12
Pajakumbuh, Indon. 148 B3
Pajala, Swed. 120 E2
Paján, Ec., 1,757 104 A2
Pajaral, Mex. 93 H4
Pajarito, Col. 100 D5
Pajarito, N. Mex. 79 B4
Pajarito Mtn., N. Mex. 79 C5
Pajarito Pk., N. Mex. 79 B4
Pajaro, r., Calif. 83 f14
Pajaros, Farallon de, i., Mar. Is. 170 D3
Pájaros, P., Mex. 93 J4
Pajaros Pt., V.I. 97 4
Pajęczno, Pol., 2,984 127 C3
Pajo, Phil., 1,169 153 h15
Páka, Hung., 1,241 126 C3
Paka, Malay., 2,211 148 B1
Paka, r., Malay. 147 p14
Pakan, Alta., Can. 43 c6
Pakanbaru, Indon., 70,821 148 B2
Pakaraima Mts., Guyana 101 K5
Pakaur, India 144 f13
Pakawau, N.Z. 175 g6
Pak Beng, Laos 146 C3
Pak Chong, Thai. 147 d4
Pakenga, Pte., Is. Wallis 175 7
Pakenham, Ont., Can. 47 H3
Pakesley, Ont., Can. 46 D3
Pa Kha, N. Viet. 146 D2
Pak Hin Boun, Laos 146 D3
Pakhna, Cyp., 1,606 142 d10
Pakhotnyy, U.S.S.R. 137 q12
Pakhtusovo, U.S.S.R. 134 F2
Pakin, atoll, Car. Is. 176 18
Pakis, Indon. 148 a7
Pakistan, ctry., 105,044,000* 144-145
Paklay, Laos 146 C3
Paklow = Pei-liu
Pak Nam Pho, Thai. 147 d4
Pakokku, Burma, 30,943 146 A2
Pakość, Pol., 4,038 127 B2
Pak Ou, Laos 146 C2
Pākpattan, Pak., 27,974 145 D3
Pak Phanang, Thai., 11,963 146 C5
Pak Phil, Thai. 147 d4
Pakrac, Yug., 3,988 125 C2
Paks, Hung., 12,162 126 D3
Pakse, Laos 146 D4
Pak Seng, Laos 146 C2
Pak Tho, Thai. 147 c5
Pak Thong Chai, Thai. 147 d4
Paku, Terr. Papua 174 e2
Pakuanadji, Indon. 148 a6
Pakwach, Uganda 164 E1
Pala, Chad, 6,050, 162 G4
Pala, Calif. 82 E6
Pala, Cimon della, mtn., It. 123 C1
Palabuhan, Indon. 148 b7
Palacios, Tex., 3,676 77 P5
Palafrugell, Sp., 9,123 122 G2
Palaiá Epídhavros, Gr., 1,071 129 D6
Palaiókastron, Gr. 129 F7
Palaiokhóra, Gr. 129 D7
Pálairos, Gr., 1,995 129 C5
Palaiseau, Fr., 16,382 117 D2
Palali, Mt., Phil. 153 c6
Palamás, Gr., 5,840 129 D5
Palamedo, Indon. 149 G5
Palamós, Sp., 7,639 122 G2
Palampas, Phil., 15,877 153 e11
Palana, U.S.S.R., 1,500 135 P4
Palanas, Phil, 1,998 153 h15
Palanga, U.S.S.R., 6,000 136 A2
Palanpur, India, 29,139 145 D4
Palaoa Pt., Hawaii 84 D3
Palapag, Phil., 4,671 153 C2
Palapye, Bots., 5,137 164 D5
Pālas, Pak. 145 D2
Palāsbāri, Pak. 144 g13
Palatine, Ill., 11,504 68 D1
Palatine Bridge, N.Y., 578 59 M6
Palatka, Fla., 11,028 65 H3
Palau, Mex., 7,629 92 E2
Palau, is., Car. Is. 170 C4
Palauig, Phil. 153 a7
Palaui I., Phil. 153 B1
Palauk, Burma 146 B4
Palauli, W. Samoa 177 38
Palauli Bay, W. Samoa 177 38
Palaw, Burma, 5,804 146 B4
Palawan, i., Phil. 153 A3
Palawan Passage, Phil. 153 A3
Palayamkottai, India, 51,002 145 k21
Palazzolo sull'Oglio, It., 13,841 123 B2
Palca, Bol., 9,387 102 b10
Palca, Chile 102 a11
Palcamayo, Peru, 2,478 104 C4
Palco, Kans., 575 75 F4
Paldau, Aust., 1,119 124 M7
Paldiski, U.S.S.R., 3,400 136 A1
Pale, Burma, 1,406 147 f7
Pale, Yug. 125 D3
Paleisheuwel, S. Af. 164 a8
Paleleh, Indon. 149 G2
Palembang, Indon., 474,971 148 C3
Palena, Chile 105 A6
Palencia, Guat., 3,832 94 c9
Palencia, Sp., 48,216 122 C1
Palenque, Mex. 93 H5
Palenque, r., Ec. 104 c10
Palenque, ruins, Mex. 93 H5
Palered, Indon. 148 b7
Palermo, Ont., Can. 46 c14
Palermo, Col. 100 C6
Palermo, It., 591,041 123 D5
Palermo, Me. 55 C4
Palermo, N.Y. 59 q22
Palermo, N. Dak., 188 74 A1
Palermo, Urug. 105 d11
Palestina, Col. 101 d14
Palestine, Ark., 532 73 D3
Palestine, Ill., 1,564 68 E4
Palestine, Tex., 13,974 77 Q4
Palestine, W. Va. 62 C3
Palestine, reg., Isr.-Jor. 142 C4
Palestrina, It., 10,167 123 b8
Palestro, Alg., 10,758 160 c5
Palestro, It., 2,872 122 b5
Paletwa, Burma 146 A2
Palghat, India, 77,620 145 E8
Palgrave, Ont., Can. 46 E5
Palgrave, Mt., Austl. 172 A3
Palhais, Port., 4,689 122 i10
P'a-li, China 150 C4
Pali, India, 33,303 145 D4
Paliat, P., Indon. 148 f7
Pa-li-han-tien-tzu, China 151 C2
Palikea, pk., Hawaii 84 b7
Pa-li-k'un, China 150 C2
Palimé, Togo, 11,925 162 E4
Palin, Guat., 4,864 94 c9
Pa-lin-tso-ch'i, China 150 F2
Palinuro, Capo, It. 123 E4
Pa-lin-yu-ch'i, China 151 C2
Paliománina, Gr., 1,529 129 C5
Paliomonastíri, Gr., 1,470 129 C5
Palioúri, Gr., 1,189 129 F4
Palisade, Minn., 180 74 F2
Palisade, Nebr., 544 75 E3
Palisade, Nev. 83 B2
Palisades, Ill. 69 c10
Palisades, Wash. 80 D2
Palisades, N.J.-N.Y. 61 •
Palisades Park, N.J. 58 d13
Palisades Res., Idaho-Wyo. 81 D4
Palit, Kep i, Alb. 125 D4
Palitana, India, 24,581 145 D5
Palito Blanco, Tex. 77 O6
Palitos, r., Mex. 93 a8
Palizada, Camp., Mex., 2,333 93 H4
Palizada, Méx., Mex., 1,600 93 d10
Palk Bay, India 145 m21
Palkonda, India, 13,780 145 G6
Palk Str., Cey.-India 145 F8
Pal Lahara, India 145 G5
Pallasca, Peru, 1,908 104 B4
Pallas Grean, Ire. 113 B5
Pallas-Ounastunturin Kansallis-puisto, Fin. 120 E1
Pallasovka, U.S.S.R., 10,300 134 D5
Pallastunturi, mt., Fin. 120 F1
Palling, Br. Col., Can. 42 E2
Pallinup, r., Austl. 172 B5
Palliser, C., N.Z. 175 g6
Pall Mall, Tenn. 71 G5
Palma, Braz., 2,391 103 e17
Palma, Moz. 164 F3
Palma, Sp., 159,084 122 G3
Palma, de la, r., Cuba 96 c1
Palma del Río, Sp., 18,757 122 C4
Palma di Montechiaro, It., 20,572 123 D6
Palmar de Varela, Col. 100 C2
Palmares, Braz., 17,327 103 b15
Palmares do Sul, Braz., 1,288 103 F8
Palmarito, Cuba, 1,985 96 f2
Palmarito, Ven., 1,167 100 E4
Palmas, Braz., 5,540 103 F7
Palmas, B., Mex. 92 C3
Palmas, C., Af. 162 C5
Palma Soriano, Cuba, 25,421 96 e2
Palm Bay, Fla., 2,808 65 J4
Palm Beach, co., Fla., 228,106 65 J6
Palm Beach, Fla., 6,055 65 K6
Palm Beach Shores, Fla., 885 65 b8
Palm City, Fla. 65 J5
Palmdale, Calif., 11,522 82 D5
Palmdale, Fla. 65 H6
Palm Desert, Calif., 1,295 82 E6
Palme, Morne, Haiti 96 k6
Palmeira dos Índios, Braz., 15,642 103 a15
Palmela, Port., 6,487 122 A3
Palmer, Alaska, 1,181 85 G3
Palmer, Ill., 265 68 C4
Palmer, Iowa, 271 72 C2
Palmer, Kans., 169 75 H4
Palmer, Mass., 10,358(T) 56 G4
Palmer, Mich. 66 F2
Palmer, Nebr., 418 75 G2
Palmer, Tenn., 1,069 71 F6
Palmer, Tex., 613 76 f10
Palmer, r., Mass. 57 L5
Palmer Center (part of Palmer), Mass. 56 G4
Palmer Lake, Colo., 542 79 C2
Palmer Pen. = Antarctic Pen.
Palmer Springs, Va. 62 F6
Palmerston, Ont., Can., 1,525 46 D5
Palmerston, N.Z. 175 f7
Palmerston, i., Cook Is. 171 H6
Palmerston North, N.Z., 41,014 175 g6
Palmerton, Pa., 5,942 61 L4
Palmetto, Fla., 5,556 65 G5
Palmetto, Ga., 1,466 64 E2
Palmetto, La., 430 73 D7
Palmetto Point, Barbuda 97 8
Palm Harbor, Fla. 65 G4
Palmi, It., 19,868 123 E5
Palmilla, Chile, 1,136 104 f14
Palmillas, Mex., 1,164 93 F3
Palmira, Col. 100 B6
Palmira, Cuba, 6,261 96 c1
Palmira, Ec. 104 c11
Palm River, Fla. 65 d12
Palms, Mich. 67 L5
Palm Springs, Calif., 13,468 82 E6
Palm Valley, Fla. 65 H2
Palmyra, Syr. = Tudmur
Palmyra, Ill. 811 68 B4
Palmyra, Ind., 470 70 C4
Palmyra, Me. 55 C4
Palmyra, Mich. 67 K7
Palmyra, Mo., 2,933 72 F5
Palmyra, Nebr., 377 75 J3
Palmyra, N.J., 7,036 61 A3
Palmyra, N.Y., 3,476 58 F5
Palmyra, Pa., 6,999 60 J5
Palmyra, Tenn. 71 D5
Palmyra, Va. 62 F5
Palmyra, Wis., 1,000 66 E6
Palmyra, i., Line Is. 171 H4
Palni, India, 39,832 145 k20
Pal'niki, U.S.S.R. 137 h6
Palo, Phil., 8,916 153 f10
Palo, Mich. 67 J5
Palo Alto, Calif., 52,287 82 C4
Palo Alto, co., Iowa, 14,736 72 C1
Palo Blanco, Arg. 105 B3
Palo Duro Cr., Okla.-Tex. 76 N1
Palo Duro Cr., Tex. 76 N2
Paloh, Indon. 148 D2
Paloh, Malay., 2,776 147 p15
Palomar, P.R. 96 s10
Palomas, Col. 101 d14
Palombara Sabina, It., 6,291 123 b8
Palomino, Col. 100 D2
Palompon, Phil., 6,399 153 C3
Palo Negro, Ven., 11,040 101 b11
Palo Pinto, co., Tex., 20,516 77 O3
Palo Pinto, Tex. 77 O3
Palopo, Indon. 149 G3
Palos, C. de, Sp. 122 E4
Palos de la Frontera, Sp., 2,540 122 B4
Palo Seco, Trin. and Tob., 1,417* 96 g5
Palos Heights, Ill., 5,303 69 c10
Palos Hills, Ill., 3,766 69 c10
Palos Park, Ill., 2,169 69 c10
Palos Verdes Estates, Calif., 9,564 83 g16
Palouse, Wash., 926 80 E2
Palouse, r., Wash. 80 D2
Palouse Falls, Wash. 80 D2
Palo Verde, Calif. 82 F6
Palpa, Peru, 2,509 104 C5
Paltamo, Fin. 120 G2
Palu, Indon. 149 F3
Palu, Turk., 3,470 142 D2
Paluan, Phil., 2,399 153 B2
Palusawa, Burma 147 f6
Paluxy, Tex. 76 d10
Paluxy Cr., Tex. 76 d10
Palwal, India, 27,863 145 E3
Pam, N. Caled. 174 i8
Pa-ma, China 152 B2
Pama, Upper Volta, 1,191 162 E4
Pamangkat, Indon. 148 D2
Pamanukan, Indon. 148 C4
Pambujan, Phil., 2,667 153 C2
Pamekasan, Indon. 148 e7
Pamel, Belg., 5,223 115 C4
Pameungpeuk, Indon. 148 C4
Pamfou, Fr. 116 k12
Pamhagen, Aust., 2,129 124 N6
Pa-mien-ch'eng, China 151 D2
Pamiers, Fr., 13,953 117 D5
Pamir, r., U.S.S.R. 137 g5
Pamirs, mts., U.S.S.R. 134 G6
Pamlico, co., N.C., 9,850 63 H2
Pamlico, r., N.C. 63 H2
Pamlico Sd., N.C. 63 H2
Pa Mok, Thai., 8,886 146 C4
Pampa, Tex., 24,664 76 N2
Pampa Aullagas, Bol., 2,196 102 b11
Pampacolca, Peru, 1,906 104 C5
Pampán, Ven., 4,881 100 E3
Pampanga, r., Phil. 153 B2
Pampanua, Indon. 149 G4
Pampas, Peru, 2,520 104 C5
Pampas, plain, Arg. 99 C6
Pampas, r., Peru 104 C5
Pampilhosa da Serra, Port., 3,549 122 B2
Pamplemousses, Maurit. 165 c12
Pamplico, S.C., 988 63 E3
Pamplin, Va., 312 62 F5
Pamplona, Col. 100 D4
Pamplona, Phil., 3,357 153 d12
Pamplona, Sp., 97,880 122 E1
Pana, Ill., 6,432 68 C4
Panabo, Phil., 5,539 153 C4
Panaca, Nev. 83 C4
Panacan, Phil., 1,410 153 A3
Panacea, Fla. 65 E2
Panadura, Cey., 20,395 145 m22
Panaete, i., Terr. Papua 174 3
Panagyurishte, Bulg., 14,000 128 E3
Panahan, Indon. 148 E3
Panaitan, P., Indon. 148 C4
Panajachel, Guat., 2,452 94 b9
Panama, ctry., 1,287,000* 94 G6
Panamá, Pan., 273,440 94 H6
Panama, Ill., 487 68 C4
Panama, Iowa, 257 72 B3
Panama, N.Y., 450 58 A7
Panama, Okla., 937 76 J2
Panamá, B. de, Pan. 94 H6
Panamá, G. de, Pan. 94 H7
Panamá, Istmo de, Pan. 94 H6
Panama Can., C.Z. 94 f12
Panama City, Fla., 33,275 65 D2
Panamint Ra., Calif. 82 E4
Panamint Springs, Calif. 82 E4
P'an-an, China 152 F1
Pananaw, Phil., 2,117 153 B4
Panao, Peru, 1,900 104 C4
Panaon I., Phil. 153 C3
Panapompom, i., Terr. Papua 174 3
Panaquire, Ven., 1,067 100 G2
Panarea, Isola, It. 123 E5
Panaro, r., It. 122 e6
Panasia, i., Terr. Papua 174 3
Pana Tinani, i., Terr. Papua 174 g3
Pana-wina, i., Terr. Papua 174 3
Panay, i., Phil. 153 B3
Panay G., Phil. 153 B3
Panayía, Gr., 1,225 129 E4
Panayía, Gr. 129 E5
Panay I., Phil. 153 i14
Pancake, Pa. 60 b9
Pancake Ra., Nev. 83 B3
Pancalieri, It., 1,803 122 a6
Pančevo, Yug., 46,000* 125 E2
Panchimalco, El Salv., 4,409 94 d10
Panciu, Rum., 7,679 128 F2
Pancorbo, Sp. 122 m12
Panda, D.R.Congo 165 n19
Panda, Moz. 164 E6
Pandale, Tex. 77 N4
Panda-ma-Tenga, Bots. 164 D5
Pandan, Malay. 148 E2
Pandan, Phil., 1,516 153 B3
Pandan, Phil., 4,669 153 C2
Pandan, Tg., Indon. 148 C3
Pandawmi, Burma 147 b2
Pandeglang, Indon. 148 a7
Pandharpur, India, 45,421 145 E6
Pandhurna, India, 17,808 145 F5
Pandino, It., 4,974 122 c5
Pandjang, Indon. 148 a6
Pandjang, Selat, Indon. 147 o16
Pando, Urug., 10,000* 105 d12
Pandora, Ohio, 782 70 F2
Pandrup, Den. 121 B3
Panducan I., Phil. 153 B4
Panevėžys, U.S.S.R., 41,100 136 B2
Panfilov, U.S.S.R. 12,400 134 H5
Pangaimotu, i., Tonga 177 36
Pangalanes, Can. des, Malag. Rep. 165 H5
Pangandaran, Indon. 148 D4
Pangani, Tanz. 164 F2
Pangani, r., Tanz. 164 F2
Pangbourne, U.K., 1,953 114 F8
Pangburn, Ark., 489 73 D2
Pange, Fr. 116 b8
Pang-fou, China, 330,000* 150 F3
Pangi, D.R.Congo 164 D2
Pangian, Indon. 149 F3
Pangkadjene, Indon. 149 F4
Pangkalanbrandan, Indon. 148 A1
Pangkalanbuun, Indon. 148 D3
Pangkalandjambi, Indon. 147 o16
Pangkalpinang, Indon., 60,283 148 C3
Pangkor, Malay., 2,580 147 o14
Panglao, Phil., 2,059 153 e12
Panglao I., Phil. 153 B3
Pangnirtung, N.W.T., Can. 41 Q4
Pango Pango, Amer. Samoa, 1,251 177 37
Pango Pango Hbr., Tutuila 177 39
Pangrango, G., Indon. 148 b7
Pangsau Pass, Burma-India 146 B1
Pangtara, Burma 147 g7
Panguipulli, Chile, 4,708 105 A5
Panguipulli, L., Chile 105 e14
Panguitch, Utah, 1,435 78 B3
Panguruan, Indon. 148 A2
Pangutaran Group, is., Phil. 153 B4
Pang-Yang, Burma 146 B2
Panhandle, Tex., 1,958 76 N2
P'an-hsien, China 152 B2
Pania-Mutombo, D.R.Congo 164 D2
Paniau, Mt., Hawaii 84 •
Panié, Mt., N. Caled. 174 i8
Panimávida, Chile 104 f15
Panindícuaro, Mex., 4,453 93 c10
Panipat, India, 67,026 145 E3
Paniqui, Phil., 6,492 153 b7
Panitian, Phil., 1,391 153 A3
Panjang, Hon, S. Viet. 146 C5
Panjao, Afghan. 144 C2
Panjgūr, Pak., 2,032 144 B4
Panjim, India 145 D7
Panjumpa, Indon. 148 E3
Panke, r., Ger.D.R. 119 e10
Pankrushikha, U.S.S.R. 137 p11
Pankshin, Nigeria 162 F4
P'an-lung, r., China-N. Viet. 152 B3
Pan-ma, China 150 D3
P'anmunjŏm, N. Kor. 151 E3
Panna, India, 16,737 144 c13
Panny, r., Alta., Can. 42 J1
Panola, Ala. 64 A3
Panola, Ill., 43 68 D3
Panola, co., Miss., 28,791 73 E3
Panola, Okla. 76 H3
Panola, co., Tex., 16,870 77 Q3
Pano Lefkara, Cyp., 2,168 142 e10
Panopah, Indon. 148 D3
Pano Platres, Cyp. 142 d10
Panora, Iowa, 1,019 72 C3
Pánormon, Gr. 129 E7
Pánormos, Gr. 129 E6
Pan-p'u, China 151 C4
P'an-shan, China 151 D2
P'an-shih, China 151 E2
P'an-shun, China 152 a6
Pant, U.K. 114 B5
Pantabañgan, Phil., 3,004 153 c7
Pantai, Indon. 148 F3
Pantai, Malay., 1,292 147 p15
Pantai Remis, Malay., 2,639 147 o14
Pantanaw, Burma, 4,687 147 a2
Pantao, Phil., 2,297 153 h14
Pantar, P., Indon. 149 H5
Pantego, N.C., 262 63 H2
Pantelleria, It., 10,057 123 C6
Pantelleria, Isola di, It. 123 C6
Pantepec, Mex., 2,399 93 f9
Pantex, Tex. 76 N2
Panther, Ky. 71 D4
Panther, Pa. 61 p16
Panther Mtn., N.Y. 59 L7
Panthersville, Ga. 64 h10
Pantin, Fr., 46,401 116 h11
Pantoja, Peru 104 C2
Panton, Vt. 54 A3
Pánuco, Mex., 8,688 93 F4
Pánuco, r., Mex. 93 F3
P'an-yü, China 152 a6
Pao, r., Ven. 100 F3
Pao, r., Ven. 101 b11
Pao, r., Ven. 101 H3
Pao-an, China 152 D3
Pao-an-chen, China 151 A4
Pao-chi, China, 180,000* 150 E3
Pao-chia-tun, China 151 D4
Pao-ch'ing, China 151 F1
Pao-ching, China 152 C1
Pao-k'ang, China 152 C1
Paoki = Pao-chi
Pao-kuo-t'u, China 151 D2
Paola, It., 18,497 123 F5
Paola, Kans., 4,784 75 L5
Paoli, Colo., 81 79 D1
Paoli, Ind., 2,754 70 C4
Paoli, Okla., 358 76 F3
Paoli, Pa., 5,100* 61 L5
Paoli, Wis. 66 D6
Paonia, Colo., 1,083 79 B2
Paopao, B. de, Moorea 177 44
Pao-shan, Chiang-Su, China 152 F1
Pao-shan, Y-n., China 150 D4
Pao-te, China 151 A3
Pao-ti, China 151 C3
Pao-ting, China, 220,000* 150 F3
Pao-t'ing, China 152 C4
Pao-t'ou, China, 1,500,000* 150 E2
Paotow = Pao-t'ou
Paoua, C.A.R., 3,669 162 G4
Paouignan, Dahom. 162 e8
Pao-ying, China 151 C4
Pápa, Hung., 25,629 126 C3
Papa, Hawaii 84 F4
Papaaloa, Hawaii, 449 84 F4
Papadhiánika, Gr., 1,642 129 D6
Papagaio, r., Braz. 102 E4
Papagayo, G. del, C.R. 94 E5
Papai, Hawaii 84 G4
Papaikou, Hawaii, 1,591 84 F4
Papakura, N.Z., 7,997 175 g5
Papalaulelei, C., W. Samoa 177 38
Papaloa, Hawaii 84 F4
Papantla, Mex., 18,579 93 F4
Papao, Tahiti 177 44
Papar, Malay. 148 F1
Paparoa, N.Z. 175 g5
Papa Stour, i., U.K. 112 F1
Papatlatla, Mex., 1,380 93 f9
Papatoetoe, N.Z., 17,924 175 g5
Papa Westray, i., U.K. 112 E2
Papayal, Col. 101 d15
Papeete, Tahiti, 20,200 177 44
Papelón, Ven. 100 F3
Papenburg, F.R.Ger., 15,098 118 A2
Papendrecht, Neth., 9,000 115 b7
Papenoo, Tahiti 177 44
Papenoo, Pte. de, Tahiti 177 44
Papetoai, Moorea 177 44
Papetoai, B. de, Moorea 177 44
Paphos, Cyp., 7,283 142 C3
Papigochic, r., Mex. 92 C2
Papillion, Nebr., 2,235 75 J2
Papineau, Ill., 169 68 E3
Papineauville, Qué., Can., 1,273 47 J3
Papinsville, Mo., 29 72 C6
Papua, Terr. of, 573,000* 170 D5
Papua, G. of, Terr. Papua 170 D5
Papua Passage, Rarotonga 177 34
Papun, Burma 147 b1
Papuri, r., Braz.-Col. 100 F7
Păpuşa, mt., Rum. 128 D2
Paquette, Ont., Can. 67 g16
Pará, st., Braz., 1,550,935 103 E3
Pará, R. do, Braz. 103 G2
Parabel', U.S.S.R. 134 H4
Paracale, Phil., 3,867 153 B2
Paracambi, Braz., 4,618 103 e18
Paracas, Peru 104 B5
Paracatu, Braz., 10,677 103 G5
Paracatu, r., Braz. 103 G5
Paracel Is. = Hsi-sha Ch'ün-tao
Parachim, Ger.D.R., 18,895 118 C2
Pārachinār, Pak., 22,953 145 D2
Paracho, Mex., 6,210 93 b10
Paraćin, Yug., 16,000* 125 E3
Paracotos, Ven., 1,213 101 b11
Parácuaro, Mex., 4,079 93 d9
Parád, Hung., 3,011 126 D3
Parade, S. Dak. 74 B3
Paradera, Aruba 97 15
Paradise, Guyana 101 L5
Paradise, Calif., 8,268 82 C3
Paradise, Kans., 134 75 F4
Paradise, Mich. 67 H2
Paradise, Pa. 61 K5
Paradise, Tex. 76 d8
Paradise, Utah, 368 78 c7
Paradise, r., Newf., Can. 45 P4
Paradise Hill, Sask., Can. 43 B4
Paradise Pond, Newf., Can. 45 b10
Paradise Valley, Nev. 83 B2
Parado, Indon. 149 F5
Paradox L., N.Y. 59 N4
Paragon, Ind., 560 70 C3
Paragonah, Utah, 300 78 B3
Paragould, Ark., 10,053 73 E1
Paraguá, r., Bol. 102 D4
Paragua, r., Ven. 101 J4
Paraguaçu, Braz., 5,961 103 d17
Paraguaçu, r., Braz. 103 H4
Paraguai, r., Braz. 102 E5
Paraguaipoa, Ven., 3,884 100 E2
Paraguaná, Pen. de, Ven. 100 E1
Paraguarí, Para., 5,040 105 D3
Paraguay, ctry., 1,816,890 105
Paraguay, r., Arg.-Para. 105 D2
Parahoué, Dahom. 162 d8
Paraíba, st., Braz., 2,018,023 103 J3
Paraíba, r., Braz. 103 b14
Paraíba, r., Braz. 103 H6
Paraíba do Sul, Braz., 7,675 103 e18
Paraibuna, Braz., 2,384 103 d18
Parainen = Pargas
Paraingkareha, Indon. 149 F5
Paraíso, Braz. 103 F5
Paraíso, C.Z., 3,113 94 g12
Paraíso, C.R., 4,427 94 F6
Paraíso, Dom. Rep., 1,665 96 m7
Paraíso, Mex., 4,094 93 G4
Paraíso, Phil., 8,423 153 e11
Paraisópolis, Braz., 6,582 103 d18
Parajimarú, Col. 100 E1
Parakhino-Poddub'ye, U.S.S.R., 12,300 136 D1
Parakoila, Gr., 1,394 129 F5
Parakou, Dahom., 10,593 162 E4
Paralaya, Phil., 2,505 153 b7
Paralimni, Cyp., 3,082 142 f9
Parallel, Kans. 75 J4
Paraloma, Ark., 94 73 A4
Param, i., Ponape 176 29
Param, i., Truk 176 19
Paramaribo, Sur., 122,634* 101 N5
Parámirim, r., Braz. 103 H4
Paramithiá, Gr., 2,827 129 C5
Paramonga, Peru 104 B4
Paramount, Calif., 27,249 83 h16
Paramus, N.J., 23,238 61 C2
Paramushir, O., U.S.S.R. 135 P4
Paran, wadi, Isr. 142 C4
Paraná, Arg., 108,078 105 C4
Paraná, st., Braz., 4,277,763 103 F6
Paranã, Braz. 103 G4
Paraná, r., S. Amer. 99 D5
Paranaguá, Braz., 27,728 103 G7
Paranaíba, Braz., 3,853 103 F5
Paranaíba, r., Braz. 103 F5
Paranaidji, Braz., 1,745 103 G3
Paranam, Sur., 1,674* 101 N5
Paranapanema, r., Braz. 103 F6
Paranavaí, Braz., 22,141 103 F6
Paranéstion, Gr., 1,244 129 E4
Parang, Phil., 1,974 153 B4
Parang, Phil., 5,894 153 C4
Parang, P., Indon. 148 d6
Parangaba, Braz., 92,534 103 J2
Paranhos, Braz. 103 E6
Paraoa, atoll, Tuam. Arch. 177 42
Paraoir, Phil., 1,217 153 b6
Paraopeba, r., Braz. 103 d17
Parapara, Ven. 101 b12
Parapóla, i., Gr. 129 D6
Parás, Mex. 93 F2
Parasca, Nic. 94 E4
Parati, Braz., 3,046 103 d18
Parati-Mirim, Braz., 3,014 103 d18
Paratinga, Braz., 2,403 103 H4
Paravóla, Gr., 1,357 129 C5
Paray-le-Monial, Fr., 9,835 117 F3
Parbati, r., India 145 E5
Pārbatipur, Pak., 27,188 144 g13
Parbhani, India, 36,795 145 E6
Parchment, Mich., 1,565 67 H6
Parczew, Pol., 8,227 127 E3
Pardee, Va. 62 B5
Pardeeville, Wis., 1,331 66 D5
Pardes Hanna, Isr., 7,320 142 a7
Pardi, India, 10,553 145 h16
Pardillal, Ven. 101 b12
Pardo, r., Braz. 103 F6
Pardo, r., Braz. 103 H5
Pardubice, Czech., 54,746 126 B1
Pare, Indon. 148 e7
Parecis, Sa. dos, Braz. 102 D4
Parede, Port, 8,811 122 i10
Paredones, Chile 104 f14
Parelhas, Braz., 3,821 103 a14
Paren', U.S.S.R. 135 Q3
Parent, Qué., Can., 1,270 44 K6
Parentis-en-Born, Fr., 2,493 117 C4
Pareora, N.Z. 175 f7
Parepare, Indon. 67,992 149 F4
Parfënovo, U.S.S.R. 137 q11
Parfen'yevo, U.S.S.R. 136 F1
Párga, Gr., 1,586 129 C5
Pargas, Fin. 120 E3
Pargolovo, U.S.S.R., 22,600 136 C1
Parham, Antigua, 1,123 97 9
Paria, G. of, Trin. and Tob.-Ven. 101 J2
Paria, Pen. de, Ven. 101 K2
Paria, r., Ariz.-Utah 78 C3
Pariaguán, Ven., 6,094 101 H3
Pariaman, Indon. 148 A3
Parichi, U.S.S.R. 136 C2
Paricutin, vol., Mex. 92 E4
Parigi, Indon. 149 G3
Parika, Guyana 101 L4
Parikkala, Fin. 120 G3
Parima, Sa., Ven. 102 D1
Parinari, Peru 104 C3
Parincea, Rum. 128 F1
Parintins, Braz., 9,068 103 E2
Paris, Ont., Can., 5,769 46 D5
Paris, Christmas Atoll 177 40
Paris, Fr., 2,811,171 117 E2
Paris, Ark., 3,007 73 B2
Paris, Idaho, 746 81 D4
Paris, Ill., 9,823 68 E4
Paris, Ky., 7,791 71 G3
Paris, Mich. 67 H5
Paris, Mo., 1,393 72 F5
Paris, Ohio 70 H2
Paris, Tenn., 9,325 71 C5
Paris, Tex., 20,977 77 Q3
Paris, Wis. 66 E6
Parish, N.Y., 567 59 H5
Parish, Urug. 105 c11
Parishville, N.Y. 59 L2
Parisienne, I., Ont., Can. 67 J2
Parismina, C.R. 94 F5
Parisville, Qué., Can. 47 N2
Parisville, Mich. 67 L5
Parit, Malay., 3,439 147 o14
Parita, Pan., 1,464 94 G7
Parita, G. de, Pan. 94 G6
Parit Buntar, Malay., 4,012 147 o14
Parit Jawa, Malay., 2,497 147 p16
Parit Sulong, Malay., 1,984 147 p16
Parizhakaya Kommuna, U.S.S.R., 32,300 136 f7
Park, co., Colo., 1,822 79 C2
Park, Kans., 218 75 E4
Park, co., Mont., 13,168 81 D3
Park, co., Wyo., 16,874 81 E3
Park, r., N. Dak. 74 D1
Parkano, Fin. 120 E3
Park City, Ill., 1,408 69 c7
Park City, Ky., 497 71 E4
Park City, Mont. 81 E3
Park City, Utah, 1,366 78 C1
Parkdale, Ark., 448 73 D4

Parkdale—Pembroke · 275

Parkdale, Oreg. 80 C3
Parke, co., Ind., 14,804 70 B3
Parker, Ont., Can. 46 a13
Parker, Ariz., 1,642 78 A4
Parker, Colo. 79 C2
Parker, Fla., 2,669 65 D2
Parker, Ind., 1,181 70 D2
Parker, Okla. 76 G3
Parker, Pa., 945 60 C3
Parker, S. Dak., 1,142 74 D4
Parker, co., Tex., 22,880 77 P3
Parker, Tex. 76 e10
Parker, Wash. 80 C2
Parker, L., Fla. 65 d11
Parker, r., Mass. 57 N2
Parker Dam, Calif. 82 F5
Parker Dam, Ariz.-Calif. 82 F5
Parker Ford, Pa. 60 e11
Parker Pd., Me. 55 B4
Parkersburg, Ill., 253 68 D5
Parkersburg, Iowa, 1,468 72 E2
Parkersburg, N.C., 65 63 F3
Parkersburg, W. Va., 44,797 62 C3
Parkers Corners, Mich. 67 J6
Parkers Prairie, Minn., 884 74 E2
Parkerville, Kans., 59 75 J5
Parkes, Austl., 7,973 173 G5
Parkesburg, Pa., 2,759 61 L6
Park Falls, Wis., 2,919 66 C3
Parkfield, Calif. 82 C5
Park Forest, Ill., 29,993 68 E2
Park Hall, Md. 62 H4
Parkhar, U.S.S.R. 137 f5
Parkhill, Ont., Can., 1,151 44 G7
Park Hills, Ky., 4,076 71 h11
Parkin, Ark., 1,489 73 E2
Parkland, Okla. 76 G2
Parkland, Wash. 80 B2
Parkman, Me. 55 C3
Parknasilla, Ire. 113 B6
Park Ra., Col. 79 ·
Park Rapids, Minn., 3,047 74 E2
Park Ridge, Ill., 32,659 68 E2
Park Ridge, N.J., 6,389 61 C1
Park Ridge, Wis., 504 66 D4
Park River, N. Dak., 1,813 74 D1
Parkrose, Oreg. 80 a6
Parks, Ariz. 78 B4
Parks, Ark. 73 B3
Parks, Nebr. 75 D3
Parkside, Sask., Can. 43 C4
Parkside, Pa., 2,426 60 f12
Parksley, Va., 850 62 J5
Parkston, S. Dak., 1,514 74 D4
Parksville, Br. Col., Can., 1,117 42 F4
Parksville, N.Y. 59 L8
Parksville, S.C., 164 63 B4
Parkton, N.C., 906 63 F3
Park Valley, Utah 78 B1
Park View, N. Mex. 79 B3
Parkview, Ohio, 2,018 70 d9
Parkville, Md. 62 d7
Parkville, Mich. 67 H6
Parkville, Mo., 1,229 72 C5
Parkville, Pa., 4,516 60 J6
Parlakimedi, India 145 G6
Parlakot, India 145 F6
Parli, India, 19,691 145 E6
Parlier, Calif., 1,366 82 D4
Parlin, Colo. 79 B2
Parma, It., 134,878 123 C2
Parma, Idaho, 1,295 81 A4
Parma, Mich., 770 67 J6
Parma, Mo., 1,060 72 H8
Parma, Ohio, 82,845 70 H1
Parma Center, N.Y. 58 E5
Parmachenee L., Me. 54 E1
Parma Heights, Ohio, 18,100 70 H1
Parmain, Fr., 1,859 116 g10
Parmele, N.C., 323 63 G2
Parmelee, S. Dak. 74 B4
Parmer, co., Tex., 9,583 77 M2
Parnaíba, Braz., 39,951 103 H2
Parnaíba, r., Braz. 103 G3
Parnassós, mt., Gr. 129 D5
Parnassus, Va. 62 E4
Parnassus = Parnassós
Parndana, Austl. 172 E5
Parnell, Iowa, 200 72 F3
Parnell, Mo., 260 72 C4
Pärnu, U.S.S.R., 38,000 134 B4
Paro Dzong, Bhutan 144 g12
Parole, Md. 62 c9
Paroo, r., Austl. 173 F4
Paropamisus, ra., Afghan. 144 B2
Páros, Gr., 1,886 129 E6
Páros, i., Gr. 129 E6
Parottee Point, Jam. 96 p9
Parowan, Utah, 1,486 78 B3
Parr, Ind. 70 B1
Parr, S.C. 63 C3
Parral, Chile, 14,610 105 A5
Parral, R. del, Mex. 92 D2
Parras, Mex., 19,499 92 E3
Parravicini, Arg. 105 b13
Parrett, r., U.K. 114 B8
Parrish, Ala., 1,608 64 B2
Parrish, Fla. 65 G5
Parrish, Wis. 66 D3
Parris I., S.C. 63 D5
Parrita, C.R. 94 E6
Parrita, Mex. 92 D2
Parrott, Ga., 280 64 E4
Parrott, Va. 62 D5
Parrottsville, Tenn., 91 71 H5
Parroy, Fr. 116 c9
Parrsboro, N.S., Can., 1,795 45 N6
Parry, i., Eniwetok 176 28
Parry Bay, N.W.T., Can. 41 N4
Parry Chan., N.W.T., Can. 108 F2
Parry I., Ont., Can. 46 D3
Parry Is., N.W.T., Can. 41 G2
Parry Sound, Ont. Can., 5,887 44 H6
Parry Sd., Ont., Can. 46 D3
Parryville, Pa., 580 61 L4
Parsa, India 144 d14
Parsad, India 145 D4
Parsberg, F.R.Ger., 2,566 118 C4
Parsęta, r., Pol. 127 B2
Parshall, N. Dak., 1,216 74 A2
Parsippany, N.J., 3,600* 61 C2
Parsnip, r., Br. Col., Can. 42 F2
Parson, Br. Col., Can. 42 J3
Parsons, Kans., 13,929 75 K6
Parsons, Tenn., 1,859 71 C6
Parsons, W. Va., 1,798 62 E3
Parsonsburg, Md. 62 J4
Parsonsfield, Me. 55 B5
Parsons Pt., India 146 A6
Parsteiner See, Ger.D.R. 118 D2
Partabpur, India 144 d14
Partello, Mich. 67 J6
Partenstein, F.R.Ger., 2,221 119 H4
Parthenay, Fr., 10,077 117 C3
Partinico, It., 26,230 123 D5
Partizánske, Czech. 126 D2
Partlow, Va. 62 G4
Parton, U.K., 1,395 114 A1
Partoun, Utah 78 B2
Partridge, r., Ont., Can. 44 H5
Paru, r., Braz. 103 F2
Parucito, r., Ven. 100 H5
Parur, India, 20,852 145 k20
Parvatipuram, India, 25,281 145 G6
Parwān, Pak. 144 B4
Parwich, U.K. 114 E4
Parys, S. Af., 12,673 165 i17
Pas, R. de., Qué., Can. 45 N3
Pasadena, Calif., 116,407 82 E5
Pasadena, Md. 62 c8
Pasadena, Tex., 58,737 77 Q5
Pasado, C., Ec. 104 A2
Pasaje, Ec., 13,195 104 B2
Pasak, r., Thai. 146 C3
Pasamonte, N. Mex. 79 D3
Pasangkaju, Indon. 149 F3
Pasarbantal, Indon. 148 B3
Pasarseluma, Indon. 148 B4
Pasarwadjo, Indon. 149 G4
Pasawahan, Indon. 148 b7
Pasay, Phil., 132,673 153 B2
Pasca, Col. 101 e15
Pascagoula, Miss., 17,155 73 G7
Pascagoula, r., Miss. 73 G7
Paşcani, Rum., 15,008 128 F1
Pasco, co., Fla., 36,785 65 G4
Pasco, Ohio 70 E2
Pasco, Wash., 14,522 80 D2
Pascoag, R.I., 2,983 57 K5
Pascoag Res., R.I. 57 K5
Pascoe Inlet, Austl. 172 E2
Pascola, Mo., 228 72 H8
Pascua, Isla de = Easter I.
Pasewalk, Ger.D.R., 12,350 118 E2
Pasfield L., Sask., Can. 43 C2
Pasha, r., U.S.S.R. 136 D1
Pashiya, U.S.S.R. 137 i7
Pashkovskiy, U.S.S.R. 136 E4
Pasión, R. de la, Guat. 94 B2
Pasirian, Indon. 148 e8
Pasir Mas, Malay., 7,859 147 p13
Pasirpengarajan, Indon. 148 B2
Pasir Pinji, Malay., 13,950 147 o14
Pasir Puteh, Malay., 2,189 148 B1
Pasi Shāh, Afghan. 145 D1
Pasi Shaw, U.S.S.R. 137 f5
Paskenta, Calif. 82 B3
Pasłęk, Pol., 6,732 127 C1
Pasłęka, r., Pol. 127 C1
Pasni, Pak., 7,483 144 B4
Paso de la Cruz, Urug. 105 c11
Paso de Lajas, Nic. 94 E5
Paso del Cerro, Urug. 105 c10
Paso de los Libres, Arg., 14,500* 105 D3
Paso de los Toros, Urug., 8,000* 105 c11
Paso del Sapo, Arg. 105 B6
Paso Real, C.R. 94 F6
Paso Real de San Diego, Cuba, 1,436 96 b1
Paso Robles, Calif., 6,677 82 C5
Paspébiac, Qué., Can. 45 N5
Pasque I., Mass. 57 N7
Pasquia, r., Man.-Sask., Can. 43 E4
Pasquotank, co., N.C., 25,630 63 H1
Passaconaway, N.H. 54 E4
Passaconaway, Mt., N.H. 54 E4
Passadumkeag Mtn., Me. 55 D3
Passage I., Mich. 66 b3
Passage Is., Falk. Is. 108 3
Passage West, Ire., 2,638 113 B6
Passaic, co., N.J., 406,618 61 C1
Passaic, N.J., 53,963 61 C2
Passaic, r., N.J. 61 C2
Passamaquoddy Bay, Can.-U.S. 55 E3
Passa Quatro, Braz., 5,691 103 d18
Passa Tempo, Braz., 2,647 103 d17
Passau, F.R.Ger., 32,913 118 D4
Pass Christian, Miss., 3,881 73 F7
Pass Cr., S. Dak. 74 B4
Passero, Capo, It. 123 E6
Passing, Va. 62 G4
Passmore, Br. Col., Can. 42 H4
Passo Fundo, Braz., 47,299 103 F7
Passos, Braz., 28,555 103 G6
Passumpsic, Vt. 54 C3
Passumpsic, r., Vt. 54 D2
Passy, Fr., 10,670 117 G4
Pastaza, r., Ec.-Peru 104 B2
Pasto, Col. 100 B7
Pastol Bay, Alaska 85 D3
Pastora Pk., Ariz. 78 D3
Pastrana, Sp., 2,546 122 D2
Pastura, N. Mex. 79 C4
Pa-su, China 150 D4
Pasuquin, Phil., 4,624 153 B1
Pasuruan, Indon., 63,408 148 E4
Pásztó, Hung., 8,119 126 D3
Pata, Bol. 102 C4
Patacayma, Bol. 102 b10
Patagonia, Ariz., 540 78 C6
Patagonia, region, Arg. 99 B7
Patah, G., Indon. 148 B4
Patamban, Mex., 3,176 93 b10
Patan, Guj., India, 51,953 145 D5
Patan, M.P., India, 5,617 144 b14
Patan, Mah., India 145 h18
Pātan, Nepal 144 e12
Patanemo, Ven. 101 b11
Pa-t'ang, China 150 D4
Patapédia, r., Qué., Can. 47 S9
Patapsco, r., Md. 62 b7
Patapsco Res., Md. 62 b7
Patargān, Daqq-e, salt pan, Iran 143 F2
Pataskala, Ohio, 1,046 70 G2
Patate, r., Ec. 104 c10
Patay, Fr., 1,861 117 D2
Patch Grove, Wis., 208 66 C6
Patchogue, N.Y., 8,838 59 P10
Patea, N.Z., 1,989 175 g5
Patea, r., N.Z. 175 g5
Pategi, Nigeria 162 f7
Pateley Bridge, U.K., 2,375 113 F4
Paternion, Aust., 5,602 124 K7
Paternò, It., 42,140 123 E6
Pateros, Wash., 673 80 C1
Paterson, N.J., 143,663 61 C2
Paterswolde, Neth., 3,000 115 E1
Patetown, N.C. 63 G2
Pathé, Mex. 93 e9
Pathfinder Res., Wyo. 81 F4
Pathfork, Ky. 71 H5
Pathum Thani, Thai., 3,013 147 d5
Pati, Indon. 148 d7
Patía, Col. 100 B6
Patiala, India, 125,234 145 E3
Patience, Fr. Guiana 101 O6
Patillas, P.R., 1,888 96 t10
Patinti, Selat, Indon. 149 H3
Pati Pt., Guam 176 24
Pativilca, r., Peru 104 B4
Patjenan, Tg., Indon. 148 E4
Patjitan, Indon. 148 D5
Patkai Ra., Burma-India 146 A1
Pátmos, Gr. 129 F6
Pátmos, i., Gr. 129 F6
Patna, Bihar, India, 363,700 145 G4
Patna, Ori., India, 7,592 145 G5
Patnai, Terr. Papua 174 3
Patnanongan I., Phil. 153 B2
Patnoñgon, Phil., 2,957 153 B3
Patnos, Turk., 3,487 142 E2
Pato, Col. 100 C4
Pato Branco, Braz., 7,195 103 F7
Patoka, Ill., 601 68 C5
Patoka, Ind., 579 70 B4
Patoka, r., Ind. 70 B4
Patomskoye Nagor'ye, U.S.S.R. 133 L4
Paton, Iowa, 370 72 C2
Patos, Braz., 27,275 103 J3
Patos, Lag. de, Mex. 77 K4
Patos, Lag. dos, Braz. 103 F8
Patos de Minas, Braz., 31,471 103 G5
Pátrai, Gr., 95,364 129 C5
Patraïkós Kólpos, Gr. 129 C5
Patras = Pátrai
Patricia, Alta., Can. 42 K4
Patricia, Tex. 77 M3
Patrick, S.C., 393 63 D3
Patrick, co., Va., 15,282 62 D6
Patrick Brompton, U.K. 114 E2
Patrick Creek, Calif. 82 B2
Patrick's Cove, Newf., Can. 45 a10
Patrick Springs, Va. 62 D6
Patrington, U.K., 1,724 114 H3
Patriot, Ind. 70 E4
Patrocínio, Braz., 13,933 103 G5
Patronville, Ind. 70 B5
Patsaliga Creek, Ala. 64 C4
Pattada, It., 5,411 123 B4
Pattani, Thai., 16,804 146 C6
Pattani, r., Thai. 146 C6
Patten, Me., 1,099 55 D2
Pattensen, F.R.Ger., 1,132 119 b9
Patterson, Calif., 2,246 82 C4
Patterson, Ga., 719 64 G4
Patterson, Idaho, 24 81 C3
Patterson, Iowa, 157 72 D3
Patterson, La., 2,923 73 D8
Patterson, N.Y. 59 N9
Patterson, N.C., 265 63 C1
Patterson, Ohio, 184 70 F2
Patterson, Okla. 76 H3
Patterson, Va. 62 D6
Patterson Gardens, Mich., 1,747 67 K7
Patterson Heights, Pa., 816 60 a7
Patterson L., Sask., Can. 43 B2
Pattersons Creek, W. Va. 62 F3
Pattersonville, N.Y. 59 M6
Patteson Passage, New Hebr. 174 m5
Pattison, Miss. 73 E6
Pattison, C., N.Z. 175 14
Patton, Ind. 70 C2
Patton, Pa., 2,880 60 E4
Pattonsburg, Mo., 753 72 D4
Pattukkottai, India, 24,726 145 m20
Patu, Braz., 2,367 103 J3
Patuca, P., Hond. 94 E3
Patuca, r., Hond. 94 E3
Patulul, Guat., 2,611 94 b9
Pa-tung, China 152 C1
Patutahi, N.Z. 175 h5
Patuxent, Md. 62 c8
Patuxent, r., Md. 62 H4
Patzau, Wis. 66 A2
Pátzcuaro, Mex., 14,281 92 E4
Pátzcuaro, L. de, Mex. 93 c10
Patzicía, Guat., 6,332 94 c9
Patzún, Guat., 6,477 94 c9
Pau, Fr., 61,468 117 C5
Pauillac, Fr., 5,725 117 C4
Pauini, Braz. 102 C3
Pauini, r., Braz. 102 C3
Pauk, Burma, 2,863 146 A2
Paukaa, Hawaii 84 F4
Paukkaung, Burma, 3,205 146 A3
Pauktaw, Burma, 2,956 146 A2
Paul, Idaho, 731 81 C4
Paula, Arg. 105 a13
Paulatuk, N.W.T., Can. 40 E4
Paulaya, r., Hond. 94 E3
Paulden, Ariz. 78 B4
Paulding, co., Ga., 13,101 64 E2
Paulding, Mich. 66 D2
Paulding, co., Ohio, 16,792 70 E1
Paulding, Ohio, 2,936 70 E1
Paulding B., Ant. 180 U6
Paulina, Oreg. 80 D3
Paulina Pk., Oreg. 80 C4
Paulins Kill, r., N.J. 61 A2
Paulis, D.R.Congo, 17,430 164 D1
Paulista, Braz., 18,370 103 b14
Paulistana, Braz., 1,105 103 H3
Paull, U.K. 114 H3
Paullina, Iowa, 1,329 72 E2
Paullo, It., 4,162 122 c5
Paulo Afonso, Braz., 19,469 103 J3
Pauloff Harbor, Alaska, 77 85 D5
Paulsboro, N.J., 8,121 61 A4
Paul Smiths, N.Y. 59 M3
Paul Str., Vt. 54 D2
Pauls Valley, Okla., 6,856 76 F3
Paulton, U.K., 2,790 114 C8
Pauma Valley, Calif. 82 E6
Paung, Burma, 6,880 146 B3
Paungbyin, Burma, 1,307 146 A1
Paungdawthi, Burma, 3,825 147 b2
Paungde, Burma, 17,286 146 A3
Paungwe, Burma, 6,525 147 b2
Paupack, Pa. 61 M3
Pauri, India, 7,484 144 b10
Paurito, Bol., 1,493 102 D5
Pausa, Ger.D.R. 126 a6
Pausa, Peru, 1,800 104 C5
Pautabusna, Hond. 94 E3
Paute, Ec., 1,462 104 c11
Paute, r., Ec. 104 c11
Pauto, r., Col. 100 E5
Pavaiai, Tutuila 177 39
Pavarandocito, Col. 100 B4
Pavda, U.S.S.R. 137 i7
Pavia, It., 73,326 123 B2
Pavilion, Br. Col., Can. 42 G4
Pavilion, N.Y. 58 E6
Pavillion, Wyo., 190 81 E4
Pāvilosta, U.S.S.R., 1,100 136 A1
Pavlikeni, Bulg., 9,278 128 E3
Pavlodar, U.S.S.R., 107,000 134 G4
Pavlof, Alaska 85 D5
Pavlof Harbor = Pauloff Harbor
Pavlof Vol., Alaska 85 D5
Pavlograd, U.S.S.R., 45,800 136 D3
Pavlogradka, U.S.S.R. 137 o11
Pávlon, Gr., 1,749 129 D5
Pavlovka, U.S.S.R. 137 h8
Pavlovo, U.S.S.R., 53,000 136 F2
Pavlovsk, U.S.S.R., 10,700 134 H4
Pavlovsk, U.S.S.R., 12,000 136 F3
Pavlovskaya, U.S.S.R. 136 E4
Pavlovskiy, U.S.S.R. 137 h7
Pavlovskiy Posad, U.S.S.R., 58,000 136 c6
Pavlovskoye Vdkhr., U.S.S.R. 137 h8
Pavo, Ga., 817 64 F5
Pavullo nel Frignano, It., 14,697 123 C2
Pavuvu, i., Sol. Is. 175 b3
Pawan, r., Indon. 148 D3
Pawayan, India, 7,383 144 c11
Pawcatuck, Conn., 4,389 57 J7
Pawcatuck, r., Conn.-R.I. 57 J7
Pawhuska, Okla., 5,414 76 G1
Pawlet, Vt. 54 A5
Pawleys Island, S.C. 63 E4
Pawling, N.Y., 1,734 59 N8
Pawnee, Ill., 1,517 68 C4
Pawnee, co., Kans., 10,254 75 F5
Pawnee, co., Nebr., 5,356 75 J3
Pawnee, co., Okla., 10,884 76 G1
Pawnee, Okla., 2,303 76 G1
Pawnee, r., Kans. 75 F5
Pawnee City, Nebr., 1,343 75 J3
Pawnee Cr., Colo. 79 D1
Pawnee Rock, Kans., 380 75 G5
Pawonków, Pol. 127 h6
Paw Paw, Ill., 725 68 C2
Paw Paw, Mich., 2,970 67 H6
Paw Paw, W. Va., 789 62 F3
Paw Paw, r., Mich. 67 G6
Paw Paw Lake, Mich., 3,518 67 G6
Pawtuckaway Pd., N.H. 54 E5
Pawtucket, R.I., 81,001 57 L5
Pawtuxet (part of Warwick and Cranston), R.I. 57 L5
Pawut, Burma 146 B4
Pax, W. Va., 408 62 C5
Paxico, Kans., 276 75 J4
Paxoi, i., Gr. 129 C5
Paxson, Alaska 85 H3
Paxtlán, Mex., 1,577 93 F5
Paxton, Austl. 173 h9
Paxton, Fla., 215 65 C2
Paxton, Ill., 4,370 68 D3
Paxton, Ind. 70 B3
Paxton, Mass., 2,399(T) 56 J3
Paxton, Nebr., 566 75 D2
Paxville, S.C., 216 63 D4
Paya, Hond. 94 E3
Paya, r., Ven. 101 b12
Payabila, Hond. 94 E3
Payagyi, Burma, 3,616 147 b2
Pa-yen, China 151 E1
Pa-yen-k'a-la Shan, China 150 D3
Pa-yen-kao-lo, China 151 A2
Payen Matrus Co., Arg. 105 B5
Payerne, Switz., 6,024 124 A2
Payette, co., Idaho, 12,363 81 A3
Payette, Idaho, 4,451 81 A3
Payette, r., Idaho 81 A3
Pay-Khoy, Khr., U.S.S.R. 132 F3
Payne, Ga., 346 64 F3
Payne, Ohio, 1,287 70 E1
Payne, co., Okla., 44,231 76 F1
Payne, r., Qué., Can. 44 L1
Payne Bay, Qué., Can. 45 L1
Payne L., Qué., Can. 41 P6
Paynes, Miss. 73 E4
Paynesville, Mich. 66 D2
Paynesville, Minn., 1,754 74 E3
Paynton, Sask., Can. 43 B4
Paysandú, Urug., 52,000* 105 D4
Payson, Ariz. 78 C4
Payson, Ill., 502 68 A4
Payson, Utah, 4,237 78 C1
Pay-Yer, G., U.S.S.R. 134 F3
Paz, Arg., 4,300* 105 a11
Paz, R. de, Guat. 94 B4
Pazardzhik, Bulg., 39,499 128 E3
Pazin, Yug., 2,450 125 A2
Pčinja, r., Yug. 125 F3
Pe, Burma 146 B4
Pea, Tonga 177 36
Pea, r., Ala. 64 D4
Peabiru, Braz., 5,358 103 F6
Peabody, Kans., 1,309 75 J5
Peabody, Mass., 32,202 57 N2
Peace, r., Alta.-Br. Col., Can. 42 K1
Peace, r., Fla. 65 H5
Peace Dale, R.I. 57 L7
Peace River, Alta., Can., 2,446 42 J2
Peach, co., Ga., 13,846 64 F3
Peacham, Vt. 54 C3
Peach Cr., Tex. 77 i8
Peachland, Br. Col., Can. 42 G4
Peachland, N.C., 563 63 D2
Peach Orchard, Ark., 348 73 E1
Peach Springs, Ariz. 78 B4
Peachtree, N.C. 63 b7
Peachtree City, Ga., 416 64 f11
Peachtree Cr., Ga. 64 g9
Peacock, Mich. 67 H4
Peacock Hills, N.W.T., Can. 38 H4
Peacock Pt., Wake I. 176 26
Peaima Fall, Guyana 101 K4
Peak, The = Kinder Scout
Peak, The, Ascension 109 6
Peake, Austl. 172 e8
Peaked Mtn., Me. 55 C2
Peaked Mtn., Me. 55 D2
Peak Hill, Austl., 1,409 173 g9
Peakville, N.Y. 59 K8
Peale, i., Wake I. 176 26
Peale, Mt., Utah 78 D2
Peam Amleang, Camb. 147 k11
Peapack-Gladstone, N.J., 1,804 61 B2
Pearblossom, Calif. 82 E5
Pearce, Ariz. 78 D6
Pearcy, Ark. 73 B3
Pea Ridge Nat. Mil. Pk., Ark. 73 A1
Pearisburg, Va., 2,268 62 D5
Pearl, Ont., Can. 44 E5
Pearl, Ill., 348 68 B4
Pearl, r., La.-Miss. 73 E6
Pearland, Tex. 1,497 77 i9
Pearl and Hermes Reef, Hawaii 84 f9
Pearl Beach, Mich., 1,224 67 L6
Pearl City, Hawaii, 8,250* 84 C2
Pearl City, Ill., 488 68 C1
Pearl Hbr., Hawaii 84 C2
Pearlington, Miss. 73 F7
Pearl Pk., Nev. 83 C2
Pearl River, La., 964 73 F7
Pearl River, co., Miss., 22,411 73 F7
Pearl River, N.Y. 58 c12
Pear Ridge, Tex., 3,470 77 n9
Pearsall, Tex., 4,957 77 O5
Pearsall Pk., Oreg. 80 A4
Pearson, Ga., 1,615 64 G4
Pearson, Okla. 76 G2
Pearson, Wis. 66 D3
Pearsonia, Okla. 76 G1
Pearson Is., Austl. 172 a7
Peary Chan., N.W.T., Can. 41 J2
Pease, r., Tex. 77 O2
Peasedown St. John, U.K., 3,238 114 D8
Peaster, Tex. 75 d9
Pebane, Moz. 164 F4
Pebas, Peru 104 D2
Pebble Beach, Calif. 83 e14
Pebble I., Falk. Is. 108 3
Peć, Yug., 28,000* 125 E3
Pećane, Yug. 125 B2
Pecatonica, Ill., 1,659 68 C1
Pecatonica, r., Ill. 68 C1
Peccia, Switz. 124 C2
Pécel, Hung., 8,735 126 D3
Pechea, Rum. 128 F2
Pechenga, U.S.S.R., 3,500 134 C3
Pechora, U.S.S.R., 30,600 134 E3
Pechora, r., U.S.S.R. 134 E3
Pechorskaya G., U.S.S.R. 134 E3
Pechory, U.S.S.R., 10,000 136 B1
Pecica, Rum. 128 C1
Pećigrad, Yug. 125 B2
Peck, Idaho, 186 81 A2
Peck, Mich., 548 67 L5
Pecka, Yug. 125 D2
Peckelsheim, F.R.Ger., 1,739 118 B3
Peckerwood L., Ark. 73 D3
Peckham, Colo. 79 c7
Pečky, Czech. 127 e6
Peconic Bay, N.Y. 59 P10
Pecos, N. Mex. 584 79 C4
Pecos, co., Tex., 11,957 77 M4
Pecos, Tex., 12,728 77 M4
Pecos, r., N. Mex.-Tex. 52 F4
Pecq, Belg., 2,075 116 a6
Pecquencourt, Fr., 8,854 116 a7
Pecqueuse, Fr. 116 g12
Pécs, Hung., 114,713 126 D3
Peculiar, Mo., 458 72 C6
Pedasí, Pan. 94 G7
Peddocks I., Mass. 57 N3
Pedernal, N. Mex. 79 C4
Pedernales, Arg., 2,195 105 b12
Pedernales, Dom. Rep., 2,466 96 m6
Pedernales, Ec. 104 A1
Pedernales, Mex., 2,767 93 c10
Pedernales, Ven. 101 J3
Pedernales, r., Tex. 77 O4
Pedernales, Salar de, Chile 105 B3
Pedersborg, Den., 1,378 121 D5
Pedhoulas, Cyp., 1,289 142 d10
Pedieos, r., Cyp. 142 e9
Pedley, Calif. 83 k16
Pedra Azul, Braz., 8,238 103 H5
Pedra Lume, C. Verde I. 109 5
Pedras Negras, Braz. 102 D4
Pedraza, Col. 100 C2
Pedregal, r., Ven. 101 c12
Pedreira, Braz., 7,286 103 c18
Pedreiras, Braz., 10,189 103 H2
Pedrera, Col. 100 F8
Pedricktown, N.J. 61 A4
Pedro, S. Dak. 74 A3
Pedro Afonso, Braz., 3,175 103 G3
Pedro Avelino, Braz., 1,399 103 a13
Pedro Bay, Alaska, 53 85 F4
Pedro Betancourt, Cuba, 6,863 96 c1
Pedro Cays, Jam. 95 C3
Pedro II, Braz., 3,160 103 H2
Pedro Escobedo, Mex., 1,317 93 d9
Pedro Gomes, Braz., 1,427 103 E5
Pedro J. Montero, Ec. 104 c11
Pedro Juan Caballero, Para., 4,984 105 D2
Pedro Luro, Arg., 5,000* 105 C5
Pedro Miguel, C.Z. 94 g12
Pedro Miguel Locks, C.Z. 94 g12
Pedro Point = North West Point
Pedro Velho, Braz., 2,320 103 b14
Peebinga, Austl. 172 F5
Peebles, co., U.K., 14,117 112 E4
Peebles, U.K., 5,545 112 E4
Peebles, Ohio, 1,601 70 F4
Peebles, Wis. 66 E5
Pee Dee, r., N.C.-S.C. 63 E3
Peekskill, N.Y., 18,737 59 N9
Peel, N.B., Can. 47 S10
Peel, U.K., 2,612 113 D4
Peel, r., N.W.T., Can. 40 B4
Pe Ell, Wash., 593 80 B2
Peel Sd., N.W.T., Can. 40 K3
Peeltown, Tex. 76 g10
Peelwood, Austl. 173 g10
Peene, r., Ger.D.R. 118 D2
Peenemünde, Ger.D.R. 118 D1
Peer, Belg., 5,379 115 D3
Peera Peera Poolanna L., Austl. 172 E4
Peerless, Mont. 81 F1
Peerless Lake, Alta., Can. 42 J2
Peerless L., Alta., Can. 42 J2
Peers, Alta., Can. 42 J3
Peetz, Colo., 218 79 D1
Peever, S. Dak., 208 74 D3
Pefferlaw, Ont., Can. 46 E4
Pegasus, Port, N.Z. 175 e7
Pegasus Bay, N.Z. 175 g6
Pegau, Ger.D.R. 126 b5
Peggau, Aust., 1,713 124 M6
Peggs, Okla., 28 76 H1
Pegnitz, F.R.Ger., 7,589 118 C4
Pego, Sp., 8,291 122 E3
Pegognaga, It., 7,840 122 d6
Pégomas, Fr., 1,332 116 m13
Pegu, Burma, 47,378 146 B3
Pegu, r., Burma 146 B3
Pegueros, Mex., 1,038 93 b9
Pegu Yoma, Burma 147 ·
Pehowa, India, 6,159 144 a10
Pehuajó, Arg., 17,875 105 C5
Pei, r., China 150 F5
Pei-an, China 150 G1
Pei-cha, China 152 a6
Pei-chen, China 150 G2
Pei-chiang, Taiwan, 45,171 152 F3
Pei-chien Shan, China 152 a7
Pei-ching, China, 6,800,000* 150 F3
Pei-ching Shih, mun., China 150 F2
Pei-ch'uan, China 152 B1
Pei-fei, r., China 151 C4
Pei-hai, China 150 E5
P'ei-hsien, China 151 C4
Pei-liu, China 152 C3
Peine, F.R.Ger., 28,775 118 C2
Peine, Pt., a, Dominica 97 13
Peinzalok, Burma, 3,574 147 b1
Pei-p'an, r., China 152 B2
Pei-p'ei, China 152 B1
Pei-p'iao, China 151 D2
Peiping = Pei-ching
Peipus, L. = Chudskoye Oz.
Peissenberg, F.R.Ger., 8,716 118 C5
Peiting, F.R.Ger., 7,322 118 C5
Peitz, Ger.D.R. 118 E3
Pei Wan, China 151 D3
Peixe, Braz. 103 G4
Pek, r., Yug. 125 E2
Pekalongan, Indon., 102,380 148 D4
Pekan, Malay., 2,070 148 B2
Pekan Ayer Panas, Malay., 1,502 147 p15
Pekan Gurney, Malay., 3,829 147 o14
Pekan Nanas, Malay., 7,127 147 p16
Pekelmeer, l., Bon. 97 17
Pekhü Tsho, l., China 144 e11
Pekin, Ill., 28,146 68 C3
Pekin, N.Y. 58 k18
Pekin, N. Dak., 180 74 C2
Peking = Pei-ching
Peking Municipality = Pei-ching Shih, mun.
Pelagie, Isole, It. 123 D7
Pélagos, i., Gr. 129 E5
Pelahatchie, Miss., 1,066 73 F5
Pelaihari, Indon. 148 E3
Pelak Entr., Yap 176 20
Pelalawan, Indon. 148 B2
Pelarco, Chile, 1,003 104 f15
Pelasyía, Gr., 1,775 129 D5
Pelat, Mt., Fr. 117 G4
Pelau, i., Sol. Is. 175 c1
Pelayo, Ven. 101 J3
Pełczyce, Pol., 1,648 127 A2
Pelechuco, Bol., 3,772 102 C4
Peleduy, U.S.S.R., 5,000 135 L4
Pelée, Montagne, Mart. 97 12
Pelee Island, Ont., Can. 46 B7
Pelee I., Ont., Can. 46 B7
Pelee Pt., Ont., Can. 44 G8
Peleliu, i., Palau 176 21
Pelendria, Cyp., 1,674 142 e10
Peleng, P., Indon. 149 G3
Peleng, Selat, Indon. 149 G3
Pelham, Ala. 64 C2
Pelham, Ga., 4,609 64 E4
Pelham, N.H., 54 E6
Pelham, N.C. 63 E1
Pelham, S.C. 63 B3
Pelham Manor, N.Y., 6,114 58 d13
Pelhřimov, Czech., 7,737 126 B2
Pelican, Alaska, 135 85 K4
Pelican, La. 73 B6
Pelican Bay, Barbuda 97 8
Pelican Lake, Wis. 66 D3
Pelican L., Man., Can. 74 C1
Pelican L., Qué., Can. 44 K2
Pelican L., Minn. 74 F1
Pelican L., Wis. 66 D3
Pelican Lakes, Minn., 134 74 E2
Pelican Narrows, Sask., Can. 43 D3
Pelican Pt., La. 73 F7
Pelican Portage, Alta., Can. 42 K2
Pelican Rapids, Man., Can. 43 E4
Pelican Rapids, Minn., 1,693 74 D2
Peligre, Lac de, Haiti 96 m6
Pelileo, Ec., 2,201 104 c10
Pelion, S.C., 233 63 C4
Pelister, mt., Yug. 125 E4
Peljekaise Nat. Pk., Swed. 120 D2
Pelkie, Mich. 66 E2
Pelkosenniemi, Fin. 120 F2
Pella, Iowa, 5,198 72 D3
Pella, Wis. 66 E4
Pélla, ruins, Gr. 129 D4
Pell City, Ala., 4,165 64 C2
Pellegrino, Monte, It. 123 D5
Pellegrino Parmense, It., 3,457 122 c6
Pellestrina, It. 122 f5
Pellines, Chile 104 e15
Pell Lake, Wis. 66 c13
Pello, Fin. 120 F2
Pellston, Mich., 429 67 J3
Pelluhue, Chile 104 e15
Pellville, Ky. 71 E4
Pellworm, i., F.R.Ger. 118 B1
Pelly, Sask., Can. 43 E4
Pelly, r., Yukon, Can. 40 C5
Pelly Bay, N.W.T., Can. 40 M4
Pelly Bay, N.W.T., Can. 40 M4
Pelly Crossing, Yukon, Can. 40 B5
Pelly L., N.W.T., Can. 40 J4
Pelly Mts., Yukon, Can. 40 C5
Pelm, F.R.Ger. 119 B4
Pelona Mtn., N. Mex. 79 A5
Peloncillo Mts., Ariz.-N. Mex. 78 D5
Pelopónnisos, reg., Gr. 129 C6
Pelotas, Braz., 121,280 103 F8
Pelotas, r., Braz. 103 F7
Pel'ovo, Bulg., 6,671 128 E3
Pelplin, Pol., 5,232 127 C2
Pelton, Ont., Can. 67 g16
Pelton, U.K., 5,826 112 g10
Pélussin, Fr., 2,839 116 p16
Pelym, U.S.S.R. 137 k7
Pelym, r., U.S.S.R. 137 k6
Pelymskiy Tuman, Oz., U.S.S.R. 137 k6
Pelzer, Ind. 70 B4
Pelzer, S.C., 106 63 B3
Pemadumcook L., Me. 55 C3
Pemalang, Indon. 148 c7
Pemalang, Udjung, Indon. 148 c7
Pemaquid, Me. 55 C5
Pemaquid Point, Me. 55 C5
Pemaquid Pd., Me. 55 C4
Pematang, Indon. 148 B3
Pematangsiantar, Indon., 114,820 148 A2
Pemba, i., Tanz. 164 F2
Pemberian, Malay. 147 p14
Pemberton, Austl., 1,257 172 A5
Pemberton, Br. Col., Can. 42 F4
Pemberton, N.J., 1,250 61 B4
Pemberville, Ohio, 1,237 70 F1
Pembina, co., N. Dak., 12,946 74 D1
Pembina, N. Dak., 625 74 D1
Pembina, r., Can.-U.S. 74 C1
Pembina, r., Alta., Can. 42 J3
Pembina Mtn., Man., Can. 43 f10
Pembine, Wis. 66 F3
Pembrey, U.K., 6,103 113 D6
Pembridge, U.K. 114 C6
Pembroke, Ont., Can., 16,862 44 J6

276 · Pembroke—Phum Choeu

Pembroke, St. Vinc. 97 19
Pembroke, U.K., 12,751 113 D6
Pembroke, Ga., 1,450 64 H3
Pembroke, Ky., 517 71 D5
Pembroke, Mass., 4,919(T) 57 N4
Pembroke, N.C., 1,372 63 E3
Pembroke, Va., 1,038 62 D5
Pembroke, C., Falk. Is. 108 3
Pembrokeshire, co., U.K., 94,124 113 D6
Pemigewasset, r., N.H. 54 D4
Pemiscot, co., Mo., 38,095 72 H8
Pemuco, Chile, 1,667 104 e16
Penacook L., N.H. 54 D5
Penafiel, Port., 6,022 122 A2
Peñafiel, Sp., 5,795 122 C2
Peñaflor, Chile, 10,699 104 f13
Penage, L., Ont., Can. 46 C2
Peñalara, pk., Sp. 122 D2
Penalva, Braz., 5,339 103 G2
Penandjung, Teluk, Indon. 148 c7
Penang=George Town, Malay.
Penang, i., Malay. 148 A1
Peñaranda de Bracamonte, Sp., 5,943 122 C2
Pen Argyl, Pa., 3,693 61 M4
Peñarroya-Pueblonuevo, Sp., 24,152 122 C3
Penarth, U.K., 20,896 114 B8
Peñas, Bol., 4,764 102 a10
Peñas, C., Sp. 122 C1
Penas, G. de, Chile 105 A7
Penasco, N. Mex. 79 C3
Peñasco, r., N. Mex. 79 C5
Penasse, Minn. 74 E1
Penawawa, Wash. 80 E2
Pencahue, Chile 104 f15
Pence, Ind. 70 B2
Pencer, Minn. 74 E1
Penchard, Fr. 116 k11
Pen-ch'i, China, 449,000* 150 G2
Pencil Bluff, Ark. 73 B3
Penco, Chile, 15,483 104 e16
Pencoed, U.K., 3,948 114 A7
Pendálofon, Gr. 129 C4
Pendálofos, Gr., 1,615 129 F4
Pendang, Malay. 147 o13
Pendembu, Sa. Leone 162 C4
Pender, Nebr., 1,165 75 J1
Pender, co., N.C., 18,508 63 F3
Pender Bay, Austl. 172 B2
Penderyn, U.K., 2,015 114 A7
Pendleton, Ind., 2,472 70 D3
Pendleton, co., Ky., 9,968 71 G3
Pendleton, N.Y. 58 C5
Pendleton, Oreg., 14,434 80 D3
Pendleton, S.C., 2,358 63 B3
Pendleton, co., W. Va., 8,093 62 E4
Pendleton Bay, Br. Col., Can. 42 F2
Pend Oreille, co., Wash., 6,914 80 E1
Pend Oreille, r., Idaho-Wash. 80 E1
Pend Oreille L., Idaho 81 A1
Pendroy, Mont. 81 C1
Pendzhikent, U.S.S.R., 10,800 137 e4
Penedo, Braz., 17,084 103 a16
Penelope, Tex., 226 77 P4
Penetanguishene, Ont., Can., 5,240 44 H7
Peneus=Piniós
Penfield, Ill. 68 D3
Penfield, N.Y. 58 F5
Penfield, Pa. 60 E3
Penfield Center, N.Y. 58 o20
Penfield Junction, Ohio 70 c9
P'eng-chia Hsü, Taiwan 152 F2
P'eng-hsien, China 152 A1
P'eng-hu, Taiwan, 37,454 152 E3
P'eng-hu Lieh tao, is., Taiwan 152 E3
P'eng-lai, China 150 F3
Pengpu=Pang-fou
P'eng-shui, China 152 C1
P'eng-tse, China 152 E1
Penhill, U.K. 114 E2
Penhold, Alta., Can. 42 K3
Penhook, Va. 62 E6
Peniche, Port., 11,388 122 A3
Penicuik, U.K., 5,824 112 E4
Penida, Nusa, Indon. 148 E5
Penig, Ger.D.R. 118 D3
Penikese I., Mass. 57 N7
Peninsula, Ohio, 644 70 e9
Peñíscola, Sp., 2,530 122 F2
Penistone, U.K., 7,071 114 E3
Peñitas, Mex. 93 c9
Penitente, Sa. do, Braz. 103 G3
Penjamillo, Mex., 3,168 93 c9
Pénjamo, Mex., 11,522 92 E4
Penju, Kep., Indon. 149 G3
Penju, Kep., Indon. 149 H4
Penju, Teluk, Indon. 148 c7
Penkridge, U.K., 2,518 114 D5
Penkun, Ger.D.R. 118 E2
Penland, N.C. 63 B2
Penley, U.K. 114 C5
Penmarch, Fr., 7,667 116 A3
Penn, Mich. 67 H7
Penn, Nebr. 75 C2
Penn, N. Dak. 74 C1
Penn, Pa., 858 60 d8
Pennant, Sask., Can. 43 B5
Penn Cr., Pa. 60 H4
Penndel, Pa., 2,158 60 g11
Penne, It., 14,046 123 D3
Pennell, Mt., Utah 78 C3
Pennellville, N.Y. 59 H5
Penner, r., India 145 F7
Penneshaw, Austl. 172 b8
Penney Farms, Fla., 545 65 H3
Penngrove, Calif. 83 d11
Penn Hills, Pa., 51,512 60 c8
Pennine Alps, Switz. 124 B2
Pennines, mtn. ra., U.K. 113 E4
Pennington, Ala. 64 B3
Pennington, co., Minn., 12,468 74 D1
Pennington, Minn. 74 E2
Pennington, N.J., 2,063 61 B3
Pennington, co., S. Dak., 58,195 74 A4
Pennington, Tex. 77 Q4
Pennington Gap, Va., 1,799 62 A6
Pennsauken, N.J., 33,771(T) 61 A4
Pennsboro, W. Va., 1,660 62 C3
Pennsburg, Pa., 1,698 61 M5
Penns Grove, N.J., 6,176 61 A4
Pennside, Pa., 3,200* 61 h14
Penns Park, Pa. 60 g10
Pennsville, N.J., 7,200* 61 A4
Pennsylvania, st., U.S., 11,583,000* 60-61
Pennville, Ind., 730 70 D2
Penny, Br. Col., Can. 42 G3
Penn Yan, N.Y., 5,770 58 F6
Pennycutaway, r., Man., Can. 43 G3
Penny Highland, N.W.T., Can. 41 Q4
Pennypack Cr., Pa. 60 f11
Penny Str., N.W.T., Can. 41 K2
Peno, U.S.S.R., 6,100 136 D1
Penobscot, co., Me., 126,346 55 D3
Penobscot, Me. 55 D4
Penobscot, r., Me. 55 D4
Penobscot Bay, Me. 55 D4
Penobscot L., Me. 55 B3
Penobsquis, N.B., Can. 47 T11
Penola, Austl., 1,263 172 F5
Peñón Blanco, Mex., 3,277 92 D3
Penong, Austl. 172 D4
Penonomé, Pan., 4,266 94 G6
Penot, Mt., New Hebr. 174 k6
Penrhyn=Tongareva
Penrith, Austl., 17,924 173 h9
Penrith, U.K., 10,931 113 E4
Penrod, Ky. 71 E4
Penryn, U.K., 4,451 113 D6
Penryn, Calif. 82 b7
Pensacola, Fla., 56,762 65 B2
Pensacola, N.C. 63 B2
Pensacola, Okla., 55 76 H1
Pensacola Beach, Fla. 65 B2
Pensacola Mts., Ant. 180 N4
Pensaukee, Wis. 66 F4
Pense, Sask., Can. 43 D5
Penshaw, U.K. 112 g10
Penshurst, Austl., 1,026 173 F5
Pensiangan, Malay. 148 F1
Pensilvania, Col. 101 d14
Pentagon Mtn., Mont. 81 C2
Pentecost=Raga
Pentecoste, Braz., 5,620 103 H2
Penticton, Br. Col., Can., 13,481 42 H4
Pentire Pt., U.K. 113 D6
Pentland, Austl. 173 F3
Pentland Firth, U.K. 112 E2
Pentland Hills, U.K. 112 d8
Pentoga, Mich. 66 E2
Penton, Ala. 64 D2
Pentwater, Mich., 1,030 67 G5
Peñuelas, P.R., 2,261 96 s10
Peñuelas, Cerrote de, mtn., P.R. 96 s10
Peñuelas, Emb. de, Chile 104 f13
Penuguan, Indon. 148 C3
Penukonda, India, 13,978 145 E7
Penwegon, Burma, 5,460 147 b1
Penwell, Tex. 77 M4
Penza, U.S.S.R., 277,000 134 D4
Penzance, U.K., 19,281 113 D6
Penzberg, F.R.Ger., 10,128 118 C5
Penzhina, r., U.S.S.R. 135 Q3
Penzhino, U.S.S.R. 135 Q3
Penzhinskaya G., U.S.S.R. 135 Q3
Penzhinskiy Khr., U.S.S.R. 135 Q3
Penzlin, Ger.D.R. 118 D2
People's Republic of China=China
Peoria, Ariz., 2,593 78 B5
Peoria, co., Ill., 189,044 68 C3
Peoria, Ill., 103,162 68 C3
Peoria, Okla., 156 76 J1
Peoria Heights, Ill., 7,064 68 C3
Peotone, Ill., 1,788 68 E2
Pep, N. Mex. 79 D5
Pepacton Res., N.Y. 59 L7
Pepe, Cabo, Cuba 96 b2
Pepeekeo, Hawaii 84 F4
Pepel, Sa. Leone 162 B4
Pepillo Salcedo, Dom. Rep., 3,966 96 m6
Pepin, co., Wis., 7,332 66 A4
Pepin, Wis., 825 66 A4
Pepin, L., Minn.-Wis. 66 A4
Péplos, Gr., 1,575 129 F4
Pepperell, Mass., 4,336(T) 57 K2
Pepper Pike, Ohio, 3,217 70 f9
Pepperton, Ga., 523 64 F2
Pepperwood, Calif. 82 B2
Pequabuck (part of Plymouth), Conn. 56 E6
Pequabuck, r., Conn. 56 E6
Pequaket, N.H. 54 E4
Pequaming, Mich. 66 E2
Pequannock, N.J. 58 b13
Pequannock, r., N.J. 58 b12
Peque, Col. 100 B4
Pequea Cr., Pa. 61 K6
Pequeri, r., Braz. 103 F6
Pequest, r., N.J. 61 A2
Pequop Mts., Nev. 83 C2
Pequot Lakes, Minn., 461 74 E2
Perabumulih, Indon. 148 C3
Perai-Tepuy, Ven. 101 K5
Perak, r., Malay. 147 o15
Perakhóra, Gr., 1,823 129 D5
Peralillo, Chile, 2,064 104 f14
Peralta, N. Mex. 79 B4
Pérama, Gr. 129 E7
Perambalur, India, 11,168 145 m20
Perawang, Indon. 148 B2
Percé, Qué., Can. 45 N5
Perch, r., Mich. 66 E2
Perche Cr., Mo. 72 E6
Perch L., Mich. 66 E2
Perchtoldsdorf, Aust., 10,766 124 c10
Percival Lakes, Austl. 172 C3
Percy, Fr., 2,391 117 C2
Percy, Ill., 810 68 C5
Percy, Miss. 73 E4
Percy, N.H. 54 E2
Pérdhika, Gr., 1,521 129 C5
Perdido, Ala. 64 B4
Perdido, r., Ala.-Fla. 64 B5
Perdido, Mte., Fr.-Sp. 122 F1
Perdido Beach, Ala. 64 B5
Perdões, Braz., 4,756 103 d17
Perdue, Sask., Can. 43 C4
Perdue Hill, Ala. 64 B4
Perechin, U.S.S.R., 3,900 136 A3
Pereira, Col. 100 C5
Perelazovskiy, U.S.S.R. 136 F3
Pere Marquette, r., Mich. 67 G5
Pérenchies, Fr., 5,050 116 a6
Perené, r., Peru 104 C4
Perenjori, Austl. 172 B4
Pereslavl'-Zalesskiy, U.S.S.R., 23,100 136 E1
Pereyaslav-Khmel'nitskiy, U.S.S.R., 14,300 136 C3
Pérez, Arg., 4,216 105 a11
Perez, Phil., 1,765 153 c8
Perga, ruins, Turk. 142 B2
Pergamino, Arg., 30,898 105 C4
Pergamum=Bergama
Perham, Me. 55 D2
Perham, Minn., 2,019 74 E2
Perhentian Is., Malay. 147 p14
Perho, Fin. 120 F3
Perhonjoki, r., Fin. 120 F3
Peri, r., Turk. 142 E2
Periam, Rum. 128 C1
Peribán, Mex., 3,511 93 b10
Péribonca, r., Qué., Can. 45 L5
Perico, Col. 101 e14
Perico, Cuba, 6,041 96 c1
Perico, Tex. 76 M1
Pericos, Mex., 2,911 92 D3
Périers, Fr., 2,728 117 C2
Périgueux, Fr., 41,134 117 D4
Perilla, Co., Chile 104 f17
Peringat, Malay., 9,577 147 p13
Peripa, r., Ec. 104 c10
Perişoru, Rum. 128 D2
Perithórion, Gr., 1,431 129 D4
Perito Moreno, Arg., 3,500* 105 A7
Periyakulam, India, 36,335 145 k20
Perkasie, Pa., 4,650 61 M5
Perkins, Calif. 82 b7
Perkins, Ga. 64 H3
Perkins, Mich. 66 F3
Perkins, Mo., 153 72 H7
Perkins, co., Nebr., 4,189 75 D3
Perkins, Okla., 769 76 F2
Perkins, co., S. Dak., 5,977 74 A3
Perkins, Mt., Ariz. 78 A4
Perkinston, Miss. 73 F7
Perkinstown, Wis. 66 C3
Perkinsville, Ariz. 78 B4
Perkinsville, N.Y. 58 E6
Perkinsville, Vt., 167 54 B5
Perkiomen Cr., Pa. 61 L5
Perkiomen Heights, Pa. 60 e10
Perky, Fla. 65 f15
Perlas, Arch. de las, Pan. 94 H6
Perlas, Lag. de, Nic. 94 F4
Perlas, P. de, Nic. 94 F4
Perlé, Lux. 115 D5
Perleberg, Ger.D.R., 13,495 118 C2
Perley, Minn., 165 74 D2
Perm', U.S.S.R., 678,000 134 E4
Permas Kechil, Malay. 147 p16
Përmet, Alb., 3,700 125 E4
Pernambuco, st., Braz., 4,136,900 103 H3
Pernell, Okla. 76 F3
Perniö, Fin. 120 E3
Pernis, Neth. 115 a7
Pernitz, Aust., 2,574 124 M6
Péronne, Fr., 5,628 117 E2
Perote, Mex., 9,701 93 F4
Perow, Br. Col., Can. 42 E2
Perpignan, Fr., 86,156 117 E5
Perquilauquén, r., Chile 104 f16
Perquimans, co., N.C., 9,178 63 H1
Perranzabuloe, U.K., 3,623 113 D6
Perreux, Fr., 1,893 117 F3
Perrin, Tex. 77 O3
Perrine, Fla., 6,424 65 J7
Perrineville, N.J. 61 C3
Perrinton, Mich., 424 67 J5
Perris, Calif., 2,950 82 E6
Perro, Lag. del, N. Mex. 79 C4
Perronville, Mich. 66 F3
Perros, Bahia, Cuba 96 d1
Perros-Guirec, Fr., 6,061 116 B2
Perrot, Î., Qué., Can. 47 o18
Perry, co., Ala., 17,358 64 B3
Perry, co., Ark., 4,927 73 C2
Perry, Ark., 224 73 C2
Perry, Fla., 8,030 65 F2
Perry, Ga., 6,032 64 F3
Perry, co., Ill., 19,184 68 C5
Perry, Ill., 442 68 B4
Perry, co., Ind., 17,232 70 C4
Perry, Iowa, 6,442 72 D3
Perry, Kans., 495 75 K4
Perry, co., Ky., 34,961 71 H4
Perry, Me. 55 E4
Perry, Mich., 1,370 67 J6
Perry, co., Miss., 8,745 73 F6
Perry, co., Mo., 14,642 72 H7
Perry, Mo., 802 72 F5
Perry, N.Y., 4,629 58 D6
Perry, co., Ohio, 27,864 70 G3
Perry, Ohio, 885 70 H1
Perry, Okla., 5,210 76 F1
Perry, co., Pa., 26,582 60 H5
Perry, S.C., 194 63 C4
Perry, co., Tenn., 5,273 71 D6
Perry, Utah, 587 78 b8
Perry, W. Va. 62 F4
Perry, r., N.W.T., Can. 40 J4
Perry Center, N.Y. 58 D6
Perrydale, Oreg. 80 B3
Perryopolis, Pa., 1,799 60 C5
Perry Res., Kans. 75 K4
Perry River, N.W.T., Can. 40 J4
Perrysburg, Ohio, 5,519 70 F1
Perrys Corner (part of Rehoboth), Mass. 57 M5
Perry Str., N.H. 54 E1
Perry's Victory and Int. Peace Mem. Nat. Mon., Ohio 70 G1
Perrysville, Ind., 497 70 B2
Perrysville, Ohio, 769 70 G2
Perrysville, Pa. 60 b7
Perryton, Tex., 7,903 76 N1
Perryville, Alaska, 93 85 E4
Perryville, Ark., 719 73 C3
Perryville, Mo., 5,117 72 H7
Perryville, N.Y. 59 J6
Perryville, R.I. 57 K7
Perschling, r., Aust. 124 b10
Persepolis, ruins, Iran 143 E3
Perseverance Bay, V.I. 97 4
Pershagen, Swed. 120 e8
Pershing, co., Nev., 3,199 83 A2
Pershing, Okla. 76 G1
Pershore, U.K., 4,094 114 D6
Persia=Iran
Persia, Iowa, 322 72 B3
Persian G., Asia 143 E3
Persimmon Gap, Tex. 77 M5
Persimmons Cr., Okla. 76 D1
Person, co., N.C., 26,394 63 E1
Perstorp, Swed. 120 C4
Pertang, Malay., 1,511 147 p15
Pertek, Turk., 3,085 142 D2
Perth, Austl., 348,647 172 A4
Perth, N.B., Can. 45 M6
Perth, Ont., Can., 5,260 44 J7
Perth, co., U.K., 127,018 112 D3
Perth, U.K., 41,199 112 E3
Perth, Kans. 75 H6
Perth, N.Y. 59 M5
Perth, N. Dak., 73 74 C1
Perth Amboy, N.J., 38,007 61 C2
Perthes, Fr. 116 i12
Perthshire, Miss. 73 D4
Pertoltice, Czech. 127 e6
Pertuis, Fr., 6,777 117 F5
Pertusato, C., Fr. 116 r18
Peru, ctry., 12,012,000* 104
Peru, Ill., 10,460 68 C2
Peru, Ind., 14,453 70 C2
Peru, Kans., 340 75 J6
Peru, Me. 55 B4
Peru, Mass., 197(T) 56 D3
Peru, Nebr., 1,151 75 K3
Peru, N.Y. 59 N2
Peru, Vt. 54 B5
Peru Basin, Pac. Oc. 169 J3
Peruc, Czech. 126 d6
Peru-Chile Trench, Pac. Oc. 169 K4
Perugia, It., 109,531 123 D3
Perugorría, Arg., 5,850 105 D3
Perušić, Yug. 125 B2
Péruwelz, Belg., 7,779 115 B4
Pervomayka, U.S.S.R. 137 n12
Pervomaysk, R.S.F.S.R., U.S.S.R., 13,700 136 F2
Pervomaysk, Ukr.S.S.R., U.S.S.R., 44,300 134 B5
Pervomaysk, Ukr.S.S.R., U.S.S.R., 43,600 136 f7
Pervomayskiy, U.S.S.R. 137 h9
Pervomayskiy, U.S.S.R. 137 k8
Pervoural'sk, U.S.S.R., 101,000 134 E4
Perwez, Belg., 2,695 115 C4
Pesagi, G., Indon. 148 C4
Pesaro, It., 63,099 123 D3
Pescadero, Mex. 92 C3
Pescadero, Calif. 83 e13
Pescadero Cr., Calif. 83 e13
Pescadero Pt., Calif. 83 e13
Pescadores=P'eng-hu Lieh-tao
Pescara, It., 83,035 123 E3
Pescara, r., It. 123 E3
Peschanaya, r., U.S.S.R. 137 r12
Peschanyy, O., U.S.S.R. 135 L2
Peschiera del Garda, It., 5,863 122 d5
Pescia, It., 20,586 123 C3
Peseux, Switz., 4,933 124 A2
Peshastin, Wash. 80 C2
Peshāwar, Pak., 218,691 145 D2
Peshkopi, Alb., 4,100 125 E4
Peshkovskoye, U.S.S.R. 137 k9
Peshtera, Bulg., 13,777 128 E3
Peshtigo, Wis., 2,504 66 F3
Peshtigo, r., Wis. 66 E3
Peski, Kaz.S.S.R., U.S.S.R. 137 m11
Peski, R.S.F.S.R., U.S.S.R. 136 c6
Peskovka, U.S.S.R., 9,800 134 E4
Pesochnoye, U.S.S.R., 6,100 136 E1
Peso da Régua, Port., 5,563 122 B2
Pesotum, Ill., 468 68 D4
Pespire, Hond., 1,696 94 D4
Pesqueira, Braz., 19,778 103 a15
Pessac, Fr., 24,849 117 C4
Peşteana Jiu, Rum. 128 D2
Pestovo, U.S.S.R., 14,200 136 D1
Pešurići, Yug. 125 D3
Petah Tiqva, Isr., 54,000 142 a7
Petal, Miss., 4,007 73 F6
Petalcingo, Mex., 2,950 93 G5
Petalidhion, Gr., 1,634 129 C6
Petaling, Indon. 148 C3
Petaling, Malay.=Petaling Jaya
Petaling Jaya, Malay., 16,575 147 o15
Petaluma, Calif., 14,035 82 B3
Petaluma, r., Calif. 83 d11
Pétange, Lux., 11,623 115 D5
Petare, Ven., 75,441 100 G2
Petatlán, Mex., 4,875 92 E5
Petauke, Zambia 164 E4
Petawaga, L., Qué., Can. 47 J1
Petawawa, Ont., Can., 1,808 44 J6
Petawawa, r., Ont., Can. 46 F3
Petegem, Belg., 5,567 115 B4
Petén Itzá, Lag. de, Guat. 94 B2
Petenwell Flowage, Wis. 66 D4
Peterbell, Ont., Can. 44 G5
Peterborough, Austl., 3,473 172 E5
Peterborough, Ont., Can., 46,455 44 H7
Peterborough, U.K., 62,340 113 F5
Peterborough, N.H., 1,931 54 D6
Peterchurch, U.K. 114 B6
Peterculter, U.K. 112 E3
Peter I Island, Ant. 180 Y6
Peterhead, U.K., 12,497 112 F3
Peter I., V.I. 97 4
Peterman, Ala. 64 B4
Peteroa, Vol., Chile 104 g15
Peter Pond L., Sask., Can. 43 B3
Peters, Fla. 65 a10
Peters, Mich. 67 L6
Petersbach, Fr. 116 d9
Petersburg, Ont., Can. 46 a14
Petersburg, Alaska, 1,502 85 L4
Petersburg, Ill., 2,359 68 B4
Petersburg, Ind., 2,939 70 B4
Petersburg, Ky., 390 71 F2
Petersburg, Mich., 1,018 67 K7
Petersburg, Nebr., 400 75 G2
Petersburg, N.Y. 59 O6
Petersburg, N. Dak., 272 74 C2
Petersburg, Ohio 70 J2
Petersburg, Okla. 76 F4
Petersburg, Pa., 552 60 F4
Petersburg, Tenn., 423 71 E6
Petersburg, Tex., 1,400 77 N3
Petersburg, Va., 36,750 62 G5
Petersburg, W. Va., 2,079 62 E4
Petersburg Nat. Mil. Pk., Va. 62 G5
Petersfield, Man., Can. 43 h9
Petersfield, U.K., 7,380 113 F6
Petershagen, F.R.Ger., 3,673 118 B2
Petershagen, Ger.D.R. 119 f10
Petersham, Mass., 890(T) 56 H3
Peterson, Iowa, 565 72 B2
Peterson, Utah 78 c8
Peter's River, Newf., Can. 45 b11
Peterstown, W. Va., 616 62 D5
Petersville, Ky. 71 H3
Petilia Policastro, It., 12,831 123 F5
Pétionville, Haiti, 10,239 96 k6
Petit Bois I., Miss. 73 G7
Petit-Bourg, Guad., 1,684 97 14
Petit-Canal, Guad. 97 14
Petitcodiac, N.B., Can. 45 N6
Petit Cul-de-Sac Marin, bay, Guad. 97 14
Petit-de-Grat Bridge, N.S., Can. 47 V11
Petite Montréal, r., Qué., Can. 47 p18
Petite-Rivière-de-l'Artibonite, Haiti, 4,766 96 k6
Petite Rivière Noire, Piton de la, Maurit. 165 c12
Petite-Rosselle, Fr., 8,984 116 c8
Petite Terre, Îles de la, Guad. 97 14
Petit-Goâve, Haiti, 5,847 96 k6
Petit Jean Cr., Ark. 73 B2
Petit Mustique I., Gren. Is. 97 20
Petitot, r., Br. Col., Can. 42 G1
Petit Piton, mtn., St. Lucia 97 11
Petit-Popo=Anécho
Petit-Réderching, Fr., 1,174 116 d8
Petit Rocher, N.B., Can. 47 S10
Petit Savanne, pt., Dominica 97 13
Petitsikapau L., Newf., Can. 45 M3
Petlalcingo, Mex., 3,290 93 F4
Peto, Mex., 6,995 93 H4
Petorca, Chile, 1,395 105 A4
Petoskey, Mich., 6,138 67 H3
Petra=Baṭrā
Petra, O-va., U.S.S.R. 135 L2
Petralica, Yug. 125 F3
Petra Velikogo, Zal., U.S.S.R. 135 N5
Petre, Pt., Ont., Can. 46 G5
Petre Bay, N.Z. 175 14
Petreto-Bicchisano, Fr., 1,518 116 r18
Petrey, Ala., 165 64 C4
Petrich, Bulg., 16,401 129 D4
Petrified Forest Nat. Mon., Ariz. 78 D4
Petrikov, U.S.S.R., 7,200 136 C2
Petrila, Rum., 19,955 128 D2
Petrinja, Yug., 5,461 125 C2
Petrodvorets, U.S.S.R., 21,700 136 C1
Petrokrepost', U.S.S.R., 7,100 136 C1
Petrólea, Col. 100 D3
Petroleum, co., Mont., 894 81 E2
Petroleum, Tex. 77 O6
Petroleum, W. Va. 62 C3
Petrolia, Ont., Can., 3,655 46 B6
Petrolia, Calif. 82 A2
Petrolia, Kans. 75 K6
Petrolia, Pa., 527 60 C3
Petrolia, Tex., 631 77 O3
Petrolina, Braz., 14,652 103 H3
Petrona, P., P.R. 96 t11
Petropavlovsk, U.S.S.R., 140,000 134 F4
Petropavlovsk-Kamchatskiy, U.S.S.R., 96,000 135 P4
Petrópolis, Braz., 93,849 103 H6
Petros, Tenn. 71 G5
Petroşeni, Rum., 23,052 128 D2
Petroso, Monte, It. 123 E4
Petroúsa, Gr., 2,697 129 E4
Petrovac, Crna G., Yug. 125 D3
Petrovac, Srba., Yug. 125 E2
Petrovec, Yug. 125 E4
Petrovgrad=Zrenjanin
Petrovka, R.S.F.S.R., U.S.S.R. 151 F2
Petrovka, Ukr.S.S.R., U.S.S.R. 136 E3
Petrovsk, U.S.S.R., 25,000 136 G2
Petrovskaya, U.S.S.R. 136 E4
Petrovskoye, U.S.S.R. 136 F4
Petrovskoye, U.S.S.R. 137 h9
Petrovsk-Zabaykal'skiy, U.S.S.R., 29,800 135 K4
Petrozavodsk, U.S.S.R., 139,000 134 C3
Petřvald, Czech., 10,811 127 h7
Petsamo=Pechenga
Pettendorf, Aust. 124 c10
Pettibone, N. Dak., 205 74 C2
Pettigoe, Ire. 113 B4
Pettigrew, Ark. 73 B2
Pettinain, U.K. 112 c8
Pettis, co., Mo., 35,120 72 D6
Pettit, Miss. 73 D4
Pettus, Ark. 73 D3
Pettus, Tex. 77 P5
Petty Harbour, Newf., Can. 45 c10
Petukhovo, U.S.S.R., 13,000 137 m11
Petworth, U.K., 2,347 113 F6
Peu, Sta. Cruz. Is. 175 6
Peuerbach, Aust., 2,105 124 K5
Peukankuala, Indon. 148 A1
Peumo, Chile, 2,574 104 f14
Pevek, U.S.S.R., 5,800 135 R3
Pevely, Mo., 416 72 G6
Pevensey, U.K., 2,151 113 G6
Peveto, Tex. 77 n8
Pewamo, Mich., 415 67 J6
Pewaukee, Wis., 2,484 66 E5
Pewaukee, L., Wis. 66 c11
Pewee Valley, Ky., 881 71 F3
Pewsey, U.K., 2,542 114 E8
Peymeinade, Fr., 1,247 116 m13
Peyrehorade, Fr., 2,711 117 C5
Peyula, Mex. 93 f8
Pézenas, Fr., 7,656 117 E5
Pezinok, Czech., 10,898 126 C2
Pfaffenhofen, F.R.Ger., 7,892 118 C4
Pfaffenhoffen, Fr., 1,802 116 d9
Pfäffikon, Switz., 5,735 124 C1
Pfalzdorf, F.R.Ger., 3,655 119 A1
Pfalzel, F.R.Ger., 5,228 119 B5
Pfälzer Bergland, mts., F.R.Ger. 119 C5
Pfälzerwald, mts., F.R.Ger. 119 D6
Pfalzgrafenweiler, F.R.Ger., 2,196 119 F7
Pfarrkirchen, F.R.Ger., 5,942 118 D4
Pfeddersheim, F.R.Ger., 4,249 119 E5
Pfedelbach, F.R.Ger., 2,382 119 H6
Pfeiffer, Ohio 70 F2
Pfinz, r., F.R.Ger. 119 E6
Pflugerville, Tex. 76 c5
Pforzheim, F.R.Ger., 71,684 118 B4
Pfrimmbach, r., F.R.Ger. 119 E5
Pfronten, F.R.Ger., 6,120 118 C5
Pfullendorf, F.R.Ger., 3,438 118 B5
Pfullingen, F.R.Ger., 12,350 118 B4
Pfunds, Aust., 1,792 124 G7
Pfungstadt, F.R.Ger., 11,681 118 B4
Pfyn, Switz., 1,048 124 C1
Phachi, Thai. 147 d4
Phaëton, Port, Tahiti 177 44
Phai, Thai. 146 C3
Phai, Ko, Thai. 147 d5
Phai Sali, Thai. 147 d4
Phak Hai, Thai. 147 d4
Phalen, L., Minn. 74 c6
Phalodi, India, 15,722 145 D4
Phalsbourg, Fr., 3,763 117 G2
Phaltan, India, 19,003 145 E6
Phan, Thai. 146 B3
Phanat Nikhom, Thai., 9,307 146 C4
Phangan, Ko, Thai. 146 C5
Phang Nga, Thai., 4,782 146 B5
Phan Ly Cham, S. Viet., 2,575 147 n11
Phanom Sarakham, Thai. 147 d5
Phanom Thuan, Thai. 147 c4
Phan Rang, S. Viet., 20,525 146 E5
Phan Thiet, S. Viet., 55,181 146 E5
Phan Thong, Thai. 147 d5
Pharr, Tex., 14,106 77 O6
Phasi Charoen, Thai. 147 d5
Phat Diem, N. Viet. 147 h9
Phato, Thai. 146 B5
Phatthalung, Thai., 10,420 146 B6
Phayakkhaphum Phisai, Thai. 146 C4
Phayao, Thai., 17,959 146 B3
Phayuha Khiri, Thai. 147 d4
Pheba, Miss. 73 G4
Phelan, Calif. 83 i15
Phelps, Ky., 725 71 J4
Phelps, co., Mo., 25,396 72 F7
Phelps, co., Nebr., 9,800 75 F3
Phelps, N.Y., 1,887 58 F6
Phelps, Wis. 66 D2
Phelps City, Mo., 81 72 B4
Phelps L., Sask., Can. 43 D2
Phelps L., N.C. 63 H2
Phen, Thai. 146 C3
Phenix, Va., 259 62 F5
Phenix City, Ala., 27,630 64 D3
Phet Buri, r., Thai. 147 c5
Phetchabun, Thai., 5,887 146 C3
Phetchaburi, Thai., 24,654 146 B4
Phiafay, Laos 146 D4
Phibun Mangsahan, Thai., 7,401 146 D4
Phichit, Thai., 9,257 146 C3
Philadelphia, Jordan='Ammān
Philadelphia, Miss., 5,017 73 F5
Philadelphia, Mo. 72 F5
Philadelphia, N.Y., 868 59 J3
Philadelphia, co., Pa., 2,002,512 61 M6
Philadelphia, Pa., 2,002,512 61 M5
Philadelphia, Tenn. 71 G6
Philae, ruins, U.A.R. 161 K4
Phil Campbell, Ala., 898 64 B1
Philip, S. Dak., 1,114 74 B3
Philip Edward I., Ont., Can. 46 C3
Philippeville=Skikda
Philippeville, Belg., 1,570 115 C4
Philippi, W. Va., 2,228 62 E3
Philippi, L., Austl. 172 E3
Philippines, ctry., 33,477,000* 153
Philippine Sea, Asia 170 C3
Philippine Trench, Phil. Sea 168 E2
Philippolis, S. Af., 2,078 164 D7
Philipsburg, St. Maarten, 1,166 97 7
Philipsburg, Mont., 1,107 81 C2
Philipsburg, Pa., 3,872 60 F4
Philip Smith Mts., Alaska 85 G1
Phillaur, India, 11,058 144 a10
Phillip Bluff, Lord Howe I. 175 12
Phillips, co., Ark., 43,997 73 E3
Phillips, co., Colo., 4,440 79 D1
Phillips, co., Kans., 8,709 75 F4
Phillips, Me. 55 B4
Phillips, co., Mont., 6,027 81 E1
Phillips, Nebr., 192 75 G3
Phillips, Okla., 91 76 G3
Phillips, Tex., 3,605 76 N2
Phillips, Wis., 1,524 66 C3
Phillips Bay, N.W.T., Can. 41 L1
Phillips Bk., Mass. 56 J2
Phillips Bk., N.H. 54 E2
Phillipsburg, Ga., 2,037 64 F4
Phillipsburg, Kans., 3,233 75 F4
Phillipsburg, Mo., 142 72 E7
Phillipsburg, N.J., 18,502 61 A2
Phillipston, Mass., 695(T) 56 H2
Phillipstown, Ill., 69 68 D5
Philmont, N.Y., 1,750 59 N7
Philo, Calif. 82 B3
Philo, Ill., 740 68 D3
Philo, Ohio, 913 70 H3
Philomath, Oreg., 1,359 80 B3
Philomena, Alta., Can. 42 K2
Philpots I., N.W.T., Can. 41 O3
Philpott, Va. 62 E6
Philpott L., Va. 62 D6
Phimai, Thai. 147 e4
Phippsburg, Colo. 79 B1
Phippsburg, Me. 55 C5
Phitsanulok, Thai., 30,364 146 C3
Phlox, Wis. 66 D3
Phnom Kus, Camb. 147 k11
Phnom Penh, Camb., 403,500 146 D5
Pho Binh Gia, N. Viet. 147 i8
Phoenicia, N.Y. 59 M7
Phoenix, Ariz., 439,170 78 C5
Phoenix, Ill., 4,203 69 d10
Phoenix, La. 73 F8
Phoenix, Mich. 66 E1
Phoenix, N.Y., 2,408 59 H5
Phoenix, Oreg., 769 80 B4
Phoenix, atoll, Phoenix Is. 170 G5
Phoenix Is., Gilb. and Ellice Is. 170 G5
Phoenixville (part of Eastford), Conn. 56 H5
Phoenixville, Pa., 13,797 61 L5
Phon, Thai., 7,402 146 C4
Phong, r., Thai. 146 C3
Phong Loc, N. Viet. 146 D3
Phong Phu, S. Viet., 19,211 147 k11
Phong Saly, Laos 146 C2
Phong Tho, N. Viet. 146 C2
Phong Y, N. Viet. 147 h9
Phon Phisai, Thai. 146 C3
Phon Tiou, Laos 146 D3
Phopāgaon, Nepal 144 d11
Photharam, Thai., 8,215 147 c5
Phou Khao Khouai, Laos 146 C3
Phrae, Thai., 16,006 146 C3
Phra Nakhon Si Ayutthaya, Thai., 32,368 146 B4
Phrao, Thai. 146 B3
Phra Phuttabat, Thai. 147 d4
Phra Pradaeng, Thai., 7,195 147 d5
Phrasaeng, Thai. 146 B5
Phrom Buri, Thai. 147 d4
Phroso, Okla. 76 E1
Phsar Oudong, Camb. 147 k11
Phu Cat, S. Viet. 146 E4
Phu Cuong, S. Viet., 27,812 146 D5
Phuc Yen, N. Viet. 147 h8
Phu Giao, S. Viet., 3,750 147 m11
Phu Huu, N. Viet. 146 D3
Phuket, Thai., 28,033 146 B6
Phuket, Ko, Thai. 146 B5
Phu Khieo, Thai. 146 C3
Phu Khuong, S. Viet., 18,259 146 D5
Phulbani, India 145 G5
Phu Loc, S. Viet., 8,740 146 D3
Phu Ly, N. Viet. 146 D2
Phum Chhoeu Kach, Camb. 147 k11
Phum Choeu Khmau, Camb. 147 k11

Phum Damrey—Plain City · 277

Phum Damrey Phong, Camb. 147 m10
Phu Mieng, S. Viet. 147 m11
Phumiphol Dam, Thai. 146 B3
Phum Kanchriech, Camb. 146 D5
Phum Kandol Chrum, Camb. 147 k11
Phum Koky, Camb. 147 m11
Phum Mong, Camb. 147 m11
Phum Pra Moi, Camb. 146 C4
Phum Prek Dach, Camb. 147 k11
Phum Prey Phnau, Camb. 147 k11
Phum Ro Kar Popram, Camb. 147 k10
Rhum Rovieng, Camb. 146 D4
Phum Samrong Thom, Camb. 147 k11
Phum Siembauk, Camb. 146 D4
Phum Tani, Camb. 147 k11
Phu My, S. Viet., 1,276 146 E4
Phung, r., China 144 f11
Phung Hiep, S. Viet., 22,377 147 k12
Phunphin, Thai. 146 B5
Phuntsholing, Bhutan 144 g12
Phuoc Binh, S. Viet., 5,884 147 m11
Phuoc Hoa, S. Viet. 147 m10
Phuoc Le, S. Viet., 6,554 147 m11
Phuoc Long, S. Viet. 147 k12
Phuoc Tin, S. Viet. 147 m11
Phuoc Vinh, S. Viet., 3,000 147 m11
Phu Qui, N. Viet. 146 D3
Phu Quoc, Dao, i., S. Viet. 146 C5
Phu Rieng, S. Viet. 147 m11
Phu Tho, N. Viet., 10,888 147 h8
Phu Tho, N. Viet. 147 h9
Phu Truong, S. Viet. 147 n11
Phu Vinh, S. Viet., 33,790 146 D5
Phu Wiang, Thai. 146 C3
Phu Yen, N. Viet. 147 h9
Phyra, Aust., 2,434 124 M5
P'i, r., China 152 E1
Piaçabuçu, Braz., 4,864 103 a16
Piacenza, It., 84,475 123 B2
Piacoa, Ven. 101 J3
Piadena, It., 4,014 122 d5
Piakan, Phil., 2,380 153 B4
Pialba, Austl., 3,544 173 H3
Piana, Fr. 116 r17
Pianello Val Tidone, It., 3,411 122 c6
Pianosa, Isola, It. 123 C3
Pianosa, Isola, It. 123 E3
Piapot, Sask., Can. 43 B5
Pias, Port., 6,408 122 B4
Piaseczno, Pol., 14,738 127 D2
Piaski, Pol. 127 E3
Piatra, Rum. 128 E3
Piatra Neamţ, Rum., 32,648 128 F1
Piatt, co., Ill., 14,960 68 D4
Piau, Braz., 1,288 103 e17
Piauí, st., Braz., 1,263,368 103 H3
Piauí, r., Braz. 103 H3
Piauí, Sa. do, Braz. 103 H3
Piave, Miss. 73 G6
Piave, r., It. 123 D1
Piaxtla, r., Mex. 92 D3
Piazza Armerina, It., 28,191 123 E6
Piazzola sul Brenta, It., 10,291 122 e5
Piblange, Fr., 1,122 116 b8
Pibor Post, Sudan 163 K4
Pibroch, Alta., Can. 43 b6
Pic, r., Ont., Can. 44 F5
Pica, Chile, 1,646 105 B2
Pica, Nic. 94 F4
Picacho, Ariz. 78 C5
Picacho, N. Mex. 79 C5
Picanoc, r., Qué., Can. 47 H3
Picara Pt., V.I. 97 4
Picardville, Alta., Can. 43 b6
Picayune, Miss., 7,834 73 F7
Piceance Cr., Colo. 79 A2
Pichátaro, Mex., 2,750 93 c10
Picher, Okla., 2,553 76 J1
Pi-chiang, China 150 D4
Pichidegua, Chile, 12,103 104 f14
Pi-chieh, China 150 E4
Pichilemu, Chile, 2,227 105 A4
Pichilinque, Mex. 92 C3
Pichimávida, Chile 104 e16
Pichincha, mtn., Ec. 104 c10
Pichingal, Chile 104 f15
Pichucalco, Mex., 2,978 93 G5
Pickaway, co., Ohio, 35,855 70 F3
Pickaway, W. Va. 62 D5
Pick City, N. Dak., 101 74 B2
Pickens, co., Ala., 21,882 64 A2
Pickens, Ark. 73 D4
Pickens, co., Ga., 8,903 64 E1
Pickens, Miss., 727 73 E5
Pickens, Okla. 76 H3
Pickens, co., S.C., 46,030 63 B3
Pickens, S.C., 2,198 63 B3
Pickens, W. Va. 62 D4
Pickensville, Ala. 64 A2
Pickerel, Ont., Can. 46 D3
Pickerel, Wis. 66 E3
Pickerel, r., Ont., Can. 46 D3
Pickerel L., Ont., Can. 74 G1
Pickerel L., Wis. 66 E3
Pickerel River, Ont., Can. 46 D3
Pickering, Ont., Can., 1,728 46 E5
Pickering, U.K., 4,186 113 F4
Pickering, Mo., 234 72 C4
Pickerington, Ohio, 634 70 G3
Pickett, co., Tenn., 4,431 71 F5
Pickett, Wis. 66 E5
Pickford, Mich. 67 J2
Pickle Crow, Ont., Can. 44 E4
Pickleville, Utah, 94 78 C1
Pickrell, Nebr., 130 75 J3
Pickstown, S. Dak. 74 C4
Pickwick L., Ala.-Miss.-Tenn. 71 C7
Pickwick Landing Dam, Tenn. 71 C6
Picnic, Fla. 65 d12
Pico, i., Azores 108 2
Pico, mtn., C. Verde Is. 109 5
Picones, Mex. 93 c8
Pico Pk., Vt. 54 B4
Pico Rivera, Calif., 49,150 83 h16
Picos, Braz., 8,176 103 H3
Pico Truncado, Arg. 105 B7
Picquigny, Fr., 1,195 117 E2
Picton, Austl., 1,234 173 h10
Picton, Ont., Can., 4,654 44 J7
Picton, N.Z., 2,315 175 g6
Pictou, N.S., Can., 4,472 45 O6
Pictou I., N.S., Can. 47 U11
Picture Butte, Alta., Can. 42 K4
Picture Rock Pass, Oreg. 80 C4
Picture Rocks, Pa., 594 60 J3
Picúa, P., P.R. 96 u10
Picuí, Braz., 3,105 103 a14
Picún-Leufú, Arg. 105 B5
Pidurutalagala, mtn., Cey. 145 F9
Piechowice, Pol., 3,491 127 e6
Piedecuesta, Col. 100 D4
Piedimonte d'Alife, It., 10,348 123 E4
Piedmont, Ala., 4,794 64 D2
Piedmont, Calif., 11,117 83 e12
Piedmont, Kans. 75 J6
Piedmont, Mo., 1,555 72 G7
Piedmont, Okla., 146 76 F2
Piedmont, S.C., 2,108 63 B3
Piedmont, S. Dak. 74 A3
Piedmont, W. Va., 2,307 62 E3
Piedmont L., Ohio 70 H2
Piedmont Plat., U.S. 51 K3
Piedra, r., Colo. 79 B3
Piedrabuena, Sp., 6,210 122 C3
Piedra del Águila, Arg. 105 B5
Piedrahita, Sp., 2,854 122 C2
Piedras, R. de las, Peru 104 D4
Piedras Blancas Pt., Calif. 82 C5
Piedras Coloradas, Urug. 105 c11
Piedras Negras, Mex., 42,649 93 E2
Piedra Sola, Urug. 105 c11
Piedrecitas, Cuba, 1,619 96 d2
Pie I., Ont., Can. 66 b8
Piekary Śląskie, Pol., 32,000* 127 i6
Pieksämäki, Fin. 120 F3
Pielavesi, Fin. 120 F3
Pielavesi, l., Fin. 120 F3
Pielinen, l., Fin. 120 G3
Pielisjärvi, Fin. 120 G3
Piemonte, reg., It. 122 a6
Piendamó, Col. 100 B6
P'ien-kuan, China 151 A3
Pien-pa, China 150 C4
Pieńsk, Pol., 4,286 127 A3
Pierce, Colo., 424 79 C1
Pierce, Fla. 65 d12
Pierce, co., Ga., 9,678 64 G4
Pierce, Idaho, 522 81 B2
Pierce, co., Nebr., 8,722 75 H1
Pierce, Nebr., 1,216 75 H1
Pierce, co., N. Dak., 7,394 74 B1
Pierce, co., Wash., 321,590 80 B2
Pierce, co., Wis., 22,503 66 A4
Pierce Bridge, N.H. 54 D3
Pierce City, Mo., 1,006 72 D8
Pierce Ferry, Ariz. 78 B3
Piercefield, N.Y. 59 L3
Pierceland, Sask., Can. 43 B3
Pierce Pds., Me. 55 B3
Pierceton, Ind., 1,186 70 D1
Pierceville, Kans. 75 E6
Piercy, Calif. 82 B3
Piermont, N.H. 54 C4
Piermont, N.Y., 1,906 58 d12
Pierowall, U.K. 112 E2
Pierpont, Ohio 70 J1
Pierpont, S. Dak., 258 74 D3
Pierre, S. Dak., 10,088 74 B3
Pierre, Bayou, Miss. 73 E6
Pierrefitte-sur-Seine, Fr., 14,826 116 h11
Pierrefort, Fr., 1,153 117 E4
Pierrelaye, Fr., 3,890 116 g10
Pierrepont Manor, N.Y. 59 J4
Pierreville, Qué., Can., 1,547 47 M2
Pierron, Ill., 451 68 C5
Piershil, Neth. 115 a7
Pierson, Man., Can. 43 E5
Pierson, Fla., 716 65 H3
Pierson, Iowa, 425 72 B2
Pierson, Mich., 219 67 H5
Pierson, C., Terr. Papua 174 3
Pierz, Minn., 816 74 E3
Pieštany, Czech., 19,552 126 C2
Piesting, r., Aust. 124 c10
Pieszyce, Pol., 8,070 127 f6
Pietarsaari = Jakobstad
Pietermaritzburg, S. Af., 95,124 164 E6
Pietersburg, S. Af., 27,835 164 D5
Pie Town, N. Mex. 79 A4
Pietrasanta, It., 23,811 123 C3
Piet Retief, S. Af., 8,604 164 D6
Pietrosul, mtn., Rum. 128 E1
Pietrowice, Pol. 127 g6
Pieve del Cairo, It., 2,945 122 b5
Pifo, Ec. 104 c10
Pigádhia, Gr., 1,281 129 F7
Pigeon, La. 73 D7
Pigeon, Mich., 1,191 67 K5
Pigeon, r., Man., Can. 43 F4
Pigeon, r., Can.-U.S. 53 H1
Pigeon, r., Ind.-Mich. 67 H7
Pigeon, r., Mich. 67 K5
Pigeon, r., N.C.-Tenn. 63 A2
Pigeon Bay, Ont., Can. 46 B7
Pigeon Cove, Mass., 1,064 57 O2
Pigeon Cr., Ala. 64 C4
Pigeon Cr., Ind. 70 B4
Pigeon Falls, Wis., 207 66 B4
Pigeon Forge, Tenn. 71 H6
Pigeon I., St. Lucia 97 11
Pigeon Key, Fla. 65 g15
Pigeon L., Alta., Can. 43 a7
Pigeon L., Ont., Can. 46 F4
Pigeon Pk., Trin. and Tob. 96 h4
Pigeon Pt., Calif. 83 e13
Pigeon River, Ont., Can. 44 E5
Pigg, r., Va. 62 E6
Piggott, Ark., 2,776 73 E1
Pignataro Maggiore, It., 6,080 123 c9
Pignon, Haiti, 1,681 96 k6
Pigs, Bay of = Cochinos, Bahía de
Pigs Eye L., Minn. 74 c6
Pigüé, Arg., 12,000* 105 C5
Pihaa, Tahiti 177 44
Pihani, India, 10,716 144 c12
P'i-hsien, China 152 A1
Pihtipudas, Fin. 120 F3
Pihuamo, Mex., 4,170 92 E4
Piihonua, Hawaii 84 F4
Piirai, i., Eniwetok 176 28
Pijao, Col. 101 d15
Pijijiapan, Mex., 4,105 93 G5
Pijnacker, Neth., 5,400 115 a6
Pikalëvo, U.S.S.R., 14,800 136 D1
Pikangikum L., Ont., Can. 44 C4
Pike, co., Ala., 25,987 64 D4
Pike, co., Ark., 7,864 73 B3
Pike, co., Ga., 7,138 64 E2
Pike, co., Ill., 20,552 68 B4
Pike, Ill. 68 B4
Pike, co., Ind., 12,797 70 B4
Pike, co., Ky., 68,264 71 J4
Pike, co., Miss., 35,063 73 E6
Pike, co., Mo., 16,706 72 F5
Pike, N.H. 54 C3
Pike, N.Y., 345 58 D6
Pike, co., Ohio, 19,380 70 F3
Pike, co., Pa., 9,158 61 M3
Pike, r., Wis. 66 d13
Pike, r., Wis. 66 E3
Pike City, Ark. 73 B3
Pike Creek, Ont., Can. 67 g15
Pike L., Wis. 66 C3
Pikelot, i., Car. Is. 176 18
Pike Road, Ala. 64 C3
Pikes Creek, Pa. 61 n16
Pikes Pk., Colo. 79 b10
Pikesville, Md., 18,737 62 H3
Piketberg, S. Af., 3,312 164 C7
Piketon, Ohio, 1,244 70 G3
Pikeview, Colo. 79 c10
Pikeville, Ky., 4,754 71 J4
Pikeville, N.C., 525 63 G2
Pikeville, Tenn., 951 71 F6
Pikhtovka, U.S.S.R. 137 q11
Pi-k'ou, China 152 B1
Pikwitonei, Man., Can. 43 F3
Pila, Arg., 1,500* 105 b12
Pila, Czech. 126 b6
Pila, It. 122 f6
Piła, Pol., 34,000* 127 B2
Pilalo, Ec. 104 c10
Pilanawa, Guyana 101 L6
Pilão Arcado, Braz., 1,457 103 H4
Pilar, Braz., 7,201 103 b15
Pilar, Para., 7,136 105 D3
Pilat, Mt., Fr. 116 p16
Piława, r., Pol. 127 B2
Piława Górna, Pol., 6,318 127 f6
Pilaya, r., Bol. 102 c12
Pilbarra Pt., New Hebr. 174 m7
Pilcaya, Mex., 1,867 93 e11
Pilchowice, Pol. 127 e6
Pilcomayo, Pq. Nac., Arg. 105 D2
Pile Bay, Alaska 85 F4
Pileni, i., Swallow Is. 175 6
Pilger, Nebr., 491 75 J1
Pilgerzell, F.R.Ger., 1,263 119 H3
Pil'gyn, U.S.S.R. 135 R3
Pilibhit, India, 57,527 144 b11
Pilica, r., Pol. 127 C3
Pililla, Phil., 4,217 153 c8
Pilis, Hung., 8,445 126 D3
Pilisvörösvár, Hung., 9,636 126 D3
Pillager, Minn., 338 74 E2
Pillar, mtn., U.K. 114 B1
Pillaro, Ec., 2,224 104 B2
Pillar Pt., Calif. 83 d13
Pillichsdorf, Aust., 1,105 124 d10
Pilling, U.K., 1,505 114 C3
Pillories, The, is., Gren. Is. 97 20
Pillow, Pa. 60 J4
Pillsbury Sd., V.I. 97 4
Pilmaiquen, r., Chile 105 e15
Pilón, Mex. 93 e8
Pilos, Gr., 2,434 129 C6
Pilot, Va. 62 D5
Pilot, The, mtn., Austl. 173 g11
Pilote, r., Mart. 97 12
Pilot Grove, Mo., 680 72 E6
Pilot Hill, Calif. 82 b7
Pilot Knob, Mo., 524 72 G7
Pilot Knob, Colo. 79 B1
Pilot Mound, Man., Can. 43 F5
Pilot Mound, Iowa, 196 72 D2
Pilot Mountain, N.C., 1,310 63 D1
Pilot Point, Alaska, 61 85 E4
Pilot Point, Tex., 1,254 77 P3
Pilot Rock, Oreg., 1,695 80 D3
Pilot Station, Alaska, 219 85 D3
Pilsen = Plzeň
Pilštanj, Yug. 125 B1
Pilszcz, Pol. 127 g6
Piltene, U.S.S.R., 2,000 136 A1
Piltown, Ire. 113 C5
Pilu, r., Burma 146 B2
Pilzno, Pol., 2,964 127 D4
Pima, Jap. 154 f15
Pima, co., Ariz., 265,660 78 B5
Pima, Ariz., 1,072 78 D5
Pimba, Austl. 172 E4
Pimentel, Dom. Rep., 5,258 96 m6
Pimentel, Peru, 5,966 104 A3
Pimento, Ind. 70 B3
Pimichín, Ven. 100 G6
Pina, Cuba, 3,667 96 d1
Pina, Sp., 2,255 122 E2
Piña, r., C.Z.-Pan. 94 f11
Pinacate, Co., Mex. 92 B1
Pinaki, atoll, Tuam. Arch. 177 42
Pinal, co., Ariz., 62,673 78 C5
Pinamalayan, Phil., 6,236 153 B2
Pinamar, Arg. 105 c13
Pinarbaşi, Turk., 5,804 142 D2
Pinar del Río, Cuba, 38,885 96 b1
Piñas, Ec., 3,333 104 B2
Pinayag, Phil. 153 b6
Pinch, W. Va. 62 C4
Pincher Creek, Alta., Can., 2,908 42 J4
Pin-ch'uan, China 150 D4
Pinckard, Ala., 578 64 D4
Pinckney, Mich., 732 67 K6
Pinckneyville, Ill., 3,085 68 C5
Pinckneyville, Miss. 73 D6
Pinconning, Mich., 1,329 67 K5
Pîncota, Rum. 128 C1
Pincourt, Qué., Can., 2,629 47 o17
Pińczów, Pol., 4,798 127 D3
Pindall, Ark. 73 C1
Pindamonhangaba, Braz., 19,144 103 d18
Pindaré, r., Braz. 103 G2
Pindaré-Mirim, Braz., 4,542 103 G2
Píndhos Óros, Gr. 129 C5
Pindi Gheb, Pak., 12,416 145 D2
Pindo, r., Ec. 104 B2
Pindstrup, Den. 121 C4
Pindus = Píndhos Óros
Pindus Mts. = Píndhos Óros
Pine, Ariz. 78 C4
Pine, Colo. 79 b9
Pine, co., Minn., 17,004 74 F2
Pine, Mo. 72 F8
Pine, r., Br. Col., Can. 42 G2
Pine, r., Mich. 67 H4
Pine, r., Mich. 67 J2
Pine, r., Mich. 67 J5
Pine, r., Mich. 67 K4
Pine, r., Wis. 66 E3
Pine, C., Newf., Can. 45 R6
Pine Aire, N.Y. 58 f13
Pine Apple, Ala., 355 64 C4
Pine Beach, N.J., 985 61 C4
Pine Bluff, Ark., 44,037 73 D3
Pinebluff, N.C., 509 63 E2
Pine Bluffs, Wyo., 1,121 81 G5
Pine Bush, N.Y., 1,016 59 M8
Pine City, Minn., 1,972 74 F3
Pinecliffe, Colo. 79 a8
Pine Creek, Mich. 67 H6
Pine Cr., Nev. 83 B2
Pine Cr., Pa. 60 H3
Pinecrest, Calif. 82 D3
Pinecrest, Fla. 65 d12
Pinedale, Ariz. 78 C4
Pinedale, Calif. 82 D4
Pinedale, Wyo., 965 81 E4
Pine Dock, Man., Can. 43 F4
Pine Falls, Man., Can., 1,082 43 G5
Pine Flat Res., Calif. 82 D4
Pine Forest Ra., Nev. 83 A2
Pinega, r., U.S.S.R. 134 D3
Pine Grove, Ont., Can. 46 c13
Pine Grove, Ark. 73 C4
Pine Grove, La. 73 E7
Pine Grove, Pa., 2,267 61 K4
Pine Grove, W. Va., 760 62 D3
Pine Grove Mills, Pa. 60 G4
Pine Hall, N.C. 63 D1
Pine Hill, Ala., 367 64 B4
Pine Hill, N.J., 3,939 61 B4
Pinehouse Lake, Sask., Can. 43 C3
Pinehouse L., Sask., Can. 43 C3
Pinehurst, Ga., 457 64 F3
Pinehurst, Idaho, 1,432 81 A2
Pinehurst, Md. 62 d8
Pinehurst, Mass., 1,991 57 L2
Pinehurst, N.C., 1,124 63 E2
Pinehurst, Montgomery Co., Tex. 77 Q4
Pinehurst, Orange Co., Tex., 1,703 77 n8
Pinehurst, Wash., 3,989 81 b7
Pine Island, Fla. 65 G4
Pine Island, Minn., 1,308 74 F3
Pine I., Fla. 65 G6
Pine Island Bayou, Tex. 77 k8
Pine Is., Fla. 65 f15
Pine Knot, Ky. 71 G5
Pine Lake, Ga. 738 64 h9
Pine Lake (part of Sudbury), Mass. 57 L3
Pine L., Ind. 69 g10
Pine L., Wis. 66 E3
Pine Lake Park, N.J. 58 b17
Pineland, Tex., 1,236 77 R4
Pine Lawn, Mo., 5,943 72 b11
Pine Level, Ala. 64 C3
Pine Level, Fla. 65 d13
Pine Level, N.C., 833 63 F2
Pinellas, co., Fla., 374,665 65 G4
Pinellas Park, Fla., 10,848 65 c12
Pine Lodge, N. Mex. 79 C5
Pine Meadow (part of New Hartford), Conn. 56 E5
Pine Mount, Fla. 65 F2
Pine Mountain, Ga. 64 F1
Pineora, Ga., 210 64 H3
Pine Orchard (part of Branford), Conn. 56 E7
Pine Orchard, Md. 62 b7
Pine Park, Ga., 82 64 E5
Pine Plains, N.Y. 59 N8
Pine Point, N.W.T., Can. 40 G5
Pine Prairie, La., 387 73 C7
Piner, Ky. 71 G3
Piñera, Urug. 105 c11
Pine Rest (part of Sudbury), Mass. 57 L3
Pine Ridge, Ky. 71 H4
Pine Ridge, S. Dak., 1,256 74 A4
Pine River, Man., Can. 43 E4
Pine River, Sask., Can. 43 C3
Pine River, Mich. 67 K5
Pine River, Minn., 775 74 E2
Pine River, Wis. 66 D4
Pine River Pd., N.H. 54 E4
Pinerolo, It., 27,732 123 A2
Piñeros, I., P.R. 96 u10
Pines, Isle of = Pinos, Isla de
Pine Springs, Minn., 142 74 d5
Pine Springs, Tex. 77 L4
Pinetop, Ariz. 78 D4
Pinetops, N.C., 1,372 63 G2
Pinetown, S. Af., 12,776 164 E7
Pinetown, N.C., 215 63 H2
Pine Tree, Wyo. 81 G4
Pinetta, Fla. 65 F2
Pine Valley, Br. Col., Can. 42 G2
Pine Valley, Calif. 82 E6
Pine Valley, N.Y. 58 G7
Pineview, Ga. 64 F3
Pineview, N.C. 63 E2
Pine Village, Ind., 309 70 B2
Pineville, Ky., 3,181 71 H5
Pineville, La., 8,636 73 C6
Pineville, Mo., 454 72 C8
Pineville, N.C., 1,514 63 D2
Pineville, Pa. 60 g10
Pineville, S.C. 63 D4
Pineville, W. Va., 1,137 62 C5
Pinewood, Ont., Can. 44 C5
Pinewood, Minn. 74 E2
Pinewood, S.C., 570 63 D4
Piney, Fr., 1,032 117 F2
Piney, r., Mo. 72 E7
Piney Green, N.C. 63 G3
Piney Point, Md. 62 H4
Piney Point, Tex., 1,790 77 i9
Piney Woods, Miss. 73 F5
Ping, r., Thai. 146 B3
P'ing-an-chen, China 151 D1
P'ing-ch'ang, China 152 B1
P'ing-chiang, China 150 F4
P'ing-ch'üan, China 151 C2
Pingelap, i., Car. Is. 176 E4
Pingelly, Austl. 172 B5
Pinggau, Aust., 2,678 124 N6
P'ing-ho, China 152 E2
P'ing-hsiang, Ch-hsi, China 152 D2
P'ing-hsiang, K-hsi, China, 7,000* 152 B3
P'ing-hsing Kuan, China 151 B3
P'ing-hu, China 152 F1
P'ing-hui, China 151 C4
P'ing-ku, China 151 C2
P'ing-kuo, China 152 B3
P'ing-lan, China 152 a6
Pinglap, i., Jaluit 176 30
Pingle, Alta., Can. 42 K2
P'ing-li, China 151 A4
P'ing-liang, China, 61,000* 150 E3
P'ing-lo, K-hsi, China 150 E4
P'ing-lo, N-h., China 150 E3
P'ing-lu, China 151 B3
P'ing-nan, F-ch., China 152 E2
P'ing-nan, K-hsi, China 152 C3
P'ing-pa, China 152 B2
P'ing-pien, China 152 A3
Pingree, N. Dak., 151 74 C2
Pingrup, Austl. 172 B5
Pingryville (part of Littleton and Ayer), Mass. 57 K2
P'ing-shan, Ho-p., China 151 B3
P'ing-shan, S-ch., China 152 A1
Ping Shan, H.K. 152 a6
P'ing-shan-hsü, China 152 b6
P'ing-shun, China 151 B3
P'ing-t'an, China 152 E2
P'ing-t'ang, China 152 B2
P'ing-ting, China 151 B3
P'ing-ting-shan, China, 150,000* 150 E3
P'ing-tu, China 151 D3
P'ing-tung, Taiwan, 108,141 152 F3
P'ing-wu, China 152 B1
P'ing-yang, China 152 F2
P'ing-yao, China 150 F3
P'ing-yin, China 151 C3
P'ing-yüan, K-t., China 152 E2
P'ing-yüan, Shant., China 151 C3
Pin-hai, China 150 G3
Pinhal, Braz., 14,260 103 c18
Pinhal Novo, Port., 7,708 122 k10
Pinheiro, Braz., 6,537 103 G2
Pinhel, Port., 3,273 122 B2
Pinhook, Ind. 69 g10
Pin-hsien, H-l-ch., China 151 E1
Pin-hsien, Shen-hsi, China 151 A4
Pini, P., Indon. 148 A2
Piñicuaro, Mex., 1,125 93 c9
Pinili, Phil., 1,633 153 B1
Pinillos, Col. 100 C3
Piniós, r., Gr. 129 C5
Piniós, r., Gr. 129 C6
Pinipel, i., Sol. Is. 175 a1
Pinjarra, Austl. 172 B5
Pink, Okla. 76 F2
Pinkafeld, Aust., 3,816 124 N6
Pink Cliffs, Utah 78
Pinkham Notch, N.H. 54 E3
Pink Hill, N.C., 457 63 G2
Pink Mountain, Br. Col., Can. 42 G2
Pinkstaff, Ill. 68 E5
Pinnacle, N.C. 63 D1
Pinnacle, mtn., N.Y. 59 M5
Pinnacles Nat. Mon., Calif. 82 C4
Pinnaroo, Austl. 172 F5
Pinnau, r., F.R.Ger. 119 a8
Pinneberg, F.R.Ger., 25,518 118 B2
Pinnebog, Mich. 67 K5
Pinola, Ind. 69 g10
Pinola, Miss., 116 73 F6
Pinole, Calif., 6,064 83 e12
Pinon, Ariz. 78 C3
Piñon, N. Mex. 79 C5
Pinos, Mex., 3,125 92 E3
Pinos, Isla de, Cuba 96 b2
Pinos, Mt., Calif. 82 D5
Pinos Wells, N. Mex. 79 C4
Pinotepa Nacional, Mex., 6,456 93 F5
Pinrang, Indon. 149 F3
Pins, C. des, Loy. Is. 174 k8
Pins, Î. des, N. Caled. 174 k9
Pins, Pt. aux, Ont., Can. 46 C6
Pinsk, U.S.S.R., 41,500 134 B4
Pinson, Tenn. 71 C6
Pinta, I., Colón, Arch. de 104 a7
Pintendre, Qué., Can. 47 n16
Pintlalla Cr., Ala. 64 C3
Pinto, Chile 104 f16
Pinto Butte, Sask., Can. 43 C5
Pin-yang, China 152 C3
Pinyug, U.S.S.R., 8,100 134 D3
Pinzón, I., Colón, Arch. de 104 a8
Pioche, Nev. 83 C4
Piombino, It., 35,456 123 C3
Pioneer, Iowa, 448 72 C2
Pioneer, La., 154 73 D5
Pioneer, Ohio, 855 70 E1
Pioneer Mts., Mont. 50 D1
Pioneerville, Idaho 81 B4
Pioner, U.S.S.R. 137 r11
Pioner, O., U.S.S.R. 135 H2
Pionierbivak, Indon. 149 L3
Pionki, Pol., 10,956 127 D3
Pionsat, Fr., 1,310 117 E3
Piora, Mt., Terr. New Guin. 174 e2
Piori, Terr. Papua 174 3
Piotrków Trybunalski, Pol., 53,000* 127 C3
Pio V. Corpuz, Phil., 2,737 153 C3
Piove di Sacco, It., 14,790 123 C2
Pipanaco, Salar de, Arg. 105 B3
Pipar, India, 12,557 145 D4
Piparia, India, 13,037 144 b14
Pipe, Wis. 66 E5
Pipecreek, Tex. 77 O5
Piper Bk., Conn. 56 E6
Piper City, Ill., 807 68 D3
Pipéri, i., Gr. 129 E5
Pipers Gap, Va. 62 D6
Piper's Hole, r., Newf., Can. 45 a9
Pipe Spring Nat. Mon., Ariz. 78 B3
Pipestone, Man., Can. 43 E5
Pipestone, co., Minn., 13,605 74 D4
Pipestone, Minn., 5,324 74 D4
Pipestone, r., Ont., Can. 44 D4
Pipestone Cr., Alta., Can. 43 b7
Pipestone Nat. Mon., Minn. 74 D3
Pipinas, Arg., 2,500* 105 c12
Piploda, India 144 a15
Pipmuacan L., Qué., Can. 45 L5
Pipriac, Fr., 2,804 117 B3
Piqua, Kans. 75 K6
Piqua, Ohio, 19,219 70 E2
Piquete, Braz., 10,543 103 d18
Pira, Dahom. 162 d7
Piracaia, Braz., 2,674 103 c18
Piracanjuba, Braz., 3,869 103 G5
Piracicaba, Braz., 80,670 103 G6
Piracuruca, Braz., 4,320 103 H2
Piraeus = Piraiévs
Piraiévs, Gr., 183,877 129 D6
Piramidal'nyy, Pik, U.S.S.R. 137 f4
Pirané, Arg., 6,000* 105 D3
Piranga, Braz., 2,169 103 e17
Piranga, r., Braz. 103 e17
Piranhas, Braz., 1,526 103 F5
Piranhas, r., Braz. 103 J3
Pirapetinga, Braz., 2,334 103 e17
Pirapora, Braz., 13,772 103 H5
Pirata, Mte., P.R. 96 u10
Pirdop, Bulg., 5,551 128 E3
Pirehueico, L., Chile 105 f14
Pires do Rio, Braz., 8,390 103 G5
Pireway, N.C. 63 F3
Pirgos, Gr., 20,558 129 C6
Pirgovo, Bulg., 3,396 128 E3
Piriá, Pan. 94 H6
Pirimapon, Indon. 149 L4
Pirin, mts., Bulg. 129 D4
Piripiri, Braz., 9,635 103 H2
Piritu, Ven., 1,854 100 F2
Píritu, Ven., 4,438 100 F3
Pirmasens, F.R.Ger., 50,480 118 A4
Pirna, Ger.D.R., 41,111 118 D3
Pirojpur, Pak., 15,754 144 g14
Pirot, Yug., 19,000* 125 F3
Pir Panjal Ra., India 145 E2
Pirtleville, Ariz. 78 D6
Piru, Indon. 149 J3
Piryatin, U.S.S.R., 15,200 136 D3
Piryi, Gr., 1,914 129 F5
Pis, i., Truk 176 19
Pisa, It., 87,575 123 C3
Pisa, r., Pol. 127 D2
Pisagua, Chile 105 A1
Piscadera B., Cur. 97 16
Piscataqua, r., Me.-N.H. 55 B5
Piscataquis, co., Me., 17,379 55 C3
Piscataquis, r., Me. 55 C3
Piscataquog, r., N.H. 54 D5
Piscatosin, L., Qué., Can. 47 J2
Pischelsdorf, Aust. 124 b10
Pischelsdorf, Aust., 1,873 124 M6
Pisco, Peru, 22,192 104 B5
Piseco, N.Y. 59 M5
Pisek, Czech., 20,213 126 B2
Pisek, N. Dak., 176 74 D1
Pisgah, Ala., 214 64 D1
Pisgah, Iowa, 343 72 B3
Pisgah, Miss. 73 F5
Pisgah, Mt., N.Y. 59 L7
Pisgah, Mt., Pa. 60 J2
Pisgah, Mt., Vt. 54 D2
Pisgah Forest, N.C. 63 B2
Pisgah Mtn., Me. 55 B3
P'i-shan, China 150 A3
Pi-shan, China 152 B1
Pishīn, Pak., 2,906 144 C3
Pising, Indon. 149 G4
Pisinimo, Ariz. 78 B5
Piskorzów, Pol. 127 g6
Pismo Beach, Calif., 1,762 82 C5
Pisoniano, It., 1,736 123 b8
Pissis, Co., Arg. 105 B3
Pissos, Fr. 117 C4
Pistakee, Ill. 69 b7
Pistakee L., Ill. 69 b7
Pisticci, It., 15,581 123 F4
Pistoia, It., 82,424 123 C3
Pistol River, Oreg. 80 A4
Pisuerga, r., Sp. 122 C1
Pisz, Pol., 6,274 127 D2
Piszczac, Pol. 127 E3
Pit, r., Calif. 82 C2
Pita, Guin., 2,000* 162 B4
Pital, Col. 100 C6
Pitalito, Col. 100 C7
Pitama, Chile 104 f13
Pitanga, Braz., 2,959 103 F6
Pitarpunga L., Austl. 173 d10
Pitcairn, N.Y. 59 K3
Pitcairn, Pa., 5,383 60 C5
Pitcairn I., Pac. Oc. 171 K6
Pitcher, N.Y. 59 J6
Pitch Lake, Trin. and Tob. 96 g5
Piteå, Swed. 120 E2
Piteälv, r., Swed. 120 D2
Piteşti, Rum., 38,330 128 E2
Pit-Gorodok, U.S.S.R. 135 J4
Pithion, Gr., 1,535 129 F4
Pithiviers, Fr., 7,646 117 E2
Piti, Guam 176 24
Pitiquito, Mex., 1,383 92 C1
Pitkin, co., Colo., 2,381 79 B2
Pitkin, Colo., 94 79 B2
Pitkin, La. 73 B7
Pitkyaranta, U.S.S.R., 6,200 134 C3
Pitlochry, U.K., 2,501 112 E3
Pitman, N.J., 8,644 61 A4
Pitogo, Phil., 2,908 153 c9
Pitogo, Phil., 2,349 153 f11
Pitomača, Yug., 6,114 125 C2
Pitrufquén, Chile, 6,472 105 e14
Pitt, co., N.C., 69,942 63 G2
Pitten, r., Aust. 124 M6
Pittenween, U.K., 1,576 112 e7
Pitt I., Br. Col., Can. 42 D3
Pitt I., N.Z. 170 G7
Pitt L., Br. Col., Can. 42 d6
Pittman, Alaska 85 c7
Pittock, Pa. 60 b8
Pitton, U.K. 113 i12
Pitts, Ga., 388 64 F4
Pittsboro, Ind., 826 70 C3
Pittsboro, Miss., 205 73 F4
Pittsboro, N.C., 1,215 63 E2
Pittsburg, Calif., 19,062 82 C4
Pittsburg, Ill., 485 68 D6
Pittsburg, Ind. 70 C2
Pittsburg, Kans., 18,678 75 L6
Pittsburg, Ky. 71 G4
Pittsburg, N.H. 54 E1
Pittsburg, co., Okla., 34,360 76 H2
Pittsburg, Okla., 195 76 H3
Pittsburg, Tex., 3,796 77 Q3
Pittsburgh, Pa., 604,332 60 C5
Pittsfield, Ill., 4,089 68 B4
Pittsfield, Me., 3,232 55 C4
Pittsfield, Mass., 57,879 56 D3
Pittsfield, Mich. 67 K6
Pittsfield, N.H., 1,407 54 E5
Pittsfield, Pa. 60 D2
Pittsfield, Vt. 54 B4
Pittsford, Mich. 67 J7
Pittsford, N.Y., 1,749 58 n20
Pittsford, Vt., 671 54 A4
Pittsford Mills, Vt. 54 B4
Pittston, Me. 55 C4
Pittston, Pa., 12,407 61 L3
Pittstown, N.J. 61 B2
Pittsview, Ala. 64 D3
Pittsville, Md., 488 62 J4
Pittsville, Wis., 661 66 C4
Pittsworth, Austl., 1,401 173 G4
Pittsylvania, co., Va., 58,296 62 E6
Pittwood, Ill. 68 E3
Pitu, Indon. 149 J2
Pium, Braz., 1,166 103 G4
Piura, Peru, 39,765 104 A3
Piura, r., Peru 104 A3
Piute, co., Utah, 1,436 78 B2
Piuthān, Nepal 144 d11
Piva, r., Yug. 125 D3
Pivka, Yug. 125 B2
Pivot, Alta., Can. 42 L4
Piwniczna, Pol., 4,523 127 D4
Pixley, Calif., 1,327 82 D5
Pixoyal, Mex. 93 H4
Pi-yang, China 151 B4
Pizarro, Col. 100 B5
Pizhma, U.S.S.R. 136 G1
Pizzighettone, It., 7,700 122 c5
Pizzo, It., 10,088 123 F5
Placedo, Tex. 77 P5
Placentia, Newf., Can., 1,603 45 R6
Placentia, Calif., 5,861 83 i16
Placentia Bay, Newf., Can. 45 Q6
Placentia Sd., Newf., Can. 45 a10
Placer, Phil., 4,298 153 B3
Placer, co., Calif., 56,998 82 C3
Placerville, Calif., 4,439 82 C3
Placerville, Colo. 79 A2
Placetas, Cuba, 25,226 96 d1
Placid, L., N.Y. 59 M3
Plácido de Castro, Braz. 102 C3
Placilla, Chile, 1,495 104 f13
Placilla, Chile, 1,047 104 f14
Placilla, Chile 104 f16
Pladju, Indon. 148 C3
Plaffeien, Switz., 1,352 124 B2
Plaidt, F.R.Ger., 4,195 119 C4
Plailly, Fr. 116 i10
Plain, Wash. 80 C2
Plain, Wis., 677 66 C5
Plain City, Ohio, 2,146 70 F2

278 · Plain City—Poplar

Plain City, Utah, 1,152 78 B1
Plain Dealing, La., 1,357 73 B5
Plainedge, N.Y., 21,973 58 e14
Plainfield, Conn., 2,044;8,884(T) 56 J6
Plainfield, Ga., 84 64 F3
Plainfield, Ill., 2,183 68 D2
Plainfield, Ind., 5,460 70 C3
Plainfield, Iowa, 445 72 E2
Plainfield, Mass., 237(T) 56 E2
Plainfield, Mich. 67 J6
Plainfield, N.H. 54 C4
Plainfield, N.J., 45,330 61 C2
Plainfield, Vt., 507 54 C3
Plainfield, Wis., 660 66 D4
Plainfield Heights, Mich. 67 H5
Plains, Ga., 572 64 E3
Plains, Kans. 75 E6
Plains, Mont., 769 81 B2
Plains, Tex., 1,195 77 M3
Plainsboro, N.J. 61 B3
Plains of San Agustin, N. Mex. 79 A5
Plainsville, Mass., 3,810(T) 57 L4
Plainview, Ark., 548 73 B3
Plainview, Ill. 68 C4
Plainview, Minn., 1,833 74 F3
Plainview, Nebr., 1,467 75 H1
Plainview, N.Y., 27,710 58 f13
Plainview, Okla. 76 D2
Plainview, S. Dak. 74 A3
Plainview, Tex., 18,735 77 M2
Plain View, Va. 62 H5
Plainville, Conn., 13,149(T) 56 E6
Plainville, Ill., 227 68 A4
Plainville, Ind., 545 70 B4
Plainville, Kans., 3,104 75 F4
Plainville, N.Y. 59 q23
Plainville, Ohio 71 i11
Plainwell, Mich., 3,125 67 H6
Plaisance, Fr., 1,490 117 D5
Plaisance, Haiti, 1,840 96 k6
Plaisir, Fr., 3,852 116 f11
Plaisted, Me. 55 D1
Plaistow, N.H. 54 E6
Plamondon, Alta., Can. 42 K2
Plamondon, Ill. 69 b9
Planá, Czech. 126 A2
Plana, Yug., 2,024 125 D3
Planada, Calif., 1,704 82 C4
Plan-de-la-Tour, Fr. 116 m14
Plandište, Yug., 3,096 125 E2
Plandome, N.Y., 1,379 58 d13
Planeta Rica, Col. 100 C3
Plank, Aust. 124 b9
Planken, Liecht. 124 a8
Plankinton, S. Dak., 644 74 C4
Plano, Ill., 3,343 68 D2
Plano, Iowa, 87 72 D4
Plano, Tex., 3,695 77 P3
Plantagenet, Ont., Can. 47 J3
Plantation, Fla., 4,772 65 a9
Plantation Key, Fla. 65 h15
Plant City, Fla., 15,711 65 G4
Plantersville, Ala. 64 B3
Plantersville, Miss., 572 73 G3
Plantersville, S.C. 63 E4
Plantsite, Ariz. 1,556 78 D5
Plantsville, Conn., 2,793 56 E6
Plaquemine, La., 7,689 73 D7
Plaquemines, parish, La., 22,545 73 F8
Plaridel, Phil., 2,170 153 B3
Plaridel, Phil., 2,365 153 f11
Plasencia, Sp., 21,297 122 B3
Plaški, Yug. 125 B2
Plassey, India 144 g14
Plast, U.S.S.R., 25,900 134 F4
Plaster Rock, N.B., Can., 1,267 45 M6
Plata, R. de la, Arg.-Urug. 105 D5
Plata, R. de la, P.R. 96 t10
Platanal, Peru 104 D6
Platanistós, Gr. 129 E5
Plátanos, r., Mex. 93 b10
Platea, Pa., 357 60 B2
Plateau Cr., Colo. 79 A2
Plateros, Mex., 1,565 92 E3
Platí, Gr., 1,897 129 D4
Platillón, Co., Ven. 101 b12
Platina, Calif. 82 B2
Platinum, Alaska, 43 85 D4
Plato, Sask., Can. 43 B4
Plato, Col. 100 C3
Plato, Mo. 72 E7
Platón Sánchez, Mex., 4,127 93 f8
Platoro, Colo. 79 B3
Platos, Mex. 93 a9
Platte, co., Mo., 23,350 72 C5
Platte, co., Nebr., 23,992 75 H2
Platte, S. Dak., 1,167 74 C4
Platte, co., Wyo., 7,195 81 G5
Platte, r., U.S. 50 G2
Platte, r., Iowa-Mo. 72 C4
Platte, r., Wis. 66 C6
Platte Center, Nebr., 402 75 H2
Platte City, Mo., 1,188 72 C5
Platte Cr., S. Dak. 74 C4
Platte L., Mich. 67 G4
Platteville, Colo., 582 79 C1
Platteville, Wis., 6,957 66 C6
Platte Woods, Mo., 393 75 a7
Plattling, F.R.Ger., 7,961 118 D4
Platt Nat. Pk., Okla. 76 G3
Plattsburg, Miss. 73 F5
Plattsburg, Mo., 1,663 72 C5
Plattsburgh, N.Y., 20,172 59 O2
Plattsmouth, Nebr., 6,244 75 K3
Plattsville, Ont., Can. 46 a14
Plau, Ger.D.R. 118 D2
Plaue, Ger.D.R. 118 D2
Plauen, Ger.D.R., 79,056 118 D3
Plauer See, Ger.D.R. 118 D2
Plavnica, Yug. 125 D3
Pławno, Pol. 127 C3
Playa Azul, Mex. 92 E4
Playa de Ponce, P.R., 3,500* 96 s11
Playa Grandi, Cur. 97 16
Playas, Ec. 104 A2
Playas L., N. Mex. 79 A6
Playa Vicente, Mex., 3,284 93 G5
Playgreen L., Man., Can. 43 F4
Playitas, Ven. 100 D3
Plaza, N. Dak., 385 74 B1
Plaza Huincul, Arg., 8,000* 105 B5
Pleasant, Mt., Va. 62 E5
Pleasant, r., Me. 55 C3
Pleasant, r., Me. 55 E4
Pleasant Bay, N.S., Can. 47 V10
Pleasant Bay, Mass. 57 R6
Pleasant Bend, Ohio 70 E1
Pleasant Dale, Nebr., 190 75 J3
Pleasant Gap, Pa., 1,389 60 G4
Pleasant Garden, N.C. 63 E2
Pleasant Grove, Ala., 3,097 64 b8
Pleasant Grove, Calif. 82 a7
Pleasant Grove, Utah, 4,772 78 c10
Pleasant Grove Cr., Calif. 82 b7
Pleasant Hill, Ala. 64 C3
Pleasant Hill, Calif., 23,844 83 e12
Pleasant Hill, Ill., 950 68 B4
Pleasant Hill, La., 907 73 B6
Pleasant Hill, Mo., 2,689 72 C6
Pleasant Hill, Ohio, 1,060 70 E2
Pleasant Hill, Pa. 60 B4
Pleasant Hill, S.C. 63 D3
Pleasant Hill, Tenn., 267 71 F6
Pleasant Lake, Ind. 70 D1
Pleasant Lake, N. Dak. 74 C1
Pleasant L., Me. 55 C4
Pleasant L., Me. 55 D2
Pleasant L., Me. 55 E3
Pleasant L., N.H. 54 D5
Pleasant Mount, Pa. 61 M2
Pleasanton, Iowa, 103 72 D4
Pleasanton, Calif., 4,203 83 f12
Pleasanton, Kans., 1,098 75 L5
Pleasanton, Nebr., 199 75 F3
Pleasanton, Tex., 3,467 77 O5
Pleasant Park, Ont., Can. 67 g16
Pleasant Plain, Iowa, 147 72 F3
Pleasant Plains, Ark., 112 73 D2
Pleasant Plains, Ill., 518 68 C4
Pleasant Plains, N.J. 58 c16
Pleasant Point, Man., Can. 43 e10
Pleasant Pond, Me. 55 C3
Pleasant Pd., Me. 55 C4
Pleasant Prairie, Wis. 66 d13
Pleasants, co., W. Va., 7,124 62 C3
Pleasant Site, Ala. 64 B1
Pleasant Valley (part of Barkhamsted), Conn. 56 D5
Pleasant Valley, Mich. 67 J5
Pleasant Valley, Mo., 1,109 75 a7
Pleasant Valley, N.Y. 59 N8
Pleasant Valley, Okla. 76 F1
Pleasant Valley, Oreg. 80 E3
Pleasant Valley, Pa. 61 k18
Pleasant View, Jefferson Co., Colo. 79 b8
Pleasant View, Montezuma Co., Colo. 79 A3
Pleasant View, Ill. 68 B3
Pleasant View, Ky. 71 G5
Pleasant View, Tenn. 71 E5
Pleasant View, Utah, 927 78 C1
Pleasantville, Ind. 70 B4
Pleasantville, Iowa, 1,025 72 D3
Pleasantville, N.J., 15,172 61 B5
Pleasantville, N.Y., 5,877 59 N9
Pleasantville, Ohio, 741 70 G3
Pleasantville, Bedford Co., Pa., 300 60 E5
Pleasantville, Venango Co., Pa., 940 60 C2
Pleasantville, Tenn. 71 D6
Pleasure Beach, Conn., 1,264 56 H7
Pleaux, Fr., 1,873 117 E4
Pledger, Tex. 77 Q5
Pleiku, S. Viet., 7,200 146 D4
Pléneuf, Fr., 3,665 116 B2
Pleniţa, Rum. 128 D2
Plenty, Sask., Can. 43 B4
Plenty, Bay of, N.Z. 175 h5
Plentywood, Mont., 2,121 81 G1
Plérin, Fr., 7,757 116 B2
Plës, U.S.S.R., 4,000 136 F1
Plesetsk, U.S.S.R., 15,700 134 D3
Plessisville, Qué., Can., 6,509 44 K6
Pleszew, Pol., 10,793 127 B3
Pletipi L., Qué., Can. 45 L4
Plettenberg, F.R.Ger., 25,637 118 A3
Pleumartin, Fr., 1,348 117 D3
Pleven, Bulg., 57,555 128 E3
Plevna, Rum. 128 F2
Plevna, Ind. 70 C2
Plevna, Mont., 263 81 G2
Plibo, Lib. 162 C5
Pliny, W. Va. 62 B4
Plješevica, mts., Yug. 125 B2
Pljevlja, Yug., 11,000* 125 D3
Ploaghe, It., 5,141 123 B4
Plochingen, F.R.Ger., 9,812 118 B4
Płock, Pol., 42,000* 127 C2
Plöcken Pass, Aust.-It. 124 K7
Ploemeur, Fr., 6,735 116 B3
Ploërmel, Fr., 6,837 116 B3
Ploeşti, Rum., 114,544 128 E2
Ploeuc, Fr., 3,123 116 B2
Plomárion, Gr., 5,172 129 F5
Plomb du Cantal, mtn., Fr. 117 E4
Plön, F.R.Ger., 9,159 118 C1
Plonge, L. la, Sask., Can. 43 C3
Plonia, r., Pol. 127 A2
Płońsk, Pol., 10,135 127 D2
Płoty, Pol., 2,748 127 A2
Ploučnice, r., Czech. 126 d6
Plougastel, Fr., 5,652 116 A2
Plouguerneau, Fr., 6,069 116 A2
Plouha, Fr., 4,584 116 B2
Plovdiv, Bulg., 161,836 128 E3
Plover, Wis. 66 D4
Plover, r., Wis. 66 D4
Pluckemin, N.J. 61 B2
Plüderhausen, F.R.Ger., 4,538 119 H7
Plugari, Rum. 128 F1
Plum, r., Ill. 68 B1
Plumas, Man., Can. 43 F5
Plumas, co., Calif., 11,620 82 C3
Plumb, Wash. 80 B2
Plum Branch, S.C., 139 63 B4
Plum City, Wis., 384 66 A4
Plum Coulee, Man., Can. 43 g10
Plum Cr., Colo. 79 c9
Plum Cr., Nebr. 75 E1
Plum Cr., Ohio 70 d9
Plumerville, Ark., 586 73 C2
Plum Hill, Ill. 68 C5
Plum I., Mass. 57 N1
Plum I., N.Y. 59 Q9
Plum L., Wis. 66 D2
Plummer, Idaho, 344 81 A2
Plummer, Minn., 283 74 E2
Plummer Corners (part of Northbridge), Mass. 57 K4
Plum Point, Md. 62 H4
Plumsteadville, Pa. 60 f10
Plumtree, Rhod., 1,210 164 D5
Plumville, Pa., 401 60 D4
Plumwood, Ohio 70 F2
Plungė, U.S.S.R., 8,700 136 A2
Plunkettville, Okla. 76 J3
Plus, r., Malay. 147 o14
Plush, Oreg. 80 C4
Plymouth, Montserrat, 1,520 97 5
Plymouth, U.K., 204,409 113 D6
Plymouth, Calif., 489 82 C3
Plymouth, Conn., 8,981(T) 56 D6
Plymouth, Ill., 781 68 A3
Plymouth, Ind., 7,558 70 C1
Plymouth, co., Iowa, 23,906 72 A2
Plymouth, Iowa, 422 72 D1
Plymouth, Kans. 75 J5
Plymouth, Me. 55 C4
Plymouth, co., Mass., 248,449 57 N5
Plymouth, Mass., 14,445(T) 57 O5
Plymouth, Mich., 8,766 67 e15
Plymouth, Minn., 13,064 74 a5
Plymouth, N.H., 2,244 54 D4
Plymouth, N.Y. 59 J6
Plymouth, N.C., 4,666 63 H2
Plymouth, Ohio, 1,822 70 G1
Plymouth, Pa., 10,401 61 K3
Plymouth, Utah, 231 78 b7
Plymouth, Vt. 54 B4
Plymouth, Wis., 5,128 66 E5
Plymouth Bay, Mass. 57 O5
Plymouth Meeting, Pa., 4,050* 60 f11
Plymouth Union, Vt. 54 B4
Plympton, Mass., 821(T) 57 N5
Plympton St. Mary, U.K., 10,600 113 E6
Plymstock, U.K., 14,700 113 D6
Plyussa, r., U.S.S.R. 136 C1
Plzeň, Czech., 141,583 126 A2
Pniewy, Pol., 4,044 127 B2
Pô, Upper Volta, 4,383 162 D4
Po, r., It. 123 C2
Po, Foci del, river mouth, It. 123 D2
Poá, Braz., 15,419 103 c18
Po-ai, China 151 B4
Poamoho Camp, Hawaii 84 b6
Poamoho Str., Hawaii 84 b6
Poané, B. de, Loy. Is. 174 m8
Poarta Albă, Rum. 128 G2
Poás, Vol., C.R. 94 E5
Pobé, Dahom., 6,547 162 e8
Pobeda, G., U.S.S.R. 133 O3
Pobedy, Pik, U.S.S.R. 134 H5
Pobiedziska, Pol., 4,806 127 B2
Pobla de Segur, Sp., 3,288 122 F1
Poblet, Arg. 105 b12
Poca, W. Va., 607 62 C4
Pocahontas, Ark., 3,665 73 D1
Pocahontas, Ill., 718 68 C5
Pocahontas, co., Iowa, 14,234 72 C2
Pocahontas, Iowa, 2,011 72 C2
Pocahontas, Va., 1,313 62 C5
Pocahontas, co., W. Va., 10,136 62 D4
Pocasset (part of Bourne), Mass. 57 O6
Pocasset, Okla. 76 F2
Pocatalico, W. Va. 62 C4
Pocataligo, S.C. 63 D5
Pocatello, Idaho, 28,534 81 C4
Počátky, Czech. 126 B2
Pochëp, U.S.S.R., 15,700 136 D2
Pochinok, U.S.S.R., 7,600 136 D2
Pöchlarn, Aust., 2,923 124 M5
Pochutla, Mex., 3,084 93 F5
Pocking, F.R.Ger., 3,678 118 D4
Pocklington, U.K., 3,452 114 G3
Pocoata, Bol., 14,921 102 C5
Poções, Braz., 6,115 103 H4
Pocomoke, r., Md. 62 J4
Pocomoke City, Md., 3,329 62 J4
Pocomoke Sd., Md.-Va. 62 J5
Poconé, Braz., 4,702 103 E5
Pocono Cr., Pa. 61 M3
Pocono Lake, Pa. 61 L3
Pocono Manor, Pa. 61 M3
Pocono Mts., Pa. 61 M3
Poços de Caldas, Braz., 32,291 103 G6
Pocotopaug, L., Conn. 56 F6
Pocrí, Pan. 94 G7
Pocwock Str., Me. 55 C1
Podareš, Yug. 125 F4
Podbořany, Czech. 126 c6
Podchinnyy, U.S.S.R. 136 G3
Podgórze, Pol., 3,053 127 C3
Poděbrady, Czech., 13,188 126 B1
Podgaytsy, U.S.S.R., 13,000 136 B3
Podgorac, Yug., 2,961 125 E3
Podgorica = Titograd
Podhokhóri, Gr., 1,128 129 E4
Podkamennaya Tunguska, r., U.S.S.R. 135 J3
Podlesí, Czech. 126 b6
Podol'sk, U.S.S.R., 139,000 134 C4
Podor, Sen. 162 B3
Podravska Slatina, Yug., 5,616 125 C2
Podtësovo, U.S.S.R., 6,100 135 J4
Podu Iloaie, Rum. 128 F1
Podu Turcului, Rum. 128 F1
Poe, Alta., Can. 43 c7
Poeldijk, Neth., 4,200 115 C2
Po-erh, China 151 C4
Po-erh-k'o, r., China 151 C2
Poestenkill, N.Y. 59 w29
Pofadder, S. Af., 2,030 164 C6
Poga, Wai, r., Indon. 149 L3
Pogamasing, Ont., Can. 46 C2
Pogar, U.S.S.R., 6,200 136 D2
Poge, C., Mass. 57 P7
Poggibonsi, It., 17,169 123 C3
Poggio Renatico, It., 8,912 122 e6
Poggio Rusco, It., 7,014 122 e6
Pöggstall, Aust. 124 M5
Pogil-to, S. Kor. 151 E4
Pogoanele, Rum. 128 F2
Pogonianí, Gr. 129 C4
Pogoreloye Gorodishche, U.S.S.R. 136 a5
Pogradec, Alb., 8,200 125 E4
Pogranichnyy, U.S.S.R. 135 N5
Pogromni Vol., Alaska 85 C5
Po Hai, China 150 F3
Po-hai Hai-hsia, China 151 D3
Po-hai Wan, China 151 C3
Pohakapu, Hawaii, 1,125* 84 d7
Pohakea Pass, Hawaii 84 b7
P'ohang, S. Kor., 59,555 151 F3
Pohoiki, Hawaii 84 G4
Pohořelice, Czech. 126 C2
Po-hsien, China 150 F3
Pohue Bay, Hawaii 84 F4
Poiana Mare, Rum. 128 D3
Poiana Stampei, Rum. 128 E1
Poindimié, N. Caled., 2,152 174 i8
Poinsett, co., Ark., 30,834 73 E2
Poinsett, L., S. Dak. 74 D3
Point Arena, Calif., 596 82 B3
Point Baker, Alaska 85 L4
Point Barrow, Alaska 85 F1
Pointblank, Tex. 77 Q4
Point Breeze, N.Y. 58 D5
Point Cloates, Austl. 172 A3
Point Comfort, Tex., 1,453 77 P5
Point du Bois, Man., Can. 43 G5
Pointe a la Hache, La. 73 F8
Pointe-à-Pitre, Guad., 25,300 97 14
Point Eastern, Va. 62 G5
Pointe au Baril Station, Ont., Can. 46 D3
Pointe Au Fer I., La. 73 D8
Pointe-au-Pic, Qué., Can., 1,328 47 Q10
Pointe Aux Pins, Mich. 67 J3
Pointe-aux-Trembles, Qué., Can., 21,472 47 p17
Pointe-Claire, Qué., Can., 22,370 47 o18
Pointe Coupee, parish, La., 22,488 73 D7
Pointe-du-Chêne, N.B., Can. 47 T10
Pointe-du-Lac, Qué., Can. 47 M2
Point Edward, Ont., Can., 2,723 46 B5
Pointe-Gatineau, Qué., Can., 8,757 47 J3
Pointe-Noire, Qué., Can. 45 M5
Pointe-Noire, Congo, 55,600 164 A2
Pointe Verte, N.B., Can. 47 S10
Point Fortin, Trin. and Tob., 8,169† 96 g5
Point Hope, Alaska, 324 85 B1
Point Judith (part of Narragansett), R.I. 57 L7
Point L., N.W.T., Can. 40 G4
Point Lay, Alaska 85 D1
Point Lookout, Md. 62 H4
Point Marion, Pa., 1,853 60 C6
Point of Rocks, Md., 326 62 G3
Pt. of Rocks, mtn., N. Mex. 79 B5
Point Pedro, Cey. 145 F8
Pt. Pelee Nat. Pk., Ont., Can. 46 B7
Point Peninsula, N.Y. 59 H3
Point Pleasant, N.J., 10,182 61 C3
Point Pleasant, Ohio 70 E4
Point Pleasant, Pa. 61 N5
Point Pleasant, W. Va., 5,785 62 B4
Point Pleasant Beach, N.J., 3,873 58 c16
Pt. Reyes Nat. Seashore, Calif. 82 B4
Point Roberts, Wash. 80 B1
Points, W. Va. 62 F3
Point Washington, Fla. 65 C2
Poipet, Camb. 147 e5
Poirino, It., 5,391 122 a6
Poisson-Blanc, L., Qué., Can. 47 J3
Poissy, Fr., 28,616 117 D2
Poitiers, Fr., 66,222 117 D3
Poix, Fr., 1,513 117 D2
Pojezierze Mazurskie, reg., Pol. 126 ·
Pojezierze Wielkopolsko-Kujawskie, reg., Pol. 126 ·
Pok, Ponape 176 29
Pokai Bay, Hawaii 84 a7
Pokaran, India, 5,284 145 D4
Pokegama L., Barron Co., Wis. 66 B3
Pokegama L., Washburn Co., Wis. 66 B2
Poke-O-Moonshine Mt., N.Y. 59 O3
Pokhara, Nepal 145 G3
Pokhodsk, U.S.S.R. 135 P3
Poko, D.R.Congo 164 D1
Pokój, Pol. 127 g6
Pokok Asam, Malay., 8,023 147 o14
Pokrov, U.S.S.R., 6,800 136 c6
Pokrovsk, U.S.S.R. 135 M3
Pokrovskoye, U.S.S.R. 136 E4
Pokrzywna, Pol. 127 g6
Pokur, U.S.S.R. 134 G3
Pola, Phil., 2,418 153 B2
Pola, Yug. = Pula
Pola, i., Tutuila 177 39
Pola, r., U.S.S.R. 136 C1
Polacca, Ariz. 78 C4
Poland, ctry., 31,551,000* 127
Poland, Christmas I. 177 40
Poland, Ind. 70 C3
Poland, Me. 55 B4
Poland, N.Y., 564 59 K5
Poland, Ohio, 2,766 70 J1
Poland Spring, Me. 55 B4
Polangui, Phil., 3,472 153 h14
Polanica-Zdrój, Pol., 4,132 127 f6
Połaniec, Pol. 127 D3
Polanów, Pol., 1,822 127 B1
Polar, Wis. 66 D3
Polar Subglacial Basin 180 ·
Polatlı, Turk., 20,319 142 C2
Polch, F.R.Ger., 3,517 118 A3
Polcura, r., Chile 104 f17
Połczyn Zdrój, Pol., 7,619 127 B2
Polémie, Fr. Guiana 101 O5
Polenia B., New Hebr. 174 m7
Pole of Inaccessibility, Ant. 180 S4
Polesella, It., 4,132 122 e6
Polessk, U.S.S.R., 5,400 136 A2
Pole Station, Ant. 180 P4
Polesworth, U.K., 4,020 114 E5
Poles'ye, reg., U.S.S.R. 134 B4
Polevskoy, U.S.S.R., 47,100 137 k8
Polewali, Indon. 149 F3
Polgár, Hung., 9,344 126 E3
Poli, Cam. 162 G4
P'o-li, China 150 H2
Poliçan, Alb. 125 E4
Policastro, Golfo di, It. 123 E5
Police, Pol., 6,981 127 A2
Polička, Czech. 126 C2
Polídhroson, Gr., 1,511 129 D5
Polignac, Alg. 161 F3
Poligny, Fr., 4,750 117 F3
Políkastron, Gr., 3,821 129 D4
Políkhnitos, Gr., 5,131 129 E5
Polillo, Phil., 4,152 153 B2
Polillo I., Phil. 153 B2
Polillo Is., Phil. 153 B2
Polillo Str., Phil. 153 B2
Polis, Cyp., 1,727 142 d9
Polist', r., U.S.S.R. 136 C1
Polistena, It., 11,809 123 F5
Politiká, Gr., 1,184 129 D5
Políyiros, Gr., 3,541 129 D4
Poljana, Yug., 2,867 125 E2
Polk, co., Ark., 11,981 73 A3
Polk, co., Fla., 195,139 65 H4
Polk, co., Ga., 28,015 64 D2
Polk, co., Iowa, 266,315 72 D3
Polk, co., Minn., 36,182 74 D2
Polk, co., Mo., 13,753 72 D7
Polk, co., Nebr., 7,210 75 H2
Polk, Nebr., 433 75 H2
Polk, co., N.C., 11,395 63 B2
Polk, Ohio, 358 70 G2
Polk, co., Oreg., 26,523 80 B3
Polk, Pa., 3,574 60 C3
Polk, co., Tenn., 12,160 71 G6
Polk, co., Tex., 13,861 77 Q4
Polk, co., Wis., 24,968 66 A3
Polk City, Iowa, 567 72 D3
Polkowice, Pol. 127 e5
Polkton, N.C., 530 63 D2
Polkville, N.C. 63 C2
Pollachi, India, 54,369 145 k20
Pollard, Ala., 210 64 B4
Pollard, Ark., 170 73 E1
Pöllau, Aust., 1,616 124 M6
Pollegio, Switz. 124 C2
Pollensa, Sp., 8,975 122 G3
Pollino, Monte, It. 123 F5
Pollionay, Fr. 116 p15
Pollock, Idaho 81 A3
Pollock, La., 366 73 C6
Pollock, Mo. 72 E4
Pollock, S. Dak., 417 74 B3
Pollock Pines, Calif. 82 C3
Pollocksville, N.C., 416 63 G2
Polmak, Nor. 120 G1
Po-lo, Hs-Ch., China 150 B2
Po-lo, K-t., China 152 D3
Polo, Ill., 2,551 68 C2
Polo, Mo., 469 72 C5
Poloa, Tutuila 177 39
Polochic, r., Guat. 94 C3
Pologi, U.S.S.R., 16,500 136 E4
Polonia, Wis. 66 D4
Polonnaruwa, Cey. 145 n21
Polonnoye, U.S.S.R., 21,000 136 B3
Polotitlán, Mex., 1,022 93 e9
Polotnyanyy, U.S.S.R., 7,500 136 b6
Polotsk, U.S.S.R., 44,000 134 B4
Polousnyy, Khr., U.S.S.R. 135 N3
Poloy-poloy, Phil., 2,518 153 C4
Polpis (part of Nantucket), Mass. 57 Q7
Polsbroek, Neth. 115 b7
Polski Trŭmbesh, Bulg., 4,231 128 E3
Polson, Mont., 2,314 81 B2
Polsum, F.R.Ger., 5,952 119 C1
Poltava, U.S.S.R., 150,000 134 C5
Poltavka, U.S.S.R. 137 n11
Poltavka, U.S.S.R. 151 F1
Polumir, Yug. 125 E3
Polunochnoye, U.S.S.R., 7,700 134 F3
Polur, India, 14,764 145 m19
Polvijärvi, Fin. 120 G3
Polya, r., U.S.S.R. 136 c6
Polyanovgrad, Bulg., 14,516 128 F3
Polyarnyy, U.S.S.R., 11,300 134 C3
Polynesia, reg., Pac. Oc. 170 G3
Polynésie Française = French Polynesia
Polysayevo, U.S.S.R., 33,600 137 r11
Pomabamba, Peru, 2,580 104 B4
Pomacanchi, Peru, 2,980 104 D5
Pomán, Arg., 1,600* 105 B3
Pomarance, It., 9,969 123 C3
Pomaria, S.C., 230 63 C3
Pomata, Peru, 1,630 104 D6
Pomato Pt., V.I. 97 4
Pomazkino, U.S.S.R. 135 P3
Pomba, r., Braz. 103 e17
Pombal, Port., 9,973 122 A3
Pómbia, Gr., 1,730 129 E7
Pomerania, reg., Ger.D.R.-Pol. 118 E2
Pomeranian Bay, Ger.D.R.-Pol. 118 E1
Pomerene, Ariz. 78 C5
Pomeroy, Iowa, 816 72 C2
Pomeroy, Ohio, 3,345 70 H3
Pomeroy, Pa., 1,085 61 L6
Pomeroy, Wash., 1,677 80 E2
Pomezia, It., 9,033 123 b8
Pomfret, Conn., 2,316(T) 56 J5
Pomfret, Md. 62 H4
Po-mi, China 150 D4
Pomigliano d'Arco, It., 22,186 123 c10
Pomio, Terr. New Guin. 174 f2
Pomme de Terre, r., Minn. 74 E3
Pomme de Terre, r., Mo. 72 D7
Pomme de Terre Res., Mo. 72 D7
Pomona, S.-W. Afr. 164 B6
Pomona, Calif., 67,157 82 E5
Pomona, Ga. 64 g11
Pomona, Ill. 68 C6
Pomona, Kans., 489 75 K5
Pomona Park, Fla., 516 65 H3
Pomona Res., Kan. 75 K5
Pomonkey, Md. 62 G4
Pomorie, Bulg., 6,015 128 F3
Pomorze = Pomerania
Pomoshnaya, U.S.S.R., 11,900 136 C3
Pomo Tsho, China 150 C4
Pompano Beach, Fla., 15,992 65 J6
Pompanoosuc, Vt. 54 C4
Pompei, It., 19,130 123 d10
Pompei, ruins, It. 123 c10
Pompeii, Mich. 67 J5
Pomperaug, r., Conn. 56 D7
Pompey, Fr., 5,464 116 b9
Pompey, N.Y. 59 r24
Pompeys Pillar, Mont. 81 F3
Pomposa, It. 122 f6
Pompton, r., N.J. 58 b13
Pompton Lakes, N.J., 9,445 61 C2
Pompton Plains, N.J. 58 b13
Pomuch, Mex., 3,195 93 H4
Ponaganset, r., R.I. 57 K5
Ponaganset Res., R.I. 57 J5
Ponape = Colonia
Ponape, i., Car. Is. 170 E4
Ponazyrevo, U.S.S.R. 136 G1
Ponca, Nebr., 924 75 J1
Ponca City, Okla., 24,411 76 F1
Ponca Cr., Nebr.-S. Dak. 74 C4
Ponce, P.R., 114,286 96 s10
Ponce de Leon, Fla. 65 D2
Poncha Springs, Colo., 201 79 B2
Ponchatoula, La., 4,727 73 E7
Poncitlán, Mex., 4,840 93 b9
Pond, Calif. 82 D5
Pond, r., Ky. 71 D4
Pond Creek, Okla., 934 76 F1
Pond Cr., Okla. 76 F1
Pond Eddy, N.Y. 59 L9
Ponder, Tex. 76 e8
Pondera, co., Mont., 7,653 81 C1
Ponderay, Idaho, 231 81 A1
Ponders Corner, Wash. 81 a8
Pondicherry, India, 40,421 145 F8
Pond Inlet, N.W.T., Can. 41 O3
Pondoklabu, Indon. 148 F3
Pondosa, Calif. 82 C2
Pondosa, Oreg. 80 E3
Pondville (part of Norfolk), Mass. 57 L4
Ponemah, Minn. 74 E1
Ponemah, N.H. 54 D6
Ponérihouen, N. Caled. 174 i8
Poneto, Ind., 289 70 D2
Ponferrada, Sp., 37,053 122 B1
Pong, Thai., 4,681 146 C3
Ponghwa-ri, N. Kor. 151 F2
Pong Nam Ron, Thai. 147 e5
Pong Tuk, Camb. 147 k11
Ponhea Lu, Camb. 147 k11
Poniatowa, Pol., 3,849 127 E3
Poniec, Pol., 2,649 127 B3
Ponkapoag (part of Canton), Mass. 57 M4
Ponnagyun, Burma 146 A2
Ponnaiyar, r., India 145 m19
Ponnani, India, 22,977 145 E8
Ponnyadaung, mts., Burma 147 ·
Ponoka, Alta., Can., 3,907 42 K3
Ponomarevka, U.S.S.R. 137 h9
Ponorogo, Indon. 148 d7
Ponot, Phil., 2,177 153 B3
Ponoy, U.S.S.R. 134 D3
Ponoy, r., U.S.S.R. 134 C3
Pons, Fr., 5,108 117 C4
Pons, Sp., 1,715 122 F2
Ponset (part of Haddam), Conn. 56 F7
Ponsford, Minn. 74 E2
Ponson I., Phil. 153 f11
Pont, r., U.K. 112 g9
Pont-à-Celles, Belg., 5,148 115 C4
Ponta Delgada, Azores, 24,091 108 2
Ponta de Pedras, Braz., 1,907 103 G2
Ponta do Sol, C. Verde Is. 109 5
Ponta Grossa, Braz., 77,803 103 G7
Pont-à-Marcq, Fr., 1,492 116 a6
Pont-à-Mousson, Fr., 13,037 117 F2
Ponta Porã, Braz., 9,610 103 E6
Pontarlier, Fr., 16,205 117 G3
Pont-Audemer, Fr., 8,542 117 D2
Pontault-Combault, Fr., 7,511 116 i11
Pont Canavese, It., 5,476 122 a5
Pontcarré, Fr. 116 i11
Pontcharra-sur-Turdine, Fr., 1,436 116 p15
Pontchartrain, L., La. 73 E7
Pontchâteau, Fr., 5,482 117 C3
Pont-d'Ain, Fr., 1,824 117 F3
Pont-de-Vaux, Fr., 2,141 117 F3
Ponte Alta do Norte, Braz. 103 G4
Ponte Branca, Braz. 103 F5
Pontecagnano, It., 15,236 123 E4
Pontecorvo, It., 13,690 123 D4
Ponte da Barca, Port., 1,262 122 A2
Ponte dell'Olio, It., 5,692 122 c6
Pontedera, It., 22,456 123 C3
Ponte de Sor, Port., 13,010 122 B3
Ponte do Lima, Port., 3,030 122 A2
Pontefract, U.K., 27,114 114 F3
Ponteix, Sask., Can. 43 C5
Ponteland, U.K., 1,481 112 g9
Pontelandolfo, It., 6,615 123 d9
Pontelongo, It., 4,595 122 f5
Ponte Nova, Braz., 22,536 103 H6
Pontenure, It., 4,852 122 c6
Pontesbury, U.K., 3,039 114 C5
Pontestura, It., 2,572 122 b5
Pontevedra, Phil., 6,476 153 d11
Pontevedra, Sp., 50,483 122 A1
Ponte Vedra, Fla. 65 H2
Ponte Vedra Beach, Fla. 65 H2
Pontével, Port., 5,113 122 k9
Pont-Evêque, Fr., 1,881 116 p15
Pontevico, It., 7,913 122 d5
Ponthierville, D.R.Congo 164 D2
Pontiac, Ill., 8,435 68 D3
Pontiac, Mich., 82,223 67 K6
Pontiac (part of Warwick), R.I. 57 L6
Pontianak, Indon., 150,220 148 D3
Pontian Kechil, Malay., 8,450 148 B2
Pontine Is. = Ponza, I. di
Pontivy, Fr., 11,815 116 B2
Pont-l'Abbé, Fr., 7,167 116 A3
Pontllanfraith, U.K., 7,636 114 B7
Pontoise, Fr., 17,947 117 E2
Ponton, r., Alta., Can. 42 J1
Pontook Res., N.H. 54 E2
Pontoon Beach, Ill., 1,107 72 b11
Pontoosuc, Ill., 210 68 A3
Pontoosuc L., Mass. 56 C3
Pontorson, Fr., 3,687 117 C2
Pontotoc, co., Miss., 17,232 73 F3
Pontotoc, Miss., 2,108 73 F3
Pontotoc, co., Okla., 28,089 76 G3
Pontotoc, Tex. 77 O4
Pontremoli, It., 13,734 123 C2
Pontresina, Switz., 1,067 124 D2
Pont-Rouge, Qué., Can., 2,982 47 N2
Pont-St-Esprit, Fr., 5,822 117 F4
Pont-Ste-Maxence, Fr., 7,444 117 E2
Pont-Viau, Qué., Can. 47 o17
Pontycymmer, U.K., 3,485 114 A7
Pontypool, Ont., Can. 46 F4
Pontypool, U.K., 39,930 113 E6
Pontypridd, U.K., 35,494 113 E6
Ponuga, Pan. 94 G7
Ponza, Isola di, It. 123 D4
Poochera, Austl. 172 E5
Pool, U.K., 1,315 114 E3
Poole, U.K., 92,111 113 E6
Poole Bay, U.K. 113 i13
Pooler, Ga., 1,073 64 H3
Poolesville, Md., 298 62 G3
Poolewe, U.K. 112 D3
Poolowanna L., Austl. 172 E4
Poolville, N.Y. 59 K6
Poolville, Tex. 76 d9
Poona, India, 597,562 145 E6
Poopó, Bol., 6,506 102 C5
Poopó, L. de, Bol. 102 C5
Poor Knights Is., N.Z. 175 g4
Poorman, Alaska 85 E2
Poos di Wanga, Cur. 97 16
Popa Hill, Burma 147 f7
Po-pai, China 150 E5
Popasnaya, U.S.S.R., 31,000 136 f7
Popayán, Col. 100 B6
Pope, co., Ark., 21,177 73 B2
Pope, co., Ill., 4,061 68 D6
Pope, co., Minn., 11,914 74 E3
Pope, Miss., 246 73 F3
Pope Cr., Ill. 68 B2
Popejoy, Iowa, 190 72 D2
Poperinge, Belg., 12,396 115 A4
Popham Beach, Me. 55 C5
Popina, Bulg., 2,699 128 F2
Poplar, Calif., 1,478 82 D4
Poplar, Mont., 1,565 81 G1
Poplar, N.C. 63 B1
Poplar, Wis., 475 66 B2
Poplar, r., Man., Can. 43 F4

Poplar—Presa El Palmito · 279

Poplar, r., Mont. 81 G1
Poplar Bluff, Mo., 15,926 72 G8
Poplar Branch, N.C. 63 J1
Poplar City, Ill. 68 B3
Poplar Cr., Ill. 69 b8
Poplar Grove, Ill., 460 68 D1
Poplar Plains, Ky. 71 H3
Poplar Point, Man., Can. 43 f9
Poplar Ridge, N.Y. 59 G6
Poplar Springs, Md. 62 a7
Poplarville, Miss., 2,136 73 F7
Popocatépetl, vol., Mex. 93 f11
Popogia, Mt., Sta. Cruz Is. 175 6
Popoh, Indon. 148 D5
Popoia I., Hawaii 84 d7
Popokabaka, D.R.Congo 164 B2
Popolá, Mex., 1,052 93 H4
Popomanasiu, Mt., Sol. Is. 175 c3
Popondetta, Terr. Papua 174 f3
Popoo Gulch, r., Hawaii 84 F4
Popote, Fr. Guiana 101 O6
Popovača, Yug. 125 C2
Popovo, Bulg., 10,597 128 F3
Poppberg, F.R.Ger. 118 C4
Popple, r., Wis. 66 E3
Poprad, Czech., 14,890 126 E2
Poprad, r., Pol. 127 D4
Poptún, Guat., 1,942 94 C2
Poquetanuck, Conn. 56 H7
Poquonock (part of Windsor), Conn. 56 F5
Poquonock Bridge (part of Groton), Conn. 56 H7
Poquoson, Va., 4,278 62 H5
Poquott, N.Y., 295 58 g13
Poraj, Pol. 127 i6
Porangatu, Braz., 2,886 103 G4
Porbandar, India, 75,081 144 C5
Porcher I., Br. Col., Can. 42 D2
Porciúncula, Braz., 4,868 103 e17
Porco, Bol., 2,877 102 b11
Porcos, I. dos, Braz. 103 d18
Porcuna, Sp., 10,516 122 C4
Porcupine, C., Newf., Can. 45 P4
Porcupine, r., Sask., Can. 43 D2
Porcupine, r., Alaska 85 J2
Porcupine Bank, Atl. Oc. 108 M3
Porcupine Mtn., Sask., Can. 43 E4
Porcupine Mts., Mich. 66 D2
Porcupine Plain, Sask., Can. 43 D4
Pordenone, It., 32,657 123 D1
Pore, Col. 100 E5
Poręba, Pol., 6,535 127 C3
Poreč, Yug., 2,488 125 A2
Porech'ye, U.S.S.R. 136 a6
Porech'ye Rybnoye, U.S.S.R., 2,800 136 E1
Porée, L., Qué., Can. 45 L3
Porga, Dahom. 162 E4
Pori, Fin., 57,229 120 E3
Porirua, N.Z., 9,614 175 g6
Porjus, Swed. 120 E2
Porkhov, U.S.S.R., 7,600 136 C1
Porkkala, Fin. 120 F4
Porlamar, Ven., 20,807 101 J2
Porlock, U.K., 1,307 114 A8
Pornic, Fr., 2,833 117 B3
Poro I., Phil. 153 f11
Poromo, Chile 102 a11
Poronaysk, U.S.S.R., 21,900 135 O5
Póros, Gr., 4,392 129 D6
Poroshiri-dake, Jap. 155 K8
Porpoise B., Ant. 180 U6
Porrau, Aust. 124 c9
Porrentruy, Switz., 7,095 124 A1
Porsangen, fj., Nor. 120 F1
Porsangerhalvöya, pen., Nor. 120 F1
Porsgrunn, Nor., 10,607 120 B4
Pörsten, Ger.D.R. 126 b5
Port, Okla. 76 D2
Portachuelo, Bol., 6,044 102 D5
Port Acres, Tex. 77 n9
Portadown, U.K., 18,605 113 C4
Portaferry, U.K., 1,275 113 D4
Portage, Alaska, 71 85 c7
Portage, Ind., 11,822 69 f10
Portage, Me. 55 D2
Portage, Mich. 67 H6
Portage, co., Ohio, 91,798 70 H1
Portage, Ohio, 420 70 F1
Portage, Pa., 3,933 60 E5
Portage, Utah, 189 78 B1
Portage, co., Wis., 36,964 66 D4
Portage, Wis., 7,822 66 D5
Portage, r., Mich. 67 H6
Portage, r., Ohio 70 F1
Portage Cr., Pa. 60 F2
Portage Des Sioux, Mo., 371 72 a10
Portage L., Me. 55 D2
Portage L., Mich. 66 E1
Portage L., Mich. 67 G4
Portage la Prairie, Man., Can., 12,223 43 F5
Portageville, Mo., 2,505 72 H8
Portageville, N.Y. 58 D6
Portal, Ariz. 78 D6
Portal, Ga., 494 64 G3
Portal, N. Dak., 351 74 A1
Port Alberni, Br. Col., Can., 11,260 42 F4
Portalegre, Port., 13,374 122 B3
Portales, N. Mex., 9,695 79 D4
Port Alexander, Alaska, 18 85 L4
Port-Alfred, Qué., Can., 8,975 45 L5
Port Alfred, S. Af., 6,171 164 D7
Port Alice, Br. Col., Can., 1,073 42 E4
Port Allegany, Pa., 2,742 60 F2
Port Allen, La., 5,026 73 D7
Port Alsworth, Alaska 85 F3
Port Andrews, Wis. 66 C5
Port Angeles, Wash., 12,653 80 B1
Port Antonio, Jam., 7,830 96 q8
Port-à-Piment, Haiti, 2,525 96 i6
Port Aransas, Tex., 824 77 P6
Portarlington, Ire., 2,720 113 C5
Port Arthur, Austl. 173 f14
Port Arthur, Ont., Can., 44,404 44 E5
Port Arthur, China = Lü-shun-k'ou
Port Arthur, Tex., 66,676 77 Q5
Port Askaig, U.K. 112 C4
Port Augusta, Austl., 6,704 172 E5
Port au Port, Newf., Can. 45 P5
Port-au-Prince, Haiti, 145,824 96 k6
Port-au-Prince, Baie de, Haiti 96 k6
Port Austin, Mich., 706 67 K4
Port Barre, La., 1,876 73 D7
Port Bell, Uganda 164 E1
Port-Bergé, Malag. Rep., 3,854 165 H4
Port Blair, India 14,075 146 A5
Port Blakely, Wash. 81 b7
Port Blandford, Newf., Can. 45 Q5
Port Bolivar, Tex. 77 k10
Port-Bou, Sp., 2,236 122 G1
Port-Bouet, Iv. Coast 162 a9
Port Broughton, Austl. 172 c7
Port Burwell, N.W.T., Can. 45 N1
Port Burwell, Ont., Can. 46 D6
Port Byron, Ill., 1,153 68 B2
Port Byron, N.Y., 1,201 59 G5
Port Campbell, Austl. 173 F6
Port Carbon, Pa., 2,775 61 K4
Port Carling, Ont., Can. 44 H6
Port Cartier, Qué., Can., 3,434 45 M5
Port Chalmers, N.Z., 3,120 175 f7
Port Charlotte, U.K. 112 C4
Port Charlotte, Fla., 3,197 65 G5
Portchester (part of Fareham), U.K., 12,224 113 k13
Port Chester, N.Y., 24,960 59 N10
Port Chicago, Calif., 1,746 83 e11
Port Chilkoot, Alaska, 120 85 L4
Port Cland, Seych. 165 a10
Port Clements, Br. Col., Can. 42 D3
Port Clinton, Ohio, 6,870 70 G1
Port Clinton, Pa., 739 61 L4
Port Colborne, Ont., Can., 14,716 44 H7
Port Coquitlam, Br. Col., Can., 7,996 42 d6
Port Credit, Ont., Can., 6,925 46 c13
Port Dalhousie, Ont., Can., 3,087 46 d15
Port-Daniel, Qué., Can. 45 N5
Port-de-Paix, Haiti, 6,964 96 k6
Port Deposit, Md., 953 62 H3
Port Dickinson, N.Y., 2,295 59 J7
Port Dickson, Malay., 4,416 147 o15
Port Dover, Ont., Can., 3,042 46 D6
Porte des Morts Str., Wis. 66 F3
Port Edward, Br. Col., Can. 42 D2
Port Edwards, Wis., 1,849 66 D4
Port Egmont Settlement, Falk. Is. 108 3
Portel, Braz., 1,821 103 F2
Portel, Port., 3,621 122 B3
Port Elgin, Ont. Can., 1,621 44 G7
Port Elizabeth, S. Af., 270,815 164 D7
Port Elizabeth, N.J. 61 B5
Port Ellen, U.K. 112 C4
Porter, Ala. 64 b7
Porter, co., Ind., 60,279 70 B1
Porter, Ind., 2,189 70 B1
Porter, Mich. 67 J5
Porter, Minn., 261 74 D3
Porter, N. Mex. 79 D4
Porter, Ohio 70 G4
Porter, Okla., 492 76 H2
Porter, Tex. 77 i8
Porter, Va. 62 F5
Porter, Wash. 80 B2
Porterdale, Ga., 2,365 64 E2
Porterfield, Wis. 66 F3
Port Erin, U.K., 1,435 113 D4
Porter Landing, Br. Col., Can. 42 D1
Porter Pt., St. Vinc. 97 19
Porter Springs, Ga. 64 E1
Portersville, Pa., 344 60 B4
Portersville, Utah 78 c9
Porterville, S. Af., 2,536 164 a8
Porterville, Calif., 7,991 82 D4
Porterville, Miss. 73 G5
Port Essington, Br. Col., Can. 42 D2
Port-Étienne, Maur., 5,300 162 A2
Port Ewen, N.Y., 2,622 59 M8
Portezuelo, Chile 105 A5
Portezuelo, Mex., 2,551 93 b9
Port-Francqui, D.R.Congo 164 C2
Port Gamble, Wash. 80 B2
Port-Gentil, Gabon 164 A2
Port Germein, Austl. 172 c7
Port Gibson, Miss., 2,861 73 D6
Port Gibson, N.Y. 58 F5
Port Glasgow, U.K., 22,551 112 a8
Port Graham, Alaska, 139 85 G4
Port-Gueydon, Alg., 1,265 160 d5
Port Hammond, Br. Col., Can., 2,000 42 d6
Port Harcourt, Nigeria, 82,379 162 E5
Port Hardy, Br. Col., Can. 42 E4
Port Harrison, Qué., Can. 44 J2
Port Hawkesbury, N.S., Can., 1,315 45 O6
Port Haywood, Va. 62 H5
Porthcawl, U.K., 11,086 113 E6
Port Hedland, Austl. 172 B3
Port Heiden, Alaska 85 E4
Port Henry, N.Y., 1,767 59 N3
Port Herald, Malawi 164 E4
Porthill, Idaho 81 A1
Port Hood, N.S., Can. 45 O6
Port Hope, Ont., Can., 8,015 44 H7
Port Hope, Mich., 349 67 L5
Port Hueneme, Calif., 11,067 82 D5
Port Huron, Mich., 36,084 67 L5
Portia, Br. Col., Can. 42 G4
Portia, Ark., 333 73 D1
Portillo, Chile 105 A4
Portimão, Port., 17,145 122 A4
Portis, Kans., 232 75 G4
Port Isabel, Tex., 3,575 77 P6
Portishead, U.K., 6,538 114 C8
Port Jefferson, N.Y., 4,440 59 O10
Port Jervis, N.Y., 9,268 59 L9
Port Kembla, Austl., 6,570 173 G5
Port Kenny, Austl. 172 a7
Port Kent, N.Y. 59 O2
Port Lambton, Ont., Can. 46 B6
Portland, N.S.W., Austl., 2,558 173 h9
Portland, Vict., Austl., 4,759 172 F6
Portland, Ark., 566 73 D4
Portland, Colo., 73 79 C2
Portland, Conn., 5,587;7,496(T) 56 F6
Portland, Fla. 65 C2
Portland, Ind., 6,999 70 E2
Portland, Me., 72,566 55 B5
Portland, Mich., 3,330 67 H6
Portland, Mo. 72 F6
Portland, N.Y. 58 A7
Portland, N. Dak., 606 74 D2
Portland, Ohio 70 H3
Portland, Oreg., 372,676 80 B3
Portland, Pa., 589 61 M4
Portland, Tenn., 2,424 71 E5
Portland, Tex., 2,538 77 P6
Portland, Wis. 66 C5
Portland, Bill of, pt., U.K. 113 E6
Portland, i., U.K. 113 E6
Portland Bay, Austl. 172 F6
Portland Can., Can.-U.S. 42 D2
Portland Mills, Pa. 60 E3
Portland Pt., Ascension 109 6
Portland Pt., Jam. 96 p9
Portland Promontory, Qué., Can. 44 J2
Portlandville, N.Y. 59 K6
Portlaoighise, Ire., 5,561 113 C5
Port Lavaca, Tex., 8,864 77 P5
Portlaw, Ire. 113 C5
Port Leyden, N.Y., 898 59 K4
Port Lincoln, Austl., 5,871 172 E5
Portlock, Hawaii 84 d8
Port Lockroy, Ant. 180 N6
Port Loko, Sa. Leone 162 B4
Port-Louis, Guad., 2,041 97 14
Port Louis, Maurit., 121,750 165 c12
Port Ludlow, Wash. 80 B2
Port Lyautey = Kénitra
Port McNicoll, Ont., Can., 1,035 46 E4
Port Macquarie, Austl., 4,408 173 H4
Portmadoc, U.K., 3,960 113 D5
Portmahomack, U.K. 112 E3
Port Maitland, N.S., Can. 47 T12
Port Maitland, Ont., Can. 46 E6
Port Mansfield, Tex. 77 P6
Port Margot, Haiti, 1,697 96 k6
Port Maria, Jam., 3,998 96 q8
Port Matilda, Pa., 697 60 F4
Port Mayaca, Fla. 65 J6
Port Menier, Qué., Can. 45 N5
Port Moller, Alaska 85 D4
Port Monmouth, N.J. 58 c15
Port Moody, Br. Col., Can., 4,744 42 c6
Port Morant, Jam., 2,284 96 q9
Port Moresby, Terr. Papua, 28,500 174 e3
Port Morien, N.S., Can. 47 W10
Port Mourant, Guyana 101 M4
Port Mouton, N.S., Can. 47 T12
Port Murray, N.J. 61 B2
Portnahaven, U.K. 112 C4
Port Neches, Tex., 8,696 77 n8
Port Neill, Austl. 172 b8
Port Nelson, Man., Can. 43 G2
Port Nelson, Ont., Can., 1,619 46 c14
Portneuf, Qué., Can., 1,372 47 N2
Port Nolloth, S. Af., 2,592 164 B6
Port Norris, N.J., 1,789 61 B5
Portnyagino, Oz., U.S.S.R. 135 K2
Porto, Port., 303,424 122 A2
Pôrto Alegre, Braz., 617,629 103 F8
Porto Alexandre, Ang. 164 A4
Porto Amboim, Ang. 164 B3
Porto Amélia, Moz., 21,027 164 F4
Portobelo, Pan. 94 H6
Pôrto Calvo, Braz., 3,876 103 b15
Porto Civitanova, It., 24,858 123 D3
Port O'Connor, Tex. 77 P5
Pôrto de Moz, Braz. 103 F2
Pôrto dos Meinacos, Braz. 103 F4
Pôrto Esperidião, Braz. 102 E5
Portoferraio, It., 10,303 123 C3
Port of Ness, U.K. 112 C2
Pôrto Franco, Braz., 1,750 103 G3
Port-of-Spain, Trin. and Tob., 93,954 96 g5
Porto Garibaldi, It. 122 f6
Porto Gouveia, C. Verde Is. 109 5
Pôrto Grande, Braz. 103 F1
Portogruaro, It., 22,020 123 D2
Porto Inglês, C. Verde Is. 109 5
Pôrto-Khéli, Gr. 129 D6
Portola, Calif., 1,874 82 C3
Portomaggiore, It., 24,007 123 C2
Pôrto Murtinho, Braz., 4,476 105 D2
Pôrto Nacional, Braz., 4,926 103 G4
Porto Novo, Dahom., 58,800 162 E4
Porto Novo, India, 15,139 145 m20
Port Orange, Fla., 1,801 65 J3
Port Orchard, Wash., 2,778 80 B2
Port Orford, Oreg., 1,171 80 A4
Pôrto Santo, i., Madeira Is. 109 4
Pôrto Seguro, Braz., 2,697 103 J5
Porto Séguro, Togo 162 d8
Porto Tolle, It., 18,176 122 f6
Porto Torres, It., 11,088 123 B4
Pôrto União, Braz., 9,954 103 F7
Pôrto Valter, Braz. 102 B3
Porto-Vecchio, Fr., 5,601 116 r18
Pôrto Velho, Braz., 19,387 102 D3
Portovenere, It., 5,734 123 B2
Portoviejo, Ec., 31,835 104 A2
Port Patteson, New Hebr. 174 k4
Port Penn, Del. 62 J3
Port Perry, Ont., Can., 2,238 46 F4
Port Phillip Bay, Austl. 173 F6
Port Pirie, Austl., 14,223 172 E5
Port Progress, Br. Col., Can. 42 E3
Port Radium, N.W.T., Can. 40 F4
Port Reading, N.J. 58 b14
Portree, U.K. 112 C3
Port Renfrew, Br. Col., Can. 42 b7
Port Republic, N.J., 561 61 C4
Port Republic, Va. 62 F4
Port Richey, Fla., 1,931 65 G4
Portrillo Mts., N. Mex. 79 B6
Port Robinson, Ont., Can. 58 i18
Port Rowan, Ont., Can. 46 D6
Port Royal, Jam. 96 q9
Port Royal, Pa., 805 60 H4
Port Royal, S.C. 686 63 D5
Port Royal, Va., 128 62 G4
Port Royal B., Berm. Is. 108 1
Port Royal Sd., S.C. 63 D5
Portrush, U.K., 4,263 113 C4
Port Said = Bûr Sa'îd
Port St. Joe, Fla., 4,271 65 D3
Port St. Johns, S. Af., 1,172 164 E7
Port-St-Louis, Fr., 6,278 117 F5
Port St. Mary, U.K., 1,403 113 D4
Port Salerno, Fla. 65 J5
Port Sanilac, Mich., 361 67 L5
Port San Vicente, Phil., 2,329 153 B1
Port Saunders, Newf., Can. 45 P5
Port Seton, U.K., 3,462 112 d8
Port Shepstone, S. Af., 4,238 164 E7
Portskewett, U.K., 1,295 114 C7
Portsmouth, Dominica, 2,243 97 13
Portsmouth, U.K., 215,077 113 F6
Portsmouth, Iowa, 232 72 B3
Portsmouth, N.H., 25,833 54 F5
Portsmouth, Ohio, 33,637 70 F4
Portsmouth, R.I., 10,664(T) 57 M6
Portsmouth, Va., 114,773 62 H6
Portsoy, U.K., 1,690 112 E3
Port Stanley, Ont., Can., 1,481 46 C6
Port Stephens, Falk. Is. 108 3
Portstewart, U.K., 3,950 113 C4
Port Sudan = Bûr Sûdân
Port Sulphur, La., 2,868 73 F8
Port Swettenham, Malay. 147 o15
Port Sydney, Ont., Can. 46 E3
Port Talbot, U.K., 51,322 113 E6
Port Townsend, Wash., 5,074 80 B1
Port Trevorton, Pa. 60 J4
Portugal, ctry., 9,255,000* 122
Portugal Cove, Newf., Can., 1,141 45 c10
Portugal Cove South, Newf., Can. 45 b11
Portugalete, Sp., 22,584 122 m11
Portugália, Ang. 164 C3
Portuguesa, r., Ven. 100 F3
Portuguese Guinea, 527,000* 162 B3
Portuguese Timor, overseas terr., 554,000* 149 H5
Portumna, Ire. 113 B5
Port-Vendres, Fr., 5,085 117 E5
Port Victoria, Austl. 172 b8
Port Victoria, Kenya 165 g13
Portville, N.Y., 1,336 58 D7
Port Vue, Pa., 6,535 60 c8
Port Wakefield, Austl. 172 b8
Port Washington, N.Y., 15,657 59 N10
Port Washington, Ohio, 526 70 H2
Port Washington, Wis., 5,984 66 F5
Port Weld, Malay., 2,260 147 o14
Port Weller, Ont., Can. 46 d15
Port Wentworth, Ga., 3,705 64 H3
Port William, Ohio, 360 70 F3
Port Wing, Wis. 66 B2
Porum, Okla., 573 76 H2
Porus, Jam., 2,723 96 p8
Porvenir, Bol., 1,008 102 C4
Porvenir, Chile, 1,956 105 B8
Porvenir, Guat. 94 B3
Porvenir, Pan. 94 H6
Porvenir, Urug. 105 b11
Porvoo = Borgå
Porz, F.R.Ger., 39,647 118 A3
Porzuna, Sp., 8 189 122 C3
Posadas, Arg., 73,071 105 D3
Poschiavo, Switz., 3,743 124 E2
Poseh = Pai-se
Posen, Ill., 4,517 69 d10
Posen, Mich., 341 67 K3
Posevnaya, U.S.S.R. 137 q11
Posey, co., Ind., 19,214 70 B4
Poseyville, Ind. 997 70 B4
Poseyville, Mich. 67 J5
Po-shan = Tzu-po
Poshekhon'ye-Volodarsk, U.S.S.R., 8,200 136 E1
Posieux, Switz. 124 B2
Posio, Fin. 120 F2
Positano, It., 2,760 123 d10
Poskin, Wis. 66 B3
Poso, Indon. 149 G3
Poso, Danau, Indon. 149 G3
Posŏng, S. Kor. 19,577 151 E4
Pospelikha, U.S.S.R. 137 q12
Posse, Braz., 1,953 103 G4
Possession, Wash. 81 b7
Possession I., Ind. Oc. 168 B4
Possession, Pt., Alaska 85 c7
Pössneck, Ger.D.R., 19,565 118 C3
Possum Kingdom L., Tex. 77 O3
Post, Oreg. 80 C3
Post, Tex., 4,663 77 N3
Post Arinda, Guyana 101 L5
Postavy, U.S.S.R., 10,500 136 B2
Poste, R. du, Qué., Can. 47 L2
Poste Deshayes, Camb. 146 D4
Postell, N.C. 63 a7
Post Falls, Idaho, 1,983 81 A2
Postmasburg, S. Af., 4,701 164 C6
Post Mills, Vt. 54 C4
Postojna, Yug., 4,081 125 B2
Postoloprty, Czech. 126 c6
Poston, Ariz. 78 A5
Poston, S.C. 63 E4
Postville, Iowa, 1,554 72 F1
Pos'yet, U.S.S.R. 151 F2
Potagannissing Bay, Mich. 67 K2
Potam, Mex., 2,656 92 C2
Potamoi, Gr. 129 E4
Potaro, r., Guyana 101 L5
Potash, La. 73 F8
Potato Creek, S. Dak. 74 A4
Potato Cr., Pa. 60 F2
Potchefstroom, S. Af., 41,701 164 D6
Poteau, Okla., 4 428 76 J2
Poteau, r., Ark.-Okla. 76 J3
Potecasi, N.C. 63 G1
Poteet, Tex., 2,811 77 O5
Potekhino, U.S.S.R. 135 M4
Potelu, L., Rum. 128 E3
Potenza, It., 39,654 123 E4
Poteriteri, L., N.Z. 175 e7
Potes, Sp., 1,364 122 C1
Potgietersrus, S. Af., 11,433 164 D6
Poth, Tex., 1,119 77 O5
Potherie, L. la, Qué., Can. 44 K2
Potholes Res., Wash. 80 D2
Poti, U.S.S.R., 43,000 134 D5
Potiskum, Nigeria 162 F4
Potlatch, Idaho, 800 81 A2
Potlatch, Wash. 80 B2
Potlogi, Rum. 128 E2
Potomac, Ill., 661 68 E3
Potomac, r., Md.-Va. 62 H4
Potonico, El Salv., 1,054 94 e10
Potosí, Bol., 53,527 102 C5
Potosi, Mo., 2,805 72 G7
Potosi, Wis., 585 66 C6
Potosí, Co., Mex. 93 E3
Pototan, Phil., 5 475 153 B3
Potrerillos, Chile, 6,168 105 A3
Potrerillos, Hond., 2,132 94 C3
Potrerillos, Mex., 1,002 93 e8
Potsdam, Ger.D.R., 115,004 118 D2
Potsdam, N.Y., 7,765 59 L2
Potštejn, Czech. 127 f6
Pott, I., N. Caled. 174 h7
Pottawatomie, co., Kans., 11,957 75 J4
Pottawatomie, co., Okla., 41,486 76 G2
Pottawattamie, co., Iowa, 83,102 72 B3
Pottawattamie Hills, Ill. 69 d10
Pottawattamie Park, Ind., 292 69 g10
Pottenbrunn, Aust., 1,798 124 b10
Pottendorf, Aust., 2,943 124 c11
Pottenstein, Aust., 2,491 124 M6
Potter, Alaska 85 c7
Potter, Kans. 75 K4
Potter, Nebr., 554 75 B2
Potter, N.Y. 58 F6
Potter, co., Pa., 16,483 60 G2
Potter, co., S. Dak., 4,926 74 B3
Potter, co., Tex., 115,580 76 M2
Potter, Wis. 66 E4
Potter Hill (part of Westerly), R.I. 57 J7
Potter Mtn., Oreg. 80 B4
Potterne, U.K., 1,218 114 E8
Potters Bar, U.K., 23,376 114 H7
Potter's Flowage, Wis. 66 C4
Potterspury, U.K. 114 G6
Pottersville (part of Somerset), Mass. 57 M5
Pottersville, Mo. 72 F8
Pottersville, N.Y. 59 N4
Potterville, Ga. 64 E3
Potterville, Mich., 1,028 67 J6
Potterville (part of Coventry), R.I. 57 K6
Pöttmes, F.R.Ger., 2,355 118 C4
Potton, U.K., 2,070 114 H6
Potts, Nev. 83 B3
Pottsboro, Tex., 640 77 P3
Potts Camp, Miss., 429 73 F3
Pottstown, Pa., 26,144 61 L5
Pottsville, Pa., 21,659 61 K4
Pottuvil, Cey. 145 n22
Potwin, Kans., 635 75 J6
P'o-tzu, Taiwan, 34,972 152 F3
Pouancé, Fr., 3,244 117 C3
Pouaréti, C., N. Caled. 174 k9
Pouce Coupé, Br. Col., Can. 42 H2
Pouch Cove, Newf., Can., 1,324 45 c10
Pouébo, N. Caled., 1,294 174 i8
Pouembout, N. Caled. 174 i8
Poughkeepsie, N.Y., 38,330 59 N8
Poughquag, N.Y. 59 N8
Pouillon, Fr., 2,502 117 C5
Poulan, Ga., 736 64 F4
Poulo Condore = Con Son
Poulo Obi, I. = Khoai, Hon
Poulsbo, Wash., 1,505 80 B2
Poultney, Vt., 1,810 54 A4
Poultney, r., N.Y.-Vt. 54 A4
Poulton-le-Fylde, U.K., 12,767 114 B3
Poume, N. Caled. 174 i8
Pound, Va., 1,135 62 B5
Pound, Wis., 273 66 F3
Pourtalé, Arg., 1,482* 105 a13
Pouso Alegre, Braz., 18,852 103 d18
Pouss, Cam. 164 G4
Poutasi, W. Samoa 177 38
Pouzauges, Fr., 4,239 117 C3
Považská Bystrica, Czech., 12,658 126 D2
Poverty Bay, N.Z. 175 h5
Povoação Velha, C. Verde Is. 109 5
Póvoa de Varzim, Port., 17,696 122 A2
Povorino, U.S.S.R., 20,000 136 F3
Povungnituk, Qué., Can. 44 J1
Povungnituk, r., Qué., Can. 44 J1
Powassan, Ont., Can., 1,043 44 H6
Poway, Calif., 1,921 82 E6
Powder, r., Mont.-Wyo. 81 G3
Powder, r., Oreg. 80 E3
Powder River, co., Mont., 2,485 81 G3
Powder Springs, Ga., 746 64 f9
Powderville, Mont. 81 G3
Powder Wash, Colo. 79 A1
Powell, co., Ky., 6,674 71 H4
Powell, co., Mont., 7,002 81 C2
Powell, Nebr. 75 H3
Powell, Pa. 60 J2
Powell, Tex. 76 g10
Powell, Wis. 66 D2
Powell, Wyo., 4,740 81 E3
Powell, L., Utah 78 C3
Powell, r., Tenn.-Va. 71 H5
Powell Butte, Oreg. 80 C3
Powell Creek, Austl. 172 D2
Powell L., Br. Col., Can. 42 b5
Powell River, Br. Col., Can., 5,700 42 F4
Powellsville, N.C., 259 63 H1
Powellton, W. Va., 1,256 62 C4
Powellville, Md. 62 J4
Power, co., Idaho, 4,111 81 C4
Powers, Mich., 383 66 F3
Powers, Oreg., 1,366 80 A4
Powers Lake, N. Dak., 633 74 A1
Powers Lake, Wis. 66 c13
Powers L., Minn. 74 d6
Powersville, Mo., 189 72 D4
Powerville, N.J. 58 b13
Poweshiek, co., Iowa, 19,300 72 E3
Powhatan, Ala. 64 b7
Powhatan, Ark., 136 73 D1
Powhatan, La. 73 B6
Powhatan, co., Va., 6,747 62 F5
Powhatan, Va. 62 F5
Powhatan Point, Ohio, 2,147 70 J3
Powhattan, Kans., 128 75 K4
Powick, U.K., 2,888 114 D6
Powley Place, N.Y. 59 L5
Pownal, Me. 55 B5
Pownal, Vt. 54 A6
Poxoreu, Braz., 3,315 103 F5
Poya, N. Caled., 1,066 174 i8
P'o-yang, China 150 F4
P'o-yang Hu, China 150 F4
Poyen, Ark., 312 73 C3
Poygan, L., Wis. 66 E4
Poynette, Wis., 1,090 66 D5
Poynton, U.K., 5,393 114 D4
Poysbrunn, Aust. 124 N5
Poysdorf, Aust., 2,740 124 N5
Poy Sippi, Wis. 66 E4
Poza de la Sal, Sp., 1039 122 m12
Pozantı, Turk., 2,473 142 C2
Požarevac, Yug., 24,000* 125 E2
Poza Rica, Mex., 19,175 93 F4
Požega, Yug., 2,710 125 E3
Poznań, Pol., 408,000* 127 B2
Pozo Almonte, Chile, 1,174 105 A2
Pozoblanco, Sp., 16,020 122 C3
Pozo del Tigre, Arg., 2,600* 105 C2
Pozos, Mex. 93 d8
Pozzolo Formigaro, It., 4,148 122 b6
Pozzuoli, It., 49,663 123 c10
Pra, r., Ghana 162 c9
Pra, r., U.S.S.R. 136 d6
Prabuty, Pol., 5,229 127 C2
Prachantakham, Thai. 147 d4
Prachatice, Czech., 5,228 126 A2
Prachin Buri, Thai., 13,420 146 C4
Prachuap Khiri Khan, Thai., 6,228 146 C5
Praděd, pk., Czech. 127 g6
Pradera, Col. 100 B6
Prades, Fr., 6,035 117 E5
Pradjekan, Indon. 148 f7
Prądła, Pol. 127 i6
Prądnik, r., Pol. 127 i6
Prado, Braz., 2,200 103 J5
Pradoluengo, Sp., 2,090 122 D1
Præstø, Den., 1,528 121 E5
Praga, r., Indon. 148 d7
Prague, Czech. = Praha
Prague, Nebr., 372 75 J2
Prague, Okla., 1,545 76 G2
Praha, Czech., 1,003,341 126 B1
Prahova, r., Rum. 128 E2
Praia, C. Verde Is., 13,142 109 5
Praia da Vitoria, Azores, 7,265 108 2
Prairie, Austl. 173 F3
Prairie, co., Ark., 10,515 73 D3
Prairie, Miss., 112 73 G4
Prairie, co., Mont., 2,318 81 G2
Prairie, Wash. 80 B1
Prairieburg, Iowa, 226 72 F2
Prairie City, Ill., 613 68 B3
Prairie City, Iowa, 943 72 D3
Prairie City, Oreg., 801 80 D3
Prairie City, S. Dak. 74 A3
Prairie Creek, Ind. 70 B3
Prairie Dog Cr., Kans. 75 E4
Prairie du Chien, Wis., 5,649 66 B5
Prairie du Rocher, Ill., 679 68 B5
Prairie du Sac, Wis., 1,676 66 D5
Prairie Farm, Wis. 350 66 B3
Prairie Grove, Man., Can. 43 h10
Prairie Grove, Ark., 1,056 73 A2
Prairie Hill, Okla. 76 D3
Prairie Home, Mo., 213 72 E6
Prairie L., Wis. 66 B3
Prairie Lea, Tex. 76 c6
Prairies, R. des, Qué., Can. 47 o17
Prairieton, Ind. 70 B3
Prairie View, Ill. 69 c8
Prairie View, Kans., 188 75 F4
Prairie View, Tex., 2,326 77 Q4
Prairie Village, Kans., 25,356 75 a8
Prairieville, Mich. 67 H6
Prairieville, Tex. 76 g10
Prakhon Chai, Thai. 146 C4
Pralboino, It., 3,153 122 d5
Pralormo, It., 1,114 122 a6
Prámanda, Gr. 129 C5
Prameny, Czech. 126 b6
Prampram, Ghana 162 d9
Pran Buri, Thai. 146 B4
Prangins, Switz., 1,123 124 A2
Prapat, Indon. 148 A2
Praslin I., Seych. 165 a10
Praszka, Pol., 2,657 127 C3
Prata, Braz., 4,725 103 G5
Pratas I. = Tung-sha Tao
Prathai, Thai. 147 e4
Prato, It., 102,323 123 C3
Pratola Peligna, It., 10,714 123 D3
Prats-de-Mollo-la-Preste, Fr. 117 E5
Pratt, Man., Can. 43 e10
Pratt, co., Kans., 12,122 75 G6
Pratt, Kans., 8,156 75 G6
Pratt, Mo. 72 G8
Pratteln, Switz., 9,492 124 B1
Prattsburg, N.Y., 690 58 F6
Prattsville, N.Y. 59 L7
Prattsville, Ohio 70 G3
Prattville, Ala., 6,616 64 C3
Prattville (part of Raynham), Mass. 57 M5
Prattville, Mich. 67 J7
Pravdinsk, U.S.S.R., 17,600 136 F1
Pravdinskiy, U.S.S.R. 136 b5
Pravia, Sp., 11,421 122 B1
Prawle Pt., U.K. 113 E6
Preble, N.Y. 59 H6
Preble, co., Ohio, 32,498 70 E3
Prechistoye, U.S.S.R. 136 a6
Precinct (part of Lakeville), Mass. 57 N5
Predeal, Rum., 5,121 128 E2
Predejane, Yug. 125 E3
Predivinsk, U.S.S.R., 2,800 135 J4
Predolje, Yug. 125 D3
Predosa, It., 2,826 122 b6
Preeceville, Sask., Can. 43 D4
Pré-en-Pail, Fr., 2,211 117 C2
Prees, U.K., 2,128 114 C5
Preesall, U.K., 2,356 114 C3
Preetz, F.R.Ger., 12,156 118 C1
Pregnall, S.C. 63 D4
Pregonero, Ven., 2,867 100 E3
Preguica, C. Verde Is. 109 5
Prek Kak, Camb. 147 k10
Preko, Yug., 2,399 125 B2
Preksandek, Camb. 147 k11
Prek Trameak, Camb. 147 k11
Prelate, Sask., Can. 43 B5
Přelouč, Czech. 127 e6
Premćani, Yug. 125 D3
Prémery, Fr., 2,815 117 E3
Premier, Br. Col., Can. 42 D2
Premio, Qué., Can. 45 N4
Premnitz, Ger.D.R. 118 D2
Premont, Tex., 3,049 77 O6
Premuda, i., Yug. 125 B2
Prenter, W. Va. 62 C4
Prentice, Wis., 427 66 C3
Prentiss, Me. 55 D3
Prentiss, co., Miss., 17,949 73 G3
Prentiss, Miss., 1,321 73 F6
Prenzlau, Ger.D.R., 19,737 118 D2
Preobrazhenka, U.S.S.R. 135 K3
Preparis I., Burma 146 A4
Preparis North Chan., Burma 146 A4
Preparis South Chan., Burma 146 A4
Přerov, Czech., 31,015 126 C2
Presa El Palmito, Mex., 1,200* 92 D3

Pusei—Raman · 281

Pusei, New Hebr. **174** k5
Pushaw L., Me. **55** D4
Pushkin, U.S.S.R., 51,000 **134** C4
Pushkino, U.S.S.R., 32,200 **136** b5
Pushmataha, Ala. **64** A3
Pushmataha, co., Okla., 9,088 **76** H3
Pusing, Malay., 6,937 **148** B1
Puslinch, Ont., Can. **46** b14
Püspökladány, Hung., 15,735 **126** E3
Pustoshka, U.S.S.R., 3,300 **136** C1
Pustunich, Mex. **93** H4
Puszczykowo, Pol., 6,399 **127** B2
Putaendo, Chile, 3,997 **104** g12
Putahow L., Man., Can. **43** E2
Pu-tai, Taiwan, 42,631 **152** F3
Putao, Burma **146** B1
Putaruru, N.Z., 3,551 **175** g5
Putbus, Ger.D.R. **118** D1
Pu-t'e-ha-ch'i, China **150** G2
Puţeni, Rum. **128** F2
P'u-t'ien, China **150** F4
Putignano, It., 19,890 **123** F4
Putina, Peru, 3,157 **104** D5
Put-in-Bay, Ohio, 357 **70** G1
P'u-ting, China **152** B2
Puting, Tg., Indon. **148** D3
Putingkahoy, Phil., 2,016 **153** c9
Putivl', U.S.S.R., 9,100 **136** D3
Putla, Mex., 3,458 **93** F5
Putlitz, Ger.D.R. **118** D2
Putna, Rum. **128** E1
Putna, r., Rum. **128** F2
Putnam, Ala. **64** A3
Putnam, Conn., 6,952;8,412(T) **56** J5
Putnam, co., Fla., 32,212 **65** H3
Putnam, co., Ga., 7,798 **64** F2
Putnam, co., Ill., 4,570 **68** C2
Putnam, co., Ind., 24,927 **70** C3
Putnam, co., Mo., 6,999 **72** D4
Putnam, co., N.Y., 31,722 **59** N9
Putnam, co., Ohio, 28,331 **70** E1
Putnam, Okla., 83 **76** E2
Putnam, co., Tenn., 29,236 **71** F5
Putnam, Tex., 203 **77** O3
Putnam, co., W. Va., 23,561 **62** C4
Putnamville, Ind. **70** C3
Putnamville, Vt. **54** B3
Putney, Ky. **71** H5
Putney, S. Dak. **74** C3
Putney, Vt. **54** B6
Putnok, Hung., 6,470 **126** E2
P'u-t'o, China **152** F1
Putorana, Gory, U.S.S.R. **135** J3
Putre, Chile **105** B1
Pütscheid, Lux. **119** A5
Puttalam, Cey., 10,237 **145** F8
Putte, Belg., 6,634 **115** e8
Puttelange, Fr., 2,013 **117** G2
Putten, Neth., 6,000 **115** D2
Putten, i., Neth. **115** C3
Püttlingen, F.R.Ger., 14,284 **116** c8
Puttur, India, 12,498 **145** E7
Putú, Chile **104** e15
P'u-tu, r., China **152** A2
Putumayo, Ec. **104** C1
Putumayo, r., S. Amer. **100** E9
Putuputua, i., Tonga **177** 36
Putussibau, Indon. **148** E2
Pütz, F.R.Ger., 3,897 **119** B3
Pu-tzu-hsü, China **152** b6
Puuanahulu, Hawaii **84** F4
Puu Hapapa, pk., Hawaii **84** b7
Puuiki, Hawaii **84** F3
Puu Kaaumakua, pk., Hawaii **84** c6
Puu Kamana, pk., Hawaii **84** c7
Puu Kaua, pk., Hawaii **84** b7
Puu Keaau, pk., Hawaii **84** a7
Puu Ki, pk., Hawaii **84** c5
Puukolii, Hawaii, 418 **84** E3
Puu Konahuanui, pk., Hawaii **84** d7
Puu Lanipo, pk., Hawaii **84** d8
Puulavesi, l., Fin. **120** F3
Puu Mailiilii, pk., Hawaii **84** a7
Puu Makakilo, pk., Hawaii **84** b7
Puumala, Fin. **120** G3
Puu Manawahua, pk., Hawaii **84** b7
Puunene, Hawaii, 3,054 **84** E3
Puu Palailai, pk., Hawaii **84** b7
Puu Pueo, pk., Hawaii **84** a6
Puurs, Belg., 6,412 **115** d8
Puu Waawaa, pk., Hawaii **84** F4
Puuwai, Hawaii **84** A2
Puxico, Mo., 743 **72** G8
Puyallup, Wash., 12,063 **80** B2
Puyallup, r., Wash. **80** C2
P'u-yang, China **151** B4
P'u-yang, r., China **152** F1
Puyehue, L., Chile **105** e15
Puylaurens, Fr., 3,083 **117** D5
Puy-l'Évêque, Fr., 2,349 **117** D4
Puyo, Ec., 2,248 **104** B2
Puysegur Pt., N.Z. **175** e7
Pwela, Burma **147** g7
Pweto, D.R.Congo **164** D3
Pwllheli, U.K., 3,647 **113** D5
P'yagina, P-ov., U.S.S.R. **135** P4
Pyakupur, r., U.S.S.R. **134** G3
Pyamalaw, r., Burma **147** a2
P'yana, r., U.S.S.R. **136** G2
Pyandzh, r., Afghan.-U.S.S.R. **134** F6
Pyanteg, U.S.S.R. **137** h6
Pyaozero, Oz., U.S.S.R. **134** B3
Pyapon, Burma, 19,174 **146** A3
Pyasina, r., U.S.S.R. **135** J2
Pyasino, Oz., U.S.S.R. **135** H2
Pyatigorsk, U.S.S.R., 73,000 **136** F4
Pyatikhatki, U.S.S.R., 21,400 **136** D3
Pyatt, Ark., 144 **73** C1
Pyawbwe, Burma, 9,502 **146** B2
Pyhäjärvi, Fin. **120** F3
Pyhäjärvi, l., Fin. **120** E3
Pyhäjärvi, l., Fin. **120** F3
Pyhäjoki, Fin. **120** F2
Pyhäjoki, r., Fin. **120** F2
Pyhäntä, Fin. **120** F2
Pyhätunturin Kansallispuisto, Fin. **120** F2
Pyhra, Aust. **124** c9
Pyinbongyi, Burma, 2,880 **147** b2
Pyingaing, Burma **146** A2
Pyinkayaing, Burma **147** a3
Pyinmadow, Burma **147** b2
Pyinmana, Burma, 22,066 **146** B3
Pymatuning Res., Ohio-Pa. **60** B2
Pyŏktong, N. Kor. **151** E2
P'yŏnggang, N. Kor. **151** E3
Pyŏnggok, S. Kor. **151** F3
P'yŏnghae, S. Kor., 20,173 **151** F3
P'yŏngsan, N. Kor. **151** E3
P'yŏngt'aek, S. Kor., 25,163 **151** E3
P'yŏngyang, N. Kor., 940,000* **151** E3
Pyŏrha-ri, N. Kor. **151** E2
Pyote, Tex., 420 **77** M4
Pyramid, Nev. **83** A2
Pyramid Corner, Okla. **76** H1
Pyramides, Pte. des, Is. de Horne **175** 9
Pyramid I., N.Z. **175** 14
Pyramid L., Nev. **83** A2
Pyramid Mts., N. Mex. **79** A5
Pyramul, Austl. **173** g9
Pyrenees, mts., Fr.-Sp. **117** C5
Pyrzyce, Pol., 5,083 **127** A2
Pyshma, r., U.S.S.R. **137** k8
Pyskowice, Pol., 21,000* **127** h6
Pytalovo, U.S.S.R., 3,600 **136** C1
Pythonga, L., Qué., Can. **47** H2
Pyu, Burma, 10,443 **146** B3
Pyuntaza, Burma, 9,170 **147** b2
Pyzdry, Pol., 3,310 **127** B2

Q

Qabb Ilyās, Leb., 3,489 **142** b6
Qābis, Tun., 24,420 **161** F2
Qābis, Khalīj, Tun. **161** F2
Qafarah, Saudi Ar. **143** D4
Qafşah, Tun., 24,345 **161** F2
Qa'fūr, Tun., 6,583 **160** f5
Qahferokh, Iran, 8,829 **143** E2
Qala'an Naḩl, Sudan, 3,083 **163** K3
Qala Nau, Afghan. **144** B2
Qala Panja, Afghan. **145** D1
Qala Panja, U.S.S.R. **137** g5
Qala Shahārak, Afghan. **144** B2
Qal'at Bīshah, Saudi Ar. **143** C4
Qallābāt, Sudan **163** K3
Qalqīlyah, Jor., 11,402 **142** b7
Qalyūb, U.A.R. **161** i7
Qamar, Ghubbat al, bay, S. Ar. **143** E5
Qamīnis, Libya **161** H2
Qanţarah, Jabal, U.A.R. **161** h8
Qanţarat al Fahş, Tun., 3,121 **160** g5
Qareh Sū, r., Iran **143** D1
Qarqannah, Juzur, is., Tun. **160** g6
Qarţājannah, Tun., 8,232 **160** g5
Qārūn, Birkat, U.A.R. **161** i8
Qaşr al Azraq, ruins, Jor. **142** D4
Qaşr al Mushattā, ruins, Jor. **142** c8
Qaşr Banī Walīd, Libya **161** G2
Qaşr-e Shīrīn, Iran, 23,901 **143** D2
Qaşr Hallāl, Tun., 12,224 **160** g6
Qaţanā, Syr., 7,715 **142** c6
Qatar, ctry., 71,000* **143** E3
Qaţrānī, Jabal, U.A.R. **161** i8
Qattara Depression = Qaţţārah, Munkhafaḑ al
Qaţţārah, Munkhafaḑ al, U.A.R. **161** J3
Qawām al Ḩamzah, Iraq, 8,463 **143** D2
Qawz Rajab, Sudan **163** K3
Qāyen, Iran, 4,414 **143** F2
Qazvīn, Iran, 66,420 **143** D1
Qena = Qinā
Qeshm, Iran, 2,356 **143** F3
Qeys, i., Iran **143** E3
Qezel Owzan, r., Iran **143** D1
Qift, U.A.R. **161** K3
Qila Lādgasht, Pak. **144** B4
Qila Saifullāh, Pak. **144** C3
Qinā, U.A.R., 58,000 **161** K3
Qiryat Gat, Isr., 10,111 **142** a8
Qiryat Shemona, Isr., 11,796 **142** b6
Qiryat Yam, Isr., 10,311 **142** a7
Qishon, r., Isr. **142** b7
Qīzān, Saudi Ar., 5,000* **143** C5
Qom, Iran, 96,499 **143** E2
Qormi, Malta, 14,869 **123** f12
Qorveh, Iran, 2,029 **143** D1
Quabbin Dike, Mass. **56** G3
Quabbin Res., Mass. **56** G3
Quaboag, r., Mass. **56** G3
Quaboag Pd., Mass. **56** H4
Quaddick Res., Conn. **57** J5
Quail, Tex. **76** N2
Quainton, U.K. **114** G7
Quairading, Austl. **172** B4
Quakenbrück, F.R.Ger., 8,096 **118** A2
Quaker City, Ohio, 583 **70** H3
Quaker Hill, Conn., 1,671 **56** H7
Quaker Hill, N.Y. **59** O8
Quaker Ridge (part of Greenwich), Conn. **56** B8
Quaker Springs, N.Y. **59** w27
Quakertown, Mich., 482 **67** e15
Quakertown, Pa., 6,305 **61** M5
Qualicum Beach, Br. Col., Can. **42** F4
Quality, Ky. **71** E4
Quamba, Minn., 95 **74** F3
Quambatook, Austl. **173** d10
Quamby, Austl. **172** E3
Quanah, Tex., 4,564 **77** O2
Quandialla, Austl. **173** g10
Quang Dien, S. Viet., 10,212 **146** D3
Quang Ngai, S. Viet., 10,064 **146** E4
Quang Tri, S. Viet., 11,818 **146** D3
Quang Xuyen, S. Viet. **147** m11
Quang Yen, N. Viet. **147** i9
Quanicassee, Mich. **67** K5
Quan Long, S. Viet., 17,977 **146** D5
Quantico, Md. **62** J4
Quantico, Va., 1,015 **62** G4
Quapaw, Okla., 850 **76** J1
Qu'Appelle, Sask., Can. **43** D5
Qu'Appelle, r., Sask., Can. **43** D5
Quaraí, Braz., 10,575 **103** E8
Quaregnon, Belg., 18,846 **115** B4
Quarry Heights, N.Y. **58** e12
Quarryville, N.B., Can. **47** S10
Quarryville, Pa., 1,427 **61** K6
Quartu Sant'Elena, It., 22,532 **123** B5
Quartz Mountain, Nev. **83** A3
Quartz Mtn., Oreg. **80** B4
Quartz Mtn., Wash. **80** C2
Quartz Mtn. Pass, Oreg. **80** C4
Quartzsite, Ariz. **78** A5
Quasqueton, Iowa, 373 **72** F2
Quassapaug L., Conn. **56** D6
Quatis, Braz., 1,719 **103** d18
Quatre, I., Gren. Is. **97** 20
Quatre Bornes, Maurit. **165** c12
Quay, co., N. Mex., 12,279 **79** D4
Quay, N. Mex. **79** D4
Quay, Okla., 51 **76** G1
Qūchān, Iran, 21,250 **143** F1
Quealy, Wyo., 42 **81** E5
Queanbeyan, Austl., 7,310 **173** G5
Québec, prov., Can., 5,657,000* **44** K4
Québec, Qué., Can., 167,600 **45** L6
Québec-Ouest, Qué., Can., 8,681 **47** n16
Quebracho, Urug. **105** c10
Quebradillas, P.R., 2,131 **96** r10
Quebrangulo, Braz., 4,227 **103** a15
Quecedo, Sp. **122** m12
Quechee, Vt. **54** C4
Quedgeley, U.K., 1,121 **114** D7
Quedlinburg, Ger.D.R., 30,965 **118** C3
Queen Anne, Md., 283 **62** H4
Queen Annes, co., Md., 16,569 **62** H3
Queen Bess, Mt., Br. Col., Can. **42** F3
Queen Charlotte, Br. Col., Can. **42** D3
Queen Charlotte B., Falk. Is. **108** 3
Queen Charlotte Is., Br. Col., Can. **42** D3
Queen Charlotte Sd., Br. Col., Can. **42** D3
Queen Charlotte Str., Br. Col., Can. **42** E3
Queen City, Mo., 599 **72** E4
Queen City, Tex., 1,081 **77** R3
Queen Creek, Ariz. **78** C5
Queen Elizabeth Is., N.W.T., Can. **41** K1
Queen Elizabeth Nat. Pk., Uganda **164** E2
Queen Mary Coast, Ant. **180** T6
Queen Maud G., N.W.T., Can. **40** J4
Queen Maud Land, Ant. **180** R5
Queen Maud Ra., Ant. **180** W4
Queens, co., N.Y., 1,809,578 **59** N10
Queensborough, Ont., Can. **46** G4
Queensbury, U.K., 9,268 **114** E3
Queens Chan., Austl. **172** D2
Queens Chan., N.W.T., Can. **41** K2
Queenscliffe, Austl., 2,551 **173** e12
Queensferry, U.K., 2,929 **112** d8
Queensland, st., Austl., 1,661,240 **173** F3
Queenston, Ont., Can. **46** d15
Queenstown, Austl., 3,458 **173** F6
Queenstown, N.Z., 1,321 **175** f7
Queenstown, S. Af., 33,126 **164** D7
Queensville, Ont., Can. **46** E4
Queets, Wash. **80** A2
Queets, r., Wash. **80** B2
Queguay Grande, r., Urug. **105** c11
Quehanna, Pa. **60** F3
Queich, r., F.R.Ger. **119** E6
Queilén, Chile **105** A6
Queimadas, Braz., 3,553 **103** H4
Quela, Ang. **164** B3
Quelimane, Moz., 64,183 **164** F4
Quellón, Chile **104** e16
Quelpart = Cheju-do
Queluz, Port., 15,746 **122** i10
Quemado, N. Mex. **79** A4
Quemado, Tex. **77** N5
Quemado de Güines, Cuba, 4,840 **96** c1
Quemoy I. = Chin-men Tao
Queniquea, Ven., 1,140 **100** E4
Quentins-Corners, Ill. **69** b8
Que Que, Rhod., 11,600 **164** D5
Quequén, Arg., 4,000* **105** D5
Querendaro, Mex., 5,884 **93** d10
Querétaro, st., Mex., 355,045 **93** F4
Querétaro, Baja Calif. S., Mex. **92** B3
Querétaro, Qro., Mex., 67,277 **93** E4
Querfurt, Ger.D.R. **118** C3
Quesada, Sp., 10,997 **122** D4
Quesnel, Br. Col., Can., 4,701 **42** G3
Quesnel L., Br. Col., Can. **42** G3
Que Son, S. Viet. **146** E4
Questa, N. Mex. **79** C3
Quetame, Col. **101** f15
Quetta, Pak., 106,633 **144** C3
Quetzalapa, Mex. **93** f9
Quevedo, Ec., 19,789 **104** B2
Quezaltenango, Guat., 37,722 **94** B3
Quezaltepeque, El Salv., 8,471 **94** d10
Quezaltepeque, Guat., 2,051 **94** d9
Quezon, Phil., 3,402 **153** B2
Quezon, Phil., 11,082 **153** B3
Quezon, Phil., 2,500 **153** c5
Quezon City, Phil., 397,990 **153** B2
Quiaios, Port., 5,785 **122** A2
Quibala, Ang. **164** B3
Quibaxi, Ang. **164** B3
Quibdó, Col. **100** B5
Quiberon, Fr., 4,540 **116** B3
Quíbor, Ven., 5,772 **100** F3
Qui Chau, N. Viet. **146** D3
Quiché, Guat., 5,793 **94** B3
Quick, Br. Col., Can. **42** E2
Quickborn, F.R.Ger., 8,452 **118** B2
Quiculungo, Ang. **164** B3
Quidnet (part of Nantucket), Mass. **57** R7
Quiebra Hacha, Cuba, 1,584 **96** b1
Quiévrain, Belg., 5,771 **115** B4
Quigley, Alta., Can. **42** L2
Quijotoa, Ariz. **78** B5
Quila, Mex., 1,200* **92** D3
Quilalí, Nic. **94** E4
Quilán, C., Chile **105** A6
Quilcene, Wash. **80** B2
Quilengues, Ang. **164** B4
Quilino, Arg., 3,870 **105** C4
Quillacollo, Bol., 16,017 **102** b10
Quillan, Fr., 4,768 **117** E5
Quilleco, Chile, 1,005 **104** f17
Quill Lakes, Sask., Can. **43** D4
Quillón, Chile, 1,569 **104** e16
Quillota, Chile, 29,447 **104** f12
Quilmaná, Peru, 1,915 **104** B5
Quilmes, Arg. **105** b12
Quilon, India, 91,018 **145** E8
Quilpie, Austl. **173** F4
Quilpolemo, Chile **104** e16
Quilpué, Chile, 26,588 **104** f13
Quimari, Alto de, mtn., Col. **100** B3
Quimbaya, Col. **101** d15
Quimbele, Ang. **164** B3
Quimby, Iowa, 369 **72** B2
Quimby, Me. **55** D2
Quime, Bol., 2,398 **102** b10
Quimiac, Ec. **104** c10
Quimichis, Mex., 3,981 **92** D3
Quimilí, Arg., 6,050* **105** C3
Quimistán, Hond. **94** C3
Quimper, Fr., 50,670 **116** A2
Quimperlé, Fr., 11,163 **116** B3
Qui My, N. Viet. **147** h9
Quinalasag I., Phil. **153** h14
Quinault, Wash. **80** B2
Quinault, r., Wash. **80** A2
Quincemil, Peru **104** D5
Quinchía, Col. **101** d14
Quincieux, Fr., 1,246 **116** p15
Quincoces, Sp. **122** m12
Quincy, Calif. **82** C3
Quincy, Fla., 8,874 **65** E2
Quincy, Ill., 43,793 **68** A4
Quincy, Ind. **70** C3
Quincy, Ky. **71** H3
Quincy, Mass., 87,409 **57** N3
Quincy, Mich., 1,602 **67** J7
Quincy, Ohio, 668 **70** F2
Quincy, Oreg. **80** B2
Quincy, Wash., 3,269 **80** D2
Quincy-sous-Sénart, Fr., 2,723 **116** i12
Quincy-Voisins, Fr., 1,385 **116** k11
Quindío, Nev. del, Col. **101** d15
Quinebaug (part of Thompson), Conn. **56** H4
Quinebaug, r., Conn.-Mass. **56** J4
Quines, Arg., 7,000* **105** B4
Quinhagak, Alaska **85** D4
Qui Nhon, S. Viet., 32,027 **146** E4
Quinindé, r., Ec. **104** c10
Quinlan, Okla., 75 **76** E1
Quinlan, Tex., 621 **76** g9
Quinn, S. Dak., 162 **74** A3
Quinn, r., Nev. **83** A2
Quinnipiac, r., Conn. **56** E7
Quinn River Crossing, Nev. **83** A2
Quinnville, R.I. **57** L5
Quinsigamond, L., Mass. **57** K3
Quinta, Chile **104** f14
Quintana-Martín Galíndez, Sp. **122** m12
Quintanar de la Orden, Sp., 9,483 **122** D3
Quintanar del Rey, Sp., 5,287 **122** E3
Quintana Roo, terr., Mex., 50,169 **93** H4
Quintay, Chile **104** f13
Quinter, Kans., 776 **75** E4
Quintero, Chile, 6,486 **104** f12
Quintin, Fr., 3,152 **116** B2
Quinto, Sp., 2,536 **122** E2
Quinton, Ala. **64** B7
Quinton, N.J. **61** A4
Quinton, Okla., 898 **76** H2
Quinwood, W. Va., 506 **62** D4
Quinzáu, Ang. **164** B3
Quipapá, Braz., 3,421 **103** b15
Quipile, Col. **101** e15
Quiquiritza, Co., Ven. **101** H6
Quiriguá, Guat., 2,563 **94** d8
Quirihue, Chile, 3,462 **104** e16
Quirindi, Austl., 2,735 **173** G4
Quiringuícharo, Mex., 1,185 **93** b9
Quirinópolis, Braz., 3,239 **103** F5
Quiripital, Ven. **101** c11
Quiriquina, Chile **104** e16
Quiriquire, Ven., 7,520 **101** J3
Quirke L., Ont., Can. **46** B2
Quiroga, Mex., 5,318 **93** c10
Quiroga, Sp., 7,115 **122** B1
Quiros, C., New Hebr. **174** k5
Quiruvilca, Peru, 7,500 **104** B3
Quisibis Mtn., N.B., Can. **55** E1
Quisicedo, Sp. **122** m11
Quisiro, Ven., 1,277 **100** E2
Quissanga, Moz. **164** F4
Quissico, Moz. **164** E6
Quistello, It., 8,124 **122** e5
Quitaque, Tex., 585 **77** N2
Quitman, Ark., 305 **73** C2
Quitman, co., Ga., 2,432 **64** D4
Quitman, Ga., 5,071 **64** F5
Quitman, La., 185 **73** C5
Quitman, co., Miss., 21,019 **73** E3
Quitman, Miss., 2,030 **73** G5
Quitman, Mo., 113 **72** B4
Quitman, Tex., 1,237 **77** Q3
Quito, Ec., 348,151 **104** B2
Quitupan, Mex., 1,552 **93** b10
Quixadá, Braz., 8,747 **103** J3
Qukës-Shkumbin, Alb. **125** E4
Qulaybīyah, Tun., 11,259 **160** g5
Qulin, Mo., 587 **72** G8
Quoich, r., N.W.T., Can. **40** L5
Quoigs, U.K. **112** c7
Quonochontaug (part of Charlestown), R.I. **57** K7
Quorn, Austl. **172** E5
Quorndon, U.K., 3,355 **114** F5
Quranbāliyah, Tun., 6,276 **161** F1
Qurbah, Tun., 13,100 **160** g5
Qurnat as Sawdā', mtn., Leb. **142** C3
Qurţabā, Leb., 3,873 **142** b5
Quşūr as Sāf, Tun., 11,341 **160** g6
Quţaynah, Sudan **163** K3
Quynh Nhai, N. Viet. **146** C2
Quyon, Qué., Can. **47** H3
Quyquyó, Para., 1,452 **105** D3

R

Raad, Guyana **101** L6
Raahe, Fin., 4,949 **120** F2
Rääkkylä, Fin. **120** G3
Raalte, Neth., 5,500 **115** E2
Raamsdonk, Neth. **115** b7
Raamsdonksveer, Neth., 5,800 **115** b7
Raas, P., Indon. **148** E4
Raasay, i., U.K. **112** C3
Raasay, Sd. of, U.K. **112** C3
Raasdorf, Aust. **124** d10
Rab, i., Yug. **125** B2
Raba, Indon. **149** F5
Rába, r., Hung. **126** C3
Raba, r., Pol. **127** D4
Rabastens, Fr., 4,162 **117** D5
Rabat, Malta, 12,792 **123** f12
Rabat, Mor., 227,445 **160** C2
Rabaul, Terr. New Guin. **174** f2
Rabbit Cr., S. Dak. **74** A3
Rabbit Lake, Sask., Can. **43** C4
Rabenau, Ger.D.R. **126** c5
Rabenstein, Aust., 2,191 **124** M5
Raber, Mich. **67** J2
Rábida, I., Colón, Arch. de **104** a8
Rābigh, Saudi Ar. **143** B4
Rabinal, Guat., 3,953 **94** c8
Rabka, Pol., 9,589 **127** D4
Raboet Pru, Thai. **147** e4
Rābor, Iran, 2,519 **143** F3
Rabun, co., Ga., 7,456 **64** F1
Råby, Den. **121** C4
Råby-Rönö, Swed. **120** d9
Rača, Yug. **125** E3
Răcăciuni, Rum. **128** F1
Răcari, Rum. **128** E2
Racconigi, It., 8,595 **122** a6
Raccoon, Pa. **60** a8
Raccoon Cr., N.J. **61** A4
Raccoon Cr., Ohio **70** G4
Raccoon Cr., Pa. **60** B5
Race, C., Newf., Can. **45** R6
Race, The, str., Conn.-N.Y. **56** H8
Race Course, Jam., 1,377 **96** p9
Raceland, Ky., 1,115 **71** J3
Raceland, La., 3,666 **73** E8
Race Pt., Mass. **57** P4
Racepond, Ga. **64** G5
Rachal, Tex. **77** O6
Rach Gia, S. Viet., 40,085 **146** D5
Raciąż, Pol., 3,591 **127** D2
Racibórz, Pol., 32,000* **127** C3
Racine, Ohio, 499 **70** H4
Racine, W. Va. **62** C4
Racine, co., Wis., 141,781 **66** E6
Racine, Wis., 89,144 **66** F6
Racine de Bouleau, r., Qué., Can. **45** M4
Racing, r., Br. Col., Can. **42** F1
Raciożnica, r., Pol. **127** C2
Ráckeve, Hung., 7,454 **126** D3
Racławice, Pol. **127** k6
Racławice Śląskie, Pol. **127** g6
Raco, Mich. **67** J2
Radačići, Yug. **125** D2
Rădăuţi, Rum., 15,949 **128** E1
Radawie, Pol. **127** h6
Radbuza, r., Czech. **126** A2
Radcliff, Ky., 3,384 **71** F4
Radcliff, Ohio **70** G3
Radcliffe, Lancs., Eng., U.K., 26,720 **114** D3
Radcliffe, Northumb., Eng., U.K. **112** g9
Radcliffe, Iowa, 615 **72** D2
Radcliffe on Trent, U.K., 6,468 **114** G5
Radd, r., Syr. **142** E2
Råde, Nor. **121** C1
Radeberg, Ger.D.R., 16,344 **126** d5
Radebeul, Ger.D.R., 40,349 **118** D3
Radeburg, Ger.D.R. **126** c5
Radenthein, Aust., 5,638 **124** K7
Radersburg, Mont. **81** D2
Radevormwald, F.R.Ger., 19,496 **119** C2
Radew, r., Pol. **127** B1
Radford, Va., 9,371 **62** D5
Radhakishorepur, India, 8,778 **145** J5
Radibor, Ger.D.R. **126** d5
Radisson, Sask., Can. **43** C4
Radisson, Wis., 179 **66** B3
Radium, Kans., 64 **75** F5
Radium Hot Springs, Br. Col., Can. **42** J4
Radium Springs, N. Mex. **79** B5
Radix, Pt., Trin. and Tob. **96** h5
Radja, Udjung, Indon. **148** A2
Radjik, Indon. **148** C3
Radkersburg, Aust., 1,745 **124** N7
Radków, Pol., 1,947 **127** f6
Radlbrunn, Aust. **124** b9
Radlin, Pol., 16,105 **127** C3
Radłów, Pol. **127** h6
Radmer, Aust., 1,179 **124** L6
Radna, Rum. **128** C1
Radnevo, Bulg., 4,208 **128** E3
Radnice, Czech. **126** c7
Radnor, Pa., 1,100* **60** f11
Radnor, W. Va. **62** B4
Radnor Forest, U.K. **114** B6
Radnorshire, co., U.K., 18,471 **113** E5
Radolfzell, F.R.Ger., 11,789 **118** B5
Radom, Pol., 130,000* **127** D3
Radom, Ill., 137 **68** C5
Radomir, Bulg., 6,685 **128** D3
Radomka, r., Pol. **127** D3
Radomsko, Pol., 27,000* **127** C3
Radomyshl', U.S.S.R., 10,900 **136** C3
Radomyśl Wielki, Pol., 1,085 **127** D3
Radonia, Pol. **127** k5
Radoszyce, Pol. **127** k5
Radoviš, Yug., 5,255 **125** F4
Radovitsy, U.S.S.R. **136** c6
Radstadt, Aust., 3,305 **124** K6
Radstock, C., Austl. **172** D5
Răducăneni, Rum. **128** F1
Radujevac, Yug., 2,700 **125** F2
Radunia, r., Pol. **127** C1
Radviliškis, U.S.S.R., 12,500 **136** A2
Radville, Sask., Can., 1,041 **43** D5
Radway, Alta., Can. **43** b6
Radymno, Pol., 3,250 **127** E4
Radziejów, Pol., 3,574 **127** C2
Radzionków, Pol., 24,000* **127** h6
Radzyń Chełmiński, Pol., 1,772 **127** C2
Radzyń Podlaski, Pol., 5,941 **127** E3
Rae, N.W.T., Can. **40** F5
Rae, Mt., Alta., Can. **42** J4
Rae Bareli, India, 29,940 **144** c12
Raechester, U.K. **112** f9
Raeford, N.C., 3,058 **63** E3
Raetihi, N.Z. **175** g5
Raevavae, i., Fr. Poly. **171** J6
Raeville, Nebr. **75** G2
Rafaela, Arg., 40,000* **105** C4
Rafael Reyes, Col. **101** e15
Rafael Village, Calif. **83** d11
Rafaḩ, U.A.R. **161** K2
Rafaï, C.A.R., 1,512 **163** H5
Rafḩā', Saudi Ar. **143** C3
Rafīd, Syr. **142** b7
Räfis, Switz. **124** a8
Rafsanjān, Iran, 9,212 **143** F2
Rafz, Switz., 1,925 **124** C1
Raga, China **144** e11
Raga, Sudan **163** J4
Raga, i., New Hebrides **174** m5
Ragan, Nebr., 90 **75** F3
Ragay G., Phil. **153** B2
Ragersville, Ohio **70** H2
Ragged, Mt., Austl. **172** C5
Ragged I., Bah. Is. **95** D2
Ragged I., Me. **55** D5
Ragged Keys, Fla. **65** b10
Ragged L., Me. **55** C3
Ragged Pt., Barb. **97** 10
Raghugarh, India, 6,365 **144** a13
Raglan, N.Z., 1,019 **175** g5
Raglan, U.K., 1,222 **114** C7
Ragland, Ala., 1,166 **64** C2
Ragland, N. Mex. **79** D4
Ragley, La. **73** B7
Ragonvalia, Col. **100** D4
Ragsdale, Ind. **70** B4
Raguba, Libya **161** H3
Ragueneau, Qué., Can. **45** M5
Ragunda, Swed. **120** D3
Ragusa, It., 56,177 **123** E6
Ragusa, Yug. = Dubrovnik
Raha, Indon. **149** G4
Rahad, Nahr ar, Eth.-Sudan **163** K3
Rahaeng = Tak
Rahang, Malay., 2,026 **147** p15
Rahatgarh, India, 6,070 **144** b14
Rahns, Pa. **60** f11
Rahouia, Alg., 4,654 **160** b6
Rahue, r., Chile **105** e15
Rahway, N.J., 27,699 **61** C2
Rahway, r., N.J. **58** b14
Rai, Hon, S. Viet. **146** D5
Raiatea, i., Soc. Is. **177** 42
Raíces Oeste, Arg. **105** b10
Raichur, India, 63,329 **145** E6
Raiford, Fla. **65** G2
Raiganj, India, 32,290 **144** g13
Raigarh, M.P., India, 36,933 **145** G5
Raigarh, Ori., India **145** G6
Raikot, India, 11,239 **144** a10
Railton, Austl. **173** f13
Rain, F.R.Ger., 3,031 **118** C4
Rainbow, Alaska **85** c7
Rainbow (part of Windsor), Conn. **56** F5
Rainbow, Utah **78** D2
Rainbow Bridge Nat. Mon., Utah **78** C3
Rainbow City, C.Z., 3,688 **94** f11
Rainbow L., Me. **55** C3
Rainbow L., Wis. **66** D3
Rainbow Lodge, Ariz. **78** C3
Rainelle, W. Va., 649 **62** D5
Rainford, U.K., 5,385 **114** C3
Rainier, Alta., Can. **42** K4
Rainier, Oreg., 1,152 **80** B2
Rainier, Wash., 245 **80** B2
Rainier, Mt., Wash. **80** C2
Rains, S.C. **63** E3
Rains, co., Tex., 2,993 **77** Q3
Rainsburg, Pa., 209 **60** F6
Rainsville, Ala., 398 **64** D1
Rainsville, N. Mex. **79** C3
Rainy, r., Can.-U.S. **44** C5
Rainy, r., Mich. **67** J3
Rainy L., Can.-U.S. **53** H1
Rainy River, Ont., Can., 1,168 **44** C5
Raipur, India, 139,792 **145** F5
Raisen, India, 5,962 **144** a14
Raisin, r., Ont., Can. **47** K3
Raisin, r., Mich. **67** K7
Raisio, Fin. **120** E3
Raismes, Fr., 18,737 **116** a7
Raiti, Nic. **94** E3
Raja, Indon. **148** F2
Rajahmundry, India, 130,002 **145** F6
Rajang, Malay., 1,349 **148** D2
Rajang, r., Malay. **148** E2
Rajaori, India **145** E2
Rajapalaiyam, India, 71,203 **145** E8
Rajapur, Mah., India, 8,270 **145** h18
Rajapur, U.P., India, 5,089 **144** c13
Rajasthan, st., India, 20,155,602 **145** D4
Rajauli, India **144** e13
Rajen, China **144** d10
Rajevo Selo, Yug. **125** D2
Rajgarh, M.P., India, 9,095 **144** a14
Rajgarh, Raj., India, 12,048 **144** a12
Rajgarh, Raj., India, 18,136 **145** E3
Rajgir, India, 9,033 **144** e13
Rajgród, Pol., 1,670 **127** E2
Rajkot, India, 193,498 **144** D5
Rajmahal, India, 6,801 **144** f13
Raj Nandgaon, India, 44,678 **145** F5
Rajpipla, India, 21,426 **145** D5
Rajpura, India, 27,925 **144** a10
Rājshāhi, Pak., 56,885 **144** g13
Rakahanga, i., Cook Is. **171** H5
Rakai, Uganda **165** e14
Rakaia, r., N.Z. **175** f6
Rakamaz, Hung., 5,420 **126** E2
Rakan, Ra's, pt., Qatar **143** E3
Rakas Tal, l., China **150** B4
Rake, Iowa, 328 **72** D1
Rakha La, China-Nepal **144** f12
Rakhes, Gr. **129** D5
Rakhov, U.S.S.R., 10,800 **136** A3
Rakita, Yug. **125** F3
Rakitovo, Bulg., 6,681 **128** E4
Rakkeby, Den. **121** B3
Rakkestad, Nor. **121** D1
Rakoniewice, Pol., 2,064 **127** B2
Rakops, Bots., 1,878 **164** D5
Rakovitsa, Bulg., 2,788 **128** D3
Rakovník, Czech., 11,879 **126** A1
Rakovo, Bulg. **128** D3
Rakvere, U.S.S.R., 15,400 **134** B4
Raleigh, Newf., Can. **45** Q4
Raleigh, Ill., 225 **68** D6
Raleigh, Ind. **70** D3
Raleigh, Miss., 614 **73** F5
Raleigh, N.C., 93,931 **63** F2
Raleigh, N. Dak. **74** B2
Raleigh, co., W. Va., 77,826 **62** C5
Ralik Chain, is., Marsh. Is. **170** E4
Ralls, co., Mo., 8,078 **72** F5
Ralls, Tex., 2,229 **77** N3
Ralph, Ala. **64** B2
Ralph, Mich. **66** F2
Ralph, S. Dak. **74** A3
Ralston, Iowa, 143 **72** C2
Ralston, Nebr., 2,977 **75** K2
Ralston, Okla., 411 **76** G1
Ralston, Pa. **60** J2
Ralston Cr., Colo. **79** b8
Rama, Sask., Can. **43** D4
Rama, Nic. **94** E4
Rama, r., Nic. **94** E5
Ramādah, Tun. **161** F2
Ramadilla, Chile **104** e16
Ramage, W. Va. **62** C4
Ramah, Newf., Can. **45** N2
Ramah, Colo., 109 **79** C2
Ramah, N. Mex. **79** A4
Ramales de la Victoria, Sp., 2,468 **122** m11
Ramalhal, Port., 2,608 **122** i9
Rām Allāh, Jor., 14,759 **142** b8
Ramallo, Arg., 5,000* **105** b11
Raman, Turk. **142** E2

282 · Ramanthapuram—Reilly

Ramanthapuram, India, 26,890 **145** m21
Ramanujganj, India, 3,172 **145** G5
Ramapo, r., N.J.-N.Y. **61** C1
Ramapo Deep, Pac. Oc. **168** E1
Ramapo Mtn., N.J. **58** b12
Ramat Gan, Isr., 90,841 **142** a7
Rambervillers, Fr., 7,060 **117** G2
Rambi, i., Fiji **174** 4
Rambouillet, Fr., 12,593 **117** D2
Rambutyo, i., Terr. New Guin. **174** f1
Rame Head, U.K. **113** D6
Ramenskoye, U.S.S.R., 41,600 **136** c6
Ramer, Ala. **64** C3
Ramer, Tenn., 358 **71** C6
Rameswaram, India, 6,801 **145** F8
Ramet, Belg., 5,034 **115** D4
Ramey, Pa., 558 **60** F4
Ramgarh, India, 20,041 **144** e14
Rāmhormoz, Iran, 7,258 **143** E2
Ramiere, Punta, It. **123** A2
Ramiriqui, Col. **100** D5
Ramla, Isr., 22,852 **142** a8
Ramlösa, Swed. **121** b7
Ramm, Jabal, Jor. **142** C4
Ramme, Den., 1,186 **121** A4
Rammelsbach, F.R.Ger., 2,104 **119** D5
Rammenau, Ger.D.R. **126** d5
Ramnagar, M.P., India **144** c13
Ramnagar, U.P., India, 16,088 **144** b11
Ramnes, Nor. **121** C1
Ramon', U.S.S.R., 5,700 **136** E3
Ramon, N. Mex. **79** C4
Ramona, Calif., 2,449 **82** E6
Ramona, Kans., 132 **75** H5
Ramona, Okla., 546 **76** H1
Ramona, S. Dak., 247 **74** D3
Ramón Castilla, Peru, 1,199 **104** D3
Ramor, L., Ire. **113** C5
Ramore, Ont., Can. **44** H5
Ramos, Mex., 1,511 **92** E3
Ramos, R. de, Mex. **92** D3
Ramos Arizpe, Mex., 3,925 **93** E3
Ramosch, Switz. **124** E2
Ramos I., Sol. Is. **175** c2
Ramos Otero, Arg., 2,200* **105** b13
Rampart, Alaska, 49 **85** G2
Rampton, U.K., 1,875 **114** G4
Rampur, H.P., India, 2,079 **144** a10
Rampur, U.P., India, 135,407 **145** F3
Rampur Hat, India, 19,897 **144** f13
Ramree, Burma, 3,892 **146** A3
Ramree I., Burma **146** A3
Rāmsar, Iran, 7,460 **143** E1
Ramsay, Ont., Can. **44** G6
Ramsay, Mich., 1,158 **66** D2
Ramsay L., Ont., Can. **44** G6
Ramsbeck, F.R.Ger., 2,903 **119** E2
Ramsbottom, U.K., 13,813 **114** D3
Ramsbury, U.K., 1,468 **114** E8
Ramsele, Swed. **120** C3
Ramsen, Switz., 1,181 **124** C1
Ramseur, N.C., 1,258 **63** E2
Ramsey, Hunts., Eng., U.K., 5,697 **113** F5
Ramsey, Isle of Man, U.K., 4,621 **113** D4
Ramsey, Ill., 815 **68** C4
Ramsey, co., Minn., 422,525 **74** F3
Ramsey, N.J., 9,527 **61** C1
Ramsey, co., N. Dak., 13,443 **74** C1
Ramsey Bk., N.J. **58** c12
Ramsey I., U.K. **113** D6
Ramsgate, U.K., 36,914 **113** G6
Ramstein, F.R.Ger., 5,532 **119** D6
Ramtek, India, 11,758 **144** b15
Ramu, r., Terr. New Guin. **174** e2
Ramville, Ilet, Mart. **97** 12
Ranaghat, India, 35,266 **144** g14
Ranai, Indon. **148** D2
Rana Kao, Vol., Easter I. **177** 46
Ranau, Malay. **148** F1
Rancagua, Chile, 53,318 **105** A4
Rance, Belg., 1,558 **115** C4
Rancheria, Yukon, Can. **40** C5
Ranchester, Wyo., 235 **81** F3
Ranchi, India, 122,416 **145** G5
Rancho Cordova, Calif., 7,429 **82** b7
Rancho Grande, Pq. Nac., Ven. **100** G2
Rancho Nuevo, Mex. **93** c9
Ranchos de Taos, N. Mex., 1,668 **79** C3
Rancho Veloz, Cuba, 1,943 **96** c1
Ranchuelo, Cuba, 4,288 **96** c1
Ranchville, Alta., Can. **42** L4
Ranco, L., Chile **105** e15
Rancocas Cr., N.J. **60** g11
Rançonnières, Fr. **117** F3
Rand, Austl. **173** f10
Rand, Colo. **79** B1
Randa, Switz. **124** B2
Randall, Ark. **73** C3
Randall, Kans., 201 **75** G4
Randall, Minn., 516 **74** E2
Randall, co., Tex., 33,913 **76** M2
Randall L., Mich. **67** H7
Randallstown, Md. **62** b7
Randalstown, U.K., 1,577 **113** C4
Randazzo, It., 13,475 **123** E6
Randers, Den., 42,238 **121** C4
Randers Fjord, bay, Den. **121** C4
Randfontein, S. Af., 41,310 **165** i17
Randijaur, l., Swed. **120** D2
Randleman, N.C., 2,232 **63** E2
Randlett, Okla., 356 **76** E3
Randolph, co., Ala., 19,477 **64** D2
Randolph, Ala. **64** C3
Randolph, Ariz. **78** C5
Randolph, co., Ark., 12,520 **73** D1
Randolph, co., Ga., 11,078 **64** E4
Randolph, co., Ill., 29,988 **68** C5
Randolph, co., Ind., 28,434 **70** D2
Randolph, Iowa, 257 **72** B4
Randolph, Me., 1,585 **55** C4
Randolph, Mass., 18,900(T) **57** M4
Randolph, Miss., 131 **73** F3
Randolph, co., Mo., 22,014 **72** E5
Randolph, Nebr., 1,063 **75** H1
Randolph, N.H. **54** E3
Randolph, N.Y., 1,414 **58** C7
Randolph, co., N.C., 61,497 **63** E2
Randolph, Utah, 537 **78** C1
Randolph, Vt., 2,122 **54** B4
Randolph, Va. **62** F6
Randolph, co., W. Va., 26,349 **62** D4
Randolph, Wis., 1,507 **66** D5
Randolph Center, Vt. **54** B4
Random Lake, Wis., 858 **66** F5
Random Sound, Newf., Can. **45** b9
Randsburg, Calif. **82** E5
Råneå, Swed. **120** E2
Ranfurly, N.Z. **175** f7
Ranfurly, U.K. **112** a8
Rāngāmāti, Pak., 6,416 **145** J5
Rangeley, Me. **55** B4
Rangeley L., Me. **55** B4
Rangely, Colo., 1,464 **79** A1
Ranger, N.C. **63** a7
Ranger, Tex., 3,313 **77** O3
Ranger, W. Va. **62** B4
Ranger Lake, Ont., Can. **46** A2
Rangiora, N.Z., 3,540 **175** g6
Rangiroa, atoll, Tuam. Arch. **177** 42
Rangitaiki, r., N.Z. **175** h5
Rangitata, r., N.Z. **175** f6
Rangitikei, r., N.Z. **175** g5
Rangitira I., N.Z. **175** 14
Rang-Kul', U.S.S.R. **137** g5
Rangoon, Burma, 737,079 **146** A3
Rangoon, r., Burma **147** b2
Rangpur, Pak., 40,634 **144** g13
Rangsang, P., Indon. **148** B2
Rånguil, Chile **104** f14
Ranibennur, India, 31,304 **145** E7
Ranier, Minn., 262 **74** F1
Raniganj, India, 30,113 **144** f14
Ranikhet, India, 10,642 **144** b11
Rankin, Ill., 761 **68** E3
Rankin, Mich. **67** K6
Rankin, co., Miss., 34,322 **73** E5
Rankin, Okla. **76** D2
Rankin, Pa., 5,164 **60** c8
Rankin, Tex., 1,214 **77** M4
Rankin Inlet, N.W.T., Can. **40** L5
Rankin Inlet, N.W.T., Can. **40** L5
Rankins Springs, Austl. **173** f9
Rankoshi, Jap., 13,228 **155** J8
Rankweil, Aust., 6,454 **124** F6
Rannersdorf, Aust. **124** d9
Rannoch, Loch, U.K. **112** D3
Rannoch Moor, U.K. **112** D3
Ranong, Thai., 5,993 **146** B5
Ranot, Thai. **146** C6
Ransbach, F.R.Ger., 2,773 **119** D4
Ransiki, Indon. **149** K3
Ransom, Ill., 415 **68** D2
Ransom, Kans., 387 **75** E5
Ransom, Mich. **66** F2
Ransom, co., N. Dak., 8,078 **74** D2
Ransom, Pa. **61** o16
Ransomville, N.Y. **58** C5
Ranson, W. Va., 1,974 **62** G3
Ranstadt, F.R.Ger., 1,164 **119** F4
Rantekombola, Bulu, Indon. **149** G3
Rantem, Newf., Can. **45** b10
Rantoul, Ill., 22,116 **68** D3
Rantoul, Kans., 157 **75** K5
Rantsila, Fin. **120** F2
Ranua, Fin. **120** F2
Ranum, Den., 1,782 **121** B4
Raon-l'Étape, Fr., 7,731 **117** G2
Raoul I., N.Z. **170** G6
Rapa, i., Fr. Poly. **171** J6
Rapallo, It., 19,362 **123** B2
Rapang, Indon. **149** G3
Rapa Nui = Easter I.
Rapel, Chile **104** f13
Rapel, r., Chile **104** f14
Rapelje, Mont. **81** E2
Raper, C., N.W.T., Can. **41** Q4
Raper, C., Chile **105** A7
Raphoe, Ire. **113** C4
Rapid, r., Mich. **66** F2
Rapid, N. Br., r., Minn. **74** E1
Rapidan, Va. **62** F4
Rapidan, r., Va. **62** G4
Rapid City, Man., Can. **43** E5
Rapid City, Mich. **67** H4
Rapid City, S. Dak., 42,399 **74** A3
Rapid Cr., S. Dak. **74** A3
Rapide Blanc, Qué., Can **44** K6
Rapides, parish, La., 111,351 **73** C6
Rapid Pt., Gren. Is. **97** 20
Rapid River, Mich. **66** G3
Rapids, Ky. **71** E5
Rapids, N.Y. **58** C5
Rapids City, Ill., 675 **68** B2
Rapoka, i., Aitutaki **177** 35
Rappahannock, co., Va., 5,368 **62** F4
Rappahannock, r., Va. **62** H4
Rapperswil, Switz., 7,585 **124** C1
Rappottenstein, Aust. **124** M5
Rapsáni, Gr., 2,032 **129** D5
Rapti, r., India-Nepal **144** d12
Rapu-Rapu, Phil., 2,704 **153** i14
Rapu Rapu I., Phil. **153** i14
Raquette, r., N.Y. **59** L2
Raquette Lake, N.Y. **59** L4
Raquette L., N.Y. **59** L4
Raraka, atoll, Tuam. Arch. **177** 42
Rarden, Ohio, 250 **70** F4
Rardin, Ill. **68** D4
Rari, Chile **104** f15
Rarinco, r., Chile **104** e17
Raritan, Ill., 182 **68** B3
Raritan, N.J., 6,137 **61** B2
Raritan, r., N.J. **61** B2
Raritan Bay, N.J.-N.Y. **58** C15
Raroia, i., Tuam. Arch. **171** J6
Raron, Switz., 1,077 **124** B2
Rarotonga, i., Cook Is. **171** H6
Rårup, Den., 2,182 **121** B5
Rasah, Malay., 2,262 **147** o15
Ra's al Jabal, Tun., 9,705 **160** g4
Ra's an Naqb, Jor. **142** C4
Ra's Ba'labakk, Leb., 3,284 **142** c5
Rascón, Mex. **93** F4
Raseiniai, U.S.S.R., 6,200 **136** A2
Ras Gharib, U.A.R., 14,000 **161** K3
Rashād, Sudan, 1,683 **163** K4
Rasharkin, U.K. **113** C4
Rāshayyā, Leb. **142** b6
Rashīd, U.A.R., 25,000* **161** i7
Rashoop, S. Af. **165** i16
Rasht, Iran, 109,491 **143** D1
Raşinari, Rum. **128** D2
Rasinja, Yug. **125** C1
Rasipur, India, 23,871 **145** m20
Råskot, Nepal **144** c11
Rasmus, Mich. **67** J4
Rasmussen Basin, N.W.T., Can. **40** K4
Raso, C., Braz. **103** G1
Raso, C., Port. **122** i10
Rason L., Austl. **172** C4
Rasra, India, 12,025 **144** d13
Rasskazovo, U.S.S.R., 38,500 **134** D4
Rastatt, F.R.Ger., 22,108 **118** B4
Rastede, F.R.Ger., 13,616 **118** B2
Råsvani, Rum. **128** F2
Rat, r., Man., Can. **43** E3
Rat, r., Man., Can. **43** h10
Rat, r., Wis. **66** E3
Rataje nad Sazavou, Czech. **127** e7
Ratak Chain, is., Marsh. Is. **170** F4
Rätan, Swed. **120** C3
Ratangarh, India, 26,631 **145** D3
Ratchaburi, Thai., 20,380 **146** B4
Ratcliff, Ark., 147 **73** B2
Ratcliff, Tex. **77** Q4
Ratekau, F.R.Ger., 8,564 **118** C2
Rath, India, 17,419 **144** b13
Rathbone, N.Y. **58** F7
Rathdowney, Ire. **113** C5
Rathdrum, Ire. **113** C5
Rathdrum, Idaho, 710 **81** A2
Rathedaung, Burma, 2,983 **146** A2
Rathenow, Ger.D.R., 28,598 **118** D2
Rathfryland, U.K., 1,558 **113** C4
Rathkeale, Ire. **113** B5
Rathlin I., U.K. **113** C4
Ráth Luirc, Ire., 1,986 **113** B5
Rathmore, Ire. **113** B5
Ratho, U.K. **112** d8
Rathwell, Man., Can. **43** f10
Ratingen, F.R.Ger., 32,003 **119** B2
Ratisbon = Regensburg
Rat I., Alaska **85** e8
Rat L., Man., Can. **43** E3
Ratlam, India, 87,472 **145** E5
Ratliff City, Okla. **76** F3
Ratmanova, O., U.S.S.R. **135** S3
Ratnagiri, India, 31,091 **145** D6
Ratnapura, Cey., 16,598 **145** F9
Ratoath, Ire. **113** C5
Ratodena, Indon. **149** G3
Raton, N. Mex., 8,146 **79** C3
Raton Pass, Colo.-N. Mex. **79** C3
Rat River, N.W.T., Can. **40** G5
Rattakadokoru, i., Palau **176** 21
Rattan, Okla. **76** H3
Rattaphum, Thai. **146** B6
Rattlesnake Butte, Ziebach Co., S. Dak. **74** A3
Rattlesnake Butte, Corson Co., S. Dak. **74** B3
Rattlesnake Cr., Oreg. **80** E4
Rattlesnake Ra., Wyo. **81** F4
Rattray Head, U.K. **112** F3
Rättvik, Swed. **120** C3
Ratu, Palabuhan, bay, Indon. **148** b7
Ratz, Mt., Br. Col., Can. **42** C1
Ratzeburg, F.R.Ger., 11,414 **118** C2
Ratzeburger See, F.R.Ger. **119** c8
Raub, Malay., 15,370 **148** B2
Raub, Ind. **70** B2
Raub, N. Dak. **74** A2
Raubach, F.R.Ger. **119** D3
Raubsville, Pa. **61** m18
Rauch, Arg., 6,820 **105** D5
Rauco, Chile **104** f14
Raufarhöfn, Ice. **120** b6
Raufoss, Nor. **120** B3
Rauhe Alb, mts., F.R.Ger. **119** H7
Rauland, Nor. **120** A4
Raul Soares, Braz., 6,194 **103** e17
Rauma, Fin., 22,481 **120** E3
Rauma, r., Nor. **120** B3
Raumo = Rauma
Raunds, U.K., 4,595 **114** G6
Raung, G., Indon. **148** f7
Raurimu, N.Z. **175** g5
Rauris, Aust., 2,315 **124** J6
Raus, Swed. **121** b7
Rausu, Jap., 5,947 **155** L7
Rausu-dake, Jap. **155** L7
Rautalampi, Fin. **120** F3
Rautavaara, Fin. **120** G3
Rauwiller, Fr. **116** d9
Ravahere, atoll, Tuam. Arch. **177** 42
Ravalli, co., Mont., 12,341 **81** B2
Ravalli, Mont. **81** B2
Ravanna, Mo., 127 **72** D4
Ravanusa, It., 16,323 **123** E6
Rāvar, Iran, 5,074 **143** F2
Rava-Russkaya, U.S.S.R., 6,500 **136** A3
Ravello, It., 2,578 **123** d10
Ravelsbach, Aust. **124** M5
Ravena, N.Y., 2,718 **59** N7
Ravendale, Calif. **82** C2
Ravenden, Ark., 231 **73** D1
Ravenel, S.C., 527 **63** D5
Ravenna, It., 109,799 **123** D2
Ravenna, Calif. **83** h15
Ravenna, Ky., 921 **71** G4
Ravenna, Mich., 801 **67** G5
Ravenna, Nebr., 1,417 **75** F3
Ravenna, Ohio, 10,918 **70** H1
Ravenna, Tex., 145 **77** P3
Ravensburg, F.R.Ger., 29,098 **118** B5
Ravenscar, U.K. **144** G2
Ravenshoe, Austl., 1,264 **173** F2
Ravensthorpe, Austl. **172** B5
Ravenswood, Austl. **173** G3
Ravenswood, W. Va., 3,410 **62** C4
Ravenwood, Mo., 282 **72** C4
Raver, India, 13,188 **144** a15
Ravia, Okla., 307 **76** G3
Ravinia, S. Dak., 164 **74** C4
Ravne na Koroškem, Yug., 3,635 **125** B1
Rāwalpindi, Pak., 340,175 **145** D2
Rawa Mazowiecka, Pol., 7,880 **127** D3
Rawāndūz, Iraq, 8,144 **143** C1
Rawang, Malay., 4,688 **147** o15
Rawcliffe, U.K., 2,435 **114** G3
Rawdon, Qué., Can., 2,311 **47** L2
Rawicz, Pol., 12,267 **127** B3
Rawka, r., Pol. **127** D3
Rawlinna, Austl. **172** C4
Rawlins, co., Kans., 5,279 **75** D4
Rawlins, Wyo., 8,968 **81** F5
Rawmarsh, U.K., 19,603 **114** F4
Rawson, Arg., 2,500* **105** C6
Rawson, N. Dak., 28 **74** A2
Rawson, Ohio, 407 **70** F2
Rawtenstall, U.K., 23,869 **114** D3
Raxaul, India, 9,699 **144** e12
Ray, Ariz., 1,468 **78** C5
Ray, Ill. **68** B3
Ray, Minn. **74** F1
Ray, co., Mo., 16,075 **72** D5
Ray, N. Dak., 1,049 **74** A1
Ray, C., Newf., Can. **45** P6
Rayadrug, India, 23,779 **145** E7
Ray Brook, N.Y. **59** M3
Raychikhinsk, U.S.S.R., 27,500 **135** M5
Ray City, Ga., 713 **64** F4
Rāyen, Iran, 3,395 **143** F3
Rayevskiy, U.S.S.R. **137** h8
Raygorodok, U.S.S.R., 5,700 **136** e7
Rayle, Ga. **64** G2
Raymer, Colo., 91 **79** D1
Raymond, Alta., Can., 2,325 **42** K4
Raymond, Calif. **82** C4
Raymond, Colo. **79** b7
Raymond, Ga. **64** f11
Raymond, Ill., 871 **68** C4
Raymond, Ind. **70** E3
Raymond, Kans., 143 **75** G5
Raymond, Me. **55** B5
Raymond, Miss., 1,381 **73** E5
Raymond, Mont. **81** G1
Raymond, Nebr., 223 **75** J3
Raymond, N.H. **54** E5
Raymond, Ohio **70** F2
Raymond, S. Dak., 168 **74** D3
Raymond, Wash., 3,301 **80** B2
Raymond Terrace, Austl., 2,726 **173** h9
Raymondville, Mo., 202 **72** F7
Raymondville, N.Y. **59** L2
Raymondville, Tex., 9,385 **77** P6
Raymore, Sask., Can. **43** D4
Ray Mts., Alaska **85** F2
Rayne, La., 8,634 **73** C7
Raynham, Mass., 4,150(T) **57** M5
Raynham Center (part of Raynham), Mass. **57** M5
Rayón, S.L.P., Mex., 4,593 **93** F4
Rayón, Son., Mex., 1,351 **92** C2
Rayong, Thai., 9,701 **146** C4
Raystown Branch, r., Pa. **60** F5
Rayton, S. Af. **165** k16
Raytown, Mo., 17,083 **75** b8
Rayville, La., 4,052 **73** D5
Rayville, Mo., 200 **72** D5
Raywood, Tex. **77** k8
Raz, Pte. du, Fr. **116** ·
Razan, Iran, 1,412 **143** D1
Războeni, Rum. **128** F1
Razdel'naya, U.S.S.R., 9,700 **136** C4
Razdolinsk, U.S.S.R. **135** J4
Razdol'noye, U.S.S.R. **151** F2
Razelm, L., Rum. **128** G2
Razgrad, Bulg., 18,389 **128** F3
Razih, Jabal, Saudi Ar. **143** C5
Razlog, Bulg., 8,611 **128** D4
Re, Cu Lao, i., S. Viet. **146** E4
Ré, Î. de, Fr. **117** C3
Rea, Mo., 90 **72** C4
Rea, Pa. **60** a8
Reaburn, Man., Can. **43** g9
Reader, Ark., 86 **73** B4
Readfield, Me. **55** C4
Reading, U.K., 119,937 **113** F6
Reading, Kans., 249 **75** J5
Reading, Mass., 19,259(T) **57** M2
Reading, Mich., 1,128 **67** J7
Reading, Ohio, 12,832 **71** i10
Reading, Pa., 98,177 **61** L5
Reading, Vt. **54** B5
Reading Center, N.Y. **58** G7
Reading Prong, N.J. **61** ·
Read Island, N.W.T., Can. **40** G4
Readland, Ark. **73** D4
Readlyn, Iowa, 547 **72** E2
Readsboro, Vt., 577 **54** A6
Readstown, Wis., 469 **66** C5
Readyville, Tenn. **71** E6
Reagan, Okla. **76** G3
Reagan, Tenn. **71** C6
Reagan, co., Tex., 3,782 **77** N4
Reager, Kans. **75** E4
Reagor Springs, Tex. **76** f10
Real, Phil., 2,147 **153** c8
Real, co., Tex., 2,079 **77** O5
Real Audiencia, Arg. **105** b13
Real del Castillo, Mex. **92** A1
Realitos, Tex. **77** O6
Ream, Camb. **146** C5
Reamstown, Pa. **61** K5
Reamsville, Kans. **75** F4
Reao, atoll, Tuam. Arch. **177** 42
Reardan, Wash., 474 **80** D2
Réau, Fr. **116** i12
Rebecca, Ga., 278 **64** F4
Rebecca, L., Austl. **172** B4
Rebecca, Mt., Austl. **172** A4
Rebel Creek, Nev. **83** B2
Rebersburg, Pa. **60** H4
Rebiana, Libya **161** H3
Rebild, Den. **121** B4
Rebrikha, U.S.S.R. **137** q11
Rebstein, Switz., 2,734 **124** D1
Rebun-jima, Jap. **155** J7
Recanati, It., 17,977 **123** D3
Recaş, Rum. **128** C2
Recea, Rum. **128** E2
Recherche, Arch. of the, Austl. **172** C5
Recherche, C., Sol. Is. **175** c3
Rechesnoi, Mt., Alaska **85** B5
Réchicourt-le-Château, Fr., 1,029 **116** c9
Rechitsa, U.S.S.R., 30,600 **136** C2
Rechnitz, Aust., 3,363 **124** N6
Recht, Belg., 1,386 **119** A4
Recife, Braz., 788,569 **103** K3
Recke, F.R.Ger., 6,323 **118** A2
Reckingen, Switz. **124** C2
Recklinghausen, F.R.Ger., 123,835 **118** A3
Recknitz, r., Ger.D.R. **118** D1
Reconquista, Arg., 26,605 **105** C3
Recreio, Braz., 5,463 **103** e17
Rector, Ark., 1,757 **73** E1
Recz, Pol., 1,857 **127** A2
Red, r., Can.-U.S. **43** F5
Red, China = Yüan
Red, China-N. Viet. = Hong
Red, r., U.S. **53** H4
Red, r., Ky.-Tenn. **71** D5
Red, r., Ky. **71** H4
Red, r., La. **73** B5
Red, Elm Fk., r., Okla. **76** D3
Red, Prairie Dog Town Fk., r., Tex. **77** N2
Red, Salt Fk. of, r., Tex. **76** N2
Reda, Pol., 4,297 **127** C1
Redang, Pulau, Malay. **147** p14
Redange, Lux. **115** D5
Red Bank, N.J., 12,482 **61** C3
Red Bank, S.C. **63** C4
Redbank Cr., Pa. **60** D3
Red Bank-White Oak, Tenn., 11,737 **71** F6
Red Bay, Newf., Can. **45** Q4
Red Bay, Ala., 1,954 **64** A1
Redbay, Fla. **65** C2
Red Bays, Bah. Is. **95** a7
Red Bird, Mo. **72** F6
Redbird, Nebr. **75** G1
Red Bird, Ohio **70** H1
Red Bird, Okla., 310 **76** H2
Red Bluff, Calif., 7,202 **82** B2
Red Bluff L., Tex. **77** M4
Red Boiling Springs, Tenn., 597 **71** F5
Redbridge (part of South-ampton) U.K., 18,458 **113** k13
Red Bridge (part of Ludlow), Mass. **56** G4
Red Bud, Ill., 1,942 **68** B5
Red Bush, Ky. **71** J4
Redby, Minn. **74** E2
Redcar, U.K., 31,460 **113** F4
Red Cedar, r., Mich. **67** J6
Red Cedar, r., Wis. **66** B3
Red Cedar L., Ont., Can. **46** E2
Red Cedar L., Wis. **66** B3
Red Clay Cr., Del. **62** e10
Redcliff, Alta., Can., 2,206 **42** K4
Redcliff, Colo., 586 **79** B2
Redcliff, Wis. **66** C2
Redcliffe, Austl., 13,857 **173** H4
Redcliffe, Mt., Austl. **172** B4
Red Cliffs, Austl., 2,361 **173** F5
Red Cloud, Nebr., 1,525 **75** G3
Redcloud Pk., Colo. **79** B3
Red Creek, N.Y., 689 **59** G5
Red Creek, W. Va. **62** E4
Red Deer, Alta., Can., 19,147 **42** K3
Red Deer, r., Alta., Can. **42** K3
Red Deer, r., Sask., Can. **43** D4
Red Deer L., Alta., Can. **43** b8
Red Deer L., Man., Can. **43** E4
Reddell, La. **73** C7
Redden, Okla. **76** H3
Red Devil, Alaska, 152 **85** E3
Reddick, Fla., 594 **65** G3
Reddick, Ill., 205 **68** D2
Redding, Calif., 12,773 **82** B2
Redding, Conn., 3,359(T) **56** C7
Redding, Iowa, 129 **72** C4
Redding Ridge (part of Redding), Conn. **56** C7
Redditch, U.K., 34,077 **113** F5
Redditt, Ont., Can. **44** C5
Redelinghuys, S. Af. **164** a8
Redfield, Ark., 242 **73** C3
Redfield, Iowa, 966 **72** C3
Redfield, Kans., 133 **75** L6
Redfield, N.Y. **59** J4
Redfield, S. Dak., 2,952 **74** C3
Redford, N.Y. **59** N2
Redford, Tex. **77** L5
Redgranite, Wis., 588 **66** D4
Red Head, Fla. **65** D2
Red Head, Newf., Can. **45** b11
Red Head Cove., Newf., Can. **45** b9
Redhill, U.K., 20,338 **114** H8
Red Hill, N. Mex. **79** A4
Red Hill, Okla. **76** H2
Red Hill, Pa., 1,086 **60** f10
Red Hill, Newf., Can. **45** b11
Red Hill, Hawaii **84** E3
Red Hook, N.Y., 1,719 **59** N8
Red House, N.Y. **58** C7
Red House, W. Va. **62** B4
Redig, S. Dak. **74** A3
Red Indian L., Newf., Can. **45** Q5
Redington, Ariz. **78** C5
Redington, Nebr. **75** B2
Redington Beach, 1,368 **65** c12
Red Island, Newf., Can. **45** a10
Redkey, Ind., 1,746 **70** D2
Redkino, U.S.S.R., 8,400 **136** D1
Red Lake, Ont., Can., 2,051 **44** C5
Red Lake, Ariz. **78** B4
Red Lake, co., Minn., 5,830 **74** D2
Redlake, Minn. **74** E2
Red Lake, r., Minn. **74** D1
Red L., Ont., Can. **44** C4
Red L., Ariz. **83** C5
Red L., S. Dak. **74** C4
Red Lake Falls, Minn., 1,520 **74** D2
Red Lake Road, Ont., Can. **44** C5
Redland, Md. **62** a8
Redlands, Calif., 26,829 **82** E5
Red Level, Ala., 327 **64** C4
Red Lion, Pa., 5,594 **60** J6
Red Lodge, Mont., 2,278 **81** E3
Redlynch, U.K., 2,148 **113** F6
Redman, Mich. **67** L5
Redmesa, Colo. **79** A3
Redmire, U.K. **114** E2
Redmon, Ill., 175 **68** E4
Redmond, Oreg., 3,340 **80** C3
Redmond, Utah, 413 **78** B2
Redmond, Wash., 1,426 **81** b7
Red Mound, Wis. **66** B5
Red Mountain, Calif. **82** E5
Red Mtn., Calif. **82** B2
Rednitz, r., F.R.Ger. **118** C4
Red Oak, Ga. **64** g10
Red Oak, Iowa, 6,421 **72** B3
Red Oak, Mich. **67** J4
Red Oak, N.C. **63** F1
Red Oak, Okla., 453 **76** H3
Red Oak, Pa. **61** p16
Red Oak, Tex., 415 **76** f10
Redoak, Va. **62** F6
Red Oaks Mill, N.Y. **59** N8
Redon, Fr., 10,151 **117** B3
Redonda, i., W.I. **95** G3
Redonda Bay, Br. Col., Can. **42** b5
Redondela, Sp., 17,206 **122** A1
Redondesco, It., 2,191 **122** d5
Redondo, Port., 8,925 **122** B3
Redondo, Wash. **81** b8
Redondo Beach, Calif., 46,986 **83** g16
Redoubt Vol., Alaska **85** F3
Redowl, S. Dak. **74** A3
Red Pass, Br. Col., Can. **42** H3
Red Pine Mtn., Utah **78** b10
Red Pt., U.K. **112** D3
Red River, parish, La., 9,978 **73** B5
Red River, N. Mex. **79** C3
Red River, S.C., 255 **63** D3
Red River, co., Tex., 15,682 **77** Q3
Red R. of the N., Can.-U.S. **52** G1
Red Rock, Br. Col., Can. **42** G3
Red Rock, Ont., Can., 1,316 **44** E5
Red Rock, Apache Co., Ariz. **78** D3
Red Rock, Pinal Co., Ariz. **78** C5
Redrock, N. Mex. **79** A5
Red Rock, N.Y. **59** q23
Red Rock, Okla., 262 **76** F1
Red Rock, r., Mont. **81** C3
Red Rock Cr., Okla. **76** F1
Redruth, U.K., 9,794 **113** D6
Red Sea, Af.-Asia **140** B4
Red Sea Hills, Eth. **163** L2
Red Shirt, S. Dak. **74** A4
Red Springs, N.C., 2,767 **63** E3
Red Springs, Tex. **77** O3
Redstone, Br. Col., Can. **42** F3
Redstone, Colo. **79** B2
Redstone, N.H. **54** E3
Redstone Cr., S. Dak. **74** D3
Red Sucker, r., Man., Can. **43** G3
Red Sucker Lake, Man., Can. **43** G3
Red Sucker L., Man., Can. **43** G3
Red Sulphur Springs, W. Va. **62** D5
Redvale, Colo. **79** A2
Redvers, Sask., Can. **43** E5
Redwater, Alta., Can., 1,123 **42** K2
Redwater, r., Alta., Can. **43** b6
Redway, Calif. **82** B2
Red Wharf Bay, U.K. **113** D5
Red Willow, co., Nebr., 12,940 **75** E3
Red Willow Cr., Nebr. **75** E3
Red Wine, r., Newf., Can. **45** O4
Red Wing, Minn., 10,528 **74** F3
Redwood, co., Minn., 21,718 **74** E3
Redwood, Miss. **73** E5
Redwood, N.Y. **59** J3
Redwood, Tex. **76** c6
Redwood, r., Minn. **74** E3
Redwood City, Calif., 46,290 **82** B4
Redwood Estates, Calif. **83** e13
Redwood Falls, Minn., 4,285 **74** E3
Ree, L., Ire. **113** C5
Reece, Kans. **75** J6
Reed, Ky. **71** D4
Reed, Me. **55** D3
Reed, Okla. **76** D3
Reed City, Mich., 2,184 **67** H5
Reeder, N. Dak., 321 **74** A2
Reed L., Man., Can. **43** E3
Reedley, Calif., 5,850 **82** D4
Reedpoint, Mont. **81** E3
Reeds, Mo., 185 **72** C7
Reeds Bay, N.J. **61** C5
Reedsburg, Wis., 4,371 **66** D5
Reeds Ferry, N.H. **54** D6
Reedsport, Oreg., 2,998 **80** A4
Reeds Spring, Mo., 327 **72** D8
Reedsville, Ohio **70** H3
Reedsville, Pa. **60** G4
Reedsville, W. Va., 398 **62** E3
Reedsville, Wis., 830 **66** F4
Reedtown, Ohio **70** G1
Reedville, Tex. **76** c6
Reedville, Va. **62** H5
Reedy, W. Va., 352 **62** C4
Reedy r., S.C. **63** B3
Reef Islets, New Hebr. **174** k4
Reefton, N.Z., 1,750 **175** f6
Ree Heights, S. Dak., 188 **74** C3
Reelfoot L., Tenn. **71** B5
Reeman, Mich. **67** H5
Rees, F.R.Ger., 4,953 **118** A3
Reese, Mich., 711 **67** K5
Reese, Ohio **70** b7
Reese, Utah **78** b8
Reese, r., Nev. **83** B3
Reeseville, Wis., 491 **66** E5
Reeth, U.K. **112** g11
Reeves, La., 151 **73** C7
Reeves, co., Tex., 17,644 **77** M4
Reevesville, Ill. **68** D6
Reevesville, S.C., 268 **63** D4
Reform, Ala., 1,241 **64** A2
Reform, Miss. **73** F4
Refuge Cove, Br. Col., Can. **42** F4
Refugio, co., Tex., 10,975 **77** P5
Refugio, Tex., 4,944 **77** P5
Rega, r., Pol. **127** A2
Regalbuto, It., 12,039 **123** E6
Regan, N. Dak., 104 **74** B2
Regar, U.S.S.R., 13,600 **137** e5
Regelsbrunn, Aust. **124** d10
Regen, F.R.Ger., 5,054 **118** D4
Regen, r., F.R.Ger. **118** D4
Regensburg, F.R.Ger., 120,324 **118** D4
Regensdorf, Switz., 4,997 **124** C1
Regenstauf, F.R.Ger., 3,628 **118** D4
Regent, N. Dak., 388 **74** A2
Reggan, Alg. **160** E3
Reggio, La. **73** F8
Reggio di Calabria, It., 152,343 **123** E5
Reggiolo, It., 7,062 **122** d6
Reggio nell'Emilia, It., 113,568 **123** C2
Reghin, Rum., 18,091 **128** E1
Regina, Sask., Can., 110,281 **43** D5
Régina, Fr. Guiana **101** O5
Regina, N. Mex. **79** B3
Regina Beach, Sask., Can. **43** C5
Regis-Breitingen, Ger.D.R. **126** b5
Registān, reg., Afghan. **144** B3
Register, Ga. **64** H3
Regnitz, r., F.R.Ger. **118** C4
Reguengos de Monsaraz, Port., 7,107 **122** B3
Rehau, F.R.Ger., 10,046 **118** D3
Rehli, India, 6,442 **144** b14
Rehna, Ger.D.R. **118** C2
Rehoboth, Isr. = Rehovot
Rehoboth, S.-W. Afr., 2,954 **164** B5
Rehoboth, Mass., 4,953(T) **57** L5
Rehoboth, N. Mex. **79** A4
Rehoboth Beach, Del., 1,507 **62** J4
Rehovot, Isr., 29,003 **142** a8
Reichelsheim, F.R.Ger., 2,536 **119** F5
Reichenbach, Ger.D.R., 29,598 **118** D3
Reichenbach, Ger.D.R., 3,150 **127** d5
Reichenbach, Switz., 2,829 **124** B2
Reicholzheim, F.R.Ger., 1,455 **119** G5
Reichraming, Aust., 2,183 **124** L6
Reichshoffen, Fr., 4,030 **116** e9
Reid, Austl. **172** D4
Reid, Miss. **73** F4
Reideburg, Ger.D.R. **118** D3
Reiden, Switz., 2,795 **124** B1
Reid Lake, Br. Col., Can. **42** F3
Reidsville, Ga., 1,229 **64** G3
Reidsville, N.C., 14,267 **63** E1
Reigate, U.K., 53,751 **113** F6
Reigoldswil, Switz., 1,192 **124** B1
Reijen, Neth., 7,100 **115** b7
Reil, F.R.Ger., 1,625 **119** C4
Reilly, Ill. **68** E3
Reilly L., Minn. **74** a6

Reily—Rio Linda · 283

Reily, Ohio 70 E3
Reims, Fr., 138,576 117 E2
Reinach, Switz., 5,174 124 C1
Reinbeck, Iowa, 1,621 72 E2
Reinbek, F.R.Ger., 9,461 118 C2
Reindeer, r., Sask., Can. 43 D3
Reindeer Depot, N.W.T., Can. 40 C4
Reindeer I., Man., Can. 43 F4
Reindeer L., Sask., Can. 43 D2
Reindeer Station, Alaska 85 D2
Reine, Nor. 120 C2
Reinfeld, F.R.Ger., 5,561 119 b8
Reinheim, F.R.Ger., 3,892 119 F5
Reinosa, Mex., 74,113 93 F2
Reinosa, Sp., 10,044 122 C1
Reinthal, Aust. 124 N5
Reisalpe, Aust. 124 b11
Reisenberg, Aust., 1,003 124 c11
Reisterstown, Md. 62 H3
Reit diep, r., Neth. 115 E1
Reitfontein, S. Af. 164 C6
Reit im Winkl, F.R.Ger., 2,219 118 D5
Reitoru, atoll, Tuam. Arch. 177 42
Reitz, S. Af., 4,990 164 D6
Rejaf, Sudan 163 K5
Rejowiec, Pol. 127 E3
Reka Devnya, Bulg., 3,449 128 F3
Rekareka, i., Tuam. Arch. 177 42
Rekarne, Swed. 120 d8
Rekata Bay, Sol. Is. 175 b2
Rekinniki, U.S.S.R. 135 Q3
Relay, Md. 62 c8
Reliance, N.W.T., Can. 40 H5
Reliance, S. Dak., 201 74 C4
Reliance, Tenn. 71 G6
Reliance, Wyo. 81 E5
Relizane = Ighil Izane
Reloca, Chile 104 e15
Reloncaví, Seno, Chile 105 e15
Remagen, F.R.Ger., 6,831 118 A3
Remanso, Braz., 5,125 103 H3
Remarkable, Mt., Austl. 172 b7
Rembang, Indon. 148 D4
Rembau, Malay., 1,239 147 p15
Rembert, S.C. 63 D3
Rembrandt, Iowa, 265 72 B2
Remchi, Alg., 5,767 160 a6
Remedios, Col. 100 C4
Remedios, Cuba, 10,602 96 d1
Remedios, Mex. 93 e9
Remedios, Pan., 1,125 94 F6
Remedios, P., El Salv. 94 d10
Remer, Minn., 492 74 E2
Remerton, Ga., 571 64 F5
Remich, Lux., 1,801 115 E5
Rémilly, Fr., 1,214 116 b8
Remington, Ind., 1,207 70 B2
Remington, Va., 288 62 G4
Rémire, Fr. Guiana 101 O5
Remiremont, Fr., 10,328 117 G2
Remmel Mtn., Wash. 80 C1
Remontnoye, U.S.S.R. 136 F4
Remote, Oreg. 80 B4
Rems, r., F.R.Ger. 119 H7
Remscheid, F.R.Ger., 118,161 118 A3
Remsen, Iowa, 1,338 72 B2
Remsen, N.Y., 567 59 K5
Remus, Mich. 67 H5
Ren, i., Jaluit 176 30
Rena, Nor. 120 B3
Rena, r., Nor. 120 B3
Renaix = Ronse
Renaker, Ky. 71 G3
Renault, Ill. 68 B5
Rench, r., F.R.Ger. 119 E7
Renchen, F.R.Ger., 2,954 119 E7
Rencona, N. Mex. 79 C4
Rende, It., 13,406 123 F5
Rendezvous Bay, Anguilla 97 7
Rendína, Gr., 1,064 129 C5
Rendova, i., Sol. Is. 175 b2
Rendsburg, F.R.Ger., 34,635 118 B1
Rendville, Ohio, 197 70 G3
Renedo, Sp. 122 m11
Renens, Switz., 10,698 124 A2
Renews, Newf., Can. 45 b11
Renfrew, Ont., Can., 8,935 44 J6
Renfrew, co., U.K., 338,815 112 D4
Renfrew, U.K., 17,946 112 b8
Renfrew (part of Adams), Mass. 56 D2
Renfrow, Okla., 38 76 F1
Rengam, Malay., 2,275 147 p16
Rengat, Indon. 148 B3
Rengit, Malay., 1,816 147 p16
Rengo, Chile, 10,989 105 A4
Reni, U.S.S.R., 16,200 136 C4
Renick, Mo., 190 72 E5
Renick, W. Va. 62 D5
Renish Pt., U.K. 112 C3
Renkum, Neth., 7,900 115 D3
Renmark, Austl., 1,979 172 F5
Rennell, i., Sol. Is. 170 E5
Rennell Sd., Br. Col., Can. 42 C3
Renner, S. Dak. 74 D4
Renner, Tex., 212 76 f8
Rennerod, F.R.Ger., 1,742 119 E3
Rennert, N.C. 63 E3
Rennes, Fr., 157,692 117 C2
Rennie, Man., Can. 43 G5
Renningen, F.R.Ger., 4,422 119 F7
Renno, S.C. 63 C3
Reno, co., Kans., 59,055 75 G6
Reno, Nev., 51,470 83 A3
Reno, Ohio 70 H3
Reno, Pa. 60 C3
Reno, Tex. 76 d9
Reno, r., It. 123 C2
Reno Beach, Ohio 70 F1
Renovo, Pa., 3,316 60 G3
Rensburgdorp, S. Af., 1,775 165 k17
Rensselaer, Ind., 4,740 70 B2
Rensselaer, co., N.Y., 142,585 59 N6
Rensselaer, N.Y., 10,506 59 N6
Rensselaer Falls, N.Y., 375 59 K2
Rensselaerville, N.Y. 59 M6
Rentería, Sp., 18,642 122 o11
Rentiesville, Okla., 122 76 H2
Renton, U.K. 112 a8
Renton, Wash., 18,453 80 B2
Rentz, Ga., 307 64 F3
Renville, co., Minn., 23,249 74 E3
Renville, Minn., 1,373 74 E3
Renville, co., N. Dak., 4,698 74 B1
Renwick, Iowa, 477 72 D2
Renwick, L., Ill. 69 b10
Reo, Indon. 149 G5
Répcelak, Hung., 1,580 126 C3
Repelón, Col. 100 C2
Repentigny, Qué., Can., 9,067 47 p17
Repino, U.S.S.R., 3,500 136 C1
Reporoa, N.Z. 175 h5
Represa, Calif. 82 b7
Repton, U.K., 1,850 114 E5
Republic, co., Kans., 9,768 75 H4
Republic, Kans., 333 75 H4
Republic, Mich. 66 E2
Republic, Mo., 1,519 72 D7
Republic, Ohio, 729 70 F1
Republic, Pa., 1,921 60 C6
Republic, Wash., 1,064 80 D1
Republican, S. Fk., r., Colo. 79 D2
Republican, r., Kans.-Nebr. 75 G3
Republiek, Sur. 101 N5
Repulse Bay, N.W.T., Can. 41 M4
Repulse Bay, Austl. 173 G3
Repulse Bay, N.W.T., Can. 41 M4
Requena, Peru, 3,901 104 C3
Requena, Sp., 18,933 122 E3
Requinoa, Chile, 1,646 104 g14
Réquista, Fr., 2,643 117 E4
Rere, i., Jaluit 176 30
Rescue L., Vt. 54 B5
Resedensia, S. Af. 165 i17
Resende, Braz., 13,544 103 d18
Resende Costa, Braz., 2,385 103 d17
Reserve, Sask., Can. 43 D4
Reserve, Kans., 138 75 K4
Reserve, La., 5,297 73 E7
Reserve, Mont. 81 G1
Reserve, N. Mex. 79 A5
Reserve, Wis. 66 B3
Reserve Mines, N.S., Can., 2,789 47 W10
Reshetilovka, U.S.S.R., 8,700 136 D3
Resia, Passo di, Aust.-It. 124 G7
Resina, It., 45,852 123 c10
Resistencia, Arg., 94,389 105 D3
Reşiţa, Rum., 41,234 128 C2
Resko, Pol., 3,297 127 A2
Resolute, N.W.T., Can. 40 L3
Resolution Island, N.W.T., Can. 41 Q5
Resolution I., N.W.T., Can. 45 N1
Resolution I., N.Z. 175 e7
Resolven, U.K., 2,973 114 A7
Resplandes, Braz. 103 G3
Restauración, Dom. Rep., 1,363 96 m6
Resteröd, Swed. 121 D2
Restigouche, Qué., Can. 47 S9
Restigouche, r., N.B., Can. 47 S10
Reston, Man., Can. 43 E5
Reston, Va. 62 G4
Restrepo, Col. 100 D5
Reszel, Pol., 3,852 127 D1
Retalhuleu, Guat., 13,464 94 B3
Retelimba, New Hebr. 174 k6
Retenue, L. de, D.R.Congo 165 n19
Rethel, Fr., 7,856 117 F2
Rethem, F.R.Ger., 2,032 118 B2
Réthimnon, Gr., 14,999 129 E7
Retie, Belg., 5,420 115 D3
Retiers, Fr., 2,878 117 C3
Retiro, Chile 104 f16
Retiro, Col. 101 d13
Retonfey, Fr. 116 b8
Retournac, Fr., 2,784 117 E4
Retrop, Okla. 76 D2
Retsof, N.Y. 58 E6
Retz, Aust., 2,942 124 N5
Retzbach, F.R.Ger., 1,517 119 H5
Reuland, Belg., 1,860 115 E4
Reumen, Chile, 1,027 105 e14
Reus, Sp., 41,014 122 F2
Reusel, Neth., 3,800 115 D3
Reuss, r., Switz. 124 C1
Reutlingen, F.R.Ger., 60,481 118 B4
Reutov, U.S.S.R., 24,600 136 b6
Reutte, Aust., 4,277 124 G6
Reuver, Neth., 4,300 115 E3
Reva, S. Dak. 74 A3
Revda, U.S.S.R., 57,000 137 i8
Revel, Fr., 6,589 117 D5
Revelganj, India, 12,684 144 e13
Revelstoke, Br. Col., Can., 3,566 42 H4
Revel-Tourdan, Fr. 116 p16
Revenge Lag., Br. Hond. 94 C2
Revere, Mass., 40,080 57 N3
Revere, Mo., 190 72 F4
Revigny, Fr., 3,327 117 F2
Revillagigedo, Is. de, Mexico 92 b7
Revillo, S. Dak., 202 74 D3
Revin, Fr., 11,260 117 F2
Revinge, Swed. 121 F5
Revloc, Pa. 60 E4
Řevnice, Czech. 126 d7
Revolyutsii, Pik, U.S.S.R. 137 g5
Revúca, Czech. 126 E2
Revúè, r., Moz. 164 E5
Rewa, India, 43,065 145 F4
Rewa, r., Fiji 174 4
Rewari, India, 36,994 144 a11
Rewey, Wis., 219 66 C6
Rex, N.C. 63 E3
Rex, Mt., Ant. 180 N5
Rexburg, Idaho, 4,767 81 C4
Rexford, Kans., 245 75 E4
Rexford, Mont. 81 B1
Rexford, N.Y. 59 v28
Rexmount, Br. Col., Can. 42 G4
Rexton, N.B., Can. 47 T10
Rexton, Mich. 67 H2
Rexville, Ind. 70 D4
Rexville, N.Y. 58 E7
Rey, Iran, 22,327 143 E1
Rey, I del, Pan. 94 H6
Reydell, Ark. 73 D3
Reydon, Okla., 183 76 D2
Reyersdorf, Aust. 124 d10
Reyes, Bol., 5,002 102 C4
Reyes, P., Col. 100 A6
Reyes, Pt., Calif. 52 B3
Reyhanlı, Turk., 12,305 142 D2
Reykjanes Ridge, Atl. Oc. 108 K3
Reykjavík, Ice., 74,978 120 a6
Reynaldo Cullen, Arg., 8,838 105 C4
Reyno, Ark., 348 73 E1
Reynolds, Ga., 1,087 64 E3
Reynolds, Ill., 494 68 B2
Reynolds, Ind., 547 70 C2
Reynolds, co., Mo., 5,161 72 F7
Reynolds, Mo. 72 F7
Reynolds, Nebr., 131 75 H3
Reynolds, N. Dak., 269 74 D2
Reynolds Bridge (part of Thomaston), Conn. 56 D6
Reynoldsburg, Ohio, 7,793 70 G3
Reynoldsville, Ga. 64 E5
Reynoldsville, Pa., 3,158 60 D3
Reyrieux, Fr., 1,162 116 p15
Rezā'īyeh, Iran, 67,605 143 C1
Rezā'īyeh, Daryācheh-ye, Iran 143 C1
Rezé, Fr., 28,419 117 C3
Rēzekne, U.S.S.R., 21,400 136 B1
Rezh, U.S.S.R., 21,300 137 k7
Rezh, r., U.S.S.R. 137 k7
Rezina, U.S.S.R., 6,900 136 C4
Rezzato, It., 7,420 122 d5
Rgotina, Yug., 2,331 125 F3
Rhade, F.R.Ger., 1,634 119 B1
Rhaetian Alps, Aust.-Switz. 124 D2
Rhame, N. Dak., 254 74 A2
Rhanu Woralaksaburi, Thai. 147 c4
Rhätikon, mts. Aust.-Switz. 124 D1
Rhaunen, F.R.Ger., 1,366 119 C5
Rhayader, U.K. 114 A6
Rhea, Okla. 76 D2
Rhea, co., Tenn., 15,863 71 G6
Rheda, F.R.Ger., 11,655 118 B3
Rheden, Neth., 6,700 115 E3
Rhein, Sask., Can. 43 D4
Rhein, r., F.R.Ger. 118 A3
Rhein, r., Switz. 124 C1
Rhein = Rhine
Rheinbach, F.R.Ger., 6,076 119 B3
Rheinberg, F.R.Ger., 8,394 119 B1
Rheinböllen, F.R.Ger., 1,579 119 D4
Rheinbrohl, F.R.Ger., 3,820 119 C4
Rheine, F.R.Ger., 43,035 118 A2
Rheineck, Switz., 3,047 124 D1
Rheinfelden, F.R.Ger., 12,292 118 A5
Rheingaugebirge, mtn., F.R.Ger. 119 D4
Rheinhausen, F.R.Ger., 62,542 118 A3
Rhein-Herne-Kanal, F.R.Ger. 119 B2
Rheinkamp, F.R.Ger., 27,563 119 B2
Rheinland-Pfalz, st., F.R.Ger., 3,545,000* 118 A4
Rheinsberg, Ger.D.R. 118 D2
Rheinzabern, F.R.Ger., 2,870 119 E6
Rhenen, Neth., 7,800 115 D3
Rhens, F.R.Ger., 2,783 119 D4
Rheydt, F.R.Ger., 89,029 118 A3
Rhin, r., Fr. 116 e9
Rhin, Fr. = Rhine
Rhin, r., Ger.D.R. 118 D2
Rhine, Ga., 485 64 F4
Rhine = Rhin, Fr.
Rhine = Rhein, F.R.Ger.
Rhine = Rhein, Switz.
Rhinebeck, N.Y., 2,093 59 N8
Rhinecliff, N.Y. 59 N8
Rhinelander, Wis., 8,790 66 D3
Rhineland-Palatinate = Rheinland-Pfalz
Rhinkanal, Ger.D.R. 118 D2
Rhin-Marne-Can., Fr. 119 C7
Rhino Camp, Uganda 164 E1
Rhiwlas, U.K. 114 B5
Rho, It., 31,030 122 c5
Rho, Loy. Is. 174 k8
Rhode Island, st., U.S., 891,000* 57
Rhode Island Sd., R.I. 57 L7
Rhodell, W. Va., 626 62 C5
Rhodes, Gr. = Ródhos
Rhodes, Iowa, 358 72 D3
Rhodes, Mich. 67 J5
Rhodesia, ctry., 3,618,150 164 D5
Rhodes Pk., Idaho 81 B2
Rhodhiss, N.C., 837 63 C2
Rhododendron, Oreg. 80 C3
Rhodope Mts., Bulg.-Gr. 129 E4
Rhome, Tex., 412 76 e8
Rhön, mts., F.R.Ger. 118 B3
Rhondda, U.K., 100,287 113 E6
Rhône, r., Fr.-Switz. 117 F5
Rhoon, Neth., 3,800 115 a7
Rhosllanerchrugog, U.K., 9,482 114 B4
Rhu, U.K. 112 a7
Rhuddlan, U.K., 2,164 114 B4
Rhum, i., U.K. 112 C3
Rhur, r., F.R.Ger. 118 A3
Rhyddhywel, mtn., U.K. 114 A6
Rhyl, U.K., 21,737 113 E5
Rhymney, U.K., 8,861 114 B7
Riachão, Braz., 1,907 103 G3
Riaillé, Fr., 1,720 117 C3
Riala, Swed. 120 f8
Rialto, Calif., 18,567 83 k15
Riaño, Sp., 1,656 122 C1
Riaza, Sp., 1,419 122 D2
Ribadavia, Sp., 7,571 122 A1
Ribadeo, Sp., 9,138 122 B1
Ribadesella, Sp., 7,845 122 C1
Ribas do Rio Pardo, Braz., 1,175 103 F6
Ribáuè, Moz. 164 F4
Ribble, r., U.K. 113 E5
Ribchester, U.K., 1,421 114 C3
Ribe, Den., 7,809 121 A5
Ribeauvillé, Fr., 4,701 117 G2
Ribécourt, Fr., 2,210 117 E2
Ribeira da Barca, C. Verde Is. 109 5
Ribeira do Pombal, Braz., 4,254 103 J4
Ribeira Grande, Azores, 8,314 108 2
Ribeira Grande, C. Verde Is. 109 5
Ribeirão, Braz., 9,707 103 b15
Ribeirão Prêto, Braz., 116,153 103 G6
Ribeiro Gonçalves, Braz. 103 H3
Ribera, It., 19,055 123 D6
Ribera, N. Mex. 79 C4
Ribérac, Fr., 4,060 117 D4
Riberalta, Bol., 9,411 102 C4
Rib Lake, Wis., 794 66 C3
Ribnica, B.-H., Yug. 125 D2
Ribnica, Slvja., Yug. 125 B2
Ribnica, Srba., Yug., 2,180 125 D3
Ribnitz-Damgarten, Ger.D.R., 14,838 118 D1
Ribon, i., Jaluit 176 30
Říčany, Czech. 126 B2
Ricardo, Tex. 77 O6
Ricardo Flores Magón, Mex., 2,596 92 D2
Ricaurte, Col. 100 B7
Riccal, r., U.K. 114 F2
Riccall, U.K. 114 F3
Riccarton, U.K. 112 a8
Riccione, It., 18,295 123 D2
Rice, Calif. 82 F5
Rice, Ill. 68 B1
Rice, co., Kans., 13,909 75 G5
Rice, co., Minn., 38,988 74 F3
Rice, Minn., 387 74 E3
Rice, Ohio 70 E1
Rice, Tex., 295 76 f10
Rice, Va. 62 F5
Riceboro, Ga., 259 64 H4
Rice City (part of Coventry), R.I. 57 K6
Rice Hill, Vt. 54 B6
Rice Lake, Wis., 7,303 66 B3
Rice L., Ont., Can. 46 F4
Rice L., Mich. 66 E1
Rice L., Minn. 74 F2
Rice L., Wis. 66 B3
Rice Mtn., N.H. 54 E2
Rices Junction, Calif. 83 e13
Riceville, Iowa, 898 72 E1
Riceville, Pa. 60 C2
Riceville, Tenn. 71 G6
Rich, co., Utah, 1,685 78 C1
Richard Collinson Inlet, N.W.T., Can. 40 G3
Richards, Mo., 133 72 C7
Richards, Tex. 77 Q4
Richards Castle, U.K. 114 C6
Richards Deep, Pac. Oc. 99 B5
Richards Landing, Ont., Can. 69 A
Richardson, Alaska 85 H2
Richardson, co., Nebr., 13,903 75 K3
Richardson, Tex., 16,810 77 P3
Richardson, r., Alta., Can. 42 L1
Richardson Bay, Calif. 83 e12
Richardson L., Alta., Can. 42 L1
Richardson Lakes, Me. 55 B4
Richardson Mts., Yukon-N.W.T., Can. 38 B4
Richardson Springs, Calif. 82 B3
Richardsville, Ky. 71 E4
Richard-Toll, Sen. 162 B3
Richardton, N. Dak., 792 74 A2
Richboro, Pa. 60 g11
Richburg, N.Y., 493 58 D7
Richburg, S.C. 63 C3
Rich Creek, Va., 748 62 D5
Richelieu, Qué., Can., 1,563 47 p18
Richelieu, Fr., 2,018 117 D3
Richelieu, r., Qué., Can. 47 L3
Richey, Mont., 480 81 G2
Richfield, Idaho, 329 81 B4
Richfield, Kans., 122 75 D6
Richfield, Minn., 42,523 74 b6
Richfield, N.C., 293 63 D2
Richfield, Pa. 60 H4
Richfield, Utah, 4,412 78 B2
Richfield, Wis. 66 c10
Richfield Center, Mich. 67 K5
Richfield Springs, N.Y., 1,630 59 L6
Richford, N.Y. 59 H7
Richford, Vt., 1,663 54 B2
Richford, Wis. 66 D4
Rich Fountain, Mo. 72 F6
Richgrove, Calif. 82 D5
Rich Hill, Mo., 1,699 72 C6
Richibucto, N.B., Can., 1,375 45 N6
Richland, Ga., 1,472 64 E3
Richland, co., Ill., 16,299 68 D5
Richland, Iowa, 546 72 F3
Richland, parish, La., 23,824 73 D5
Richland, Mich., 511 67 H6
Richland, Mo., 1,662 72 E7
Richland, co., Mont., 10,504 81 G2
Richland, Nebr., 139 75 H2
Richland, N.Y. 59 H4
Richland, co., N. Dak., 18,824 74 D2
Richland, co., Ohio, 117,761 70 G2
Richland, Oreg., 228 80 E3
Richland, Pa., 1,276 61 K5
Richland, co., S.C., 200,102 63 D3
Richland, S.C. 63 A3
Richland, Tex., 287 77 P4
Richland, Wash., 23,548 80 D2
Richland, co., Wis., 17,684 66 C5
Richland Balsam, mtn., N.C. 63 B2
Richland Center, Wis., 4,746 66 C5
Richland Hills, Tex., 7,804 76 e9
Richlands, N.C., 1,079 63 G3
Richlands, Va., 4,963 62 C5
Richland Springs, Tex., 331 77 O4
Richlandtown, Pa., 741 61 M5
Richlea, Man., Can. 43 B4
Richmond, N.S.W., Austl., 35,213 173 G5
Richmond, Queensland, Austl. 173 F3
Richmond, Ont., Can., 1,204 47 H3
Richmond, Qué., Can., 3,999 47 M3
Richmond, N.Z., 3,482 175 g6
Richmond, London, U.K. 114 H8
Richmond, York., Eng., U.K., 5,776 113 F4
Richmond, Calif., 71,854 82 B4
Richmond, co., Ga., 135,601 64 G2
Richmond, Ill., 855 69 a7
Richmond, Ind., 44,149 70 E3
Richmond, Kans., 352 75 K5
Richmond, Ky., 12,168 71 G4
Richmond, Me., 1,412 55 C4
Richmond, Mass., 890(T) 56 C3
Richmond, Mich., 2,667 67 L6
Richmond, Minn., 751 74 E3
Richmond, Mo., 4,604 72 D5
Richmond, N.H. 54 C6
Richmond, co., N.Y., 221,991 59 M10
Richmond, co., N.C., 39,202 63 E2
Richmond, Ohio, 728 70 J2
Richmond, Okla. 76 D1
Richmond, Tex., 3,668 77 Q5
Richmond, Utah, 977 78 c7
Richmond, Vt., 765 54 B3
Richmond, co., Va., 6,375 62 H4
Richmond, Va., 219,958 62 G5
Richmond, Wis. 66 E6
Richmond, r., St. Vinc. 97 19
Richmond Beach, Wash. 81 a7
Richmond Dale, Ohio 70 G3
Richmond Furnace (part of Richmond), Mass. 56 C3
Richmond Furnace, Pa. 60 G6
Richmond G., Qué., Can. 44 J3
Richmond Heights, Mo., 15,622 72 a11
Richmond Heights, Ohio, 5,068 70 e8
Richmond Highlands, Wash. 81 b7
Richmond Hill, Ont., Can., 16,191 44 H7
Richmond Hill, Ga. 64 H4
Richmond I., Me. 55 B5
Richmond Park, Alta., Can. 42 K2
Richmond Pk., St. Vinc. 97 19
Richmond Pd., Mass. 56 C3
Richmondville, Mich. 67 L5
Richmondville, N.Y., 743 59 L6
Richmound, Sask., Can. 43 B5
Rich Mtn., Okla. 76 J3
Rich Pond, Ky. 71 E5
Rich Square, N.C., 1,134 63 G1
Richterswil, Switz., 5,842 124 C1
Richton, Miss., 1,089 73 G6
Richvale, Calif. 82 C3
Richville, Mich. 67 K5
Richville, Mo. 72 E8
Richville, N.Y., 292 59 K3
Richwood, Ont., Can. 46 a15
Richwood, N.J. 60 f13
Richwood, Ohio, 2,137 70 F2
Richwood, W. Va., 4,110 62 D4
Richwood, Wis. 66 E5
Richwoods, Mo. 72 F6
Ricketts, Iowa, 133 72 B2
Rickman, Tenn. 71 F5
Rickmansworth, U.K., 28,549 114 G7
Rickreall, Oreg. 80 B3
Rico, Colo., 353 79 A3
Ridā', Yemen, 25,000* 143 D6
Ridderkerk, Neth., 10,000 115 b7
Riddle, Idaho 81 A4
Riddle, Oreg., 992 80 B4
Riddlesburg, Pa. 60 F5
Rideau L., Ont., Can. 47 H4
Rideau Lakes, Ont., Can. 59 H2
Rideau River & Can., Ont., Can. 47 J4
Ridge, N.Y. 58 h13
Ridgecrest, Calif., 5,099 82 E5
Ridge Farm, Ill., 894 68 E4
Ridgefield, Conn., 2,954;8,165(T) 56 C7
Ridgefield, Wash., 823 80 B3
Ridgefield Park, N.J., 12,701 58 c13
Ridgeland, Miss., 875 73 E5
Ridgeland, Ohio 70 G3
Ridgeland, S.C., 1,192 63 C5
Ridgeland, Wis., 288 66 B3
Ridgeley, W. Va., 1,229 62 F3
Ridgely, Md., 886 62 J4
Ridgely, Tenn., 1,464 71 B5
Ridge Spring, S.C., 649 63 C4
Ridgetown, Ont., Can., 2,539 46 C6
Ridgeview, S. Dak. 74 B3
Ridgeville, Man., Can. 43 g10
Ridgeville, Ind., 950 70 E2
Ridgeville, Md. 62 a7
Ridgeville, S.C., 611 63 D4
Ridgeville Corners, Ohio 70 E1
Ridgeway, Ont., Can., 1,571 46 E6
Ridgeway, Iowa, 267 72 F1
Ridgeway, Md. 62 c8
Ridgeway, Mich. 67 K7
Ridgeway, Mo., 470 72 D4
Ridgeway, N.J. 58 b16
Ridgeway, N.C. 63 F1
Ridgeway, S.C., 417 63 D3
Ridgeway, Va., 524 62 E6
Ridgeway, Wis., 455 66 D6
Ridgeway Br., N.J. 58 b16
Ridgewood, Ill. 69 b10
Ridgewood, N.J., 25,391 61 C2
Ridgway, Colo., 254 79 B2
Ridgway, Ill., 1,055 68 D6
Ridgway, Pa., 6,387 60 E3
Riding Mtn. Nat. Pk., Man., Can. 43 E5
Ridley Park, Pa., 7,387 60 f12
Ridott, Ill., 221 68 C1
Ridsdale, U.K. 112 f9
Riebeek Wes, S. Af., 1,265 164 a8
Riecito, r., Ven. 100 F4
Ried, Aust., 9,375 124 K5
Riedisheim, Fr., 8,555 117 G3
Riedlingen, F.R.Ger., 4,560 118 B4
Riegelsberg, F.R.Ger., 10,506 116 c8
Riegelsville, N.J. 61 A2
Riegelsville, Pa., 953 61 M4
Rieglewood, N.C. 63 F3
Riehen, Switz., 18,077 124 B1
Rieneck, F.R.Ger., 2,159 119 H4
Rienzi, Miss., 375 73 G3
Riesa, Ger.D.R., 36,769 118 D3
Rieseby, F.R.Ger., 2,148 118 B1
Riesel, Tex., 503 77 P4
Rietberg, F.R.Ger., 5,175 119 E1
Rieth, Oreg. 80 D3
Rieti, It., 35,450 123 D3
Rieumes, Fr., 1,772 117 D5
Rieupeyroux, Fr., 2,606 117 E4
Rif, Cur. 97 16
Rif, ra., Mor. 160 D2
Riffe, Wash. 80 B2
Rifle, Colo., 2,135 79 B2
Rifle, r., Mich. 67 J4
Rift Valley = Eastern Rift Valley
Rift Valley = Western Rift Valley
Rig, W. Va. 62 E3
Rīga, U.S.S.R., 620,000 134 B4
Riga, Mich. 67 K7
Riga, G. of, U.S.S.R. 136 A1
Rīgas Jūrmala, U.S.S.R., 35,300 136 A1
Rigaud, Qué., Can., 1,969 47 K3
Rigaud, r., Ont., Can. 47 K3
Rigby, Idaho, 2,281 81 D4
Rigdon, Ind. 70 D2
Riggins, Idaho, 588 81 A3
Riggisberg, Switz., 1,949 124 B2
Rigili, i., Eniwetok 176 28
Rignold, Man., Can. 43 f9
Rigo, Terr. Papua 174 e3
Rigolet, Newf., Can. 45 P3
Rig Rig, Chad 162 G3
Rigside, U.K. 112 c8
Rihand, r., India 144 d14
Rihand Dam, India 144 d13
Riihimäki, Fin., 20,860 120 F3
Riíto, Mex. 92 B1
Riječki Zaliv, Yug. 125 B2
Rijeka, Yug., 100,000* 125 B2
Rijkevorsel, Belg., 7,111 115 C3
Rijnsburg, Neth., 6,300 115 a6
Rijsoord, Neth., 3,000 115 b7
Rijssen, Neth., 13,400 115 E2
Rijswijk, Neth., 34,500 115 a6
Rikuchū-Kaigan-ktk., Jap. 155 G2
Rikumbetsu, Jap. 155 K8
Rikuzen-Takada, Jap., 32,833 155 G2
Rila, Bulg., 4,400 128 D3
Rila, mts., Bulg. 128 D3
Riley, Ind., 248 70 B3
Riley, co., Kans., 41,914 75 J4
Riley, Kans., 575 75 J4
Riley, N. Mex. 79 B4
Riley, Oreg. 80 D4
Rileyville, Va. 62 F4
Rillieux, Fr., 3,281 116 p15
Rillington, U.K. 114 G2
Rillito, Ariz. 78 C5
Rillton, Pa. 60 d8
Rimāḥ, Tall, hill, Jor. 142 D3
Rimatara, i., Is. Tubuai 177 42
Rimavská Sobota, Czech., 10,927 126 E2
Rimbach, F.R.Ger., 3,193 119 F5
Rimbey, Alta., Can., 1,249 42 J3
Rimbo, Swed. 120 D4
Rimersburg, Pa., 1,323 60 D3
Rimini, It., 88,199 123 D2
Rimnic, r., Rum. 128 F2
Rîmnicu Sărat, Rum., 19,095 128 F2
Rîmnicu Vîlcea, Rum., 18,984 128 E2
Rimouski, Qué., Can., 17,000 45 M5
Rimouski-Est, Qué., Can., 1,565 47 R9
Rimrock, Ariz. 78 C4
Rinard, Ill. 68 D5
Rincon, Bon. 97 17
Rincón, P.R., 1,094 96 r10
Rincon, Ga., 1,057 64 H3
Rincon, N. Mex. 79 B5
Rincón, B. de, P.R. 96 t11
Rinconada, Chile 104 e15
Rincón de Nogoyá, Arg., 3,000* 105 b11
Rincón de Romos, Mex., 5,856 92 E3
Rindge, N.H. 54 D6
Rindjani, G., Indon. 148 F5
Rineyville, Ky. 71 E4
Ringana, Sol. Is. 175 b2
Ringarooma Bay, Austl. 173 f13
Ringe, Den., 4,750 121 C5
Ringebu, Nor. 120 B3
Ringgold, Ga., 1,311 64 D1
Ringgold, co., Iowa, 7,910 72 C4
Ringgold, La., 953 73 B5
Ringgold, Nebr. 75 E2
Ringgold, Tenn. 71 D5
Ringgold Is., Fiji 174 4
Ringim, Nigeria 162 F3
Ringkøbing, Den., 4,869 121 A4
Ringkøbing Fjord, lag., Den. 121 A4
Ringle, Wis. 66 D4
Ringling, Mont. 81 D2
Ringling, Okla., 1,170 76 F3
Ringoes, N.J. 61 B3
Ringold, Okla. 76 H3
Ringsted, Den., 9,694 121 D5
Ringsted, Iowa, 559 72 C1
Ringvaart, can., Neth. 115 b6
Ringvassöy, i., Nor. 120 D1
Ringville (part of Worthington), Mass. 56 E3
Ringwood, U.K., 7,971 113 F6
Ringwood, Ill. 69 a7
Ringwood, N.J., 4,182 61 C1
Ringwood, N.C. 63 G1
Ringwood, Okla., 232 76 E1
Rinia, i., Gr. 129 E6
Riñihue, L., Chile 105 e14
Riñinahue, Chile 105 e15
Rinkerode, F.R.Ger., 2,403 119 D1
Rinteln, F.R.Ger., 9,948 118 B2
Rinya-Patak, r., Hung. 126 C3
Rînzeşti, Rum. 128 F1
Rio, Fla. 65 J5
Rio, Ill., 177 68 B2
Rio, La. 73 F7
Rio, W. Va. 62 F3
Rio, Wis., 788 66 D5
Rio Acima, Braz., 2,955 103 e17
Rio Arriba, co., N. Mex., 24,193 79 B3
Riobamba, Ec., 41,417 104 B2
Río Blanco, Guat., 1,821 94 b8
Río Blanco, Mex. 93 e8
Rio Blanco, co., Colo., 5,150 79 A2
Rio Blanco, Colo. 79 A2
Rio Bonito, Braz., 11,916 103 e18
Rio Branco, Braz., 17,245 102 C4
Río Branco, Urug., 4,000* 105 E4
Río Bravo, Guat., 8,348 94 b9
Río Bravo, Mex., 4,630 93 F3
Rio Brilhante, Braz. 103 F6
Río Bueno, Chile, 7,544 105 A6
Rio Bueno, Jam. 96 p8
Río Caribe, Ven., 7,188 101 J2
Rio Casca, Braz., 4,360 103 e17
Río Chico, Arg. 105 B7
Río Chico, Ven., 2,584 100 H2
Rio Claro, R. de J., Braz., 1,416 103 d18
Rio Claro, S.P., Braz., 48,548 103 G6
Río Claro, Chile, 1,023 104 e17
Río Claro, Chile 104 f15
Rio Claro, Trin. and Tob., 2,740* 96 g5
Río Colorado, Arg., 10,000* 105 C5
Río Corrientes, Ec. 104 B2
Rio Creek, Wis. 66 F4
Río Cuarto, Arg., 80,000* 105 B4
Rio de Janeiro, st., Braz., 3,402,728 103 H6
Rio de Janeiro, Braz., 3,223,408 103 H6
Río de Jesús, Pan., 1,086 94 G7
Rio Dell, Calif., 3,222 82 A2
Rio do Sul, Braz., 13,433 103 G7
Rio Espera, Braz., 1,580 103 e17
Río Frío, Mex., 1,311 93 f10
Río Gallegos, Arg., 15,000* 105 B8
Río Grande, Arg., 2,500* 105 B8
Río Grande, Bol. 102 b12
Rio Grande, Braz., 83,189 103 F8
Rio Grande, Alta., Can. 42 G2
Río Grande, Mex., 8,208 92 E3
Río Grande, Nic. 94 F4
Río Grande, P.R., 2,763 96 u10
Rio Grande, co., Colo., 11,160 79 B3
Rio Grande, N.J. 61 B5
Rio Grande, Ohio, 333 70 G4
Rio Grande, r., Mex.-U.S. 52 G5
Rio Grande City, Tex., 5,835 77 O6
Río Grande de Loíza, L., P.R. 96 u10
Rio Grande do Norte, st., Braz., 1,157,258 103 J3
Rio Grande do Sul, st., Braz., 5,448,823 103 F7
Rio Grande Pyramid, pk., Colo. 79 B3
Rio Grande Rise, Atl. Oc. 99 F6
Ríohacha, Col. 100 D2
Río Hato, Pan. 94 H6
Río Hondo, Guat., 1,090 94 d8
Rio Hondo, Tex., 1,344 77 P6
Río Lagartos, Mex. 93 J4
Rio Largo, Braz., 16,749 103 b15
Rio Linda, Calif., 2,189 82 a7

284 · Riom—Ronchin

Riom, Fr., 15,416 117 E4
Rio Maior, Port., 9,032 122 A3
Río Mayo, Arg., 1,000* 105 A7
Riom-ès-Montagnes, Fr., 3,707 117 E4
Río Mulatos, Bol. 102 b11
Río Muni, prov., Sp. 164 A1
Rion, S.C. 63 C3
Riondel, Br. Col., Can. 42 J4
Río Negro, Bol. 102 C3
Rio Negro, Mo. Gro., Braz. 103 E5
Rio Negro, Paraná, Braz., 10,225 103 G7
Río Negro, Chile, 3,661 105 e15
Ríonegro, Col. 101 d13
Río Negro, Emb. del, Urug. 105 D4
Rionero in Vulture, It., 15,303 123 E4
Rioni, r., U.S.S.R. 137 b1
Rio Nôvo, Braz., 3,826 103 e17
Rio Oso, Calif. 82 a7
Riópar, Sp., 2,280 122 D3
Rio Piracicaba, Braz., 2,941 103 e17
Rio Pomba, Braz., 6,083 103 e17
Rio Prêto, Braz., 2,527 103 d18
Rio Res., N.Y. 61 N2
Río San Juan, Dom. Rep., 1,912 96 m6
Río Seco, Cuba, 1,615 96 f2
Riosucio, Col. 100 B4
Riosucio, Col. 100 C5
Río Tercero, Arg., 25,000* 105 C4
Río Tigre, Ec. 104 B2
Rio Tinto, Braz., 16,811 103 K3
Rio Tinto, Nev. 83 B2
Río Tocuyo, Ven., 1,650 100 F2
Rio Tuba, Phil., 1,956 153 A3
Riou L., Sask., Can. 43 C2
Riouw, Kep., Indon. 148 C2
Rio Verde, Braz., 11,268 103 F5
Río Verde, Chile 105 A8
Rioverde, Mex., 14,294 93 E4
Rio Verde de Mato Grosso, Braz., 9,535 103 E5
Rio Vista, Calif., 2,616 83 f11
Rio Vista, Tex., 284 76 e10
Riozinho, r., Braz. 102 C2
Ripanj, Yug., 8,255 125 E2
Ripley, Ont., Can. 44 G7
Ripley, Derby., Eng., U.K., 17,617 114 F4
Ripley, York., Eng., U.K. 114 E2
Ripley, Ill., 167 68 B3
Ripley, co., Ind., 20,641 70 D3
Ripley, Me. 55 C4
Ripley, Miss., 2,668 73 G3
Ripley, co., Mo., 9,096 72 G8
Ripley, N.Y., 1,247 58 A7
Ripley, Ohio, 2,174 70 F4
Ripley, Okla., 263 76 G1
Ripley, Tenn., 3,782 71 B6
Ripley, W. Va., 2,756 62 C4
Riplinger, Wis. 66 C4
Ripoll, Sp., 9,034 122 G1
Ripon, Qué., Can. 47 J3
Ripon, U.K., 10,490 113 F4
Ripon, Calif., 1,894 82 C4
Ripon, Wis., 6,163 66 E5
Riposto, It., 12,894 123 E6
Rippey, Iowa, 331 72 C3
Rippon, W. Va. 62 G3
Ripponden, U.K., 5,765 114 E3
Rippowam, r., Conn.-N.Y. 56 B8
Ripsa, Swed. 120 d9
Ripton, Vt. 54 A4
Riṣāfah, ruins, Syr. 142 D3
Risan, Yug. 125 D3
Risaralda, Col. 101 d14
Risbäck, Swed. 120 C2
Risca, U.K., 13,955 114 B7
Risch, Switz., 2,038 124 C1
Risco, Mo., 502 72 H8
Riseley, U.K. 114 H6
Risher, Ark. 73 E2
Rishikesh, India, 10,925 144 b10
Rishiri-tō, Jap. 155 J7
Rishon Le Zion, Isr., 27,887 142 a8
Rising City, Nebr., 308 75 H2
Risingdale (part of Great Barrington), Mass. 56 C4
Rising Star, Tex., 997 77 O3
Rising Sun, Ind., 2,230 70 E4
Rising Sun, Md., 824 62 H3
Risingsun, Ohio, 815 70 F1
Risk, Ill. 68 D3
Riske Creek, Br. Col., Can. 42 G3
Risle, r., Fr. 117 D2
Risley = Estell Manor
Rişnov, Rum., 7,974 128 E2
Rison, Ark., 889 73 C4
Risör, Nor., 3,061 120 B4
Ris-Orangis, Fr., 9,247 116 h12
Risöyhamn, Nor. 120 C1
Riṣṣū, Jabal, U.A.R. 161 i8
Ristijärvi, Fin. 120 G2
Rita, La. 73 E8
Rita Blanca Cr., Tex. 76 M2
Ritchey, Mo., 128 72 C8
Ritchie, Md. 62 b9
Ritchie, co., W. Va., 10,877 62 C3
Ritidian Pt., Guam 176 24
Ritter, Oreg. 80 D3
Ritter, Mt., Calif. 82 D4
Rittersdorf, F.R.Ger., 1,008 119 A4
Rittman, Ohio, 5,410 70 H1
Ritzville, Wash., 2,173 80 D2
Riu, Mt., Terr. Papua 174 3
Riung, Indon. 149 G5
Riva, It., 10,664 123 C2
Riva, Md. 62 c9
Rivadavia, Arg. 105 B4
Rivadavia, Arg., 6,240 105 C5
Rivare, Ind. 70 E2
Rivarolo Canavese, It., 8,069 122 a5
Rivarolo Mantovano, It., 3,573 122 d5
Rivas, Nic., 7,176 94 D5
Rivas, Urug. 105 c10
Riva San Vitale, Switz., 1,358 124 C3
Rive-de-Gier, Fr., 16,677 116 p15
Rivera, Arg., 5,800* 105 C5
Rivera, Col. 100 C6
Rivera, Ec. 104 c11
Rivera, Urug., 35,000* 105 D4
Riverbank, Calif., 2,786 82 C4
River Canard, Ont., Can 67 f16
River Cess, Lib. 162 C5
Riverdale, Ga., 1,045 64 g10
Riverdale, Ill., 12,008 69 d10
Riverdale, Md., 4,389 62 b9
Riverdale (part of Northbridge), Mass. 57 K4
Riverdale, Mich. 67 J5
Riverdale, Nebr., 144 75 F3
Riverdale, N.J., 2,596 58 b13
Riverdale, N. Dak., 1,055 74 B2
Riverdale, Utah, 1,848 78 b8
Riverdale, Va. 62 E6
River Edge, N.J., 13,264 58 c13
River Falls, Ala., 401 64 C4
River Falls, Wis., 4,857 66 A4
River Forest, Ill., 12,695 69 c9
Rivergaro, It., 4,634 122 c6
River Grove, Ill., 8,464 69 c9
Riverhead, Newf., Can. 45 b11
Riverhead, N.Y., 5,830 59 P10
River Hébert, N.S., Can., 1,549 47 T11
River Heights, Utah, 880 78 c7
River Hills, Wis., 1,257 66 d11
Riverhurst, Sask., Can. 43 C5
Riverina, plain, Austl. 173 F5
River John, N.S., Can. 47 U11
River Jordan, Br. Col., Can. 42 c7
Riverlea, Ohio, 625 70 a6
River Oaks, Tex., 8,444 76 e9
River Point (part of W. Warwick), R.I. 57 L6
Riverport, N.S., Can. 47 T11
River Rouge, Mich., 18,147 67 f15
Rivers, Man., Can., 1,498 43 E5
Riversdale, S. Af., 5,071 164 C7
Riverside, Ont., Can., 18,000 44 G7
Riverside, co., Calif., 306,191 82 E6
Riverside, Calif., 84,332 82 E6
Riverside (part of Greenwich), Conn. 56 B8
Riverside (part of Oxford), Conn. 56 D7
Riverside, Ga., 329 64 F4
Riverside, Ill., 9,750 69 c9
Riverside, Iowa, 656 72 F3
Riverside (part of Gill), Mass. 56 F2
Riverside, Mo., 1,315 75 a7
Riverside, Nev. 83 C4
Riverside, N.J., 8,474(T) 61 A3
Riverside, N.Y., 1,030 58 F7
Riverside, Oreg. 80 D4
Riverside, Pa., 1,580 60 J4
Riverside (part of E. Providence), R.I. 57 L5
Riverside, Tex. 77 Q4
Riverside, Utah 78 b7
Riverside, Wash., 201 80 D1
Riverside, Wyo., 87 81 F5
Riverside Res., Colo. 79 C1
Rivers Inlet, Br. Col., Can. 42 E3
Riverton, Austl., 1,500* 172 c8
Riverton, Man., Can. 43 F4
Riverton, N.Z., 1,225 175 e7
Riverton (part of Barkhamsted), Conn. 56 D5
Riverton, Ill., 1,536 68 C4
Riverton, Iowa, 399 72 B4
Riverton, La. 73 C5
Riverton, Nebr., 303 75 G3
Riverton, N.J., 3,324 61 B3
Riverton, Oreg. 80 A4
Riverton, Utah, 1,993 78 B1
Riverton, Vt. 54 B3
Riverton, Va. 62 F4
Riverton, W. Va. 62 E4
Riverton, Wyo., 6,845 81 E4
Riverton Heights, Wash. 81 b8
River View, Ala., 1,171 64 D3
Riverview, Fla. 65 H2
Riverview, Mich., 7,237 67 f16
Riverview, Mo., 3,706 72 b11
Riverview, Nebr. 75 F1
Riverview Heights, N.B., Can., 2,666 47 T10
Riverville, Va. 62 F5
Riverwoods, Ill., 96 69 c8
Rives, Fr., 3,922 117 F4
Rivesaltes, Fr., 6,262 117 E5
Rives Junction, Mich. 67 J6
Rivesville, W. Va., 1,191 62 D3
Riviera, Tex. 77 P6
Riviera, coast, Fr.-It. 117 G5
Riviera Beach, Fla., 13,046 65 K6
Riviera Beach, Md., 4,902 62 H3
Rivière-à-Pierre, Qué., Can. 47 M1
Rivière-au-Renard, Qué., Can., 1,772 45 N5
Rivière Bleue, Qué., Can., 1,501 47 R10
Rivière des Anguilles, Maurit. 165 c12
Rivière-des-Prairies, Qué., Can., 8,548 47 p17
Rivière-du-Loup, Qué., Can., 11,057 45 L6
Rivière du Rempart, Maurit. 165 c12
Rivière-Pentecôte, Qué., Can. 45 M5
Rivière-Pilote, Mart., 1,502 97 12
Rivière-Quelle, Qué., Can. 47 Q10
Rivière Salée, Mart., 1,049 97 12
Rivoli, It., 17,831 123 A2
Rivolta d'Adda, It., 6,621 122 c5
Riwaka, N.Z. 175 g6
Rixford, Pa. 60 E2
Riyadh = Ar Riyāḍ
Rizal, Phil., 6,114 153 c7
Rize, Turk., 22,261 142 E1
Rizokarpaso, Cyp., 3,667 142 C3
Rizzuto, Capo, It. 123 F5
Rjukan, Nor. 120 B4
Roa, Sp., 2,898 122 D2
Roachdale, Ind., 927 70 C3
Roach Pds., Me. 55 C3
Roade, U.K., 1,534 114 G6
Road Town, V.I. 97 4
Roan Cliffs, Utah 78 ·
Roan Cr., Colo. 79 A2
Roane, co., Tenn., 39,133 71 G6
Roane, Tex. 76 g10
Roane, co., W. Va., 15,720 62 C4
Roan Mountain, Tenn. 71 J5
Roann, Ind., 478 70 D2
Roanne, Fr., 53,203 117 E3
Roanoke, Ala., 5,288 64 D2
Roanoke, Ill., 1,821 68 C3
Roanoke, Ind., 935 70 D2
Roanoke, Tex., 585 76 e8
Roanoke, co., Va., 61,693 62 D5
Roanoke, Va., 97,110 62 E5
Roanoke, W. Va. 62 D4
Roanoke, r., N.C.-Va. 53 L3
Roanoke Rapids, N.C., 13,320 63 G1
Roanoke Rapids L., N.C. 62 G6
Roan Plat., Colo. 50 E3
Roaring Bk., Conn. 56 F6
Roaring Fk., r., Colo. 79 B2
Roaring River, N.C. 63 C1
Roaring Spring, Pa., 2,937 60 F5
Roaring Springs, Tex., 398 77 N3
Roatán, Hond., 1,171 94 D2
Roatán, I. de, Hond. 94 D2
Robāt, Afghan. 144 B2
Robbins, Calif. 82 a7
Robbins, Ill., 7,511 69 d10
Robbins, N.C., 1,294 63 E2
Robbins, Tenn. 71 G5
Robbinsdale, Minn., 16,381 74 b5
Robbins I., Austl. 173 e13
Robbinston, Me. 55 E3
Robbinsville, N.C., 587 63 b7
Robbio, It., 7,175 122 b5
Robbs, Ill. 68 D6
Robe, Austl. 172 E5
Röbel, Ger.D.R. 118 D2
Robeline, La., 308 73 B6
Roberdel, N.C., 379 63 E2
Robersonville, N.C., 1,684 63 G2
Robert, Havre du, Mart. 97 12
Roberta, Ga., 714 64 E3
Robert Lee, Tex., 990 77 N4
Roberto Payán, Col. 100 B7
Roberts, Idaho, 422 81 C4
Roberts, Ill., 504 68 D3
Roberts, Mont. 81 E3
Roberts, Okla. 76 G4
Roberts, co., S. Dak., 13,190 74 D3
Roberts, co., Tex., 1,075 76 N2
Roberts, Wis., 308 66 A4
Robertsburg, W. Va. 62 B4
Roberts Creek, Br. Col., Can. 42 c6
Robertsdale, Ala., 1,474 64 B5
Robertsdale, Pa. 60 F5
Robertsfors, Swed. 120 E2
Robertsganj, India, 6,584 145 G4
Robertson, S. Af., 8,166 164 a8
Robertson, co., Ky., 2,443 71 G3
Robertson, co., Tenn., 27,335 71 E5
Robertson, co., Tex., 16,157 77 P4
Robertsonville, Qué., Can., 1,136 47 N2
Robertsport, Lib. 162 B4
Robertsville, Calif. 83 f13
Robertsville, Ohio 70 H2
Robertville, Belg., 1,686 119 A4
Roberval, Qué., Can., 7,597 44 K5
Robeson, co., N.C., 89,102 63 E3
Robeson Chan., Can.-Greenl. 180 F1
Robesonia, Pa., 1,579 61 K5
Robinson, Alta., Can. 42 L4
Robinson, Yukon, Can. 40 B5
Robinson, Ill., 7,226 68 E4
Robinson, Kans., 317 75 K4
Robinson, N. Dak., 155 74 C2
Robinson, Tex., 2,111 77 P4
Robinson, L., S.C. 63 D3
Robinsons, Me. 55 E2
Roblin, Man., Can., 1,425 43 E4
Roboré, Bol., 6,403 102 E5
Rob Roy I., Sol. Is. 175 b2
Robsart, Sask., Can. 43 B5
Robson, Mt., Br. Col., Can. 42 H3
Robstown, Tex., 10,266 77 P6
Roby, Mo. 72 E7
Roby, Tex., 913 77 N3
Roca, Nebr., 123 75 J3
Roca, C. da, Port. 122 i10
Rocafuerte, Ec., 4,383 104 A2
Rocafuerte, Ec. 104 B2
Roca Kong, Camb. 147 k11
Roca Partida, I., Mex. 92 b7
Rocas de Sto. Domingo, Chile 104 f13
Rocca di Papa, It., 7,291 123 b8
Roccamonfina, It., 5,311 123 c9
Roccastrada, It., 14,499 123 C3
Rocester, U.K., 1,234 114 E5
Rocha, Urug., 18,000* 105 E4
Rochdale, U.K., 85,785 113 E5
Rochdale, Mass., 1,058 56 J4
Roche, Switz. 124 A2
Rochechouart, Fr., 4,093 117 D4
Rochedo, Braz. 103 E5
Rochefort, Belg., 3,956 115 D4
Rochefort, Fr., 33,584 117 C4
Rochefort-en-Yvelines, Fr. 116 f12
Rochelle, Ga., 1,235 64 F4
Rochelle, Ill., 7,008 68 C2
Rochelle, Tex. 77 O4
Rochelle, Va. 62 F4
Rocheport, Mo., 375 72 E5
Rocher River, N.W.T., Can. 40 G5
Roches Point, Ont., Can. 46 E4
Rochester, Austl., 1,791 173 e11
Rochester, Alta., Can. 42 K2
Rochester, U.K., 50,143 113 G6
Rochester, Ill., 1,265 68 C4
Rochester, Ind., 4,883 70 C1
Rochester, Mass., 1,559(T) 57 N6
Rochester, Mich., 5,431 67 K6
Rochester, Minn., 40,663 74 F4
Rochester, N.H., 15,927 54 E5
Rochester, N.Y., 318,611 58 E5
Rochester, Pa., 5,952 60 B4
Rochester, Tex., 625 77 O3
Rochester, Vt. 54 B4
Rochester, Wash. 80 B2
Rochester, Wis., 413 66 c13
Rochester Mills, Pa. 60 D4
Rochetaillée, Fr. 116 O16
Rochlitz, Ger.D.R. 126 b5
Rock, Kans. 75 J6
Rock (part of Middleboro), Mass. 57 N5
Rock, Mich. 66 F2
Rock, co., Minn., 11,864 74 D4
Rock, co., Nebr., 2,554 75 F1
Rock, co., Wis., 113,913 66 D6
Rock, r., Br. Col.-Yukon, Can. 42 E1
Rock, r., Qué.-Vt. 54 A1
Rock, r., Ill.-Wis. 53 J2
Rock, r., Iowa-Minn. 72 A1
Rock, r., Vt. 54 B6
Rockall, i., Atl. Oc. 108 M3
Rockaway, N.J., 5,413 61 C2
Rockaway, Oreg., 771 80 A3
Rockaway, r., N.J. 61 B2
Rockaway Beach, Mo., 177 72 D8
Rockaway Park (part of N.Y.C.), N.Y. 58 d14
Rockaway Pt., N.Y. 58 d14
Rock Bay, Br. Col., Can. 42 F4
Rockbridge, Ill., 253 68 B4
Rockbridge, Mo. 72 E8
Rockbridge, co., Va., 24,039 62 E5
Rockbridge Baths, Va. 62 E5
Rockcastle, co., Ky., 12,334 71 G4
Rockcastle, r., Ky. 71 G4
Rock Cave, W. Va. 62 D4
Rock City Falls, N.Y. 59 v27
Rockcliffe Park, Ont., Can., 2,022 47 J3
Rock Creek, Ohio, 673 70 J1
Rock Creek, Baker Co., Oreg. 80 D3
Rock Creek, Gilliam Co., Oreg. 80 C3
Rock Cr., D.C.-Md. 62 a8
Rock Cr., Ill. 68 B2
Rock Cr., Pa. 60 H6
Rock Cr., S. Dak. 74 D4
Rock Cr., Utah 78 C1
Rock Cr., Wash. 80 E2
Rock Cr. Butte, Oreg. 80 D3
Rockdale, co., Ga., 10,572 64 E2
Rockdale, Ill., 1,272 69 b10
Rockdale, Md. 62 c7
Rockdale, N.Y. 59 J7
Rockdale, Tex., 4,481 77 P4
Rockdale, Wis., 191 66 D6
Rock Elm, Wis. 66 A4
Rockenberg, F.R.Ger., 2,402 119 F4
Rockenhausen, F.R.Ger., 2,960 119 D5
Rockerville, S. Dak. 74 A4
Rockfall (part of Middlefield), Conn. 56 F6
Rock Falls, Ill., 10,261 68 C2
Rock Falls, Iowa, 156 72 D1
Rock Falls, Wis. 66 B4
Rockfield, Ky. 71 E5
Rockfield, Wis. 66 c10
Rockfish, Va. 62 F5
Rockford, Ala., 328 64 C3
Rockford, Ill., 126,706 68 D1
Rockford, Iowa, 941 72 D1
Rockford, Mich., 2,074 67 H5
Rockford, Ohio, 1,155 70 E2
Rockford, Tenn. 71 H6
Rockford, Wash., 369 80 E2
Rockglen, Sask., Can. 43 C5
Rock Hall, Md., 1,073 62 H3
Rockham, S. Dak., 197 74 C3
Rockhampton, Austl., 40,670 173 G3
Rock Harbor (part of Orleans), Mass. 57 Q5
Rock Hbr., Mich. 66 b8
Rock Harbor Lodge, Mich. 66 b8
Rockhaven, Sask., Can. 43 B4
Rock Hill, Mo., 6,523 72 a11
Rock Hill, N.Y. 59 L8
Rock Hill, S.C., 29,404 63 C3
Rockhill Furnace, Pa. 60 G5
Rockholds, Ky. 71 G5
Rockingham, Austl., 1,022 172 A5
Rockingham, N.S., Can., 1,451 47 U11
Rockingham, U.K. 114 G5
Rockingham, co., N.H., 99,029 54 E5
Rockingham, Ga. 64 G4
Rockingham, co., N.C., 69,629 63 E1
Rockingham, N.C., 5,512 63 E3
Rockingham, co., Va., 40,485 62 E4
Rockingham B., Austl. 173 G2
Rock Island, Qué., Can., 1,589 47 M4
Rock Island, co., Ill., 150,991 68 B2
Rock Island, Ill., 51,863 68 B2
Rock Island, Okla. 76 J2
Rock Island, Wash., 260 80 C2
Rock Lake, N. Dak., 350 74 C1
Rock L., Man., Can. 74 C1
Rockland, Ont., Can., 3,041 47 J3
Rockland (part of Madison), Conn. 56 F7
Rockland, Del. 62 e10
Rockland, Idaho, 258 81 C4
Rockland, Me., 8,769 55 C4
Rockland, Mass., 13,119(T) 57 N4
Rockland, Mich. 66 D2
Rockland, co., N.Y., 136,802 59 M9
Rockland, N.Y. 59 L8
Rockland, Wis., 257 66 C5
Rockledge, Fla., 3,481 65 J4
Rockledge, Pa., 2,587 60 f11
Rocklin, Calif., 1,495 82 b7
Rocklyn, Wash. 80 D2
Rockmart, Ga., 3,938 64 D1
Rock Point, Ariz. 78 D3
Rock Point, Md. 62 H4
Rockport, Calif. 82 B3
Rockport, Ill. 68 A4
Rockport, Ind., 2,474 70 B5
Rockport, Me. 55 C4
Rockport, Mass., 3,511; 4,616(T) 57 O2
Rockport, Miss. 73 E6
Rock Port, Mo., 1,310 72 B4
Rockport, Tex., 2,989 77 P5
Rockport, Wash. 80 C1
Rock Rapids, Iowa, 2,780 72 A1
Rock Rift, N.Y. 59 K7
Rock River, Wyo., 497 81 F5
Rock Run, Ala. 64 D1
Rock Sound, Bah. Is. 95 D1
Rocksprings, Tex., 1,182 77 N4
Rock Springs, Wis., 463 66 D5
Rock Springs, Wyo., 10,371 81 E5
Rockton, Ont., Can. 46 b14
Rockton, Ill., 1,833 68 C1
Rockton, Pa. 60 E3
Rockton, Wis. 66 C5
Rockvale, Colo., 413 79 C2
Rock Valley, Iowa, 1,693 72 A1
Rockville, Calif. 83 e11
Rockville, Conn., 9,478 56 G5
Rockville, Ind., 2,756 70 B3
Rockville, Md., 26,090 62 G3
Rockville, Mo., 255 72 D6
Rockville, Nebr., 153 75 G2
Rockville (part of Hopkinton), R.I. 57 J6
Rockville, S.C. 63 D5
Rockville, Wis. 66 C6
Rockville Centre, N.Y., 26,355 59 N10
Rockwall, co., Tex., 5,878 77 P3
Rockwall, Tex., 2,166 76 g9
Rockwell, Iowa, 772 72 D2
Rockwell, N.C., 948 63 D2
Rockwell City, Iowa, 2,313 72 C2
Rockwood, Ont., Can. 46 b13
Rockwood, Ala. 64 B1
Rockwood, Colo. 79 A3
Rockwood, Ill., 98 68 C6
Rockwood, Me. 55 C3
Rockwood, Mich., 2,026 67 e16
Rockwood, Oreg. 80 a6
Rockwood, Pa., 1,101 60 D6
Rockwood, Tenn., 5,345 71 G6
Rocky, Okla., 343 76 D2
Rocky, r., Newf., Can. 45 b10
Rocky, r., N.C. 63 D2
Rocky, r., N.C. 63 E2
Rocky, r., Ohio 70 d9
Rocky, r., S.C. 63 B3
Rocky Comfort, Mo., 151 72 C8
Rocky Comfort Cr., Ga. 64 G2
Rockyford, Alta., Can. 42 K3
Rocky Ford, Colo., 4,929 79 D2
Rocky Ford, Ga., 241 64 H3
Rocky Fork, r., Ohio 70 b6
Rocky Fork L., Ohio 70 F3
Rocky Gorge Res., Md. 62 b8
Rocky Grove, Pa., 3,168 60 C3
Rocky Hill, Conn., 7,404(T) 56 F6
Rocky Hill, N.J., 528 61 B3
Rocky I., Wis. 66 C1
Rocky Island L., Ont., Can. 44 G6
Rocky L., Man., Can. 43 E3
Rocky L., Me. 55 E4
Rocky Mount, Ga., 83 64 f12
Rocky Mount, N.C., 32,147 63 G2
Rocky Mount, Va., 1,412 62 E5
Rocky Mtn., Me. 55 C1
Rocky Mountain House, Alta., Can., 2,258 42 J3
Rocky Mtn. Nat. Pk., Colo. 79 C1
Rocky Mts., Can.-U.S. 34 D4
Rocky Mtn. Trench, Br. Col., Can. 38 E6
Rocky Point, N.Y., 2,261 59 P10
Rocky Point, Jam. 96 p9
Rocky Pt., Norfolk I. 175 11
Rocky Pt., Tutuila 177 39
Rocky Point, N.C. 63 G3
Rocky Ridge, Ala. 64 d8
Rockyridge, Ohio, 441 70 F1
Rocky River, Ohio, 18,097 70 d9
Ročov, Czech. 126 c6
Rocroi, Fr., 2,870 117 F2
Roda, Va. 62 B6
Rodalben, F.R.Ger., 6,513 119 D6
Rodanthe, N.C. 63 J2
Rodas, Cuba, 4,569 96 c1
Rødby, Den., 3,551 121 D6
Rødby Havn, Den. 121 D6
Rodd, New Hebr. 174 m6
Rodden, Ill. 68 B1
Roddickton, Newf., Can., 1,185 45 Q5
Rødding, Den. 121 A4
Rodding, Den. 121 B5
Röddinge, Swed. 121 F5
Rødekro, Den. 121 B5
Roden, Neth. 115 E1
Roden, r., U.K. 114 C5
Rodenkirchen, F.R.Ger., 3,360 118 B2
Rodeo, Mex., 1,105 92 D3
Rodeo, Calif. 83 e11
Rodeo, N. Mex. 79 A6
Röderau, Ger.D.R. 126 c5
Rodessa, La. 73 A5
Rodewisch, Ger.D.R., 12,828 126 b6
Rodez, Fr., 24,352 117 E4
Rodheim, F.R.Ger., 2,567 119 F4
Rodholivos, Gr., 4,021 129 D4
Rodhópolis, Gr. 129 D4
Ródhos, Gr., 37,393 129 G6
Ródhos, i., Gr. 129 G6
Roding, F.R.Ger., 2,878 118 D4
Roding, r., U.K. 114 J7
Rödingen, F.R.Ger., 2,253 119 A3
Rodington, U.K. 114 C5
Rodino, U.S.S.R. 137 q11
Rodionovo-Nesvetayskoye, U.S.S.R. 136 f8
Rodman, Iowa, 144 72 C1
Rodman, N.Y. 59 J4
Rodna, Rum. 128 E1
Rodney, Ont., Can., 1,036 46 C6
Rodney, Iowa, 94 72 B2
Rodney, Mich. 67 H5
Rodney, Miss. 73 D6
Rodniki, U.S.S.R., 29,200 136 F1
Rodnikovskiy, U.S.S.R. 137 i10
Rodonit, Kep i, Alb. 125 D4
Rødvig, Den., 1,862 121 E5
Roe, r., U.K. 113 C4
Roebling, N.J., 3,272 61 B3
Roebourne, Austl. 172 B3
Roebuck Bay, Austl. 172 B2
Roeland Park, Kans., 8,949 75 a7
Roelofarendsveen, Neth., 4,200 115 b6
Roer, r., F.R.Ger.-Neth. 119 A2
Roermond, Neth., 31,400 115 D3
Roeselare, Belg., 34,953 115 B4
Roes Welcome Sd., N.W.T., Can. 41 M5
Roetgen, F.R.Ger., 2,785 119 A3
Roff, Okla., 638 76 G3
Rogachëv, U.S.S.R., 10,000 136 C2
Rogačica, Yug. 125 D2
Rogans Seat, mtn., U.K. 114 D2
Rogate, U.K., 1,394 113 m12
Rogatec, Yug. 125 B1
Rogatica, Yug., 2,585 125 D3
Roger, Mt., Br. Col., Can. 42 H3
Roger Mills, co., Okla., 5,090 76 D2
Rogers, Ark., 5,700 73 A1
Rogers (part of Killingly), Conn. 56 J5
Rogers, La. 73 C6
Rogers, Nebr., 162 75 J2
Rogers, N. Mex. 79 D4
Rogers, N. Dak., 119 74 C2
Rogers, co., Okla., 20,614 76 H1
Rogers, Tex., 936 77 P4
Rogers, Mt., Va. 62 C6
Rogers City, Mich., 4,722 67 K3
Rogers L., Calif. 82 E5
Rogerson, Idaho 81 B4
Rogerstone, U.K., 5,931 114 B7
Rogersville, N.B., Can., 1,040 47 T10
Rogersville, Ala., 766 64 B1
Rogersville, Mo., 447 72 E7
Rogersville, Tenn., 3,121 71 H5
Roggan, r., Qué., Can. 44 H3
Roggendorf, Aust. 124 c9
Roggewein, C., Easter I. 177 46
Roggiano Gravina, It., 8,056 123 F5
Roggwil, Switz., 3,420 124 B1
Rogliano, Fr. 116 r17
Rognan, Nor. 120 C2
Rogoaguado, L., Bol. 102 C4
Rogodjampi, Indon. 148 f8
Rogozna, mts., Yug. 125 E3
Rogoźnica, Pol. 127 f5
Rogoznica, Yug. 125 B3
Rogoźno, Pol., 7,257 127 B2
Rogue, r., Oreg. 80 A4
Rogue I., Me. 55 E4
Rogue River, Oreg., 520 80 B4
Roha, India, 7,553 145 h17
Rohan, Fr. 116 B2
Rohnerville, Calif., 2,268 82 B2
Rohr, Aust. 124 b11
Röhr, r., F.R.Ger. 119 E2
Rohrau, Aust. 124 N5
Rohrbach, Aust., 1,320 124 b10
Rohrbach, Aust., 1,668 124 K5
Rohrbach, Aust., 2,300 124 N6
Rohrbach, Fr., 1,517 116 d8
Rohrbach, F.R.Ger., 1,492 119 E6
Rohri, Pak., 19,072 144 C4
Rohtak, India, 88,193 144 a11
Rohunta, L., Mass. 56 G2
Roi, i., Kwajalein 176 25
Roi Baudouin, Ant. 180 Q6
Roi Et, Thai., 13,055 146 C3
Roisel, Fr., 1,843 117 E2
Roissy, Fr., 1,900 116 i11
Roissy-en-France, Fr., 1,243 116 i10
Rojas, Arg., 10,371 105 C4
Rojo, C., Dom. Rep. 96 m7
Rojo, C., Mex. 93 F4
Rojo, C., P.R. 96 r11
Rojoa, i., Eniwetok 176 28
Rokan, r., Indon. 148 B2
Rokiškis, U.S.S.R., 5,500 136 B2
Rokitki, Pol. 127 e5
Rokugō, Jap., 9,354 155 G2
Rokycany, Czech., 12,050 126 A2
Rokytnice nad Jizerou, Czech. 127 e6
Roland, Man., Can. 43 f10
Roland, Iowa, 748 72 D2
Roland, Okla., 100 76 J2
Rölanda, Swed. 121 D2
Röldal, Nor. 120 A4
Roldán, Arg., 6,500* 105 a11
Roldanillo, Col. 100 B5
Rolde, Neth. 115 E2
Rolesville, N.C., 358 63 F2
Rolette, co., N. Dak., 10,641 74 C1
Rolette, N. Dak., 524 74 C1
Rolfe, Iowa, 819 72 C2
Rolfe, Pa. 60 E2
Roll, Ariz. 78 A5
Roll, Okla. 76 D2
Rolla, Br. Col., Can. 42 G2
Rolla, Kans., 464 75 D6
Rolla, Mo., 11,132 72 F7
Rolla, N. Dak., 1,398 74 C1
Rolla, Tex. 76 N2
Rolle, Switz., 2,942 124 A2
Rolle, C., St. Vinc. 97 19
Rolleston, Austl. 173 G4
Rolleville, Bah. Is. 95 c8
Rollin, Mich. 67 J7
Rolling Fork, Miss., 1,619 73 E5
Rolling Fk., r., Ky. 71 F4
Rolling Hills, Alta., Can. 42 K4
Rolling Hills, Calif., 1,664 83 h16
Rolling Hills Estates, Calif., 3,941 83 g16
Rolling Meadows, Ill., 10,879 69 c8
Rolling Prairie, Ind. 70 C1
Rollingstone, Austl. 173 F2
Rollingstone, Minn., 392 74 G3
Rollingwood, Tex. 76 c5
Rollins, Ill. 69 b7
Rollinsford, N.H., 1,210 54 F5
Rollinsville, Colo. 79 a8
Rollo Head = Ronar, Point
Rolvsöya, i., Nor. 120 E1
Roma, Austl., 4,248 173 G4
Roma, It., 1,983,286 123 D4
Romaine, r., Qué., Can. 45 N4
Roma-Los Saenz, Tex., 1,496 77 O6
Roman, Rum., 27,948 128 F1
Romanche Gap, Atl. Oc. 109 L7
Romang, P., Indon. 149 H4
Romania = Rumania
Roman-Kosh, G., U.S.S.R. 136 D4
Romano, Cayo, Cuba 96 e1
Romano di Lombardia, It., 10,350 122 c5
Romanovka, U.S.S.R. 136 F3
Romanshorn, Switz., 7,755 124 D1
Romans-sur-Isère, Fr., 27,662 117 F4
Romanzof, C., Alaska 85 C3
Rombas, Fr., 10,492 116 b8
Rombauer, Mo. 72 G8
Romblon, Phil., 3,342 153 B2
Rombo, Ilhéus do, C. Verde Is. 109 5
Rome, It. = Roma
Rome, Ga., 32,226 64 D1
Rome, Ill., 1,347 68 C3
Rome, Ind. 70 C5
Rome, Me. 55 C4
Rome, Miss., 279 73 E4
Rome, N.Y., 51,646 59 J5
Rome, Ashtabula Co., Ohio 70 J1
Rome, Richland Co., Ohio 70 G2
Rome, Oreg. 80 E4
Rome, Pa., 274 61 K2
Rome, Tenn. 71 E5
Rome, Wis. 66 E6
Rome City, Ind. 70 D1
Romeo, Colo., 339 79 B3
Romeo, Fla. 65 G3
Romeo, Mich., 3,327 67 L6
Romeoville, Ill., 6,358 69 b10
Romeral, Chile, 1,232 104 f14
Romero, Tex. 76 M2
Romeroville, N. Mex. 79 C4
Romford, London, U.K. 114 J7
Romilly, Fr., 15,966 117 E2
Romilly, Terr. Papua 174 e2
Romita, Mex., 10,377 93 c9
Rommerskirchen, F.R.Ger., 3,760 119 B2
Rommerz, F.R.Ger., 1,220 119 H4
Romney, Ind. 70 C2
Romney, W. Va., 2,203 62 F3
Romney Marsh, U.K. 113 G6
Romny, U.S.S.R., 34,500 136 D3
Rømø, i., Den. 121 A5
Romodan, U.S.S.R., 5,700 136 D3
Rømø Kirkeby, Den. 121 A5
Romoland, Calif. 83 k16
Romona, Ind. 70 C3
Romont, Switz., 2,892 124 A2
Romoos, Switz., 1,028 124 B1
Romorantin-Lanthenay, Fr., 11,984 117 D3
Rompin, r., Malay. 147 p15
Romsey, U.K., 6,350 113 k13
Romulus, Mich., 1,798 67 e16
Romulus, N.Y. 59 G6
Ron, N. Viet. 146 D3
Ron, Mui, c., N. Viet. 146 D3
Rona, i., U.K. 112 D3
Ronald, Wash. 80 C2
Ronan, Mont., 1,334 81 B2
Ronas Hill, U.K. 112 F1
Ronay, i., U.K. 112 C3
Roncador, Sa. do, Braz. 103 F4
Roncador Reef, Sol. Is. 175 c2
Roncesvalles, Sp. 122 E1
Ronceverte, W. Va., 1,882 62 D5
Ronchin, Fr., 11,690 116 a6

Roncq—Russellton · 285

Roncq, Fr., 7,536 116 a6
Ronda, Sp., 28,831 122 C4
Ronda, N.C., 501 63 C1
Rønde, Den. 121 C4
Ronde, Point, Dominica 97 13
Rondeau Park, Ont., Can. 46 C6
Ronde I., Gren. Is. 97 20
Rondo, Ark., 219 73 E3
Rondón, Col. 100 E4
Rondônia, terr., Braz., 70,783 102 D4
Rondônia, Braz., 1,293 102 D4
Rondonópolis, Braz., 4,345 103 E5
Rondorf, F.R.Ger., 23,459 119 B3
Rondout, Ill. 69 c7
Rondout Res., N.Y. 59 M8
Rong, Koh, i., Camb. 146 C5
Ronge, L. la, Sask., Can. 43 D3
Rongelap, atoll, Marsh. Is. 170 F4
Rongerik, atoll, Marsh. Is. 176 22
Roniu, pk., Tahiti 177 44
Ronkiti, Ponape 176 29
Ronkonkoma, N.Y., 4,220 58 g13
Rønne, Den., 13,195 121 G5
Ronneburg, Ger.D.R., 11,987 126 b6
Ronneby, Swed. 120 C4
Ronne Entr., Ant. 180 N5
Rönninge, Swed. 120 e8
Ron Phibun, Thai., 2,176 146 C5
Ronse, Belg., 25,178 115 B4
Ronsecco, It., 1,339 122 b5
Ronuro, r., Braz. 103 F4
Roodepoort, S. Af., 94,740 165 i17
Roodhouse, Ill., 2,352 68 B4
Rookhope, U.K. 112 f10
Rooks, co., Kans., 9,734 75 F4
Roon, P., Indon. 149 K3
Roopville, Ga., 203 64 D2
Roorkee, India, 33,651 145 F3
Roos, U.K. 114 H3
Roosendaal, Neth., 32,800 115 C3
Roosevelt, La. 73 D5
Roosevelt, Minn., 145 74 E1
Roosevelt, co., Mont., 11,731 81 G1
Roosevelt, N.J., 764 61 C3
Roosevelt, co., N. Mex., 16,198 79 D5
Roosevelt, N.Y., 12,883 58 e14
Roosevelt, Okla., 495 76 D3
Roosevelt, Tex. 77 N4
Roosevelt, Utah, 1,812 78 C1
Roosevelt, Wash. 80 C3
Roosevelt, Mt., Br. Col., Can. 42 F1
Roosevelt, r., Braz. 102 D3
Roosevelt I., Ant. 180 W4
Roosevelt Park, Mich., 2,578 67 G5
Root, Switz., 2,537 124 C1
Root, r., Minn. 74 G4
Root, r., Wis. 66 F6
Ropczyce, Pol., 3,709 127 D3
Rope, The, cliff, Pitc. I. 177 45
Roper, Kans. 75 K6
Roper, N.C., 771 63 H2
Roper, r., Austl. 172 E2
Ropesville, Tex., 423 77 M3
Ropi, mt., Fin. 120 E1
Ropley, U.K., 1,210 113 k12
Ropotovo, Yug. 125 E4
Ropsley, U.K. 114 H5
Roquebillière, Fr., 1,530 117 G4
Roquebrune-Cap-Martin, Fr., 6,605 116 n13
Roquebrune-sur-Argens, Fr., 2,873 116 m14
Roquefort, Fr., 2,111 117 C4
Roque Pérez, Arg., 4,550 105 b12
Roquetas de Mar, Sp., 7,013 122 D4
Rora Head, U.K. 112 E2
Roraima, terr., Braz., 29,489 102 D1
Roraima, Mt., S. Amer. 101 K5
Rorketon, Man., Can. 43 E4
Röros, Nor. 120 B3
Rorosi, Sol. Is. 175 b2
Rorschach, Switz., 12,759 124 D1
Rörum, Swed. 121 G5
Rörvik, Nor. 120 B2
Rosa, P., Mex. 92 C2
Rosales, Mex., 2,839 92 D2
Rosalia, Kans. 75 J6
Rosalia, Wash., 585 80 E2
Rosalia, P., Easter I. 177 46
Rosalie, Dominica 97 13
Rosalie, Nebr., 182 75 J1
Rosalind, Alta., Can. 43 c8
Rosamond, Calif. 82 D5
Rosamond, Ill. 68 C4
Rosamond L., Calif. 82 D5
Rosamorada, Mex., 1,664 92 D3
Rosario, Arg., 604,084* 105 C4
Rosário, Braz., 6,999 103 H2
Rosario, Baja Calif., Mex. 92 B1
Rosario, Sin., Mex., 11,608 92 D3
Rosario, Para., 1,854 105 D2
Rosario, Phil., 2,396 153 b6
Rosario, Phil., 3,122 153 b8
Rosario, Phil., 3,424 153 c9
Rosario, Urug., 8,000* 105 c12
Rosario, Ven., 10,482 100 D2
Rosario, Cayo, Cuba 96 c2
Rosario, Sierra del, Cuba 96 b1
Rosario de la Frontera, Arg., 5,900* 105 C3
Rosário do Sul, Braz., 15,786 103 E8
Rosário Oeste, Braz., 2,607 103 E4
Rosario Tala, Arg., 17,995 105 b11
Rosarno, It., 18,393 123 F5
Rosas, Arg. 105 b12
Rosas, Las, Mex., 7,771 93 G5
Rosas, Sp., 3,575 122 G1
Rosate, It., 3,124 122 b5
Rosa Zárate, Ec. 104 B1
Rosbach, F.R.Ger., 5,927 119 D3
Rosboro, Ark. 73 B3
Rosburg, Wash. 80 B2
Roscoe, Ill. 68 C1
Roscoe, Mo., 125 72 D7
Roscoe, Nebr. 75 D2
Roscoe, N.Y. 59 L8
Roscoe, Ohio 70 H2
Roscoe, Pa., 1,315 60 c9
Roscoe, S. Dak., 532 74 C3
Roscoe, Tex., 1,490 77 N3
Roscoff, Fr., 4,030 116 B2
Roscommon, co., Ire., 63,710 113 B5
Roscommon, Ire., 1,800 113 B5
Roscommon, co., Mich., 7,200 67 J4
Roscommon, Mich., 867 67 J4
Roscrea, Ire., 3,095 113 C5
Rose, Kans. 75 K6
Rose, Nebr. 75 F1
Rose, N.Y. 58 G5
Rose, Okla. 76 H1
Rose, Pte. de la, Mart. 97 12
Roseau, Dominica, 10,422 97 13
Roseau, co., Minn., 12,154 74 E1
Roseau, Minn., 2,146 74 E1
Roseau, r., Man., Can. 43 g10
Roseau, r., Dominica 97 13
Roseau, r., St. Lucia 97 11
Roseau, r., Minn. 74 D1
Rose au Rue, Newf., Can. 45 a10
Rosebery, Austl., 1,460 173 F6
Rose Blanche, Newf., Can. 45 P6
Roseboro, N.C., 1,354 63 F3
Rosebud, Austl., 1,694 173 e12
Rose Bud, Ark. 73 C2
Rosebud, Mo., 288 72 F6
Rosebud, co., Mont., 6,187 81 F2
Rosebud, Mont. 81 F2
Rosebud, S. Dak. 74 B4
Rosebud, Tex., 1,644 77 P4
Roseburg, Mich. 67 L5
Roseburg, Oreg., 11,467 80 B4
Rosebush, Mich. 67 J5
Rose Canyon, Calif. 82 c9
Rose City, Mich., 435 67 J4
Rosecrans, Ill. 69 c7
Rosedale, Austl. 173 G3
Rosedale, Colo. 79 b8
Rosedale, Ill. 68 B4
Rosedale, Ind., 726 70 B3
Rosedale, Mich. 67 J2
Rosedale, Miss., 2,339 73 E4
Rosedale, N.J. 60 g10
Rosedale, Ohio, 8,204 70 G2
Rosedale, Okla., 88 76 F3
Rosedale, Wash. 81 a8
Rosedale, W. Va. 62 C4
Roseglen, N. Dak. 74 B2
Rosehearty, U.K., 1,140 112 E3
Rose Hill, Ill., 117 68 D4
Rose Hill, Iowa, 223 72 E3
Rose Hill, Miss. 73 F5
Rose Hill, N.Y. 59 q24
Rose Hill, N.C., 1,292 63 F3
Rose Hill, Tex. 76 f9
Rose Hill, Va. 62 A6
Rose I., Amer. Samoa 177 37
Rose I., Bah. Is. 95 b7
Roseisle, Man., Can. 43 f10
Roseland, Ont., Can. 67 g15
Roseland, La., 1,254 73 E7
Roseland, Nebr., 163 75 G3
Roseland, N.J., 2,804 58 b13
Roseland, Va. 62 F5
Roselawn, Ind. 70 B1
Roselle, Ill., 3,581 68 D2
Roselle, N.J., 21,032 58 c14
Roselle Park, N.J., 12,546 58 c14
Rose Lodge, Oreg. 80 B3
Rosemary, Alta., Can. 42 K4
Rosemead, Calif., 15,476 83 h15
Rosemère, Qué., Can., 6,077 47 o17
Rosemont, Ariz. 78 C6
Rosemont, Cook Co., Ill., 2,283 69 c9
Rosemont, St. Clair Co., Ill. 72 b11
Rosemont, Pa., 3,600* 60 f11
Rosemount, Minn., 1,068 74 F3
Rosenberg, Tex., 9,698 77 Q5
Rosendale, Mo., 234 72 C4
Rosendale, N.Y., 1,033 59 M8
Rosendale, Wis., 415 66 E5
Roseneath, Ont., Can. 46 F4
Rosenfeld, Man., Can. 43 g10
Rosenhayn, N.J. 61 A5
Rosenheim, F.R.Ger., 30,472 118 D5
Rose Pk, Ariz. 78 D5
Rosepine, La., 414 73 B7
Rose Prairie, Br. Col., Can. 42 G2
Röser, Lux. 119 A5
Rosersberg, Swed. 120 e8
Roseţi, Rum. 128 F2
Roseto, Pa., 1,630 61 M4
Roseto degli Abruzzi, It., 15,185 123 E3
Rosetown, Sask., Can., 2,413 43 B4
Rosetta, U.A.R.=Rashīd
Rosetta, Ark. 73 B2
Rosette, Utah 78 B1
Rose Valley, Sask., Can. 43 D4
Roseville, Ont., Can. 46 b14
Roseville, Calif., 13,421 82 C3
Roseville, Ill., 1,065 68 B3
Roseville, Mich., 50,195 67 g14
Roseville, Minn., 29,581 74 c5
Roseville, Ohio, 1,749 70 G3
Roseville, Pa., 162 60 J2
Rosewood, Austl. 173 g10
Rosewood, Ind. 70 D4
Rosewood, N.C. 63 F2
Rosewood, Ohio 70 E2
Rosewood Heights, Ill., 4,572 72 b10
Roshal', U.S.S.R., 21,300 136 c6
Rosharon, Tex. 77 Q5
Rosheim, Fr., 3,004 119 C7
Rosholt, S. Dak., 423 74 D3
Rosholt, Wis., 497 66 D4
Roşia Montana, Rum. 128 D1
Rosice, Czech. 126 C2
Rosiclare, Ill., 1,700 68 D6
Rosières-aux-Salines, Fr., 2,550 116 b9
Rosignano Marittimo, It., 27,005 123 C3
Rosignol, Guyana 101 M4
Roşiori de Vede, Rum., 17,320 128 E2
Rositsa, r., Bulg. 128 E3
Roskilde, Den., 31,928 121 E5
Roskilde Fjord, bay, Den. 121 E5
Roslavl', U.S.S.R., 37,400 134 C4
Roslev, Den., 1,252 121 B4
Roslyatino, U.S.S.R. 136 G1
Roslyn, Austl. 173 g10
Roslyn, N.Y., 2,681 58 e13
Roslyn, Pa., 8,575* 60 f11
Roslyn, S. Dak., 256 74 D3
Roslyn, Wash., 1,283 80 C2
Rosmalen, Neth. 115 D3
Rosman, N.C., 419 63 B2
Røsnæs, pen., Den. 121 C5
Rosneath, U.K. 112 a7
Rosny-sous-Bois, Fr., 21,090 116 i11
Rosolini, It., 17,288 123 E6
Rosport, Lux. 115 E5
Rospuda, r., Pol. 127 E2
Rösrath, F.R.Ger., 12,799 119 C3
Ross, N.Z. 175 f6
Ross, Calif., 2,551 83 d12
Ross, Ind. 69 e10
Ross, Ohio 70 E3
Ross, N. Dak., 167 74 A1
Ross, co., Ohio, 61,215 70 F3
Ross', r., U.S.S.R. 136 C3
Ross, Mt., N.Z. 175 g6
Ross, Pt., Norfolk I. 175 11
Rossall Pt., U.K. 114 B3
Ross and Cromarty, co., U.K., 57,067 112 D3
Rossano, It., 22,910 123 F5
Rossan Pt., Ire. 113 B4
Rossatz, Aust. 124 b10
Ross Barnett Res., Miss. 73 F5
Rossburg, Ohio, 295 70 E2
Rossburn, Man., Can. 43 E5
Rossdorf, F.R.Ger., 5,297 119 F5
Rosseau, Ont., Can. 44 H6
Rosseau L., Ont., Can. 46 E3
Rosseau Road, Ont., Can. 46 E3
Rossel, C., Loy. Is. 174 k8
Rossel, Mt., Terr. Papua 174 3
Rossel I., Terr. Papua 174 g3
Rossel Lag., Terr. Papua 174 3
Rosserdale, Man., Can. 43 f10
Rosser, Tex. 76 g10
Rossford, Ohio, 4,406 70 F1
Ross Ice Shelf, Ant. 180 W4
Rossie, Iowa, 102 72 B1
Rossie, N.Y. 59 J3
Rossignol, L., N.S., Can. 47 T11
Rossinière, Switz. 124 B2
Ross I., Ant. 180 V5
Ross I., Burma 146 B4
Rossiter, Pa. 60 E4
Rossiyskaya Sovetskaya Federativnaya Sotsialisticheskaya Respublika, U.S.S.R., 125,800,000* 134-5
Ross L., Wash. 80 C1
Rossland, Br. Col., Can., 4,305 42 H4
Rosslare, Ire. 113 C5
Rosslau, Ger.D.R., 16,042 118 D3
Rosso, Maur., 5,000 162 B3
Ross-on-Wye, U.K., 5,641 113 E6
Rossosh', U.S.S.R., 30,100 134 C4
Rossport, Ont., Can. 44 E5
Ross River, Yukon, Can. 40 C5
Ross Sea, Ant. 180 W5
Rosston, Ark. 73 B4
Rosston, Okla. 76 D1
Rossville, Austl. 173 F2
Rossville, Ga., 4,665 64 D1
Rossville, Ill., 1,470 68 E3
Rossville, Ind., 831 70 C2
Rossville, Kans., 797 75 K4
Rossville, Tex. 77 O5
Rosswein, Ger.D.R., 10,343 118 D3
Rosthern, Sask., Can., 1,255 43 C4
Rostock, Ger.D.R., 158,630 118 D1
Rostov, U.S.S.R., 29,200 134 C4
Rostov-na-Donu, U.S.S.R., 662,000 134 D5
Rostrenen, Fr., 2,793 116 B2
Rosult, Fr., 1,215 116 a7
Rösvatnet, l., Nor. 120 C2
Roswell, Ga., 2,983 64 E1
Roswell, N. Mex., 39,593 79 C5
Roswell, S. Dak., 39 74 D4
Rosyth, U.K. 112 d7
Rot, F.R.Ger., 3,536 119 F6
Rota, Sp., 16,856 122 B4
Rota, i., Mar. Is. 170 D4
Rotan, Tex., 2,788 77 N3
Rotava, Czech. 126 b6
Rot-Bach, r., F.R.Ger. 119 B3
Rotebro, Swed. 120 e8
Rotenburg, Hess., F.R.Ger., 7,322 118 B3
Rotenburg, Ndrsachs., F.R.Ger., 13,586 118 B2
Rotenfels, F.R.Ger., 3,098 119 E7
Roth, F.R.Ger., 9,429 118 C4
Rötha, Ger.D.R. 126 b5
Rothaargebirge, F.R.Ger. 118 B3
Rothbury, U.K., 1,648 113 E4
Rothbury, Mich. 67 G5
Rothenberg, F.R.Ger., 1,322 119 F5
Rothenburg, Ger.D.R. 118 E3
Rothenburg ob der Tauber, F.R.Ger., 11,258 118 C4
Rother, r., U.K. 113 F6
Rother, r., U.K. 113 G6
Rotherham, U.K., 85,346 113 F5
Rothes, U.K., 1,105 112 E3
Rothesay, N.B., Can. 45 N6
Rothesay, U.K., 7,656 112 D4
Rothleiten, Aust., 1,991 124 M6
Rothsay, Minn., 457 74 D2
Rothschild, Wis., 2,550 66 D4
Rothwell, N.B., Can., 1,190 47 T10
Rothwell, Lincs., Eng., U.K 114 H4
Rothwell, Northants., Eng., U.K., 4,763 113 F5
Rothwell, York., Eng., U.K., 25,360 114 E3
Roti, P., Indon. 149 G5
Roto, Austl. 173 F5
Rotondo, Mt., Fr. 116 r17
Rotorua, N.Z., 19,360 175 h5
Rott, F.R.Ger., 2,300 118 D5
Rott, r., F.R.Ger. 118 D4
Rotte, r., Neth. 115 b7
Rottenburg, Bay., F.R.Ger., 2,313 118 D4
Rottenburg, Bad.-Württ., F.R.Ger., 10,046 118 B4
Rottenegg, Aust. 124 L5
Rottenmann, Aust., 4,124 124 L6
Rotterdam, Neth., 711,800 115 C3
Rotterdam, N.Y., 16,871 59 v28
Rotterdam Junction, N.Y. 59 M6
Rottumeroog, i., Neth. 115 E1
Rottweil, F.R.Ger., 16,674 118 B4
Rotwakakura, i., Aitutaki 177 35
Rotui, Mt., Moorea 177 44
Rotuma, i., Fiji 170 F5
Roubaix, Fr., 113,163 117 E1
Roudnice nad Labem, Czech. 126 B1
Rouen, Fr., 123,474 117 D2
Rouffach, Fr., 5,002 117 G3
Rouge, r., Qué., Can. 47 K3
Rouge, r., Mich. 67 K6
Rouge Hill, Ont., Can. 46 E5
Rougemont, Fr., 1,076 117 G3
Rougemont, Switz. 124 B2
Rougemont, N.C. 63 E1
Rough, r., Ky. 71 E4
Rough Pt., V.I. 97 4
Rough Run, W. Va. 62 E4
Roughty, r., Ire. 113 B6
Rouillac, Fr., 1,612 117 C4
Rouku, Terr. Papua 174 d3
Rouleau, Sask., Can. 43 D5
Roulers=Roeselare
Roulette, Pa. 60 F2
Round Hill, Alta., Can. 43 c7
Round Hill, N.S., Can. 47 T11
Round Hill (part of Greenwich), Conn. 56 B8
Round Hill, Va., 430 62 G3
Round Hill Pt., Mass. 57 N6
Round I., Mauris. 165 c12
Round Island Passage, Fiji 174 4
Round Knob, Ill. 68 D6
Round Lake, Ill., 997 69 b7
Round Lake, N.Y. 59 v28
Round L., Ont., Can. 46 G3
Round L., Mich. 67 H4
Round L., N. Dak. 74 B1
Round L., Sawyer Co., Wis. 66 B2
Round L., Price Co., Wis. 66 C3
Round Lake Beach, Ill., 5,011 69 b7
Round Lake Park, Ill., 2,565 69 b7
Round Mountain, Calif. 82 C2
Round Mountain, Nev. 83 B3
Round Mountain, Tex. 77 O4
Round Mtn., Austl. 173 ·
Round Mtn., Me. 55 D2
Round Mtn., N.J. 61 B2
Round Mtn., Vt. 54 D2
Round Mts., Calif. 82 C2
Round Oak, Ga. 64 F2
Round Pd., Me. 55 C2
Round Rock, Tex., 1,878 77 O4
Round Top, Tex., 124 77 P4
Round Top, mtn. Mass. 56 D3
Roundup, Mont., 2,842 81 E2
Roura, Fr. Guiana 101 O5
Rourkela, India, 90,287 145 G5
Rousay, i., U.K. 112 E2
Rouses Point, N.Y., 2,160 59 O2
Rouseville, Pa., 923 60 C3
Rousham, U.K. 114 F7
Roussillon, Fr., 6,588 117 F4
Roussin, C., Loy. Is. 174 m8
Routier, Calif. 82 b7
Routt, co., Colo., 5,900 79 B1
Rouvroy, Fr., 9,853 116 a7
Rouyn, Qué., Can., 18,390 44 H5
Rouzerville, Pa. 60 H6
Rovaniemi, Fin., 23,199 120 F2
Rovato, It., 11,939 122 d5
Roven'ki, U.S.S.R., 31,500 136 f7
Rover, Ga. 64 g12
Rover, Tenn. 71 E6
Roverchiara, It., 3,445 122 e5
Rovereto, It., 24,178 123 C2
Rovigo, It., 46,251 123 C2
Rovine, Rum. 128 F2
Rovinj, Yug., 5,712 125 A2
Rovira, Col. 100 C5
Rovno, U.S.S.R., 68,000 134 B4
Rowa=Reef Islets
Rowan, Iowa, 273 72 D2
Rowan, co., Ky., 12,808 71 H3
Rowan, co., N.C., 82,817 63 D2
Rowan L., Ont., Can. 44 C5
Rowayton (part of Norwalk), Conn. 56 C8
Rowe, Mass., 231(T) 56 E2
Rowe, N. Mex. 79 C4
Rowena, Austl. 173 G4
Rowena, Colo. 79 b7
Rowena, Tex. 77 N4
Rowesville, S.C., 398 63 D4
Rowland, Nev. 83 C2
Rowland, N.C., 1,408 63 E3
Rowland, Tex. 77 P3
Rowland's Gill, U.K., 5,050 112 g10
Rowlesburg, W. Va., 970 62 E3
Rowlett, Tex., 1,015 76 f9
Rowlett Cr., Tex. 76 f8
Rowley, Iowa, 234 72 F2
Rowley, Mass., 1,223;2,783(T) 57 N2
Rowley Bay, Wis. 66 G3
Rowley I., N.W.T., Can. 41 O4
Rowley Shoals, Austl. 172 B2
Roworante, Indon. 148 e8
Roxana, Ill., 2,090 68 C5
Roxas, Palawan, Phil., 1,317 153 A3
Roxas, Luzon, Phil., 5,612 153 B1
Roxas, Panay, Phil., 14,167 153 B3
Roxboro, Qué., Can., 5,864 47 o17
Roxboro, N.C., 5,147 63 E1
Roxboro, Wash. 80 D2
Roxburgh, N.Z. 175 f7
Roxburgh, co., U.K., 43,171 112 E4
Roxbury, Fairfield Co., Conn. 58 e12
Roxbury, Litchfield Co., Conn., 912(T) 56 C6
Roxbury, Kans. 75 H5
Roxbury, Me. 55 B4
Roxbury, N.Y. 59 L7
Roxbury, Pa. 60 G5
Roxbury, Vt. 54 B3
Roxbury Falls (part of Roxbury), Conn. 56 C6
Roxen, l., Swed. 120 C4
Roxheim, F.R.Ger., 3,316 119 E5
Roxie, Miss., 585 73 D6
Roxobel, N.C., 452 63 G1
Roxton, Okla. 76 E2
Roxton, Tex. 77 Q3
Roxton Falls, Qué., Can. 47 M3
Roy, Br. Col., Can. 42 F4
Roy, Mont. 81 E2
Roy, N. Mex., 633 79 C4
Roy, Utah, 9,239 78 B1
Roy, Wash., 246 81 a8
Royal, Ill., 171 68 E3
Royal, Iowa, 475 72 B1
Royal, Nebr., 93 75 G1
Royal, N.C. 63 H2
Royal, r., Me. 55 B5
Royal Can., Ire. 113 C5
Royal Center, Ind., 966 70 C2
Royal City, Wash. 80 D2
Royale, I., Mich. 66 b8
Royal Glades Can., Fla. 65 a10
Royal Gorge, Colo. 79 ·
Royal Oak, Md. 62 J4
Royal Oak, Mich., 80,612 67 K6
Royal Palm Beach, Fla., 1 65 a8
Royal Park, Alta., Can. 43 c7
Royalston, Mass., 800(T) 56 H2
Royalton, Ill., 1,225 68 C6
Royalton, Ky. 71 H4
Royalton, Minn. 580 74 E3
Royalton, Ohio 70 G3
Royalton, Vt. 54 B4
Royalton, Wis. 66 E4
Royal Tunbridge Wells, U.K., 39,869 113 G6
Royalty, Tex. 77 M4
Royan, Fr., 17,232 117 C4
Royaumont, Fr. 117 E2
Roybon, Fr., 1,345 117 F4
Royce, Alta., Can. 42 H2
Roydon, U.K., 2,828 114 J7
Roye, Fr., 5,106 117 E2
Royersford, Pa., 3,969 61 M5
Royerton, Ind. 70 D2
Royse City, Tex., 1,274 76 g9
Royston, Herts., Eng., U.K., 6,166 113 F5
Royston, York., Eng., U.K., 8,490 114 F3
Royston, Ga., 2,333 64 F1
Różan, Pol., 1,632 127 D2
Rožanstvo, Yug. 125 D3
Rožďalovice, Czech. 127 e6
Rozel, Kans., 207 75 F5
Rozellville, Wis. 66 C4
Rozewie, Przylądek, Pol. 127 C1
Rozhishche, U.S.S.R., 5,900 136 B3
Rozino, Bulg., 2,546 128 E3
Rožňava, Czech. 10,566 126 E2
Roznov, Rum. 128 F1
Rozovka, U.S.S.R., 6,000 136 E4
Roztoka, Pol. 127 f6
Roztoky, Czech. 126 d6
Rozwadów, Pol., 3,637 127 E3
Rrogozhinë, Alb., 3,150 125 D4
Rtishchevo, U.S.S.R., 32,700 136 G2
Ruabon, U.K., 3,377 114 B5
Ruacanà Falls, Ang.-S.-W. Af. 164 B4
Ruapehu, pk., N.Z. 175 g5
Ruapuke I., N.Z. 175 f7
Ruashi, D.R.Congo 165 n19
Rubelles, Fr. 116 i12
Rubeshibe, Jap., 19,923 155 K8
Rubezhnoye, U.S.S.R., 45,200 136 E3
Rubha a'Mhail, c., U.K. 112 C4
Rubha Ardvule, pt., U.K. 112 C3
Rubha Coigeach, pt., U.K. 112 D2
Rubha Hunish, c., U.K. 112 C3
Rubha Réidh, c., U.K. 112 D3
Rubi, r., D.R.Congo 164 D1
Rubicon, Wis. 66 E5
Rubidoux, Calif. 83 k15
Rubiera, It., 7,043 122 d6
Rubik, Alb. 125 D4
Rubio, Ven., 11,813 100 D4
Rubondo I., Tanz. 165 e15
Rubonia, Fla. 65 G5
Rubtsovsk, U.S.S.R., 123,000 134 H4
Ruby, Alaska, 157 85 F2
Ruby, Ariz. 78 C6
Ruby, Nev. 83 C2
Ruby, S.C., 284 63 D3
Ruby L., Nev. 83 C2
Ruby Mts., Nev. 83 C2
Ruby Ra., Mont. 81 C3
Ruby Valley, Nev. 83 C2
Ruciane, Pol., 2,190 127 D2
Rückers, F.R.Ger., 1,387 119 H4
Ruda, r., Pol. 127 h6
Rudabánya, Hung., 3,595 126 E2
Rudall, Austl. 172 E5
Ruda Maleniecka, Pol. 127 k5
Ruda Śląska, Pol., 131,000* 127 C3
Rudauli, India, 15,491 144 c12
Rūdbār, Afghan. 144 B3
Rudbøl, Den. 121 A6
Rudd, Iowa, 436 72 E1
Ruddington, U.K., 5,158 114 F5
Rudersberg, F.R.Ger., 3,531 119 H7
Rudersdorf, Aust., 1,380 124 N6
Rüdersdorf, Ger.D.R., 12,505 118 D2
Rüderswil, Switz., 2,209 124 B2
Rudesheim, F.R.Ger., 6,830 118 A4
Rudkøbing, Den., 4,336 121 C6
Rudmanns, Aust. 124 M5
Rudná, Czech. 126 d6
Rudna, Pol. 127 f5
Rudnichnyy, U.S.S.R. 137 k7
Rudnik, Bulg., 5,258 128 F3
Rudnik, Pol., 5,589 127 E3
Rudnik, Yug. 125 E2
Rudnik, Yug. 125 E3
Rudnya, U.S.S.R., 8,200 136 C2
Rudnyy, U.S.S.R., 55,000 134 F4
Rudolf, L., Kenya 164 F1
Rudol'fa, O., U.S.S.R. 134 E1
Rudolph, Wis. 66 D4
Rudolstadt, Ger.D.R., 27,678 118 C3
Rudozem, Bulg., 6,108 129 E4
Rudston, U.K. 114 H2
Ruds-Vedby, Den., 1,462 121 D5
Rudy, Ark., 113 73 A2
Rudyard, Mich. 67 J2
Rudyard, Mont. 81 D1
Rue, Fr., 3,020 117 D1
Rüegsau, Switz., 2,816 124 B1
Rueil-Malmaison, Fr., 56,024 116 g11
Ruelle, Fr., 5,997 117 D4
Ruen, Bulg., 1,803 128 F3
Rueras, Switz. 124 C2
Rueun, Switz. 124 D2
Rufā'ah, Sudan, 9,137 163 K3
Rufe, Okla. 76 H3
Ruffec, Fr., 4,354 117 D3
Ruffin, N.C. 63 E1
Ruffin, S.C. 63 D4
Ruffling Pt., V.I. 97 4
Rufiji, r., Tanz. 164 F3
Rufino, Arg., 14,000* 105 C4
Rufisque, Sen., 45,900 162 B3
Rufus, Oreg. 80 C3
Rugarama, Rwanda 165 e14
Rugby, Austl. 173 g10
Rugby, U.K., 51,651 113 F5
Rugby, N. Dak., 2,972 74 B1
Rugeley, U.K., 13,012 113 F5
Rügen, i., Ger.D.R. 118 D1
Ruggell, Liecht. 124 a8
Ruggles, Pa. 61 n16
Ruggs, Oreg. 80 D3
Rugles, Fr., 2,680 117 D2
Ruhengeri, Rwanda 165 d14
Ruhla, Ger.D.R. 118 C3
Ruhland, Ger.D.R. 118 D3
Ruhner Berge, Ger.D.R. 118 C2
Ruhpolding, F.R.Ger., 5,239 118 D5
Ruhr, reg., F.R.Ger. 118 A3
Ruhunu Nat. Pk., Cey. 145 F9
Ruidosa, Tex. 77 L4
Ruidoso, N. Mex., 1,557 79 C5
Ruidoso Downs, N. Mex., 407 79 C5
Ruindi, D.R.Congo 165 d14
Ruinen, Neth. 115 E2
Ruiselede, Belg., 5,256 115 B3
Ruiz, Mex., 6,490 92 D4
Ruiz, Nev. del, Col. 101 d15
Rujen, mtn., Bulg.-Yug. 128 D3
Rūjiena, U.S.S.R., 4,600 136 B1
Rujiyoru, i., Eniwetok 176 28
Ruki, r., D.R.Congo 164 C2
Rukumkot, Nepal 145 F3
Rukungiri, Uganda 165 d14
Rukwa, L., Tanz. 164 E3
Rule, Tex., 1,347 77 O3
Ruleton, Kans. 75 D4
Ruleville, Miss., 1,902 73 E4
Rulhieres, C., Austl. 172 C1
Rulo, Nebr., 412 75 K3
Rülzheim, F.R.Ger., 4,520 119 E6
Rum, r., Minn. 74 F3
Ruma, Ill., 138 68 B5
Ruma, Yug., 20,000* 125 D2
Rumania, ctry., 19,105,056 128
Rumbek, Sudan, 2,934 163 J4
Rumberpon, P., Indon. 149 K3
Rumburk, Czech. 126 B1
Rum Cay, i., Bah. Is. 95 D2
Rumegies, Fr., 1,187 116 a7
Rumeln-Kaldenhausen, F.R.Ger., 6,739 119 B2
Rumford, Me., 7,233 55 B4
Rumford (part of E. Providence), R.I. 57 L5
Rumford, Va. 62 G5
Rumia, Pol., 13,360 127 C1
Rumigny, Fr. 117 F2
Rumilly, Fr., 6,270 117 F4
Rummah, Wādī ar, Saudi Ar. 143 C3
Rumney, N.H. 54 D4
Rumney Depot, N.H. 54 D4
Rumoi, Jap., 35,818 155 J8
Rump Mtn., Me. 55 A3
Rum Pt., Grand Cayman 97 3
Rumpt, Neth. 115 c7
Rumsey, Alta., Can. 42 K3
Rumska, Yug. 125 D2
Rumson, N.J., 6,405 61 D3
Rumst, Belg., 5,783 115 d8
Rumung, i., Yap 176 20
Rumuruti, Kenya 165 h13
Runacraig, U.K. 112 b7
Runanga, N.Z., 1,735 175 f6
Runaway, C., N.Z. 175 h5
Runaway Bay, Jam., 1,219 96 p8
Runcorn, U.K., 26,035 114 C4
Runcu, Rum. 128 D2
Ründeroth, F.R.Ger., 7,281 119 C2
Rundvik, Swed. 120 D3
Runge, Tex., 1,036 77 P5
Rungwa, Tanz. 164 E3
Rungwa, r., Tanz. 164 E3
Rungwe, mtn., Tanz. 164 E3
Runnells, Iowa, 322 72 D3
Runnels, co., Tex., 15,016 77 N4
Runnemede, N.J., 8,396 60 f12
Running Springs, Calif. 83 k15
Rünthe, F.R.Ger., 7,958 119 D1
Runu, Yap 176 20
Ruokolahti, Fin. 120 G3
Ruovesi, Fin. 120 F3
Rupanco, L., Chile 105 e15
Rupar, India, 14,136 144 a10
Rupat, P., Indon. 148 B2
Rupat, Selat, Indon. 147 o16
Rupauli, India 144 f13
Rupea, Rum., 4,691 128 E1
Rupel, r., Belg. 115 d8
Rupert, Idaho, 4,153 81 C4
Rupert, Vt. 54 A5
Rupert, W. Va., 921 62 D5
Rupert, r., Qué., Can. 44 J4
Rupert Bay, Qué., Can. 44 H4
Rupert House, Qué., Can. 44 H4
Ruppichteroth, F.R.Ger., 4,078 119 C3
Ruppiner See, Ger.D.R. 118 D2
Rupununi, r., Guyana 101 L6
Rur, r., F.R.Ger. 119 A2
Rural, Wis. 66 D4
Rural Hall, N.C., 1,503 63 D1
Rural Hill, Miss. 73 F4
Rural Retreat, Va., 413 62 C6
Rural Ridge, Pa. 60 c7
Rural Valley, Pa., 860 60 D4
Rurrenabaque, Bol., 2,369 102 C4
Rurutu, i., Is. Tubuai 171 H6
Rusape, Rhod., 1,680 164 E5
Rusca Montană, Rum. 128 D2
Ruscom, r., Ont., Can. 46 B6
Ruse, Bulg., 87,584 128 F3
Rusengo, Burundi 165 e15
Rusera, India, 13,142 144 f13
Rush, Ire., 2,007 113 C5
Rush, Ark. 73 C1
Rush, Colo. 79 C2
Rush, co., Ind., 20,393 70 D3
Rush, co., Kans., 6,160 75 F5
Rush, N.Y. 58 n21
Rushanskiy Khr., U.S.S.R. 137 f5
Rush Center, Kans., 278 75 F5
Rush City, Minn., 1,108 74 F3
Rush Cr., Colo. 79 D2
Rush Cr., Nebr. 75 B2
Rushden, U.K., 17,377 114 G6
Rushford, Minn., 1,335 74 G4
Rushford, N.Y. 58 D7
Rushing, Ark. 73 C2
Rush Lake, Sask., Can. 43 C5
Rush Lake, Wis. 66 E5
Rush L., Minn. 74 E2
Rush L., Wis. 66 E5
Rush Springs, Okla., 1,303 76 F3
Rushsylvania, Ohio, 601 70 F2
Rushville, Ill., 2,819 68 B3
Rushville, Ind., 7,264 70 D3
Rushville, Mo., 253 72 B5
Rushville, Nebr., 1,228 75 C1
Rushville, N.Y., 465 58 F6
Rusiec, Pol. 127 h5
Rusinga I., Kenya 165 f14
Rusk, co., Tex., 36,421 77 Q3
Rusk, Tex., 4,900 77 Q4
Rusk, co., Wis., 14,794 66 B3
Ruskin, Fla., 1,894 65 G5
Ruskin, Nebr., 203 75 H3
Ruskington, U.K., 2,462 114 H4
Ruso, N. Dak., 31 74 B2
Rusokastro, Bulg., 2,090 128 F3
Russas, Braz., 7,102 103 J2
Russell, Man., Can., 1,227 43 E5
Russell, Ont., Can. 47 J3
Russell, N.Z. 175 g4
Russell, co., Ala., 46,351 64 D3
Russell, Ark., 203 73 D2
Russell, Fla. 65 H2
Russell, Ill. 69 c7
Russell, Iowa, 577 72 D4
Russell, co., Kans., 11,348 75 G5
Russell, Kans., 6,113 75 G5
Russell, co., Ky., 11,076 71 F4
Russell, Ky., 1,458 71 J3
Russell, Mass., 1,366(T) 56 E4
Russell, N.Y. 59 K3
Russell, Ohio 70 f9
Russell, Okla. 76 D3
Russell, Pa. 60 D2
Russell, co., Va., 26,290 62 B6
Russell Cave Nat. Mon., Ala. 64 D1
Russell Cr., Ky. 71 F4
Russell Gulch, Colo. 79 a8
Russell I., N.W.T., Can. 40 K3
Russell Is., Sol. Is. 175 c2
Russell L., Man., Can. 43 E3
Russell Mtn., Me. 55 C2
Russells Point, Ohio, 1,110 70 F2
Russell Springs, Kans., 93 75 D5
Russell Springs, Ky., 1,125 71 F4
Russell Str., Me. 55 C2
Russellton, Pa., 1,613 60 C4

286 · Russellville—Ste-Geneviève

Russellville, Ala., 6,628 64 B1
Russellville, Ark., 10,525 73 B2
Russellville, Ill., 197 68 E5
Russellville, Ind., 372 70 C3
Russellville, Ky., 5,861 71 E5
Russellville (part of Southampton), Mass. 56 E4
Russellville, Mo., 442 72 E6
Russellville, Ohio, 412 70 F4
Russellville, Tenn. 71 H5
Russel Pt., N.W.T., Can. 40 G3
Rüsselsheim, F.R.Ger., 30,113 118 B3
Russenes, Nor. 120 F1
Russian, r., Calif. 82 B3
Russian Mission, Alaska, 102 85 D3
Russian Mission, Alaska 85 E3
Russiaville, Ind., 1,064 70 C2
Russkaya Gavan', U.S.S.R. 134 E2
Russkaya Polyana, U.S.S.R. 137 o11
Russkiy, O., U.S.S.R. 135 J2
Russkiy, O., U.S.S.R. 151 F2
Russko-Ust'Inskoye, U.S.S.R. 135 O2
Rust, Aust. 124 b10
Rust, Aust., 1,697 124 d11
Rustak, Afghan. 145 D1
Rustavi, U.S.S.R., 70,000 137 c1
Rustburg, Va. 62 E5
Rustenburg, S. Af., 20,866 164 D6
Rustic, Colo. 79 C1
Ruston, La., 13,991 73 C5
Ruston, Wash., 699 81 a8
Ruswil, Switz., 4,657 124 C1
Ruszów, Pol. 127 e5
Rutaki Passage, Rarotonga 177 34
Ruteng, Indon. 149 G5
Rutesheim, F.R.Ger., 3,542 119 F7
Ruth, Calif. 82 B2
Ruth, Ky. 71 G4
Ruth, Mich. 67 L5
Ruth, Miss. 73 E6
Ruth, Nev. 83 C3
Ruth, N.C., 529 63 C2
Rüthen, F.R.Ger., 3,779 119 E1
Rutherford, N.J., 20,473 61 C2
Rutherford, co., N.C., 45,091 63 B2
Rutherford, co., Tenn., 52,368 71 E6
Rutherford, Tenn., 983 71 C5
Rutherfordton, N.C., 3,392 63 C2
Rutherglen, Ont., Can. 46 F2
Rutherglen, U.K., 25,067 112 b8
Ruthin, U.K., 3,502 113 E5
Ruths Pt., Berm. Is.=Cove Pt.
Ruthton, Minn., 476 74 D3
Ruthven, Ont., Can. 46 B6
Ruthven, Iowa, 712 72 B1
Rüti, Switz., 8,282 124 C1
Rüti, Switz. 124 D2
Rutland, Ill., 509 68 C3
Rutland, Mass., 1,774;3,253(T) 56 J3
Rutland, Ohio, 687 70 G3
Rutland, N. Dak., 308 74 D2
Rutland, co., Vt., 46,719 54 A4
Rutland, Vt., 18,325 54 B4
Rutland I., India 146 A5
Rutlandshire, co., U.K., 23,504 113 F5
Rutledge, Ala., 276 64 C4
Rutledge, Minn., 146 74 F2
Rutledge, Mo., 158 72 E4
Rutledge, Tenn., 793 71 H5
Rutshuru, D.R.Congo 164 D2
Rutter, Ont., Can. 46 D2
Rutzendorf, Aust. 124 d10
Ruurlo, Neth. 115 E2
Ru'ūs al Jibāl, pen., Asia 140 D4
Ruvo di Puglia, It., 24,432 123 F4
Ruvu, Tanz. 164 F3
Ruvu, r., Tanz. 164 F3
Ruvubo, r., Burundi 165 e15
Ruvuma, r., Moz.-Tanz. 164 F3
Ruwe, D.R.Congo 165 m19
Ruwenzori, mts., D.R.Congo-Uganda 164 D1
Ruwer, F.R.Ger., 1,863 119 B5
Ruwer, r., F.R.Ger. 119 B5
Ruxton, Md. 62 c7
Ruyigi, Burundi 165 e15
Ruza, U.S.S.R., 6,000 136 b6
Ruza, r., U.S.S.R. 136 a6
Ruzayevka, Kaz.S.S.R., U.S.S.R. 134 F4
Ruzayevka, R.S.F.S.R., U.S.S.R., 24,900 136 G2
Ružomberok, Czech., 20,589 126 D2
Rwanda, ctry., 3,018,000* 164 D2
Ryabiki, U.S.S.R. 136 a6
Ryabinino, U.S.S.R. 137 h6
Ryakhovo, Bulg., 3,612 128 F3
Ryan, Iowa, 347 72 F2
Ryan, Okla., 978 76 F3
Ryan, L., U.K. 113 D4
Ryan Pk., Idaho 81 B4
Ryazan', U.S.S.R., 240,000 134 D4
Ryazhsk, U.S.S.R., 7,400 136 F2
Rybach'ye, U.S.S.R., 18,600 134 G5
Rybinsk, U.S.S.R., 206,000 134 C4
Rybinskoye Vdkhr., U.S.S.R. 134 C4
Rybnik, Pol., 34,000* 127 C3
Rybnitsa, U.S.S.R., 18,600 136 C4
Rybnoye, U.S.S.R., 13,600 136 c6
Rychnov, Czech. 127 e6
Rychnov nad Kněžnou, Czech., 6,455 126 C1
Rychwał, Pol., 1,433 127 C2
Rycroft, Alta., Can. 42 H2
Ryde, U.K., 19,845 113 F6
Ryder, N. Dak., 264 74 B2
Ryderwood, Wash. 80 B2
Rydsgård, Swed. 121 F5
Rydułtowy, Pol., 15,814 127 C3
Rye, Den. 121 B4
Rye, U.K., 4,438 113 G6
Rye, Ark. 73 D4
Rye, Colo., 179 79 C3
Rye, N.H. 54 F5
Rye, N.Y., 14,255 59 N10
Rye, Tex. 77 Q4
Rye, r., Den. 121 B3
Rye, r., U.K. 113 F4
Rye Beach, N.H. 54 F6
Ryegate, Mont., 314 81 E2
Ryegate Corner, Vt. 54 C3
Rye L., N.Y. 58 e12
Rye North Beach, N.H. 54 F5
Rye Patch Res., Nev. 83 A2
Ryer I., Calif. 83 e11
Rye Water, r., U.K. 112 a8
Rygge, Nor. 121 C1
Ryhall, U.K., 1,052 114 G5
Ryhope, U.K., 10,116 112 h10
Rylestone, Austl. 173 g9
Ryley, Alta., Can. 43 c7
Ryl'sk, U.S.S.R., 12,700 134 C4
Rymanów, Pol., 2,181 127 D4
Rýmařov, Czech. 126 C2
Ryn, Pol., 1,613 127 D2
Rynfield, S. Af. 165 k17
Ryn-Peski, U.S.S.R. 134 D5
Ryōtsu, Jap., 28,892 155 F2
Rypin, Pol., 8,743 127 C2
Ryrkaypiy, U.S.S.R. 135 S3
Ryslinge, Den., 1,568 121 C5
Rysy, pk., Pol. 127 C4
Ryton, U.K., 13,485 112 g10
Ryūgasaki, Jap., 33,581 155 G4
Ryukyu Is.=Nansei-shotō
Ryus, Kans. 75 D6
Rzepin, Pol., 4,098 127 A2
Rzeszów, Pol., 62,000* 127 E3
Rzhev, U.S.S.R., 54,000 134 C4
Rzhishchev, U.S.S.R., 7,000 136 C3

S

Sa, Thai. 146 C3
Saa, Sol. Is. 175 c3
Saalach, r., Aust.-F.R.Ger. 124 J6
Saalan, Indon. 148 F2
Saalbach, r., F.R.Ger. 119 F6
Saalburg, Ger.D.R. 126 a6
Saale, r., Ger.D.R. 118 C3
Saaler B., Ger.D.R. 118 D1
Saalfeld, Ger.D.R., 26,876 118 C3
Saalfelden, Aust., 8,900 124 J6
Saanen, Switz., 5,649 124 B2
Saar, r., F.R.Ger. 119 B5
Saarbrücken, F.R.Ger., 123,504 118 A4
Saarburg, F.R.Ger., 5,229 118 A4
Saaremaa, i., U.S.S.R. 134 B4
Saarhölzbach, F.R.Ger., 1,569 116 c8
Saarijärvi, Fin. 120 F3
Saarland, st., F.R.Ger., 1,117,000* 118 A4
Saarlouis, F.R.Ger., 34,076 118 A4
Saas, Switz. 124 D2
Saas Almagell, Switz. 124 B2
Saas Grund, Switz. 124 B2
Saba, i., W.I. 95 G3
Šabac, Yug., 26,000* 125 D2
Sabadell, Sp., 105,152 122 G2
Sabae, Jap., 49,045 155 E4
Sabael, N.Y. 59 M4
Sabah (part of Malay.), 549,000* 148 F1
Sabak, Malay., 3,626 147 o15
Sabal, Indon. 149 G3
Sabalgarh, India, 7,482 145 E4
Sabana-Camagüey, Arch. de, Cuba 96 c1
Sabana de la Mar, Dom. Rep., 4,032 96 n6
Sabana de Mendoza, Ven., 3,439 100 E3
Sabana Grande, Hond., 2,213 94 D4
Sabana Grande, P.R., 3,318 96 s10
Sabana Grande de Boyá, Dom. Rep., 2,857 96 m6
Sabana Grande de Palenque, Dom. Rep., 1,509 96 n6
Sabanalarga, Col. 100 B4
Sabanalarga, Col. 100 C2
Sabana Westpunt, Cur. 97 16
Sabancuy, Mex., 1,039 93 H4
Sabaneta, Ven. 100 F2
Sabaneta, Ven., 1,714 100 F3
Sabang, Indon. 148 A1
Sabang, Phil., 1,495 153 c7
Sabangan, Phil., 3,608 153 B1
Săbăoani, Rum. 128 F1
Sabará, Braz., 10,004 103 e17
Sabarmati, r., India 145 D5
Sabattus, Me. 55 B4
Sabattus Pd., Me. 55 B4
Sabaya, Bol., 1,940 102 a11
Sabbatia, L., Mass. 57 M5
Sab'Biyār, Syr. 142 D3
Sabderat, Eth. 163 L3
Săbed, Rum. 128 E1
Saberang Takir, Malay., 3,952 147 p14
Saberania, Indon. 149 L3
Sāberī, Hāmūn-e, Afghan.-Iran 143 G2
Sabetha, Kans., 2,318 75 K4
Sabhah, Libya 161 G3
Sabhah, Wāhat, oasis, Libya 161 G3
Sabie, S. Af., 4,100 164 E6
Sabillasville, Md. 62 G3
Sabin, Minn., 251 74 D2
Sabina, Ill. 68 D3
Sabina, Ohio, 2,313 70 F3
Sabina, r., Tex. 77 O5
Sabinal, Tex., 1,747 77 O5
Sabinal, Cayo, Cuba 96 e2
Sabiñánigo, Sp., 6,184 122 E1
Sabinas, Mex., 15,953 92 E2
Sabinas, r., Mex. 93 E2
Sabinas Hidalgo, Mex., 11,558 93 E2
Sabine, parish, La., 18,564 73 B6
Sabine, co., Tex., 7,302 77 R4
Sabine, Tex. 77 n9
Sabine, Mt., Ant. 180 V6
Sabine, r., La.-Tex. 53 H4
Sabine L., La.-Tex. 73 B8
Sabine Pass, Tex. 77 Q5
Sabinoso, N. Mex. 79 C4
Sabinov, Czech. 126 E2
Sabinsville, Pa. 60 G2
Sabirabad, U.S.S.R., 8,900 137 d2
Sable, C., N.S., Can. 45 N7
Sable, C., Fla. 65 H7
Sable, Î. de, Marq. Is. 177 42
Sable I., N.S., Can. 45 P7
Sable I. Bank, Can. 39 R9
Sables, L. aux, Ont., Can. 46 B2
Sables, R. aux, Ont., Can. 46 B2
Sables, R. aux, Ont., Can. 46 C5
Sablé-sur-Sarthe, Fr., 7,367 117 C3
Sabor, r., Port. 122 B2
Saboyá, Col. 101 f14
Sabrathah, ruins, Libya 161 G2
Sabres, Fr., 1,341 117 C4
Sabrina Coast, Ant. 180 U6
Sabtang, Phil. 153 g13
Sabtang I., Phil. 153 g13
Sabugal, Port., 2,908 122 B2
Sabula, Iowa, 894 72 G2
Sabzevār, Iran, 30,545 143 F1
Sabzvārān, Iran, 2,480 143 F3
Sac, co., Iowa, 17,007 72 B2
Sac, r., Mo. 72 D7
Sacaba, Bol., 12,875 102 c10
Sacaca, Bol., 12,438 102 b11
Sacajawea Pk., Oreg. 80 E3
Sacandaga, W., Br., r., N.Y. 59 M5
Sacandaga Res., N.Y. 59 M5
Sacapulas, Guat., 1,450 94 b8
Sacaton, Ariz. 78 C5
Sacavém, Port., 10,624 122 i10
Sac City, Iowa, 3,354 72 B2
Sacedón, Sp., 1,856 122 D2
Săcel, Rum. 128 E1
Săcele, Rum., 18,365 128 E2
Sachigo, r., Ont., Can. 44 D3
Sachigo L., Ont., Can. 44 D4
Sachse, Tex., 359 76 f9
Sachseln, Switz., 2,721 124 C2
Sachsen, reg., Ger.D.R. 118 D3
Sachsenburg, Aust., 1,366 124 K7
Sachs Harbour, N.W.T., Can. 40 E3
Sacile, It., 12,782 123 D1
Sackets Harbor, N.Y., 1,279 59 H4
Säckingen, F.R.Ger., 9,671 118 B5
Sackville, N.B., Can., 2,899 45 N6
Saclay, Fr., 1,667 116 g12
Saco, Me., 10,515 55 B5
Saco, Mont., 490 81 F1
Saco, r., Me.-N.H. 55 B5
Saco, Rocky Br., r., N.H. 54 E3
Sacramento, co., Calif., 502,778 82 C3
Sacramento, Calif., 191,667 82 C3
Sacramento, r., Calif. 82 C3
Sacramento Mts., N. Mex. 79 C5
Sacramento Valley, Calif. 82 B2
Sacré-Coeur-de-Jésus, Qué., Can., 1,089 47 Q9
Sacred Falls, Hawaii 84 c6
Sacred Heart, Minn., 696 74 E3
Sacriston, U.K. 112 g10
Săcueni, Rum. 128 D1
Sacupana, Ven. 101 K3
Sada, Jap. 154 g14
Sádaba, Sp., 3,126 122 E1
Sadabad, India, 6,572 144 b12
Sá da Bandeira, Ang., 13,867 164 B4
Şa'dah, Yemen, 25,000* 143 C5
Sadamitsu, Jap., 6,779 154 f15
Sadao, Thai., 6,360 146 C6
Sadaung, Burma 147 f6
Sadberge, U.K. 114 E1
Saddle, r., N.J. 61 C1
Saddleback Mtn., Franklin Co., Me. 55 B4
Saddleback Mtn., Aroostook Co., Me. 55 D2
Saddleback Mtn., N.Y. 59 N3
Saddlebunch Keys, Fla. 65 f15
Saddle Buttes, N. Dak. 74 A2
Saddle Buttes, S. Dak. 74 B3
Saddle Hill, Nevis 97 6
Saddle I., New Hebr. 174 k4
Saddle Mountain, Okla. 76 E3
Saddle Mtn., Colo. 79 C2
Saddle Mtn., Wyo. 81 E3
Saddle Pk., India 146 A4
Saddle River, N.J., 1,776 58 c12
Saddleworth, U.K., 17,010 114 E3
Sa Dec, S. Viet., 15,935 147 k11
Sadhoowa, Trin. and Tob. 96 g5
Sadieville, Ky., 276 71 G3
Sadina, Bulg., 3,702 128 F3
Sadiya, India 145 K4
Sa'diyah, Hawr as, l., Iraq 143 D2
Sado, i., Jap. 155 F2
Sado, r., Port. 122 A3
Sadohara, Jap., 10,371 154 B5
Sadon, Burma 146 B1
Sadorus, Ill., 384 68 D3
Sadová, Czech. 127 e6
Sadovets, Bulg., 5,004 128 E3
Sadovoye, U.S.S.R. 136 G4
Sadská, Czech. 127 d6
Sæby, Den., 3,669 121 C3
Saegertown, Pa., 1,131 60 B2
Saeki, Jap., 51,369 154 B5
Saeki-wan, Jap. 154 C5
Saeul, Lux. 119 A5
Safad, Isr., 10,710 142 b7
Safaniya, Saudi Ar. 143 D3
Şafāqis, Tun., 65,635 161 F2
Safar, Afghan. 144 B3
Şafarābād, Iran 137 c2
Safata Hbr., W. Samoa 177 38
Safed Khirs, mts., Afghan. 137 f5
Safety Harbor, Fla., 1,787 65 c11
Saffell, Ark. 73 D2
Säffle, Swed. 120 C4
Safford, Ariz., 5,165 78 D5
Saffron Walden, U.K., 7,817 113 G5
Safi, Mor., 81,072 160 C2
Sāfīd, r., Iran 143 D1
Safidon, India, 9,223 144 a11
Safipur, India 144 c12
Şāfītā, Syr., 8,118 142 D3
Safonovo, U.S.S.R. 134 D3
Safonovo, U.S.S.R., 34,700 136 D2
Safotu, W. Samoa, 1,052 177 37
Safranbolu, Turk., 7,352 142 C1
Saga, Jap., 129,888 154 B5
Saga, Jap., 6,313 155 C5
Sagada, Phil., 2,832 153 b5
Sagadahoc, co., Me., 22,793 55 C4
Sagae, Jap., 40,015 155 G2
Sagaing, Burma, 15,439 147 f7
Sagami, r., Jap. 155 m20
Sagamihara, Jap., 101,655 155 F4
Sagami-nada, Jap. 155 F4
Sagami-wan, Jap. 155 m20
Sagamore (part of Bourne), Mass. 57 O5
Sagamore, Pa. 60 D4
Sagamore Beach (part of Bourne), Mass. 57 O5
Sagamore Hills, Ohio 70 e9
Saganaga L., Can.-U.S. 44 D5
Saganashkee Slough, Ill. 69 c10
Saganing, Mich. 67 K5
Saganoseki, Jap., 25,841 154 C5
Sagar, M.P., India, 104,676 145 F5
Sagar, Mys., India, 20,414 145 E7
Sagara, Jap., 29,596 155 F4
Sagard, Ger.D.R. 118 D1
Sagar I., India 144 f15
Sagauli, India, 10,447 144 e12
Sagavanirktok, r., Alaska 85 G1
Sag Bridge, Ill. 69 c10
Sagerton, Tex. 77 O3
Sageville, Iowa, 110 72 G2
Sag Harbor, N.Y., 2,346 59 Q9
Sagil, Malay., 2,074 147 p15
Saginaw, co., Mich., 190,752 67 J5
Saginaw, Mich., 98,265 67 K5
Saginaw, Oreg. 80 B4
Saginaw, Tex., 1,001 76 e9
Saginaw, r., Mich. 67 K5
Saginaw Bay, Mich. 67 K5
Sagiz, U.S.S.R., 1,300 134 E5
Saglek Bay, Newf., Can. 45 O2
Sagola, Mich. 66 E2
Sagres, Port., 1,001 122 A4
Sag Sag, Terr. New Guin. 174 f2
Sagu, Burma, 5,152 146 A2
Sagu, Indon. 149 G5
Saguache, co., Colo., 4,473 79 B2
Saguache, Colo., 722 79 B2
Sagua de Tánamo, Cuba, 7,604 96 f2
Sagua la Grande, Cuba, 26,187 96 c1
Sagua la Grande, r., Cuba 96 c1
Saguaro Nat. Mon., Ariz. 78 C5
Saguenay, r., Qué., Can. 47 R9
Sagunto, Sp., 40,293 122 E3
Sagy, Fr. 116 f10
Sahagún, Col. 100 C3
Sahagún, Sp., 3,122 122 C1
Sahara, des., Af. 158 C2
Saharanpur, India, 185,213 145 E3
Saharsa, India, 14,803 144 f13
Sahaswan, India, 23,293 144 b11
Sahibganj, India, 31,409 144 f13
Sahuaripa, Mex., 4,114 92 C2
Sahuarita, Ariz. 78 C6
Sahuayo, Mex., 25,673 92 E4
Sai, Jap., 5,642 155 G1
Sai, r., India 144 c12
Sai, r., Jap. 155 E3
Saibai, i., Austl. 174 d3
Sai Buri, Thai., 5,945 146 C6
Sai Buri, r., Thai. 147 o13
Saïda, Alg., 21,396 160 E2
Sa'īdābād, Iran, 12,160 143 F3
Saidaiji, Jap., 45,984 154 f15
Saidapet, India 145 n19
Saidor, Terr. New Guin. 174 e2
Saidora, Ill. 68 B3
Saidpur, India, 8,007 144 d13
Saidpur, Pak., 60,628 145 H4
Saidu, Pak., 15,920 145 D2
Saignelégier, Switz., 1,636 124 A1
Saigō, Jap., 16,199 155 C3
Saigon, S. Viet.=Sai Gon
Sai Gon, S. Viet., 1,400,000* 146 D5
Sai Gon, r., S. Viet. 147 m11
Saijō, Jap., 11,842 155 C4
Saijō, Jap., 17,598 155 C4
Saijō, Jap., 53,187 155 C5
Saikai-kōk., Jap. 154 A5
Saiki, Jap. 154 f15
Saikū, Jap. 154 h15
Sai Kung, H.K., 3,805 152 b6
Saileen, Indon. 149 J3
Saillans, Fr., 1,071 117 F4
Sailly, Fr. 116 f10
Sailor Springs, Ill., 187 68 D5
Saimaa, l., Fin. 120 F3
Saimaa Can., Fin.-U.S.S.R. 120 G3
Sai-ma-chi, China 151 E2
Sain, Chenal, str., Horne, Îs. de 175 9
Sain-Bel, Fr., 1,851 116 p15
Saindak, Pak. 144 A3
Saio=Dembidollo
Saipan, i., Mar. Is. 170 D3
Saipan Chan., Mariana Is. 176 23
St. Abb's Head, U.K. 112 F4
Ste-Adèle, Qué., Can., 1,285 47 K3
St-Adelphe, Qué., Can. 47 M2
St. Adolphe, Man., Can. 43 h10
St-Affrique, Fr., 8,023 117 E5
St-Agapit, Qué., Can., 1,117 47 N2
St. Agatha, Me. 55 D1
Ste. Agathe, Man., Can. 43 F5
Ste-Agathe, Qué., Can. 47 N2
Ste-Agathe-des-Monts, Qué., Can., 5,716 47 K2
St. Agnes, U.K., 4,221 113 D6
St. Agnes, i., U.K. 113 C7
St-Aignan, Fr. 117 D3
St-Aimé, Qué., Can. 47 M3
St-Alban, Qué., Can. 47 M2
St. Alban's, Newf., Can., 1,547 45 Q6
St. Albans, U.K., 50,293 113 F6
St. Albans, Me. 55 C4
St. Albans, Vt., 8,806 54 A2
St. Albans, W. Va., 15,103 62 C4
St. Albans Bay, Vt. 54 A2
St. Alban's Head, U.K. 113 F6
St. Albert, Alta., Can., 3,982 42 K3
St-Alexandre, Qué., Can. 47 R10
St-Alexis-des-Monts, Qué., Can., 1,298 47 L2
St-Amable, Qué., Can. 47 p17
St-Amand-les-Eaux, Fr., 17,041 116 a7
St-Amand-Mont-Rond, Fr., 11,383 117 E3
St. Ambroise, Man., Can. 43 f9
St-Amour, Fr., 2,501 117 F3
St-Anaclet, Qué., Can. 47 R9
St-André, Fr., 10,070 116 a6
St-André, La Réunion, 1,501 165 b11
St-André, C., Malag. Rep. 165 G4
St-André-Avellin, Qué., Can., 1,040 47 J3
St-André-de-Corcy, Fr. 116 p15
St-André-de-Cubzac, Fr., 4,315 117 C4
St. Andrews, N.B., Can., 1,511 47 S11
St. Andrew's, Newf., Can. 45 P6
St. Andrews, U.K., 9,888 112 E3
St. Andrews, Ill. 69 b9
St. Andrews Bay, U.K. 112 e7
St. Andrews Major, U.K., 4,789 114 B8
Ste-Angèle, Qué., Can. 47 p18
Ste-Angèle-de-Mérici, Qué., Can. 47 S9
St-Anicet, Qué., Can. 69 D
St. Ann, Mo., 12,155 72 a11
Ste-Anne, Guad., 2,384 97 14
Ste-Anne, Mart. 97 12
St. Anne, Ill., 1,378 68 E2
Ste-Anne, r., Qué., Can. 47 N1
Ste-Anne-de-Beaupré, Qué., Can., 1,846 47 N1
Ste-Anne-de-Bellevue, Qué., Can., 3,732 47 o18
Ste-Anne-de-la-Pérade, Qué., Can., 1,282 47 M2
Ste-Anne-de-la-Pocatière, Qué., Can., 4,253 47 R10
Ste-Anne-de-Portneuf, Qué., Can. 47 R9
Ste. Anne des Chênes, Man., Can. 43 h10
Ste-Anne-des-Monts, Qué., Can., 1,906 45 M5
Ste-Anne-des-Plaines, Qué., Can. 47 o17
St. Anne's, U.K. 113 E5
St. Anns, Ont., Can. 46 d15
St. Anns Bay, Jam., 5,087 96 p8
St. Ann's Head, U.K. 113 D6
St-Anselme, Qué., Can., 1,115 47 O2
St. Ansgar, Iowa, 1,014 72 E1
St. Anthonis, Neth. 115 D3
St. Anthony, N.B., Can. 47 T10
St. Anthony, Newf., Can., 1,799 45 Q4
St. Anthony, Idaho, 2,700 81 D4
St. Anthony, Iowa, 130 72 D2
St. Anthony, Minn., 5,084 74 b5
St. Anthony, N. Dak. 74 B2
St. Anthony's Pk., St. Christopher 97 6
St-Antoine-des-Laurentides, Qué., Can. 47 o17
St-Antoine-sur-Richelieu, Qué., Can. 47 p17
St-Apollinaire, Qué., Can. 47 N2
Ste-Apolline, Qué., Can. 47 O2
St. Arnaud, Austl., 3,037 173 d11
St-Arnoult-en-Yvelines, Fr., 1,384 116 f12
St. Asaph, U.K., 2,238 114 B4
St-Astier, Fr., 4,445 117 D4
St. Athan, U.K., 3,268 114 B8
St-Aubert, Qué., Can. 47 Q10
St-Aubert, Fr., 1,871 116 a7
St-Aubin, Switz. 124 A2
St-Aubin-du-Cormier, Fr., 2,556 117 C2
St-Augustin, Qué., Can. 47 n16
St-Augustin, Qué., Can. 47 o17
St. Augustine, Fla., 14,734 65 H3
St. Augustine, Ill., 201 68 B3
St. Augustine, r., Qué.-Newf., Can. 45 P4
St. Augustine Beach, Fla., 396 65 H3
St-Augustin-Saguenay, Qué., Can. 45 P4
St. Austell, U.K., 25,074 113 D6
St-Avold, Fr., 15,443 117 G2
St-Aygulf, Fr. 116 m14
St. Barbe Is., Newf., Can. 45 Q5
St-Barnabé, Qué., Can. 47 L2
St-Barthélemy, Qué., Can. 47 L2
St-Barthélemy, i., Lesser Ant. 97 7
St-Basile, Qué., Can., 1,729 47 N2
St-Basile, Qué., Can., 1,064 47 p17
St. Bees Head, U.K. 113 E4
St-Benjamin, Qué., Can. 47 O2
St-Benoît, Qué., Can. 47 K3
St-Benoît, La Réunion, 4,095 165 b11
St-Bernard, Qué., Can. 47 O2
St. Bernard, parish, La., 32,186 73 F8
St. Bernard, Ohio, 6,778 71 i11
St. Bernice, Ind. 70 B3
St-Blaise, Switz., 2,412 124 A1
Ste-Blandine, Qué., Can. 47 R9
St. Boniface, Man., Can., 37,247 43 F5
St-Boniface, Qué., Can. 47 M2
St-Bonnet-en-Champsaur, Fr., 1,244 117 F4
St-Brais, Switz. 124 B1
St. Briavels, U.K., 1,087 114 C7
St. Bride's, Newf., Can. 45 a11
St. Brides Bay, U.K. 113 D6
St. Bride's Major, U.K., 1,500 114 A8
St. Bridget Beckermet, U.K., 1,019 114 A2
St-Brieuc, Fr., 47,307 116 B2
St. Brieux, Sask., Can. 43 D4
St-Bruno, Qué., Can., 1,129 47 p17
St-Calais, Fr., 4,213 117 D3
St-Camille, Qué., Can. 47 O2
St-Casimir, Qué., Can., 1,345 47 M2
St. Catharines, Ont., Can., 83,412 44 H7
Ste-Catherine, Fr. 116 p15
St. Catherine, L., Vt. 54 A5
St. Catherine, Mt., Gren. 97 18
St. Catherine's, Newf., Can. 45 b10
St. Catherines I., Ga. 64 H4
St. Catherine's Pt., U.K. 113 k13
St-Céré, Fr., 3,690 117 D4
St-Cernin, Fr., 1,777 117 E4
St-Césaire, Qué., Can., 2,067 47 L3
St-Chamond, Fr., 17,256 117 F4
St-Charles, Qué., Can. 47 N2
St-Charles, Qué., Can. 47 p17
St. Charles, Ark., 255 73 D3
St. Charles, Idaho, 300 81 D4
St. Charles, Ill., 11,158 68 D2
St. Charles, Iowa, 355 72 D3
St. Charles, Ky., 421 71 D4
St. Charles, parish, La., 21,219 73 E8
St. Charles, Mich., 1,959 67 J5
St. Charles, Minn., 1,882 74 G4
St. Charles, co., Mo., 52,970 72 G6
St. Charles, Mo., 21,189 72 G6
St. Charles, Va., 368 62 A6
St. Charles, r., Colo. 79 C2
St-Chély-d'Apcher, Fr., 5,026 117 E4
St-Chéron, Fr., 2,236 116 g12
St. Christopher, i., Lesser Ant. 97 6
St.-Chrysostôme, Qué., Can. 47 L3
St. Clair, co., Ala., 25,388 64 C2
St. Clair, co., Ill., 262,509 68 B5
St. Clair, co., Mich., 107,201 67 L5
St. Clair, Mich., 4,538 67 L6
St. Clair, co., Mo., 8,421 72 D6
St. Clair, Mo., 2,711 72 G6
St. Clair, Pa., 5,159 61 K4
St. Clair, r., Can.-U.S. 67 L6
St. Clair, L., Can.-U.S. 67 L6
St. Clair Beach, Ont., Can., 1,459 46 B6
St. Clair Bottom, Va. 62 C6
Ste-Claire, Qué., Can., 1,122 47 O2
St. Clair Shores, Mich., 76,657 67 L6
St. Clairsville, Ohio, 3,865 70 H2
St. Clairsville, Pa., 115 60 F5
St. Claude, Man., Can. 43 f10
St-Claude, Fr., 12,649 117 F3
St-Claude, Guad., 1,988 97 14
St. Clears, U.K., 1,937 113 D6
St-Clément, Fr. 116 c9
St. Clements, Ont., Can. 46 a13
St-Cloud, Fr., 26,746 116 g11
St. Cloud, Fla., 4,353 65 H4
St. Cloud, Minn., 33,815 74 F3
St. Cloud, Wis., 530 66 E5
Ste-Colombe, Fr., 2,018 116 p15
St-Côme, Qué., Can. 47 L2
St-Côme, Qué., Can., 1,264 47 O2
St-Constant, Qué., Can., 2,739 47 o18
Ste-Croix, Qué., Can., 1,440 47 N2
Ste-Croix, Switz., 6,925 124 A2
St. Croix, Ind. 70 C4
St. Croix, co., Wis., 29,164 66 A3
St. Croix, i., Lesser Ant. 97 1
St. Croix, r., Can.-U.S. 55 E3
St. Croix, r., Minn.-Wis. 66 A3
St. Croix Falls, Wis., 1,249 66 A3
St. Croix Flowage, Wis. 66 A2
St. Croix Str., Me. 55 D2
St-Cuthbert, Qué., Can. 47 L2
St-Cyprien, Qué., Can. 47 R10
St-Cyrille, Qué., Can., 1,110 47 M3
St-Cyrille, Qué., Can. 47 O1
St-Cyr-l'École, Fr., 9,610 116 g11
St-Cyr-sous-Dourdan, Fr. 116 g12
St-Damien, Qué., Can., 1,396 47 O2
St. David, Ariz. 78 C6
St. David, Ill., 862 68 B3
St. David, Me. 55 D1
St. David Bay, Dominica 97 13
St. David's, U.K., 1,690 113 D6
St. David's Head, U.K. 113 D6
St. Davids I., Berm. Is. 108 1
St-Denis, Qué., Can., 1,042 47 p17
St-Denis, Fr., 95,072 117 E2
St-Denis, La Réunion, 37,047 165 b11
St. Dennis, U.K., 2,370 113 D6
St-Dié, Fr., 24,373 117 G2
St-Dizier, Fr., 36,361 117 F2
St-Dominique, Qué., Can. 47 M3
Ste-Dorothée, Qué., Can. 47 o17
St-Édouard, Qué., Can. 47 N2
St. Edward, Nebr., 777 75 G2
St-Eleuthère, Qué., Can., 1,033 47 R10
St. Elias, C., Alaska 85 J4
St. Elias, Mt., Can.-U.S. 85 J3
St. Elias Mts., Can.-U.S. 42 A1
St-Élie, Qué., Can. 47 L2
St-Elie, Fr. Guiana 101 O5
Ste. Elizabeth, Man., Can. 43 F5
Ste-Élizabeth, Qué., Can. 47 L2
St. Elmo, Ill., 1,503 68 D4
St-Eloi, Qué., Can. 47 R9
St-Éloy-les-Mines, Fr., 6,898 117 E3
Ste-Emélie-de-l'Energie, Qué., Can. 47 K2
St-Émile, Qué., Can., 1,793 47 n16
Ste-Enimie, Fr. 117 E4
St-Ephrem, Qué., Can. 47 O2
Saintes, Fr., 27,159 117 C4
Saintes, Îles des, Guad. 97 14
St-Esprit, Mart., 1,614 97 12
St-Étienne, Fr., 203,633 117 F4
St-Étienne-de-Baïgorry, Fr., 2,181 117 C5
St-Étienne-des-Grès, Qué., Can. 47 M2
St-Étienne-de-Tinée, Fr., 1,551 117 G4
St. Eugène, Ont., Can. 47 K3
St-Eugène, Qué., Can., 1,000 47 O1
Ste-Euphemie, Qué., Can. 47 O2
St. Eustache, Man., Can. 43 g10
St-Eustache, Qué., Can., 5,359 47 o17
St-Eustache-sur-le-Lac, Qué., Can., 7,236 47 o17
St. Eustatius, i., Lesser Ant. 97 6
St-Fabien, Qué., Can., 1,200 45 M5
St-Fargeau, Fr., 4,135 116 h12
St-Faustin, Qué., Can. 47 K2
St-Félicien, Qué., Can., 5,008 44 K5
Ste-Félicité, Qué., Can., 1,002 45 M5
St-Félix-de-Valois, Qué., Can., 1,387 47 L2
St. Fillans, U.K. 112 b7
St-Flavien, Qué., Can. 47 N2
Ste-Flore, Qué., Can. 47 M2
Ste-Florence, Qué., Can., 1,218 47 S9
St-Florent-en-Corse, Fr. 116 r17
St-Florentin, Fr., 4,243 117 E3
St-Florent-sur-Cher, Fr., 5,453 117 E3
St-Flour, Fr., 6,898 117 E4
St-Fons, Fr., 13,081 116 p15
St-Forgeux, Fr. 116 o15
Ste-Foy, Qué., Can., 29,185 47 n16
St. Francis, co., Ark., 33,303 73 E2
St. Francis, Kans., 1,594 75 D4
St. Francis, Ky. 71 F4
St. Francis, Me. 55 D1
St. Francis, S. Dak., 421 74 B4
St. Francis, Wis., 10,065 66 d12
St. Francis, r., Ark.-Mo. 53 H3
St. Francis, r., Me. 55 C1
St. Francis, C., Newf., Can. 45 c10
St. Francis, C., S. Af. 164 D7
St. Francisville, Ill., 1,040 68 E5
St. Francisville, La., 1,661 73 D7
St. Francisville, Mo. 72 F4
St-François, Qué., Can. 47 O2
St-François, Guad., 2,501 97 14
St. Francois, co., Mo., 36,516 72 G7
St-François, r., Qué., Can. 47 M3
St-François, L., Qué., Can. 47 K3
St-François, L., Qué., Can. 47 N3
St-François-de-Laval, Qué., Can. 47 o17
St. François de Madawaska, N.B., Can. 47 R10
St-François-du-Lac, Qué., Can. 47 M2
Ste-Françoise, Qué., Can. 47 R9
St. Francois Mts., Mo. 72 G7
St. Froid L., Me. 55 D2
St-Gabriel, Qué., Can., 1,157 47 S9
St. Gabriel, La. 73 D7
St-Gabriel-de-Brandon, Qué., Can., 3,402 47 L2
St-Gaudens, Fr., 11,435 117 D5
St-Gédéon, Qué., Can. 47 O3
Ste-Geneviève, Qué., Can., 2,331 47 o18
Ste. Genevieve, co., Mo., 12,116 72 G7
Ste. Genevieve, Mo., 4,443 72 H7
Ste-Geneviève-de-Batiscan, Qué., Can. 47 M2
Ste-Geneviève-des-Bois, Fr., 17,660 116 h12

St-Geniez-d'Olt—Salcajá · 287

St-Geniez-d'Olt, Fr., 2,445 117 E4
St-Genis-Laval, Fr., 6,584 116 p15
St. Gennys, U.K. 113 D6
St. George, Austl., 1,698 173 G4
St. George, Berm. Is., 1,926 108 1
St. George, N.B., Can., 1,125 45 M6
St. George, Ont., Can. 46 b14
St. George, Alaska 85 B4
St. George, Ga. 64 H5
St. George, Kans., 259 75 J4
St. George, Me. 55 C4
St. George, Mo., 1,323 72 a11
St. George (part of N.Y.C.), N.Y. 58 c14
St. George, S.C., 1,833 63 D4
St. George, Utah, 5,130 78 B3
St. George, W. Va. 62 E3
St. George, C., Terr. New Guin. 174 g2
St. George, C., Fla. 65 E3
St. George, Pt., Calif. 82 A2
St. George I., Alaska 85 B4
St. George I., Fla. 65 E3
St-Georges, Belg., 5,936 115 D4
St. George's, Newf., Can., 1,181 45 P5
St-Georges, Qué., Can., 4,006 45 L6
St-Georges, Qué., Can., 1,765 47 M2
St-Georges, Fr. Guiana 101 O6
St. Georges, Gren., 7,305 97 18
St. George's Bay, Newf., Can. 45 P5
St. George's Chan., Ire.-U.K. 113 D5
St. Georges Chan., Terr. New Guin. 174 g1
St. Georges Hbr., Berm. Is. 108 1
St. Georges Island, Md. 62 H4
St. Georges I., Berm. Is. 108 1
St-Georges-Ouest, Qué., Can., 4,714 47 O2
St-Gérard, Belg., 1,670 115 C4
St-Gérard, Qué., Can. 47 N3
St-Germain, Qué., Can., 1,008 47 M3
St. Germain, Wis. 66 D3
St-Germain-au-Mont-d'Or, Fr., 1,775 116 p15
St-Germain-en-Laye, Fr., 37,391 116 g11
St-Germain-Laxis, Fr. 116 i12
St-Germain-lès-Corbeil, Fr. 116 i12
St-Gervais, Qué., Can., 1,000 47 O2
St-Gervais-d'Auvergne, Fr., 1,714 117 E3
St-Gilles, Fr., 7,034 117 F5
St-Gilles-sur-Vie, Fr., 3,387 117 C3
St-Gingolph, Switz. 124 A2
St-Girons, Fr., 7,977 117 D5
St. Gotthard Pass, Switz. 124 C2
St. Govan's Head, U.K. 113 D6
St-Grégoire, Qué., Can. 47 M2
St-Grégoire, Qué., Can. 47 p18
St-Guillaume, Qué., Can. 47 M3
St. Harmon, U.K. 114 A6
St-Héand, Fr., 2,317 116 o15
St. Hedwig, Tex., 589 76 b7
St. Helen, Mich. 67 J4
St. Helen, L., Mich. 67 J4
St. Helena, Atl. Oc., 5,000* 109 M8
St. Helena, Calif., 2,722 82 B3
St. Helena, parish, La., 9,162 73 E7
St. Helena, N.C. 63 F3
St. Helena Bay, S. Af. 164 a8
St. Helena I., S.C. 63 D5
Ste-Hélène, Qué., Can. 47 R10
St. Helens, Austl. 173 g13
St. Helens, Lancs., U.K., 108,348 113 E5
St. Helen's (part of Ryde), U.K., 2,395 113 k13
St. Helens, Oreg., 5,022 80 B3
St. Helens, Mt., Wash. 80 B2
St. Helier, U.K., 13,355 117 B2
Ste-Hénédine, Qué., Can. 47 O2
St-Henri, Qué., Can. 47 n16
St. Henry, Ohio, 978 70 E2
Ste-Hermine, Fr., 1,717 117 C3
St-Hilaire, Qué., Can., 2,867 47 p17
St. Hilaire, Minn., 270 74 D1
St-Hilaire-du-Harcouët, Fr., 4,321 117 C2
St-Hippolyte-du-Fort, Fr., 3,363 117 E5
St-Honoré, Qué., Can. 47 O3
St-Hubert, Belg., 3,100 115 D4
St-Hubert, Qué., Can., 14,067 47 p18
St-Hubert, Qué., Can. 47 R10
St. Huberts, N.Y. 59 N3
St-Hyacinthe, Qué., Can., 21,647 44 K6
St. Ignace, Mich., 3,334 67 J3
St. Ignace, I., Ont., Can. 44 E5
St. Ignatius, Mont., 940 81 B2
St-Imier, Switz., 6,704 124 A1
St-Irénée, Qué., Can. 47 Q10
St-Isidore, Qué., Can. 47 O2
St-Isidore, Qué., Can. 47 o18
St. Ives, Corn., Eng., U.K., 9,346 113 D6
St. Ives, Hants., Eng., U.K. 113 i13
St. Ives, Hunts., Eng., U.K., 4,082 113 F5
St. Jacobiparochie, Neth. 115 D1
St. Jacobs, Ont., Can. 46 a13
St. Jacques, N.B., Can. 47 R10
St-Jacques, Qué., Can., 2,007 47 L3
St-Jacques-des-Piles, Qué., Can. 47 M2
St. James, Man., Can., 33,644 43 F5
St-James, Fr., 2,437 117 C2
St. James, Ill. 68 D5
St. James, parish, La., 18,369 73 E7
St. James, Mich. 67 H3
St. James, Minn., 4,174 74 E4
St. James, Mo., 2,384 72 F6
St. James, N.Y., 3,524 58 g13
St. James City, Fla. 65 G6
St-Janvier, Qué., Can., 1,811 47 o17
St-Jean, Qué., Can., 26,181 44 K6
St-Jean, Qué., Can., 1,579 47 N2
St-Jean, Fr. Guiana 101 O5
St-Jean, B., St-Barthélemy 97 7
St-Jean, L., Qué., Can. 44 K5
St. Jean Baptiste, Man., Can., 1,200 43 F5
St-Jean-Baptiste, Qué., Can. 47 p17
St-Jean-Cap-Ferrat, Fr., 2,416 116 n13
St-Jean-Chrysostôme, Qué., Can. 47 n16
St-Jean-d'Angély, Fr., 9,374 117 C4
St-Jean-de-Dieu, Qué., Can., 1,009 47 R10
St-Jean-de-Luz, Fr., 10,417 117 C5
St-Jean-de-Matha, Qué., Can., 1,016 47 L2
St-Jean-de-Maurienne, Fr., 7,926 117 G4
St-Jean-de-Monts, Fr., 4,818 117 C3
St-Jeannet, Fr., 1,079 116 n13
St-Jean-Pied-de-Port, Fr., 1,673 117 C5
St-Jean-Port-Joli, Qué., Can., 1,615 45 L6
St-Jérôme, Qué., Can., 24,329 44 K6
St. Jo, Tex., 977 77 P3
St-Joachim, Qué., Can. 47 O1
St. Joe, Ark. 73 C1
St. Joe, Ind., 499 70 E1
St. Joe, r., Idaho 81 B2
St. John, N.B., Can., 53,640 45 N6
St. John, Ind., 1,128 70 B1
St. John, Kans., 1,753 75 G5
St. John, Mo., 7,342 72 a11
St. John, N. Dak., 420 74 C1
St. John, Utah 78 B1
St. John, Wash., 545 80 E2
St. John, C., Newf., Can. 45 Q5
St. John, i., V.I. 97 4
St. John, r., Can.-U.S. 45 M6
St. John Pd., Me. 55 C2
Saint Johns, Antigua, 21,637 97 9
St. John's, Newf., Can., 61,738 45 R6
St. Johns, Qué., Can. = St-Jean
St. Johns, Ariz., 1,310 78 D4
St. Johns, co., Fla., 30,034 65 H3
St. Johns, Ill., 206 68 C5
St. Johns, Mich., 5,629 67 J6
St. Johns, r., Fla. 65 H3
St. Johnsburg, N.Y. 58 k18
St. Johnsbury, Vt., 6,809 54 D3
St. Johnsbury Center, Vt. 54 D3
St. Johns Harbour, Antigua 97 9
St. John's Pt., Ire. 113 B4
St. Johns Pt., Jam. 96 o8
St. Johnsville, N.Y., 2,196 59 L5
St. John the Baptist, parish, La., 18,439 73 E7
St. Jones, r., Del. 61 A5
St-Joseph, Qué., Can., 2,568 45 L6
St-Joseph, Qué., Can., 3,545 47 L2
St-Joseph, Qué., Can., 3,772 47 M3
St. Joseph, Dominica, 2,044 97 13
St-Joseph, Fr., 1,059 116 p15
St-Joseph, La Réunion, 5,969 165 b11
St-Joseph, Mart. 97 12
St. Joseph, Ill., 1,210 68 E3
St. Joseph, co., Ind., 238,614 70 C1
St. Joseph, La., 1,653 73 D6
St. Joseph, co., Mich., 42,332 67 H7
St. Joseph, Mich., 11,755 67 G6
St. Joseph, Minn., 1,487 74 E3
St. Joseph, Mo., 79,673 72 B5
St. Joseph, Tenn., 547 71 D6
St. Joseph, Wis. 66 B5
St. Joseph, r., Ind.-Mich. 67 G7
St. Joseph, r., Ind.-Ohio 70 E1
St. Joseph, L., Ont., Can. 44 D4
St. Joseph I., Ont., Can. 44 F6
St. Joseph Pt., Fla. 65 D3
St-Jovite, Qué., Can., 2,636 44 K6
Ste-Julienne, Qué., Can. 47 L3
St-Junien, Fr., 11,424 117 D4
St. Just, P.R. 96 u10
St. Just, U.K., 3,642 113 D6
St-Just-en-Chaussée, Fr., 3,575 117 E2
St-Justin, Qué., Can. 47 L2
St. Kitts = St. Christopher
St-Lambert, Qué., Can. 47 N2
St-Lambert, Qué., Can., 14,211 47 p17
St-Lambert, Fr. 116 g12
St-Lambert, Fr. 116 m13
St-Lambert Lock, Qué., Can. 69 D
St. Landry, parish, La., 81,493 73 D7
St. Laurent, Man., Can. 43 g9
St-Laurent, Qué., Can., 50,421 47 L3
St-Laurent, Fr., 8,213 116 n13
St-Laurent, Fr. Guiana 2,827* 101 O5
St-Laurent = St. Lawrence
St-Laurent-de-Chamousset, Fr., 1,319 116 o15
St-Laurent-de-la-Salanque, Fr., 3,338 117 E5
St. Lawrence, Austl. 173 G3
St. Lawrence, Newf., Can., 2,113 45 Q6
St. Lawrence, co., N.Y., 111,239 59 K3
St. Lawrence, N.Y. 59 H3
St. Lawrence, Pa., 929 61 h14
St. Lawrence, S. Dak., 290 74 C3
St. Lawrence, G. of, Can. 45 O5
St. Lawrence, r., Can.-U.S. 44-5
St. Lawrence I., Alaska 85 B3
St. Lawrence Is. Nat. Pk., Ont., Can. 47 H4
St. Lazare, Man., Can. 43 E5
St. Leo, Fla., 278 65 G4
St. Leo, Kans. 75 G6
St. Leo, Minn., 129 74 E3
St. Leonard, N.B., Can., 1,646 45 M6
St-Léonard, Qué., Can. 47 M2
St-Léonard, Fr., 6,002 117 D4
St. Leonard, Md. 62 H4
St-Léonard-de-Port-Maurice, Que., Can., 4,893 47 o17
St-Léonard-de-Portneuf, Qué., Can. 47 M2
St-Leu, La Réunion, 1,447 165 b11
St-Leu-la-Forêt, Fr., 8,839 116 h10
St. Lewis, r., Newf., Can. 45 P4
St-Liboire, Qué., Can. 47 M3
St-Lin, Qué., Can., 1,495 47 L3
Ste-Livrade-sur-Lot, Fr., 5,452 117 D4
St-Lô, Fr., 16,072 117 C2
St-Louis, Fr., 12,511 117 G3
St-Louis, Guad., 1,017 97 14
St-Louis, La Réunion, 7,753 165 b11
St. Louis, Sen., 58,000 162 B3
St. Louis, Mich., 3,808 67 J5
St. Louis, co., Minn., 231,588 74 F2
St. Louis, co., Mo., 703,532 72 G6
St. Louis, Mo., 750,026 72 G6
St. Louis, Okla., 76 76 G2
St-Louis, r., Qué., Can. 69 D
St-Louis, r., Guad. 97 14
St. Louis, r., Minn. 74 F2
St-Louis, L., Qué., Can. 47 o18
St-Louis-de-Gonzague, Qué., Can. 47 K3
St. Louis-de-Kent, N.B., Can. 47 T10
St-Louis-du-Ha! Ha!, Qué., Can., 47 R10
St-Louis-du-Nord, Haiti, 3,130 96 k6
Ste-Louise, Qué., Can. 47 R10
St. Louis Heights, Hawaii 84 d8
St. Louis Park, Minn., 43,310 74 b6
St. Louisville, Ohio, 349 70 G2
St-Loup, Fr., 2,864 117 G3
St-Luc, Qué., Can. 47 p18
St-Luc, Qué., Can., 47 S9
Ste-Luce, Mart. 97 12
St. Lucia, i., Lesser Ant. 97 11
St. Lucia Channel, W.I. 95 G4
St. Lucie, co., Fla., 39,294 65 J5
St. Lucie, Fla. 65 J5
St. Lucie Can., Fla. 65 J5
St. Luke's I., Burma 146 B5
St-Lys, Fr., 1,426 117 D5
Ste-Madeleine, Qué., Can. 47 p17
St-Magloire, Qué., Can. 47 O2
St. Magnus Bay, U.K. 112 F1
St-Maixent, Fr., 8,180 117 C3
St-Malachie, Qué., Can. 47 O2
St. Malo, Man., Can. 43 h10
St-Malo, Fr., 17,800 117 B2
St-Malo, G. de, Fr. 117 C2
St-Mandé, Fr., 24,769 116 h11
St-Marc, Qué., Can. 47 p17
St-Marc, Haiti, 10,222 96 k6
St-Marc, Canal de, Haiti 96 k6
St-Marc, Cap, Haiti 96 k6
St-Marc-des-Carrières, Qué., Can., 2,591 47 M2
St-Marcel, Mt., Fr. Guiana 101 O6
St-Marcellin, Fr., 5,570 117 F4
St-Mard, Belg., 2,382 115 D5
St-Mard, Fr., 1,073 116 i10
St-Margaret Mtn., Qué., Can. 47 O1
St. Margaret's Hope, U.K. 112 E2
Ste-Marguerite, Qué., Can. 47 L2
Ste-Marie, Qué., Can., 3,599 45 L6
Ste-Marie, La Réunion, 2,200 165 b11
Ste-Marie, Mart., 2,197 97 12
Ste-Marie, C., Malag. Rep. 165 G6
Ste-Marie, Î., Malag. Rep. 165 H4
Ste-Marie-aux-Mines, Fr., 7,923 117 G2
St. Maries, Idaho, 2,435 81 A2
St. Marks, Fla. 65 E2
St. Marks, r., Fla. 65 E2
St-Martin, Qué., Can., 1,176 47 O3
St-Martin, Switz., 1,155 124 B2
St. Martin, parish, La., 29,063 73 D7
St. Martin, Minn., 215 74 E3
St. Martin, Ohio, 152 70 F3
St. Martin, i., W.I. 95 G3
St. Martin, L., Man., Can. 43 F4
St-Martin-de-Ré, Fr., 2,304 117 C3
St-Martin-du-Tertre, Fr., 1,731 116 h10
Ste-Martine, Qué., Can., 1,436 69 D
St. Martin I., Mich. 67 G3
San-Martino-di-Lota, Fr., 1,235 116 r17
St. Martins, N.B., Can. 47 T11
St. Martin's, U.K., 1,970 114 C5
St. Martin's, i., U.K. 113 C7
St-Martin-Vésubie, Fr., 1,131 117 G4
St. Martinville, La., 6,468 73 D7
St. Mary, Ill. 68 A3
St. Mary, Ky. 71 F4
St. Mary, parish, La., 48,833 73 D8
St. Mary Bourne, U.K. 1,271 114 F8
St. Mary Pk., Austl. 172 E4
St. Marys, Austl. 73 g13
St. Mary's, Newf., Can. 45 R6
St. Mary's, Ont., Can., 4,437 46 C5
St. Marys, Alaska 85 C3
St. Marys, Ga., 3,272 64 H5
St. Marys, Kans., 1,509 75 K4
St. Marys, co., Md., 38,915 62 H4
St. Marys, Ohio, 7,737 70 E2
St. Marys, Pa., 8,065 60 E3
St. Marys, W. Va., 2,443 62 C3
St. Mary's, i., U.K. 113 C7
St. Marys, r., Can.-U.S. 67 J2
St. Marys, r., Fla.-Ga. 64 G5
St. Marys, r., Ind.-Ohio 70 E2
St. Mary's, C., Newf., Can. 45 a11
St. Mary's Bay, Newf., Can. 45 Q6
St. Mary's Bay, N.S., Can. 47 S11
St. Marys City, Md. 62 H4
St. Mary's Point, Minn. 74 d6
St-Mathias, Que., Can. 47 p18
St-Mathieu, Qué., Can. 47 p18
St-Mathieu, Fr. 1,711 117 D4
St-Mathieu, Pte., Fr. 116 A2
St. Matthew I., Alaska 85 A3
St. Matthews, Ky., 10,796 71 F3
St. Matthews, S.C., 2,433 63 D4
St. Matthews I., Burma 146 B5
St. Matthias Group, is., Terr. New Guin. 174 f1
St-Maur-des-Fossés, Fr., 70,681 116 i11
St-Maurice, Qué., Can. 47 M2
St-Maurice, Switz., 3,196 124 A2
St-Maurice, r., Qué., Can. 44 K6
St-Max, Fr., 8,528 116 b9
Ste-Maxime, Fr., 3,937 116 m14
St-Méen, Fr., 3,018 117 B2
St. Meinrad, Ind. 70 C4
St. Mellons, U.K., 1,035 114 B7
Ste-Menehould, Fr., 4,374 117 F2
Ste-Mère-Église, Fr., 1,221 117 C2
St-Méry, Fr. 115 k12
St-Mesmes, Fr. 116 i11
St-Méthode-de-Frontenac, Qué., Can. 47 O2
St. Michael, Alta., Can. 43 c7
St. Michael, Alaska, 205 85 D3
St. Michael, Nebr. 75 G2
St. Michael, Pa., 1,292 60 E5
St. Michaels, Ariz. 78 D4
St. Michaels, Md., 1,484 62 H4
St-Michel, Qué., Can., 52,719 47 L3
St-Michel-de-l'Atalaye, Haiti, 2,431 96 k6
St-Michel-des-Saints, Qué., Can., 1,637 47 K2
St-Michel-sur-Orge, Fr., 3,730 116 h12
St. Michielsgestel, Neth., 4,500 115 D3
St-Mihiel, Fr., 5,366 117 F2
St. Monance, U.K., 1,406 112 e7
Ste-Monique-des-Saules, Qué., Can., 4,066 47 n16
St-Narcisse, Qué., Can. 47 M2
St-Nazaire, Fr., 59,181 117 C3
St. Nazianz, Wis., 669 66 F4
St. Neots, U.K., 5,554 114 H6
St-Nicolas, Qué., Can. 47 n16
St-Nicolas-de-Port, Fr., 5,761 117 G2
St-Nicolas-du-Pélem, Fr., 2,403 116 B2
St-Noël, Qué., Can., 1,094 47 S9
St. Norbert, Man., Can. 43 g10
Ste-Odile, Qué., Can., 1,173 47 R9
St. Oedenrode, Neth., 4,500 115 D3
St-Omer, Fr., 20,911 117 E1
St. Onge, S. Dak. 74 A3
St-Ouen-l'Aumône, Fr., 7,102 116 g10
St-Ours, Qué., Can. 47 L3
St-Pacôme, Qué., Can., 1,212 45 L6
St-Pamphile, Qué., Can., 1,534 47 P2
St. Paris, Ohio, 1,460 70 F2
St-Pascal, Qué., Can., 2,083 45 L6
St-Pathus, Fr. 116 k10
St-Patrice, Qué., Can. 47 N2
St-Patrice, L., Qué., Can. 46 G2
St. Paul, Alta., Can., 2,797 42 K2
St-Paul, Fr., 1,461 116 n13
St-Paul, Fr., 5,037 117 C5
St-Paul, La Réunion, 5,624 165 b11
St. Paul, Alaska, 378 85 B4
St. Paul, Ark., 118 73 B2
St. Paul, Ind., 702 70 D3
St. Paul, Kans., 675 75 K6
St. Paul, Minn., 313,411 74 F3
St. Paul, Nebr., 1,714 75 G2
St. Paul, Oreg., 254 80 B3
St. Paul, Va., 1,156 62 B6
St. Paul, r., Newf.-Qué., Can. 45 P4
St-Paul, Île, Ind. Oc. 168 C4
St-Paul-de-Montminy, Qué., Can. 47 O2
St-Paul-du-Nord, Qué., Can. 45 L5
St-Paul-en-Forêt, Fr. 116 m13
St-Paulin, Qué., Can. 47 L2
St. Paul I., N.S., Can. 45 O6
St. Paul I., Alaska 85 B4
St-Paul-l'Ermite, Qué., Can., 2,935 47 o17
St. Paul Park, Minn., 5,111 74 c6
St. Pauls, N.C., 2,249 63 F3
St. Paul's Bay, Malta, 3,040 123 f12
St. Paul's Church Nat. Hist. Site, N.Y. 58 d13
St. Pauls Pt., Pitc. I. 177 45
St-Péray, Fr., 3,097 117 F4
Ste-Perpétue, Qué., Can. 47 P1
St. Peter, Ill., 397 68 D5
St. Peter, Kans. 75 E4
St. Peter, Minn., 8,484 74 E3
St. Peter and St. Paul Rocks, Atl. Oc. 109 K6
St. Peter Port, Channel Islands, U.K., 16,849 116 B2
St. Peters, N.S., Can. 47 V11
St. Peters, P.E.I., Can. 47 U10
St. Peters, Mo., 404 72 G6
St. Peters, Pa. 60 e11
St. Petersburg, Colo. 79 D1
St. Petersburg, Fla., 181,298 65 G5
St. Petersburg, Pa., 417 60 C3
St. Petersburg Beach, Fla., 6,268 65 G5
Ste-Pétronille, Qué., Can. 47 n16
St-Philémon, Qué., Can. 47 O2
St. Philip and St. James B., New Hebr. 174 k5
St-Philippe, Qué., Can. 47 R10
St-Philippe, Qué., Can. 47 p18
St-Philippe, La Réunion 165 b11
St. Phillip, Ind. 70 B4
St. Phillips, Newf., Can. 45 c10
Ste-Philomène, Qué., Can. 47 o18
St-Pie, Qué., Can., 1,406 47 M3
St. Pierre, Man., Can. 43 F5
St-Pierre, Qué., Can., 1,200 47 O2
St-Pierre, Qué., Can. 47 n16
St-Pierre, Qué., Can., 6,657 47 o18
St-Pierre, La Réunion, 8,752 165 b11
St-Pierre, Mart., 3,942 97 12
St-Pierre, i., N. Amer. 45 Q6
St-Pierre, L., Qué., Can. 47 M2
St-Pierre, Rade de, Mart. 97 12
St-Pierre-de-Bœuf, Fr., 1,145 116 p16
St-Pierre-d'Oléron, Fr., 4,025 117 C4
St-Pierre-Église, Fr., 1,683 117 C2
St-Pierre-sur-Dives, Fr., 3,521 117 C2
St-Pol-de-Léon, Fr., 8,899 116 B2
St-Polycarpe, Qué., Can. 47 K3
St-Pons, Fr., 3,508 117 E5
St-Pourçain, Fr., 4,887 117 E3
St-Prex, Switz., 1,897 124 A2
St-Priest, Fr., 10,932 116 p15
St-Priest-en-Jarez, Fr., 3,512 116 o16
St-Prosper, Que., Can., 1,277 47 O2
Ste-Prudentienne, Qué., Can. 47 M3
St. Quentin, N.B., Can., 2,089 45 M6
St-Quentin, Fr., 62,579 117 E2
St-Quirin, Fr. 116 d9
St. Quivox, U.K. 112 a8
St-Raphaël, Qué., Can., 1,125 47 O2
St-Raphaël, Fr., 13,787 116 m14
St-Raphaël, Haiti, 1,586 96 k6
St-Raymond, Qué., Can., 3,883 47 N2
St-Rédempteur, Qué., Can., 1,030 47 n16
St. Regis, Mont. 81 B2
St. Regis, N.Y. 59 L2
St. Regis, r., N.Y. 59 L2
St. Regis Falls, N.Y. 59 M2
St-Regis I., Qué., Can. 69 C
St-Rémi, Qué., Can. 47 K2
St-Rémy-lès-Chevreuse, Fr., 3,116 116 g12
St-Rémy-l'Honoré, Fr. 116 f11
St-Robert, Qué., Can. 47 M3
St. Robert, Mo., 860 72 E7
St. Roch Basin, N.W.T., Can. 40 K4
St-Roch-de-l'Achigan, Qué., Can. 47 L3
St-Roch-de-Richelieu, Qué., Can. 47 L3
St-Romain-les-Atheux, Fr. 116 o16
St-Romuald, Qué., Can., 5,183 47 n16
Ste-Rosalie, Qué., Can., 1,251 47 M3
Ste-Rose, Qué. Can. 47 o17
Ste-Rose, Guad., 1,288 97 14
Ste-Rose, La Réunion 165 b11
Ste-Rose-du-Dégelé, Qué., Can., 1,943 45 M6
Ste. Rose du Lac, Man., Can. 43 E4
Saintry-sur-Seine, Fr., 1,558 116 i12
St-Saëns, Fr., 2,479 117 D2
St-Samuel, Qué., Can. 47 N3
St-Sauveur, Qué., Can., 1,663 47 K3
St-Sauveur, Fr., 1,282 117 E3
St-Sauveur-sur-École, Fr. 116 i12
Ste-Savine, Fr., 12,022 117 E2
Ste-Scholastique, Qué., Can. 47 L3
St-Sébastien, Qué., Can. 47 O3
St-Sébastien, C., Malag. Rep. 165 G4
St-Servais, Belg., 9,014 115 C4
St-Servan, Fr., 15,275 117 C2
St-Sever, Fr., 3,983 117 C5
St. Shott's, Newf., Can. 45 b11
St-Siméon, Qué., Can., 1,169 45 L6
St. Simons, Ga., 3,199 64 H4
St. Simons I., Ga. 64 H4
Stes-Maries-de-la-Mer, Fr., 2,179 117 F5
Ste-Sophie, Qué., Can. 47 N2
St-Souplet, Fr., 1,447 116 a7
St-Soupplets, Fr. 116 k10
St-Stanislas, Qué., Can. 47 M2
St. Stanislas Bay, Christmas Atoll 177 40
St. Stephen, N.B., Can., 3,260 45 M6
St. Stephen, S.C., 1,462 63 E4
Ste-Suzanne, La Réunion 165 b11
St-Sylvestre, Qué., Can. 47 N2
St-Symphorien, Fr., 2,447 116 p15
St-Symphorien, Fr., 1,537 117 C4
St-Symphorien, Fr., 12,780 117 D3
St-Symphorien-sur-Coise, Fr., 2,960 116 o15
St. Tammany, parish, La., 38,643 73 E7
Ste-Thècle, Qué., Can., 1,950 47 M2
St-Théophile, Qué., Can. 47 M2
Ste-Thérèse, Qué., Can., 11,420 47 o17
St. Thomas, Ont., Can., 22,095 44 G7
St-Thomas, Qué., Can. 47 L2
St. Thomas, Ind. 70 B4
St. Thomas, N. Dak., 660 74 D1
St. Thomas, Pa. 60 G6
St. Thomas, i., V.I. 97 4
St. Thomas Mount, India, 15,790 145 n19
St-Thuribe, Qué., Can. 47 M2
St-Timothée, Qué., Can. 47 L3
St-Timothée, Qué., Can. 47 M2
St-Tite, Qué., Can., 3,192 47 M2
St-Tite-des-Caps, Qué., Can. 47 N1
St-Trond = Sint-Truiden
St-Tropez, Fr., 5,689 117 G5
St-Tropez, G. de, Fr. 116 m14
St-Ubald, Qué., Can. 47 M2
St-Ulric, Qué., Can. 47 S9
St-Urbain, Qué., Can. 47 Q10
St-Ursanne, Switz., 1,304 124 B1
St-Valéry-en-Caux, Fr., 2,979 117 D2
St-Valery-sur-Somme, Fr., 3,176 117 D1
St-Vallier, Qué., Can. 47 O2
St-Vallier, Fr., 4,420 117 F4
St-Vallier-de-Thiey, Fr. 116 m13
St-Varent, Fr., 2,480 117 C3
St-Vaury, Fr., 2,142 117 D3
St-Victor, Qué., Can. 47 N2
St-Vincent, N. Caled. 174 i9
St. Vincent, Minn., 217 74 D1
St-Vincent, B. de, N. Caled. 174 i9
St. Vincent, C., Austl. 173 e14
St-Vincent, C., Malag. Rep. 164 G5
St. Vincent, Gulf, Austl. 172 E5
St. Vincent, i., Lesser Ant. 97 19
St-Vincent-de-Paul, Qué., Can. 47 o17
St-Vincent-de-Tyrosse, Fr., 2,945 117 C5
St. Vincent I., Fla. 65 D3
St. Vincent Passage, W.I. 95 G4
St. Vincent's, Newf., Can. 45 b11
St-Vith, Belg., 2,688 115 E4
St-Vivien-de-Médoc, Fr., 1,027 117 C4
St-Vrain, Fr. 116 h12
St. Vrain, N. Mex. 79 D4
St. Vrain, r., Colo. 79 b7
St. Walburg, Sask., Can. 43 B4
St. Willebrord, Neth., 6,400 115 C3
St. Williams, Ont., Can. 46 D6
St-Witz, Fr. 116 i10
St. Xavier, Mont. 81 E3
St-Yrieix, Fr., 7,689 117 D4
St-Zacharie, Qué., Can., 1,367 47 O2
St-Zotique, Qué., Can. 69 D
Sairs, L., Qué., Can. 46 F2
Saiteli, Turk., 6,781 142 C2
Saito, Jap., 37,661 154 B5
Sai Yol, Thai. 147 c4
Sai Yong, Thai. 147 e4
Saja, India 144 c15
Sajama, Bol. 102 a11
Sajama, Nev., Bol. 102 C5
Saji, Jap. 154 g14
Sajószentpéter, Hung., 11,300 126 E2
Sajyang Pass, Burma-China 146 B1
Sa-ka, China 150 B4
Saka, Jap. 154 A4
Sakado, Jap., 23,962 155 m19
Sa Kaeo, Thai. 147 e5
Sakahara, Jap. 154 g14
Sakai, Jap., 339,863 155 D4
Sakaide, Jap., 62,142 155 C4
Sakaiminato, Jap., 32,714 155 C4
Sakaino, Jap. 154 g15
Sakākā, Saudi Ar. 143 C3
Sakami, r., Qué., Can. 44 J4
Sakami L., Qué., Can. 44 J4
Sakamoto, Jap. 154 g15
Sakamoto, Jap. 155 m19
Sakania, D.R.Congo 164 D4
Sakar, i., Terr. New Guin. 174 f2
Sakaraha, Malag. Rep. 165 G5
Sakari, Jap. 155 G2
Sakarya, r., Turk. 142 B1
Sakashita, Jap., 6,376 155 E4
Sakata, Jap., 97,671 155 F2
Sakau, New Hebr. 174 m6
Sakau, i., New Hebr. 174 k5
Sakawa, Jap., 18,785 155 C5
Sakawa, Jap. 155 m20
Sakawa, r., Jap. 155 m20
Sakchu, N. Kor. 151 E2
Sakété, Dahom., 13,873 162 e8
Sakhalin, O., U.S.S.R. 135 O4
Sakhalinskiy Zal., U.S.S.R. 135 O4
Sakhnin, Isr., 5,150 142 b7
Saki, U.S.S.R., 18,100 136 D4
Sakinohama, Jap. 155 D5
Sakishima-guntō, Ryukyu Is. 154 c13
Sakmara, U.S.S.R. 137 h9
Sakmara, r., U.S.S.R. 137 i9
Sako, Jap. 154 g15
Sakodo, Jap. 154 e16
Sa-koi, Burma 146 B3
Sakon Nakhon, Thai., 15,997 146 C3
Sakonnet (part of Little Compton), R.I. 57 M7
Sakonnet, r., R.I. 57 M6
Sakonnet Pt., R.I. 57 M7
Sakoshi, Jap. 154 f15
Sakota, Eth. 163 L3
Sakrand, Pak. 144 C4
Saksaul'skiy, U.S.S.R. 134 F5
Sakskøbing, Den., 2,526 121 D6
Sakuhata, Jap. 154 f14
Sakura, Jap. 154 h15
Sakura, Jap., 35,298 155 n19
Sakurai, Jap. 154 e15
Sakurai, Jap., 35,924 154 g15
Säkylä, Fin. 120 E3
Sal, i., C. Verde Is. 109 5
Sal, r., U.S.S.R. 136 F4
Sala, Swed. 120 D4
Salacgrīva, U.S.S.R., 4,500 136 A1
Sala Consilina, It., 11,522 123 E4
Salada, Lag., Mex. 92 B1
Saladas, Arg., 8,477 105 D3
Saladillo, Arg., 9,612 105 a12
Salado, Col. 101 d15
Salado, r., Arg. 105 B5
Salado, r., Arg. 105 C3
Salado, r., Arg. 105 c12
Salado, r., Mex. 92 F2
Salado, r., N. Mex. 79 B4
Salaga, Ghana 162 D4
Salaguí, Col. 100 B4
Salailua, W. Samoa 177 38
Salailua Bay, W. Samoa 177 38
Salair, U.S.S.R., 17,500 137 r11
Salajar, P., Indon. 148 G4
Salak South, Malay., 5,596 147 o15
Salala, Lib. 162 C4
Şalālah, Muscat and Oman 143 E5
Salālah, Sudan 163 L2
Salamá, Guat., 3,809 94 B3
Salamá, Hond., 1,712 94 D3
Salamanca, Chile, 3,197 105 A4
Salamanca, Mex., 32,192 92 E4
Salamanca, Peru, 1,469 104 C5
Salamanca, Sp., 90,498 122 C2
Salamanca, N.Y., 8,480 58 C7
Salamat, Bahr, Chad 163 H4
Salamaua, Terr. New Guin. 174 e2
Salamina, Col. 101 d14
Salamís, Gr., 11,161 129 D6
Salamis, i., Gr. 129 D6
Salamis, ruins, Cyp. 142 e9
Salamīyah, Syr., 22,863 142 D3
Salamo, Terr. Papua 174 3
Salamonia, Ind., 142 70 E2
Salamonie, r., Ind. 70 D2
Salamumu, W. Samoa 177 38
Salang, Indon. 148 F1
Salangen, Nor. 120 D1
Salang Kotal, pass, Afghan. 144 C2
Salani, W. Samoa 177 38
Sala Phya Ong, Laos 146 D4
Salara, It., 1,964 122 e6
Salard, Rum. 128 C1
Salas, Sp., 11,977 122 B1
Salas de los Infantes, Sp., 1,848 122 D1
Salat, i., Truk 176 19
Sălățig, Rum. 128 D1
Salatiga, Indon., 58,135 148 D4
Salavat, U.S.S.R., 68,000 134 E4
Salaverry, Peru, 4,514 104 B4
Salawati, P., Indon. 149 J3
Salay, Phil., 3,887 153 C3
Sala y Gómez, I., Pac. Oc. 171 M6
Sala y Gomez Ridge, Pac. Oc. 169 J3
Salazar, Ang. 164 B3
Salazar, Col. 100 D4
Salbris, Fr., 5,227 117 D3
Salcajá, Guat., 4,300 94 b9

288 · Salcedo—San Fernando

Salcedo, Dom. Rep., 6,175 96 m6
Salcedo, Phil., 1,300 153 b5
Salcedo, Phil., 2,671 153 C3
Salcha, r., Alaska 85 H2
Salcia, Rum. 128 E3
Salcombe, U.K., 2,549 113 E6
Saldaña, Sp., 2,433 122 C1
Saldanha, S. Af., 2,195 164 a8
Saldungaray, Arg., 3,000* 105 C5
Saldus, U.S.S.R., 7,800 136 A1
Sale, Austl., 6,537 173 G5
Sale, It., 5,505 122 b6
Salé, Mor., 75,799 160 C2
Sale, U.K., 51,317 114 D4
Sale, r., Man., Can. 43 g10
Salebabu, P., Indon. 149 H2
Sale City, Ga., 275 64 F4
Sale Creek, Tenn. 71 F6
Salée, chan., Guad. 97 14
Saleimoa, W. Samoa 177 38
Salekhard, U.S.S.R., 16,600 134 F3
Salelologa, W. Samoa, 1,089 177 38
Salem, Ont., Can. 46 b13
Salem, India, 249,145 145 F8
Salem, Montserrat 97 5
Salem, Ala. 64 D3
Salem, Ark., 713 73 D1
Salem, Conn., 925(T) 56 G7
Salem, Fla. 65 F3
Salem, Ill., 6,165 68 D5
Salem, Ind., 4,546 70 C4
Salem, Iowa, 442 72 F4
Salem, Ky. 71 C4
Salem, Me. 55 B4
Salem, Mass., 39,211 57 N2
Salem, Mich. 67 K6
Salem, Mo., 3,870 72 F7
Salem, Nebr., 261 75 K3
Salem, N.H. 54 E6
Salem, co., N.J., 58,711 61 A4
Salem, N.J., 8,941 61 A4
Salem, N. Mex. 79 B5
Salem, N.Y., 1,076 59 O5
Salem, Ohio, 13,854 70 J2
Salem, Oreg., 49,142 80 B3
Salem, S.C., 206 63 A3
Salem, S. Dak., 1,188 74 D4
Salem, Utah, 920 78 c10
Salem, Va., 16,058 62 D5
Salem, W. Va., 2,366 62 D3
Salem, Wis. 66 c13
Salem, r., N.J. 61 A4
Salemburg, N.C., 569 63 F2
Salem Depot, N.H., 2,523 54 E6
Salem Heights, Oreg., 10,770 80 B3
Salemi, It., 16,527 123 D6
Salem Maritime Nat. Hist. Site., Mass. 57 N2
Salem Plat., Mo. 72 ·
Salen, U.K. 112 C3
Salento, Col. 101 d15
Salernes, Fr., 2,269 117 G5
Salerno, It., 110,953 123 E4
Salerno, Golfo di, It. 123 E4
Sales Cay, Bah. Is. 95 a6
Salesville, Tex. 76 d9
Salford, U.K., 154,963 114 D4
Salgar, Col. 100 C5
Salgir, r., U.S.S.R. 136 D4
Salgótarján, Hung., 26,682 126 D2
Salgueiro, Braz., 8,936 103 J3
Salice, Fr. 116 r17
Salida, Calif., 1,109 82 C4
Salida, Colo., 4,560 79 C2
Salies-de-Béarn, Fr., 5,816 117 C5
Salihli, Turk., 24,114 142 B2
Salima, Malawi 164 E4
Salīmah, Wāḥat, Sudan 163 J2
Salimbatu, Indon. 148 F2
Salin, Burma, 6,604 146 A2
Salina, Kans., 43,202 75 H5
Salina, Okla., 972 76 H1
Salina, Utah, 1,618 78 C2
Salina, Isola, It. 123 E5
Salina Cruz, Mex., 14,881 93 G5
Salinas, Braz., 5,186 103 H5
Salinas, Ec., 5,395 104 A2
Salinas, Guat. 94 B3
Salinas, Mex., 6,626 92 E3
Salinas, P.R., 3,666 96 t11
Salinas, Calif., 28,957 82 C4
Salinas, r., Calif. 82 C4
Salinas, P., Dom. Rep. 96 m6
Salinas, P., P.R. 96 t10
Salinas de Garci Mendoza, Bol., 2,993 102 a11
Salinas Pk., N. Mex. 79 B5
Salinas Victoria, Mex., 2,152 93 E2
Saline, U.K. 112 c7
Saline, co., Ark., 28,956 73 C3
Saline, co., Ill., 26,227 68 D6
Saline, co., Kans., 54,715 75 H5
Saline, La., 329 73 C5
Saline, Mich., 2,334 67 K6
Saline, co., Mo., 25,148 72 D5
Saline, co., Nebr., 12,542 75 H3
Saline, r., Ark. 73 A3
Saline, r., Ark. 73 C3
Saline, r., Ill. 68 D6
Saline, r., Kans. 75 F4
Saline I., Gren Is. 97 20
Saline L., La. 73 C6
Saline, Pt., Gren. 97 18
Salineno, Tex. 77 O6
Salineville, Ohio, 1,898 70 J2
Salingyi, Burma, 2,458 147 f7
Salino, U.S.S.R. 136 a5
Salinópolis, Braz., 4,101 103 G2
Salins-les-Bains, Fr., 4,827 117 F3
Salinungan, Phil., 2,919 153 c6
Salisbury, Austl., 2,619 172 c8
Salisbury, N.B., Can. 47 T10
Salisbury, Guam 176 24
Salisbury, Rhod., 277,000 164 E4
Salisbury, U.K., 35,492 113 F6
Salisbury, Conn., 3,309(T) 56 C5
Salisbury, Md., 16,302 62 J4
Salisbury, Mass., 3,154(T) 57 N1
Salisbury, Mo., 1,787 72 E5
Salisbury, N.H. 54 D5
Salisbury, N.C., 21,297 63 D2
Salisbury, Pa., 862 60 D6
Salisbury, Vt. 54 A4
Salisbury Beach (part of Salisbury), Mass. 57 N1
Salisbury Center, N.Y. 59 L5
Salisbury Heights, N.H. 54 D5
Salisbury I., Austl. 172 C5
Salisbury I., N.W.T., Can. 41 O5
Salisbury Plain, U.K. 113 E6
Sălişte, Rum. 128 D2
Salix, Iowa, 394 72 A2
Salkehatchie, r., S.C. 63 C4
Şalkhad, Syr., 5,323 142 D3
Salkum, Wash. 80 B2
Salla, Fin. 120 G2
Salladasburg, Pa., 255 60 H3
Sallanches, Fr., 4,807 117 G4
Sallent, Sp., 9,227 122 F2
Salles-Curan, Fr., 1,655 117 E4
Salley, S.C., 403 63 C4
Salliqueló, Arg., 8,350 105 C5
Sallis, Miss., 223 73 F4
Sallisaw, Okla., 3,351 76 J2
Sallyāna, Nepal 144 d11
Sal'm, O., U.S.S.R. 134 F2
Salm-Bach, r., F.R.Ger. 119 B5
Salmo, Br. Col., Can. 42 H4
Salmo, Wis. 66 C2
Salmon, Idaho, 2,944 81 B3
Salmon, r., Br. Col., Can. 42 F2
Salmon, r., Br. Col., Can. 42 H4
Salmon, r., N.B., Can. 47 T10
Salmon, r., Ont., Can. 46 G4
Salmon, r., Conn. 56 G6
Salmon, r., Idaho 81 B3
Salmon, r., Franklin Co., N.Y. 59 M2
Salmon, r., Clinton Co., N.Y. 59 N2
Salmon Arm, Br. Col., Can., 1,228 42 H4
Salmon Bk., Conn. 56 E5
Salmon Bk., Mass.-N.H. 57 L2
Salmon Cove, Newf., Can. 45 b10
Salmon Cr., Conn. 56 C5
Salmon Falls, r., Me.-N.H 54 F5
Salmon Falls Cr., Idaho-Nev. 81 B4
Salmon Gums, Austl. 172 B5
Salmon Mts., Calif. 82 ·
Salmon Res., N.Y. 59 J4
Salmon River, N.S., Can. 47 S11
Salmon River Mts., Idaho 81 B3
Salmon Valley, Br. Col., Can. 42 F2
Salmsh, r., U.S.S.R. 137 h9
Salmünster, F.R.Ger., 2,583 119 G4
Salo, Fin., 11,005 120 E3
Salò, It., 8,642 122 d5
Salogon, Phil., 1,076 153 A3
Salol, Minn. 74 E1
Salome, Ariz. 78 B5
Salomon, C., Mart. 97 12
Salon, Fr., 22,629 117 F5
Salon, India 144 c12
Salong, Phil., 28,734 153 B3
Salonga, r., D.R.Congo 164 C2
Salonica = Thessaloníki
Salonika, G. of = Thermaïkós Kólpos
Salonta, Rum., 16,276 128 C1
Saloum, r., Sen. 162 B3
Sal Rei, C. Verde Is., 1,085 109 5
Salsipuedes, Guat. 94 C2
Sal'sk, U.S.S.R., 37,000 134 D5
Salso, r., It. 123 E6
Salsomaggiore, It., 17,645 123 B2
Salt, r., Alta., Can. 42 K1
Salt, r., Ariz. 78 C5
Salt, r., Ky. 71 E3
Salt, r., Mo. 72 E5
Salt, Mid. Fk., r., Mo. 72 E5
Salta, Arg., 93,694 105 B2
Saltaim, Oz., U.S.S.R. 137 n11
Saltair, Utah 78 b9
Saltash, U.K., 7,425 113 D6
Saltburn, U.K., 5,708 114 G1
Saltcoats, Sask., Can. 43 D4
Saltcoats, U.K., 14,187 112 D4
Salt Cr., Austl. 173 d12
Salt Cr., Ill. 68 D3
Salt Cr., Ill. 69 c9
Salt Cr., Ind. 69 f10
Saltee Is., Ire. 113 C5
Salter Path, N.C. 63 G3
Salters, S.C. 63 E4
Saltery Bay, Br. Col., Can. 42 b6
Salt Flat, Tex. 77 L4
Salt Fork, Okla. 76 F1
Salt Fk., r., Ill. 68 D3
Saltholm, i., Den. 121 b7
Saltillo, Mex., 99,101 93 E3
Saltillo, Ind. 121 70 C4
Saltillo, Miss., 536 73 G3
Saltillo, Ohio 70 G3
Saltillo, Pa., 395 60 F5
Saltillo, Tenn., 397 71 C6
Salt I., V.I. 97 4
Salt Island Passage, V.I. 97 4
Salt Lake, N. Mex. 79 A4
Salt Lake, co., Utah, 383,035 78 B1
Salt L., Austl. 172 A3
Salt L., Hawaii 84 c7
Salt Lake City, Utah, 189,454 78 B1
Salt Lakes, Tex. 77 L4
Saltney, U.K., 11,900 114 C4
Salto, Arg., 15,000* 105 C4
Salto, Braz., 12,643 103 c18
Salto, Urug., 52,000* 105 D4
Salto de Agua, Mex., 1,598 93 G5
Salton Sea, Calif. 82 F6
Saltpond, Ghana, 9,866 162 c9
Salt Pond, St. Christopher 97 6
Salt River, N.W.T., Can. 40 G5
Salt Rock, W. Va. 62 B4
Saltrou, Haiti, 1,203 96 k6
Saltsburg, Pa., 1,054 60 D4
Saltsjöbaden, Swed. 120 f8
Saltspring I., Br. Col., Can. 42 c7
Saltville, Va., 2,844 62 C6
Salt Wells, Nev. 83 A3
Saluafata, W. Samoa 177 38
Salud, Pan. 94 G6
Saluda, N.C., 570 63 B2
Saluda, co., S.C., 14,554 63 C3
Saluda, S.C., 2,089 63 C4
Saluda, Va. 62 H5
Saluda, r., S.C. 63 B3
Salur, India, 26,111 145 G6
Salus, Ark. 73 B2
Salussola, It., 2,519 122 b5
Salut, Îs. du, Fr. Guiana 101 O5
Saluzzo, It., 16,425 123 A2
Salvador, Braz., 630,878 103 J4
Salvador, Sask., Can. 43 B4
Salvador, Cuba, 1,520 96 e2
Salvador, L., La. 73 E8
Salvador, Port, inlet, Falk. Is. 108 3
Salvador María, Arg., 2,036 105 b12
Salvage Pt., Newf., Can. 45 b9
Salvaterra, Braz., 1,422 103 G2
Salvaterra de Magos, Port., 6,867 122 A3
Salvatierra, Mex., 14,417 93 E4
Salvisa, Ky. 71 G4
Salvo, N.C. 63 J2
Salween, r., Burma-China 141 H5
Sal'yany, U.S.S.R., 17,200 137 d2
Salybia, Dominica 97 13
Salyersville, Ky., 1,173 71 H4
Salza, r., Aust. 124 M6
Salzach, r., Aust.-F.R.Ger. 124 J6
Salzburg, Aust., 106,892 124 J6
Salzgitter, F.R.Ger., 100,294 118 C2
Salzgitter-Wattenstedt = Salzgitter
Salzhausen, F.R.Ger., 1,506 119 b9
Salzkammergut, reg. Aust. 124 K6
Salzkotten, F.R.Ger., 5,841 119 F1
Salzwedel, Ger.D.R., 20,683 118 C2
Sama, Peru 104 D6
Sama, Sp., 65,806 122 C1
Samac, Phil., 1,759 153 e12
Samagaltay, U.S.S.R. 135 J4
Samak, Tg., Indon. 148 C3
Samalanga, Indon. 148 A1
Samales Group, is., Phil. 153 B4
Samalkot, India, 31,924 145 G6
Samaná, Col. 101 d14
Samaná, Dom. Rep., 3,309 96 n6
Samaná, Bahía de, Dom. Rep. 96 n6
Samaná, C., Dom. Rep. 96 n6
Samaná, r., Col. 101 e14
Samana Cay, i., Bah. Is. 95 D2
Samanco, Peru, 2,052 104 B4
Samandağ, Turk., 13,922 142 C2
Samani, Jap., 10,163 155 K8
Samaniego, Col. 100 B7
Samaqua, r., Qué., Can. 44 K5
Samar, i., Phil. 153 C2
Samara, r., U.S.S.R. 136 E3
Samarai, Terr. Papua, 1,115 174 f3
Samaria, reg., Jor. 142 b7
Samarinda, Indon., 69,715 148 F3
Samarkand, U.S.S.R., 215,000 134 F6
Sāmarrā', Iraq, 16,398 143 C2
Samar Sea, Phil. 153 C2
Samastipur, India, 25,726 145 H4
Samataitai, W. Samoa 177 38
Samatan, Fr., 2,050 117 D5
Samba, India, 4,361 145 E2
Sambalpur, India, 38,915 145 G5
Sambar, Tg., Indon. 148 D3
Sambas, Indon. 148 D2
Sambava, Malag. Rep., 2,544 165 H4
Samberbaba, Indon. 149 L3
Sambhal, India, 68,940 145 F3
Sambhar, India, 14,139 145 E4
Sambhar L., India 145 E4
Sambiase, It., 20,324 123 F5
Samboan, Phil., 2,310 153 e12
Sambongi, Jap., 45,362 155 G1
Sambonyanagi, Jap. 154 h15
Sambor, Camb. 146 D4
Sambor, U.S.S.R., 23,600 136 A3
Samborombón, B., Arg. 105 D5
Samborondón, Ec., 3,800 104 B2
Sambre, r., Belg.-Fr. 115 C4
Sambro, N.S., Can. 47 U11
Sambú, r., Pan. 94 H7
Samburg, Tenn., 451 71 B5
Samch'ŏk, S. Kor., 30,169 151 F3
Samch'ŏnp'o, S. Kor., 50,301 151 F4
Sam Chuk, Thai. 147 c4
Same, Tanz. 164 F2
Samedan, Switz., 2,106 124 D2
Sameikkon, Burma, 3,099 147 f7
Samer, Fr., 2,563 117 D1
Samfya, Zambia 164 D3
Sámi, Gr., 1,065 129 C5
Samina, r., Aust.-Liecht. 124 a8
Samka, Burma 146 B2
Sam Khok, Thai. 147 d4
Sammamish, L., Wash. 81 b7
Samnaun, Switz. 124 E2
Samneua, Laos 146 C2
Samoa Is., Pac. Oc. 177 37
Samobor, Yug., 4,665 125 B2
Samoded, U.S.S.R., 4,200 134 D3
Samois-sur-Seine, Fr., 1,424 116 i12
Samokov, Bulg., 16,748 128 D3
Samos, Va. 62 H5
Sámos, i., Gr. 129 F6
Samoset, Fla., 4,824 65 G5
Samothrace = Samothráki
Samothrace = Samothráki
Samothráki, Gr., 1,555 129 E4
Samothráki, i., Gr. 129 E4
Samothráki, i., Gr. 129 B5
Samouco, Port., 1,823 122 k10
Sampa, Ghana 162 b8
Sampacho, Arg., 6,300* 105 B4
Sampaga, Indon. 149 F3
Sampaloc, Phil., 5,373 153 c8
Sampang, Indon. 148 e7
Sampit, Indon. 148 E3
Sampson, co., N.C., 48,013 63 F3
Sampués, Col. 100 C3
Sampwe, D.R.Congo 165 n18
Sam Rayburn Res., Texas 77 Q4
Samreboi, Ghana 162 b9
Samrong, Camb. 146 C4
Samrong, Camb. 147 k11
Samrong, Thai. 147 e4
Samsø, i., Den. 121 C5
Samsø Bælt, Den. 121 C5
Sam Son, N. Viet. 146 D3
Samson, Ala., 1,932 64 C4
Samsonville, N.Y. 59 M8
Samsun, Turk., 87,311 142 D1
Samthar, India, 9,449 144 b13
Samtredia, U.S.S.R., 20,500 137 b1
Samuel, Mt., Austl. 172 E2
Samuels, Ky. 71 F4
Samui, Ko, Thai. 146 C5
Samur, r., U.S.S.R. 137 d1
Samus', U.S.S.R., 6,500 137 r11
Samusele, D.R.Congo 164 C3
Samut Prakan, Thai., 21,766 147 d5
Samut Sakhon, Thai., 27,602 146 C4
Samut Songkhram, Thai., 12,801 147 d5
Samye La, China 144 e11
San, Mali, 9,764 162 D3
San, r., Camb. 146 D4
San, r., Pol. 127 D3
Şan'ā', Yemen, 55,000* 143 C5
Sana, r., Yug. 125 C2
Sanabria, Col. 100 B6
Sanae, Ant. 180 P6
Sanaga, r., Cam. 162 G5
Sanagu, Jap. 154 h15
San Agustín, Col. 100 B7
San Agustín, C., Phil. 153 C4
San Agustín Acasaguastlán, Guat., 3,571 94 c9
San Agustín de Valle Fértil, Arg., 3,872* 105 B4
Sanak I., Alaska 85 D5
San Ambrosio, I., Chile 171 N6
Sanana, Indon. 149 H3
Sanana, P., Indon. 149 H3
Sanandaj, Iran, 40,641 143 D1
Sanandita, Bol., 2,113 102 D6
San Andreas, Calif., 1,416 82 C3
San Andrés, Bol., 1,155 102 D4
San Andrés, Col. 100 C4
San Andrés, Col. 100 D4
San Andrés, Guat., 1,383 94 C2
San Andrés, Peru, 3,256 104 B5
San Andrés, Co., Mex. 93 d10
San Andrés, I. de, Col. 94 G4
San Andres de Giles, Arg., 6,124 105 b12
San Andrés Itzapa, Guat., 5,139 94 c9
San Andres Mts., N. Mex. 79 B5
San Andres Pk., N. Mex. 79 B5
San Andrés Tuxtla, Mex., 19,830 93 G4
San Angel, Col. 100 C3
San Angelo, Tex., 58,815 77 N4
San Angelo Res., Texas 77 N4
San Anselmo, Calif., 11,584 83 d12
San Antero, Col. 100 C3
San Antonio, Br. Hond. 94 C2
San Antonio, Chile, 26,749 105 A4
San Antonio, Col. 100 C6
San Antonio, Col. 100 D2
San Antonio, Cuba, 1,300 96 f2
San Antonio, Guat. 94 B3
San Antonio, Mex. 92 C3
San Antonio, Phil., 8,717 153 A2
San Antonio, Phil., 1,843 153 i15
San Antonio, Fla., 479 65 G4
San Antonio, N. Mex. 79 B5
San Antonio, Tex., 587,718 77 O5
San Antonio, Urug., 1,000* 105 c10
San Antonio, Ven., 14,697 100 D4
San Antonio, Ven., 2,115 100 E3
San Antonio, Ven. 100 G6
San Antonio, Ven. 101 c11
San Antonio, r., Tex. 77 P5
San Antonio, C., Arg. 105 D5
San Antonio, C., Cuba 96 a2
San Antonio Abad, Sp., 5,635 122 F3
San Antonio Bay, Tex. 77 P5
San Antonio de Areco, Arg., 8,300* 105 b12
San Antonio de Cabezas, Cuba, 2,309 96 c1
San Antonio de Caparo, Ven., 1,403 100 E4
San Antonio de Esquilache, Peru, 1,149 104 D5
San Antonio del Golfo, Ven., 1,331 101 J2
San Antonio de Lípez, Bol. 102 C6
San Antonio de los Baños, Cuba, 17,783 96 b1
San Antonio de los Cobres, Arg., 3,000* 105 B2
San Antonio de Tabasca, Ven. 101 J3
San Antonio Heights, Calif. 83 i15
San Antonio Mtn., Tex. 77 L4
San Antonio Oeste, Arg., 6,000* 105 B6
San Antonio Pajonal, El Salv., 1,233 94 d9
San Antonio Pk., Calif. 83 i15
San Antonio Pk., N. Mex. 79 B3
San Antonio Villalongin, Mex., 1,337 93 d10
San Antonito, N. Mex. 79 B4
Sanarate, Guat., 4,415 94 c9
San Ardo, Calif. 82 C4
Sanariapo, Ven. 100 G5
Sanaroa, i., Terr. Papua 174 3
Sanatorium, N.C. = McCain
Sanatorium, Tex. 77 N4
San Augustine, co., Tex., 7,722 77 Q4
San Augustine, Tex., 2,585 77 Q4
Sanawad, India, 11,130 144 a14
San Bartolo, Baja Calif. S., Mex. 92 C3
San Bartolo, Gto., Mex., 1,925 93 c8
San Bartolome, Mex., 1,781 93 d9
San Bartolomeo in Galdo, It., 10,210 123 E4
San Benedetto del Tronto, It., 30,055 123 D3
San Benedetto Po, It., 11,527 122 d5
San Benedicto, I., Mex. 92 b7
San Benito, Col. 100 C3
San Benito, Guat., 2,696 94 B2
San Benito, co., Calif., 15,396 82 C4
San Benito, Tex., 16,422 77 P6
San Benito, Is., Mex. 92 B2
San Benito, r., Calif. 82 C4
San Bernard, r., Tex. 77 P5
San Bernardino, co., Calif., 503,591 82 E5
San Bernardino, Calif., 91,922 82 E5
San Bernardino Mts., Calif. 50 C4
San Bernardino Pass, Switz. 124 D2
San Bernardino Str., Phil. 153 C2
San Bernardo, Arg., 4,000* 105 C3
San Bernardo, Chile, 45,207 104 g13
San Bernardo, Col. 100 C5
San Bernardo, Col. 101 d15
San Bernardo, Baja Calif. S., Mex. 92 C3
San Bernardo, Dgo., Mex., 1,093 92 D2
San Blas, Nay., Mex., 2,631 92 D4
San Blas, Sin., Mex., 4,220 92 C2
San Blas, C., Fla. 65 D3
San Blas, Cord. de, Pan. 94 H6
San Blas, G. de, Pan. 94 H6
San Blas, P., Pan. 100 A3
San Bonifacio, It., 10,754 122 e5
San Borja, Bol., 5,584 102 C4
Sanborn, Iowa, 1,323 72 B1
Sanborn, Minn., 521 74 E3
Sanborn, N.Y. 58 k18
Sanborn, N. Dak., 263 74 C2
Sanborn, co., S. Dak., 4,641 74 C4
Sanborn, Wis. 66 C2
Sanbornton, N.H. 54 D4
Sanbornville, N.H. 54 E4
San Bruno, Calif., 29,063 83 e12
San Buenaventura, Mex., 5,790 92 E2
San Carlos, Arg. 105 B3
San Carlos, Bol., 4,545 102 D5
San Carlos, Chile, 13,598 104 e16
San Carlos, Col. 100 C4
San Carlos, Chih., Mex., 1,340 92 D2
San Carlos, Micho., Mex. 93 d11
San Carlos, Tam., Mex. 93 F3
San Carlos, Nic., 1,722 94 E5
San Carlos, Pan. 94 H6
San Carlos, Phil., 9,779 153 B2
San Carlos, Phil., 21,144 153 B3
San Carlos, Ariz. 78 C5
San Carlos, Calif., 21,370 83 e13
San Carlos, Ven., 11,656 100 F3
San Carlos, r., C.R. 94 E5
San Carlos, r., Ariz. 78 C5
San Carlos Centro, Arg., 5,500* 105 a10
San Carlos de Bariloche, Arg., 20,000* 105 A6
San Carlos de la Rápita, Sp., 7,320 122 F2
San Carlos del Zulia, Ven., 14,478 100 D3
San Carlos de Río Negro, Ven. 100 G7
San Carlos L., Ariz. 78 C5
San Carlos Sija, Guat., 1,179 94 b9
San Casimiro, Ven., 3,415 101 b11
San Cataldo, It., 25,317 123 D6
San Cayetano, Arg., 15,000* 105 D5
San Cayetano, Col. 101 e14
Sancerre, Fr., 2,695 117 E3
San-ch'a, r., China 152 B2
Sánchez, Dom. Rep., 4,587 96 n6
Sánchez Magallanes, Mex., 1,008 93 G4
Sánchez Román, Mex., 7,165 92 E4
Sanchi, India 145 E5
San-chiang, China 152 C2
San-ch'uan, r., China 151 A3
San-ch'ung, Taiwan, 81,036 152 F2
Sanchursk, U.S.S.R. 136 G1
San Clemente, Chile, 2,507 104 f15
San Clemente, Sp., 6,948 122 D3
San Clemente, Calif., 13,167 82 E6
San Clemente Canyon, Calif. 82 c9
San Clemente del Tuyú, Arg., 1,500* 105 c13
San Clemente I., Calif. 82 D6
Sancoins, Fr., 3,666 117 E3
San Colombano al Lambro, It., 8,449 122 c5
San Cristóbal, Arg., 15,000* 105 C4
San Cristóbal, Cuba, 4,638 96 b1
San Cristóbal, Dom. Rep., 15,525 96 m6
San Cristóbal, Guat., 3,873 94 B3
San Cristóbal, Mex. 93 e9
San Cristóbal, Pan. 94 G6
San Cristóbal, Ven., 96,102 100 D4
San Cristóbal, i., Sol. Is. 170 E5
San Cristóbal, B. de, Mex. 92 B2
San Cristóbal, I., Colón, Arch. de 104 b8
San Cristóbal, Vol., Nic. 94 D4
San Cristóbal de las Casas, Mex., 23,355 93 G5
San Cristobal Wash, Ariz. 78 B5
Sancti Spíritus, Cuba, 37,741 96 d2
Sancy, Puy de, Fr. 117 E4
Sand, Nor. 120 A4
Sand, r., Alta., Can. 42 K2
Sanda, Jap., 32,528 155 D4
Sandai, Indon. 148 D3
Sanda I., U.K. 113 D4
Sandakan, Malay., 29,291 148 F1
Sandal, B. du, Loy. Is. 174 k8
San Damiano d'Asti, It., 6,637 122 b6
Sandane, Nor. 120 A3
Sandanski, Bulg., 10,630 129 D4
Sanday, i., U.K. 112 E2
Sanday Sd., U.K. 112 E2
Sandbach, U.K., 9,856 114 D4
Sandbank, U.K. 112 a8
Sandborn, Ind., 547 70 B4
Sand Cliff Pt., Lesser Caymans 97 2
Sand Creek, Okla. 76 E1
Sand Creek, Wis. 66 B3
Sand Cr., Ind. 70 D3
Sand Cr., Okla. 76 A1
Sand Cr., Okla. 76 G1
Sand Cr., S. Dak. 74 C3
Sande, F.R.Ger., 7,114 118 B2
Sandefjord, Nor. 121 C1
Sanders, Ariz. 78 D4
Sanders, co., Mont., 6,880 81 B2
Sanderson, Fla. 65 G2
Sanderson, Tex., 2,189 77 M4
Sandersville, Ga., 5,425 64 G2
Sandersville, Miss., 657 73 G6
Sandford, Ind. 70 B3
Sandgap, Ky. 71 G4
Sandgate, Vt. 54 A5
Sandhausen, F.R.Ger., 7,341 119 F6
Sandhead, U.K. 113 D4
Sand Hill, r., Minn. 74 D2
Sand Hill Region, Neb. 50 F2
Sand Hills, Nebr. 75 C2
Sandhorst, F.R.Ger., 3,162 118 A2
Sandhurst, U.K., 6,445 114 G8
Sandi, India, 9,103 144 c12
Sandia, Peru, 3,787 104 D5
Sandia, Tex. 77 O5
Sandiacre, U.K., 6,794 114 F5
Sandia Pk., N. Mex. 79 B4
San Diego, Guat. 94 d9
San Diego, co., Calif., 1,033,011 82 E6
San Diego, Calif., 573,224 82 E6
San Diego, Tex., 4,351 77 O6
San Diego, Ven., 1,507 101 b11
San Diego, Ven. 101 c11
San Diego, r., Calif. 82 c9
San Diego, C., Arg. 105 C8
San Diego Bay, Calif. 82 c10
San Diego de Cabrutica, Ven. 101 H3
San Diego de la Unión, Mex., 4,135 93 d8
Sandigo, Austl. 173 f10
Sandıklı, Turk., 9,384 142 B2
Sandila, India, 18,407 144 c12
San Dimas, Mex. 92 D3
San Dimas, Calif., 11,520 83 i15
San Dionisio, Phil., 2,049 153 e10
Sandisfield, Mass., 536(T) 56 D4
Sand I., Amer. Samoa 177 37
Sand I., Swallow Is. 175 6
Sand I., Hawaii 84 c8
Sand I., Wis. 66 B2
Sand Key, Fla. 65 f15
Sand Lake, Mich., 394 67 H5
Sand Lake, N.Y. 59 w29
Sand Lake, Oreg. 80 A3
Sand L., Minn. 74 F2
Sand L., Wis. 66 A3
Sand Mtn., Ala.-Ga. 64 D1
Sandnes, Nor., 3,985 120 A4
Sandnes, Nor. 121 A2
Sandnessjöen, Nor. 120 B2
Sandoa, D.R.Congo 164 C3
Sandomierz, Pol., 10,891 127 D3
Sandoná, Col. 100 B7
San Donà di Piave, It., 25,463 123 D2
Sándorfalva, Hung., 5,815 126 D3
Sandoval, Mex., 1,284 93 F3
Sandoval, Ill., 1,356 68 C5
Sandoval, co., N. Mex., 14,201 79 B4
Sandoway, Burma, 5,172 146 A3
Sandown, U.K., 7,892 113 F6
Sandown, N.H. 54 E6
Sandown Bay, U.K. 113 k13
Sandoy, i., Faeroe Is. 120 c7
Sand Point, Alaska, 254 85 D5
Sandpoint, Idaho, 4,355 81 A1
Sand Pt., U.K. 114 C8
Sand Pt., Mich. 67 K5
Sandray, i., U.K. 112 C3
Sandridge, Man., Can. 43 g9
Sand River, Mich. 66 F2
Sands, Mich. 66 F2
Sands Key, Fla. 65 b10
Sandspit, Br. Col., Can. 42 D3
Sands Point, N.Y., 2,161 58 d13
Sand Springs, Okla., 7,754 76 G1
Sandston, Va. 62 G5
Sandstone, Austl. 172 B4
Sandstone, Minn., 1,552 74 F2
Sandstone, W. Va. 62 D5
Sandusky, Ind. 70 D3
Sandusky, Mich., 2,066 67 L5
Sandusky, N.Y. 58 D7
Sandusky, co., Ohio, 56,486 70 F1
Sandusky, Ohio, 31,989 70 G1
Sandusky, r., Ohio 70 F2
Sandusky Bay, Ohio 70 G1
Sandvig, Den. 121 G5
Sandviken, Swed. 120 D3
Sandwich, Ill., 3,842 68 D2
Sandwich, Mass., 1,099;2,082(T) 57 P5
Sandwich, N.H. 54 E4
Sandwich Bay, Newf., Can. 45 P4
Sandwich Dome, N.H. 54 D4
Sandwick, Br. Col., Can., 1,029 42 a6
Sandy, U.K., 3,963 114 H6
Sandy, Fla. 65 G5
Sandy, Nev. 83 C5
Sandy, Oreg., 1,147 80 B3
Sandy, Pa., 2,070 60 E3
Sandy, Tex. 76 a5
Sandy, Utah, 3,322 78 c9
Sandy, r., Qué., Can. 45 M3
Sandy, r., Me. 55 B4
Sandy Bay Mtn., Me.-Qué. 55 B3
Sandy Beach (part of Rutland), Mass. 56 J3
Sandy Bk., Conn.-Mass. 56 D4
Sandy C., Austl. 173 H3
Sandy Creek, N.Y., 697 59 H4
Sandy Cr., N.Y. 59 H4
Sandy Cr., Pa. 60 B3
Sandy Cr., Wyo. 81 E4
Sandy Des., Pak. 144 B3
Sandyhill Bay, Anguilla 97 7
Sandy Hook, Man., Can. 43 g9
Sandy Hook (part of Newtown), Conn. 56 C7
Sandy Hook, Ky., 195 71 H3
Sandy Hook, Miss. 73 F6
Sandy Hook, N.J. 61 D3
Sandy Hook Bay, N.J. 58 c15
Sandykachi, U.S.S.R., 4,900 134 F6
Sandy Key, Fla. 65 g14
Sandy Lake, Alta., Can. 42 K2
Sandy Lake, Sask., Can. 43 C3
Sandy Lake, Pa., 838 60 B3
Sandy L., Alta., Can. 43 a7
Sandy L., Ont., Can. 44 D4
Sandy Lick Cr., Pa. 60 E3
Sandy Point, St. Christopher, 3,608 97 6
Sandy Point, Me. 55 D4
Sandy Point, Tex. 77 i10
Sandy Pt., Bah. Is. 95 b6
Sandy Pt., St. Christopher 97 6
Sandy Pt., R.I. 57 K8
Sandy Ridge, Ala. 64 C3
Sandy Ridge, N.C. 63 D1
Sandy Spring, Md. 62 a8
Sandy Springs, Ga. 64 g9
Sandy Str., Me. 55 B3
Sandyville, Iowa, 115 72 D3
Sandyville, W. Va. 62 C4
Sanem, Lux., 7,021 115 D5
San Elizario, Tex., 1,064 77 K4
San Emilio, Phil., 2,981 153 B1
San Enrique, Chile 104 f13
San Enrique, Phil., 4,052 153 d11
San Estanislao, Para., 3,022 105 D2
San Estebán, Chile 104 e15
San Esteban, Hond., 2,366 94 E3
San Esteban, Mex. 93 a9
San Esteban, I., Mex. 92 B2
San Esteban de Gormaz, Sp., 2,246 122 D2
San Felice sul Panaro, It., 10,080 122 e6
San Felipe, Chile, 19,048 105 A4
San Felipe, Guat. 94 c9
San Felipe, Baja Calif., Mex. 92 B1
San Felipe, Gto., Mex., 8,553 93 c8
San Felipe, Phil., 5,900 153 A2
San Felipe, N. Mex., 1,034 79 B4
San Felipe, Ven., 27,774 100 F2
San Felipe, r., Cuba 96 b1
San Felipe, Cayos de, Cuba 96 b1
San Felipe Aztatán, Mex., 2,826 92 D3
San Feliú de Guixols, Sp., 10,307 122 G2
San Feliú de Llobregat, Sp., 10,201 122 F2
San Félix, Col. 101 d14
San Félix, Ven. = Sto. Tomé de Guayana
San Félix, I., Chile 171 N6
San Fernando, Chile, 21,774 105 A4
San Fernando, Col. 101 e13
San Fernando, Hond., 1,241 94 C3
San Fernando, Chis., Mex., 3,737 93 G5
San Fernando, Tam., Mex., 3,904 93 F3
San Fernando, Phil., 4,427 153 B1
San Fernando, Phil., 3,273 153 B2
San Fernando, Phil., 4,486 153 b7

San Fernando—San Secondo · 289

San Fernando, Phil., 3,210 **153** e11
San Fernando, Phil., 2,527 **153** h14
San Fernando, Phil., 4,416 **153** h15
San Fernando, Sp., 52,389 **122** B4
San Fernando, Trin. and Tob., 39,830 **96** g5
San Fernando, Calif., 16,093 **83** h15
San Fernando, r., Mex. **93** F3
San Fernando de Apure, Ven., 21,544 **100** G4
San Fernando de Atabapo, Ven. **100** G5
San Filipe Cr., Calif. **83** f13
Sånfjället, mt., Swed. **120** C3
Sanford, Man., Can. **43** g10
Sanford, Ala., 247 **64** C4
Sanford, Colo., 679 **79** C3
Sanford, Fla., 19,175 **65** H4
Sanford, Me., 10,936 **55** B5
Sanford, Mich. **67** J5
Sanford, Miss. **73** F6
Sanford, N.C., 12,253 **63** E2
Sanford, Tex. **76** N2
Sanford, Mt., Alaska **85** J3
San Francisco, Bol., 1,005 **102** C5
San Francisco, Col. **101** e15
San Francisco, Guat., 1,167 **94** C2
San Francisco, Hond., 1,615 **94** D3
San Francisco, Nic. **94** E5
San Francisco, Pan. **94** G6
San Francisco, Phil., 2,991 **153** C3
San Francisco, Phil., 4,219 **153** f11
San Francisco, co., Calif., 740,316 **83** e12
San Francisco, Calif., 740,316 **82** B4
San Francisco, Ven. **100** E2
San Francisco, I., Mex. **92** C3
San Francisco, r., Ariz.-N. Mex. **78** D5
San Francisco Bay, Calif. **83** e12
San Francisco Chilpan, Mex., 3,149 **93** e10
San Francisco Cr., Tex. **77** M5
San Francisco de Asís, Ven., 2,875 **101** b11
San Francisco de Becerra, Hond., 1,192 **94** E3
San Francisco de Borja, Mex., 1,015 **92** D2
San Francisco de Cara, Ven. **101** b12
San Francisco de La Paz, Hond., 1,961 **94** D3
San Francisco del Chañar, Arg., 1,560 **105** C3
San Francisco del Monte de Oro, Arg., 4,000* **105** B4
San Francisco del Oro, Mex., 11,317 **92** D2
San Francisco del Rincón, Mex., 20,846 **93** c9
San Francisco del Valle, Hond., 1,310 **94** e9
San Francisco de Macaira, Ven. **100** G3
San Francisco de Macorís, Dom. Rep., 26,000 **96** m6
San Francisco de Mostazal, Chile, 3,257 **104** g13
San Francisco de Yare, Ven., 1,531 **101** c11
San Francisco Gotera, El Salv., 3,661 **94** C4
San Gabriel, Ec., 6,603 **104** B1
San Gabriel, Calif., 22,561 **83** h15
San Gabriel, r., Calif. **83** h16
San Gabriel, r., Tex. **77** P4
San Gabriel, P., Mex. **92** B2
San Gabriel Mts., Calif. **83** h15
San Gabriel Res., Calif. **83** i15
Sangallán, I., Peru **104** B5
Sangamner, India, 21,729 **145** i17
Sangamon, co., Ill., 146,539 **68** C4
Sangamon, r., Ill. **68** D4
Sang-ang-ch'ü, China **150** D4
Sangar, U.S.S.R. **135** M3
Sangasanga-dalan, Indon. **148** F3
San Gavino Monreale, It., 8,509 **123** B5
Sangay, mtn., Ec. **104** c11
Sang-chih, China **152** C1
Sangeang, P., Indon. **149** F5
Sanger, Calif., 8,072 **82** D4
Sanger, Tex., 1,190 **77** P3
Sangerhausen, Ger.D.R., 23,778 **118** C3
San Germán, Cuba, 5,802 **96** e2
San Germán, P.R., 7,790 **96** r10
Sangerville, Me. **55** C3
Sanggau, Indon. **148** D2
Sangha, r., Congo **164** B1
San Giacomo, Passo di, It.-Switz. **123** B1
Sangihe, Kep., Indon. **149** H2
Sangihe, P., Indon. **149** H2
San Gil, Col. **100** D4
Sang-i-Māsha, Afghan. **144** C2
San Gimignano, It., 10,369 **123** C3
San Giorgio di Piano, It., 5,069 **122** e6
San Giovanni, S. Mar. **123** e11
San Giovanni in Fiore, It., 21,106 **123** F5
San Giovanni in Persiceto, It., 21,335 **123** C2
San Giovanni Lupatoto, It., 12,976 **122** e5
San Giovanni Rotondo, It., 19,864 **123** E4
San Giovanni Valdarno, It., 15,772 **123** C3
Sangitan, Phil., 3,783 **153** c7
San Giuliano Terme, It., 22,649 **123** C3
San Giuseppe Vesuviano, It., 20,711 **123** d10
Sangju, S. Kor., 46,925 **151** F3
Sang-kan, r., China **151** B3
Sangkapura, Indon. **148** e6
Sangkha, Thai. **146** C4
Sangkhlaburi, Thai. **146** B4
Sang-kou Wan, China **151** D3
Sangkulirang, Indon. **148** F2
Sangli, India, 73,838 **145** E6
Sangmélima, Cam., 7,500* **162** G5
Sangnamsŏk, N. Kor. **151** F2
Sang-ni, N. Kor. **151** F2
Sango Bay, Uganda **165** e14
Sangod, India **144** a13
Sangolquí, Ec., 5,407 **104** B2
San Gorgonio Mtn., Calif. **82** E5
Sangre de Cristo Mts., Colo. **79** B2
Sangre de Cristo Mts., N. Mex. **79** C4
San Gregorio, Arg., 2,600* **105** C4
San Gregorio, Chile **105** A8
San Gregorio, Calif. **83** e13
San Gregorio, Urug., 3,000* **105** d11
Sangre Grande, Trin. and Tob., 2,000* **96** h5
Sangro, r., It. **123** E4
Sangrur, India, 28,344 **144** a10
Sangsŏng-ni, N. Kor. **151** E3
Sangudo, Alta., Can. **42** J3
Sangue, R. do, Braz. **102** E4
Sangüesa, Sp., 4,323 **122** E1
San Guillermo, Arg., 1,508 **105** C4
San Hipólito, B., Mex. **92** B2
San Hipólito, P., Mex. **92** B2
San-ho, China **151** C3
Sanibel I., Fla. **65** G6
Sanice, Pol. **127** e5
San Ignacio, Arg. **105** b13
San Ignacio, Arg., 3,500* **105** D3
San Ignacio, Bol., 7,319 **102** C4
San Ignacio, Bol., 4,558 **102** D5
San Ignacio, Bol., 2,379 **102** d10
San Ignacio, Chile, 1,489 **104** f16
San Ignacio, Baja Calif. S., Mex. **92** B2
San Ignacio, Gto., Mex. **93** d8
San Ignacio, Jal., Mex., 1,451 **93** b9
San Ignacio, Peru, 1,370 **104** B3
San Ignacio, Lag., Mex. **92** B2
San Ignacio, P., Mex. **92** C3
Sanilac, co., Mich., 32,314 **67** L5
San Ildefonso, Guat., 1,501 **94** B3
San Ildefonso, Mex., 1,839 **93** d9
San Ildefonso, I., Mex. **92** C2
San Ildefonso Pen., Phil. **153** B1
San Isabel, Colo. **79** C3
San Isidro, Mex., 1,022 **93** a9
San Isidro, Phil., 2,778 **153** f10
San Isidro, Phil. **153** f11
San Isidro, Tex. **77** O6
San Isidro del General = Ureña
Sanislău, Rum. **128** D1
San Jacinto, Col. **100** C3
San Jacinto, Nic. **94** F5
San Jacinto, Phil., 5,120 **153** B2
San Jacinto, Calif., 2,553 **82** E6
San Jacinto, Nev. **83** C2
San Jacinto, co., Tex., 6,153 **77** Q4
San Jacinto, r., Calif. **83** k16
San Jacinto, E. Fk., r., Tex. **77** Q4
San Jacinto, Mt., Calif. **82** E6
San Jacinto, W. Fk., r., Tex. **77** Q4
San Jacinto Mts., Calif. **82** •
San Javier, Arg., 4,000* **105** E3
San Javier, Bol., 4,271 **102** D5
San Javier, Chile, 8,541 **104** f15
San Javier, Mex. **93** e9
San Javier, Sp., 10,284 **122** E4
San Javier, Urug., 3,500* **105** c11
San Jeronimito, Mex., 1,367 **92** E5
San Jerónimo, Col. **101** d13
San Jerónimo, Guat. **94** b9
San Jerónimo, Guat., 1,298 **94** c8
San Jerónimo, Hond., 1,592 **94** d9
San Jerónimo, Mex., 4,186 **93** E5
San Jerónimo, Peru, 3,552 **104** D5
Sanjō, Jap., 71,594 **155** F3
San Joaquín, Bol., 4,100 **102** C4
San Joaquín, Mex. **93** e9
San Joaquin, Phil., 2,730 **153** C2
San Joaquin, co., Calif., 249,989 **82** C4
San Joaquin, Calif., 879 **82** C4
San Joaquín, Ven., 5,264 **101** b11
San Joaquín, Ven., 1,231 **101** H3
San Joaquin, r., Calif. **82** C4
San Joaquin Hills, Calif. **83** i16
San Joaquin Valley, Calif. **82** C4
San Jon, N. Mex., 411 **79** D4
San Jorge, Arg., 1,000* **105** a13
San Jorge, Arg., 9,500* **105** C4
San Jorge, Nic., 1,902 **94** E5
San Jorge, B. de, Mex. **92** B1
San Jorge, G., Arg. **105** B7
San Jorge, r., Col. **100** C4
San Jorge I., Sol. Is. **175** c2
San José, Chile **104** e17
San José, Col. **100** D1
San José, C.R., 167,309 **94** E6
San José, Ec., 3,030 **104** c10
San José, Guat. **94** B2
San José, Guat., 4,447 **94** B4
San José, Hond., 1,949 **94** e9
San José, Mex., 2,798 **92** C2
San Jose, Phil., 10,353 **153** B2
San Jose, Phil., 4,247 **153** B2
San Jose, Phil., 6,364 **153** B3
San Jose, Phil., 2,104 **153** h14
San José, Sp., 5,076 **122** F3
San Jose, Calif., 204,196 **82** C4
San Jose, Ill., 1,093 **68** C3
San José, Urug., 28,000* **105** D4
San José, Ven., 2,991 **100** D3
San Jose, r., N. Mex. **79** B4
San José, r., Urug. **105** c11
San José, I., Mex. **92** C3
San José, I., Pan. **94** H6
San José, Lag., P.R. **96** u10
San José de Amacuro, Ven. **101** K3
San José de Ayala, Mex. **93** c9
San José de Chiquitos, Bol., 3,871 **102** D5
San José de Feliciano, Arg., 7,187 **105** D4
San José de Gracia, Jal., Mex., 2,717 **93** b9
San José de Gracia, Micho., Mex., 3,827 **93** a10
San José de Guaribe, Ven., 2,164 **100** H3
San José de la Mariquina, Chile, 2,878 **105** e14
San José de la Parrilla, Mex., 1,930 **92** D3
San José de las Matas, Dom. Rep., 2,305 **96** m6
San José del Cabo, Mex., 1,838 **92** C3
San José del Guaviare, Col. **100** D6
San José del Rincon, Arg., 3,000* **105** a10
San José de Ocoa, Dom. Rep., 5,591 **96** m6
San José de Ocuné, Col. **100** E5
San José de Unare, Ven. **100** H3
San José La Arada, Guat. **94** d9
San José Ojetenán, Guat. **94** b8
San José Poaquil, Guat., 1,327 **94** b9
San José Purúa, Mex. **93** d9
San Juan, Arg., 106,746 **105** B4
San Juan, Bol., 1,488 **102** E5
San Juan, Col. **100** B3
San Juan, Col. **100** B6
San Juán, Col. **100** D6
San Juan, Dom. Rep., 20,449 **96** m6
San Juan, Peru **104** C5
San Juan, Peru, 1,683 **104** D5
San Juan, Phil., 1,887 **153** b6
San Juan, Phil., 2,777 **153** c9
San Juan, P.R., 432,377 **96** t10
San Juan, co., Colo., 849 **79** B3
San Juan, co., N. Mex., 53,306 **79** A3
San Juan, co., Utah, 9,040 **78** C3
San Juan, co., Wash., 2,872 **80** B1
San Juan, r., Bol. **102** c12
San Juan, r., Br. Col., Can. **42** b7
San Juan, r., Col. **100** B5
San Juan, r., C.R.-Nic. **94** E5
San Juan, r., Dom. Rep. **96** m6
San Juan, r., Mex. **93** F3
San Juan, r., Colo.-N. Mex.-Utah **52** D3
San Juan, Cabezas de, P.R. **96** u10
San Juan, Cayo, Cuba **96** b2
San Juan, Loma, hill, Cuba **96** c2
San Juan, P., Easter I. **177** 46
San Juan Bautista, Para., 5,351 **105** D3
San Juan Bautista, Calif., 1,046 **82** C4
San Juan Capistrano, Calif., 1,120 **83** i16
San Juan Cotzal, Guat., 3,428 **94** B3
San Juan Cr., Calif. **82** C5
San Juan de César, Col. **100** D2
San Juan de Colón, Ven., 8,910 **100** D3
San Juan de Guadalupe, Mex., 2,875 **92** E3
San Juan de Guia, C. de, Col. **100** D2
San Juan de la Maguana = San Juan, Dom. Rep. =
San Juan de las Galdonas, Ven., 1,093 **101** J2
San Juan de La Virgen, Peru **104** A2
San Juan de Limay, Nic., 1,839 **94** D4
San Juan del Norte, Nic. **94** F5
San Juan del Norte, B. de, Nic. **94** F5
San Juan de los Cayos, Ven., 1,192 **100** F2
San Juan de los Lagos, Mex., 22,713 **92** E4
San Juan de los Lagos, r., Mex. **93** b8
San Juan de los Morros, Ven., 25,821 **100** G3
San Juan del Río, Dgo., Mex., 3,010 **92** D3
San Juan del Río, Qro., Mex., 11,179 **93** E4
San Juand del Rio, r., Mex. **93** e9
San Juan del Sur, Nic., 1,874 **94** D5
San Juan de Opoa, Hond., 1,442 **94** e9
San Juan de Payara, Ven. **100** G4
San Juan de Rioseco, Col. **101** e15
San Juan Guarita, Hond., 1,068 **94** e9
San Juanico, Mex., 1,092 **93** e10
San Juan I., Wash. **80** B1
San Juanito, B., Mex. **92** B2
San Juanito, I., Mex. **92** D4
San Juan Mts., Colo. **79** B3
San Juan Nat. Hist. Site, P.R. **96** t10
San Juan Nepomuceno, Col. **100** C3
San Juan Nonualco, El Salv., 3,231 **94** e10
San Juan Sacatepéquez, Guat., 4,922 **94** B3
San Juan Tecuaco, Guat., 1,005 **94** c9
San Juan y Martínez, Cuba, 4,865 **96** b1
San Julián, Arg., 5,500* **105** B7
San Julián, Mex., 3,690 **93** b9
San Julian, Phil., 2,259 **153** C3
San Justo, Arg., 12,000* **105** C4
Sankaty Head (part of Nantucket), Mass. **57** R7
Sankeimō, Ryukyu Is. **154** a10
Sankhaburi, Thai. **147** c4
Sankosh, r., Bhutan **144** g12
Sankt Aegyd, Aust., 3,204 **124** M6
Sankt Andrä, Aust., 1,077 **124** c10
Sankt Andrä, Aust., 2,134 **124** L7
Sankt Andrä, Aust., 1,426 **124** N6
Sankt Anton, Aust., 1,757 **124** G6
Sankt Blasien, F.R.Ger., 3,814 **118** B5
Sankt Christophen, Aust. **124** b10
Sankt Corona, Aust. **124** b10
Sankt Gallen, Aust., 1,625 **124** L6
Sankt Gallen, Switz., 76,279 **124** D1
Sankt Georgen, Aust., 2,841 **124** b10
Sankt Georgen, Aust. **124** L6
Sankt Georgen, Aust., 1,018 **124** M7
Sankt Gilgen, Aust., 2,789 **124** K6
Sankt Goar, F.R.Ger., 2,077 **118** A3
Sankt Goarshausen, F.R.Ger., 2,002 **119** D4
Sankt Hubert, F.R.Ger., 4,947 **119** A2
Sankt Ilgen, Aust. **124** M6
Sankt Ingbert, F.R.Ger., 27,118 **118** A4
Sankt Johann, Aust., 4,664 **124** J6
Sankt Johann, Aust., 5,775 **124** K6
Sankt Johann, Aust. **124** L6
Sankt Lambrecht, Aust., 2,223 **124** L6
Sankt Leonhard, Aust., 1,559 **124** L5
Sankt Mang, F.R.Ger., 7,899 **118** C5
Sankt Marein, Aust., 1,081 **124** M6
Sankt Margarethen, Aust., 2,364 **124** d11
Sankt Margrethen, Switz., 4,286 **124** D1
Sankt Martin, Aust. **124** J6
Sankt Michael, Aust., 2,421 **124** K6
Sankt Michael, Aust. **124** N6
Sankt Michel = Mikkeli
Sankt Moritz, Switz., 3,751 **124** D2
Sankt Moritz Bad, Switz. **124** D2
Sankt Niklaus, Switz., 2,071 **124** B2
Sankt Nikolai, Aust. **124** L6
Sankt Oswald, F.R.Ger., 3,115 **118** D4
Sankt Paul, Aust., 1,806 **124** L7
Sankt Peter, Aust. **124** L6
Sankt Peter, F.R.Ger., 3,032 **118** B1
Sankt Pölten, Aust., 40,319 **124** M5
Sankt Salvator, Aust., 2,101 **124** L7
Sankt Stephan, Switz., 1,227 **124** B2
Sankt Tönis, F.R.Ger., 11,559 **119** A2
Sankt Veit, Aust., 10,952 **124** L7
Sankt Veit, Aust., 3,712 **124** M5
Sankt Wendel, F.R.Ger., 10,540 **118** A4
Sankt Wolfgang, Aust., 2,234 **124** K6
Sankuru, r., D.R.Congo **164** C2
San Lázaro, C., Mex. **92** B3
San Leandro, Calif., 65,962 **82** B4
San Leandro Res., Calif. **83** e12
San Leonardo, Phil., 4,054 **153** c7
San Leonardo, Sp., 1,866 **122** D2
San Lorenzo, Arg., 11,500* **105** a11
San Lorenzo, Bol. **102** C4
San Lorenzo, Bol., 2,950 **102** C5
San Lorenzo, Bol., 1,683 **102** D6
San Lorenzo, Ec. **104** B1
San Lorenzo, El Salv. **94** d9
San Lorenzo, Guat., 3,156 **94** b8
San Lorenzo, Guat. **94** C2
San Lorenzo, Hond., 3,799 **94** D3
San Lorenzo, Chih., Mex., 1,021 **92** D2
San Lorenzo, Coah., Mex., 1,049 **92** E3
San Lorenzo, Méx., Mex. **93** e9
San Lorenzo, P.R., 5,551 **96** t10
San Lorenzo, Calif., 23,773 **83** e12
San Lorenzo, Ven., 1,544 **100** E3
San Lorenzo, r., Mex. **92** D3
San Lorenzo, I., Mex. **92** B2
San Lorenzo de El Escorial, Sp., 7,965 **122** B4
Sanlúcar de Barrameda, Sp., 40,335 **122** B4
Sanlúcar la Mayor, Sp., 6,379 **122** B4
San Lucas, Baja Calif. S., Mex. **92** C3
San Lucas, Gto., Mex., 1,004 **93** d9
San Lucas, Hgo., Mex. **93** e9
San Lucas, Méx., Mex., 1,240 **93** d11
San Lucas, Méx., Mex., 1,552 **93** e9
San Lucas, Micho., Mex., 1,674 **93** d11
San Lucas, Calif. **82** C4
San Lucas Tolimán, Guat., 3,513 **94** b9
San Luis, Arg., 40,000* **105** B4
San Luis, Col. **101** e13
San Luis, Cuba, 2,735 **96** b1
San Luis, Cuba, 11,110 **96** f2
San Luis, Guat. **94** C2
San Luis, Mex., 28,336 **92** B1
San Luis, Pima Co., Ariz. **78** A5
San Luis, Yuma Co., Ariz. **78** C5
San Luis, Colo. **79** C3
San Luis, I., Mex. **92** B1
San Luis, L. de, Bol. **102** D4
San Luis Cr., Colo. **79** C2
San Luis de la Paz, Mex., 8,268 **93** E4
San Luis del Cordero, Mex., 2,545 **92** D3
San Luis Gonzaga, B., Mex. **92** B2
San Luis Jilotepeque, Guat., 5,800 **94** d9
San Luis Obispo, co., Calif., 81,044 **82** C5
San Luis Obispo, Calif., 20,437 **82** C5
San Luis Obispo Bay, Calif. **82** C5
San Luis Potosí, st., Mex., 1,048,297 **92** E3
San Luis Potosí, Mex., 159,640 **93** E3
San Luis Rey, Calif. **82** E6
San Luis Rey, r., Calif. **82** E6
San Luis Soyatlán, Mex., 2,682 **93** a9
San Luis Valley, Colo. **59** E3
Sanluri, It., 8,191 **123** B5
San Manuel, Cuba, 2,105 **96** e2
San Manuel, Ariz., 4,524 **78** C5
San Marcelino, Phil., 6,841 **153** b8
San Marcial, N. Mex. **79** B5
San Marco de Cavoti, It., 5,375 **123** d9
San Marco in Lamis, It., 22,468 **123** E4
San Marcos, Col. **100** C3
San Marcos, El Salv., 7,080 **94** d10
San Marcos, Guat., 5,160 **94** B3
San Marcos, Hond. **94** e9
San Marcos, Mex., 5,060 **93** F5
San Marcos, Tex., 12,713 **77** O5
San Marcos, r., Tex. **76** e6
San Marcos, I., Mex. **92** C2
San Marcos, Lag. de, Mex. **93** a9
San Marcos de Colón, Hond., 4,227 **94** D4
San Margherita, Ohio **70** a6
San Mariano, Phil., 1,516 **153** c6
San Marino, ctry., 17,000* **123** f11
San Marino, S. Mar., 3,400 **123** e11
San Marino, Calif., 13,658 **83** h15
San Marino, Torrente di, S. Mar. **123** e11
San Martín, Col. **100** D5
San Martín, Micho., Mex., 1,233 **93** c9
San Martín, S.L.P., Mex., 1,782 **93** f8
San Martín, Zac., Mex., 1,889 **92** E3
San Martin, Calif., 1,162 **82** C4
San Martin, Urug. **105** c11
San Martín, r., Bol. **102** D4
San Martín, L., Arg.-Chile **105** A7
San Martín de Aguarás, Cuba, 2,020 **96** e2
San Martín de Elines, Sp. **122** m12
San Martín de los Andes, Arg., 4,500* **105** A6
San Martín de Valdeiglesias, Sp., 3,994 **122** C2
San Martín Hidalgo, Mex., 5,249 **92** D4
San Martín Jilotepeque, Guat., 2,906 **94** c9
San Mateo, Méx., Mex., 1,129 **93** d10
San Mateo, Zac., Mex., 1,612 **92** E3
San Mateo, Phil., 3,468 **153** B1
San Mateo, Sp., 2,452 **122** E2
San Mateo, co., Calif., 444,387 **82** B4
San Mateo, Calif., 69,870 **82** B4
San Mateo, Fla. **65** H3
San Mateo, N. Mex. **79** B4
San Mateo, Ven., 10,419 **101** b11
San Mateo, Ven., 1,829 **101** H3
San Mateo Ixtatán, Guat., 2,989 **94** B3
San Mateo Mts., N. Mex. **79** B5
San Mateo Pk., N. Mex. **79** B5
San Matías, G., Arg. **105** C6
Sanmaur, Qué., Can. **44** K6
San-men, China **152** F1
San-men-hsia, China **150** E3
San-men Wan, China **152** F1
San Miguel, Bol., 4,158 **102** D5
San Miguel, Ec., 2,135 **104** c10
San Miguel, El Salv., 38,330 **94** C4
San Miguel, Guat. **94** C2
San Miguel, Pan., 1,071 **94** H6
San Miguel, Phil., 8,498 **153** b7
San Miguel, Phil., 15,909 **153** C3
San Miguel, Ariz. **78** C6
San Miguel, Calif. **82** C5
San Miguel, co., Colo., 2,944 **79** A3
San Miguel, co., N. Mex., 23,468 **79** C4
San Miguel, N. Mex. **79** B5
San Miguel, Ven. **100** F2
San Miguel, Ven. **101** H3
San Miguel, B., Bol. **102** D5
San Miguel, r., Ec. **104** B1
San Miguel, r., Son., Mex. **92** C2
San Miguel, r., Chih., Mex. **92** D2
San Miguel, r., Colo. **79** A2
San Miguel, Co., Bol. **102** D5
San Miguel, G. de, Pan. **94** H6
San Miguel, R. de, Mex. **93** b8
San Miguel, Vol. de, El Salv. **94** •
San Miguel Acatán, Guat., 1,696 **94** A3
San Miguel Bay, Phil. **153** B2
San Miguel Chicaj, Guat., 1,002 **94** c8
San Miguel de Allende, Mex., 14,853 **93** E4
San Miguel de Hauchi, Bol. **102** b9
San Miguel de la Paz, Mex. **93** b9
San Miguel del Monte, Arg., 3,156 **105** b12
San Miguel de Salcedo, Ec., 3,464 **104** c10
San Miguel de Tucumán, Arg., 280,075 **105** C3
San Miguel I., Calif. **82** C5
San Miguel Is., Phil. **153** A4
San Miguelito, Nic. **94** E5
San Miguel Pk., N. Mex. **79** B4
San Miguel Uspantán, Guat., 1,663 **94** c8
San-ming, China **152** E2
San Miniato, It., 21,794 **123** C3
Sannār, Sudan, 8,093 **163** K3
San Narciso, Phil., **153** b7
Sannazzaro de'Burgondi, It., 4,468 **122** b5
Sanne, Swed. **121** D2
Sannicandro Garganico, It., 18,144 **123** E4
San Nicolao, Fr. **116** r17
San Nicolás, Arg., 40,000* **105** a11
San Nicolas, Aruba = Sint Nicolaas
San Nicolás, Chile **104** e16
San Nicolás, Hond., 3,172 **94** e9
San Nicolás, Gro., Mex., 1,021 **93** F5
San Nicolás, Jal., Mex. **93** a9
San Nicolás, Peru **104** C5
San Nicolas, Phil., **153** A3
San Nicolas, Phil., 11,632 **153** B1
San Nicolas, Phil., 14,722 **153** e11
San Nicolás, B., Mex. **92** C2
San Nicolás de los Garzas, Mex., 15,313 **93** E3
San Nicolas I., Calif. **82** D6
Sannikova, Prol., U.S.S.R. **135** O2
Sannohe, Jap., 17,764 **155** G1
Sannois, Fr., 16,707 **116** g11
Sano, Jap. **154** f15
Sano, Jap., 68,461 **155** F3
Sanok, Pol., 15,319 **127** E4
San Onofre, Col. **100** C3
Sanostee, N. Mex. **79** A3
San Pablito, Mex., 1,596 **93** f9
San Pablo, Chile, 1,112 **105** e15
San Pablo, Col. **100** B6
San Pablo, Guat. **94** a9
San Pablo, Mex., 1,030 **93** d9
San Pablo, Mex., 1,359 **93** e9
San Pablo, Peru, 2,882 **104** B3
San Pablo, Phil., 29,990 **153** c8
San Pablo, Calif., 19,687 **83** e12
San Pablo, Colo. **79** C3
San Pablo, Sa. de, Hond. **94** •
San Pablo, Vol., Chile **105** B2
San Pablo Balleza, Mex. **92** D2
San Pablo Bay, Calif. **83** e11
San Pablo Res., Calif. **83** e12
San Pascual, Phil., 1,246 **153** B2
San Pascual, Phil., 4,028 **153** f12
San Patricio, co., Tex., 45,021 **77** P5
San Pedro, Arg., 13,253 **105** B2
San Pedro, Arg., 20,100* **105** b11
San Pedro, Arg., 1,000* **105** E3
San Pedro, Bol., 1,446 **102** D4
San Pedro, Br. Hond. **94** C3
San Pedro, Col. **101** d13
San Pedro, C. R., 14,466 **94** E6
San Pedro, Cur. **97** 16
San Pedro, Baja Calif. S., Mex. **92** C3
San Pedro, Hgo., Mex., 1,318 **93** f9
San Pedro, Son., Mex., 1,476 **92** C2
San Pedro, Nic. **94** E4
San Pedro, Para., 3,135 **105** D2
San Pedro, (part of Los Angeles), Calif. **83** h15
San Pedro, Tex., 7,634 **77** P6
San Pedro, Ven., 1,005 **101** b11
San Pedro, r., Chile **105** e14
San Pedro, r., Cuba **96** d2
San Pedro, r., Guat.-Mex. **94** B2
San Pedro, r., Mex. **92** D2
San Pedro, r., Ariz. **78** C5
San Pedro Arriba, Mex., 3,118 **93** e10
San Pedro Ayampuc, Guat., 3,695 **94** c9
San Pedro Bay, Calif. **83** h16
San Pedro Chan., Calif. **83** h16
San Pedro de Arimena, Col. **100** E5
San Pedro de Atacama, Chile **105** B2
San Pedro de las Colonias, Mex., 25,183 **92** E3
San Pedro del Gallo, Mex., 1,484 **92** D3
San Pedro de Lloc, Peru, 7,594 **104** A3
San Pedro de los Incas, Peru, 3,751 **104** A2
San Pedro de Macorís, Dom. Rep., 22,935 **96** n6
San Pedro el Alto, Méx., Mex., 1,874 **93** e10
San Pedro el Alto, Oax., Mex., 1,061 **93** F5
San Pedro La Laguna, Guat., 3,396 **94** b9
San Pedro Mártir, I., Mex. **92** B2
San Pedro Mártir, Sa., Mex. **92** B1
San Pedro Mtn., N. Mex. **79** B3
San Pedro Necta, Guat., 1,347 **94** A3
San Pedro Pinula, Guat., 2,631 **94** d9
San Pedro Pt., Calif. **83** d12
San Pedro Sacatepéquez, Guat., 8,316 **94** b9
San Pedro Soloma, Guat., 1,279 **94** B3
San Pedro Sula, Hond., 32,793 **94** D3
San Pedro Tenango, Mex., 1,317 **93** d9
San Pedro Totoltepec, Mex., 4,255 **93** e10
San Pedro Yepocapa, Guat., 2,907 **94** b9
San Pelayo, Col. **100** B3
San Perlita, Tex., 348 **77** P6
Sanpete, co., Utah, 11,053 **78** C2
Sanphaya, Thai. **147** d4
San Pierre, Ind. **70** C1
San Pietro in Casale, It., 8,175 **122** e6
San Pitch, r., Utah **78** C2
Sanpoil, r., Wash. **80** D1
Sanquhar, U.K., 2,182 **113** E4
San Quintín, Mex. **92** B1
San Quintin, Phil., 2,037 **153** b7
San Quintín, C., Mex. **92** A1
San Rafael, Arg., 46,000* **105** B4
San Rafael, Chile **104** e16
San Rafael, Chile, 1,156 **104** f15
San Rafael, Col. **100** F5
San Rafael, Col. **101** e13
San Rafael, El Salv., 1,471 **94** d9
San Rafael, Phil., 1,331 **153** c7
San Rafael, Ariz. **78** C6
San Rafael, Calif., 20,460 **82** B4
San Rafael, N. Mex. **79** A4
San Rafael, Ven., 7,110 **100** D2
San Rafael, C., Dom. Rep. **96** n6
San Rafael, r., Utah **78** C2
San Rafael de Atamaica, Ven. **100** G4
San Rafael de la Cuesta, Guat., 1,382 **94** b9
San Rafael de Orituco, Ven. **101** c12
San Rafael Knob, Utah **78** C2
San Rafael Mts., Calif. **82** D5
San Rafael Saltán, Guat. **94** c9
San Rafael Swell, Utah **78** •
San Ramón, Bol., 2,173 **102** D4
San Ramón, Cuba, 1,037 **96** e2
San Ramón, Peru, 3,030 **104** C4
San Ramon, Calif. **83** f12
San Ramón, Urug., 6,000* **105** d12
San Ramón de la Nueva Orán, Arg., 12,000* **105** C2
San Remo, It., 52,092 **123** A3
Sanrizuka, Jap. **155** n19
San Román, C., Ven. **100** F1
San Roque, Arg., 8,000* **105** D3
San Roque, Col. **101** e13
San Roque, Mex., 1,003 **93** c9
San Roque, Sp., 17,126 **122** C4
San Rosendo, Chile, 3,744 **105** A5
San Saba, co., Tex., 6,381 **77** O4
San Saba, Tex., 2,728 **77** O4
San Saba, r., Tex. **77** O4
San Salvador, Arg., 5,105 **105** D4
San Salvador, Col. **100** E4
San Salvador, El Salv., 248,100 **94** C4
San Salvador, I., Colón, Arch. de **104** a8
San Salvador de Jujuy, Arg., 72,150 **105** C2
San Salvador I., Bah. Is. **95** D1
San Salvatore Monferrato, It., 4,836 **122** b6
Sansanding, Mali, 5,366 **162** C3
Sansanné-Mango, Togo, 6,016 **162** D4
Sansapor, Indon. **149** J3
Sansare, Guat., 1,516 **94** c9
Sansbois Mtn., Okla. **76** H2
San Sebastián, Can. Is. **109** 4
San Sebastián, Col. **100** B7
San Sebastián, El Salv., 4,595 **94** e10
San Sebastián, Guat., 4,173 **94** b9
San Sebastián, Jal., Mex., 1,036 **93** b8
San Sebastián, Qro., Mex. **93** d9
San Sebastián, P.R., 4,019 **96** s10
San Sebastián, Sp., 135,149 **122** D1
San Sebastián, Ven., 4,024 **100** G3
San Sebastián, B., Arg. **105** B8
San Secondo Parmense, It., 5,267 **122** d6

290 · Sansepolcro—Sarrebourg

Sansepolcro, It., 14,611 123 D3
San Severino Marche, It., 15,067 123 D3
San Severo, It., 53,095 123 E4
San-sha Wan, China 152 F2
San-shui, China 152 D3
San Silvestre, Ven. 100 E3
San Simeon, Calif. 82 C5
San Simón, Méx., Mex. 93 e11
San Simón, Micho., Mex., 1,043 93 b9
San Simon, Ariz. 78 D5
San Simon, r., Ariz. 78 D5
San Simon Val., Ariz. 78 D5
Sanski Most, Yug., 3,540 125 C2
Sansom Park Village, Tex., 4,175 76 e9
San Souci, St. Vinc. 97 19
Sans Souci, Mich. 67 L6
Sans Toucher, Mt., Guad. 97 14
San-sui, China 150 E4
Santa, Peru, 3,809 104 B4
Santa, r., Peru 104 B4
Sta. Ana, Arg. 105 b10
Sta. Ana, Bol., 7,990 102 C4
Sta. Ana, Col. 100 E1
Sta. Ana, Ec., 4,220 104 A2
Sta. Ana, El Salv., 73,864 94 C3
Sta. Ana, Hgo., Mex., 1,462 93 f9
Sta. Ana, Micho., Mex., 1,514 93 d10
Sta. Ana., Son., Mex., 5,896 92 C1
Sta. Ana, Tab., Mex., 2,612 93 G4
Sta. Ana, Calif., 100,350 82 E6
Sta. Ana, Urug. 105 c10
Sta. Ana, Ven., 3,103 100 D4
Sta. Ana, Ven., 1,609 100 E3
Sta. Ana, Ven., 3,584 101 H3
Sta. Ana, r., Calif. 83 i16
Sta. Ana, Cuch. de, Braz. 99 D6
Sta. Ana, Pico, P.R. 96 r10
Sta. Ana, Vol. de, El Salv. 94 C4
Sta. Ana I., Sol. Is. 175 d3
Sta. Ana Maya, Mex., 3,784 93 d10
Sta. Anita, Arg., 8,500* 105 b11
Sta. Anita, Chih., Mex. 92 D2
Sta. Anita, Jal., Mex., 4,807 93 a9
Sta. Anna, Tex., 1,320 77 O4
Sta. Bárbara, Col. 100 C5
Sta. Bárbara, Guat. 94 b8
Sta. Bárbara, Hond., 4,551 94 C3
Sta. Bárbara, Chih., Mex., 15,892 92 D2
Sta. Bárbara, Gto., Mex., 1,395 93 c8
Sta. Bárbara, Micho., Mex. 93 c10
Sta. Barbara, Phil., 6,256 153 d11
Sta. Barbara, co., Calif., 168,962 82 C5
Sta. Barbara, Calif., 58,768 82 D5
Sta. Bárbara, Ven., 1,751 100 E4
Sta. Bárbara, Ven. 100 G6
Sta. Bárbara, Ven., 4,680 101 J3
Sta. Barbara Chan., Calif. 82 C5
Sta. Bárbara de Samaná = Samaná, Dom. Rep.
Sta. Barbara I., Calif. 82 D6
Sta. Branca, Braz., 2,532 103 d18
Sta. Catalina, Arg. 105 B2
Sta. Catalina, Pan. 94 G6
Sta. Catalina, Phil., 3,733 153 d12
Sta. Catalina, Urug., 1,500* 105 c11
Sta. Catalina, Ven. 100 F4
Sta. Catalina, Ven. 101 K3
Sta. Catalina, Gulf of, Calif. 82 D6
Sta. Catalina, I., Mex. 92 C3
Sta. Catalina I., Sol. Is. 175 d3
Sta. Catalina I., Calif. 82 D6
Sta. Catalina Mts., Ariz. 78 •
Sta. Catarina, st., Braz., 2,146,909 103 F7
Sta. Catarina, I. de, Braz. 103 G7
Sta. Catarina Loxicha, Mex., 1,781 93 F5
Sta. Catarina Mita, Guat., 3,272 94 d9
Sta. Catharina, Cur. 97 16
Sta. Clara, Chile 104 e16
Sta. Clara, Chile 104 e17
Sta. Clara, Col. 100 F9
Sta. Clara, Cuba, 77,398 96 d1
Sta. Clara, Dgo., Mex., 2,967 92 E3
Sta. Clara, Micho., Mex., 3,505 93 b10
Sta. Clara, co., Calif., 642,315 82 C4
Sta. Clara, Calif., 58,880 82 B4
Sta. Clara, N.Y. 59 M2
Sta. Clara, Utah, 291 78 B3
Sta. Clara, Ven. 101 H3
Sta. Clara La Laguna, Guat., 1,612 94 b9
Sta. Claus, Ariz. 78 A4
Sta. Clotilde, Peru 104 C2
Sta. Cruz, Arg., 1,300* 105 B8
Sta. Cruz, Aruba 97 15
Sta. Cruz, Flores, Azores, 1,898 108 2
Sta. Cruz, Graciosa, Azores, 2,104 108 2
Sta. Cruz, Bol., 66,548 102 D5
Sta. Cruz, Braz., 5,286 103 b14
Sta. Cruz, Chile, 5,905 104 f14
Sta. Cruz, C. R., 3,849 94 E5
Sta. Cruz, Guat. 94 C2
Sta. Cruz, Jam., 1,426 96 p8
Sta. Cruz, Peru 104 C3
Sta. Cruz, Phil., 3,538 153 A2
Sta. Cruz, Phil., 4,770 153 B2
Sta. Cruz, Phil., 1,627 153 b5
Sta. Cruz, Phil., 6,456 153 C4
Sta. Cruz, Phil., 8,962 153 d12
Sta. Cruz, co., Ariz., 10,808 78 C6
Sta. Cruz, co., Calif., 84,219 82 B4
Sta. Cruz, Calif., 25,596 82 B4
Sta. Cruz, N. Mex. 79 B4
Sta. Cruz, Ven., 1,919 100 D2
Sta. Cruz, Ven., 3,190 100 E3
Sta. Cruz, Ven., 4,145 101 b11
Sta. Cruz, I., Colón, Arch. de 104 a8
Sta. Cruz, I., Mex. 92 C3
Sta. Cruz, r., Arg. 105 B8
Sta. Cruz, r., Ariz.-Mex. 78 C5
Sta. Cruz de Bucaral, Ven., 1,871 100 F2
Sta. Cruz de la Palma, Can. Is. 109 4
Santa Cruz de la Zarza, Sp., 5,588 122 D3
Sta. Cruz del Norte, Cuba, 3,537 96 c1
Sta. Cruz del Sur, Cuba, 2,781 96 e2
Sta. Cruz de Mudela, Sp., 8,740 122 D3
Sta. Cruz de Orinoco, Ven. 101 H3
Sta. Cruz de Tenerife, Can. Is., 141,557 109 4
Sta. Cruz I., Calif. 82 D6
Sta. Cruz Is., Sol. Is. 170 F5
Sta. Cruz Mts., Jam. 96 p9
Sta. Cruz Mts., Calif. 82 •
Sta. Elena, Arg., 12,000* 105 b10
Sta. Elena, Ec., 5,049 104 A2
Sta. Elena, Peru 104 C3
Sta. Elena, Tex. 77 O6
Sta. Elena, Ven. 101 K5
Sta. Elena, B. de, C.R. 94 D5
Sta. Elena, C., C.R. 94 D5
Santa Fe, Arg., 199,179 105 C4
Santa Fé, Chile, 1,588 104 e17
Santa Fe, Hond. 94 D3
Santa Fe, Pan. 94 G6
Santa Fe, Phil., 3,756 153 B1
Santa Fe, Phil. 153 B2
Santa Fe, Phil., 2,974 153 e10
Santafé, Sp., 9,803 122 D4
Santa Fe, co., N. Mex., 44,970 79 B4
Santa Fe, N. Mex., 34,676 79 B4
Santa Fe, Tenn. 71 D6
Sta. Fe, I., Colón, Arch. de 104 b8
Sta. Fe, L., Fla. 65 G3
Sta. Fe, r., Fla. 65 G3
Sta. Fe Park, Ill. 69 c10
Sta. Fe Springs, Calif., 16,342 83 h16
Sant'Agata de' Goti, It., 12,188 123 d9
Sant'Agostino, It., 9,541 122 e6
Sāntāhār, Pak., 8,292 144 g13
San-t'ai, China 150 E4
Sta. Inés, Ven. 101 H3
Sta. Inés, B., Mex. 92 C2
Sta. Inés, I., Chile 105 A8
Sta. Isabel, Arg. 105 B5
Sta. Isabel, Braz., 4,631 103 c18
Sta. Isabel, Col. 101 d15
Sta. Isabel, Ec., 1,603 104 B2
Sta. Isabel, Fern. Póo, 19,869 164 A1
Sta. Isabel, Guat. 94 C2
Sta. Isabel, Peru 104 C3
Sta. Isabel, Peru 104 D5
Sta. Isabel, P.R., 4,712 96 t11
Sta. Isabel, i., Sol. Is. 170 E5
Sta. Isabel de las Lajas, Cuba, 5,362 96 c1
Sta. Isabel do Araguaia, Braz. 103 G3
San-t'ai Shan, China 152 A2
Sta. Juana, Chile, 2,020 104 e17
Santakheza, U.S.S.R. 151 F1
Sta. Lucía, Cuba, 1,698 96 a1
Sta. Lucía, Nic. 94 D4
Sta. Lucía, Peru, 1,071 104 D5
Sta. Lucía, Phil., 2,118 153 b5
Sta. Lucía, Phil., 3,975 153 b8
Sta. Lucía, Urug., 8,500* 105 D4
Sta. Lucía, Ven. 100 F3
Sta. Lucía, Ven., 3,035 101 c11
Sta-Lucia-di-Tallano, Fr., 1,520 116 r18
Sta. Lucia Ra., Calif. 82 C4
Sta. Lucrecia, Mex. 93 G5
Sta. Luzia, i., C. Verde Is. 109 5
Sta. Magdalena, Phil., 5,155 153 i15
Sta. Magdalena, I., Mex. 92 B3
Sta. Margarita, Calif. 82 C5
Sta. Margarita, I., Mex. 92 B3
Sta. Margherita Ligure, It., 11,576 123 B2
Sta. María, Arg., 2,555 105 B3
Sta. Maria, Braz., 78,682 103 F7
Santa Maria, C. Verde I. 109 5
Sta. María, Chile, 1,580 104 g12
Sta. María, C.R. 94 F6
Sta. María, Hond. 94 D3
Sta. María, Gro., Mex., 1,132 93 F5
Sta. María, Hgo., Mex. 93 e9
Sta. Maria, Phil., 2,554 153 B1
Sta. Maria, Phil., 1,654 153 c5
Sta. Maria, Switz. 124 E2
Sta. Maria, Calif., 20,027 82 C5
Sta. Maria, Tex., 281 77 P6
Sta. María, Ven. 101 H3
Sta. Maria, i., Azores 108 2
Sta. Maria, i., New Hebr. 174 k5
Sta. María, r., Mex. 92 D1
Sta. María, r., Mex. 93 e8
Sta. María, r., Pan. 94 G6
Sta. Maria, r., Ariz. 78 B4
Sta. María, B., Mex. 92 B3
Sta. Maria, C. de, Ang. 164 A4
Sta. Maria, C. de, Moz. 164 E6
Sta. Maria, C. de, Port. 122 B4
Sta. María, Cayo, Cuba 96 d1
Sta. María, I., Colón, Arch. de, 104 a8
Sta. María, Lag. de, Mex. 92 D1
Sta. María, Vol., Guat. 94 b9
Sta. Maria Capua Vetere, It., 30,878 123 c9
Sta. Maria das Barrieras, Braz. 103 F3
Sta. Maria da Vitória, Braz., 3,208 103 H4
Sta. María de Ipire, Ven., 3,110 100 H3
Sta. María del Oro, Mex., 4,224 92 D2
Sta. María del Río, Mex., 4,841 93 E4
Sta. María de Nanay, Peru 104 C2
Sta. Maria di Leuca, Capo, It. 123 G5
Sta. Maria Madalena, Braz., 1,530 103 f17
Sta. Marta, Col. 100 C2
Sta. Marta, Sp., 5,142 122 B3
Sta. Marta, C. de, Ang. 164 A4
Sta. Monica, Calif., 83,249 82 D6
Sta. Monica Bay, Calif. 82 D6
Sta. Monica Mts., Calif. 83 g15
Santan, Indon. 148 F3
Santana, Braz., 4,357 103 H4
Santana do Livramento, Braz., 37,666 103 E8
Santana do Matos, Braz., 2,036 103 a13
Santander, Phil., 1,025 153 B3
Santander, Sp., 118,435 122 D1
Santander de Quilichao, Col. 100 B6
Sant'Angelo Lodigiano, It., 10,634 122 c5
Santanilla, P., Dom. Rep. 96 m6
Sant'Antioco, It., 11,060 123 B5
Sant'Antioco, Isola di, It. 123 B5
Santañy, Sp., 5,082 122 G3
Sta. Paula, Calif., 13,279 82 D5
Santaquin, Utah, 1,183 78 C2
Sant'Arcangelo, It., 6,723 123 E4
Sant'Arcangelo di Romagna, It., 13,197 123 C2
Santarém, Braz., 24,924 103 F2
Santarém, Port., 18,635 122 A3
Santaren Channel, W.I. 95 C2
Sta. Rita, Braz., 20,623 103 b14
Sta. Rita, Cuba, 1,655 96 e2
Sta. Rita, Guam, 1,630 176 24
Sta. Rita, Guat. 94 B2
Sta. Rita, Hond., 1,759 94 D3
Sta. Rita, Mex., 2,134 93 b9
Sta. Rita, Phil., 3,672 153 C3
Sta. Rita, N. Mex., 1,772 79 B5
Sta. Rita, Ven., 11,623 100 E2
Sta. Rita de Jacutinga, Braz., 2,292 103 d18
Sta. Rita do Sapucaí, Braz., 8,464 103 d18
Sta. Rita do Weil, Braz. 102 C2
Sta. Rita Pk., Calif. 82 C4
Sta. Rosa, Arg., 23,699* 105 B5
Sta. Rosa, Arg., 6,800* 105 C4
Sta. Rosa, Bol. 102 C4
Sta. Rosa, Bol. 102 d12
Sta. Rosa, Goiás, Braz., 1,271 103 G5
Sta. Rosa, R.G. do S., Braz., 12,283 103 F7
Sta. Rosa, Col. 100 B7
Sta. Rosa, Gto., Mex., 1,009 93 c8
Sta. Rosa, Gto., Mex. 93 d8
Sta. Rosa, Méx., Mex., 3,054 93 d10
Sta. Rosa, Qro., Mex., 3,022 93 E4
Sta. Rosa, Peru, 2,047 104 D5
Sta. Rosa, Phil., 3,730 153 c7
Sta. Rosa, Phil. 153 g13
Sta. Rosa, Calif., 31,027 82 B3
Sta. Rosa, co., Fla., 29,547 65 B2
Sta. Rosa, N. Mex., 2,220 79 C4
Sta. Rosa, Urug., 5,000* 105 d12
Sta. Rosa, Ven., 1,016 100 F3
Sta. Rosa, Ven. 101 H3
Sta. Rosa, Mt., Guam 176 24
Sta. Rosa de Aguán, Hond. 94 E3
Sta. Rosa de Amanadona, Ven. 100 G7
Sta. Rosa de Cabal, Col. 101 d15
Sta. Rosa de Copán, Hond., 9,078 94 C3
Sta. Rosa de Lima, El Salv., 4,563 94 D4
Sta. Rosa de Lima, Guat., 1,039 94 c9
Sta. Rosa de Osos, Col. 100 C4
Sta. Rosa de Río Primero, Arg., 6,000* 105 C4
Sta. Rosa de Sucumbio, Col. 100 B7
Sta. Rosa de Viterbo, Col. 100 D5
Sta. Rosa I., Calif. 82 C6
Sta. Rosa I., Fla. 65 C2
Sta. Rosalía, Mex., 5,361 92 B2
Sta. Rosalía, Ven., 1,194 100 F3
Sta. Rosalía, Ven. 100 H4
Sta. Rosalía, P., Mex. 92 B2
Sta. Rosa Pk., Nev. 52 C2
Sta. Rosa Ra., Nev. 83 B2
Sta. Susana, Calif., 2,310 83 g15
Sta. Susana Mts., Calif. 83 g15
Sta. Tecla, El Salv., 26,911 94 C4
Sta. Teresa, Arg., 2,900* 105 a11
Sta. Teresa, Chile 104 e17
Sta. Teresa, Mex. 93 e8
Sta. Teresa, Phil., 2,294 153 d11
Sta. Teresa, Ven., 6,939 101 c11
Sta. Teresa, Pantano de, Sp. 122 C2
Sta. Teresita, Arg. 105 c13
Sta. Vitória do Palmar, Braz., 8,224 103 F8
Santee, Calif. 82 c9
Santee, Nebr. 75 H1
Santee, S.C., 105 63 D4
Santee, r., S.C. 63 E4
Santeetlah, N.C. 63 b7
Sant'Elena, It., 1,903 122 e5
San Telmo, Mex. 92 A1
Santena, It., 4,284 122 a6
Santeny, Fr. 116 i12
San Teodoro, Phil., 1,430 153 B2
Santeramo in Colle, It., 20,812 123 F4
Sant'Eufemia, Golfo di, It. 123 E5
Santhià, It., 7,457 122 b5
Santiago, Braz., 15,140 103 F7
Santiago, C. Verde Is. 109 5
Santiago, Chile, 646,731 105 A4
Santiago, Dom. Rep., 83,523 96 m6
Santiago, Mex. 92 C3
Santiago, Pan., 8,746 94 G6
Santiago, Peru, 1,457 104 C5
Santiago, Phil., 4,243 153 B1
Santiago, Sp., 57,165 122 A1
Santiago, Mich. 67 K4
Santiago, r., Peru 104 B2
Santiago, C., Phil. 153 b9
Santiago, Snia. de, Bol. 102 E5
Santiago Astata, Mex., 1,022 93 G5
Santiago Atitlán, Guat., 8,822 94 b9
Santiago de Chocorvos, Peru 104 C5
Santiago de Chuco, Peru, 6,292 104 B4
Santiago de Cuba, Cuba, 163,237 96 f3
Santiago de Hauta, Bol., 20,244 102 a10
Santiago de la Peña, Mex., 3,686 93 F4
Santiago del Estero, Arg., 108,466 105 C3
Santiago de María, El Salv., 7,143 94 e10
Santiago do Cacém, Port., 6,939 122 A3
Santiago Ixcuintla, Mex., 10,985 92 D4
Santiago Mts., Texas 50 F4
Santiago Nonualco, El Salv., 3,138 94 d10
Santiago Oxtempan, Mex., 1,708 93 d10
Santiago Papasquiaro, Mex., 5,317 92 D3
Santiago Pk., Calif. 83 k16
Santiago Pk., Tex. 77 M5
Santiago Res., Calif. 83 i16
Santiago Rodríguez, Dom. Rep., 3,590 96 m6
Santiago Tezontlale, Mex., 1,864 93 e9
Santiago Tuxtla, Mex., 7,390 93 G4
Santiago Yeché, Mex., 2,719 93 e10
Santiaguillo, Mex. 93 d8
Santiaguito, Mex., 3,185 93 c10
Santiam Junction, Oreg. 80 C3
Santigi, Indon. 149 G2
Sant' Ilario d'Enza, It., 5,251 122 d6
Santillana, Sp., 3,703 122 m11
Santipur, India, 51,190 144 g14
Santiurde de Reinosa, Sp. 122 m11
Sant Julià, Andorra, 1,592 122 g7
Sto. Aleixo, Braz., 9,227 103 e18
Sto. Amaro, Braz., 17,226 103 J4
Sto. André, Braz., 230,196 103 G6
Sto. Ângelo, Braz., 25,415 103 E7
Sto. Antão, i., C. Verde Is. 109 5
Sto. Antônio, Braz., 2,978 103 b14
Sto. Antônio de Jesus, Braz., 14,902 103 H4
Sto. Antônio de Pádua, Braz., 6,173 103 e17
Sto. Antônio do Amparo, Braz., 2,797 103 d17
Sto. Antônio do Içá, Braz. 102 C2
Sto. Antônio do Leverger, Braz., 2,028 103 E5
Sto. Antônio do Zaire, Ang. 164 A3
Sto. Corazón, Bol. 102 E5
Sto. Cristo, Phil., 4,889 153 c7
Sto. Domingo, Arg., 1,060* 105 c13
Sto. Domingo, Col. 101 d13
Sto. Domingo, Cuba, 4,728 96 c1
Sto. Domingo, Dom. Rep., 367,053 96 n6
Sto. Domingo, Ec. 104 c10
Sto. Domingo, Baja Calif., Mex. 92 B2
Sto. Domingo, Coah., Mex. 92 E2
Sto. Domingo, Jal., Mex. 93 c8
Sto. Domingo, S.L.P., Mex. 93 E4
Sto. Domingo, Nic., 3,821 94 E4
Sto. Domingo, Phil., 3,583 153 h14
Sto. Domingo, r., Ven. 100 F3
Sto. Domingo, P., Mex. 92 B2
Sto. Domingo de Guzmán, El Salv., 2,726 94 d10
Sto. Domingo de la Calzada, Sp., 5,436 122 D1
Sto. Eduardo, Braz., 1,565 103 f17
Sto. Isidoro, Port., 2,515 122 i10
San Tomé, Ven., 4,138 101 H3
Santoña, Sp., 9,082 122 D1
Santonia, Fr. Guiana 101 N5
Santos, Braz., 262,048 103 G6
Santos Dumont, Amaz., Braz. 102 C3
Santos Dumont, Ms. Gs., Braz., 20,414 103 H6
Sto. Tirso, Port., 10,754 122 A2
Sto. Tomás, Col. 100 C2
Sto. Tomás, Baja Calif., Mex. 92 A1
Sto. Tomás, Hgo., Mex., 1,053 93 f10
Sto. Tomás, Nic., 1,012 94 E4
Sto. Tomás, Peru, 1,181 104 B3
Sto. Tomás, Peru, 1,661 104 D5
Sto. Tomas, Phil., 1,199 153 b6
Sto. Tomas, Phil., 9,450 153 C4
Sto. Tomás, P., Mex. 92 A1
Sto. Tomé, Arg. 105 a10
Sto. Tomé, Arg., 8,882 105 D3
Sto. Tomé de Guayana, Ven., 65,000* 101 J3
Santpoort, Neth., 15,000 115 C2
San-tsao, i., China 152 a7
San-tu, China 152 B2
Santuario, Col. 101 d13
Santuario, Mex. 93 e9
Santuit (part of Barnstable), Mass. 57 P6
Sanuki, Jap. 155 m20
Sanuma, Jap. 155 G2
San Valentín, Co., Chile 105 A7
San Vicente, Bol. 102 a10
San Vicente, Chile, 4,447 104 f14
San Vicente, Col. 100 D4
San Vicente, Col. 101 d13
San Vicente, Ec. 104 A2
San Vicente, El Salv., 15,189 94 C4
San Vicente, Baja Calif., Mex. 92 A1
San Vicente, S.L.P., Mex. 93 F4
San Vicente, Phil., 3,389 153 B1
San Vicente, Ven. 100 F4
San Vicente, Vol. de, El Salv. 94 e10
San Vicente de la Barquera, Sp., 3,673 122 C1
San Vicente Pacaya, Guat., 2,510 94 c9
Sanvignes-les-Mines, Fr., 6,707 117 F3
San Vito, Capo, It. 123 D5
San Vito dei Normanni, It., 19,144 123 F4
Sanya, Jap. 154 g16
San Ygnacio, Tex. 77 O6
San Ysidro, Calif. 82 c10
San Ysidro, N. Mex. 79 B4
San-yüan, China 151 A4
Sanza Pombo, Ang. 164 B3
Sanzey, Fr. 116 b9
São Bartolomeu de Messines, Port., 10,459 122 A4
São Bento, Braz., 7,094 103 G2
São Bento do Una, Braz., 5,096 103 a15
São Bernardo do Campo, Braz., 61,645 103 c18
São Borja, Braz., 20,339 103 E7
São Caetano do Sul, Braz., 114,039 103 c18
São Carlos, Braz., 50,010 103 G6
São Domingos, Braz. 103 G4
São Domingos do Maranhão, Braz., 3,966 103 H3
São Félix, Mo. Gro., Braz. 103 F4
São Félix, Pará, Braz. 103 F3
São Fidélis, Braz., 6,145 103 f17
São Filipe, C. Verde Is., 1,785 109 5
São Francisco, Braz., 4,074 103 H5
São Francisco, r., Braz. 103 H4
São Francisco do Sul, Braz., 11,593 103 G7
São Gabriel, Braz., 22,967 103 F8
São Gonçalo, Braz., 63,776 103 e18
São Gonçalo do Sapucaí, Braz., 7,215 103 d17
Sao Hai, Thai. 147 d4
Sao Hill, Tanz. 164 E3
São João da Barra, Braz., 3,441 103 f17
São João da Boa Vista, Braz., 25,226 103 G6
São João da Madeira, Port., 11,921 122 A2
São João das Lampas, Port., 4,946 122 i10
São João del Rei, Braz., 34,654 103 H6
São João do Piauí, Braz., 2,688 103 H3
São João dos Patos, Braz., 2,590 103 H3
São Jorge, i., Azores 108 2
São José da Laje, Braz., 5,822 103 b15
São José de Anauá, Braz. 102 D1
São José de Mipibu, Braz., 5,179 103 b14
São José do Calçado, Braz., 2,637 103 f17
São José do Campestre, Braz., 3,288 103 b14
São José do Goiabal, Braz., 1,793 103 e17
São José do Rio Prêto, R. de J., Braz., 3,287 103 e18
São José do Rio Prêto, S.P., Braz., 66,476 103 F6
São José dos Campos, Braz., 55,349 103 c18
São Leopoldo, Braz., 41,023 103 F7
São Lourenço, Braz., 14,680 103 d18
São Lourenço, r., Braz. 103 E5
São Lourenço do Sul, Braz., 6,877 103 F8
São Luís, Braz., 124,606 103 H2
São Luís, Port., 4,345 122 A4
São Luís do Paraitinga, Braz., 2,153 103 d18
São Luís do Quitunde, Braz., 3,359 103 b15
São Manuel = Teles Pires
São Marcos, r., Braz. 103 G5
São Mateus, Azores, 1,319 108 2
São Mateus, Braz., 6,075 103 J5
São Miguel, i., Azores 108 2
São Miguel do Araguaia, Braz., 1,873 103 F4
São Miguel do Campos, Braz., 6,511 103 J3
Saona, Isla, Dom. Rep. 96 n6
Saône, r., Fr. 117 F3
Saonek, Indon. 149 J3
Saoner, India, 10,186 144 b15
São Nicolau, i., C. Verde Is. 109 5
São Paulo, st., Braz., 12,974,699 103 G6
São Paulo, Braz., 3,164,804 103 G6
São Paulo de Olivença, Braz., 1,157 102 C2
São Paulo do Potengi, Braz., 2,197 103 a13
São Pedro da Aldeia, Braz., 2,436 103 e18
São Pedro dos Ferros, Braz., 4,276 103 e17
São Pedro do Sul, Port., 3,649 122 B2
São Raimundo das Mangabeiras, Braz., 1,736 103 G3
São Raimundo Nonato, Braz., 3,751 103 H3
São Romão, Braz., 1,438 103 G5
São Roque, Braz., 12,409 103 c18
São Roque, C. de, Braz. 103 b13
São Salvador do Congo, Ang. 164 B3
São Sebastião, Braz., 3,490 103 d18
São Sebastião, I. de, Braz. 103 d18
São Sepé, Braz., 5,026 103 F8
São Tiago, Braz., 2,505 103 d17
São Tiago, i., C. Verde Is. 109 5
São Tomé, Braz., 2,406 103 a13
São Tomé, São Tomé, 7,817 162 F5
São Tomé, i., Afr. 164 A1
São Tomé, C., Braz. 103 f18
São Vicente, Braz., 73,578 103 c18
São Vicente, i., C. Verde Is. 109 5
São Vicente, C. de, Port. 122 A4
São Vicente de Minas, Braz., 2,441 103 d17
Sap, r., Camb. 147 k11
Sap, Tonle, Camb. 146 C4
Sapahaqui, Bol. 102 b10
Sápai, Gr., 2,589 129 E4
Sapé, Braz., 10,602 103 b14
Sapele, Nigeria, 39,020 162 E5
Sapello, N. Mex. 79 C4
Sapelo I., Ga. 64 H4
Sapeza, D.R.Congo 165 m18
Sapian, Phil., 2,033 153 B3
Sapiéntza, i., Gr. 129 C6
Sapinero, Colo. 79 B2
Sapo, Snia del, Pan. 94 •
Sapocoy, Mt., Phil. 153 B1
Saponac, Me. 55 D3
Saponé, Upper Volta, 1,395 162 D3
Saposoa, Peru, 4,462 104 B3
Sapotille, Fr. Guiana 101 O5
Sapozhok, U.S.S.R., 4,300 136 F2
Sappa Cr., Kans.-Nebr. 75 E4
Sappho, Wash. 80 A1
Sappington, Mo. 72 a11
Sapporo, Jap., 523,839 155 J8
Sapucaia, Braz., 2,836 103 e17
Sapudi, P., Indon. 148 E4
Sapudi, Selat, Indon. 148 f7
Sapulpa, Okla., 14,282 76 G1
Sapulu, Indon. 148 e7
Sapulut, Malay. 148 F1
Sapwe, D.R.Congo 165 o19
Sāqiyat Az Zayt, Tun., 8,716 160 g6
Şaqqārah, ruins, U.A.R. 161 i8
Saqqez, Iran, 12,907 143 D1
Saquena, Peru 104 C3
Saquisilí, Ec., 2,378 104 c10
Sara, Phil., 3,433 153 B3
Sarāb, Iran, 13,086 143 D1
Saraburi, Thai., 18,861 146 C4
Sarafiré, Mali, 1,943 162 D3
Saragosa, Tex. 77 M4
Saragossa = Zaragoza, Sp.
Saraguro, Ec., 1,571 104 B2
Sarah, Miss. 73 E3
Sarahsville, Ohio, 164 70 H3
Sarajevo, Yug., 198,000* 125 D3
Saraktash, U.S.S.R., 12,500 134 E4
Sarala, U.S.S.R. 137 s11
Saraland, Ala., 4,595 64 A5
Saramacca, r., Sur. 101 N5
Saramati, pk., Burma-India 146 A1
Saran', U.S.S.R., 51,700 134 G5
Sarana, U.S.S.R. 137 i8
Saranac, Mich., 1,081 67 H6
Saranac, N.Y. 59 N2
Saranac, r., N.Y. 59 N2
Saranac Lake, N.Y., 6,421 59 M3
Saranac Lakes, N.Y. 59 M3
Sarandë, Alb., 6,800 125 E4
Sarandi, Braz., 3,858 103 F7
Sarandí del Yi, Urug., 6,000* 105 d11
Sarandí de Navarro, Urug. 105 c11
Sarandí Grande, Urug. 105 c11
Sarangani Bay, Phil. 153 C4
Sarangani I., Phil. 153 C4
Sarangani Is., Phil. 153 C4
Sarangpur, India, 11,263 144 a14
Saranpaul', U.S.S.R. 134 F3
Saransk, U.S.S.R., 108,000 134 D4
Sarany, U.S.S.R. 137 i7
Saraphi, Thai. 146 B3
Sarapul, U.S.S.R., 76,000 134 E4
Sarare, Ven., 2,490 100 F3
Sarare, r., Ven. 100 E4
Sarasota, co., Fla., 76,895 65 G5
Sarasota, Fla., 34,083 65 G5
Sarasota Bay, Fla. 65 c13
Sărata, r., Rum. 128 F2
Sărata-Monteoru, Rum. 128 F2
Saratani, Jap. 154 h14
Saratoga, Ark., 62 73 A4
Saratoga, Calif., 14,861 82 B4
Saratoga, Ind., 363 70 E2
Saratoga, co., N.Y., 89,096 59 N5
Saratoga, N.C., 409 63 G2
Saratoga, Tex. 77 Q4
Saratoga, Wash. 81 b6
Saratoga, Wyo., 1,133 81 F5
Saratoga Lake, N.Y. 59 w25
Saratoga L., N.Y. 59 N5
Saratoga Nat. Hist. Pk., N.Y. 59 w27
Saratoga Springs, N.Y., 16,630 59 N5
Saratok, Malay., 1,340 148 D2
Saratov, U.S.S.R., 631,000 134 D4
Saraurcu, mtn., Ec. 104 d10
Saravan, Iran, 4,012 143 G3
Saravane, Laos 146 D4
Sarawak (part of Malay.), 838,000* 148 E2
Sarayacu, Ec. 104 B2
Sarayköy, Turk., 6,914 142 B2
Sarayönü, Turk., 5,389 142 C2
Sarben, Nebr. 75 D2
Sárbogárd, Hung., 6,859 126 D3
Sarcelle, Passe de la, N. Caled. 174 k9
Sarcelles, Fr., 36,028 116 h11
Sarcoxie, Mo., 1,056 72 C7
Sarda, r., India 144 c11
Sardalas, Libya 161 F3
Sardarshahr, India, 32,072 145 E3
Sardegna, i., It. 123 B4
Sardinal, C.R. 94 E5
Sardinata, Col. 100 D3
Sardinia, It. = Sardegna
Sardinia, N.Y. 58 C6
Sardinia, S.C. 63 D4
Sardinia, Ohio, 799 70 F4
Sardis, Ala. 64 C3
Sardis, Ga., 829 64 H3
Sardis, Ky., 190 71 H3
Sardis, Miss., 2,098 73 F3
Sardis, Ohio 70 J3
Sardis, S.C. 63 E3
Sardis, Tenn., 274 71 C6
Sardis L., Miss. 73 F3
Sardo, Eth. 163 L3
Sare, Kenya 165 g14
Sareks Nat. Pk., Swed. 120 D2
Sarepta, La., 737 73 B5
Sarera, Teluk, Indon. 149 K3
Sarezskoye Oz., U.S.S.R. 137 g5
Sargans, Switz., 2,571 124 D1
Sargasso Sea, Atl. Oc. 108 H4
Sargatskoye, U.S.S.R. 137 o11
Sargent, Nebr., 876 75 F2
Sargent, co., N. Dak., 6,856 74 D2
Sargent, Tex. 77 Q5
Sargents, Colo. 79 B2
Sargentville, Me. 55 D4
Sargodha, Pak., 129,291 145 D2
Sargur, India, 4,599 145 k19
Sārī, Iran, 26,278 143 E1
Saria, i., Gr. 129 F7
Sariaya, Phil., 7,110 153 c9
Sariba, i., Terr. Papua 174 3
Sari-d'Orcino, Fr. 116 r17
Sarigan, i., Mariana Is. 176 23
Sarıkamış, Turk., 17,573 142 E1
Sarikei, Malay., 4,204 148 D2
Sarime, Sol. Is. 175 a1
Sarina, Austl., 1,983 173 G3
Sariñena, Sp., 3,389 122 E2
Sar-i-Pul, Afghan. 144 C1
Sarita, Tex. 77 P6
Sarita River, Br. Col., Can. 42 b7
Sariwŏn, N. Kor. 151 E3
Sarıyar Barajı, Turk. 142 B1
Sarıyer, Turk., 23,978 142 B1
Sarjektjåkko, mt., Swed. 120 D2
Sarju, r., India 144 c12
Sark, i., U.K. 117 C2
Sarkad, Hung., 12,336 126 E3
Şarkışla, Turk., 6,646 142 D2
Sarlat, Fr., 7,976 117 D4
Sarleinsbach, Aust., 2,048 124 K5
Sarles, N. Dak., 225 74 C1
Sarlyk, G., U.S.S.R. 137 r12
Sărmaş, Rum. 128 E1
Sármellék, Hung., 2,806 126 C3
Sarmi, Indon. 149 L3
Sarmiento, Arg., 6,000* 105 B7
Sarmizegetusa, Rum. 128 D2
Särna, Swed. 120 C3
Sarnath, India 144 d13
Sarnen, Switz., 6,554 124 C2
Sarnersee, Switz. 124 C2
Sarnia, Ont., Can., 50,308 44 G7
Sarno, It., 30,298 123 d10
Sarnowa, Pol., 1,525 127 B3
Sarny, U.S.S.R., 12,200 134 B4
Sarolangun, Indon. 148 B3
Saroma, Jap., 10,232 155 K7
Saroma-ko, Jap. 155 K7
Sarona, Wis. 66 B3
Saronikós Kólpos, Gr. 129 D6
Saronno, It., 24,210 122 c5
Sáros = Saria
Saros Körfezi, Turk. 129 F4
Sárospatak, Hung., 12,917 126 E2
Šar Planina, Yug. 125 E3
Sarpsborg, Nor., 13,347 120 B4
Sarpy, co., Nebr., 31,281 75 J2
Sarralbe, Fr., 4,235 116 d9
Sarrat, Phil., 4,186 153 B1
Sarre, r., Fr. 117 G2
Sarrebourg, Fr., 13,280 117 G2

Sarreguemines—Sealark · 291

Sarreguemines, Fr., 18,135 117 G2
Sarre-Union, Fr., 2,645 117 G2
Sarria, Sp., 14,759 122 B1
Sarrión, Sp., 1,688 122 E2
Sarsang, Iraq 143 C1
Sarstedt, F.R.Ger., 9,620 118 B2
Sarstún, r., Br. Hond.-Guat. 94 C3
Sartang, r., U.S.S.R. 135 N3
Sartell, Minn., 791 74 E3
Sartène, Fr., 5,935 116 r18
Sarthe, r., Fr. 117 C3
Sartilly, Fr., 1,058 117 C2
Sartinville, Miss. 73 E6
Sartirana Lomellina, It., 3,125 122 b5
Sartlan, Oz., U.S.S.R. 137 p11
Sartrouville, Fr., 31,284 116 g11
Sartyn'ya, U.S.S.R. 134 F3
Saru, L., Terr. Papua 174 d3
Sarufutsu, Jap., 8,871 155 K7
Sarum, China 144 e11
Sárvár, Hung., 11,021 126 C3
Sarver, Pa. 60 d7
Sárviz, r., Hung. 126 D3
Sarych, M., U.S.S.R. 136 D4
Sary-Ishikotrau, Peski, U.S.S.R. 134 G5
Sary-Ozek, U.S.S.R., 14,500 134 G5
Sary-Shagan, U.S.S.R. 134 G5
Sarysu, r., U.S.S.R. 134 F5
Sary-Tash, U.S.S.R. 137 g4
Sarzana, It., 17,098 123 B2
Sarzeau, Fr., 3,759 116 B3
Sarzyna, Pol., 1,919 127 E3
Sasabe, Ariz. 78 C6
Sasae, Jap. 154 g14
Sasaima, Col. 101 e15
Sasak, Indon. 148 A2
Sasakwa, Okla., 253 76 G3
Sasamungga Mission, Sol. Is. 175 b2
Sasao, Jap. 154 g15
Sasaram, India, 37,782 144 d13
Sasayama, Jap., 16,828 155 D4
Sasca Montană, Rum. 128 C2
Sásd, Hung., 2,640 126 C3
Sasebo, Jap., 262,484 154 A5
Saseginaga, L., Qué., Can. 46 F1
Sasina, W. Samoa 177 38
Saskatchewan, prov., Can., 951,000* 43
Saskatchewan, r., Can. 40 J7
Saskatoon, Sask., Can., 92,367 43 C4
Saskylakh, U.S.S.R. 135 L2
Saslaya, Co., Nic. 94 E4
Sasolburg, S. Af., 12,557 165 D6
Sasovo, U.S.S.R., 23,000 136 F2
Saspamco, Tex. 77 O5
Sassabaneh, Eth. 163 M4
Sassafras Mtn., S.C. 63 B2
Sassandra, Iv. Coast, 5,300 162 D5
Sassandra, r., Iv. Coast 162 C5
Sassari, It., 86,425 123 B4
Sassenheim, Neth., 9,300 115 b6
Sasser, Ga., 382 64 E4
Sassnitz, Ger.D.R., 13,413 118 D1
Sasso Feltrio, It., 1,600 123 e11
Sassuolo, It., 21,593 123 C2
Sastown, Lib. 162 C5
Sas-Tyube, U.S.S.R., 3,700 137 f3
Sasuna, Jap. 154 A4
Sasvad, India, 8,498 145 i17
Sas van Gent, Neth., 3,800 115 B3
Sasyk, Oz., U.S.S.R. 136 C4
Sasykkol', Oz., U.S.S.R. 134 H5
Sata, Jap., 11,239 154 B6
Satadougou, Mali 162 C3
Satalo, W. Samoa 177 38
Sata-misaki, Jap. 154 B6
Satanta, Kans., 686 75 E6
Satapuala, W. Samoa 177 37
Satara, India, 48,709 145 D6
Satartia, Miss., 126 73 E5
Sataua, W. Samoa 177 37
Sataua Bay, W. Samoa 177 38
Satawal, i., Car. Is. 176 18
Satawan, atoll, Car. Is. 176 18
Satellite Beach, Fla., 825 65 J4
Säter, Swed. 120 C3
Satigny, Switz., 1,594 124 A2
Satilla, r., Ga. 64 H4
Satillieu, Fr., 2,198 117 F4
Satka, U.S.S.R., 45,500 134 E4
Sätkhira, Pak., 20,169 144 g14
Satna, India, 38,046 145 F4
Sato, Jap., 3,692 154 A6
Sato, Jap. 154 h15
Sato-Hami, Jap. 154 g14
Sátoraljaújhely, Hung., 16,197 126 E2
Satpura Ra., India 144 ·
Satrup, F.R.Ger., 1,750 118 B1
Satsop, Mid. Fk., r., Wash. 80 B2
Satsuma, Jap. 154 h14
Satsuma, Ala., 1,491 64 A5
Satsuma, Tex. 77 h9
Sattahip, Thai. 146 C4
Satte, Jap., 23,378 155 m18
Sattel, Switz., 1,012 124 C1
Sattler, Tex. 76 b6
Satuk, Thai. 146 C4
Satulung, Rum. 128 D1
Satu-Lung, Rum. 128 E2
Satu Mare, Rum., 52,096 128 D1
Satun, Thai., 4,369 146 B6
Satupa'itea, W. Samoa 177 38
Saturna I., Br. Col., Can. 42 c7
Satus Cr., Wash. 80 C2
Satyamangalam, India, 19,236 145 k20
Saualpe, Aust. 125 ·
Sauble, r., Ont., Can. 46 C4
Sauce, Arg., 8,500* 105 D4
Sauceda, Mex. 92 E3
Sauce de Luna, Arg., 1,500* 105 b10
Saucedo, Urug. 105 c10
Saucier, Miss. 73 F7
Saucillo, Chih., Mex., 6,820 92 D2
Saucillo, Qro., Mex. 93 e8
Sauda, Nor. 120 A4
Saudhárkrókur, Ice., 1,302 120 a6
Saudi Arabia, ctry., 6,750,000* 143
Sauer, r., F.R.Ger.-Fr. 119 E7
Sauer = Sûre
Sauerbrunn, Aust., 1,696 124 c11
Saugatuck (part of Westport), Conn. 56 C8
Saugatuck, Mich., 927 67 G6
Saugatuck, r., Conn. 56 C7
Saugatuck Res., Conn. 56 C7
Saugeen, r., Ont., Can. 46 C4
Saugerties, N.Y., 4,286 59 M7
Saughall, U.K., 1,518 114 C4
Saugues, Fr., 2,709 117 E4
Saugus, Calif. 83 g15
Saugus, Mass., 20,666(T) 57 M3
Sauherad, Nor. 121 B1
Saujon, Fr., 3,428 117 C4
Sauk, co., Wis., 36,179 66 D5
Sauk, r., Wash. 80 C1
Sauk Centre, Minn., 3,573 74 E3
Sauk City, Wis., 2,095 66 D5
Saukea, Terr. Papua 174 3
Sau Ki Wan, H.K., 136,184 152 b6
Saukorem, Indon. 149 K3
Sauk Rapids, Minn., 4,038 74 E3
Sauk Village, Ill., 5,774 69 d10
Saukville, Wis., 1,038 66 F5
Saül, Fr. Guiana 101 O6
Sauldre, r., Fr. 117 E3
Saulgau, F.R.Ger., 8,541 118 B4
Şăulia, Rum. 128 E1
Saulich, Alaska 85 a6
Saulieu, Fr., 3,511 117 F3
Saulnierville, N.S., Can. 45 M7
Saulsbury, Tenn., 141 71 B6
Sault-au-Mouton, Qué., Can. 47 R9
Sault Ste. Marie, Ont., Can., 42,354 44 F6
Sault Ste. Marie, Mich., 18,722 67 J2
Sault Ste. Marie Canals, Can.-U.S. 69 A
Saulzoir, Fr., 2,010 116 a7
Saumâtre, Étang, Haiti 96 m6
Saumlakki, Indon. 149 J4
Saumon, R. au, Qué., Can. 55 A3
Saumsville, Va. 62 F4
Saumur, Fr., 22,876 117 C3
Saunders, Kans. 75 D6
Saunders, co., Nebr., 17,270 75 J2
Saunders, Mt., Austl. 172 D1
Saunders, Pt., Austl. 172 C4
Saunders I., Falk. Is. 108 3
Saunderstown, R.I. 57 L6
Saunemin, Ill., 392 68 D3
Saupon Pt., Guam 176 24
Sauquoit, N.Y., 1,715 59 K5
Sauriwaunawa, Guyana 101 K6
Sausalito, Calif., 5,331 83 d12
Sausu, Indon. 149 G3
Sautatá, Col. 100 B4
Saut d'Eau = Ville Bonheur
Sauteurs, Gren. 97 18
Sauxillanges, Fr., 1,166 117 E4
Sauzal, Chile 104 e15
Sava, It., 15,912 123 F4
Sava, r., Yug. 125 C2
Savage, Md., 1,341 62 H3
Savage, Mont. 81 G2
Savaia, Terr. Papua 174 3
Savai'i, i., W. Samoa 177 37
Savalou, Dahom., 5,015 162 E4
Savana I., V.I. 97 4
Savaneta, Aruba 97 15
Savanna, Ill., 5,190 68 B1
Savanna, Okla., 620 76 H3
Savannah, Ga., 149,245 64 H3
Savannah, Mo., 2,455 72 C5
Savannah, N.Y., 602 59 G5
Savannah, Ohio, 409 70 G2
Savannah, Tenn., 4,315 71 C6
Savannah, r., Ga.-S.C. 63 C4
Savannah Beach, Ga., 1,385 64 J4
Savannah Sound, Bah. Is. 95 d7
Savannakhet, Laos 146 D3
Savanna-la-Mar, Jam., 9,789 96 o8
Savant Lake, Ont., Can. 44 D5
Savant L., Ont., Can. 44 D5
Savantvadi, India, 15,120 145 D7
Sävar, Swed. 120 E3
Savda, India, 13,124 144 a15
Savé, Dahom., 6,000* 162 E4
Säve, Swed. 121 D3
Save, r., Fr. 117 D5
Save, r., Moz. 164 E5
Säveh, Iran, 14,537 143 E1
Savelugu, Ghana 162 D4
Săveni, Rum. 128 F1
Saverne, Fr., 9,382 117 G2
Saverton, Mo. 72 F5
Savigliano, It., 17,752 123 A2
Savigneux, Fr., 1,586 117 E4
Savigny, Fr. 116 p15
Savigny-le-Temple, Fr. 116 i12
Savigny-sur-Braye, Fr., 2,282 117 D3
Savigny-sur-Orge, Fr., 24,333 116 h12
Saville Dam, Conn. 56 E5
Savinja, r., Yug. 125 B1
Săvîrşin, Rum. 128 D1
Šavnik, Yug. 125 D3
Savo, i., Sol. Is. 175 c3
Savoie, reg., Fr. 117 G4
Savona, It., 71,458 123 B2
Savona, N.Y., 904 58 F7
Savonet, Cur. 97 16
Savonlinna, Fin., 14,728 120 G3
Savonranta, Fin. 120 G3
Savoonga, Alaska 85 B3
Savoy = Savoie
Savoy, Ill., 339 68 D3
Savoy, Mass., 277(T) 56 D2
Savoy Center (part of Savoy), Mass. 56 D2
Sävsjö, Swed. 120 C4
Savukoski, Fin. 120 G2
Savur, Turk., 3,393 142 E2
Savusavu Bay, Fiji 174 4
Savu Sea, Indon. 149 G5
Saw, Burma, 1,277 146 A2
Sawabe, Jap. 155 G2
Sawaengna, Thai. 147 d4
Sawah, Indon. 148 E2
Sawahlunto, Indon., 12,276 148 B3
Sawai Madhopur, India, 20,952 144 a13
Sawākin, Sudan, 4,228 163 L2
Sawang Arom, Thai. 146 B3
Sawangtungku, Indon. 148 B3
Sawankhalok, Thai., 7,873 146 C3
Sawansaku, i., Kusaie 176 31
Sawara, Jap. 154 h15
Sawara, Jap., 49,564 155 G4
Sawara, Jap., 7,559 155 J8
Sawatch Mts., Colo. 50 E3
Sawayan Pt., Qué., Can. 44 H4
Sawazaki-bana, Jap. 155 E3
Sawbill, Man., Can. 43 E2
Sawbill, Newf., Can. 45 M4
Sawbill Landing, Minn. 74 G2
Sawbridgeworth, U.K., 4,634 114 J7
Sawdā', Jabal as, Libya 161 G3
Sawdirī, Sudan 163 J3
Sawe, Indon. 148 A2
Sawhāj, U.A.R., 62,000 161 K3
Sawla, Ghana 162 b7
Sawmill, Apache Co., Ariz. 78 D4
Sawmill, Gila Co., Ariz. 78 C5
Sawmill, r., Mass. 56 F2
Saw Mill, r., N.Y. 58 d12
Sawpit, Colo., 30 79 B3
Sawston, U.K., 3,277 114 J6
Sawtooth Range, Idaho 81 B3
Sawtry, U.K. 114 H6
Sawu, P., Indon. 149 G5
Şawwān, Tall aş, mound, Jor. 142 D4
Sawyer, Kans., 192 75 G6
Sawyer, Mich. 67 G7
Sawyer, N. Dak., 390 74 B1
Sawyer, Okla. 76 H3
Sawyer, co., Wis., 9,475 66 B3
Sawyers Bar, Calif. 82 B2
Sawyerville, Qué., Can. 47 N3
Saxapahaw, N.C. 63 E2
Saxby, r., Austl. 173 F2
Saxby All Saints, U.K. 114 H3
Saxe, Va. 62 F6
Saxeville, Wis. 66 D4
Saxilby, U.K. 114 G4
Saxis, Va., 577 62 J5
Saxman, Kans. 75 G5
Saxon, Calif. 82 a8
Saxon, Wis. 66 C2
Saxonburg, Pa., 876 60 C4
Saxony = Sachsen
Saxton, Pa., 977 60 F5
Saxtons, r., Vt. 54 B5
Saxtons River, Vt., 725 54 B5
Saxtorp, Swed. 121 b7
Say, Niger, 2,316 162 E3
Sayabec, Qué., Can., 2,243 45 M5
Sayaboury, Laos 146 C3
Sayapullo, Peru, 1,391 104 B3
Sayausí, Ec. 104 c11
Saybrook, Ill., 859 68 D3
Saybrook, Ohio 70 J1
Saybrook Manor (part of Old Saybrook), Conn. 56 G7
Saybrook Point, Conn. 56 G7
Sayda, Ger.D.R. 126 c6
Şaydā, Leb., 22,441 142 C3
Sayers, Tex. 76 b7
Sayers L., Austl. 173 d9
Saykhen-Daban, Per., U.S.S.R. 135 J4
Saylesville, R.I. 57 L5
Saylorsburg, Pa. 61 M4
Saymo L., Ont., Can. 46 A1
Sayner, Wis. 66 D3
Sayn Shanda, Mong. 150 E2
Sayo, Jap., 13,298 155 D4
Sayram, U.S.S.R. 137 f3
Sayre, Ala. 64 c7
Sayre, Ohio 70 G3
Sayre, Okla., 2,913 76 D2
Sayre, Pa., 7,917 60 J2
Sayreville, N.J., 22,553 61 C3
Sayre Woods, N.J. 58 b15
Sayula, Jal., Mex., 11,596 92 E4
Sayula, Ver. C., Mex., 4,107 93 G5
Say'ūn, S. Ar., 10,000* 143 D5
Sayville, N.Y. 59 O10
Saywers Hill, Newf., Can. 45 a10
Sayylyk, U.S.S.R. 135 L3
Sazan, i., Alb. 125 D4
Sázava, r., Czech. 126 B2
Scaër, Fr., 7,530 116 B2
Scafell Pike, mts., U.K. 113 E4
Scaggsville, Md. 62 b8
Scalasaig, U.K. 112 C3
Scalby, U.K., 7,251 113 F4
Scald Law, mtn., U.K. 112 d8
Scales Mound, Ill., 399 68 B1
Scalford, U.K. 114 G5
Scalloway, U.K. 112 F1
Scalpay, i., U.K. 112 C3
Scalpay, i., U.K. 112 D3
Scalp Level, Pa., 1,445 60 E5
Scaly, N.C. 63 A2
Scamander, Austl. 173 g13
Scammon, Kans., 429 75 L6
Scammon Bay, Alaska, 115 85 C3
Scandia, Kans., 643 75 H4
Scandinavia, Wis., 266 66 D4
Scandinavian Pen., Eur. 110 E2
Scandolara Ravara, It., 2,615 122 d5
Scanlon, Minn., 1,126 74 F2
Scanterbury, Man., Can. 43 h9
Scantic, Conn. 56 F5
Scantic, r., Conn. 56 F5
Scapa Flow, U.K. 112 E2
Scapegoat Mtn., Mont. 81 C2
Scappoose, Oreg., 923 80 B3
Scarba, i., U.K. 112 D3
Scarboro, Ga. 64 H3
Scarboro, Me. 55 B5
Scarborough, Ont., Can. 46 d13
Scarborough, Trin. and Tob., 15,000* 96 h4
Scarborough, U.K., 43,061 113 F4
Scargill, U.K. 112 g10
Scarinish, U.K. 112 C3
Scarisbrick, U.K., 2,952 114 C3
Scarp, i., U.K. 112 C2
Scarpe, r., Fr. 116 a7
Scarriff, Ire. 113 B5
Scarsdale, N.Y., 17,968 59 N10
Sceaux, Fr., 19,527 116 h11
Ščedro, i., Yug. 125 C3
Scenic, S. Dak. 74 A4
Sceptre, Sask., Can. 43 B5
Scey-sur-Saône, Fr., 1,442 117 F3
Schaafheim, F.R.Ger., 3,290 119 F5
Schaale, r., Ger.D.R. 118 C2
Schaalsee, F.R.Ger. 118 C2
Schaan, Liecht., 3,604 124 a8
Schaarbeek = Schaerbeek
Schaefferstown, Pa. 61 K5
Schaerbeek, Belg., 118,495 115 d9
Schaffer, Mich. 66 F3
Schaffhausen, Switz., 30,904 124 C1
Schafstädt, Ger.D.R. 126 a5
Schagen, Neth., 4,300 115 C2
Schaghticoke, N.Y., 720 59 w28
Schalbach, Fr. 116 d9
Schaller, Iowa, 896 72 B2
Schanck, C., Austl. 173 e12
Schangnau, Switz., 1,030 124 B2
Schänis, Switz., 2,328 124 D1
Schärding, Aust., 5,711 124 K5
Scharhörn, i., F.R.Ger. 118 B2
Schattdorf, Switz., 2,754 124 C2
Schattendorf, Aust., 2,526 124 N6
Schauenstein, F.R.Ger., 1,723 126 a6
Schaumburg Center, Ill., 986 69 b8
Scheessel, F.R.Ger., 4,102 118 B2
Schefferville, Qué., Can., 2,799 45 M3
Scheibbs, Aust., 3,228 124 L5
Scheiben, Aust. 124 L6
Scheinfeld, F.R.Ger., 2,481 118 C4
Schela, Rum. 128 D2
Schelde, r., Eur. 115 C3
Schell City, Mo., 343 72 C7
Schell Cr., N. Pk., Nev. 83 C3
Schell Cr. Ra., Nev. 83 C3
Schell Cr. S. Pk., Nev. 83 C3
Schellenberg, Liecht. 124 a8
Schellsburg, Pa., 288 60 E5
Schellville, Calif. 83 e11
Schenectady, co., N.Y., 152,896 59 M6
Schenectady, N.Y., 81,682 59 N6
Schenefeld, F.R.Ger., 7,058 119 a8
Schenevus, N.Y., 493 59 L6
Schenevus Cr., N.Y. 59 L6
Schenkenbrunn, Aust. 124 b10
Schenley, Pa. 60 d7
Schenob Bk., Mass. 56 C4
Schererville, Ind., 2,875 69 e10
Scherfede, F.R.Ger., 2,647 118 B3
Schermbeck, F.R.Ger., 1,796 119 B1
Scherpenheuvel, Belg., 5,925 115 C4
Scherpenzeel, Neth., 3,200 115 D2
Scherr, W. Va. 62 E3
Schertz, Tex., 2,281 77 O5
Scherzingen, Switz., 1,370 124 D1
Schesslitz, F.R.Ger., 1,833 118 C3
Scheveningen, Neth. 115 a6
Schicks Crossing, Ill. 69 b9
Schiedam, Neth., 75,400 115 C3
Schiefbahn, F.R.Ger., 6,532 119 B2
Schie kan., Neth. 115 a7
Schiermonnikoog, Neth. 115 E1
Schiermonnikoog, i., Neth. 115 E1
Schiers, Switz., 2,363 124 D2
Schifferstadt, F.R.Ger., 14,659 119 E6
Schijndel, Neth., 9,400 115 D3
Schildau Gneisenaustadt, Ger.D.R. 126 b5
Schildwolde, Neth. 115 E1
Schiller Park, Ill., 5,687 69 c9
Schiltern, Aust. 124 b9
Schiltigheim, Fr., 25,165 116 e9
Schinznach Dorf, Switz., 1,081 124 C1
Schio, It., 27,863 123 C2
Schipbeek, r., F.R.Ger.-Neth. 115 E2
Schipluiden, Neth. 115 a7
Schirgiswalde, Ger.D.R. 126 d5
Schirmeck, Fr., 2,415 117 G2
Schitu-Goleşti, Rum. 128 E2
Schkeuditz, Ger.D.R., 18,300 118 D3
Schkölen, Ger.D.R. 126 a5
Schladming, Aust., 3,250 124 K6
Schlarigna = Celerina
Schlei, r., F.R.Ger. 118 B1
Schleicher, co., Tex., 2,791 77 N4
Schleiden, F.R.Ger., 3,087 118 A3
Schleithal, Fr., 1,473 119 E7
Schleiz, Ger.D.R. 118 C3
Schleswig, F.R.Ger., 32,616 118 B1
Schleswig, Iowa, 785 72 B2
Schleswig-Holstein, st. F.R.Ger., 2,406,000* 118 B1
Schlettau, Ger.D.R. 126 c6
Schleusingen, Ger.D.R. 118 C3
Schley, co., Ga., 3,256 64 E3
Schley, Va. 62 H5
Schlieben, Ger.D.R., 2,402 118 D3
Schlieren, Switz., 10,043 124 C1
Schliersee, F.R.Ger., 6,036 118 C5
Schlitz, F.R.Ger., 4,895 118 B3
Schlotheim, Ger.D.R., 5,527 118 C3
Schlüchtern, F.R.Ger., 5,773 118 B3
Schlüsselfeld, F.R.Ger. 118 C4
Schmalkalden, Ger.D.R., 14,022 118 C3
Schmallenberg, F.R.Ger., 3,910 119 E2
Schmelz, F.R.Ger., 6,356 116 c8
Schmiden, F.R.Ger., 5,013 119 G7
Schmölln, Ger.D.R., 13,827 118 D3
Schneeberg, Ger.D.R., 21,595 118 D3
Schneeberg, F.R.Ger. 118 C3
Schneekoppe, pk., Czech.-Pol. 126 B1
Schneider, Ind., 405 70 B1
Schneiders Prairie, Wash. 81 a8
Schneifel, mts., F.R.Ger. 119 A4
Schneverdingen, F.R.Ger., 5,910 118 B2
Schodack Landing, N.Y. 59 N7
Schöder, Aust., 1,133 124 K6
Schoelcher, Mart. 97 12
Schoenchen, Kans., 188 75 F5
Schofield, Wis., 3,038 66 D4
Schofield Barracks, Hawaii 84 b7
Schoharie, co., N.Y., 22,616 59 L6
Schoharie, N.Y., 1,168 59 M6
Schoharie Cr., N.Y. 59 M6
Schoharie Res., N.Y. 59 M7
Scholle, N. Mex. 79 B4
Schöllkrippen, F.R.Ger., 1,710 119 G4
Schomberg, Ont., Can. 46 E4
Schönaich, F.R.Ger., 5,088 119 G7
Schönberg, Ger.D.R. 118 C2
Schondra, F.R.Ger. 119 H4
Schönebeck, Ger.D.R., 44,366 118 C2
Schöneberg, F.R.Ger., 1,325 119 C3
Schönecken, F.R.Ger., 1,145 118 A3
Schöneiche, Ger.D.R., 10,790 119 f11
Schönenwerd, Switz., 4,561 124 B1
Schönewalde, Ger.D.R. 118 D3
Schongau, F.R.Ger., 7,629 118 C5
Schönhausen, Ger.D.R. 118 D2
Schönholthausen, F.R.Ger., 10,724 119 D2
Schöningen, F.R.Ger., 16,103 118 C2
Schönkirchen, Aust. 124 d10
Schönningstedt, F.R.Ger., 3,720 119 b8
Schoodic L., Me. 55 D3
Schoodic Pt., Me. 55 D4
Schoolcraft, co., Mich., 8,953 67 G2
Schoolcraft, Mich., 1,205 67 H6
Schooleys Mtn., N.J. 61 B2
Schoolmarm Mtn., Colo. 79 a9
Schoolton, Okla. 76 G2
Schoonebeek, Neth. 115 F2
Schoonhoven, Neth., 6,100 115 C3
Schopp, F.R.Ger., 1,044 119 D6
Schorndorf, F.R.Ger., 15,913 119 H7
Schottegat, Inlet, Cur. 97 16
Schotten, F.R.Ger., 3,434 119 G3
Schottwien, Aust. 124 M6
Schötz, Switz., 1,890 124 B1
Schouten, Kep., Indon. 149 K3
Schouten I., Austl. 173 g14
Schouten Is., Terr. New Guin. 174 e1
Schouwen, i., Neth. 115 B3
Schrader Cr., Pa. 60 J2
Schramberg, F.R.Ger., 17,544 118 B4
Schram City, Ill., 698 68 C4
Schraplau, Ger.D.R. 126 a5
Schreiber, Ont., Can., 2,230 44 E5
Schrems, Aust., 3,077 124 M5
Schrick, Aust. 124 d9
Schriesheim, F.R.Ger., 6,758 119 F6
Schrobenhausen, F.R.Ger., 8,264 118 C4
Schroeder, Minn. 74 G2
Schroeder, Tex. 77 P5
Schroon Lake, N.Y. 59 N4
Schroon L., N.Y. 59 N4
Schrozberg, F.R.Ger., 2,242 118 B4
Schruns, Aust., 3,281 124 G6
Schübelbach, Switz., 3,206 124 C1
Schulenburg, Tex., 2,207 77 P5
Schuler, Alta., Can. 42 L4
Schuls = Scuol
Schulter, Okla. 76 G2
Schulzendorf, Ger.D.R. 118 D2
Schüpfheim, Switz., 3,771 124 C2
Schurz, Nev. 83 A3
Schussen, r., F.R.Ger. 118 B5
Schussenried, F.R.Ger., 5,006 118 B4
Schutterwald, F.R.Ger., 4,272 118 A4
Schuyler, co., Ill., 8,746 68 B3
Schuyler, co., Mo., 5,052 72 E4
Schuyler, Nebr., 3,096 75 H2
Schuyler, co., N.Y., 15,044 58 F7
Schuyler, Va. 62 F5
Schuyler Falls, N.Y. 59 O2
Schuyler Lake, N.Y. 59 L6
Schuylerville, N.Y., 1,361 59 N5
Schuylkill, co., Pa., 173,027 61 K4
Schuylkill, r., Pa. 61 L5
Schuylkill Haven, Pa., 6,470 61 K4
Schwaan, Ger.D.R. 118 C2
Schwabach, F.R.Ger., 21,438 118 C4
Schwäbische Alb, mts., F.R.Ger. 118 B4
Schwäbisch Gmünd, F.R.Ger., 36,046 118 B4
Schwäbisch Hall, F.R.Ger., 20,229 118 B4
Schwabmünchen, F.R.Ger., 6,380 118 C4
Schwägalp, Switz. 124 D1
Schwaigern, F.R.Ger., 3,635 119 F6
Schwaikheim, F.R.Ger., 4,205 119 G7
Schwalm, r., F.R.Ger. 119 A2
Schwanberg, Aust., 1,474 124 M7
Schwanden, Switz., 3,020 124 D1
Schwändi, Switz. 124 D1
Schwandorf, F.R.Ger., 14,634 118 D4
Schwanebeck, Ger.D.R. 119 f10
Schwarmstedt, F.R.Ger., 2,964 118 B2
Schwarz Bach, r., F.R.Ger. 119 D6
Schwarzbach, r., F.R.Ger. 119 F5
Schwarze Elster, r., Ger.D.R. 118 D3
Schwarzenbach, F.R.Ger., 7,467 118 D3
Schwarzenbek, F.R.Ger., 7,282 118 C2
Schwarzenberg, Ger.D.R., 14,877 118 D3
Schwarzenburg, Switz. 124 B2
Schwarzenfeld, F.R.Ger., 4,773 118 D4
Schwarzensee, Aust. 124 c11
Schwarzwald, mts., F.R.Ger. 118 B4
Schwatka Mts., Alaska 85 E2
Schwaz, Aust., 9,467 124 H6
Schwechat, Aust., 13,404 124 N5
Schwedt, Ger.D.R. 118 E2
Schweich, F.R.Ger., 4,159 119 B5
Schweiggers, Aust. 124 L5
Schweighouse-sur-Moder, Fr., 2,640 116 e9
Schweinfurt, F.R.Ger., 52,774 118 B3
Schwelm, F.R.Ger., 32,422 119 C2
Schwenksville, Pa., 620 60 f10
Schwenningen, F.R.Ger., 29,280 118 B4
Schwepnitz, Ger.D.R. 126 d5
Schwerin, Ger.D.R., 92,508 118 C2
Schweriner See, Ger.D.R. 118 C2
Schwerte, F.R.Ger., 23,654 119 D2
Schwetzingen, F.R.Ger., 14,749 119 F6
Schweyen, Fr. 116 d8
Schwielow-See, Ger.D.R. 119 d11
Schwyz, Switz., 11,007 124 C1
Sciacca, It., 32,006 123 D6
Science Hill, Ky., 463 71 G4
Scilly, atoll, Soc. Is. 177 42
Scilly, Is. of, U.K. 113 C7
Ścinawa, Pol., 3,125 127 f5
Ścinawa, r., Pol. 127 g6
Ścinawa Mała, Pol. 127 g6
Scînteia, Rum. 128 F1
Scio, N.Y. 58 E7
Scio, Ohio, 1,135 70 H2
Scio, Oreg., 441 80 B3
Sciota, Ill., 120 68 B3
Scioto, co., Ohio, 84,216 70 F4
Scioto, r., Ohio 70 F2
Sciotodale, Ohio, 1,113 70 G4
Scipio, Ind. 70 D3
Scipio, Okla. 76 G2
Scipio, Utah, 328 78 B2
Scitico (part of Enfield), Conn. 56 F5
Scituate, Mass., 3,229;11,214(T) 57 O4
Scituate Center (part of Scituate), Mass. 57 O4
Scituate Res., R.I. 57 K5
Scoarţa, Rum. 128 D2
Scobey, Mont., 1,726 81 G1
Scofield, Mich. 67 e16
Scofield, Utah, 158 78 C2
Scone, Austl., 3,351 173 G5
Scone, U.K., 2,559 112 d7
Sconticut Pt., Mass. 57 N6
Scooba, Miss., 513 73 G5
Scorpion Bight, Austl. 172 C5
Scorţeni, Rum. 128 F1
Scorton, Lancs., Eng., U.K. 114 C3
Scorton, York., Eng., U.K. 112 g11
Scorzè, It., 9,791 122 f5
Scossa, Nev. 83 A2
Scotch Plains, N.J., 18,491(T) 58 b14
Scotia, Ont., Can. 46 E3
Scotia, Calif., 1,122 82 B2
Scotia, Nebr., 350 75 G2
Scotia, N.Y., 7,625 59 M6
Scotia, S.C., 102 63 C5
Scotia Bay, Br. Col., Can. 42 C1
Scotia Ridge, Atl. Oc. 109 K10
Scotia Sea, Atl. Oc. 99 D8
Scotland, Ont., Can. 46 D5
Scotland, U.K., 5,204,000* 112 D3
Scotland, Ark. 73 C2
Scotland, Conn., 684(T) 56 H6
Scotland, Ga., 236 64 G3
Scotland (part of Bridgewater), Mass. 57 N5
Scotland, co., Mo., 6,484 72 E4
Scotland, co., N.C., 25,183 63 E3
Scotland, Pa. 60 G6
Scotland, S. Dak., 1,077 74 D4
Scotland Neck, N.C., 2,974 63 G1
Scotlandville, La. 73 D7
Scotstown, Qué., Can., 1,023 45 L6
Scott, Ant. 180 V5
Scott, Sask., Can. 43 B4
Scott, co., Ark., 7,297 73 A3
Scott, Ark. 73 C3
Scott, Ga., 149 64 G3
Scott, co., Ill., 6,377 68 B4
Scott, co., Ind., 14,643 70 D4
Scott, Ind. 70 D1
Scott, co., Iowa, 119,067 72 G3
Scott, co., Kans., 5,228 75 E5
Scott, co., Ky., 15,376 71 G3
Scott, co., Minn., 21,909 74 F3
Scott, co., Miss., 21,187 73 F5
Scott, Miss. 73 D4
Scott, co., Mo., 32,748 72 H7
Scott, N.Y. 59 H6
Scott, Ohio, 365 70 E2
Scott, co., Tenn., 15,413 71 G5
Scott, co., Va., 25,813 62 B6
Scott, Mt., Oreg. 80 C4
Scott Bay, Lesser Caymans 97 2
Scottburgh, S. Af., 1,708 164 E7
Scott City, Kans., 3,555 75 E5
Scott City, Mo., 1,963 72 H7
Scottdale, Ga. 64 g9
Scottdale, Pa., 6,244 60 C5
Scott I., Ant. 180 W6
Scott Is., Br. Col., Can. 42 E4
Scott L., N.W.T.-Sask., Can. 43 C2
Scott Reef, Austl. 172 B2
Scotts, Mich. 67 H6
Scotts Bluff, co., Nebr., 33,809 75 B2
Scottsbluff, Nebr., 13,377 75 B2
Scotts Bluff Nat. Mon., Nebr. 75 B2
Scottsboro, Ala., 6,449 64 D1
Scottsburg, Ind., 3,810 70 D4
Scottsburg, N.Y. 58 E6
Scottsburg, Oreg. 80 A4
Scottsburg, Va., 188 62 F6
Scottsdale, Austl., 1,462 173 f13
Scottsdale, Ariz., 54,504 78 C5
Scotts Head, pt., Dominica 97 13
Scotts Hill, N.C. 63 G3
Scotts Hill, Tenn., 298 71 C6
Scotts Mills, Oreg., 155 80 B3
Scottsmoor, Fla. 65 J4
Scotts Valley, Calif. 83 f13
Scottsville, Ky., 3,324 71 E5
Scottsville, N.Y., 1,863 58 E5
Scottsville, Va., 353 62 F5
Scottville, Ill., 186 68 B4
Scottville, Mich., 1,245 67 G5
Scottville, N.C. 63 C1
Scourie, U.K. 112 D2
Scrabster, U.K. 112 E2
Scraggly L., Me. 55 D2
Scranton, Iowa, 865 72 C2
Scranton, Kans., 576 75 K5
Scranton, N.Y., 1,078 58 k19
Scranton, N. Dak., 358 74 A2
Scranton, Pa., 111,443 61 L3
Scranton, S.C., 613 63 E4
Scraper-Moecherville, Ill. 69 a10
Screven, co., Ga., 14,919 64 H3
Screven, Ga., 1,010 64 H4
Screw Auger Falls, Me. 54 F2
Scriba, N.Y. 59 H5
Scribner, Nebr., 1,021 75 J2
Scridain, Loch, U.K. 112 C3
Scrivia, r., It. 122 b6
Scrub I., Lesser Ant. 97 7
Scrub I., V.I. 97 4
Scugog, L., Ont., Can. 46 F4
Scullin, Okla., 27 76 G3
Sculthorpe, U.K., 3,238 113 G5
Scunthorpe, U.K., 67,324 113 F5
Scuol, Switz., 1,429 124 E2
Scurrival Pt., U.K. 112 C3
Scurry, co., Tex., 20,369 77 N3
Scurry, Tex. 76 g10
Scusciuban, Som. Rep., 1,318* 163 N4
Scutari = Shkodër
Scutari, L., Alb.-Yug. 125 D3
Seabeck, Wash. 80 B2
Seaboard, N.C., 624 63 G1
Sea Breeze, N.Y. 58 n20
Sea Bright, N.J., 1,138 61 D3
Seabrook, Ga. 64 H4
Seabrook, N.H. 54 F6
Seabrook, N.J., 1,798 61 A5
Seabrook, Tex. 77 k9
Seabrook, L., Austl. 172 B4
Sea Cliff, N.Y., 5,669 58 e13
Seadrift, Tex., 1,082 77 P6
Seaford, Del., 4,430 62 J4
Seaford, N.Y., 14,718 58 f14
Seaford, Va. 62 H5
Seaforth, Ont., Can., 2,272 44 G7
Sea Girt, N.J., 1,798 61 D3
Seagoville, Tex., 3,745 76 g9
Seagraves, Tex., 2,307 77 M3
Seagrove, N.C., 323 63 E2
Seagrove Beach, Fla. 65 C2
Seaham, U.K., 26,048 113 F4
Sea Island, Ga. 64 H4
Sea Isle City, N.J., 1,393 61 B5
Seal, r., Man., Can. 43 F2
Sea Lake, Austl. 173 d10
Sealark Chan., Sol. Is. 175 c3

292 · Seal Beach—Shag Rocks

Seal Beach, Calif., 6,994 83 h16
Seal Cove, N.B., Can. 47 S11
Seale, Ala. 64 D3
Sealevel, N.C. 63 H3
Sea Lion I., Falk. Is. 108 3
Seal I., N.S., Can. 45 M7
Seal I., Lesser Ant. 97 7
Seal L., Newf., Can. 45 O3
Seal Rock, Oreg. 80 A3
Sealy, Tex., 2,328 77 P5
Seaman, Ohio, 714 70 F4
Seamer, U.K., 1,205 114 H2
Searchlight, Nev. 83 C5
Searchmont, Ont., Can. 44 G6
Searcy, co., Ark., 8,124 73 C2
Searcy, Ark., 7,272 73 D2
Searles, Ala. 64 a8
Searles L., Calif. 82 E5
Sears, Mich. 67 H5
Searsboro, Iowa, 165 72 E3
Searsburg, Vt. 54 A6
Searsmont, Me. 55 C4
Searsport, Me. 55 D4
Seascale, U.K., 1,328 113 E4
Seaside, Calif., 19,353 82 C4
Seaside, Oreg., 3,877 80 B3
Seaside Heights, N.J., 954 61 C4
Seaside Park, N.J., 1,054 61 C4
Seaton, Ill., 235 68 B2
Seaton Delaval, U.K. 112 h9
Seat Pleasant, Md., 5,365 62 b9
Seattle, Wash., 557,087 80 B2
Seattle, Mt., Can.-U.S. 85 K3
Seaview, Va. 62 J5
Seaview, Wash. 80 A2
Seba, Indon. 149 G5
Seba Beach, Alta., Can. 42 J3
Sébaco, Nic., 1,652 94 D4
Sebago, Me. 55 B5
Sebago Lake, Me. 55 B5
Sebago L., Me. 55 B5
Sebakung, Indon. 148 F3
Sebanga, Indon. 148 B2
Sebangan, Teluk, Indon. 148 E3
Sebangka, P., Indon. 148 C2
Sebasco Estates, Me. 55 C5
Sebastian, co., Ark., 66,685 73 A2
Sebastian, Fla., 698 65 J5
Sebastián Elcano, Arg., 1,700* 105 C4
Sebastián Vizcaíno, B., Mex. 92 B2
Sebasticook L., Me. 55 C4
Sebastopol, Austl., 3,265 173 d11
Sebastopol, Calif., 2,694 82 B3
Sebastopol, Miss., 343 73 F5
Sebastopol, Tex. 77 Q4
Sebauh, Malay. 148 E2
Sebba, Upper Volta, 2,045 162 E3
Sebdou, Alg., 8,039 160 D2
Sebec, Me. 55 C3
Sebec Lake, Me. 55 C3
Sebec L., Me. 55 C3
Sebedau, Indon. 148 D3
Sebeka, Minn., 823 74 E2
Sebeş, Rum., 11,628 128 D2
Sebesi, P., Indon. 148 a6
Sebewaing, Mich., 2,026 67 K5
Sebezh, U.S.S.R., 7,200 136 C1
Şebinkarahisar, Turk., 8,771 142 D1
Sebiş, Rum. 128 D1
Seblat, Indon. 148 B3
Sebnitz, Ger.D.R., 14,782 118 E3
Seboeis, Me. 55 D3
Seboeis, r., Me. 55 D2
Seboeis, r., Me. 55 D3
Seboeis L., Me. 55 D2
Seboeis L., Me. 55 D3
Seboomook L., Me. 55 C3
Seboruco, Ven., 2,422 100 D3
Sebree, Ky., 1,139 71 D4
Sebrell, Va. 62 G6
Sebring, Fla., 6,939 65 H5
Sebring, Ohio, 4,439 70 J2
Sebringville, Ont., Can. 46 C5
Sebuku, P., Indon. 148 a6
Sebuku, P., Indon. 148 F3
Sebutuia, Terr. Papua 174 3
Sebuyau, Malay., 1,901 148 D2
Seč, Czech. 127 e7
Secaucus, N.J., 12,154 58 c13
Secchia, r., It. 123 C2
Secemin, Pol. 127 i6
Sechelt, Br. Col., Can. 42 F4
Sechtem, F.R.Ger., 8,567 119 B3
Sechura, Peru, 5,137 104 A3
Sechura, Des. de, Peru 104 A3
Seckach, F.R.Ger., 1,668 119 G6
Seckach, r., F.R.Ger. 119 G6
Seckau, Aust., 1,242 124 L6
Seclin, Fr., 9,459 116 a6
Seco, Ky., 531 71 J4
Seco, r., Mex. 92 C1
Second Cataract, Sudan 163 K2
Second Connecticut L., N.H. 54 E1
Secondigny, Fr., 2,053 117 C3
Second L., Me. 55 D2
Second Nasab Slough, Calif. 83 e11
Secor, Ill., 427 68 C3
Secos, Ilhêus=Rombo, Ilhéus do
Secourt, Fr. 116 b9
Sečovce, Czech. 126 E2
Secretary, Md., 351 62 H4
Secretary I., N.Z. 175 e7
Section, Ala., 595 64 D1
Secunderabad, India, 78,412 145 F6
Sécure, r., Bol. 102 b9
Security, Colo., 9,017 79 C2
Sedalia, Colo. 79 C2
Sedalia, Ky., 258 71 C5
Sedalia, Mo., 23,874 72 D6
Sedan, Fr., 21,766 117 F2
Sedan, Kans., 1,677 75 J6
Sedan, N. Mex. 79 D3
Sedanka I., Alaska 85 C5
Sedano, Sp. 122 D1
Sedari, Tg., Indon. 148 b6
Sedaw, Burma 147 f6
Sedaw, Burma 147 g6
Sedbergh, U.K., 2,330 114 D2
Seddon, N.Z. 175 g6
Sederot, Isr. 142 a8
Sedgeberrow, U.K. 114 D6
Sedgefield, U.K., 4,748 112 h10
Sedgewick, Alta., Can. 42 K3
Sedgewickville, Mo., 91 72 G7
Sedgwick, co., Colo., 4,242 79 D1
Sedgwick, Colo., 299 79 D1
Sedgwick, co., Kans., 343,231 75 H6
Sedgwick, Kans., 1,095 75 H6
Sedgwick, Me. 55 D4
Sedhiou, Sen., 2,419 162 B3
Sedjaka, Indon. 148 F3
Sedlčany, Czech. 126 B2
Sedley, Sask., Can. 43 D5
Sedley, Ind. 69 f10
Sedley, Va. 62 H6
Sedom, Isr. 142 b8
Sedona, Ariz. 78 C4
Sedova, Pik, U.S.S.R. 134 E2
Sedrata, Alg., 10,327 160 e5
Sedro Woolley, Wash., 3,705 80 B1
Sedrun, Switz. 124 C2
Sędziszów, Pol., 2,789 127 D3
Seebert, W. Va. 62 D4
Seeboden, Aust., 3,348 124 K7
Seefeld, Aust., 1,800 124 H6
Seehausen, Ger.D.R. 118 C2
Seeheim, F.R.Ger., 4,076 119 F5
Seeheim, S.-W. Afr. 164 C6
Seekonk, Mass., 8,399(T) 57 L5
Seeley, Wis. 66 B2
Seeley Lake, Mont. 81 C2
Seelow, Ger.D.R. 118 E2
Seelyville, Ind., 1,114 70 B3
Sées, Fr., 4,592 117 D2
Seesen, F.R.Ger., 11,557 118 C3
Seetaler Alpen, Aust. 125 •
Seetanga, Tutuila 177 39
Seeve, r., F.R.Ger. 119 b9
Seez, r., Switz. 124 D1
Seffner, Fla. 65 d12
Sefrou, Mor., 21,478 160 D2
Segama, r., Malay. 153 A4
Segamat, Malay., 18,451 148 B2
Segarcea, Rum. 128 D2
Ségbana, Dahom., 1,224 162 E4
Segesta, ruins, It. 123 D6
Seget, Indon. 149 J3
Segezha, U.S.S.R., 21,000 134 C3
Seghill, U.K. 112 g9
Segl=Sils im Engadin
Segni, It., 9,158 123 b8
Sego, Ohio 70 G3
Sego, Utah 78 D2
Segorbe, Sp., 7,538 122 E3
Ségou, Mali, 29,000 162 C3
Segovia, Col. 100 C4
Segovia, Sp., 33,360 122 C2
Segovia, Tex. 77 O4
Segovia=Coco
Segré, Fr., 5,800 117 C3
Segre, r., Sp. 122 F1
Segreganset (part of Dighton), Mass. 57 M5
Seguam I., Alaska 85 g8
Seguam Pass, Alaska 85 g8
Seguédine, Niger 162 G2
Séguéla, Iv. Coast, 4,620 162 C4
Seguí, Arg., 3,500* 105 a10
Seguin, Kans. 75 E4
Seguin, Tex., 14,299 77 P5
Seguntur, Indon. 148 F2
Segura, r., Sp. 122 D3
Sehore, India, 28,489 145 E5
Sehwān, Pak., 4,169 144 C4
Seia, Port., 3,457 122 B2
Seiad Valley, Calif. 82 B2
Seibersdorf, Aust. 124 c11
Seibert, Colo., 210 79 D2
Şeica Mare, Rum. 128 E1
Seiches, Fr., 2,260 117 C3
Seighford, U.K., 1,178 114 D5
Seigling, S.C. 63 C4
Seignelay, r., Qué., Can. 45 L4
Seikpyu, Burma 146 A2
Seil, i., U.K. 112 D3
Seiland, i., Nor. 120 E1
Seiling, Okla., 910 76 E1
Seillans, Fr. 116 m13
Seille, r., Fr. 116 b9
Seille, r., Fr. 117 F3
Sein, Î. de, Fr. 116 A2
Seinäjoki, Fin., 15,834 120 E3
Seine, r., Man., Can. 43 h10
Seine, r., Ont., Can. 74 G1
Seine, r., Fr. 117 D2
Seine, B. de la, Fr. 116 •
Seine Bight Village, Br. Hond. 94 C2
Seine-Port, Fr., 1,075 116 i12
Seini, Rum. 128 D1
Seixal, Port., 4,036 122 i10
Sejerø, i., Den. 121 D5
Sejerø Bugt, Den. 121 D5
Sejny, Pol., 2,486 127 E1
Sekaju, Indon. 148 C3
Seke, Tanz. 165 f15
Sekenke, Tanz. 164 E2
Seki, Jap. 154 f14
Seki, Jap., 8,554 154 h15
Seki, Jap., 43,187 155 E4
Seki, Jap. 155 n20
Sekinchang, Malay., 4,605 147 o15
Sekiu, Wash. 80 A1
Sekodi, Indon. 147 p16
Sekondi, Ghana, 34,323 162 D5
Selah, Wash., 2,824 80 C2
Selama, Malay., 3,355 147 o14
Selandar, Malay., 1,010 147 p15
Selangor, r., Malay. 147 o15
Selaön, i., Swed. 120 e8
Selaru, P., Indon. 149 J5
Selatan, Tg., Indon. 148 E4
Selatan Timur, Kep., Indon. 149 J4
Selatpampang, Indon. 148 D3
Selawik, Alaska, 348 85 E2
Selawik L., Alaska 85 D2
Selb, F.R.Ger., 19,083 118 D3
Selbitz, F.R.Ger., 3,973 126 a6
Selborne, U.K., 1,034 113 k12
Selbu, Nor. 120 B3
Selby, U.K., 9,869 113 F5
Selby, S. Dak., 979 74 C3
Selbyville, Del., 1,080 62 J4
Selca, Yug. 125 B1
Selçuk, Turk., 9,097 142 A2
Selden, Kans., 347 75 E4
Selden, Me. 55 E3
Selden, N.Y., 1,604 58 g13
Seldovia, Alaska, 460 85 F4
Sele, r., It. 123 E4
Selemdzha, r., U.S.S.R. 135 N4
Selenduma, U.S.S.R. 135 K4
Selenga, r., U.S.S.R. 135 K4
Selenge, r., Mong. 150 E1
Selennyakh, r., U.S.S.R. 135 O3
Selenter See, F.R.Ger. 118 C1
Sélestat, Fr., 14,049 117 G2
Selety, r., U.S.S.R. 137 o11
Seletytengiz, Oz., U.S.S.R. 137 o11
Seleucia, ruins, Iraq 143 C2
Selfoss, Ice., 1,597 120 a6
Selfridge, N. Dak., 371 74 B2
Sélibaby, Maur., 2,800 162 C3
Selidovo, U.S.S.R., 15,700 136 e7
Seligenstadt, F.R.Ger., 9,126 119 F4
Seliger, Oz., U.S.S.R. 136 D1
Seligman, Ariz. 78 B4
Seligman, Mo., 387 72 D8
Selimbau, Indon. 148 E2
Selimiye, Turk. 142 B2
Seling Tsho, China 150 C4
Selinsgrove, Pa., 3,948 60 J4
Selinunte, ruins, It. 123 D6
Selizharovo, U.S.S.R., 4,500 136 D1
Selkirk, Man., Can. 43 F5
Selkirk, Ont., Can. 46 E6
Selkirk, co., U.K., 21,055 112 E4
Selkirk, U.K., 5,634 112 E4
Selkirk, Kans. 75 D5
Selkirk, Mich. 67 J4
Selkirk, N.Y. 59 v29
Selkirk Mts., Br. Col., Can. 42 H3
Selle, Massif de la, mts., Haiti 96 k6
Selleck, Wash. 80 C2
Sellers, Ill. 68 D3
Sellers, S.C., 431 63 E3
Sellersburg, Ind., 2,679 70 D4
Sellersville, Pa., 2,497 60 f10
Selles-sur-Cher, Fr., 3,886 117 D3
Selliá, Gr. 129 E7
Sellore I., Burma 146 B4
Sells, Ariz. 78 C6
Sellye, Hung., 2,517 126 C4
Selm, F.R.Ger., 13,705 119 C1
Selma, Ala., 28,385 64 B3
Selma, Ark. 73 D4
Selma, Calif., 6,934 82 D4
Selma, Kans. 75 K5
Selma, Miss. 73 D6
Selma, N.C., 3,102 63 F2
Selma, Oreg. 80 B4
Selma, Tex. 76 b6
Selmah, N.S., Can. 47 U11
Selman, Okla. 76 D1
Selmer, Tenn., 1,897 71 C6
Selongey, Fr., 1,774 117 F3
Selsey, U.K., 4,007 113 m13
Selsey Bill, pt., U.K. 113 m13
Selston, U.K., 9,904 114 F4
Selters, F.R.Ger., 1,753 119 D3
Sel'tsy, U.S.S.R. 136 c6
Seltz, Fr., 2,150 117 G2
Selukwe, Rhod., 3,960 164 E5
Selva, It., 2,356 122 e5
Selvagens, is., Madeira Is. 109 4
Selvas, reg., Braz. 98 C3
Selvazzano Dentro, It., 5,712 122 e5
Selvin, Ind. 70 B4
Selway, r., Idaho 81 B3
Selwyn L., N.W.T.-Sask., Can. 43 C1
Selwyn Mts., Yukon, Can. 40 C5
Selwyn Range, Austl. 172 E3
Selwyn Str., New Hebr. 174 m6
Selz, N. Dak. 74 C2
Selz, r., F.R.Ger. 119 E5
Selzach, Switz., 2,636 124 B1
Sem, Nor. 121 C1
Seman, r., Alb. 125 D4
Semans, Sask., Can. 43 D4
Semanu, Indon. 148 D5
Semara, Sp. Sah. 160 C3
Semarang, Indon., 503,153 148 D4
Semaria, India 144 c13
Sembabule, Uganda 165 e14
Sembé, Congo 164 B1
Sembodjalama, Indon. 148 F3
Sembrancher, Switz. 124 B2
Sembrong, r., Malay. 147 p15
Semënov, U.S.S.R., 19,800 136 G1
Semënovka, U.S.S.R., 10,300 136 D2
Semënovskiy, O., U.S.S.R. 135 N2
Semenyih, Malay., 5,450 148 B2
Semichi Is., Alaska 85 d8
Semidi Is., Alaska 85 E4
Semikarakorskiy, U.S.S.R. 136 g8
Semiling, Malay., 1,930 147 o14
Semiluki, U.S.S.R., 13,400 136 E3
Semily, Czech., 6,989 127 e6
Seminary, Miss., 288 73 F6
Seminoe Res., Wyo. 81 F4
Seminole, co., Fla., 54,947 65 H4
Seminole, co., Ga., 6,802 64 E5
Seminole, co., Okla., 28,066 76 G2
Seminole, Okla., 11,464 76 G2
Seminole, Tex., 5,737 77 M3
Seminole, L., Fla.-Ga. 64 D5
Seminole, L., Fla. 65 c12
Semipalatinsk, U.S.S.R., 177,000 134 H4
Semirara Is., Phil. 153 B3
Semisopochnoi I., Alaska 85 f8
Semitau, Indon. 148 E2
Semiyarskoye, U.S.S.R. 137 p12
Semmaya, Jap., 7,168 155 G2
Semna, Sudan 163 K2
Semnān, Iran, 29,036 143 E1
Semo, Indon. 149 H3
Semois, r., Belg. 115 D5
Semora, N.C. 63 E1
Sempachersee, Switz. 124 C1
Semriach, Aust., 1,774 124 M6
Sem Tripa, Braz. 103 F2
Semur-en-Auxios, Fr., 4,167 117 F3
Sen, r., Camb. 146 D4
Sena, Bol. 102 C4
Sena, Moz. 164 E4
Sena, Thai., 5,201 147 d4
Senado, Cuba, 1,314 96 e2
Senador Firmino, Braz., 2,073 103 e17
Senador Pompeu, Braz., 8,210 103 J3
Senai, Malay., 3,782 147 p16
Senaja, Malay. 148 F1
Senajo, Indon. 149 L5
Sena Madureira, Braz., 1,962 102 C3
Senanayaka Samudra, l., Cey. 145 n22
Senanga, Zambia 164 C4
Senath, Mo., 1,369 72 G8
Senatobia, Miss., 3,259 73 F3
Senda, Jap. 154 e15
Sendai, Jap., 61,322 154 B6
Sendai, Jap., 425,272 155 G2
Senden, F.R.Ger., 4,087 119 C1
Sendenhorst, F.R.Ger., 3,848 119 D1
Senebui, Indon. 147 o15
Senec, Czech. 126 C2
Seneca, Ariz. 78 C5
Seneca, Ill., 1,719 68 D2
Seneca, Kans., 2,072 75 K4
Seneca, Mich. 67 J7
Seneca, Mo., 1,478 72 C8
Seneca, Nebr., 160 75 E1
Seneca, N. Mex. 79 D3
Seneca, co., N.Y., 31,984 58 G6
Seneca, co., Ohio, 59,326 70 F1
Seneca, Oreg. 80 D3
Seneca, Pa. 60 C3
Seneca, S.C., 5,227 63 B3
Seneca, S. Dak., 161 74 C3
Seneca, Wis. 66 B5
Seneca, r., N.Y. 59 q23
Seneca Castle, N.Y. 58 F6
Seneca Falls, N.Y., 7,439 58 G6
Seneca Hill, N.Y. 59 q22
Seneca L., N.Y. 58 G6
Seneca L., Ohio 70 H3
Senecaville, Ohio, 575 70 H3
Senegal, ctry., 3,490,000* 162 B3
Sénégal, r., Af. 162 B3
Seney, Mich. 67 H2
Senftenberg, Aust., 1,001 124 b10
Senftenberg, Ger.D.R., 20,959 118 E3
Sengeløse, Den., 1,435 121 a7
Senggarang, Malay., 2,045 147 p16
Sengiley, U.S.S.R., 10,700 134 D4
Senheim, F.R.Ger. 119 C4
Senhor do Bonfim, Braz., 13,958 103 H4
Senhōshi, Jap. 155 J7
Senica, Czech., 6,370 126 C2
Senigallia, It., 35,606 123 D3
Senirkent, Turk., 7,991 142 B2
Senise, It., 7,464 123 F4
Senj, Yug., 3,093 125 B2
Senja, i., Nor. 120 D1
Senju, Jap., 4,687 155 F3
Senlis, Fr., 10,121 117 E2
Senlisse, Fr. 116 f12
Sennah, Indon. 147 o15
Senneterre, Qué., Can., 3,150 44 J5
Sennett, N.Y. 59 H6
Senneville, Qué., Can., 1,188 47 o18
Sennfeld, F.R.Ger., 1,122 119 G6
Senno, U.S.S.R., 4,100 136 C2
Sennori, It., 5,638 123 B4
Sennwald, Switz., 2,754 124 D1
Sennybridge, U.K. 114 A7
Senoia, Ga., 782 64 E2
Senonches, Fr., 2,706 117 D2
Senoo, Jap., 9,756 154 e15
Senquerr, r., Arg. 105 A6
Sens, Fr., 21,742 117 E2
Sensuntepeque, El Salv., 5,517 94 C4
Sent, Switz. 124 E2
Senta, Yug., 21,000* 125 E2
Sentinel, Ariz. 78 B5
Sentinel, Okla., 1,154 76 D2
Sentinel Butte, N. Dak., 160 74 A2
Sentinel Butte, N. Dak. 74 A2
Sento Sé, Braz., 1,842 103 H3
Sentry Hill, St. Maarten 97 7
Senyavin Is., Car. Is. 176 18
Senzu, Jap. 155 m20
Seo de Urgel, Sp., 7,195 122 F1
Seohara, India 144 b11
Seondha, India 144 b12
Seoni, India, 30,274 145 F5
Seoni Malwa, India, 9,118 144 a14
Seoul=Sŏul
Sepahat, Indon. 147 o16
Sepandjang, P., Indon. 148 f7
Sepang, Indon. 148 E3
Separ, N. Mex. 79 A5
Separation Pt., N.Z. 175 g6
Sepasu, Indon. 148 F2
Sepetiba, B. de, Braz. 103 d18
Sepi, Sol. Is. 175 c2
Sepik, r., Terr. New Guin. 174 d2
Sep'o, N. Kor. 151 E3
Sępólno Krajeńskie, Pol., 5,112 127 B2
Sépone, Laos 146 D3
Sępopol, Pol. 127 D1
Seppenrade, F.R.Ger., 4,012 119 C1
Seppensen, F.R.Ger., 1,184 119 a9
Septème, Fr. 116 q15
Septemvri, Bulg., 5,796 128 E3
Sept-Îles, Qué., Can., 12,776 45 M5
Sepulga, r., Ala. 64 C4
Sepúlveda, Sp., 1,338 122 D2
Seputih, r., Indon. 148 a6
Sequatchie, co., Tenn., 5,915 71 F6
Sequatchie, r., Tenn. 71 F6
Sequeros, Sp. 122 B2
Sequim, Wash., 1,164 80 B1
Sequoia Nat. Pk., Calif. 82 D4
Sequoyah, co., Okla., 18,001 76 J2
Serafimovich, U.S.S.R., 8,900 136 F3
Seraincourt, Fr. 116 f10
Seraing, Belg., 42,155 115 D4
Seraju, r., Indon. 148 c7
Seram, i., Indon. 149 J3
Serampore, India, 91,521 144 f14
Serang, Indon. 148 C4
Séranon, Fr. 116 m13
Serasan, P., Indon. 148 D2
Serasan Passage, Indon. 148 D2
Serbia=Srbija
Şercaia, Rum. 128 E2
Serdang, Malay., 3,596 147 o14
Serdang, Malay., 10,029 147 o15
Serdang, Tg., Indon. 148 C4
Serdobsk, U.S.S.R., 26,100 136 G2
Serebryanka, U.S.S.R., 16,500 134 H5
Sered', Czech. 126 C2
Sereda, U.S.S.R. 136 a6
Seredina-Buda, U.S.S.R., 7,800 136 D2
Serednikovo, U.S.S.R. 136 c6
Şereflikoçhisar, Turk., 8,739 142 C2
Seregno, It., 26,993 123 B2
Serein, r., Fr. 117 E3
Seremban, Malay., 52,020 148 B2
Serena, Ill. 68 D2
Serengeti Nat. Pk., Tanz. 164 E2
Serengeti Plain, Tanz. 164 E2
Serenje, Zambia 164 E4
Serenli, Som. Rep. 163 L5
Serfaus, Aust. 124 G6
Ser'ga, U.S.S.R. 137 i7
Sergach, U.S.S.R., 8,200 136 G2
Sergeant Bluff, Iowa, 813 72 A2
Sergeya Kirova, O-va., U.S.S.R. 135 J2
Sergeyevka, U.S.S.R. 151 F2
Sergeyevskiy, U.S.S.R. 137 h6
Sergipe, st., Braz., 760,273 103 J4
Seria, Brunei 148 E1
Serian, Malay., 1,236 148 D2
Seribu, Kep., Indon. 148 b6
Sérifos, i., Gr. 129 E6
Sérigny, r., Qué., Can. 45 L3
Serik, Turk., 4,895 142 B2
Seringapatam Reef, Austl. 172 C1
Serio, r., It. 122 c5
Sermaise, Fr. 116 g12
Sermata, P., Indon. 149 J5
Sermide, It., 9,989 122 e6
Sernyy Zavod, U.S.S.R., 2,200 134 E6
Serock, Pol., 2,259 127 D2
Serodino, Arg., 6,900* 105 a11
Seronera, Tanz. 165 g15
Serooskerke, Neth. 115 B3
Serov, U.S.S.R., 102,000 134 F4
Serowe, Bots. 164 D5
Serpa, Port., 10,967 122 B4
Serpa Pinto, Ang. 164 C4
Serpentine Lakes, Austl. 172 D4
Serpents Mouth, Trin. and Tob.-Ven. 101 K3
Serpukhov, U.S.S.R., 111,000 136 E2
Serra Branca, Braz., 1,558 103 a14
Serra do Navio, Braz. 103 F1
Sérrai, Gr., 40,063 129 D4
Serramanna, It., 7,747 123 B5
Serra Negra, Braz., 5,221 103 c18
Serranópolis, Braz. 103 F5
Serrat, C., Tun. 160 f5
Serra Talhada, Braz., 12,164 103 J3
Serravalle, S. Mar., 3,700 123 e11
Serres, Fr., 1,066 117 F4
Serrig, F.R.Ger., 1,552 119 B5
Serrinha, Braz., 10,284 103 J4
Serris, Fr. 116 k11
Sertã, Port., 6,879 122 A3
Sertânia, Braz., 7,556 103 J3
Sertung, P., Indon. 148 a7
Serua, P., Indon. 149 J4
Serui, Indon. 149 K3
Sérvia, Gr., 4,132 129 C4
Servia, W. Va. 62 C4
Service Creek, Oreg. 80 C3
Servon, Fr. 116 i12
Sesajap-lama, Indon. 148 F2
Seseganaga L., Ont., Can. 44 D5
Sese Is., Uganda 164 E2
Sesepe, Indon. 149 J3
Sesfontein, S.-W. Afr. 164 B5
Sesheke, Zambia 164 D4
Sesia, r., It. 123 B2
Sesibu, Indon. 148 F1
Sesquilé, Col. 101 f14
Sessa Aurunca, It., 29,351 123 c9
Sesser, Ill., 1,764 68 C5
Sessok, Indon. 149 F5
Sestao, Sp., 24,992 122 m11
Sesto Fiorentino, It., 21,113 123 C3
Sesto San Giovanni, It., 62,436 122 c5
Sestra, r., U.S.S.R. 136 b5
Sestri Levante, It., 18,639 123 B2
Sestroretsk, U.S.S.R., 25,200 136 C1
Sesvenna, Piz, mtn., Switz. 124 E2
Setaka, Jap., 29,260 154 B5
Setana, Jap., 6,023 155 H8
Sète, Fr., 36,816 117 E5
Sete Lagoas, Braz., 36,302 103 H5
Sete Quedas Falls, Braz.-Para. 103 F6
Seth, W. Va. 62 C4
Seth Ward, Tex., 1,328 77 N2
Seti, r., Nepal 145 F3
Sétif, Alg., 82,340 160 E1
Seto, Jap. 154 A5
Seto, Jap., 11,929 154 f15
Seto, Jap., 82,101 154 i14
Seto, Jap. 154 i14
Setoda, Jap., 13,073 154 e15
Seto-naikai, Jap. 155 C4
Setonaikai-ktk., Jap. 154 f15
Setsan, Burma 147 a2
Settat, Mor., 29,617 160 C2
Setté Cama, Gabon 164 A2
Sette-Daban, Khr., U.S.S.R. 135 N4
Settimo Torinese, It., 16,147 122 a5
Setting L., Man., Can. 43 E3
Settle, U.K., 2,297 114 D2
Setúbal, Port., 50,966 122 A3
Setúbal, B. de, Port. 122 A3
Seugne, r., Fr. 117 C4
Seul, L., Ont., Can. 44 D5
Seulimeum, Indon. 148 A1
Seurre, Fr., 2,396 117 F3
Seuzach, Switz., 2,484 124 C1
Sevan, Oz., U.S.S.R. 137 c1
Sevaruyo, Bol. 102 b11
Sevastopol', U.S.S.R., 163,000 134 C5
Sevelen, F.R.Ger., 3,173 119 A2
Sevelen, Switz., 2,370 124 a8
Seven, r., U.K. 114 G2
Seven Hills, Ohio, 5,708 70 e9
Seven Lakes, N. Mex. 79 A4
Sevenoaks, U.K., 17,645 113 G6
Seven Pagodas, India 145 n19
Seven Sisters, Tex. 77 O5
Seven Springs, N.C., 207 63 G2
Seven Troughs, Nev. 83 A2
Sevenum, Neth. 119 A2
Seven Valleys, Pa., 515 60 J6
Sévérac-le-Château, Fr., 3,178 117 E4
Severance, Colo., 70 79 C1
Severance, Kans., 146 75 K4
Severance, N.H. 54 E5
Severance, N.Y. 59 N4
Severin, Yug. 125 C2
Severn, Md. 62 c8
Severn, N.C., 310 63 G1
Severn, Va. 62 H5
Severn, r., Ont., Can. 44 D3
Severn, r., U.K. 113 E6
Severn, r., Md. 62 c8
Severna Park, Md., 3,728 62 H3
Severnaya Dvina, r., U.S.S.R. 134 D3
Severnaya Sos'va, r., U.S.S.R. 134 F3
Severnaya Zemlya, U.S.S.R. 135 J1
Severn Bridge, Ont., Can. 46 E4
Severn L., Ont., Can. 44 D3
Severnoye, U.S.S.R. 134 G4
Severnyy Anyuyskiy Khr., U.S.S.R. 135 Q3
Severnyye Uvaly, hills, U.S.S.R. 132 D4
Severnyy Kommunar, U.S.S.R. 137 h7
Severodvinsk, U.S.S.R., 91,000 134 C3
Severo-Kuril'sk, U.S.S.R., 7,700 135 P4
Severomorsk, U.S.S.R., 32,200 134 C3
Severo-Sibirskaya Nizm., U.S.S.R. 135 H2
Severoural'sk, U.S.S.R., 25,900 137 i6
Severo-Yeniseyskiy, U.S.S.R. 135 J3
Severo-Zadonsk, U.S.S.R., 23,200 136 E2
Severskiy Donets, r., U.S.S.R. 134 C4
Severy, Kans., 492 75 J6
Sevier, co., Ark., 10,156 73 A3
Sevier, co., Tenn., 24,251 71 H6
Sevier, co., Utah, 10,565 78 C2
Sevier, r., Utah 78 B2
Sevier Bridge Res., Utah 78 B2
Sevier Des., Utah 50 D3
Sevier Lake, Utah 78 B2
Sevier Plat., Utah 78 •
Sevierville, Tenn., 2,890 71 H6
Sevigné, Arg., 1,350* 105 c13
Sevilla, Col. 100 C5
Sevilla, Sp., 442,300 122 B4
Sevilla, r., Cuba 96 e2
Sevilla Arriba, Cuba 96 e3
Seville, Sp.=Sevilla
Seville, Fla., 623 65 H3
Seville, Ohio, 1,190 70 H1
Sevina, Mex., 1,053 93 c10
Sevlievo, Bulg., 14,381 128 E3
Sevnica, Yug. 125 B1
Sevran, Fr., 17,972 116 i11
Sèvre, r., Fr. 117 C3
Sèvre Nantaise, r., Fr. 117 C3
Sèvres, Fr., 20,292 117 E2
Sevsk, U.S.S.R., 6,100 136 D2
Sewa B., Terr. Papua 174 3
Sewai, Terr. Papua 174 3
Sewanee, Tenn., 1,464 71 F6
Seward, Alaska, 1,891 85 G3
Seward, co., Kans., 15,930 75 E6
Seward, Kans., 92 75 G5
Seward, co., Nebr., 13,581 75 H3
Seward, Nebr., 4,208 75 H3
Seward, Okla., 49 76 F2
Seward, Pa., 754 60 D5
Seward Mtn., N.Y. 59 M3
Seward Pen., Alaska 85 C2
Sewellton, Ky. 71 F5
Sewickley, Pa., 6,157 60 B4
Sexsmith, Alta., Can. 42 H2
Sextonville, Wis. 66 C5
Seybaplaya, Mex., 3,352 93 H4
Seychelles, is. group, Ind. Oc., 48,000* 165 H2
Seychelles-Mauritius Ridge, Ind. Oc. 168 B3
Seydhisfjördhur, Ice. 120 b6
Seydişehir, Turk., 6,311 142 B2
Seyfert, Pa. 61 h14
Seyhan, r., Turk. 142 C2
Seym, r., U.S.S.R. 134 C4
Seymchan, U.S.S.R., 4,100 135 P3
Seymour, Austl., 3,736 173 F5
Seymour, Conn., 10,100(T) 56 D7
Seymour, Ill. 68 D3
Seymour, Ind., 11,629 70 D4
Seymour, Iowa, 1,117 72 D4
Seymour, Mo., 1,046 72 E7
Seymour, Tex., 3,789 77 O3
Seymour, Wis., 2,045 66 E4
Seymour Corners, Wis. 66 C6
Seymour L., Vt. 54 D2
Seymour Pt., Conn. 56 C8
Seymour Pd., Mass. 57 Q6
Seymourville, La., 1,788 73 D7
Seyne-les-Alpes, Fr., 1,267 117 G4
Seyring, Aust. 124 d10
Seyssuel, Fr. 116 p15
Sezaki, Jap. 154 g14
Sežana, Yug. 125 A2
Sézanne, Fr., 5,521 117 E2
Sezimbra, Port., 16,837 122 A3
Sezzàdio, It., 2,098 122 b6
Sezze, It., 18,388 123 D4
Sfax=Şafāqis
Sfîntu Gheorghe, Rum., 17,638 128 E2
Sfîntu Gheorghe, Braţul, Rum. 128 G2
Sfisef, Alg., 12,841 160 a6
's-Graveland, Neth. 115 c6
's-Gravendeel, Neth., 4,600 115 b7
's Gravenhage, Neth., 603,300 115 C2
's Gravenzande, Neth., 6,600 115 C2
Sgùrr Alasdair, mtn., U.K. 112 C3
Sgùrr Mòr, mtn., U.K. 112 D3
Sgùrr na Ciche, mtn., U.K. 112 D3
Sgùrr na Lapaich, mtn., U.K. 112 D3
Sha, r., China 151 B3
Sha, r., China 151 B4
Sha, r., China 152 E2
Shabani, Rhod., 11,774 164 D5
Shabbona, Ill., 690 68 C2
Shabbona Grove, Ill. 68 D2
Shabla, Bulg., 3,788 128 G3
Shabo, Newf., Can. 45 M4
Shabogamo L., Newf., Can. 45 M4
Shabunaren, i., Jaluit 176 30
Shabunda, D.R.Congo 164 D2
Sha-ch'i, China 152 a6
Sha-ching, China 152 a6
Sha-ch'ung, China 152 a6
Shackelford, co., Tex., 3,990 77 O3
Shackleton Ice Shelf, Ant. 180 T6
Shaddick Pt., Anguilla 97 7
Shade, Ohio 70 H3
Shade Gap, Pa., 140 60 G5
Shadehill, S. Dak. 74 A3
Shadehill Res., S. Dak. 74 A3
Shadeville, Ohio 70 b7
Shadforth, U.K., 2,197 112 h10
Shadow Mtn. Nat. Rec. Area, Colo. 79 B1
Shadrinsk, U.S.S.R., 59,000 134 F4
Shaduzup, Burma 146 B1
Shadwell, Va. 62 F5
Shadybrook, Oreg. 80 a6
Shady Cove, Oreg. 80 B4
Shady Dale, Ga., 201 64 F2
Shady Grove, Fla. 65 F2
Shadygrove, Pa. 60 G6
Shady Oak L., Minn. 74 b6
Shady Side, Md. 62 H4
Shadyside, Ohio, 5,028 70 J3
Shady Valley, Tenn. 71 K5
Shafer, L., Ind. 68 E3
Shaffer, Kans. 75 F5
Shaffers Crossing, Colo. 79 b9
Shafranovo, U.S.S.R., 3,800 137 h9
Shafter, Calif., 5,312 82 D5
Shafter, Nev. 83 C2
Shafter, Tex. 77 L5
Shaftesbury, U.K., 3,372 113 E6
Shaftsburg, Mich. 67 J6
Shaftsbury, Vt. 54 A5
Shaftsbury Center, Vt. 54 A6
Shagamu, Nigeria, 34,915 162 E4
Shagany, Oz., U.S.S.R. 136 C4
Shageluk, Alaska, 155 85 E3
Shaglytengiz, Oz., U.S.S.R. 137 n11
Shagonar, U.S.S.R., 4,200 137 t12
Shag Rocks, Atl. Oc. 99 E8

Shahabad—Shoalwater · 293

Shahabad, Pun., India, 18,975 144 a10
Shahabad, U.P., India, 28,399 144 b12
Shāhābād, Iran, 4,346 143 D2
Shahbā', Syr., 2,922 142 D3
Shāhdādpur, Pak., 21,537 144 C4
Shahdol, India, 22,196 145 F5
Shah Fuladi, mtn., Afghan. 144 C2
Shahganj, India, 8,139 144 d12
Shaḥḥāt, Libya 161 H2
Shāhī, Iran, 23,055 143 E1
Shaḥīm, Leb., 5,316 142 b6
Shāhīn Dezh, Iran, 4,195 143 D1
Shahjahanpur, India, 110,432 145 F4
Sha-ho, China 151 B3
Shahpur, India 144 a14
Shāhpūr, Iran, 13,161 143 C1
Shahpura, M.P., India 144 c14
Shahpura, Raj., India, 12,155 145 E4
Shahreẓā, Iran, 29,311 143 E2
Shahr Kord, Iran, 15,476 143 E2
Shāhrūd, Iran, 17,058 143 F1
Shahsavār, Iran, 7,626 143 E1
Sha-hsien, China 150 F4
Sha-hu-k'ou, China 151 A1
Shailerville (part of Haddam), Conn. 56 G7
Shaim, U.S.S.R. 134 F3
Shajapur, India, 17,317 144 a14
Sha-kang-hsü, China 152 b6
Shaker Heights, Ohio, 36,460 70 H1
Shakespeare, Ont., Can. 46 D5
Shakhdara, r., U.S.S.R. 137 f5
Shakhovskaya, U.S.S.R. 136 a6
Shakhrisyabz, U.S.S.R., 22,000 134 F6
Shakhta, U.S.S.R. 137 i7
Shakhtërsk, R.S.F.S.R., U.S.S.R., 11,300 135 O5
Shakhtërsk, Ukr. S.S.R., U.S.S.R., 37,100 136 f8
Shakhty, U.S.S.R., 241,000 134 D5
Shakhun'ya, U.S.S.R., 21,100 134 D4
Shaki, Nigeria, 26,660 162 e7
Shaklefords, Va. 62 H5
Shakopee, Minn., 5,201 74 F3
Shakotan-misaki, Jap. 155 J8
Shaktoolik, Alaska, 187 85 D2
Shakushi, Jap. 154 g14
Shala, L., Eth. 163 L4
Shalakusha, U.S.S.R. 134 D3
Sha-lan-chen, China 151 F1
Shalbourne, U.K. 114 E8
Shaler Mts., N.W.T., Can. 40 G3
Shalfleet, U.K., 1,136 113 k13
Shalford, U.K., 3,939 114 G8
Shali, U.S.S.R. 137 c1
Sha-li, r., China 152 b6
Shalimar, Fla., 754 65 C2
Shalkar-Yega-Kara, Oz., U.S.S.R. 137 k10
Shallop, Qué., Can. 45 O5
Shallotte, N.C., 480 63 F4
Shallowater, Tex., 1,001 77 M3
Shallow Lag., Grand Cayman 97 3
Shallow Lake, Ont., Can. 46 C4
Shallow L., Me. 55 C2
Shallow Water, Kans. 75 D5
Shalya, U.S.S.R. 137 i7
Shalym, U.S.S.R. 137 r11
Shām, Bādiyat ash, des., Asia 143 B2
Shama, Ghana 162 c9
Shamalān, Afghan. 144 B3
Shamary, U.S.S.R. 137 i7
Shamattawa, Man., Can. 43 H3
Shamattawa, r., Ont., Can. 44 F3
Shambāt, Sudan, 6,611 163 K3
Shambaugh, Iowa, 206 72 C4
Sham Chun, r., China-H.K. 152 b6
Shamīṣṭār, Leb., 4,417 142 c6
Shamkhor, U.S.S.R., 9,200 137 c1
Shamli, India, 26,397 144 a11
Shamo=Gobi
Shamokin, Pa., 13,674 60 J4
Shamokin Dam, Pa., 1,093* 60 J4
Skamokawa, Wash. 80 B2
Shamrock, Fla. 65 F3
Shamrock, Okla., 211 76 G2
Shamrock, Tex., 3,113 76 N2
Shamsang, China 144 d10
Sha'nabī, Jabal Ash, Tun. 160 f6
Shan-ch'ang, China 152 a6
Shan-ch'eng-chen, China 151 E2
Shanchi, U.S.S.R. 137 s12
Shand, Afghan. 144 B3
Shandaken, N.Y. 59 M7
Shandon, Calif. 82 C5
Shandī, Sudan, 11,031 163 K3
Shanesville, Pa. 60 e10
Shangani, r., Rhod. 164 D5
Shang-ch'eng, China 152 D1
Shang-chih, China 151 F1
Shang-ching, China 151 A4
Shang-ch'iu, China, 160,000* 150 F3
Shang-ch'uan Shan, China 152 D3
Shanghai=Shang-hai
Shang-hai, China, 7,000,000* 150 G4
Shanghai Municipality=Shang-hai Shih
Shang-hai Shih, mun., China 150 G4
Shang-hang, China 152 E2
Shang-ho, China 151 C3
Shang-hsien, China 151 A4
Shang-jao, China 150 F4
Shang-kao, China 152 D1
Shang-lien-wan, China 152 a6
Shang-lin, China 152 C3
Shang-nan, China 151 A4
Shangolume, D.R.Congo 165 n19
Shangrila, L., Wis. 69 b7
Shang-shui, China 150 F3
Shang-ssu, China 152 C3
Shang-ts'ai, China 151 B4
Shang-tu-hsiang-huang-ch'i, China 150 F2
Shang-yu, China 152 D2
Shang-yü, China 152 F1
Shan-hai-kuan, China 151 D3
Shan-ho, China 150 B3
Shan-hsi, prov., China, 15,960,000 150 E3
Shan-hsien, Ho-n., China 151 A4
Shan-hsien, Shant., China 151 C4
Shan-hua, Taiwan, 30,177 152 F3
Shaniko, Oreg., 39 80 C3
Shank L., Mich. 66 E2
Shanklin, U.K., 6,494 113 k13
Shanksville, Pa., 314 60 E5
Shannock, R.I. 57 K7
Shannon, N.Z., 1,398 175 g6
Shannon, Ga., 1,629 64 E1
Shannon, Ill., 766 68 C1
Shannon, Miss., 554 73 G3
Shannon, co., Mo., 7,087 72 F7
Shannon, N.C. 63 E3
Shannon, co., S. Dak., 6,000 74 A4
Shannon, r., Ire. 113 B5
Shannon, Mouth of the, Ire. 113 B5
Shannon City, Iowa, 127 72 C4
Shannonville, Ont., Can. 46 G4
Shan Plat., Burma 146 B2
Shan-shan, China 150 C2
Shansi=Shan-hsi
Shan-tan, China 150 D3
Shantarskiye O-va., U.S.S.R. 135 N4
Shan-t'ou, China, 440,000* 150 F5
Shan-tung, prov., China, 54,030,000 150 F3
Shan-tung Pan-tao, China 150 G3
Shantytown, Wis. 66 D4
Shan-yang, China 151 A4
Shan-yin, China 151 B3
Shao-hsing, China 150 G4
Shao-kuan, China, 75,000* 150 F4
Shao-tung, China 152 C2
Shao-wu, China 152 E2
Shao-yang, China, 250,000* 150 F4
Shap, U.K., 1,152 113 E4
Shapinsay, i., U.K. 112 E2
Shapio L., Newf., Can. 45 O3
Sharan, U.S.S.R. 137 h8
Sharbot Lake, Ont., Can. 46 H4
Shardara, Step', U.S.S.R. 137 e4
Shargorod, U.S.S.R. 136 C3
Shari, Jap., 17,468 155 L8
Shari, r., Af. 158 E3
Shari-dake, Jap. 155 L8
Sharīk, Jazīrat, pen., Tun. 161 F1
Shark, r., N.J. 58 c16
Sharkan, U.S.S.R. 137 h7
Sharkar, Afghan. 145 D1
Shark Bay, Austl. 172 A3
Shark Bay, Austl. 172 A3
Sharkey, co., Miss., 10,738 73 E5
Sharkovshchina, U.S.S.R. 136 B2
Sharlyk, U.S.S.R. 137 h9
Sharm ash Shaykh, is. Saudi Ar. 161 K3
Sharnbrook, U.K., 1,053 114 G6
Sharnūb, U.A.R. 161 i7
Sharon, Conn., 2,141(T) 56 C5
Sharon, Ind. 70 C2
Sharon, Mass., 5,888;10,070(T) 57 M4
Sharon, Mich. 67 H4
Sharon, Miss. 73 F5
Sharon, N.H. 54 D6
Sharon, N. Dak., 251 74 D2
Sharon, Ohio 70 H3
Sharon, Okla., 97 76 D1
Sharon, Pa., 25,267 60 B3
Sharon, S.C., 280 63 C3
Sharon, Tenn., 966 71 C5
Sharon, Vt. 54 C4
Sharon, Wis., 1,167 66 E6
Sharon Grove, Ky. 71 D5
Sharon Hill, Pa., 7,123 60 f12
Sharon Springs, Kans., 966 75 D5
Sharon Springs, N.Y., 351 59 L6
Sharon Valley, Conn. 56 B5
Sharonville, Ohio, 6,457 71 i10
Sharp, co., Ark., 6,319 73 D1
Sharpe, Kans. 75 K5
Sharpe, L., Austl. 172 B5
Sharpe L., Man., Can. 43 G3
Sharpes, Fla. 65 J4
Sharps, Va. 62 H5
Sharpsburg, Ga., 155 64 f11
Sharpsburg, Iowa, 130 72 C4
Sharpsburg, Ky., 311 71 H3
Sharpsburg, Md., 861 62 G3
Sharpsburg, N.C., 490 63 G2
Sharpsburg, Pa., 6,096 60 c7
Sharpstown, N.J. 61 A4
Sharpsville, Ind., 663 70 C2
Sharpsville, Pa., 6,061 60 B3
Sharptown, Md., 651 62 J4
Sharqī, Al Jabal ash, Leb.-Syr. 142 b6
Sharqīyah, Aṣ Ṣaḥrā' ash, U.A.R. 161 K3
Shar'ya, U.S.S.R., 33,000 134 D4
Sha-shih, China, 120,000* 150 E4
Shasta, co., Calif., 59,468 82 B2
Shasta, Calif. 82 B2
Shasta, Mt., Calif. 82 B2
Shasta L., Calif. 82 B2
Sha Tau Kok, H.K. 152 b6
Sha Tin, H.K., 5,944 152 b6
Sha-ting, China 150 C4
Shatsk, U.S.S.R., 5,100 136 F2
Shattuck, Okla., 1,625 76 D1
Shattuckville (part of Colrain), Mass. 56 F2
Shatura, U.S.S.R., 18,600 136 c6
Shaturtorf, U.S.S.R., 6,400 136 c6
Shaunavon, Sask., Can., 2,128 43 B5
Shaver Cr., Pa. 60 G4
Shaver Lake, Calif. 82 D4
Shavers Fk., r., W. Va. 62 E4
Shavington, U.K. 114 D4
Shaw, Colo. 79 D2
Shaw, Miss., 2,062 73 E4
Shaw, Mt., N.H. 54 E4
Sha-wan, China 150 B2
Shawanaga, Ont., Can. 46 D3
Shawanese, Pa. 61 n16
Shawangunk Kill, r., N.Y. 59 M8
Shawangunk Mts., N.Y. 61 N3
Shawano, co., Wis., 34,351 66 E4
Shawano, Wis., 6,103 66 E4
Shawano L., Wis. 66 E4
Shawboro, N.C. 63 H1
Shawbridge, Qué., Can., 1,029 47 K3
Shawbury, U.K., 2,366 114 C5
Shawinigan, Qué., Can., 31,496 44 K6
Shawinigan-Sud, Qué., Can., 12,417 47 M2
Shawnee, Colo. 79 a9
Shawnee, co., Kans., 141,286 75 K5
Shawnee, Kans., 9,072 75 a7
Shawnee, N.Y. 58 k18
Shawnee, Ohio, 1,000 70 G3
Shawnee, Okla., 24,326 76 G2
Shawnee Hills, Ohio, 394 70 F2
Shawneetown, Ill., 1,280 68 D6
Shawsheen, r., Mass. 57 M2
Shawsheen Village (part of Andover), Mass. 57 M2
Shawsville, Md. 62 H3
Shawsville, Va. 62 D5
Shawville, Qué., Can., 1,521 47 H3
Sha-ya, China 150 B2
Sha-yang, China 152 D1
Shaykh, Jabal ash, Leb.-Syr. 142 D3
Shaykh Miskīn, Syr. 142 c7
Shchara, r., U.S.S.R. 136 B2
Shchëkino, U.S.S.R., 42,400 136 E2
Shchëlkovo, U.S.S.R., 65,000 136 E2
Shcherbinka, U.S.S.R. 136 b6
Shchigry, U.S.S.R., 9,200 136 E3
Shchors, U.S.S.R., 9,000 136 C3
Shchorsk, U.S.S.R., 3,200 136 D3
Shchuchinsk, U.S.S.R., 35,800 137 n11
Shchuch'ye, U.S.S.R., 10,100 137 k8
Shchuch'ye Ozero, U.S.S.R. 137 h8
Shea, Guyana 101 L6
Sheakleyville, Pa., 138 60 B3
Shearer Dale, Br. Col., Can. 42 G2
Sheaville, Oreg. 80 E4
Sheba, Mt., Br. Col., Can. 42 G2
Shebalino, U.S.S.R. 137 r12
Shebandowan L., Ont., Can. 74 G1
Shebbear, U.K. 113 D6
Shebekino, U.S.S.R., 14,000 136 E3
Shebeli, Webi, Eth.-Som. Rep. 163 M5
Sheboygan, co., Wis., 86,484 66 E5
Sheboygan, Wis., 45,747 66 F5
Sheboygan Falls, Wis., 4,061 66 F5
Shedd, Oreg. 80 B3
Shedden, Ont., Can. 46 C6
Shedfield, U.K., 2,142 113 k13
Shediac, N.B., Can., 2,119 45 N6
Sheelin, L., Ire. 113 C5
Sheenborough, Qué., Can. 46 G3
Sheenjek, r., Alaska 85 H2
Sheep Butte, N. Dak. 74 A2
Sheep Mtn., Colo. 79 B2
Sheep Mtn., S. Dak. 74 A3
Sheep Pk., Nev. 83 C4
Sheep Ra., Nev. 83 C4
Sheepscot Pd., Me. 55 C4
Sheep's Head, Ire. 113 A6
Sheep Springs, N. Mex. 79 A3
's-Heerenberg, Neth., 5,100 115 E3
's Heerenloo, Neth. 115 D2
Sheerin, Tex. 76 N2
Sheering, U.K., 1,457 114 J7
Sheet Harbour, N.S., Can., 1,073 45 O7
Sheffield, Ont., Can. 46 b14
Sheffield, U.K., 493,954 113 F5
Sheffield, Ala., 13,491 64 B1
Sheffield, Ill., 1,078 68 C2
Sheffield, Iowa, 1,156 72 D2
Sheffield, Mass., 2,138(T) 56 C4
Sheffield, Ohio, 1,664 70 c9
Sheffield, Pa., 1,971 60 D2
Sheffield, Tex. 77 M4
Sheffield, Vt. 54 C2
Sheffield Center, Ohio 70 J1
Sheffield Lake, Ohio, 6,884 70 c9
Sheffry Hills, Ire. 113 B5
Shegarka, r., U.S.S.R. 137 q11
Sheho, Sask., Can. 43 D4
She-hsien, A-h., China 152 E1
She-hsien, Shan-hsi, China 151 B3
She-hung, China 152 B1
Shehy Mts., Ire. 113 B6
Sheikh, Som. Rep. 163 M4
Sheikhpura, India, 16,758 144 e13
Shekhūpura, Pak., 41,635 145 D3
Shek Kip Mei, H.K., 239,550 152 b6
Sheksna, U.S.S.R. 136 E1
Shelagskiy, M., U.S.S.R. 135 R2
Shelbina, Mo., 2,067 72 F5
Shelburn, Ind., 1,299 70 B3
Shelburne, N.S., Can., 2,317 45 N7
Shelburne, Ont., Can., 1,218 46 D4
Shelburne, Mass., 1,739(T) 56 F2
Shelburne, N.H. 54 E3
Shelburne, Vt. 54 A3
Shelburne Bay, Austl. 173 F1
Shelburne Falls, Mass., 2,097 56 E2
Shelburne Pd., Vt. 54 A3
Shelby, co., Ala., 32,132 64 C2
Shelby, co., Ill., 23,404 68 D4
Shelby, co., Ind., 34,093 70 D3
Shelby, Ind. 70 B1
Shelby, co., Iowa, 15,825 72 B3
Shelby, Iowa, 533 72 B3
Shelby, co., Ky., 18,493 71 F3
Shelby, Mich., 1,603 67 G5
Shelby, Miss., 2,384 73 E4
Shelby, co., Mo., 9,063 72 E5
Shelby, Mont., 4,017 81 D1
Shelby, Nebr., 613 75 H2
Shelby, N.Y. 58 D5
Shelby, N.C., 17,698 63 C2
Shelby, co., Ohio, 33,586 70 E2
Shelby, Ohio, 9,106 70 G2
Shelby, co., Tenn., 627,019 71 B6
Shelby, co., Tex., 20,479 77 Q4
Shelbyville, Ill., 4,821 68 D4
Shelbyville, Ind., 14,317 70 D3
Shelbyville, Ky., 4,525 71 F3
Shelbyville, Mich. 67 H6
Shelbyville, Mo., 657 72 E5
Shelbyville, Tenn., 10,466 71 E6
Shelbyville, Tex. 77 Q4
Sheldon, Calif. 82 b8
Sheldon, Ill., 1,137 68 E3
Sheldon, Iowa, 4,251 72 B1
Sheldon, Minn. 74 G4
Sheldon, Mo., 434 72 C7
Sheldon, N. Dak., 221 74 D2
Sheldon, S.C. 63 D5
Sheldon, Tex. 77 i9
Sheldon, Vt. 54 B2
Sheldon, Wis., 240 66 B3
Sheldon Junction, Vt. 54 B2
Sheldon Point, Alaska, 110 85 C3
Sheldon Springs, Vt. 54 A2
Sheldonville (part of Wrentham), Mass. 57 L4
Sheldrake, N.Y. 59 G6
Shelekov, U.S.S.R. 135 K4
Shelikhova, Zal., U.S.S.R. 135 P4
Shelikof Str., Alaska 85 F4
Shellbrook, Sask., Can., 1,038 43 C4
Shell Creek, Tenn. 71 K5
Shelldrake, Mich. 67 H2
Shelley, Br. Col., Can. 42 G3
Shelley, Idaho, 2,612 81 C4
Shellharbour, Austl., 5,523 173 G5
Shell Lake, Sask., Can. 43 C4
Shell Lake, Wis., 1,016 66 A3
Shell L., Wis. 66 B3
Shellman, Ga., 1,050 64 E4
Shellpot Cr., Del. 62 e10
Shell Rock, Iowa, 1,112 72 E2
Shellrock, r., Iowa 72 E2
Shellsburg, Iowa, 625 72 F2
Shelly, Minn., 310 74 D2
Shelocta, Pa., 89 60 D4
Shelon', r., U.S.S.R. 136 C1
Shelter Bay, Qué., Can. 45 M5
Shelter Island, N.Y. 59 Q9
Shelter I., N.Y. 56 G8
Shelton, Conn., 18,190 56 D7
Shelton, Nebr., 904 75 G3
Shelton, S.C. 63 C3
Shelton, Wash., 5,651 80 B2
Shemakha, U.S.S.R., 13,200 137 d1
Shemonaikha, U.S.S.R., 16,500 137 q12
Shenandoah, Iowa, 6,567 72 B4
Shenandoah, Ohio 70 G2
Shenandoah, Pa., 11,073 61 K4
Shenandoah, co., Va., 21,825 62 F4
Shenandoah, Va., 1,839 62 F4
Shenandoah, r., Va.-W. Va. 62 F4
Shenandoah Nat. Pk., Va. 62 F4
Shenango, r., Pa. 60 B3
Shen-cha, China 150 C4
Shen-ch'ih, China 151 A3
Shendam, Nigeria 162 F4
Shen-hsi, prov., China, 18,130,000 150 E3
Shenipsit L., Conn. 56 G5
Shenkursk, U.S.S.R., 5,400 134 D3
Shen-mu, China 151 A3
Shensi=Shen-hsi
Shenton, Mt., Austl. 172 C4
Shen-wan, China 152 a6
Shen-yang, China, 3,100,000* 150 G2
Sheo, India 145 D4
Sheopur, India, 14,591 144 a13
Shep, Tex. 77 N3
Shepard Is., New Hebr. 174 m6
Shepardsville, Mich. 67 J5
Shepaug, r., Conn. 56 C6
Sheperdsville, Ky., 1,525 71 F4
Shepetkovo, U.S.S.R. 135 Q3
Shepetovka, U.S.S.R., 31,600 136 B3
Shepherd, Mich., 1,293 67 J5
Shepherd, Tex. 77 Q4
Shepherd Brook Mtn., Me. 55 C2
Shepherd Is., New Hebr. 174 m6
Sheppards, Va. 62 F5
Shepparton, Austl., 10,848 173 F5
Shepperd, L., Austl. 172 C4
Sheppton, Pa. 61 K4
Shepshed, U.K., 7,179 114 F5
Shepton Mallet, U.K., 5,517 114 D8
Sherando, Va. 62 F5
Sherbakul', U.S.S.R. 137 o11
Sherborn, Mass., 1,806(T) 57 L4
Sherborne, U.K., 6,053 113 E6
Sherborne St John, U.K., 2,855 114 F8
Sherbro I., Sa. Leone 162 B4
Sherbrooke, N.S., Can. 45 O6
Sherbrooke, Qué., Can., 66,363 44 K6
Sherburn, U.K. 114 H2
Sherburn, Minn., 1,227 74 E4
Sherburne, co., Minn., 12,861 74 F3
Sherburne, N.Y., 1,647 59 K6
Sherburne, Vt. 54 B4
Sherburne Four Corners, N.Y. 59 J6
Shercock, Ire. 113 C5
Shere, Br. Col., Can. 42 H3
Shere, U.K., 3,876 114 H8
Sheregesh, U.S.S.R. 137 s11
Shereshevo, U.S.S.R. 136 B2
Sherfield English, U.K., 1,194 113 i13
Sherghati, India, 8,925 144 e13
Sheridan, Ont., Can. 46 c13
Sheridan, Ark., 1,938 73 C3
Sheridan, Colo., 3,559 79 b8
Sheridan, Ill., 704 68 D2
Sheridan, Ind., 2,165 70 C2
Sheridan, co., Kans., 4,267 75 E4
Sheridan, Me. 55 D2
Sheridan, Mich., 606 67 H5
Sheridan, Mo., 277 72 C4
Sheridan, co., Mont., 6,458 81 G1
Sheridan, Mont., 539 81 C3
Sheridan, co., Nebr., 9,049 75 C1
Sheridan, N.Y. 58 B7
Sheridan, co., N. Dak., 4,350 74 B2
Sheridan, Oreg., 1,763 80 B3
Sheridan, Wis. 66 D4
Sheridan, co., Wyo., 18,989 81 F3
Sheridan, Wyo., 11,651 81 F3
Sheridan, Mt., Wyo. 81 D3
Sheridan Lake, Colo., 90 79 D2
Sheriff Hutton, U.K. 114 G2
Sheringham, U.K., 4,846 113 G5
Sherkston, Ont., Can. 58 i19
Sherman, Conn., 825(T) 56 C6
Sherman, Fla. 65 J5
Sherman, Ill., 209 68 C4
Sherman, co., Kans., 6,682 75 D4
Sherman, Kans. 75 L6
Sherman, Mich. 67 H4
Sherman, Miss., 403 73 G3
Sherman, co., Nebr., 5,382 75 F2
Sherman, N.Y., 873 58 A7
Sherman, Okla. 76 E1
Sherman, co., Oreg., 2,446 80 C3
Sherman, co., Tex., 2,605 76 M1
Sherman, Tex., 24,988 77 P3
Sherman, Mt., Colo. 79 B2
Sherman Basin, N.W.T., Can. 40 K4
Sherman Cr., Pa. 60 H5
Sherman Mills, Me. 55 D3
Sherman Pass, Wash. 80 D1
Sherman Res., Nebr. 75 G2
Sherman Sta., Me. 55 D3
Sherpur, Pak., 24,924 144 g13
Sherpur, Pak., 4,812 144 g13
Sherrard, Ill., 574 68 B2
Sherridon, Man., Can., 1,500 43 E3
Sherrill, Ark., 241 73 D3
Sherrill, N.Y., 2,922 59 J5
Sherry, Wis. 66 D4
Sherston, U.K., 1,184 114 D7
Shertally, India, 31,155 145 k21
's-Hertogenbosch, Neth., 71,700 115 D3
Sherwood, Mich., 356 67 H7
Sherwood, N.C. 63 C1
Sherwood, N. Dak., 360 74 B1
Sherwood, Ohio, 578 70 E1
Sherwood, Oreg., 680 80 B3
Sherwood, Tenn. 71 E6
Sherwood, Wis. 66 E4
Sherwood Forest, Md. 62 c8
Sherwood Forest, U.K. 114 F4
Sherwood Park=Campbelltown, Alta., Can.
Sheshabee, Minn. 74 F2
Sheslay, Br. Col., Can. 42 D1
Sheslay, r., Br. Col., Can. 42 C1
Shetek, L., Minn. 74 E3
Shetland Is., U.K. 112 F1
Shetucket, r., Conn. 56 H6
Sheung Shui, H.K. 152 b6
Shevlin, Minn., 203 74 E2
Sheyenne, N. Dak., 423 74 C2
Sheyenne, r., N. Dak. 74 C2
Sheykh Sho'eyb, i., Iran 143 E3
Shiant Is., U.K. 112 C3
Shiashkotan, O., U.S.S.R. 135 P5
Shiawassee, co., Mich., 53,446 67 J5
Shiawassee, r., Mich. 67 J5
Shibām, S. Ar., 8,000* 143 D5
Shibarghān, Afghan., 48,000* 144 B1
Shibar Pass, Afghan. 144 C2
Shibata, Jap., 73,886 155 F3
Shibecha, Jap., 16,831 155 L8
Shibetsu, Jap., 38,951 155 K7
Shibetsu, Jap., 7,442 155 L8
Shibīn al Kawm, U.A.R., 55,000 161 i7
Shibukawa, Jap., 39,851 155 F3
Shibushi, Jap., 26,061 154 B6
Shichinohe, Jap., 13,908 155 G1
Shickley, Nebr., 371 75 H3
Shickshinny, Pa., 1,843 61 K3
Shickshock Mts., Qué., Can. 47 S9
Shiderty, r., U.S.S.R. 137 o12
Shidler, Okla., 870 76 G1
Shido, Jap., 15,164 154 f15
Shiel, Loch, U.K. 112 D3
Shields, Kans. 75 E5
Shields, Mich. 67 J5
Shields, N. Dak. 74 B2
Shifnal, U.K., 3,896 114 D5
Shigatse=Jih-k'o-tse
Shigei, Jap. 154 e15
Shih, r., China 152 D1
Shih-ch'eng, China 152 D2
Shih-ch'eng Tao, China 151 D3
Shih-ch'i, China 152 a6
Shih-chia-chuang, China, 503,000* 150 F3
Shih-ch'ien, China 152 B2
Shih-chiu Hu, China 152 E1
Shih-chiu-so, China 151 C4
Shih-chu, China 152 C1
Shih-ch'ü, China 150 D3
Shih-ch'üan, China 151 A4
Shih-ho-tzu, China, 60,000* 150 B2
Shih-hsing, China 152 D2
Shihkiachwang=Shih-chia-chuang
Shih-lou, China 151 A3
Shih-lung, K-hsi, China 152 C3
Shih-lung, K-t., China 152 a5
Shih-men, China 152 C1
Shih-men-tzu-t'sun, China 151 F2
Shih-mien, China, 50,000* 152 A1
Shih-ping, China 152 C2
Shih-p'ing, China 152 A3
Shih-p'u, China 152 F1
Shih-shou, China 152 D1
Shih-tai, China 152 E1
Shih-tao, China 151 D3
Shih-tsui-shan, China 150 E3
Shih-tsung, China 152 B2
Shih-tu, China 150 D4
Shijak, Alb., 4,600 125 D4
Shikabe, Jap., 5,096 155 J8
Shikama, Jap. 154 f15
Shikaoi, Jap., 10,059 155 K8
Shikārpur, Pak., 53,910 144 C4
Shiki, Jap. 155 m19
Shikisai, Jap. 154 f15
Shikizu, Jap. 154 h15
Shikohabad, India, 23,458 144 b12
Shikoku, i., Jap. 155 C5
Shikoku Basin, Pac. Oc. 133 N6
Shikotsu-ko, Jap. 155 J8
Shikotsu-Tōya-ktk., Jap. 155 J8
Shilbottle, U.K., 1,378 113 F4
Shildon, U.K., 14,372 112 g10
Shilka, U.S.S.R., 17,900 135 L4
Shilka, r., U.S.S.R. 135 L4
Shilkan, U.S.S.R. 135 O4
Shillington, Pa., 5,639 61 L5
Shillong, India, 83,786 145 J4
Shiloh, Ark., 6 73 C2
Shiloh, Fla. 65 J4
Shiloh, Ill., 701 68 C5
Shiloh, N.J., 554 61 A5
Shiloh, N.C. 63 H1
Shiloh, Ohio, 724 70 G2
Shiloh, Tenn. 71 D5
Shiloh Nat. Mil. Pk., Tenn. 71 C6
Shilovo, U.S.S.R. 136 F2
Shima, Jap. 154 h14
Shimabara, Jap., 45,205 154 B5
Shimada, Jap., 53,900 155 F4
Shimagahara, Jap., 3,726 154 g15
Shima-hantō, Jap. 154 h15
Shimakatsu, Jap. 154 h15
Shimanovsk, U.S.S.R., 23,000 135 M4
Shimizu, Jap., 142,983 155 F4
Shimizu, Jap., 12,723 155 K8
Shimizu, Jap. 154 g15
Shimmachi, Jap. 155 n20
Shimminato, Jap., 47,882 155 E3
Shimmyō, Jap. 154 e15
Shimo-Asō, Jap., 1,924 154 i14
Shimobuchi, Jap. 154 g15
Shimoda, Jap., 27,387 155 F4
Shimoda, Jap. 154 g15
Shimoda, Jap. 155 C5
Shimodate, Jap., 51,257 155 G3
Shimo-Furano, Jap., 29,253 155 K8
Shimoga, India, 63,764 145 E7
Shimoichiba, Jap. 155 n19
Shimo-Izumi, Jap. 155 n20
Shimokawa, Jap., 15,018 155 K7
Shimokōchi, Jap. 154 h15
Shimo-Koshiki, Jap., 9,918 154 A6
Shimo-Koshiki-shima, Jap. 154 A6
Shimoku, Jap. 154 g14
Shimonoseki, Jap., 246,941 154 B4
Shimonoseki-kaikyō, Jap. 154 B5
Shimono-shima, Jap. 154 A4
Shimosami, Jap. 154 i14
Shimosato, Jap., 4,447 155 E5
Shimotsu, Jap., 18,593 155 D4
Shimotsui, Jap. 154 e15
Shimo-Tsuma, Jap., 30,011 155 G3
Shimo-Tsuruma, Jap. 155 m20
Shimoyaku, Jap., 10,022 154 k17
Shimoyama, Jap. 154 g14
Shimoyama, Jap. 154 h14
Shimo-Yamaguchi, Jap. 155 m20
Shimo-Yūbetsu, Jap., 13,719 155 K7
Shimsk, U.S.S.R. 136 C1
Shin, L., U.K. 112 D2
Shinano, r., Jap. 155 F3
Shindand, Afghan. 144 A2
Shinden, Jap. 154 i14
Shindō, Jap. 154 h15
Shine, Wash. 81 a7
Shiner, Tex., 1,945 77 P5
Shinfield, U.K., 5,187 114 F8
Shingbwiyang, Burma 146 A1
Shinglehouse, Pa., 1,298 60 F2
Shingler, Ga. 64 F4
Shingleton, Mich. 67 G2
Shingletown, Calif. 82 C2
Shingū, Jap. 154 e16
Shingū, Jap., 17,506 155 D4
Shingū, Jap., 39,114 155 E5
Shinhopple, N.Y. 59 K7
Shinji, Jap., 10,513 155 C4
Shinjō, Jap. 154 h15
Shinjō, Jap., 43,550 155 G2
Shinjuku, Jap. 155 n19
Shinnston, W. Va., 2,724 62 D3
Shinonoi, Jap., 23,361 155 E3
Shin Pond, Me. 55 D2
Shinshiro, Jap., 33,022 155 E4
Shintoku, Jap., 15,525 155 K8
Shinyanga, Tanz. 164 E2
Shiobara, Jap., 5,969 155 F3
Shiocton, Wis., 685 66 E4
Shioe, Jap. 154 f14
Shiogama, Jap., 55,325 155 G2
Shiojiri, Jap., 32,857 155 F3
Shionoe, Jap. 154 f15
Shionoha, Jap. 154 h15
Shiono-misaki, Jap. 155 D5
Shiosawa, Jap., 9,377 155 F3
Shioya, Jap. 155 m18
Ship Bottom, N.J., 717 61 C4
Ship Cove, Newf., Can. 45 a10
Ship Harbour, Newf., Can. 45 b10
Ship Harbour, N.S., Can. 47 U11
Ship I., Miss. 73 G7
Shipki La, pass, China-India 145 F3
Shiplake, U.K., 1,365 114 G8
Shipley, U.K., 29,762 114 E3
Shipman, Ill., 417 68 C4
Shipman, Va. 62 F5
Shippensburg, Pa., 6,138 60 G5
Shippenville, Pa., 599 60 D3
Shippigan, N.B., Can., 1,617 45 N6
Shippigan I., N.B., Can. 45 N6
Shippingport, Pa., 383 60 B4
Ship Rock, N. Mex. 79 A3
Shiprock Pk., N. Mex. 79 A3
Shipshewana, Ind., 312 70 D1
Shipston on Stour, U.K., 1,585 114 E6
Shipton Bellinger, U.K., 1,003 114 E8
Shipyard, Br. Hond., 1,116 94 C2
Shira, U.S.S.R., 10,400 137 s11
Shirahama, Jap., 9,013 155 F4
Shirakami-saki, Jap. 155 H9
Shirakawa, Jap., 41,196 155 G3
Shirane-san, mtn., Jap. 155 F3
Shiranuka, Jap., 17,412 155 K8
Shiraoi, Jap., 11,083 155 J8
Shiraoka, Jap., 15,655 155 m18
Shiratani, Jap. 154 h14
Shirati, Tanz. 165 f14
Shīrāz, Iran, 170,659 143 E3
Shirbīn, U.A.R. 161 i7
Shire, r., Malawi-Moz. 164 E4
Shirebrook, U.K., 11,635 114 F4
Shired Island, Fla. 65 F3
Shiretoko-hantō, Jap. 155 L7
Shiretoko-misaki, Jap. 155 L7
Shiriuchi, Jap., 9,735 155 J9
Shiriya-saki, Jap. 155 G1
Shirkishinai, Jap., 10,205 155 J9
Shīr Kūh, mtn., Turk. 132 E6
Shirland, Ill. 68 C1
Shirley, Ark., 197 73 C2
Shirley, Ill. 68 C3
Shirley, Ind., 1,038 70 D3
Shirley, Mass., 1,762;5,202(T) 57 K2
Shirley, N.Y. 58 h13
Shirley, Wis. 66 F4
Shirley Center (part of Shirley), Mass. 57 K2
Shirley Mills, Me. 55 C3
Shirleysburg, Pa., 170 60 G5
Shirlovaya Gora, U.S.S.R., 12,500 135 L4
Shiroi, Jap. 155 n19
Shiroishi, Jap., 43,911 155 G2
Shirokaya, G., U.S.S.R. 137 i7
Shirokochō, Jap. 154 h15
Shirone, Jap., 35,658 155 F3
Shirotori, Jap., 14,499 154 f15
Shirotori, Jap., 6,043 155 E4
Shirpur, India, 20,846 145 E5
Shīrvān, Iran, 6,906 143 F1
Shirwa, L., Malawi-Moz. 164 F4
Shishaldin Vol., Alaska 85 C5
Shishimi, Jap. 154 A4
Shishmaref, Alaska, 217 85 C2
Shiveluch, S., U.S.S.R. 135 Q4
Shively, Ky., 15,155 71 E3
Shivers, Miss. 73 F6
Shivpuri, India, 28,681 145 E4
Shizugawa, Jap., 18,316 155 G2
Shizuki, Jap. 154 f15
Shizunai, Jap., 22,095 155 K8
Shizuoka, Jap., 328,819 155 F4
Shkapovo, U.S.S.R. 137 h9
Shkin', U.S.S.R. 136 c6
Shklov, U.S.S.R., 7,700 136 C2
Shkodër, Alb., 44,900 125 D3
Shkotovo, U.S.S.R., 8,000 135 N5
Shkumbin, r., Alb. 125 D4
Shmidta, M., U.S.S.R. 135 S3
Shmidta, O., U.S.S.R. 135 H1
Shō, r., Jap. 155 E3
Shoa Ghimirra, Eth. 163 K4
Shoal, r., Fla. 65 C2
Shoal Cr., Alta., Can. 43 a6
Shoal Cr., Ill. 68 C5
Shoal Cr., Mo. 72 C5
Shoal Cr., Mo. 75 a7
Shoal Harbor, Newf., Can. 45 a9
Shoal Lake, Man., Can. 43 E5
Shoals, Ind., 1,022 70 C4
Shoals, Okla. 76 H4
Shoals Junction, S.C. 63 B3
Shoalwater Bay, Austl. 173 G3

294 · Shōbara—Si Songkhram

Shōbara, Jap., 30,663 155 C4
Shobonier, Ill. 68 C5
Shōbu, Jap., 16,718 155 m18
Shōbudani, Jap. 154 h14
Shōdo-shima, Jap. 154 f15
Shoemakersville, Pa., 1,464 61 K4
Shoffner, Ark. 73 D2
Shohola, Pa. 61 N3
Shohola Cr., Pa. 61 M3
Shōjō, Jap. 154 f15
Shokal'skogo, O., U.S.S.R. 134 G2
Shokal'skogo, Prol., U.S.S.R. 135 K2
Shokambetsu-dake, Jap. 155 J8
Sholapur, India, 337,583 145 E6
Shol Plat., Som. Rep. 163 N4
Shōnai, r., Jap. 154 i14
Shongopovi, Ariz. 78 C4
Shonō, Jap. 154 i14
Shonto, Ariz. 78 C3
Shopton, Ala. 64 D3
Shoptykul', U.S.S.R. 137 o12
Shoranur, India, 14,307 145 k20
Shore Acres, Calif., 3,093 83 f11
Shore Acres, Md. 62 c8
Shore Acres, N.J. 58 c16
Shore Acres, R.I. 57 L6
Shore Acres, Tex., 518 77 i9
Shoreham, Mich., 443 67 G6
Shoreham, N.Y., 164 58 h13
Shoreham, Vt. 54 A4
Shores, Va. 62 F5
Shoreview, Minn., 7,157 74 c5
Shorewood, Ill., 358 68 D2
Shorewood, Wis., 15,990 66 d11
Shorkot, Pak., 7,197 145 D3
Short, Okla. 76 J2
Shortandy, U.S.S.R. 137 n12
Short Beach (part of Branford), Conn. 56 E8
Short Creek, Ala. 64 b7
Shorter, Ala. 64 D3
Shorterville, Ala. 64 D4
Short Falls, N.H. 54 E5
Short Hills, N.J. 58 b13
Shortland, i., Sol. Is. 175 a2
Shortsville, N.Y., 1,382 58 F6
Short Tract, N.Y. 58 E7
Shosambetsu, Jap., 5,640 155 J7
Shoshone, Calif. 82 E5
Shoshone, co., Idaho, 20,876 81 B2
Shoshone, Idaho, 1,416 81 B4
Shoshone, Nev. 83 C3
Shoshone, r., Wyo. 81 E3
Shoshone L., Wyo. 81 D3
Shoshone Mts., Nev. 83 B3
Shoshone Pk. S., Nev. 83 B3
Shoshoni, Wyo., 766 81 F4
Shostka, U.S.S.R., 40,000 136 D3
Shotley Bridge, U.K. 112 g10
Shō-Tombetsu, Jap. 155 K7
Shotton, U.K., 7,144 112 h10
Shotts, U.K. 112 c8
Shou-chang, China 151 B3
Shou-ch'ang, China 152 E1
Shou-hsien, China 151 C4
Shou-kuang, China 151 C3
Shou-ning, China 152 E2
Shouns, Tenn. 71 K5
Shou-yang, China 151 B3
Shoveltown, Mo. 72 b10
Showa, Ant. 180 R6
Show Low, Ariz., 1,625 78 C4
Shoyna, U.S.S.R. 134 D3
Shpola, U.S.S.R., 16,100 136 C3
Shreve, Ohio, 1,617 70 G2
Shreveport, La., 164,372 73 B5
Shrewsbury, U.K., 49,566 113 E5
Shrewsbury, Ky. 71 E4
Shrewsbury, Mass., 16,622(T) 57 K3
Shrewsbury, N.J., 3,222 58 c15
Shrewsbury, Pa., 943 60 J6
Shrewsbury, r., N.J. 58 c15
Shrewton, U.K., 1,283 114 E8
Shrivenham, U.K., 2,016 114 E7
Shropshire, co., U.K., 297,466 113 E5
Shroud Cays, Bah. Is. 95 c8
Shrub Oak, N.Y., 1,874 59 N9
Shrüle, Ire. 113 B5
Shu, r., China 151 C4
Shua-ching-szu, China, 5,000* 152 A1
Shuang, r., China 152 E2
Shuang-ch'eng, China 150 G2
Shuang-feng, China 152 D2
Shuang-feng Tao, China 152 F2
Shuang-kou, China 151 C4
Shuang-liao, China 150 G2
Shuang-liu, China 152 B1
Shuang-pai, China 152 A2
Shuang-shan, China 151 C2
Shuang-yang, China 151 E2
Shuang-ya-shan, China, 110,000* 150 H2
Shubar-Kuduk, U.S.S.R., 8,400 134 E5
Shubenacadie, N.S., Can. 47 U11
Shubert, Nebr., 231 75 K3
Shubuta, Miss., 718 73 G6
Shu-ch'eng, China 152 E1
Shūchi, Jap. 154 g14
Shugnou, U.S.S.R. 137 f5
Shui-ch'eng, China 150 E4
Shui-kou-t'ou, China 151 D3
Shujāābād, Pak., 16,815 145 D3
Shujalpur, India, 13,690 144 a14
Shuksan, Mt., Wash. 80 C1
Shuku, Jap. 155 m19
Shu-lan, China 151 E1
Shuler, Ark. 73 C4
Shullsburg, Wis., 1,324 66 C6
Shumagin Is., Alaska 85 D5
Shuman House, Alaska 85 J2
Shumarinai, Jap. 155 J7
Shumerlya, U.S.S.R., 30,100 136 G2
Shumikhinskiy, U.S.S.R. 137 h7
Shumilinskaya, U.S.S.R. 136 F3
Shumshu, O., U.S.S.R. 135 P4
Shumway, Ill., 212 68 D4
Shun-an, China 152 E1
Shun-ch'ang, China 152 E2
Shungnak Alaska, 135 85 E2
Shungru Truga, China 144 e11
Shun-hua, China 151 A4
Shunk, Pa. 60 J2
Shuo-hsien, China 151 B3
Shupiyan, India, 6,005 145 E2
Shuqrā', S. Ar. 143 D6
Shuqualak, Miss., 550 73 G5
Shurab, U.S.S.R., 10,300 137 f4
Shuri, Ryukyu Is. 154 a11
Shuru Tsho, China 145 H3
Shuryshkary, U.S.S.R. 134 F3
Shūsh, Iran 143 D2
Shusha, U.S.S.R., 5,700 137 c2
Shushal, India 145 F2
Shushan, N.Y. 59 O5
Shushenskoye, U.S.S.R. 135 J4
Shūshtar, Iran, 18,527 143 D2
Shuswap L., Br. Col., Can. 42 H4
Shutesbury, Mass., 265(T) 56 G3
Shuwak, Sudan, 2,171 163 K3
Shuya, U.S.S.R., 67,000 136 F1
Shuyak I., Alaska 85 F4
Shu-yang, China 151 C4
Shuyskoye, U.S.S.R. 136 F1
Shūzan, Jap. 154 g14
Shuzenji, Jap., 7,921 155 F4
Shwebo, Burma, 17,842 146 A2
Shwedaung, Burma, 9,044 146 A3
Shwegu, Burma 146 B1
Shwegun, Burma 147 b2
Shwegyin, Burma, 5,439 147 b2
Shwelaung, Burma, 1,200 147 a2
Shweli, r., Burma 146 B2
Siabu, Indon. 148 A2
Siachoque, Col. 100 D5
Siagne, r., Fr. 116 m13
Siālkot, Pak., 143,889 145 E2
Siam=Thailand
Siam, Ohio 70 G1
Siam, G. of, Camb.-Thai. 146 C5
Sian, Ch-l.=Liao-yüan
Sian, Shen-hsi=Hsi-an
Siangtan=Hsiang-t'an
Sianów, Pol., 3,315 127 B1
Siapo, r., Ven. 100 H7
Siargao I., Phil. 153 C3
Siasconset (part of Nantucket), Mass. 57 R7
Siasi I., Phil. 153 B4
Siátista, Gr., 4,737 129 C4
Siaton, Phil., 2,862 153 e12
Siau, P., Indon. 149 H2
Šiauliai, U.S.S.R., 70,000 134 B4
Siay, Phil., 2,497 153 B4
Siazan', U.S.S.R., 10,700 137 d1
Sibalom, Phil., 3,486 153 B3
Sibambe, Ec. 104 c11
Sibanicú, Cuba, 3,378 96 e2
Sibay, U.S.S.R., 34,000 134 E4
Šibenik, Yug., 26,000* 125 C3
Sibert, Ky. 71 H4
Siberut, P., Indon. 148 A3
Siberut, Selat, Indon. 148 A3
Sibi, Pak., 13,327 144 C3
Sibigo, Indon. 148 A2
Sibil, Indon. 149 L4
Sibiryakova, O., U.S.S.R. 134 G2
Sibiti, Congo 164 B2
Sibiu, Rum., 90,475 128 E2
Sibley, Ill., 386 68 D3
Sibley, Iowa, 2,852 72 B1
Sibley, Lincoln Parish, La. 73 C5
Sibley, Webster Parish, La., 595 73 B5
Sibley, co., Minn., 16,228 74 E3
Sibley, Miss. 73 D6
Sibolga, Indon., 38,655 148 A2
Sibonga, Phil., 2,695 153 e11
Sibsagar, India, 15,106 145 K4
Sibsey, U.K., 1,023 114 H4
Sibu, Malay., 29,249 148 D2
Sibuguey Bay, Phil. 153 B4
Sibuku, Indon. 148 F1
Sibul Spring, Phil., 3,579 153 c7
Sibun, r., Br. Hond. 94 C2
Sibutu I., Phil. 153 A4
Sibutu Passage, Phil. 153 A4
Sibuyan I., Phil. 153 B2
Sibuyan Sea, Phil. 153 B2
Sichang, Ko, Thai. 147 d5
Sichon, Thai. 146 B5
Sicié, C., Fr. 117 F5
Sicilia, i., It. 123 D6
Sicily=Sicilia
Sicily, Str. of, It. 123 C6
Sicily Island, La., 761 73 D6
Sickles, Okla. 76 E2
Sico, r., Hond. 94 E3
Sicuani, Peru, 10,663 104 D5
Šid, Yug., 7,268 125 D2
Sidas, Indon. 148 D2
Sidate, Indon. 149 H2
Sideburen, Neth. 115 E1
Siddipett, India, 18,719 145 F6
Sideia, i., Terr. Papua 174 f3
Sideling Hill Cr., Pa. 60 F6
Sidell, Ill., 614 68 E4
Siderno Marina, It., 17,465 123 F5
Sideview, Ky. 71 G3
Sidheros, Ákra, Gr. 129 F7
Sidhi, India, 5,021 145 G4
Sidhirókastron, Gr., 8,177 129 D4
Sidhpur, India, 33,850 145 D5
Sidi, India 144 c14
Sīdī Barrānī, U.A.R., 15,000 161 J2
Sidi-Bel-Abbès, Alg., 96,608 160 D2
Sidi-Bennour, Mor., 5,479 160 C2
Sīdī Bū Zayd, Tun., 1,918 160 f6
Sidi Ifni, Ifni, 8,311 160 C3
Sidi-Kacem, Mor., 19,478 160 D2
Sidikalang, Indon. 148 A2
Sidi-Mohamed-Ben-Aouda, Alg. 160 b6
Sidi-Okba, Alg., 7,980 160 e6
Sidley, Mt., Ant. 180 X5
Sidmouth, U.K., 10,890 113 E6
Sidnaw, Mich. 66 E2
Sidney, Br. Col., Can., 1,489 42 F4
Sidney, Man., Can. 43 e10
Sidney, Ark., 97 73 D1
Sidney, Ill., 686 68 D4
Sidney, Iowa, 1,057 72 B4
Sidney, Mich. 67 H5
Sidney, Mont., 4,564 81 G2
Sidney, Nebr., 8,004 75 C2
Sidney, N.Y., 5,157 59 K7
Sidney, Ohio, 14,663 70 E2
Sidney, Tex. 77 O4
Sidney Center, N.Y. 59 K7
Sidney Lanier, L., Ga. 64 E1
Sidoardjo, Indon. 148 e7
Sidon, Leb.=Ṣaydā
Sidon, Miss., 410 73 E4
Sidra, Pol. 127 E2
Sidra, G. of=Surt, Khalīj
Sidrolândia, Braz., 1,510 103 F6
Siebenhirten, Aust. 124 d10
Siebenlehn, Ger.D.R. 126 c5
Siedlce, Pol., 32,000* 127 E2
Siedlinghausen, F.R.Ger., 1,844 119 E2
Sieg, r., F.R.Ger. 119 D3
Siegburg, F.R.Ger., 29,093. 118 A3
Siegen, F.R.Ger., 45,173 118 B3
Siegendorf, Aust., 2,397 124 d11
Sieghartskirchen, Aust., 1,489 124 M5
Sieglar, F.R.Ger., 16,556 119 C3
Siegmar-Schönau, Ger.D.R. 126 b6
Siemiatycze, Pol., 4,891 127 E2
Siemionówka, Pol. 127 F2
Siem Pang, Camb. 146 D4
Siem Reap, Camb., 10,230 146 D4
Siena, It., 59,492 123 C3
Sieniawa, Pol., 1,166 127 E3
Sieppijärvi, Fin. 120 F2
Sieradz, Pol., 12,997 127 C3
Sieraków, Pol., 4,205 127 B2
Sieraków, Pol. 127 h6
Sierck-les-Bains, Fr., 1,993 116 b8
Sierndorf, Aust. 124 M5
Sierning, Aust., 7,535 124 L5
Siero, Sp., 34,574 122 C1
Sierpc, Pol., 10,609 127 C2
Sierra, co., Calif., 2,247 82 C3
Sierra, co., N. Mex., 6,409 79 B5
Sierra Blanca, Tex. 77 L4
Sierra Chica, Arg., 3,160 105 a13
Sierra City, Calif. 82 C3
Sierra Colorada, Arg. 105 B6
Sierra Gorda, Chile 105 B2
Sierra Grande, Arg., 1,000* 105 B6
Sierra Leone, ctry., 2,180,355 162 C4
Sierra Leone Basin, Atl. Oc. 109 L6
Sierra Leone Rise, Atl. Oc. 109 L6
Sierra Madre, Calif., 9,732 83 h15
Sierra Madre Mts., Calif. 82 D5
Sierra Nevada, mts., Calif. 82 C3
Sierra Pailemán, Arg. 105 B6
Sierras Bayas, Arg., 2,601 105 b13
Sierraville, Calif. 82 C3
Sierra Vista, Ariz., 3,121 78 C6
Sierre, Switz., 8,690 124 B2
Siersburg, F.R.Ger., 2,987 116 c8
Siershahn, F.R.Ger., 2,335 119 D4
Şieu, Rum. 128 E1
Sievi, Fin. 120 F3
Siewier, Pol., 3,932 127 i6
Sífnos, i., Gr. 129 E6
Sifton, Man., Can., 1,000 43 E4
Sig, Alg., 26,452 160 a6
Sig, r., Alg. 160 a6
Sigave, Îs. de Horne 175 9
Sigave, Anse de, Is. de Horne 175 9
Sigchos, Ec. 104 c10
Sigean, Fr., 2,555 117 E5
Sigel, Ill., 387 68 D4
Sigel, Pa. 60 D3
Sigep, Indon. 148 A3
Sighet, Rum., 22,361 128 D1
Sighişoara, Rum., 20,363 128 E1
Sigiriya, Cey. 145 n22
Sigli, Indon. 148 A1
Siglufjördhur, Ice., 2,625 120 a6
Sigmaringen, F.R.Ger., 7,517 118 B4
Signal, Ariz. 78 B4
Signal Hill, Calif., 4,627 83 h16
Signal Hill, Ill. 72 b11
Signal Mountain, Tenn., 3,413 71 F6
Signau, Switz., 2,555 124 B2
Signy-l'Abbaye, Fr., 1,779 117 F2
Signy Island, Ant. 180 O6
Sigourney, Iowa, 2,387 72 E3
Sigriswil, Switz., 3,739 124 B2
Sigsig, Ec., 1,071 104 B2
Sigsipamba, Ec. 104 d9
Sigtuna, Swed. 120 e8
Siguanea, Ens. de la, Cuba 96 b2
Siguatepeque, Hond., 6,486 94 C3
Sigüenza, Sp., 4,620 122 D2
Siguinalá, Guat. 94 b9
Siguiri, Guin., 11,761 162 C4
Sigulda, U.S.S.R., 4,800 136 B1
Sigurd, Utah, 339 78 C2
Sihanoukville, Camb. 146 C5
Sihlsee, Switz. 124 C1
Sihochac, Mex. 93 H4
Sihora, India, 14,194 145 F5
Sihuas, Peru, 1,329 104 B4
Siikajoki, r., Fin. 120 F2
Siilinjärvi, Fin. 120 G3
Siirt, Turk., 22,898 142 E2
Sik, Malay., 1,408 147 o14
Sikandarabad, India, 26,290 144 a11
Sikandra, India 144 a12
Sikandra Rao, India, 13,899 144 b12
Sikanni Chief, Br. Col., Can. 42 G1
Sikanni Chief, r., Br. Col., Can. 42 G1
Sikar, India, 50,636 145 E4
Sikasso, Mali, 22,000 162 D4
Sikéa, Gr., 1,318 129 D6
Sikeli, Indon. 149 G4
Sikes, La., 233 73 C5
Sikeston, Mo., 13,765 72 H8
Sikhiu, Thai. 147 d4
Sikhote-Alin', Khr., U.S.S.R. 135 N5
Sikiá, Gr., 2,456 129 D4
Siking=Hsi-an
Síkinos, i., Gr. 129 E6
Sikión, Gr. 129 D5
Sikkim, Indian Prot., 176,000* 145 H4
Siklós, Hung., 5,095 126 D4
Sikoúrion, Gr., 2,454 129 D5
Siktyakh, U.S.S.R. 135 M3
Sil, r., Sp. 122 B1
Silao, Mex., 24,138 92 E4
Silas, Ala., 353 64 A4
Silat, Indon. 148 D2
Silay, Phil., 16,927 153 B3
Silba, i., Yug. 125 B2
Silcayoapan, ruins, Mex. 93 F5
Silchar, India, 41,062 145 J4
Silcox, Man., Can. 43 G2
Şilea, Rum 128 E1
Silenen, Switz., 2,261 124 C2
Siler, Ky. 71 H5
Siler City, N.C., 4,455 63 E2
Silesia=Śląsk
Siletz, Oreg., 583 80 B3
Siletz, r., Oreg. 80 B3
Silex, Mo., 176 72 F5
Silgarhi-Doti, Nepal 144 c11
Silhouette I., Seych. 165 a10
Silifke, Turk., 9,162 142 C2
Siliguri, India, 65,471 145 H4
Siliştea, Rum. 128 E2
Silistra, Bulg., 20,350 128 F2
Siljan, Nor. 121 B1
Siljan, l., Swed. 120 C3
Silkeborg, Den., 24,465 121 B4
Silkworth, Pa. 61 n16
Silleda, Sp., 11,758 122 A1
Sillegny, Fr. 116 b9
Sillé-le-Guillaume, Fr., 2,792 117 C2
Sillery, Qué., Can., 13,918 47 n16
Sillian, Aust., 1,951 124 J7
Silloth, U.K., 3,081 113 E4
Silly-le-Long, Fr. 116 k10
Siloam, N.C. 63 D1
Siloam Springs, Ark., 3,953 73 A1
Silsbee, Tex., 6,277 77 Q4
Silsden, U.K., 5,142 114 E3
Sils im Engadin, Switz. 124 D2
Silt, Colo., 384 79 B2
Siltcoos, Oreg. 80 B4
Siluko, Nigeria 162 f8
Siluria, Ala., 736 64 C2
Šilutė, U.S.S.R., 10,000 136 A2
Silva, N. Dak. 74 C1
Silva, Recife do, Braz. 103 H2
Silvana, Wash. 80 B1
Silvania, Col. 101 e15
Silvano d'Orba, It., 2,066 122 b6
Silvaplana, Switz. 124 D2
Silva Porto, Ang., 12,146 164 B4
Silveira, Port., 3,327 122 i9
Silver, Tex. 77 N3
Silver, r., Mich. 66 E2
Silverado, Calif. 83 i16
Silver Bay, Minn., 3,723 74 G2
Silver Bay, N.Y. 59 N4
Silver Bell, Ariz. 78 C5
Silver Bow, co., Mont., 46,454 81 C3
Silver City, Iowa, 281 72 B3
Silver City, Mich. 66 D2
Silver City, Miss., 431 73 E4
Silver City, Nev. 83 A3
Silver City, N. Mex., 6,972 79 A5
Silver City, Okla. 76 G1
Silver City, S. Dak. 74 A3
Silver City, Utah 78 b11
Silver Cliff, Colo., 153 79 C2
Silver Creek, Miss., 229 73 E6
Silver Creek, Nebr., 431 75 H2
Silver Creek, N.Y., 3,310 58 B6
Silver Creek, Wash. 80 B2
Silverdale, N.C. 63 G3
Silverdale, Pa., 489 60 f10
Silverdale, Wash. 81 a7
Silverhill, Ala., 417 64 B5
Silver Lake, Calif. 82 E5
Silver Lake, Ind., 514 70 D1
Silver Lake (part of Kingston), Mass. 57 N4
Silver Lake, N.H. 54 E4
Silver Lake, Oreg. 80 C4
Silverlake, Utah 78 c9
Silver Lake, Wash. 80 B2
Silver Lake, Kenosha Co., Wis., 1,077 66 E6
Silver Lake, Waushara Co., Wis. 66 D4
Silver L., Mass. 57 N4
Silver L., Mich. 66 E2
Silver L., Mo. 72 D5
Silver L., Oreg. 80 D4
Silver L., Oreg. 80 C4
Silver L., Wis. 66 a13
Silver Lakes, Ill. 69 b8
Silvermine (part of Norwalk, New Canaan), Conn. 56 C8
Silverpeak, Nev. 83 B4
Silver Pk. Ra., Nev. 83 B4
Silver Run, Miss. 73 F7
Silver Spring, Md., 66,348 62 H3
Silver Springs, Colo. 79 b9
Silver Springs, Nev. 83 A3
Silver Springs, N.Y., 726 58 D6
Silverstone, U.K., 1,067 114 F6
Silverstreet, S.C., 181 63 C3
Silverton, Austl. 172 F4
Silverton, Br. Col., Can. 42 H4
Silverton, S. Af., 4,809 165 k16
Silverton, Colo., 822 79 B3
Silverton, N.J. 58 c16
Silverton, Ohio, 6,682 71 i10
Silverton, Oreg., 3,081 80 B3
Silverton, Tex., 1,098 77 N2
Silvertown, Ga. 64 E3
Silverwood, Mich. 67 K5
Silves, Braz. 102 E2
Silves, Port., 9,014 122 A4
Silvia, Col. 100 B6
Silvianópolis, Braz., 2,156 103 d18
Silvícola, Port. Timor 149 H5
Silvies, r., Oreg. 80 D4
Silvis, Ill., 3,973 68 B2
Silvituc, Mex. 93 H4
Silvolde, Neth., 3,300 115 E3
Silyānah, Tun., 3,431 160 f5
Sim, U.S.S.R., 13,900 137 i8
Sima, Burma 146 B1
Simacota, Col. 100 D4
Si Maha Phot, Thai. 147 d5
Simakalo, Indon. 148 B3
Simanggang, Malay., 5,648 148 D2
Šimanovci, Yug. 125 E2
Simão Dias, Braz., 5,334 103 J4
Simav, Turk., 6,337 142 B2
Simav, r., Turk. 142 B2
Simba, D.R.Congo 164 C1
Simbach, F.R.Ger., 6,892 118 D4
Simbahan, Phil., 1,341 153 B4
Simbo, i., Sol. Is. 175 b2
Simbukhovo, U.S.S.R. 136 b6
Simcoe, Ont., Can., 8,618 46 D6
Simcoe, L., Ont., Can. 44 H7
Simcoe Mtn., Wash. 80 C2
Simdega, India, 10,438 145 G5
Simen Mts., Eth. 163 L3
Simeonof I., Alaska 85 E5
Simeulue, P., Indon. 148 A2
Simferopol', U.S.S.R., 196,000 134 C5
Sími, Gr., 2,982 129 F6
Simi, Calif., 2,107 83 g15
Sími, i., Gr. 129 F6
Simijaca, Col. 100 C5
Simikot, Nepal 145 F3
Similkameen, r., Br. Col., Can. 42 G4
Simití, Col. 100 C4
Simitli, Bulg., 2,871 128 D4
Simla, India, 42,597 145 E3
Simla, Colo., 450 79 C2
Şimleu Silvaniei, Rum., 8,560 128 D1
Simme, r., Switz. 124 B2
Simmer, r., F.R.Ger. 119 C5
Simmerath, F.R.Ger., 2,444 119 A3
Simmern, F.R.Ger., 4,851 119 C5
Simmesport, La., 2,125 73 D7
Simmons, Mo. 72 F7
Simms, Mont. 81 D2
Simms Str., N.H. 54 E2
Simnasho, Oreg. 80 C3
Simo, Fin. 120 F2
Simojärvi, l., Fin. 120 F2
Simojoki, r., Fin. 120 F2
Simojovel, Mex., 3,739 93 G5
Simon, L., Qué., Can. 47 J3
Simón Bolivar, Pq. Nac., Ven. 100 E3
Simonésia, Braz., 1,568 103 e17
Simonikha, U.S.S.R. 137 h8
Simonstorp, Swed. 120 d9
Simonstown, S. Af., 8,272 164 B7
Simoom Sound, Br. Col., Can. 42 E4
Simpang, Indon. 148 B2
Simpang Ampat, Malay., 1,258 147 o13
Simpang Rengam, Malay., 2,366 147 p16
Simpele, Fin. 120 G3
Simplício Mendes, Braz., 1,682 103 H3
Simplon, Switz. 124 C2
Simplon Pass, Switz. 124 B2
Simpson, Sask., Can. 43 C4
Simpson, Kans., 154 75 H4
Simpson, co., Ky., 11,548 71 E5
Simpson, La. 73 B6
Simpson, co., Miss., 20,454 73 F6
Simpson, Nev. 83 A3
Simpson, N.C., 302 63 G2
Simpson, Pa., 1,900* 61 L2
Simpson Desert, Austl. 172 E3
Simpsonville, S.C., 2,282 63 B3
Simral, India 144 a14
Simrishamn, Swed. 120 C5
Sims, Ill., 376 68 D5
Sims, N.C., 205 63 F2
Simsboro, La., 363 73 C5
Simsbury, Conn., 2,745;10,138(T) 56 E5
Simsonbaai, St. Maarten 97 7
Simten, F.R.Ger., 2,061 119 D6
Simtustus, L., Oreg. 80 C3
Simunul I., Phil. 153 A4
Simushir, O., U.S.S.R. 135 P5
Sinabang, Indon. 148 A2
Sinai, S. Dak., 166 74 D3
Sinai, Mt.=Mūsā Jabal
Sinai, pen., U.A.R. 161 K3
Sinaia, Rum., 9,006 128 E2
Sinajana, Guam, 2,861 176 24
Sinaloa, st., Mex., 838,404 92 C2
Sinaloa, r., Mex. 92 C3
Sinaloa de Leyva, Mex., 1,284 92 C3
Sinamar, Phil., 2,366 153 c6
Sînandrei, Rum. 128 C2
Sinanju, N. Kor. 151 E3
Sinara, r., U.S.S.R. 137 k8
Sinarádhes, Gr., 1,316 129 B5
Sinaung Myauk, Burma 146 A2
Sīnāwan, Libya 161 F2
Sinbaungwe, Burma, 3,186 146 A3
Sinbo, Burma 146 B1
Sinbyugyun, Burma, 4,369 146 A2
Sincelejo, Col. 100 C3
Sincerín, Col. 100 C2
Sinch'ang, N. Kor. 151 F2
Sinch'ang, S. Kor., 14,657 151 E3
Sinch'ŏn, N. Kor. 151 E3
Sinclair, Me. 55 D1
Sinclair, Wyo., 621 81 F5
Sinclair, L., Ga. 64 F2
Sinclair Mills, Br. Col., Can. 42 G2
Sinclair's Bay, U.K. 112 E2
Sinclairville, N.Y., 726 58 B7
Sindal, Den., 2,317 121 C3
Sindañgan, Phil., 5,867 153 B3
Sindangbarang, Indon. 148 C4
Sindelfingen, F.R.Ger., 17,661 118 B4
Sindeya, U.S.S.R. 137 k6
Sindh, r., India 144 b13
Síndhos, Gr., 4,132 129 D4
Sindhūli Garhi, Nepal 144 e12
Sindi, U.S.S.R., 3,300 136 B1
Sındırgı, Turk., 5,077 142 B2
Sindjai, Indon. 149 G4
Sîndominic, Rum. 128 E1
Sindri, India, 41,315 144 f14
Sinegorskiy, U.S.S.R. 136 g8
Sines, Port., 8,866 122 A4
Sines, C. de, Port. 122 A4
Sinfães, Port., 3,961 122 B2
Sinfra, Iv. Coast, 5,342 162 D4
Singa, Peru, 1,268 104 B4
Singac, N.J. 58 b13
Singac Bk., N.J. 58 b13
Singaingmyo, Burma, 1,721 147 g7
Singapore, ctry., 1,891,000* 148 C2
Singaradja, Indon. 148 E5
Singatoka, Fiji 174 4
Singatoka, r., Fiji 174 4
Singavi, Mt., Îs. de Horne 175 9
Sing Buri, Thai., 8,322 146 B4
Singen, F.R.Ger., 28,364 118 B5
Sîngeorz-Băi, Rum. 128 E1
Singer, La. 73 B7
Singers Glen, Va., 102 62 E4
Singhampton, Ont., Can. 46 D4
Singhofen, F.R.Ger., 1,027 119 D4
Singida, Tanz. 164 E2
Singitikós Kólpos, Gr. 129 D4
Singkaling Hkamti, Burma 146 A1
Singkang, Indon. 149 G4
Singkawang, Indon. 148 D2
Singkep, P., Indon. 148 C3
Singkil, Indon. 148 A2
Singkuang, Indon. 148 A2
Singleton, Austl., 4,506 173 h9
Singleton, Mt., Austl. 172 D3
Singora=Songkhla
Singu, Burma, 4,069 147 f7
Singu, Burma 147 g6
Singuilucan, Mex., 1,522 93 f10
Sin'gye, N. Kor. 151 E3
Sinhailien=Hsin-hai-lien
Sinhŭng, N. Kor. 151 E2
Sinhyo-ri, S. Kor. 151 E4
Sining=Hsi-ning
Siniscola, It., 6,754 123 B4
Sinissippi L., Wis. 66 E5
Sinj, Yug., 3,319 125 C3
Sinjah, Sudan, 9,437 163 K3
Sinjār, Iraq, 4,988 143 C1
Sinkāt, Sudan, 5,175 163 L2
Sinkiang=Hsin-chiang-wei-wu-erh Tzu-chih-ch'ü
Sinkiang Uighur Autonomous Region=Hsin-chiang-wei-wu-erh Tzu-chih-ch'ü
Sinking Spring, Ohio, 202 70 F3
Sinking Spring, Pa., 2,244 61 h14
Sin-le-Noble, Fr., 14,794 116 a7
Sinmak, N. Kor. 151 E3
Sinn, F.R.Ger., 3,514 119 E3
Sinn, r., F.R.Ger. 119 H4
Sinnamary, Fr. Guiana 1,563* 101 O5
Sinnamary, r., Fr. Guiana 101 O5
Sinnar, India, 17,092 145 i17
Sinnemahoning, Pa. 60 F3
Sinnemahoning Cr., Pa. 60 F3
Sînnicolau Mare, Rum., 9,956 128 C1
Sinnūris, U.A.R. 161 i8
Sinoe, Rum. 128 G2
Sinoe, L., Rum. 128 G2
Sinoia, Rhod., 2,444 164 D4
Sinop, Turk., 9,899 142 C1
Sinp'o, N. Kor. 151 F2
Sinp'ung-dong, N. Kor. 151 F2
Sinp'yŏng, N. Kor. 151 E3
Sinsang, N. Kor. 151 E3
Sinsheim, F.R.Ger., 6,112 118 B4
Sinsinawa, Wis. 66 C6
Sinskoye, U.S.S.R. 135 M3
Sint-Amands, Belg., 4,076 115 d8
Sint-Amandsberg, Belg., 23,726 115 B3
Sînta Maria, Rum. 128 F1
Sîntana, Rum. 128 C1
Sintang, Indon. 148 D2
Sint Christoffelberg, mtn., Cur. 97 16
Sint-Denijs, Belg., 2,642 116 a6
Sint-Genesius-Rode, Belg., 10,287 115 C4
Sint-Gillis-bij-Dendermonde, Belg., 10,282 115 C3
Sint-Gillis-Waas, Belg., 5,801 115 C3
Sint Jan, Cur. 97 16
Sint Joris B., Cur. 97 16
Sint Josefsdal, Cur. 97 16
Sint-Katelijne-Waver, Belg., 11,314 115 e8
Sint-Kruis, Belg., 10,129 115 B3
Sint Kruis, Cur. 97 16
Sint Maarten, i., Lesser Ant. 97 7
Sint Martha B., Cur. 97 16
Sint-Michiels, Belg., 8,085 115 B3
Sint Nicolaas, Aruba, 20,000* 97 15
Sint Nicolaas, Cur. 97 16
Sint-Niklaas, Belg., 47,015 115 C3
Sinton, Tex., 6,008 77 P5
Sintong, Indon. 147 o16
Sint-Pieters-Leeuw, Belg., 13,609 115 C4
Sintra, Port., 19,930 122 A3
Sint-Truiden, Belg., 20,552 115 D4
Sinú, r., Col. 100 B3
Sinuapa, Hond. 94 d9
Sinŭiju, N. Kor. 151 E2
Sinyaya, r., U.S.S.R. 136 C1
Sinyukha, r., U.S.S.R. 136 C3
Sinzheim, F.R.Ger., 5,093 118 B4
Sinzig, F.R.Ger., 5,830 119 C3
Sio, Terr. New Guin. 174 e2
Sió, r., Hung. 126 D3
Siocon, Phil., 1,667 153 B4
Siófok, Hung., 9,832 126 D3
Sion, Switz., 16,051 124 B2
Sion Mills, U.K., 1,623 113 C4
Sioule, r., Fr. 117 E4
Sioux, co., Iowa, 26,375 72 A1
Sioux, co., Nebr., 2,575 75 B1
Sioux, co., N. Dak., 3,662 74 B2
Sioux Center, Iowa, 2,275 72 A1
Sioux City, Iowa, 89,159 72 A2
Sioux Falls, S. Dak., 65,466 74 D4
Sioux Lookout, Ont., Can. 44 D5
Sioux Narrows, Ont., Can. 44 C5
Sioux Rapids, Iowa, 962 72 B2
Sipalay, Phil., 3,740 153 B3
Sipapo, r., Ven. 100 G5
Siparia, Trin. and Tob., 5,940* 96 g5
Sipesville, Pa. 60 D5
Sipiwesk, Man., Can. 43 F3
Sipiwesk L., Man., Can. 43 F3
Siple, Mt., Ant. 180 X5
Sipocot, Phil., 5,914 153 B2
Sipolilo, Rhod. 164 E4
Şipote, Rum. 128 F1
Sippola, Fin. 120 F3
Si Pranchan, Thai. 147 c4
Sipsey, r., Ala. 64 B2
Sip Song Chau Thai, reg., N. Viet. 147 ·
Sipul, Terr. New Guin. 174 f2
Sipura, P., Indon. 148 A3
Siqueros, Mex., 1,306 92 D3
Siquia, r., Nic. 94 E4
Siquijor, Phil. 153 e12
Siquijor I., Phil. 153 B3
Siquirres, C.R., 2,157 94 F5
Siquisique, Ven., 2,354 100 F2
Sira, India, 15,408 145 E7
Sira, r., Nor. 120 A4
Sirač, Yug. 125 C2
Si Racha, Thai., 10,472 146 C4
Siracusa, It., 82,944 123 E6
Sirājganj, Pak., 47,152 145 H4
Siraway, Phil., 3,000 153 B4
Sir Edward Pellew Group, is., Austl. 172 E2
Sireköpinge, Swed. 121 c7
Siren, Wis., 679 66 A3
Siret, Rum., 5,664 128 E1
Siretul, r., Rum. 128 F1
Sir Francis Drake Chan., V.I. 97 4
Sirha, Nepal, 2,546 145 H4
Sirḥān, Wādī as, val., Saudi Ar. 143 B2
Siri, C., Terr. Papua 174 3
Şiria, Rum. 128 C1
Sirik, Tg., Malay. 148 D2
Sirina, i., Gr. 129 F6
Sir James MacBrien, Mt., N.W.T., Can. 40 D5
Sīrjan=Sa'īdābād
Sirmans, Fla. 65 F2
Sirmione, It., 2,356 122 d5
Sirnach, Switz., 3,075 124 C1
Şırnak, Turk., 4,060 142 E2
Sirnitz, Aust. 124 K7
Sirohi, India, 14,451 145 D4
Sirombu, Indon. 148 A2
Sironcha, India 145 F6
Sironj, India, 17,288 145 E4
Síros, i., Gr. 129 E6
Sirsa, India, 33,363 145 E3
Sir Sanford, Mt., Br. Col., Can. 42 H3
Sirsi, India, 21,240 145 E7
Sirte=Surt
Siruela, Sp., 5,132 122 C3
Sirur, India, 6,234 145 i17
Sir Wilfrid Laurier, Mt., Br. Col., Can. 42 H3
Sisak, Yug., 26,000* 125 C2
Si Saket, Thai., 9,517 146 D4
Sisal, Mex. 93 H4
Sisante, Sp., 3,277 122 D3
Si Sawat, Thai. 147 c4
Sisim, r., U.S.S.R. 137 t11
Sisipuk L., Man.-Sask., Can. 43 E3
Siskiwit Bay, Mich. 66 b9
Siskiwit L., Mich. 66 b8
Siskiyou, co., Calif., 32,885 82 B2
Siskiyou Mts., Calif.-Oreg. 82 B2
Sison, Phil., 2,288 153 b6
Si Songkhram, Thai. 146 C3

Sisophon—Sombrerete · 295

Sisophon, Camb. 146 C4
Sisquoc, r., Calif. 82 D5
Sissach, Switz., 4,574 124 B1
Sissano, Terr. New Guin. 174 d1
Sisseton, S. Dak., 3,218 74 D3
Sissonne, Fr., 4,439 117 E2
Sissonville, W. Va. 62 C4
Sīstān, Daryācheh-ye, Iran 143 F2
Sister Bay, Wis., 520 66 F3
Sister Lakes, Mich. 67 G6
Sisteron, Fr., 5,689 117 F4
Sisters, Oreg., 602 80 C3
Sisters, The, is., Gren. Is. 97 20
Sisters, The, is., N.Z. 175 14
Sisters, The, is., Seych. 165 a10
Sisters Pk., Ascension 109 6
Sistersville, W. Va. 62 C3
Sitamarhi, India, 17,873 144 e12
Sitangkai, Phil., 3,328 153 A4
Sitapur, India, 53,884 145 F4
Sitges, Sp., 10,491 122 F2
Sithonía, pen., Gr. 129 D4
Sitía, Gr., 5,327 129 F7
Sitka, Alaska, 3,237 85 L4
Sitka, Kans. 75 F6
Sitka Nat. Mon., Alaska 85 L4
Sitkinak I., Alaska 85 F4
Sitkum, Oreg. 80 B4
Sitkwin, Burma, 4,597 147 a2
Sitnica, r., Yug. 125 E3
Sitrah, U.A.R. 161 J3
Sittang, r., Burma 146 B3
Sittard, Neth., 27,300 115 D3
Sittaung, Burma 146 A1
Sitter, r., Switz. 124 D1
Sittersdorf, Aust., 2,003 124 L7
Situbondo, Indon. 148 f7
Sitzenberg, Aust. 124 b10
Sitzendorf, Aust. 124 b9
Si-u, Burma 146 B2
Siuslaw, r., Oreg. 80 B4
Siutu, W. Samoa 177 38
Siva, U.S.S.R. 137 h7
Sivac, Yug., 11,105 125 D2
Sivaganga, India, 15,642 145 m21
Sivakasi, India, 30,690 145 k21
Sivaki, U.S.S.R. 135 M4
Sivas, Turk., 93,849 142 D2
Siverek, Turk., 26,071 142 D2
Sivrihisar, Turk., 7,186 142 B2
Sivry, Belg., 1,485 115 C4
Sivry-Courtry, Fr. 116 k12
Sivuch, U.S.S.R. 135 P4
Sīwah, U.A.R. 161 J3
Sīwah, Wāḥāt, oasis, U.A.R. 161 J3
Siwālik Hills, Nepal 144 c11
Siwalkis, mtn. ra., Asia 140 F3
Siwan, India, 27,370 144 e12
Siwa Oasis=Sīwah, Wāḥāt
Sixaola, r., C.R. 94 F6
Six Corners, Ill. 69 b10
Sixes, Oreg. 80 A4
Sixlakes, Mich. 67 H5
Six Mile, S.C., 218 63 B3
Six Mile L., La. 73 D8
Six Run Cr., N.C. 63 F2
Sixteen Acres (part of Springfield), Mass. 56 G4
Sixteen Mile Cr., Ont., Can. 46 d15
Sixth Cataract, Sudan 163 K3
Sizandro, r., Port. 122 i9
Sizerville, Pa. 60 F2
Sjælland, i., Den. 121 D5
Sjællands Odde, Den. 121 D5
Själevad, Swed. 120 D3
Sjenica, Yug., 4,801 125 D3
Sjørring, Den., 1,377 121 A4
Sjösa, Swed. 120 e9
Skabersjö, Swed. 121 F5
Skadovsk, U.S.S.R. 136 D4
Skælskør, Den., 2,889 121 D5
Skærbæk, Den., 2,646 121 A5
Skafså, Nor. 121 A1
Skagen, Den., 10,390 121 C3
Skagens Odde=Grenen
Skagerrak, str., Eur. 120 B4
Skagit, co., Wash., 51,350 80 C1
Skagit, r., Wash. 80 C1
Skagway, Alaska, 659 85 L4
Skála, Gr., 2,343 129 D6
Skálavík, Faeroe Is. 120 c7
Skalbmierz, Pol., 1,702 127 D3
Skälderviken, bay, Swed. 121 E4
Skalica, Czech. 126 C2
Skal'nyy, U.S.S.R. 137 i7
Skals, Den., 1,414 121 B4
Skamania, co., Wash., 5,207 80 B2
Skanderbeut, Mal i, Alb. 125 D4
Skanderborg, Den., 5,482 121 C4
Skandia, Mich. 66 F2
Skaneateles, N.Y., 2,921 59 H6
Skaneateles Falls, N.Y. 59 q24
Skaneateles L., N.Y. 59 H6
Skanee, Mich. 66 E2
Skanör, Swed. 121 E5
Skantzoúra, i., Gr. 129 E5
Skara, Swed. 120 C4
Skärdu, Pak. 145 E2
Skarnes, Nor. 120 B3
Skarrild, Den. 121 A5
Skarszewy, Pol., 3,454 127 C1
Skårup, Den., 2,260 121 C5
Skaryszew, Pol., 2,355 127 D3
Skarżysko-Kamienna, Pol., 35,000* 127 D3
Skåtöy, Nor. 121 B2
Skavaig, Loch, U.K. 112 C3
Skaw, The=Grenen
Skawa, r., Pol. 127 i7
Skawce, Pol. 127 i7
Skawina, Pol., 9,452 127 C4
Skebokvarn, Swed. 120 d8
Skedans, Br. Col., Can. 42 D3
Skedee, Okla., 128 76 G1
Skee, Swed. 121 D2
Skeels, Mich. 67 J4
Skeena, r., Br. Col., Can. 42 E2
Skeerpoort, S. Af. 165 i16
Skegness, U.K., 12,847 113 G5
Skela, Yug., 2,064 125 E2
Skeldon, Guyana, 4,367 101 M5
Skeleton Cr., Okla. 76 F1
Skeleton L., Ont., Can. 46 E3
Skellefteå, Swed., 22,730 120 E2
Skellefteälv, r., Swed. 120 D2
Skelleftehamn, Swed. 120 E2
Skellingthorpe, U.K., 1,328 114 G4
Skellytown, Tex., 967 76 N2
Skelmersdale, U.K., 6,308 114 C3
Skelmorlie, U.K. 112 a8
Skelton, U.K., 4,059 114 F1
Skelum, Den., 1,612 121 C4
Skene, Swed. 120 C4
Skępe, Pol. 127 C2
Skerries, Ire., 2,450 113 C5
Skerryvore, i., U.K. 112 C3
Skhimatárion, Gr., 1,161 129 D5
Skhiza, i., Gr. 129 C6
Skhodnya, U.S.S.R., 16,000 136 b6
Skhoinoúsa, i., Gr. 129 E6
Ski, Nor. 120 B4
Skiathos, Gr., 3,042 129 D5
Skiatook, Okla., 2,503 76 G1
Skibbereen, Ire., 2,202 113 B6
Skibotn, Nor. 120 E1
Skiddy, Kans. 75 J5
Skidel', U.S.S.R., 4,800 136 B2
Skidhra, Gr., 3,172 129 D4
Skidmore, Md. 62 d8
Skidmore, Mo., 425 72 B4
Skidmore, Tex. 77 P5
Skien, Nor., 15,505 120 B4
Skierniewice, Pol., 22,000* 127 D3
Skikda, Alg., 80,281 160 E1
Skillet Fk., r., Ill. 68 D5
Skillinge, Swed. 121 G5
Skinnskatteberg, Swed. 120 C4
Skinquarter, Va. 62 G5
Skippack, Pa. 60 f11
Skippers, Va. 62 G6
Skipsea, U.K. 114 H3
Skipton, U.K., 12,988 113 F5
Skipton-on-Swale, U.K. 114 F2
Skipwith, Va. 62 F6
Skíros, Gr., 2,411 129 E5
Skíros, i., Gr. 129 E5
Skivarp, Swed. 121 F5
Skive, Den., 15,558 121 A4
Skjeberg, Nor. 121 D1
Skjern, Den., 5,349 121 A5
Sklíthron, Gr., 1,084 129 C4
Skočivir, Yug. 125 E4
Skoczów, Pol., 6,298 127 C4
Skodborg, Den., 1,705 121 B5
Skodsborg, Den. 121 b7
Škofja Loka, Yug., 3,360 125 B1
Skogstorp, Swed. 120 d8
Skoki, Pol., 2,457 127 B2
Skokie, Ill., 59,364 69 d8
Skokie, r., Ill. 69 c8
Skokie Lagoons, Ill. 69 c8
Sköldinge, Swed. 120 d8
Skole, U.S.S.R., 5,600 136 A3
Skomer I., U.K. 113 D6
Skookumchuck, Br. Col., Can. 42 J4
Skópelos, Gr., 2,955 129 D5
Skópelos, Gr., 2,762 129 F5
Skópelos, i., Gr. 129 D5
Skopin, U.S.S.R., 18,000 136 E2
Skopje, Yug., 168,000* 125 E4
Skórcz, Pol., 2,375 127 C2
Skórkowice, Pol. 129 D3
Skorogoszcz, Pol. 127 g6
Skoroszyce, Pol. 127 g6
Skørping, Den. 121 B4
Skotfoss, Nor. 121 B1
Skoun, Camb. 147 k10
Skövde, Swed. 120 C4
Skovlunde, Den. 121 a7
Skovorodino, U.S.S.R., 15,100 135 M4
Skovsgård, Den. 121 B3
Skowhegan, Me., 6,667 55 C4
Skownan, Man., Can. 43 E4
Skradin, Yug. 125 B3
Skromberga, Swed. 121 b7
Skrwa, r., Pol. 127 C2
Skryje, Czech. 126 c7
Skudai, Malay., 1,982 147 p16
Skudeneshavn, Nor., 1,383 120 A4
Skull Valley, Ariz. 78 B4
Skultuna, Swed. 120 D4
Skummeslöv, Swed. 121 E4
Skuna, r., Miss. 73 F4
Skunk, r., Iowa 72 F4
Skuratovskiy, U.S.S.R., 21,200 136 E2
Skurup, Swed. 121 F5
Skuteč, Czech. 127 e7
Skutskär, Swed. 120 D3
Skúvoy, i., Faeroe Is. 120 c7
Skvira, U.S.S.R., 12,800 136 C3
Skwentna, Alaska 85 G3
Skwierzyna, Pol., 5,718 127 A2
Skye, I. of, U.K. 112 C3
Skykomish, Wash., 366 80 C2
Skykomish, r., Wash. 80 C2
Skyland, N.C. 63 B2
Skylight, Mt., N.Y. 59 N3
Skyring, Seno de, Chile 105 A8
Skytop, Pa. 61 M3
Slade, Ky. 71 H4
Slade Pt., Austl. 172 a7
Slades Corners, Wis. 66 c13
Sladesville, N.C. 63 H2
Slættaratindur, mt., Faeroe Is. 120 c7
Slagelse, Den., 20,562 121 D5
Slagle, La. 73 B6
Slagslunde, Den. 121 a7
Slaithwaite, U.K., 4,989 114 E3
Slaley, U.K. 112 f10
Slamannan, U.K., 2,959 112 c8
Slamet, G., Indon. 148 c7
Slana, Alaska 85 J3
Slaney, r., Ire. 113 C5
Slangerup, Den., 2,077 121 E4
Slănic, Rum., 6,842 128 F2
Slano, Yug. 125 C3
Slaný, Czech., 12,056 126 A1
Slåp, Swed. 121 D3
Slapout, Okla. 76 C1
Slapy, Czech. 126 d7
Ślęsk, reg., Pol. 127 B3
Slate, W. Va. 62 C3
Slatedale, Pa. 61 L4
Slater, Colo. 79 B1
Slater, Iowa, 717 72 D2
Slater, Mo., 2,767 72 D5
Slater, S.C. 63 B2
Slatersville, R.I. 57 K4
Slate Run, Pa. 60 H3
Slaterville Springs, N.Y. 59 H7
Slate Spring, Miss., 123 73 F4
Slatina, Rum., 13,381 128 E2
Slatington, Pa., 4,316 61 L4
Slaton, Tex., 6,568 77 N3
Slaty Fork, W. Va. 62 D4
Slaughter, La. 73 D7
Slaughter Beach, Del., 107 62 J4
Slaung, Indon. 148 d8
Slautnoye, U.S.S.R. 135 Q3
Slave, r., Alta., Can. 42 K1
Slave Falls, Man., Can. 43 G5
Slave Lake, Alta., Can. 42 J2
Slavgorod, Bel.S.S.R., U.S.S.R., 6,400 136 C2
Slavgorod, R.S.F.S.R., U.S.S.R., 38,400 134 G4
Slavgorod, Ukr.S.S.R., U.S.S.R., 4,800 136 D3
Slavonice, Czech. 126 B2
Slavonska Požega, Yug., 13,000* 125 C2
Slavonski Brod, Yug., 25,000* 125 C2
Slavuta, U.S.S.R., 25,000 136 B3
Slavyanka, U.S.S.R. 151 F2
Slavyanovo, Bulg., 6,513 128 E3
Slavyansk, U.S.S.R., 86,000 136 E3
Slavyansk-na-Kubani, U.S.S.R., 39,000 136 E4
Sławatycze, Pol. 127 E3
Slawi, Indon. 148 c7
Sławniowice, Pol. 127 g6
Sławno, Pol., 8,101 127 B1
Slayden, Miss. 73 F3
Slayden, Tenn., 101 71 D5
Slayton, Minn., 2,487 74 E4
Sleaford, U.K., 7,844 113 F5
Sleaford Bay, Austl. 172 a8
Sleat, Pt. of, U.K. 112 C3
Sleat, Sd. of, U.K. 112 D3
Sledge, Miss., 440 73 E3
Sled L., Sask., Can. 43 C3
Sledmere, U.K. 114 G2
Sleekburn, U.K. 112 g9
Sleeman, Ont., Can. 44 C5
Sleeper, Mo., 111 72 E7
Sleeper Is., N.W.T., Can. 44 H2
Sleepy Eye, Minn., 3,492 74 E3
Sleepy Hollow, Ill., 311 69 a8
Sleetmute, Alaska, 122 85 E3
Ślesin, Pol., 1,920 127 C2
Sletten, Den. 121 b7
Slettetrhage, pt., Den. 121 C4
Sleża, r., Pol. 127 f6
Sliabh Gaoil, mtn., U.K. 112 D4
Slick, Okla., 151 76 G2
Slick Rock, Colo. 79 A2
Slickville, Pa. 60 C5
Slidell, La., 6,356 73 F7
Slide Mtn., N.Y. 59 M8
Sliedrecht, Neth., 16,800 115 b7
Sliema, Malta, 23,399 123 f12
Slieve Aughty Mts., Ire. 113 B5
Slieve Mish Mts., Ire. 113 B5
Sligo, co., Ire., 56,850 113 B4
Sligo, Ire., 12,947 113 B4
Sligo, Pa., 814 60 D3
Sligo Bay, Ire. 113 B4
Slikkerveer, Neth., 8,000 115 b7
Slim, Malay., 2,255 147 o15
Slimbridge, U.K. 114 D7
Slim River, Malay., 3,728 147 o15
Slinger, Wis., 1,141 66 E5
Slingerlands, N.Y. 59 v29
Slipčići, Yug. 125 C3
Slippery Rock, Pa., 2,563 60 B3
Slippery Rock Cr., Pa. 60 B4
Slite, Swed. 120 D4
Sliven, Bulg., 46,175 128 F3
Slivileşti, Rum. 128 D2
Slivnitsa, Bulg., 4,862 128 D3
Sloan, Iowa, 704 72 A2
Sloan, Nev. 83 C5
Sloan, N.Y., 5,803 58 C6
Sloan Pk., Wash. 80 C1
Sloansville, N.Y. 59 M6
Sloat, Calif. 82 C3
Sloatsburg, N.Y., 2,565 59 M9
Sloboda, U.S.S.R. 136 D2
Slobodskoy, U.S.S.R., 34,300 134 D4
Slobozia, Rum., 9,632 128 E3
Slobozia, Rum. 128 F2
Slocan, Br. Col., Can. 42 H4
Slocan L., Br. Col., Can. 42 H4
Slocomb, Ala., 1,368 64 D4
Slocum, R.I. 57 K6
Slöinge, Swed. 121 E4
Słomniki, Pol., 4,496 127 C3
Slonim, U.S.S.R., 17,500 136 B2
Slope, co., N. Dak., 1,893 74 A2
Slot, The, sd., Sol. Is. 170 E5
Slotermeer, Neth. 115 D2
Slough, U.K., 80,781 114 G7
Sloughhouse, Calif. 82 b8
Slovakia=Slovensko
Slovan, Pa., 1,018 60 B5
Slovenia=Slovenija
Slovenija, st., Yug., 1,591,523 125 B2
Slovenska Bistrica, Yug., 2,570 125 B1
Slovenské Rudohorie, mts., Czech. 126 D2
Slovensko, reg., Czech. 126 D2
Slow Fork Kuskokwim, r., Alaska 85 F3
Słubice, Pol., 7,204 127 A2
Sluch', r., U.S.S.R. 136 B2
Sluch', r., U.S.S.R. 136 B3
Sluiskil, Neth., 3,200 115 B3
Šluknov, Czech. 126 d5
Slunj, Yug. 125 B2
Słupca, Pol., 4,880 127 B2
Słupia, r., Pol. 127 B1
Słupsk, Pol., 53,000* 127 B1
Slutsk, U.S.S.R., 22,700 136 B2
Slyne, U.K. 114 C2
Slyne Head, Ire. 113 A5
Slyudyanka, U.S.S.R., 21,400 135 K4
Smackover, Ark., 2,434 73 C4
Småland, reg., Swed. 120 C4
Smålandsfarvandet, sd., Den. 121 D5
Smart Mtn., Me. 55 B3
Smarts Mtn., N.H. 54 C4
Smeaton, Sask., Can. 43 C4
Smečno, Czech. 126 d6
Smederevo, Yug., 27,000* 125 E2
Smederevska Palanka, Yug., 13,000* 125 E2
Smedstorp, Swed. 121 G5
Smela, U.S.S.R., 46,000 136 D3
Smelterville, Idaho, 1,127 81 A2
Smethport, N.C. 63 C1
Smethport, Pa., 1,725 60 E2
Smethwick, U.K., 68,372 114 E6
Smicksburg, Pa., 80 60 D4
Smidary, Czech. 127 e6
Smidovich, U.S.S.R., 9,200 135 N5
Smidovich, U.S.S.R. 134 E2
Smilde, Neth., 5,800 115 E2
Smiley, Sask., Can. 43 B4
Smiley, Tex., 455 77 P5
Smiltene, U.S.S.R., 6,400 136 B1
Smilyan, Bulg., 1,229 129 E4
Smiřice, Czech. 127 e6
Smirnovskiy, U.S.S.R. 137 n11
Smith, Alta., Can. 42 K2
Smith, co., Kans., 7,776 75 G4
Smith, co., Miss., 14,303 73 F5
Smith, Nev. 83 A3
Smith, co., Tenn., 12,059 71 F5
Smith, co., Tex., 86,350 77 Q3
Smith, r., Mont. 81 D2
Smith, r., N.H. 54 D4
Smith, r., Oreg. 80 B4
Smith, r., Va. 62 E6
Smith and Sayles Res., R.I. 57 K5
Smith Arm, N.W.T., Can. 40 E4
Smith Bay, N.W.T., Can. 41 O2
Smith Bay, Alaska 85 F1
Smithboro, Ill., 213 68 C5
Smithboro, N.Y. 59 G7
Smithburg, N.J. 58 b16
Smith Center, Kans., 2,379 75 G4
Smith Cr., S. Dak. 74 C4
Smithers, Br. Col., Can., 2,457 42 E2
Smithers, W. Va., 1,696 62 C4
Smithfield, S. Af., 2,824 164 D7
Smithfield, Ill., 329 68 B3
Smithfield, Me. 55 C4
Smithfield, Nebr., 85 75 F3
Smithfield, N.C., 6,117 63 F2
Smithfield, Ohio, 1,312 70 J2
Smithfield, Pa., 939 60 C6
Smithfield, R.I., 9,442(T) 57 K5
Smithfield, Utah, 2,512 78 C1
Smithfield, Va., 917 62 H6
Smithfield, W. Va., 361 62 D3
Smith I., N.W.T., Can. 44 H1
Smithland, Iowa, 349 72 A2
Smithland, Ky., 541 71 C4
Smithmill, Pa. 60 F4
Smith Pk., Idaho 81 A1
Smith Point, Tex. 77 k9
Smith Pt., Mass. 57 P7
Smith River, Br. Col., Can. 42 E1
Smith River, Calif. 82 A2
Smithsburg, Md., 586 62 G3
Smiths Creek, Mich. 67 L6
Smiths Falls, Ont., Can., 9,488 44 J7
Smiths Ferry, Idaho 81 B3
Smiths Ferry (part of Holyoke), Mass. 56 F3
Smiths Grove, Ky., 613 71 E4
Smiths I., Berm. Is. 108 1
Smiths Mills=North Dartmouth
Smith Sound, Newf., Can. 45 b9
Smith Sd., Can.-Greenl. 180 F2
Smithton, Austl., 2,506 173 F6
Smithton, Ill., 629 68 B5
Smithton, Mo., 395 72 D6
Smithton, Pa., 649 60 C5
Smithtown, Austl. 173 H4
Smith Town, Ky. 71 G5
Smithtown, N.Y. 58 g13
Smithtown, N.C., 199 63 D1
Smithtown Bay, N.Y. 58 f13
Smithville, Ont., Can. 46 c15
Smithville, Ga., 732 64 E4
Smithville, Ind. 70 C3
Smithville, Miss., 489 73 G3
Smithville, Mo., 1,254 72 C5
Smithville, Ohio, 1,024 70 H2
Smithville, Okla., 110 76 J3
Smithville, Tenn., 2,348 71 F6
Smithville, Tex., 2,933 77 P5
Smithville Flats, N.Y. 59 J7
Smithwick, S. Dak. 74 A4
Smoaks, S.C., 145 63 D4
Smock, Pa., 1,012 60 C6
Smokemont, N.C. 63 A2
Smoky, r., Alta., Can. 42 H2
Smoky Bay, Austl. 172 E5
Smoky Bay, Austl. 172 D5
Smoky Hill, r., Kans. 75 G5
Smoky Hill, N. Fk., r., Colo. 79 D2
Smoky Hill, S. Fk., r., Colo. 79 D2
Smoky Hills, Kans. 50 G3
Smoky Lake, Alta., Can. 42 K2
Smoky L., Alta., Can. 43 c6
Smoky Ordinary, Va. 62 G6
Smöla, i., Nor. 120 A3
Smolensk, U.S.S.R., 159,000 134 C4
Smolensko-Moskovskaya Voz., U.S.S.R. 136 D2
Smoljana, Yug. 125 C2
Smolyan, Bulg., 5,113 129 E4
Smolyanovtsi, Bulg., 2,750 128 D3
Smoot, Wyo. 81 D4
Smooth Rock Falls, Ont., Can., 1,080 44 G5
Smoothstone, r., Sask., Can. 43 C3
Smoothstone L., Sask., Can. 43 C3
Smorgon', U.S.S.R., 6,500 136 B2
Smrk, pk., Czech.-Pol. 127 e6
Smugglers Notch, Vt. 54 B2
Smyadovo, Bulg., 5,916 128 F3
Smychka, U.S.S.R. 136 b5
Smyge, Swed. 121 F5
Smyków, Pol. 127 k5
Smyrna, Del., 3,241 62 J3
Smyrna, Ga., 10,157 64 E2
Smyrna, Mich. 67 H5
Smyrna, N.Y., 286 59 J6
Smyrna, Tenn., 3,612 71 E6
Smyrna, r., Del. 61 A5
Smyrna Mills, Me. 55 D2
Smyth, co., Va., 31,066 62 C6
Snaefell, mtn., U.K. 113 D4
Snag, Yukon, Can. 40 A5
Snagov, Rum. 128 F2
Snainton, U.K. 114 G2
Snaipol, Camb. 147 k11
Snaith, U.K., 1,118 114 F3
Snake, r., U.S. 52 C1
Snake, r., Minn. 74 D1
Snake, r., Minn. 74 F3
Snake, r., Nebr. 75 D1
Snake Buttes, N. Dak. 74 A2
Snake Cr., S. Dak. 74 C3
Snake Cr., N. Fk., S. Dak. 74 C3
Snake Mtn., Vt. 54 A3
Snake Ra., Nev. 83 C3
Snake R. Plain, Idaho 50 C2
Snape, U.K. 114 E2
Snapper Cr. Can., Fla. 65 a10
Snare River, N.W.T., Can. 40 F5
Snares, The, is., N.Z. 170 F8
Snåsa, Nor. 120 C2
Snåsavatnet, l., Nor. 120 B2
Sneads, Fla., 1,399 65 D2
Sneads Ferry, N.C. 63 G3
Snedsted, Den., 1,991 121 A4
Sneedville, Tenn., 799 71 H5
Sneek, Neth., 20,600 115 D1
Sneeker meer, Neth. 115 D1
Snegamook L., Newf., Can. 45 O3
Snekkersten, Den. 121 b7
Snelgrove, Ont., Can. 46 c13
Snell, Va. 62 G4
Snelling, Calif. 82 C4
Snelling, S.C., 100 63 C4
Snell Lock, N.Y. 69 C
Snettisham, U.K., 1,671 114 J5
Snezhnoye, U.S.S.R., 25,700 136 f8
Sneżnik, mt., Yug. 125 B2
Sniardwy, Jez., Pol. 127 D2
Snicarte, Ill. 68 B3
Snina, Czech. 126 F2
Snipatuit Pd., Mass. 57 N5
Snipe Keys, Fla. 65 f13
Snizort, Loch, U.K. 112 C3
Snodland, U.K., 3,834 114 J8
Snohomish, co., Wash., 172,199 80 C1
Snohomish, Wash., 3,894 80 C2
Snook, Tex. 77 P4
Snoqualmie, Wash., 1,216 80 C2
Snoqualmie, r., Wash. 81 b7
Snoqualmie Pass, Wash. 80 C2
Snötinden, pk., Nor. 120 C2
Snover, Mich. 67 L5
Snow, Okla. 76 H3
Snowball, Ark. 73 C2
Snowbank L., Minn. 74 G1
Snow Camp, N.C. 63 E2
Snowcap Mtn., Alaska 85 F3
Snowden, Sask., Can. 43 D4
Snowdon, mtn., U.K. 113 E5
Snowdoun, Ala. 64 C3
Snowdrift, N.W.T., Can. 40 G5
Snowflake, Man., Can. 43 f10
Snowflake, Ariz., 1,723 78 C4
Snow Hill, Md., 2,311 62 J4
Snow Hill, N.C., 1,043 63 G2
Snow Lake, Man., Can. 43 E3
Snow Mtn., Me. 55 B3
Snow Mtn., Oreg. 80 D4
Snow Mtn. East, Calif. 82 B3
Snowshoe, Br. Col., Can. 42 G3
Snow Shoe, Pa., 714 60 G3
Snowshoe L., Me. 55 D2
Snowshoe Pk., Mont. 81 B1
Snowtown, Austl. 172 E5
Snowville, N.H. 54 E4
Snowville, Utah, 159 78 B1
Snowville, Va. 62 D5
Snow Water L., Nev. 83 C2
Snowy, r., Austl. 173 g11
Snowy Mts., Austl. 173 g11
Snug Harbour, Newf., Can. 45 Q4
Snug Harbor, R.I. 57 L7
Snuol, Camb. 146 D4
Snyatyn, U.S.S.R., 6,200 136 B3
Snyder, Ont., Can. 58 i19
Snyder, Ark. 73 D4
Snyder, Nebr., 325 75 J2
Snyder, Okla., 1,663 76 E3
Snyder, co., Pa., 25,922 60 H4
Snyder, Tex., 13,850 77 N3
Snydertown, Pa., 278 60 J4
Soacha, Col. 100 C5
Soalala, Malag. Rep. 165 G4
Soalary, Malag. Rep. 165 G5
Soan-kundo, S. Kor. 151 E4
Soap Lake, Wash., 1,591 80 D2
Soar, r., U.K. 114 F5
Soatá, Col. 100 D4
Soavinandriana, Malag. Rep., 2,478 165 G5
Soay, i., U.K. 113 C3
Soazza, Switz. 124 D2
Sobat, r., Sudan 163 K4
Sobe, Ryukyu Is. 154 a11
Sobernheim, F.R.Ger., 5,469 119 D5
Sobger, r., Indon. 149 L3
Soběslav, Czech. 126 B2
Sobieski, Wis. 66 E4
Sobieszów, Pol., 4,515 127 e6
Sobinka, U.S.S.R., 19,800 136 d6
Sobków, Pol. 127 k6
Sobotka, Czech. 127 e6
Sobótka, Pol., 2,695 127 f6
Sobów, Pol. 127 D3
Sobo-zan, mtn., Jap. 154 B5
Sobral, Braz., 32,281 103 H2
Sobral de Monte Agraço, Port., 1,793 122 i9
Sobreira Formosa, Port., 5,122 122 B3
Søby, Den. 121 C6
Soča, r., Yug. 125 A1
Socha, Col. 100 D5
Sochaczew, Pol., 15,810 127 D2
So-ch'e, China 150 A3
Sochi, U.S.S.R., 101,000 134 C5
Sŏch'ŏn, S. Kor., 17,718 151 E3
Social Circle, Ga., 1,780 64 F2
Société, Îs. de la, Fr. Poly. 171 H6
Society Hill, Ala. 64 D3
Society Hill, S.C., 677 63 D3
Society Is.=Société, Îs. de la
Socompa, Arg. 105 B2
Socorro, Braz., 6,402 103 c18
Socorro, Col. 100 D4
Socorro, Phil., 2,785 153 C3
Socorro, co., N. Mex., 10,168 79 B4
Socorro, N. Mex., 5,271 79 B4
Socorro, I., Mex. 92 b7
Socotra, i., Af. 159 J3
Socrum, Fla. 65 H4
Soc Trang=Khanh Hung
Socuéllamos, Sp., 14,828 122 D3
Sod, W. Va. 62 C4
Soda L., Calif. 82 E5
Sodankylä, Fin. 120 F2
Soda Springs, Calif. 82 C3
Soda Springs, Idaho, 2,424 81 D4
Sodaville, Nev. 83 A3
Sodaville, Oreg., 145 80 B3
Soddu, Eth. 163 L4
Soddy, Tenn., 2,206 71 F6
Söderhamn, Swed., 13,010 120 D3
Söderköping, Swed. 120 D4
Södertälje, Swed., 33,152 120 D4
Sod House, Nev. 83 A2
Sodom=Sedom
Södra Mellby, Swed. 121 G5
Södra Rörum, Swed. 121 F5
Södra Sandby, Swed. 121 F5
Sodus, N.Y., 1,645 58 F5
Sodus Point, N.Y., 868 58 F5
Soekmakaar, S. Af., 1,285 164 D5
Soest, F.R.Ger., 31,989 118 B3
Soest, Neth., 15,000 115 D2
Soestdijk, Neth., 5,400 115 c6
Soesterberg, Neth., 4,600 115 c6
Sofádhes, Gr., 4,771 129 D5
Sofadhítikos, r., Gr. 129 D5
Sofia, Bulg.=Sofiya
Sofia, N. Mex. 79 D3
Sofikón, Gr., 1,984 129 D6
Sofiya, Bulg., 592,845 128 D3
Sofiysk, U.S.S.R. 135 N4
Sōfu-gan, i., Japan 170 D3
Sogamoso, Col. 100 D5
Sogan, Indon. 148 d8
Sogang-ni, N. Kor. 151 E3
Sögel, F.R.Ger., 2,909 118 A2
Sognafjorden, Nor. 120 A3
Sogndal, Nor. 120 A3
Søgne, Nor. 121 A2
Sohāg=Sawhāj
Sohagpur, India, 9,382 144 b14
Soham, U.K., 5,077 113 G5
Sohara, Jap. 154 h14
Sohm Plain, Atl. Oc. 108 J4
Sohna, India, 6,889 144 a11
Sŏho-ri, N. Kor. 151 F2
Sohren, F.R.Ger., 1,739 119 C5
So-hsien, China 150 C4
Sohŭksan-do, S. Kor. 151 E4
Soignies, Belg., 10,919 115 B4
Soignolles-en-Brie, Fr. 116 i12
Soissons, Fr., 24,359 117 E2
Soisy-sur-Seine, Fr., 2,246 116 h12
Sōja, Jap., 36,413 155 C4
Sojat, India, 16,548 145 D4
Sŏjosŏn-man, N. Kor. 151 E3
Sŏka, Jap., 38,533 155 m19
Sokal', U.S.S.R., 9,400 136 B3
Söke, Turk., 23,442 142 A2
Sokele, D.R.Congo 165 m18
Soko Banja, Yug., 3,984 125 E3
Sokodé, Togo, 14,756 162 E4
Sokol, U.S.S.R., 46,000 134 D4
Sokolac, Yug. 125 D3
Sokolany, Pol. 127 E2
Sokółka, Pol., 7,263 127 E2
Sokolo, Mali, 3,458 162 D3
Sokolov, Czech., 18,330 126 A1
Sokolovo-Kundryuchenskoye, U.S.S.R. 136 f8
Sokołów Małopolski, Pol., 2,342 127 E3
Sokołów Podlaski, Pol., 9,669 127 E2
Sokosti, mt., Fin. 120 G1
Sokoto, Nigeria, 55,742 162 E3
Sokoto, r., Nigeria 162 E3
Sol, Costa del, Sp. 122 C4
Sola, Cuba, 1,724 96 e2
Sola, r., Pol. 127 i7
Sola de Vega, Mex., 1,882 93 F5
Solai, Kenya 165 h13
Solana, Phil., 2,428 153 c5
Solander I., N.Z. 175 e7
Solânea, Braz., 5,707 103 b14
Solanet, Arg. 105 b13
Solano, Phil., 12,095 153 c6
Solano, co., Calif., 134,597 82 C3
Solano, N. Mex. 79 C4
Solano, P., Col. 100 B4
Solaro, Fr. 116 r18
Solbad Hall, Aust., 10,680 124 H6
Solberg, Swed. 120 D3
Solberg L., Wis. 66 C3
Solca, Rum., 2,384 128 E1
Soldatna, Alaska, 32 85 G3
Soldier, Iowa, 284 72 B3
Soldier, Kans., 171 75 K4
Soldier Key, Fla. 65 b10
Soldier Pt., V.I. 97 4
Soldiers Grove, Wis., 663 66 C5
Soldier Summit, Utah, 33 78 C2
Soe, Indon. 149 H5
Solebury, Pa. 60 f10
Solec Kujawski, Pol., 6,940 127 C2
Soledad, Cuba, 1,245 96 e2
Soledad, Calif., 2,837 82 C4
Soledad, Ven., 5,259 101 J3
Soledade, Braz. 102 C3
Soledade, Braz., 7,211 103 F7
Soleduck, r., Wash. 80 A2
Solemint, Calif. 83 h15
Solen, N. Dak. 74 B2
Solent, The, chan., U.K. 113 k13
Solero, It., 2,481 122 b6
Solers-les-Etards, Fr. 116 i12
Solesmes, Fr., 6,369 116 a7
Solgne, Fr. 116 b9
Soliera, It., 9,945 122 d6
Soligalich, U.S.S.R., 5,800 136 F1
Solihull, U.K., 96,010 113 F5
Solikamsk, U.S.S.R., 84,000 137 i7
Sol'-Iletsk, U.S.S.R., 21,600 134 E4
Solimán, P., Mex. 93 J4
Solimões, Braz.=Amazonas
Solingen, F.R.Ger., 161,353 118 A3
Solís, Presa, res., Mex. 93 d10
Söll, Aust., 2,008 124 J6
Sollefteå, Swed. 120 D3
Sollenau, Aust., 2,503 124 N6
Sollentuna, Swed. 120 e8
Sóller, Sp., 9,473 122 G3
Søllested, Den., 1,143 121 D6
Solling, mtn., F.R.Ger. 118 B3
Solna, Swed. 120 e8
Solnechnogorsk, U.S.S.R., 22,800 136 D1
Solnice, Czech. 127 f6
Solo=Surakarta
Solo, r., Indon. 148 D4
Solok, Indon. 148 B3
Sololá, Guat., 4,291 94 b9
Solomea, W. Samoa 177 38
Solomon, Alaska 85 C2
Solomon, Ariz. 78 D5
Solomon, Kans., 1,008 75 H5
Solomon, r., Kans. 75 H4
Solomon Is., Terr. New Guin.-Terr. Papua 170 E5
Solomons, Md., 183 62 H4
Solomon Sea 170 E5
Solon, Ohio, 6,333 70 H1
Solon, Iowa, 604 72 F3
Solon, Me. 55 C4
Solon, Mich. 67 H4
Solon Mills, Ill. 69 a7
Solon Springs, Wis., 530 66 A2
Solopaca, It., 5,880 123 d9
Solor, P., Indon. 149 G5
Solothurn, Switz., 18,394 124 B1
Solov'yëvsk, U.S.S.R. 135 M4
Sølrod, Den., 1,369 121 E5
Solsberi, O., U.S.S.R. 134 E1
Solsberry, Ind. 70 C3
Solsona, Sp., 4,956 122 F1
Solt, Hung., 7,153 126 D3
Šolta, i., Yug. 125 C3
Soltau, F.R.Ger., 14,498 118 B2
Solton, U.S.S.R. 137 r11
Sol'tsy, U.S.S.R., 9,100 136 C1
Soltvadkert, Hung., 8,233 126 D3
Solum, Nor. 121 B1
So-lun, China 151 D1
Solunska Glava, mt., Yug. 125 E4
Solvang, Calif., 1,325 82 C5
Solvay, N.Y., 8,732 59 H5
Sölvesborg, Swed. 120 C4
Sol'vychegodsk, U.S.S.R., 3,500 134 D3
Solway Firth, U.K. 113 E4
Solwezi, Zambia 164 D4
Sōma, Jap., 41,352 155 G3
Soma, Turk., 13,119 142 A2
Somain, Fr., 15,241 116 a7
Somakimata, Jap. 154 h15
Somali Basin, Ind. Oc. 168 B2
Somali Republic, ctry., 2,500,000* 163 M5
Somaruma, Rochers, rocks, Horne, Îs. de 175 9
Sombor, Yug., 29,000* 125 D2
Somborn, F.R.Ger., 3,916 119 G4
Sombra, Ont., Can. 46 B6
Sombrerete, Qro., Mex. 93 e9

296 · Sombrerete—South Woodstock

Sombrerete, Zac., Mex., 9,260 92 E3
Sombrero, i., W.I. 95 G3
Sombrero Chan., India 146 A6
Şomcuta Mare, Rum. 128 D1
Somenos, Br. Col., Can. 42 c7
Someo, Switz. 124 C2
Somerby, U.K. 114 G5
Someren, Neth., 3,900 115 D3
Somero, Fin. 120 E3
Somers, Conn., 3,702(T) 56 G5
Somers, Iowa, 203 72 C2
Somers, Mont. 81 B1
Somers, Wis. 66 d13
Somersby, U.K. 114 J4
Somerset, Berm. Is. 108 1
Somerset, Man., Can. 43 f10
Somerset, Kans. 75 L5
Somerset, Ky., 7,112 71 G4
Somerset, co., Me., 39,749 55 B3
Somerset, co., Md., 19,623 62 J4
Somerset, Mass., 12,196(T) 57 M5
Somerset, co., N.J., 143,913 61 B2
Somerset, Ohio, 1,361 70 G3
Somerset, co., Pa., 77,450 60 D6
Somerset, Pa., 6,347 60 D6
Somerset, Va. 62 F4
Somerset, Wis., 729 66 A3
Somerset Center, Mich. 67 J6
Somerset East, S. Af., 9,779 164 D7
Somerset I., Berm. Is. 108 1
Somerset I., N.W.T., Can. 40 L3
Somerset Res., Vt. 54 B5
Somerset West, S. Af., 8,243 164 a9
Somersetshire, co., U.K., 599,046 113 E6
Somersham, U.K., 1,401 114 H6
Somers Point, N.J., 4,504 61 B5
Somersville (part of Somers), Conn. 56 G5
Somersworth, N.H. 54 F5
Somerton, U.K., 2,182 113 E6
Somerton, Ariz., 1,613 78 A5
Somerton, Ohio 70 H3
Somerton, Va. 62 H6
Somervell, co., Tex., 2,577 77 P3
Somerville, Ind., 317 70 B4
Somerville, Me. 55 C4
Somerville, Mass., 94,697 57 M3
Somerville, N.J., 12,458 61 B2
Somerville, Ohio, 478 70 E3
Somerville, Tenn., 1,820 71 B6
Somerville, Tex., 1,177 77 P4
Somesbar, Calif. 82 B2
Someşul, r., Rum. 128 D1
Someşul Mare, r., Rum. 128 E1
Somesville, Me. 55 D4
Sommacampagna, It., 7,624 122 d5
Sommariva del Bosco, It., 5,144 122 a6
Somma Vesuviana, It., 17,974 123 c10
Somme, r., Fr. 117 D1
Sommelsdijk, Neth., 3,100 115 C3
Sommen, l., Swed. 120 C4
Sömmerda, Ger.D.R., 13,811 118 C3
Sommerein, Aust., 1,507 124 d10
Sommersted, Den., 1,525 121 B5
Sommesous, Fr. 117 E2
Sommières, Fr., 3,323 117 E5
Somnath, India, 13,927 144 C5
Somonauk, Ill., 899 68 D2
Somosomo Str., Fiji 174 4
Somotillo, Nic., 1,384 94 D4
Somoto, Nic., 3,260 94 D4
Sompolno, Pol., 3,493 127 C2
Somvix, Switz., 2,004 124 C2
Son, r., India 145 F4
Soná, Pan., 3,176 94 G6
Sona, r., Pol. 127 D2
Sonaguera, Hond., 3,740 94 D3
Sonamukhi, India, 15,027 144 f14
Sonar, r., India 144 b13
Sonchamp, Fr. 116 f12
Sŏnch'ŏn, Japan 151 E3
Soncillo, Sp. 122 m12
Soncino, It., 8,759 122 c5
Søndbjerg, Den. 121 A4
Søndera, r., Den. 121 B6
Sønderborg, Den., 20,653 121 B6
Sønder Broby, Den., 1,371 121 C5
Sønder Felding, Den., 2,080 121 A5
Sønderho, Den. 121 A5
Sønder Omme, Den., 2,885 121 A5
Sondershausen, Ger.D.R., 19,191 118 C3
Søndersø, Den., 1,299 121 C5
Søndervig, Den. 121 A4
Sondheimer, La. 73 D5
Sondo, r., Kenya 165 g14
Sondrio, It., 17,527 123 B1
Sonenji, Jap. 154 g15
Sonepat, India, 45,882 144 a11
Song, Malay. 148 E2
Song Cau, S. Viet., 2,337 146 E4
Sŏngch'ŏn, N. Kor. 151 E3
Songea, Tanz. 164 E3
Songjŏng, S. Kor., 29,821 151 E4
Songkhla, Thai., 31,014 146 C6
Song Khon, Thai. 146 D3
Songkhram, r., Thai. 146 C3
Songnim, N. Kor. 151 E3
Song Ong Doc, S. Viet. 147 k12
Song Phi Nong, Thai., 6,660 146 C4
Son Ha, S. Viet. 146 E4
Sonkach, India, 6,540 144 a14
Sonkajärvi, Fin. 120 F3
Sonkovo, U.S.S.R., 4,900 136 E1
Son-Kul', Oz., U.S.S.R. 137 g4
Son La, N. Viet. 146 C2
Sonmiāni Bay, Pak. 144 B4
Sonnberg, Aust. 124 c9
Sonneberg, Ger.D.R., 28,936 118 C3
Sono, R. do, Braz. 103 G4
Sonobe, Jap., 15,734 154 g14
Sonogi, Jap., 7,372 154 A5
Sonogno, Switz. 124 C2
Sonoita, Ariz. 78 C6
Sonoma, co., Calif., 147,375 82 B3
Sonoma, Calif., 3,023 83 e11
Sonoma, Tex. 76 f10
Sonoma Cr., Calif. 83 e11
Sonora, st., Mex., 783,378 92 B1
Sonora, Mex., 1,125 92 B1
Sonora, Ariz., 1,244 78 C5
Sonora, Calif., 2,725 82 C4
Sonora, Tex., 2,619 77 N4
Sonora, r., Mex. 92 C1
Sonoyta, Mex., 1,275 92 B1
Sonoyta, r., Mex. 92 B1
Sonpur, India, 7,108 145 G5
Sonqor, Iran, 12,126 143 D2
Sŏnsan, S. Kor., 17,084 151 F3
Sonsbeck, F.R.Ger., 2,378 119 A1
Sonseca, Sp., 6,076 122 C3
Sonsón, Col. 100 C5
Sonsonate, El Salv., 23,137 94 C4
Sonsorol, i., Car. Is. 170 C4
Sontag, Miss. 73 E6
Son Tay, N. Viet., 19,213 146 D2
Sonthofen, F.R.Ger., 11,991 118 C5
Sontra, F.R.Ger., 5,206 118 B3
Sonvico, Switz., 1,005 124 D2
Sonyea, N.Y. 58 E6
Soochow = Su-chou
Sooghmeghat, Alaska 85 B3
Soo Junction, Mich. 67 H2
Sooke, Br. Col., Can., 1,121 42 c7
Soo Locks, Can.-U.S. 69 A
Soos Cr., Wash. 81 b8
Sooss, Aust. 124 c11
Sopchoppy, Fla., 450 65 E2
Sopchoppy, r., Fla. 65 E2
Soper, Okla., 309 76 H3
Soperton, Ga., 2,317 64 G3
Soperton, Wis. 66 E3
Sopetrán, Col. 100 C4
Sop Hao, Laos 146 D2
Sophia, N.C. 63 E2
Sophia, W. Va., 1,284 62 C5
Sop Khao, Laos 146 C3
Sopley, U.K., 1,063 113 i13
Sopó, Col. 101 e15
Sopot, Pol., 44,000* 127 C1
Sop Prap, Thai. 146 B3
Sopris, Colo. 79 C3
Sopron, Hung., 41,246 126 C3
Sopur, India, 18,987 145 E2
Soquel, Calif. 83 f14
Sora, It., 24,904 123 D4
Soraba, Guyana 101 K5
Sŏrak-san, S. Kor. 151 F3
Sorata, Bol., 7,874 102 a9
Sorbas, Sp., 5,132 122 D4
Sorbey, Fr. 116 b8
Sorbolo, It., 6,210 122 d6
Sorbo, Fr. 117 C4
Sorel, Qué., Can., 17,045 44 K6
Sorell, Austl. 173 G6
Sorell, C., Austl. 173 e14
Soresina, It., 10,787 122 c5
Sorento, Ill., 681 68 C5
Sörfold, Nor. 120 C2
Sorgues, Fr., 10,578 117 F4
Soria, Mex., 1,544 93 d9
Soria, Sp., 19,301 122 D2
Soriano, Urug., 2,500* 105 b11
Sorikmarapi, G., Indon. 148 A2
Sörli, Nor. 120 C2
Sorø, Den., 5,494 121 D5
Sorocaba, Braz., 109,258 103 G6
Sorochinsk, U.S.S.R., 20,200 134 E4
Soroki, U.S.S.R., 15,200 136 C3
Sorol, atoll, Car. Is. 170 D4
Sorong, Indon. 149 J3
Soroní, Gr. 129 F6
Soroti, Uganda, 6,645 164 E1
Sörøya, i., Nor. 120 E1
Sorraia, r., Port. 122 A3
Sorrento, It., 11,882 123 c10
Sorrento, La., 1,151 73 E7
Sorrento, Me. 55 D4
Sorsatunturi, mt., Fin. 120 G2
Sorsele, Swed. 120 D2
Sorso, It., 9,554 123 B4
Sorsogon, Phil., 13,983 153 C2
Sorsogon Bay, Phil. 153 h15
Sort, Sp., 1,209 122 F1
Sortavala, U.S.S.R., 17,600 134 C3
Sortland, Nor. 120 C1
Sorum, S. Dak. 74 A3
Sorunda, Swed. 120 e8
Sørvágur, Faeroe Is. 120 c7
Sörve Poolsaar, pen., U.S.S.R. 136 A1
Sŏsan, S. Kor., 27,607 151 E3
Sos del Rey Católico, Sp., 2,183 122 E1
Sosna, r., U.S.S.R. 136 E2
Sośnica, Pol. 127 E4
Sosnogorsk, U.S.S.R., 18,000 134 E3
Sosnovoborsk, U.S.S.R., 5,900 136 G2
Sosnovo-Ozërskoye, U.S.S.R. 135 L4
Sosnowiec, Pol., 132,000* 127 C3
Soso, Miss. 73 F6
Soso Bay, Fiji 174 4
Sospel, Fr., 2,321 117 G5
Sospiro, It., 4,172 122 d5
Sosúa, Dom, Rep., 1,808 96 m6
Sŏsura-ri, N. Kor. 151 F2
Sos'va, U.S.S.R. 134 F4
Sos'va, r., U.S.S.R. 137 k7
Sosyka, r., U.S.S.R. 136 E4
So Ta, N. Viet. 147 h8
Sōtani, Jap. 154 g15
Sötern, F.R.Ger., 1,204 119 C5
Sotik, Kenya 165 g14
Sotillo de la Adrada, Sp., 2,966 122 C2
Sotkamo, Fin. 120 G2
Soto la Marina, Mex. 93 F3
Sotta, Fr., 1,352 116 r18
Sotteville, Fr., 33,719 117 D2
Sottomarina, It. 122 f5
Souanké, Congo 164 B1
Soubré, Iv. Coast 162 C5
Soucht, Fr., 1,231 116 d9
Soucook, r., N.H. 54 E5
Soudan, Minn. 74 F2
Souderton, Pa., 5,381 61 M5
Soufflenheim, Fr., 3,868 119 D7
Souflíon, Gr., 6,693 129 F4
Soufrière, St. Lucia, 2,723 97 11
Soufrière, mtn., Guad. 97 14
Soufrière Bay, Dominica 97 13
Soufrière Hills, Montserrat 97 5
Soufrière Mts., St. Vinc. 97 19
Souhegan, r., N.H. 54 D6
Souillac, Fr., 3,394 117 D4
Souillac, Maurit. 165 c12
Souilly, Fr. 117 F2
Souk-Ahras, Alg., 23,120 160 f5
Souk-el-Arba-du-Rharb, Mor., 11,624 160 C2
Sŏul, S. Kor., 2,444,883 151 E3
Soulac, Fr., 2,120 117 C4
Soulanges Can., Qué., Can. 69 D
Soulby, U.K. 114 D2
Soultz-sous-Forêts, Fr., 1,698 119 D7
Sound Beach, N.Y., 1,625 59 P10
Sound Island, Newf., Can. 45 a10
Soúnion, ruins, Gr. 129 D6
Soupading, Nic. 94 E4
Souppes, Fr., 3,612 117 E2
Sourbrodt, Belg. 119 A4
Sourd, R. du, Qué., Can. 47 J2
Sourdeval, Fr., 3,278 117 C2
Soure, Braz., 6,666 103 G2
Soure, Port., 9,655 122 A2
Sour-el-Chozlane, Alg., 7,365 160 c5
Souris, Man., Can., 1,746 43 E5
Souris, P.E.I., Can., 1,479 45 O6
Souris, N. Dak., 213 74 B1
Souris, r., Can.-U.S. 52 F1
Souris, r., N. Dak. 74 B1
Sour Lake, Tex., 1,602 77 Q4
Sourland Mtn., N.J. 61 B3
Soúrpi, Gr., 2,032 129 D5
Soûs, r., Mor. 160 C2
Sousa, Braz., 12,350 103 J3
Sous le Vent, Îs., Soc. Is. 177 42
Sousse = Sūsah
Soustons, Fr., 4,242 117 C5
South, r., Ont., Can. 46 E3
South, r., Ga. 64 h10
South, r., Iowa 72 D3
South, r., Md. 62 c9
South, r., Mass. 56 E2
South, r., Mass. 57 O4
South, r., N.J. 58 b15
South, r., N.C. 63 F3
South Acton, Mass., 1,114 57 L3
South Acworth, N.H. 54 C5
South Africa, ctry., 17,867,000* 164 C6
South Albany, Vt. 54 C2
Southall, London, U.K. 114 H8
South Alligator, r., Austl. 172 D1
Southam, U.K., 1,881 114 F6
South Amboy, N.J., 8,422 61 C3
South Amherst (part of Amherst), Mass. 56 G3
South Amherst, Ohio, 1,657 70 c9
Southampton, Ont., Can., 1,785 46 C4
Southampton, U.K., 204,822 113 F6
Southampton, Mass., 2,192(T) 56 F4
Southampton, N.Y., 4,582 59 Q10
Southampton, Pa., 4,575* 60 N5
Southampton, co., Va., 27,195 62 G6
Southampton, C., N.W.T., Can. 44 G2
Southampton I., N.W.T., Can. 41 M5
Southampton Water, chan., U.K. 113 k13
South Andaman, i., India 146 A5
South Arabia, Prot. of, ctry., 1,099,000* 143 D5
South Arabia, Prot. of (Eastern part) 143 E5
South Arabia, Prot. of (Western part) 143 D6
Southard, N.J. 58 c16
Southard, Okla. 76 E1
South Ashfield (part of Ashfield), Mass. 56 E2
South Athol (part of Athol), Mass. 56 H2
South Attleboro (part of Attleboro), Mass. 57 L5
South Aulatsivik I., Newf., Can. 45 O3
South Australia, st., Austl., 1,090,723 172 D4
South Australian Basin, Ind. Oc. 168 E4
South Baldy, mtn., N. Mex. 79 B4
Southbank, Br. Col., Can. 42 F3
South Barnstead, N.H. 54 E5
South Barre (part of Barre), Mass. 56 H3
South Barre, Vt. 54 B3
South Barrington, Ill., 473 69 b8
South Bass I., Ohio 70 G1
South Bay, Fla., 1,631 65 J6
South Bay, N.W.T., Can. 41 N5
South Bay, Ont., Can. 46 C3
South Baymouth, Ont., Can. 46 B3
South Beach, Oreg. 80 A3
South Belmar, N.J., 1,537 58 c16
South Beloit, Ill., 3,781 68 D1
South Bend, Ind., 132,445 70 C1
South Bend, Wash., 1,671 80 B2
South Berwick, Me., 1,773 55 B5
South Bethlehem, N.Y. 59 N6
South Bight, Bah. Is. 95 b8
South Boardman, Mich. 67 H4
Southboro, Mass., 1,114;3,996(T) 57 K3
Southborough, U.K., 9,771 114 J8
South Boston, Va., 5,974 62 F6
South Bound Brook, N.J., 3,626 58 b14
South Braintree (part of Braintree), Mass. 57 N4
Southbranch, Mich. 67 J4
South Branch Cr., Del. 62 f10
South Branch L., Me. 55 D3
South Brewster (part of Brewster), Mass. 57 Q6
Southbridge, Mass., 15,889; 16,523(T) 56 H4
South Britain (part of Southbury), Conn. 56 C7
South Bruny, i., Austl. 173 f14
South Burlington, Vt. 54 A3
Southbury, Conn., 5,186(T) 56 D7
South Butte, Idaho 81 B2
South Byfield (part of Newbury), Mass. 57 N2
South Byron, N.Y. 58 D5
South Byron, Wis. 66 E5
South Canaan (part of Canaan), Conn. 56 C5
South Canaan, Pa. 61 p15
South C., New Hebr. 174 k5
South C., Hawaii = Ka Lae
South Carolina, st., U.S., 2,550,000* 63
South Carver (part of Carver), Mass. 57 O5
South Casco, Me. 55 B5
South Cave, U.K., 1,521 114 G3
South Cerney, U.K., 1,772 114 E7
South Chan., Eniwetok 176 28
South Chaplin (part of Chaplin), Conn. 56 H5
South Charleston, Ohio, 1,505 70 F3
South Charleston, W. Va., 19,180 62 C4
South Charlestown, N.H. 54 C5
South Chatham (part of Chatham), Mass. 57 Q6
South Cheek, pt., U.K. 114 H2
South Chelmsford (part of Chelmsford), Mass. 57 L2
South China, Me. 55 C4
South China Basin, Asia 141 K5
South China Sea, Asia 141 J6
South Cle Elum, Wash., 383 80 C2
South Coffeyville, Okla., 622 76 H1
South Colby, Wash. 81 a7
South Colton, N.Y. 59 L2
South Corning, N.Y., 1,448 58 F7
South Cornish, N.H. 54 C5
South Coventry, Conn., 3,568 56 G5
South Dakota, st., U.S., 686,000* 74
South Danbury, N.H. 54 D5
South Dansville, N.Y. 58 E7
South Dartmouth (part of Dartmouth), Mass. 57 N6
South Dayton, N.Y., 696 58 B7
South Deerfield, Mass., 1,253 56 F3
South Deerfield, N.H. 54 E5
South Dennis (part of Dennis), Mass. 57 Q6
South Diamond Pk., Nev. 83 B3
South Dorset, Vt. 54 A5
South Downs, reg., U.K. 112 ·
South Duxbury (part of Duxbury), Mass. 57 O4
South East C., Austl. 173 G6
South East Head, Ascension 109 6
South East Loch, Hawaii 84 c7
South East Mtn., Gren. 97 18
South Easton (part of Easton), Mass. 57 M4
Southeast Indian Rise, Ind. Oc. 168 D4
Southeast Pass, Jaluit 176 30
South East Pt., Austl. 173 f12
South East Pt., Christmas Atoll 177 40
South East Pt., Jam. 96 q9
Southeast Pt., R.I. 57 K8
South East Range, St. Christopher 97 6
South Eaton, Pa. 61 o16
South Edisto, r., S.C. 63 C4
South Effingham, N.H. 54 E4
South Egremont, Mass. 56 C4
South Elgin, Ill., 2,624 68 D2
South Eliot, Me., 1,730 55 B5
South El Monte, Calif., 4,850 83 h15
Southend, Sask., Can. 43 D3
Southend-on-Sea, U.K., 165,093 113 G6
South English, Iowa, 217 72 E3
Southern Alps, N.Z. 175 f6
Southern Cross, Austl. 172 B4
Southern Indian L., Man., Can. 43 F2
Southern Pines, N.C., 5,198 63 E2
Southern Rhodesia = Rhodesia
Southern View, Ill., 1,667 68 C4
Southery, U.K., 1,209 114 J5
South Esk, r., Austl. 173 f13
South Esk, r., U.K. 112 d8
South Esk, r., U.K. 112 E3
South Essex (part of Essex), Mass. 57 O2
South Euclid, Ohio, 27,569 70 e8
Southey, Sask., Can. 43 D5
South Fabius, r., Mo. 72 F5
South Fallsburg, N.Y., 1,290 59 L8
South Farmingdale, N.Y., 16,318 58 f14
Southfield (part of New Marlborough), Mass. 56 D4
Southfield, Mich., 31,501 67 f15
South Fiji Basin, Ind. Oc. 169 F3
Southford (part of Southbury), Conn. 56 D7
South Foreland, U.K. 113 G6
South Fork, Pa., 2,053 60 E5
South Fort Mitchell, Ky., 4,086 71 h11
South Foster (part of Foster), R.I. 57 K5
South Fox I., Mich. 67 H3
South Fulton, Tenn., 2,512 71 C5
South Gardiner, Me. 55 C4
South Gardner (part of Gardner), Mass. 56 J2
South Gate, Calif., 53,831 83 h16
Southgate, Mich., 29,404 67 e16
South Glastonbury (part of Glastonbury), Conn. 56 F6
South Glens Falls, N.Y., 4,129 59 N5
South Grand, r., Mo. 72 C6
South Greenfield, Mo., 179 72 D7
South Greenwood, S.C., 2,520 63 B3
South Groveland (part of Groveland), Mass. 57 M2
South Hadley, Mass., 14,956(T) 56 F4
South Hadley Falls (part of S. Hadley), Mass. 56 F4
South Halawa Str., Hawaii 84 c7
South Hamilton, Mass. 57 N2
South Hannibal, N.Y. 59 q22
South Harwich (part of Harwich), Mass. 57 Q6
South Haven, Kans., 408 75 H6
South Haven, Mich., 6,149 67 G6
South Haven, N.Y. 58 h13
South Heights, Pa., 740 60 a7
South Henik L., N.W.T., Can. 40 K5
South Hero, Vt. 54 A2
South Hill, Anguilla 97 7
South Hill, Va., 2,569 62 F6
South Hiram, Me. 55 B5
South Hole Sound, Lesser Caymans 97 2
South Holland, Ill., 10,412 69 d10
South Holston L., Tenn.-Va. 62 C6
South Hooksett, N.H. 54 E5
South Hope, Me. 55 C4
South Horr, Kenya 164 F1
South Houston, Tex., 7,523 77 i9
South Huntington, N.Y., 7,084 58 f13
South Hutchinson, Kans., 1,672 75 G5
South Indian Basin, Ind. Oc. 168 D4
South Indian Lake, Man., Can. 43 F3
Southington, Conn., 9,952; 22,797(T) 56 E6
South International Falls, Minn., 2,479 74 F1
South I., N.Z. 175 g7
South I., Truk 176 19
South Jacksonville, Ill., 2,654 68 B4
South Jefferson, Me. 55 C4
South Jordan, Utah, 1,354 78 c9
South Kenosha, Wis. 66 d13
South Kent (part of Kent), Conn. 56 C6
South Killingly (part of Killingly), Conn. 57 J5
South Kirkby, U.K., 11,490 114 F3
South Knife, r., Man., Can. 43 F2
South Korea, ctry., 28,377,000* 151
South Kortright, N.Y. 59 L7
Southlake, Tex., 1,023 76 e9
South Laguna, Calif., 2,000 83 i16
South Lancaster, Mass., 1,891 57 K3
Southland, Tex., 153 77 N3
South La Porte, Ind. 69 h10
South Lebanon, Me. 55 B5
South Lebanon, Ohio, 2,720 70 E3
South Lee (part of Lee), Mass. 56 C3
South Liberty, Mo. 75 b7
South Lima, N.Y. 58 E6
South Lincoln, Me. 55 D3
South Lincoln (part of Lincoln), Mass. 57 L3
South Lincoln, Vt. 54 B3
South Lineville, Mo., 76 72 D4
South Livonia, N.Y. 58 n21
South Llano, r., Tex. 77 N4
South Londonderry, Vt. 54 B5
South Loup, r., Nebr. 75 F2
South Lunenburg, Vt. 54 D3
South Lyme (part of Old Lyme), Conn. 56 G7
South Lyndeboro, N.H. 54 D6
South Lyon, Mich., 1,753 67 K6
South Magnetic Pole, Ant. 180 U6
South Manistique L., Mich. 67 H2
South Manitou I., Mich. 67 G3
South Mansfield, La., 616 73 B5
South Mashpee (part of Mashpee), Mass. 57 P6
South Medwin, r., U.K. 112 c8
South Meriden (part of Meriden), Conn. 56 E6
South Merrimack, N.H. 54 D6
South Miami, Fla., 9,846 65 a10
South Middleboro (part of Middleboro), Mass. 57 N5
South Mills, N.C. 63 H1
South Milwaukee, Wis., 20,307 66 F6
Southminster, U.K., 1,897 113 G6
South Molton, U.K., 2,993 113 E6
South Monroe, Mich., 2,919 67 K7
South Monson (part of Monson), Mass. 56 G4
Southmont, N.C. 63 D2
South Moreau Cr., Mo. 72 E6
Southmost, Tex. 77 P7
South Mountain, Pa. 60 G6
South Mtn., Pa. 60 H6
South Negril Point, Jam. 96 o8
South Nahanni, N.W.T., Can. 40 E5
South Nahanni, r., N.W.T., Can. 40 D5
South Naknek, Alaska, 33 85 E4
South Natick (part of Natick), Mass. 57 L3
South Nation, r., Ont., Can. 47 J4
South New Berlin, N.Y. 59 K6
South Newbury, N.H. 54 D5
South Newbury, Vt. 54 C3
South Newfane, Vt. 54 B6
South New River Can., Fla. 65 J6
South Normanton, U.K., 6,946 114 F4
South Nyack, N.Y., 3,113 58 d12
South Ogden, Utah, 7,405 78 c8
Southold, N.Y. 59 P9
South Orange, N.J., 16,175 58 b14
South Orkney Is. Atl. Oc. 109 K11
South Orleans (part of Orleans), Mass. 57 R6
South Otselic, N.Y. 59 J6
South Otterington, U.K. 114 F2
South Oyster Bay, N.Y. 58 f14
South Paris, Me., 2,063 55 B4
South Park, Ill. 69 a10
South Park, Kans. 75 a7
South Pk., basin, Colo. 79 ·
South Pasadena, Calif., 19,706 83 h15
South Pass, Kwajalein 176 25
South Pass, Wyo. 81 E4
South Peacham, Vt. 54 C3
South Pk., Utah 78 A1
South Pekin, Ill., 1,007 68 C3
South Penobscot, Me. 55 D4
South Pittsburg, Tenn., 4,130 71 F6
South Plainfield, N.J., 17,879 58 b14
South Platte, Colo. 79 b9
South Platte, r., Colo. 52 F2
South Platte, N. Fk., r., Colo. 79 a9
South Point, Ohio, 1,663 70 G4
South Point, Wash. 81 a7
South Pt., Ascension 109 6
South Pt., Barb. 97 10
South Pt., Jaluit 176 30
South Pt., Mich. 67 K4
South Pole, Ant. 180 V4
South Pomfret, Vt. 54 B4
South Pd., Mass. 57 O5
South Ponte Vedra Beach, Fla. 65 H2
South Porcupine, Ont., Can., 5,144 44 G5
Southport, Austl., 8,134 173 H4
Southport, U.K., 81,976 113 E5
Southport (part of Fairfield), Conn. 56 C8
Southport, Fla. 65 D2
Southport, Ind., 892 70 C3
Southport, N.Y., 6,698 58 G7
Southport, N.C., 2,034 63 G4
South Portland, Me., 22,788 55 B5
South Portsmouth, Ky. 71 H3
South Prairie, Wash., 214 81 b8
South Raisin, r., Ont., Can. 69 C
South Range, Mich., 760 66 E1
South Range, Wis. 66 A2
South Reading, Vt. 54 B5
South Renovo, Pa., 777 60 G3
South River, Ont., Can., 1,021 44 H6
South River, N.J., 13,397 61 C3
South Rockwood, Mich., 1,337 67 e16
South Ronaldsay, i., U.K. 112 E2
South Roxana, Ill., 2,010 68 C5
South Royalston (part of Royalston), Mass. 56 H2
South Royalton, Vt. 54 C4
South Ryegate, Vt. 54 C3
South Sacramento, Calif. 82 b7
South St. Paul, Minn., 22,032 74 c6
South Salem, Ohio, 180 70 F3
South Salt Lake, Utah, 9,520 78 c9
South Sandisfield (part of Sandisfield), Mass. 56 D4
South Sandwich Is., Atl. Oc. 109 L10
South Sandwich Trench, Atl. Oc. 109 L10
South San Francisco, Calif., 39,418 83 d12
South Santiam, r., Oreg. 80 B3
South Saskatchewan, r., Alta.-Sask., Can. 40 H7
South Schroon, N.Y. 59 N4
South Seal, r., Man., Can. 43 E2
South Seekonk (part of Seekonk), Mass. 57 L5
South Shaftsbury, Vt. 54 A6
South Shetland Is., Ant. 109 J11
South Shields, U.K., 109,533 113 F4
South Shore, S. Dak., 259 74 D3
South Shore Can., Qué., Can. 69 D
Southside, Tenn. 71 D5
Southside, W. Va. 62 B4
South Side Place, Tex., 1,282 77 i9
South Sioux City, Nebr., 7,200 75 J1
South Sister, mtn., Oreg. 80 C3
South Solon, Ohio, 414 70 F3
South Somercotes, U.K. 114 J4
South Sd., Ire. 113 B5
South Sd., V.I. 97 4
South Spencer (part of Spencer), Mass. 56 H4
South Stoke, U.K. 114 F7
South Strafford, Vt. 54 C4
South Sterling, Pa. 61 M3
South Superior, Wyo., 401 81 E5
South Sutton (part of Sutton), Mass. 57 K4
South Sutton, N.H. 54 D5
South Tamworth, N.H. 54 E4
South Taranaki Bight, N.Z. 175 g5
South Toe, r., N.C. 63 B2
South Trap, i., N.Z. 175 e7
South Trenton, N.Y. 59 u26
South Trescott, Me. 55 E4
South Truro (part of Truro), Mass. 57 Q5
South Tucson, Ariz., 7,004 78 C5
South Tunbridge, Vt. 54 C4
South Twin I., N.W.T., Can. 44 H4
South Twin Mtn., N.H. 54 D3
South Uist, i., U.K. 112 C3
South Umpqua, r., Oreg. 80 B4
South Union, Wash. 81 a9
South Vernon, Vt. 54 B6
South Vienna, Ohio 70 F3
South Viet-Nam, ctry, 14,200,000* 146
Southville (part of Southboro), Mass. 57 K3
South Vineland, N.J. 61 B5
South Wales, N.Y. 58 C6
South Wallingford, Vt. 54 A5
South Walpole (part of Walpole), Mass. 57 M4
South Wareham (part of Wareham), Mass. 57 N5
South Warren, Me. 55 C4
South Waterford, Me. 55 B4
South Waverly, Pa., 1,382 60 J2
South Wayne, Wis., 354 66 D6
South Weare, N.H. 54 D5
South Webster, Ohio, 803 70 G4
Southwell, U.K., 4,301 114 G4
South Wellesley Is., Austl. 172 E2
South Wellfleet (part of Wellfleet), Mass. 57 R5
South Wellington, Br. Col., Can. 42 b6
South Werribee, Austl., 1,480 173 e12
South-West Africa, terr. adm. by S. Af., 574,000* 164 B5
South West Arm, Newf., Can. 45 b9
Southwest Brook, Newf., Can. 45 a9
South West C., Austl. 173 F6
Southwest C., N.Z. 175 e7
Southwest C., St. Croix 97 1
South West City, Mo., 504 72 C8
South West Fargo, N. Dak., 3,328 74 D2
Southwest Harbor, Me. 55 D4
Southwest Miramichi, r., N.B., Can. 47 S10
Southwest Oswego, N.Y. 59 p22
Southwest Pass, Jaluit 176 30
Southwest Passage, Eniwetok 176 28
Southwest Pt., Bah. Is. 95 a6
Southwest Pt., Bah. Is. 95 b7
South West Pt., Christmas Atoll 177 40
Southwest Pt., Grand Cayman 97 3
South West Pt., Gren. Is. 97 20
Southwest Pt., Lesser Caymans 97 2
South West Pt., Lesser Caymans 97 2
South Westport (part of Westport), Mass. 57 M6
South West Sd., Grand Cayman 97 3
South Weymouth (part of Weymouth), Mass. 57 N4
South Whitley, Ind., 1,325 70 D1
Southwick, Ont., Can. 67 f16
Southwick, U.K. 113 k13
Southwick, Mass., 1,242;5,139(T) 56 E4
South Williamsport, Pa., 6,972 60 H3
South Williamstown (part of Williamstown), Mass. 56 D2
South Willington (part of Willington), Conn. 56 G5
South Wilmington, Ill., 730 68 D2
South Wilton (part of Wilton), Conn. 56 C8
South Windham, Me., 1,142 55 B5
South Windham, Vt. 54 B5
South Windsor, Conn., 9,460(T) 56 F5
South Windsor, Me. 55 C4
Southwold, U.K., 2,234 113 G5
South Woodbury, Vt. 54 C3
South Woodstock, Vt. 54 B4

South Worthington—Steele · 297

South Worthington (part of Worthington), Mass. 56 E3
South Yarmouth, Mass., 2,029 57 Q6
South Yolla Bolly, pk., Calif. 82 B2
Souvigny, Fr., 2,259 117 E3
Souzel, Port., 3,859 122 B3
Sovata, Rum., 6,498 128 E1
Soveja, Rum. 128 F1
Sövestad, Swed. 121 F5
Sovetsk, U.S.S.R., 15,500 134 D4
Sovetsk, U.S.S.R., 31,900 136 A2
Sovetskaya, G., U.S.S.R. 135 R2
Sovetskaya Gavan', U.S.S.R., 50,000 135 O5
Sovići, Yug., 3,027 125 C3
Sowerby, U.K., 2,471 114 F2
Soy, Kenya 165 g13
Sōya, Jap. 155 J7
Sōya-misaki, Jap. 155 K7
Soyapango, El Salv., 12,427 94 d10
Soyatal, Mex. 93 e9
Soyaux, Fr., 6,588 117 D4
Sōya-wan, Jap. 155 J7
Soyopa, Mex. 92 C2
Sozh, r., U.S.S.R. 136 C2
Sozopol, Bulg., 3,257 128 F3
Spa, Belg., 8,661 115 D4
Spain, ctry., 31,871,000* 122
Spakenburg, Neth., 5,300 115 D2
Spalding, Austl. 172 c7
Spalding, Sask., Can. 43 D4
Spalding, U.K., 14,824 113 F5
Spalding, co., Ga., 35,404 64 E2
Spalding, Mich. 66 F3
Spalding, Nebr., 683 75 G2
Spaldings, Jam., 1,959 96 p8
Spaldington, U.K. 114 G3
Spalt, F.R.Ger., 2,759 118 C4
Spanaway, Wash. 80 B2
Spangle, Wash., 208 80 E2
Spangler, Pa., 2,658 60 E4
Spangsville, Pa. 60 e10
Spaniard's Bay, Newf., Can., 1,289 45 b10
Spanish, Ont., Can., 1,536 46 B2
Spanish, r., Ont., Can. 46 C2
Spanish Equatorial Region=Equatorial Guinea
Spanish Fork, Utah, 6,472 78 C1
Spanish Guinea=Equatorial Guinea
Spanish Lake, Mo. 72 b10
Spanish Pt., Barbuda 97 8
Spanish Pt., Berm. Is. 108 1
Spanish Sahara (part of Sp.), 48,000* 160 B4
Spanish Town, Jam., 14,706 96 p8
Spanish Wells, Bah. Is. 95 c7
Spannberg, Aust. 124 d10
Sparanise, It., 5,594 123 c9
Spar City, Colo. 79 B3
Sparenberg, Tex. 77 N3
Sparkman, Ark., 787 73 C4
Sparks, Ga., 1,158 64 F4
Sparks, Nebr. 75 E1
Sparks, Nev., 16,618 83 A3
Sparks, Okla., 186 76 G2
Sparland, Ill., 534 68 C2
Sparlingville, Mich., 1,877 67 L6
Sparr, Fla. 65 G3
Sparr, Mich. 67 J3
Sparreholm, Swed. 120 d8
Sparrow Bush, N.Y. 59 L9
Sparrowhawk Hill, Lesser Caymans 97 2
Sparrow L., Ont., Can. 46 E4
Sparrows Point, Md. 62 H3
Sparta, Ont., Can. 46 C6
Sparta, Gr.=Spárti
Sparta, Ga., 1,921 64 G2
Sparta, Ill., 3,452 68 C5
Sparta, Mich., 2,749 67 H5
Sparta, Mo., 272 72 D7
Sparta, N.J. 61 B1
Sparta, N.C., 1,047 63 C1
Sparta, Oreg. 80 E3
Sparta, Tenn., 4,510 71 F6
Sparta, Wis., 6,080 66 C5
Spartanburg, co., S.C., 156,830 63 B3
Spartanburg, S.C., 44,352 63 C3
Spartansburg, Pa., 500 60 C2
Spárti, Gr., 10,412 129 D6
Spartivento, Capo, It. 123 F6
Spas-Demensk, U.S.S.R., 6,100 136 D2
Spas-Klepiki, U.S.S.R., 5,100 136 d6
Spassk-Dal'niy, U.S.S.R., 42,000 135 N5
Spassk-Ryazanskiy, U.S.S.R., 8,000 136 F2
Spátha, Ákra, Gr. 129 D7
Spatsizi, r., Br. Col., Can. 42 E1
Spaulding, Cook Co., Ill. 68 b8
Spaulding, Sangamon Co., Ill., 178 69 C4
Spaulding, Okla. 76 G2
Spavinaw, Okla., 319 76 H1
Spavinaw Lakes, Okla. 76 J1
Speaks, Tex. 77 P5
Spear, C., Newf., Can. 45 c10
Spearfish, S. Dak., 3,682 74 A3
Spearman, Tex., 3,555 76 N1
Spearsville, Ind. 70 C3
Spearsville, La. 73 C5
Spearville, Kans., 602 75 F6
Speckled Mtn., Me. 55 B4
Spectacle Pd., Me. 55 D4
Speculator, N.Y., 372 59 M4
Spedden, Alta., Can. 43 d6
Speed, Ind. 70 D4
Speed, Kans., 75 75 F4
Speed, N.C., 142 63 G2
Speed, r., Ont., Can. 46 D5
Speedsville, N.Y. 59 H7
Speedway, Ind., 11,319 70 C3
Speedwell, Va. 62 C6
Speedwell I., Falk. Is. 108 3
Speen, U.K., 1,247 114 F8
Speer, Ill. 68 C2
Speers, Pa., 1,479 60 c9
Speicher, F.R.Ger., 2,743 119 B5
Speightstown, Barb., 3,500* 97 10
Speke G., Tanz. 165 f15
Spekholzerheide, Neth., 9,400 115 E4
Spenard, Alaska, 9,074 85 G3
Spence Bay, N.W.T., Can. 40 L4
Spencer, Mass., 5,593;7,838(T) 56 H4
Spencer, Idaho, 100 81 C3
Spencer, Ill. 69 c10
Spencer, co., Ind., 16,074 70 C4
Spencer, Ind., 2,557 70 C3
Spencer, Iowa, 8,864 72 B1
Spencer, co., Ky., 5,680 71 F3
Spencer, La. 73 C5
Spencer, Me. 55 B3
Spencer, Mich. 67 H4
Spencer, Nebr., 671 75 G1
Spencer, N.Y., 767 59 H7
Spencer, N.C., 2,904 63 D2
Spencer, Ohio, 742 70 G1
Spencer, S. Dak., 460 74 D3
Spencer, Tenn., 870 71 F6
Spencer, Va. 62 D6
Spencer, W. Va., 2,660 62 C4
Spencer, Wis., 897 66 C4
Spencer, C., Austl. 172 E5
Spencer Cr., Ont., Can. 46 b14
Spencer Gulf, Austl. 172 E5
Spencerport, N.Y., 2,676 58 E5
Spencer's Cove, Newf., Can. 45 a10
Spencer Settlement, N.Y. 59 s26
Spencer Str., Me. 55 B3
Spencertown, N.Y. 59 O7
Spencerville, Ind. 70 E1
Spencerville, Ohio, 2,061 70 E2
Spencerville, Okla. 76 H3
Spennymoor, U.K., 19,104 112 g10
Sperkhiás, Gr., 2,656 129 C5
Sperkhiós, r., Gr. 129 D5
Sperling, Man., Can. 43 g10
Sperone, Capo, It. 123 B5
Sperry, Okla., 883 76 G1
Sperryville, Va. 62 F4
Spessart, mts., F.R.Ger. 118 B4
Spétsai, i., Gr. 129 D6
Spey, r., U.K. 112 E3
Spey Bay, U.K. 112 E3
Speyer, F.R.Ger., 35,405 118 B4
Speyer, r., F.R.Ger. 119 E6
Speyside, Ont., Can. 46 c13
Sphinx Pk., Mont. 81 C2
Spiceland, Ind., 863 70 D3
Spicer, Minn., 589 74 E3
Spickards=Spickardsville
Spickardsville, Mo., 450 72 D4
Spiddal, Ire. 113 B5
Spider L., Me. 55 C2
Spiekeroog, i., F.R.Ger. 118 A2
Spiess Seamount, Atl. Oc. 109 M10
Spiez, Switz., 8,168 124 B2
Spijk, Neth. 115 E1
Spijkenisse, Neth., 3,300 115 a7
Spíli, Gr. 129 E7
Spilimbergo, It., 11,074 123 D1
Spillern, Aust. 124 c10
Spillimacheen, Br. Col., Can. 42 J4
Spilsby, U.K., 1,665 114 J4
Spin Baldak, Afghan. 144 B3
Spincourt, Fr. 117 F2
Spindale, N.C., 4,082 63 B2
Spink, co., S. Dak., 11,706 74 C3
Spinuș, Rum. 128 D1
Spirit, Wis. 66 C3
Spirit, r., Wis. 66 D3
Spirit Lake, Idaho, 693 81 A2
Spirit Lake, Iowa, 2,685 72 B1
Spirit L., Iowa 72 B1
Spirit L., Wash. 80 B2
Spirit L., Wis. 66 A3
Spirit L., Wis. 66 C3
Spirit River, Alta., Can. 42 H2
Spiritwood, Sask., Can. 43 C4
Spiritwood, N. Dak. 74 C2
Spiro, Okla., 1,450 76 J2
Spišská Belá, Czech. 126 E2
Spišská Nová Ves, Czech., 16,926 126 E2
Spitak, U.S.S.R., 8,300 137 c1
Spital, Aust., 2,413 124 M6
Spithead, chan., U.K. 113 k13
Spit Pt., Austl. 172 B3
Spitsbergen=Svalbard
Spittal, Aust., 10,034 124 K7
Spivey, Kans., 98 75 G6
Spjald, Den. 120 A4
Splendora, Tex. 77 Q4
Split, Yug., 99,000* 125 C3
Split Lake, Man., Can. 43 F3
Split L., Man., Can. 43 F3
Splitlog, Ont., Can. 67 f16
Splitrock Res., N.J. 58 b13
Splügen, Switz. 124 D2
Splügen Pass, Switz. 124 D2
Spofford, N.H. 54 C6
Spofford, Tex., 138 77 N5
Spofford L., N.H. 54 C6
Spofforth, U.K. 114 F3
Spokane, co., Wash., 278,333 80 E2
Spokane, Wash., 181,608 80 E2
Spokane, r., Idaho-Wash. 80 D2
Spokoynyy, U.S.S.R. 135 M4
Spoleto, It., 39,769 123 D3
Spondon, U.K., 11,541 114 F5
Spoolde, Neth. 115 D2
Spoon, r., Ill. 68 B3
Spooner, Wis., 2,398 66 B3
Spooner L., Wis. 66 B3
Sporades=Sporádhes
Sporádhes, is., Gr. 129 F6
Spornoye, U.S.S.R. 135 O3
Spotswood, N.J., 5,788 61 C3
Spotsylvania, co., Va., 13,819 62 G4
Spotsylvania, Va. 62 G4
Spotted Islands, Newf., Can. 45 Q4
Spottswood, Va. 62 E5
Spout Spring, Va. 62 F5
Spragge, Ont., Can. 46 B2
Sprague, Man., Can. 43 G5
Sprague, Nebr., 120 75 J3
Sprague, Wash., 597 80 D2
Sprague, W. Va., 3,073 62 C5
Sprague, Wis. 66 C4
Sprague, r., Oreg. 80 C4
Sprague River, Oreg. 80 C4
Spratt, Mich. 67 K4
Spratton, U.K. 114 F6
Spray, N.C., 4,656 63 E1
Spray, Oreg., 194 80 D3
Spray Beach, N.J. 61 C4
Spraytown, Ind. 70 C3
Spread Eagle, Wis. 66 E3
Spreča, r., Yug. 125 D2
Spreckelsville, Hawaii 84 E3
Spreckles, Calif. 83 f14
Spree, r., Ger.D.R. 118 E3
Spremberg, Ger.D.R., 22,865 118 E3
Sprendlingen, Hess., F.R.Ger., 12,009 119 F4
Sprendlingen, Rhein.-Pfalz, F.R.Ger., 3,140 119 E5
Sprent, Mt., Austl. 173 e14
Sprimont, Belg., 3,921 115 D4
Spring, Kans. 75 G6
Spring, Tex. 77 Q4
Spring, r., Ark.-Mo. 72 F8
Spring, r., Mo. 72 C7
Spring Arbor, Mich. 67 J6
Spring Bay, Ill., 285 68 C3
Springbok, S. Af., 3,111 164 C6
Springboro, Pa., 583 60 B2
Spring Branch, Tex. 76 b6
Springbrook, Iowa, 139 72 G2
Spring Brook, N.Y. 58 m19
Spring Brook, N. Dak., 35 74 A1
Spring Brook, Pa. 61 o16
Springbrook, Wis. 66 B3
Spring Bk., N.Y. 58 n21
Spring Brook Mtn., Me. 55 D4
Spring City, Pa., 3,162 61 L5
Spring City, Tenn., 1,800 71 F6
Spring City, Utah, 463 78 C2
Spring Creek, Fla. 65 E2
Springcreek, La. 73 E7
Spring Creek, Okla. 76 E2
Spring Creek, Tenn. 71 C6
Spring Cr., Ga. 64 E4
Spring Cr., Ill. 68 D3
Spring Cr., Ill. 69 b8
Spring Cr., Ill. 69 c10
Spring Cr., Nebr. 75 D3
Spring Cr., N. Dak. 74 A2
Spring Cr., S. Dak. 74 B3
Spring Cr., Tex. 77 i8
Springdale, Alta., Can. 43 a8
Springdale, Newf., Can., 1,638 45 Q5
Springdale, Ala. 64 d7
Springdale, Ark., 10,076 73 A1
Springdale (part of Stamford), Conn. 56 B8
Springdale, Mont. 81 D3
Springdale, Ohio, 3,556 70 E3
Springdale, Pa., 5,602 60 C4
Springdale, Utah, 248 78 B3
Springdale, Wash., 254 80 E1
Spring Dale, W. Va. 62 D5
Springe, F.R.Ger., 8,941 118 B2
Springer, N. Mex., 1,564 79 C3
Springer, Okla., 212 76 F3
Springerton, Ill., 232 68 D5
Springerville, Ariz., 719 78 D4
Springfield, Ont., Can. 46 C6
Springfield, U.K. 112 d7
Springfield, Colo., 1,791 79 D3
Springfield, Fla., 4,628 65 D2
Springfield, Ga., 858 64 H3
Springfield, Idaho 81 C4
Springfield, Ill., 83,271 68 C4
Springfield, Ky., 2,382 71 F4
Springfield, La. 73 E7
Springfield, Me. 55 D3
Springfield, Mass., 174,463 56 F4
Springfield, Mich., 4,605 67 H6
Springfield, Minn., 2,701 74 E3
Springfield, Mo., 95,865 72 D7
Springfield, Nebr., 506 75 J2
Springfield, N.H. 54 C4
Springfield, N.J., 14,467 58 b14
Springfield, Ohio, 82,723 70 F3
Springfield, Oreg., 19,616 80 B3
Springfield, Pa., 26,733(T) 61 M6
Springfield, S.C., 787 63 C4
Springfield, S. Dak., 1,194 74 C4
Springfield, Tenn., 9,221 71 E5
Springfield, Vt., 6,600 54 B5
Springfield, Va., 10,783 62 a9
Springfield, W. Va. 62 F3
Springfield, Wis. 66 c13
Springfield, L., Ill. 68 C4
Springfield Center, N.Y. 59 L6
Springfield Corners, Wis. 66 D5
Springfield Plat., Mo. 72 ·
Springfield Res., Mass. 56 G4
Springford, Ont., Can. 46 D6
Spring Garden, Guyana 101 L4
Spring Garden, Va. 62 E6
Spring Green, Wis., 1,146 66 C5
Spring Grove, Ill., 301 69 b7
Spring Grove, Minn., 1,342 74 G4
Spring Grove, Pa., 1,675 60 J6
Spring Hall, Barb. 97 10
Springhill, N.S., Can., 5,644 45 N6
Spring Hill, Ala. 64 D4
Spring Hill, Ark. 73 B4
Spring Hill (part of Mansfield), Conn. 56 H5
Spring Hill, Iowa, 111 72 D3
Spring Hill, Kans., 909 75 L5
Springhill, La., 6,437 73 B4
Spring Hill, Pa., 1,127 60 E5
Spring Hill, Tenn., 689 71 E6
Spring Hope, N.C., 1,336 63 F2
Spring House, Pa. 60 f11
Spring Lake, Mich., 2,063 67 G5
Spring Lake, N.J., 2,922 61 D3
Spring Lake, N.Y. 59 p23
Spring Lake, N.C., 4,110 63 F2
Springlake, Tex., 245 77 M2
Spring Lake Heights, N.J., 3,309 58 c16
Springlands, Guyana 101 M5
Spring Mill, Pa. 60 f11
Spring Mills, Pa. 60 G4
Spring Mts., Nev. 82 ·
Springport, Ind., 253 70 D2
Springport, Mich., 693 67 J5
Spring Prairie, Wis. 66 E6
Springs, S. Af., 135,231 164 D6
Springs, Pa. 60 D6
Springside, Sask., Can. 43 D4
Springsure, Austl. 173 G3
Springton Res., Pa. 60 f12
Springtown, Pa. 61 M4
Springtown, Tex., 859 77 P3
Springvale, Me., 2,379 55 B5
Spring Valley, Calif. 82 c9
Spring Valley, Ill., 5,371 68 C2
Spring Valley, Minn., 2,628 74 F4
Spring Valley, N.Y., 6,538 59 M9
Spring Valley, Ohio, 678 70 F3
Spring Valley, Tex., 3,004 77 h9
Spring Valley, Wis., 977 66 A4
Springview, Nebr., 281 75 F1
Springville, Ala., 822 64 C2
Springville, Calif. 82 D4
Springville, Ind. 69 h10
Springville, N.Y., 3,852 58 C6
Springville, Pa. 61 K2
Springville, Utah, 7,913 78 C1
Springwater, N.Y. 58 E6
Sprinkle, Tex. 76 c5
Sproat L., Br. Col., Can. 42 a6
Sprowston, U.K., 9,609 113 G5
Sproxton, U.K. 114 G5
Spruce, Mich. 67 K4
Spruce, Wis. 66 E4
Spruce Creek, Pa. 60 F4
Sprucedale, Ont., Can. 46 E3
Spruce Grove, Alta., Can. 43 b7
Spruce Knob, mtn., W. Va. 62 E4
Spruce Lake, Sask., Can. 43 B4
Sprucemont, Nev. 83 C2
Spruce Mtn., Nev. 83 C2
Spruce Mtn., Vt. 54 C3
Spruce Pine, Ala. 64 B1
Spruce Pine, N.C., 2,504 63 C2
Spui, r., Neth. 115 a7
Spur, Tex., 2,170 77 N3
Spurfield, Alta., Can. 42 J2
Spurgeon, Ind., 269 70 B4
Spurn Head, pt., U.K. 113 G5
Spurr, Mt., Alaska 85 F3
Spuzzum, Br. Col., Can. 42 G4
Spy, Belg., 3,381 115 C4
Squamish, Br. Col., Can., 1,536 42 G4
Squamish, r., Br. Col., Can. 42 F4
Squam L., N.H. 54 D4
Squankum, N.J. 58 c16
Squannacook, r., Mass. 57 K2
Squapan, Me. 55 D2
Squapan Knob, Me. 55 D2
Squapan L., Me. 55 D2
Square Butte, N. Dak. 74 A2
Square Head, Tutuila 177 39
Square Island Harbour, Newf., Can. 45 Q4
Square L., Me. 55 D1
Square Pd., Me. 55 B5
Squaw Cr., Ill. 69 b7
Squaw Lake, Minn., 129 74 E2
Squaw Mtn., Me. 55 C3
Squibnocket, Mass. 57 O7
Squillace, Golfo di, It. 123 F5
Squire, W. Va. 62 C5
Squires, Mt., Austl. 172 C4
Squirrel L., Wis. 66 D3
Sragen, Indon. 148 d7
Srbac, Yug. 125 C2
Srbija, reg., Yug. 125 E2
Srbobran, Yug. 125 D2
Srebrino, Bulg., 2,821 128 E3
Srebrnik, Yug. 125 D2
Sredets, Bulg. 128 E3
Sredetska, r., Bulg. 128 F3
Sredinnyy Khr., U.S.S.R. 135 P4
Sredna Gore, mts., Bulg. 128 D3
Sredne-Kamchatsk, U.S.S.R. 135 Q4
Sredne-Kolymsk, U.S.S.R., 2,100 135 P3
Sredne-Russkaya Vozvyshennost', U.S.S.R. 134 C4
Sredne-Sibirskoye Plos., U.S.S.R. 135 K3
Sredne-Ural'sk, U.S.S.R., 13,100 137 k7
Sredne-Vilyuysk, U.S.S.R. 135 M3
Sredniy Ural, mts., U.S.S.R. 137 i8
Sredniy Urgal, U.S.S.R. 135 N4
Sredniy Vasyugan, U.S.S.R. 134 G4
Sre Khlong, Camb. 147 k11
Sre Khtum, Camb. 146 D4
Śrem, Pol., 10,413 127 B2
Sremska Mitrovica, Yug., 21,000* 125 D2
Sremski Karlovci, Yug., 5,628 125 E2
Sreng, r., Camb. 146 C4
Srepok, r., Camb. 146 D4
Sretensk, U.S.S.R., 15,100 135 L4
Sre Umbell, Camb. 146 C5
Srikakulam, India, 35,071 145 G6
Srinagar, India, 285,257 145 E2
Sripur, Pak. 144 g13
Srirangam, India, 41,949 145 m20
Srirangapatna, India, 11,423 145 k19
Srivardhan, India, 10,344 145 h17
Srivilliputtur, India, 46,816 145 k21
Srnetica, Yug. 125 C2
Środa, Pol., 12,693 127 B2
Środa Śląska, Pol., 5,516 127 B3
Srostki, U.S.S.R. 137 r11
Ssu-ch'uan, prov., China, 72,160,000 150 D4
Ssu-ch'uan P'en-ti, reg., China 152 B1
Ssu-hsien, China 151 C4
Ssu-hui, China 152 D3
Ssu-mao, China 150 D5
Ssu-nan, China 150 E4
Ssu-p'ing, China, 153,600* 150 G2
Ssu-shui, China 151 C4
Ssu-tzu-wang-ch'i, China 150 F2
Staasdorf, Aust. 124 c10
Staaten, r., Austl. 173 F2
Staatz, Aust. 124 N5
Stabroek, Belg., 5,181 115 C3
Staby, Den., 1,065 121 A4
Stacey, N.C. 63 E1
Stacy, Ky. 71 H4
Stacy, N.C. 63 H3
Stacyville, Me. 55 D3
Stacyville, Iowa, 588 72 E1
Stad-Delden, Neth., 4,400 115 E2
Stade, F.R.Ger., 30,477 118 B2
Staden, Belg., 5,547 115 A4
Stadil, Den. 121 A4
Stadskanaal, Neth., 19,500 115 F2
Stads kan., Neth. 115 E2
Stadthagen, F.R.Ger., 13,654 118 B2
Stadtlohn, F.R.Ger., 7,615 118 A3
Stadtoldendorf, F.R.Ger., 6,761 118 B3
Stadtroda, Ger.D.R. 118 C3
Stäfa, Switz., 6,947 124 C1
Staffanstorp, Swed. 121 F5
Staffelstein, F.R.Ger., 4,101 118 C3
Staffora, r., It. 122 c6
Stafford, U.K., 47,814 113 E5
Stafford, Conn., 7,476(T) 56 G5
Stafford, co., Kans., 7,451 75 G5
Stafford, Kans., 1,862 75 G6
Stafford, Ohio, 113 70 H3
Stafford, Okla. 76 D2
Stafford, Tex., 1,485 77 h9
Stafford, co., Va., 16,876 62 G4
Stafford, Va. 62 G4
Stafford, L., Fla. 65 G3
Staffordshire, co., U.K., 1,733,887 113 E5
Stafford Springs, Conn., 3,322 56 G5
Staffordsville, Ky. 71 H4
Staffordsville, Va. 62 D5
Staffordville (part of Stafford), Conn. 56 H5
Stagno Lombardo, It., 2,989 122 d5
Stahnsdorf, Ger.D.R. 119 e11
Stainach, Aust., 1,785 124 K6
Staindrop, U.K., 7,209 113 F4
Staines, U.K., 49,838 114 H8
Stainforth, U.K., 7,126 114 G3
Stains, Fr., 27,503 116 h11
Stainz, Aust., 1,461 124 M7
Stakeford, U.K., 2,315 112 g9
Stakes Bay, Lesser Caymans 97 2
Stakes Bay Pt., Lesser Caymans 97 2
Stala, Swed. 121 D2
Stålboga, Swed. 120 d8
Štalcerji, Yug. 125 B2
Stalden, Switz., 1,007 124 B2
Staley, N.C., 260 63 E2
Stalin, Alb., 11,100 125 D4
Stalingrad=Volgograd
Stalinstadt=Eisenhüttenstadt
Stallarholmen, Swed. 120 e8
Stallworthy, C., N.W.T., Can. 41 K1
Stalowa Wola, Pol., 23,000* 127 E3
Stalwart, Mich. 67 J2
Stambaugh, Mich., 1,876 66 E2
Stamford, Austl. 173 F3
Stamford, Ont., Can., 1,255 46 d15
Stamford, U.K., 11,743 113 F5
Stamford, Conn., 92,713 56 B8
Stamford, Nebr., 220 75 F3
Stamford, N.Y., 1,166 59 L7
Stamford, S. Dak. 74 B4
Stamford, Tex., 5,259 77 O3
Stamford, L., Tex. 77 O3
Stamford Bridge, U.K. 114 G3
Stammheim, F.R.Ger., 2,327 119 F7
Stamná, Gr., 1,754 129 C5
Stampa, Switz. 124 D2
Stampersgat, Neth. 115 a7
Stamping Ground, Ky., 353 71 G3
Stampriet, S.-W. Afr. 164 C6
Stamps, Ark., 2,591 73 B4
Stamsund, Nor. 120 C1
Stanardsville, Va., 283 62 F4
Stanberry, Mo., 1,409 72 C4
Stâncuța, Rum. 128 F2
Standard, Alta., Can. 42 K3
Standard, Alaska 85 a6
Standard, Ill., 282 68 C2
Standard City, Ill., 182 68 C4
Standerton, S. Af., 16,868 164 D6
Standing Stone Cr., Pa. 60 G4
Standish, Calif. 82 C2
Standish, Mich., 1,214 67 J5
Standish, N.Y. 59 M2
Standley L., Colo. 79 b8
Standon, U.K., 2,763 114 J7
Standrod, Utah 78 B1
Stanfield, Ariz. 78 B5
Stanfield, N.C., 471 63 D2
Stanfield, Oreg., 745 80 D3
Stanford, S. Af. 164 a9
Stanford, Ill., 479 68 C3
Stanford, Ind. 70 C3
Stanford, Ky., 2,019 71 G4
Stanford, Mont., 615 81 D2
Stanford le Hope (part of Thurrock), U.K., 8,654 114 J7
Stanfordville, N.Y. 59 N8
Stangelville, Wis. 66 F4
Stanghella, It., 4,781 122 e5
Stanhope, U.K., 5,854 113 E4
Stanhope, Iowa, 461 72 D2
Stanhope, N.J., 1,814 61 B2
Stanhope, N.C. 63 F2
Staniard Creek, Bah. Is. 95 a8
Stanichno-Luganskoye, U.S.S.R., 11,000 136 f7
Stanišić, Yug., 7,814 125 D2
Stanislaus, co., Calif., 157,294 82 C4
Stanislaus, r., Calif. 82 C3
Stanke Dimitrov, Bulg., 25,466 128 D3
Stankovci, Yug. 125 B3
Stanley, Austl. 173 e13
Stanley, Br. Col., Can. 42 G3
Stanley, N.B., Can. 47 S10
Stanley, Falkland Is., 1,074 108 3
Stanley, U.K., 46,280 113 F4
Stanley, Idaho, 35 81 B3
Stanley, Iowa, 156 72 F2
Stanley, Kans. 75 L5
Stanley, Ky. 71 D4
Stanley, La., 234 73 B6
Stanley, N. Mex. 79 C4
Stanley, N.Y. 58 F6
Stanley, N.C., 1,980 63 C2
Stanley, N. Dak., 1,795 74 A1
Stanley, Okla. 76 H3
Stanley, co., S. Dak., 4,085 74 B3
Stanley, Va., 1,039 62 F4
Stanley, Wis., 2,014 66 C4
Stanley, Mt., Austl. 172 D3
Stanley Falls, D.R.Congo 164 D1
Stanley Mission, Sask., Can. 43 D3
Stanley Pool, Congo-D.R.Congo 164 B2
Stanley Res., India 145 m20
Stanleyville, D.R.Congo=Kisangani
Stanleyville, N.C., 1,138 63 D1
Stanly, co., N.C., 40,873 63 D2
Stannard, Vt. 54 C2
Stann Creek, Br. Hond., 5,287 94 C2
Stannington, Northumb., Eng., U.K., 2,573 112 g9
Stannington, York., Eng., U.K., 5,157 114 E4
Stanovoye Nag., U.S.S.R. 135 L4
Stanovoy Khr., U.S.S.R. 135 M4
Stans, Switz., 4,337 124 C2
Stansbury Mts., Utah 78 b9
Stanstead, Qué., Can., 1,120 47 M3
Stansted Mountfitchet, U.K., 3,376 114 J7
Stanthorpe, Austl., 2,907 173 G4
Stanton, N.W.T., Can. 40 D4
Stanton, U.K., 1,252 113 G5
Stanton, Ala. 64 C3
Stanton, Calif., 11,163 83 i16
Stanton, Del. 62 e11
Stanton, Iowa, 514 72 C4
Stanton, co., Kans., 2,108 75 D6
Stanton, Ky., 753 71 H4
Stanton, Mich., 1,139 67 J5
Stanton, co., Nebr., 5,783 75 H2
Stanton, Nebr., 1,317 75 H2
Stanton, N. Dak., 409 74 B2
Stanton, Tenn., 458 71 B6
Stanton, Tex., 2,228 77 M3
Stanton Lacy, U.K. 114 C6
Stantonsburg, N.C., 897 63 G2
Stanwich (part of Greenwich), Conn. 56 B8
Stanwix, N.Y. 59 t26
Stanwood, Iowa, 598 72 F3
Stanwood, Mich., 205 67 H5
Stanwood, Wash., 646 80 B1
Stanzach, Aust. 124 G6
Stapar, Yug. 125 D2
Staphorst, Neth., 5,500 115 E2
Stapleford, U.K., 13,307 114 F5
Staplehurst, Nebr., 240 75 H3
Staples, Ont., Can. 46 B6
Staples, Minn., 2,706 74 E2
Staples, Tex. 76 c6
Staples Corner, Ill. 69 b8
Stapleton, Ala. 64 B5
Stapleton, Ga., 356 64 G2
Stapleton, Nebr., 359 75 E2
Staporków, Pol., 3,301 127 k5
Stapp, Okla. 76 J3
Star, Alta., Can. 43 c7
Star, Miss. 73 E5
Star, N.C., 745 63 E2
Starachowice, Pol., 36,000* 127 D3
Stará L'ubovňa, Czech. 126 E2
Stara Pazova, Yug., 12,000* 125 E2
Stara Planina, mts., Bulg. 128 D3
Staraya Russa, U.S.S.R., 24,300 134 B4
Stara Zagora, Bulg., 56,177 128 E3
Starboard, Me. 55 E4
Starbuck, Man., Can. 43 g10
Starbuck, Minn., 1,099 74 E3
Starbuck, Wash., 161 80 D2
Starbuck I., Line Is. 171 H5
Star City, Sask., Can. 43 D4
Star City, Ark., 1,573 73 D4
Star City, Ind. 70 C2
Star City, W. Va., 1,236 62 E3
Stare Budkowice, Pol. 127 h6
Starford, Pa., 60 E4
Stargard Szczeciński, Pol., 31,000* 127 A2
Star Hbr., Sol. Is. 175 d3
Starigrad, Yug. 125 B2
Staritsa, U.S.S.R., 4,700 136 D1
Star Junction, Pa., 1,142 60 c9
Stark, co., Ill., 8,152 68 C2
Stark, Kans., 96 75 K6
Stark, N.H. 54 E2
Stark, co., N. Dak., 18,451 74 A2
Stark, co., Ohio, 340,345 70 H2
Starke, Fla., 4,806 65 G3
Starke, co., Ind., 17,911 70 C1
Starks, La. 73 B7
Starks, Me. 55 B4
Starks, Wis. 66 D3
Starksboro, Vt. 54 A3
Starkville, Colo., 261 79 C3
Starkville, Miss., 9,041 73 G4
Starkweather, N. Dak., 223 74 C1
Star Lake, N.Y. 59 K3
Starlake, Wis. 66 D2
Starnberg, F.R.Ger., 9,899 118 C5
Staro-Baltachevo, U.S.S.R. 137 h8
Starobel'sk, U.S.S.R., 18,700 136 E3
Staro-Beshevo, U.S.S.R. 136 e8
Starobin, U.S.S.R., 5,700 136 B2
Starodub, U.S.S.R., 11,600 136 D2
Starogard Gdański, Pol., 26,000* 127 C2
Starokadomskogo, O., U.S.S.R. 135 K2
Staro-Konstantinov, U.S.S.R., 16,400 136 B3
Staro-Minskaya, U.S.S.R. 136 E4
Staro Petrovo Selo, Yug., 2,332 125 C2
Staro-Shcherbinovskaya, U.S.S.R. 136 E4
Starosoldatskoye, U.S.S.R. 137 o11
Staro-Subkhangulovo, U.S.S.R. 137 i9
Star Prairie, Wis., 331 66 A3
Starr, Ohio 70 G3
Starr, S.C., 243 63 B3
Starr, co., Tex., 17,137 77 O6
Starring L., Minn. 74 b6
Starrucca, Pa., 330 61 M2
Start Bay, U.K. 113 E6
Startex, S.C. 63 B3
Startforth, U.K., 1,162 112 f10
Start Pt., Eng., U.K. 113 E6
Start Pt., Scot., U.K. 112 E2
Stary Sącz, Pol., 5,788 127 D4
Staryy Krym, U.S.S.R., 6,800 136 D4
Staryy Oskol, U.S.S.R., 26,400 136 E3
Stassfurt, Ger.D.R., 26,259 118 C3
Staszów, Pol., 5,534 127 D3
State Bridge, Colo. 79 B2
Stateburg, S.C. 63 D4
State Center, Iowa, 1,142 72 D2
State College, Miss. 73 G4
State College, Pa., 27,584 60 G4
State Farm (part of Bridgewater), Mass. 57 N5
Stateline, Calif. 82 D3
State Line, Ind., 171 70 B2
State Line (part of W. Stockbridge), Mass. 56 C3
State Line, Miss., 653 73 G6
Staten I., N.Y. 59 M10
Statenville, Ga. 64 F5
State Road, N.C. 63 D1
Statesboro, Ga., 8,356 64 H3
Statesville, N.C., 19,844 63 D2
Statham, Ga., 711 64 F2
Stathern, U.K. 114 G5
Statue of Liberty Nat. Mon., N.Y. 58 c14
Statzendorf, Aust., 1,115 124 b10
Staufen, F.R.Ger., 3,024 118 A5
Staunton, Ill., 4,228 68 C4
Staunton, Va., 22,232 62 E4
Stavanger, Nor., 52,799 120 A4
Stave Falls, Br. Col., Can. 42 d6
Staveley, U.K., 18,070 114 F4
Stavelot, Belg., 4,729 115 D4
Stavely, Alta., Can. 42 K4
Stavenhagen, Ger.D.R., 6,521 118 D2
Staveren, Neth. 115 D2
Stavern, Nor. 121 C2
Staverton, U.K. 114 D7
Stavropol', U.S.S.R., 123,400 134 D4
Stavropol', U.S.S.R., 158,000 134 D5
Stavropol'skaya Voz., U.S.S.R. 136 F4
Stavroúpolis, Gr., 1,375 129 E4
Stavrovo, U.S.S.R. 136 c5
Stawell, Austl., 5,463 173 F5
Stawiski, Pol., 1,986 127 E2
Stawiszyn, Pol., 1,434 127 C3
Stayner, Ont., Can., 1,653 44 H7
Stayton, Oreg., 2,108 80 B3
Stead, N. Mex. 79 D3
Steamboat Canyon, Ariz. 78 D4
Steamboat Rock, Iowa, 426 72 D2
Steamboat Springs, Colo., 1,843 79 B1
Stearns, Ky. 71 G5
Stearns, co., Minn., 80,345 74 E3
Stebbing, U.K., 1,035 114 J7
Stebbins, Alaska, 158 85 D3
Štěchovice, Czech. 126 d7
Steckborn, Switz., 3,514 124 D1
Stecker, Okla. 76 E3
Stedman, N.C., 463 63 F2
Stedum, Neth. 115 E1
Steele, Ala., 625 64 C2
Steele, co., Minn., 25,029 74 F4

298 · Steele—Süchow

Steele, Mo., 2,301 72 H8
Steele, co., N. Dak., 4,719 74 D2
Steele, N. Dak., 847 74 C2
Steele City, Nebr., 173 75 J3
Steeleville, Ill., 1,569 68 C5
Steels Pt., Norfolk I. 175 11
Steelton, Pa., 11,266 60 J5
Steelville, Mo., 1,127 72 F7
Steen, Sask., Can. 43 D4
Steen, r., Alta., Can. 42 H1
Steenbergen, Neth., 5,600 115 C3
Steenhuffel, Belg., 2,482 115 d9
Steenkool, Indon. 149 K3
Steensby Inlet, N.W.T., Can. 41 O3
Steens Mtn., Oreg. 50 C2
Steenwijk, Neth., 10,500 115 E2
Steep Falls, Me. 55 B5
Steep Holme, i., U.K. 114 B8
Steeping, r., U.K. 114 J4
Steeple Bumpstead, U.K. 114 J6
Steeple Claydon, U.K., 1,079 114 F7
Steeple Morden, U.K. 114 H6
Steep Rock, Man., Can. 43 F4
Steep Rock Lake, Ont. Can. 44 D5
Ştefăneşti-Tîrg, Rum. 128 F1
Stefanie, L., Eth.-Kenya 163 L5
Stefanovo, Bulg., 1,023 128 F3
Stefansson I., N.W.T., Can. 40 H3
Steffeln, F.R.Ger. 119 B4
Steffenville, Mo. 72 F5
Steffisburg, Switz., 10,757 124 B2
Stege, Den., 2,620 121 E6
Steger, Ill., 6,432 68 E2
Stehekin, Wash. 80 C1
Ştei, Rum., 5,874 128 D1
Steigerwald, mts., F.R.Ger. 118 C4
Steijl, Neth. 115 E3
Steilacoom, Wash., 1,569 80 B2
Steinabrückl, Aust. 124 c11
Steinach, Aust., 2,155 124 H6
Steinach, Ger.D.R. 118 C3
Stein am Rhein, Switz., 2,588 124 C1
Steinau, F.R.Ger., 3,879 119 G4
Steinbach, Man., Can. 43 F5
Steinbach, F.R.Ger., 2,566 119 E7
Steinbeck, F.R.Ger., 1,025 119 a9
Steinberg, Aust. 124 N6
Steinfeld, Aust., 2,705 124 K7
Steinfeld, Bay., F.R.Ger., 1,125 119 H5
Steinfeld, Ndrsachs., F.R.Ger., 5,470 118 B2
Steingaden, F.R.Ger., 2,592 118 C5
Steinhagen, Ger.D.R. 118 D1
Steinhatchee, Fla. 65 F3
Steinhausen, F.R.Ger., 1,837 119 E1
Steinheim, F.R.Ger., 5,801 118 B3
Steinhuder M., F.R.Ger. 118 B2
Steinkjer, Nor., 4,122 120 B2
Steinkopf, S. Af. 164 B6
Steins, N. Mex. 79 A5
Stekene, Belg., 8,931 115 C3
Stella, Mo., 166 72 C8
Stella, Nebr., 262 75 K3
Stellarton, N.S., Can., 5,227 47 U11
Stelle, F.R.Ger., 2,985 119 b9
Stellenbosch, S. Af., 22,233 164 a8
Steller, Mt., Alaska 85 J3
Stelton = Edison, N.J.
Stem, N.C., 221 63 F1
Stemwarde, F.R.Ger. 119 b8
Stenay, Fr., 3,883 117 F2
Stendal, Ger.D.R., 36,975 118 C2
Stenderup, Den. 121 A5
Stene, Belg., 6,164 115 A3
Stenen, Sask., Can. 43 D4
Stenhouse Bay, Austl. 172 b8
Stenkyrka, Swed. 121 D3
Stenlille, Den., 1,652 121 D5
Stenløse, Den. 121 a7
Stensele, Swed. 120 D2
Stenstrup, Den., 1,916 121 C5
Stenungsund, Swed. 120 B4
Stepanakert, U.S.S.R., 22,000 137 c2
Stepanavan, U.S.S.R., 9,900 137 c1
Stephan, S. Dak. 74 C3
Stephen, Minn., 858 74 D1
Stephens, Ark., 1,275 73 C4
Stephens, co., Ga., 18,391 64 F1
Stephens, co., Okla., 37,990 76 F3
Stephens, co., Tex., 8,885 77 O3
Stephens, C., N.Z. 175 g6
Stephens, Port, Falk. Is. 108 3
Stephens City, Va., 876 62 F3
Stephens Creek, Austl. 173 F4
Stephens Mills, N.Y. 58 E7
Stephenson, co., Ill., 46,207 68 C1
Stephenson, Mich., 820 66 F3
Stephensport, Ky. 71 E4
Stephensville, Wis. 66 E4
Stephentown, N.Y. 59 O6
Stephenville, Newf., Can., 6,001 45 P5
Stephenville, Tex., 7,359 77 O3
Stepnyak, U.S.S.R., 12,800 134 G4
Steppsville, Tenn. 71 F6
Steps Pt., Tutuila 177 39
Steptoe, Wash. 80 E2
Sterbfritz, F.R.Ger., 1,799 119 H4
Sterlibashevo, U.S.S.R. 137 h9
Sterling, Alaska, 460 85 G3
Sterling, Colo., 10,751 79 D1
Sterling, Idaho 81 C4
Sterling, Ill., 15,688 68 C2
Sterling, Kans., 2,303 75 G5
Sterling, Mass., 3,193(T) 57 K3
Sterling, Mich., 470 67 J4
Sterling, Nebr., 471 75 J3
Sterling, N.Y. 59 p22
Sterling, N. Dak. 74 B2
Sterling, Okla., 562 76 E3
Sterling, Pa. 61 p16
Sterling, co., Tex., 1,177 77 N4
Sterling, Utah, 137 78 C2
Sterling City, Tex., 854 77 N4
Sterling Cr., N.Y. 59 p23
Sterling Hill, Conn. 57 J6
Sterling Res., Colo. 79 D1
Sterling Run, Pa. 60 F3
Sterling Station, Conn. 57 J6
Sterlington, La. 73 C5
Sterling Valley, N.Y. 59 p22
Sterling Valley Cr., N.Y. 59 p22
Sterlitamak, U.S.S.R., 131,000 134 E4
Sternalice, Pol. 127 h6
Sternberg, Ger.D.R. 118 C2
Šternberk, Czech., 11,833 126 C2
Stérnes, Gr., 1,377 129 E7
Sterrett, Ala. 64 e8
Sterrett, Tex. 76 f10
Štětí, Czech. 126 d6
Stetlersville, Pa. 61 i18
Stetson, Me. 55 C4
Stetsonville, Wis., 319 66 C3
Stettin = Szczecin
Stettin Lag., Ger.D.R.-Pol. 118 E2
Stettler, Alta., Can., 3,553 42 K3
Steuben, co., Ind., 17,184 70 D1
Steuben, Me. 55 E4
Steuben, Mich. 67 G2
Steuben, co., N.Y., 97,691 58 E7
Steuben, Wis., 193 66 C5
Steubenville, Ohio, 32,495 70 J2
Stevenage, U.K., 42,968 113 F6
Stevens, Ont., Can. 44 F5
Stevens, Alaska = Stevens Village
Stevens, co., Kans., 4,400 75 D6
Stevens, co., Minn., 11,262 74 D3
Stevens, co., Wash., 17,884 80 E1
Stevens Bk., N.H. 54 D5
Stevens Mills, Vt. 54 B2
Stevenson, Ala., 1,456 64 D1
Stevenson, Wash., 927 80 B3
Stevenson L., Man., Can. 43 F4
Stevens Pass, Wash. 80 C2
Stevens Point, Wis., 17,837 66 D4
Stevens Pottery, Ga. 64 F3
Stevenston, U.K., 10,174 112 a8
Stevens Village, Alaska 85 G2
Stevensville, Ont., Can. 46 F6
Stevensville, Mich., 697 67 G6
Stevensville, Mont., 784 81 C2
Stevensville, Pa. 61 K2
Stevensville, Va. 62 H5
Stever, r., F.R.Ger. 119 C1
Steveston, Br. Col., Can., 2,207 42 c6
Steward, Ill., 264 68 D2
Stewardson, Ill., 656 68 D4
Stewart, Br. Col., Can. 42 D2
Stewart, Cuba, 1,943 96 d2
Stewart, co., Ga., 7,371 64 E3
Stewart, Miss., 162 73 F4
Stewart, Nev. 83 A3
Stewart, Ohio 70 H3
Stewart, co., Tenn., 7,851 71 D5
Stewart, C., Austl. 172 E1
Stewart, r., Yukon, Can. 40 C5
Stewart Corners, N.Y. 59 u26
Stewart I., N.Z. 175 f7
Stewart Is., Sol. Is. 175 d2
Stewart Mtn., Me. 55 B3
Stewarton, U.K., 3,387 112 a8
Stewart Pk., Colo. 79 B2
Stewart River, Yukon, Can. 40 A5
Stewarts Point, Calif. 82 B3
Stewartstown, N.H. 54 E2
Stewartstown, Pa., 1,164 60 J6
Stewartstown Hollow, N.H. 54 E2
Stewartsville, Mo., 466 72 C5
Stewartsville, N.J. 61 A2
Stewart Town, Jam. 96 p8
Stewart Valley, Sask., Can. 43 C5
Stewartville (part of Colrain), Mass. 56 F2
Stewartville, Minn., 1,670 74 F4
Stewiacke, N.S., Can., 1,015 45 N6
Stewkley, U.K., 1,016 114 G7
Steyr, Aust., 38,105 124 L5
Steyr, r., Aust. 124 L6
Stibnite, Idaho 81 B3
Stickney, N.B., Can. 47 S10
Stickney, Ill., 6,239 69 c9
Stickney, S. Dak., 456 74 C4
Stidham, Okla., 88 76 H2
Stiefern, Aust. 124 b9
Stierva, Switz. 124 D2
Stigler, Okla., 1,923 76 H2
Stigliano, It., 10,513 123 F4
Stigtomta, Swed. 120 d9
Stikine, r., Can.-U.S. 42 D1
Stikine Mts., Br. Col., Can. 42 D1
Stikine Plat., Br. Col., Can. 42 C1
Stiles, N.C. 63 b7
Stiles, Tex. 77 N4
Stiles, Wis. 66 E4
Stilís, Gr., 4,673 129 D5
Still, r., Conn. 56 C7
Still, r., Conn. 56 D5
Stilling, Den. 121 C4
Stillington, Dur., Eng., U.K. 112 g10
Stillington, York., Eng., U.K. 114 F2
Stillman Valley, Ill., 598 68 C1
Stillmore, Ga., 354 64 G3
Still River (part of New Milford), Conn. 56 C6
Still River (part of Harvard), Mass. 57 K3
Stillwater, Br. Col., Can. 42 b6
Stillwater, Minn., 8,310 74 F3
Stillwater, co., Mont., 5,526 81 E3
Stillwater, Nev. 83 A3
Stillwater, N.J. 61 B1
Stillwater, N.Y., 1,398 59 N6
Stillwater, Okla., 23,965 76 F1
Stillwater, Pa., 193 61 K3
Stillwater (part of Smithfield), R.I. 57 K5
Stillwater Center, N.Y. 59 w28
Stillwater Cr., Okla. 76 F1
Stillwater Ra., Nev. 83 A3
Stillwell, Ind. 70 C1
Stilton, U.K. 114 H6
Stilwell, Kans. 75 L5
Stilwell, Okla., 1,916 76 J2
Štimlje, Yug. 125 E3
Stinesville, Ind., 288 70 C3
Stinnett, Tex., 2,695 76 N2
Stinson Beach, Calif. 83 d12
Stinson Lake, N.H. 54 D4
Štip, Yug., 19,000* 125 F4
Stíra, Gr. 129 E5
Stiring-Wendel, Fr., 15,028 116 c8
Stirling, Alta., Can. 42 K4
Stirling, N.S., Can. 47 V11
Stirling, Ont., Can., 1,281 46 G4
Stirling, co., U.K., 194,858 112 D3
Stirling, U.K., 27,553 112 D3
Stirling, N.J., 1,382 58 a14
Stirling City, Calif. 82 C3
Stirum, N. Dak. 74 D2
Stites, Idaho, 299 81 B2
Stith, Ala. 64 a7
Stittsville, Ont., Can., 1,459· 47 H3
Stittville, N.Y. 59 K5
Štíty, Czech. 127 f7
Stitzer, Wis. 66 C6
Stjärnhov, Swed. 120 d8
Stjernöya, i., Nor. 120 E1
Stjördalshalsen, Nor. 120 B3
Stöbber-Bach, r., Ger.D.R. 119 f11
Stobrawa, r., Pol. 127 g6
Stock, Ég. du, Fr. 116 c9
Stockach, F.R.Ger., 4,869 118 B5
Stockbridge, Ga., 1,201 64 E2
Stockbridge, Mass., 2,161(T) 56 C3
Stockbridge, Mich., 1,097 67 J6
Stockbridge, Vt. 54 B4
Stockbridge, Wis., 476 66 E4
Stockdale, Ohio 70 G4
Stockdale, Pa., 815 60 c9
Stockdale, Tex., 1,111 77 P5
Stockelsdorf, F.R.Ger., 9,571 119 c8
Stockerau, Aust., 11,824 124 N5
Stockertown, Pa., 777 61 M4
Stockett, Mont. 81 D2
Stockholm, Swed., 806,903 120 D4
Stockholm, Me. 55 D1
Stockholm, N.J. 58 a12
Stockholm, S. Dak., 155 74 D3
Stockholm, Wis., 106 66 A4
Stockhorn, mtn. Switz. 124 B2
Stockport, U.K., 142,469 113 E5
Stockport, Iowa, 342 72 F4
Stockport, N.Y. 59 N7
Stockport, Ohio, 458 70 H3
Stocksbridge, U.K., 11,137 114 E4
Stockstadt, F.R.Ger., 4,561 119 G5
Stocksville, N.C. 63 B2
Stockton, Ala. 64 B5
Stockton, Calif., 86,321 82 C4
Stockton, Ga. 64 G5
Stockton, Ill., 1,800 68 C1
Stockton, Kans., 2,073 75 F4
Stockton, Md. 62 J4
Stockton, Mo., 838 72 D7
Stockton, N.J., 520 61 A3
Stockton, N.Y. 58 B7
Stockton, Utah, 362 78 B1
Stockton I., Wis. 66 C2
Stockton-on-Tees, U.K., 81,198 113 F4
Stockton Springs, Me. 55 D4
Stockum, F.R.Ger., 1,230 119 D2
Stockville, Nebr., 91 75 E3
Stoczek Łukowski, Pol., 1,750 127 E3
Stod, Czech. 126 A2
Stoddard, co., Mo., 29,490 72 H8
Stoddard, N.H. 54 C5
Stoddard, Wis., 552 66 B5
Stöde, Swed. 120 D3
Stoer, Pt. of, U.K. 112 D2
Stofberg, S. Af. 165 k17
Stogursey, U.K., 1,391 114 B8
Stoholm, Den. 121 B4
Stoke Ferry, U.K. 114 J5
Stokenchurch, U.K., 2,794 114 G7
Stoke-on-Trent, U.K., 265,506 113 E5
Stoke Prior, U.K., 2,329 114 D6
Stokes, N.Y. 59 t25
Stokes, co., N.C., 22,314 63 D1
Stokes, N.C., 195 63 G2
Stokesdale, N.C. 63 E1
Stokesley, U.K., 2,529 112 h11
Stokke, Nor. 121 C1
Stokken, Nor. 121 A2
Stokkmarknes, Nor. 120 C1
Stokksund, Nor. 120 B2
Stolac, Yug., 2,369 125 C3
Stolberg, F.R.Ger., 34,828 118 A3
Stolberg, Ger.D.R. 118 C3
Stolbovaya, U.S.S.R. 136 b6
Stolbovoy, O., U.S.S.R. 135 N2
Stolbtsy, U.S.S.R., 5,400 136 B2
Stolica, pk., Czech. 126 E2
Stolin, U.S.S.R., 5,000 136 B3
Stollberg, Ger.D.R., 13,035 118 D3
Stolpen, Ger.D.R. 126 d5
Stolwijk, Neth. 115 b7
Stolzenau, F.R.Ger., 2,868 118 B2
Stommeln, F.R.Ger., 3,672 119 B2
Stompneusbaai, S. Af. 164 a8
Ston, Yug. 125 C3
Stone, Bucks., Eng., U.K., 2,106 114 G7
Stone, Staffs., Eng., U.K., 8,791 113 E5
Stone, co., Ark., 6,294 73 C2
Stone, Idaho 78 b7
Stone, Ky. 71 J4
Stone, co., Miss., 7,013 73 F7
Stone, co., Mo., 8,176 72 D8
Stone Bank, Wis. 66 c11
Stone Bluff, Okla. 76 H2
Stoneboro, Pa., 1,267 60 B3
Stoneboro, S.C. 63 D3
Stone City, Colo. 79 C2
Stonecliffe, Ont., Can. 46 F2
Stonecoal, W. Va. 62 B5
Stone Corral L., Oreg. 80 D4
Stonefort, Ill., 349 68 D6
Stonega, Va. 62 B6
Stoneham, Colo. 79 D1
Stoneham, Mass., 17,821(T) 57 M3
Stone Harbor, N.J., 834 61 B5
Stonehaven, U.K., 4,500 112 E3
Stonehenge, Austl. 173 F3
Stonehenge, ruins, U.K. 114 E8
Stone Hill, Mo. 72 F7
Stonehouse, Eng., U.K., 5,311 114 D7
Stonehouse, Scot., U.K. 112 b8
Stone Lake, Wis. 66 B3
Stoneleigh, U.K., 3,724 114 F6
Stoneleigh, Md. 62 c7
Stone Mountain, Ga., 1,976 64 E2
Stone Mtn., Ga. 64 h9
Stone Mtn., Vt. 54 D2
Stone Park, Ill., 3,038 69 c9
Stoner, Colo. 79 A3
Stonersville, Pa. 60 e10
Stones, E. Fk., r., Tenn. 71 E6
Stones, W. Fk., r., Tenn. 71 E6
Stoneville (part of Auburn), Mass. 57 J4
Stoneville, N.C., 951 63 E1
Stoneville, S. Dak. 74 A3
Stonewall, Man., Can., 1,395 43 F5
Stonewall, Ga. 64 f10
Stonewall, Miss., 1,126 73 G5
Stonewall, N.C., 214 63 H2
Stonewall, Okla., 584 76 G3
Stonewall, co., Tex., 3,017 77 N3
Stonewall, Tex. 76 a5
Stonewood, W. Va., 2,202 62 D3
Stoney Creek, Ont., Can., 5,845 46 E5
Stoney Ground, Anguilla 97 7
Stonington, Colo. 79 D3
Stonington, Conn., 1,622; 13,969(T) 56 J7
Stonington, Ill., 1,076 68 C4
Stonington, Me. 55 D4
Stonington, Mich. 66 G3
Stonington Is., Ant. 180 N6
Stony, r., Alaska 85 F3
Stony Brook, N.Y., 3,548 58 g13
Stony Brook, N.J. 60 g10
Stony Butte, N. Dak. 74 A2
Stony Creek (part of Branford), Conn. 56 F7
Stony Creek, N.Y. 59 M5
Stony Creek, Va., 437 62 G6
Stony Cr., Pa. 60 E5
Stony Cr., Pa. 60 J5
Stony Crossing, Austl. 173 d10
Stonyford, Calif. 82 B3
Stony I., Mich. 67 K5
Stony I., N.Y. 59 H4
Stony L., Man., Can. 43 F2
Stony L., Ont., Can. 46 F4
Stony Mountain, Man., Can., 1,071 43 g9
Stony Plain, Alta., Can., 1,292 42 J3
Stony Point, N.Y., 3,330 59 M9
Stony Point, N.C., 1,015 63 D2
Stony Point, Okla. 76 J2
Stony Rapids, Sask., Can. 43 C2
Stony Stratford, U.K., 3,449 114 G6
Stooping, r., Ont., Can. 44 G4
Storå, r., Den. 121 A4
Stora Le, l., Swed. 121 D1
Stora Lulevatten, l., Swed. 120 D2
Stora Sjöfallet, falls, Swed. 120 D2
Stora Sjöfallets Nat. Pk., Swed. 120 D2
Storavan, l., Swed. 120 D2
Stora Vika, Swed. 120 e9
Stord, i., Nor. 120 A4
Store Bælt, Den. 121 C5
Store-Heddinge, Den., 2,082 121 E5
Store Magleby, Den., 3,789 121 b7
Stören, Nor. 120 B3
Storey, co., Nev., 568 83 A3
Storfjorden, Nor. 134 A2
Stör Kan., Ger.D.R. 118 C2
Storlien, Swed. 120 C3
Storm Bay, Austl. 173 f14
Storm Lake, Iowa, 7,728 72 B2
Storm L., Iowa 72 B2
Stornoway, U.K., 5,221 112 C2
Storr, The, mtn., U.K. 112 C3
Storrs, Conn., 6,054 56 G5
Storsjön, l., Swed. 120 C3
Stort, r., U.K. 114 J7
Storuman, Swed. 120 D2
Storuman, l., Swed. 120 D2
Storvätteshågna, pk., Swed. 120 C3
Storvorde, Den. 121 C4
Story, Ind. 70 C3
Story, co., Iowa, 49,327 72 D2
Story, Okla. 76 F3
Story City, Iowa, 1,773 72 D2
Stössen, Ger.D.R. 126 a5
Stössing, Aust. 124 b10
Stotesbury, Mo., 64 72 C7
Stotfold, U.K., 5,334 114 H6
Stotts City, Mo., 221 72 D7
Stottville, N.Y., 1,040 59 N7
Stotzing, Aust. 124 d11
Stouffville, Ont., Can., 3,159 46 E4
Stoughton, Sask., Can. 43 D5
Stoughton, U.K. 113 m13
Stoughton, Mass., 16,328(T) 57 M4
Stoughton, Wis., 5,555 66 D6
Stour, r., U.K. 113 E6
Stour, r., U.K. 113 G6
Stourbridge, U.K., 43,917 113 E5
Stourport-on-Severn, U.K., 11,751 114 D6
Stout, Iowa, 145 72 E2
Stout, Ohio 70 F4
Stout L., Ont., Can. 44 C4
Stoutland, Mo., 172 72 E7
Stoutsville, Mo. 109 72 F5
Stoutsville, Ohio 70 G3
Stovall, N.C., 570 63 F1
Stover, Mo., 757 72 E6
Støvring, Den. 121 B4
Stow, Eng., U.K. 114 B6
Stow, Scot., U.K. 112 e8
Stow, Mass., 2,573(T) 57 K3
Stow, Ohio, 12,194 70 H1
Stowe, U.K., 1,068 114 D5
Stowe, Pa., 2,765 61 L5
Stowe, Vt., 534 54 B3
Stowell, Tex. 77 m9
Stowmarket, U.K., 7,795 113 G5
Stow on the Wold, U.K., 1,780 114 E7
Stoyanovo, Bulg., 2,682 128 E3
Stoyba, U.S.S.R. 135 N4
Stoystown, Pa., 360 60 D5
Strabane, U.K., 7,786 113 C4
Strachur, U.K. 112 D3
Stradella, It., 10,331 122 c5
Straelen, F.R.Ger., 8,402 119 A2
Strafford, co., N.H., 59,799 54 E5
Strafford, N.H. 54 E5
Strafford, Vt. 54 C4
Strafford P.O., N.H. 54 E5
Stragari, Yug. 125 E2
Strahan, Austl. 173 e14
Straitsville (part of Naugatuck), Conn. 56 D7
Strakonice, Czech., 14,739 126 A2
Straldzha, Bulg., 5,963 128 F3
Stralsund, Ger.D.R., 65,758 118 D1
Strand, Nor. 120 A4
Strand, S. Af., 13,313 164 C7
Stranda, Nor. 120 A3
Strandburg, S. Dak., 105 74 D3
Strandby, Den., 1,178 121 C3
Strandquist, Minn., 160 74 D1
Strang, Okla., 176 76 H1
Strangford L., U.K. 113 D4
Strängnäs, Swed. 120 e8
Strångsjö, Swed. 120 d9
Straning, Aust. 124 b9
Stranraer, U.K., 9,249 113 D4
Stranzendorf, Aust. 124 c10
Strasbourg, Sask., Can. 43 D4
Strasbourg, Fr., 233,549 117 G2
Strasburg, Ger.D.R. 118 D2
Strasburg, Ill., 467 68 D4
Strasburg, Mo., 213 72 C6
Strasburg, N. Dak., 612 74 B2
Strasburg, Ohio, 1,687 70 H2
Strasburg, Pa., 1,416 61 K6
Strasburg, Va., 2,428 62 F4
Strassburg, Aust., 3,036 124 L7
Strasshof, Aust., 3,627 124 d10
Stratford, Ont., Can., 20,067 44 G7
Stratford, Qué., Can. 47 N3
Stratford, N.Z., 5,273 175 g5
Stratford, Calif. 82 D4
Stratford, Conn., 45,012(T) 56 D8
Stratford, Iowa, 703 72 D2
Stratford, N.H. 54 D2
Stratford, N.J., 4,308 60 f12
Stratford, N.Y. 59 L5
Stratford, Okla., 1,058 76 F3
Stratford, S. Dak., 109 74 C3
Stratford, Tex., 1,380 76 M1
Stratford, Wis., 1,106 66 C4
Stratford on Avon, U.K., 16,847 113 F5
Strathalbyn, Austl., 1,334 172 c8
Stratham, N.H. 54 F5
Strathaven, U.K. 112 b8
Strathclair, Man., Can. 43 E5
Strathcona, Minn., 64 74 D1
Strathkinness, U.K. 112 e7
Strathmiglo, U.K. 112 d7
Strathmore, Alta., Can. 42 K3
Strathmore, Calif., 1,095 82 D4
Strathnaver, Br. Col., Can. 42 G3
Strathroy, Ont., Can., 5,043 46 C6
Strathy Pt., U.K. 112 D2
Strathyre, U.K. 112 D3
Stratoniki, Gr., 1,346 129 D4
Strattanville, Pa., 547 60 D3
Stratton, Ont., Can. 44 C5
Stratton, U.K., 1,167 113 D6
Stratton, Colo., 680 79 D2
Stratton, Ill. 68 D5
Stratton, Me. 55 B3
Stratton, Miss. 73 F5
Stratton, Nebr., 492 75 D3
Stratton, Ohio, 311 70 J2
Stratton Mtn., Vt. 54 B5
Stratton on the Fosse, U.K., 1,025 114 C8
Stratton St. Margaret, U.K., 11,191 114 E7
Stratton's Corner, Ont., Can. 46 b13
Straubing, F.R.Ger., 36,282 118 D4
Straubville, N. Dak. 74 C2
Straumen, Nor. 120 C2
Strausberg, Ger.D.R., 13,767 118 D2
Strausstown, Pa., 380 61 K5
Strawberry, Ark., 200 73 D2
Strawberry, r., Ark. 73 D1
Strawberry, r., Utah 78 C1
Strawberry Cr., Alta., Can. 43 a7
Strawberry Mtn., Oreg. 80 D3
Strawberry Point, Iowa, 1,303 72 F2
Strawberry Res., Utah 78 C1
Strawn, Ill., 152 68 D3
Strawn, Kans. 75 K5
Strawn, Tex., 817 77 O3
Strayhorn, Miss. 73 E3
Strážnice, Czech. 126 C2
Streaky Bay, Austl. 172 a7
Streaky Bay, Austl. 172 D5
Streamwood, Ill., 10,252 69 b8
Streatham, Br. Col., Can. 42 E3
Streatley, U.K. 114 F7
Streator, Ill., 16,868 68 D2
Street, U.K., 6,666 113 E6
Streeter, N. Dak., 491 74 C2
Streeter, Tex. 77 O4
Streetman, Tex., 300 77 P4
Streetsboro, Ohio 70 f9
Streetsville, Ont., Can., 4,740 46 E5
Strehaia, Rum. 128 D2
Strehla, Ger.D.R. 118 D3
Streich Mound, Austl. 172 C4
Střela, r., Czech. 126 c6
Strelcha, Bulg., 5,309 128 E3
Strelka, U.S.S.R. 135 J4
Strelka-Chunya, U.S.S.R. 135 K3
Strem, Aust. 124 N6
Strengberg, Aust., 1,714 124 L5
Strengen, Nor. 121 B1
Strensall, U.K., 1,138 114 F2
Stresa, It., 4,839 123 B2
Stretford, U.K., 60,331 114 D4
Stretton, Ches., Eng., U.K., 1,083 114 C4
Stretton, Staffs., Eng., U.K., 1,934 114 E5
Streymoy, i., Faeroe Is. 120 c7
Strib, Den. 121 B5
Stříbrná Skalice, Czech. 127 d7
Stříbro, Czech. 126 A2
Strichen, U.K. 112 E3
Strickland, Me. 55 B4
Strickland, r., Terr. Papua 174 d2
Strijen, Neth. 115 b7
Strimón, r., Gr. 129 D4
Strimonikós Kólpos, Gr. 129 E4
Stringer, Miss. 73 F6
Stringtown, Okla., 414 76 H3
Strizhëva, O., U.S.S.R. 135 N2
Strobl, Aust., 2,203 124 K6
Stroeder, Arg., 3,310 105 C6
Stroeşti, Rum. 128 D2
Strofádhes, is., Gr. 129 C6
Stroh, Ind. 70 D1
Ströhen, F.R.Ger., 2,274 118 B2
Strokestown, Ire. 113 B5
Stroma, i., U.K. 112 E2
Strombeek-Bever, Belg., 7,738 115 d9
Stromberg, F.R.Ger., 1,808 119 D5
Stromboli, vol., It. 123 ·
Stromboli, Isola, It. 123 E5
Strome, Alta., Can. 43 d8
Stromeferry, U.K. 112 D3
Stromness, U.K., 1,477 112 E2
Stromsburg, Nebr., 1,244 75 H2
Strömsholm, Swed. 120 d8
Strömstad, Swed. 120 B4
Strömsund, Swed. 120 C3
Ströms Vattudal, l., Swed. 120 C2
Stronach, Mich. 67 G4
Stronachlachar, U.K. 112 a7
Strong, Ark., 741 73 C4
Strong, Me. 55 B4
Strong, Miss. 73 G4
Strong, r., Miss. 73 F5
Strong City, Kans., 659 75 J5
Strong City, Okla., 51 76 D2
Strongfield, Sask., Can. 43 C4
Stronghurst, Ill., 815 68 A3
Strongs, Mich. 67 J2
Strongs Corners, Mich. 67 J2
Strongsville, Ohio, 8,504 70 H1
Stronie Śląska, Pol. 127 f6
Stronsay, i., U.K. 112 E1
Stronsay Firth, U.K. 112 E2
Strontian, U.K. 112 D3
Strood, (part of Rochester), U.K., 5,913 114 J8
Stropkov, Czech. 126 E2
Stroppiana, It., 1,863 122 b5
Stroud, Austl. 173 H5
Stroud, Ont., Can. 46 E4
Stroud, U.K., 17,468 113 E6
Stroud, Okla., 2,456 76 G2
Stroudsburg, Pa., 6,070 61 M4
Struble, Iowa, 74 72 A2
Struer, Den., 8,335 121 A4
Struga, Yug., 4,996 125 E4
Strugi Krasnyye, U.S.S.R. 136 C1
Strum, Wis., 663 66 B4
Struma, r., Bulg. 128 D3
Strumble Head, U.K. 113 D5
Strumica, Yug., 16,000* 125 F4
Strumica, r., Yug. 125 F4
Strumień, Pol., 2,055 127 h7
Strunino, U.S.S.R., 19,200 136 c5
Struthers, Ohio, 15,631 70 J1
Struvenhütten, F.R.Ger. 119 b8
Stryama, r., Bulg. 128 E3
Strydenburg, S. Af. 164 c7
Stryker, Ohio, 1,205 70 E1
Strykersville, N.Y. 58 C6
Stryków, Pol., 3,238 127 C3
Stryy, U.S.S.R., 36,100 136 A3
Strzegom, Pol., 10,546 127 B3
Strzegomka, r., Pol. 127 f5
Strzelce Krajeńskie, Pol., 4,063 127 A2
Strzelce Opolskie, Pol., 10,875 127 C3
Strzelin, Pol., 8,280 127 B3
Strzelno, Pol., 5,328 127 C2
Strzybnica, Pol. 127 h6
Strzyżów, Pol., 3,300 127 D4
Strzyżów, Pol. 127 F3
Stuart, Fla., 4,791 65 J5
Stuart, Iowa, 1,486 72 C3
Stuart, Nebr., 794 75 F1
Stuart, Okla., 271 76 G3
Stuart, Va., 974 62 D6
Stuart, r., Br. Col., Can. 42 F2
Stuart, Mt., Wash. 80 C2
Stuartburn, Man., Can. 43 h10
Stuart I., Alaska 85 D3
Stuart L., Br. Col., Can. 42 F2
Stuart Ra., Austl. 172 E4
Stuarts Draft, Va. 62 E4
Stubaier Alpen, Aust. 124 H6
Stubbekøbing, Den., 2,097 121 E6
Stuben, Aust. 124 G6
Stubenberg, Aust. 124 M6
Studenci, Yug., 2,126 125 C3
Studina, Rum. 128 E3
Studland, U.K. 113 i13
Studland Bay, U.K. 113 i13
Studley, U.K., 3,928 114 E6
Studley, Kans. 75 E4
Studsvik, Swed. 120 e9
Study Butte, Tex. 77 M5
Stugun, Swed. 120 C3
Stuie, Br. Col., Can. 42 F3
Stull, r., Man., Can. 43 H3
Stull L., Man.-Ont., Can. 43 H3
Stumm, Aust. 124 H6
Stump Creek, Pa. 60 E3
Stump L., N. Dak. 74 C2
Stumpy Point, N.C. 63 J2
Stung Treng, Camb., 3,369 146 D4
Stupart, r., Man., Can. 43 G3
Stupino, U.S.S.R., 49,000 136 E2
Sturbridge, Mass., 3,604(T) 56 H4
Sturgeon, Mo., 619 72 E5
Sturgeon, Pa. 60 a8
Sturgeon, r., Alta., Can. 43 a7
Sturgeon, r., Ont., Can. 46 D1
Sturgeon, r., Mich. 66 E2
Sturgeon, r., Mich. 66 F3
Sturgeon, r., Mich. 67 G2
Sturgeon, r., Mich. 67 J3
Sturgeon, r., Minn. 74 F2
Sturgeon Bay, Wis., 7,353 66 F4
Sturgeon Bay, Mich. 67 H3
Sturgeon Bay, Wis. 66 F4
Sturgeon Falls, Ont., Can., 6,176 44 H6
Sturgeon Lake, Minn., 151 74 F2
Sturgeon L., Ont., Can. 44 D5
Sturgeon L., Ont., Can. 46 F4
Sturgeon L., Ont., Can. 74 G1
Sturgeon Landing, Sask., Can. 43 D3
Sturgeon Pt., Mich. 67 K4
Sturgeon R. Falls, Mich. 66 E2
Sturgis, Sask., Can. 43 D4
Sturgis, Ky., 2,209 71 D4
Sturgis, Mich., 8,915 67 H7
Sturgis, Miss., 358 73 F4
Sturgis, Okla. 76 A1
Sturgis, S. Dak., 4,639 74 A3
Sturt Cr., Austl. 172 D2
Sturtevant, Wis., 1,488 66 F6
Sturton, U.K. 114 G4
Stutsman, co., N. Dak., 25,137 74 C2
Stutsmanville, Mich. 67 H3
Stutterheim, S. Af., 9,015 164 D7
Stuttgart, F.R.Ger., 601,115 118 B4
Stuttgart, Ark., 10,252 73 D3
Stuttgart, Kans. 75 F4
Stutts Cr., N. Br., Mich. 67 G2
Stuyvesant, N.Y. 59 N7
Stuyvesant Falls, N.Y. 59 N7
Stykkishólmur, Ice. 120 a6
Styr', r., U.S.S.R. 136 B3
Styrvoll, Nor. 121 B1
Styx, r., Ala. 64 B5
Suai, Malay. 148 E2
Suakin = Sawākin
Suamico, Wis. 66 E4
Suan, N. Kor. 151 E3
Suances, Sp., 4,846 122 m11
Suan Pung, Thai. 147 c5
Su-ao, Taiwan, 35,237 152 F2
Suaqui, Mex., 1,453 92 C2
Suaza, Col. 100 C7
Suba, Col. 101 e15
Subachoque, Col. 101 e15
Subang, Indon. 148 D4
Subansiri, r., India 145 K3
Subarnarekha, r., India 144 f14
Subaytilah, Tun., 3,409 161 F2
Subiaco, It., 9,105 123 D4
Subi-besar, P., Indon. 148 D2
Subic Bay, Phil. 153 b8
Sublette, Ill., 306 68 C2
Sublette, Kans., 1,077 75 E6
Sublette, co., Wyo., 3,778 81 D4
Sublimity, Oreg., 490 80 B3
Subotica, Yug., 78,000* 125 D1
Suburban Gardens, Ind. 69 e10
Succasunna, N.J., 2,550* 61 B2
Success, Sask., Can. 43 B5
Success, Ark., 226 73 E1
Success, Mo. 72 F7
Success, Mt., N.H. 54 E3
Success L., N.J. 58 b16
Suceava, Rum., 20,949 128 F1
Suceava, r., Rum. 128 F1
Sucha, Pol., 6,553 127 C4
Suchań, Pol., 1,108 127 A2
Suchan, U.S.S.R., 47,600 135 N5
Suchedniów, Pol., 7,826 127 D3
Suches, Ga. 64 F1
Suchiapa, Mex., 3,891 93 G5
Su-ch'ien, China 150 F3
Suchitoto, El Salv., 4,380 94 d10
Su-chou, China, 633,000* 150 G4
Süchow = Hsü-chou

300 · Swan—Tamashima

Swan, r., Austl. 172 B4
Swan, r., Man.-Sask., Can. 43 E4
Swan, r., Mont. 81 C2
Swanage, U.K., 8,120 113 F6
Swan Creek, Ill. 68 B3
Swan Cr., S. Dak. 74 B3
Swan Hill, Austl., 5,197 173 F5
Swan Hills, Alta., Can. 42 J2
Swanington, Ind. 70 B2
Swan Is., Caribbean Sea 95 B3
Swan Lake, Ark. 73 D3
Swanlake, Idaho 81 C4
Swan Lake, N.Y. 59 L8
Swan L., Me. 55 C4
Swan L., Minn. 74 E3
Swan L., Wis. 66 D5
Swan L., Man., Can. 43 f10
Swan L., Man., Can. 43 E4
Swanley, U.K., 12,707 114 J8
Swanlinbar, Ire. 113 C4
Swanmore, U.K., 1,678 113 k13
Swannanoa, N.C., 2,189 63 B2
Swan Quarter, N. Car. 63 H2
Swan Reach, Austl. 172 c8
Swan River, Man., Can., 2,955 43 E4
Swan River, Minn. 74 F2
Swansboro, N.C., 1,104 63 G3
Swansea, N.S.W., Austl., 3,672 173 h9
Swansea, Tasm., Austl. 173 f14
Swansea, Ont., Can., 9,544 46 d13
Swansea, U.K., 167,332 113 D6
Swansea, Ill., 3,018 68 B5
Swansea, Mass., 9,916(T) 57 M6
Swansea, S.C., 776 63 C4
Swans Island, Me. 55 D4
Swanson Bay, Br. Col., Can. 42 E3
Swanson L., Nebr. 75 D3
Swanton, Ohio, 2,306 70 F1
Swanton, Vt., 2,390 54 A2
Swan Valley, Idaho, 217 81 D4
Swanville, Me. 55 C4
Swanville, Minn., 342 74 E3
Swanzey, N.H. 54 C6
Swarthmore, Pa., 5,753 60 f12
Swartswood L., N.J. 61 B1
Swartz Creek, Mich., 3,006 67 K6
Swarzędz, Pol., 8,894 127 B2
Swasey Pk., Utah 78 B2
Swastika, Ont., Can. 44 H5
Swatara, Minn. 74 F2
Swatara Cr., Pa. 60 J4
Swatow = Shan-t'ou
Sway, U.K., 2,289 113 i13
Swayzee, Ind., 863 70 D2
Swaziland (Br. prot.), 389,492 164 E6
Swea City, Iowa, 805 72 C1
Sweatman, Miss. 73 F4
Sweden, ctry., 7,773,000* 120
Sweden, Me. 55 D2
Swedesboro, N.J., 2,449 61 A4
Swedru, Ghana, 18,700 162 c9
Sweeden, Ky. 71 E4
Sweeney, Tex., 3,087 77 Q5
Sweeney L., Minn. 74 b6
Sweet Briar, Va. 62 E5
Sweet Grass, co., Mont., 3,290 81 E3
Sweetgrass, Mont. 81 C1
Sweet Home, Ark. 73 C3
Sweet Home, Oreg., 3,353 80 B3
Sweethope Loughs, U.K. 112 f9
Sweets, Antigua, 1,132 97 9
Sweetsburg, Qué., Can. 47 M3
Sweetsers, Ind., 896 70 D2
Sweet Springs, Mo., 1,452 72 D6
Sweet Springs, W. Va. 62 D5
Sweet Valley, Pa. 61 K3
Sweet Water, Ala. 64 B3
Sweetwater, Nev. 83 A3
Sweetwater, Okla. 76 D2
Sweetwater, Tenn., 4,145 71 G6
Sweetwater, Tex., 13,914 77 N3
Sweetwater, co., Wyo., 17,920 81 E5
Sweetwater, r., Calif. 82 c10
Sweetwater, r., Wyo. 81 E4
Sweetwater Res., Calif. 82 c10
Swellendam, S. Af., 4,896 164 C7
Swenson, Tex. 77 N3
Swepsonville, N.C. 63 E1
Świdnica, Pol., 39,000* 127 B3
Świdnik, Pol., 11,595 127 E3
Świdwin, Pol., 9,715 127 A2
Świebodzice, Pol., 14,740 127 B3
Świebodzin, Pol., 12,238 127 A2
Świecie, Pol., 10,286 127 C2
Świeradów Zdrój, Pol., 2,787 127 e6
Świerczów, Pol. 127 g6
Świerzawa, Pol., 1,784 127 B3
Święta Anna, Pol. 127 i6
Świętokrzyskie, Góry, Pol. 126 ·
Swift, co., Minn., 14,936 74 E3
Swift, r., Alaska 85 F3
Swift, r., Me. 55 B4
Swift, r., N.H. 54 E4
Swift Cr. Res., Wash. 80 B2
Swift Current, Newf., Can. 45 a10
Swift Current, Sask., Can., 11,883 43 B5
Swiftcurrent Cr., Sask., Can. 43 B5
Swift Diamond, r., N.H. 54 E2
Swifton, Ark., 601 73 D2
Swift River, Yukon, Can. 40 C6
Swift River (part of Cummington), Mass. 56 E3
Swift Run, Va. 62 F4
Swiftwater, Pa. 61 M3
Swilly, L., Ire. 113 C4
Swilly, r., Ire. 113 C4
Swindon, U.K., 91,739 113 F6
Swinefleet, U.K., 1,220 114 G3
Swineshead, U.K., 1,824 114 H5
Swinford, Ire. 113 B5
Swinging Bridge Res., N.Y. 61 N2
Swingle, Calif. 82 a7
Swink, Colo., 348 79 D2
Swink, Okla. 76 H4
Swinoujście, Pol., 10,646 127 A2
Swinstead, U.K. 114 H5
Swisher, Iowa, 271 72 F3
Swisher, co., Tex., 10,607 77 N2
Swiss, N.C. 63 B2
Swiss, W. Va. 62 C4
Swisshome, Oreg. 80 B3
Swissvale, Pa., 15,089 60 c8
Swist Bach, r., F.R.Ger. 119 C3
Switz City, Ind., 339 70 B3
Switzer, S.C. 63 C3
Switzer, W. Va., 1,131 62 B5
Switzerland, ctry., 5,945,000* 124
Switzerland, co., Ind., 7,092 70 D4
Swords, Ire., 1,629 113 C5
Swormville, N.Y. 58 k18
Swoyersville, Pa., 6,751 61 L3
Swynnerton, U.K., 3,716 114 D5
Syābru Bensi, Nepal 144 e11
Syalakh, U.S.S.R. 135 M3
Syāng, Nepal 144 d11
Syas', r., U.S.S.R. 136 D1
Syas'stroy, U.S.S.R., 7,200 136 D1
Syava, U.S.S.R. 136 G1
Sybil Pt., Ire. 113 A5
Sycamore, Ga., 501 64 F4
Sycamore, Ill., 6,961 68 D2
Sycamore, Kans. 75 K6
Sycamore, Mo. 72 E8
Sycamore, Ohio, 998 70 F2
Sycamore, Okla. 76 J1
Sycamore, S.C., 401 63 C4
Sycamore, Va. 62 E5
Sycan, r., Oreg. 80 C4
Sychëvka, U.S.S.R., 6,500 136 D2
Syców, Pol., 3,643 127 g5
Syda, r., U.S.S.R. 137 s11
Sydenham, Ont., Can. 47 H4
Sydenham, r., Ont., Can. 46 C6
Sydney, Austl., 1,863,161 173 G5
Sydney, N.S., Can., 33,201 45 O6
Sydney, Fla. 65 d12
Sydney, atoll, Phoenix Is. 170 G5
Sydney Bay, Norfolk I. 175 11
Sydney L., Ont., Can. 44 C5
Sydney Mines, N.S., Can., 8,948 47 V10
Sydney Pt., Ocean I. 175 16
Sydnorsville, Va. 62 E6
Syke, F.R.Ger., 6,582 118 B2
Sykeston, N. Dak., 236 74 C2
Sykesville, Md., 1,196 62 G3
Sykesville, Pa., 1,479 60 E3
Syktyvkar, U.S.S.R., 84,000 134 E3
Sylacauga, Ala., 12,857 64 C2
Sylamore, Ark. 73 C2
Sylarna, mt., Nor.-Swed. 120 C3
Sylhet, Pak., 37,740 145 J4
Sylt, i., F.R.Ger. 118 B1
Sylva, U.S.S.R. 137 h7
Sylva, N.C., 1,564 63 A2
Sylva, r., U.S.S.R. 137 h7
Sylvan, Wis. 66 C5
Sylvan Beach, N.Y. 59 J5
Sylvan Grove, Kans., 400 75 G5
Sylvania, Ga., 3,469 64 H3
Sylvania, Ind. 70 B3
Sylvania, Ohio, 5,187 70 F1
Sylvania, Pa., 243 60 J2
Sylvan Lake, Alta., Can., 1,337 42 J3
Sylvan Lake, Mich., 2,004 67 e14
Sylvarena, Miss., 69 73 F5
Sylvatus, Va. 62 D6
Sylvester, Ga., 3,610 64 F4
Sylvester, Tex. 77 N3
Sylvester, Mt., Newf., Can. 45 Q5
Sylvia, Kans., 402 75 G6
Sym, U.S.S.R. 134 H3
Symco, Wis. 66 E4
Symerton, Ill., 123 68 D2
Symington, Ayr, Scot., U.K. 112 a8
Symington, Lnrk., Scot., U.K. 112 c8
Symsonia, Ky. 71 C5
Syntasty, r., U.S.S.R. 137 k9
Syosset, N.Y. 58 f13
Syracuse, It. = Siracusa
Syracuse, Ind., 1,595 70 D1
Syracuse, Kans., 1,888 75 D5
Syracuse, Mo., 180 72 E6
Syracuse, Nebr., 1,261 75 J3
Syracuse, N.Y., 216,038 59 H5
Syracuse, Ohio, 731 70 H3
Syracuse, Utah, 1,061 78 b8
Syr-Dar'inskiy, U.S.S.R. 137 e4
Syr-Dar'ya, r., U.S.S.R. 134 F5
Syre, r., Lux. 119 A5
Syresham, U.K. 114 F6
Syria, ctry., 5,300,000* 142
Syria, Va. 62 F4
Syriam, Burma, 15,296 147 b2
Syrian Des. = Shām, Bādiyat ash
Syssert', U.S.S.R.; 19,200 137 k8
Sysmä, Fin. 120 F3
Syston, U.K., 6,455 114 F5
Syzran', U.S.S.R., 159,000 154 D4
Szabadszállás, Hung., 8,818 126 D3
Szakcs, Hung., 2,504 126 C3
Szamocin, Pol., 2,794 127 B2
Szamos, r., Hung. 126 F3
Szamotuły, Pol., 11,578 127 B2
Szany, Hung., 3,308 126 C3
Szarvas, Hung., 18,946 126 E3
Szczawnica, Pol., 4,822 127 D4
Szczawno-Zdrój, Pol., 8,148 127 f6
Szczebrzeszyn, Pol., 5,137 127 E3
Szczecin, Pol., 269,000* 127 A2
Szczecinek, Pol., 23,000* 127 B2
Szczekociny, Pol., 3,696 127 C3
Szczerców, Pol. 127 i5
Szczuczyn, Pol., 3,142 127 E2
Szczyrk, Pol., 4,132 127 i7
Szczyrzyc, Pol. 127 k7
Szczytna, Pol. 127 f6
Szczytno, Pol., 12,191 127 D2
Szechwan = Ssu-ch'uan
Szechwan Basin = Ssu-ch'uan P'en-ti
Szeged, Hung., 99,061 126 D3
Szeghalom, Hung., 10,327 126 E3
Székesfehérvár, Hung., 55,934 126 D3
Szekszárd, Hung., 19,347 126 D3
Szendrő, Hung., 3,778 126 E2
Szentendre, Hung., 10,307 126 D3
Szentes, Hung., 31,175 126 E3
Szentgotthárd, Hung., 5,403 126 C3
Szerencs, Hung., 7,812 126 E2
Szigetvár, Hung., 7,395 126 C3
Szikszó, Hung., 6,036 126 E2
Szklarska Poręba, Pol. 127 e6
Szkwa, r., Pol. 127 D2
Szlachta, Pol. 127 C2
Szolnok, Hung., 45,553 126 D3
Szombathely, Hung., 54,465 126 C3
Szprotawa, Pol., 9,378 127 A3
Szreniawa, r., Pol. 127 D3
Sztum, Pol., 5,037 127 C2
Szubin, Pol., 4,873 127 B2
Szydłów, Pol. 127 D3
Szydłów, Pol. 127 g6
Szydłowiec, Pol., 5,137 127 D3
Szypliszki, Pol. 127 E1

T

Ta, Jap. 154 g15
Taakoka, i., Rarotonga 177 34
Taal, L., Phil. 153 c9
Tab, Ind. 70 B2
Tabaco, Phil., 11,599 153 B2
Tabacundo, Ec. 104 c9
Tabanan, Indon. 148 f8
Taban Bogdo Uula, Mong. 150 B1
Tabaquite, Trin. and Tob. 96 g5
Tabara, Jap. 154 e15
Tábara, Sp., 1,629 122 B2
Tabar Is., Terr. New Guin. 174 g1
Ṭabarqah, Tun. 161 F1
Ṭabas, Iran, 7,413 143 F2
Ṭabas, Iran 143 G2
Tabasará, Snía. de, Pan. 94 G6
Tabasco, Hond. 94 E4
Tabasco, st., Mex., 496,340 93 G4
Tabasco, Mex., 2,555 92 B1
Tabayin, Burma 147 f6
Tabayoo, Mt., Phil. 153 c6
Tabbita, Austl. 173 e10
Tabelbala, Alg., 1,038 160 D3
Tabeng, Camb. 146 D4
Taber, Alta., Can., 3,865 42 K4
Taberg, N.Y. 59 J5
Tabernas, Sp., 4,366 122 D4
Tabernes de Valldigna, Sp., 12,890 122 E3
Tabiang, Ocean I. 175 16
Tabiang, Tarawa 175 15
Tabik, i., Kwajalein 176 25
Tabika, Jap. 154 h14
Tabio, Col. 101 e15
Tabiona, Utah, 167 78 C1
Tabira, Braz., 3,446 103 J3
Tabiteuea, Tarawa 175 15
Tabiteuea, i., Gilb. Is. 175 10
Tab Kwang, Thai. 147 d4
Tablan, Thai. 147 d4
Tablas I., Phil. 153 B2
Tablas Str., Phil. 153 B2
Table C., N.Z. 175 h5
Table Grove, Ill., 500 68 B3
Table Mtn., S. Dak. 74 A3
Tabler, Okla. 76 F2
Table Rock, Nebr., 422 75 J3
Table Rock Res., Mo. 72 D8
Tabligbo, Togo, 2,821* 162 d8
Taboada, Sp., 7,123 122 B1
Taboga, Pan. 94 H6
Tabon, Phil., 1,639 153 A3
Tábor, Czech., 20,142 126 B2
Tabor, Iowa, 909 72 B4
Tabor, Minn. 74 D1
Tabor, S. Dak., 378 74 D4
Tabor, Wis. 66 d12
Tabor, Mt., Vt. 54 B5
Tabora, Tanz., 15,361 164 E2
Tabor City, N.C., 2,338 63 F3
Taborda, Ven. 101 a11
Tabossi, Arg., 4,500* 105 b10
Tabou, Iv. Coast, 3,028 162 C5
Tabrīz, Iran, 289,996 143 D1
Tabu, Motu, i., Christmas Atoll 177 40
Tabuelan, Phil., 3,583 153 e11
Tabujung, Indon. 148 A2
Tabuk, Phil., 3,378 153 B1
Tabūk, Saudi Ar., 8,000* 143 B3
Tabunco, Chile 104 f15
Tabunifi, Yap 176 20
Ṭaburbah, Tun., 6,103 160 f5
Tabursuq, Tun., 7,177 161 F1
Tabwemasana, Mt., New Hebr. 174 k5
Täby, Swed. 120 D4
Tacajó, Cuba, 1,298 96 e2
Tacámbaro, Mex., 7,286 93 c10
Tacámbaro, r., Mex. 93 c11
Tacaná, Guat., 1,195 94 a8
Tacaná, Vol., Guat.-Mex. 93 H5
Tacaratu, Braz., 2,723 103 J3
Tacarigua, Ven., 2,569 100 G2
Tácata, Ven. 101 c11
Tacátzcuaro, Mex., 1,720 93 b10
Ta-ch'ai-tan, China 150 C3
Ta-ch'an Wan = Tai Shan Bay
Ta-ch'eng, China 150 B2
Ta-ch'eng, China 151 C3
Tachi, Jap. 154 g14
Ta-ch'i, Taiwan, 39,683 152 F2
Ta-chia, Taiwan, 41,816 152 F2
Ta-chia, r., Taiwan 152 F2
Ta-chiao-t'ou Tao, China 152 a6
Tachibana, Jap., 21,031 154 f16
Ta-chih Chou, China 152 a6
Ta-ch'ih-k'an, China 152 a6
Tachikawa, Jap., 67,949 155 F4
Ta-chin, r., China 152 A1
Ta-ch'ing, r., China 151 B3
Ta-ch'ing Shan, China 151 A2
Tachino, Jap. 155 m19
Ta-chou, China 152 b5
Tachov, Czech., 5,381 126 A2
Ta-chu, China 152 B1
Ta-chu-ho, China 152 C1
Ta-ch'ung, China 152 a6
Tacks Beach, Newf., Can. 45 a10
Tacloban, Phil., 35,974 153 C3
Taclobo, Phil., 3,366 153 e12
Tacna, Peru, 26,212 104 D6
Tacna, Ariz. 78 B5
Tacoma, Wash., 147,979 80 B2
Taconic (part of Salisbury), Conn. 56 C4
Taconic Mts., Mass.-N.Y.-Vt. 54 A5
Tacora, Vol., Chile 105 A1
Tacuarembó, Urug., 22,000* 105 D4
Tacurong, Phil., 6,413 153 C4
Tacutu = Takutu
Tadanoumi, Jap., 8,800 154 e15
Tada-u, Burma, 4,241 147 f7
Tadcaster, U.K., 4,933 114 F3
Tademaït, Plat. de, Alg. 160 E3
Tadinou, Loy. Is. 174 m8
Tadjoura, Fr. Som., 1,612 163 M4
Tadley, U.K., 4,443 114 F8
Tadó, Col. 100 B5
Tadoshi, Jap., 6,900 155 K8
Tadotsu, Jap., 21,899 154 e15
Tadoule L., Man., Can. 43 F2
Tadoussac, Qué., Can., 1,062 45 L5
Tadpatri, India, 23,129 145 F7
Tadten, Aust., 1,565 124 O6
Tadzhik S.S.R. = Tadzhikskaya S.S.R.
Tadzhikskaya S.S.R., U.S.S.R., 2,432,000* 134 F6
T'aebaek-sanmaek, S. Kor. 151 F3
Taech'ŏn, S. Kor., 22,676 151 E3
Taedong, r., N. Kor. 151 E3
Taedong-man, N. Kor. 151 E3
Taegang-got, N. Kor. 151 E3
Taegu, S. Kor., 678,277 151 F4
T'aeha, S. Kor. 151 F3
Taehŭksan-do, S. Kor. 151 E4
Taehŭng, N. Kor. 151 E2
Taejŏn, S. Kor., 229,393 151 E3
Taep'o-ri, S. Kor. 151 F3
Tafahi, i., Tonga 170 G6
Tafalla, Sp., 7,320 122 E1
Ṭafas, Syr. 142 c7
Tafers, Switz., 1,621 124 B2
Taff, r., U.K. 114 B8
Tafilalt, oasis, Mor. 160 D2
Tafí Viejo, Arg., 18,500* 105 B3
Ta-fou, China 151 C4
Tafoya, N. Mex. 79 C3
Taft, Calif., 3,822 82 D5
Taft, Fla., 1,214 65 H4
Taft, Okla., 386 76 H2
Taft, Oreg., 557 80 A3
Taft, Tenn. 71 E6
Taft, Tex., 3,463 77 P5
Tafton, Pa. 61 M3
Taftville (part of Norwich), Conn. 56 H6
Tafuna, Tutuila 177 39
Ṭaga, Rum. 128 E1
Taga Dzong, Bhutan 144 g12
Tagama, reg., Niger 162 F3
Tagana-an, Phil., 3,853 153 C3
Taganrog, U.S.S.R., 220,000 134 C5
Taganrogskiy Zal., U.S.S.R. 136 E4
Tagant, reg., Maur. 162 C2
Tagappan, Phil., 1,902 153 c6
Tågarp, Swed. 121 b7
Tagaung, Burma 146 B2
Tagawa, Jap., 95,911 154 B5
Tagaytay, Phil., 7,203 153 B2
Tagbilaran, Phil., 7,206 153 C3
Tagegu, Terr. Papua 174 d2
Taghum, Br. Col., Can. 42 H4
Tagil, r., U.S.S.R. 137 k7
Tagkawayan, Phil., 3,555 153 B2
Tagliamento, r., It. 123 D1
Taglio di Po, It., 11,347 122 f6
Tago, Phil., 3,953 153 C3
Tagounite, Mor. 160 D2
Tagū, Jap. 155 n19
Tagua, r., Col. 100 C6
Taguac, Guam 176 24
Taguaiguai, Embalse, Ven. 101 b11
Taguasco, Cuba, 2,642 96 d2
Taguatinga, Braz., 1,496 103 G4
Taguay, Ven. 101 c12
Taguay, r., Ven. 101 c12
Taguchi, Jap., 5,243 155 E4
Tagudin, Phil., 3,020 153 b6
Tagula, i., Terr. Papua 174 g3
Tagum, Phil., 5,263 153 C4
Tagus, N. Dak., 72 74 B1
Tagus = Tajo, Sp.
Tagus = Tejo, Port.
Tahaltan, Br. Col., Can. 42 D1
Tahan, G., Malay. 148 B1
Tahanea, atoll, Tuam. Arch. 177 42
Tahara, Jap., 27,010 155 E4
Tahat, Mt., Alg. 160 E4
Tahawus, N.Y. 59 M3
Taheke, N.Z. 175 g4
Tahiti, i., Fr. Poly. 171 J6
Tahlequah, Okla., 5,840 76 H2
Tahoe, L., Calif. 82 C3
Tahoe City, Calif. 82 C3
Tahoe Valley, Calif. 82 D3
Tahoka, Tex., 3,012 77 M3
Taholah, Wash. 80 A2
Tahonsaku, Kusaie 176 31
Tahoua, Niger, 13,056 162 E3
Tahoutoumah, pt., Pitc. I. 177 45
Tahquamenon, r., Mich. 67 H2
Tahquamenon Falls, Mich. 67 H2
Ta-hsien, China 150 E4
Ta-hsin, China 152 B3
Ta-hsing-an-ling Shan-mo, China 150 G1
Ta-hsing-kou, China 151 F2
Ta-hsin-tien, China 151 D3
Ta-hsi Shui-tao, chan., China 152 a6
Ta-hsüeh Shan, China 150 D4
Ṭahṭā, U.A.R., 36,000 161 K3
Tahtsa L., Br. Col., Can. 42 E3
Tahua, Co. de, Bol. 102 b11
Ta-hua-te, China 152 a6
Tahuamanu, Peru, 1,452 104 D4
Tahuata, i., Marq. Is. 177 42
Tahulandang, P., Indon. 149 H2
Tahuna, Indon. 149 H2
Ta-hung Shan, China 152 D1
Tahuya, Wash. 81 a8
Ṭahwāy, U.A.R. 161 i7
Tai, r., China 152 E2
T'ai-an, L-n., China 151 D2
T'ai-an, Shant., China 151 C3
Taiarapu, Presqu'île de, Tahiti 177 44
Taiaro, atoll, Tuam. Arch. 177 42
Taiaroa Head, N.Z. 175 f7
Taiban, N. Mex. 79 D4
T'ai-chiang, China 152 C2
T'ai-chou, China 150 G3
T'ai-chou Lieh-tao, China 152 F1
T'ai-chou Wan, China 152 F1
T'ai-chung, Taiwan, 260,902 150 G4
T'ai-erh-chuang, China 151 C4
Taieri, r., N.Z. 175 f7
Tai Hai, China 151 B2
T'ai-Hang Shan, China 151 B3
Taihape, N.Z., 2,682 175 g5
T'ai-ho, A-h., China 151 B4
T'ai-ho, Ch-hsi, China 152 D2
Taiho, Ryukyu Is. 154 b10
Tai-hsien, China 151 B3
T'ai-hsing, China 152 F1
T'ai-hu, China 152 E1
T'ai Hu, China 150 F4
T'ai-k'ang, China 151 B4
Taiki, Jap., 11,296 155 K8
Taikkyi, Burma, 8,720 146 B3
T'ai-ku, China 151 B3
T'ai-lai, China 151 D1
Taileleo, Indon. 148 A3
Tailem Bend, Austl., 1,952 172 E5
T'ai-ling, China 151 F1
Tain, U.K., 1,699 112 E3
T'ai-nan, Taiwan, 299,851 150 F5
Tainaron, Ákra, Gr. 129 D6
T'ai-ning, China 152 E2
Tain-l'Hermitage, Fr., 5,097 117 F4
Tainter L., Wis. 66 B4
Taintignies, Belg., 2,922 116 a6
Tai O, H.K., 5,516 152 a6
T'ai-pai-chen, China 151 A4
T'ai-pai Shan, China 151 A4
Taipe, Sta. Cruz Is. 175 6
T'ai-pei, Taiwan, 963,640 150 G4
T'ai-p'ing, China 152 E1
Taiping, Malay., 48,183 148 B1
T'ai-p'ing-fang, China 151 D2
Tai Po, H.K., 16,957 152 b6
Taipu, Braz., 1,638 103 b13
T'ai-p'u-ssu-ch'i, China 150 F2
Taira, Jap., 5,690 154 A5
Taira, Jap., 71,115 155 G3
Tairadate, Jap., 6,140 155 G1
Tais, Indon. 148 B3
Taisha, Jap., 20,181 155 C4
T'ai-shan, China 150 F5
Tai-shan, China 152 F1
T'ai Shan, China 151 C3
Tai Shan Bay, China-H.K. 152 D3
T'ai-shan Lieh-tao, China 152 F2
Taishō, Jap., 5,873 155 K8
T'ai-shun, China 152 E2
Taitao, Pen. de, Chile 105 A7
Tai-tung, Taiwan, 46,303 150 G5
T'ai-tzu, r., China 151 D2
Taivalkoski, Fin. 120 F2
Taiwan, ctry., 12,791,000* 150
T'ai-wan Hai-hsia = Formosa Str.
Taiwara, Afghan. 144 B2
Taïyetos, Óros, Gr. 129 D6
Taiyiba, Isr., 7,569 142 a7
T'ai-yüan, China, 1,500,000* 150 E3
Taiza, Jap. 154 g14
Ta'izz, Yemen, 35,000* 143 C6
Tajan, Indon. 148 D2
Tajarḥī, Libya 161 G3
Ta-jih, China 150 D3
Tajima, Jap., 21,093 155 F3
Tajimechō, Jap. 154 g15
Tajimi, Jap., 53,793 155 E4
Tajin-dong, N. Kor. 151 F2
Tājirwīn, Tun., 3,531 160 f6
Tajo, r., Sp. 122 D2
Tajrīsh, Iran, 26,525 143 E1
Taju, Indon. 148 D4
Tajumulco, Vol., Guat. 94 A3
Tajuña, r., Sp. 122 D2
Tājūrā, Libya 161 G2
Tak, Thai., 13,398 146 B3
Taka, Jap. 154 g15
Taka, atoll, Marsh. Is. 176 22
Takabanare-jima, Ryukyu Is. 154 b11
Takachiho, Jap., 12,554 154 B5
Takada, Jap. 154 h14
Takada, Jap., 73,238 155 F3
Takada, Jap., 23,025 155 F3
Takafuta, Jap. 154 e15
Takahagi, Jap., 32,816 155 G3
Takahagi, Jap. 155 m19
Takahama, Jap., 12,772 155 D4
Takahama, Jap., 6,202 155 E3
Takahashi, Jap., 34,478 155 C4
Takahashi, r., Jap. 154 e15
Takahata, Jap., 35,333 155 G3
Takaikami-jima, Jap. 154 e15
Takajō, Jap., 17,437 154 B6
Takaka, N.Z. 175 g6
Takamatsu, Jap. 154 i15
Takamatsu, Jap., 228,172 155 D4
Takamatsu, Jap., 10,441 155 E3
Takamiya, Jap., 3,865 154 h14
Takamori, Jap., 10,888 154 B5
Takanabe, Jap., 19,906 154 B5
Takano, Jap. 154 g16
Takanosu, Jap., 27,240 155 G1
Takaoka, Jap., 17,106 154 B6
Takaoka, Jap., 23,184 155 C5
Takaoka, Jap., 135,190 155 E3
Takapoto, atoll, Tuam. Arch. 177 42
Takapuna, N.Z., 20,394 175 g5
Takara-jima, Jap. 154 d12
Takaroa, atoll, Tuam. Arch. 177 42
Takasago, Jap., 53,565 154 f15
Takasaki, Jap., 142,152 155 F3
Takatik, i., Ponape 176 29
Takatō, Jap., 4,872 155 F4
Takatomi, Jap. 154 h14
Takatsuki, Jap. 154 h14
Takatsuki, Jap., 79,043 155 D4
Takaya, Jap. 154 e15
Takayama, Jap., 50,588 155 E3
Takazu, Jap. 154 e16
Takazze, r., Eth. 163 L3
Takchiyan, U.S.S.R., 4,100 137 e5
Takeda, Jap., 34,911 154 B5
Takeda, Jap., 4,680 154 f14
Takefu, Jap., 62,610 155 E4
Takenami, Jap. 154 g14
Takeno, Jap., 8,328 155 D4
Takeo, Camb., 11,312 146 D5
Takeo, Jap., 39,437 154 A5
Take-shima, Jap. 154 k17
Takeshita, Jap. 155 m19
Tākestān, Iran, 10,534 143 D1
Taketazu, Jap., 3,356 154 B5
Taketoyo, Jap., 17,103 154 h15
Takhil, Thai. 146 C4
Takhini, r., Yukon, Can. 85 K3
Takhmau, Camb. 147 k11
Takhta, U.S.S.R. 135 N4
Takhta-Bazar, U.S.S.R. 134 F6
Takhtabrod, U.S.S.R. 137 m11
Taki, Jap., 11,278 154 B6
Taki, Jap. 155 n19
Taki, Sol. Is. 175 a2
Takidai, Jap. 155 n19
Takikawa, Jap., 35,093 155 J8
Takingeun, Indon. 148 A1
Takinomiya, Jap. 154 e15
Takinoue, Jap., 13,465 155 K7
Takipy, Man., Can. 43 E3
Takla L., Br. Col., Can. 42 F2
Takla Landing, Br. Col., Can. 42 F2
Takla Makan, des., China 150 B3
Taklau, Thai. 147 d4
Tako, Jap., 21,578 155 n19
Takob, Thai. 147 d4
Takob, U.S.S.R., 1,800 137 e5
Ta-ko-chen, China 151 C2
Takoma Park, Md., 16,799 62 a9
Takoradi, Ghana, 55,639 162 D5
Takotna, Alaska, 40 85 E3
Takōtsu, Jap. 154 g15
Takshak, Alaska 85 D3
Taku, Br. Col., Can. 42 c1
Ta-ku, China 151 C3
Taku, Jap., 45,346 154 B5
Taku, r., Br. Col., Can. 42 C1
Ta-ku, r., China 151 D3
Ta-kuan, China 152 A2
Takua Pa, Thai., 6,282 146 B5
Takua Thung, Thai. 146 B5
Takum, Nigeria 162 F4
Takuma, Jap., 20,391 154 e15
Takume, atoll, Tuam. Arch. 177 42
Takutea, i., Cook Is. 177 33
Takutu, r., Braz.-Guyana 101 L6
Tāl, Pak. 145 D2
Tala, Arg. 105 B3
Tala, India 144 c14
Tala, Mex., 12,541 92 E4
Tala, Urug. 105 c11
Talacogon, Phil., 2,883 153 C3
Talaga, Phil., 2,204 153 b9
Talagang, Pak., 10,818 145 D2
Talagante, Chile, 11,560 104 g13
Talaguton, Phil., 4,740 153 C4
Tālah, Tun., 4,301 161 F2
Ta-lai, China 151 E1
Ta Lai, S. Viet. 147 m11
Talak, reg., Niger 162 E3
Talakmau, G., Indon. 148 B2
Talala, Okla., 147 76 H1
Talamanca, Cord. de, C.R. 94 F6
Talang, G., Indon. 148 B3
Talanga, Hond., 3,453 94 D3
Talange, Fr., 5,246 116 b8
Talanqueras, Col. 100 C6
Talara, Peru, 26,486 104 A3
Talas, U.S.S.R., 13,600 134 G5
Talasea, Terr. New Guin. 174 f2
Talass, r., U.S.S.R. 137 f3
Talasskiy Alatau, Khr., U.S.S.R. 137 f3
Ta-la-t'e-ch'i, China 151 A2
Talaud, Kep., Indon. 149 H1
Talavera, Peru, 3,750 104 C5
Talavera, Phil., 5,217 153 b7
Talavera de la Reina, Sp., 31,900 122 C3
Talawdī, Sudan, 2,736 163 K4
Talbot, co., Ga., 7,127 64 E3
Talbot, Ind. 70 B2
Talbot, co., Md., 21,578 62 H4
Talbot, Mt., Austl. 172 C3
Talbot L., Man., Can. 43 E3
Talbotton, Ga., 1,163 64 E3
Talca, Chile, 68,148 105 A5
Talcahuano, Chile, 83,609 104 e16
Talcamávida, Chile 104 e17
Talco, Tex., 1,024 77 Q3
Talcott, W. Va. 62 D5
Talcottville, Conn. 56 G5
Taldom, U.S.S.R., 10,600 136 E1
Taldy-Kurgan, U.S.S.R., 41,000 134 G5
Taldysay, U.S.S.R. 137 k10
Talegaon, India, 11,753 145 D6
Talent, Oreg., 868 80 B4
Talgarth, U.K., 1,876 114 B7
Ta-li, Shen-hsi, China 151 A4
Ta-li, Y-n., China 150 D4
Ta-li, r., China 151 A3
Taliabu, P., Indon. 149 H3
Taliaferro, co., Ga., 3,370 64 G2
Ta-liang Shan, China 152 A1
Talibon, Phil., 2,061 153 f11
Ta-lien = Lü-ta
Talihina, Okla., 1,048 76 H3
Ta-ling, r., China 151 D2
Taling Chan, Thai., 3,831 147 d5
Taling Sung, Thai. 147 c4
Talip, S. Viet. 147 n11
Talisay, Phil., 1,120 153 A4
Talisay, Phil., 2,047 153 B2
Talisay, Phil., 2,581 153 b8
Talisay, Phil., 20,254 153 e11
Talisayan, Phil., 4,195 153 f12
Talitsa, U.S.S.R., 16,800 134 F4
Taliwang, Indon. 148 F5
Talkeetna, Alaska, 76 85 G3
Talkeetna Mts., Alaska 85 G3
Ṭalkhā, U.A.R. 161 i7
Talkheh, r., Iran 143 D1
Tall Abyaḍ, Syr. 142 D2
Talladega, co., Ala., 65,495 64 C2
Talladega, Ala., 17,742 64 C2
Tall'Afar, Iraq, 25,543 143 C1
Tallaght, Ire. 113 C5
Tallahassee, Fla., 58,022 65 E2
Tallahatchie, co., Miss., 24,081 73 E4
Tallahatchie, r., Miss. 73 E3
Tall al-'Amarna, ruins, U.A.R. 161 K3
Tallangatta, Austl. 173 f11
Tallant, Okla. 76 G1
Tallapoosa, co., Ala., 35,007 64 D3
Tallapoosa, Ga., 2,744 64 D2
Tallapoosa, r., Ala.-Ga. 64 D2
Tallassee, Ala., 4,934 64 C3
Tallevast, Fla. 65 c13
Talley Cavey, Pa. 60 c7
Talleyville, Del. 62 e10
Tallimba, Austl. 173 f10
Tallinn, U.S.S.R., 320,000 134 B4
Tall Kalakh, Syr., 5,470 142 c5
Tall Kūshik, Syr. 142 E2
Tallmadge, Ohio, 10,246 70 H1
Tallman, Mich. 67 G5
Tallman, N.Y. 58 c12
Tall Pines, Sask., Can. 43 D4
Tallula, Ill., 547 68 C4
Tallulah, La., 9,413 73 D5
Talma, Ind. 70 C1
Talmage, Kans. 75 H4
Talmage, Nebr., 361 75 K3
Talmalmo, Austl. 173 f10
Tal'menka, U.S.S.R. 137 q11
Talmont, Fr., 1,046 117 C3
Tal'noye, U.S.S.R., 13,000 136 C3
Talofofo, Guam 176 24
Talofofo, r., Guam 176 24
Talofofo Bay, Guam 176 24
Taloga, Okla., 322 76 E1
Talok, Indon. 149 F2
Talomako, New Hebr. 174 k5
Talomo, Phil., 10,384 153 C4
Ta-lou Shan, China 152 B1
Talovaya, U.S.S.R. 136 F3
Talowah, Miss. 73 F6
Talpa, Rum. 128 E2
Talpa, Tex., 195 77 O4
Talpa de Allende, Mex., 3,587 92 D4
Talquin, L., Fla. 65 E2
Talsarnau, U.K. 113 E5
Talsi, U.S.S.R., 7,000 136 A1
Taltal, Chile, 5,291 105 A3
Taltson, r., N.W.T., Can. 40 G5
Taludaa, Indon. 149 G2
Taluk, Indon. 148 B3
Taluyers, Fr. 116 p15
Talvik, Nor. 120 E1
Tama, co., Iowa, 21,413 72 E2
Tama, Iowa, 2,925 72 E3
Tama, r., Jap. 155 m19
Tamaha, Okla., 80 76 H2
Tamahú, Guat. 94 c8
Tamakautoga, Niue 177 32
Tamalameque, Col. 100 D3
Tamalco, Ill. 68 C5
Tamale, Ghana, 49,123 162 D4
Tamames, Sp., 1,786 122 C2
Tamana, Jap., 47,736 154 B5
Tamana, i., Gilb. Is. 170 F5
Tamani, Mali, 3,800 162 C3
Taman Negara, nat. pk., Malay. 148 B1
Tamano, Jap., 65,292 155 D4
Tamanoura, Jap., 7,323 154 A5
Tamanrasset, Alg., 1,547 160 E4
Tamanthi, Burma 146 A1
Ta-mao-wei, China 152 b6
Tamaqua, Pa., 10,173 61 L4
Tamar, r., Austl. 173 f13
Tamar, r., U.K. 116 A1
Támara, Col. 100 D5
Tamarack, Minn., 112 74 F2
Tamarike, Indon. 149 L5
Tamarin, Maurit. 165 c12
Tamarite de Litera, Sp., 4,707 122 F2
Tamaroa, Ill., 696 68 C5
Tamasee, S.C. 63 A3
Tamashima, Jap., 51,928 155 C4

Tamási—Tecolote · 301

Tamási, Hung., 7,701 126 D3
Tamatave, Malag. Rep., 39,627 165 H5
Tamaulipas, st., Mex., 1,024,182 93 F3
Tamaulipas, Sa. de, Mex. 93 F3
Tamaya, r., Peru 104 C4
Tamayo, Dom. Rep., 3,613 96 m6
Tamazula de Gordiano, Mex., 10,784 92 E4
Tamazulapan, Mex., 3,390 93 F5
Tamazunchale, Mex., 8,393 93 F4
Tambach, Kenya 165 g13
Tambacounda, Sen., 4,824 162 B3
Tambalan, Indon. 148 E2
També, Braz., 4,149 103 b14
Tambea, Indon. 149 G4
Tambelan, Kep., Indon. 148 C2
Tambellup, Austl. 172 B5
Tambey, U.S.S.R. 134 F2
Tambilahan, Indon. 148 B3
Tambillo, Ec. 104 c10
Tam Binh, S. Viet., 5,994 147 m12
Tambisan, Malay. 149 F1
Tambo, Austl. 173 G3
Tambo, Col. 100 B5
Tambo, D.R.Congo 165 n18
Tambo, r., Peru 104 D6
Tambobamba, Peru, 3,580 104 C5
Tambopata, r., Peru 104 D5
Tambora, G., Indon. 148 F5
Tambores, Urug., 2,000* 105 D4
Tamboril, Dom. Rep., 2,286 96 m6
Tamboryacu, r., Peru 104 C2
Tambov, U.S.S.R., 186,000 134 D4
Tambre, r., Sp. 122 A1
Tambura, Sudan 163 J5
Tamchakett, Maur. 162 C3
Tam Dao, N. Viet. 147 h8
Tamdy-Bulak, U.S.S.R. 134 F5
Tame, Col. 100 E4
Tame, r., U.K. 114 E5
Tâmega, r., Port. 122 B2
Tamentit, Alg. 160 D3
Tamesi, r., Mex. 93 F3
Támesis, Col. 101 d14
Tamgak, mt., Niger 162 F2
Tamiahua, Mex., 3,824 93 F4
Tamiahua, Lag. de, Mex. 93 F4
Tamiami Can., Fla. 65 J6
Ta-miao-shan, China 152 C2
Taminango, Col. 100 B7
Ta-ming, China 151 B3
Tamins, Switz. 124 D2
Tamiš, r., Yug. 125 E2
Tam Ky, S. Viet. 146 E4
Tamluk, India, 17,986 144 f14
Tammerfors = Tampere
Tammisaari = Ekenäs
Tamms, Ill., 548 68 C6
Tampa, Fla., 274,970 65 G5
Tampa, Kans., 145 75 H5
Tampa Bay, Fla. 65 G5
Tampang, Indon. 148 C4
Tampate, Mex., 1,951 93 F4
Tampere, Fin., 133,406 120 F3
Tampico, Mex., 122,197 93 F3
Tampico, Ill., 790 68 C2
Tampico, Ind. 70 C4
Tampico, Wash. 80 C2
Tampin, Malay., 3,928 148 B2
Tamra, Isr., 5,324 142 b7
Tamrah, Saudi Ar. 143 C4
Tams, W. Va. 62 C5
Tamsag Bulag, Mong. 150 F2
Tamshiyacu, Peru 104 C3
Tamsweg, Aust., 4,429 124 K6
Tam Tan, S. Viet. 147 m11
Tamu, Burma, 1,687 146 A1
Tamuín, Mex., 4,151 93 F3
Tamuning, Guam, 5,380 176 24
Tamur, r., Nepal 144 f12
Tamworth, Austl., 13,641 173 G4
Tamworth, Ont., Can. 46 H4
Tamworth, U.K., 13,555 114 E5
Tamworth, N.H. 54 E4
Tamyang, S. Kor., 14,201 151 E4
Tan, r., China 151 A4
Tana, Nor. 120 F1
Tana, i., New Hebr. 170 F6
Tana, r., Kenya 164 F2
Tana, r., Nor. 120 F1
Tana, L., Eth. 163 L3
Tanabashi, Jap. 154 h15
Tanabe, Jap., 48,673 155 D5
Tanabu, Jap., 23,248 155 G1
Tanaco, Mex., 1,148 93 b10
Tanacross, Alaska, 102 85 J3
Tanafjorden, Nor. 120 G1
Tanaga I., Alaska 85 f8
Tanaga Vol., Alaska 85 f8
Tanah, Tg., Indon. 148 c7
Tanahbala, P., Indon. 148 A3
Tanahdjampea, P., Indon. 149 G4
Tanahgrogot, Indon. 148 F3
Tanahmasa, P., Indon. 148 A3
Tanahmerah, Kalimantan, Indon. 148 F2
Tanahmerah, Irian Barat, Indon. 149 L4
Tanahputih, Indon. 148 B2
Tanah Rata, Malay., 4,186 147 o14
Tanaka, Jap. 154 g14
Tanakeke, P., Indon. 149 F4
Tanakpur, India 144 c11
Tanakura, Jap., 19,443 155 G3
Tanalyk, r., U.S.S.R. 137 i9
Tanamá, r., P.R. 96 s10
Tan An, S. Viet., 12,836 146 D5
Tanana, Alaska, 349 85 F2
Tanana, r., Alaska 85 H3
Tananarive, Malag. Rep., 254,271 165 G5
Tanapag, Saipan 176 27
Tanapag Hbr., Saipan 176 27
Tanaro, r., It. 123 B2
Tanashi, Jap., 31,323 155 m19
Tanauan, Phil., 7,145 153 B2
Tanay, Phil., 11,123 153 B2
Tan Binh, S. Viet., 103,832 146 D5
Tan-chai, China 152 C2
Tan Chau, S. Viet., 11,936 146 D5
T'an-ch'eng, China 151 C4
Tanch'ŏn, N. Kor. 151 F2
T'an-chou-hsü, China 152 a6
Tan-chou Shui-Tao, chan., China 152 a6
Tancítaro, Mex., 3,246 93 b10
Tancítaro, P. de, Mex. 93 b10
Tancoyol, Mex. 93 e8
Tanda, India, 32,687 145 G4
Tanda, Iv. Coast, 1,200 162 b8
Tandag, Phil., 3,501 153 C3
Tandaho, Eth. 163 L4
Tandaltī, Sudan, 7,388 163 K3
Ţăndărei, Rum. 128 F2
Tandil, Arg., 41,115 105 D5
Tandjung, Indon. 148 E3
Tandjungbalai, Indon., 29,152 148 B2
Tandjungbatu, Indon. 148 F2
Tandjungpandan, Indon. 148 D3
Tandjungpriok, Indon. 148 b7
Tandjungpusu, Indon. 148 E2
Tandjungradja, Indon. 148 C3
Tandjungrusa, Indon. 148 D3
Tando Ādam, Pak., 31,246 144 C4
Tando Allāhyār, Pak., 17,273 144 C4
Tandoc, Phil., 1,767 153 h14
Tanduan, Phil., 1,633 153 A4
Tanega-shima, Jap. 154 k17
Tanegashima-kaikyō, Jap. 154 k17
Tanen Taunggyi, Burma-Thai. 146 B3
Tanew, r., Pol. 127 E3
Taney, co., Mo., 10,238 72 D8
Taneytown, Md., 1,519 62 H3
Taneyville, Mo., 134 72 E8
Tanezrouft, des., Alg.-Mali 160 D4
Tan-feng, China 150 E3
Tanfi, r., Ghana 162 c8
Tang, Kas, Camb. 146 C5
T'ang, r., Ho-p., China 151 B3
T'ang, r., Ho-n., China 151 B4
T'ang, r., A-h., China 151 C4
Tanga, Tanz., 38,053 164 F2
Tanga, W. Samoa 177 38
Tangahka, Burma 146 B1
Tangail, Pak., 23,688 144 g13
Tanga Is., Terr. New Guin. 174 g1
Tangalla, Cey., 6,823 145 n22
Tangancícuaro, Mex., 9,408 93 b10
Tanganyika = Tanzania
Tanganyika, L., Af. 164 E2
Tanganyika and Zanzibar = Tanzania
Tangarare, Sol. Is. 175 c3
T'ang-ch'i, China 152 E1
Tang-chin Shan-k'ou, China 150 C3
Tangent, Alta., Can. 42 H2
Tangent, Oreg. 80 B3
Tanger, Mor., 141,714 160 C2
Tangerang, Indon. 148 b7
Tangerhütte, Ger.D.R. 118 C2
Tangermünde, Ger.D.R., 13,840 118 C2
T'ang-ho, China 151 B4
T'ang-hsien, China 151 B3
Tangier, N.S., Can. 47 u11
Tangier, Mor. = Tanger
Tangier, Ind. 70 B3
Tangier, Va., 876 62 J5
Tangier Sd., Md. 62 J4
Tangipahoa, parish, La., 59,434 73 E7
Tangipahoa, La., 465 73 E7
Tangipahoa, r., La. 73 E6
Tangkak, Malay., 9,013 147 p15
Tangla, India, 4,319 145 J4
T'ang-li-hsü, China 152 b6
Tang Paloch, Camb. 147 k11
Tangra Tsho, China 150 B4
T'ang-shan, China, 788,000* 150 F3
Tang-shan, China 151 C4
T'ang-t'ou, China 151 C4
T'ang-t'ou-hsia, China 152 b6
Tang-t'u, China 152 E1
Tangua, Col. 100 B7
Tangub, Phil., 3,039 153 B3
Tanguiéta, Dahom., 3,194 162 E4
Tanguisson Pt., Guam 176 24
Tangyan, Burma 146 B2
Tang-yang, China 150 E4
T'ang-yin, China 151 B4
T'ang-yüan, China 151 F1
Tanh Linh, S. Viet., 1,278 147 m11
Tan-hsien, China 152 C4
Taniai, Jap. 154 h14
Tanimbar, Kep., Indon. 149 K4
Ta-ning, China 151 A3
Täning, Den. 121 B4
Taninul, Mex. 93 F3
Taniyama, Jap., 38,640 154 B6
Taniyama, Jap. 154 f16
Tanjay, Phil., 12,355 153 B3
Tanjong Malim, Malay., 7,006 148 B2
Tanjong Piandang, Malay., 3,236 147 o14
Tanjong Sepat, Malay., 5,051 148 B2
Tanjungpinang, Indon. 148 C2
Tānk, Pak., 10,582 145 D2
Tanka-jima, Jap. 154 f15
Tan-kan Shan, China 152 b6
Tankersly, Tex. 77 N4
Tank Pk., Colo. 79 A1
Tan-leng, China 152 A1
Tann, F.R.Ger., 1,759 118 C3
Tanna, Ger.D.R. 126 a6
Tanner, Ala. 64 C1
Tanneron, Fr. 116 m13
Tanners L., Minn. 74 d6
Tannersville, N.Y., 580 59 M7
Tannersville, Pa. 61 M3
Tanner Williams, Ala. 64 A5
Tännforsen, falls, Swed. 120 C3
Tannheim, Aust. 124 G6
Tannis Bugt, Den. 121 C3
Tannu-Ola, Khr., U.S.S.R. 132 J4
Tannūrah, Ra's at, c., Saudi Ar. 143 E3
Tano, r., Ghana 162 b8
Tañon Str., Phil. 153 B3
Tanoriki, New Hebr. 174 m5
Tanout, Niger, 1,205 162 F3
Tan-pa, China 152 A1
Tanque, Ariz. 78 D5
Tanque Verde, Ariz., 1,053 78 C5
Tanquián, Mex., 1,907 93 F4
Tan-shui, China 152 b6
Tan-shui, Taiwan, 36,431 152 F2
Tan-shui, China 152 b6
Tänsing, Nepal 144 d12
Tansley, Ont., Can. 46 c14
Ţanţā, U.A.R., 184,000 161 K2
Tantabin, Burma, 3,703 146 B3
Tantalus, Mt., Hawaii 84 d7
Tan Thanh, S. Viet. 147 k11
Tantoyuca, Mex., 7,476 93 F4
Tan Tru, S. Viet., 1,050 147 m11
Tanu, Br. Col., Can. 42 D3
Tanum, Swed. 120 B4
Tanum, r., Malay. 147 p14
Tanunak = Tununak
Tanunda, Austl., 1,626 172 c8
Tan Uyen, S. Viet. 147 m11
Tanworth, U.K., 2,354 114 E6
Tan Xion, S. Viet. 147 m11
Tan-yang, China 152 E1
Tanyang, S. Kor., 11,662 151 F3
Tan Yong Mat, Thai. 147 o13
Tanzania, ctry., 10,567,000* 164 E2
Tanzawa-yama, Jap. 155 m20
Tao, N. Caled. 174 i8
Tao, Ko, Thai. 146 B5
T'ao, r., K-su, China 150 D3
T'ao, r., Ch-hsi, China 152 D2
T'ao-an, China 151 D1
Tao-chen, China 152 B1
Tao-ch'eng, China 150 D4
T'ao-chiang, China 152 C1
T'ao-erh, r., China 151 D1
Tao-fu, China 152 A1
Tao-hsien, China 152 C2
T'ao Hu, China 152 E1
T'ao-lo, China 151 C4
Taongi, atoll, Marsh. Is. 170 F4
Taormina, It., 8,072 123 E6
Taos, co., N. Mex., 15,934 79 C3
Taos, N. Mex., 2,163 79 C3
Taos Pueblo, N. Mex. 79 C3
T'ao-ts'un, China 151 D3
Taoudenni, Mali 162 D2
Taourirt, Mor., 7,343 160 D2
T'ao-yüan, China 152 C1
T'ao-yüan, Taiwan, 55,311 152 F2
Tapa, U.S.S.R., 8,100 136 B1
Tapaan Passage, Phil. 153 B4
Tapachula, Mex., 41,701 93 G5
Tapah, Malay., 9,599 148 B1
Tapajós, r., Braz. 103 E2
Tapak, i., Ponape 176 29
Tapakkuda, Indon. 148 A2
Tapaktuan, Indon. 148 A2
Tapalang, Indon. 149 F3
Tapalquén, Arg., 3,824 105 a13
Tapanahoni, r., Sur. 101 N6
Tapanatepec, Mex., 3,702 93 G5
Tapanga, C., W. Samoa 177 37
Tapanshang = Pa-lin-yu-ch'i
Ta-pa Shan, China 152 C1
Tapauá, Braz. 102 D3
Tapauá, r., Braz. 102 C3
Tapaz, Phil., 2,289 153 B3
Tapdrup, Den. 121 B4
Ta-p'eng, China 152 b6
Taperoá, Braz., 2,984 103 a14
Tapes, Braz., 5,074 103 F8
Taphan Hin, Thai., 11,412 146 C3
Taphoen, r., Thai. 147 c4
Tapi, r., Thai. 146 B5
Tapiche, r., Peru 104 C3
Tapicito Cr., N. Mex. 79 B3
Ta-pieh Shan, China 152 D1
Tapilon, Phil., 3,166 153 f10
Tapini, Terr. Papua 174 e3
Tápió, r., Hung. 126 D3
Tapiola, Mich. 66 E2
Tapipa, Ven. 101 c11
Tapiwa, Ocean I. 175 16
Täplejung, Nepal 144 f12
Tapoco, N.C. 63 a7
Tapolca, Hung., 8,577 126 C3
Tapotchau, pk., Saipan 176 27
Tappahannock, Va., 1,086 62 H5
Tappan L., Ohio 70 H2
Tappan Zee, N.Y. 58 d12
Tappen, N. Dak., 326 74 C2
Tappi-saki, Jap. 155 G1
Tappita, Lib. 162 C4
Tapps, L., Wash. 81 b8
Tapti, r., India 145 E5
Ta-pu, China 152 E2
Tapuaenuku, pk., N.Z. 175 g6
Ta-pu-chan-ko, China 151 A3
Tapul Group, is., Phil. 153 B4
Tapun, Burma, 2,327 147 a1
Tapung, India 146 A5
Taputapu, C., Tutuila 177 39
Taputimu, Tutuila 177 39
Taquara, Braz., 11,282 103 F7
Taquari, Braz. 103 F5
Taquari, r., Mo.Gro., Braz. 103 E5
Taquari, r., R.G.do.S., Braz. 103 F7
Tar, r., U.S.S.R. 137 g4
Tar, r., N.C. 63 F1
Tara, Austl. 173 G4
Tara, Ont., Can. 46 C4
Tara, U.S.S.R., 22,800 134 G4
Tara, r., U.S.S.R. 137 p11
Tara, r., Yug. 125 D3
Tarabuco, Bol., 11,345 102 D5
Ţarābulus, Leb., 76,074 142 C3
Ţarābulus, prov. Libya, 291,236 161 G2
Ţarābulus, Libya, 129,728 161 G2
Taradale, N.Z., 4,846 175 h5
Tarakan, Indon. 148 F2
Taraki, Jap., 20,091 154 B5
Taralga, Austl. 173 g10
Taramakau, r., N.Z. 175 f6
Taran, U.S.S.R. 134 G2
Tarana, India, 10,805 144 a14
Tarancón, Sp., 7,714 122 D2
Tarangnan, Phil., 2,135 153 C3
Taransay, i., U.K. 112 C3
Taranto, It., 192,821 123 F4
Taranto, Golfo di, It. 123 F4
Tarapacá, Col. 100 E9
Tarapoto, Peru, 13,741 104 B3
Taraquá, Braz. 102 C2
Tarare, Fr., 12,298 117 F4
Tarascon, Fr., 8,910 117 F5
Tarascon-sur-Ariège, Fr., 3,680 117 D5
Tarasovskiy, U.S.S.R. 136 g7
Tarat, Alg. 161 F3
Tarata, Bol., 8,031 102 C5
Tarata, Peru 2,676 104 D6
Tarauacá, Braz., 2,292 102 B3
Tarauacá, r., Braz. 102 B3
Taravao, B. de, Tahiti 177 44
Taravao, Isthme de, Tahiti 177 44
Tarawa, atol, Gilb. Is. 170 F4
Tarawera, N.Z. 175 h5
Tarawera, Mt., N.Z. 175 h5
Tarazin, Burma 147 c5
Tarazit, Massif de, Niger 162 F2
Tarazona, Sp., 12,059 122 D2
Tårbæk, Den., 2,739 121 b7
Tarbagatay, Khr., China-U.S.S.R. 132 H5
Tarbat Ness, U.K. 112 E3
Tarbert, Arg., Scot., U.K. 112 D4
Tarbert, Inv., Scot., U.K. 112 C3
Tarbes, Fr., 50,715 117 C5
Tarbet, U.K. 112 a7
Tarbolton, U.K. 112 b8
Tarboro, Ga. 64 H4
Tarboro, N.C., 8,411 63 G2
Tarcento, It., 11,142 123 D1
Tarcoola, Austl. 172 E4
Tarcutta, Austl. 173 f10
Tardets-Sorholus, Fr., 1,107 117 C5
Tardoire, r., Fr. 117 D4
Tardoki-Yani, G., U.S.S.R. 135 N5
Tarecuato, Mex., 3,486 93 b10
Taree, Austl., 7,408 173 H4
Tärendö, Swed. 120 E2
Tarengo, Mex., 1,250 93 b9
Tarentum, Pa., 8,232 60 C4
Taretán, Mex., 2,059 93 b10
Tarevo, Yug. 125 D2
Tareya, U.S.S.R. 135 J2
Tarfaya, Mor., 1,521 160 B3
Targhee Pass, Idaho 81 •
Targuist, Mor., 2,297 160 D2
Tarhauş, mts., Rum. 128 F1
Tarhit, Alg. 160 D2
Tarhūnah, Libya 161 G2
Tari, Terr. Papua 174 d2
Tàriba, Ven., 9,481 100 D4
Tarica, Nic. 94 E4
Tarifa, Sp., 18,042 122 C4
Tariffville (part of Simsbury), Conn. 56 E5
Tarija, Bol., 20,127 102 C6
Tarik, i., Truk 176 19
Tarīm, S. Ar., 10,000* 143 D5
Tarim, plair, China 150 B3
Tarim, r., China 150 B2
Tarimbaro, Mex., 1,412 93 c10
Tarime, Tanz. 165 g14
Tarimoro, Mex., 6,718 93 d9
Taritai, i., Tarawa 175 15
Taritipan, Malay. 148 F1
Tarkhankut, M., U.S.S.R. 136 C4
Tarkio, Mo., 2,160 72 B4
Tarkio, r., Mo. 72 B4
Tarko-Sale, U.S.S.R. 134 G3
Tarkwa, Ghana, 13,066 162 c9
Tarlac, Phil., 1,764 153 B2
Tarleton, U.K., 2,774 114 C3
Tarleton, L., N.H. 54 D4
Tarlton, S. Af. 165 i17
Tarlton, Ohio, 377 70 G3
Tarlton, Tenn. 71 F6
Tarm, Den. 121 A5
Tarma, Peru, 15,404 104 C4
Tarn, r., Fr. 117 E4
Tarna, r., Hung. 126 E2
Tärnaby, Swed. 120 C2
Tarnāk, r., Afghan. 144 C2
Tårnby, Den., 42,688 121 E5
Tarnobrzeg, Pol., 5,108 127 D3
Tarnov, Nebr., 70 75 H2
Tarnów, Pol., 71,000* 127 D3
Tarnowskie Góry, Pol., 28,000* 127 h6
Tarn Taran, India, 20,961 145 E3
Taro, r., It. 123 B2
Taroa, Col. 100 E1
Tarobi, Terr. New Guin. 174 f2
Taroka, Mt., Sol. Is. 175 a2
Taroom, Austl. 173 G3
Taroudannt, Mor., 17,141 160 C2
Tarpley, Tex. 77 O5
Tarpon, L., Fla. 65 c11
Tarpon Springs, Fla., 6,768 65 G4
Tarporley, U.K., 1,538 114 C4
Tarpum Bay, Bah. Is. 95 c7
Tarqui, r., Ec. 104 c11
Tarquinia, It., 11,856 123 C3
Tarrafal, Sto. Antão, C. Verde Is. 109 5
Tarrafal, São Tiago, C. Verde Is. 109 5
Tarragona, Sp., 43,519 122 F2
Tarrant, Ala., 7,810 64 C2
Tarrant, co., Tex., 538,495 77 P3
Tarrasa, Sp., 92,234 122 F2
Tàrrega, Sp., 7,317 122 F2
Tarryall, Colo. 79 C2
Tarryall Cr., Colo. 79 C2
Tarryall Mts., Colo. 79 b9
Tarrytown, Ga., 191 64 G3
Tarrytown, N.Y., 11,109 59 N9
Târs, Den. 121 C3
Tarsus, Turk., 51,310 142 C2
Tartagal, Arg., 20,000* 105 C2
Tartaro, Phil., 3,744 153 b7
Tartaro, r., It. 122 e5
Tartas, Fr., 3,134 117 C5
Tartas, r., U.S.S.R. 137 p11
Tartu, U.S.S.R., 76,000 134 B4
Ţarţūs, Syr., 15,573 142 C3
Tarui, Jap., 19,748 154 h14
Tarui, Jap., 5,722 155 D4
Taruma, Jap. 154 e15
Tarumi, Jap., 111,028 154 g15
Tarumizu, Jap., 37,316 154 B6
Tarumovka, U.S.S.R. 137 c1
Tarusa, U.S.S.R., 5,000 136 b6
Ta Ru Tao, Ko, Thai. 146 B6
Tarutung, Indon. 148 A2
Tarver, Ga. 64 G5
Tarvisio, It., 7,044 123 D1
Tarxien, Malta, 7,706 123 f12
Tasch, Switz. 124 B2
Tasco, Kans. 75 E4
Tascosa, Tex. 76 M2
Taseko, r., Br. Col., Can. 42 F3
Taseko, Mt., Br. Col., Can. 42 F3
Tasgaon, India, 16,649 145 i18
Tashauz, U.S.S.R., 45,000 134 E5
Ta-she-t'ai, China 151 A2
Tashi Gang Dzong, Bhutan 145 J4
T'a-shih-k'u-erh-kan, China 150 A3
Ta-shih-t'ou, China 151 F2
Tashiro, Jap. 155 m19
Tashkent, U.S.S.R., 1,061,000 134 F5
Tashkumyr, U.S.S.R., 18,400 137 g4
Tashkurghan, Afghan. 144 C1
Tashota, Ont., Can. 44 E5
Tashtagol, U.S.S.R., 16,500 134 H4
Tashurghan, U.S.S.R. 137 e5
Tasiat L., Qué., Can. 44 J2
Tasikmalaja, Indon. 148 D4
Tåsinge, i., Den. 121 C6
Tasitel, Terr. New Guin. 174 f1
Taskan, U.S.S.R. 135 P3
Taşköprü, Turk., 5,721 142 C1
Taskul, Terr. New Guin. 174 f1
Tas-Kysta-Bys, Khr., U.S.S.R. 135 O3
Tasman Basin, Tasman Sea 168 F4
Tasman Bay, N.Z. 175 g6
Tasmania, st., Austl., 371,217 173 G6
Tasman Pen., Austl. 173 G6
Tasman Sea 170 E7
Tåsnad, Rum. 128 D1
Tasquillo, Mex., 1,440 93 e9
Tassajara, Calif. 83 f12
Tassialuk, L., Qué., Can. 44 K2
Tassili du Hoggar, plat., Alg. 160 E4
Tassil n'Ajjer, plat., Alg. 160 F3
Tåstrup, Den. 121 a7
Tastür, Tun., 5,527 160 f5
Tata, Hung., 17,333 126 D3
Tata, Mor. 160 C3
Tataa, Pte., Tahiti 177 44
Tataba, Indon. 149 G3
Tatabánya, Hung., 52,044 126 D3
Tatakoto, i., Tuam. Arch 171 J6
Tatala, Terr. Papua 174 3
Tatalrose, Er. Col., Can. 42 F3
Tatamagouche, N.S., Can. 47 U11
Tatamy, Pa., 762 61 M4
Tatarsk, U.S.S.R., 29,000 134 G4
Tatarskaya Karabolka, U.S.S.R. 137 k8
Tatarskiy Proliv, U.S.S.R. 135 O4
Tatau, Malay. 148 E2
Tate, co., Miss., 18,138 73 E3
Tatebayashi, Jap., 55,684 155 F3
Tateishi-saki, Jap. 154 g14
Tate Mountain Estates, Ga. 64 E1
Tateyama, Jap., 57,643 155 F4
Tate-yama, Jap. 155 E3
Tathlina L., N.W.T., Can. 40 F5
Tathlīth, Wādī, Saudi Ar. 163 M2
Ta-t'ien, China 152 E2
Ta-ting, China 152 B2
Tatitlek, Alaska, 96 85 H3
Tatkon, Burma, 2,696 146 B2
Tatla Lake, Br. Col., Can. 42 F3
Tatlayoko Lake, Br. Col., Can. 42 F3
Tatlow, Mt., Br. Col., Can. 42 F3
Tatnam, C., Man., Can. 43 H2
Tatnuck (part of Worcester), Mass. 57 J3
Tatow Knob, Utah 78 B2
Tatshenshini, r., Can.-U.S. 42 B1
Tatsienlu = K'ang-ting
Ta-tsu, China 152 B1
Tatsuno, Jap., 34,966 154 f15
Tatsuruhama, Jap., 6,796 155 E3
Tatsutori, Jap. 155 n20
Tatta, Pak., 12,786 144 C4
Tattenhall, U.K., 1,049 114 C4
Tattnall, co., Ga., 15,837 64 G4
Ta-tu, r., China 152 A1
Tatui, Braz., 22,550 103 G6
Tatum, N. Mex., 1,168 79 D5
Tatum, S.C., 132 63 E3
Tatum, Tex., 542 77 Q3
Tatum Cr., Ga. 64 G5
Ta-t'ung, A-h., China 150 F4
Ta-t'ung, Shan-hsi, China, 270,000* 150 F3
Ta-t'ung, China 150 D3
Ta-t'ung-chen, China 151 E1
Tatura, Austl., 1,929 173 e11
Tatvan, Turk., 6,549 142 E2
Ta-tzu, China 150 C4
Tau, i., Amer. Samoa 177 37
Tau, i., Tonga 177 36
Tauá, Braz., 4,904 103 H3
Taubaté, Braz., 64,863 103 d18
Tauber, r., F.R.Ger. 118 B4
Tauberbischofsheim, F.R.Ger., 6,036 118 B4
Taucha, Ger.D.R., 15,576 118 D3
Tauchik, U.S.S.R. 134 E5
Tauere, i., Tuam. Arch. 171 J6
Täuffelen, Switz., 1,500 124 B1
Taufkirchen, F.R.Ger., 3,025 118 C4
Taufstein, pk., F.R.Ger. 119 G3
Tauka, Aust. 124 M7
Taula, i., Tonga 177 36
Taulihawa, Nepal 144 d12
Taumarunui, N.Z., 4,961 175 g5
Taum Sauk Mtn., Mo. 72 G7
Taungdwingyi, Burma, 16,233 146 A3
Taunggaung, Burma 147 g6
Taunggyi, Burma, 8,652 146 B2
Taungnyo Ra., Burma 147 b3
Taungtha, Burma, 5,418 146 A2
Taungup, Burma, 4,117 146 A3
Taunsa Bge., Pak. 145 D3
Taunton, U.K., 35,192 113 E6
Taunton, Mass., 41,132 57 M5
Taunton, r., Mass. 57 M5
Taunton Lake, N.J. 60 g12
Taunus, mts., F.R.Ger. 118 B3
Taupo, N.Z., 5,261 175 h5
Taupo, L., N.Z. 175 g5
Tauragė, U.S.S.R., 12,100 136 A2
Tauramena, Col. 100 D5
Tauranga, N.Z., 13,468 175 g5
Taureau, L., Qué., Can. 47 L2
Täureni, Rum. 128 E1
Taurianova, It., 20,433 123 F5
Tauroa Pt., N.Z. 175 g4
Taurus Mts. = *Toros Dağları*
Tausa, Col. 101 f14
Tauste, Sp., 6,634 122 E2
Tautendorf, Aust. 124 b9
Tautira, Tahiti 177 44
Tauu Is., Sol. Is. 175 b1
Tauyskaya G., U.S.S.R. 135 O4
Tavani, N.W.T., Can. 40 L5
Tavannes, Switz., 3,939 124 B1
Tavares, Fla., 2,724 65 H4
Tavastehus = Hämeenlinna
Tavatum, U.S.S.R. 135 P3
Tavda, U.S.S.R., 50,000 134 F4
Tavda, r., U.S.S.R. 134 F4
Tavernier, Fla. 65 h14
Taverny, Fr., 8,898 116 g10
Tavesurhlava, Mt., New Hebr. 174 k4
Taveta, Kenya 164 F2
Taveuni, i., Fiji 174 4
Tavignano, r., Fr. 116 r17
Tavira, Port., 12,046 122 B4
Tavistock, Ont., Can., 1,213 46 D5
Tavistock, U.K., 6,088 113 D6
Tavolzhan, U.S.S.R. 137 p11
Tavoy, Burma, 40,312 146 B4
Tavoy I., Burma 146 B4
Tavoy Pt., Burma 146 B4
Tavrichanka, U.S.S.R. 151 F2
Tavşanlı, Turk., 11,538 142 B2
Tavua, Fiji 174 4
Taw, r., U.K. 113 E6
Tawa, Burma, 1,233 147 b2
Tawai, India 145 K4
Tawakoni, L., Tex. 76 g9
Tawang, India 145 J4
Ta-wan Shan, China 152 a7
Tawaramoto, Jap., 4,585 154 g15
Tawas City, Mich., 1,810 67 K4
Tawas Pt., Mich. 67 K4
Tawatinaw, Alta., Can. 43 b6
Tawatinaw, r., Alta., Can. 43 b6
Tawau, Malay. 148 F1
Ta-wen, r., China 151 C3
Tawgywe-in, Burma, 1,498 147 b1
Tawitawi Group, is., Phil. 153 B4
Tawitawi I., Phil. 153 A4
Ţawkar, Sudan, 16,801 163 L2
Tawku, Burma 147 b2
Tawnghkam, Burma 147 g6
Tawonga, Austl. 173 f11
Ta-wu, China 152 D1
Ta-wu, Taiwan 152 F3
Tawzar, Tun., 11,820 161 F2
Ta Xa, N. Viet. 147 i9
Taxco, Mex., 16,604 93 F4
Taxenbach, Aust., 2,714 124 K6
Taxila, ruins, India 145 D2
Taxisco, Guat., 2,555 94 c9
Tay, r., Ont., Can. 47 H4
Tay, r., U.K. 112 E3
Tay, Firth of, U.K. 112 E3
Tay, Loch, U.K. 112 D3
Tayabamba, Peru, 7,230 104 B4
Tayabas, Phil., 9,272 153 c8
Tayabas Bay, Phil. 153 c9
Ta-yao, China 152 A2
Ta-yao-shan, China 152 C2
Tayasan, Phil., 2,041 153 e12
Ta-ya Wan, China 152 D3
Taycheedah, Wis. 66 E5
Ta-yeh, China 152 D1
Tayga, U.S.S.R., 31,700 134 H4
Taygonos, M., U.S.S.R. 135 P3
Taygonos, P-ov., U.S.S.R. 135 Q3
Taylor, Br. Col., Can. 42 G2
Taylor, Alaska 85 C2
Taylor, Ariz. 78 D4
Taylor, Ark., 734 73 B4
Taylor, co., Fla., 13,168 65 F3
Taylor, Fla. 65 G2
Taylor, co., Ga., 8,311 64 E3
Taylor, co., Iowa, 10,288 72 C4
Taylor, co., Ky., 16,285 71 F4
Taylor, Miss., 122 73 F3
Taylor, Nebr., 280 75 F2
Taylor, N. Dak., 215 74 A2
Taylor, Okla. 76 E3
Taylor, Pa., 6,148 61 o16
Taylor, co., Tex., 101,078 77 O3
Taylor, Tex., 9,434 77 P4
Taylor, co., W. Va., 15,010 62 D3
Taylor, co., Wis., 17,843 66 C3
Taylor, Wis., 334 66 B4
Taylor, r., Colo. 79 B2
Taylor, Mt., N. Mex. 52 E3
Taylor Bayou, Tex. 77 m9
Taylor Center, Mich. 67 e16
Taylor Cr., Ohio 71 h10
Taylor Mtn., Idaho 81 B3
Taylor Mts., Alaska 85 E3
Taylor Park, Colo. 79 B2
Taylor Pk., Colo. 79 a7
Taylors, S.C., 1,071 63 B3
Taylors Creek, Ohio 71 g10
Taylors Falls, Minn., 546 74 F3
Taylorsport, Ky. 71 g11
Taylor Springs, N. Mex. 79 C3
Taylor Station, Ohio 70 b7
Taylorstown, Pa. 60 a9
Taylorsville, Ky., 937 71 F3
Taylorsville, Miss., 1,132 73 F6
Taylorsville, N.C., 1,470 63 C2
Taylorsville, Utah 78 c9
Taylortown, La. 73 B5
Taylorville, Ill., 8,801 68 C4
Taymā', Saudi Ar. 143 B3
Taymouth, N.B., Can. 47 S10
Taymura, r., U.S.S.R. 135 K3
Taymylyr, U.S.S.R. 135 M2
Taymyr, O., U.S.S.R. 135 J2
Taymyr, O., U.S.S.R. 135 K2
Taymyr, P-ov., U.S.S.R. 135 H2
Tayncha, U.S.S.R., 11,000 134 F4
Tay Ninh, S. Viet., 14,672 147 m11
Tayoltita, Mex., 1,810 92 D3
Tayport, U.K., 3,151 112 E3
Tayshet, U.S.S.R., 34,500 135 J4
Taytay, Palawan, Phil. 153 A3
Taytay, Luzon, Phil., 21,747 153 c8
Ta-yü, China 152 D2
Tayug, Phil., 5,629 153 b6
Ta-yung, China 150 E4
Taz, r., U.S.S.R. 134 H3
Taza, Mor., 31,667 160 D2
Tazadit, Maur. 162 C2
Tazawa-ko, Jap. 155 G2
Taze, Burma 147 f6
Tazewell, Ga., 112 64 E3
Tazewell, co., Ill., 99,789 68 C3
Tazewell, Tenn., 1,264 71 H5
Tazewell, co., Va., 44,791 62 C5
Tazewell, Va., 3,000 62 C5
Tazin, r., Sask., Can. 43 B2
Tazin L., Sask., Can. 43 B2
Tazlina L., Alaska 85 H3
Tazovskaya G., U.S.S.R. 134 G3
Tazovskoye, U.S.S.R. 134 G3
Tbilisi, U.S.S.R., 724,000 134 D5
Tchaourou, Dahom. 162 e7
Tchibanga, Gabon 164 A2
Tchien, Lib. 162 C5
Tchollire, Cam., 1,600* 162 G4
Tchula, Miss., 882 73 E4
Tczew, Pol., 34,000* 127 C1
Tea, S. Dak., 188 74 D4
Teaca, Rum. 128 E1
Teacheys, N.C., 187 63 F3
Teague, Tex., 2,728 77 P4
Teaharoa, Moorea 177 44
Teahupoo, Tahiti 177 44
Teaiti Pt., Rarotonga 177 34
Teal Inlet, Falk. Is. 108 3
Teal L., Wis. 66 B2
Te-an, China 152 D1
Te Anau, L., N.Z. 175 e7
Teaneck, N.J., 42,085(T) 61 D2
Teano, It., 16,477 123 c9
Teapa, Mex., 4,083 93 G5
Te Araroa, N.Z. 175 h5
Te Aroha, N.Z., 3,060 175 g5
Teasdale, Utah 78 C2
Teaticket (part of Falmouth), Mass. 57 O6
Te Atu Kura, pk., Rarotonga 177 34
Teavanui, Passe, Bora-Bora 177 43
Te Awamutu, N.Z., 5,425 175 g5
Tebaida, Col. 101 d15
Tebay, U.K. 114 C2
Tébessa, Alg., 26,622 160 e6
Tebingtinggi, Indon., 26,228 148 A2
Tebingtinggi, Indon. 148 B3
Tebingtinggi, P., Indon. 148 B2
Tecali, Mex., 1,541 93 f11
Tecate, Mex., 7,074 92 A1
Techa, r., U.S.S.R. 137 k8
Techaluta, Mex., 1,636 93 a9
Te-ch'ang, China 150 D4
Teche, Bayou, La. 73 D7
Te-chiang, China 152 B1
Techiman, Ghana 162 c8
Te-ch'in, China 150 D4
Te-ch'ing, Ch-ch., China 152 E1
Te-ch'ing, K-t., China 152 C3
Te-ch'ing, N-h., China 150 C4
Techirghiol, Rum., 2,705 128 G2
Techny, Ill. 69 c8
Te-chou, China 151 C3
Teckomatorp, Swed. 121 b7
Tecolote, Lincoln Co., N. Mex. 79 C4

302 · Tecolote—Thoeng

Tecolote, San Miguel Co., N. Mex. 79 C4
Tecolotlán, Mex., 4,831 92 D4
Tecolutla, Mex. 93 F4
Tecomán, Mex., 14,374 92 D4
Tecopa, Calif. 82 E5
Tecoripa, Mex. 92 C2
Tecozautla, Mex., 3,257 93 F4
Tecpán, Guat., 4,644 94 c9
Tecpan, Mex., 5,835 93 E5
Tecuala, Mex., 10,747 92 D3
Tecuci, Rum., 23,400 128 F2
Teculután, Guat., 1,260 94 d9
Tecumseh, Ont., Can., 4,435 46 B6
Tecumseh, Kans. 75 K4
Tecumseh, Mich., 7,045 67 K6
Tecumseh, Mo. 72 E8
Tecumseh, Nebr., 1,887 75 J3
Tecumseh, Okla., 2,630 76 F2
Tecumseh, Mt., N.H. 54 D4
Tedjakule, Indon. 148 f8
Tedrow, Ohio 70 E1
Tedzhen, U.S.S.R., 15,600 134 F6
Teec Nos Pos, Ariz. 78 D3
Tee Harbor, Alaska 85 L4
Tee Lake, Qué., Can. 46 F2
Tees, r., U.K. 113 F4
Tees Bay, U.K. 112 h10
Teeswater, Ont., Can. 46 C5
Teeswater, r., Ont., Can. 46 C4
Tefé, Braz., 2,781 102 D2
Tefé, r., Braz. 102 C2
Tefenni, Turk., 2,928 142 B2
Tefft, Ind. 70 C1
Tefle, Ghana 162 d9
Tegal, Indon., 89,016 148 D4
Tega-numa, l., Jap. 155 m19
Tegarden, Okla. 76 E1
Tegelen, Neth., 16,400 115 E3
Tegeler See, F.R.Ger. 119 e10
Tegernsee, F.R.Ger., 4,426 118 C5
Tegneby, Swed. 121 D2
Tegua, i., New Hebr. 174 k4
Tegualda, Chile 105 e15
Tegucigalpa, Hond., 107,571 94 D3
Tegul'det, U.S.S.R. 134 H4
Tehachapi, Calif., 3,161 82 D5
Tehachapi Mts., Calif. 82 D5
Tehama, co., Calif., 25,305 82 B2
Tehama, Calif., 261 82 B2
Te Hapua, N.Z. 175 g4
Tehek L., N.W.T., Can. 40 K4
Teheran, Iran = Tehrān
Teheran, Ill. 68 C3
Téhini, Iv. Coast 162 D4
Tehrān, Iran, 1,512,082 143 E1
Tehri, India, 4,508 144 b10
Te-hsing, China 152 E1
Te-hua, China 152 E2
Tehuacán, Mex., 31,724 93 F4
Tehuantepec, Mex., 13,440 93 G5
Tehuantepec, Golfo de, Mex. 93 G5
Tehuantepec, Istmo de, Mex. 93 G5
Tehuantepec, r., Mex. 93 F5
Te-hui, China 151 E1
Tehuitzingo, Mex., 4,212 93 F4
Tehuixtla, Mex., 3,178 93 e11
Teide, Pico de, Can. Is. 109 4
Teifi, r., U.K. 113 D5
Teignmouth, U.K., 11,528 113 E6
Teith, r., U.K. 112 D3
Teiuş, Rum. 128 D1
Teixeiras, Braz., 2,930 103 e17
Tejerías, Ven. 101 b11
Tejo, r., Port. 122 B3
Te-jung, China 150 D4
Tejupilco, Mex., 3,083 93 d11
Tejutla, Guat., 1,096 94 b8
Tekai, r., Malay. 147 p14
Tekamah, Nebr., 1,788 75 J2
Te Kao, N.Z. 175 g4
Tekapo, r., N.Z. 175 f7
Tekari, India, 7,392 144 e13
Tekax, Mex., 7,797 93 H4
Teke, Oz., U.S.S.R. 137 o11
Tekeli, U.S.S.R., 32,000 134 G5
Tekes, r., China 150 B2
Tekija, Yug. 125 F2
Tekirdağ, Turk., 23,905 142 A1
Te-ko, China 150 D4
Tekoa, Wash., 911 80 E2
Tekom, Mex., 1,053 93 H4
Tekonsha, Mich., 744 67 J6
T'e-k'o-ssu, China 150 B2
Teku, Indon. 149 G3
Te Kuiti, N.Z., 4,492 175 g5
Tel, r., India 145 G5
Tela, D.R.Congo 165 o20
Tela, Hond., 18,476 94 D3
Telagh, le, Alg., 5,847 160 a6
T'e-la-to-mu, China 150 B4
Telavi, U.S.S.R., 14,700 137 c1
Tel Aviv-Yafo, Isr., 386,070 142 C3
Telchac, Mex., 2,695 93 H4
Telciu, Rum. 128 E1
Telde, Can Is. 109 4
Telegraph Creek, Br. Col., Can. 42 D1
Telekhany, U.S.S.R. 136 B2
Telekihaapai, i., Tonga 177 36
Telekitonga, i., Tonga 177 36
Telekivavau, i., Tonga 177 36
Telemark, reg., Nor. 120 B4
Telemong, Malay., 1,560 147 p15
Telen, r., Indon. 148 F2
Teleorman, r., Rum. 128 E2
Telerig, Bulg., 1,728 128 F3
Telescope Pt., Gren. 97 18
Teles Pires, r., Braz. 102 E3
Teletskoye Oz., U.S.S.R. 137 r12
Telfair, co., Ga., 11,715 64 G4
Telford, Pa., 2,763 61 M5
Telfs, Aust., 5,410 124 G6
Teli, U.S.S.R. 137 s12
Telico, Tex. 76 g10
Telida, Alaska 85 F3
Télimélé, Guin., 7,000 162 B4
Te-ling-ha, China 150 B3
Telkwa, Br. Col., Can. 42 E2
Tell, Tex. 77 N2
Tell Atlas, mts., Afr. 161 •
Tell City, Ind., 6,609 70 C5
Teller, Alaska, 217 85 C2
Teller, co., Colo., 2,495 79 C2
Teller Mission, Alaska, 77 85 C2
Téllez, Mex., 1,050 93 f10
Tellicherry, India, 44,763 145 E8
Tellico Plains, Tenn., 794 71 G6
Tellier, Arg. 105 B7
Tello, Col. 100 C6
Telluride, Colo., 677 79 B3
Telma, Wash. 80 C2
Tel'manovo, U.S.S.R. 136 e8
Telocaset, Oreg. 80 D3
Telogia, Fla. 65 E2
Telok Anson, Malay., 37,040 148 B2
Teloloapan, Mex., 7,297 93 E4
Telom, r., Malay. 147 o14
Telos L., Me. 55 C2
Telpaneca, Nic. 94 D4
Telsen, Arg. 105 B6
Telšiai, U.S.S.R., 16,000 136 A1
Teltow, Ger.D.R., 11,304 118 D2
Teluk Bajur, Indon. 148 A3
Telukbajur, Indon. 148 F2
Telukbatang, Indon. 148 D3
Telukbetung, Indon. 148 C4
Telukbutun, Indon. 148 C1
Telukdalam, Indon. 148 A2
Teluklandjut, Indon. 148 B2
Telukmerbau, Indon. 147 o15
Teluknjirih, Indon. 148 B2
Tema, Ghana, 14,341 162 E5
Témacine, Alg. 160 E2
Temalacacingo, Mex., 2,885 93 F5
Temangan, Malay., 2,298 147 p14
Temanggung, Indon. 148 d7
Temanu, Mt., Bora-Bora 177 43
Temassinine = Fort Flatters
Tematangi, i., Tuam. Arch. 171 J6
Tembeling, r., Malay. 147 p14
Tembenchi, r., U.S.S.R. 135 J3
Temblador, Ven., 2,035 101 J3
Temblor Ra., Calif. 82 C5
Tembok, Indon. 148 f8
Teme, r., U.K. 114 D6
Temecula, Calif. 83 k16
Temengor, Malay. 147 o14
Temerin, Yug., 11,621 125 D2
Temerloh, Malay., 12,278 148 B2
Teminabuan, Indon. 149 J3
Temir, U.S.S.R., 3,700 134 E5
Temir-Tau, Kaz.S.S.R., U.S.S.R., 113,000 134 G4
Temir-Tau, R.S.F.S.R., U.S.S.R., 15,200 134 H4
Témiscouata, L., Qué., Can. 47 R10
Témiskaming, Qué., Can., 2,501 44 H6
Temixco, Mex., 4,025 93 e11
Temkino, U.S.S.R. 136 D2
Temnikov, U.S.S.R., 6,100 136 F2
Temoac, Mex., 1,705 93 f11
Temoe, Tuam. Arch. 177 42
Temora, Austl., 4,567 173 G5
Temósachic, Mex., 1,164 92 D2
Te Mot Noi = Lord Howe I.
Te Motu, i., Sta. Cruz Is. 175 6
Tempe, Ariz., 24,897 78 C5
Temperance, Ga. 64 F4
Temperance, Mich., 2,215 67 K7
Temperanceville, Va. 62 J5
Tempino, Indon. 148 B3
Tempio Pausania, It., 17,284 123 B4
Tempisque, r., C.R. 94 E5
Tempiute, Nev. 83 C4
Templanza, Phil., 2,462 153 f11
Temple, Me. 55 B4
Temple, Mich. 67 H4
Temple, N.H. 54 D6
Temple, N. Dak. 74 A1
Temple, Okla., 1,282 76 E3
Temple, Pa., 1,633 61 L5
Temple, Tex., 30,419 77 P4
Temple Bay, Austl. 173 F1
Temple City, Calif., 31,838 83 h15
Templemore, Ire., 1,934 113 B5
Temple Mtn., Utah 78 C2
Temple Terrace, Fla., 3,812 65 G4
Templeton, Calif. 82 C5
Templeton, Iowa, 354 72 B3
Templeton, Mass., 5,371(T) 56 H2
Templeton, Pa. 60 D4
Templeuve, Belg., 3,461 115 B4
Templeuve, Fr., 3,879 116 a6
Templin, Ger.D.R., 11,558 118 D2
Templiner See, Ger.D.R. 119 e11
Tempoal, r., Mex. 93 f8
Temryuk, U.S.S.R., 22,300 136 E4
Temse, Belg., 14,165 115 d8
Temska, Yug., 2,224 125 F3
Temuco, Chile, 72,132 105 A5
Temuka, N.Z., 2,431 175 f7
Temvik, N. Dak. 74 B2
Ten, Col. 100 D5
Tena, Col. 101 e15
Tena, Ec., 1,010 104 B2
Tenabó, Mex., 2,739 93 H4
Ténado, Upper Volta, 2,885 162 D3
Tenafly, N.J., 14,264 58 d13
Tenaha, Tex., 1,097 77 Q4
Tenakee Springs, Alaska, 60 85 L4
Tenali, India, 78,525 145 F6
Te Namu, N.Z. 175 g6
Tenancingo, El Salv., 1,483 94 e10
Tenancingo, Mex., 14,769 93 E4
Tenango, Mex., 7,536 93 F4
Tenant Mtn., N.Y. 59 M5
Tenants Harbor, Me. 55 C5
Tenasserim, Burma, 1,194 146 B4
Ten Brook, Mo. 72 a12
Tenbury, U.K., 1,918 113 E5
Tenby, U.K., 4,752 113 D6
Tence, Fr., 3,000 117 F4
Tenczynek, Pol. 127 i6
Tenda, China 144 f11
Tende, Fr., 2,071 117 G4
Ten Degree Chan., India 146 A5
Tenderovskaya K., U.S.S.R. 136 C4
Tendō, Jap., 32,909 155 G2
Tendoy, Idaho 81 C3
Ténenkou, Mali, 3,200 162 D3
Ténéré, reg., Niger 162 F2
Tenerife, i., Can. Is. 109 4
Ténès, Alg., 8,386 160 E1
Ténès, C., Alg. 160 b5
Tenevo, Bulg., 3,339 128 F3
Tenexpa, Mex., 2,525 93 E5
Teng, r., Burma 146 B2
Tengeru, Tanz. 165 h15
Teng-feng, China 151 B4
Te Nggano, l., Sol. Is. 175 c3
Tenggarong, Indon. 148 F3
Tenghilan, Malay. 148 E1
Teng-hsien, China 151 A4
T'eng-hsien, K-hsi, China 152 C3
T'eng-hsien, Shant., China 150 F3
Tengiz, Oz., U.S.S.R. 134 F4
Teng-k'o, China 150 D3
Téniet-El-Haâd, Alg., 9,591 160 E2
Tenino, Wash., 836 80 B2
Tenjin, Jap. 154 g15
Tenjo, Col. 101 e15
Tenke, D.R.Congo 164 D3
Tenkiller Ferry Res., Okla. 76 J2
Tenkodogo, Upper Volta, 5,852 162 E4
Tenmile, Oreg. 80 B4
Tenmile Cr., Pa. 60 B5
Ten Mile L., Minn. 74 E2
Tennant, Calif. 82 C2
Tennant Creek, Austl. 172 E2
Tennent, N.J. 58 b15
Tennessee, st., U.S., 3,850,000* 71
Tennessee, Ill., 206 68 B3
Tennessee, r., U.S. 53 J3
Tennessee City, Tenn. 71 D5
Tennessee Pass, Colo. 79 •
Tennessee Ridge, Tenn., 324 71 D5
Tennille, Ga., 1,837 64 G3
Tennyson, Ind., 312 70 B4
Tennyson, Tex. 77 N4
Tennyson, Wis., 314 66 C6
Teno, Chile, 2,501 104 f14
Teno, r., Chile 104 g14
Tenojoki, r., Fin. 120 F1
Tenos, Pte., Mart. 97 12
Tenosique, Mex., 6,423 93 H5
Tenri, Jap., 53,131 155 D4
Tenryū, r., Jap. 155 E4
Tensas, parish, La., 11,796 73 D5
Tensas, r., La. 73 D5
Tensaw, r., Ala. 64 B5
Tensed, Idaho, 184 81 A2
Tensift, r., Mor. 160 C2
Ten Sleep, Wyo., 314 81 F3
Tenstrike, Minn., 147 74 E2
Tenterden, U.K., 4,948 113 G6
Tenterfield, Austl., 3,268 173 H4
Ten Thousand Is., Fla. 65 H7
Tentolomatinan, G., Indon. 149 G2
Teocaltiche, Mex., 11,066 92 E4
Teocuitatlán, Mex., 3,999 93 a9
Teófilo Otoni, Braz., 41,013 103 H5
Teopisca, Mex., 3,646 93 G5
Teorama, Col. 100 D3
Teotepec, Co., Mex. 93 E5
Teotepeque, El Salv., 1,146 94 d10
Teotihuacán, ruins, Mex. 93 e10
Teotitlán, Mex., 2,897 93 F4
Tepa, Indon. 149 J4
Tepache, Mex., 1,059 92 C2
Tepako, Pte., Is. Wallis 175 7
Tepalcatepec, r., Mex. 92 E4
Tepalcingo, Mex., 3,665 93 f11
Te-pao, China 152 B3
Tepatepec, Mex., 5,199 93 e9
Tepatitlán, Mex., 19,609 92 E4
Tepeapulco, Mex., 3,076 93 f10
Tepechitlán, Mex., 2,589 92 E4
Tepee Buttes, N. Dak. 74 A2
Tepee Cr., Okla. 76 B1
Tepehuanes, Mex., 1,835 92 D3
Tepeji del Río, Mex., 9,245 93 F4
Tepelenë, Alb., 2,150 125 E4
Tepenené, Mex., 1,332 93 f9
Tepetitla, Mex., 2,859 93 f10
Tepetzintla, Mex., 1,488 93 f8
Tepeyahualco, Mex., 1,159 93 f10
Tepic, Mex., 53,995 92 D4
Te-p'ing, China 151 C3
Teplá, Czech. 126 b7
Téplaya Gora, U.S.S.R., 7,200 137 i7
Teplice, Czech., 44,136 126 A1
Teplice nad Metují, Czech. 127 f6
Tepoca, C., Mex. 92 B2
Tepoto, i., Tuam. Arch. 177 42
Tepotzotlán, Mex., 2,648 93 e10
Tepoztlán, Mex., 4,314 93 e11
Te Puke, N.Z., 2,298 175 h5
Tepungan, Guam 176 24
Tepus, Indon. 148 d8
Tepuxtepec, Presa, res., Mex. 93 d9
Tequendama, Salto de, Col. 100 C5
Tequexquipan, Mex., 2,881 93 e10
Tequila, Mex., 7,381 92 E4
Tequisquiapan, Mex., 2,043 93 e9
Ter, r., Sp. 122 G1
Téra, Niger, 5,835 162 E3
Ter Aar, Neth. 115 b6
Terada, Jap. 154 g15
Teradai, Jap. 155 n20
Teradomari, Jap., 12,181 155 F3
Te Raki Pt., N.Z. 175 14
Teramo, It., 42,761 123 D3
Terán, Mex., 3,305 93 G5
Terang, Austl., 2,365 173 d12
Terao, Jap. 154 g14
Ter Apel, Neth., 7,500 115 E2
Terceira, i., Azores 108 2
Terebovlya, U.S.S.R., 6,300 136 B3
Teregova, Rum. 128 D2
Terehe, Tahiti 177 44
Terek, U.S.S.R., 6,500 137 c1
Terek, r., U.S.S.R. 134 D5
Terekli-Mekteb, U.S.S.R. 137 c1
Terence Bay, N.S., Can., 1,055 47 U11
Terenos, Braz., 1,257 103 E6
Teresina, Braz., 100,006 103 H3
Teresita, Col. 110 F7
Teresita, Okla. 76 J1
Teresópolis, Braz., 29,540 103 e18
Terespol, Pol., 3,995 127 E2
Teressa I., India 146 A5
Terevaka, Co., Easter I. 177 46
Terezín, Czech. 126 d6
Tergnier, Fr., 5,868 117 E2
Terheijden, Neth. 115 b7
Terinam Tsho, China 150 B4
Terisakkan, r., U.S.S.R. 137 m12
Terlingua, Tex. 77 M5
Terlingua Cr., Tex. 77 M5
Terlizzi, It., 22,280 123 F4
Terlton, Okla., 90 76 G1
Termas de Catillo, Chile 104 f16
Termas de Chillán, Chile 104 f16
Termas de Mamiña, Chile 105 B2
Terme, Turk., 6,998 142 D1
Termeil, Austl. 173 h10
Termen, Switz. 124 C2
Termet, Niger 162 F3
Termez, Afghan. 144 C1
Termez, U.S.S.R., 27,000 134 F6
Termination I., Austl. 172 B5
Termini Imerese, It., 25,784 123 D6
Términos, Lag. de, Mex. 93 H4
Termo, Calif. 82 C2
Termoli, It., 11,213 123 E4
Ternate, Indon. 149 H2
Ternate, Phil., 2,807 153 b8
Ternay, Fr., 1,470 116 p15
Ternberg, Aust., 2,815 124 L6
Terndrup, Den. 121 C4
Terneuzen, Neth., 12,000 115 B3
Terney, U.S.S.R. 135 N5
Terni, It., 94,825 123 D3
Ternitz, Aust., 9,043 124 M6
Ternopol', U.S.S.R., 56,000 134 B5
Terowie, Austl. 172 c7
Terpeniya, M., U.S.S.R. 135 O5
Terpeniya, Zaliv, U.S.S.R. 133 O5
Terra Alta, W. Va., 1,504 62 E3
Terra Bella, Calif. 82 D5
Terrace, Br. Col., Can., 4,682 42 E2
Terrace Bay, Ont., Can., 1,901 44 E5
Terra Ceia, Fla. 65 c12
Terra Ceia, N.C. 63 H2
Terrace Mts., Utah 78 B1
Terracina, It., 29,190 123 D4
Terra Cotta, Ont., Can. 46 c13
Terra Cotta, Ill. 69 a7
Terral, Okla., 585 76 F4
Terralba, It., 9,075 123 B5
Terra Nova, Newf., Can. 45 Q5
Terrasson, Fr., 4,148 117 D4
Terrebonne, Qué., Can., 6,167 47 o17
Terrebonne, parish, La., 60,771 73 D8
Terrebonne, Oreg. 80 C3
Terrebonne Bay, La. 73 E8
Terre d'en Bas, i., Guad. 97 14
Terre d'en Haut, i., Guad. 97 14
Terre Haute, Ind., 72,500 70 B3
Terre Hill, Pa., 1,129 61 K5
Terrell, co., Ga., 12,742 64 E4
Terrell, Tenn. 71 B5
Terrell, co., Tex., 2,600 77 M4
Terrell, Tex., 13,803 77 P3
Terrell Hills, Tex., 5,572 76 b7
Terrenate, Mex., 1,175 93 f10
Terrenceville, Newf., Can. 45 Q6
Terrero Blanco, Hond. 94 E3
Terres Basses, Pén. des, St-Martin 97 7
Terrigal, Austl., 1,105 173 h9
Terril, Iowa, 382 72 C1
Terrington St. Clement, U.K., 3,038 114 J5
Terrugem, Port., 2,694 122 i10
Terry, La. 73 D5
Terry, Miss., 585 73 E5
Terry, Mont., 1,140 81 G2
Terry, co., Tex., 16,286 77 M3
Terryville, Conn., 5,231 56 D6
Terryville, N.Y. 58 g13
Tersa, r., U.S.S.R. 136 F3
Terschelling, i., Neth. 115 D1
Terskey-Alatau, Khr., U.S.S.R. 132 G5
Teruel, Sp., 19,726 122 E2
Tervel, Bulg., 4,682 128 F3
Tervola, Fin. 120 F2
Teryayevo, U.S.S.R. 136 b5
Tescott, Kans., 396 75 H4
Tesha, r., U.S.S.R. 136 G2
Teshekpuk L., Alaska 85 F1
Teshikaga, Jap., 12,961 155 L8
Teshima, Jap. 154 e15
Teshio, Jap., 10,019 155 J7
Teshio, r., Jap. 155 K7
Teshio-dake, Jap. 155 K7
Teshio-sammyaku, Jap. 155 J7
Tesiin = Tes-Khem
Tesiin, r., Mong-U.S.S.R. 150 D1
Tesissat Falls, Eth. 163 L3
Tesistán, Mex., 1,633 93 a9
Tes-Khem = Tesiin
Tes-Khem, r., Mong.-U.S.S.R. 135 J4
Teslić, Yug., 3,190 125 C2
Teslin, Yukon, Can. 40 C5
Teslin, r., Yukon, Can. 38 C5
Teslin L., Br. Col.-Yukon, Can. 42 C1
Tesouro, Braz., 1,239 103 F5
Tësovo-Netyl'skiy, U.S.S.R., 8,100 136 C1
Tespe, F.R.Ger., 1,018 119 b9
Tessalit, Mali 162 E2
Tessaoua, Niger, 5,882 162 F3
Tess Corners, Wis. 66 c12
Tessenderlo, Belg., 9,242 115 C3
Tessenei, Eth. 163 L3
Tesserete, Switz. 124 C2
Tessin, Ger.D.R. 118 D1
Test, r., U.K. 113 k13
Testa, Capo, It. 123 B4
Tesuque, N. Mex. 79 C4
Tét, Hung., 4,877 126 C3
Têt, r., Fr. 117 E5
Tetbury, U.K., 3,117 114 D7
Tete, Moz., 38,183 164 E4
Tête Jaune Cache, Br. Col., Can. 42 G3
Teterev, r., U.S.S.R. 136 C3
Teteringen, Neth. 115 b7
Teterow, Ger.D.R., 11,125 118 D2
Teterville, Kans. 75 J5
Teteven, Bulg., 7,995 128 E3
Tetiaroa, atoll, Soc. Is. 177 42
Tetipari, i., Sol. Is. 175 b2
Tetlán, Mex., 1,111 93 a9
Tetlin, Alaska, 122 85 J3
Tetlin L., Alaska 85 J3
Teton, co., Idaho, 2,639 81 D4
Teton, Idaho, 399 81 D4
Teton, co., Mont., 7,295 81 C2
Teton, co., Wyo., 3,062 81 D4
Tetonia, Idaho, 194 81 D4
Teton Ra., Idaho-Wyo. 81 •
Tetouan, Mor., 101,352 160 D2
Tetovo, Bulg., 4,341 128 F3
Tetovo, Yug., 25,000* 125 E3
Tetyukhe, U.S.S.R., 23,000 135 N5
Teuchern, Ger.D.R. 126 b5
Teuco, r., Arg. 105 C2
Teufen, Switz., 5,110 124 D1
Teufenthal, Switz., 1,350 124 B1
Teul, Mex., 1,616 92 E4
Teulada, It., 6,070 123 B5
Teulada, Capo, It. 123 B5
Teulon, Man., Can. 43 F5
Teun, P., Indon. 149 J4
Teupitz, Ger.D.R. 118 D2
Teuri-tō, Jap. 155 J7
Teustepe, Nic. 94 E4
Teutoburger Wald, F.R.Ger. 118 B2
Teutopolis, Ill., 1,140 68 D4
Teuvâ, Fin. 120 E3
Te Vaakauta, pk., Rarotonga 177 34
Tevai, i., Sta. Cruz Is. 175 6
Tevere, r., It. 123 D3
Teveren, F.R.Ger., 2,253 119 A3
Tevriz, U.S.S.R. 134 G4
Te Waewae Bay, N.Z. 175 e7
Tewah, Indon. 148 E3
Te Whanga Lagoon, N.Z. 175 14
Tewkesbury, U.K., 5,822 113 E6
Tewksbury, Mass., 1,151; 15,902(T) 57 M2
Te-wu-lu, China 150 D3
Texada I., Br. Col., Can. 42 b6
Texanna, Okla. 76 H2
Texarkana, Ark.-Tex., 50,006 73 A4
Texarkana, L., Tex. 77 Q3
Texas, Austl. 173 G4
Texas, st., U.S., 10,591,000* 76-7
Texas, co., Mo., 17,758 72 E7
Texas, N.Y. 59 H4
Texas, co., Okla., 14,162 76 B1
Texas City, Tex., 32,065 77 Q5
Texas Creek, Colo. 79 C2
Texcaltitlán, Mex., 3,404 93 e11
Texcoco, Mex., 10,935 93 F4
Texcoco, L. de, Mex. 93 f10
Texel, i., Neth. 115 C1
Texhoma City, Tex. 77 O3
Texico, N. Mex., 889 79 D4
Texistepeque, El Salv., 1,337 94 d9
Texline, Tex., 430 76 M1
Texmelucan, Mex., 15,378 93 f10
Texola, Okla., 202 76 D2
Texoma, Okla.-Tex., 1,261 76 N1
Texoma, L., Okla.-Tex. 77 P3
Texon, Tex. 77 N4
Te-yang, China 152 B1
Teykovo, U.S.S.R., 28,000 136 F1
Teziutlán, Mex., 17,384 93 F4
Tezontepec, Mex., 6,900 93 e9
Tezontepec, Mex. 93 f10
Tezpur, India, 24,159 145 J4
Tha, r., Laos 146 C2
Tha-Anne, r., N.W.T., Can. 40 K5
Thabaung, Burma 147 a2
Thabazimbi, S. Af., 5,597 164 D6
Thabeikkyin, Burma 147 g6
Tha Bo, Thai. 146 C3
Tha Chang, Thai. 147 d4
Tha Chin, r., Thai. 147 d4
Thackerville, Okla., 185 76 F4
Thac Nham, N. Viet. 147 i8
Tha Deua, Laos 146 C3
Thagala, Burma, 4,095 147 b2
Thagchhab Gangri, China 150 B3
Thai Binh, N. Viet., 14,739 146 D2
Thai Binh, r., N. Viet. 147 i9
Thailand, ctry., 30,591,000* 146 C4
Thailand, G. of = Siam, G. of
Thai Nguyen, N. Viet., 21,846 146 D2
Thakhek, Laos 146 D3
Thākurgaon, Pak., 7,039 144 g12
Thal, Pak., 11,747 145 D2
Thalabarivat, Camb. 146 D4
Thalang, Thai. 146 B5
Thaleischweiler, F.R.Ger., 2,725 119 D6
Thalfang, F.R.Ger., 1,057 119 B5
Thalgau, Aust., 2,856 124 K6
Tha Li, Thai. 146 C3
Thalia, Tex. 77 O3
Thallon, Austl. 173 G4
Thalmann, Ga. 64 H4
Tha Mai, Thai., 5,688 146 C4
Tha Maka, Thai. 147 c5
Thame, U.K., 4,207 114 G7
Thame, r., U.K. 114 F7
Thames, N.Z., 5,315 175 g5
Thames, r., Ont., Can. 46 B6
Thames, r., U.K. 113 G6
Thames, r., Conn. 56 H7
Thamesford, Ont., Can. 46 C5
Thamesville, Ont., Can., 1,030 46 C6
Tha Muang, Thai. 146 B5
Tha Muang, Thai. 147 c5
Thana, India, 101,107 145 D6
Thanatpin, Burma, 6,805 147 b2
Thanesar, India, 16,828 144 a10
Thanglango, pass, China 150 C3
Thanglha Ri, mts., China 150 C3
Thanh Binh, S. Viet., 1,936 147 k11
Thanh Hoa, N. Viet., 31,211 146 D3
Thanh Phu, S. Viet., 1,697 147 m12
Thanh Thuy, N. Viet. 146 D2
Thanh Tri, S. Viet., 6,000* 146 D5
Thanjavur, India, 111,099 145 F8
Thankerton, U.K. 112 c8
Thann, Fr., 7,736 117 G3
Thanyaburi, Thai. 147 d4
Thaon-les-Vosges, Fr., 8,312 117 G2
Tha Pla, Thai. 146 C3
Thap Put, Thai. 146 B5
Thap Sakae, Thai. 146 B5
Thap Than, Thai. 147 c4
Tharad, India, 7,566 145 D4
Tharandt, Ger.D.R. 126 c6
Thar Des. = Great Indian Des.
Thargomindah, Austl. 173 F4
Tharrawaddy, Burma, 8,977 147 a2
Tharrawaw, Burma, 3,753 147 a2
Tharthār, Wādī ath, Iraq 143 C1
Tha Rua, Thai., 5,189 147 d4
Tha Sae, Thai. 146 B5
Tha Sala, Thai. 146 C5
Tha Song Yang, Thai. 146 B3
Tha Song Yang, Thai. 147 b2
Thásos, Gr., 1,875 129 E4
Thásos, i., Gr. 129 E4
Tha Tako, Thai. 147 d4
Thatcham, U.K., 7,483 114 F8
Thatcher, Ariz., 1,581 78 D5
Thatcher, Colo. 79 C3
Thatcher, Idaho 81 D4
Thatcher, Utah 78 b7
That Khe, N. Viet. 146 D2
Thaton, Burma, 38,047 146 B3
Tha Tum, Thai. 146 C4
Thaungdut, Burma 146 A1
Thaungyin, r., Burma 146 B3
Tha Uthen, Thai. 146 D3
Tha Wung, Thai. 147 d4
Thawville, Ill., 246 68 D3
Thaxted, U.K., 1,905 114 J7
Thaxton, Miss. 73 F3
Thaxton, Va. 62 E5
Tha Yang, Thai. 147 c5
Thayawe, Burma 147 a2
Thayer, Ill., 649 68 C4
Thayer, Ind. 70 B1
Thayer, Iowa, 101 72 D3
Thayer, Kans., 396 75 K6
Thayer, Mo., 1,713 72 F8
Thayer, co., Nebr., 9,118 75 H3
Thayer, Nebr., 78 75 H3
Thayetchaung, Burma 146 B4
Thayetmyo, Burma, 11,649 146 A3
Thayetta, Burma 146 B1
Thayne, Wyo., 214 81 D4
Thazi, Burma, 7,552 146 B2
Theale, U.K., 1,638 114 F8
Theba, Ariz. 78 B5
Thebes, Gr. = Thívai
Thebes, Ark. 73 D4
Thebes, Ill., 471 68 C6
Thebes, ruins, U.A.R. 161 K3
The Bluff, Bah. Is. 95 c7
The Cheviot, mtn., U.K. 112 E4
The Coorong, lagoon, Aust. 172 c8
The Coteau, hills, Sask., Can. 43 C4
The Dalles, Oreg., 10,493 80 C3
Thedaw, Burma, 3,080 147 g7
The Deeps, U.K. 112 F1
Thedford, Ont., Can. 46 B5
Thedford, Nebr., 303 75 E2
The Dome, mtn., Vt. 54 A6
The Everglades, Fla. 65 J6
The Father, pk. Terr. New Guin. 174 F2
The Flatts Village, Berm. Is. 108 1
The Forks, Colo. 79 C1
The Forks, Me. 55 C3
The Gap, Ariz. 78 C3
Thegon, Burma, 1,505 146 A3
The Grove, Tex. 77 P4
The Hague = 's Gravenhage
Thelma, Alta., Can. 42 L4
Thelon, r., N.W.T., Can. 40 J5
Them, Den., 3,426 121 B4
Théméricourt, Fr. 116 f10
The Mumbles (part of Swansea), U.K., 11,983 113 D6
The Narrows, chan., St. Christopher-Nevis 97 6
The Narrows, str., N.Y. 58 c14
The Naze, Nor. = Lindesnes
The Naze, promontory, U.K. 113 G6
Thendara, N.Y. 59 K4
Thenneberg, Aust. 124 b11
The North Sd., U.K. 112 E2
Theodore, Austl. 173 G3
Theodore, Sask., Can. 43 D4
Theodore, Ala. 64 A5
Theodore Roosevelt L., Ariz. 78 C5
Theodore Roosevelt Nat. Mem. Pk., N. Dak. 74 A2
Theodosia Arm, Br. Col., Can. 42 b5
Theollogo, Alb. 125 E4
Théoule-sur-Mer, Fr. 116 m14
The Pas, Man., Can., 4,521 43 E4
The Peak = Kinder Scout
Thepha, Thai. 146 C6
The Pillories, is., Gren. Is. 97 20
The Plains, Ohio, 1,148 70 G3
The Plains, Va., 484 62 G4
The Race, str., Conn.-N.Y. 56 H8
Thérain, r., Fr. 117 D2
Theresa, N.Y., 956 59 J3
Theresa, Wis., 576 66 E5
Theriot, La. 73 E8
Thermaïkós Kólpos, Gr. 129 D4
Thermal, Calif. 82 E6
Thérmi, Gr., 1,750 129 D4
Thermí, Gr., 1,110 129 F5
Thérmon, Gr., 2,109 129 C5
Thermopílai, pass, Gr. 129 D5
Thermopolis, Wyo., 3,955 81 E4
Thermopylae = Thermopílai
The Rock, Austl. 173 f10
Théroaune, r., Fr. 116 k10
Thesiger B., N.W.T., Can. 40 D3
The Sisters, is., Gren. Is. 97 20
The Sisters, is., N.Z. 175 14
The Sisters, is., Seych. 165 a10
The Skaw = Grenen
The Slot, sd., Sol. Is. 170 E5
The Snares, is., N.Z. 170 F8
The Solent, chan., U.K. 113 k13
The Sound, Den.-Swed. 121 E5
Thesprotikón, Gr., 2,126 129 C5
Thessalía, reg., Gr. 129 D5
Thessalon, Ont., Can., 1,751 44 G6
Thessalon, r., Ont., Can. 46 A2
Thessaloníki, Gr., 250,920 129 D4
Thessaly = Thessalía
The Storr, mtn., U.K. 112 C3
Theta, Tenn. 71 D6
Thetford, U.K., 5,399 113 G5
Thetford Center, Vt. 54 C4
Thetford Mines, Qué., Can., 21,314 45 L6
The Triangle, reg., Burma 146 B1
The Twelve Pins, mtn.ra., Ire., 113 B5
The Twins, mtn., Austl. 173 f11
The Two Rivers, Sask., Can. 43 D3
Theun, r., Laos 146 D3
Theup, S. Viet. 147 n11
Theux, Belg., 5,384 115 D4
The Village, Okla., 12,118 76 F2
The Wash, estuary, U.K. 113 G5
Thiais, Fr., 15,360 116 h11
Thiamis, r., Gr. 129 C5
Thiaucourt, Fr., 1,158 116 b9
Thibodaux, La., 13,403 73 E8
Thicket Portage, Man., Can. 43 F3
Thief, r., Minn. 74 D1
Thief L., Minn. 74 E1
Thief River Falls, Minn., 7,151 74 D1
Thielsen, Mt., Oreg. 80 C4
Thiensville, Wis., 2,507 66 d11
Thiers, Fr., 17,442 117 E4
Thiès, Sen., 61,000 162 B3
Thieux, Fr. 116 i10
Thika, Kenya 164 F2
Thikombia, i., Fiji 174 4
Thil, Fr., 3,210 116 b8
Thimbu, Bhutan 145 H4
Thingangyun, Burma, 17,761 147 b2
Thingeyri, Ice. 120 a6
Thio, N. Caled., 1,776 174 k8
Thionville, Fr., 33,669 117 G2
Thíra, Gr., 1,481 129 E6
Thíra, i., Gr. 129 E6
Thirasía, i., Gr. 129 E6
Third Cataract, Sudan 163 J2
Thirlestane, U.K. 112 e8
Thirsk, U.K., 2,856 113 F4
Thisted, Den., 8,768 121 A4
Thistle, Utah 78 C1
Thistle Creek, Yukon, Can. 40 B5
Thistle Cr., Utah 78 c11
Thistle I., Austl. 172 b8
Thistletown, Ont., Can., 1,496 46 c13
Thíthia, i., Fiji 174 4
Thívai, Gr., 15,779 129 D5
Thiverval-Grignon, Fr. 116 f11
Thiviers, Fr., 3,781 117 D4
Thjórsa, r., Ice. 120 a6
Thlewiaza, r., N.W.T., Can. 40 K5
Thoai Huong, S. Viet. 147 m11
Thoen, Thai. 146 B3
Thoeng, Thai. 146 B3

Thoi Binh—Tocantinópolis · 303

Thoi Binh, S. Viet., 1,110 147 k12
Thoiry, Fr. 116 f11
Thoissey, Fr., 1,210 117 F3
Thok Jalung=Cha-lun
Tholen, Neth. 115 C3
Tholen, i., Neth. 115 C3
Tholey, F.R.Ger., 1,651 116 d8
Thomas, co., Ga., 34,319 64 F5
Thomas, co., Kans., 7,358 75 D4
Thomas, co., Nebr., 1,078 75 E2
Thomas, Okla., 1,211 76 E2
Thomas, Pa. 60 b9
Thomas, W. Va., 830 62 E3
Thomas, L., Tex. 77 N3
Thomasboro, Ill., 458 68 D3
Thomasburg, F.R.Ger. 119 c9
Thomaston, Ala., 857 64 B3
Thomaston, Conn., 3,579; 5,850(T) 56 D6
Thomaston, Ga., 9,336 64 E3
Thomaston, Me., 2,342 55 C4
Thomaston, Mich. 66 D2
Thomaston, N.Y., 2,767 58 d13
Thomaston, Tex. 77 P5
Thomastown, Ire. 113 C5
Thomastown, Miss. 73 F5
Thomasville, Ala., 3,182 64 B4
Thomasville, Colo. 79 B2
Thomasville, Ga., 18,246 64 F5
Thomasville, N.C., 15,190 63 D2
Thom Bay, N.W.T., Can. 40 L3
Thommen, Belg., 2,237 119 A4
Thompson, Man., Can. 43 F3
Thompson, Conn., 6,217(T) 56 J5
Thompson, Iowa, 689 72 D1
Thompson, Delta Co., Mich. 66 F2
Thompson, Schoolcraft Co., Mich. 67 G3
Thompson, N. Dak., 211 74 D2
Thompson, Pa., 286 61 L2
Thompson, Utah 78 D2
Thompson, Wis. 66 c10
Thompson, L., S. Dak. 74 D3
Thompson, r., Br. Col., Can. 42 G4
Thompson, r., Iowa 72 C3
Thompson Falls, Mont., 1,274 81 B2
Thompson L., Me. 55 B4
Thompson Landing, N.W.T., Can. 40 G5
Thompson Pk., Calif. 82 B2
Thompsons, Tex. 77 h10
Thompsontown, Pa., 713 60 H4
Thompsonville (part of Enfield), Conn. 56 F4
Thompsonville, Ill., 428 68 D6
Thompsonville, Mich., 243 67 G4
Thompsonville, Tex. 77 O6
Thomson, Ga., 4,522 64 G2
Thomson, Ill., 543 68 B2
Thomson, N.Y. 59 N5
Thomson, r., Austl. 173 F3
Thomsons Falls, Kenya 165 h13
Thon Buri, Thai., 403,818 146 C4
Thônes, Fr., 3,008 117 G4
Thongwa, Burma, 10,829 146 B3
Thonon, Fr., 18,501 117 G3
Thonotosassa, Fla. 65 d11
Thonze, Burma, 14,443 146 B3
Thor, Iowa, 234 72 C2
Thorburn, N.S., Can., 1,000 47 U11
Thoreau, N. Mex. 79 A4
Thorhild, Alta., Can. 43 b6
Thorigny-sur-Marne, Fr., 3,727 116 i11
Thornaby-on-Tees, U.K., 22,793 112 h10
Thornapple, r., Mich. 67 H6
Thornapple, r., Wis. 66 C3
Thornburg, Ark. 73 C3
Thornbury, Ont., Can., 1,071 44 H7
Thornbury, U.K., 3,473 114 D7
Thorn Cr., Ill. 69 d10
Thorndale, Ont., Can. 46 C5
Thorndale, Pa. 60 e11
Thorndale, Tex., 995 77 F4
Thorndike, Me. 55 C4
Thorndike (part of Palmer), Mass. 56 G4
Thorne, U.K., 14,462 113 F5
Thorne, Nev. 83 A3
Thorne, N. Dak. 74 C1
Thorner, U.K., 1,099 114 F3
Thorney, U.K., 2,142 114 H5
Thornfield, Mo. 72 E8
Thornham, U.K. 114 J5
Thornhill, Man., Can. 43 f10
Thornhill, Ont., Can., 1,135 46 E5
Thornhill, Dumf., Scot., U.K. 113 E4
Thornhill, Perth, Scot., U.K. 112 b7
Thorn Hollow, Oreg. 80 D3
Thornhurst, Pa. 61 o17
Thornlea, Newf., Can. 45 b10
Thornley, U.K., 4,755 112 g10
Thornloe, Ont., Can. 44 H6
Thornton, U.K. 114 B3
Thornton, Ark., 658 73 C4
Thornton, Colo., 11,353 79 C2
Thornton, Ill., 2,895 69 d10
Thornton, Iowa, 449 72 D2
Thornton, Miss. 73 E4
Thornton, N.H. 54 D4
Thornton (part of Cranston), R.I. 57 K5
Thornton, Tex., 504 77 P4
Thornton, W. Va. 62 E3
Thornton, Wis. 66 E4
Thornton Dale, U.K., 1,199 114 G2
Thorntons Ferry, N.H. 54 D6
Thorntown, Ind., 1,486 70 C2
Thornville, Ohio, 521 70 G3
Thornwood, N.Y. 58 d12
Thorofare, N.J., 1,200* 60 f12
Thorold, Ont., Can., 8,560 46 E5
Thorp, Wash. 80 C2
Thorp, Wis., 1,496 66 C4
Thorpe L., N.C. 63 A2
Thorp Spring, Tex. 76 d10
Thørsager, Den., 1,282 121 C4
Thorsby, Alta., Can. 42 J3
Thorsby, Ala., 968 64 C3
Thórshöfn, Ice. 120 b6
Thorsminde, Den. 121 A4
Thorsø, Den. 121 B4
Thot Not, S. Viet., 2,550 147 k11
Thouars, Fr., 11,983 117 C3
Thouet, r., Fr. 117 C3
Thousand Is., Can.-U.S. 59 H3
Thousand Oaks, Calif., 2,934 82 D5
Thrace, reg., Gr. 129 E4
Thrall, Kans. 75 J5
Thrall, Tex., 631 77 P4
Thrapsanós, Gr., 1,466 129 E7
Thrapston, U.K., 1,994 114 G6
Thrasher, Miss. 73 G3
Three Bridges, N.J. 61 B2
Three Churches, W. Va. 62 F3
Three Creeks, Alta., Can. 42 J2
Three Creeks, Ark. 73 B4
Threeforks, Ky. 71 E5
Three Forks, Mont., 1,161 81 D3
Three Forks, W. Va. 62 D4
Three Hills, Alta., Can., 1,486 42 K3
Three Hummock I., Austl. 173 e13
Three Kings Is., N.Z. 175 g4
Three Lakes, Wis. 66 D3
Three Mile Bay, N.Y. 59 H3
Three Mile Plains, N.S., Can., 1,414 47 U11
Three Oaks, Mich., 1,763 67 G7
Three Pagodas Pass, Burma-Thai. 146 B4
Three Point, Calif. 82 D5
Three Points, C., Ghana 162 D5
Three Rivers, Calif. 82 D4
Three Rivers, Mass., 3,082 56 G4
Three Rivers, Mich., 7,092 67 H7
Three Rivers, N. Mex. 79 B5
Three Rivers, N.Y. 59 q23
Three Rivers, Tex., 1,932 77 O5
Three Springs, Austl. 172 A4
Three Springs, Pa., 475 60 G5
Thrift, N.C. 63 D2
Throat, r., Ont., Can. 44 C4
Throckmorton, co., Tex., 2,767 77 O3
Throckmorton, Tex., 1,299 77 O3
Throop, Pa., 4,732 61 L3
Throopsville, N.Y. 59 p24
Throssell, L., Austl. 172 C4
Thu Duc, S. Viet., 16,626 147 m11
Thueyts, Fr., 1,017 117 F4
Thuiller, Mt., India 146 A6
Thuin, Belg., 5,783 115 C4
Thuir, Fr., 3,717 117 E5
Thule, Mt., N.W.T., Can. 39 O3
Thum, Ger.D.R. 126 b6
Thumbs, The, pk., N.Z. 175 f6
Thumeries, Fr., 3,553 116 a7
Thun, Switz., 29,034 124 B2
Thunder Bay, Mich. 67 K4
Thunder Bay, r., Mich. 67 K3
Thunderbolt, Ga., 1,925 64 J3
Thunder Butte, S. Dak. 74 B3
Thunder Butte, S. Dak. 74 B3
Thunder Butte Cr., S. Dak. 74 A3
Thunder Hawk, S. Dak. 74 B3
Thunder L., Wis. 66 D3
Thunersee, Switz. 124 B2
Thüngersheim, F.R.Ger., 2,199 199 H5
Thung Song, Thai., 10,286 146 B5
Thunkar, Bhutan 145 J4
Thuong, r., N. Viet. 147 i8
Thur, r., Switz. 124 D1
Thüringen, reg., Ger.D.R. 118 C3
Thüringer Wald, Ger.D.R. 118 C3
Thurins, Fr., 1,537 116 p15
Thurlby, U.K. 114 H5
Thurles, Ire., 6,573 113 B5
Thurlow Dam, Ala. 64 D3
Thurlstone, U.K., 1,862 114 E3
Thurman, Colo. 79 D2
Thurman, Iowa, 268 72 B4
Thurman, N.Y. 59 M4
Thurmont, Md., 1,998 62 G3
Thurø By, Den. 121 C5
Thurrock, U.K., 114,263 113 G6
Thursby, U.K. 113 E4
Thursday I., Pac. Oc. 173 F1
Thurso, Qué., Can., 3,306 47 J3
Thurso, U.K., 8,038 112 E2
Thurso, r., U.K. 112 E2
Thurston, co., Nebr., 7,237 75 J1
Thurston, Nebr., 140 75 J1
Thurston, co., Wash., 55,049 80 B2
Thurston I., Ant. 180 Y5
Thusis, Switz., 1,998 124 D2
Thutade L., Br. Col., Can. 42 E2
Thu Thua, S. Viet., 2,936 147 m11
Thyra, Austl. 173 e10
Thyregod, Den., 2,068 121 B5
Thysville, D.R.Congo, 16,369 164 B2
Tiabaya, Peru, 3,056 104 C6
Tiahuanacu, Bol., 10,577 102 a10
Tiahura, i., Moorea 177 44
Tia Juana, Ven. 100 E2
Tia Juana, r., Calif. 82 c10
Tianguá, Braz., 4,228 103 H2
Tianguistengo, Mex., 1,169 93 f9
Tiara, Ven. 101 b11
Tiarei, Tahiti 177 44
Tiaret, Alg., 36,322 160 E2
Ti'avea, W. Samoa 177 38
Tiawah, Okla. 76 H1
Tibaji, r., Braz. 103 F6
Tibasti, Sarīr, des., Libya 161 G4
Tibati, Cam., 3,000* 162 G4
Tibbie, Ala. 64 A4
Tiber=Tevere
Tiberias, Isr., 20,792 142 b7
Tiberias, L.=Kinneret, Yam
Tiber Res., Mont. 81 D1
Tibesti, mts., Chad 163 G2
Tibet=Hsi-tsang Tzu-chih-ch'ü
Tibetan Autonomous Reg.=Hsi-tsang Tzu-chih-ch'ü
Tibnīn, Leb., 2,211 142 b6
Tibooburra, Austl. 173 F4
Tibrikot, Nepal 144 d11
Tibú, Col. 100 D3
Tiburon, Haiti, 1,468 96 i6
Tiburon, Calif. 83 e12
Tiburón, I., Mex. 92 B2
Ticaco, Peru, 1,205 104 D6
Ticao I., Phil. 153 B2
Ticao Pass, Phil. 153 h15
Tice, Fla., 4,377 65 H6
Tice, Kans. 75 E6
Ticha, Bulg., 1,178 128 F3
Tichá Orlice, r., Czech. 127 f6
Tichigan, Wis. 66 c12
Tichigan L., Wis. 66 c12
Tichitt, Maur., 1,000 162 C2
Tichla, Sp. Sah. 160 B4
Tichnor, Ark. 73 D3
Ticino, r., It.-Switz. 123 B2
Tickfaw, La., 317 73 E7
Tickhill, U.K., 2,584 114 F4
Tickle Bay, Newf., Can. 45 b10
Ticonderoga, N.Y., 3,568 59 O4
Ticul, Mex., 10,809 93 H4
Tidaholm, Swed. 120 C4
Tidal, Man., Can. 43 G2
Tiddim, Burma 146 A2
Tidehead, N.B., Can. 47 S10
Tidenham, U.K., 4,195 114 C7
Tideswell, U.K., 1,829 114 E4
Tidewater, Fla. 65 G3
Tidewater, Oreg. 80 B3
Tidikelt, Plaine du, Alg. 160 E3
Tidioute, Pa., 860 60 D2
Tidjikja, Maur., 5,907 162 C2
Tidore, P., Indon. 149 H2
Tidwell, Tex. 76 g8
Tiefencastel, Switz. 124 D2
Tieffenbach, Fr. 116 d9
T'ieh-kang, China 152 b5
T'ieh-li, China 151 F1
T'ieh-ling, China 151 E2
Tieh-mu-ch'o-k'o, China 150 A3
Tiel, Neth., 16,000 115 D3
Tielt, Belg., 13,227 115 B3
Tiempo, Phil., 1,276 153 b5
T'ien-chen, China 151 B2
T'ien-chi, China 151 D3
Tien Ch'ih, China 152 A2
T'ien-ching, China, 2,900,000* 150 F3
T'ien-chu, China 152 C2
T'ien-ch'üan, China 152 A1
T'ien-chuang-t'ai, China 151 D2
T'ien-chün, China 150 D3
Tienen, Belg., 22,685 115 C4
Tiengemeten, i., Neth. 115 a7
Tiengen, F.R.Ger., 6,537 118 B5
Tien Giang=Mekong
Tienhoven, Neth. 115 c6
T'ien-lin, China 152 B2
T'ien-men, China 150 F4
Tien Nong, N. Viet. 147 i9
T'ien-o, China 152 B2
T'ien-pai, China 152 C3
Tien Shan, China-U.S.S.R. 150 A2
T'ien-shui, China, 65,000* 150 E3
T'ien-t'ai, China 152 F1
T'ien-teng, China 152 B3
Tientsin=T'ien-ching
T'ien-tung, China 152 B3
T'ien-yang, China 152 B3
Tien Yen, N. Viet. 146 D2
Tie Plant, Miss., 1,491 73 F4
Tiercé, Fr., 1,968 117 C3
Tiernan, Oreg. 80 A3
Tierp, Swed. 120 D3
Tierra Amarilla, Chile, 1,830* 105 A3
Tierra Amarilla, N. Mex. 79 B3
Tierra Blanca, Mex., 16,474 93 F4
Tierrablanca, Mex. 93 d8
Tierra Colorada, Mex. 93 F5
Tierra del Fuego, I. Gde. de, Arg.-Chile 105 B8
Tierralta, Col. 100 C3
Tierranueva, Mex., 1,696 93 E4
Tieschen, Aust., 1,481 124 N7
Tiétar, r., Sp. 122 C2
Tietê, r., Braz. 103 G6
Tieton, Wash., 479 80 C2
Tieton, r., Wash. 80 C2
Tieu Can, S. Viet., 1,922 147 m12
Tifariti, Sp. Sah. 160 C3
Tiffany, Wis. 66 E6
Tiffin, Iowa, 311 72 F3
Tiffin, Ohio, 21,478 70 F1
Tiffin, r., Ohio 70 E1
Tiflis=Tbilisi
Tifore, P., Indon. 149 H2
Tift, co., Ga., 23,487 64 F4
Tifton, Ga., 9,903 64 F4
Tiga, I., Loy. Is. 174 k8
Ţigăneşti, Rum. 128 E3
Ţigăneşti, Rum. 128 F2
Tigaon, Phil., 2,798 153 h14
Tigbauan, Phil., 4,942 153 d11
Tigeaux, Fr. 116 k11
Tiger, Wash. 80 E1
Tigerton, Wis., 781 66 D4
Tigerville, S.C. 63 B2
Tighennif, Alg., 14,080 160 b6
Tigieglo, Som. Rep., 1,015* 163 M5
Tigil', U.S.S.R. 135 P4
Tignall, Ga., 556 64 G2
Tignère, Cam., 3,000*, 162 G4
Tignish, P.E.I., Can. 45 N6
Tigre, r., Peru 104 C2
Tigre, r., Ven. 101 J3
Tigrett, Tenn. 71 B6
Tigris=Dicle, Turk.
Tigris=Dijlah, Iraq
Tiguabos, Cuba, 1,286 96 f2
Tiguentourine, Alg. 161 F3
Tigyaing, Burma, 2,615 146 B2
Tihany, Hung., 1,315 126 C3
Tihuatlán, Mex., 4,460 93 F4
Tijeras, N. Mex. 79 B4
Tijuana, Mex., 151,939 92 A1
Tijuco, r., Braz. 103 G5
Tika, Qué., Can. 45 N5
Tikal, ruins, Guat. 94 C2
Tikamgarh, India, 20,469 144 b13
Tikchik L., Alaska 85 E4
Tikehau, atoll, Tuam. Arch. 177 42
Tikhoretsk, U.S.S.R., 52,000 134 D5
Tikhvin, U.S.S.R., 18,300 136 D1
Tikhvinka, r., U.S.S.R. 136 D1
Tikhvinskaya Gryada, U.S.S.R. 136 D1
Tikikluk, Alaska 85 E1
Tikitiki, N.Z. 175 h5
Tiko, Cam., 26,000*, 162 F5
Tikøb, Den. 121 a7
Tikopia, i., Sta. Cruz Is. 170 F5
Tikrīt, Iraq, 7,678 143 C2
Tiksi, U.S.S.R., 6,000 135 M2
Tilamuta, Indon. 149 G2
Tilapa, Mex., 1,227 93 f11
Tilburg, Neth., 135,300 115 D3
Tilbury, Ont., Can., 3,009 46 B6
Tilbury, (part of Thurrock), U.K., 18,387 114 J8
Tilcara, Arg., 2,532 105 B2
Tilden, Ill., 308 68 C5
Tilden, Nebr., 917 75 H1
Tilden, Tex. 77 O5
Tileagd, Rum. 128 D1
Tilghman, Md. 62 H4
Tilichiki, U.S.S.R. 135 Q3
Tiligul'skiy Liman, estuary, U.S.S.R. 136 C4
Tilin, Burma 146 A2
Tilissos, Gr., 1,372 129 E7
Tillabéri, Niger, 1,632 162 E3
Tillamook, co., Oreg., 18,955 80 B3
Tillamook, Oreg., 4,244 80 B3
Tillanchong, i., India 146 A5
Tillar, Ark., 232 73 D4
Tillatoba, Miss., 102 73 E4
Tilleda, Wis. 66 E4
Tiller, Oreg. 80 B4
Tillery, N.C. 63 G1
Tillery, L., N.C. 63 D2
Tilley, Alta., Can. 42 K4
Tillia, Niger 162 E3
Tillicoultry, U.K., 3,963 112 c7
Tillicum, Wash. 80 B2
Tillman, co., Okla., 14,654 76 D3
Tillman, S.C. 63 C5
Tilloo Cay, Bah. Is. 95 c6
Tillsonburg, Ont., Can., 6,473 44 G7
Tilly, L., Qué., Can. 44 K3
Tilomar, Port. Timor 149 H5
Tilos, i., Gr. 129 F6
Tilpa, Austl. 173 F4
Tilshead, U.K. 114 E8
Tiltil, Chile, 1,825 104 g13
Tilton, Ill., 2,598 68 E3
Tilton, N.H., 1,129 54 D5
Tiltonsville, Ohio, 2,454 70 J2
Timagami, Ont., Can. 44 H6
Timagami, L., Ont., Can. 44 H6
Timahoe, Ire. 113 C5
Timaná, Col. 100 B6
Timane, r., Para. 105 C2
Timanskiy Kr., U.S.S.R. 134 E3
Timaru, N.Z., 24,821 175 f7
Timashevskaya, U.S.S.R. 136 E4
Timax, Guat. 94 C2
Timbákion, Gr., 2,816 129 E7
Timbaúba, Braz., 21,019 103 b14
Timbédra, Maur. 162 C3
Timber, Oreg. 80 B3
Timberlake, N.C. 63 F1
Timberlake, Ohio, 670 70 H1
Timber Lake, S. Dak., 624 74 B3
Timber Mtn., Tex. 77 M4
Timberville, Va., 412 62 F4
Timberwolf Mtn., Wash. 80 C2
Timbío, Col. 100 B6
Timbiquí, Col. 100 B6
Timblin, Pa., 240 60 D4
Timbo, Guin. 162 C4
Timbo, Ark. 73 C2
Timboon, Austl. 173 d12
Timboroa, Kenya 165 g13
Timbuktu=Tombouctou
Time, Ill., 45 68 B4
Timewell, Ill. 68 B4
Timfristós, Óros, Gr. 129 C5
Timgad, ruins, Alg. 160 e6
Timimoun, Alg., 3,038 160 E3
Timiris, C.=Mirik, C.
Timiryazevskiy, U.S.S.R. 137 r11
Timiş, r., Rum. 128 C2
Timiskaming, L., Ont.-Qué. 44 H6
Timişoara, Rum., 142,257 128 C2
Timken, Kans., 147 75 F5
Timmins, Ont., Can., 28,797 44 G5
Timmonsville, S.C., 2,178 63 E3
Timok, r., Yug. 125 F2
Timon, Braz., 7,077 103 H3
Timonium, Md. 62 c7
Timor, i., Indon. 149 H5
Timor Sea, Austl.-Indon. 170 C5
Timotes, Ven., 2,489 100 E3
Timpah, Indon. 148 E3
Timpanogos Cave Nat. Mon., Utah 78 C1
Timpas, Colo. 79 D3
Timpie, Utah 78 B1
Timpson, Tex., 1,120 77 Q4
Timrå, Swed. 120 D3
Timsbury, U.K., 1,587 114 D8
Timsher, r., U.S.S.R. 137 h6
Tim's Hill, Wis. 66 C3
Tīn, Ra's at, Libya 161 H2
Tina, Mo., 199 72 D5
Tinaco, Ven., 4,497 100 F3
Tinahely, Ire. 113 C5
Tinajones, r., Pan. 94 f12
Tinakula, i. Sta. Cruz. Is. 175 6
Tinambac, Phil., 2,800 153 h14
Tinaquillo, Ven., 8,305 100 F3
Tinca, Rum. 128 C1
Tinchebray, Fr., 3,238 117 C2
Tincup, Colo. 79 B2
Tindivanam, India 34,342 145 F7
Tindjil, P., Indon. 148 a7
Tindouf, Alg., 1,209 160 C3
Tineo, Sp., 20,347 122 B1
T'ing, r., China 152 E2
Tingambato, Mex., 3,370 93 b10
Ting-an, China 152 C4
Ting-chieh, China 144 f11
Ting-ch'ing, China 150 C4
Tingewick, U.K. 114 F7
Tinggi, Puleu, Malay. 147 p15
Tinghert, Ḥammādat, upland, Alg.-Libya 161 F3
Ting-hsi, China, 6,000* 150 E3
Ting-hsiang, China 150 E3
Ting-hsien, China 150 F3
Ting-jih, China 144 f11
Ting-k'ou-chen, China 151 A3
Tinglev, Den. 121 B6
Tingley, Iowa, 278 72 C4
Tingloy, Phil., 1,558 153 b9
Tingmerkpuk Mtn., Alaska 85 D1
Ting-nan, China 152 D2
Tingo María, Peru 104 C4
Ting-pien, China 150 E3
Tingsryd, Swed. 120 C4
Tingstäde, Swed. 120 D4
Ting-t'ao, China 151 D4
Tingüindín, Mex., 3,548 93 b10
Tinguipaya, Bol., 18,229 102 b11
Tinguiririca, r., Chile 104 f14
Tingvoll, Nor. 120 A3
Tingwick, Qué., Can. 47 M3
Ting-yüan, China 151 C4
Tinh Bien, S. Viet., 3,426 147 k11
Tinian, Tinian 176 27
Tinian, i., Mar. Is. 170 D4
Tinian Chan., Mariana Is. 176 23
Tinib, Phil., 2,635 153 c6
Tinitian, Phil. 153 A3
Tinkers Cr., Ohio 70 e9
Tinkisso, r., Guin. 162 C4
Tinley Park, Ill., 6,392 68 E2
Tinmouth, Vt. 54 A5
Tinnie, N. Mex. 79 C5
Tinniswood, Mt., Br. Col., Can. 42 c5
Tinnoset, Nor. 120 B4
Tinogasta, Arg. 105 B3
Tinos, Gr., 2,888 129 E6
Tinos, i., Gr. 129 E6
Tinsman, Ark. 73 C4
Tinsukia, India, 28,468 145 K4
Tintagel, U.K., 1,300 113 D6
Tintah, Minn., 228 74 D3
Tintamarre, Îlot, St-Martin 97 7
Tinténiac, Fr., 2,229 117 C2
Tintern Abbey, ruins, U.K. 114 C7
Tintic Mtn., Utah 78 b11
Tintina, Arg., 4,443 105 C3
Tinto, mtn., U.K. 112 E4
Tinwald, N.Z. 175 f7
Tiny Town, Colo. 79 b8
Tin Zaouaten, Alg. 160 E4
Tioga, Ill. 68 A3
Tioga, co., N.Y., 37,802 59 H7
Tioga, N. Dak., 2,087 74 A1
Tioga, co., Pa., 36,614 60 H2
Tioga, Pa., 597 60 H2
Tioga, Tex., 403 77 P3
Tioga, W. Va. 62 D4
Tioga, r., Pa. 60 H2
Tioga Center, N.Y. 59 H7
Tioga Pass, Calif. 82 D4
Tioman, P., Malay. 148 C2
Tiona, Pa. 60 D2
Tione, r., It. 122 d5
Tionesta, Pa., 778 60 C2
Tionesta Cr., Pa. 60 D2
Tiong, G., Malay. 147 p15
Tioro, Selat, Indon. 149 G4
Tiosa, Ind. 70 C1
Tioughnioga, r., N.Y. 59 H6
Tipa, pt., Niue 177 32
Tipana, Col. 100 B3
Tipitapa, Nic., 2,485 94 E4
Tipler, Wis. 66 E3
Tiplersville, Miss. 73 F3
Tippah, co., Miss., 15,093 73 G3
Tipp City, Ohio, 4,267 70 E3
Tippecanoe, co., Ind., 39,122 70 C2
Tippecanoe, r., Ind. 70 C2
Tipperary, co., Ire., 129,415 113 C5
Tipperary, Ire., 4,790 113 B5
Tipton, U.K., 38,091 114 D5
Tipton, Calif. 82 D4
Tipton, co., Ind., 15,856 70 C2
Tipton, Ind., 5,604 70 C2
Tipton, Iowa, 2,862 72 F3
Tipton, Kans., 252 75 G4
Tipton, Mich. 67 J6
Tipton, Mo., 1,639 72 E6
Tipton, Okla., 1,117 76 D3
Tipton, Pa. 60 F4
Tipton, co., Tenn., 28,564 71 B6
Tipton, Mt., Ariz. 78 A4
Tiptonville, Tenn., 2,068 71 B5
Tip Top, Va. 62 C5
Tip Top Hill, Ont., Can. 44 F5
Tipuani, Bo., 102 a9
Tiquicheo, Mex. 93 E4
Tiquisate, Guat., 7,255 94 B3
Tiracambu, Sa. do, Braz. 103 G2
Tīrān, Jazīrat, i., Saudi Ar. 143 A3
Tirana=Tiranë
Tiranë, Alb., 146,500 125 D4
Tirano, It., 7,393 123 C1
Tiraque, Bol., 2,026 102 c10
Tiraspol', U.S.S.R., 72,000 134 C5
Tirat Karmel, Isr., 10,995 142 a7
Tire, Turk., 26,530 142 A2
Tiree, i., U.K. 112 C3
Tîrgovişte, Rum., 24,360 128 E2
Tîrgu Cărbuneşti, Rum. 128 D2
Tîrgu Frumos, Rum. 128 F1
Tîrgu Jiu, Rum., 19,618 128 D2
Tîrgu Mureş, Rum., 65,194 128 E1
Tîrgu Neamţ, Rum., 10,373 128 F1
Tîrgu Ocna, Rum., 11,277 128 F1
Tîrgu Secuesc, Rum. 128 F2
Tirich Mīr, mtn., Pak. 145 D1
Tiripetío, Mex., 1,724 93 c10
Tirke, Guyana 101 L5
Tirlemont=Tienen
Tirlyanskiy, U.S.S.R. 137 i8
Tîrnava Mare, r., Rum. 128 E1
Tîrnava Mică, r., Rum. 128 E1
Tîrnăveni, Rum., 14,883 128 E1
Tirnavos, Gr., 10,805 129 D5
Tiro, Ohio, 334 70 G2
Tirodi, India, 8,807 144 b15
Tirpul, Afghan. 144 A2
Tirschenreuth, F.R.Ger., 7,796 118 D4
Tirso, r., It. 123 B5
Tirstrup, Den. 121 C4
Tiruchengodu, India, 21,386 145 m20
Tiruchirapalli, India, 249,862 145 E8
Tirukkalikundram, India, 12,881 145 n19
Tirumangalam, India, 17,633 145 k21
Tirumayam, India, 2,522 145 m20
Tirunelveli, India, 87,988 145 E8
Tiruntán, Peru 104 C3
Tirupati, India, 35,845 145 F7
Tiruppattur, India, 30,799 145 F7
Tiruppur, India, 79,773 145 k20
Tiruvallur, India, 19,757 145 m19
Tiruvannamalai, India 46,441 145 F7
Tiruvattipuram, India, 15,386 145 m19
Tisa, r., Yug. 125 E2
Tisbury, U.K., 1,656 113 E6
Tisbury Great Pd., Mass. 57 O7
Tisch Mills, Wis. 66 F4
Tisdale, Sask., Can., 2,379 43 D4
Tishomingo, co., Miss., 13,889 73 G3
Tishomingo, Miss., 415 73 G3
Tishomingo, Okla., 2,381 76 G3
Tiskilwa, Ill., 951 68 C2
Tiskoli, India 144 d14
Tismana, Rum. 128 D2
Tišnov, Czech. 126 C2
Tisovec, Czech. 126 D2
Tissø, l., Den. 121 D5
Tista, r., India-Pak. 144 g13
Tistrup, Den., 1,876 121 A5
Tisza, r., Hung. 126 F2
Tiszacsege, Hung., 7,011 126 E3
Tiszaföldvár, Hung., 12,517 126 E3
Tiszafüred, Hung., 11,577 126 E3
Tiszakécske, Hung., 13,149 126 E3
Tiszalök, Hung., 6,117 126 E2
Tiszapalkonya, Hung. 126 E3
Tiszavasvári, Hung., 12,355 126 E3
Tit, Alg. 160 E4
Titanic, Okla. 76 J2
Titano, Monte, S. Mar., 123 e11
Tit-Ary, U.S.S.R. 135 M2
Titel, Yug., 5,481 125 E2
Titeşti, Rum. 128 E2
Titi, Malay., 3,133 147 p15
Titicaca, L., Bol.-Peru 104 D5
Titicus (part of Ridgefield), Conn. 56 B7
Titikaveka, Rarotonga 177 34
Titilagarh, India, 7,433 145 G5
Titiribí, Col. 101 d13
Titograd, Yug., 30,000* 125 D3
Titonka, Iowa, 647 72 C1
Titovo Užice, Yug., 20,000* 125 D3
Titov Veles, Yug., 27,000* 125 E4
Tittabawassee, r., Mich. 67 J5
Tittling, F.R.Ger., 3,373 118 D4
Titule, D.R.Congo 164 D1
Titus, Ala. 64 C3
Titus, co., Tex., 16,785 77 Q3
Titusville, Fla., 6,410 65 J4
Titusville, N.J. 60 g10
Titusville, Pa., 8,356 60 C2
Titu-Tîrg, Rum. 128 E2
Titz, F.R.Ger., 2,991 119 A2
Tivaouane, Sen., 8,000 162 B3
Tivat, Yug., 2,835 125 D3
Tiverton, N.S., Can. 47 S11
Tiverton, Ont., Can. 46 C4
Tiverton, U.K., 12,397 113 E6
Tiverton, R.I., 9,461(T) 57 M6
Tiverton Center, Ohio 70 G2
Tiverton Four Corners (part of Tiverton), R.I. 57 M6
Tivoli, Gren. 97 18
Tivoli, It., 33,193 123 D4
Tivoli, N.Y., 732 59 N7
Tivoli, Tex. 77 P5
Tiv'on, Isr., 9,518 142 b7
Tiwi, Phil., 1,581 153 h14
Tixcacalcupul, Mex., 1,051 93 H4
Tixmucuy, Mex. 93 H4
Tixtla, Mex., 8,542 93 F5
Tizatlán, ruins, Mex. 93 f10
Tizayuca, Mex., 4,692 93 F4
Tizimín, Mex., 14,100 93 H4
Tizi-Ouzou, Alg., 25,367 160 E1
Tiznados, r., Ven. 100 G3
Tiznit, Mor., 7,694 160 C3
Tjæreborg, Den., 1,360 121 A5
Tjalang, Indon. 148 A1
Tjampurdarat, Indon. 148 e8
Tjapalulu, Selat, Indon. 149 H3
Tjaremai, G., Indon. 148 c7
Tjenrana, Indon. 149 F3
Tjepu, Indon. 148 d7
Tjeukemeer, Neth. 115 D2
Tjiamis, Indon. 148 c7
Tjiandjur, Indon. 148 b7
Tjiandur, Indon. 148 C4
Tjibatu, Indon. 148 c7
Tjibuni, r., Indon. 148 b7
Tjidaun, Indon. 148 b7
Tjidjulang, Indon. 148 D4
Tjidurian, r., Indon. 148 b7
Tjihara, Indon. 148 b7
Tjikadjang, Indon. 148 c7
Tjikalong, Indon. 148 c7
Tjikampek, Indon. 148 b7
Tjilatjap, Indon. 148 D4
Tjiledug, Indon. 148 c7
Tjimahi, Indon. 148 b7
Tjimanuk, r., Indon. 148 b7
Tjimari, Indon. 148 b7
Tjipatudja, Indon. 148 b7
Tjirebon, Indon., 158,299 148 D4
Tjitanduj, r., Indon. 148 c7
Tjitarum, r., Indon. 148 C4
Tjiudjung, r., Indon. 148 b7
Tjölling, Nor. 121 C1
Tjöme, Nor. 121 C1
Tjonger kan., Neth. 115 E2
Tjörn, i., Swed. 121 D2
Tkibuli, U.S.S.R., 22,700 137 b1
Tkvarcheli, U.S.S.R., 28,700 137 b1
Tlacolula, Mex., 7,546 93 F5
Tlacotalpan, Mex., 6,382 93 G4
Tlacuitapa, Mex., 1,467 93 b8
Tlajomulco, Mex., 5,292 93 a9
T Lake Mtn., N.Y. 59 L5
Tlalancaleca, Mex., 4,344 93 f10
Tlalcotepec, Mex., 1,195 93 d10
Tlalnepantla, Mex., 23,886 93 e10
Tlalpan, Mex., 18,141 93 e10
Tlalpujahua, Mex., 2,283 93 d10
Tlaltepingo, Mex. 93 f9
Tlanalapa, Mex. 93 f10
Tlanchinol, Mex. 93 f9
Tlapa, Mex., 4,453 93 F5
Tlapacoyan, Mex., 8,511 93 F4
Tlapanalá, Mex., 1,128 93 f11
Tlaquepaque, Mex., 37,249 92 E4
Tlaquilpan, Mex., 1,321 93 f10
Tlaquiltenango, Mex., 6,723 93 e11
Tlatlaya, Mex. 93 d11
Tlaxcala, st., Mex., 346,699 93 F4
Tlaxcala, Mex., 7,646 93 F4
Tlaxcalancingo, Mex., 2,880 93 f10
Tlaxcalilla, Mex., 1,797 93 e9
Tlaxco, Pue., Mex., 1,252 93 f9
Tlaxco, Tlax., Mex., 4,885 93 F4
Tlaxcoapan, Mex., 4,258 93 e9
Tlaxiaca, Mex., 2,702 93 f9
Tlaxiaco, Mex., 6,123 93 F5
Tlazazalca, Mex., 5,323 93 b10
Tlemcen, Alg., 70,930 160 D2
Tleń, Pol. 127 C2
Tłuszcz, Pol., 3,944 127 D2
Tmassah, Libya 161 G3
Tmiet, i., Jaluit 176 30
T'o, r., S-ch., China 152 B1
T'o, r., K-t., China 152 E3
Toa, r., Cuba 96 f2
Toa, Cuchillas de, Cuba 96 f2
Toa Alta, P.R., 1,284 96 t10
Toa Baja, P.R., 1,084 96 t10
Toachi, r., Ec. 104 B1
Toad, r., Br. Col., Can. 42 F1
Toad River, Br. Col., Can. 42 F1
Toana Ra., Nev. 83 C2
Toano, Va. 62 H5
Toanoano, Tahiti 177 44
Toast, N.C., 2,023 63 D1
Toau, atoll, Tuam. Arch. 177 42
Toay, Arg., 4,000* 105 C5
Toba, Jap., 30,521 155 E4
Toba, Danau, Indon. 148 A2
Toba, r., Br. Col., Can. 42 b5
Tobacco, N. Br., r., Mich. 67 J5
Tobacco, S. Br., r., Mich. 67 J5
Tobacco Root Mts., Mont. 50 D1
Tobadi, Indon. 149 L3
Tobago, i., Trin. & Tob. 96 h4
Tobago Cays, Gren. Is. 97 20
Tobago I., V.I. 97 4
Toba Inlet, Br. Col., Can. 42 F4
Tobarra, Sp., 11,114 122 E3
Tobe, Colo. 79 D3
Tobelo, Indon. 149 J2
Tobercurry, Ire. 113 B4
Tobermory, Ont., Can. 44 G6
Tobermory, U.K. 112 C3
Tōbetsu, Jap., 18,969 155 J8
Tobi, i., Car. Is. 170 C4
Tobias, Nebr., 202 75 H3
Tobias Barreto, Braz., 4,527 103 J4
Tobin, Wis. 69 c7
Tobin, Mt., Nev. 83 B2
Tobin L., Austl. 172 C3
Tobin Ra., Nev. 83 B2
Tobinsport, Ind. 70 C5
Tobique, r., N.B., Can. 47 S10
Toboali, Indon. 148 C3
Tobol, U.S.S.R. 134 F4
Tobol, r., U.S.S.R. 134 F4
Toboli, Indon. 149 G3
Tobol'sk, U.S.S.R., 39,000 134 F4
Toboso, Phil., 5,401 153 B3
Tobruk=Ṭubruq
Tobyhanna, Pa. 61 L3
Tocaima, Col. 100 C5
Tocantínia, Braz., 1,414 103 G3
Tocantinópolis, Braz., 4,927 103 G3

304 · Tocantins—Trelde

Tocantins, Braz., 2,986 **103** e17
Tocantins, r., Braz. **103** G2
Toccoa, Ga., 7,303 **64** F1
Toche, r., Col. **101** d15
Tochibora, Jap. **154** i14
Tochidani, Jap. **154** g16
Tochigi, Jap., 73,436 **155** F3
Tochimilco, Mex., 3,157 **93** f11
Tochimoto, Jap. **154** f14
To-ch'in, r., China **151** D1
Tochio, Jap., 37,681 **155** F3
T'o-chi Tao, China **151** D3
Tochū, Jap. **154** g14
Toco, Chile **105** B2
Toco, Trin. and Tob. **96** h5
Tocoa, Hond., 1,666 **94** E3
Tocopilla, Chile, 21,580 **105** A2
Tocorpuri, Co. de, Bol.-Chile **102** C6
Tocumbo, Mex., 1,974 **93** b10
Tocumwal, Austl., 1,389 **173** F5
Tocuyito, Ven., 5,811 **100** G2
Tocuyo, r., Ven. **100** F2
Tocuyo de la Costa, Ven., 3,355 **100** F2
Toda Bhim, India, 8,653 **144** a12
Todasana, Ven. **101** c11
Todd, co., Ky., 11,364 **71** D5
Todd, co., Minn., 23,119 **74** E3
Todd, co., S. Dak., 4,661 **74** B4
Todds Hbr., Mich. **66** b8
Todds Road, Trin. and Tob. **96** g5
Toddsville, N.Y. **59** K6
Toddy Pd., Me. **55** D4
Todeli, Indon. **149** H3
Todi, It., 20,659 **123** D3
Todjo, Indon. **149** G3
Todmorden, U.K., 17,416 **114** D3
Todohokke, Jap., 3,799 **155** J9
Todor Ikonomov, Bulg., 3,133 **128** F3
Todoroki, Jap. **154** g15
Todos Los Santos, L., Chile **105** e15
Todos Santos, Bol., 2,366 **102** D5
Todos Santos, Mex., 1,886 **92** C3
Todos Santos, B., Mex. **82** E6
Todos Santos Cuchumatán, Guat., 2,165 **94** B3
Todtnau, F.R.Ger., 2,861 **118** B5
Toe Head, Ire. **113** B6
Toe Head, U.K. **112** C3
Toetoes Bay, N.Z. **175** f7
Toffen, Switz. **124** B2
Tofield, Alta., Can. **43** c7
Tofino, Br. Col., Can. **42** E4
Tofte, Minn. **74** G2
Töftedal, Swed. **121** D2
Toftlund, Den. **121** B5
Tofua, i., Tonga **177** 36
Toga, i., New Hebr. **174** k4
Tōgane, Jap., 34,495 **155** n19
Togawa, Jap. **154** e15
Togchhen, China **144** c10
Togi, Jap., 16,327 **155** E3
Togiak, Alaska, 220 **85** D4
Togiak, r., Alaska **85** D4
Togiak Bay, Alaska **85** D4
Togo, ctry., 1,682,000* **162** E4
Togo, Sask., Can. **43** E4
Tōgō, Jap. **154** h14
Toguchin, U.S.S.R., 19,200 **134** H4
Toguzak, r., U.S.S.R. **137** k9
Togwotee Pass, Wyo. **81** E4
Tohatchi, N. Mex. **79** A4
Tohautu, Tahiti **177** 44
Tohickon Cr., Pa. **61** M5
Tohivea, Mt., Moorea **177** 44
Tohma, r., Turk. **142** D2
Tohmajärvi, Fin. **120** G3
Tohopekaliga, L., Fla. **65** H4
Toi, Jap., 8,041 **155** J9
Toi, Niue **177** 32
Toiavea, mtn., W. Samoa **177** 38
Toijala, Fin. **120** E3
Toi-misaki, Jap. **154** B6
Toiny, Pte., St-Barthélemy **97** 7
Toivola, Mich. **66** E1
Toiyabe Pk., Nev. **83** B3
Toiyabe Ra., Nev. **83** B3
Tōjō, Jap., 21,713 **155** C4
Tok, r., U.S.S.R. **137** h9
Tokaanu, N.Z. **175** g5
Tokachi, r., Jap. **155** K8
Tokachi-dake, Jap. **155** K8
Tokai, Malay., 1,182 **147** o13
Tokaj, Hung., 5,031 **126** E2
Tōkamachi, Jap., 42,223 **155** F3
Tokanui, N.Z., 1,490 **175** f7
Tokara-guntō, Jap. **154** d12
Tokara-kaikyō, Jap. **154** k17
Tokat, Turk., 32,725 **142** D1
Tŏkchŏk-kundo, S. Kor. **151** E3
Tŏkch'ŏn, N. Kor. **151** E3
Tokeen, Alaska **85** L5
Tokelau Is., Pac. Oc., **170** G5
Toki, Jap., 55,198 **155** E4
Tokio, N. Dak. **74** C2
Toki Pt., Wake I. **176** 26
Tok Junction, Alaska **85** H3
Tokke, l., Nor. **121** B1
Tokko, U.S.S.R. **135** M4
Toklat, r., Alaska **85** G2
Tokmak, U.S.S.R., 29,100 **134** G5
T'o-k'o-hsün, China **150** B2
Tokomaru Bay, N.Z. **175** h5
Tokoname, Jap., 51,919 **155** E4
Tokoro, Jap., 9,705 **155** L7
Tokoro, r., Jap. **155** K8
Tokoroa, N.Z., 7,104 **175** g5
Tokorozawa, Jap., 65,903 **155** F4
Tokose, Jap. **154** f14
T'o-k'o-t'o, China **151** A2
Toktogul, U.S.S.R. **137** g4
Toku, i., Tonga **177** 36
Tokulu, i., Tonga **177** 36
Tokung, Indon. **148** E3
Tokuno-shima, Jap. **154** d12
Tokushima, Jap., 182,782 **155** D4
Tokuyama, Jap., 77,246 **154** B4
Tokuyama, Jap. **154** h14
Tōkyō, Jap., 9,683,802 **155** F4
Tōkyō-wan, Jap. **155** F4
Tol, i., Truk **176** 19
Tolaga Bay, N.Z. **175** h5
Tolageak, Alaska **85** D1
Tolala, Indon. **149** G3
Tolånga, Swed. **121** F5
Tolar, Tex., 283 **76** d10
Tolbazy, U.S.S.R. **137** h8
Tolbert, Tex. **77** O2
Tolbukhin, Bulg., 42,661 **128** F3
Tolcayuca, Mex., 2,103 **93** e10
Tolé, Pan. **94** G6
Toledo, Bol., 7,443 **102** b11
Toledo, Col. **100** C4
Toledo, Col. **100** D4
Toledo, Phil., 4,913 **153** e11
Toledo, Sp., 40,651 **122** C3
Toledo, Ill., 998 **68** D4
Toledo, Iowa, 2,850 **72** E2
Toledo, Ohio, 318,003 **70** F1
Toledo, Oreg., 3,053 **80** B3
Toledo, Wash., 499 **80** B2
Tolentino, It., 15,407 **123** D3
Tolga, Alg., 6,479 **160** d6
T'o-li, China **150** B2
Tolimán, Mex. **93** e9
Tolitoli = Kampungbaru
Tolkomicko, Pol., 2,282 **127** C1
Tolland, Colo. **79** a8
Tolland, co., Conn., 68,737 **56** G5
Tolland, Conn., 2,950(T) **56** G5
Tolland, Mass., 101(T) **56** D4
Tollense, r., Ger.D.R. **118** D2
Tollense See, Ger.D.R. **118** D2
Tollerton, U.K. **114** F2
Tollesboro, Ky. **71** H3
Tolleson, Ariz., 3,886 **78** B5
Tolley, N. Dak., 189 **74** B1
Tølløse, Den., 2,586 **121** D5
Tolmezzo, It., 9,649 **123** D1
Tolmin, Yug. **125** A1
Tolna, Hung., 8,748 **126** D3
Tolna, N. Dak., 291 **74** C2
Tolo, Teluk, Indon. **149** G3
Toloa, Houma, pt., Tonga **177** 36
Tolocolme Pk., Ponape **176** 29
Tolokiwa, i., Terr. New Guin. **174** e2
Tolomosita, Bol., 2,343 **102** D6
Tolono, Ill., 1,539 **68** D4
Tolosa, Sp., 16,281 **122** E1
Tolovana, Alaska **85** G2
Tolovana, r., Alaska **85** G2
Tolovana Park, Oreg. **80** A3
Tolsan-do, S. Kor. **151** E4
Tolsta Head, U.K. **112** C2
Tolstoi, Man., Can. **43** h10
Tolstoy, S. Dak., 142 **74** C3
Tolstoy, M., U.S.S.R. **135** P4
Toltec, Ariz. **78** C5
Toltén, Chile **105** e14
Toltén, r., Chile **105** e14
Tolú, Col. **100** C3
Tolu, Ky. **71** C4
Toluca, Mex., 76,871 **93** F4
Toluca, Ill., 1,352 **68** C2
Toluca, N.C. **63** C2
Toluca, Nev. de, Mex. **93** e10
To-lun, China **150** F2
Tolybay, U.S.S.R. **137** k10
Tom, Okla. **76** J4
Tom', r., U.S.S.R. **134** H4
Tōma, Jap., 14,226 **155** K8
Tomah, Wis., 5,321 **66** C5
Tomahawk, Wis., 3,348 **66** D3
Tomahawk L., Wis. **66** D3
Tomah Str., Me. **55** E3
Tomakomai, Jap., 62,384 **155** J8
Tomalá, Hond., 1,029 **94** e9
Tomales, Calif. **82** B3
Tomamae, Jap., 11,696 **155** J7
Tomanivi, Mt., Fiji **174** 4
Tomar, Port., 12,974 **122** A3
Tomari, Jap. **155** E3
Tomari, Jap. **155** G1
Tomari, Jap., 8,916 **155** J8
Tomari, U.S.S.R., 9,200 **135** O5
Tomás Barrón, Bol. **102** b10
Tomasiri, Peru **104** D6
Tomaszów Lubelski, Pol., 7,830 **127** E3
Tomaszów Mazowiecki, Pol., 49,000* **127** D3
Tomatlán, Jal., Mex., 1,059 **92** D4
Tomatlán, Pue., Mex., 1,714 **93** f10
Tomayapo, Bol., 1,369 **102** C6
Tombador, Sa. do, Braz. **102** E4
Tomball, Tex., 1,713 **77** Q4
Tombe, Sol. Is. **175** b2
Tombigbee, r., Ala.-Miss. **64** A4
Tomblaine, Fr., 5,247 **116** b9
Tombôco, Ang. **164** B3
Tombos, Braz., 3,925 **103** f17
Tombouctou, Mali, 7,000 **162** D3
Tombstone, Ariz., 1,283 **78** D6
Tomé, Chile, 26,942 **104** e16
Tomé-Açu, Braz., 1,130 **103** G2
Tomelilla, Swed. **120** C5
Tomelloso, Sp., 27,815 **122** D3
Tomendán, Mex. **93** c10
Tomerong, Austl. **173** h10
Tom Green, co., Tex., 64,630 **77** N4
Tomhannock Res., N.Y. **59** w28
Tomichi Cr., Colo. **79** B2
Tomie, Jap., 15,112 **154** A5
Tomifobia, r., Qué., Can. **54** C1
Tomiko, Ont., Can. **46** E2
Tomiko, r., Ont., Can. **46** E2
Tomil, Yap **176** 20
Tomil Hbr., Yap **176** 20
Tomina, Bol., 5,645 **102** c11
Tomini, Indon. **149** G2
Tomini, Teluk, Indon. **149** G3
Tomintoul, U.K. **112** E3
Tomioka, Jap. **154** A5
Tomioka, Jap., 45,039 **155** F3
Tomioka, Jap., 13,117 **155** G3
Tomiuchi, Jap. **155** K8
Tomiura, Jap., 8,351 **155** F4
Tomlison Corners, N.Y. **58** n21
Tømmerup, Den., 3,068 **121** b7
Tommot, U.S.S.R., 8,700 **135** M4
Tomo, Jap. **154** e15
Tomo, N. Caled. **174** k8
Tomo, r., Col. **100** F5
Tomochi, Jap., 15,169 **154** B5
Tomóchic, r., Mex. **92** D2
Tomoda, Jap. **154** h15
Tomo-Oku, Jap. **155** D5
Tomori, Ryukyu Is. **154** a11
Tomorrit, Mal i, Alb. **125** E4
Tompkins, Sask., Can. **43** B5
Tompkins, co., N.Y. 66,164 **59** G7
Tompkins Center, Mich. **67** J6
Tompkinsville, Ky., 2,091 **71** F5
Tompkinsville, Md. **62** H4
Tompo, Indon. **149** F2
Tompo, U.S.S.R. **135** N3
Tompo, r., U.S.S.R. **135** N3
Toms, r., N.J. **61** C3
Toms Brook, Va., 244 **62** F4
Tomsk, U.S.S.R., 269,000 **134** H4
Toms River, N.J., 6,062 **61** C4
Tonalá, Mex., 12,204 **93** G5
Tonalá, r., Mex. **93** G5
Tonalea, Ariz. **78** C3
Tonami, Jap., 36,377 **155** E3
Tonasket, Wash., 958 **80** D1
Tonatico, Mex., 3,104 **93** e11
Tonawanda, N.Y., 21,561 **58** B6
Tonawanda Cr., N.Y. **58** D5
Tonbridge, U.K., 22,146 **113** G6
Tonda, Terr. Papua **174** d3
Tonda, r., Jap. **154** g16
Tondabayashi, Jap., 36,261 **155** D4
Tondano, Indon. **149** H2
Tondela, Port., 3,198 **122** A2
Tønder, Den., 7,192 **121** A6
Tondi, India, 6,422 **145** m21
Tondol, Phil., 2,406 **153** b6
Tone, r., Jap. **155** G4
Tonga, ctry., 74,000* **170** G6
Tonga, Sudan **163** K4
Tonga Is., Tonga **177** 36
Tonga Trench, Pac. Oc. **169** G3
Tonganoxie, Kans., 1,354 **75** K4
Tongareva, i., Cook Is. **171** H5
Tongariki, i., New Hebr. **174** m6
Tongariro Nat. Pk., N.Z. **175** g5
Tongas, Indon. **148** e7
Tongatapu, i., Tonga **177** 36
Tongatapu Group, is., Tonga **170** G6
Tongeren, Belg., 15,552 **115** D4
Tongjosŏn-man, N. Kor. **151** F3
Tonglau, Burma **146** B2
Tongnae, S. Kor. **151** F4
Tongoa, i., New Hebr. **174** m6
Tongres = Tongeren
Tongsa Dzong, Bhutan **144** g12
Tongue, U.K. **112** D2
Tongue, r., Mont.-Wyo. **81** F3
Tongue of the Ocean, Bah. Is. **95** C1
Tongyi, Burma, 1,923 **147** b2
T'o-niang, r., China **152** B2
Tonica, Ill., 750 **68** C2
Tonila, Mex., 2,805 **92** E4
Tonilco, Mex. **93** a8
Tonj, Sudan, 2,071 **163** J4
Tonj, r., Sudan **163** J4
Tonk, India, 43,413 **145** E4
Tonkawa, Okla., 3,415 **76** F1
Tonkin, G. of, China-N. Viet. **146** E2
Tonle Sap, Camb. **146** C4
Tonnay-Charente, Fr., 5,765 **117** C4
Tonneins, Fr., 7,987 **117** D4
Tonnerre, Fr., 5,760 **117** E3
Tönning, F.R.Ger., 4,789 **118** B1
Tōno, Jap., 36,923 **155** G2
Tonopah, Ariz. **78** B5
Tonopah, Nev., 1,679 **83** B3
Tonoshō, Jap., 24,879 **155** D4
Tonosi, Pan. **94** G7
Tons, r., India **144** c13
Tönsberg, Nor., 12,583 **120** B4
Tonstad, Nor. **120** A4
Ton Tan, Thai. **147** c4
Tontitown, Ark., 209 **73** A1
Tonto Nat. Mon., Ariz. **78** C5
Tontouta, N. Caled. **174** k8
Tonumea, i., Tonga **177** 36
Tony, Wis., 162 **66** C3
Tonzona, r., Alaska **85** F3
Toodyay, Austl. **172** A4
Tooele, co., Utah, 17,868 **78** B1
Tooele, Utah, 9,133 **78** B1
Toole, co., Mont., 7,904 **81** D1
Toombs, co., Ga., 16,837 **64** G3
Toomsboro, Ga., 764 **64** F3
Toomyvara, Ire. **113** B5
Toone, Tenn., 202 **71** C6
Toonerville, Colo. **79** D3
Toopua, i., Bora-Bora **177** 43
Toowoomba, Austl., 43,149 **173** G4
Topagoruk, r., Alaska **85** F1
Topaipí, Col. **101** e14
Topalu, Rum. **128** G2
Topanga, Calif. **83** g15
Topanga Beach, Calif. **83** g15
Topawa, Ariz. **78** C6
Topaz, Calif. **82** D3
Topaz Mtn., Utah **78** B2
Topeka, Ill., 77 **68** C3
Topeka, Ind., 600 **70** D1
Topeka, Kans., 119,484 **75** K4
Topinabee, Mich. **67** J3
Topit, Gur i, Alb. **125** E4
Topki, U.S.S.R., 26,200 **137** r11
Topl'a, r., Czech. **126** E2
Topleţ, Rum. **128** D2
Topley, Br. Col., Can. **42** E2
Topley Landing, Br. Col., Can. **42** F2
Toplica, r., Yug. **125** E3
Topliţa, Rum., 8,944 **128** E1
Topocalma, Chile **104** e14
Topock, Ariz. **78** A4
Topola, Yug. **125** E2
Topol'čany, Czech., 10,556 **126** D2
Topolo, Yug. **125** C3
Topolobampo, Mex., 1,738 **92** C3
Topolog, Rum. **128** G2
Topolovăţu Mare, Rum. **128** C2
Topoloveni, Rum. **128** E2
Topolovgrad, Bulg., 6,958 **128** F3
Toponas, Colo. **79** B1
Topozero, Oz., U.S.S.R. **134** C3
Toppenish, Wash., 5,667 **80** C2
Toppenish Cr., Wash. **80** C2
Topraisar, Rum. **128** G2
Topsail, Newf., Can., 1,066 **45** c10
Topsey, Tex. **77** P4
Topsfield, Me. **55** E3
Topsfield, Mass., 3,351(T) **57** N2
Topsham, U.K., 3,963 **113** E6
Topsham, Me., 2,240 **55** B5
Topstone (part of Redding, Ridgefield), Conn. **56** C7
Topsy, Okla. **76** J1
Topton, N.C. **63** b7
Topton, Pa., 1,684 **61** L5
Topura, Terr. Papua **174** 3
Topusko, Yug. **125** B2
Toquepala, Peru **104** D6
Toquerville, Utah, 197 **78** B3
Toquima Ra., Nev. **83** B3
Tor, Sp. **122** g7
Tora-Khem, U.S.S.R. **135** J4
Torbalı, Turk., 7,973 **142** A2
Torbat-e Ḩeydarīyeh, Iran, 19,830 **143** F1
Torbat-e Jām, Iran, 6,756 **143** G1
Torbay, Newf., Can., 1,445 **45** c10
Torbay, N.S., Can. **47** V11
Törbel, Switz. **124** B2
Torch, Ohio **70** H3
Torch Keys, Fla. **65** f15
Torch Lake, Mich. **67** H3
Torch L., Mich. **67** H3
Torcy, Fr., 3,221 **116** i11
Tördal, Nor. **121** A1
Tordesillas, Sp., 5,836 **122** C2
Tordino, r., It. **123** D3
Töre, Swed. **120** E2
Töreboda, Swed. **120** C4
Torfou, Fr. **116** g12
Torgau, Ger.D.R., 19,690 **118** D3
Torgelow, Ger.D.R., 14,421 **118** D2
Torhout, Belg., 13,115 **115** B3
Toribulu, Indon. **149** G3
Toride, Jap., 22,582 **155** n19
Toril, Phil., 8,094 **153** C4
Torino, It., 946,029 **123** A2
Tori-shima, Japan **170** D2
Torit, Sudan, 2,353 **163** K5
Toritama, Braz., 3,578 **103** a14
Torixoreu, Braz. **103** F5
Toriya, Jap., 7,306 **155** E3
Tormes, r., Sp. **122** C2
Tornacuxtla, Mex., 1,468 **93** f9
Tornby, Den. **121** B3
Torneälven = Tornionjoki, Fin.
Torneälven, r., Swed. **120** E2
Tornesch, F.R.Ger., 6,110 **119** a8
Torneträsk, l., Swed. **120** D1
Torngat Mts., Newf., Can. **45** N2
Tornillo, Tex. **77** L4
Tornio, Fin., 5,517 **120** F2
Tornionjoki = Torneälven, Swed.
Tornionjoki, r., Fin. **120** F2
Tornquist, Arg., 5,300* **105** C5
Tōro, Jap. **155** L8
Toro, Sp., 10,218 **122** C2
Torö, Swed. **120** e9
Toro, La. **73** B6
Toro, Co. del, Arg.-Chile **105** A3
Torokina, Sol. Is. **175** a2
Törökszentmiklós, Hung., 23,576 **126** E3
Toronaios Kólpos, Gr. **129** D4
Toronto, Ont., Can., 657,452 **44** H7
Toronto, Kans., 524 **75** K6
Toronto, Ohio, 7,780 **70** J2
Toronto, S. Dak., 268 **74** D3
Toronto, L., Mex. **92** D2
Toronto Res., Kans. **75** K6
Toropets, U.S.S.R., 14,500 **136** C1
Tororo, Uganda, 6,365 **164** E1
Toros Dağları, Turk. **142** C2
Torquay, Sask., Can. **43** D5
Torquay, U.K., 54,046 **113** E6
Torrance, Calif., 100,991 **82** D6
Torrance, co., N. Mex., 6,497 **79** B4
Torrance, N. Mex. **79** C4
Torrão, Port., 6,088 **122** A3
Torre Annunziata, It., 58,476 **123** c10
Torreblanca, Sp., 3,809 **122** F2
Torre Cerredo, mtn., Sp. **122** C1
Torrecilla, pk., Sp. **122** C4
Torrecilla en Cameros, Sp., 1,347 **122** D1
Torre del Greco, It., 76,074 **123** c10
Torre de Moncorvo, Port., 2,757 **122** B2
Torreglia, It., 4,165 **122** e5
Torrejoncillo, Sp., 5,499 **122** B3
Torrelaguna, Sp., 2,509 **122** D2
Torrelavega, Sp., 31,021 **122** D1
Torremolinos, Sp., **122** C4
Torrens, L., Austl. **172** E4
Torrens Creek, Austl. **173** F3
Torrente, Sp., 24,042 **122** E3
Torreón, Mex., 179,955 **92** E3
Torreon, N. Mex. **79** B4
Torre-Pacheco, Sp., 11,184 **122** E4
Tôrres, Braz., 4,729 **103** G7
Torres, i., Truk **176** 19
Torresandino, Sp., 1,408 **122** C2
Torres Is., New Hebr. **174** k4
Torres Novas, Port., 11,974 **122** A3
Torres Str., Austl. **173** F1
Torres Vedras, Port., 13,091 **122** A3
Torrey, Utah, 128 **78** C2
Torrey Mtn., Mont. **81** C3
Torridon, Loch, U.K. **112** D3
Torrijos, Sp., 5,163 **122** C2
Torringford (part of Torrington), Conn. **56** D5
Tørring Stationsby, Den., 1,367 **121** B5
Torrington, Conn., 30,045 **56** D5
Torrington, Wyo., 4,188 **81** G4
Torrlösa, Swed. **121** c7
Torröjen, l., Swed. **120** C3
Torrox, Sp., 8,069 **122** D4
Torsby, Swed. **120** C3
Tor's Cove, Newf., Can. **45** c10
Torshälla, Swed. **120** d8
Tórshavn, Faeroe Is., 6,067 **120** c7
Torsken, Nor. **120** D1
Torsnes, Nor. **121** D1
Torsvi, Swed. **120** e8
Tortilla Flat, Ariz. **78** C5
Tortola, i., V.I. **97** 4
Tortona, It., 25,046 **123** B2
Tortosa, Sp., 43,267 **122** F2
Tortosa, C., Sp. **122** F2
Tortue, Canal de la, Haiti **96** k6
Tortue, Île de la, Haiti **96** k6
Tortuga I. = Tortue, Île de la
Toruń, Pol., 105,000* **127** C2
Torunos, Ven. **100** E3
Torup, Swed. **120** C4
Torup, Swed. **121** c7
Tory Hill, Ont., Can. **46** F4
Tory I., Ire. **113** B4
Torysa, r., Czech. **126** E2
Tory Sd., Ire. **113** B4
Torzhok, U.S.S.R., 34,900 **136** D1
Tosa, Jap. **154** g15
Tosamaganga, Tanz. **164** E3
Tosa-Shimizu, Jap., 29,944 **155** C5
Tosa-wan, Jap. **155** C5
Tōsens, Aust. **124** G6
Tōshi, Jap. **154** h15
Toshima, Jap. **154** f15
To-shima, Jap. **155** F4
Töss, r., Switz. **124** C1
Tossene, Swed. **121** D2
Tosson Hill, U.K. **112** f9
Tosterön, i., Swed. **120** d8
Toston, Mont. **81** D2
Tosu, Jap., 41,870 **154** B5
Tosya, Turk., 13,690 **142** C1
Toszek, Pol., 3,397 **127** h6
Totana, Sp., 14,281 **122** E4
Totare, r., Col. **101** e15
Totimehuacán, Mex., 4,618 **93** f11
Tótkomlós, Hung., 9,364 **126** E3
Totland, U.K., 1,724 **113** i13
Totley, U.K. **114** E4
Tot'ma, U.S.S.R., 7,900 **136** F1
Totnes, U.K., 5,502 **113** E6
Totness, Sur., 1,325* **101** M5
Toto, Guam **176** 24
Totogatic L., Wis. **66** B2
Totolan, Indon. **147** o16
Totonicapán, Guat., 8,103 **94** B3
Totora, Bol. **102** a10
Totora, Bol., 7,362 **102** c10
Totoral, Urug. **105** D4
Tototlán, Mex., 6,421 **93** b9
Totowa, N.J., 10,897 **61** C2
Totoya, i., Fiji **174** 4
Totsu, r., Jap. **154** g15
Totsukachō, Jap. **155** m20
Totten Gl., Ant. **180** T6
Tottenham, Ont., Can. **46** E4
Tottenham, London, U.K. **114** H7
Totten Inlet, Wash. **81** a8
Tottori, Jap., 104,833 **155** D4
Tou, r., China **152** C3
Tou, Motu, i., Rarotonga **177** 34
Touba, Iv. Coast, 1,217 **162** C4
Toub Roos, Nic. **94** E3
Touchet, Wash. **80** D2
Touchet, r., Wash. **80** D2
Touchwood L., Man., Can. **43** G3
Toucy, Fr., 2,631 **117** E3
T'ou-fen, Taiwan, 33,560 **152** F2
Tougaloo, Miss. **73** E5
Tougan, Upper Volta, 5,014 **162** D3
Touggourt, Alg., 17,305 **160** F2
Toughkenamon, Pa. **60** e12
Tougouri, Upper Volta, 2,400 **162** D3
Tougué, Guin. **162** C4
Touho, N. Caled., 1,332 **174** i8
Toukoto, Mali, 1,820 **162** C3
Toul, Fr., 15,031 **117** F2
Toulépleu, Iv. Coast, 2,415 **162** C4
Toulnustouc, r., Qué., Can. **45** M5
Toulon, Fr., 172,586 **117** G5
Toulon, Ill., 1,213 **68** C2
Toulouse, Fr., 330,570 **117** D5
Tou Morong, S. Viet. **146** D4
Tou-nan, Taiwan, 34,661 **152** F3
Tounassine, Alg. **162** D1
Toungoo, Burma, 31,589 **146** B3
Tounj, Yug. **125** B2
Toupéti, I., N. Caled. **174** k8
Tourakom, Laos **146** C3
Tourane = Da Nang
Tourcoing, Fr., 90,105 **116** a6
Tourette-Levens, Fr., 2,035 **116** n13
Tourlaville, Fr., 11,607 **117** C2
Tournai, Belg., 33,414 **115** B4
Tournan-en-Brie, Fr., 2,908 **116** k12
Tournon, Fr., 8,127 **117** F4
Tournus, Fr., 6,180 **117** F3
Touros, Braz., 1,550 **103** J3
Tourouvre, Fr., 1,581 **117** D2
Tourrettes, Fr. **116** m13
Tours, Fr., 96,472 **117** D3
Tourville, Qué., Can. **47** P1
Toušeň, Czech. **126** d6
Touside, Pic, Chad **162** G2
Toussine, Fr. Guiana **101** O5
Toutle, r., Wash. **80** B2
Touwsrivier, S. Af., 5,458 **164** C7
Toužim, Czech. **126** c6
Tovar, Ven., 8,827 **100** E3
Tovdal, Nor. **121** A2
Tovdalsåna, r., Nor. **121** A2
Towaco, N.J. **58** b13
Towada-Hachimantai-ktk., Jap. **155** G1
Towada-ko, Jap. **155** G1
Towaliga, r., Ga. **64** F2
Towanda, Ill., 586 **68** D3
Towanda, Kans., 1,031 **75** H6
Towanda, Pa., 4,283 **61** K2
Towanda Cr., Pa. **60** J2
Towaninie, Austl. **173** d11
Towaoc, Colo. **79** A3
Towari, Indon. **149** G4
Towcester, U.K., 2,743 **113** F5
Tower, Mich. **67** J3
Tower, Minn., 878 **74** F2
Tower City, N. Dak., 300 **74** D2
Tower City, Pa., 1,968 **60** J4
Tower Hill, Ill., 700 **68** D4
Tower Pt., mtn., Oreg. **80** C3
Tow Law, U.K., 2,920 **112** g10
Town Creek, Ala., 810 **64** B1
Town Creek, N.C. **63** F3
Towner, co., N. Dak., 5,624 **74** C1
Towner, N. Dak., 948 **74** B1
Townley, Ala. **64** B2
Town of Pines, Ind., 939 **69** f10
Towns, co., Ga., 4,538 **64** F1
Towns, Ga., 91 **64** G3
Townsend, Del., 434 **62** J3
Townsend, Mass., 1,101;3,650(T) **57** K2
Townsend, Mont., 1,528 **81** D2
Townsend, Va. **62** H5
Townsend, Wis. **66** E3
Townsend Harbor (part of Townsend), Mass. **57** K2
Townsend's Inlet, N.J. **61** B5
Townshend, Vt., 170 **54** B5
Townsville, Austl., 40,471 **173** F2
Townsville, N.C., 195 **63** F1
Townville, Pa., 361 **60** C2
Towson, Md., 19,090 **62** H3
Towuti, Danau, Indon. **149** G3
Towyn, U.K., 1,929 **113** D5
Toxey, Ala., 157 **64** A4
Toyah, Tex., 294 **77** M4
Toyah Cr., Tex. **77** M4
Toyah L., Tex. **77** M4
Toyahvale, Tex. **77** M4
Tōya-ko, Jap. **155** J8
Toyama, Jap., 207,266 **155** E3
Toyama-wan, Jap. **155** E3
Toyofusa, Jap. **155** n20
Toyohama, Jap., 11,881 **155** C4
Toyohama, Jap., 9,190 **155** E4
Toyohashi, Jap., 212,515 **155** E4
Toyohira, Jap., 77,312 **155** J8
Toyokawa, Jap., 65,313 **155** E4
Toyokoro, Jap., 10,725 **155** K8
Toyoma, Jap., 10,350 **155** G2
Toyonaka, Jap., 199,065 **155** D4
Toyooka, Jap., 42,569 **155** D4
Toyooka, Jap., 12,326 **155** m19
Toyotomi, Jap. **155** J7
Toyoura, Jap., 11,005 **155** J8
Tozitna, r., Alaska **85** G2
Trabanca, Sp. **122** B2
Traben Trarbach, F.R.Ger., 5,771 **118** A3
Trabzon, Turk., 52,680 **142** D1
Tracadie, N.B., Can., 1,357 **45** N6
Tracadie, N.S., Can. **47** V11
Tra Cu, S. Viet. **147** m12
Tracy, N.B., Can. **47** S11
Tracy, Qué., Can., 8,106 **47** L2
Tracy, Calif., 11,289 **82** C4
Tracy, Minn., 2,862 **74** E3
Tracy, Mo., 208 **72** C5
Tracy City, Tenn., 1,577 **71** F6
Tracy Mtn., N. Dak. **74** A2
Tracyton, Wash. **81** a7
Trade, Tenn. **71** K5
Tradewater, r., Ky. **71** D4
Traer, Iowa, 1,623 **72** E2
Traer, Kans. **75** E4
Trafalgar, Ind., 459 **70** C3
Trafford, Ala., 529 **64** C2
Trafford, Pa., 4,330 **60** d8
Trafford, L., Fla. **65** H6
Trafúl, L., Arg. **105** f15
Traganón, Gr., 2,099 **129** C6
Traian, Rum. **128** F2
Traiguén, Chile, 9,990 **105** A5
Trail, Br. Col., Can., 11,242 **42** H4
Trail, Minn., 100 **74** E2
Trail, Oreg. **80** B4
Trail City, S. Dak. **74** B3
Trail Creek, Ind., 1,552 **70** C1
Trail Cr., Colo. **79** b9
Traill, co., N. Dak., 10,583 **74** D2
Trail Pt., Utah **78** C2
Trainer, Pa., 2,358 **60** f12
Traisen, Aust., 3,358 **124** b10
Traisen, r., Aust. **124** M5
Traiskirchen, Aust., 7,023 **124** c10
Traismauer, Aust., 3,358 **124** M5
Trakai, U.S.S.R., 3,000 **136** B2
Trakiszki, Pol. **127** E1
Trakiyska Nizina, plain, Bulg. **128** ·
Träkvista, Swed. **120** e8
Tralee, Ire., 11,612 **113** B5
Tralee Bay, Ire. **113** A5
Tramelan, Switz., 5,567 **124** B1
Tramén-Tepui, mtn., Ven. **101** J5
Tram Khnar, Camb. **147** k11
Tramm, F.R.Ger. **119** c8
Trammel, Va. **62** B5
Tramore, Ire., 2,919 **113** C5
Tramping Lake, Sask., Can. **43** B4
Tramway, N.C. **63** E2
Tranås, Swed. **120** C4
Trancoso, Mex., 3,827 **92** E3
Tranebjerg, Den., 2,554 **121** C5
Tranent, U.K., 6,317 **112** e8
Trang, Thai., 17,158 **146** B6
Trangan, P., Indon. **149** K4
Trang Bang, S. Viet. **147** m11
Trani, It., 38,223 **123** F4
Trangie, Austl., 1,400 **173** G4
Tranninh, Plat. du, Laos **146** C3
Tranquebar, India, 14,754 **145** m20
Tranqueras, Urug., 2,000* **105** D4
Tranquillity, Calif. **82** C4
Transcona, Man., Can., 14,171 **43** F5
Trans-en-Provence, Fr., 1,290 **116** m13
Transilvania, reg., Rum. **128** C1
Transkei, reg., S. Af. **164** D7
Transtrand, Swed. **120** C3
Transvaal, prov., S. Af. **164** D6
Transylvania, co., N.C., 16,372 **63** B2
Transylvania, La. **73** D5
Transylvania, Rum. = Transilvania
Tra On, S. Viet., 3,949 **147** k12
Trapaeng Kraleng, Camb. **147** k11
Trapani, It., 77,795 **123** D6
Trapeang Chong, Camb. **146** C4
Trap Falls Res., Conn. **56** D7
Trap Hill, N.C. **63** C1
Trappe, Md., 358 **62** H4
Trappe, Pa., 1,264 **60** f11
Trapper Pk., Mont. **81** B3
Traralgon, Austl., 8,845 **173** G6
Trarza, reg., Maur. **162** B3
Trasimeno, Lago, It., **123** D3
Trask, r., Oreg. **80** B3
Traskwood, Ark., 205 **73** C3
Träslöv, Swed. **121** E3
Trat, Thai., 3,813 **146** C4
Traun, Aust., 16,037 **124** L5
Traun, r., Aust. **124** L5
Traunik, Mich. **66** G2
Traunreut, F.R.Ger., 3,802 **118** D5
Traunsee, Aust. **124** K6
Traunstein, Aust. **124** M5
Traunstein, F.R.Ger., 14,540 **118** D5
Travagliato, It., 7,640 **122** d5
Trave, r., F.R.Ger. **119** c8
Travelers Rest, S.C., 1,973 **63** B3
Travers, Switz., 1,550 **124** A2
Travers, Mt., N.Z. **175** g6
Traverse, co., Minn., 7,503 **74** D3
Traverse, L., S. Dak. **74** D3
Traverse City, Mich., 18,432 **67** H4
Traverse Mts., Utah **78** c10
Traverse Pt., Mich. **66** E1
Travessão, Braz., 1,006 **103** f17
Travis, co., Tex., 212,136 **77** P4
Travis, L., Tex. **77** O4
Travnik, Yug., 10,000* **125** C2
Travo, It., 4,037 **122** c6
Trbovlje, Yug., 16,000* **125** B1
Treadwell, N.Y. **59** K7
Treasure, co., Mont., 1,345 **81** F2
Treasure Beach, Jam., 1,465 **96** p9
Treasure Island, Fla., 3,506 **65** G5
Treasury Is., Sol. Is. **175** a2
Treaty, Ind. **70** D2
Trebbia, r., It. **123** B2
Třebechovice pod Orebem, Czech. **127** f6
Trebel, r., Ger.D.R. **118** D2
Trebelsee, Ger.D.R. **119** d11
Třebětín, Czech. **127** e7
Třebíč, Czech., 20,102 **126** B2
Trebinje, Yug., 3,445 **125** D3
Trebisacce, It., 6,072 **123** F5
Trebišnica, r., Yug. **125** D3
Trebišov, Czech., 9,198 **126** E2
Trebižat, r., Yug. **125** C3
Třeboň, Czech. **126** B2
Třebovice, Czech. **127** f7
Trebsen, Ger.D.R. **126** b5
Trebur, F.R.Ger., 3,555 **119** E5
Trecate, It., 11,698 **122** b5
Trece Martires, Phil., 4,422 **153** b8
Trecenta, It., 5,496 **122** e5
Tredegar, U.K., 19,835 **114** B7
Treene, r., F.R.Ger. **118** B1
Trefeglwys, U.K. **114** A6
Trefnant, U.K. **114** B4
Tregaron, U.K. **113** E5
Treglwang, Aust. **124** L6
Trego, co., Kans., 5,473 **75** F5
Trego, Wis. **66** B3
Trego Center, Kans. **75** E5
Treguaco, Chile **105** e14
Treguaco, Chile **104** e16
Tréguier, Fr., 3,600 **116** B2
Trégunc, Fr., 5,081 **116** B3
Tregynon, U.K. **114** B5
Treherne, Man., Can. **43** f10
Treichlers, Pa. **61** i18
Treignac, Fr., 1,942 **117** D4
Treinta-y-uno de Janeiro, Ang. **164** B3
Treinta y Tres, Urug., 18,000* **105** E4
Treis, F.R.Ger., 1,900 **119** C4
Trélazé, Fr., 9,583 **117** C3
Trelde Næs, pen., Den. **121** B5

Trelew—Tunstall · 305

Trelew, Arg., 12,000* **105** B6
Trelleborg, Swed., 19,209 **120** C5
Trelleck, U.K., 1,954 **114** C7
Trélon, Fr., 3,344 **117** E1
Tremadoc Bay, U.K. **113** D5
Tremblant, Mt., Qué., Can. **47** K2
Tremblay-lès-Gonesse, Fr., 13,788 **116** i11
Trembleur L., Br. Col., Can. **42** F2
Tremembé, Braz., 4,478 **103** d18
Trementina, N. Mex. **79** C4
Třemešná, Czech. **127** g6
Tremiti, Isole di, It. **123** E3
Tremont, Calif. **82** a8
Tremont, Ill., 1,558 **68** C3
Tremont, Ind. **69** f10
Tremont (part of Wareham), Mass. **57** N5
Tremont, Miss. **73** G3
Tremont, Pa., 1,893 **61** K4
Tremont City, Ohio, 414 **70** F2
Tremonton, Utah, 2,115 **78** B1
Třemošnice, Czech. **127** e7
Tremp, Sp., 4,466 **122** F1
Trempealeau, co., Wis., 23,377 **66** B4
Trempealeau, Wis., 704 **66** B4
Trempealeau, r., Wis. **66** B4
Trenary, Mich. **66** G2
Trenčín, Czech., 24,222 **126** D2
Trengganu, r., Malay. **147** p14
Trenholm, Va. **62** F5
Trenque Lauquen, Arg., 17,873 **105** C5
Trent, S. Dak., 232 **74** D4
Trent, Tex., 298 **77** N3
Trent, r., Ont., Can. **46** G4
Trent, r., U.K. **113** F5
Trent, r., N.C. **63** G2
Trente-et-un-milles, L. des, Qué., Can. **47** H2
Trento, It., 71,226 **123** C1
Trenton, N.S., Can., 3,090 **47** U11
Trenton, Ont., Can., 12,809 **44** J7
Trenton, Fla., 941 **65** G3
Trenton, Ga., 1,301 **64** D1
Trenton, Ill., 1,866 **68** C5
Trenton, Mich., 18,439 **67** K6
Trenton, Mo., 6,262 **72** D4
Trenton, Nebr., 914 **75** D3
Trenton, N.J., 114,167 **61** B3
Trenton, N.Y., 363 **59** u25
Trenton, N.C., 404 **63** G2
Trenton, N. Dak. **74** A1
Trenton, Ohio, 3,064 **70** E3
Trenton, S.C., 314 **63** C4
Trenton, Tenn., 4,225 **71** B6
Trenton, Utah, 448 **78** c7
Trentwood, Wash., 1,387 **80** E2
Trent Woods, N.C., 517 **63** G2
Trepassey, Newf., Can. **45** R6
Trepassey Bay, Newf., Can. **45** b11
Trepča, Yug. **125** E3
Tres Arboles, Urug. **105** c11
Tres Arroyos, Arg., 40,000* **105** C5
Três Casas, Braz. **102** D3
Tresco, i., U.K. **113** C7
Três Corações, Brazil, 17,498 **103** d17
Tres Cruces, Arg., 1,500* **105** B2
Tres Cruces, Co., Mex. **93** G5
Tres Esquinas, Col. **100** C7
Tres Hermanas Mts., N. Mex. **79** B5
Treshnish Is., U.K. **112** C3
Treska, r., Yug. **125** E4
Treskavica, mt., Yug. **125** D3
Três Lagoas, Braz., 14,520 **103** F6
Tres Marias, Is., Mex. **92** D4
Três Marias, Represa, Braz. **103** G5
Tres Montes, G., Chile **105** A7
Tres Morros, Alto, mtn., Col. **100** B4
Tres Palos, Mex., 1,492 **93** F5
Tres Piedras, N. Mex. **79** B3
Tres Pinos, Calif. **82** C4
Três Pontas, Braz., 11,534 **103** d17
Três Rios, Braz., 22,246 **103** e18
Třešť, Czech. **126** B2
Treuchtlingen, F.R.Ger., 6,346 **118** C4
Treuddyn, U.K., 1,230 **114** B4
Treuen, Ger.D.R., 10,093 **126** b6
Treuenbrietzen, Ger.D.R. **118** D2
Treungen, Nor. **121** A2
Treutlen, co., Ga., 5,874 **64** G3
Trèves = Trier
Treveskyn, Pa., 1,450* **60** b8
Treviglio, It., 22,719 **122** c5
Trevilians, Va. **62** F4
Treviño, Sp. **122** n12
Treviso, It., 73,898 **123** D2
Trevor, Wis. **66** c13
Trevorton, Pa., 2,597 **60** J4
Trevose Head, U.K. **113** D6
Trévoux, Fr., 3,866 **116** p15
Treynor, Iowa, 368 **72** B3
Treysa, F.R.Ger., 7,520 **118** B3
Trezevant, Tenn., 944 **71** C5
Trezzo sull'Adda, It., 8,692 **122** c5
Trhové Sviny, Czech. **126** B2
Triabunna, Austl. **173** f14
Triadelphia, W. Va., 600 **62** D2
Triadelphia L., Md. **62** a8
Triánda, Gr., 2,918 **129** G6
Triang, Malay., 3,412 **147** p15
Triangle, Idaho **81** A4
Triangle, Va., 2,948 **62** G4
Triangle, The, reg., Burma **146** B1
Triángulos, Arrecifes, Mex. **93** G4
Triberg, F.R.Ger., 5,769 **118** B4
Tribes Hill, N.Y. **59** M6
Tribsees, Ger.D.R. **118** D1
Tribune, Kans., 1,036 **75** D5
Tricase, It., 13,011 **123** G5
Trichur, India, 73,038 **145** E8
Trida, Austl. **173** e9
Tridell, Utah **78** D1
Triel, Fr., 4,812 **116** g11
Trier, F.R.Ger., 84,869 **118** A4
Triesen, Liecht., 1,762 **124** a8
Triesenberg, Liecht., 1,387 **124** a8
Trieste, It., 282,776 **123** D2
Trieste, Gulf of, It. **123** D2
Trieste Deep, Pac. Oc. **168** E2
Triesting, r., Aust. **124** c10
Trigg, co., Ky., 8,870 **71** D5
Triggiano, It., 16,266 **123** F4
Triglav, mt., Yug. **125** A1
Trignac, Fr., 6,917 **117** B3
Trikeri, Gr., 1,198 **129** D5
Trikhonis, Límni, Gr. **129** C5
Trikkala, Gr., 27,876 **129** C5
Trikomo, Cyp., 2,080 **142** e9
Trilbardou, Fr. **116** k11
Trilby, Fla. **65** G4
Trilby, Ohio **70** F1
Trilla, Ill. **68** D4
Trilport, Fr., 1,460 **116** k11
Trim, Ire., 1,786 **113** C5
Trimbach, Switz., 5,784 **124** B1
Trimble, Ill. **68** E4
Trimble, co., Ky., 5,102 **71** F3
Trimble, Mo., 185 **72** C5
Trimble, Tenn., 581 **71** B5
Trimdon, U.K., 5,423 **112** h10
Trimont, Minn., 942 **74** E4
Trinchera, Colo. **79** C3
Trinchera Pk., Colo. **79** C3
Trincomalee, Cey., 26,356 **145** F8
Trindade, Braz., 7,015 **103** F5
Trindade, i., Atl. Oc. **109** K8
Třinec, Czech., 24,705 **126** D2
Tring, U.K., 6,051 **114** G7
Tring-Jonction, Qué., Can., 1,203 **47** N2
Trinidad, Bol., 13,800 **102** D4
Trinidad, Col. **100** E5
Trinidad, Cuba, 16,756 **96** c2
Trinidad, Hond., 2,984 **94** C3
Trinidad, Mex. **92** C3
Trinidad, Calif., 289 **82** A2
Trinidad, Colo., 10,691 **79** C3
Trinidad, Tex., 786 **77** P3
Trinidad, Wash. **80** D2
Trinidad, Urug., 15,000* **105** D4
Trinidad, i., Trin. and Tob. **96** g5
Trinidad, Sierra de, Cuba **96** c2
Trinidad and Tobago, ctry., 975,000* **96**
Trinidad Bay, Pan. **94** f12
Trinil, Indon. **148** d7
Trinitapoli, It., 14,938 **123** F4
Trinity, Newf., Can. **45** R5
Trinity, Ala., 454 **64** B1
Trinity, co., Calif., 9,706 **82** B2
Trinity, Ky. **71** H3
Trinity, N.C., 881 **63** E2
Trinity, co., Tex., 7,539 **77** Q4
Trinity, Tex., 1,787 **77** Q4
Trinity, Va. **62** E5
Trinity, r., Calif. **82** B2
Trinity, r., Tex. **77** Q4
Trinity Bay, Newf., Can. **45** R5
Trinity Bay, Tex. **77** k9
Trinity Center, Calif. **82** B2
Trinity Is., Alaska **85** F4
Trinity Mts., Calif. **82** ·
Trinity Res., Calif. **82** B2
Trinity Springs, Ind. **70** C4
Trinkitat, Sudan **163** L2
Trino, It., 9,151 **122** b5
Trio, S.C. **63** E4
Trion, Ga., 2,227 **64** D1
Triplett, Mo., 231 **72** D5
Tripoli, Leb. = Ṭarābulus
Tripoli, Libya = Ṭarābulus
Tripoli, Iowa, 1,179 **72** E2
Tripoli, Wis. **66** D3
Tripolis, Gr., 18,500 **129** D6
Tripolitania, Libya = Ṭarābulus
Tripótamon, Gr. **129** C5
Tripp, co., S. Dak., 8,761 **74** B4
Tripp, S. Dak., 873 **74** D4
Trippstadt, F.R.Ger., 1,783 **119** D6
Triptis, Ger.D.R. **126** a6
Tripura, un. terr., India, 1,142,005 **145** J4
Trischen, i., F.R.Ger. **118** B1
Tristan da Cunha Group, is., Atl. Oc. **109** M9
Trith-St-Léger, Fr., 7,098 **116** a7
Tri Ton, S. Viet., 7,878 **147** k11
Trittau, F.R.Ger., 4,283 **119** b8
Triune, Tenn. **71** E6
Trivandrum, India, 239,815 **145** E8
Trnava, Czech., 32,594 **126** C2
Trobriand Is., Terr. Papua **170** E5
Trochtelfingen, F.R.Ger., 1,606 **118** B4
Trochu, Alta., Can. **42** K3
Trocomán, r., Arg. **104** g17
Trofaiach, Aust., 6,920 **124** M6
Trofarello, It., 5,171 **122** a6
Trofimovsk, U.S.S.R. **135** M2
Trogen, Switz., 2,101 **124** D1
Trogir, Yug., 4,348 **125** C3
Troia, It., 11,234 **123** E4
Trois Bassins, La Réunion **165** b11
Troisdorf, F.R.Ger., 15,308 **119** C3
Trois-Îlets, Mart. **97** 12
Trois-Pistoles, Qué., Can., 4,278 **45** M5
Trois-Rivières, Qué., Can., 52,387 **44** K6
Trois-Rivières, Guad. **97** 14
Troisvierges, Lux. **115** E4
Troitsk, R.S.F.S.R., U.S.S.R., 79,000 **134** F4
Troitsk, Ukr.S.S.R., U.S.S.R. **136** E3
Troitsko-Pechorsk, U.S.S.R. **134** E3
Troitskoye, U.S.S.R. **137** h9
Troitskoye, U.S.S.R. **137** r11
Trolak, Malay. **147** o15
Troldhede, Den. **121** A5
Trollhättan, Swed. **120** C4
Trollheimen, mts., Nor. **120** B3
Trombetas, r., Braz. **103** E1
Trombly, Mich. **66** F2
Tromelin, Île, Ind. Oc. **168** B3
Tromöy, Nor. **121** A2
Tromsö, Nor., 12,316 **120** D1
Trona, Calif., 1,138 **82** E5
Trondheim, Nor., 59,271 **120** B3
Trondheimsfjorden, Nor. **120** B3
Trong, Malay., 1,463 **147** o14
Trönninge, Swed. **121** E4
Tronto, r., It. **123** D3
Tronzano Vercellese, It., 4,497 **122** b5
Troon, U.K., 9,932 **112** D4
Trooper, Pa. **60** f11
Tropic, Utah, 382 **78** B3
Tropojë, Alb. **125** D3
Trosa, Swed. **120** e9
Trostberg, F.R.Ger., 6,872 **118** D4
Trostyanets, U.S.S.R., 17,800 **136** D3
Trotuș, r., Rum. **128** F1
Trotwood, Ohio, 4,992 **70** E3
Troup, co., Ga., 47,189 **64** D3
Troup, Tex., 1,667 **77** Q3
Troupsburg, N.Y. **58** E7
Trousdale, Kans. **75** F6
Trousdale, co., Tenn., 4,914 **71** E5
Trousers L., N.B., Can. **55** F2
Trout, La. **73** C6
Trout, r., N.W.T., Can. **40** E5
Trout, r., Vt. **54** B2
Trout Creek, Ont., Can. **46** E3
Trout Creek, Mich. **66** D2
Trout Creek, N.Y. **59** K7
Trout Creek, Utah **78** B2
Trout Cr., Colo. **79** b9
Trout Cr., Oreg. **80** C3
Trout Cr., Oreg. **80** D4
Trout Creek Hills, Colo. **79** B2
Troutdale, Oreg., 522 **80** b6
Trout Dale, Va., 273 **62** C6
Trout Lake, Alta., Can. **42** J2
Trout Lake, Mich. **67** H2
Trout L., N.W.T., Can. **40** E5
Trout L., Ont., Can. **44** C4
Trout L., Wis. **66** D2
Troutman, N.C., 648 **63** D2
Trout Pk., Wyo. **81** E3
Trout River, Newf., Can. **45** P5
Trout Run, Pa. **60** H3
Troutville, Pa., 209 **60** E3
Troutville, Va., 524 **62** D5
Trouville, Fr., 6,822 **117** D2
Trovaharabesi, ruins, Turk. **142** A1
Trowbridge, U.K., 15,844 **113** E6
Trowbridge, Calif. **82** b7
Troy, Ont., Can. **46** b14
Troy, Ala., 10,234 **64** C4
Troy, Idaho, 555 **81** A2
Troy, Ill., 1,778 **68** C5
Troy, Ind., 528 **70** C4
Troy, Kans., 1,051 **75** K4
Troy, Me. **55** C4
Troy, Mich., 19,058 **67** f14
Troy, Miss. **73** G3
Troy, Mo., 1,779 **72** F6
Troy, Mont., 855 **81** B1
Troy, N.H. **54** C6
Troy, N.Y., 67,492 **59** N6
Troy, N.C., 2,346 **63** E2
Troy, Ohio, 13,685 **70** E2
Troy, Okla. **76** G3
Troy, Oreg. **80** E3
Troy, Pa., 1,478 **60** J2
Troy, S.C., 260 **63** B4
Troy, Tenn., 587 **71** B5
Troy, Tex. **77** P4
Troy, Vt. **54** C2
Troy, W. Va. **62** D3
Troy, Wis. **66** E6
Troy, Turk. = *Trovaharabesi*
Troyan, Bulg., 9,946 **128** E3
Troy Bk., N.J. **58** b13
Troy Center, Wis. **66** E6
Troyes, Fr., 68,898 **117** F2
Troy Grove, Ill., 271 **68** C2
Troy Pk., Nev. **83** C3
Trpezi, Yug. **125** E3
Trstená, Czech. **126** D2
Trstenik, Yug., 3,856 **125** E3
Truax, Sask., Can. **43** D5
Trub, Switz., 1,981 **124** B2
Trübbach, Switz. **124** a8
Trubchëvsk, U.S.S.R., 9,400 **136** D2
Trubjela, Yug. **125** D3
Trubschacher, Switz., 1,665 **124** B2
Truby, Tex. **77** N3
Truchas, N. Mex. **79** C3
Trucial States, ctry., 130,000* **143** E4
Truckee, Calif. **82** C3
Truckee, r., Nev. **83** A3
Truckton, Colo. **79** C2
Trudovets, Bulg., 2,675 **128** D3
Trudovoye, U.S.S.R. **151** F2
Truesdale, Iowa, 153 **72** B2
Truesdell, Wis. **66** d13
Trufant, Mich. **67** H5
Trujillo, Col. **100** B5
Trujillo, Hond., 4,101 **94** E3
Trujillo, Peru, 99,808 **104** B4
Trujillo, Sp., 13,326 **122** C3
Trujillo, N. Mex. **79** C4
Trujillo, Ven., 19,358 **100** E3
Trujillo Alto, P.R., 1,297 **96** u10
Trujin, Lag. de, Dom. Rep. **96** m7
Truk, is., Car. Is. **170** E4
Truman, Minn., 1,256 **74** E4
Trumann, Ark., 5,013 **73** E2
Trumansburg, N.Y., 1,768 **59** G6
Trumbull, Conn., 20,379(T) **56** C8
Trumbull, Nebr., 173 **75** G3
Trumbull, co., Ohio, 208,526 **70** J1
Trumbull, Tex. **76** f10
Trumbull, Mt., Ariz. **78** B3
Trumon, Indon. **148** A2
Trŭn, Bulg., 2,922 **128** D3
Trun, Switz., 1,583 **124** C2
Trundle, Austl. **173** f9
Trung Dong, N. Viet. **147** i9
Trung Khanh Phu, N. Viet. **146** D2
Trung Luong, S. Viet., 1,151 **146** D3
Truquilemo, Chile **104** e15
Truro, N.S., Can., 12,098 **45** N6
Truro, U.K., 13,336 **113** D6
Truro, Ill. **68** B3
Truro, Iowa, 338 **72** D3
Truro, Mass., 1,002(T) **57** Q5
Truscott, Tex. **77** O3
Trușești, Rum. **128** F1
Truskavets, U.S.S.R., 10,000 **136** A3
Trussville, Ala., 2,510 **64** C2
Trŭstenik, Bulg., 6,680 **128** E3
Trŭstenik, Bulg., 3,510 **128** E3
Trustrup, Den. **121** C4
Trutch, Br. Col., Can. **42** G1
Truth or Consequences, N. Mex., 4,269 **79** B5
Trutnov, Czech., 23,016 **127** e6
Truxton, N.Y. **59** J6
Truyère, r., Fr. **117** E4
Tryavna, Bulg., 5,965 **128** E3
Tryon, Nebr. **75** D2
Tryon, Okla., 254 **76** F2
Tryonville, Pa. **60** C2
Trysilelva, r., Nor. **120** C3
Trzcianka, Pol., 8,815 **127** B2
Trzciel, Pol., 2,254 **127** A2
Trzcińsko Zdrój, Pol., 2,058 **127** A2
Trzebiatów, Pol., 7,360 **127** A1
Trzebień, Pol. **127** e5
Trzebinia, Pol., 6,773 **127** C3
Trzebnica, Pol., 5,928 **127** B3
Trzemeszno, Pol., 4,494 **127** C2
Trzepizury, Pol. **127** i6
Tsaidam, salt marsh, China **150** C3
Tsáktso, mt., Swed. **120** E1
Tsala Apopka L., Fla. **65** G4
Tsangarádha, Gr. **129** D5
Ts'ang-ch'i, China **152** B1
Ts'ang-hsien, China **150** F3
Ts'ang-k'ou, China **151** D3
Tsangwu = Wu-chou
Ts'ang-yüan, China **150** D5
Ts'ao-hsien, China **151** B4
Ts'ao-o, r., China **152** F1
Ts'ao-t'ang, China **152** a6
Ts'ao-tu, r., China **152** B2
Tsao-yang, China **152** D1
Tsar, Mt., Br. Col., Can. **42** H3
Tsaratanana, Malag. Rep., 1,447 **165** G4
Tsaratanana, Mt. = Maromokotro
Tsarev Brod, Bulg., 2,885 **128** F3
Tsasata Bogdo Uulc, Mong. **150** C2
Tsa-to, China **150** C3
Tsavo Nat. Pk., Kenya **164** F2
Tschida, L., N. Dak. **74** B2
Tschierv, Switz. **124** E2
Ts'e-heng, China **152** B2
Tselina, U.S.S.R. **136** F4
Tselinnoye, U.S.S.R. **137** r11
Tselinograd, U.S.S.R., 139,000 **134** G4
Ts'e-lo, China **150** B3
Tsen-ch'i, China **152** C3
Tseng-ch'eng, China **152** D3
Ts'eng-shan, China **151** C4
Ts'en-kung, China **152** C2
Tsentral'no-Yakutskaya Nizm., U.S.S.R. **135** M3
Tsentral'nyy, U.S.S.R. **137** r11
Tsentral'nyy-Kospashskiy, U.S.S.R. **137** i7
Tse-p'u, China **150** A3
Tse-tang, China **150** C4
Tsetseng, Bots. **164** C5
Tsetserlig, Mong. **150** D2
Tsévié, Togo, 9,000* **162** d8
Tshabong, Bots. **164** C6
Tshane, Bots. **164** C6
Tshela, D.R.Congo **164** B2
Tshikapa, D.R.Congo **164** C3
Tshilongo, D.R.Congo **165** m19
Tshinsenda, D.R.Congo **165** c20
Tshipasa, D.R.Congo **165** m18
Tshofa, D.R.Congo **164** D2
Tshuapa, r., D.R.Congo **164** C2
Tsimlyanskiy, U.S.S.R., 10,100 **136** F4
Tsimlyanskoye Vdkhr., U.S.S.R. **136** F3
Tsinan = Chi-nan
Tsinghai = Ch'ing-hai
Tsingtao = Ch'ing-tao
Tsingyüan = Pao-ting
Tsinh Ho, N. Viet. **146** C2
Tsining = Chi-ning
Tsipikan, U.S.S.R. **135** L4
Tsiribihina, r., Malag. Rep. **165** G5
Tsiroanomandidy, Malag. Rep., 4,125 **165** G5
Tsis, i., Truk **176** 19
Tsiteli-Tskaro, U.S.S.R., 8,600 **137** c1
Tsitsihar = Ch'i-ch'i-ha-erh
Tsitsutl Pk., Br. Col., Can. **42** F3
Tsivory, Malag. Rep. **165** G5
Tskhinvali, U.S.S.R., 24,000 **137** c1
Tsna, r., U.S.S.R. **136** e6
Tsna, r., U.S.S.R. **136** F2
Tso-ch'üan, China **151** B3
Tso-kung, China **150** D4
Tsomotretung, l., China **144** g11
Tso-shui, China **151** A4
Tsotílion, Gr., 1,554 **129** C4
Tsou-hsien, China **151** C4
Tso-yün, China **151** B3
Tsu, Jap., 113,900 **155** E4
Tsubame, Jap., 37,547 **155** F3
Tsubata, Jap., 18,157 **155** E3
Tsubetsu, Jap., 15,471 **155** L8
Tsuchimaru, Jap. **154** g15
Tsuchiura, Jap., 71,474 **155** G3
Tsuchiyama, Jap., 11,255 **154** h15
Tsuchizakiminato, Jap. **155** F2
Tsuda, Jap., 7,796 **155** D4
Tsudaehō, Jap. **154** f15
Tsuegayabu, Jap. **154** g15
Tsuen-Wan, H.K., 61,106 **152** b6
Tsugaru-kaikyō, Jap. **155** G1
Tsugawa, Jap., 10,414 **155** F3
Ts'ui-wei, China **152** a6
Tsuji, Jap., 5,188 **154** e15
Tsukahara, Jap. **155** n20
Tsukamoto, Jap. **154** f15
Tsuker-jima, Ryukyu Is. **154** b11
Tsukigata, Jap., 8,995 **155** J8
Tsukizaki, Jap. **155** n20
Tsukumi, Jap., 37,164 **154** B5
Tsuma, Jap., 4,240 **155** C3
Tsumai, Jap. **154** f14
Tsumeb, S.-W. Afr., 7,796 **164** B5
Tsu-mu-tsung, China **150** C4
Ts'ung-chiang, China **152** C2
Ts'ung-hua, China **152** D3
Ts'ung-yang, China **152** E1
Tsun-i, China **150** E4
Tsunō, Jap., 15,480 **154** B5
Tsuno-shima, Jap. **154** B4
Tsurasaku, Ryukyu Is. **154** b10
Tsuru, Jap., 29,262 **155** F4
Tsuruga, Jap., 53,493 **155** E4
Tsurugaoka, Jap. **154** g14
Tsuruga-wan, Jap. **154** h14
Tsurugi, Jap. **154** h14
Tsurugi, Jap., 12,397 **155** E3
Tsurugi-san, mtn., Jap. **154** f16
Tsurumai, Jap. **155** n20
Tsurumi-zaki, Jap. **154** C5
Tsurucka, Jap., 83,149 **155** F2
Tsurusaki, Jap., 27,755 **154** B5
Tsushi, Jap. **154** f15
Tsushima, Jap., 43,198 **155** E4
Tsushima, is., Jap. **154** A4
Tsushima-kaikyo, Jap. **154** A4
Tsutsu, Jap., 2,993 **154** A4
Tsuwano, Jap., 13,262 **154** B4
Tsuyama, Jap., 78,549 **155** D4
Tsuyazaki, Jap., 11,546 **154** B5
Tsuyung = Ch'u-hsiung
Tsyurupinsk, U.S.S.R., 11,700 **136** D4
Tua, r., Port. **122** B2
Tuakau, N.Z., 1,521 **175** g5
Tual, Indon. **149** K4
Tuam, Ire., 4,789 **113** B5
Tuamotu Arch. = Tuamotu, Îs.
Tuamotu, Îs., Fr. Poly. **171** J6
Tu-an, China **152** B2
Tuan Giao, N. Viet. **146** C2
Tuangku, P., Indon. **148** A2
Tuao, Phil., 5,556 **153** c5
Tuapa, Niue **177** 32
Tuapí, Nic. **94** F3
Tuapse, U.S.S.R., 37,000 **134** C5
Tuaran, Malay. **148** E1
Tuasivi, W. Samoa **177** 38
Tuasivi, C., W. Samoa **177** 38
Tuba, r., U.S.S.R. **137** s11
Tubac, Ariz. **78** C6
Tuba City, Ariz. **78** C3
Tubai, i., Soc. Is. **177** 42
Tuba L., Christmas Atoll **177** 40
Tubal, Wādī at, Iraq **142** E3
Tuban, Indon. **148** E4
Tubarão, Braz., 29,615 **103** G7
Ṭūbās, Jor., 5,709 **142** b7
Tubay, Phil., 1,793 **153** C3
Ṭubayq, Jabal at, Jor. **142** D4
Tubbataha Reefs, Phil. **153** B3
Tubbs I., Calif. **83** e11
Tubigon, Phil., 1,612 **153** e12
Tübingen, F.R.Ger., 44,264 **118** B4
Tubinskiy, U.S.S.R. **137** i9
Tubize, Belg., 9,260 **115** C4
Ṭubruq, Libya, 4,995 **151** J2
Tubuai, Îs. Tubuai **171** J6
Tubuai, Îs., Fr. Poly. **171** H6
Tubuai-Manu, i., Soc. Is. **177** 42
Tuburan, Phil., 4,161 **153** e11
Tucacas, Ven., 3,783 **100** F2
Tucannon, r., Wash. **80** E2
Tucano, Braz., 4,007 **103** J4
Tucapel, Chile, 1,065 **104** f17
Tuchan, Fr., 1,014 **117** E5
Tu-ch'ang, China **152** E1
T'u-ch'eng-tzu, China **151** C2
Tuchola, Pol., 7,854 **127** B2
Tuchomie, Pol. **127** B1
Tuchów, Pol. 3,430 **127** D4
Tuckahoe, N.J. **61** B5
Tuckahoe, N.Y., 6,423 **58** d13
Tuckahoe, r., N.J. **61** B5
Tuckaseigee, r., U.S. **63** A2
Tucker, Ark. **73** C3
Tucker, Ga. **64** h9
Tucker, co., W. Va., 7,750 **62** E3
Tuckerman, Ark., 1,539 **73** D2
Tuckernuck I., Mass. **57** P7
Tuckers Town, Berm. Is. **108** 1
Tuckerton, N.J., 1,536 **61** C4
Tuc Mac, N. Viet. **147** h9
Tucquegnieux, Fr., 5,440 **116** b8
Tucson, Ariz., 212,892 **78** C5
Tucumcari, N. Mex., 8,143 **79** C4
Tucumcari Mtn., N. Mex. **79** D4
Tucunaré, Braz. **103** E3
Tucupido, Ven. **100** F2
Tucupido, Ven., 6,763 **100** G3
Tucupita, Ven., 9,900 **101** K3
Tucuruí, Braz., 3,403 **103** F2
Tucutí, Pan. **94** J7
Tuczno, Pol., 1,706 **127** B2
Tuczno, Pol. **127** C2
Tudela, Sp., 16,456 **122** E1
Tudmur, Syr., 9,489 **142** D3
Tudor, L., Qué., Can. **45** N3
Tu-erh-po-t'e, China **151** E1
Tuffé, Fr. **117** D2
Tufi, Terr. Papua **174** f3
Tuftonboro, N.H. **54** E4
Tugaske, Sask., Can. **43** C5
Tugby, U.K. **114** G5
Tugela, r., S. Af. **164** E6
Tug Fk., r., Ky.-W. Va. **62** B4
Tugidak I., Alaska **85** F4
Tug Mtn., Me. **55** E4
Tugpan, Phil. **153** c8
Tuguegarao, Phil., 10,497 **153** B1
Tugur, U.S.S.R. **135** N4
Tuht, Turk., 8,393 **142** C1
Tuilá, Guat. **94** C3
Tuim, U.S.S.R. **137** s11
Tui-mien-pu, China **152** b6
Tuineje, Can. Is. **109** 4
Tuira, r., Pan. **94** J7
Tuitán, Mex., 1,350 **92** D3
Tujunga Cr., Calif. **83** h15
Tuka, Indon. **148** A2
Tukan, U.S.S.R. **137** i9
Tukangbesi, Kep., Indon. **149** H4
Ṭūkh, U.A.R. **161** i7
Tuk Khleang, Camb. **147** k11
Tuk Meas, Camb. **147** k11
Tūkrah, Libya **161** H2
Tuksum, China **144** d10
Tuktoyaktuk, N.W.T., Can. **40** C4
Tukums, U.S.S.R., 11,900 **136** A1
Tukuyu, Tanz. **164** E3
Tukwila, Wash., 1,804 **81** b8
Tula, Hgo., Mex., 7,559 **93** F4
Tula, Tam., Mex., 4,210 **93** F3
Tula, Tutuila **177** 39
Tula, U.S.S.R., 351,000 **134** C4
Tula, Miss. **73** F3
Tula, r., Mex. **93** e9
Tulagi, Sol. Is. **175** c3
Tulak, Afghan. **144** B2
Tulalip, Wash. **81** b6
Tu-lan, China **150** D3
Tulancingo, Mex., 26,663 **93** F4
Tulare, co., Calif., 168,403 **82** D4
Tulare, Calif., 13,824 **82** D4
Tulare, S. Dak., 225 **74** C3
Tularosa, N. Mex., 3,200 **79** B5
Tulbagh, S. Af., 1,938 **164** a8
Tulcán, Ec., 16,752 **104** B1
Tulcea, Rum., 24,639 **128** G2
Tul'chin, U.S.S.R., 10,500 **136** C3
Tuléar, Malag. Rep., 33,850 **165** G5
Tulelake, Calif., 950 **82** C2
Tule L., Calif. **82** C2
Tulemalu L., N.W.T., Can. **40** J5
Tulgheș, Rum. **128** E1
Tulia, Tex., 4,410 **77** N2
Tulip, Ark. **73** C3
Tuliszków, Pol., 2,001 **127** C2
Ṭūl Karm, Jor., 20,688 **142** b7
Tulla, Ire. **113** B5
Tullah, Austl. **173** e13
Tullahassee, Okla., 199 **76** H2
Tullahoma, Tenn., 12,242 **71** E6
Tullamore, Austl. **173** f9
Tullamore, Ire., 6,147 **113** C5
Tulle, Fr., 20,790 **117** D4
Tullibigeal, Austl. **173** f9
Tullinge, Swed. **120** e8
Tullins, Fr., 4,880 **117** F4
Tulln, Aust., 6,286 **124** c10
Tullos, La., 594 **73** C6
Tullow, Ire., 1,838 **113** C5
Tully, Austl., 2,808 **173** F2
Tully (part of Orange), Mass. **56** H2
Tully, N.Y., 803 **59** H6
Tullytown, Pa., 2,452 **60** g11
Tulmaythah, Libya **161** H2
Tulpehocken Cr., Pa. **61** K5
Tulpfontein, S. Af., **164** a8
Tulsa, co., Okla., 346,038 **76** H1
Tulsa, Okla., 261,685 **76** G1
Tulsequah, Br. Col., Can. **42** C1
Tulstrup, Den. **121** B4
Tultitlán, Mex. **93** e9
Tuluá, Col. **100** B5
T'u-lu-fan, China **150** C2
T'u-lu-fan P'en-ti, depression, China **150** C2
Tuluksak, Alaska, 137 **85** D3
Tulum, ruins, Mex. **93** J4
Tulun, U.S.S.R., 59,000 **135** K4
Tulungagung, Indon. **148** d8
Tulva, r., U.S.S.R. **137** h8
Tuły, Pol. **127** h6
Tuma, U.S.S.R. **136** F2
Tuma, i., Terr. Papua **174** f3
Tuma, r., Nic. **94** E4
Tumacacori Nat. Mon., Ariz. **78** C6
Tumaco, Col. **100** A7
Tumaco, Rada de, Col. **100** A7
Tumalo, Oreg. **80** C3
Tumany, U.S.S.R. **135** P3
Tumarbong, Phil., 1,070 **153** A3
Tumatumari, Guyana **101** L5
Tumauini, Phil., 3,497 **153** B1
Tumba, Swed. **120** e8
Tumba, L., D.R.Congo **164** C2
Tumbador, Guat. **94** a9
Tumbarumba, Austl., 1,293 **173** G5
Tumbes, Peru, 19,033 **104** A2
Tumbiscatío, Mex., 1,115 **92** E4
Tumbledown Mtn., Me. **55** B3
Tumbwe, D.R.Congo **165** n19
Tumby Bay, Austl. **172** E5
T'u-men, China **151** F2
Tumen, r., China-Korea **150** H2
Tumeremo, Ven., 3,121 **101** K4
Tumkur, India, 47,277 **145** E7
Tummel, r., U.K. **112** E3
Tummo = Bi'r al Wa'r
Tumon Bay, Guam **176** 24
T'u-mo-t'e-ch'i, China **150** E2
Tumpat, Malay., 8,947 **147** p13
Tumsar, India, 24,910 **144** b15
Tumtum, Wash. **80** E2
Tumu, Ghana **162** D4
Tumuc-Humac Mts., Braz. **103** E1
Tumu Pt., Ponape **176** 29
Tumureng, Guyana **101** L4
Tumusla, Bol. **102** b12
Tumut, Austl., 3,012 **173** f10
Tumwater, Wash., 3,885 **80** B2
Tuna, P., P.R. **96** u11
Tuna, r., Col. **100** C7
Tunapui, Ven., 2,637 **101** J2
Tunapuna, Trin. and Tob., 9,770* **96** g5
Tunas de Zaza, Cuba, 1,380 **96** d2
Tunbridge, Vt. **54** C4
T'un-ch'ang, China **152** C4
T'un-ch'i, China **150** F4
Tunda, P., Indon. **148** b6
Tunduma, Zamb. **164** E3
Tunduru, Tanz. **164** F3
Tundzha, r., Bulg. **128** E3
Tunel, Pol. **127** i6
Tung, r., China **150** F4
Tungabhadra, r., India **145** E7
Tung-an, China **150** E4
T'ung-an, China **152** E2
Tung-ao, i., China **152** a6
Tungareo, Mex., 1,363 **93** d10
T'ung-ch'eng, A-h., China **152** E1
T'ung-ch'eng, Hu-p., China **152** D1
T'ung-chiang, China **152** B1
Tung-chiang, Taiwan, 30,181 **152** F3
Tung-ching, China **152** a6
Tung-ching-ch'eng, China **151** F1
T'ung-ch'uan, China **150** E3
Tung-ch'uan, China **152** A2
Tungelsta, Swed. **120** f8
Tung-fang, China **152** C4
Tung-feng, China **151** E2
T'ung-hai, China **150** D5
Tung-hai Tao, China **152** C3
T'ung-ho, China **151** F1
T'ung-hsiang, China **152** F1
T'ung-hsiang, China **152** F1
T'ung-hsien, China **151** C3
T'ung-hsing, China **152** C3
T'ung Hu, China **152** b5
T'ung-hua, China **150** G2
T'ung-jen, Ch-hai, China **150** D3
T'ung-jen, K-ch., China **152** C2
Tung-k'ou, China **152** C2
Tung Kratum, Thai. **147** c4
T'ung-ku, China **152** D1
Tungku, Malay. **149** F1
T'ung-kuan, China **151** A4
Tung-kuan, China **152** D3
Tung-kuang, China **151** C3
Tungla, Nic. **94** E4
Tung-lan, China **152** B2
T'ung-liang, China **152** B1
T'ung-liao, China **150** G2
T'ung-ling, China **152** E1
Tung-liu, China **152** E1
T'ung-lu, China **150** F4
Tung-ming, China **151** B4
Tung-ning, China **151** F1
Tungokochen, U.S.S.R. **135** L4
Tung-pai, China **152** D1
T'ung-pai Shan, China **152** D1
Tung-p'ing, China **151** C4
Tung-p'ing Hu, China **151** C3
Tungsan-got, N. Kor. **151** E3
T'ung-shan, China **152** D1
Tung-shan, China **152** E3
Tung-sha Tao, China **152** E3
Tung-sheng, China **151** A3
Tung-shih, China **151** C4
Tung-shih, Taiwan, 40,679 **152** F2
Tungsten, Nev. **83** A2
Tung-t'ai, China **151** D4
T'ung-tao, China **152** C2
T'ung-te, China **150** D3
T'ung-t'ien, r., China **150** C3
Tung-t'ing Hu, China **150** F4
Tung-t'ou Shan, China **152** F2
T'ung-tzu, China **150** E4
Tungua, i., Tonga **177** 36
Tungurahua, mtn., Ec. **104** c10
T'ung-wei, China **150** E3
Tung-wu-chu-mu-ch'in-ch'i, China **151** C1
Tung-yang, China **152** F1
Tun-hua, China **150** H2
Tun-huang, China **150** C2
Tunica, La. **73** D7
Tunica, co., Miss., 16,826 **73** E3
Tunica, Miss., 1,445 **73** E3
Tūnis, Tun., 410,000 **161** F1
Tūnis, Khalīj, Tun. **160** g5
Tunisia, ctry., 4,675,000* **160–1**
Tunja, Col. **100** D5
Tunjang, Malay., 2,305 **147** o13
Tunker, Ind. **70** D1
Tunkhannock, Pa., 2,297 **61** K2
Tunkhannock Cr., Pa. **61** L2
Tunk L., Me. **55** D4
Tunk Mtn., Wash. **80** D1
T'un-liu, China **151** B3
Tunnel City, Wis. **66** C4
Tunnel Hill, Ill. **68** D6
Tunnelton, W. Va., 359 **62** E3
Tunnsjöen, l., Nor. **120** C2
Tunø, i., Den. **121** C5
Tunor, U.S.S.R. **135** K3
Tunstall, Dur., Eng., U.K., 5,637 **112** h10
Tunstall, Staffs., Eng., U.K., 11,622 **114** D4

306 · Tuntatuliag—Union City

Tuntatuliag, Alaska, 144 85 D3
Tuntulara, Hond. 94 F3
Tunulik, r., Qué., Can. 45 M2
Tununak, Alaska 85 C3
Tunuyán, Arg., 20,000* 105 B4
Tunuyán, r., Arg. 105 B4
Tuobuya, U.S.S.R. 135 M3
Tuolumne, co., Calif., 14,404 82 D3
Tuolumne, Calif., 1,403 82 C4
Tuolumne, r., Calif. 82 C4
Tuoy-Khaya, U.S.S.R. 135 L3
Tupã, Braz., 28,723 103 F6
Tupaciguara, Braz., 10,642 103 G5
Tu-p'ang Ling, China 152 C2
Tupelo, Ark., 201 73 D2
Tupelo, Miss., 17,221 73 G3
Tupelo, Okla., 261 76 G3
Tupelo Nat. Btfld. Site, Miss. 73 G3
Tupí, Hond. 94 F3
Tupilac, Phil., 2,480 153 B4
Tupinambaranas, I., Braz. 102 E2
Tupinier, C., Kusaie 176 31
Tupiratins, Braz. 103 G3
Tupiza, Bol., 10,013 102 C6
Tupman, Calif. 82 D5
Tupper, Br. Col., Can. 42 G2
Tupper Lake, N.Y., 5,200 59 M3
Tupper L., N.Y. 59 L3
Tupsan, Phil., 1,961 153 f12
Tupungato, Arg., 10,800* 105 B4
Tupungato, Co., Arg.-Chile 105 •
Tupure, Ven. 100 E2
Túquerres, Col. 100 B7
Tura, India, 8,888 145 J4
Tura, U.S.S.R., 3,000 135 J3
Tura, r., U.S.S.R. 134 F4
Turabah, Saudi Ar., 6,864 143 C4
Turagua, Co., Ven. 101 H4
Turama, r., Terr. Papua 174 d2
Turan, U.S.S.R., 4,500 135 J4
Turanskaya Nizm., U.S.S.R. 134 E5
Turawa, Pol. 127 h6
Turawskie, Jez., Pol. 127 h6
Turbaco, Col. 100 C2
Turbat, Pak., 4,578 144 B4
Turbenthal, Switz., 2,685 124 C1
Turbeville, S.C., 355 63 E4
Turbeville, Va. 62 E6
Turbo, Col. 100 B3
Turbotville, Pa., 612 60 J3
Turceni, Rum. 128 D2
Turco, Bol. 102 a11
Turda, Rum., 33,614 128 D1
Tureia, atoll, Tuam. Arch. 177 42
Turek, Pol., 10,320 127 C2
Turema, St. Vinc. 97 19
Turfan = T'u-lu-fan
Turfan Depression = T'u-lu-fan P'en-ti
Turgay, U.S.S.R. 134 F5
Turgay, U.S.S.R. 137 o12
Turgay, r., U.S.S.R. 134 F5
Turgayskaya Dolina, val., U.S.S.R. 132 F4
Turgayskaya Stolovaya Strana, U.S.S.R. 134 F4
Turgeon, r., Qué., Can. 44 H5
Tŭrgovishte, Bulg., 14,193 128 F3
Turgutlu, Turk., 31,697 142 A2
Turhal, Turk., 17,159 142 D1
Türi, U.S.S.R., 5,700 136 B1
Turia, Rum. 128 F1
Turia, r., Sp. 122 E3
Turiaçu, Braz., 1,826 103 G2
Turicuaro, Mex. 93 c10
Turin, El Salv., 1,915 94 d10
Turin, It. = Torino
Turin, Ga., 183 64 f11
Turin, Iowa, 163 72 B2
Turin, Mich. = McFarland
Turin, N.Y. 59 K4
Turinsk, U.S.S.R., 18,000 134 F4
Turiy Rog, U.S.S.R. 151 F1
Türje, Hung., 2,589 126 C3
Turka, U.S.S.R., 5,700 136 A3
Turkestan, U.S.S.R., 10,600 134 F5
Turkestanskiy Khr., U.S.S.R. 132 F6
Túrkeve, Hung., 12,505 126 E3
Turkey, ctry., 31,391,207 142
Turkey, N.C., 199 63 F3
Turkey, Tex., 813 77 N2
Turkey, r., Iowa 72 F1
Turkey Creek, Ind. 69 e10
Turkey Creek, La., 279 73 C7
Turkey Cr., Ala. 64 d7
Turkey Cr., Okla. 76 F1
Turkey Flat, Ariz. 78 D5
Turkmen S.S.R. = Turkmenskaya S.S.R.
Turkmenskaya S.S.R., U.S.S.R., 1,862,000* 134 E5
Turks Is., W.I. 95 E2
Turku, Fin., 130,844 120 E3
Turkwel, r., Kenya 164 E1
Turlock, Calif., 9,116 82 C4
Turmero, Ven., 8,101 101 b11
Turnagain, r., Br. Col., Can. 42 E1
Turnagain, C., N.Z. 175 h6
Turnagain Arm, Alaska 85 c7
Turnberry, Man., Can. 43 E4
Turnbull, Mt., Austl. 172 D3
Turneffe Is., Br. Hond. 94 C2
Turner, co., Ga., 8,439 64 F4
Turner, Kans. 75 a7
Turner, Me. 55 B4
Turner, Mich., 206 67 K4
Turner, Mont. 81 E1
Turner, Oreg., 770 80 B3
Turner, co., S. Dak., 11,159 74 D4
Turners Falls, Mass., 4,917 56 F2
Turners Hall, Barb. 97 10
Turnersville, N.J. 60 f12
Turner Valley, Alta., Can. 42 J4
Turney, Mo., 144 72 C5
Turnhout, Belg., 35,165 115 D3
Türnich, F.R.Ger., 12,795 119 B3
Türnitz, Aust., 2,397 124 M6
Turn of River (part of Stamford), Conn. 56 B8
Turnor L., Sask., Can. 43 B3
Turnov, Czech., 11,636 126 B1
Tŭrnovo, Bulg., 24,648 128 E3
Turnpike (part of Shrewsbury), Mass. 57 K3
Turnu Măgurele, Rum., 18,055 128 E3
Turnu Roşu, Pasul, Rum. 128 E2
Turnu Severin, Rum., 32,486 128 D2
Turobin, Pol. 127 E3
Turochak, U.S.S.R. 137 r11
Turon, Kans., 559 75 G6
Turowo, Pol. 127 E2
Turpin, Okla. 76 C1
Turpo, Peru, 1,200 104 C5
Turquino, Pico, Cuba 96 e3
Turrell, Ark., 794 73 E2
Turret Pk., Ariz. 78 C4
Turrialba, C.R., 8,629 94 F6
Turriff, U.K., 2,686 112 E3
Tursi, It., 6,476 123 F4
Turtkul', U.S.S.R., 10,400 134 F5
Turtle, N. Br., r., N. Dak. 74 D1
Turtle, r., S. Dak. 74 C3
Turtle Creek, Pa., 10,607 60 c8
Turtleford, Sask., Can. 43 B4
Turtle Is., Phil. 153 A4
Turtle Lake, N. Dak., 792 74 B2
Turtle Lake, Wis., 691 66 A3
Turtle Mtn., Man., Can. 43 E5
Turtmann, Switz. 124 B2
Turtok, Pak. 145 E2
Turton, U.K., 13,673 114 D3
Turton, S. Dak., 140 74 C3
Turug Art Dawan, pass, China-U.S.S.R. 150 A2
Turukhansk, U.S.S.R. 134 H3
Turulung, Rum. 128 D1
Turzovka, Czech. 126 D2
Tus, ruins, Iran 143 F1
Tuscahoma, Okla. 76 H3
Tuscaloosa, co., Ala., 109,047 64 B2
Tuscaloosa, Ala., 63,370 64 B2
Tuscarawas, co., Ohio, 76,789 70 H2
Tuscarawas, Ohio, 817 70 H2
Tuscarora, Nev. 83 B2
Tuscarora, N.Y. 58 E6
Tuscarora Cr., Pa. 60 G5
Tuscarora Mtn., Pa. 60 G5
Tuscarora Mts., Nev. 83 B2
Tuscola, Ill., 3,875 68 D4
Tuscola, co., Mich., 43,305 67 K5
Tuscola, Mich. 67 K5
Tuscola, Tex., 414 77 O3
Tusculum, Ga. 64 H3
Tusculum, Tenn., 1,433 71 J5
Tuscumbia, Ala., 8,994 64 B1
Tuscumbia, Mo., 231 72 E6
Tu-shan, China 150 E4
Tu-shan-tzu, China 150 B2
Tushar Mts., Utah 78 B2
Tushka, Okla. 76 G3
Tuskegee, Ala., 1,750 64 D3
Tuskegee, Okla. 76 G2
Tuşnad, Rum. 128 E1
Tussey Mtn., Pa. 60 F4
Tussy, Okla. 76 F3
Tustin, Calif., 2,006 83 i16
Tustin, Mich., 248 67 H4
Tustumena L., Alaska 85 G3
Tuszyn, Pol., 6,866 127 C3
Tutayev, U.S.S.R., 17,700 136 E1
Tutbury, U.K., 2,274 114 E5
Tuthill, S. Dak. 74 B4
Tuticorin, India, 124,230 145 F8
Tutin, Yug. 125 E3
Tutira, N.Z. 175 h5
Tutóia, Braz., 3,337 103 H2
Tutrakan, Bulg., 9,592 128 F3
Tuttle, N. Dak., 255 74 C2
Tuttle, Okla., 855 76 F2
Tuttle Cr., Res., Kans. 75 J4
Tuttlingen, F.R.Ger., 23,828 118 B4
Tutuaca, Mex., 1,335 92 D2
Tutuba, i., New Hebr. 174 k5
Tutuila, i., Amer. Samoa 170 G5
Tututepec, Mex., 2,025 93 F5
Tutwiler, Miss., 912 73 E3
Tuula, r., Mong. 150 E2
Tuupovaara, Fin. 120 G3
Tuutapu, Co., Easter I. 177 46
Tu Vu, N. Viet. 147 h8
Tuvutha, i., Fiji 174 4
Ţuwayq, Jabal, Saudi Ar. 143 C4
Tuweep, Ariz. 78 B3
Tuxcueca, Mex., 1,261 93 a9
Tuxedo, Man., Can., 1,624 43 g10
Tuxedo, N.C. 63 B2
Tuxedo Park, N.Y., 723 59 M9
Tuxford, U.K., 1,510 114 G4
Tuxpan, Jal., Mex., 10,871 92 E4
Tuxpan, Micho., Mex., 3,580 93 d10
Tuxpan, Nay., Mex., 14,863 92 D4
Tuxpan, Ver. C., Mex., 23,222 93 F4
Tuxpan, r., Mex. 93 d10
Tuxtla Chico, Mex., 3,359 93 G5
Tuxtla Gutiérrez, Mex., 41,532 93 G5
Tuy, Sp., 12,671 122 A1
Tuy, r., Ven. 100 G2
Tuya, r., Br. Col., Can. 42 D1
Tuya L., Br. Col., Can. 42 D1
Tuy Duc, S. Viet. 147 m10
Tuyen Binh, S. Viet., 2,556 147 k11
Tuyen Hoa, N. Viet. 146 D3
Tuyen Nhon, S. Viet., 1,490 147 m11
Tuyen Quang, N. Viet. 146 D2
Tuy Hoa, S. Viet., 15,509 146 E4
Tuy Phong, S. Viet., 9,693 146 E5
Tūysarkān, Iran, 11,323 143 D2
Tu-yün, China, 120,000* 150 E4
Tuzantla, Mex., 1,212 93 d10
Tuz Gölü, Turk. 142 C2
Tuzi, Yug. 125 D3
Tuzigoot Nat. Mon., Ariz. 78 C4
Tuzkan, Oz., U.S.S.R. 137 e4
Ţūz Khurmātū, Iraq, 9,144 143 C1
Tuzla, Yug., 52,000* 125 D2
Tuzla, r., Turk. 137 b2
Tuzlov, r., U.S.S.R. 136 f8
Tvååker, Swed. 121 E3
Tved, Den. 121 C4
Tvedestrand, Nor. 121 A2
Tveit, Nor. 121 A2
Tveitsund, Nor. 121 A1
Tversted, Den., 1,697 121 C3
Tvis, Den., 1,504 121 A4
Tvørovri, Faeroe Is. 120 c7
Tvŭrditsa, Bulg., 4,689 128 E3
Twain Harte, Calif. 82 C3
Twante, Burma, 6,949 147 b2
Twardogóra, Pol., 3,069 127 B3
Tweed, Ont., Can., 1,761 44 J7
Tweed, r., Dominica 97 13
Tweed, r., U.K. 112 E4
Tweede Exloërmond, Neth., 6,200 115 E2
Twelve Pins, The, mtn. ra., Ire. 113 B5
Twenthe kan., Neth. 115 E2
25 de Mayo, Arg., 12,964 105 D5
Twenty Mile Cr., Ont., Can. 46 c15
Twentynine Palms, Calif. 82 F5
Twickenham, London, U.K. 114 H8
Twiggs, co., Ga., 7,935 64 F3
Twilight Cove, Austl. 172 C5
Twillingate, Newf., Can. 45 Q5
Twin, Ala. 64 B2
Twin Bridges, Mont., 509 81 C3
Twin Butte Cr., Kans. 75 D5
Twin City, Ga., 1,095 64 G3
Twin Falls, co., Idaho, 41,842 81 B4
Twin Falls, Idaho, 20,126 81 B4
Twinhsing, Mich., 199 67 K4
Twin Lake, Mich. 67 G5
Twin Lake, Wis., 1,497 66 c13
Twin Lakes, Conn. 56 C4
Twin Lakes, Me. 55 D3
Twin Lakes, Minn. 74 b5
Twin Lakes, Nebr. 75 C1
Twin Mountain, N.H. 54 D3
Twin Mtn., Alaska 85 H2
Twin Mts., Tex. 77 L4
Twin Oaks, Okla. 76 J1
Twin Rocks, Pa. 60 E4
Twinsburg, Ohio, 4,098 70 H1
Twins, The, mtn., Austl. 173 f11
Twin Sisters, Tex. 76 a5
Twin Valley, Minn., 841 74 D2
Twisp, Wash., 750 80 C1
Twist, Ark. 73 E2
Twistringen, F.R.Ger., 5,472 118 B2
Twitchell Res., Calif. 82 C5
Twitty, Tex. 76 N2
Two Buttes, Colo., 111 79 D3
Two Buttes, Colo. 79 D3
Two Buttes Cr., Colo. 79 D3
Two Friends = Canaries
Two Harbors, Minn., 4,695 74 G2
Two Hearted, N. Br., r., Mich. 67 H2
Two Hills, Alta., Can. 42 K3
Two Rivers, Br. Col., Can. 42 G2
Two Rivers, Wis., 12,393 66 F4
Two Rivers, S. Br., Minn. 74 D1
Two Rivers Res., N. Mex. 79 C5
Two Sister Lakes, Wis. 66 D3
Twyford, U.K., 1,411 113 k12
Tyao, r., Burma-India. 146 A2
Tybee I., Ga. 64 J4
Tybo, Nev. 83 B3
Tyborøn, Den. 121 A4
Tychy, Pol., 50,000* 127 C3
Tyczyn, Pol., 2,427 127 E4
Tydd St. Giles, U.K. 114 J5
Tye, Tex., 521 77 O3
Tygart L., W. Va. 62 E3
Tygarts Cr., Ky. 71 H3
Tygda, U.S.S.R. 135 M4
Tygelsjö, Swed. 121 E5
Tygh Valley, Oreg. 80 C3
Tyin, Nor. 120 B3
Tyler, Minn., 1,138 74 D3
Tyler, Pa. 60 E3
Tyler, co., Tex., 10,666 77 Q4
Tyler, Tex., 51,230 77 Q3
Tyler, Wash. 80 E2
Tyler, co., W. Va., 10,026 62 D3
Tylersport, Pa. 60 f10
Tylersville, Pa. 60 H4
Tylertown, Miss., 1,532 73 E6
Tylerville (part of Haddam), Conn. 56 G7
Tylstrup, Den. 121 B3
Tym, r., U.S.S.R. 134 H3
Tymowa, Pol. 127 k7
Tynan, Tex. 77 P5
Tynant, U.K. 114 A5
Tyndall, Man., Can. 43 h9
Tyndall, S. Dak., 1,262 74 D4
Tyndinskiy, U.S.S.R. 135 M4
Tyne, r., Eng., U.K. 113 E4
Tyne, r., Scot., U.K. 112 e8
Týnec nad Sázavou, Czech. 126 d7
Tynemouth, U.K., 70,112 113 F4
Tyner, Ind. 70 C1
Tyner, Ky. 71 H4
Tyner, N.C. 63 H1
Tynewydd, U.K., 5,206 114 A7
Tyngsboro, Mass., 3,302(T) 57 L2
Tyniec, Pol. 127 i6
Tyninghame, U.K. 112 e7
Týniště nad Orlicí, Czech. 127 e6
Týn nad Vltavou, Czech. 126 B2
Tynset, Nor. 120 B3
Tyonek, Alaska, 187 85 F3
Tyre = Şūr
Tyrifjorden, l., Nor. 120 B3
Tyringham, Mass., 197(T) 56 D3
Tyro, Ark. 73 D4
Tyro, Miss. 73 F3
Tyro, Va. 62 E5
Tyron, N.C., 2,223 63 B2
Tyrone, co., U.K., 133,930 113 C4
Tyrone, Colo. 79 C3
Tyrone, Ga., 124 64 f11
Tyrone, Ky. 71 G3
Tyrone, Mo. 72 F7
Tyrone, N. Mex. 79 A5
Tyrone, Okla., 456 76 B1
Tyrone, Pa., 7,792 60 F4
Tyronza, Ark., 601 73 E2
Tyrrell, co., N.C., 4,520 63 H2
Tysoe, U.K. 114 E6
Tyson, Vt. 54 B5
Tystberga, Swed. 120 e9
Tyszowce, Pol. 127 E3
Ty Ty, Ga., 461 64 F4
Tyukalinsk, U.S.S.R., 10,400 134 G4
Tyul'kino, U.S.S.R. 137 h7
Tyul'kubas, U.S.S.R., 8,200 137 f3
Tyumen', U.S.S.R., 168,000 134 F4
Tyumen'-Aryk, U.S.S.R. 137 e3
Tyumentsevo, U.S.S.R. 137 q11
Tyundyk, r., U.S.S.R. 137 p12
Tyung, r., U.S.S.R. 135 L3
Tzaneen, S. Af., 6,209 164 E5
Tzekung = Tzu-kung
Tzimol, Mex., 2,588 93 G5
Tzu, r., China 152 C1
Tzu-ch'ang, China 151 A3
Tzu-ch'i, China 152 E2
Tz'u-ch'i, China 152 F1
Tzu-chin, China 152 D3
Tzu-chou, China 151 A3
Tzu-ch'uan, China 151 C3
Tzu-chung, China 152 B1
Tzu-hsing, China 152 D2
Tz'u-kao Shan, Taiwan 152 F2
Tzu-kuei, China 152 C1
Tzu-kung, China 152 B1
Tz'u-li, China 152 C1
Tzu-po, China, 1,200,000* 150 F3
Tzu-t'ung, China 152 B1
Tz'u-t'ung-chiao, Taiwan 152 F3
Tzuya, r., China 151 C3
Tzu-yang, Shen-hsi, China 151 A4
Tzu-yang, S-ch., China 152 B1
Tzu-yüan, China 152 C2
Tzu-yün, China 152 B2

U

Uaboe (dist.), Nauru 175 17
Uadaura-Parú-Ta, Ven. 101 K5
Ua Huka, i., Marq. Is. 171 J5
Uala, N. Caled. 174 h7
Uanle Uen, Som. Rep., 9,445* 163 M5
Uapao, C., Loy. Is. 174 k8
Ua Pu, i., Marq. Is. 177 42
Uatio, Passe de, N. Caled. 174 k9
Uatumã, r., Braz. 102 E2
Uauá, Braz., 1,361 103 J3
Uaupés, Braz. 102 C2
Uaupés, r., Braz. 102 C1
Ub, Yug., 2,176 125 D2
Ubá, Braz., 21,767 103 e17
Uba, r., U.S.S.R. 137 q12
Übach-Palenberg, F.R.Ger., 22,256 119 A3
Ubagan, r., U.S.S.R. 134 F4
Ubangi, r., Af. 164 C1
Ubaque, Col. 101 e15
Ubara, Jap. 154 g14
Ubaté, Col. 100 D5
Ubatuba, Braz., 3,748 103 d18
Ubay, Phil., 3,875 153 C3
Ubayyiḑ, Wādī al, Iraq 143 C2
Ubby, Den., 1,492 121 D5
Ube, Jap., 166,632 154 B5
Ubeda, Sp., 28,956 122 D3
Übelbach, Aust., 2,460 124 M6
Uberaba, Braz., 72,053 103 G5
Uberlândia, Braz., 70,719 103 G5
Überlingen, F.R.Ger., 8,998 118 B5
Ubiaja, Nigeria, 7,790 162 g8
Ubinskoye Oz., U.S.S.R. 137 p11
Ubly, Mich., 819 67 L5
Ubombo, S. Af. 164 E6
Ubon Ratchathani, Thai., 27,222 146 D4
Ubort', r., U.S.S.R. 136 B3
Ubrique, Sp., 9,669 122 C4
Ubrub, Indon. 149 L3
Ubsa Nuur, Mong. 150 C1
Ubud, Indon. 148 f8
Ucareo, Mex., 1,615 93 d10
Ucayali, r., Peru 104 C3
Uccle, Belg., 69,126 115 d9
Uchanie, Pol. 127 E3
Uchigō, Jap., 38,820 155 G3
Uchiko, Jap., 20,764 155 C5
Uchinoura, Jap., 11,792 154 B6
Uchinskoye Vdkhr., U.S.S.R. 136 b5
Uchiura-wan, Jap. 155 J8
Uchte, F.R.Ger., 2,942 118 B2
Uchur, r., U.S.S.R. 135 N4
Uckange, Fr., 7,861 116 D2
Uckerath, F.R.Ger., 4,065 119 C3
Ucluelet, Br. Col., Can. 42 F4
Ucolo, Utah 78 D3
Ucon, Idaho, 532 81 D4
Uda, Rum. 128 E2
Uda, r., U.S.S.R. 135 N4
Udaipur, India, 111,139 145 D4
Udaipur Garhi, Nepal 144 f12
Udamalpet, India, 28,345 145 k20
Udaquiola, Arg. 105 b13
Udbina, Yug. 125 B2
Uddevalla, Swed., 34,290 120 C4
Uddiawan, Phil., 1,733 153 c6
Uddingston, U.K. 112 b8
Uddjaur, l., Swed. 120 D2
Uden, Neth., 7,400 115 D3
Udenbreth, F.R.Ger. 119 A4
Udenhout, Neth., 3,300 115 c7
Udhampur, India, 10,263 145 E2
Udine, It., 83,300 123 D1
Udipi, India, 24,610 145 E7
Udjunggading, Indon. 147 o16
Udon Thani, Thai., 30,884 146 C3
Udot, i., Truk 176 19
Udskaya G., U.S.S.R. 135 N4
Ueberstorf, Switz., 1,536 124 B2
Uecker, r., Ger.D.R. 118 D2
Ueckermünde, Ger.D.R., 11,859 118 E2
Ueda, Jap., 70,186 155 F3
Uedem, F.R.Ger., 3,421 119 A1
Uehling, Nebr., 231 75 J2
Ueki, Jap., 2,303 154 B5
Uele, r., D.R.Congo 164 D1
Uelen, U.S.S.R. 135 S3
Uel'kal', U.S.S.R. 135 R3
Ueloi, Yap 176 20
Uelzen, F.R.Ger., 24,617 118 C2
Uenfra, Yap 176 20
Uenishi, Jap. 154 g15
Ueno, Jap. 154 g16
Ueno, Jap., 60,725 155 E4
Uenohara, Jap., 27,004 155 m19
Uenota, Jap. 154 i14
Uere, r., D.R.Congo 164 D1
Uesugi, Jap. 154 g14
Uetersen, F.R.Ger., 14,971 118 B2
Ufa, U.S.S.R., 651,000 134 E4
Ufa, r., U.S.S.R. 134 E4
Uffenheim, F.R.Ger., 4,242 118 C4
Ufimskoye Plato, U.S.S.R. 137 i8
Ugalla, r., Tanz. 164 E2
Uganda, ctry., 7,551,000* 164 E1
Ugashik, Alaska, 36 85 E4
Ugashik Lakes, Alaska 85 E4
Ugchelen, Neth. 115 D2
Uggeløse, Den., 1,480 121 a7
Uggerby, Den. 121 C3
Ughelli, Nigeria 162 g9
Ugi, i., Sol. Is. 175 c3
Ugíjar, Sp., 2,527 122 D4
Ugimi, Ryukyu Is. 154 b10
Ugine, Fr., 7,746 117 G4
Uglegorsk, U.S.S.R., 17,500 135 O5
Ugleural'skiy, U.S.S.R. 137 i7
Uglich, U.S.S.R., 28,000 136 E1
Ugljan, i., Yug. 125 B3
Uglovoye, U.S.S.R. 151 F2
Uglovskoye, U.S.S.R. 137 q12
Ugra, r., U.S.S.R. 136 D2
Ugŭrchin, Bulg., 6,906 128 E3
Uherské Hradiště, Czech., 13,790 126 C2
Uherský Brod, Czech. 126 C2
Uhingen, F.R.Ger., 7,202 119 H7
Uhland, Tex. 76 c6
Uhlířské Janovice, Czech. 127 e7
Uhrichsville, Ohio, 6,201 70 H2
Uhříněves, Czech. 126 d6
Uhyst, Ger.D.R. 118 E3
Ŭich'ang, S. Kor. 151 F3
Uig, U.K. 112 C3
Uiha, i., Tonga 177 36
Ŭijŏnbu, S. Kor., 51,855 151 E3
Uil, U.S.S.R. 134 E5
Uiñamarca, L., Bol.-Peru 104 D6
Uinskoye, U.S.S.R. 137 h8
Uinta, co., Wyo., 7,484 81 D5
Uinta, r., Utah 78 C1
Uintah, co., Utah, 11,582 78 D1
Uintah, Utah, 344 78 c8
Uinta Mts., Utah-Wyo. 78 C1
Ŭiryŏng, S. Kor. 151 F4
Ŭisŏng, S. Kor., 22,853 151 F3
Uitenhage, S. Af., 48,146 164 D7
Uithoorn, Neth. 115 b6
Uithuizen, Neth., 3,700 115 E1
Uithuizermeeden, Neth. 115 E1
Uitkerke, Belg., 3,123 115 B3
Uitvlugt, Guyana, 3,529 101 L4
Uivuk, C., Newf., Can. 45 O2
Ujae, atoll, Marsh. Is. 176 22
Ujazd, Pol. 127 C3
Ujazd, Pol., 3,066 127 h6
Ujelang, atoll, Marsh. Is. 170 E4
Újfehértó, Hung., 14,847 126 E3
Ujhani, India, 17,542 144 b12
Uji, Jap., 47,336 154 g15
Uji-guntō, Jap. 154 A6
Ujiji, Tanz., 12,011 164 D2
Ujina, Chile 102 a12
Ujjain, India, 144,161 145 E5
Ujście, Pol., 2,483 127 B2
Újszász, Hung., 6,738 126 D3
Uka, Ryukyu Is. 154 b10
Uka, U.S.S.R. 135 Q4
Ukara I., Tanz. 165 f14
Ukerewe I., Tanz. 165 f14
Ukhta, U.S.S.R. 134 C3
Ukhta, U.S.S.R., 35,000 134 E3
Ukiah, Calif., 9,900 82 B3
Ukiah, Oreg. 80 D3
Ukmergė, U.S.S.R., 16,200 136 B2
Ukrainian S.S.R. = Ukrainskaya S.S.R.
Ukrainskaya S.S.R., U.S.S.R., 45,516,000* 134 B5
Uksukalik, Alaska 85 C3
Uku, Ryukyu Is. 154 b10
Uku-shima, Jap. 154 A5
Ula, Turk., 4,237 142 B2
Ulaan Baatar, Mong., 160,000* 150 E1
Ulaan Goom, Mong. 150 C1
Ulaga, U.S.S.R. 135 N3
Ulakhan Sis, Khr., U.S.S.R. 135 P3
Ulak I., Alaska 85 f8
Ulalu, i., Truk 176 19
Ulan Bator = Ulaan Baatar
Ulan Hoto = Wu-lan-hao-t'e
Ulanów, Pol., 1,479 127 E3
Ulan-Ude, U.S.S.R., 201,000 135 K4
Ulawa, i., Sol. Is. 175 c3
Ul'banskiy Zal., U.S.S.R. 135 N4
Ulceby, U.K. 114 J4
Ulchin, S. Kor., 24,221 151 F3
Ulcinj, Yug., 4,919 125 D4
Uldum, Den., 1,098 121 B5
Uleåborg = Oulu
Ulefoss, Nor. 121 B1
Ulen, Ind., 130 70 C2
Ulen, Minn., 481 74 D2
Ulfa, F.R.Ger., 1,380 119 G4
Ulfborg, Den., 1,989 121 A4
Ulft, Neth., 6,400 115 E3
Ulgham, U.K., 2,083 113 F4
Uliassutai = Jibhalanta
Ulindi, r., D.R.Congo 164 D2
Ulingan, Terr. New Guin. 174 e2
Ulithi, atoll, Car. Is. 170 D4
Uljma, Yug., 3,933 125 E2
Ulkatcho, Br. Col., Can. 42 F3
Ul'kenkaroy, Oz., U.S.S.R. 137 n11
Ulla, U.S.S.R. 136 C2
Ulla, r., Sp. 122 B1
Ulladulla, Austl., 1,210 173 h10
Ullapool, U.K. 112 D3
Ullared, Swed. 121 E3
Ulldecona, Sp., 5,186 122 F2
Ullensvang, Nor. 120 A3
Ullerslev, Den., 1,450 121 C5
Ullesthorpe, U.K. 114 F6
Ullin, Ill., 577 68 C6
Ulloa, Col. 101 d15
Ullsfjorden, Nor. 120 E1
Ullswater, l., U.K. 113 E4
Ullŭng-do, S. Kor. 151 F3
Ulm, F.R.Ger., 90,530 118 B4
Ulm, Ark., 140 73 D3
Ulmarra, Austl., 1,499 173 H4
Ulmbach, F.R.Ger., 1,336 119 G4
Ulmeni, Rum. 128 F2
Ulmen-Meiserich, F.R.Ger., 1,446 119 C4
Ulmers, S.C., 168 63 C4
Ulmu, Rum. 128 F2
Ulog, Yug. 125 D3
Ulovo, U.S.S.R. 135 P2
Ulricehamn, Swed. 120 C4
Ulrichskirchen, Aust. 124 c10
Ulrum, Neth. 115 E1
Ulsan, S. Kor., 29,992 151 F4
Ulsted, Den., 1,558 121 C3
Ulster, prov., Ire.-U.K., 1,661,325 113 C4
Ulster, co., N.Y., 118,804 59 M8
Ulster, Pa. 60 J2
Ulster Park, N.Y. 59 M8
Ulster Spring, Jam. 96 p8
Ulstrup, Den., 1,624 121 B4
Ultima, Austl. 173 d10
Ulúa, r., Hond. 94 C3
Ulu Bakar, G., Malay. 147 p14
Ulubat Gölü, Turk. 142 B1
Ulu Bernam, Malay., 3,165 147 o15
Ulu Dağ, Turk. 142 B2
Ulugh Muz Tagh, pk., China 150 B3
Uluinggalau, pk., Fiji 174 4
Ulumawao, pk., Hawaii 84 d7
Ulunga, U.S.S.R. 135 N5
Ulupalakua, Hawaii 84 E3
Ulupau Head, Hawaii 84 d7
Ulu Tiram, Malay., 2,778 147 p16
Ulu Titi Basah, G., Malay. 147 o14
Ulu Yam Bharu, Malay., 1,386 147 o15
Ulva, i., U.K. 112 C3
Ulverston, U.K., 10,515 113 E4
Ulverstone, Austl., 5,005 173 G6
Ulvik, Nor. 120 A3
Ul'ya, U.S.S.R. 135 O4
Ul'yanovsk, U.S.S.R., 247,000 134 D4
Ulysses, Kans., 3,157 75 D6
Ulysses, Nebr., 357 75 H2
Ulysses, Pa. = Lewisville
Umag, Yug., 2,616 125 A2
Umaji, Jap. 154 e15
Umala, Bol. 102 b10
Umán, Mex., 6,435 93 H4
Uman', U.S.S.R., 53,000 134 C5
Uman, i., Truk 176 19
Umapine, Oreg. 80 D3
Umar, Indon. 149 K4
Umaria, India, 11,277 145 F5
Umarkot, Pak., 5,878 144 C4
Umatac, Guam 176 24
Umatac Bay, Guam 176 24
Umatilla, Fla., 1,717 65 H4
Umatilla, co., Oreg., 44,352 80 D3
Umatilla, Oreg., 617 80 D3
Umatilla, r., Oreg. 80 D3
Umauma Cr., Hawaii 84 F4
Umbagog L., Me.-N.H. 54 E2
Umbarger, Tex. 76 M2
Umbazooksus L., Me. 55 C2
Umbertide, It., 15,798 123 D3
Umboi, i., Terr. New Guin. 174 e2
Umbrella Point, Jam. 96 p8
Umbukul, Terr. New Guin. 174 f1
Umeå, Swed., 22,623 120 E3
Umeälv, r., Swed. 120 D2
Umeura, Jap. 154 g14
Umiat, Alaska 85 F1
Umikoa, Hawaii 84 F4
Umingan, Phil., 4,050 153 b7
Umm al'Abīd, Libya 161 G3
Umm al Arānib, Libya 161 G3
Umm al Jimāl, ruins, Jor. 142 c7
Umm Bel, Sudan 163 J3
Umm Durmān, Sudan, 113,551 163 K3
Umm el Fahm, Isr., 7,492 142 b7
Umm Kaddādah, Sudan 163 J3
Umm Qays, Jor. 142 b7
Umm Ruwābah, Sudan, 7,805 163 K3
Umnak, Alaska 85 B5
Umnak I., Alaska 85 B5
Umnäs, Swed. 120 C2
Umniati, r., Rhod. 164 E5
Umphang, Thai. 146 B3
Umpire, Ark., 64 73 A3
Umpqua, Oreg. 80 B4
Umpqua, r., Oreg. 80 B4
'Umrān, Yemen 143 C5
Umsaskis L., Me. 55 C2
Umtali, Rhod., 36,000 164 E5
Umtata, S. Af., 12,287 164 D7
Una, Braz., 1,102 103 J5
Una, India, 16,098 145 D5
Una, r., Yug. 125 C2
Unac, r., Yug. 125 C2
Unadilla, Ga., 1,304 64 F3
Unadilla, Mich. 67 J6
Unadilla, N.Y., 1,586 59 K7
Unadilla Forks, N.Y. 59 K6
Unaí, Braz., 4,214 103 G5
Unalakleet, Alaska, 547 85 D3
Unalaska, Alaska, 218 85 C5
Unalaska I., Alaska 85 C5
Unare, r., Ven. 101 H3
'Unayzah, Saudi Ar. 143 C3
'Unayzah, Jabal, Asia 143 B2
Uncas, Alta., Can. 43 c7
Uncasville, Conn., 1,381 56 H7
Uncia, Bol., 8,810 102 C5
Uncompahgre, r., Colo. 79 B2
Uncompahgre Pk., Colo. 79 B2
Uncompahgre Plat., Colo. 79 A2
Underhill, Wis. 66 E4
Underhill Center, Vt. 54 B3
Underhill Flats, Vt. 54 B2
Underwood, Ind. 70 D4
Underwood, Iowa, 337 72 B3
Underwood, N.Y. 59 N3
Underwood, N. Dak., 819 74 B2
Underwood, Wash. 80 C3
Undu, C., Fiji 174 4
Undy, U.K. 114 C7
Une, Col. 101 e15
Unea I., Terr. New Guin. 174 f2
Unehata, Jap. 154 g16
Úněšov, Czech. 126 c7
Unga, Alaska, 43 85 D5
Unga I., Alaska 85 D5
Ungalik, r., Alaska 85 D2
Ungarie, Austl. 173 f9
Ungarra, Austl. 172 b8
Ungeny, U.S.S.R., 10,800 136 B4
Unger, Okla. 76 H4
Unggi, N. Kor. 151 F2
Ungkharak, Thai. 147 d4
Unhošť, Czech. 126 d6
União, Braz., 4,296 103 H2
União da Vitória, Braz., 15,822 103 F7
União dos Palmares, Braz., 10,406 103 J3
Uniara, India, 5,760 144 a13
Unicoi, co., Tenn., 15,082 71 J5
Unicoi, Tenn. 71 J5
Uničov, Czech. 127 g7
Unije, i., Yug. 125 B2
Unilla, r., Col. 100 C6
Unimak I., Alaska 85 C5
Unimak Pass, Alaska 85 C5
Union, Ala. 64 B2
Union, co., Ark., 49,518 73 C4
Union, co., Fla., 6,043 65 G2
Union, co., Ga., 6,510 64 F1
Union, co., Ill., 17,645 68 C6
Union, Ill. 68 C3
Union, co., Ind., 6,457 70 E3
Union, Ind. 70 B4
Union, co., Iowa, 13,712 72 C3
Union, Iowa, 534 72 D2
Union, co., Ky., 14,537 71 C4
Union, Ky. 71 G3
Union, parish, La., 17,624 73 C5
Union, La. 73 E7
Union, Me. 55 C4
Union, Mich. 67 H7
Union, co., Miss., 18,904 73 F3
Union, Miss., 1,726 73 F5
Union, Mo., 3,937 72 G6
Union, Nebr., 303 75 K3
Union, N.H. 54 E4
Union, co., N.J., 504,255 61 C2
Union, N.J., 51,499(T) 61 C2
Union, co., N. Mex., 6,068 79 D3
Union, co., N.C., 44,670 63 D3
Union, N.C. 63 G1
Union, co., Ohio, 22,853 70 F2
Union, Ohio, 1,072 70 E3
Union, Okla., 329 76 F2
Union, co., Oreg., 18,180 80 D3
Union, Oreg., 1,490 80 E3
Union, co., Pa., 25,646 60 H4
Union, co., S.C., 30,015 63 C3
Union, S.C., 10,191 63 C3
Union, co., S. Dak., 10,197 74 D4
Union, co., Tenn., 8,498 71 H5
Union, Tenn. 71 B6
Union, Utah 78 c9
Union, Wash. 80 B2
Union, W. Va., 411 62 D5
Union, r., Me. 55 D4
Union Bay, Br. Col., Can. 42 a6
Union Beach, N.J., 5,862 61 C3
Union Bridge, Md., 833 62 G3
Union Center, Ind. 69 h10
Union Center, S. Dak. 74 A3
Union Center, Wis., 252 66 C5
Union City, Calif., 6,618 83 e12
Union City (part of Naugatuck), Conn. 56 D6
Union City, Ga., 2,118 64 f10

Union City—Vals · 307

Union City, Ind.-Ohio, 5,704 70 E2
Union City, Mich., 1,669 67 H6
Union City, N.J., 52,180 61 C2
Union City, Pa., 3,819 60 C2
Union City, Tenn., 8,837 71 C5
Union Creek, Oreg. 80 B4
Uniondale, Ind., 311 70 D2
Union Dale, Pa., 287 61 M2
Unión de Reyes, Cuba, 5,351 96 c1
Unión de San Antonio, Mex., 1,997 93 b8
Unión de Tula, Mex., 5,584 92 D4
Union Flat Cr., Idaho-Wash. 80 E2
Union Furnace, Ohio 70 G3
Union Gap, Wash., 2,100 80 C2
Union Grove, Wis., 1,970 66 F6
Unión Hidalgo, Mex., 7,792 93 G5
Union Hill, Ill., 80 68 D2
Union Hill, N.Y. 58 o20
Union I., Gren. Is. 97 20
Union Lake, Mich. 67 e14
Union Lake, N.J. 61 A5
Union Level, Va. 62 F6
Union Mills, Ind. 70 C1
Union Mills, N.C. 63 B2
Union of South Africa = South Africa
Union of Soviet Socialist Republics, ctry., 233,200,000* 134-5
Union Pier, Mich. 67 G7
Union Point, Man., Can. 43 g10
Union Point, Ga., 1,615 64 F2
Unionport, Ind. 70 D2
Union Springs, Ala., 3,704 64 D3
Union Springs, N.Y., 1,066 59 G6
Union Star, Mo., 392 72 C5
Uniontown, Ala., 1,993 64 B3
Uniontown, Ky., 1,255 71 D4
Uniontown, Md. 62 G3
Uniontown, Mo. 72 H7
Uniontown, Pa., 17,942 60 C6
Uniontown, Wash., 242 80 E2
Union Valley, Tex. 76 g9
Union Village, R.I. 57 K5
Union Village, Vt. 54 C4
Unionville, Ont., Can. 46 E5
Unionville, Conn., 2,246 56 E5
Unionville, Ind. 70 C3
Unionville, Iowa, 185 72 E4
Unionville, Me. 55 E4
Unionville (part of Franklin), Mass. 57 L4
Unionville, Mich., 629 67 K5
Unionville, Mo., 1,896 72 E4
Unionville, Nev. 83 A2
Unionville, Albany co., N.Y. 59 v29
Unionville, Orange co., N.Y., 511 59 L9
Unionville, N.C., 119 63 D2
Unionville, Beaver Co., Pa. 60 b7
Unionville, Centre Co., Pa., 371 60 G4
Unionville, Chester Co., Pa. 60 e12
Unionville, Va. 62 G4
Unisan, Phil., 2,707 153 c9
Uništa, Yug. 125 C2
United, Pa., 2,044 60 D5
United Arab Republic, ctry., 30,053,861 161 J3
United Kingdom, ctry., 54,436,000* 112-3
United States, ctry., 197,967,000* 52-3
U.S. Air Force Academy, Colo. 79 c9
United States Range, N.W.T., Can. 41 N1
Unity, Sask., Can., 1,877 43 B4
Unity, Me. 55 C4
Unity, Md. 62 a8
Unity, N.H. 54 C5
Unity, Oreg. 80 D3
Unity, Wis., 386 66 C4
Unity Pd., Me. 55 C4
Unity Village, Mo., 153 75 b8
Universal, Ind., 424 70 B3
Universal City, Tex. 76 b6
Universales, Montes, Sp. 122 •
University, Miss., 3,597 73 F3
University City, Mo., 51,249 72 G6
University Heights, Iowa, 841 72 F3
University Heights, Ohio, 16,641 70 e9
University Park, Iowa, 569 72 E3
University Park, Md., 3,098 62 a9
University Park, N. Mex. 79 B5
University Park, Pa. = State College
University Park, Tex., 23,202 76 f9
Unkel, F.R.Ger., 2,789 119 C3
Unken, Aust., 1,544 124 J6
Unna, F.R.Ger., 29,684 119 D1
Unnao, India, 29,780 145 F4
Uno, Mich. 67 G2
Uno, Va. 62 F4
Unra, Jap. 154 h14
Unst, i., U.K. 112 F1
Unstrut, r., Ger.D.R. 118 C3
Unterägeri, Switz., 3,832 124 C1
Untergrombach, F.R.Ger., 3,876 119 F6
Unteriberg, Switz., 1,251 124 C1
Unterjettingen, F.R.Ger., 1,586 119 F7
Unterlüss, F.R.Ger., 3,941 118 C2
Unteröwisheim, F.R.Ger., 2,508 119 F6
Untersee, F.R.Ger.-Switz. 125 •
Unterseen, Switz., 3,783 124 B2
Unţeşti, Rum. 128 F1
Unuk, r., Can.-U.S. 42 D2
Ünye, Turk., 11,366 142 D1
Unzen-Amakusa-ktk., Jap. 154 B5
Unzha, r., U.S.S.R. 136 G1
Unzmarkt, Aust. 124 L6
Uo, I., Loy. Is. 174 k8
Uo-jima, Jap. 154 e15
Uoleva, i., Tonga 177 36
Uomi, Jap. 154 h14
Uozu, Jap., 47,309 155 E3
Upa, r., U.S.S.R. 136 E2
Upano, r., Ec. 104 B2
Upata, Ven., 12,421 101 J3
Upatoie Cr., Ga. 64 E3
Upavon, U.K., 1,521 114 E8
Upemba, L., D.R.Congo 164 D3
Upemba, Parc Nat. de l', D.R.Congo 164 D3
Upeo, Chile 104 f15
Uphall, U.K. 112 c8
Upham, N.B., Can. 47 T11
Upham, N. Dak., 333 74 B1
Uphill, U.K., 4,230 114 C8
Upi, Guam 176 24
Úpice, Czech. 127 e6
Upington, S. Af., 20,249 164 C6
Upland, Calif., 15,918 83 i15
Upland, Ind., 1,999 70 D2
Upland, Nebr., 237 75 G3
Upland, Pa., 4,343 60 f12
Upolu, i., W. Samoa 177 37
Upolu Pt., Hawaii 84 F3
Upou, Motu, i., Christmas Atoll 177 40
Uppåkra, Swed. 121 c7
Upper Ammonoosuc, r., N.H. 54 E2
Upper Arlington, Ohio, 28,486 70 F2
Upper Arrow L., Br. Col., Can. 42 H4
Upper Blackville, N.B., Can. 47 T10
Upper Brookville, N.Y., 1,045 58 e13
Upper Chateaugay L., N.Y. 59 M2
Upper Darby, Pa., 50,000* 61 M6
Upper Des Lacs L., N. Dak. 74 B1
Upper Hay River, Alta., Can. 42 H1
Upper Heyford, U.K., 2,190 114 F7
Upper Hutt, N.Z. 16,861 175 g6
Upper Iowa, r., Iowa 72 F1
Upper Island Cove, Newf., Can., 1,668 45 b10
Upper Jay, N.Y. 59 N3
Upper Kapuas Mts., Malay. 148 E2
Upper Keith, U.K. 112 e8
Upper Kent, N.B., Can. 47 S10
Upper Klamath L., Oreg. 80 B4
Upper Laberge, Yukon, Can. 40 C5
Upper Lake, Calif. 82 B3
Upper L., Calif. 82 C2
Upper Lough Erne, U.K. 113 C4
Upper Marlboro, Md., 673 62 H4
Upper Matecumbe Key, Fla. 65 h15
Upper Musquodoboit, N.S., Can. 47 U11
Upper N.Y. Bay, N.J.-N.Y. 58 c14
Upper Nyack, N.Y., 1,838 58 d12
Upper Red L., Minn. 74 E1
Upper Rice L., Minn. 74 E2
Upper Richardson L., Me. 54 F2
Upper Saddle River, N.J., 3,570 58 c12
Upper St. Croix L., Wis. 66 B2
Upper St. Johns Pd., Me. 55 C2
Upper Sandusky, Ohio, 4,941 70 F2
Upper Stepney (part of Monroe), Conn. 56 C7
Upper Sysladobsis L., Me. 55 D3
Upper Tract, W. Va. 62 E4
Upperville, Va. 62 G3
Upper Volta, ctry., 4,955,000* 162 D3
Upper Wire Village (part of Spencer), Mass. 56 J3
Uppingham, U.K., 1,940 114 G5
Upplands Väsby, Swed. 120 e8
Uppsala, Swed., 77,518 120 D4
Upsala, Ont., Can. 44 D5
Upsala, Minn., 356 74 E3
Upsalquitch, r., N.B., Can. 47 S10
Upshur, co., Tex., 19,793 77 Q3
Upshur, co., W. Va., 18,292 62 D4
Upson, co., Ga., 23,800 64 E3
Upson, Wis. 66 C2
Upstart, C., Austl. 173 G2
Upton, Qué., Can. 47 M3
Upton, U.K., 7,234 114 C4
Upton, Ky., 547 71 F4
Upton, Me. 55 B4
Upton, Mass., 3,127(T) 57 K4
Upton, Mo. 72 F7
Upton, co., Tex., 6,239 77 M4
Upton, Wyo., 1,224 81 G3
Upton upon Severn, U.K., 2,035 114 D6
Upwell, U.K., 1,883 114 J5
Uquilla, Bol. 102 a12
Ur, ruins, Iraq 143 D2
Urabá, G. de, Col. 100 B3
Urach, F.R.Ger., 8,111 119 G7
Uracoa, Ven. 101 J3
Uradome, Jap. 155 D4
Uraga, Jap. 155 m20
Uraga-suidō, Jap. 155 m20
Urahoro, Jap., 13,214 155 K8
Urakawa, Jap., 21,915 155 K8
Ural, r., U.S.S.R. 134 E5
Uralla, Austl., 1,121 173 G4
Ural'sk, U.S.S.R., 111,000 134 E4
Ural'skiye Gory, U.S.S.R. 134 E4
Urambo, Tanz. 164 E2
Urana, Austl. 173 G5
Urana, L., Austl. 173 e10
Urandangi, Austl. 172 E3
Urandi, Braz., 1,497 103 H4
Urania, La., 1,063 73 C6
Uran-Islampur, India, 20,817 145 i18
Uranium City, Sask., Can., 1,794 43 B2
Uranium Pk., Colo. 79 B1
Uraricoera, Braz., 1,075 102 D1
Uraricuera, r., Braz. 102 D1
Urasalakh, U.S.S.R. 135 O3
Urasi, i., Terr. Papua 174 3
Ura-Tyube, U.S.S.R., 30,000 134 F6
Urausu, Jap., 7,151 155 J8
Uravan, Colo., 1,005 79 A2
Urawa, Jap., 168,757 155 F4
Urayasu, Jap., 16,847 155 m19
Urbana, Ark. 73 C4
Urbana, Ill., 27,294 68 D3
Urbana, Ind. 70 D2
Urbana, Iowa, 544 72 F2
Urbana, Mo., 348 72 D7
Urbana, N.Y. 58 F7
Urbana, Ohio, 10,461 70 F2
Urbancrest, Ohio, 1,029 70 a7
Urbandale, Iowa, 10,310 72 D3
Urbanna, Va., 512 62 H5
Urbett, i., Jaluit 176 30
Urbina, Paso de, Ec. 104 c10
Urbino, It., 20,548 123 D3
Urbiztondo, Phil., 2,364 153 b7
Urcos, Peru, 2,939 104 D5
Urcuquí, Ec. 104 c9
Urcusique, Col. 100 B7
Urda, U.S.S.R. 134 D5
Urdinarrain, Arg., 7,437 105 D4
Ure, r., U.K. 113 F4
Uren', U.S.S.R. 136 G1
Ureña, C.R., 5,353 94 F6
Urengoy, U.S.S.R. 134 G3
Urenui, N.Z. 175 g5
Ureparapara, i., New Hebr. 174 k4
Ures, Mex., 3,174 92 C2
Ureterp, Neth. 115 E1
Urewera Nat. Pk., N.Z. 175 h5
Urfa, Turk., 59,910 142 D2
Urft, r., F.R.Ger. 119 B3
Urgench, U.S.S.R., 55,000 134 F5
Urgün, Afghan. 144 C2
Ürgüp, Turk., 5,018 142 C2
Uriah, Ala. 64 B4
Uriah, Mt., N.Z. 175 f6
Uriangato, Mex., 10,075 93 c9
Uribia, Col. 100 D2
Urich, Mo., 408 72 C6
Urimán, Ven. 101 J5
Urique, r., Mex. 92 D2
Uritskoye, U.S.S.R. 137 m11
Urititua, Tahiti 177 44
Urk, Neth., 5,700 115 D2
Úrkút, Hung., 2,825 126 C3
Urla, Turk., 10,796 142 A2
Urlaţi, Rum., 8,658 128 F2
Urle, Pol. 127 D2
Urlingford, Ire. 113 C5
Urloffen, F.R.Ger., 3,027 119 D7
Urmia, L. = Rezā'īyeh, Daryācheh-ye
Urnäsch, Switz., 2,330 124 D1
Uromi, Nigeria 162 g8
Uroševac, Yug., 12,000 125 E3
Uroyán, Montañas de, P.R. 96 r10
Urrao, Col. 100 B4
Ursa, Ill. 68 A3
Ursat'yevskaya, U.S.S.R. 137 e4
Ursina, Pa., 313 60 D6
Ursine, Nev. 83 C4
Ursus, Pol., 18,718 127 D2
Urtazym, U.S.S.R. 137 i9
Urtenen, Switz., 1,619 124 B1
Uruaçu, Braz., 4,392 103 G4
Uruana, Braz., 4,380 103 G5
Uruapan, Mex., 45,580 92 E4
Urubamba, Peru, 7,850 104 C5
Urubamba, r., Peru 104 C4
Urubu, r., Braz. 102 E2
Urucará, Braz., 1,203 102 E2
Uruçuí, Braz., 2,253 103 H3
Uruguai, r., Braz. 103 F7
Uruguaiana, Braz., 48,358 103 E7
Uruguay, ctry., 2,592,563 105
Uruguay, r., S. Amer. 105 D4
Uruido, Jap. 155 n19
Urukthapel, i., Palau 176 21
Urumaco, Ven. 100 E2
Urumchi = Wu-lu-mu-ch'i
Urungu, r., China 150 C2
Uruno Pt., Guam 176 24
Urup, O., U.S.S.R. 135 O5
Urus-Martan, U.S.S.R. 137 c1
Uruzgān, Afghan. 144 C2
Uryū, Jap., 7,225 155 J8
Uryū, r., Jap. 155 K8
Uryū-ko, Jap. 155 K7
Uryung-Khaya, U.S.S.R. 135 L2
Uryupinsk, U.S.S.R., 31,200 134 D4
Urzhum, U.S.S.R., 10,500 134 E4
Urziceni, Rum., 6,061 128 F2
Ürzig, F.R.Ger., 1,308 119 B4
Us, r., U.S.S.R. 137 t11
Usa, Jap., 7,904 155 C5
Usa, r., F.R.Ger. 119 F4
Usa, r., U.S.S.R. 134 E3
Uşak, Turk., 28,927 142 B2
Usakos, S.-W. Afr., 4,242 164 B5
Usambara Mts., Tanz. 164 F2
Usaquén, Col. 101 f15
Usarkopf, F.R.Ger. 119 C5
Usborne, Mt., Falk. Is. 108 3
Ušće, Yug. 125 E3
Uście Solne, Pol. 127 k6
Usedom, Ger.D.R. 118 E2
Usedom, i., Ger.D.R.-Pol. 118 E1
Usetsu, Jap. 155 E3
Ushachi, U.S.S.R. 136 C2
Ushakova, O., U.S.S.R. 135 H1
Ushakovskiy, U.S.S.R. 135 S2
Ushibuka, Jap., 34,700 154 A5
Ushiku, Jap. 155 n20
Ushimado, Jap., 12,328 154 f15
Ushi Pt., Tinian 176 27
Ush-Tobe, U.S.S.R., 24,000 134 G5
Ushuaia, Arg., 3,472* 105 B8
Ushumun, U.S.S.R. 135 M4
Usicayos, Peru, 1,018 104 D5
Usingen, F.R.Ger., 3,639 119 E4
Usk, Br. Col., Can. 42 E2
Usk, U.K., 1,869 114 C7
Usk, Wash. 80 E1
Usk, r., U.K. 114 C7
Uslar, F.R.Ger., 6,229 118 B3
Usman', U.S.S.R., 10,100 136 E2
Usmun, U.S.S.R. 135 M4
Usol'ye, U.S.S.R., 15,000 137 h7
Usol'ye-Sibirskoye, U.S.S.R., 64,000 135 K4
Uson, Phil., 2,857 153 h15
Uspanapa, r., Mex. 93 G5
Uspenka, U.S.S.R. 137 p11
Uspenskiy, U.S.S.R. 134 G5
Usquepaug, R.I. 57 K6
Ussel, Fr., 8,236 117 E4
Ussher Cr., Ont., Can. 58 i18
Ussuri, r., China-U.S.S.R. 150 H2
Ussuriysk, U.S.S.R., 113,000 135 N5
Ussurka, U.S.S.R. 151 F1
Ust'-Abakan, U.S.S.R. 137 s11
Ust'-Amginskoye, U.S.S.R. 135 N3
Ust'-Barguzin, U.S.S.R., 8,100 135 K4
Ust'-Belaya, U.S.S.R. 135 R3
Ust'-Bol'sheretsk, U.S.S.R. 135 P4
Ust'-Charyshskaya Pristan', U.S.S.R. 137 q11
Ust'-Chaun, U.S.S.R. 135 R3
Úštěk, Czech. 126 d6
Uster, Switz., 17,252 124 C1
Ustibar, Yug. 125 D3
Ustica, Isola d', It., 123 D5
Ust'-Ilimpeya, U.S.S.R. 135 K3
Ust'Labinsk, U.S.S.R., 34,500 136 E4
Ústí nad Labem, Czech., 66,410 126 B1
Ústí nad Orlicí, Czech., 11,435 126 C2
Ust'-Ishim, U.S.S.R. 134 G4
Ustka, Pol., 5,648 127 B1
Ust'-Kalmanka, U.S.S.R. 137 q11
Ust'-Kamchatsk, U.S.S.R., 10,900 135 Q4
Ust'-Kamenogorsk, U.S.S.R., 173,000 134 H5
Ust'-Kan, U.S.S.R. 137 r12
Ust'-Karsk, U.S.S.R. 135 L4
Ust'-Katav, U.S.S.R., 23,100 137 i8
Ust'-Khayryuzovo, U.S.S.R. 135 P4
Ust'-Kishert', U.S.S.R. 137 i7
Ust'-Koksa, U.S.S.R. 137 r12
Ust'-Kureyka, U.S.S.R. 134 H3
Ust'-Kut, U.S.S.R., 28,300 135 K4
Ust'-Maya, U.S.S.R. 135 N3
Ust'-Mil', U.S.S.R. 135 N4
Ust'-Nera, U.S.S.R. 135 O3
Ust'-Olenëk, U.S.S.R. 135 L2
Ust'-Onolva, U.S.S.R. 137 h7
Ust'-Ordynskiy, U.S.S.R., 7,500 135 K4
Ust'-Omchug, U.S.S.R. 135 O3
Ustovo, Bulg., 2,359 129 E4
Ust'-Ozërnoye, U.S.S.R. 134 H4
Ust'-Port, U.S.S.R. 134 H3
Ustrem, Bulg., 2,962 128 F3
Ustroń, Pol., 7,528 127 C4
Ustrzyki Dolne, Pol., 3,219 127 E4
Ust'-Tara, U.S.S.R. 137 o11
Ust'-Tarka, U.S.S.R. 137 o11
Ust'-Tsil'ma, U.S.S.R. 134 E3
Ust'-Ulagan, U.S.S.R. 134 H4
Ust'-Uls, U.S.S.R. 137 i6
Ust'-Usa, U.S.S.R. 134 E3
Ust'-Usa, U.S.S.R. 137 t11
Ust'-Voyampolka, U.S.S.R. 135 P4
Ust'-Yerba, U.S.S.R. 137 s11
Ustyurt, Plato, U.S.S.R. 134 E5
Ustyuzhna, U.S.S.R., 8,900 136 D1
Usudai, Jap. 154 f16
Usujiri, Jap., 7,527 155 J9
Usuki, Jap., 45,421 154 B5
Usulután, El Salv., 12,094 94 C4
Usumacinta, r., Guat.-Mex. 94 B2
Usumatlán, Guat. 94 d9
Usur, India 145 F6
Us'va, r., U.S.S.R. 137 i7
Usworth, U.K. 112 g10
Utah, st., U.S., 994,000* 78
Utah, co., Utah, 106,991 78 C1
Utah L., Utah 78 B1
Utajärvi, Fin. 120 F2
Utan Melintang, Malay. 147 o15
Utashinai, Jap., 38,002 155 K8
Utazu, Jap., 8,990 154 e15
Ute, Iowa, 511 72 B2
Ute Cr., N. Mex. 79 D3
Utena, U.S.S.R., 7,900 136 B2
Ute Pk., Colo. 79 B2
Úterý, Czech. 126 b7
Utete, Tanz. 164 F3
Uthai, Thai. 147 d4
Uthai Thani, Thai., 10,729 146 B4
U Thong, Thai. 147 c4
Utiariti, Braz. 102 E4
Utica, Col. 101 e14
Utica, Ill. 68 D2
Utica, Kans., 322 75 E5
Utica, Ky. 71 D4
Utica, Mich., 1,454 67 L6
Utica, Miss., 764 73 E5
Utica, Mo. 72 D5
Utica, Nebr., 564 75 H3
Utica, N.Y., 100,410 59 K5
Utica, Ohio, 1,854 70 G2
Utica, Pa., 274 60 B3
Utica, ruins, Tun. 160 f5
Utiel, Sp., 12,542 122 E3
Utik L., Man., Can. 43 F3
Utikuma L., Alta., Can. 42 J2
Utila, I. de, Hond. 94 D2
Utinga, Braz., 1,875 103 H4
Utique, Tun. = Utica
Utirik, atoll, Marsh. Is. 170 F4
Utiroa, Gilb. Is. 175 10
Utleyville, Colo. 79 D3
Uto, Jap., 25,792 154 B5
Utö, Swed. 120 f9
Utopia, Tex. 77 O5
Utraula, India, 10,065 144 d12
Utrecht, Neth., 247,500 115 D2
Utrera, Sp., 41,126 122 C4
Utsayantha, Mt., N.Y. 59 M7
Utsjoki, Fin. 120 F1
Utsumi, Jap., 7,123 154 h15
Utsunomiya, Jap., 239,007 155 G3
Uttaradit, Thai., 9,109 146 C3
Uttar Pradesh, st., India, 73,746,401 145 E3
Utterby, U.K. 114 H4
Utterson, Ont., Can. 46 E3
Uttoxeter, U.K., 8,168 114 E5
Utuado, P.R., 9,870 96 s10
Utukok, r., Alaska 85 D1
Utupua, i., Vanikoro Is. 175 6
Utzenstorf, Switz., 2,821 124 B1
Uuldza, Mong. 150 F1
Uuldza, r., Mong. 150 F1
Uusikaarlepyy = Nykarleby
Uusikaupunki, Fin., 4,531 120 E3
Uva, r., Col. 100 E6
Uvac, r., Yug. 125 D3
Uvalda, Ga., 589 64 G3
Uvalde, co., Tex., 16,814 77 O5
Uvalde, Tex., 10,293 77 O5
Úvaly, Czech. 126 d6
Uvarovka, U.S.S.R. 136 a6
Uvarovo, U.S.S.R. 136 F2
Uvat, U.S.S.R. 134 F4
Uvéa, B. de, Loy. Is. 174 k8
Uvéa, I., Loy. Is. 174 k8
Uvéa, I., Is. Wallis 175 7
Uvel'ka, r., U.S.S.R. 137 k8
Uvelse, Den. 121 a7
Uvel'skiy, U.S.S.R. 137 k8
Uverito, Ven. 101 H3
Uvinza, Tanz. 164 E2
Uvira, D.R.Congo 164 D2
Uwajima, Jap., 68,106 155 C5
Uwano, Jap. 154 h16
Uwayl, Sudan 163 J4
'Uwaynat, Jabal al, Sudan 163 J2
Uwharrie, r., N.C. 63 D2
Uwimmerah, r., Indon. 149 L4
Uxbridge, Ont., Can., 2,262 46 E4
Uxbridge, London, U.K. 114 H7
Uxbridge, Mass., 3,377; 7,789(T) 57 K4
Uxmal, ruins, Mex. 93 H4
Uy, r., U.S.S.R. 137 k8
Uyandina, r., U.S.S.R. 135 O3
Uyar, U.S.S.R., 20,500 137 t11
Uyea, i., U.K. 112 F1
Uyedineniya, O., U.S.S.R. 135 H2
Uyu, r., Burma 146 A1
Uyuni, Bol., 7,635 102 b12
Uyuni, Salar de, Bol. 102 C6
Uzbek S.S.R. = Uzbekskaya S.S.R.
Uzbekskaya S.S.R., U.S.S.R., 10,130,000* 134 F5
Uzdowo, Pol. 127 D2
Uzerche, Fr. 3,551 117 D4
Uzès, Fr., 6,058 117 F4
Uzgen, U.S.S.R., 16,400 137 g4
Uzhgorod, U.S.S.R., 52,000 134 B5
Uzhur, U.S.S.R., 22,400 137 s11
Uzinki = Ouzinkie
Uzlovaya, U.S.S.R., 54,000 136 E2
Uznach, Switz., 3,173 124 D1
Uzunköprü, Turk., 18,510 142 A1
Uzuto, Jap. 154 e15

V

Vaal, r., S. Af. 164 D6
Vaala, Fin. 120 F2
Vaaldam, res., S. Af. 165 k17
Vaals, Neth., 6,800 115 D4
Vaalserberg, mt., Neth. 115 E4
Vaasa, Fin., 44,436 120 E3
Vaassen, Neth., 4,500 115 D2
Vabre, Fr., 1,415 117 E5
Vác, Hung., 24,748 126 D3
Vaca, Key, Fla. 65 g15
Vacaria, Braz., 15,488 103 F7
Vacaville, Calif., 10,898 82 C3
Vacha, U.S.S.R., 5,200 136 F2
Vache, Île à, Haiti 96 k6
Vacoas, Maurit. 165 c12
Vada, Ga. 64 E4
Vader, Wash., 380 80 B2
Vadnais, L., Minn. 74 c5
Vadnais Heights, Minn., 2,459 74 c5
Vado, N. Mex. 79 B5
Vado Ligure, It., 10,007 123 B2
Vadsbro, Swed. 120 d9
Vadsö, Nor., 3,077 120 G1
Vadstena, Swed. 120 C4
Vaduz, Liecht., 3,369 124 D1
Værløse, Den., 8,072 121 a7
Væröy, i., Nor. 120 C2
Vágafjørdhur, sd., Faeroe Is. 120 c7
Vaganjski Vrh, mt., Yug. 125 B2
Vágar, i., Faeroe Is. 120 c7
Vagnhärad, Swed. 120 e9
Vagos, Port., 8,281 122 A2
Vágur, Faeroe Is. 120 c7
Váh, r., Czech. 126 D2
Vahitahi, atoll, Tuam. Arch. 177 42
Vaiden, Miss., 475 73 F4
Vaiere, B., Moorea 177 44
Vaigai, r., India 145 m21
Vaigalu, W. Samoa 177 38
Vaihingen, F.R.Ger., 5,730 119 F7
Vail, Ariz. 78 C5
Vail, Iowa, 473 72 B2
Vail, Wash. 80 B2
Vaila, i., U.K. 112 F1
Vaileka, Fiji 174 4
Vailly-sur-Aisne, Fr., 1,589 117 E2
Vail Mills, N.Y. 59 M5
Vaipae, Aitutaki 177 35
Vairaatea, atoll, Tuam. Arch. 177 42
Vaires-sur-Marne, Fr., 6,908 116 i11
Vaison-la-Romaine, Fr., 3,865 117 F4
Vaitape, Bora-Bora 177 43
Vaitongi, Tutuila 177 39
Vaitupu, i., Ellice Is. 170 F5
Vakh, r., U.S.S.R. 134 H3
Vakhanskiy Khr., U.S.S.R. 137 g5
Vakhsh, r., U.S.S.R. 134 F6
Vakhtan, U.S.S.R. 136 G1
Vakuta, Terr. Papua 174 3
Vakuta, i., Terr. Papua 174 3
Valašské Meziříčí, Czech., 12,695 126 D2
Valahia, reg., Rum. 128 E2
Valatie, N.Y., 1,237 59 N7
Val-Barrette, Qué., Can. 47 J2
Valbonne, Fr., 1,332 116 n13
Valbo-Ryr, Swed. 121 D2
Val-Brillant, Qué., Can. 47 S9
Valcartier, Qué., Can. 47 n16
Valchava, Switz. 124 E2
Valcheta, Arg., 6,000* 105 B6
Valcour I., N.Y. 54 A2
Valdagno, It., 27,205 123 C2
Val-David, Qué., Can., 1,109 47 K2
Valday, U.S.S.R., 9,700 136 D1
Valdayskaya Voz., U.S.S.R. 134 C4
Valdegovia, Sp. 122 m12
Valdemārpils, U.S.S.R., 2,100 136 A1
Valdemarsvik, Swed. 120 D4
Valdepeñas, Sp., 25,706 122 D3
Valderas, Sp., 3,982 122 C1
Valderrama, Phil., 2,345 153 B3
Valderrama, Sp. 122 m12
Valderrobres, Sp., 2,280 122 E2
Valders, Wis., 622 66 F4
Valdés, Pen., Arg. 105 C6
Valdese, N.C., 2,941 63 C2
Valdes I., Br. Col., Can. 42 c6
Val d'Esquières, Fr. 116 m14
Valdez, Ec., 3,064 104 B1
Valdez, Alaska, 555 85 H3
Valdez, Colo. 79 C3
Valdivia, Chile, 61,334 105 A5
Valdivia, Col. 100 C4
Valdobbiadene, It., 11,122 123 C2
Val-d'Or, Qué., Can., 10,415 44 J5
Val D'Or, Malay., 3,064 147 o14
Valdosta, Ga., 30,652 64 F5
Vale, Oreg., 1,491 80 E4
Vale, S. Dak. 74 A3
Valea lui Mihai, Rum. 128 D1
Valea Lungă, Rum. 128 E1
Valea Mare, Rum. 128 E2
Valea Vişeului, Rum. 128 E1
Valeggio sul Mincio, It., 8,516 122 d5
Valemount, Br. Col., Can. 42 H3
Valença, Bahia, Braz., 17,137 103 J4
Valença, R. de J., Braz., 18,935 103 e18
Valença do Piauí, Braz., 3,046 103 H3
Valençay, Fr., 2,732 117 D3
Valence, Fr., 55,023 117 F4
Valence-en-Brie, Fr. 116 k12
Valencia, Ec. 104 c10
Valencia, Phil., Mindanao, 2,881 153 C4
Valencia, Phil., Cebu, 2,032 153 e12
Valencia, Sp., 505,066 122 E3
Valencia, co., N. Mex., 39,085 79 A4
Valencia, N. Mex. 79 B4
Valencia, Pa., 310 60 c7
Valencia, Ven., 161,413 100 F2
Valencia, reg., Sp. 122 E3
Valencia, G. de, Sp. 122 F3
Valencia, L. de, Ven. 101 b11
Valencia de Alcántara, Sp., 13,159 122 B3
Valencia de Don Juan, Sp., 3,879 122 C1
Valencia I., Ire. 113 A6
Valenciennes, Fr., 46,643 117 E1
Văleni, Rum. 128 E2
Vălenii de Munte, Rum., 5,472 128 F2
Valens, Ont., Can. 46 b14
Valentine, Ariz. 78 B4
Valentine, Ind. 70 D1
Valentine, Nebr., 2,875 75 E1
Valentine, Tex., 420 77 L4
Valentines, Va. 62 G6
Valenton, Fr., 7,716 116 h11
Valenza, It., 17,881 123 B2
Valera, Ven., 44,566 100 E3
Valga, U.S.S.R., 13,600 136 B1
Val Gagné, Ont., Can. 44 H5
Valguarnera Caropepe, It., 16,584 123 E6
Valhalla, N.Y. 58 d12
Valhalla, N.C. 63 H1
Valiente Pen., Pan. 94 G6
Valier, Mont., 724 81 C1
Valier, Pa. 60 D4
Valinge, Swed. 121 E3
Valinhos, Braz., 10,104 103 c18
Valira, r., Andorra-Sp. 122 g7
Valjevo, Yug., 25,000* 125 D2
Valka, U.S.S.R., 4,900 136 B1
Valkeakoski, Fin. 120 F3
Valkenburg, Neth., 5,600 115 D4
Valkenswaard, Neth., 16,100 115 D3
Valladolid, Mex., 9,306 93 H4
Valladolid, Sp., 151,807 122 C2
Vallåkra, Swed. 121 b7
Vallauris, Fr., 11,135 116 n13
Vall de Uxó, Sp., 18,596 122 E3
Valle, Nor. 120 A4
Valle, Sp., 1,837 122 C1
Valle, Ariz. 78 B4
Vallecitos, N. Mex. 79 B3
Valle de Allende, Mex., 3,104 92 D2
Valle de Banderas, Mex., 1,489 92 D4
Valle de Bravo, Mex., 3,847 93 E4
Valle de Guadalupe, Mex., 1,560 93 b8
Valle de la Pascua, Ven., 24,051 100 G3
Valle de la Trinidad, Mex. 92 B1
Valle de Morín, Ven. 101 c12
Valle de Santiago, Mex., 20,879 93 c9
Valle de Zaragoza, Mex. 92 D2
Valledupar, Col. 100 D2
Vallée-Jonction, Qué., Can., 1,381 47 O2
Valle Grande, Bol., 9,111 102 D5
Valle Hermoso, Mex., 15,793 93 F3
Vallejo, Calif., 60,877 82 B3
Valle Nacional, Mex., 1,521 93 F5
Vallenar, Chile, 15,693 105 A3
Vallendar, F.R.Ger., 6,822 119 D4
Vallensbæk, Den., 1,834 121 a7
Vallentuna, Swed. 120 f8
Valleraugue, Fr., 1,047 117 E4
Vallersville (part of Plymouth), Mass. 57 O5
Valles, Mex., 23,620 93 F4
Valles Mines, Mo. 72 G6
Vallet, Fr., 4,476 117 C3
Valletta, Malta, 18,202 123 E7
Valley, Anguilla 97 7
Valley, co., Idaho, 3,663 81 B3
Valley, co., Mont., 17,080 81 F1
Valley, co., Nebr., 6,590 75 F2
Valley, Nebr., 1,452 75 J2
Valley, Wash. 80 E1
Valley, Wis. 66 C5
Valley Bend, W. Va. 62 D4
Valley Center, Calif. 82 E6
Valley Center, Kans., 2,570 75 H6
Valley City, Ill., 109 68 B4
Valley City, N. Dak., 7,809 74 C2
Valley Cr., Ala. 64 b8
Valley Falls, Kans., 1,193 75 K4
Valley Falls, N.Y., 589 59 N6
Valley Falls, R.I. 57 L5
Valley Falls, S.C. 63 B2
Valleyfield, Qué., Can., 28,256 47 K3
Valleyford, Wash. 80 E2
Valley Forge, Pa. 61 L5
Valley Grove, W. Va., 548 62 D2
Valley Head, Ala. 64 D1
Valley Head, W. Va. 62 E4
Valley Junction, Wis. 66 C4
Valley Lee, Md. 62 H4
Valley Mills, Tex., 1,061 77 P4
Valley Springs, S. Dak., 472 74 D4
Valley Stream, N.Y., 38,629 59 N10
Valleyview, Alta., Can., 1,027 42 H2
Valley View, Ill., 1,741 69 a9
Valley View, Ky. 71 G4
Valley View, Mo. 72 G6
Valley View, Cuyahoga Co., Ohio, 1,221 70 e9
Valleyview, Franklin Co., Ohio, 790 70 a7
Valley View, Pa., 1,540 60 J4
Valley View, Tex. 77 P3
Valley Wells, Tex. 77 O5
Valliant, Okla., 477 76 H3
Vallimanca, Arg., 1,150* 105 a13
Vallimanca, r., Arg. 105 C5
Vallo della Lucania, It., 7,104 123 E4
Vallonia, Ind. 70 C4
Vallorbe, Switz., 3,990 124 A2
Valls, Sp., 11,886 122 F2
Val Marie, Sask., Can. 43 C5
Valmaseda, Sp., 5,798 122 D1
Valmeyer, Ill., 709 68 B5
Valmiera, U.S.S.R., 11,800 136 B1
Valmondois, Fr. 116 g10
Valmont, N. Mex. 79 C5
Valmontone, It., 8,215 123 b8
Valmy, Nev. 83 B2
Valmy, Wis. 66 F4
Valognes, Fr., 5,743 117 C2
Valona = Vlorë
Valpaços, Port., 3,460 122 B2
Valparaíso, Chile, 252,865 105 A4
Valparaíso, Col. 101 d14
Valparaíso, Mex., 5,083 92 E3
Valparaiso, Fla., 5,975 65 C2
Valparaiso, Ind., 15,227 70 B1
Valparaiso, Nebr., 394 75 J2
Valpovo, Yug. 125 D2
Valréas, Fr., 6,701 117 F4
Valrita, Ont., Can. 44 G5
Vals, Switz. 124 D2
Vals, Tg., Indon. 149 L5

310 · Voghera—Walton

Voghera, It., 35,286 **123** B2
Vogošća, Yug., 3,744 **125** D3
Voh, N. Caled., 1,328 **174** i8
Vohemar, Malag. Rep., 2,241 **165** H4
Vohenstrauss, F.R.Ger., 3,772 **118** D4
Vohipeno, Malag. Rep., 3,092 **165** H5
Võhma, U.S.S.R. **136** A1
Vöhringen, F.R.Ger., 7,038 **118** B4
Voi, Kenya **164** F2
Voiceşti, Rum. **128** E2
Void, Fr., 1,118 **117** F2
Voil, Loch, U.K. **112** b7
Voila, Rum. **128** E2
Voineşti, Rum. **128** F1
Voinjama, Lib. **162** C4
Voiron, Fr., 15,585 **117** F4
Voisenon, Fr. **116** i12
Voisins-le-Bretonneux, Fr. **116** g11
Voislova, Rum. **128** D2
Voitsberg, Aust., 6,236 **124** M6
Voïviïs, Límni, Gr. **129** D5
Vojens, Den. **121** B5
Vokhma, U.S.S.R. **136** G1
Voládha, Gr. **129** F7
Volano, It. **122** f6
Volant, Pa., 213 **60** B3
Volary, Czech. **126** A2
Volcano, W. Va. **62** C3
Volcano I., Phil. **153** b8
Volcano Is., Pac. Oc. **170** D3
Volchansk, R.S.F.S.R., U.S.S.R., 25,200 **137** k7
Volchansk, Ukr.S.S.R., U.S.S.R., 20,500 **136** E3
Volchikha, U.S.S.R. **137** q11
Volch'ya, r., U.S.S.R. **136** e8
Volda, Nor. **120** A3
Volendam, Neth., 10,100 **115** D2
Volens, Va. **62** F6
Volga, Ind. **70** D4
Volga, Iowa **72** F2
Volga, S. Dak., 780 **74** D3
Volga, r., U.S.S.R. **134** D5
Volgodonsk, U.S.S.R., 16,000 **136** F4
Volgo-Donskoy Kan., U.S.S.R. **136** F3
Volgograd, U.S.S.R., 632,000 **134** D5
Volgogradskoye Vdkhr., U.S.S.R. **134** D4
Volin, S. Dak., 171 **74** D4
Volissós, Gr. **129** E5
Völkermarkt, Aust., 3,682 **124** L7
Volkhov, U.S.S.R., 37,700 **136** D1
Volkhov, r., U.S.S.R. **134** C4
Völklingen, F.R.Ger., 41,094 **118** A4
Volkmarsen, F.R.Ger., 4,040 **118** B3
Volkovysk, U.S.S.R., 16,400 **136** B2
Volksrust, S. Af., 8,096 **164** E6
Vollsjö, Swed. **121** F5
Volmarstein, F.R.Ger., 9,802 **119** C2
Volme, r., F.R.Ger. **119** D2
Volmer, Alta., Can. **43** b7
Volmunster, Fr. **116** d8
Volney, N.Y. **59** q22
Volney, Va. **62** C6
Volnovakha, U.S.S.R., 20,000 **136** E4
Volo, Ill. **69** b7
Volochanka, U.S.S.R. **135** J2
Vologda, U.S.S.R., 148,000 **134** D4
Volokolamsk, U.S.S.R., 7,800 **136** D1
Vólos, Gr., 49,221 **129** D5
Voloshino, U.S.S.R. **136** g7
Volpiano, It., 5,212 **122** a5
Vol'sk, U.S.S.R., 66,000 **134** D4
Volta, r., Ghana **162** d8
Volta, Pte. de, Îs. de Horne **175** 9
Voltaire, N. Dak., 70 **74** B2
Volta Mantovana, It., 5,263 **122** d5
Volta Redonda, Braz., 83,973 **103** H6
Volterra, It., 17,137 **123** C3
Volturno, r., It. **123** E4
Volubilis, Mor. **160** D2
Voluntad, Arg. **105** a13
Volunteer Pt., Falk. Is. **108** 3
Voluntown, Conn., 1,028(T) **56** J6
Volusia, co., Fla., 125,319 **65** H3
Vólvi, Límni, Gr. **129** D4
Volyně, Czech. **126** A2
Volyno-Podol'skaya Voz., U.S.S.R. **136** B3
Volzhskiy, U.S.S.R., 71,000 **136** G3
Vom, Nigeria **162** F4
Vona, Colo., 130 **79** D2
Vonda, Sask., Can. **43** C4
Vónitsa, Gr., 2,996 **129** C5
Vonore, Tenn. **71** G6
Von Ormy, Tex. **76** a7
Voorburg, Neth., 44,300 **115** a6
Voorheesville, N.Y., 1,228 **59** M6
Voorhout, Neth., 3,100 **115** b6
Voorne, i., Neth. **115** C3
Voorschoten, Neth., 12,900 **115** a6
Voorthuizen, Neth. **115** D2
Vòras Óros, Gr. **129** C4
Vorau, Aust., 1,206 **124** M6
Vorbasse, Den., 1,984 **121** A5
Vörden, F.R.Ger., 1,554 **118** B2
Vorden, Neth. **115** E2
Vordernberg, Aust., 2,896 **124** M6
Vorderrhein, r., Switz. **124** C2
Vordingborg, Den., 11,780 **121** D5
Vorhelm, F.R.Ger., 2,464 **119** D1
Vöringsfoss, falls, Nor. **120** A3
Vórios Evvoïkós Kólpos, Gr **129** D5
Vorkuta, U.S.S.R., 59,000 **134** F3
Vormsi, i., U.S.S.R. **136** A1
Vorona, r., U.S.S.R. **136** F2
Voronezh, U.S.S.R., 496,000 **134** C4
Voronezh, r., U.S.S.R. **136** E2
Voroniha, O., U.S.S.R. **135** J2
Voronin Trough **133** H2
Voronovo, U.S.S.R. **136** B2
Vorså, Den. **121** C3
Vorskla, r., U.S.S.R. **136** D3
Vorsma, U.S.S.R., 9,800 **136** F2
Vörterkaka, mtn., Ant. **180** Q5
Vörts-Järv, l., U.S.S.R. **136** B1
Võru, U.S.S.R., 11,500 **136** B1
Vose (part of Groton), Mass. **57** K2
Vosges, mts., Fr. **117** G2
Voskopojë, Alb. **125** E4
Voskresensk, U.S.S.R., 43,200 **136** E2
Voskresenskoye, U.S.S.R. **136** E1
Voss, Nor. **120** A3
Voss, Tex. **77** O4
Vosselaar, Belg., 4,848 **115** C3
Vossenack, F.R.Ger., 1,347 **119** A3
Vostochno Evropeyskaya Ravnina, U.S.S.R. **111** G2
Vostochno-Sibirskoye More, U.S.S.R. **135** P2
Vostochnyy, U.S.S.R. **137** k7
Vostochnyy Chink, ridge, U.S.S.R. **132** E5
Vostochnyy Sayan, mts., U.S.S.R. **135** J4
Vostok, Ant. **180** T5
Vostok I., Line Is. **171** H5
Votice, Czech. **126** B2
Votkinsk, U.S.S.R., 65,000 **137** h7
Votuporanga, Braz., 18,722 **103** G6
Vouga, Ang. **164** B4
Vouga, r., Port. **122** A2
Vouillé, Fr., 1,574 **117** D3
Vouvry, Switz., 1,368 **124** A2
Vouziers, Fr., 4,445 **117** F2
Voves, Fr., 2,371 **117** D2
Voy-Vozh, U.S.S.R. **134** E3
Vozhe, Oz., U.S.S.R. **134** D3
Voznesensk, U.S.S.R. **137** n11
Voznesenskoye, U.S.S.R., 31,000 **136** C4
Vrå, Den., 2,697 **121** B3
Vráble, Czech. **126** D2
Vrachesh, Bulg., 3,945 **128** D3
Vrådal, Nor. **121** A1
Vrads, Den. **121** B4
Vraňany, Czech. **126** d6
Vranduk, Yug. **125** D2
Vrangelya, O., U.S.S.R. **135** S2
Vranje, Yug., 16,000* **125** E3
Vranjska Banja, Yug., 2,362 **125** F3
Vranov, Czech. **126** E2
Vransko, Yug. **125** B1
Vratarnica, Yug. **125** F3
Vratimov, Czech. **127** h7
Vratsa, Bulg., 26,582 **128** D3
Vråvatnet, l., Nor. **121** A1
Vrbanja, Yug., 3,440 **125** D2
Vrbanja, r., Yug. **125** C2
Vrbas, Yug., 19,000* **125** D2
Vrbas, r., Yug. **125** C2
Vrbnik, Yug., 2,174 **125** B2
Vrbno, Czech. **127** g6
Vrbovsko, Yug. **125** B2
Vrchlabí, Czech., 10,582 **126** B1
Vrdy, Czech. **127** e7
Vrede, S. Af., 6,770 **164** D6
Vredefort, S. Af., 2,515 **165** i17
Vreden, F.R.Ger., 6,271 **118** A2
Vredenburg, S. Af., 2,140 **164** B7
Vredenburgh, Ala., 632 **64** B4
Vreed-en-Hoop, Guyana 3,156 **101** L4
Vreeland, Neth. **115** c6
Vreeswijk, Neth., 3,100 **115** c6
Vrela, Yug. **125** E3
Vrena, Swed. **120** d9
Vrensted, Den., 1,234 **121** B3
Vrginmost, Yug. **125** B2
Vrgorac, Yug. **125** C3
Vrhnika, Yug., 3,347 **125** B2
Vriddhachalam, India, 14,350 **145** m20
Vriezenveen, Neth., 6,500 **115** E2
Vrindaban, India, 25,138 **144** a12
Vrises, Gr. **129** E7
Vrlika, Yug. **125** C3
Vrondádhes, Gr., 4,685 **129** F5
Vroomshoop, Neth., 4,500 **115** E2
Vrpolje, Yug. **125** D2
Vršac, Yug., 32,000* **125** E2
Vrútky, Czech. **126** D2
Vryburg, S. Af., 14,597 **164** D6
Vryheid, S. Af., 10,753 **164** E6
Všetaty, Czech. **126** d6
Vsetín, Czech., 19,045 **126** C2
Vučitrn, Yug., 6,691 **125** E3
Vught, Neth., 16,900 **115** D3
Vuka, Yug. **125** D2
Vukovar, Yug., 24,000* **125** D2
Vulcan, Alta., Can., 1,297 **42** K4
Vulcan, Rum., 14,859 **128** D2
Vulcan, Mich. **66** F3
Vulcano, Isola, It. **123** E5
Vŭlchedrŭma, Bulg., 8,351 **128** D3
Vu Liet, N. Viet. **146** D3
Vultureşti, Rum. **128** E2
Vung Liem, S. Viet., 10,290 **147** m11
Vung Tau, S. Viet., 13,900 **146** D5
Vunindawa, Fiji **174** 4
Vunisea, Fiji **174** 4
Vunmarama, New Hebr. **174** m5
Vuohijärvi, l., Fin. **120** F3
Vuoitaspakte, mt., Swed. **120** D1
Vuokatti, Fin. **120** F3
Vuollerim, Swed. **120** E2
Vuotso, Fin. **120** F1
Vŭrbitsa, Bulg., 2,616 **128** F3
Vurnary, U.S.S.R., 7,200 **136** G2
Vŭrshets, Bulg., 3,435 **128** D3
Vutcani, Rum. **128** F1
Vuya Pt., Fiji **174** 4
Vya, Nev. **83** A2
Vyatka, r., U.S.S.R. **134** D4
Vyatskiye Polyany, U.S.S.R., 25,800 **134** D4
Vyazemskiy, U.S.S.R., 21,300 **135** N5
Vyaz'ma, U.S.S.R., 34,100 **134** C4
Vyazniki, U.S.S.R., 38,000 **136** F1
Vyborg, U.S.S.R., 56,000 **134** B3
Vychegda, r., U.S.S.R. **134** D3
Vygozero, Oz., U.S.S.R. **134** C3
Vyksa, U.S.S.R., 38,500 **136** F2
Vyrnwy, L., U.K. **114** B5
Vyrnwy, r., U.K. **114** B5
Vyselki, U.S.S.R. **136** E4
Vysha, r., U.S.S.R. **136** F2
Vyshniy Volochëk, U.S.S.R., 70,000 **134** C4
Vyškov, Czech., 12,160 **126** C2
Vysoké Mýto, Czech. **127** f7
Vysokinichi, U.S.S.R. **136** b6
Vysokovsk, U.S.S.R., 11,000 **136** b5
Vysokoye, U.S.S.R. **136** A2
Vysotsk, U.S.S.R., 11,000 **136** C1
Vyšší Brod, Czech. **126** B2
Vytegra, U.S.S.R., 11,000 **134** C3

W

Wa, Ghana, 14,479 **162** D4
Wa, Jap. **154** h15
Waal, r., Neth. **115** D3
Waalwijk, Neth., 17,300 **115** D3
Waar, Mios, i., Indon. **149** K3
Waas, Mt., Utah **78** D2
Waardenburg, Neth. **115** c7
Waarschoot, Belg., 7,860 **115** B3
Waasmunster, Belg., 6,958 **115** C3
Wabana, Newf., Can., 8,013 **45** b10
Wabasca, Alta., Can. **42** K2
Wabasca, r., Alta., Can. **42** J1
Wabash, Ark. **73** E3
Wabash, co., Ill., 14,047 **68** E5
Wabash, co., Ind., 32,605 **70** D2
Wabash, Ind., 12,621 **70** D2
Wabash, r., Ill.-Ind. **70** B4
Wabasha, co., Minn., 17,007 **74** F3
Wabasha, Minn., 2,500 **74** G3
Wabasso, Fla. **65** J5
Wabasso, Minn., 789 **74** E3
Wabaunsee, co., Kans., 6,648 **75** J5
Wabek, N. Dak., 14 **74** B2
Wabeno, Wis. **66** E3
Wabigoon, Ont., Can. **44** D5
Wabomat, i., Terr. Papua **174** 3
Wabowden, Man., Can. **43** F3
Wąbrzeźno, Pol., 10,844 **127** C2
Wabuk Pt., Ont., Can. **44** F3
Wabush, Newf., Can. **45** M4
Wabuska, Nev. **83** A3
Waccamaw, L., N.C. **63** F3
Waccamaw, r., N.C.-S.C. **63** E4
Wachapreague, Va., 509 **62** J5
Wachenheim, F.R.Ger., 2,806 **119** E6
Wachibara, Jap. **154** i14
Wachtebeke, Belg., 5,134 **115** B3
Wachtendonk, F.R.Ger. **119** A2
Wächtersbach, F.R.Ger., 3,508 **119** G4
Wachusett Mtn., Mass. **56** J1
Wachusett Res., Mass. **57** K3
Wacissa, Fla. **65** F2
Wacker, Ill. **68** B1
Waco, Qué., Can. **45** N4
Waco, Ga., 381 **64** D2
Waco, Ky. **71** G4
Waco, Mo. 143 **72** C7
Waco, Nebr., 166 **75** H3
Waco, Tenn. **71** D6
Waco, Tex., 97,808 **77** P4
Waconia, Minn., 2,048 **74** F3
Wacousta, Mich. **67** J6
Wada, Jap. **154** g15
Wada, Jap., 6,487 **155** D4
Wada, Jap., 6,754 **155** G4
Wada, Jap., 5,935 **155** L8
Wadakkancherry, India, 11,506 **145** k20
Wadan, Burma **147** f6
Wadayama, Jap., 6,480 **155** D4
Wad Bandah, Sudan **163** J3
Waddān, Libya **161** G3
Waddenzee, Neth. **115** D1
Waddesdon, U.K., 1,583 **114** F7
Waddingham, U.K. **114** H4
Waddington, Lincs., Eng., U.K., 4,193 **113** F5
Waddington, York., Eng., U.K. **114** C3
Waddington, N.Y., 921 **59** K2
Waddington, Mt., Br. Col., Can. **42** F3
Waddinxveen, Neth., 8,800 **115** b6
Wade, N.C. **63** F2
Wade, Ohio **70** H3
Wadebridge, U.K., 2,998 **113** D6
Wadena, Sask., Can., 1,292 **43** D4
Wadena, Ind. **70** B2
Wadena, Iowa, 275 **72** F2
Wadena, co., Minn., 12,199 **74** E2
Wadena, Minn., 4,381 **74** E2
Wadena, Okla. **76** H3
Wädenswil, Switz., 11,677 **124** C1
Wadern, F.R.Ger., 1,559 **118** A4
Wadersloh, F.R.Ger., 5,066 **119** E1
Wadesboro, N.C., 3,744 **63** D3
Wadeville, N.C. **63** E2
Wadhams, Br. Col., Can. **42** E3
Wadhams, N.Y. **59** O3
Wadhope, Man., Can. **43** G5
Wādī Ḥalfā, Sudan, 11,007 **163** K2
Wading, r., N.J. **61** B4
Wading River, N.Y. **58** h13
Wadlew, Pol. **127** i5
Wadley, Ala., 605 **64** D2
Wadley, Ga., 1,898 **64** G3
Wad Madanī, Sudan, 47,677 **163** K3
Wadomari, Jap., 12,564 **154** d12
Wadowice, Pol., 9,858 **127** C4
Wadrill, F.R.Ger., 1,329 **119** B5
Wadsworth, Ill. **69** c7
Wadsworth, Nev. **83** A3
Wadsworth, Ohio, 10,635 **70** H1
Wadsworth, Tex. **77** Q5
Wae, Jap. **154** g14
Waelder, Tex., 1,270 **77** P5
Wa-fang-tien, China **151** A4
Wa-fou Hu, China **152** E1
Wagan, Burma **147** f7
Wagap, N. Caled. **174** i8
Wagarville, Ala. **64** A4
Wagenberg, Neth. **115** b7
Wagenborgen, Neth. **115** F1
Wagener, S.C., 614 **63** C4
Wageningen, Neth., 19,900 **115** D3
Wageningen, Sur., 1,500* **101** M5
Wager Bay, N.W.T., Can. **40** M4
Wagga Wagga, Austl., 19,235 **173** G5
Waggoner, Ill., 219 **68** C4
Wagin, Austl., 1,526 **172** B5
Wagina, i., Sol. Is. **175** b2
Wagner, S. Dak., 1,586 **74** C4
Wagoner, co., Okla., 15,673 **76** H2
Wagoner, Okla., 4,469 **76** H2
Wagon Mound, N. Mex., 760 **79** C4
Wagram, Aust. **124** d10
Wagram, N.C., 562 **63** E3
Wągrowiec, Pol., 12,099 **127** B2
Wagu, Jap. **154** h15
Wag Water, r., Jam. **96** q8
Waha, Libya **161** H3
Wahai, Indon. **149** J3
Wahalak, Miss. **73** G5
Wahiawa, Hawaii, 15,512 **84** D2
Wahiawa Res., Hawaii **84** b7
Wahjamega, Mich. **67** K5
Wah Keeney Park, Colo. **79** a8
Wahkiacus, Wash. **80** C3
Wahkiakum, co., Wash., 3,426 **80** B2
Wahkon, Minn., 172 **74** F2
Wahlen, F.R.Ger., 2,160 **119** B4
Wahlscheid, F.R.Ger., 3,687 **119** C3
Wahoo, Nebr., 3,610 **75** J2
Wahpeton, N. Dak., 5,876 **74** D2
Wahrenholz, F.R.Ger., 1,864 **118** C2
Wahsatch, Utah **78** C1
Wah Wah Mts., Utah **78** B2
Wai, India, 17,826 **145** h18
Wai, Poulo, Camb. **146** C5
Waiahukini, Hawaii **84** F4
Waiakoa, Hawaii, 416 **84** E3
Waialee, Hawaii **84** b5
Waialua, Honolulu Co., Hawaii, 2,689 **84** C2
Waialua, Maui Co., Hawaii **84** E2
Waialua Bay, Hawaii **84** C2
Waianae, Hawaii, 4,100* **84** C2
Waianae Ra., Hawaii **84** a6
Waiau, r., N.Z. **175** e7
Waiau, r., N.Z. **175** g6
Waiawa Str., Hawaii **84** c7
Waibeem, Indon. **149** K3
Waiblingen, F.R.Ger., 19,017 **119** G7
Waibstadt, F.R.Ger., 2,987 **119** F6
Waidhofen, Aust., 5,582 **124** L6
Waidhofen, Aust., 3,746 **124** M5
Waigama, Indon. **149** J3
Waigen Lakes, Austl. **172** C4
Waigeo, P., Indon. **149** J2
Waiharara, N.Z. **175** g4
Waihee, Hawaii, 436 **84** E3
Waiheke I., N.Z. **175** g5
Waihi, N.Z., 3,164 **175** h5
Waihou, r., N.Z. **175** g5
Waikabubak, Indon. **149** F5
Waikakalaua Str., Hawaii **84** c7
Waikalo, Indon. **149** F5
Waikane, Hawaii **84** c7
Waikapu, Hawaii, 513 **84** E3
Waikare Moana, L., N.Z. **175** h5
Waikari, N.Z. **175** g6
Waikato, r., N.Z. **175** g5
Waikele Str., Hawaii **84** b7
Waikerie, Austl. **172** F5
Waikii, Hawaii **84** F4
Waikiki Beach, Hawaii **84** c8
Waikiwi, N.Z., 1,961 **175** f7
Waikouaiti, N.Z. **175** f7
Wailea Pt., Hawaii **84** d7
Wai-ling-ting, i., China **152** b6
Wailua, Hawaii, 1,129 **84** B1
Wailuku, Hawaii, 6,969 **84** E3
Wailuku, r., Hawaii **84** F4
Waimakariri, r., N.Z. **175** f6
Waimalu Str., Hawaii **84** c7
Waimamaku, N.Z. **175** g4
Waimanalo, Hawaii, 3,011 **84** D2
Waimanalo Bay, Hawaii **84** d7
Waimanalo Beach, Hawaii **84** d7
Waimanalo Village, Hawaii **84** b8
Waimano Str., Hawaii **84** c7
Waimate, N.Z., 3,310 **175** f7
Waimea, Hawaii Co., Hawaii = Kamuela
Waimea, Honolulu Co., Hawaii **84** b6
Waimea, Kauai co., Hawaii, 1,312 **84** B2
Waimea, r., Hawaii **84** B1
Waimea Bay, Hawaii **84** b6
Waimea Camp, Hawaii **84** b6
Waimes, Belg., 2,640 **115** E4
Waimuli, Indon. **148** a6
Wainfleet, Ont., Can. **46** E6
Wainiha, Hawaii **84** B1
Wainfleet All Saints, U.K., 1,184 **114** J4
Wainganga, r., India **144** b15
Waingapu, Indon. **149** G5
Waini, r., Guyana **101** L4
Wainunu Bay, Fiji **174** 4
Wainwright, Alta., Can., 3,313 **42** L3
Wainwright, Alaska, 253 **85** D1
Wainwright, Okla., 114 **76** H2
Waiohinu, Hawaii **84** F4
Waipa, r., N.Z. **175** g5
Waipahu, Hawaii, 7,600* **84** C2
Waipara, N.Z. **175** g6
Waipawa, N.Z., 1,714 **175** h5
Waipio, Hawaii **84** F3
Waipio Acres, Hawaii, 1,158 **84** b7
Waipu, N.Z. **175** g4
Waipukurau, N.Z., 3,250 **175** h6
Wairau, r., N.Z. **175** g6
Wairio, N.Z. **175** f7
Wairoa, N.Z., 4,303 **175** h5
Wairoa, r., N.Z. **175** g4
Wairoa, r., N.Z. **175** h5
Wairokai, Sol. Is. **175** c3
Waisai, Indon. **149** J3
Waisenberg, Aust., 2,672 **124** L7
Waitaki, r., N.Z. **175** f7
Waitangi, Chatham Is. **175** 14
Waitangi, N.Z. **175** g4
Waitara, N.Z., 4,372 **175** g5
Waite, Me. **55** E3
Waite Hill, Ohio, 360 **70** f8
Waite Park, Minn., 2,016 **74** E3
Waiteville, W. Va. **62** D5
Waitomo Caves, N.Z. **175** g5
Waits, r., Vt. **54** C3
Waitsburg, Wash., 1,010 **80** D2
Waitsfield, Vt. **54** B3
Waits River, Vt. **54** C3
Waiwai, Guyana **101** L6
Waizenkirchen, Aust., 3,414 **124** K5
Wajabula, Indon. **149** J2
Wajiki, Jap., 4,930 **154** f16
Wajima, Jap., 38,754 **155** E3
Wajir, Kenya **164** F1
Waka, Eth. **163** L4
Waka, Tex. **76** N1
Wakaf Bharu, Malay., 1,075 **147** p13
Wakapp, Mt., Kusaie **176** 31
Wakarusa, Ind., 1,145 **70** D1
Wakasa, Jap., 9,522 **155** D4
Wakasa-wan, Jap. **155** D4
Wakatipu, L., N.Z. **175** f7
Wakaw, Sask., Can. **43** C4
Wakaya, i., Fiji **174** 4
Wakayama, Jap., 285,155 **155** D4
Wakayanagi, Jap., 20,830 **155** G2
Wake, Jap., 14,185 **155** D4
Wake, co., N.C., 169,082 **63** F2
Wakeby (part of Sandwich), Mass. **57** P6
WaKeeney, Kans., 2,808 **75** F4
Wakefield, U.K., 61,591 **113** F5
Wakefield, Ill. **68** D5
Wakefield, Kans., 603 **75** H4
Wakefield, Mass. 24,295(T) **57** M3
Wakefield, Mich., 3,231 **66** D2
Wakefield, Nebr., 1,068 **75** J1
Wakefield, N.H. **54** E4
Wakefield, Ohio **70** G4
Wakefield, Pa. **61** K6
Wakefield, R.I. **57** L7
Wakefield, Va., 1,015 **62** G6
Wake Forest, N.C., 2,664 **63** F1
Wakeham Bay, Qué., Can. **44** L1
Wake I., Pac. Oc. **170** F3
Wakema, Burma, 20,716 **147** a2
Wakeman, Ohio, 728 **70** G1
Wakenda, Mo., 146 **72** D5
Wakenitz, r., F.R.Ger. **119** c8
Wake Village, Tex., 1,140 **77** Q3
Waki, Jap., 7,754 **155** D4
Wakide, Jap. **154** h15
Wakinosawa, Jap., 4,788 **155** G1
Wakita, Okla., 452 **76** F1
Wakkanai, Jap., 51,113 **155** J7
Wakomata L., Ont., Can. **46** A2
Wakonassin, r., Ont., Can. **46** B2
Wakonda, S. Dak., 382 **74** D4
Wakool, Austl. **173** e10
Wakpala, S. Dak. **74** B3
Wakuach L., Qué., Can. **45** M3
Wakulla, co., Fla., 5,257 **65** E2
Wakulla, Fla. **65** E2
Wakulla Beach, Fla. **65** E2
Wakunai, Sol. Is. **175** a1
Wakuya, Jap., 23,604 **155** G2
Wakwayowkastic, r., Ont., Can. **44** H5
Wakwekobi L., Ont., Can. **67** K2
Walachia = Valahia
Walakpa, Alaska **85** E1
Walapai, Ariz. **78** B4
Walbeck, F.R.Ger., 3,013 **119** A2
Walbridge, Ohio, 2,142 **70** F1
Wałbrzych, Pol., 117,000* **127** B3
Walbury Hill, U.K. **114** F8
Walchen-See, F.R.Ger. **118** C5
Walcheren, i., Neth. **115** B3
Walcott, Iowa, 664 **72** G3
Walcott, L., Idaho **81** C4
Walcourt, Belg., 2,030 **115** C4
Wałcz, Pol., 15,637 **127** B2
Wald, Aust. **124** b10
Wald, Switz., 7,778 **124** C1
Waldbreitbach, F.R.Ger., 1,509 **119** C3
Waldbröl, F.R.Ger., 11,269 **118** A3
Waldbüttelbrunn, F.R.Ger., 2,590 **119** H5
Waldeck, Sask., Can. **43** C5
Waldegg, Aust., 1,580 **124** c11
Walden, Colo., 809 **79** B1
Walden, N.Y., 5,015 **59** M8
Walden, Vt. **54** C3
Waldenbuch, F.R.Ger., 3,915 **119** G7
Waldenburg, F.R.Ger., 1,433 **119** H6
Waldenburg, Switz., 1,284 **124** B1
Waldenburg, Mich. **67** g14
Walderston, Jam. **96** p8
Waldfischbach, F.R.Ger., 4,124 **119** D6
Waldhausen, Aust. **124** M5
Waldheim, Sask., Can. **43** C4
Waldheim, Ger.D.R., 11,387 **118** D3
Waldkraiburg, F.R.Ger., 5,561 **118** D4
Waldmohr, F.R.Ger., 2,885 **119** C6
Waldmünchen, F.R.Ger., 4,192 **118** D4
Waldniel, F.R.Ger., 6,956 **119** A2
Waldo, Ark., 1,722 **73** B4
Waldo, Fla., 735 **65** G3
Waldo, Kans., 178 **75** G4
Waldo, Ohio, 374 **70** F2
Waldo, co., Me., 22,632 **55** C4
Waldo, Wis., 403 **66** F5
Waldoboro, Me. **55** C4
Waldo L., Oreg. **80** B4
Waldorf, Md., 1,048 **62** H4
Waldport, Oreg., 667 **80** A3
Waldrach, F.R.Ger., 1,808 **119** B5
Waldron, Ark., 1,619 **73** A3
Waldron, Ind. **70** D3
Waldron, Mich., 454 **67** J7
Waldrup, Miss. **73** F6
Waldsassen, F.R.Ger., 7,928 **118** D3
Waldshut, F.R.Ger., 10,412 **118** B5
Waldstatt, Switz., 1,536 **124** D1
Waldwick, N.J., 10,495 **61** C1
Waldwisse, Fr. **116** b8
Walensee, Switz. **124** D1
Walenstadt, Switz., 3,296 **124** D1
Wales, div., U.K., 2,693,000* **113** E5
Wales, U.K., 4,548 **114** F4
Wales, Alaska, 128 **85** C2
Wales, Me. **55** B4
Wales, Mass., 659(T) **56** H4
Wales, Minn. **74** G2
Wales, N. Dak., 151 **74** C1
Wales, Tenn. **71** D6
Wales, Utah, 130 **78** C2
Wales, Wis., 356 **66** c11
Walesboro, Ind. **70** D3
Wales Center, N.Y. **58** D6
Wales I., N.W.T., Can. **41** M4
Waleska, Ga., 479 **64** E1
Walferdange, Lux., 3,008 **115** E5
Walford, Ont., Can. **46** B2
Walford, U.K., 1,153 **114** C7
Walford, Iowa, 264 **72** F3
Walgett, Austl., 1,348 **173** G4
Walhalla, Mich. **67** G5
Walhalla, N. Dak., 1,432 **74** D1
Walhalla, S.C., 3,431 **63** A3
Walheim, F.R.Ger., 5,245 **119** A3
Walhorn, Belg., 1,094 **119** A3
Walichnowy, Pol. **127** h5
Walikale, D.R.Congo **164** D2
Walikukun, Indon. **148** d7
Walim, Pol., 3,015 **127** f6
Walincourt, Fr., 2,143 **116** a7
Walk, L., Tex. **77** N5
Walkaway, Austl. **172** A4
Walker, co., Ala., 54,211 **64** B2
Walker, co., Ga., 45,264 **64** D1
Walker, Iowa, 584 **72** F2
Walker, La., 912 **73** E7
Walker, Minn., 1,180 **74** E2
Walker, Mo., 235 **72** C7
Walker, N.Y. **58** E5
Walker, S. Dak. **74** B3
Walker, co., Tex., 21,475 **77** Q4
Walker, r., Nev. **83** A3
Walker, W., r., Calif.-Nev. **82** D3
Walker Creek, Falk. Is. **108** 3
Walker L., Man., Can. **43** F3
Walker L., Alaska **85** F2
Walker L., Nev. **83** A3
Walkern, U.K. **114** H7
Walker Springs, Ala. **64** B4
Walkersville, Md., 1,020 **62** G3
Walkersville, W. Va. **62** D4
Walkerton, Ont., Can., 3,785 **44** H7
Walkerton, Ind., 2,044 **70** C1
Walkerton, Va. **62** H5
Walkertown, N.C., 1,240 **63** D1
Walker Valley, N.Y. **59** M8
Walkerville, S. Af. **165** i17
Walkerville, Mich., 261 **67** G5
Walkerville, Mont., 1,453 **81** C3
Walkington, U.K., 1,336 **114** G3
Wall, S. Dak., 629 **74** A4
Wallace, N.S., Can. **47** U11
Wallace, Ala. **64** B4
Wallace, Idaho, 2,412 **81** A2
Wallace, Ind., 122 **70** B2
Wallace, co., Kans., 2,069 **75** D4
Wallace, Kans., 110 **75** D5
Wallace, Mich. **66** F3
Wallace, Nebr., 293 **75** D3
Wallace, N.Y. **58** F7
Wallace, N.C., 2,285 **63** G3
Wallace, S.C. **63** E3
Wallace, S. Dak., 132 **74** D3
Wallace, Va. **62** B6
Wallace, W. Va. **62** D3
Wallaceburg, Ont., Can., 7,790 **44** G7
Wallaceton, Pa., 429 **60** F4
Wallacetown, U.K. **112** a8
Wallagrass L., Me. **55** D1
Walland, Tenn. **71** H6
Wallaroo, Austl., 2,403 **172** E5
Wallasey, U.K., 103,213 **114** B4
Wallau, F.R.Ger., 3,229 **119** F3
Walla-Walla, Austl. **173** f10
Walla Walla, co., Wash., 42,195 **80** D2
Walla Walla, Wash., 24,536 **80** D2
Walla Walla, r., Oreg.-Wash. **80** D2
Wallburg, N.C. **63** D1
Walldorf, Bad.-Württ., F.R.Ger., 6,350 **119** F6
Walldorf, Hess., F.R.Ger., 8,158 **119** F4
Walldürn, F.R.Ger., 6,238 **118** B4
Walled Lake, Mich., 3,550 **67** K6
Wallel, pk., Eth. **163** K4
Wallen, Ind. **70** D1
Wallenpaupack L., Pa. **61** M3
Wallenstein, Ont., Can. **46** a13
Waller, co., Tex., 12,071 **77** P5
Waller, Tex., 900 **77** Q5
Wallers, Fr., 7,558 **116** a7
Wallersdorf, F.R.Ger., 3,010 **118** D4
Wallersheim, F.R.Ger. **119** B4
Wallibu, St. Vinc. **97** 19
Wallingford, U.K., 4,833 **114** F7
Wallingford, Conn., 29,920(T) **56** E7
Wallingford, Iowa, 228 **72** C1
Wallingford, Vt. **54** B5
Walling Mtn., Mass. **56** D3
Wallis, Tex. **77** P5
Wallis, Îs., Wallis and Futuna **170** G5
Wallis and Futuna, is., Pac. Oc., 8,326 **170** G5
Wallisellen, Switz., 8,601 **124** C1
Wallis Res., Mass. **57** J4
Wallisville, Tex. **77** k9
Wallkill, N.Y., 1,215 **59** M8
Wallkill, r., N.J.-N.Y. **59** L9
Wall Lake, Iowa, 812 **72** B2
Wallonia, Ky. **71** D5
Walloomsac, r., Vt. **54** A6
Walloon Lake, Mich. **67** J3
Walloon L., Mich. **67** J3
Wallops I., Md. **62** J5
Wallowa, co., Oreg., 7,102 **80** E3
Wallowa, Oreg., 989 **80** E3
Wallowa, r., Oreg. **80** E3
Wallowa Mts., Oreg. **50** C1
Walls, Miss. **73** E3
Wallsend, U.K., 49,785 **112** g9
Wall Springs, Fla. **65** c11
Wallula, Wash. **80** D2
Wallumbilla, Austl. **173** G4
Wallum Lake, R.I. **57** K5
Wallum L., Mass.-R.I. **57** K4
Walney, I. of, U.K. **114** B2
Walnut, Calif., 934 **83** i15
Walnut, Ill., 1,192 **68** C2
Walnut, Ind. **70** C1
Walnut, Iowa, 777 **72** B3
Walnut, Kans., 381 **75** K6
Walnut, Miss., 390 **73** G3
Walnut, N.C. **63** B2
Walnut, r., Kans. **75** J6
Walnut Bottom, Pa. **60** H5
Walnut Canyon Nat. Mon., Ariz. **78** C4
Walnut Cove, N.C., 1,288 **63** D1
Walnut Creek, Calif., 23,328 **83** e12
Walnut Cr., Kans. **75** F5
Walnut Grove, Ala., 237 **64** C1
Walnut Grove, Minn., 886 **74** E3
Walnut Grove, Miss., 433 **73** F5
Walnut Grove, Mo., 373 **72** D7
Walnut Hill, Fla. **65** B2
Walnutport, Pa., 1,609 **61** L4
Walnut Ridge, Ark., 3,547 **73** E1
Walnut Springs, Tex., 490 **77** P3
Walpole, Mass., 14,068(T) **57** L4
Walpole, N.H. **54** C5
Walpole St. Peter, U.K., 1,581 **114** J5
Wals, Aust., 6,331 **124** J6
Walsall, U.K., 117,836 **113** F5
Walschbronn, Fr. **116** e8
Walsenburg, Colo., 5,071 **79** C3
Walsh, Colo., 856 **79** D3
Walsh, co., N. Dak., 17,997 **74** D1
Walsingham, Fla. **65** c12
Walsrode, F.R.Ger., 12,831 **118** B2
Walston, U.K. **112** d8
Walsum, F.R.Ger., 38,575 **119** B1
Walterboro, S.C., 5,417 **63** D5
Walters, Okla., 2,825 **76** E3
Walters, Va. **62** H6
Waltershausen, Ger.D.R., 13,365 **118** C3
Walterville, Oreg. **80** B3
Walthall, co., Miss., 13,512 **73** E6
Walthall, Miss., 153 **73** F4
Waltham, Qué., Can. **46** G3
Waltham, U.K., 3,015 **114** H3
Waltham, Me. **55** D4
Waltham, Mass., 55,413 **57** L3
Waltham on the Wolds, U.K. **114** G5
Walthamstow, London, U.K. **114** J7
Walthill, Nebr., 844 **75** J1
Walthourville, Ga. **64** H4
Walton, Ont., Can. **46** C5
Walton, U.K., 3,626 **113** G6
Walton, co., Fla., 15,576 **65** C2
Walton, Fla. **65** J5
Walton, co., Ga., 20,481 **64** F2
Walton, Ind., 1,079 **70** C2
Walton, Kans., 225 **75** H5

Walton—Wayne · 311

Walton, Ky., 1,530 71 G3
Walton, Mich. 67 H4
Walton, N.Y., 3,855 59 K7
Walton, W. Va. 62 C4
Walton Hills, Ohio, 1,776 70 e9
Walton-le-Dale, U.K., 19,061 114 C3
Waltonville, Ill., 394 68 C5
Waltreak, Ark. 73 B3
Waltz, Mich. 67 e16
Walvis Bay, S. Af., 12,165 164 B5
Walvis Ridge, Atl. Oc. 109 N8
Wal Wal, Eth. 163 M4
Walworth, N.Y. 58 F5
Walworth, co., S. Dak., 8,097 74 B3
Walworth, co., Wis., 52,368 66 E6
Walworth, Wis., 1,494 66 E6
Wamac, Ill., 1,394 68 C5
Wamala, L., Uganda 165 e13
Wamba, D.R.Congo, 3,640 164 D1
Wamba, r., D.R.Congo 164 B3
Wambrechies, Fr., 6,031 116 a6
Wamea, i., Terr. Papua 174 3
Wamego, Kans., 2,363 75 J4
Wamgumbaug L., Conn. 56 G5
Wamic, Oreg. 80 C3
Wamlana, Indon. 149 H3
Wampsville, N.Y., 564 59 J5
Wampum, Pa., 1,085 60 B4
Wamsutter, Wyo., 110 81 E5
Wan, Indon. 149 L5
Wanaaring, Austl. 173 F4
Wanaka, L., N.Z. 175 f7
Wanakah, N.Y. 58 B6
Wanamie, Pa. 61 n17
Wanamingo, Minn., 540 74 F3
Wan-an, China 152 D2
Wanapitei, r., Ont., Can. 46 D2
Wanapitei L., Ont., Can. 46 D2
Wanaque, N.J. 58 b12
Wanaque Res., N.J. 61 C1
Wanatah, Ind. 70 B1
Wanawana, i., Sol. Is. 175 b2
Wanblee, S. Dak. 74 B4
Wanchese, N.C. 63 J2
Wan-ch'üan, China 151 B2
Wan-ch'üan, r., China 152 C4
Wandaik, Guyana 101 L5
Wandell, Okla. 76 F2
Wandels Sea, Greenl. 180 D1
Wandering River, Alta., Can. 42 K2
Wanderoos, Wis. 66 A3
Wanderup, F.R.Ger., 1,343 118 B1
Wandiwash, India, 12,546 145 m19
Wando, S. Kor., 17,302 151 E4
Wando, r., S.C. 63 E5
Wandoan, Austl. 173 G4
Waneta, W. Va. 62 D4
Wanette, Okla., 381 76 F3
Wanfried, F.R.Ger., 3,928 118 C3
Wan-fu, China 151 D3
Wan-fu, r., China 151 C4
Wan-fu-chuang, China 151 D2
Wang, r., Thai. 146 B3
Wanganella, Austl. 173 e10
Wanganui, N.Z. 33,316 175 g5
Wanganui, r., N.Z. 175 g5
Wang A Pong, Thai. 147 e4
Wangaratta, Austl., 10,715 173 G5
Wang-ch'eng, China 152 D1
Wang-chiang, China 152 E1
Wang-ch'ing, China 150 H2
Wangdu Phodrang, Bhutan 144 g12
Wangen, F.R.Ger., 12,095 118 B5
Wangen, F.R.Ger., 1,809 119 H7
Wangerooge, F.R.Ger., 1,524 118 B2
Wanggava, i., Fiji 174 4
Wang-k'uei, China 151 E1
Wang-mo, China 152 B2
Wang Noi, Thai. 147 d4
Wang Saphung, Thai. 146 C3
Wang-ts'ang, China 152 B1
Wanham, Alta., Can. 42 H2
Wan-hsien, Ho-p., China 151 B3
Wan-hsien, S-ch., China 150 E4
Wan-hu-yü, China 151 A3
Wan-jung, China 151 A4
Wankie, Rhod., 22,450 164 D5
Wankie Nat. Pk., Rhod. 164 D5
Wanless, Man., Can. 43 E3
Wann, Okla., 157 76 H1
Wanna Lakes, Austl. 172 C4
Wannamassa, N.J. 58 c16
Wannaska, Minn. 74 E1
Wanne-Eickel, F.R.Ger., 101,758 119 C1
Wan-nien, China 152 E1
Wan-ning, China 150 E5
Wannweil, F.R.Ger., 2,969 119 G7
Wansbeck, r., U.K. 112 g9
Wantage, U.K., 5,949 113 F6
Wantagh, N.Y., 34,172 58 e14
Wan-ta Shan-mo, China 151 F1
Wan-t'ing, China 150 D4
Wan-tsai, China 152 D1
Wantzenau, Fr., 3,051 119 D7
Wan-tzu, China 152 a6
Wanup, Ont., Can. 46 D2
Wanwyksvlei, S. Af. 164 C7
Wan-yin, Burma 146 B2
Wan-yüan, China 150 E3
Wanzleben, Ger.D.R. 118 C2
Wapakoneta, Ohio, 6,756 70 E2
Wapanucka, Okla., 459 76 G3
Wapato, Wash., 3,137 80 C2
Wapawekka Hills, Sask., Can. 43 D3
Wapawekka L., Sask., Can. 43 D3
Wapella, Sask., Can. 43 E5
Wapella, Ill., 526 68 D3
Wapello, co., Iowa, 46,126 72 E4
Wapello, Iowa, 1,745 72 F3
Wapiti, r., Alta., Can. 42 H2
Waples, Tex. 76 d10
Wapogasset L., Wis. 66 A3
Wappapello Res., Mo. 72 G8
Wappasening Cr., Pa. 61 K2
Wapping (part of S. Windsor), Conn. 56 F5
Wapping (part of Deerfield), Mass. 56 F2
Wappinger Cr., N.Y. 59 N8
Wappingers Falls, N.Y., 4,447 59 N8
Wapsipinicon, r., Iowa 72 E1
Wapskehegan, r., N.B., Can. 55 E2
Wapwallopen, Pa. 61 K3
Waquoit (part of Falmouth), Mass. 57 O6
War, W. Va., 3,006 62 C5
Warabi, Jap., 50,952 155 m19
Waraigar, r., Indon. 149 K3
Waramaug, L., Conn. 56 C6
Warangal, India, 156,106 145 F6
Wara Seoni, India, 11,308 144 c15
Waratah, Austl. 173 e13
Waratah Bay, Austl. 173 e12
Warba, Minn., 162 74 F2
Warboys, U.K., 1,950 114 H6
Warburg, Alta., Can. 42 J3
Warburg, F.R.Ger., 9,618 118 B3
Warburn, Austl. 173 f10
Warburton, Austl., 1,320 173 e11
Ward, Ark., 470 73 D3
Ward, Colo., 9 79 a7
Ward, co., N. Dak., 47,072 74 B1
Ward, S.C., 162 63 C4
Ward, S. Dak., 74 74 D3
Ward, co., Tex., 14,917 77 M4
Ward, W. Va., 1,109 62 C4
Ward, Mt., N.Z. 175 f6
Wardell, Mo., 331 72 H8
Wardell, Va. 62 C5
Warden, U.K. 112 f9
Warden, Wash., 949 80 D2
Wardensville, W. Va., 289 62 F3
Wardere, Eth. 163 M4
Wardha, India, 49,113 145 F5
Ward Hill, U.K. 112 E2
Ward Hunt Str., Terr. Papua 174 f3
Wardington, U.K. 114 F6
Ward Mtn., Nev. 83 C3
Wardner, Br. Col., Can. 42 J4
Wardner, Idaho, 577 81 A2
Ward's Stone, mtn., U.K. 114 C2
Wardsville, Ont., Can. 46 C6
Wardt, F.R.Ger., 2,267 119 A1
Wardville, La., 1,086 73 C6
Wardville, Okla. 76 H3
Ware, Br. Col., Can. 42 F1
Ware, U.K., 9,987 114 H7
Ware, co., Ga., 34,219 64 G4
Ware, Mass., 6,650; 7,517(T) 56 H3
Ware, Tex. 76 M1
Ware, r., Mass. 56 H3
War Eagle, W. Va. 62 C5
Ware Center (part of Ware), Mass. 56 G3
Waregem, Belg., 15,157 115 B4
Wareham, Mass., 1,739; 9,461(T) 57 N5
Warehouse Point, Conn., 1,936 56 F5
Waremme, Belg., 6,115 115 D4
Waren, Ger.D.R., 19,664 118 D2
Waren, Indon. 149 K3
Warenai, r., Indon. 149 L3
Warendorf, F.R.Ger., 15,229 118 A2
Ware Shoals, S.C., 2,671 63 B3
Waretown, N.J. 61 C4
Warffum, Neth. 115 E1
Warfield, Va. 62 G6
Warfordsburg, Pa. 60 F6
Wargrave, U.K., 2,895 114 G8
Wari, i., Terr. Papua 174 3
Warialda, Austl., 1,254 173 G4
Warin, Ger.D.R. 118 C2
Warin Chamrap, Thai., 7,067 146 D4
Warka, Pol., 5,404 127 D3
Warkworth, Ont., Can. 46 G4
Warkworth, N.Z. 175 g5
Warkworth, U.K. 112 g9
Warman, Sask., Can. 43 C4
Warmandi, Indon. 149 K3
Warmbad, S. Af., 6,351 164 D6
Warmbad, S.-W. Afr. 164 C6
Warm Beach, Wash. 80 B1
Warmensteinach, F.R.Ger., 1,929 126 a7
Warmington, U.K. 114 G5
Warminster, U.K., 9,860 113 E6
Warminster, Pa., 3,100* 61 M5
Warmond, Neth., 3,900 115 a6
Warm River, Idaho, 20 81 D3
Warm Springs, Ga., 538 64 E3
Warmsprings, Mont. 81 C2
Warm Springs, Nev. 83 B3
Warm Springs, Oreg. 80 C3
Warm Springs, Va. 62 E4
Warm Sprs., r., Oreg. 80 C3
Warm Sprs. Res., Oreg. 80 D4
Warne, N.C. 63 b7
Warner, Alta., Can. 42 K4
Warner, N.H. 54 D5
Warner, Ohio 70 H3
Warner, Okla., 881 76 H2
Warner, S. Dak. 74 C3
Warner, Va. 62 H5
Warner Mts., Calif. 82 ·
Warner Robins, Ga., 18,633 64 F3
Warner Springs, Calif. 82 E6
Warner Valley, Oreg. 80 C4
Warnerville, Nebr. 75 H2
Warnerville, N.Y. 59 L6
Warnes, Arg., 1,482 105 a12
Warneton, Fr. 116 a6
Warnow, r., Ger.D.R. 118 D2
Warnsveld, Neth., 3,000 115 E2
Waroona, Austl. 172 A5
Warora, India, 14,148 145 F5
Warracknabeal, Austl., 3,009 173 F5
Warragul, Austl., 5,324 173 F6
Warramboo, Austl. 172 a7
Warrego, r., Austl. 173 F4
Warrego Range, Austl. 173 F3
Warren, Austl., 1,828 173 G4
Warren, Man., Can. 43 g9
Warren, Ont., Can. 44 H6
Warren, Ark., 6,752 73 D4
Warren, Conn., 600(T) 56 C5
Warren, co., Ga., 7,360 64 G2
Warren, Idaho 81 B3
Warren, co., Ill., 21,587 68 B3
Warren, Ill., 1,470 68 C1
Warren, co., Ind., 8,545 70 B2
Warren, Ind., 1,241 70 D2
Warren, co., Iowa, 20,829 72 D3
Warren, co., Ky., 45,491 71 E4
Warren, Me. 55 C4
Warren, Mass., 1,616; 3,383(T) 56 H4
Warren, Mich., 89,246 67 K6
Warren, Minn., 2,007 74 D1
Warren, co., Miss., 42,206 73 E5
Warren, co., Mo., 8,750 72 F6
Warren, N.H. 54 D4
Warren, co., N.J., 63,220 61 A2
Warren, co., N.Y., 44,002 59 N4
Warren, co., N.C., 19,652 63 F1
Warren, co., Ohio, 65,711 70 E3
Warren, Ohio, 59,648 70 J1
Warren, Okla. 76 D3
Warren, Oreg. 80 B3
Warren, co., Pa., 45,582 60 D2
Warren, Pa., 14,505 60 D2
Warren, R.I., 8,750(T) 57 L6
Warren, co., Tenn., 23,102 71 F6
Warren, Tex. 77 Q4
Warren, Vt. 54 B3
Warren, co., Va., 14,655 62 F4
Warren Center, Pa. 61 K2
Warrendale, Pa. 60 b7
Warren Glen, N.J. 61 A2
Warrenhurst, Ill. 69 b9
Warren Landing, Man., Can. 43 F4
Warren Pk., Calif. 82 C2
Warrenpoint, U.K., 3,238 113 C4
Warrens, Wis. 66 C4
Warrensburg, Ill., 681 68 C4
Warrensburg, Mo., 9,689 72 D6
Warrensburg, N.Y., 2,240 59 N4
Warrens Corner, N.Y. 58 k18
Warrensville, Pa. 60 J3
Warrensville Heights, Ohio, 10,609 70 H1
Warrenton, S. Af., 5,980 164 D6
Warrenton, Ga., 1,770 64 G2
Warrenton, Mo., 1,869 72 F6
Warrenton, N.C., 1,124 63 F1
Warrenton, Oreg., 1,717 80 A2
Warrenton, Va., 3,522 62 F4
Warrentown (part of Middleboro), Mass. 57 N5
Warrenville (part of Ashford), Conn. 56 H5
Warrenville, Ill., 3,134 69 b9
Warrenville, S.C., 1,128 63 C4
Warri, Nigeria, 22,650 162 E5
Warrick, co., Ind., 23,577 70 B4
Warrington, U.K., 75,533 113 E5
Warrington, Fla., 16,752 65 B2
Warrior, Ala., 2,448 64 C2
Warrior Dam, Ala. 64 B3
Warrior Run, Pa., 833 61 o17
Warriors Mark, Pa. 60 F4
Warrnambool, Austl., 10,850 173 F6
Warroad, Minn., 1,309 74 E1
Warsaw, Ont., Can. 46 F4
Warsaw, Pol.=Warszawa
Warsaw, Ill., 1,938 68 A3
Warsaw, Ind., 7,234 70 D1
Warsaw, Ky., 981 71 G3
Warsaw, Mo., 1,054 72 D6
Warsaw, N.Y., 3,653 58 D6
Warsaw, N.C., 2,221 63 F2
Warsaw, Ohio, 594 70 G2
Warsaw, Va., 549 62 H5
Warsingsfehn, F.R.Ger., 3,555 118 A2
Warspite, Alta., Can. 42 K2
Warstein, F.R.Ger., 8,314 118 B3
Warszawa, Pol., 1,136,000* 127 D2
Warszów, Pol., 2,726 127 A2
Warta, Pol., 2,976 127 C3
Warta, r., Pol. 127 A2
Wartburg, Tenn. 71 G5
Warthen, Ga. 64 G2
Warton, Lancs., Eng., U.K. 114 C2
Warton, Lancs., Eng., U.K., 1,671 114 C3
Warton, Northumb., Eng., U.K. 112 g9
Wartrace, Tenn., 545 71 E6
Waru, Indon. 149 J3
Waruta, r., Indon. 149 L3
Warwick, Austl., 9,151 173 G4
Warwick, Alta., Can. 43 c7
Warwick, Qué., Can., 2,433 47 N3
Warwick, U.K., 16,032 113 F5
Warwick, Ga., 434 64 E4
Warwick, Mass., 426(T) 56 G2
Warwick, N.Y., 3,218 59 M9
Warwick, N. Dak., 204 74 C2
Warwick, Okla. 76 G2
Warwick, Pa. 60 e11
Warwick, R.I., 68,504 57 L6
Warwickshire, co., U.K., 2,023,289 113 F5
Wasaga Beach, Ont., Can. 46 E4
Wasatch, co., Utah, 5,308 78 C1
Wasatch Plat., Utah 50 D3
Wasatch Ra., Utah-Idaho 78 c8
Wasco, Calif., 6,841 82 D5
Wasco, co., Oreg., 20,205 80 C3
Wasco, Oreg., 348 80 C3
Wascott, Wis. 66 B2
Waseca, Sask., Can. 43 B4
Waseca, co., Minn., 16,041 74 F4
Waseca, Minn., 5,898 74 F3
Wasekamio L., Sask., Can. 43 B3
Washabaugh, co., S. Dak., 1,042 74 B4
Washago, Ont., Can. 46 E4
Washakie, co., Wyo., 8,883 81 F4
Washakie Needles, mtn., Wyo. 81 E4
Washburn, Ill., 1,064 68 C3
Washburn, Me., 1,055 55 D2
Washburn, N. Dak., 993 74 B2
Washburn, Tex. 76 N2
Washburn, W. Va. 62 D3
Washburn, co., Wis., 10,301 66 B2
Washburn, Wis., 1,896 66 B2
Washburn, Mt., Wyo. 81 D3
Washika, Jap. 154 g15
Washimi, Jap. 154 h14
Washington, U K., 18,772 112 h10
Washington, st., U.S., 2,973,000* 80
Washington, co., Ala., 15,372 64 A4
Washington, co., Ark., 55,797 73 A2
Washington, Ark., 321 73 B4
Washington, co., Colo., 6,625 79 D2
Washington, Conn., 2,603(T) 56 C6
Washington, District of Columbia, 763,956 62 H4
Washington, co., Fla., 11,249 65 D2
Washington, co., Ga., 18,903 64 G2
Washington, Ga., 4,440 64 G2
Washington, co., Idaho, 8,378 81 A3
Washington, co., Ill., 13,569 68 C5
Washington, Ill., 5,919 68 C3
Washington, co., Ind., 17,819 70 C4
Washington, Ind., 10,846 70 B4
Washington, co., Iowa, 19,406 72 F3
Washington, Iowa, 6,037 72 F3
Washington, co., Kans., 10,739 75 H4
Washington, Kans., 1,506 75 J4
Washington, co., Ky., 11,168 71 F4
Washington, parish, La., 44,015 73 E7
Washington, La., 1,291 73 C7
Washington, co., Me., 32,908 55 E3
Washington, co., Md., 91,219 62 G3
Washington, Mass., 290(T) 56 D3
Washington, Mich. 67 K6
Washington, co., Minn., 52,432 74 F3
Washington, co., Miss., 78,638 73 E4
Washington, co., Mo., 14,346 72 G6
Washington, Mo., 7,961 72 F6
Washington, co., Nebr., 12,103 75 J2
Washington, N.H. 54 C5
Washington, N.J., 5,723 61 A2
Washington, co., N.Y., 48,476 59 O5
Washington, co., N.C., 13,488 63 H2
Washington, N.C., 9,939 63 H2
Washington, co., Ohio, 51,689 70 H3
Washington, co., Okla., 42,347 76 H1
Washington, Okla., 278 76 F3
Washington, co., Oreg., 92,237 80 B3
Washington, co., Pa., 217,271 60 B5
Washington, Pa., 23,545 60 B5
Washington, co., R.I., 59,054 57 K7
Washington (part of Coventry), R.I. 57 K6
Washington, co., Tenn., 54,832 71 J5
Washington, co., Tex., 19,145 77 P4
Washington, Tex. 77 P4
Washington, co., Utah, 10,271 78 B3
Washington, Utah, 445 78 B3
Washington, co., Vt., 42,860 54 B3
Washington, Vt. 54 C3
Washington, co., Va., 38,076 62 B6
Washington, Va., 255 62 F4
Washington, W. Va. 62 C3
Washington, co., Wis., 46,119 66 E5
Washington, C., Fiji 174 4
Washington, L., Wash. 80 B2
Washington, Mt., St. Croix 97 1
Washington, Mt., N.H. 54 E3
Washington Birthplace Nat. Mon., Va. 62 H4
Washington Court House, Ohio, 12,388 70 F3
Washington Crossing, N.J. 60 g10
Washington Depot (part of Washington), Conn. 56 C6
Washington Grove, Md., 576 62 a8
Washington Hbr., Mich. 66 a9
Washington Island, Wis. 66 F3
Washington I., Line Is. 171 H4
Washington I., Wis. 66 G3
Washington Mills, N.Y. 59 u26
Washington Park, Ill., 6,601 68 B5
Washington Ter., Utah, 6,441 78 c8
Washingtonville, N.Y., 1,178 59 M9
Washingtonville, Pa., 198 60 J3
Washita, co., Okla., 18,121 76 D2
Washita, Okla. 76 E2
Washita, r., Okla.-Tex. 76 F3
Washoe, Mont. 81 E3
Washoe, co., Nev., 84,743 83 A2
Washougal, Wash., 2,672 80 B3
Washta, Iowa, 310 72 B2
Washtenaw, co., Mich., 172,440 67 K6
Washtucna, Wash., 331 80 D2
Washunga, Okla., 60 76 G1
Wasian, Indon. 149 K3
Wasilków, Pol., 3,785 127 E2
Wasilla, Alaska, 112 85 G3
Wasimu, i., Terr. Papua 174 3
Wasior, Indon. 149 K3
Waskada, Man., Can. 43 E5
Waskaiowaka L., Man., Can. 43 F3
Waskatenau, Alta., Can. 43 c6
Waskerley, U.K. 112 f10
Waskesiu Lake, Sask., Can. 43 C4
Waskish, Minn. 74 E1
Waskom, Tex., 1,336 77 R3
Wasmes, Belg., 14,688 115 B4
Wasola, Mo. 72 E8
Waspán, Nic. 94 E3
Waspik, Neth. 115 b7
Wasquehal, Fr., 13,634 116 a6
Wasque Pt., Mass. 57 P7
Wassaic, N.Y. 59 N8
Wassamu, Jap., 11,636 155 K7
Wassataquoik Str., Me. 55 D3
Wasselonne, Fr., 3,655 116 d9
Wassen, Switz. 124 C2
Wassenaar, Neth., 23,600 115 C2
Wassenberg, F.R.Ger., 4,301 119 A2
Wasseralfingen, F.R.Ger., 9,364 118 C4
Wasserburg, F.R.Ger., 6,438 118 D4
Wasserkuppe, mt., F.R.Ger. 118 B3
Wassertrüdingen, F.R.Ger., 3,076 118 C4
Wassuk Ra., Nev. 83 A3
Wassy, Fr., 3,391 117 F2
Wasta, S. Dak., 196 74 A3
Wast Water, l., U.K. 114 B2
Wasum, Terr. New Guin. 174 f2
Waswanipi, Qué., Can. 44 J5
Wataga, Ill., 570 68 B2
Watampone, Indon. 149 G4
Watansoppeng, Indon. 149 F4
Watari, Jap., 27,277 155 G2
Watauga, co., N.C., 17,529 63 C1
Watauga, S. Dak. 74 B3
Watauga, r., N.C.-Tenn. 63 B1
Watauga L., Tenn. 71 K5
Watchaug Pd., R.I. 57 K7
Watchet, U.K., 2,597 113 E6
Watch Hill (part of Westerly), R.I. 57 J7
Watchorn, Okla. 76 G1
Watchung, N.J., 3,312 58 b14
Watchung Mts., N.J. 61 ·
Waterbeach, U.K., 2,561 114 J6
Waterboro, Me. 55 B5
Waterboro Center, Me. 55 B5
Waterbury, Conn., 107,130 56 D6
Waterbury, Vt., 2,984 54 B3
Waterbury Center, Vt. 54 B3
Waterbury Dam, Vt. 54 B3
Waterbury L., Sask., Can. 43 D2
Water Cap, pk., Terr. New Guin. 174 d2
Water Cays, Bah. Is. 95 a8
Waterdown, Ont., Can., 1,808 46 D5
Wateree, r., S.C. 63 D4
Wateree Pd., S.C. 63 D3
Waterford, Ont., Can., 2,199 46 D6
Waterford, co., Ire., 74,031 113 C5
Waterford, Ire., 28,878 113 C5
Waterford, Calif., 1,780 82 C4
Waterford, Conn., 15,391(T) 56 H7
Waterford, Ind. 69 g10
Waterford, Mich. 67 K6
Waterford, Miss. 73 F3
Waterford, N.Y., 2,915 59 N6
Waterford, Pa., 1,390 60 B2
Waterford, Va. 62 G3
Waterford, Wis., 1,500 66 E6
Waterford Works, N.J. 61 B4
Waterhen, r., Sask., Can. 43 B3
Waterhen L., Man., Can. 43 E4
Waterhen L., Sask., Can. 43 B3
Wateringen, Neth., 6,100 115 a6
Water I., V.I. 97 4
Waterlick, Va. 62 F4
Waterloo, Belg., 10,476 115 C4
Waterloo, Ont., Can., 21,214 46 D5
Waterloo, Qué., Can., 4,494 47 M3
Waterloo, Ala., 215 64 B1
Waterloo, Ark. 73 B4
Waterloo, Ill., 3,739 68 B5
Waterloo, Ind., 1,432 70 D1
Waterloo, Iowa, 71,755 72 E2
Waterloo, Kans. 75 H6
Waterloo, Md. 62 b8
Waterloo, Mich. 67 J6
Waterloo, Nebr., 516 75 J2
Waterloo, N.Y., 5,098 58 G6
Waterloo, Ohio 70 G4
Waterloo, Oreg., 151 80 B3
Waterloo, S.C., 148 63 C3
Waterloo, Wis., 1,947 66 E5
Waterlooville (incl. Havant), U.K., 74,552 113 m13
Waterman, Ill., 916 68 D2
Waterman, Ind. 70 B3
Waterman Mtn., Calif. 83 i15
Water of Leith, r., U.K. 112 d8
Waterproof, La., 1,412 73 D6
Waters, Mich. 67 J4
Waterside, U.K. 112 b8
Watersmeet, Mich. 66 D2
Watersville, Md. 62 a7
Waterton Lakes Nat. Pk., Alta., Can. 42 J4
Watertown, Conn., 14,837(T) 56 D6
Watertown, Fla., 2,109 65 G2
Watertown, Mass., 39,092(T) 57 M3
Watertown, Mich. 67 L5
Watertown, Minn., 1,046 74 E3
Watertown, N.Y., 33,306 59 J4
Watertown, Ohio 70 H3
Watertown, S. Dak., 14,077 74 D3
Watertown, Tenn., 919 71 E5
Watertown, Wis., 13,943 66 E5
Water Valley, Ky., 267 71 C5
Water Valley, Miss., 3,206 73 F3
Water Village, N.H. 54 E4
Waterville, N.S., Can. 47 T11
Waterville, Qué., Can., 1,329 47 N3
Waterville (part of Waterbury), Conn. 56 D6
Waterville, Iowa, 184 72 F1
Waterville, Kans., 700 75 J4
Waterville, Me., 18,695 55 C4
Waterville (part of Winchendon), Mass. 56 H2
Waterville, Minn., 1,623 74 F3
Waterville, N.Y., 1,901 59 K6
Waterville, Ohio, 1,856 70 F1
Waterville, Pa. 60 H3
Waterville, Vt. 54 B2
Waterville, Wash., 1,013 80 D2
Waterville Valley, N.H. 54 E4
Watervliet, Mich., 1,818 67 G6
Watervliet, N.Y., 13,917 59 N6
Waterways, Alta., Can. 42 K2
Wates, Indon. 148 E4
Watford, Ont., Can., 1,283 46 B6
Watford, U.K., 75,622 113 F6
Watford City, N. Dak., 1,865 74 A2
Watford I., Berm. Is. 108 1
Wa'th, Sudan 163 K4
Watha, N.C., 174 63 G3
Wathaman, r., Sask., Can. 43 D3
Wathaman L., Sask., Can. 43 D2
Wathena, Kans., 837 75 K4
Watheroo, Austl. 172 A4
Watino, Alta., Can. 42 H2
Watkins, Minn., 744 74 E3
Watkins Glen, N.Y., 2,813 58 F7
Watkinsville, Ga., 758 64 F2
Watlam=Yü-lin
Watling I.=San Salvador I.
Watlington, Norfolk, Eng., U.K. 114 J5
Watlington, Oxon., Eng., U.K., 1,791 114 F7
Watonga, Okla., 3,252 76 E2
Watonwan, co., Minn., 14,460 74 E4
Watonwan, r., Minn. 74 E3
Watota, i., Terr. Papua 174 3
Watova, Okla. 76 H1
Wat Phleng, Thai. 147 c5
Watrous, Sask., Can., 1,446 43 C4
Watrous, N. Mex. 79 C4
Watrousville, Mich. 67 K5
Watrus Res., Pa. 61 o16
Watsa, D.R.Congo, 6,077 164 D1
Watseka, Ill., 5,219 68 E3
Watsi Kengo, D.R.Congo 164 C2
Wat Sing, Thai., 4,041 147 c4
Watson, Sask., Can. 43 D4
Watson, Ark., 312 73 D4
Watson, Ill., 247 68 D4
Watson (part of Ashfield), Mass. 56 E2
Watson, Minn., 267 74 E3
Watson, Mo., 181 72 B4
Watson, N.Y. 59 K4
Watson, Okla. 76 J3
Watson, Utah 78 D2
Watson Chapel, Ark. 73 C3
Watson Lake, Yukon, Can. 40 D5
Watsons Corner, Mich. 67 H2
Watsontown, Pa., 2,431 60 J3
Watsonville, Calif., 13,293 82 C4
Watt, Morne, Dominica 97 13
Watten, U.K. 112 E2
Wattenberg, Colo. 79 c7
Wattens, Aust., 5,280 124 H6
Wattenscheid, F.R.Ger., 74,943 119 C2
Wattenwil, Switz., 2,269 124 B2
Watthana Nakhon, Thai. 147 e5
Wattignies, Fr., 5,965 116 a6
Watton, Mich. 66 E2
Wattrelos, Fr., 41,319 116 a6
Watts, Okla., 268 76 J1
Watts, C., Terr. Papua 174 3
Watts Bar L., Tenn. 71 G6
Wattsburg, Pa., 401 60 C1
Watts Mills, S.C., 1,438 63 C3
Wattsville, Ala. 64 c7
Wattwil, Switz., 7,480 124 D1
Watuppa Pd., Mass. 57 M6
Watzenborn-Steinberg, F.R.Ger., 3,855 119 F3
Watzmann, pk., F.R.Ger. 118 D5
Waubach, Neth., 7,600 115 E4
Waubamick, Ont., Can. 46 E3
Waubaushene, Ont., Can. 46 E4
Waubay, S. Dak., 851 74 D3
Waubay L., S. Dak. 74 D3
Waubesa, L., Wis. 66 D5
Waubun, Minn., 350 74 E2
Wauchope, N.S.W., Austl., 2,498 173 G4
Wauchope, N. Terr., Austl. 172 E3
Wauchula, Fla., 3,411 65 H5
Waucoma, Iowa, 364 72 F1
Wauconda, Ill., 3,227 68 D1
Wauconda, Wash. 80 D1
Waugh, Man., Can. 43 G5
Waugoshance Pt., Mich. 67 H3
Waukarlycarly, L., Austl. 172 C3
Waukau, Wis. 66 E5
Waukeenah, Fla. 65 F2
Waukegan, Ill., 55,719 68 E1
Waukesha, co., Wis., 158,249 66 E6
Waukesha, Wis., 30,004 66 E5
Waukewan, L., N.H. 54 D4
Waukomis, Okla., 516 76 F1
Waukon, Iowa, 3,639 72 F1
Waukon, Wash. 80 E2
Waumandee, Wis. 66 B4
Wauna, Oreg. 80 B2
Wauna, Wash. 81 a8
Waunakee, Wis., 1,611 66 D5
Wauneta, Kans. 75 J6
Wauneta, Nebr., 794 75 D3
Waun Fach, U.K. 114 B7
Waupaca, co., Wis., 35,340 66 D4
Waupaca, Wis., 3,984 66 D4
Waupun, Wis., 7,935 66 E5
Wauregan (part of Plainfield), Conn. 56 J5
Waurika, Okla., 1,933 76 E3
Wausa, Nebr., 724 75 H1
Wausau, Fla. 65 D2
Wausau, Wis., 31,943 66 D4
Wausaukee, Wis., 608 66 E3
Wauseon, Ohio, 4,311 70 E1
Waushara, co., Wis., 13,497 66 D4
Wautoma, Wis., 1,466 66 D4
Wauwatosa, Wis., 56,923 66 c11
Wauwinet (part of Nantucket), Mass. 57 R7
Wauzeka, Wis., 494 66 C5
Wave Hill, Austl. 172 D2
Waveland, Ind., 549 70 B3
Waveland, Miss., 1,106 73 F7
Waverly, Ala., 250 64 D3
Waverly, Ga. 64 H4
Waverly, Ill., 1,375 68 B4
Waverly, Ind. 70 C3
Waverly, Iowa, 6,357 72 E2
Waverly, Kans., 381 75 K5
Waverly, Ky., 331 71 D4
Waverly, Mo., 837 72 D5
Waverly, Nebr., 511 75 J3
Waverly, N.Y., 5,950 59 H7
Waverly, Ohio, 3,830 70 G3
Waverly, Pa. 61 o15
Waverly, Tenn., 2,891 71 D5
Waverly, Tex. 77 Q4
Waverly, Va., 1,601 62 G5
Waverly, Wash., 108 80 E2
Waverly, W. Va. 62 C3
Waverly Hall, Ga., 712 64 E3
Waves, N.C. 63 J2
Wavre, Belg., 9,119 115 C4
Wavrin, Fr., 5,308 116 a6
Wavy L., Alta., Can. 43 d8
Waw, Burma, 6,978 147 b2
Waw, Sudan, 8,009 163 J4
Wāw, Nahr, Sudan 163 J4
Wawa, Ont., Can., 2,897 44 F5
Wawa, Nigeria 162 f7
Wawa, Phil., 3,418 153 b8
Wawaka, Ind. 70 D1
Wāw al Kabīr, Libya 161 G3
Wawasee, L., Ind. 70 D1
Wawayanda Mtn., N.J. 61 C1
Wawiwa, i., Terr. Papua 174 3
Wawne, U.K. 114 H3
Wawo, Indon. 149 G3
Wawoi, r., Terr. Papua 174 d2
Wawona, Calif. 82 D4
Wawota, Sask., Can. 43 D5
Waxahachie, Tex., 12,749 77 P3
Waxhaw, N.C., 729 63 D3
Waxweiler, F.R.Ger., 1,028 119 A4
Way, Miss. 73 E5
Way, L., Austl. 172 B4
Waya, i., Fiji 174 4
Waycross, Ga., 20,944 64 G4
Wayland, Iowa, 597 72 F3
Wayland, Ky., 1,340 71 J4
Wayland, Mass., 10,444(T) 57 L3
Wayland, Mich., 2,019 67 H6
Wayland, Mo., 384 72 F4
Wayland, N.Y., 2,003 58 E6
Waymart, Pa., 1,106 61 M2
Wayne, co., Ga., 17,921 64 H4
Wayne, co., Ill., 19,008 68 D5
Wayne, Ill., 373 69 b9
Wayne, co., Ind., 74,039 70 D3
Wayne, co., Iowa, 9,800 72 D4
Wayne, co., Ky., 14,700 71 G5
Wayne, Me. 55 B4
Wayne, co., Mich., 2,666,297 67 K6
Wayne, Mich., 16,034 67 e15
Wayne, co., Miss., 16,258 73 G6
Wayne, co., Mo., 8,638 72 G7
Wayne, co., Nebr., 9,959 75 H1
Wayne, Nebr., 4,217 75 J1
Wayne, co., N.Y., 67,989 58 F5
Wayne, N.Y. 58 F7
Wayne, co., N.C., 82,059 63 F2
Wayne, co., Ohio, 75,497 70 H2
Wayne, Ashtabula Co., Ohio 70 J1
Wayne, Wood Co., Ohio, 949 70 F1
Wayne, Okla., 517 76 F3
Wayne, co., Pa., 28,237 61 M2
Wayne, Pa., 10,125* 60 f11
Wayne, co., Tenn., 11,908 71 D6
Wayne, co., Utah, 1,728 78 C2
Wayne, co., W. Va., 38,977 62 B4

312 · Wayne—West Liberty

Wayne, W. Va., 1,274 62 B4
Wayne Center, Ill. 69 b9
Wayne City, Ill., 903 68 D5
Waynesboro, Ga., 5,359 64 G2
Waynesboro, Miss., 3,892 73 G6
Waynesboro, Pa., 10,427 60 G6
Waynesboro, Tenn., 1,343 71 C6
Waynesboro, Va., 15,694 62 E4
Waynesburg, Ky. 71 G4
Waynesburg, Ohio, 1,442 70 H2
Waynesburg, Pa., 5,188 60 B6
Waynes Corner, Del. 62 f10
Waynesfield, Ohio, 765 70 E2
Waynesville, Ga. 64 H4
Waynesville, Ill., 510 68 C3
Waynesville, Mo., 2,377 72 E7
Waynesville, N.C., 6,159 63 B2
Waynesville, Ohio, 1,298 70 E3
Waynetown, Ind., 933 70 B2
Waynoka, Okla., 1,794 76 E1
Wayside, Miss. 73 E4
Wayside, Nebr. 75 B1
Wayside, N.J. 58 c15
Wayside, Tex. 76 N2
Wayside, Wis. 66 F4
Wayzata, Minn., 3,219 74 b6
Waziers, Fr., 10,507 116 a7
Wazi Khwa, Afghan. 144 C2
Wda, r., Pol. 127 C2
We, P., Indon. 148 A1
Weagamow L., Ont., Can. 44 D4
Weakley, co., Tenn., 24,227 71 C5
Weam, Terr. Papua 174 d3
Wear, r., U.K. 113 F4
Weare, N.H. 54 D5
Weare Res., N.H. 54 D5
Weary Hill, Lesser Caymans 97 2
Weatherby, Mo., 450 72 C5
Weatherby L., Mo. 75 a7
Weatherford, Okla., 4,499 76 E2
Weatherford, Tex., 9,759 77 P3
Weather Law, mtn., U.K. 112 g10
Weatherly, Pa., 2,591 61 L4
Weathersby, Miss., 80 73 F6
Weaubleau, Mo., 349 72 D7
Weaver, Ala., 1,401 64 D2
Weaver, r., U.K. 114 C4
Weaverham, U.K., 6,617 114 C4
Weaver L., Man., Can. 43 F4
Weaverthorpe, U.K. 114 G2
Weaverville, Calif., 1,736 82 B2
Weaverville, N.C., 1,041 63 B2
Webb, Sask., Can. 43 B5
Webb, Iowa, 236 72 C2
Webb, Miss., 686 73 E4
Webb, co., Tex., 64,791 77 O6
Webb, Tarrant Co., Tex. 76 e9
Webb, Webb Co., Tex. 77 O6
Webb, W. Va. 62 B5
Webb, L., Me. 55 B4
Webb City, Mo., 6,740 72 C7
Webb City, Okla., 233 76 G1
Webber L., Man., Can. 43 G3
Webbers Falls, Okla., 441 76 H2
Webberville, Mich., 664 67 J6
Webb Lake, Wis. 66 A2
Webb Mills, N.Y. 58 F7
Webbville, Ky. 71 J3
Webbwood, Ont., Can. 46 B2
Weber, Ga. 64 F4
Weber, co., Utah, 110,744 78 C1
Weber, r., Utah 78 C1
Weber City, N. Mex. 79 D4
Weber City, Va., 1,274 62 B6
Webhannet, Me. 55 B5
Webster, Alta., Can. 42 H2
Webster, Calif. 82 a7
Webster, Fla., 366 65 H4
Webster, co., Ga., 3,247 64 E3
Webster, co., Iowa, 47,810 72 C2
Webster, co., Ky., 14,244 71 D4
Webster, parish, La., 39,701 73 B5
Webster, Me., 4,747 55 B4
Webster, Mass., 12,072; 13,680(T) 56 J4
Webster, co., Miss., 10,580 73 F4
Webster, co., Mo., 13,753 72 E7
Webster, co., Nebr., 6,224 75 G3
Webster, N.H. 54 D5
Webster, N.Y., 3,060 58 F5
Webster, N. Dak. 74 C1
Webster, Pa. 60 c9
Webster, S. Dak., 2,409 74 D3
Webster, co., W. Va., 13,719 62 D4
Webster, Wis., 514 66 A3
Webster, L., Mass. 57 J4
Webster City, Iowa, 8,520 72 D2
Webster Groves, Mo., 28,990 72 G6
Webster L., N.H. 54 D5
Webster Res., Kans. 75 F4
Webster Springs, W. Va., 1,132 62 D4
Websterville, Vt. 54 B3
Wechsel, ridge, Aust. 125 •
Wecota, S. Dak. 74 C3
Weda, Indon. 149 J2
Weddelbrook, F.R.Ger. 119 a8
Weddell I., Falk. Is. 108 3
Weddell Sea, Ant. 180 O5
Wedderburn, Austl. 173 d11
Wedderburn, Oreg. 80 A4
Weddington, N.C. 63 D2
Wedel, F.R.Ger., 19,620 118 B2
Wedge, Mt., Austl. 172 a7
Wedgefield, S.C. 63 D4
Wedgeport, N.S., Can. 47 T12
Wedges Corner, Ill. 69 c7
Wedgworth, Ala. 64 B3
Wedmore, U.K., 2,191 114 C8
Wedowee, Ala., 917 64 D2
Wedron, Ill. 68 D2
Wedza, Rhod. 164 E5
Weed, Calif., 3,223 82 B2
Weed, N. Mex. 79 C5
Weed Heights, Nev., 1,092 83 A3
Weedon, Qué., Can., 1,410 45 L6
Weedon Bec, U.K., 1,489 114 F6
Weedsport, N.Y., 1,731 59 G5
Wee Jasper, Austl. 173 g10
Weekapaug (part of Westerly), R.I. 57 K7
Weekeepeemee, r., Conn. 56 D6
Weeks, La., 1,138 73 D8
Weeks, Nev. 83 A3
Weeksbury, Ky. 71 J4
Weeksville, N.C. 63 H1
Weelde, Bdg., 2,649 115 C3
Weems, Ala. 64 d7
Weende, F.R.Ger., 6,007 118 B3
Weener, F.R.Ger., 5,366 118 A2
Weepah, Nev. 83 B4
Weeping Water, Nebr., 1,048 75 J3
Weert, Neth., 19,100 115 D3
Weesp, Neth., 10,700 115 c6
Weethalle, Austl. 173 f9
Weeton, U.K. 114 C3
Wee Waa, Austl., 1,075 173 G4
Weeze, F.R.Ger., 7,263 119 A1
Weferlingen, Ger.D.R. 118 C2
Wegberg, F.R.Ger., 11,762 119 A2
Weggis, Switz., 2,243 124 C1
Weggs, C., Qué., Can. 44 K1
Węglewice, Pol. 127 h5
Węgliniec, Pol., 4,931 127 A3
Węgorzewo, Pol., 6,467 127 D1
Węgorzyno, Pol., 1,832 127 A2
Węgra, Ala. 64 b7
Węgrów, Pol., 5,170 127 E2
Wehen, F.R.Ger., 2,054 118 B3
W.F. George Dam, Ala.-Ga. 64 E4
Wei, r., China 150 E3
Wei, r., China 151 C3
Weibern, F.R.Ger., 1,313 119 C4
Wei-ch'ang, China 150 F2
Wei-chou Tao, China 152 C3
Wei-ch'uan, China 151 B4
Weida, Ger.D.R., 12,025 118 C3
Weiden, F.R.Ger., 40,429 118 D4
Weidenau, F.R.Ger., 17,407 119 E3
Weidenhausen, F.R.Ger., 2,123 119 E3
Weidman, Mich. 67 H5
Weierbach, F.R.Ger., 2,319 119 C5
Wei-fang, China, 149,000* 150 F3
Wei-hai, China 151 D3
Weiher, F.R.Ger., 2,311 119 F6
Wei-ho, China 151 F1
Wei-hsi, China 150 D4
Wei-hsin, China 152 B2
Weikersdorf, Aust. 124 b10
Weikersdorf, Aust. 124 c11
Weikwabinonaw L., Ont., Can. 74 G1
Weil, F.R.Ger., 14,602 118 A5
Weil, r., F.R.Ger. 119 E4
Weilbach, F.R.Ger., 1,380 119 G5
Weilburg, F.R.Ger., 6,153 118 B3
Weilerbach, F.R.Ger., 2,192 119 D6
Weilerswist, F.R.Ger., 2,857 119 B3
Weilheim, Bad.-Württ., F.R.Ger., 5,236 119 H7
Weilheim, Bay., F.R.Ger., 11,803 118 C5
Wei-li, China 150 B2
Weil im Schönbuch, 3,779 119 G7
Weilmünster, F.R.Ger., 4,120 118 B3
Weimar, Ger.D.R., 63,943 118 C3
Weimar, Calif. 82 C3
Weimar, Tex., 2,006 77 P5
Wei-nan, China 151 A4
Weinböhla, Ger.D.R., 10,278 118 D3
Weiner, Ark., 669 73 E2
Weinfelden, Switz., 6,954 124 C1
Weingarten, F.R.Ger., 7,448 118 B5
Weingarten, F.R.Ger. 119 F6
Weingarten, Mo. 72 G7
Weinheim, F.R.Ger., 26,343 118 B4
Wei-ning, China 152 B2
Weinsberg, F.R.Ger., 8,280 118 B4
Weippe, Idaho 81 B2
Weir, Kans., 699 75 L6
Weir, Miss., 522 73 F4
Weir, L., Fla. 65 H3
Weir, r., Man., Can. 43 G3
Weir River, Man., Can. 43 G3
Weirton, W. Va., 28,201 62 D2
Weisbrook, Ill. 69 b9
Weisenheim, F.R.Ger., 3,224 119 E5
Weiser, Idaho, 4,208 81 A3
Weiser, r., Idaho 80 E3
Wei-shan, China 150 D4
Wei-shan Hu, China 151 C4
Weissach, F.R.Ger., 2,057 119 F7
Weisse Elster, r., Ger.D.R. 118 D3
Weissen-Berg, F.R.Ger. 119 D6
Weissenburg, F.R.Ger., 13,930 118 C4
Weissenfels, Ger.D.R., 45,856 118 D3
Weissenhorn, F.R.Ger., 5,491 118 C4
Weissenstadt, F.R.Ger., 3,888 126 a6
Weissenthurm, F.R.Ger., 6,064 119 C4
Weissert, Nebr. 75 F2
Weisskugel, mtn. Aust.-It. 124 G7
Weissport, Pa., 625 61 L4
Weisswasser, Ger.D.R., 14,071 118 E3
Weiswampach, Lux. 119 A4
Weisweiler, F.R.Ger., 4,585 119 A3
Weitchpec, Calif. 82 B2
Weitensfeld, Aust., 2,970 124 K7
Weitersfeld, Aust. 124 M5
Weitersfelden, Aust., 1,368 124 L5
Weiterstadt, F.R.Ger., 4,058 119 F5
Weitje, Cur. 97 16
Weitra, Aust., 1,882 124 L5
Wei-yüan, China 152 B1
Weiz, Aust., 8,145 124 M6
Wejherowo, Pol., 25,000* 127 C1
Wekusko, Man., Can. 43 E3
Wekusko L., Man., Can. 43 E3
Wekuwa P., Bon. 97 17
Welaka, Fla., 526 65 H3
Welaung, Burma 147 f7
Welborn, Kans. 75 a7
Welbury, U.K. 112 h11
Welch, Okla., 557 76 H1
Welch, Tex. 77 M3
Welch, W. Va., 5,313 62 C5
Welche Pt., Conn. 56 D8
Welcome, N.C. 63 D2
Weld, co., Colo., 72,344 79 C1
Weld, Me. 55 B4
Weldon, Sask., Can. 43 C4
Weldon, Ark., 150 73 D2
Weldon, Ill., 449 68 D3
Weldon, Iowa, 202 72 D4
Weldon, N.C., 2,165 63 G1
Weldon Spring, Mo. 72 G6
Weleetka, Okla., 1,231 76 G2
Weleri, Indon. 148 D4
Welford, U.K. 114 F6
Welge, Ill. 68 C6
Welgedag, S. Af. 165 k17
Welgelegen, D.R.Congo 165 n20
Weligama, Cey., 12,834 145 n22
Welkenraedt, Belg., 5,128 115 E4
Welkom, S. Af., 47,768 164 D6
Welland, Ont., Can., 35,607 44 H7
Welland, r., Ont., Can. 46 E5
Welland, r., U.K. 113 F5
Welland Can., Ont., Can. 58 B5
Welland Junction, Ont., Can., 1,066 46 E6
Wellandport, Ont., Can. 46 E5
Wellborn, Fla. 65 G2
Wellborn, Tex. 77 P4
Wellersburg, Pa., 303 60 E6
Wellesbourne Mountford, U.K., 1,054 114 E6
Wellesley, Ont., Can. 46 a14
Wellesley, Mass., 26,071(T) 57 L3
Wellesley Hills (part of Wellesley), Mass. 57 L3
Wellesley I., N.Y. 59 J3
Wellesley Is., Austl. 172 E2
Wellfleet, Mass., 1,404(T) 57 Q5
Wellfleet, Nebr., 67 75 E3
Wellfleet Hbr., Mass. 57 Q5
Wellford, S.C., 1,040 63 B3
Wellin, Belg., 1,054 115 D4
Wellingborough, U.K., 30,583 113 F5
Wellingore, U.K. 114 G4
Wellington, Austl., 5,213 173 G5
Wellington, Ont., Can., 1,064 44 J7
Wellington, P.E.I., Can. 47 T10
Wellington, N.Z., 123,969 175 g6
Wellington, S. Af., 10,330 164 a8
Wellington, Herefs., Eng., U.K. 114 C6
Wellington, Salop., Eng., U.K., 13,654 113 E5
Wellington, Somerset., Eng., U.K., 7,531 113 E6
Wellington, Colo., 532 79 C1
Wellington, Ill., 334 68 E3
Wellington, Kans., 8,809 75 H6
Wellington, Me. 55 C3
Wellington, Mo., 651 72 D5
Wellington, Nev. 83 A3
Wellington, Ohio, 3,599 70 G1
Wellington, Tex., 3,137 76 N2
Wellington, Utah, 1,066 78 C2
Wellington, I., Chile 105 A7
Wellington, L., Austl. 173 f12
Wellington Chan., N.W.T., Can. 40 L2
Wellman, Iowa, 1,085 72 F3
Wellman, Tex. 77 M3
Wellpinit, Wash. 80 D2
Wells, Br. Col., Can. 42 G3
Wells, U.K., 6,715 113 E6
Wells, co., Ind., 21,220 70 D2
Wells, Kans. 75 H4
Wells, Me. 55 B5
Wells, Mich. 66 F3
Wells, Minn., 2,897 74 F4
Wells, Nev., 1,071 83 C2
Wells, N.Y. 59 M5
Wells, co., N. Dak., 9,237 74 C2
Wells, Cherokee Co., Tex., 544 77 Q4
Wells, Lynn Co., Tex. 77 N3
Wells, Vt. 54 A5
Wells, L., Austl. 172 C4
Wells, r., Vt. 54 C3
Wellsboro, Ind. 69 g10
Wellsboro, Pa., 4,369 60 H2
Wells Bridge, N.Y. 59 K7
Wellsburg, Iowa, 827 72 E2
Wellsburg, N.Y., 643 59 G7
Wellsburg, N. Dak. 74 C2
Wellsburg, W. Va., 5,514 62 D2
Wellsford, N.Z. 175 g5
Wellsford, Kans., 24 75 F6
Wells L., Man., Can. 43 E2
Wells-next-the-Sea, U.K., 2,491 113 G5
Wells River, Vt., 472 54 C3
Wellston, Mich. 67 H4
Wellston, Mo., 7,979 72 a11
Wellston, Ohio, 5,728 70 G3
Wellston, Okla., 630 76 F2
Wellsville, Kans., 984 75 L5
Wellsville, Mo., 1,523 72 F5
Wellsville, N.Y., 5,967 58 E7
Wellsville, Ohio, 7,117 70 J2
Wellsville, Pa., 320 60 H5
Wellsville, Utah, 1,106 78 B1
Wellton, Ariz. 78 A5
Wellville (part of Ashburnham), Mass. 56 J2
Wełna, r., Pol. 127 B2
Welper, F.R.Ger., 9,399 119 C2
Wels, Aust., 41,060 124 K5
Welser Heide, reg., Aust. 125 •
Welsh, La., 3,332 73 C7
Welshpool, U.K., 6,330 113 E5
Welton, U.K. 112 g9
Welwyn, U.K., 6,612 114 H7
Welwyn Garden City, U.K., 35,179 113 F6
Welzheim, F.R.Ger., 5,539 119 H7
Wem, U.K., 2,606 113 E5
Wembere, r., Tanz. 164 E2
Wembi, Indon. 149 L3
Wembley, Alta., Can. 42 H2
Wembley, London, U.K. 114 H7
Wemding, F.R.Ger., 4,114 118 C4
Wemme, Oreg. 80 B3
Wemmel, Belg., 8,644 115 d9
Wemyss Bight, Bah. Is. 95 c8
Wenatchee, Wash., 16,726 80 C2
Wen-ch'ang, China 150 E5
Wen-ch'eng, China 152 E2
Wenchi, Ghana, 10,632 162 D4
Wen-chou, China, 250,000* 150 G4
Wenchow = Wen-chou
Wen-ch'üan, Hs-ch., China 150 B2
Wen-ch'üan, N-m-k., China 151 D1
Wendell, Idaho, 1,232 81 B4
Wendell, Mass., 292(T) 56 G2
Wendell, Minn., 253 74 E2
Wendell, N.C., 1,620 63 F2
Wendell Depot (part of Wendell), Mass. 56 G2
Wenden, F.R.Ger., 8,872 119 D3
Wenden, Ariz. 78 B5
Wendlingen, F.R.Ger., 8,710 119 G7
Wendover, U.K., 6,151 114 G7
Wendover, Nev. 83 C2
Wendover, Utah, 609 78 B1
Wendte, S. Dak. 74 B3
Wenebegon, r., Ont., Can. 67 K1
Weng-an, China 152 B2
Wengen, Switz. 124 B2
Weng-niu-t'e-ch'i, China 150 F2
Weng-yüan, China 152 D2
Wenham, Mass., 2,798(T) 57 N2
Wen-hsi, China 151 A4
Wen-hsien, China 151 B4
Wen-ling, China 152 F1
Wenlock, r., Austl. 173 F1
Wenlock Edge, ridge, U.K. 114 C5
Wenman, I., Colón, Arch. de 104 a7
Wenne, r., F.R.Ger. 119 E2
Wenona, Ga. 64 F4
Wenona, Ill., 1,005 68 D2
Wenona, Md. 62 H4
Wenona Beach, Mich. 67 K5
Wenonah, Ala. 64 c8
Wenonah, Ill., 102 68 C4
Wenonah, N.J., 2,100 61 A4
Wen-shan, China 152 B3
Wen-shang, China 151 C4
Wen-shui, China 151 A3
Wensley, U.K. 114 E4
Wen-teng, China 151 D3
Wentorf, F.R.Ger., 4,836 119 b9
Wentworth, Austl., 4,034 173 F5
Wentworth, Mo., 174 72 D7
Wentworth, N.H. 54 D4
Wentworth, N.C. 63 E1
Wentworth, S. Dak., 211 74 D3
Wentworth, Wis. 66 B2
Wentworth, L., N.H. 54 E4
Wentzville, Mo., 2,742 72 G6
Wenvoe, U.K. 114 B8
Weobley, U.K. 114 C6
Weogufka, Ala. 64 C2
Weott, Calif. 82 A2
Wepawaug, r., Conn. 56 D7
Wepener, S. Af., 3,911 164 D6
Wépion, Belg., 3,345 115 C4
Wequaquet L., Mass. 57 P6
Werbkowice, Pol. 127 E3
Werdau, Ger.D.R., 24,539 118 D3
Werder, Ger.D.R., 10,333 118 D2
Werdohl, F.R.Ger., 20,622 119 D2
Werfen, Aust., 3,102 124 K6
Werkendam, Neth., 5,500 115 b7
Werl, F.R.Ger., 15,957 118 A3
Wermelskirchen, F.R.Ger., 22,086 119 C2
Wernau, F.R.Ger., 7,140 119 G7
Werne, F.R.Ger., 18,675 118 A3
Wernersville, Pa., 1,462 61 K5
Wernigerode, Ger.D.R., 33,059 118 C3
Werra, r., F.R.Ger.-Ger.D.R. 118 C3
Werribee, Austl., 4,335 173 F5
Werris Creek, Austl., 2,409 173 G4
Werse, r., F.R.Ger. 119 D1
Wershofen, F.R.Ger. 119 B4
Wertach, r., F.R.Ger. 118 C4
Wertheim, F.R.Ger., 10,967 118 B4
Wertingen, F.R.Ger., 3,239 118 C4
Wervik, Belg., 12,377 115 A4
Wescosville, Pa. 61 i18
Wesel, F.R.Ger., 26,045 118 A3
Wesenberg, Ger.D.R. 118 D2
Weser, r., F.R.Ger. 118 B2
Weser-Elbe Kan., F.R.Ger.-Ger.D.R. 118 C2
Weskan, Kans. 75 D5
Weslaco, Tex., 15,649 77 P6
Weslemkoon L., Ont., Can. 46 G3
Wesley, Dominica, 1,446 97 13
Wesley, Iowa, 514 72 C1
Wesley, Me. 55 E4
Wesley Chapel, Fla. 65 d11
Wesleyville, Newf., Can., 1,264 45 R5
Wesleyville, Pa., 3,534 60 C1
Wesoła, Pol., 5,068 127 D2
Wesoła, Pol., 7,016 127 i6
Wessel, C., Austl. 172 E1
Wesselburen, F.R.Ger., 3,720 118 B1
Wesseling, F.R.Ger., 14,073 119 C3
Wessel Is., Austl. 172 E1
Wesserunsett, L., Me. 55 C4
Wesserunsett Str., Me. 55 C4
Wessex, reg., U.K. 113 E6
Wessington, S. Dak., 378 74 C3
Wessington Springs, S. Dak., 1,488 74 C3
Wesson, Ark. 73 C4
Wesson, Miss., 1,157 73 E6
West, Tex., 2,352 77 P4
West, r., Conn. 56 E7
West, r., Vt. 54 B5
West Acton (part of Acton), Mass. 57 K3
West Alexander, Pa., 468 60 B5
West Alexandria, Ohio, 1,524 70 E3
West Allis, Wis., 68,157 66 c12
West Alton, Mo. 72 b10
West Alton, N.H. 54 E4
West Andover (part of Andover), Mass. 57 M2
West Aspetuck, r., Conn. 56 C6
West Athens, Me. 55 C4
West Augusta, Va. 62 E4
West Avon (part of Avon), Conn. 56 E5
West Baden Springs, Ind., 879 70 C4
West Baldwin, Me. 55 B5
West Bamitz Cr., Okla. 76 D2
West Baraboo, Wis., 613 66 D5
West Barnet, Vt., 113 54 C3
West Barnstable (part of Barnstable), Mass. 57 P6
West Barrington (part of Barrington), R.I. 57 L6
West Baton Rouge, parish, La., 14,796 73 D7
West Bay, Newf., Can. 45 P3
West Bay, Grand Cayman, 2,082 97 3
Westbay, Fla. 65 D2
West Bay, Ont., Can. 46 B3
West Bay, Grand Cayman 97 3
West Bay, Tex. 77 i10
West Bedford (part of Bedford), Mass. 57 L3
West Bend, Iowa, 910 72 C2
West Bend, Wis., 9,969 66 E5
West Bengal, st., India, 34,926,279 145 H5
West Berkshire, Vt. 54 B2
West-Berlin, F.R.Ger., 2,201,000* 118 D2
West Berlin (part of Berlin), Mass. 57 K3
West Berlin, N.J., 3,578 60 g12
West Blocton, Ala., 1,156 64 B2
West Bloomfield, N.Y. 58 E6
West Bolton, Vt. 54 B3
Westboro, Mass., 4,011;9,599(T) 57 K3
Westboro, Mo., 262 72 B4
Westboro, Wis. 66 C3
West Bountiful, Utah, 945 78 c9
Westbourne, Man., Can. 43 f9
Westbourne, U.K., 6,096 113 m13
West Boxford, Mass. 57 M2
West Boylston, Mass., 5,526(T) 57 J3
West Braintree, Vt. 54 B4
West Branch, Iowa, 1,053 72 F3
West Branch, Mich., 2,025 67 J4
West Br. Res., N.Y. 56 A7
West Brewster (part of Brewster), Mass. 57 Q6
West Bridgewater, Mass., 5,061(T) 57 M4
West Bridgewater, Pa., 1,300* 60 a7
West Bridgewater, Vt. 54 B4
West Bridgford, U.K., 26,973 114 F5
West Bromwich, U.K., 95,909 114 E5
Westbrook, Conn., 2,399(T) 56 G7
Westbrook, Me., 13,820 55 B5
Westbrook, Minn., 1,012 74 E3
Westbrook, Tex., 214 77 N3
West Brookfield, Mass., 1,250; 2,053(T) 56 H4
West Brooklyn, Ill., 182 68 C2
Westbrookville, N.Y. 59 L8
West Burke, Vt., 369 54 D2
West Burlington, Iowa, 2,560 72 F4
West Burra, i., U.K. 112 F1
Westbury, Salop., Eng., U.K. 114 C5
Westbury, Wilts., Eng., U.K., 5,417 114 D8
Westbury, Cayuga co., N.Y. 59 p23
Westbury, Nassau co., N.Y., 14,757 59 N10
West Buxton, Me. 55 B5
Westby, Mont., 309 81 H1
Westby, Wis., 1,544 66 C5
West Cache Cr., Okla. 76 E3
West Calder, U.K. 112 c8
West Caldwell, N.J., 8,314 58 b13
West Campton, N.H. 54 D4
West Canada Cr., N.Y. 59 L5
West Canada Mtn., N.Y. 59 L4
West C., N.Z. 175 e7
West C., Sol. Is. 175 c3
West Cape Howe, Austl. 172 B5
West Carroll, parish, La., 14,177 73 D5
West Carrollton, Ohio, 4,749 70 E3
West Carthage, N.Y., 2,167 59 J4
West Charleston, Vt. 54 C2
West Chatham (part of Chatham), Mass. 57 R6
West Chazy, N.Y. 59 N2
Westchester (part of Colchester), Conn. 56 G6
Westchester, Ill., 18,092 69 c9
West Chester, Iowa, 253 72 F3
Westchester, co., N.Y., 808,891 59 N9
West Chester, Pa., 15,705 61 L6
West Chesterfield (part of Chesterfield), Mass. 56 E3
West Chesterfield, N.H. 54 C6
West Chicago, Ill., 6,854 69 b9
West City, Ill., 814 68 C5
West Clarksville, N.Y. 58 D7
Westcliffe, Colo., 306 79 C2
West Columbia, S.C., 6,410 63 C3
West Columbia, Tex., 2,947 77 h10
West Concord, Mass., 1,556 57 L3
West Concord, Minn., 810 74 F3
Westconnaug Res., R.I. 57 K5
West Cornwall (part of Cornwall), Conn. 56 C5
West Cornwall, Vt. 54 A4
West Covina, Calif., 50,645 82 D5
Westcreek, Colo. 79 b9
West Creek, N.J. 61 C4
West Cr., Pa. 60 F3
West Cummington (part of Cummington), Mass. 56 E3
Westdale, La. 73 B5
Westdale, N.Y. 59 J5
West Danville, Vt. 54 C3
West Davenport, N.Y. 59 L7
West Dean, U.K. 113 m13
West Decatur, Pa. 60 F4
West Dennis (part of Dennis), Mass. 57 Q6
West Derry, N.H., 4,468 54 E6
West Des Moines, Iowa, 11,949 72 D3
West Dover, Vt. 54 B6
West Dresden, Me. 55 C4
West Dudley (part of Dudley), Mass. 56 H4
West Dummerston, Vt. 54 B6
West Dundee, Ill., 2,530 68 D1
West Eaton, N.Y. 59 J6
West Edmeston, N.Y. 59 K6
Westeinder plassen, l., Neth. 115 b6
West Elizabeth, Pa., 921 60 c8
West Elk Pk., Colo. 79 B2
West End, Anguilla 97 7
West End, Bah. Is. 95 C1
West End, U.K., 5,064 113 k13
West End, V.I. 97 4
Westend, Calif. 82 E5
West End, Ill. 68 d6
West End, N.C. 63 E2
Westende, Belg., 2,293 115 A3
Westend Saltpond, St. Croix 97 1
West Enfield, Me. 55 D3
West Enosburg, Vt. 54 B2
West Entr., Palau 176 21
West Epping, N.H. 54 E5
Westerbork, Neth. 115 E2
Westerburg, F.R.Ger., 2,313 118 A3
Westerems, esturary, Ger.-Neth. 115 E1
Westerham, U.K., 4,228 114 J8
Westerholt, F.R.Ger., 10,567 119 B1
Westerland, F.R.Ger., 8,244 118 B1
Westerlo, Belg., 7,087 115 C3
Westerlo, N.Y. 59 N6
Westerly, R.I., 14,267(T) 57 J7
Western, Nebr., 351 75 H3
Western Australia, st., Austl., 835,570 172 B3
Western Bay, Newf., Can. 45 b10
Western Chan., Jap.-Kor. 154 A4
Western Duck I., Ont., Can. 67 K3
Western Ghats, ra., India 145 D6 •
Western Grove, Ark., 148 73 B1
Western Hills, Colo. 79 b8
Westernport, Md., 3,559 62 F3
Western Rift Valley, Afr. 159
Western Samoa, ctry., 130,000* 170 G5
Western Shore, N.S., Can. 47 T11
Western Springs, Ill., 10,838 69 c9
Westernville, N.Y. 59 t25
Wester Schelde, chan., Neth. 115 B3
Westersche Veld, Neth. 115 E2
Westerstede, F.R.Ger., 15,157 118 A2
Westervelt, Ill. 68 D4
Westerville, Nebr. 75 F2
Westerville, Ohio, 7,011 70 F2
Westerwald, mts., F.R.Ger. 118 A3
West European Basin, Atl. Oc. 108 L3
West Exeter, N.Y. 59 K6
West Fairlee, Vt. 54 C4
West Fairview, Pa., 1,718 60 H5
West Falkland, i., Falkland Is. 108 3
Westfall, Kans. 75 G5
Westfall, Oreg., 8 80 E3
West Falls, N.Y. 58 C6
West Falmouth (part of Falmouth), Mass. 57 O6
West Farmington, Ohio, 614 70 H1
West Farms, N.J. 58 c16
West Fayu, atoll, Car. Is. 176 18
West Feliciana, parish, La., 12,395 73 D7
West Felton, U.K. 114 C5
Westfield (part of Middletown), Conn. 56 F6
Westfield, Ill., 636 68 E4
Westfield, Ind., 1,217 70 C2
Westfield, Iowa, 187 72 A2
Westfield, Me. 55 D2
Westfield, Mass., 26,302 56 F4
Westfield, N.J., 31,447 61 C2
Westfield, N.Y., 3,878 58 A7
Westfield, N.C. 63 D1
Westfield, N. Dak. 74 B2
Westfield, Pa., 1,333 60 H2
Westfield, Tex. 77 i8
Westfield, Vt. 54 C2
Westfield, Wis., 919 66 D5
Westfield, r., Mass. 56 E4
West Finley, Pa. 60 B6
Westfir, Oreg. 80 B4
West Fitchburg (part of Fitchburg), Mass. 57 J2
Westford (part of Ashford), Conn. 56 H5
Westford, Mass., 6,261(T) 57 L2
Westford, N.Y. 59 L6
Westford, Vt. 54 B2
West Fork, Ark., 350 73 A2
West Frankfort, Ill., 9,027 68 D6
West Friendship, Md. 62 b7
West Fulton, N.Y. 59 L6
Westgate, Alaska 85 b6
West Germany = Germany, Federal Republic of
West Gilgo Beach, N.Y. 58 f14
West Glacier, Mont. 81 C1
West Glocester, R.I. 57 J5
West Gloucester (part of Gloucester), Mass. 57 N2
West Glover, Vt., 64 54 C2
West Goshen (part of Goshen), Conn. 56 C5
West Granville (part of Granville), Mass. 56 E4
West Green, Ga. 64 G4
West Greenwich Center, R.I. 57 K6
West Groton (part of Groton), Mass. 57 K2
West Grove, Pa., 1,607 61 L6
West Haddam (part of Haddam), Conn. 56 F7
West Halifax, Vt. 54 B6
West Ham, London, U.K. 114 J7
West Hamlin, W. Va., 788 62 B4
Westhampton, Mass., 583(T) 56 F3
Westhampton Beach, N.Y., 1,460 59 P10
West Hanover (part of Hanover), Mass. 57 N4
West Harbour, Jam. 96 p9
West Hartford, Conn., 62,382(T) 56 E5
West Hartford, Vt. 54 C4
West Hartland, Conn. 56 E4
West Hartlepool, U.K., 77,073 113 F4
West Harwich (part of Harwich), Mass. 57 Q6
West Haven, Conn., 43,002(T) 56 E7
West Haverstraw, N.Y., 6,770 59 M9
West Hawley (part of Hawley), Mass. 56 E2
West Hebron, N.Y. 59 O5
Westheim, F.R.Ger., 1,609 119 H6
West Helena, Ark., 8,385 73 E3
West Henrietta, N.Y. 58 n20
West Hickory, Pa. 60 D2
West Hill, Ont., Can. 46 d13
Westhofen, F.R.Ger., 4,488 119 C2
Westhoff, Tex. 77 P5
Westhoffen, Fr., 1,322 115 d9
Westhope, N. Dak., 824 74 B1
West Hopkinton, N.H. 54 D5
West Ice Shelf, Ant. 180 S6
West I., Mass. 57 N6
West Jefferson, N.C. 63 C1
West Jefferson, Ohio, 2,747 70 a7
West Jonesport, Me. 55 E4
West Jordan, Utah, 3,009 78 b9
West Kankakee, Ill., 3,197 68 E2
West Kennebunk, Me. 55 B5
West Kilbride, U.K. 112 a8
West Kill, N.Y. 59 M7
West Kingston, R.I. 57 K7
West Kirby, U.K., 17,892 114 B4
West Lafayette, Ind., 12,680 70 B2
West Lafayette, Ohio, 1,476 70 H2
Westlake, La., 3,311 73 B7
Westlake, Ohio, 12,906 70 d9
Westlake, Oreg. 80 A4
Westlake, Wash., 298 80 D2
West Lake Hills, Tex. 76 c5
Westland, Pa. 60 a8
Westland Nat. Pk., N.Z. 175 f6
West Lawn, Pa., 2,059 61 h14
West Lebanon, Ind., 720 70 B2
West Lebanon, N.H. 54 C4
West Leesport, Pa. 61 h14
West Leominster (part of Leominster), Mass. 57 J2
West Leyden (part of Leyden), Mass. 56 F2
West Leyden, N.Y. 59 K5
West Liberty, Ill. 68 D5
West Liberty, Iowa, 2,042 72 F3
West Liberty, Ky., 1,165 71 H4
West Liberty, Ohio, 1,522 70 F2

West Liberty—Wiener Wald · 313

West Liberty, Pa., 201 **60** B3
West Liberty, W. Va. **62** D2
West Lima, Wis. **66** C5
West Lincoln, Vt. **54** A3
Westline, Pa. **60** E2
West Linn, Oreg., 3,933 **80** B3
West Linton, U.K. **112** d8
West Loch, Hawaii **84** b7
West Loch Roag, U.K. **112** C2
West Loch Tarbert, U.K. **112** C3
Westlock, Alta., Can., 1,782 **42** K2
West Lomond, mtn., U.K. **112** d7
West Long Branch, N.J. **58** d15
West Lorne, Ont., Can., 1,056 **46** C6
West Lothian, co., U.K., 92,764 **112** E4
West Lubec, Me. **55** E4
West Lunga, r., Zambia **164** D4
West Mansfield, Ohio, 791 **70** F2
West Mayfield, Pa., 2,201 **60** B4
Westmeath, Ont., Can. **46** G3
Westmeath, co., Ire., 54,122 **113** C5
West Medway, Mass., 1,818 **57** L4
West Memphis, Ark., 19,374 **73** E2
Westmeon, U.K. **113** k12
West Mersea, U.K., 3,140 **113** G6
West Miami, Fla., 5,296 **65** a10
West Middlesex, Pa., 1,301 **60** B3
West Mifflin, Pa., 27,289 **60** c8
West Milan, N.H. **54** E2
West Milford, N.J. **61** C1
West Mills, Me. **55** B4
West Milton, Ohio, 2,972 **70** E3
West Milton, Pa. **60** J3
West Milwaukee, Wis., 5,043 **66** c11
Westminster, London, U.K. **114** H7
Westminster, Colo., 13,850 **79** b8
West Minot, Me. **55** B4
Westminster, Calif., 25,750 **83** h16
Westminster (part of Canterbury), Conn. **56** H6
Westminster, Md., 6,123 **62** H3
Westminster, Mass., 1,047; 4,022(T) **56** J2
Westminster, S.C., 2,413 **63** A3
Westminster, Vt., 333 **54** B5
Westminster Station, Vt. **54** B5
West Monroe, La., 15,215 **73** C5
Westmont, Pa., 6,573 **60** D5
West Monterey, Pa. **60** C3
Westmont Hills, Ill., 5,997 **69** c9
West Montrose, Ont., Can. **46** a13
Westmore, Vt. **54** C2
Westmoreland, Kans., 460 **75** J4
Westmoreland, N.H. **54** C6
Westmoreland, N.Y. **59** t26
Westmoreland, co., Pa., 352,629 **60** D5
Westmoreland, Tenn., 865 **71** E5
Westmoreland, co., Va., 11,042 **62** H4
Westmorland, co., U.K., 67,222 **113** E4
Westmorland, Calif., 1,404 **82** F6
Westmount, Qué., Can., 24,050 **47** o18
West Mtn., Me. **55** B4
West Mtn., Mass. **56** E2
West Mtn., Vt. **54** D2
West Mystic, Conn., 3,268 **56** J7
West Nanticoke, Pa., 1,025* **61** n17
West New Boston (part of Sandisfield), Mass. **56** D4
West Newbury, Mass., 1,844(T) **57** N1
West Newbury, Vt. **54** C3
West New Guinea = Irian Barat
West Newton, U.K. **114** J5
West Newton, Pa., 3,982 **60** C5
West New York, N.J., 35,547 **61** D2
West Nicholson, Rhod. **164** D5
West Nishnabotna, r., Iowa **72** B3
West Northfield (part of Northfield), Mass. **56** F2
West Nottingham, N.H. **54** E5
West Nueces, r., Tex. **77** N5
West Olive, Mich. **67** G6
Weston, Ont., Can., 9,557 **46** c13
Weston, Malay. **148** E1
Weston, Ches., Eng., U.K. **114** C4
Weston, Herts., Eng., U.K. **114** H7
Weston, Lincs., Eng., U.K., 1,364 **114** H5
Weston, Somerset, Eng., U.K., 7,559 **114** D8
Weston, Colo. **79** C3
Weston, Conn., 4,039(T) **56** C8
Weston, Ga., 120 **64** E4
Weston, Idaho, 284 **81** C4
Weston, Me. **55** E3
Weston, Mass., 8,261(T) **57** L3
Weston, Mich. **67** J7
Weston, Mo., 1,057 **72** B5
Weston, Nebr., 340 **75** J2
Weston, N.Y. **58** F7
Weston, Ohio, 1,075 **70** F1
Weston, Oreg., 783 **80** D3
Weston, Vt. **54** B5
Weston, W. Va., 8,754 **62** D3
Weston, co., Wyo., 7,929 **81** G4
Westonaria, S. Af., 26,514 **165** i17
West Oneonta, N.Y. **59** K7
Weston Rhyn, U.K., 1,934 **114** B5
Westons Mills, N.Y. **58** D7
Weston-super-Mare, U.K., 43,938 **113** E6
West Orange (part of Orange), Mass. **56** G2
West Orange, N.J., 39,895 **58** b13
West Orange, Tex., 4,848 **77** n8
West Ossipee, N.H. **54** E4
West Otis (part of Otis), Mass. **56** D4
Westover, Ont., Can. **46** b14
Westover, Ala. **64** d8
Westover, Md. **62** J4
Westover, N.Y. **59** J7
Westover, Pa., 492 **60** E4
Westover, Tenn. **71** B6
Westover, W. Va., 4,749 **62** D3
West Oxford (part of Oxford), Mass. **56** J4
West Palm Beach, Fla., 56,208 **65** J6
West Palm Beach Can., Fla. **65** J6
West Paris, Me. **55** B4
West Parley, U.K., 2,002 **113** i13
West Passage, Palau **176** 21
West Passage, R.I. **57** L6
West Paterson, N.J., 7,602 **58** c13
West Pawlet, Vt. **54** A5
West Pearl, r., La. **73** F7
West Pelham, Mass. **56** G3
West Peru, Me. **55** B4
West Peterborough, N.H. **54** C6
Westphalia, Iowa, 131 **72** B3
Westphalia, Kans., 249 **75** K5
Westphalia, Mich., 560 **67** J6
West Pittsburg, Calif., 5,188 **83** f11
West Pittsfield (part of Pittsfield), Mass. **56** C3
West Plains, Mo., 5,836 **72** F8
West Point, Ga., 4,610 **64** D2
West Point, Ill., 234 **68** A3
West Point, Iowa, 758 **72** F4
West Point, Ky., 1,957 **71** E3
West Point, Miss., 8,550 **73** G4
West Point, Nebr., 2,921 **75** J2
West Point, N.Y. **59** N9
West Point, Ohio **70** J2
West Point, Pa. **60** f11
West Point, Tenn. **71** D6
West Point, Utah, 599 **78** b8
West Point, Va., 1,678 **62** H5
West Pt., Austl. **172** a8
West Pt., Austl. **173** e13
West Pt., Jaluit **176** 30
West Pt., St. Helena **109** 7
West Pt., Terr. Papua **174** 3
West Pt., Alaska **85** H2
Westpoint I., Falk. Is. **108** 3
Westport, Ont., Can. **47** H4
Westport, Ire., 2,947 **113** B5
Westport, N.Z., 5,460 **175** f6
Westport, Calif. **82** B3
Westport, Conn., 20,955(T) **56** C8
Westport, Ind., 833 **70** D3
Westport, Mass., 6,641(T) **57** M6
Westport, N.H. **54** C6
Westport, N.Y., 723 **59** N3
Westport, Oreg. **80** B2
Westport, Pa. **60** G3
Westport, S. Dak. **74** C3
Westport, Wash., 976 **80** A2
Westport, Wis. **66** C5
Westport, E. Br., r., Mass. **57** M6
West Portland, Oreg. **80** a7
Westport Point (part of Westport), Mass. **57** M6
West Portsmouth, Ohio, 3,100 **70** F4
West Rainton, U.K., 2,353 **112** h10
Westray, Man., Can. **43** E4
Westray, i., U.K. **112** E2
Westray Firth, U.K. **112** E2
West Redding (part of Redding), Conn. **56** C7
Westree, Ont., Can. **44** G6
West Richland, Wash., 1,347 **80** D2
West Riding (admin. part of Yorkshire), U.K., 3,641,228 **113** F5
West Rindge, N.H. **54** D6
West River, Md. **62** c9
West River St. Mary's, N.S., Can. **47** U11
West Riverside = Rubidoux
West Road, r., Br. Col., Can. **42** F3
West Rockport, Me. **55** C4
West Royalston (part of Royalston), Mass. **56** G2
West Rupert, Vt. **54** A5
West Rush, N.Y. **58** n21
Westruther, U.K. **112** e8
West Rutland, Vt., 1,991 **54** A4
West Sacramento, Calif. **82** C3
West St. Paul, Minn., 13,101 **74** c6
West Salem, Ill., 956 **68** D5
West Salem, Ohio, 1,017 **70** G2
West Salem, Wis., 1,707 **66** B5
West Salt Cr., Colo. **79** A2
West Sand Lake, N.Y. **59** w29
West Sayville, N.Y. **58** g14
West Scarboro, Me. **55** B5
West Schuyler, N.Y. **59** u26
West Scotia Basin, Atl. Oc. **109** J10
West Seneca, N.Y., 23,138 **58** C6
West Shoal L., Man., Can. **43** g9
Westside, Iowa, 367 **72** B2
West Sidney, Me. **55** C4
West Simsbury (part of Simsbury), Conn. **56** E5
West Slope, Oreg. **80** a6
West Spit, Eniwetok **176** 28
West Springfield, Mass., 24,924(T) **56** F4
West Springfield, N.H. **54** C5
West Sterling (part of Sterling), Mass. **57** J3
West Stewartstown, N.H. **54** E2
West Stockbridge, Mass., 1,244(T) **56** C3
West Stockholm, N.Y. **59** K2
West Stoughton (part of Stoughton), Mass. **57** M4
West Sumner, Me. **55** B4
West Sunbury, Pa., 252 **60** C4
West Sutton (part of Sutton), Mass. **57** J4
West Swamp Cr., Pa. **60** e10
West Swanton, Vt. **54** A2
West Swanzey, N.H. **54** C6
West Tanfield, U.K. **114** E2
West Tatnuck (part of Worcester), Mass. **56** J3
West Tavaputs Plat., Utah **78** C2
West Terre Haute, Ind., 3,006 **70** B3
West-Terschelling, Neth. **115** D1
West Thorney, U.K., 1,124 **113** m13
West Thornton, N.H. **54** D4
West Topsham, Vt. **54** C3
Westtown, N.Y. **59** M9
Westtown, Pa. **61** L6
West Townsend (part of Townsend), Mass. **57** K2
West Townshend, Vt. **54** B5
West Trenton, Me. **55** D4
West Trenton, N.J., 1,600* **61** B3
West Twin, r., Wis. **66** F4
West Union, Ill. **68** E4
West Union, Iowa, 2,551 **72** F2
West Union, Ohio, 1,762 **70** F4
West Union, Oreg. **80** a6
West Union, S.C., 443 **63** A3
West Union, W. Va., 1,186 **62** D3
West Unity, Ohio, 1,192 **70** E1
West University Place, Tex., 14,628 **77** i9
West Valley, N.Y. **58** C7
West Vancouver, Br. Col., Can., 25,454 **42** G4
Westview, Br. Col., Can., 4,000 **42** F4
Westview, Ill. **72** b11
Westview, Ohio, 1,303 **70** H1
West View, Pa., 8,079 **60** b7
Westville, N.S., Can., 4,091 **47** U11
Westville, Fla. **65** C2
Westville, Ill., 3,497 **68** E3
Westville, Ind., 789 **70** B1
Westville (part of Taunton), Mass. **57** M5
Westville, N.J., 4,951 **60** f12
Westville, Okla., 727 **76** J1
Westville, Pa. **60** E3
Westville, S.C. **63** D3
West Virginia, st., U.S., 1,815,000* **62**
West Walworth, N.Y. **58** o20
West Wardsboro, Vt. **54** B5
West Wareham (part of Wareham), Mass. **57** O5
West Warren, Mass., 1,124 **56** G4
West Warwick, R.I. 21,414(T) **57** K6
Westwater, Utah **78** D2
West Webster, N.Y. **58** o20
Westwego, La., 9,815 **73** E8
West Whately (part of Whately), Mass. **56** F3
West Willington (part of Willington), Conn. **56** G5
West Wilton, N.H. **54** D6
West Winfield, N.Y. **59** K6
Westwood, Calif., 1,209 **82** C2
Westwood, Kans., 2,040 **75** a7
Westwood, Mass., 10,354(T) **57** L4
Westwood, N.J., 9,046 **61** C2
West Woodstock, Vt. **54** B4
Westworth, Tex., 3,321 **76** e9
West Wrentham (part of Wrentham), Mass. **57** L4
West Wyalong, Austl., 2,490 **173** G5
West Yarmouth, Mass., 1,365 **57** Q6
West Yellowstone, Mont. **81** D3
West York, Ill. **68** E4
West York, Pa., 5,526 **60** J6
Wetar, i., Indon. **149** H4
Wetar Str., Indon. **149** H5
Wetaskiwin, Alta., Can., 5,250 **42** K3
Wete, Tanz., 7,507 **164** F2
Wet Glaize, Mo. **72** E7
Wetherby, U.K., 4,237 **114** F3
Wethersfield, U.K., 2,774 **113** G6
Wethersfield, Conn., 20,561(T) **56** F6
Wetlet, Burma, 3,802 **146** A2
Wetlu, Burma **147** f7
Wetmore, Colo. **79** C2
Wetmore, Kans., 390 **75** K4
Wetmore, Mich. **67** G2
Wetmore, Tenn. **71** G6
Wetmore, Tex. **76** a6
Wetonka, S. Dak., 46 **74** C3
Wetten, F.R.Ger., 1,991 **119** A1
Wetter, Hess., F.R.Ger., 2,575 **118** B3
Wetter, Nrh.-Wf., F.R.Ger., 13,633 **119** C2
Wetter, r., F.R.Ger. **119** F4
Wetteren, Belg., 19,928 **115** B4
Wettin, Ger.D.R. **118** C3
Wettingen, Switz., 17,613 **124** C1
Wetumka, Okla., 1,798 **76** G2
Wetumpka, Ala., 3,672 **64** C3
Wetwang, U.K. **114** G2
Wetzel, co., W. Va., 19,347 **62** D3
Wetzikon, Switz., 10,421 **124** C1
Wetzlar, F.R.Ger., 32,244 **118** B3
Wevelgem, Belg., 12,825 **115** B4
Wevertown, N.Y. **59** M4
Wewahitchka, Fla., 1,436 **65** D2
Wewak, Terr. New Guin. **174** d1
Weweantic, r., Mass. **57** N5
Wewela, S. Dak. **74** C4
Wewoka, Okla., 5,954 **76** G2
Wewoka Cr., Okla. **76** G2
Wexford, Ont., Can. **46** d13
Wexford, co., Ire., 87,259 **113** C5
Wexford, Ire., 11,840 **113** C5
Wexford, co., Mich., 18,466 **67** H4
Wexford, Pa. **60** b7
Weyauwega, Wis., 1,239 **66** E4
Weybridge, U.K., 7,635 **114** G8
Weybridge, Vt. **54** A3
Weyburn, Sask., Can., 8,998 **43** D5
Weyer, F.R.Ger., 1,145 **119** B3
Weyerhauser, Wis., 339 **66** B3
Weyer Markt, Aust., 2,369 **124** L6
Weyers Cave, Va. **62** F4
Weyersheim, Fr., 2,275 **116** e9
Weymouth, N.S., Can. **45** N7
Weymouth, U.K., 34,527 **113** E6
Weymouth, Mass., 48,177(T) **57** N4
Weymouth, NJ **61** B4
Weymouth, Ohio **70** H1
Wezep, Neth. **115** D2
Whakatane, N.Z., 7,167 **175** h5
Whale, r., Qué., Can. **45** M2
Whale Bay, Burma **146** B5
Whale Cay, Bah. Is. **95** b7
Whaletown, Br. Col., Can. **42** a5
Whaley Bridge, U.K., 5,290 **114** E4
Whaleysville, Va., 402 **62** H6
Whalom (part of Lunenburg and Leominster), Mass. **57** K2
Whalsay, i., U.K. **112** F1
Whalton, U.K. **112** g9
Whanganui Inlet, N.Z. **175** g6
Whangarei, N.Z., 17,880 **175** g4
Whangarei Hbr., N.Z. **175** g4
Whaplode Drove, U.K., 2,452 **114** H5
Wharfe, r., U.K. **113** E4
Wharncliffe, W. Va. **62** B5
Wharton, N.J., 5,006 **61** B2
Wharton, Ohio, 463 **70** F2
Wharton, co., Tex., 38,152 **77** P5
Wharton, Tex., 5,734 **77** P5
Wharton, W. Va., 1,055 **62** C5
Wharton Basin, Ind. Oc. **168** D3
Wharton L., N.W.T., Can. **40** J5
Whataroa, N.Z. **175** f6
What Cheer, Iowa, 956 **72** E3
Whatcom, co., Wash., 70,317 **80** B1
Whatley, Ala. **64** B4
Whately, Mass., 1,037(T) **56** F3
Wheatfield, Ind., 679 **70** B1
Wheatland, Calif., 813 **82** C3
Wheatland, Ind., 614 **70** B4
Wheatland, Iowa, 643 **72** G3
Wheatland, Mo., 305 **72** D7
Wheatland, co., Mont., 3,026 **81** E2
Wheatland, N. Mex. **79** D4
Wheatland, Pa., 1,813 **60** A3
Wheatland, Wis. **66** c13
Wheatland, Wyo., 2,350 **81** G4
Wheatley, Ont., Can., 1,345 **46** B6
Wheatley, U.K., 2,208 **114** F7
Wheatley, Ark., 443 **73** D3
Wheaton, Ill., 26,263 **68** D2
Wheaton, Kans., 114 **75** J4
Wheaton, Md., 54,635 **62** G3
Wheaton, Minn., 2,102 **74** D3
Wheaton, Mo., 341 **72** C8
Wheaton Aston, U.K. **114** D5
Wheaton Springs, Calif. **82** F5
Wheat Ridge, Colo., 21,619 **79** b8
Wheelbarrow Pk., Nev. **83** C4
Wheeler, co., Ga., 5,342 **64** G3
Wheeler, Ill., 173 **68** D4
Wheeler, Ind. **69** f10
Wheeler, Kans. **75** D4
Wheeler, Mich. **67** J5
Wheeler, Miss. **73** G3
Wheeler, co., Nebr., 1,297 **75** G2
Wheeler, co., Oreg., 2,722 **80** C3
Wheeler, Oreg., 237 **80** B3
Wheeler, co., Tex., 7,947 **76** N2
Wheeler, Tex., 1,174 **76** N2
Wheeler, Wis. 227 **66** B3
Wheeler, r., Qué., Can. **45** M3
Wheeler L., Ala. **64** B1
Wheeler Lake, Mich. **67** H2
Wheeler Pk., Nev. **83** C3
Wheeler Pk., N. Mex. **79** C3
Wheeler Ridge, Calif. **82** D5
Wheelersburg, Ohio, 2,682 **70** G4
Wheeless, Okla. **76** A1
Wheeling, Ill., 11,756 **68** D1
Wheeling, W. Va., 53,400 **62** D2
Wheelock, Me. **55** D1
Wheelock, N. Dak., 32 **74** A1
Wheelock, Vt. **54** C2
Wheelock Mtn., Vt. **54** C2
Wheelockville (part of Uxbridge), Mass. **57** K4
Wheelwright, Ky., 1,518 **71** J4
Wheelwright (part of Hardwick), Mass. **56** H3
Whelen Springs, Ark., 155 **73** B4
Whernside, mtn., U.K. **114** D2
Wherwell, U.K. **114** E8
Whetstone Bk., Vt. **54** B6
Whickham, U.K., 24,791 **112** g10
Whidbey, Pt., Austl. **172** E5
Whidbey Is., Austl. **172** a8
Whigham, Ga., 463 **64** E5
Whigville (part of Burlington), Conn. **56** E6
Whippany, N.J., 6,100* **61** C2
Whippleville, N.Y. **59** M2
Whiskey Jack L., Man., Can. **43** E2
Whiskey Jack Landing, Man., Can. **43** F3
Whissendine, U.K. **114** G5
Whitakers, N.C., 1,004 **63** G1
Whitakerville, Mo. **72** D6
Whitburn, Dur., Eng., U.K., 6,419 **112** h10
Whitburn, W.L., Scot., U.K., 5,902 **112** c8
Whitby, Ont., Can., 14,515 **46** F5
Whitby, U.K. 11,675 **113** F4
Whitchurch, Glam., Wales, U.K., 27,325 **113** E6
Whitchurch, Hants., Eng., U.K., 2,699 **114** F8
Whitchurch, Herefs., Eng., U.K. **114** C7
Whitchurch, Salop., Eng., U.K., 7,165 **114** C5
Whitcomb Mtn., N.H. **54** E2
White, co., Ark., 32,745 **73** D2
White, co., Ga., 6,935 **64** F1
White, co., Ill., 19,373 **68** D5
White, co., Ind., 19,709 **70** C2
White, S. Dak., 417 **74** D3
White, co., Tenn., 15,577 **71** F6
White, r., Yukon, Can. **85** J3
White, r., Ariz. **78** C5
White, r., Ark. **73** D3
White, r., Colo.-Utah **79** A1
White, r., Ind. **70** B4
White, r., Mich. **67** G5
White, N. Fk., r., Mo. **72** E8
White, r., Nebr.-S. Dak. **74** A4
White, r., Nev. **83** C4
White, r., Oreg. **80** C3
White, r., Tex. **77** N3
White, r., Vt. **54** B4
White, r., Wash. **80** C2
White, r., Wis. **66** C2
White, r., Wis. **66** c13
White Bay, Newf., Can. **45** Q5
White Bear Lake, Minn., 12,849 **74** c5
White Bear L., Minn. **74** c5
White Bird, Idaho, 253 **81** A3
White Bluff, Tenn., 486 **71** D5
White Butte, N. Dak. **74** A2
White Cap Mtn., Franklin Co., Me. **55** B3
White Cap Mtn., Piscataquis Co., Me. **55** C3
White Cart Water, r., U.K. **112** b8
White Castle, La., 2,253 **73** D7
White City, Gulf Co., Fla. **65** D3
White City, St. Lucie Co., Fla. **65** J5
White City, Kans., 459 **75** J5
White City, Mich. **66** D2
White City, Oreg. **80** B4
Whiteclay, Nebr. **75** C1
White Clay Cr., Pa. **61** L6
White Cliffs, Austl. **173** F4
White Cloud, Kans., 238 **75** K4
White Cloud, Mich., 1,001 **67** H5
Whitecourt, Alta., Can. **42** J2
White Creek, N.Y. **59** C6
White Deer, Tex., 1,057 **76** N2
White Deer Cr., Pa. **60** H3
White Eagle, Okla. **76** F1
White Earth, Minn. **74** E2
White Earth, N. Dak., 208 **74** A1
White Earth, r., N. Dak. **74** A1
Whiteface, N.H. **54** E4
Whiteface, Tex., 535 **77** M3
Whiteface Mtn., N.Y. **59** N3
Whiteface Mtn., Vt. **54** B2
Whitefield, Me. **55** C4
Whitefield, N.H., 1,244 **54** D3
Whitefield, Okla. **76** H2
Whitefish, Ont., Can. **46** C2
Whitefish, Mont., 2,965 **81** B1
Whitefish, r., Mich. **66** G2
Whitefish Bay, Wis., 18,390 **66** F5
Whitefish B., Ont., Can. **53** K1
Whitefish Bay, Mich. **67** J2
Whitefish Falls, Ont., Can. **46** C2
Whitefish L., N.W.T., Can. **40** H5
Whitefish Point, Mich. **67** H2
Whitefish Pt., Mich. **67** J2
Whiteford, Md. **62** H3
White Fox, Sask., Can. **43** D4
Whitegate, Ire. **113** B6
White Gull L., Qué., Can. **45** N3
White Hall, Ala. **64** C3
Whitehall, Jefferson Co., Ark., 1,257 **73** C3
Whitehall, Poinsett Co., Ark. **73** E2
White Hall, Ill., 3,012 **68** B4
Whitehall, Mich., 2,590 **67** G5
Whitehall, Mont., 898 **81** C3
Whitehall, N.Y., 4,016 **59** O4
Whitehall, Ohio, 20,818 **70** b7
Whitehall, Pa., 16,075 **60** b8
Whitehall, S.C. **63** D5
Whitehall, Wis., 1,446 **66** B4
Whitehall, N.C. = Seven Springs
Whitehaven, U.K., 27,541 **113** E4
White Haven, Pa., 1,778 **61** L3
Whitehaven, Tenn., 13,894 **71** A6
Whitehead, U.K., 2,174 **113** D4
Whitehead, N.C. **63** C1
Whitehorse, Yukon, Can., 4,833 **40** C5
Whitehorse, S. Dak. **74** B3
White Horse, Val., U.K. **114** E7
White Horse Beach (part of Plymouth), Mass. **57** O5
Whitehorse L., Me. **55** D2
Whitehouse, Ohio, 1,135 **70** F1
Whitehouse, Tex., 842 **77** Q3
Whitehouse Station, N.J. **61** B2
White Lake, N.C., 130 **63** F3
White Lake, S. Dak., 357 **74** C4
White Lake, Wis., 325 **66** E3
White, L., Austl. **172** D3
White L., Ont., Can. **47** H3
White L., La. **73** C8
White L., Mich. **67** G5
White L., N. Dak. **74** A1
White L., S. Dak. **74** C4
White L., Wis. **66** E4
Whiteland, Ind., 1,368 **70** C3
Whitelaw, Alta., Can. **42** H2
Whitelaw, Kans. **75** D5
Whitelaw, Wis., 420 **66** F4
Whiteman Cr., Ont., Can. **46** b15
Whitemark, Austl. **173** G6
White Marsh, Md. **62** d7
White Mills, Pa. **61** M2
White Mountain, Alaska, 151 **85** C2
White Mtn. Pk., Calif. **82** D4
White Mts., Alaska **85** H2
White Mts. Calif. **50** C3
White Mts., N.H. **54** D3
Whitemouth, Man., Can. **43** G5
Whitemouth, r., Man., Can. **43** G5
Whitemouth L., Man., Can. **43** G5
Whitemud, r., Man., Can. **43** f9
Whiten Head, U.K. **112** D2
White Nile, Sudan = Jabal, Bahr al
White Oak, Ill. **68** C4
White Oak, N.C. **63** F3
White Oak, Pa., 9,047 **60** c8
White Oak, S.C. **63** C3
White Oak, r., N.C. **63** G3
White Oak Bayou, Tex. **77** Q3
White Oaks (part of Williamstown), Mass. **56** D2
White Otter L., Ont., Can. **74** F1
Whiteparish, U.K. **113** i12
White Pass, Br. Col., Can. **42** B1
White Pigeon, Mich., 1,399 **67** H7
White Pine, Mich. **66** D2
White Pine, co., Nev., 9,808 **83** C3
White Pine, Tenn., 1,035 **71** H5
White Pine Mts., Nev. **83** C3
White Plains, Ga., 273 **64** F2
White Plains, N.Y., 50,485 **59** N9
White Plains, N.C. **63** D1
White Pond, S.C. **63** C4
White Potato L., Wis. **66** E3
White River, Ont., Can. **44** F5
Whiteriver, Ariz. **78** D5
White River, S. Dak., 583 **74** B4
White River Junction, Vt., 2,546 **54** C4
White Rock, Br. Col., Can., 6,127 **42** G4
White Rock, Calif. **82** B7
White Rock, Mich. **67** L5
White Rock, Nev. **83** B2
White Rock, S.C. **63** C3
White Rock, S. Dak., 76 **74** D3
White Rock, mtn., Vt. **54** B5
White Rock, pk., Utah **78** a10
White Rock Cr., Kans. **75** G4
White Rock Cr., Tex. **76** f8
White Rock L., Tex. **76** f9
White Rock Mtn., Ark. **73** B2
White Rocks Mtn., Vt. **54** B4
White Russian S.S.R. = Belorusskaya S.S.R.
Whitesail L., Br. Col., Can. **42** E3
White Salmon, Wash., 1,590 **80** C3
Whitesands, New Hebr. **174** m7
Whitesand, r., Alta., Can. **42** J1
Whitesand Bay, U.K. **113** D6
White Sand L., Wis. **66** D2
White Sands, area, N. Mex. **52** E4
White Sands Nat. Mon., N. Mex. **79** B5
Whitesbog, N.J. **58** b17
Whitesboro, N.J. **61** B5
Whitesboro, N.Y., 4,784 **59** K5
Whitesboro, Okla. **76** J3
Whitesboro, Tex., 2,485 **77** P3
Whitesburg, Ky., 1,774 **71** H4
Whitesburg, Tenn. **71** H5
Whites City, N. Mex. **79** C5
White Sea = Beloye More
White Settlement, Tex., 11,513 **76** d9
Whiteside, co., Ill., 59,887 **68** B2
Whiteside, Mo., 122 **72** G5
White Signal, N. Mex. **79** A5
White Springs, Fla., 633 **65** G2
White Stone, Va., 395 **62** H5
Whitestown, Ind. **70** C2
White Sulphur Springs, Mont., 1,519 **81** D2
White Sulphur Springs, W. Va., 2,676 **62** D5
Whitesville, Ky., 713 **71** D4
Whitesville, N.J. **61** C3
Whitesville, N.Y. **58** E7
Whitesville, W. Va., 774 **62** C5
White Swan, Wash. **80** C2
Whiteswan Lakes, Sask., Can. **43** D3
Whitetail, Mont. **81** G1
White Tail, N. Mex. **79** C5
White Valley Ra., Utah **78** B2
Whiteville, N.C., 4,683 **63** F3
Whiteville, Tenn., 757 **71** B6
White Volta, r., Ghana-Upper Volta **162** D4
Whitewater, Colo. **79** A2
Whitewater, Kans., 499 **75** H6
Whitewater, Mo., 169 **72** H7
Whitewater, N. Mex. **79** A5
Whitewater, Wis., 10,353 **66** E6
Whitewater, r., Ind. **70** E3
Whitewater, r., Mo. **72** G7
Whitewater Baldy, mtn., N. Mex. **79** A5
Whitewater L., Ont., Can. **44** E5
Whitewood, Sask., Can. **43** D5
Whitewood, S. Dak., 470 **74** A3
Whitewright, Tex., 1,315 **77** P3
Whitfell, mtn., U.K. **114** B2
Whitfield, co., Ga., 42,109 **64** E1
Whitford, Alta., Can. **43** c7
Whitford, U.K., 3,823 **114** B4
Whitford L., Alta., Can. **43** c7
Whithorn, U.K. **113** D4
Whitianga, N.Z. **175** g5
Whiting, Ind., 8,137 **70** B1
Whiting, Iowa, 595 **72** A2
Whiting, Kans., 233 **75** K4
Whiting, Me. **55** E4
Whiting, N.J. **61** C4
Whiting, Vt. **54** A4
Whiting, Wis., 1,193 **66** D4
Whitingham, Vt. **54** B6
Whitingham, L., Vt. **54** B6
Whitinsville, Mass., 5,102 **57** K4
Whitley, co., Ind., 20,954 **70** D1
Whitley, co., Ky., 25,815 **71** G5
Whitley Bay, U.K., 36,519 **112** h9
Whitley City, Ky., 1,034 **71** G5
Whitman, Mass., 10,485(T) **57** N4
Whitman, Nebr. **75** D1
Whitman, N. Dak. **74** C1
Whitman, co., Wash., 31,263 **80** E2
Whitman Nat. Mon., Wash. **80** D2
Whitmanville (part of Westminster), Mass. **56** J2
Whitmell, Va. **62** E6
Whitmer, W. Va. **62** E4
Whitmire, S.C., 2,663 **63** C3
Whitmore, Hawaii, 1,820 **84** b6
Whitmore Lake, Mich. **67** K6
Whitmore Mts., Ant. **180** Y4
Whitnash, U.K., 1,682 **114** F6
Whitnel, N.C., 1,232 **63** C2
Whitney, Ont., Can. **44** H6
Whitney, Calif. **82** C3
Whitney, Idaho **78** c7
Whitney, Nebr. **75** B1
Whitney, Pa. **60** D5
Whitney, Tex., 1,050 **77** P4
Whitney, L., Tex. **77** P4
Whitney, Mt., Calif. **82** D4
Whitney Point, N.Y., 1,049 **59** J7
Whitsett, Tex. **77** O5
Whitstable, U.K., 19,571 **113** G6
Whitsunday I., Austl. **173** G3
Whitt, Tex. **76** d9
Whittaker, Mich. **67** K6
Whittemore, Iowa, 741 **72** C1
Whittemore, Mich., 460 **67** K4
Whittier, Alaska, 809 **85** G3
Whittier, Calif., 33,663 **83** h16
Whittier, N.H. **54** E4
Whittier, N.C. **63** A2
Whittingham, U.K. **112** g9
Whittington, U.K., 4,524 **113** E5
Whittlesey, U.K., 9,322 **113** F5
Whittlesey, Wis. **66** C3
Whittonstall, U.K. **112** g10
Whitwell, U.K., 4,847 **114** F4
Whitwell, Tenn., 1,857 **71** F6
Whitwick, U.K., 6,526 **114** F5
Whixley, U.K. **114** F2
Wholdaia L., N.W.T., Can. **40** H5
Whyalla, Austl., 8,598 **172** E5
Whynot, Miss. **73** G5
Wianno (part of Barnstable), Mass. **57** P6
Wiarton, Ont., Can., 2,063 **46** C4
Wiawso, Ghana **162** b8
Wiay, i., U.K. **112** C3
Wiązów, Pol., 1,886 **127** B3
Wibaux, co., Mont., 1,698 **81** G2
Wibaux, Mont., 766 **81** G2
Wichabai, Guyana **101** L6
Wichian Buri, Thai. **147** d4
Wichita, co., Kans., 2,765 **75** D5
Wichita, Kans., 254,698 **75** H6
Wichita, Oreg. **80** a7
Wichita, co., Tex., 123,528 **77** O2
Wichita, r., Tex. **77** O3
Wichita Falls, Tex., 101,724 **77** O3
Wichita Mts., Okla. **76** E3
Wick, U.K., 7,397 **112** E2
Wickaboag Pd., Mass. **56** H4
Wickatunk, N.J. **58** c15
Wickede, F.R.Ger., 5,997 **119** D1
Wickenburg, Ariz., 2,445 **78** B5
Wickepin, Austl. **172** B5
Wickersham, Wash. **80** B1
Wickes, Ark., 368 **73** A3
Wickett, Tex. **77** M4
Wickford, R.I., 2,934 **57** L6
Wickford Junction, R.I. **57** K6
Wickham, U.K., 3,586 **113** k13
Wickiup Res., Oreg. **80** C4
Wickliffe, Ky., 917 **71** B5
Wickliffe, Ohio, 15,760 **70** f8
Wicklow, co., Ire., 59,906 **113** C5
Wicklow, Ire., 3,070 **113** D5
Wicklow Head, Ire. **113** D5
Wicklow Mts., Ire. **113** C5
Wickrath, F.R.Ger., 10,492 **119** A2
Wicksville, S. Dak. **74** A3
Wickwar, U.K. **114** D7
Wicomico, co., Md., 49,050 **62** J4
Wicomico Church, Va. **62** H5
Wiconisco, Pa., 1,402 **60** J4
Wiconisco Cr., Pa. **60** J4
Widawa, Pol. **127** h5
Widawa, r., Pol. **127** B3
Widawka, r., Pol. **127** i5
Widdern, F.R.Ger., 1,107 **119** G6
Widdrington, U.K. **112** g9
Wide, r., F.R.Ger. **119** D3
Wide B., Terr. New Guin. **174** g2
Widen, W. Va. **62** D4
Wide Ruin, Ariz. **78** D4
Widgeon, Va. **62** G4
Widgiemooltha, Austl. **172** B4
Widnes, U.K., 52,168 **114** C4
Więcbork, Pol., 4,430 **127** B2
Wiedenbrück, F.R.Ger., 13,483 **118** B3
Wiehl, F.R.Ger., 9,840 **118** A3
Wiehl, r., F.R.Ger. **119** D3
Wielbark, Pol. **127** D2
Wieleń, Pol., 3,820 **127** B2
Wielgomłyny, Pol. **127** C3
Wieliczka, Pol., 12,142 **127** D4
Wieluń, Pol., 11,735 **127** C3
Wien, Aust., 1,627,034 **125** N5
Wiener Neustadt, Aust., 33,836 **124** N6
Wiener Wald, mts. Aust. **124** b10

314 · Wieprz—Wixhausen

Wieprz, r., Pol. 127 E3
Wieprza, r., Pol. 127 B1
Wieprz-Krzna, Kan., Pol. 127 E3
Wierden, Neth., 5,600 115 E2
Wiergate, Tex. 77 R4
Wieringerwaard, Neth. 115 C2
Wiers, Belg., 3,073 115 B4
Wieruszów, Pol., 3,212 127 C3
Wierzbica, Pol. 127 E3
Wierzyca, r., Pol. 127 C1
Wies, Aust., 1,506 124 M7
Wiesau, F.R.Ger., 3,918 126 b7
Wiesbaden, F.R.Ger., 244,994 118 A3
Wieselburg, Aust., 2,555 124 M5
Wiesensteig, F.R.Ger., 2,212 119 H7
Wiesental, F.R.Ger., 6,208 119 F6
Wiesloch, F.R.Ger., 11,940 118 B4
Wiesmoor, F.R.Ger., 5,210 118 A2
Wietze, F.R.Ger., 4,143 118 B2
Wietzen, F.R.Ger., 2,016 118 B2
Wieżyca, pk., Pol. 127 B1
Wigan, U.K., 78,702 113 E5
Wigger, r. Switz. 124 C1
Wiggins, Colo. 79 C1
Wiggins, Leake Co., Miss. 73 F5
Wiggins, Stone Co., Miss., 1,591 73 F7
Wigginsville, Tex. 77 i8
Wight, I. of, U.K. 113 F6
Wigry, Jez., Pol. 127 E2
Wigston, U.K., 21,415 113 F5
Wigton, U.K., 4,085 113 E4
Wigtown, co., U.K., 29,107 113 D4
Wigtown, U.K., 1,201 113 D4
Wigtown Bay, U.K. 113 D4
Wihan Daeng, Thai. 147 d4
Wijchen, Neth., 5,800 115 D3
Wijhe, Neth., 3,100 115 E2
Wijk, Neth. 115 c7
Wijnegem, Belg., 7,782 115 e8
Wikieup, Ariz. 78 B4
Wikwemikong, Ont., Can. 46 C3
Wil, Switz., 10,927 124 D1
Wilamowice, Pol., 2,123 127 i7
Wilbarger, co., Tex., 17,748 77 O3
Wilber, Nebr., 1,358 75 H3
Wilberforce, Ont., Can. 44 H7
Wilberforce, Ohio 70 F3
Wilberforce, C., Austl. 172 E1
Wilbraham, Mass., 7,387(T) 56 G4
Wilbur, Ind. 70 C3
Wilbur, Oreg. 80 B4
Wilbur, Wash., 1,138 80 D2
Wilburton, Kans. 75 D6
Wilburton, Okla., 1,772 76 H3
Wilcannia, Austl. 173 F4
Wilchingen, Switz., 1,061 124 C1
Wilcox, Sask., Can. 43 D5
Wilcox, co., Ala., 18,739 64 B3
Wilcox, Fla. 65 G3
Wilcox, co., Ga., 7,905 64 F4
Wilcox, Nebr., 260 75 F3
Wilcox, Pa. 60 E2
Wilcze Gardło, Pol., 1,624 127 h6
Wild, r., N.H. 54 E3
Wild Acres, R.I. 57 L6
Wildalpen, Aust. 124 L6
Wild Ammonoosuc, r., N.H. 54 D3
Wildau, Ger.D.R. 119 f11
Wildbad, F.R.Ger., 5,967 119 F7
Wildberg, F.R.Ger., 1,656 119 F7
Wildcat, Okla., 142 76 H2
Wildcat Cr., Ind. 70 C2
Wildcat Mtn., Nebr. 75 B2
Wildcat Pk., Nev. 83 B3
Wilder, Idaho, 603 81 A4
Wilder, Tenn. 71 F5
Wilder, Vt., 1,322 54 C4
Wilder Dam, N.H.-Vt. 54 C4
Wilders, Ind. 70 C1
Wildersville, Tenn. 71 C6
Wildervank, Neth., 5,300 115 E1
Wilderville, Oreg. 80 B4
Wildeshausen, F.R.Ger., 8,646 118 B2
Wildhaus, Switz., 1,179 124 D1
Wild Horse, Colo. 79 D2
Wildhorse, Okla. 76 G1
Wildhorse Cr., Okla. 76 F3
Wild Horse Hill, Nebr. 75 D2
Wildomar, Calif. 83 k16
Wildon, Aust., 2,011 124 M7
Wildorado, Tex. 76 M2
Wild Rice, r., Minn. 74 E2
Wild Rice, r., N. Dak. 74 D2
Wild Rice L., Wis. 66 D2
Wildrose, Calif. 82 E4
Wildrose, N. Dak., 361 74 A1
Wild Rose, Wis., 594 66 D4
Wildspitze, mtn., Aust. 124 G7
Wildstrubel, mtn., Switz. 124 B2
Wildsville, La. 73 D6
Wildwood, Alta., Can. 42 J3
Wildwood, Calif. 82 B2
Wildwood, Fla., 2,170 65 G4
Wildwood, N.J., 4,690 61 B6
Wildwood, Pa., 2,500* 60 b7
Wildwood Crest, N.J., 3,011 61 B6
Wiley, Colo., 383 79 D2
Wiley, Mich. 67 G5
Wilga, Pol. 127 D3
Wilgersdorf, F.R.Ger., 1,671 119 E3
Wilgus, Ohio 70 G4
Wilhelm, Mt., Terr. New Guin. 174 e2
Wilhelminagebergte, Sur. 101 M6
Wilhelmina kan., Neth. 115 C3
Wilhelmina Rise, Hawaii 84 d8
Wilhelmsburg, Aust., 6,200 124 M5
Wilhelm II Coast, Ant. 180 T6
Wilhelmshaven, F.R.Ger., 98,374 118 A2
Wilhoit, Ariz. 78 B4
Wilkau-Hasslau, Ger.D.R., 13,826 126 b6
Wilkes, Ant. 180 T6
Wilkes, co., Ga., 10,961 64 G2
Wilkes, co., N.C., 45,269 63 C1
Wilkes, i., Wake I. 176 26
Wilkes-Barre, Pa., 63,551 61 L3
Wilkesboro, N.C., 1,568 63 C1
Wilkes Land, Ant. 180 U5
Wilkeson, Wash., 412 80 C2
Wilkes Subglacial Basin 180 ·
Wilkesville, Ohio, 190 70 G3
Wilkie, Sask., Can., 1,568 43 B4
Wilkin, co., Minn., 10,650 74 D2
Wilkins, Nev. 83 C2
Wilkinsburg, Pa., 30,066 60 C5
Wilkinson, co., Ga., 9,250 64 F3
Wilkinson, Ind., 388 70 D3
Wilkinson, co., Miss., 13,235 73 D6
Wilkinson, Miss. 73 D6
Wilkinson Lakes, Austl. 172 D4
Wilkins Str., N.W.T., Can. 41 G2
Wilków, Pol., 1,489 127 B3
Wilków, Pol. 127 D3
Will, co., Ill., 191,617 68 E2
Willacoochee, Ga., 1,061 64 F4
Willacy, co., Tex., 20,084 77 P6
Willamette, r., Oreg. 80 B3
Willamina, Oreg., 960 80 B3
Willandra Billabong Cr., Austl. 173 e9
Willapa, r., Wash. 80 B2
Willapa Bay, Wash. 80 B2
Willara, L., Austl. 172 F4
Willard, Ill. 68 C6
Willard, Ky., 164 71 J3
Willard, Mich. 67 J5
Willard, Mo., 357 72 D7
Willard, Mont. 81 G2
Willard, N. Mex., 294 79 C4
Willard, N.Y. 58 G6
Willard, N.C. 63 F3
Willard, Ohio, 5,457 70 G1
Willard, Okla. 76 D1
Willard, Utah, 814 78 B1
Willard, Wis. 66 C4
Willards, Md., 531 62 J4
Willaumez Pen., Terr. New Guin. 174 f2
Willaura, Austl. 173 d11
Willcox, Ariz., 3,018 78 D5
Willcox Playa, Ariz. 78 C5
Willebroek, Belg., 15,380 115 d8
Willemstad, Cur., 44,560 97 16
Willemstad, Neth. 115 a7
Willendorf, Aust. 124 b11
Willenhall, U.K., 32,317 114 D5
Willernie, Minn., 664 74 d5
Willesden, London, U.K. 114 H7
Willeskop, Neth. 115 b6
Willet, N.Y. 59 J7
Willette, Tenn. 71 F5
William, r., Sask., Can. 43 B2
William L., Man., Can. 43 E4
Williams, Ariz., 3,559 78 B4
Williams, Calif., 1,370 82 B3
Williams, Iowa, 490 72 D2
Williams, Minn., 317 74 E1
Williams, co., N. Dak., 22,051 74 A1
Williams, co., Ohio, 29,968 70 E1
Williams, Oreg. 80 B4
Williams, S.C., 194 63 D4
Williams, Mt., New Hebr. 174 m7
Williams, r., Mass. 56 C3
Williams, r., Vt. 54 B5
Williams Bay, Wis., 1,347 66 E6
Williamsburg, Iowa, 1,342 72 F3
Williamsburg, Ky., 3,478 71 G5
Williamsburg, Mass., 2,186(T) 56 F3
Williamsburg, Mich. 67 H4
Williamsburg, Ohio, 1,956 70 E3
Williamsburg, Pa., 1,792 60 F5
Williamsburg, co., S.C., 40,932 63 E4
Williamsburg, Va., 6,832 62 H5
Williamsburg, W. Va. 62 D5
Williamsfield, Ill., 548 68 C3
Williamsford, Ont., Can. 46 C4
Williams Fk., r., Colo. 79 B1
Williams I., Bah. Is. 95 a8
Williams Lake, Br. Col., Can., 2,051 42 G3
Williams Mtn., Okla. 76 J3
Williamson, Ga., 215 64 E2
Williamson, co., Ill., 46,117 68 D6
Williamson, Iowa, 262 72 D3
Williamson, N.Y., 1,690 58 F5
Williamson, co., Tenn., 25,267 71 D6
Williamson, co., Tex., 35,044 77 P4
Williamson, W. Va., 6,746 62 B5
Williamson, r., Oreg. 80 C4
Williams Park, Ill. 69 b7
Williamsport, Ind., 1,353 70 B2
Williamsport, Md., 1,853 62 G3
Williamsport, Morrow Co., Ohio 70 G2
Williamsport, Pickaway Co., Ohio, 840 70 F3
Williamsport, Pa., 41,967 60 H3
Williamston, Mich., 2,214 67 J6
Williamston, N.C., 6,924 63 G2
Williamston, S.C., 3,721 63 B3
Williamstown, Ont., Can. 47 K3
Williamstown, Ky., 1,611 71 G3
Williamstown, Mass., 5,428; 7,322(T) 56 C2
Williamstown, N.J., 2,722 61 B4
Williamstown, N.Y. 59 J5
Williamstown, Pa., 2,097 60 J4
Williamstown, Vt. 54 B3
Williamstown, W. Va., 2,632 62 C3
Williamsville, Ill., 735 68 C4
Williamsville (part of Hubbardston), Mass. 56 H3
Williamsville (part of Stockbridge), Mass. 56 C3
Williamsville, Mich. 67 H7
Williamsville, Mo., 412 72 G7
Williamsville, N.Y., 6,316 58 m19
Williamsville, Vt. 54 B6
Williamsville, Va. 62 E4
Willich, F.R.Ger., 11,253 119 B2
Williford, Ark., 195 73 D1
Willikies Village, Antigua, 1,330 97 9
Willimansett (part of Chicopee), Mass. 56 F4
Willimantic, Conn., 13,881 56 H6
Willimantic, r., Conn. 56 G5
Willimantic Res., Conn. 56 G5
Willingboro, N.J., 11,861 61 B3
Willingdon, Alta., Can. 42 K3
Willingdon, Mt., Alta., Can. 42 J3
Willingham, U.K., 1,766 114 J6
Willington (incl. Crook), U.K., 25,218 112 g10
Willington, Conn., 2,005(T) 56 G5
Willis, Mich. 67 K6
Willis, Okla. 76 G4
Willis, Tex., 975 77 Q4
Willisau, Switz., 5,774 124 C1
Willisburg, Ky. 71 F4
Williston, S. Af., 2,873 164 C7
Williston, Fla., 1,582 65 G3
Williston, N. Dak., 11,866 74 A1
Williston, S.C., 2,722 63 C4
Williston, Tenn. 71 B6
Williston, Vt. 54 A3
Williston Park, N.Y., 8,255 58 e13
Willisville, Ark. 73 B4
Willisville, Ill., 532 68 C6
Willis Wharf, Va. 62 J5
Willits, Calif., 3,410 82 B3
Willmar, Minn., 10,417 74 E3
Willoughby, Ohio, 15,058 70 H1
Willoughby, C., Austl. 172 c8
Willoughby, L., Vt. 54 C2
Willoughby, Mt., Austl. 172 E4
Willoughby Bay, Antigua 97 9
Willoughby Hills, Ohio, 4,241 70 f8
Willow, Alaska, 78 85 G3
Willow, Ark. 73 C3
Willow, Ky. 71 G3
Willow, Mich. 67 e16
Willow, Okla., 187 76 D2
Willow, r., Mich. 67 L5
Willowbrook, Ill., 157 69 c9
Willow Bunch, Sask., Can. 43 C5
Willow Bunch L., Sask., Can. 43 C5
Willow City, N. Dak., 494 74 B1
Willow City, Tex. 76 a5
Willow Creek, Calif. 82 B2
Willowcreek, Oreg. 80 E3
Willow Cr., Oreg. 80 E3
Willow Cr., Utah 78 D2
Willowdale, Nebr. 75 H1
Willowemoc Cr., N.Y. 61 N2
Willow Grove, Pa., 10,150* 61 M5
Willow Hill, Ill., 335 68 D4
Willowick, Ohio, 18,749 70 H1
Willowie, Austl. 172 c7
Willow Island, Nebr. 75 E3
Willow Lake, S. Dak., 467 74 D3
Willowmore, S. Af., 3,454 164 C7
Willow Ranch, Calif. 82 C2
Willow Res., Wis. 66 D3
Willow River, Br. Col., Can. 42 G2
Willow River, Minn., 343 74 F2
Willow Run, Mich. 67 K6
Willows, Calif., 4,139 82 B3
Willow Spring, N.C. 63 F2
Willow Springs, Calif. 82 D5
Willow Springs, Ill., 2,348 69 c10
Willow Springs, Mo., 1,913 72 E7
Willow Springs, Utah 78 B1
Willowvale, N.Y. 59 t26
Willow View, Okla. 76 F2
Wills, L., Austl. 172 D3
Willsboro, N.Y. 59 O3
Wills Cr., Ohio 70 H2
Wills Cr., Pa. 60 E6
Willseyville, N.Y. 59 G7
Willshire, Ohio, 601 70 E2
Wills Mtn., Pa. 60 E6
Wills Point, Tex., 2,281 77 Q3
Willunga, Austl. 172 E5
Wilma, Fla. 65 E2
Wilmar, Ark., 718 73 D4
Wilmer, Br. Col., Can. 42 J4
Wilmer, Ala. 64 A5
Wilmer, Tex., 1,785 76 f9
Wilmerding, Pa., 4,349 60 c8
Wilmette, Ill., 28,268 68 E1
Wilmington, Austl. 172 E5
Wilmington, Del., 95,827 62 J3
Wilmington, Ill., 4,210 68 D2
Wilmington, Mass., 2,250; 12,475(T) 57 M2
Wilmington, N.Y. 59 N3
Wilmington, N.C., 44,103 63 G3
Wilmington, Ohio, 8,915 70 F3
Wilmington, Vt., 591 54 B6
Wilmington Beach, N.C. 63 G3
Wilmington Manor, Del. 62 e11
Wilmont, Ark., 1,005 73 D4
Wilmont, Minn., 473 74 D4
Wilmore, Kans., 99 75 F6
Wilmore, Ky., 2,773 71 G4
Wilmot, Mich. 67 K5
Wilmot, N.H. 54 D5
Wilmot, S. Dak., 545 74 D3
Wilmot, Wis. 66 c13
Wilmot Flat, N.H. 54 D5
Wilmslow, U.K., 21,393 113 E5
Wilna, N. Mex. 79 A5
Wilnecote, U.K. 114 E5
Wilnis, Neth. 115 b6
Wilno, Ont., Can. 46 G3
Wilpattu Nat. Pk., Cey. 145 F8
Wilpen, Pa. 60 D5
Wilpshire, U.K., 1,733 114 C3
Wilrijk, Belg., 32,688 115 C3
Wilsall, Mont. 81 D2
Wilsdruff, Ger.D.R. 126 c5
Wilseder Berg, F.R.Ger. 118 B2
Wilsey, Kans., 224 75 J5
Wilseyville, Calif. 82 C3
Wilshamstead, U.K., 1,095 114 H6
Wilson, Ark., 1,191 73 E2
Wilson (part of Windsor), Conn. 56 F5
Wilson, Ill. 69 c7
Wilson, co., Kans., 13,077 75 K6
Wilson, Kans., 905 75 G5
Wilson, La. 73 D7
Wilson, Mich. 66 F3
Wilson, N.Y., 1,320 58 C5
Wilson, co., N.C., 57,716 63 G2
Wilson, N.C. 28,753 63 F2
Wilson, Okla., 1,647 76 F3
Wilson, Pa., 8,465 61 k18
Wilson, co., Tenn., 27,668 71 E5
Wilson, co., Tex., 13,267 77 O5
Wilson, Tex., 403 77 N3
Wilson, Wis. 140 66 A4
Wilson, Mt., Calif. 83 h15
Wilson, Mt., Colo. 79 B3
Wilson, Mt., Nev. 83 C3
Wilson City, Bah. Is. 95 c6
Wilson Creek, Wash., 252 80 D2
Wilson Cr. Ra., Nev. 82 ·
Wilson L., Ala. 64 B1
Wilson Mill I., N.Y. 69 C
Wilson Mills, N.C., 280 63 F2
Wilson Res., Kans. 75 G5
Wilsons, Va. 62 G5
Wilsons Mills, Me. 55 B4
Wilsons Promontory, Austl. 173 G6
Wilsons Promontory Nat. Pk., Austl. 173 G6
Wilsonville, Ala., 683 64 C2
Wilsonville, Ill., 688 68 C4
Wilsonville, Nebr., 289 75 E3
Wilster, F.R.Ger., 5,093 118 B2
Wilthen, Ger.D.R. 118 E3
Wiltingen, F.R.Ger., 1,354 119 B5
Wilton, U.K., 3,402 113 E6
Wilton, Ala., 428 64 C2
Wilton, Ark., 329 73 A4
Wilton, Calif. 82 b8
Wilton, Conn., 8,026(T) 56 C8
Wilton, Me., 1,761 55 B4
Wilton, Minn., 112 74 E2
Wilton, N.H., 1,425 54 D6
Wilton, N.Y. 59 N5
Wilton, N. Dak., 739 74 B2
Wilton, Wis., 578 66 C5
Wilton, r., Austl. 172 E1
Wilton Junction, Iowa 72 G3
Wilton Manors, Fla., 8,257 65 b9
Wiltshire, co., U.K., 422,985 113 E6
Wiltz, Lux., 1,551 115 D5
Wiluna, Austl. 172 B4
Wimauma, Fla. 65 d12
Wimberly, Tex. 76 b5
Wimbledon, London, U.K. 114 H8
Wimbledon, N. Dak., 402 74 C2
Wimblington, U.K., 1,365 114 H5
Wimborne Minster, U.K., 4,158 113 F6
Wimer, Oreg. 80 B4
Wimmis, Switz., 1,756 124 B2
Winamac, Ind., 2,375 70 C1
Winameg, Ohio 70 E1
Winburne, Pa. 60 F4
Winchcombe, U.K., 3,047 114 E7
Winchell, Tex. 77 O4
Winchendon, Mass., 3,839; 6,237(T) 56 H2
Winchendon Center (part of Winchendon), Mass. 56 H2
Winchendon Springs (part of Winchendon), Mass. 56 J2
Wincheringen, F.R.Ger., 1,244 119 A5
Winchester, Ont., Can., 1,491 44 J6
Winchester, U.K., 28,770 113 F6
Winchester, Ark., 185 73 D4
Winchester, Calif. 83 k16
Winchester, Idaho, 427 81 A2
Winchester, Ill., 1,657 68 B4
Winchester, Ind., 5,742 70 E2
Winchester, Kans., 458 75 K4
Winchester, Ky., 10,187 71 G4
Winchester, Mass., 19,376(T) 57 M3
Winchester, N.H. 54 C6
Winchester, Ohio, 788 70 F4
Winchester, Oreg. 80 B4
Winchester, Tenn., 4,760 71 E6
Winchester, Va., 15,110 62 F3
Winchester, Vilas Co., Wis. 66 D2
Winchester, Winnebago Co., Wis. 66 E4
Winchester Bay, Oreg. 80 A4
Winchester Center, Conn. 56 D5
Windber, Pa., 6,994 60 E5
Wind Cave Nat. Pk., S. Dak. 74 A4
Windecken, F.R.Ger., 2,748 119 F4
Windehsi, Indon. 149 K3
Winder, Ga., 5,555 64 F1
Windermere, U.K., 6,556 113 E4
Windermere, l., U.K. 114 C2
Windfall, Ind., 1,135 70 D2
Wind Gap, Pa., 1,930 61 M4
Windham, co., Conn., 68,572 56 H5
Windham, Conn., 16,973(T) 56 H6
Windham, N.Y. 59 M7
Windham, Ohio, 3,777 70 H1
Windham, co., Vt., 29,776 54 B5
Windham, Vt. 54 B5
Windham Center, Me. 55 B5
Windham Depot, N.H. 54 E6
Windham Springs, Ala. 64 B2
Windhoek, S.-W. Afr., 36,051 164 B5
Windhorst, Kans. 75 F6
Windigo, Qué., Can. 44 K6
Windigsteig, Aust. 124 M5
Windischeschenbach, F.R.Ger., 4,644 118 C4
Windischgarsten, Aust., 1,728 124 L6
Wind Lake, Wis., 1,305 66 E6
Wind L., Wis. 66 c12
Windlass Bight, V.I. 97 4
Windlestraw Law, mtn., U.K. 112 d8
Windom, Kans., 168 75 H5
Windom, Minn., 3,691 74 E4
Windom, N.Y. 58 k19
Windom Pk., Colo. 79 B3
Windorah, Austl. 173 F3
Window Rock, Ariz. 78 D4
Wind Point, Wis., 463 66 d12
Wind Pt., Wis. 66 F6
Wind Ridge, Pa. 60 B6
Wind River Pk., Wyo. 81 E4
Wind River Ra., Wyo. 81 E4
Windrush, r., U.K. 114 F7
Windsheim, F.R.Ger., 7,898 118 C4
Windsor, Austl., 9,867 173 h9
Windsor, Newf., Can., 5,478 45 Q5
Windsor, N.S., Can., 3,496 45 N6
Windsor, Ont., Can., 113,036 44 G7
Windsor, Qué., Can., 6,593 44 K6
Windsor, U.K., 15,665 113 F6
Windsor, Colo., 1,509 79 C1
Windsor, Conn., 19,467(T) 56 F5
Windsor, Fla. 65 G3
Windsor, Ill., 1,021 68 D4
Windsor, Me. 55 C4
Windsor, Mass., 384(T) 56 D2
Windsor, Mo., 2,714 72 D6
Windsor, N.J. 58 a16
Windsor, N.Y., 1,026 59 J7
Windsor, N.C., 1,813 63 G1
Windsor, Pa., 1,029 60 J6
Windsor, S.C. 63 C4
Windsor, Va., 579 62 H6
Windsor, co., Vt., 42,483 54 B4
Windsor, Vt., 3,256 54 C5
Windsor, Wis. 66 D5
Windsor Beach, N.Y. 58 n20
Windsor Heights, Iowa, 6,409 72 D3
Windsor Locks, Conn., 11,411(T) 56 F5
Windsorville, Conn. 56 F5
Windthorst, Tex. 77 O3
Windward Is., Lesser Antilles 95 G4
Windward Passage, W.I. 95 D3
Windy Hill Beach, S.C., 233 63 F4
Windy Hill Pt., Nevis 97 6
Windy Point, Br. Col., Can. 42 G2
Winefred L., Alta., Can. 42 L2
Winegars, Mich. 67 J5
Winema Beach, Oreg. 80 A3
Winenne, Belg., 1,089 115 C4
Winfall, N.C., 269 63 H1
Winfield, Br. Col., Can. 42 H4
Winfield, Ont., Can. 46 a13
Winfield, Ala., 2,907 64 B2
Winfield, Ill., 1,575 69 b9
Winfield, Kans., 11,117 75 J6
Winfield, Mo., 564 72 G5
Winfield, Pa. 60 J4
Winfield, Tenn. 71 G5
Winfield, Tex., 251 77 Q3
Winfield, W. Va., 318 62 B4
Winford, U.K., 1,309 114 C8
Winfred, S. Dak., 137 74 D4
Wing, U.K., 1,719 114 G7
Wing, Ala. 64 C4
Wing, N. Dak., 303 74 B2
Wingate, U.K., 12,688 113 F4
Wingate, Md. 62 H4
Wingate, N.C., 1,304 63 D3
Wingates, U.K. 112 g9
Wingdale, N.Y. 59 N8
Wingene, Belg., 7,140 115 B3
Wingen-sur-Moder, Fr., 1,239 116 d9
Winger, Minn., 292 74 D2
Wingham, Austl., 2,591 173 G4
Wingham, Ont., Can., 2,878 44 G7
Wingst, F.R.Ger., 2,767 118 B2
Winhall, r., Vt. 54 B5
Winifred, Mont., 220 81 E2
Winisk, Ont., Can. 44 F3
Winisk, r., Ont., Can. 44 F3
Winisk L., Ont., Can. 44 E4
Wink, Tex., 1,863 77 M4
Winkelman, Ariz., 1,123 78 C5
Winkle, Ohio 70 F3
Winkleigh, U.K. 113 E6
Winkler, Man., Can., 2,409 43 F5
Winkler, co., Tex., 13,652 77 M4
Winklern, Aust. 124 L6
Winlaw, Br. Col., Can. 42 H4
Winlock, Oreg. 80 D3
Winlock, Wash., 808 80 B2
Winmana, Burma 147 f6
Winn, parish, La., 16,034 73 C5
Winn, Me. 55 D3
Winn, Mich. 67 J5
Winnabow, N.C. 63 F3
Winneba, Ghana, 25,292 162 D5
Winnebago, co., Ill., 209,765 68 C1
Winnebago, Ill., 1,059 68 C1
Winnebago, co., Iowa, 13,099 72 D1
Winnebago, Minn., 2,088 74 F4
Winnebago, Nebr., 682 75 J1
Winnebago, co., Wis., 107,928 66 E4
Winnebago, Wis. 66 E4
Winnebago, L., Wis. 66 E4
Winnebago, r., Iowa 72 D1
Winnecke, Mt., Austl. 172 E3
Winneconne, Wis., 1,273 66 E4
Winneconnet (part of Norton), Mass. 57 M5
Winnecook, Me. 55 C4
Winnemucca, Nev., 3,453 83 A2
Winnemucca L., Nev. 83 A2
Winnenden, F.R.Ger., 10,194 119 G7
Winner, S. Dak., 3,705 74 C4
Winneshiek, co., Iowa, 21,651 72 F1
Winnetka, Ill., 13,368 68 E1
Winnetoon, Nebr., 85 75 G1
Winnett, Mont., 360 81 E2
Winnetuxet, r., Mass. 57 N5
Winnfield, La., 7,022 73 C6
Winnibigoshish, L., Minn. 74 F2
Winnie, Tex., 1,114 77 Q5
Winnipeg, Man., Can., 260,391 43 F5
Winnipeg, L., Man., Can. 43 F4
Winnipeg, r., Man.-Ont., Can. 43 G5
Winnipeg Beach, Man., Can. 43 F5
Winnipegosis, Man., Can. 43 E4
Winnipegosis, L., Man., Can. 43 E4
Winnipesaukee, L., N.H. 54 E4
Winnisquam, N.H. 54 E5
Winnisquam L., N.H. 54 D4
Winnsboro, La., 4,437 73 D5
Winnsboro, S.C., 3,479 63 C3
Winnsboro, Tex., 2,675 77 Q3
Winnweiler, F.R.Ger., 1,854 119 D5
Winokapau L., Newf., Can. 45 O4
Winokur, Ga. 64 G4
Winona, Ont., Can. 46 c15
Winona, Ariz. 78 C4
Winona, Ind. 70 C1
Winona, Kans., 393 75 D4
Winona, Mich. 66 E2
Winona, co., Minn., 40,937 74 G3
Winona, Minn., 24,895 74 G3
Winona, Miss., 4,282 73 F4
Winona, Mo., 562 72 F7
Winona Lake, Ind., 1,928 70 D1
Winooski, Vt., 7,420 54 A2
Winooski, r., Vt. 54 B3
Winooski, Kingsbury Br., r., Vt. 54 C3
Winschoten, Neth., 14,700 115 F1
Winschoter diep, can., Neth. 115 E1
Winscombe, U.K., 2,553 114 C8
Winsen, F.R.Ger., 3,319 118 B2
Winsen, F.R.Ger., 9,158 118 C2
Winsford, U.K., 12,738 113 E5
Winside, Nebr., 416 75 H1
Wińsko, Pol. 127 f5
Winslow, U.K., 2,072 114 G7
Winslow, Ariz., 8,862 78 C4
Winslow, Ark., 183 73 A2
Winslow, Ill., 366 68 C1
Winslow, Ind., 1,089 70 B4
Winslow, Me., 3,640 55 C4
Winslow, Nebr., 136 75 J2
Winslow, N.J. 61 B4
Winslow, Wash., 919 81 b7
Winslow Reef, Phoenix Is. 175 8
Winsor Dam, Mass. 56 G3
Winsted, Conn., 8,136 56 D5
Winsted, Minn., 1,163 74 E3
Winston, U.K., 1,091 112 g10
Winston, co., Ala., 14,858 64 B1
Winston, Fla. 65 d11
Winston, Ky. 71 G4
Winston, co., Miss., 19,246 73 F4
Winston, Mo., 236 72 C5
Winston, N. Mex. 79 B5
Winston, Oreg., 2,395 80 B4
Winston-Salem, N.C., 111,135 63 D1
Winsum, Neth. 115 E1
Winter, Wis. 66 C3
Winter Beach, Fla. 65 J5
Winterberg, F.R.Ger., 3,215 118 B3
Winterbourne, Ont., Can. 46 b13
Winter Garden, Fla., 5,513 65 H4
Winter Harbor, Me. 55 D4
Winterhaven, Calif. 82 F6
Winter Haven, Fla., 16,277 65 H5
Winter Park, Colo. 79 C2
Winter Park, Fla., 17,162 65 H4
Winterpock, Va. 62 G5
Winterport, Me., 1,000 55 D4
Winters, Calif., 1,700 82 B3
Winters, Tex., 3,266 77 O4
Winterscheid, F.R.Ger., 1,497 119 C3
Winterset, Iowa, 3,639 72 C3
Winterslow, U.K., 1,070 113 i12
Winterspelt, F.R.Ger. 119 A4
Wintersville, Ohio, 3,597 70 J2
Winterswijk, Neth., 16,100 115 E3
Winterthur, Switz., 80,352 124 C1
Winterthur, Del. 62 e10
Winterton, Newf., Can. 45 b10
Winterton, U.K., 2,688 114 G3
Winterville, Me. 55 D2
Winterville, Miss. 73 E4
Winterville, N.C., 1,418 63 G2
Winthrop, Ark., 225 73 A4
Winthrop (part of Deep River), Conn. 56 G7
Winthrop, Iowa, 649 72 F2
Winthrop, Me., 2,260 55 C4
Winthrop, Mass., 20,303(T) 57 N3
Winthrop, Minn., 1,381 74 E3
Winthrop, Wash., 359 80 C1
Winthrop Harbor, Ill., 3,848 68 E1
Winton, Austl., 1,398 173 F3
Winton, N.Z., 1,473 175 f7
Winton, Minn., 182 74 G2
Winton, N.C., 835 63 G1
Winton, Pa., 5,456 61 L3
Wintzenheim, Fr., 5,365 117 G2
Winyah Bay, S.C. 63 E4
Wiota, Iowa, 195 72 C3
Wiota, Wis. 66 D6
Wipper, r., F.R.Ger. 119 C2
Wipper, r., Ger.D.R. 118 C3
Wipperfürth, F.R.Ger., 11,631 119 C2
Wirges, F.R.Ger., 4,631 119 D4
Wirksworth, U.K., 4,931 114 E4
Wirrulla, Austl. 172 E5
Wirt, Ind. 70 D4
Wirt, Minn. 74 F2
Wirt, Okla. 76 F3
Wirt, co., W. Va., 4,391 62 C3
Wirtz, Va. 62 E5
Wisacky, S.C. 63 D3
Wisbech, U.K., 17,528 113 F5
Wiscasset, Me. 55 C5
Wisconsin, st., U.S., 4,140,000* 66
Wisconsin, L., Wis. 66 D5
Wisconsin, r., Wis. 66 D5
Wisconsin Dells, Wis., 2,105 66 D5
Wisconsin, Dells of the, Wis. 67 ·
Wisconsin Rapids, Wis., 15,042 66 D4
Wiscoy, N.Y. 58 D6
Wisdom, Mo. 72 D6
Wisdom, Mont. 81 C3
Wisdom, L., Terr. New Guin. 174 e2
Wise, N.C. 63 F1
Wise, co., Tex., 17,012 77 P3
Wise, Tex. 76 g9
Wise, co., Va., 43,579 62 B6
Wise, Va., 2,614 62 B5
Wiseman, Alaska 85 G2
Wiseman, Ark. 73 D1
Wise River, Mont. 81 C3
Wiset Chaichan, Thai. 147 d4
Wiseton, Sask., Can. 43 C4
Wishart, Sask., Can. 43 D4
Wishaw (incl. Motherwell), 72,799 112 c8
Wishek, N. Dak., 1,290 74 C2
Wishram, Wash. 80 C3
Wiske, r., U.K. 112 h11
Wisła, r., Pol. 127 C1
Wisłok, r., Pol. 127 D4
Wisłoka, r., Pol. 127 D4
Wismar, Guyana 101 L4
Wismar, Ger.D.R., 55,400 118 C2
Wisner, La., 1,254 73 D6
Wisner, Mich. 67 K5
Wisner, Nebr., 1,192 75 J2
Wiśnicz Nowy, Pol. 127 k7
Wissahickon Cr., Pa. 60 f11
Wissembourg, Fr., 5,298 117 G2
Wissen, F.R.Ger., 7,043 118 A3
Wissey, r., U.K. 114 J5
Wissota, L., Wis. 66 B4
Wistanstow, U.K. 114 C6
Wistaria, Br. Col., Can. 42 E3
Wistaston, U.K., 2,818 114 C4
Wister, Okla., 592 76 J3
Wister, L., Okla. 76 J3
Wistow, U.K. 114 F3
Wisznice, Pol. 127 E3
Witbank, S. Af., 24,510 164 D6
Witch Lake, Mich. 66 F2
Witham, U.K., 9,459 113 G6
Witham, r., U.K. 113 F5
Withamsville, Ohio, 2,811 70 E4
Withee, Wis., 442 66 C4
Witherbee, N.Y. 59 N3
Withern, U.K. 114 J4
Withernsea, U.K., 4,981 113 G5
Withington, Glos., U.K. 114 E7
Withington, Herefs., U.K. 114 C6
Withington, Mt., N. Mex. 79 B5
Withlacoochee, r., Fla. 65 G4
Withlacoochee, r., Fla.-Ga. 65 F2
Withnell, U.K., 2,840 114 C3
Withrow, Wash. 80 D2
Witków, Pol. 127 E3
Witkowo, Pol., 4,129 127 B2
Witless Bay, Newf., Can. 45 c10
Witmarsum, Neth. 115 D1
Witney, U.K., 9,219 113 F6
Witnica, Pol., 5,362 127 A2
Witosławice, Pol. 127 h6
Witt, Ill., 1,101 68 C4
Witten, F.R.Ger., 91,706 119 C2
Witten, S. Dak. 74 B4
Wittenberg, Ger.D.R., 45,965 118 D3
Wittenberg, Wis., 892 66 D4
Wittenberge, Ger.D.R., 31,609 118 C2
Wittenburg, Ger.D.R. 118 C2
Wittenheim, Fr., 9,297 117 G3
Wittenoom, Austl. 172 B3
Witterschlick, F.R.Ger., 3,103 119 B3
Wittichenau, Ger.D.R. 118 E3
Wittingen, F.R.Ger., 5,045 118 C2
Wittlich, F.R.Ger., 8,902 118 A3
Wittman, Ariz. 78 B5
Wittmannsdorf, Aust. 124 M7
Wittmund, F.R.Ger., 4,233 118 A2
Witton Park, U.K. 112 g10
Wittstock, Ger.D.R. 118 D2
Witu, Kenya 164 F2
Witvlei, S.-W. Afr. 164 B5
Witwatersrand, reg., S. Af. 165 i17
Witzenhausen, F.R.Ger., 8,005 118 B3
Wivenhoe, Man., Can. 43 G3
Wiwŏn, N. Kor. 151 E2
Wixhausen, F.R.Ger., 3,407 119 F5